MAJOR ◆
20th- ◆
CENTURY ◆
WRITERS ◆

MAJOR 20th-CENTURY WRITERS

A Selection of Sketches from *Contemporary Authors*

Contains more than one thousand entries on the most widely studied twentieth-century writers, all originally written or updated for this set.

First Edition

Bryan Ryan, Editor

Volume 1: A–D

 Gale Research Inc. • *DETROIT* • *LONDON*

STAFF

Bryan Ryan, **Editor**

Marilyn K. Basel, Barbara Carlisle Bigelow, Christa Brelin, Carol Lynn DeKane, Janice E. Drane,
Kevin S. Hile, Thomas Kozikowski, Sharon Malinowski, Emily J. McMurray,
Michael E. Mueller, Kenneth R. Shepherd, Les Stone, Diane Telgen,
Polly A. Vedder, and Thomas Wiloch, **Associate Editors**

Marian Gonsior, Katherine Huebl, James F. Kamp, Margaret Mazurkiewicz,
Jani Prescott, and Neil R. Schlager, **Assistant Editors**

Anne Janette Johnson, Donna Olendorf, and Curtis Skinner, **Contributing Sketchwriters**

Hal May, **Senior Editor,** *Contemporary Authors*

Mary Rose Bonk, **Research Supervisor, Biography Division**

Jane Cousins, Andrew Guy Malonis, and Norma Sawaya, **Editorial Associates**

Reginald A. Carlton, Shirley Gates, Sharon McGilvray,
Diane Linda Sevigny, and Tracey Head Turbett, **Editorial Assistants**

Mary Beth Trimper, **Production Manager**
Evi Seoud, **Assistant Production Manager**

Arthur Chartow, **Art Director**
Kathleen A. Mouzakis, **Graphic Designer**
C. J. Jonik, **Keyliner**

∞™ This book is printed on acid-free paper that meets the minimum
requirements of American National Standard for Information Sciences
Permanence Paper for Printed Library Materials, ANSI Z39.48-1984.

♺ This book is printed on recycled paper that meets Environmental
Protection Agency standards.

Library of Congress Catalog Card Number: 90-84380
ISBN 0-8103-7766-7 (Set)
ISBN 0-8103-7912-0 (Volume 1)

Printed in the United States of America.

Published simultaneously in the United Kingdom
by Gale Research International Limited
(An affiliated company of Gale Research Inc.)

CONTENTS

INTRODUCTION

An Important Information Source on 20th-Century Literature and Culture

Major 20th-Century Writers provides students, educators, librarians, researchers, and general readers with an affordable and comprehensive source of biographical and bibliographical information on more than 1,000 of the most influential authors of our time. Of primary focus are novelists, short story writers, poets, and dramatists from the United States and the United Kingdom, but prominent writers from over sixty other nations have also been included. Important figures from beyond the literary realm, nonfiction writers who have influenced twentieth-century thought, are also found here.

The vast majority of the entries in *Major 20th-Century Writers* were selected from Gale's acclaimed *Contemporary Authors* series and completely updated for this publication. About 40 sketches on important authors not already in *CA* were written especially for this four-volume set to furnish readers with the most comprehensive coverage possible. These newly written entries will also appear in future volumes of *Contemporary Authors*.

International Advisory Board

Before preparing *Major 20th-Century Writers*, the editors of *Contemporary Authors* conducted a telephone survey of librarians and mailed a print survey to more than four thousand libraries to help determine the kind of reference tool libraries wanted. Once it was clear that a comprehensive, yet affordable source of information on the best 20th-century writers was needed to serve small and medium-sized libraries, a wide range of resources was consulted: national surveys of books taught in American high schools and universities; British secondary school syllabi; reference works such as the *New York Public Library Desk Reference*, *Reading Lists for College-Bound Students: The Books Most Recommended by America's Top Colleges*, *The List of Books*, E. D. Hirsch's *Cultural Literacy*, and volumes in Gale's Literary Criticism series and *Dictionary of Literary Biography*.

A preliminary list of authors drawn from these sources was then sent to an advisory board of librarians and teaching professionals in both the United States and Great Britain. The recommendations made by these advisors helped define the scope of the project and the final list of authors to be included in the four-volume set. Stephen T. Willis, Social Sciences Librarian at the Manchester Central Library in Manchester, England, focused on the literary and nonliterary writers of most interest to British school libraries and public libraries, with special consideration for those authors who are relevant to the GCSE and A-level public examinations. Jacqueline G. Morris of the Indiana Department of Education provided input from an American secondary school perspective; Tim LaBorie of St. Joseph University in Philadelphia and Rev. John P. Schlegel, S.J., the Executive and Academic Vice President of John Carroll University in Cleveland, reviewed the list with college students in mind.

Broad Coverage in a Single Source

Built upon these suggestions, *Major 20th-Century Writers* provides single-source coverage of the most influential writers of our time, including:

- *Novelists and short story writers*: James Baldwin, Saul Bellow, Willa Cather, James Joyce, Franz Kafka, Thomas Mann, Flannery O'Connor, George Orwell, Eudora Welty, and Edith Wharton.

- *Dramatists*: Samuel Beckett, Bertolt Brecht, Eugene O'Neill, and Tennessee Williams.

- *Poets*: W. H. Auden, T. S. Eliot, Robert Frost, Ezra Pound, and William Butler Yeats.

- *Contemporary literary figures*: Chinua Achebe, Don DeLillo, Gabriel Garcia Marquez, Nadine Gordimer, Guenter Grass, John Irving, Toni Morrison, V. S. Naipaul, Joyce Carol Oates, and Thomas Pynchon.

- *Genre writers*: Isaac Asimov, Agatha Christie, Tom Clancy, Stephen King, Louis L'Amour, John le Carre, Ursula K. Le Guin, Danielle Steel, and J. R. R. Tolkien.

- *20th-Century thinkers*: Hannah Arendt, Bruno Bettelheim, Joseph Campbell, Albert Einstein, Sigmund Freud, Mohandas Gandhi, Margaret Mead, Jean Piaget, Bertrand Russell, and Jean-Paul Sartre.

Easy Access to Information

Both the newly written and the completely updated entries in *Major 20th-Century Writers* provide in-depth information in a format designed for ease of use. Individual paragraphs within each entry, labeled with descriptive rubrics, ensure that a reader seeking specific information can quickly focus on the pertinent portion of an entry.

A typical entry in *Major 20th-Century Writers* contains the following, clearly labeled information sections:

- *PERSONAL:* dates and places of birth and death; parents' names and occupations; name(s) of spouse(s), date(s) of marriage(s); names of children; colleges attended and degrees earned; political and religious affiliation when known.

- *ADDRESSES:* complete home, office, and agent's addresses.

- *CAREER:* name of employer, position, and dates for each career post; résumé of other vocational achievements; military service.

- *MEMBER:* memberships and offices held in professional and civic organizations.

- *AWARDS, HONORS:* literary and professional awards received and dates.

- *WRITINGS:* title-by-title chronological bibliography of books written and edited, listed by genre when known; list of other notable publications, such as plays, screenplays, and periodical contributions.

- *WORK IN PROGRESS:* description of projects in progress.

- *SIDELIGHTS:* a biographical portrait of the author's development; information about the critical reception of the author's works; revealing comments, often by the author, on personal interests, aspirations, motivations, and thoughts on writing.

- *BIOGRAPHICAL/CRITICAL SOURCES:* books, feature articles, and reviews in which the writer's work has been treated.

Nationality Index Reveals International Scope

Authors included in *Major 20th-Century Writers* appear alphabetically in an index organized by country of birth and/or citizenship. More than 60 nations are represented, reflecting the international scope of this set.

Genre/Subject Index Indicates Range of Writers' Works

The written works composed by the authors collected in this four-volume set represent not only literary novels, short stories, plays, and poems, but also over 25 other genres and subject areas of fiction and nonfiction.

Acknowledgments

The editor wishes to thank: Barbara Carlisle Bigelow for her editorial assistance; Kenneth R. Shepherd for his technical assistance; and James G. Lesniak and Susan M. Trosky, editors of the *Contemporary Authors* series, for their cooperation and assistance, and for that of their staffs.

Comments Are Appreciated

Major 20th-Century Writers is intended to serve as a useful reference tool for a wide audience, so your comments about this work are encouraged. Suggestions of authors to include in future editions of *Major 20th-Century Writers* are also welcome. Send comments and suggestions to: The Editor, *Major 20th-Century Writers*, Gale Research Inc., 835 Penobscot Bldg., Detroit, MI 48226–4094. Or, call toll-free at 1–800–347–GALE.

MAJOR 20th-CENTURY WRITERS

VOLUME 1: A-D

Abe, Kobo 1924-
Abrahams, Peter 1919-
Achebe, Chinua 1930-
Adamov, Arthur 1908-1970
Adams, Alice 1926-
Adams, Richard 1920-
Adamson, Joy 1910-1980
Adler, Mortimer J. 1902-
Adler, Renata 1938-
Agnon, S. Y. 1888-1970
Aiken, Conrad 1889-1973
Aiken, Joan 1924-
Aitmatov, Chingiz 1928-
Akhmatova, Anna 1888-1966
Albee, Edward 1928-
Alcayaga, Lucila Godoy
   See Godoy Alcayaga, Lucila
Aldiss, Brian W. 1925-
Aleixandre, Vicente 1898-1984
Alexander, Lloyd 1924-
Algren, Nelson 1909-1981
Allen, Woody 1935-
Allende, Isabel 1942-
Allingham, Margery 1904-1966
Alther, Lisa 1944-
Amado, Jorge 1912-
Ambler, Eric 1909-
Amichai, Yehuda 1924-
Amis, Kingsley 1922-
Ammons, A. R. 1926-
Anand, Mulk Raj 1905-
Anaya, Rudolfo A. 1937-
Andersch, Alfred 1914-1980
Anderson, Poul 1926-
Anderson, Sherwood 1876-1941
Andrews, V. C. ?-1986
Andric, Ivo 1892-1975
Angelou, Maya 1928-
Anouilh, Jean 1910-1987
Anthony, Piers 1934-
Antschel, Paul 1920-1970
Aragon, Louis 1897-1982
Arden, John 1930-
Arendt, Hannah 1906-1975
Armah, Ayi Kwei 1939-
Arnow, Harriette Simpson 1908-
   1986
Ashbery, John 1927-
Ashton-Warner, Sylvia 1908-1984
Asimov, Isaac 1920-

Asturias, Miguel Angel 1899-1974
Atwood, Margaret 1939-
Auchincloss, Louis 1917-
Auden, W. H. 1907-1973
Avison, Margaret 1918-
Ayckbourn, Alan 1939-
Azuela, Mariano 1873-1952
Bach, Richard 1936-
Bachman, Richard
   See King, Stephen
Bainbridge, Beryl 1933-
Baker, Russell 1925-
Baldwin, James 1924-1987
Ballard, J. G. 1930-
Bambara, Toni Cade 1939-
Baraka, Amiri 1934-
Barker, Clive 1952-
Barker, George Granville 1913-
Barnes, Djuna 1892-1982
Barnes, Peter 1931-
Barth, John 1930-
Barthelme, Donald 1931-1989
Barthes, Roland 1915-1980
Bashevis, Isaac
   See Singer, Isaac Bashevis
Bassani, Giorgio 1916-
Bates, H. E. 1905-1974
Baum, L. Frank 1856-1919
Baumbach, Jonathan 1933-
Beattie, Ann 1947-
Beauvoir, Simone de 1908-1986
Beckett, Samuel 1906-1989
Behan, Brendan 1923-1964
Bell, Clive 1881-1964
Bell, Marvin 1937-
Bellow, Saul 1915-
Benavente, Jacinto 1866-1954
Benchley, Peter 1940-
Bennett, Alan 1934-
Berger, Thomas 1924-
Berne, Eric 1910-1970
Bernhard, Thomas 1931-1989
Berryman, John 1914-1972
Bester, Alfred 1913-1987
Beti, Mongo
   See Biyidi, Alexandre
Betjeman, John 1906-1984
Bettelheim, Bruno 1903-1990
Bioy Casares, Adolfo 1914-
Birney, Earle 1904-

Bishop, Elizabeth 1911-1979
bissett, bill 1939-
Biyidi, Alexandre 1932-
Blackwood, Caroline 1931-
Blair, Eric 1903-1950
Blais, Marie-Claire 1939-
Blasco Ibanez, Vicente 1867-1928
Blish, James 1921-1975
Blixen, Karen 1885-1962
Blount, Roy, Jr. 1941-
Blume, Judy 1938-
Blunden, Edmund 1896-1974
Bly, Robert 1926-
Bodet, Jaime Torres
   See Torres Bodet, Jaime
Boell, Heinrich 1917-1985
Bogan, Louise 1897-1970
Boll, Heinrich
   See Boell, Heinrich
Bolt, Robert 1924-
Bombeck, Erma 1927-
Bond, Edward 1934-
Bonnefoy, Yves 1923-
Bontemps, Arna 1902-1973
Borges, Jorge Luis 1899-1986
Bova, Ben 1932-
Bowen, Elizabeth 1899-1973
Bowles, Paul 1910-
Boyle, Kay 1902-
Bradbury, Malcolm 1932-
Bradbury, Ray 1920-
Bradford, Barbara Taylor 1933-
Bradley, Marion Zimmer 1930-
Braine, John 1922-1986
Brautigan, Richard 1935-1984
Brecht, Bertolt 1898-1956
Brenton, Howard 1942-
Breslin, James 1930-
Breslin, Jimmy
   See Breslin, James
Breton, Andre 1896-1966
Brink, Andre 1935-
Brittain, Vera 1893(?)-1970
Brodsky, Iosif Alexandrovich 1940-
Brodsky, Joseph
   See Brodsky, Iosif Alexandrovich
Brook, Peter 1925-
Brooke, Rupert 1887-1915
Brookner, Anita 1938-
Brooks, Cleanth 1906-

Brooks, Gwendolyn 1917-
Brophy, Brigid 1929-
Brother Antoninus
   See Everson, William
Brown, Dee 1908-
Brown, George Mackay 1921-
Brown, Rita Mae 1944-
Brown, Sterling Allen 1901-1989
Brownmiller, Susan 1935-
Brunner, John 1934-
Buber, Martin 1878-1965
Buchwald, Art 1925-
Buck, Pearl S. 1892-1973
Buckley, William F., Jr. 1925-
Buechner, Frederick 1926-
Buero Vallejo, Antonio 1916-
Bukowski, Charles 1920-
Bullins, Ed 1935-
Bultmann, Rudolf Karl 1884-1976
Burgess, Anthony
   See Wilson, John Burgess
Burke, Kenneth 1897-
Burroughs, Edgar Rice 1875-1950
Burroughs, William S. 1914-
Bustos Domecq, H.
   See Bioy Casares, Adolfo
   and Borges, Jorge Luis
Butler, Octavia E. 1947-
Butor, Michel 1926-
Byars, Betsy 1928-
Byatt, A. S. 1936-
Cabrera Infante, G. 1929-
Cade, Toni
   See Bambara, Toni Cade
Cain, Guillermo
   See Cabrera Infante, G.
Cain, James M. 1892-1977
Calder, Nigel 1931-
Caldicott, Helen 1938-
Caldwell, Erskine 1903-1987
Calisher, Hortense 1911-
Callaghan, Morley Edward 1903-
   1990
Calvino, Italo 1923-1985
Cameron, Eleanor 1912-
Campbell, John W. 1910-1971
Campbell, Joseph 1904-1987
Camus, Albert 1913-1960
Canetti, Elias 1905-
Capote, Truman 1924-1984
Card, Orson Scott 1951-
Cardenal, Ernesto 1925-
Carey, Peter 1943-
Carr, John Dickson 1906-1977
Carruth, Hayden 1921-
Carson, Rachel Louise 1907-1964
Carter, Angela 1940-
Carter, James Earl, Jr. 1924-
Carter, Jimmy
   See Carter, James Earl, Jr.
Cartland, Barbara 1901-

Carver, Raymond 1938-1988
Casares, Adolfo Bioy
   See Bioy Casares, Adolfo
Castaneda, Carlos 1931(?)-
Cather, Willa
   See Cather, Willa Sibert
Cather, Willa Sibert 1873-1947
Causley, Charles 1917-
Cela, Camilo Jose 1916-
Celan, Paul
   See Antschel, Paul
Celine, Louis-Ferdinand
   See Destouches, Louis-Ferdinand
Cendrars, Blaise
   See Sauser-Hall, Frederic
Cesaire, Aime 1913-
Chandler, Raymond 1888-1959
Char, Rene 1907-1988
Charyn, Jerome 1937-
Cheever, John 1912-1982
Chesnutt, Charles W. 1858-1932
Chesterton, G. K. 1874-1936
Ch'ien Chung-shu 1910-
Childress, Alice 1920-
Chomsky, Noam 1928-
Christie, Agatha 1890-1976
Churchill, Caryl 1938-
Churchill, Winston 1874-1965
Ciardi, John 1916-1986
Cixous, Helene 1937-
Clancy, Thomas L., Jr. 1947-
Clancy, Tom
   See Clancy, Thomas L., Jr.
Clark, Kenneth 1903-1983
Clark, Mary Higgins 1929-
Clarke, Arthur C. 1917-
Clavell, James 1925-
Cleary, Beverly 1916-
Cleese, John 1939-
Clifton, Lucille 1936-
Clutha, Janet Paterson Frame 1924-
Cocteau, Jean 1889-1963
Coetzee, J. M. 1940-
Cohen, Leonard 1934-
Colegate, Isabel 1931-
Colette 1873-1954
Colum, Padraic 1881-1972
Colwin, Laurie 1944-
Commager, Henry Steele 1902-
Commoner, Barry 1917-
Compton-Burnett, I. 1884(?)-1969
Condon, Richard 1915-
Connell, Evan S., Jr. 1924-
Connolly, Cyril 1903-1974
Conrad, Joseph 1857-1924
Conran, Shirley 1932-
Conroy, Pat 1945-
Cookson, Catherine 1906-
Coover, Robert 1932-
Cormier, Robert 1925-
Cornwell, David 1931-

Corso, Gregory 1930-
Cortazar, Julio 1914-1984
Cousins, Norman 1915-
Cousteau, Jacques-Yves 1910-
Coward, Noel 1899-1973
Cowley, Malcolm 1898-1989
Cox, William Trevor 1928-
Cozzens, James Gould 1903-1978
Crane, Hart 1899-1932
Creasey, John 1908-1973
Creeley, Robert 1926-
Crews, Harry 1935-
Crichton, Michael 1942-
Cullen, Countee 1903-1946
Cummings, E. E. 1894-1962
Dahl, Roald 1916-
Dahlberg, Edward 1900-1977
Dailey, Janet 1944-
Daly, Mary 1928-
Dannay, Frederic 1905-1982
Dario, Ruben 1867-1916
Davie, Donald 1922-
Davies, Robertson 1913-
Day Lewis, C. 1904-1972
de Beauvoir, Simone
   See Beauvoir, Simone de
de Bono, Edward 1933-
de Filippo, Eduardo 1900-1984
Deighton, Len
   See Deighton, Leonard Cyril
Deighton, Leonard Cyril 1929-
Delaney, Shelagh 1939-
Delany, Samuel R. 1942-
Delibes, Miguel
   See Delibes Setien, Miguel
Delibes Setien, Miguel 1920-
DeLillo, Don 1936-
Deloria, Vine, Jr. 1933-
del Rey, Lester 1915-
de Man, Paul 1919-1983
de Montherlant, Henry
   See Montherlant, Henry de
Dennis, Nigel 1912-
Desai, Anita 1937-
Destouches, Louis-
   Ferdinand 1894-1961
De Vries, Peter 1910-
Dexter, Pete 1943-
Dick, Philip K. 1928-1982
Dickey, James 1923-
Dickson, Carter
   See Carr, John Dickson
Didion, Joan 1934-
Dillard, Annie 1945-
Dinesen, Isak
   See Blixen, Karen
Diop, Birago 1906-1989
Disch, Thomas M. 1940-
Doctorow, E. L. 1931-
Donleavy, J. P. 1926-
Donoso, Jose 1924-

Doolittle, Hilda 1886-1961
Dos Passos, John 1896-1970
Doyle, Arthur Conan 1859-1930
Drabble, Margaret 1939-
Dreiser, Theodore 1871-1945
Du Bois, W. E. B. 1868-1963
Duerrenmatt, Friedrich 1921-
Duffy, Maureen 1933-
Duhamel, Georges 1884-1966

du Maurier, Daphne 1907-1989
Dunbar, Alice
  See Nelson, Alice Ruth Moore
  Dunbar
Dunbar-Nelson, Alice
  See Nelson, Alice Ruth Moore
  Dunbar
Duncan, Robert 1919-1988

Dunn, Douglas 1942-
Durant, Will 1885-1981
Duras, Marguerite 1914-
Durrell, Gerald 1925-
Durrell, Lawrence 1912-
Durrenmatt, Friedrich
  See Duerrenmatt, Friedrich
Dworkin, Andrea 1946-

VOLUME 2: E-K

Eagleton, Terence 1943-
Eagleton, Terry
  See Eagleton, Terence
Eberhart, Richard 1904-
Echegaray, Jose 1832-1916
Eco, Umberto 1932-
Edgar, David 1948-
Ehrenreich, Barbara 1941-
Einstein, Albert 1879-1955
Ekwensi, Cyprian 1921-
Eliade, Mircea 1907-1986
Eliot, T. S. 1888-1965
Elkin, Stanley L. 1930-
Ellin, Stanley 1916-1986
Ellison, Harlan 1934-
Ellison, Ralph 1914-
Ellmann, Richard 1918-1987
Elytis, Odysseus 1911-
Emecheta, Buchi 1944-
Empson, William 1906-1984
Endo, Shusaku 1923-
Erdrich, Louise 1954-
Erikson, Erik H. 1902-
Esslin, Martin 1918-
Estleman, Loren D. 1952-
Everson, William 1912-
Ewart, Gavin 1916-
Fallaci, Oriana 1930-
Farmer, Philip Jose 1918-
Farrell, J. G. 1935-1979
Farrell, James T. 1904-1979
Faulkner, William 1897-1962
Feiffer, Jules 1929-
Feinstein, Elaine 1930-
Ferber, Edna 1887-1968
Ferlinghetti, Lawrence 1919(?)-
Fermor, Patrick Leigh
  See Leigh Fermor, Patrick
Feynman, Richard Phillips 1918-
  1988
Fiedler, Leslie A. 1917-
Filippo, Eduardo de
  See de Filippo, Eduardo
Fitzgerald, F. Scott 1896-1940
Flanagan, Thomas 1923-
Fleming, Ian 1908-1964
Fo, Dario 1926-
Follett, Ken 1949-
Ford, Ford Madox 1873-1939

Fornes, Maria Irene 1930-
Forster, E. M. 1879-1970
Forsyth, Frederick 1938-
Fossey, Dian 1932-1985
Foucault, Michel 1926-1984
Fowles, John 1926-
Fox, Paula 1923-
Frame, Janet
  See Clutha, Janet Paterson
  Frame
France, Anatole
  See Thibault, Jacques Anatole
  Francois
Francis, Dick 1920-
Frank, Anne 1929-1945
Fraser, Antonia 1932-
Frayn, Michael 1933-
French, Marilyn 1929-
Freud, Anna 1895-1982
Freud, Sigmund 1856-1939
Friday, Nancy 1937-
Friedan, Betty 1921-
Friedman, Milton 1912-
Friel, Brian 1929-
Frisch, Max 1911-
Fromm, Erich 1900-1980
Frost, Robert 1874-1963
Fry, Christopher 1907-
Frye, Northrop 1912-
Fuentes, Carlos 1928-
Fugard, Athol 1932-
Fuller, Buckminster
  See Fuller, R. Buckminster
Fuller, Charles 1939-
Fuller, R. Buckminster 1895-1983
Fussell, Paul 1924-
Gaddis, William 1922-
Gaines, Ernest J. 1933-
Galbraith, John Kenneth 1908-
Gallant, Mavis 1922-
Gallegos, Romulo 1884-1969
Gandhi, Mahatma
  See Gandhi, Mohandas Karam-
  chand
Gandhi, Mohandas Karamchand
  1869-1948
Garcia Lorca, Federico 1898-1936
Garcia Marquez, Gabriel 1928-
Gardam, Jane 1928-

Gardner, Erle Stanley 1889-1970
Gardner, John 1926-
Gardner, John, Jr. 1933-1982
Garner, Alan 1934-
Gascoyne, David 1916-
Gass, William H. 1924-
Gasset, Jose Ortega y
  See Ortega y Gasset, Jose
Geisel, Theodor Seuss 1904-
Genet, Jean 1910-1986
Gide, Andre 1869-1951
Gilbert, Sandra M. 1936-
Gilchrist, Ellen 1935-
Gill, Brendan 1914-
Ginsberg, Allen 1926-
Ginzburg, Natalia 1916-
Giono, Jean 1895-1970
Giovanni, Nikki 1943-
Godoy Alcayaga, Lucila 1889-1957
Godwin, Gail 1937-
Golding, William 1911-
Goodall, Jane 1934-
Goodman, Paul 1911-1972
Gorbachev, Mikhail 1931-
Gordimer, Nadine 1923-
Gordon, Caroline 1895-1981
Gordon, Mary 1949-
Gordone, Charles 1925-
Gould, Lois
Gould, Stephen Jay 1941-
Gouldner, Alvin W. 1920-1980
Goytisolo, Juan 1931-
Grass, Guenter 1927-
Grau, Shirley Ann 1929-
Graves, Robert 1895-1985
Gray, Alasdair 1934-
Gray, Francine du Plessix 1930-
Gray, Simon 1936-
Greeley, Andrew M. 1928-
Green, Julien 1900-
Greene, Graham 1904-
Greer, Germaine 1939-
Grey, Zane 1872-1939
Grieve, C. M. 1892-1978
Grigson, Geoffrey 1905-1985
Grimes, Martha
Grizzard, Lewis 1946-
Grossman, Vasily 1905-1964
Guare, John 1938-

VOLUME 3: L-Q

Lagerkvist, Paer 1891-1974
La Guma, Alex 1925-1985
Laing, R. D. 1927-1989
Lamming, George 1927-
L'Amour, Louis 1908-1988
Langer, Susanne K. 1895-1985
Lardner, Ring
  See Lardner, Ring W.
Lardner, Ring W. 1885-1933
Larkin, Philip 1922-1985
Lasch, Christopher 1932-
Laurence, Margaret 1926-1987
Lavin, Mary 1912-
Lawrence, D. H. 1885-1930
Laye, Camara 1928-1980
Layton, Irving 1912-
Leakey, Louis S. B. 1903-1972
Leary, Timothy 1920-
Leavis, F. R. 1895-1978
Lebowitz, Fran 1951(?)-
le Carre, John
  See Cornwell, David
Lee, Harper 1926-
Lee, Laurie 1914-
Leger, Alexis Saint-Leger 1887-1975
Le Guin, Ursula K. 1929-
Leiber, Fritz 1910-
Leigh Fermor, Patrick 1915-
Lem, Stanislaw 1921-
L'Engle, Madeleine 1918-
Leonard, Elmore 1925-
Leonov, Leonid 1899-
Lessing, Doris 1919-
Levertov, Denise 1923-
Levi, Primo 1919-1987
Levin, Ira 1929-
Levi-Strauss, Claude 1908-
Lewis, C. S. 1898-1963
Lewis, Norman 1918-
Lewis, Sinclair 1885-1951
Lindbergh, Anne Morrow 1906-
Lippmann, Walter 1889-1974
Little, Malcolm 1925-1965
Lively, Penelope 1933-
Livesay, Dorothy 1909-
Llosa, Mario Vargas
  See Vargas Llosa, Mario
Lodge, David 1935-
London, Jack
  See London, John Griffith
London, John Griffith 1876-1916
Lopez, Barry Holstun 1945-
Lorca, Federico Garcia
  See Garcia Lorca, Federico
Lorde, Audre 1934-
Lorenz, Konrad Zacharias 1903-
Lovecraft, H. P. 1890-1937
Lovelace, Earl 1935-

Lovesey, Peter 1936-
Lowell, Robert 1917-1977
Lowry, Malcolm 1909-1957
Luce, Henry R. 1898-1967
Ludlum, Robert 1927-
Lukacs, George
  See Lukacs, Gyorgy
Lukacs, Gyorgy 1885-1971
Lukas, J. Anthony 1933-
Luria, Alexander R. 1902-1977
Lurie, Alison 1926-
MacBeth, George 1932-
MacDiarmid, Hugh
  See Grieve, C. M.
MacDonald, John D. 1916-1986
Macdonald, Ross
  See Millar, Kenneth
MacInnes, Colin 1914-1976
MacInnes, Helen 1907-1985
MacLean, Alistair 1922(?)-1987
MacLeish, Archibald 1892-1982
MacLennan, Hugh 1907-
MacNeice, Louis 1907-1963
Madden, David 1933-
Mahfouz, Naguib 1911(?)-
Mahfuz, Najib
  See Mahfouz, Naguib
Mailer, Norman 1923-
Mais, Roger 1905-1955
Malamud, Bernard 1914-1986
Malcolm X
  See Little, Malcolm
Malraux, Andre 1901-1976
Mamet, David 1947-
Manchester, William 1922-
Mann, Thomas 1875-1955
Manning, Olivia 1915-1980
Mao Tse-tung 1893-1976
Marcel, Gabriel Honore 1889-1973
Marsh, Ngaio 1899-1982
Marshall, Paule 1929-
Martin, Steve 1945-
Masefield, John 1878-1967
Maslow, Abraham H. 1908-1970
Mason, Bobbie Ann 1940-
Masters, Edgar Lee 1868-1950
Matthews, Patricia 1927-
Matthiessen, Peter 1927-
Matute, Ana Maria 1925-
Maugham, W. Somerset
  See Maugham, William Somerset
Maugham, William Somerset 1874-1965
Mauriac, Francois 1885-1970
Maurois, Andre 1885-1967
Maxwell, Gavin 1914-1969
McBain, Ed
  See Hunter, Evan
McCaffrey, Anne 1926-

McCarthy, Mary 1912-1989
McCullers, Carson 1917-1967
McCullough, Colleen 1938(?)-
McEwan, Ian 1948-
McGahern, John 1934-
McGrath, Thomas 1916-
McGuane, Thomas 1939-
McIntyre, Vonda N. 1948-
McKay, Claude
  See McKay, Festus Claudius
McKay, Festus Claudius 1889-1948
McKillip, Patricia A. 1948-
McLuhan, Marshall 1911-1980
McMurtry, Larry 1936-
McPhee, John 1931-
McPherson, James Alan 1943-
McPherson, James M. 1936-
Mead, Margaret 1901-1978
Meaker, Marijane 1927-
Mehta, Ved 1934-
Mencken, H. L. 1880-1956
Menninger, Karl 1893-1990
Mercer, David 1928-1980
Merril, Judith 1923-
Merrill, James 1926-
Merton, Thomas 1915-1968
Merwin, W. S. 1927-
Michaels, Leonard 1933-
Michener, James A. 1907(?)-
Millar, Kenneth 1915-1983
Millay, Edna St. Vincent 1892-1950
Miller, Arthur 1915-
Miller, Henry 1891-1980
Millett, Kate 1934-
Milligan, Spike
  See Milligan, Terence Alan
Milligan, Terence Alan 1918-
Milne, A. A. 1882-1956
Milner, Ron 1938-
Milosz, Czeslaw 1911-
Mishima, Yukio
  See Hiraoka, Kimitake
Mistral, Gabriela
  See Godoy Alcayaga, Lucila
Mitchell, Margaret 1900-1949
Mo, Timothy 1950(?)-
Momaday, N. Scott 1934-
Montague, John 1929-
Montale, Eugenio 1896-1981
Montherlant, Henry de 1896-1972
Moorcock, Michael 1939-
Moore, Brian 1921-
Moore, Marianne 1887-1972
Morante, Elsa 1918-1985
Moravia, Alberto
  See Pincherle, Alberto
Morgan, Robin 1941-
Morris, Desmond 1928-

Morris, James
  See Morris, Jan
Morris, Jan 1926-
Morris, Wright 1910-
Morrison, Toni 1931-
Mortimer, John 1923-
Mowat, Farley 1921-
Mrozek, Slawomir 1930-
Muggeridge, Malcolm 1903-
Mukherjee, Bharati 1940-
Munro, Alice 1931-
Munro, H. H. 1870-1916
Murdoch, Iris 1919-
Nabokov, Vladimir 1899-1977
Naipaul, Shiva 1945-1985
Naipaul, V. S. 1932-
Narayan, R. K. 1906-
Nash, Ogden 1902-1971
Naughton, Bill 1910-
Naylor, Gloria 1950-
Nehru, Jawaharlal 1889-1964
Nelson, Alice Ruth Moore Dunbar
  1875-1935
Nemerov, Howard 1920-
Neruda, Pablo 1904-1973
Newby, P. H. 1918-
Ngugi, James T.
  See Ngugi wa Thiong'o
Ngugi wa Thiong'o 1938-
Nichols, Peter 1927-
Nin, Anais 1903-1977
Niven, Larry
  See Niven, Laurence Van Cott
Niven, Laurence Van Cott 1938-
Nixon, Richard M. 1913-
Norton, Andre 1912-
Nye, Robert 1939-
Oates, Joyce Carol 1938-
O'Brien, Edna 1936-
O'Casey, Sean 1880-1964
O'Cathasaigh, Sean
  See O'Casey, Sean
O'Connor, Flannery 1925-1964
Odets, Clifford 1906-1963
Oe, Kenzaburo 1935-
O'Faolain, Julia 1932-
O'Faolain, Sean 1900-
O'Flaherty, Liam 1896-1984
O'Hara, Frank 1926-1966
O'Hara, John 1905-1970

Okigbo, Christopher 1932-1967
Olsen, Tillie 1913-
Olson, Charles 1910-1970
O'Neill, Eugene 1888-1953
Onetti, Juan Carlos 1909-
Oppenheimer, J. Robert 1904-1967
Ortega y Gasset, Jose 1883-1955
Orton, Joe
  See Orton, John Kingsley
Orton, John Kingsley 1933-1967
Orwell, George
  See Blair, Eric
Osborne, John 1929-
Ousmane, Sembene 1923-
Oz, Amos 1939-
Ozick, Cynthia 1928-
Page, P. K. 1916-
Pagnol, Marcel 1895-1974
Paley, Grace 1922-
Panova, Vera 1905-1973
Pargeter, Edith Mary 1913-
Parker, Dorothy 1893-1967
Parker, Robert B. 1932-
Parra, Nicanor 1914-
Parsons, Talcott 1902-1979
Pasolini, Pier Paolo 1922-1975
Pasternak, Boris 1890-1960
Patchen, Kenneth 1911-1972
Paterson, Katherine 1932-
Paton, Alan 1903-1988
Patterson, Harry 1929-
Pauling, Linus 1901-
Paz, Octavio 1914-
p'Bitek, Okot 1931-1982
Peake, Mervyn 1911-1968
Peale, Norman Vincent 1898-
Pearson, Andrew Russell 1897-
  1969
Pearson, Drew
  See Pearson, Andrew Russell
Pedersen, Knut 1859-1952
Percy, Walker 1916-1990
Perelman, S. J. 1904-1979
Perse, Saint-John
  See Leger, Alexis Saint-Leger
Peters, Ellis
  See Pargeter, Edith Mary
Petry, Ann 1908-
Pevsner, Nikolaus 1902-1983

Phillips, Jayne Anne 1952-
Piaget, Jean 1896-1980
Piercy, Marge 1936-
Pilcher, Rosamunde 1924-
Pincherle, Alberto 1907-
Pinter, Harold 1930-
Pirsig, Robert M. 1928-
Plante, David 1940-
Plath, Sylvia 1932-1963
Plimpton, George 1927-
Plomer, William Charles Franklin
  1903-1973
Plowman, Piers
  See Kavanagh, Patrick
Pohl, Frederik 1919-
Pollitt, Katha 1949-
Popper, Karl R. 1902-
Porter, Katherine Anne 1890-1980
Porter, William Sydney 1862-1910
Potok, Chaim 1929-
Potter, Dennis 1935-
Potter, Stephen 1900-1969
Pound, Ezra 1885-1972
Powell, Anthony 1905-
Powers, J. F. 1917-
Powys, John Cowper 1872-1963
Prevert, Jacques 1900-1977
Prichard, Katharine Susannah
  1883-1969
Priestley, J. B. 1894-1984
Pritchett, V. S. 1900-
Proust, Marcel 1871-1922
Puig, Manuel 1932-1990
Purdy, James 1923-
Puzo, Mario 1920-
Pym, Barbara 1913-1980
Pynchon, Thomas 1937-
Python, Monty
  See Cleese, John
Qian Zhongshu
  See Ch'ien Chung-shu
Quasimodo, Salvatore 1901-1968
Queen, Ellery
  See Dannay, Frederic
  and Sturgeon, Theodore
  and Vance, John Holbrook
Queneau, Raymond 1903-1976
Quiroga, Horacio 1878-1937
Quoirez, Francoise 1935-

VOLUME 4: R-Z

Raine, Kathleen 1908-
Rand, Ayn 1905-1982
Ransom, John Crowe 1888-1974
Rao, Raja 1909-
Rattigan, Terence 1911-1977
Ravitch, Diane 1938-
Reed, Ishmael 1938-
Remarque, Erich Maria 1898-1970

Rendell, Ruth 1930-
Rexroth, Kenneth 1905-1982
Rhys, Jean 1894-1979
Rice, Elmer 1892-1967
Rich, Adrienne 1929-
Richler, Mordecai 1931-
Richter, Conrad 1890-1968
Rilke, Rainer Maria 1875-1926

Ritsos, Giannes
  See Ritsos, Yannis
Ritsos, Yannis 1909-
Robbe-Grillet, Alain 1922-
Robbins, Harold 1916-
Robbins, Thomas Eugene 1936-
Robbins, Tom
  See Robbins, Thomas Eugene

Robinson, Edwin Arlington 1869–
1935
Robinson, Joan 1903–1983
Rodd, Kylie Tennant 1912–1988
Roethke, Theodore 1908–1963
Rogers, Carl R. 1902–1987
Rogers, Rosemary 1932–
Romains, Jules 1885–1972
Rooney, Andrew A. 1919–
Rooney, Andy
  See Rooney, Andrew A.
Rossner, Judith 1935–
Rostand, Edmond 1868–1918
Roth, Henry 1906–
Roth, Philip 1933–
Roy, Gabrielle 1909–1983
Rozewicz, Tadeusz 1921–
Rubens, Bernice 1923–
Rukeyser, Muriel 1913–1980
Rulfo, Juan 1918–1986
Rushdie, Salman 1947–
Russ, Joanna 1937–
Russell, Bertrand 1872–1970
Sabato, Ernesto 1911–
Saberhagen, Fred 1930–
Sacks, Oliver 1933–
Sackville-West, V. 1892–1962
Sagan, Carl 1934–
Sagan, Francoise
  See Quoirez, Francoise
Saint-Exupery, Antoine de 1900–
1944
Saki
  See Munro, H. H.
Salinger, J. D. 1919–
Salisbury, Harrison E. 1908–
Sanchez, Sonia 1934–
Sandburg, Carl 1878–1967
Sanders, Lawrence 1920–
Sandoz, Mari 1896–1966
Sansom, William 1912–1976
Santmyer, Helen Hooven 1895–
1986
Saroyan, William 1908–1981
Sarraute, Nathalie 1900–
Sarton, May 1912–
Sartre, Jean-Paul 1905–1980
Sassoon, Siegfried 1886–1967
Sauser-Hall, Frederic 1887–1961
Sayers, Dorothy L. 1893–1957
Schaeffer, Susan Fromberg 1941–
Schlafly, Phyllis 1924–
Schlesinger, Arthur M., Jr. 1917–
Schmitz, Aron Hector 1861–1928
Schwartz, Delmore 1913–1966
Sciascia, Leonardo 1921–1989
Scott, Paul 1920–1978
Seferiades, Giorgos
  Stylianou 1900–1971
Seferis, George
  See Seferiades, Giorgos
  Stylianou

Segal, Erich 1937–
Seifert, Jaroslav 1901–1986
Selvon, Samuel 1923–
Sendak, Maurice 1928–
Sender, Ramon 1902–1982
Senghor, Leopold Sedar 1906–
Sepheriades, Georgios
  See Seferiades, Giorgos
  Stylianou
Setien, Miguel Delibes
  See Delibes Setien, Miguel
Seuss, Dr.
  See Geisel, Theodor Seuss
Sexton, Anne 1928–1974
Shaffer, Peter 1926–
Shange, Ntozake 1948–
Shapiro, Karl 1913–
Shaw, George Bernard 1856–1950
Shaw, Irwin 1913–1984
Sheed, Wilfrid 1930–
Sheehy, Gail 1936(?)–
Sheen, Fulton J. 1895–1979
Sheldon, Alice Hastings Bradley
  1915–1987
Sheldon, Sidney 1917–
Shepard, Sam 1943–
Shirer, William L. 1904–
Sholokhov, Mikhail 1905–1984
Siddons, Anne Rivers 1936–
Sillanpaa, Frans Eemil 1888–1964
Sillitoe, Alan 1928–
Silone, Ignazio 1900–1978
Silverberg, Robert 1935–
Simak, Clifford D. 1904–1988
Simenon, Georges 1903–1989
Simon, Claude 1913–
Simon, Kate 1912–1990
Simon, Neil 1927–
Simpson, Dorothy 1933–
Simpson, George Gaylord 1902–
1984
Simpson, Harriette
  See Arnow, Harriette Simpson
Simpson, Louis 1923–
Sinclair, Andrew 1935–
Sinclair, Upton 1878–1968
Singer, Isaac Bashevis 1904–
Sitwell, Dame Edith 1887–1964
Skinner, B. F. 1904–1990
Skvorecky, Josef 1924–
Smith, Florence Margaret 1902–
1971
Smith, Stevie
  See Smith, Florence Margaret
Smith, Wilbur 1933–
Snodgrass, William D. 1926–
Snow, C. P. 1905–1980
Solzhenitsyn, Aleksandr I. 1918–
Sontag, Susan 1933–
Soyinka, Wole 1934–
Spark, Muriel 1918–

Spencer, Elizabeth 1921–
Spender, Stephen 1909–
Spillane, Frank Morrison 1918–
Spillane, Mickey
  See Spillane, Frank Morrison
Spock, Benjamin 1903–
Stafford, Jean 1915–1979
Stead, Christina 1902–1983
Steel, Danielle 1947–
Stegner, Wallace 1909–
Stein, Gertrude 1874–1946
Steinbeck, John 1902–1968
Steinem, Gloria 1934–
Steiner, George 1929–
Stevens, Wallace 1879–1955
Stevenson, Anne 1933–
Stewart, J. I. M. 1906–
Stone, Irving 1903–1989
Stone, Robert 1937–
Stoppard, Tom 1937–
Storey, David 1933–
Stow, Randolph 1935–
Straub, Peter 1943–
Sturgeon, Theodore 1918–1985
Styron, William 1925–
Susann, Jacqueline 1921–1974
Suzuki, D. T.
  See Suzuki, Daisetz Teitaro
Suzuki, Daisetz Teitaro 1870–1966
Svevo, Italo
  See Schmitz, Aron Hector
Swenson, May 1919–1989
Symons, Julian 1912–
Tagore, Rabindranath 1861–1941
Talese, Gay 1932–
Tate, Allen 1899–1979
Taylor, A. J. P. 1906–
Taylor, Elizabeth 1912–1975
Taylor, Peter 1917–
Taylor, Telford 1908–
Teller, Edward 1908–
Tennant, Kylie
  See Rodd, Kylie Tennant
Terkel, Louis 1912–
Terkel, Studs
  See Terkel, Louis
Theroux, Paul 1941–
Thibault, Jacques Anatole Francois
  1844–1924
Thomas, Audrey 1935–
Thomas, D. M. 1935–
Thomas, Dylan 1914–1953
Thomas, Joyce Carol 1938–
Thomas, Lewis 1913–
Thomas, R. S. 1913–
Thompson, Hunter S. 1939–
Thurber, James 1894–1961
Tillich, Paul 1886–1965
Tiptree, James, Jr.
  See Sheldon, Alice Hastings
  Bradley

Toffler, Alvin 1928-
Toland, John 1912-
Tolkien, J. R. R. 1892-1973
Toomer, Jean 1894-1967
Torres Bodet, Jaime 1902-1974
Torsvan, Ben Traven
    See Traven, B.
Tournier, Michel 1924-
Townsend, Sue 1946-
Traven, B. ?-1969
Tremblay, Michel 1942-
Trevor, William
    See Cox, William Trevor
Trifonov, Yuri 1925-1981
Trillin, Calvin 1935-
Trilling, Diane 1905-
Trilling, Lionel 1905-1975
Troyat, Henri 1911-
Truman, Margaret 1924-
Tryon, Thomas 1926-
Tsvetaeva, Marina 1892-1941
Tuchman, Barbara W. 1912-1989
Tutuola, Amos 1920-
Tyler, Anne 1941-
Tynan, Kenneth 1927-1980
Uchida, Yoshiko 1921-
Unamuno, Miguel de 1864-1936
Undset, Sigrid 1882-1949
Updike, John 1932-
Uris, Leon 1924-
Valery, Paul 1871-1945
Vallejo, Antonio Buero
    See Buero Vallejo, Antonio
Vance, Jack
    See Vance, John Holbrook
Vance, John Holbrook 1916-
Van Doren, Mark 1894-1972
van Lawick-Goodall, Jane
    See Goodall, Jane
Vargas Llosa, Mario 1936-
Vendler, Helen 1933-
Vidal, Gore 1925-
Vine, Barbara
    See Rendell, Ruth
Voinovich, Vladimir 1932-

von Hayek, Friedrich August
    See Hayek, F. A.
Vonnegut, Kurt, Jr. 1922-
Voznesensky, Andrei 1933-
Wain, John 1925-
Walcott, Derek 1930-
Walker, Alice 1944-
Walker, Margaret 1915-
Wallace, Irving 1916-1990
Wallant, Edward Lewis 1926-1962
Wambaugh, Joseph 1937-
Warner, Sylvia Ashton
    See Ashton-Warner, Sylvia
Warner, Sylvia Townsend 1893-
    1978
Warren, Robert Penn 1905-1989
Waruk, Kona
    See Harris, Wilson
Waterhouse, Keith 1929-
Waugh, Evelyn 1903-1966
Wedgwood, C. V. 1910-
Weinstein, Nathan
    See West, Nathanael
Weldon, Fay 1933(?)-
Wells, H. G. 1866-1946
Welty, Eudora 1909-
Wesker, Arnold 1932-
Wesley, Mary 1912-
West, Jessamyn 1902-1984
West, Morris L. 1916-
West, Nathanael 1903-1940
West, Rebecca 1892-1983
Wharton, Edith 1862-1937
Wheatley, Dennis 1897-1977
White, E. B. 1899-1985
White, Edmund 1940-
White, Patrick 1912-
White, Phyllis Dorothy James 1920-
White, Theodore H. 1915-1986
Wiesel, Elie 1928-
Wilbur, Richard 1921-
Wilder, Thornton 1897-1975
Wilhelm, Kate
    See Wilhelm, Katie Gertrude

Wilhelm, Katie Gertrude 1928-
Will, George F. 1941-
Willard, Nancy 1936-
Williams, Emlyn 1905-1987
Williams, Raymond 1921-1988
Williams, Tennessee 1911-1983
Williams, William Carlos 1883-
    1963
Williamson, Henry 1895-1977
Willingham, Calder 1922-
Wilson, Angus 1913-
Wilson, August 1945-
Wilson, Colin 1931-
Wilson, Edmund 1895-1972
Wilson, Edward O. 1929-
Wilson, Ethel Davis 1888(?)-1980
Wilson, John Burgess 1917-
Wilson, Robert M. 1944-
Winters, Yvor 1900-1968
Wodehouse, P. G. 1881-1975
Wolf, Christa 1929-
Wolfe, Thomas 1900-1938
Wolfe, Thomas Kennerly, Jr. 1931-
Wolfe, Tom
    See Wolfe, Thomas Kennerly, Jr.
Woodiwiss, Kathleen E. 1939-
Woodward, Bob
    See Woodward, Robert Upshur
Woodward, Robert Upshur 1943-
Woolf, Virginia 1882-1941
Wouk, Herman 1915-
Wright, Charles 1935-
Wright, James 1927-1980
Wright, Judith 1915-
Wright, Richard 1908-1960
Yeats, William Butler 1865-1939
Yerby, Frank G. 1916-
Yevtushenko, Yevgeny 1933-
Yezierska, Anzia 1885(?)-1970
Yglesias, Helen 1915-
Yourcenar, Marguerite 1903-1987
Zelazny, Roger 1937-
Zindel, Paul 1936-
Zukofsky, Louis 1904-1978

MAJOR 20th- CENTURY WRITERS

Volume 1: A-D

A

ABE, Kobo 1924-

PERSONAL: Born March 7, 1924, in Tokyo, Japan; son of Asakichi (a doctor) and Yorimi Abe; married Machi Yamada (an artist), March, 1947; children: Neri (daughter). *Education:* Tokyo University, M.D., 1948.

ADDRESSES: Home—1-22-10 Wakaba Cho, Chofu City, Tokyo, Japan.

CAREER: Novelist and playwright. Director and producer of the Kobo Theatre Workshop in Tokyo, Japan, beginning in 1973.

AWARDS, HONORS: Post-war literature prize, 1950; Akutagawa prize, 1951, for *Kabe-S karumashi no hanzai;* Kishida prize for drama, 1958; Yomiuri literature prize, 1962; special jury prize from Cannes Film Festival, 1964, for film "Woman in the Dunes"; Tanizaki prize for drama, 1967.

WRITINGS:

NOVELS IN ENGLISH TRANSLATION

Daiyon Kampyoki, Kodan-sha, 1959, translation by E. Dale Saunders published as *Inter Ice Age Four,* Knopf, 1970.
Suna no onna, Shincho-sha, 1962, translation by Saunders published as *The Woman in the Dunes,* Knopf, 1964, adapted screenplay with Hiroshi Teshigahara published under same title, Phaedra, 1966, 2nd edition, 1971.
Tanin no kao, Kodan-sha, 1964, translation by Saunders published as *The Face of Another,* Knopf, 1966.
Moetsukita chizu, Shincho-sha, 1967, translation by Saunders published as *The Ruined Map,* Knopf, 1969.
Hakootoko, Shincho-sha, 1973, translation published as *The Box Man,* Knopf, 1975.
Mikkai, 1977, translation by Juliet W. Carpenter published as *Secret Rendezvous,* Knopf, 1979.
The Ark Sakura, translated by Carpenter, Knopf, 1988.

OTHER NOVELS

Owarishi michino shirubeni (title means "The Road Sign at the End of the Road"), Shinzenbi-sha, 1948.
Kabe-S karumashi no hanzai (title means "The Crimes of S. Karma"), Getsuyo-syobo, 1951.
Kiga domei (title means "Hunger Union"), Kodan-sha, 1954.
Kemonotachi wa kokyo o mezasu (title means "Animals Are Forwarding to Their Natives"), Kodan-sha, 1957.

Ishi no me (title means "Eyes of Stone"), Shincho-sha, 1960.
Omaenimo tsumi ga aru (title means "You Are Guilty Too"), Gakusyukenkyusha, 1965.
Enomoto Buyo (title means "Enomoto Buyo"), Tyuokaron-sha, 1965.

PLAYS IN ENGLISH TRANSLATION

Tomodachi, Enemoto Takeaki, Kawade-syobo, 1967, translation by Donald Keene published as *Friends,* Grove, 1969.
Bo ni natta otoko, Shincho-sha, 1969, translation by Keene published as *The Man Who Turned into a Stick* (produced in New York City at Playhouse 46, May, 1986), University of Tokyo Press, 1975.

OTHER PLAYS

Seifuku (title means "The Uniform"), Aokisyoten, 1955.
Yurei wa kokoniiru (title means "Here Is a Ghost"), Shincho-sha, 1959.
Abe Kobe gikyoku zenshu (title means "The Collected Plays of Kobo Abe"), Shincho-sha, 1970.
Mihitsu no koi (title means "Willful Negligence"), Shincho-sha, 1971.
Ai no megane wa irogarasu (title means "Love's Spectacles Are Colored Glass"), Shincho-sha, 1973.
Midoriiro no stocking (title means "Green Stocking"), Shincho-sha, 1974.
Ue (title means "The Cry of the Fierce Animals"), Shincho-sha, 1975.

OTHER WORKS

Suichu toshi (short stories; title means "The City in Water"), Togen-sha, 1964.
Yume no tobo (short stories; title means "Runaway in the Dream"), Tokuma-syoten, 1968.
Uchinaro henkyo (essays; title means "Inner Border"), Tyuokoron-sha, 1971.
Abe Kobo zensakuhin (title means "The Collected Works of Kobo Abe"), fifteen volumes, Shincho-sha, 1972-73.
Han gekiteki ningen (collected lectures; title means "Anti-Dramatic Man"), Tyuokoron-sha, 1973.
Hasso no shuhen (lectures; title means "Circumference of Inspiration"), Shincho-sha, 1974.
Warau Tsuki (short stories; title means "The Laughing Moon"), Shincho-sha, 1975.

Ningen sokkuri, Shincho hunko, 1976.

SIDELIGHTS: Kobo Abe's fiction bears little resemblance to the traditional literature of Abe's native country, Japan. With its existential themes and what *Saturday Review* contributor Thomas Fitzsimmons describes as its "bizarre situations loaded with metaphysical overtones," Abe's work has more in common with that of Samuel Beckett and Franz Kafka, to whom he is often compared. His preoccupation with modern man's sense of displacement originated during his childhood. Abe grew up in the ancient Manchurian city of Mukden, which was seized from China by the Japanese in 1931. According to the *Washington Post*'s David Remnick, Abe "was fascinated by the Chinese quality of the town and was appalled by the behavior of the Japanese army during occupation. As a testament to his ambivalence about Japan, he changed his name from Kimfusa to the more Chinese rendering, Kobo. Abe was in high school during the war and though he once said, 'I longed to be a little fascist,' he never accepted the perverse nationalism of his country in the '40s. When he heard of Japan's imminent defeat in late 1944, he was 'overjoyed.' " The author's strong feelings against nationalism remain with him to this day, and he told Remnick, "Place has no role for me. I am rootless." Many critics believe that Abe's alienation from his own country is also the key to his international popularity. As Hisaaki Yamanouchi says in his book *The Search for Authenticity in Modern Japanese Literature,* "It enabled him to create a literary universe which transcends the author's nationality. He is probably the first Japanese writer whose works, having no distinctly Japanese qualities, are of interest to the Western audience because of their universal relevance."

Abe's first novel to be translated into English was *Suna no onna* (*The Woman in the Dunes*). In this story, a schoolteacher and amateur entomologist goes to the country for a weekend of insect-hunting. He stumbles upon a primitive tribe living in sand pits and becomes their prisoner. Escape is his obsession for a time, but when it is finally possible, he has lost the desire to return to his former identity. Critics praise Abe for both his metaphysical insights and his engrossing description of life in the sand pits. "The story can be taken at many levels," reports a *Times Literary Supplement* reviewer. "It is an allegory, it shares elements with *Pincher Martin* and Kafka; . . . and it also has the suspense, the realism, and the obsessive regard for detail of a superb thriller. . . . It is a brilliantly original work, which cannot easily be fitted into any category or given any clear literary ancestors. The claustrophobic horror, the sense of physical degradation and bestiality, are conveyed in a prose as distinct and sharp as the sandgrains which dominate the book." Thomas Lask summarizes, "Mr. Abe put together a tale that combined a Crusoe-like fascination with survival with the larger issues of liberty and obligation."

The central theme of *The Woman in the Dunes*—loss of identity—reoccurs in most of Abe's subsequent novels. *Moetsukita chizu,* translated as *The Ruined Map,* uses the conventions of detective novels as a framework. Flight and pursuit merge as a private investigator gradually takes on the persona of the very man he has been hired to track down. Earl Mine finds *The Ruined Map*'s "combination of the macabre and the realistic" similar to that of *The Woman in the Dunes.* "Although less hallucinatory in its effect, *The Ruined Map* is in the end more terrifying, . . ." finds Miner. "Abe has a remarkable talent for creating fables of contemporary experience that manage to be at once rooted in minute detail and expressive of man's plight; but in none of his previous work have the detail and the larger meaning combined so perfectly. The sheer force of accumulating realities is what drives man to madness, what leads him to abscond from himself since he cannot otherwise abscond from the modern world. It is astonishing how successfully Abe renders this effacing of human consciousness in the very mind that is lost." Shane Stevens also reserves high praise for *The Ruined Map,* calling it in the *New York Times Book Review* "a brilliant display of pyrotechnics, a compelling tour de force that seems to have been built lovingly, word by word, sentence by sentence, by a master jeweler of polished prose."

Although Abe's attitudes and concerns are far from those of a typical Japanese writer, some reviewers point out that the author's work is not completely outside his cultural tradition. *The Face of Another* and *Secret Rendezvous* are both presented in the form of journals and letters, a style that dates back to the tenth century in Japan. Furthermore, points out William Currie in *Approaches to the Modern Japanese Novel,* "Abe shows a meticulous care for concrete detail worthy of the most confirmed naturalist or realist. His precision and concreteness give the impression of reality to the dream or nightmare. In this regard, Abe, who is sometimes considered thoroughly Western in his approach to literature, is solidly in the Japanese tradition with his emphasis on the concrete and the particular."

A *New Republic* contributor refers to another aspect in which Abe's writing differs from most Western literature. "The Japanese seem to embrace the unspeakable openly, as a form of release, accepting the facets of the imagination Americans often skirt—even in the most lurid popular fiction," states the writer in his review of Abe's novel *Mikkai,* translated as *Secret Rendezvous. Secret Rendezvous* relates the story of a man's search for his wife, who has been taken to the hospital although she was not sick. The man discovers that the hospital is run by an "incestuous circle of rapists, voyeurs, 13-year-old nymphomaniacs, testtube babies and centaurs." Abe's graphic descriptions of their activities drew negative reactions from many Western critics. Sidney DeVere Brown declares in *World Literature Today,* "The novel would be pornography but for the sterile laboratory in which the explicit scenes are placed." D. J. Enright protests in the *New York Review of Books:* "The paths whether of pursuit or of flight lead through turds, urine, phlegm, vomit, the stench of dead animals. A master of the seedy, Abe seems ambitious to erect it into a universal law." Concludes the *New Republic* reviewer: "Kobo Abe delights in the excessive and the perverse. With its surrealistic setting, its claustrophobic atmosphere, and its increasingly distressing scenes of sexual decadence and violence, *Secret Rendezvous* disturbs rather than titillates."

Doug Lang defends *Secret Rendezvous,* however. His *Washington Post Book World* review calls the plot incoherent, but continues, "fortunately, the novel does not depend on plot for its momentum. It depends much more on the ever-expanding circles of [the protagonist's] nightmarish experience, as Abe propels his main character to the outer perimeters of his existence, where he is confronted with the terrifying absurdity of his life. . . . The hospital is a metaphor for modern Japanese life. . . . *Secret Rendezvous* is very convincing. There is passion in it and a great deal of very bleak humor. Abe's view of things is not a pretty one, but it is well worth our attention." Howard Hibbitt concludes in *Saturday Review* that Abe is the master of the "philosophical thriller" and summarizes the strengths of his novels: "Brilliant narrative, rich description and invention, [and] vital moral and intellectual concerns."

BIOGRAPHICAL/CRITICAL SOURCES:

BOOKS

Contemporary Literary Criticism, Gale, Volume 8, 1978, Volume 22, 1982, Volume 53, 1989.
Janiera, Armando Martins, *Japanese and Western Literature,* Tuttle, 1970.
Tsurutu, Kinya, editor, *Approaches to the Modern Japanese Novel,* Sophia University, 1976.
Yamanouchi, Hisaaki, *The Search for Authenticity in Modern Japanese Literature,* Cambridge University Press, 1978.

PERIODICALS

Atlantic, October, 1979.
Chicago Tribune Book World, October 7, 1979.
Commonweal, December 21, 1979.
Globe and Mail (Toronto), May 7, 1988.
International Fiction Review, summer, 1979.
Los Angeles Times Book Review, April 17, 1988.
New Republic, September 22, 1979.
New York Review of Books, January 14, 1964, September 27, 1979.
New York Times, September 27, 1966, June 3, 1969, December 31, 1974, May 25, 1986.
New York Times Book Review, September 18, 1966, August 3, 1969, December 8, 1974, September 9, 1979, April, 10, 1988.
New York Times Magazine, November 17, 1974.
Saturday Review, September 5, 1964, September 10, 1966, October 11, 1969, September 26, 1970.
Spectator, March 18, 1972.
Times (London), August 4, 1988.
Times Literary Supplement, March 18, 1965, March 6, 1969, September 3, 1971, March 17, 1972, August 12, 1988.
Tribune Books (Chicago), April 24, 1988.
Washington Post, January 20, 1986.
Washington Post Book World, February 21, 1971, October 28, 1979, March 27, 1988.
World Literature Today, winter, 1981.

*   *   *

ABRAHAMS, Peter (Henry)   1919-

PERSONAL: Born March 19, 1919, at Vrededorp, near Johannesburg, South Africa; son of James Henry and Angelina (DuPlessis) Abrahams; married Dorothy Pennington, 1942 (marriage dissolved, 1948); married Daphne Elizabeth Miller (an artist), June 1, 1948; children: (second marriage) Anne, Aron, Naomi. *Education:* Attended St. Peter's College and Teacher's Training College. *Avocational interests:* Gardening, tennis, walking, conversation, reading, travel.

ADDRESSES: Home—Red Hills, St. Andrew, Jamaica, West Indies. *Agent*—Faber & Faber Ltd., 3 Queen Sq., London WC1N 3AU, England; and 50 Cross St., Winchester, Mass.

CAREER: Began working, as a tinsmith's helper, at the age of nine; attended schools between periods of working at jobs such as kitchen helper, dishwasher, porter, and clerk; failed in his attempt to start a school near Capetown for poor Africans; for a short time worked as an editor in Durban; in 1939, to reach England, he took work as a stoker, and spent two years at sea; correspondent in Kenya and South Africa for the London *Observer* and the *New York Herald Tribune* (New York and Paris), 1952-54; commissioned by British Government in 1955 to write a book on Jamaica; emigrated to Jamaica in 1956; regular radio news commentator in Jamaica, 1957—; editor of the *West Indian Economist,* Jamaica, 1958-62, and radio commentator and controller for the "West Indian News" Program, 1958-62; full-time writer, 1964—. Radio Jamaica chairman, set up a new ownership structure, making major interest groups into shareholders, 1978-80.

MEMBER: International PEN, Society of Authors, Authors League.

WRITINGS:

NOVELS

Song of the City, Dorothy Crisp, 1945.
Mine Boy, Dorothy Crisp, 1946, Knopf, 1955, Collier Books, 1970.
The Path of Thunder, Harper, 1948, Chatham Bookseller, 1975.
Wild Conquest (historical fiction), Harper, 1950, Anchor Books, 1970.
A Wreath for Udomo, Knopf, 1956, Collier Books, 1971.
A Night of Their Own, Knopf, 1965.
This Island Now, Faber, 1966, Knopf, 1967, revised edition, Faber & Faber, 1985.
The View from Coyaba (historical fiction), Faber & Faber, 1985.
Tongues of Fire, Pocket Books, 1985
Hard Rain, Dutton, 1988.

OTHER

A Blackman Speaks of Freedom (poetry), Universal Printing Works (Durban, South Africa), 1941.
Dark Testament (short stories), Allen and Unwin, 1942, Kraus Reprint, 1970.
Return to Goli (autobiography), Faber & Faber, 1953.
Tell Freedom (autobiography), Knopf, 1954, published as *Tell Freedom: Memories of Africa,* Knopf, 1969, abridged edition, Macmillan, 1970.
Jamaica: An Island Mosaic (travel), H.M.S.O., 1957.
(And editor) *Souvenir Pictorial Review of the West Indies Federation, 1947-57,* Edna Manley (Kingston, Jamaica), c. 1958.
(With the staff of *Holiday* magazine and others) *The World of Mankind,* Golden Press, 1962.
(With others) *History of the Pan-African Congress,* Hammersmith Bookshop, 1963.

Contributor to *Modern African Prose,* edited by Richard Rive and to *Schwarze Ballade,* edited by Janheinz Jahn. Also author of radio scripts for British Broadcasting Corp. during the 1950s. Contributor to *Holiday* and *Cape Standard.*

ADAPTATIONS: Abrahams' novel *Mine Boy* was adapted as a play; the novel *Path of Thunder* was made into a movie and a ballet in the Soviet Union.

SIDELIGHTS: Peter Abrahams, the son of an Ethiopian father and a mother of mixed French and African ancestry, published his first book at a time when nearly all the novelists in South Africa were white. Abrahams himself was considered Colored, a legal designation referring to the descendents from blacks and early white settlers. The Colored people had traditionally remained aloof from blacks, but Abrahams took a unique step by siding with black South Africans. Abrahams also stood apart by being one of South Africa's first non-whites to make a living as a writer. And whether using fiction or autobiography, his focus has remained on the non-whites' struggle for respect and political power. In the book *Peter Abrahams,* Michael Wade writes that "Peter Abrahams is a novelist of ideas. He writes about the machinery of politics and power, but he uses his considerable grasp of this area of activity to serve his central interest, which is the problem of individual freedom in contemporary affairs."

Abrahams grew up in the slums of Johannesburg, where illiteracy was common. He didn't learn to read until he was nine years old, but thereafter immersed himself in books. He sought out British classics, including Shakespeare, and found works by black American authors in the local library. At the age of eleven, he started writing short stories. Abrahams left school early and tried to support himself as a journalist, but jobs were hard to find for a non-white; almost every door seemed closed to him. While he considered himself a Marxist, editors sharing his political beliefs found him too restrained, while black editors thought him too left-wing to hire for black newspapers. At twenty, Abrahams decided he had to leave South Africa. In his autobiographical *Return to Goli,* he explains, "I had to escape or slip into that negative destructiveness that is the offspring of bitterness and frustration." He worked his way to England as a ship's stoker, later moving to France, and then to Jamaica, which became his permanent home. After emigrating, he only returned to South Africa as a visitor.

While Abrahams has always felt strongly about the problems of non-whites in Africa, when writing his early works he restrained his anger toward the government. In *Return to Goli,* he explains that he had "purged himself of hatred," since "art and beauty come of love, not hate." Believing that love was necessary to overcome racial prejudice, Abrahams frequently incorporated mixed-race love affairs in his early novels. These relationships and their resulting children represented a new order, where the individual would not be judged by his color. In *An African Treasury,* Abrahams claims that this perception comes from tribal Africa, where "the attitude to colour is healthy and normal. Colour does not matter. Colour is an act of God that neither confers privileges nor imposes handicaps on a man. . . . What does matter to the tribal African, what is important, is the complex pattern of his position within his own group and his relations with the other members of the group. . . . The important things in his life are anything but race and colour until they are forced on him."

And yet at the same time, Abrahams felt that the great influence of African tribalism on contemporary blacks was a handicap. He embraced Western culture, because, as he wrote in an issue of *International Affairs,* "The true motive forces of Western culture are to be found in the first place in the teachings of the Christ who taught a new concept of men's relations with their God and with each other, a concept that cuts across tribal gods and tribal loyalties and embraces all men in all lands offering them a common brotherhood." In his novel, *A Night of Their Own,* Abrahams emphasizes the common goals of South African Indians and blacks. Both groups work together to change their tyrannical government. While the setting is fictional, Abrahams tied it to contemporary issues by dedicating the book to imprisoned South African activists Walter Sisulu and Nelson Mandela.

Although critics praise Abrahams' handling of political issues, they often fault his characterization. In the *New York Times Book Review,* Martin Levin says, "What is rich in this novel is the complexity of its political climate," but adds that "what snarls matters is the author's tendency to spell out his characters' thinking." In *The Writing of Peter Abrahams,* Kolawole Ogungbesan voices a similar concern: "The tone of [*A Night of Their Own*] is uncompromisingly noble and determinedly serious, making the characters' gestures as stagey as their dialogues. But the cumulative effect is powerful."

In *This Island Now,* Abrahams turns from his early call for a pluralistic society to insisting that blacks first establish their own identity, socially and politically, as free men. He also stops looking to Western civilization for solutions. The plot concerns a left-wing black leader who rises to power on a fictional island. But according to Ogungbesan "There is no doubt that the physical terrain of *This Island Now* is largely that of Jamaica as described in [Abrahams'] essay, *The Real Jamaica,* . . . [with] the political terrain of Haiti." *New York Times Book Review* contributor Peter Buitenhuis comments, "As an analysis of this kind of political process, [*This Island Now*] throws light on the motivations of black leaders who have risen to power in recent years in the Caribbean and elsewhere. Unfortunately [Abrahams'] attempt to make this material into a novel has not been too successful. He has tried to embody each interest—political, journalistic, financial, etc.—in a different character, and as a result, the book is overpopulated and over-schematic." But Ogungbesan feels the book's strengths and weaknesses are inseparable, and that it must be regarded as a purely political work. He remarks, "The book is a serious political novel precisely because it avoids the easy banalities that its theme . . . might provoke. . . . Abrahams is so preoccupied with the political conflict that everything else recedes to the background."

The View from Coyaba is the work that reflects Abrahams' thorough disenchantment with what he calls "destructive Westernism." Some critics, however, find Abrahams' work closer to a tract or treatise than a novel. While *Times Literary Supplement* contributor David Wright considers the book "highminded, sincere, committed," he thinks that "as a philosophic and humane survey of the history of black emancipation since the British abolition of slavery, his book may be recommended; as a novel, not." Judith Wilson, writing in the *New York Times Book Review,* agrees in finding *The View from Coyaba* "unmistakably didactic fiction." However, she finds that "the originality of Mr. Abrahams' message, its global sweep and political urgency exert their own force. . . . Peter Abrahams challenges us to rethink a large chunk of modern history and to question many of our current ideological assumptions." But Andrew Salkey in *World Literature Today* never questions whether the work is a true novel, as Abrahams has produced, he states, "the most dramatically resonant writing I have read in many years. . . . It is not only a composite novelistic picture, but also a reverberating metaphor."

While Abrahams' books may not point to any definite means of eliminating racism, they contain hope that conditions will improve. Ogungbesan affirms, "Himself such an incurable optimist, all his books are open to the future, based on his belief that change is inevitable, a natural process. This is why the image of the day assumes such symbolic significance in his novels. The implication is that although the black people in South Africa are passing through a long night, their ordeal will not last for ever: after the night inevitably comes the dawn. Abrahams thinks that it will be a glorious dawn if the whites and the blacks can cooperate peacefully to work towards that day."

BIOGRAPHICAL/CRITICAL SOURCES:

BOOKS

Abrahams, Peter, *Return to Goli,* Faber, 1953.
Barnett, Ursula A., *A Vision of Order: A Study of Black South African Literature in English (1914-1980),* University of Massachusetts Press, 1983.
Contemporary Literary Criticism, Volume 4, Gale, 1975.
Hughes, Langston, editor, *An African Treasury,* Gollancz, 1961.
Lindfors, Bernth, *Early Nigerian Literature,* Africana Publishing, 1982.

Ogungbesan, Kolawole, *The Writing of Peter Abrahams,* Africana Publishing, 1979.

Tucker, Martin, *Africa in Modern Literature: A Survey of Contemporary Writing in English,* Ungar, 1967.

Wade, Michael, *Peter Abrahams,* Evans Brothers, 1971.

PERIODICALS

Critique, Volume XI, number 1, 1968.

Los Angeles Times Book Review, July 14, 1985.

New Statesman, February 22, 1985.

New Yorker, September 25, 1965.

New York Times Book Review, April 11, 1965, September 24, 1967, April 2, 1972, May 26, 1985.

Observer, February 17, 1985.

Times Literary Supplement, March 25, 1965, October 20, 1966, March 22, 1985.

World Literature Today, fall, 1985.

* * *

ACHEBE, (Albert) Chinua(lumogu) 1930-

PERSONAL: Born November 16, 1930, in Ogidi, Nigeria; son of Isaiah Okafo (a Christian churchman) and Janet N. (Iloegbunam) Achebe; married Christie Chinwe Okoli, September 10, 1961; children: Chinelo (daughter), Ikechukwu (son), Chidi (son), Nwando (daughter). *Education:* Attended Government College, Umuahia, 1944-47; attended University College, Ibadan, 1948-53; London University, B.A., 1953; studied broadcasting at the British Broadcasting Corp., London, 1956.

ADDRESSES: Home—33 Umunkanka St., Nsukka, Anambra State, Nigeria. *Office*—Institute of African Studies, University of Nigeria, Nsukka, Anambra State, Nigeria; and University of Massachusetts, Amherst, Mass. 01003.

CAREER: Writer. Nigerian Broadcasting Corp., Lagos, Nigeria, talks producer, 1954-57, controller of Eastern Region in Enugu, 1958-61, founder, and director of Voice of Nigeria, 1961-66; University of Nigeria, Nsukka, senior research fellow, 1967-72, professor of English, 1976-81, professor emeritus, 1985—; Anambra State University of Technology, Enugu, pro-chancellor and chairman of council, 1986—; University of Massachusetts—Amherst, professor, 1987-88. Served on diplomatic missions for Biafra during the Nigerian Civil War, 1967-69. Visiting professor of English at University of Massachusetts—Amherst, 1972-75, and University of Connecticut, 1975-76. Lecturer at University of California, Los Angeles, and at universities in Nigeria and the United States; speaker at events in numerous countries throughout the world. Chairman, Citadel Books Ltd., Enugu, Nigeria, 1967; director, Heinemann Educational Books Ltd., Ibadan, Nigeria, 1970—; director, Nwamife Publishers Ltd., Enugu, Nigeria, 1970—. Founder, and publisher, *Uwa Ndi Igbo: A Bilingual Journal of Igbo Life and Arts,* 1984—. Governor, Newsconcern International Foundation, 1983. Member, University of Lagos Council, 1966, East Central State Library Board, 1971-72, Anambra State Arts Council, 1977-79, and National Festival Committee, 1983; director, Okike Arts Centre, Nsukka, 1984—. Deputy national president of People's Redemption Party, 1983; president of town union, Ogidi, Nigeria, 1986—.

MEMBER: International Social Prospects Academy (Geneva), Writers and Scholars International (London), Writers and Scholars Educational Trust (London), Commonwealth Arts Organization (member of executive committee, 1981—), Association of Nigerian Authors (founder; president, 1981-86), Ghana

Association of Writers (fellow), Royal Society of Literature (London), Modern Language Association of America (honorary fellow), American Academy and Institute of Arts and Letters (honorary member).

AWARDS, HONORS: Margaret Wrong Memorial Prize, 1959, for *Things Fall Apart;* Rockefeller travel fellowship to East and Central Africa, 1960; Nigerian National Trophy, 1961, for *No Longer at Ease;* UNESCO fellowship for creative artists for travel to United States and Brazil, 1963; Jock Campbell/*New Statesman* Award, 1965, for *Arrow of God;* D.Litt., Dartmouth College, 1972, University of Southampton, 1975, University of Ife, 1978, University of Nigeria, Nsukka, 1981, University of Kent, 1982, Mount Allison University, 1984, University of Guelph, 1984, and Franklin Pierce College, 1985; Commonwealth Poetry Prize, 1972, for *Beware, Soul-Brother, and Other Poems;* D.Univ., University of Stirling, 1975; Neil Gunn international fellow, Scottish Arts Council, 1975; Lotus Award for Afro-Asian Writers, 1975; LL.D., University of Prince Edward Island, 1976; D.H.L., University of Massachusetts—Amherst, 1977; Nigerian National Merit Award, 1979; named to the Order of the Federal Republic of Nigeria, 1979; Commonwealth Foundation senior visiting practitioner award, 1984; *A Man of the People* was cited in Anthony Burgess's 1984 book *Ninety-nine Novels: The Best in England since 1939;* Booker Prize nomination, 1987, for *Anthills of the Savannah.*

WRITINGS:

Things Fall Apart (novel), Heinemann, 1958, McDowell Obolensky, 1959, reprinted, Fawcett, 1988.

No Longer at Ease (novel), Heinemann, 1960, Obolensky, 1961, 2nd edition, Fawcett, 1988.

The Sacrificial Egg, and Other Stories, Etudo (Onitsha, Nigeria), 1962.

Arrow of God (novel), Heinemann, 1964, John Day, 1967.

A Man of the People (novel), John Day, 1966, published with an introduction by K. W. J. Post, Doubleday, 1967.

Chike and the River (juvenile), Cambridge University Press, 1966.

Beware, Soul-Brother, and Other Poems, Nwankwo-Ifejika (Enugu, Nigeria), 1971, Doubleday, 1972, revised edition, Heinemann, 1972.

(With John Iroaganachi) *How the Leopard Got His Claws* (juvenile), Nwankwo-Ifejika, 1972, (bound with *Lament of the Deer,* by Christopher Okigbo), Third Press, 1973.

Girls at War (short stories), Heinemann, 1973, reprinted, Fawcett, 1988.

Christmas in Biafra, and Other Poems, Doubleday, 1973.

Morning Yet on Creation Day (essays), Doubleday, 1975.

The Flute (juvenile), Fourth Dimension Publishers (Enugu), 1978.

The Drum (juvenile), Fourth Dimension Publishers, 1978.

(Editor with Dubem Okafor) *Don't Let Him Die: An Anthology of Memorial Poems for Christopher Okigbo,* Fourth Dimension Publishers, 1978.

(Co-editor) *Aka Weta: An Anthology of Igbo Poetry,* Okike (Nsukka, Nigeria), 1982.

The Trouble with Nigeria (essays), Fourth Dimension Publishers, 1983, Heinemann, 1984.

(Editor with C. L. Innes) *African Short Stories,* Heinemann, 1984.

Anthills of the Savannah (novel), Anchor Books, 1988.

Hopes and Impediments (essays), Heinemann, 1988.

CONTRIBUTOR

Ellis Ayitey Komey and Ezekiel Mphahlele, editors, *Modern African Stories,* Faber, 1964.

Neville Denny, compiler, *Pan African Stories,* Nelson, 1966.

Paul Edwards, compiler, *Through African Eyes,* two volumes, Cambridge University Press, 1966.

Mphahlele, editor, *African Writing Today,* Penguin Books (Baltimore), 1967.

Barbara Nolen, editor, *Africa and Its People: Firsthand Accounts from Contemporary Africa,* Dutton, 1967.

Ime Ikiddeh, compiler, *Drum Beats: An Anthology of African Writing,* E. J. Arnold, 1968.

Ulli Beier, editor, *Political Spider: An Anthology of Stories from "Black Orpheus,"* Africana Publishing, 1969.

John P. Berry, editor, *Africa Speaks: A Prose Anthology with Comprehension and Summary Passages,* Evans, 1970.

Joseph Conrad, Heart of Darkness, edited by Robert Kimbrough, 3rd edition, Norton, 1987.

OTHER

Founding editor, "African Writers Series," Heinemann, 1962-72. Editor, *Okike: A Nigerian Journal of New Writing,* 1971—; editor, *Nsukkascope,* a campus magazine. *Things Fall Apart* has been translated into forty-five languages.

SIDELIGHTS: Since the 1950s, Nigeria has witnessed "the flourishing of a new literature which has drawn sustenance both from traditional oral literature and from the present and rapidly changing society," writes Margaret Laurence in her book *Long Drums and Cannons: Nigerian Dramatists and Novelists.* Thirty years ago, Chinua Achebe was among the founders of this new literature and over the years many critics have come to consider him the finest of the Nigerian novelists. His achievement has not been limited to his native country or continent, however. As Laurence maintains in her 1968 study of his novels, "Chinua Achebe's careful and confident craftsmanship, his firm grasp of his material and his ability to create memorable and living characters place him among the best novelists now writing in any country in the English language."

Unlike some African writers struggling for acceptance among contemporary English-language novelists, Achebe has been able to avoid imitating the trends in English literature. Rejecting the European notion "that art should be accountable to no one, and [needs] to justify itself to nobody," as he puts it in his book of essays, *Morning Yet on Creation Day,* Achebe has embraced instead the idea at the heart of the African oral tradition: that "art is, and always was, at the service of man. Our ancestors created their myths and legends and told their stories for a human purpose." For this reason, Achebe believes that "any good story, any good novel, should have a message, should have a purpose."

Achebe's feel for the African context has influenced his aesthetic of the novel as well as the technical aspects of his works. As Bruce King comments in *Introduction to Nigerian Literature:* "Achebe was the first Nigerian writer to successfully transmute the conventions of the novel, a European art form, into African literature." In an Achebe novel, King notes, "European character study is subordinated to the portrayal of communal life; European economy of form is replaced by an aesthetic appropriate to the rhythms of traditional tribal life." Kofi Awoonor writes in *The Breast of the Earth* that in wrapping this borrowed literary form in African garb "he created a new novel that possesses its own autonomy and transcends the limits set by both his African and European teachers."

On the level of ideas, Achebe's "prose writing reflects three essential and related concerns," observes G. D. Killam in his book *The Novels of Chinua Achebe,* "first, with the legacy of colonialism at both the individual and societal level; secondly, with the *fact* of English as a language of national and international exchange; thirdly, with the obligations and responsibilities of the writer both to the society in which he lives and to his art." Over the past century, Africa has been caught in a war for its identity between the forces of tradition, colonialism, and independence. This war has prevented many nations from raising themselves above political and social chaos to achieve true independence. "Most of the problems we see in our politics derive from the moment when we lost our initiative to other people, to colonizers," Achebe observes in his book of essays. He goes on to explain: "What I think is the basic problem of a new African country like Nigeria is really what you might call a 'crisis in the soul.' We have been subjected—we have subjected ourselves too—to this period during which we have accepted everything alien as good and practically everything local or native as inferior."

In order to reestablish the virtues of precolonial Nigeria, chronicle the impact of colonialism on native cultures, expose present day corruption, and communicate these to his fellow countrymen and to those outside his country, Achebe must make use of English, the language of colonialism. The ways in which he transforms language to achieve his particular ends distinguishes his writing from the writing of other English-language novelists. To convey the flavor of traditional Nigeria, Achebe translates Ibo proverbs into English and weaves them into his stories. "Among the Ibo the art of conversation is regarded very highly," he writes in his novel *Things Fall Apart,* "and proverbs are the palm-oil with which words are eaten." "Proverbs are cherished by Achebe's people as tribal heirlooms, the treasure boxes of their cultural heritage," explains Adrian A. Roscoe in his book *Mother Is Gold: A Study of West African Literature.* "Through them traditions are received and handed on; and when they disappear or fall into disuse . . . it is a sign that a particular tradition, or indeed a whole way of life, is passing away." Achebe's use of proverbs also has an artistic aim, as Bernth Lindfors suggests in *Folklore in Nigerian Literature.* "Achebe's proverbs can serve as keys to an understanding of his novels," comments the critic, "because he uses them not merely to add touches of local color but to sound and reiterate themes, to sharpen characterization, to clarify conflict, and to focus on the values of the society he is portraying."

To engender an appreciation for African culture in those unfamiliar with it, Achebe alters English to reflect native Nigerian languages in use. "Without seriously distorting the nature of the English," observes Eustace Palmer in *The Growth the African Novel,* "Achebe deliberately introduces the rhythms, speech patterns, idioms and other verbal nuances of Ibo. . . . The effect of this is that while everyone who knows English will be able to understand the work and find few signs of awkwardness, the reader also has a sense, not just of black men using English, but of black Africans speaking and living in a genuinely black African rural situation." In the opinion of *Busara* contributor R. Angogo, this "ability to shape and mould English to suit character and event and yet still give the impression of an African story is one of the greatest of Achebe's achievements." The reason, adds the reviewer, is that "it puts into the reader a kind of emotive effect, an interest, and a thirst which so to say awakens the reader."

Finally, Achebe uses language, which he sees as a writer's best resource, to expose and combat the propaganda generated by African politicians to manipulate their own people. "Language is our tool," he told Anthony Appiah in a *Times Literary Supplement* interview, "and language is the tool of the politicians. We are like two sides in a very hostile game. And I think that the attempt to deceive with words is countered by the efforts of the writer to go behind the words, to show the meaning."

Faced with his people's growing inferiority complex and his leaders' disregard for the truth, the African writer cannot turn his back on his culture, Achebe believes. "A writer has a responsibility to try and stop [these damaging trends] because unless our culture begins to take itself seriously it will never . . . get off the ground." He states his mission in his essay "The Novelist as Teacher": "Here then is an adequate revolution for me to espouse—to help my society regain belief in itself and to put away the complexes of the years of denigration and self-abasement. And it is essentially a question of education, in the best sense of that word. Here, I think, my aims and the deepest aspirations of society meet."

Although he has also written poetry, short stories, and essays—both literary and political—Achebe is best known for his novels: *Things Fall Apart, No Longer at Ease, Arrow of God, A Man of the People,* and *Anthills of the Savannah.* Considering Achebe's novels, Anthony Daniels writes in the *Spectator,* "In spare prose of great elegance, without any technical distraction, he has been able to illuminate two emotionally irreconcilable facets of modern African life: the humiliations visited on Africans by colonialism, and the utter moral worthlessness of what replaced colonial rule." Set in this historical context, Achebe's novels develop the theme of "tradition verses change," and offer, as Palmer observes, "a powerful presentation of the beauty, strength and validity of traditional life and values and the disruptiveness of change." Even so, the author does not appeal for a return to the ways of the past. Palmer notes that "while deploring the imperialists' brutality and condescension, [Achebe] seems to suggest that change is inevitable and wise men . . . reconcile themselves to accommodating change. It is the diehards . . . who resist and are destroyed in the process."

Two of Achebe's novels—*Things Fall Apart* and *Arrow of God*—focus on Nigeria's early experience with colonialism, from first contact with the British to widespread British administration. "With remarkable unity of the word with the deed, the character, the time and the place, Chinua Achebe creates in these two novels a coherent picture of coherence being lost, of the tragic consequences of the African-European collision," offers Robert McDowell in a special issue of *Studies in Black Literature* dedicated to Achebe's work. "There is an artistic unity of all things in these books which is rare anywhere in modern English fiction."

Things Fall Apart, Achebe's first novel, was published in 1958 in the midst of the Nigerian renaissance. Achebe explained his motivation to begin writing at this time in an interview with Lewis Nkosi published in *African Writers Talking: A Collection of Radio Interviews:* "One of the things that set me thinking [about writing] was Joyce Cary's novel set in Nigeria, *Mr Johnson,* which was praised so much, and it was clear to me that this was a most superficial picture . . . not only of the country, but even of the Nigerian character. . . . I thought if this was famous, then perhaps someone ought to try and look at this from the inside." Charles R. Larson, in his book *The Emergence of African Fiction,* details the success of Achebe's effort, both in investing his novel of Africa with an African sensibility and in making this view available to African readers. "In 1964, . . . *Things Fall Apart* became the first novel by an African writer to be included in the required syllabus for African second-

ary school students throughout the English-speaking portions of the continent." Later in that decade, it "became recognized by African and non-African literary critics as the first 'classic' in English from tropical Africa," adds Larson.

The novel tells the story of an Ibo village of the late 1800s and one of its great men, Okonkwo. Although the son of a ne'er-do-well, Okonkwo has achieved much in his life. He is a champion wrestler, a wealthy farmer, a husband to three wives, a title-holder among his people, and a member of the select *egwugwu* whose members impersonate ancestral spirits at tribal rituals. "The most impressive achievement of *Things Fall Apart . . .,*" maintains David Carroll in his book *Chinua Achebe,* "is the vivid picture it provides of Ibo society at the end of the nineteenth century." He explains: "Here is a clan in the full vigor of its traditional way of life, unperplexed by the present and without nostalgia for the past. Through its rituals the life of the community and the life of the individual are merged into significance and order."

This order is disrupted, however, with the appearance of the white man in Africa and with the introduction of his religion. "The conflict in the novel, vested in Okonkwo, derives from the series of crushing blows which are levelled at traditional values by an alien and more powerful culture causing, in the end, the traditional society to fall apart," observes Killam. Okonkwo is unable to adapt to the changes that accompany colonialism. In the end, in frustration, he kills an African employed by the British, and then commits suicide, a sin against the tradition to which he had long clung. The novel thus presents "two main, closely intertwined tragedies," writes Arthur Ravenscroft in his study *Chinua Achebe,* "the personal tragedy of Okonkwo . . . and the public tragedy of the eclipse of one culture by another."

Although the author emphasizes the message in his novels, he still receives praise for his artistic achievement. As Palmer comments, "Chinua Achebe's *Things Fall Apart . . .* demonstrates a mastery of plot and structure, strength of characterization, competence in the manipulation of language and consistency and depth of thematic exploration which is rarely found in a first novel." Achebe also achieves balance in recreating the tragic consequences of the clash of two cultures. Killam notes that "in showing Ibo society before and after the coming of the white man he avoids the temptation to present the past as idealized and the present as ugly and unsatisfactory." And, as Killam concludes, Achebe's "success proceeds from his ability to create a sense of real life and real issues in the book and to see his subject from the point of view which is neither idealistic nor dishonest."

Arrow of God, the second of Achebe's novels of colonialism, takes place in the 1920s after the British have established a presence in Nigeria. The "arrow of god" mentioned in the title is Ezeulu, the chief priest of the god Ulu who is the patron deity of an Ibo village. As chief priest, Ezeulu is responsible for initiating the rituals that structure village life, a position vested with a great deal of power. In fact, the central theme of this novel, as Laurence points out, is power: "Ezeulu's testing of his own power and the power of his god, and his effort to maintain his own and his god's authority in the face of village factions and of the [Christian] mission and the British administration." "This, then, is a political novel in which different systems of power are examined and their dependence upon myth and ritual compared," writes Carroll. "Of necessity it is also a study in the psychology of power."

In Ezeulu, Achebe presents a study of the loss of power. After his village rejects his advice to avoid war with a neighboring village, Ezeulu finds himself at odds with his own people and praised by the British administrators. The British, seeking a candidate to install as village chieftain, make him an offer, which he refuses. Caught in the middle with no allies, Ezeulu slowly loses his grip on reality and slips into senility. "As in Achebe's other novels," observes Gerald Moore in *Seven African Writers*, "it is the strong-willed man of tradition who cannot adapt, and who is crushed by his virtues in the war between the new, more worldly order, and the old, conservative values of an isolated society."

The artistry displayed in *Arrow of God,* Achebe's second portrait of cultures in collision, has drawn a great deal of attention, adding to the esteem in which the writer is held. Charles Miller comments in a *Saturday Review* article that Achebe's "approach to the written word is completely unencumbered with verbiage. He never strives for the exalted phrase, he never once raises his voice; even in the most emotion-charged passages the tone is absolutely unruffled, the control impeccable." Concludes this reviewer, "It is a measure of Achebe's creative gift that he has no need whatever for prose fireworks to light the flame of his intense drama."

Killam recognizes this novel as more than a vehicle for Achebe's commentary on colonialism. He suggests in his study that "Achebe's overall intention is to explore the depths of the human condition and in this other more important sense *Arrow of God* transcends its setting and shows us characters whose values, motivations, actions and qualities are permanent in human kind." Laurence offers this evaluation in her 1968 book: "*Arrow of God,* in which [Achebe] comes into full maturity as a novelist, . . . is probably one of the best novels written anywhere in the past decade."

Achebe's three other novels—*No Longer at Ease, A Man of the People,* and *Anthills of the Savannah*—examine Africa in the era of independence. This is an Africa less and less under direct European administration, yet still deeply affected by it, an Africa struggling to regain its footing in order to stand on its own two feet. Standing in the way of realizing its goal of true independence is the corruption pervasive in modern Africa, an obstacle Achebe scrutinizes in each of these novels.

In *No Longer at Ease,* set in Nigeria just prior to independence, Achebe extends his history of the Okonkwo family. Here the central character is Obi Okonkwo, grandson of the tragic hero of *Things Fall Apart.* This Okonkwo has been raised a Christian and educated at the university in England. Like many of his peers, he has left the bush behind for a position as a civil servant in Lagos, Nigeria's largest city. "*No Longer at Ease* deals with the plight of [this] new generation of Nigerians," observes Palmer, "who, having been exposed to education in the western world and therefore largely cut off from their roots in traditional society, discover, on their return, that the demands of tradition are still strong, and are hopelessly caught in the clash between the old and the new."

Many, faced with this internal conflict, succumb to corruption. Obi is no exception. "The novel opens with Obi on trial for accepting bribes when a civil servant," notes Killam, "and the book takes the form of a long flashback." "In a world which is the result of the intermingling of Europe and Africa . . . Achebe traces the decline of his hero from brilliant student to civil servant convicted of bribery and corruption," writes Carroll. "It reads like a postscript to the earlier novel [*Things Fall Apart*] because the same forces are at work but in a confused, diluted, and blurred form." In *This Africa: Novels by West Africans in English and French,* Judith Illsley Gleason points out how the imagery of each book depicts the changes in the Okonkwo family and the Nigeria they represent. As she points out, "The career of the

grandson Okonkwo ends not with a machet's swing but with a gavel's tap."

Here again in this novel Achebe carefully shapes language, to inform, but also to transport the reader to Africa. "It is through [his characters'] use of language that we are able to enter their world and to share their experiences," writes Shatto Arthur Gakwandi in *The Novel and Contemporary Experience in Africa.* Gakwandi adds: "Through [Achebe's] keen sensitivity to the way people express themselves and his delicate choice of idiom the author illuminates for us the thoughts and attitudes of the whole range of Nigerian social strata." The impact of Achebe's style is such that, as John Coleman observes in the *Spectator,* his "novel moves towards its inevitable catastrophe with classic directness. Nothing is wasted and it is only after the sad, understated close that one realises, once again how much of the Nigerian context has been touched in, from the prejudice and corruption of Lagos to the warm, homiletic simplicities of life."

A Man of the People is "the story of the yokel who visits the sinful city and emerges from it scathed but victorious," writes Martin Tucker in *Africa in Modern Literature,* "while the so-called 'sophisticates' and 'sinners' suffer their just desserts." In this novel, Achebe casts his eye on African politics, taking on, as Moore notes, "the corruption of Nigerians in high places in the central government." The author's eyepiece is the book's narrator Odili, a schoolteacher; the object of his scrutiny is Chief the Honorable M. A. Nanga, Member of Parliament, Odili's former teacher and a popular bush politician who has risen to the post of Minister of Culture in his West African homeland.

At first, Odili is charmed by the politician; but eventually he recognizes the extent of Nanga's abuses and decides to oppose the minister in an election. Odili is beaten, both physically and politically, his appeal to the people heard but ignored. The novel demonstrates, according to Gakwandi, that "the society has been invaded by a wide range of values which have destroyed the traditional balance between the material and the spiritual spheres of life, which has led inevitably to the hypocrisy of double standards." Odili is a victim of these double standards.

Despite his political victory, Nanga, along with the rest of the government, is ousted by a coup. "The novel is a carefully plotted and unified piece of writing," writes Killam. "Achebe achieves balance and proportion in the treatment of his theme of political corruption by evoking both the absurdity of the behavior of the principal characters while at the same time suggesting the serious and destructive consequences of their behavior to the commonwealth." The seriousness of the fictional situation portrayed in *A Man of the People* became real very soon after the novel was first published in 1966 when Nigeria itself was racked by a coup.

Two decades passed between the publications of *A Man of the People* and Achebe's most recent novel, *Anthills of the Savannah.* During this period, the novelist wrote poetry, short stories, and essays. He also became involved in Nigeria's political struggle, a struggle marked by five coups, a civil war, elections marred by violence, and a number of attempts to return to civilian rule. *Anthills of the Savannah* represents Achebe's return to the novel, and as Nadine Gordimer comments in the *New York Times Book Review,* "it is a work in which 22 years of harsh experience, intellectual growth, self-criticism, deepening understanding and mustered discipline of skill open wide a subject to which Mr. Achebe is now magnificently equal." It also represents a return to the themes informing Achebe's earlier novels of independent Africa. "This is a study of how power corrupts itself and by doing so begins to die," writes *Observer* contributor Ben Okri. "It is also about dissent, and love."

Three former schoolmates have risen to positions of power in an imaginary West African nation, Kangan. Ikem is editor of the state-owned newspaper; Chris is the country's minister of information; Sam is a military man become head of state. Sam's quest to have himself voted president for life sends the lives of these three and the lives of all Kangan citizens into turmoil. "In this new novel . . . Chinua Achebe says, with implacable honesty, that Africa itself is to blame," notes Neal Ascherson in the *New York Review of Books,* "and that there is no safety in excuses that place the fault in the colonial past or in the commercial and political manipulations of the First World." Ascherson continues that the novel becomes "a tale about responsibility, and the ways in which men who should know better betray and evade that responsibility."

The turmoil comes to a head in the novel's final pages. All three of the central characters are dead. Ikem, who spoke out against the abuses of the government, is murdered by Sam's secret police. Chris, who flees into the bush to begin a journey of transformation among the people, is shot attempting to stop a rape. Sam is kidnapped and murdered in a coup. "The three murders, senseless as they are, represent the departure of a generation that compromised its own enlightenment for the sake of power," writes Ascherson. And, as Okri observes, "The novel closes with the suggestion that power should reside not within an elite but within the awakened spirit of the people." Here is the hope offered in the novel, hope that is also suggested in its title, as Charles Trueheart relates in the *Washington Post:* "When the brush fires sweep across the savanna, scorching the earth, they leave behind only anthills, and inside the anthills, the surviving memories of the fires and all that came before."

Anthills of the Savannah has been well received and has earned for Achebe a nomination for the Booker Prize. In Larson's estimation, printed in the Chicago *Tribune Books,* "No other novel in many years has bitten to the core, swallowed and regurgitated contemporary Africa's miseries and expectations as profoundly as 'Anthills of the Savannah.'" It has also enhanced Achebe's reputation as an artist; as *New Statesman* contributor Margaret Busby writes, "Reading [this novel] is like watching a master carver skilfully chiselling away from every angle at a solid block of wood: at first there is simply fascination at the sureness with which he works, according to a plan apparent to himself. But the point of all this activity gradually begins to emerge—until at last it is possible to step back and admire the image created."

In his novels, Achebe offers a close and balanced examination of contemporary Africa and the historical forces that have shaped it. "His distinction is to have [looked back] without any trace either of chauvinistic idealism or of neurotic rejection, those twin poles of so much African mythologizing," maintains Moore. "Instead, he has recreated for us a way of life which has almost disappeared, and has done so with understanding, with justice and with realism." And Busby commends the author's achievement in "charting the socio-political development of contemporary Nigeria." However, Achebe's writing reverberates beyond the borders of Nigeria and beyond the arenas of anthropology, sociology, and political science. As literature, it deals with universal qualities. And, as Killam writes in his study: "Achebe's novels offer a vision of life which is essentially tragic, compounded of success and failure, informed by knowledge and understanding, relieved by humour and tempered by sympathy, embued with an awareness of human suffering and the human capacity to endure." Concludes the critic, "Sometimes his char-

acters meet with success, more often with defeat and despair. Through it all the spirit of man and the belief in the possibility of triumph endures."

MEDIA ADAPTATIONS: Things Fall Apart was adapted for the stage and produced by Eldred Fiberesima in Lagos, Nigeria; it was also adapted for radio and produced by the British Broadcasting Corp. in 1983, and for television in English and Igbo and produced by the Nigerian Television Authority in 1985.

AVOCATIONAL INTERESTS: Music.

BIOGRAPHICAL/CRITICAL SOURCES:

BOOKS

Achebe, Chinua, *A Man of the People,* introduction by K. W. J. Post, Doubleday, 1967.
Achebe, Chinua, *Morning Yet on Creation Day,* Doubleday, 1975.
Achebe, Chinua, *Things Fall Apart,* Fawcett, 1977.
Awoonor, Kofi, *The Breast of the Earth,* Doubleday, 1975.
Baldwin, Claudia, *Nigerian Literature: A Bibliography of Criticism,* G. K. Hall, 1980.
Carroll, David, *Chinua Achebe,* Twayne, 1970.
Contemporary Literary Criticism, Gale, Volume 1, 1973, Volume 3, 1975, Volume 5, 1976, Volume 7, 1977, Volume 11, 1979, Volume 26, 1983, Volume 51, 1988.
Duerden, Dennis and Cosmo Pieterse, editors, *African Writers Talking: A Collection of Radio Interviews,* Africana Publishing, 1972.
Gakwandi, Shatto Arthur, *The Novel and Contemporary Experience in Africa,* Africana Publishing, 1977.
Gleason, Judith Illsley, *This Africa: Novels by West Africans in English and French,* Northwestern University Press, 1965.
Killam, G. D., *The Novels of Chinua Achebe,* Africana Publishing, 1969.
King, Bruce, *Introduction to Nigerian Literature,* Africana Publishing, 1972.
King, Bruce, *The New English Literatures: Cultural Nationalism in a Changing World,* Macmillan, 1980.
Larson, Charles R., *The Emergence of African Fiction,* Indiana University Press, 1972.
Laurence, Margaret, *Long Drums and Cannons: Nigerian Dramatists and Novelists,* Praeger, 1968.
Lindfors, Bernth, *Folklore in Nigerian Literature,* Africana Publishing, 1973.
McEwan, Neil, *Africa and the Novel,* Humanities Press, 1983.
Moore, Gerald, *Seven African Writers,* Oxford University Press, 1962.
Njoku, Benedict Chiaka, *The Four Novels of Chinua Achebe: A Critical Study,* Peter Lang, 1984.
Palmer, Eustace, *The Growth of the African Novel,* Heinemann, 1979.
Ravenscroft, Arthur, *Chinua Achebe,* Longmans, Green, for the British Council, 1969.
Roscoe, Adrian A., *Mother Is Gold: A Study of West African Literature,* Cambridge University Press, 1971.
Tucker, Martin, *Africa in Modern Literature,* Ungar, 1967.
Wren, Robert M., *Achebe's World: The Historical and Cultural Context of the Novels,* Three Continents, 1980.

PERIODICALS

Boston Globe, March 9, 1988.
Busara, Volume VII, number 2, 1975.
Commonweal, December 1, 1967.
Economist, October 24, 1987.
English Studies in Africa, September, 1971.

Listener, October 15, 1987.
Lively Arts and Book Review, April 30, 1961.
London Review of Books, August 7, 1986, October 15, 1981.
Los Angeles Times Book Review, February 28, 1988.
Michigan Quarterly Review, fall, 1970.
Nation, October 11, 1965, April 16, 1988.
New Statesman, January 4, 1985, September 25, 1987.
New York Review of Books, March 3, 1988.
New York Times, August 10, 1966, February 16, 1988.
New York Times Book Review, December 17, 1967, May 13, 1973, August 11, 1985, February 21, 1988.
Observer, September 20, 1987.
Saturday Review, January 6, 1968.
Spectator, October 21, 1960, September 26, 1987.
Studies in Black Literature: Special Issue; Chinua Achebe, spring, 1971.
Times Educational Supplement, January 25, 1985.
Times Literary Supplement, February 3, 1966, March 3, 1972, May 4, 1973, February 26, 1982, October 12, 1984, October 9, 1987.
Tribune Books (Chicago), February 21, 1988.
Village Voice, March 15, 1988.
Wall Street Journal, February 23, 1988.
Washington Post, February 16, 1988.
Washington Post Book World, February 7, 1988.
World Literature Today, summer, 1985.
World Literature Written in English, November, 1978.

* * *

ADAMOV, Arthur   1908-1970

PERSONAL: Born August 23, 1908, in Kislovodsk, Russia (now U.S.S.R.); immigrated to Paris, c. 1920; died March 16, 1970, in Paris, France; son of Sourene (an oil-well proprietor) and Helene (Bagatourov) Adamov; married Jacqueline Austrusseau. *Education:* Educated in Switzerland and in Mainz, Germany.

ADDRESSES: Home—52 rue de Seine, Paris 6, France.

CAREER: Author and playwright. Member of Surrealist circles in Paris, France, and editor of avant-garde periodical *Discontinuite.* Also edited *L'Heure Nouvelle* following World War II.

WRITINGS:

PLAYS

La Parodie [and] *L'Invasion* ("L'Invasion" [title means "The Invasion"], produced, 1950; "La Parodie" [title means "The Parody"], produced, 1952), Charlot, 1950.
La Grande et la petite manoeuvre (produced, 1950), [Paris], 1950.
Tous contre tous (title means "All Against All"; produced, 1953), L'Avantscene (Paris), 1952.
Theatre I (contains "La Parodie," "L'Invasion," "La Grande et la petite manoeuvre," "Tous contre tous," and "Le Professeur Taranne" [produced, 1953]), Gallimard, 1953, new edition, 1970.
Theatre II (contains "Le Sens de la marche" [produced, 1953], "Les Retrouvailles," and "Le Ping-pong" [produced, 1955]), Gallimard, 1955.
Paolo Paoli (produced, 1956), Gallimard, 1957.
(With Guy Demoy and Maurice Regnaut) *Theatre de societe* (contains "Intimite," "Je ne suis pas francais," and "La Complainte du ridicule"), Editeurs Francais Reunis, 1958.
Les Ames mortes (based on the poem by Nikolai Gogol; produced, 1963), Gallimard, 1960.
Le Printemps 71 (produced, 1963), Gallimard, 1961.

Theatre III (contains "Paolo Paoli," "La Politique des restes," and "Sainte Europe"), Gallimard, 1966.
Theatre IV (contains "M. le Modere" and "Le Printemps 71"), Gallimard, 1968.
Off Limits (produced, 1969), Gallimard, 1969.
Si l'ete revenait, Gallimard, 1970.

Also author of "Comme nous avons ete," published in *Nouvelle Revue Francaise,* March, 1953, translation by Richard Howard published as "As We Were," in *Evergreen Review,* number 4, 1957; author of radio play "En Fiacre," 1959.

ENGLISH TRANSLATIONS

Ping-pong (produced in New York), translated by Richard Howard, Grove, 1959.
Paolo Paoli, translated by Geoffrey Brereton, J. Calder, 1959.
"Professor Taranne," published in *Four Modern French Comedies,* Capricorn, 1960.
Two Plays (contains "Professor Taranne," translated by Peter Meyer, and "Ping-pong," translated by Derek Prouse), J. Calder, 1962.
Adamov: Collected Plays, Volume I: *Parody; Invasion; All Against All, Professor Taranne,* edited and translated by Meyer and others, Riverrun Press, 1989.

OTHER

(Editor) Claudine Chonez, *Il est temps,* Editions de l'Ilot, 1941.
L'aveu (autobiographical confession), Editions du Sagittaire, 1946 (one section translated by Richard Howard and published as "The Endless Humiliation," in *Evergreen Review,* spring, 1958).
(Adaptor) George Buechner, "La Mort de Danton," produced, 1948.
(Author of preface) August Strindberg, *Inferno,* Editions du Griffon, 1948.
(With Maurice Gravier) *August Strindberg, Dramaturge,* L'Arche, 1955. (Author of introduction) Roger Gilbert-Lecomte, *Testament,* Gallimard, 1955.
(Adaptor) Strindberg, *Le Pelican,* [France], 1956.
(Adaptor) Maxim Gorki, *Les Petits bourgeois* (produced, 1959), Editions de l'Arche, 1958.
(Editor) *La Commune de Paris,* Editions Sociales, 1959.
(With others) *Connaissance de Don Ramon Maria del Valle-Inclan,* Julliard, 1963.
Ici et maintenant, Gallimard, 1964.
L'Homme et l'enfant (autobiographical), Gallimard, 1968.
Je ils, Gallimard, 1969.
(Contributor with others) *Antonin Artaud et le theatre de notre temps,* new edition, Gallimard, 1969.

TRANSLATOR

Carl Jung, *Le Moi et l'inconscient,* Nouvelle Revue Francaise, 1938.
(With Marie Geringer) Rainer Maria Rilke, *Le Livre de la pauvrete et de la mort,* Bonnard (Lausanne), 1941.
(With Marthe Robert) George Buechner, *Theatre Complet,* Editions de l'Arche, 1953.
Kleist, "La Cruche cassee," in *Theatre Populaire,* March-April, 1954.
Fyodor Dostoyevsky, *Crime et Chatiment,* Club Francaise du Livre, 1956. Nikolai Gogol, *Les Aventures de Tchitchikov; ou, Les Ames mortes,* La Guilde du Livre (Lausanne), 1956.
Gogol, *Le Revisor,* Editions de l'Arche, 1958.
Maxim Gorki, *Vassa Geleznova,* Editions de l'Arche, 1958.
Anton Chekhov, *L'Esprit des bois,* Gallimard, 1958.
Gorki, *La Mere,* Club Francais du Livre, 1958.

Chekhov, *Theatre,* Club Francais du Livre, 1958.

August Strindberg, *Le Pere,* Editions de l'Arche, 1958.

Ivan Gontcharov, *Oblomov* (novel), Club Francais du Livre, 1959.

Gogol, *Cinq Recits,* Club des Libraires de France, 1961.

(With Claude Sebisch) Erwin Piscator, *Le Theatre politique,* Editions de l'Arche, 1962.

Gorki, *Theatre Complet,* Volumes I and II (with Genia Cannac and Georges Daniel), Editions de l'Arche, 1963, Volume IV (with Cannac), 1964.

Contributor of articles to *L'Heure Nouvelle, Theatre Populaire,* and *Cahiers de la Compagnie M. Renaud—Jean-Louis Barrault.*

SIDELIGHTS: Arthur Adamov's plays may be divided for convenience of analysis into the absurdist, surrealistic dramas he wrote prior to 1957 and the epic, realistic dramas he wrote after that point. The genesis of the earlier plays, of which "Ping-pong" is the acknowledged masterpiece, was an incident that occurred when he was first reading the works of Swedish modernist writer August Strindberg. Adamov began to see loneliness everywhere and to listen to snatches of conversation between people who passed him on the street. One day he saw a blind beggar ignored by two girls who were singing a peculiar song. He said, "I had closed my eyes, it was wonderful!" This led him to want to portray "on the stage, as crudely and as visibly as possible, the loneliness of man, the absence of communication." He once wrote that "a stage play ought to be the point of intersection between the visible and invisible worlds, or, in other words, the display, the manifestation of the hidden, latent contents that form the shell around the seeds of drama." In 1938 he stated that "the words in our aging vocabularies are like very sick people. Some may be able to survive, others are incurable." He did his best to rectify this situation. Jean Vilar praised him for renouncing "the lace ornaments of dialogue and intrigue, for having given back to the drama its stark purity."

Adamov evolved a theory of the theatre which emphasized human isolation, the impossibility of any real communication or sympathy between people, and the absurdity of death. George Wellwarth wrote that in Adamov's plays, "nothing decisive ever happens, except the inevitable, meaningless and reasonless death at the end. . . . During the play the characters move aimlessly in mutually exclusive spheres running on courses unfathomable to their occupants." David I. Grossvogel noted that each person in the playwright's works "is hardly more than a negative quantity, a victim whose capacity to exist is real only to the extent that the physical instruments of his torture are real and will be used on him: it is only by comparison with these instruments that he is found to have significance greater than that of the rudimentary and static object."

Adamov wrote in "The Endless Humiliation": "I want to make this truth contagious, virulent: every private fault, every individual guilt, whether the guilty person is conscious of it or not, transcends the individual to identify itself with the fault of all men everywhere and forever—the great original prevarication which is named Separation. . . . I do not know what name to give what I am separated from, but I am separated from it. Once it was called God. Now there is no longer any name. . . . When a terrifying vision assails me and I become a prey to fear, I perform a ritual of exorcism to conquer it, and my fear diminishes. But the legions of multiform terrors all derive from a single principle: the fear of death." In *La Parodie,* a character says that everyone is dead. Wallace Fowlie believed this "summarizes two major characteristics of Adamov's world as reflected in his [early] plays: everything moves toward death, and death has no

reason. Adamov seems to be preparing the advent of tragedy and at the same time denying the authenticity or the competence of tragedy. In this sense, his world is a 'parody.' If fate is the same for everyone, then there is no fate." Wellwarth noted that for Adamov, "the climax of a human event must always involve the relentless destruction of the hero." Yet even this is futile, for, said Adamov, "in this life of which the basic circumstances themselves are terrifying, where the same situations fatally recur, all we can do is destroy, and too late at that, what we consider . . . mistakenly . . . to be the real obstacle, but what in fact is merely the last item in a maleficent series."

While the general outlook may remind one of the works of Franz Kafka, Adamov denied that his theatre derived from Kafka or that it strived for metaphysical allusions. Adamov had been accused of unallayed pessimism, but he wrote in the 1940s: "We are accused of pessimism, as though pessimism were but one among a number of possible attitudes, as if man were capable of choosing between two alternatives—optimism and pessimism." He believed, rather, that the crisis of the time was "essentially a religious crisis. It is a matter of life or death. . . . From whatever point he starts, whatever path he follows, modern man comes to the same conclusion: behind its visible appearances, life hides a meaning that is eternally inaccessible to penetration by the spirit that seeks for its discovery, caught in the dilemma of being aware that it is impossible to find it, and yet also impossible to renounce the hopeless quest." Esslin wrote that Adamov believed that this was not, "strictly speaking, a philosophy of the absurd, because it still presupposes the conviction that the world *has* a meaning, although it is of necessity outside the reach of human consciousness."

After the mid-1950s, however, Adamov, in effect, rejected all the plays that could be classified as belonging to the "Theatre of the Absurd." He maintained that "the theatre must show, simultaneously but well-differentiated, both the curable and the incurable aspect of things. The incurable aspect, we all know, is that of the inevitability of death. The curable aspect is the social one." Wellwarth noted that "with this step Adamov leaves the death-oriented hopelessness that is the avant-garde drama's chief philosophical standpoint and returns to a belief in the temporal hopes that exist in the illusion-laden world of social humanity. . . . Adamov has abandoned the deterministic play for a more flexible psychological drama. The characters are no longer helpless automatons but human beings endowed with free will." Esslin wrote that Adamov regarded Bertold Brecht as his mentor, and "puts him next to Shakespeare, Chekhov, and Buechner among the dramatists of world literature he admires most." Esslin continued: "Adamov has become the main spokesman of the committed political theatre in France. At the same time, he is regarded as one of the masters of a noncommitted, anti-political theatre of the soul. Like one of his own characters, he is the embodiment of two conflicting tendencies coexisting within the same person."

Esslin spoke of two Adamovs, "Adamov the dramatist of dream, neurosis, and futility, and Adamov the Brechtian epic realist, [both of which] may not be so far apart as they appear. It is only too easy to understand why Adamov should repudiate his earlier plays today. They are the expression of a past he has outgrown, the fossilized remains of a former self that he is only too happy to have put behind him." Also, Adamov "regards his [early] plays from *La Parodie* to *Les Retrouvailles* as too schematic, crude, and lacking in a proper appreciation of the needs and prospects of remedial revolutionary action in the face of social injustice. Yet these criticisms, even if they were entirely relevant, miss the point—these plays are true and have a powerful impact because they are the genuine expressions of a soul in torment [which was] real when it was felt—and it remains a very profound insight into the workings of the human mind and retains the power of all deeply felt poetic statements. It was, after all, Adamov himself, who pointed out that neurosis sharpens the perceptions and enables the sufferer to look into depths not usually open to the healthy eye. The works inspired by Adamov's neurosis may be more profound than those of an Adamov reconciled to the world, though still determined to change its institutions." Esslin also believed that the more recent Adamov plays combined the elements of the absurdist theatre and the more conventional theatre, and cited as an example the three short pieces he contributed to *Theatre de societe,* two being allegorical and one realistic, and the latter an acknowledged failure.

In the 1940s Adamov turned to Communism. But, wrote Esslin, "He finds in Communism no supernatural, sacred element. Its ideology confines itself to purely human terms, and for him it remains open to question 'whether anything that confines itself to the human sphere could ever attain anything but the subhuman. . . . If we turn to Communism nevertheless, it is merely because one day, when it will seem quite close to the realization of its highest aim—the victory over all the contradictions that impede the exchange of goods among men—it will meet, inevitably, the great "no" of the nature of things, which it thought it could ignore in its struggle.' " Esslin reported that after 1958 and the emergence in France of General Charles de Gaulle, Adamov more actively supported the extreme Left. Yet in 1960, the playwright said he still subscribed to what he had written earlier on this subject.

BIOGRAPHICAL/CRITICAL SOURCES:

BOOKS

Beigbeder, Marc, *Le Theatre en France depuis la liberation,* Bordas, 1959.
Bradby, D., *Adamov,* [London], 1975.
Contemporary Literary Criticism, Gale, Volume 4, 1975, Volume 25, 1983.
Esslin, Martin, *The Theatre of the Absurd,* Doubleday, 1961.
Fowlie, Wallace, *Dionysus in Paris,* Meridian, 1960.
Grossvogel, David I., *The Self-Conscious Stage,* Columbia University Press, 1958.
Lumley, Frederick, *Trends in Twentieth-Century Drama,* Barrie & Rockliff, 1956.
Pronko, L. C., *Avant-Garde: The Experimental Theatre in France,* University of California Press, 1962.
Wellwarth, George, *The Theatre of Protest and Paradox,* New York University Press, 1964.

PERIODICALS

Yale French Studies, winter, 1954-55.

* * *

ADAMS, Alice (Boyd) 1926-

PERSONAL: Born in Fredericksburg, Va., August 14, 1926; daughter of Nicholson (a professor) and Agatha (a writer; maiden name, Boyd); married Mark Linenthal, Jr. (a professor), 1946 (divorced, 1958); children: Peter. *Education:* Radcliffe College, B.A., 1946.

ADDRESSES: Home—2661 Clay St., San Francisco, Calif. 94115. *Agent*—Lynn Nesbit, International Creative Management, 40 West 57th St., New York, N.Y. 10019.

CAREER: Writer. Has held various office jobs, including secretary, clerk, and bookkeeper. Instructor at the University of Cali-

fornia at Davis, 1980, University of California at Berkeley, and Stanford University.

AWARDS, HONORS: O. Henry Awards, Doubleday & Co., 1971-82 and 1984-88, for short stories; National Book Critics Circle Award nomination, 1975, for *Families and Survivors;* National Endowment for the Arts fiction grant, 1976; Guggenheim fellowship, 1978; O. Henry Special Award for Continuing Achievement, 1982.

WRITINGS:

Careless Love, New American Library, 1966 (published in England as *The Fall of Daisy Duke,* Constable, 1967).
Families and Survivors (novel), Knopf, 1975.
Listening to Billie (novel), Knopf, 1978.
Beautiful Girl (short stories), Knopf, 1979.
Rich Rewards (novel), Knopf, 1980.
To See You Again (short stories), Knopf, 1982.
Molly's Dog (short stories), Ewert, 1983.
Superior Women (novel), Knopf, 1984.
Return Trips (short stories), Knopf, 1985.
Second Chances (novel), Knopf, 1988.
After You've Gone (short stories), Knopf, 1989.

Contributor of short stories to anthologies, including *Best American Short Stories,* 1976, and *Prize Stories: The O. Henry Awards,* 1971-82, and 1984-88. Contributor to periodicals, including *New Yorker, Atlantic, Shenandoah, Crosscurrents, Grand Street, Mademoiselle, Virginia Quarterly Review, New York Times Book Review, Vogue, Redbook, McCall's,* and *Paris Review.*

SIDELIGHTS: In many of her short stories and novels, Alice Adams writes about women struggling to find their place in the world. Adams challenges her characters, whether they live alone or with a partner, to establish meaningful lives, working creatively with both life's blessings and its disappointments. Robert Phillips writes in *Commonweal:* "The usual Adams character does not give in to his or her fate, but attempts to shape it, however misguidedly. . . . Women become aware not only of missed opportunities, but also of life's endless possibilities." While men occupy important positions in the female characters' lives, Adams's books tend to focus on the women's own struggles with identity. "The conflict—not the outward conflict between men and women, but the private and inward conflict of individual women—runs through all Adams' work," notes Stephen Goodwin in the *Washington Post Book World.* "Her women value men, but prize their own independence." Adams's women generally find true contentment in work and the freedom to make their own choices. According to William L. Stull in the *Dictionary of Literary Biography Yearbook,* "Each of her novels concerns a woman's search for satisfying work as a means to economic, artistic, and finally political independence."

And yet the experience of romantic love constantly recurs in Adams's work. Beverly Lowry maintains in the *New York Times Book Review* that "nobody writes better about falling in love than Alice Adams. The protagonists of her stories . . . fall with eyes open, knowing full well that the man in question might be inappropriate. . . . Such women think they should know better. They do know better. That is the glory of an Adams heroine, she is that smart and still goes on. 'Ah,' she says to herself, sighing, 'this again: love.' And plunges in." While the romantic pairings may or may not work out, "Adams' women often learn, in the course of her novels, that the stereotyped 'happy ending' is not feasible and that they must focus on work and on developing a healthy respect for themselves," writes Larry T. Blades in *Critique.* "These are perhaps the ultimate rich rewards."

Beautiful Girl was Adams's first published collection of short fiction. Although half of the stories had won the O. Henry Award, the tales did not fully satisfy *New York Times Book Review* critic Katha Pollitt. While praising Adams's gifts as a storyteller, Pollitt laments the ubiquitous presence of one "recognizable type" of heroine in the collection: "I kept waiting for Miss Adams to flash an ironic smile toward these supremely sheltered, idle, unexamined people. . . . She never does." *Hudson Review* contributor Dean Flowers believes that in *Beautiful Girl,* Adams portrays difficult problems with too much ease: "At their best these stories explore complex relationships in a quick, deceptively offhand manner. They tend to begin with a tense problem (a wife dying, a divorce impending, a moment of wrath, an anxious move to a new place) and unravel gradually, without much climax except a muted sense of recovered balance and diminished expectation. . . . One feels neither gladness nor sorrow in such conclusions, but rather an implicit appeal of stylish melancholy." Still, the intensity of her characters' feelings can belie the author's seemingly neat appraisals of their lives. Susan Schindehette comments in her *Saturday Review* appraisal of the stories collected in *Return Trips,* "It is Adams' gift to reveal the tremendous inner workings beneath the apparent tranquility and make characters come to life in her spare, elegant style."

Reviewers frequently praise Adams's concise, understated use of language. "Some writers have such lovely voices they always make you want to hum along. Alice Adams is like that; she is fond of the word 'perfect,' and it suits her," writes Lois Gould in the *New York Times Book Review.* She continues, "For Miss Adams, applying her elegant, rhythmic style to the form, the challenge lies in making it new, fitting it to her own literary place and our time." Adams's sure touch conveys the rough sides of life as well as the tender. Douglas Hill observes in the Toronto *Globe and Mail,* "Adams writes decidedly grown-up fiction, though it's by no means X-rated. She uses language almost surgically, and can be quite candid and direct about matters sexual and vulgar. Her characteristic tone is light, even at times airy. But there's always a hint of darkness underneath; for Adams the course of adult affection and love is always at greatest risk when it seems safest and most placid." Critics also like the compactness of Adams's writing and the careful use of detail. "The typical Alice Adams short story announces itself in the very first sentence as a thing of edgy wit and compressed narrative power," says Pollitt. And Phillips in *Commonweal* notes that Adams "suppresses and condenses, allowing the reader to make vital connections between situation and character."

In *Rich Rewards,* Adams focuses on a middle-aged woman who has spent her life in a series of disappointing and often addictive relationships with men. At the novel's beginning the heroine, Daphne, having recently broken off a relationship with an abusive lover, intends to immerse herself in her work as an interior decorator. But the plot carries her to San Francisco and into a friend's troubled marriage. By the book's conclusion, she finds herself unexpectedly reunited with a lover from her youth. According to Blades, "*Rich Rewards* chronicles the maturation of Daphne from a woman who devotes her life to punishing and humiliating sexual encounters into a woman who can establish a productive love relationship because she has first learned to respect herself." In the *New York Times Book Review,* Anne Tyler says, "This is a marvelously readable book. It's mysterious in the best sense—not a setup, artificial mystery but a real one, in which we wonder along with the heroine just what all the chaotic events are leading up to." *Chicago Tribune Book World* contributor Lynne Sharon Schwartz calls *Rich Rewards* "a stringent story elegantly told, and enhanced by a keen moral judg-

ment. . . . As in her earlier novels, . . . Alice Adams is concerned with the shards of broken families and with the quickly severed ties that spring up in place of families. But in *Rich Rewards* the harshness latent in such tenuous relations is more overt than before. . . . It takes a sort of magician to render hope from the brew of pain, muddle, and anomie that Alice Adams has managed charmingly to concoct: Once again she brings it off with panache."

But some critics have faulted the author's "reward" for Daphne the protagonist and have called the ending of *Rich Rewards* unrealistic compared to the rest of the book. Blades admits that "the novelistic contrivances used to bring the lovers back together also suggest the unrealistic nature of the resolution. There is the sense of enchantment, of a fairy godmother waving her wand and saying, 'Let Daphne and Jean-Paul fall in love again, and let the plot be twisted to accomplish this.'" However, he defends Adams's choice: "Readers who complain about Adams' use of coincidence in *Rich Rewards* have recognized an element conspicuously present in the author's overall purpose. 'This is a novel,' Alice Adams seems to say, 'and since I'm writing it, I can create a happy ending. Real life might end differently.'" Considering Daphne's growth as a character, Tyler writes that the ending fits the story: "If the conclusion seems a bit sudden and easy, lacking the texture of the rest of the story, it is also the 'rich reward' that Daphne deserves. Draw a moral, if you like: Daphne is one of the most admirable female characters in recent fiction."

Adams moved to California in the fifties, and the state and its residents figure prominently in her work. *To See You Again* is a "collection of 19 short stories [that] may surprise readers who have been led to think that all fictional California women are angst-ridden, sex-crazed or mellowed-out," writes Paul Gray in *Time.* Some reviewers have taken issue with the book's even tone. While Benjamin DeMott admires the irony and understatement in the collection, he notes in the *New York Times Book Review:* "Life in this book is indeed lived, . . . in easygoing obedience to the key emotional imperative of the age (Change Your Life). None of Miss Adams's people ever tears a passion to tatters. . . . But these stories do suffer from a lack of tonal variety." Mary Morris, in a *Chicago Tribune Book World* article, says that "[Adams] has spared us the fights, she has spared us the asking of the unaskable, the struggle to love. And in the end she has also spared us what we want most, the drama." Morris claims that "the protagonists' inability to achieve involvement" frustrates the reader. Adams's characters in *To See You Again* "don't reach out, they don't fight back. What they do is leave, remember or fantasize." But the strength of the book, Linda Pastan writes in the *American Book Review,* lies in "the cumulative effect" that makes "the reader feel as though he knows the San Francisco of Alice Adams in the special way one knows a place inhabited by friends."

Superior Women concerns the relationship among four young women during their years at Radcliffe and afterwards. The novel has frequently been compared to Mary McCarthy's *The Group,* which describes the lives of eight women who attended Vassar in the thirties. As in *The Group, Superior Women* takes its characters through graduation and into the outside world, showing how political and social events affect their lives. This technique has met with some criticism. "The effects of viewing a whole age through gauze in this fashion is pretty deadening," claims Michael Wood in the *London Review of Books.* Jonathan Yardley, a *Washington Post Book World* contributor, states: "What we . . . have is a shopping list of public events, causes and fads. As the women leave Radcliffe and enter the world, Adams dutifully trots them through everything from civil rights to Watergate."

And yet other critics found Adams's usual style, allied with a swifter pace, produced a highly satisfactory work. John Updike in the *New Yorker* writes, "The novel . . . reads easily, even breathlessly; one looks forward, in the chain of coincidences, to the next encounter, knowing that this author always comes to the point from an unexpected angle, without fuss." And Barbara Koenig Quart remarks in *Ms.* that Adams's talent holds the reader through any weak points: "Not at all systematically, to be sure, and with fairly thin references to the extraordinary events of those turbulent decades, still, Adams holds us firmly with a lively narrative pace. She creates an almost gossipy interest in what happens to her characters; and she can't write a bad sentence, though hers is the kind of fine unobtrusive style that you notice only if you're looking for it."

Some reviewers have questioned the "superiority" of the young students in *Superior Women*. Their experiences are similar to those of other young coeds of the time, and their discussions usually revolve around sex. *West Coast Review of Books* contributor Dorothy Sinclair doubts their credibility: "There is so little that is believable about these young women that one suspects the usually deep and honest Adams of running amuck. Certainly there seems to be nothing 'superior' or original about their endless chatter of 'necking.' (Do they, or don't they 'do it'? They never tell.)" Annabel Edwards in *Books and Bookmen* objects to "the very use of the title *Superior Women* with apparently no ironic overtones at all." Wood, however, feels that the women display an above average concern for each other: "Her characters are genuinely kind and easy, anxious about each other. . . . Certainly Adams's characters, men and women, are nicer than most folks in fiction, or in fact."

Adams earned ample praise with her 1985 collection of stories, *Return Trips,* which "shows a master writer at the height of her powers," says Stull. He relates, "The title is apt in every way, from the dedication [to Adams's son, Peter Adams Linenthal] to the travel motifs that link these fifteen accounts of women recalling or revisiting people and places that shaped their lives." All the stories in the collection depict women struggling along on a physical or spiritual journey. According to Isabel Raphael in the London *Times:* "To make a return trip, [Adams] seems to be saying, you must leave where you are, and there is no guarantee that things will be the same when you come back, or that you yourself will be unaffected by the journey. But with a solid experience of love in your life on which to base a sense of identity, you will not lose your way." And Elaine Kendall concludes in the *Los Angeles Times* that in *Return Trips,* "unburdened by complex rigging, her imagination sails swiftly and gracefully over a sea of contemporary emotional experience, sounding unexpected depths."

Adams's novel *Second Chances* portrays the lives of men and women who face the onset of their sixties and the stigma of "old age." Like Adams's other characters, they worry about relationships and suffer losses, but in this book a marriage that dissolves through death forces them to evaluate their own lives. Adams told Mervyn Rothstein in an interview for the *New York Times:* "The novel grew out of the fact I was getting toward being 60 myself. It struck me that 60 is not middle-age. I do not know a lot of people who are 120. . . . I began looking at people who are 10 to 15 years older. The book is for me a kind of exploration." *Second Chances* also gave Adams a chance to speak truthfully about aging. In an interview with Kim Heron for the *New York Times Book Review*, Adams said, "I have the perception that people talk about old age in two ways. One is to focus on the horrors of it, not that they should be underestimated, and the other is to romanticize it."

The book starts with a group of long-term friends, all of them examining changes in their relationships. The scene soon changes to memory, and the reader is filled in on the characters' sometimes highly intricate lives. Barbara Williamson relates in the *Washington Post Book World* that "the backward and forward motion of time in the novel happily captures the way old people tell wistful, probably falsified tales of when they were young and beautiful. And the stories of their youth are the liveliest parts of the novel." But Williamson also finds that the characters' very gracefulness inhibits Adams's attempts to portray old age truthfully: "The picture presented in this novel seems too kind, too pretty. Old age, we suspect, is not a gentle stroll on the beach at twilight with kind and caring friends. Where, we ask, is the 'rage against the dying of the light'?" But *Los Angeles Times Book Review* contributor Joanna Barnes praises the depiction of the pain that exists in all relationships, whether among the young or the old. Barnes writes: "In a larger sense, it is the nature of friendship under Adams' delicate examination here. She re-creates, too, the haunting undertone of the loneliness present in all human intercourse, that separateness which, despite the presence of kindly acquaintances and lovers, can never be bridged nor breached."

Second Chances "is both the richest and the most satisfying novel that Adams . . . has produced," writes Diane Cole in *Chicago Tribune Books*. She adds, "Throughout, Adams demonstrates her gift for capturing the telling detail—the apartment decor, conversation topics, or fears left unsaid—that defines a particular era, setting or social milieu. . . . She has succeeded in painting a moving group portrait of friendship through the ages." *New York Times Book Review* contributor DeMott also feels that *Second Chances* is Adams's strongest work. DeMott believes "the strength flows partly from Ms. Adams's capacity to evoke fellow feeling, kindness and devotion as entirely natural inclinations of the heart. Her people care intensely for one another, and, although not beyond rage, seem beyond meanness. Equally important to the book's success is her grasp of conditions of feeling that are special to the middle classes just now entering their 60's and 70's. . . . [*Second Chances*] is a touching, subtle, truth-filled book."

As Elizabeth Ward observes in the *Washington Post Book World,* "Alice Adams' reputation is as a connoisseur of contemporary American relationships, a specialist in the affairs of white, middle- or upper middle-class, well-educated, well-traveled women." *Washington Post Book World* contributor Goodwin sees in Adams a "worldliness," which is "more than an attitude, a matter of style or sophistication; it amounts to a metaphysics, the wisdom of the world. Adams casts a cold eye on romance, nostalgia, anything that smacks of sentiment. She is staunchly on the side of those who believe that happiness, if it lies anywhere, lies in reality." Adams's future as a writer remains bright, writes Hill in the Toronto *Globe and Mail,* since she "is one of a number of productive American writers . . . whose fictional accomplishments are substantial now and will likely loom even larger in years to come."

BIOGRAPHICAL/CRITICAL SOURCES:

BOOKS

Contemporary Literary Criticism, Gale, Volume 6, 1976, Volume 13, 1980, Volume 46, 1988.
Dictionary of Literary Biography Yearbook: 1986, Gale, 1987.

PERIODICALS

American Book Review, July, 1983.

Booklist, December 15, 1978, January 15, 1982, June 15, 1984, July, 1985.
Books and Bookmen, March, 1985, February, 1986.
Chicago Tribune, September 1, 1985.
Chicago Tribune Book World, September 14, 1980, May 2, 1982.
Christian Science Monitor, February 20, 1975, October 16, 1985.
Commonweal, March 25, 1983.
Critique, summer, 1986.
Globe and Mail (Toronto), November 10, 1984.
Harvard Magazine, February, 1975.
Hudson Review, summer, 1979, spring, 1985.
Listener, January 29, 1976.
London Review of Books, February 21, 1985.
Los Angeles Times, April 13, 1982, August 19, 1985, October 10, 1989.
Los Angeles Times Book Review, November 16, 1980, May 8, 1988.
Ms., September, 1984.
New England Review, autumn, 1986.
New Leader, March 27, 1978.
New Republic, February 4, 1978.
New Statesman, January 16, 1976.
Newsweek, February 3, 1975.
New Yorker, February 10, 1975, November 5, 1984.
New York Times, January 30, 1975, January 10, 1978, August 21, 1985, May 19, 1988.
New York Times Book Review, March 16, 1975, February 26, 1978, January 14, 1979, September 14, 1980, April 11, 1982, September 23, 1984, September 1, 1985, May 1, 1988, October 8, 1989.
Observer (London), January 18, 1976.
People, April 3, 1978.
Publishers Weekly, January 16, 1978.
Rolling Stone, April 20, 1978.
San Francisco Review of Books, spring, 1985.
Saturday Review, November-December, 1985.
StoryQuarterly, Number 11, 1980.
Time, December 26, 1977, April 19, 1982.
Times (London), January 9, 1986.
Times Literary Supplement, January 16, 1976, January 31, 1986.
Tribune Books (Chicago), May 1, 1988, September 3, 1989.
Village Voice, January 9, 1978.
Washington Post Book World, February 23, 1975, January 13, 1978, January 21, 1979, October 12, 1980, May 9, 1982, September 2, 1984, September 15, 1985, May 6, 1988, October 24, 1989.
West Coast Review of Books, March, 1978, November, 1984.

*   *   *

ADAMS, Richard (George) 1920-

PERSONAL: Born May 9, 1920, in Newbury, Berkshire, England: son of Evelyn George Beadon (a surgeon) and Lilian Rosa (Button) Adams; married Barbara Elizabeth Acland, September 26, 1949; children: Juliet, Rosamond. *Education:* Worcester College, Oxford, M.A., 1948. *Religion:* Church of England.

ADDRESSES: Home—Knocksharry House, Lhergy Dhoo, Peel, Isle of Man, United Kingdom. *Agent*—David Higham Associates Ltd., 5-8 Lower John St., London W1R 4HA, England.

CAREER: British Home Higher Civil Service, 1948-74, serving in Ministry of Housing and Local Government until its amalgamation as part of Department of Environment, assistant secretary of Department of Environment, 1968-74; full-time writer, 1974—. Writer-in-residence at University of Florida, 1975, and Hollins College, 1976. *Military service:* British Army, 1940-45.

MEMBER: Royal Society of Literature (honorary fellow), Royal Society for the Prevention of Cruelty to Animals (vice-president).

AWARDS, HONORS: Guardian Award for children's literature, and Carnegie Medal, both 1972, both for *Watership Down;* California Young Readers' Association Medal, 1977.

WRITINGS:

NOVELS

Watership Down, Rex Collings, 1972, Macmillan, 1974.
Shardik, Rex Collings, 1974, Simon & Schuster, 1975.
The Plague Dogs, illustrated by A. Wainwright, Allen Lane, 1977, Knopf, 1978.
The Girl in a Swing, Knopf, 1980.
Maia, Knopf, 1985.
Traveller, Knopf, 1988.

OTHER

(With Max Hooper) *Nature through the Seasons,* illustrated by David A. Goddard and Adrian Williams, Simon & Schuster, 1975.
The Tyger Voyage, illustrated by Bayley, Knopf, 1976.
The Adventures and Brave Deeds of the Ship's Cat on the Spanish Maine: Together With the Most Lamentable Losse of the Alcestis and Triumphant Firing of the Port of Chagres, illustrated by Alan Aldridge and Harry Willock, Knopf, 1977.
(With Hooper) *Nature Day and Night,* illustrated by Goddard and Stephen Lee, Viking, 1978.
(Compiler) *Sinister and Supernatural Stories,* Ward Locke, 1978.
(Author of introduction) Georgi Vladimov, *Faithful Ruslan,* translation by Michael Glenn, Simon & Schuster, 1979.
The Iron Wolf and Other Stories, Allen Lane, 1980.
(Adaptor) *The Unbroken Web: Stories and Fables* (collection of nineteen folk tales), Crown, 1980.

Story anthologized in *Kingdoms of Sorcery,* edited by Lin Carter, Doubleday, 1976.

SIDELIGHTS: While still a civil servant in Britain's Department of Environment, Richard Adams began writing *Watership Down.* The story was told originally to amuse his two young daughters; at their insistence, Adams began to write down the tale. The manuscript, which took two years to complete, was rejected by four publishers and three authors' agents. Because he wanted to deliver a book into his daughters' hands, Adams was on the verge of having the novel printed at his own expense when he read of a small publisher who had just reissued an out-of-print animal fantasy; Adams contacted Rex Collings who accepted *Watership Down* for a limited first edition of 2,000 copies. Later reprinted by Penguin as a juvenile, the novel was a surprising success, winning the Guardian Award and Carnegie Medal. The American publisher, Macmillan, marketed the novel as an adult title, and the sales and reviews were again rewarding.

Watership Down relates the adventures of a group of rabbits who must set out in search of a new home because their warren is being razed by a developer who plans to gas all its animal inhabitants. P. S. Prescott of *Newsweek* calls the book "an adventure story of an epic. . . . It is a story of exile and survival, of heroism and political responsibility, of the making of a leader and of a community. . . . Adams has constructed a complete civilization, with its own governments, language and mythology." Writing in *New York,* Eliot Fremont-Smith comments: "There are a lot of things that make this book work, including the traditional and here expertly employed device of cliff-hanging chapter endings. But mainly it is Richard Adams's wonderfully rich imagination, together with an extraordinary and totally disarming respect for his material. Tone is all-important in a tale like this, and Adams's is straight, confidently controlled, never maudlin."

Janet Adam Smith writes in the *New York Review of Books* that she believes Adams "is a master of menace and suspense," but she adds: "I much prefer Mr. Adams when he is plain—'where the turf ended, the sky began' conveys in a flash the rabbits' view from the down—or in his high style, as when he meditates on moonlight. . . . Such passages are more than decoration; they (and the chapter headings from Aeschylus, the Psalms, and the Epic of Gilgamesh) dignify the action, making it not just the trek of a bunch of rabbits, but a movement of creatures who are no less part of nature than we are, and whose humble disasters and migrations have a claim to the attention of men, for all the greater scale of *theirs*."

Smith feels that Macmillan's labeling of the book as simply a novel rather than a juvenile novel "may well encourage readers to go looking for the wrong things. For who would write a novel for adults about rabbits—unless the tale were a fable or a myth? . . . Certainly, it appears at a time when we are becoming increasingly skeptical of our species' ability to live its life decently; there is an inclination to look, if only in fancy, for alternative models in other species, other worlds. . . . In as much as Mr. Adams has a message for his readers, I'd say it is to make them more sensitive to the complex balance of nature, more aware of the needs and ways of other species (and the effect of human actions on them), more mindful that we are creatures too, and must live in harmony with the others who share our world." Agreeing with Smith is the author himself, who has consistently said that *Watership Down* should not be taken as allegory. As quoted by the *Pittsburgh Press*, Adams comments: "A lot of people have said this is a political fable or even a religious fable or social comment. I promise you it is not a fable or an allegory or a parable of any kind. It is a story about rabbits, that is all."

Despite the reviewers' praise and the public's acceptance, the novel has its critics. An example of negative criticism directed against *Watership Down* comes from *National Review*'s D. Keith Mano, who questions the complimentary reviews the book has received. Mano writes: " 'An exceptional book, a true original.' 'It doesn't fit any known formula, thank goodness.' Nonsense: it fits five or six. This bunny squad could be a John Wayne platoon of GIs. The foresighted, tactful rabbit leader. The fast rabbit. The clever rabbit. The blustery, hard-fighting noncom rabbit. Athos, Porthos, and D'Artagnan on a diet of grass. *Watership Down* is pleasant enough, but it has about the same intellectual firepower as *Dumbo.* 'Refreshes a reader's feeling for the world of man.' Apparently more than one reviewer has been rabbited out of his critical faculties. After all, if your dog started speaking French you'd be loath to criticize his pronunciation. Yet if Hazel and Bigwig and Dandelion were men, they'd make very commonplace characters. What seems a moral, an insight, is just a novelty. . . . *Watership Down* is an adventure story, no more than that: rather a swashbuckling, crude one to boot. There are virtuous rabbits and bad rab-bits: if that's allegory, *Bonanza* is an allegory. . . . This is an okay book; well enough written. But it is grossly overrated."

Although Mano and others may feel *Watership Down* has been overrated, they cannot question the book's commercial success. Penguin sold more than one and one-quarter million copies of their edition, and the hardcover edition by Macmillan was pur-

chased by more than seven-hundred thousand customers. Alison Lurie of the *New York Review of Books* feels that *Watership Down* has been so successful "not just because it was well written and original. It was attractive also because it celebrated qualities many serious novelists are currently afraid or embarrassed to write about. The heroes and heroines of most contemporary novels (including mine) are sad, bumbling failures; hysterical combatants in the sex war; or self-deceptive men and women of ill-will. What a relief to read of characters who have honor and courage and dignity, who will risk their lives for others, whose love for their families and friends and community is enduring and effective—even if they look like Flopsy, Mopsy, and Benjamin Bunny."

Lurie writes that Adams's second novel, *Shardik,* did not receive as much acclaim as *Watership Down* partly because in it Adams is "attempting something more difficult." The novel is set in a mythical country and time; the natives worship a giant bear, Shardik. Lurie comments that like *Watership Down, Shardik* can be viewed as "an allegory and history of the relationship of human beings to the physical world." But she believes *Shardik* to be much more than an ecological allegory; she thinks the novel is really a study of how human beings choose and follow their gods. The great bear, Lurie continues, "is not really a magical being; he is not anthropomorphized. All that he does is within the range of normal animal behavior; only to those who believe in him does it seem symbolical, an Act of God. Because of this belief, however, lives are changed utterly; hundreds of men, women, and children die; a barbaric empire is destroyed and rebuilt and destroyed again, and finally brought a little nearer to civilized humanism. . . . In *Shardik,* belief causes men to act cruelly and destructively as well as nobly; the bear is a kind of test which brings out hidden strengths and weaknesses, even in those who do not believe in him."

Like Lurie, Bruce Allen believes *Shardik*'s major theme is the effect of religious belief on human beings. He writes in the *Saturday Review:* "[*Shardik* is] a powerfully compelling prose epic that recreates the fortunate fall of unaccommodated man. . . . Among this book's greatest strengths is its rejection of the modern novel's emphasis on subjective uncertainty. It urges that truth is knowable, and that our intelligences must accept what they recognize for revealed truth—even if it be partial and unsatisfying. Surely, this points to its Christian framework. But isn't there something more, something stretching back still farther? . . . In reading *Shardik,* we seem to hear again the old stories that were told to us by old people remembering them from past years, knowing we must be made to hear them, that our survival depends upon them. This is a new story, but it has the satisfying wholeness of the great ones it dares to rival; it should be told, and retold, for many generations."

Newsweek's Arthur Cooper also points to the religious element in *Shardik,* calling the novel "an exploration of the way an incarnate god works on the human psyche. . . . Beneath the rich vein of allegory and symbolism, Adams is concerned with how a society worships its gods, chooses its values and raises its children. Adams is a splendid descriptive writer whose only flaw—a minor one—is a fondness for the extended Homeric simile. . . . This is a marvelous novel of epic dimension, more ambitious, deeper, darker and more richly textured than *Watership [Down].*"

Praising *Shardik*'s "majestic language, heroic theme and sustained power," Peter Wolf writes in the *New Republic:* "Its achievement is awesome: some of its effects move us so deeply that we're surprised to find them made up of words on a printed page. . . . No estimate of *Shardik* can overlook how well

Adams's firmly cadenced sentences knit with its epical theme, how his style brings to life his uncanny knowledge of bears—their anatomy, feeding and sleeping habits, and reactions to stress. *Shardik* is both the power of God and a dangerous, wounded animal, half-crazed by hunger, fire and hunters' arrows. Adams makes the great shambling bear a figure of terror and savage grandeur even in his physical ruin."

As with *Watership Down,* the reviewers' praise for *Shardik* was not unanimous. Webster Schott of *Washington Post Book World* writes: "There is one good thing to say for *Shardik.* Adams writes about nature—trees, plants, animals, stones, bug—as though he grew in ground next to wild onions. He talks the natural world into life. But there are few of the usual reasons for reading fiction in *Shardik.* We learn nothing about ourselves here; Adams's people belong with Snow White. . . . The novel is a fake antique, a sexless, humorless, dull facsimile of an epic without historical or psychological relevance. Contrary to Adams's wish, *Shardik* transmits no information we need, want, or can use about how we have chosen or employed our deities. *Shardik* is a long-winded Victorian fantasy, a piece of literary furniture properly destined to be unread by tens of thousands of book-club check writers."

John Skow of *Time* also dislikes the novel; he comments: "There is no iron to this Iron Age fable. The grimness is fake, the fascination with virginity is a naughty bore, and the monstrous figure of Shardik is cheapened by watery supernaturalism. . . . The author spins out his romance entertainingly, but without dealing seriously with the questions he raises: of belief and its perversion, of authority and its corruption. Good as he is at nature walks, Adams does not venture far into the forests of the mind." The *Listener*'s Kenneth Graham complains that *Shardik* "is too long, and too uneven. There is no real grasp of the inward reaches of character, only of the grand simplicities of archetype." Despite this, Graham adds that "there can be few books on which more loving, energetic inventiveness has been expended than on *Shardik.* . . . There is enough creative endeavour, careful planning, integrity and sheer multifarious detail in *Shardik* to make a dozen ordinary novels."

Adams's third novel, *The Plague Dogs,* harks back to *Watership Down* in its anthropomorphic use of animals. The novel tells of the adventures of two dogs who have escaped from an animal experimentation laboratory in the English Lake District. In an interview with Jan Rodger of Toronto's *Globe and Mail,* Adams says of the book: "*The Plague Dogs* is not just an attack on animal experimentation. . . . It is about the way in which, in modern life, almost all of us have a motive for what we do which is other than a simple, direct, honest motive, straightforward hunger or love. . . . If you are put off by tracts, you are probably not going to like *The Plague Dogs.* But I do feel very indignant about animal experimentation and perhaps my indignation got the better of me."

The *New York Times*'s John Leonard disliked Adams's third novel. "On the one hand, *The Plague Dogs* fairly reeks of literary self-consciousness. In the grand manner of the English novel, it is discursive and coy. It pauses every 12 pages for an afflatus or a tantrum or a pun. It is not above stopping to doggerel and parody," Leonard writes. "On the other hand, *The Plague Dogs* must carry around a big load of philosophical heavy water. It is a polemic on the nature of freedom and illusion, the confusion between objective and subjective states of reality, the meaning of Auschwitz and the iniquities of modern science. . . . Mr. Adams's oddly sexless world is full of contempt—for science, for politics, for journalism. What is so far missing from that world are the marvelous people who came along with the discursive style in the great English novels he cannibalizes. I finished *Watership Down* in tears at the death of Hazel, the warrior-rabbit. I finished *The Plague Dogs* dry-eyed, having been manipulated."

William Safire takes the opposite point of view in the *New York Times Book Review.* Safire comments that while he disliked *Watership Down,* "in *The Plague Dogs* Richard Adams drags the reluctant reader into his world, entices him into accepting its conventions and atmosphere, and peppers him with hard-to-forget images and messages. . . . Once hooked by the dogs'-eye view of life, the dogs' fear of 'whitecoats,' and the drama of the chase, the reader is ready for Adams's sermons on animal slavery, on the power of hope to increase endurance, and on the cruelty that freedom demands of fugitives. . . . Adams is madcap-serious, usually controlled in his outrage, and knows how to evoke a sense of place. It matters not whose ox he allegories. *The Plague Dogs* is a savage snarl of a satire, a world created with a purpose clear in the writer's mind. It puts the reader on the scent of himself."

Time's Paul Gray notes that "even Adams's fervent admirers admit that he can be spotty: at best an artful cataloguer of flora and fauna, at worst a windy sentimentalist. . . . Adams overwrites almost every scene, but he manages to turn that fault into a virtue. Length can lull disbelief and make the unlikely seem familiar." Joseph McLellan agrees that *The Plague Dogs* is not a perfect novel, but further comments in the *Washington Post:* "By his repeatedly felt presence behind the scenes, manipulating the action and commenting on it, Adams underlines a fact that is already apparent: like them or not, his novels differ from all others being written. . . . As the book weathers into a classic (if it does, and it well may) the idiosyncrasies that are a distraction on its first appearance will become part of its charm. And the prospect for the foreseeable future is that its central image—that of two creatures victimized by society, unable to live by its rules but also unable to work out and live by their own outlaw code—is one in which many people will see reflected some part of themselves."

With *The Girl in a Swing,* Adams turns from his former animal heroes to contemporary human characters. The novel relates the meeting and marriage of a young conventional Englishman, Alan Desland, and a beautiful and mysterious German woman named Kathe. As with *Shardik,* this fourth novel involves the supernatural, and here Adams belies the complaint by Leonard and other reviewers that his fictional world is sexless. P. D. James of the *Washington Post Book World* comments: "Two of the most difficult tasks which a novelist can set himself are to write an erotic novel and to deal convincingly with the supernatural, and a writer who attempts both in the same book, particularly when the attempt marks a new direction of his talent, at least deserves an accolade for courage. But Richard Adams . . . deserves more. With *The Girl in a Swing* we acclaim success."

James's only complaint about the novel is that she would have liked to know more about Kathe's past and her motivation for marrying Alan Desland. She writes: "The deed which lies at the heart of the book's haunting tragedy is so horrible, at once a symbol of evil and its manifestation, that felt the need to understand something of the desperation, the moral corruption or the yearning for security from which it sprang." But, she adds: "There may be readers for whom this reticence about Kathe's motives and the details of her past life provides an intensification of the mystery which surrounds her; the horror is rendered more horrible because we can only guess at the psychological springs from which it flows."

Robert Kiely presents no reservations in his complimentary assessment of *The Girl in a Swing.* He writes in the *New York Times Book Review:* "Richard Adams turns his commonplace man into the hero-victim of a tale of fatal passion. . . . Alan never ceases being the solid, decent chap he was brought up to be. He remains completely believable throughout. The love scenes between him and Kathe are presented with lyrical beauty, a touch of humor and increasing obsessiveness. Kathe's ability to enchant is never in doubt. Finally, the ghost story is absolutely terrifying, as gripping and psychological penetrating as anything in James or Poe. Richard Adams has written, with marvelous tact and narrative power, a strange, beautiful, haunting book."

Adams next novel, *Maia,* is a tale of adventure and romance set in the magical land of the Bekland Empire. Of this novel, Robert Hughes remarks in the *Chicago Tribune:* "*Maia* is a major work dealing with the adventures of a magnificently beautiful peasant girl sold into slavery, degraded beyond belief, and surviving to become the heroine of her people. There is no gainsaying the power of the narrative. It sweeps along through halls of grandeur and sloughs of despair, interrupted only by the necessity of referring occasionally to a long list of exotically named characters to see who is who, and by textual reminders of their relationships." Joy Fielding also believes *Maia* is a real treat to read. She writes in Toronto's *Globe and Mail:* "There is rarely a dull moment, and more than a few moments of genuine suspense. . . . Richard Adams maintains that the essence of fiction is that the reader wants to keep turning those pages."

In Adams's sixth novel, *Traveller,* the hero is once again an animal. *Traveller* recounts the events of the Civil War as seen through the eyes of General Robert E. Lee's horse. Michiko Kakutani comments in the *New York Times:* "As in Mr. Adams's earlier books, the follies of human beings—especially their penchant for killing one another—are lamented by the ever-so-much-wiser animals." "Traveller," Kakutani elsewhere notes, "is supposedly relating his memories of the war to his stablemate, a cat by the name of Tom; and like many old soldiers' stories, his account is filled with examples of the thrill of victory and the agony of defeat. . . . Mainly, though, Traveller's story is a tribute to his master."

MEDIA ADAPTATIONS: Watership Down was produced as a motion picture by Avco-Embassy in 1978; *The Girl in a Swing* was produced as a motion picture in 1989.

BIOGRAPHICAL/CRITICAL SOURCES:

BOOKS

Authors in the News, Gale, Volume 1, 1976, Volume 2, 1976.
Contemporary Literary Criticism, Gale, Volume 4, 1975, Volume 5, 1976, Volume 18, 1981.

PERIODICALS

Atlantic, April, 1978.
Chicago Tribune, February 17, 1985.
Commonweal, September 27, 1974.
Detroit News, February 24, 1985.
Globe and Mail (Toronto), November 16, 1977, February 23, 1985.
Harper's, May, 1975.
Listener, January 2, 1975, September 22, 1977.
London Times, November 8, 1974.
Los Angeles Times, July 20, 1975.
National Review, April 26, 1974.

New Republic, March 23, 1974, May 3, 1975.
Newsweek, March 18, 1974, April 28, 1975, March 13, 1978.
New York, March 4, 1974.
New York Review of Books, April 18, 1974, June 12, 1975.
New York Times, March 7, 1978, May 28, 1988.
New York Times Book Review, March 24, 1974, June 30, 1974, May 4, 1975, March 12, 1978, April 27, 1980, June 5, 1988.
Pittsburgh Press, March 20, 1974.
Saturday Review, May 31, 1975, March 4, 1978.
Times Literary Supplement, December 8, 1972, November 15, 1974, September 30, 1977, October 24, 1980.
Village Voice, March 21, 1974.
Virginia Quarterly Review, summer, 1974.
Washington Post, November 8, 1978, December 2, 1980.
Washington Post Book World, May 25, 1975, February 26, 1978, May 11, 1980, June 5, 1988.

*　　*　　*

ADAMSON, Joy(-Friederike Victoria)　1910-1980

PERSONAL: Born January 20, 1910, in Troppau, Silesia (now Opava, Czechoslovakia); died January 3, 1980, in Kenya, of stab wounds inflicted by a former employee; daughter of Victor (an architect and urban planner) and Traute (Greipel) Gessner; married Victor von Klarwill, 1935 (divorced, 1937); married Peter Bally, 1938 (divorced, 1942); married George Adamson (a game warden), January, 1943. *Education:* Educated in Vienna, Austria, 1933-35. *Religion:* Protestant.

ADDRESSES: Home—P.O. Box 254, Naivasha, Kenya. *Office*—Elsa Wild Animal Appeal, P.O. Box 30029, Nairobi, Kenya.

CAREER: Illustrator of African botany texts and painter, 1938-80, work has been exhibited by Kenya National Museum and Tryon Gallery in Nairobi and Fort Jesus Museum in Mombasa; ethologist, 1956-80; author, 1958-80. Founder and head of Elsa Wild Animal Appeal in England, 1961, United States, 1969, Canada, 1971, and Japan, 1976.

MEMBER: Nanyuki Club, Nairobi Club.

AWARDS, HONORS: Gold Grenfall medal from Royal Horticulture Society, 1947; award of merit from government of Czechoslovakia, 1970; Joseph Wood Krutch medal from U.S. Humane Society, 1971; Ehrenkreutz fuer Kunst und Wissenschaft (Austria), 1977.

WRITINGS:

ADULT NONFICTION

Born Free: A Lioness of Two Worlds (also see below), Pantheon, 1960, reprinted, 1987.
Living Free (also see below), Harcourt, 1961.
Forever Free (also see below), Harcourt, 1962 (published in England as *Forever Free: Elsa's Pride,* Harvell, 1962).
The Story of Elsa (includes *Born Free, Living Free,* and *Forever Free*), Harcourt, 1966.
The Peoples of Kenya, self-illustrated, Harcourt, 1967.
The Spotted Sphinx, Harcourt, 1969.
Pippa's Challenge, Harcourt, 1972.
Joy Adamson's Africa, self-illustrated, Harcourt, 1972.
The Searching Spirit: An Autobiography, foreword by Elspeth Huxley, Collins & Harvill, 1978, Harcourt, 1979.
(Contributor) *Such Agreeable Friends: Adventures with Animals,* Universe Books, 1978.
Queen of Shaba: The Story of an African Leopard, Harcourt, 1980.

Friends from the Forest, foreword by Juliette Huxley, Harcourt, 1981.

JUVENILE NONFICTION

Elsa: The True Story of a Lioness, Pantheon, 1961.
Elsa and Her Cubs, Harcourt, 1965.
Pippa the Cheetah and Her Cubs, Harcourt, 1970.

ILLUSTRATOR

Arthur J. Jex-Blake, editor, *Gardening in East Africa,* Longmans, 2nd edition (Adamson was not associated with 1st edition), 1939, 4th edition, 1957.
Muriel Jex-Blake, *Some Wild Flowers of Kenya,* Longmans, 1948.
Flore des spermatophytes, National Parc de Congo Belge, 1955.
W. J. Eggeling, *Indigenous Trees of the Uganda Protectorate,* Government Printer (Entebbe, Uganda), 1957.
Ivan R. Dale and Percy J. Greenway, *Kenya Trees and Shrubs,* Hatchards (London) for Buchanan's Kenya Estates (Nairobi), 1961.

OTHER

Contributor of articles to magazines, including *Journal of the Royal Geographical Society, Country Life,* and *Geographical Journal.*

Joy Adamson's works have been translated into more than thirty-five languages.

WORK IN PROGRESS: Research on the lion, cheetah, and leopard.

SIDELIGHTS: Author Joy Adamson spent the last thirty years of her life rehabilitating African wildlife in Kenya's game reserves. Her efforts, chronicled in such best-selling works as *Born Free: A Lioness of Two Worlds, Living Free,* and *The Spotted Sphinx,* brought the daily travails of wildlife conservation to a worldwide audience. Adamson herself became an international celebrity when she successfully returned to the wild human-reared cats such as Elsa, a lioness, Pippa, a cheetah, and Penny, a leopard. Through books and films her adventures with the big cats "attracted the attention of famous scientists and zoologists, and alerted the world to an animal kingdom that without care can be lost forever," according to Peggy Crane in *Books and Bookmen.* As Gerald Durrell notes in the *New York Times Book Review,* Adamson's pioneering relationship with Elsa "must surely be one of the most remarkable cases on record of human association with a wild animal."

"In Mrs. Adamson's vocabulary," writes *Book World* contributor Alfred C. Ames, " 'rehabilitating' means successfully encouraging an animal to go wild, though starting life under circumstances leading almost inevitably to roles as a confined pet or a zoo exhibit or both in succession." An estimated thirteen million readers followed Adamson's patient attempts to return the loving cub Elsa to a life independent of human contact. Proceeds from the books and movies based on the experiment provided the initial funds for Adamson's Elsa Wildlife Trust, a foundation that has raised millions of dollars to aid conservation causes. According to Richard M. Weintraub in the *Washington Post,* Adamson's well-publicized activities "lent force to a then nascent movement to preserve African wildlife." Weintraub adds: "On another level, the popularity of her work is often cited as a premier example of man's continuing pull toward basic relationships in nature during a time increasingly complicated by industrial and technological growth."

Adamson was born and raised in Austria, the daughter of a wealthy architect. She spent her early childhood years at her mother's family's estate near Troppau, Silesia, where she enjoyed following the gamekeeper on his rounds. Career choices proved difficult for Adamson as she matured; she earned a state diploma in piano but also pursued metalwork, poster and book jacket design, dressmaking, singing, art history, drawing, shorthand, typing, and wood sculpting. For a brief period she even studied psychoanalysis and medicine, but she never qualified for university entrance. In 1935 she married Victor von Klarwill, an Austrian businessman. The marriage ended in divorce after von Klarwill sent her to explore possible living arrangements in East Africa. She fell in love with Kenya and with Peter Bally, a botanist she met on the outward voyage.

During her marriage to Bally, Adamson discovered a career that allowed her to explore wide regions of her adopted homeland—she began to paint pictures of Kenya's indigenous plant life. "For ten years," she told the *New York Post,* "I did nothing but paint flowers. There are seven times more plants in Kenya than in all of Europe." Gradually Adamson began to diversify the subjects of her paintings. She recorded on canvas scenes from Kenyan tribal life, insects, reptiles, and landscapes. Several hundred of her works are displayed in the National Museum and the State House in Nairobi and in Mombasa's Fort Jesus Museum. Adamson also illustrated two of her books about life in Kenya, *The Peoples of Kenya* and *Joy Adamson's Africa. Saturday Review* contributor Charles L. Miller suggests that to peruse *The Peoples of Kenya* is "to enjoy the weird and beautiful experience of a journey through a lost dimension of time." Although Adamson will be best remembered for her work with wildlife, critics claim her paintings of the major cultural groups in Kenya form a lasting record of lifestyles that have been undermined by modernization.

The diversification of the author's painting subjects coincided with her 1943 marriage to George Adamson, a senior game warden in the Kenyan park service. Together the Adamsons traveled the length and breadth of Kenya on safaris and in a Land Rover, supervising, among other things, the care of orphaned wild animals. In January of 1956, Mr. Adamson took responsibility for three lion cubs whose mother he had killed in self-defense. Two of the cubs were eventually sent to a zoo, but the third, Elsa, remained with the Adamsons. In an unprecedented and heart-wrenching experiment, the Adamsons taught Elsa to hunt her food in preparation for a return to the wild. They kept written records of their progress and detailed the setbacks and difficulties that arose during the twenty-seven-month project. In the *Washington Post,* Faith McNulty writes: "The education of Elsa, the lioness, transforming her from an oversized tame cat to a fully capable wild animal, was a complex task. In doing it the Adamsons broke new ground, recording lion behavior as it had never been recorded before. Wild lions had been described, and tame lions had been described. It was Elsa's transition from one to the other that was so enormously revealing."

Born Free: A Lioness of Two Worlds and its sequels *Living Free* and *Forever Free* have received enthusiastic comments from critics. *Chicago Tribune* contributor Charles Paul May contends that the reader of *Born Free* "gets a feeling for nature in Kenya, and, in slight degree, for human life as well." Durrell calls the work "a moving and incredible story," and he notes that Adamson "writes well, without excess sentimentality, and with a nice, dry humor." *Living Free,* the account of Elsa's independent life with her own cubs, also has pleased reviewers. In the *New Statesman,* Ted Hughes makes the observation that *Living Free* "is the perfect kind of children's book. It has the ideal ingredients: close friendship with a wild animal, . . . baby lions in their day-to-day growing up, . . . villains, suspense, . . . a passionately involved narrator, beautiful photographs, and it all really happened. But more than that it has genuine educational virtues: clear, firm, vivid prose, sensitive observation, courage and patience, intense sympathy for life, no padding, no details politely muffed." A *Times Literary Supplement* reviewer writes: "[There] is something rather mysterious about the extent of Mrs. Adamson's impact on her readers. . . . It is the tender relationship between Mrs. Adamson and Elsa that holds the key." The reviewer suggests that Adamson's story of a human mother preparing her spoiled leonine offspring for an independent wild life is symbolic of any parent-child relationship, but the tale of Elsa remains powerful because "Mrs. Adamson's anecdotes are not distorted to suit the demands of human sentimentality." Hughes concludes: "That a lioness, one of the great moody aggressors, should be brought to display such qualities as Elsa's, is a step not so much in the education of lions as in the civilization of men. . . . [Living Free] is a small gospel."

The experiments in wildlife repatriation were not always successful. After Elsa's death, her cubs began to slaughter domestic animals and had to be removed to an isolated game park. A lion that appeared in the film version of *Born Free* had to be shot after it mauled a child and killed one of the Adamsons' servants. Joy Adamson persisted, however, in her attempts to return big carnivores to independence. In 1964 she assumed responsibility for an eight-month-old cheetah, Pippa, the pet of a British army officer. Pippa's rehabilitation took four and a half years and required Adamson to make long treks with meat for sustenance as the cat learned to fend for herself. Pippa's adventures appear in *The Spotted Sphinx, Pippa's Challenge,* and a children's book called *Pippa the Cheetah and Her Cubs.* In the last three years of her life, Adamson devoted herself to restoring a testy leopard named Penny to life as a free-ranging wild cat. Her book *Queen of Shaba: The Story of an African Leopard* arrived at the publisher ten days after her death. In his *New York Times Book Review* piece on the work, John W. Miller concludes: "Though Penny's survival is the driving force of this book, its richness comes from Mrs. Adamson herself. While our attention is focused on her single-minded mission and on the details of leopard behavior, we also get a picture of the last three years of a woman as unselfconscious as the animals she observed."

Preliminary reports on Adamson's death suggested that she had been fatally mauled by a lion as she walked alone a few hundred yards from her back country camp. A subsequent investigation revealed mortal stab wounds, and a former employee of Adamson's was charged with her murder. Wildlife expert Roger Caras told *People* magazine that Adamson "was an incredible woman, but very difficult to get along with." He added: "Rarely did she have any long-lasting personal relationships. She was so stubborn and unyielding and people did not live up to her expectations. She rarely met anyone as strong as herself." Although she worked with several physical disabilities right until she was killed, Adamson openly preferred a solitary life; from 1971 onward, she and her husband lived hundreds of miles apart and communicated by shortwave radio once a week. While friends and aides claimed that Adamson had become intemperate and alienating to humans and concurrently more devoted to wild animals as she aged, they nonetheless conceded that she contributed greatly to international awareness of conservation. Faith Mc-Nulty concluded: "Within a simple narrative, 'Born Free' subtly introduced primary lessons in ethology together with a new view of 'savage' predators that transformed the attitude of millions of readers. It may have done for the cause of wildlife what [Harriet

Beecher Stowe's abolitionist novel] 'Uncle Tom's Cabin' did for the antislavery crusade." *New York Times Book Review* contributor Harold Hayes called Adamson "an altogether admirable person" who "has lived a rambunctious, large-scale, productive life."

As founder of the Elsa Wild Animal Appeal, Adamson urged everyone to "save the wild cats of Africa and the world . . . by boycotting the trade of furs and other organic parts of the animal's body sold as jewelry or trinkets." She especially urged writers to "help the wild animals of the U.S.S.R., Poland, Hungary, Czechoslovakia, Roumania, and Bulgaria with book royalties sold in those countries."

Mrs. Adamson once told *CA:* "The more I learn from wild animals, the more I am convinced that they communicate by thought communication—which we humans may also have possessed before we developed speech and mechanical means of communication. Our telepathy gradually atrophied, except in very rare cases. I had it with Elsa and Pippa, but not with humans."

MEDIA ADAPTATIONS: Films—"Born Free," British Lion Films Ltd., 1964; "Living Free," Columbia Productions Ltd., 1971; "Joy Adamson," based on *The Searching Spirit: An Autobiography,* was filmed in 1978. *Television*—"Born Free," National Broadcasting Company (NBC), 1974. *Filmstrip*—"Joy Adamson's Africa," 1972.

AVOCATIONAL INTERESTS: Riding, skiing, tennis, mountaineering, and swimming.

BIOGRAPHICAL/CRITICAL SOURCES:

BOOKS

Adamson, Joy, *The Searching Spirit: An Autobiography,* foreword by Elspeth Huxley, Collins & Harvill, 1978, Harcourt, 1979.
Contemporary Literary Criticism, Volume 17, Gale, 1981.
Newquist, Roy, *Counterpoint,* Simon & Schuster, 1964.

PERIODICALS

Atlantic, November, 1961.
Books and Bookmen, May, 1979.
Book World, October 19, 1969.
Chicago Tribune, April 24, 1960.
Christian Science Monitor, March 28, 1963, July 13, 1969, July 13, 1979, December 17, 1980.
Good Housekeeping, February, 1972.
Horn Book, December, 1969.
Junior Bookshelf, August, 1972.
New Statesman, November 10, 1961.
New York Post, May 29, 1966, October 11, 1969.
New York Times, August 14, 1972.
New York Times Book Review, May 22, 1960, October 15, 1961, April 22, 1979, October 26, 1980.
People, October 4, 1976.
Saturday Review, December 23, 1967, August, 1981.
Times Literary Supplement, April 22, 1960, December 22, 1961, December 7, 1967, January 29, 1970.
Washington Post, April 21, 1979.

OBITUARIES:

PERIODICALS

Los Angeles Times, February 9, 1980.
New York Times, January 5, 1980, January 7, 1980.
People, January 21, 1980.

Publishers Weekly, January 18, 1980.
Time, January 21, 1980.
Washington Post, January 5, 1980.

* * *

ADLER, Mortimer J(erome) 1902-

PERSONAL: Born December 28, 1902, in New York, N.Y.;. son of Ignatz (a jewelry salesman) and Clarissa (a school teacher; maiden name, Manheim) Adler; married Helen Leavenworth Boyton, May 2, 1927 (divorced, 1961); married Caroline Sage Pring, February, 1963; children: (first marriage) Mark Arthur, Michael Boyton; (second marriage) Douglas Robert, Philip Pring. *Education:* Columbia University, Ph.D., 1928, B.A., 1983.

ADDRESSES: Office—Institute for Philosophical Research, 101 East Ontario St., Chicago, Ill. 60611.

CAREER: New York Sun, New York City, secretary to editor, 1915-17; Columbia University, New York City, instructor in psychology, 1923-30; University of Chicago, Chicago, Ill., associate professor, 1930-42, professor of philosophy of law, 1942-52; Institute for Philosophical Research, Chicago, president and director, 1952—; San Francisco Productions, Inc., Chicago, president, 1954—. Lecturer and assistant director of People's Institute (New York City), 1927-29; visiting lecturer, City College (now City College of the City University of New York), 1927, St. John's College (Annapolis, Md.), 1936, and University of Chicago, 1963-68; university professor, University of North Carolina at Chapel Hill, 1988—; lecturer for U.S. Air Transport Command. Consultant to Ford Foundation, 1952-56. Honorary trustee, Aspen Institute for Humanistic Studies, 1974—.

MEMBER: American Catholic Philosophical Association, American Philosophical Association, Phi Beta Kappa.

AWARDS, HONORS: Aquinas Medal, American Catholic Philosophical Association, 1976; Graduate Faculties Alumni Award for Excellence, Columbia University, 1977; Wilma and Roswell Messing Award, 1978.

WRITINGS:

Dialectic, Harcourt, 1927.
(With Maude Phelps Hutchins) *Diagrammatics,* Random House, 1932.
(With Jerome Michael) *Crime, Law, and Social Science,* Harcourt, 1933, reprinted, Patterson Smith, 1971.
Art and Prudence: A Study in Practical Philosophy, Longmans, Green, 1937, reprinted, Arrio, 1978, revised edition published as *Poetry and Politics,* Duquesne University Press, 1965.
What Man Has Made of Man: A Study of the Consequences of Platonism and Positivism in Psychology, Longmans, Green, 1937, reprinted, Ungar, 1957.
Saint Thomas and the Gentiles, Marquette University Press, 1938.
Problems for Thomists: The Problem of Species, Sheed, 1940.
(Editor) *The Philosophy and Science of Man as a Foundation for Ethics and Politics,* University of Chicago, 1940.
(Editor of translation) *Jacques Maritain, Scholasticism and Politics,* Macmillan, 1940, 3rd edition, Bles, 1954.
How to Read a Book: The Art of Getting a Liberal Education, Simon & Schuster, 1940, revised and enlarged edition (with Charles Van Doren), 1972.
Hierarchy, College of St. Thomas (St. Paul, Minn.), 1940.
A Dialetic of Morals: Toward the Foundations of Political Philosophy, University of Notre Dame, 1941.

How to Think about War and Peace, Simon & Schuster, 1944.
(Associate editor) *The Great Ideas: A Syntopicon of Great Books of the Western World,* two volumes, Encyclopaedia Britannica, 1952.
The Democratic Revolution, Industrial Indemnity, 1956.
The Capitalistic Revolution, Industrial Indemnity, 1957.
Liberal Education in an Industrial Democracy, Industrial Indemnity, 1957.
(With Louis O. Kelso) *The Capitalist Manifesto,* Random House, 1958, reprinted, Greenwood, 1975.
(With Milton Mayer) *The Revolution in Education,* University of Chicago Press, 1958.
The Idea of Freedom, Doubleday, Volume I: *A Dialectical Examination of the Conceptions of Freedom,* 1958, Volume II: *A Dialectical Examination of the Controversies About Freedom,* 1961.
Family Participation Plan for Reading and Discussing the Great Books of the Western World, with reading guides, Encyclopaedia Britannica, 1959.
(With Kelso) *The New Capitalists: A Proposal to Free Economic Growth from the Slavery of Savings,* Random House, 1961.
Great Ideas from the Great Books, Washington Square Press, 1961, revised and enlarged edition, 1963.
(Contributor) Arthur Allen Cohen, editor, *Humanistic Education and Western Civilization: Essays for Robert M. Hutchins,* Holt, 1964.
The Conditions of Philosophy: Its Checkered Past, Its Present Disorder, and Its Future Promise, Atheneum, 1965.
The Greeks, the West, and World Culture, New York Public Library, 1966.
The Difference of Man and the Difference It Makes, Holt, 1967.
Freedom: A Study of the Development of the Concept in the English and American Traditions of Philosophy, Magi Books, 1968.
(Editor with Van Doren) *The Negro in American History,* three volumes, Encyclopaedia Britannica Educational Corp., 1969.
The Time of Our Lives: the Ethics of Common Sense, Holt, 1970.
The Common Sense of Politics, Holt, 1971.
(With William Gorman) *The American Testament,* Praeger, 1975.
Some Questions about Language, Open Court, 1976.
Reforming Education: The Schooling of a People and Their Education Beyond Schooling, Westview, 1977.
Philosopher at Large: An Intellectual Autobiography, Macmillan, 1977.
(With Van Doren) *The Great Treasury of Western Thought: A Compendium of Important Statements and Comments on Man and His Institutions by the Great Thinkers in Western History,* Bowker, 1977.
Aristotle for Everybody: Difficult Thought Made Easy, Macmillan, 1978.
How to Think about God: A Guide for the Twentieth-Century Pagan, Macmillan, 1980.
Six Great Ideas, Macmillan, 1981.
The Angels and Us, Macmillan, 1982.
The Paideia Proposal: An Educational Manifesto, Macmillan, 1982.
How to Speak/How to Listen: A Guide to Pleasurable and Profitable Conversation, Macmillan, 1983.
Paideia Problems and Possibilities, Macmillan, 1983.
The Paideia Program: An Educational Syllabus, Macmillan, 1984.
A Vision of the Future: Twelve Ideas for a Better Life and a Better Society, Macmillan, 1984.

Ten Philosophical Mistakes, Macmillan, 1985.

A Guidebook to Learning: For the Lifelong Pursuit of Wisdom, 1986.

We Hold These Truths: Understanding the Ideas and Ideals of the Constitution, Macmillan, 1987.

Reforming Education: The Opening of the American Mind (collected essays), Macmillan, 1989.

Intellect: Mind Over Matter, Macmillan, 1990.

"THE GREAT IDEAS PROGRAM" SERIES, PUBLISHED BY ENCYCLOPAEDIA BRITANNICA

(With Peter Wolff) *A General Introduction to the Great Books and to a Liberal Education,* 1959.

(With Wolff) *The Development of Political Theory and Government,* 1959.

(With Wolff) *Foundations of Science and Mathematics,* 1960.

(With Seymour Cain) *Religion and Theology,* 1961.

(With Wolff) *Philosophy of Law and Jurisprudence,* 1961.

(With Cain) *Imaginative Literature,* Volume I: *From Homer to Shakespeare,* 1961, Volume II: *From Cervantes to Dostoevsky,* 1962.

(With Cain) *Ethics: The Study of Moral Values,* 1962.

(With V. J. McGill) *Biology, Psychology, and Medicine,* 1963.

(With Cain) *Philosophy,* 1963.

OTHER

Associate editor, "Great Books of the Western World" series, fifty-four volumes, Encyclopaedia Britannica, 1952; editor-in-chief with Robert M. Hutchins, "The Great Ideas Today" series, Encyclopaedia Britannica, beginning 1961; editor with Hutchins, "Gateway to the Great Books" series, ten volumes, Encyclopaedia Britannica, 1963; editor, "The Annals of America" series, twenty-three volumes, Encyclopaedia Britannica, 1968—. Contributor to professional journals and popular magazines, including *Commonweal, Social Frontier, New Scholasticism, Thomist, Review of Literature, Harper's,* and *Ladies' Home Journal.* Encyclopaedia Britannica, Inc., director of editorial planning, 1966—, chairman of the board of editors, 1974—.

WORK IN PROGRESS: Several new books, including *What There Is: The Metaphysics of Common Sense.*

SIDELIGHTS: America's John W. Donohue describes Mortimer Adler and John Dewey as "the two most widely known American practitioners of philosophy since the death of William James in 1910, although their scholarly reputations are unequal." A disciple of Aristotle and Aquinas, a believer in absolute and universal truths and values, Adler has fought against the pragmatism of Dewey—the dominant influence on twentieth-century American thought and education—for over fifty years. Best known as the progenitor of the Great Books Program, he has attempted to popularize reading of the classics and to persuade others of the universal truths they contain. The attempts have made him a popular philosopher at large but have alienated him from many members of the academic community.

A high school dropout who was nevertheless an omnivorous reader, Adler decided to become a philosopher at age fifteen when he discovered Plato while reading John Stuart Mill's *Autobiography.* To this end, he attended Columbia University on a scholarship, finished the four-year program in three years, received a Phi Beta Kappa key, but failed to receive a B.A. degree because he refused to take the required swimming test. Nevertheless, he was appointed instructor in psychology at Columbia and after five years of teaching wrote his doctoral dissertation on the measurement of music appreciation. As John Murray Cuddihy wrote in the *New York Times Book Review,* Adler had become

"the only Ph.D. in America with no B.A., no M.A., not even a high school diploma." (In 1983—sixty years late—Columbia relented, waived the swimming requirement, and gave Adler his bachelor's degree. He was delighted to attend his graduation.)

While an undergraduate at Columbia, Adler launched his philosophical attack on pragmatism—the position that truth is whatever is useful to a given society at a specific stage in its history—and its leading spokesman, John Dewey, who was also one of Adler's teachers. A *Time* writer says that Adler "became a bulldozer for truth. In class he bombarded John Dewey with lone letters pointing out ambiguities and contradictions in his lectures." Influenced by the philosophy of Aristotle and St. Thomas Aquinas, Adler affirmed his belief in absolute and universal truths and values, charging that the failure to recognize their existence results from the application of the scientific method in areas where it is inappropriate. He argued that pragmatism, with its view of the scientific method as the preeminent model for all useful thought, creates moral and intellectual chaos, an effect that Adler considered apparent in progressive education.

After leaving Columbia for the University of Chicago at the invitation of Robert Maynard Hutchins, Adler expounded in numerous articles, books, and lectures his belief that a good education for all people everywhere (just because they are human) is to be found in the moral and intellectual disciplines that nurture the ability to think clearly and to exercise free will wisely. He asserted that progressive education, which emphasizes individual expression through a system of electives, is misguided and ultimately harmful: its subjectivity and relativity encourage aimlessness and superficiality. His ideas attracted attention, as evidenced by the success of his best-selling *How to Read a Book: The Art of Getting a Liberal Education.* Though some educators, according to the *Time* writer, "attacked him as a brash upstart who advocated a philosophical 'return to the Middle Ages,'" others supported him, particularly at Catholic colleges and universities where, John Donohue claims, "he was a legend" during the 1930s and 1940s.

At the University of Chicago, Adler put his educational theory to practice. He and Hutchins, the university's president and Adler's intellectual comrade-at-arms, managed to change academic requirements in favor of a broad training in the humanities, an education based primarily on close reading of the classics of Western civilization, the "Great Books." In 1946 they organized the Great Books Program, which brought together adults from all walks of life to discuss one of the classics every two weeks. To facilitate the project, 443 Great Books were reprinted in a 54-volume set by Encyclopaedia Britannica, Inc. Moreover, Adler directed production of the *Syntopicon* ("synthesis of topics"), an index to 102 "Great Ideas" in the Great Books. Donohue writes that "under Adler's generalship, a staff of thirty indexers [including the young Saul Bellow] and sixty clerical helpers took ten years to produce this remarkable tool at the cost of one million dollars. Ever since it appeared, it has refreshed the writers of term papers and has perhaps been surreptitiously consulted by their professors."

Since the Great Books Program, Adler has continued to promote public enlightenment, earning such nicknames as the "super-salesman of philosophy" and, according to John Murray Cuddihy, "the Charles Atlas of Western Intellection." "The underestimation of the human intelligence is the worst sin of our time," Adler told Michiko Kakutani of the *New York Times,* and he sees his task as the restoration of philosophy "to its proper place in our culture," to make it accessible to the person in the street. This goal is readily apparent in such works as *The Angels and*

Us and *Aristotle for Everybody,* though in a *Washington Post* review of the latter, Carole Horn expresses surprise at one of Adler's statements: "Aristotle's books are much too difficult for beginners." In the *Chicago Tribune Book World,* Victor Power recommends *Six Great Ideas* "as a layman's tour of six philosophical concepts that hold within them the kernels of deeper thought. By examining the concepts of truth, goodness, beauty, justice, equality, and liberty, the layman may be tempted, as I was, to re-examine what Plato, Aristotle, Augustine, Aquinas, Hume, and others said about the assumption of their societies. . . . The object of this study is to remind us all of our common vocation to become thoughtful human beings." Partly because of his efforts to popularize philosophy, Adler has largely been ignored by the philosophical establishment, which Kakutani asserts "tends to regard any sort of popularization—as well as the attendant commercial success—with distrust, even disdain." He admits being "run out of the academy" to Kakutani, but says he is not bothered by it: "I thumbed my nose at them—so why should they pay any attention to me? They think you're spoonfeeding if you write something free of jargon and footnotes. But you're not spoon-feeding—you're simply avoiding putting obstacles in people's path."

But Adler's ostracism from the philosophical establishment is also due to his unfashionable Aristotelian-Thomistic line of thought. Adler, says the *Time* writer, "relishes dismissing most of philosophy since Thomas Aquinas as being snarled with pseudo problems. Modern philosophy, [he] claims . . . , got off to 'a very bad start' when Descartes and Locke committed the 'besetting sin of modern thought': they ignored Aristotle. Many contemporary philosophers would disagree." Theologian Robert Short, for example, does. Reviewing *How to Think about God* in the *Chicago Tribune Book World,* Short calls the book "an anachronism" and takes issue with Adler's lack of concern for modern philosophy: "Sixty years ago such a book might not have surprised us. But since that time the easy assumptions of classical Western philosophy have been questioned and shaken by one of the strongest anti-philosophical movements ever seen—existentialism. It is as though Adler is entirely unaware of the scathingly anti-philosophical attacks of such giants as Kierkegaard, Nietzsche, Dostoevsky, Heidegger, and Sartre. More probably, Adler hopes that by ignoring them they'll simply go away."

Despite such criticism, Adler remains true to the convictions formulated early in his life. Consistent with his belief that truth is absolute and not subject to change due to events in the world, he continues to attack the pervasive influence of pragmatism: "The twentieth century, for the most part, is an age in which relativism, skepticism, and subjectivism are rampant," he told Kakutani, "and that's what I'm mainly fighting against."

MEDIA ADAPTATIONS: Six Great Ideas was adapted for a television series of the same title, featuring Adler and Bill Moyers, Public Broadcasting Service, 1982.

BIOGRAPHICAL/CRITICAL SOURCES:

BOOKS

Adler, Mortimer J., *Philosopher at Large: An Intellectual Autobiography,* Macmillan, 1977.

PERIODICALS

America, April 29, 1978.
Chicago Tribune, January 5, 1983, March 25, 1987, November 27, 1988, March 20, 1989.

Chicago Tribune Book World, March 9, 1980, May 3, 1981, April 11, 1982, September 26, 1982.
Commonweal, June 7, 1940, June 20, 1958.
Globe & Mail (Toronto), August 24, 1985.
Los Angeles Times, June 10, 1982, November 1, 1982.
Los Angeles Times Book Review, September 12, 1982.
New Statesman and Nation, January 4, 1941.
New Yorker, March 9, 1940.
New York Times, December 14, 1982.
New York Times Book Review, August 14, 1977, April 28, 1985.
Saturday Review, May 24, 1958.
Saturday Review of Literature, March 9, 1940.
Time, March 18, 1940, March 17, 1952, April 6, 1959, July 25, 1977, May 30, 1983, May 4, 1987.
Times Literary Supplement, October 14, 1977.
Washington Post, May 25, 1978, April 3, 1980, May 8, 1982.
Washington Post Book World, November 14, 1982, June 26, 1983, September 18, 1983.
Yale Review, autumn, 1940.

*   *   *

ADLER, Renata   1938-
(Brett Daniels)

PERSONAL: Born October 19, 1938, in Milan, Italy; daughter of Frederick L. and Erna (Strauss) Adler. *Education:* Bryn Mawr College, A.B., 1959; Sorbonne, University of Paris, D.d'E.S., 1961; Harvard University, M.A., 1962; Yale University, J.D., 1979.

ADDRESSES: Agent—Lynn Nesbit, International Creative Management, 40 West 57th St., New York, N.Y. 10019.

CAREER: Novelist, journalist, film critic. *New Yorker,* New York City, writer-reporter, 1962-68 and 1970-82; *New York Times,* New York City, film critic, 1968-69. Fellow of Trumbull College, Yale University, 1969-72; associate professor of theatre and cinema, Hunter College of City University of New York, 1972-73. Judge in arts and letters for National Book Awards, 1969.

MEMBER: PEN (member of executive board, 1964-70).

AWARDS, HONORS: Guggenheim fellow, 1973-74; first prize in O. Henry Short Story Awards, Doubleday & Co., 1974; American Academy and Institute of Arts and Letters Award, 1976; Ernest Hemingway Prize, 1976, for best first novel; elected to American Academy and Institute of Arts and Letters, 1987.

WRITINGS:

Toward a Radical Middle: Fourteen Pieces of Reporting and Criticism, Random House, 1969.
A Year in the Dark: Journal of a Film Critic, 1968-1969, Random House, 1970.
Reckless Disregard; Westmoreland v. CBS et al.; Sharon v. Time, Knopf, 1986.

NOVELS

Speedboat, Random House, 1976.
Pitch Dark, Knopf, 1983.

OTHER

Contributor of articles and short stories, sometimes under pseudonym Brett Daniels, to *National Review, Vanity Fair, New Yorker, Harper's Bazaar, Commentary, Atlantic,* and other periodicals. Member of editorial board, *American Scholar,* 1969-75; consulting editor, *Vanity Fair,* 1983.

SIDELIGHTS: With just five books to her credit, Renata Adler has distinguished herself as a gifted prose writer with a unique sensibility and an analytical mind. Trained as a journalist, Adler worked for twenty years at the *New Yorker,* and her first two books were collections of essays and reviews written on assignment for that magazine and for the *New York Times,* where she worked one year as a film critic. In 1969, having had "about enough" of film reviewing and convinced, as she told *New York* contributor Jesse Kornbluth, "that if you're going to write, after a certain point some of it better be fiction," Adler turned to short stories. Her early work surfaced in the *New Yorker,* and she eventually collected and reshaped much of this short fiction into her award-winning first novel, *Speedboat.* Seven years later her second novel, *Pitch Dark,* appeared. Well before its 1983 publication, however, Adler had decided that "you can't really be a journalist and not know the law," as she told Kornbluth. She enrolled at the Yale Law School. The influence of her legal training is apparent in her 1986 book, an exhaustive investigation into shoddy news reporting practices entitled *Reckless Disregard: Westmoreland v. CBS et al.; Sharon v. Time.*

Despite the scope of her interests, Adler brings a constancy of outlook to all her writing. She grew up during the postwar Eisenhower years, "part of an age group," she once told *CA,* "that through being skipped, through never having had a generational voice, was forced into the broadest possible America. . . . We have no journals we publish, no exile we share, no brawls, no anecdotes, no way, no solidarity, no mark. In a way . . . we are the last custodians of language . . . because history, in our time, has rung so many changes on the meaning of terms, and we, having never generationally perpetuated anything, have no commitment to any distortion of them." Adler's careful use of language, her insistence on factual accuracy, and her original way of thinking have established her as a cultural critic whose work often contains what Kornbluth calls "bombshells."

Among these bombshells are Adler's provocative but generally negative film reviews, which so angered the moviemaking industry that in 1968 United Artists took out a full-page *New York Times* ad denouncing her. She further outraged the film community in 1979 by publishing a scathing *New York Review of Books* critique of colleague Pauline Kael's work. Her review of Kael's *When the Lights Go Down* pronounced the collection of film reviews "jarringly, piece by piece, line by line, and without interruption, worthless," and created a minor scandal within the film community. But even when she's dealing in the realm of imagination rather than analysis, Adler's work can provoke literary controversy, as evidenced by critical reaction to her first book of fiction, *Speedboat.*

Labeled a novel by its publisher, *Speedboat* defies many novelistic conventions. *Atlantic* reviewer Richard Todd believes "calling it a novel perhaps stretches a point. It is a gathering of stories. . . . And the stories themselves are assemblages of small moments that lack the coherence of plot but nevertheless overlap and iridesce like the scales of a fish." The episodes vary in length from a few lines to several pages and seem to be organized in random fashion. In one incident (from which the novel takes its name), a young woman takes a joyride in a new speedboat and exaggerates each bounce of the boat against the waves until she breaks her back. In another, a different woman imagines that she is being followed by rats.

By juxtaposing episodes like these with personal observations, Adler creates a disturbing portrait of contemporary urban life.

But, unlike a traditional novel that builds to a climax, *Speedboat* offers neither "engrossing narrative" nor "sustained psychological rendering of character," *New York Times Book Review* contributor Robert Towers believes. What holds the book together is the sensibility of Jen Fain, its fictional narrator. Patterned, critics believe, after Adler herself, Fain is a career woman about 35 years of age, living in New York and working at a newspaper while also teaching college part-time. Just as Adler grew up in the fifties, so does her narrator represent that age group in *Speedboat.* "Associate Professor Fain (to use her part-time academic title) epitomizes a whole generation of educationally privileged Americans who came of age at the end of the Eisenhower era. She often writes as a historian of this generation, as a survivor," writes Towers. Like her reticent creator, "Fain does not declare herself; she has to be pieced together by the reader from what she chooses to report and generalize about," John Leonard observes in *Harper's* magazine.

Though written in the first person, *Speedboat,* according to critics, is cool, dispassionate, and always carefully controlled. "For all its attention to modern woes, *Speedboat* is free of stock response," notes Todd. "No lamentations of vulgarity. No intimations of systematic evil. No love of madness, no chic despair. It is the work of someone who simply won't relinquish the right to say . . . 'how strange.'" Other reviewers also note Adler's unique way of recording events. Her voice, "although in the familiar tradition of wise, witty, perceptive, resigned New York cool, is original in its avoidance . . . of the mawkishly tough or languidly hysterical, in the exact grace of its prose and its vigilant self-scrutiny," notes *Times Literary Supplement* contributor Eric Korn. Describing the book as "wonderfully fresh and thoughtful," *New Republic* contributor Anne Tyler surmises that *Speedboat* was "written as if the author neither knew nor cared how other people wrote; she would proceed in her own remarkable way."

Because it is composed of unrelated incidents, *Speedboat* presents some structural challenges that not all reviewers believe Adler has overcome. For instance, in one of the few truly negative reviews of the book, *New York Times* critic Anatole Broyard dismisses *Speedboat* as "little more than a series of witty jottings, a collection of small, contemporary curiosities set down one after another in the conviction that they would all eventually work in apposition. . . . It is all extremely clever, but, in my opinion, it is not what I mean—and I decline the semantic challenge—by a novel. I do not believe that 'Speedboat' is important either." More representative of critical opinion is *Saturday Review* contributor Jane Larkin Crain's assertion that "as a series of sketches, vignettes, tableaus, the novel has already more force and stature than is ordinarily found in contemporary fiction, even in those offerings that attend faithfully, as Adler's work does not, to narrative conventions." Towers recommends reading the book in parts, "one section at a sitting, with frequent pauses for rereading," to relieve any "clogging effect."

The literary controversy that attended publication of Adler's first novel resumed in earnest when her second book of fiction, *Pitch Dark,* appeared in 1983. Variously described as an "antinovel" in the *New York Times,* a "meditation on writing a novel" in *Harper's,* and a "genre unto itself" in the *New York Times Book Review, Pitch Dark* emerged as one of the most widely discussed books of the year. Similar in style and structure to her first novel, *Pitch Dark* is also related by a first-person narrator who resembles Adler. Furthermore, according to Tyler, "it conveys the same sense of freshness, or originality practiced not for its own sake but because the author is absolutely desperate to tell us how . . . her heroine feels." In this book Adler narrows her focus from the general malaise of city life to the private pain accompanying the end of a love affair.

The plot, which is skeletal, revolves around narrator Kate Ennis's attempts to break off an extended affair with a married man. "Though the situation is essentially banal, Kate's methods of coping with emotional crises are so extraordinary that the book becomes a series of excursions into history, literature, philosophy, human relations, memory and fantasy," writes Elaine Kendall in the *Los Angeles Times Book Review.* "Some of these are hilarious; others ominous; several so remote from the matter at hand they seem imported from another book entirely."

To convey her story, Adler creates three loosely connected sections, the first and third of which are comprised of diverse episodes, reflections, and observations arranged non-chronologically, almost like journal entries reflecting what's on her mind. The longest episode in the first part is a five-page parable about an ailing raccoon that seems to overcome its wildness and takes up residence on Kate's stove. "I thought he was growing to trust me, when in fact he was dying," Kate writes. Developing this incident into a metaphor for her relationship to Jake, she continues: "So are we all, of course. But we do not normally mistake progressions of weakness, the loss of the simple capacity to escape, for the onset of love." *Village Voice* contributor Eliot Fremont-Smith describes the narrator's agonizing over the raccoon's fate as "a typical rumination in the book" and points out that "there are as many of these as there are half-mind's of Kate." In fact, the novel is studded with incidents that "at the time seemed only peripherally connected or connected not at all to the love affair," but in memory become "inextricably and painfully bound up with it," writes Steven Simmons in *Harper's.*

In the second section, Adler shifts to a more traditional narrative, chronicling a visit Kate makes to an Irish castle to get her mind off Jake. Adopting the tone of a thriller, this segment "is sensationally effective," according to Simmons. "The Irish passages by turns scary and funny, brilliantly evoke a very modern sense of paranoia, and they also reveal Adler's real and rather old-fashioned gift for sketching characters vividly and economically." It is here, as Kate plots a surreptitious departure from Ireland, that her identity and Adler's temporarily merge. At the airport, while trying to convince herself that adopting a false name would provide good cover, Kate writes: "I should make the name as like my own as possible to account for the mistake. Alder, I thought." After she experiments with variations, the name she eventually chooses is Hadley, but as *New York Times Book Review* contributor Muriel Spark notes: "Her own name is Ennis, and Alder, Haddock, Hadley do not resemble Ennis, could not possibly pose as either a visual or aural mistake. . . . Does Miss Adler mean to suggest that she herself is Kate Ennis? Illogical characters are fine, but this has the effect of professional illogic. It breaks the fiction and, for a brief moment, we have autobiography."

One strategy for deciphering the story, suggests Toronto *Globe and Mail* contributor Gale Garnett, is to read it as "a long letter from one lover to another, filled with all of the accumulated grievances, angers and desires that pile up over the course of a long alliance with a very busy married man. . . . He knows all the details of the relationship so, if it is to him that our author-protagonist is writing, it would be redundant to chronicle them here. Instead she gives him what she believes he does not know: her feelings, her thoughts, her frustrations at his perpetually unfulfilled promise to take her to New Orleans. Toward the end, she even becomes bored with sustaining the existence of 'Kate Ennis' and tells a story of selecting 'Hadley' as a pseud-

onym. . . . Perhaps Adler intended that the reader do some inductive and deductive sleuthing through her printed words."

By forcing the reader to piece her story together from fragments, Adler is affirming what Roger Shattuck calls "the 'innarratability principle.' You cannot tell your essential story straight out; Adler-Ennis quotes Emily Dickinson on telling it 'slant.' As the symbolist poets hesitated to name anything for fear of destroying the fragile essence of the object so rudely named, Adler fears to narrate. She proceeds by indirection, giving us only glancing views of the breakup with Jake," he writes in the *New York Review of Books.*

Critics typically associate this kind of minimalist approach with modernist fiction. But Adler, in an interview with *New York Times* reporter Samuel G. Freedman, expresses a wariness about aligning herself with that sophisticated school: "I think 'Pitch Dark' either works emotionally or it doesn't work at all. . . . If it is modernist in form, then I hope that form can accommodate a certain amount of feeling, because the relationship of modernism to feeling has been, at best, skittish. Modernism might be comic. It might be rueful. But it's all astringent. Someone said my writing was ironic. I don't think there's any irony, because in irony, there's a certain safety and reserve."

Arguing that Adler does indeed take risks in the novel, *New York Times* critic Michiko Kakutani concludes that "in the end, Kate's personality and voice—which, one suspects, closely echoes Miss Adler's own—help 'Pitch Dark' transcend the limits of its structure; they make the book not only engaging intellectually, but also emotionally compelling."

Between the publication of her first and second novels, Adler enrolled at Yale University to study jurisprudence, and by the time *Pitch Dark* was published, she had earned her law degree. Her fifth book reflects that legal training. In *Reckless Disregard: Westmoreland v. CBS et al.; Sharon v. Time,* Adler abandons the imaginary drama of fiction to portray the real-life theatrics of courtroom law. Her most controversial book to date, *Reckless Disregard* has been criticized less for how it is written than for what it implies. The book took shape when, through an unusual coincidence, two military leaders filed separate, but remarkably similar, libel suits charging that their reputations had been wrongfully damaged by major news organizations. Both suits were filed in the U.S. District Court of Manhattan between October, 1984, and February, 1985, and both defendants were represented by what Adler calls "the large and powerful New York law firm, Cravath, Swaine & Moore."

In the Sharon case, former Defense Minister of Israel General Ariel Sharon filed suit against Time, Inc., to protest a news story in *Time* magazine's February 21, 1983, issue suggesting that Sharon had abetted the massacre of civilian Palestinians by Lebanese Christian Phalangists. That story, which claimed that Sharon had "reportedly discussed . . . the need for the Phalangists to take revenge," was judged "false and defamatory" by the jury. But because Sharon had not, in the court's eyes, "proved by clear and convincing evidence" that *Time* knew the story was false before publishing it, "actual malice" could not be proved. Despite being cleared of libel charges, *Time* correspondent David Halevy, who filed the story, was singled out by the jury in an amplifying statement for having "acted negligently and carelessly."

In the Westmoreland case, former commander of American forces in South Vietnam General William Westmoreland filed charges against CBS, news reporter Mike Wallace, and others because of a documentary aired January 23, 1982. Entitled "The

Uncounted Enemy: A Vietnam Deception," the program suggested that "a conspiracy at the highest levels of American military intelligence" had resulted in underestimating the number of North Vietnamese forces in 1967-68 so that it would look like the war was being won. Unlike *Time,* which had simply neglected to verify information provided by its correspondent, CBS was guilty of deliberate misrepresentation, Adler believes. "They took a thesis; found witnesses more or less to support it; interviewed those witnesses, and cut those parts of the interviews which did not support the thesis," she argues at length, concluding that "in short, they were acting not as press but as producers and directors casting for a piece of theatre." Despite the apparent merit of his case, Westmoreland dropped the charges before they reached a jury.

As she investigated both cases, Adler became convinced that the defendants had refused to acknowledge even the possibility of error, that their lawyers had behaved with what she called "almost mindless aggressiveness," and that together they displayed "a concerted disregard for the fundamental . . . goals of truth and accuracy," to use *New York Times Book Review* contributor Marvin E. Frankel's words. Her conclusions so angered CBS in particular that the network had Cravath file a fifty-plus-page document charging that *Reckless Disregard* represented "plainly false, gross misrepresentations and distortions of the record" and should be withdrawn. Publication of the manuscript, though delayed for several months, was ultimately effected without requiring a single factual change.

Adler's clash with Cravath was closely followed by the press, and syndicated columnist Edwin M. Yoder, Jr., dubbed it "the publishing scandal of the fall." When *Reckless Disregard* finally appeared in November, 1986, there were some scattered objections to specific minor issues, such as whether *Time* and CBS could even be considered as legitimate news sources and whether Adler were truly as impartial as she appeared to be. Several critics also noted her affinity for complex sentences, studded with dependent clauses and parenthetical asides. "Is there no editor at *The New Yorker* or Knopf who dares cry, 'Block that parenthesis!'?" *Washington Post Book World* critic William V. Shannon asks in frustration. In general, however, most critics applauded Adler's courage and firmly endorsed her book.

" 'Reckless Disregard' is the best book about American journalism of our time . . . yet another parable of how law, in our overly litigious society, can overcome and even devour professional and ethical scruples," Yoder writes in the *Washington Post.* Shannon describes it as "brilliant in its analysis, relentlessly argued, and unsparing in its moral and professional journalistic judgments. Adler leaves in shreds and tatters the professional reputations of both *Time* and CBS and their respective employees involved in these two cases. She proves that both organizations were wrong in their original news presentations, refused when challenged to admit error, and deployed their huge financial and legal resources to obscure the truth and defeat justice." Concludes *Chicago Tribune Books* reviewer Edward P. Bassett, "Given the apparent breakdown in ethics in a number of fields today, the journalist (and lawyer?) and citizen interested in encouraging those in our society to discourse should read this book and take pains to understand the author's messages."

BIOGRAPHICAL/CRITICAL SOURCES:

BOOKS

Contemporary Literary Criticism, Gale, Volume 8, 1978, Volume 31, 1985.

PERIODICALS

Atlantic, October, 1976.
Chicago Tribune, October 28, 1986.
Chicago Tribune Books, December 14, 1986.
Commentary, June, 1984.
Detroit News, January 29, 1984.
Globe and Mail (Toronto), January 28, 1984.
Harper's, November, 1976, February, 1984.
Los Angeles Times, November 18, 1986.
Los Angeles Times Book Review, December 18, 1983, December 7, 1986.
Ms., November, 1976.
Nation, November 6, 1976, February 18, 1984.
New Republic, December 5, 1983.
Newsweek, October 11, 1976, December 19, 1983, November 10, 1986.
New York, December 12, 1983.
New York Review of Books, August 14, 1980, March 15, 1984.
New York Times, January 28, 1970, September 23, 1976, December 5, 1983, December 27, 1983, August 28, 1986, October 25, 1986, November 6, 1986.
New York Times Book Review, March 29, 1970, September 26, 1976, December 18, 1983, November 9, 1986.
Saturday Review, April 4, 1970, October 2, 1976.
Spectator, September 10, 1977.
Time, October 11, 1976, December 5, 1983.
Times (London), July 19, 1984.
Times Literary Supplement, August 26, 1977, July 20, 1984.
Village Voice, October 11, 1976.
Voice Literary Supplement, December, 1983.
Washington Post, August 18, 1984, November 4, 1986, November 14, 1986, November 23, 1986, May 10, 1988.
Washington Post Book World, October 24, 1976, December 25, 1983, November 9, 1986.

*   *   *

AGHILL, Gordon
   See SILVERBERG, Robert

*   *   *

AGNON, S(hmuel) Y(osef Halevi)   1888-1970

PERSONAL: Name originally Shmuel Yosef Czaczkes; born July 17, 1888, in Buczacz, Galicia (then Austria-Hungary, now Poland); immigrated to Palestine (now Israel); died February 17, 1970, in Tel Aviv, Israel; son of Shalom Mordecai (an ordained rabbi, merchant, and scholar) and Esther (Farb-Hacohen) Czaczkes; married Esther Marx, May 6, 1919; children: Emuna (daughter), Shalom Mordecai Hemdat. *Education:* Spent six years in various private hadarim and a short period at the Baron Hirsch School. *Religion:* Jewish.

CAREER: Lived in Galicia, 1888-1908; his first published verses appeared in Hebrew and Yiddish when he was fifteen; first went to Jaffa, Palestine, c. 1908, and became first secretary of the Jewish court in Jaffa and secretary of the National Jewish Council; went to Germany, 1913, and was a lecturer in Hebrew literature, 1920-1924, and a tutor in Hebrew; returned to Palestine in 1924 to settle there permanently.

MEMBER: Hebrew Language Academy, Mekitzei Nirdanim (society for the publication of ancient manuscripts; president, 1950-70).

AWARDS, HONORS: Fellow, Bar Ilan University; Bialik Prize for Literature, 1934, for *Bi-levav Yamin (In the Heart of the*

Seas), and again in the 1950s; D.H.L., Jewish Theological Seminary of America, 1936; Hakhnasat Kala, 1937; Ussishkin Prize, 1950, for *Tmol Shilshom;* Israel Prize, 1958; Ph.D., Hebrew University, Jerusalem, 1959; was made an honorary citizen of Jerusalem, 1962; Nobel Prize for Literature, 1966.

WRITINGS:

Ve-Hayah he-'Akov le-Mishor, [Jaffa], 1911/12, Juedischer Verlag (Berlin), 1919.

(Editor with Ahron Eliasberg) *Das Buch von den Polnischen Juden* (folk tales), Juedischer Verlag, 1916.

(Editor) *Moaus Zur: Ein Chanukkahbuch,* Juedischer Verlag, 1918.

Giv 'at ha-Hol, Juedischer Verlag, 1919.

Sipur ha-Shanim ha-Tovot (II Title: *Ma'aseh ha-Rav Veha-Orah*), [Tel Aviv], c. 1920.

Be-Sod Yesharim, Juedischer Verlag, 1921.

Me-Hamat ha-Metsik, Juedischer Verlag, 1921.

'Al Kupot ha-Man'ul, Juedischer Verlag, 1922.

Polin (fiction), Hedim (Tel Aviv), 1924/25.

Ma'aseh ha-meshulah me-erets ha-Kedosha, [Tel Aviv], 1924/25.

Ma'aseh rabi Gadiel ha-Tinok, [Berlin], 1925.

Agadat ha-sofer, [Tel Aviv], 1929.

Laylot, [Tel Aviv], 1930/31.

Bi-levav Yamim, Schocken (Berlin), 1935, translation by Israel Meir Lask published as *In the Heart of the Seas: A Story of a Journey to the Land of Israel,* Schocken (New York), 1948, reprinted, 1980.

Kovets Sipurim, [New York], 1937.

Yamim Nora'im, Schocken (Jerusalem and Berlin), 1938, 4th edition, Schocken (New York), 1956, translation by Maurice T. Galpert, revised by Jacob Sloan, published as *Days of Awe: Being a Treasury of Traditions, Legends and Learned Commentaries Concerning Rosh ha-Shanah, Yom Kippur and the Days Between, Culled from Three Hundred Volumes, Ancient and New,* condensed and edited by Nahum N. Glatzer, Schocken, 1948.

Pi Shenaim o me-Husar Yom, [Tel Aviv], 1939.

Shevu'ath Emunim, [Jerusalem], 1943, translation by Walter Lever published as "Betrothed" in *Two Tales: Betrothed* [and] *Edo and Enam,* Schocken, 1966, reprinted, 1986.

Sipurim ve-Agadot, edited by Jehiel Ben-Num, [Tel Aviv], 1944.

'Al Berl Kazenelson, [Tel Aviv], 1944.

Sipurim, [Jerusalem, Tel Aviv], 1945.

Edo ve-Enam, Schocken (Jerusalem), 1950, translation by Walter Lever published as "Edo and Enam" in *Two Tales: Betrothed* [and] *Edo and Enam,* Schocken, 1966, reprinted, 1986.

Sifrehem shel Anshe Butshatsh (reprinted from "Sefer Butsats"), [Tel Aviv], 1956.

(With others) *Tehilla, and Other Israeli Tales,* Abelard, 1956.

(Editor) *Atem re'item,* [Jerusalem], 1959.

Kelev Hutsot, [Jerusalem], 1960.

(Compiler) *Sifrehem shel Tsadikim,* [Jerusalem], 1961.

Ha-Esh ve-Ha'etsim, Schocken, 1962.

Ve-Hayah he-Akov le-Mishor, edited by Naftali Ginaton, [Israel], 1966.

Sipurim, [Israel], 1966.

Sipurim, edited by Ginaton, [Israel], 1967.

Sipure Yom ha-Kipurim, edited by Ginaton, [Israel], 1967.

Selected Stories of S. Y. Agnon (Hebrew text), edited, with introduction, interpretations, and vocabulary, by Samuel Leiter, Tarbuth Foundation, 1970.

Twenty-One Stories, edited by Nahum N. Glatzer, Schocken (New York), 1970.

Shirah, [Israel], 1971, translation by Zeva Shapiro published as *Shira,* Schocken, 1989.

Ir u-Melo'ah, [Israel], 1973.

Kol Sipurav (collected works), eleven volumes, Schocken (Berlin, Tel Aviv, and Jerusalem), Volumes 1 and 2: *Hakhnasath Kallah,* 1931, translation by I. M. Lask published as *The Bridal Canopy,* Doubleday, 1937, reprinted, Gollancz, 1968; Volume 3: *Me-Az ume-Ata,* 1931; Volume 4: *Sippurei Ahayim,* 1931; Volume 5: *Sipur Pashut,* 1935, translation by Hillel Halkin published as *A Simple Story,* Schocken (New York), 1985; Volume 6: *Be-Shuva u-ve-Natat,* 1935; Volume 7: *Ore'ah Nata Lalun,* 1937, translation by Misha Louvish and others published as *A Guest for the Night,* Schocken (New York), 1968; Volume 8: *Elu va-Elu,* 1941 (later published in a revised edition as Volume 2 of collected works), translation by J. Weinberg and H. Russell published as *A Dwelling Place of My People: Sixteen Stories of the Chassidim,* Scottish Academic Press, 1983; Volume 9: *Tmol Shilshom,* 1945 (a section of this was published as *Kelev Hutsot,* [Merhavya], 1950); Volume 10: *Samukh ve-Nireh,* 1950; Volume 11: *Ad Heinah,* 1953; volumes issued under title *Kol Sipurav Shel Agnon,* [Jerusalem, Tel Aviv], beginning in 1947, 4th edition, Schocken, 1957, standard edition, edited by Agnon, Schocken, 1953-62.

Also author of *Ha-Nidah,* 1926, and *Ad olam,* 1954 (translated as *Forever More,* 1961).

Contributor to numerous books, including *Festschrift fuer A. Freimann,* [Berlin], 1935; *Minhah Ledavid,* [Jerusalem], 1935; *Sefer ha'Shanah shel Eretz Yisrael,* [Tel Aviv], 1935; *Jewish Studies . . . in Honour . . . of J. L. Lendau,* [Tel Aviv], 1936; *Sefer ha-Shabbat,* [Tel Aviv], 1936; Leo W. Schwarz, editor, *A Golden Treasury of Jewish Literature,* Farrar & Rinehart, 1937; *Luah ha-Arets,* [Tel Aviv], 1944; *Sefer Hashabat,* [New York], 1947; *Me-otuar ha-Sifrut ha-Hadashah,* [New York], 1948; Philip Goodman, editor, *The Purim Anthology,* Jewish Publication Society, 1949; Nathan Ausubel, editor, *A Treasury of Jewish Humor,* Doubleday, 1952; Azriel Eisenberg, editor, *The Bar Mitzvah Treasury,* Behrman, 1952; Abraham E. Millgram, editor, *Sabbath: The Day of Delight,* Jewish Publication Society, 1952; Joseph Leftwich, editor, *Yisroel,* Behrman, 1952; Azriel Eisenberg, editor, *The Confirmation Reader,* Behrman, 1953; M. Z. Frank, editor, *Sound the Great Trumpet,* Whittier Books, 1955; Sholom J. Kahn, editor, *A Whole Loaf: Stories from Israel,* Vanguard, 1962; Joel Blocker, editor, *Israeli Stories,* Schocken, 1962; Saul Bellow, editor, *Great Jewish Short Stories,* Dell, 1963; Samuel Sobel, editor, *A Treasury of Jewish Sea Stories,* Jonathan David, 1965; Leo W. Schwarz, editor, *The Jewish Caravan,* Farrar, Straus, 1965; S. Y. Penueli and A. Ukhmani, editors, *Hebrew Short Stories,* Volume 1, Institute for the Translation of Hebrew Literature, and Megiddo Publishing Co. (Tel Aviv), 1965.

Contributor to *Haaretz* (daily newspaper), *Palestine Review, Commentary, Gazith, Congress Bi-Weekly,* and other publications.

Agnon's works have been translated into at least sixteen languages.

SIDELIGHTS: "I am not a modern writer," S. Y. Agnon once commented. "I am astounded that I have even one reader. I don't see the reader before me. . . . I never wanted to know the reader. I wanted to work in my own way." It is true that, though Agnon was the dominant figure among Hebrew fiction writers for many years, and though his works are considered classics, he was, until he won the Nobel Prize, virtually unknown outside the Jewish reading public. Yet his advent as a writer early in the twentieth century reversed the trend of Jewish literature from what Menachem Ribalow called "the general European spirit." Agnon "reversed the trend from Europe homeward again, from alien ways back to the native road. . . . He said not a single word *pro* or *contra*. He simply began to write in a different manner, different from all other Hebrew writers of that time. His novelty lay in his old-fashionedness. His uniqueness consisted in his return to the old sources, to the folk-character and its traits of simplicity and sincerity, purity and piety."

Agnon had sensed the alien aspects of European culture and initiated a return to Jewish folk material, to Medieval Hebrew, and to the traditions and laws that he found in ancient sources. His prose, which is lyrical, ironic, humorous, and deceptively simple, reads as though it had been written ages ago. "With Agnon," wrote Ribalow, "the Hebrew short story reaches artistic heights. He has the secret of the perfect blend of content and form, style and rhythm, inner beauty and outer grace. He has tapped new sources of Jewish ethical and esthetic values, revealing the spiritual grandeur in Jewish life. He has done what others have sought in vain to do: to convert simplicity and folk-naivete into a thing of consummate art and beauty. To the jangled nerves of this troubled generation, Agnon's stories bring balm and comfort." Edmund Wilson considered him "a man of unquestionable genius."

Agnon revived ancient forms of storytelling, forms unlike those of the modern Hebrew "realistic" story. Rueben Wallenrod said that "because of its [apparent] lack of frame, Agnon's story flows without effort, and events follow one another in loose sequence. The time of the events is very seldom indicated. In the continuous shift of his relationships, he lives mainly within his memories, and the boundary between the actual and the imaginary has become blurred to such an extent that the confines of time are gone." According to David Patterson, "The first impressions of apparent simplicity soon give way to a realization of the overtones, references and allusions arising from the author's complete familiarity with the whole vast corpus of Hebrew literature. The ancient vocabulary of Hebrew is pregnant with associations of all kinds, and the skillful juxtaposition of words and phrases can be made to yield a variety of nuances. Linguistically, as well as thematically, Agnon's writings can be read at different levels."

Arnold J. Band wrote: "For some readers, Agnon is the epitome of traditional Jewish folk-literature; for others, he is the most daring of modernists. For the older reader, Agnon conjures up memories of Jewish life in Eastern Europe; for the younger reader, he wrestles with the central universal problems of our agonized century." Band took issue with those who saw Agnon as merely a reviver of Jewish folk material and techniques. He pointed out that Agnon read widely in German and Scandinavian literatures, and also read Russian and French novelists in German translation. "To attribute Agnon's literary technique to Jewish folk-literature alone, as many tend to do, is sheer nonsense; Agnon was well-acquainted with the best in modern European literature at a relatively early age."

Agnon's characters are the pious and the humble men of faith whom he endowed "with divine qualities without making an effort to emphasize the mystical," wrote Ribalow. He, as well as his characters, believed that righteousness will ultimately triumph and that the cruel aspects of reality can be transcended by pity and love. He wrote about the dispossessed of the earth, he himself having twice lost his home in a fire. Robert Alter wrote that in 1924 Agnon's home in Hamburg burned down, "and ev-

erything he owned went up in the flames, including his library of four thousand books and the manuscript of an autobiographical novel (which he never attempted to begin again)." Other manuscripts, all unpublished, were also destroyed. In 1929, his home in Jerusalem was ravaged by Arab rioters, and a good part of his library was lost. In 1948, during the Israeli liberation, Agnon had to evacuate his home in Talpiot. He returned after the end of the hostilities.

Agnon took his pen name, which later became his legal name, from the title of his first published story, "Agunot," which appeared in Jaffa in 1909. Baruch Hochman explained that the Hebrew word *agunah* refers to a Jewish grass widow, i.e., a woman who is separated from her husband. "Owing to conditions of life in the Diaspora, war, plague and political accident carried men off, leaving the *agunah* as living testament to the vicissitudes of both life in the Diaspora and the rigors of the impersonal Law. It would seem no accident that Agnon took his name from the tale. The very word is redolent of loss, but also of the infinite yearning and ineffable tenderness elicited by loss. All of Agnon's work was to pivot on such feeling. First there was the sort of loss rendered in this tale: of loved ones torn away in the midst of life, by chance, by fate, by death or desire. Then there was historical loss: the submergence of the world of origins to which one's feelings are bound, in the abyss of history. Finally, there was metaphysical loss: of transcendent objects of desire in the bewilderment of modernity."

His work has been compared to that of Miguel de Cervantes and, even more frequently, to Franz Kafka's, though his relation with the former is tenuous, and Agnon had reportedly denied any knowledge of Kafka. Alter noted that Agnon was not unlike Kafka in that he possessed "something of the same sense of a world where terrible things are waiting to spring out from the shadows of experience. Also . . . his Hebrew has much the same unexcited, deliberately restrained tone of narration as Kafka's German, and achieves a very convincing Kafkaesque *frisson*, often through the imagery of sounds." But Kafka's world, unlike Agnon's, was amoral, and the distinction between good and evil was vague.

Agnon once stated his reasons for writing in Hebrew: "Out of affection for our language and love of the holy, I burn midnight oil over the teachings of the Torah and deny myself food for the words of our sages that I may store them up within me to be ready upon my lips. If the Temple were standing, I would take my place on the platform with my fellow choristers and would recite each day the song that the Levites used to say in the Holy Temple. [Agnon traced his ancestry to the tribe of Levi.] But since the Temple is destroyed and we have neither Priests in their service nor Levites in their chorus and song, I devote myself to the Torah, the Prophets, the latter Scriptures, the Mishnah, Halachah and Aggada, the Tosefta, rabbinical commentaries and textual glosses. When I look at their words and see that of all our precious possessions in ancient times only the memory is left us, I am filled with sorrow. And that sorrow makes my heart tremble. And from that trembling I write stories, like a man banished from his father's palace who builds himself a small shelter and sits there telling the glory of his ancestral home." Alter noted that "like generations of Jews before him, Agnon regards Hebrew as the Jew's indispensable means of entrance into the sphere of sanctity." For Agnon, the Hebrew characters comprised "the alphabet of holiness."

Although Agnon's stories reflect the tragedy and death that lurk in the background, David Patterson wrote that "one positive element alone remains constant—Jerusalem herself, which in

Agnon's stories is endowed with a personality of her own, and becomes a symbol for all that is meaningful and permanent and harmonious in life. It is as though the holy city alone contains the seeds which might restore that wholeness of spirit and oneness [with the world] that are slipping through the nerveless fingers of our unhappy generation."

After his immigration in 1924 until his death, Agnon wrote about life in Israel. The style remained the same, wrote Ribalow, "epically quiet and midrashically wise. But more and more do present realities play a part, together with all of their difficulties and sufferings, their problems and contradictions." And Wallenrod observed that "the new form of Agnon's stories has not changed the former content. The criterion for the human being is still his humaneness."

Agnon's entire life had been devoted to writing, and, with a permanent annual stipend from his publisher, Schocken Books, he was able to support himself on his writings alone. (In 1916 Salman Schocken promised to find a publisher for Agnon, and he redeemed this promise by becoming a publisher in order to issue Agnon's writings.) He was known to be a perfectionist who sometimes set aside a story for as long as fifteen years before he felt ready to rework it and submit it for publication. Agnon revised stories he had published more than thirty years previously. He described his writing habits for the *New York Times:* "When I was healthy I used to work standing. I felt myself fresh and good and sometimes worked that way all day and into the night. I recommend it to every writer. But now I must sit to work and keep this [nitroglycerine] for the heart condition I have had for fifteen years." The street in Talpiot on which he lived was closed to traffic, and a sign at the head of the street read: "Quiet. Agnon is Writing."

Agnon read less in his later years, his vision failing, but when he did it was to the Talmud that he turned. He apologized to one American interviewer for not being able to speak English, and added: "I made a contract with the Almighty, that for every language I did not learn he would give me a few words in Hebrew. . . . [Also], in order that I shouldn't have to go many places, I don't learn English." One place he wanted to, and did, visit, however, was Stockholm to receive the Nobel Prize from the king. It would be a rare pleasure, Agnon said beforehand, "because there is a special benediction one says before a king, and I have never met a king."

BIOGRAPHICAL/CRITICAL SOURCES:

BOOKS

Band, Arnold J., *Nostalgia and Nightmare: A Study in the Fiction of S. Y. Agnon,* University of California Press, 1968.
Contemporary Literary Criticism, Gale, Volume 4, 1975, Volume 8, 1978, Volume 14, 1980.
Hojman, B., *The Fiction of S. Y. Agnon,* Cornell University Press, 1970.
Hurwicz, Elias, *Aus Agnons dichterischen Schaffen,* [Berlin], 1936.
Kaufmann, Fritz Mordechai, *Vier Essais Ueber ostjuedische Dichtung und Kultur,* [Berlin], 1919.
Kimhi, Dob, *Soferim,* J. Sreberk (Tel Aviv), 1953.
Kurzweil, Baruch, *Masekhet ha-Roman,* [Tel Aviv], 1953.
Malachi, Eliezer Raphael, *Dr. Sh. Y. Agnon,* Hadoar (New York), 1935/36.
Penuell, S. I., *Yetsirato shel Sh. Y. Agnon,* [Tel Aviv], 1960.
Ribalow, Menachem, *Dichter und Shafer fuer neu-Hebraish,* [New York], 1936.

Ribalow, Menachem, *The Flowering of Modern Hebrew Literature,* Twayne, 1959.
Sadan, Dob, *Al Shai Agnon,* [Tel Aviv], 1959.
Seh-Lavan, Yosef, *Shmuel Yosef Agnon,* [Tel Aviv], 1947.
Wallenrod, Rueben, *The Literature of Modern Israel,* Abelard, 1956.
Zoref, Ephraim, *Sh. Y. Agnon,* [Tel Aviv], 1957.

PERIODICALS

Adam International Review, Number 307-8-9, 1966.
Ariel (Jerusalem), Number 11, 1965, Number 17, 1966/67.
Commentary, August, 1961, December, 1966.
Congress Bi-Weekly, November 7, 1966.
Daedalus, fall, 1966.
Nation, December 12, 1966.
New Statesman, December 9, 1966.
New York Times, October 21, 1966.
New York Times Book Review, September 18, 1966.

*   *   *

AIKEN, Conrad (Potter)   1889-1973
(Samuel Jeake, Jr.)

PERSONAL: Born August 5, 1889, in Savannah, Ga.; died August 17, 1973, in Savannah, Ga.; son of William Ford (a physician) and Anna (Potter) Aiken; married Jessie McDonald, August 25, 1912 (divorced, 1930); married Clarice Lorenz, February, 1930 (divorced, 1937); married Mary Hoover, August 7, 1937; children: (first marriage) John Kempton, Jane Kempton, Joan Delano. *Education:* Harvard University, A.B., 1911.

ADDRESSES: Home—Forty-one Doors, Stony Brook Rd., Brewster, Mass.; and Savannah, Ga.

CAREER: Poet, essayist, novelist, and short-story writer. President of Harvard's *Advocate* while in college; placed on probation for irregular class attendance in his senior year at Harvard and left for his first trip to Europe, 1911; made several trips abroad between 1916 and 1922 and met Ezra Pound, T. S. Eliot, and Amy Lowell; at this time he also became a reviewer for *New Republic, Poetry, Chicago Daily News, Poetry Journal,* and *Dial* (for which he was a contributing editor, 1917-18); wrote "Letters from America" to *Athenaeum* and *London Mercury;* settled in England, 1922 ("I didn't stay all the time," he says. "I went and came."); returned to America, 1925; tutor in English at Harvard University, 1925-26; under pseudonym Samuel Jeake, Jr., was London correspondent to *New Yorker,* 1934-36; consultant in poetry, Library of Congress, 1950-52.

MEMBER: American Academy of Arts and Letters, Harvard Club (Boston).

AWARDS, HONORS: Pulitzer Prize, 1930, for *Selected Poems;* Shelley Memorial Award, 1930; Guggenheim fellowship, 1934; named fellow in American letters, 1947; Bryher Award, 1952; National Book Award, 1954, for *Collected Poems;* Bollingen Prize in Poetry, 1956; Academy of American Poets fellowship, 1957; National Institute of Arts and Letters Gold Medal, 1958; Huntington Hartford Foundation Award, 1961; St. Botolph Award, 1965; Gold Medal of Achievement, Brandeis University Creative Awards Commission, 1967; National Medal for Literature, 1969, Poet Laureate of Georgia, 1973.

WRITINGS:

POETRY

Earth Triumphant, and Other Tales in Verse, Macmillan, 1914, reprinted, St. Martin's, 1975.

The Jig of Forslin: A Symphony, Four Seas, 1916, reprinted, International Pocket Library, 1965.

Turns and Movies, and Other Tales in Verse, Houghton, 1916, reprinted, R. West, 1976.

Nocturne of Remembered Spring, and Other Poems, Four Seas, 1917.

The Charnel Rose, Senlin: A Biography, and Other Poems, Four Seas, 1918, reprinted, Haskell House, 1971.

The House of Dust: A Symphony, Four Seas, 1920.

Punch: The Immortal Liar, Documents in His History, Knopf, 1921.

Priapus and the Pool (also see below), Dunster House, 1922.

The Pilgrimage of Festus, Knopf, 1923.

Senlin: A Biography, Hogarth Press, 1925.

Priapus and the Pool, and Other Poems, Boni & Liveright, 1925.

Conrad Aiken, edited by Louis Untermeyer, Simon & Schuster, 1928.

Selected Poems, Scribner, 1929.

Prelude, Random House, 1929.

Gehenna, Random House, 1930, reprinted, R. West, 1977.

John Deth: A Metaphysical Legend, and Other Poems, Scribner, 1930.

Preludes for Memnon; or, Preludes to Attitude (also see below), Scribner, 1931.

The Coming Forth by Day of Osiris Jones, Scribner, 1931.

Prelude: A Poem, Equinox, 1932, reprinted, Arden Library, 1978.

And in the Hanging Gardens, Lineweave Limited Editions (Baltimore), 1933.

Landscape West of Eden, Dent, 1934, Scribner, 1935.

Time in the Rock: Preludes to Definition (also see below), Scribner, 1936.

And in the Human Heart, Duell, Sloan & Pearce, 1940.

Brownstone Eclogues, and Other Poems, Duell, Sloan & Pearce, 1942.

The Soldier: A Poem, New Directions, 1944.

The Kid, Duell, Sloan & Pearce, 1947.

The Divine Pilgrim, University of Georgia Press, 1949.

Skylight One: Fifteen Poems, Oxford University Press, 1949.

Collected Poems, Oxford University Press, 1953, 2nd edition, 1970.

A Letter from Li Po, and Other Poems, Oxford University Press, 1955.

The Fluteplayer, privately printed, 1956.

Sheepfold Hill: Fifteen Poems, Sagamore Press, 1958.

Selected Poems (new selection), Oxford University Press, 1961.

The Morning Song of Lord Zero: Poems Old and New, Oxford University Press, 1963.

A Seizure of Limericks, Holt, 1964.

Cats and Bats and Things with Wings (poems for children), Atheneum, 1965.

Tom, Sue, and the Clock (poem for children), Macmillan, 1965.

Preludes (contains *Preludes for Memnon* and *Time in the Rock*), Oxford University Press, 1966.

Thee: A Poem, illustrations by Leonard Baskin, Braziller, 1967, published with illustrations by Gillian Ruff, limited edition, Inca Books, 1973.

The Clerk's Journal; Being the Diary of a Queer Man: An Undergraduate Poem, Together with a Brief Memoir of Harvard, Dean Briggs, and T. S. Eliot, Eakins Press, 1971.

A Little Who's Zoo of Mild Animals, Atheneum, 1977.

SHORT STORIES

Bring! Bring!, and Other Stories, Boni & Liveright, 1925 (published in England as *Bring! Bring!,* Secker, 1925).

Costumes by Eros, Scribner, 1928.

Among the Lost People, Scribner, 1934.

The Short Stories of Conrad Aiken, Duell, Sloan & Pearce, 1950.

The Collected Short Stories of Conrad Aiken, World Publishing, 1960, published with preface by Walter Allen, Heinemann, 1966.

NOVELS

Blue Voyage (also see below), Scribner, 1927.

Great Circle (also see below), Scribner, 1933.

King Coffin (also see below), Scribner, 1935.

A Heart for the Gods of Mexico, Secker, 1939, reprinted, R. West, 1977.

Conversation; or, Pilgrims' Progress, Duell, Sloan & Pearce, 1940.

The Collected Novels of Conrad Aiken (contains *Blue Voyage, Great Circle, King Coffin,* and *A Heart for the Gods of Mexico*), introduction by R. P. Blackmur, Holt, 1964.

Three Novels: Blue Voyage, Great Circle, King Coffin, preface by Aiken, McGraw, 1965.

EDITOR OR COMPILER

(And author of preface) *Modern American Poets,* Secker, 1922, revised edition with new preface, Modern Library, 1927, enlarged as *Twentieth Century American Poetry,* with augmented preface, 1945, revised edition, 1963.

(And author of preface) Emily Dickinson, *Selected Poems,* J. Cape, 1924, reprinted, Modern Library, 1948.

(And author of preface) *American Poetry, 1671-1928: A Comprehensive Anthology,* Modern Library, 1929, enlarged as *A Comprehensive Anthology of American Poetry,* 1944, revised, 1963.

(With William Rose Benet) *An Anthology of Famous English and American Poetry,* Modern Library, 1945.

OTHER

Scepticisms: Notes on Contemporary Poetry, Knopf, 1919, reprinted, Folcroft, 1969.

(Author of foreword) Thomas Hardy, *Two Wessex Tales,* Four Seasons, 1919.

Ushant: An Essay (autobiography), Duell, Sloan & Pearce/ Little, Brown, 1952.

Mr. Arcularis: A Play (first published in *Among the Lost People;* produced as "Fear No More" in London, 1946; produced in Washington, D.C., 1951), Harvard University Press, 1957.

A Reviewer's ABC: Collected Criticism of Conrad Aiken from 1916 to the Present, edited by Rufus A. Blanshard, Meridian, 1958, published as *Collected Criticism,* preface by I. A. Richards, Oxford University Press, 1968.

(Contributor) Howard Nemerov, editor, *Poets on Poetry,* Basic Books, 1965.

Selected Letters of Conrad Aiken, edited by Joseph Killorin, Yale University Press, 1978.

Contributor to *Massachusetts: A Guide to Its Places and People,* 1937. Aiken's papers are collected at the Huntington Library in San Marino, California, and the Houghton Library at Harvard University.

SIDELIGHTS: Although he received the most prestigious of literary awards, along with the critical acclaim of some of the most respected writers and critics of his time, Conrad Aiken never became a truly popular poet. This fact puzzled his admirers and, indeed, Aiken himself, who never lost his self-confidence and who always denied the charge that his poetry might be too difficult. Benjamin DeMott considered possibilities for Aiken's lack of exposure in a *Saturday Review* article: "The reasons for the neglect aren't so far to seek as might be supposed. They have to do partly with this poet's reluctance to break with certain nineteenth-century conventions of sound and posture. . . . Aiken has often flown against [dominant taste], writing heavy music, laying out gorgeous sound, providing no clear 'speaker,' no definable 'dramatic situation,' and pruning no modifiers." According to Alden Whitman of the *New York Times,* Louis Untermeyer once commented that "the poet made no effort to popularize himself or make himself in fashion." Aiken noted one curious phenomenon about his critical reception. He wrote to Malcolm Cowley that "each new book is panned—but in the background is the implication that all the previous ones were good."

A childhood tragedy left an indelible impression on Aiken. When he was eleven, his father shot first Aiken's mother and then himself. Aiken related the circumstances of his parents' death in his autobiography, *Ushant:* "After the desultory early-morning quarrel, came the half-stifled scream, and the sound of his father's voice counting three, and the two loud pistol shots and he tiptoed into the dark room, where the two bodies lay motionless, and apart, and, finding them dead, found himself possessed of them forever." It has been suggested that much of Aiken's interest in psychology stemmed from that shattering incident. Aiken once said that his short story "Silent Snow, Secret Snow" (a psychological portrait of a disturbed boy) was "a projection of my own inclination to insanity." According to Richard Hauer Costa, writing in the *Nation,* Aiken was "at all times an 'I' writer. He neither could nor wished to separate his life from his work." Aiken imbued much of his writing with psychological themes, frequently using the metaphor of a voyage to signify a journey to self-knowledge. Jennifer Aldrich noted in the *Sewanee Review:* "Three of Aiken's five novels, many of his short stories, and his first long poetic series, *The Divine Pilgrim,* as well as some of the later poems, were all written in the physical form of a journey. The actual vehicles of these journeys seem . . . to be in some way a symbol for consciousness; and the goal is the self." Throughout his career, Aiken measured his characters' progress along the voyage with a Freudian yardstick. Psychological themes were sometimes explored in unconventional formal structures. In a preface to his *Three Novels: Blue Voyage, Great Circle, King Coffin,* Aiken commented: "*Great Circle,* written five years after *Blue Voyage,* is just as insistently psychological in its approach to its theme, but less closely tethered to my own personality than its predecessor. . . . My early and continued preoccupation with musical form was allowed greater play."

Other early impressions reflected in Aiken's philosophy and writing were formed at Harvard, where he showed interest in the work of—among others—Henry and William James, Walt Whitman, the Symbolists, and the English Romanticists. In one case, an admired writer's style was baldly reproduced in Aiken's work. Alden Whitman reported in the *New York Times* that in his maturity Aiken called his first book of verse, *Earth Triumphant, and Other Tales in Verse,* "a dead steal from [John] Masefield." Aiken was aware that critics considered his style imitative, and at times he responded humorously to such suggestions. In 1918, for example, he wrote a dream dialogue in which Ezra Pound said, "Swinburne plus Fletcher minus Aiken equals Aiken," and Louis Untermeyer responded, "Eliot plus Masters minus Aiken equals Aiken." Aiken discussed the issue of influence more seriously with Robert Hunter Wilbur in a *Paris Review* interview. The work of T. S. Eliot, a friend from Harvard days, had had a "tremendous influence" on him, said Aiken; but

there had also been "a lot of interchange" in their relationship. As Aiken phrased it, "the juices went both ways."

A Harvard acquaintance to whom Aiken gave great credit was a professor of his, George Santayana. In the *Paris Review* interview, Aiken asserted that it was Santayana who shaped his "view of what poetry would ultimately be." Santayana's personal philosophy and his emphasis on the philosophical content of poetry were enormously appealing to Aiken. According to Jennifer Aldrich in the *Sewanee Review,* when Aiken was " 'invited to give his notions of what poetry should be' " he "turned to the following passage from Santayana's *Three Philosophical Poets:* 'Focus a little experience, give some scope and depth to your feeling, and it grows imaginative; give it more scope and more depth, focus all experience within it, make it a philosopher's vision of the world, and it will grow more imaginative in a superlative degree, and be supremely poetical. . . . Poetry, then, is not poetical for being short-winded or incidental, but on the contrary, for being comprehensive and having range. If too much matters renders it heavy, that is the fault of the poet's weak intellect, not of the outstretched world.' "

While Aiken admired many writers early in his career, that number decreased sharply with the passing years. His views, always vehement, became increasingly vitriolic. In an interview with Harvey Breit in 1950, he called William Faulkner "the great American genius, the only adult writer of fiction we've had in the last twenty years on a major scale." In 1969, he could name no such leader. He told Alden Whitman of the *New York Times:* "I think we're going through a very depressing decline in taste. . . . I don't think there is any first-rate fiction, and I mean to include everybody in that—Nabokov, Bellow, and so on." In Whitman's opinion, Aiken had "scarcely a kind word for anybody or anything except comic strips, martinis and Conrad Aiken."

Poets fared no better than novelists in Aiken's assessment of the state of writing. In 1968 he told Wilbur in the *Paris Review:* "I think we've come to a kind of splinter period in poetry. These tiny little bright fragments of observation—and not produced under sufficient pressure—some of it's very skillful, but I don't think there's anywhere a major poet in the process of emerging." Aiken had strong words, too, for anything resembling clubbiness. He once wrote that poets "really stink. Especially in large numbers, when herding." Patricia Reynolds Willis, writing for the *Georgia Review,* recorded his feelings about writers' colonies: "One writer by himself is bad enough, but if you get five in a room, it's terrible. And I doubt if anything good comes of it. It's much better to just go and hire a room in a lodging house and sequester yourself there in the city, and just get lost. But at those places, you've got a little sacred cabin out in the woods and have your own little lunch put at your doorstep at one p.m., and you are supposed to sit there and produce like a hen in a hen factory."

I. A. Richards felt that Aiken was more gracious than the above comments would indicate. Richards wrote in a *Times Literary Supplement* review of the *Selected Letters of Conrad Aiken:* "Few poets can have made greater efforts or faced more reasonably deprivation of recognition. His truly prodigious output met with curiously intermittent appreciation, periods of long neglect being taken with unflagging endurance and resolution. Along with this went a truly noteworthy immunity to those infections of jealousy and envy which afflict so many of us." The kindness Aiken showed to Malcolm Lowry, acting as a sort of father figure to the young writer, was noted by critics; and Richards noted that "his joy when he can really go all out in praise knows no bounds." Confident of his stature among peers, Aiken was modest when it came to the question of his place in history. Replying to a schoolboy who had praised his work, Aiken once wrote: "No, I don't have any great notion about where I stand as a poet. That will be taken care of by those wiser people who come later on the scene than we do. Thus, as in their turn, those opinions too will be revalued over and over. None of us knows in what direction poetry and those other arts will turn—that's part of the cruel fascination of being interested in the arts as you are, and keeping your head about it."

BIOGRAPHICAL/CRITICAL SOURCES:

BOOKS

Aiken, Conrad, *Ushant: An Essay,* Duell, Sloan & Pearce, 1952.
Aiken, Conrad, *A Reviewer's ABC: Collected Criticism,* Meridian, 1958, published as *Collected Criticism,* Oxford University Press, 1968.
Aiken, Conrad, *Three Novels: Blue Voyage, Great Circle, King Coffin,* preface by Aiken, McGraw, 1963.
Aiken, Conrad, *Selected Letters of Conrad Aiken,* edited by Joseph Killorin, Yale University Press, 1978.
Allen, Walter, *The Modern Novel,* Dutton, 1965.
Bonnell, F. W., and F. C. Bonnell, *Conrad Aiken: A Bibliography (1902-1978),* Huntington Library, 1982.
Breit, Harvey, *The Writer Observed,* World Publishing, 1956.
Concise Dictionary of Literary Biography, The Age of Maturity, 1929-1941, Gale, 1989.
Contemporary Literary Criticism, Gale, Volume 1, 1973, Volume 3, 1975, Volume 5, 1976, Volume 10, 1979, Volume 52, 1989.
Denney, Reuel, *Conrad Aiken,* University of Minnesota Press, 1964.
Dictionary of Literary Biography, Gale, Volume 9: *American Novelists, 1910-1945,* 1981, Volume 45: *American Poets, 1880-1945,* 1986.
Harris, Catherine, *Conrad Aiken: Critical Recognition, 1914-1981; A Bibliographic Guide,* Garland, 1983.
Hoffman, Frederick J., *Conrad Aiken,* Twayne, 1962.
Lorenz, Clarissa, *Lorelei Two: My Life with Conrad Aiken,* University of Georgia Press, 1983.
Martin, Jay, *Conrad Aiken: A Life of His Art,* Princeton University Press, 1962.
Peterson, Houston, *The Melody of Chaos,* Longmans, Green, 1931.

PERIODICALS

Atlanta Journal and Constitution Magazine, May 5, 1963.
Georgia Review, spring, 1968.
Nation, June 26, 1967.
New York Times, August 5, 1969, August 19, 1973.
New York Times Book Review, May 14, 1978.
Paris Review, winter-spring, 1968.
Rebel, winter, 1965.
Saturday Review, January 30, 1971, May 27, 1978.
Sewanee Review, summer, 1967.
Shenandoah, autumn, 1963.
Studies in the Literary Imagination, fall, 1980 (Aiken issue).
Times Literary Supplement, July 7, 1978.
Wake, Volume 11, 1952 (Aiken issue).
Washington Post Book World, May 16, 1982.

*   *   *

AIKEN, Joan (Delano) 1924-

PERSONAL: Born September 4, 1924, in Rye, Sussex, England; daughter of Conrad Potter (a poet) and Jessie (MacDonald) Aiken; married Ronald George Brown (a journalist), July 7, 1945 (died, 1955); married Julius Goldstein (a painter), September 2, 1976; children: (first marriage) John Sebastian, Elizabeth Delano. *Politics:* Liberal. *Religion:* Agnostic.

ADDRESSES: Home—The Hermitage, East St., Petworth, West Sussex GU28 0AB, England; New York, New York. *Agent*—Brandt & Brandt, 1501 Broadway, New York, NY 10036.

CAREER: Associated with British Broadcasting Corp., 1942-43, and United Nations Information Office, London, England, 1943-49; feature editor, *Argosy* magazine, 1955-60; copywriter, J. Walter Thompson Advertising Agency, 1961; full-time writer, 1961—.

MEMBER: Writers Guild, Society of Authors, Mystery Writers of America, Crime Writers Association.

AWARDS, HONORS: Guardian award, and runner-up for Carnegie Award, 1969, for *The Whispering Mountain;* Mystery Writers of America award, 1972, for *Night Fall.*

WRITINGS:

JUVENILE FICTION

All You've Ever Wanted (also see below), J. Cape, 1953.
More Than You Bargained For (also see below), J. Cape, 1955, Abelard, 1957.
The Kingdom and the Cave, Abelard, 1960.
The Wolves of Willoughby Chase, J. Cape, 1962, Doubleday, 1963, reprinted, 1989.
Black Hearts in Battersea, Doubleday, 1964, reprinted, Dell, 1987.
Nightbirds on Nantucket, Doubleday, 1966, reprinted, Dell, 1981.
The Whispering Mountain, J. Cape, 1968, Doubleday, 1969.
A Necklace of Raindrops, and Other Stories, J. Cape, 1968, Doubleday, 1969.
A Small Pinch of Weather, and Other Stories, J. Cape, 1969.
Night Fall, Macmillan (London), 1969, Holt, 1970, reprinted, Dell, 1988.
Armitage, Armitage, Fly away Home, Doubleday, 1970.
Smoke from Cromwell's Time, and Other Stories, Doubleday, 1970.
The Cuckoo Tree, Doubleday, 1971, reprinted, Dell, 1988.
The Kingdom under the Sea, J. Cape, 1971, reprinted, Penguin, 1986.
All and More (short stories; includes *All You've Ever Wanted* and *More Than You Bargained For*), J. Cape, 1971.
Winterthing: A Child's Play (first produced in London, England, by Puffin Drama Group at Young Vic Theatre, 1970), Holt, 1972.
Arabel's Raven, BBC Publications, 1972, hardcover edition published as *Tales of Arabel's Raven,* J. Cape, 1974, published under original title, Doubleday, 1974.
A Harp of Fishbones (stories), J. Cape, 1972.
The Mooncusser's Daughter (play; first produced in London at Unicorn Theatre, 1973), Viking, 1973.
The Escaped Black Mambo, BBC Publications, 1973.
The Bread Bin, BBC Publications, 1974.
Midnight Is a Place, Viking, 1974.
Not What You Expected (stories), Doubleday, 1974.
Tale of a One-Way Street (stories), J. Cape, 1976, Doubleday, 1980.
The Skin Spinners (poems), Viking, 1976.
A Bundle of Nerves (horror stories), Gollancz, 1976.
Mortimer's Tie, BBC Publications, 1976.
Go Saddle the Sea, Doubleday, 1977.

The Faithless Lollybird (stories), J. Cape, 1977, Doubleday, 1978.

Mice and Mendelson, J. Cape, 1978.

Street (play; first produced in 1977), Viking, 1978.

The Spiral Stair, BBC Publications, 1979.

Mortimer and the Sword Excalibur, BBC Publications, 1979.

Arabel and Mortimer, BBC Publications, 1980.

The Shadow Guests, Delacorte, 1980.

A Touch of Chill, Delacourt, 1980.

The Stolen Lake, Delacorte, 1981.

"Moon Mill" (play), first produced in London at Unicorn Theatre, 1982.

Mortimer's Portrait on Glass (also see below), BBC Publications, 1982.

The Mystery of Mr. Jones's Disappearing Taxi (also see below), BBC Publications, 1982.

Bridle the Wind, Delacorte, 1983.

Mortimer's Cross (also contains *Mortimer's Portrait on Glass* and *The Mystery of Mr. Jones's Disappearing Taxi*), J. Cape, 1983, Harper, 1984.

The Kitchen Warriors (stories), BBC Publications, 1984.

Up the Chimney Down (stories), J. Cape, 1984, Harper, 1985.

Fog Hounds, Wind Cat, Sea Mice (stories), Macmillan, 1984.

Mortimer Says Nothing (stories), J. Cape, 1985, Harper, 1986.

The Last Slice of Rainbow: And Other Stories, J. Cape, 1985.

Past Eight O'Clock (stories), J. Cape, 1986.

Dido and Pa, Delacorte, 1986.

The Teeth of the Gale, Harper, 1988.

The Moon's Revenge, Knopf, 1988.

The Erl King's Daughter, Barron, 1989.

Give Yourself a Fright, Delacorte, 1989.

Return to Harken House, Delacorte, 1990.

A Foot in the Grave, J. Cape, 1990.

A Goose on Your Grave, Gollancz, in press.

ADULT FICTION

The Silence of Herondale, Doubleday, 1964.

The Fortune Hunters, Doubleday, 1965.

Beware of the Bouquet, Doubleday, 1966 (published in England as *The Trouble with Product X,* Gollancz, 1966, reprinted, State Mutual Book, 1987).

Dark Interval, Doubleday, 1967 (published in England as *Hate Begins at Home,* Gollancz, 1967).

The Ribs of Death, Gollancz, 1967, reprinted, State Mutual Book, 1988, published as *The Crystal Crow,* Doubleday, 1968.

The Windscreen Weepers, and Other Tales of Horror and Suspense, Gollancz, 1969, published as *Green Flash, and Other Tales of Horror, Suspense, and Fantasy,* Holt, 1971.

The Embroidered Sunset, Doubleday, 1970.

The Butterfly Picnic, Gollancz, 1970, reprinted, State Mutual Book, 1988, published as *A Cluster of Separate Sparks,* Doubleday, 1972.

Nightly Deadshade, Macmillan, 1971.

Died on a Rainy Sunday, Holt, 1972, reprinted, Dell, 1988.

Voices in an Empty House, Doubleday, 1975.

Castle Barebane, Viking, 1976.

Last Movement, Doubleday, 1977.

The Five-Minute Marriage, Gollancz, 1977, Doubleday, 1978.

The Smile of the Stranger, Doubleday, 1978.

A Touch of the Chili: Tales for Sleepless Nights (honor stories), Gollancz, 1979, Delacorte, 1980.

The Weeping Ash, Doubleday, 1980.

The Girl from Paris, Doubleday, 1982 (published in England as *The Young Lady from Paris,* Gollancz, 1982).

A Whisper in the Night: Tales of Terror and Suspense, Gollancz, 1982, Delacorte, 1983.

Foul Matter, Doubleday, 1983.

Mansfield Revisited, Gollancz, 1984, Doubleday, 1985.

If I Were You, Doubleday, 1987.

Deception, Gollancz, 1987.

Blackground, Doubleday, 1989..

SOUND RECORDINGS

"The Wolves of Willoughby Chase," Caedmon, 1978.

"A Necklace of Raindrops," Caedmon, 1978.

OTHER

(Translator from the French) Sophie De Segur, *The Angel Inn,* J. Cape, 1976, Stemmer House, 1978.

The Way to Write for Children, Elm Tree Books, 1982, St. Martin's, 1983.

Contributor to periodicals, including *New Statesman, Times Literary Supplement, Times Educational Supplement, Washington Post, Good Housekeeping, Woman's Journal, Children's Literature in Education,* and *Quarterly Bulletin of the Library of Congress.*

MEDIA ADAPTATIONS: An adaptation of *Midnight Is a Place,* directed by Chris McMaster, was produced by Southern Television, 1977.

SIDELIGHTS: Joan Aiken is best known for inventing the "unhistorical romance, . . . a new genre which far outdoes its conventional counterpart in inventiveness and wit," according to *New Statesman* contributor Patricia Craig. These tales combine traditional elements of fairy tale, romance, and myth with fast-paced action and humor. They are set in an imaginary time period during the reign of King James III in England, described by Susan Dooley in the *Washington Post Book World* as "a surreal version of Dickens' 19th century." Aiken began her alternate history in *The Wolves of Willoughby Chase* and continued it in several other novels, including *Black Hearts in Battersea, Nightbirds on Nantucket,* and *The Stolen Lake.*

As the daughter of the American poet Conrad Aiken and the stepdaughter of the English writer Martin Armstrong, Joan Aiken was surrounded by literary models from birth. At the age of five she decided upon a literary career and began writing her first stories and poems. Her first acceptance came while she was still in school; two of her poems were published in a prestigious little magazine, the *Abinger Chronicle,* edited by E. M. Forster, Sylvia Sprigge, and Max Beerbohm. "They printed my poems but never paid me, which gave me the idea that poetry was not a remunerative occupation," notes Aiken in the *Something about the Author Autobiography Series.*

Aiken continued to develop her writing after her marriage to journalist Ron Brown, selling several radio scripts and some short stories. When Brown's death in 1955 left her with large debts and two children to support, she went to work as an editor for the short story magazine *Argosy.* To supplement her editor's wages, she also contributed many short stories to this publication and others. "I worked like a beaver, selling stories to *John Bull, Housewife, Vogue,* any magazine that would take fiction other than the woman's sob-type," the author relates in the *SATA Autobiography Series.* These stories, collected in the volumes *More Than You Bargained For* and *All You've Ever Wanted,* became Aiken's first published books. But writing short stories was beginning to seem like "an uneconomic use of time," she continues in the *SATA Autobiography Series.* "I wanted to write longer pieces of fiction that would sell for large sums." With that goal in mind she unearthed the manuscript of a novel written at the age of seventeen. Carefully revised, that manuscript became her first published novel, *The Kingdom and the Cave.*

Aiken began creating her scrambled history of England in her next novel, *The Wolves of Willoughby Chase.* Here she introduced what would become the standard elements of several of her novels: an English countryside terrorized by wolves, a colorful London underworld, the Stuart king James III, and the Hanoverian rebels determined to assassinate him. Although *The Wolves of Willoughby Chase* was marketed as a children's book, it was read and enjoyed by adults as well. Its success enabled Aiken to devote herself to writing full-time.

In their book *You're a Brick, Angela! A New Look at Girls' Fiction from 1839 to 1975,* Patricia Craig and Mary Cadogan offer an analysis of Aiken's "unhistorical adventure stories." They believe that these stories have "an exuberance, a pantomimic largeness which is . . . effective. There is nothing original about her plots, but she has brought to bear on them a sensibility which *is* original, if only because of its ability to assimilate, re-channel, enliven, send up, make good use of elements and conventions already traditional. She has effected a fusion of Gothic with Baroque, set off by a manneristic flair for detail."

Cadogan and Craig comment on Aiken's invented time setting: "This device has a great economy: events which take place in an imaginary era obviously are not governed by restrictions of plausibility, either social or temperamental. The period's non-existence serves mainly to emphasize that the stories are not meant to be pegged to the ground, their purpose is to take off as stylishly as possible. In a time that never happened, anything *can* happen."

Aiken's horror and suspense stories have been as highly praised as her fantasy adventures. Georgess McHargue writes of *Died on a Rainy Sunday* in the *New York Times Book Review:* "A thriller by Joan Aiken is like an ice cream cone. Both must be consumed at a single sitting and both leave a cold but pleasurable feeling in the pit of the stomach." *Washington Post Book World* contributor Natalie Babbitt explains that Aiken's stories in this genre "do not, any of them, go in much for the blood and gore that passes for horror in the movies these days, nor do any of them deal flat-out with the supernatural, also a common movie gimmick. Rather they run on the gray edge between order and chaos called so aptly the 'twilight zone' by the old television series."

In any genre, it is Aiken's professional craftsmanship that lifts her stories to the level of fine entertainment, writes *Washington Post Book World* contributor Michael Dirda. He concludes: "Joan Aiken can turn her hand to almost anything—mystery, fantasy, suspense, comedy—and nearly always come up with a winner." Reflecting on her earliest aspirations in her *SATA Autobiography Series* essay, Aiken notes, "With over sixty books listed on the British Public Lending Right register I feel I have achieved my ambition to be a professional writer. I know that my books vary. Some I am proud of; some are mere jobs of work, money-earners; a couple now fill me with slight embarrassment. Which do I love best? A pair of books with Spanish settings—*Go Saddle the Sea* and *Bridle the Wind.* Sometimes when you write a book you can feel it take off and lift away from you into unexplored regions—I felt those two did that."

BIOGRAPHICAL/CRITICAL SOURCES:

BOOKS

Authors and Artists for Young Adults, Volume 1, Gale, 1989.

Books for Children, 1960-1965, American Library Association, 1966.
Cadogan, Mary, and Patricia Craig, *You're a Brick, Angela! A New Look at Girls' Fiction from 1839 to 1975,* Gollancz, 1976.
The Children's Bookshelf, Child Study Association of America, Bantam, 1966.
Children's Literature Review, Volume 1, Gale, 1976.
Contemporary Literary Criticism, Volume 35, Gale, 1985.
Eadkin, Mark K., editor, *Good Books for Children,* Phoenix Books, 1966.
Jones, Cornelia, and Olivia R. Way, *British Children's Authors: Interviews at Home,* American Library Association, 1976.
Larrick, Nancy, *A Parent's Guide to Children's Reading,* 3rd edition, Doubleday, 1969.
Something about the Author Autobiography Series, Volume 1, Gale, 1986.
Townsend, John Rowe, *A Sense of Story: Essays on Contemporary Writers for Children,* Lippincott, 1971.

PERIODICALS

British Book News, August, 1982.
Calendar, March-October, 1979.
Chicago Tribune, November 9, 1980.
Horn Book, October, 1970, October, 1973, April, 1974, December, 1976.
Junior Bookshelf, August, 1974, June, 1976, October, 1982.
National Observer, September 23, 1968.
New Statesman, December 4, 1981.
New York Times, December 3, 1987.
New York Times Book Review, July 23, 1967, March 24, 1968, July 23, 1972, May 5, 1974, April 27, 1980, February 14, 1982.
Observer, April 18, 1982.
Punch, August 15, 1984.
Saturday Review, April 18, 1970, April 17, 1971, May 20, 1972.
Times (London), March 5, 1980, February 8, 1982, August 25, 1983, December 27, 1984, October 22, 1988, February 3, 1990.
Times Educational Supplement, June 5, 1981.
Times Literary Supplement, June 15, 1967, July 2, 1971, March 28, 1980, July 10, 1987, July 31, 1987.
Tribune Books (Chicago), July 10, 1988.
Washington Post, July 17, 1987.
Washington Post Book World, January 8, 1978, May 22, 1980, July 13, 1980, January 13, 1985, June 9, 1985, November 4, 1986, August 14, 1988, October 9, 1988, February 11, 1990.
Writer, March, 1980, May, 1982.

*   *   *

AITMATOV, Chingiz   1928-

PERSONAL: Born December 12, 1928, in Sheker Village, Kirghizia, U.S.S.R.; son of Torekul and Nahima Aitmatov; married wife, Keres (a physician); children: two sons. *Education:* Received degree in animal husbandry from Kirghiz Agricultural Institute; attended Moscow Literary Institute of the Union of Soviet Writers.

ADDRESSES: Home—43 Dzerzhinsky Flat 1, Frunze Kirghiz Soviet Socialist Republic, U.S.S.R. *Office*—c/o Kirghiz Branch of the Union of Writers of the U.S.S.R., Ulitsa Pushkina 52, Frunze, U.S.S.R.

CAREER: Novelist, short story writer, and playwright, 1952—. Communist Party of the Soviet Union, assistant to the secretary of Sheker Village Soviet, c. 1943, member, 1959—; People's Writer of Kirghiz Soviet Socialist Republic, 1968. Candidate member of Central Committee of Kirghiz Soviet Socialist Republic; vice-chairman of committee of Solidarity With Peoples of Asian and African Countries; deputy of U.S.S.R. Supreme Soviet. Cinema Union of Kirghiz Soviet Socialist Republic, first secretary, 1964-69, chairman, 1969—.

AWARDS, HONORS: Lenin Prize for literature and the fine arts, 1963, for *Tales of the Mountains and Steppes;* Order of the Red Banner of Labor (twice); U.S.S.R. State Prize, 1968; Hero of Socialist Labor, 1978.

WRITINGS:

IN ENGLISH TRANSLATION

Dzhamilia (novel), Pravda, 1959, translation published as *Jamila,* Foreign Languages Publishing House (Moscow).

Povesti gor i stepei, Sovetskii Pisatel, 1963, translation published as *Proschai, Gul'sary!* (novella), Molodia Guardiia, 1967, translation by John French published as *Farewell, Gulsary!,* Hodder & Stoughton, 1970.

Tales of the Mountains and Steppes, Progress Publishers, 1969.

Posle skazki, Belyi parokhod (novel), 1970, translation by Mirra Ginsburg published as *The White Ship,* Crown, 1972 (translation by Tatyana Feifer and George Feifer published in England as *The White Steamship,* Hodder & Stoughton, 1972).

(With Kaltai Mukhamedzhanov) *Voskhozhdenie na Fudzhiamu* (play; produced in Moscow, U.S.S.R., 1973; produced as "The Ascent of Mount Fuji" in Washington, D.C., at Kreeger Theatre, 1975), translation by Nicholas Bethell published as *The Ascent of Mount Fuji,* Farrar, Straus, 1975.

The Day Lasts More than a Hundred Years, translated by John French, Macdonald, 1983.

The Place of the Skull (novel), translated by Natasha Ward, Grove, 1989.

Also author of *Tri povesti* (novel), translation published as *Short Novels,* Progress Publishers.

OTHER

Rasskazy (title means "Stories"), Sovetskii Pisatel, 1958.

Verbliuzhii glaz (short stories and novellas; title means "The Camel's Eye"), Sovetskii Pisatel, 1962.

Materinskoe Pole (novel; title means "The Field of Mothers"), Pravda, 1963.

Samanchy zholu (short stories and novellas), Basmasy, 1963.

Povesti (title means "Novellas"), Izvestia, 1967.

Pervyi uchitel (novel; title means "The First Master"), Detskaia Literatura, 1967.

Atadan kalgan tuiak, Mektep, 1970.

Povesti i rasskazy (title means "Novellas and Stories"), Molodaia Guardiia, 1970.

Pegil pes, begushchij kraem moria, Sovetskii Pisatel, 1977.

V soavtostve s zemleiu i vodoiu (essays and lectures), Kyrgyzstan, 1978.

(With others) *You Have to Treat Your Heart,* Imported Publications, 1986.

A Time to Speak, International Publishing, 1989.

Contributor of articles to *Pravada* and other major newspapers and periodicals.

SIDELIGHTS: Unlike such dissident Soviet writers as Solzhenitsyn and Tsabour, Chingiz Aitmatov has managed to remain in the U.S.S.R. and write of life in the republic of his birth, Kirghizia. A member of one of the Soviet Union's central Asian minorities, he is the first Kirghiz author to become known throughout the world. His books have been widely translated, with several appearing in French, German, Polish, English, and Arabic editions. His work has also been the focus of several Soviet films.

Aitmatov is an active and prominent member of the Communist party. Nevertheless, as *Newsweek*'s Jay Axelbank noted, he "tries to steer clear of political ideology and concentrate on psychological portraits" in his writing. He incorporates aspects of the Kirghiz oral tradition into the reality of Soviet society and culture.

One of the best examples of this quality of Aitmatov's work is to be found in *Farewell, Gulsary!* This novella recounts the story of an old draughthorse, once a magnificent steed, and his aged master, Tanabai. The tale is strongly reminiscent of the old oral epics that focus on the cultural importance of horses and horseback riding. As Gulsary and his master contemplate their shared past, Aitmatov illustrates the interwoven destinies of man and animal, the concordance of man and nature so vital to the Kirghiz oral heritage. The horse suffers a long, agonizing death which prompts deep soul searching in his master. In the end, Tanabai accepts the passing of his old companion and the passing of the old days.

Underlying Aitmatov's support of the Soviet system is a strong determination to uphold the freedom of artistic expression. "Clearly among the things he believes," said Frank Getlein of *Commonweal,* "is the efficacy of facing facts, however unpleasant." These two aspects of Aitmatov's character have led him, occasionally, to violate certain literary taboos of the Soviet state. In *The White Ship,* for example, Aitmatov depicts the suicide of a seven-year-old boy who becomes despondent after witnessing the brutal slaying and consumption of a rare deer.

Some Soviet readers were offended by the pessimism of the story, and the outcry against it prompted the author to defend his artistic integrity in the *Literaturnaya Gazeta.* Countering suggested changes in the tale, Aitmatov was quoted in the *New York Times:* "I had a choice, either to write or not to write the story. And if to write it, then only as I did." The author also asserted that evil is inexorable and, lacking the capacity to overcome the adult evil surrounding him, the boy had to sacrifice his life or his childhood ideals. As Rosemarie Keiffer explained in *Books Abroad,* Aitmatov intended to provoke thought by allowing the young protagonist to take his own life: "The boy's fate is aimed at elucidating certain human faults: Who has been faithful to the most positive of childhood dreams? Who has measured up to the moral aspirations of adolescence? Who has remained truthful in his relations with children? Aitmatov does not pretend here to teach men how to live up to their most cherished and human ideals, only to prick their consciences with the disparities between those ideals and the realities of most people's lives."

Another of Aitmatov's more daring works is "The Ascent of Mount Fuji," a play he co-authored with Kaltai Mikhamedzhanov, another native of Kirghizia. This drama caused a sensation when it premiered in Moscow in 1973 because it openly treats the delicate subject of Soviet suppression of dissidents. The drama does not recount the many horrors suffered by dissidents in the Soviet state; instead, it is a psychological study of betrayal and quiescence. Four old schoolmates meet on a mountaintop to renew their friendship but find they must first confront and reconcile the absence of a fifth friend, Sabur, a poet who questioned some Red Army tactics. Sabur had been betrayed by one of his four friends while the other three remained silent. Each must now acknowledge his own portion of guilt in the case.

Assessing Aitmatov's appeal for both Western and Eastern readers, Rosemarie Keiffer declared: "Like the classical poets and epic bards, he is a patriot and a historian of his nation. He is an ardent lover of life and nature, possesses a deep understanding of such varied human passions as love and despair, admires the Leninist society's ideals of order and progress, and is optimistic about that society's potential for bringing prosperity to his native region. And permeating all his writing is a serene harmony between past and present, between man and nature, between joy and sadness, a spirit which unequivocally condemns such aberrations of the human ideal as war or personal cruelty but which also holds to the hope that such ideals will at least endure and possibly one day even be attained."

BIOGRAPHICAL/CRITICAL SOURCES:

PERIODICALS

Books Abroad, summer, 1975.
Commonweal, July 18, 1975.
Globe and Mail (Toronto), July 8, 1989.
Los Angeles Times Book Review, June 18, 1989.
Newsweek, June 24, 1974, June 30, 1975.
New York Times, July 30, 1970, May 6, 1989.
New York Times Book Review, April 30, 1989.
Times (London), August 18, 1983.
UNESCO Courier, October, 1972.

* * *

AKERS, Floyd
See BAUM, L(yman) Frank

* * *

AKHMATOVA, Anna 1888-1966

PERSONAL: Born June 23, 1888, in Bolshoy Fontan, near Odessa, Russia; real name Anna Andreyevna Gorenko (she took her great-grandmother's name, Akhmatova, as a pen name); died, March 5, 1966; daughter of an officer in the merchant marine; married Nicholas G. Gumilyov (a major Acmeist poet; shot in 1921 for complicity in an anti-Bolshevik plot), 1910 (divorced, 1918); married Vladimir Silejko; married four times in all; children: (with first husband) Lev Nikolaevich, one daughter from a later marriage. *Education:* Attended Carskoe Selo and the Smolny Institute, St. Petersburg (now Leningrad); completed secondary education in Kiev; attended colleges in Kiev and St. Petersburg, including Zhenskie Kursy.

ADDRESSES: Home—Komarovo, on the Gulf of Finland, northwest of Leningrad, U.S.S.R.; and Ulitsa Vorovskovo 52, Moskva, U.S.S.R.

CAREER: Poet and translator. Lived in Paris, France, spring, 1910-11; joined Acmeist movement and the Guild of Poets (Acmeist society), St. Petersburg, 1912; toured northern Italy, 1912, again in 1964; from 1922 to 1940 she was not allowed to publish officially (although some scholarly articles appeared), but her poems re-appeared in state-sanctioned periodicals during World War II; during the siege of Leningrad, 1941, she was evacuated to Tashkent where she remained until 1944; went to Moscow, 1944-45, before returning to Leningrad; in 1946 her work was declared dangerous and subversive by Zhdanov, the Soviet cultural leader; following this attack, she again did not publish and lived in considerable poverty until her work reappeared in Soviet periodicals in 1953, following the death of Stalin; in 1965 she traveled to England.

MEMBER: Union of Soviet Writers (expelled, 1946), Writers' Union (honorary; elected to presidium, 1965).

AWARDS, HONORS: Candidate for the Nobel Prize, 1958 (won by Boris Pasternak) and 1965 (won by Mikhail Sholokov); Taormina Prize for poetry (Catagna, Italy), 1964; D.Litt., Oxford University, 1965.

WRITINGS:

POETRY

Vecher (title means "Evening"; also see below), Guild of Poets, 1912.
Chetki (title means "The Rosary"; also see below), Izdatelstvo Giperborey (organ of Guild of Poets), 1914, reprinted, Ardis (Ann Arbor, Michigan), 1972.
Belaya Staya (title means "The White Flock"; also see below), Izdatelstvo Giperborey, 1917, reprinted, Ardis, 1979.
Skrizhal Sbornik (title means "Ecstasy Collection"), [Russia], 1918.
U Samogo Morya (title means "At the Very Edge of the Sea"), Alkonost, (St. Petersburg), 1921, reprinted, Berkley Slavic Specialties, 1977.
Podorozhnik (title means "Plaintain"; also see below), Petropolis Printers (St. Petersburg), 1921.
Anno Domini MCMXXI (also see below), Petropolis Printers, 1921.
Stikhi (title means "Poems"), [Russia], 1940.
Iz Shesti Knig (title means "From Six Books"; includes a group of new poems entitled "Iva," which means "The Willow"), Izdatelstvo Sovetskii Pisatel (Moscow), 1940.
Izbrannie Stikhi (title means "Selected Poems"), Izdatelstvo Sovetskii Pisatel (Tashkent), 1943, reprinted, 1974.
Tashkentskie Stikhi (title means "Tashkent Poems"), [Tashkent], 1944. *Izbrannie Stikhotvoreniya* (title means "Selected Poems"), Chekova (New York), 1952.
Stikhotvoreniya, 1909-1957, edited by A. A. Surkov, Izdatelstvo Khudozhestvennaya Literatura (Moscow), 1958, reprinted, 1976.
Poema Bez Geroya; Triptykh (originally published in *Vozdushnye puti;* title means "Poem Without a Hero; Triptych"), [New York], 1960, reprinted, Ardis, 1978.
Stikhi, 1909-1960, [Russia], 1961.
Stikhotvoreniya, [Moscow], 1961.
Collected Poems: 1912-1963 (Russian language), edited by Virginia E. Van Wynen, privately printed, 1963.
50 Stikhotvorenii, YMCA Press (Paris), 1963.
Rekviem: Tsikl Stikhotvorenii (title means "Requiem: A Cycle of Poems"; also see below), Possev-Verlag (Frankfurt am Main), 1964, reprinted, Inter-Language Literary Associates, 1967, new edition edited by Borys Oleksandriv, [Suchasnist], 1973.
Poeziya (title means "Poetry"), Vilnyus Vaga, 1964.
Beg Vremeni (poems, 1909-1965; title means "Race of Time"; includes poems from *Vecher, Chetki, Belaya Staya, Podorozhnik, Anna Domini MCMXXI,* and two new groups entitled "Trostnik" [means "Cane"] and "Sedmaya Kniga" [means "Seventh Book"]), Izdatelstvo Sovetskii Pisatel, 1965, reprinted, Mastatskaya Litaratura, 1983.
Stikhotvoreniya, 1909-1965, [Moscow], 1965.
Sochineniya, 2 volumes, Inter-Language Literary Associates (Washington, D.C.), 1965, 1968.
Tainy remesla, "Sov. Rossiia," 1986.
Sochineniya v dvukh tomakh, Khudozhestvennaya Literatura, 1986.

Works also collected in *Stikhi i proza,* edited by B. G. Druian, 1976, and *Stikhi, perepiska, vospominaniya, ikongrafiya,* edited by Carl R. Proffer, 1977.

TRANSLATOR

Koreiskaya Klassicheskaya Poeziya (title means "Korean Classical Poetry"), edited by A. A. Kholodovich, Izdatelstvo Khudozhestvennaya Literatura, 1956.

(With Vera Potapova) *Lirika Drevnevo Egipta* (title means "Ancient Egyptian Lyrics"), Izdatelstvo Khudozhestvennaya Literatura, 1965.

Golosa Poetov (anthology; title means "Voices of the Poets"), Izdatelstvo Progress (Moscow), 1965.

Klassicheskya poeziya Vostoka, (title means "Classical Poetry of the East") [Moscow], 1969.

Also translator of works from French, Chinese, Rumanian, Bengali, Polish, Hebrew, and other languages.

ENGLISH TRANSLATIONS

Forty-Seven Love Poems, translation by Natalie Doddington, J. Cape, 1927.

Selected Poems, translation and introduction by Richard McKane, Penguin, 1969, reprinted, Bloodaxe Books, 1989.

Poems of Akhmatova, translation and introduction by Stanley Kunitz and Max Hayward, Little, Brown, 1973.

A Poem Without a Hero (also see below), translation of *Poema bez Geroya* by Carl R. Proffer and Assya Humesky, Ardis Publishers, 1973.

Moscow Trefoil, Australian National University Press, 1975.

Requiem [and] *Poem Without A Hero,* translation of *Rekviem* and *Poema Bez Geroya* by D. M. Thomas, Ohio University Press, 1976.

Selected Poems (includes *A Poem Without A Hero* by Proffer and *Requiem* translated by Robin Kemball), edited and translated by Walter Arndt, Ardis, 1976.

The White Flock, edited by Geoffrey Thurley, Oasis Books, 1978.

Way of All the Earth, translation by D. M. Thomas, Ohio University Press, 1979.

Three Russian Women Poets, translation by Mary Maddock, Crossing Press, 1983.

Poems, translation by Lyn Coffin, Norton, 1983.

You Will Hear Thunder, translation by Thomas, Ohio University Press, 1985.

Twenty Poems, Eighties Press/Ally Press, 1985.

Northern Elegies, Firefly Press, 1985.

Selected Poems, translation by Thomas, Penguin International Poets Series, 1988.

CONTRIBUTOR

Modern Poems from Russia, translated by Gerard Shelley, Allen & Unwin, 1942.

A Book of Russian Verse, edited by Cecil Wm. Bowra, Macmillan (London), 1943.

Sbornik Stikhov (title means "A Collection of Poems"), compiled by Vasilii Kazin and Viktor Pertsov, Goslitizdat (Moscow), 1943.

A Treasury of Russian Verse, translated and edited by Avrahm Yarmolinsky, Macmillan, 1949.

Soviet Russian Verse (Russian language), edited by R. R. Milner-Gulland, Pergamon, 1964.

Stikhotvoreniya, Letchworth, 1965.

Modern European Poetry, edited by Willis Barnstone, Bantam, 1966.

A collection of short poems originally published in Russian periodicals was published in German as part of *Geschichte der Sowjetliteratur,* three volumes (title means "A History of Soviet Literature"; Volumes 1395-1397 of *Goldmanns Gelbe Taschenbuecher*), edited and translated by Gleb Struve and B. Filippov, Goldmann (Munich), 1966. Also author of twenty-five essays about Pushkin, written between 1926 and 1936. Contributor to *Sirus* (edited by her first husband, Nicholas A. Gumilyov), *Apollon, Krasnaya Nov, Zvezda, Novy Mir, Znamya, Ogonyok,* and other periodicals.

SIDELIGHTS: In 1964 R. R. Milner-Gulland noted in *Soviet Russian Verse: An Anthology* that Anna Akhmatova had been called "the greatest living Russian poet." When she was young, critics called her work brilliant and original, and while still in her twenties she became, with her husband Gumilyov and the poet [Osip] Mandelstam, one of the three leading figures in the Acmeist movement, which predominated, with Russian futurism, in Russian poetry from about 1910 to 1917. The movement was a reaction against the mysticism and vagueness of style employed by the symbolists; the precision of Akhmatova's language and her clear, concrete imagery were considered exemplary by Acmeist theoreticians.

Akhmatova's theme was always love. When she was young, she was happy, and the simple lyricism with which she developed her theme is unequaled in contemporary Russian verse. During the revolution and, later, the war years, she became intense and bitter. Her only son was arrested during the thirties and sent to a concentration camp for more than fifteen years, she herself was shamed, and her work was banned in her own country. After her former husband's execution in 1921, she burned a number of her poems, and new poems were not written down, but memorized by her friends. But her theme was still love, if love turned to hatred and remaining alive only in reminiscence. During these years she wrote "Requiem" and "Poem Without a Hero," and the critics, when she was again allowed to publish, called this work great poetry. Sam Driver wrote in *Great Foreign Language Writers,* " 'Poem Without a Hero' is a retrospective of Akhmatova's own world from the Petersburg in 1913 to the nightmare of World War II and beyond. It is her judgment on an age and also her retribution for her own suffering. By the time she added the last touches to the poem in 1962, Akhmatova had become for Russian poetry the very symbol of moral rectitude and artistic integrity in the face of intolerable personal hardship and official persecution." But she had passed 65 when she wrote her finest poems, those in which she resolved her early lyricism with her mature pathos and despair and finally became, in *Nation* critic Alexander Werth's words, the "tragic queen" of Russian poetry.

Akhmatova began writing poems in 1907 and her husband Gumilyov was the first to publish them. Although he considered her earliest work to be the insignificant pastime of a young wife, his review of her second book exemplifies his increasing awareness of her talent and importance. Leonid I. Strakhovsky, author of *Craftsmen of the World, Three Poets of Modern Russia: Gumilyov, Akhmatova, Mandelstam,* quoted from Gumilyov's review: "The most outstanding factor in Akhmatova's poetry is her style: she almost never explains, she demonstrates. . . . There are many definitions of color in Akhmatova's poems and most often these are of yellow and gray, until now the rarest in poetry." Another critic of her early work, according to Strakhovsky, wrote: "Anna Akhmatova knows how to follow the highway of contemporary artistic culture with such primitive independence of her personal life as if this highway were merely a whimsical path in her own private garden. . . . Revery feeds the poetry of Anna Akhmatova, a deeply sad revery often romantic in its content. However, we call a romantic a man who sees in reality merely a pretext for revery, but a woman who wants to abandon herself to revery is not a romantic but simply—a woman." Werth noted that "her second book, *The Rosary*, . . . became immensely popular, especially with women readers who were fascinated by the music of her verse, its epigrammatic conciseness, and by her strangely varying female moods, ranging from feminine humility to haughtiness and feminine arrogance; from timid uncertainty to full self-assurance; from sensuality to a kind of intellectually amorous detachment." Werth continues: "Akhmatova was happiest in her youth, before the revolution, and she scarcely ever made any secret of it. She loved Russia, but was always out of step with the Soviet Union except—and the exception is significant—during World War II when 'Russia' and the 'Soviet Union' became one for her."

Essentially, Akhmatova was an urban poet. Strakhovsky wrote: "All told, cities predominate in Akhmatova's poetry. It seems that man-made structures attract her more than nature's landscapes." And throughout her life she wrote with deepest affection for pre-revolutionary St. Petersburg. But whether her poems spoke of city or country, peace or war, love or hatred (although, Strakhovsky noted, "her hate is only another form of her love"), it was the manner in which she developed her poetic subject that was most distinctive. Her poetry is fundamentally subjective, approaching the fact of the poem by an analysis of her own interpretation of it. Strakhovsky wrote: "She assembles artistically the particulars of a given moment which are often unnoticeable to others; she notices everything anew so that her internal world is not merely framed by the external world, but they combine into one solid and organic wholeness of life."

It was the perfection of this technique—the interpretation of reality in terms of experience—that made her achievement in the last poems truly remarkable. Werth wrote: "Unlike her early love lyrics, unlike her tragic, intensely bitter 'Requiem,' unlike her war poems with their exaltation, pathos and infinite human pity—above all, for the martyred children of Leningrad—her last poems are marked by the serenity, wisdom and resignation of old age. They combine a deep love of art, music, nature and, again, St. Petersburg-Leningrad and Tsarskoye Selo, the one associated with her whole life, the other with her happy youth." Akhmatova, citing "Midnight Verses," a cycle of very short poems written between 1963 and 1964, chose her own favorites from among these most recent poems. The last poems, too, were written when she had finally been recognized by her country, and it is possible that the state's acceptance of her after so many years contributed to the inner harmony and peacefulness that is often expressed in these poems. Werth noted: "Even the official obituary published by the Writers' Union paid tribute to a 're-markable Soviet poet': 'For more than half a century she devoted herself to the noble service of Russian poetic speech, of the homeland, and of Soviet society building a new world.' "

Akhmatova wrote poems for 59 years. Thus, to study the body of her work is to understand the remarkable achievement of her life. The *Books Abroad* reviewer writes: "Akhmatova was one of the first to use the elements of genuine popular speech in Russian poetry; with utmost simplicity and depth she developed the great lyrical theme of love, jealousy, parting and death, as if writing her own diary—though a diary crystallized into art; and what is even more, she introduced a great historiosophic theme. In her last works . . . there is a deep perception of the meaning of our times and of our historical trials, as well as perfection of form." Michael Klimenko added: "Akhmatova did not write much, but

everything she wrote bears the stamp of finely-chiseled, most intimate, aesthetic and emotional experience."

BIOGRAPHICAL/CRITICAL SOURCES:

BOOKS

Contemporary Literary Criticism, Gale, Volume 11, 1979, Volume 25, 1983.
Barnstone, Willis, editor, *Modern European Poetry*, Bantam, 1966.
Driver, Sam N., *Anna Akhmatova*, Twayne, 1972.
Great Foreign Language Writers, St. Martin's, 1984.
Haight, Amanda, *Anna Akhmatova: A Poetic Pilgrimage*, Oxford University Press, 1976.
Hingley, Ronald, *Nightingale Fever: Russian Poets in Revolution*, Knopf, 1981.
Leiter, Sharon, *Akhmatova's Petersburg*, University of Pennsylvania Press, 1983.
Milner-Gulland, R. R., editor, *Soviet Russian Verse: An Anthology*, Pergamon, 1964.
Religious Theme in the Poetry of Anna Akhmatova: "Prince, the Fool, and The Nunnery", Gower Press, 1987.
Sinyavski, Andrei, *For Freedom of Imagination*, Holt, 1971.
Strakhovsky, Leonid I., *Craftsmen of the World, Three Poets of Modern Russia: Gumilyov, Akhmatova, Mandelstam*, Harvard University Press, 1949, reprinted, Greenwood Press, 1969.
Terry, *Anna Akhmatova: A Bibliography, 1889-1989*, Astra Press, 1989.

PERIODICALS

Literaturnaya Gazeta (official publication of the Union of Soviet Writers), November 24, 1945 (interview).
Literaturnaia Rossiia, winter, 1979-80.
Nation, August 22, 1966.
New York Review of Books, August 9, 1973.
New York Times Book Review, April 17, 1966.
New York Times Magazine, May 28, 1967.
Times Literary Supplement, July 10, 1969, April 16, 1976.

OBITUARIES:

PERIODICALS

Antiquarian Bookman, April 11, 1966.
Books Abroad, spring, 1967.
Newsweek, March 14, 1966.
New York Herald Tribune, March 6, 1966.
New York Times, March 6, 1966.
Time, March 18, 1966.

*   *   *

ALBEE, Edward (Franklin III) 1928-

PERSONAL: Surname is pronounced "*All*-bee"; born March 12, 1928, probably in Virginia; adopted son of Reed A. (part-owner of Keith-Albee theatre circuit) and Frances (Cotter) Albee. *Education:* Attended Trinity College, Hartford, Conn., 1946-47. *Religion:* Christian.

ADDRESSES: Home—Irvine, Calif.

CAREER: Writer, producer, and director of plays. Worked as continuity writer for WNYC-radio, office boy for Warwick & Legler (advertising agency), record salesman for G. Schirmer, Inc. (music publishers), and counterman in luncheonette of Manhattan Towers Hotel; messenger for Western Union, 1955-58. Producer, with Richard Barr and Clinton Wilder, New

Playwrights Unit Workshop, 1963—; director of touring retrospective of his one-act plays including, "The Zoo Story," "The American Dream," "Fam and Yam," "The Sandbox," "Box," "Quotations from Chairman Mao Tse-Tung," "Counting the Ways," and "Listening," produced as "Albee Directs Albee," 1978-79; co-director of Vivian Beaumont Theatre at Lincoln Center for the Performing Arts, New York, N.Y., 1979—. Founder of William Flanagan Center for Creative Persons in Mountauk, N.Y., 1971. Member of National Endowment grant-giving council; member of governing commission of New York State Council for the Arts. Lecturer at college campuses. Cultural exchange visitor to U.S.S.R. and Latin American countries for U.S. State Department.

AWARDS, HONORS: Berlin Festival Award, 1959, for "The Zoo Story," and 1961, for "The Death of Bessie Smith"; Vernon Rice Memorial Award, and Obie Award, 1960, and Argentine Critics Circle Award, 1961, all for "The Zoo Story"; "The Death of Bessie Smith" and "The American Dream" chosen as best plays of the 1960-61 season by Foreign Press Association, 1961; Lola D'Annunzio Award, 1961, for "The American Dream"; selected as most promising playwright of 1962-63 season by New York Drama Critics, 1963; New York Drama Critics Circle Award, Foreign Press Association Award, Antoinette Perry ("Tony") Award, Outer Circle Award, *Saturday Review* Drama Critics Award, and *Variety* Drama Critics' Poll Award, 1963, and *Evening Standard* Award, 1964, all for "Who's Afraid of Virginia Woolf?"; with Richard Barr and Clinton Wilder, recipient of Margo Jones Award, 1965, for encouraging new playwrights; Pulitzer Prize, 1967, for "A Delicate Balance," and 1975, for "Seascape"; D.Litt., Emerson College, 1967, and Trinity College, 1974; American Academy and Institute of Arts and Letters Gold Medal, 1980.

WRITINGS:

PLAYS

The Zoo Story, The Death of Bessie Smith, The Sandbox: Three Plays ("The Zoo Story" [also see below], first produced [in German] in Berlin at Schiller Theater Werkstaat, September 28, 1959, produced Off-Broadway at Provincetown Playhouse, January 14, 1960; "The Death of Bessie Smith" [also see below], first produced in Berlin at Schlosspark Theater, April 21, 1960, produced Off-Broadway at York Playhouse, March 1, 1961; "The Sandbox" [also see below], first produced in New York City at Jazz Gallery, April 15, 1960, produced Off-Broadway at Cherry Lane Theatre, February, 1962, directed by author), Coward, 1960.

The American Dream (also see below; produced Off-Broadway at York Playhouse, January 24, 1961), with introduction by the author, Coward, 1961.

Fam and Yam (also see below; first produced in Westport, Conn., at White Barn Theatre, August 27, 1960), Dramatists Play Service, 1961.

Who's Afraid of Virginia Woolf? (produced on Broadway at Billy Rose Theatre, October 13, 1962; revival produced in Los Angeles at the U.C.L.A. James A. Doolittle Theatre, November, 1989, directed by Albee), Atheneum, 1962.

The Ballad of the Sad Cafe (also see below; adaptation of novella of same title by Carson McCullers; produced on Broadway at Martin Beck Theatre, October 30, 1963), Houghton, 1963.

Tiny Alice (also see below; produced on Broadway at Billy Rose Theatre, December 29, 1964), Atheneum, 1965.

Malcolm (also see below; adaptation of novel of same title by James Purdy; produced on Broadway at Shubert Theatre, January 11, 1966), Atheneum, 1966.

A Delicate Balance (also see below; produced on Broadway at Martin Beck Theatre, September 22, 1966), Atheneum, 1966.

"Breakfast at Tiffany's" (musical; adaptation of story of same title by Truman Capote; music by Bob Merrill), produced in Philadelphia, 1966; produced on Broadway at Majestic Theatre, December, 1966.

Everything in the Garden (also see below; based on play by Giles Cooper; produced on Broadway at Plymouth Theatre, November 16, 1967), Atheneum, 1968.

Box [and] *Quotations from Chairman Mao Tse-Tung* (also see below; two interrelated plays; first produced in Buffalo, N.Y., at Studio Arena Theater, March 6, 1968; produced on Broadway at Billy Rose Theatre, September 30, 1968), Atheneum, 1969.

All Over (also see below; produced on Broadway at Martin Beck Theatre, January 26, 1971; produced in London by Royal Shakespeare Co. at Aldwych Theatre, January 31, 1972), Atheneum, 1971.

Seascape (also see below; produced on Broadway at Shubert Theatre, January 26, 1975, directed by author), Atheneum, 1975.

Counting the Ways [and] *Listening* ("Counting the Ways" [also see below], first produced in London at National Theatre, 1976, produced in Hartford by Hartford Stage Co., January 28, 1977; "Listening: A Chamber Play" [also see below; produced as radio play by British Broadcasting Corp. (BBC), 1976], first produced on stage in Hartford by Hartford Stage Co., January 28, 1977), Atheneum, 1977.

The Lady from Dubuque (produced on Broadway at Morosco Theatre, January 31, 1980), Atheneum, 1979.

The Plays, Volume 1 (contains *The Zoo Story, The Death of Bessie Smith, The Sandbox,* and *The American Dream*), Coward, 1981, Volume 2 (contains *Tiny Alice, A Delicate Balance, Box,* and *Quotations from Chairman Mao Tse-Tung*), Atheneum, 1981, Volume 3 (contains *All Over, Seascape, Counting the Ways,* and *Listening*), Atheneum, 1982, Volume 4 (contains *Everything in the Garden, Malcolm,* and *The Ballad of the Sad Cafe*), Atheneum, 1983.

Lolita (adaptation of novel of same title by Vladimir Nabokov; first produced in Boston at Wilbur Theatre, January 15, 1981; produced on Broadway at Brooks Atkinson Theatre, March 19, 1981), Dramatists Play Service, 1984.

The Man Who Had Three Arms (first produced in Miami, Fla., at New World Festival, June 10, 1982, directed by the author; produced in Chicago, at Goodman Theater, October 4, 1982, directed by the author), Atheneum, 1987.

"The Marriage Play," first produced in Vienna, May, 1987; produced in San Diego at the Hahn Cosmopolitan Theatre, March, 1989.

AUTHOR OF INTRODUCTION

Noel Coward, *Three Plays by Noel Coward: Blithe Spirit, Hay Fever,* [and] *Private Lives,* Delta, 1965.

Phyllis Johnson Kaye, editor, *National Playwrights Directory,* 2nd edition, Eugene O'Neill Theater Center (Waterford, Conn.), 1981.

(With Sabina Lietzmann) *New York,* Vendome Press, 1981.

Louise Nevelson: Atmospheres and Environments, Clarkson N. Potter, Inc., 1981.

OTHER

(Author of libretto with James Hinton, Jr.) "Bartleby" (opera; adaptation of story by Herman Melville; music by William Flanagan), produced Off-Broadway at York Playhouse, January 24, 1961.

Also author of screenplays, including an adaptation of *Le locataire* (title means "The Tenant"), a novel by Roland Topor, an adaptation of his "The Death of Bessie Smith," one about the life of Nijinsky, and one about Stanford White and Evelyn Nesbitt. Also contributor of articles to magazines.

WORK IN PROGRESS: Two plays, "Attila the Hun" and "Quitting."

SIDELIGHTS: Reviewing the numerous commentaries written about Edward Albee's plays, C. W. E. Bigsby notes in *Edward Albee: A Collection of Critical Essays* that in comparison to Albee "few playwrights . . . have been so frequently and mischievously misunderstood, misrepresented, overpraised, denigrated, and precipitately dismissed." Capsulizing the changing tone of Albee criticism since the early sixties (when his first play appeared), Bigsby offers this overview: "Canonized after . . . *The Zoo Story,* [Albee] found himself in swift succession billed as America's most promising playwright, leading dramatist, and then, with astonishing suddenness, a 'one-hit' writer. . . . The progression was essentially that suggested by George in [Albee's] *Who's Afraid of Virginia Woolf?,* 'better, best, bested.'"

To symbolize the curve of Albee's reputation as a dramatist, Bigsby chooses this phrase from a play designated by many critics as a dividing line in the playwright's career. T. E. Kalem, for example, in *Time* remarks: "Albee almost seems to have lived through two careers, one very exciting, the other increasingly depressing. From *The Zoo Story* through *The American Dream* to *Who's Afraid of Virginia Woolf?,* he displayed great gusto, waspish humor and feral power. In the succeeding . . . years, he has foundered in murky metaphysics, . . . dabbled in adaptations, . . . and gone down experimental blind alleys." Stanley Kauffmann gives a similar evaluation in *New Republic:* "Ever since . . . *Virginia Woolf*—Albee's last good play—all we've been getting . . . are abortions: two plays and three adaptations that are all varyingly bad and two one-act plays [as of 1971] that are Absurdist imitations."

However, many critics have praised these same plays. Albee continues to win awards; he received two Pulitzer Prizes since *Virginia Woolf,* one in 1967 for *A Delicate Balance,* and one in 1975, for *Seascape.* Walter Wagner in *The Playwrights Speak* notes, "[Albee] is a successful dramatist because of his intelligence, perceptions, talent and willingness to treat questions that few American playwrights examined before him." Brian Way, in *American Theatre,* while conceding what he judges to be limitations in the scope of Albee's writing, also praises the dramatist: "It is only fair that one should return to an assertion of the importance of Albee's good qualities in the American theatre. If it is true that he inhabits a finite world, he does so with brilliance, inventiveness, intelligence, and moral courage." And, according to Ruby Cohn in *Dialogue in American Drama,* Albee is "the most skillful composer of dialogue that America has produced."

Bigsby offers an explanation of the ongoing critical attacks on Albee's ability as a playwright: "There is no doubt that the Broadway production of . . . *Virginia Woolf* provided the basis for Albee's amazing popular reputation; . . . equally certainly, it was also the primary reason for the suspicion with which some reviewers and critics approached his work. . . . The success of *Virginia Woolf* established Albee's reputation around the world. . . . And now, public and reviewers alike expected him to repeat his earlier success. [But] the truth was that Albee has remained at heart a product of Off-Broadway, claiming the same freedom to experiment and, indeed, fail, which is the special strength of that theatre."

The playwright, in spite of negative criticism, has not been "bested" by the critics. He continues in his role as dramatist, writing usually one play a year. In a *Washington Post* interview with David Richards, Albee explains his own reaction to the critics: "I have been both overpraised and underpraised. I assume by the time I finish writing—and I plan to go on writing until I'm ninety or gaga—it will all equal itself out. . . . You can't involve yourself with the vicissitudes of fashion or critical response. I'm fairly confident that my work is going to be around for a while."

Although stylistically varied, Albee's plays are thematically connected. Gerald Weales in *The Jumping Off Place: American Drama in the 1960's* notes: "Each new Albee play seems to be an experiment in form, in style . . ., and yet there is unity to his work as a whole. This is apparent in the devices and the characters that recur, modified according to context, but it is most obvious in the repetition of theme, in the basic assumptions about the human condition that underlie all his work."

Reviewing Albee's touring retrospective of eight of his one-act plays, "Albee Directs Albee," Sylvie Drake of the *Los Angeles Times* observes: "This condensation of work reveals Albee's consistent and enduring concern with loss. . . . 'Pain is understanding,' says someone in [Albee's play] 'Counting the Ways.' 'It's really loss.' Yes. These plays are *all* about loss." In her analysis of Albee's plays Drake also discovers the following themes: "the chasm between people, [and] their inability to connect except through pain."

John MacNicholas, writing in *Dictionary of Literary Biography,* says the development of these themes in Albee's plays started with his very first play, *The Zoo Story.* According to Way, this play, a tale of a fairly prosperous married man and his confrontation on a Central Park bench with a totally alienated young drifter, "is an exploration of the farce and agony of human isolation." George Wellwarth, in *The Theater of Protest and Paradox,* explains the play's thematic content in more detail: "[Albee] is exemplifying or demonstrating a theme. That theme is the enormous and usually insuperable difficulty that human beings find in communicating with each other. More precisely, it is about the maddening effect that the enforced loneliness of the human existence condition has on the person who is cursed (for in our society it undoubtedly is a curse) with an infinite capacity for love."

Albee's thematic preoccupation with loss of contact between individuals is tied to the playwright's desire to make a statement about American values, as Weales points out. "In much of his work," according to the critic, "there is a suggestion . . . that the emptiness and loneliness of the characters are somehow the result of a collapse of values in the Western world, in general, in the United States, in particular." Albee finds the feelings of loss and emptiness prevalent in the society that surrounds him. Howard Schneider elaborates on this idea in a *Pittsburgh Press* article: "[Albee] hammers incessantly [at this theme] when he talks at college campuses. The 'disengagement' of the population. The passivity of Americans drawn to a television set six hours a day. The religious, political and social structures that men have created to 'illusion' themselves from the world and each other." Schneider quotes Albee's own explanation of the themes present in his work: "People who are passive and who are careless contribute to the decline of the system, especially in a democracy. . . . People still refuse to think and act honorably with each other. They are still mean and vicious and these are the subjects of my plays."

Following *The Zoo Story*, three Albee plays opened in New York during 1960-61. All of these—*The Sandbox, The American Dream,* and *The Death of Bessie Smith*—"attack certain features in American society," according to MacNicholas. *The Death of Bessie Smith*, for example, deals with the death of the black singer who bled to death after an automobile accident, apparently because she was denied care at a nearby all-white hospital. *The American Dream* and *The Sandbox* share the same characters—Mommy, Daddy, and Grandma. MacNicholas feels that these two plays "form a continuum in subject matter and technique; both attack indifference to love, pity, and compassion. In both . . ., the characters . . . live in a kind of moral narcosis."

Allan Lewis, in *American Plays and Playwrights of the Contemporary Theatre*, comments: "*The American Dream* is a wildly imaginative caricature of the American family. . . . [In this play] Albee is the angry young man, tearing apart the antiseptic mirage of American middle-class happiness." The American family of the play is comprised of characters known only as "Mommy" (a domineering shrew), "Daddy" (a weak henpecked husband), and "Grandma" (an older version of "Mommy"). Set in the family's stuffy apartment, the play includes the story of the couple's adoption of a "bumble of joy" whom they destroy after discovering his various defects. (For example, they cut out his tongue when he says a dirty word.) As he grows up, Mommy and Daddy complain that the baby has no head on his shoulders, is spineless, and has feet of clay. They complain again when he dies after having already been paid for. Near the end of the play, the baby's twin appears. He is a handsome young man who describes himself as a "clean-cut midwest farm boy type, almost insultingly good-looking in a typically American way." "The young man," as Frederick Lumley notes in *New Trends in Twentieth Century Drama*, "feels that he is incomplete, he doesn't know what has happened to something within him, but he has no touch, he is unable to make love, to see anything with pity; in fact he has no feeling."

Continuing his interpretation of the play, Lewis states: "The American Dream [of the title] is the young man who is all appearance and no feelings. . . . He says: 'I cannot touch another person and feel love . . . I have no emotions. . . . I have now only my person my body my face. . . . I let people love me. . . . I feel nothing.'" In his preface to *The American Dream*, Albee explains the play's content: "The play is an examination of the American Scene, an attack on the substitution of artificial for real values in our society, a condemnation of complacency, cruelty, emasculation and vacuity; it is a stand against the fiction that everything in this slipping land of ours is peachy-keen."

According to MacNicholas, Albee continues his critique of American society in his first three-act play, *Who's Afraid of Virginia Woolf?*. Critics note a relationship between this play and *The American Dream*. Martin Esslin, writing in *The Theatre of the Absurd*, comments: "A closer inspection reveals elements which clearly . . . relate [*Virginia Woolf*] to Albee's earlier work. . . . George and Martha [a couple in the play] (there are echoes here of George and Martha Washington) have an imaginary child which they treat as real, until in the cold dawn of that wild night [in which the action of the play takes place] they decide to 'kill' it by abandoning their joint fantasy. Here the connection to *The American Dream* with its horrid dream-child of

the ideal all-American boy becomes clear. . . . Is the dream-child which cannot become real among people torn by ambition and lust something like the American ideal itself?" Drake finds George and Martha of *Virginia Woolf* directly related to Mommy and Daddy of *The American Dream*. Lumley describes this evolution: "The Mommy and Daddy of . . . *Virginia Woolf* are this time given names, Martha and George, thus becoming individuals instead of abstract characters. . . . They have been unable to have children; so that their love is mixed-up sexual humiliation, a strong love-hate relationship which makes them want to hurt and claw and wound each other because they know each other and cannot do without one another."

In the *Arizona Quarterly*, James P. Quinn describes the combination of social criticism and the theme of human isolation in *Virginia Woolf*: "In [the play] the author parodies the ideals of western civilization. . . . Thus, romantic love, marriage, sex, the family, status, competition, power all the 'illusions' man has erected to eliminate the differences between self and others and to escape the . . . burden of his freedom and loneliness come under attack."

Critics also note a continuation of theme and social awareness in Albee's more recent plays. For example, Harold Clurman, in his *Nation* review of *All Over*, writes: "Albee is saying [in this play] that despite all the hasty bickering, the fierce hostility and the mutual misunderstandings which separate us, we need one another. We cry out in agony when we are cut off." Bigsby, commenting on the same play, concludes: "Albee's concern in *All Over* is essentially that of his earlier work. He remains intent on penetrating the bland urbanities of social life in an attempt to identify the crucial failure of nerve which has brought individual men and whole societies to the point of not merely soulless anomie but even of apocalypse."

Bigsby also finds similar characteristics in Albee's play *Box*, calling it "a protest against the dangerously declining quality of life—a decline marked . . . by the growth of an amoral technology with a momentum and direction of its own." And, MacNicholas notes Albee's preoccupation with loss in *A Delicate Balance*: "[The play] concerns itself with loss: not loss which occurs in one swift traumatic stroke, but that which evolves slowly in increments of gentle and lethal acquiescence."

Although Albee has not achieved commercial success with all his plays, his impact on twentieth-century American drama is undeniable, according to Richards. He comments, "Despite what [the playwright] calls 'the ritual slaughter of Albee' each time he unveils a new play, he remains one of the key reference points of American theater." Alan Schneider, in *Tulane Drama Review*, finds that Albee's impact is due to his ability to touch people emotionally with his plays. The critic remarks, "Anyone who has read any portion of any play [Albee] has ever written surely must sense the depth of his purpose and recognize . . . the power of the talent which is at his disposal; certainly no . . . individual today can fail to recognize somewhere in Albee's characters and moods the stirring of his own viscera, the shadow of his own self-knowledge" In conclusion, MacNicholas writes, "Albee's ideals about man and art and his formidable technical skills representing them on stage unquestionably place him in the first rank of the dramatists of this century."

MEDIA ADAPTATIONS: Who's Afraid of Virginia Woolf was adapted and filmed by Warner Bros. in 1966.

AVOCATIONAL INTERESTS: Travel, playing the harpsichord.

BIOGRAPHICAL/CRITICAL SOURCES:

BOOKS

Albee, Edward, *The American Dream,* Coward, 1961.
Amacher, Richard E., *Edward Albee,* Twayne, 1969, revised edition, 1982.
Authors in the News, Volume 1, Gale, 1976.
Bigsby, C. W. E., *Albee,* Oliver & Boyd, 1969.
Bigsby, C. W. E., editor, *Edward Albee: A Collection of Critical Essays,* Prentice-Hall, 1975.
Bloom, Harold, editor, *Edward Albee,* Chelsea House, 1987.
Brown, John Russell, and Bernard Harris, editors, *American Theatre,* Edward Arnold, 1967.
Cohn, Ruby, *Edward Albee,* University of Minnesota Press, 1969.
Cohn, Ruby, *Dialogue in American Drama,* Indiana University Press, 1971.
Contemporary Authors Bibliographic Series, Volume 3: *American Dramatists,* Gale, 1989.
Contemporary Literary Criticism, Gale, Volume 1, 1973, Volume 2, 1974, Volume 3, 1975, Volume 5, 1976, Volume 9, 1978, Volume 11, 1979, Volume 13, 1980, Volume 25, 1983, Volume 53, 1989.
Debusscher, Gilbert, *Edward Albee: Tradition and Renewal,* American Studies Center (Brussels), 1967.
Dictionary of Literary Biography, Volume 7: *Twentieth-Century American Dramatists,* Gale, 1981.
Downer, Alan S., editor, *American Drama and Its Critics,* University of Chicago Press, 1965.
Esslin, Martin, *The Theatre of the Absurd,* Doubleday, 1969.
Giantvalley, Scott, *Edward Albee: A Reference Guide,* Hall, 1987.
Hughes, Catharine, *American Playwrights, 1945-1975,* Pitman, 1976.
Kolin, Philip C., and J. Madison Davis, editors, *Critical Essays on Edward Albee,* Hall, 1986.
Kolin, editor, *Conversations with Edward Albee,* University Press of Mississippi, 1988.
Kostelanetz, Richard, *On Contemporary Literature,* Avon, 1964.
Lewis, Allan, *American Plays and Playwrights in the Contemporary Theatre,* Crown, 1965.
Lumley, Frederick, *New Trends in Twentieth Century Drama,* 4th edition, Oxford University Press, 1972.
McCarthy, Gerry, *Edward Albee,* St. Martin's, 1987.
Paolucci, Anne, *From Tension to Tonic: The Plays of Edward Albee,* Southern Illinois University Press, 1972.
Roudane, Matthew C., *Understanding Edward Albee,* University of South Carolina Press, 1987.
Rutenberg, Michael E., *Edward Albee: Playwright in Protest,* Avon, 1969.
Wagner, Walter, editor, *The Playwrights Speak,* Delacorte, 1967.
Wassermann, Julian N., editor, *Edward Albee: An Interview and Essays,* University of St. Thomas, 1983.
Weales, Gerald, *The Jumping Off Place: American Drama in the 1960's,* Macmillan, 1969.
Wellwarth, George, *The Theater of Protest and Paradox: Development in the*
Avant-Garde Drama, New York University Press, 1964.

PERIODICALS

Arizona Quarterly, autumn, 1974.
Atlantic, April, 1965.
Books, July, 1966.
Boston Globe, March 14, 1976.

Chicago Tribune, March 26, 1979, September 26, 1982, March 14, 1985, September 17, 1985.
Chicago Tribune Book World, September 26, 1982.
Commonweal, January 22, 1965.
Contemporary Literature, spring, 1968.
Detroit News, June 27, 1982.
Hudson Review, spring, 1965, winter, 1966-67.
Life, October 28, 1966, May 26, 1967, February 2, 1968.
London Magazine, March, 1969.
Los Angeles Times, October 18, 1978, October 24, 1982, May 22, 1984, May 26, 1984, February 14, 1987, March 26, 1989, October 6, 1989.
Miami Herald, March 16, 1986.
Nation, December 18, 1967, March 25, 1968, April 12, 1971, February 23, 1980, April 18, 1981.
National Observer, December 4, 1967.
New Leader, December 18, 1967, April 19, 1971.
New Republic, January 23, 1965, April 17, 1971, February 2, 1975, April 11, 1981.
Newsday, March 26, 1971.
New Statesman, January 23, 1970.
Newsweek, January 4, 1965, March 18, 1968, April 5, 1971, February 10, 1975, March 30, 1981, April 6, 1983, April 9, 1983.
New York, August 22, 1983.
New Yorker, January 22, 1966, April 3, 1971, March 3, 1980, May 30, 1981.
New York Times, December 27, 1964, January 21, 1965, January 13, 1966, August 16, 1966, September 18, 1966, September 24, 1966, October 2, 1966, August 20, 1967, November 26, 1967, April 4, 1971, April 18, 1971, January 27, 1975, February 4, 1977, May 23, 1978, January 27, 1980, March 1, 1981, March 20, 1981, March 29, 1981.
New York Times Magazine, February 25, 1962.
New York World Journal Tribune, September 22, 1966, October 2, 1966.
Observer Review, January 19, 1969.
Paris Review, fall, 1966.
People, February 25, 1980, April 6, 1981.
Pittsburgh Press, February 3, 1974.
Prairie Schooner, fall, 1965.
Reporter, December 28, 1967.
Saturday Review, June 4, 1966, April 17, 1971, March 8, 1975, May, 1981.
Theatre Arts, March, 1961.
Time, April 5, 1971, February 10, 1975.
Times (London), May 5, 1983, February 20, 1987, March 14, 1989.
Transatlantic Review, summer, 1963.
Tulane Drama Review, spring, 1963, summer, 1965.
Village Voice, December 7, 1967, March 21, 1968, October 31, 1968.
Washington Post, February 18, 1979, November 19, 1989.
Writer's Digest, October, 1980.

*   *   *

ALCAYAGA, Lucila Godoy
   See GODOY ALCAYAGA, Lucila

*   *   *

ALDISS, Brian W(ilson) 1925-
   (C. C. Shackleton)

PERSONAL: Born August 8, 1925, in East Dereham, Norfolk, England; son of Stanley (an outfitter) and May (Wilson) Aldiss;

married second wife, Margaret Christie Manson, December 11, 1965; children: (first marriage) Clive, Caroline Wendy; (second marriage) Timothy Nicholas, Charlotte May. *Education:* Attended Framlingham College.

ADDRESSES: Home—Woodlands, Boars Hill, Oxford OX1 5DL, England. *Agent*—A. P. Watt Ltd., 26/28 Bedford Row, London WC1, England, and Robin Straus, 229 East 79th St., New York, N.Y. 10021 (literary); Frank Hatherly, 35 Fishers Lane, London W4 1RX, England (media).

CAREER: Writer, editor, critic, bookseller. *Oxford Mail,* Oxford, England, literary editor, 1957-69; Penguin Books, Ltd., London, England, editor of science fiction novels, 1961-64; *The Guardian,* London, art correspondent, 1971—. Judge for Booker-McConnell Prize, 1981. *Military service:* British Army, four years, including service with Royal Corps of Signals; attached to Indian Army, 1945-46; received Burma Star.

MEMBER: International Institute for the Study of Time, International Organization for the Fantastic in the Arts (permanent guest), World Science Fiction Society (president, 1982-84), British Science Fiction Association (president, 1960-64), Science Fiction Writers of America, Science Fiction Research Association, Society of Authors (chairman, 1977-78), PEN, Arts Council of Great Britain (literature panelist, 1978-80), Cultural Exchanges Committee (chairman).

AWARDS, HONORS: Observer book award for science fiction, 1956; named most promising new author of the year, 1958, World Science Fiction Convention; Hugo Award for best short fiction, World Science Fiction Convention, 1962, for *Hothouse;* special British Science Fiction Association Award for Britain's most popular science fiction author, 1964; Nebula Award for best novella, Science Fiction Writers of America, 1966, for *The Saliva Tree, and Other Strange Growths;* Ditmar Award for world's best contemporary science fiction author, 1970; British Science Fiction Association Award, 1972, for *The Moment of Eclipse;* Eurocon III Award, 1976, for *Billion Year Spree: The History of Science Fiction;* James Blish Award for excellence in science fiction criticism, 1977; Ferrara Silver Comet, 1977, for *Science Fiction Art;* Prix Jules Verne, 1977, for *Non-Stop;* Science Fiction Research Association Pilgrim Award, 1978; John W. Campbell Memorial Award for best novel of 1982, British Science Fiction Association Award for best fiction of 1982, and Kur Lasswitz Award, 1984, all for *Helliconia Spring;* first Inter-American Foundation for the Arts distinguished scholarship award, 1986; Eaton Award for best criticism, 1988.

WRITINGS:

NOVELS

The Brightfount Diaries, Faber, 1955.
Non-Stop, Faber, 1958, Pan Books, 1976, published as *Starship,* Criterion, 1959.
Equator, Digit Books, 1958, published as *Vanguard From Alpha,* Ace, 1959.
Bow Down to Nul, Ace, 1960 (published in England as *The Interpreter,* Digit Books, 1961).
The Male Response, Ballantine, 1961.
The Primal Urge, Ballantine, 1961.
Long Afternoon of Earth, Signet, 1962 (published in England as *Hothouse,* Faber, 1962).
The Dark Light Years, Harcourt, 1964.
Greybeard, Harcourt, 1964.
Earthworks, Faber, 1965, Doubleday, 1966.
The Saliva Tree, and Other Strange Growths, Faber, 1966.
An Age, Faber, 1967, published as *Cryptozoic!,* Doubleday, 1968.

Report on Probability A, Faber, 1968, Doubleday, 1969.
A Brian Aldiss Omnibus, Sidgwick & Jackson, 1969.
Barefoot in the Head: A European Fantasia, Faber, 1969, Doubleday, 1970.
The Hand-Reared Boy, McCall, 1970.
A Soldier Erect, Coward, 1971 (published in England as *A Soldier Erect; or, Further Adventures of the Hand-Reared Boy,* Weidenfeld & Nicolson, 1971).
Brian Aldiss Omnibus 2, Sidgwick & Jackson, 1971.
Frankenstein Unbound (also see below), Random House, 1973.
The Eighty-Minute Hour: A Space Opera, Doubleday, 1974.
The Malacia Tapestry, J. Cape, 1976, Harper, 1977.
Brothers of the Head, illustrated by Ian Pollock, Pierrot, 1977.
A Rude Awakening, Weidenfeld & Nicolson, 1978, Random House, 1979.
Enemies of the System: A Tale of Homo Uniformis, Harper, 1978.
Life in the West, Weidenfeld & Nicolson, 1980.
Moreau's Other Island, J. Cape, 1980, published as *An Island Called Moreau,* Simon & Schuster, 1981.
Helliconia Spring, Atheneum, 1982.
Helliconia Summer, Atheneum, 1983.
Helliconia Winter, Atheneum, 1985.
The Year Before Yesterday: A Novel in Three Acts, F. Watts, 1987.
Ruins, Century Hutchinson (London), 1987.
Forgotten Life, Gollancz, 1988, Atheneum, 1989.

NONFICTION

Cities and Stones: A Traveller's Yugoslavia, Faber, 1966.
The Shape of Further Things, Doubleday, 1970.
Billion Year Spree: The History of Science Fiction, Doubleday, 1973.
Science Fiction Art, New English Library, 1975.
This World and Nearer Ones: Essays Exploring the Familiar, Weidenfeld & Nicolson, 1979, Kent State University Press, 1981.
Pile: Petals From St. Klaed's Computer, illustrations by Mike Wilks, J. Cape, 1979, Holt, 1980.
The Pale Shadow of Science, Serconia, 1985.
. . . And the Lurid Glare of the Comet, Serconia, 1986.
(With David Wingrove) *Trillion Year Spree: The History of Science Fiction,* Atheneum, 1986.

STORY COLLECTIONS

Space, Time and Nathaniel, Faber, 1957.
The Canopy of Time, Faber, 1959.
No Time Like Tomorrow, Signet, 1959.
Galaxies Like Grains of Sand, Signet, 1960, reprinted with new introduction by Norman Spinrad, Gregg, 1977.
The Airs of Earth, Faber, 1963.
Starswarm, Signet, 1964.
Best Science Fiction Stories of Brian Aldiss, Faber, 1965, revised edition, 1971, published as *Who Can Replace a Man?,* Harcourt, 1966.
Intangibles Inc., and Other Stories: Five Novellas, Faber, 1969.
Neanderthal Planet, Avon, 1969.
(Contributor) *The Inner Landscape,* Allison & Busby, 1969.
The Moment of Eclipse, Faber, 1971, Doubleday, 1972.
The Book of Brian Aldiss, DAW Books, 1972 (published in England as *Comic Inferno,* New English Library, 1973).
Last Orders and Other Stories, J. Cape, 1977.
New Arrivals, Old Encounters, Harper, 1979.
Foreign Bodies, Chapman (Singapore), 1981.
Seasons in Flight, J. Cape, 1984, Atheneum, 1986.

Best SF Stories of Brian W. Aldiss, Gollancz, 1988, Atheneum, 1989 (published in England as *Man in His Time: Best SF Stories of Brian W. Aldiss,* with new introduction by author, Gollancz, 1989).

Science Fiction Blues: The Show That Brian Aldiss Took on the Road, Avernus, 1988.

A Romance of the Equator: Best Fantasy Stories of Brian W. Aldiss, Atheneum, 1990.

EDITOR

Penguin Science Fiction, Penguin, 1961.

More Penguin Science Fiction: An Anthology, Penguin, 1962.

Best Fantasy Stories, Faber, 1962.

Science Fiction Horizons, Numbers 1-2, Arno Press, 1964-65.

Yet More Penguin Science Fiction, Penguin, 1964.

Introducing Science Fiction: A Science Fiction Anthology, Faber, 1964.

(With Harry Harrison) *Nebula Award Stories II,* Doubleday, 1967.

(With Harrison) *All About Venus: A Revelation of the Planet Venus in Fact and Fiction,* Dell, 1968 (published in England as *Farewell Fantastic Venus! A History of the Planet Venus in Fact and Fiction,* Macdonald, 1968).

(With Harrison) *The Astounding Analog Reader,* two volumes, Doubleday, 1973.

Penguin Science Fiction Omnibus: An Anthology, Penguin, 1973.

Space Opera: An Anthology of Way-Back-When Futures, Weidenfeld & Nicolson, 1974, Doubleday, 1975.

(With Harrison) *Hell's Cartographers: Some Personal Histories of Science Fiction Writers,* Doubleday, 1975.

Space Odysseys, Weidenfeld & Nicolson, 1975, Doubleday, 1976.

Evil Earths, Weidenfeld & Nicolson, 1975, Avon, 1979.

Galactic Empires, two volumes, Weidenfeld & Nicolson, 1976, St. Martin's, 1977.

(With Harrison) *Decade: The 1940s,* Pan Books, 1977, St. Martin's, 1978.

(With Harrison) *Decade: The 1950s,* Pan Books, 1977, St. Martin's, 1978.

(With Harrison) *Decade: The 1960s,* Macmillan, 1977.

Perilous Planets, Weidenfeld & Nicolson, 1978, Avon, 1980.

The Penguin World Omnibus of Science Fiction, Penguin Books, 1986.

Also co-editor of "SF Master" series, New English Library, 1976-79.

EDITOR WITH HARRY HARRISON; "BEST SCIENCE FICTION" ANNUALS

Best Science Fiction: 1967, Berkley Publishing, 1968 (published in England as *The Year's Best Science Fiction 1,* Sphere, 1968).

Best Science Fiction: 1968, Putnam, 1969 (published in England as *The Year's Best Science Fiction 2,* Sphere, 1969).

Best Science Fiction: 1969, Putnam, 1970 (published in England as *The Year's Best Science Fiction 3,* Sphere, 1970).

Best Science Fiction: 1970, Putnam, 1971 (published in England as *The Year's Best Science Fiction 4,* Sphere, 1971).

Best Science Fiction: 1971, Putnam, 1972.

Best Science Fiction: 1972, Putnam, 1973.

Best Science Fiction: 1973, Putnam, 1974.

Best Science Fiction: 1974, Putnam, 1975 (published in England as *The Year's Best Science Fiction,* Sphere, 1975).

Best Science Fiction: 1975, Putnam, 1976 (published in England as *The Year's Best Science Fiction,* Sphere, 1976).

OTHER

"Frankenstein Unbound" (radio play based on the novel of the same title), British Broadcasting Corp. (BBC-Radio), 1974, abridged version released as a sound recording by Alternate World Recordings, 1976.

Author of articles and reviews under pseudonym C. C. Shackleton.

WORK IN PROGRESS: Bury My Heart at W. H. Smith's, a book on authorship.

SIDELIGHTS: Brian W. Aldiss is a prolific British author who has published criticism, essays, travelogues, short stories, and traditional novels, but who remains best known for his science fiction writing. Since the appearance of his first science fiction novel, *Non-Stop,* in 1958, Aldiss has garnered virtually every major award in the field, including a Hugo Award for *Hothouse,* a Nebula Award for *The Saliva Tree,* a John W. Campbell Memorial Award for *Helliconia Spring,* and a James Blish Award for excellence in science fiction criticism. Unlike many of his colleagues, Aldiss approaches science fiction from a humanist point of view, focusing on character and theme rather than gadget-oriented technology. He demands an authorial autonomy that is rare in the field, and he typically discards worn-out formulas in favor of riskier, creative experiments.

As a critic, Aldiss campaigns for the acceptance of science fiction as a legitimate genre. He argues that science fiction is not just a fad, but will remain a permanent fixture in literature. According to Jonathan White in *Publishers Weekly,* Aldiss believes that science fiction has the potential to evolve, while other genres inevitably disappear after running their courses. The author explains to White: "I don't look upon science fiction as a genre at all; rather, it *contains* genres. For a bit it was the space opera that was in vogue. Then the catastrophe novel. For every kind of story that gets used up, another will always take its place." His comprehensive history of this genre, *Trillion Year Spree: The History of Science Fiction,* written with David Wingrove, testifies to his vision of science fiction as a serious literary endeavor.

Aldiss has himself experimented with different types of science fiction. *An Age,* for example, deals with the theme of time travel, but it is also "an amalgam . . . of detective story, psychological thriller and visionary fantasy," writes a *Times Literary Supplement* reviewer. *The Eighty-Minute Hour* "joyously resurrects old SF stereotypes," but it does so with "an amused self-consciousness, stylistic flair and dexterity, and a double-edged humor based in the comic multiple meanings of language," declares Richard Mathews in his *Aldiss Unbound: The Science Fiction of Brian W. Aldiss.* Two of the author's books, *Report on Probability A* and *Barefoot in the Head: A European Fantasia,* are experimental works which are meant to challenge the reader intellectually, Aldiss tells White. *Barefoot* describes a war fought with hallucinogenic drugs, while *Report* is "a kind of fantasy *nouveau roman* of voyeurism," as a *Chicago Tribune Book World* reviewer calls it. Aldiss says in a *Contemporary Authors Autobiography Series* entry that *Report* marks his "commitment to bringing art and artistic concerns into SF." Neither novel was accepted with much critical or public enthusiasm upon publication, but both, especially the repeatedly reissued *Report,* have enjoyed some success since then.

After exploring the many features of the genre in over a dozen books, Aldiss felt he had "written himself out of science fiction," relates Mathews. He ventured into what he terms "ordinary fiction" with the novel *The Hand-Reared Boy* and its two sequels, *A Soldier Erect* and *A Rude Awakening.* Mathews argues that the adjective "ordinary," far from having any negative connotation, is "used in its best sense" because the book, which records the "male rites of passage before the [Second World War,] is one with which any man can identify." It is, the reviewer suggests, far from ordinary in its ability to reach its audience. *The Hand-Reared Boy* is the story of Horatio Stubbs's experiences at a private (or, in British usage, public) boarding school for boys in England. Its sequel, *A Soldier Erect,* follows Stubbs into military service. Mathews finds that "these novels are significant in marking [Aldiss's] return to standard fiction devices, without the aid of stylistic inventions or SF gimmicks."

The frankness of Aldiss's approach to this trilogy, which strongly emphasizes Horatio's sexual exploits, has inspired strong reactions from critics, who either find the characters refreshing or vulgar. A *Times Literary Supplement* reviewer notes that *The Hand-Reared Boy* may seem like "an erotic fantasy. Yet it rings true—however surprising to young readers educated at day-schools." And Valentine Cunningham remarks in the *Times Literary Supplement* that "even a taste for the tasteless has a way of sliding into tastefulness" in *A Rude Awakening,* the last Horatio book. She feels that the postwar wisdom Horatio expresses toward the end of the book is the most tasteful part, though she believes Aldiss wades through too many "bodily fluids" before offering anything of literary substance to his text. *New York Times Book Review* critic Martin Levin also has mixed feelings about the Horatio Stubbs trilogy. Reviewing *The Hand-Reared Boy,* Levin believes that the "disarming keynote" of an otherwise sexually preoccupied book is the "spirit of joyful exuberance" with which Horatio recalls his childhood memories. Levin expresses little tolerance for Horatio's "zest for whoring [which] declines only during bouts of dysentery," but he praises Aldiss's portrayal of war in the China-Burma-India theater. The vividness of this part of the book comes from the author's personal experiences in Asia during the Second World War. "Mr. Aldiss brings to life this long-dead war, with its vanished mystique and its forgiven and forgotten enemies," declares Levin. Balancing out the blunt corporeal language and situations of this trilogy, this aspect of the Horatio novels has helped mitigate criticism of these publicly well-received books.

Aldiss's *Forgotten Life,* published in 1988, contains descriptions of life in wartime Burma and Sumatra which echo those of the Asian war theater in the Horatio books, but any similarities between this and those earlier works end there. *Forgotten Life* deals with the relationships between mature people rather than with the maturation processes of a single character. It is concerned with three people, explains *Glasgow Herald* contributor Ian Bell: Clement Winter, an Oxford psychoanalyst who is struggling "for an emotional life of his own," his wife Sheila, a successful science fiction/fantasy novelist, who is "living half her life in a fantasy world," and Clement's brother Joseph, who is striving "to form a lasting relationship free from the rejection he endured at his mother's hands." Jonathan Keates claims in an *Observer* review that "the true protagonist here is Joseph," whose tale is told when Clement reads his brother's journals after the latter's death. "Aldiss's skill," continues Keates, "lies in sustaining [Joseph] in a continuing duel with Clement." Contrary to this opinion, *Punch* critic Simon Brett believes that "too great a percentage of the book is devoted to [Joseph]. And the author has created a self-regarding style for Joseph's writings which, while entirely appropriate for the character, does become a little wearing for the reader."

The organization of the book is complex, shifting in viewpoint as it involves the reader in Joseph's journal, Clement's life in north Oxford, the brothers' childhood lives, and the present-day relationships between Clement and his brother's mistress, and Sheila and her American editor. *Times Literary Supplement* contributor John Melmoth believes this approach "fails to cohere," making it a "frustrating experience." But Isabel Quigley writes in the London *Financial Times* that "all these shifts of viewpoint, method, sympathy, place and time . . . [form a] whole and [achieve] a pattern, likeable, solid and satisfying." Sophia Watson, a *Literary Review* critic, similarly remarks that *Forgotten Life* is "a good read," but she does not believe it should be considered a major work of fiction. Ian Bell feels more strongly about the novel's merits, however, asserting that "this is a fine and satisfying novel of a type which Mr. Aldiss, masterly SF writer that he is, should try more often."

Despite praise for his mainstream fiction, the author has concentrated most of his efforts on science fiction. His most ambitious effort in this genre is the much-critiqued Helliconia trilogy, which Gerald Jonas says in the *New York Times Book Review* "truly deserves the label 'epic.' " The novels, *Helliconia Spring, Helliconia Summer,* and *Helliconia Winter,* are set on a world in a binary star system. The 2,592-year orbit of Helliconia's sun Batalix around the larger sun Freyr "subjects Helliconia to a Great Year whose seasons last for centuries," summarizes Colin Greenland in a *Times Literary Supplement* review of *Summer.* The extremity of the weather on the planet dictates to a great extent the rise and fall of civilizations, the relationship between the humans and beast-like "Phagors," and the biology of the planet's inhabitants (including humans).

Helliconia Spring starts at the end of Helliconia's 600-year-long barbaric ice age and follows the story of Yuli and his descendants as they begin to reestablish civilization in the town of Embruddock, which Yuli renames Oldorando. As the town grows, the men vie for power and battle the Phagors, while the women, led by the sorceress Shay Tal, establish an academy of science and discover how their planet behaves in its solar system. Aldiss fills his alien setting with descriptions of bizarre species of flora and fauna, a feature of the novel which *Los Angeles Times* contributor Carolyn See believes is distracting to the story line. In defense of this part of his trilogy, the author told *CA* that these details of life on Helliconia were "brought about by the joy of invention. The uses of strange species and alien planets were densely related; yet there is hardly a plant or animal which does not have its parallel on Earth."

In a review of *Spring,* Greenland also raises the objection that the plot of the novel depends too much on coincidence and is "overburdened with slabs of undigested science." But these are complaints which critics like See believe to be outweighed by the book's strengths. "For use of climate as character, for making the very long view palatable to the reader, for creating an entire universe that pulses and hums and crackles with life, Aldiss deserves full marks," concludes See. Michael Bishop adds that "Aldiss' unflagging narrative energy, his gift for drawing character, . . . and the many overt or subtle hints of larger, more portentous mysteries underlying the Viking-saga surface of his story" make the novel well worth while.

In the trilogy's second book, *Helliconia Summer,* the author focuses on a time period of only a few months. The Phagors have been subjugated (at least temporarily) and the story focuses on JandolAnganol, King of Borlien, and the intrigue and politics between his country and neighboring Oldorando. It is a tale which, according to London *Times* critic Nicholas Shakespeare, "smacks less of science fiction than medieval romance," though the plot also follows the society's progress as the priesthood becomes more and more involved in scientific studies. The concluding book of the series, *Helliconia Winter*, "combines the best of the Helliconia volumes—the breadth, scope, and historical sweep of *Spring* with the finely crafted details and narrow focus of *Summer*," says *Fantasy Review* contributor Michael R. Collins. In a review of *Helliconia Winter*, Greenland writes that the trilogy signifies "fatalism, fundamentality, the brute biology of it all. Everything comes back to nature, which endures." As civilization struggles to survive the oncoming winter, the reader follows the adventures of Luterin Shokerandit as he goes to war, is imprisoned in the Great Wheel of Kharnabar, and survives the "Fat Death," a disease transmitted by ticks which infest the Phagors and cause the victim's body to change drastically. Strangely enough and unknown to the Helliconians, the virus actually has a beneficial side effect which allows humankind to survive the harsh winter.

While all this is taking place, the importance of the space station Avernus (which was also mentioned in the earlier books) is made more apparent to the reader in *Helliconia Winter*. The purpose of the station is to transmit messages back to Earth about every event that occurs on Helliconia's surface. On Earth, viewing "the social and cultural evolution of other worlds has become our children's children's grandiose equivalent of watching *Dallas*," remarks Michael Bishop. Greenland feels that Aldiss's inclusion of the events on Avernus and Earth do not add to the story of Helliconia. This parallel story seems "like a dissonant dream, almost trivial beside the main drama," says Greenland. In contrast, an *Extrapolation* reviewer holds that the stories of Earth and Helliconia present a unifying theme of hope for humanity which is finally brought together in the last book. "The endless pictures coming from Helliconia [are] an example from which humanity might learn," suggests the article. The review concludes that as the people on Earth achieve a "new consciousness" which provides "humanity with a new unity instead of the old isolation," the highly technological station Avernus, which is also, in turn, a place of isolation for its caretakers, is replaced by higher, empathic communications. Humanity finds peace and understanding at last through the unification of the people of Earth with the Helliconians.

In a *Los Angeles Times* article, Sue Martin expresses her feeling that overall the trilogy is only "semicompelling" because there are "no real twists" in the plot. In response to this remark, Aldiss told *CA* that he considers such criticism to be imperceptive, since he "was not writing a detective novel." Indeed, many critics believe the Helliconia trilogy to be a considerable achievement. "Though science fiction often has this scope," asserts Greenland, "it has never had this grandeur." Gerald Jonas feels these books comprise "a splendid work of imagination that weds grandeur of concept to a mastery of detail and a sense of style unmatched in modern science fiction." Aldiss says in *Publishers Weekly* that the importance of these books to him is that they signify his attempt "to get on my horse again and write a big, solid novel that *no* one could say wasn't SF. And I think I've managed to do that." According to his own definition of science fiction quoted in the *New York Times Book Review*, this means that he has written a work which attempts "to build some sort of philosophical and metaphysical framework around the immense changes of our times brought about by technological development." The trilogy addresses all these aspects by including a scope of time encompassing thousands of years, the description of technology and its effect on Avernus and Earth, and, in *Science Fiction and Fantasy Book Review* contributor Willis E. McNelly's words, the "artistic, intellectual, theological, even teleological sustenance" which Helliconia offers to Earth.

The trilogy is the author's most ambitious effort to give science fiction credibility as a form of serious literature. *Fantasy Review* contributor Michael R. Collings remarks that "only an author such as Aldiss, who has immersed himself in questions of stasis and change, entropy, ecological balance, and definitions of what it is to be human—and has explored their possibilities for almost three decades—could have completed such a vision" as the Helliconia trilogy. Discussing Aldiss's science fiction work in general, critic Robert E. Colbert writes in *Extrapolation* that Aldiss's "concern for the dearth of ordinary human feeling in so much genre science fiction, its lack of warmth and compassion, is clear. And the specific literary benefits of the reintroduction of such concerns are also clear: an art which renders situations, depicts characters, closer to the more immediate human concerns can only benefit artistically." A number of critics believe that for these reasons, Brian Aldiss's contributions to science fiction have done much to improve its respectability. According to Greenland, Aldiss "continues to represent the acceptable face of science fiction to those literati who still cannot bring themselves to acknowledge the genre."

BIOGRAPHICAL/CRITICAL SOURCES:

BOOKS

Aldiss, Margaret, compiler, *Brian W. Aldiss: A Bibliography, 1954-1988*, Borgo, 1989.
Contemporary Authors Autobiography Series, Volume 2, Gale, 1985.
Contemporary Literary Criticism, Gale, Volume 5, 1976, Volume 14, 1980, Volume 40, 1986.
Dictionary of Literary Biography, Volume 14, *British Novelists since 1960*, Gale, 1983.
Griffin, Brian and David Wingrove, *Apertures: A Study of the Writings of Brian W. Aldiss*, Greenwood Press, 1984.
Mathews, Richard, *Aldiss Unbound: The Science Fiction of Brian W. Aldiss*, Borgo, 1977.
Platt, Charles, editor, *Dream Makers: The Uncommon People Who Write Science Fiction*, Berkley Publishing, 1980.

PERIODICALS

Chicago Tribune Book World, January 25, 1981, February 28, 1982.
Extrapolation, winter, 1982, spring, 1986.
Fantasy Review, April, 1985.
Financial Times (London), October 1, 1988.
Foundation, winter, 1985/86.
Glasgow Herald, October 8, 1988.
Listener, March 25, 1971, July 22, 1976.
Literary Review, September, 1988.
London Magazine, March, 1982.
Los Angeles Times, February 12, 1981, February 25, 1982.
Los Angeles Times Book Review, August 18, 1985, June 4, 1989.
New Statesman, November 2, 1973.
New York Times, February 17, 1981.
New York Times Book Review, April 19, 1970, August 22, 1971, September 12, 1976, February 26, 1984, April 28, 1985, April 30, 1989, May 21, 1989.
Observer (London), September 25, 1988.
Publishers Weekly, April 19, 1985.
Punch, September 30, 1988.
Science Fiction and Fantasy Book Review, June, 1982.
Science Fiction Studies, Volume 1, number 2, 1973.
Spectator, November 10, 1973, May 27, 1978, May 8, 1980, August 22, 1980.
Times (London), December 8, 1983.

Times Literary Supplement, September 21, 1967, January 22, 1970, May 19, 1978, March 7, 1980, December 2, 1983, September 30, 1988.

Washington Post Book World, March 22, 1981, August 28, 1988, May 14, 1989, April 29, 1990.

*   *   *

ALDRICH, Ann
See MEAKER, Marijane (Agnes)

*   *   *

ALEIXANDRE, Vicente   1898-1984

PERSONAL: Born April 26, 1898, in Seville, Spain; died of kidney failure and shock from intestinal hemorrhage, December 14, 1984, in Madrid, Spain; son of Cirilo (an engineer) and Elvira (Merlo) Aleixandre. *Education:* Attended University of Seville; University of Madrid, license in law and diploma in business, both 1919.

CAREER: Poet and writer, 1925-84. Central School of Commerce, Madrid, Spain, associate professor, 1919-21; Residencia de Estudiantes, Madrid, teacher of business terminology, 1921; worked for Ferrocarriles andaluces (railroad company), 1921-25. Lecturer at Oxford University and University of London, 1950, and in Morocco, 1953.

MEMBER: Real Academia Espanola, American Association of Teachers of Spanish and Portuguese (honorary fellow), Hispanic Society of America, Monde Latin Academy (Paris); corresponding member of Malaga Arts Academy, Academy of Science and Arts (Puerto Rico), and Hispanic-American Academy (Bogota).

AWARDS, HONORS: National Literary Prize (Spain), 1933, for *La destruccion o el amor;* Spanish Critics' Prize, 1963, 1969, and 1975; Nobel Prize in Literature, Swedish Academy, 1977; Grand Cross of the Order of Carlos III, 1977; Gold Medal of the City of Madrid, 1984.

WRITINGS:

IN ENGLISH TRANSLATION; POEMS

La destruccion o el amor, Signo (Madrid), 1935, 2nd edition, 1967, translation by Stephen Kessler of selected poems published as *Destruction or Love: A Selection From La destruccion o el amor of Vicente Aleixandre,* Green Horse Three (Santa Cruz, Calif.), 1976.
Mundo a solas, Clan (Madrid), 1950, translation by Lewis Hyde and David Unger published as *World Alone/Mundo a solas* (bilingual edition), Penmaen Press (Great Barrington, Mass.), 1982.
Poems (bilingual edition), translations by Ben Belitt, Alan Brilliant, and others, Department of English, Ohio University, 1969.
Vicente Aleixandre and Luis Cernuda: Selected Poems (bilingual edition), translations by Linda Lehrer and others, Copper Beach Press (Providence, R.I.), 1974.
The Cave of Night: Poems (bilingual edition), translation by Joeffrey Bartman, Solo Press (San Luis Obispo, Calif.), 1976.
Twenty Poems, edited by Hyde, translations by Hyde and Robert Bly, Seventies Press (Madison, Minn.), 1977.
Poems-Poemas (bilingual edition), Unicorn Press, 1978.
A Longing for the Light: Selected Poems of Vicente Aleixandre, edited by Hyde, translations by Kessler and others, Harper, 1979.

The Crackling Sun: Selected Poems of the Nobel Prize Recipient, 1977, translated and introduced by Louis Bourne, Sociedad General Espanola de la Libreria (Madrid), 1981.
A Bird of Paper: Poems of Vicente Aleixandre, translated by Willis Barnstone and David Garrison, Ohio University Press, 1982.

IN SPANISH; POEMS

Ambito (title means "Ambit"), Litoral (Malaga), 1928, reprinted, Raiz (Madrid), 1950.
Espadas como labios (title means "Swords Like Lips"; also see below), Espasa-Calpe (Madrid), 1932, reprinted, Losada (Buenos Aires), 1957.
Pasion de la tierra (title means "Passion of the Earth"; also see below), Fabula (Mexico), 1935, revised edition, Adonais (Madrid), 1946, critical edition with notes and commentary by Luis Antonio de Villena, Narceu, 1976.
Sombra del paraiso (also see below), Adan (Madrid), 1944, reprinted, Castalia, 1976, translation by Hugh Harter published as *Shadow of Paradise: Sombra del paraiso,* University of California Press, 1987.
Poemas paradisiacos (title means "Poems of Paradise"; includes selections from *Sombra del paraiso*), [Malaga], 1952, 3rd edition, edited by Jose Luis Cano, Catedra, 1981.
Nacimiento ultimo (title means "Final Birth"), Insula (Madrid), 1953.
Historia del corazon (title means "History of a Heart"), Espasa-Calpe, 1954, critical edition with prologue by Cano, 1983.
Antigua casa madrilena (title means "Ancient Madrid House"; also see below), Hermanos Bedia (Santander, Spain), 1961.
Picasso (long poem) [Malaga], 1961.
En un vasto dominio (title means "In a Vast Dominion"; includes *Antigua casa madrilena*), Revista de Occidente, 1962.
Retratos con nombres (title means "Portraits With Names"), El Bardo, 1965.
Poemas de la consumacion (title means "Poems of Consummation"), Plaza y Janes (Barcelona), 1968.
Sonido de la guerra, Fomento de Cultura Ediciones (Valencia), 1972.
Dialogos del conocimiento (title means "Dialogues of Knowledge"), Plaza y Janes, 1974.

OMNIBUS VOLUMES IN SPANISH

Mis poemas mejores (title means "My Best Poems"), Gredos (Madrid), 1956, revised edition, 1976.
Espadas como labios [and] *Pasion de la tierra,* Losada, 1957, critical edition with notes and introduction by Cano, Castalia, 1977.
Poemas amorosos: Antologia (title means "Love Poems: Anthology"), Losada, 1960.
Poesias completas (title means "Complete Poems"), introduction by Carlos Bousono, Aguilar, 1960.
Presencias (title means "Presences"; limited edition), Seix Barral (Barcelona), 1965.
Obras completas (title means "Complete Works"), introduction by Bousono, Aguilar, 1968, revised edition published in two volumes, 1977.
Poesia superrealista (title means "Surrealistic Poetry"), Barral Editores, 1971.
Antologia del mar y de la noche (title means "Anthology of the Sea and the Night"), edited by Javier Lostale, Al-Borak, 1971.
Antologia total (title means "Total Anthology"), compiled by Pere Gimferrer, Seix Barral, 1975.

Antologia poetica (title means "Poetry Anthology"), edited by Leopoldo de Luis, Castalia, 1976.
Aleixandre para ninos (title means "Aleixandre for Children"; juvenile), Ediciones de la Torre (Madrid), 1984.

AUTHOR OF PROLOGUE IN SPANISH

Bousono, *La primavera de la muerte,* Adonais, 1946.
Gregoria Prieto, *Poesia en linea,* Adonais, 1948.
Fernando Charry Lara, *Nocturnos y otros suenos,* [Bogota], 1948.
Adonais: Segunda antologia, Rialp (Madrid), 1962.

CONTRIBUTOR TO ANTHOLOGIES

Eleanor Laurelle Turnbull, editor, *Contemporary Spanish Poetry: Selections From Ten Poets* (bilingual edition), Johns Hopkins University Press, 1945.
Penguin Book of Spanish Verse, Penguin, 1956.
Willis Barnstone, editor, *Modern European Poetry,* Bantam, 1966.
Hardie St. Martin, editor, *Roots and Wings, Poetry From Spain: A Bilingual Anthology,* Harper, 1976.

OTHER

Algunos caracteres de la poesia espanola contemporanea (title means "Some Characteristics of Contemporary Spanish Poetry"; criticism), Imprenta Gongora (Madrid), 1955.
Los encuentros (title means "The Meetings"; critical/biographical sketches), Guadarrama (Madrid), 1958.
(Contributor) Francisco Sabadett Lopez, *Desnudos,* [Valladolid], 1961.
(Author of epilogue) Federico Garcia Lorca, *Obras completas,* Aguilar, 1963.
(Contributor) Jose Angeles, editor, *Estudios sobre Antonio Machado,* Ariel, 1977.

Contributor of poetry and articles to Spanish journals. Co-editor, *Revista de Economia,* 1920-22; staff member, *La Semana Financiera* (financial magazine), ending 1927.

SIDELIGHTS: Poet Vicente Aleixandre was a member of Spain's Generation of 1927, which Manuel Duran described in a *World Literature Today* essay as "perhaps the brightest and most original poetic generation in twentieth-century Western Europe." Along with Aleixandre, the group included many of modern Spain's most influential writers, such as Jorge Guillen, Gerardo Diego, and Rafael Alberti.

Although nearly unknown outside his native country before receiving the Nobel Prize for Literature in 1977, Aleixandre had much in common with the generation's best-known poet, Federico Garcia Lorca. The two men were from the same region in Spain—the southernmost Andalusia—and revealed the same sources of inspiration in their poetry: Spanish writing of the fifteenth and sixteenth centuries, popular folk rhythms of their native Andalusia, and surrealism. But, while Lorca's death at the hands of Franco's forces at the beginning of the Spanish Civil War catapulted him into international recognition, Aleixandre's name was known only in Spanish circles. He survived both having his house nearly destroyed in a Civil War bomb attack—an autographed book of Lorca's was one of the only items recovered from his gutted library—and having his work banned by government censors for nearly five years after the war to become one of Spain's most prominent poets.

Most critics of Aleixandre's work commented on the thematic and stylistic evolution evident in his poetry. In *Contemporary Spanish Poetry (1898-1963),* for example, Carl W. Cobb noted that in Aleixandre's early poems the poet "rejected the historical

and social world around him and created from his elemental passions a vast domain of cosmic and telluric forces anterior to man himself." In contrast, Cobb described the poet's later work as being focused "directly in the historical reality of his pueblo, his 'people.' "

Other critics, such as Diana Der Hovanessian, Arthur Terry, and Kessel Schwartz, echoed Cobb's assessment. In the *Christian Science Monitor,* for instance, Der Hovanessian noted: "Some of [Aleixandre's] early poetry might tax a reader with its mysticism and disjointed style. But Aleixandre's poetry loses much of the disconnectedness in later years, and begins to address people directly." Terry similarly stated in the *Times Literary Supplement* that while Aleixandre's early poems were "Surrealist-influenced," in later poems "emphasis shifts to the contemplation of man in his human context." Schwartz described the poet's work in *Vicente Aleixandre* as a movement from "the chaotic maelstrom" of his early work to a new poetry in which Aleixandre "became aware of historical man, the temporal man, that is, man in time and space."

Dario Fernandez-Morera explained the transformation in Aleixandre's poetry in light of the dramatic change in Spanish society following the Civil War. In *Symposium* the critic stated: "Before [the war], poets had lived in an atmosphere of continuity, of relative intellectual security; therefore they could be concerned with their own psyches rather than with the world they lived in. . . . But the growing turmoil made this attitude no longer feasible."

The selection of Aleixandre as a Nobel laureate was controversial, since the complexity of his surrealistic poetry made it unintelligible to many critics and most readers. A *Washington Post* writer quoted a translated line of poetry from Aleixandre's second book, *Pasion de la tierra* (title means "Passion of the Earth") as an example of what the reviewer called Aleixandre's "puzzling" verse: "To sleep when my time comes on a conscience without a pillowcase."

G. G. Brown referred to the same book of poetry in *A Literary History of Spain* as "a collection of largely incomprehensible prose-poems, whose private subconscious ramblings Aleixandre tried to excuse later by calling them Freudian." And in *A Longing for the Light: Selected Poems of Vicente Aleixandre,* Lewis Hyde noted that the poems in *Pasion de la tierra* were "written in an almost hermetic dream-language."

According to Hyde, Aleixandre agreed with critics who called *Pasion de la tierra* difficult, but he nevertheless defended the book's worth. Hyde translated the poet's comments: "I have always thought I could see in its chasm-like layers the sudden start of my poetry's evolution, which, from its earliest, has been . . . a longing for the light. This book has therefore produced in me a double, complicated feeling: of aversion, because of its difficulty, which contradicts the call, the appeal it makes to basic levels, common to all of us; and of affection, for the maternal *humus* from which it grew."

Although Fernandez-Morera pointed out that "Aleixandre's surrealist phase is perhaps [his] most publicized," the poet's Nobel Prize was awarded largely for his later, more accessible, work. This was evident, Pablo Beltran de Heredia observed in the *Texas Quarterly,* "when [the Swedish Academy] stated, during the award ceremonies, that the work of this Spanish poet 'illuminates the condition of man in the cosmos and in our present-day society.' "

Cobb noted that "it is perhaps with a feeling of relief that the reader turns from the difficult and turbulent world of Aleixandre's first period . . . to the quieter and simpler but no less moving world of his second phase. . . . His major theme becomes human solidarity, with compassion toward all human beings living in time." Cobb singled out *Historia del corazon* (title means "History of the Heart") published in 1954 as Aleixandre's first book of this new style of poetry. Abandoning the obscurity of his early poems, Aleixandre came to believe that poetry was essentially communication. In general, the prose-poems gave way to what a *New York Times* writer called "carefully cadenced free verse." The nightmarish images were replaced by portraits of everyday life. According to Duran, "*Historia del corazon* is basically the story of a love affair, in its daily moments of joy and anguish, and also the story of a growing awareness, a solidarity: the poet realizes that he is only one member of a vast society, the Spanish people, and that ultimately he is a part of mankind."

Beltran de Heredia pointed out that Aleixandre expressed a fondness for this simpler poetry, preferring *Historia del corazon* among his books and—from that same collection—"En la plaza" (title means "On the Square") among his poems. Both Santiago Daydi-Tolson in *The Post-Civil War Spanish Poets* and Duran emphasized the importance of this same poem. Aleixandre "uses the image of the public square," Daydi-Tolson observed, "to represent the greatness of human solidarity." According to the critic, the plaza, the axis around which society revolves in every Spanish city, is the perfect embodiment of the essence of Spanish life. In the symbol of the public square the poet "feels and understands this essential communal quality of man's existence."

Duran saw the poem as an encapsulated portrait of Aleixandre's evolution from personal to communal poet. Duran explained the imagery of the poem: "After being long confined in his room, the poet goes out into the street, to the square, in order to mingle with other human beings and be part of humanity." Duran illustrated his point with a translation from the poem: "It is a beautiful feeling, beautifully humble and buoyant, life-giving and deep,/ to feel yourself beneath the sun among other people."

Aleixandre is important for his own poetry but also for his influence on the poetry of subsequent generations. As one of the few poets to remain in Spain during the Civil War, he was a symbol of hope to younger poets. In a *New York Times Book Review* essay, Robert Bly suggested that after the war "the younger writers felt abandoned, dead, in despair. It turned out that Aleixandre's decision to stay helped all that. He represented the wild energy still alive on Spanish soil."

A *London Times* writer noted that although Aleixandre "was privately distressed at the low quality of verse of Falangist poets [members of Franco's party], . . . he encouraged them as he encouraged every other poet, seeking with a noble magnanimity of spirit to unify all factions. He worked behind the scenes to obtain the release of imprisoned writers, and was more responsible than any other single person for creating the relaxed [Spanish] censorship of the middle and late 1960s, which led to better things."

In Aleixandre's prologue to the second edition of *La destruccion o el amor,* the Spaniard summarized his ideas on poets and poetry. The prologue, written in 1944 shortly before the poet began work on *La historia del corazon* and translated by David Pritchard in the *Paris Review,* ends with a short explanation of Aleixandre's poetics. "Some poets . . .," he wrote, "are poets 'of the few.' They are artists . . . who address themselves to men by attending, so they say, to exquisite and narrow obsessions. . . . Other poets . . . address themselves to what is permanent in man. Not to the details that set us apart, but to the essence that brings us together. . . . These poets are radical poets and they speak to what is primordial, to what is elemental in humanity.

They cannot *feel* themselves to be poets of the few. I am one of these."

BIOGRAPHICAL/CRITICAL SOURCES:

BOOKS

Aleixandre, Vicente, *Twenty Poems,* edited by Lewis Hyde, Seventies Press, 1977.

Aleixandre, Vicente, *A Longing for the Light: Selected Poems of Vicente Aleixandre,* edited by Lewis Hyde, Copper Canyon Press, 1985.

Alonso, Damaso, *Ensayos sobre poesia espanola,* Revista de Occidente, 1946.

Bousono, Carlos, *La poesia de Vicente Aleixandre,* Insula, 1950, revised edition, 1977.

Brown, G. G., *A Literary History of Spain,* Barnes & Noble, 1972.

Cabrera, Vicente and Harriet Boyer, editors, *Critical Views on Vicente Aleixandre's Poetry,* Society of Spanish and Spanish-American Studies (Lincoln, Neb.), 1979.

Cobb, Carl W., *Contemporary Spanish Poetry (1898-1963),* Twayne, 1976.

Contemporary Literary Criticism, Gale, Volume 9, 1978, Volume 36, 1986.

Daydi-Tolson, Santiago, editor, *Vicente Aleixandre: A Critical Appraisal,* Bilingual Press, 1981.

Daydi-Tolson, Santiago, *The Post-Civil War Spanish Poets,* Twayne, 1983.

Jimenez, Jose Olivio, *Cinco poetas del tiempo,* Insula, 1964.

Jimenez, Jose Olivio, *Vicente Aleixandre: Una aventura hacia el conocimiento,* Ediciones Jucar (Madrid), 1982.

Ley, Charles David, *Spanish Poetry Since 1939,* Catholic University of America Press, 1962.

Morris, C. B., *A Generation of Spanish Poets: 1920-1936,* Cambridge University Press, 1969.

Schwartz, Kessel, *Vicente Aleixandre,* Twayne, 1970.

PERIODICALS

Christian Science Monitor, January 2, 1980.
Hispania, May, 1967.
Hispanic Journal, fall, 1982.
Hudson Review, winter, 1978-79.
Nation, March 4, 1978.
New Republic, December 24-31, 1977.
Newsweek, October 17, 1977.
New York Times, October 7, 1977.
New York Times Book Review, October 30, 1977.
Paris Review, fall, 1978.
Parnassus: Poetry in Review, fall/winter, 1979.
Poetry, April, 1980.
Symposium, summer, 1979.
Texas Quarterly, winter, 1978.
Time, October 17, 1977.
Times (London), December 15, 1984.
Times Literary Supplement, May 17, 1957, November 2, 1958, July 10, 1969, May 23, 1975.
Washington Post, December 15, 1984.
World Literature Today, spring, 1975.

OBITUARIES:

PERIODICALS

AB Bookman's Weekly, January 21, 1985.
Chicago Tribune, December 26, 1984.
Los Angeles Times, December 16, 1984.
Time, December 24, 1984.

Times (London), December 15, 1984.

—Sketch by Marian Gonsior

*   *   *

ALEXANDER, Lloyd (Chudley) 1924-

PERSONAL: Born January 30, 1924, in Philadelphia, Pa.; son of Alan Audley (a stockbroker and importer) and Edna (Chudley) Alexander; married Janine Denni, January 8, 1946; children: Madeleine (Mrs. Zohair Khalil). *Education:* Attended West Chester State Teachers College, 1942; Lafayette College, 1943; earned degree at Sorbonne, University of Paris, 1946.

ADDRESSES: Home—1005 Drexel Ave., Drexel Hill, Pa. 19026. *Agent*—Brandt & Brandt, 1501 Broadway, New York, N.Y. 10036.

CAREER: Author of children's books; free-lance writer and translator, 1946—. Author-in-residence, Temple University, 1970-74. Also worked as cartoonist, layout artist, advertising copywriter, and editor of an industrial magazine. *Military service:* U.S. Army, Intelligence, 1942-46; became staff sergeant.

MEMBER: Authors Guild, Authors League of America, PEN, Amnesty International, Carpenter Lane Chamber Music Society (member of board of directors).

AWARDS, HONORS: Isaac Siegel Memorial Juvenile Award, 1959, for *Border Hawk: August Bondi;* American Library Association notable book citation, 1964, for *The Book of Three;* Newbery Honor Book Award, American Library Association, 1965, for *The Black Cauldron; School Library Journal* Best Books of the Year citation, 1967, for *Taran Wanderer;* American Institute of Graphic Arts Children's Books citation, 1967-68, for *The Truthful Harp;* Child Study Association of America Children's Books of the Year citation, 1968, for *The High King,* 1971, for *The King's Fountain,* 1973, for *The Cat Who Wished to Be a Man,* 1974, for *The Foundling and Other Tales of Prydain,* 1975, for *The Wizard in the Tree,* 1982, for *The Kestrel,* and 1985, for *The Black Cauldron* and *Time Cat;* National Book Award nomination, and Newbery Medal, American Library Association, both 1969, both for *The High King;* Library of Congress Best Books of the Year citation, 1970, and National Book Award, 1971, both for *The Marvelous Misadventures of Sebastian; School Library Journal* Best Books for Spring citation, 1971, for *The King's Fountain;* Drexel Award, 1972 and 1976, for outstanding contributions to literature for children; *Boston Globe/Horn Book* award, 1973, for *The Cat Who Wished to Be a Man; New York Times* Outstanding Books of the Year Citation, 1973, for *The Foundling and Other Tales of Prydain;* Laura Ingalls Wilder Award nomination, 1975; CRABbery Award from Oxon Hill Branch of Prince George's County Library (Maryland), 1979, National Book Award nomination 1979, Silver Pencil Award, 1981, and Austrian Children's Book Award, 1984, all for *The First Two Lives of Lukas-Kasha;* American Book Award nomination, 1980, for *The High King,* and 1982, for *The Wizard in the Tree;* American Library Association Best Books for Young Adults citation, 1981, for *Westmark,* 1982, for *The Kestrel,* and 1984, for *The Beggar Queen;* American Book Award, 1982, for *Westmark;* Parents' Choice Award, 1982, for *The Kestrel,* 1984, for *The Beggar Queen,* and 1986, for *The Illyrian Adventure; School Library Journal* Best Books for Young Adults citation, 1982, and Best of the Best Books, 1970-1983 citation, both for *Westmark;* Golden Cat Award, Sjoestrands Foerlag (Swedish publisher), 1984, for excellence in children's literature; Regina Medal, Catholic Library Association, 1986; Church and Syna-

gogue Library Association Award, 1987; Field Award, Pennsylvania Library Association, 1987, for *The Illyrian Adventure;* Helen Keating Ott award, 1987.

WRITINGS:

And Let the Credit Go, Crowell, 1955.
My Five Tigers, Crowell, 1956.
Janine Is French, Crowell, 1958.
My Love Affair with Music, Crowell, 1960.
(With Louis Camuti) *Park Avenue Vet,* Holt, 1962.
Fifty Years in the Doghouse, Putnam, 1963 (published in England as *Send for Ryan!,* W. H. Allen, 1965).
My Cats and Me: The Story of an Understanding, Running Press, 1989.

JUVENILES

Border Hawk: August Bondi (biography), Farrar, Straus, 1959.
Aaron Lopez and Flagship Hope (biography), Farrar, Straus, 1960.
Time Cat, Holt, 1963 (published in England as *Nine Lives,* Cassell, 1963).
Coll and His White Pig, Holt, 1965.
The Truthful Harp, Holt, 1967.
The Marvelous Misadventures of Sebastian, Dutton, 1970.
The King's Fountain, Dutton, 1971.
The Four Donkeys, Holt, 1972.
The Foundling and Other Tales of Prydain, Holt, 1973.
The Cat Who Wished to Be a Man, Dutton, 1973.
The Wizard in the Tree, Dutton, 1975.
The Town Cats and Other Tales, Dutton, 1977.
The First Two Lives of Lukas-Kasha, Dutton, 1978.

THE "PRYDAIN CHRONICLES" SERIES

The Book of Three, Holt, 1964.
The Black Cauldron, Holt, 1965.
The Castle of Llyr, Holt, 1966.
Taran Wanderer, Holt, 1967.
The High King, Holt, 1968.

THE WESTMARK TRILOGY

Westmark, Dutton, 1981.
The Kestrel, Dutton, 1982.
The Beggar Queen, Dutton, 1984.

THE VESPER HOLLY ADVENTURES

The Illyrian Adventure, Dutton, 1986.
The El Dorado Adventure, Dutton, 1987.
The Drackenberg Adventure, Dutton, 1988.
The Jedera Adventure, Dutton, 1989.

TRANSLATOR FROM THE FRENCH

Jean-Paul Sartre, *The Wall and Other Stories,* New Directions, 1948, published as *Intimacy and Other Stories,* Peter Nevill, 1949, New Directions, 1952.
Sartre, *Nausea,* New Directions, 1949 (published in England as *The Diary of Antoine Roquentin,* Lehmann, 1949).
Paul Eluard, *Selected Writings,* New Directions, 1951, published as *Uninterrupted Poetry: Selected Writings,* 1975.
Paul Vialar, *The Sea Rose,* Neville Spearman, 1951.

CONTRIBUTOR

Elinor Whitney Field, editor, *Horn Book Reflections on Children's Books and Reading,* Horn Book, 1969.
Cricket's Choice, Open Court, 1974.

OTHER

Also author of afterword to *Five Children* and *It* by E. Nesbit. Work included in New Directions anthologies. Contributor to *Contemporary Poetry;* also contributor of articles to *School Library Journal, Harper's Bazaar, Horn Book,* and other periodicals. Member of editorial board, *Cricket.*

SIDELIGHTS: Lloyd Alexander's childhood fascination with Welsh and Arthurian legend is clearly reflected in many of his novels. Blending these and other early literary influences with his own brand of humor and adventure, Alexander has successfully created several of his own mythological worlds for young readers, leading *Dictionary of Literary Biography* contributor Laura Ingram to call him "a master in the field of modern children's literature."

Alexander's earliest literary ambition was to be a poet. He announced this on the eve of his high school graduation at the age of fifteen. His family was far from wealthy, and they were unimpressed with the idea. "Poetry, my father warned, was no practical career," Alexander told *CA.* "I would do well to forget it. My mother came to my rescue. At her urging, my father agreed I might have a try, on condition that I also find some sort of useful work."

Alexander worked as a messenger boy in a bank until he had saved enough money to enroll in West Chester State Teachers College. After only one term there, he decided that college was not the way for him to become a writer. A life of action seemed a more promising route; so, in 1942, Alexander enlisted in the army. To his disappointment, he was initially sent to Texas where he served as a cymbal player and chapel organist. Eventually, however, he was sent to Paris as part of a counterintelligence unit. He met and married his wife, Janine, during his stay in the French capital; he also earned a degree from the Sorbonne before the couple returned to settle near Alexander's hometown of Philadelphia, Pennsylvania.

Alexander's determination to be a published author remained strong, but the three novels he wrote in the next seven years only brought him rejection slips. He described this period to *CA:* "I had been writing grimly . . . , in a stubborn kind of hopeless hopefulness, ready to admit I was no writer at all." Eventually the cheerlessness of his attitude began to seem ridiculous to him. That change in attitude brought a change in his fortunes as well: "Looking back on those days, what seemed a catastrophe now struck me as deeply funny, I was able to laugh at it; and at myself. And enjoy it. I wrote a novel about it, as my fourth and last attempt. The novel was published." And *Let the Credit Go* appeared in 1955. Alexander followed this light, anecdotal account of his life with three more books in the same vein: *My Five Tigers, Janine Is French,* and *My Love Affair with Music.* His first books for children were *Border Hawk: August Bondi* and *Aaron Lopez and Flagship Hope,* biographies of two important though little-known Jewish-American patriots. The themes of faith and personal freedom Alexander emphasized in these biographies would also be important elements in the children's fantasies that soon would bring him national attention.

Alexander's first experiment with fantasy was *Time Cat,* a juvenile novel about a boy's adventures with his cat. "I realize now that *Time Cat* is an example of a fantasy perhaps more realistic than otherwise," reflects Alexander in an essay for *Horn Book.* "Basically, only one fantastic premise moved the story: that Gareth, a black cat, could take the young boy Jason into nine historical periods." Reviewers praised *Time Cat* as an entertaining introduction to history as well as an enjoyable tale. "Filled with

excitement and humor the book also leaves the receptive reader with some interesting reflections on human conduct," notes *New York Times Book Review* writer Ellen Lewis Buell.

Time Cat was originally to have included a Welsh episode. While researching that chapter, however, the author rediscovered his strong childhood feelings for the old Welsh myths and decided to devote a whole book to their retelling. Despite his enthusiasm for the project, he found that it was slow to take shape. "Sifting the material, hoping to find whatever I was groping for, I accumulated box after box of file cards covered with notes, names, relationships, and I learned them cold," he remembers in *Horn Book.* "With great pains I began constructing a kind of family tree or genealogical chart of mythical heroes. . . . Nothing suited my purposes. At that point, the Muse in Charge of Fantasy, seductive in extremely filmy garments, sidled into my work room. 'Not making much headway, are you? How would it be,' she murmured huskily, 'if you invented your own mythology? Isn't that what you really want to do?' "

Alexander found that his research served him well even when he abandoned his original goal of faithfully retelling the Welsh stories. "It had given me roots, suggestions, possibilities," he writes in *Horn Book.* Once the author began the creation of his original fantasy, set in a land called Prydain, it grew to include five books: *The Book of Three, The Black Cauldron, The Castle of Llyr, Taran Wanderer,* and *The High King.* Despite the importance of the Welsh material to Alexander's work, "Prydain grew into something much more than a thinly disguised ancient Wales," asserts Ingram. "Undeniably, it was similar to that land, but reshaped by the addition of contemporary realism, modern values, and a generous dose of humor, as well as the special depth and insight provided by characters who not only act, but think, feel, and struggle with the same kinds of problems that confuse and trouble people in the twentieth century."

As *The Book of Three* opens, Alexander's young protagonist Taran is shown as an Assistant Pig-Keeper who longs for glory and heroism. He gets more excitement than he ever wished for when his search for a runaway pig leads him into a magical battle between the forces of good and evil. Taran learns much about the true nature of heroism during the course of his adventures. Humor is provided by his companions, including Fflewddur Fflam, the minstrel, and the sarcastic princess Eilonwy. Alexander's tone becomes increasingly serious in the subsequent Prydain novels. Taran and Eilonwy endure many trials, and in the process, they grow and mature until they are ready to lead Prydain into a new age in *The High King.* The authors of *Fantasy Literature: A Core Collection and Reference Guide* believe that on the merits of his Prydain novels, "Lloyd Alexander ranks as one of the best writers of high fantasy to emerge since Tolkien. . . . [He creates] a successful blend of tragedy and comedy with a resultant wisdom."

Many other reviewers also praise Alexander's deft, imaginative blend of action, humor, and philosophy. In her book *The Green and Burning Tree: On the Writing and Enjoyment of Children's Books,* Eleanor Cameron remarks, "Each episode of Taran's quest is absorbingly told and freshly seen (not an easy task considering that the tale of quest has such a long and distinguished tradition), and the truth of each episode brought out in such a way as to build strongly toward the moment of Taran's final illumination." *Washington Post Book World* contributor Houston L. Maples summarizes, "The author's total creation is a remarkable achievement, a rich and varied tapestry of brooding evil, heroic action and great natural beauty, vividly conceived, romantic in mood yet curiously contemporary in its immediacy and fast action."

Alexander followed his "Prydain chronicles" with several simple, lively tales for younger children. Some of these supplemented or retold stories of Prydain, including *Coll and His White Pig, The Truthful Harp,* and *The Foundling and Other Tales of Prydain.* Ingram finds that "Alexander's understated satire and valuable, if sometimes obvious morals are conveyed easily and effectively in . . . simple and engaging fashion." Jean Fritz recommends these stories for all readers in the *New York Times Book Review,* saying, "Read these tales before or after the chronicles, or independently no matter. The important thing is to go to Prydain."

In 1981 Alexander published what *Horn Book* reviewer Ethel L. Heins terms his "most inventive book in many years," *Westmark.* Like the Prydain books, *Westmark* combines a fast-paced plot, humor, and philosophical questions. Some reviewers suggest that in *Westmark,* the author even surpasses the narrative skill he displayed in his Prydain cycle. Fritz writes in another *New York Times Book Review* article: "Lloyd Alexander is obviously a bard who has traveled the roads of many kingdoms, perfecting the art of storytelling and becoming ever more wise in the ways of humankind. Like a juggler, he keeps four stories going at once in [*Westmark*]: tossing them lightly apart, calling them together, crisscrossing their paths until at last he has described a complete circle."

Alexander's kingdom of *Westmark* is described by Ingram as "an imaginary place which seems to be a cross between colonial America and feudal Europe." Other than that setting, there is no fantasy in *Westmark* or its two companion volumes *The Kestrel* and *The Beggar Queen.* Instead, Alexander explores in these books the political evolution of *Westmark.* The three books have been as highly praised for their thoughtful content as for their lively storylines. Ingram writes that *Westmark*'s "adroitly controlled complex plot . . . often delves into the wide gray areas between good and evil." And *School Library Journal* contributor Hazel Rochman asserts, "The fast-paced plot, subtleties of character, ironic wit, quiet understatement and pervasive animal imagery—all work with superb concentration to undercut the heroics of war, its slogans, uniforms, and myths of comradeship and glory."

Ingram quotes Alexander as saying, "Writing realism or fantasy, my concerns are the same: how we learn to become genuine human beings." In writing fantasy, states Alexander in a *Horn Book* essay, one "presents the world as it should be. . . . Sometimes heartbreaking, but never hopeless, the fantasy world as it 'should be' is one in which good is ultimately stronger than evil, where courage, justice, love, and mercy actually function. Thus, it may often appear quite different from our own. In the long run, perhaps not. Fantasy does not promise Utopia. But if we listen carefully, it may tell us what we someday may be capable of achieving."

MEDIA ADAPTATIONS: The Cat Who Wished to Be a Man and *The Wizard in the Tree* have been produced on stage in Japan. *The Marvelous Misadventures of Sebastian* was produced as a television serial in Japan. "The Black Cauldron," an animated film produced by Walt Disney Productions in 1985, is based on parts of Alexander's Prydain novels.

AVOCATIONAL INTERESTS: Music (particularly violin, piano, and guitar), printmaking.

BIOGRAPHICAL/CRITICAL SOURCES:

BOOKS

Attebery, Brian, *The Fantasy Tradition in American Literature: From Irving to LeGuin,* Indiana University Press, 1980.
Cameron, Eleanor, *The Green and Burning Tree: On the Writing and Enjoyment of Children's Books,* Little, Brown, 1962.
Children's Literature Review, Gale, Volume 1, 1976, Volume 5, 1983.
Contemporary Literary Criticism, Volume 35, Gale, 1985.
Crouch, Marcus, *The Nesbit Tradition: The Children's Novel in England, 1945-1970,* Rowman, 1972.
Dictionary of Literary Biography, Volume 52: *American Writers for Children since 1960: Fiction,* Gale, 1986.
Field, Elinor Whitney, editor, *Horn Book Reflections on Children's Books and Reading,* Horn Book, 1969.
Fisher, Margery, *Who's Who in Children's Books: A Treasury of the Familiar Characters of Childhood,* Holt, 1975.
Hopkins, Lee Bennett, *More Books by More People,* Citation, 1974.
Livingston, Myra Cohn, *A Tribute to Lloyd Alexander,* Drexel Institute, 1976.
Sebesta, Sam Leaton and William J. Iverson, *Literature for Thursday's Child,* Science Research Associates, 1975.
Sutherland, Zena and others, *Children and Books,* 6th edition, Scott, Foresman, 1981.
Townsend, John Rowe, *Written for Children: An Outline of English Language Children's Literature,* revised edition, Lippincott, 1974.
Tymn, Marshall B. and others, *Fantasy Literature: A Core Collection and Reference Guide,* Bowker, 1979.
Wintle, Justin and Emma Fisher, editors, *The Pied Pipers: Interviews with the Influential Creators of Children's Literature,* Paddington Press, 1974.

PERIODICALS

Chicago Tribune Book World, November 26, 1967.
Christian Science Monitor, May 2, 1968, November 7, 1973.
Cricket, January, 1974, December, 1976, September, 1983.
Elementary English, December, 1971.
Horn Book, October, 1964, April, 1965, June, 1965, December, 1965, June, 1966, June, 1967, April, 1968, December, 1970, August, 1971, October, 1971, December, 1972, October, 1973, August, 1975, February, 1978, August, 1981, August, 1982, August, 1983, August, 1984, October, 1984.
Junior Bookshelf, October, 1966, June, 1967.
Language Arts, October, 1981, April, 1984.
Los Angeles Times, July 24, 1985, July 27, 1985.
National Observer, September 23, 1968.
New Statesman, November 8, 1963.
New Yorker, December 3, 1973.
New York Review of Books, December 3, 1964.
New York Times Book Review, March 23, 1958, April 14, 1963, December 3, 1964, June 19, 1966, April 9, 1967, March 24, 1968, November 15, 1970, July 25, 1971, November 5, 1972, September 30, 1973, November 4, 1973, May 4, 1975, November 13, 1977, December 10, 1978, May 10, 1981, April 25, 1982, June 7, 1987.
Philadelphia Sunday Bulletin, March 22, 1959.
Psychology Today, May, 1974.
Saturday Review, March 18, 1967, April 20, 1968, June 19, 1971.
School Library Journal, December, 1967, February, 1968, October, 1970, December, 1972, May, 1975, November, 1977, May, 1981, April, 1982.

Times Literary Supplement, November 24, 1966, May 25, 1967, October 3, 1968, April 6, 1973.
Top of the News, November, 1968.
Washington Post Book World, August 21, 1966, May 5, 1968, November 8, 1970, November 12, 1978, May 10, 1981, January 9, 1983.
Wilson Library Bulletin, October, 1970, June, 1974.
Writer, May, 1971.
Writer's Digest, April, 1973.

*   *   *

ALGREN, Nelson   1909-1981

PERSONAL: Given name Nelson Ahlgren Abraham; name legally changed to Nelson Algren; born March 28, 1909, in Detroit, Mich.; died of a heart attack, May 9, 1981, in Sag Harbor, N.Y.; married Amanda Kontowicz, 1936 (divorced, 1939); married Betty Ann Jones, 1965 (divorced, 1967). *Education:* University of Illinois, B.A., 1931.

CAREER: Salesman (sold coffee door to door for a time) and migratory worker in the South and Southwest during the Depression; worked at a gas station in Rio Hondo, Tex., 1933, which eventually led to the writing of his first published story; worked briefly for a W.P.A. writers' project; worked on venereal-disease control for the Chicago Board of Health; edited, with Jack Conroy, an experimental magazine called *The New Anvil,* 1939-41; author and journalist, 1941-81, including coverage of the Vietnam war, 1969. *Military service:* U.S. Army, 1942-45; medical corpsman.

MEMBER: American Academy and Institute of Arts and Letters.

AWARDS, HONORS: National Institute of Arts and Letters fellowship, 1947, and Newberry Library fellowship, both for the writing of *The Man With the Golden Arm;* National Book Award, 1950, for *The Man With the Golden Arm;* National Institute of Arts and Letters medal of merit, 1974; "Nelson Algren fiction contest" established in author's memory by *Chicago Magazine,* 1982, continued by *Chicago Tribune,* 1986—; "PEN/Nelson Algren Fiction Award" established in author's memory by PEN American Center, 1983—.

WRITINGS:

Somebody in Boots (novel), Vanguard, 1935, reprinted with new preface, Berkley Publishing, 1965.
Never Come Morning (novel), Harper, 1942, reprinted, Berkley Publishing, 1968.
The Neon Wilderness (short stories), Doubleday, 1947, reprinted with afterword by Studs Terkel and a 1955 *Paris Review* interview, Writing and Readers, 1986.
The Man With the Golden Arm (novel), Doubleday, 1949, reprinted, Robert Bentley, 1978.
Chicago: City on the Make (prose poem), Doubleday, 1951, University of Chicago Press, 1987.
A Walk on the Wild Side (novel; also see below), Farrar, Strauss, 1956, reprinted, Greenwood Press, 1978.
(With Jay Landesman, Fran Landesman and Tommy Wolf) "A Walk on the Wild Side" (three-act musical play), first produced at Crystal Palace Theatre, St. Louis, 1960.
Who Lost an American? (nonfiction), Macmillan, 1963.
(Author of foreword and contributor) *Nelson Algren's Own Book of Lonesome Monsters* (short story anthology), Lancer Books, 1962, Bernard Geis, 1963.
Notes from a Sea Diary: Hemingway All the Way (nonfiction), Putnam, 1965.

(Author of introduction) Jan I. Fortune, editor, *The True Story of Bonnie and Clyde: As Told by Bonnie's Mother and Clyde's Sister,* Signet, 1968.
The Last Carousel (collection of short pieces), Putnam, 1973.
Calhoun: Roman eines Verbrechens, edited and translated by Carl Weissner, Zweitausendeins, 1981, original English language edition published as *The Devil's Stocking,* Arbor House, 1983.

CONTRIBUTOR TO ANTHOLOGIES

Galena Guide, Works Progress Administration, 1937.
Herschell Brickell, editor, *O. Henry Memorial Award Prize Stories of 1941,* Doubleday, 1941.
Martha Foley, editor, *Best American Short Stories 1942,* Houghton, 1942.
Modern Reading, Wells, Gardner, Darton, 1943.
Cross Section, Simon & Schuster, 1947.
John Lehmann, editor, *The Penguin New Writing,* Penguin Books, 1948.
New World Writing, New American Library, 1956.
Taboo, New Classics House, 1964.
Focus/Media, Chandler, 1972.

OTHER

Contributor of short stories, essays, articles and reviews to numerous periodicals, including *Story, Nation, Life, Saturday Evening Post, American Mercury, Atlantic, Chicago Tribune, Partisan Review, Playboy,* and *Rolling Stone.* A collection of Nelson Algren's papers are at the Ohio State University Library, Columbus, Ohio.

SIDELIGHTS: The late Nelson Algren's casts of hopeless drifters, prostitutes, petty thieves, con men, addicts and derelicts earned him the designation "poet of the Chicago slums," but he preferred to call himself "the tin whistle of American letters." Algren's novels, including *A Walk on the Wild Side, Never Come Morning,* and the National Book Award-winning *The Man with the Golden Arm,* explore life situations in the seamy sections of town with emphasis on humanity battered by abject poverty and social indifference. As Chester E. Eisinger notes in *Fiction of the Forties,* Algren was "the poet of the jail and the whorehouse; he has made a close study of the cockroach, the drunkard, and the pimp, the garbage in the street and the spittle on the chin. He has a truly cloacal vision of the American experience." Though Algren worked as a journalist, essayist and reviewer most of his life, Eisinger suggests the author earned a reputation for writing fiction that attacked the "bluebird vision of America." According to Eisinger, the criticism in Algren's novels "is not in any sense ideological. It is a compound of resentment and perversity, of feelings; it is a conviction that the respectable classes ought to have their noses rubbed in the poverty and degradation of American life as an antidote to their self-satisfaction; it is a conviction that the poor are just as good as the rich, and more fun to boot; it is sheer sentimental sympathy for the under-dog."

Critics such as Ralph J. Gleason and Sheldon Norman Grebstein feel that Algren took a singular responsibility for exploding the myths of opportunity and democracy generated by and for the American middle class. In *Rolling Stone,* Gleason writes: "Up until Algren, no American writer had really combined a poetic gift for words and a vision of truth about the textbook democracy." Grebstein elaborates in *The Forties: Fiction, Poetry, Drama,* noting that Algren's work "depicts but three milieux: life on the road or in the jails of the South-west in the 1930's; life in the slums, bars, and whorehouses of New Orleans of the '30's; life in the poorer working-class neighborhoods . . . in the Chicago of the 1930's and '40's. . . . Nowhere in Algren are there people vibrantly healthy, free of guilt, clean, fulfilled, content." Grebstein concludes that Algren's central theme is "the refutation of what has been among the hallowed official truths of American society, a truth which Algren considers the blackest lie: the belief that the individual retains the power of choice, of deciding between two alternatives, in plotting his destiny."

Kenneth G. McCollum reflects on Algren's vision of hopelessness in the *Dictionary of Literary Biography,* claiming that Algren's stories and novels are "often loose and rambling, partly because the lives of the characters are uncertain and disconnected. . . . Algren deals with man in a world of chance in a universe that is indifferent or even hostile to his microcosmic sense of himself." Eisinger likewise cites Algren's "unheroic hero who comes to a blank end in a hostile world," trapped by his own fallible nature and by social circumstances. McCollum contends that this existential viewpoint entered Algren's fiction without the author's conscious philosophical design. "Algren's works abound with manifestations of such existential terms as *dread, anxiety, despair, nothingness, alienation,* and the *absurd,*" concludes McCollum. Often an Algren protagonist finds momentary redemption or meaning through love, as George Bluestone notes in the *Western Review:* "[In] Algren's central vision, self-destruction becomes operative only after the destruction of some loved object. The moment a central character becomes responsible for such ruin, he is irrevocably doomed. That 'irrational, destructive force,' then, is the impulse to destroy love which is tantamount to death." Eisinger sees Algren as "insisting that nothing can kill the aspiration for a more meaningful life than it is possible for his people to attain. And he is insisting most of all upon the survival of love, not as the romantic passion that men die for but as the only source of warmth in the lives of the hopeless."

Algren wrote for more than forty years, but a conviction that novels require an "all out" singleminded dedication limited his output of longer fiction. In *Conversations with Nelson Algren,* the author told H. E. F. Donohue about his approach to the craft: "If you do the big book there's no way—at least I have no way—of doing a big book and doing anything else. . . . In fact you don't do much of anything but get a scene and you live within the scene and keep pushing that particular scene. . . . You've got to cut everything else out. You're never free. And you've got to do that for a couple of years before you can make a pattern or cut a scene that nobody else has touched." Algren added that he required firsthand experience of his fictional milieux in order to create a novel: "The only way I can write is to try to make something that hasn't been done before, and in order to do that you can't just take notes. You have to *be* there. You write about your own reactions to the scene. You identify yourself with the scene. And you have to get all the details that nobody knows about. You have to be specific." In their study entitled *Nelson Algren,* Martha Heasley Cox and Wayne Chatterton cite Algren for "style and language that are drawn from the world he depicts." They also record Algren's often-quoted assertion about his realistic yet poetic prose: "My most successful poetry, the lines people threw back at me years after they were written, were lines I never wrote. They were lines I heard, and repeated, usually by someone who never read and couldn't write."

Algren indeed spent a great deal of time in the company of the homeless and the illiterate. He was born in Detroit but was raised in a working class section of Chicago, the only son of a machinist. Despite an undistinguished high school career, he enrolled in college at the University of Illinois and majored in journalism. When he graduated in 1931, work was unobtainable; he searched

for a job for a year and then began to hitchhike south. The following two years were extremely difficult ones for Algren. He spent some months in New Orleans, selling coffee and bogus beauty parlor discount certificates door-to-door. For a time he accepted responsibility for an all-but-deserted gas station in Rio Hondo, Texas, until an unscrupulous partner began to abscond with the gasoline. Algren then hopped a freight train to El Paso, where he was arrested for vagrancy, thrown in jail and fined five dollars. When he was released he moved to Alpine, Texas and discovered that he could use the typewriters at the understaffed Alpine Teachers College without detection. He began to write short stories and letters that he mailed back to Chicago, and it was from among these Depression-era experiences that his early fiction was culled.

Eventually Algren decided to return to Chicago. He chose a typewriter from the Alpine Teachers College and attempted to mail it north. Then he jumped into a boxcar himself, but he only got as far as San Antonio before he was arrested for the theft of the typewriter. He spent the next four months in jail, awaiting trial with a circuit-riding judge. This incident involving rural law enforcement is reflected throughout Algren's fiction, most notably in *The Neon Wilderness, Somebody in Boots,* and *A Walk on the Wild Side.* After his trial, Algren left Texas immediately, riding freight trains and hitchhiking back to Chicago.

In *Conversations with Nelson Algren,* the author reminisced about why he decided to write fiction: "I wanted to be a writer in the literary sense That is, I wanted to find a place in the literary world. . . . But the experience on the road gave me something to write about. It was just an accidental, just a fortuitous thing. I didn't go on the road in order to have something to write about. You do see what it's like, what a man in shock who is dying looks like. . . . Or you're waiting for a boxcar and it seems to be going a little too fast and some kid makes a try for it and you see him miss and then you get the smell of blood and you go over and you see it sliced off his arm. And all the whores in New Orleans. And all the tens of thousands of Americans literally milling around at that time trying to survive. . . . All these scenes, one after another, piled up into something that made me not just want to write but to really say it, to find out that this thing was all upside down."

Somebody in Boots, Algren's first novel, was published in 1935. The book's emphasis, writes Maxwell Geismar in *American Moderns: From Rebellion to Conformity,* lies in its "scenes of brutality which mark the life of the 'lumpen proletariat,' the social scum, the passively rotting mass of people who lie at the bottom of the social scale." The hero of *Somebody in Boots,* Cass McKay, is driven from his home in a Texas border town by violence and poverty; the narrative follows the youth's misadventures as a homeless, freight-hopping hobo. Bluestone calls the work "the most uneven and least satisfying, but in some ways the most revealing of [Algren's] books." Eisinger a]so finds the novel revealing in its "Marxist-angled social criticism," but he adds: "[Algren] displays an unreasoning hatred for the respectable, property-owning classes in America, but unfortunately nothing of what he says has relevance in his story. In this inability to integrate such criticism and the themes of his novel one may find a reason for Algren's surrender of the techniques of frontal attack on social issues." Bluestone likewise cites "parenthetical broadsides" in the novel that are "purely didactic intrusions," but he concludes that *Somebody in Boots* "reveals certain inclinations which will become more important later on: the choice of fallen, barely articulate characters; a narrative sensibility aware of verbal complexity; a prose appropriation of poetic devices; a piecing together of previously published pieces; . . . [and] a central concern with love and survival in the face of loneliness and death."

Much of the critical commentary on *Somebody in Boots* is retrospective, for the book was not widely reviewed or commercially successful when first released. This lack of public enthusiasm for his work led Algren to concentrate on short stories and journalism for nearly five years. He worked as a staff writer for the Works Progress Administration and helped to edit a small leftist magazine, the *New Anvil,* while publishing occasional poems in other magazines. In 1940 he returned to work on longer fiction, and the resulting novel, *Never Come Morning,* was published in 1942 to immediate critical acclaim. Set in a Polish community of the Chicago slums, the story revolves around Bruno Bicek, an aspiring boxer who turns to criminal activity and murder after allowing his street gang friends to rape his girlfriend. According to McCollum, the book's theme of physical conquest devoid of love is "symbolic of the differences between Algren's perception and the middle-class idea of what was going on in America. To Algren, niceness, purity, and fairness were part of a myth that disguised the strong taking from the weak."

Never Come Morning established Algren as a "Chicago novelist" as well as a practitioner of the style known as native American realism. *New Republic* contributor Malcolm Cowley writes: "It is the poetry of familiar things that is missing in the other Chicago novels and that shows the direction of Algren's talent. In spite of the violent story he tells—and tells convincingly—he is not by instinct a novelist. He is a poet of the Chicago slums, and he might well be Sandburg's successor." According to Philip Rahv in *Nation, Never Come Morning* "is pervaded by a feeling of loss rather than of bitterness or horror. And Algren's realism is so paced as to avoid the tedium of the naturalistic stereotype, of the literal copying of surfaces. He knows how to select, how to employ factual details without letting himself be swamped by them, and, finally, how to put the slang his characters speak to creative uses so that it ceases to be an element of mere documentation and turns into an element of style." Bluestone concludes that, in *Never Come Morning,* "Algren's characteristic symbolism and indirection endow the action with pity and concealed prophecy. . . . [One finds] here, woven into the matrix of the prose, those haunting images of deserted cities, symbolizing the characters' life-in-death, which becomes increasingly typical of Algren. . . . More important than any plot or character development is the general doom implicit from the start. Only, the powerful voice behind the events insists on our attention."

Algren served in the U.S. Army as a medical corpsman from 1942 until 1945. After his discharge he began his most productive decade as a fiction writer—between 1947 and 1956 he published a short story collection, *The Neon Wilderness,* a lengthy prose poem, *Chicago: City on the Make,* and two highly acclaimed novels, *The Man with the Golden Arm* and *A Walk on the Wild Side.* It was also during this period that Algren began to undertake the extensive travels that would form a basis for much of his nonfiction. Sometimes accompanied by the French novelist Simone de Beauvoir, he visited Europe, Central America, and many regions of the United States. Through de Beauvoir Algren met members of prominent Parisian literary circles, including Jean-Paul Sartre. Algren continued to reside primarily in Chicago, however, usually renting a small furnished flat in which he could write through the night.

The Man with the Golden Arm, published in 1949, propelled Algren to the literary forefront. He won the first National Book Award for the work, and it was also a bestseller. Once again centered in the Chicago slums, *The Man with the Golden Arm* details the downfall of Frankie Machine, a card dealer with a morphine addiction who is inevitably pursued by the law. The reaction of the book's reviewers is almost universally positive. Grebstein writes: "Not only is Algren's novel the first serious treatment in our literature of the drug addict, it is also a profoundly felt and profoundly moving book. . . . This novel marks the culmination of Algren's identification with characters the 'normal' man might think beneath or beyond his sympathies, yet such is Algren's craft that he extends the norm." *New York Times* contributor A. C. Spectorsky claims that *The Man with the Golden Arm* "is a powerful book, illuminated by flashes of Algren's grisly, antic, almost horrifying humor, by passages of finely poetic writing, and by his love and understanding, which are, at times, almost morbidly compassionate." A critic for *Time* concludes: "Readers with queasy stomachs may shrink from an environment in which the unbelievably sordid has become a way of life. They will also come away with some of Algren's own tender concern for his wretched, confused and hopelessly degenerate cast of characters. In that, Writer Algren scores a true novelist's triumph."

Critics of *The Man with the Golden Arm* cite a strong portrayal of Algren's recurring theme of love, guilt and death. "The particular conflict here," Grebstein writes, "is that between self-sacrifice and self-preservation, a conflict knotted into the relationship between Frankie Machine and his wife Sophie, his friend Sparrow, and his girl Molly. These are the dynamic relationships which fluctuate with the condition of the participants. Such is Algren's version of the whole truth that his people tend to prey on one another, whether in friendship or love." McCollum likewise contends that in *The Man with the Golden Arm* "the personal interactions of the characters have more impact on the progression of the plot than does the effect of the total environment." McCollum also notes an absence of didacticism in the work despite its elucidation of the pernicious nature of slum life. "The personal tragedy of Frankie Machine," McCollum concludes, "is not death, but loneliness and isolation in an environment where everybody hustles and everybody is on the take." Bluestone offers a similar assessment: "Algren's final image, despite the humor, despite the intensity, despite the struggle to survive, is one of hopelessness and desolation. In this world, death is inescapable. What possible approaches are open to the narrator who wishes to communicate such a vision? He can laugh; or he can lament. Algren does both supremely well. But the laughter is edged with bitterness; before the reality of death, it sadly falls away."

Algren was known to recycle material, especially memorable lines and scenes. His 1956 novel, *A Walk on the Wild Side,* bears a strong thematic resemblance to *Somebody in Boots.* The protagonist of *A Walk on the Wild Side* is once again a young illiterate Texan who drifts to Depression-era New Orleans and becomes involved in a sordid sex show in a house of prostitution. In his appraisal of Algren's work, Bluestone writes: "At first glance, *A Walk on the Wild Side* seems to be a mere rewriting of *Somebody in Boots.* . . . From the point of view of Algren's entire output, however, it represents a fascinating reappraisal of his central theme. Ultimately the differences between the two books are more striking than the resemblances. The narrative alternates between a mood of savage tenderness and one of broad burlesque, but this time the comic mood is strongest. . . . Out of the poetic exploration of this marginal, half-lit world there emerges the image of a universe in which human action must inevitably seem absurd. And yet, within that world, there co-exists a real belief that human action can have validity and meaning."

This belief, Bluestone concludes, contrasts with the nihilistic tones and outcomes of Algren's earlier works.

Critics are divided on the quality of *A Walk on the Wild Side*. *New York Times* contributor Alfred Kazin states: "It is impossible to feel that [Algren] really cares about these people, that he is interested in them, that these are human beings he has observed. What I object to most in this book is the plainly contrived quality of this pretended feeling about characters whom Mr. Algren writes about not because they are 'lost,' but because they are freaks." In his *New Yorker* review, Norman Podhoretz finds the book "more in the spirit of the boozy sentimentality of the broken-down Shakespearean actor declaiming to the boys on the barroom floor than an expression of Rabelaisian exuberance." Cox and Chatterton express a different opinion in their study of Algren's work: "One of Algren's most remarkable achievements in *A Walk on the Wild Side* is his convincing, compassionate treatment of a group of characters who could, in less skillful hands, be little more than a gallery of freaks and sheer grotesques. . . . The impressive verbal mortar which binds the other stylistic properties is still the concreteness and specificity of detail; the accurate terminology of road, gutter, bar, and brothel; the keen and comprehensive ear for dialect; the eye for significant idiosyncrasies of dress and behavior; the quick grasp of obsessive quirks of thought—the ring of authority." In the *New York Herald Tribune Book Review,* Milton Rugoff concludes that the novel "is an American tradition of emotional gigantism: its comedy is farce, its joys are orgies, the feats of its characters Bunyanesque, their sexuality is prodigious, their sorrow a wild keening almost too high for ordinary ears. . . . In a period that hasn't lacked for novels of degeneracy and cruelty, . . . 'A Walk on the Wild Side' is almost without peer."

Algren's shorter works—fiction, nonfiction and poetry—reflect many of the same concerns that motivated him to write novels. Cox and Chatterton call the author's short stories "a considerable achievement," adding: "The stories in *The Neon Wilderness* have elicited unexpected discipline from an author so often charged with looseness and with over-rhapsodizing in his novels. . . . Nowhere outside the short stories has Algren been so free to exercise his ability to construct a tale from the single, self-revelatory catch-phrase. . . . Nowhere else has he controlled so stringently his tendency to blend the sordid and poetic; as a result the short stories have largely escaped the adverse reaction which such a controversial mixture has brought against his novels." Geismar likewise writes: "Algren's powerful effects are usually in his big scenes rather than in the portrayal or development of character. He is almost at his best in . . . short stories where he can suggest the whole contour of a human life in a few terse pages."

The "blend of sordid and poetic" that Cox and Chatterton note finds further elucidation in *Chicago: City on the Make,* Algren's best-known prose poem. Commissioned by *Holiday* magazine as the lead article for a Chicago theme issue, the completed poem "was so unflattering that it was relegated to rear pages," according to Jack Conroy in the *Dictionary of Literary Biography Yearbook.* The work was subsequently published in book form in 1951. In a *Saturday Review* assessment, Emmett Dedmon states: "The qualities of Nelson Algren's prose essay on Chicago are those of fine poetry—vivid images, richness of language, economy of form, and most importantly, poetic vision. It is necessary to go back to the 'Chicago Poems' of Carl Sandburg . . . to find a book about the city comparable to Algren's." Bluestone feels that Algren's impressions of Chicago are "typical of a new and sympathetic look at urban life which goes beyond recoil and horror. Much of what we have seen in the stories and novels appears

here, too: a pervasive sense of loss and loneliness, an image of urban desolation, an eye for graphic detail, incantory prose. . . . This author knows that in urban society there is vertical as well as horizontal mobility, that Skid Row is merely the ugliest manifestation of tendencies embedded in all strata of city life."

Most of Algren's output in the 1960s and 1970s was nonfiction, some of it distilled from magazine and newspaper pieces. He published two travelogues, *Who Lost an American?* and *Notes from a Sea Diary: Hemingway All the Way,* both of which combine travel experiences with commentary on other authors and their works. Algren's most notable book from this period is *The Last Carousel,* a chrestomathy of thirty-seven pieces from 1947 to 1972, including short fiction, unpublished bits of novels, and nonfiction essays on a variety of subjects. In the *New York Times Book Review,* James R. Frakes calls *The Last Carousel* a "catch-all volume" with moments at which Algren is "at the top of his form, with his hallmark stamped on every link." Tom Carson gives a concurrent opinion in the *Voice Literary Supplement:* "Ironically, losing his sense of obligation to an audience he had decided wasn't there freed Algren; the loosened responsibilities of who-gives-a-damn product allowed him to express himself more idiosyncratically and directly than ever. And his wonderful ear, that spinning-against-the-way-it-drives colloid of highly charged poetic language and colloquial closed-mouthedness, survives in even his most occasional pieces."

In 1974 Algren was commissioned to write an article about Rubin "Hurricane" Carter for *Esquire* magazine. Carter, a former boxer who had been convicted on three counts of murder, received a second trial that year when two witnesses denied their previous testimony. Leaving Chicago behind, Algren moved to Paterson, New Jersey, where he immersed himself in the case. When Carter lost in the second trial, *Esquire* dropped the story. Algren, however, did not. As James Hardin notes in the *Dictionary of Literary Biography Yearbook,* Algren "thought of himself as a fighter, a reporter who championed the rights of the outsiders." Hardin claims additionally that "the social milieu of the case appealed to Algren, not merely the opportunity to expose an injustice." Algren eventually fictionalized the events for a novel entitled *The Devil's Stocking.* Hardin writes: "All the figures of the novel have or had their counterparts in real life, among them Algren himself. It is a world of prostitutes, gangsters, jaded barkeeps—the fringes of society—but it also describes the brief rise in the fortunes of the [boxer Ruby Calhoun] and gives a glimpse of the life that might have been, of the loser who was on the way to the big time."

The Devil's Stocking appeared in German translation before it was released in the United States. By the time it saw American publication in 1983, Algren had been dead for two years. Critical reaction to the work is mixed; some reviewers feel Algren would have served the material more faithfully had he maintained nonfictional accuracy. "Since most of the work is patently based on fact," Hardin contends, "it could be argued that a 'documentary'—Algren's original plan—would have been more effective, more disquieting." Hardin admits, however, that the novel "is an excellent example of unpretentious reportage. The conversations have the ring of authenticity. It is a hard-nosed piece of writing." John W. Aldridge expresses similar sentiments in the *New York Times Book Review:* "Algren . . . seems not to have aged but only matured and to be, as never before, in firm possession of his subject. His language throughout the novel is precise, controlled, almost entirely free of the lush lyrical excesses of the past, but nonetheless genuinely warm and alive. The story is recognizable as belonging in the classic Algren repertoire, yet is also freshly conceived and carried forward with an easy assurance that indicates Algren had it in him to write five or six more novels in the same vein."

Algren died of a heart attack on May 9, 1981, just weeks before his formal induction into the prestigious American Academy and Institute of Arts and Letters. His eulogists, including Carson, suggest that his work has not received sufficient critical attention and respect. "Algren's story isn't that of a once-fashionable writer gone out of season," Carson states. "He never was all that fashionable. Bad timing, for one thing: a '30s novelist shouldn't do his best work in the '40s and '50s. Then there's the problem of being a Chicago novelist—Algren saw himself extending the midwestern tradition . . . at a time when New York was establishing a near-total literary hegemony and thanking God it'd gotten the rough boys out. And after popular success finally came, Algren's reaction was to deny the worth of writing fiction at all. What that adds up to is a career spent entirely on the fringe; and the center, nettled by his sense of its irrelevance, ended up returning the favor." In a *Chicago Tribune Book World* retrospective, Budd Schulberg writes: "To his honor, Algren never denied himself the pain endured by the victims who were his heroes in book after book. . . . Nor did he deny himself the risk of failure in a fickle, success-ridden America that might reward him with fame and fortune for one book . . . and then turn its back on him because he would not play the game of the Eastern Literary Establishment, . . . the 'club' that decides from its high and haughty platforms which writers are in and which are out. Let the Eastern literati praise him, damn him, or neglect him, the Nelson Algren I knew really didn't give a damn."

If literary critics tend to ignore Algren, many of his fellow writers have accorded him a great deal of recognition. Authors such as Ernest Hemingway, Carl Sandburg, Studs Terkel and Richard Wright have praised Algren for his contribution to the body of twentieth century American letters. Hemingway, for instance, once listed Algren as one of the two most notable authors of his generation. In a foreword to *Nelson Algren: A Checklist,* Terkel suggests: "My hunch is [Algren's] writings will be read long after acclaimed works of the Academe's darlings, yellowed on coffee tables, will be replaced by acclaimed works of other Academe's darlings." Ross Macdonald also offers plaudits in the *New York Times Book Review:* "Algren's Chicago and the people who live in its shadows are still there. Algren is their tragic poet, enabling those who can read him to feel pain. . . . The intensity of his feeling, the accuracy of his thought, make me wonder if any other writer of our time has shown us more exactly the human basis of our democracy."

The author who has given American literature such memorable phrases as "monkey on my back," "Never play cards with a man named Doc," and "I'm the girl that men forget" is memorialized by two annual fiction contests that bear his name. Eisinger, who calls Algren "the twentieth century man of feeling, inexplicably caught in the city slums," contends that the writer gave his characters "yearnings for love or pride in themselves as separate and identifiable individuals—yearnings that reveal a tender concern for them as human beings." In *American Moderns,* Geismar comments: "Nelson Algren . . . represents a solid and enduring part of the American literary heritage. . . . And Algren is a writer who carries with him our hope and concern for something more than entertainment." "Algren's ambitions as a social novelist notwithstanding," Grebstein concludes, "his ambition to write 'influential' books, books that ameliorate unfair conditions, he has perhaps already accomplished something more important for literature: the scenes he has created have become part of our imaginative life, and his people are now among those we know."

MEDIA ADAPTATIONS: The Man with the Golden Arm was produced as a film under the same title by United Artists, 1955. *A Walk on the Wild Side* was produced as a film under the same title by Columbia Pictures, 1962, and as a musical play under the same title at New York's Musical Theater Workshop and later at the Back Alley Theatre in Van Nuys, California, 1988. (Algren did not approve of the productions.)

AVOCATIONAL INTERESTS: Boxing, horse racing, poker and other card games.

BIOGRAPHICAL/CRITICAL SOURCES:

BOOKS

Algren, Nelson, *Who Lost an American?,* Macmillan, 1963.
Algren, Nelson, *Notes from a Sea Diary: Hemingway All the Way,* Putnam, 1965.
Algren, Nelson, *The Last Carousel,* Putnam, 1973.
Beauvoir, Simone de, *America Day by Day,* Duckworth, 1952, Grove, 1953.
Beauvoir, Simone de, *The Force of Circumstance,* translated by Richard Howard, Putnam, 1965.
Contemporary Literary Criticism, Gale, Volume 4, 1975, Volume 10, 1979, Volume 33, 1985.
Cowley, Malcolm, editor, *Writers at Work: The "Paris Review" Interviews,* Viking, 1958.
Cox, Martha H. and Wayne Chatterton, *Nelson Algren,* Twayne, 1975.
Dictionary of Literary Biography, Volume 9: *American Novelists 1910-1945,* Gale, 1981.
Dictionary of Literary Biography Yearbook 1982, Gale, 1983.
Donohue, H. E. F., *Conversations with Nelson Algren,* Hill & Wang, 1964.
Drew, Bettina, *Nelson Algren: A Life on the Wild Side,* Putnam, 1989.
Eisinger, Chester E., *Fiction of the Forties,* University of Chicago Press, 1963.
French, Warren, editor, *The Forties: Fiction, Poetry, Drama,* Everett/Edwards, 1969.
Geismar, Maxwell, *American Moderns: From Rebellion to Conformity,* Hill & Wang, 1958.
McCollum, Kenneth G., *Nelson Algren: A Checklist,* Gale, 1973.

PERIODICALS

Atlantic, June, 1963, October, 1964, August, 1965, October, 1983.
Books, April 26, 1942.
Book Week, November 1, 1964, August 15, 1965.
Chicago Sun Book Week, February 2, 1947.
Chicago Sun-Times, March 26, 1973.
Chicago Tribune, September 11, 1985.
Chicago Tribune Book World, August 21, 1983.
Chicago Tribune Magazine, September 14, 1986.
Commonweal, February 8, 1974.
Critic, October, 1965, January-February, 1973.
Current History, August, 1942.
Harper's, May, 1965.
Life, May 18, 1964.
Los Angeles Times, September 2, 1988.
Los Angeles Times Book Review, October 30, 1983.
Nation, April 18, 1942, October 17, 1953, June 1, 1964, September 21, 1964, October 25, 1965.
New Republic, July 17, 1935, May 4, 1942, May 21, 1956, January 19, 1974.
Newsweek, May 13, 1963, October 26, 1964, August 16, 1965.
New Yorker, June 2, 1956.

New York Herald Tribune Book Review, October 21, 1951, May 20, 1956.
New York Herald Tribune Weekly Book Review, September 11, 1949.
New York Times, April 7, 1935, May 10, 1942, February 2, 1947, September 11, 1949, October 21, 1951, May 20, 1956, August 24, 1965, August 28, 1968, November 1, 1973, October 25, 1989.
New York Times Book Review, October 2, 1949, June 2, 1963, October 25, 1964, August 22, 1965, December 4, 1977, October 9, 1983.
Reporter, June 11, 1959, June 20, 1963.
Rolling Stone, August 6, 1970.
San Francisco Chronicle, October 9, 1949, May 27, 1956.
Saturday Review, May 26, 1956.
Saturday Review of Literature, April 18, 1942, February 8, 1947, October 8, 1949, December 8, 1951.
Time, September 12, 1949, May 28, 1956, May 31, 1963.
Times Literary Supplement, September 29, 1966.
Tribune Books, May 10, 1987.
Voice Literary Supplement, November, 1983.
Western Review, autumn, 1957.
Writer, March, 1943.

OBITUARIES

BOOKS

Dictionary of Literary Biography Yearbook 1981, Gale, 1982.

PERIODICALS

Detroit News, May 17, 1981.
Los Angeles Times Book Review, June 7, 1981.
New York Times, May 10, 1981.
Publishers Weekly, May 22, 1981.
Times (London), May 1, 1981.

*   *   *

ALLEN, Roland
   See AYCKBOURN, Alan

*   *   *

ALLEN, Woody   1935-

PERSONAL: Given name, Allen Stewart Konigsberg; born December 1, 1935, in Brooklyn, N.Y.; son of Martin (a waiter and jewelry engraver) and Nettie (Cherry) Konigsberg; married Harlene Rosen, 1954 (divorced, 1960); married Louise Lasser (an actress), February 2, 1966 (divorced); currently living with Mia Farrow (an actress); children: (with Farrow) Satchel. *Education:* Attended New York University and City College (now City College of the City University of New York), 1953. *Politics:* Democrat.

ADDRESSES: Office—Orion Pictures, 9 West 57th St., New York, N.Y. 10019. *Agent*—Jack Rollins, Rollins, Joffe, Morra & Brezner Productions, 130 West 57th St., New York, N.Y. 10019.

CAREER: Comedian, actor, director, and writer for television, films, and the stage. Began writing jokes for columnists and celebrities while in high school; regular staff writer for National Broadcasting Corp., 1952, writing for such personalities as Herb Shriner, Sid Caesar, Art Carney, Kaye Ballard, Buddy Hackett, Carol Channing, Pat Boone, Jack Paar, and Garry Moore. Performer in nightclubs, on television, and on the stage in 1960s.

AWARDS, HONORS: Sylvania Award, 1957, for script of a "Sid Caesar Show"; Academy Awards for best director and best original screenplay from the Academy of Motion Picture Arts and Sciences, National Society of Film Critics award, and New York Film Critics Circle award, all 1977, for "Annie Hall"; British Academy Award and New York Film Critics award, both 1979, for "Manhattan"; Academy Award nomination for best director, 1984, for "Broadway Danny Rose"; Academy Award for best original screenplay, Golden Globe Award for best motion picture comedy or musical, New York Film Critics award, and Los Angeles Film Critics award, all 1987, for "Hannah and Her Sisters"; Academy Award nominations for best director and best original screenplay, both 1989, for "Crimes and Misdemeanors."

WRITINGS:

Getting Even (humor collection), Random House, 1971.
Without Feathers (humor collection), Random House, 1975.
Non-Being and Somethingness (collections from comic strip "Inside Woody Allen"), Random House, 1978.
Side Effects (humor collection), Random House, 1980.

SCREENPLAYS

(And actor) "What's New, Pussycat?," United Artists, 1965.
(With Frank Buxton, Len Maxwell, Louise Lasser, and Mickey Rose, and actor) "What's Up, Tiger Lily?," American International, 1966.
(With Rose, and actor and director) "Take the Money and Run," Palomar, 1969.
(With Rose, and actor and director) "Bananas" (also see below), United Artists, 1971.
(And actor and director) "Everything You Always Wanted to Know about Sex But Were Afraid to Ask" (based on the book by David Ruben), United Artists, 1972.
(And actor) "Play It Again, Sam" (also see below; based on the play), Paramount, 1972.
(With Marshall Brickman, and actor and director) "Sleeper" (also see below), United Artists, 1973.
(And actor and director) "Love and Death" (also see below), United Artists, 1975.
(With Brickman, and actor and director) "Annie Hall" (also see below), United Artists, 1977.
(And director) "Interiors" (also see below), United Artists, 1978.
Four Screenplays: Sleeper, Love and Death, Bananas, Annie Hall, Random House, 1978.
(With Brickman, and actor and director) "Manhattan" (also see below), United Artists, 1979.
(And actor and director) "Stardust Memories" (also see below), United Artists, 1980.
(And actor and director) "A Midsummer Night's Sex Comedy," Warner Brothers, 1982.
Four Films of Woody Allen (includes "Annie Hall," "Manhattan," "Stardust Memories," and "Interiors"), Random House, 1982.
(And actor and director) "Zelig," Orion, 1983.
(And actor and director) "Broadway Danny Rose," Orion, 1984.
(And director) "The Purple Rose of Cairo," Orion, 1985.
(And actor and director) *Hannah and Her Sisters* (produced by Orion, 1986), Random House, 1986.
(And narrator and director) "Radio Days," Orion, 1987.
(And director) "September," Orion, 1987.
(And director) "Another Woman," Orion, 1988.
(And actor and director) "Oedipus Wrecks" in "New York Stories," Touchstone, 1989.

(And actor and director) "Crimes and Misdemeanors," Orion, 1989.

PLAYS

(With Herbert Farjeon, Hermoine Gingold, and others) "From A to Z," produced in New York at Plymouth Theatre, April 20, 1960.

Don't Drink the Water (produced in New York at Morosco Theatre, November 17, 1966), Samuel French, 1967.

Play It Again, Sam (produced on Broadway at Broadhurst Theatre, February 12, 1969), Random House, 1969.

Death: A Comedy in One Act, Samuel French, 1975.

God: A Comedy in One Act, Samuel French, 1975.

The Floating Light Bulb (produced in New York at Vivian Beaumont Theatre, April 27, 1981), Random House, 1982.

Author of radio production of "God," produced by National Radio Theatre of Chicago, 1978. Featured on recording "Woody Allen, Stand-up Comic: 1964-1968," United Artists Records, 1978.

WORK IN PROGRESS: Another film.

SIDELIGHTS: Woody Allen falls into one of the most rarified categories of artist—the *auteur* filmmaker, one whose vision pervades every aspect of his work. Allen is also one of the world's best-recognized cinematic figures; indeed, he has more "name value" as a writer or director than do many of the stars of his pictures. But for all his acclaim and fame, he maintains a relatively balanced perspective on his own importance. As he told Natalie Gittelson in a *New York Times* piece, "I'm not holed up in my apartment every night poring over Russian literature and certain Danish philosophers. I'm really hardly a recluse. When a half-dozen *paparazzi* follow me down the street, naturally I don't like that very much. But I do go out all the time—to movies, to shop, to walk around in the street, to those parties I think I'll enjoy."

The object of substantial media attention was born Allen Stewart Konigsberg in pre-World War II Brooklyn, New York. In many ways, the growing boy resembled his peers: "I was out in the streets from 8 o'clock in the morning," Allen tells *Newsweek*'s Jack Kroll, "playing baseball and basketball. At lunchtime I'd race into the house, eat a tuna-fish sandwich by myself and read a comic book—Superman, Batman or Mickey Mouse. I'd run back out on the street and play ball. Then I'd run back in for dinner, read another comic book, run back out again for two hours, come in and watch the St. Louis Cardinals beat the Dodgers on television."

Young Allen hated school. In a *Rolling Stone* interview, the writer recalls the "equally bad" experience of attending public school and Hebrew school, in a neighborhood that, though primarily Jewish, was filled with "teachers [who] were backward and anti-Semitic." With that kind of academic background, it's not surprising that Allen shunned higher education as well. He briefly attended New York's City College and entered into an equally brief teenage marriage to childhood sweetheart Harlene Rosen.

By this time Allen was also submitting jokes and one-liners, some of which caught the attention of columnists like Earl Wilson. From there it was a quick foray into television, where Allen was among the youngest—and quietest—staff writers for shows starring Sid Caesar, Art Carney, and Jack Paar, among others. During the early 1960s Allen worked as a comedian in nightclubs, where he began to create the persona that would bring him fame—that of the intellectual bumbler, unlucky in love, adver-

sary of nature and small appliances, a perpetual victim of his own urban angst. His comedy was embraced by a generation of city sophisticates, but the persona didn't exactly reflect its creator. "People always associated me with Greenwich Village and sweaters with holes in them and things like that," Allen remarks to Tom Shales in an *Esquire* piece. "And I've never been that kind of person. Never. I never lived in the Village. I always lived on the Upper East Side of Manhattan."

Film producer Charles Feldman discovered Allen in 1964 and offered him a screenwriting job on a movie called "What's New, Pussycat?" The story of a man who simply cannot stay faithful to the woman he loves, the movie also marked Allen's acting debut as a neurotic psychiatric patient. In a *Dictionary of Literary Biography* profile, Alan S. Horowitz notes that even in this knockabout farce, the "conflict between security and freedom, and its related problem of freedom versus commitment, recurs in later Allen films."

While "What's New, Pussycat?" "was a great financial success, Allen was not entirely pleased with the finished film," continues Horowitz. The writer "began looking for a project over which he would have more creative control. He acquired the Japanese-made spy film 'Dagi no Kagi' (1964), reedited it, and dubbed in a sound track written and performed by himself, [second wife Louise] Lasser, Frank Buxton, and Len Maxwell, changing the film to a spy spoof about a search for an egg salad recipe." The film, "What's Up, Tiger Lily?," has enjoyed cult status to this day.

The success of Allen's first two films marked the onset of an era, between the late 1960s and the mid-1970s, that saw him writing, directing, and/or starring in six more freewheeling comedies. Beginning with "Take the Money and Run," the comedies reinforced the Allen persona, a kind of modern version of Charlie Chaplin's Little Tramp. "Bananas," Allen's next outing, features him as products-tester Fielding Mellish, who rises—through a series of misadventures—from soldier to president of the tiny banana-republic San Marcos (a country that "leads the world in hernias").

"Both 'Bananas' and 'Take the Money and Run' boast sharp bits of parody (of prison movies, TV commercials, courtroom dramas), with Allen kidnapping the cliches and transporting them into wildly inappropriate settings," finds *Film Comment*'s Richard Zoglin, who adds: "The underlying message of Allen's comedy is the tyranny of the cliche, which threatens to dehumanize us, to turn us into reflexive automatons. This is not random gagwriting but social comedy of a subtle subversiveness."

Allen the playwright had written and starred in the Broadway production of "Play It Again, Sam," a romantic farce about identity and commitment, with Allen's character, Allan Felix, fantasizing about being as tough and irresistible as Humphrey Bogart. When Felix finds himself increasingly attracted to his best friend's wife, the spirit of the real Bogey appears periodically to explain the mysteries of the female mind. "Play It Again, Sam" enjoyed a prosperous stage run and was adapted by Allen for his fifth produced screenplay.

1972, the same year of the film "Play It Again, Sam," was also the year of "Everything You Always Wanted to Know about Sex But Were Afraid to Ask," Allen's film derived—only slightly—from Dr. David Ruben's controversial bestseller. Allen's film takes an anecdotal approach: "Do Aphrodisiacs Work?," for instance, features Allen as a medieval court jester who uses a love potion to get his hands on "the royal tomatoes" (i.e., the queen). According to *Film Comment* contributor Michael Dempsey,

Allen's version of "Sex" approximates a "savage dissection of sexual absurdity."

Allen's next film, "Sleeper," presents him as health-food store owner Miles Monroe, whose disastrous ulcer operation results in his being frozen alive. "Sleeper" recounts what happens when this urban specimen defrosts 200 years later. In 2173 technology has taken over, with robots serving as servants, Jewish-accented tailors, and even cordial home pets. The time-traveling Miles, with his memory of a more natural earth, is perceived as a threat by the dictatorial government. Miles joins a rebel force that includes Luna (Diane Keaton), an anthem-spouting free spirit who helps him escape his foes.

"Sleeper" explores themes familiar to Allen works, including the search for cultural identity (Miles has to be cued to his time by being shown artifacts of his own epoch, including a beauty pageant and a picture of Richard Nixon, whom Miles cannot identify). Sex also plays a role in Miles's identity crisis-after Luna comments that he has gone two hundred years without it, Miles corrects her: "Two hundred and four, if you count my marriage." But in the new age, sex has been replaced by machinery-made stimuli, a concept that Miles samples but ultimately rejects. "During the conclusion of 'Sleeper' Miles Monroe comes right out with his total disbelief in science and politics, opting for 'sex and death, two things which come once in my life—but at least after death you're not nauseous,' " as Dempsey quotes.

Allen's next movie, "Love and Death," is both a spoof of Russian literature and an examination into the meaning of life. The movie opens in nineteenth-century Czarist Russia, where the citizens of a small village are preparing to join in the fight against Emperor Napoleon's invading forces—all except Boris (Allen), a "militant coward" in love with his cousin Sonia (Keaton). Pressured into joining the army after Sonia decides to marry the town's herring merchant, Boris, as klutzy as ever, becomes a quite inadvertent war hero ("*You* should have such inadvertent heroism," he sniffs to a rival). By this time Sonia is again unmarried, for the herring merchant has expired. She and Boris marry and each finds happiness—until they devise a plot to kill the visiting Napoleon. The plan backfires, Boris is captured, and is sentenced to die the next morning at six o'clock. "It was supposed to be five o'clock, but I had a smart lawyer," he remarks. At film's end, the dead Boris dances with Death.

"Although the story sounds tragic, 'Love and Death' is a comedy," Horowitz says. "The dead Boris appears at the beginning, joking about death and setting the story in flashback. By letting the audience know what Boris's fate will be, Allen makes the film lighter and more amenable to humor." The critic also finds that "Love and Death" has "other literary and theatrical devices which Allen has used in many of his films. Frequently he speaks directly to the audience in absurdist fashion. The film is filled with allusions to Russian literature [specifically, the works of Leo Tolstoy and Feyodor Dostoevsky] and to the films of Ingmar Bergman, one of Allen's favorite filmmakers. Finally, Allen's discussion of death leads him to examine the rationale behind death, which brings him to explore the existence and nature of God."

In "Annie Hall" Allen wrestled further with serious themes. The setting for this film is contemporary New York, the characters are witty and self-motivated, and the plot goes back farther than *Pygmalion:* a highly sophisticated man uses education and culture to create the perfect mate out of a simple, small-town woman and then watches in mounting disbelief as the newly liberated female breaks from his influence and forms a life of her own. With its insights into the way romances blossom and wilt in the 1970s, "Annie Hall" was embraced by many as a representative film of its age. The movie, declares *Newsweek*'s Janet Maslin, "is a perverse self-help manual about How to Be Your Own Worst Enemy, and even its most uproarious moments ride an undercurrent of wistfulness."

Allen himself noted "Annie Hall"'s biggest departure from his previous works in the interview with Natalie Gittelson: " 'Sleeper' and 'Love and Death' were cartoon-style films. I was still struggling to develop a sense of cinema, a better feeling for technique. But even though those films tried for some satirical content, they were still cartoon. I had intended to be very serious in 'Love and Death.' But the serious intent underlying the humor was not very apparent to most audiences. Laughter submerges everything else. That's why I felt that, with 'Annie Hall,' I would have to reduce some of the laughter. I didn't want to destroy the credibility for the sake of the laugh."

Allen's efforts were richly rewarded, for "Annie Hall" swept the 1978 Academy Awards, taking best picture, best director for Allen, best original screenplay for Allen and Marshall Brickman, and best actress for Keaton. America's newest *auteur,* however, made headlines as much for his boycotting of the ceremony as for his Oscar triumphs. While Allen had made no secret of his disregard for awards, he noted that the Oscars were held on Monday and thus conflicted with his previous commitment playing clarinet with the New Orleans Funeral and Ragtime Band at a New York City nightclub.

In his next film, "Interiors," Allen broke completely from comedy. The film deals with a family in trouble: The parents, Eve and Arthur, are at the breaking point in their marriage. Their three enigmatic daughters, Flyn, Joey, and Renata, "are like [Anton] Chekhov's *Three Sisters*," as *Dictionary of Literary Biography*'s Horowitz sees it. "Chekhov's women talk about 'going to Moscow' but never go anywhere. Allen's women talk of becoming artists and achieving self-fulfillment, yet manage only to wallow in their own despair. Arthur leaves Eve and romances vivacious and lively Pearl. . . . The family, particularly Eve, cannot accept this, and Eve commits suicide." Horowitz echoes many critics in his view that with this work Allen's "conscious avoidance of laughter gives the film a stilted, unnatural quality, and his dialogue is unrealistic, filled with psychological jargon."

"Manhattan," released in 1979, is the movie many people see as a truer follow-up to "Annie Hall." Certainly there are many similarities. Like "Annie Hall," "Manhattan" follows the romantic foibles of New York's intellectual elite. The movie again stars Allen and Keaton as nervous lovers; this time, however, Allen plays a disgruntled television hack yearning to write the Great American Novel, and Keaton portrays an overeducated critic who cranks out movie novelizations on the side. Their romance is doomed, though, by the lovers and ex-spouses who surround them: Keaton's Mary Wilke has had a long-running affair with a married college professor; Allen's Issac Davis must cope with a 17-year-old girlfriend as well as an ex-wife (bisexual when they married, but who left Issac shortly afterward for another woman) publishing a tell-all account of their relationship called *Marriage, Divorce and Selfhood.*

In *New York Times* critic Vincent Canby's opinion, "Manhattan" "moves on from both 'Interiors' and 'Annie Hall,' being more effectively critical and more compassionate than the first and more witty and clear-eyed than the second." As Canby adds, the film is "mostly about Issac's efforts to get some purchase on his life after he initiates a breakup with his illegal, teenage mistress . . . and his attempt to forge a relationship with the deeply troubled Mary Wilke. Unlike all of his friends except the still-learning [teenager] Tracy, Issac believes in monogamy. 'I think people should mate for life,' he says, 'like pigeons and Catholics.' "

Most critics and scholars considered "Annie Hall" and "Manhattan" Allen's two best films to date. But the movie Allen himself is most proud of, from that period, is one that offended many of his fans. "The best film I ever did, really, was *Stardust Memories,*" the director tells Tom Shales. "It was my least popular film. That may automatically mean it was my best film. It was the closest that I came to achieving what I set out to achieve." In "Stardust Memories," famous film director Sandy Bates (played by Allen) spends a weekend at an upstate New York resort where a collection of critics and fans pay homage to his work. Along the way he meets a mysterious woman and anticipates a visit from his French mistress (married with children, but no less accessible to Sandy's advances). He also confronts his current girlfriend, a neurotic actress. Besieged, Sandy contemplates his future while every one in his life pulls him in opposite directions. Eventually, fantasy and reality become a blur.

Whether meant satirically or sincerely, "Stardust Memories" nonetheless bore the wrath of insulted patrons. Critics generally panned the film, citing uneven pacing and overall sourness. One *Washington Post* writer calls the work an example of the "self-pitying tradition" of Federico Fellini's "8 1/2," which "Stardust Memories" distinctly resembles. The critic adds that the spectacle of "the celebrity artist [envisioning] himself as a potential victim of this freak show of admirers and supplicants" doesn't help Allen's case. "Allen even shows [Sandy] Bates fantasizing his own murder at the hands of some blandly psychotic fan. There's no satiric distancing to soften or contradict the impression of fundamental distaste."

Whether or not Allen was truly influenced by the negative press he received for "Stardust Memories," his next effort, "A Midsummer Night's Sex Comedy," certainly marked a departure in another direction. This film is a pastoral comedy centering on love, adultery, and the spirit world in a turn-of-the-century setting. Appraising the story of a crackpot inventor, played by Allen, who brings a group of friends and lovers to a country retreat where couplings and recouplings abound, critics generally agreed that "Midsummer Night's" is a pleasant diversion. *New York Times* writer Janet Maslin even commended Allen for his willingness to pursue new directions.

1983's "Zelig" showed Allen once again trying to broaden his artistry. This film presents Allen as a rather nondescript urban Jew who amazingly adopts the looks and characteristics of any distinct individual or group he encounters. Among fat men, for instance, Zelig's weight balloons; among black jazz musicians, Zelig's skin darkens. Eventually, "The Human Chameleon" catches the fancy of a fickle Roaring Twenties America, and Leonard finds himself the subject of songs, dances, and movies. Exploited by his ruthless sister, however, Leonard is miserable. Then a psychiatrist, Eudora Fletcher, becomes convinced that she can cure Zelig of his tendencies. But his public doesn't want cured the man who inspired the hit tune "You May Be Six People But I Love You." The resulting backlash drives Leonard out of the country and into Nazi Germany—in effect an entire nation of conformists, led by Hitler. Fortunately for Leonard, Eudora spots his face among the masses in a newsreel film and embarks on a daring rescue.

"Zelig," set in the 1920s, used a myriad of modern technological magic to evoke the jumpy, crackling film footage of that era. By shooting black-and-white film and then running it through a gauntlet of edits and scratches, Allen and cinematographer Gor-

don Willis created authentic looking action. Willis also succeeded in editing Allen's image into actual old footage, thus showing the character of Leonard Zelig with such notables as Babe Ruth, Calvin Coolidge, and even Adolph Hitler.

Critics disagreed on the merits of "Zelig." John Simon finds it "a curious example of a film with too much cleverness for its own good." Assessing the film in *National Review,* Simon goes on to say that "though the kaleidoscopic fortunes of the protagonist are aptly mirrored in the collage-like quality of the movie, the art of assemblage, instead of enhancing the semblance of reality, proves an inadequate way of dissembling: the cunningly joined snippets challenge us to peer behind them and discover the central hollowness." London *Times* writer David Robinson, however, finds no reason not to include "Zelig" in the company "of great comedies, like *Candide* or *Verdoux* or *Viridiana,*" adding that in all such narratives the "seemingly transparent simplicity leave you with quite as many questions about the condition of man as do great tragedies. When you recover from the laughter, this pure, perfect, beautiful comedy leaves a trail of reflections about truth and fiction and the difficulty of preserving one's own personality in a society which offers so many off-the-peg models for being which are so much easier to wear."

Embarking on yet another narrative form, Allen next brought out "Broadway Danny Rose." A Damon Runyonesque showbiz romance, "Broadway Danny Rose" features Allen as Danny Rose, a very-small-time theatrical agent to such acts as a skating rabbi, a blind xylophonist, a woman who plays the rims of drinking glasses, and a parrot who warbles standards like "I Gotta Be Me." The film's heroine is Tina Vitale, ex-moll of an unsuccessful gangster, current girlfriend of Lou Canova, an Italian lounge-singer whose career Danny is trying to resuscitate. Lou is married, so he asks Danny to be his stand-in and accompany Tina to a nightclub opening where Lou is making a comeback. A series of misunderstandings and betrayals results in Danny and Tina on the run from the mob, discovering their feelings for one another in the process.

Some critics see "Broadway Danny Rose" as a throwback to Allen's earlier comedies like "Sleeper"; others find it gratifying in a way they hadn't expected from such a modern filmmaker. Richard Corliss, for one, thinks the movie "is free of the Post-Funny School's hip condescension toward mediocrity. In the melancholy perseverance of these 'entertainers,' Danny and Woody find something admirable, even lovable. So should the movie audience," says the *Time* reviewer. Similarly, Canby observes that the movie "is a love letter not only to American comedy stars and to all of those pushy hopefuls who never quite make it to the top in show biz, but also to the kind of comedy that nourished the particular genius of Woody Allen."

For "The Purple Rose of Cairo," his fifteenth film, Allen turned to Depression-era New Jersey. The film centers on Cecilia, a destitute and abused wife who consoles herself by repeatedly seeing the adventure film "The Purple Rose of Cairo." One day, the film's clean-cut hero, Tom Baxter, actually leaves the screen and enters Cecilia's life. Finding herself the love interest of a fictional character proves both confusing and exhilarating to Cecilia. But back in Hollywood, studio executives are panicked. It seems that Tom Baxters have begun to leave their movies all across America. The executives decide that only Gil Shepard, the actor who plays Tom, might convince the make-believe adventurer to return to the "Purple Rose" so that the movie can proceed. Gil is dispatched to New Jersey, where he quickly becomes Tom's rival for Cecilia's love. She accepts Gil's invitation to follow him back to Hollywood. Rebuffed, Tom Baxter returns to the "Purple

Rose" movie. But when Cecilia, bags packed, goes to the movie house to meet Gil, he doesn't show up. He has left without her. Evidently he only pretended to love Cecilia in order to get Tom Baxter to return to the big screen. The movie's final image is of Cecilia, sitting in the audience once again, waiting for a movie to bring her out of her misery.

Canby wrote in the *New York Times* that "The Purple Rose of Cairo" is "pure enchantment[, a] sweet, lyrically funny, multilayered work that again demonstrates that Woody Allen is our premier film maker." To *Time*'s Schickel, the comedy "is not merely one of the best movies about movies ever made. It is still more unusual, because it comes at its subject the hard way, from the front of the house, instead of from behind the scenes. Its subject is not how movies work but how they work on the audience. Or more accurately, how they once did." And *New Yorker*'s Pauline Kael declares "Purple Rose" to be "the most purely charming" of Allen's films to date, perhaps "the fullest expression yet of his style of humor."

"Hannah and Her Sisters," a 1986 comedy-drama, proved yet another high point of Allen's career. It tells the story of how shifting allegiances and marital strife affect the lives of three grown sisters and their families. Hannah, the eldest, is a Broadway actress married to Elliott, a financial adviser. Elliott, however, has a desperate passion for Lee, the youngest sister, who herself lives with an alienated artist, Frederick. Holly, the middle sister, aspires to both acting and writing, depending on her mood. She ends up in a romance with Mickey, Hannah's first husband and, as played by Allen, a rampant hypochondriac.

Several critics praise "Hannah and Her Sisters" as a full-bodied, uplifting work. In *Washington Post* Paul Attanasio deems the movie "an encyclopedia of the emotions of ordinary life, not a movie so much as a prayer, if prayers could be so funny and tortured and full of love." "It is one of the extraordinary aspects of the film that 'Hannah and Her Sisters' is most secure when it's being least self-consciously funny," notes Canby in his *New York Times* column. *Newsweek*'s David Ansen wrote, "Anyone bemoaning the disappearance of adult matter from the movies need look no farther," he writes. "Here Allen singlehandedly restores glamour and substance to middle age. He juggles these overlapping stories with novelistic finesse, counterpointing hilarity and pathos with almost faultless tact."

It is generally believed that "Radio Days," Allen's next self-directed screenplay, is pulled from events in its creator's early years. But, as usual, Allen wasn't telling the press how much of the movie was fact and how much fiction. An anecdotal film with Allen providing a voice-over narration, "Radio Days" follows two narratives: one featuring young Joe and his family, the other tracing the rise of Sally White, a cigarette girl with more spunk than talent but one who nonetheless becomes the toast of radio high-society, thanks to some influential friends and a brace of elocution lessons. With "Radio Days," Canby is once again among Allen's most vocal supporters. "Never has Mr. Allen been so steadily in control," he wrote, "as 'Radio Days' slides from low blackout sketch to high satire to family drama that's as funny as it is moving," he writes in the *New York Times*. Devoting two articles to "Radio Days," Canby also states that the film "is so densely packed with vivid detail of place, time, music, event and character that it's virtually impossible to take them all in in one sitting."

But even Canby admits that the director's next feature, "September," "has big problems." This straight drama is notable for the fact that Allen, after seeing a first version of the film, "went out and filmed it all over again—rethought, rewritten and . . . sub-

stantially recast," as Eric Lax relates in a *New York Times* report. But to hear critics tell it, the new version is no more successful. "Gloomy" and "claustrophobic" are common adjectives the reviewers use to describe "September," which takes place in one house and centers around infidelity, suicide, and scandal. *New Yorker*'s Kael calls it "profoundly derivative and second-rate." She added: "When [a character] lifts up a large bouquet of wilting wildflowers and complains that her mother picked them but didn't bother to put them in water, some part of you refuses to believe that Woody Allen thought this up and that it survived the months of writing and shooting and reshooting and editing."

"Another Woman," Allen's similarly ponderous account of a philosophy professor who realizes a greater understanding and acceptance of life, fared better with critics, some of whom found it more relaxed, less stilted. Much better received was "Oedipus Wrecks," Allen's contribution to the 1988 omnibus "New York Stories." In his contribution, Allen plays a lawyer beleaguered by his hyper-critical mother. After the woman vanishes during a botched magic trick, she reappears—to her son's considerable mortification—as a giant figure in the New York sky. There she continues to offer her humiliating recollections and criticisms of her son.

Even more successful was Allen's 1989 work, "Crimes and Misdemeanors," which comprises both dramatic and comedic storylines. The dramatic narrative concerns an ophthalmologist plagued with a destructive mistress. The comedic plot deals with the efforts of a modest filmmaker (played by Allen) to complete a serious documentary—about a philosophy professor—while begrudgingly preparing a film about his egomaniacal brother-in-law, a successful television producer. This film, which many critics consider one of Allen's finest, earned several Oscar nominations, including one for best film. Michael Wilmington, in his *Los Angeles Times* review, hails "Crimes and Misdemeanors" as "a film that stands apart" and adds that it consists of "real comic savagery and dramatic grace."

While Allen has made himself known in many artistic categories—not just films, but television, theatre, print, and others—the movies are his most familiar and longstanding tradition. And yet the writer-director-actor has said that he doesn't enjoy the physical process of filmmaking, the early hours, the reshooting. "I wish somebody would come in and tell me I can't make films anymore," Allen revealed to Tom Shales in *Esquire*. He also told Shales, "There's never been a film of mine that I've been really satisfied with," and he added that he won't watch his films once their released because "I think I would hate them."

BIOGRAPHICAL/CRITICAL SOURCES:

BOOKS

Adler, Bill and Jeff Feinman, *Woody Allen: Clown Prince of American Humor,* Pinnacle, 1975.

Anobile, Richard, editor, *Woody Allen's "Play It Again, Sam,"* Grosset, 1977.

Brode, Douglas, *Woody Allen: His Films and Career,* Citadel, 1985.

Contemporary Literary Criticism, Volume 16, Gale, 1981.

De Navacelle, Thierry, *Woody Allen on Location,* Morrow, 1987.

Dictionary of Literary Biography, Volume 44: *American Screenwriters, Second Series,* Gale, 1986.

Guthrie, Lee, *Woody Allen: A Biography,* Drake, 1978.

Hirsch, F., *Love, Sex, Death, and the Meaning of Life: Woody Allen's Comedy,* McGraw, 1981.

Kael, Pauline, *Reeling,* Little, Brown, 1976.

Lax, Eric, *On Being Funny: Woody Allen and Comedy,* Charterhouse, 1975.

Palmer, M., *Woody Allen,* Proteus Press, 1980.

Yacowar, Maurice, *Loser Take All: The Comic Art of Woody Allen,* Ungar, 1979.

PERIODICALS

Atlantic, August, 1971, December, 1982, May, 1985.

Chicago Tribune, April 30, 1977, May 11, 1979, October 3, 1980, April 30, 1981, May 31, 1981, June 1, 1981, August 19, 1983, January 27, 1984, January 29, 1984, March 25, 1985, February 7, 1986, February 4, 1987.

Commentary, July, 1979, June, 1982, November, 1983.

Commonweal, September 24, 1982, September 9, 1983, March 23, 1984, April 19, 1985, March 14, 1986, February 27, 1987.

Dissent, fall, 1985.

Esquire, April, 1987.

Film Comment, March/April, 1974, March/April, 1978, May/June, 1979, May/June, 1986.

Film Quarterly, winter, 1972, March/April, 1987.

Los Angeles Times, June 24, 1982, March 22, 1983, July 29, 1983, March 1, 1985, January 30, 1987, December 18, 1987, October 22, 1989.

Nation, September 11, 1982, September 17, 1983, March 17, 1984, February 21, 1987.

National Review, June 22, 1979, September 17, 1982, August 5, 1983, May 3, 1985, March 14, 1986, March 27, 1987.

New Republic, August 16, 1982, August 15, 1983, February 20, 1984, April 1, 1985, February 10, 1986, March 9, 1987.

Newsweek, June 23, 1975, May 2, 1977, April 24, 1978, July 19, 1982, July 18, 1983, January 30, 1984, February 25, 1985, February 3, 1986, February 2, 1987, January 4, 1988.

New Yorker, May 15, 1971, June 16, 1975, April 25, 1977, July 26, 1982, July 8, 1983, February 6, 1984, March 25, 1985, February 24, 1986, March 9, 1987, January 25, 1988.

New York Times, June 29, 1975, August 2, 1978, April 29, 1979, September 19, 1980, September 20, 1980, September 28, 1980, October 19, 1980, March 19, 1981, July 16, 1982, July 25, 1982, October 19, 1982, July 15, 1983, July 17, 1983, July 18, 1983, January 27, 1984, January 29, 1984, June 4, 1984, March 1, 1985, February 7, 1986, February 9, 1986, January 25, 1987, January 30, 1987, February 1, 1987, May 14, 1987, November 24, 1987, December 16, 1987, December 18, 1987.

New York Times Magazine, January 7, 1973, April 22, 1979, January 19, 1986.

Rolling Stone, April 9, 1987.

Saturday Review, January 6, 1979, May, 1986.

Time, April 25, 1977, April 30, 1979, August 2, 1982, July 11, 1983, January 23, 1984, March 4, 1985, February 3, 1986, February 2, 1987, December 21, 1987.

Washington Post, May 2, 1979, September 25, 1979, October 3, 1980, June 2, 1981, August 7, 1983, January 27, 1984, March 22, 1985, February 7, 1986, January 30, 1987, April 1, 1987, March 11, 1988.

*   *   *

ALLENDE, Isabel   1942-

PERSONAL: Surname is pronounced "Ah-*yen*-day"; born August 2, 1942, in Lima, Peru; daughter of Tomas (a Chilean diplomat) and Francisca (Llona Barros) Allende; married Miguel Frias (an engineer), September 8, 1962 (divorced, 1987); married William Gordon (a lawyer), July 17, 1988; children: (first marriage) Paula, Nicolas; Scott (stepson). *Education:* Graduated from a private high school in Santiago, Chile, at age 16.

ADDRESSES: Home—15 Nightingale Lane, San Rafael, Calif. 94901. *Agent*—Carmen Balcells, Diagonal 580, Barcelona 21, Spain.

CAREER: United Nations Food and Agricultural Organization, Santiago, Chile, secretary, 1959-65; *Paula* (magazine), Santiago, journalist, editor, and advice columnist, 1967-74; *Mampato* (magazine), Santiago, journalist, 1969-74; Canal 13/Canal 7 (television station), television interviewer, 1970-75; worked on movie newsreels, 1973-75; Colegio Marroco, Caracas, Venezuela, administrator, 1979-82; writer. Guest teacher at Montclair State College, N.J., spring, 1985, and University of Virginia, fall, 1988; Gildersleeve Lecturer, Barnard College, spring, 1988; teacher of creative writing, University of California, Berkeley, spring, 1989.

AWARDS, HONORS: Quality Paperback Book Club New Voice Award nomination, 1986, for *The House of the Spirits; Los Angeles Times* Book Prize nomination, 1987, for *Of Love and Shadows; Eva Luna* was named one of *Library Journal*'s Best Books of 1988.

WRITINGS:

Civilice a su troglodita: Los impertinentes de Isabel Allende (humor), Lord Cochran (Santiago), 1974.

La casa de los espiritus, Plaza y Janes (Barcelona), 1982, translation by Magda Bogin published as *The House of the Spirits,* Knopf, 1985.

La gorda de porcelana (juvenile; title means "The Fat Porcelain Lady"), Alfaguara (Madrid), 1984.

De amor y de sombra, Plaza y Janes, 1984, translation by Margaret Sayers Peden published as *Of Love and Shadows,* Knopf, 1987.

Eva Luna, Plaza y Janes, 1987, translation by Peden published under same title, Knopf, 1988.

Also author of several plays and stories for children. Author of weekly newspaper column for *El Nacional* (Caracas), 1976-83.

WORK IN PROGRESS: Stories of Eva Luna, a collection of short stories.

SIDELIGHTS: When Chilean president Salvador Allende was assassinated in 1973 as part of a military coup against his socialist government, it had a profound effect on his niece, novelist Isabel Allende. "I think I have divided my life [into] before that day and after that day," Allende told *Publishers Weekly* interviewer Amanda Smith. "In that moment, I realized that everything was possible—that violence was a dimension that was always around you." At first, Allende and her family didn't believe that a dictatorship could last in Chile; they soon found it too dangerous to remain in the country, however, and fled to Venezuela. Although she had been a noted journalist in Chile, Allende found it difficult to get a job in Venezuela and didn't write for several years; but after receiving word from her grandfather, a nearly one-hundred-year-old man who had remained in Chile, she began to write again in a letter to him. "My grandfather thought people died only when you forgot them," the author explained to Harriet Shapiro in *People.* "I wanted to prove to him that I had forgotten nothing, that his spirit was going to live with us forever." Allende never sent the letter to her grandfather, who soon died, but her memories of her family and her country became the genesis of *The House of the Spirits,* her first novel. "When you lose everything, everything that is dear to you . . . memory becomes more important," Allende commented to

Mother Jones writer Douglas Foster. With *The House of the Spirits,* the author added, "[I achieved] the recovery of those memories that were being blown by the wind, by the wind of exile."

Following three generations of the Trueba family and their domestic and political conflicts, *The House of the Spirits* "is a novel of peace and reconciliation, in spite of the fact that it tells of bloody, tragic events," claims *New York Times Book Review* contributor Alexander Coleman. "The author has accomplished this not only by plumbing her memory for the familial and political textures of the continent, but also by turning practically every major Latin American novel on its head," the critic continues. The patriarch of the family, Esteban Trueba, is a strict, conservative man who exploits his workers and allows his uncompromising beliefs to distance him from his wife and children, even in the face of tremendous events.

Allende's grand scope and use of fantastic elements and characters have led many critics to place *The House of the Spirits* in the category of the Latin American novel of "magic realism," and they compare it specifically to Nobel winner Gabriel Garcia Marquez's *One Hundred Years of Solitude.* "Allende has her own distinctive voice, however," notes a *Publishers Weekly* reviewer; "while her prose lacks the incandescent brilliance of the master's, it has a whimsical charm, besides being clearer, more accessible and more explicit about the contemporary situation in South America." In contrast, *Village Voice* contributor Enrique Fernandez believes that "only the dullest reader can fail to be distracted by the shameless cloning from *One Hundred Years of Solitude.* . . . Allende writes like one of the many earnest minor authors that began aping Gabo after his success, except she's better at it than most." Although Lori M. Carlson agrees that *The House of the Spirits* is too reminiscent of Garcia Marquez's masterpiece, she writes in *Review* that "Allende's novel does remain compelling, nevertheless. Technique is polished, imagination full." "Isabel Allende is very much under the influence of Gabriel Garcia Marquez, but she is scarcely an imitator," remarks the *Washington Post Book World*'s Jonathan Yardley, concluding that "she is most certainly a novelist in her own right and, for a first novelist, a startlingly skillful, confident one."

While *The House of the Spirits* contains some of the magic realism that is characteristic of much Latin American fiction, it is counterbalanced by the political realities that Allende recounts. *Times Literary Supplement* reviewer Antony Beevor states that whereas the early chapters of *The House of the Spirits* seem "to belong firmly in the school of magical realism," a closer reading "suggests that Isabel Allende's tongue is lightly in her cheek. It soon becomes clear that she has taken the genre to flip it over," the critic elaborates. "The metaphorical house, the themes of time and power, the *machista* violence and the unstoppable merry-go-round of history: all of these are reworked and then examined from the other side—from a woman's perspective." Other critics, however, fault Allende for trying to combine the magical and the political; Richard Eder of the *Los Angeles Times* feels that the author "rarely manages to integrate her magic and her message," while *Nation* contributor Paul West says that the political story is "the book Allende probably wanted to write, and would have had she not felt obliged to toe the line of magical realism." But others maintain that the contrast between the fantastic and political segments is effective, as Harriet Waugh of the *Spectator* explains: "[The] magic gradually dies away as a terrible political reality engulfs the people of the country. Ghosts, the gift of foretelling the future and the ability to make the pepper and salt cellars move around the dining-room table cannot survive terror, mass-murder and torture."

Christian Science Monitor reviewer Marjorie Agosin presents a similar assessment: "Part of the [book's] power comes from the fact that real events form the background for the fictional story. The unbridled fantasy of the protagonists and their enchanted spirits is played out against the story of the demented and tragic country once free, now possessed by the evil spirits of a military dictatorship." When members of the Trueba family become increasingly involved in their nation's politics, "Allende here begins to exercise her skills as a journalist as she evokes the turbulent events she witnessed during the Marxists' electrifying rise and precipitous fall," remarks Patricia Blake in her *Time* review. "Not surprisingly, magic subsides and realism takes over. Allende deftly turns her characters into archetypes of Latin America's left and right." Despite this metaphorical aspect, notes Beevor, "there is too much humanity in her book for the characters to become ossified by symbolism; the story-telling is so natural that one risks overlooking the richness of allusion." "Finally," concludes *New York Times* critic Christopher Lehmann-Haupt, "what is fabulous in the story works to give it its extraordinary character. . . . It is also these spirits that help to lift the novel out of the realm of local political allegory, and lend it a feeling of extraterritorial truth." "*The House of the Spirits* does contain a certain amount of rather predictable politics, but the only cause it wholly embraces is that of humanity, and it does so with such passion, humor and wisdom that in the end it transcends politics," asserts Yardley; "it is also a genuine rarity, a work of fiction that is both an impressive literary accomplishment and a mesmerizing story fully accessible to a general readership."

Although *The House of the Spirits* includes political approaches similar to other Latin American works, it also contains "an original feminist argument that suggests [a] women's monopoly on powers that oppose the violent 'paternalism' from which countries like Chile continue to suffer," according to *Chicago Tribune* contributor Bruce Allen. Alberto Manguel likewise considers important Allende's "depiction of woman as a colonial object," as he writes in the Toronto *Globe and Mail,* a depiction reinforced by Esteban Trueba's cruel treatment of his wife, daughter, and female workers. But despite the concentration on female characters and "the fact that Esteban rapes, pillages, kills and conspires, he never entirely loses the reader's sympathy," comments Waugh. "It is a remarkable achievement to make the old monster lovable not just to his wife, daughter, and granddaughter, and the other women in his life, but also to the reader," Philip Howard contends in the London *Times.* "It is a fairminded book, that pities and understands people on both sides of the politics." Allen concurs: "The most remarkable feature of this remarkable book is the way in which its strong political sentiments are made to coexist with its extravagant and fascinating narrative. . . . Despite its undeniable debt to 'One Hundred Years of Solitude,' " the critic concludes, *The House of the Spirits* "is an original and important work; along with Garcia Marquez's masterpiece, it's one of the best novels of the postwar period, and a major contribution to our understanding of societies riddled by ceaseless conflict and violent change. It is a great achievement, and it cries out to be read."

With *Of Love and Shadows,* which *Detroit Free Press* contributor Anne Janette Johnson calls "a frightening, powerful work," Allende "proves her continued capacity for generating excellent fiction. She has talent, sensitivity, and a subject matter that provides both high drama and an urgent political message." The novel begins "matter-of-factly, almost humorously," with the switching of two baby girls, as Charles R. Larson describes it in the *Detroit News.* The story becomes more complex, however, when one of the babies grows up to become the focus of a journalist's investigation; after a reporter and photographer expose the political murder of the girl, they are forced to flee the country. "And so," Larson observes, "Allende begins with vignettes of magical realism, only to pull the rug out from under our feet once we have been hooked by her enchanting tale. What she does, in fact, is turn her story into a thriller." "Love and struggle à la 'Casablanca'—it's all there," Gene H. Bell-Villada likewise states in the *New York Times Book Review*. "Ms. Allende skillfully evokes both the terrors of daily life under military rule and the subtler form of resistance in the hidden corners and 'shadows' of her title." But while political action comprises a large part of the story, "above all, this is a love story of two young people sharing the fate of their historical circumstances, meeting the challenge of discovering the truth, and determined to live their life fully, accepting their world of love and shadows," Agosin declares. With *Of Love and Shadows* "Allende has mastered the craft of being able to intertwine the turbulent political history of Latin America with the everyday lives of her fictional characters caught up in recognizable, contemporary events."

Rosemary Sullivan, however, feels that Allende is not as successful in blending magical and realistic elements in this novel; she remarks in the Toronto *Globe and Mail* that "Allende has some difficulty getting her novel started because she has to weave two stories separately, and seems to be relying initially too much on her skills as a journalist." *New York Times* critic Michiko Kakutani similarly relates that the book is "more literal in a way that points up the author's tendency to cast everything in terms of white and black, good and evil, love and shadows." This leads to what Beevor perceives as a lack of "emotional distance"; the author's characters, "in spite of their lack of depth, are all perfectly convincing until she burdens them with interior monologues, giving them superfluous roles in a Greek chorus." But Johnson believes that Allende's characters, "major and minor, brim with the vagaries of human nature. Allende hops from one personality to another . . . with a gentle grace that is quite endearing," the critic continues. "When her tale descends to horror, which inevitably it must, she never relinquishes the warm, confiding tone, like that used between old friends." "One of [the book's] many strengths is that Allende sees no person and no issue in simplistic terms," Yardley likewise contends; "she always tries to understand what makes people think and behave as they do, even when she disagrees with them or dislikes them, and thus her work contains depths of empathy and compassion rarely found in fiction that embraces a political cause. . . . [Allende] is a writer of deep conviction, but she knows that in the end it is people, not issues, who matter most," the critic concludes. "The people in *Of Love and Shadows* are so real, their triumphs and defeats are so faithful to the truth of human existence, that we see the world in miniature. This is precisely what fiction should do."

"Fears that Isabel Allende might be a 'one-book' writer, that her first success . . . would be her only one, ought to be quashed by *Eva Luna*," asserts Abigail E. Lee in the *Times Literary Supplement*. "The eponymous protagonist and narrator of this, her third novel, has an engaging personality, a motley collection of interesting acquaintances and an interesting angle on political upheavals in the unnamed Latin American republic in which she lives." Born illegitimate and later orphaned, Eva Luna, a scriptwriter and storyteller, becomes involved with a filmmaker—Rolf Carle, an Austrian emigre haunted by his Nazi father—and his subjects, a troop of revolutionary guerrillas. "In 'Eva Luna,' Allende moves between the personal and the political, between realism and fantasy, weaving two exotic coming-of-age stories— Eva Luna's and Rolf Carle's—into the turbulent coming of age

of her unnamed South American country," Elizabeth Benedict summarizes in Chicago *Tribune Books*. Switching between the stories of the two protagonists, *Eva Luna* is "filled with a multitude of characters and tales," recounts *Washington Post Book World* contributor Alan Ryan. Allende's work is "a remarkable novel," the critic elaborates, "one in which a cascade of stories tumbles out before the reader, stories vivid and passionate and human enough to engage, in their own right, all the reader's attention and sympathy."

Perhaps due to this abundance of stories and characters, John Krich thinks that "few of the cast of characters emerge as distinctive or entirely believable," as he comments in the *New York Times Book Review*. "Too often, we find Eva Luna's compatriots revealed through generalized attributions rather than their own actions. . . . Is this magic realism à la Garcia Marquez or Hollywood magic à la Judith Krantz? We can only marvel at how thin the line becomes between the two, and give Ms. Allende the benefit of the doubt." London *Times* writer Stuart Evans, however, praises Allende's "range of eccentric or idiosyncratic characters who are always credible," and adds: "Packed with action, prodigal in invention, vivid in description and metaphor, this cleverly plotted novel is enhanced by its flowing prose and absolute assurance." "*Eva Luna* is a great read that *El Nobel* [Garcia Marquez] couldn't hope to write," claims Dan Bellm in the *Voice Literary Supplement*, for the women "get the best political debate scenes, not the men." Lee also sees a serious political side to the novel, noting "an interesting juxtaposition in *Eva Luna* of feminism and revolutionary politics. . . . In all the depictions of women and their relationships with men, though, one feels not a militant or aggressive feminism—rather a sympathetic awareness of the injustices inherent in traditional gender roles." The critic continues, remarking that *Eva Luna* "is an accomplished novel, skilfully blending humour and pathos; its woman's perspective on Latin American is a refreshing one, but it is enjoyable above all for its sensitivity and charm." "Reading this novel is like asking your favorite storyteller to tell you a story and getting a hundred stories instead of one . . . and then an explanation of how the stories were invented . . . and then hearing the storyteller's life as well," concludes Ryan. "Does it have a happy ending? What do you think?"

MEDIA ADAPTATIONS: The House of the Spirits will be filmed in English by Bille August, the Danish director of "Pelle the Conqueror."

BIOGRAPHICAL/CRITICAL SOURCES:

BOOKS

Coddou, Marcelio, editor, *Los libros tienen sus propios espiritus: Estudios sobre Isabel Allende*, Universidad Veracruzana, 1986.
Contemporary Literary Criticism, Volume 39, Gale, 1986.

PERIODICALS

Chicago Tribune, May 19, 1985.
Christian Science Monitor, June 7, 1985, May 27, 1987.
Detroit Free Press, June 7, 1987.
Detroit News, June 14, 1987.
Globe and Mail (Toronto), June 24, 1985, June 27, 1987.
Los Angeles Times, February 10, 1988.
Los Angeles Times Book Review, June 16, 1985, May 31, 1987.
Mother Jones, December, 1988.
Nation, July 20, 1985.
New Statesman, July 5, 1985.
Newsweek, May 13, 1985.
New York Review of Books, July 18, 1985.

New York Times, May 2, 1985, May 20, 1987, February 4, 1988.
New York Times Book Review, May 12, 1985, July 12, 1987, October 23, 1988.
People, June 10, 1985, June 1, 1987.
Publishers Weekly, March 1, 1985, May 17, 1985.
Review, January-June, 1985.
Spectator, August 3, 1985.
Time, May 20, 1985.
Times (London), July 4, 1985, July 9, 1987, March 22, 1989, March 23, 1989.
Times Literary Supplement, July 5, 1985, July 10, 1987, April 7-13, 1989.
Tribune Books (Chicago), October 9, 1988.
U.S. News and World Report, November 21, 1988.
Village Voice, June 7, 1985.
Voice Literary Supplement, December, 1988.
Washington Post Book World, May 12, 1985, May 24, 1987, October 9, 1988.

—Sketch by Diane Telgen

*   *   *

ALLINGHAM, Margery (Louise)   1904-1966

PERSONAL: Born May 20, 1904, in London, England; died June 30, 1966; daughter of Hebert John (a writer) and Emily Jane (Hughes) Allingham; married Philip Youngman Carter (an artist; formerly editor of the *Tatler,* a British magazine), 1927.

ADDRESSES: Home—D'Arcy House, Tolleshunt D'Arcy, Essex, England.

CAREER: Writer of detective novels.

WRITINGS:

Blackkerchief Dick, Doubleday, 1923.
The Black Dudley Murder, Doubleday, 1929 (published in England as *Crime at Black Dudley,* Jarrolds, 1929).
Mystery Mile, Doubleday, 1930.
Police at the Funeral, Heinemann, 1931, Doubleday, 1932.
The Gyrth Chalice Mystery, Doubleday, 1931 (published in England as *Look to the Lady,* Jarrolds, 1931).
Kingdom of Death, Doubleday, 1933 (published in England as *Sweet Danger,* Heinemann, 1933).
Death of a Ghost, Doubleday, 1934.
(Contributor) *Six Against Scotland Yard,* Doubleday, 1936.
Flower for the Judge, Doubleday, 1936.
The Case of the Late Pig, Hodder & Stoughton, 1937.
Mr. Campion, Criminologist (short stories), Doubleday, 1937.
Dancers in Mourning, Doubleday, 1937, published as *Who Killed Chloe?,* Avon, 1943.
The Fashion in Shrouds, Doubleday, 1938.
Black Plumes, Doubleday, 1940.
Traitor's Purse, Doubleday, 1941.
The Oaken Heart (nonfiction), Doubleday, 1941.
The Galantrys, Little, Brown, 1943 (published in England as *Dance of the Years,* M. Joseph, 1943).
Pearls Before Swine, Doubleday, 1945 (published in England as *Coroner's Pidgin,* Heinemann, 1945).
The Case Book of Mr. Campion, American Mercury, 1947.
Deadly Duo, Doubleday, 1949 (published in England as *Take Two at Bedtime,* World's Work, 1950).
More Work for the Undertaker, Doubleday, 1949.
The Tiger in the Smoke, Doubleday, 1952.
No Love Lost: Two Stories of Suspense, Doubleday, 1954.

The Estate of the Beckoning Lady, Doubleday, 1955 (published in England as *The Beckoning Lady* (also see below), Chatto & Windus, 1955.
Tether's End, Doubleday, 1958.
Hide My Eyes (also see below), Chatto & Windus, 1958.
Crime and Mr. Campion (contains *Death of a Ghost, Flowers for the Judge,* and *Dancers in Mourning*), Doubleday, 1959.
Three Cases for Mr. Campion, Doubleday, 1961.
The China Governess, Doubleday, 1962.
The Mysterious Mr. Campion (omnibus), Chatto & Windus, 1963.
The Mind Readers, Morrow, 1965.
Mr. Campion's Lady (omnibus), Chatto & Windus, 1965.
Mr. Campion's Clowns (anthology), Doubleday, 1966.
The Mysterious Mr. Campion (anthology), Doubleday, 1966.
Cargo of Eagles, Morrow, 1967.
Mr. Campion and Others, Heinemann, 1967.
The Allingham Case-Book, Morrow, 1969.
The Allingham Minibus, Morrow, 1973.
The White Cottage Mystery, Chatto & Windus, 1975.
The Fear Sign, Manor, 1976.
Hide My Eyes [and] *The Beckoning Lady,* Hogarth, 1985.
The Return of Mr. Campion, St. Martin's, 1990.

Also author of *Water in a Sieve; A Fantasy in One Act,* French, Toronto, and of short stories, serials, and book reviews.

SIDELIGHTS: One of England's leading mystery writers, Margery Allingham was the creator of the mild-mannered sleuth, Mr. Albert Campion. The character became popular immediately after his introduction in *The Crime at Black Dudley* in 1929. The *New York Times* reported that "for the first 22 years of her writing career, Miss Allingham wrote a novel almost every year. These are considered classics in their genre, charming works of manners and milieus." Phyllis McGinley, Pulitzer Prize winner and author of light verse, said Allingham was "sufficiently talented to write graceful and perceptive prose, sensitive enough to character to make human beings out of victim, criminal and detective alike." Although the *Times Literary Supplement* maintained that she "reached her apogee in 1949 with *More Work for the Undertaker,*" a *Best Sellers* critic contended that her last book, *The Mind Readers,* proved her to be "an acknowledged master of her craft." After Allingham's death, her husband, Philip Carter, continued her series and completed *Cargo of Eagles.*

BIOGRAPHICAL/CRITICAL SOURCES:

BOOKS

Dictionary of Literary Biography, Volume 77: *British Mystery Writers, 1920-1939,* Gale, 1989.

PERIODICALS

Best Sellers, July 1, 1965.
Book World, October 12, 1969.
Los Angeles Times Book Review, April 15, 1990.
New York Times, July 1, 1966.
New York Times Book Review, March 20, 1949, June 2, 1968, October 26, 1969.
Punch, February 14, 1968.
Saturday Evening Review, September 29, 1951.
Times (London), June 6, 1987, September 24, 1988, February 10, 1990.
Times Literary Supplement, April 19, 1963, January 5, 1990.
Wilson Library Bulletin, March, 1939.

ALTHER, Lisa 1944-

PERSONAL: Born July 23, 1944, in Tennessee; daughter of John Shelton (a surgeon) and Alice Margaret (Greene) Reed; married Richard Philip Alther (a painter), August 26, 1966; children: Sara Halsey. *Education:* Wellesley College, B.A., 1966. *Politics:* None. *Religion:* None.

ADDRESSES: c/o Alfred A. Knopf, Inc., 201 East 50th St., New York, N.Y. 10022.

CAREER: Atheneum Publishers, New York, N.Y., secretary and editorial assistant, 1967; free-lance writer, 1967—. Writer for Garden Way, Inc., Charlotte, Vt., 1970-71. Member of board of directors of Planned Parenthood of Champlain Valley, 1972.

MEMBER: PEN, National Writers' Union, Authors Guild, Authors League of America.

WRITINGS:

Kinflicks (novel), Knopf, 1976.
(Author of introduction) Flannery O'Connor, *A Good Man Is Hard to Find*, Women's Press, 1980.
Original Sins (novel), Knopf, 1981.
Other Women (novel), Knopf, 1984.

Also contributor of a short story, "Termites," to *Homewords*, edited by Douglas Paschell and Alice Swanson. Contributor of articles and stories to national magazines, including *Vogue, Cosmopolitan, Natural History, New Society, Yankee, Vermont Freeman, New Englander, New York Times Magazine*, and *New York Times Book Review*.

WORK IN PROGRESS: A novel.

SIDELIGHTS: Lisa Alther's *Kinflicks* made publishing news. Instead of a small press run, the novel boasted an initial printing of 30,000 hardback copies; it quickly ascended to the bestseller lists and was widely and favorably reviewed. In fact, Alther's satiric portrayal of a young woman's coming of age in the sixties so captivated the critics that it was immediately elevated to the company of J. D. Salinger's classic apprenticeship novel, *Catcher in the Rye.*

This comparison stems largely from the similarity between the novels' protagonists. In her search for a meaningful existence, Ginny Babcock emerges as a female Holden Caulfield. Like him, she is a survivor, and while the story of how adolescents survive is now a familiar one, Alther's graphic depiction of Ginny's Tennessee teens, her flight north, and subsequent return south to her mother's deathbed rescues the novel from predictability. As a *New Yorker* critic puts it: "A number of other excellent writers have covered various parts of the turf covered here," but "no other writer has yet synthesized this material as well as Miss Alther has. In fact, it would not be an exaggeration to say that her cynical, clear-eyed, well-heeled, disaster-prone heroine, Ginny Babcock, can easily take her place alongside Holden Caulfield as a symbol of everything that is right and wrong about a generation." Furthermore, notes Valentine Cunningham in the *New Statesman*, "her account is often to be caught uproariously in the rye."

In her second novel, *Original Sins*, Alther covers much the same territory she did in her first, only this time there are five protagonists. "*Kinflicks* followed a single heroine from her Tennessee upbringing through a series of wacky encounters up North with the countercultures of the '60s," Paul Gray explains in *Time.* "*Original Sins* quintuples its predecessor, offering five main characters, all Southerners, who try to grow up in a region and a country that are changing even faster than they are."

Alther chronicles the relocation of three of the five to the North while painting a broad social history of the sixties and seventies. Women's liberation, Vietnam, black power, civil rights, and the counterculture movement are among her subjects, and the portrait that emerges is unsatisfactory to some. Several critics charge that in her attempt to cover so much ground, Alther has sacrificed her characters' individuality. "The reader is haunted by the thought that the central characters, with the exception, perhaps, of the obstinately individualistic Emily, exist chiefly in order to illustrate differently developing states of political consciousness, as their progress from childhood to maturity is traced in often absorbing but sometimes oppressive detail," a *Times Literary Supplement* reviewer notes.

Whereas her first novel is a burlesque satire bordering on farce, *Original Sins* "is a protest novel of a conventional sort, a compound of outrage and doctrine," according to Mark Schechner. "It is an all-out assault on the South for its rigidly maintained double standards on matters of race, sex, and class and for its failures to live up to its deficiencies," he continues in his *New Republic* review.

Critics find fault in Alther's use of dialect and in what some refer to as a didactic tone. "The essential problem with those nearly 600 pages," Susan Wood writes in the *Washington Post Book World*, "is that they present every cliche you've ever heard about the South or about the political movements of the last two decades as though they are really, truly true: that is, with no sense of the complexities of individual lives, with no sympathy for the characters." Wood adds that such characters, like stick figures, are difficult to perceive as real people. Gray suggests, "Alther takes risks that sometimes fail. She is willing to sacrifice plausibility for comic effect, to put her characters through paces that occasionally seem dictated rather than inevitable. But such lapses are more than offset by the novel's page-turning verve and intelligence." Alther "gives generously, both to her readers and to the children of her imagination," Gray concludes. Cyra McFadden maintains that Alther's "excesses are those of overflowing talent and high spirits," and in her *Chicago Tribune Book World* review, proclaims *Original Sins* "a thoroughly endearing book."

Other Women examines how women relate to each other in various roles, as friends, lovers, and patient-to-therapist. Heroine Caroline Kelley is a doctor's ex-wife who gives up on men for women, and after a disappointing affair with a female friend, seeks aid in psychotherapy. Suspense builds around the question of what her sexual preference will be after analysis. Caroline and therapist Hannah Burke are "believable characters with real problems and realistic attitudes," notes Merle Rubin in a *Los Angeles Times* review. According to critics, elements in the novel identified as problematic are balanced against its positive features. Isabel Raphael of the London *Times*, for example, takes particular delight in Alther's portrait of Caroline's parents, two self-sacrificing people who give so much of themselves to others that they have little left to offer their own children. In addition, says Raphael, *Other Women* has "some sharp insights and a disarmingly fluent style."

BIOGRAPHICAL/CRITICAL SOURCES:

BOOKS

Contemporary Literary Criticism, Gale, Volume 7, 1977, Volume 41, 1987.

PERIODICALS

Chicago Tribune Book World, June 14, 1981, December 9, 1984.

Harper's, May, 1976.
Los Angeles Times, June 4, 1981, December 20, 1984.
Ms., May, 1981.
Nation, April 25, 1981.
New Republic, June 13, 1981.
New Statesman, August 27, 1976, May 29, 1981.
New Yorker, March 29, 1976, May 4, 1981.
New York Review of Books, April 1, 1976.
New York Times, March 16, 1976, December 10, 1984.
New York Times Book Review, March 14, 1976, May 3, 1981,
    November 11, 1984.
Time, March 22, 1976, April 27, 1981.
Times (London), February 28, 1985.
Times Literary Supplement, June 26, 1981.
Village Voice, March 8, 1976, December 18, 1984.
Washington Post Book World, March 28, 1976, May 31, 1981.

*   *   *

ALVAREZ, John
See del REY, Lester

*   *   *

AMADO, Jorge   1912-

PERSONAL: Born August 10, 1912, in Itabuna, Bahia, Brazil;
son of Joao Amado de Faria (a plantation owner) and Eulalia
(Leal) Amado; married Zelia Gattai, July 14, 1945; children:
Joao Jorge, Paloma. *Education:* Federal University of Rio de Janeiro, J.D., 1935.

ADDRESSES: Home—Rua Alagoinhas 33, Rio Vermelho-
Salvador, Bahia, Brazil.

CAREER: Writer. Imprisoned for political reasons, 1935, exiled,
1937, 1941-43, 1948-52. Federal deputy of Brazilian parliament,
1946-48; *Para Todos* (cultural periodical), Rio de Janeiro, Brazil,
editor, 1956-59.

MEMBER: Brazilian Association of Writers, Brazilian Academy of Letters.

AWARDS, HONORS: Stalin International Peace Prize, 1951;
Calouste Gulbenkian Prize, Academie du Monde Latin, 1971;
candidate for Neustadt International Prize for Literature, 1984;
National Literary Prize (Brazil); Nonnino Literary Prize (Italy);
Commander, Legion d'Honneur (France).

WRITINGS:

IN ENGLISH TRANSLATION

Jubiaba, J. Olympio, 1935, translation by Margaret A. Neves
    published as *Jubiaba,* Avon, 1984.
Mar morto, J. Olympio, 1936, translation by Gregory Rabassa
    published as *Sea of Death,* Avon, 1984.
Capitaes da areia, J. Olympio, 1937, translation by Rabassa pub-
    lished as *Captains of the Sands,* Avon, 1988.
Terras do sem fim, Martins, 1942, translation by Samuel Putnam
    published as *The Violent Land,* Knopf, 1945, revised edi-
    tion, 1965.
Gabriela, cravo e canela, Martins, 1958, translation by James L.
    Taylor and William L. Grossman published as *Gabriela,
    Clove and Cinnamon,* Knopf, 1962.
Os velhos marinheiros, Martins, 1961, translation by Harriett de
    Onis published as *Home Is the Sailor,* Knopf, 1964.
A morte e a morte de Quincas Berro Dagua, Sociedade dos Cem
    Bibliofilos do Brasil, 1962, translation by Barbara Shelby

published as *The Two Deaths of Quincas Wateryell,* Knopf,
    1965.
Os pastores da noite, Martins, 1964, translation by de Onis pub-
    lished as *Shepherds of the Night,* Knopf, 1966.
Dona Flor e seus dois maridos: Historia moral e de amor, Martins,
    1966, translation by de Onis published as *Dona Flor and
    Her Two Husbands: A Moral and Amorous Tale,* Knopf,
    1969.
Tenda dos milagres, Martins, 1969, translation by Shelby pub-
    lished as *Tent of Miracles,* Knopf, 1971.
Bahia (bilingual Portuguese-English edition), Graficos Brunner,
    1971.
Tereza Batista cansada de guerra, Martins, 1972, translation by
    Shelby published as *Tereza Batista: Home from the Wars,*
    Knopf, 1975.
O gato malhado e a andorinha Sinha, Editora Record, 1976,
    translation by Barbara Shelby Merello published as *The
    Swallow and the Tom Cat: A Love Story,* Delacorte, 1982.
*Tieta do agreste, pastora de cabras; ou, A volta da filha prodiga:
    Melodramatico folhetim em cinco sensacionais episodios e
    comovente epilogo, emocao e suspense!,* Editora Record,
    1977, translation by Shelby Merello published as *Tieta, the
    Goat Girl; or, The Return of the Prodigal Daughter: Melo-
    dramatic Serial Novel in Five Sensational Episodes, with a
    Touching Epilogue, Thrills and Suspense!,* Knopf, 1979.
*Farda, fardao, camisola de dormir: Fabula para acender uma es-
    peranca,* Editora Record, 1979, translation by Helen R.
    Lane published as *Pen, Sword, Camisole: A Fable to Kindle
    a Hope,* D. R. Godine, 1985.
The Miracle of the Birds, Targ Editions, 1982.
Tocaia grande, Editora Record, 1984, translation by Rabassa
    published as *Showdown,* Bantam, 1988.

OTHER

O paiz do carnaval (title means "Carnival Land"), Schmidt,
    1932.
Suor (title means "Sweat"), J. Olympio, 1936.
Cacau (title means "Cocoa"), J. Olympio, 1936.
A B C de Castro Alves (title means "The Life of Castro Alves"),
    Martins, 1941.
Vida de Luiz Carlos Prestes, o cavaleiro da esperanca (title means
    "The Life of Luiz Carlos Prestes"), Martins, 1942.
Sao Jorge dos Ilheus (title means "St. George of Ilheus"), Mar-
    tins, 1944.
O pais do carnaval [and] *Cacau* [and] *Suor,* Martins, 1944.
Obras (collected works), seventeen volumes, Martins, beginning
    1944.
*Bahia de Todos os Santos: Guia das ruas e dos misterios da cidade
    do Salvador* (title means "Bahia: A Guide to the Streets and
    Mysteries of Salvador"), Martins, 1945.
Seara vermelha (title means "Red Harvest"), Martins, 1946.
Homens e coisas do Partido Comunista (title means "Men and
    Facts of the Communist Party"), Edicoes Horizonte, 1946.
O amor de Castro Alves (title means "Castro Alves's Love"), Edi-
    coes do Povo, 1947, published as *O amor do soldado* (title
    means "The Soldier's Love"), Martins, 1958.
O mundo da paz: Uniao Sovietica e democracias populares (title
    means "The World of Peace: Soviet Union and Popular De-
    mocracies"), Editorial Vitoria, 1952.
Os subterraneos da liberdade (title means "The Subterraneans of
    Freedom"; contains *Os asperos tempos, Agonia da noite,* and
    A luz no tunel), Martins, 1954.
Jorge Amado: Trinta anos de literatura (title means "Jorge
    Amado: Thirty Years of Literature"), Martins, 1961.
Agonia da noite (title means "Night's Agony"), Martins, 1961.

Os asperos tempos (title means "Harsh Times"), Martins, 1963.

A luz no tunel (title means "A Light in the Tunnel"), Martins, 1963.

O poeta Ze Trindade (title means "Ze Trindade: A Poet"), J. Ozon, 1965.

Bahia boa terra Bahia (title means "Bahia Sweet Land"), Image (Rio de Janeiro), 1967.

O compadre de Ogun, Sociedade dos Cem Bibliofilos do Brasil, 1969.

Jorge Amado, povo e terra: Quarenta anos de literatura (title means "Jorge Amado, His Land and People: Forty Years of Literature"), Martins, 1972.

(With others) *Brandao entre o mar e o amor* (title means "Swinging between Love and Sea"), Martins, 1973.

(With others) *Gente boa* (title means "The Good People"), Editora Brasilial/Rio, 1975.

(With Luis Viana Filho and Jeanine Warnod) *Porto Seguro recriado por Sergio Telles* (title means "Porto Seguro in the Painting of Sergio Telles"), Bolsa de Arte do Rio de Janeiro, 1976.

Conheca o escritor brasileiro Jorge Amado: Textos para estudantes com exercicios de compreensao e dabate (title means "Know the Writer Jorge Amado: Texts for Students"), edited by Lygia Marina Moraes, Editora Record, 1977.

O menino grapiuna, Editora Record, 1981.

Jorge Amado (selected works), Abril Educacao, 1981.

Also author of *Bolaeo Goleiro,* 1984.

Amado's works have been translated into as many as fifty languages.

SIDELIGHTS: Ranked as one of the greatest contemporary Brazilian novelists, Amado has written prolifically of his homeland and his fellow countrymen. "Bahia surely has no greater poet than Jorge Amado," wrote D. A. Yates. Critics emphasize the influence of Amado's Marxist political views on his early novels, which depict the downtrodden masses on the plantations and in the cities of Brazil. John Duncan expressed the views of many critics in his response to *Shepherds of the Night:* "Amado's world is that of the People. In this world, everyone is poor, healthy and happy. The poor are the ones who live. The rich are sick. . . . The difficulty, even now, seems to be that he is as much an ideologist as a novelist. He sees classes, not individuals. . . . His is a world where instinct, impulse and animal exuberance become the ultimate value, while the whole range of thinking man remains unexamined."

In a review of *Dona Flor and Her Two Husbands,* L. L. Barrow noted the evolution of Amado's work: "In most of his earlier novels Jorge Amado showed great concern for the social problems of Brazil, offering rather rigid socialist solutions. His later works have subtler social themes, subordinated to the overall work. In his later novels, Amado's philosophy gives each person his own life, his own love and his own madness." Amado discussed the change in his writing in an interview for the *New York Times.* "As a young man I sought to put revolution into all my books and I always had a theoretical speech included. I did not realize that the reality was much more powerful than I could be," he said. When asked about the root of his success, he replied: "I write about Brazilian problems from the side of the people and I'm antielitist. I use popular language, I am no James Joyce. And in my works the people always win. I am very proud of that. My message is one of hope instead of despair."

In his novel *Showdown,* Amado tells the lively history of a town founded on the Brazilian frontier, and the rural people that inhabit it. "*Showdown* is a second look at the terrain Amado cov-

ered in *The Violent Land,*" comments Pat Aufderheide in the *Washington Post Book World.* "It has the plot drive that has kept people reading the latest Amado novel all these years; it's loaded with sex and violence; and the picaresque characters all share their inner lives with the reader through Amado's ominscient narration." Paul West in the *New York Times Book Review* calls *Showdown* "a vital novel, more complex than it seems at first, written in a long series of ebullient lunges, none of them stylish or notably elegant or eloquent, but in sum haunting and massive. . . . [Amado] creates something fecund and funny, tender and burly, as if his lively social conscience, under pressure, . . . yet again had to take the side of the human race."

MEDIA ADAPTATIONS: Gabriela, Clove and Cinnamon was adapted as the 1984 film *Gabriela,* released by Metro-Goldwyn-Mayer/United Artists. *Dona Flor and Her Two Husbands: A Moral and Amorous Tale* was adapted as the Broadway play *Sarava.*

BIOGRAPHICAL/CRITICAL SOURCES:

BOOKS

Contemporary Literary Criticism, Gale, Volume 13, 1980, Volume 40, 1986.

Ellison, Fred P., *Brazil's New Novel: Four Northeastern Masters,* University of California Press, 1954.

Peden, Margaret Sayers, editor, *The Latin American Short Story: A Critical History,* Twayne, 1983.

PERIODICALS

Americas, May-June, 1984.
Book World, August 24, 1969.
Chicago Tribune Book World, September 9, 1979.
Hispania, May, 1968, September, 1978.
Los Angeles Times Book Review, February 28, 1988, March 27, 1988.
Nation, June 5, 1967.
New York Review of Books, May 4, 1967,
New York Times, February 26, 1970, October 1, 1977, January 12, 1985, January 24, 1988.
New York Times Book Review, November 28, 1965, January 22, 1967, August 17, 1969, October 24, 1971, September 21, 1975, July 1, 1979, October 28, 1984, May 19, 1985, February 7, 1988.
Publishers Weekly, November 21, 1980.
Saturday Review, January 8, 1966, February 4, 1967, August 16, 1969, August 28, 1971, August 28, 1971.
Times Literary Supplement, July 2, 1970, October 2, 1981, November 12, 1982, January 20-26, 1989.
Tribune Books (Chicago), January 24, 1988.
Washington Post, December 29, 1984.
Washington Post Book World, September 12, 1971, January 10, 1988.

* * *

AMBLER, Eric 1909-
(Eliot Reed, a joint pseudonym)

PERSONAL: Born June 28, 1909, in London, England; son of Alfred Percy (a music hall performer) and Amy Madeline (Andrews) Ambler; married Louise Crombie, October 5, 1939 (divorced May, 1958); married Joan Harrison, October 11, 1958. *Education:* Attended University of London, 1924-27.

ADDRESSES: Home—Avenue Eugene Rambert 20, 1815 Clarens, Switzerland. *Agent*—Linder AG, Jupiterstrasse 1, 8032 Zurich, Switzerland.

CAREER: Writer, 1937—. Engineering apprentice, London, England, 1927-28; actor, comedian, and songwriter in vaudeville, 1929-30; advertising copywriter and agency director, 1930-37. Producer of several films, including "October Man," 1947; worked on 96 educational and training films for the British Army. *Military service:* British Army, Artillery, 1940-46; served in North Africa and Italy; assistant director of Army Kinematography, 1944-46; became lieutenant colonel; awarded Bronze Star.

MEMBER: Authors League of America, Writers Guild of America, West (council member, 1961-64), Garrick Club (London).

AWARDS, HONORS: Academy Award nomination, 1953, for screenplay "The Cruel Sea"; Golden Dagger Award, Crime Writers Association, 1959, for *A Passage of Arms,* 1962, for *The Light of Day,* 1967, for *Dirty Story,* and 1973, for *The Levanter;* Mystery Writers of America, Edgar Allan Poe Award for best mystery novel, 1963, for *The Light of Day,* and for best critical/biographical work, 1987, for *Here Lies: An Autobiography;* Grand Master Award, Mystery Writers of America, 1975; Svenska Deckarakademins Grand Master Award, 1975; Order of the British Empire, 1981; Golden Dagger Award (first presented), Veterans of the OSS (Office of Strategic Services), 1989.

WRITINGS:

The Dark Frontier, Hodder & Stoughton, 1936.
Background to Danger (also see below), Knopf, 1937, reprinted, Berkley Publishing, 1985 (published in England as *Uncommon Danger,* Hodder & Stoughton, 1937).
Cause for Alarm (also see below), Hodder & Stoughton, 1938, Knopf, 1939, reprinted, Berkley Publishing, 1985.
Epitaph for a Spy, Hodder & Stoughton, 1938, Knopf, 1952, reprinted, Berkley Publishing, 1987.
(Contributor) *The Queen's Book of the Red Cross,* Hodder & Stoughton, 1939.
A Coffin for Dimitrios (Book-of-the-Month Club selection; also see below), Knopf, 1939 (published in England as *The Mask of Dimitrios,* Hodder & Stoughton, 1939).
Journey Into Fear (also see below), Knopf, 1940, reprinted, Berkley Publishing, 1987.
Intrigue (contains *Journey Into Fear, A Coffin for Dimitrios, Cause for Alarm,* and *Background to Danger*), introduction by Alfred Hitchcock, Knopf, 1943.
Eric Ambler's Double Decker, World Publishing, 1945.
Judgment on Deltchev (also see below), Knopf, 1951, reprinted, Berkley Publishing, 1985.
The Schirmer Inheritance (also see below), Knopf, 1953, reprinted, Berkley Publishing, 1984.
State of Siege (also see below), Knopf, 1956, reprinted, Berkley Publishing, 1985 (published in England as *The Night-Comers,* Heinemann, 1956).
Passage of Arms (also see below), Heinemann, 1959, Knopf, 1960, reprinted, Berkley Publishing, 1985.
The Light of Day, Heinemann, 1962, Knopf, 1963, reprinted, Berkley Publishing, 1985, published as *Topkapi,* Bantam, 1964.
The Ability to Kill, and Other Pieces (essays), Bodley Head, 1963, reprinted, Mysterious Press, 1987.
A Kind of Anger, Atheneum, 1964.
(Editor, author of introduction, and contributor) *To Catch a Spy: An Anthology of Favourite Spy Stories,* Bodley Head, 1964, Atheneum, 1965.

The Intriguers: A Second Omnibus (contains *A Passage of Arms, State of Siege, The Schirmer Inheritance,* and *Judgment on Deltchev*), Knopf, 1965.
Dirty Story: A Further Account of the Life and Adventures of Arthur Abdel Simpson (Literary Guild alternate selection), Atheneum, 1967.
The Intercom Conspiracy, Atheneum, 1969, reprinted, Berkley Publishing, 1987.
(Contributor of essay) Dorothy Salisbury Davis, editor, *Crime Without Murder: An Anthology of Stories by the Mystery Writers of America,* Scribner, 1970.
(Contributor) George Hardinge, editor, *Winter's Crimes 2,* Macmillan, 1970.
The Levanter (also see below), Atheneum, 1972.
(Author of introduction) Arthur Conan Doyle, *The Adventures of Sherlock Holmes,* Murray-Cape, 1974.
Doctor Frigo (also see below), Atheneum, 1974.
The Siege of the Villa Lipp, Random House, 1977 (published in England as *Send No More Roses,* Weidenfeld & Nicolson, 1977).
The Care of Time, Farrar, Straus, 1981.
The Levanter [and] *Dr. Frigo,* Atheneum, 1982.
Here Lies: An Autobiography, Weidenfeld & Nicolson, 1985, Farrar, Straus, 1986.

Contributor of articles and short stories to *London Times, Sketch,* and other publications.

SCREENPLAYS

(With Peter Ustinov) "The Way Ahead," Two Cities, 1944.
"United States," British Army, 1945.
"The October Man," Two Cities, 1947.
(With David Lean and Stanley Haynes) "One Woman's Story," Cineguild, 1949 (released in England as "The Passionate Friends").
"Highly Dangerous," J. Arthur Rank Organization, 1950.
"The Clouded Yellow," General Film Distributors, 1950.
(With others) "Encore," Paramount, 1951.
"The Magic Box," J. Arthur Rank Organization, 1951.
"The Promoter," Universal, 1952 (released in England as "The Card").
"Shoot First," United Artists, 1953 (released in England as "Rough Shoot").
"The Cruel Sea" (based on the novel by Nicholas Monsairat), Ealing Pictures, 1953.
"Lease of Life," Ealing Pictures, 1954.
"The Purple Plain," United Artists, 1954.
"Battle Hell," Distributors Corp. of America, 1957 (released in England as "Yangtse Incident").
"A Night to Remember," J. Arthur Rank Organization, 1958.
"The Wreck of the Mary Deare," Metro-Goldwyn-Mayer, 1960.
"Love, Hate, Love," American Broadcasting Company, 1970.

Creator of television series "Checkmate," 1961-62.

WITH CHARLES RODDA UNDER JOINT PSEUDONYM ELIOT REED

Skytip, Doubleday, 1950.
Tender to Danger, Doubleday, 1951 (published in England as *Tender to Moonlight,* Hodder & Stoughton, 1952).
The Maras Affair, Doubleday, 1953.
Passport to Panic, Collins, 1958.

OTHER

A collection of Ambler's manuscripts, correspondence, and reviews is at the Department of Special Collections, Mugar Memorial Library, Boston University.

SIDELIGHTS: In the field of espionage fiction Eric Ambler is known as the writer who first created realistic stories about intelligence operations. Writing in the *Hollins Critic,* Paxton Davis states: "Ambler's world, far from being the projection of an adolescent's fantasies of spies who foil master-plots while they wallow in booze and broads, is very much the world we live in. It is Eric Ambler's distinctive contribution to 20th-century fiction that he was able both to discard [the espionage genre's] preposterous conventions, which were strangling the literature of espionage, and to establish a believable world, shabby, gritty, devious, threatening, but compellingly interesting, to replace them." As Joan DelFattore explains in the *Dictionary of Literary Biography,* "In Ambler's world people do things to gain something or to avoid something. There are very few real idealists or patriots in these stories, and their survival rate is close to zero."

It was in his first six novels that Ambler established his reputation as a writer of this new kind of espionage story. "He acquired," Julian Symons writes in *Critical Occasions,* "the sort of reputation that has about it almost a legendary nature." George Grella writes that Ambler "occupies an enviable position in the field of suspense literature. Along with Somerset Maugham and Graham Greene, he changed the spy novel from the jolly-good-fellows, sporting tale of hearty English Fascism to a sophisticated examination of the methods and moralities of modern international intrigue." Grella particularly notes Ambler's "disenchanted, liberal political views which were innovative in a form previously dominated by a provincial, upper-class vision—the world through a monocle." Symons also sees Ambler's political stance as something new to the genre. "Writers of spy stories, from John Buchan onwards," Symons writes, "have almost always been staunch right wingers, proudly unaware of political subtleties: Mr. Ambler seemed to many readers refreshingly aware of the world's changed political climate." In his book *Mortal Consequences,* Symons elaborates further on Ambler's political perspective. Ambler, he writes, "infused warmth and political color into the spy story by using it to express a Left Wing point of view." Ralph Harper points out in *The World of the Thriller* that Ambler was the first in his genre to display "a critical attitude toward capitalism." Robert Gillespie of *Salmagundi* judges all of Ambler's books to be "political and economic novels but they are something else first. Before they are socialist realism they are democratic realism and before that they are romances."

Over the years, Ambler's political views have changed and his novels have reflected this evolution. "In the 1930s a staunch anti-Fascist, in the 1950s suspicious in turn of Soviet policy," Davis writes, "Ambler [revealed] himself in 1969 [with *The Intercom Conspiracy*] as purged of faith in the wisdom, good intentions or competence of either of the great post-war powers, . . . echoing the antipathy to political action that has become so common, East and West, in these post-Hungary, post-Vietnam years."

Although his politics have evolved over the years, Ambler's novels usually concern "invariably decent, intelligent, well bred men more or less unwittingly enmeshed in Gorgonian webs of political and financial conspiracy," as a reviewer for *Time* notes. Symons sees a recurring situation in Ambler's novels. "The central character," he writes in *Mortal Consequences,* "is an innocent figure mixed up in violent events who slowly comes to realize that the agents and spies working on both sides are for the most part unpleasant but not important men. They murder casually

and without passion on behalf of some immense corporation or firm of armaments manufacturers whose interests are threatened. These, rather than any national group, are the enemy."

Some reviewers find this use of a non-professional spy to be one reason for the popularity of Ambler's work. "The amateur as protagonist," Ronald Ambrosetti writes in *Dimensions of Detective Fiction,* "succeeds for Ambler by reducing all of the angst of international intrigue to a very personal level. Ambler gets the edge on suspense by making his spy-detective an average person—the reader identifies easily. In this sense, the Ambler novel is more of a 'thriller' than the . . . professional-spy novels."

In evaluations of his career as a writer, Ambler is often referred to as a "master of suspense" or a "Grand Master." His influence in the genre of espionage fiction has been substantial for many years, and his work has received the highest awards the field has to offer. "To say he is held in high esteem by his writing colleagues would be an understatement," Symons remarks in an article for the London *Times.* At a lunch held in honor of Ambler, Symons reports, such writers as John le Carre, Frederick Forsyth, Gavin Lyall, and Lionel Davidson were in attendance. Le Carre said that Ambler's novels "were the well into which everybody had dipped," while Graham Greene cabled a greeting: "To the master from one of his disciples."

Phoebe Adams of *Atlantic* claims that "Ambler probably could not write badly if he tried." In similar terms, Frederick Busch of the *Chicago Tribune Book World* states: "I think that Ambler cannot write a seriously flawed novel. And I think that his best are among the genre's best." In conclusion, Busch believes that "Ambler has magnificently stood the test of time."

MEDIA ADAPTATIONS: Journey into Fear was filmed by RKO in 1942; *Background to Danger* was filmed by Warner Brothers in 1943; *The Mask of Dimitrios* was filmed by Warner Brothers in 1944; *Epitaph for a Spy* was filmed as "Hotel Reserve" by RKO in 1944; *The Light of Day* was filmed as "Topkapi" by United Artists in 1964; *Epitaph for a Spy* appeared as a television episode of the "Climax!" series for the Columbia Broadcasting System.

BIOGRAPHICAL/CRITICAL SOURCES:

BOOKS

Contemporary Literary Criticism, Gale, Volume 4, 1975, Volume 6, 1976, Volume 9, 1978.
Dictionary of Literary Biography, Volume 77: *British Mystery Writers, 1920-1939,* Gale, 1989.
Eames, Hugh, *Sleuths, Inc.,* Lippincott, 1978.
Haffmans, Gerd, editor, *Uber Eric Ambler,* Diogenes (Zurich), 1979.
Harper, Ralph, *The World of the Thriller,* Press of Case Western Reserve University, 1969.
Lambert, Gavin, *The Dangerous Edge,* Grossman, 1976.
Landrum, Larry N., Pat Browne, and Ray B. Browne, editors, *Dimensions of Detective Fiction,* Popular Press, 1976.
Symons, Julian, *Critical Occasions,* Hamish Hamilton, 1966.
Symons, *Mortal Consequences: A History—From the Detective Story to the Crime Novel,* Harper, 1972.

PERIODICALS

Atlantic, January, 1941, July, 1972, October, 1974.
Best Sellers, September 15, 1969, September, 1977.
Books, October 22, 1939, October 13, 1940, April, 1970.
Books and Bookmen, April, 1970.
Boston Transcript, September 18, 1937.
Chicago Tribune, August 7, 1986.

Chicago Tribune Book World, September 13, 1981, October 28, 1981, March 14, 1982.
Commonweal, August 7, 1953.
Economist, January 13, 1973.
Globe & Mail (Toronto), November 16, 1985.
Guardian, February 2, 1970, September 23, 1972.
Hollins Critic, February, 1971.
Journal of Popular Culture, fall, 1975.
Life, January 23, 1972.
Listener, August 31, 1972, December 8, 1977.
Manchester Guardian, August 13, 1940.
National Observer, October 16, 1967, September 22, 1969.
National Review, December 20, 1974.
New Review, September, 1974.
New Statesman, February 20, 1970, July 1, 1977.
Newsweek, June 12, 1961, July 10, 1972, October 14, 1974, June 20, 1977, August 31, 1981.
New Yorker, January 28, 1939, October 19, 1940, March 2, 1963, November 21, 1964, July 15, 1972, October 7, 1974, June 20, 1977.
New York Herald Tribune Book Review, March 23, 1952, August 2, 1953, September 16, 1956.
New York Times, August 8, 1937, January 29, 1939, October 22, 1939, July 18, 1943, September 23, 1956, September 16, 1969, July 3, 1972, November 16, 1974, June 6, 1977, September 11, 1981, July 29, 1986.
New York Times Book Review, October 18, 1964, October 8, 1967, September 21, 1969, July 16, 1972, September 13, 1981.
Observer, February 22, 1970, August 27, 1972, November 17, 1974, June 26, 1977.
Publishers Weekly, July 24, 1967, September 9, 1974.
Punch, March 11, 1970.
Rolling Stone, March 25, 1976.
Salmagundi, summer, 1970.
Saturday Review, September 18, 1937, January 28, 1939, October 25, 1969, August 5, 1972.
Spectator, July 19, 1940, February 28, 1970.
Time, June 26, 1972, November 11, 1974, June 6, 1977, September 14, 1981.
Times (London), January 7, 1970, June 13, 1985, June 23, 1989.
Times Literary Supplement, July 20, 1956, March 5, 1970, November 10, 1972, November 22, 1974, July 29, 1977.
Washington Post, October 22, 1981.
Washington Post Book World, January 14, 1968, July 20, 1969, September 14, 1969, July 2, 1972, September 29, 1974, September 6, 1981.
Weekly Book Review, February 28, 1943.
Wilson Library Bulletin, June, 1943.

*   *   *

AMICHAI, Yehuda 1924-

PERSONAL: First name sometimes listed as Yehudah; born in 1924 in Germany; immigrated to Palestine in 1936; naturalized Israeli citizen.

CAREER: Poet and writer. *Military service:* Served with Israeli defense forces during 1948 war.

WRITINGS:

IN ENGLISH

Lo me-'akhshav, Lo mi-kan (novel), [Tel Aviv], 1963, translation by Shlomo Katz published as *Not of This Time, Not of This Place,* Harper, 1968.

Selected Poems, translation from the original Hebrew by Assia Gutmann, Cape Goliard Press, 1968, published as *Poems,* introduction by Michael Hamburger, Harper, 1969.
Selected Poems of Yehuda Amichai, translation from the original Hebrew by Gutmann, Harold Schimmel, and Ted Hughes, Penguin, 1971.
Songs of Jerusalem and Myself (poetry), translation from the original Hebrew by Schimmel, Harper, 1973.
Amen (poetry), translation from the original Hebrew by the author and Hughes, Harper, 1977.
(Editor with Allen Mandelbaum) Avoth Yeshurun, *The Syrian-African Rift, and Other Poems,* translation by Harold Schimmel, Jewish Publications Society of America, 1980.
Love Poems, translation from the original Hebrew by Glenda Abramson and Tudor Parfitt, Harper, 1981.
(Editor with Mandelbaum) Dan Pagis, *Points of Departure,* translation from the original Hebrew by Stephen Mitchell, Jewish Publications Society of America, 1982.
Great Tranquilities: Questions and Answers, translation from the original Hebrew by Abramson and Parfitt, Harper, 1983.
The World Is a Room, and Other Stories, Jewish Publications Society of America, 1984.
Travels (bilingual edition), translation from the original Hebrew by Ruth Nevo, Sheep Meadow, 1986.
The Selected Poetry of Yehudah Amichai, translation from the original Hebrew by Mitchell and Chana Bloch, Harper, 1986.
Poems of Jerusalem, Harper, 1988.

IN HEBREW

Akhshav uba-yamim na-aherim (poetry; title means "Now and in the Other Days"), [Tel Aviv], 1955.
Ba-ginah ha-tsiburit (poetry; title means "In the Park"), [Jerusalem], 1958-59.
Be-merhak shete tikrot (poetry), [Tel Aviv], 1958.
Be-ruah ha-nora'ah ha-zot (stories), Merhavya, 1961.
Masa' le-Ninveh (play; title means "Journey to Nineveh"), 1962.
Shirim, 1948-1962 (title means "Poetry, 1948-1962"), [Jerusalem], 1962-63.

Also author of *'Akshav ba-ra'nsh,* 1968, *Mah she-karah le-Roni bi-Nyu-York,* 1968, *Pa 'amonim ve-rakavot,* 1968, *Mi yitneni malon* (title means "Hotel in the Wilderness"), 1972, *Ve-lo 'al menat lizkor* (poetry), 1971, and *Me-ahore kol zeh mistater osher gadol* (poetry), 1974.

Translator of German works into Hebrew.

SIDELIGHTS: According to M. L. Rosenthal, Yehuda Amichai "is Israel's best-known living poet." Born in Germany, Amichai left that country in 1936 with his family and journeyed to Palestine. During the 1948 war, he fought with the Israeli defense forces prior to the creation of the state and the Israeli Army. In his novel, *Not of This Time, Not of This Place,* Amichai struggles with "the torment of being buried alive in the irrelevant past." The novel's hero is torn between returning to the German town where he grew up and staying in Jerusalem and "immersing himself in a love affair with an outsider who has had no part in it." Anthony West in his review of the novel in *New Yorker* explained: "The alternatives are both impossibilities. The past is still going on back in Germany, and it is inescapable in Israel: the knowledge of what men are and what they can do that was acquired in the years of Hitler's 'final solution' cannot be discarded or ignored, and it is no easier to live with when one is in the country of the ex-butchers than it is in that of the ex-victims."

In his review, Amos Elon highlighted the theme of struggle for identity in *Not of This Time, Not of This Place:* "Amichai has been brought up in Israel, but the question of his identity sits heavily on his mind as much as with his Jewish-American fellow writers. He attempts a synoptic view of modern Jewish existence; its keys are ambivalence and disintegration, rather than clarity, unity or nationalistic simplicities." The treatment of this identity struggle is different, however, from other novels dealing with Holocaust themes. Robert Alter observed: "The fact of his German childhood, his awareness of kin and earliest friends murdered by the Nazis, clearly determines the broad direction of the sections of his novel set in Germany, and yet the general attempt of the book to make moral contact with the destruction and its perpetrators is eminently that of an Israeli beyond the experience, not of a European Jew actually torn by it. Indeed, the peculiar structure of the novel—a brilliant but not fully worked out invention of Amichai's—provides a kind of diagrammatic illustration of the difficulties Israeli writers have in trying to imagine this ultimate catastrophe and how one can live with the knowledge of it."

Leon Wieseltier commented that "Amichai's poems must compel the attention not only of devotees of modern Hebrew literature, but of anyone concerned with the state of contemporary poetry in general." In a review of *Poems,* Aaron Kramer wrote: "[Amichai] makes us leap from association to association, metaphor to metaphor—arriving finally at the hush of understanding. His sense of disorientation, noncommunication, and despair at times seems too pervasive—perilously close to self-pity. But the volcanic lyricism of this German-born Israeli poet bursts through again and again. There are many superlative songs of love, war, and loss."

Chad Walsh of the *Washington Post Book World* commented: "A Jewish poet, like a Greek, has the enormous advantage of an immense history and tradition which he can handle with an easy familiarity, and play with as a foil to the homogenized culture that is spreading over the globe like a universal parking lot. This combination of the old and the new speaks very powerfully in Amichai's poetry and makes him, as it were, a contemporary simultaneously of King David the psalmist and Eric Sevareid."

Reviewing the poetry collection *Amen,* Rochelle Ratner wrote: "The most important thing that Amichai teaches us is that the universal can only be approached through one's most personal experience. There is no anger and little guilt in these poems, only a quiet acceptance and a depression which strives to fill itself with love and caring. In many poems, the poet is alone, remembering and regretting, but silence doesn't have to be empty— Amichai knows that."

BIOGRAPHICAL/CRITICAL SOURCES:

BOOKS

Alter, Robert, *After the Tradition: Essays on Modern Jewish Writing,* Dutton, 1969.
Contemporary Literary Criticism, Gale, Volume 9, 1978, Volume 22, 1982.

PERIODICALS

Commentary, May, 1974.
Library Journal, July, 1969, July, 1977.
New Yorker, May 3, 1969.
New York Times Book Review, August 4, 1965, July 3, 1977.
New York Times Magazine, June 8, 1986.
Washington Post Book World, February 15, 1970.*

AMIS, Kingsley (William) 1922-
(Robert Markham, William Tanner)

PERSONAL: Born April 16, 1922, in London, England; son of William Robert (an office clerk) and Rosa Annie (Lucas) Amis; married Hilary Ann Bardwell, 1948 (divorced, 1965); married Elizabeth Jane Howard (a novelist), 1965 (divorced, 1983); children: (first marriage) Philip Nicol William, Martin Louis, Sally Myfanwy. *Education:* St. John's College, Oxford, B.A. (with first class honors in English), 1947, M.A., 1948.

ADDRESSES: Home—186 Leighton Rd., London NW5, England. *Agent*—Jonathan Clowes Ltd., 22 Prince Albert Rd., London NW1 7ST, England.

CAREER: University College of Swansea, Swansea, Glamorganshire, Wales, lecturer in English, 1949-61; Cambridge University, Peterhouse, Cambridge, England, fellow, 1961-63; full-time writer, 1963—. Visiting fellow in creative writing, Princeton University, 1958-59; visiting professor of English, Vanderbilt University, 1967-68. *Military service:* British Army, Royal Signal Corps, 1942-45; became lieutenant.

MEMBER: Authors' Club (London), Bristol Channel Yacht Club.

AWARDS, HONORS: Somerset Maugham Award, 1955, for *Lucky Jim;* M.A., Cambridge University, 1961; Booker Prize nomination and *Yorkshire Post* Book of the Year Award, both 1974, for *Ending Up;* John W. Campbell Memorial Award, 1977, for *The Alteration;* Commander of the British Empire, 1981; Booker-McConnell Prize for Fiction from Great Britain's Book Trust, 1986, for *The Old Devils.*

WRITINGS:

Socialism and the Intellectuals, Fabian Society (London), 1957.
(Author of introduction) Oscar Wilde, *Essays and Poems,* Norton, 1959.
New Maps of Hell: A Survey of Science Fiction, Harcourt, 1960, reprinted, Arno, 1975.
My Enemy's Enemy (short stories; also see below), Gollancz, 1962, Harcourt, 1963, Penguin, 1980.
(Under pseudonym William Tanner) *The Book of Bond, or Every Man His Own 007,* Viking, 1965.
The James Bond Dossier, New American Library, 1965.
Lucky Jim's Politics, Conservative Political Centre (London), 1968.
What Became of Jane Austen? and Other Questions (essays), J. Cape, 1970, Harcourt, 1971, published as *What Became of Jane Austen and Other Essays,* Penguin, 1981.
Dear Illusion (short stories; also see below), Covent Garden Press, 1972.
On Drink (also see below), illustrations by Nicolas Bentley, J. Cape, 1972, Harcourt, 1973.
First Aid for ABA Conventioneers (excerpt from *On Drink*), Harcourt, 1973.
Rudyard Kipling and His World, Scribner, 1975.
(Author of introduction) Arthur Hutchings, *Mozart: The Man, the Music,* Schirmer, 1976.
Interesting Things, edited by Michael Swan, Cambridge University Press, 1977.
The Darkwater Hall Mystery (also see below), illustrations by Elspeth Sojka, Tragara Press, 1978.
An Arts Policy?, Centre for Policy Studies, 1979.
Collected Short Stories (includes *My Enemy's Enemy, Dear Illusion,* and *The Darkwater Hall Mystery*), Hutchinson, 1980, Penguin, 1983, revised edition, 1987.

Every Day Drinking, illustrations by Merrily Harper, Hutchinson, 1983.

How's Your Glass? A Quizzical Look at Drinks and Drinking, Weidenfeld & Nicolson, 1984, edition with cartoons by Michael Heath, Arrow, 1986.

The Amis Anthology, Century Hutchinson, 1988.

NOVELS

Lucky Jim, Doubleday, 1954 (though title page of first printing reads 1953), reprinted, Queens House, 1976, Gollancz, 1984, edited and abridged edition by D. K. Swan, illustrations by William Burnard, Longmans, 1963, abridged edition with glossary and notes by R. M. Oldnall, Macmillan, 1967.

That Uncertain Feeling, Gollancz, 1955, Harcourt, 1956, reprinted, Panther Books, 1975.

I Like It Here, Harcourt, 1958, reprinted, Panther Books, 1975, Gollancz, 1984.

Take a Girl Like You, Gollancz, 1960, Harcourt, 1961, reprinted, Penguin, 1976.

One Fat Englishman, Gollancz, 1963, Harcourt, 1964, Penguin, 1980.

(With Robert Conquest) *The Egyptologists,* J. Cape, 1965, Random House, 1966, Panther Books, 1975.

The Anti-Death League, Harcourt, 1966, Gollancz, 1978, Penguin, 1980.

(Under pseudonym Robert Markham) *Colonel Sun: A James Bond Adventure,* Harper, 1968.

I Want It Now, J. Cape, 1968, collected edition, 1976, Harcourt, 1969.

The Green Man, J. Cape, 1969, Harcourt, 1970, Academy Chicago, 1986.

Girl, 20, J. Cape, 1971, Harcourt, 1972.

The Riverside Villas Murder, Harcourt, 1973.

Ending Up, Harcourt, 1974.

The Alteration, J. Cape, 1976, Viking, 1977.

Jake's Thing (also see below), Hutchinson, 1978, Viking, 1979.

Russian Hide-and-Seek: A Melodrama, Hutchinson, 1980, Penguin, 1981.

Stanley and the Women (also see below), Hutchinson, 1984, Summit Books, 1985.

The Old Devils (also see below), Hutchinson, 1986, Summit Books, 1987.

The Crime of the Century, Dent, 1987.

A Kingsley Amis Omnibus (includes *Jake's Thing, The Old Devils,* and *Stanley and the Women*), Hutchinson, 1987.

Difficulties With Girls, Summit Books, 1989.

The Folks That Live on the Hill, Hutchinson, 1990.

POETRY

Bright November, Fortune Press, 1947.

A Frame of Mind: Eighteen Poems, School of Art, Reading University, 1953.

Poems, Oxford University Poetry Society, 1954.

Kingsley Amis, Fantasy Press, 1954.

A Case of Samples: Poems, 1946-1956, Gollancz, 1956, Harcourt, 1957.

(With Dom Moraes and Peter Porter) *Penguin Modern Poets 2,* Penguin, 1962.

The Evans Country, Fantasy Press, 1962.

A Look Round the Estate: Poems 1957-1967, J. Cape, 1967, Harcourt, 1968.

Collected Poems: 1944-1979, Hutchinson, 1979, Viking, 1980.

OTHER

Also author of a science fiction radio play, "Something Strange," and of television plays "A Question About Hell," 1964, "The Importance of Being Harry," 1971, "Dr. Watson and the Darkwater Hall Mystery," 1974, and "See What You've Done," 1974. Author of recordings, "Reading His Own Poems," Listen, 1962, and with Thomas Blackburn, "Poems," Jupiter, 1962. Author of column on beverages in *Penthouse.* Editor of and contributor to literary anthologies. Contributor to periodicals, including *Spectator, Encounter, New Statesman, Listener, Observer,* and *London Magazine.*

SIDELIGHTS: "I think of myself like a sort of mid- or late-Victorian person," says Kingsley Amis in *Contemporary Literature,* "not in outlook but in the position of writing a bit of poetry (we forget that George Eliot also wrote verse), writing novels, being interested in questions of the day and occasionally writing about them, and being interested in the work of other writers and occasionally writing about that. I'm not exactly an entertainer pure and simple, not exactly an artist pure and simple, certainly not an incisive critic of society, and certainly not a political figure though I'm interested in politics. I think I'm just a combination of some of those things." Though an eclectic man of letters, Amis is best known as a prolific novelist who, in the words of Blake Morrison in the *Times Literary Supplement,* has the "ability to go on surprising us." He won critical acclaim in 1954 with the publication of his first novel, *Lucky Jim,* and after producing three other comic works was quickly characterized as a comic novelist writing in the tradition of P. G. Wodehouse and Evelyn Waugh. Since his early works, however, Amis has produced a spate of novels that vary radically in genre and seriousness of theme. He keeps "experimenting with ways of confounding the reader who hopes for a single focus," claims William Hutchings in *Critical Quarterly,* though Clancy Sigal suggests in *National Review* that Amis simply "has the virtue, rare in England, of refusing to accept an imposed definition of what a Serious Writer ought to write about."

Amis, who admits in *Contemporary Literature* that he considers poetry a "higher art" than prose writing, was publishing poems before novels. "I would have been a poet entirely if I had had my way," Amis told *CA* interviewer Jean W. Ross. A respected poet influenced by Philip Larkin, Amis not only eschews the grandiose subject matter and lofty tones of romanticism; as editor of several collections of British verse, he encourages his peers to do the same. Because his poems focus on the realities of contemporary life, which he renders with "innovative technique," Amis has a place in British poetry as an important minor poet, Neil Brennan notes in a *Dictionary of Literary Biography* essay.

Clive James, writing in the *New Statesman,* suggests, "Only the fact that he is so marvellously readable can now stop Kingsley Amis from being placed in the front rank of contemporary poets." Yet it was through his early novels that Amis became widely known and respected as a writer. When *Lucky Jim* first appeared, it attracted unusually wide review attention and led to a Somerset Maugham Award, a successful film, and a paperback sale of over a million copies in America. Edmund Fuller praised it in the *New York Times* as "written with the cool, detached, sardonic style which is the trademark of the British satirical novelist. *Lucky Jim* is funny in something approaching the Wodehouse vein, but it cuts a bit deeper." Other critics also likened it to P. G. Wodehouse's works, and Walter Allen in *The Modern Novel* called it "the funniest first novel since [Evelyn Waugh's] *Decline and Fall.*" William Van O'Connor summed up the book's virtues this way in *The New University Wits and the*

End of Modernism, "The characterizations are extremely good, the dialogue is natural, the narrative pacing is excellent, and Jim himself is not only a wonderfully funny character, he is almost archetypical."

Jim Dixon, the protagonist, is, according to Anthony Burgess in *The Novel Now,* "the most popular anti-hero of our time." Though a junior lecturer at a provincial university, Jim has no desire to be an intellectual—or a "gentleman"—because of his profound, almost physical, hatred of the social and cultural affectations of university life. This characteristic of Jim's has led several critics to conclude that he is a philistine, and, moreover, that beneath the comic effects, Amis is really attacking culture and is himself a philistine. Brigid Brophy, for example, writes in *Don't Never Forget: Collected Views and Reviews* that the "apex of philistinism" is reached "when Jim hears a tune by the composer whom either he or Mr. Amis . . . thinks of as 'filthy Mozart.' "

Ralph Caplan, however, claims in Charles Shapiro's *Contemporary British Novelists* that *Lucky Jim* "never [promises] anything more than unmitigated pleasure and insight, and these it keeps on delivering. The book [is] not promise but fulfillment, a commodity we confront too seldom to know how to behave when it is achieved. This seems to be true particularly when the achievement is comic. Have we forgotten how to take humor straight? Unable to exit laughing, the contemporary reader looks over his shoulder for Something More. The trouble is that by now he knows how to find it."

Amis himself states in a *Publishers Weekly* interview that to see *Lucky Jim* as a polemic on culture is to misinterpret it: "This is the great misunderstanding of it. People said I was part of an emergent group of angry young men writing novels of protest. But the idea that Jim was an 'outsider' just won't do. He was an *insider.* This still eludes people, especially Americans." As to the charges of philistinism, Amis says to Dale Salwak in *Contemporary Literature:* "Jim and I have taken a lot of bad mouthing for being philistine, aggressively philistine, and saying, 'Well, as long as I've got me blonde and me pint of beer and me packet of fags and me seat at the cinema, I'm all right.' I don't think either of us would say that. It's nice to have a pretty girl with large breasts rather than some fearful woman who's going to talk to you about Ezra Pound and hasn't got large breasts and probably doesn't wash much. And better to have a pint of beer than to have to talk to your host about the burgundy you're drinking. And better to go to see nonsensical art exhibitions that nobody's really going to enjoy. So it's appealing to common sense if you like, and it's a way of trying to denounce affectation."

Critics generally see the three novels that followed *Lucky Jim* as variations on this theme of appealing to common sense and denouncing affectation. Discussing *Lucky Jim, That Uncertain Feeling, I Like It Here,* and *Take a Girl Like You* in the *Hudson Review,* James P. Degnan states: "In the comically outraged voice of his angry young heroes—e.g., Jim Dixon of *Lucky Jim* and John Lewis of *That Uncertain Feeling*—Amis [lampoons] what C. P. Snow . . . labeled the 'traditional culture,' the 'culture of the literary intellectuals,' of the 'gentleman's world.' " James Gindin notes in *Postwar British Fiction* that the similarity of purpose is reflected in a corresponding similarity of technique: "Each of the [four] novels is distinguished by a thick verbal texture that is essential comic. The novels are full of word play and verbal jokes. . . . All Amis's heroes are mimics: Jim Dixon parodies the accent of Professor Welch, his phony and genteel professor, in *Lucky Jim;* Patrick Standish, in *Take a Girl Like You,* deliberately echoes the Hollywood version of the Southern

Negro's accent. John Lewis, the hero of *That Uncertain Feeling,* also mimics accents and satirically characterizes other people by the words and phrases they use."

The heroes in these four novels are in fact so much alike that Brigid Brophy charges Amis with "rewriting much the same novel under different titles and with different names for the characters," although Walter Allen insists that the "young man recognizably akin to Lucky Jim, the Amis man as he might be called, . . . has been increasingly explored in depth." Consistent with her assessment of Jim Dixon in *Lucky Jim,* Brophy sees the other three Amis heroes also as "militant philistines," a view that is not shared by Caplan, Burgess, or Degnan. Caplan explains that though the Amis hero in these novels is seemingly anti-intellectual, he is nonetheless "always cerebral," and Burgess points out that the hero "always earns his living by purveying culture as teacher, librarian, journalist, or publisher." Representing a commonsensical approach to life, the Amis protagonist, according to Degnan, is an inversion of a major convention of the hero "as 'sensitive soul,' the convention of the 'alienated' young man of artistic or philosophical pretensions struggling pitifully and hopelessly against an insensitive, middle-class, materialistic world. . . . In place of the sensitive soul as hero, Amis creates in his early novels a hero radically new to serious contemporary fiction: a middle-class hero who is also an intellectual, an intellectual who is unabashedly middle-brow. He is a hero . . . whose chief virtues, as he expresses them, are: 'politeness, friendly interest, ordinary concern and a good natured willingness to be imposed upon. . . .' Suspicious of all pretentiousness, of all heroic posturing, the Amis hero . . . voices all that is best of the 'lower middle class, of the non-gentlemanly' conscience."

Degnan, however, does believe that Patrick Standish in *Take a Girl Like You* comes dangerously close to "the kind of anti-hero—e.g., blase, irresponsible, hedonistic—that Amis's first three novels attack," and that this weakens the satirical aspect of the novel. Echoing this observation in *The Reaction Against Experiment in the English Novel, 1950-1960,* Rubin Rabinovitz detects an uncertainty as to what "vice and folly" really are and who possesses them: "In *Take a Girl Like You* Amis satirizes both Patrick's lechery and Jenny's persistence in preserving her virginity. . . . The satire in *Lucky Jim* is not divided this way: Jim Dixon mocks the hypocrisy of his colleagues in the university and refuses to be subverted by it. [In *Lucky Jim*] the satire is more powerful because the things being satirized are more boldly defined."

After *Take a Girl Like You,* Amis produced several other "straight" novels, as *Time*'s Christopher Porterfield describes them, as well as a James Bond spy thriller, written under the pseudonym of Robert Markham, called *Colonel Sun: A James Bond Adventure;* a work of science fiction, *The Anti-Death League;* and a ghost story, *The Green Man.* When Gildrose Productions, the firm to which the James Bond copyright was sold after Ian Fleming's death, awarded the first non-Fleming sequel to Amis, the literary world received the news with a mixture of apprehension and interest. Earlier, Amis had done an analysis of the nature of Fleming's hero, *The James Bond Dossier,* and he appeared to be a logical successor to Bond's creator. But the reactions to *Colonel Sun* have been mixed. Though Clara Siggins states in *Best Sellers* that Amis has "produced an exciting narrative with the expertise and verve of Fleming himself," S. K. Oberbeck claims in the *Washington Post Book World* that the changes Amis makes "on Bond's essential character throw the formula askew. . . . In humanizing Bond, in netting him back into the channel of real contemporary events, Amis somehow deprives him of the very ingredients that made his barely believable adventures so rewarding." Similarly, David Lodge, discussing the book in *The Novelist at the Crossroads and Other Essays on Fiction and Criticism,* considers *Colonel Sun* "more realistic" yet "duller" than most of the Fleming novels, because "the whole enterprise, undertaken, apparently, in a spirit of pious imitation, required Amis to keep in check his natural talent for parody and deflating comic realism."

Amis's comic spirit, so prominent in his first four novels and muted in *Colonel Sun,* is noticeably absent from *The Anti-Death League,* which was published two years before the Bond adventure. Bernard Bergonzi comments in *The Situation of the Novel* that in *The Anti-Death League* Amis "has written a more generalised kind of fiction, with more clearly symbolic implications, than in any of his earlier novels. There is still a trace of sardonic humor, and his ear remains alert to the placing details of individual speech; but Amis has here abandoned the incisive social mimicry, the memorable responses to the specificity of a person's appearance or the look of a room that have previously characterized his fiction."

The story concerns a British army officer who becomes convinced that a nonhuman force of unlimited malignancy, called God, is responsible for a pattern of seemingly undeserving deaths. Bergonzi views the work as a provocative, antitheological novel of ideas, and maintains that it "represents Amis's immersion in the nightmare that flickers at the edges of his earlier fiction." He does, however, find one shortcoming in the novel: "*The Anti-Death League* . . . is intensely concerned with the questions that lead to tragedy—death, cruelty, loss of every kind—while lacking the ontological supports—whether religious or humanistic—that can sustain the tragic view of life." A *Times Literary Supplement* reviewer admits that the rebellion against the facts of pain and death "seems rather juvenile, like kicking God's ankle for doing such things to people," but asserts: "[Amis] takes the argument to more audacious and hopeful lengths. . . . We do care about his creatures; the agents intrigue us and the victims concern us. The handling is vastly less pompous than the theme: oracular, yes, but eloquent and earthly and even moving."

Amis followed *The Anti-Death League* with *The Green Man* and *Girl, 20,* a comic novel with serious overtones. Like Burgess's assessment of the former, Paul Schleuter views the latter as a harmonious addition to Amis's body of work. He writes in *Saturday Review* that in *Girl, 20* Amis's "talent for creating humorous situations, characters, and dialogue is as fresh as ever. . . . Amis also has a distinct undercurrent of pathos, darkness, and trauma. The result is not really a 'new' Amis so much as a more mature examination of human foibles and excesses than was the case in his earlier novels." But Amis's next novel, *The Riverside Villas Murder,* "offers no comfort to those who look for consistency in [his] work," according to a *Times Literary Supplement* reviewer.

A departure from Amis's previous works, *The Riverside Villas Murder* is a detective story, though there is some debate among critics whether it is to be read "straight" or as a parody of the genre. Patrick Cosgrave, for example, claims in *Saturday Review/World* that the book is "a straight detective story, with a murder, several puzzles, clues, a great detective, and an eminently satisfying and unexpected villain. So bald a statement is a necessary introduction in order to ensure that nobody will be tempted to pore over *The Riverside Villas Murder* in search of portentiousness, significance, ambiguity, or any of the more tiresome characteristics too often found in the work of a straight novelist who has turned aside from the main road of his work into the byways of such subgenres as crime and adventure. More,

the book is straight detection because Amis intended it to be such: It is written out of a great love of the detective form and deliberately set in a period—the Thirties—when that form was . . . most popular." The *Times Literary Supplement* reviewer, however, considers the book "something more and less than a period detective story. Mr. Amis is not one to take any convention too seriously, and on one plane he is simply having fun." Patricia Coyne, writing in the *National Review,* and *Time's* T. E. Kalem express similar opinions. Coyne describes the story as "a boy discovers sex against a murder-mystery backdrop," and Kalem concludes that by making a fourteen-year-old boy the hero of the novel, "Amis cleverly combines, in mild parody, two ultra-British literary forms—the mystery thriller with the boyhood adventure yarn."

Some critics consider the plot of *The Riverside Villas Murder* weak, but the characterization and style particularly strong. Angus Wilson writes in the *New York Times Book Review* that the "mechanism of the murder, who did it and how, is at once creaky, obvious, and entirely improbable" yet he believes that the book contains "an almost perfect creation of the character of a young adolescent boy." Moreover, Wilson lauds Amis's prose as "probably the most pleasant to read of any good writers of English today. I know no other writer who can forgo all ornament without either aridity or pseudo-simplicity. . . . Each sentence, each paragraph, each chapter is organized to do its job, and the whole is therefore always satisfactory within its limits." Coyne, who also maintains that the mystery is not engaging enough, finds the characterization and the style of the highest quality: "[Amis's] may be the best secondary characters—most notably, his old men—since Dickens. And equally satisfying is his style, the often complex sentences falling clear and true with that deceptive ease that marks the master craftsman."

Almost as if to befuddle readers searching for consistency in his work, Amis followed his detective story *The Riverside Villas Murder* with a straight novel, *Ending Up,* before producing *The Alteration,* which *Time's* Paul Gray says "flits quirkily between satire, science fiction, boy's adventure, and travelogue. The result is what *Nineteen Eighty-Four* might have been like if Lewis Carroll had written it: not a classic, certainly, but an oddity well worth an evening's attention." According to Bruce Cook in *Saturday Review, The Alteration* belongs to a rare subgenre of science fiction: "the so-called counterfeit- or alternative-world novel." Though set in the twentieth century (1976), the book has as its premise that the Protestant Reformation never occurred and, as a result, that the world is essentially Catholic. The plot centers on the discovery of a brilliant boy soprano, the Church's plans to preserve his gift by "altering" his anatomy through castration, and the debate on the justice of this decision.

Thomas R. Edwards notes in the *New York Review of Books* that though "Amis isn't famous for his compassion," in *The Alteration* he "affectingly catches and respects a child's puzzlement about the threatened loss of something he knows about only from descriptions." John Carey insists in the *New Statesman* that the book "has almost nothing expectable about it, except that it is a study of tyranny." What Carey refers to is the destructive power of the pontifical hierarchy to emasculate life and art, which he sees as the theme of the novel. Bruce Cook shares this interpretation. Calling *The Alteration* "the most overtly and specifically theological of all [Amis's] books," Cook argues: "Fundamentally, *The Alteration* is another of Kingsley Amis's angry screeds against the Catholic faith and the Catholic idea of God. And it is not just what Amis sees as the life-hating, sex-hating aspect of High Christianity—something that made possible such monstrous phenomena as the castrati—that concerns him here

[but] . . . Christianity itself. At the end of *The Anti-Death League,* his oddest and most extreme book and in some ways his best, Amis allows some talk of reconciliation, of forgiving God the wrongs He has done humanity. But there is none of that in *The Alteration.* It is an almost bitter book by a man grown angry in middle age."

W. Hutchings, however, does not regard the novel as an attack on Catholicism. Despite sharing Cook's conviction that Amis's concern in his works since *The Anti-Death League* has been increasingly metaphysical, even theological, Hutchings maintains that the novel presents Amis with a way of making sense of a world "both absurd and threatening. Death, which dominates much of his fiction (for example, *The Anti-Death League, The Green Man,* and *Ending Up*), may be meaningless, but it cannot be viewed dispassionately. If death is horrible and God, should he exist, is either cruel or teasing, life has all the more to be lived for its present values. If we don't want it now, we'll never get it. . . . It is here that *The Alteration* represents a fascinating new step in Amis's career. If art is to have any value in such a world, then it must be part of the reason for wanting it now. The structure of the novel and its use of a musically talented main character bring a consciousness of the importance of art directly into its presentation of some problems of life."

From *The Alteration* to *Jake's Thing,* Amis again made the transition from science fiction to "comic diatribe," according to V. S. Pritchett in the *New York Review of Books.* Pritchett considers *Jake's Thing* "a very funny book, less for its action or its talk than its prose. . . . Mr. Amis is a master of laconic mimicry and of the vernacular drift." A reviewer writes in *Choice* that this is "the Amis of *Lucky Jim,* an older and wiser comic writer who is making a serious statement about the human condition."

The story focuses on Jake Richardson, a sixty-year-old reader in early Mediterranean history at Oxford who in the past has been to bed with well over a hundred women but now suffers from a loss of libido. Referred to sex therapist Dr. Proinsias (Celtic, pronounced "Francis") Rosenberg, Jake, says *Nation*'s Amy Wilentz, "is caught up in the supermarket of contemporary life. The novel is filled with encounter groups, free love, women's liberation, and such electronic contrivances as the 'nocturnal mensurator,' which measures the level of a man's arousal as he sleeps." Christopher Lehmann-Haupt of the *New York Times* notes that Amis "makes the most of all the comic possibilities here. Just imagine sensible, civilized Jake coming home from Dr. Rosenberg's office with . . . assignments to study 'pictorial pornographic material' and to 'write out a sexual fantasy in not less than six hundred words.' Consider Jake struggling to find seventy-three more words, or contemplating the nudes in *Mezzanine* magazine, which 'had an exotic appearance, like the inside of a giraffe's ear or a tropical fruit not much prized by the locals."

But for all the hilarity, there is an undercurrent of seriousness running through the novel. "It comes bubbling up," writes Lehmann-Haupt, "when Jake finally grows fed up with Dr. Rosenberg and his experiments." Wilentz argues that the novel expresses "outrage at, and defeat at the hands of, modernity, whose graceless intrusion on one's privacy is embodied in Dr. Rosenberg's constantly repeated question, 'I take it you've no objection to exposing your genitals in public?' " Malcolm Bradbury shares this interpretation, writing in the *New Statesman:* "Amis, watching [history's] collectivising, behaviourist, depersonalizing progress, would like nice things to win and certain sense to prevail. Indeed, a humanist common sense—along with attention to farts—is to his world view roughly what post-Heideggerian existentialism is to Jean-Paul Sartre's."

John Updike, however, offers another interpretation. Reviewing the book in the *New Yorker,* he calls the satire "more horrifying than biting, more pathetic than amusing." Updike claims that the book does not demonstrate that Dr. Rosenberg, in peddling the ideas and techniques of sex therapy, is a charlatan, "though Jake comes to believe so, and the English reader might be disposed to expect so. To an American, conditioned to tolerance of all sorts of craziness on behalf of the soul, the exercises of group therapy seem at least a gallant attack upon virtually intractable forms of human loneliness and mental misery." Updike views *Jake's Thing* as a portrait of a man infuriated by the times in which he lives. As such, he concludes it is "satisfyingly ambiguous, relentless, and full. Jake has more complaints than the similarly indisposed Alexander Portnoy [in *Portnoy's Complaint* by Philip Roth]. . . . He suffers from moments of seeing 'the world in its true light, as a place where nothing had ever been any good and nothing of significance done.' He is in a rage. Yet he is also dutiful, loyal in his fashion, and beset; we accept him as a good fellow, an honest godless citizen of the late twentieth century, trying hard to cope with the heretical possibility that sex isn't everything."

After the problems of libido in *Jake's Thing,* writes Blake Morrison in the *Times Literary Supplement, Russian Hide-and-Seek* "signals the return of the young, uncomplicated, highly sexed Amis male; . . . the more important connection, however, is with Amis's earlier novel, *The Alteration.*" Another example of the "alternative world" novel, *Russian Hide-and-Seek* depicts an England, fifty years hence, that has been overrun by the Soviet Union; oddly enough, though, the Soviets have abandoned Marxism and returned to the style of Russia under the czars. Paul Binding describes the book in the *New Statesman* as "at once a pastiche of certain aspects of nineteenth-century Russian fiction and an exercise in cloak-and-dagger adventure. The two genres unite to form a work far more ambitious than those earlier *jeux*—a fictional expression of the author's obsessive conviction that, whatever its avatar, Russian culture is beastly, thriving on conscious exploitation, enamoured of brutality."

Binding considers the indictment of Russian culture only moderately successful, citing as a weakness Amis's characterizations: "For the most part he has accorded his twenty-first-century Russians only the outward rituals and attitudes—and indeed attitudinisings—of their ancestors. . . . If Amis believes that [the ideologies and social structure of the Soviet Union] now contain the germinating seeds of reversion, then—even in a fictional parable—evidence should be given." Morrison admits *Russian Hide-and-Seek* "is not all it might be" but maintains it is a novel "of interest and subtlety." He believes that along with *The Alteration, Russian Hide-and-Seek* confirms in Amis's body of work "a development away from the provincial, lower-middle class comic novels of the 1950s and the metropolitan, upper-middle, satirical ones of the 1960s and early 1970s towards an interest in serious politico-historical fiction (*The Anti-Death League* was an early forerunner)."

Amis placed himself at the center of political controversy with his next novel, *Stanley and the Women.* Published first and well received in England, the book was rejected by publishing houses in the United States twice because of objections to its main character's misogyny, say some sources. "When rumors that one of Britain's most prominent and popular postwar novelists was being censored Stateside by a feminist cabal hit print [in early 1985], the literary flap echoed on both sides of the Atlantic for weeks," reports *Time*'s Paul Gray. After the book found an American publisher a critical debate ensued, with some reviewers condemning its uniformly negative depiction of women, and others defending the book's value nonetheless.

In a *Washington Post Book World* review, Jonathan Yardley charges, "Amis has stacked the deck against women, reducing them to caricatures who reinforce the damning judgments made by Stanley and his chums." Though Yardley feels that "much else in the novel is exceedingly well done," he also feels that its "cranky mysogynism" is too prominent to be ignored. Indeed, Stanley casts himself as the victim of a gang of female villains: a self-centered ex-wife; a current wife who stabs herself and accuses Stanley's emotionally unstable son; and a psychiatrist who deliberately mishandles the son's case and blames Stanley for the son's schizophrenia. On the other hand, "the men in the novel hardly fare any better," remarks Kakutani of the *New York Times*. In her view, shared by Susan Fromberg Schaeffer in the *New York Times Book Review, Stanley and the Women* proves Amis to be "not just a misogynist, but a misanthrope as well. Practically every character in the novel is either an idiot or a scheming hypocrite." Amis, who observes that British women take less offense from the book, claims it is not anti-female; *Time* presents his statement that "all comedy, . . . all humor is unfair. . . . There is a beady-eyed view of women in the book, certainly . . . . But a novel is not a report or a biographical statement or a confession. If it is a good novel, it dramatizes thoughts that some people, somewhere, have had."

Viewing the book from this perspective, some critics find it laudable. *Spectator* contributor Harriet Waugh argues, "It does have to be admitted . . . that Mr. Amis's portrayal of Stanley's wives as female monsters is funny and convincing. Most readers will recognise aspects of them in women they know . . . . [Amis] has written a true account of the intolerableness of women in relation to men." Such a tract, she feels, is comparable in many respects to novels by women that show women "downtrodden" by men. Writes Gray, "Amis has excelled at rattling preconceptions ever since the appearance of his classically comic first novel, *Lucky Jim* . . . . Is this novel unfair to women? Probably. Is the question worth asking? No. . . . The females in the world of this book all commit 'offences . . .', at least in the eyes of Stanley, who is . . . nobody's idea of a deep thinker." In the *Times Literary Supplement,* J. K. L. Walker concludes, "*Stanley and the Women* reveals Kingsley Amis in the full flood of his talent and should survive its ritual burning in William IV Street unscathed."

The author's next novel, *The Old Devils,* "manifests little of the female bashing that made the satiric *Stanley and the Women* (1985) so scandalous. In fact, dissatisfied wives are given some tart remarks to make about their variously unsatisfactory husbands. . . . Even so, these concessions never denature Amis's characteristic bite," writes Gray. In a London *Times* review, Victoria Glendinning concurs, "This is vintage Kingsley Amis, 50 percent alcohol, with splashes of savagery about getting old, and about the state of the sex-war in marriages of thirty or more years' standing." Reviewers most admire the book's major female character; Amis gives her a relationship with her daughter "so close, candid and trusting that the most ardent feminist must applaud," notes Champlin in the *Los Angeles Times Book Review.* Her husband, Alun, an aggressive womanizer, draws the most disfavor. In what Gray feels is the author's "wisest and most humane work," both sexes enjoy their best and worst moments. "This is one of Amis's strengths as a novelist, not noticeably to the fore in recent work but making a welcome return here: 'bad' characters are allowed their victories and 'good' characters their defeats. Yet Amis comes down against Alun in a

firmly 'moral' conclusion," comments Morrison in the *Times Literary Supplement.*

Alun's funeral near the close of the book is balanced with "the reconciliation of two of the feuding older generation, and the marriage of two of the younger," such that the ending has "an almost Shakespearean symmetry," relates Morrison. But the mood, he warns, is not exactly one of celebration. He explains that the character Amis seems to most approve "belongs in that tradition of the Amis hero who would like to believe but can't," whose "disappointed scepticism" keeps him from seeing a romantic encouragement behind a pleasant scene. "Finally," reflects Bryan Appleyard in the London *Times,* "it is this sense of an empty, somewhat vacuous age which seems to come close to the heart of all [Amis's] work. His novels are no-nonsense, well-made, good-humored products. They are about the struggle to get by in the gutter and their heroes seldom roll over to gaze at the stars. Like Larkin he is awestruck by the *idea* of religion but he cannot subscribe. Instead, his novels are happily committed to the obliteration of cant without thought of what to put in its place."

For *The Old Devils,* Amis received the Booker-McConnell Prize for Fiction, the most prestigious book award in England. Among critics who feel the prize was well-deserved is Champlin, who refers to "its sheer storytelling expertise, and its qualities of wit, humanity, and observation." In the *New York Times Book Review,* William H. Pritchard recognizes *The Old Devils* as Amis's "most ambitious and one of his longest books, . . . neither a sendup nor an exercise in some established genre. It sets forth, with full realistic detail, a large cast of characters at least six of whom are rendered in depth . . . . 'The Old Devils' is also Mr. Amis's most inclusive novel, encompassing kinds of feeling and tone that move from sardonic gloom to lyric tenderness." Also to the author's credit, says Pritchard, "one is constantly surprised by something extra, a twist or seeming afterthought signifying an originality of mind that is inseparable from the novelist's originality of language." Adds Champlin, "For long-term admirers of the Amis of 'Lucky Jim' and after, 'The Old Devils' is welcome evidence that the master remains masterful, able now to conjoin the mischievous with the mellow. As always, he is an insightful guide through the terrain where what is said is not meant and what is felt is not said, but where much of life is lived."

Amis continues to elude categorization partly because he actively fights it. "He loves to bait his readers," observes Frederick Busch in a *Chicago Tribune Book World* review of *Stanley and the Women.* More importantly, Amis loves to explore his own capabilities as a novelist. "I agree with Kipling," he explains in a *Publishers Weekly* interview, that "as soon as you find you can do something, try something you can't. As a professional writer one should range as widely as possible." Reflecting on efforts to categorize him and on his excursions into new areas of fiction, Amis muses in *Contemporary Literature:* "So I'm a funny writer, am I? [*Ending Up*], you'll have to admit, is quite serious. Oh, so I'm primarily a comic writer with some serious overtones and undertones? Try that with *The Anti-Death League* and see how that fits. So I'm a writer about society, twentieth-century man and our problems? Try that one on *The Green Man.* Except for one satirical portrait, that of the clergyman, it is about something quite different. So there is a lot of sex? Try that on [*Ending Up*], in which sexual things [are] referred to, but they've all taken place in the past because of the five central characters the youngest is seventy-one. So you dislike the youth of today, Mr. Amis, as in *Girl, 20?* Try that on [*Ending Up*] where all the young people are sympathetic and all the old people are unsympathetic.

This can be silly, but I think it helps to prevent one from repeating oneself, and [Robert] Graves [said] the most dreadful thing in the world is that you're writing a book you've written before. Awful. I haven't quite done that yet, but it's certainly something to guard against."

For *CA* interview with this author, see earlier entry in *CANR*-8.

MEDIA ADAPTATIONS: British Lion filmed *Lucky Jim* in 1957 and *That Uncertain Feeling,* renamed "Only Two Can Play" and starring Peter Sellers, in 1961. Columbia produced *Take a Girl Like You* in 1971.

AVOCATIONAL INTERESTS: Music (jazz, Mozart), thrillers, television, science fiction.

BIOGRAPHICAL/CRITICAL SOURCES:

BOOKS

Allen, Walter, *The Modern Novel,* Dutton, 1984.
Allsop, Kenneth, *The Angry Decade,* P. Owen, 1958.
Authors in the News, Volume 2, Gale, 1976.
Bergonzi, Bernard, *The Situation of the Novel,* University of Pittsburgh Press, 1970.
Brophy, Brigid, *Don't Never Forget: Collected Views and Reviews,* Holt, 1967.
Burgess, Anthony, *The Novel Now: A Guide to Contemporary Fiction,* Norton, 1967.
Contemporary Literary Criticism, Gale, Volume 1, 1973, Volume 2, 1974, Volume 3, 1975, Volume 5, 1976, Volume 8, 1978, Volume 13, 1980, Volume 40, 1987, Volume 44, 1988.
Dictionary of Literary Biography, Gale, Volume 15. *British Novelists, 1930-1959,* 1983, Volume 27: *Poets of Great Britain and Ireland, 1945-1960,* 1984.
Dictionary of Literary Biography Yearbook, 1986, Gale, 1987.
Feldman, Gene and Max Gartenberg, editors, *The Beat Generation and the Angry Young Men,* Citadel, 1958.
Gardner, Philip, *Kingsley Amis,* Twayne, 1981.
Gindin, James, *Postwar British Fiction,* University of California Press, 1962.
Gooden, Philip, *Makers of Modern Culture,* Facts on File, 1981.
Johnson, William, compiler, *Focus on the Science Fiction Film,* Prentice-Hall, 1972.
Karl, Frederick R., *The Contemporary English Novel,* Farrar, Straus, 1962.
Lodge, David, *Language of Fiction,* Columbia University Press, 1966.
Lodge, David, *The Novelist at the Crossroads and Other Essays on Fiction and Criticism,* Cornell University Press, 1971.
Nemerov, Howard, *Poetry and Fiction: Essays,* Rutgers University Press, 1963.
Rabinovitz, Rubin, *The Reaction against Experiment in the English Novel, 1950-1960,* Columbia University Press, 1967.
Shapiro, Charles, editor, *Contemporary British Novelists,* Southern Illinois University Press, 1963.
Wilson, Edmund, *The Bit Between My Teeth: A Literary Chronicle of 1950-1965,* Farrar, Straus, 1965.

PERIODICALS

America, May 7, 1977.
Atlantic, April, 1956, April, 1958, July, 1965, June, 1968, June, 1970, February, 1977, November, 1985.
Best Sellers, May 15, 1968, April 4, 1969.
Books and Bookmen, December, 1965, July, 1968, January, 1969, September, 1969, October, 1978.
Bookseller, November 11, 1970.
British Book News, June, 1981.
Chicago Tribune, August 1, 1989.
Chicago Tribune Book World, October 13, 1985.
Choice, November, 1979.
Christian Science Monitor, January 16, 1958, September 24, 1970, September 11, 1985, March 10, 1987.
Commonweal, March 21, 1958.
Contemporary Literature, winter, 1975.
Critical Quarterly, summer, 1977.
Critique, spring-summer, 1966, Volume IX, number 1, 1968, summer, 1977.
Encounter, November, 1974, January, 1979, September/October, 1984.
Essays in Criticism, January, 1980.
Hudson Review, summer, 1972, winter, 1973-74, winter, 1974-75, winter, 1980-81.
Library Journal, July, 1970.
Life, May 3, 1968, March 14, 1969, August 28, 1970.
Listener, November 9, 1967, January 11, 1968, November 26, 1970, May 30, 1974, October 7, 1976, May 22, 1980, October 23, 1980, May 24, 1984, October 16, 1986.
London Magazine, January, 1968, August, 1968, October, 1968, January, 1970, January, 1981, October, 1986.
London Review of Books, June 7-20, 1984, September 18, 1986, December 4, 1986, April 2, 1987.
Los Angeles Times, September 25, 1985, July 6, 1989.
Los Angeles Times Book Review, May 4, 1980, April 26, 1987.
Manchester Guardian, February 2, 1954, August 23, 1955, November 30, 1956.
Nation, January 30, 1954, August 20, 1955, April 28, 1969, May 5, 1969, October 5, 1970, April 7, 1979.
National Observer, September 15, 1969, June 29, 1977.
National Review, June 18, 1968, June 3, 1969, August 25, 1970, October 27, 1973, February 1, 1974, March 14, 1975, October 27, 1983, February 22, 1985, May 8, 1987.
New Leader, September 21, 1970, December 6, 1976.
New Republic, March 24, 1958, September 19, 1970, October 12, 1974, May 28, 1977, November 26, 1977, February 25, 1985, May 30, 1987.
New Statesman, January 30, 1954, August 20, 1955, January 18, 1958, September 24, 1960, November 28, 1963, July 7, 1967, December 1, 1967, October 11, 1968, November 21, 1975, October 8, 1976, September 15, 1978, April 13, 1979, May 23, 1980, December 5, 1980, September 19, 1986.
Newsweek, March 2, 1964, May 8, 1967, May 6, 1968, September 14, 1970, September 30, 1974, January 17, 1977, February 4, 1985.
New Yorker, March 6, 1954, March 24, 1958, April 26, 1969, September 13, 1969, October 21, 1974, March 14, 1977, August 20, 1979, April 27, 1987.
New York Review of Books, October 6, 1966, August 1, 1968, March 9, 1972, March 20, 1975, April 15, 1976, March 3, 1977, May 17, 1979, March 26, 1987.
New York Times, January 31, 1954, February 26, 1956, February 23, 1958, April 25, 1967, April 25, 1968, March 12, 1969, August 17, 1970, January 6, 1972, May 11, 1979, September 14, 1985, October 8, 1985, November 8, 1986, February 25, 1987, March 28, 1989.
New York Times Book Review, April 28, 1963, July 25, 1965, April 28, 1968, May 19, 1968, March 23, 1969, August 23, 1970, November 11, 1973, October 20, 1974, April 18, 1976, January 30, 1977, May 13, 1979, January 13, 1985, June 13, 1985, September 22, 1985, March 22, 1987, April 2, 1989.
Observer (London), October 10, 1976, December 12, 1976, February 12, 1978, July 23, 1978.
Observer Review, November 12, 1967, October 6, 1968.

Paris Review, winter, 1975.
Poetry, spring, 1968, July, 1969.
Publishers Weekly, October 28, 1974.
Punch, April 24, 1968, August 28, 1968, October 12, 1968, October 22, 1969, November 18, 1970, October 4, 1978.
Saturday Review, February 20, 1954, May 7, 1955, February 25, 1956, July 27, 1957, March 8, 1958, April 6, 1963, April 5, 1969, February 5, 1977, May/June, 1985.
Saturday Review/World, May 8, 1973.
Spectator, January 29, 1954, September 2, 1955, January 17, 1958, September 23, 1960, October 11, 1969, October 9, 1976, June 2, 1984, September 13, 1986, November 29, 1986, December 6, 1986.
Sunday Times (London), September 28, 1986.
Time, May 27, 1957, August 31, 1970, September 10, 1973, September 30, 1974, January 3, 1977, June 12, 1978, September 20, 1985, September 30, 1985, March 9, 1987.
Times (London), May 15, 1980, December 31, 1980, May 17, 1984, May 24, 1984, December 15, 1984, September 4, 1986, September 11, 1986, October 23, 1986, December 12, 1987, March 26, 1988, March 31, 1990.
Times Literary Supplement, February 12, 1954, September 16, 1955, January 17, 1958, September 21, 1962, November 23, 1967, March 28, 1968, September 24, 1971, April 6, 1973, October 8, 1976, September 22, 1978, May 16, 1980, October 24, 1980, November 27, 1981, May 25, 1984, September 12, 1986, December 26, 1986.
Tribune Books (Chicago), March 8, 1987.
Vanity Fair, May, 1987.
Village Voice, October 25, 1973.
Washington Post, September 10, 1973.
Washington Post Book World, May 5, 1968, August 8, 1968, October 20, 1968, September 1, 1985, March 1, 1987, March 26, 1989.
Wilson Library Bulletin, May, 1958, May, 1965.
World, May 8, 1973.
World Literature Today, summer, 1977, winter, 1977.
Yale Review, autumn, 1969, summer, 1975.

*   *   *

AMMONS, A(rchie) R(andolph) 1926-

PERSONAL: Born February 18, 1926, in Whiteville, N.C.; son of Willie M. and Lucy Della (McKee) Ammons; married Phyllis Plumbo, November 26, 1949; children: John Randolph. *Education:* Wake Forest College (now University), B.S., 1949; University of California, Berkeley, studies in English, 1950-52.

ADDRESSES: Office—Cornell University, Ithaca, N.Y. 14850.

CAREER: Poet and painter. Elementary school principal in Hatteras, North Carolina, 1949-64; Frederich & Dimmock, Inc. (manufacturer of biological glassware), Atlantic City, N.J., executive vice-president, 1952-61; Cornell University, Ithaca, N.Y., teacher of creative writing, 1964—, currently Goldwin Smith Professor. *Military service:* U.S. Naval Reserve, 1944-46; served in South Pacific.

AWARDS, HONORS: Scholarship in poetry, Bread Loaf Writers' Conference, 1961; John Simon Guggenheim fellowship, 1966; American Academy of Arts and Letters traveling fellowship, 1967; Levinson Prize, 1970; D.Litt., Wake Forest University, 1972, and University of North Carolina at Chapel Hill; National Book Award in Poetry, 1973, for *Collected Poems: 1951-1971;* Bollingen Prize, Yale University, 1974-75; American Book Award nomination and National Book Critics Circle Award,

1982, for *A Coast of Trees;* MacArthur Prize fellowship, 1981-86; North Carolina Award for Literature, 1986; National Institute of Arts and Letters Award.

WRITINGS:

POETRY

Ommateum, with Doxology, Dorrance, 1955.
Expressions of Sea Level, Ohio State University Press, 1964.
Corsons Inlet: A Book of Poems, Cornell University Press, 1965.
Tape for the Turn of the Year (book-length poem not included in later collections), Cornell University Press, 1965.
Northfield Poems, Cornell University Press, 1966.
Selected Poems, Cornell University Press, 1968.
Uplands, Norton, 1970.
Briefings, Norton, 1971.
Collected Poems, 1951-1971, Norton, 1972.
Sphere: The Form of a Motion, Norton, 1973.
Diversifications: Poems, Norton, 1975.
For Doyle Fosso, Press for Privacy (Winston-Salem, N.C.), 1977.
Highgate Road, Inkling X Press, 1977.
The Snow Poems, Norton, 1977.
The Selected Poems: 1951-1977, Norton, 1977, expanded edition, 1987.
Breaking Out, Palaemon, 1978.
Six-Piece Suite, Palaemon, 1978.
Selected Longer Poems, Norton, 1980.
Changing Things, Palaemon, 1981.
A Coast of Trees: Poems, Norton, 1981.
Worldly Hopes: Poems, Norton, 1982.
Lake Effect Country: Poems, Norton, 1982.
Sumerian Vistas: Poems, 1987, Norton, 1987.

Contributor to *Hudson Review, Poetry, Carleton Miscellany,* and other periodicals. Poetry editor, *Nation,* 1963.

SIDELIGHTS: A. R. Ammons once told the *Winston-Salem Journal & Sentinel:* "I never dreamed of being a Poet poet. I think I always wanted to be an amateur poet." But critics recognized him as more than an amateur, and today he is considered a major American poet. The measure of critics' esteem is implied by the stature of the poets to whom they compare Ammons. Tracing his creative geneology, they are apt to begin with Emerson and Thoreau and work chronologically forward through Whitman, Pound, Frost, Stevens, and Williams. Of those poets, Harold Bloom feels that Emerson and Whitman have influenced Ammons the most. He contends in his book *The Ringers in the Tower: Studies in Romantic Tradition* that "the line of descent from Emerson and Whitman to the early poetry of Ammons is direct, and even the Poundian elements in [Ammons's poem] *Ommateum* derive from that part of Pound that is itself Whitmanian." Bloom also believes that Ammons "illuminates Emerson and all his progeny as much as he needs them for illumination." Daniel Hoffman, writing in the *New York Times Book Review,* agrees that Ammons's poetry "is founded on an implied Emersonian division of experience into Nature and the Soul," adding that it "sometimes consciously echo[es] familiar lines from Emerson, Whitman and Dickinson."

While they acknowledge Ammons' debt to other writers, reviewers find that he has forged a style that is distinctly his own. Jascha Kessler writes in *Kayak,* "[Ammons] makes his daily American rounds about lawn and meadow, wood, hill, stream, in an easy, articulate, flat, utterly uneventful expository syntax. Altogether unlike Thoreau's sinewy, exacting, apothegmatic prose, and unlike that suavely undulant later Stevens from whom he borrows some of his stanza structures or envelopes, transmogrifying the Master of Imagination into a freshman-text writer who uses the colon for endless, undigestible linkages, never daring Stevens' comma, or venturing Thoreau's period." Other critics join Kessler in objecting to Ammons's sparse punctuation, but David Kirby defends Ammons, writing in the *Times Literary Supplement* that "his short lines, his overall brevity, his avoidance of punctuation marks other than the occasional comma and that quick stop-and-go colon are hallmarks of his minimalism, his exquisitely unencumbered technique."

Peter Stevens believes that Ammons's punctuation and form serve his intents well in some cases, poorly in others. Writing in the *Ontario Review,* he argues that the "ongoing flux" in *Tape for the Turn of the Year* (a long poem composed on an adding machine tape) works as "an almost perfect method to allow his notion of organic form to function," but that "no such wedding of form and content" occurs in another long poem, *Sphere: The Form of a Motion.* In the latter work, says Stevens, "the looseness that Ammons believes in derives from the use of a form the poet has tried before. [The poem is] written in three-or four-line stanzas, though there seems to be nothing definite about such paragraphing, running on as they do indiscriminately, often with no periods. Breathing space is provided by commas and colons only. Such a form fits snugly into Ammons' concern with flux and motion, and yet somehow the form seems too arbitrary."

Ammons is concerned with change both in nature and in daily life. William Logan notes in the *Chicago Tribune Book World* that in these interests, Ammons's work is "reminiscent of Frost on one side and Williams on the other, and in the work of both men, as in the [some] dozen books of their heir, intellect copes with its surroundings." According to Robert Shaw in *Poetry,* Ammons does more than describe; he forces the reader to involve himself. "The interest in an Ammons poem," he writes, "is less in the thing perceived than in the imaginative effort of the perceiver." Richard Howard explains further in his *Alone with America: Essays on the Art of Poetry in the United States since 1950* that "Ammons rehearses a marginal, a transitional experience[;] he is a littoralist of the imagination because the shore, the beach, or the coastal creek is not a *place* but an *event,* a transaction where land and water create and destroy each other, where life and death are exchanged, where shape and chaos are won and lost."

M. L. Rosenthal feels that although Ammons shares Wallace Stevens's desire to intellectualize rather than simply describe, he falls short of Stevens's success. Rosenthal writes in *Shenandoah:* "Ammons does have certain advantages over Stevens: his knowledge of geological phenomena and his ability to use language informally and to create open rhythms. Everything he writes has the authority of his intelligence, of his humor, and of his plastic control of materials. What he lacks as compared to Stevens, is a certain passionate confrontation of the implicit issues such as makes Stevens' music a richer deeper force. There is a great deal of feeling in Ammons; but in the interest of ironic self-control he seems afraid of letting the feeling have its way [as Stevens does]." Paul Zweig agrees that "unlike Eliot or Stevens, Ammons does not write well about ideas." He feels that "only when his poem plunges into the moment itself does it gain the exhilarating clarity which is Ammons' best quality." Writing in *Partisan Review,* Zweig asserts that Ammons's strength is in his form. "At first glance," he writes, "Ammons . . . seems to be a maverick, working vigorously against the limitations of the plain style, making a case in his work for a new intricacy of conception. Yet his best poems are closer to the plain style than one might think. It is when one hears William Carlos Williams in the background

of his voice that the poems work clearly and solidly, not when one hears Hopkins or Stevens."

Harold Bloom suggests that while readers may indeed hear other voices in the background, Ammons's poems are uniquely valuable because of the personal voice that not only borrows from but also adds to the poetic tradition. Bloom writes: "Ammons's poetry does for me what Stevens's did earlier, and the High Romantics [Bloom's term for Blake, Wordsworth, Coleridge, Shelley, Keats, and Byron] before that; it helps me to live my life. If Ammons is, as I think, the central poet of my generation, because he alone has made a heterocosm, a second nature in his poetry, I deprecate no other poet by this naming. . . . A solitary artist, nurtured by the strength available for him only in extreme isolation, carrying on the Emersonian tradition with a quietness directly contrary to nearly all its other current avatars, he has emerged as an extraordinary master, comparable to the Stevens of *Ideas of Order* and *The Man With the Blue Guitar.* To track him persistently [through his oeuvre] is to be found by not only a complete possibility of imaginative experience, but by a renewed sense of the whole line of Emerson, the vitalizing and much maligned tradition that has accounted for most that matters in American poetry."

BIOGRAPHICAL/CRITICAL SOURCES:

BOOKS

Authors in the News, Volume 1, Gale, 1976.
Bloom, Harold, *The Ringers in the Tower: Studies in Romantic Tradition,* University of Chicago Press, 1971.
Bloom, *Figures of Capable Imagination,* Seabury-Continuum, 1976.
Bloom, editor, *A. R. Ammons,* Chelsea House, 1986.
Contemporary Literary Criticism, Gale, Volume 2, 1974, Volume 3, 1975, Volume 5, 1976, Volume 8, 1978, Volume 9, 1978, Volume 25, 1983.
Dictionary of Literary Biography, Volume 5: *American Poets since World War II,* Gale, 1980.
Holder, Alan, *A. R. Ammons,* Twayne, 1978.
Howard, Richard, *Alone with America: Essays on the Art of Poetry in the United States since 1950,* Atheneum, 1969, enlarged edition, 1980.
Waggoner, Hyatt H., *American Visionary Poetry,* Louisiana State University Press, 1982.

PERIODICALS

Book Week, February 20, 1966.
Chicago Tribune Book World, July 26, 1981, June 12, 1983.
Contemporary Literature, winter, 1968.
Diacritics, winter, 1973.
Hudson Review, summer, 1967.
Kayak, summer, 1973.
Los Angeles Times Book Review, May 16, 1982.
Nation, April 24, 1967, January 18, 1971.
New York Times, November 10, 1972.
New York Times Book Review, December 14, 1969, May 10, 1981, January 17, 1982, September 4, 1983.
Ontario Review, fall-winter, 1975-76.
Partisan Review, Volume XLI, No. 4, 1974.
Pembroke Magazine, No. 18 (special Ammons issue), 1986.
Poetry, April, 1969, November, 1973.
Prairie Schooner, fall, 1967.
Shenandoah, fall, 1972.
Time, July 12, 1971.
Times Literary Supplement, April 24, 1981, October 23, 1981, May 25, 1984.

Winston-Salem Journal & Sentinel, December 1, 1974.

*   *   *

ANAND, Mulk Raj   1905-

PERSONAL: Born December 12, 1905, in Peshawar, India; son of Lal Chand (a coppersmith and soldier) and Ishwar (Kaur) Anand; married Kathleen Van Gelder (an actress), 1939 (divorced, 1948); married Shirin Vajifdar (a classical dancer), 1949; children: one daughter. *Education:* University of Punjab, B.A. (with honors), 1924; University College, London, Ph.D., 1929; additional study at Cambridge University, 1929-30.

ADDRESSES: Home—Jassim House, 25 Cuffe Parade, Colaba, Bombay 400 005, India. *Office*—MARG Publications, Army & Navy Bldg., 148, Mahatma Gandhi Rd., Bombay 400 023, India.

CAREER: Novelist, essayist, and lecturer. Fought with Republicans in Spanish Civil War, 1937-38; helped found the Progressive Writer's Movement in India, 1938; lecturer in literature and philosophy at London County Council Adult Education Schools, and broadcaster and scriptwriter in films division for British Broadcasting Corp., 1939-45; lecturer at various Indian universities, 1948-63; Tagore Professor of Fine Arts at University of Punjab, 1963-66; visiting professor at Institute of Advanced Studies in Simla, 1967-68; president of Lokayata Trust (an organization developing community and cultural centers in India), 1970—. Editor, *MARG* (Indian art quarterly), Bombay, India, 1946—.

MEMBER: Indian National Academy of Letters (fellow), Indian National Academy of Art (fellow), Indian National Council of Arts, Sahitya Academy (fellow), Lalit Kala Academy (fellow).

AWARDS, HONORS: Leverhulme fellow, 1940-42; International Peace Prize, World Council of Peace, 1952, for promoting understanding among nations; Padma Bhusan award from the President of India, 1968; honorary doctorates from Indian universities in Delhi, Benares, Andhra, Patiala, and Shantiniketan.

WRITINGS:

Persian Painting, Faber, 1931.
The Golden Breath: Studies in Five Poets of the New India, Dutton, 1933.
The Hindu View of Art, Allen & Unwin, 1933, 2nd edition published as *The Hindu View of Art with an Introductory Essay on Art and Reality by Eric Gill,* Asia Publishing House, 1957, 3rd edition, Arnold Publishers (New Delhi), 1988.
Apology for Heroism: A Brief Autobiography of Ideas, Drummond, 1934, 2nd edition, Kutub-Popular (Bombay), 1947.
Letters on India, Transatlantic, 1942.
"India Speaks" (play), first produced in London at the Unity Theatre, 1943.
Homage to Tagore, Sangam (Lahore, India), 1946.
(With Krishna Hutheesing) *The Bride's Book of Beauty,* Kutub-Popular, 1947, published as *The Book of Indian Beauty,* Tuttle (Tokyo), 1981.
On Education, Hind Kitabs (Bombay), 1947.
The Story of India (juvenile history), Kutub-Popular, 1948.
The King-Emperor's English; or, The Role of the English Language in Free India, Hind Kitabs, 1948.
Lines Written to an Indian Air: Essays, Nalanda (Bombay), 1949.
The Indian Theatre, illustrated by Usha Rani, Dobson, 1950, Roy, 1951.
The Story of Man (juvenile natural history), Sikh (Amritsar, India), 1954.
The Dancing Foot, Publications Division, Indian Ministry of Information & Broadcasting (Delhi), 1957.

Kama Kala: Some Notes on the Philosophical Basis of Hindu Erotic Sculpture, Nagel, 1958, Lyle Stuart, 1962.
(Author of introduction and text) *India in Color,* McGraw, 1958.
(With Stella Kramrisch) *Homage to Khajuraho,* MARG Publications (Bombay), 1960, 2nd edition, 1962.
Is There a Contemporary Indian Civilisation?, Asia Publishing House, 1963.
The Third Eye: A Lecture on the Appreciation of Art, edited by Diwan Chand Sharma, privately printed for the University of Punjab, 1963.
(With Hebbar) *The Singing Line,* Western Printers & Publishers, 1964.
(With others) *Inde, Napal, Ceylan* (French guidebook), Editions Vilo (Paris), 1965.
The Story of Chacha Nehru (juvenile), Rajpal, 1965.
Bombay, MARG Publications, 1965.
Design for Living, MARG Publications, 1967.
The Volcano: Some Comments on the Development of Rabindranath Tagore's Aesthetic Theories and Art Practice, Maharaja Sayajirao University of Baroda, 1967.
The Humanism of M. K. Gandhi, Three Lectures, University of Punjab, 1967.
(With others) *Konorak,* MARG Publications, 1968.
Indian Ivories, MARG Publications, 1970.
(Author of text) *Ajanta,* photographs by R. R. Bhurdwaj, MARG Publications/McGraw, 1971.
Roots and Flowers: Two Lectures on the Metamorphosis of Technique and Content in the Indian-English Novel, Karnatak University (Dharwar), 1972.
Mora, National Book Trust (New Delhi), 1972.
Album of Indian Paintings, National Book Trust, 1973.
Author to Critic: The Letters of Mulk Raj Anand, edited by Saros Cowasjee, Writers Workshop (Calcutta), 1973.
Folk Tales of Punjab, Sterling (New Delhi), 1974.
Lepakshi, MARG Publications, c. 1977.
(With others) *Persian Painting, Fifteenth Century,* Arnold-Heinemann/MARG Publications (India), 1977.
Seven Little-Known Birds of the Inner Eye, Tuttle, 1978.
The Humanism of Jawaharlal Nehru, Visva-Bharati (Calcutta), 1978.
The Humanism of Rabindranath Tagore, Marathwada University (Aurangabad, India), 1979.
Album of Indian Paintings, Auromere, 1979.
Maya of Mohenjo-Daro (juvenile), 3rd edition, Auromere, 1980.
Conversations in Bloomsbury (reminiscences), Arnold-Heinemann, 1981.
Madhubani Painting, Publications Division, Ministry of Information and Broadcasting, 1984.
Ghandhian Thought and Indo-Anglican Novelists, Chanakya Publications (India), 1984.
Poet-Painter: Paintings by Rabindranath Tagore, Abhinav Publications (New Delhi), 1985.
Pilpali Sahab: The Story of a Childhood under the Raj (autobiography), Arnold-Heinemann, 1985.
Aesop's Fables, Apt Books, 1987.

NOVELS

Untouchable, preface by E. M. Forster, Wishart, 1935, Hutchinson, 1947, revised edition, Bodley Head, 1970, reprinted, Penguin, 1989.
The Coolie, Lawrence & Wishart, 1936, Liberty Press, 1952, new revised edition, Bodley Head, 1972.
Two Leaves and a Bud, Lawrence & Wishart, 1937, Liberty Press, 1954, Ind-US, 1979.

Lament on the Death of a Master of Arts, Naya Sansar (Lucknow, India), 1938.

The Village, J. Cape, 1939.

Across the Black Waters, J. Cape, 1940, Ind-US, 1980.

The Sword and the Sickle, J. Cape, 1942, Ind-US, 1984.

The Big Heart, Hutchinson, 1945, Ind-US, 1980.

Seven Summers: The Story of an Indian Childhood (first book of autobiographical septet, "Seven Ages of Man"), Hutchinson, 1951, Ind-US, 1973.

Private Life of an Indian Prince, Hutchinson, 1953, revised edition, Bodley Head, 1970.

The Old Woman and the Cow, Kutub-Popular, 1960, published as *Gauri,* Arnold-Heinemann, 1987.

The Road, Sterling, 1961, reprinted, 1989.

Death of a Hero: Epitaph for Maqbool Sherwani, Kutub-Popular, 1963, reprinted, Arnold-Heinemann, 1988.

Morning Face (second book of autobiographical septet, "Seven Ages of Man"), Kutub-Popular, 1968, Ind-US, 1976.

Confessions of a Lover (third book of autobiographical septet, "Seven Ages of Man"), Arnold-Heinemann, 1984.

The Bubble (fourth book of autobiographical septet, "Seven Ages of Man"), Arnold-Heinemann, 1984.

STORY COLLECTIONS

The Lost Child and Other Stories (also see below), J. A. Allen, 1934.

The Barber's Trade Union and Other Stories (includes the stories from *The Lost Child and Other Stories*), J. Cape, 1944, Ind-US, 1983.

Indian Fairy Tales: Retold, Kutub-Popular, 1946, 2nd edition, 1966.

The Tractor and the Corn Goddess and Other Stories, Thacker (Bombay), 1947, reprinted, Arnold-Heinemann, 1987.

Reflections on the Golden Bed and Other Stories, Current Book House (Bombay), 1954, reprinted, Arnold Publishers, 1984.

The Power of Darkness and Other Stories, Jaico (Bombay), 1959.

More Indian Fairy Tales, Kutub-Popular, 1961.

Lajwanti and Other Stories, Sterling, 1973.

Between Tears and Laughter, Sterling, 1973, Ind-US, 1974.

Selected Short Stories of Mulk Raj Anand, edited by M. K. Naik, Arnold-Heinemann, 1977.

EDITOR

Marx and Engels on India, Socialist Book Club (Allahabad, India), 1933.

(With Iqbal Singh) *Indian Short Stories,* New India (London), 1946.

Ananda Kentish Coomaraswamy, *Introduction to Indian Art,* Theosophical Publishing, 1956.

Annals of Childhood, Kranchalson (Agra, India), 1968.

Experiments: Contemporary Indian Short Stories, Kranchalson, 1968.

Grassroots (short stories), Kranchalson, 1968.

Contemporary World Sculpture, MARG Publications, 1968.

Homage to Jaipur, MARG Publications, 1977.

Homage to Amritsar, MARG Publications, 1977.

Tales from Tolstoy, Arnold-Heinemann, 1978.

Alampur, MARG Publications, 1978.

Homage to Kalamkari, MARG Publications, 1979.

Splendours of Kerala, MARG Publications, 1980.

Golden Goa, MARG Publications, 1980.

Splendours of the Vijayanagara, MARG Publications, 1980.

Treasures of Everyday Art, MARG Publications, 1981.

Maharaja Ranjit Singh as Patron of the Arts, MARG Publications, 1981, Humanities, 1982.

(With Lance Dane) *Kama Sutra of Vatsyayana* (from a translation by Richard Burton and F. F. Arbuthnot), Humanities, 1982.

(With S. Balu Rao) *Panorama: An Anthology of Modern Indian Short Stories,* Sterling, 1986.

(And author of background essay) *The Historic Trial of Mahatma Gandhi,* National Council of Educational Research and Training (New Delhi), 1987.

OTHER

Editor of numerous magazines and journals, 1930—.

WORK IN PROGRESS: The last three books of the septet, "Seven Ages of Man," tentatively titled *And So He Plays His Part, A World Too Wide,* and *Last Scene;* a Tagore lecture on Indian fiction, *A Novel Form in the Ocean of Story,* for Punjab University Publication Bureau; a third edition of *Apology for Heroism: A Brief Autobiography of Ideas,* for Arnold Publishers.

SIDELIGHTS: A champion of the underprivileged classes in India, Mulk Raj Anand attacks religious bigotry and established institutions in his numerous novels and short stories. His basic philosophy mixes humanism and socialism into the concept of "bhakti." Bhakti, explains Margaret Berry in her *Mulk Raj Anand: The Man and the Novelist,* is "the relation of personal, efficacious love between the members of the units of society—family, community, nation, or world. It is the maintenance of loving service which constitutes the 'wholeness' of Anand's ideal man. It is, indeed, . . . a new religion, i.e. a new value system supplanting 'superstitious' personal devotion to God by rational devotion to man."

As the author once told *CA:* "I believe in the only ism possible in our age—humanism. I feel that man can grow into the highest consciousness from insights into the nature of human experience derived through creative art and literature. The piling up of these insights may make a man survive at some level of the quality of life, in our tragic age. I believe in co-existence among human beings and co-discovery of cultures. I believe the world must end the arms race and get five percent disarmament to give resources for building basic plenty throughout the world by the year 2000. I believe, though man has fallen very low at various times in history, he is not so bad that he will not survive on this planet—as long as the earth does not grow cold. I always dream the earth is not flat, but round."

Anand's devotion to socialism and humanism has had a dual effect on his writing. According to Berry, the author's "humanism gives effective formal expression to the dignity of the individual person in the lowest ranks of society, struggling to realize his potential—though in doing so the author often forgets the dignity and the value of persons who are rich." Berry continues by saying Anand's humanism lends more artistry to the value of his works, while his belief in socialism tends to detract from their literary worth. "Anand is technically unable to cope with the dangers of 'writing for a cause,' " asserts Berry, and this results in a certain amount of stereotyping against such people as "Brahmans, schoolteachers, Capitalists, moneylenders, [and] landlords."

However, critics like Krishna Nandan Sinha note that Anand's integration of characterization with situation has improved over the years. In his *Mulk Raj Anand,* Sinha comments that "while the [author's] earlier novels show a sense of horror and disgust against social and economic ills, the novels of the middle period show a greater concern for and with the human heart. It is, however, in the later novels that a healthy synthesis of the social and personal concerns is achieved. Thus, the art of Anand gradually gains much in confidence. . . . While the later novels retain the passion for social justice, they sound greater emotional depths.''

Anand's short stories suffer from problems similar to those in his novels, say several critics. M. K. Naik, for example, points out in his *Mulk Raj Anand* that ''time and again, his compassion for the underdog bowls him over; his indignation at the injustice of traditional practices erupts into hysteria; and he can seldom resist the temptation to squeeze the last tear out of a pathetic situation.'' Nevertheless, Anand's short stories have many strengths as well. ''His range is wider than that of Raja Rao,'' attests Naik, comparing Anand to other Indian authors, ''and his work exhibits a greater variety of mood and tone and a greater complexity than R. K. Narayan's short stories evince.'' *World Literature Today* contributor Shyam M. Asnani adds that ''Anand writes about Indians much as Chekhov writes about Russians, or Sean O'Faolain or Frank O'Connor about the Irish.'' ''In the field of Indian writers of short stories,'' Asnani later concludes, ''he is still matchless.''

For his realistic portrayals of the social and economic problems suffered by Indians at the hands of the British, as well as those of other more affluent and powerful Indians, Anand is accepted by several critics as one of India's best writers. The value of his novels, concludes Berry, ''is the witness they offer of India's agonizing attempt to break out of massive stagnation and create a society in which men and women are free and equal.'' Other virtues of the author's work, according to Berry, include Anand's portrayal ''of the modern educated Indian's struggle to identify with himself and his country'' and Anand's search for ''a principle of unity,'' which the writer considers to be bhakti. Because of these strengths in his writings, critics like Sinha esteem Anand to be ''the most authentic interpreter of responsible human experience *here* and *now*. His vision of the vast human concourse, his serene contemplation of characters and situations, his control of words and sentences, and, above all, his choice between alternatives make him perhaps the foremost and most significant novelist of today's India.''

BIOGRAPHICAL/CRITICAL SOURCES:

BOOKS

Berry, Margaret, *Mulk Raj Anand: The Man and the Novelist,* Oriental Press, 1971.
Contemporary Literary Criticism, Volume 23, Gale, 1983.
Cowasjee, Saros, *So Many Freedoms: A Study of the Major Fiction of Mulk Raj Anand,* Oxford University Press (Delhi), 1977.
Fisher, Marlene, *Wisdom of the Heart,* Sterling, 1980.
Iyengar, K. R. Srinivasa, *Indian Writing in English,* Asia Publishing House, 1962.
Kaul, Premila, *The Novels of Mulk Raj Anand: A Thematic Study,* Sterling, 1983.
Lindsay, Jack, *The Lotus and the Elephant,* Kutub-Popular, 1954.
Naik, M. K., *Mulk Raj Anand,* Arnold-Heinemann, 1973.
Niven, Alastair, *The Yoke of Pity,* Arnold-Heinemann, 1978.
Riemenschneider, D., *The Ideal of Man in Anand's Novels,* Kutub-Popular, 1969.
Sinha, Krishna Nandan, *Mulk Raj Anand,* Twayne, 1972.

PERIODICALS

Contemporary Indian Literature, December, 1965.
Scrutiny, June, 1935.
World Literature Today, summer, 1978.

World Literature Written in English, November, 1975, spring, 1980.

—Sketch by Kevin S. Hile

*   *   *

ANAYA, Rudolfo A(lfonso) 1937-

PERSONAL: Born October 30, 1937, in Pastura, N.M.; son of Martin (a laborer) and Rafaelita (Mares) Anaya; married Patricia Lawless (a counselor), July 21, 1966. *Education:* Attended Browning Business School, 1956-58; University of New Mexico, B.A. (English), 1963, M.A. (English), 1968, M.A. (guidance and counseling), 1972.

ADDRESSES: Home—5324 Canada Vista N.W., Albuquerque, N.M. 87120. *Office*—Department of English, University of New Mexico, Albuquerque, N.M. 87131.

CAREER: Public school teacher in Albuquerque, N.M., 1963-70; University of Albuquerque, Albuquerque, N.M., director of counseling, 1971-73; University of New Mexico, Albuquerque, associate professor, 1974-88, professor of English, 1988—. Teacher, New Mexico Writers Workshop, summers, 1977-79. Lecturer, Universidad Anahuac, Mexico City, Mexico, summer, 1974; lecturer at other universities, including Yale University, University of Michigan, Michigan State University, University of California, Los Angeles, University of Indiana, and University of Texas at Houston. Board member, El Norte Publications/Academia; consultant.

MEMBER: Modern Language Association of America, American Association of University Professors, National Council of Teachers of English, Trinity Forum, Coordinating Council of Literary Magazines (vice president, 1974-80), Rio Grande Writers Association (founder and first president), La Academia Society, La Compania de Teatro de Albuquerque, Multi-Ethnic Literary Association (New York, N.Y.), Before Columbus Foundation (Berkeley, Calif.), Santa Fe Writers Co-op, Sigma Delta Pi (honorary member).

AWARDS, HONORS: Premio Quinto Sol literary award, 1971, for *Bless Me, Ultima;* University of New Mexico Mesa Chicana literary award, 1977; City of Los Angeles award, 1977; New Mexico Governor's Public Service Award, 1978 and 1980; National Chicano Council on Higher Education fellowship, 1978-79; National Endowment for the Arts fellowships, 1979, 1980; Before Columbus American Book Award, Before Columbus Foundation, 1980, for *Tortuga;* New Mexico Governor's Award for Excellence and Achievement in Literature, 1980; literature award, Delta Kappa Gamma (New Mexico chapter), 1981; D.H.L., University of Albuquerque, 1981; Corporation for Public Broadcasting script development award, 1982, for ''Rosa Linda''; Award for Achievement in Chicano Literature, Hispanic Caucus of Teachers of English, 1983; Kellogg Foundation fellowship, 1983-85; D.H.L., Marycrest College, 1984; Mexican Medal of Friendship, Mexican Consulate of Albuquerque, N.M., 1986.

WRITINGS:

Bless Me, Ultima (novel; also see below), Tonatiuh International, 1972.
Heart of Aztlan (novel), Editorial Justa, 1976.
Bilingualism: Promise for Tomorrow (screenplay), Bilingual Educational Services, 1976.
(Editor with Jim Fisher, and contributor) *Voices from the Rio Grande,* Rio Grande Writers Association Press, 1976.

(Contributor) Charlotte I. Lee and Frank Galati, editors, *Oral Interpretations*, 5th edition, Houghton, 1977.

(Contributor) *New Voices 4 in Literature, Language and Composition*, Ginn, 1978.

(Author of introduction) Sabine Ulibarri, *Mi abuela fumaba puros*, Tonatiuh International, 1978.

(Contributor) *Anuario de letras chicanas*, Editorial Justa, 1979.

(Contributor) *Grito del sol*, Quinto Sol Publications, 1979.

Tortuga (novel), Editorial Justa, 1979.

"The Season of La Llorona" (one-act play), first produced in Albuquerque, N.M., at El Teatro de la Compania de Albuquerque, October 14, 1979.

(Translator) *Cuentos: Tales from the Hispanic Southwest, Based on Stories Originally Collected by Juan B. Rael*, edited by Jose Griego y Maestas, Museum of New Mexico Press, 1980.

(Editor with Antonio Marquez) *Cuentos Chicanos: A Short Story Anthology*, University of New Mexico Press, 1980.

(Editor with Simon J. Ortiz) *A Ceremony of Brotherhood, 1680-1980*, Academia Press, 1981.

The Silence of the Llano (short stories), Tonatiuh/Quinto Sol International, 1982.

The Legend of La Llorona (novel), Tonatiuh/Quinto Sol International, 1984.

The Adventures of Juan Chicaspatas (epic poem), Arte Publico, 1985.

A Chicano in China (nonfiction), University of New Mexico Press, 1986.

The Farolitos of Christmas: A New Mexican Christmas Story (juvenile), New Mexico Magazine, 1987.

Lord of the Dawn: The Legend of Quetzacoatl, University of New Mexico Press, 1987.

(Editor) *Voces: An Anthology of Nuevo Mexicano Writers*, University of New Mexico Press, 1987.

"Who Killed Don Jose" (play), first produced in Albuquerque, N.M., at La Compania Menval High School Theatre, July, 1987.

"The Farolitos of Christmas" (play), first produced in Albuquerque, N.M., at La Compania Menval High School Theatre, December, 1987.

Selected from "Bless Me, Ultima," Literary Volumes of New York City, 1989.

(Editor with Francisco Lomeli) *Aztlan: Essays on the Chicano Homeland*, El Norte, 1989.

(Editor) *Tierra: Contemporary Fiction of New Mexico* (short story collection), Cinco Puntos, 1989.

Author of unproduced play "Rosa Linda," for the Corporation for Public Broadcasting; author of unpublished and unproduced dramas for the Visions Project, KCET-TV (Los Angeles). Contributor of short stories, articles, essays, and reviews to periodicals in the United States and abroad, including *La Luz, Bilingual Review-Revista Bilingue, New Mexico Magazine, La Confluencia, Contact II, Before Columbus Review, L'Umano Avventura, 2 Plus 2*, and *Literatura Uchioba;* contributor to *Albuquerque News*. Editor, *Blue Mesa Review;* associate editor, *American Book Review*, 1980-85, and *Escolios;* regional editor, *Viaztlan* and *International Chicano Journal of Arts and Letters;* member of advisory board, *Puerto Del Sol Literary Magazine*. Anaya's manuscript collection is available at the Zimmerman Museum, University of New Mexico, Albuquerque.

SIDELIGHTS: Best known for his first novel, *Bless Me, Ultima,* Rudolfo A. Anaya's writing stems from his New Mexican background and his fascination with the oral tradition of Spanish *cuentos* (stories). The mystical nature of these folk tales has had

a significant influence on his novels, which portray the experiences of Hispanics in the American Southwest. But the novelist's books are also about faith and the loss of faith. As Anaya explains in his *Contemporary Authors Autobiography Series* entry, his education at the University of New Mexico caused him to question his religious beliefs, and this, in turn, led him to write poetry and prose in order to "fill the void." "I lost faith in my God," Anaya writes, "and if there was no God there was no meaning, no secure road to salvation. . . . The depth of loss one feels is linked to one's salvation. That may be why I write. It is easier to ascribe those times and their bittersweet emotions to my characters."

Bless Me, Ultima, "a unique American novel that deserves to be better known," in *Revista Chicano-Riquena* contributor Vernon Lattin's opinion, leans heavily on Anaya's background in folklore in its depiction of the war between the evil Tenorio Trementina and the benevolent *curandera* (healer) Ultima. Several critics, such as *Latin American Literary Review*'s Daniel Testa, have praised Anaya's use of old Spanish-American tales in his book. "What seems to be quite extraordinary," avers Testa, " . . . is the variety of materials in Anaya's work. He intersperses the legendary, folkloric, stylized, or allegorized material with the detailed descriptions that help to create a density of realistic portrayal."

The novel is also a *bildungsroman* about a young boy, named Antonio, who grows up in a small village in New Mexico around the time of World War II. Most of Antonio's maturation is linked with a struggle with his religious faith and his trouble in choosing between the nomadic way of life of his father's family, and the agricultural lifestyle of his mother's. Reviewers of *Bless Me, Ultima* have lauded Anaya for his depiction of these dilemmas in the life of a young Mexican-American. For example, in *Chicano Perspectives in Literature: A Critical and Annotated Bibliography*, authors Francisco A. Lomeli and Donaldo W. Urioste call this work "an unforgettable novel . . . already becoming a classic for its uniqueness in story, narrative technique and structure." And *America* contributor Scott Wood remarks: "Anaya offers a valuable gift to the American scene, a scene which often seems as spiritually barren as some parched plateau in New Mexico."

Anaya's next novel, *Heart of Aztlan*, is a more political work about a family that moves from a rural community to the city; but as with its predecessor, Anaya mixes in some mystical elements along with the book's social concern for the Chicano worker in capitalist America. Reception of this second book has been somewhat less enthusiastic than it was for *Bless Me, Ultima*. Marvin A. Lewis observes in *Revista Chicano-Requena* that "on the surface, the outcome [of *Heart of Aztlan*] is a shallow, romantic, adolescent novel which nearly overshadows the treatment of adult problems. The novel does have redeeming qualities, however, in its treatment of the urban experience and the problems inherent therein, as well as in its attempt to define the mythic dimension of the Chicano experience." Similarly, *World Literature Today* critic Charles R. Larson feels that *Heart of Aztlan*, along with *Bless Me, Ultima*, "provide[s] us with a vivid sense of Chicano Life since World War II."

Tortuga, Anaya's third novel, continues in the mythical vein of the author's other works. The novel concerns a young boy who must undergo therapy for his paralysis and wear a body cast, hence his nickname "Tortuga," which means turtle. "Tortuga," however, also "refers . . . to the 'magic mountain' (with a nod here to Thomas Mann) that towers over the hospital for paralytic children," according to Angelo Restivo in *Fiction International*.

While staying at the Crippled Children and Orphans Hospital, Tortuga becomes more spiritually and psychologically mature, and the novel ends when he returns home after his year-long ordeal. As with the novelist's other books, *Tortuga* is a story about growing up; indeed, *Bless Me, Ultima, Heart of Aztlan,* and *Tortuga* form a loosely-tied trilogy that depicts the Hispanic experience in America over a period of several decades. As the author once told *CA*, these novels "are a definite trilogy in my mind. They are not only about growing up in New Mexico, they are about life."

All of Anaya's novels attempt to find the answers to life's questions, doing so from the perspective of his own personal cultural background. "If we as Chicanos do have a distinctive perspective on life," he tells John David Bruce-Novoa in *Chicano Authors: Inquiry by Interview,* "I believe that perspective will be defined when we challenge the very basic questions which mankind has always asked itself: What is my relationship to the universe, the cosmos? Who am I and why am I here? If there is a Godhead, what is its nature and function? What is the nature of mankind?" These questions echo the doubts that the author has had all his life, and that he links closely to American mythology. Anaya explains to Bruce-Novoa, "All literature, and certainly Chicano literature, reflects, in its more formal aspects, the mythos of the people, and the writings speak to the underlying philosophical assumptions which form the particular world view of culture. . . . In a real sense, the mythologies of the Americas are the only mythologies of all of us, whether we are newly arrived or whether we have been here for centuries. The land and the people force this mythology on us. I gladly accept it; many or most of the American newcomers have resisted it."

BIOGRAPHICAL/CRITICAL SOURCES:

BOOKS

Bruce-Novoa, John David, *Chicano Authors: Inquiry by Interview,* University of Texas Press, 1980.
Contemporary Authors Autobiography Series, Volume 4, Gale, 1986.
Contemporary Literary Criticism, Volume 23, Gale, 1983.
Dictionary of Literary Biography, Volume 82: *Chicano Writers, First Series,* Gale, 1989.
Lomeli, Francisco A. and Donaldo W. Urioste, *Chicano Perspectives in Literature: A Critical and Annotated Bibliography,* Pajarito, 1976.

PERIODICALS

America, January 27, 1973.
American Book Review, March-April, 1979.
Fiction International, Number 12, 1980.
Hispania, September, 1985.
La Luz, May, 1973.
Latin American Literary Review, spring-summer, 1978.
Revista Chicano-Riquena, spring, 1978, summer, 1981.
University of Albuquerque Alumni Magazine, January, 1973.
University of New Mexico Alumni Magazine, January, 1973.
World Literature Today, spring, 1979.

—*Sketch by Kevin S. Hile*

*   *   *

ANDERSCH, Alfred   1914-1980

PERSONAL: Born February 4, 1914, in Munich, Germany; immigrated to Switzerland, 1958; naturalized citizen, 1973; died February 21, 1980, in Berzona, Switzerland; son of Alfred A. and Hedwig (Watzek) Andersch; married Gisela Dichgans (a painter), 1950; children: Michael, Martin, Annette. *Education:* Attended Wittelsbacher Gymnasium, Munich.

ADDRESSES: Home—6611 Berzona, Ticino, Switzerland.

CAREER: Writer of novels, essays, short stories, radio scripts, and travel books. Worked in a Munich publishing house as a young man to learn book trade; because of his involvement in a Communist youth organization, in 1933 he spent six months in the Dachau Concentration Camp; after release worked in industry; following World War II was a newspaper editor, working on *Der Ruf* and later on *Texte und Zeichen;* radio broadcaster, 1948-60; leader of an Arctic expedition for German television, 1965. Co-founder with Heinrich Boell and Guenter Grass of Gruppe 47. *Military service:* Drafted into the German Army, 1940; deserted in 1944 on the Italian Front and became an American prisoner-of-war.

MEMBER: Deutsche Akademie fuer Sprache und Dichtkunst, Bayerische Akademie der Schoenen Kuenste, P.E.N.

AWARDS, HONORS: Deutscher Kritiker-Preis, 1958, for *Sansibar;* Nelly Sachs-Preis, 1968; Prix Charles Veillon, 1968, for *Efraim;* Literaturpris der Bayerisken Academic der Schoeuen Knuste.

WRITINGS:

Deutsche Literatur in der Entscheidung (essays), Volk & Zeit, 1948.
(Editor) *Europaeische Avantgarde* (anthology), Verlag der Frankfurter Hefte, 1949.
Kirschen der Freiheit: Ein Bericht (autobiographical), Frankfurter Verlagsanstalt, 1952.
Piazza San Gaetano: Suite (narrative), Walter-Verlag, 1957.
Sansibar: Oder, der letzte Grund (novel), Walter-Verlag, 1957, translation by Michael Bullock published as *Flight to Afar,* Coward, 1958, edition in German with introduction and notes by Walter G. Hesse, published in England under original title, Harrap, 1964.
Geister und Leute, Walter-Verlag, 1958, translation by Christa Armstrong published as *The Night of the Giraffe and Other Stories,* Random House, 1964.
Fahrerflucht (radio play), Hans Bredow-Institut, 1958, published with three other radio plays under same title, Deutcher Taschenbuch Verlag, 1956.
Die Rote (novel), Walter-Verlag, 1960, translation by Bullock published as *The Redhead,* Pantheon, 1961.
Der Tod des James Dean (radio play; text adapted from John Dos Passos and others), Tschudy, 1960.
Paris ist eine ernste Stadt (narrative), Olten, 1961.
Wanderungen im Norden (travel narrative), illustrated with color pictures by wife, Gisela Andersch, Walter-Verlag, 1962.
Ein Liebhaber des Halbschattens (stories), Walter-Verlag, 1963.
Die Blindheit des Kunstwerks und andere Aufsaetze (essays and other writings), Suhrkamp, 1965.
Bericht, Roman, Erzaehlungen (collection with bibliography of Andersch's works), Walter-Verlag, 1965.
Aus Einem roemischen Winter (travel narrative), Walter-Verlag, 1966.
Efraim (novel), Diogenes Verlag, 1967, translation by Ralph Manheim published as *Efraim's Book,* Doubleday, 1970.
(Contributor) Wolfgang Tschechne, editor, *Geliebte Staedte,* Fackeltraeger-Verlag, 1967.
Ein Auftrag fuer Lord Glouster (collection), Signal-Verlag, 1968.

Hohe Breitengrade (travel narrative on Arctic expedition), Diogenes Verlag, 1968.

Mein Verschwinden in Providence (nine stories), Diogenes Verlag, 1971, translation by Manheim published as *My Disappearance in Providence,* Doubleday, 1978.

Norden, Sueden, rechis and links (essays), Diogenes Verlag, 1972.

Winterspelt, translation by Clara Winston and Richard Winston, Doubleday, 1978, published as *Winterspelt: A Novel about the Last Days of World War II,* Dufour, 1980.

Also author of numerous unpublished radio scripts, including: "Strahlende Melancholie," 1953, "Synnoeves Halsband," 1958, "Von Ratten und Evangelisten," 1960, and "Russisches Roulette," 1961.

MEDIA ADAPTATIONS: Die Rote was made into a film in Germany.

SIDELIGHTS: Until his death in 1980, Alfred Andersch was recognized as one of the most influential spokespersons of his generation. Involved at an earlier age in political causes, Andersch expressed his various opinions, including his early opposition to the Nazi Regime, in various formats. As editor of two respected periodicals, *Der Ruf* and *Texte und Zeichen,* writer of such novels discussing moral responsibilities as *Sansibar; oder, Der letze Grund (Flight to Afar), Mein Verschwinden in Providence (My Disappearance in Providence and Other Stories),* and radio broadcaster, Andersch reached millions of people worldwide.

In *Dictionary of Literary Biography: Contemporary German Fiction Writers, First Series,* Michael Winkler states: "Flight into freedom and withdrawal into the world of artistic creation are dominant themes in all of Andersch's works, and his personal experiences, re-created with intellectual honesty, are the source of inspiration for his fiction." Winkler goes on to write that Andersch "was an accomplished storyteller whose best work shows a subtle ability to capture human frailty and to portray the complicated situations in which think people have to make decisions."

Reviewing Andersch's *Efraim's Book,* Charles Markmann writes in the *Nation:* "It is not always easy to follow, but it is an impressively convincing synthesis of the simultaneous levels of his narrator so that past and present and even future and potential, desired and hated and feared, are elements that in every successful work of art strikes one as inevitable."

Andersch's novels, *Sansibar* and *Die Rote,* are the most widely reprinted of his works.

BIOGRAPHICAL/CRITICAL SOURCES:

BOOKS

Dictionary of Literary Biography, Volume 69: *Contemporary German Fiction Writers, First Series,* Gale, 1988.

PERIODICALS

Nation, December 13, 1971.
New York Times, May 6, 1978, July 4, 1978.

OBITUARIES:

PERIODICALS

New York Times, February 23, 1980.
Times (London), March 10, 1980.

ANDERSON, C. Farley
See MENCKEN, H(enry) L(ouis)

*   *   *

ANDERSON, Poul (William)   1926-
(A. A. Craig, Michael Karageorge, Winston P. Sanders)

PERSONAL: Born November 25, 1926, in Bristol, Pa.; son of Anton William and Astrid (Hertz) Anderson; married Karen J. M. Kruse, December 12, 1953; children: Astrid May. *Education:* University of Minnesota, B.S., 1948.

ADDRESSES: Home—3 Las Palomas, Orinda, Calif. 94563. *Agent*—Scott Meredith Literary Agency, 845 Third Ave., New York, N.Y. 10022.

CAREER: Free-lance writer, except for occasional temporary jobs, 1948—.

MEMBER: Institute for Twenty-First Century Studies, Science Fiction Writers of America (president, 1972-73), American Association for the Advancement of Science, Mystery Writers of America (northern California regional vice chairman, 1959) Scowrers (secretary, 1957-62), Elves, Gnomes, and Little Men's Science Fiction Chowder and Marching Society.

AWARDS, HONORS: First annual Cock Robin Mystery Award, 1959, for *Perish by the Sword;* Guest of Honor, World Science Fiction Convention, 1959; Hugo Award, World Science Fiction Convention, for best short fiction, 1961, for "The Longest Voyage," 1964, for "No Truce with Kings," 1969, for "The Sharing of Flesh," 1972, for "The Queen of Air and Darkness," 1973, for "Goat Song," and 1979, for "Hunter's Moon"; Nebula Award, Science Fiction Writers of America, 1971, for "The Queen of Air and Darkness," and 1972, for "Goat Song"; August Derleth Award, British Fantasy Society, 1974, for *Hrolf Kraki's Saga;* Gandalf Award, Grand Master of Fantasy, World Science Fiction Convention, 1978.

WRITINGS:

SCIENCE FICTION NOVELS

Vault of the Ages, Winston, 1952, reprinted, Avon, 1969.
Brain Wave, Ballantine, 1954, reprinted, Ballantine, 1985.
The Broken Sword, Abelard, 1954, reprinted, Baen Books, 1988.
No World of Their Own (bound with *The 1,000 Year Plan* by Isaac Asimov), Ace Books, 1955, published separately as *The Long Way Home,* Gregg, 1978.
Planet of No Return (also see below), Ace Books, 1956, published as *Question and Answer* (also see below), 1978.
Star Ways, Avalon, 1957, published as *The Peregrine,* Ace Books, 1978.
War of the Wing-Men, Ace Books, 1958, reprinted, 1976, published as *The Man Who Counts,* 1978.
The Snows of Ganymede, Ace Books, 1958.
Virgin Planet, Avalon, 1959.
The Enemy Stars, Lippincott, 1959, reprinted, Baen Books, 1987.
The War of Two Worlds (also see below), Ace Books, 1959, reprinted, Dobson, 1974.
We Claim These Stars! (also see below; bound with *The Planet Killers* by Robert Silverberg), Ace Books, 1959.
Earthman, Go Home! (also see below; bound with *To the Tombaugh Station* by Wilson Tucker), Ace Books, 1960.
The High Crusade, Doubleday, 1960, reprinted, Manor Publishing, 1975.
Twilight World, Torquil, 1960, reprinted, Tor Books, 1983.

Mayday Orbit (also see below; bound with *No Man's World* by Kenneth Bulmer), Ace Books, 1961.

Three Hearts and Three Lions, Doubleday, 1961, reprinted, Berkley Publishing, 1978.

Orbit Unlimited, Pyramid Publications, 1961, reprinted, Panther House, 1976.

The Makeshift Rocket (also see below), Ace Books, 1962.

After Doomsday, Ballantine, 1962, reprinted, Baen Books, 1986.

Shield, Berkley Publishing, 1963.

Let the Spacemen Beware! (bound with *The Wizard of Starship Poseidon* by Kenneth Bulmer), Ace Books, 1963, published separately as *The Night Face* (also see below), 1978.

Three Worlds to Conquer, Pyramid Publications, 1964.

The Star Fox, Doubleday, 1965.

The Corridors of Time, Doubleday, 1965.

Ensign Flandry, Chilton, 1966.

World without Stars (also see below), Ace Books, 1966.

Satan's World, Doubleday, 1969.

The Rebel Worlds, Signet, 1969 (published in England as *Commander Flandry,* Severn House, 1978).

A Circus of Hells, Signet, 1970.

Tau Zero, Doubleday, 1970.

The Byworlder, Signet, 1971.

Operation Chaos, Doubleday, 1971.

The Dancer from Atlantis, Doubleday, 1971.

There Will Be Time, Doubleday, 1972.

Hrolf Kraki's Saga, Ballantine, 1973, reprinted, Baen Books, 1988.

The Day of Their Return, Doubleday, 1973.

The People of the Wind, Signet, 1973.

Fire Time, Doubleday, 1974.

A Knight of Ghosts and Shadows, Doubleday, 1974 (published in England as *Knight Flandry,* Severn House, 1980).

A Midsummer Tempest, Doubleday, 1974.

(With Gordon Ecklund) *Inheritors of Earth,* Chilton, 1974.

The Worlds of Poul Anderson (contains *Planet of No Return, The War of Two Worlds,* and *World without Stars*), Ace Books, 1974.

(With Gordon Dickson) *Star Prince Charlie* (juvenile), Putnam, 1975.

The Winter of the World, Doubleday, 1975.

Mirkheim, Berkley Publishing, 1977.

The Avatar, Putnam, 1978.

Two Worlds (contains *Question and Answer* and *World without Stars*), Gregg, 1978.

The Merman's Children, Putnam, 1979.

A Stone in Heaven, Ace Books, 1979.

The Devil's Game, Pocket Books, 1980.

The Road of the Sea Horse, Zebra Books, 1980.

Conan the Rebel #5, Bantam, 1980.

(With Mildred D. Broxon) *The Demon of Scattery,* Ace Books, 1980.

The Last Viking: Book One, The Golden Horn, Zebra Books, 1980.

The Sign of the Raven, Zebra Books, 1980.

Cold Victory, Pinnacle Books, 1982.

The Gods Laughed, Pinnacle Books, 1982.

Maurai and Kith, Tor Books, 1982.

New America, Pinnacle Books, 1983.

The Long Night, Pinnacle Books, 1983.

Orion Shall Rise, Pocket Books, 1983.

Agent of Vega, Ace Books, 1983.

Conflict, Pinnacle Books, 1983.

Time Patrolman, Pinnacle Books, 1983.

Bat-Twenty-One, Bantam, 1983.

(With Dickson) *Hoka!,* Simon & Schuster, 1983.

(With wife, Karen Anderson) *The Unicorn Trade,* Tor Books, 1984.

Dialogue with Darkness, Tor Books, 1985.

The Game of Empire, Pocket Books, 1985.

The Psychotechnic League, Tor Books, 1985.

(With K. Anderson) *The King of Ys,* Baen Books, Book 1: *Roma Mater,* 1986, Book 2: *Gallicenae,* 1988, Book 3: *Dahut,* 1988, Book 4: *The Dog and the Wolf,* 1988.

The Year of the Ransom, Walker & Co., 1988.

Conan the Rebel #17, Ace Books, c. 1989.

No Truce with Kings (bound with *Ship of Shadows* by Fritz Leiber), Tor Books, 1989.

The Boat of a Million Years, Tor Books, 1989.

SHORT STORY COLLECTIONS

(With Dickson) *Earthman's Burden,* Gnome Press, 1957, reprinted, Avon, 1985.

Guardians of Time, Ballantine, 1960, revised edition, Pinnacle Books, 1981.

Strangers from Earth: Eight Tales of Vaulting Imagination, Ballantine, 1961, reprinted, Baen Books, 1987.

Un-Man and Other Novellas (bound with *The Makeshift Rocket*), Ace Books, 1962.

Trader to the Stars, Doubleday, 1964.

Time and Stars, Doubleday, 1964.

Agent of the Terran Empire (includes *We Claim These Stars!*), Chilton, 1965.

Flandry of Terra (includes *Earthman, Go Home!* and *Mayday Orbit*), Chilton, 1965.

The Trouble Twisters, Doubleday, 1966.

The Horn of Time, Signet, 1968.

Beyond the Beyond, Signet, 1969.

Seven Conquests: An Adventure in Science Fiction, Macmillan, 1969, reprinted, Pocket Books, 1984.

Tales of the Flying Mountains, Macmillan, 1970.

The Queen of Air and Darkness and Other Stories, Signet, 1973.

The Many Worlds of Poul Anderson, Chilton, 1974, published as *The Book of Poul Anderson,* DAW Books, 1975.

Homeward and Beyond, Doubleday, 1975.

Homebrew, National Education Field Service Association Press, 1976.

The Best of Poul Anderson, Pocket Books, 1976.

The Earth Book of Stormgate, Putnam, 1978.

The Night Face and Other Stories (includes *The Night Face*), Gregg, 1978.

The Dark between the Stars, Berkley Publications, 1980.

Explorations, Pinnacle Books, 1981.

Fantasy, Pinnacle Books, 1981.

Winners, Pinnacle Books, 1981.

Starship, Pinnacle Books, 1982.

Past Times, Tor Books, 1984.

OTHER NOVELS

Perish by the Sword, Macmillan, 1959.

Murder in Black Letter, Macmillan, 1960.

The Golden Slave, Avon, 1960, reprinted, Zebra Books, 1980.

Rogue Sword, Avon, 1960, reprinted, Zebra Books, 1980.

Murder Bound, Macmillan, 1962.

NONFICTION

Is There Life on Other Worlds?, Crowell, 1963.

Thermonuclear Warfare, Monarch, 1963.

The Infinite Voyage: Man's Future in Space, Macmillan, 1969.

CONTRIBUTOR

Martin Greenberg, editor, *All about the Future,* Gnome Press, 1955.

The Day the Sun Stood Still: Three Original Novellas of Science Fiction, Thomas Nelson, 1972.

Reginald Bretnor, editor, *Science Fiction: Today and Tomorrow,* Harper, 1974.

Bretnor, editor, *The Craft of Science Fiction,* Harper, 1976.

Damon Knight, editor, *Turning Points: Essays on the Art of Science Fiction,* Harper, 1977.

Andrew J. Offutt, editor, *Swords against Darkness,* Zebra Books, Volume 1, 1977, Volume 3, 1978, Volume 4, 1979.

L. Sprague de Camp, editor, *The Blade of Conan,* Ace Books, 1979.

Space Wars (short stories), edited by Charles Waugh and Martin H. Greenberg, Tor Books, 1988.

OTHER

(Adaptor) Christian Molbech, *The Fox, the Dog, and the Griffin,* Doubleday, 1966.

(Author of introduction) *The Best of L. Sprague de Camp,* Ballantine, 1978.

Time Wars (short stories), Tor Books, 1986.

Space Folk (short stories), Baen Books, 1989.

Work appears in numerous anthologies, including: *Possible Worlds of Science Fiction,* edited by Groff Conklin, Vanguard, 1951; *A Treasury of Great Science Fiction,* edited by Anthony Boucher, Doubleday, 1959; *The Hugo Winners,* edited by Isaac Asimov, Doubleday, 1962; *Space, Time, and Crime,* edited by Miriam Allen de Ford, Paperback Library, 1964; *Masters of Science Fiction,* Belmont Books, 1964; *The Science Fiction Hall of Fame,* edited by Ben Bova, Doubleday, 1973; *The Future at War,* edited by Bretnor, Ace Books, 1979. Contributor of short stories, some under pseudonyms A. A. Craig and Winston P. Sanders, to *Magazine of Fantasy and Science Fiction, Galaxy, Analog Science Fiction/Science Fact, Isaac Asimov's Science Fiction Magazine,* and other publications.

SIDELIGHTS: Although he is often referred to as a writer of "hard" science fiction—science fiction with a scrupulously accurate scientific basis—Poul Anderson is also known for his creation of plausible fantasy worlds, often based on Nordic mythology. His "recognition of the inevitability of sorrow and death and of the limitations of human powers (but not human spirit) in the face of the immense inhumanity of the universe," Russell Letson of the *Science Fiction and Fantasy Book Review* believes, "lifts Anderson's fiction above its flaws." "It is increasingly clear," writes Michael W. McClintock in the *Dictionary of Literary Biography,* "that [Anderson] is one of the five or six most important writers to appear during the science-fiction publishing boom of the decade following the end of World War II."

The novel *Tau Zero* is one of Anderson's best works of hard science fiction. It presents a simple scientific possibility—a space ship uncontrollably accelerating at a steady one gravity—and develops the consequences in a relentlessly logical and scientifically plausible manner. Sandra Miesel, writing in her *Against Time's Arrow: The High Crusade of Poul Anderson,* finds the novel's structure a key to its effectiveness. "To convey the numbing immensities of the time and distance traversed [during the novel]," Miesel writes, "Anderson begins slowly, letting a few hours elapse at the normal rate in the first chapter. Thereafter, the tempo quickens at an exponential rate until eons fleet by in heartbeats and the reader unquestioningly accepts all the marvels described." James Blish calls *Tau Zero* "the ultimate 'hard' science

fiction novel." Blish goes on, in his review of the book for the *Magazine of Fantasy and Science Fiction,* to say that "everybody else who has been trying to write this kind of thing can now fold up his tent and creep silently away. . . . Overall, [*Tau Zero*] is a monument to what a born novelist and poet can do with authentic scientific materials. And as is usual with recent Anderson, the poet is as important as the novelist."

Anderson's scientific accuracy is reflected in the carefully constructed backgrounds he creates for his stories. He has set about fifty of his science fiction novels and short stories in a consistent "future history" of his own devising. This history concerns the exploration of outer space by the *Technic Civilization,* and each story explores a different event within this history. Although other science fiction writers have also used the future history idea, McClintock believes Anderson "has utilized it more extensively—and arguably to better advantage—than any other writer."

In his fantasy works, too, Anderson constructs imaginary worlds that are logical and coherent. These worlds are often based on Nordic sagas or contain elements from Nordic history. His prize-winning story "The Queen of Air and Darkness" is set in an arctic wilderness that is, Miesel states, "a scientifically plausible Elfland." In *Operation Chaos,* Miesel notes, magic is "a perfectly rational, orderly activity." The novel *The Merman's Children* is based on a medieval Danish ballad about the decline of the world of Faerie. Set in Denmark in the Middle Ages, the novel tells of the struggle between the mermen and the Christian church. The conflict arises because the mermen, an older and less developed species, do not possess souls. "One might guess the book," writes Gerald Jonas in the *New York Times Book Review,* "to be either a fantasy or a 'historical' novel. Yet Poul Anderson . . . has produced a genuine hybrid." Anderson, McClintock states, "is consistent and logical in constructing backgrounds." Anderson's "sensibility is mythic," McClintock further states, "and strongly influenced by the Nordic Edda and sagas that are part of his heritage. . . . At his best, Anderson evokes responses, not unlike those appropriate to *Beowulf* or the *Volsungasaga.*"

Over the years, Anderson has dealt with "overpopulation, conflict between cultures, man's biological imperatives, and depleted natural resources," writes Michael Pottow in the *Science Fiction and Fantasy Book Review,* "but in the final analysis each of the stories is about people." A recurring theme in his work is the importance of individual liberty and free will. Anderson admits to Jeffey M. Elliot in *Science Fiction Voices #2:* "If I preach at all, it's probably in the direction of individual liberty, which is a theme that looms large in my work." Miesel sees Anderson as primarily concerned with the question, "How should mortal man in a finite universe *act?* Rejecting passivity, [Anderson] asserts that free action is both possible and necessary. . . . Mortals must resist entropy in both its guises, tyrannical stasis or anarchic chaos. The fight is all the more valiant for its utter hopelessness."

Because of his emphasis on liberty, Anderson has gained a reputation in science-fiction circles "as being fairly far to the right," Charles Platt states in *Dream Makers, Volume 2: The Uncommon Men and Woman Who Write Science Fiction,* "and has been called a reactionary." When asked about this, Anderson told Platt to "just look at what I'm reacting against. . . . If I had to call myself something, it would be either a conservative libertarian or a libertarian conservative. . . . Basically, I feel that the concepts of liberty that were expressed . . . by people like the Founding Fathers were actually the radically bold concepts from which people have been retreating ever since. And I don't believe that it's necessarily reactionary to say so."

When asked to comment on the role of science fiction in relation to other types of literature, Anderson told *CA:* "I have written quite a lot of it, and am proud to have done so, because science fiction is and always has been part of literature. Its long isolation, strictly a twentieth-century phenomenon, is ending; its special concepts and techniques are becoming common property, employed not only by the mass media but by some of our most respected writers; in turn, it is shedding artistic parochialism and thus starting to communicate beyond a small circle of enthusiasts. This is good, because the particular concerns of science fiction never have been parochial; they have included, or tried to include, all of space, time, and fate. Not that I wish to make exaggerated claims. I merely set forth that science fiction is one human accomplishment, among countless others, which has something to offer the world. Lest even this sound too pompous let me say that at the very least it is often a lot of fun."

BIOGRAPHICAL/CRITICAL SOURCES:

BOOKS

Contemporary Authors Autobiography Series, Volume 2, Gale, 1985.
Contemporary Literary Criticism, Volume 15, Gale, 1980.
Dictionary of Literary Biography, Volume 8: *Twentieth-Century American Science-Fiction Writers,* Gale, 1981.
Elliot, Jeffrey M., *Science Fiction Voices #2,* Borgo, 1979.
Miesel, Sandra, *Against Time's Arrow: The High Crusade of Poul Anderson,* Borgo, 1978.
Peyton, Roger C., *A Checklist of Poul Anderson,* privately printed, 1965.
Platt, Charles, *Dream Makers, Volume 2: The Uncommon Men and Women Who Write Science Fiction,* Berkley Publishing, 1983.
Stever, David, and Andrew Adams Whyte, *The Collector's Poul Anderson,* privately printed, 1976.
Walker, Paul, *Speaking of Science Fiction: The Paul Walker Interviews,* Luna Publications, 1978.

PERIODICALS

Algol, summer-fall, 1978.
Books and Bookmen, August, 1972.
Globe and Mail (Toronto), November 18, 1989.
Luna Monthly, June, 1972.
Magazine of Fantasy and Science Fiction, March, 1971, December, 1971.
National Review, January 2, 1964.
New York Times Book Review, October 28, 1979.
Science Fiction and Fantasy Book Review, April, 1982.
Science Fiction Review, May, 1978.
Washington Post Book World, February 24, 1980, May 29, 1983.

*   *   *

ANDERSON, Sherwood   1876-1941

PERSONAL: Born September 13, 1876, in Camden, Ohio; died of peritonitis, March 8, 1941, in Cristobal (one source says Colon), Panama Canal Zone; son of Irwin M. (a harnessmaker) and Emma (Smith) Anderson; married Cornelia Lane, 1904 (divorced, 1916); married Tennessee Mitchell, 1916 (divorced, 1924); married Elizabeth Prall, 1924 (divorced, 1932); married Eleanor Copenhaver, 1933; children: two sons, one daughter. *Education:* Attended Wittenberg Academy, 1899.

CAREER: Writer. Worked as copywriter for advertising firm in Chicago, Ill., 1900; president of United Factories Co., in Cleveland, Ohio, 1906, and of Anderson Manufacturing Co., in Elyria, Ohio, 1907-12; advertising copywriter in Chicago, 1913; editor of two newspapers in Marion, Va., 1927-29; lecturer. *Military service:* U.S. Army, 1899; served in Cuba.

AWARDS, HONORS: Prize from *Dial,* 1921.

WRITINGS:

Windy McPherson's Son (novel), John Lane, 1916, revised edition, B. W. Huebsch, 1922, reprinted, University of Chicago Press, 1965.
Marching Men (novel), John Lane, 1917, reprinted as *Marching Men: A Critical Text,* edited by Ray Lewis White, Press of Case Western Reserve University, 1972.
Mid-American Chants (poems), John Lane, 1918, reprinted, Frontier Press, 1972.
Winesburg, Ohio: A Group of Tales of Ohio Small Town Life, B. W. Huebsch, 1919, New American Library, 1956, reprinted with introduction by Malcolm Cowley, Viking, 1960, reprinted as *Winesburg, Ohio: Text and Criticism,* edited by John G. Ferres, Viking, 1966.
Poor White (novel), B. W. Huebsch, 1920, reprinted with an introduction by Walter B. Rideout, Viking, 1966.
The Triumph of the Egg: A Book of Impressions From American Life in Tales and Poems, B. W. Huebsch, 1921, new edition with an introduction by Herbert Gold, Four Walls Eight Windows, 1988.
Many Marriages (novel), B. W. Huebsch, 1923, reprinted as *Many Marriages: A Critical Edition,* edited by Douglas G. Rogers, Scarecrow, 1978.
Horses and Men: Tales, Long and Short, B. W. Huebsch, 1923.
A Story-Teller's Story: The Tale of an American Writer's Journey Through His Own Imaginative World and Through the World of Facts, With Many of His Experiences and Impressions Among Other Writers—Told in Many Notes—in Four Books and an Epilogue, B. W. Huebsch, 1924, reprinted as *A Story Teller's Story: A Critical Text,* edited by White, Press of Case Western Reserve University, 1968, revised edition with preface by Rideout, Viking, 1969, recent edition published as *A Story-Teller's Story,* Penguin, 1989.
Dark Laughter (novel), Boni & Liveright, 1925, reprinted with introduction by Howard Mumford Jones, Liveright, 1925.
Hands and Other Stories (selections from *Winesburg, Ohio;* also see above), Haldeman-Julius, 1925.
The Modern Writer (nonfiction), Lantern Press, 1925, reprinted, Folcroft, 1976.
Sherwood Anderson's Notebook: Containing Articles Written During the Author's Life as a Story Teller, and Notes of His Impressions From Life Scattered Through the Book, Boni & Liveright, 1926, reprinted, P. P. Appel, 1970.
Tar: A Midwest Childhood (semi-autobiography), Boni & Liveright, 1926, reprinted as *Tar: A Midwest Childhood; A Critical Text,* edited by White, Press of Case Western Reserve University, 1969.
A New Testament (prose poems), Boni & Liveright, 1927.
Alice [and] *The Lost Novel,* E. Mathews & Marrot, 1929, reprinted, Folcroft, 1973.
Hello Towns! (collection of newspaper articles), Liveright, 1929, reprinted, Dynamic Learning, 1980.
Nearer the Grass Roots [and] *An Account of a Journey, Elizabethton* (essays), Westgate Press, 1929, reprinted, Folcroft, 1976.
Perhaps Women (essays), Liveright, 1931, reprinted, P. P. Appel, 1970.

Beyond Desire (novel), Liveright, 1932, reprinted with introduction by Rideout, Liveright, 1961.

Death in the Woods and Other Stories, Liveright, 1933, recent edition, 1986.

No Swank (articles), Centaur Press, 1934, reprinted, Appel, 1970.

Puzzled America (articles), Scribner, 1935.

Kit Brandon (novel), Scribner, 1936.

Plays: Winesburg and Others (includes "Jaspar Deeter, a Dedication," "Winesburg," "The Triumph of the Egg," "Mother," and "They Married Later"), Scribner, 1937.

Home Town (nonfiction), Alliance Book Corp., 1940, reprinted, P. P. Appel, 1975.

Sherwood Anderson's Memoirs, Harcourt, 1942, reprinted as *Sherwood Anderson's Memoirs: A Critical Edition,* edited by White, University of North Carolina Press, 1969.

The Sherwood Anderson Reader, edited by Paul Rosenfeld, Houghton, 1947.

The Portable Sherwood Anderson, edited by Horace Gregory, Viking, 1949, Penguin, 1970.

Letters of Sherwood Anderson, edited by Rideout and Howard Mumford Jones, Little, Brown, 1953.

The Short Stories of Sherwood Anderson, edited by Maxwell Geismar, Hill & Wang, 1962.

Return to Winesburg: Selections From Four Years of Writing for a Country Newspaper, edited by White, University of North Carolina Press, 1967.

Buck Fever Papers (articles), edited by D. Welford Taylor, University Press of Virginia, 1971.

Sherwood Anderson: Selected Letters, edited by Charles E. Modlin, University of Tennessee Press, 1984.

Work represented in anthologies. Contributor to periodicals, including *Harper's.*

SIDELIGHTS: While Sherwood Anderson did his best creative work in prose fiction, he created not only a distinctive, repetitive persona in his stories but also a public role. Giving impetus both to his fiction and to his life was a profound autobiographical need expressed in the lyrical nature of his fiction and in the creation of the public myth as well as in three major autobiographical works *A Story-Teller's Story, Tar: A Midwest Childhood,* and his *Memoirs.* Anderson's contributions to twentieth-century American letters are both defined and circumscribed by this need to express his intense personal vision.

Anderson's critical reputation has been a subject of much debate. However, in at least three areas his literary impact has been considerable. First, he was very active in helping other writers. For example, writer Ernest Hemingway carried Anderson's letter of introduction with him to writer Gertrude Stein's influential salon in Paris, and clearly such stories as Hemingway's "My Old Man" suggest how Hemingway found inspiration in Anderson's racetrack stories. More candid in acknowledging Anderson's influence was Nobel laureate writer William Faulkner, who in 1950 recalled how Anderson helped him publish his first novel, *Soldier's Pay* (1926), and provided an attractive example of a writer's lifestyle when they spent time together in the New Orleans French Quarter. In a statement made before he quarreled with Anderson, writer Thomas Wolfe declared that Anderson was the only man in America who taught him anything; the pervasiveness of the "aloneness" theme in the fictions of both writers is apparent to even the most casual reader. While these instances suggest Anderson's roles in the careers of our foremost novelists, they are but a few of the many instances of how, in literally thousands of letters, lectures, and essays, Anderson promoted the craft.

Another, more elusive aspect of Anderson's influence is found in the development of the short story form. Many studies of modern story theory and short story anthologies allude to his technique in and his pronouncements about fictive form. While Anderson's statements about his art do not add up to a clear, conscious sense of design, they are consistent and can be characterized as "expressive"—focusing on the writer in his art of creation, not on the fidelity of his imitation or the response of the audience. His notion of form is central to his aesthetics; and form for him was subjective and organic, as he stressed in a letter to a friend: "You see, Pearson, I have the belief that, in this matter of form, it is largely a matter of depth of feeling. How deeply do you feel it? Feel it deeply enough and you will be torn inside and driven on until form comes." Such an approach to artistic form can be more vulnerable to failure than is an aesthetic that is self-conscious and dependent on willed techniques. Certainly Anderson experienced many periods when form did not come—or came imperfectly—while he seemed powerless to change the imperfections.

Two important ramifications of his aesthetic stance are his views of plot and characterization. He bitterly attacked the stories of O. Henry and others for their "poison plots"—stories that sacrificed characterization and fidelity to life for the sake of a striking turn of events. In an almost perverse way Anderson expected a writer to have utter loyalty to the characters in his imagination. His typical stories, then—both unique and typically modern in eschewing strict plots—offered a compelling model for other writers.

Most importantly, Anderson was the creator of some of the finest American stories. *Winesburg, Ohio* (1919), his masterpiece, remains a durable classic, and half a dozen or more individual stories, such as "The Egg," "I Want to Know Why," "The Man Who Became a Woman," and "Death in the Woods," are among the finest products of the American short story tradition. *Winesburg, Ohio* is a hybrid form, unified by setting, theme, and character; but clearly the stories are also discreet and are further evidence that Anderson's genius lay in the short form. He wrote seven novels, but not one is completely satisfactory, as his invention flagged in creating the larger structures. Some of Anderson's best writing appears in the mixed genres such as *A Story-Teller's Story* (1924) and his *Memoirs* (1942), but certainly his lasting achievement is in his short fiction.

Because of the nature of Anderson's art, as outlined above, some survey of his life is of more than usual concern in assessing his literary achievement. The outline is familiar to most Anderson scholars: early boyhood in Ohio, mainly Clyde, Ohio; his "conventional" period when he became a businessman, husband to a better-educated, more sophisticated woman, and when he became father of three children; the break from commercial life into the greatest period of his artistic development and achievement—the decade after 1912; most of the 1920's when, despite a few exceptions and interludes of professional contentment, he struggled to maintain the level of earlier achievement; and a final period until his death in 1941, when from a base in southwestern Virginia, his writing turned increasingly toward social commentary, and he appeared to reach a state of relative equanimity, content in his fourth marriage and in the role as elder statesman in the writing community.

The richest lode of material for Anderson's best fiction was comprised of his experiences growing up in the Ohio small towns. While many of the characters in *Winesburg, Ohio* were based on people he met in an apartment house in Chicago, the fictional Winesburg is essentially Clyde, Ohio, in the 1890's. Critic Walter

Rideout has shown how fully Anderson evokes the Clyde setting. Like the book's protagonist, George Willard, Anderson left his hometown after his mother's death in 1895 broke up the family, and both were budding writers. Furthermore, Tom and Elizabeth Willard are important creations in a long series of veiled portraits of and responses to Anderson's own parents. The trajectory of his coming to terms with his father's life can be traced from his first novel, *Windy McPherson's Son* (1916), through *Winesburg, Ohio* to a kind of acceptance in *A Story-Teller's Story*. His deepest feelings about his mother impel the characterizations of many of his women; but especially noteworthy are Elizabeth Willard, who figures so prominently in *Winesburg,* and, in a kind of apotheosis, the old woman in "Death in the Woods," one of his finest stories.

Anderson, like George Willard, was perhaps an incipient artist when he left his hometown, but the creative fires were banked while he pursued the American dream of business success. After short tenures as a Chicago laborer, as a soldier in the Spanish American War, and as a student at Wittenberg Academy, he began working for a Chicago advertising firm in sales and copywriting. He did similar work in Cleveland, Ohio, and Elyria, Ohio; but despite his apparent success and growing family responsibilities—children born in 1917, 1908, and 1911—Anderson had begun to write fiction and to feel the warring claims of artistic creation and business values. Finally Anderson left the Anderson Manufacturing Company in November, 1912, as he said, in the middle of dictating a letter. He was found a few days later in a Cleveland hospital and did return briefly to the business world, but that day proved to be the great watershed of his career. When Anderson wrote of the urban settings, the business world, and businessmen in his fiction, it was usually to satirize corrupting materialism.

It was fortuitous that the Chicago to which Anderson returned provided an exciting milieu for writers—the so-called Chicago Renaissance. He met and was encouraged by such men and women as Floyd Dell, Margery Currey, Margaret Anderson, Ben Hecht, Carl Sandburg, Burton Rascoe, Lewis Galantiere, Harry Hansen, Ferdinand Schevill, and Robert Moss Lovett. He heard discourses on socialism, on the pioneering psychoanalytic theories of Sigmund Freud, and on writers such as Fedor Dostoevsky, August Strindberg, Gertrude Stein, and James Joyce. And he began playing the bohemian role not only in appearance, but also in his second, "modern" marriage to Tennessee Mitchell. More importantly, he sounded the thematic notes of his writing career and discovered the distinctive voice of his best writing.

As critic Irving Howe has noted, Anderson continued to be under great pressure, not only the pressure of guilt for failing to meet family responsibilities but also that of his sense of inadequacy. In 1919, the year that *Winesburg, Ohio* appeared, he was a forty-three-year old, ill-educated ex-salesman. But it was exhilarating to try to catch up. His first published story appeared in *Harper's,* in July, 1914; and two of the novels he had been working on in Elyria were published soon after: *Windy McPherson's Son* in 1916 and *Marching Men* in 1917.

Windy McPherson's Son foreshadows the materials and themes of later, better works. Sam McPherson, the novel's title character, rises from humble, small-town beginnings to become a business executive and to marry the boss's daughter. But in an act that recurs in Anderson's fiction and career, Sam rejects the business world to find happiness in love rather than money. Simplistic, didactic, and very awkwardly written, this first novel did not augur well for future novels. Nor is *Marching Men* a successful novel, for in addition to the book's wooden dialogue and gen-

erally inept construction and style, Anderson's notion of a marching men movement, whether suggestive of fascism or not, is a simplistic, irresponsible response to the complex problems of a materialistic world. These earlier works did little to prepare readers for the immense leap in artistic quality represented by *Winesburg, Ohio* published in 1919.

As critic William Phillips demonstrated, *Winesburg* was written in a burst of concentrated creation in 1915 and 1916. A number of the individual stories appeared in periodicals before 1919. But, perhaps taking a clue from Edgar Lee Masters's *Spoon River Anthology,* a collection of poetic vignettes, Anderson probably discovered in his Winesburg stories a firmer unity as the project developed, and rounded off the collection with the unifying plotting of the final three stories.

Winesburg is not a novel; what unity it has is often tenuous. However, the book is tied together by four important elements: the common setting, the episodic story of George Willard's development, the "aloneness" theme, and the tone. All of the stories take place in or around a small rural Ohio community in the last decade of the nineteenth century. The community of about eighteen hundred inhabitants depends on the fertile cabbage and strawberry fields of nearby farms and boasts a train depot, a hotel, fairgrounds, and a prominent Presbyterian church. But, significantly, much is missing—the stories present very little dramatization of community life or even family life; much of the action takes place at night or at least in shadowy and private surroundings; and the characters themselves are hardly typical.

George Willard appears first in "Hands," and after the death of his mother and the climactic experiences of "Sophistication," he leaves Winesburg. In his eighteen years he has learned something about women in a progression from the first furtive experience in "Nobody Knows" through the rueful lesson of "An Awakening" to tentative sophistication in the story with that title. The young *Winesburg Eagle* reporter is also the auditor of the secret stories of many of the grotesques. His teacher, Kate Swift, most directly encourages him as a writer; but others not only pour out to George their most intimate truths in therapeutic release but also want him to perpetuate their truths. Dr. Parcival, for example, wants everyone to know that all men are Christ in that their love is rejected and they are crucified. One of the most important lessons George learns is that of silence, for, alter the prodigality of his expression in, for example, "An Awakening," George seems to have learned Kate Swift's lesson, as he walks "in dignified silence" with Helen White on the fair grounds. Except that the omniscient narrator and George share virtually the same Andersonian sensibility, no trace of George emerges in a number of stories; but his development is a thread seen frequently in the *Wineburg* fabric.

A third unifying motif is the aloneness theme, a main element in the "grotesque" concept. The title of the first story written, "The Book of the Grotesque," was also a title Anderson considered for the whole book. The implication is that *Winesburg* would be a collection of brief biographical sketches of people, many of whom are grotesque. The complete titles in the table of contents suggest the approach, as for example, "Hands"—concerning Wing Biddlebaum."

Anderson's concept of the grotesque, set forth in only a limited way in "The Book of the Grotesque," has been variously interpreted by such important scholars as Irving Howe, Malcolm Cowley, Edwin Fussell, and David Anderson, but among the most searching analyses is Ralph Ciancio's. Ciancio concluded that to Anderson grotesqueness "was nothing more than a metaphor of the natural condition of man, of his being at cross-purposes with himself, of his compulsive hearkening to the infinite call of transcendence which his finitude makes impassible from the start." Some of the grotesques are, indeed, horrible; but the largest group are motivated by genuine human emotions. Included in this group of *Winesburg* characters are Wash Williams, who seeks love beyond the physical, Curtis Hartman, who strives to reconcile his religion with his erotic feelings, and Elmer Cowley, who wants to belong. Grotesqueness can thus be seen as an imbalance—not that the thrust of an individual's fanaticism is intrinsically wrong but rather that any single note sounded exclusively repels the auditor. In describing what he perceives to be common to all of the "grotesques," Malcolm Cowley stresses their inability to communicate. This view plausibly accounts for typical behavior in Winesburg, however, as the above remarks suggest, chronic, crippling failures in communication may merely be symptomatic of the ineffable aloneness dramatized hyperbolically in these twisted beings. Whatever the case, the fairgrounds scene in "Sophistication" is climactic not only in George's development, but also in suggesting that only through others can we mitigate the "sadness of sophistication," consciousness of our cosmic limitations and aloneness.

Finally, complementing and sustaining *Winesburg*'s theme is its tone. The omniscient narrator-seemingly fumbling along, arranging ill-fitting blocks of information, and complaining of his lack of art—provides a sympathetic continuo for the sad tales. This unity of feeling in the book Howe called "the accents of love."

The advance in the simplicity, directness, and evocative power of the language in *Winesburg* over the earlier work is remarkable. Gertrude Stein's stylistic experiments, as in *Tender Buttons* (1914), are often cited as a major influence on Anderson's style. In his *Memoirs* Anderson credited her example for making him conscious of his own vocabulary and how he might convey emotions through "a kind of word color, a march of simple words, simple sentence structures. The style of *Winesburg* became a staple of his best work. When he experimented with a very loose, impressionistic style in the twenties, the result compounded the blurred thinking that weakened too much of his later storytelling.

As critic Rex Burbank suggested in *Sherwood Anderson,* the stories of the hero and the heroine in *Poor White* (1920) are juxtaposed awkwardly, and too often the narrative loses effect by relying on assertion instead of dramatization. Nevertheless, *Poor White* is probably Anderson's best novel. The idea of industrialization's impact on a small midwestern town sustains the novel when the narrative falters. Hugh McVey, one of the novel's main characters, progresses from innocence, to naive inventor in Bidwell, Ohio, to the realization that the new industrial society to which he contributes distorts community values, to a final, more fulfilling aesthetic and humane view of life. This progress is a more searching and cogent dramatization than those appearing in Anderson's first two novels. Unfortunately, the novel's parallel story of Clara Butterworth is awkwardly juxtaposed with Hugh's tale of development.

Poor White reflects both the influence of American writer Mark Twain and Anderson's lifelong critique of the values of the industrial society. His affinity for Twain and Twain's fiction is explained in part by Anderson's projection of his own sense of his career into the career of the older writer. For Anderson, both Twain and U.S. president Abraham Lincoln were midwestern primitives whose innocence and integrity clashed with the intellectually more complex and morally more ambiguous eastern culture. The very first sentence of *Poor White* conjures up the set-

ting of Twain's classic *Huckleberry Finn,* and the early characterization of Hugh suggests the character and situation of Twain's protagonist Huck.

In *Winesburg* the "Godliness" sequence provides the context of the impact of the post-Civil War industrialism on villages such as Winesburg, but most of Anderson's best work in fiction, including *Winesburg,* is more concerned with the personal and the psychological, rather than the socio-economic issues. However, in *Poor White* the battle is engaged against the dehumanizing machine age that later in Anderson's career would command much more of his attention.

Anderson's major single work was published in 1919, and his arguably best novel in 1920. While he wrote a number of good stories during the remainder of his career, the publication of the two story collections *The Triumph of the Egg* (1921) and *Horses and Men* (1923) marked the close of his major creative period. "Death in the Woods," a story that Anderson did not publish until 1926, was created from a fragmentary version he had written on the back of the *Winesburg* manuscript possibly before the publication of *Winesburg* and it epitomizes the best of his narrative art.

The narrative point of view is one of the most distinctive features of Anderson's stories and is especially salient in "Death in the Woods." *Winesburg, Ohio* and *Poor White* are narrated in the third person. The speaking voice in each of these works is unique. For example, the speaker in *Winesburg* is a groping, seemingly artless storyteller outside the story action, who constantly invites attention to how he is crafting the story—"it needs a poet there"; "It will, however, be necessary to talk a little of young Hal so that you will get into the spirit of it." In contrast, the first-person, frustrated speaker in "I'm a Fool" is the chief character in this tale of poignant social failure. However, there is a sense in most of Anderson's stories of an oral tradition, a convention that presumes a sympathetic audience and invites the reader to share in the epistemological search for the essence of a particular character.

What needs to be underscored in "Death in the Woods" is that the narrator is not an adolescent like the youths in "I'm a Fool" and "I Want to Know Why," but a mature person who is recalling not only a striking event of his youth but also subsequent experiences that modify his understanding of the event. The story contains a double theme: the significance of the old woman's complete life *and* the nature of the artistic process.

Like the *Winesburg* stories, "Death in the Woods" is not conventionally plotted. It is fabricated of a number of related episodes, of which the chief is the course of an old woman's winter day. The woman, Ma Grimes, walks to town to trade a few eggs for "some salt pork, a little sugar, and some coffee perhaps" and liver and meat bones. Trudging home through the heavy snow, she decides to take a short cut through the woods, and there in a clearing she sits down to rest and freezes to death. The dogs which have accompanied her seize the grain bag tied to her back and drag her body into the center of the clearing. A hunter finds the body, its dress torn off, and returns to inform the town. The crowd that returns to the clearing includes the young narrator upon whose consciousness the sight of the frozen, naked woman in the middle of that scene—the men, the tracks made by the circling dogs, the white fragments of clouds above—is impressed indelibly. As he says, the scene was the "foundation for the real story I am now trying to tell." It is the epiphany, like many of those illuminated moments in *Winesburg*—such as Alice Hindman running naked in the rain, Wash Williams attacking his mother-in-law, Ray Pearson running in the fields—moments that epitomize the character because the context of the character's life has informed the epiphany.

At one level "Death in the Woods" is about Ma Grimes, whose life is so wholly concentrated on feeding animal life that it takes on mythic dimensions. Throughout her joyless life she is preyed upon, by the farmer in whose home she is a hound girl and then by her vicious husband, children, and dogs, all of whom exploit her remorselessly. She is, to a degree, grotesque; but, reinforced by the repetitive, ritualistic language of the story, the reader is led to perceive her as an earth mother, an incarnate principle of that which feeds carnal need. In unpublished statements Anderson expressed his intent to stress her fundamental role in the community. Indirectly, through the orchestration of the narrator, the reader shares the narrator's respect and awe before the absolute purity and even beauty of her unified life.

But the other important character is the narrator himself, who is a variation of the character type who appears most frequently in Anderson's fiction: the artistic man. To be sure, as William Scheick has emphasized, an element of sexual guilt or at least sexual ambivalence exists in the narrator's make up—this, too, is a familiar motif in many of Anderson's stories that may contribute to his anxiety. However, at a level that respects the full data of the story, the source of the narrator's frustration is, more plausibly, his struggle for artistic expression. He is driven to tell the story. He has collected all of the experiences—the epiphany scene, gossipy stories about Ma Grimes, and even more oblique experiences such as the time when he saw dogs running in the circle—and he seeks to bring them all to artistic form. What he and the story say about the significance of Ma Grimes's life is a truth, "music heard from far off"; but both the "mystery of life" and artistic perfection lie beyond human grasp.

A few stories, including "Death in the Woods" and *Winesburg, Ohio,* then, created during the decade after he left his Elyria paint business, appear to be Anderson's most durable achievements; but he would go on to write four more novels and a number of good stories. One need not agree with Anderson's harshest critics, who stress a precipitous decline in his career after 1923, to nevertheless recognize that Anderson struggled often unsuccessfully with his craft in the later 1920's. He had received recognition: the *Dial* award in 1921 and growing praise for his fiction both in the United States and abroad. But he was never to be secure financially; he was forced to depend on advertising writing through most of the period of his greatest achievements and then on lecturing, a generous allowance from publisher and theatre producer Horace Liveright, and the patronage of Burton Emmett to supplement his income in the 1920's. Furthermore, since income and status came with success in writing novels, Anderson directed much of his energies to a form uncongenial with his artistic gifts. The bizarre fable of *Many Marriages* (1923) alienated critics, publishers, and general readers; while *Dark Laughter* (1925) was the only commercial success among his novels, it did little to restore his critical reputation and even inspired Hemingway's parody *Torrents of Spring.*

In 1923, a year in which he was dissolving his second marriage in Reno, Nevada, Anderson's fourth novel, *Many Marriages,* appeared. This story of a man's rebellion against puritan repression of sexual expression has been called "irresponsible" by Rex Burbank, despite the validity of Anderson's motive and thesis. The acts of John Webster, the book's main character, are grotesque in a negative sense, featuring a scene with the naked Webster, his wife, and daughter that in length, symbolism, and muddled thought illustrates the novel's chief weaknesses. *Dark Laughter* also concerns sexual repression and reflects, as Burbank and

Howe have shown, the influence of D. H. Lawrence and James Joyce. Anderson was not only again assaying the longer form but also seeking to generate subject matter beyond that of his earlier successes. However, *Dark Laughter* is not much better than *Many Marriages* in execution, flawed again by the unconvincing analysis of the conflict between middle-class values and the primitive expression of feelings and additionally by the Joycean stream-of-consciousness style, which in this novel and in his later writings seems pretentious and serves to exacerbate the problems of his intellectual analysis.

More successful during this period of his career were Anderson's two fictional autobiographies. *A Story-Teller's Story* is in the tradition of mythic works or parables. Not interested in telling the whole biographical truth, the book presents stories to illustrate an argumentative position or moral. Anderson was in his element in writing this book, for he was writing both about the personality and role that is ubiquitous in his fiction and about settings and plot rooted in fact. The book is loose in form and episodic, but the stories that make up his life are often intrinsically interesting and finally unified by the narrator's personality. The exploration of such issues as craftsmanship in literature, business and artistic ethics, the impact of industrialism on human life, and the role of the American artist make *A Story-Teller's Story* profitable reading for students of American literature.

The second fictional autobiography, *Tar: A Midwest Childhood* (1926), focuses on the earliest stage of the author's life, the boyhood years when he was growing up in Clyde, Ohio. The text includes a version of "Death in the Woods" and other effective passages, but the book repeats much of the material of *A Story-Teller's Story,* and the stylistic mannerisms that seek to reflect the boy's sensibility are unsuccessful. Anderson's intent was to recapture the boyhood scenes and ideals in tales projected to be published as a series in *The Woman's Home Companion,* and, indeed, six installments were published in this magazine. His decisions about how *Tar* would be written might have been influenced by his sense of the *Companion* readers.

In 1927, Anderson's career took an unexpected turn when he bought the two newspapers in Marion, Virginia, and became a country editor. For two years these papers absorbed his energies, and apparently he found the business, the reporting, and the writing to his liking. However, his newspaper writings, some of them gathered in *Hello Towns!* (1929), could not sustain the self-esteem of one who had tasted international acclaim only a few years before. Critics Walter Rideout and Welford Taylor have examined this epoch in Anderson's career with subtlety and depth. In 1929, he turned over the papers to his son Robert, during the same year that his third marriage broke up.

While we may designate the period from 1930 to Anderson's death in 1941 as the final phase, we do so because of his developing relationship with Eleanor Copenhaver and his growing interest in the industrial South that his association with her fostered. This connection signaled a new direction in his life and career toward greater personal contentment and toward writing which reflected his developing interest in the contemporary economic, political, and social scene, a dominant but not exclusive direction for his final years.

But Anderson did not stop writing fiction. Indeed, *Death in the Woods,* published in 1933, is a story collection that includes not only the new and good "Brother Death" and the title story first published in 1926 but also other stories that give evidence that his creative power in the shorter forms was diminished but intact. The conflicts in "Brother Death," between the values represented by the younger brother who dies but maintains his freedom and those of the older brother who surrenders his spiritual freedom to secure the legacy of the farm, are quite effective symbolically but the important theme obtrudes as that element does not in the greater, earlier stories. It is important to note that Anderson's final collection of stories appeared in the middle of the Great Depression and that the bankruptcy of his publisher Liveright permitted only a technical publication of the book, without the marketing that might have bolstered Anderson's bank account and his morale.

In addition, Anderson wrote two novels in the 1930's. Divided into four books, *Beyond Desire* (1932) is Anderson's dramatization of the New South, stressing especially the southern mill workers' struggle against the established power behind the machines. Anderson's growing interest in socio-economic conflict and even his attraction to aspects of Communism lie behind the story, though Anderson's *real* concern remains, as always, with the relationships among people. Unfortunately, in structure and style the novel is confused and awkwardly written.

Kit Brandon (1936), his last published novel, is in many ways more satisfactory than *Beyond Desire*. Heroically, in the sixtieth year of his life, Anderson sought, as he told Maxwell Perkins, to be "more objective," to exercise greater control over the form. Despite technical problems in handling point of view and transitions, the novel may be, in David Anderson's words, "the best constructed of any of Anderson's long works." He published thirteen stories with a similar Appalachian setting that stressed a similar social pattern, but *Kit Brandon* is his only full treatment of the hill setting and bootlegging. The sense of place is established well, and the episodes and characters encountered as the novel traces Kit's career are effective in themselves and for what they reveal about the human cost of the mechanized culture. Kit is a southern mountain girl who is raised on a poverty-ridden farm where the chief "crop" is moonshine. She leaves her moonshining family at sixteen to take a mill job and then marries the weak son of a powerful bootlegger. After the marriage fails, Kit joins the bootleg gang and becomes a wealthy, notorious runner. Her obsession with the powerful cars she drives provides a shortlived compensation for the failures of the men she encounters. Although at the novel's end Kit has not found fulfillment, she has learned the emptiness of pursuing mere wealth and adventure, the same lesson Windy McPherson learned in Anderson's first published novel.

Beyond Desire and Kit Brandon deserve emphasis because Anderson's reputation resides not solely but primarily on his fiction; however, in addition to the posthumously published *Memoirs,* he wrote a number of journalistic pieces and four other nonfiction books during the last decade of his life: *Perhaps Women* (1931), *No Swank* (1934), *Puzzled America* (1935), and *Home Town* (1940). While Irving Howe and David Anderson, two astute critics of Anderson's social criticism, offered essentially contrasting evaluations of Anderson's social analyses, even the more adversely critical Howe found insights buried within "untenable" theses and admiration for Anderson's unique gifts. For example, Howe wrote, "*Puzzled America* is one of the few books that convey a sense of what it meant to live in depression America."

Appropriately Anderson's last important work was his *Memoirs,* published first in 1942 but more dependably edited by Ray Lewis White in 1969. This is appropriate first because, like *Winesburg, Ohio, A Story-Teller's Story,* and *Tar,* it is another maverick form: fact and fiction, biographical and mythic, unified and fragmented. Secondly, *Memoirs* is written in the natural style of his most successful works. The mannerisms of *Tar* are gone, and Anderson's "voice" is steady, informed, and mature. Finally, the

Memoirs, though unfinished, is unified once more by the Anderson myth. One last time he has put on record the anecdotal parable of the life of an American artist. Beyond the aesthetic issues, the *Memoirs* is also the record of a sensitive American who experienced the coming of the modern industrial world, its factories and advertising, and—measuring that world by the criteria of craftsmanship, brotherhood, and love—often found it wanting. In the *Memoirs* Anderson judged himself too harshly: "For all my egotism I know I am but a minor figure." Some have chosen to underscore the word minor, but such ratings can distort value. One may, as did T. S. Eliot, prefer Italian renaissance poet Dante Alighieri to William Shakespeare, but the value of such judgments should be to honor and foster what is valuable in writings of both. Sherwood Anderson wrote much that will not stand close scrutiny; however, in *Winesburg, Ohio,* in a number of short stories, and in at least parts of such works as *A Story-Teller's Story* and *Poor White,* Anderson's literary achievement is impressive.

BIOGRAPHICAL/CRITICAL SOURCES:

BOOKS

Anderson, David D., *Sherwood Anderson: An Introduction and Interpretation,* Holt, 1967.

Anderson, David D., editor, *Sherwood Anderson: Dimensions of His Literary Art,* Michigan State University Press, 1976.

Anderson, David D., editor, *Critical Essays on Sherwood Anderson,* G. K. Hall, 1981.

Anderson, Sherwood, *Winesburg, Ohio,* introduction by Malcolm Cowley, Viking, 1960.

Anderson, Sherwood, *Beyond Desire,* introduction by Walter B. Rideout, Liveright, 1961.

Anderson, Sherwood, *Poor White,* introduction by Walter B. Rideout, Viking, 1966.

Anderson, Sherwood, *Winesburg, Ohio,* edited by John G. Ferres, Viking, 1966.

Bridgman, Richard, *The Colloquial Style in America,* Oxford University Press, 1966.

Burbank, Rex, *Sherwood Anderson,* Twayne, 1964.

Dictionary of Literary Biography, Gale, Volume 4: *American Writers in Paris, 1920-1939,* 1980, Volume 9: *American Novelists, 1910-1945,* 1981.

Dictionary of Literary Biography Documentary Series, Volume 1, Gale, 1982.

Geismar, Maxwell David, *The Last of the Provincials: The American Novel, 1915-1925,* Houghton, 1947.

Howe, Irving, *Sherwood Anderson,* William Sloane Associates, 1951, reprinted, Stanford University Press, 1966.

Kazin, Alfred, *On Native Grounds,* Reynal & Hitchcock, 1942.

Rideout, Walter B., editor, *Sherwood Anderson: A Collection of Critical Essays,* Prentice-Hall, 1974.

Rosenfeld, Paul, *Port of New York,* Harcourt, 1924.

Schevill, James, *Sherwood Anderson: His Life and Work,* University of Denver Press, 1951.

Sutton, William A., *Exit to Elsinore,* Ball State University Press, 1967.

Sutton, William A., *The Road to Winesburg: A Mosaic of the Imaginative Life of Sherwood Anderson,* Scarecrow, 1972.

Taylor, Welford Dunaway, *Sherwood Anderson,* Ungar, 1977.

Townsend, Kim, *Sherwood Anderson,* Houghton, 1988.

Trilling, Lionel, *The Liberal Imagination: Essays on Literature and Society,* Viking, 1950.

Twentieth-Century Literary Criticism, Gale, Volume 1, 1978, Volume 10, 1983.

Walcutt, Charles C., *American Literary Naturalism: A Divided Stream,* University of Minnesota Press, 1956.

Weber, Brom, *Sherwood Anderson,* University of Minnesota Press, 1964.
White, Ray Lewis, editor, *The Achievement of Sherwood Anderson,* University of North Carolina Press, 1966.

PERIODICALS

Accent, Volume 16, number 2, 1956.
American Literature, Volume 23, number 1, 1951, Volume 40, number 1, 1968, Volume 41, number 1, 1969.
American Quarterly, Volume 20, number 4, 1968.
Hudson Review, Volume 10, number 4, 1957-58.
Journal of English and Germanic Philology, Volume 54, number 4, 1955.
Mark Twain Journal, Volume 11, number 2, 1960.
MidAmerica, 1, 1974.
Midcontinent American Studies Journal 3, 1962.
Modern Fiction Studies, Volume 5, number 2, 1959, Volume 5, number 4, 1959-60.
New York Times Book Review, July 10, 1988.
PMLA, Volume 74, number 3, 1959, Volume 80, number 4, 1965, Volume 87, number 5, 1972.
Studies in Short Fiction, Volume 4, number 3, 1967, Volume 11, number 2, 1974.
University of Chicago Magazine, January, 1955.

*   *   *

ANDREWS, Elton V.
See POHL, Frederik

*   *   *

ANDREWS, V(irginia) C(leo)   ?-1986

PERSONAL: Born in Portsmouth, Va.; died of cancer, December 19, 1986, in Virginia Beach, Va., buried in Portsmouth, Va.; daughter of William Henry (a tool and die maker) and Lillian Lilnora (a telephone operator; maiden name, Parker) Andrews. *Education:* Educated in Portsmouth, Va.

ADDRESSES: Home—Virginia Beach, Va. *Agent*—Anita Diamant, The Writers' Workshop, 310 Madison Ave., New York, N.Y. 10017.

CAREER: Writer. Formerly worked as a fashion illustrator, commercial artist, portrait artist, and gallery exhibitor.

WRITINGS:

NOVELS

Flowers in the Attic, Pocket Books, 1979, subsequent hardcover edition, Simon & Schuster, 1979.
Petals on the Wind, Pocket Books, 1980, simultaneous hardcover edition, Simon & Schuster, 1980.
If There Be Thorns, Pocket Books, 1981, simultaneous hardcover edition, Simon & Schuster, 1981.
My Sweet Audrina, Pocket Books, 1982, simultaneous hardcover edition, Poseidon Press, 1982.
Seeds of Yesterday, Pocket Books, 1984, simultaneous hardcover edition, Poseidon Press, 1984.
Heaven, Pocket Books, 1985, simultaneous hardcover edition, Poseidon Press, 1985.
Dark Angel, Pocket Books, simultaneous hardcover edition, Poseidon Press, 1986.
Garden of Shadows, Pocket Books, simultaneous hardcover edition, Poseidon Press, 1987.
Fallen Hearts, Pocket Books, simultaneous hardcover edition, Poseidon Press, 1988.

The Gates of Paradise, Pocket Books, simultaneous harcover edition, Poseidon Press, 1989.

WORK IN PROGRESS: A novel based in thirteenth-century France.

SIDELIGHTS: V. C. Andrews's books, described by a London *Times* critic as "her own blend of gothic horror stories crossed with fairy tales," sold millions of copies worldwide. A tale of greed, incest, and child abuse, Andrews's first novel, *Flowers in the Attic,* tells the story of the four beautiful Dollanganger children. These children, the offspring of an incestuous union, are locked in an attic because if their fundamentalist grandfather learns of their existence, he will exclude their mother from his will. Forgotten by their unfeeling mother and tormented by their sadistic grandmother, the children create their own world, turning to each other for love. The saga of the Dollangangers, including the children's subsequent revenge, continues in the next two books, *Petals on the Wind* and *If There Be Thorns.*

The success of the Dollanganger trilogy is a remarkable story in itself. Released in 1979, *Flowers in the Attic* rocketed to the best-seller lists a mere two weeks after its publication and remained there for over fourteen weeks. When word spread that there would be a sequel to *Flowers,* the demand was so great that Andrews's paperback publisher, Pocket Books, advanced the publishing date by several months. The sequel, *Petals on the Wind,* also became an instant success, rising to the number one position and remaining on the *New York Times* best-seller list for nineteen weeks. *Petals*'s popularity was so great that it even caused *Flowers* to reappear on the list for a brief stint. *If There Be Thorns,* the third part of the Dollanganger trilogy, continued Andrews's impressive track record, attaining the number two slot on most best-seller lists the second week after its release. While the books' themes of incest, misogyny, rape, and revenge have outraged some readers, others, particularly the adolescent girls who constitute the major proportion of Andrews's readership, have found the mixture irresistible. In fact, all three of the Dollanganger novels have been record breakers for Pocket Books, the first two alone selling over seven million copies within two years.

Despite their overwhelming popularity, Andrews's novels have not met with proportionate critical acclaim. In her *Washington Post Book World* review of *Flowers in the Attic,* Carolyn Banks calls the book's plot "unbelievable" and its dialogue "indigestible." She adds, "The principle of selection does not seem to have entered the author's head, nor her editor's." Reviewing *My Sweet Audrina* in the *New York Times Book Review,* Eden Ross Lipson finds the storyline difficult to follow, claiming: "Most of the brief sexual passages involve third parties watching in fascination, which gives things a little spin, I suppose. Nothing else makes much sense." However, not all the reviews of Andrews's novels have been so negative. Without dismissing the criticism leveled by other reviewers, some critics have found praiseworthy elements in Andrews's works. While she acknowledges that certain situations in *Petals on the Wind* tax credibility, Bea Maxwell, writing in the *Los Angeles Times Book Review,* praises Andrews's storytelling ability, particularly her skill in ensnaring her audience. "Andrews lulls the reader, then shocks and awakens," she says.

Dale Pollock, another *Los Angeles Times Book Review* critic, sees weak spots in *If There Be Thorns,* namely the ending, but finds the book "an absorbing narrative" in which the two speakers "emerge as credible (if pitiable) characters." Pollock also sees considerable merit in Andrews's ability to tell the story through the eyes of two adolescent boys. "Andrews excels at re-creating the confusion and frustration of being old enough to grasp the pieces of a family mystery, but too young to assemble the puzzle." London *Times* reviewer Patricia Miller seems to sum up the attitude of many of those who find themselves attracted to Andrews's books when she writes: "Virginia Andrews' writing is embarrassingly crude and naive, especially in her first books, though she has improved greatly in the course of writing four. A reviewer in the *Washington Post* said *Flowers in the Attic* was 'the worst book in the world.' I see his point, but there is a strength in her books—the bizarre plots, matched with the pathos of the entrapped, which she herself clearly feels."

Andrews spoke freely of her past and, in recounting her life story, told a tale of tragedy, courage, and even the supernatural which rivals a plot from one of her novels. Crippled in her childhood as a result of medical neglect, Andrews spent most of her adolescence on crutches and as an adult remained largely confined to a wheelchair. In spite of several painful operations during her late teens, she was able to finish high school. From there she went on to complete a four-year art course. In fact, before the huge success of *Flowers in the Attic,* Andrews supported herself quite comfortably as a commercial artist. Prior to *Flowers,* her career as a writer was unremarkable. Finding her work as a commercial artist unfulfilling ("I became an artist, and was still unsatisfied, for an artist is an artist, doing the same thing every day," she told *CA*), Andrews had been a closet writer for years, scribbling away at night in the secluded suburban home that she shared with her mother until her death. In spite of her handicap, Andrews managed to produce from thirty to forty pages a night, usually typing in bed but often writing while standing up in an awkward body brace. Despite her prodigious output, Andrews initially had little success getting her words into print. Her only sale before 1979 was a small piece in a confessions magazine. After that she wrote nine books in seven years and each of them was turned down. She remained undaunted, however, continuing to write every night.

A major breakthrough occurred when she submitted a novel entitled *The Obsessed* to a publishing company. Editors told Andrews that the 290,000-word story showed promise but was simply too long. Encouraged, she began revising extensively and came up with a shortened ninety-eight-page version she entitled *Flowers in the Attic.* The turning point came when early readers of this "new" novel suggested that Andrews get "more gutsy" and give free rein to her vivid imagination. As Andrews herself remarked in a *Washington Post* article, she was given the green light to "deal with all those unspeakable things my mother didn't want me to write about, which was exactly what I wanted to do in the first place." She then rewrote *Flowers* a second time, adding those libidinous elements she had originally omitted, dedicated the book to her mother, and sold the novel to Pocket Books for $7,500.

In order to promote the sales of a first novel by the unknown Andrews, editor Ann Patty, then associated with Pocket Books, instituted a massive publicity campaign, complete with complimentary preview editions, haunting radio advertisements, and aggressive in-store merchandising. This boost, combined with the book's chilling cover graphics and controversial themes, had an immediate and lasting impact on the book-buying public. The great success of *Flowers in the Attic* and its sequels have assured V. C. Andrews a large and faithful readership.

When asked by the *Washington Post*'s Stephen Rubin about the types of novels she writes, full of greed, incest, and horror, Andrews explained: "Why do I write about such oddball situations? Why have an imagination if you don't go that way? I guess I'm just drawn to that sort of thing. I don't like everything to be explained by scientists who say there are no little green men from Mars. I don't like that, I want them to be there. I like things out of the ordinary." In response to those who charge that her books are morbid or bleak, Andrews told Rubin: "I don't think anything that appears wonderful and shiny on its surface doesn't have a dark side to it." Elaborating on this she remarked to *CA,* "There is no beauty without ugliness, and no enjoyment without suffering; we have to have the shade in order to see the light, and that is all I do in a story, put my characters in the shade and try, before the ending, to have them in the sunlight."

When Andrews began writing one of her books, she completely immersed herself in the task. She believed so wholeheartedly in what she wrote that when one of her characters had trouble eating or sleeping, she herself could not eat or sleep. She so empathized with her characters that if one of them died, she was grief-stricken. In fact, during the composition of *Flowers in the Attic* Andrews purportedly lost twenty of her usual 110 pounds. Another one of her quirks was to mount a mirror behind her typewriter so that she could see herself as she wrote and thus "project better."

Psychic experiences played an important role in Andrews's life and writings. A firm believer in ESP and reincarnation, she claimed to have known all along that she was going to be crippled because of psychic flashes she experienced as a child. "When I was still very healthy, I saw my shadow and it had crutches," she told the London *Times.* Andrews's faith in the supernatural, in particular in her own dreams, was reflected in her books. As she explained to *CA,* "My novels are based on dreams and situations taken from my own life, in which I change the pattern so that what might have happened actually does happen—and therein lies the tale."

Andrews's great success had little effect on her work habits. She wrote each night before retiring to bed. In fact, in 1981 she told the *Washington Post* that she had already composed brief synopses for an additional sixty-three books. This dedication reflects Andrews's commitment to her work. As she told the *Washington Post:* "I always wanted to be somebody exceptional, somebody different, who did something on her own."

Andrews's books have been translated into Norwegian, Swedish, Portuguese, Dutch, Hebrew, Turkish, Italian, and German.

MEDIA ADAPTATIONS: A movie adaptation of *Flowers in the Attic* was filmed by Fries Entertainment-New World Pictures in 1987.

AVOCATIONAL INTERESTS: Ballet, classical music, chess, astrology (for personality profiles, not predictions).

BIOGRAPHICAL/CRITICAL SOURCES:

PERIODICALS

Detroit Free Press, January 18, 1987.
Los Angeles Times Book Review, October 5, 1980, August 30, 1981, April 29, 1984.
New York Times Book Review, October 3, 1982.
Times (London), September 15, 1982.
Washington Post, September 20, 1981.
Washington Post Book World, November 4, 1979.

OBITUARIES:

PERIODICALS

Chicago Tribune, December 22, 1986.
Los Angeles Times, December 21, 1986.

New York Times, December 21, 1986.
Norfolk Ledger-Star, December 20, 1986.
Washington Post, December 21, 1986.

*   *   *

ANDREZEL, Pierre
See BLIXEN, Karen (Christentze Dinesen)

*   *   *

ANDRIC, Ivo   1892-1975

PERSONAL: Born October 10, 1892, in Docu, Bosnia, Austria-Hungary (now Yugoslavia); died March 13, 1975, in Belgrade, Yugoslavia; married Milica Babic (a painter and theatre designer), 1959 (died, 1968). *Education:* Attended University of Zagreb, Yugoslavia, Vienna University, Austria, and University of Krakow, Poland; Graz University, Austria, doctorate in philosophy, 1923. *Politics:* Communist.

ADDRESSES: Home—Proleterskih brigada 2a, Belgrade, Yugoslavia.

CAREER: Political prisoner during World War I; Yugoslav diplomatic service, 1919-41, served in Rome, Geneva, Madrid, Bucharest, Trieste, Graz, Belgrade, and Berlin; full-time writer, 1941-49; Yugoslav Parliament, deputy and representative from Bosnia, 1949-55.

MEMBER: Federation of Writers of Yugoslavia (president, 1946-51), Serbian Academy.

AWARDS, HONORS: Prize for life work from Yugoslav Government, 1956; Nobel Prize for Literature, 1961; honorary doctorate, University of Krakow, 1964.

WRITINGS:

IN ENGLISH TRANSLATION; FICTION, EXCEPT AS NOTED

Gospodjica, [Yugoslavia], 1945, translation by Joseph Hitrec published as *The Woman From Sarajevo,* Knopf, 1965.
Travnicka hronika, [Yugoslavia], 1945, translation by Kenneth Johnstone published as *Bosnian Story,* Lincolns-Prager, 1958, British Book Center, 1959, translation by Hitrec published as *Bosnian Chronicle,* Knopf, 1963.
Na Drini cuprija, [Yugoslavia], 1945, translation by Lovett F. Edwards published as *The Bridge on the Drina,* Macmillan, 1959.
Prica o vezirovam slonu, Nakladni Zavod (Zagreb), 1948, translation by Drenka Willen published as *The Vizier's Elephant: Three Novellas,* Harcourt, 1962.
Prokleta avlija, [Yugoslavia], 1954, translation by Johnstone published as *Devil's Yard,* Grove, 1962.
Sabrana djela Ive Andrica (also see below) Mladost (Zagreb) 1963, partial translation by Hitrec published as *The Pasha's Concubine and Other Tales,* Knopf, 1968.
Most na Zepi, Svjetlost (Sarajevo), 1967, updated edition with text in Serbo-Croatian, English, German, and Italian published as *Most na Zepi/The Bridge on the Zepa/Die Bruecke ueber die Zepa/Il ponte sulla Zepa,* Oslobodenje (Sarajevo), 1971.
Letters, translation, editing, and introduction by Zelimir B. Juricic, Serbian Heritage Academy (Toronto), 1984.

OTHER

Ex ponto (prison meditations; title means "Restlessness"), Knjizevnog juga (Zagreb), 1918, reprinted, Univerzitetska biblioteka Svetozar Markovic, 1975.

Nemiri (poems; title means "Disquietudes"), Naklada S. Kugli, 1920, reprinted, Univerzitetska biblioteka Svetozar Markovic, 1975.
Put Alje Djerzeleza, [Yugoslavia], 1920.
Pripovetke (short stories), [Yugoslavia], Volume I, 1924, Volume II, 1931, Volume III, 1936.
Nove pripovetka (short stories), Kultura (Zagreb), 1949.
Prica o kmetu Simanu, [Yugoslavia], 1950.
Novele, Mladinska Knjiga (Ljubljana), 1951.
Pod grabicem: Pripovetke o zivotu bosanskog sela (short stories), Seljacka knjiga (Sarajevo), 1952.
Panorama: Pripovetke (short stories), Prosveta (Belgrade), 1958.
Lica (short stories), Mladost, 1960.
Izbor, Svjetlost, 1961.
Sabrana djela Ive Andrica (title means "Collected Works of Ivo Andric"), Volumes 1-10, Mladost, 1963, Volumes 11-16, Svjetlost, 1976.
Ljubav u Kasabi (short stories), Branko Donovic (Belgrade), 1963.
Bosna hikayeleri, Varlik Yayinevi (Istanbul), 1965.
Mustafa Madzar i druge price, Svjetlost, 1965.
(Contributor) *Nouvel essai yougoslave* (essays), compiled by Aleksandar V. Stefanovic, Zalozba Obzorja, 1965.
Anikina vremena (short stories), Svjetlost, 1967.
Kula i druge pripovetke (children's stories), Veselin Maslesa (Sarajevo), 1970.
Eseji i kritike (essays), Svjetlost, 1976.
Sta sanjam i sta mi se dogada: Pesme i pesme u prozi, Prosveta, 1977.
O Vuku, Rad (Belgrade), 1977.
Wegzeichen (collection of personal impressions; title means "Road Markings"), [Munich, West Germany], 1982.
Sveske, Prosveta, 1982.

Poetry represented in *An Anthology of Modern Yugoslav Poetry,* edited by Janko Lavrin, J. Calder, 1963. Member of editorial board of *Knjizevni jug,* a literary magazine.

SIDELIGHTS: In both his diplomatic and writing careers, Ivo Andric displayed a passion for politics and history. Andric was born in Bosnia, a region in Austria-Hungary that had been wracked by political turmoil for centuries. As a young man, he had joined the Mlada Bosna, a revolutionary Bosnian organization that sought the downfall of the Hapsburg regime and the establishment of an independent state for the South Slav peoples. A member of the Mlada Bosna shot and killed Archduke Ferdinand of Austria in 1914, an act that ignited World War I. Because of his association with the revolutionary group, Andric was imprisoned for three years.

Following the war, Andric entered his country's diplomatic service and continued in this capacity even after the Kingdom of the Serbs, Croats, and Slovenes became Yugoslavia in 1929. The last diplomatic post Andric held was ambassador to Nazi Germany. In 1941 he fled from Berlin only a few hours before the Germans began bombing Yugoslavia. After World War II, Andric resumed his career in politics. He joined the Communist party and became a deputy in the Yugoslav Parliament.

Andric's pen had not been idle during his years in the diplomatic service. His most fruitful creative periods, however, occurred when he was in prison during World War I and when he was under virtual house arrest during World War II. When he was first incarcerated, Andric read the works of Soren Kierkegaard, a Danish philosopher and writer on religion. Kierkegaard's vision of the world as a place of fear, isolation, and irrationality had a permanent impact on Andric's writings. Andric stated his philosophy in *Ex ponto,* a collection of his prison meditations: "There is no other truth but pain, there is no other reality but suffering, pain and suffering in every drop of water, in every blade of grass, in every grain of crystal, in every sound of living voice, in sleep and in vigil, in life, before life and perhaps also after life."

Having forged such a philosophy, Andric found his native Bosnia the perfect setting for his fiction. The people of Bosnia had been oppressed and exploited throughout their history, and the resulting torment and gloom were explored in Andric's writings. "For Andric man, set against the vast panorama of history, is insignificant—fearful of external disaster and inwardly aware of his own insecurity in a world where everything is ephemeral, however much he may long for constancy," Konstantin Bazarov explained. "The particular history of old Turkish Bosnia, with its despotism and violence, thus portrays the broader theme of man's tragic struggle against the oncoming darkness of change and death."

Andric's most memorable novels about Bosnia were written during World War II. When the Germans occupied Belgrade, Andric refused to leave. He holed up in his apartment and wrote what has come to be known as the Bosnian trilogy—*Gospodjica* (*The Woman From Sarajevo*), *Travnicka hronika* (*Bosnian Story* or *Bosnian Chronicle*), and *Na Drini cuprija* (*The Bridge on the Drina*). In *The Woman From Sarajevo,* Andric portrayed the people of Sarajevo as "already burdened with the Turkish legacy of habitual indolence and with the Slavic hankering for excesses, having lately adopted the formal Austrian notions of society and social obligations, according to which one's personal prestige and the dignity of one's class were measured by a rising scale of senseless and non-productive spending." After reading the novel in translation, William Cooper remarked that *The Woman From Sarajevo* "is so fascinating and distinguished that one feels dismayed—and ashamed—to think of the writers in lesser-known languages whose work we have never read."

Even more highly acclaimed was *Bosnian Chronicle.* Set in Travnik during the Napoleonic era, *Bosnian Chronicle* focused on the conflicts that arose between the French and Austrian consulates as they vied to win the favor of the Turkish vizier and the support of the local townspeople. In his translator's note, Joseph Hitrec declared that Andric's principal themes—"causative interplay of guilt and human suffering, the individual versus tyranny, the warping of men's destinies through historic circumstance"— were masterfully combined in *Bosnian Chronicle.* Alan Ferguson saw two major themes in the novel, the first being the clash between the private individual and his public image. He pointed out that the Austrian and French consuls had much in common yet were prevented from becoming friends by their official duties. The second theme that Ferguson discerned in *Bosnian Chronicle* was the clash between East and West. Bosnia epitomized the struggle between these two cultures because the Christians and Moslems had been fighting over the territory since the fourteenth century.

Bosnian Chronicle covered only seven years in the history of Bosnia, but *The Bridge on the Drina* spanned three and a half centuries. The Turks had constructed the bridge over the Drina River in the sixteenth century at the town of Visegrad. The novel recorded life in Visegrad from the time of the bridge's erection to shortly before World War I. Egon Hostovsky discussed the symbolic import of the bridge: "The ancient bridge is a piece of eternity, forged by human hands and baptized with the bold dreams of men. It has outlasted generations, invasions, wars, and peace. Everything around it was continually changing, rotting, dying,

being reborn; but the bridge has stood immutable, the witness of values and efforts that do not pass."

The epic proportions of *The Bridge on the Drina* have prompted many critics to liken Andric to Leo Tolstoy. Like Tolstoy, Andric was concerned with the inexorable flow of history, with the precedence that events take over the individual. Andric has also been compared to Herman Melville. Stoyan Christowe demonstrated that the elephant in "The Vizier's Elephant" was similar to Melville's fictional whale, Moby Dick, because "both personify the universal, hostile forces against which man struggles."

Comparisons to writers of the caliber of Tolstoy and Melville suggest that Andric was not just a regional writer, but an artist whose work had universal implications. Alan Ferguson commented that Andric's works were not about foreign lands but "about the 'common course of all humanity'; its fundamental similarities rather than its superficial differences." The Swedish Academy attested to Andric's universality when it awarded him the Nobel Prize for Literature in 1961 "for the epic force with which he has depicted themes and human destinies drawn from the history of his country."

One mark of Andric's greatness was his devotion to truth and morality. Although Andric was involved in politics for many years, his writing was notably free of cant. He believed that fiction "should not be poisoned with hatred nor stifled by the din of lethal weapons. It should be motivated by love and guided by the breadth and serenity of the free human spirit. Because any storyteller and his work serve nothing if they do not, in one way or another, serve man and mankind."

Some of Andric's works have been translated into German, French, Russian, Spanish, and Italian.

BIOGRAPHICAL/CRITICAL SOURCES:

BOOKS

Contemporary Literary Criticism, Volume 8, Gale, 1978.
Ivo Andric, *Bosnian Chronicle,* translation by Joseph Hitrec, Knopf, 1963.

PERIODICALS

Books and Bookmen, November, 1974.
Book World, June 30, 1968.
Christian Century, February 15, 1967.
Christian Science Monitor, August 9, 1968.
Harvard Review, autumn, 1959.
Listener, August 11, 1966.
Literary Quarterly, summer, 1965.
Modern Language Review, October, 1975.
New York Times, October 28, 1962.
New York Times Book Review, July 28, 1968.
Saturday Review, July 11, 1959.
Slavic and East European Journal, fall, 1972.
Slavic Review, September, 1964.
Slavonic and East European Review, June, 1963, July, 1970.
Times Literary Supplement, May 20, 1965.

OBITUARIES:

BOOKS

Current Biography, H. W. Wilson, 1975.

PERIODICALS

AB Bookman's Weekly, April 7, 1975.
Newsweek, March 24, 1975.
New York Times, March 14, 1975.

Washington Post, March 14, 1975.

*   *   *

ANGELOU, Maya 1928-

PERSONAL: Name originally Marguerita Johnson; surname is pronounced "*An*-ge-lo"; born April 4, 1928, in St. Louis, Mo.; daughter of Bailey (a naval dietician) and Vivian (Baxter) Johnson; married Tosh Angelos (divorced); married Paul Du Feu, December, 1973 (divorced); children: Guy. *Education:* Attended public schools in Arkansas and California; studied music privately; studied dance with Martha Graham, Pearl Primus, and Ann Halprin; studied drama with Frank Silvera and Gene Frankel.

ADDRESSES: Home—Sonoma, Calif. *Agent*—Gerald W. Purcell Associates Ltd., 133 Fifth Ave., New York, N.Y. 10003.

CAREER: Author, poet, playwright, professional stage and screen producer, director, and performer, and singer. Appeared in "Porgy and Bess" on twenty-two-nation tour sponsored by the U.S. Department of State, 1954-55; appeared in Off-Broadway plays "Calypso Heatwave," 1957, and "The Blacks," 1960; produced and performed in "Cabaret for Freedom," with Godfrey Cambridge, Off-Broadway, 1960; University of Ghana, Institute of African Studies, Legon-Accra, Ghana, assistant administrator of School of Music and Drama, 1963-66; appeared in "Mother Courage" at University of Ghana, 1964, and in "Meda" in Hollywood, 1966; made Broadway debut in "Look Away," 1973; directed film "All Day Long," 1974; directed her play "And Still I Rise" in California, 1976; directed Errol John's "Moon on a Rainbow Shawl" in London, England, 1988; appeared in film "Roots," 1977. Television narrator, interviewer, and host for Afro-American specials and theatre series, 1972. Lecturer at University of California, Los Angeles, 1966; writer in residence at University of Kansas, 1970; distinguished visiting professor at Wake Forest University, 1974, Wichita State University, 1974, and California State University, Sacramento, 1974. Northern coordinator of Southern Christian Leadership Conference, 1959-60; appointed member of American Revolution Bicentennial Council by President Gerald R. Ford, 1975-76; member of National Commission on the Observance of International Women's Year.

MEMBER: American Federation of Television and Radio Artists, American Film Institute (member of board of trustees, 1975—), Directors Guild, Equity, Women's Prison Association (member of advisory board).

AWARDS, HONORS: Nominated for National Book Award, 1970, for *I Know Why the Caged Bird Sings;* Yale University fellowship, 1970; Pulitzer Prize nomination, 1972, for *Just Give Me a Cool Drink of Water 'fore I Diiie;* Antoinette Perry ("Tony") Award nomination from League of New York Theatres and Producers, 1973, for performance in "Look Away"; Rockefeller Foundation scholar in Italy, 1975; named Woman of the Year in Communications by *Ladies' Home Journal,* 1976; Tony Award nomination for best supporting actress, 1977, for "Roots"; honorary degrees from Smith College, 1975, Mills College, 1975, and Lawrence University, 1976.

WRITINGS:

I Know Why the Caged Bird Sings (autobiography; Book-of-the-Month Club selection; also see below), Random House, 1970.
Just Give Me a Cool Drink of Water 'fore I Diiie (poetry), Random House, 1971.

Gather Together in My Name (autobiography; Book-of-the-Month Club selection), Random House, 1974.
Oh Pray My Wings Are Gonna Fit Me Well (poetry), Random House, 1975.
Singin' and Swingin' and Gettin' Merry Like Christmas (autobiography; Book-of-the-Month Club selection), Random House, 1976.
And Still I Rise (poetry; also see below), Random House, 1978.
The Heart of a Woman (autobiography; also see below), Random House, 1981.
Shaker, Why Don't You Sing? (poetry), Random House, 1983.
All God's Children Need Traveling Shoes (autobiography), Random House, 1986.
Mrs. Flowers: A Moment of Friendship (fiction), illustrations by Etienne Delessert, Redpath Press, 1986.
Poems: Maya Angelou, four volumes, Bantam, 1986.
Now Sheba Sings the Song, illustrations by Tom Feelings, Dial Books, 1987.
Selections from I Know Why the Caged Bird Sings and The Heart of A Woman, Literacy Volunteers of New York City, 1989.
I Shall Not Be Moved, Random House, 1990.

PLAYS

(With Godfrey Cambridge) "Cabaret for Freedom" (musical revue), first produced in New York at Village Gate Theatre, 1960.
"The Least of These" (two-act drama), first produced in Los Angeles, 1966.
(Adaptor) Sophocles, "Ajax" (two-act drama), first produced in Los Angeles at Mark Taper Forum, 1974.
"And Still I Rise" (one-act musical), first produced in Oakland, Calif., at Ensemble Theatre, 1976.

Also author of two-act drama "The Clawing Within," 1966, and of two-act musical "Adjoa Amissah," 1967, both as yet unproduced.

SCREENPLAYS

"Georgia, Georgia," Independent-Cinerama, 1972.
"All Day Long," American Film Institute, 1974.

TELEVISION PLAYS

"Blacks, Blues, Black" (ten one-hour programs), National Educational Television (NET-TV), 1968.
"Sister, Sister" (drama), National Broadcasting Co. (NBC-TV), 1982.

Also author of "Assignment America" series, 1975, and two Afro-American specials "The Legacy" and "The Inheritors," 1976.

RECORDINGS

Miss Calypso (songs), Liberty Records, 1957.
The Poetry of Maya Angelou, GWP Records, 1969.
Women in Business, University of Wisconsin, 1981.

OTHER

Composer of songs, including two songs for movie "For Love of Ivy," and composer of musical scores for both her screenplays. Contributor to Ghanaian Broadcasting Corp., 1963-65. Contributor of articles, short stories, and poems to periodicals, including *Harper's, Ebony, Ghanaian Times, Mademoiselle, Redbook,* and *Black Scholar.* Associate editor, *Arab Observer* (English-language news weekly in Cairo, Egypt), 1961-62; feature editor, *African Review* (Accra, Ghana), 1964-66.

SIDELIGHTS: By the time she was in her early twenties, Maya Angelou had been a Creole cook, a streetcar conductor, a cocktail waitress, a dancer, a madam, and an unwed mother. The following decades saw her emerge as a successful singer, actress, and playwright, an editor for an English-language magazine in Egypt, a lecturer and civil rights activist, and a popular author of four collections of poetry and five autobiographies.

Angelou is hailed as one of the great voices of contemporary black literature and as a remarkable Renaissance woman. She began producing books after some notable friends, including author James Baldwin, heard Angelou's stories of her childhood spent shuttling between rural, segregated Stamps, Arkansas, where her devout grandmother ran a general store, and St. Louis, Missouri, where her worldly, glamorous mother lived. *I Know Why the Caged Bird Sings,* a chronicle of her life up to age sixteen (and ending with the birth of her son, Guy) was published in 1970 with great critical and commercial success. Although many of the stories in the book are grim as in the author's revelation that she was raped at age eight by her mother's boyfriend, the volume also recounts the self-awakening of the young Angelou. "Her genius as a writer is her ability to recapture the texture of the way of life in the texture of its idioms, its idiosyncratic vocabulary and especially in its process of image-making," reports Sidonie Ann Smith in *Southern Humanities Review.* "The imagery holds the reality, giving it immediacy. That [the author] chooses to recreate the past in its own sounds suggests to the reader that she accepts the past and recognizes its beauty and its ugliness, its assets and its liabilities, its strengths and its weaknesses. Here we witness a return to the final acceptance of the past in the return to and full acceptance of its language, the language a symbolic construct of a way of life. Ultimately Maya Angelou's style testifies to her reaffirmation of self-acceptance, [which] she achieves within the pattern of the autobiography."

Her next two volumes of autobiography, *Gather Together in My Name* and *Singin' and Swingin' and Gettin' Merry Like Christmas,* take Angelou from her late adolescence, when she flirted briefly with prostitution and drug addiction, to her early adulthood as she established a reputation as a performer among the avant-garde of the early 1950s. Not as commercially successful as *I Know Why the Caged Bird Sings,* the two books were guardedly praised by some critics. Lynn Sukenick, for example, remarks in *Village Voice* that *Gather Together in My Name* is "sculpted, concise, rich with flavor and surprises, exuding a natural confidence and command." Sukenick adds, however, that one fault lies "in the tone of the book. . . . [The author's] refusal to let her earlier self get off easy, and the self-mockery which is her means to honesty, finally becomes in itself a glossing over; although her laughter at herself is witty, intelligent, and a good preventative against maudlin confession, . . . it eventually becomes a tic and a substitute for a deeper look." Annie Gottlieb has another view of *Gather Together in My Name.* In her *New York Times Book Review* article, Gottlieb states that Angelou "writes like a song, and like the truth. The wisdom, rue and humor of her storytelling are borne on a lilting rhythm completely her own, the product of a born writer's senses nourished on black church singing and preaching, soft mother talk and salty street talk, and on literature."

The year 1981 brought the publication of *The Heart of a Woman,* a book that "covers one of the most exciting periods in recent African and Afro-American history," according to Adam David Miller in *Black Scholar.* Miller refers to the era of civil rights marches, the emergence of Dr. Martin Luther King, Jr., and Malcolm X, and the upheaval in Africa following the assassination of the Congolese statesman Patrice Lumumba. The 1960s

see Angelou active in civil rights both in America and abroad; at the same time she enters into a romance with African activist Vusumzi Make, which dissolves when he cannot accept her independence or even promise fidelity. In a *Dictionary of Literary Biography* piece on Angelou, Lynn Z. Bloom considers *The Heart of a Woman* the author's best work since *I Know Why the Caged Bird Sings:* "Her enlarged focus and clear vision transcend the particulars and give this book a fascinating universality of perspective and psychological depth that almost matches the quality of [Angelou's first volume]. . . . Its motifs are commitment and betrayal."

Washington Post Book World critic David Levering Lewis also sees a universal message in *The Heart of a Woman.* "Angelou has rearranged, edited, and pointed up her coming of age and going abroad in the world with such just-rightness of timing and inner truthfulness that each of her books is a continuing autobiography of Afro-America. Her ability to shatter the opaque prisms of race and class between reader and subject is her special gift," he says. To Bloom, "it is clear from [this series of autobiographies] that Angelou is in the process of becoming a self-created Everywoman. In a literature and a culture where there are many fewer exemplary lives of women than of men, black or white, Angelou's autobiographical self, as it matures through successive volumes, is gradually assuming that exemplary stature."

In her fifth autobiographical work, *All God's Children Need Traveling Shoes,* Angelou describes her four-year stay in Ghana, "just as that African country had won its independence from European colonials," according to Barbara T. Christian in the *Chicago Tribune Book World.* Christian indicates that Angelou's "sojourn in Africa strengthens her bonds to her ancestral home even as she concretely experiences her distinctiveness as an Afro American."

This book has also received praise from reviewers. Wanda Coleman in the *Los Angeles Times Book Review* calls it "a thoroughly enjoyable segment from the life of a celebrity," while Christian describes it as "a thoughtful yet spirited account of one Afro-American woman's journey into the land of her ancestors." In Coleman's opinion, *All God's Children Need Traveling Shoes* is "an important document drawing more much needed attention to the hidden history of a people both African and American."

MEDIA ADAPTATIONS: I Know Why the Caged Bird Sings has been adapted into a television movie.

BIOGRAPHICAL/CRITICAL SOURCES:

BOOKS

Angelou, Maya, *I Know Why the Caged Bird Sings,* Random House, 1970.
Angelou, *Gather Together in My Name,* Random House, 1974.
Angelou, *Singin' and Swingin' and Gettin' Merry Like Christmas,* Random House, 1976.
Angelou, *The Heart of a Woman,* Random House, 1981.
Angelou, *All God's Children Need Traveling Shoes,* Random House, 1986.
Contemporary Literary Criticism, Gale, Volume 12, 1980, Volume 35, 1985.
Dictionary of Literary Biography, Volume 38: *Afro-American Writers after 1955: Dramatists and Prose Writers,* Gale, 1985.

PERIODICALS

Black Scholar, summer, 1982.
Black World, July, 1975.
Chicago Tribune, November 1, 1981.

Chicago Tribune Book World, March 23, 1986.
Detroit Free Press, May 9, 1986.
Harper's, November, 1972.
Harvard Educational Review, November, 1970.
Ladies' Home Journal, May, 1976.
Los Angeles Times, May 29, 1983.
Los Angeles Times Book Review, April 13, 1986, August 9, 1987.
Ms., January, 1977.
New Republic, July 6, 1974.
Newsweek, March 2, 1970.
New York Times, February 25, 1970.
New York Times Book Review, June 16, 1974.
Observer (London), April 1, 1984.
Parnassus: Poetry in Review, fall-winter, 1979.
Poetry, August, 1976.
Southern Humanities Review, fall, 1973.
Time, March 31, 1986.
Times (London), September 29, 1986.
Times Literary Supplement, February 17, 1974, June 14, 1985, January 24, 1986.
Village Voice, July 11, 1974, October 28, 1981.
Washington Post, October 13, 1981.
Washington Post Book World, October 4, 1981, June 26, 1983, May 11, 1986.

*   *   *

ANOUILH, Jean (Marie Lucien Pierre) 1910-1987

PERSONAL: Surname pronounced "Ahn-wee"; born June 23, 1910, in Bordeaux, France; died of a heart attack October 3, 1987, in Lausanne, Switzerland; son of Francois (a tailor) and Marie-Magdeleine (a pianist; maiden name, Soulue) Anouilh; married first wife, Monelle Valentin (divorced); married second wife, Nicole Lancon, July 30, 1953; children: (first marriage) Catherine; (second marriage) Caroline, Nicolas, Marie-Colombe. *Education:* College Chaptal, baccalaureate; Sorbonne, University of Paris, law student, 1931-32.

ADDRESSES: Home—7 rue Saint-James, 92200 Neuilly-sur-Seine, France.

CAREER: Writer, 1929-87. Advertising copy writer, author of publicity scripts and comic gags for films, 1929-32; secretary to theatrical company Comedie des Champs-Elysees, Paris, 1931-32. Also directed several films in France. *Military service:* Served in French Army during 1930s.

AWARDS, HONORS: Grand Prix du Cinema Francais, 1949, for film "Monsieur Vincent"; Antoinette Perry ("Tony") Award and citation from the cultural division of the French Embassy, both 1955, both for *Thieves' Carnival* (New York production); New York Drama Critics Circle Award for best foreign play of 1956-57, for *Waltz of the Toreadors;* Prix Dominique for the direction of film "Madame M.," 1959; *Evening Standard* newspaper drama award and Antoinette Perry Award for best foreign play of the year, both 1961, both for *Becket; or, The Honor of God; Evening Standard* newspaper drama award for best play of the year, 1963, for *Poor Bitos;* first prize for best play of the year, Syndicate of French Drama Critics, 1970, for *Cher Antoine; ou, l'amour rate* and *Les poissons rouges; ou, mon pere, ce heros;* Paris Critics Prize, 1971, for *Ne reveillez pas madame.*

WRITINGS:

PLAYS

(With Jean Aurenche) *Humulus le muet,* Editions Francaises Nouvelles, c. 1929.

"L'hermine," first produced in Paris at Theatre de l'Oeuvre, 1932.
"Mandarine," first produced in Paris at Theatre de l'Athenee, 1933.
"Y'avait un prisonnier" (title means "There Was a Prisoner"), first produced in Paris at Theatre des Ambassadeurs, 1935.
"Le voyageur sans bagage" (first produced in Paris at Theatre des Mathurins, 1937; English translation by Lucienne Hill produced in New York at ANTA Theatre, 1964; also see below), translation by John Whiting published as *Traveller without Luggage,* Methuen, 1959.
La sauvage (first produced in Paris at Theatre des Mathurins, 1938), translation by Hill published as *Restless Heart,* Methuen, 1957.
Le bal des voleurs (first produced in Paris at Theatre des Arts, 1938; produced in New York at Theatre des Quatre Saisons, 1938; English version produced as *Thieve's Carnival* in New York at Cherry Lane Theatre, 1955), Editions Francaises Nouvelles, 1945, translation by Hill published as *Thieves' Carnival,* Samuel French, 1952.
Rendez-vous de Senlis (first produced in Paris at Theatre de l'Atelier, 1938; produced as *Dinner with the Family,* in New York at Gramercy Arts Theatre, 1961; also see below), Editions de la Table Ronde, 1958, translation by Edwin O. Marsh published as *Dinner with the Family,* Methuen, 1958.
Leocadia (first produced at Theatre de l'Atelier, 1939; produced as *Time Remembered,* in New York at Morosco Theater, 1957; also see below), Appleton, 1965, translation by Patricia Moyes published as *Time Remembered,* Methuen, 1955.
Eurydice (first produced at Theatre de l'Atelier, 1941; produced in English in Hollywood at Coronet Theatre, 1948; also see below), annotation by Rambert George, Bordas, 1968, translation by Kitty Black published as *Point of Departure,* Samuel French, 1951, second English translation published as *Legend of Lovers,* Coward, 1952.
Antigone (first produced at Theatre de l'Atelier, 1944; produced in English in New York at Cort Theatre, 1946; also see below), Editions de la Table Ronde, 1946, translation by Lewis Galantiere, Random House, 1946; excerpts published as *Antigone: Extraits,* Bordas, 1968.
"Romeo et Jeannette" (also see below), first produced at Theatre de l'Atelier, 1946, translation by Miriam John produced as "Jeannette," in New York at Maidman Playhouse, 1960.
L'invitation au chateau (first produced at Theatre de l'Atelier, 1947; produced as *Ring around the Moon,* in New York at Martin Beck Theatre, 1950), Editions de la Table Ronde, 1948, translation by Christopher Fry published as *Ring around the Moon,* Oxford University Press, 1950.
"Episode de la vie d'un auteur" (one-act; also see below), first produced in Paris at Comedie des Champs-Elysees, 1948; translation produced as "Episode in the Life of an Author" in Buffalo, N.Y., at Studio Arena Theatre, September, 1969.
Ardele; ou, la Marguerite (first produced with *Episode de la vie d'un auteur,* at Comedie des Champs-Elysees, 1948; produced as "Cry of the Peacock," in New York at Mansfield Theatre, 1950), Editions de la Table Ronde, 1949, translation by Hill published as *Ardele,* Methuen, 1951.
Cecile; ou, l'ecole des peres (first produced at Comedie des Champs-Elysees, 1949; also see below), Editions de la Table Ronde, 1954.
La repetition; ou, l'amour puni (first produced in Paris at Theatre Marigny, 1950; produced in New York at Ziegfield Theatre, 1952), La Palatine (Geneva), 1950, critical edition, Bordas, 1970, translation by Pamela Hansford Johnson and Black published as *The Rehearsal,* Coward, 1961.

Colombe (first produced at Theatre de l'Atelier, 1951; adaptation by Denis Cannan produced in New York at Longacre Theatre, 1954), Livre de Poche, 1963, translation by Cannan published as *Colombe,* Coward, 1954.

Monsieur Vincent (dialogue), Beyerische Schuelbuch-Verlag, 1951.

La valse des toreadors (English translation produced in New York at Coronet Theatre, 1957), Editions de la Table Ronde, 1952, translation by Hill published as *The Waltz of the Toreadors,* Elek, 1956, Coward, 1957.

L'alouette (first produced in Paris at Theatre Montparnasse, 1953; adaptation by Lillian Hellman produces as "The Lark" in New York at Longacre Theatre, 1955), Editions de la Table Ronde, 1953, translation by Christopher Fry published as *The Lark,* Methuen, 1955.

Medee (first produced at Theatre de l'Atelier, 1953; also see below), Editions de la Table Ronde, 1953.

Ornifle; ou, le courant d'air (first produced at Comedie des Champs-Elysees, 1955), Editions de la Table Ronde, 1955, translation by Hill published as *Ornifle: A Play,* Hill & Wang, 1970.

Pauvre Bitos; ou, le diner de tetes (first produced at Theatre Montparnasse, 1956; produced in English in New York at Classic Stage Repertory, 1969), Editions de la Table Ronde, 1958, translation by Hill published as *Poor Bitos,* Coward, 1964.

L'hurluberlu; ou, le reactionnaire amoureux (first produced at Comedie des Champs-Elysees, 1959; produced in English in New York at ANTA Theatre, 1959), Editions de la Table Ronde, 1959, translation by Hill published as *The Fighting Cock,* Coward, 1960.

Becket; ou, l'honneur de Dieu (first produced in Paris at Theatre Montparnasse-Gaston Baty, 1959; produced as "Becket," in New York at St. James Theatre, 1960), Editions de la Table Ronde, 1959, translation by Hill published as *Becket; or, The Honor of God,* Coward, 1960.

Madame de . . . (produced with "Traveller without Luggage" in London at Arts Theatre, 1959), translation by John Whiting, Samuel French, c. 1959.

"La petite Moliere," first produced in France at Festival of Bordeaux, 1960.

La grotte (first produced at Theatre Montparnasse, 1961; produced in English in Cincinnati at Playhouse in the Park, June, 1967), Editions de la Table Ronde, 1961, translation by Hill published as *The Cavern,* Hill & Wang, 1966.

La foire d'empoigne (first produced in Paris, 1962), Editions de la Table Ronde, 1961.

"L'orchestre," first produced in Paris, 1962; produced in English in Buffalo, at Studio Arena Theatre, September, 1969.

Fables, Editions de la Table Ronde, 1962.

Le boulanger, la boulangere et le petit mitron (first produced at Comedie des Champs-Elysees, November 13, 1968; English translation by Hill produced in Newcastle, England, at University Theatre, fall, 1972), Editions de la Table Ronde, 1969.

Cher Antoine; ou, l'amour rate (first produced at Comedie des Champs-Elysees, October 1, 1969; produced in English in Cambridge, Mass., at Loeb Drama Center of Harvard University, July 20, 1973), Editions de la Table Ronde, 1969, translation by Hill published as *Dear Antoine; or, The Love That Failed,* Hill & Wang, 1971.

"Le Theatre; ou, la vie comme elle est," first produced at Comedie des Champs-Elysees, c. 1970.

Ne reveillez pas madame (first produced at Comedie des Champs-Elysees, October 21, 1970), Editions de la Table Ronde, 1970.

Les poissons rouges; ou, mon pere, ce heros (first produced at Theatre de l'Oeuvre, c. 1970), Editions de la Table Ronde, 1970.

Tu etais si gentil quand tu etais petit (first produced at Theatre Antoine, January 18, 1972), Editions de la Table Ronde, 1972.

Le directeur de l'opera, Editions de la Table Ronde, 1972.

Monsieur Barnette, avec l'orchestre, Schoenhof, 1975.

L'arrestation: piece en deux parties, Editions de la Table Ronde, 1975, translation by Hill published as *The Arrest: A Drama in Two Acts,* Samuel French, 1978.

Le scenario, Schoenhof, 1976.

Chers Zoiseaux, Schoenhof, 1977.

La culotte, Editions de la Table Ronde, 1978.

"Number One," produced in English in London at Queen's Theatre, April 24, 1984.

Also author of plays published in French periodicals, including "Attile le magnifique," 1930, "Le petit bonheur," 1935, "L'incertain," 1938, "Oreste," 1945, "Jezebel," 1946, and "Le songe du critique," 1961.

TRANSLATOR

(And editor) William Shakespeare, *Trois comedies* (contains *As You Like It, Winter's Tale,* and *Twelfth Night*), Editions de la Table Ronde, 1952.

(With wife, Nicole Anouilh) Graham Greene, *L'amant complaisant* (translation of *The Complacent Lover*) Laffont, 1962.

Shakespeare, "Richard III," performed at Theatre Montparnasse, 1964.

OMNIBUS VOLUMES IN FRENCH

Pieces roses: Le bal des voleurs, Le rendez-vous de Senlis, Leocadia, Editions Balzac, 1942, 2nd edition, with addition of *Humulus le muet,* Editions de la Table Ronde, 1958.

Pieces noires: L'hermine, La sauvage, Le voyageur sans bagage, Eurydice, Editions Balzac, 1942.

Nouvelles pieces noires: Jezebel, Antigone, Romeo et Jeannette, [et] Medee, Editions de la Table Ronde, 1946.

Antigone [et] Medee, Le Club Francais du Livre, 1948.

Pieces brillantes: L'invitation au chateau, Colombe, La repetition; ou, l'amour puni, [et] Cecile; ou, l'ecole des peres, Editions de la Table Ronde, 1951.

Deux pieces brillantes: L'invitation au chateau [et] La repetition; ou, l'amour puni, Le Club Francais du Livre, 1953.

La sauvage [et] Le bal des voleurs, Colmann-Levy, 1955.

Antigone [et] L'alouette, Livre Club de Libraire, 1956.

Pieces grincantes (includes *Ardele; ou, la Marguerite, La valse des toreadors, Ornifle; ou, le courant d'air,* and *Pauvre Bitos; ou, le diner de tetes*), Editions de la Table Ronde, 1956.

Une piece rose, deux pieces noires (includes *Le bal des voleurs, La sauvage,* and *Eurydice*), Club des Libraires de France, 1956.

Le rendez-vous de Senlis [et] Leocadia, Editions de la Table Ronde, 1958.

Le voyageur sans bagage [et] Le bal des voleurs, Editions de la Table Ronde, 1958.

Antigone, Becket, [et] Cecile, Editions de la Table Ronde, 1959.

La sauvage [et] L'invitation au chateau, Editions de la Table Ronde, 1960.

Pieces costumees (includes *L'alouette, Becket; ou, l'honneur de Dieu,* and *La foire d'empoigne*), Editions de la Table Ronde, 1960.

Theatre complet, six volumes, Editions de la Table Ronde, 1961-63.

Deux pieces roses: Le bal des voleurs [et] Le rendezvous de Senlis, Le Club Francais du Livre, 1963.

Ardele; ou, la Marguerite suivi de La valse des toreadors, Editions de la Table Ronde, 1970.

Nouvelles pieces grincantes (contains *L'hurluberlu; ou, le reactionnaire amoureux, La grotte, L'orchestre, Le boulanger, la boulangere, et le petit mitron,* and *Les poissons rouges; ou, mon pere, ce heros*), Editions de la Table Ronde, 1970.

Eurydice, suivi de Romeo et Jeannette, Editions de la Table Ronde, 1971.

Pieces baroques (includes *Cher Antoine, Ne reveillez pas madame, Le directeur de l'opera*), French & European, 1974.

Pieces secrets (includes *Tu etais si gentil quand tu etais petit, L'arrestation,* and *Le scenario*), French & European, 1977.

Also author of *La repetition; ou, L'amour puni, Leocadia [et] Eurydice,* Club des Amis.

OMNIBUS VOLUMES IN ENGLISH

Antigone [and] *Eurydice,* Methuen, 1951.

. . . *Plays,* three volumes, Hill & Wang, Volume 1: *Five Plays* (contains *Antigone, Eurydice, The Ermine, The Rehearsal,* and *Romeo and Jeannette*), 1958, Volume 2: *Five Plays* (contains *Restless Heart, Time Remembered, Ardele, Mademoiselle Colombe,* and *The Lark*), 1959, Volume 3: *Seven Plays* (contains *Thieves' Carnival, Medea, Cecile; or, The School for Fathers, Traveler without Luggage, The Orchestra, Episode in the Life of an Author,* and *Catch as Catch Can*), 1967.

Ardele [and] *Colombe,* Methuen, 1959.

Leocadia [and] *Humulus le muet,* Harrap, 1961.

Ardele [and] *Pauvre Bitos,* Dell, 1965.

The Collected Plays, Methuen, Volume 1 (contains *The Ermine, Thieves' Carnival, Restless Heart, Traveller without Luggage,* and *Dinner with the Family*), 1966, Volume 2 (contains *Time Remembered, Point of Departure, Antigone, Romeo and Jeannette,* and *Medea*), 1967.

FILMS

(With Aurenche) "Le voyageur sans bagage," 1943, released in U.S. as "Identity Unknown," Republic, 1945.

(With J. Bernard-Luc) "Monsieur Vincent," released in U.S. by Lopert, 1949.

"The End of Belle," released in U.S. as "The Passion of Slow Fire," Trans-Lux Distributing, 1962.

Also author of screenplays (with Jean Aurenche) "Les degourdis de la onzieme," 1936, (with Aurenche) "Vous n'avez rien a declarer," 1937, (with J. Duvivier and G. Morgan) "Anna Karenina," 1947, (with Bernard-Luc) "Pattes Blanches," 1948, "Un caprice de Caroline cherie," 1950, (with Monelle Valentin) "Deux sous de violettes," 1951, "Le rideau rouge (ce soir on joue Macbeth)," 1952, "Le chevalier de la nuit," 1953, "Waterloo," c. 1969, "La grain de beaute," c. 1969, and "Time for Loving," 1972.

OTHER

(With Pierre Imbourg and Andre Warnod) *Michel-Marie Poulain,* Braun, 1953.

(With Georges Neveux) *Le loup* (ballet), score by Henri Dutilleux, Editions Ricordi, 1953.

(With Leon Thoorens and others) *Le dossier Moliere,* Gerard, 1964.

Also author of ballet "Les demoiselles de la nuit," score by Jean-Rene Francaix, 1948. Contributor to anthologies, including *Contemporary Drama,* Scribner, 1956; *One-Act: Eleven Short Plays*

of the Modern Theatre, Grove, 1961; *Joan of Arc: Fact, Legend, and Literature,* Harcourt, 1964; and *Masterpieces of Modern French Theatre,* Macmillan, 1967.

SIDELIGHTS: The late Jean Anouilh was ranked among France's most successful popular playwrights for more than forty years. One of several theatrical craftsmen whose work marked an exceptionally rich era in French theatre, Anouilh authored numerous dramas that have been performed all over the world. His plays often feature moral heroes, forced to desperate confrontations with "a world fueled by cowardice, revenge and hatred," to quote *Washington Post* contributor Richard Pearson. This expressed horror at mankind's predicament led Anouilh to pen many grim dramas (he called them "black plays" and "grating plays"), but it also spawned humorous pieces that have been compared to the works of Moliere. In *Jean Anouilh: Stages in Rebellion,* B. A. Lenski wrote: "For thirty years, through bedroom as well as metaphysical farces, Anouilh has been providing us with his orchestration of the eternal debate between the body and the soul. . . . [His] voice rises in indignation before certain historical crimes and yet always remains stylized, elegant and perfectly allied to the action on the stage." Sylvie Drake put it more succinctly in the *Los Angeles Times.* Anouilh, Drake concluded, "was a man of ideas who skillfully disguised them as entertainments."

Anouilh held strong views on the purpose of the theatre. He saw drama as a temporary escape from awareness of the inevitability of death, and he therefore strove to make his work highly theatrical. A London *Times* reviewer found Anouilh's plays "compellingly watchable," with "dialogue which could be spoken easily and effectively on stage." *Nation* correspondent Harold Clurman also observed that the playwright desired "to do little more than purvey material for enjoyable theatregoing. But that is only a disguise: Anouilh [possessed] an artistic individuality, deep-rooted in his personality and in the nature of the French nation." Lenski wrote that Anouilh was "the type of playwright who [poured] all his life into his plays, crying, laughing, vituperating, battling, confessing. . . . Such theatre often exhibits cheap sentimentality, is talkative, abounds in locker-room jokes, relies on vaudeville gimmicks—yet in so doing it is only true to life." The effect of such entertainment, concluded Jack Kroll in *Newsweek,* is "like a child being held by a sage and cynical uncle who talks seductively of the bittersweet pleasure-pains of life."

Anouilh enjoyed grouping his plays in categories. He did it, he said, to satisfy the public's need for classifications—but it also helped to organize his prolific oeuvre. His categories included *pieces noires* (black plays), *pieces roses* (rosy plays), *nouvelles pieces noires* (new black plays), *pieces brillantes* (brilliant plays), *pieces grincantes* (grating plays), *pieces costumees* (costume plays), and *pieces baroques* (baroque plays). *Jean Anouilh* author Alba Della Fazia wrote: "In plays classified as 'black,' 'pink,' 'brilliant,' 'jarring,' and 'costumed,' Anouilh treats an assortment of themes that range from the soul of man to the world of men, from the heroism of the individual to the mediocrity of the masses. Some of the plays are heavy and dismal, some are light and fanciful, but all reveal the author's profound and often painful insight into the human condition."

The *pieces noires* and the *pieces roses* are similar in content—both are concerned with man's survival in an inhospitable environment. In the *pieces noires,* society triumphs over the hero's ideals, forcing the hero to seek a tragic form of escape. Lenski observed that the central characters in the *pieces noires* "are deaf to arguments in favor of a humble sort of happiness. They want all or nothing at all, and the lower they stand, the greater their claims on the Ideal, the louder their plea for help." In the *pieces roses,* the hero escapes not through death but through fantasy, illusion, and changing personality. In *The World of Jean Anouilh,* author Leonard Cabell Pronko contended that although the characters of the *pieces roses* are unheroic in their compromise with happiness, "they at least possess the noble desire for the purity of life that dares to be what it is without excuses. But they are satisfied with a happiness that Anouilh later satirizes as illusory and unworthwhile." In his book entitled *Jean Anouilh,* Lewis W. Falb concluded: "Anouilh may choose to present his observations in the guise of amusing fables, but one must not be deceived by their often pleasing surfaces; the vision underlying them is brutal and unpleasant. . . . But in his theatre, even at his most misanthropic, Anouilh offers a glimpse of an ideal, which, although faint or parodied, is not forgotten."

Over time Anouilh gradually became more grim in his theatrical treatments of his fellow men. Harold Hobson noted in *Drama* magazine that these *pieces gricantes* "certainly caused audiences and critics to say that Anouilh was a man who hated life itself." *New York Times* contributor Gerald Jonas described these "grating plays" as productions in which "moments of realism, even tragedy, alternate with moments of corrosive humor. In such plays, judgments about events on the stage and the motivations of the principals must be constantly revised in the light of new revelations. Anyone in the audience who does not feel a certain discomfort as the evening progresses is probably not paying attention." Pronko claimed that the picture "is one of compromise, and the outlook seems more pessimistic than ever. We can find no hole in the fabric of an absurd universe through which to bring in some meaning." Della Fazia, too, stated that the effect of the plays "is 'jarring' because two irreconcilables—comedy and tragedy—clash on a battlefield strewn with the castoff armor of humanity's defense mechanisms."

In his *The Theatre of Jean Anouilh,* H. G. McIntyre wrote: "It is hardly an exaggeration to say that there is only one central theme running through the whole of Anouilh's work—the eternal and universal conflict between idealism and reality. All his other themes are related to this, either as expressions of the idealistic rejection of life or as explorations of the various obstacles to idealism and self-realization in an imperfect world." Lenski felt that Anouilh judged reality "from the height of the ideal and inevitably, seen from high up, the world seems a very sad place to live. At the same time, in showing reality in black coloring, Anouilh places the ideal into proper perspective." According to Joseph Chiari in *The Contemporary French Theatre: The Flight from Naturalism,* the pessimism of Anouilh is "the revolt of a sensitive being appalled and wounded by the cruelty of life and expressing man's despair at never being able to know his true self or to meet another self in a state of purity. . . . His heroes and heroines are alone, and when they hope to escape from their loneliness through another they generally realize that there is no escape, that life soils everything and that unless they choose to live a lie, death is the only solution—or failing death, the acceptance of suffering as a refining fire which will consume the dross into the ashes of a life devoted to an ideal."

This tendency to champion nonconformity gave Anouilh's work a political edge, especially during the Second World War. During the Nazi occupation of France, Anouilh produced the play *Antigone,* a reworking of the classical story of a young woman who dies because she defies the state. With *Antigone,* Bryan Appleyard wrote in the London *Times,* Anouilh "confronted the ironic contrast between the life of the imagination and the life of the world." Resistance critics hailed the work as a position statement, but Nazi collaborators also praised it for the prag-

matic, reasoned arguments it offered in favor of capitulation. A *Times* contributor claimed, however, that *Antigone* "remains the quintessential French play of the 1940s. It combines moving if ambiguous references to the politics of the Resistance with a metaphysical despair that went straight to many an adolescent heart." After the war, Anouilh continued to pen dramas about martyrs; his best-known plays include *Becket; or, The Honor of God,* the story of an English archbishop murdered for his steadfast adherence to the church, and *The Lark,* a treatment of the life of Joan of Arc. Pronko noted that these works show a conflict between "the hero's or the heroine's aspirations and the world of compromise that they must face and in contact with which they would become sullied. . . . Contrasted to them are the mediocre who consent to play the game, and who seek happiness by hiding the truth of life's absurdity from themselves."

Anouilh died of a heart attack at the age of 77. Ironically, given his predilection for viewing himself as an entertainer, he was eulogized as a playwright of ideas. Pronko called Anouilh "a writer who [was] bound to the cause of man's freedom." Likewise, Falb praised the author for his "rich statement of a personal vision, a lucid yet entertaining exploration of themes that involve the anxieties and preoccupations of contemporary audiences." Still, Chiari maintained that it was "human reality and not systems or concepts which Anouilh [was] after, and that is why his characters, full of human contradictions, are emotionally alive. It is in fact not what they think, but above all what they feel which is the main factor." In comedies that force audiences to laugh uncomfortably at their own absurdities, and in tragedies that highlight the venality of life, Anouilh strove to reveal his deepest torments. In the process, to quote Bettina L. Knapp in *Books Abroad,* he "has given the world some very great plays." As Harold Hobson put it, "Jean Anouilh, savage and ferocious at the crucifixion of humanity's highest values, was the greatest dramatist of our time."

MEDIA ADAPTATIONS: L'alouette was adapted for television and presented as "The Lark," in the "Hallmark Hall of Fame" series, 1956-57; *Madame de . . .* was filmed in 1959; *Leocadia* was adapted for television and presented by Compass Productions as "Time Remembered" for the "Hallmark Hall of Fame" series, 1961; *La valse des toreadors* was filmed with the title "Waltz of the Toreadors," Continental Distributing, 1962; *Becket; ou, l'honneur de Dieu* was filmed with the title "Becket," Paramount Pictures, 1963; the film "Monsoon," United Artists, 1963, was based on *Romeo et Jeannette; Colombe* was produced as an opera at Opera Comique, Paris, c. 1970; *Traveller without Luggage* was adapted for NET Playhouse in 1971; *Antigone* was produced in English for "Playhouse New York," Public Broadcasting System, 1972.

BIOGRAPHICAL/CRITICAL SOURCES:

BOOKS

Archer, Marguerite, *Jean Anouilh,* Columbia University Press, 1971.

Bogard, Travis and William I. Oliver, editors, *Modern Drama: Essays in Criticism,* Oxford University Press, 1965.

Brustein, Robert, *Seasons of Discontent: Dramatic Opinions, 1959-1965,* Simon & Schuster, 1965.

Chiari, Joseph, *The Contemporary French Theatre: The Flight from Naturalism,* Gordian Press, 1970.

Chiari, Joseph, *Landmarks of Contemporary Drama,* Herbert Jenkins, 1965.

Cole, Toby, editor, *Playwrights on Playwrighting,* Hill & Wang, 1961.

Contemporary Literary Criticism, Gale, Volume 1, 1973, Volume 3, 1975, Volume 8, 1978, Volume 13, 1980, Volume 40, 1986, Volume 50, 1988.

Curtis, Anthony, *New Developments in the French Theatre: A Critical Introduction to the Plays of Jean-Paul Sartre, Simone de Beauvoir, Albert Camus and Jean Anouilh,* Curtain Press, 1948.

Della Fazia, Alba M., *Jean Anouilh,* Twayne, 1969.

de Luppe, Robert, *Jean Anouilh,* Editions Universitaires, 1959.

Falb, Lewis W., *Jean Anouilh,* Ungar, 1977.

Fowlie, Wallace, *Dionysus in Paris: A Guide to Contemporary French Theater,* World, 1960.

Gassner, John, *Theatre at the Crossroads: Plays and Playwrights of the Mid-Century American Stage,* Holt, 1960.

Gassner, John, *Dramatic Soundings: Evaluations and Retractions Culled from 30 Years of Drama Criticism,* Crown, 1968.

Grossvogel, David I., *The Self-Conscious Stage in Modern French Drama,* Columbia University Press, 1958.

Harvey, John, *Anouilh: A Study in Theatrics,* Yale University Press, 1964.

Jolivet, Phillippe, *Le Theatre de Jean Anouilh,* Michel Brient, 1963.

Kelly, K. W., *Jean Anouilh: An Annotated Bibliography,* Scarecrow, 1973.

Lenski, B. A., *Jean Anouilh: Stages in Rebellion,* Humanities Press, 1975.

Marsh, E. O., *Jean Anouilh,* British Book Centre, 1953.

McIntyre, H. G., *The Theatre of Jean Anouilh,* Barnes & Noble, 1981.

Picon, Gaetan, *Contemporary French Literature: 1945 and After,* Ungar, 1974.

Pronko, Leonard Cabell, *The World of Jean Anouilh,* University of California Press, 1961.

Smith, H. A., *Contemporary Theater,* Arnold, 1962.

Thody, P. M. W., *Anouilh,* Oliver & Boyd, 1968.

PERIODICALS

Books Abroad, autumn, 1976.
College English, March, 1955.
Nation, October 8, 1973.
New Republic, February 11, 1957.
Newsweek, September 24, 1973.
New York Times, November 7, 1979, October 13, 1985, October 17, 1985, May 29, 1989.
Plays and Players, April, 1974.
Romance Notes, fall, 1978.
Times (London), April 23, 1984.
Yale French Studies, winter, 1954-55.

OBITUARIES:

PERIODICALS

Chicago Tribune, October 6, 1987.
Drama, 1st quarter, 1988.
Los Angeles Times, October 7, 1987.
New York Times, October 5, 1987.
Times (London), October 5, 1987.
Village Voice, October 20, 1987.
Washington Post, October 5, 1987.

—*Sketch by Anne Janette Johnson*

ANTHONY, John
See CIARDI, John (Anthony)

*   *   *

ANTHONY, Peter
See SHAFFER, Peter (Levin)

*   *   *

ANTHONY, Piers 1934-
(Robert Piers, a joint pseudonym)

PERSONAL: Name originally Piers Anthony Dillingham Jacob; born August 6, 1934, in Oxford, England; came to United States, 1940, naturalized, 1958; son of Alfred Bennis and Norma (Sherlock) Jacob; married Carol Marble (a computer programmer), June 23, 1956; children: Penelope Carolyn, Cheryl. *Education:* Goddard College, B.A., 1956; University of South Florida, teaching certificate, 1964. *Politics:* Independent. *Religion:* "No preference."

ADDRESSES: Office—c/o Press Relations, Ace Books, Berkley Publishing Corp., 200 Madison Ave., New York, N.Y. 10016.

CAREER: Electronic Communications, Inc., St. Petersburg, Fla., technical writer, 1959-62; free-lance writer, 1962-63; Admiral Farragut Academy, St. Petersburg, teacher of English, 1965-66; free-lance writer, 1966—. *Military service:* U.S. Army, 1957-59.

AWARDS, HONORS: Nebula Award nomination, Science Fiction Writers of America, 1966, for short story "The Message"; Nebula Award nomination, 1967, and Hugo Award nomination, World Science Fiction Convention, 1968, both for *Chthon;* science fiction award, Pyramid Books/*Magazine of Fantasy and Science Fiction/*Kent Productions, 1967, and Hugo Award nomination, 1968, both for *Sos the Rope;* Hugo Award nomination, 1969, for novella "Getting Through University," and 1970, for *Macroscope* and for best fan writer; Nebula Award nomination, 1970, for short story "The Bridge," and 1972, for novelette "In the Barn"; British Fantasy Award, 1977, and Hugo Award nomination, 1978, both for *A Spell for Chameleon.*

WRITINGS:

Chthon (science fiction), Ballantine, 1967, reprinted, Berkley Publishing, 1982.
(With Robert E. Margroff) *The Ring,* Ace Books, 1968.
Macroscope (science fiction), Avon, 1969, reprinted, Gregg Press, 1985.
(With Margroff) *The E.S.P. Worm,* Paperback Library, 1970, reprinted, Tor Books, 1986.
(Contributor) Anthony Cheetham, editor, *Science Against Man,* Avon, 1970.
(Contributor) Harry Harrison, editor, *Nova One: An Anthology of Original Science Fiction,* Delacorte Press, 1970.
Prostho Plus (science fiction), Gollancz, 1971, Bantam, 1973.
(Contributor) Harlan Ellison, editor, *Again, Dangerous Visions,* Doubleday, 1972.
(Contributor) David Gerrold, editor, *Generation,* Dell, 1972.
Race Against Time (juvenile), Hawthorne, 1973.
Rings of Ice (science fiction), Avon, 1974.
Triple Detente (science fiction), DAW Books, 1974.
Phthor (sequel to *Chthon;* science fiction), Berkley Publishing, 1975.
(With Robert Coulson) *But What of Earth?* (science fiction), Laser (Toronto), 1976.
Steppe (science fiction), Millington, 1976, Tor Books, 1985.

Hasan (fantasy), Borgo Press, 1977.

(With Frances Hall) *The Pretender* (science fiction), Borgo Press, 1979.

God of Tarot (first section of *Tarot;* also see below), Jove, 1979.

Vision of Tarot (second section of *Tarot;* also see below), Berkley Publishing, 1980.

Faith of Tarot (third section of *Tarot;* also see below), Berkley Publishing, 1980.

Mute (science fiction), Avon, 1981.

(Contributor) Victoria Schochet and John Silbersack, editors, *The Berkley Showcase,* Berkley Publishing, 1981.

Anthonology (short stories), Tor Books, 1985.

Ghost (science fiction), Tor Books, 1986.

Shade of the Tree, St. Martin's, 1986.

(Editor with Barry Malzberg and Martin Greenberg) *Uncollected Stars* (short stories), Avon, 1986.

(With Margroff) *Dragon's Gold,* Tor Books, 1987.

Tarot (contains *God of Tarot, Vision of Tarot,* and *Faith of Tarot*), Ace Books, 1987.

Bio of an Ogre (autobiography), Ace Books, 1988.

(With Margroff) *Serpent's Silver,* Tor Books, 1988.

Balook, Underwood-Miller, 1989.

Pornucopia, Tafford Publishing, 1989.

Total Recall, Morrow, 1989.

(With Jody Lynn Nye) *Piers Anthony's Visual Guide to Xanth,* Avon, 1989.

(With Robert Kornwise) *Through the Ice,* Underwood-Miller, 1990.

"APPRENTICE ADEPT" SERIES; SCIENCE FICTION/FANTASY NOVELS

Split Infinity, Del Rey, 1980.

Blue Adept, Del Rey, 1981.

Juxtaposition, Del Rey, 1982.

Double Exposure (omnibus volume; includes *Split Infinity, Blue Adept,* and *Juxtaposition*), Doubleday, 1982.

Out of Phaze, Ace Books, 1987.

Robot Adept, Ace Books, 1988.

Unicorn Point, Ace Books, 1989.

Phase Doubt, Ace Books, in press.

"BATTLE CIRCLE" SERIES; SCIENCE FICTION NOVELS

Sos the Rope, Pyramid, 1968.

Var the Stick, Faber, 1972, Bantam, 1973.

Neq the Sword, Corgi, 1975.

Battle Circle (omnibus volume; includes *Sos the Rope, Var the Stick,* and *Neq the Sword*), Avon, 1978.

"BIO OF A SPACE TYRANT" SERIES; SCIENCE FICTION NOVELS

Refugee, Avon, 1983.

Mercenary, Avon, 1984.

Politician, Avon, 1985.

Executive, Avon, 1985.

Statesman, Avon, 1986.

"CLUSTER" SERIES; SCIENCE FANTASY NOVELS

Cluster, Avon, 1977 (published in England as *Vicinity Cluster,* Panther, 1979).

Chaining the Lady, Avon, 1978.

Kirlian Quest, Avon, 1978.

Thousandstar, Avon, 1980.

Viscous Circle, Avon, 1982.

"INCARNATIONS OF IMMORTALITY" SERIES; FANTASY NOVELS

On a Pale Horse, Del Rey, 1983.

Bearing an Hourglass, Del Rey, 1984.

With a Tangled Skein, Del Rey, 1985.

Wielding a Red Sword, Del Rey, 1987.

Being a Green Mother, Del Rey, 1987.

For Love of Evil, Morrow, 1988.

And Eternity, Morrow, 1989.

"JASON STRIKER" SERIES; WITH ROBERTO FUENTES; MARTIAL ARTS NOVELS

Kiai!, Berkley Publishing, 1974.

Mistress of Death, Berkley Publishing, 1974.

The Bamboo Bloodbath, Berkley Publishing, 1975.

Ninja's Revenge, Berkley Publishing, 1975.

Amazon Slaughter, Berkley Publishing, 1976.

"MAGIC OF XANTH" SERIES; FANTASY NOVELS

A Spell for Chameleon, Del Rey, 1977.

The Source of Magic, Del Rey, 1979.

Castle Roogna, Del Rey, 1979.

Centaur Aisle, Del Rey, 1981.

The Magic of Xanth (omnibus volume; includes *A Spell for Chameleon, The Source of Magic,* and *Castle Roogna*), Doubleday, 1981.

Ogre, Ogre, Del Rey, 1982.

Night Mare, Del Rey, 1983.

Dragon on a Pedestal, Del Rey, 1983.

Crewel Lye: A Caustic Yarn, Del Rey, 1985.

Golem in the Gears, Del Rey, 1986.

Vale of the Vole, Avon, 1987.

Heaven Cent, Avon, 1988.

Man From Mundania, Avon, 1989.

"OMNIVORE" SERIES; SCIENCE FICTION NOVELS

Omnivore, Ballantine, 1968.

Orn, Avon, 1971.

Ox, Avon, 1976.

OTHER

Contributor, with Robert Margroff, under joint pseudonym Robert Piers, of a short story to *Adam Bedside Reader.* Also contributor of short stories to science fiction periodicals, including *Analog Science Fact/Science Fiction, Fantastic, Worlds of If, Worlds of Tomorrow, Amazing, Magazine of Fantasy and Science Fiction,* and *Pandora.*

WORK IN PROGRESS: Firefly, a horror story; *Tatham Mound,* a historical novel.

SIDELIGHTS: "Piers Anthony," states Michael R. Collings in his study *Piers Anthony,* "has become one of the most prolific and controversial writers in the genre" of fantasy/science fiction. An author whose "early fiction earned him a name as a solid writer with flashes of brilliance," Anthony "survived a blackballing by publishers" to emerge in the 1980s as a highly successful novelist with a broad readership and a large output, according to Daryl Lane, Bill Vernon, and David Carson in their introduction to Anthony's interview in *The Sound of Wonder: Interviews From "The Science Fiction Radio Show," Volume 2.* His works, including the highly popular "Magic of Xanth," "Apprentice Adept," and "Bio of a Space Tyrant" series, are often enjoyed by people who do not ordinarily read science fiction or fantasy, and his novels have appeared on best-seller lists.

The author suggests, in an interview with Charles Platt published in *Dream Makers Volume II: The Uncommon Men and Women Who Write Science Fiction,* that his light fantasy is popular because his readers are "tired when they come home, they don't want to read *War and Peace,* they just want to relax and be entertained." Yet Anthony's popularity does not detract from the quality of his work. Baird Searles and his fellow editors state in *A Reader's Guide to Science Fiction,* "Piers Anthony is one of those authors who can perform magic with the ordinary; he manages to take what at first glance seems to be a fairly pedestrian plot and make of it something rather special." "He is highly imaginative, but at the same time self-consistent; much of what is said about one novel is applicable to others. He is a careful craftsman in his plotting and in creating an array of truly alien characters," declares Collings. "Anthony is a craftsman," conclude the editors of *A Reader's Guide to Science Fiction,* "and, like a skilled furniture builder who can make a chair much more than a place to sit, makes a book more than words to read. Don't be misled by plot summary of any of his works; even if it sounds like you may have read it before by another author, Anthony will give you something extra." "That something," according to Collings, "is frequently an irrepressible sense of fun, of excitement, and of energy."

Anthony's first published novel, the Nebula and Hugo Award nominee *Chthon,* and its sequel *Phthor* share characteristic structures and themes with the rest of his fiction. In these books, declares Collings, Anthony "weaves a complex tapestry of myth and legend drawn from classical antiquity; from Norseland; from the Christian Eden and Paradise Lost; from Dante's Purgatory; from the modern mythologies of psychoanalysis and psychology; from literature; and from folk tales of magicians and dragons." *Chthon* relates the adventures of Aton Five, a prisoner sentenced to dwell inside a hellish planet. Eventually he establishes contact with the planet itself—Chthon, an intelligent mineral entity—and comes to terms with it. *Phthor* tells of Aton's son, Arlo, who brings the conflict between the collected mineral and organic intelligences to a destructive conclusion. Both books showcase Anthony's representative themes and devices, says Collings: control and order in civilization, the unity of life, punning and wordplay, and fertility or sterility. "The novels are complex, convoluted, inverted—and powerful," states Collings. "In incorporating the multiple strands of technique and theme and intertwining them with pre-existent strands of mythology, Anthony has himself created an enduring and a moving myth."

Other novels also explore themes relevant to science fiction and fantasy. *Dictionary of Literary Biography* contributors Stephen Bucchleugh and Beverly Rush note, "In Anthony's best fiction, questions of man's place in the ecology of the natural universe blend with considerations of the individual's role in providing satisfactory and humane answers." This is especially evident in the "Omnivore" books, where "Anthony assesses the human race, finds it lacking in certain essential areas, and then devises a structure by which it might be guided in its progress," says Collings. *Omnivore* itself is "an overt plea for respect for all life—human and animal," he continues. The "Battle Circle" trilogy takes place in a post-nuclear war America, and underlines the need for order in a civilization. *Macroscope,* another Hugo Award-nominated novel, presents the effects of a machine that shows how unimportant humanity is in comparison to the rest of the universe, and "in doing so, it becomes an allegory on the fate of the individual diminished and possibly destroyed by mass society," declare Bucchleugh and Rush. On a less galactic level, the *Tarot* novel—originally published in three volumes as *God of Tarot, Vision of Tarot,* and *Faith of Tarot*—takes as its theme

"questions of individual belief," according to Bucchleugh and Rush. "Much of the quest here is an internal one as Brother Paul of the secular Holy Order of Vision is sent to the planet Tarot to investigate the strange animations which may represent manifestations of the deity," they continue. "Paul's journey is both inward and outward as he finds companions in his quest, confronts temptations, fails and recovers, and finally faces his own personal hell."

Characterized by a lighthearted approach and the extensive use of puns, Anthony's "Xanth" fantasy novels are perhaps his most popular work. Xanth is a magic peninsula, sometimes resembling Florida, that makes occasional contacts with the outside world, known as Mundania. Populated with a variety of curious creatures—shoe-trees that grow shoes and chocolate-chip cookie bushes, for instance, as well as dragons, ogres, centaurs and nymphs—the country provides a rich background for Anthony's questing characters. *Fantasy Review* contributor Richard Mathews calls the Xanth series "one of the happiest things to happen to fantasy in a very long time." He maintains that *Dragon on a Pedestal,* the seventh Xanth novel, "exudes energy, humor and delightful invention." "This, like all the Xanth tales, is episodic in structure, and rich in classic mythic reference," he continues. "Anthony is assembling, bit by bit, his own *Arabian Nights.*" Mathews concludes by stating his belief that "the entire Xanth series ranks with the best of American and classic fantasy literature." Bob Collins, also writing for *Fantasy Review,* echoes Mathews's assessment, comparing Xanth to L. Frank Baum's land of Oz.

Other reviewers are not so enthusiastic. They find too much sexist humor and too great a reliance on puns in the "Xanth" novels. Baird Searles and his fellow editors in the *Reader's Guide to Fantasy,* for instance, consider the Xanth novels "a wee bit cute in their humor," and suggest that they "may tend to irritate some feminists." "The punning, more subdued in earlier books, goes wild here from the title onward," asserts *Science Fiction Review* contributor Philip M. Cohen, writing about the fourth Xanth novel, *Centaur Aisle.* He concludes: "You must be prepared to suspend disbelief—by the neck, until dead—and maturity as well; the ideal audience of this book is probably fourteen-year-olds. If you do, it's fun." Paul McGuire, also of *Science Fiction Review,* says of *Crewel Lye: A Caustic Yarn,* "At times the writing can be relentlessly cute, and it takes the plot a long time to get started. On the other hand, there is a fair amount of genuine wit in addition to the endless puns, the bumbling lout who is the hero does grow on one, a peculiar logic underlies the silliness of Xanth, and Anthony is a storyteller." When ordinary fantasy fare palls, he declares, "Xanth at the very least is something different inside, and a quite pleasant read."

Anthony states in his *Sound of Wonder* interview that he conceived the "Apprentice Adept" series to challenge two mutually exclusive audiences: science fiction readers who don't like fantasy and fantasy readers who won't read science fiction. "I thought the 'fantasy as pollution' people would be angry and so would the other side," he remarks. "I don't think I received a single negative comment on it; everybody seemed to like it, and they wanted more." Indeed, many critics support Anthony's assessment. "Aliens and unicorns in the same novel!" exclaims a reviewer for the *Science Fiction Chronicle,* writing about *Out of Phaze.* "It's easily the most interesting of Anthony's recent novels." *Science Fiction and Fantasy Book Review's* Richard W. Miller declares, "In fact, Anthony shows nice growth in his treatment of women in this series; they are not so stereotyped as, say, in the Xanth series." "What Anthony has done here (also in the Xanth series, but better in this [series])," Miller continues, "is to argue effectively for the basic human need for magic. Even the dedicated SF fan is likely to find that the magical (yet natural) world of Phaze has more appeal than its parallel/adjacent scientific (and ecologically controlled) analog, Proton."

The "Bio of a Space Tyrant" and "Incarnations of Immortality" series introduce what Roland Green of *Booklist* calls "Anthony's new 'serious' phase." Although the "Incarnations" volumes are fantasy and the "Bio" sequence is space opera, Anthony uses the forms as vehicles for social commentary. For instance, the "Incarnations of Immortality" feature Death, Time, Space, War, and Nature as protagonists, involved in a conflict against Satan. Mary S. Weinkauf of *Fantasy Review* calls *On a Pale Horse,* the first volume of the "Incarnations" series, "allegorical fantasy set in a future not much different from ours except in the use of magical stones and flying carpets." The "Bio of a Space Tyrant" series is "based on the Vietnamese boat people, really," Anthony tells Platt. It chronicles the rise of a space refugee to power on Jupiter, exploring problems of contemporary America in a science fictional setting. By the end of the third novel in the sequence, says Collings in *Fantasy Review,* Anthony "has explored capital punishment, warfare as political tool, US/Soviet relations, rights for the aged, bilingual education and flaws in the current electoral system."

Anthony tells the interviewers in *The Sound of Wonder:* "I'd like to think I'm on Earth for some purpose other than just to feed my face. I want to do something and try to leave the universe a better place than it was when I came into it. If there is anything in my power I can do to improve things, then I want to do it. I try to do this through the ability that I have as a writer, so I want to write, in the guise of fiction, material that people will read and become better persons for or get ideas that they wouldn't ordinarily have. . . . I want to do something so that when I die, I can look back and say I've done something useful in the world."

BIOGRAPHICAL/CRITICAL SOURCES:

BOOKS

Anthony, Piers, *Bio of an Ogre,* Ace Books, 1988.
Collings, Michael R., *Piers Anthony,* Starmont House, 1983.
Contemporary Literary Criticism, Volume 35, Gale, 1985.
Dictionary of Literary Biography, Volume 8: *Twentieth-Century American Science Fiction Writers,* Gale, 1981.
Lane, Daryl, William Vernon, and David Carson, *The Sound of Wonder: Interviews From "The Science Fiction Radio Show,"* Volume 2, Oryx Press, 1985.
Platt, Charles, *Dream Makers Volume II. The Uncommon Men and Women Who Write Science Fiction,* Berkley Publishing, 1983.
Searles, Baird, Beth Meacham, and Michael Franklin, *A Reader's Guide to Fantasy,* Avon, 1982.
Searles, Baird, Martin Last, Beth Meacham, and Michael Franklin, *A Reader's Guide to Science Fiction,* Avon, 1979.

PERIODICALS

Analog Science Fact/Science Fiction, March 30, 1981.
Booklist, June 1, 1979, July, 1984.
Books and Bookmen, July, 1969, December, 1969, April, 1970.
Fantasy Review, March, 1984, April, 1984, June, 1984, August, 1984, October, 1984, April, 1985, October, 1985, November, 1985, December, 1985, January, 1986, March, 1986, April, 1986, May, 1986, September, 1986, October, 1986, November, 1986, December, 1986, March, 1987, July, 1987.

Los Angeles Times Book Review, August 17, 1980, December 11, 1983, January 1, 1984, March 3, 1985.
Magazine of Fantasy and Science Fiction, July, 1986.
New York Times Book Review, April 20, 1986.
Observer (London), January 10, 1971.
Punch, April 4, 1984.
Science Fiction and Fantasy Book Review, March, 1982, July, 1982, October, 1983.
Science Fiction Chronicle, July, 1985, January, 1986, July, 1986, August, 1986, October, 1986, December, 1986, November, 1987.
Science Fiction Review, November, 1977, November, 1979, August, 1982, November, 1983, February, 1985, May, 1985, November, 1985, May, 1986, August, 1986.
Science Fiction Studies, Volume 2, 1975.
Times (London), May 14, 1983.
Times Literary Supplement, May 22, 1969, February 11, 1972, July 5, 1974.

*   *   *

ANTOINE, Marc
See PROUST, (Valentin-Louis-George-Eugene-)Marcel

*   *   *

ANTSCHEL, Paul   1920-1970
(Paul Celan)

PERSONAL: Born November 23, 1920, in Cernowitz, Rumania; committed suicide by drowning, sometime in April, 1970, in France; married Gisele de Lestrange (an artist), 1950; children: Eric. *Education:* Earned licence es lettres in Paris, 1950. *Religion:* Jewish.

CAREER: Poet and translator. Lecturer at L'Ecole Normale Superieure of University of Paris, 1959-70.

AWARDS, HONORS: Literary Prize of City of Bremen, 1958; Georg Buechner Prize, German Academy of Language and Literature, 1960.

WRITINGS:

POETRY; UNDER PSEUDONYM PAUL CELAN

Der Sand aus den Urnen, Sexl (Vienna), 1948.
Mohn und Gedaechtnis: Gedichte (title means "Poppy and Memory"), Deutsche Verlags-Anstalt (Stuttgart), 1952.
Von Schwelle zu Schwelle: Gedichte (title means "From Threshold to Threshold"), Deutsche Verlags-Anstalt, 1955.
Sprachgitter, S. Fischer, 1959, translation by Joachim Neugroschel published as *Speech-Grille and Selected Poems,* Dutton, 1971.
Gedichte: Eine Auswahl, edited by Klaus Wagenbach, S. Fischer, 1959.
Der Meridian: Rede anlaesslich der Verleihung des Georg-Buechner-Preises, Darmstadt, a, 22. Oktober 1960, S. Fischer, 1961.
Die Niemandsrose (title means "The No Man's Rose"), S. Fischer, 1963.
Atemkristall, Brunidor, 1965.
Gedichte (title means "Poetry"), Moderner Buch-Club, 1966.
Atemwende: Gedichte, Suhrkamp, 1967.
Fadensonnen, Suhrkamp, 1968.
Ausgewaehlte Gedichte: Zwei Reden, Suhrkamp, 1968.
Lichtzwang, Suhrkamp, 1970.
Schneepart, Suhrkamp, 1971.

Strette. Suivis du Meridien et d'Entretien dans la montagne, Mercure de France, 1971.

Nineteen Poems, translation by Michael Hamburger, Carcanet Press, 1972.

Selected Poems, translation by Hamburger and Christopher Middleton, Penguin, 1972.

Gedichte: In zwei Banden, Suhrkamp, 1975.

Zeitgehoeft: Spaete Gedichte aus dem Nachlass, Suhrkamp, 1976.

Poesie/Paul Celan; a cura di Moshe Kahne e Marcella Bagnasco, A. Mondadori (Italy), 1976.

Paul Celan: Poems, translation by Hamburger, Persea Books, 1980, published as *Poems of Paul Celan,* 1989.

Gesammelte Werke in fuenf Baenden, 5 volumes, Suhrkamp, 1983.

Todesfuge, Edition Gunnar A. Kaldewey, 1984.

65 Poems, Raven Arts Press (Dublin), 1985.

Last Poems, translation by Katherine Washburn and Margret Guillemin, North Point Press, 1986.

Also author of *Breath Crystal: Translations of Paul Celan,* translation by Walter Billeter, Ragman Productions (Australia), and of *Conversation in the Mountains,* translation by Rosmarie Waldrop.

OTHER; UNDER PSEUDONYM PAUL CELAN

Edgar Jene und der Traum vom Traume, Agathon (Vienna), 1948.

Paul Celan: Prose Writings and Selected Poems, translation by Walter Billeter, Paper Castle (Victoria, Austrlaia), 1977.

Collected Prose, translation by Rosemarie Waldrop, Carcanet Press, 1986.

Translator of numerous works into German. Also author of works represented in anthologies, including *Modern German Poetry, 1910-1960,* edited by Hamburger and C. Middleton, 1962, *Twentieth-Century German Verse,* edited by P. Bridgewater, 1963, and *Modern European Poetry,* edited by W. Barnstone, 1966.

SIDELIGHTS: Paul Antschel, best known under his pseudonym Paul Celan, was regarded as one of the most important poets to emerge from post-World War II Europe. According to one critic, he "made a more original and substantial contribution to modern poetry than any other German-language poet of his generation." His work bears the influence of both the French surrealists and Rilke in terms of poetic devices and linguistic stylization. His thematic obsession, however, is the extermination of the Jews during World War II. A writer for the *Times Literary Supplement* wrote that Celan "makes us aware of the horror of our age in a way that is the more powerful for being oblique. The humble and familiar images . . . combine with others that suggest blinding, mutilation and empaling, burning, whipping and shooting, hunting down and shutting in with walls and barbed wire—festering memories of Auschwitz which are relevant not only to Germany and not only to an era that ended in 1945."

Celan began writing poetry shortly after the war. His first book in 1947 caused little stir in the German literary community. His second collection, "Poppy and Memory," received much more critical attention, and Celan quickly became a reputable poet. Among his most popular poems is "Death Fugue," a stark recreation of activities at Auschwitz which was featured in both of the early collections. Paul Auster called it "literally a fugue composed of words, and the incessant, rhythmical repetitions and variations of phrases evoke a nightmare more devastating than any forthright description could." This description is exemplified in the stanza which includes the lines "death is a master

from Germany / his eye is blue / he shoots you with bullets of lead / his aim is true / a man lives in the house your / golden hair Margarete / he sets his hounds on us he gives / us a grave in the air he plays with the serpent and / dreams death is a master from / Germany." Despite its high regard, "Death Fugue" was later refuted by Celan as, according to Auster, "too obvious and superficially realistic," and he disallowed its inclusion in collections.

As Celan progressed, his poetry became increasingly inaccessible. "The poems grow shorter," observed John Hollander, "denser and less easily rewarding toward the end of the poet's career, and more starkly impressive." His poetry also became less depressing. One critic wrote, "The worst, we are made to feel, has been faced, and out of despair has come a new beauty which *is* truth." The same reviewer added that the collection *Atemwende* "shows a poet projecting his breath into emptiness and feeling it return . . . charged with a numinous power." Aside from its rather positive stance, *Atemwende* was also noted for its attention to the language itself. "The author of *Atemwende* is obsessed by words and obsessed by forms," contended a writer for the *Times Literary Supplement.* The critic attributed Celan's brighter outlook to his new interest in words. "And this new reality has been uniquely embodied in language," the critic claimed: "language, in fact, has helped not just to shape it, but to bring it life."

Celan pursued his interest in economy of form in *Lichtzwang,* a collection published the same year as his death. A reviewer for the *Times Literary Supplement* wrote that "his poems are very much word-sculptures." Jerry Glenn believed that Celan was moving towards a union of his early realist style with his later structure-conscious poems. He also noted in a review of *Lichtzwang,* "There are some fine poems here, poems which will justly become a part of the permanent legacy of German literature."

Celan committed suicide by drowning in 1970. In a eulogy, Auster called him "one of the truly great poets of our time." In the same article, he observed that by reading the collected works, one could perceive a developing sense of despair within Celan. Referring to the poems, Auster wrote, "One feels both a shrinking and an expansion in them, as if, by traveling to the inmost recesses of himself, Celan had somehow vanished, joining with the greater forces beyond him, and at the same time sinking more deeply into his terrifying sense of isolation." Celan once revealed, "I have tried to write poetry in order to acquire a perspective of reality for myself." Perhaps he forecast his own fate when he wrote, "You were my death: / you I could hold / when all fell away from me."

BIOGRAPHICAL/CRITICAL SOURCES:

BOOKS

Brierley, David, *"Der Meridian": Ein Versuch zur Poetik und Dichtung Paul Celans,* Lang, 1984.

Celan, Paul, *Speech-Grille and Selected Poems,* Dutton, 1971.

Celan, Paul, *Selected Poems,* Penguin, 1972.

Chalfen, Israel, *Paul Celan: Eine Biographie seiner Jugend,* Suhrkamp, 1979.

Contemporary Literary Criticism, Gale, Volume 10, 1979, Volume 19, 1981.

Dictionary of Literary Biography, Volume 69: *Contemporary German Fiction Writers,* first series, Gale, 1988.

Glenn, Jerry, *Paul Celan,* Twayne, 1973.

Meinecke, Dietlind, editor, *Uber Paul Celan,* Suhrkamp, 1973.

Neumann, Peter Horst, *Zur Lyrik Paul Celans,* Vandenhoeck & Ruprecht, 1968.

PERIODICALS

Books Abroad, spring, 1971.
Chicago Review, Volume 29, number 3, 1978.
Commentary, February, 1976.
New York Times Book Review, July 18, 1971.
Studies in Twentieth Century Literature, fall, 1983.
Times Literary Supplement, December 7, 1967, September 18, 1970, September 29, 1984.

*   *   *

APPLETON, Lawrence
See LOVECRAFT, H(oward) P(hillips)

*   *   *

ARAGON, Louis   1897-1982
(Albert de Routisie, Arnaud de Saint Roman, Francois La Colere, Francois Lacolere)

PERSONAL: Original name Louis Andrieux; born October 3, 1897, in Neuilly, France; died December 24, 1982, in Paris, France; son of Louis Andrieux (an innkeeper) and Marguerite Toucas; married Elsa Triolet Kagan (a writer), February 28, 1939 (died June 16, 1970). *Education:* Studied medicine at the University of Paris, 1916-17. *Politics:* Communist.

CAREER: Poet and novelist. Member of staff of French Communist party newspapers, *L'Humanite* and *Commune,* in early 1930s; *Ce Soir* (French Communist party daily newspaper), Paris, France, co-director, 1937-39; editor of clandestine periodical *La Drome en armes* during World War II; Editeurs Francais Reunis (publishing house), Paris, founder and managing director, beginning 1944; *Ce Soir,* Paris, editor, 1947-53; *Les Lettres francaises* (weekly literary and political review), Paris, staff member, 1949-53, director, 1953-72. Member of central committee of French Communist party; member of Lenin Peace Prize committee; member of advisory board of *Europe* (monthly literary review), beginning 1958; member of Academie Concourt, 1967-68. *Wartime service:* Medical auxiliary with the French Army in early World War I; entered combat with 355th Infantry Regiment in 1917; awarded Croix de Guerre; during World War II, served as auxiliary doctor with French Army until the fall of Dunkirk; fought remainder of war as a member of the French Resistance; awarded Croix de Guerre and Medaille Militaire.

MEMBER: International Association of Writers for the Defense of Culture (founder, 1935; secretary of French division), Association of Combatant Writers (vice president, 1945-60), French National Committee of Authors, American Academy of Arts and Letters (honorary member).

AWARDS, HONORS: Prix Renaudot, 1936, for *Les Beaux Quartiers;* Lenin Peace Prize, 1957, for poem "Ode to Stalin"; Ph.D., University of Prague, 1963, and University of Moscow, 1965; Order of the October Revolution, 1972; Chevalier de la Legion d'Honneur, 1981.

WRITINGS:

POEMS

Feu de joie (also see below; title means "Bonfire"), Au Sans-Pareil (Paris), 1920.
Le Mouvement perpetuel (also see below; title means "Perpetual Motion"), Nouvelle Revue Francaise (Paris), 1925.
La Grande Gaite (title means "High Spirits"), with drawings by Yves Tanguy, Gallimard (Paris), 1929.
Persecute persecuteur, Editions Surrealistes (Paris), 1931.

The Red Front, translation by E. E. Cummings, Contempo Publishers, 1933.
Hourra l'Oural (title means "Hurrah, the Urals"), Denoel et Steele (Paris), 1934.
Le Creve-Coeur (title means "Heartbreak"), Gallimard, 1941, [New York], 1942, new edition, Gallimard, 1946, reprinted, 1980.
Cantique a Elsa (title means "Canticle to Elsa"), Editions de la Revue Fontaine (Algiers), 1941.
Broceliande (also see below), Editions de la Baconniere (Neuchatel, Switzerland), 1942.
Les Yeux d'Elsa (also see below; title means "Elsa's Eyes"), Cahiers du Rhone (Neuchatel), 1942, Pantheon, 1944, new edition with critical essays, P. Seghers (Paris), 1945, reprinted, 1966.
(Under pseudonym Francois La Colere) *Le Musee Grevin* (also see below; title means "The Grevin Museum"), Editions de Minuit (Paris), 1943.
France, ecoute (title means "France, Listen"), Editions de la Revue Fontaine, 1944.
En etrange pays dans mon pays lui-meme (also see below; contains *Broceliande* and *En Francais dans le texte*), P. Seghers, 1945.
(Under pseudonym Francois Lacolere) *Neuf Chansons interdites, 1942-1944* (title means "Nine Banned Songs"), Bibliotheque Francaise (Paris), 1945.
La Diane francaise (also see below; title means "The French Diana"), P. Seghers, 1945, reprinted, 1960.
Le Musee Grevin, Les Poissons noirs et quelques poems inedits (title means "The Grevin Museum, The Black Fishes and Some Unpublished Poems"), Editions de Minuit, 1946.
Le Nouveau Creve-Coeur (title means "The New Heartbreak"), Gallimard, 1948.
Les Yeux et la memoire (title means "Eyes and Memory"), Gallimard, 1954.
Mes Caravanes, et autres poemes (1948-1954) (title means "My Caravans, and Other Poems"), P. Seghers, 1954.
Le Roman inacheve (autobiographical poem; title means "The Unfinished Romance"), Gallimard, 1956, new edition, 1978.
Elsa, Gallimard, 1959.
Poesies: Anthologie, 1917-1960, Le Club de Meilleur Livre (Paris), 1960.
Les Poetes (autobiographical poem; title means "The Poets"), Gallimard, 1960, revised editions, 1969 and 1976.
Le Fou d'Elsa (title means "Elsa's Madman"), Gallimard, 1963.
Il ne m'est Paris que d'Elsa (anthology; title means "There Is Only Elsa's Paris for Me"), Laffont (Paris), 1964, new edition with photographs, 1968.
Le Voyage de Hollande, P. Seghers, 1964, 5th edition published as *Le Voyage de Hollande et autres poemes,* 1965.
Elegie a Pablo Neruda (title means "Elegy to Pablo Neruda"), Gallimard, 1966.
Les Chambres; poeme du temps qui ne passe pas, Editeurs Francais Reunis, 1969.
L'Oeuvre poetique, 15 volumes, Livre Club Diderot, 1974-81.
Mes Voyages avec un poeme unedit d'Aragon, with illustrations by Fernand Leger, Bibliographique Artes, 1976.
Les Adieux et autres poemes, Temps Actuels, 1981.
Choix de poemes, Temps Actuels, 1983.

"LE MONDE REEL" ("REAL WORLD") SERIES OF HISTORICAL NOVELS

Les Cloches de Bale, Denoel et Steele, 1934, reprinted, Gallimard, 1969, translation by Haakon M. Chevalier published as *The Bells of Basel,* Harcourt, 1936.

Les Beaux Quartiers, Denoel et Steele, 1936, reprinted, Gallimard, 1972, translation by Chevalier published as *Residential Quarter,* Harcourt, 1938.

Les Voyageurs de l'imperiale, Gallimard, 1942, translation by Hannah Josephson published as *The Century Was Young,* Duell, Sloane and Pearce, 1941 (published in England as *Passengers of Destiny,* Pilot Press, 1947), definitive French edition, Gallimard, 1947, reprinted, 1972.

Aurelien, Gallimard, 1944, reprinted, 1966, translation by Eithne Wilkins published under same title, Duell, Sloane and Pearce, 1947.

Les Communistes, six volumes, Bibliotheque Francaise, 1949-51, reprinted, Le Livre de Poche, 1967-68.

OTHER NOVELS

Anicet; ou, Le Panorama (title means "Anicet; or, The Panorama"), Nouvelle Revue Francaise, 1921, reprinted, Gallimard, 1972.

Les Aventures de Telemaque, Gallimard, 1922, new edition, 1966, translation by Renee Hubert and Judd Hubert published as *The Adventures of Telemachus,* University of Nebraska Press, 1988.

Le Paysan de Paris, Gallimard, 1926, reprinted, 1972, translation by Frederick Brown published as *Nightwalker,* Prentice-Hall, 1970, translation by Simon Watson Taylor published as *Paris Peasant,* Cape, 1971.

La Semaine sainte, Gallimard, 1958, translation by Chevalier published as *Holy Week,* Putnam, 1961.

La Mise a mort (also see below; title means "The Moment of Truth"), Gallimard, 1965.

Blanche ou l'oubli, Gallimard, 1967, published with afterword by author, 1972.

(Under pseudonym Albert de Routisie) *Irene,* L'Or du Temps (Paris), 1968.

Henri Matisse: Roman, two volumes, Gallimard, 1971, translation by Jean Stewart published as *Henri Matisse: A Novel,* Harcourt, 1972.

Theatre/Roman (also see below), Gallimard, 1974.

Aragon; ou, Les Metamorphoses (excerpts from *La Mise a mort* and *Theatre/Roman*), Gallimard, 1977.

STORY COLLECTIONS

Servitude et grandeur des Francais: Scenes des annees terribles (seven stories; title means "Servitude and Greatness of the French: Scenes from the Terrible Years"), Bibliotheque Francaise, 1945.

(Under pseudonym Arnaud de Saint Roman) *Trois Contes* (title means "Three Tales"), Burrup, Mathieson, 1945.

Shakespeare, translation by Bernard Frechtman, with illustrations by Pablo Picasso, Abrams, 1966.

Le Mentir-vrai, Gallimard, 1981.

NONFICTION

Traite du style (literary criticism and surrealist manifesto), Nouvelle Revue Francaise, 1928.

Le Peinture au defi (essays), Editions Surrealistes, 1930.

Pour un realisme socialiste (lectures), Denoel et Steele, 1935.

(With others) *Authors Take Sides on the Spanish War,* Left Review (London), 1937.

En Francais dans le texte (essay), Ides et Calendes (Paris), 1943.

Le Crime contre l'esprit (les martyrs) par le temoin des martyrs, Editions de Minuit, 1944.

Apologie de luxe (art criticism), Skira (Geneva), 1946.

L'Enseigne de Gersaint (essays), Ides et Calendes, 1946.

L'Homme communiste (title means "The Communist Man"), Gallimard, Volume 1, 1946, Volume 2, 1953.

Chroniques du bel canto (essays and lectures), Skira, 1947.

La Culture et les hommes (essays), Editions Sociales (Paris), 1947.

Hugo, poete realiste (literary criticism), Editions Sociales, 1952.

L'Exemple de Courbet (art criticism), Cercle d'Art (Paris), 1952.

Le Neveu de M. Duval, suivi d'une lettre de celui a l'auteur de ce livre (title means "The Nephew of M. Duval, Followed by a Letter from Him to the Author of This Book"), Editeurs Francais Reunis, 1953.

Journal d'une poesie nationale (critical anthology), Ecrivains Reunis (Lyons), 1954.

La Lumiere de Stendhal (essays and lectures), Denoel, 1954.

Litteratures sovietiques (essays and lectures), Denoel, 1955.

J'abats mon jeu (essays), Editeurs Francais Reunis, 1959.

(With Maurice Thorez) *Il faut appeler les choses par leur nom* [and] *Problemes de notre epoque* (addresses), Parti Communiste Francaise, 1959.

(With Andre Maurois) *Histoire parallele* (historical study of the United States and the Soviet Union), four volumes, Presses de la Cite (Paris), 1962, new edition published in five volumes as *Les Deux Geants; Histoire des Etats-Unis et de l'U.R.S.S., de 1917 a nos jours,* Editions du Pont Royal (Paris), 1962-64, translation of Volumes 1 and 2 by Patrick O'Brian published as *A History of the U.S.S.R. from Lenin to Khrushchev,* two volumes, McKay, 1964, Volumes 1 and 2 also published in three volumes as *Histoire de l'U.R.S.S., 1917 a 1960,* Union Generale d'Editions (Paris), 1972.

Les Collages (art criticism), Hermann (Paris), 1965.

(With others) *Dictionnaire abrege du surrealisme,* new edition (Aragon not associated with earlier editions), Corti (Paris), 1969.

Je n'ai jamais appris a ecrire; ou, Les Incipit, Skira, 1969.

(With others) *La Superletteratura e A. Rimbaud,* L. Lucarini (Rome), 1975.

Paris des poetes, F. Nathan, 1977.

(With others) *Les Poetes de la Revue Fontaine,* Cherche Midi, 1978.

(With others) *Essais de critique genetique,* Flammarion, 1979.

Chroniques de la pluie et du beau temps, Temps Actuels, 1979.

Essai de bibliographie, Grant & Cutler, Volume 1: *Oeuvres, 1918-59,* 1979, Volume 2: *Oeuvres, 1960-77,* 1980.

Ecrits sur l'art moderne, Flammarion, 1981.

Reflexions sur Rimbaud, Editions de Musee-Bibliotheque Arthur Rimbaud, 1983.

AUTHOR OF PREFACE OR INTRODUCTION

Exposition de collages, Jose Corti, 1930.

(Under pseudonym Francois La Colere) Jean Cassou, *33 Sonnets composes au secret,* Editions de la Baconniere, 1946.

Gilbert Debrise, *Cimetieres sans tombeaux,* Bibliotheque Francaise, 1946.

Andre Fougerson, *Dessins,* Les 13 Epis (Paris), 1947.

Pablo Picasso, *Sculptures et dessins* (exhibition catalog), Maison de la Pensee Francaise (Paris), 1952.

(And of reviews) Iurii Ianovski, *Les Cavaliers,* Gallimard, 1957.

Fernand Leger, *Contrastes: 13 Aquarelles,* Au Vent d'Arles (Paris), 1959.

Marc Chagall: Recent Paintings, 1966-68 (exhibition catalog), Pierre Matisse Gallery (New York), 1968.

OTHER

Les Plaisirs de la capitale, [Berlin], 1923.

"Au pied du mur" (play), first produced in 1924.

Le Libertinage (also see below; includes the play "L'Armoire a glace un beau soir" and essays), Nouvelle Revue Francaise, 1924, translation published as *Libertine,* Riverrun Press, 1987.

(Translator) Lewis Carroll, *La Chasse au snark: Une Agonie en huit crises,* Hours Press, 1929.

Le Temoin des martyrs, printed clandestinely in Paris, 1942.

(Under pseudonym Arnaud de Saint Roman) *Les Bons Voisins,* Editions de Minuit, 1942.

Matisse-en-France, Martin Fabiani, 1943.

Saint-Pol-Roux; ou, L'Espoir, P. Seghers, 1945.

Aragon, Poet of the French Resistance (includes translations of wartime poetry and prose and critical essays on Aragon), edited by Josephson and Malcolm Cowley, Duell, Sloane and Pearce, 1945 (published in England as *Aragon, Poet of Resurgent France,* Pilot Press, 1946).

Aragon: Une Etude (selections from his writings), edited and with a critical essay by Claude Roy, P. Seghers, 1945.

(Contributor) Gabriel Peri, *Toward Singing Tomorrows,* International Publishers, 1946.

(Translator and author of preface) *Cinq Sonnets de Petrarque,* A la Fontaine de Vaucluse, 1947.

(Contributor) *Henri Matisse: Retrospective Exhibition of Paintings, Drawings and Sculpture,* Philadelphia Museum of Art, 1948.

La Lumiere et la paix, Lettres Francaises, 1950.

(Editor and author of commentary) *Avez-vous lu Victor Hugo?,* Editeurs Francais Reunis, 1952.

La Vraie Liberte de la culture, reduire notre train de mort pour accroitre notre train de vie, Lettres Francaises, 1952.

Les Egmont d'aujourd'hui s'appellent Andre Stil, Lettres Francaises, 1952.

(Editor and author of preface) *Introduction aux litteratures sovietiques: Contes et nouvelles,* Gallimard, 1956.

(With Jean Cocteau) *Entretiens sur le Musee de Dresde,* Cercle d'Art, 1957, translation by Francis Scarfe published as *Conversations on the Dresden Gallery,* Holmes & Meier, 1982.

(Translator and author of preface) Tchinghiz Aitmatov, *Djamilia,* Editeurs Francais Reunis, 1959.

L'Un ne va pas sans l'autre: Un Perpetuel Printemps, suivi de Paroles a Saint-Denis (poetry and a speech), privately printed, 1959.

(Editor and author of critical essays) *Elsa Triolet, choisie par Aragon,* Gallimard, 1960.

La Diane francaise, suivi de En etrange pays dans mon pays lui-meme, Seghers, 1962.

Entretiens avec Francis Cremieux (ten radio interviews), Gallimard, 1964.

Ouevres romanesques croisees d'Elsa Triolet et Aragon (complete works of Aragon and his wife, Elsa Triolet), forty-two volumes, Laffont, 1964-74.

(Contributor) Michael Benedikt and George E. Wellwarth, editors, *Modern French Theatre,* Dutton, 1964.

(Contributor) Roger H. Guerrand, *L'Art nouveau en Europe,* Plon (Paris), 1965.

Aragon (selected works), edited and with an introduction by Georges Sadoul, P. Seghers, 1967.

Les Yeux d'Elsa, suivi de La Diane francaise, illustrations by Cecile Picoux, P. Seghers, 1968.

Aragon parle avec Dominique Arban, P. Seghers, 1968.

Fernand Sequin recontre Louis Aragon, Editions de l'Homme (Montreal), 1969.

(Contributor) Robert G. Marshall and Frederic C. St. Aubyn, editors, *Trois Pieces surrealists,* Appleton, 1969.

Le Mouvement perpetuel; precede de Feu de joie et suivie de Ecritures automatiques (includes *Le Mouvement perpetuel* and *Feu de joie*), Gallimard, 1970.

(Editor with Andre Breton) *La Revolution surrealiste: Collection complete de la revue (Nos. 1 a 12; 1er decembre 1924 au 15 decembre 1929),* J. Place, 1975.

(Contributor) Daniel Wallard, *Aragon: Un portrait,* Editions Cercle d'Art, 1979.

La Defense de l'infini et Les Aventures de Jean-Foutre la Bite, Gallimard, 1987.

Co-editor, *Litterature,* 1918-20; co-editor, *La Revolution surrealiste,* 1924-29.

SIDELIGHTS: Louis Aragon's long career was marked by two distinct, even contradictory phases. He began as one of the leading theorists of the avant-garde art movements of dada and surrealism, calling for uninhibited freedom for the creative imagination. In the early 1930s, however, he joined the French Communist party, rising to become a member of the party's Central Committee. For the next half century Aragon was a doctrinaire loyalist who promoted the idea of socialist realism in the arts and carefully followed the party line. This unlikely odyssey, and the drastic changes it entailed, caused Aragon to be labeled an opportunist or political hack by some observers, while his political allies praised his writings. He was best known to the French public as the "Poet of the Resistance," the poet whose stirring patriotic works inspired the nation's fight against the Nazi occupation forces of World War II. His largely nonpolitical novels *Paris Peasant (Le Paysan de Paris)* and *Holy Week (La Semaine sainte)* won critical praise as well. Because of those works, his place in twentieth-century French literature is secure. As a writer for the *New York Times* observed, "Aragon was among France's foremost men of letters in this century." Upon his death in 1982, French President Francois Mitterand announced that "France is grief-stricken by the death of one of its greatest writers. . . . I bow before his memory."

The illegitimate son of a Parisian innkeeper, Aragon spoke little of his childhood or family, usually beginning his life story with his student days at the University of Paris just before World War I. It was while studying medicine with hopes of becoming a doctor that Aragon first met fellow student Andre Breton. The two young men shared an interest in literature, particularly the experimental works of French poet Guillaume Apollinaire. After serving in the French army as a medical auxiliary and soldier, for which he was awarded a Croix de Guerre, Aragon found himself in 1918 back in Paris. Returning to school seemed pointless after the horrors he had experienced in the war. As a *National Review* writer noted, Aragon "was traumatized emotionally by his experiences." He and Breton decided to devote their time to writing. Following the lead of Tristan Tzara and other artists of the time, he and Breton called for an artistic rebellion against the society that had caused such a devastating and senseless war. As part of their rebellion, the two writers, along with poet Philippe Soupault, founded the ironically-titled magazine *Litterature.*

Litterature quickly became one of the voices for dada, a radically anti-art movement begun during the war in Zurich, Switzerland, by Tzara, Hugo Ball, and other artists. Dada was a movement of nihilistic rebellion that attacked reason, the rational mind, the established social order, and all other "causes" of World War I. It called for the abolition of museums, opposed all art theories and schools, and promoted the unrestricted expression of the creative impulse. As Sarane Alexandrian wrote in *Surrealist Art,* "Dada was a detonation of anger which showed itself in insults and buffoonery." Dadaists experimented with sound poems, simultaneous poems, and randomly assembled writings and artwork. They gave public shows wearing grotesque costumes, shouting derision at the audience, and performing senseless, mysterious acts, all accompanied by a cacophony of whistles, horns, gunshots,and drumbeats. Along with Francis Picabia and a small group of other writers and artists, Aragon and Breton were among the most active dadaists in Paris.

But by 1922, Breton had grown dissatisfied with the essential pointlessness of dada as a movement. He wanted a more serious artistic enterprise which retained many of dada's concerns but explored them in a somber and systematic manner. Dada had revealed the limitations of rational thought; Breton now wished to explore what lay beyond those limitations. Heavily influenced by the ideas of psychoanalyst Sigmund Freud, Breton called for an art which would liberate man's unconscious desires and integrate them with ordinary waking life to create a super-reality, or surreality. At the "Congress of Paris," organized in 1922 by Breton, the Paris dadaists and other avant-garde artists met to discuss this new direction. Out of this meeting was born the art movement surrealism. Aragon was a founding member of the new group.

The early surrealists experimented with a host of methods and techniques meant to free the unconscious, and Aragon played a prominent role in the research. Chance occurrences, dream analysis, the Tarot deck, the ouija board, group hypnosis sessions, psychoanalysis,. and automatic writing were all employed. Automatic writing in particular, Alexandrian wrote, "was intended to lay bare the 'mental matter' which is common to all men, and to separate it from thought, which is only one of its manifestations." The startling and spontaneous nature of such writing, which was done while the writer actively suppressed his control and allowed the sentences to form themselves, especially impressed the surrealists, who incorporated the technique into much of their written work.

Another experiment conducted at this time was the deliberate provoking of unaccustomed sensations that went beyond the rational thinking process or usual emotions. Objects of beauty were thought to be able to spur such overwhelming reactions. Roger Cardinal and Robert Stuart Short stated in *Surrealism: Permanent Revelation:* "To witness beauty as Surrealism sees it is to undergo a kind of psychic disorientation, a disturbance that affects both mind and senses." This intense, surreal moment was defined and described by Aragon and Breton. "At times," Cardinal and Short wrote, "Aragon felt this vertigo, this sense of the pavements of everyday opening up beneath his feet to reveal what he called 'magical precipices'—moments in which normality is shaken by something *other,* moments which can suggest panic, but which Aragon as a surrealist welcomes wholeheartedly."

The surrealists believed that certain locations around Paris, because of their striking, mysterious nature, were also able to provoke these intense moments. A passageway at the Paris Opera, the Tower of Saint-Jacques, and the Pon des Suicides at the Buttes-Chaumont were among the sites credited by the surrealists with special evocative powers. Aragon was especially attuned to finding such places. Years later, when speaking to Andre Parinaud in *Entretiens, 1913-1952,* Breton recalled Aragon's ability: "I can still remember him as an extraordinary walking companion. . . . No one was more skilled than Aragon in detecting the unusual in all of its forms; no one else could have

been led to such intoxicating reveries about the hidden life of the city."

Aragon used two of these sites in his surrealistic novel *Paris Peasant,* published in 1926. Several critics praised this book in the highest of terms. "The prose of *Le Paysan de Paris,*" Cardinal and Short stated, "has the freshness and conviction of a masterpiece." Lucile F. Becker, writing in her *Louis Aragon,* called the book "one of the masterpieces of French twentieth-century literature." Discussing Aragon's use of two of the surrealists' evocative sites, Cardinal and Short stated that the novel "contains a cryptic discussion of *la mythologie moderne* and *le merveilleux,* exemplified by evocations of two 'elective places' for the urban surrealist, the Passage de l'Opera and the Buttes-Chaumont park. In these innocuous corners of Paris Aragon intuits an immanent surreality almost bordering on the mystical: 'I began to discover the face of the infinite behind the concrete forms which escorted me as I walked along the pathways of this earth.' " M. Adereth, writing in *Commitment in Modern French Literature: A Brief Study of "Litterature Engagee" in the Works of Peguy, Aragon, and Sartre,* found that unlike other surrealistic prose, Aragon's novel was based on the real world. "Surrealists," Adereth noted, "tended to despise prose and the novel and to condemn descriptions of real places as incompatible with automatic writing. . . . [But *Paris Peasant* is] based, not on an imaginary city, but on the Paris which [Aragon] loved so much. . . . He revealed many unknown aspects of the capital, and although his style is in the best surrealist manner—lyrical, poetic and spontaneous—the source of his inspiration is thoroughly realistic."

In 1926 Aragon and Breton led a small group of surrealists into the French Communist party where, they hoped, the surrealist aesthetic would be adopted and the surrealist vision of a life in which the conscious and unconscious minds are integrated could be realized. A year later they left the party, angered and disillusioned by the group's pedestrian conception of the arts and hostility to surrealist ideas. For their part, the communists found the surrealists to be nothing but bohemian artists not seriously committed to the revolution. Breton and other surrealists became supporters of exiled Russian communist leader Leon Trotsky instead, creating an independent radical position in which psychic and political liberation were compatible.

But Aragon rejoined the Communist party in 1930 and made a visit to the Soviet Union that same year to attend a writers conference. The visit changed his life. "Like other foreign intellectuals before and after him," a writer for the London *Times* explained, "he was overwhelmed by his first direct experience of the 'homeland of socialism.' " Aragon agreed to renounce surrealism, admit his previous mistakes, and become a model communist. He explained publicly that his involvement with the surrealists had been a youthful error. For the next five decades Aragon was to hold true to his communist commitment. Speaking of this political conversion in his *History of Surrealism,* Maurice Nadeau reported: "Aragon merely followed the current that with increasing power swept the advanced intellectuals of every nation toward the USSR, at a time when this adherence no longer occasioned any disadvantage for those who adopted it, quite the contrary. The surrealists did not choose to regard Aragon's move as a development, but as a palinode, 'a betrayal' which they were to censure him for bitterly down through the years." As late as 1966, the surrealists, in a book entitled *Aragon au defi* or "Aragon Challenged," were still attacking him as an opportunist who had sold out his ideals.

Aragon's loyalty to the Communist party and the Soviet Union withstood onslaughts that led less committed members to defect.

During the Soviet Union's purge trials of the 1930s, in which thousands of political rivals of Soviet dictator Joseph Stalin were executed, Aragon served as Communist party apologist for the action. He was a supporter, too, of the Soviet-Nazi friendship pact and of the two countries' subsequent invasion of Poland in 1939 which triggered World War II. In 1956, when the Soviets first publicly admitted some of the crimes of the late Stalin, Aragon claimed to be "overwhelmed" by the revelations. And yet the following year he wrote the poem "Ode to Stalin," which won him the Soviet Union's Lenin Peace Prize. When, in 1968, the French Communist party broke with the Soviets over the Russian invasion of Czechoslovakia, Aragon also criticized the attack in his periodical *Les Lettres francaises.* The Soviet government responded by banning the magazine in Eastern Europe and canceling party-approved subscriptions. The magazine was forced out of business. Aragon learned his lesson. When the Soviets invaded Afghanistan in 1980, Aragon supported the move.

From the early 1930s until the end of his life, Aragon's writings were usually of a political nature and displayed little if any of his earlier surrealist style. His "Real World" series of historical novels were examples of socialist realism, a school which calls for a realistic depiction of the class struggle in literature and the arts. His six-volume novel *The Communists* told of the French Communist party's heroic role in the Resistance movement of World War II. Aragon also wrote and edited several of the official publications of the French Communist party and served on the party's Central Committee, the ruling council of the organization. David Gascoyne, writing in the *Times Literary Supplement,* reported that Aragon's apartment was even "opposite the Soviet Embassy."

Aragon's first overtly political work was a long poem entitled *The Red Front,* published in French in the early 1930s. A searing, provocative poem, *The Red Front* "brought down the wrath of the authorities upon [Aragon's] head," Philip Rahv commented in the *Nation,* "as their police minds would not put down to poetic license his open advocacy of the shooting of prominent politicians." Another of his early political works was *Hourra l'Oural,* which means "Hurrah, the Urals," a hymn of praise for the Soviet government.

With the "Real World" series of novels published during the 1930s and 1940s, Aragon turned to the history of the late nineteenth and early twentieth century for inspiration, transforming his vision of the period into effective political commentary. The first of these novels is *The Bells of Basel* (*Les Cloches de Bale*), set in France before World War I and focusing on three women of the time. Each woman comes from a different social class, so their careers illustrate the range of possibilities afforded by French society. Two of the women are fictional creations but the third, Clara Zetkin, is based on a real communist organizer of the early twentieth century. This novel, Rahv noted, "is built around the lives of three women, who become the focus of [Aragon's] insights into the society that produced them."

Aragon later admitted that he had learned how to write novels by writing *The Bells of Basel,* and some of the faults of an apprentice novel mar the work. As Frederick Brown commented in the *Southern Review,* in Aragon's novels his characters "*are* players, actors who, as the novel progresses, become increasingly aware that it and their roles must end in favor of History. . . . Aragon reveals this scheme most crudely in the first novel of *The Real World—The Bells of Basel.*" Malcolm Cowley, reviewing the novel for the *New Republic,* was "disappointed" to realize that Aragon was "a writer whose personality as revealed in his books is more brilliant and coherent than the books themselves."

More successful as fiction was the second novel in the "Real World" series, *Residential Quarter* (*Les Beaux Quartiers*). The story revolves around a young man who becomes involved in strike-breaking activity at a French automobile manufacturing plant but eventually joins the strikers. "In this novel," Cowley wrote, "there are types of writing that Aragon does supremely well—for example, satire of the middle class in its own language, lyrical apostrophes to Paris and its workers, outright melodrama. . . . *Residential Quarter* is an absorbing and brilliant novel."

In *The Century Was Young* (*Les Voyageurs de l'imperiale*), Aragon wrote of France at the turn of the century and of the attitudes which led the nation into World War I. The book argues against an aloofness to political matters and instead calls for political involvement. R. E. Roberts of the *Saturday Review of Literature* described the novel as "a pitiless portrayal of human stupidity, human corruption, human vanity, and of that astounding toughness which, in itself quite unmoral, may breed a strange nobility." Although he believed the book "doesn't quite add up," Clifton Fadiman of the *New Yorker* called Aragon potentially "one of the most important of contemporary French novelists. He is very intelligent and conscientious, with deep social sympathies, a wide culture, and great lingual dexterity." Roberts was "reminded of Dickens and Dostoievsky. . . . There is in [*The Century Was Young*] the same warm humanity, the same refusal to despise the most despicable, and the same note of warning to the smug and self-satisfied of the world."

Aurelien, the fourth of the "Real World" novels, was written during World War II and published just after the war's end. Because it tells a love story, Aragon was criticized by his political allies who felt it a frivolous work. As Adereth noted, "a number of Aragon's friends, including some narrow-minded Soviet critics, were shocked at the thought that he had found nothing better to do in those [war] years."

Yet much of Aragon's work during World War II concerned love. He wrote a series of love poems to his wife, Elsa Triolet, which were published as *Cantique a Elsa* and *Les Yeux d'Elsa.* Gascoyne noted that after first meeting Elsa in 1928, Aragon "became an adoringly one-woman man, mythologizing his companion in a number of poetic works, and using her name as a symbol of the new revolutionary woman." As late as the 1960s Aragon was still publishing poetry collections inspired by her. His patriotic war poems revealed another kind of love, his love for France. These poems, first published pseudonymously because Aragon was working underground for the French Resistance, are still among his most praised works. As Becker claimed, Aragon's poems of the 1940s about Elsa and patriotism "are among the finest written in the French language."

Many of these poems were collected in *Aragon: Poet of the French Resistance,* a book of his poems and prose from the war. Writing in the *Weekly Book Review,* Karl Shapiro called the collection "in many respects the most extraordinary example of poetic creativity to emerge from the struggle. With its thrilling lyricism, its inspired translations, and its fine emotionality, it forms a collection which is simultaneously a tribute to Aragon and an Aragon triumph." Reviewing the book for the *New York Times,* Donald Stauffer claimed that "Aragon represents such a miracle—brilliance and hope born out of war, defeat, despair."

The last of Aragon's "Real World" novels, the six-volume *The Communists,* was published in the late 1940s and early 1950s. Meant as a fictionalized account of the French Communist party's role in the Resistance of World War II, the novel was never completed. The six published volumes cover only the early history of the war; poor sales forced Aragon to abandon the project. Although Claude Roy, writing in his *Aragon,* found the novel "never a *simplistic* book" and Aragon "marvelously accurate and attentive," most critics felt that the book's political intent devalued its literary worth. Nadeau remarked in *The French Novel since the War:* "As the spokesman in France of the theory of 'socialist realism,' Aragon was obliged to set a good example. He undertook to recount in a series of novels the struggles, anxieties and victories of his political friends. However, in his [*The Communists*] . . . historical truth is so mishandled, the characters are so vague and improbable, even the writing itself so foreign to the author, that he did not persevere in his self-imposed task." "The fictional chronicle [Aragon] writes," Germaine Bree and Margaret Otis Guiton state in *An Age of Fiction: The French Novel from Gide to Camus,* "is shamelessly partial and its fictional value almost nil."

Because he had long written politically oriented fiction for a limited audience, by the 1950s Aragon was little noticed outside his political circle. "Even in France," Becker reported, "very little critical material has appeared on Aragon other than in the Communist press, which hailed all of his work indiscriminately." With the appearance of *Holy Week* in 1958, however, Aragon reached a wider critical audience. The story of French king Louis XVIII's escape from Napoleon in the nineteenth century, *Holy Week* is far less politically motivated than are other of Aragon's novels. Despite the fact that, as Leon S. Roudiez observed in the *Saturday Review,* "a philosophy of history, a social ethic, and a political ideology inform [the novel's] entire structure . . . its Marxist flavor is rarely obtrusive." Becker noted that "critics who had ignored or discounted Aragon's previous work because of his political sympathies praised what they termed his return to objectivity."

Holy Week is an exception to the usually strident propaganda tone of Aragon's later work. During the 1960s and 1970s, he published collections of political speeches he had delivered before the French Communist party, essays on political topics, and several works on Soviet history and literature. One of these, *A History of the U.S.S.R. from Lenin to Khrushchev,* was described by Harry Schwartz of the *Saturday Review* as "Soviet history as seen through the eyes of a Khrushchev supporter who obediently follows the Khrushchev line." The novel *La Mise a mort,* in which Aragon "condemns his blind acceptance of Soviet propaganda in the thirties," as Adereth reports, nonetheless ends with Aragon's continued support of communism, "despite the monstrous distortions which it suffered," as Adereth commented. Speaking of Aragon's work as director of the periodical *Les Lettres francaises,* Francois Bondy of the *New Republic* wrote that he "combined a campaign to seduce the younger 'uncommitted' writers with a most aggressive and fanatical defense of the cult of Stalinism . . ., to a degree unparalleled by any other known writer, justifying the most obviously monstrous political trials, insulting the victims of these proceedings, and slandering those who protested against them."

Critical evaluations of Aragon's career are often colored by his political activities and by the fact that he wrote prolifically, producing much work of an ephemeral nature. At the time of his death, a writer for the London *Times* said that Aragon "was a writer of undoubted distinction but curiously uneven achievement." J. W. Kneller of the *French Review* found that "the case of Louis Aragon is one of the most controversial in contemporary French letters. Aside from political matters, he has been a source of disagreement among critics on purely literary grounds. Some consider him one of the most gifted writers of his generation. Others call him an elegant failure."

Because of this continuing controversy, Aragon's stature as a writer is still largely in dispute. Most critics do credit him, however, with several notable works of lasting interest, including *Paris Peasant, Holy Week,* and his poems of World War II. A *New York Times* writer commented at the time of his death that "even those who disagreed with his politics admired his talents as a poet and as a novelist." A *National Review* writer called him "a great twentieth century poet" and "one of the relatively few genuine heroes of the Resistance." Looking back over Aragon's long and controversial career, Gascoyne believed that "in the end the renown of Louis Aragon will be that of a poet, novelist and critic who tried his best to give Communist writing in France a human face."

BIOGRAPHICAL/CRITICAL SOURCES:

BOOKS

Adereth, M., *Commitment in Modern French Literature: A Brief Study of "Litterature Engagee" in the Works of Peguy, Aragon, and Sartre,* Gollancz, 1967.
Alexandrian, Sarane, *Surrealist Art,* Praeger, 1970.
Aragon au defi, Le Terrain Vague, 1966.
Balakian, Anna, *Surrealism: The Road to the Absolute,* Dutton, 1970.
Becker, Lucille E., *Louis Aragon,* Twayne, 1971.
Bree, Germaine, and Margaret Otis Guiton, *An Age of Fiction: The French Novel from Gide to Camus,* Rutgers University Press, 1957.
Breton, Andre, *Entretiens, 1913-1952,* Gallimard, 1952.
Burnsham, Stanley, editor, *The Poem Itself,* Holt, 1960.
Cardinal, Roger, and Robert Stuart Short, *Surrealism: Permanent Revelation,* Studio Vista/Dutton, 1970.
Caute, David, *Communism and the French Intellectuals, 1914-60,* Andre Deutsch, 1964.
Contemporary Literary Criticism, Gale, Volume 3, 1975, Volume 22, 1982.
Dictionary of Literary Biography, Volume 72: *French Novelists, 1930-1960,* Gale, 1988.
Juin, Hubert, *Aragon,* Gallimard, 1960.
Lecherbonnier, Bernard, *Aragon,* Bordas, 1971.
Lindsay, Jack, *Meetings with Poets,* Ungar, 1969.
Nadeau, Maurice, *The History of Surrealism,* Macmillan, 1965.
Nadeau, Maurice, *The French Novel since the War,* Methuen, 1967.
Raymond, Marcel, *From Baudelaire to Surrealism,* Methuen, 1970.
Roy, Claude, *Aragon,* P. Seghers, 1951.
Savage, Catherine, *Malraux, Sartre, and Aragon as Political Novelists,* University of Florida Press, 1965.
Tetel, Marcel, editor, *Symbolism and Modern Literature: Studies in Honor of Wallace Fowlie,* Duke University Press, 1978.

PERIODICALS

Comparative Drama, spring, 1977.
French Review, December, 1952, May, 1965.
Mainstream, January, 1962.
Nation, September 26, 1936.
New Republic, October 7, 1936, November 23, 1938, December 25, 1961, December 16, 1972.
New Yorker, November 1, 1941.
New York Times, December 16, 1945.
Saturday Review, October 7, 1961, August 8, 1964.
Saturday Review of Literature, December 24, 1938, November 15, 1941.
Southern Review, spring, 1967.
Spectator, October 13, 1961.

Times (London), January 4, 1983.
Times Literary Supplement, January 23, 1961.
Transformation, Number 3, 1945.
Weekly Book Review, December 16, 1945.
Yale French Studies, fall-winter, 1948.
Yale Review, September, 1945.

OBITUARIES:

PERIODICALS

AB Bookman's Weekly, February 14, 1983.
National Review, January 21, 1983.
Newsweek, January 10, 1983.
New York Times, December 25, 1982.
Time, January 10, 1983.
Times (London), January 4, 1983.
Washington Post, December 25, 1982.

*   *   *

ARCHER, Herbert Winslow
See MENCKEN, H(enry) L(ouis)

*   *   *

ARCHER, Lee
See ELLISON, Harlan

*   *   *

ARDEN, John 1930-

PERSONAL: Born October 26, 1930, in Barnsley, Yorkshire, England; son of Charles Alwyn (a manager of a glass works) and Annie Elizabeth (Layland) Arden; married Margaretta Ruth D'Arcy (a playwright), 1957; children: Francis Gwalchmei (deceased), Finn, Adam, Jacob, Neuss. *Education:* King's College, Cambridge, B.A., 1953; Edinburgh College of Architecture, diploma, 1955.

ADDRESSES: Agent—Margaret Ramsay Ltd., 14a Goodwin Court, London WC2N 4LL, England.

CAREER: Architectural assistant in London, England, 1955-57; playwright, 1957—. Fellow in playwriting, University of Bristol, Bristol, England, 1959-60; visiting lecturer in politics and drama, New York University, 1967; Regents' lecturer, University of California, Davis, 1973; writer in residence, University of New England, Australia, 1975. Co-founder of Corrandulla Arts and Entertainment Club, Corrandulla, Ireland, 1971, and Galway Theatre Workshop, 1975. *Military service:* British Army, Intelligence Corps, 1949-50.

AWARDS, HONORS: British Broadcasting Corp. Northern Region prize for "The Life of Man"; *Encyclopaedia Britannica* prize, 1959, and Vernon Rice award, 1966, both for *Serjeant Musgrave's Dance: An Unhistorical Parable;* Bristol University fellowship in playwriting, 1959-60; *Evening Standard* (London) "most promising playwright" award, 1960; Trieste Festival prize, 1961, for "Soldier, Soldier"; Arts Council Award, 1973; recipient with husband John Arden, award from Arts Council, 1974, for *The Ballygombeen Bequest* and *The Island of the Mighty: A Play on a Traditional British Theme in Three Parts; The Old Man Sleeps Alone* included in *Best Radio Plays of 1982; Silence among the Weapons: Some Events at the Time of the Failure of a Republic* considered for Booker McConnell prize for fiction, 1982.

WRITINGS:

PLAYS

"All Fall Down," produced in Edinburgh, Scotland, 1955.
"The Waters of Babylon" (also see below), first produced in London at Royal Court Theatre, October 20, 1957; produced in New York City, 1958, and in Washington, D.C., at Washington Theatre Club, 1967.
"When Is a Door Not a Door?" (also see below), first produced in London at Central School of Speech and Drama, 1958.
"Live Like Pigs" (also see below), first produced in London at Royal Court Theatre, September 30, 1958; produced Off-Broadway at Actor's Playhouse, June 7, 1965.
Serjeant Musgrave's Dance: An Unhistorical Parable (also see below; first produced in London at Royal Court Theatre, October 22, 1959; produced Off-Broadway at Theatre de Lys, March 8, 1966; revised version with John McGrath produced on tour as "Serjeant Musgrave Dances On," 1972), Methuen, 1960, Grove, 1962, with notes and commentary by R. W. Ewart, Longman, 1982, with notes and commentary by Glenda Leeming, Methuen, 1982, revised 1966 script, Studio Duplicating Service, 1986.
The Workhouse Donkey: A Vulgar Melodrama (also see below; first produced in Sussex, England, at Chichester Festival Theatre, July 8, 1963), Methuen, 1964, Grove, 1967.
Ironhand (adaptation of Goethe's *Goetz von Berlichingen;* first produced in Bristol, England, at Bristol Old Vic Theatre, November 12, 1963), Methuen, 1965, Grove, 1967.
"Woyzeck" (adaptation of Alban Berg's opera "Wozzeck") first produced in London, 1964.
Armstrong's Last Goodnight: An Exercise in Diplomacy (also see below; first produced in Glasgow, Scotland, at Glasgow Citizens' Theatre, May 5, 1964; produced in Boston, 1966), Methuen, 1965, Grove, 1976.
"Fidelio" (adaptation of libretto by Joseph Sonnleithner and Friedrich Treitschke of opera by Beethoven), first produced in London, 1965.
"Play without Words," first produced in Glasgow, 1965.
Left-Handed Liberty: A Play about Magna Carta (commissioned by the City of London to celebrate the 750th anniversary of the sealing of the Magna Carta; first produced in London at Mermaid Theatre, June 14, 1965), Methuen, 1965, Grove, 1966.
"The Soldier's Tale" (adaptation of opera by Igor Stravinsky; libretto by Charles Ramuz), first produced in Bath, England, 1968.
"The True History of Squire Jonathan and His Unfortunate Treasure" (also see below), first produced in London at Ambiance Lunch Hour Theatre, June 17, 1968.

PLAYS; WITH WIFE, MARGARETTA D'ARCY

"The Happy Haven" (two-act; also see below), first produced in Bristol at Bristol University, 1960; produced in London at Royal Court Theatre, September 14, 1960; produced in New York City, 1967.
The Business of Good Government: A Christmas Play (one-act; first produced as "A Christmas Play," in Somerset, England, at Brent Knoll Church of St. Michael, December, 1960; produced in New York City, 1970), Methuen, 1963, reprinted, 1983, Grove, 1967.
Ars Longa, Vita Brevis (one-act; first produced on the West End at Aldwych Theatre by the Royal Shakespeare Co., 1964), Cassell, 1965.

"Friday's Hiding" (one-act; also see below), first produced in London, 1965; produced in Edinburgh at the Lyceum Theatre, 1966.

The Royal Pardon; or, The Soldier Who Became an Actor (first produced in Devon, England, at Beaford Arts Centre, September 1, 1966; produced in London at Arts Theatre, 1967), Methuen, 1967.

(And with Cartoon Archetypical Slogan Theatre) "Harold Muggins Is a Martyr," first produced in London at Unity Theatre Club, June, 1968.

The Hero Rises Up: A Romantic Melodrama (two-act; first produced in London at Round House Theatre, November 6, 1968), Methuen, 1969.

(And with Muswell Hill Street Theatre) "Granny Welfare and the Wolf," first produced in London at Ducketts Common, Turnpike Lane, March, 1971.

(And with Muswell Hill Street Theatre) "My Old Man's a Tory" (one-act), first produced in London at Wood Green, March, 1971.

(And with Socialist Labour League) "Two Hundred Years of Labour History" (two-act), first produced in London at Alexandra Palace, April, 1971.

(And with Writers Against Repression) "Rudi Dutschke Must Stay," first produced in London at British Museum, spring, 1971.

The Ballygombeen Bequest (first produced in Belfast, Northern Ireland, at St. Mary and St. Joseph's College Drama Society, May, 1972; produced in London at Bush Theatre, September 11, 1972), Scripts, 1972.

The Island of the Mighty: A Play on a Traditional British Theme in Three Parts (first produced on the West End at Aldwych Theatre, December 5, 1972), with illustrations by authors, Eyre Methuen, 1974.

(And with Corrandulla Arts Entertainment Club) "The Devil and the Parish Pump" (one-act), first produced in County Galway, Ireland, at Gort Roe, Corrandulla Arts Centre, April, 1974.

The Non-Stop Connolly Show: A Dramatic Cycle of Continuous Struggle in Six Parts (first produced in Dublin at Liberty Hall, March 29, 1975, produced in London at Ambiance Lunch Hour Theatre, May 17, 1976), Pluto, Parts 1 and 2: *Boyhood 1868-1889* [and] *Apprenticeship, 1889-1896,* 1977, Part 3: *Professional, 1896-1903,* Part 4: *The New World, 1903-1910,* Part 5: *The Great Lockout, 1910-1914,* and Part 6: *World War and the Rising, 1914-1916,* 1978.

(And with Galway Theatre Workshop) "The Crown Strike Play" (one-act), first produced in Galway at Eyre Square, December, 1975.

(And with Galway Theatre Workshop) "Sean O'Scrudu," first produced in Galway at Coachman Hotel, February, 1976.

(And with Galway Theatre Workshop) "The Mongrel Fox" (one-act), first produced in Galway at Regional Technical College, October, 1976.

(And with Galway Theatre Workshop) "No Room at the Inn" (one-act), first produced in Galway at Coachman Hotel, December, 1976.

(And with Galway Theatre Workshop) "Silence," first produced in Galway at Eyre Square, April, 1977.

(And with Galway Theatre Workshop) "Mary's Name" (one-act), first produced in Galway at University College, May, 1977.

(And with Galway Theatre Workshop) "Blow-In Chorus for Liam Cosgrave," first produced in Galway at Eyre Square, June, 1977.

Vandaleur's Folly: An Anglo-Irish Melodrama; The Hazard of Experiment in an Irish Co-operative, Ralahine, 1831 (two-act; first produced at Lancaster University, 1978), Eyre Methuen, 1981.

The Little Gray Home in the West: An Anglo-Irish Melodrama, Pluto, 1982.

RADIO/TELEVISION PRODUCTIONS

"Soldier, Soldier: A Comic Song for Television" (also see below), BBC, 1960.

"Wet Fish: A Professional Reminiscence for Television" (also see below), BBC, 1961.

"The Bagman; or, The Impromptu of Muswell Hill" (radio play; also see below), British Broadcasting Corp. (BBC-Radio), 1970.

(With D'Arcy) "Keep Those People Moving" (radio play), BBC-Radio, 1972.

(With D'Arcy) "Portrait of a Rebel" (television documentary about Sean O'Casey), Radio-Telefis Eireann (Dublin), 1973.

"To Put It Frankly" (radio play), BBC-Radio, 1979.

Pearl: A Play about a Play within a Play (radio play), Eyre Methuen, 1979.

The Adventures of the Ingenious Gentlemen (two-part adaptation of Cervantes' *Don Quixote*), BBC-Radio, 1980.

"Garland for a Hoar Head" (radio play), BBC-Radio, 1982.

"The Old Man Sleeps Alone" (radio play), BBC-Radio, 1982.

(With D'Arcy) *Whose Is the Kingdom?* (radio play broadcast in nine parts by BBC-Radio, 1988), Methuen, 1988.

COLLECTIONS

Three Plays (contains "The Waters of Babylon," "Live Like Pigs," and "The Happy Haven"), introduction by John Russell Taylor, Penguin, 1964, reprinted, 1984, Penguin (Baltimore), 1965.

Soldier, Soldier, and Other Plays (contains "Soldier, Soldier: A Comic Song for Television," "Wet Fish: A Professional Reminiscence for Television," "When Is a Door Not a Door?" and "Friday's Hiding"), Methuen, 1967.

Two Autobiographical Plays (contains "The True History of Squire Jonathan and His Unfortunate Treasure" and "The Bagman; or, The Impromtu of Muswell Hill"), Methuen, 1971.

Plays (includes "Serjeant Musgrave's Dance: An Unhistorical Parable," "The Workhouse Donkey: A Vulgar Melodrama," and "Armstrong's Last Goodnight: An Exercise in Diplomacy"), Methuen, 1977, Grove, 1978.

OTHER

(With D'Arcy) *To Present the Pretence: Essays on the Theatre and Its Public,* Eyre Methuen, 1977, Holmes & Meier, 1979.

Vox Pop: The Last Days of the Roman Republic (novel), Harcourt, 1982 (published in England as *Silence among the Weapons: Some Events at the Time of the Failure of a Republic,* Methuen, 1982).

Books of Bale (novel), Methuen, 1988.

(With D'Arcy) *Awkward Corners* (essays), Methuen, 1988.

Also author of "The Life of Man," 1956. Contributor to anthologies, including *New English Dramatists,* Penguin, Volume 3, 1961, Volume 4, 1962, and *Scripts 9,* 1972.

SIDELIGHTS: British playwright John Arden may not be as well-known outside his native land as are some of his contemporaries of the radical writers school that emerged during the 1950s and 1960s. But like John Osborne, author of "Look Back in

Anger," and David Edgar, whose many agitprop dramas rocked the stage, Arden takes a hard look at English life, examining the conflicts behind the traditions. As Stanley Lourdeaux describes it in a *Dictionary of Literary Biography* article, when the fledgling playwright Arden began his professional career in 1957, "critics hastily placed him with other 'angry young men' of the period. Recent critics have labeled Arden the British [Bertolt] Brecht because of his generally Marxist politics in his recent social drama. But neither his present politics nor the 'angry' nonconformity of his protagonists tells the story of why he gradually rejected the appearance of 1950s social realism for that of improvisation."

Arden's early theatrical efforts "scrutinized the basic social tension between aggressive survivors and the institutions meant to pacify them," continues Lourdeaux, who points to "The Waters of Babylon," a 1957 production, as an illustration. It is the story of Sigismanfred Krankiewicz—Krank for short—a Pole who emigrates to London as an architectural assistant (the playwright's original career). When Krank runs up against local authorities for harboring too many boarders, many of them prostitutes, at his private boardinghouse, the immigrant rebels by becoming involved in a corrupt local lottery. Krank's schemes are contrasted against his friend Paul's, who is an amateur anarchist given to building bombs in the name of Polish patriotism. But Polish patriotism "makes little sense to Krank in a world gone mad, as he explains when Paul almost shoots him after learning that he was a soldier in the German army at Buchenwald," notes Lourdeaux. Eventually, Paul does shoot Krank and kills him, though accidentally, and "the random results of the entire scene undermines Krank's clever individualism as well as social justice," Lourdeaux writes.

In his book *Anger and After: A Guide to the New British Drama*, John Russell Taylor remarks that "behind Arden's work there seems to be brooding one basic principle: not exactly the obvious one that today there are no causes—that would be altogether too facile, and in any case just not true—but that there are too many." In the opinion of Simon Trussler, in his published study *John Arden*, "The Waters of Babylon" is "extravagantly plotted, generously peopled—a scenically-shuttling kaleidoscope of down-at-heel London life in the early 1950s. Coincidence functions here not with the shyly intruding excuses of the well-made play but as a fine art in itself, a satisfaction of improbable expectations. And the characters, a racial mixture of Poles, English, Irish, and West Indians, embody in this comedy of contemporary humours many of the mythic archetypes of urban life, caught from an unexpected angle."

Another Arden work to satirically examine the conflict between the classes is "Live Like Pigs." Like "The Waters of Babylon," this play "contains earthy and zestful language and depends greatly on performance," according to Lourdeaux. "Arden presents the chaos of the gypsylike Sawney family who are forced out of their broken run-down tramcar and made to live in the local housing project. The Sawneys quickly manage to insult their new neighbors, the Jacksons, who eventually incite a vigilante group to run the unappreciative vulgar family out of the project."

"Live Like Pigs" looks "superficially naturalistic, but one has only to consider the sturdy-beggarly tongue in which the Sawneys speak to realize that Arden is here employing a device which was to become more familiar in his historical plays for distinguishing a way of life through its language," says Trussler. "The ballads which introduce the scenes, and the occasional snatches of song within them, underline the danger of approaching the play naturalistically." The purpose of song in this work, the critic continues, "is in marked contrast to the deliberately in-

terruptive purpose it usually serves in Brecht's: balladry is best regarded as another of Arden's invented languages, the problems it poses dramatic rather than musical."

Called by the Irish dramatist Sean O'Casey "far and away the finest play of the present day," "Serjeant Musgrave's Dance: An Unhistorical Parable," a 1958 Arden drama, centers on a fanatical officer of the nineteenth-century British army who exacts a bizarre revenge on the life of a soldier killed by a sniper. He in fact wants no fewer than five men to die to avenge the young private; then calls for more murders to mark another soldier's death, although that one was accidental. "Serjeant Musgrave's Dance," in M. W. Steinberg's view, "is largely an exploration of the place of violence in society and our varying responses to it." The *Dalhousie Review* writer adds that "the moral-political question is given sharpest focus and most acute and challenging dramatic expression through Serjeant Musgrave, a zealot so convinced of the absolute rightness of his cause that he is willing to adopt horrifying means to achieve his goal, and so unswerving and single-minded in his devotion to his avowed purpose that he refuses to be distracted by any consideration not immediately relevant."

"[It] would make for easier acceptance of *Serjeant Musgrave's Dance* if the fanatical sergeant were to be either wholly condemned or wholly approved of," states G. W. Brandt, the author of *Contemporary Theatre*. "But is it not disturbing to see a morally sensitive man trying to start a public massacre? It is. Does his fanaticism invalidate his moral protest as such? It does not. The contradiction between laudable indignation and reprehensible conclusions drawn from it may either alienate the spectators out of all sympathy with the play (as happened to some critics), or else it may jolt them into stirring moral speculation (as was the experience of some other critics)."

That "Serjeant Musgrave's Dance" evoked a divided, if emotional, reaction in critics proved a point of discussion to Malcolm Page: "Clearly there are grounds for uncertainty about the import of the play; difficulties in comprehension arose mainly because neither method nor subject was what the critics expected," he writes in *Drama Survey*. The play "suggests that pacifists are not sure enough about what they are trying to do, and have not understood the complexities of the world," Page says. And "there are several other ideas in the play, perhaps too many. Musgrave and his followers are obsessed with guilt at the evil in which they joined, raising the issue of how to expiate it. . . . Musgrave touches, too, on the question of what principle is: where and how can one begin to apply principles in an imperfect world; does the quest of absolute principle lead to madness?"

In another *Drama Survey* article, John Mills reacts both to "Serjeant Musgrave's Dance" and to Page's assessment of it. To Page's opinion that the work asks "why pacifist ideas have not had more influence," Mills responds that "though I agree with much of [Page's] commentary, I think that the play is a little more hopeful than he indicates. For one thing, it seems to me that *Musgrave* is less about pacifism than it is about anarchism, a doctrine [with] which the play tentatively (as Arden himself might put it) agrees."

The playwright does not lack for personal anger, "but he is the dramatist par excellence who translates that anger into situations of a strictly impersonal nature," in the words of Arnold P. Hinchcliffe in his book *British Theatre 1950-70*. "Arden's characters are primarily used as representatives, and his plots bring about conflicts between social groups. His characters, of course, exist as very colourful individuals, but their personality is shaped at all times to suggest what they stand for . . . and add to the picture of the community as a whole. Thus, isolated town or national politics reflected in local government is observed with an accurate social eye and a strong historical sense which combine to 'translate the concrete life of today into terms of poetry that shall at the one time illustrate that life and set it within the historical and legendary tradition of our culture,' " he says, quoting Arden.

To Lourdeaux, Arden "began his career in theater as a trained architect who was guided by the basic foundation of social drama only to turn more and more explicitly political material. Though at first interested in epic figures like Hitler and King Arthur, Arden tempered his taste to the smaller stature of men like Sigismanfred Krankiewicz and Serjeant Musgrave whose vivid speech and improvised actions supplanted the significance of seemingly realistic plots. With other fierce survivors like the Sawneys in *Live Like Pigs,* [the playwright] seemed to have settled on contemporary social realism."

Arden's career took another turn, though, when he began collaborating on plays with his wife, the Irish actress and playwright Margaretta D'Arcy. The professional partnership was a natural move, as Arden explains in a *Contemporary Authors Autobiography Series* article. "She was closely involved with the most progressive aspects of the theatre of that time, aspects of which I knew nothing, with my limited Shakespearean provincial orientation and my academic (and indeed pompous) attitude towards the stage. She gave me a copy of Brecht—a writer I had only heard of: she introduced me to the works of Beckett, Strindberg, Toller, Behan," he writes. "Her name now appears, sometimes first, sometimes second, together with mine, upon a great deal of published work which nonetheless the male critics, managements, publishers, and broadcasters, will insist upon referring to as 'Arden's.' Or, worse, 'the Ardens'.' It also appears on work of her own, but this did not appear until after the collaborative pieces."

The Non-Stop Connolly Show: A Dramatic Cycle of Continuous Struggle in Six Parts is a marathon collaboration between Arden and D'Arcy; a six-part cycle lasting nearly 24 hours, with a huge cast of historical characters, the production traces the life of Irish socialist leader James Connolly from boyhood through the Easter Uprising in 1916, an important and inspiring event in the history of Irish nationalism. Writing of the two traditions in Ireland, "vicious, merciless violence" and pacifism, Desmond Hogan points out in *New Statesmen* that Connolly exemplified neither, but "ultimately opted for a bloody revolution on a minor scale not so much to break from Britain but to let out his own protest against Britain's centuries of manhandling Ireland." Although Lourdeaux considers the play "too long and the characters too numerous for viewers to focus exclusively on any one character or action in this complex political tapestry," Hogan suggests that "one feels one is in the presence of great drama and that the drama was made from a cold eye, an eye which like Yeats's, penetrated lies, phobias, images which dressed other images, and came up with—even if only for moments at a stretch—a mind-boggling authenticity."

Concluding an essay on Arden in *Modern Drama,* Joan Tindale Blindheim declares the playwright "a conscious and imaginative explorer of visual effects and stage resources. His knowledge of stage history and his trained eye add dimensions to his work that are often absent from that of more 'literary' writers. There are aspects that must not be ignored when [Arden's] contribution to the drama is considered, and it is through them that he is likely to make a lasting contribution to the theatre too, in helping to

break down theatre conventions and in striving towards a richer and more active relationship between actors and audience."

BIOGRAPHICAL/CRITICAL SOURCES:

BOOKS

Anderson, Michael, *Anger and Detachment: A Study of Arden, Osborne and Pinter,* Pitman, 1976.
Armstrong, William A., general editor, *Experimental Drama,* G. Bell & Sons, 1963.
Brandt, G. W., *Contemporary Theatre,* Stratford-Upon-Avon Studies 4, Edward Arnold, 1962.
Contemporary Authors Autobiography Series, Volume 4, Gale, 1986.
Contemporary Literary Criticism, Gale, Volume 6, 1976, Volume 13, 1980, Volume 15, 1980.
Dictionary of Literary Biography, Volume 13: *British Dramatists since World War II,* Gale, 1982.
Gilman, Richard, *Common and Uncommon Masks: Writings on Theatre, 1961-1970,* Random House, 1971.
Hayman, Ronald, *John Arden,* Heinemann Educational Books, 1968.
Hinchcliffe, Arnold P., *British Theatre 1950-1970,* Rowman & Littlefield, 1974.
Hunt, Albert, *Arden: A Study of His Plays,* Eyre Methuen, 1974.
Kennedy, Andrew K., *Six Dramatists in Search of a Language: Studies in Dramatic Language,* Cambridge University Press, 1975.
Leeming, Glenda, *John Arden,* edited by Ian Scott-Kilvert, Longman, 1974.
Lowenfels, Walter, editor, *The Playwrights Speak,* Delacorte, 1967.
Lumley, Frederick, *New Trends in 20th Century Drama: A Survey since Ibsen and Shaw,* Oxford University Press, 1967.
Marowitz, Charles, *The Encore Reader: A Chronicle of New Drama,* Methuen & Co., 1965.
Roy, Emil, *British Drama since Shaw,* Southern Illinois University Press, 1972.
Taylor, John Russell, *Anger and After: A Guide to the New British Drama,* Methuen, 1962.
Trussler, Simon, *John Arden,* Columbia University Press, 1973.
Tschudin, Marcus, *A Writer's Theatre: George Devine and the English Stage Company at the Royal Court, 1956-1965,* Lang, 1972.
Wellworth, George, *The Theatre of Protest and Paradox,* New York University Press, 1964.
Williams, Raymond, *Drama from Ibsen to Brecht,* Oxford University Press, 1969.

PERIODICALS

Dalhousie Review, autumn, 1977.
Drama Survey, summer, 1967, winter, 1968.
Hibbert Journal, autumn, 1966.
Modern Drama, December, 1968, March, 1978.
New Statesman, April 11, 1980.
Times Literary Supplement, January 7, 1965, March 3, 1978, August 27, 1982.

*   *   *

ARENDT, Hannah 1906-1975

PERSONAL: Born October 14, 1906, in Hannover, Germany; came to the United States, 1941, naturalized, 1950; died December 4, 1975, of an apparent heart attack, in New York, N.Y.;

daughter of Paul (an engineer) and Martha (Cohn) Arendt; married Heinrich Bluecher (a professor of philosophy), 1940 (died, 1970). *Education:* Koenigsberg University, B.A., 1924; attended universities at Marburg and Freiburg; Heidelberg University, studied with Karl Jaspers, Ph.D. (philosophy), 1928; Notgemeinschaft der Deutschen Wissenschaft, research fellow, 1931-33. *Politics:* Independent. *Religion:* No religious affiliation.

ADDRESSES: Home—370 Riverside Dr., New York, NY 10025. *Office*—Graduate Faculty of Political and Social Science, New School for Social Research, New York, NY.

CAREER: Fled Germany for Paris in 1933; social worker for Youth Aliyah, Paris, France, 1934-40; Conference on Jewish Relations, New York City, research director, 1944-46; Schocken Books, Inc., New York City, chief editor, 1946-48; Jewish Cultural Reconstruction, New York City, executive director, 1949-52; Princeton University, Princeton, N.J., visiting professor of politics (the first woman to be appointed a full professor there), 1959; University of Chicago, Chicago, Ill., professor with committee on social thought, 1963-67; New School for Social Research, Graduate Faculty of Political and Social Science, New York City, professor, 1967-75. Visiting professor at University of California, Berkeley, 1955, Columbia University, 1960, and at Brooklyn College (now Brooklyn College of the City University of New York). Member of board of directors, Conference on Jewish Relations, Jewish Cultural Reconstruction, and Judah Magnes Foundation.

MEMBER: Institut International de Philosophic Politique, American Academy of Political and Social Science, National Institute of Arts and Letters, American Academy of Arts and Sciences (fellow), American Political Science Association, American Society of Political and Legal Philosophy, Deutsche Akademie fuer Sprache und Dichtung (corresponding member), PEN.

AWARDS, HONORS: Guggenheim fellow, 1952-53; award from National Institute of Arts and Letters, 1954; Rockefeller fellow, 1958-60 and 1969-70; Lessing Preis, Hamburg, 1959; Freud Preis from Deutsche Akademie fur Sprache und Dichtung, 1967; Emerson-Thoreau Medal from American Academy of Arts and Sciences, 1969; M. Cary Thomas Prize from Bryn Mawr College, 1971; Danish Sonning Prize, 1975; honorary degrees from numerous colleges and universities, including Yale University, 1971, Dartmouth College, 1972, and Princeton University, 1972.

WRITINGS:

Der Liebesbegriff bei Augustin, J. Springer (Berlin), 1929.
Sechs Essays, L. Schneider (Heidelberg), 1948.
(Translator with M. Greenberg) Franz Kafka, *Diaries,* edited by Max Brod, Volume 2, Schocken, 1949.
The Origins of Totalitarianism, Harcourt, 1951 (published in England as *Burden of Our Time,* Secker & Warburg, 1951), new edition, 1966, three volume edition, Volume 1: *Totalitarianism,* Volume 2: *Imperialism,* Volume 3: *Anti-Semitism,* 1968, new edition with added prefaces, 1973.
(Editor and author of introduction) Hermann Broch, *Essays,* Volume 1: *Dichten und Erkennen,* Volume 2: *Erkennen und Handeln,* Rhein-Verlag (Zurich), 1955.
Fragwuerdige Traditionsbestaende im politischen Denken der Gegenwart: Vier Essays, Europaeische Verlagsanstalt (Frankfurt am Main), 1957.
The Human Condition (lectures delivered under the title "Vita Activa"), University of Chicago Press, 1958, collector's edition, 1969.
Die Krise in der Erziehung, Angelsachsen Verlag (Bremen), 1958.

Rahen Varnhagen: The Life of a Jewess, translation by Richard and Clara Winston, East and West Library for Leo Baeck Institute, 1958, revised edition published as *Rahel Varnhagen: The Life of a Jewish Woman,* Harcourt, 1974, original German text published as *Rahel Varnhagen: Lebensgeschichte einer Deutschen Juedin aus der Romantic,* Piper (Munich), 1959.
Die ungarische Revolution und der totalitaere Imperialismus, Piper, 1958.
Wahrheit, Freiheit, und Friede: Karl Jaspers, Piper, 1958.
Elemente totaler Herrschaft, Europaeische Verlagsanstalt, 1958.
Von der Menschlichkeit in finsteren Zeiten: Rede ueber Lessing, Piper, 1960.
Between Past and Future: Six Exercises in Political Thought, Viking, 1961, enlarged edition published as *Between Past and Future: Eight Exercises in Political Thought,* 1968.
Freedom and Revolution, Connecticut College, 1961.
(Editor) Karl Jaspers, *The Great Philosophers,* translated by Ralph Manheim, Harcourt, Volume 1: *The Foundations* (also published as *Kant, Plato and Augustine,* and *Socrates, Buddha, Confucius, Jesus*), 1962, Volume 2: *The Original Thinkers,* 1966.
On Revolution, Faber, 1963.
Eichmann in Jerusalem: A Report on the Banality of Evil, Viking, 1963, revised and enlarged edition, 1964.
Men in Dark Times, Harcourt, 1968.
(Editor and author of introduction) Walter Benjamin, *Illuminations: Essays and Reflections,* translated by Harry Zohn, Harcourt, 1968.
Macht und Gewalt, Piper, 1970.
On Violence, Harcourt, 1970.
Crises of the Republic: Lying in Politics, Civil Disobedience, On Violence, Thoughts on Politics and Revolution, Harcourt, 1972.
Wahrheit und Luege in der Politik: Zwei Essays, Piper, 1972.
(Editor) *Spinoza,* translated by Ralph Manheim, Harcourt, 1974.
The Jew as Pariah: Jewish Identity and Politics in the Modern Age, Grove, 1978.
The Life of the Mind, Harcourt, Volume 1: *Thinking,* 1978, Volume 2: *Willing,* 1978, one-volume edition, 1981.
Lectures on Kant's Political Philosophy, University of Chicago Press, 1983.

CONTRIBUTOR

K. S. Pinson, editor, *Essays on Antisemitism,* 2nd edition, Conference on Jewish Relations, 1946.
William Ebenstein, editor, *Modern Political Thought,* Rinehart, 1954.
Columbia College, *Man in Contemporary Society,* Volume 2, Columbia University Press, 1956.
Carl J. Friedrich, editor, *Authority,* Harvard University Press, 1958.
Robert M. Hutchins and Mortimer J. Adler, editors, *The Great Ideas Today, 1961-1963,* Encyclopedia Britannica, 1961-1963.
Peter Demetz, editor, *Brecht,* Prentice-Hall, 1962.
Analyse d'un vertige, Societe d'Editions et de Publications, Artistiques et Litteraires, 1968.
Arthur A. Cohn, editor, *Arguments and Doctrines: A Reader of Jewish Thinking in the Aftermath of the Holocaust,* Harper, 1970.
Carl Saner, compiler, *Karl Jaspers in der Diskussion,* Piper, 1973.

OTHER

Contributor to *Contemporary Jewish Record, Review of Politics, New Yorker, New York Review of Books,* and other publications.

SIDELIGHTS: Hannah Arendt earned a reputation as one of the twentieth century's most brilliant and original political thinkers. "Her penetrating analyses of totalitarianism and democracy, the problems of mass society, the reasons for revolution and political image making are widely regarded as required reading for a thorough understanding of modern political history," observed *Washington Post* writer Stephen Klaidman. Arendt studied philosophy at the University of Heidelberg under Karl Jaspers and received her doctorate when she was only twenty-two years old. She was already established as an outstanding essayist in her own country when Hitler's ascent to power in 1933 sent her to Paris. For several years she studied and wrote there; she also was active in a relief agency that found homes in Palestine for the orphaned and homeless children of Europe. Arendt and her husband finally fled for the United States when Nazi troops began to press into France in 1940.

Arendt's first major publication in the United States was a penetrating analysis of the forces that brought Hitler to power, *The Origins of Totalitarianism.* Her contention that anti-Semitism and imperialism were at the root of totalitarianism was disputed by some, but her writing was praised even by those who disagreed with her theories. *New York Times Book Review* contributor E. H. Carr attributed Arendt's emphasis on anti-Semitism to her personal history, but concluded, "Whatever its shortcomings, however, . . . the book is the work of one who has thought as well as suffered. . . . Miss Arendt, her eyes fixed in fascination and repulsion on the horror of Nazi Germany, offers only slender hope for Western civilization to avoid this form of suicide. Yet the reader who shuns this conclusion can still be grateful for a disquieting, moving and thought-provoking book." H. Stuart Hughes believed that Arendt had exaggerated certain facts to prove her point, but he also felt that *The Origins of Totalitarianism* was "a great book. Deeply thought-out and conscientiously documented, [it] will take its place among the major writings of our times. . . . To the totalitarian threat to change 'human nature' itself she opposes an equally total declaration of human responsibility. Her book is a moving testament of solidarity with all the 'superfluous people' now living out their meaningless days in all the concentration camps of the earth."

Arendt's background led the *New Yorker* magazine to send her to Israel for the trial of Adolf Eichmann, one of Hitler's top bureaucrats. The magazine pieces she wrote from Israel evolved into her most controversial book, *Eichmann in Jerusalem: A Report of the Banality of Evil.* Eichmann was held responsible for the deaths of millions of Jews. Arendt did not excuse him for his part in the Holocaust, but she argued that to hold him personally responsible for so many deaths was to attribute him with a power that was more than any one person could ever embody. She stated that the Nazi leadership had encountered an extraordinary amount of cooperation from all levels of European society, including the Jewish leaders themselves. Her point was that the success of the Nazi regime was attributable to a general moral collapse across Europe. Eichmann she characterized not as a fanatical anti-Semite, but simply an ambitious office worker whose main concern was to provide for his family.

Her subtle arguments provoked highly emotional responses. Many critics wondered if Arendt was defending Eichmann's activities. Her statement that the cooperation of Jewish leaders had led to the deaths of millions who might otherwise have escaped infuriated many Jews; B'nai B'rith pronounced *Eichmann in Je-* *rusalem* an evil distortion of the facts. Arendt herself was suspected of anti-Semitism. Bruno Bettelheim commented in *New Republic* that her analysis was simply too objective for many to accept so soon after the horror of the Holocaust: "The issues are so vast that we do not seem to be able yet to cope with them intellectually. . . . [It is difficult to accept the incongruity] between all the horrors recounted, and this man in the dock, when essentially all he did was talk to people, write memoranda, receive and give orders from behind a desk. It is essentially the incongruity between our conception of life and the bureaucracy of the total state. Our imagination, our frame of reference, even our feelings, are simply not up to it." Bettelheim understood why *Eichmann in Jerusalem* was rejected by so many, but he insisted: "While I would recommend this book for many reasons the most important one is that our best protection against oppressive control and dehumanizing totalitarianism is still a personal understanding of events as they happen. To this end Hannah Arendt has furnished us with a richness of material."

Arendt's later works clarified her position, particularly the collection of essays called *The Jew as Pariah: Jewish Identity and Politics in the Modern Age.* "Readers of this collection will be disabused of the notion that Arendt went to Jerusalem loaded for bear against Zionism, that she was unsympathetic to the Jews, that she reproached them for collaborating and not resisting," wrote Leon Botstein in *New Republic.* "Indeed, I think that if the Eichmann book had been published with several of these essays, Arendt's primary concerns would have been clear from the start." Botstein vigorously defended Arendt against the charges of anti-Semitism that had been levelled at her, declaring: "[Her] analysis of the Jewish dilemma provides an interpretive logic for her whole life's work. [These] essays should stimulate a long overdue rehabilitation of Hannah Arendt in the Jewish community. . . . To [her], being Jewish was the decisive fact of her life as a private person and as a political thinker. It cast the mold for the thinking and willing for which she was, and will be, honored. . . . Apart from its service to the legacy of Hannah Arendt, *The Jew as Pariah* offers brilliance, eloquence, and reasoned commitment on issues where clarity and courage are in perpetually short supply."

Toward the end of her life, Arendt's focus shifted inward. Instead of analyzing political trends, she became increasingly involved in the analysis of thought itself. She planned a three-volume work exploring the three activities of the mind she considered basic—thinking, willing, and judging. She had completed the first volume and part of the second at the time of her death, and these were published posthumously as *The Life of the Mind.* Walter Clemons assessed them in *Newsweek:* " 'The Life of the Mind' is a work requiring stubborn application and a readiness to cope with abstractions more elusive than the social and political arguments advanced in 'The Origins of Totalitarianism,' 'The Human Condition,' or 'Eichmann in Jerusalem.' The reward for perseverance is contact with a passionate, humane intelligence addressing itself to the fundamental problem of how the mind operates." The ideas examined in the books are complex, Clemons observed, but "because Arendt was strongly endowed with common sense, her forays into the realm of the unverifiable are as toughly argued as her investigations, in earlier books, of violence and revolution." James M. Altman judged *The Life of the Mind* to be Arendt's greatest work, even in its incomplete state. He wrote in *New Republic,* "Few works of philosophy published today seriously confront the Western philosophical tradition as a whole. *The Life of the Mind* has that bold ambition. At a minimum, it resembles a deep mining operation, which brings to the surface the authentic insights of [the philosophical] tradition which has fragmented and lost its power to guide us. Arendt intentionally preserves those treasures by reflecting upon them anew. At its best, . . . *The Life of the Mind* succeeds in offering us new insights to illuminate our own mental experiences and an integrative vision of their profound meanings."

BIOGRAPHICAL/CRITICAL SOURCES:

BOOKS

Arendt, Hannah, *On Revolution,* Faber, 1963.
Arendt, *On Violence,* Harcourt, 1970.
Canovan, M., *The Political Thought of Hannah Arendt,* Methuen, 1977.
Contemporary Issues Criticism, Volume 1, Gale, 1982.
Essays and Reviews from the Times Literary Supplement, 1964, Oxford University Press, 1965.
Hobsbawm, E. J., *Revolutionaries: Contemporary Essays,* Weidenfeld & Nicolson, 1973.
McCarthy, Mary, *On the Contrary,* Farrar, Straus, 1961.
Podhoretz, Norman, *Doings and Undoings: The Fifties and After in American Writing,* Farrar, Straus, 1964.

PERIODICALS

American Political Science Review, September, 1980.
American Sociological Review, February, 1959.
Atlantic, March, 1963.
Commentary, September, 1963, October, 1963.
Ethics, October, 1962.
Guardian, November 3, 1961.
Nation, March 24, 1951, January 27, 1969, April 6, 1970, November 11, 1978.
New Republic, July 10, 1961, June 15, 1963, January 18, 1969, February 25, 1978, October 21, 1978, August 15, 1983.
Newsweek, March 20, 1978.
New Yorker, July 20, 1963.
New York Review of Books, November 6, 1969, October 26, 1978, February 17, 1983.
New York Times, March 28, 1970, April 3, 1978.
New York Times Book Review, March 25, 1951, May 19, 1963, November 17, 1968, April 12, 1970, May 7, 1972, November 24, 1974, January 21, 1979.
Partisan Review, summer, 1964.
Saturday Review, May 18, 1963.
Social Research, spring, 1977.
Times Literary Supplement, March 26, 1970, July 23, 1970.
Village Voice, January 6, 1975, May 15, 1978.
Washington Post Book World, March 26, 1978.

OBITUARIES:

PERIODICALS

AB Bookman's Weekly, January 1, 1976.
New York Times, December 6, 1975, December 9, 1975.
Publishers Weekly, December 15, 1975.
Time, December 15, 1975.
Washington Post, December 6, 1975.

*   *   *

ARMAH, Ayi Kwei   1939-

PERSONAL: Born in 1939 (some sources list 1938), in Takoradi, Gold Coast (now Ghana). *Education:* Harvard University, B.A. (cum laude); attended Achimota College, University of Ghana, and Columbia University.

ADDRESSES: c/o Third World Press, 7524 South Cottage Grove Rd., Chicago, Ill. 60019.

CAREER: Worked in Algiers as translator for the magazine *Revolution Africaine,* as a scriptwriter in Ghana for Ghana Television, and as a teacher of English at Navrongo School in Ghana, 1966; *Jeune Afrique* (news magazine), Paris, France, editor and translator, 1967-68; writer, 1968—. Visiting professor at Teacher's College, Dar es Salaam University, University of Massachusetts, Amherst University, University of Lesotho, and University of Wisconsin—Madison.

AWARDS, HONORS: Farfield Foundation grant.

WRITINGS:

NOVELS

The Beautyful Ones Are Not Yet Born, Houghton, 1968, reprinted with an introduction by Christina Ama Ata Aidoo, Collier Books, 1969.
Fragments, Houghton, 1970.
Why Are We So Blest?, Doubleday, 1971.
Two Thousand Seasons, East African Publishing House (Nairobi), 1973, Third World Press, 1980.
The Healers, East African Publishing House, 1978, Heinemann, 1979.

OTHER

Poetry included in anthology *Messages: Poems from Ghana,* edited by K. Awoonor and G. Adali-Mortty, Heinemann, 1970. Contributor of short stories and articles to periodicals, including *Atlantic, Harper's, New African, New York Review of Books, Okyeame, and Presence Africaine.*

SIDELIGHTS: With the publication of *The Beautyful Ones Are Not Yet Born* in 1968, Ghanaian author Ayi Kwei Armah established prominence among younger African novelists writing in English. Armah is often cited for his vivid prose as well as for his realistic portrayals of the legacy of colonialism in postindependent African society. In *The Emergence of African Fiction,* Charles R. Larson states that Armah "is the most skilled prose stylist in Anglophone Africa today, a painter whose medium happens to be prose." Armah's longer fiction falls into two categories. His first three novels, *The Beautyful Ones Are Not Yet Born, Fragments,* and *Why Are We So Blest?,* depict "an African wasteland, where corruption in the government [is] rampant and where the African intellectual, educated abroad, [feels] totally out of place, frustrated to the point of rage or despair by his inability to make any change in the system," according to Larson in the *Saturday Review.* More recently, Armah's *Two Thousand Seasons* and *The Healers* explore Africa's rich cultural heritage through fictional characters placed in historical contexts. *New Statesman* contributor S. Nyamfukudza sees these works as part of Armah's spiritual quest "to recapture as well as create a saving vision of a time when black people were one and their relationship was one of 'reciprocity' between individuals." In *African Literature Today,* Bernth Lindfors contends that the body of Armah's work presents "Africa as a victim of outside forces that it resists but cannot contain," but that through his historical fiction, "instead of merely cursing various symptoms of the colonial disease, . . . Armah now wants to work towards effecting a cure."

In his essay in *The Emergence of African Fiction,* Larson suggests that Armah's early protagonists "become alienated men—lonely, isolated individuals confronting a thoroughly dehumanized society in which everyone else seems insane, although it is usually Armah's insular protagonists who, because of their determination to dance to a different drummer, become the accused criminals or madmen." Larson finds *The Beautyful Ones Are Not Yet Born* "a richly evocative work" and "a deeply disturbing picture of the foibles of all decadent political systems—a decadence which has nothing to do with age—of all late bourgeois worlds where morals and values have been lost and even the man of good intentions begins to doubt his sanity, begins to feel that he is the guilty one for not being corrupt." Martin Tucker, reviewing *Fragments* for *New Republic,* notes that the work, "while a powerful moral indictment of the present state of [Armah's] country makes its force felt through symbolism, not direct propagandistic means. . . . The result is a wonderfully sensuous appreciation of the dissociation of life, the inward nature of each individual, the ultimate unknowingness of things."

Armah relies upon metaphor and symbolism in his early works as a means to relate individual actions to wider human and social behavior patterns. According to Gareth Griffiths in *Studies in Black Literature, The Beautyful Ones Are Not Yet Born* "operates through a series of remarkable metaphorical links which institute a set of correspondences between the body of man, his society and his landscape; between, too, the inner processes of feeding and reproduction and their social equivalents, inheritance and consumption; and, finally, between the personal rot of conscience and ideals and the physical decay and putrescence of the world in which this rot occurs." Griffiths concludes: "The man struggling in the squalor of compromise and disillusion is a vision of Ghana itself, and its whole people. . . . The novel pictures vividly the process by which in the colonial period the envy and aggression of the colonised people finds expression in a self-destructive process in which each turns upon his fellow." *Journal of Commonwealth Literature* contributor James Booth writes: "In my view Armah is attempting . . . by careful simplification and dazzling symbolism to shock his readers into accepting a crude and subjective deduction from the dubiousness and relativity of real individual experience. Armah's work gains much of its distinctive power from such emotive symbolism. He sees life instinctively in terms of brilliant, resonant images, which usually express a moral or spiritual attitude in shocking physical terms. . . . Such images are compulsive and unforgettable." Although Armah's symbolism sometimes merely reveals his particular subjective emotions, the critic nonetheless notes: "Armah asserts against the European 'I think therefore I am,' an 'African' 'I feel therefore I am.' The protagonists of his first three novels are all desperately, wincingly sensitive beings."

Critics praise Armah's first three works for their mature artistry. In *The Emergence of African Fiction,* Larson calls *The Beautyful Ones Are Not Yet Born* "a novel which burns with passion and tension, with a fire so strongly kindled that in every word and every sentence one can almost hear and smell the sizzling of the author's own branded flesh." "*Fragments* is a caustic exposure of the sickness of modern African urban life." writes M. M. Mahood in *Saturday Review.* Mahood further comments: "Essentially it is a novel, of high and consistent artistry. . . . *Fragments* lets us see many things in the mind of thoughtful West Africans today; one takes away from the book the recollection of filmlike sequences of incompetence, callousness, cynicism, concern with status. . . . *Fragments* is a novel of genuine engagement." Tucker feels that *Fragments* succeeds best as "a tone poem of powerful allegorical force." According to Booth, *Why Are We So Blest?* is "the most powerful work of a novelist of genius. . . . The disturbing power of Armah's novel is that it confronts this individual/communal dichotomy in racism and ruthlessly insists that there is no personal or individual escape."

As Nyamfukudza notes, *Two Thousand Seasons* "presents a considerable departure from what [Armah] has done before. . . . The collective racial memory of the black people is given voice through their pilgrimage of self-assertion in received versions of the long years of collision, destruction and enslavement by . . . 'the destroyers,' both Arab and Caucasian who have colonised and plundered Africa." This historical theme continues in *The Healers,* a fictional chronicle based on the history of the Ashanti people. In his work *The Novels of Ayi Kwei Armah: A Study in Polemical Fiction,* Robert Fraser claims that *The Healers* "is thus not merely a reinstatement of a neglected and misunderstood phase of the colonial past, but part of the total reclamation of history on behalf of those whose contribution received opinion has traditionally slighted or abused. . . . Armah, in pursuit of his ideal of spiritual health, has used history as a medicine for rankling sores, and hence acted as a healer of his own people." In *International Fiction Review,* Eustace Palmer comments that Armah's exercise in racial retrieval "is part of the strategy for the transformation of modern society. It is much more therefore than a complacent, self-regarding idealization of blackness and black culture. The values thus retrieved must be actively used as the leaven for humanizing contemporary society."

Critical reception of *Two Thousand Seasons* and *The Healers* reflects continuing respect for Armah's accomplishments. A study group for *Black Books Bulletin* writes of *Two Thousand Seasons:* "The sheer beauty of Armah's prose is almost enough to make this novel outstanding, but the power of his ideas is what brings this book into the realm of the extraordinary. . . . We commend [Armah] for this monumental task." Lindfors calls *The Healers* "a major attempt by a major African writer to reinterpret a major event in African history." The critic concludes: "I think it will have its major impact on young people, and this is as it should be in any remythologizing of Africa. One must aim at winning the hearts and minds of the young, imbuing them with the highest ideals and making them proud and happy to be Africans. This *The Healers* does better than any other novel Armah has written. And this is why it is potentially his most important book and certainly his healthiest."

Armah, who was educated in the United States as well as in Ghana, has been compared to fiction writers of the Western literary tradition. Larson states: "In his depiction of the stifled artist in contemporary Africa, and specifically of the writer, Armah has turned to a theme almost as old as Western fiction itself." Joyce Johnson feels, nevertheless, that as an artist, Armah evinces a sense of his responsibility to show "the extent to which the masses are responsible for perpetuating their own servile condition. . . . The Ghanaian masses, Armah suggests, . . . need to be rescued not only from the abuses of those with power but also from the destructive tendencies within themselves." Larson, in his *Saturday Review* article, contends that though Armah's criticism seems aimed at life in his native country, "indirectly it [points] away from Africa—especially at Western commercialism and neo-colonialism." Larson expresses the opinion that Armah, "this most talented of the younger African novelists," writes books that "will make people talk . . . for a long time to come."

BIOGRAPHICAL/CRITICAL SOURCES:

BOOKS

Achebe, Chinua, *Morning Yet on Creation Day: Essays,* Doubleday, 1975.

Armah, Ayi Kwei, *The Beautyful Ones Are Not Yet Born,* with an introduction by Christina Ama Ata Aidoo, Collier Books, 1969.

Contemporary Literary Criticism, Gale, Volume 5, 1976, Volume 33, 1985.

Fraser, Robert, *The Novels of Ayi Kwei Armah: A Study in Polemical Fiction,* Heinemann, 1979.

Larson, Charles R., *The Emergence of African Fiction,* revised edition, Indiana University Press, 1972.

PERIODICALS

African Literature Today, Number 11, 1980.
America, April 22, 1972.
Black Books Bulletin, winter, 1976.
Black World, March, 1974.
International Fiction Review, winter, 1981.
Journal of Commonwealth Literature, August, 1980.
National Review, November 5, 1968.
New Republic, January 31, 1970.
New Statesman, March 7, 1980.
New York Times, January 16, 1970.
New York Times Book Review, April 2, 1972.
Saturday Review, August 31, 1968, January 17, 1970, March 18, 1972.
Studies in Black Literature, summer, 1971.
Times Literary Supplement, March 27, 1969.
Washington Post Book World, April 2, 1972.
World Literature Today, spring, 1970.
World Literature Written in English, autumn, 1982.

*   *   *

ARNETTE, Robert
See SILVERBERG, Robert

*   *   *

ARNOW, Harriette (Louisa) Simpson   1908-1986
(Harriette Simpson)

PERSONAL: Born July 7, 1908, in Wayne County, Ky.; died in March, 1986, in Washtenaw County, Mich.; daughter of Elias Thomas (a teacher, farmer, and oil well driller) and Mollie Jane (a teacher; maiden name, Denney) Simpson; married Harold B. Arnow (publicity director for Michigan Heart Association), March 11, 1939; children: Marcella Jane, Thomas Louis. *Education:* Attended Berea College, 1924-26; University of Louisville, B.S., 1931.

ADDRESSES: Home— 3220 Nixon Rd., R.R. 7, Ann Arbor, Mich. 48105.

CAREER: Author.

MEMBER: Women's International League for Peace and Freedom, P.E.N., Authors Guild, Authors League of America, American Civil Liberties Union, Phi Beta Kappa (honorary).

AWARDS, HONORS: Friends of American Writers Award, runner up for National Book Award, *Saturday Review* national critics' poll co-winner for best novel, Berea College Centennial award, *Woman's Home Companion* Silver Distaff award for "unique contribution by a woman to American life," all 1955, all for *The Dollmaker;* commendation from Tennessee Historical Commission and award of merit of American Association for State and Local History, both 1961, both for *Seedtime on the Cumberland; Tennessee Historical Quarterly* prize for best article

of the year, 1962; Outstanding Alumni award, University of Louisville, College of Arts and Sciences, 1979; honorary degrees from Albion College, Transylvania College, and University of Kentucky; Mark Twain Award for distinguished Midwestern Literature, Michigan State University, 1984.

WRITINGS:

(Under name Harriette Simpson) *Mountain Path* (novel), Covici-Friede, 1936.

Hunter's Horn (novel), Macmillan, 1949, reprinted, Avon, 1979.

The Dollmaker (novel), Macmillan, 1954, reprinted, University Press of Kentucky, 1985.

Seedtime on the Cumberland (nonfiction), Macmillan, 1960.

Flowering of the Cumberland (nonfiction), Macmillan, 1963.

The Weedkiller's Daughter (novel), Knopf, 1970.

The Kentucky Trace: A Novel of the American Revolution, Knopf, 1974.

Old Burnside (nonfiction), University Press of Kentucky, 1978.

Also author of short stories in the 1930s, two of them anthologized in *O. Henry Memorial Award Prize Stories.* Contributor of articles and reviews to magazines.

SIDELIGHTS: Harriette Simpson Arnow is a Kentucky-born novelist whose work captures the erosion of rural life in the Cumberland hills. "I was aware that nothing had been written on the Southern immigrants, of what was actually happening to them and to their culture, of how they came to the cities for the first time in the 1920s, leaving their families behind," she explained to Barbara L. Baer in the *Nation.* "I began writing during the depression which had sent hill people back home again. And then, as I was still writing during the Second War, I witnessed the permanent move the men made by bringing their wives and children with them to the cities. With that last migration, hill life was gone forever, and with it, I suppose, a personal dream of community I'd had since childhood."

To recapture that sense of community, Arnow spent two decades writing her Kentucky trilogy, a series of novels which begins with a coming-of-age story called *Mountain Path,* continues with a serious adventure novel entitled *Hunter's Horn,* and culminates in *The Dollmaker,* Arnow's best known fiction and, according to Joyce Carol Oates, "our most unpretentious American masterpiece." Over the years, many labels have been to attached to these writings, but "whether the books are read today as regional, or realistic or even feminist writing, they are first of all a coherent vision in the best tradition of American fiction" in Baer's opinion. They tell the stories of men and women who see their dreams of self-sufficiency shrink and their personal freedoms foreclosed by a rapacious industrial society.

In *Mountain Path,* her first and most autobiographical novel, Arnow focuses on a young student teacher from the city and her experiences in a community of feuding mountaineers. Torn between the intellectual existence for which her education has prepared her and the pull of the earthy backwoods culture, the heroine faces a difficult decision, complicated by her love for a mountain man. Unlike earlier novelists who caricatured "hill-billies" or moralized about their violent feuds, Arnow acknowledges the individuality of her characters and the legitimacy of their ways. Even though the book was tagged a "regional" novel and eventually went out of print, it garnered enough attention to establish Arnow as "a writer of considerable talent," Glenda Hobbs reports in the *Dictionary of Literary Biography.*

In *Hunter's Horn,* the second book of her trilogy, Arnow continues her exploration of the conflict between an individual's dreams and society's demands, this time from a male point of view. Nunn Ballew, husband, father, and Kentucky farmer, becomes engrossed in the pursuit of "King Devil," an elusive red fox that has been raiding local farms and destroying livestock. Like Ahab in *Moby Dick,* Ballew will stop at nothing to catch his prey—even though his obsession triggers both personal anguish and the community's ridicule and disdain.

His family also suffers as Ballew invests money in expensive hunting dogs that could pay for his 14-year-old daughter Suse's schooling. No sooner does he kill "King Devil"—which turns out to be a female slowed down because she is carrying pups—than Suse discovers she is pregnant. An independent, high-spirited girl who wants to go north and get an education, Suse is confident that her father will support her decision not to wed.

Instead, in a riveting scene that is played out before the assembled community, Ballew capitulates to the local mores he has always scorned. Asserting that his fire will warm no bastard, he insists that Suse marry the father of the child. As Hobbs reports, "Nunn, nearly frozen with ambivalence and grief wins back the neighbors' approval in exchange for his daughter's back and heart being 'broke to the plow.' "

Reviewers consider it a mark of her excellence that Arnow sustains reader sympathy for Nunn Ballew. "However much we may resent Nunn's improvidence and his betrayal of Suse," writes a *Ms.* reviewer, "it is a testament to Arnow's extraordinary skill at characterization that almost against our will we share his anguish and cheer him on after his four-legged red whale. *Hunter's Horn* manifests Arnow's ability to create male characters as palpable and as complex as her best women. Nunn can't be written off as another hateful man."

In spite of the appeal he exerts, Nunn Ballew pales in comparison to Gertie Nevels, a character Baer describes as "larger than life, a rawboned figure hewn from some matriarchal past" and the protagonist of the third and final volume of the trilogy, *The Dollmaker.* Published at a time when strong women were a rarity in fiction, the 1954 best-seller was a critical as well as a popular success and tied for best novel in the *Saturday Review* national critics' poll. Perhaps partly because most of the novel is set outside Kentucky, critics were less tempted to call the book 'regional,' *Dictionary of Literary Biography* contributor Glenda Hobbs explains.

For thirty-one weeks the novel remained on the best-seller lists, and, when Columbia purchased the movie rights, it appeared as though the story would be filmed. But, with the passage of time, the public's interest subsided and movie executives had second thoughts about the novel's commercial appeal. They shelved the project, for reasons which *Chicago Tribune* reporter Eric Zorn details: "In a year when Ernest Hemingway won the Nobel Prize for literature and the public taste was for action, drama and romance they found onscreen in such movies as 'From Here to Eternity' and 'On the Waterfront,' Arnow offered a grim picture of the cultural collision of traditional, rural lifestyles with industrial America. It was not thrilling, uplifting, intellectually ambitious or filled with adventure, suspense or intrigue."

The story instead depicts a Kentucky woman's losing battle to retain her dignity when her family is relocated in Detroit. A simple country woman with a talent for whittling and a love of the land, Gertie Nevels seeks no greater fulfillment than raising her family on a farm of her own. But she gives up her dream to follow her husband Clovis up north when he takes a wartime job in a factory. With her she brings a magnificent block of cherry wood from which she plans to carve a religious figure—Judas,

maybe, or the laughing Christ—if, as she explains to a stranger, "I can ever hit on the right face."

In the brutal environment of the Detroit projects, inspiration never comes, and Gertie finds herself sacrificing her artistic integrity to survival. The dolls she once hand-carved for her daughter's pleasure, she now mass-produces to feed her family. And though she ultimately "adjusts," Gertie feels corrupted—her children lost to her, her self-reliance undermined. The book ends with her splintering the beloved cherry wood block so she can manufacture crude dolls for quick money.

While some critics have interpreted this ending as evidence of Gertie's defeat, Dorothy H. Lee offers a brighter interpretation. "The hidden face in the wood is that of Christ: Gertie does not contradict the scrapwood man's assumption that it is," she writes in *Critique.* "Questioned further by the man as to whether or not she could find a face for him, she responds, 'They was so many would ha done; they's millions and millions a faces plenty fine enough—fer him. . . . Why some a my neighbors down there in the alley—they would ha done.' She thus reveals that she retains her vision of Christ's humility. Further, she perceives her neighbors as crucified and, although she would not be able so to verbalize, as scapegoats of the processes of urbanization—of competition, poverty, materialism, and mechanization. She has always had compassion for others, but her vision now is less provincial. She recognizes suffering of a broader scope and understands the unity of all men who share it."

In her *Nation* article, Barbara L. Baer gauges the effect this ending has upon the reader: "In the beautiful last dialogue, as the woodcutter gives Gertie his ax, we learn what Gertie has learned; no individual face can encompass the complexity of human suffering, whether a man's or a woman's, a relative's or a stranger's, a friend's or an enemy's."

Joyce Carol Oates was so moved by the story that she chose to critique it for the *New York Times Book Review* seventeen years after it originally appeared, calling it "one of those excellent American works that have yet to be properly assessed" and rekindling the public's interest. Among the readers whose curiosity was piqued was Jane Fonda, who eventually acquired filming rights and successfully brought the story to television as an ABC-TV movie in 1984.

Though nothing else Arnow has written before or since has come close to achieving *The Dollmaker*'s acclaim, Glenda Hobbs believes that the author has earned a permanent place in American letters. "Arnow alone has rendered Kentucky highlanders' fully and fairly," she writes in the *Dictionary of Literary Biography,* "rescuing them from the literary stereotype of the lazy, suspicious, ignorant, manically violent hillbilly. Taking their dignity for granted Arnow also avoids the passionate yearning for identification with the rural poor that betrays insecurity and condescension. . . . Arnow's unique, obstinate characters, even in the face of economic ruin and spiritual exhaustion, will endure and prevail. With luck and justice, so should Arnow's place in American literature."

BIOGRAPHICAL/CRITICAL SOURCES:

BOOKS

Arnow, Harriette, *The Dollmaker,* Macmillan, 1954.
Contemporary Literary Criticism, Gale, Volume II, 1974, Volume VII, 1977, Volume XVII, 1981.
Dictionary of Literary Biography, Volume VI: *American Novelists since World War II,* Second Series, 1980.
Eckley, Wilton, *Harriette Arnow,* Twayne, 1974.

PERIODICALS

Chicago Tribune, February 10, 1983.
Critique: Studies in Modern Fiction, Volume XX, number 2, 1978.
Georgia Review, winter, 1979.
Michigan: The Magazine of the Detroit News, December 4, 1983.
Ms., December, 1979.
Nation, January 31, 1976.
New York Times, May 28, 1949.
New York Times Book Review, May 29, 1949, March 22, 1970, January 24, 1971.
New Yorker, May 1, 1954.
New Republic, August 31, 1974.

OBITUARIES:

PERIODICALS

Chicago Tribune, March 24, 1986, March 25, 1986.
Detroit Free Press, March 23, 1986.
Detroit News, March 23, 1986.
New York Times, March 25, 1986.
Time, April 7, 1986.
Times (London), March 26, 1986.

*   *   *

ASHBERY, John (Lawrence) 1927-
(Jonas Berry)

PERSONAL: Born July 28, 1927, in Rochester, N.Y.; son of Chester Frederick (a farmer) and Helen (a biology teacher at time of marriage; maiden name, Lawrence) Ashbery. *Education:* Harvard University, B.A., 1949; Columbia University, M.A., 1951; graduate study at New York University, 1957-58.

ADDRESSES: Agent—Georges Borchardt, Inc., 136 East 57th St., New York, N.Y. 10022.

CAREER: Writer, critic, and editor. Worked as reference librarian for Brooklyn Public Library, Brooklyn, N.Y.; Oxford University Press, New York City, copywriter, 1951-54; McGraw-Hill Book Co., New York City, copywriter, 1954-55; New York University, New York City, instructor in elementary French, 1957-58; *New York Herald Tribune,* European Edition, Paris, France, art critic, 1960-65; *Art News,* New York City, Paris correspondent, 1964-65, executive editor in New York City, 1966-72; Brooklyn College of the City University of New York, Brooklyn, professor of English and co-director of Master of Fine Arts Program in Creative Writing, 1974—, distinguished professor, 1980—. Art critic for *Art International* (Lugano, Switzerland), 1961-64; *New York,* 1978-80, and *Newsweek,* 1980—. Has read his poetry at the Living Theatre, New York City, and at numerous universities, including Yale University, University of Chicago, and University of Texas.

MEMBER: American Academy and Institute of Arts and Letters, 1980—.

AWARDS, HONORS: Discovery Prize co-winner, Young Men's Hebrew Association, 1952; Fulbright scholarships to France, 1955-56 and 1956-57; Yale Series of Younger Poets Prize, 1956, for *Some Trees;* Poets' Foundation grants, 1960 and 1964; Ingram-Merrill Foundation grants, 1962 and 1972; Harriet Monroe Poetry Award, *Poetry,* 1963; Union League Civic and Arts Foundation Prize, *Poetry,* 1966; National Book Award nomination, 1966, for *Rivers and Mountains;* Guggenheim fellowships, 1967 and 1973; National Endowment for the Arts grants, 1968 and 1969; National Institute of Arts and Letters Award, 1969; Shelley Memorial Award, Poetry Society of America, 1973, for *Three Poems;* Frank O'Hara Prize, Modern Poetry Association, 1974; Harriet Monroe Poetry Award, University of Chicago, 1975; Pulitzer Prize, National Book Award, and National Book Critics Circle Award, all 1976, for *Self-Portrait in a Convex Mirror;* Levinson Prize, *Poetry,* 1977; Rockefeller Foundation grant in playwriting, 1978; D. Litt., Southampton College of Long Island University, 1979; Phi Beta Kappa Poet, Harvard University, 1979; English-Speaking Union Poetry Award, 1979; American Book Award nomination, 1982, for *Shadow Train;* Academy of American Poets fellowship, 1982; The Mayor's Award of Honor for Arts and Culture, New York City, 1983; Charles Flint Kellogg Award in Arts and Letters, Bard College, 1983; co-winner of Bollingen prize, 1985, for the body of his work; Los Angeles Times Book Award nomination, 1986, for *Selected Poems;* Common Wealth Award, 1986; Lenore Marshall award, *Nation,* 1986, for *A Wave.*

WRITINGS:

Turandot and Other Poems (chapbook), Tibor de Nagy Gallery, 1953.
Some Trees (poems), foreword by W. H. Auden, Yale University Press, 1956, Ecco Press, 1978.
The Poems, Tiber Press (New York), 1960.
The Tennis Court Oath (poems), Wesleyan University Press, 1962.
Rivers and Mountains (poems), Holt, 1966.
Selected Poems, J. Cape, 1967.
Sunrise in Suburbia, Phoenix Bookshop, 1968.
Three Madrigals, Poet's Press, 1969.
(With James Schuyler) *A Nest of Ninnies* (novel), Dutton, 1969.
Fragment (poem; also see below), Black Sparrow Press, 1969.
Evening in the Country, Spanish Main Press, 1970.
The Double Dream of Spring (includes poem "Fragment," originally published in book form), Dutton, 1970.
The New Spirit, Adventures in Poetry, 1970.
(With Lee Hawood and Tom Raworth) *Penguin Modern Poets 19,* Penguin, 1971.
Three Poems, Viking, 1972.
The Serious Doll, privately printed, 1975.
(With Joe Brainard) *The Vermont Notebook* (poems), Black Sparrow Press, 1975.
Self-Portrait in a Convex Mirror (poems), Viking, 1975.
Houseboat Days (poems), Viking, 1977.
Some Trees (poems), Ecco Press, 1978.
As We Know (poems), Viking, 1979.
Shadow Train: Fifty Lyrics, Viking, 1981.
(With others) *R. B. Kitaj: Paintings, Drawings, Pastels,* Smithsonian Institution, 1981, Thames Hudson, 1986.
Fairfield Porter: Realist Painter in an Age of Abstraction, New York Graphic Society, 1983.
A Wave (poems), Viking, 1984.
Selected Poems, Viking, 1985.
April Galleons, Penguin, 1987.
The Ice Storm, Hanuman Books, 1987.
Reported Sightings (art criticism), edited by David Bergman, Knopf, 1989.

PLAYS

"The Heroes" (one-act; also see below), first produced Off-Broadway at the Living Theater Playhouse, August 5, 1952, produced in London, 1982, published in *Artists' Theater,* edited by Herbert Machiz, Grove, 1969.

"The Compromise" (three-act; also see below), produced in Cambridge, Mass., at the Poet's Theater, 1956, published in *The Hasty Papers,* Alfred Leslie, 1960.

"The Philosopher" (one-act; also see below), published in *Art and Literature,* No. 2, 1964.

Three Plays (contains "The Heroes," "The Compromise," and "The Philosopher"), Z Press, 1978.

EDITOR

(With others) *The American Literary Anthology,* Farrar, Straus, 1968.

(With Thomas B. Hess) *Light* (art book), Macmillan, 1969.

(With Hess) *Painters Painting* (art book), Newsweek, 1971.

(With Hess) *Art of the Grand Eccentrics,* Macmillan, 1971.

(With Hess) *Avant-Garde Art,* Macmillan, 1971.

Penguin Modern Poets 24: Ken Ward Elmslie, Kenneth Hoch, James Schuyler, Penguin, 1974.

Richard F. Sknow, *The Funny Place,* O'Hara (Chicago), 1975.

Bruce Marcus, *Muck Arbour,* O'Hara, 1975.

(With David Lehman) *The Best American Poetry, 1988,* Scribner, 1989.

CONTRIBUTOR TO ANTHOLOGIES

New American Poetry, 1945-1960, Grove, 1960.

Paris Leary and Robert Kelly, editors, *A Controversy of Poets,* Doubleday/Anchor, 1964.

L'Avant-Garde aujourd'hui, [Brussels], 1965.

Anthology of New York Poets, Random House, 1969.

N.Y. Amerikansk Poesi, Gyldendal (Copenhagen), 1969.

The Voice That Is Great Within Us: American Poetry of the Twentieth Century, Bantam, 1970.

Contemporary American Poetry, Houghton, 1971.

Louis Untermeyer, editor, *50 Modern American and British Poets, 1920-1970,* McKay, 1973.

Shake the Kaleidoscope: A New Anthology of Modern Poetry, Simon & Schuster, 1973.

Works also represented in other anthologies.

OTHER

Collaborator with Joe Brainard on C Comic Books; collaborator with Elliott Carter on the musical setting "Syringa," first produced in New York at Alice Tully Hall, December, 1979; verse has been set to music by Ned Rorem, Eric Salzman, Paul Reif, and James Dashow. Poetry recordings include "Treasury of 100 Modern American Poets Reading Their Poems," Volume 17, Spoken Arts, and "Poetry of John Ashbery," Jeffrey Norton. Translator, from the French, of the works of Jean-Jacques Mayoux, Jaques Dupin, Raymond Roussel, Andre Breton, Pierre Reverdy, Arthur Cravan, Max Jacob, Alfred Jarry, Antonin Artaud, Noel Vexin, Genevieve Manceron, and others. Also translator, under pseudonym Jonas Berry, of two French detective novels. Contributor of poetry to periodicals, including *New York Review of Books, Partisan Review, Harper's,* and *New Yorker;* contributor of art criticism to periodicals, including *Art International* and *Aujourd'hui;* contributor of literary criticism to *New York Review of Books, Saturday Review, Poetry, Bizarre* (Paris), and other periodicals. Editor, *Locus Solus* (Lans-en-Vercors, France), 1960-62; co-founder and editor, *Art and Literature* (Paris), 1964-66; poetry editor, *Partisan Review,* 1976—.

WORK IN PROGRESS: Poems; a play; a translation of the literary works of Belgian surrealist painter Rene Magritte.

SIDELIGHTS: "Stop anywhere you happen to be in the underground and listen: that sound you hear is the sound of Ashbery's poetic voice being mimicked—a hushed, simultaneously incomprehensible and intelligent whisper with a weird pulsating rhythm that fluctuates like a wave between peaks of sharp clarity and watery droughts of obscurity and langour," Stephen Koch commented in a 1968 *New York Times Book Review* article. Poet John Ashbery's style, once considered avant-garde, has since become "so influential that its imitators are legion," Helen Vendler observes in the *New Yorker.* After suffering through a period of critical misunderstanding, Ashbery has entered the mainstream of American poetry, becoming, as James Atlas notes in the *New York Times Sunday Magazine,* "the most widely honored poet of his generation." Ashbery's position in American letters is confirmed by his unprecedented sweep of the literary "triple crown" in 1976, as his *Self-Portrait in a Convex Mirror* won the Pulitzer Prize, the National Book Award, *and* the National Book Critics Circle Prize. According to Howard Wamsley in *Poetry,* "The chances are very good that he will dominate the last third of the century as Yeats . . . dominated the first."

A key element of Ashbery's success is his openness to change; it is both a characteristic of his development as a writer and an important thematic element in his verse. "It is a thankless and hopeless task to try and keep up with Ashbery, to try and summarize the present state of his art," Raymond Carney writes in the *Dictionary of Literary Biography.* "As [*As We Know*] shows, he will never stand still, even for the space (or time) of one poem. Emerson wrote that 'all poetry is vehicular,' and in the case of Ashbery the reader had better resign himself to a series of unending adjustments and movements. With each subsequent book of poetry we only know that he will never be standing still, for that to him is death." In a *Washington Post Book World* review of *Shadow Train,* David Young notes: "You must enjoy unpredictability if you are to like John Ashbery. . . . We must be ready for anything in reading Ashbery because this eclectic, dazzling, inventive creator of travesties and treaties is ready to and eager to include anything, say anything, go anywhere, in the service of an esthetic dedicated to liberating poetry from predictable conventions and tired traditions." And in the *New York Times Book Review,* J. M. Brinnon observes that *Self-Portrait in a Convex Mirror* is "a collection of poems of breathtaking freshness and adventure in which dazzling orchestrations of language open up whole areas of consciousness no other American poet has even begun to explore. . . . The influence of films now shows in Ashbery's deft control of just those cinematic devices a poet can most usefully appropriate. Crosscut, flashback, montage, close-up, fade-out—he employs them all to generate the kinetic excitement that starts on the first page of his book and continues to the last."

As Brinnon's analysis suggests, Ashbery's verse has taken shape under the influence of films and other art forms. The abstract expressionist movement in modern painting, stressing nonrepresentational methods of picturing reality, is an especially important presence in his work. "Modern art was the first and most powerful influence on Ashbery," Helen McNeil notes in the *Times Literary Supplement.* "When he began to write in the 1950s, American poetry was constrained and formal while American abstract-expressionist art was vigorously taking over the heroic responsibilities of the European avant garde. . . . Ashbery remarks that no one now thinks it odd that Picasso painted faces with eyes and mouth in the wrong place, while the hold of realism in literature is such that the same kind of image in a poem would still be considered shocking."

True to this influence, Ashbery's poems, according to Fred Moramarco, are a "verbal canvas" upon which the poet freely applies the techniques of expressionism. Moramarco, writing in the *Journal of Modern Literature,* finds that Ashbery's verse, maligned by many critics for being excessively obscure, becomes less difficult to understand when examined in relation to modern art. "*The Tennis Court Oath* is still a book that arouses passions in critics and readers, some of whom have criticized its purposeful obscurity. For me it becomes approachable, explicable, and even down-right lucid when read with some of the esthetic assumptions of Abstract Expressionism in mind. . . . The techniques of juxtaposition developed by the Abstract painters, particularly [Mark] Rothko and [Adolph] Gottlieb, can be related to the verbal juxtaposition we find in *The Tennis Court Oath,* where words clash and interact with one another to invigorate our sense of the creative possibilities of language. . . . What we confront [in the title poem], it seems to me, is constantly shifting verbal perceptions. . . . [Jackson] Pollock's drips, Rothko's haunting, color-drenched, luminous, rectangular shapes, and Gottlieb's spheres and explosive strokes are here, in a sense, paralleled by an imagistic scattering and emotional and intellectual verbal juxtaposition."

In the same article, Moramarco reviews "Self-Portrait in a Convex Mirror," a long poem inspired by a work by the Renaissance painter Francesco Parmigianino, and is "struck by Ashbery's unique ability to explore the verbal implications of painterly space, to capture the verbal nuances of Parmigianino's fixed and distorted image. The poem virtually resonates or extends the painter's meaning. It transforms visual impact to verbal precision. . . . It seems to me Ashbery's intention in 'Self-Portrait' is to record verbally the emotional truth contained in Parmigianino's painting. Visual images do not have to conform to verbal *thinking,* and it is this sort of universe that Ashbery's poetry has consistently evoked." And Jonathan Holden believes that "Ashbery is the first American poet to successfully carry out the possibilities of analogy between poetry and 'abstract expressionist' painting. He has succeeded so well for two reasons: he is the first poet to identify the *correct* correspondences between painting and writing; he is the first poet to explore the analogy who has possessed the *skill* to *produce* a first-rate 'abstract expressionist' poetry, a poetry as beautiful and sturdy as the paintings of William de Kooning." In the *American Poetry Review,* Holden says that "it is Ashbery's genius not only to be able to execute syntax with heft, but to perceive that syntax in writing is the equivalent of 'composition' in painting: it has an intrinsic beauty and authority almost wholly independent of any specific context. Thus, in Ashbery's poetry, the isolation of verse is analogous to the framing of a painting; and each sentence . . . is analogous to a 'brushstroke' . . . recorded in paint on a canvas."

Ashbery's experience as an art critic has strengthened his ties to abstract expressionism and instilled in his poetry a sensitivity to the interrelatedness of artistic mediums. As he once commented in an essay on the American artist and architect Saul Steinberg: "Why shouldn't a painting tell a story, or not tell it, as it sees fit? Why should poetry be intellectual and nonsensory, or the reverse? Our eyes, minds, and feelings do not exist in isolated compartments but are part of each other, constantly crosscutting, consulting and reinforcing each other. An art constructed to the above canons, or any others, will wither away since, having left one or more of the faculties out of account, it will eventually lose the attention of the others." Ashbery's poetry is open-ended and multivarious because life itself is, he told Bryan Appleyard of the London *Times:* "I don't find any direct statements in life. My poetry imitates or reproduces the way knowledge or awareness come to me, which is by fits and starts and by indirection. I don't think poetry arranged in neat patterns would reflect that situation. My poetry is disjunct, but then so is life."

Ashbery's verbal expressionism has attracted a mixed critical response. James Schevill, in a *Saturday Review* article on *The Tennis Court Oath,* writes: "The trouble with Ashbery's work is that he is influenced by modern painting to the point where he tries to apply words to the page as if they were abstract, emotional colors and shapes. . . . Consequently, his work loses coherence. . . . There is little substance to the poems in this book." In the *New York Times Book Review,* X. J. Kennedy praises the book: " 'I attempt to use words abstractly,' [Ashbery] declares, 'as an artist uses paint'. . . . If the reader can shut off that portion of the brain which insists words be related logically, he may dive with pleasure into Ashbery's stream of consciousness." And Moramarco believes Ashbery's technique has an invigorating effect: "We become caught up in the rich, vitalized verbal canvas he has painted for us, transported from the mundane and often tedious realities of our daily lives to this exotic, marvelous world. . . . Literature and art can provide these moments of revitalization for us, and although we must always return to the real world, our esthetic encounters impinge upon our sensibilities and leave us altered."

Many critics have commented on the manner in which Ashbery's fluid style has helped to convey a major concern in his poetry: the refusal to impose an arbitrary order on a world of flux and chaos. In his verse, Ashbery attempts to mirror the stream of perceptions of which human consciousness is composed. His poems move, often without continuity, from one image to the next, prompting some critics to praise his expressionist technique and others to accuse him of producing art which is unintelligible, even meaningless.

"Reality, for Ashbery, is elusive, and things are never what they seem to be. They cannot be separated from one another, isolated into component parts, but overlap, intersect, and finally merge into an enormous and constantly changing whole," Paul Auster writes in *Harper's.* "Ashbery's manner of dealing with this flux is associative rather than logical, and his pessimism about our ever really being able to know anything results, paradoxically, in a poetry that is open to everything. His language is discursive, rhetorical, and even long-winded, a kind of obsessive talking around things, suggesting a reality that refuses to come forth and let itself be known."

In the *American Poetry Review,* W. S. Di Piero states: "Ashbery wonders at the processes of change he sees in people, in the seasons, in language, but his perception of the things about him also persuades him that nothing has ever really changed. If all things, all thought and feeling, are subject to time's revisions, then what can we ever know? What events, what feelings can we ever trust? In exploring questions such as these, Ashbery has experimented with forms of dislocated language as one way of jarring things into order; his notorious twisting of syntax is really an attempt to straighten things out, to clarify the problems at hand." David Kalstone, in his book *Five Temperaments,* comments: "In his images of thwarted nature, of a discontinuity between past and present, Ashbery has tuned his agitation into a principle of composition. From the start he has looked for sentences, diction, a syntax which would make these feelings fully and fluidly available." "Robbed of their solid properties, the smallest and surest of words become part of a new geography," Kalstone writes of *The Double Dream of Spring* in the *New York Times Book Review.* To explore this "new geography," Kalstone notes, the reader must immerse himself in Ashbery's language and "learn something like a new musical scale."

Closely related to Ashbery's use of language as a "new musical scale" is his celebration of the world's various motions and drives. Under the poet's care, the most ordinary aspects of our lives leap into a new reality, a world filled with the joyous and bizarre. In his book *The Poem in Its Skin,* Paul Carroll finds that "one quality most of Ashbery's poems share is something like the peculiar excitement one feels when stepping with Alice behind the Looking Glass into a reality bizarre yet familiar in which the 'marvelous' is as near as one's breakfast coffee cup or one's shoes. His gift is to release everyday objects, experiences and fragments of dreams or hallucinations from stereotypes imposed on them by habit or preconception or belief: he presents the world as if seen for the first time." In a review of *Self-Portrait in a Convex Mirror* for *Harper's,* Paul Auster contends that "few poets today have such an uncanny ability to undermine our certainties, to articulate so fully the ambiguous zones of our consciousness. We are constantly thrown off guard as we read his poems. The ordinary becomes strange, and things that a moment ago seemed clear are cast into doubt. Everything remains in place, and yet nothing is the same." Edmund White, appraising *As We Know* in *Washington Post Book World,* writes: "As David Shapiro has pointed out in his critical study, all [of Ashbery's] long poems tend to end on a joyful note, though one harmonized with doubt and anguish. In [the conclusion of 'Litany'] the poet rejects the equation of life and text in order to acknowledge the rich messiness of experience. Like the familiar example of the bee which is aerodynamically impossible but doesn't know so and flies anyway, the poet—though faced with death, crushed under history and immersed in the fog of daily life—evinces a will to joy and thereby, becomes joyful."

Several critics have suggested that this joyful quality is sometimes contradicted by an intellectualism and obscurity present in Ashbery's verse. Victor Howes, reviewing *Houseboat Days* for the *Christian Science Monitor,* calls the poet "a kaleidoscope of Daffy Duck and Amadis de Gaul, of root beer stands and lines from Sir Thomas Wyatt and old Scotch ballads, or art-deco and scrimshaw," but, Howes asks, "does he touch the heart? Does he know the passions? My dear. My dear. Really, sometimes you ask too much." J. A. Avant of *Library Journal* argues that in *The Double Dream of Spring* "emotion has been intellectualized to the extent that it is almost nonexistent," while Pearl K. Bell comments in the *New Leader,* "Long stretches of 'Self-Portrait' read like the bland prose of an uninspired scholar, complete with references and quotations. Bleached of feeling and poetic surprise, the words gasp for air, stutter, go dead." In a *New York Review of Books* article on *The Double Dream of Spring,* Robert Mazzocco finds that "in Ashbery there has always been a catlike presence, both in the poems themselves and in the person these poems reveal: tender, curious, cunning, tremendously independent, sweet, guarded. Above all, like a cat, Ashbery is a born hunter: now prowling through deepest Africa; now chasing leaves or scraps of paper, rolling over and over, and then curling up, happily exhausted, beneath a bush. . . . But the one prime act of the cat—to spring, to pounce, to make the miraculous leap—Ashbery, for me, has yet to perform."

In *The Poem in Its Skin,* Carroll examines Ashbery's "Leaving the Atocha Station" and finds that "several close readings fail to offer a suspicion of a clue as to what it might be all about. I . . . feel annoyed: the poem makes me feel stupid. . . . [The] narrative skeleton is fleshed out by skin and features made from meaningless phrases, images and occasional sentences. In this sense, 'Leaving the Atocha Station' out-Dadas Dada: it is totally meaningless. . . . The most obvious trait is the general sense that the reader has wandered into somebody else's dream or hallucination." After suggesting several ways to read the poem, Carroll concludes that "the reader should feel free to do what-

ever he wants with the words in this poem. . . . I also suspect some readers will respond to Ashbery's invitation that the reader too become a poet as he rereads [the poem]." As Ashbery explains in an essay on Gertrude Stein in *Poetry,* a poem is "a hymn to possibility," "a general, all-purpose model which each reader can adapt to fit his own set of particulars." In the *New York Review of Books,* Irvin Ehrenpreis comments on Ashbery's assessment of the participatory nature of poetry: "The poem itself must become an exercise in re-examining the world from which the self has become alienated. We must confront its language with the same audacity that we want when confronting the darkened world within us and without. To offer a clear meaning would be to fix the reader in his place, to turn him away from the proper business of poetry by directing him to an apparent subject. . . . The act of reading must become the purpose of the poem. Consequently, the poem must stand by itself as the world stands by itself. It must change as the world changes. It must offer the same challenge as the world."

Carney contends that the possibilities inherent in an Ashbery poem often create confusion rather than interpretive freedom: "Ashbery's poetry is a continuous criticism of all the ways in which literature would tidy up experience and make the world safe for poetry. But it must be admitted that the poetry that results is frequently maddening because of Ashbery's willingness to lose himself in a sea of details and memories even if it means losing the reader. Even [a judicious critic] can be baited into a fit of pique by Ashbery's randomness." In a review of *As We Know* for the *Chicago Tribune Book World,* Joseph Parisi grants that Ashbery's " 'subject matter' remains incomprehensible, to be sure—the whole world of sensible objects, memories, and feelings, in all their profusion, variety, and flux," but nevertheless insists: "As these streams of everyday and extraordinary objects flow past us in no apparent order, but always in wondrously lyrical lines, the poems make their own curious kind of sense. After all, isn't this how we perceive 'reality'? . . . Ashbery's poems imply the improbability of finding ultimate significance amid the evanescence and transience of modern life. If however, in the process of these poems the old order is lost or irrelevant, the longing for it or some kind of meaning is not." Reflecting upon the critical response to his poem "Litany," Ashbery told *CA* interviewer , "I'm quite puzzled by my work too, along with a lot of other people. I was always intrigued by it, but at the same time a little apprehensive and sort of embarrassed about annoying the same critics who are always annoyed by my work. I'm kind of sorry that I cause so much grief."

Di Piero describes the reaction of critics to Ashbery's style as "amusing. On the one hand are those who berate him for lacking the Audenesque 'censor' (that little editing machine in a poet's head which deletes all superfluous materials) or who accuse him of simply being willfully and unreasonably perverse. On the other hand are those reviewers who, queerly enough, praise the difficulty of Ashbery's verse as if difficulty were a positive literary value in itself, while ignoring what the poet is saying. I think that Ashbery's 'difficulty' (grammatical ellipses, misapplied substantives, fragmented verb phrases, etc.) is a function of his meaning. . . . Ashbery avoids generalized declarations of his vision of our fragmented, unpredictable world. Instead, he gives us a feel for the elusive processes of change." Vendler offers this summary in the *New Yorker:* "It is Ashbery's style that has obsessed reviewers, as they alternately wrestle with its elusive impermeability and praise its power of linguistic synthesis. There have been able descriptions of its fluid syntax, its insinuating momentum, its generality of reference, its incorporation of vocabulary from all the arts and sciences. But it is popularly believed, with some reason, that the style itself is impenetrable, that it is impossible to say what an Ashbery poem is 'about.' An alternative view says that every Ashbery poem is about poetry."

This alternative view emphasizes Ashbery's concern with the nature of the creative act, particularly as it applies to the writing of poetry. This is, Peter Stitt notes, a major theme of *Houseboat Days,* a volume acclaimed by Marjorie Perloff in *Washington Post Book World* as "the most exciting, most original book of poems to have appeared in the 1970s." Ashbery shares with the abstract expressionists of painting "a preoccupation with the art process itself," Stitt writes in the *Georgia Review.* "Ashbery has come to write, in the poet's most implicitly ironic gesture, almost exclusively about his own poems, the ones he is writing as he writes about them. The artist becomes his own theoretical critic, caught in the critical lens even at the moment of conception." Roger Shattuck makes a similar point in the *New York Review of Books:* "Nearly every poem in *Houseboat Days* shows that Ashbery's phenomenological eye fixes itself not so much on ordinary living and doing as on the specific act of composing a poem. Writing on Frank O'Hara's work, Ashbery defined a poem as 'the chronicle of the creative act that produces it.' Thus every poem becomes an ars poetica of its own condition." Ashbery's examination of creativity, according to Paul Breslin in *Poetry,* is a "prison of self-reference" which detracts from the poet's "lyrical genius." *New Leader*'s Phoebe Pettingell, however, argues that "Ashbery carries the saw that 'poetry does not have subject matter because it is the subject' to its furthest limit. Just as we feel we are beginning to make sense of one of his poems, meaning eludes us again. . . . Still, we are somehow left with a sense that the conclusion is satisfactory, with a wondering delight at what we've heard. And since a primary function of poetry is giving pleasure, Ashbery ranks very high. . . . *Houseboat Days* is evidence of the transcendent power of the imagination, and one of the major works of our time."

Ashbery's poetry, as critics have observed, has evolved under a variety of influences besides modern art, becoming in the end the expression of a voice unmistakably his own. Among the influences that have been discerned in his verse are the Romantic tradition in American poetry that progresses from Whitman to Wallace Stevens, the so-called "New York School of Poets," featuring contemporaries such as Frank O'Hara and Kenneth Koch, and the French surrealist writers with whom Ashbery has dealt in his work as a critic and translator. In *The Fierce Embrace,* Charles Molesworth traces Ashbery's development: "The first few books by John Ashbery contained a large proportion of a poetry of inconsequence. Borrowing freely from the traditions of French surrealism, and from his friends Frank O'Hara and Kenneth Koch, Ashbery tried out a fairly narrow range of voices and subjects. Subject matter, or rather the absence of it, helped form the core of his aesthetic, an aesthetic that refused to maintain a consistent attitude toward any fixed phenomena. The poems tumbled out of a whimsical, detached amusement that mixed with a quizzical melancholy. . . . With the exception of *The Tennis Court Oath,* Ashbery's first four commercially published books . . . included some poems with interpretable meanings and recognizable structures. But reading the first four books together, one is struck by how precious are those poems that do make poetic sense, surrounded as they are by the incessant chatter of the poems of inconsequence. Slowly, however, it appears as if Ashbery was gaining confidence for his true project, and, as his work unfolds, an indulging reader can see how it needed those aggressively bland 'experiments' in nonsense to protect its frailty." Ashbery's "true project," Molesworth believes, is *Self-Portrait in a Convex Mirror.* Many reviewers agree with Moles-

worth that this volume, especially the long title poem, is Ashbery's "masterpiece."

Essentially a meditation of the painting "Self-Portrait in a Convex Mirror" by Parmigianino, the narrative poem focuses on many of the themes present in Ashbery's work. "I have lived with John Ashbery's 'Self-Portrait in a Convex Mirror' as with a favorite mistress for the past nine months," Laurence Lieberman declares in his book *Unassigned Frequencies.* "Often, for whole days of inhabiting the room of its dream, I have felt that it is the only poem—and Ashbery the only author—in my life. It is what I most want from a poem. Or an author." Lieberman finds that "when I put this poem down I catch myself in the act of seeing objects and events in the world as through different— though amazingly novel other eyes: the brilliantly varied other life of surfaces has been wonderfully revivified, and I take this transformation to be an accurate index of the impact of Ashbery's poetry upon the modus operandi of my perception." Like Molesworth, Lieberman believes that Ashbery's early work, though "unreadable," was an "indispensable detour that precipitated, finally, the elevated vision of Ashbery's recent work. . . . Following his many years of withdrawal and seclusion, a period of slow mellowing, this exactly appointed occasion has been granted to him. A reader feels he can bodily sense an immense weight lifting, as if Ashbery has been relieved, suddenly, of the burden of guilt and bewilderment that two decades of self-imposed ostracism that his choice of direction as an artist . . . had condemned him to, years of lonely waiting to connect with a viable audience, and to expedite human good fellowship with a widespread community of readers."

Like other critics, Lieberman believes that Ashbery was once overly concerned with examining the nature of art and creativity, with escaping into his poems and "producing forms that achieved a semblance of ideal beauty." In "Self-Portrait," Lieberman contends, "Ashbery forecloses irrevocably on the mortgage of an *ars poetica* which conceives the poem as 'exotic refuge,' and advances to an aesthetic which carries a full burden of mirroring the age's ills." Unlike Parmigianino, who retreated into his hermitage, Ashbery ventures out from "the comfortable sanctuary of the dream" to confront the world. "His new art achieves a powerful re-engagement with the human community," Lieberman concludes. "That is his honorable quest."

For an interview with this author see *Contemporary Authors, New Revision Series,* Volume 9.

BIOGRAPHICAL/CRITICAL SOURCES:

BOOKS

Ashton, Dore, *The New York School: A Cultural Reckoning,* Viking, 1973.
Carroll, Paul, *The Poem in Its Skin,* Follett, 1968.
Contemporary Literary Criticism, Gale, Volume 2, 1974, Volume 3, 1975, Volume 4, 1975, Volume 6, 1976, Volume 9, 1978, Volume 13, 1980, Volume 15, 1980, Volume 25, 1983, Volume 41, 1988.
Contemporary Poets, St. Martins, 1985.
Dictionary of Literary Biography, Gale, Volume 5: *American Poets since World War II,* 1980, *Yearbook: 1981,* 1981.
Howard, Richard, *Alone with America: Essays on the Art of Poetry in the United States since 1950,* Athenuem, 1969.
Kalstone, David, *Five Temperaments: Elizabeth Bishop, Robert Lowell, James Merrill, Adrienne Rich, John Ashbery,* Oxford University Press, 1977.
Kermani, David K., *John Ashbery: A Comprehensive Bibliography,* Garland Publishing, 1976.

Koch, Kenneth, *Rose, Where Did You Get That Red?,* Random House, 1973.
Kostelanetz, Richard, editor, *The New American Arts,* Horizon Press, 1965.
Kostelanetz, *The Old Poetries and the New,* University of Michigan Press, 1979.
Leary, Paris and Robert Kelly, editors, *A Controversy of Poets,* Doubleday, 1965.
Lehman, David, editor, *John Ashbery,* Cornell University Press, 1979.
Lehman, editor, *Beyond Amazement: New Essays on John Ashbery,* Cornell University Press, 1980.
Lieberman, Laurence, *Unassigned Frequencies: American Poetry in Review, 1964-1977,* University of Illinois Press, 1977.
Meyers, John Bernard, editor, *The Poets of the New York School,* University of Pennsylvania Press, 1969.
Molesworth, Charles, *The Fierce Embrace: A Study of Contemporary American Poetry,* University of Missouri Press, 1979.
Packard, William, editor, *The Craft of Poetry,* Doubleday, 1964.
Shapiro, David, *John Ashbery: An Introduction to the Poetry,* Columbia University Press, 1979.
Shaw, Robert B., editor, *American Poetry since 1960: Some Critical Perspectives,* Carcanet Press, 1973.
Stepanchev, Stephen, *American Poetry since 1945: A Critical Survey,* Harper, 1965.
Sutton, Walter, *American Free Verse: The Modern Revolution in Poetry,* New Directions, 1973.

PERIODICALS

American Poetry Review, August 1973, September, 1978, July, 1979, July, 1981.
Booklist, May 1, 1981.
Chicago Tribune Book World, January 27, 1980, July 26, 1981.
Christian Science Monitor, September 6, 1962, March 9, 1970, October 12, 1977, December 3, 1979.
Commentary, February, 1973.
Contemporary Literature, winter, 1968, spring, 1969.
Encounter, April, 1980.
Esquire, January, 1978.
Georgia Review, winter, 1975, winter, 1978, summer, 1980.
Harper's, April, 1970, November, 1975.
Hudson Review, spring, 1970, autumn, 1975, autumn, 1976, spring, 1978, autumn, 1980, winter, 1981.
Journal of Modern Literature, September, 1976.
Library Journal, January 1, 1970.
Listener, August 18, 1977.
Nation, December 12, 1966, April 14, 1969, September 3, 1977, November 11, 1978.
New Leader, May 26, 1975, November 7, 1977, January 29, 1981.
New Republic, June 14, 1975, November 29, 1975, November 26, 1977, December 29, 1979.
New Statesman, June 16, 1967, January 4, 1980, April 24, 1981.
Newsweek, September 26, 1977.
New York Arts Journal, November, 1977.
New Yorker, September 1, 1956, March 24, 1969, March 16, 1981.
New York Quarterly, winter, 1972.
New York Review of Books, April 14, 1966, December 14, 1973, October 16, 1975, March 23, 1978, January 24, 1980, July 16, 1981.
New York Times, April 15, 1956.
New York Times Book Review, July 15, 1962, February 11, 1968, May 4, 1969, June 8, 1969, July 5, 1970, April 9, 1972, August 2, 1975, November 13, 1977, January 6, 1980, September 6, 1981.
New York Times Sunday Magazine, May 23, 1976, February 3, 1980.
Observer, December 9, 1979, December 16, 1979.
Parnassus, fall-winter, 1972, fall-winter, 1977, spring-summer, 1978, fall-winter, 1979.
Partisan Review, fall, 1972, summer, 1976.
Poet and Critic, Volume 11, number 3, 1979.
Poetry, July, 1957, September, 1962, December, 1966, October, 1970, August, 1972, October, 1980.
Saturday Review, June 16, 1956, May 5, 1962, August 8, 1970, July 8, 1972, September 17, 1977.
Sewanee Review, April, 1976, April, 1978, July, 1980.
Southern Review, April, 1978.
Spectator, November 22, 1975.
Time, April 26, 1976.
Times (London), August 23, 1984.
Times Literary Supplement, September 14, 1967, July 25, 1975, September 1, 1978, March 14, 1980, June 5, 1981, October 8, 1982.
Village Voice, January 19, 1976, October 17, 1977, December 26, 1977.
Village Voice Literary Supplement, October, 1981.
Virginia Quarterly Review, autumn, 1970, winter, 1973, spring, 1976, spring, 1979, spring, 1980.
Washington Post Book World, May 11, 1975, October 30, 1977, December 11, 1977, November 25, 1979, June 7, 1981.
Western Humanities Review, winter, 1971.
Yale Review, October, 1969, June, 1970, winter, 1981.

*   *   *

ASHE, Gordon
See CREASEY, John

*   *   *

ASHTON-WARNER, Sylvia (Constance) 1908-1984
(Sylvia Henderson, Sylvia)

PERSONAL: Born December 17, 1904, in Stratford, New Zealand; died April 28, 1984, in Tauranga, New Zealand; married Keith Dawson Henderson (a teacher). *Education:* Attended Wairarapa College, Masterton, New Zealand, and Teachers' College, Auckland, New Zealand, 1928-29.

ADDRESSES: Home—Whenua, 5-9 Levers Rd., Otumoetai, Tuaranga, New Zealand. *Agent*—Monica McCall, International Creative Management, 1301 Avenue of the Americas, New York, N.Y. 10019.

CAREER: Writer and educator. Taught at several schools in New Zealand; former professor of education at Aspen Community School Teaching Center, Aspen, Colo.

WRITINGS:

Spinster (novel), Simon & Schuster, 1959, reprinted, 1985.
Incense to Idols (novel), Simon & Schuster, 1960.
Teacher (nonfiction), Simon & Schuster, 1963, reprinted, 1986.
Bell Call (novel), Simon & Schuster, 1964.
Greenstone (novel), Simon & Schuster, 1967.
Myself (autobiography), Simon & Schuster, 1967.
Three (novel), Knopf, 1970.
Spearpoint: Teacher in America (autobiography), Knopf, 1972.
I Passed This Way (autobiography), Knopf, 1979.

Contributor of short stories, sometimes under names Sylvia and Sylvia Henderson, and of poetry to *New Zealand Listener, New Zealand Monthly Review,* and other periodicals.

SIDELIGHTS: Sylvia Ashton-Warner's novels are set in her native New Zealand, where she spent most of her career not only writing but also teaching grammar school to white and Maori children. The challenges of teaching and the conflicts among the racial mixture served as points in her books, the most notable of them being Ashton-Warner's debut novel *Spinster,* and *Teacher,* a nonfiction work.

Spinster, the story of a New Zealand schoolteacher struggling with inner doubt, won almost unanimous applause from critics, with John Wain's remarks in a *New Yorker* review summing up many opinions: "The identity at the center of [the story], the woman who somehow preserves each day, and every minute of every day, so as to achieve some sort of two-way relationship with so many people and things, is wonderfully real and moving—a useful reminder that the novel is still a field in which the novice, given inspiration, can produce work beyond the range of the average professional, and in which there are many discoveries to be made."

With *Teacher,* Ashton-Warner examined the way children learn in New Zealand schools, written from the viewpoint of an insider. Especially in her dealings with the Maori children, the author noted the way cultural differences can influence the effectiveness of teachers. To *New York Times Book Review* critic Katharine Taylor, the book "should have great value not only for those interested in the problems of education in old cultures and new nations, but also for those concerned with the future of civilization."

In another departure, Ashton-Warner wrote three autobiographical volumes. Her last work, *I Passed This Way,* serves as a look back on a long life of teaching and writing. But Carolyn F. Ruffin saw another side to the book. The *Christian Science Monitor* critic found that "what gives this book its power is Ashton-Warner's scrap with the cautious and the blindly secure. She takes on bureaucracy of the spirit as well as red tape in institutions." Noting how the author's "wide-ranging love gives [the work] its poetry, its humor, and an array of carefully drawn human beings," Ruffin concluded that in *I Passed This Way* Ashton-Warner produced a memoir not only full of answers but brimming with questions. And to *Washington Post* reviewer Linda B. Osborne, Ashton-Warner's final book "builds her self-portrait through a series of images that hold for her a special meaning. It is autobiography as art, selective and visionary, grounded in impressions, memories and dreams as much as fact." What concerned this author, Osborne said, is "what is essential to people, what moves their spirits, fuels their imaginations and encourages their potential to be lively human beings."

MEDIA ADAPTATIONS: Spinster was adapted for film and released as "Two Loves," starring Shirley MacLaine.

BIOGRAPHICAL/CRITICAL SOURCES:

BOOKS

Ashton-Warner, Sylvia, *Teacher,* Simon & Schuster, 1963, reprinted, 1986.
Ashton-Warner, Sylvia, *Myself,* Simon & Schuster, 1967.
Ashton-Warner, Sylvia, *Spearpoint: Teacher in America,* Knopf, 1972.
Ashton-Warner, Sylvia, *I Passed This Way,* Knopf, 1979.
Contemporary Literary Criticism, Volume 19, Gale, 1981.

Hood, Lynley, *Sylvia!: The Biography of Sylvia Ashton-Warner,* Viking, 1989.

PERIODICALS

Christian Science Monitor, April 2, 1959, December 3, 1979.
Commonweal, December 9, 1960.
New Republic, September 23, 1972.
New Yorker, April 11, 1959.
New York Times Book Review, September 8, 1963, February 14, 1965, October 8, 1967.
Saturday Review, November 12, 1960, March 19, 1966.
Washington Post, January 6, 1980.

OBITUARIES:

PERIODICALS

New York Times, April 30, 1984.
Publishers Weekly, May 18, 1984.
Times (London), May 2, 1984.

*   *   *

ASIMOV, Isaac 1920-
(George E. Dale, Dr. A, Paul French)

PERSONAL: Born January 2, 1920, in Petrovichi, U.S.S.R.; brought to United States in 1923, naturalized citizen in 1928; son of Judah (a candy store owner) and Anna Rachel (Berman) Asimov; married Gertrude Blugerman, July 26, 1942 (divorced, November 16, 1973); married Janet Opal Jeppson (a psychiatrist), November 30, 1973; children: David, Robyn Joan. *Education:* Columbia University, B.S., 1939, M.A., 1941, Ph.D., 1948.

ADDRESSES: Home—10 West 66th St., Apt. 33-A, New York, N.Y. 10023.

CAREER: Writer. Boston University, School of Medicine, Boston, Mass., instructor, 1949-51, assistant professor, 1951-55, associate professor, 1955-79, professor of biochemistry, 1979—. Worked as a civilian chemist at U.S. Navy Air Experimental Station, Philadelphia, 1942-45. *Military service:* U.S. Army, 1945-46.

MEMBER: Authors League of America, Science Fiction Writers of America, National Association of Science Writers, American Chemical Society, Zero Population Growth, Population Institute, National Organization of Non-Parents, Sigma Xi, Mensa.

AWARDS, HONORS: Guest of honor at the Thirteenth World Science Fiction Convention, 1955; Edison Foundation National Mass Media Award, 1958; Blakeslee Award for nonfiction, 1960; special Hugo Award for distinguished contributions to the field, 1963, for science articles in the *Magazine of Fantasy and Science Fiction,* special Hugo Award for best all-time science fiction series, 1966, for *Foundation, Foundation and Empire,* and *Second Foundation,* Hugo Award for best novel, 1973, for *The Gods Themselves,* and 1983, for *Foundation's Edge,* Hugo Award for best short story, 1977, for "The Bicentennial Man," all from World Science Fiction Conventions; James T. Grady Award, American Chemical Society, 1965; American Association for the Advancement of Science-Westinghouse award for science writing, 1967; Nebula Award, Science Fiction Writers of America, 1973, for *The Gods Themselves,* and 1977, for "The Bicentennial Man"; Glenn Seabord Award, International Platform Association, 1979; "Nightfall" was chosen the best science fiction story of all time in a Science Fiction Writers of America poll.

WRITINGS:

SCIENCE FICTION

Pebble In the Sky (novel; also see below), Doubleday, 1950, reprinted, R. Bentley, 1982.

I, Robot (short stories), Gnome Press, 1950, reprinted, Fawcett, 1970.

The Stars, Like Dust (novel; also see below), Doubleday, 1951, published as *The Rebellious Stars* with *An Earth Gone Mad* by R. D. Aycock, Ace Books, 1954, reprinted under original title, Fawcett, 1972.

Foundation (also see below), Gnome Press, 1951, published as *The 1,000 Year Plan* with *No World of Their Own* by Poul Anderson, Ace Books, 1955, reprinted under original title, Ballantine, 1983.

(Under pseudonym Paul French) *David Starr, Space Ranger* (juvenile; also see below), Doubleday, 1952, reprinted under name Isaac Asimov, Twayne, 1978.

Foundation and Empire (also see below), Gnome Press, 1952, reprinted, Ballantine, 1983.

The Currents of Space (novel; also see below), Doubleday, 1952, reprinted, Fawcett, 1971.

Second Foundation (also see below), Gnome Press, 1953, reprinted, Ballantine, 1983.

(Under pseudonym Paul French) *Lucky Starr and the Pirates of the Asteroids* (juvenile; also see below), Doubleday, 1953, reprinted under name Isaac Asimov, Twayne, 1978.

The Caves of Steel (novel; also see below), Doubleday, 1954, reprinted, Fawcett, 1972.

(Under pseudonym Paul French) *Lucky Starr and the Oceans of Venus* (juvenile), Doubleday, 1954, reprinted under name Isaac Asimov, Twayne, 1978.

The Martian Way and Other Stories (also see below), Doubleday, 1955, reprinted, Ballantine, 1985.

The End of Eternity (novel; also see below), Doubleday, 1955, reprinted, Fawcett, 1971.

(Contributor) Groff Conklin, editor, *Science Fiction Terror Tales by Isaac Asimov and Others,* Gnome Press, 1955.

(Under pseudonym Paul French) *Lucky Starr and the Big Sun of Mercury* (juvenile), Doubleday, 1956, published under name Isaac Asimov as *The Big Sun of Mercury,* New English Library, 1974, reprinted under name Isaac Asimov under original title, Twayne, 1978.

The Naked Sun (novel; also see below), Doubleday, 1957, reprinted, Fawcett, 1972.

(Under pseudonym Paul French) *Lucky Starr and the Moons of Jupiter* (juvenile), Doubleday, 1957, reprinted under name Isaac Asimov, Twayne, 1978.

Earth Is Room Enough: Science Fiction Tales of Our Own Planet (also see below), Doubleday, 1957, reprinted, Abelard-Schuman (London), 1976.

The Robot Novels (contains *The Caves of Steel* and *The Naked Sun;* also see below), Doubleday, 1957.

(Under pseudonym Paul French) *Lucky Starr and the Rings of Saturn* (juvenile), Doubleday, 1958, reprinted under name Isaac Asimov, Twayne, 1978.

Nine Tomorrows: Tales of the Near Future, Doubleday, 1959.

Triangle: "The Currents of Space," "Pebble In the Sky," and "The Stars, Like Dust," Doubleday, 1961 (published in England as *An Isaac Asimov Second Omnibus,* Sidgwick & Jackson, 1969).

The Foundation Trilogy: Three Classics of Science Fiction (contains *Foundation, Foundation and Empire,* and *Second Foundation*), Doubleday, 1963, reprinted, Doubleday, 1982

(published in England as *An Isaac Asimov Omnibus,* Sidgwick & Jackson, 1966).

The Rest of the Robots (short stories and novels, including *The Caves of Steel* and *The Naked Sun*), Doubleday, 1964, published as *Eight Stories from the Rest of the Robots,* Pyramid Books, 1966.

Fantastic Voyage (novelization of screenplay by Harry Kleiner), Houghton, 1966.

Through a Glass Clearly, New English Library, 1967.

Asimov's Mysteries (short stories), Doubleday, 1968.

Nightfall and Other Stories, Doubleday, 1969 (published in England in two volumes, as *Nightfall One* and *Nightfall Two,* Panther Books, 1969, published as *Nightfall: Twenty SF Stories,* Rapp & Whiting, 1971).

The Best New Thing (juvenile), World Publishing, 1971.

The Gods Themselves (novel), Doubleday, 1972.

The Early Asimov: Or, Eleven Years of Trying (short stories), Doubleday, 1972.

(Contributor) Conklin, editor, *Possible Tomorrows by Isaac Asimov and Others,* Sidgwick & Jackson, 1972.

An Isaac Asimov Double: "Space Ranger" and "Pirates of the Asteroids", New English Library (London), 1972.

A Second Isaac Asimov Double: "The Big Sun of Mercury" and "The Oceans of Venus", New English Library, 1973.

The Third Isaac Asimov Double, New English Library/Times Mirror, 1973.

The Best of Isaac Asimov (short stories), Doubleday, 1974.

Have You Seen These?, NESFA Press, 1974.

Buy Jupiter and Other Stories, Doubleday, 1975.

The Heavenly Host (juvenile), Walker & Co., 1975.

The Bicentennial Man and Other Stories, Doubleday, 1976.

The Collected Fiction of Isaac Asimov, Volume 1: *The Far Ends of Time and Earth* (contains *Pebble in the Sky, Earth Is Room Enough,* and *The End of Eternity*), Doubleday, 1979, Volume 2: *Prisoners of the Stars* (contains *The Stars, Like Dust, The Martian Way and Other Stories,* and *The Currents of Space*), Doubleday, 1979.

Three by Asimov, limited edition, Targ Editions, 1981.

The Complete Robot (also see below), Doubleday, 1982.

Foundation's Edge (novel), Doubleday, 1982.

The Winds of Change and Other Stories, Doubleday, 1983.

(With wife, Janet O. Jeppson under name Janet Asimov) *Norby, the Mixed-Up Robot* (juvenile), Walker & Co., 1983.

The Robots of Dawn (novel), Doubleday, 1983.

The Robot Collection (contains *The Caves of Steel, The Naked Sun,* and *The Complete Robot*), Doubleday, 1983.

(With Janet Asimov) *Norby's Other Secret* (juvenile), Walker & Co., 1984.

Robots and Empire (novel), Doubleday, 1985.

(With Janet Asimov) *Norby and the Invaders* (juvenile), Walker & Co., 1985.

(With Janet Asimov) *Norby and the Lost Princess* (juvenile), Walker & Co., 1985.

The Best Science Fiction of Isaac Asimov, Doubleday, 1986.

The Alternative Asimovs (contains *The End of Eternity*), Doubleday, 1986.

(With Janet Asimov) *The Norby Chronicles,* Ace Books, 1986.

Foundation and Earth (novel), Doubleday, 1986.

(With Janet Asimov) *Norby and the Queen's Necklace,* Walker & Co., 1986.

(With Janet Asimov) *Norby: Robot for Hire,* Ace Books, 1987.

Fantastic Voyage II: Destination Brain, Doubleday, 1987.

(With Janet Asimov) *Norby Finds a Villain,* Walker & Co., 1987.

(With Janet Asimov) *Norby through Time and Space,* Ace Books, 1988.

Azazel, Doubleday, 1988.
Nemesis, Doubleday, 1988.
Prelude to Foundation, Doubleday, 1988.
(With Theodore Sturgeon) *The Ugly Little Boy/The Widget, the Wadget, and Boff,* Tor Books, 1989.
(With Janet Asimov) *Norby Down to Earth,* Walker & Co., 1989.
(With Janet Asimov) *Norby and Yobo's Great Adventure,* Walker & Co., 1989.

Also editor or co-editor of over eighty science fiction and fantasy anthologies.

MYSTERIES

Death Dealers (novel), Avon Publications, 1958, published as *A Whiff of Death,* Walker & Co., 1968.
Tales of the Black Widowers, Doubleday, 1974.
Murder at the ABA: A Puzzle in Four Days and Sixty Scenes (novel), Doubleday, 1976 (published in England as *Authorised Murder: A Puzzle in Four Days and Sixty Scenes,* Gollancz, 1976).
More Tales of the Black Widowers, Doubleday, 1976.
The Key Word and Other Mysteries, Walker & Co., 1977.
Casebook of the Black Widowers, Doubleday, 1980.
The Union Club Mysteries, Doubleday, 1983.
Computer Crimes and Capers, Academy Chicago Publishers, 1983.
Banquets of the Black Widowers, Doubleday, 1984.
The Disappearing Man and Other Mysteries, Walker & Co., 1985.
The Best Mysteries of Isaac Asimov, Doubleday, 1986.
Hound Dunnit, Carroll & Graf, 1987.

Also editor, with others, of several mystery anthologies.

SCIENCE FACT; ADULT

(With William C. Boyd and Burnham S. Walker) *Biochemistry and Human Metabolism,* Williams & Wilkins, 1952, 3rd edition, 1957.
The Chemicals of Life: Enzymes, Vitamins, Hormones, Abelard-Schuman, 1954.
(With Boyd) *Races and People,* Abelard-Schuman, 1955.
(With Walker and Mary K. Nicholas) *Chemistry and Human Health,* McGraw, 1956.
Inside the Atom, Abelard-Schuman, 1956, revised and updated edition, 1966.
Only a Trillion (essays), Abelard-Schuman, 1958, published as *Marvels of Science: Essays of Fact and Fancy on Life, Its Environment, Its Possibilities,* Collier Books, 1962, reprinted under original title, Ace Books, 1976.
The World of Carbon, Abelard-Schuman, 1958, revised edition, Collier Books, 1962.
The World of Nitrogen, Abelard-Schuman, 1958, revised edition, Collier Books, 1962.
The Clock We Live On, Abelard-Schuman, 1959, revised edition, 1965.
Words of Science and the History behind Them, Houghton, 1959, revised edition, Harrap, 1974.
Realm of Numbers, Houghton, 1959.
The Living River, Abelard-Schuman, 1959, published as *The Bloodstream: River of Life,* Collier Books, 1961.
The Kingdom of the Sun, Abelard-Schuman, 1960, revised edition, 1963.
Realm of Measure, Houghton, 1960.
The Wellsprings of Life, Abelard-Schuman, (London), 1960, New American Library, 1961.
The Intelligent Man's Guide to Science, two volumes, Basic Books, 1960, Volume 1 published separately as *The Intelli-

gent Man's Guide to the Physical Sciences,* Pocket Books, 1964, Volume 2 published separately as *The Intelligent Man's Guide to the Biological Sciences,* Pocket Books, 1964, revised edition published as *The New Intelligent Man's Guide to Science,* 1965, published as *Asimov's Guide to Science,* 1972, revised edition published as *Asimov's New Guide to Science,* 1984.
The Double Planet, Abelard-Schuman, 1960, revised edition, 1967.
Realm of Algebra, Houghton, 1961.
Life and Energy, Doubleday, 1962.
Fact and Fancy (essays), Doubleday, 1962.
The Search for the Elements, Basic Books, 1962.
The Genetic Code, Orion Press, 1963.
The Human Body: Its Structure and Operation (also see below), Houghton, 1963.
View from a Height, Doubleday, 1963.
The Human Brain: Its Capacities and Functions (also see below), Houghton, 1964.
A Short History of Biology, Natural History Press for the American Museum of Natural History, 1964, reprinted, Greenwood, 1980.
Quick and Easy Math, Houghton, 1964.
Adding a Dimension: Seventeen Essays on the History of Science, Doubleday, 1964.
(With Stephen H. Dole) *Planets for Man,* Random House, 1964.
Asimov's Biographical Encyclopedia of Science and Technology, Doubleday, 1964, 2nd revised edition, 1982.
A Short History of Chemistry, Doubleday, 1965.
Of Time and Space and Other Things (essays), Doubleday, 1965.
An Easy Introduction to the Slide Rule, Houghton, 1965.
The Noble Gasses, Basic Books, 1966.
The Neutrino: Ghost Particle of the Atom, Doubleday, 1966.
Understanding Physics, three volumes, Walker & Co., 1966.
The Genetic Effects of Radiation, U.S. Atomic Energy Commission, 1966.
The Universe: From Flat Earth to Quasar, Walker & Co., 1966, 3rd edition published as *The Universe: From Flat Earth to Black Holes—and Beyond,* 1980.
From Earth to Heaven (essays), Doubleday, 1966.
Environments out There, Abelard-Schuman, 1967.
Is Anyone There? (essays), Doubleday, 1967.
Science, Numbers and I (essays), Doubleday, 1968.
Photosynthesis, Basic Books, 1968.
Twentieth Century Discovery (essays), Doubleday, 1969, revised edition, Ace Books, 1976.
The Solar System and Back (essays), Doubleday, 1970.
The Stars in Their Courses (essays), Doubleday, 1971, revised edition, Ace Books, 1976.
The Left Hand of the Electron (essays), Doubleday, 1972.
Electricity and Man, U.S. Atomic Energy Commission, 1972.
Worlds within Worlds: The Story of Nuclear Energy, three volumes, U.S. Atomic Energy Commission, 1972.
A Short History of Chemistry, Heinemann, 1972.
Today and Tomorrow and . . . , Doubleday, 1973.
The Tragedy of the Moon, Doubleday, 1973.
Asimov on Astronomy (essays), Doubleday, 1974.
Our World in Space, foreword by Edwin E. Aldrin, Jr., New York Graphic Society, 1974.
Asimov on Chemistry (essays), Doubleday, 1974.
Of Matters Great and Small, Doubleday, 1975.
Science Past, Science Future, Doubleday, 1975.
Eyes on the Universe: A History of the Telescope, Houghton, 1975.
The Ends of the Earth: The Polar Regions of the World, Weybright & Talley, 1975.

Asimov on Physics (essays), Doubleday, 1976.
The Planet that Wasn't (essays), Doubleday, 1976.
The Collapsing Universe, Walker & Co., 1977.
Asimov on Numbers (essays), Doubleday, 1977.
The Beginning and the End (essays), Doubleday, 1977.
Quasar, Quasar, Burning Bright (essays), Doubleday, 1978.
Life and Time, Doubleday, 1978.
The Road to Infinity (essays), Doubleday, 1979.
A Choice of Catastrophes: The Disasters that Threaten Our World, Simon & Schuster, 1979.
Visions of the Universe, preface by Carl Sagan, Cosmos Store, 1981.
The Sun Shines Bright (essays), Doubleday, 1981.
Exploring the Earth and the Cosmos: The Growth and Future of Human Knowledge, Crown, 1982.
Counting the Eons, Doubleday, 1983.
The Roving Mind, Prometheus Books, 1983.
The Measure of the Universe, Harper, 1983.
X Stands for Unknown, Doubleday, 1984.
The History of Physics, Walker & Co., 1984.
Isaac Asimov on the Human Body and the Human Brain (contains *The Human Body: Its Structure and Operation* and *The Human Brain: Its Capacities and Functions*), Bonanza Books, 1984.
The Exploding Suns: The Secrets of the Supernovas, Dutton, 1985.
Asimov's Guide to Halley's Comet, Walker & Co., 1985.
Robots: Machines in Man's Image, Harmony Books, 1985.
The Subatomic Monster, Doubleday, 1985.
(With Karen Frenkel) *Robots: Machines in Man's Image*, Robot Institute of America, 1985.
Isaac Asimov's Wonderful Worldwide Science Bazaar: Seventy-Two Up-to-Date Reports on the State of Everything from Inside the Atom to Outside the Universe, Houghton, 1986.
Far as Human Eye Could See (essays), Doubleday, 1987.
The Relativity of Wrong, Doubleday, 1988.
Asimov on Science: A Thirty Year Retrospective, Doubleday, 1989.
Asimov's Chronology of Science and Technology: How Science Has Shaped the World and How the World Has Affected Science from 4,000,000 B.C. to the Present, Harper, 1989.
The Tyrannosaurus Prescription and One Hundred Other Essays, Prometheus Books, 1989.

SCIENCE FACT; JUVENILE

Building Blocks of the Universe, Abelard-Schuman, 1957, revised and updated edition, 1974.
Breakthroughs in Science, Houghton, 1960.
Satellites in Outer Space, Random House, 1960, revised edition, 1973.
The Moon, Follett, 1966.
To the Ends of the Universe, Walker & Co., 1967, revised edition, 1976.
Mars, Follett, 1967.
Stars, Follett, 1968.
Galaxies, Follett, 1968.
ABC's of Space, Walker & Co., 1969, published as *Space Dictionary*, Scholastic, 1970.
Great Ideas of Science, Houghton, 1969.
ABC's of the Ocean, Walker & Co., 1970.
Light, Follett, 1970.
What Makes the Sun Shine?, Little, Brown, 1971.
ABC's of the Earth, Walker & Co., 1971.
ABC's of Ecology, Walker & Co., 1972.

Ginn Science Program, Ginn, intermediate levels A, B, and C, 1972, advanced levels A and B, 1973.
Comets and Meteors, Follett, 1972.
The Sun, Follett, 1972.
Jupiter, the Largest Planet, Lothrop, 1973, revised edition, 1976.
Please Explain, Houghton, 1973.
Earth: Our Crowded Spaceship, John Day, 1974.
The Solar System, Follett, 1975.
Alpha Centauri, the Nearest Star, Lothrop, 1976.
Mars, the Red Planet, Lothrop, 1977.
Saturn and Beyond, Lothrop, 1979.
Venus: Near Neighbor of the Sun, Lothrop, 1981.
Beginnings: The Story of the Origins of Mankind, Life, the Earth, the Universe, Walker & Co., 1987.
Franchise, Creative Education, 1988.
All the Troubles of World, Creative Education, 1988.
Think about Space, Walker & Co., 1989.

Also author of over thirty volumes in the "How Did We Find Out" series, Walker & Co., 1972—, and of over twenty-five volumes in the "Isaac Asimov's Library of the Universe" series, Gareth Stevens, 1987—.

HISTORY

The Kite that Won the Revolution (juvenile), Houghton, 1963, revised edition, 1973.
The Greeks: A Great Adventure, Houghton, 1965.
The Roman Republic, Houghton, 1966.
The Roman Empire, Houghton, 1967.
The Egyptians, Houghton, 1967.
The Near East: Ten Thousand Years of History, Houghton, 1968.
The Dark Ages, Houghton, 1968.
Words from History, Houghton, 1968.
The Shaping of England, Houghton, 1969.
Constantinople: The Forgotten Empire, Houghton, 1970.
The Land of Canaan, Houghton, 1970.
The Shaping of France, Houghton, 1972.
The Shaping of North America from Earliest Times to 1763, Houghton, 1973.
The Birth of the United States, 1763-1816, Houghton, 1974.
Our Federal Union: The United States from 1816 to 1865, Houghton, 1975.
The Golden Door: The United States form 1865 to 1918, Houghton, 1977.

OTHER

Words from the Myths, Houghton, 1961.
Words in Genesis, Houghton, 1962.
Words on the Map, Houghton, 1962.
Words from Exodus, Houghton, 1963.
Asimov's Guide to the Bible, Doubleday, Volume 1: *The Old Testament*, 1968, Volume 2: *The New Testament*, 1969.
Opus 100 (selections from author's first one hundred books), Houghton, 1969.
Asimov's Guide to Shakespeare, two volumes, Doubleday, 1970, published as one volume, Avenel Books, 1981.
"Unseen World" (teleplay), American Broadcasting Co. (ABC-TV), 1970.
(Under pseudonym Dr. A) *The Sensuous Dirty Old Man*, Walker & Co., 1971.
Treasury of Humor: A Lifetime Collection of Favorite Jokes, Anecdotes, and Limericks with Copious Notes on How to Tell Them and Why, Houghton, 1971.
(With James Gunn) "The History of Science Fiction from 1938 to the Present" (filmscript), Extramural Independent Study Center, University of Kansas, 1971.

More Words of Science, Houghton, 1972.

The Story of Ruth, Doubleday, 1972.

Asimov's Annotated "Don Juan," Doubleday, 1972.

Asimov's Annotated "Paradise Lost," Doubleday, 1974.

Lecherous Limericks, Walker & Co., 1975.

"The Dream," "Benjamin's Dream," and "Benjamin's Bicentennial Blast": Three Short Stories, Printing Week in New York, 1976.

More Lecherous Limericks, Walker & Co., 1976.

Familiar Poems Annotated, Doubleday, 1977.

Still More Lecherous Limericks, Walker & Co., 1977.

Asimov's Sherlockian Limericks, New Mysterious Press, 1978.

Animals of the Bible, Doubleday, 1978.

(With John Ciardi) *Limericks Too Gross,* Norton, 1978.

Opus 200 (selections from the author's second hundred books), Houghton, 1979.

In Memory Yet Green: The Autobiography of Isaac Asimov, 1920-1954, Doubleday, 1979.

Extraterrestrial Civilizations (speculative nonfiction), Crown, 1979.

Isaac Asimov's Book of Facts, Grosset, 1979.

In Joy Still Felt: The Autobiography of Isaac Asimov, 1954-1978, Doubleday, 1980.

The Annotated "Gulliver's Travels," C. N. Potter, 1980.

In the Beginning: Science Faces God in the Book of Genesis, Crown, 1981.

Asimov on Science Fiction, Doubleday, 1981.

Change!: Seventy-One Glimpses of the Future (forecasts), Houghton, 1981.

(With Ciardi) *A Grossery of Limericks,* Norton, 1981.

Would You Believe?, Grosset, 1981.

(With Ken Fisher) *Isaac Asimov Presents Superquiz,* Dembner, 1982.

More—Would You Believe?, Grosset, 1982.

(Editor with George R. Martin) *The Science Fiction Weight-Loss Book,* Crown, 1983.

(Editor with Martin H. Greenberg and Charles G. Waugh) *Isaac Asimov Presents the Best Horror and Supernatural of the Nineteenth Century,* Beaufort Books, 1983.

(Editor) *Thirteen Horrors of Halloween,* Avon, 1983.

(Editor with Greenberg and George Zebrowski and author of introduction) *Creations: The Quest for Origins in Story and Science,* Crown, 1983.

(With Fisher) *Isaac Asimov Presents Superquiz 2,* Dembner, 1983.

Opus 300 (selections from the author's third hundred books), Houghton, 1984.

Isaac Asimov's Limericks for Children, Caedmon, 1984.

(Editor) *Living in the Future* (forecasts), Beaufort Books, 1985.

The Edge of Tomorrow, T. Doherty, 1985.

(With James Burke and Jules Bergman) *The Impact of Science on Society,* National Aeronautics and Space Administration (NASA), 1985.

Isaac Asimov, Octopus Books, 1986.

Past, Present, and Future, Prometheus Books, 1987.

Robot Dreams, edited by Bryon Preiss, Berkley, 1987.

(With Janet Asimov) *How to Enjoy Writing: A Book of Aid and Comfort,* Walker & Co., 1987.

Asimov's Annotated Gilbert and Sullivan, Doubleday, 1988.

The Alternate Asimovs, Signet/New American Library, 1988.

Isaac Asimov's Book of Science and Nature Quotations, Weidenfeld & Nicolson, 1988.

Asimov's Galaxy: Reflections on Science Fiction, Doubleday, 1989.

Also author of *The Adventures of Science Fiction,* Ameron Ltd. Author of "Science" column in *Magazine of Fantasy and Science Fiction,* 1958—. Contributor of stories to numerous science fiction anthologies, and to many science fiction magazines, including *Astounding Science Fiction, Amazing Stories, Fantastic Adventures, Science Fiction,* and *Future Fiction;* contributor of one short story under pseudonym George E. Dale to *Astounding Science Fiction.* Contributor of articles to numerous science journals and popular periodicals. Editorial director, *Isaac Asimov's Science Fiction Magazine.*

SIDELIGHTS: One of the most noteworthy features of Isaac Asimov's writing is the incredible bulk of material that he has produced. His bibliography includes more than 320 books, and this, together with innumerable short stories and nonfiction articles published in magazines, amounts to over twenty million words in print. In order to maintain the necessary writing pace, Asimov has trained himself to type ninety words per minute. He revises only once, believing, as he says in his autobiography, that "if after two typings the result proves unsatisfactory, it has always seemed to me it is better abandoned. There is less trouble and trauma involved in writing a new piece than in trying to salvage an unsatisfactory old one." Unless he is forcibly kept away from the typewriter, he works up to twelve hours a day, stopping only for meals or an occasional coffee break. He vacations infrequently and claims never to have experienced "writer's block." He also has complete control over what he describes, in his introduction to *The Bicentennial Man and Other Stories,* as "an absolutely one-man operation. I have no assistants of any kind. I have no agent, no business manager, no research aides, no secretary, no stenographer. I do all my own typing, all my own proof reading, all my own indexing, all my own research, all my own letter writing, all my own telephone answering. I like it that way. Since I don't have to deal with other people, I can concentrate more properly on my work, and get more done."

Asimov's abundant output led Newgate Callendar of the *New York Times Book Review* to label him "a writing machine"; but it is not only prolificity that makes the author unique. In addition, Asimov has tackled a tremendously wide range of topics in his nonfiction books and has become at least as well known for his elucidation of technical subjects as for science fiction. Peter Stoler explains in his *Time* article that "Simenon may have written more thrillers, Chesterton more poetry and philosophy, Pulp Romance Writer Barbara Cartland more novels. But no single author has ever written more books about more subjects than Isaac Asimov."

Asimov's interest in science fiction began when he first noticed several of the early s.f. magazines for sale on the newsstand of his family's candy store. Unfortunately the periodicals, like the candy, were forbidden to him. His father felt that young Isaac should spend his time in more serious pursuits than the reading of contemporary fiction. As a boy Isaac read, and enjoyed, numerous volumes of nonfiction as well as many of the literary "classics" (although, since modern fiction was off-limits, he claims that he had no way of knowing he was reading classical works); but he longed to explore the intriguing magazines with the glossy covers. His father, however, remained adamant, maintaining, as Asimov recalls, that fiction magazines were "junk! . . . Not fit to read. The only people who read magazines like that are bums." And bums, he explains, represented "the dregs of society, apprentice gangsters."

But in August of 1929, a new magazine appeared on the scene called *Science Wonder Stories.* Asimov knew that as long as science fiction magazines had titles like *Amazing Stories,* he would have little chance of convincing his father of their worth. The newcomer, however, had the word "science" in its title, and he says, "I had read enough about science to know that it was a mentally nourishing and spiritually wholesome study. What's more, knew that my father thought so from our occasional talks about my schoolwork." When confronted with this argument, the elder Asimov capitulated. Soon Isaac began collecting even those periodicals that didn't have "science" in the title. He notes: "I planned to maintain with all the strength at my disposal the legal position that permission for one such magazine implied permission for all the others, regardless of title. No fight was needed, however; my harassed father conceded everything." Thus Asimov was allowed to feed his appetite for science fiction "pulp" and rapidly developed into an avid fan while, at the same time, gaining valuable experience in the genre which had yet to be labeled science fiction.

Asimov wrote his first original fiction at the age of eleven. For some time he had been reading stories and then retelling them to groups of his schoolmates, adding a few personal embellishments in the process. In the fall of 1931 he decided to begin a series of books in the vein of some of the popular series of the 1920s: "The Rover Boys," "The Bobbsey Twins," and "Pee Wee Wilson." Asimov's series was called "The Greenville Chums at College," unashamedly patterned after the better known "The Darewell Chums at College," and it grew to eight chapters before he abandoned it. Asimov, in *In Memory Yet Green,* describes the flaw in his initial literary venture: "I was trying to imitate the series books without knowing anything but what I read there. Their characters were small-town boys, so mine were, for I imagined Greenville to be a town in upstate New York. Their characters went to college, so mine did. Unfortunately, a junior-high-school youngster living in a shabby neighborhood in Brooklyn knows very little about small-town life and even less about college. Even I, myself, was forced eventually to recognize the fact that I didn't know what I was talking about."

He made a similar mistake in 1934 when, in a high-school creative writing class, he attempted to write a descriptive essay about a spring day and chose, as a setting, not Brooklyn (with which he would have been familiar), but "a never-never pastoral land full of larks and daisies." To compound the error, he volunteered to read the finished work to the class; he had been writing, off and on, for several years and was eager to demonstrate his prowess to the teacher. As he tells it, "I had not read more than two paragraphs before Mr. Newfield could endure no more. 'This is shit!' he said, sending me back to my seat. . . . I never came closer in my life to giving up." But he kept writing, of course, and it was during the term of that same creative writing class that his first printed piece appeared. All the students were required to submit items for publication in the school's literary semiannual, the *Boys High Recorder,* and Asimov wrote a humorous essay entitled "Little Brother" which was accepted, he says, because it was the only funny piece anyone wrote, and the editors needed something funny.

In the summer of 1934, Asimov had a letter published in *Astounding Stories* in which he commented on several stories that had appeared in the magazine. This was the first time any of his writing had appeared in a science fiction periodical, and it led to several other letters to the editor. His continuing activities as a fan brought him to the decision to attempt a science fiction piece of his own; in 1937, at the age of seventeen, he began a story entitled "Cosmic Corkscrew." It dealt with the notion of helical time, and in it the hero was able to travel through time to certain points determined by the shape of a helix. The procedure Asimov used to formulate the plot was, he says, "typical of my science

fiction. I usually thought of some scientific gimmick and built a story about that." By the time he finished the story on June 19, 1938, *Astounding Stories* had become *Astounding Science Fiction* and was being edited by John W. Campbell, who was to influence the work of some of the most prominent authors of modern science fiction, including Arthur C. Clarke, Robert Heinlein, Poul Anderson, L. Sprague de Camp, and Theodore Sturgeon. Since Campbell was one of the best-known science fiction writers of the thirties and *Astounding* one of the most prestigious publications in its field at the time, Asimov was shocked by his father's suggestion that he submit "Cosmic Corkscrew" to the editor in person. But mailing the story would have cost twelve cents while subway fare, round trip, was only ten cents. In the interest of economy, therefore, he agreed to make the trip to the magazine's office, fully expecting to leave the manuscript with a secretary. Campbell, however, had invited many young writers to discuss their work with him, and when Asimov arrived he was shown into the editor's office. Campbell talked for over an hour and agreed to read the story; two days later Asimov received the manuscript back in the mail. It had been rejected, but Campbell offered extensive suggestions for improvement and encouraged the young man to keep trying. This began a pattern that was to continue for several years with Campbell guiding Asimov through his formative beginnings as a science fiction writer.

Asimov's association with the field of science fiction, as both an author and an editor, has been a long and distinguished one. He is generally considered to be one of the leading writers of science fiction's "Golden Age," which places him in the company of such luminaries as Heinlein, de Camp, Sturgeon, L. Ron Hubbard, and A. E. Van Vogt. Asimov is credited with the introduction of several innovative concepts into the genre, not the least of which is the formulation of the "Three Laws of Robotics." He maintains that the idea for the laws was given to him by Campbell; Campbell, on the other hand, said that he had merely picked them out of Asimov's early robot stories. In any case, it was Asimov who formalized the principles into three dicta: "1. A robot may not injure a human being or, through inaction, allow a human being to come to harm. 2. A robot must obey the orders given it by human beings except where such orders would conflict with the First Law. 3. A robot must protect its own existence as long as such protection does not conflict with the First or Second Laws." Asimov says that he used these precepts as the basis for "over two dozen short stories and three novels . . . about robots," and he feels that he is "probably more famous for them than for anything else I have written, and they are quoted even outside the science-fiction world. The very word 'robotics' was coined by me." The three laws gained general acceptance among readers and among other science fiction writers; Asimov, in his autobiography, writes that they "revolutionized" science fiction and that "no writer could write a *stupid* robot story if he used the Three Laws. The story might be bad on other counts, but it wouldn't be stupid." The laws became so popular, and seemed so logical, that many people believed real robots, if they ever were invented, would be designed according to Asimov's basic principles.

Also notable among Asimov's science fiction works, in addition to the robot stories and the Three Laws, is the "Foundation" series. This group of short stories, published in magazines in the forties and then collected into a trilogy in the early fifties, was inspired by Edward Gibbon's *Decline and Fall of the Roman Empire.* It was written as a "future history," a story being told in a society of the distant future which relates events of that society's history. The concept was not invented by Asimov, but there can be little doubt that he became a master of the technique.

Foundation, Foundation and Empire, and *Second Foundation* have achieved special standing among science fiction enthusiasts. In 1966, the World Science Fiction Convention honored them with a special Hugo Award as the best all-time science fiction series. Even thirty years after their original publication, Asimov's future history series remains popular, having sold in excess of two million copies.

Although some reviewers believe that traditional literary style, plot, and characterization in these books is scarce, as James Gunn explains in his book *Isaac Asimov: The Foundations of Science Fiction,* "story in *The Foundation Trilogy* is plentiful. Events move on a grand scale, beginning with the approaching dissolution of a galactic empire." To those in power, all seems well, but all is not well. Gunn relates the reasons: "According to the calculations of a psychologist named Hari Seldon, who has used a new science for predicting mass behavior called 'psychohistory,' the Empire will fall and be followed by 30,000 years of misery and barbarity. Seldon sets up two Foundations, one of physical scientists and a Second Foundation of psychologists . . . to shorten the oncoming dark ages to only a thousand years."

The inhabitants of Asimov's future worlds have forgotten Earth and owe allegiance to an Empire that has endured for over twelve thousand years. Still, "being a conservative writer Asimov decided that what would happen when men were in control of the Universe would be much the same as when they were in charge of a single planet: their main preoccupations would . . . be political intrigue, commercial opportunism, and back scratching, revolution and murder," observes Brian Patten in *Books and Bookmen.* New, however, is the psychohistorian's statistical forecasting and his thousand-year plan; in the unfolding of this imaginative creation, points out Maxine Moore in her contribution to *Voices for the Future: Essays on Major Science Fiction Writers,* "the Foundation group deals overtly with the problem of Free Will in deterministic universe." Moore believes that "whereas [Asimov's] robot stories reveal individual man as mechanism, the Foundation group shows society as a mechanism."

What emerges from Asimov's study of this society at once guided and trapped by a grand scheme is, as Gunn sees it, the conviction that "rationality is the one human trait that can always be trusted. . . . Sometimes rational decisions are based on insufficient information and turn out to be wrong, or the person making the decision is not intelligent enough to see the ultimate solution rather than the partial one, but nothing other than reason works at all." Gunn believes that this aspect of the "Foundation" trilogy reflects the nature of its author: "More than any other writer of his time (the Campbell era, as Asimov calls it) or even later, Asimov speaks with the voice of reason."

Asimov's achievement in writing the "Foundation" trilogy, maintains David A. Wollheim in *The Universe Makers,* rests in his application "to future history the lessons of past history. He brought to the attention of the science-fiction cosmos the fact that humanity follows patterns." Like conventional history, Asimov's "Foundation" stories are informed by the concept that "the rise of civilization follows a spiral that makes certain events seem to recur predictably but always on a new and vaster level," Wollheim suggests. And in the opinion of Jean Fiedler and Jim Mele in their book *Isaac Asimov,* "the successful transfer of this historical perspective to science fiction is, more than any other single element, one of Asimov's greatest fictional inventions."

Another of Asimov's science fiction masterpieces is a short story entitled "Nightfall." The idea for the story came from Campbell

and was inspired by a quotation from Emerson's *Nature:* "If the stars should appear one night in a thousand years, how would men believe and adore; and preserve for many generations the remembrance of the city of God." Campbell wondered how men would react to the stars if they were visible only once every thousand years; he suggested the topic to Asimov who began the story on March 18, 1941. At that time Asimov took stock of his position in the world of science fiction, and, as he says in *In Memory Yet Green:* "It was a crucial moment for me. I had, up to that moment, written thirty-one stories in not quite three years. Of these I had, as of that time, sold seventeen stories and had published fourteen, with a fifteenth about to come out. Of those thirty-one stories, published and unpublished, sold and unsold, only three were what I would now consider as three stars or better on my old zero-to-five scale, and they were positronic robot stories: 'Robbie,' 'Reason,' and 'Liar!' My status on that evening of March 18 was as nothing more than a steady and (perhaps) hopeful third-rater."

"Nightfall," written in twenty-one days by a twenty-one-year-old author, is considered by many people to be the best science fiction work of all time. Thirty years after its initial publication, in a poll conducted by the Science Fiction Writers of America, "Nightfall" finished in first place by a wide margin. It has done equally well in other polls by different organizations, and its popularity is confirmed by the numerous times it has been anthologized and reprinted. With the appearance of "Nightfall" in the September, 1941, issue of *Astounding,* Asimov was, as he says, "no longer a minor writer, hovering about the fringes of science-fiction fame. Finally . . . I was accepted as a major figure in the field." And yet he does not feel that the story is the best ever written; he doesn't even think it's the best that he's ever written. He lists three of his own short stories that he believes are better: "The Last Question," "The Bicentennial Man," and "The Ugly Little Boy." However, as he readily concedes in response to an incident described in his autobiography in which he argues an interpretation of his work delivered by a lecturer, "it became clear to me that there might well be more in a story than an author was aware of." If reader response and expert opinion are valid indicators, then "Nightfall" may be a case in point.

Asimov's first nonfiction book was a medical text entitled *Biochemistry and Human Metabolism,* begun in 1950 and written in collaboration with William Boyd and Burnham Walker, two of his colleagues at the Boston University School of Medicine. The project was Boyd's idea, and he asked Asimov, who was an instructor in biochemistry at the time, to be his co-author. Asimov, however, was working for Walker and was unable to take part in the project without his approval. When they approached Walker with the idea, he was sufficiently impressed to offer his assistance. Each of them wrote one-third of the 300,000-word text, and Asimov did the extremely detailed indexing. Although the book appears to have been fairly successful, Asimov was not terribly happy working on it, nor is he particularly satisfied with the text itself. "For one thing," he writes in *In Memory Yet Green,* "Walker and I were antithetical in style. I wanted to be chatty, colloquial, and dramatic; Walker wanted to be terse, formal, and cold. More often than not, Boyd sided with Walker, and it was not long before it seemed to me the textbook was more trouble than it was worth." He also comments that "the fact is that the textbook was a distressing failure. . . . Just about the time it came out, two other new biochemistry texts appeared. . . . Each was longer and better than ours. And even if the two competitors had not appeared on the scene, ours just wasn't good enough."

It did, however, launch Asimov into the field of nonfiction. He had recognized his ability as an explainer early in life, and he enjoyed clarifying scientific principles for his family and friends; he also discovered that he was a most able and entertaining lecturer who delighted in his work as a teacher. He told *New York Times* interviewer Israel Shenker that his talent lies in the fact that he "can read a dozen dull books and make one interesting book out of them." He also said: "I'm on fire to explain, and happiest when it's something reasonably intricate which I can make clear step by step. It's the easiest way I can clarify things in my own mind." The result is that Asimov has been phenomenally successful as a writer of science books for the general public.

He has invited his readers, adults and children, into the realms of chemistry, biology, physics, mathematics, astronomy, technology, and more in books such as *The Chemicals of Life, Only a Trillion, Great Ideas of Science, Quasar, Quasar, Burning Bright, Robots: Machines in Man's Image,* and *The Subatomic Monster.* Asimov's "strategy for explaining complex material better than any other person emerges as a simple method for luring laymen into subjects they can't fundamentally understand and making them think they do," observes Ray Sokolov in the *New York Times Book Review. New York Review of Books* contributor Martin Gardner commends Asimov's "unfailing clarity, humor, informality, and enthusiasm. Like all top science-fiction writers he knows exactly where to draw the line between serious science and fantasy." Alfred Bester characterizes him as "the finest popular science writer working today, and in my opinion . . . the finest who has ever written; prolific, encyclopedic, witty, with a gift for colorful and illuminating examples and explanations."

In recent years, Asimov has continued to produce science popularizations; he has also taken on the responsibility of editing several science fiction anthologies. Yet, perhaps more significant to his numerous fans, he has resumed writing science fiction novels after a ten-year break. During his hiatus, distanced from his imaginative worlds, the author was able to reconsider them and come to a new understanding of his fiction. "As Asimov has said," writes Gene Deweese in the *Science Fiction Review,* "his robot series, his Empire stories and his Foundation series have, to his own surprise, turned out to be three parts of a single series." With this in mind, Asimov has in his recent novels ventured to fill gaps and build bridges between his three major cycles and thereby unite his future history. Much of the critical debate surrounding his new work focuses on this unification attempt and whether or not it succeeds without damaging the integrity of his earlier works.

In *Foundation's Edge,* Asimov resumes his story of the two Foundations. One hundred twenty years have passed, and as E. F. Bleiler notes in the *Washington Post Book World,* "a crisis is at hand." Councilmen in each Foundation independently discover that "the Seldon Plan is working better than it theoretically should. This is disastrous, for it indicates the presence of outside manipulators, who must have their own aims and purposes," adds Bleiler. From opposite ends of the galaxy, the two set out to prove the existence of a manipulative power. For a majority of the first Foundation council, however, Golan Trevize and his companion—a professor in search of man's mythical origin, Earth—are simply bait to lure the Second Foundation into the open to be destroyed.

"Like the trilogy," writes Mary Ellen Burns in the *Nation,* "*Foundation's Edge* explores the nature of free will and the question of historical determinism." And it does so in Asimov's characteristic style. "In style [this novel] belongs to the 1940s—not simply to science fiction's 1940s but to Asimov's 1940s," comments James Gunn in the *Fantasy Newsletter.* "It is no novel of character . . . but a discursive novel of ideas, much like the rest of the Foundation stories." To Darrell Schweitzer, writing in the *Science Fiction Review,* this style is seen in "the scenes . . . of people sitting in nearly featureless rooms talking about the Big Situation. . . . There is little sense of place."

Asimov's storytelling technique weakens *Foundation's Edge,* according to Brian Stableford in the *Science Fiction and Fantasy Book Review:* "Asimovian characters always spend a lot of time sitting around discussing their situation, but never before has their discussion been so obsessively concerned with the issue of whether things are as they appear and, if not, what might hypothetically lie hidden within the web of appearance." In another *Science Fiction and Fantasy Book Review* article, Donald M. Hassler offers a different perspective. As he sees it, "all possibilities are carefully weighed, including the weighing of possibilities itself, before the next action is undertaken; and the whole piece orchestrates beautifully to hold the reader in suspense till the several strands of plot climax with a final question." Moreover, Gunn suggests that the characters' obsession with what is hidden behind appearances is crucial to the novel's development. He maintains that "the suspense of the novel is sustained by repeated examples of motivations within motivations, wheels within wheels." And finally, in his opinion, "the motivation-behind-motivation method is appropriate to the subject of the novel. When psychological control of people's actions and even of people's thought occurs, the hiding—and questioning—of motivation is natural."

A criticism often leveled against this sequel to the "Foundation" trilogy is that it does not complement its predecessors. "*Foundation's Edge* starts off promisingly . . . but ultimately loses itself in an overly elaborate plot," writes Burns. In her estimation, Asimov "has tampered too much with his basic material; [this novel] destroys the harmony and balance of the theme the trilogy so elegantly set up and played out." Stableford goes further, stating "it devalues by its existence the three books to which it is a belated sequel." Even Gunn, in his review, notes the differences between the sequel and the original series: "*Foundation's Edge* alters the message of the Trilogy—the message that rationality is the only human trait that can be trusted and that it will, if permitted to do so, come up with the correct solution. . . . In the new novel, however, Asimov has allowed to creep in (or purposefully has included) a significant element of mysticism."

On the other hand are critics who believe *Foundation's Edge* does live up to the standard Asimov set in the original books. "It is the first true novel in the Foundation series, the other volumes being filled with linked novelettes and novellas," observes Schweitzer. "Aside from structural differences, however, Asimov has been completely successful in recapturing the feel of the earlier books." And in the opinion of Gerald Jonas, contributor to the *New York Times Book Review,* "[Asimov] writes much better than he did 33 years ago—yet has lost none of the verve that he brought to his series when he and the galaxy were much younger."

Bleiler believes that not only has Asimov matched the accomplishment of the "Foundation" trilogy, he has surpassed it. "*Foundation's Edge* reveals many improvements over the earlier work," the reviewer writes. "The ideas are better worked out; the plotting is better; the writing is superior; and Asimov has outgrown his tendency to trick endings that didn't always work. Instead of good guys and bad guys, we now find credible motivations like arrogance, ambition, suspicion, and feelings of insecurity—all of which take form in manipulation." Schweitzer too praises Asimov's effort, commenting: "I was surprised at how enormously, almost compulsively readable this book was, when it followed none of the usual rules of dramatic storytelling." "Rare is the author who can resume a story after a pause of three decades," concludes Peter Stoler in *Time,* "but Asimov has never been predictable in anything but fecundity. This is his 260th book and one of his best."

Robots of Dawn extends and expands Asimov's robot novels toward the more distant future and toward his stories of the galactic empire. In the novel, Elijah Baley and his robot companion, R. Daneel Olivaw, are faced with a new mystery. This time they travel to Aurora, the planet on which Daneel was created, to investigate the murder of his only robotic equal. As Stableford points out in another *Science Fiction and Fantasy Book Review* article, the novel also "deals with a pivotal point in history: will the empty galaxy be settled by men from Earth, who will crowd the worlds with their shortlived kind and keep their machines in their place; or will it be settled by humaniform robots . . . dispatched . . . to build utopias which men might later use?"

The Robots of Dawn is another novel of ideas. "Asimov is . . . addressing real problems about the interaction of humans with artificial intelligences," notes John Sladek in the *Washington Post Book World.* "He may even be raising real ethical and social questions which will need answers 20 years hence. But because he chooses to bury it all in a humdrum whodunit, retrieving the message (if any) is just not worth it." Stableford believes that its flaws lie in that "much of what happens in it, and much of what is said and done by the characters, is not directed towards any internal purpose of the plot, but rather establishing coherency between this story and earlier robot stories, and between those stories and the Foundation series."

Among those with a positive analysis of the novel is a *Publishers Weekly* reviewer who admits that "Asimov's narrative technique is more dependent than ever on dialogue, but his plotting is as ingenious as always. The mystery unravels with the polished logical precision of a robot's program." *Science Fiction Review* contributor Karl Edd concurs: "As usual with Asimov there are long passages of dialog . . . and intellectual dissection of ideas, paradoxes . . . and zero base contradictions. . . . Asimov's method is never boring, usually entertaining, and always thought-provoking." With *The Robots of Dawn,* Edd concludes, Asimov has "produced the proper blend—the humor of a Jewish elf, Yankee wit, word conundrums, mental boxing practice, a bit of mind-bending, a story and a learning experience."

Asimov's third science fiction novel of the 1980s provides a bridge between his near future and far future histories. As James and Eugene Sloan put it in their *Chicago Tribune Book World* review, " 'Robots and Empire'. . . extends and unites Isaac Asimov's Robot and Foundation trilogies, pushing robots to the forefront both as characters and as vehicles for asking philosophical questions." Central to the book are Daneel and his new companion, another robot called Giskard Reventlow. "This circumstance allows Mr. Asimov to examine, in greater depth than ever before, the strengths and limitations of his Three Laws of Robotics," observes Jonas in another *New York Times Book Review* article.

The growing tension between Spacers, the original galactic explorers, and the Settlers trekking out from Earth engages the attention of the two robots. They reach the conclusion that "in order to obey their elevated concept of the First Law enjoining robots to aid humans, they must manipulate the societies within their purview, so that the vital expanding Settlers can win the

coming conflict, but peacefully," relates John Clute in the *Washington Post Book World.* Building on this, observes Jonas, "Mr. Asimov [has] once again turned an ethical dilemma into the basis of an exciting novel of suspense." "The writing [in this novel] is typical smooth Asimov, in some ways his most visual and emotionally evocative novel yet," indicates Elton T. Elliott in the *Science Fiction Review.* Adds Robert A. Collins in the *Fantasy Review:* "*Robots and Empire* is both entertaining and significant within the author's canon."

With the addition of these three recent novels plus *Foundation and Earth,* the sequel to *Foundation's Edge,* Asimov's future history now comprises sixteen books. Having closed old gaps and provided new links, the author can trace the possible changes to come from a near future into a distant future. In fact, according to Marjorie Mithoff Miller, writing in her book *Isaac Asimov,* "one of the major functions of science fiction for Asimov is to accustom its readers to the idea of change." Asimov explains to Schweitzer in *Science Fiction Voices 5* that contrary to the belief of some, science fiction "isn't intended to predict. . . . The only thing that [it] predicts is that the future is going to be different from the present, and that will always come true."

"In contemplating the possible futures presented in science fiction," continues Miller, "the reader is forced to recognize and accept the idea that things will change, and he is helped to surrender some of his traditional human passion for the status quo. Asimov sees this as a real benefit to our society, as we try to plan and implement the changes that will do the most good for humanity." Two areas in which Asimov has recently been campaigning for change are population control and space exploration. Each, he believes, will influence significantly which future comes to pass.

"My feeling is that the chance of our surviving into the twenty-first century as a working civilization is less than fifty percent but greater than zero," he tells Charles Platt in *Dream Makers: The Uncommon People Who Write Science Fiction.* "There are several items, each one of which is sufficient to do us in. Number one is the population problem." Another of his concerns is the militarization of space proposed in the Strategic Defense Initiative or "Star Wars" defense. As William J. Broad relates in the *New York Times,* Asimov "recently quit the board of governors of the L-5 Society, a space lobbying organization, because it would not take a firm stand against missile defense." Instead, Asimov advocates peaceful space colonization. One reason, he explains to Schweitzer, is that "we will have people living on a multiplicity of worlds so that if anything happens to any one of them, even to Earth, mankind will continue."

As Bester suggests in his interview with the author, Asimov, as a result of his broad knowledge and his ability to handle fiction and nonfiction with equal proficiency, "comes close to the ideal of the Renaissance Man." Brian Patten of *Books and Bookmen* dubs Asimov "the father of modern science fiction," explaining that "while others have invented supermen, supergods and superbeasts, he has remained basically a conservative author. While they have prophesised he has speculated and as a practising scientist has moved with caution, examining what is possible rather than what is fanciful. Yet still his Foundation trilogy is praised as being the corner-stone of that most fanciful craft, as being the point where it grew up. And if growing up means shedding one's belief in the utterly impossible, of losing innocence, then yes, he helped science fiction grow up." Fellow s.f. writer Theodore Sturgeon, in a *New York Times Book Review* article, concludes that "Asimov has achieved a unique status, for not only is he admired and, by many, loved for his work in s.f. and his engrossing regular science column in the *Magazine of Fantasy and Science Fiction,* but he is equally respected by professionals in some 20-odd scientific disciplines. He has become the perfect and the most inclusive interface between hard science (including math) and the layman, for he has a genius for bringing the obscure into the light."

MEDIA ADAPTATIONS: A sound recording of William Shatner reading the first eight chapters of *Foundation* was produced as *Foundation: The Psychohistorians,* Caedmon, 1976, and of Asimov reading from the same novel was produced as *The Mayors,* Caedmon, 1977; the film, "The Ugly Little Boy," from a short story of the same title, was produced by Learning Corporation of America, 1977.

BIOGRAPHICAL/CRITICAL SOURCES:

BOOKS

Asimov, Isaac, *The Bicentennial Man and Other Stories,* Doubleday, 1976.

Asimov, Isaac, *In Memory Yet Green: The Autobiography of Isaac Asimov, 1920-1954,* Doubleday, 1979.

Asimov, Isaac, *In Joy Still Felt: The Autobiography of Isaac Asimov, 1954-1979,* Doubleday, 1980.

Clareson, Thomas D., editor, *Voices for the Future: Essays on Major Science Fiction Writers,* Popular Press, 1976.

Contemporary Literary Criticism, Gale, Volume 1, 1973, Volume 3, 1975, Volume 9, 1978, Volume 19, 1981, Volume 26, 1983.

Dictionary of Literary Biography, Volume 8: *Twentieth-Century American Science Fiction Writers,* Gale, 1981.

Fiedler, Jean, and Jim Mele, *Isaac Asimov,* Ungar, 1982.

Greenberg, Marfin H., and Joseph D. Olander, editors, *Isaac Asimov,* Taplinger, 1977.

Gunn, James, *Isaac Asimov: The Foundations of Science Fiction,* Oxford University Press, 1982.

Miller, Marjorie Mithoff, *Isaac Asimov: A Checklist of Works Published in the United States,* Kent State University Press, 1972.

Patrouch, Joseph F., Jr., *The Science Fiction of Isaac Asimov,* Doubleday, 1974.

Platt, Charles, *Dream Makers: The Uncommon People Who Write Science Fiction,* Berkley Publishing, 1980.

Schweitzer, Darrell, *Science Fiction Voices 5,* Borgo Press, 1981.

Slusser, George E., *Isaac Asimov: The Foundations of His Science Fiction,* Borgo Press, 1979.

Wollheim, Donald A., *The Universe Makers,* Harper, 1971.

PERIODICALS

Books and Bookmen, July, 1968, February, 1969, July, 1973.

Chicago Tribune Book World, March 4, 1979, January 19, 1986.

Chicago Tribune Magazine, April 30, 1978.

Fantasy Newsletter, April, 1983.

Fantasy Review, September, 1985.

Globe and Mail (Toronto), August 10, 1985.

Magazine of Fantasy and Science Fiction, October, 1966, September, 1980.

Nation, March 5, 1983.

New York Review of Books, September 12, 1977, October 24, 1985.

New York Times, October 18, 1969, January 1, 1980, December 17, 1984, February 26, 1985.

New York Times Book Review, November 17, 1968, January 28, 1973, January 12, 1975, May 30, 1976, June 25, 1978, February 25, 1979, December 16, 1979, December 19, 1982, October 20, 1985.

Publishers Weekly, April 17, 1972, September 2, 1983.

Science Fiction and Fantasy Book Review, December, 1982, June, 1983, November, 1983.

Science Fiction Review, winter, 1982, spring, 1984, winter, 1985.

Time, February 26, 1979, November 15, 1982.

Times Literary Supplement, October 5, 1967, December 28, 1967.

Washington Post, April 4, 1979.

Washington Post Book World, April 1, 1979, May 25, 1980, September 26, 1982, September 27, 1983, August 25, 1985.

SOUND RECORDINGS

Isaac Asimov Talks: An Interview, Writer's Voice, 1974.

*   *   *

ASTURIAS, Miguel Angel   1899-1974

PERSONAL: Surname pronounced "As-*too*-ree-ahs"; born October 19, 1899, in Guatemala City, Guatemala; stripped of Guatemalan citizenship and forced into exile in Argentina, 1954; Guatemalan citizenship restored, 1966; died June 9, 1974, in Madrid, Spain; son of Ernesto (a supreme court magistrate, later an importer) and Maria (Rosales) Asturias; married Clemencia Amado; married second wife, Blanca Mora y Araujo; children: Rodrigo, Miguel Angel. *Education:* Universidad de San Carlos de Guatemala, Doctor of Laws, 1923; attended the Sorbonne, University of Paris, 1923-28.

CAREER: Diplomat and writer. Left Guatemala for political reasons, 1923; European correspondent for Central American and Mexican newspapers, 1923-32; returned to Guatemala, 1933; founded and worked as broadcaster for radio program "El Diario del Aire" and worked as a journalist, c. 1933-42; elected deputy to Guatemalan national congress, 1942; member of Guatemalan diplomatic service, 1945-54, cultural attache to Mexico, 1946-47, and to Argentina, 1947-51, minister-counselor to Argentina, 1951-52, diplomat in Paris, 1952-53, ambassador to El Salvador, 1953-54; correspondent for Venezuelan newspaper *El Nacional* and adviser to Editorial Losada publishers in Argentina, 1954-62; member of cultural exchange program Columbianum in Italy, 1962; Guatemalan ambassador to France, 1966-70. Co-founder of Universidad Popular de Guatemala (a free evening college), 1921, and of Associacion de Estudiantes Universitarios (Unionist party group).

MEMBER: International PEN.

AWARDS, HONORS: Premio Galvez for dissertation, and Chavez Prize, both 1923; Prix Sylla Monsegur, 1931, for *Leyendas de Guatemala;* Prix du Meilleur Roman Etranger, 1952, for *El senor presidente;* International Lenin Peace Prize from U.S.S.R., 1966, for *Viento fuerte, El papa verde,* and *Los ojos de los enterrados;* Nobel Prize for literature from Swedish Academy, 1967.

WRITINGS:

POETRY

Rayito de estrella (title means "Little Starbeam"), privately printed, 1925.

Emulo lipolidon, Typografia America (Guatemala), 1935.

Anoche, 10 de marzo de 1543, Ediciones del Aire (Guatemala), 1943.

Poesia sien de alondra, preface by Alfonso Reyes, Argos (Buenos Aires), 1949.

Ejercicios poeticos en forma de soneto sobre temas de Horacio, Botella al Mar (Buenos Aires), 1951.

Bolivar, El Salvador (San Salvador), 1955.

Nombre custodio, e imagen pasajera, La Habana, 1959.

Clarivigilia primaveral (anthology), Losada (Buenos Aires), 1965.

Also author of *Fantomina,* 1935, *Sonetos,* 1936, *Alclasan,* 1939, *Fantomina,* 1940, and *Con el rehen en los dientes,* 1946.

NOVELS

El senor presidente, Costa-Amic (Mexico), 1946, critical edition, Editions Klincksieck (Paris), 1978, translation by Frances Partridge published as *The President,* Gollancz, 1963, published as *El Senor Presidente,* Atheneum, 1964 (also see below).
Hombres de maiz, Losada, 1949, reprinted, 1968, translation by Gerald Martin published as *Men of Maize,* Delacorte, 1975.
Viento fuerte (first volume in "Banana Trilogy"), Ministerio de Educacion Publica (Guatemala), 1950, translation by Darwin Flakoll and Claribel Alegria published as *The Cyclone,* Owen, 1967, translation by Gregory Rabassa published as *Strong Wind,* Delacorte, 1968.
El papa verde (second volume in "Banana Trilogy"), Losada, 1954, reprinted, 1973, translation by Rabassa published as *The Green Pope,* Delacorte, 1971.
Los ojos de los enterrados (third volume in "Banana Trilogy"), Losada, 1960, translation by Rabassa published as *The Eyes of the Interred,* Delacorte, 1973.
Mulata de tal, Losada, 1963, translation by Rabassa published as *Mulata,* Delacorte, 1967 (published in England as *The Mulatta and Mr. Fly,* Owen, 1967).

PLAYS

Soluna: Comedia prodigiosa en dos jornados y un final, Ediciones Losange (Buenos Aires), 1955 (also see below).
La audiencia de los confines: Cronica en tres andanzas, Ariadna (Buenos Aires), 1957 (also see below).
Teatro: Chantaje, Dique seco, Soluna, La audiencia de los confines (collected plays), Losada, 1964.

OTHER

(Translator with J. M. Gonzalez de Mendoza) *Anales de los xahil de los indios cakchiqueles,* c. 1925, 2nd edition, Tipografia Nacional, 1967.
(Translator from the French with Gonzalez de Mendoza) Georges Raynaud, *Los dioses, los heroes y los hombres de Guatemala antigua, o, el libro del consejo, Popol-vuh de los indios quiches,* Paris-America (Paris), 1927, 2nd edition published as *Popul-vuh, o libro del consejo de los indios quiches,* Losada, 1969.
La arquitectura de la vida nueva (lectures; title means "The Building of a New Life"), Goubaud, 1928.
Leyendas de Guatemala (collection of Indian tales), preface by Paul Valery, Ediciones Oriente (Madrid), 1930, reprinted, Losada, 1957 (also see below).
Weekend en Guatemala (short stories), Goyanarte (Buenos Aires), 1956.
(Editor) *Poesia precolombina* (collection of Aztec and Mayan poetry), Fabril (Buenos Aires), 1960.
(With Jean Mazon and F. Diez de Medina) *Bolivia: An Undiscovered Land,* translated by Frances Hogarth-Gaute, Harrap, 1961.
El alhajadito (poem and children's stories), Goyanarte, 1961, translation by Martin Shuttleworth published as *The Bejeweled Boy,* Doubleday, 1971 (also see below).
(Editor) *Paginas de Ruben Dario,* Universitaria de Buenos Aires, 1963.
Rumania, su nueva imagen, Universidad Veracruzana, 1964.

Juan Girador, Centre de Recherches de l'Institut d'Etudes Hispaniques, 1964.
El espejo de Lida Sal, Siglo Veintiuno Editores (Mexico), 1967.
(Translator from the Rumanian) *Antologia de la prosa rumana,* Losada, 1967.
Latinoamerica y otros ensayos, Guadiana de Publicaciones (Madrid), 1968.
(With Pablo Neruda) *Comiendo en Hungria* (poems and sketches), Lumen (Barcelona), 1969, translation by Barna Balogh revised by Mary Arias and published as *Sentimental Journey around the Hungarian Cuisine,* Corvina (Budapest), 1969.
Maladron: Epopeya de los Andes verdes, Losada, 1969.
Hector Poleo, Villand & Golanis (Paris), 1969.
The Talking Machine (juvenile), translated by Beverly Koch, Doubleday, 1971.
Viernes de dolores, Losada, 1972.
America: Fabula de fabulas y otros ensayos (essays), compiled with preface by Richard J. Callan, Monte Avila (Caracas), 1972.
Sociologia guatemalteca: El problema social del indio, (dual language edition, including original Spanish text followed by English text titled *Guatemalan Sociology: The Social Problem of the Indian*), English translation by Maureen Ahern, introduction by Callan, Arizona State University Center for Latin American Studies, 1977.
Tres de cuatro soles, preface by Marcel Bataillon, introduction and notes by Dorita Nouhaud, Fondo de Cultura Economica (Madrid), 1977.
Sinceridades (essays), edited by Epaminondas Quintana, Academica Centroamericana (Guatemala), 1980.
El hombre que lo tenia todo, todo, todo, illustrations by Jacqueline Duheme, Bruguera (Barcelona), 1981.
Viajes, ensayos y fantasias (selected articles), Losada, 1981.

Founder of periodical *Tiempos Nuevos,* 1923; contributor to periodicals.

Work collected in omnibus volumes, including *Obras escogidas,* Aguilar (Madrid), 1955; *Obras completas,* three volumes, Aguilar, 1967; *Antologia de Miguel Angel Asturias,* edited by Pablo Palomina, Costa-Amic, 1968; *Miguel Angel Asturias: Semblanza para el estudio de su vida y obra, con una seleccion de poemas y prosas,* Cultural Centroamericana Libreria Proa (Guatemala), 1968; *El problema social del indio y otros textos,* edited by Claude Couffon, Centre de Recherches de l'Institut d'Etudes Hispaniques, 1971; *Novelas y cuentos de juventud,* edited by Couffon, Centre de Recherches de l'Institut d'Etudes Hispaniques, 1971; *Mi mejor obra,* Organizacion Editorial Novaro (Mexico), 1973, reissued as *Lo mejor de mi obra,* 1974; *Tres obras* (includes *Leyendas de Guatemala, El alhajadito,* and *El senor presidente*), introduction by Arturo Uslar Pietri, notes by Giuseppe Bellini, Biblioteca Ayacucho (Caracas), 1977.

SIDELIGHTS: Guatemalan statesman and Nobel laureate Miguel Angel Asturias is best known for the novels *El senor presidente,* about a Latin American dictator, and *Hombres de maiz,* about the conflicts between Guatemalan native Indians and land-exploiting farmers, as well as for a trilogy of novels about the Latin American banana industry. His writing—an extensive canon of fiction, essays, and poetry—often blends Indian myth and folklore with surrealism and satiric social commentary, and is considered to evidence his compassion for those unable to escape political or economic domination. "My work," Asturias promised when he accepted the 1967 Nobel Prize for literature, "will continue to reflect the voice of the peoples, gathering their myths and popular beliefs and at the same time seeking to give birth to a universal consciousness of Latin American problems."

Asturias was born in 1899 in Guatemala City, Guatemala, just one year after the country succumbed to the dictatorship of Manuel Estrada Cabrera. Asturias's father, a supreme court magistrate, lost his position in 1903, when he refused to convict students who protested against Estrada Cabrera's totalitarian regime. Consequently, Asturias's family was forced to leave the city for a rural area in Guatemala, where the young Asturias's interest in his country's Indian and peasant customs perhaps originated. Although his family returned to Guatemala City four years later, Asturias had nonetheless suffered the first of the many personal disruptions that autocracy and political unrest would cause throughout his career.

After attending secondary school, Asturias entered the Universidad de San Carlos to study law. As a college student, he was politically active, participating in demonstrations that helped to depose Estrada Cabrera and then serving as court secretary at the dictator's trial. Asturias also helped to found both a student association of Guatemala's Unionist party and the Universidad Popular de Guatemala, an organization that provided free evening instruction for the country's poor. In 1923, as the military gained strength and Guatemala's political climate worsened, Asturias took his law degree and shortly thereafter founded the weekly newspaper *Tiempos Nuevos,* in which he and several others began publishing articles decrying the new militarist government. Asturias fled the country the same year, his own life in danger after a colleague on the paper's writing staff was assaulted.

Asturias lived for the next five months in London, spending much of his time learning about Mayan Indian culture at the British Museum. He moved then to Paris, where he supported himself for several years as European correspondent for Mexican and Central American newspapers while he studied ancient Central American Indian civilizations at the Sorbonne. There he completed a dissertation on Mayan religion and translated sacred Indian texts, including the *Popol-vuh* and the *Anales de los xahil.*

In Paris Asturias also began his literary career. Associating with such avant-garde French poets as Andre Breton and Paul Valery, Asturias was introduced to the techniques and themes of the surrealist literary movement, which would become important elements of his writing style. In 1925 Asturias privately published *Rayito de estrella,* a book of poetry, and later, his *Leyendas de Guatemala,* a critically acclaimed collection of Indian stories and legends recalled from childhood, garnered him the 1931 Prix Sylla Monsegur.

Asturias returned to Guatemala in 1933 after further travel in Europe and the Middle East. He spent the next ten years working as a journalist and poet while Guatemala operated under the military dictatorship of Jorge Ubico Casteneda. He also founded and worked as a broadcaster for the radio program "El Diario del Aire," and between 1935 and 1940, he published several more volumes of poetry, including *Emulo lipolidon, Sonetos, Alclasan,* and *Fantomina.* Asturias first entered politics in 1942 with his election as deputy to the Guatemalan national congress. Three years later, after the fall of the Casteneda regime and the installation of the new president, Juan Jose Arevalo, Asturias joined the Guatemalan diplomatic service. The more liberal policies of the new government proved important for the author, both politically and artistically. Under Arevalo's rule, Asturias served in several ambassadorial posts in Mexico and Argentina from the early 1940s until 1952. In addition, the more tolerant

atmosphere made it possible for Asturias to publish his first novel, *El senor presidente,* in 1946.

Asturias began writing *El senor presidente* while he was a law student at San Carlos University. Based on his own and others' memories of the Estrada Cabrera administration, the novel was first conceived as a short story about a ruthless dictator—reportedly Estrada Cabrera himself—and his schemes to dispose of a political adversary in an unnamed Latin American country usually identified as Guatemala. Asturias had developed the story through numerous revisions into a novel and completed it in the early 1930s, when publication of the book under Ubico Casteneda's rule would have been too dangerous.

Translated as *The President* in 1968, *El senor presidente* was acclaimed for portraying both totalitarian government and its damaging psychological effects. Drawing from his experiences as a journalist writing under repressive conditions, Asturias employed such literary devices as satire to convey the government's transgressions and used surrealistic dream sequences to demonstrate the police state's impact on the individual psyche. Asturias also made use of colloquial Latin American dialogue to render realistically the varying perspectives of the country's social classes. Asturias's stance against all forms of injustice in Guatemala caused critics to view the author as a compassionate spokesman for the oppressed. "Asturias . . . does not see the drama of his people from the outside, as a dilettante, . . . but from the inside, as a participant," noted *Les Temps Modernes* contributor Manuel Tunon de Lara, for example. And a *Times Literary Supplement* review, also commenting on Asturias's success in portraying the country's unique political circumstances, asserted that *El senor presidente* presents "Latin American problems according to their merits and not according to preconceived stereotypes."

Proclaimed by *Los Angeles Times Book Review* contributor Eduardo Galeano as "the best novel about dictators ever written in Latin America," *El senor presidente* especially elicited praise for its representation of severe political repression. Critics expressing this view included T. B. Irving, who wrote in the *Inter-American Review of Bibliography* that Asturias "has achieved in a splendid manner a grotesque and almost asphyxiating conception of the total state." "Asturias leaves no doubt about what it is like to be tortured, or what it is like to work for a man who is both omnipotent and depraved," applauded the *Times Literary Supplement* reviewer. "When the reader puts down the novel," Irving remarked, "he does so with a feeling of compassion and, at the same time, relief that he has not had to live through similar circumstances."

Three years after the publication of *El senor presidente,* while serving as Guatemalan cultural attache in Buenos Aires, Argentina, Asturias completed and published *Hombres de Maiz,* the first of his novels explicitly to evoke the mythology of his country's ancient past. Translated as *Men of Maize* in 1975, the book abandons *El senor presidente*'s satiric approach for a poetic, surrealistic treatment of the struggle between the Guatemalan *indigenista,* or highland Indians, and the *ladinos,* peasants who, much like their conquering Spanish ancestors, attempt to usurp Indian territory in order to raise commercial corn crops. The story unfolds from the point of view of the *indigenista,* whose ancient beliefs teach that the first human was made from corn and that the grain is therefore sacred and must be grown only for tribal use. When their resistance leader, Gaspar Ilom, is assassinated, the Indians place a curse on their enemies, beginning a series of events that becomes part of the Indian mythological heritage. According to Joseph Sommers in the *Journal of Inter-*

American Studies, "the reader sees briefly . . . the concrete situation which gives rise to myth. Then . . . he witnesses the formation of legends, as the novel traces their spread and elaboration into full-fledged folklore."

While *Men of Maize* was coolly received at the time of its publication in 1949, many critics have come to view the work as Asturias's masterpiece—his most successful integration of the social and the artistic. Reviewers especially admired the author's portrayal of the contrasting *indigenista* and *ladino* conceptions of the world. "At one level," noted *Washington Post Book World* reviewer Patrick Breslin, the book is "symbolic of the Spanish conquest itself. The social and economic order violently introduced by the Spanish four and a half centuries ago is still tenuous, not only in the highlands of Guatemala, but throughout the Andes of South America as well." Other readers, such as Sommers, who criticized what he saw as the author's "baroque profusion of imagery" and frequent use of "expressive but difficult localism," praised Asturias's surrealistic combination of myth and reality as an original and insightful portrait of Indian attitudes. *Men of Maize,* Sommers explained, "transcends the former stereotype of superficial realism and frequently elementary social protest."

During his diplomatic assignments in Argentina, Asturias also worked on what has come to be known to English-speaking readers as his "Banana Trilogy"—three novels about the Latin American banana industry. Consisting of *Viento fuerte, El papa verde,* and *Los ojos de los enterrados,* the trilogy focuses on the conflicts between the labor force in an unidentified country (taken again by critics to be Guatemala), and Tropical Banana, Inc., a North American conglomerate commonly accepted as a portrait of the real-life United Fruit Company. *Viento fuerte,* translated as *The Strong Wind,* relates the attempts of the main character, former Tropical Banana official Lester Mead, to bring about cooperation between the native growers and the company by urging fairness over profit. *El papa verde,* the second volume of the trilogy translated as *The Green Pope,* depicts Mead's continued and ultimately unsuccessful efforts to convince the head of Tropical Banana—the "Green Pope"—to offer banana growers a stable market and fairer prices for their crops. The final novel, *Los ojos de los enterrados,* translated as *The Eyes of the Interred,* deals with the spread of the banana industry's turmoil into the political arena through a general strike that helps depose the country's president. Although the "Banana Trilogy" was not as critically acclaimed as either *El senor presidente* or *Hombres de maiz,* it earned Asturias the International Lenin Peace Prize from the Soviet Union, who honored the works' stance against capitalist imperialism.

Working for the government of Arevalo's successor Jacobo Arbenz Guzman in 1953, Asturias was sent as Guatemalan ambassador to El Salvador to try to prevent El Salvadorean rebels from invading Guatemala. Although he had enlisted the El Salvadorean government's aid, the rebels, with backing from the United States, nonetheless invaded Guatemala and overthrew Arbenz Guzman. Because of his support for the defeated leader, Asturias was stripped of his citizenship and exiled in 1954. Asturias later incorporated details from these El Salvadorean events in his 1956 collection of stories titled *Weekend en Guatemala.*

Asturias lived in exile, working in Argentina as a journalist for the Caracas, Venezuela, newspaper *El Nacional* until 1962, when he traveled to Italy as part of a cultural exchange program. During this period he continued to write, completing scholarly studies and publishing lectures, children's stories, and another novel, *Mulata de tal.* Asturias did not recover his Guatemalan citizenship until the election of president Cesar Mendes Montenegro's moderate government in 1966, when he accepted a job as French ambassador, the position in which he remained until 1970. Throughout his life of service and exile, Asturias remained committed to exposing through his writing the injustice and oppression plaguing his fellow Guatemalans. For his efforts, he was awarded the 1967 Nobel Prize for literature. "Latin American literature is still a literature of combat," Asturias once declared, as quoted by Robert G, Mead, Jr., in the *Saturday Review.* "The novel is the only means I have of making the needs and aspirations of my people known to the world."

MEDIA ADAPTATIONS: El senor presidente was made into a film of the same title by Imago Producciones, Argentina.

BIOGRAPHICAL/CRITICAL SOURCES:

BOOKS

Anderson-Imbert, Enrique, *Spanish American Literature: A History,* translation by John V. Falconiere, Wayne State University Press, 1963.

Callan, Richard, *Miguel Angel Asturias,* Twayne, 1970.

Contemporary Literary Criticism, Gale, Volume 3, 1975, Volume 8, 1978, Volume 13, 1980.

Dardon, Hugo Cerezo, editor, *Coloquio con Miguel Angel Asturias,* Universitario, 1968.

Miquel Angel Asturias en la literatura, Istmo (Guatemala), 1969.

Meyer, Doris, *Lives on the Line: The Testimony of Contemporary Latin American Authors,* University of California Press, 1988.

PERIODICALS

Inter-American Review of Bibliography, April-June, 1965.

Journal of Inter-American Studies, April, 1964.

Les Temps Modernes, November, 1954.

Los Angeles Times Book Review, May 28, 1989.

New Statesman, October 25, 1963, September 29, 1967, April 22, 1988.

New York Review of Books, May 22, 1969.

New York Times, October 20, 1967, January 2, 1971, June 10, 1974.

New York Times Book Review, November 19, 1967, January 26, 1979.

Saturday Review, January 25, 1969.

Times Literary Supplement, October 18, 1963, September 28, 1967, November 19, 1971.

Washington Post Book World, August 17, 1975.

OBITUARIES:

PERIODICALS

Newsweek, June 24, 1974.

New York Times, June 10, 1974.

Time, June 24, 1974.

Washington Post, June 10, 1974.

—*Sketch by Emily J. McMurray*

*   *   *

ATHELING, William
See POUND, Ezra (Weston Loomis)

*   *   *

ATHELING, William, Jr.
See BLISH, James (Benjamin)

ATHERTON, Lucius
See MASTERS, Edgar Lee

*   *   *

ATTICUS
See FLEMING, Ian (Lancaster)

*   *   *

ATWOOD, Margaret (Eleanor)   1939-

PERSONAL: Born November 18, 1939, in Ottawa, Ontario, Canada; daughter of Carl Edmund (an entomologist) and Margaret (Killam) Atwood; married Graeme Gibson (a writer); children: Jess. *Education:* University of Toronto, B.A., 1961; Radcliffe College, A.M., 1962; Harvard University, graduate study, 1962-63, and 1965-67. *Politics:* "William Morrisite." *Religion:* "Immanent Transcendentalist."

ADDRESSES: Agent—Phoebe Larmore, 2814 Third St., Santa Monica, Calif. 90405.

CAREER: Writer. University of British Columbia, Vancouver, lecturer in English literature, 1964-65; Sir George Williams University, Montreal, Quebec, lecturer in English literature, 1967-68; York University, Toronto, Ontario, assistant professor of English literature, 1971-72; House of Anansi Press, Toronto, editor and member of board of directors, 1971-73; University of Toronto, Toronto, writer-in-residence, 1972-73; University of Alabama, Tuscaloosa, writer-in-residence, 1985; New York University, New York, N.Y., Berg Visiting Professor of English, 1986; Macquarie University, North Ryde, Australia, writer-in-residence, 1987.

MEMBER: Amnesty International, Writers' Union of Canada (vice-chairman, 1980-81), Royal Society of Canada (fellow), Canadian Civil Liberties Association (member of board, 1973-75), PEN International, Canadian Centre, American Academy of Arts and Sciences (honorary member), Anglophone (president, 1984-85).

AWARDS, HONORS: E. J. Pratt Medal, 1961, for *Double Persephone;* President's Medal, University of Western Ontario, 1965; YWCA Women of Distinction Award, 1966; Governor General's Award, 1966, for *The Circle Game,* and 1986, for *The Handmaid's Tale;* first prize in Canadian Centennial Commission Poetry Competition, 1967; Union Prize, *Poetry,* 1969; Bess Hoskins Prize, *Poetry,* 1969 and 1974; D.Litt., Trent University, 1973, Concordia University, 1980, Smith College, 1982, University of Toronto, 1983, Mount Holyoke College, 1985, University of Waterloo, 1985, and University of Guelph, 1985; LL.D., Queen's University, 1974; City of Toronto Book Award, 1977; Canadian Booksellers' Association Award, 1977; Periodical Distributors of Canada Short Fiction Award, 1977; St. Lawrence Award for fiction, 1978; Radcliffe Medal, 1980; *Life before Man* named notable book of 1980 by the American Library Association; Molson Award, 1981; Guggenheim fellowship, 1981; named Companion of the Order of Canada, 1981; International Writer's Prize, Welsh Arts Council, 1982; Book of the Year Award, Periodical Distributors of Canada and the Foundation for the Advancement of Canadian Letters, 1983; Ida Nudel Humanitarian Award, 1986; Toronto Arts Award for writing and editing, 1986; *Los Angeles Times* Book Award, 1986, for *The Handmaid's Tale;* named Woman of the Year, *Ms.* magazine, 1986; Arthur C. Clarke Award, 1987; Commonwealth Literature Prize, 1987; Council for the Advancement and Support of Education silver medal, 1987; named *Chatelaine* magazine's Woman of the Year.

WRITINGS:

POEMS

Double Persephone, Hawkshead Press, 1961.
The Circle Game, Cranbrook Academy of Art (Bloomfield Hills, Mich.), 1964, revised edition, Contact Press, 1966.
Kaleidoscopes Baroque: A Poem, Cranbrook Academy of Art, 1965.
Talismans for Children, Cranbrook Academy of Art, 1965.
Speeches for Doctor Frankenstein, Cranbrook Academy of Art, 1966.
The Animals in That Country, Oxford University Press (Toronto), 1968, Atlantic-Little, Brown, 1969.
The Journals of Susanna Moodie, Oxford University Press, 1970.
Procedures for Underground, Atlantic-Little, Brown, 1970.
Power Politics, House of Anansi Press, 1971, Harper, 1973.
You Are Happy, Harper, 1974.
Selected Poems, 1965-1975, Oxford University Press, 1976, Simon & Schuster, 1978.
Marsh Hawk, Dreadnaught, 1977.
Two-Headed Poems, Oxford University Press, 1978, Simon & Schuster, 1981.
Notes Toward a Poem That Can Never Be Written, Salamander Press, 1981.
True Stories, Oxford University Press, 1981, Simon & Schuster, 1982.
Snake Poems, Salamander Press, 1983.
Interlunar, Oxford University Press, 1984.
Selected Poems II: Poems Selected and New, 1976-1986, Oxford University Press, 1986.

Also author of *Expeditions,* 1966, and *What Was in the Garden,* 1969.

NOVELS

The Edible Woman, McClelland & Stewart, 1969, Atlantic-Little, Brown, 1970.
Surfacing, McClelland & Stewart, 1972, Simon & Schuster 1973.
Lady Oracle, Simon & Schuster, 1976.
Life before Man, McClelland & Stewart, 1979, Simon & Schuster, 1980.
Bodily Harm, McClelland & Stewart, 1981, Simon & Schuster, 1982.
Encounters with the Element Man, Ewert, 1982.
Unearthing Suite, Grand Union Press, 1983.
The Handmaid's Tale, McClelland & Stewart, 1985, Houghton, 1986.
Cat's Eye, Doubleday, 1989.

STORY COLLECTIONS

Dancing Girls and Other Stories, McClelland & Stewart, 1977, Simon & Schuster, 1982.
Bluebeard's Egg and Other Stories, McClelland & Stewart, 1983, Fawcett, 1987.
Murder in the Dark: Short Fictions and Prose Poems, Coach House Press, 1983.

OTHER

The Trumpets of Summer (radio play), Canadian Broadcasting Corporation (CBC), 1964.
Survival: A Thematic Guide to Canadian Literature, House of Anansi Press, 1972.
The Servant Girl (teleplay), CBC-TV, 1974.
Days of the Rebels, 1815-1840, Natural Science Library, 1976.
The Poetry and Voice of Margaret Atwood (recording), Caedmon, 1977.

Up in the Tree (juvenile), McClelland & Stewart, 1978.

(Author of introduction) Catherine M. Young, *To See Our World*, GLC Publishers, 1979, Morrow, 1980.

(With Joyce Barkhouse) *Anna's Pet* (juvenile), James Lorimer, 1980.

Snowbird (teleplay), CBC-TV, 1981.

Second Words: Selected Critical Prose, House of Anansi Press, 1982.

(Editor) *The New Oxford Book of Canadian Verse in English*, Oxford University Press, 1982.

(Editor with Robert Weaver) *The Oxford Book of Canadian Short Stories in English*, Oxford University Press, 1986.

(With Peter Pearson) *Heaven on Earth* (teleplay), CBC-TV, 1986.

(Editor) *The Canlit Foodbook*, Totem, 1987.

(Editor with Shannon Ravenal) *The Best American Short Stories, 1989,* Houghton, 1989.

Contributor to anthologies, including *Five Modern Canadian Poets,* 1970, *The Canadian Imagination: Dimensions of a Literary Culture,* Harvard University Press, 1977, and *Women on Women,* 1978; contributor to periodicals, including *Atlantic, Poetry, Kayak, New Yorker, Harper's, New York Times Book Review, Saturday Night, Tamarack Review, Canadian Forum,* and other publications.

MEDIA ADAPTATIONS: The Handmaid's Tale was filmed by Cinecom Entertainment Group, 1990.

SIDELIGHTS: As a poet, novelist, story writer, and essayist, Margaret Atwood holds a unique position in contemporary Canadian literature. Her books have received critical acclaim in the United States, Europe, and her native Canada, and she has been the recipient of numerous literary awards. Ann Marie Lipinski, writing in the *Chicago Tribune,* describes Atwood as "one of the leading literary luminaries, a national heroine of the arts, the *rara avis* of Canadian letters." Atwood's critical popularity is matched by her popularity with readers. She is a frequent guest on Canadian television and radio, her books are best-sellers, and "people follow her on the streets and in stores," as Judy Klemesrud reports in the *New York Times.* Atwood, Roy MacGregor of *Maclean's* explains, "is to Canadian literature as Gordon Lightfoot is to Canadian music, more institution than individual." Atwood's popularity with both critics and the reading public has surprised her. "It's an accident that I'm a successful writer," she tells MacGregor. "I think I'm kind of an odd phenomenon in that I'm a serious writer and I never expected to become a popular one, and I never did anything in order to become a popular one."

Atwood first came to public attention as a poet in the 1960s with her collections *Double Persephone,* winner of the E. J. Pratt Medal, and *The Circle Game,* winner of a Governor General's Award. These two books marked out the terrain which all of Atwood's later poetry would explore. *Double Persephone* concerns "the contrast between the flux of life or nature and the fixity of man's artificial creations," as Linda Hutcheon explains in the *Dictionary of Literary Biography. The Circle Game* takes this opposition further, setting such human constructs as games, literature, and love against the instability of nature. Human constructs are presented as both traps and shelters, the fluidity of nature as both dangerous and liberating. Sherrill Grace, writing in her *Violent Duality: A Study of Margaret Atwood,* sees the central tension in all of Atwood's work as "the pull towards art on one hand and towards life on the other." This tension is expressed in a series of "violent dualities," as Grace terms it. Atwood "is constantly aware of opposites—self/other, subject/ object, male/female, nature/man—and of the need to accept and work within them," Grace explains. "To create, Atwood chooses violent dualities, and her art re-works, probes, and dramatizes the ability to see double."

Linda W. Wagner, writing in *The Art of Margaret Atwood: Essays in Criticism,* believes that in Atwood's poetry "duality [is] presented as separation." This separation leads her characters to be isolated from one another and from the natural world, resulting in their inability to communicate, to break free of exploitative social relationships, or to understand their place in the natural order. "In her early poetry," Gloria Onley writes in the *West Coast Review,* ". . . [Atwood] is acutely aware of the problem of alienation, the need for real human communication and the establishment of genuine human community—real as opposed to mechanical or manipulative; genuine as opposed to the counterfeit community of the body politic." Speaking of *The Circle Game,* Wagner writes that "the personae of those poems never did make contact, never did anything but lament the human condition. . . . Relationships in these poems are sterile if not destructive."

Atwood's sense of desolation, especially evident in her early poems, and her use of frequently violent images, moves Helen Vendler of the *New York Times Book Review* to claim that Atwood has a "sense of life as mostly wounds given and received." Speaking of *The Circle Game* and *Procedures for Underground,* Peter Stevens notes in *Canadian Literature* that both collections contain "images of drowning, buried life, still life, dreams, journeys and returns." In a review of *True Stories* for *Canadian Forum,* Chaviva Hosek states that the poems "range over such topics as murder, genocide, rape, dismemberment, instruments of torture, forms of torture, genital mutilation, abortion, and forcible hysterectomy," although Robert Sward of *Quill and Quire* explains that many reviewers of the book have exaggerated the violence and give "the false impression that all 38 poems . . . are about torture." Yet, Scott Lauder of *Canadian Forum* speaks of "the painful world we have come to expect from Atwood."

Suffering is common for the female characters in Atwood's poems, although they are never passive victims. In more recent works they take active measures to improve their situations. Atwood's poems, Onley states, concern "modern woman's anguish at finding herself isolated and exploited (although also exploiting) by the imposition of a sex role power structure." Speaking to Klemesrud, Atwood explains that her suffering characters come from real life: "My women suffer because most of the women I talk to seem to have suffered." By the early 1970s, this stance had made Atwood into "a cult author to faithful feminist readers," as Lipinski reports. Atwood's popularity in the feminist community was unsought. "I began as a profoundly apolitical writer," she tells Lindsy Van Gelder of *Ms.,* "but then I began to do what all novelists and some poets do: I began to describe the world around me."

Atwood's feminist concerns are evident in her novels as well, particularly in *The Edible Woman, Surfacing, Life before Man, Bodily Harm,* and *The Handmaid's Tale.* These novels feature female characters who are, Klemesrud reports, "intelligent, self-absorbed modern women searching for identity. . . . [They] hunt, split logs, make campfires and become successful in their careers, while men often cook and take care of their households." Like her poems, however, Atwood's novels "are populated by pained and confused people whose lives hold a mirror to both the front page fears—cancer, divorce, violence—and those that persist quietly, naggingly—solitude, loneliness, desperation," Lipinski writes.

The Edible Woman tells the story of Marian McAlpin, a young woman engaged to be married, who rebels against her upcoming marriage. Her fiance seems too stable, too ordinary, and the role of wife too fixed and limiting. Her rejection of marriage is accompanied by her body's rejection of food. Even a spare vegetarian diet cannot be eaten. Eventually Marian bakes a sponge cake in the shape of a woman and feeds it to her fiance because, she explains, "You've been trying to assimilate me." After the engagement is broken, she is able to eat some of the cake herself.

Reaction to *The Edible Woman* was divided, with some reviewers pointing to flaws commonly found in first novels. John Stedmond of *Canadian Forum*, for example, believes that "the characters, though cleverly sketched, do not quite jell, and the narrative techniques creak a little." Linda Rogers of *Canadian Literature* finds that "one of the reasons *The Edible Woman* fails as a novel is the awkwardness of the dialogue." But other critics note Atwood's at least partial success. Tom Marshall, writing in his *Harsh and Lovely Land: The Major Canadian Poets and the Making of a Canadian Tradition*, calls *The Edible Woman* "a largely successful comic novel, even if the mechanics are sometimes a little clumsy, the satirical accounts of consumerism a little drawn out." Millicent Bell of the *New York Times Book Review* calls it "a work of feminist black humor" and claims that Atwood's "comic distortion veers at times into surreal meaningfulness." And Hutcheon describes *The Edible Woman* as "very much a social novel about the possibilities for personal female identity in a capitalistic consumer society."

Surfacing, Atwood's second novel, is "a psychological ghost story," as Marshall explains it, in which a young woman confronts and accepts her past during a visit to her rural home. She comes to realize that she has repressed disturbing events from her memory, including an abortion and her father's death. While swimming in a local lake, she has a vision of her drowned father which "drives her to a healing madness," Marshall states. Hutcheon explains that "*Surfacing* tells of the coming to terms with the haunting, separated parts of the narrator's being . . . after surfacing from a dive, a symbolic as well as a real descent under water, where she has experienced a revealing and personally apocalyptic vision."

Many of the concerns found in Atwood's poetry reappear in *Surfacing.* The novel, Roberta Rubenstein writes in *Modern Fiction Studies,* "synthesizes a number of motifs that have dominated [Atwood's] consciousness since her earliest poems: the elusiveness and variety of 'language' in its several senses; the continuum between human and animal, human being and nature; the significance of one's heritage . . . ; the search for a location (in both time and place); the brutalizations and victimizations of love; drowning and surviving." Margaret Wimsatt of *Commonweal* agrees with this assessment. "The novel," Wimsatt writes, "picks up themes brooded over in the poetry, and knits them together coherently." Marshall believes that both *The Edible Woman* and *Surfacing* "are enlargements upon the themes of [Atwood's] poems. In each of them a young woman is driven to rebellion against what seems to be her fate in the modern technological 'Americanized' world and to psychic breakdown and breakthrough."

In *Life before Man,* Atwood dissects the relationships between three characters: Elizabeth, a married woman who mourns the recent suicide of her lover; Elizabeth's husband, Nate, who is unable to choose between his wife and his lover; and Lesje, Nate's lover, who works with Elizabeth at a museum of natural history. All three characters are isolated from one another and unable to experience their own emotions. The fossils and dinosaur bones on display at the museum are compared throughout the novel with the sterility of the characters' lives. As Laurie Stone notes in the *Village Voice, Life before Man* "is full of variations on the theme of extinction." Similarly, Rubenstein writes in the *Chicago Tribune* that the novel is a "superb living exhibit in which the artifacts are unique (but representative) lives in progress."

Although *Life before Man* is what Rosellen Brown of *Saturday Review* calls an "anatomy of melancholy," MacGregor sees a tempering humor in the novel as well. *Life before Man,* MacGregor writes, "is not so much a story as it is the discarded negatives of a family album, the thoughts so dark they defy any flash short of Atwood's remarkable, and often very funny, insight." Comparing the novel's characters to museum pieces and commenting on the analytical examination to which Atwood subjects them, Peter S. Prescott of *Newsweek* finds that "with chilly compassion and an even colder wit, Atwood exposes the interior lives of her specimens." Writing in the *New York Times Book Review,* Marilyn French makes clear that in *Life before Man,* Atwood "combines several talents—powerful introspection, honesty, satire and a taut, limpid style—to create a splendid, fully integrated work."

The novel's title, French believes, relates to the characters' isolation from themselves, their history, and from one another. They have not yet achieved truly human stature. "This novel suggests," French writes, "that we are still living life before man, before the human—as we like to define it—has evolved." Prescott raises the same point. The novel's characters, he writes, "do not communicate; each, in the presence of another, is locked into his own thoughts and feelings. Is such isolation and indeterminacy what Atwood means when she calls her story 'Life before Man'?" This concern is also found in Atwood's previous novels, French argues, all of which depict "the search for identity . . . a search for a better way to be—for a way of life that both satisfies the passionate, needy self and yet is decent, humane and natural."

Atwood further explores this idea in *Bodily Harm.* In this novel Rennie Wilford is a Toronto journalist who specializes in light, trivial pieces for magazines. She is, Anne Tyler explains in the *Detroit News,* "a cataloguer of current fads and fancies." Isabel Raphael of the London *Times* calls Rennie someone who "deals only in surfaces; her journalism is of the most trivial and transitory kind, her relationship with a live-in lover limited to sex, and most of her friends 'really just contacts.'" Following a partial mastectomy, which causes her lover to abandon her, Rennie begins to feel dissatisfied with her life. She takes on an assignment to the Caribbean island of St. Antoine in an effort to get away from things for a while. Her planned magazine story focusing on the island's beaches, tennis courts, and restaurants is distinctly facile in comparison to the political violence she finds on St. Antoine. When Rennie is arrested and jailed, the experience brings her to a self-realization about her life. "Death," Nancy Ramsey remarks in the *San Francisco Review of Books,* "rather than the modern sense of ennui, threatens Rennie and the people around her, and ultimately gives her life a meaning she hadn't known before."

Bodily Harm, Frank Davey of the *Canadian Forum* believes, follows the same pattern set in Atwood's earlier novels: "Alienation from natural order . . . , followed by descent into a more primitive but healing reality . . . , and finally some reestablishment of order." Although Davey is "troubled" by the similarities between the novels and believes that "Atwood doesn't risk much with this book," he concludes that "these reservations aside, *Bodily Harm* is still a pleasure to read." Other critics have few such reservations about the book. Anatole Broyard of the *New York Times,* for example, claims that "the only way to describe my response to [*Bodily Harm*] is to say that it knocked me out. Atwood seems to be able to do just about everything: people, places, problems, a perfect ear, an exactly-right voice and she tosses off terrific scenes with a casualness that leaves you utterly unprepared for the way these scenes seize you." Tyler calls Atwood "an uncommonly skillful and perceptive writer," and goes on to state that, because of its subject matter, *Bodily Harm* "is not always easy to read. There are times when it's downright unpleasant, but it's also intelligent, provocative, and in the end—against all expectations—uplifting."

In *The Handmaid's Tale* Atwood turns to speculative fiction, creating the dystopia of Gilead, a future America in which Fundamentalist Christians have killed the president and members of Congress and imposed their own dictatorial rule. In this future world, polluted by toxic chemicals and nuclear radiation, few women can bear children; the birthrate has dropped alarmingly. Those women who can bear children are forced to become Handmaids, the official breeders for society. All other women have been reduced to chattel under a repressive religious hierarchy run by men.

The Handmaid's Tale is a radical departure from Atwood's previous novels. Her strong feminism was evident in earlier books, but *The Handmaid's Tale* is dominated by the theme. As Barbara Holliday writes in the *Detroit Free Press,* Atwood "has been concerned in her fiction with the painful psychic warfare between men and women. In 'The Handmaid's Tale,' a futuristic satire, she casts subtlety aside, exposing woman's primal fear of being used and helpless." Atwood's creation of an imaginary world is also new. As Mary Battiata notes in the *Washington Post, The Handmaid's Tale* is the first of Atwood's novels "not set in a worried corner of contemporary Canada."

Atwood was moved to write her story only after images and scenes from the book had been appearing to her for three years. She admits to Mervyn Rothstein of the *New York Times,* "I delayed writing it . . . because I felt it was too crazy." But she eventually became convinced that her vision of Gilead was not far from reality. Some of the anti-female measures she had imagined for the novel actually exist. "There is a sect now, a Catholic charismatic spinoff sect, which calls the women handmaids," Atwood tells Rothstein. "A law in Canada," Battiata reports, "[requires] a woman to have her husband's permission before obtaining an abortion." And Atwood, speaking to Battiata, points to repressive laws in effect as late as 1988 in the totalitarian state of Romania as well: "No abortion, no birth control, and compulsory pregnancy testing, once a month." *The Handmaid's Tale,* Elaine Kendall explains in the *Los Angeles Times Book Review,* depicts "a future firmly based upon actuality, beginning with events that have already taken place and extending them a bit beyond the inevitable conclusions. 'The Handmaid's Tale' does not depend upon hypothetical scenarios, omens, or straws in the wind, but upon documented occurrences and public pronouncements; all matters of record." Stephen McCabe of the *Humanist* calls the novel "a chilling vision of the future extrapolated from the present."

Yet, several critics voice a disbelief in the basic assumptions of *The Handmaid's Tale.* Mary McCarthy, in her review for the *New York Times Book Review,* complains that "I just can't see the intolerance of the far right . . . as leading to a super-biblical puritanism." And although agreeing that "the author has carefully drawn her projections from current trends," McCarthy believes that "perhaps that is the trouble: the projections are too

neatly penciled in. The details . . . all raise their hands announcing themselves present. At the same time, the Republic of Gilead itself, whatever in it that is not a projection, is insufficiently imagined." Richard Grenier of *Insight* objects that the Fundamentalist-run Gilead does not seem Christian: "There seems to be no Father, no Son, no Holy Ghost, no apparent belief in redemption, resurrection, eternal life. No one in this excruciatingly hierarchized new clerical state . . . appears to believe in God." Grenier also finds it improbable that "while the United States has hurtled off into this morbid, feminist nightmare, the rest of the democratic world has been blissfully unaffected." Writing in the Toronto *Globe and Mail,* William French states that Atwood's "reach exceeds her grasp" in *The Handmaid's Tale,* "and in the end we're not clear what we're being warned against." Atwood seems to warn of the dangers of religious fanaticism, of the effects of pollution on the birthrate, and of a possible backlash to militant feminist demands. The novel, French states, "is in fact a cautionary tale about *all* these things . . . but in her scenario, they interact in an implausible way."

Despite this flaw, French sees *The Handmaid's Tale* as being "in the honorable tradition of *Brave New World* and other warnings of dystopia. It's imaginative, even audacious, and conveys a chilling sense of fear and menace." Prescott also compares *The Handmaid's Tale* to other dystopian novels. It belongs, he writes, "to that breed of visionary fiction in which a metaphor is extended to elaborate a warning. . . . Wells, Huxley and Orwell popularized the tradition with books like 'The Time Machine,' 'Brave New World' and '1984'—yet Atwood is a better novelist than they." Christopher Lehmann-Haupt sees *The Handmaid's Tale* as a book that goes far beyond its feminist concerns. Writing in the *New York Times,* Lehmann-Haupt explains that the novel "is a political tract deploring nuclear energy, environmental waste, and antifeminist attitudes. But it [is] so much more than that—a taut thriller, a psychological study, a play on words." Van Gelder agrees. The novel, she writes, "ultimately succeeds on multiple levels: as a page-turning thriller, as a powerful political statement, and as an exquisite piece of writing." Lehmann-Haupt concludes that *The Handmaid's Tale* "is easily Margaret Atwood's best novel to date."

Just as *The Handmaid's Tale* is Atwood's most direct expression of her feminism, *Survival: A Thematic Guide to Canadian Literature* is the most direct presentation of her strong belief in Canadian nationalism. In the book Atwood discerns a uniquely Canadian literature, distinct from its American and British counterparts, and she discusses the dominant themes to be found in it. Canadian literature, she argues, is primarily concerned with victims and with the victim's ability to survive. Atwood, Onley explains, "perceives a strong sado-masochistic patterning in Canadian literature as a whole. She believes that there is a national fictional tendency to participate, usually at some level as Victim, in a Victor/Victim basic pattern." But "despite its stress on victimization," Hutcheon writes "this study is not a revelation of, or a reveling in, [masochism]." What Atwood argues, Onley believes, is that "every country or culture has a single unifying and informing symbol at its core: for America, the Frontier; for England, the Island; for Canada, Survival."

Several critics find that Atwood's own work exemplifies this primary theme of Canadian literature. Her examination of destructive sex roles and her nationalistic concern over the subordinate role Canada plays to the United States are variations on the victor/victim theme. As Marge Piercy explains in the *American Poetry Review,* Atwood believes that a writer must consciously work within his or her nation's literary tradition. Atwood argues in *Survival,* Piercy writes, "that discovery of a writer's tradition may be of use, in that it makes available a conscious choice of how to deal with that body of themes. She suggests that exploring a given tradition consciously can lead to writing in new and more interesting ways." Because Atwood's own work closely parallels the themes she sees as common to the Canadian literary tradition, *Survival* "has served as the context in which critics have subsequently discussed [Atwood's] works," Hutcheon states.

Atwood's prominent stature in Canadian letters rests as much on her published works as on her efforts to define and give value to her nation's literature. "Atwood," Susan Wood states in the *Washington Post Book World,* "has emerged as a champion of Canadian literature and of the peculiarly Canadian experience of isolation and survival." Hutcheon notes Atwood's "important impact on Canadian culture" and believes that her books, "internationally known through translations, stand as testimony to Atwood's significant position in a contemporary literature which must deal with defining its own identity and defending its value."

Although she has been labelled a Canadian nationalist, a feminist, and even a gothic writer, Atwood incorporates and transcends these categories. Writing in *Saturday Night* of Atwood's several perceived roles as a writer, Linda Sandler concludes that "Atwood is all things to all people . . . a nationalist . . . a feminist or a psychologist or a comedian . . . a maker and breaker of myths . . . a gothic writer. She's all these things, but finally she's unaccountably Other. Her writing has the discipline of a social purpose but it remains elusive, complex, passionate. It has all the intensity of an act of exorcism." Atwood's work finally succeeds because it speaks of universal concerns. As Piercy explains, "Atwood is a large and remarkable writer. Her concerns are nowhere petty. Her novels and poems move and engage me deeply, can matter to people who read them."

BIOGRAPHICAL/CRITICAL SOURCES:

BOOKS

Atwood, Margaret, *The Edible Woman,* McClelland & Stewart, 1969, Atlantic-Little, Brown, 1970.
Contemporary Literary Criticism, Gale, Volume 2, 1974, Volume 3, 1975, Volume 4, 1975, Volume 8, 1978, Volume 13, 1980, Volume 15, 1980, Volume 25, 1983, Volume 44, 1987.
Davidson, Arnold E. and Cathy N. Davidson, editors, *The Art of Margaret Atwood: Essays in Criticism,* House of Anansi Press, 1981.
Dictionary of Literary Biography, Volume 53: *Canadian Writers since 1960,* Gale, 1986.
Gibson, Graeme, *Eleven Canadian Novelists,* House of Anansi Press, 1973.
Grace, Sherrill, *Violent Duality: A Study of Margaret Atwood,* Vehicule Press, 1980.
Grace, Sherrill and Lorraine Weir, editors, *Margaret Atwood: Language, Text and System,* University of British Columbia Press, 1983.
Lecker, Robert and Jack David, editors, *The Annotated Bibliography of Canada's Major Authors,* ECW, 1980.
Marshall, Tom, *Harsh and Lovely Land: The Major Canadian Poets and the Making of a Canadian Tradition,* University of British Columbia Press, 1978.
Sandler, Linda, editor, *Margaret Atwood: A Symposium,* University of British Columbia, 1977.
Twigg, Alan, *For Openers: Conversations with 24 Canadian Writers,* Harbour, 1981.
Woodcock, George, *The Canadian Novel in the Twentieth Century,* McClelland & Stewart, 1975.

PERIODICALS

American Poetry Review, November/December, 1973, March/April, 1977, September/October, 1979.
Atlantic, April, 1973.
Book Forum, Volume 4, number 1, 1978.
Books in Canada, January, 1979, June/July, 1980, March, 1981.
Canadian Forum, February, 1970, January, 1973, November/December, 1974, December/January, 1977-78, June/July, 1981, December/January, 1981-82.
Canadian Literature, autumn, 1971, spring, 1972, winter, 1973, spring, 1974, spring, 1977.
Chicago Tribune, January 27, 1980, February 3, 1980, May 16, 1982, March 19, 1989.
Chicago Tribune Book World, January 26, 1986.
Christian Science Monitor, June 12, 1977.
Commonweal, July 9, 1973.
Communique, May, 1975.
Detroit Free Press, January 26, 1986.
Detroit News, April 4, 1982.
Essays on Canadian Writing, spring, 1977.
Globe and Mail (Toronto), July 7, 1984, October 5, 1985, October 19, 1985, February 15, 1986, November 15, 1986, November 29, 1986, November 14, 1987.
Hudson Review, autumn, 1973, spring, 1975.
Humanist, September/October, 1986.
Insight, March 24, 1986.
Journal of Canadian Fiction, Volume 1, number 4, 1972.
Los Angeles Times, March 2, 1982, April, 22, 1982, May 9, 1986, January 12, 1987.
Los Angeles Times Book Review, October 17, 1982, February 9, 1986, December 23, 1987.
Maclean's, January 15, 1979, October 15, 1979, March 30, 1981.
Malahat Review, January, 1977.
Manna, Number 2, 1972.
Meanjin, Volume 37, number 2, 1978.
Modern Fiction Studies, autumn, 1976.
Ms., January, 1987.
New Leader, September 3, 1973.
New Orleans Review, Volume 5, number 3, 1977.
Newsweek, February 18, 1980, February 17, 1986.
New York Times, December 23, 1976, January 10, 1980, February 8, 1980, March 6, 1982, March 28, 1982, September 15, 1982, January 27, 1986, February 17, 1986, November 5, 1986.
New York Times Book Review, October 18, 1970, March 4, 1973, April 6, 1975, September 26, 1976, May 21, 1978, February 3, 1980, October 11, 1981, February 9, 1986.
Observer, June 13, 1982.
Ontario Review, spring/summer, 1975.
Open Letter, summer, 1973.
Parnassus: Poetry in Review, spring/summer, 1974.
People, May 19, 1980.
Poetry, March, 1970, July, 1972, May, 1982.
Publishers Weekly, August 23, 1976.
Quill and Quire, April, 1981, September, 1984.
Room of One's Own, summer, 1975.
San Francisco Review of Books, January, 1982, summer, 1982.
Saturday Night, May, 1971, July/August, 1976, September, 1976, May, 1981.
Saturday Review, September 18, 1976, February 2, 1980.
Saturday Review of the Arts, April, 1973.
Shenandoah, Volume 37, number 2, 1987.
Studies in Canadian Literature, summer, 1977.
This Magazine Is about Schools, winter, 1973.
Time, October 11, 1976.

Times (London), March 13, 1986, June 4, 1987, June 10, 1987.
Times Literary Supplement, March 21, 1986, June 12, 1987.
University of Toronto Quarterly, summer, 1978.
Village Voice, January 7, 1980.
Vogue, January, 1986.
Washington Post, April 6, 1986.
Washington Post Book World, September 26, 1976, December 3, 1978, January 27, 1980, March 14, 1982, February 2, 1986.
Waves, autumn, 1975.
West Coast Review, January, 1973.

*   *   *

AUBIGNY, Pierre d'
See MENCKEN, H(enry) L(ouis)

*   *   *

AUCHINCLOSS, Louis (Stanton) 1917-
(Andrew Lee)

PERSONAL: Surname is pronounced "*Auk*-in-klaus"; born September 27, 1917, in New York, N.Y.; son of Joseph Howland (a corporate lawyer) and Priscilla (Stanton) Auchincloss; married Adele Lawrence, 1957; children: John Winthrop, Blake Leay, Andrew Sloane. *Education:* Attended Yale University, 1935-39; University of Virginia Law School, LL.B., 1941. *Religion:* Episcopalian.

ADDRESSES: Home—1111 Park Ave., Apt. 14-D, New York, N.Y. 10128; and Claryville, N.Y. *Agent*—Curtis Brown Ltd., Ten Astor Place, New York, N.Y. 10003.

CAREER: Admitted to the Bar of New York State, 1941; Sullivan & Cromwell (law firm), New York City, associate, 1941-51; Hawkins, Delafield & Wood (law firm), New York City, associate, 1954-58, partner, 1958-86. President, Museum of the City of New York; trustee, Josiah Macy, Jr., Foundation; former trustee, St. Barnard's School and New York Society Library; life fellow, Pierpont Morgan Library; former member of administrative committee, Dumbarton Oaks Research Library. *Military service:* U.S. Navy, 1941-45; served in Naval Intelligence and as gunnery officer; became lieutenant senior grade.

MEMBER: National Institute of Arts and Letters, Association of the Bar of the City of New York (former member of executive committee), Phi Beta Kappa, Century Association.

AWARDS, HONORS: D.Litt., New York University, 1974, Pace University, 1979, University of the South, 1986; New York State Governor's Art Award.

WRITINGS:

NOVELS

(Under pseudonym Andrew Lee) *The Indifferent Children,* Prentice-Hall, 1947.
Sybil, Houghton, 1952, reprinted, Greenwood, 1972.
A Law for the Lion, Houghton, 1953.
The Great World and Timothy Colt, Houghton, 1956, reprinted, McGraw, 1987.
Venus in Sparta, Houghton, 1958.
Pursuit of the Prodigal, Houghton, 1959, reprinted, Avon, 1977.
The House of Five Talents, Houghton, 1960.
Portrait in Brownstone, Houghton, 1962, reprinted, McGraw, 1987.
The Rector of Justin, Houghton, 1964, reprinted, Hill & Co. Press, 1987.
The Embezzler, Houghton, 1966.

A World of Profit, Houghton, 1968.
I Come as a Thief, Houghton, 1972.
The Dark Lady, Houghton, 1977.
The Country Cousin, Houghton, 1978.
The House of the Prophet, Houghton, 1980.
The Cat and the King, Houghton, 1981.
Watchfires, Houghton, 1982.
Exit Lady Masham, Houghton, 1983.
The Book Class, Houghton, 1984.
Honourable Men, Houghton, 1986.
Diary of a Yuppie, Houghton, 1987.
The Golden Calves, Houghton, 1988.
Fellow Passengers: A Novel in Portraits, Houghton, 1989.
The Lady of Situations, Houghton, 1990.

SHORT STORIES

The Injustice Collectors, Houghton, 1950.
The Romantic Egoists, Houghton, 1954.
Powers of Attorney, Houghton, 1963.
Tales of Manhattan, Houghton, 1967.
Second Chance: Tales of Two Generations, Houghton, 1970.
The Partners, Houghton, 1974.
The Winthrop Covenant, Houghton, 1976.
Narcissa and Other Fables, Houghton, 1982.
Skinny Island: More Tales of Manhattan, Houghton, 1987.

Contributor of stories to *New Yorker, Harper's, Good Housekeeping, Town and Country,* and *Atlantic.*

BIOGRAPHICAL AND CRITICAL STUDIES

Reflections of a Jacobite (essays), Houghton, 1961.
Pioneers and Caretakers: A Study of Nine American Women Novelists, University of Minnesota Press, 1965, reprinted, G. K. Hall, 1985.
On Sister Carrie, University of Minnesota Press, 1968.
Motiveless Malignity (essays), Houghton, 1969.
Edith Wharton: A Woman in Her Time (biography), Viking, 1972.
Richelieu (biography), Viking, 1972.
A Writer's Capital (autobiography), University of Minnesota Press, 1974.
Reading Henry James (essays), University of Minnesota Press, 1975.
Life, Law and Letters (essays), Houghton, 1979.
Persons of Consequence: Queen Victoria and Her Circle, Random House, 1979.
Three "Perfect Novels" and What They Have in Common (lecture; first delivered at Pierpont Morgan Library, January, 1981), Bruccoli Clark, 1981.
(Editor) Adele Florence Sloane, *Maverick in Mauve: The Diary of a Romantic Age,* Doubleday, 1983.
(Editor) *Quotations from Henry James,* University Press of Virginia, 1984.
False Dawn: Women in the Age of the Sun King, Anchor Press, 1985.
The Vanderbilt Era: Profiles of a Gilded Age, Scribner, 1989.
(Editor) *The Hone and Strong Diaries of Old Manhattan,* Abbeville Press, 1989.

Also author of pamphlets, *Edith Wharton,* 1961, *Ellen Glasgow,* 1964, and *Henry Adams,* 1971, all published by University of Minnesota Press. Contributor of essays to *Partisan Review* and the *Nation.* Member of advisory board, *Dictionary of Literary Biography.*

OTHER

(Editor) Edith Wharton, *An Edith Wharton Reader,* Scribner, 1965, reprinted, Macmillan, 1989.

"The Club Bedroom" (one-act play; published in *Esquire,* December, 1966), produced on television, 1966, and Off-Off Broadway at The Playwright's Unit, 1967.

(Editor) Anthony Trollope, *The Warden* [and] *Barchester Towers,* Houghton, 1966.

(Editor) *Fables of Wit and Elegance,* Scribner, 1972.

Author of four unproduced full-length plays and several one-act plays.

SIDELIGHTS: Although he also writes short stories and criticism, Louis Auchincloss has established himself as a highly prolific novelist of manners, the chronicler of New York City's "aristocracy." According to *New York Times* contributor Charlotte Curtis, "Louis Auchincloss . . . is the nearest we have to a Henry James or an Edith Wharton of the East Coast's WASP upper classes. . . . Aside from his books' literary quality, their value has always been the detailed sociological reporting of what life inside these largely invisible families, their networks, their clubs and work places is like." Ronald Bryden in the *Spectator* also compares Auchincloss to Wharton, and feels that the "mantle of Edith Wharton, or whatever she wore, is now firmly [Auchincloss's] and only these two have made New York so real a place."

But critics have faulted the author for portraying an outmoded way of life. In the *Dictionary of Literary Biography Yearbook: 1980,* Patricia Kane observes how his choice of genre has affected his popularity: "Auchincloss's reputation as a writer has been influenced by factors somewhat external to it. Both the novel of manners and the fictional characters called WASPs are not fashionable." In the *New York Times Book Review* Webster Schott concurs when he states that Auchincloss "is far from the swarming hot center of American literary intellectualism; he's a museum of all that American writing valued before its World War I baptism of despair. . . . Buried in its own riches, his world exists like Shangri-La, lost to inhabitation." But Gore Vidal, writing in the *New York Review of Books,* disagrees: "The world Auchincloss writes about, the domain of Wall Street bankers and lawyers and stockbrokers, is thought to be irrelevant, a faded and fading genteel-gentile enclave when, in actual fact, this little world comprises the altogether too vigorous and self-renewing ruling class of the United States. . . . Of all our novelists, Auchincloss is the only one who tells us how our rulers behave in their banks and their boardrooms, their law offices and their clubs." And Sandra Salmans reports in the *New York Times* that "some academics and publishers praise him as one of the few authors who write about the business world with a real understanding of its complexities and conflicts."

The family as a social unit is important to Auchincloss's novels, many of which are multigenerational sagas. *The House of Five Talents,* which *New York Herald Tribune Book Review* critic E. C. Dunn calls "the story of human beings, their complexity, their insecurity, [and] their magnificent failure to grasp and hold the full meaning of life," takes an originally middle-class New York family from 1873 to 1948, from a social-climbing grandfather to his heiress granddaughter. In another novel, *Portrait in Brownstone,* the author relates the history of the Denison family from the turn of the century to 1951. Granville Hicks states in the *Saturday Review* that Auchincloss "tells the story in a neat, dry style that repeatedly gives great pleasure. . . . What distinguishes the novel is its subtlety." And Fanny Butcher writes in the *Chicago Sunday Tribune:* "The warmth of the family ties, the family tra-

ditions make the novel a happy reading experience. . . . when 'Portrait in Brownstone' is good it is very good. The author has a sensitive eye for human foibles, a sensitive ear for conversation, and a sensitive mind that ferrets out human emotions." Citing an occasionally disjointed plot, however, Butcher adds: "If the book were more technically cohesive, it would be a fine novel instead of just a good one."

With *The Rector of Justin,* which critics regard as one of his best works, Auchincloss relates the story of the dead hero, Francis Prescott, through the testimony of friends, coworkers, and relations. Hicks explains in another issue of the *Saturday Review* that "the subject of *The Rector of Justin* does not seem to promise excitement—the octogenarian headmaster of a small private school—and yet I was swept along by it, for the revelation of Prescott's character is fascinating. . . . We do come to feel the reality, the complicated reality, of Francis Prescott." *The House of the Prophet* also uses the testimony of other characters to portray Felix Leitner (based, some critics claim, on editor and journalist Walter Lippmann), a lawyer, columnist, and public figure who, in his later years, leaves his wife and betrays his best friend. While admitting that Auchincloss's style and "formal prose [are] so well crafted, so consistent, and so entertaining that you forgive him lapses you wouldn't forgive in a less talented writer," *Christian Science Monitor* reviewer Anne Bernays contends that "the people in this novel . . . don't really breathe; they carry ideas, rather than blood, in their veins." However, *Times Literary Supplement* contributor Charles Wheeler speaks of the novel as "a taut and elegant study of a distinguished American whose closest friends cannot decide whether they like or detest him."

Two of Auchincloss's more recent novels draw on his own background. In *The Book Class,* he exposes the power held by "unliberated" upper-class New York City wives in the early twentieth century. The story shows the inner workings of a book club's members; the tale is related by the son of the now-deceased founder, through the reminiscences of surviving members. *Washington Post Book World* contributor Jonathan Yardley claims that while the women "get affectionate and clear-eyed tribute in *The Book Class* . . . Auchincloss never manages to make the reader care about them; they never seem to matter, to be of real consequence, and thus in the end neither does the book. Intelligent and craftsmanlike though it is, *The Book Class* is Auchincloss going through the motions, sticking to his last." But *Los Angeles Tribune* contributor Carolyn See, who compares the book favorably to Helen Hooven Santmyer's . . . *And Ladies of the Club,* states: " 'The Book Class' really is a *book class,* a compact history of literature as we use it today. It's dazzling."

With *Honorable Men,* Auchincloss attempted "to come to grips with a long-standing American obsession—how the values, if not the beliefs, of our Puritan forefathers still permeate some of their descendants, and what is won and lost by adhering to them," writes A. R. Gurney in the *New York Times Book Review.* In a *New York Times Book Review* interview with Herbert Mitgang, Auchincloss explained: "I used to say to my father, 'Everything would be all right if only my class at Yale ran the country.' Well, they did run the country during the Vietnam War and look what happened. . . . [*Honorable Men*] is my ultimate explanation of the Puritan ethic in our time." According to Yardley in the *Washington Post, Honorable Men* is "a novel about politics, but in no way is it a political novel. What concerns Auchincloss is . . . what shaped the men who determined the nature of [America's role in Vietnam] and pressed their cause even against clamorous public opinion. He is considering in fiction, in other words, the same men whom David Halberstam analyzed journalistically in 'The Best and the Brightest.' " And while Gurney sees "a tendency toward stuffiness in the writing that can occasionally settle over the book like dust," he adds that with *Honorable Men* "Mr. Auchincloss adds a significant work to his long and considerable canon."

Diary of a Yuppie focuses on anti-hero Robert Service, a man determined to succeed in the world of corporate takeovers and double crosses. Rory Quirk writes in the *Washington Post Book World:* "Auchincloss unfolds this delightful and disquieting tale with his characteristic deftness, allowing Service to destroy himself in his own words through his damning diary entries. . . . This is contemporary fiction of the absolute first rank. It is fiction, isn't it?" As with some of his other books, *Diary of a Yuppie* has prompted critics to compare Auchincloss to his predecessors. According to London *Times* contributor Andrew Sinclair: "Not since rereading *The Great Gatsby* have I felt a whole new class so economically taken apart. . . . [*Diary of a Yuppie* is] the most significant novel Mr. Auchincloss has written in his distinguished career."

Critics also consider the author a skilled short story writer. *Skinny Island* involves a frequently implemented Auchincloss technique: that of revolving a collection of short stories around a central theme, in this case the "skinny island" of Manhattan. Paul Gray in *Time* suggests another unifying link: "The pieces are not just connected chronologically and geographically but by a common concern as well: the dilemma faced by comfortable people when they must choose between honor and expediency." And *Washington Post Book World* contributor James K. Glassman feels the work "conveys the insular, claustrophobic, dignified and rigid world that obsesses Auchincloss: Old New York." Glassman continues, "the death of society has always been one of Auchincloss' themes, but regular readers will find him here utterly pessimistic, his irony turned to cynicism. This writing on the edge of despair gives *Skinny Island* an urgency and an emotional kick that bring it close to his best books."

A story collection that also stands as a novel, *Fellow Passengers* reveals that the rich "are no different, emotionally or morally, from the rest of us; they just have money left in their checking accounts at the end of the month," according to Edward Hawley in *Tribune Books*. *Washington Post* contributor Bruce Bawer calls the stories "witty, charming and economical" and states that "these tales have the pithiness of biblical parables or Aesopian fables," while also delivering a criticism frequently leveled at Auchincloss: "At times the dialogue feels not only formal but unnaturally stilted; and some of the characters' off-the-cuff literary references are hard to buy." Bawer concludes, however: "But no matter. This book—novel, memoir, short-story collection, or what-have-you—is at once a triumph of storytelling and an exemplary meditation upon the standards of conduct by which we live. Auchincloss accomplishes something that's not easy: Even as he delightfully celebrates the voyage of life, he delivers a serious reminder of the responsibilities we all have toward our fellow passengers on the trip." And Hawley advocates: "Readers familiar with Auchincloss' rich body of work will find much pleasure in 'Fellow Passengers,' which is full of his characteristic insight and irony. For those who aren't, this is a good place to start."

BIOGRAPHICAL/CRITICAL SOURCES:

BOOKS

Auchincloss, Louis, *A Writer's Capital,* University of Minnesota Press, 1974.
Contemporary Literary Criticism, Gale, Volume 4, 1975, Volume 6, 1976, Volume 9, 1978, Volume 18, 1981, Volume 45, 1987.

Dictionary of Literary Biography, Volume 2: *American Novelists since World War II,* Gale, 1978.
Dictionary of Literary Biography Yearbook: 1980, Gale, 1981.

PERIODICALS

Chicago Sunday Tribune, July 15, 1962.
Christian Science Monitor, May 7, 1980.
Los Angeles Times, September 3, 1984.
New York Herald Tribune Book Review, September 11, 1960.
New York Review of Books, July 18, 1974.
New York Times, October 28, 1985, April 22, 1986, December 21, 1989.
New York Times Book Review, March 19, 1967, October 13, 1985.
Saturday Review, July 14, 1962, July 11, 1964.
Spectator, March 4, 1960.
Time, May 11, 1987.
Times (London), January 29, 1987.
Times Literary Supplement, May 2, 1980.
Tribune Books (Chicago), March 19, 1989.
Washington Post, September 11, 1985, September 28, 1986, March 28, 1989.
Washington Post Book World, July 22, 1984, September 28, 1986, May 17, 1987, June 11, 1989.

*   *   *

AUDEN, W(ystan) H(ugh)   1907-1973

PERSONAL: Born February 21, 1907, in York, England; came to the United States in 1939, became U.S. citizen in April, 1946; died September 28, 1973, in Vienna, Austria; son of George Augustus (a medical officer) and Constance Rosalie (a nurse; maiden name, Bicknell) Auden; married Erika Mann (a writer; daughter of Thomas Mann), 1935, in order to provide her with a British passport (divorced). *Education:* Attended Christ Church, Oxford, 1925-28. *Religion:* Episcopal.

ADDRESSES: Home—All Souls College, Oxford University, Oxford, England; and No. 6 Hinterholz, Kirschstetten, St. Poelten, Austria. *Agent*—Curtis Brown Ltd., 575 Madison Ave., New York, N.Y. 10022.

CAREER: Poet, playwright, librettist, critic, editor, and translator. Larchfield Academy, Helensburgh, Scotland, and Downs School, Colwall, near Malvern, England, schoolmaster, 1930-35; with Rupert Doone, Robert Medley, and others, founded the Group Theatre, 1932; worked with General Post Office film unit, 1935, collaborating on such films as "Night Mail" and "Coal-Face"; made trip to Iceland with Louis MacNeice, 1936; went to Spain as stretcher-bearer for Loyalists during Spanish Revolution, 1937; made trip to China with Christopher Isherwood, 1938; taught at St. Mark's School, Southborough, Mass., 1939-40; faculty member of American Writers League Writers School, 1939; taught at New School for Social Research, 1940-41 and 1946-47; faculty member of University of Michigan, 1941-42, Swarthmore College, 1942-45, Bryn Mawr College, 1943-45, Bennington College, 1946, and Barnard College, 1947; with Lionel Trilling and Jacques Barzun, founded The Reader's Subscription Book Club, 1951, associated with Club until 1959, wrote occasionally for its publication, *The Griffin,* 1951-58; Smith College, Northampton, Mass., W. A. Neilson Research Professor, 1953; Oxford University, Oxford, England, professor of poetry, 1956-61; with Jacques Barzun and Lionel Trilling, established the Mid-Century Book Society, 1959, wrote occasionally for its periodical, *The Mid-Century,* 1959-63.

MEMBER: American Academy of Arts and Letters.

AWARDS, HONORS: King's Gold Medal for poetry, 1937; Guggenheim fellowships, 1942 and 1945; Award of Merit Medal, American Academy of Arts and Letters, 1945; Pulitzer Prize in Poetry, 1948, for *The Age of Anxiety;* Bollingen Prize in Poetry, 1954; National Book Award, 1956, for *The Shield of Achilles;* Feltrinelli Prize (Rome), 1957; Alexander Droutzkoy Memorial Award, 1959; shared Guiness Poetry Award (Ireland) with Robert Lowell and Edith Sitwell, 1959; honored on Chicago Poetry Day, 1960; Honorary Student (Fellow), Christ College, Oxford University, 1962-73; Austrian State Prize for European Literature, 1966; National Medal for Literature of National Book Committee, 1967, for total contributions to literature; Gold Medal of National Institute of Arts and Letters, 1968.

WRITINGS:

COLLECTED WORKS

Complete Works of W. H. Auden, Princeton University Press, 1989—.

POETRY

Poems, hand printed by Stephen Spender, 1928, Faber, 1930, 2nd edition, 1933, Random House, 1934, revised edition, Faber, 1960, revised, with new foreword by Spender, for Elliston Poetry Foundation of the University of Cincinnati, 1965.

The Orators: An English Study (includes prose), Faber, 1932, revised edition with new foreword, Random House, 1967.

Look, Stranger!, Faber, 1936, published as *On This Island,* Random House, 1937.

(With Louis MacNeice) *Letters from Iceland,* Random House, 1937, revised edition, 1969.

Selected Poems, Faber, 1938.

(With Christopher Isherwood) *Journey to a War,* Random House, 1939, reprinted, Hippocrene Books, 1972, revised edition, Faber, 1973.

Another Time, Random House, 1940.

Some Poems, Random House, 1940.

Three Songs for St. Cecilia's Day, privately printed, 1941.

The Double Man, Random House, 1941 (published in England as *New Year Letter,* Faber, 1941).

For the Time Being, Random House, 1944.

The Collected Poetry of W. H. Auden, Random House, 1945.

The Age of Anxiety: A Baroque Eclogue (performed Off-Broadway at the Attic Theatre, March 18, 1954), Random House, 1947.

Collected Shorter Poems, 1930-44, Random House, 1951.

The Shield of Achilles, Random House, 1955.

The Old Man's Road, Voyages Press, 1956.

A Gobble Poem ("snatched from the notebooks of W. H. Auden and now believed to be in the Morgan Library"), [London], 1957.

Selected Poetry, Modern Library, 1959, 2nd edition, Vintage, 1971.

Homage to Clio, Random House, 1960.

W. Auden, A Selection, with notes and critical essay by Richard Hoggart, Hutchinson, 1961.

The Common Life (written in German), translation by Dieter Leisegang, Blaeschke, 1964.

The Cave of the Making (written in German), translation by Leisegang, Blaeschke, 1965.

Half-Way, limited edition, Lowell-Adams House Printers, 1965.

About the House, Random House, 1965.

The Platonic Blow, [New York], 1965.

Collected Shorter Poems, 1927-57, Faber, 1966, Random House, 1967.

Portraits, Apiary Press, 1966.

Marginalia, Ibex Press, 1966.

A Selection by the Author, Faber, 1967.

Selected Poems, Faber, 1968, revised edition, Random House, 1979.

Two Songs, Phoenix Book Shop, 1968.

Collected Longer Poems, Faber, 1968, Random House, 1969.

City without Walls, and Many Other Poems, Random House, 1969.

Academic Graffiti, Faber, 1971, Random House, 1972.

(With Leif Sjoeberg) *Selected Poems,* Pantheon, 1972.

Epistle to a Godson, and Other Poems, Random House, 1972.

Poems and Lithographs, edited by John Russell, British Museum, 1974.

Poems, lithographs by Henry Moore, edited by Vera Lindsay, Petersburg Press, 1974.

Thank You Fog: Last Poems, Random House, 1974.

Collected Poems, edited by Edward Mendelson, Random House, 1976.

Sue, Sycamore Press, 1977.

The English Auden: Poems, Essays, and Dramatic Writings, edited by Mendelson, Faber, 1977, Random House, 1978.

PLAYS

The Dance of Death (produced in London, 1934; produced in New York City, 1935; produced in Poughkeepsie, N.Y., as "Come out into the Sun," 1935), Faber, 1933, 2nd edition, 1935.

(With Isherwood) *The Dog beneath the Skin; or, Where Is Francis?* (also see below; produced in London, 1936; revised version produced in New York City, 1947), Faber, 1935, reprinted, Random House, 1968.

The Ascent of F6: A Tragedy in Two Acts (also see below; produced in London, 1931; produced in New York City, 1939), Faber, 1936, 2nd edition, 1957, published as *The Ascent of F6,* Random House, 1937, 2nd edition, 1956.

(Adaptor with Edward Crankshaw) Ernst Toller, *No More Peace! A Thoughtful Comedy* (produced in London, 1936; produced in New York City, 1937), Farrar & Rinehart, 1937.

On the Frontier: A Melodrama in Three Acts (produced in London, 1939), Random House, 1938.

(With Isherwood) *Two Great Plays* (contains "The Dog Beneath the Skin" and "The Ascent of F6"), Random House, 1959.

Also author of documentary screenplays in verse, including "Night Mail," 1936, "Coal-Face," 1936, and "The Londoners," 1938; author of radio plays, including "Hadrian's Wall," 1937, "The Dark Valley," 1940, and "The Rocking-Horse Winner" (adapted from the short story by D. H. Lawrence).

CRITICISM AND ESSAYS

(With T. C. Worley) *Education, Today, and Tomorrow,* Hogarth, 1939.

Address on Henry James (booklet), [New York], 1947.

The Enchafed Flood: The Romantic Iconography of the Sea, Random House, 1950.

Making, Knowing, and Judging, Clarendon Press, 1956.

The Dyer's Hand, and Other Essays, Random House, 1962.

Louis MacNeice (memorial address), Faber, 1963.

Shakespeare, Fuenf Augsaetze, [Frankfurt am Main], 1964.

Selected Essays, Faber, 1964.

Secondary Worlds (T. S. Eliot Memorial Lectures at University of Kent, 1967), Faber, 1968, Random House, 1969.

A Certain World: A Commonplace Book (annotated personal anthology), Viking, 1970.

Forewords and Afterwords, edited by Mendelson, Random House, 1973.

EDITOR

(With Charles Plumb) *Oxford Poetry, 1926,* Basil Blackwell, 1926.
(With C. Day Lewis) *Oxford Poetry, 1927,* Appleton, 1927.
(With John Garrett) *The Poet's Tongue,* G. Bell, 1935.
(With Arthur Elton) *Mechanics,* Longmans, Green, 1936.
(And author of introduction) *Oxford Book of Light Verse,* Oxford University Press, 1938.
(And author of introduction) *A Selection of the Poems of Alfred Lord Tennyson,* Doubleday, 1944 (published in England as *Tennyson: An Introduction and a Selection,* Phoenix House, 1946).
(And author of introduction) Henry James, *American Scene,* Scribner, 1946.
(And author of introduction) John Betjeman, *Slick but Not Streamlined,* Doubleday, 1947.
(And author of introduction) *The Portable Greek Reader,* Viking, 1948.
(And author of introduction) Edgar Allan Poe, *Selected Prose and Poetry,* Rinehart, 1950, revised edition, 1957.
(With Norman Holmes Pearson) *Poets of the English Language,* Viking, 1950, reprinted, Penguin, 1977, Volume 1: *Medieval and Renaissance Poets: Langland to Spenser,* Volume 2: *Elizabethan and Jacobean Poets: Marlowe to Marvell,* Volume 3: *Restoration and Augustan Poets: Milton to Goldsmith,* Volume 4: *Romantic Poets: Blake to Poe,* Volume 5: *Victorian and Edwardian Poets: Tennyson to Yeats.*
(And author of introduction) *The Living Thoughts of Kierkegaard,* McKay, 1952 (published in England as *Kierkegaard,* Cassell, 1955).
(With Marianne Moore and Karl Shapiro) *Riverside Poetry 1953: Poems by Students in Colleges and Universities in New York City,* Association Press, 1953.
(With Chester Kallman and Noah Greenberg) *An Elizabethan Song Book: Lute Songs, Madrigals, and Rounds,* Doubleday, 1956, published as *An Anthology of Elizabethan Lute Songs, Madrigals, and Rounds,* Norton, 1970.
(And author of introduction) *Selected Writings of Sydney Smith,* Farrar, Straus, 1956.
(And author of introduction) *The Criterion Book of Modern American Verse,* Criterion, 1956 (published in England as *The Faber Book of Modern American Verse,* Faber, 1956).
Van Gogh: A Self Portrait (selected letters), New York Graphic Society, 1961.
Joseph Jacobs, *The Pied Piper, and Other Fairy Tales,* Macmillan, 1963.
(With Louis Kronenberger) *The Viking Book of Aphorisms,* Viking, 1963 (published in England as *The Faber Book of Aphorisms,* Faber, 1964).
Walter de la Mare, *A Choice of de la Mare's Verse,* Faber, 1963.
Selected Poems of Louis MacNeice, Faber, 1964.
(And author of introduction) *Nineteenth Century British Minor Poets,* Delacorte, 1966 (published in England as *Nineteenth Century Minor Poets,* Faber, 1967).
(With John Lawlor) *To Nevill Coghill From Friends,* Faber, 1966.
Selected Poetry and Prose of George Gordon, Lord Byron, New American Library, 1966.
MacNeice, *Persons from Porlock, and Other Plays for Radio,* BBC Productions, 1969.
G. K. Chesterton: A Selection from His Non-Fictional Prose, Faber, 1970.

George Herbert, Penguin, 1973.
(And author of preface) *Selected Songs of Thomas Campion,* Godine, 1973.

Also editor and author of foreword of "Yale Series of Younger Poets," 1947-59. Co-editor of "The Looking Glass Library" series of children's books.

CONTRIBUTOR

Clifton Fadiman, editor, *I Believe,* Simon & Schuster, 1939, revised edition, G. Allen, 1941.
Donald A. Stauffer, editor, *The Intent of the Critic,* Princeton University Press, 1941.
Rudolf Arnheim, editor, *Poets at Work,* introduction by Charles D. Abbott, Harcourt, 1948.
Marvin Halvorsen, editor, *Religious Drama,* Volume 1, Peter Smith, 1957.
Igor Stravinsky, *Memories and Commentaries* (letters), Faber, 1960.
Raymond Mortimer, compiler, *The Seven Deadly Sins,* Sunday Times Publications, 1962.
Norman Davis and C. C. Wrenn, editors, *English and Medieval Studies* (tribute to J. R. R. Tolkien), Allen & Unwin, 1962.
A. Ostroff, editor, *The Contemporary Poet as Artist and Critic,* Little, Brown, 1964.
Eric W. White, editor, *Poems by W. H. Auden and Others,* Poetry Book Society, 1966.
C. B. Cox and A. E. Dyson, editors, *Word in the Desert,* Oxford University Press, 1968.
G. F. Kennan, editor, *Democracy and the Student Left,* Little, Brown, 1968.

Contributor to periodicals, including *Botteghe Obscure, Poetry, New Verse, New Republic, The Griffin, Trace, Listener, Times Literary Supplement, New Statesman, Mid-Century, Texas Quarterly, Nation, New York Times Book Review, Atlantic, Spectator, Kenyon Review, Reporter, Horn Book, New Yorker, Harper's, Mademoiselle, Partisan Review, Christian Scholar, Encounter, Vogue, Tulane Drama Review, Esquire, Delos, New York Review of Books,* and *Quest.*

AUTHOR OF INTRODUCTION OR AFTERWORD

(With others) Robert Frost, *Selected Poems of Robert Frost,* J. Cape, 1936.
Baudelaire, *Intimate Journals,* Methuen, 1949.
Charles Williams, *The Descent of the Dove,* Meridian Books, 1956.
Iwan Goll, *Jean sans Terre,* Yoseloff, 1958.
William Shakespeare, *Romeo and Juliet,* edited by Francis Fergusson, Dell, 1958.
John Hollander, *A Crackling of Thorns,* Yale University Press, 1958, reprinted, AMS Press, 1974.
Phyllis McGinley, *Times Three: Selected Poems From Three Decades,* Viking, 1960.
Henrik Ibsen, *Brand,* Anchor, 1960.
Konstantinos P. Kabaphes, *The Complete Poems of Cavafy,* Harcourt, 1961.
M. F. K. Fisher, *The Art of Eating,* Faber, 1963.
William Burto, editor, *Shakespeare: The Sonnets,* New American Library, 1964.
Anne Fremantle, editor, *The Protestant Mystics,* Little, Brown, 1964.
Oscar Wilde, *De Profundis and The Ballad of Reading Gaol,* Avon, 1964.
B. C. Bloomfield, *W. H. Auden: A Bibliography,* University Press of Virginia, 1964.

Sister Mary Immaculate, *The Tree and the Master: An Anthology of Literature on the Cross of Christ,* Random House, 1965.

Victor Yanovsky, *No Man's Time* (novel), Weybright & Talley, 1967.

George McDonald, *The Golden Key,* Farrar & Straus, 1967.

G. Handley-Taylor and T. d'A. Smith, compilers, *Cecil Day Lewis, The Poet Laureate,* St. James Press, 1968.

Eugen Rosenblock-Huessy, *I Am an Impure Thinker,* Argo Books, 1970.

TRANSLATOR

(With others) *Adam Mickiewicz, 1798-1855: Selected Poems,* Noonday Press, 1956.

(With Kallman) Bertolt Brecht and Kurt Weill, "The Seven Deadly Sins" (ballet cantata), performed at New York City Center, 1959.

Jean Cocteau, "The Knights of the Round Table," 1957, published in *The Infernal Machine, and Other Plays,* New Directions, 1973.

(With others) Brecht, "The Caucasian Chalk Circle," published in *Bertolt Brecht Plays,* Volume 1, Methuen, 1960.

St. John Perse (pseudonym of Alexis Saint-Leger Leger) *On Poetry,* Pantheon, 1961, also published in *Two Addresses* (also see below).

(With Elizabeth Mayer) Johann Wolfgang von Goethe, *Italian Journey,* Pantheon, 1962.

(With Sjoeberg, and author of foreword) Dag Hammarskjoeld, *Markings,* Knopf, 1964.

Perse, *Two Addresses,* Pantheon, 1966.

(With others, and author of foreword) Andrei Voznesenski, *Antiworlds,* Basic Books, 1966, bilingual edition including additional Voznesenski work published as *Antiworlds, and the Fifth Ace,* 1967.

(With Paul Beekman Taylor) *Voeluspa: The Song of the Sybil,* Windhover Press, 1968.

(With Taylor) Edda Saemundar, *The Elder Edda: A Selection,* Random House, 1969.

Perse, *Collected Poems,* Princeton University Press, 1971.

Goethe, *The Sorrows of Young Werther,* Random House, 1971.

(With Sjoeberg) Gunnar Ekeloef, *Selected Poems,* Pantheon, 1972.

(With Sjoeberg) Paer Lagerkvist, *Evening Land,* Wayne State University Press, 1975.

(With Kallman) Brecht, *The Rise and Fall of the City of Mahagonny,* Godine, 1976.

Also translator, with Kallman, of opera libretto *The Magic Flute* (music by Wolfgang Amadeus Mozart), Random House, 1956, and (with others) *The Great Operas of Mozart,* Grossett, 1962.

LIBRETTOS AND LYRICS

Our Hunting Fathers, music by Benjamin Britten, Boosey & Hawkes, 1936.

Fish in the Unruffled Lakes, music by Britten, Boosey & Hawkes, 1937.

On This Island, music by Britten, Boosey & Hawkes, 1937.

Two Ballads, Boosey & Hawkes, 1937.

Now through the Night's Caressing Grip, music by Britten, Boosey & Hawkes, 1938.

Ballad of Heroes, music by Britten, Boosey & Hawkes, 1939.

Hymn to St. Cecilia for S.S.A.T.B., music by Britten, Boosey & Hawkes, 1942.

For the Time Being: A Christmas Oratorio (first produced at Carnegie Hall, New York, December 7, 1959), music by Marvin David Levy, [New York], 1944.

(With Brecht and H. R. Hays) "The Duchess," music by John Webster, performed in New York, 1946.

(With Kallman) *The Rake's Progress,* music by Igor Stravinsky, Boosey & Hawkes, 1951.

(With Kallman) "Delia; or, A Masque of Night," published in *Botteghe Obscure,* 1953.

(With Greenberg) *The Play of Daniel: A Thirteenth Century Musical Drama,* Oxford University Press, 1959.

Five Poems (produced in New York, March, 1959), music by Lennox Berkeley, J. & W. Chester, 1960.

(With Kallman) *Elegy for Young Lovers,* music by Hans Werner Henze, Schott (Mainz), 1961.

(Adapter with Kallman) Lorenzo Da Ponte, *Don Giovanni,* music by Mozart, Schirmer, 1961.

Elegy for J.F.K., music by Stravinsky, Boosey & Hawkes, 1964.

The Twelve: Anthem for the Feast Day of Any Apostle, music by William Walton, Oxford University Press, 1966.

(With Kallman) *The Bassarids* (based on Euripides' "The Bacchae"; produced in German at Salzburg Festival, 1966; produced in Santa Fe, N.M., August, 1966), Schott, 1966.

Moralities: Three Scenic Plays from Fables by Aesop, music by Henze, Schott, 1969.

(With Kallman) "Love's Labour's Lost" (adapted from the play by William Shakespeare), music by Nicholas Nabokov, first performed at 25th Edinburgh International Festival, Scotland, 1971.

Paul Bunyan (performed at Columbia University, New York, 1941), music by Britten, Faber, 1976.

OTHER

(With others) "Time Cycle, for Soprano and Orchestra," performed by New York Philharmonic, directed by Leonard Bernstein, at Carnegie Hall, New York, October 21, 1960.

(Adapter with Kallman) "Arcifanfano, King of Fools," for its first performance since 1778, held at Town Hall, New York, November, 1965.

Also composed narrative for "The Ballad of Barnaby" (adapted from Anatole France's version of "Our Lady's Juggler"), for music written by students of Wykeham Rise School under the direction of Charles Turner, first performed at St. John's Episcopal Church, Washington, Conn., May, 1969.

SIDELIGHTS: It was W. H. Auden—poet, playwright, librettist, critic, editor, and translator—who characterized the thirties as "the age of anxiety." His poem by that title, wrote Monroe K. Spears in his *Poetry of W. H. Auden,* was a "sympathetic satire on the attempts of human beings to escape, through their own efforts, the anxiety of our age." Auden struck an extraordinarily receptive chord in readers with his timely treatment of the moral and political issues that directly affected them. Harold Bloom suggested in the *New Republic* that "Auden [was] accepted as not only a great poet but also a Christian humanist sage not because of any conspiracy among moralizing neo-Christian academicians, but because the age require[d] such a figure."

Auden possessed a formidable technique and an acute ear. In her book *Auden,* Barbara Everett commented on the poet's facility: "In his verse, Auden can argue, reflect, joke, gossip, sing, analyse, lecture, hector, and simply talk; he can sound, at will, like a psychologist on a political platform, like a theologian at a party, or like a geologist in love; he can give dignity and authority to nonsensical theories, and make newspaper headlines sound both true and melodious." Jeremy Robson noted in *Encounter:* "The influence of music on Auden's verse . . . has always been salient: even his worst lines often 'sound' impressive." Everett found that a musical sensibility marked Auden's work from the very beginning, and she felt that when "he turned more and more, in the latter part of his career, to the kind of literary work that demands free exercise of verbal and rhythmic talent—for instance, to the writing of libretti—[he developed] that side of his artistic nature which was from the beginning the strongest."

Auden's linguistic innovations, renowned enough to spawn the adjective "Audenesque," were described by Karl Shapiro in his *In Defense of Ignorance* as "the modernization of diction, [and] the enlarging of dictional language to permit a more contemporary-sounding speech." As his career progressed, however, Auden was more often chastised than praised for his idiosyncratic use of language. James Fenton wrote in the *New Statesman:* "For years—for over forty years—the technical experimentation started by Auden enlarged and enriched the scope of English verse. He rediscovered and invented more than any other modern poet. . . . And yet there grew up . . . a number of mannerisms, such as the use of nouns as verbs, or the employment of embarrassingly outdated slang, or the ransacking of the OED [Oxford English Dictionary], which became in the end a hindrance to his work."

Some critics have suggested that Auden's unusual style germinated in the social climate of his childhood. Robert Bloom, writing in *PMLA,* commented that in Auden's writing in 1930 "the omission of articles, demonstrative adjectives, subjects, conjunctions, relative pronouns, auxiliary verbs—form a language of extremity and urgency. Like telegraphese . . . it has time and patience only for the most important words." In his *W. H. Auden as a Social Poet,* Frederick Buell identified the roots of this terse style in the private, codified language in which Auden and his circle of schoolboy friends conversed. Buell quoted Christopher Isherwood, one of those friends and later a collaborator with Auden, who described a typical conversation between two members of the group: "We were each other's ideal audience; nothing, not the slightest innuendo or the subtlest shade of meaning, was lost between us. A joke which, if I had been speaking to a stranger, world have taken five minutes to lead up to and elaborate and explain, could be conveyed by the faintest hint. . . . Our conversation would have been hardly intelligible to anyone who had happened to overhear it; it was a rigamarole of private slang, deliberate misquotations, bad puns, bits of parody, and preparatory school smut." Peter E. Firchow felt that the nature of Auden's friendships affected not only his style but also his political views. In *PMLA,* Firchow noted that Auden thought of his friends "as a 'gang' into which new members were periodically recruited," pointing out that Auden, "while never a Fascist, came at times remarkably close to accepting some characteristically Fascist ideas, especially those having to do with a mistrust of the intellect, the primacy of the group over the individual, the fascination with a strong leader (who expresses the will of the group), and the worship of youth."

The extent to which Auden believed in various political theories is still debated; what is clear to some critics, though, is that Auden habitually revised his writing to accommodate any shifts in faith. Hannah Arendt considered Auden's changes of heart to be a natural response to the flux of the times. She wrote in the *New Yorker:* "In the Forties, there were many who turned against their old beliefs. . . . They simply changed trains, as it were; the train of Socialism and Communism had been wrong, and they changed to the train of Capitalism or Freudianism or some refined Marxism." Auden apparently changed trains frequently. In the case of his poem "Spain 1937," a denouncement of Fascism in the Spanish Civil War, Auden later wrote that "it would have been bad enough if I had ever held this wicked doctrine [of Marxism], but that I should have stated it simply be-

cause it sounded to me rhetorically effective is quite inexcusable." Although in *Yale Review* Frank Kermode acknowledged that Auden "denied that his revision and rejections had an ideological motive," Kermode asserted that "his earlier rhetoric failed later ethical tests." Robert Greacen supported the latter claim, noting in *Books and Bookmen* that the poems of *Journey to a War* were "extensively revised because Auden was 'shocked to discover how carelessly [he] had written them.' " Greacen reported that Auden had found his work "preachy," and had commented that "if he were to preach the same sermon today he would do it in a very different way."

Buell drew a parallel between the political activism of Auden and that of playwright Bertolt Brecht, noting that both men were "attempting to find an artistic voice for a left-wing polemic." Arendt supported Buell's assertion, writing that "[Auden] once mentioned as a 'disease' his 'early addiction to German usages,' but much more prominent than these, and less easy to get rid of, was the obvious influence of Bertolt Brecht with whom he had more in common than he was ever ready to admit. . . . What made this influence possible was that [Auden and Brecht] both belonged to the post-First World War generation, with its curious mixture of despair and *joie de vivre.*" Buell found stylistic as well as political similarities: "The techniques of Brecht's epic theatre and Verfremdungseffekt [alienation-effect; a method of dramatic presentation calculated to alert the audience to the unreality of a performance and to jolt them to political activism] correlate with a number of Auden's specific rhetorical practices: Auden's own propensity to quick changes in and explosions of poetic mood, his use of a wide range of rhetoric and diction that calls attention to itself as such, and his cultivation of a poetic structure that is intentionally nonorganic would be the most important examples."

Bernard Bergonzi, writing in *Encounter,* contended that ideologies were only tools to serve Auden's foremost interest: understanding the workings of the world. For Auden, said Bergonzi, Marxism and psychoanalysis alike were "attractive as techniques of explanation." Bergonzi posited that Auden perceived reality as "actually or potentially known and intelligible, without mysteries or uncertainty," and that he considered experience to be a complex entity which could be "reduced to classifiable elements, as a necessary preliminary to diagnosis and prescription." Auden expressed his desire for order in his preface to *Oxford Poetry 1927:* "All genuine poetry is in a sense the formation of private spheres out of a public chaos." Bergonzi was one of many critics who felt that Auden succeeded in giving his readers a feeling of the well-ordered "private sphere." He wrote: "At a time of world economic depression there was something reassuring in Auden's calm demonstration, mediated as much by style as by content, that reality was intelligible, and could be studied like a map or a catalogue, or seen in temporal terms as an inexorable historical process. . . . It was the last time that any British poet was to have such a global influence on poetry in English."

BIOGRAPHICAL/CRITICAL SOURCES:

BOOKS

Auden, W. H., *A Certain World: A Commonplace Book,* Viking, 1970.

Bahlke, G. W., *The Later Auden,* Rutgers University Press, 1970.

Beach, Joseph Warren, *The Making of the Auden Canon,* University of Minnesota Press, 1957.

Blair, J. G., *The Poetic Art of W. H. Auden,* Princeton University Press, 1965.

Bloom, Harold, *Ringers in the Tower: Studies in Romantic Tradition,* University of Chicago Press, 1971.

Bloomfield, B. C., *W. H. Auden: A Bibliography,* University Press of Virginia, 1964, 2nd edition, 1972.

Brophy, J. D., *W. H. Auden,* Columbia University Press, 1970.

Buell, Frederick, *W. H. Auden as a Social Poet,* Cornell University Press, 1973.

Callan, Edward, *An Annotated Check List of the Works of W. H. Auden,* A. Swallow, 1958.

Contemporary Literary Criticism, Gale, Volume 1, 1973, Volume 2, 1974, Volume 3, 1975, Volume 4, 1975, Volume 6, 1976, Volume 9, 1978, Volume 11, 1979, Volume 14, 1980, Volume 43, 1987.

Davidson, D., *W. H. Auden,* Evans, 1970.

Dictionary of Literary Biography, Gale, Volume 10: *Modern British Dramatists, 1940-45,* 1982, Volume 20, *British Poets, 1914-1945,* 1983.

Everett, Barbara, *Auden,* Oliver & Boyd, 1964.

Fuller, J., *A Reader's Guide to W. H. Auden,* Thames & Hudson, 1970.

Greenberg, Herbert, *Quest for the Necessary: W. H. Auden and the Dilemma of Divided Consciousness,* Harvard University Press, 1969.

Hoggart, Richard, *Auden: An Introductory Essay,* Yale University Press, 1951.

Mitchell, Donald, *Britten and Auden in the Thirties,* Faber, 1981.

Nelson, G., *Changes of Heart: A Study of the Poetry of W. H. Auden,* University of California Press, 1969.

Osborne, C. W. H., *W. H. Auden,* Harcourt, 1979.

Pike, James Albert, editor, *Modern Canterbury Pilgrims,* Morehouse, 1956.

Replogle, J. M., *Auden's Poetry,* Methuen, 1969, University of Washington Press, 1971.

Scarfe, Francois, *Auden and After,* Routledge, 1942, reprinted, Norwood, 1978.

Shapiro, Karl, *In Defense of Ignorance,* Random House, 1960.

Spears, Monroe K., *The Poetry of W. H. Auden: The Disenchanted Island,* Oxford University Press, 1963.

Spender, Stephen, *W. H. Auden,* Macmillan, 1975.

Srivastava, N., *W. H. Auden: A Poet of Ideas,* Chand, 1978.

Untermeyer, Louis, *Lives of the Poets,* Simon & Schuster, 1959.

Wright, G. T. W., *W. H. Auden,* Twayne, 1969.

PERIODICALS

Atlantic Monthly, August, 1966.
Books and Bookmen, June, 1969.
Carleton Miscellany, fall, 1969.
Chicago Tribune Book World, January 18, 1981.
Choice, April, 1972.
Christian Science Monitor, January 8, 1970, December 30, 1976.
Commentary, July, 1968.
Comparative Literature, spring, 1970.
Encounter, January, 1970, February, 1975.
Harper's, April, 1970.
Holiday, June, 1969.
Hudson Review, spring, 1968.
Life, June 30, 1970.
Listener, March 17, 1966, May 4, 1967, November 9, 1967, May 28, 1970, December 24, 1970.
London Magazine, January, 1961, March, 1968, February, 1969, October, 1969.
Nation, February 9, 1970, March 19, 1978.
New Leader, October 27, 1969.
New Republic, April 23, 1956.

New Statesman, January 28, 1956, June 9, 1956, July 19, 1958, December 13, 1968, September 26, 1969, September 27, 1974.
Newsweek, May 20, 1968, July 28, 1969.
New Yorker, August 4, 1956.
New York Times, October 26, 1967, January 24, 1970.
New York Times Book Review, February 15, 1968, July 20, 1969, March 18, 1973, April 29, 1979.
Observer, June 28, 1970, May 2, 1971.
Philological Quarterly, January, 1960.
Playboy, December, 1970.
PMLA, June, 1968.
Poetry, March, 1961, January, 1969.
Prairie Schooner, summer, 1970.
Publishers Weekly, October 15, 1973, August 11, 1975.
Punch, October 1, 1969.
Reporter, January 31, 1963.
Shenandoah, winter, 1967.
Time, May 3, 1960, May 31, 1968, January 26, 1970, July 6, 1970.
Times Literary Supplement, June 7, 1963, December 7, 1967, January 23, 1969, June 26, 1969, February 15, 1980, November 21, 1980.
Twentieth Century, September, 1960.
Twentieth Century Literature, January, 1970.
Variety, July 26, 1972.
Village Voice, February 10, 1972.
Virginia Quarterly Review, spring, 1966, spring, 1969.
Washington Post Book World, November 19, 1967, July 27, 1969, November 26, 1972.
Yale Review, autumn, 1968.

*　　*　　*

AVISON, Margaret   1918-

PERSONAL: Born April 23, 1918, in Galt, Ontario, Canada; daughter of Harold Wilson (a clergyman) and Mabel (Kirkland) Avison. *Education:* University of Toronto, B.A., 1940, M.A., 1964.

ADDRESSES: Home—17 Lascelles Blvd., Apt. 108, Toronto, Ontario, Canada M4V 2B6.

CAREER: Poet. Has held various positions, such as secretary, librarian, lecturer, researcher, and social worker.

AWARDS, HONORS: Guggenheim fellowship, 1956; Governor General's Literary Award for poetry, 1960.

WRITINGS:

Winter Sun, Routledge & Kegan Paul, 1960.
The Research Compendium, University of Toronto Press, 1964.
The Dumbfounding, Norton, 1966.
Silverick, Ganglia Press, 1969.
The Cosmic Chef, Oberon Press, 1970.
Sunblue, Lancelot Press, 1978.

Contributor to anthologies, including *The Book of Canadian Poetry,* University of Chicago Press, 1943, *Recent Canadian Verse,* Jackson Press, 1959, and *The Country of the Risen King: An Anthology of Christian Poetry,* Baker Books, 1978. Also contributor to periodicals and literary magazines, including *Canadian Forum, Manitoba Arts Review,* and *Origin.*

SIDELIGHTS: Although Margaret Avison is recognized by many critics as one of Canada's finest and most sensitive poets, she is relatively unknown internationally. Several reasons have been suggested for her lack of fame and attention. A very private person, Avison has not actively promoted her books. Another factor contributing to her lack of public recognition can be attributed to the fact that several of her books are hard to find—either published by a small press or not widely distributed by the publisher.

In *Dictionary of Literary Biography,* Ernest H. Redekop explains: "Margaret Avison has always been a relatively unknown poet, except among readers and critics of Canadian verse. Since 1966, critical essays on her work have increased, but the verbal and imaginative complexities of her poems have not won over many casual readers. . . . Her stature as a Canadian poet, to judge from the distribution of her poems today, is low; but those readers who have taken the trouble to study her work acknowledge the scope of her intelligence, the uniqueness of her imagination, and a virtuosity in the use of language perhaps unparalleled among contemporary Canadian poets."

Daniel W. Doerksen comments on Avison's poems in *Canadian Literature:* "Their rich sensitivity to all aspects of life, amounting to a wholesome 'secularity', their deep and incisive engagement in the world of thought and meaning, their full exploitation of all the modern resources of language and technique—all these mark them with the vitality which is the essence of true poetry."

BIOGRAPHICAL/CRITICAL SOURCES:

BOOKS

Contemporary Literary Criticism, Volume 2, 1974, Volume 4, 1975.
Dictionary of Literary Biography, Volume 53: *Canadian Writers Since 1960,* Gale, 1986.

PERIODICALS

Canadian Literature, spring, 1974.
Twentieth Century Literature, July, 1970.

* * *

AXTON, David
See KOONTZ, Dean R(ay)

* * *

AYCKBOURN, Alan 1939-
(Roland Allen)

PERSONAL: Surname is pronounced Ache-born; born April 12, 1939, in Hampstead, London, England; son of Horace (a concert musician) and Irene (Worley) Ayckbourn; married Christine Roland, May 9, 1959; children: Steven Paul, Philip Nicholas. *Education:* Attended Haileybury and Imperial Service College, Hertfordshire, England, 1952-57.

ADDRESSES: Office—Stephen Joseph Theatre-in-the-Round, Valley Bridge Parade, Scarborough YO11 2PL, England. *Agent*—Margaret Ramsay Ltd., 14 A, Goodwin's Ct., St. Martin's Lane, London WC2N 4LL, England.

CAREER: Stephen Joseph Theatre-in-the-Round Company, Scarborough, England, stage manager and actor, 1957-59, writer and director, 1959-61; Victoria Theatre, Stoke-on-Trent, England, actor, writer, and director, 1961-64; British Broadcasting Corporation (BBC), Leeds, Yorkshire, England, drama producer, 1965-70; Stephen Joseph Theatre-in-the-Round Company, writer and artistic director, 1970—. Visiting playwright

and director, National Theatre, London, England, 1977, 1980, 1986-88. Also acted with several British repertory companies.

AWARDS, HONORS: London Evening Standard best comedy award, 1973, for *Absurd Person Singular,* best play awards, 1974, for *The Norman Conquests,* 1977, for *Just Between Ourselves,* and 1987, for *A Small Family Business; Plays and Players* best new play awards, 1974, for *The Norman Conquests,* and 1985, for *A Chorus of Disapproval;* named "playwright of the year" by Variety Club of Great Britain, 1974; D.Litt, University of Hull, 1981, University of Keele, 1987, and University of Leeds, 1987; *London Evening Standard* Award, Olivier Award, and *Drama* Award, all 1985, for *A Chorus of Disapproval;* named Commander of the British Empire, 1987; Director of the Year Award, *Plays and Players,* 1987, for production of Arthur Miller's *A View from the Bridge.*

WRITINGS:

PLAYS

(Under pseudonym Roland Allen) "The Square Cat," first produced in Scarborough at Library Theatre, June, 1959.
(Under pseudonym Roland Allen) "Love after All," first produced in Scarborough at Library Theatre, December, 1959.
(Under pseudonym Roland Allen) "Dad's Tale," first produced in Scarborough at Library Theatre, December 19, 1960.
(Under pseudonym Roland Allen) "Standing Room Only," first produced in Scarborough at Library Theatre, July 13, 1961.
"Xmas v. Mastermind," first produced in Stoke-on-Trent, England at Victoria Theatre, December 26, 1962.
"Mr. Whatnot," first produced in Stoke-on-Trent at Victoria Theatre, November 12, 1963, revised version produced in London at Arts Theatre, August 6, 1964.
"The Sparrow," first produced in Scarborough at the Library Theatre, July 13, 1967.
Relatively Speaking (first produced as "Meet My Father" in Scarborough at Library Theatre, July 8, 1965, produced on the West End at Duke of York's Theatre, March 29, 1967), Samuel French, 1968.
We Who Are About To . . . (one-act; includes "Countdown"; first produced in London at Hampstead Theatre Club, February 6, 1969; also see below), published in *Mixed Doubles: An Entertainment on Marriage,* Methuen, 1970.
Mixed Doubles: An Entertainment on Marriage (includes "Countdown," and *We Who Are About to . . .*; first produced on the West End at Comedy Theatre, April 9, 1969), Methuen, 1970.
How the Other Half Loves (first produced in Scarborough at Library Theatre, July 31, 1969, produced on the West End at Lyric Theatre, August 5, 1970), Samuel French, 1971.
"The Story So Far," produced in Scarborough at Library Theatre, August 20, 1970, revised version as "Me Times Me Times Me," produced on tour March 13, 1972, second revised version as "Family Circles," produced in Richmond, England at Orange Tree Theatre, November 17, 1978.
Ernie's Incredible Illucinations (first produced in London, 1971), Samuel French, 1969.
Time and Time Again (first produced in Scarborough at Library Theatre, July 8, 1971, produced on the West End at Comedy Theatre, August 16, 1972), Samuel French, 1973.
Absurd Person Singular (first produced in Scarborough at Library Theatre, June 26, 1972, produced on the West End at Criterion Theatre, July 4, 1973), Samuel French, 1974.
Mother Figure (one-act; first produced in Horsham, Sussex, England at Capitol Theatre, 1973, produced on the West End

at Apollo Theatre, May 19, 1976; also see below), published in *Confusions,* Samuel French, 1977.

The Norman Conquests (trilogy; composed of *Table Manners, Living Together,* and *Round and Round the Garden;* first produced in Scarborough at Library Theatre June, 1973, produced on the West End at Globe Theatre, August 1, 1974), Samuel French, 1975.

Absent Friends (first produced in Scarborough at Library Theatre, June 17, 1974, produced on the West End at Garrick Theatre, July 23, 1975), Samuel French, 1975.

"Service Not Included" (television script), produced by British Broadcasting Corporation (BBC), 1974.

Confusions (one-acts; includes *Mother Figure, Drinking Companion, Between Mouthfuls, Gosforth's Fete,* and *A Talk in the Park;* first produced in Scarborough at Library Theatre, September 30, 1974, produced on the West End at Apollo Theatre, May 19, 1976), Samuel French, 1977.

(Author of book and lyrics) "Jeeves" (musical; adapted from stories by P. G. Wodehouse), music by Andrew Lloyd Webber, first produced on the West End at Her Majesty's Theatre, April 22, 1975.

Bedroom Farce (first produced in Scarborough at the Library Theatre, June 16, 1975, produced on the West End at Prince of Wales's Theatre, November 7, 1978, produced on Broadway at Brooks Atkinson Theatre, 1979; also see below), Samuel French, 1977.

Just Between Ourselves (first produced in Scarborough at Library Theatre, January 28, 1976, produced on the West End at Queen's Theatre, April 22, 1977; also see below), Samuel French, 1978.

Ten Times Table (first produced in Scarborough at Stephen Joseph Theatre-in-the-Round, January 18, 1977, produced on the West End at Globe Theatre, April 5, 1978; also see below), Samuel French, 1979.

Joking Apart (first produced in Scarborough at Stephen Joseph Theatre-in-the-Round, January 11, 1978, produced on the West End at Globe Theatre, March 7, 1979), Samuel French, 1979.

(Author of book and lyrics) "Men on Women on Men" (musical), music by Paul Todd, first produced in Scarborough at Stephen Joseph Theatre-in-the-Round, June 17, 1978.

Sisterly Feelings (first produced in Scarborough at Stephen Joseph Theatre-in-the-Round, January 10, 1979, produced on the West End at Olivier Theatre, June 3, 1980; also see below), Samuel French, 1981.

Taking Steps (first produced in Scarborough at Stephen Joseph Theatre-in-the-Round, September 27, 1979, produced on the West End at Lyric Theatre, September 2, 1980), Samuel French, 1981.

(Author of book and lyrics) *Suburban Strains* (musical; first produced in Scarborough at Stephen Joseph Theatre-in-the-Round, January 20, 1980, produced in London at Round House Theatre, February 2, 1981), music by Todd, Samuel French, 1981.

Season's Greetings (first produced in Scarborough at Stephen Joseph Theatre-in-the-Round, September 24, 1980, revised version first produced in Greenwich, England at Greenwich Theatre, January 27, 1982, produced on the West End at Apollo Theatre, March 29, 1982), Samuel French, 1982.

(Author of book and lyrics) "Me, Myself, and I" (musical), music by Todd, first produced in Scarborough at Stephen Joseph Theatre-in-the-Round, June, 1981.

Way Upstream (first produced in Scarborough at Stephen Joseph Theatre-in-the-Round, October, 1981, produced in London

at National Theatre, October 4, 1982), Samuel French, 1983.

(Author of book and lyrics) "Making Tracks" (musical), music by Todd, first produced in Scarborough at Stephen Joseph Theatre-in-the-Round, December 16, 1981.

Intimate Exchanges (first produced in Scarborough at Stephen Joseph Theatre-in-the-Round, June 3, 1982, produced on the West End at the Ambassadors Theatre, August 14, 1984), Samuel French, 1985.

"It Could Be Any One of Us," first produced in Scarborough at Stephen Joseph Theatre-in-the-Round, October 9, 1983.

A Chorus of Disapproval (first produced in Scarborough at Stephen Joseph Theatre-in-the-Round, May 3, 1984, produced on the West End at the Lyric Theatre, June 11, 1986), Samuel French, 1985.

Woman in Mind (first produced in Scarborough at Stephen Joseph Theatre-in-the-Round, June 3, 1985, produced on the West End at Vaudeville Theatre, September 3, 1986), Faber, 1986, Samuel French, 1987.

"The Westwoods," first produced in Scarborough at Stephen Joseph Theatre-in-the-Round, May 1984, produced in London at Etcetera Theatre, May 31, 1987.

A Small Family Business (first produced on the West End at Olivier Theatre, June 5, 1987), Faber, 1987, Samuel French, 1988.

Henceforward . . . (first produced in Scarborough at Stephen Joseph Theatre-in-the-Round, July 30, 1987, produced on the West End at Vaudeville Theatre, November 21, 1988), Faber, 1989.

"Man of the Moment," first produced in Scarborough at Stephen Joseph Theatre-in-the-Round, August 10, 1988.

Mr. A's Amazing Maze Plays (first produced in Scarborough at Stephen Joseph Theatre-in-the-Round, November 30, 1988), Faber, 1989.

"The Revenger's Comedies," first produced in Scarborough at Stephen Joseph Theatre-in-the-Round, June 13, 1989.

OMNIBUS VOLUMES

Three Plays (contains *Absurd Person Singular, Absent Friends,* and *Bedroom Farce*), Grove, 1979.

Joking Apart and Other Plays (includes *Joking Apart, Just Between Ourselves,* and *Ten Times Table*), Chatto & Windus, 1979.

Sisterly Feelings and Taking Steps, Chatto & Windus, 1981.

SIDELIGHTS: Alan Ayckbourn is generally considered Great Britain's most successful living playwright. For well over two decades Ayckbourn comedies have been appearing regularly in London's West End theatres, earning the author handsome royalties as well as an international reputation. London *Times* reviewer Anthony Masters observes that Ayckbourn's work since the mid-1960s "is rich in major and minor masterpieces that will certainly live and are now overdue for revival." A prolific writer who often crafts his dramas just shortly before they are due to be staged, Ayckbourn extracts wry and disenchanted humor from the dull rituals of English middle-class life. To quote *Nation* contributor Harold Clurman, the dramatist is "a master hand at turning the bitter apathy, the stale absurdity which most English playwrights now find characteristic of Britain's lower-middle-class existence into hilarious comedy." *Dictionary of Literary Biography* essayist Albert E. Kalson describes a typical Ayckbourn play as an "intricately staged domestic comedy with a half-dozen intertwined characters who reflect the audience's own unattainable dreams and disappointments while moving them to laughter with at least a suggestion of a tear." In the London *Times,* Andrew Hislop comments that the plays, translated into two dozen languages, "are probably watched by more people in the world than those of any other living dramatist."

Kalson suggests that Ayckbourn's work "is rooted in the Home Counties, his characters' speech patterns reflecting his upbringing." Indeed, although Ayckbourn was born in London, he was raised in a succession of small Sussex towns by his mother and her second husband, a provincial bank manager. Ayckbourn told the *New York Times* that his childhood was not comfortable or cheery. "I was surrounded by relationships that weren't altogether stable, the air was often blue, and things were sometimes flying across the kitchen," he said. *New York Times* contributor Benedict Nightingale finds this youthful insecurity reflected in Ayckbourn's writings, since the characters "often come close to destroying each other, though more commonly through insensitivity than obvious malice." At seventeen Ayckbourn determined that he wanted to be an actor. After several years with small repertory companies, during which he learned stage managing as well as acting techniques, he took a position with the Stephen Joseph Company in Scarborough. According to Kalson, his continuing association with that group "eventually turned a minor actor into a major playwright." Nightingale is philosophical about Ayckbourn's creative development. "If he had been a happier man," the critic writes, ". . . he wouldn't have wanted to write plays. If he had been a more successful actor, he would have had no need to do so. If he'd known happier people in his early life, his plays wouldn't be so interesting. And if he had not been an actor at all, it would have taken him much longer to learn how to construct his plots, prepare his effects and time his jokes."

Ayckbourn began his tenure at Scarborough as an actor and stage manager. He has described the company as "the first of the fringe theatres," with interests in experimental theatre-in-the-round work and other so-called underground techniques. As he gained experience, Ayckbourn began to agitate for larger roles. The group leader, Stephen Joseph, had other ideas, however. In *Drama,* Ayckbourn reminisced about his earliest attempts at playwrighting. Joseph told him, "If you want a better part, you'd better write one for yourself. You write a play, I'll do it. If it's any good. . . . Write yourself a main part." Ayckbourn appreciated the latter advice especially, calling it "a very shrewd remark, because presumably, if the play had not worked at all, there was no way I as an actor was going to risk my neck in it." Ayckbourn actually wrote several plays that were staged at Scarborough in the early 1960s—pseudonymous works such as "The Square Cat," "Love after All," "Dad's Tale," and "Standing Room Only." According to Ian Watson in *Drama,* these "belong to Ayckbourn's workshop period, and today he is careful to ensure that nobody reads them, and certainly nobody produces them."

Eventually Ayckbourn gave up acting when he discovered his particular muse—the fears and foibles of Britain's middle classes. As he began to experience success outside of Scarborough, however, he continued to craft his work specifically for that company and its small theatre-in-the-round. A large majority of his plays have debuted there, despite the lure of the West End. "My plays are what one would expect from someone who runs a small theater in a community such as Scarborough," Ayckbourn told the *Chicago Tribune.* "That means the cost for the play is about the budget for one production in the company's season, and the subject matter offers the audience a chance to see something they know, to laugh at jokes they've heard before." Kalson likewise notes that the playwright "bears in mind the requirements of the Scarborough audience, many of them his neighbors, upon whom he depends for the testing of his work.

He will neither insult nor shock them, respecting their desire to be entertained. He provides them with plays about the life he observes around him, sometimes even his own." *Los Angeles Times* correspondent Sylvie Drake writes: "Alan Ayckbourn is a blithe spirit. He has been writing plays for actors he knows in a theater in Scarborough, England, without much concern for the rest of the world. Since that 'rest of the world' admires nothing more than someone with the audacity to pay it no attention, it promptly embraced his idiosyncratic comedies and totally personal style."

Ayckbourn's early plays "succeeded in resuscitating that most comatose of genres, the 'farcical comedy,' " according to Nightingale in *New Statesman.* In *Modern Drama,* Malcolm Page similarly characterizes the early works as "the lightest and purest of comedies, giving [Ayckbourn] the reputation of being the most undemanding of entertainers." Plays such as *Relatively Speaking, How the Other Half Loves,* and *Absurd Person Singular* "abound with the basic element of theatrical humor, that is incongruity, the association of unassociable elements," to quote Guido Almansi in *Encounter.* Typically revolving around extramarital affairs or class conflicts, the comedies begin with a peculiar situation that grows inexorably out of control, with mistaken identities, unclarified misunderstandings, and overlooked clues. *New York Times* commentator Walter Goodman writes: "How Mr. Ayckbourn contrives to get his people into such states and persuade us to believe that they are reasonable is a secret of his comic flair." With the enthusiastic reception for *Relatively Speaking,* concludes Oleg Kerensky in *The New British Drama: Fourteen Playwrights since Osborne and Pinter,* Ayckbourn established himself "as a writer of ingenious farcical comedy, with an ear for dialogue and with a penchant for complex situations . . . and ingenious plots." That reputation led some critics to question Ayckbourn's lasting contribution to the theatre, but subsequent plays have clarified the author's more serious intentions. Kalson concludes: "Beyond the easy jokes, the mistaken identities, the intricate staging, Ayckbourn was learning a craft that would enable him, always within the framework of bourgeois comedy, to illuminate the tedium, the pain, even the horror of daily life recognizable not only in England's Home Counties, . . . or in gruffer, heartier northern England, . . . but all over the world."

Throughout his years of playwrighting, Ayckbourn has taken risks not easily reconciled with popular comedy. Some American critics have labeled him "the British Neil Simon," but in fact his characters often must contend with an undercurrent of humiliation, mediocrity, and embarrassment that Simon does not address. In the *Chicago Tribune,* Howard Reich writes: "The best of Ayckbourn's work . . . is funny not only for what its characters say but because of what they don't. Between the wisecracks and rejoinders, there breathe characters who are crumbling beneath the strictures of British society." Ayckbourn may pillory the manners and social conventions of the middle classes, but he also concerns himself with the defeats that define ordinary, often hopeless, lives. According to Alan Brien in *Plays and Players,* the author "shows . . . that what is funny to the audience can be tragic to the characters, and that there is no lump in the throat to equal a swallowed laugh which turns sour." *New York* magazine contributor John Simon suggests that Ayckbourn "extends the range of farce, without cheating, to cover situations that are not farcical—the fibrillations of the heart under the feverish laughter. And he keeps his characters characters, not walking stacks of interchangeable jokebooks." As Guido Almansi notes in *Encounter,* the playwright "knows how to operate dramatically on what seems to be utterly banal: which is certainly more difficult than the exploitation of the sublime."

A favorite Ayckbourn theme is the pitfalls of marriage, an institution in which the playwright finds little joy. *New Yorker* correspondent Brendan Gill contends that the author "regards human relationships in general and the marriage relationship in particular as little more than a pailful of cozily hissing snakes." Richard Eder elaborates in the *New York Times:* "His characters are simply people for whom the shortest distance between two emotional points is a tangle; and who are too beset by doubts, timidities and chronic self-complication to have time for anything as straightforward as sex." Harold Hobson also observes in *Drama* that behind Ayckbourn's foolery "he has this sad conviction that marriage is a thing that will not endure. Men and women may get instant satisfaction from life, but it is not a satisfaction that will last long. . . . It is when Ayckbourn sees the tears of life, its underlying, ineradicable sadness, that he is at his superb best." *Bedroom Farce* and *Absurd Person Singular* both tackle the thorny side of marriage; the two plays are among Ayckbourn's most successful. In *New Statesman,* Nightingale concludes that in both works Ayckbourn "allows his people to have feelings, that these feelings can be hurt, and that this is cause for regret. . . . There are few sadder things than the slow destruction of youthful optimism, not to mention love, trust and other tender shoots: Mr. Ayckbourn makes sure we realise it."

Throughout his career Ayckbourn has demonstrated a reluctance to be limited by conventional staging techniques. This tendency, born in the Scarborough theatre-in-the-round atmosphere, has become an abiding factor in the playwright's work. "Alan Ayckbourn's comedies have become such money-spinners and he himself has won such general critical acclaim that it is difficult to think of him as an experimental dramatist," writes Shorter. "He has however probably done as much as any other living playwright to use the stage with an original sense of its scope—to stretch its scenic and dramatic possibilities." Some Ayckbourn plays juxtapose several floors of a house—or several different houses—in one set; others offer alternative scenes decided at random by the actors or by a flip of a coin. According to J. W. Lambert in *Drama,* Ayckbourn's "ingenuity in thus constructing the plays positively makes the head spin if dwelt upon; but of course it should not be dwelt upon, for however valuable the challenge may have been to his inventive powers, it is to us only an incidental pleasure. The value of the work lies elsewhere—in its knife-sharp insights into the long littleness of life and in its unflagging comic exhilaration." Page likewise insists that while his staging skills "are frequently dazzling, Ayckbourn claims our attention for his insights about people: he prompts us to laugh, then to care about the character and to make a connection with ourselves, our own behavior, and possibly beyond to the world in which we live."

The Norman Conquests, first produced in 1973, combines Ayckbourn's theme of the frailty of relationships with an experimental structure. The piece is actually a trilogy of plays, any one of which can be seen on its own for an understanding of the story. Together, however, the three parts cover completely several hours in the day of an unscrupulous character named Norman, whose "conquests" are generally restricted to the seduction of women. In the *Chicago Tribune,* Richard Christiansen suggests that the three plays "fit together like Chinese boxes. Each comedy has the same cast of characters, the same time frame and the same house as a setting; but what the audience sees on stage in the dining room in one play may happen off stage in the living room in another, and vice versa. Though each play can be enjoyed on its own, much of the fun relies on the audience knowing

what is going on in the other two plays." Almansi writes: "As we view the second and then the third play of the trilogy, our awareness of what is going on in the rest of the house and likewise the satisfaction of our curiosity grow concurrently. We enjoy guessing what preceded or what will follow the entrance or the exit of the actor from the garden to the lounge, or from the latter to the kitchen, and we slowly build up a complete picture of the proceedings, as if we were Big Brother enjoying a panoptic and all-embracing vision. I dare surmise that this innovation will count in the future development of theatrical technique." Gill comments that despite its length, the farce "is likely to make you laugh far more often than it is likely to make you look at your watch."

Page, among others, sees a gradual darkening of Ayckbourn's vision over the years. The author's plays, writes Page, "challenge an accepted rule of contemporary comedy: that the audience does not take home the sorrows of the characters after the show. This convention—a matter of both the dramatist's style and the audience's expectations—verges on breakdown when Ayckbourn shifts from farce to real people in real trouble." London *Times* reviewer Bryan Appleyard similarly contends that in recent Ayckbourn dramas "the signs are all there. Encroaching middle age and visionary pessimism are beginning to mark [his] work." This is not to suggest that the author's plays are no longer funny; they simply address such themes as loneliness, adultery, family quarrels, and the twists of fate with candor and sincerity. "Up to now, we have thought of Ayckbourn as the purveyor of amusing plays about suburban bumblers," writes Dan Sullivan in a *Los Angeles Times* review of Ayckbourn's futuristic comedy *Henceforward.* "Here we see him as a thoughtful and painfully honest reporter of the crooked human heart—more crooked every year, it seems." Appleyard observes that Ayckbourn "appears to be entering a visionary middle age and the long-term effect on his plays is liable to be stronger polarization. Villains will really be villains . . . and heroes may well at last begin to be heroes." Indeed, Ayckbourn seems to have become interested in the acceleration of moral decay in his country; plays such as *Way Upstream, A Chorus of Disapproval,* and *A Small Family Business* explore small communities where extreme selfishness holds sway. In the *Chicago Tribune,* for instance, Matthew Wolf calls *A Small Family Business* "a strong study of one man's seduction into a milieu of moral filth." Christiansen concludes that the cumulative effect of these plays puts Ayckbourn "into his rightful place as an agile and insightful playwright in the front ranks of contemporary theatre."

Drama essayist Anthony Curtis declares that Ayckbourn's career "is shining proof that the well-made play is alive and well." Now entering his fourth decade as a playwright, Ayckbourn continues to craft at least one full-length work a year; he also directs his own and others' works in Scarborough and at London's National Theatre. In *Drama,* Michael Leech writes: "There are those who compare [Ayckbourn] to a latterday Moliere, those who say he is a mere play factory, others who might opine that he veers violently between the two extremes. Certainly he is one of our most prolific and gifted writers of comedy, with characters pinned to the page with the finesse and exactness of a collector of unusual butterflies. . . . And he can look back on a body of work that for most writers would be a life-time's effort." London *Times* commentator Andrew Hislop finds Ayckbourn "at the summit of his career. . . . The security of his Scarborough nest has enabled him to continue his work remarkably unaffected by those who have overpraised him, comparing him to Shakespeare, and those who have unjustly reviled him, regarding him as a vacuous, right-wing boulevardier." Certainly Ayckbourn has more champions than critics, both in England and abroad. Hobson, for one, concludes that the public responds to Ayckbourn's work "because he is both a highly comic writer and, dramatically speaking, a first-class conjuror. The tricks he plays in some of his work are stupendous. They are miracles of human ingenuity." Shorter also observes that as a playwright, Ayckbourn is "homely," "comforting," "immediately accessible," and "easily enjoyed." The critic adds: "Witness the crowded audiences of laughing shirt-sleeved holiday-makers. . . . They are never made to frown or allowed to yawn. . . . They are too busy . . . recognizing themselves, or at any rate each other. They are in fact what Mr. Ayckbourn calls his 'source material,' and he means to stick close to it, despite his popular success and the wealth it has brought him."

Ayckbourn told the *Los Angeles Times* that his ambition is to write "totally effortless, totally truthful, unforced comedy shaped like a flawless diamond in which one can see a million reflections, both one's own and other people's." He also commented in the London *Times* that the best part of his work "is not the clapping, it's the feeling at the end of the evening, that you have given the most wonderful party and those five hundred strangers who came in are feeling better. . . . I don't know, but they are sort of unified into a whole and that is marvelous. That's really like shutting the door on a good party and thinking—that went well!"

MEDIA ADAPTATIONS: A Chorus of Disapproval was produced as a feature film in Great Britain in 1989.

BIOGRAPHICAL/CRITICAL SOURCES:

BOOKS

Contemporary Literary Criticism, Gale, Volume 5, 1976, Volume 8, 1978, Volume 18, 1981, Volume 33, 1985.
Dictionary of Literary Biography, Volume 13: *British Dramatists since World War II,* Gale, 1982.
Elsom, John, *Post-War British Theatre,* Routledge & Kegan Paul, 1976.
Hayman, Ronald, *British Theatre since 1955: A Reassessment,* Oxford University Press, 1979.
Joseph, Stephen, *Theatre in the Round,* Barrie & Rockcliff, 1967.
Kerensky, Oleg, *The New British Drama: Fourteen Playwrights since Osborne and Pinter,* Hamish Hamilton, 1977.
Taylor, John Russell, *The Second Wave: British Drama for the Seventies,* Methuen, 1971.
Taylor, John Russell, *Contemporary English Drama,* Holmes & Meier, 1981.
Watson, Ian, *Alan Ayckbourn: Bibliography, Biography, Playography, Theatre Checklist, No. 21,* T.Q. Publications, 1980.
Watson, Ian, *Conversations with Ayckbourn,* Macmillan (London), 1981.
White, Sidney Howard, *Alan Ayckbourn,* Twayne, 1985.

PERIODICALS

Chicago Tribune, July 17, 1982, July 15, 1983, August 2, 1987.
Drama, autumn, 1974, summer, 1978, spring, 1979, summer, 1979, January, 1980, October, 1980, first quarter, 1981, second quarter, 1981, autumn, 1981, spring, 1982, summer, 1982, winter, 1982, Volume 162, 1986.
Encounter, December, 1974, April, 1978.
Guardian, August 7, 1970, August 14, 1974.
Listener, May 23, 1974.
Los Angeles Times, January 20, 1983, March 6, 1984, March 30, 1987, October 28, 1987.
Modern Drama, March, 1983.
Nation, March 8, 1975, December 27, 1975, April 21, 1979.

New Republic, November 9, 1974.
New Statesman, May 31, 1974, July 5, 1974, December 1, 1978, June 13, 1980.
Newsweek, October 21, 1974.
New York, October 28, 1974, December 22, 1975, April 16, 1979, April 2, 1984.
New Yorker, October 21, 1974, December 22, 1975, April 9, 1979.
New York Times, October 20, 1974, February 16, 1977, April 4, 1977, March 25, 1979, March 30, 1979, March 31, 1979, May 1, 1979, October 16, 1981, May 29, 1986, June 15, 1986, June 25, 1986, October 3, 1986, October 29, 1986, November 26, 1986, July 20, 1987, April 15, 1988, June 5, 1988.
Plays and Players, September, 1972, September, 1975, January, 1983, May, 1983, April, 1987.
Observer, February 13, 1977, March 4, 1979.
Sunday Times (London), June 3, 1973, June 8, 1980.
Sunday Times Magazine, February 20, 1977.
Time, May 9, 1979, August 13, 1984.
Times (London), January 5, 1976, January 19, 1980, February 4, 1981, February 2, 1982, June 7, 1982, August 18, 1982, October 6, 1982, October 10, 1983, May 4, 1984, June 4, 1985, April 9, 1986, September 5, 1986, November 5, 1986, December 15, 1986, June 1, 1987, June 8, 1987, June 27, 1987, February 10, 1988, November 23, 1988.
Tribune, February 13, 1981.
Washington Post, July 10, 1977.

—*Sketch by Anne Janette Johnson*

*   *   *

AZUELA, Mariano 1873-1952
(Beleno)

PERSONAL: Born January 1, 1873, in Lagos de Moreno, Jalisco, Mexico; died of a heart attack, March 1, 1952, in Mexico City, Mexico; buried in the Rotonda de Hombres Ilustres, Mexico City, Mexico; son of Evaristo Azuela and Paulina Gonzalez; married Carmen Rivera; children: Salvador, Mariano, Carmen, Julia, Paulina, Maria de la Luz, Augustin, Esperanza, Antonio, Enrique. *Education:* Faculty of Medicine and Pharmacy of Guadalajara, degree of doctor, 1898.

ADDRESSES: Home—Mexico City, Mexico.

CAREER: Physician, 1898-1952, and writer, 1907-1952. Director of public education in Jalisco province under government of Francisco ("Pancho") Villa. *Wartime service:* Physician with Villa's army during Mexican Revolution.

AWARDS, HONORS: National Prize for Literature, 1949; *The Underdogs* won a prize for drama, 1950.

WRITINGS:

NOVELS AND NOVELLAS

Maria Luisa, first published in 1907, 2nd edition, Botas, 1938.
Los fracasados (title means "The Failures"), first published in 1908, 4th edition, Botas, 1939.
Mala yerba: Novela de costumbres nacionales, first published in 1909, reprinted, R. Terrazas, 1924, translation by Anita Brenner published as *Marcela: A Mexican Love Story,* foreword by Waldo Frank, Farrar & Rinehart, 1932.
Andres Perez, maderista, Botas, 1911.
Sin amor, first published in 1912, 2nd edition, Botas, 1945.
Los de abajo: Novela de la revolucion mexicana, first published in 1916, translation by E. Munguia, Jr., published as *The*

Under Dogs, preface by Carleton Beals, illustrations by J. C. Orozco, Brentano's, 1929; published as *The Underdogs: A Novel of the Mexican Revolution,* foreword by Harriet de Onis, illustrations by Orozco, New American Library, 1963; translation by Frances K. Hendricks and Beatrice Berler published as *The Underdogs* in *Two Novels of the Mexican Revolution: The Trials of a Respectable Family and The Underdogs,* Principia Press of Trinity University, 1963 (also see below).

Los caciques, first published in 1917, translation by Lesley Byrd Simpson published as *The Bosses* in *Two Novels of Mexico: The Flies. The Bosses,* University of California Press, 1956 (also see below).

Las moscas [and] *Domitilo quiere ser diputado* [and] *De como al fin lloro Juan Pablo,* Tip de A. Carranza e Hijos, 1918, translation of *Las moscas* by Simpson published as *The Flies* in *Two Novels of Mexico: The Flies. The Bosses,* University of California Press, 1956 (also see below).

Las tribulaciones de una familia decente, first published in 1918, 2nd edition, Botas, 1938, translation by Hendricks and Berler published as *The Trials of a Respectable Family* in *Two Novels of the Mexican Revolution: The Trials of a Respectable Family and The Underdogs,* Trinity University Press, 1963 (also see below).

La malhora, first published in 1923, 3rd edition published with 2nd edition of *El desquite,* Botas, 1941 (also see below).

El desquite, first published in 1925, 2nd edition published with 3rd edition of *La malhora,* Botas, 1941.

La luciernaga, Espasa-Calpe (Madrid), 1932, translation by Hendricks and Berler published as *The Firefly* in *Three Novels of Mariano Azuela,* Trinity University Press, 1979 (also see below).

Pedro Moreno, el insurgente: Biografia novelada, Ediciones Ercilla (Santiago, Chile), 1935.

Precursores, Ediciones Ercilla, 1935.

El camarada Pantoja, Botas, 1937.

San Gabriel de Valdivias, comunidad indigena, Ediciones Ercilla, 1938.

Regina Landa, Botas, 1939.

Avanzada, Botas, 1940.

Nueva burguesia, Club del Libro Amigos del Libro Americano (Buenos Aires), 1941, recent edition, Secretaria de Educacion Publica, Cultura, Fondo de Cultura Economica, 1985.

El padre don Agustin Rivera, Botas, 1942.

La marchanta, Seminario de Cultura Mexicana, Secretaria de Educacion Publica, 1944.

La mujer domada, El Colegio Nacional, 1946.

Sendas perdidas, Botas, 1949.

La maldicion, Fondo de Cultura Economica, 1955.

Esa sangre, Fondo de Cultura Economica, 1956.

Also author of *Madero: Biografia novelada.*

WORKS IN TRANSLATION

Two Novels of Mexico: The Flies. The Bosses, translation with preface by Simpson, University of California Press, 1956.

Two Novels of the Mexican Revolution: The Trials of a Respectable Family and The Underdogs, translation by Hendricks and Berler, introduction by Hendricks, Principia Press of Trinity University, 1963.

Three Novels by Mariano Azuela (contains *The Trials of a Respectable Family, The Underdogs,* and *The Firefly*), translation by Hendricks and Berler, introduction by Luis Leal, Trinity University Press, 1979.

OTHER

Teatro: Los de abajo, El buho en la noche, Del llano hnos. (plays), Botas, 1938.

Cien anos de novela mexicana (criticism), Botas, 1947.

Obras completas (title means "Complete Works"), three volumes, prologue by Francisco Monterde, Fondo de Cultura Economica, 1958-60, recent edition, 1976.

Introduccion al estudio del amparo: Lecciones, Department de Bibliotecas, Universidad de Nuevo Leon, 1968.

Epistolario y archivo, compiled with notes and appendices by Berler, Centro de Estudios Literarios, Universidad Nacional Autonoma de Mexico, 1969.

Also author of works under the pseudonym Beleno. Contributor to periodicals.

SIDELIGHTS: Mariano Azuela was one of the leading writers of twentieth-century Mexico and the foremost chronicler of that country's revolution. During his forty-year literary career he wrote more than twenty novels describing the volatile Mexican political scene, including *Las tribulaciones de una familia decente* (*The Trials of a Respectable Family*), and an account of his experiences with Francisco ("Pancho") Villa's army of revolutionaries, *Los de abajo* (*The Underdogs*). A physician, he dedicated his life to alleviating the suffering of the poor and oppressed, and through his novels he strove to rectify social inequality. His works, imbued with his pessimistic view of Mexico's future, expose the sources of the oppression that brought about the revolution, the false idealism and brutality of many of the politicians and military leaders during the war years, and the anarchy that pervaded postrevolutionary Mexican society.

Azuela was originally compelled to write by the desperate conditions he encountered while practicing medicine in the Mexico City slums. His first novel, *Maria Luisa,* was based on a story about a woman forced to choose between becoming a factory worker or a student's mistress. The composition of this novice work, published in 1907 when Azuela was thirty-four, displays the strengths and weaknesses of his subsequent writings. While creating vivid social and cultural scenes, he pays little attention to plot and structure. He forms his characters by concentrating on a few actions or other outstanding physical features, a technique some critics contend is dangerously close to caricature. And his characters, though well-rounded, are often stereotypical: villains are rich, conservative, and ruthless, while heroes are poor and seek only social equality. Although he wrote about both the lower and middle classes throughout Mexico, most commentators label his provincial characters—rich and poor—his most believable and interesting.

Maria Luisa also displays Azuela's hallmark use of dialogue. The author is consistently praised for mimicking speech patterns and idioms particular to specific social classes, professions, and provinces. He writes with few subordinate clauses, and his sentence structure is straightforward but lyrical, especially when describing nature and, ironically, the horrors of war. He is also noted for his concision. Jefferson Rea Spell in *Contemporary Spanish-American Fiction* assessed that it is Azuela's "mastery of the art of selection and condensation . . . whether he is describing nature, persons, or the man-made world," that distinguishes him as a literary artist.

In his early novels—*Los fracasados* ("The Failures"), *Mala yerba* (*Marcela: A Mexican Love Story*), and *Sin amor*—Azuela outlines the social and political circumstances that led to the revolution. *Los fracasados* excoriates Porfirio Diaz, Mexico's notoriously corrupt dictator who, during his thirty-five year tenure, rewarded his political allies with lands taken from the peasants. Azuela condemns the provincial landowners and the middle class—Diaz's chief supporters—by satirizing their greed and pettiness. Some critics, including Spell, however, complained that in the novel Azuela seems "less concerned with telling a story than with exposing the iniquity of certain inhabitants of Alamos." Although reviewers found the novel technically and artistically lacking, most agreed with Spell, who claimed that the work "is significant in that it portrays the intolerable conditions in a Mexican town that gave rise to the brutality of the underlings when they rose a few years later against their masters."

Azuela continued his attack on rural bourgeois society in *Marcela* and *Sin amor,* two books exploring the differences between the wealthy landowners and the wretched peasants who worked the estates. Spell noted that *Sin amor* successfully depicts "the great gulf between those that have and those that have not; the resentment of the latter toward the former; and the scorn of the wealthy for the poor."

Azuela's novels written during the Mexican Revolution unflinchingly portray war and display his growing disgust as the violence escalated. The revolution began with Diaz's overthrow by liberal leader Francisco I. Madero in 1910, and Madero's subsequent assassination by an opposing faction. During the consequent struggle for succession, which lasted seven years and embroiled the whole country, Azuela supported Villa. When the guerrilla army led by Venustiano Carranza gained the upper hand in government, however, Azuela was forced to flee with Villa's band to Texas. After the war Azuela returned to Mexico, where he practiced medicine and chronicled the revolution in five novels, *Andres Perez, maderista, The Underdogs, Los caciques* (*The Bosses*), *Las moscas* (*The Flies*), and *The Trials of a Respectable Family.*

Andres Perez, maderista recounts the chaos and confusion of the initial battles of the revolution and analyzes the various motives of some of Madera's followers, including an altruistic ideologist, a landowner whose property had been seized, and a political opportunist. "Ideologically, [*Andres Perez, maderista*] is one of his most significant novels," John E. Englekirk and Lawrence B. Kiddle observed in their introduction to Azuela's *Los de abajo.* "Conceived during those very months when Azuela already foresaw the tragic turn the revolt of the idealist Madero was soon to take, . . . it is the work of one who boldly, fearlessly, and prophetically [decried the revolution]."

The Underdogs, considered Azuela's masterwork, followed. He wrote it in 1915 while a fugitive in El Paso, Texas, with Villa's band. By presenting the experiences of a common soldier during the conflict, Azuela condemned the gratuitous violence, the sociopolitical forces that drove the Mexican people into poverty, and the opportunism that contradicted the goals of the revolution. The novel follows poor country boy Demetrio Macias's rise to the rank of general in Villa's revolutionary army. Opening in a battle in Juchipila Canyon, where Demetrio's forces deftly triumph, the drama and violence escalate until Macias is killed in the same canyon. Azuela depicts him as being defeated by the same forces—corruption and greed—that were bastardizing the revolution.

Azuela's despair for the future of his country permeates *The Underdogs.* Citing the "brutality" of many of his scenes, *Bookman* contributor Carleton Beals likened Azuela's writing to that of Russian revolutionary author Maxim Gorki. The critic pointed out, however, that the Mexican shares "Gorki's terrific pessimism [but] none of [his] revolutionary optimism." Spell also re-

marked on *The Underdogs*'s "intense and varied emotive power," extrapolating: "while the author arouses pity for the downtrodden peasants, he also horrifies the reader with the crimes that some of them, in their ignorance and bestiality, commit." Beals noted that Azuela's "language is the language of reality . . . crude, often vile, truculent, fiendish."

The Bosses is a pessimistic account of life in a small western town owned and run by a family of wealthy Diaz supporters who viciously defend their privileged position by making war against the peasants. "Azuela is writing in white-hot anger against the cruelty and injustice of a system," Lesley Byrd Simpson wrote in the preface to *Two Novels of Mexico,* "and uses the effective device of extreme caricature to point up his thesis." Spell agreed, noting that Azuela's apparent intention for writing *The Bosses*—to expose the oppressors—applies to all of his novels of the war in general: "Through the injustice that it lays bare, the book affords a vindication, in a measure, of those who committed the most shocking atrocities against the lives and property of the privileged classes when the Revolution broke."

Azuela continues in the same vein with *The Flies,* considered one of his finest works. The action opens as a panicked throng of middle-class merchants are crowding onto trains in a Mexico City railway station to escape imminent slaughter by guerrilla leader Alvaro Obregon's ferocious troops. Throughout the night the characters reveal their thoughts and fears, and, Simpson wrote, condemn themselves. "The choppy, fragmentary dialogue," the critic noted, "the abrupt shifts, the callousness of some, the maudlin drunkenness of others, and the prodigious silliness of the frightened mother and her gold-digging family, together give us an etching of civil war not easily forgotten."

Azuela's last war novel, *Trials of a Respectable Family,* is an uncharacteristically sensitive study of the plight of the bourgeoisie during the revolution. Some critics surmise he wrote this novel after realizing that during war "good" men are as capable of atrocities as "bad" men. When affluent provincials heard reports of slaughters and pilfering by the revolutionaries, they fled to Mexico City, where they faced hardship in a city overrun by barbarous gangs. Azuela portrays the refugees' suffering as ennobling. Today *Trials of a Respectable Family* is considered second only to *The Underdogs* in the canon of Mexican revolutionary literature, although when it was published in 1918—directly following the revolution—it was ignored by critics who were perhaps unwilling to review a book sympathetic to the bourgeoisie.

Some critics claim that Azuela next produced three experimental novels, *La malhora, El desquite,* and *La luciernaga* (*The Firefly*), in response to this lack of contemporary critical attention. Published in 1923, 1925, and 1932, these novels are difficult to read, due to thick, obscure, and sometimes incomprehensible imagery, heavy symbolism, and distorted sentence structure. "Azuela's striving for inordinate effects has definitely marred the work," Englekirk and Kiddle assessed in their critique of *La malhora.* They also complained that Azuela's continual digressions overwhelmed the main narrative threads. Other commentators noted that Azuela's dialogue was exaggerated and ill-suited to his characters.

Yet the sentiment that *La malhora, El desquite,* and *The Firefly* purvey, critical of postrevolutionary society, is undoubtedly true to Azuela's social philosophy. According to Englekirk and Kiddle, "the picture Azuela paints for us here is a somber one indeed . . . in the sordidness and the physical and mental degeneracy it portrays." His last radical novel, *The Firefly,* is his only work that can be called a psychological study. In it he contrasts two brothers, a guilt-ridden thief and a drug addict.

Azuela abandoned his experimental style and addressed national problems clearly in his next novels, *El camarada Pantoja, San Gabriel de Valdivias, Regina Landa, Avanzada,* and *Nueva burguesia,* which are nonetheless steeped in his characteristic pessimism. In subsequent works he shifted his focus away from society to the individual, a trend foreshadowed in *The Firefly.* In these works, *La marchanta, La mujer domada, Sendas perdidas, La maldicion, Esa sangre,* and *Madero,* he forsakes his depiction of traditional provincial life for an exploration of hectic urban life.

Luis Leal suggested in *Mariano Azuela* that these latest novels are his least effective, perhaps due to Azuela's becoming "a stern critic of new social order" rather than remaining "an objective recorder of social change." A probable cause for his change in style was his growing disillusionment with Mexico's notoriously corrupt government. Critics contend that Azuela's literary reputation rests not on his plots or imagery or characterization, but on his ability to analyze Mexico's changing social and political scene and its players.

BIOGRAPHICAL/CRITICAL SOURCES:

BOOKS

Azuela, Mariano, *Los de abajo: Novela de la revolucion mexicana,* edited with introduction by John E. Englekirk and Lawrence B. Kiddle, reprinted, Prentice-Hall, 1971.
Azuela, Mariano, *Two Novels of Mexico: The Flies. The Bosses,* translated with preface by Lesley Byrd Simpson, University of California Press, 1956.
Leal, Luis, *Mariano Azuela,* Twayne, 1971.
Robe, Stanley Linn, *Azuela and the Mexican Underdogs,* University of California Press, 1979.
Spell, Jefferson Rea, *Contemporary Spanish-American Fiction,* reprinted, Biblo & Tannen, 1968.
Twentieth-Century Literary Criticism, Volume 3, Gale, 1980.

PERIODICALS

Bookman, May, 1929.
Books Abroad, autumn, 1953.
Hispania, February, 1935, February, 1952, May, 1967, March, 1972, December, 1980.
Modern Language Journal, May, 1951, October, 1968.
New Republic, October 23, 1929.

—*Sketch by Carol Lynn DeKane*

B

BACH, Richard (David) 1936-

PERSONAL: Born in 1936 in Oak Park, Ill.; son of Roland Robert and Ruth Helen (Shaw) Bach; married Leslie Parrish, 1977. *Education:* Attended Long Beach State College (now California State University, Long Beach), 1955.

ADDRESSES: c/o William Morrow & Co., 105 Madison Ave., New York, N.Y. 10016.

CAREER: Writer. U.S. Air Force, pilot, 1956-59, 1961-62, became captain; *Flying* (magazine) New York, N.Y., and Beverly Hills, Calif., 1961-64, began as associate editor, became West Coast editor; charter pilot, flight instructor, aviation mechanic, and barnstormer in Iowa and the Midwest, 1965-70.

AWARDS, HONORS: Nene Award, 1974, for *Jonathan Livingston Seagull;* American Book Award nomination, 1980, for *Illusions: The Adventures of a Reluctant Messiah.*

WRITINGS:

Stranger to the Ground, Harper, 1963, reprinted, Macmillan, 1983.
Biplane, Harper, 1966, reprinted, Macmillan, 1983.
Nothing by Chance: A Gypsy Pilot's Adventures in Modern America, Morrow, 1969, reprinted Macmillan, 1983.
Jonathan Livingston Seagull, Macmillan, 1970.
A Gift of Wings, Delacorte, 1974.
Illusions: The Adventures of a Reluctant Messiah, Delacorte, 1977.
There's No Such Place as Far Away, Delacorte, 1979.
The Bridge across Forever: A Lovestory, Morrow, 1984.
One, Morrow, 1988.

Contributor of about one hundred articles, most of them about flying, to *Flying, Air Facts, Argosy, Holiday, Writer,* and other magazines.

SIDELIGHTS: A direct descendant of Johann Sebastian Bach and an aviation enthusiast (Bach once allowed his family car to be repossessed while he still owned an airplane), Richard Bach has said that his best-selling and by far most popular book, *Jonathan Livingston Seagull,* is the result of a vision. "I realized," he said in a *Life* interview, "that I was meant to write it all down, not just watch it." Midway through the writing of the book the vision disappeared. Bach explained to Alden Whitman of the *New York Times* that the vision "stopped like fireworks gone

cold in the sky. I tried to invent an ending and just couldn't." Then, after several years, he reports, "this strange visionesque thing picked up just where it had left off. And there was the end of the story."

For a book that was rejected by numerous publishers before Macmillan cautiously printed 7,500 copies, *Jonathan Livingston Seagull* took the industry by storm. Although Macmillan launched the book with a very limited advertising campaign, word-of-mouth praise brought Bach's book to the attention of many more readers. Best-seller status, foreign language translations, television talk-show appearances, and film offers followed.

Bach's novel tells the story of a spirited and brave seagull, Jonathan, who dreams of flying for grace and speed instead of mere survival. After much experimenting and practicing, Jonathan learns to do this. Rejected by the other seagulls, who like Jonathan's father believe "the reason that you fly is to eat," Jonathan lives and flies in solitude until two radiant gulls appear and begin to teach him to transcend the limits of his beliefs in space and time. He then returns to his original flock to try to share what he found.

When asked about the popularity of his novel, Bach remarked to Judith Wagner in the *Toledo Blade:* "Something invisible guides any ideal into communication. Jonathan came in the '70s when people needed to hear what he is saying to them. If I had finished the manuscript in the late '50s when I started it, the book probably would not have been accepted." Bach continues: "Jonathan is a crystal sphere in which we can see glimpses of our past and our future. He is true for anyone who finds him true. He believes in doing things that matter. He has his dark times and his bright times, just like all of us. To me, he is saying 'I'm going to live the way I want to live, the way that is right for me. If you are going to destroy me for that, OK. But as long as I'm able I will follow my own direction.'"

The enormous popularity of the book sometimes leads Bach to wish that he had written it under a pseudonym. He has been deluged with mail from readers wanting to know the underlying metaphysical philosophy behind the story of the seagull who deviates from the behavior of his flock. Paul S. Nathan mentions in *Publishers Weekly* that "Buddhists . . . say the story of the seagull who strives for perfection in flying, and progresses through different states of being in his quest, perfectly captures the spirit of Buddhism." A bishop denounced the book as being an example of the sin of pride. A group of reformed alcoholics used it for inspiration. Timothy Foote reports in *Time* that "a columnist, dismissing the whole thing as 'half-baked fantasy,' offered its success as proof that America's brains are addled." Bach's own interpretation of the book: "Find out what you love to do, and do your darndest to make it happen."

As proof of the fact that he did not really write *Jonathan Livingston Seagull,* Bach points to the differences in style between it and his earlier books. Foote explains: "His normal style is highly personal and full of description. As a parable, *Jonathan* is little more than a narrative skeleton supporting a number of inspirational and philosophic assertions. Bach also points out that he disagrees entirely with Jonathan's decision to abandon the pursuit of private perfection in favor of returning to the dumb old flock and encouraging its members toward higher wisdom. 'Self-sacrifice,' says Bach, 'is a word I cannot stand.' "

While *Jonathan Livingston Seagull* has been extremely well received by readers, many reviewers dismissed the novel as being shallow and pretentious. For example, a *Publishers Weekly* reviewer comments that it is a pity that "Bach has chosen to deck [his idea] out in a wispy little fable about a brave and individualistic seagull which elects to go against the rules of the flock and becomes first an exile, then a hero. It is when Jonathan Livingston Seagull begins to be known as the Son of the Great Gull that the prose gets a mite too icky poo for comfort." And John Carey remarks in the *Listener* that *Jonathan Livingston Seagull* "is for those who think the world would be a lovely place if it were full of chummy people and tame animals. Needless to say, such beliefs are for the most part readily divorceable from their owners' actual conduct. It's of interest that Jonathan's spiritual aviation should prove so endearing to a nation [then] using its own air power to crush North Vietnam."

However, Jean Caffey Lyles states in the *Christian Century:* "Clearly, here is a work that transcends not only age but culture and politics. . . . *Moby Dick* it's not; nor am I prepared to class it with *The Old Man and the Sea.* . . . The great virtue of this book is that it means precisely what you want it to mean. . . . No matter what your age, sex, race, annual income, religion or politics, somewhere in the context of your life you can find a use for *Jonathan*'s message that there are 'no limits.' "

When asked by Wagner if he was bothered by the fact that *Jonathan Livingston Seagull* "has received precious little critical acclaim," Bach answered: "No. At first I was upset when I read bad reviews. I wanted to say, 'Poor fellows, you really missed the boat, didn't you?' But now that doesn't matter either. Book reviewers tend to be literary, very intellectual, and quite sophisticated. Jonathan is none of these things. *Jonathan,* the book, is the archetype Cinderella story. The depth of Jonathan's touch is as unique as the people who read his story. I wrote him for myself and for anyone else who finds special space for him in their lives."

Foote describes Bach as having "a remarkable gift for saying tentatively, and with disarming humor, things that ought to sound pretentious or phony or both, but instead convince and captivate his listeners. The result is that after meeting Bach, even the veriest cynic is likely to find himself shamelessly rooting for Jonathan Livingston Seagull and curiously willing to forgive the book its literary trespasses. . . . Whether his book raises tingles at the back of your neck or curdles your vichysoisse, it is hard not to believe that somebody up there loves Richard Bach. Maybe even the Great Gull himself."

Although they never achieved the commercial success of *Jonathan Livingston Seagull,* Bach's next three books, *A Gift of Wings, Illusions: The Adventures of a Reluctant Messiah,* and *There's No Such Place as Far Away,* were also perceived as inspirational by many readers. *A Gift of Wings* is a collection of forty-six essays, most of which have some connection with flying or other aspects of aviation. Bach described this book to *Publishers Weekly*'s editor, Mildred Sola Neely, as a compilation of stories "of friendship and joy and of beauty and love and of living, really living." He added that these stories are based on "whatever sad times, bright times, strange fantasies struck me as I flew." And Bach's former editor, Eleanor Friede, remarked to *Publishers Weekly* that *A Gift of Wings* "has many parallels to the theme in [*Jonathan Livingston*] *Seagull.*"

Arthur G. Hansen writes in the *Saturday Evening Post* that *A Gift of Wings* "is an accounting of one man's feelings about life and the things that make life worth living. Flying is the means for expression rather than an end in itself. . . . Flying is aimed at finding life itself and of living it in the present. It is the challenge of independence." Hansen continues: "One suspects that the main issue under discussion in *A Gift of Wings* is the never-ending search for transcendence. This was also the core of *Jonathan*—we really can be more than we are if we try hard enough. We all have the means to do so. What we need is the will, an adventuresome spirit, and an idea of what we might eventually become with practice and effort."

Illusions: The Adventures of a Reluctant Messiah and *There's No Such Place as Far Away* have also been compared to the seagull's quest for fulfillment in Bach's earlier novel. *Illusions: The Adventures of a Reluctant Messiah* attempts to find the answers to the age-old questions concerning the true meaning of life through the main character's encounters with a fictional messiah. Joseph McLellan of the *Washington Post Book World* comments that *Illusions* contains "enlightenment, miracles, reincarnations [and] out-of-body experiences." And according to Richard R. Lingeman in the *New York Times,* "the general pitch seems to be that the world is an illusion, death is an illusion [and that] happiness lies inside you anyway, not outside you in so-called reality."

In *There's No Such Place as Far Away,* a young child learns about the meaning of life from a hummingbird, an owl, an eagle, a hawk, and a seagull. Explains a reviewer for *Publishers Weekly:* "On his/her way to [a] birthday party . . . the narrator is uplifted and instructed by the spiritual logic of five feathered friends. . . . They utter bromides about the unity of all life and experience in a universe unfettered by time, space and the corporeal body."

Bach's next novel, *The Bridge across Forever: A Lovestory,* is the story of "one man's obsessive search for his soulmate and what happened after he found her," according to Phyllis Butler in the *Los Angeles Times Book Review. The Bridge across Forever* is an account of Bach's life since the publication of *Jonathan Livingston Seagull.* Nancy Wigston writes in *Globe & Mail* that the work "zooms around Bach's life as an adventurer on the road in search of true love. It's a serious enough issue, the business of finding a soul-mate, and Bach is serious to the point of obsession." Concludes Butler: "Bach's successful love quest is probably what many of us secretly hope will happen to us, fulfilling the promises of a dozen relationships and romantic love seminars."

In Bach's 1988 best-selling novel, *One,* he and his wife, Leslie, are flying from Los Angeles to Santa Monica when they find themselves traveling through time. At each point in time they discover the impact of their past decisions on their own lives and the lives of others. By the journey's end, Bach has realized the unity or "oneness" of all people. In *One,* writes a reviewer for *Publishers Weekly,* "Bach again displays an inventive imagination and inspirational zeal." Added Katherine Green of the *Detroit Free Press:* "There are human lessons to be learned on this trip. . . . The Bachs take their passengers on a strange trip through the space of consciousness, but it could be worthwhile for those willing to take a chance."

MEDIA ADAPTATIONS: Jonathan Livingston Seagull was produced as a film of the same title by Paramount in 1973; a 1974 film documentary was based on *Nothing by Chance.*

BIOGRAPHICAL/CRITICAL SOURCES:

BOOKS

Authors in the News, Volume I, Gale, 1976.
Bestsellers 89, Issue 2, Gale, 1989.
Contemporary Literary Criticism, Volume XXIV, Gale, 1983.

PERIODICALS

Booklist, August, 1984
Book World, April 23, 1972.
Christian Century, November 22, 1972.
Detroit Free Press, November 13, 1988.
Globe & Mail, February 23, 1985.
Library Journal, December 1, 1970, December 15, 1972, November 15, 1974, August, 1984.
Life, March 3, 1972.
Listener, December 7, 1972, December 15, 1972.
Los Angeles Times Book Review, November 4, 1984.
New Statesman, November 4, 1984.
Newsweek, February 2, 1976.
New York Times, January 18, 1972, April 1, 1977.
New York Times Book Review, April 10, 1977, November 27, 1988.
Publishers Weekly, February 17, 1969, August 3, 1970, October 18, 1971, December 4, 1972, April 29, 1974, June 17, 1974, February 14, 1977, March 12, 1979, July 13, 1984, August 12, 1988.
Time, November 13, 1972, April 16, 1977.
Toledo Blade, March 24, 1974.
Saturday Evening Post, April, 1975.
Saturday Review, November/December, 1984.
Washington Post, April 24, 1977.
Washington Post Book World, April 24, 1977.

* * *

BACHMAN, Richard
See KING, Stephen (Edwin)

* * *

BAINBRIDGE, Beryl (Margaret) 1933-

PERSONAL: Born November 21, 1933, in Liverpool, England; daughter of Richard (a salesman) and Winifred (Baines) Bainbridge; married Austin Davies (an artist), April 24, 1954 (divorced); children: Aaron Paul, Johanna Harriet, Ruth Emmanuella. *Education:* Attended Merchant Taylor's School, Great Crosby, England. *Politics:* Socialist. *Religion:* "Lapsed Catholic." *Avocational interests:* Painting.

ADDRESSES: Home—42 Albert St., Camden Town, London NW1 7NU, England.

CAREER: Actress in England on radio and in repertory theatre, 1943-56; writer, 1956-68 and 1972—. Also has worked in a wine-bottling factory, as a clerk for Gerald Duckworth & Company publishers, and as a host for the British Broadcasting Corporation series "English Journey," 1983, and "Forever England," 1986.

MEMBER: Royal Society of Literature (fellow).

AWARDS, HONORS: Booker Prize nomination, 1973, for *The Dressmaker;* Booker Prize nomination and Guardian Fiction Award, both 1974, both for *The Bottle Factory Outing;* Whitbread Award, 1977, for *Injury Time;* Litt.D. from University of Liverpool, 1986.

WRITINGS:

FICTION

A Weekend with Claud (novel), Hutchinson, 1967, revised edition published as *A Weekend with Claude,* Duckworth, 1981.
Another Part of the Wood (novel), Hutchinson, 1968, revised edition, Duckworth, 1979, Braziller, 1980.
Harriet Said (novel), Duckworth, 1972, Braziller, 1973.
The Dressmaker (novel), Duckworth, 1973, published as *The Secret Glass,* Braziller, 1973.
The Bottle Factory Outing (novel), Braziller, 1974.
Sweet William (novel), Braziller, 1975.
A Quiet Life (novel; also see below), Duckworth, 1976, Braziller, 1977.
Injury Time (novel; also see below), Braziller, 1977.
Young Adolf (novel), Duckworth, 1978, Braziller, 1979.
Winter Garden (novel), Duckworth, 1980, Braziller, 1981.
Watson's Apology (novel), Duckworth, 1984, McGraw, 1985.
Mum and Mr. Armitage (short stories), Duckworth, 1985.
Filthy Lucre, or The Tragedy of Andrew Ledwhistle and Richard Soleway (novel), Duckworth, 1986.

NONFICTION

English Journey, or The Road to Milton Keynes, Duckworth, 1984.
Forever England: North and South, Duckworth, 1987.

TELEVISION SCRIPTS

"Sweet William" (based on the novel of the same title), produced by British Broadcasting Corporation (BBC), 1979.
"A Quiet Life" (based on the novel of the same title), BBC, 1980.
(With Phillip Seville) "The Journal of Bridget Hitler," BBC, 1980.

Also author of "Tiptoe through the Tulips," 1976, "Blue Skies from Now On," 1977, "The Warrior's Return," 1977, "It's Lovely Day Tomorrow," 1977, "Words Fail Me," 1979, and "Somewhere More Central," 1981.

OTHER

(Contributor) Emma Tennant, editor, *Bananas,* Quartet Books, 1977.
(Contributor) A. D. Maclean, editor, *Winter's Tales 26,* Macmillan (London), 1980, St. Martin's, 1981.
(Editor) *New Stories 6* (anthology), Hutchinson, 1981.

Contributor to periodicals, including *Spectator, Listener, Times Literary Supplement,* and *Sunday Times Magazine.*

MEDIA ADAPTATIONS: The Dressmaker, a film adapted from Bainbridge's novel, was released by Fine Arts, 1988.

SIDELIGHTS: Beryl Bainbridge "is one of the half-dozen most inventive and interesting novelists working in Britain today," according to Julian Symons in the *New York Review of Books.* A native of Liverpool who now lives in London, Bainbridge has won critical acclaim and a wide readership on two continents for her black humor chronicles of the lives and neuroses of the English lower middle classes. Reviewers cite the unassuming author for her satiric but naturalistic portrayals of the drab and desperate British poor, of "the hidden springs of anarchy that bedevil the least adventurous of us, booby-trapping our lives and making them the occasion of violent and dangerous humor," in the words of *Spectator* contributor Harriet Waugh. Bainbridge's tales of urban wildness often stray into the realm of violence and nightmare, where trapped spirits collide with thwarted ambition and the bosom of the family offers more grief than relief. *Newsweek* correspondent Margo Jefferson writes, "Bainbridge's books are melancholy, provincial landscapes in which violence, like a thunderstorm, always threatens, sometimes strikes." *New York Times* columnist Anatole Broyard suggests that Bainbridge "has established herself as the high priestess of the rueful. She has opened a thrift shop in English literature, a home for frayed, faded, out-of-fashion and inexpensive people. The name of her shop might be Things Out of Joint. . . . Miss Bainbridge's people have all missed the train, or boat, the main chance. They are stranded in themselves, left behind by a world rushing toward the gratification of desire."

Their dark subject matter notwithstanding, Bainbridge's novels have achieved a cult following, largely because the author juxtaposes horror and comedy with precision. As Anne Duchene notes in the *Times Literary Supplement,* reading a Bainbridge novel "has always been a special kind of experience, at once very funny, abrasive and intimate—rather like having a nasty sticking-plaster pulled off for you by an old friend: jokes, and the little unpleasantness briskly but tenderly dealt with, then drinks of relief all around." In the *Detroit News,* Anne Tyler writes: "Bainbridge addicts settle gleefully into her genteel parlors, knowing that shortly everything will fall apart. There'll be bodies in the hedge, baked apples behind the refrigerator. A grown man, in a fit of temper, will set fire to a chair arm. A woman will try to sleep while teenaged boys clamber over her bed in search of ping-pong balls. Like a schoolgirl fighting off the giggles, Beryl Bainbridge begins her stories with a determinedly straight face, plods virtuously forward—and then her sharp eye is snagged by some unlikely detail and all is lost. How can I stay serious, she seems to be asking, when people behave so absurdly?" *Books and Bookmen* reviewer James Brockway detects yet another level to Bainbridge's appeal. "The more I read her," he claims, "the more I suspect that the grip her work has taken on us, the ease with which she has won us, the enthusiasm with which the critics (most of them) greet her work, the more I suspect that this is not merely due to her being an exquisite entertainer—a star performer, who can get away with anything, . . . a deliciously preposterous humorist and a very, very clever writer, but also to the powerful *subconscious* appeal of her subject matter: our present parlous postwar condition."

Bainbridge told the *New York Times Book Review* that she writes in order to make sense of her own childhood experiences. "Childhood is a thing that happens so early you don't forget it," she said. "Everything else you grow out of, but you never recover from childhood. So I go over it again and again." By all accounts, Bainbridge's youth was spent in an extremely tense environment where bitter disputes between her parents developed frequently. *Dictionary of Literary Biography* contributor Barbara C. Millard notes that Bainbridge's mother's "preoccupation with class distinction" and her father's "manic temper" and financial insolvency precipitated quarrels during which Bainbridge defended her mother "by jumping on her father's back and bring-

ing him to the ground." According to Willa Petschek in the *New York Times Book Review,* the family "stayed together for appearances' sake, but their tiny house was full of frightening emotions." It was this climate of strain, played out in the working-class neighborhoods of Liverpool, that Bainbridge has sought to duplicate in her fiction. She told the *Dictionary of Literary Biography* that confronting the pain has helped her to exorcise it, although the process did not begin until she was nearing middle age. "Fortunately I did it late enough," she said. "If I had done it twenty years ago, I wouldn't have been neurotic for twenty years and so I wouldn't have written."

Fiction writing is indeed Bainbridge's second career; during her teen and early adult years she worked as an actress on the radio and in repertory theatres, and as late as 1972 she was still performing professionally. At sixteen she met and fell in love with her future husband, artist Austin Davies. They were married in 1954, although Bainbridge had misgivings about the match. While awaiting the birth of her first child in 1956, Bainbridge began to write a novel. She derived the plot from a newspaper story about two girls who had murdered their mother, but drew on her own childhood experiences to enhance and alter the details. The resulting work, *Harriet Said,* was completed in 1958 but went unpublished until 1972. Millard notes: "When Bainbridge submitted the manuscript to publishers in 1959, she received outraged response, including the comment that the book was 'too indecent and unpleasant even for these lax days.'" Editors were aghast at Bainbridge's tale of juvenile sexuality, voyeurism, and murder; their response so daunted Bainbridge that she returned to the stage. In 1959 her marriage ended, and she took her two young children back to Liverpool to live. Soon thereafter, however, she moved to London and started writing again. Her second novel, *A Weekend with Claud,* was published in 1967.

"Beryl Bainbridge's publishing history is perhaps the kind of thing you'd expect of a writer who is preoccupied with the idea of isolation," notes Karl Miller in the *New York Review of Books.* "It may be that this portrayer of shyness and constraint, who appears to be no punctuator, found it difficult to cope with the embarrassment of a debut, and of getting herself properly published." Indeed, Bainbridge has since revised both of her first two books to go into print, *A Weekend with Claud* (revised as *A Weekend with Claude*) and *Another Part of the Wood.* In a piece for the London *Times,* Bainbridge attributes her success as an author to her acquaintance, in 1970, with Anna Haycraft, fiction editor for Gerald Duckworth & Company publishers. Bainbridge writes of Haycraft: "She had read my two published books, didn't like them all that much ('rotten' was the word she used) and wanted to know if I had written anything else. I showed her *Harriet Said.* . . . Duckworth published it, employed me in the office for a year, put me on a monthly salary—an arrangement that still exists—and suggested I write another novel as soon as possible." Bainbridge stresses that her editor's encouragement helped her to find her authorial voice: "It was she who told me to abandon the flowery and obscure style of my two later books and return to the simpler structure of the first. She pointed out that, in my case, clarity came from writing from my own experience. . . . I gradually learnt the best way, for me, of expressing what I wanted to say, and wrote a novel a year from then on."

Critics suggest that although *A Weekend with Claud, Another Part of the Wood,* and *Harriet Said* lack the polish of later Bainbridge works, they nonetheless demonstrate a burgeoning talent at work. *New York Times Book Review* contributor Gail Godwin observes that *Harriet Said* "certainly ranks in content with the more celebrated thrillers of corrupt childhood, but it has literary and psychological virtues as well. The architecture of its narrative would have satisfied Poe: every incident advances the design. The language, though simple, often has the effect of poetry . . . [and] there are also several remarkable passages which reveal, so accurately, adolescence's frequent, unpredictable swing between mature and infantile behavior." Assessing *A Weekend with Claud,* Millard writes: "In *Claud,* Bainbridge presents the first of her predatory men. He is tigerlike in his ruthless wooing and possession of women, and he creates what will become a familiar tension between the vulnerable female and the exploitative male. The novel lacks the author's characteristic crispness; its fuzzy prose is rescued only by the pointed imagery which projects an exact vision of the despair and folly of love and lovemaking." A *Washington Post* reviewer finds *Another Part of the Wood* "a scrupulously detailed, wryly witty and ultimately harrowing study of manners in the British middle and working classes, of the effects of dependency on a variety of weak people and of the lies we all tell ourselves to make life bearable and the deadly passions that lie buried under the dull surface of our daily banalities. . . . This slow-moving book does acquire a cumulative momentum, pointing toward an effective, quietly powerful end, and much of the detail work is exquisite."

Petschek contends that Bainbridge "can date the onset of happiness back to the year she published the first of her . . . successful novels; what really happened, she says, is that . . . it dawned on her that the wretched tensions of childhood were not her fault, that her parents' unhappiness had not been caused by her." What Bainbridge also discovered was that her own life, past and present, could be mined for fiction. She began to mingle autobiography and imagination to depict, in *New York Times* reviewer Michiko Kakutani's words, a "drab, depressing" England "where lives are circumscribed and expectations diminished. Families tend to be the source of suffocation rather than sustenance; and romance, too, has a way of dwindling into comedy instead of blossoming into hope." Judith Gies elaborates in the *New York Times Book Review:* "When [Bainbridge's] characters are not meeting violent ends, their psyches are being pummeled. Drawn largely from the English lower middle class, they exist in a stifling and dangerous atmosphere of claustrophobic domesticity, crippling gentility and pretension. Her protagonists (generally women) make fumbling, gallant attempts to get out from under their bell jars—usually through love. But Bainbridge's characters never quite connect; they talk *through* each other. . . . The disturbing edge this produces is intensified by the author's use of naturalism—with its careful attention to detail—and the grotesque details she chooses to use. Her vision is as glittering and as narrow as a needle."

Perhaps as an inevitable consequence of her perspective and aspirations, Bainbridge writes principally about love, or the lack thereof, between families or sexual partners. Miller suggests that her novels "are adamant that intimacy and teaming-up conceal hostility, desperation, and an outcast condition. And yet they also contribute a good deal in the way of qualifying evidence, in the way of relief. There are occasions when people help each other, when need answers need. . . . Bleak as it can be at times, her fiction has in it ties of affection. It has saving instances, merciful exceptions, thoughtfully averted glances." *Times Literary Supplement* contributor Carol Rumens observes that Bainbridge's central characters, often though not always female, "express, with the fragile authority of the wounded, the ravenous need of love that underlies adult pretensions and ideals." Millard explains how Bainbridge's microcosmic views of individuals can reveal wider cultural and emotional difficulties: "The Bain-

bridgean female, alternately silly and wise, loving and self-absorbed, rebellious and conformist, deluded and perceptive—but always accommodating and vulnerable—has been interpreted as the image of a befuddled and helpless postwar England, and finally, as the image of modern humanity perplexed in the extreme. Her men and women are in the same modern fix—having escaped the old repressive rules of Victorian middle-class respectability, they yet seek normality but end up adrift in a sea of too many choices. Criticized early in her career for her 'dark view' of a violent world, Bainbridge is now credited with having identified, accurately, moral and cultural confusion as the contemporary malaise." Yet, Millard concludes, "her characters have remained resilient, and the books have retained their good humor."

Most critics agree that Bainbridge's prose style contributes significantly to the impact her novels make on readers. In the *New York Times Book Review,* Julia O'Faolain writes: "It is Miss Bainbridge's style that makes her a seductive writer—her manner, not her matter, that is so good. Summaries do her no justice. Her genius is for a tapestry of ephemera. Detail is a component that she handles with a miniaturist's skill, often in a close-up so obsessive as to create a tension between her naturalistic accuracy and queerness of perspective." According to Mary Hope in *The Nation,* the *"faux naivete,* one of the distinguishing marks of Bainbridge's writing, hides consummate technical comic skill. Bainbridge has you crying with laughter while the blood freezes in your veins. This close relationship between farce and horror often depends on extreme physical, as well as emotional, propinquity between the characters. . . . Her dialogue is always wildly funny, and she uses it most intricately to depict social anxiety and emotional turmoil or sterility. As in all great English writing, class discomfiture is used to pinpoint and give strength to the farcical situation." *Ms.* magazine reviewer Norma Rosen notes that Bainbridge "writes brilliant detail into even the prettiest of her characters. It is all done with perfect timing and tone—though the language is resolutely plain." Edith Milton, in a *New Republic* essay, describes the cumulative effect of Bainbridge's prose: "When the laughter is over, what remains is almost an abstraction, a rather novel view over a well-known landscape. The scale and clarity of its perspective are astonishing."

The Dressmaker, published in America as *The Secret Glass,* remains one of Bainbridge's best-known works. Set in Liverpool during the Second World War, the novel explores the painful and claustrophobic existence of a young woman who lives with her two unmarried aunts. Millard suggests that the book "depicts the cramped, impoverished lives of working-class Liverpudlians during the darker days of 1944. The psychological realism of the novel goes beyond reminiscence and proves Bainbridge a master of detail and atmosphere." Godwin feels that *The Dressmaker* "will attract readers not for its suspense-entertainment but for its sharp character study and unrelenting Naturalism. . . . The author is painstaking in her evocation of era and perceptive about the world of manners in working-class Liverpool. She has much to tell us about those pressure cookers of family life and limited means. And she creates memorable portraits of her people." A *Times Literary Supplement* reviewer writes: "To have disinterred so many nasty things in the woodshed and yet evoked a workaday image of Liverpudlian optimism and resilience, in so few claustrophobic pages, is a remarkable achievement. Miss Bainbridge's imagination pushes her towards nightmare, and her eye for detail is macabre; but because she writes with taut, matter-of-fact simplicity this seems as authentic as any contemporary image the camera has preserved of that mercifully vanished past."

In recent years Bainbridge has moved away from the autobiographical ground situations that form such books as *The Dressmaker, The Bottle Factory Outing, Sweet William,* and *A Quiet Life,* and has instead let her imagination be piqued by history and travel. Her 1978 novel *Young Adolf,* for instance, describes a family reunion in Liverpool between Adolf Hitler and his half-brother Alois, who did indeed live in England. Broyard contends in a *New York Times* column that the book "has all the improbability of history. It is funny in a way that will make you shudder, sad in a way that will astonish you with unwanted feelings of sympathy. In making Hitler human, Miss Bainbridge has reminded us once again that it is persons, not abstract forces, that engender our disasters." *Christian Science Monitor* contributor Bruce Allen likewise asserts that the novel's best effects "rise out of Bainbridge's genius for finding latent menace in the dreariest everydayness. . . . Bainbridge's real subject is less a portrayal of an embryonic monster than a subtle revelation of the social enfeeblement that let him grow and prosper." *Winter Garden,* published in 1980, weaves a satirical tale of a group of artists who visit the Soviet Union by invitation. In the *New York Times Book Review,* Valerie Brooks comments that the work "is razor sharp, most appealing and somewhat resembles a quicksilver Stravinsky-Balanchine ballet. An unusual combination of characters and events creates mystery and tension." Marital discord proves the theme of *Watson's Apology,* Bainbridge's 1984 novel based on a notorious Victorian murder trial. According to Merle Rubin in the *Chicago Tribune Book World,* using the framework of documents surrounding the court case, "Bainbridge weaves her fictional fabrication: thickly detailed, redolent of the specific time and place, and suffused in the grimly desperate atmosphere of a misbegotten marriage."

Critics find much to praise in Bainbridge's many works of fiction. Edith Milton notes that the author "mocks at the same time our lives' drab imitation of fiction, and our fictions' bright imitation of life. Though her impact is that of satire, and though her joke is really very good, her method has the purity of certain photographs, where a closeness of focus, a magnification of detail, turns organic confusion and the ugliness of the familiar into geometry." *Times Literary Supplement* reviewer Diane Johnson writes of the Bainbridge novels: "Like a family of gifted eccentrics, they are diverse, yet there are strong similarities, as there always must be in the work of an original and accomplished writer. . . . The plots each with its lurking catastrophe are similar, the characters, each so memorable in his way, are similar too. . . . Her characters don't have illusions, they have bruises—always bruises of the spirit, often literal bruises, and sometimes lacerations." In *The Spectator,* Peter Ackroyd concludes that Bainbridge "observes the margins, she patrols the corners, where the great events of the day—where even 'life' itself—are seen only as a dusty and wayward reflection. This meant that her novels were always strikingly odd, and she has earned a well deserved reputation as one of our funniest writers."

Bainbridge has also adapted several of her novels for the screen and has served as a host-commentator on two British Broadcasting Corporation travel serials. Answering the demands of her growing readership, she has traveled widely in Great Britain, Europe, and the United States, always expressing a willingness to discuss the wellsprings from which her works have sprung. She once told *CA* that she writes to work out her own "personal obsessions," because she believes that writing, "like old photographs, gives a record by which past experience can be remembered." *New York Review of Books* essayist Frank Kermode characterizes Bainbridge's ability as "an odd and in a muted way fantastic talent, as is perhaps necessary in modern English writ-

ers who manage to escape the rather stifling conditions of normal contemporary competence." In the *New York Times Book Review,* Guy Davenport makes the observation that Bainbridge "has her comic eye on cultural confusion. She makes us see that it goes deeper than we think and touches more widely than we had imagined. The most appalling muddles can still be laughed at, and laughter is a kind of understanding."

BIOGRAPHICAL/CRITICAL SOURCES:

BOOKS

Contemporary Literary Criticism, Gale, Volume IV, 1975, Volume V, 1976, Volume VIII, 1978, Volume X, 1979, Volume XIV, 1980, Volume XVIII, 1981, Volume XXII, 1982.
Dictionary of Literary Biography, Volume XIV: *British Novelists since 1960,* Gale, 1983.

PERIODICALS

Albion, Volume XI, 1979.
Antioch Review, fall, 1979.
Atlantic, March, 1979.
Books and Bookmen, January, 1974, December, 1977, November, 1978, February, 1980.
Chicago Tribune Book World, April 8, 1979, January 12, 1986.
Christian Science Monitor, April 9, 1979.
Detroit News, April 29, 1979, April 27, 1980.
Encounter, February, 1975, February, 1976.
Hudson Review, winter, 1977-78.
Listener, November 29, 1973, November 20, 1980.
London Magazine, January, 1978, April-May, 1979.
London Review of Books, November 20-December 3, 1980.
Los Angeles Times, July 12, 1983, December 16, 1988.
Los Angeles Times Book Review, May 18, 1980, April 25, 1982, September 9, 1984, January 12, 1986.
Ms., December, 1974, August, 1977.
National Review, September 17, 1976.
New Republic, September 28, 1974, May 24, 1975, March 25, 1978, June 16, 1979.
New Review, November, 1977.
New Statesman, November 1, 1974, November 10, 1978, December 21-28, 1979, November 25, 1985.
Newsweek, August 12, 1974, March 19, 1979, April 7, 1979.
New Yorker, April 25, 1977.
New York Review of Books, May 16, 1974, July 15, 1976, April 5, 1979, July 17, 1980, October 26, 1984.
New York Times, August 21, 1974, May 26, 1975, March 17, 1976, March 1, 1978, March 7, 1979, May 18, 1979, March 5, 1980, March 13, 1981, September 6, 1984, July 11, 1987.
New York Times Book Review, September 30, 1973, September 15, 1974, June 8, 1975, May 16, 1976, March 20, 1977, February 26, 1978, March 11, 1979, April 13, 1980, March 1, 1981, March 21, 1982, September 23, 1984, October 20, 1985.
Publishers Weekly, March 15, 1976, April 9, 1979.
Saturday Review, July 26, 1975, April 2, 1977.
Spectator, November 2, 1974, October 11, 1975, October 9, 1976, October 1, 1977, November 11, 1978, December 8, 1979, November 1, 1980, April 28, 1984, November 3, 1984.
Sunday Times Magazine, February 17, 1980.
Time, November 11, 1974.
Times (London), September 3, 1981, April 5, 1984, August 17, 1984, October 4, 1984.
Times Literary Supplement, October 6, 1972, September 28, 1973, November 1, 1974, October 3, 1975, November 3, 1978, December 1, 1978, February 29, 1980, October 31,

1980, August 14, 1981, September 11, 1981, October 5, 1984, December 20, 1985, October 17, 1986, April 24, 1987.
Voice Literary Supplement, October, 1985.
Washington Post, April 8, 1980, March 5, 1981, February 10, 1989.
Washington Post Book World, December 4, 1977, August 20, 1978, April 15, 1979, September 23, 1984, November 17, 1985, July 26, 1987.
Yale Review, winter, 1978.

*   *   *

BAKER, Russell (Wayne) 1925-

PERSONAL: Born August 14, 1925, in Morrisonville, Loudoun County, Va.; son of Benjamin Rex and Lucy Elizabeth (Robinson) Baker; married Miriam Emily Nash, March 11, 1950; children: Kathleen Leland, Allen Nash, Michael Lee. *Education:* Johns Hopkins University, B.A., 1947.

ADDRESSES: Office—New York Times, 229 West 43rd St., New York, N.Y. 10036.

CAREER: Sun, Baltimore, Md., member of staff, 1947-53, London bureau chief, 1953-54; *New York Times,* New York, N.Y., member of Washington, D.C. bureau, 1954-62, author of "Observer" column, 1962—. *Military service:* U.S. Naval Reserve, 1943-45.

MEMBER: American Academy and Institute of Arts and Letters.

AWARDS, HONORS: L.H.D. from Hamilton College, Princeton University, Johns Hopkins University, and Franklin Pierce College; D.Litt., Wake Forest University; LL.D., Union College; Frank Sullivan Memorial Award, 1976; George Polk Award for commentary, 1979; Pulitzer Prize, 1979, for distinguished commentary, and 1983, for *Growing Up;* Elmer Holmes Bobst Prize for nonfiction, 1983; Fourth Estate Award from National Press Club, 1989.

WRITINGS:

(Author of text) *Washington: City on the Potomac,* Arts, 1958.
An American in Washington, Knopf, 1961.
No Cause for Panic (collection of newspaper articles), Lippincott, 1964.
Baker's Dozen (collection of newspaper articles), New York Times Co., 1964.
All Things Considered (collection of newspaper articles), Lippincott, 1965, reprinted, Greenwood, 1981.
Our Next President: The Incredible Story of What Happened in the 1968 Elections (fiction), Atheneum, 1968.
Poor Russell's Almanac (collection of newspaper articles), Doubleday, 1972, revised edition, 1981.
The Upside Down Man (children's book), McGraw, 1977.
So This Is Depravity (collection of newspaper articles), Congdon & Lattes, 1980.
Growing Up (autobiography), Congdon & Weed, 1982.
The Rescue of Miss Yaskell and Other Pipe Dreams (collection of newspaper articles), Congdon & Weed, 1983.
(Editor) *The Norton Book of Light Verse,* Norton, 1986.
The Good Times (autobiography), Morrow, 1989.

Also co-author of musical play "Home Again," 1979. Contributor to periodicals, including *Saturday Evening Post, New York Times Magazine, Sports Illustrated, Ladies Home Journal, Holiday, Theatre Arts, Mademoiselle, Life, Look,* and *McCalls.*

SIDELIGHTS: "I didn't set out in life to be a humorist," Russell Baker once told Israel Shenker in the *New York Times Book Re-*view. "I set out in life to be a novelist, and I look like a novelist. Art Buchwald looks like a humorist. . . . I don't look like him and most of the time I don't even look like myself." Nevertheless, Baker is regarded today as one of America's most literate and successful humorists. His thrice-weekly "Observer" column has been running in the *New York Times* since 1962 and is syndicated to the more than 450 newspapers that subscribe to the Times News Service. He is also the recipient of two Pulitzer Prizes: the first in commentary, for ten columns published in 1979; the second in biography, for his bittersweet account of his early years, *Growing Up,* published in 1982.

Baker was born in rural Morrisonville, Virginia, in 1925, "issued uneventfully into the governance of Calvin Coolidge," as he puts it in *Growing Up,* adding, "World War I was seven years past, the Russian revolution was eight years old, and the music on my grandmother's wind-up Victrola was 'Yes, We Have No Bananas.' " Baker's father, Benjamin, died at age 33, during the Depression, of diabetes. His mother, the stalwart Lucy Elizabeth Baker, after handing over her youngest child, Audrey, to more affluent relatives, began a new life with five-year-old Russell and his three-year-old sister, Doris, that included periods of residence in Virginia, New Jersey, and Baltimore, Maryland.

Baker began his newspaper career in 1947 as a reporter for the Baltimore *Sun,* eventually ending up in London, writing a spirited weekly series for that paper, "From a Window on Fleet Street." In 1954 he joined the *New York Times* staff in Washington, D.C., and covered the White House, State Department, politics and Congressional activities for the *Times* for eight years until, as he tells John Skow of *Time* magazine, "I just got bored. I had done enough reporting. I began to feel like Willy Loman in 'Death of a Salesman,' carrying that typewriter in one hand and that suitcase in the other and a dirty old raincoat into one more hotel lobby. It came to seem that this wasn't a worthy way for a grown man to spend his life. You have good seats, sure, but you're always on the sidelines. You're not making anything." The last straw came, Skow reports, one afternoon when Baker had spent several hours sitting on a hallway floor of the Senate Office Building, outside a closed meeting of the Armed Services Committee. "I began to wonder," Baker says, "why, at the age of 37, I was wearing out my hams waiting for somebody to come out and lie to me."

Offered the "Observer" column by the *Times* as an incentive to stay at the paper, Baker accepted and soon produced his first piece, a farcical version of a John F. Kennedy press conference. He quickly established himself as an adroit political satirist and stayed in Washington throughout the Kennedy, Johnson, and Nixon administrations. By 1974, though, Baker felt he'd written all he could about politics and relocated to New York City. It was there that his articles expanded in subject matter; he won a 1979 Pulitzer Prize for columns covering such topics as tax reform, trends, inflation, Norman Rockwell, fear, and the death of *New Times* magazine.

In his *Time* profile of Baker, Skow says that the columnist "walks the high wire between light humor and substantive comment, a balancing act so punishingly difficult that in the entire country there are not a dozen men and women who can be said to have the hang of the thing." "At his best," observes R. Z. Sheppard in his *Time* review of *Poor Russell's Almanac,* a collection of columns, "Baker fills his allotted space . . . with bizarre, often bleak fantasies about human foolishness. At his second best, he holds a funhouse mirror up to the nature of the consumer state. . . . Baker is a man of range, sensitive intellect and fertile imagination. He is also a fine stylist whose columns frequently unfurl to defend the language against corruption. . . . Russell Baker can then be best appreciated doing what a good humorist has always done: writing to preserve his sanity for at least one more day."

"I'm basically a guy with a yearning for the past," Baker told Thomas Chastain in a 1972 *Publishers Weekly* interview, "a time when things were better. Life was better when there were trains. It's probably a sign of the hardening of the mental arteries, this yearning for boyhood, the kind of thing I dislike when I hear it from other people." Ten years later the writer realized his need to connect with the past through his autobiography, *Growing Up.* Baker remarks in the book: "I wondered about the disconnections between children and parents that prevent them from knowing each other while there is still time. Children ought to know what went into their making, to know that life is a braided cord of humanity stretching up from time long gone. I thought that, when I am beyond explaining, they would want to know what the world was like when my mother was young and I was younger and we two relics passed together through strange times."

Richard Lingeman, writing about *Growing Up* in the *New York Times Book Review,* comments that he "approached [the book] with high anticipation, expecting a heartening read about someone more miserable than I am. Alas, I was deeply disappointed. . . . This is not the kind of book one can put down with a contented sigh: 'that poor son of a bitch.' Instead of being a grim tale of drunken stepmothers and battered stepfathers, *Growing Up* is touching and funny, a hopeless muddle of sadness and laughter that bears a suspicious resemblance to real life." "This is not the dirt-poor South of easy fiction," offers *Los Angeles Times Book Review* critic Mary Lee Settle. She adds: "With sensuous grace, incisive recall and an evocation of daily language that is the poetry of the inarticulate, [Baker] recreates a place where there is dignity and ambition and an inflexible social and economic hierarchy run by women." Noting that "there are scenes as funny and as touching as Mark Twain's" and that the "acute simplicity of the scene of the father's death is a masterpiece," Settle concludes that *Growing Up* is "a wondrous book, funny, sad and strong. Above all, it can make us see that the family cruelties we have suffered are often cultural and not personal—and that to recognize this is to begin to forgive."

According to Jonathan Yardley, writing in the *Washington Post Book World,* Growing Up is "a work as deeply rooted in what we know as the 'American experience' as anything [James] Thurber wrote; moreover, it leaves no doubt that Baker must not merely be compared with Thurber, as he has been in the past, but ranked with him as well." The author "has accomplished the memorialist's task: to find shape and meaning in his own life, and to make it interesting and pertinent to the reader. In lovely, haunting prose, he has told a story that is deeply in the American grain, one in which countless readers will find echoes of their own, yet in the end it is very much his own." Finally, *Detroit News* critic Leola Floren notes that "too often autobiographers exhibit an unfortunate compulsion to chronicle a thousand anecdotes, of which only a handful are either significant or interesting." But not Baker: his "timing is exquisite; he exits humbly into the wings with a smile and a wink at those of us pleading for encores. Bravo."

A few years after the publication of *Growing Up,* Baker followed with a sequel—*The Good Times*—that describes his early years as a reporter for the the *New York Times* and the Baltimore *Sun.* As the book makes clear, "The Good Times" for Baker involved the spirit of youthful adventure that he felt as a young man at the beginning of his career. He especially enjoyed his years in England, which he covered as a "big, gaudy feature story" while polishing his writing style by reading famous English papers such as the *Manchester Guardian.* "*The Good Times* offers . . . an insider's view of modern American journalism that illuminates both the author and his trade," observed Robert Shogan in the *Los Angeles Times Book Review.* "[It] is a superb autobiography, wonderfully told, often hilarious, always intelligent and unsparing," wrote the *New York Times Book Review*'s Ward Just, who particularly enjoyed the book's "whisper of misanthropy, indispensable equipment for the nonconforming serious humorist."

MEDIA ADAPTATIONS: One of Baker's columns, "How to Hypnotize Yourself into Forgetting the Vietnam War," was dramatized and filmed in 1971 by Eli Wallach for Public Broadcasting System's "The Great American Dream Machine."

BIOGRAPHICAL/CRITICAL SOURCES:

BOOKS

Baker, Russell, *Growing Up,* Congdon & Weed, 1982.
Baker, Russell, *The Good Times,* Morrow, 1989.
Contemporary Literary Criticism, Volume 31, Gale, 1985.

PERIODICALS

Chicago Tribune, January 16, 1987.
Detroit Free Press, June 27, 1989.
Detroit News, November 7, 1982, July 9, 1989.
Globe and Mail (Toronto), June 24, 1989.
Los Angeles Times, December 7, 1980, January 22, 1984, March 17, 1988.
Los Angeles Times Book Review, October 10, 1982, November 30, 1986, June 11, 1989.
Newsweek, September 29, 1980, November 8, 1982.
New York Times, January 30, 1972, October 6, 1982, May 23, 1989.
New York Times Book Review, January 30, 1972, October 18, 1982, May 28, 1989.
New York Times Magazine, September 12, 1982.
People, December 20, 1982.
Publishers Weekly, January 24, 1972.
Time, January 19, 1968, January 17, 1972, June 4, 1979, November 1, 1982.
Tribune Books, May 21, 1989.
Washington Post, July 25, 1989.
Washington Post Book World, October 5, 1980, October 3, 1982, October 9, 1983, January 18, 1987, May 28, 1989.

*   *   *

BALBUS
See HUXLEY, Julian (Sorell)

*   *   *

BALDWIN, James (Arthur) 1924-1987

PERSONAL: Born August 2, 1924, in New York, N.Y.; died of stomach cancer December 1 (some sources say November 30), 1987, in St. Paul de Vence, France; son of David (a clergyman and factory worker) and Berdis (Jones) Baldwin. *Education:* Graduate of De Witt Clinton High School, New York, N.Y., 1942.

ADDRESSES: Home—St. Paul de Vence, France. *Agent*—Edward Acton, Inc., 17 Grove St., New York, N.Y. 10014.

CAREER: Writer, 1944-87. Youth minister at Fireside Pentecostal Assembly, New York, N.Y., 1938-42; variously employed as handyman, dishwasher, waiter, and office boy in New York City, and in defense work in Belle Meade, N.J., 1942-46. Lecturer on racial issues at universities in the United States and Europe, 1957-87. Director of play, "Fortune and Men's Eyes," in Istanbul, Turkey, 1970, and film, "The Inheritance," 1973.

MEMBER: Congress on Racial Equality (member of national advisory board), American Academy and Institute of Arts and Letters, Authors League, International PEN, Dramatists Guild, Actors' Studio, National Committee for a Sane Nuclear Policy.

AWARDS, HONORS: Eugene F. Saxton fellowship, 1945; Rosenwald fellowship, 1948; Guggenheim fellowship, 1954; National Institute of Arts and Letters grant for literature, 1956; Ford Foundation grant, 1959; National Conference of Christians and Jews Brotherhood Award, 1962, for *Nobody Knows My Name: More Notes of a Native Son;* George Polk Memorial Award, 1963, for magazine articles; Foreign Drama Critics Award, 1964, for *Blues for Mister Charlie;* D.Litt. from the University of British Columbia, Vancouver, 1964; National Association of Independent Schools Award, 1964, for *The Fire Next Time;* American Book Award nomination, 1980, for *Just Above My Head;* named Commander of the Legion of Honor (France), 1986.

WRITINGS:

FICTION

Go Tell It on the Mountain (novel), Knopf, 1953.
Giovanni's Room (novel; also see below), Dial, 1956, reprinted, Transworld, 1977.
Another Country (novel), Dial, 1962.
Going to Meet the Man (short stories), Dial, 1965.
(Contributor) *American Negro Short Stories,* Hill & Wang, 1966.
Tell Me How Long the Train's Been Gone (novel), Dial, 1968.
If Beale Street Could Talk (novel), Dial, 1974.
Little Man, Little Man: A Story of Childhood (juvenile), M. Joseph, 1976, Dial, 1977.
Just above My Head (novel), Dial, 1979.

Also author of *Harlem Quartet* (novel), 1987.

NONFICTION

Autobiographical Notes, Knopf, 1953.
Notes of a Native Son (essays), Beacon Press, 1955.
Nobody Knows My Name: More Notes of a Native Son (essays), Dial, 1961.
The Fire Next Time, Dial, 1963.
(Author of text) Richard Avedon, *Nothing Personal* (photographic portraits), Atheneum, 1964.
(With others) *Black Anti-Semitism and Jewish Racism,* R. W. Baron, 1969.
(With Kenneth Kaunda) Carl Ordung, editor, *Menschenwuerde und Gerechtigkeit* (essays delivered at the fourth assembly of the World Council of Churches), Union-Verlag, 1969.
(With Margaret Mead) *A Rap on Race* (transcribed conversation), Lippincott, 1971.
No Name in the Street (essays), Dial, 1972.
(With Francoise Giroud) *Cesar: Compressions d'or,* Hachette, 1973.
(With Nikki Giovanni) *A Dialogue* (transcribed conversation), Lippincott, 1973.
The Devil Finds Work (essays), Dial, 1976.
(With others) John Henrik Clarke, editor, *Harlem, U.S.A.: The Story of a City Within a City,* Seven Seas [Berlin], 1976.

The Evidence of Things Not Seen, Holt, 1985.
The Price of the Ticket: Collected Nonfiction 1948-1985, St. Martin's, 1985.
(With others) Michael J. Weber, editor, *Perspectives: Angles on African Art,* Center for African Art, 1987.

PLAYS

The Amen Corner (first produced in Washington, D.C. at Howard University, 1955; produced on Broadway at Ethel Barrymore Theatre, April 15, 1965), Dial, 1968.
"Giovanni's Room" (based on novel of same title), first produced in New York City at Actors' Studio, 1957.
Blues for Mister Charlie (first produced on Broadway at ANTA Theatre, April 23, 1964), Dial, 1964.
One Day, When I Was Lost: A Scenario (screenplay; based on *The Autobiography of Malcolm X,* by Alex Haley), M. Joseph, 1972, Dial, 1973.
"A Deed for the King of Spain," first produced in New York City at American Center for Stanislavski Theatre Art, January 24, 1974.

Also author of "The Welcome Table," 1987.

OTHER

Jimmy's Blues: Selected Poems, M. Joseph, 1983, St. Martin's, 1985.

Contributor of book reviews and essays to numerous periodicals in the United States and abroad, including *Harper's, Nation, Esquire, Playboy, Partisan Review, Mademoiselle,* and *New Yorker.*

WORK IN PROGRESS: A study of the life of Martin Luther King, Jr.

SIDELIGHTS: A novelist and essayist of considerable renown, James Baldwin bore articulate witness to the unhappy consequences of American racial strife. Baldwin's writing career began in the last years of legislated segregation; his fame as a social observer grew in tandem with the civil rights movement as he mirrored blacks' aspirations, disappointments, and coping strategies in a hostile society. *Tri-Quarterly* contributor Robert A. Bone declared that Baldwin's publications "have had a stunning impact on our cultural life" because the author ". . . succeeded in transposing the entire discussion of American race relations to the interior plane; it is a major breakthrough for the American imagination." In his novels, plays, and essays alike, Baldwin explored the psychological implications of racism for both the oppressed and the oppressor. Best-sellers such as *Nobody Knows My Name: More Notes of a Native Son* and *The Fire Next Time* acquainted wide audiences with his highly personal observations and his sense of urgency in the face of rising black bitterness. As Juan Williams noted in the *Washington Post,* long before Baldwin's death, his writings "became a standard of literary realism. . . . Given the messy nature of racial hatred, of the half-truths, blasphemies and lies that make up American life, Baldwin's accuracy in reproducing that world stands as a remarkable achievement. . . . Black people reading Baldwin knew he wrote the truth. White people reading Baldwin sensed his truth about the lives of black people and the sins of a racist nation."

Critics accorded Baldwin high praise for both his style and his themes. "Baldwin has carved a literary niche through his exploration of 'the mystery of the human being' in his art," observed Louis H. Pratt in *James Baldwin.* "His short stories, novels, and plays shed the light of reality upon the darkness of our illusions, while the essays bring a boldness, courage, and cool logic to bear on the most crucial questions of humanity with which this country has yet to be faced." In the *College Language Association Journal,* Therman B. O'Daniel called Baldwin "the gifted professor of that primary element, genuine talent. . . . Secondly he is a very intelligent and deeply perceptive observer of our multifarious contemporary society. . . . In the third place, Baldwin is a bold and courageous writer who is not afraid to search into the dark corners of our social consciences, and to force out into public view many of the hidden, sordid skeletons of our society. . . . Then, of course, there is Baldwin's literary style which is a fourth major reason for his success as a writer. His prose . . . possesses a crystal clearness and a passionately poetic rhythm that makes it most appealing." *Saturday Review* correspondent Benjamin De Mott concluded that Baldwin "retains a place in an extremely select group: That composed of the few genuinely indispensable American writers. He owes his rank partly to the qualities of responsiveness that have marked his work from the beginning. . . . Time and time over in fiction as in reportage, Baldwin tears himself free of his rhetorical fastenings and stands forth on the page utterly absorbed in the reality of the person before him, strung with his nerves, riveted to his feelings, breathing his breath."

Baldwin's central preoccupation as a writer lay in "his insistence on removing, layer by layer, the hardened skin with which Americans shield themselves from their country," according to Orde Coombs in the *New York Times Book Review.* The author saw himself as a "disturber of the peace"—one who revealed uncomfortable truths to a society mired in complacency. Pratt found Baldwin "engaged in a perpetual battle to overrule our objections and continue his probe into the very depths of our past. His constant concern is the catastrophic failure of the American Dream and the devastating inability of the American people to deal with that calamity." Pratt uncovered a further assumption in Baldwin's work; namely, that all of mankind is united by virtue of common humanity. "Consequently," Pratt stated, "the ultimate purpose of the writer, from Baldwin's perspective, is to discover that sphere of commonality where, although differences exist, those dissimilarities are stripped of their power to block communication and stifle human intercourse." The major impediment in this search for commonality, according to Baldwin, is white society's entrenched moral cowardice, a condition that through longstanding tradition equates blackness with dark impulses, carnality and chaos. By denying blacks' essential humanity so simplistically, the author argued, whites inflict psychic damage on blacks and suffer self-estrangement—a "fatal bewilderment," to quote Bone. Baldwin's essays exposed the dangerous implications of this destructive way of thinking; his fictional characters occasionally achieve interracial harmony after having made the bold leap of understanding he advocated. In the *British Journal of Sociology,* Beau Fly Jones claimed that Baldwin was one of the first black writers "to discuss with such insight the psychological handicaps that most Negroes must face; and to realize the complexities of Negro-white relations in so many different contexts. In redefining what has been called the Negro problem as white, he has forced the majority race to look at the damage it has done, and its own role in that destruction."

Dictionary of Literary Biography essayist John W. Roberts felt that Baldwin's "evolution as a writer of the first order constitutes a narrative as dramatic and compelling as his best story." Baldwin was born and raised in Harlem under very trying circumstances. His stepfather, an evangelical preacher, struggled to support a large family and demanded the most rigorous religious behavior from his nine children. Roberts wrote: "Baldwin's ambivalent relationship with his stepfather served as a constant source of tension during his formative years and informs some of his best mature writings. . . . The demands of caring for younger siblings and his stepfather's religious convictions in large part shielded the boy from the harsh realities of Harlem street life during the 1930s." As a youth Baldwin read constantly and even tried writing; he was an excellent student who sought escape from his environment through literature, movies, and theatre. During the summer of his fourteenth birthday he underwent a dramatic religious conversion, partly in response to his nascent sexuality and partly as a further buffer against the ever-present temptations of drugs and crime. He served as a junior minister for three years at the Fireside Pentecostal Assembly, but gradually he lost his desire to preach as he began to question blacks' acceptance of Christian tenets that had, in essence, been used to enslave them.

Shortly after he graduated from high school in 1942, Baldwin was compelled to find work in order to help support his brothers and sisters; mental instability had incapacitated his stepfather. Baldwin took a job in the defense industry in Belle Meade, New Jersey, and there, not for the first time, he was confronted with racism, discrimination, and the debilitating regulations of segregation. The experiences in New Jersey were closely followed by his stepfather's death, after which Baldwin determined to make writing his sole profession. He moved to Greenwich Village and began to write a novel, supporting himself by performing a variety of odd jobs. In 1944 he met author Richard Wright, who helped him to land the 1945 Eugene F. Saxton fellowship. Despite the financial freedom the fellowship provided, Baldwin was unable to complete his novel that year. He found the social tenor of the United States increasingly stifling even though such prestigious periodicals as the *Nation, New Leader,* and *Commentary* began to accept his essays and short stories for publication. Eventually, in 1948, he moved to Paris, using funds from a Rosenwald Foundation fellowship to pay his passage. Most critics feel that this journey abroad was fundamental to Baldwin's development as an author.

"Once I found myself on the other side of the ocean," Baldwin told the *New York Times,* "I could see where I came from very clearly, and I could see that I carried myself, which is my home, with me. You can never escape that. I am the grandson of a slave, and I am a writer. I must deal with both." Through some difficult financial and emotional periods, Baldwin undertook a process of self-realization that included both an acceptance of his heritage and an admittance of his bisexuality. Bone noted that Europe gave the young author many things: "It gave him a world perspective from which to approach the question of his own identity. It gave him a tender love affair which would dominate the pages of his later fiction. But above all, Europe gave him back himself. The immediate fruit of self-recovery was a great creative outburst. First came two [works] of reconciliation with his racial heritage. *Go Tell It on the Mountain* and *The Amen Corner* represent a search for roots, a surrender to tradition, an acceptance of the Negro past. Then came a series of essays which probe, deeper than anyone has dared, the psychic history of this nation. They are a moving record of a man's struggle to define the forces that have shaped him, in order that he may accept himself."

Many critics view Baldwin's essays as his most significant contribution to American literature. Works such as *Notes of a Native Son, Nobody Knows My Name, The Fire Next Time, No Name in the Street,* and *The Evidence of Things Not Seen* "serve to illuminate the condition of the black man in twentieth-century America," according to Pratt. Highly personal and analytical, the essays probe deeper than the mere provincial problems of white versus black to uncover the essential issues of self-determination, identity, and reality. "An artist is a sort of emotional or spiritual historian," Baldwin told *Life* magazine. "His role is to make you realize the doom and glory of knowing who you are and what you are. He has to tell, because nobody else *can* tell, what it is like to be alive." *South Atlantic Quarterly* contributor Fred L. Standley asserted that this quest for personal identity "is indispensable in Baldwin's opinion and the failure to experience such is indicative of a fatal weakness in human life." C. W. E. Bigsby elaborated in *The Fifties: Fiction, Poetry, Drama:* "Baldwin's central theme is the need to accept reality as a necessary foundation for individual identity and thus a logical prerequisite for the kind of saving love in which he places his whole faith. For some this reality is one's racial or sexual nature, for others it is the ineluctable fact of death. . . . Baldwin sees this simple progression as an urgent formula not only for the redemption of individual men but for the survival of mankind. In this at least black and white are as one and the Negro's much-vaunted search for identity can be seen as part and parcel of the American's long-standing need for self-definition."

Inevitably, however, Baldwin's assessments of the "sweet" and "bitter" experiences in his own life led him to describe "the exact place where private chaos and social outrage meet," according to Alfred Kazin in *Contemporaries.* Eugenia Collier described this confrontation in *Black World:* "On all levels personal and political . . . life is a wild chaos of paradox, hidden meanings, and dilemmas. This chaos arises from man's inability—or reluctance to face the truth about his own nature. As a result of this self-imposed blindness, men erect an elaborate facade of myth, tradition, and ritual behind which crouch, invisible, their true selves. It is this blindness on the part of Euro-Americans which has created and perpetuated the vicious racism which threatens to destroy this nation." In his essays on the 1950s and early 1960s, Baldwin sought to explain black experiences to a white readership as he warned whites about the potential destruction their psychic blindness might wreak. *Massachusetts Review* contributor David Levin noted that the author came to represent "for 'white' Americans, the eloquent, indignant prophet of an oppressed people, a voice speaking . . . in an all but desperate, final effort to bring us out of what he calls our innocence before it is (if it is not already) too late. This voice calls us to our immediate duty for the sake of our own humanity as well as our own safety. It demands that we stop regarding the Negro as an abstraction, an invisible man; that we begin to recognize each Negro in his 'full weight and complexity' as a human being; that we face the horrible reality of our past and present treatment of Negroes—a reality we do not know and do not want to know." In *Ebony* magazine, Allan Morrison observed that Baldwin evinced an awareness "that the audience for most of his nonfictional writings is white and he uses every forum at his disposal to drive home the basic truths of Negro-white relations in America as he sees them. His function here is to interpret whites to themselves and at the same time voice the Negro's protest against his role in a Jim Crow society."

Because Baldwin sought to inform and confront whites, and because his fiction contains interracial love affairs—both homosexual and heterosexual—he came under attack from the writers of the Black Arts Movement, who called for a literature exclusively by and for blacks. Baldwin refused to align himself with the movement; he continued to call himself an "American writer" as opposed to a "black writer" and continued to confront the issues facing a multi-racial society. Eldridge Cleaver, in his book *Soul on Ice,* accused Baldwin of a hatred of blacks and "a shameful, fanatical fawning" love of whites. What Cleaver saw as complicity with whites, Baldwin saw rather as an attempt to alter the real daily environment with which American blacks have been faced all their lives. Pratt noted, however, that Baldwin's efforts to "shake up" his white readers put him "at odds with current white literary trends" as well as with the Black Arts Movement. Pratt explained that Baldwin labored under the belief "that mainstream art is directed toward a complacent and apathetic audience, and it is designed to confirm and reinforce that sense of well-being. . . . Baldwin's writings are, by their very nature, iconoclastic. While Black Arts focuses on a black-oriented artistry, Baldwin is concerned with the destruction of the fantasies and delusions of a contented audience which is determined to avoid reality." As the civil rights movement gained momentum, Baldwin escalated his attacks on white complacency from the speaking platform as well as from the pages of books and magazines. *Nobody Knows My Name* and *The Fire Next Time* both sold more than a million copies; both were cited for their predictions of black violence in desperate response to white oppression. In *Encounter,* Colin MacInnes concluded that the reason "why Baldwin speaks to us of another race is that he still believes us worthy of a warning: he has not yet despaired of making us feel the dilemma we all chat about so glibly, . . . and of trying to save us from the agonies that we too will suffer if the Negro people are driven beyond the ultimate point of desperation."

Retrospective analyses of Baldwin's essays highlight the characteristic prose style that gives his works literary merit beyond the mere dissemination of ideas. In *A World More Attractive: A View of Modern Literature and Politics,* Irving Howe placed the author among "the two or three greatest essayists this country has ever produced." Howe claimed that Baldwin "has brought a new luster to the essay as an art form, a form with possibilities for discursive reflection and concrete drama. . . . The style of these essays is a remarkable instance of the way in which a grave and sustained eloquence—the rhythm of oratory, . . . held firm and hard—can be employed in an age deeply suspicious of rhetorical prowess." "Baldwin has shown more concern for the painful exactness of prose style than any other modern American writer," noted David Littlejohn in *Black on White: A Critical Survey of Writing by American Negroes.* "He picks up words with heavy care, then sets them, one by one, with a cool and loving precision that one can feel in the reading. . . . The exhilarating exhaustion of reading his best essays—which in itself may be a proof of their honesty and value—demands that the reader measure up, and forces him to learn."

Baldwin's fiction expanded his exploration of the "full weight and complexity" of the individual in a society prone to callousness and categorization. His loosely autobiographical works probed the milieus with which he was most familiar—black evangelical churches, jazz clubs, stifling Southern towns, and the Harlem ghetto. In *The Black American Writer: Fiction,* Brian Lee maintained that Baldwin's "essays explore the ambiguities and ironies of a life lived on two levels—that of the Negro and that of the man—and they have spoken eloquently to and for a whole generation. But Baldwin's feelings about the condition—alternating moods of sadness and bitterness—are best expressed in the paradoxes confronting the haunted heroes of his novels and stories. The possible modes of existence for anyone seeking refuge from a society which refuses to acknowledge one's humanity are necessarily limited, and Baldwin has explored with some thoroughness the various emotional and spiritual alternatives available to his retreating protagonists." Pratt felt that Baldwin's fictive artistry "not only documents the dilemma of the black man in American society, but it also bears witness to the struggle of the artist against the overwhelming forces of oppression. Almost invariably, his protagonists are artists. . . . Each character is engaged in the pursuit of artistic fulfillment which, for Baldwin, becomes symbolic of the quest for identity."

Love, both sexual and spiritual, was an essential component of Baldwin's characters' quests for self-realization. John W. Aldridge observed in the Saturday Review that sexual love "emerges in his novels as a kind of universal anodyne for the disease of racial separatism, as a means not only of achieving personal identity but also of transcending false categories of color and gender." Homosexual encounters emerged as the principal means to achieve important revelations; as Bigsby explained, Baldwin felt that "it is the homosexual, virtually alone, who can offer a selfless and genuine love because he alone has a real sense of himself, having accepted his own nature." Baldwin did not see love as a "saving grace," however; his vision, given the circumstances of the lives he encountered, was more cynical than optimistic. In his introduction to *James Baldwin: A Collection of Critical Essays,* Kenneth Kinnamon wrote: "If the search for love has its origin in the desire of a child for emotional security, its arena is an adult world which involves it in struggle and pain. Stasis must yield to motion, innocence to experience, security to risk. This is the lesson that . . . saves Baldwin's central fictional theme from sentimentality. . . . Similarly, love as an agent of racial reconciliation and national survival is not for Baldwin a vague yearning for an innocuous brotherhood, but an agonized confrontation with reality, leading to the struggle to transform it. It is a quest for truth through a recognition of the primacy of suffering and injustice in the American past." Pratt also concluded that in Baldwin's novels, "love is often extended, frequently denied, seldom fulfilled. As reflections of our contemporary American society, the novels stand as forthright indictments of the intolerable conditions that we have accepted unquestioningly as a way of life."

Black family life—the charged emotional atmosphere between parents and children, brothers and sisters—provided another major theme in Baldwin's fiction. This was especially apparent in his first and best-known novel, *Go Tell It on the Mountain,* the story of a Harlem teenager's struggles with a repressive father and with religious conversion. According to Roberts, *Go Tell It on the Mountain* "proved that James Baldwin had become a writer of enormous power and skill. [It] was an essential book for Baldwin. Although clearly a fictional work, it chronicles two of the most problematic aspects of his existence as a young man: a son's relationship to his stepfather and the impact of fundamentalist religion on the consciousness of a young boy." In her work entitled *James Baldwin,* Carolyn Wedin Sylvander praised Baldwin's family chronicle particularly because the author "is dealing comprehensively and emotionally with the hot issue of race relations in the United States at a time . . . when neither white ignorance and prejudice nor black powerlessness is conducive to holistic depictions of black experience." Indeed, the overt confrontation between the races that characterizes Baldwin's later work was here portrayed as a peripheral threat, a danger greater than, but less immediate than, the potential damage inflicted by parents on children. Sylvander wrote: "It is painfully, dramatically, structurally clear throughout *Go Tell It on the Mountain* that the struggles every individual faces—with sexuality, with guilt, with pain, with love—are passed on, generation to generation." Littlejohn described Baldwin's treatment of this essential American theme as "autobiography-as-exorcism, . . . a lyrical, painful, ritual exercise whose necessity and intensity the reader feels." Pratt likewise stated that *Go Tell It on the Mountain* "stands as an honest, intensive, self-analysis, functioning simultaneously to illuminate self, society, and mankind as a whole."

In addition to his numerous books, Baldwin was one of the few black authors to have had more than one of his plays produced on Broadway. Both *The Amen Corner,* another treatment of storefront pentecostal religion, and *Blues for Mister Charlie,* a drama based on the racially-motivated murder of Emmett Till in 1955, had successful Broadway runs and numerous revivals. Standley commented in the *Dictionary of Literary Biography* that in both plays, "as in his other literary works, Baldwin explores a variety of thematic concerns: the historical significance and the potential explosiveness in black-white relations; the necessity for developing a sexual and psychological consciousness and identity; the intertwining of love and power in the universal scheme of existence as well as in the structures of society; the misplaced priorities in the value systems in America; and the responsibility of the artist to promote the evolution of the individual and the society." In *The Black American Writer: Poetry and Drama,* Walter Meserve offered remarks on Baldwin's abilities as a playwright. "Baldwin tries to use the theatre as a pulpit for his ideas," Meserve stated. "Mainly his plays are thesis plays—talky, over-written, and cliche dialogue and some stereotypes, preachy, and argumentative. Essentially, Baldwin is not particularly dramatic, but he can be extremely eloquent, compelling, and sometimes irritating as a playwright committed to his approach to life." Meserve added, however, that although the author was criticized for creating stereotypes, "his major characters are the most successful and memorable aspects of his plays. People are important to Baldwin, and their problems, generally embedded in their agonizing souls, stimulate him to write. . . . A humanitarian, sensitive to the needs and struggles of man, he writes of inner turmoil, spiritual disruption, the consequence upon people of the burdens of the world, both White and Black."

Baldwin's oratorical prowess—honed in the pulpit as a youth—brought him into great demand as a speaker during the civil rights era. Sylvander observed that national attention "began to turn toward him as a spokesperson for blacks, not as much because of his novels as his essays, debates, interviews, panel discussions." Baldwin embraced his role as racial spokesman reluctantly and grew increasingly disillusioned as the American public "disarmed him with celebrity, [fell] in love with his eccentricities, and institutionalized his outrage . . . into prime-time entertainment," to quote Aldridge. Nor was Baldwin able to feel that his speeches and essays were producing social change—the assassinations of three of his associates, Medgar Evers, Martin Luther King, Jr., and Malcolm X, shattered his remaining hopes for racial reconciliation. Kinnamon remarked that by 1972, the year Baldwin published *No Name in the Street,* "the redemptive possibilities of love seemed exhausted in that terrible decade of assassination, riot, and repression. . . . Social love had now become for Baldwin more a rueful memory than an alternative to disaster." *London Magazine* contributor James Campbell also noted that by 1972 "Baldwin the saviour had turned into Baldwin the soldier. What [observers] failed to notice was that he was still the preacher and the prophet, that his passion and rage were mingled with detachment, and that his gloomy prognostications were based on powerful observation and an understanding of the past which compelled their pessimism."

Many critics took Baldwin to task for the stridency and gloom that overtook his writings. "To function as a voice of outrage month after month for a decade and more strains heart and mind, and rhetoric as well," declared Benjamin De Mott in the *Saturday Review.* "The consequence is a writing style ever on the edge of being winded by too many summonses to intensity." *New Republic* correspondent Nathan Glazer likewise stated that Baldwin had become "an accusing voice, but the accusation is so broad, so general, so all-embracing, that the rhetoric disappears into the wind." Stephen Donadio offered a similar opinion in the *Partisan Review:* "As his notoriety increased, his personality was oversimplified, appropriated, and consumed. . . . Mr. Baldwin created a situation in which the eye of the audience was fixed on the author as a performer, and the urgency of the race problem in America became a backdrop for elaborate rhetorical assaults which could be dutifully acknowledged but forgotten with a sigh."

Baldwin's passionate detractors were offset by equally passionate defenders, however. Sylvander wrote: "Wading through vehement and sometimes shallow reactions to the deep water of the statements and works themselves, one is struck repeatedly by the power of Baldwin's prose, and by our continuing need, as readers and as citizens, for his steadying apocalyptic vision. Finally, in his fantastic, experientially various, wide-ranging, searching, and committed life, one can find a vigorous model for venturing beyond charted areas." Charles Newman made two points in *James Baldwin: A Collection of Critical Essays.* First, Newman noted that Baldwin's experience is "unique among our artists in that his artistic achievements mesh so precisely with his historical circumstances. He is that nostalgic type—an artist speaking for a genuinely visible revolution." Second, Newman maintained that as an observer of this painful revolution, "almost alone [Baldwin] continued to confront the unmanageable questions of modern society, rather than creating a nuclear family in which semantic fantasies may be enacted with no reference to the larger world except that it stinks." Kinnamon concluded: "James Baldwin has always been concerned with the most personal and intimate areas of experience and also with the broadest questions of national and global destiny—and with the intricate interrelationships between the two. Whatever the final assessment of his literary achievement, it is clear that his voice—simultaneously that of victim, witness, and prophet—has been among the most urgent of our time."

At the time of his death from cancer late in 1987, Baldwin was still working on two projects—a play, "The Welcome Table," and a biography of Martin Luther King, Jr. Although he lived primarily in France, he had never relinquished his United States citizenship and preferred to think of himself as a "commuter" rather than as an expatriate. The publication of his collected essays, *The Price of the Ticket: Collected Nonfiction 1948-1985,* and his subsequent death sparked reassessments of his career and comments on the quality of his lasting legacy. "Mr. Baldwin has become a kind of prophet, a man who has been able to give a public issue all its deeper moral, historical, and personal significance," remarked Robert F. Sayre in *Contemporary American Novelists.* "Certainly one mark of his achievement, . . . is that whatever deeper comprehension of the race issue Americans now possess has been in some way shaped by him. And this is to have shaped their comprehension of themselves as well." Sylvander asserted that what emerges from the whole of Baldwin's work is "a kind of absolute conviction and passion and honesty that is nothing less than courageous. . . . Baldwin has shared his struggle with his readers for a purpose—to demonstrate that our suffering is our bridge to one another."

Perhaps the most telling demonstration of the results of Baldwin's achievement came from other black writers. Orde Coombs, for instance, concluded: "Because he existed we felt that the racial miasma that swirled around us would not consume us, and it is not too much to say that this man saved our lives, or at least, gave us the necessary ammunition to face what we knew would continue to be a hostile and condescending

world." Playwright Amiri Baraka phrased a similar assessment even more eloquently in his funeral eulogy to Baldwin. "This man traveled the earth like its history and its biographer," Baraka said. "He reported, criticized, made beautiful, analyzed, cajoled, lyricized, attacked, sang, made us think, made us better, made us consciously human. . . . He made us feel . . . that we could defend ourselves or define ourselves, that we were in the world not merely as animate slaves, but as terrifyingly sensitive measurers of what is good or evil, beautiful or ugly. This is the power of his spirit. This is the bond which created our love for him." In a posthumous profile for the *Washington Post,* Juan Williams wrote: "The success of Baldwin's effort as the witness is evidenced time and again by the people, black and white, gay and straight, famous and anonymous, whose humanity he unveiled in his writings. America and the literary world are far richer for his witness. The proof of a shared humanity across the divides of race, class and more is the testament that the preacher's son, James Arthur Baldwin, has left us."

MEDIA ADAPTATIONS: The Amen Corner was adapted as a musical stage play, "Amen Corner," by Garry Sherman, Peter Udell and Philip Rose, and produced on Broadway at the Nederlander Theater, November 10, 1983. *Go Tell It on the Mountain* was dramatized under the same title for the Public Broadcasting System's "American Playhouse" series, January 14, 1985.

BIOGRAPHICAL/CRITICAL SOURCES:

BOOKS

Balakian, Nona, and Charles Simmons, editors, *The Creative Present: Notes on Contemporary Fiction,* Doubleday, 1963.

Bigsby, C. W. E., *Confrontation and Commitment: A Study of Contemporary American Drama,* University of Missouri Press, 1967.

Bigsby, C. W. E., editor, *The Black American Writer,* Volume I: *Fiction,* Volume II: *Poetry and Drama,* Everett/Edwards, 1969.

Bone, Robert, *The Negro Novel in America,* Yale University Press, 1965.

Brustein, Robert, *Seasons of Discontent: Dramatic Opinions 1959-1965,* Simon & Schuster, 1965.

Burgess, Anthony, *The Novel Now: A Guide to Contemporary Fiction,* Norton, 1967.

Chapman, Abraham, editor, *Black Voices: An Anthology of Afro-American Literature,* New American Library, 1968.

Cleaver, Eldridge, *Soul on Ice,* McGraw-Hill, 1968.

Cohn, Ruby, *Dialogue in American Drama,* Indiana University Press, 1971.

Concise Dictionary of American Literary Biography: The New Consciousness, 1941-1968, Gale, 1987.

Contemporary Authors Bibliographical Series, Volume I: *American Novelists,* Gale, 1986.

Contemporary Literary Criticism, Gale, Volume I, 1973, Volume II, 1974, Volume III, 1975, Volume IV, 1975, Volume V, 1976, Volume VIII, 1978, Volume XIII, 1980, Volume XV, 1980, Volume XVII, 1981, Volume XLII, 1987, Volume L, 1988.

Cook, M. G., editor, *Modern Black Novelists: A Collection of Critical Essays,* Prentice-Hall, 1971.

Culture for the Millions, Van Nostrand, 1959.

Dance, Daryl, *Black American Writers: Bibliographical Essays,* St. Martin's, 1978.

Dictionary of Literary Biography, Gale, Volume II: *American Novelists since World War II,* 1978, Volume VIII: *Twentieth-Century American Dramatists,* 1981, Volume XXXIII: *Afro-American Fiction Writers after 1955,* 1984.

Eckman, Fern Marja, *The Furious Passage of James Baldwin,* M. Evans, 1966.

Dictionary of Literary Biography Yearbook: 1987, Gale, 1988.

French, Warren, editor, *The Fifties: Fiction, Poetry, Drama,* Everett/Edwards, 1970.

Frost, David, *The Americans,* Stein & Day, 1970.

Gayle, Addison, Jr., *The Way of the World: The Black Novel in America,* Anchor Press, 1975.

Gibson, Donald B., editor, *Five Black Writers: Essays on Wright, Ellison, Baldwin, Hughes, and LeRoi Jones,* New York University Press, 1970.

Hesse, H. Ober, editor, *The Nature of a Humane Society,* Fortress, 1976.

Hill, Herbert, editor, *Anger and Beyond,* Harper, 1966.

Howe, Irving, *A World More Attractive: A View of Modern Literature and Politics,* Horizon Press, 1963.

Hyman, Stanley Edgar, *Standards: A Chronicle of Books for Our Time,* Horizon Press, 1966.

Kazin, Alfred, *Bright Book of Life: American Novelists & Storytellers from Hemingway to Mailer,* Little, Brown, 1973.

Kazin, Alfred, *Contemporaries,* Little, Brown, 1962.

King, Malcolm, *Baldwin: Three Interviews,* Wesleyan University Press, 1985.

Kinnamon, Kenneth, editor, *James Baldwin: A Collection of Critical Essays,* Prentice-Hall, 1974.

Klein, Marcus, *After Alienation: American Novels in Mid-Century,* World Publishing, 1964.

Littlejohn, David, *Black on White: A Critical Survey of Writing by American Negroes,* Viking, 1966.

Lumley, Frederick, *New Trends in 20th Century Drama: A Survey Since Ibsen and Shaw,* Oxford University Press, 1967.

Macebuh, Stanley, *James Baldwin: A Critical Study,* Joseph Okpaku, 1973.

Major, Clarence, *The Dark and Feeling: Black American Writers and Their Work,* Joseph Okpaku, 1974.

Moeller, Karin, *The Theme of Identity in the Essays of James Baldwin,* Acta Universitatis Gotoburgensis, 1975.

Moore, Harry T., editor, *Contemporary American Novelists,* Southern Illinois University Press, 1964.

O'Daniel, Therman B., *James Baldwin: A Critical Evaluation,* Howard University Press, 1977.

Panichas, George A., *The Politics of Twentieth-Century Novelists,* Hawthorn, 1971.

Podhoretz, Norman, *Doings and Undoings,* Farrar, Straus, 1964.

Pratt, Louis Hill, *James Baldwin,* Twayne, 1978.

Rosenblatt, Roger, *Black Fiction,* Harvard University Press, 1974.

Sheed, Wilfrid, *The Morning After,* Farrar, Straus, 1971.

Simon, John, *Uneasy Stages: Chronicle of the New York Theatre,* Random House, 1975.

Sontag, Susan, *Against Interpretation and Other Essays,* Farrar, Straus, 1966.

Standley, Fred and Nancy Standley, *James Baldwin: A Reference Guide,* G. K. Hall, 1980.

Standley, Fred and Nancy Standley, editors, *Critical Essays on James Baldwin,* G. K. Hall, 1981.

Sylvander, Carolyn Wedin, *James Baldwin,* Frederick Ungar, 1980.

Turner, Darwin T., *Afro-American Writers,* Appleton, 1970.

Weatherby, William J., *Squaring Off: Mailer vs. Baldwin,* Mason/Charter, 1977.

Williams, John A. and Charles F. Harris, editors, *Amistad I: Writings on Black History and Culture,* Random House, 1970.

Williams, Sherley Anne, *Give Birth to Brightness: A Thematic Study in Neo-Black Literature,* Dial, 1972.

PERIODICALS

America, March 16, 1963.

Atlanta Constitution, May 19, 1976.

Atlantic, July, 1961, July, 1962, March, 1963, July, 1968, June, 1972.

Atlas, March, 1967.

Black Scholar, December, 1973-January, 1974.

Black World, June, 1972, December, 1974.

Books and Bookmen, August, 1968, September, 1972, December, 1979.

Book Week, May 31, 1964, September 26, 1965.

British Journal of Sociology, June, 1966.

Bulletin of Bibliography, January-April, 1965, May-August, 1968.

Chicago Tribune, September 16, 1979, October 10, 1979, November 15, 1985, December 16, 1987, November 15, 1989.

Christian Science Monitor, July 19, 1962.

College Language Association Journal, Number 7, 1964, Number 10, 1966, March, 1967.

Commentary, November, 1953, January, 1957, December, 1961, June, 1968, December, 1979, December, 1985.

Commonweal, May 22, 1953, December 8, 1961, October 26, 1962, December 7, 1962, October 12, 1973, June 24, 1977.

Critical Quarterly, summer, 1964.

Critique, winter, 1964-65.

Cross Currents, summer, 1961.

Ebony, October, 1961.

Ecumenical Review, October, 1968.

Encounter, August, 1963, July, 1965.

English Journal, May, 1973.

Esquire, July, 1968.

Freedomways, summer, 1963.

Globe & Mail (Toronto), January 11, 1986.

Harper's, March, 1963, September, 1968.

Hollins Critic, December, 1965.

Hudson Review, autumn, 1964, autumn, 1968.

Intellectual Digest, July, 1972.

Life, May 24, 1963, June 7, 1968, June 4, 1971, July 30, 1971.

Listener, July 25, 1974.

London Magazine, December, 1979-January, 1980.

Lone Star Book Review, January-February, 1980.

Look, July 23, 1968.

Los Angeles Times Book Review, December 1, 1985.

Mademoiselle, May, 1963.

Massachusetts Review, winter, 1964.

Midcontinent American Studies Journal, fall, 1963.

Muhammad Speaks, September 8, 1973, September 15, 1973, September 29, 1973, October 6, 1973.

Nation, July 14, 1962, November 17, 1962, March 2, 1963, December 13, 1965, April 10, 1972, June 10, 1968, July 3, 1976, November 3, 1979.

National Observer, March 6, 1967, June 3, 1968.

National Review, May 21, 1963, July 7, 1972.

Negro American Literature Forum, spring, 1969, winter, 1972.

Negro Digest, June, 1963, October, 1966, April, 1967.

New Leader, June 3, 1968, May 27, 1974, May 24, 1976.

New Republic, December 17, 1956, August 7, 1961, August 27, 1962, November 27, 1965, August 17, 1968, June 15, 1974, November 24, 1979, December 30, 1985.

New Statesman, July 13, 1962, July 19, 1963, December 4, 1964, November 3, 1972, June 28, 1974, February 25, 1977, November 29, 1985.

Newsweek, February 4, 1963, June 3, 1969, May 27, 1974.

New Yorker, June 20, 1953, November 25, 1961, August 4, 1962, July 8, 1974, November 26, 1979.

New York Herald Tribune Book Review, June 17, 1962.

New York Review of Books, May 28, 1964, December 17, 1964, December 9, 1965, June 29, 1972, June 13, 1974, December 6, 1979, January 21, 1988.

New York Times, May 3, 1964, April 16, 1965, May 31, 1968, February 2, 1969, May 21, 1971, May 17, 1974, June 4, 1976, September 4, 1977, September 21, 1979, September 23, 1979, November 11, 1983, January 10, 1985, January 14, 1985, June 22, 1989.

New York Times Book Review, February 26, 1956, July 2, 1961, June 24, 1962, December 12, 1965, June 2, 1968, June 23, 1968, May 28, 1972, May 19, 1974, May 2, 1976, September 23, 1979, May 24, 1984.

New York Times Magazine, March 7, 1965.

Nickel Review, February 27, 1970.

Observer, November 24, 1985, April 6, 1986.

Partisan Review, summer, 1963, winter, 1966.

People, January 7, 1980.

Progressive, August, 1972.

Queen's Quarterly, summer, 1965.

San Francisco Chronicle, June 28, 1962.

Saturday Review, December 1, 1956, July 1, 1961, July 7, 1962, February 2, 1963, February 8, 1964, May 2, 1964, November 6, 1965, June 1, 1968, May 27, 1972, June 15, 1974, January 5, 1980.

Sight and Sound, autumn, 1976.

South Atlantic Quarterly, summer, 1966.

Southern Humanities Review, winter, 1970.

Southern Review, summer, 1985.

Spectator, July 12, 1968, July 6, 1974, January 11, 1986, April 26, 1986.

Studies in Short Fiction, summer, 1975, fall, 1977.

Time, June 30, 1961, June 29, 1962, November 6, 1964, June 7, 1968, June 10, 1974.

Times (London), May 15, 1986, January 19, 1987, January 22, 1987, January 31, 1989.

Times Educational Supplement, December 27, 1985.

Times Literary Supplement, July 26, 1963, December 10, 1964, October 28, 1965, July 4, 1968, April 28, 1972, November 17, 1972, June 21, 1974, December 21, 1979, August 2, 1984, January 24, 1986, September 19, 1986.

Tri-Quarterly, winter, 1965.

Twentieth-Century Literature, April, 1967.

Village Voice, October 29, 1979, January 12, 1988.

Vogue, July, 1964.

Washington Post, September 23, 1979, October 15, 1979, September 9, 1983, September 25, 1983, August 14, 1989.

Washington Post Book World, September 11, 1977, September 23, 1979, October 27, 1985, December 9, 1987.

Western Humanities Review, spring, 1968.

World Literature Today, spring, 1980.

Yale Review, October, 1966.

OBITUARIES:

PERIODICALS

Chicago Tribune, December 2, 1987.

Detroit Free Press, December 2, 1987, December 8, 1987.

Los Angeles Times, December 2, 1987.

New York Times, December 2, 1987, December 9, 1987.

Philadelphia Inquirer, December 2, 1987, December 9, 1987, December 14, 1987.

Times (London), December 2, 1987.

Washington Post, December 2, 1987.

*   *   *

BALLARD, J(ames) G(raham)   1930-

PERSONAL: Born November 15, 1930, in Shanghai, China; son of James (a chemist and business executive) and Edna (Johnstone) Ballard; married Helen Mary Matthews, 1953 (died, 1964); children: James, Fay, Beatrice. *Education:* Studied medicine at King's College, Cambridge, 1949-51.

ADDRESSES: Home—36 Charlton Rd., Shepperton, Middlesex, England. *Agent*—Margaret Hanbury, 27 Walcot Sq., London S.E. 11, England.

CAREER: Writer. Trustee, Institute for Research in Art and Technology. *Military service:* Royal Air Force, c. 1954-57; became pilot.

AWARDS, HONORS: Guardian Fiction Prize, 1984, James Tait Black Memorial Prize, 1985, and nomination for Booker Prize, 1984, all for *Empire of the Sun.*

WRITINGS:

(Editor with others) *Best Science Fiction From "New Worlds,"* Medallion, 1968.

(Contributor) *The Inner Landscape,* Allison & Busby, 1969.

"The Assassination Weapon" (play), produced in London, 1969.

(Author of introduction) *Salvador Dali,* Ballantine, 1974.

(Author of introduction) Brian Ash, editor, *The Visual Encyclopaedia of Science Fiction,* Pan Books, 1977.

(Contributor) V. Vale and Andre Juno, editors, *Re/Search: J. G. Ballard,* Re/Search Publishing, 1984.

NOVELS

The Wind From Nowhere (also see below), Berkley Publishing, 1962.

The Drowned World (also see below), Berkley Publishing, 1962.

The Burning World, Berkley Publishing, 1964 (revised edition published in England as *The Drought,* J. Cape, 1965).

The Drowned World [and] *The Wind From Nowhere,* Doubleday, 1965.

The Crystal World, Farrar, Straus, 1966.

Crash, J. Cape, 1972, Farrar, Straus, 1973.

Concrete Island, Farrar, Straus, 1974.

High-Rise, J. Cape, 1975, Holt, 1977.

The Unlimited Dream Company, Holt, 1979.

Hello America, J. Cape, 1981.

Empire of the Sun, Simon & Schuster, 1984.

The Day of Creation, Gollancz, 1987, published as *The Act of Creation,* Farrar, Straus, 1988.

Running Wild, Hutchinson, 1989.

STORY COLLECTIONS

The Voices of Time and Other Stories, Berkley Publishing, 1962.

Billenium and Other Stories, Berkley Publishing, 1962.

The Four-Dimensional Nightmare, Gollancz, 1963, revised edition, 1974.

Passport to Eternity and Other Stories, Berkley Publishing, 1963.

Terminal Beach, Berkley Publishing, 1964 (revised edition published as *The Terminal Beach,* Gollancz, 1964).

The Impossible Man and Other Stories, Berkley Publishing, 1966.

The Disaster Area, J. Cape, 1967.

By Day Fantastic Birds Flew Through the Petrified Forests, Esographics for Firebird Visions, 1967.

The Day of Forever, Panther Books, 1967, revised edition, 1971.

The Overloaded Man, Panther Books, 1968.

The Atrocity Exhibition, J. Cape, 1970, published as *Love and Napalm: Export U.S.A.,* Grove Press, 1972.
Vermilion Sands, Berkley Publishing, 1971.
Chronopolis and Other Stories, Putnam, 1971.
Low-Flying Aircraft and Other Stories, J. Cape, 1976.
The Best of J. G. Ballard, Futura Publications, 1977, revised edition published as *The Best Short Stories of J. G. Ballard,* Holt, 1978.
The Venus Hunters, Granada, 1980.
Myths of the Near Future, J. Cape, 1982.
Memories of the Space Age, Arkham House, 1988.

Contributor to *New Worlds, Ambit, Guardian, Transatlantic Review, Triquarterly, Playboy, Encounter, Evergreen Review,* and other publications. Prose editor, *Ambit.*

SIDELIGHTS: J. G. Ballard uses the language and symbols of science fiction to "explore the collective unconscious, the externalized psyche, which is plainly visible around us and which belongs to us all," as David Pringle states in his study *Earth Is the Alien Planet: J. G. Ballard's Four-Dimensional Nightmare.* Ballard's obsessive characters—searching "for a reality beyond 'normal' life," as Douglas Winter describes it in the *Washington Post Book World*—attempt to manifest their private visions in landscapes which seem to reflect their own mental states. Whether he uses post-holocaust or electronic media landscapes, what characterizes this surreal fusion of environment and the unconscious, Ballard writes in an essay for *New Worlds,* "is its redemptive and therapeutic power. To move through these landscapes is a journey of return to one's innermost being."

This idea is echoed by Joseph Lanz who, in an article for *Re/Search: J. G. Ballard,* also points out the neurotic nature of Ballard's characters. Ballard's science fiction, Lanz writes, "replaces the intergalactic journey with excursions into the convoluted psyche. In Ballard's realm, neurosis is an ultracivilized version of primitive ritual where object and subject meld into an alchemical union. The outside world is just a projection of private fetishes." Pringle claims that Ballard's characters "are driven by obsessions" and often choose "to strand themselves in some bizarre terrain which reflects their states of mind." Ballard addresses this question in an interview with Douglas Reed in *Books and Bookmen.* "My psychological landscapes," he explains, "are the sort that might be perceived by people during major mental crises—not literally, of course, but they represent similar disturbed states of mind." Speaking with Thomas Frick for *Paris Review,* Ballard further explains his intentions: "I quite consciously rely on my obsessions in all my work, . . . I deliberately set up an obsessional state of mind."

This obsessional quality is reflected in Ballard's recurring use of a few powerful symbols—symbols which have become so closely associated with his work that some critics label them "Ballardian." Dunes, abandoned buildings, crashed automobiles, low-flying airplanes, drained swimming pools, and beaches are found in story after story. They are used, Charles Platt writes in *Dream Makers: The Uncommon People Who Write Science Fiction,* "as signposts, keys to the meaning of technology, the structure of the unconscious, and the promise of the Future." Noting the repetitive use of these symbols, Galen Strawson of the *Times Literary Supplement* observes that "sometimes it seems as if Ballard's oeuvre is just the systematic extrapolation . . . of an initial fixed set of possibilities, obsessions, and palmary symbols."

Ballard's richly metaphoric prose and his emphasis on psychological and technological themes make him a unique and important figure on the contemporary literary scene. Malcolm Bradbury, writing in the *New York Times Book Review,* stresses the psychological insights in Ballard's work. Ballard is, Bradbury believes, "an explorer of the displacements produced in modern consciousness by the blank ecology of stark architecture, bare high-rises, dead super-highways, and featureless technology." In similar terms, Emma Tennant writes in the *New Statesman* that "Ballard's talent . . . is to show us what we refuse to see—the extraordinary mixture of old ideas and modern architecture, the self-contradictory expectation of 'human' responses in a landscape constructed to submerge all traces of identity—and to prove that it is only by knowing ourselves that we can understand the technology we have created."

Ballard began his writing career in the 1950s, selling his short stories to science fiction magazines in his native England and in the United States. "But Ballard," Platt relates, "never showed any interest in the usual subject matter of science fiction—rockets, aliens, and other planets." Encouraged by E. J. Carnell, the editor of *New Worlds,* to follow his own inclinations, Ballard soon adopted a distinctive style and choice of subject matter. "By the late 1950's," Robert Silverberg writes in *Galactic Dreamers: Science Fiction as Visionary Literature,* Ballard "was dazzling and perplexing science-fiction readers with his dark and hypnotic stories and novels, typified by intelligent though passive characters in the grips of inexplicable cosmic catastrophes."

In his first four novels, Ballard depicts global catastrophes that destroy modern civilization: high winds in *The Wind From Nowhere,* melting ice caps in *The Drowned World,* drought in *The Burning World,* and a spreading, cancerous mutation in *The Crystal World.* These catastrophes alter the perceptions of Ballard's protagonists who, feeling a kinship with the destruction around them, respond by embracing it. Ballard's heroes, writes Platt, are "solitary figures, courting the apocalypse and ultimately seduced by it. To them, a private, mystical union with a ruined world [is] more attractive than the pretense of a 'normal' lifestyle among organized bands of survivors."

Although some critics see these early novels as pessimistic because of their seemingly passive and self-destructive characters, Ballard does not agree. "I haven't got any sort of 'deathwish,' " he tells Reed. "This aspect of my work parallels the self-destructive but curiously consistent logic of people enduring severe mental illness. There is a unique set of laws governing their actions, laws as constant as those controlling sane behavior but based on different criteria." Speaking to Platt on the same topic, Ballard claims his work is not pessimistic. "It's a *fiction of psychological fulfillment,*" he clarifies. "The hero of *The Drowned World,* who goes south toward the sun and self-oblivion, is choosing a sensible course of action that will result in absolute psychological fulfillment for himself. . . . All my fiction describes the merging of the self in the ultimate metaphor, the ultimate image, and that's psychologically fulfilling." Graeme Revell, writing in *Re/Search: J. G. Ballard,* sees these books as " 'transformation' rather than 'disaster' stories, involving not a material solution, but one of psychic fulfillment of the hero. . . . The hero is the only one who pursues a meaningful course of action—instead of escaping or trying to adapt to the material environment, he stays and comes to terms with the changes taking place within it and, by implication, within himself."

These early novels, particularly *The Drowned World* and *The Crystal World,* "helped make [Ballard's] name as a topographer of post-cataclysmic landscape," according to a reviewer for the *Times Literary Supplement.* This reputation changed in the late 1960s when Ballard became a leading spokesman for the "New Wave" in science fiction, a movement seeking to introduce experimental literary techniques and more sophisticated subject matter into the science fiction field. In an editorial he wrote for *New Worlds* at that time, Ballard states: "It is *inner* space, not outer, that needs to be explored." In his own work Ballard began to explore the media landscape of modern society through a non-linear writing style, entering his most experimental period. Many of the stories from this time are found in *The Atrocity Exhibition*. In this collection, Ballard explains to Reed, he writes of "a doctor who's had a mental break-down. He has been shocked and numbed by events like the deaths of the Kennedys and Marilyn Monroe. To make sense of the modern world he wants to immerse himself in its most destructive elements. He creates a series of psycho-dramas that produce grim paradoxes." As a critic for the *Times Literary Supplement* sees it, in *The Atrocity Exhibition* Ballard "presents extreme examples of the private psyche being invaded by public events." In a preface to the American edition of the book, William S. Burroughs calls it "profound and disquieting. . . . The nonsexual roots of sexuality are explored with a surgeon's precision."

Because of objections to some of the book's content—in particular, a story entitled "Why I Want to F—— Ronald Reagan" and certain references to consumer activist Ralph Nader—two American publishers accepted and then rejected the book before Grove Press brought it out in the United States in 1972. Called by Joseph W. Palmer of *Library Journal* an "ugly, nauseating, brilliant, and profound" book, *The Atrocity Exhibition* is a collection of nonlinear stories composed of short dreamlike narrative fragments assembled in collage fashion. The book "might well be considered," Jerome Tarshis claims in the *Evergreen Review,* "a long poem on metaphysical themes. That is the difficult part; the horrifying part is that this philosophical investigation is conducted in terms of violent death and perverse sexuality." This opinion is echoed by Paul Theroux of the *New York Times Book Review*. *The Atrocity Exhibition,* he writes, "is a kind of toying with horror, a stylish anatomy of outrage. . . . It is not [Ballard's] choice of subject, but his celebration of it, that is monstrous."

The sex and violence of *The Atrocity Exhibition* are also found in three novels of the early 1970s—*Crash, Concrete Island,* and *High-Rise*—each of which presents an urban disaster and deals with the perverse violence of modern society. *Crash,* an attempt to discover the "true significance of the automobile crash," as one character states, tells the story of crash victim James Ballard and photographer Vaughan, a man obsessed with the idea of dying in an auto crash with Elizabeth Taylor, the two of them receiving identical wounds to their genitalia. It is, writes the *Times Literary Supplement* critic, "a fetishist's book. . . . Ballard's endless reiteration of crashes—of the famous, on acid, with dummies, on film—begins to seem like a frantic litany, grotesque mantras in a private meditation." John Fletcher of the *Dictionary of Literary Biography* calls *Crash* "an unsentimental scrutiny of the dehumanized eroticism and the brutality that [Ballard] feels are inseparable from the new technologies."

Critical reaction to *Crash* is sometimes extremely harsh. D. Keith Mano, for example, writes in the *New York Times Book Review* that *Crash* is "the most repulsive book I've yet to come across. . . . J. G. Ballard choreographs a crazed, morbid roundelay of dismemberment and sexual perversion. 'Crash' is well written: credit given where due. But I could not, in conscience, recommend it." A critic for the *Times Literary Supplement* believes that with *The Atrocity Exhibition* and *Crash,* Ballard "produced a compendium of twentieth-century pathological imagery which earned him the disparaging reputation of being the intellectual of avant-garde science fiction." Revell observes that *The Atrocity Exhibition* and *Crash* seemed to many critics of the time

to be "some kind of perverse aberration in the career of their author. . . . These new works developed previously latent ideas to a malignancy which burst out of the confines of science fiction. The fiction seemed to have become real, too real, and there were dangerous questions: moral, existential, even political."

The idea for *Crash* originated in a scene from *The Atrocity Exhibition*. One of the psycho-dramas staged by Ballard's protagonist in that book was an art exhibit consisting of crashed cars. Before beginning *Crash,* Ballard also staged an exhibit of crashed cars at the New Arts Laboratory in London. "I had an opening party at the gallery," *Studio International* quotes Ballard as saying. "I'd never seen 100 people get drunk so quickly. Now, this had something to do with the cars on display. I also had a topless girl interviewing people on closed circuit TV, so that people could see themselves being interviewed around the crashed cars by this topless girl. This was clearly too much. I was the only sober person there. Wine was poured over the crashed cars, glasses were broken, the topless girl was nearly raped. . . . It was not so much an exhibition of sculpture as almost of experimental psychology using the medium of the fine art show. People were unnerved, you see. There was enormous hostility." Two weeks after completing *Crash,* Ballard was involved in a serious car accident in which his car rolled over and into the oncoming traffic lane. "This is," Ballard tells James Goddard of *Cypher,* "an extreme case of nature imitating art."

Concrete Island again concerns a car crash. In this novel, Robert Maitland has an accident on the freeway and is stranded on an isolated strip of land between the interweaving lanes of an interchange. Because of his injuries, Maitland cannot climb the embankment to get out. After a time, he finds survival more important than escape and comes to accept his situation. "Ballard plays two themes," Martin Levin of the *New York Times Book Review* believes, "in this compact little book. The external theme is the Robinson Crusoe gambit. . . . The internal theme is the search-for-self motif." *Concrete Island,* writes the *Times Literary Supplement* reviewer, "is a most intelligent and interesting book. . . . [Ballard] reveals undertones of savagery and desolation beneath a metaphor of apparent neutrality . . . [Ballard is] our foremost iconographer of landscape."

Ballard's next novel, *High-Rise,* is set in a forty-story apartment block. The residents of this block revert to tribal savagery after a power failure, transforming their building into a recreation of man's prehistoric past. The apartments are ruled, Fletcher states, "by the brutally simple law of the jungle: to survive one must prey on others and keep out of the way of those who would prey upon oneself." In a review for *Listener,* Neil Hepburn finds the novel "well stocked with bizarre and imaginative strokes . . ., but requiring such an effort for the suspension of disbelief as to become tiresome." Mel Watkins sees little merit in *High-Rise.* In his review for the *New York Times Book Review* he claims that the novel "exploits both technology and human emotion in a compulsively vulgar manner." But, according to Pringle, *High-Rise* "makes the point that the high-rise building is not so much a machine for living in as a brutal playground full of essentially solitary children. It is a concrete den which encourages every anti-social impulse in its inhabitants rather than serving as a physical framework for a genuine social structure."

The catastrophes and ruined landscapes of Ballard's fiction find their roots in his childhood, which was spent in Shanghai during the Second World War. The son of a British businessman, Ballard was a child when the war began and the Japanese conquered the city. After several months of separation from his parents, during which he wandered the city alone, Ballard was reunited with his family in a prisoner-of-war camp. The startling inversions brought about by the war and occupation, the empty or ruined buildings, the sudden evacuations, and the societal instability are all echoed in his fiction. He tells Platt that the abandoned buildings and drained swimming pools found in his fiction are based on Shanghai's luxury hotels, which were closed for the duration of the war. Once, when he went to visit a friend, Ballard tells Platt, the building had been evacuated during the night and "I remember going there and suddenly finding that the building was totally empty, and wandering around all those empty flats with the furniture still in place, total silence, just the odd window swinging in the wind." Incidents like this, Ballard goes on to say, formed his vision of society. "Conventional life," he says, "places its own glaze over everything, a sort of varnish through which the reality is muffled. In Shanghai, what had been a conventional world for me was exposed as no more than a stage set whose cast could disappear overnight; so I saw the fragility of everything, the transience of everything, but also, in a way, the *reality* of everything."

It wasn't until *Empire of the Sun* that Ballard dealt directly with his childhood experiences. "Perhaps," he muses to Frick, "I've always been trying to return to the Shanghai landscape, to some sort of truth that I glimpsed there." Telling the semiautobiographical story of a young boy on his own in war-torn Shanghai, the novel has received high praise from reviewers in England and the United States. It has also hit the best-seller charts in England. Reviewing *Empire of the Sun* for *Newsweek*, David Lehman and Donna Foote place the book "on anyone's short list of outstanding novels inspired by the second world war. . . . [It] combines the exactness of an autobiographical testament with the hallucinatory atmosphere of twilight-zone fiction." Although *Empire of the Sun* is more realistic than any of Ballard's other writings, John Gross of the *New York Times* "still hesitates to call [the book] a conventional novel . . . because many of the scenes in it are so lurid and bizarre, so very nearly out of this world. Among other things, they help to explain why in his work up till now Mr. Ballard should have been repeatedly drawn to apocalyptic themes." "It's ironic," write Lehman and Foote, "that 'Empire of the Sun'—Ballard's first fictional foray into the past—has earned him accolades denied to his earlier 'disaster novels,' since it has more in common with them than immediately meets the eye. Like its predecessors, the book explores the zone of 'inner space' that Ballard sees as 'the true domain of science fiction.'" Winter sees *Empire of the Sun* as something new for Ballard, "a union of apparent irreconcilables—autobiography, naturalistic storytelling, and surrealism. Ballard has not only transcended science fiction, he has pushed at the limits of fiction itself, producing a dream of his own life that is both self-critique and story, an entertainment that enriches our understanding of the fact and fantasy in all our lives."

It is just this examination of fact and fantasy—the relationships between the private fantasies of his characters and the public events and images of their environments—that makes Ballard's work uniquely important. "The 20th century has seen a psychologization of man and his environment," Revell writes. "Ballard, of course, is not alone in confronting this challenge, but he has gone by far the furthest in adapting the new language of science and technology to positive ends." Winter describes Ballard as "one of the most imaginative and idiosyncratic of modern writers, a visionary in both style and substance." Pringle predicts that "Ballard's reputation will grow in the decades to come, and he is likely to become recognized as by far and away the most important literary figure associated with the field of science fiction. More than that: he will be seen as one of the major imagina-

tive writers of the second half of the 20th century—an author for our times, and for the future."

MEDIA ADAPTATIONS: A film entitled "The Unlimited Dream Company," in which Ballard talks about his life and work while a lost pilot wanders through the landscapes of his fiction, was produced by the Royal College of Art School of Film and Television in 1983; *Empire of the Sun* was adapted as a film by screenwriter Tom Stoppard, produced and directed by Steven Spielberg, in 1987.

BIOGRAPHICAL/CRITICAL SOURCES:

BOOKS

Aldiss, Brian and Harry Harrison, editors, *SF Horizons,* two volumes, Arno Press, 1975.

Ballard, J. G., *Crash,* J. Cape, 1970, Farrar, Straus, 1973.

Ballard, *The Atrocity Exhibition,* J. Cape, 1970, published as *Love and Napalm: Export U.S.A.,* Grove Press, 1972.

Burns, Alan, and Charles Sugnet, editors, *The Imagination on Trial: British and American Writers Discuss Their Working Methods,* Allison & Busby, 1981.

Clareson, Thomas D., editor, *SF: The Other Side of Realism—Essays on Modern Fantasy and Science Fiction,* Bowling Green University, 1971.

Clareson, editor, *Voices for the Future: Essays on Major Science Fiction Writers,* Bowling Green University, Volume I, 1976, Volume II, 1979.

Contemporary Fiction in America and England, 1950-1970, Gale, 1976.

Contemporary Literary Criticism, Gale, Volume 3, 1975, Volume 6, 1976, Volume 14, 1980, Volume 36, 1986.

Dictionary of Literary Biography, Volume 14: *British Novelists since 1960,* two volumes, Gale, 1983.

Goddard, James and David Pringle, editors, *J. G. Ballard: The First Twenty Years,* Bran's Head Books, 1976.

James, Langdon, editor, *The New Science Fiction,* Hutchinson, 1969.

Neilson, Keith, editor, *Survey of Science Fiction Literature,* Salem Press, 1979.

Platt, Charles, *Dream Makers: The Uncommon People Who Write Science Fiction,* Berkley Publishing, 1980.

Pringle, *Earth Is the Alien Planet: J. G. Ballard's Four-Dimensional Nightmare,* Borgo Press, 1979.

Pringle, *J. G. Ballard: A Primary and Secondary Bibliography,* G. K. Hall, 1984.

Rose, Mark, *Alien Encounters: Anatomy of Science Fiction,* Harvard University Press, 1981.

Ross, Lois, and Stephen Ross, *The Shattered Ring: Science Fiction and the Quest for Meaning,* John Knox Press, 1970.

Short Story Criticism, Volume 1, Gale, 1988.

Silverberg, Robert, editor, *The Mirror of Infinity,* Harper, 1970.

Silverberg, editor, *Galactic Dreamers: Science Fiction as Visionary Literature,* Random House, 1977.

Vale, V., and Andrea Juno, editors, *Re/Search: J. G. Ballard,* Re/Search Publishing, 1984.

PERIODICALS

Books and Bookmen, April, 1971, March, 1977.

Chicago Tribune, December 11, 1987.

Cypher, October, 1973.

Evergreen Review, spring, 1973.

Foundation, November, 1975, February, 1982.

Globe and Mail (Toronto), November 7, 1987.

Hudson Review, winter, 1973-74.

Library Journal, July, 1970.

Listener, December 11, 1975.
Los Angeles Times, October 20, 1988.
Los Angeles Times Book Review, October 20, 1985, May 1, 1988.
Magazine Litteraire, April, 1974.
Magazine of Fantasy and Science Fiction, September, 1976.
New Review, May, 1974.
New Statesman, May 10, 1974, November 15, 1975.
Newsweek, January 28, 1985.
New Worlds, November, 1959, May, 1962, July, 1966, October, 1966.
New York Review of Books, January 25, 1979.
New York Times, May 11, 1977, October 13, 1984, April 5, 1988.
New York Times Book Review, September 23, 1973, December 1, 1974, December 9, 1979, November 11, 1984, May 15, 1988, October 16, 1988, December 17, 1989.
Paris Review, winter, 1984.
Penthouse, September, 1970, April, 1979.
Publishers Weekly, March 11, 1988.
Rolling Stone, November 19, 1987.
Search and Destroy, Number 10, 1978.
Studio International, October, 1971.
Thrust: Science Fiction In Review, winter, 1980.
Times (London), September 20, 1984, September 10, 1987.
Times Literary Supplement, July 9, 1970, November 30, 1973, April 26, 1974, December 5, 1975, November 30, 1979, June 12, 1981, September 14, 1984, September 11, 1987, January 13-19, 1989.
Transatlantic Review, spring, 1971.
Tribune Books, April 10, 1988.
Vector, January, 1980.
Washington Post, February 21, 1989.
Washington Post Book World, November 25, 1979, October 28, 1984, July 26, 1987, April 17, 1988, June 12, 1988.
Writer, June, 1973.

*   *   *

BAMBARA, Toni Cade   1939-
(Toni Cade)

PERSONAL: Surname originally Cade, name legally changed in 1970; born March 25, 1939, in New York, N.Y.; daughter of Helen Brent Henderson Cade. *Education:* Queens College (now Queens College of the City University of New York), B.A., 1959; University of Florence, studied Commedia dell'Arte, 1961; student at Ecole de Mime Etienne Decroux in Paris, 1961, New York, 1963; City College of the City University of New York, M.A., 1964; additional study in linguistics at New York University and New School for Social Research. Also attended Katherine Dunham Dance Studio, Syvilla Fort School of Dance, Clark Center of Performing Arts, 1958-69, and Studio Museum of Harlem Film Institute, 1970.

ADDRESSES: Home—5720 Wissahickon Ave., Apt. E12, Philadelphia, Pa. 19144.

CAREER: Free-lance writer and lecturer. Social investigator, New York State Department of Welfare, 1959-61; director of recreation in psychiatry department, Metropolitan Hospital, New York City, 1961-62; program director, Colony House Community Center, New York City, 1962-65; English instructor in SEEK Program, City College of the City University of New York, New York City, 1965-69, and in New Careers Program of Newark, N.J., 1969; assistant professor, Livingston College, Rutgers University, New Brunswick, N.J., 1969-74; visiting professor of African American studies, Stephens College, Columbia,

Mo., 1975; Atlanta University, visiting professor, 1977, research mentor and instructor, School of Social Work, 1977, 1979. Founder and director of Pamoja Writers Collective, 1976-85. Production artist-in-residence for Neighborhood Arts Center, 1975-79, Stephens College, 1976, and Spelman College, 1978-79. Production consultant, WHYY-TV, Philadelphia, Pa. Has conducted numerous workshops on writing, self-publishing, and community organizing for community centers, museums, prisons, libraries, and universities. Has lectured and conducted literary readings at many institutions, including the Library of Congress, Smithsonian Institute, Afro-American Museum of History and Culture and for numerous other organizations and universities. Humanities consultant to New Jersey Department of Corrections, 1974, Institute of Language Arts, Emory University, 1980, and New York Institute for Human Services Training, 1978. Art consultant to New York State Arts Council, 1974, Georgia State Arts Council, 1976, 1981, National Endowment for the Arts, 1980, and the Black Arts South Conference, 1981. Member of board of directors of Sojourner Productions, SISSA, and Meridian.

MEMBER: National Association of Third World Writers, Screen Writers Guild of America, African American Film Society, Sisters in Support of South African Sisterhood.

AWARDS, HONORS: Peter Pauper Press Award, 1958; John Golden Award for Fiction from Queens College (now Queens College of the City University of New York), 1959; Theatre of Black Experience award, 1969; Rutgers University research fellowship, 1972; *Tales and Short Stories for Black Folks* named outstanding book of 1972 in juvenile literature by *New York Times;* Black Child Development Institute service award, 1973; Black Rose Award from *Encore,* 1973, for *Gorilla, My Love;* Black Community Award from Livingston College, Rutgers University, 1974; award from the National Association of Negro Business and Professional Women's Club League; George Washington Carver Distinguished African American Lecturer Award from Simpson College; *Ebony*'s Achievement in the Arts Award; Black Arts Award from University of Missouri; literature grant from National Endowment for the Arts, 1980; American Book Award, 1981, for *The Salt Eaters;* Best Documentary of 1986 Award from Pennsylvania Association of Broadcasters and Documentary Award from National Black Programming Consortium, both 1986, for "The Bombing of Osage"; Langston Hughes Medallion from Langston Hughes Society of City College of the City University of New York, 1986; Zora Hurston Award from Morgan State College, 1986; Bronze Jubilee Award for Literature from WETV.

WRITINGS:

Gorilla, My Love (short stories), Random House, 1972.
The Sea Birds Are Still Alive (short stories), Random House, 1977.
The Salt Eaters (novel), Random House, 1980.
(Author of preface) Cecelia Smith, *Cracks,* Select Press, 1980.
(Author of foreword) Cherrie Moraga and Gloria Anzaldua, editors, *This Bridge Called My Back: Radical Women of Color,* Persephone Press, 1981.
(Author of foreword) *The Sanctified Church: Collected Essays by Zora Neale Hurston,* Turtle Island, 1982.
If Blessing Comes (novel), Random House, 1987.

SCREENPLAYS

"Zora," produced by WGBH-TV, 1971.
"The Johnson Girls," produced by National Educational Television, 1972.

"Transactions," produced by School of Social Work, Atlanta University, 1979.

"The Long Night," produced by American Broadcasting Co., 1981.

"Epitaph for Willie," produced by K. Heran Productions, Inc., 1982.

"Tar Baby" (based on Toni Morrison's novel), produced by Sanger/Brooks Film Productions, 1984.

"Raymond's Run," produced by Public Broadcasting System, 1985.

"The Bombing of Osage," produced by WHYY-TV, 1986.

"Cecil B. Moore: Master Tactician of Direct Action," produced by WHYY-TV, 1987.

EDITOR

(And contributor, under name Toni Cade) *The Black Woman,* New American Library, 1970.

(And contributor) *Tales and Stories for Black Folks,* Doubleday, 1971.

(With Leah Wise) *Southern Black Utterances Today,* Institute for Southern Studies, 1975.

CONTRIBUTOR

Addison Gayle, Jr., editor, *Black Expression: Essays by and about Black Americans in the Creative Arts,* Weybright, 1969.

Jules Chametsky, editor, *Black and White in American Culture,* University of Massachusetts Press, 1970.

Ruth Miller, *Backgrounds to Blackamerican Literature,* Chandler Publishing, 1971.

Janet Sternburg, editor, *The Writer on Her Work,* Norton, 1980.

Paul H. Connolly, editor, *On Essays: A Reader for Writers,* Harper, 1981.

Howe, editor, *Women Working,* Feminist Press, 1982.

Mari Evans, editor, *Black Women Writers (1950-1980): A Critical Evaluation,* Doubleday, 1984.

Baraka and Baraka, editors, *Confirmations,* Morrow, 1984.

Claudia Tate, editor, *The Black Writer at Work,* Howard University Press, 1984.

OTHER

Contributor to *What's Happnin, Somethin Else,* and *Another Eye,* all readers published by Scott, Foresman, 1969-70. Contributor of articles and book and film reviews to *Massachusetts Review, Negro Digest, Liberator, Prairie Schooner, Redbook, Audience, Black Works, Umbra, Onyx,* and other periodicals. Guest editor of special issue of *Southern Exposure,* summer, 1976, devoted to new southern black writers and visual artists.

SIDELIGHTS: Toni Cade Bambara is a well known and respected civil rights activist, professor of English and of African American studies, editor of two anthologies of black literature, and author of short stories and a novel. According to Alice A. Deck in the *Dictionary of Literary Biography,* "in many ways Toni Cade Bambara is one of the best representatives of the group of Afro-American writers who, during the 1960s, became directly involved in the cultural and sociopolitical activities in urban communities across the country." However, Deck points out that "Bambara is one of the few who continued to work within the black urban communities (filming, lecturing, organizing, and reading from her works at rallies and conferences), producing imaginative reenactments of these experiences in her fiction. In addition, Bambara established herself over the years as an educator, teaching in colleges and independent community schools in various cities on the East Coast."

Bambara's first two books of fiction, *Gorilla, My Love* and *The Sea Birds Are Still Alive,* are collections of her short stories. Susan Lardner remarks in the *New Yorker* that the stories in these two works, "describing the lives of black people in the North and the South, could be more exactly typed as vignettes and significant anecdotes, although a few of them are fairly long. . . . All are notable for their purposefulness, a more or less explicit inspirational angle, and a distinctive motion of the prose, which swings from colloquial narrative to precarious metaphorical heights and over to street talk, at which Bambara is unbeatable."

In a review of *Gorilla, My Love,* for example, a writer remarks in the *Saturday Review* that the stories "are among the best portraits of black life to have appeared in some time. [They are] written in a breezy, engaging style that owes a good deal to street dialect." A critic writing in *Newsweek* makes a similar observation, describing Bambara's second collection of short stories, *The Sea Birds Are Still Alive,* in this manner: "Bambara directs her vigorous sense and sensibility to black neighborhoods in big cities, with occasional trips to small Southern towns. . . . The stories start and stop like rapid-fire conversations conducted in a rhythmic, black-inflected, sweet-and-sour language." In fact, according to Anne Tyler in the *Washington Post Book World,* Bambara's particular style of narration is one of the most distinctive qualities of her writing. "What pulls us along is the language of [her] characters, which is startlingly beautiful without once striking a false note," notes Tyler. "Everything these people say, you feel, ordinary, real-life people are saying right now on any street corner. It's only that the rest of us didn't realize it was sheer poetry they were speaking."

In terms of plot, Bambara tends to avoid linear development in favor of presenting "situations that build like improvisations of a melody," as a *Newsweek* reviewer explains. Commenting on *Gorilla, My Love,* Bell Gale Chevigny observes in the *Village Voice* that despite the "often sketchy" plots, the stories are always "lavish in their strokes—here are elaborate illustrations, soaring asides, aggressive sub-plots. They are never didactic, but they abound in far-out common sense, exotic home truths."

Numerous reviewers have also remarked on Bambara's sensitive portrayals of her characters and the handling of their situations, portrayals that are marked by an affectionate warmth and pride. Laura Marcus writes in the *Times Literary Supplement* that Bambara "presents black culture as embattled but unbowed. . . . Bambara depicts black communities in which ties of blood and friendship are fiercely defended." Deck expands on this idea, remarking that "the basic implication of all of Toni Cade Bambara's stories is that there is an undercurrent of caring for one's neighbors that sustains black Americans. In her view the presence of those individuals who intend to do harm to people is counterbalanced by as many if not more persons who have a genuine concern for other people."

C. D. B. Bryan admires this expression of the author's concern for other people, declaring in the *New York Times Book Review* that "Bambara tells me more about being black through her quiet, proud, silly, tender, hip, acute, loving stories than any amount of literary polemicizing could hope to do. She writes about love: a love for one's family, one's friends, one's race, one's neighborhood and it is the sort of love that comes with maturity and inner peace." According to Bryan, "All of [Bambara's] stories share the affection that their narrator feels for the subject, an affection that is sometimes terribly painful, at other times fiercely proud. But at all times it is an affection that is so genuinely *genus homo sapiens* that her stories are not only black stories."

In 1980, Bambara published her first novel, a generally well-received work entitled *The Salt Eaters*. Written in an almost dream-like style, *The Salt Eaters* explores the relationship between two women with totally different backgrounds and lifestyles brought together by a suicide attempt by one of the women. John Leonard, who describes the book as "extraordinary," writes in the *New York Times* that *The Salt Eaters* "is almost an incantation, poem-drunk, myth-happy, mudcaked, jazz-ridden, prodigal in meanings, a kite and a mask. It astonishes because Toni Cade Bambara is so adept at switching from politics to legend, from particularities of character to prehistorical song, from LaSalle Street to voodoo. It is as if she jived the very stones to groan."

In a *Times Literary Supplement* review, Carol Rumens states that *The Salt Eaters* "is a hymn to individual courage, a sombre message of hope that has confronted the late twentieth-century pathology of racist violence and is still able to articulate its faith in 'the dream.' " And John Wideman notes in the *New York Times Book Review*: "In her highly acclaimed fiction and in lectures, [Bambara] emphasizes the necessity for black people to maintain their best traditions, to remain healthy and whole as they struggle for political power. *The Salt Eaters*, her first novel, eloquently summarizes and extends the abiding concerns of her previous work."

MEDIA ADAPTATIONS: Three of Bambara's short stories, "Gorilla, My Love," "Medley," and "Witchbird," have been adapted for film.

BIOGRAPHICAL/CRITICAL SOURCES:

BOOKS

Contemporary Literary Criticism, Volume 19, Gale, 1984.
Dictionary of Literary Biography, Volume 38: *Afro-American Writers after 1955: Dramatists and Prose Writers,* Gale, 1985.
Parker, Bell and Beverly Guy-Sheftall, *Sturdy Black Bridges: Visions of Black Women in Literature,* Doubleday, 1979.
Prenshaw, Peggy Whitman, editor, *Women Writers of the Contemporary South,* University Press of Mississippi, 1984.
Tate, Claudia, editor, *Black Women Writers at Work,* Continuum, 1983.

PERIODICALS

Black World, July, 1973.
Books of the Times, June, 1980.
Chicago Tribune Book World, March 23, 1980.
Drum, spring, 1982.
First World, Volume 2, number 4, 1980.
Los Angeles Times Book Review, May 4, 1980.
Ms., July, 1977, July, 1980.
National Observer, May 9, 1977.
Newsweek, May 2, 1977.
New Yorker, May 5, 1980.
New York Times, October 11, 1972, October 15, 1972, April 4, 1980.
New York Times Book Review, February 21, 1971, May 2, 1971, November 7, 1971, October 15, 1972, December 3, 1972, March 27, 1977, June 1, 1980, November 1, 1981.
Saturday Review, November 18, 1972, December 2, 1972, April 12, 1980.
Sewanee Review, November 18, 1972, December 2, 1972.
Times Literary Supplement, June 18, 1982, September 27, 1985.

Village Voice, April 12, 1973.
Washington Post Book World, November 18, 1973, March 30, 1980.

*   *   *

BANCROFT, Laura
See BAUM, L(yman) Frank

*   *   *

BARAKA, Amiri   1934-
(LeRoi Jones)

PERSONAL: Born October 7, 1934, in Newark, N.J.; original name Everett LeRoi Jones; name changed to Imamu ("spiritual leader") Ameer ("blessed") Baraka ("prince"); later modified to Amiri Baraka; son of Coyette Leroy (a postman and elevator operator) and Anna Lois (Russ) Jones; married (divorced, August, 1965); married Sylvia Robinson (Bibi Amina Baraka), 1966; children: (first marriage) Kellie Elisabeth, Lisa Victoria Chapman; (second marriage) Obalaji Malik Ali, Ras Jua Al Aziz, Shani Isis, Amiri Seku, Ahi Mwenge. *Education:* Attended Rutgers University, 1951-52; Howard University, B.A., 1954; Columbia University, M.A. in philosophy; New School for Social Research, M.A. in German literature.

ADDRESSES: Office—Department of Africana Studies, State University of New York, Long Island, NY 11794-4340. *Agent*—Joan Brandt, Sterling Lord Agency, 660 Madison Ave., New York, NY 10021.

CAREER: Founded *Yugen* magazine and Totem Press, 1958, New School for Social Research, New York City, instructor, 1961-64; State University of New York at Stony Brook, associate professor, 1983-85, professor of Afro-American studies, 1985—. Visiting professor, University of Buffalo, summer, 1964, Columbia University, fall, 1964, and 1966-67, Yale University, 1977-78, George Washington University, 1978-79, Rutgers University, 1988, and San Francisco State University. Founder and director, 1964-66, of Black Arts Repertory Theatre (disbanded, 1966); currently director of Spirit House (a black community theater; also known as Heckalu Community Center), and head of advisory group at Treat Elementary School, both in Newark. Member, Political Prisoners Relief Fund, and African Liberation Day Commission. Candidate, Newark community council, 1968. *Military service:* U.S. Air Force, 1954-57; weather-gunner; stationed for two and a half years in Puerto Rico with intervening trips to Europe, Africa, and the Middle East.

MEMBER: All African Games, Pan African Federation, Black Academy of Arts and Letters, National Black Political Assembly (secretary general; co-governor), National Black United Front, Congress of African People (co-founder, chairman), Black Writers' Union, League of Revolutionary Struggle, United Brothers (Newark), Newark Writers Collective.

AWARDS, HONORS: Longview Best Essay of the Year award, 1961, for "Cuba Libre"; John Whitney Foundation fellowship for poetry and fiction, 1962; Obie Award, Best American Off-Broadway Play, 1964, for *Dutchman;* Guggenheim fellowship, 1965-66; Yoruba Academy fellow, 1965; second prize, International Art Festival, Dakar, 1966, for *The Slave;* National Endowment for the Arts grant, 1966; Doctorate of Humane Letters, Malcolm X College, Chicago, Ill., 1972; Rockefeller Foundation fellow (drama), 1981; Poetry Award, National Endowment for the Arts, 1981; New Jersey Council for the Arts award, 1982;

American Book Award, Before Columbus Foundation, 1984, for *Confirmation: An Anthology of African-American Women;* Drama Award, 1985.

WRITINGS:

UNDER NAME LEROI JONES UNTIL 1967; PLAYS

"A Good Girl Is Hard to Find," produced in Montclair, N.J. at Sterington House, 1958.

"Dante" (one act; an excerpt from the novel *The System of Dante's Hell;* also see below), produced in New York at Off-Bowery Theatre, 1961; produced again as "The Eighth Ditch," at the New Bowery Theatre, 1964.

Dutchman, (also see below; produced Off-Broadway at Village South Theatre, 1964; produced Off-Broadway at Cherry Lane Theater, 1964; produced in London, 1967), Faber & Faber, 1967.

The Baptism: A Comedy in One Act (also see below; produced Off-Broadway at Writers' Stage Theatre, 1964, produced in London, 1970-71), Sterling Lord, 1966.

The Toilet (also see below; produced with "The Slave: A Fable" Off-Broadway at St. Mark's Playhouse, 1964; produced at International Festival of Negro Arts at Dakar, Senegal, 1966), Sterling Lord, 1964.

J-E-L-L-O (one act comedy; also see below; produced in New York by Black Arts Repertory Theatre, 1965), Third World Press, 1970.

"Experimental Death Unit #1" (one act; also see below), produced Off-Broadway at St. Mark's Playhouse, 1965.

"The Death of Malcolm X" (one act), produced in Newark at Spirit House, 1965, published in *New Plays from the Black Theatre,* edited by Ed Bullins, Bantam, 1969.

"A Black Mass" (also see below), produced in Newark at Proctor's Theatre, 1966.

Slave Ship (also see below; produced as "Slave Ship: A Historical Pageant" at Spirit House, 1967; produced in New York City, 1969), Jihad, 1967.

"Madheart: Morality Drama" (one act; also see below), produced at San Francisco State College, May, 1967.

Arm Yourself, or Harm Yourself, A One-Act Play (also see below; produced at Spirit House, 1967), Jihad, 1967.

"Great Goodness of Life (A Coon Show)" (one act; also see below), produced at Spirit House, 1967; produced Off-Broadway at Tambellini's Gate Theater, 1969.

"Home on the Range" (one act comedy; also see below), first produced at Spirit House, 1968; produced in New York City at a Town Hall rally, 1968.

"Junkies Are Full of SHHH . . .," produced at Spirit House, 1968; produced with "Bloodrites" (also see below) Off-Broadway at Henry Street Playhouse, 1970.

"Board of Education" (children's play), produced at Spirit House, 1968.

"Resurrection in Life" (one act pantomime) produced under the title "Insurrection" in Harlem, N.Y., 1969.

"Black Dada Nihilism" (one act), produced Off-Broadway at Afro-American Studio, 1971.

"A Recent Killing" (three acts), produced Off-Broadway at the New Federal Theatre, 1973.

"Columbia the Gem of the Ocean," produced in Washington, D.C., by Howard University Spirit House Movers, 1973.

"The New Ark's A-Moverin," produced in Newark, February, 1974.

The Sidnee Poet Heroical, in Twenty-Nine Scenes, (one act comedy; also see below; produced Off-Broadway at the New Federal Theatre, 1975), Reed & Cannon, 1979.

"S-1: A Play with Music in 26 Scenes" (also see below), produced in New York at Washington Square Methodist Church, 1976, produced at Afro-American Studio, August, 1976.

(With Frank Chin and Leslie Silko) "America More or Less" (musical), produced in San Francisco at Marine's Memorial Theater, 1976.

"The Motion of History" (four acts; also see below), produced at New York City Theatre Ensemble, 1977.

What Was the Relationship of the Lone Ranger to the Means of Production?: A Play in One Act, (also see below; produced in New York at Ladies Fort, 1979), Anti-Imperialist Cultural Union, 1978.

"Money: Jazz Opera" (libretto), produced in New York at Kool Jazz Festival, 1982.

"Dim Cracker Party Convention," produced in New York at Columbia University, 1980.

"Boy and Tarzan Appear in a Clearing," produced Off-Broadway at New Federal Theatre, 1981.

"Money," produced Off-Broadway at La Mama Experimental Theatre Club, 1982.

"Song: A One Act Play about the Relationship of Art to Real Life," produced in Jamaica, N.Y., 1983.

Also author of the plays "Home on the Range" and "Police," published in *Drama Review,* summer, 1968; "Rockgroup," published in *Cricket,* December, 1969; "Black Power Chant," published in *Drama Review,* December, 1972; "The Coronation of the Black Queen," published in *Black Scholar,* June, 1970; "Vomit and the Jungle Bunnies," unpublished; and of "Revolt of the Moonflowers," 1969, lost in manuscript.

PLAY COLLECTIONS

Dutchman [and] *The Slave,* Morrow, 1964.

The Baptism [and] *The Toilet,* Grove, 1967.

Four Black Revolutionary Plays: All Praises to the Black Man (contains "Experimental Death Unit # 1," "A Black Mass," "Great Goodness of Life," and "Madheart"), Bobbs-Merrill, 1969.

(Contributor) Woodie King and Ron Milner, editors, *Black Drama Anthology* (includes "Bloodrites" and "Junkies Are Full of SHHH . . ."), New American Library, 1971.

(Contributor) Rochelle Owens, editor, *Spontaneous Combustion: Eight New American Plays* (includes "Ba-Ra-Ka"), Winter House, 1972.

The Motion of History and Other Plays (contains "Slave Ship" and "S-1"), Morrow, 1978.

Selected Plays and Prose of LeRoi Jones/Amiri Baraka, Morrow, 1979.

SCREENPLAYS

"Dutchman," Gene Persson Enterprises, Ltd., 1967.

Black Spring, Jihad Productions, 1968.

"A Fable" (based on "The Slave"), MFR Productions, 1971.

"Supercoon," Gene Persson Enterprises, Ltd., 1971.

POETRY

April 13 (broadside Number 133), Penny Poems (New Haven), 1959.

Spring & So Forth (broadside Number 141), Penny Poems, 1960.

Preface to a Twenty Volume Suicide Note, Totem/Corinth, 1961.

The Disguise (broadside), [New Haven], 1961.

The Dead Lecturer (also see below), Grove, 1964.

Black Art (also see below), Jihad, 1966.

Black Magic (also see below), Morrow, 1967.

A Poem for Black Hearts, Broadside Press, 1967.

Black Magic: Sabotage; Target Study; Black Art; Collected Poetry, 1961-1967, Bobbs-Merrill, 1969.

It's Nation Time, Third World Press, 1970.

Spirit Reach, Jihad, 1972.

Afrikan Revolution: A Poem, Jihad, 1973.

Hard Facts: Excerpts, People's War, 1975, 2nd edition, Revolutionary Communist League, 1975.

Spring Song, Baraka, 1979.
AM/TRAK, Phoenix Bookship, 1979.

Selected Poetry of Amiri Baraka/Leroi Jones (includes "Poetry for the Advanced"), Morrow, 1979.

In the Tradition: For Black Arthur Blythe, Jihad, 1980.

Reggae or Not! Poems, Contact Two, 1982.

ESSAYS

Cuba Libre, Fair Play for Cuba Committee (New York City), 1961.

Blues People: Negro Music in White America, Morrow, 1963, reprinted, Greenwood Press, 1980, published in England as *Negro Music in White America,* MacGibbon & Kee, 1965.

Home: Social Essays (contains "Cuba Libre," "The Myth of a 'Negro Literature,'" "Expressive Language," "the legacy of malcolm x, and the coming of the black nation," and "state/meant"), Morrow, 1966.

Black Music, Morrow, 1968, reprinted, Greenwood Press, 1980.

Raise, Race, Rays, Raze: Essays since 1965, Random House, 1971.

Strategy and Tactics of a Pan-African Nationalist Party, Jihad, 1971.

Kawaida Studies: The New Nationalism, Third World Press, 1972.

Crisis in Boston!, Vita Wa Watu People's War, 1974.

Daggers and Javelins: Essays, 1974-1979, Morrow, 1984.

(With wife, Amina Baraka) *The Music: Reflections on Jazz and Blues,* Morrow, 1987.

EDITOR

January 1st 1959: Fidel Castro, Totem, 1959.

Four Young Lady Poets, Corinth, 1962.

(And author of introduction) *The Moderns: An Anthology of New Writing in America,* 1963, published as *The Moderns: New Fiction in America,* 1964.

(And co-author) *In-formation,* Totem, 1965.

Gilbert Sorrentino, *Black & White,* Corinth, 1965.

Edward Dorn, *Hands Up!,* Corinth, 1965.

(And contributor) *Afro-American Festival of the Arts Magazine,* Jihad, 1966, published as *Anthology of Our Black Selves,* 1969.

(With Larry Neal and A. B. Spellman) *The Cricket: Black Music in Evolution,* Jihad, 1968, published as *Trippin': A Need for Change,* New Ark, 1969.

(And contributor, with Larry Neal) *Black Fire: An Anthology of Afro-American Writing,* Morrow, 1968.

A Black Value System, Jihad, 1970.

(With Billy Abernathy under pseudonym Fundi) *In Our Terribleness (Some Elements of Meaning in Black Style),* Bobbs-Merrill, 1970.

(And author of introduction) *African Congress: A Documentary of the First Modern Pan-African Congress,* Morrow, 1972.

(With Diane DiPrima) *The Floating Bear, A Newsletter, No.1-37, 1961-1969,* McGilvery, 1974.

(With Amina Baraka) *Confirmation: An Anthology of Afro-American Women,* Morrow, 1983.

OTHER

(Contributor) Herbert Hill, editor, *Soon, One Morning,* Knopf, 1963.

The System of Dante's Hell (novel; includes the play "Dante"), Grove, 1965.

(Author of introduction) David Henderson, *Felix of the Silent Forest,* Poets Press, 1967.

Striptease, Parallax, 1967.

Tales (short stories), Grove, 1967.

(Author of preface), *Black Boogaloo (Notes on Black Liberation),* Journal of Black Poetry Press, 1969.

"Focus on Amiri Baraka: Playwright LeRoi Jones Analyzes the 1st National Black Political Convention" (sound recording), Center for Cassette Studies, 1973.

Three Books by Imamu Amiri Baraka (LeRoi Jones) (contains *The System of Dante's Hell, Tales,* and *The Dead Lecturer*), Grove, 1975.

The Autobiography of LeRoi Jones/Amiri Baraka, Freundlich, 1984.

Works represented in more than seventy-five anthologies, including *A Broadside Treasury, For Malcolm, The New Black Poetry, Nommo,* and *The Trembling Lamb.* Baraka's works have been translated into German, French, and Spanish. Contributor to *Evergreen Review, Poetry, Downbeat, Metronome, Nation, Negro Digest, Saturday Review,* and other periodicals. Editor with Diane Di Prima, *The Floating Bear,* 1961-1963.

WORK IN PROGRESS: "Why's/Wise," an epic poem; four books of poetry.

SIDELIGHTS: Amiri Baraka (formerly LeRoi Jones) is a major and controversial author. He is a maverick who has produced a large body of work that is highly critical of American civilization. Perhaps moreso than fellow mavericks Allen Ginsberg or Norman Mailer, Baraka continues to be an irritant to the American literary establishment. Baraka may be the most difficult American author to evaluate dispassionately since the modernist poet Ezra Pound, another important writer whose work still evokes volatile critical response. Like Pound, Baraka has dared to bring radical politics into the world of literature and to deliver his explosive ideas in an inflammatory style.

Critical opinion about Baraka is highly divided. In *Dissent,* Stanley Kauffman calls Baraka "the luckiest man of our times, a writer who . . . would be less than lightly held if he did not happen to be a Negro at this moment in American history." Kimberly Benston, on the other hand, asserts in *Baraka: The Renegade and the Mask,* "Imamu Amiri Baraka is one of the foremost American artists of our century." Baraka demands that his audience accept his Afro-American identity as central to his art. Furthermore, he is an avant-garde writer whose variety of forms, including poetry, drama, music criticism, fiction, autobiography, and the essay, makes him difficult to categorize. Moreover, Baraka's stormy history clouds critical objectivity. No armchair artist, he has gone through a series of dramatic stages, from wild Beatnik ranting against the square world in the late 1950s through early 1960s, to black cultural nationalist renouncing the white world in the mid-1960s through mid-1970s, to Marxist-Leninist rejecting monopoly capitalism since the mid-1970s. Beyond Baraka's talents as a creative writer, his ideas and art, especially as the primary architect of the Black Arts Movement of the 1960s, have had a profound influence on the direction of black literature. Therefore, when Arnold Rampersad claims in *American Book Review* that Baraka "stands with [Phillis] Wheatley, [Frederick] Douglass, [Paul Laurence] Dunbar, [Langston] Hughes, [Zora Neale] Hurston, [Richard] Wright and [Ralph] Ellison as one of the eight figures . . . who have significantly affected the course of African-American literary culture," he does not exaggerate.

During his Beat period, when he was known as LeRoi Jones, Baraka lived in New York's Greenwich Village and Lower East Side, where he published important little magazines such as *Yugen* and *Floating Bear* and socialized with such figures as Ginsberg, Frank O'Hara, and Gilbert Sorrentino. He was greatly influenced by the white avant-garde: Charles Olson, O'Hara and Ginsberg, in particular, shaped his conception of a poem as being exploratory and open in form. Donald Allen records in *The New American Poetry: 1945-1960* Baraka's Beat-period views on form: "There must not be any preconceived notion or design for what a poem ought to be. 'Who knows what a poem ought to sound like? Until it's thar' says Charles Olson . . . & I follow closely with that. I'm not interested in writing sonnets, sestina or anything . . . only poems."

Baraka's first book, *Preface to a Twenty Volume Suicide Note,* met with general critical approval. In *The New Poets: American and British Poetry since World War II,* M. L. Rosenthal says that the early Jones/Baraka "has a natural gift for quick, vivid imagery and spontaneous humor, and his poems are filled with sardonic or sensuous or slangily knowledgeable passages." Theodore Hudson, in *From Leroi Jones to Amiri Baraka: The Literary Works,* observes: "All things considered, *Preface* was an auspicious beginning for LeRoi Jones the poet."

At first glance *Preface* looks like a typical product of integrated Bohemia; in fact, it ends: "You are / as any other sad man here / american." Yet there is a "blues feeling" throughout—an infusion of black culture and reference. The reader can hear the "moaning . . . [of] Bessie Smith" in the book's lines, although blackness is not its principal focus. As David Ossman reports in *The Sullen Art: Interviews with Modern American Poets,* Baraka remarked in early 1960: "I'm fully conscious all the time that I am an American Negro, because it's part of my life. But I know also that if I want to say, 'I see a bus full of people,' I don't have to say, 'I am a Negro seeing a bus full of people.' I would deal with it when it has to do directly with the poem, and not as a kind of broad generalization that doesn't have much to do with a lot of young writers today who are Negroes." This view proved to be transitory. With the Civil Rights movement, Martin Luther King, and the black political upsurge of the late 1960s, Baraka's attitude toward race and art changed; he found that being black was integral to his art. Furthermore, with the coming of ethnic consciousness came political consciousness and the slow and painful rejection of Bohemia.

In July 1960 Baraka visited Castro's Cuba. In *The Autobiography of LeRoi Jones/Amiri Baraka,* Baraka refers to this visit as "a turning point in my life." While in Cuba he met politically committed Third World artists and intellectuals who challenged him to reconsider his apolitical stance. They attacked him for being an American; he tried to defend himself in "Cuba Libre," an essay reprinted in *Home: Social Essays,* by saying: "Look, why jump on me? . . . I'm in complete agreement with you. I'm a poet . . . what can I do? I write, that's all, I'm not even interested in politics." The Mexican poet, Jaime Shelley, answered him: "You want to cultivate your soul? In that ugliness you live in, you want to cultivate your soul? Well, we've got millions of starving people to feed, and that moves me enough to make poems out of." In Cuba the young intellectuals seemed to be doing something concrete to create a more humane world. Baraka felt that the Cuban government, unlike that of the United States, was actually being run by young intellectuals and idealists. This trip was the beginning of Baraka's radical political art and his identification with Third World artists.

Although Baraka started publishing in the early 1960s, he did not achieve fame until the 1964 publication of his play *Dutchman,* which won the *Village Voice*'s Obie Award. Werner Sollors notes in *Amiri Baraka/LeRoi Jones: The Quest for a "Populist Modernism"* that Norman Mailer called it "the best play in America." It has often been reprinted and performed, and was adapted for a film in Britain by Anthony Harvey. (The play also provides scenes for Jean-Luc Godard's movie *Masculine-Feminine.*) In *Dutchman* Baraka no longer presents the melancholy hipster world where, as he declared in *Preface,* "Nobody sings anymore," but instead a realm where an angry young man fights for his ethnic identity and his manhood. The white woman Lula, the symbolic agent of the white state, sent out to find the latent murderer in the assimilated middle-class Negro Clay, locates and kills him. The play is highly stylized, reflecting the 1960s movement to propel black literature away from naturalism (the principal mode from the 1940s to 1960s) to a more experimental avant-garde art.

In a 1979 *New York Times Book Review* Darryl Pinckney commends Baraka's skill as a playwright: "He is a highly gifted dramatist. Much of the black protest literature of the 60's now seems diminished in power, even sentimental. But 'Dutchman' immediately seizes the imagination. It is radically economical in structure, striking in the vivacity of its language and rapid shifts of mood."

The Dead Lecturer, Baraka's second book of poetry, is the work of a black man who wants to leave white music and the white world behind. As civil rights activities intensified, Baraka became more and more disappointed with his white friends; in fact, the word "friends" becomes ironic in this second volume. In "Black Dada Nihilismus," for example, he realizes that he must escape their influence and vision. Baraka demands violence in himself and his people to escape the white consciousness. He no longer wants to be the *Dead Lecturer;* he wants life. In this book of poetry he attempts to reject the "quiet verse" of the Beat Generation and claim the black chant of political commitment.

This politicalization of Baraka's art is formal as well as thematic. The poetic line becomes longer as the verse imitates the chant. In the poem "Rhythm and Blues," Baraka claims he does not want to become a martyr for Western art. Richard Howard, writing in the *Nation,* finds the Baraka of *The Dead Lecturer* "much surer of his own voice. . . . These are the agonized poems of a man writing to save his skin, or at least to settle in it, and so urgent is their purpose that not one of them can trouble to be perfect." In a negative review of *The Dead Lecturer* in *Salmagundi,* Rosenthal anticipates the far more political art of Baraka's Black Arts and Marxist periods: "No American poet since Pound has come closer to making poetry and politics reciprocal forms of action." As Baraka wrote to his friend, Black Mountain poet Edward Dorn, in a 1961 letter: " 'Moral earnestness'. . . ought [to] be transformed into action. . . . I know we think that to write a poem, and be Aristotle's God is sufficient. But I can't sleep. . . . There is a right and a wrong. And it's up to me, you, all of the so called minds, to find out. It is only knowledge of things that will bring this 'moral earnestness'."

Baraka had joined the Beat Generation because he regarded its members as spiritual outsiders who were against white middle-class America. Yet as time progressed, disengagement was no longer enough for Baraka, who notes in the essay "Cuba Libre": "The rebels among us have become merely people like myself who grow beards and will not participate in politics. Drugs, juvenile delinquency, complete isolation from the vapid mores of the country, are a few current ways out. But name an alternative here."

During this transitional period Baraka produced his only serious efforts in fiction: *The System of Dante's Hell,* a novel, and *Tales,* a collection of short stories. As Sollors points out, the sections of the novel parallel the themes and even passages found in *Preface, The Dead Lecturer,* and the early uncollected poems. Although *System* was published in 1965 it was mostly written in the early 1960s. Baraka commented on the book and the times to Kimberly Benston in an interview published in *Boundary 2:* "I was really writing defensively. I was trying to get away from the influence of people like Creeley and Olson. I was living in New York then and the whole Creeley-Olson influence was beginning to beat me up. I was in a very closed circle—that was about the time I went to Cuba and I felt the need to break out of the type of form that I was using then. I guess this was not only because of the form itself but because of the content which was not my politics."

Tales, published in 1967, treats the years 1963 through 1967, a time of radical change in Baraka's life, and reflects the themes of the poetry in *Black Magic,* which also appeared in 1967. Both works try to convey a sense of the ethnic self apart from the world of white culture. In *Conscientious Sorcerers: The Black Postmodernist Fiction of LeRoi Jones/Baraka, Ishmael Reed and Samuel R. Delany,* Robert Elliot Fox remarks: "However, the essential energy linking these two works which recount and re-evaluate his life up to that time is a relentless momentum deeper into blackness. These fugitive narratives describe the harried flight of an intensely self-conscious Afro-American artist/intellectual from neo-slavery of blinding, neutralizing whiteness, where the arena of struggle is basically within the mind." In *Tales* Baraka describes the posture and course he wishes to adopt: that of "The straight ahead people, who think when that's what's called for, who don't when they don't have to. Not the Hamlet burden, which is white bullshit, to always be weighing and analyzing, and reflecting." Baraka wants action, and the story "Screamers" casts action in musical terms. In this tale blacks riot in the streets because of the wild music of Lynn Hope, a jazz saxophonist: "We screamed at the clear image of ourselves as we should always be. Ecstatic, completed, involved in a secret communal expression. It would be the sweetest revolution, to hucklebuck into the fallen capital, and let the oppressors lindy hop out."

During the early 1960s Baraka composed his major study of black music in America, *Blues People: Negro Music in White America.* A history, it begins in slavery and ends with contemporary avant-garde jazz (John Coltrane, Ornette Coleman, and Cecil Taylor). Baraka argues that since Emancipation the blues have been an essential feature of black American music and that this form was born from the union of the American and the African experience; as Baraka says, "Undoubtedly, none of the African prisoners broke out into 'St. James Infirmary' the minute the first of them was herded off the ship." *Blues People* allowed Baraka to meditate on a profound and sophisticated art form created by blacks and to do so during a time when he was trying to find a model for his own art that was not white avant-garde. Although he later retracted his evaluation, he had temporarily rejected black literature as mediocre and middle-brow. In his *Home* essay "The Myth of a 'Negro Literature,' " he declares: "Only in music, and most notably in blues, jazz, and spirituals, *i.e.,* 'Negro Music,' has there been a significantly profound contribution by American Negroes." In the *New York Times Book Review,* Jason Berry calls Baraka "an eloquent jazz critic; his 1963 study, *Blues People: Negro Music in White America* is a classic." Furthermore, Clyde Taylor maintains in James B. Gwynne's *Amiri Baraka: The Kaleidoscopic Torch,* "The connection he nailed down between the many faces of black music, the sociological sets that nurtured them, and their symbiotic evolutions through socio-economic changes, in *Blues People,* is his most durable conception, as well as probably the one most indispensable thing said about black music."

Baraka has published two other collections containing important essays on the Afro-American music: *Black Music,* written from a black nationalist perspective, and *The Music: Reflections on Jazz and Blues,* written from a Marxist one. In *Black Music* Baraka crystallizes the idea of John Coltrane as the prime model for the new black art: "Trane is a mature swan whose wing span was a whole world. But he also shows us how to murder the popular song. To do away with weak Western forms. He is a beautiful philosopher." Lloyd Brown asserts in *Amiri Baraka:* "As an essayist Baraka's performance is decidedly uneven. The writings on music are always an exception. As historian, musicological analyst, or as a journalist covering a particular performance Baraka always commands attention because of his obvious knowledge of the subject and because of a style that is engaging and persuasive even when the sentiments are questionable and controversial." In *Amiri Baraka: The Kaleidoscopic Torch* Joe Weixlmann states: "Baraka's expertise as an interpreter of Afro-American music is, of course, well-known. Had he never done any belletristic writing or political organizing, he would be remembered as the author of *Blues People . . .* and *Black Music*."

In 1965, following the assassination of Black Muslim leader Malcolm X, Baraka left Greenwich Village and moved uptown to Harlem and a new life as a cultural nationalist. He argued in "the legacy of malcolm x, and the coming of the black nation" (collected in *Home*) that "black People are a race, a culture, a Nation." Turning his back on the white world, he established the Black Arts Repertory Theatre/School in Harlem, an influential model that inspired black theaters throughout the country. In 1967, he published his black nationalist collection of poetry, *Black Magic,* which traces his painful exit from the white world. Unfortunately, his exorcism of white consciousness and values included a ten-year period of intense hatred of whites and most especially Jews; in "A POEM SOME PEOPLE WILL HAVE TO UNDERSTAND," Baraka expressed his impatience with liberals and Bohemians, and he requests: "Will the machinegunners please step forward?" Espousing political action and political art, he declares, "We want poems that kill." After a year in Harlem, he returned home to his birthplace, Newark, New Jersey, where he continued his cultural nationalist activities. In 1967 he changed his name from LeRoi Jones to the Bantuized Muslim appellation Imamu ("spiritual leader," later dropped) Ameer (later Amiri, "blessed") Baraka ("prince"), to confirm his pride in his blackness.

While in Harlem Baraka had become the main theorist of the Black Aesthetic, defined by Houston Baker in *Black American Literature Forum* as "a distinctive code for the creation and evaluation of black art." The aesthetician felt that the black artist must express his American experience in forms that spring from his own unique culture and that his art must be evaluated by standards that grow out of his own culture. Baraka writes in "Expressive Language," an essay in *Home:* "Words' meanings, but also the rhythm and syntax that frame and propel their concatenation, seek their culture as the final reference for what they are describing of the world." In his *Home* essay, "state/meant" Baraka declares fiercely: "The Black Artist's role in America is to aid in the destruction of America as he knows it. His role is to report . . . so precisely the nature of the society, and of himself in that society, that other men will be moved by the exactness of his rendering and, if they are black men, grow strong through this moving, having seen their own strength, and weakness; and if they are white men, tremble, curse, and go mad, because they will be drenched with the filth of their evil." Or, as Baraka writes in his essay "the legacy of malcolm x," "The song title 'A White Man's Heaven Is a Black Man's Hell' describes how complete an image reversal is necessary in the West."

In *Understanding the New Black Poetry: Black Speech and Black Music as Poetic References,* Stephen Henderson observes, "[Baraka] is the central figure of the new black poetry awakening"; in an essay collected in *Modern Black Poets,* Arthur P. Davis calls him "the high priest of this new Black literary renaissance and one who has done most to shape its course." Baraka dominated the Black Arts Period of the late 1960s both as a theorist and artist. In the 1960s Baraka was the pioneer of black experimental fiction, probably the most important since Jean Toomer who had written during the Harlem Renaissance of the 1920s. Furthermore, *Black Arts* had its impact on other ethnic groups primarily through the person of Baraka. The Native American author Maurice Kenny writes of Baraka in *Amiri Baraka: The Kaleidoscopic Torch:* "He opened tightly guarded doors for not only Blacks but poor whites as well and, of course, Native Americans, Latinos and Asian-Americans. We'd all still be waiting the invitation from the *New Yorker* without him. He

taught us all how to claim it and take it." In the same book, Clyde Taylor says of Baraka's poems of the Black Arts period: "There are enough brilliant poems of such variety in *Black Magic* and *In Our Terribleness* to establish the unique identity and claim for respect of several poets. But it is beside the point that Baraka is probably the finest poet, black or white, writing in this country these days." However, some felt that the political purpose of the poetry was a liability. In *With Eye and Ear,* Kenneth Rexroth contended: "In recent years he [Baraka] has succumbed to the temptation to become a professional Race Man of the most irresponsible sort. . . . His loss to literature is more serious than any literary casualty of the Second War."

In 1966 Baraka published *Home,* an important book of essays, in which the reader sees Baraka becoming more radical in each essay. The collection includes the famous "Cuba Libre," which documents his trip to Cuba and his awakening to Third-World conceptions of art and political activism. A spiritual autobiography, *Home* assumes the same importance in Baraka's career as *Advertisements for Myself* does in Mailer's. The poet Sterling D. Plumpp observes in *Amiri Baraka: The Kaleidoscopic Torch* that he regards *Home* as a major work "for its forthrightness and daring courage to call for 'revolutionary changes,' [and moreover it] . . . is unsurpassed for its seminal ideas regarding black art which is excellent and people-centered."

Baraka's years in Greenwich Village had made him a master of avant-garde technique that he utilized in his own work and passed on to younger black artists such as Nikki Giovanni and Don L. Lee [now Haki R. Madhubuti]. Avant-garde ideas of form cohered perfectly with the new black artist's need to express his or her own oral traditions; the free verse and the eccentric typography of the white avant-garde were ideal vehicles for black oral expression and experience. Unlike Harlem Renaissance poets such as Claude McKay—who constantly battled the rigid, archaic form of the English sonnet replete with nineteenth-century diction and conventions to express 1920s black American language and life—the Black Arts poet had the flexibility of contemporary forms, forms committed to the oral tradition and polyrhythms. In a 1971 issue of *Black World* Dudley Randall observes: "The younger poets have a teacher of great talent, and while they think they are rejecting white standards, they are learning from LeRoi Jones, a man versed in German philosophy, conscious of literary traditions . . . who uses the structure of Dante's *Divine Comedy* in his *The System of Dante's Hell* and the punctuation, spelling and line divisions of sophisticated contemporary poets." Rampersad maintains in *American Book Review:* "Among all the major writers who helped to wean younger black writers away from imitation and compulsive traditionalism and toward modernism, Baraka has been almost certainly the most influential. . . . In speaking of his modernizing influence on younger black poets, one does not mean that Baraka taught them to imitate or even to admire the verse of Pound and Eliot, Stevens and Williams, Ginsberg and Kerouac, all of whose poetry he himself attempted to absorb. More than any other black poet, however, he taught younger black poets of the generation past how to respond poetically to their lived experience, rather than to depend as artists on embalmed reputations and outmoded rhetorical strategies derived from a culture often substantially different from their own." In the 1970s and 1980s Baraka has been joined by a band of younger experimental black writers, including Ishmael Reed, Clarence Major, and Charles Johnson.

In 1974, dramatically reversing himself, Baraka rejected black nationalism as racist and became a Third World Socialist. He declared, in the *New York Times:* "It is a narrow nationalism that says the white man is the enemy. . . . Nationalism, so-called, when it says 'all non-blacks are our enemies,' is sickness or criminality, in fact, a form of fascism." Since 1974 he has produced a number of Marxist poetry collections and plays. He has also published a book of Marxist essays, *Daggers and Javelins.* The goal of his socialist art is the destruction of the capitalist state and the creation of a socialist community. In *The Poetry and Poetics of Amiri Baraka: The Jazz Aesthetic,* William J. Harris records Baraka's assessment of his goals as a Third World Socialist: "I think fundamentally my intentions are similar to those I had when I was a Nationalist. That might seem contradictory, but they were similar in the sense I see art as a weapon . . . of revolution. It's just now that I define revolution in Marxist terms. I once defined revolution in Nationalist terms. But I came to my Marxist view as a result of having struggled as a Nationalist and found certain dead ends theoretically and ideologically, as far as Nationalism was concerned, and had to reach out for a communist ideology."

Baraka's socialist works have not fared well in the establishment press. In the *New York Times Book Review* Pinckney comments that Baraka has "sacrificed artistic vitality on the altar of his political faith. . . . his early work is far better than his recent efforts: he now seems content to express his Marxism in the most reductive, shrill propaganda." Henry C. Lacey, in his 1981 book *To Raise, Destroy, and Create: The Poetry, Drama, and Fiction of Imamu Amiri Baraka (LeRoi Jones),* ignores the Marxist work entirely; Fox, in his 1987 study, says, "The Marxist work is intellectually determined, whereas the cultural-nationalist pieces are emotionally felt." On the other hand, E. San Juan, an exiled Filipino leftist intellectual, writes in *Amiri Baraka: The Kaleidoscopic Torch* that he finds the "Lone Ranger" "the most significant theatrical achievement of 1978 in the Western hemisphere." Weixlmann responds in *Amiri Baraka: The Kaleidoscopic Torch* to the tendency to categorize the radical Baraka instead of analyze him: "At the very least, dismissing someone with a label does not make for very satisfactory scholarship. Initially, Baraka's reputation as a writer and thinker derived from a recognition of the talents with which he is so obviously endowed. The assaults on that reputation have, too frequently, derived from concerns which should be extrinsic to informed criticism."

As the critical climate cools, critics find merit in the recent poetry, especially the long *In the Tradition: For Black Arthur Blythe,* and the epic-in-progress, "Why's/Wise." Also with the 1984 publication of *The Autobiography* Baraka has joined the great tradition of the black autobiography, which runs from Frederick Douglass to W. E. B. DuBois to Richard Wright to Malcolm X. Like other authors in this tradition, in the act of making sense of his life, Baraka makes sense of American culture. Rampersad comments on Baraka and his autobiography in *Amiri Baraka: The Kaleidoscopic Torch:* "His change of heart and head is testimony to his honesty, energy, and relentless search for meaning, as demonstrated recently once again with the publication of his brilliant *The Autobiography of LeRoi Jones.*"

In a piece on Miles Davis in *The Music: Reflections on Jazz and Blues,* Baraka quotes the contemporary trombonist, Craig Harris: "Miles is gonna do what Miles wants to do. And everybody else can follow, if they feel like it." Like Davis, Baraka is going his own way; he is an original, and others can follow if they like. He is a black writer who has taken the techniques and notions of the white avant-garde and made them his own; like the great bop musicians before him, he has united avant-garde art with the black voice, creating a singular expressive mode. Baraka has created a major art, not by trying to blend into Western tradition but by trying to be true to himself and his culture. He speaks out

of a web of personal and communal experience, minimizing the so-called universal features he shared with the white world and focusing on the black cultural difference what has made the black experience unique in the West. Out of this experience Baraka fashions his art, his style, his distinctive vision of the world.

Papers by and about Amiri Baraka/LeRoi Jones are housed in the Dr. Martin Sukov Collection at Yale University's Beinecke Rare Book and Manuscript Library; numerous letters to and from the author, and several of Baraka's manuscripts are collected at Indiana University's Lilly Library; the author's letters to Charles Olson are housed at the University of Connecticut's Special Collections Library; other manuscripts and materials are collected at Syracuse University's George Arents Research Library.

BIOGRAPHICAL/CRITICAL SOURCES:

BOOKS

Allen, Donald M., and Warren Tallman, editors, *Poetics of the New American Poetry,* Grove, 1973.

Baraka, Amiri, *Tales,* Grove, 1967.

Baraka, and Larry Neal, editors, *Black Fire: An Anthology of Afro-American Writing,* Morrow, 1968.

Baraka, *Black Magic: Sabotage; Target Study; Black Art; Collected Poetry, 1961-1967,* Bobbs-Merrill, 1969.

Baraka, *The Autobiography of LeRoi Jones/Amiri Baraka,* Freundlich Books, 1984.

Benston, Kimberly A., editor, *Baraka: The Renegade and the Mask,* Yale University Press, 1976.

Benston, *Imamu Amiri Baraka (LeRoi Jones): A Collection of Critical Essays,* Prentice-Hall, 1978.

Bigsby, C. W. E., *Confrontation and Commitment: A Study of Contemporary American Drama, 1959-66,* University of Missouri Press, 1968.

Bigsby, editor, *The Black American Writer, Volume II: Poetry and Drama,* Everett/Edwards, 1970, Penguin, 1971.

Bigsby, *The Second Black Renaissance: Essays in Black Literature,* Greenwood Press, 1980.

Birnebaum, William M., *Something for Everybody Is Not Enough,* Random House, 1972.

Brown, Lloyd W., *Amiri Baraka,* Twayne, 1980.

Concise Dictionary of American Literary Biography, Volume 1: *The New Consciousness,* Gale, 1987.

Contemporary Literary Criticism, Gale, Volume 1, 1973, Volume 2, 1974, Volume 3, 1975, Volume 5, 1976, Volume 10, 1979, Volume 14, 1980, Volume 33, 1985.

Cook, Bruce, *The Beat Generation,* Scribner, 1971.

Dace, Letitia, *LeRoi Jones (Imamu Amiri Baraka): A Checklist of Works by and about Him,* Nether Press, 1971.

Dace, and Wallace Dace, *The Theatre Student: Modern Theatre and Drama,* Richards Rosen Press, 1973.

Dictionary of Literary Biography, Gale, Volume 5: *American Poets since World War II,* 1980, Volume 7: *Twentieth Century American Dramatists,* 1981, Volume 16: *The Beats; Literary Bohemians in Postwar America,* 1983, Volume 38: *Afro-American Writers after 1955: Dramatists and Prose Writers,* 1985.

Dukore, Bernard F., *Drama and Revolution,* Holt, 1971.

Ellison, Ralph, *Shadow and Act,* New American Library, 1966.

Emanuel, James A., and Theodore L. Gross, editors, *Dark Symphony: Negro Literature in America,* Free Press, 1968.

Fox, Robert Elliot, *Conscientious Sorcerers: The Black Postmodernist Fiction of LeRoi Jones/Baraka, Ishmael Reed and Samuel R. Delany,* Greenwood Press, 1987.

Frost, David, *The Americans,* Stein & Day, 1970.
Gayle, Addison, editor, *Black Expression: Essays by and about Black Americans in the Creative Arts,* Weybright & Talley, 1969.
Gayle, *The Way of the New World: The Black Novel in America,* Anchor/Doubleday, 1975.
Gwynne, James B., editor, *Amiri Baraka: The Kaleidoscopic Torch,* Steppingstones Press, 1985.
Hall, Veronica, *Chicorel Theater Index to Plays in Anthologies, Periodicals, Discs and Tapes,* Chicorel Library Publishing, 1970.
Harris, William J., *The Poetry and Poetics of Amiri Baraka: The Jazz Aesthetic,* University of Missouri Press, 1985.
Haskins, James, *Black Theater in America,* Crowell, 1982.
Hatch, James V., *Black Image on the American Stage: A Bibliography of Plays and Musicals, 1770-1970,* Drama Book Specialists, 1970.
Hatch, editor, *Black Theatre, U.S.A.,* Free Press, 1974.
Henderson, Stephen E., *Understanding the New Black Poetry: Black Speech and Black Music as Poetic References,* Morrow, 1973.
Hill, Herbert, *Soon, One Morning,* Knopf, 1963.
Hill, editor, *Anger, and Beyond: The Negro Writer in the United States,* Harper, 1966.
Hudson, Theodore, *From LeRoi Jones to Amiri Baraka: The Literary Works,* Duke University Press, 1973.
Jones, LeRoi, *Preface to a Twenty Volume Suicide Note,* Totem Press/Corinth Books, 1961.
Jones, *The Dead Lecturer,* Grove, 1964.
Jones, *Blues People: Negro Music in White America,* Morrow, 1963.
Jones, *Home: Social Essays,* Morrow, 1966.
Keil, Charles, *Urban Blues,* University of Chicago Press, 1966.
King, Woodie, and Ron Milner, editors, *Black Drama Anthology,* New American Library, 1971.
Knight, Arthur and Kit Knight, editors, *The Beat Vision,* Paragon House, 1987.
Kofsky, Frank, *Black Nationalism and the Revolution in Music,* Pathfinder, 1970.
Lacey, Henry C., *To Raise, Destroy, and Create: The Poetry, Drama, and Fiction of Imamu Amiri Baraka (LeRoi Jones),* The Whitson Publishing Company, 1981.
Lewis, Allan, *American Plays and Playwrights,* Crown, 1965.
Littlejohn, David, *Black on White: A Critical Survey of Writing by American Negroes,* Viking, 1966.
O'Brien, John, *Interviews with Black Writers,* Liveright, 1973.
Ossman, David, *The Sullen Art: Interviews with Modern American Poets,* Corinth, 1963.
Rexroth, Kenneth, *With Eye and Ear,* Herder and Herder, 1970.
Rosenthal, M. L., *The New Poets: American and British Poetry since World War II,* Oxford University Press, 1967.
Sollors, Werner, *Amiri Baraka/LeRoi Jones: The Quest for a "Populist Modernism,"* Columbia University Press, 1978.
Stepanchev, Stephen, *American Poetry since 1945,* Harper, 1965.
Weales, Gerald, *The Jumping-Off Place: American Drama in the 1960s,* Macmillan, 1969.
Whitlow, Roger, *Black American Literature: A Critical History,* Nelson Hall, 1973.
Williams, Martin, *The Jazz Tradition,* New American Library, 1971.
Williams, Sherley Anne, *Give Birth to Brightness: A Thematic Study in Neo-Black Literature,* Dial, 1972.

PERIODICALS

American Book Review, February, 1980, May-June, 1985.
Atlantic, January, 1966, May, 1966.
Avant Garde, September, 1968.
Black American Literature Forum, spring, 1980, spring, 1981, fall, 1982, spring, 1983, winter, 1985.
Black World, volume 29, number 6, April, 1971, December, 1971, November, 1974, July, 1975.
Book Week, December 24, 1967.
Book World, October 28, 1979.
Boundary 2, number 6, 1978.
Chicago Defender, January 11, 1965.
Chicago Tribune, October 4, 1968.
Contemporary Literature, volume 12, 1971.
Detroit Free Press, January 31, 1965.
Detroit News, January 15, 1984, August 12, 1984.
Dissent, spring, 1965.
Ebony, August, 1967, August, 1969, February, 1971.
Educational Theatre Journal, March, 1968, March, 1970, March, 1976.
Esquire, June, 1966.
Essence, September, 1970, May, 1984, September, 1984, May, 1985.
Jazz Review, June, 1959.
Journal of Black Poetry, fall, 1968, spring, 1969, summer, 1969, fall, 1969.
Los Angeles Free Press, volume 5, number 18, May 3, 1968.
Los Angeles Times, April 20, 1990.
Los Angeles Times Book Review, May 15, 1983, March 29, 1987.
Nation, October 14, 1961, November 14, 1961, March 13, 1964, April 13, 1964, January 4, 1965, March 15, 1965, January 22, 1968, February 2, 1970.
Negro American Literature Forum, March, 1966, winter, 1973.
Negro Digest, December, 1963, February, 1964, Volume 13, number 19, August, 1964, March, 1965, April, 1965, March, 1966, April, 1966, June, 1966, April, 1967, April, 1968, January, 1969, April, 1969.
Newsweek, March 13, 1964, April 13, 1964, November 22, 1965, May 2, 1966, March 6, 1967, December 4, 1967, December 1, 1969, February 19, 1973.
New York, November 5, 1979.
New Yorker, April 4, 1964, December 26, 1964, March 4, 1967, December 30, 1972.
New York Herald Tribune, March 25, 1964, April 2, 1964, December 13, 1964, October 27, 1965.
New York Post, March 16, 1964, March 24, 1964, January 15, 1965, March 18, 1965.
New York Review of Books, January 20, 1966, May 22, 1964, July 2, 1970, October 17, 1974, June 11, 1984, June 14, 1984.
New York Times, April 28, 1966, May 8, 1966, August 10, 1966, September 14, 1966, October 5, 1966, January 20, 1967, February 28, 1967, July 15, 1967, January 5, 1968, January 6, 1968, January 9, 1968, January 10, 1968, February 7, 1968, April 14, 1968, August 16, 1968, November 27, 1968, December 24, 1968, August 26, 1969, November 23, 1969, February 6, 1970, May 11, 1972, June 11, 1972, November 11, 1972, November 14, 1972, November 23, 1972, December 5, 1972, December 27, 1974, December 29, 1974, November 19, 1979, October 15, 1981, January 23, 1984.
New York Times Book Review, January 31, 1965, November 28, 1965, May 8, 1966, February 4, 1968, March 17, 1968, February 14, 1971, June 6, 1971, June 27, 1971, December 5, 1971, March 12, 1972, December 16, 1979, March 11, 1984, July 5, 1987, December 20, 1987.
New York Times Magazine, February 5, 1984.
Salmagundi, spring-summer, 1973.

Saturday Review, April 20, 1963, January 11, 1964, January 9, 1965, December 11, 1965, December 9, 1967, October 2, 1971, July 12, 1975.

Studies in Black Literature, spring, 1970, Volume 1, number 2, 1970, Volume 3, number 2, 1972, Volume 3, number 3, 1972, Volume 4, number 1, 1973.

Sunday News (New York), January 21, 1973.

Time, December 25, 1964, November 19, 1965, May 6, 1966, January 12, 1968, April 26, 1968, June 28, 1968, June 28, 1971.

Times Literary Supplement, November 25, 1965, September 1, 1966, September 11, 1969, October 9, 1969.

Tribune Books, March 29, 1987.

Village Voice, December 17, 1964, May 6, 1965, May 19, 1965, August 30, 1976, August 1, 1977, December 17-23, 1980, October 2, 1984.

Washington Post, August 15, 1968, September 12, 1968, November 27, 1968, December 5, 1980, January 23, 1981, June 29, 1987.

Washington Post Book World, December 24, 1967, May 22, 1983.

*   *   *

BARCLAY, Bill
See MOORCOCK, Michael (John)

*   *   *

BARCLAY, William Ewert
See MOORCOCK, Michael (John)

*   *   *

BARKER, Clive   1952-

PERSONAL: Born in 1952 in Liverpool, England; son of Len (a personnel director) and Joan (a school welfare officer) Barker. *Education:* Received degree from University of Liverpool.

ADDRESSES: Home—36 Wimpole St., London W2, England.

CAREER: Illustrator, painter, actor, playwright, and author. Executive producer of motion pictures, including "Hellbound: Hellraiser II," 1989.

AWARDS, HONORS: Two British Fantasy awards from British Fantasy Society; World Fantasy Award for best anthology/collection, World Fantasy Convention, 1985, for *Clive Barker's Books of Blood.*

WRITINGS:

SHORT STORIES AND NOVELLAS

Clive Barker's Books of Blood, Volume One, Sphere, 1984, Berkley Publishing, 1986; *Volume Two,* Sphere, 1984, Berkley Publishing, 1986; *Volume Three* (includes "Rawhead Rex"), Sphere, 1984, Berkley Publishing, 1986; published as *Books of Blood,* Volumes 1-3, Weidenfeld & Nicolson, 1985, one-volume edition, Scream/Press, 1985.

Clive Barker's Books of Blood, Volume Four, Sphere, 1985, published in the United States as *The Inhuman Condition: Tales of Terror,* Poseidon, 1986; *Volume Five,* Sphere, 1985, published in the United States as *In The Flesh: Tales of Terror,* Poseidon, 1986; *Volume Six* (selections published in the United States with the novel *Cabal* [also see below]),

Sphere, 1985; published as *Books of Blood,* Volumes 4-6, Weidenfeld & Nicolson, 1986.

(Contributor) *Night Visions 3* (includes "The Hellbound Heart"), edited by George R. R. Martin, Dark Harvest, 1986.

The Hellbound Heart, Simon & Schuster, 1988.

Work represented in anthologies, including *Cutting Edge,* Futura.

NOVELS

The Damnation Game, Weidenfeld & Nicolson, 1985, Putnam, 1987.

Weaveworld, Poseidon, 1987, special edition, self-illustrated, Collins, 1987.

Cabal (includes novel *Cabal,* and shorter works from *Clive Barker's Books of Blood, Volume Six*), Poseidon, 1988.

The Great and Secret Show, Collins, 1989.

SCREENPLAYS

"Underworld," Limehouse Pictures, 1985.

"Rawhead Rex" (adapted from his short story of the same title), Empire, 1987.

(And director) "Hellraiser" (adapted from his novella "The Hellbound Heart"), New World, 1987.

"Nightbreed" (adapted from his novel *Cabal*), Twentieth Century-Fox, 1990.

OTHER

(Author of introduction) Ramsey Campbell, *Scared Stiff: Tales of Sex and Death,* Scream/Press, 1987.

(Author of introduction) *Night Visions 4* (anthology), Dark Harvest, 1987.

Also author of plays, including "Frankenstein in Love," "The History of the Devil," "Subtle Bodies," and "The Secret Life of Cartoons." Contributor to periodicals, including *American Film* and *Omni.*

SIDELIGHTS: In the mid-1980s Clive Barker, a young British playwright, burst into the world of horror fiction with the publication of six volumes of short stories known as the *Books of Blood.* These works, which combine unprecedented ugliness with literary skill, drew the attention of some of the world's best-known horror writers. "I have seen the future of the horror genre, and his name is Clive Barker," said Stephen King, quoted in *Publishers Weekly.* "What Barker does makes the rest of us look like we've been asleep for 10 years." Fellow Briton Ramsey Campbell, according to *Books and Bookmen,* termed Barker "the first true voice of the next generation of horror writers."

Journalists who meet Barker observe that despite his nightmarish imagination, he seems very well-adjusted—smiling, personable, and boyishly enthusiastic. Nor did Barker always intend to write horrific short stories. After graduating from college he moved to London, where he worked in the theater, did illustrations, and sometimes lived on welfare. The public saw his fantasy plays, such as "The History of the Devil" and "Frankenstein in Love," but only friends saw his short fiction. That changed after Barker read *Dark Forces,* a 1980 anthology edited by Stephen King's agent, Kirby McCauley. Barker perceived an audience for a new, more audacious horror writing, and he quickly penned the first three *Books of Blood.* Initially he was only published in England, but his work caused such a stir among fantasy fans in North America that U.S. publishers soon produced their own editions. His subsequent horror novel, *The Damnation Game,* made the *New York Times* best-seller list within a week of its publication.

Barker's stories, reviewers warn, are relentlessly graphic. Many consider such lack of restraint to be his trademark and his chief innovation. The author "never averts his gaze, no matter how gruesome the scene," wrote Beth Levine of *Publishers Weekly.* "He follows every story through to its logical end, never flinching from detail. The result is mesmerizing, disturbing and elating, all at once." The story "In the Hills, the Cities" depicts an ancient quarrel between a pair of Yugoslavian towns: the townspeople abjure their individuality and form themselves into two lumbering giants who do battle. The title character of "Rawhead Rex," a flesh-eating monster, lingers indulgently over his evening meal: a freshly killed child. Rex especially enjoys the kidneys. As Mikal Gilmore wrote in *Rolling Stone,* "Barker's willingness to enter the sensibilities of his characters—to make their terrible desires comprehensible, even sympathetic—raises questions about both his work and modern horror in general. Namely, does it merely appeal to the meanness of the modern spirit?"

Barker and his admirers would respond that tales of terror can be valid as works of art and as social commentary. "I feel that horror literature is touching upon the big issues time and time again," the author told *Omni:* "death and life after death, sex after death, insanity, loneliness, anxiety. Horror writers are addressing the deepest concerns of the human condition." In *Publishers Weekly* he rejected the common view of horror fiction as a defender of social norms, in which the monster is an outsider who is reassuringly destroyed. "I don't believe that's true of the world," he said. "We can't destroy the monster because the monster is us." Accordingly, as Michael Morrison suggested in *Fantasy Review,* Barker's stories become a strongly worded commentary on human nature. In "Jaqueline Ess: Her Will and Testament," an embittered, suicidal woman discovers that psychokinetic powers can liberate her from the tyranny of men but not from her own hatred of life. In "The Skins of the Fathers," the monsters who approach a small town to reclaim their half-human child seem less repugnant than the cold, tough Americans who oppose them. Writers such as Barker, said Kim Newman of *New Statesman,* "raise the possibility that horror fiction is the most apt form for dealing with the subject of life in the late 20th century."

Admirers consider Barker a fine writer as well as a maker of nightmares. He has been compared not only to Stephen King and Peter Straub, two of his highly popular contemporaries, but also to more literary predecessors such as Henry James and Edith Wharton. *The Damnation Game,* Barker's first full-length novel, seemed to confirm his talent. The book depicts two criminals with supernatural powers who pursue each other across modern Europe for decades. Writing in *Washington Post Book World,* Laurence Coven praised Barker for such details as his "remarkably powerful portrait" of the menacing ruins of Warsaw at the end of World War II. "In pure descriptive power," Coven averred, "there is no one writing horror fiction now who can match him." Algis Budrys of the *Magazine of Fantasy and Science Fiction* said *The Damnation Game* was better written than the typical novel by King or Straub, though he felt that Barker's colleagues could easily improve their style if readers desired. Nevertheless Budrys praised the book, calling it "a masterly novel that even a lit. professor couldn't help but be impressed by."

While he relishes horror stories, Barker remains determined not to be confined to a single genre. He told *Books and Bookmen* that his work belongs to a broader category—"imaginative fiction"—which is a valid part of the larger literary tradition. "Mainstream" writers, Barker contended, readily use the techniques of imaginative literature, though they may not admit it. Barker's American hardback publisher, Poseidon Press, made a point of marketing his work to a broad audience. When Barker wrote his first fantasy novel, *Weaveworld,* he switched publishers in England in order to ensure such treatment in his home country. Though *Weaveworld* is punctuated by Barker's characteristically graphic writing, it is fundamentally a romance. In the book a race of magicians, who hide their blissful world in the weave of a magic carpet, defend themselves against sinister intruders. Gilmore wrote that *Weaveworld* "is clearly Barker's loveliest, most hopeful work, and in its themes and its tone it is somewhat akin to the best fantasy literature of J. R. R. Tolkein," the acclaimed author of *Lord of the Rings.*

Barker continues to display a broad range of artistic interests. Already an illustrator, he designed the cover art for British printings of the *Books of Blood* and illustrated a special British edition of *Weaveworld.* He wrote two screenplays that were directed by others—"Underworld" and an adaptation of "Rawhead Rex"—but he agreed with film reviewers who found the results disappointing. Barker felt the remedy was greater creative control, and so he directed the next script himself—"Hellraiser," adapted from his novella "The Hellbound Heart." *Video*'s Daniel Schweiger thought that "Hellraiser" adeptly delivered the "excited chill" that audiences want in a horror movie, but he also considered the film "as excessive as any . . . in cinema's gross-me-out school." Gilmore emphasized the movie's philosophical qualities, calling it "less memorable for its hideous demons than for how it echoes [French existentialist] Jean-Paul Sartre's bleak dictum 'Hell is other people.' "

When interviewers wonder how Barker can express such pessimism and yet remain so cheerful, he suggests that an interest in horror can be natural and healthy. "Within the circle of your skull you have an immense imaginative freedom," he told Gilmore. "For Christ's sake, use it to understand your response to death . . . eroticism . . . all the things that come to haunt you and attract you and repulse you in your dreams. Because as soon as you relinquish control and lay your head down on the pillow, those things are going to come anyway."

MEDIA ADAPTATIONS: Some of Barker's work has been abridged and dramatized for audio cassette, including *The Body Politic,* Simon & Schuster, 1987, and *The Damnation Game,* Warner, 1987.

BIOGRAPHICAL/CRITICAL SOURCES:

BOOKS

Contemporary Literary Criticism, Volume 52, Gale, 1989.
McCauley, Kirby, editor, *Dark Forces: New Stories of Suspense and Supernatural Horror,* Bantam, 1980.

PERIODICALS

Books and Bookmen, July, 1985, September, 1987.
Chicago Tribune, September 15, 1987.
Detroit Free Press, December 23, 1988.
Fantasy Review, February, 1985, June, 1985, August, 1985, September, 1985, October, 1986, April, 1987.
Los Angeles Times, February 19, 1990.
Los Angeles Times Book Review, August 10, 1986, June 14, 1987.
Magazine of Fantasy and Science Fiction, August, 1987.
New Statesman, July 18, 1986.
New York, May 26, 1986.

New York Times, September 20, 1987.
New York Times Book Review, September 21, 1986, February 15, 1987, June 21, 1987.
Omni, October, 1986.
People, June 15, 1987.
Publishers Weekly, December 13, 1985, July 4, 1986.
Rolling Stone, February 11, 1988.
Times (London), October 17, 1986.
Times Literary Supplement, February 12, 1988.
Tribune Books (Chicago), September 14, 1986, April 26, 1987.
USA Weekend, October 9-11, 1987.
Video, April, 1988.
Washington Post, September 30, 1987, November 17, 1988.
Washington Post Book World, August 24, 1986, June 28, 1987, September 27, 1987.

*   *   *

BARKER, George Granville   1913-

PERSONAL: Born February 26, 1913, in Essex, England; son of George and Marion Frances (Taaffe) Barker; married Jessica Woodward, 1935 (divorced, 1940); married 1942; wife's name, Elizabeth; married Elspeth Langlands, January 10, 1964; children: Raffaella-Flora, Alescander, Roderick, Samuel. *Education:* Attended Regents Street Polytechnic, 1927-30. *Politics:* None. *Religion:* Roman Catholic.

ADDRESSES: Home—Bintry House, Itteringham, Aylsham, Norfolk, England. *Agent*—John Johnson, 51-54 Goschen Bldg., 12-13 Henitetta St., London WC2E 8LF, England.

CAREER: Writer. Professor of English literature, Imperial Tohoku University, Sendai, Japan, 1939-41; visiting professor of English literature, State University of New York College at Buffalo, 1965-66, University of Wisconsin, 1971-72, and Florida International University, 1974. Arts fellow, York University, 1966.

AWARDS, HONORS: Royal Society of Literature bursary, 1950; Guiness Prize, 1962; Levinson Prize from *Poetry* magazine, 1965; Borestone Mountain Poetry Award, 1967; Arts Council bursary, 1968.

WRITINGS:

Thirty Preliminary Poems, Archer Press, 1933.
Alanna Autumnal, Wishart & Co., 1933.
Janus (stories), Faber, 1935.
Poems, Faber, 1935.
Calamiterror (poems), Faber, 1937.
Elegy on Spain, Contemporary Bookshop, 1939.
Lament and Triumph (poems), Faber, 1940.
Selected Poems, Macmillan, 1941.
Sacred and Secular Elegies, New Directions, 1943.
Eros in Dogma (poems), Faber, 1944.
Love Poems, Dial, 1947.
News of the World (poems), Faber, 1950.
The Dead Seagull (novel), Lehmann, 1950, Farrar, Straus, 1951.
The True Confession of George Barker (poem), Fore Publications, 1950, New American Library, 1964.
A Vision of Beasts and Gods, Faber, 1954.
Collected Poems, 1930-1955, Faber, 1957, Criterion, 1958.
Two Plays (contains "Seraphina" and "In the Shade of the Old Apple Tree"), Faber, 1958.
The View from a Blind I (poems), Faber, 1962.
(With Martin Bell and Charles Causley) *Penguin Modern Poets Number Three,* Penguin, 1962.
(Author of foreword) Alfred, Lord Tennyson, *Idylls of the King, and a Selection of Poems,* New American Library, 1962.

Collected Poems, 1930-1965, October House, 1965.
Dreams of a Summer Night (poems), Faber, 1966.
The Golden Chains, Faber, 1968.
Runes and Rhymes and Tunes and Chimes, Faber, 1969.
At Thurgarton Church: A Poem with Drawings, Trigram Press, 1969.
Essays, Macgibbon & Kee, 1970.
What Is Mercy and a Voice, Poem-of-the-Month Club, 1970.
To Aylsham Fair (poems), Faber, 1970.
Poems of People and Places, Faber, 1971.
(Author of introduction) Maurice Carpenter, *The Black Ballads and the Love Words,* Quaker Press, 1971.
III Hallucination Poems, Helikon Press, 1972.
The Alphabetical Zoo, Faber, 1972.
In Memory of David Archer (poems), Faber, 1973.
Dialogues, Merrimack Book Service, 1976 (published in England as *Dialogues Etc.,* Faber, 1976).
Seven Poems, Greville Press, 1977.
Villa Stellar, Faber, 1978, Merrimack Book Service, 1979.
Anno Domini, Faber, 1983.
Collected Poems, Faber, 1987.
Seventeen, Greville, 1988.

SIDELIGHTS: George Granville Barker "must be the oldest living enfant terrible in the world," according to Robert Nye in the London *Times.* A writer and poet who began publishing at the age of twenty, Barker's work is marked by rebellion, erotic imagery, and a high romantic outlook. Though sometimes criticized for his lack of consistency, Barker's best works have been described as being among the finest written in the English language. In his review of *Collected Poems* for *Agenda,* Jonathan Barker notes that "even Barker's staunchest admirers do not dispute the unevenness of his writing, but he is also one of those few English poets who need to be read entire for the full range and comprehensiveness of his vision to be properly appreciated. [Barker] remains a major figure for me, one of the few living poets in our language whose best work really matters and is sure to endure."

Throughout much of his work, Barker deals with such themes as sexuality, uncertainty, and despair. *Poetry* critic E. G. Burrows comments in his review of *The True Confession of George Barker:* "Barker confesses in middle-age to those typical ills of mid-twentieth century man: the failure to relate to one's fellowman, the obsession with and distortion of sex, rootlessness and Godlessness, the loss of human love and its effect on art. These are the weightiest of themes and though Barker treats them jocularly and without respect at times, we know that he knows he is whistling in the dark. Behind the clever lines there is a tense battle being waged and it is Barker's genius to show us the value of this struggle and the toll it has taken even in the midst of his most urbane verses."

Many reviewers feel that one of Barker's most impressive traits as a writer is the emotional intensity he brings to his work. It is this emotional intensity that grabs the reader, drawing him in and involving him in the experience of the poetry. Terry Eagleton writes in *Stand* that "the authenticity of the emotional impulse is impressive. Barker is willing to reveal himself, and while the unstaunched flow of that confessionalism leaves a good many ragged edges, it also conveys the sense of an individual voice rather than of an anonymous ('timeless') Naturepoet." Commenting in the festschrift *Homage to George Barker on His Sixtieth Birthday,* Paul Potts notes that Barker's writings truly reflect the man as well as the poet. As Potts writes, Barker "is capable of spoiling a good poem by a noisy line, but never of trying to make one out of any emotion that is not an integral part of his own deep feeling."

Religion also plays an important role in Barker's writings. In the chapter he contributed to *Homage to George Barker on His Sixtieth Birthday*, Patrick Swift writes: "I doubt if it is possible to discuss Barker's work at all seriously without penetrating to some extent into the world of religious belief. He himself asserts the supreme importance of religion. For him poetry cannot usurp the responsibilities of religion. The poet cannot operate without the sanction of the religious man, whereas the religious man can pray without reference to the poet. The category of prayer being of a higher order than that of the poem." Swift goes on to suggest that Barker's play *In the Shade of the Old Apple Tree* "places [Barker] so close to the orthodox Catholic view of good and evil, that he may as well be called a 'Catholic' poet. In the work of Barker I see a deeply religious nature break silence in anguish."

However, Roger Garfitt of *London Magazine* claims that "Barker's quality as a religious poet is that he is an impenitent, as most of us are. The poems hold in tension the conflicts basic to any relationship, spiritual or personal: the recognition of need, for instance, and the reaction of defiance that immediately follows." And Potts writes that "the world of George Barker is a place for sinners. It is not a street of barricades, nor is it a house where one prays. Yet the nature of the poetry in him is the plentifulness of forgiveness. His is original without being unique. He is very much of this world, in so far as it is a vale of tears, without being seduced by worldliness. His technique is in advance of his maturity. He is married to poetry, he is not just having an affair with words. But he is still waiting for the cock to crop whereas, according to the calendar of his achievements, he should be getting ready for the gift of tongues."

In an evaluation of Barker's poetry for *PN Review*, David Gascoyne states: "I recognise and salute in George Barker a poet whose work has never ceased to develop, who has been almost uninterruptedly prolific, whose themes have been basic and perennial, and who has remained faithful to his exceptional gift, enriching our language and literature to an extent that remains to be estimated." In a review for *London Magazine* of Barker's *Collected Poems, 1930-1955*, Anthony Cronin notes that "the best of these verses can stand comparison with the best poetry of our time, with Yeats and Auden. . . . They seem to me to be, at their best, among the most honest and agonizing, and therefore reconciling, consolatory and elating poems written in English in this century."

BIOGRAPHICAL/CRITICAL SOURCES:

BOOKS

Contemporary Literary Criticism, Gale, Volume 8, 1978, Volume 48, 1988.
Dictionary of Literary Biography, Volume 20: *British Poets, 1914-1945*, Gale, 1983.
Feder, Lillian, *Ancient Myth in Modern Poetry*, Princeton University Press, 1971.
Fodaski, Martha, *George Barker*, Twayne, 1969.
Heath-Stubbs, John and Martin Green, editors, *Homage to George Barker on His Sixtieth Birthday*, Martin Brian & O'Keefe, 1973.

PERIODICALS

Agenda, summer, 1987.
Library Journal, February 1, 1979.
London Magazine, May, 1958, May, 1968, August/September, 1976.

New Statesman, September 25, 1970.
PN Review, Volume 9, number 5, 1983.
Poetry, December, 1964.
Punch, March 27, 1968.
Saturday Review, July 4, 1964, December 25, 1965.
Sewanee Review, summer, 1968.
Stand, Volume XV, number 4, 1974.
Times (London), June 25, 1987.
Times Literary Supplement, April 14, 1966, April 16, 1970.

*   *   *

BARNES, Djuna   1892-1982
(Lydia Steptoe)

PERSONAL: Born January 12, 1892, in Cornwall-on-Hudson, N.Y.; died June 18(?), 1982, in New York, N.Y.; daughter of Henry Budington (later changed name to Wald) and Elizabeth (Chappell) Barnes; married Courtenay Lemon, 1917 (divorced, 1919). *Education:* Attended Pratt Institute and Art Students' League.

CAREER: Journalist, 1913-31. Trustee, Dag Hammarskjoeld Foundation, beginning 1961.

MEMBER: National Institute of Arts and Letters.

AWARDS, HONORS: National Endowment for the Arts senior fellowship, 1981.

WRITINGS:

The Book of Repulsive Women: 8 Rhythms and 5 Drawings, Bruno Chap Books, 1915.
(Self-illustrated) *A Book* (includes "Three from the Earth" [one-act play; first produced by the Provincetown Players, 1919], "Kurzy of the Sea" [one-act play; first produced by the Provincetown Players, 1919], "An Irish Triangle" [one-act play; first produced by the Provincetown Players, 1919], and "The Dove" [first produced by the Studio Theatre of Smith College, 1926]), Boni & Liveright, 1923, enlarged edition published as *A Night among the Horses,* 1929, abridged edition published as *Spillway* (also see below), Faber, 1962, Harper, 1972.
(Self-illustrated) *Ladies Almanack: Showing Their Signs and Their Tides; Their Moons and Their Changes; the Seasons as It Is with Them; Their Eclipses and Equinoxes; as Well as a Full Record of Diurnal and Nocturnal Distempers* (published anonymously), privately printed, 1928, reprinted (under name Djuna Barnes), Harper, 1972.
(Self-illustrated) *Ryder* (novel), Liveright, 1928, St. Martin's, 1979.
Nightwood (also see below; novel), with introduction by T. S. Eliot, Faber, 1936, Harcourt, 1937, 2nd edition, Faber, 1950, New Directions, 1961.
The Antiphon (also see below; verse play; first produced at Royal Theatre, Stockholm, February, 1961), Farrar, Straus, 1958.
Selected Works: Spillway, The Antiphon, Nightwood, Farrar, Straus, 1962, published as *Selected Works of Djuna Barnes: Spillway, The Antiphon, Nightwood,* Farrar, Straus, 1980.
Vagaries Malicieux: Two Stories, Frank Hallman, 1974.
Greenwich Village as It Is, edited by Robert A. Wilson, Phoenix Book Shop, 1978.
Creatures in an Alphabet (poems), Dial, 1983.
Smoke and Other Early Stories, edited by Douglas Messerli, Sun & Moon, 1983.
Interviews (interviews conducted by Barnes), edited by Alyce Barry, Sun & Moon, 1985.

I Could Never Be Lonely without a Husband (interviews conducted by Barnes), edited by Alyce Barry, Virago, 1987.
New York (newspaper articles), edited by Alyce Barry, Sun & Moon, 1989.

Work appears in anthologies, including *Unmuzzled Ox Anthology,* edited by Michael Andre, Unmuzzled Ox Press, 1974. Contributor, sometimes under pseudonym Lydia Steptoe, to *Dial, Vanity Fair, Smart Set, Town and Country, New Republic, New Yorker, transatlantic review,* and other publications.

SIDELIGHTS: A major figure on the Paris literary scene of the 1920s and 1930s, Djuna Barnes was best known for her experimental novel *Nightwood,* one of the most influential works of modernist fiction. Described by Elizabeth Hardwick of the *Times Literary Supplement* as "a writer of wild and original gifts," Barnes was acclaimed by such writers as "Graham Greene, Samuel Beckett, Janet Flanner, Laurence Durrell, Kenneth Burke, Sir Herbert Read, and Dylan Thomas," Andrew Field pointed out in the *New York Times Book Review.* Field noted, too, that "a list just as long could be made of important writers who borrowed heavily from her." Barnes was at various times a poet, journalist, playwright, theatrical columnist, and novelist. But her prolific career was brought to a voluntary end in the 1930s when Barnes virtually gave up writing and retreated into nearly half a century of silence. She lived like a recluse, "a form of Trappist," Louis F. Kannenstine quoted her as saying in the *Dictionary of Literary Biography,* refusing to grant interviews or to approve the reprinting of most of her early writings. Because of this silence, Barnes's work is still not as widely celebrated as is that of many of her contemporaries.

Born in 1892 in Cornwall-on-Hudson, New York, Barnes began writing at an early age to support her mother and three brothers. She contributed frequently to New York City newspapers and to such magazines as *Smart Set* and *Vanity Fair.* In 1915, her first collection, *The Book of Repulsive Women: 8 Rhythms and 5 Drawings,* appeared as a chapbook. With the production in 1919 of three one-act plays by Eugene O'Neill's Provincetown Players, Barnes first gained serious recognition for her work. Her contributions to modernist publications of the day established her reputation among the avant-garde community. In 1920, Barnes left New York for Paris, where she was to live for the next twenty years and write the "relatively small body of work" upon which her "literary reputation must ultimately rest," as Kannenstine stated. This small body of work consists of four volumes: *A Book, Ladies Almanack, Ryder,* and *Nightwood.*

A Book, a collection of Barnes's plays, short stories, poems, and drawings, appeared in 1923. The plays produced by the Provincetown Players are collected here, as well as early stories set in Paris and inspired by the people Barnes knew there. The poet Raymond Radiguet, who died at the age of twenty, is the inspiration for one story. Two Dutch sisters, friends of Barnes and fixtures of Paris cafe society, inspire two other stories. All of these characters "are restless, estranged from society and themselves," Kannenstine wrote. Later editions of *A Book* were published as *A Night among the Horses* and *Spillway. Horses* adds several short stories to the original collection, while *Spillway* consists only of the short stories from the original collection.

In *Ladies Almanack,* published in 1928, Barnes based her characters on prominent lesbian writers of 1920s Paris, particularly those in author Natalie Barney's circle of friends. Written in Elizabethan prose, the book depicts a lesbian society in which one woman is sainted. Barnes described the book as "a slight satiric wigging," as Hardwick quoted her. The satire, however, is

gentle and amiable. "The primary intention of *Ladies Almanack,*" Kannenstine believed, "is to confront the anomaly of sexual identity." The book was privately printed and distributed in Paris.

Barnes's first novel, *Ryder,* was also published in 1928. As in *Ladies Almanack,* there is an element of satire in the book. Barnes parodies "biblical language, Chaucer, heroic couplets, mystical literature, the epistolary novel, mock-epic tales, and other forms," Donald J. Greiner explained in the *Dictionary of Literary Biography. Ryder* is ostensibly a family chronicle revolving around Wendell Ryder, his wife, mother, and mistress. Ryder brings misery to all the women in his life because of his conviction that he has a mission to love women. Told in nonchronological chapters, many of which could stand on their own, *Ryder* is a "kaleidoscope of moods and styles," Joseph Frank wrote in *Sewanee Review.* Many of the qualities for which Barnes is known are first displayed in *Ryder.* "Of the fantastical quality of her imagination; of the gift for imagery, . . . ; of the epigrammatic incisiveness of her phrasing and her penchant, akin to the Elizabethans, for dealing with the more scabrous manifestations of human fallibility—of all these there is evidence in *Ryder,*" Frank stated. Greiner believed that the publication of *Ryder* moved Barnes into the ranks of important literary innovators. "With *Ryder,*" he noted, "she joined [James] Joyce, [T. S.] Eliot, and [Ezra] Pound in breaking through the conservative restrictions on poetry and fiction by looking over her shoulder at past literary models while stepping toward the future with experiments in technique and structure that would influence writing for the next fifty years."

Although *Ryder* was considered a bold experiment, it is *Nightwood,* Barnes's second novel, that most critics believed to be her most successful and important work. It is, Stephen Koch wrote in the *Washington Post Book World,* "a recognized masterpiece of modernism." *Nightwood* combines comedy and horror in a fiction without narrative structure or conventionally developed characters. "It would be more appropriate," Kannenstine believed, "to speak of *Nightwood*'s situation than its plot." *Nightwood,* Frank explained, "lacks a narrative structure in the ordinary sense." It is, however, organized according to nonliterary models. Various critics have demonstrated that *Nightwood* borrows its structure from poetry, music, drama, psychology, or the visual arts, but Kannenstine maintained that no one explanation of its structure was correct. Instead, "all are correct: all of these function simultaneously," he declared. "The novel is essentially transgeneric." It also incorporates a broad spectrum of literary styles, including that of the Elizabethans and Jacobeans, the writers of the Old Testament, and the Surrealists, while "parodying the venerable traditions of plot, character, setting, and theme, and maintaining extreme authorial detachment," as Greiner wrote in the *Dictionary of Literary Biography.*

The book traces the love affairs of the young woman Robin Vote in 1920s Paris. She first marries Felix Volkbien, but leaves him for the journalist Nora Flood. She then leaves Nora for Jenny Petherbridge. Brokenhearted, Nora turns to Dr. Matthew O'Connor, but he is unable to relieve her suffering and eventually breaks down. "The plot relates little more than the theft of one person's lover by another," Sharon Spencer observed in *Space, Time and Structure in the Modern Novel.* "Yet, through the heightened intensity of its language, and through the adroit structuring of its disjunct elements, *Nightwood* leaves the reader with a coherent and powerful impression of spiritual agony." This agony is commented on by Stanley Edgar Hyman in *Standards: A Chronicle of Books for Our Time.* Hyman compared *Nightwood* to Nathanael West's *Miss Lonelyhearts,* another tragic novel of the 1930s. "In the years since the 30s," Hyman wrote, "we have had nothing to equal those two great cries of pain, in their combination of emotional power and formal artistry." "For all its power," Koch said of *Nightwood,* "this is the bleakest modernism of all, a modernism like a wailing wall."

Although *Nightwood* has a tragic and even nightmarish side, it is also a humorous novel. Elizabeth Pochoda, commenting in *Twentieth Century Literature,* called *Nightwood* "a tremendously funny book in a desperately surgical sort of way." The novel's humor lies in its wit and its use of paradox and hoax, Pochoda argued, and all actions in the novel "are reduced to their initial hoax. Only then is sympathy allowable. The apparently touching love story of Robin and Nora is also a kind of hoaxing, and we are not permitted to weep with Nora over her loss. Once the bloodthirsty nature of such love is uncovered we are allowed the sympathy appropriate to such an inevitable delusion." Greiner, writing in *Critique: Studies in Modern Fiction,* saw the paradoxical combination of humor and sadness as fundamental to all black humor. Barnes's "sense of humor is evident from the beginning," Greiner wrote, "and her use of funny elements with a depressing theme reflects the perplexing mixture so vital to black humor." *Nightwood,* Greiner concluded, "remains the most successful early example of the American black humor novel."

While interweaving humor and horror, *Nightwood* explores the theme of "man's separation from his primitive, yet more fundamental animal nature," Greiner observed in the *Dictionary of Literary Biography.* This separation between human and animal is expressed by Dr. O'Connor who, at one point in the novel, states that man "was born damned and innocent from the start, and wretchedly—as he must—on these two themes—whistles his tune." As Pochoda saw it, the reduction of all actions in *Nightwood* to "their initial hoax" eventually reveals the futility of language to communicate truth. Beginning with a historical allusion, the novel "turns its back on history, on faith in coherent expression, and finally on words themselves," Pochoda stated. "The novel bows down before its own impotence to express truths." In the last scene of the novel, Robin is transformed into a dog. This scene of devolution into beast is written, in contrast to the exuberance of the rest of the book, in a plain and unenergetic style to show the ultimate failure of language to overcome the animal within man. "The novel," Pochoda noted, "ends in wordlessness and failure, with the impasse of life intact and its contradictions nicely exposed."

Writing in the *International Fiction Review,* Robert L. Nadeau had a Freudian explanation for the devolution in *Nightwood.* He argued that the novel "does not depict human interaction on the level of conscious, waking existence. It is rather a dream world in which the embattled forces of the human personality take the form of characters representing aspects of that personality at different levels of its functioning." The transformation of Robin into an animal takes place, Nadeau wrote, "after she divests herself of the demands of the superego, or that whole complex of forms and values known as 'civilization,'. . . . She is an animal—pure and simple."

In his biography *Djuna: The Life and Times of Djuna Barnes,* Field showed that much of *Nightwood* is autobiographical. He identified the main characters as friends of Barnes in Paris and found that Barnes herself was the character Nora. Robin was identified as Thelma Wood, a woman with whom Barnes had a love affair. But how much of the novel is taken from life is unclear. Field's account, Koch maintained, "is sometimes impossibly evasive, especially on matters sexual." Hardwick saw the bi-

ography as being "under considerable strain" because Barnes "was noted for her silence."

Shortly after publishing *Nightwood,* Barnes ceased writing and, in 1940, she returned to New York City. For the rest of her life she lived in a small apartment in Greenwich Village and published only one play and two poems. Her withdrawal from the literary world caused her reputation to pale. And Barnes's refusal to allow much of her earlier work for magazines to be reprinted kept the scope of her achievement unknown. In her book *Shakespeare and Company,* Sylvia Beach admitted that Barnes "was not one to cry her wares."

Despite her reserve, Barnes maintained a secure place in American letters because of *Nightwood,* which has been in print since it first appeared in 1936. *Nightwood,* Greiner wrote in the *Dictionary of Literary Biography,* "stands high in the list of significant twentieth-century American novels." Nadeau described it as "a truly great piece of American fiction," while Dylan Thomas, according to Field in the *New York Times Book Review,* called *Nightwood* "one of the three great prose books ever written by a woman." Hardwick believed that to Barnes's name "there is always to be attached the splendor of *Nightwood,* a lasting achievement of her great gifts and eccentricities." Barnes was, Koch maintained, a "strange and impossible genius." Since the 1970s, some of Barnes's earlier writings have been found and reprinted in book form and a bibliography of her work has been assembled by Douglas Messerli. Greiner believed that "Djuna Barnes's work will eventually receive the attention it deserves."

BIOGRAPHICAL/CRITICAL SOURCES:

BOOKS

Baldwin, Kenneth H. and David K. Kirby, editors, *Individual and Community: Variations on a Theme in American Fiction,* Duke University Press, 1975.

Beach, Sylvia, *Shakespeare and Company,* Harcourt, 1959.

Broe, Mary Lynn, editor, *Silence and Power: A Re-evaluation of Barnes,* Southern Illinois University Press, 1986.

Cohn, Ruby, *Dialogue in American Drama,* Indiana University Press, 1971.

Contemporary Literary Criticism, Gale, Volume 3, 1975, Volume 4, 1975, Volume 8, 1978, Volume 9, 1979, Volume 29, 1984.

Cook, Albert, *The Meaning of Fiction,* Wayne State University Press, 1960.

Dictionary of Literary Biography, Gale, Volume 4: *American Writers in Paris, 1920-1939,* 1980, volume 9: *American Novelists, 1910-1945,* 1981.

Field, Andrew, *Djuna: The Life and Times of Djuna Barnes,* Putnam, 1983 (published in England as *The Formidable Miss Barnes: The Life of Djuna Barnes,* Secker & Warburg, 1983).

Fowlie, Wallace, *Love in Literature: Studies in Symbolic Expression,* Indiana University Press, 1965.

Frank, Joseph, *The Widening Gyre: Crisis and Mastery in Modern Literature,* Rutgers University Press, 1963.

Friedman, Melvin, *Stream of Consciousness: A Study in Literary Method,* Yale University Press, 1955.

Gildzen, Alex, editor, *A Festschrift for Djuna Barnes on Her 80th Birthday,* Kent State University Libraries, 1972.

Hyman, Stanley Edgar, *Standards: A Chronicle of Books for Our Time,* Horizon Press, 1966.

Kannenstine, Louis F., *The Art of Djuna Barnes: Duality and Damnation,* New York University Press, 1977.

Messerli, Douglas, *Djuna Barnes: A Bibliography,* David Lewis, 1975.

Muir, Edwin, *The Present Age from 1914,* Cresset Press, 1939.

Nemerov, Howard, *Reflexions on Poetry & Poetics,* Rutgers University Press, 1972.
Nin, Anais, *The Novel of the Future,* Macmillan, 1968.
Scott, James B., *Djuna Barnes,* Twayne, 1976.
Spencer, Sharon, *Space, Time and Structure in the Modern Novel,* New York University Press, 1971.
Taylor, William E., editor, *Modern American Drama: Essays in Criticism,* Everett/Edwards, 1968.

PERIODICALS

Atlantic, May, 1962.
Berkeley Daily Gazette, March 31, 1961.
Chapel Hill Weekly, September 9, 1962.
Chicago Sunday Tribune, April 8, 1962.
Critique: Studies in Modern Fiction, spring, 1964, August, 1975.
Hollins Critic, June, 1981.
International Fiction Review, July, 1975.
Journal of Aesthetics, September, 1957.
Massachusetts Review, summer, 1962.
Modern Fiction Studies, winter, 1973-74.
Nation, January 2, 1924, April 3, 1937.
New Statesman, October 17, 1936, February 8, 1958.
New York Herald Tribune Book Review, October 14, 1923, March 7, 1937, April 29, 1962.
New York Times, April 20, 1958, June 28, 1980.
New York Times Book Review, April 29, 1962, January 9, 1983, December 1, 1985.
Northwest Review, summer, 1958.
Renascence, fall, 1962.
San Francisco Chronicle, April 13, 1958.
Saturday Review, November 17, 1928.
Sewanee Review, summer, 1945, summer, 1968.
Southern Review, Number 2, 1966-67, January, 1969.
Time, April 20, 1962.
Times Literary Supplement, April 4, 1958, September 12, 1980, January 21, 1983, October 7, 1983, March 20, 1987.
Twentieth Century Literature, May, 1976
Virginia Quarterly Review, autumn, 1958.
Washington Post Book World, February 1, 1981, June 12, 1983.

OBITUARIES:

PERIODICALS

Chicago Tribune, June 21, 1982.
Newsweek, July 5, 1982.
New York Times, June 20, 1982.
Publishers Weekly, July 2, 1982.
Times (London), June 21, 1982.
Washington Post, June 21, 1982.

* * *

BARNES, Peter 1931-

PERSONAL: Born January 10, 1931, in London, England; son of Frederick and Martha (Miller) Barnes; married Charlotte Beck, 1960.

ADDRESSES: Home—7 Archery Close, Connaught St., London W2 2BE, England. *Agent*—Margaret Ramsay Ltd., 14-A Goodwin's Court, London WC2 4LL, England.

CAREER: Films and Filming magazine, London, England, critic, 1954; Warwick Film Productions Ltd., London, story editor, 1956; playwright, 1963—; stage director, 1970—.

AWARDS, HONORS: John Whiting Playwrights Award, 1968, for *The Ruling Class; Evening Standard* Annual Drama Award for most promising playwright, 1969; The London *Observer* named "Red Noses" best new play, 1985; Olivier Award, 1985.

WRITINGS:

PLAYS

"The Time of the Barracudas" (two-act), first produced in San Francisco at Curran Theatre, 1963.
"Sclerosis" (one-act), first produced in Edinburgh, Scotland, at Traverse Theatre, 1963.
The Ruling Class (two-act; first produced in Nottingham, England, at Playhouse Theatre, 1968; produced in Washington, D.C., at Kreeger Theatre, 1971), Grove, 1969.
Leonardo's Last Supper and Noonday Demons (two one-acts; both first produced in London at Open Space Theatre, 1969), Heinemann, 1970.
Lulu (adaptation and consolidation of two plays by Frank Wedekind; two-act; first produced in Nottingham at Playhouse Theatre, 1970), Heinemann, 1971.
"The Devil Is an Ass" (adaptation of play by Ben Jonson; two-act), first produced in Nottingham at Playhouse Theatre, 1973.
The Bewitched (two-act; first produced in London by Royal Shakespeare Company at Aldwych Theatre, 1974), Heinemann, 1974.
(And director) *The Frontiers of Farce* (adaptation of plays *The Purging* by Georges Feydeau and *The Singer* by Wedekind; first produced in London, 1976), Heinemann, 1977.
(And director) "For All Those Who Get Despondent" (cabaret; adaptation of works by Bertolt Brecht and Wedekind), produced in London, 1977.
Laughter! (produced in London at Royal Court Theatre, 1978), Heinemann, 1978.
(And director) "Antonio" (adaptation of John Marston's plays *Antonio and Mellida* and *Antonio's Revenge*), produced in Nottingham, 1979.
(And director) "The Devil Himself " (revue; adaptation of works by Wedekind), produced in London, 1980.
Barnes' People: Seven Monologues (broadcast, 1981), published in *Collected Plays,* Heinemann, 1981 (also see below).
Collected Plays, Heinemann, 1981.
(And director) "Somersaults" (revue), produced in Leicester, England, at Haymarket Theatre, 1981.
Barnes' People II: Seven Duologues (broadcast, 1984), Heinemann, 1984.
Red Noses (produced in London, 1985), Faber, 1986.
"Scenes from a Marriage" (adaptation of Feydeau's play), produced in London at the Barbican, 1986.
Real Long John Silver and Other Plays: Barnes' People III, Faber, 1986.
(And director) "Bartholomew Fair" (adaptation of Ben Jonson's play), produced in London, 1987.

Also author and adapter of plays for radio broadcasts.

SCREENPLAYS

"Violent Moment," Anglo Amalgamated, 1958.
"The White Trap," Anglo Amalgamated, 1959.
"Breakout," Anglo Amalgamated, 1959.
"The Professionals," Anglo Amalgamated, 1961.
"Off Beat," British Lion, 1961.
"Ring of Spies," British Lion, 1965.
"Not With My Wife, You Don't," Warner Bros., 1966.
"The Ruling Class" (adaptation of own play), United Artists, 1972.

Barnes's screenplays also include "Leonardo's Last Supper," 1977, and "Spaghetti House," 1983.

OTHER

"The Man with a Feather in His Hat" (television script), British ABC, 1960.

SIDELIGHTS: David William, director of the American premier of Barnes' award winning drama *The Ruling Class* wrote: "Just as *Streetcar* [*Named Desire*] is about America, although not only about America, so *The Ruling Class* is about England, although not only England. England provides the local habitation and the name. But beneath the vivid, specific narrative surface of the play swirl the dangerous currents of fantasy and the subconscious. One of the special triumphs of the play is the vision and the wit with which the dramatist has incarnated the life of the psyche: its tensions and paradox, hilarity and horror. For the play is both funny and frightening: a playful nightmare.

"The appalling injury that can be done by society and the individual (or both, acting in some dreadful collusion) to society and the individual in order to perpetuate a status quo regardless of the demands of humanity and truth—this is the material out of which Peter Barnes has shaped a swift and resonant play. The silhouette never shrinks to one of propaganda; the spell is the artist's, unique and surprising."

BIOGRAPHICAL/CRITICAL SOURCES:

BOOKS

Contemporary Literary Criticism, Gale, Volume 5, 1976, Volume 56, 1989.
Dictionary of Literary Biography, Volume 13: *British Dramatists Since World War II,* Gale, 1982.
Dukore, Bernard F., *The Theatre of Peter Barnes,* Heinemann, 1981.

PERIODICALS

Times (London), October 25, 1986, June 3, 1987.

*   *   *

BARON, David
   See PINTER, Harold

*   *   *

BARRINGTON, Michael
   See MOORCOCK, Michael (John)

*   *   *

BARTH, John (Simmons)   1930-

PERSONAL: Born May 27, 1930, in Cambridge, Md.; son of John Jacob and Georgia (Simmons) Barth; married (Harriette) Anne Strickland, January 11, 1950 (divorced, 1969); married Shelly I. Rosenberg (a teacher), December 27, 1970; children: (first marriage) Christine Anne, John Strickland, Daniel Stephen. *Education:* Attended Juilliard School of Music; Johns Hopkins University, A.B., 1951, M.A., 1952.

ADDRESSES: *Home*—Baltimore, Md. *Office*—Writing Seminars, Johns Hopkins University, Baltimore, Md. 21218. *Agent*—International Creative Management, 40 West 57th St., New York, N.Y. 10019.

CAREER: Pennsylvania State University, University Park, instructor, 1953-56, assistant professor, 1957-60, associate profes-

sor of English, 1960-65; State University of New York at Buffalo, professor of English, 1965-71, Edward H. Butler Professor of English, 1971-73; Johns Hopkins University, Baltimore, Md., Alumni Centennial Professor of English and Creative Writing, 1973.

MEMBER: American Academy and Institute of Arts and Letters, American Academy of Arts and Sciences.

AWARDS, HONORS: National Book Award nominations, 1956, for *The Floating Opera,* and 1968, for *Lost in the Funhouse;* Brandeis University Creative Arts Award, 1965; Rockefeller Foundation grant, 1965-66; National Institute of Arts and Letters grant, 1966, for *Giles, Goat-Boy; or, The Revised New Syllabus;* Litt.D., University of Maryland, 1969; National Book Award, 1973, for *Chimera.*

WRITINGS:

NOVELS

The Floating Opera, Appleton-Century-Crofts, 1956, revised edition, Doubleday, 1967, with new foreword by the author, Doubleday-Anchor, 1988.
The End of the Road, Doubleday, 1958, revised edition, 1967, with new foreword by the author, Doubleday/Anchor, 1988.
The Sot-Weed Factor, Doubleday, 1960, revised edition, 1967, with new foreword by the author, Doubleday/Anchor, 1988.
Giles, Goat-Boy; or, The Revised New Syllabus, Doubleday, 1966, with new foreword by the author, Doubleday-Anchor, 1988.
LETTERS, Putnam, 1979.
Sabbatical: A Romance, Putnam, 1982.
Tidewater Tales: A Novel, Putnam, 1987.

OTHER

Lost in the Funhouse: Fiction for Print, Tape, Live Voice (short stories), Doubleday, 1968, with new foreword by the author, Doubleday-Anchor, 1988.
(Contributor) Quinn, editor, *The Sense of the '60s,* Free Press, 1968.
Chimera (novellas), Random House, 1972.
(Contributor) Weintraub and Young, editors, *Directions in Literary Criticism,* Pennsylvania State University Press, 1973.
The Literature of Exhaustion, and The Literature of Replenishment (essays), Lord John Press, 1982.
The Friday Book: Essays and Other Nonfiction, Putnam, 1984.
Don't Count on It: A Note on the Number of the 1001 Nights, Lord John Press, 1984.

Contributor to numerous periodicals, including *Atlantic, Hopkins Review, Esquire, Kenyon Review,* and *Johns Hopkins Magazine.*

SIDELIGHTS: Master of contemporary fiction John Barth often defines himself as a "concocter of comic novels," an inventor of universes who is, above all, a lover of storytelling. For almost forty years, the Maryland-born author has displayed his command of many fictional forms, including short experimental fiction, the novella, and both the short and the long novel. Barth has also produced important nonfiction. His essay "The Literature of Exhaustion" is "one of the more influential pieces to come out of an American fiction writer of Barth's generation," Jack Fuller reports in the *Chicago Tribune Book World.* Barth's literary rank is a subject of critical debate, but "in his fascinated commitment to the art—and to the criticism—of storytelling, he has no rival," declares William Pritchard in the *New York Times*

Book Review. Noting the author's other characteristics, John Barth author E. P. Walkiewicz names the subject of his study a "writer who throughout his career has exhibited great versatility, technical virtuosity, learning, and wit."

Introducing Barth as the "most cerebral of novelists," Curt Suplee goes on to state in the *Washington Post* that Barth has reaped "a madcap eminence (and occasional odium) for huge and bawdy intellectual fables, philosophical vaudeville, [and] rococo parodies of antique literary forms." Barth's first novel, *The Floating Opera,* was second-runner-up for the National Book Award in 1956; *Lost in the Funhouse: Fiction for Print, Tape, Live Voice* was nominated for the same award in 1968, and *Chimera* won it in 1973. In addition, every year on his birthday, the author hears from a nationwide fan club, The Society for the Celebration of Barthomania. "Fortunately for the size of one's ego, there are always at least as many critics telling you to go back to [the] marsh and stick your head in it," Barth remarked to Suplee. The unpredictable author's encyclopedic fictions have baffled some critics and bored others, yet nearly all reviewers recognize his genius even when pronouncing his novels unreadable or tedious. A typically mixed response printed in the *Times Literary Supplement* rates *The Sot-Weed Factor, Giles, Goat-Boy; or, The Revised New Syllabus,* and *Chimera* "easily the best worst in modern fiction." Their author, critics have found, is just as difficult to assess. Efforts to place Barth in a literary category are futile, Walkiewicz explains, due to "the formal complexity, verbal richness, and eclectic content" of the books.

Multiple puns, literary jokes and labyrinthine plots reminiscent of Vladimir Nabokov and Jorge Luis Borges secure Barth's standing with "the great sportsmen of contemporary fiction," to quote *City of Words: American Fiction, 1950-1970* author Tony Tanner. Frank D. McConnell's study, *Four Postwar Novelists: Bellow, Mailer, Barth, and Pynchon,* notes the difference between the pure sport of Nabokov's *Pale Fire* and Barth's fiction, which combines lexical play with "the stuff of history, of change and the dynamic flux of ideas." The heroes in Barth's "preposterous fictions" attempt to find "a philosophical justification for life, search for values and a basis for action in a relativistic cosmos, [and] concern themselves with . . . the question of whether character and external reality are stable or floating phenomena," Gerhard Joseph summarizes in *John Barth.* Furthermore, indicates Walkiewicz, in all the books, Barth "has undermined the foundations of his own authority, and has toyed with a profound skepticism that calls into question . . . all systems of ethics and philosophy." In *The Contemporary Writer,* L. S. Dembo and Cyrena N. Pondrom affirm, "It is appropriate that Barth should refuse to see himself as a part of any intellectual tradition, including nihilism, while remaining one of the best comic-absurdists of his time." The books are not strictly novels of ideas, say critics, who point to an exuberant comic sexuality and a pervasive concern with aesthetics as the dominating features of Barth's work.

Notions about the theory and practice of fiction figure prominently in Barth's canon. One of these ideas, expressed in "The Literature of Exhaustion," is the difficulty of achieving originality in the twentieth century after so many narrative possibilities have been used by other storytellers. Barth's preoccupation, as he told Annie Le Rebeller in a *Caliban* interview, is to "keep a foot in two doors," to be original, "and, at the same time, explore especially the oldest conventions of the medium for their possible present usefulness." This engagement with the history of fiction binds Barth to "a crucial phase in the evolution of modern literature generally," McConnell reports. Writing in *Twentieth Century Literature,* Manfred Puetz deems Barth's writings "epitomes of contemporary American fiction: they expose some of its

key problems and they test representative strategies for solving them." "Almost all commentators" saw Barth's first novel, *The Floating Opera,* "as a philosophical work," Frank Gado generalized in an interview with Barth published in *First Person: Conversations on Writers and Writing.* Barth admitted he was engrossed in certain problems, particularly suicide and nihilism (the view that all beliefs and values are relative and that life is meaningless). He planned to write a comic "philosophical minstrel show" informed by memories of a showboat he had seen as a child. "The plan grew; . . . I decided to write three novels, all dealing with the problem of nihilism." For the first one, he told Gado, "my notion was to take a man who . . . decides to commit suicide" for "ostensibly logical" reasons. The narrator-protagonist Todd Andrews realizes that if there are no absolutes, then one's own version of reality is merely one of numerous other possibilities; even one's own identity is not certifiable in such a world. On the other hand, shifts in philosophical positions do nothing to alleviate the arbitrariness and finality of biological facts such as his own potentially fatal heart condition. Finding no way to overcome such facts, and seeing no ultimate justification for any action, Andrews decides to blow up the Floating Opera with himself aboard during one of its performances. "*The Floating Opera* is not merely an account of Todd's Hamlet-like musings," *Dictionary of Literary Biography* contributor Arthur D. Casciato relates. Citing Andrews from within the narrative, Casciato elaborates, "the story is 'fraught with curiosities, melodrama, spectacle, instruction, and entertainment.' Its digressive plot includes a grisly World War I foxhole scene in which Todd bayonets a German soldier, an adulterous *menage a trois,* and a hilariously complicated legal dispute complete with seventeen wills and 129 jars of human excrement." By the end of the story, Andrews "comes to the conclusion, by the same operation of reason, that there's no more reason to kill himself than not to kill himself; that indeed, there's no reason to do anything," Barth told Gado.

The End of the Road, as the second novel to treat nihilism according to Barth's plan, "would begin with the conclusion of the first as its premise but come to completely different conclusions—horrifying conclusions, where people who shouldn't die do die, where people are destroyed by their own and other people's ideas," the author explained to Gado. Andrews of *The Floating Opera* "reveals that he has only been able to move and act at all by adopting a series of masks," and he recognizes that the people in his life are equally inauthentic, notes Tanner. Jacob Homer of *The End of the Road* promotes these views to Rennie, the wife of Joe Morgan, "a fanatical ideologue whose philosophical wrestling match" against Homer "ends disastrously," Joseph reports. Morgan, who has married Rennie because he can make her a disciple of his ethical system, deliberately introduces her to Homer "as an ethical experiment," to quote from the novel. Homer undermines Rennie's faith in her husband's authenticity, then sleeps with her. She conceives a child who may be either Morgan's or Homer's, then decides to have an abortion. Barth's all-pervasive humor dismisses "the ordinary moral and psychological implications" of these events, says Beverly Gross in the *Chicago Review.* But then, the novel "repudiates itself, or rather it repudiates what would seem to be its glib ability to deal with, and therefore dismiss, ugliness, pain, and despair" when Rennie chokes to death on her own vomit during the abortion. "Rennie's hemorrhaging corpse cannot be transformed into comedy, nor does Barth try. That is the second stage of undercutting: having reduced everything to comedy," Barth exposes humor's inadequacy, maintains Gross. Barth repeats this strategy in other books, "working steadily against an initial premise or turning a literary tradition against itself," Gado notes.

The premise destroyed at the end of *The Sot-Weed Factor* is the radical innocence of the seventeenth-century poet Ebenezer Cooke. At the outset of this mock-epic, Cooke determines to remain a virgin but later finds that he must consummate his marriage to a whore and contract her social disease if he is to regain his estate from her in the morally and politically corrupt colony of Maryland. Cooke's tutor and ethical opposite, Henry Burlingame, promotes an unbridled sexuality and radical cynicism perhaps no more viable than the virgin poet's innocence, remarks *Saturday Review* contributor Granville Hicks, who relates that Burlingame's impotence is one of many ironies in the book. In *Forum-Service,* Leslie Fiedler notes that Barth "distorts the recognitions and reversals of popular literature, first in the direction of travesty and then of nightmare: . . . the tomahawked and drowned corpses in one chapter revive in the next. Yet somehow the parody remains utterly serious, the farce and melodrama evoke terror and pity, and the flagrant mockery of a happy ending constricts the heart. And all the while one *laughs,* at a pitch somewhere between hysteria and sheer delight. The book is a joke book, an endless series of gags. But the biggest joke of all is that Barth seems finally to have written something closer to the 'Great American Novel' than any other book of the last decade." In a *Book Week* poll, two hundred literary professionals confirmed this estimate by listing *The Sot-Weed Factor* among the twenty best novels written between 1945 and 1965.

Among the book's achievements is a plot more complicated and more completely resolved than that of *Tom Jones,* many critics observe. Moreover, as Joseph Featherstone quips in a *New Republic* review, Barth "pinch[es] the behind of Bawd history." Others remark that he proves himself a competent pasticheur of eighteenth-century literature from *Don Quixote* and *Candide* to *Tristram Shandy* and *Fanny Hill.* In Fiedler's view, *The Sot-Weed Factor* is "no mere pastiche, but a piece of ingenious linguistic play, a joyous series of raids on half-forgotten resources of the language, largely obscene." "At one point in the book," Tanner says, "two women exchange terms of sexual abuse for seven pages. Ludicrous as a piece of history, this minor verbal gesture reflects a major mood of the book, namely the dominance of words over things. . . . Like these good ladies, or rather the author behind them, you can call each fact a hundred names—indeed, you can proliferate names quite independently of facts. . . . The substantiality of fact melts away as we watch him at his brilliant rhetorical play."

Surely, "the notion of any serious historical inquiry is undermined" in *The Sot-Weed Factor,* Tanner maintains; the book reminds us that American history is the result of "storytelling," one of "our attempts to name and control the world around us," McConnell concurs. Furthermore, "for Heide Ziegler, *The Sot-Weed Factor* is, 'a, or even *the,* decisive landmark in the development of postmodern fiction,' since it marks a 'shift in commitment from the realm of reality to the realm of the imagination,' " *Contemporary Authors Bibliographical Series* contributor Joseph Weixlmann writes in a commentary on Ziegler's *Amerikastudien* essay. "Ziegler insists that, by treating both fictional and 'historical' events as stories, Barth deconstructs the traditional notion of reality and provides for its reconstruction on his own terms."

Barth indeed reinvents the universe, making it a University, in *Giles, Goat-Boy; or, The Revised New Syllabus.* With it, he "became a key figure in what was seen by many critics as a revolt against realism in the . . . American novel of the 1960's," David Lodge indicates in the *Times Literary Supplement.* This revolt, says Gado, is "the most fundamental revolution in fiction in the last two hundred years." In a *Wisconsin Studies* interview with John Enck, Barth said he set out to write a "comic Old Testa-

ment," or "souped-up Bible" after reviewers had alerted him to parallels between Ebenezer Cooke and the archetypal hero of world mythology. In preparation, Barth studied the works of comparative mythologists who had seen certain events and conditions recur in the life stories of many ritual heroes. These events include a period of testing and a descent into the dark underworld to achieve immortality for oneself and sometimes for others—a sequence symbolic of the stages of development common to every human life, Campbell suggests. Giles "was for better or worse the conscious and ironic orchestration" of this archetype, the author discloses in *Chimera,* which would further exploit ritual hero myths.

In this "wildly rambunctious" novel, as *New York Times Book Review* contributor Guy Davenport describes it, George Giles, raised as the goat Billy Bockfuss, sets out to become the savior, or Grand Tutor, of his world. "The narrative requires Giles to work out a viable ethical position for himself and his potential tutees" and to descend into the belly of the computer that controls the University to either Pass or Fail, Robert Scholes sums up in the *New York Times Book Review.* "[Giles] first tries the two extremes of ethical absolutism, maintaining on one tour of the campus that good and evil are totally separate, and on another that they are indistinguishable. When both of these doctrines have disastrous results, he is forced to a third position, in which he sees the problem as too subtle for formulation," says Scholes in his synopsis. Along the way, Barth supplies "sometimes sacrilegious imitations and distortions of . . . demigod heroes from Dionysius and Oedipus to Moses and Christ," McConnell notes. Tanner suggests that "it is perhaps another of Barth's ironies that it has taken over 700 pages to bring his hero to a realization that truth lies beyond terms."

If Barth debunks all orthodoxies and academic guideposts in *Giles,* as Scholes's study *The Fabulators* states, he also undercuts his own authority by enclosing the text in a frame of introductory publisher's and author's disclaimers, and several endnotes that question the testament's validity. Tanner comments, "We become aware of a writer going to perverse lengths . . . not only to demonstrate what he can invent—and that is prodigious—but to demonstrate how he can equivocate about, trivialize, and undermine his own inventions." The book's point, Gross speculates, is "to expose the fraudulence of [narrative] art."

Giles was Barth's first commercial success. Sales of his "souped-up Bible" doubled and redoubled the combined sales of previous books, which had brought him critical acclaim and a largely academic underground following, but only modest financial rewards. The widespread popularity of *Giles* seemed to generate a tidal wave of good fortune for Barth, who received a formal recognition for achievement in fiction from Brandeis University's Creative Arts Commission and a $2,500 grant from the National Institute of Arts and Letters. Doubleday capitalized on the new momentum and reissued Barth's complete works to date, but not before their author had trimmed and polished *The End of the Road* and *The Sot-Weed Factor* and restored the ending of *The Floating Opera.* Back in 1955, the young author had rewritten the ending of the manuscript to satisfy an editor in order to see the book published, but the amendment had displeased the critics. The 1967 edition contains the ending as it was originally conceived.

"The Literature of Exhaustion," also published in 1967, increased Barth's fame. The seminal essay, first printed in the *Atlantic,* has been "reprinted, quoted, and 'explained' by any number of critics and teachers anxious to clarify and celebrate the fiction, not only of Barth, but of his contemporaries," McConnell reports. It was often misunderstood, claims Barth in a later essay, "The Literature of Replenishment." Perceived as another "death of the novel" treatise akin to the statements of Louis D. Rubin, Susan Sontag, and others, it was actually a state-of-the-art message that proposed various keys to the novel's survival in the face of exhausted possibilities. The misread essay, Barth goes on, "was really about . . . the effective 'exhaustion' not of language or literature, but of the aesthetic of high modernism: that admirable, not-to-be repudiated, but essentially completed 'program' " that had produced masterpieces of erudition and technique such as James Joyce's *Ulysses.* Speaking to Phyllis Meras of the *New York Times Book Review,* Barth explained, "the old masters of 20th-century fiction—especially [James] Joyce and [Franz] Kafka in their various ways—brought prose narrative to a kind of ultimacy." The next generation had not yet produced the work that would be the next stage in the genre's history, and critics had begun to talk of the art form's death. But "a few people—like Beckett and the Argentinian, Borges, and Nabokov, for example—have been able to turn this ultimacy against itself in order to produce new work," Barth told Meras. This view puts the novelist "in competition with the accumulated best of human history," and one response to this problem, Barth later remarked to Gado, "is to ignore it." Barth has instead found a number of ways to meet this challenge.

One way is "to write a novel about it," Barth's 1967 essay states. "Fiction" that aspires to become "part of the history of fiction," as Barth demonstrates in *The Friday Book,* "is almost always about itself," whatever else may be its concerns. Another way to go beyond the achievements of past novelists without repudiating their accomplishments, he adds, is to parody them. "Far from disowning a received way of doing something difficult, [parody] is meant to show rather that it can be done easily and for sport," Richard Poirier explains in his study of postmodern fiction, *The Performing Self.* The writer can also move out of realism (which has been outdone by cinema and electronic media) into irrealism, to bring fiction up to date with "painting, music, and . . . the age," Joe David Bellamy notes in *The New Fiction: Interviews with Innovative American Writers.* Another way to extend the life of the novel is to seize upon one of the last resources of originality left to the modern artist, "the voice, the authorial instrument that shapes the retelling," in Joseph's words; or, as Paul Gray of *Time* magazine puts it, "to exalt artifice and make the telling the subject of the tale." Such writing must be "comic about its own self-consciousness" to be interesting, Barth expressed to Bellamy in a *New American Review* interview. A writer can also revive an exhausted genre by going, as Barth often says, "back to the roots" of a tradition, or to the roots of storytelling itself, to discover unused possibilities or received stories that may be reshaped to fit his own purpose.

Barth's characters dramatize these solutions in *Lost in the Funhouse* and *Chimera,* two collections of shorter fiction that explore "the oral narrative tradition from which printed fiction evolved," according to his article, "Getting Oriented" in *The New York Times Book Review.* McConnell points out that "neither book is, finally, a 'collection.' Both are a series of tales which, in their order of telling and their explicit comments upon each other, are something like novels." When seen as novels, their "plot" is "what happens to the storyteller himself as he moves through the series" of related short stories and novellas.

The stories in *Funhouse* depict characters lost in the mazes of refracting and distorting mirrors and echo chambers; their confusions express "the condition of disorientation" that Barth identifies in "Getting Oriented" as his own "fictionary stock in trade. Intellectual and spiritual disorientation is the family disease of all my main characters—a disease usually complicated by ontological disorientation, since knowing where you're at is often contingent upon knowing who you are." Puetz relates this concern to contemporary views on personality. "The novel of the sixties has celebrated . . . the second coming of Proteus, the archetypal shape-shifter. . . . If change itself is the defining feature of human existence, the argument goes, then why not . . . become a whole spectrum of varying selves?" This shape-shifting, Tanner feels, brings Barth to an "impasse" in which the author "can no longer get hold of any 'reality' at all; everything he touches turns into fictions," or the sound of his own voice. "To find an exit from a world of self-generated fictions . . . demands an intense effort," Puetz writes. "The feasibility and the formal implications of such an effort as much as the increasing worries about the exit from the maze of fiction prove to be the opening themes of . . . *Funhouse* and *Chimera.*"

Chimera contains three novellas, the retellings of three myths whose heroes, like Barth, are in the process of reorientation to discern their future: Bellerophon, who learns that one does not become a hero by merely imitating heroes; Dunyazade, who, after witnessing countless permutations of narrative and sexual expression while stationed at the foot of her sister Scheherazade's bed, must make her future out of whatever is left; and Perseus, whose walk into the future takes him past the scenes of his life so far, depicted on the walls of his temple, which is shaped like a nautilus shell. Unlike a closed circle, the temple spirals outward, allowing Perseus to move forward by retracing his own history. Barth explained in the *Caliban* interview how the image further relates to his oeuvre: "When the chambered nautilus adds a new chamber to itself, that chamber is determined somewhat by its predecessors, but it's where the beast is living presently, and he's a larger animal for it." Each new room is a gnomon, "something you can *add* to an already existing figure to change its size without changing its basic shape." This structural principle, "and logarithmic spirals in general, winds through the *Chimera* novellas," says Barth, who points out in *The Friday Book* that the length of each novella is proportioned to the next one according to logarithmic measurements. This structure replicates "the way I like to think about my past, present, and future work," he says in the interview; in other words, each new novel will be his endeavor "to see what new changes I can ring around some old concerns without falling into complete self-parody." Though many reviewers see *Funhouse* and *Chimera* as proof that Barth has been swallowed up by his own self-conscious obsession, others concur with McConnell that the author's attempt "to write himself out of a corner" generally succeeds. Subsequent books, they maintain, demonstrate Barth's ability to invent new work by recycling traditional literature, and his own.

LETTERS—larger and more complex than its predecessors, "brilliant, witty . . . and damn near unreadable as well," to quote Peter S. Prescott of *Newsweek*—rehearses Barth's literary past in letters he ostensibly receives from characters in previous novels. At the same time, scholars note, it carries the author beyond the "impasse" of predominantly aesthetic concerns into the world of public events. *LETTERS* sums up the decade of the seventies along with Barth's collected works, observes Frederick R. Karl in his *American Fictions, 1940-1980: A Comprehensive History and Critical Evaluation.* Because the book "put[s] the weight of the past on every present activity" and offers the War of 1812 as "the major clue to American history," Karl deems it "invaluable" as a cultural document despite complexities that bar a general readership. Writing in the *Washington Post Book World,* Tanner praises a plot that intertwines plots from the lives of his previous characters with plots brought forward from the American Revolution, further braided with plots "which are active in contemporary America" relevant to "a 'second revolution.'" *LETTERS,* says Benjamin De Mott in an *Atlantic* review "is by turns a brain-buster, a marathon, an exasperation, a frustration, a provocation to earnest thought. Barth is preaching, wittily but with total conviction, on the limits of our kind, on the sanity of doubting that we know where, in our lives, fiction stops."

"A condensed overview cannot begin to suggest the wealth of stories and word play, the complications and correspondences that 'Letters' affords," claims Prescott, who lists among the book's embellishments "all manner of alphabetical, anagrammatical, and numerological games." For example, as Thomas R. Edwards notes in the *New York Times Book Review,* the first letters of the book's epistles, when arranged on a calendar for the dates on which they were composed, "spell out the story's secret subtitle . . . in a shape that itself spells out 'LETTERS'!" Such devices, claims Karl, disclose "the anagrammatic quality not only of a given work but of an entire career," an intricate pattern from which the author struggles to break free. "He announces that he would like to . . . re-establish the cordial relations once enjoyed between the novel and 'reality,' whether psychologically, sexually, socially, or politically understood. The book is really about mid-life crisis," McConnell concludes in a *Books & Arts* review, "the mid-life crisis of literature itself, of Western (particularly American) civilization, and of John Barth, middle-aged novelist." McConnell believes that "this self-confrontation at mid-career may be the single finest achievement of this exceptionally fine, very important book." Many other reviews were not as complimentary. *LETTERS* "received a very poor press," reports Karl, who esteems it "with all its excesses, an uncanny fiction, a capping of Barth's career and the entire postwar era."

The Friday Book: Essays and Other Nonfiction is "required reading for any serious student of Barth's canon," Weixlmann says. Its contents constitute "a resume of my Stories" from *The Floating Opera* to *The Tidewater Tales: A Novel* "and an account of what I believe I have been up to in writing them," Barth says in the introduction to one of its pieces. The book begins with "Some Reasons Why I Tell the Stories I Tell . . . ," an essay that reveals the elements of his personal history that have become part of his unique aesthetic. His books "tend to come in pairs" because he was born an opposite-sex twin. "In myth, twins signified whatever dualisms a culture entered: . . . good/evil, creation/destruction, what had they." In Western culture, he explains, they signify the divided or alienated self in search of the missing half. Thus he is a writer "in part because I no longer have my twin to be wordless with." And since twins share "a language before . . . and beyond speech," they acquire language primarily for "dealing with the outsiders," a factor that explains why Barth is "perhaps unnaturally conscious" of language, "forever at it, tinkering, foregrounding it." If being a twin underscored life's dualities, living in the landscape of tidewater Maryland where borders are always shifting blurred the distinctions between them. Barth remarks, "Your web-foot amphibious marsh-nurtured writer will likely by mere reflex regard many conventional boundaries and distinctions as arbitrary, fluid, negotiable: form versus content, realism versus irrealism, fact versus fiction, life versus art." The unimpeded flatness of the marshland, he claims, partly accounts for his drive to become distinguished at something.

As a young man with this goal in mind, Barth went to the Juilliard School of Music in New York to become a famous jazz arranger. Instead, he found himself a talented amateur among professionals, and "went home to think of some other way to become distinguished." There he discovered he had won a

scholarship to Johns Hopkins University and accepted it. As an undergraduate, he filed books in the Classics Department and the stacks of the Oriental seminary, and became enchanted with the tenth-century Sanskrit *Ocean of Story* and Richard Burton's annotated *Arabian Nights*—two reservoirs of frame-tale literature that were to inspire him throughout his career. Barth is particularly moved by Scheherazade, whose tales told at night to her misogynist ruler prevented him from executing her in the morning. She is, he says in "Getting Oriented," a fit metaphor for "the condition of narrative artists in general and of artists who work on University campuses in particular," who must literally "publish or perish." Her example also suggested to him several ways to survive twentieth-century pressures on the novel, and a justification for writing self-reflexive fiction. As he reasons in *The Friday Book,* "We tell stories and listen to them because we live stories and live in them. Narrative equals language equals life: To cease to narrate . . . is to die. . . . If this is true, then not only is all fiction fiction about fiction, but all fiction about fiction is in fact fiction about life."

Barth graduated with a commitment to become a writer and meanwhile earn a living by teaching, a choice he came to by means of "passionate default or heartfelt lack of alternatives." He has taught at Pennsylvania State University, the State University of New York at Buffalo, and at his alma mater. Partly due to these affiliations, Barth has been called an academic writer. Though he resisted this label at first, his mid-life orientation brought him to recognize, as he says in "Getting Oriented," that all of his novels are about education—or rather, "imperfect or misfired education." In *Harper's,* he writes, "There is chalk dust on the sleeve of my soul. . . . I have never been away from classrooms for longer than a few months. . . . I believe I know my strengths and limitations as a teacher the way I know them as a writer: doubtful of my accomplishments in both metiers, I am not doubtful at all that they are my metiers, for good or ill." However, Barth remains an arranger at heart, as he says in *The Friday Book,* and his "chief pleasure is to take a received melody—an old narrative poem, a classical myth, a shopworn literary convention . . .—and, improvising like a jazzman within its contraints, reorchestrating it to its present purpose."

With *Sabbatical: A Romance,* Barth "resume[s] a romance with realism," he intimates to Suplee. Shorter than previous novels and less obsessed with comments on his craft, the book stresses certain apocalyptic elements that Barth has carried from the beginning. "Todd Andrews in 'The Floating Opera' (and again in 'Letters') wonders sentence by sentence whether his heart will carry him from subject to predicate; in 'Sabbatical,' set on Chesapeake Bay in 1980, the background question is whether the world will end before the novel does," Barth states in the *New York Times Book Review.* On their sabbatical, narrator-protagonists Fenwick Turner and Susan Seckler cruise to the Caribbean and return to Chesapeake Bay. The possibly CIA-related death of Fenwick's twin brother is one of several mysteries they encounter along the way, and "the story fills up with the rough contemporary world," Michael Wood relates in the *New York Times Book Review.* In fact, the book "was occasioned" by the mysterious death of ex-CIA official John Paisley, whose corpse was found in Barth's "home waters" in 1978, as he told Suplee. Suplee notes, "This literal intrusion of the real world becomes a ditto in the novel: Barth simply reprints 20 pages of Paisley stories from *The Baltimore Sun.*"

Sabbatical nonetheless retains some familiar Barth trademarks, notes Charles Trueheart in a *Washington Post Book World* review. It "is the record of its own composition" and "Fenn and Susan argue incessantly about the proper way to tell the story

. . . and remind one another of the literary traditions into which their narrative falls." John W. Aldridge, also writing in the *Washington Post Book World,* approves Barth's new tack toward realism: "While to be sure the story does contain elements indicating that the familiar temporizing mind of John Barth is still hard at work, they are effectively subordinated to the strong realistic thrust of the narrative and so provide the book with an agreeable controlled complexity instead of burying it beneath the old fog-bank of endless equivocation."

By design, *Tidewater Tales: A Novel* was to be "a sort of opposite-sex twin to *Sabbatical,*" featuring a married couple afloat on the same bay, whose situation, Barth reveals in *The Friday Book,* was to be "rather the reverse of Fenwick's and Susan's." Whereas Susan of *Sabbatical* wonders how she can bring children into the world at this late hour and aborts twins, Katharine Sagamore of *Tidewater Tales* happily carries and delivers twins, not fully knowing what to make of the fact that people still desire to procreate in a threatened world. Again, two lines of interest develop: one, a plot entangled with the problematical real world on the verge of apocalypse; and the other, related to stories from classical literature that parallel the Sagamore's voyage. Toronto *Globe & Mail* reviewer Douglas Hill praises the book's "dizzying . . . manipulations of literary forms and traditions." Aldridge concurs that it is the "richest, most ebullient and technically daring" of Barth's canon to date, "crowded" as it is "with grand virtuosic effects that seem to have nothing to do with the action except to interrupt it, . . . offered simply because they are such fun." The stories of Odysseus, Don Quixote, Scheherazade, Huck Finn, and more resurface here, their retelling facilitated by events in the realistic narrative. Some reviewers find the tales improved in the retelling while others, such as *New York Times Book Review* contributor William Pritchard, are less enamored. Pritchard qualifies his opinion by saying that "Barth gives ample food to please or displease everyone's taste." Moved by the book's "richness as a love story—marital, filial, domestic—and also its love of a place, of a country, even as place and country are scarred by human depredations," Pritchard leaves it to the reader to decide "whether the novel's ending—or its various coves and shallows sailed into along the way—give us something more rich and strange than a funhouse."

"Barth has now written the same novel twice," using materials already employed in previous works, notes *Los Angeles Times Book Review* contributor Richard Lehan, who wonders what kind of work can follow. More nonfiction, perhaps; or fiction that investigates "the way that evil comes into being and how we best cope with it," a theme suggested in *Sabbatical* and *Tidewater Tales.* Barth speculated to Israel Shenker for the *New York Times Book Review,* "Maybe when I'm 90 I'll be as grave as Sophocles at 90. More likely, Zeus willing, I'll be writing comedy in my 80's as Thomas Mann did, and die laughing."

In any case, Barth has parlayed his talents into a permanent place in literary history; commentary proliferates in the wake of each new offering from Barth, and criticism of his entire oeuvre shows no signs of abatement, according to a *Mississippi Quarterly* overview by Charles B. Harris. As of 1986, writes Walkiewicz, "Barth's 'significance,' his place in the tradition remain, of course, matters very much under consideration or open to debate." Poirier explains why that place is not clear; he allows that Barth is "perhaps more intellectually attuned, . . . and surely more philosophically adroit than all but a few of the exclusively literary critics now writing in America or Europe." At the same time, however, Poirier goes on to observe, "admiration for [his] thinking about literature must very often contend with the experience of reading [his] novels. . . . We sit in a favorite chair . . .

and we open, let us say, *Giles, Goat-Boy.* Several days later we're probably no longer infatuated with repeated illustrations that literary and philosophical structures are really put-ons, and that what we are doing is kind of silly."

"While there are those who, as always, are of the opinion that [Barth] has reduced the art of fiction to the chronicling 'of minstrel misery,' there are also many who are willing to affirm that he has added a number of 'minstrel masterpieces' . . . to the treasury," Walkiewicz notes. He adds that "if Barth has earned the high praise he . . . has received from some, if he deserves to be called the 'best writer of fiction we have at present, and one of the best we have ever had,' it is because he has given form and substance to a body of work that is traditional, contemporary, and trail-blazing, consistent and evolutionary, self-affirming and self-questioning, that acknowledges contradictions and contrarieties and enlists them in the service of art and humanity." Weixlmann comments, "Barth has, on various occasions, indicated that the true measure of his authorial success will not be taken for decades, even centuries; that his attempt, as a writer, is to rival Shakespeare and Cervantes rather than his contemporaries. In this context, Barth scholarship is in its infancy, despite the fact that much serious critical attention has already been focused on his work." Barth criticism has itself become the subject of several compendiums, including *Critical Essays on John Barth* by Joseph J. Waldmeir. In one essay collected by Waldmeir, Richard W. Noland concludes that Barth's "most interesting and important achievement [as of 1966] is the embodiment of philosophical ideas in a form both tragic and comic. . . . He considers each of the ways in which Western man has attempted to fill his life with value after the death of the old gods . . . only to find all of them inadequate." All inadequate, perhaps, except for storytelling, Josephine Hendin contends in *Harper's.* Her survey of Barth's work as far as *Chimera* distills Barth's message that "storytelling is life's means and only prize. And no one has written more glitteringly than John Barth of the worthlessness of the heart, or the great munificence of language in bestowing so much grandeur, so much richness, so many pearly epigrams on all us swine."

MEDIA ADAPTATIONS: The End of the Road was made into a film.

BIOGRAPHICAL/CRITICAL SOURCES:

BOOKS

Adams, Robert Martin, *After Joyce: Studies in Fiction after "Ulysses,"* Oxford University Press, 1977.

Allen, Mary, *The Necessary Blankness: Women in Major American Fiction of the Sixties,* University of Illinois Press, 1976.

Authors in the News, Gale, Volumes 1 and 2, 1976.

Baldwin, Kenneth H. and David K. Kirby, editors, *Individual and Community: Variations on a Theme in American Fiction,* Duke University Press, 1975.

Barth, John, *The Floating Opera,* Appleton-Century-Crofts, 1956, reprinted, 1988.

Barth, *The End of the Road,* Doubleday, 1958, revised edition, 1967, reprinted, 1988.

Barth, *The Sot-Weed Factor,* Doubleday, 1960, reprinted, 1988.

Barth, *Lost in the Funhouse: Fiction for Print, Tape, Live Voice,* Doubleday, 1968, reprinted, 1988.

Barth, *Chimera,* Random House, 1972.

Barth, *LETTERS,* Putnam, 1979.

Barth, *The Friday Book: Essays and Other Nonfiction,* Putnam, 1984.

Bellamy, Joe David, *The New Fiction: Interviews with Innovative American Writers,* University of Illinois Press, 1974.

Bergonzi, Bernard, *The Situation of the Novel,* University of Pittsburgh Press, 1970.

Bryant, Jerry, *The Open Decision: The Contemporary American Novel and its Intellectual Background,* Free Press, 1970.

Caramello, Charles, *Silverless Mirrors: Self and Postmodern American Fiction,* University Presses of Florida, 1983.

Contemporary Authors Bibliographical Series, Volume 1: *American Novelists,* Gale, 1986.

Contemporary Literary Criticism, Gale, Volume 1, 1973, Volume 2, 1974, Volume 3, 1975, Volume 5, 1976, Volume 7, 1977, Volume 9, 1978, Volume 10, 1979, Volume 14, 1980, Volume 27, 1984, Volume 51, 1988.

Dembo, L. S. and Cyrena N. Pondrom, editors, *The Contemporary Writer,* University of Wisconsin Press, 1972.

D'Haen, Theo, *Text to Reader: a Communicative Approach to Fawles, Barth, Cartazar, and Boon,* John Benjamins, 1983.

Dictionary of Literary Biography, Volume 2: *American Novelists since World War II,* Gale, 1978.

Gado, Frank, *First Person: Conversations an Writers and Writing,* Union College Press, 1973.

Gardner, John, *On Moral Fiction,* Basic Books, 1978.

Harris, Charles B., *Contemporary American Novelists of the Absurd,* College and University Press, 1971.

Harris, *Passionate Virtuosity: The Fiction of John Barth,* University of Illinois Press, 1983.

Hassan, Ihab, *The Dismemberment of Orpheus,* Oxford University Press, 1971.

Hauck, Richard Boyd, *A Cheerful Nihilism: Confidence and "The Absurd" in American Humorous Fiction,* Indiana University Press, 1971.

Hipkiss, Robert A., *The American Absurd: Pynchon, Vonnegut, and Barth,* Associated Faculty Press, 1984.

Hyman, Stanley Edgar, *Standards: A Chronicle of Books for Our Time,* Horizon, 1966.

Joseph, Gerhard, *John Barth,* University of Minnesota Press, 1970.

Karl, Frederick R., *American Fictions, 1940-1980: A Comprehensive History and Critical Evaluation,* Harper, 1983.

Kennard, Jean E., *Number and Nightmare,* Archon, 1975.

Klinkowitz, Jerome, *Literary Disruptions: The Making of a Post-Contemporary American Fiction,* University of Illinois Press, 1975.

Klinkowitz, *Literary Subversions: New American Fiction and the Practice of Criticism,* Southern Illinois University Press, 1985.

Kostelanetz, Richard, editor, *American Writing Today,* Forum Books/Voice of America Editions, 1982.

Kostelanetz, editor, *On Contemporary Literature,* Avon, 1964.

McConnell, Frank D., *Four Postwar American Novelists: Bellow, Mailer, Barth, and Pynchon,* University of Chicago Press, 1976.

Morrell, David, *John Barth: An Introduction,* Pennsylvania State University Press, 1976.

Olderman, Raymond M., *Beyond the Waste Land: A Study of the American Novel in the Nineteen-Sixties,* Yale University Press, 1972.

Poirier, Richard, *The Performing Self,* Oxford University Press, 1971.

Porush, David, *The Soft Machine: Cybernetic Fiction,* Methuen, 1985.

Raban, Jonathan, *The Technique of Modern Fiction,* Edward Arnold, 1966.

Scholes, Robert, *The Fabulators,* Oxford University Press, 1967.

Schulz, Max F., *Black Humor Fiction of the Sixties: A Pluralistic Definition of Man and His World,* Ohio University Press, 1973.

Stark, John O., *The Literature of Exhaustion: Borges, Nabokov, Barth,* Duke University Press, 1974.

Tanner, Tony, *City of Words: American Fiction, 1950-1970,* Harper, 1971.

Tharpe, Jac, *John Barth: The Comic Sublimity of Paradox,* Southern Illinois University Press, 1974.

Tilton, John W., *Cosmic Satire in the Contemporary Novel,* Bucknell University Press, 1977.

Vidal, Gore, *Matters of Fact and Fiction: Essays, 1973-1976,* Random House, 1977.

Vine, Richard Allan, *John Barth: An Annotated Bibliography,* Scarecrow, 1977.

Waldmeir, Joseph J., editor, *Critical Essays on John Barth,* G. K. Hall, 1980.

Walkiewicz, E. P., *John Barth,* G. K. Hall, 1986.

Weixlmann, Joseph, *John Barth: A Bibliography,* Garland Publishing, 1976.

Werner, Craig Hansen, *Paradoxical Resolutions: American Fiction since Joyce,* University of Illinois Press, 1982.

Ziegler, Heide and Christopher Bigsby, editors, *The Radical Imagination and the Liberal Tradition: Interviews with English and American Novelists,* Junction, 1982.

PERIODICALS

America, September 17, 1966, November 26, 1966, October 7, 1972, November 18, 1972.

Amerikastudien, Volume 25, number 2, 1980.

Antioch Review, spring, 1980, fall, 1982.

Atlantic, August, 1967, July 1968, October, 1968, October, 1972, November, 1979, June, 1982.

Best Sellers, October 1, 1966, October 15, 1968, November 1, 1973.

Books & Arts, October 26, 1979.

Books and Bookmen, April, 1967, November, 1968.

Book Week, September 26, 1965, August 7, 1966.

Buffalo Courier Express Magazine, September 12, 1976.

Caliban, Volume 12, 1975.

Chicago Review, winter-spring, 1959, November, 1968.

Chicago Tribune, August 21, 1960, September 15, 1968, June 7, 1987.

Chicago Tribune Book World, November 11, 1979, May 30, 1982, January 13, 1985.

Contemporary Literature, winter, 1971, winter, 1981.

Criticism, winter, 1970.

Critique, fall, 1963, winter, 1965-66, Volume 9, number 1, 1966, Volume 13, number 3, 1972, Volume 17, number 1, 1975, Volume 18, number 2, 1976.

Detroit News, September 17, 1972, September 30, 1979.

Encounter, June, 1967.

Esquire, October, 1979.

Forum-Service, January 7, 1961.

Globe & Mail (Toronto), September 3, 1966, January 26, 1985, July 4, 1987.

Harper's, September, 1972, September, 1973, November, 1986.

Harrisburg Patriot (Pennsylvania), March 30, 1965.

Hudson Review, autumn, 1967, spring, 1969, winter, 1972-73.

Illustrated London News, April 8, 1967.

Journal of Narrative Technique, winter, 1978, winter, 1981.

Listener, March 30, 1967, October 3, 1968, September 18, 1969.

London Magazine, May, 1967, December, 1969.

Los Angeles Times Book Review, November 18, 1984, June 28, 1987.

Massachusetts Review, May, 1960.

Mississippi Quarterly, spring, 1979.

Modern Fiction Studies, winter, 1968-69, spring, 1973, autumn, 1974, summer, 1976, summer, 1979.

MOSAIC: A Journal for the Study of Literature and Ideas, Volume 3, number 2, 1970, fall, 1974.

Nation, November 19, 1960, September 5, 1966, October 28, 1968, December 18, 1972, October 13, 1979.

National Observer, August 1, 1966, August 29, 1966, September 16, 1968, February 23, 1970, October 7, 1972.

National Review, December 3, 1968, October 13, 1972.

New American Review, April, 1972.

New Leader, February 13, 1961, March 2, 1964, April 12, 1965.

New Republic, September 3, 1966, November 23, 1968, December 1, 1979.

New Statesman, October 13, 1961, March 31, 1967, September 19, 1969, July 19, 1974.

Newsweek, August 8, 1966, December 19, 1966, September 30, 1968, February 16, 1970, October 9, 1972, January 1, 1973, October 1, 1979, May 24, 1982.

New Yorker, December 10, 1966, September 30, 1972, December 31, 1979, June 7, 1982.

New York Herald Tribune Book Review, July 20, 1958, September 26, 1965.

New York Review of Books, August 18, 1966, October 19, 1972, July 15, 1976, December 20, 1979, June 10, 1982.

New York Times, August 3, 1966, November 21, 1967, October 16, 1968, February 9, 1969, February 11, 1970, March 18, 1970, November 21, 1970, September 20, 1972, October 1, 1979, May 27, 1982, June 28, 1982.

New York Times Book Review, August 21, 1960, June 6, 1965, May 8, 1966, August 7, 1966, October 20, 1968, September 24, 1972, December 3, 1972, April 1, 1979, July 15, 1979, September 30, 1979, May 9, 1982, June 20, 1982, September 16, 1984, November 18, 1984, January 5, 1986, June 28, 1987.

Novel: A Forum on Fiction, October 20, 1968, winter, 1971, September 24, 1972, December 3, 1972, July 15, 1979, September 30, 1979.

Observer, October 10, 1965, April 2, 1967, September 29, 1968, September 14, 1969, July 21, 1974, May 29, 1977.

Partisan Review, winter, 1967, summer, 1968, spring, 1969, summer 1983.

Prairie Schooner, summer, 1969.

Publishers Weekly, October 22, 1979.

Punch, April 5, 1967, October 2, 1968.

Saturday Review, November 26, 1960, July 3, 1965, August 6, 1966, September 30, 1967, September 28, 1978, October 13, 1979.

South Atlantic Quarterly, summer, 1969.

Spectator, March 31, 1967, September 20, 1969, July 20, 1974, May 10, 1980, August 7, 1982.

Studies in Short Fiction, fall, 1973, fall, 1974, summer, 1975.

Time, July 21, 1958, September 5, 1960, February 12, 1965, May 17, 1967, September 27, 1968, February 23, 1970, October 2, 1972, October 8, 1979, May 31, 1982.

Times Literary Supplement, October 27, 1961, March 30, 1967, October 10, 1968, September 18, 1969, July 26, 1974, May 30, 1980, July 23, 1982.

Tri-Quarterly, winter, 1967, winter, 1968, spring, 1975, fall, 1981.

Twentieth Century Literature, April, 1973, December, 1975, December, 1976.

Virginia Quarterly Review, autumn, 1969, winter, 1972.

Washington Post, June 17, 1966, September 26, 1968, June 17, 1982.

Washington Post Book World, September 17, 1967, September 15, 1968, May 18, 1969, August 6, 1972, November 18, 1973, September 30, 1979, May 23, 1982, November 18, 1984, June 7, 1987.

Washington Post Potomac, September 3, 1967.

Wisconsin Studies in Contemporary Literature, winter, 1965, autumn, 1966.

*   *   *

BARTHELME, Donald   1931-1989

PERSONAL: Born April 7, 1931, in Philadelphia, Pa.; son of Donald (an architect) and Helen (Bechtold) Barthelme; married wife Birgit; married second wife, Marion; children: (first marriage) Anne Katharine.

ADDRESSES: Agent—Lynn Nesbit, International Creative Management, 40 West 57th St., New York, N.Y. 10019.

CAREER: Writer of short fiction and novels. Worked as a newspaper reporter for the *Houston Post;* managing editor of *Location,* an art and literature review; and director of Contemporary Arts Museum, Houston, Tex., 1961-62. Distinguished visiting professor of English, City College of the City University of New York, 1974-75; visiting professor at University of Houston, 1981—. *Military service:* U.S. Army, 1953-55; served in Korea and Japan.

MEMBER: American Academy and Institute of Arts and Letters, Authors League of America, Authors Guild, PEN.

AWARDS, HONORS: Guggenheim fellowship, 1966; *Time* magazine's Best Books of the Year list, 1971, for *City Life;* National Book Award for children's literature, 1972, for *The Slightly Irregular Fire Engine or the Hithering Thithering Djinn;* Morton Dauwen Zabel Award from the National Institute of Arts and Letters, 1972; Jesse H. Jones Award from Texas Institute of Letters, 1976, for *The Dead Father;* nominated for National Book Critics Circle Award, PEN/Faulkner Award for Fiction, *Los Angeles Times* Book Prize, all for *Sixty Stories,* all in 1982; "Basil From Her Garden" was included in *Prize Stories 1987: The O. Henry Awards;* Rea Award from Dungannon Foundation, 1988.

WRITINGS:

Come Back, Dr. Caligari (stories), Little, Brown, 1964.

Snow White (novel; first published in *New Yorker,* February 18, 1967), Atheneum, 1967.

Unspeakable Practices, Unnatural Acts (stories), Farrar, Straus, 1968.

City Life (stories), Farrar, Straus, 1970.

The Slightly Irregular Fire Engine or the Hithering Thithering Djinn (children's book), Farrar, Straus, 1971.

Sadness (stories), Farrar, Straus, 1972.

Guilty Pleasures (parodies and satire), Farrar, Straus, 1974.

The Dead Father (novel), Farrar, Straus, 1975.

Amateurs (stories), Farrar, Straus, 1976.

Great Days (stories; also see below), Farrar, Straus, 1979.

Sixty Stories (stories), Putnam, 1981.

Overnight to Many Distant Cities (stories), Putnam, 1983.

"Great Days" (play; based on his story of the same title), first produced off-Broadway at American Place Theater, 1983.

Paradise (novel), Putnam, 1986.

Forty Stories (stories), Putnam, 1987.

Regular contributor to *New Yorker.*

SIDELIGHTS: Donald Barthelme, widely acknowledged as the most original and influential American writer of short fiction since Ernest Hemingway, came to the short story after varied experience in the other arts. The son of an avant-garde architect, Barthelme grew up in Texas with a sense that his father was "something of an anomaly," a man whose concerns "were to say the least somewhat different from those of the other people we knew. His mind was elsewhere." In an interview collected in *The New Fiction: Interviews with Innovative American Writers,* Barthelme also told Jerome Klinkowitz that "in the late thirties my father built a house for us, something not too dissimilar to Mies's Tugendhat house. It was wonderful to live in but strange to see on the Texas prairie. On Sundays people used to park their cars on the street and stare."

Even after becoming a writer, Barthelme retained an interest in problems of physical structure and spatial design. "I could very cheerfully be a typographer," he told Klinkowitz, and the graphics in several stories in *City Life* and *Guilty Pleasures* and in his children's book, *The Slightly Irregular Fire Engine or the Hithering Thithering Djinn,* attest to his continuing fascination with the integration of older design into new structures he called "collages." Glossing his statement to Richard Schickel in the *New York Times Magazine* that "the principal of collage is the central principle of all art in the twentieth century in all media," Barthelme suggested to Klinkowitz that "New York City is or can be regarded as a collage, as opposed to, say, a tribal village in which all of the huts . . . are the same hut, duplicated. The point of collage is that unlike things are stuck together to make, in the best case, a new reality."

Before turning to short fiction, Barthelme wrote poetry, essays, and reviews for his high school and college newspapers and for the *Houston Post;* later, he served as editor of *Forum* and *Location* and, briefly, as the director of the Contemporary Arts Museum in Houston. His first published story, "The Darling Duckling at School" (later revised and reprinted as "Me and Miss Mandible"), did not appear until 1961, but by the end of 1963 he had published four stories in the *New Yorker,* a magazine which would become closely identified with and influenced by his work, and in 1964 his first book, *Come Back, Dr. Caligari,* appeared. Barthelme's critical success was immediate; popular success followed with his 1967 novel *Snow White,* which sold over 200,000 copies in paperback. Richard Gilman, in a representative statement reprinted in *The Confusion of Realms,* calls Barthelme "one of a handful of American writers who are working to replenish and extend the art of fiction instead of trying to add to the stock of entertainments, visions and human documents that fiction keeps piling up." Recognizing *Snow White* both as a retelling of a familiar story and as a meditation on the nature of fiction, scholars unite in characterizing Barthelme's work as self-reflexive, or centered on the art of writing itself. But Barthelme usually manages to escape the charges of elitism and obscurantism often leveled at such other self-reflexive writers as Ronald Sukenick and Raymond Federman.

Barthelme's critical reputation reached a peak with the 1970 publication of *City Life,* his most brilliant, audacious, and experimental collection of stories, which included the collages "At the Tolstoy Museum" and "Brain Damage." Thereafter his stories are less marked by spectacular technical effects, and a new strain becomes dominant. Beginning with the aptly titled collection *Sadness* and continuing in *Amateurs,* which J. D. O'Hara describes in his *Library Journal* review as a collection of stories "about lovers who are not very good at what they are doing," Barthelme's fiction is pervaded by a melancholy gaiety which,

together with his technical experimentation, has become his hallmark.

Although he is best known as a master of short fiction, Barthelme has also written three novels, *Snow White, The Dead Father,* and *Paradise,* all of which characteristically use mythic narratives as structures within which non-mythic characters, objects, and episodes strain at probability, break the rules of the given story, and otherwise compete for the audience's attention. The world of his fiction, despite widespread imitation, remains unique: it could never be mistaken for the world of any other writer or, for that matter, the world of Greenwich Village, where Barthelme lives and works, or for any other actual location. William H. Gass observes in *Fiction and the Figures of Life* that there is "nothing surrealistic about him, his dislocations are real, his material quite actual" but also acknowledges that each of Barthelme's books "has seemed unnatural: certainly none speaks." This sense of unnaturalness or unreality is produced by Barthelme's striking omissions. Regis Durand concludes in *Donald Barthelme* that "Barthelme's is an art of absences," and Lois Gordon elaborates this idea in her Twayne volume, *Donald Barthelme:* "He rejects traditional chronology, plot, character, time, space, grammar, syntax, metaphor, and simile, as well as the traditional distinctions between fact and fiction. What used to organize reality—time, space, and the structure of language—is now often disjointed, and *language,* and the difficulties in 'using' it, becomes the very subject of his art. Most obvious is . . . its refusal to be an orderly reflection of, and comment upon, a stable, external world."

Bizarre incidents abound in Barthelme's world: a thirty-five year old man is placed by some inexplicable error in a sixth-grade class, a woman attempts to open a car rental agency in a city whose every building is a church, the nonsense poet Edward Lear invites friends to witness his death. But such experiences are all pointedly disengaged from the voice that recounts them and from the audience's emotional sympathies. Even the characters in the stories take the wildest dislocations for granted. When King Kong, "now an adjunct professor of art history at Rutgers," breaks through a window in "The Patty," the guests simply utter "loud exclamations of fatigue and disgust, examining the situation in the light of their own needs and emotions, hoping that the ape was real or papier-mache according to their temperaments, or wondering whether other excitements were possible out in the crisp, white night." As Maurice Couturier notes in *Donald Barthelme,* the writer's idiom is marked by a "high degree of impersonality. . . . 'Sadness' and 'equanimity' appear to refer to essences which the characters accidentally happen to run across. Man is like a chance visitor in a world teeming with universals." Charles Molesworth, writing in *Donald Barthelme's Fiction: The Ironist Saved from Drowning,* agrees: "For the typical Barthelme character, it is just the variousness of the world that spells defeat, since the variety is both a form of plenitude and the sign of its absence. The realm of brand names, historical allusions, 'current events,' and fashionable topics exists in a world whose fullness results from the absence of any strong hierarchical sense of values, and the causal randomness of such things both blurs and signals how any appeal to a rigorous, ordering value system would be futile."

Underlying what Molesworth calls Barthelme's three chief subjects—"the futility of work in a post-industrial society, the emotional disorientation of divorce (in both literal and metaphoric terms), and the impotent double-mindedness of the artist"—many critics perceive a horrified fascination with the dreck of cultural disintegration: advertising slogans, facts from the public media, objects arrayed like trash on a junkpile, and opinions and actions unmoored from any system of belief that might give them meaning. Barthelme's contradictory attitude toward the cultural debris his work both celebrates and deplores is best revealed in an often-cited passage from *Snow White,* in which the "stuffing" of ordinary language is compared to trash by virtue of its leading qualities: "(1) an 'endless' quality and (2) a 'sludge' quality." The proportion of "stuffing" in language, the novel contends, is constantly increasing, like "the per-capita production of trash in this country," which "is up from 2.75 pounds per day in 1920 to 4.5 pounds per day in 1965 . . . and is increasing at the rate of about four percent a year. . . . We may very well reach a point where it's 100 percent. Now at such a point, you will agree, the question turns from a question of disposing of this 'trash' to a question of appreciating its qualities, because, after all, it's 100 percent, right? And there can no longer be any question of 'disposing' of it, because it's all there is, and we will simply have to learn to 'dig' it—that's slang, but peculiarly appropriate here."

Like the character who draws this analogy, Barthelme seems determined, as Gass and other critics observed, to place himself "on the leading edge of this trash phenomenon." Such a position is clearly perilous: even in his best stories, Barthelme is constantly in danger of being engulfed by the cultural dreck—second-hand language, second-hand beliefs, second-hand emotions—he invariably takes as his subject so that his world sometimes appears as a symptom of cultural malaise rather than a response to it. Noting that "anything dropped in the dreck *is* dreck, at once, as an uneaten porkchop mislaid in the garbage," Gass contends that Barthelme's work sometimes suffers from a lack of "seriousness about his subject," a seriousness which is necessary because "the idea is to *use* dreck, not write about it." Hence early critical discussion of Barthelme focused on the question of his relation to his subjects: was he celebrating or condemning the vacuous fragmentation of his characters' experience? How seriously did he take his material and his project?

In *Bright Book of Life: American Novelists and Story Tellers from Hemingway to Mailer,* Alfred Kazin relates Barthelme's revulsion from and dependence on cultural rubbish to the writer's equally contradictory attitude toward the institutions of form and subject behind his stories; Kazin describes Barthelme as an "antinovelist" who "operates by countermeasures only. . . . [He] is outside everything he writes in a way that a humorist like Perelman could never be. He is under the terrible discipline that the system inflicts on those who are most fascinated with its relentlessness."

Such critical judgments, however, give no indication of the exhilarating quality of Barthelme's best writing, the sheer comic exuberance found in "The Falling Dog," "The Sandman," "The Abduction from the Seraglio," or dozens of other stories. Because his work is frequently strongest when his satire is laced with parody, as in "Robert Kennedy Saved from Drowning," his funniest stories are often his most effective, and even his simplest parodies have an ambiguous edge. When Barthelme collected two dozen of his parodies and other fugitive pieces in *Guilty Pleasures,* the critical consensus was that the collection was slighter than his earlier volumes but not so much slighter as to constitute a different kind of writing. The publication of *Guilty Pleasures* ten years earlier might well have proclaimed Barthelme simply a gifted mimic and parodist. By 1974, most reviewers recognized the essential continuity between Barthelme the essayist and the writer of short stories. In both cases he takes off from a series of artifacts or voices of modern culture and elaborates, exaggerates, or propounds implications, which seldom have more than a passing relation with the empathetic characters and revelatory plots of more traditional stories.

The 1981 publication of *Sixty Stories,* a collection of previously printed works, corresponded with a turning point in Barthelme's career and in the critical reception of his work. Within a twelve-month period, three books and many scholarly articles on Barthelme appeared. The earlier critical debate over whether his ironic stance made him a master manipulator or simply another casualty of the cultural debris he catalogued assumed another form. Academic critics who regarded Barthelme's mastery of his material as self-evident asked whether his affinities were with post-modernists like Vladimir Nabokov and John Barth, as earlier critics had assumed, or with more conservative modernists like Joseph Conrad and James Joyce, whose work had embodied a specifically moral criticism of social reality. These critics addressed a central question: Does Barthelme primarily criticize or celebrate modern culture?

Jerome Klinkowitz, the foremost proponent of the former view, writes in *Literary Disruptions: The Making of a Post-Contemporary American Fiction* that Barthelme is a "counterrevolutionary" who opposes "the new language of technology and manipulation with pleas for old-fashioned interest and imagination. In a new world, old values must be expressed in new form." Charles Molesworth agrees that "Barthelme's work can be read as an attack on the false consciousness generated by meretricious sources of information that are accepted as commonplace in the modern, technologized, urban society of mass man." But he adds, "This is . . . to read the stories as more morally pointed than they are intended." For Molesworth, "The stories are built with a divided consciousness that says first of all that all the formats of information and narrative are compromised, if not actively corrupt. The possible response is then twofold: either use these available formats since the audience is reachable by no other, or demonstrate by a parodic 'de-creation' of the formats that no real binding or altering force is left to the narrative imagination in today's world."

In *The Metafictional Muse: The Works of Robert Coover, Donald Barthelme, and William H. Gass,* Larry McCaffery similarly distinguishes Barthelme's irony from that of the modernists: "If there is a sense of optimism in his work, it does not derive from the familiar modernist belief that art offers the possibility of escape from the disorders of the modern world or that art can change existing conditions; Barthelme overtly mocks these beliefs along with most other modern credos. Instead Barthelme posits a less lofty function for art with his suggestion that it is valuable simply because it gives man a chance to create a space in which the deadening effects of ordinary living can be momentarily defied." Regis Durand goes still further in arguing that "Barthelme is and is not an ironist": "He is, inasmuch as through various personae and fictional voices and garbs he plays the game of dressing up with nimble versatility. He is not, in the sense that his constantly shifting positions are no longer linked to a 'fundamental I' but only to an endless displacement. Where irony preserves a fixed point of reference, humour describes what happens in the post-modernist text when the core vanishes." Durand distinguishes Barthelme's irony in "Robert Kennedy Saved from Drowning" from "the confident irony of modernism, which never stops believing in its own power, even when at its grimmest" by urging that Barthelme's work calls into question "not simply the failure to decipher and narrate the subject or referent (the hypothetical 'Robert Kennedy'), but the activity of reference itself." What therefore is "at stake is a radical questioning of the symbolic process itself."

Other critics have applied a variety of labels to Barthelme in an attempt to place him accurately in the context of contemporary fiction. Alfred Kazin calls him an "antinovelist"; Frederick R.

Karl a "minimalist"; Jack Hicks and Larry McCaffery, a "meta-fictionist." Molesworth, titling him "perhaps the final post-Enlightenment writer," locates him on the frontier between modernism and post-modernism: "An absurdist like [Samuel] Beckett maintains the world is fundamentally ambiguous, whereas a playful surrealist like [Richard] Brautigan suggests it is ambivalent. For Barthelme, it is both. . . . Nowhere does Barthelme's fiction wholly reject or wholly assent to the contemporary world. The world is always subject in these stories to an endless figuration, to unceasing impulses toward romance and fantasy. So if narrative doesn't adequately or accurately reflect the world, it doesn't bow down before it either."

Sixty Stories encourages such generalizations about Barthelme's career because it presents most of his best writing over a period of nearly twenty years. Always a severe critic of his own work, an author who continues to revise his fiction even after its publication, Barthelme excluded stories which were slight, like "The Joker's Greatest Triumph"; modish, like "Edward and Pia"; or merely obscure, like "Bone Bubbles." With one notable exception ("Engineer-Private Paul Klee Misplaces an Aircraft between Milbertshofen and Cambrai, March 1916"), he chose to reprint all of his most successful stories: "Me and Miss Mandible," "A Shower of Gold," "The Indian Uprising," "Robert Kennedy Saved from Drowning," "Views of My Father Weeping," "Kierkegaard Unfair to Schlegel," "Daumier," "Nothing: A Preliminary Account," "A Manual for Sons," "At the End of the Mechanical Age," and "The Abduction from the Seraglio." Taken as a body, the work collected in *Sixty Stories* suggests a definite pattern to Barthelme's career. The stories from *Come Back, Dr. Caligari* represent preparatory efforts in which Barthelme's distinctive voice is often obscured by a tendency to random cataloguing and aimless clowning quite different from the pointed clowning and cataloguing of the later work. In early stories like "Florence Green Is 81" and "The Big Broadcast of 1938," Barthelme constructs what Gass calls "a single plane of truth, of relevance, of style, of value—a flatland junkyard." Like the later "Edward and Pia" and "City Life," for which it is clearly a preparation, "Will You Tell Me?" attempts to dramatize the banality of modern urban life by presenting a series of uninflected observations and events: a love affair, a trip to Canada, the loss of ten thousand dollars, and a list of people who have not written letters that morning are all described with the same deadpan economy. Such stories read like compressed novels, or outlines for novels.

In *Snow White* and *Unspeakable Practices, Unnatural Acts*, Barthelme experiments with an opposite procedure. Instead of attempting to compress modern sensibility or modern experience into a single uninflected catalogue, he focuses on metaphors for this experience, explores their implications, and ultimately undermines their explanatory power. In "The Balloon," "The Dolt," "Robert Kennedy Saved from Drowning," and "The Indian Uprising," Barthelme examines single metaphorical figures whose significance the stories consider without conclusively establishing. This tendency to break down the significance of cultural codes is the structural—or anti-structural—principle behind Barthelme's two novels, *Snow White* and *The Dead Father*. Each of these works turns a familiar narrative pattern inside out by exposing its internal contradictions and absurdities, by adding new absurdities, and by undermining the assumptions on which the original narrative rests; Snow White, for example, showers with the seven dwarfs, some of whom suffer from anomie—a condition of isolation, disorientation, and anxiety.

Snow White points the way toward the method and theme of Barthelme's most significant stories. Given the presence of so many objects, opinions, and habits that persist despite the lack of any rationale—given, that is, the modern world as a cultural junkyard—Barthelme tends to concentrate on a single bit of junk and speculate on its range of implications. This preoccupation underlies many of the stories in *City Life*—"The Falling Dog," "The Policeman's Ball," "The Glass Mountain," "On Angels,"—and persists in such later stories as "The Sandman," "The Party," "The Captured Woman," "Our Work and Why We Do It," "Cortes and Montezuma," and "The Leap." Some critics have called Barthelme a miniaturist whose talent is essentially uncongenial to the novel for several reasons: the development of action and psychology fundamental to the novel is foreign to Barthelme's fiction; the social and cultural references characteristic of most novels are easily accommodated by the shorter form of his stories; and his most distinctive stories typically focus on a single figure or situation, as characters and readers alike try to come to terms with it. Barthelme's eye for the unexamined assumptions that sap the life from a culture recalls Henrik Ibsen's *Ghosts;* but Barthelme's work, unlike Ibsen's, remains predominantly comic because he is more interested in the marvelous absurdities of particular images and institutions than in their stifling effect on particular people. When he does examine an individual character's struggle with the deadening effects of the modern world, as in his most ambitious stories, "Views of My Father Weeping" and "Daumier," the effect is at once comic and elegiac.

Having demonstrated the range of his technical and thematic concerns in *City Life,* Barthelme has largely continued to explore the same territory in his later work. The melancholy fantasy of *Sadness* and *Amateurs* is already implicit in "Views of My Father Weeping"; the dialogues dominating *Great Days* do not mark a clear advance over the earlier "The Explanation" and "Kierkegaard Unfair to Schlegel" in *City Life*. In Barthelme's *Overnight to Many Distant Cities,* a collection that in structure echoes Hemingway's *In Our Time,* the stories are almost uniformly accomplished but break no new ground. Within his chosen range, however, Barthelme's mastery has never been seriously challenged.

The very different literary personalities exemplified by the wildly comic invention of *City Life* and the melancholy fantasy of *Sadness* are complementary aspects of a single humorous personality dominated by a characteristic sensibility, a way of seeing the world. Barthelme is ultimately a humorist not only because his work is almost always funny but because its comedy stems from a deadpan sensibility recognizing its mirror image in the absurdly fragmented languages and activities of talk-show hosts, conceptual artists, urban planners, military bureaucrats, and married couples. Despite John Gardner's remark to Joe David Bellamy in *The New Fiction* that "*Nobody* could have predicted Barthelme. . . . He wasn't a possibility," Barthelme's precursors are numerous. They include Francois Rabelais, Heinrich von Kleist, Arthur Rimbaud, Franz Kafka, Gertrude Stein, and Flann O'Brien, as well as Jorge Luis Borges, to whom he is often compared, and Lewis Carroll, who of all earlier writers most strikingly anticipates Barthelme's combination of fantasy and literal-mindedness. On the other hand, Barthelme's structural innovations, even if they are less original than they are often taken to be, are still radical and profound. More than any other writer in English, he has freed the short story from its dependence on a linear plot, a clarifying design, and a psychological conception of character; he has illustrated, instead, the affinities of short fiction with the parody, the monologue, the sketch, and other plotless and apparently ephemeral kinds of writing.

Guilty Pleasures, apparently Barthelme's most derivative and impersonal book, is in fact almost uncomfortably self-revealing in its intimations of the artist at work transforming cultural debris into narrative discourse. Whether a parody of *Cosmopolitan,* a series of speculations about an aging Playmate's "loss of bunny image," or a straight-faced account of one episode of the "Ed Sullivan Show," each piece nearly turns into a Donald Barthelme story. In "Nothing: A Preliminary Account," he exhibits his ability to make a narrative from a list of all the things nothing is not. In "The Question Party," collected in *Great Days,* he manages, with only one major change, to make a characteristic story out of an account of a parlor game first published in *Godey's Lady's Book* in 1850. What apparently constitutes Barthelme's stories as stories depends less on the nature of their conflicts and resolutions than on the relationship between the author and his audience. Once that relationship is established, the audience will be ready to assist Barthelme in constructing a story out of any materials whatsoever—even out of literally nothing at all.

By offering an alternative to the short story organized in terms of a traditional plot, characters, conflict, and resolution—a model which, after all, had dominated short fiction only since Edgar Allan Poe—Barthelme's fiction persuasively demonstrates the comparatively superficial dependence of the short story on these conventions. Because his own work, however, has typically resisted new descriptive categories, it is easier to define the formal tradition with which he is breaking than to say exactly what he is creating in its place. But the leading characteristic of all Barthelme's work is clearly its antithetical stance toward its materials, a stance that, without necessarily expressing hostility toward the world, frees the stories from commitment to the truth of any representation of that world. Lois Gordon suggests that Barthelme's most striking formal technique is a "shifting from one voice of authority to another, or manipulation or literalization of metaphor or cliche, or creation of open-ended or seemingly nonfixed situations" that "is noticeably *dislocating* (or disorienting)." She adds that "because of the open-ended quality of his language—which always begins with a logical albeit extraordinarily unusual connection before it splits and widens into its several, moving parts—one never feels he 'finishes' a Barthelme story." As Molesworth writes, "For Barthelme the highest success is not if the story strikes us as true, but rather if it shows us how it works." Maurice Couturier, in his remarks on "The Explanation," argues further that Barthelme "is composing a fiction which is so saturated with motley fragments of recognizable discourses that it eventually becomes non-discursive": the stories reveal characters so encrusted with cultural debris that their very individuality—and by extension the whole notion of an independent personal consciousness—has become suspect.

Whether or not they concur with Couturier's analysis of Barthelme's early work, most critics would agree that Barthelme's work since *City Life* has been less pyrotechnical, less formally innovative, and more acquiescent to the institutions and the relations it satirizes. Scholars have disagreed sharply, however, over the implications of this change in Barthelme's temper. Jack Hicks finds a fundamental continuity between Barthelme's earlier, more overtly experimental work and his more recent collections: "Though *Amateurs* and *Great Days* have turned more to the prickly conditions of modern urban human society, his path continues to be the creation of an essentially private fiction." Josephine Hendin, however, finds Barthelme's work far less private. His best stories, she suggests in *Vulnerable People: A View of American Fiction since 1945,* "are those with the strongest emotional charge. But his strongest emotion is anger." For Morris Dickstein in *Gates of Eden: American Culture in the Sixties,* the

lessening of that anger in Barthelme's work since *City Life* and his increased disinclination to tackle a subject as ambitious or consequential as Robert Kennedy have cut his work off from the sources of its power: "Barthelme needs a great subject, an immediate subject, to draw him at least halfway out of his irony and aesthetic detachment. The feverish immediacy of life in the late sixties, the energy and pressure and swirl . . . worked their way into his fiction with a fascinating indirection. . . . Without that stimulus, without the pull of social ferment and spiritual possibility, Barthelme's work in *Sadness* looks the same but feels listless and remote." And *The Dead Father,* which deals with a problematical subject without engaging its volatile aspects openly, "is better but not much better," Dickstein believes.

By contrast, Alan Wilde, agreeing with Alfred Kazin that Barthelme's early stories posit a thematic and methodological impasse for fiction, believes the stories in *Amateurs* suggest an escape from that impasse. Arguing in *Boundary 2* that throughout his work "Barthelme remains part of the world he perceives, approaching it through a process of interrogation to which he opens himself as well," Wilde finds the writer essentially pessimistic: "Life, as he sees it, not only refuses to offer up assurances and answers; it continues to be in large part, for human beings trying to make their way through it, frustrating, disjointed, and drab." Still, "there is, at the least, a change of emphasis in Barthelme's later work: a sense that . . . an alternative, the possibility of assent, does exist." Wilde sees in this openness to assent a leading example of "the recovery of depth" by postmodern writers who look beyond "the aesthetics of surface."

John Romano, reviewing *Sixty Stories* in the *New York Times Book Review,* adopts still another perspective. Regretting the author's drift away from corrosive satire toward an homage to "the lyric and trivial," Romano finds Barthelme less impressive as a metaphysician than an entertainer: "The chief thing to say about Barthelme . . . is that he is fiercely committed to showing us a good time. . . . Although there is avant-gardist flair, and broken lines and paragraphs, and an air of experiment everywhere in his prose, nothing much is finally challenged, no walls are even so much as asked politely to fall down."

If Barthelme is finally considered a humorist rather than a theoretician of postmodernism, the label does not make his work less consequential: his own favorite comedians, he told Klinkowitz, are "the government." And although his deadpan treatment of absurdity, which was the trademark of so much of the *New Yorker*'s fiction for the ten years following 1965, has been eclipsed by the more intimate studies of social disintegration by Ann Beattie and Barthelme's brother Frederick, Donald Barthelme's achievement—apart from questions of modishness and immediate influence—seems likely to be recognized as enduring and substantial.

BIOGRAPHICAL/CRITICAL SOURCES:

BOOKS

Bellamy, Joe David, editor, *The New Fiction: Interviews with Innovative American Writers,* University of Illinois Press, 1974.

Bruss, Paul, *Victims: Textual Strategies in Recent American Fiction,* Bucknell University Press, 1981.

Contemporary Fiction in America and England, 1950-1970, Gale, 1976.

Contemporary Literary Criticism, Gale, Volume 1, 1973, Volume 2, 1974, Volume 3, 1975, Volume 5, 1976, Volume 6, 1976, Volume 8, 1978, Volume 13, 1980, Volume 23, 1983, Volume 46, 1988.

Couturier, Maurice and Regis Durand, *Donald Barthelme,* Methuen, 1982.

The Devil in the Fire: Retrospective Essays on American Literature and Culture, Harper's Magazine Press, 1972.

Dickstein, Morris, *Gates of Eden: American Culture in the Sixties,* Basic Books, 1977.

Dictionary of Literary Biography, Volume II: *American Novelists since World War II,* Gale, 1978.

Dictionary of Literary Biography Yearbook: 1980, Gale, 1981.

Fiction and the Figures of Life, Knopf, 1970.

Gilman, Richard, *The Confusion of Realms,* Random House, 1969.

Gordon, Lois, *Donald Barthelme,* Twayne, 1981.

Graff, Gerald, *Literature against Itself: Literary Ideas in Modern Society,* University of Chicago Press, 1979.

Harris, Charles B., *Contemporary American Novelists of the Absurd,* College and University Press, 1971.

Hendin, Josephine, *Vulnerable People: A View of American Fiction since 1945,* Oxford University Press, 1978.

Hicks, Jack, *In the Singer's Temple: Prose Fictions of Barthelme, Gaines, Brautigan, Piercy, Kesey, and Kosinski,* University of North Carolina Press, 1981.

Karl, Frederick R., *American Fictions, 1940-1980: A Comprehensive History and Critical Evaluation,* Harper, 1983.

Kazin, Alfred, *Bright Book of Life: American Novelists and Story Tellers from Hemingway to Mailer,* Atlantic/Little, Brown, 1973.

Klinkowitz, Jerome, *The American 1960s: Imaginative Arts in a Decade of Change,* Iowa State University Press, 1980.

Klinkowitz, Jerome, *Literary Disruptions: The Making of a Post-Contemporary American Fiction,* 2nd edition, University of Illinois Press, 1980.

Klinkowitz, Jerome, *The Self-Apparent Word: Fiction as Language/Language as Fiction,* Southern Illinois University Press, 1984.

Klinkowitz, Jerome and others, editors, *Donald Barthelme: A Comprehensive Bibliography and Annotated Secondary Checklist,* Shoe String, 1977.

McCaffery, Larry, *The Metafictional Muse: The Works of Robert Coover, Donald Barthelme, and William H. Gass,* University of Pittsburgh Press, 1982.

Molesworth, Charles, *Donald Barthelme's Fiction: The Ironist Saved from Drowning,* University of Missouri Press, 1982.

Peden, William, *The American Short Story,* Houghton, 1975.

Scholes, Robert, *Fabulation and Metafiction,* University of Illinois Press, 1971.

Short Story Criticism, Volume 2, Gale, 1989.

Stengel, Wayne B., *The Shape of Art in the Short Stories of Donald Barthelme,* Louisiana State University Press, 1985.

Tanner, Tony, *City of Words: American Fiction, 1950-1970,* Harper, 1971.

Weaver, Gordon, editor, *The American Short Story, 1945-1980,* Twayne, 1983.

Wemer, Braig Hansen, *Paradoxical Resolutions: American Fiction since James Joyce,* University of Illinois Press, 1982.

PERIODICALS

America, December 10, 1981.
Antioch Review, spring, 1970.
Books, April, 1967.
Books and Bookmen, February, 1974.
Book Week, May 21, 1967, February 4, 1979.
Boundary 2, fall, 1976, spring, 1977.
Chicago Review, Number 1, 1973.
Chicago Tribune, November 27, 1986, October 23, 1987.

Chicago Tribune Book World, January 28, 1979, September 27, 1981, October 17, 1982.
Christian Science Monitor, June 1, 1967.
Commentary, November, 1975, August, 1976.
Commonweal, December 29, 1967, June 21, 1968.
Critique: Studies in Modern Fiction, Number 3, 1969, Number 3, 1975.
Denver Quarterly, winter, 1979.
Detroit News, October 4, 1981, December 1, 1983.
Fiction International, Number 4/5, 1975.
Georgia Review, summer, 1974.
Harper's, January, 1973.
Hudson Review, autumn, 1967.
International Fiction Review, Number 6, 1979.
Journal of Narrative Theory, spring, 1982.
Kenyon Review, spring, 1967.
Language and Style, spring, 1975.
Library Journal, December 15, 1976.
Linguistics in Literature, Number 2, 1977.
Listener, December 6, 1973.
Los Angeles Times, December 7, 1983.
Los Angeles Times Book Review, October 8, 1981, October 24, 1982, November 2, 1986, October 18, 1987.
Life, May 26, 1967.
Michigan Quarterly Review, spring, 1977.
Milwaukee Journal, February 4, 1973.
Minnesota Review, fall, 1971, fall, 1977.
Modern Fiction Studies, spring, 1982.
Nation, June 19, 1967, April 7, 1979, October 17, 1981.
National Review, March 28, 1975.
New Leader, February 26, 1979.
New Orleans Review, summer, 1981.
New Republic, May 2, 1964, June 3, 1967, December 14, 1974, February 17, 1979.
New Statesman, December 7, 1973.
Newsweek, May 22, 1967, May 6, 1968, November 25, 1974, October 12, 1981, November 3, 1986.
New York Review of Books, April 30, 1964, August 24, 1967, April 25, 1968, December 14, 1972, December 1, 1975.
New York Times, April 24, 1968, January 31, 1979, October 24, 1981, February 18, 1982, June 18, 1983, December 9, 1983, October 22, 1986, April 9, 1988.
New York Times Book Review, September 27, 1964, May 21, 1967, May 12, 1968, November 7, 1971, September 3, 1972, November 5, 1972, December 23, 1973, December 19, 1976, February 4, 1979, October 4, 1981, October 10, 1982, December 8, 1983, October 26, 1986, October 25, 1987.
New York Times Magazine, August 16, 1970.
Orbis Litterarum, Number 38, 1983.
Partisan Review, Number 3, 1973.
Philological Quarterly, fall, 1983.
Prospects, Number 1, 1975.
Publishers Weekly, March 18, 1968, November 1, 1974.
Resources for American Literary Study, Number 7, 1977.
Saturday Review, May 9, 1970, November 25, 1972, March 3, 1979, September, 1981.
Sewanee Review, summer, 1970.
Southwest Review, spring, 1982.
Spectator, December 8, 1973.
Studies in Short Fiction, winter, 1981.
Style, summer, 1975.
Time, May 26, 1967, November 1, 1974, September 21, 1981.
Times (London), April 6, 1989.
Times Literary Supplement, June 17, 1977, May 13, 1988.
Tri Quarterly, winter, 1973, spring, 1974, spring, 1975.

Twentieth Century Literature, January, 1972.
Virginia Quarterly Review, spring, 1975.
Washington Post Book World, November 5, 1972, November 3, 1974, November 28, 1976, February 1, 1979, October 25, 1981, December 14, 1986, October 11, 1987.
Xavier Review, Number 1, 1980-81.
Yale Review, spring, 1976.

*   *   *

BARTHES, Roland (Gerard) 1915-1980

PERSONAL: Born November 12, 1915, in Cherbourg, France; died of chest injuries sustained in an automobile accident, March 25, 1980, in Paris, France; son of Louis (a naval officer) and Henriette (Binger) Barthes; *Education:* Sorbonne, University of Paris, *licence* (classical letters), 1939, *diplome d'etudes,* 1939, *licence* (grammar and philology), 1943.

ADDRESSES: Home—11 rue Servandoni, Paris 6, France.

CAREER: Teacher in Bayonne, France, 1939-40, and Paris, France, 1940-41; French Institute, Bucharest, Romania, teacher, 1948-49; University of Alexandria, Alexandria, Egypt, reader in French, 1950; cultural attache in 1950s; Centre Nationale de Recherche Scientifique, teaching fellow in lexicology, 1952-54, research fellow in sociology, 1955-59; Ecole Pratique des Hautes Etudes, began in 1960 as *chef de travaux,* became director of studies; College de France, professor of semiological literature, 1976-80. Visiting professor at Johns Hopkins University, 1967. Co-founder of *Theatre populaire* (periodical).

WRITINGS:

Le Degre zero de l'ecriture, Editions du Seuil, 1953, translation by Annette Lavers and Colin Smith published as *Writing Degree Zero,* J. Cape, 1967, reprinted with preface by Susan Sontag, Hill & Wang, 1968.
(Editor) Jules Michelet, *Michelet par lui-meme* (title means "Michelet by Himself"), Editions du Seuil, 1954, translation by Richard Howard published as *Michelet,* Hill & Wang, 1987.
Mythologies, Editions du Seuil, 1957, translation by Lavers published as *Mythologies,* Hill & Wang, 1972.
Sur Racine (criticism), 1963, translation by Howard published as *On Racine,* Hill & Wang, 1964.
(With Andre Martin) *La Voyageuse de nuit,* [France], 1964.
Essais critiques (includes "Le Monde objet," "Litterature objective," and "Litterature litterale"), Editions du Seuil, 1964, translation by Howard published as *Critical Essays,* Northwestern University Press, 1972.
(With Martin) *La Tour Eiffel,* Delpire, 1964, translation by Howard published as *The Eiffel Tower, and Other Mythologies,* Hill & Wang, 1979.
Critique et verite, Editions du Seuil, 1966, translation by Katrine Pilcher Keuneman published as *Criticism and Truth,* foreword by Philip Thody, University of Minnesota Press, 1987.
Systeme de la mode, Editions du Seuil, 1967, translation by Matthew Ward and Howard published as *The Fashion System,* Hill & Wang, 1983.
Elements de semiologie, 1967, translation by Lavers and Smith published as *Elements of Semiology,* Hill & Wang, 1968.
L'Empire des signes, Albert Skira, 1970, translation by Howard published as *Empire of Signs,* J. Cape, 1982.
S/Z, Editions du Seuil, 1970, translation by Richard Miller published as *S/Z,* Hill & Wang, 1974.
Sade, Fourier, Loyola, Editions du Seuil, 1971, translation by Miller published as *Sade, Fourier, Loyola,* Hill & Wang, 1976.

Nouveaux Essais critiques, 1972, translation by Howard published as *New Critical Essays,* Hill & Wang, 1980.
(Contributor) *L'Express va plus loin avec. . . ,* R. Laffont, 1973.
Le Plaisir du texte, Editions du Seuil, 1973, translation by Miller published as *The Pleasure of the Text,* note by Howard, Hill & Wang, 1975.
Alors la Chine?, C. Bourgois, 1975.
Roland Barthes par Roland Barthes, Editions du Seuil, 1975, translation by Howard published as *Roland Barthes by Roland Barthes,* Hill & Wang, 1977.
Graphies, Transedition, 1976.
Fragments d'un discours amoureux, Editions du Seuil, 1977, translation by Howard published as *A Lover's Discourse: Fragments,* Hill & Wang, 1978.
Lecon, Editions du Seuil, 1978.
Image, Music, Text, selected and translated by Stephen Heath, Hill & Wang, 1978.
Sollers ecrivain, Editions du Seuil, 1979, translation by Philip Tody published as *Writer Sollers,* University of Minnesota Press, 1987.
La Claire Chambre: Note sur la photographie, Cahiers du Cinema, 1980, translation by Howard published as *Camera Lucida: Reflections on Photography,* Hill & Wang, 1981.
Arcimboldi, translated by John Shepley, with essay by Achille Bonito Oliva, F. M. Ricci, 1980.
Recherche de Proust, Editions du Seuil, 1980.
(Contributor) *L'Analyse structurale du recit,* Editions du Seuil, 1981.
Le Grain de la voix: Entretiens, 1962-1980, Editions du Seuil, 1981, translation by Linda Coverdale published as *The Grain of the Voice,* Hill & Wang, 1985.
A Barthes Reader, edited with introduction by Sontag, Hill & Wang, 1982.
Litterature et realite, Editions du Seuil, 1982.
Obvie et l'obtus, Editions du Seuil, 1982, translation by Howard published as *The Responsibility of Forms: Critical Essays on Music, Art, and Representation,* Basil Blackwell, 1984.
All Except You, Galerie Maeght, 1983.
Michelangelo Antonioni, C. Hanser, 1984.
Le Bruissement de la langue, Editions du Seuil, 1984, translation by Howard published as *The Rustle of Language,* Hill & Wang, 1986.
L'Aventure semiologique, Seuil, 1985.
Le Texte et l'image, Edition Paris Musees, 1986.

Also author of *Combat,* 1947. Author of introductions to editions of works by various writers, including Jean Baptiste Racine. Essays included in editions of works by various writers, including Lord Auch. Works also published in multi-title volumes and represented in anthologies.

Contributor to periodicals, including *Communications, La Quinzaine Litteraire, Les Lettres Nouvelles,* and *Tel Quel.*

SIDELIGHTS: Roland Barthes was a leading figure in semiology, a critical method that analyzes expression—from the artistic to the merely communicative—as a system of signs. His principal subject was, inevitably, language itself, and his principal theme was the imprecision of language as a means of communicating a fixed idea. For Barthes, any literary work yields a multiplicity of interpretations, and even literary interpretations of a given work are open to varied readings. Therefore, a reduction of Barthes's own work is somewhat paradoxical: His basic premise is that there is no such thing as one basic premise. As John Updike wrote in *New Yorker:* "Barthes compels our respect more by what he demands than by what he delivers; his criticism lacks only the quality of inspiring trust. It is never *relaxed.* He teaches us to see multiple layers of reader-writer interaction hovering above every page; above his own pages there is, faint but obscuring, a frosted layer of irony that blurs opus and commentary into a single plane."

Barthes's first important work is *Le Degre zero de l'ecriture* (*Writing Degree Zero*), in which he considers both language and literature within historical contexts. Prior to the class upheavals of the mid-nineteenth century, Barthes claims, all literature adhered to basic premises of logic and continuity. In the alienating, chaotic twentieth century, however, literature fragmented into various dissimilar styles. For Barthes, the only response to this confusing state, in which a work's style becomes its content, is to promote a colorless, "objective" literature—what he called "writing degree zero"—as exemplified by such writers as Albert Camus and Alain Robbe-Grillet.

With *Writing Degree Zero* Barthes showed himself a provocative critical theorist. Laurent LeSage, for instance, wrote in *The French New Criticism* that Barthes had produced "a dazzling piece of argumentation." But some critics accused Barthes of introducing little more than a different way of considering a vogue subject. "The notion of a literature so reduced to silence is already fashionable," wrote Frank Kermode in *Listener*, "and Barthes can only give us a new way of talking about it if we want to." A more balanced appraisal was proffered by Susan Sontag in her preface to the English-language edition. "*Writing Degree Zero* probably isn't the easiest text with which to start an acquaintance with Barthes," she wrote. "The book is compact to the point of ellipsis, often arcane." But she also found it worthwhile as an assemblage of new, necessary "myths" about literature. "Measured on this scale of need," Sontag asserted, "the myths about literature proposed in *Writing Degree Zero* seem to me sturdy, subtle, and highly serviceable."

Among Barthes's next important works is the essay collection *Mythologies*. Included in this volume is "Myth Today," in which Barthes explicates and elaborates his notion of myth as a form of expression within a historical context. He sees such phenomena as professional wrestling and the fashion industry as contemporary myths, and he finds these myths consistent with the increasing prevalence of bourgeois ideology, which he disdains. But the political left, he laments, offers little alternative, tied as it is to socio-political issues. "The same intelligence that permits Barthes to see through . . . the bourgeois myths or codes," Updike wrote in *New Yorker*, "exposes to his vision the mysterious negativity, the terrible thinness, of the revolutionary alternative."

In *Mythologies* Barthes discussed a wide range of topics, and in subsequent books he continued to apply himself broadly. In *Elements de semiologie* (*Elements of Semiology*), he outlined semiology as a method for perceiving virtually anything—even physical movements or noises—as systems. Another work, *Systeme de la mode* (*The Fashion System*), examines fashion magazines for their semiological content, and in the radical *S/Z* Barthes devoted himself to an exhaustive semiological analysis of Honore de Balzac's story "Sarrasine." In so thoroughly analyzing Balzac's tale, Barthes elucidated the actual act of reading. "Only when we know . . . what we are doing when we read, are we free to enjoy what we read," summarized Richard Howard in his preface to the English-language edition of *S/Z*. "As long as our enjoyment is—or is said to be—instinctive it is not enjoyment, it is terrorism." For Howard, *S/Z* proved "the most useful, the most intimate, and the most suggestive book I have ever read about why I have ever read a book."

Barthes further explored reading in *Le Plaisir du texte* (*The Pleasure of the Text*), a relatively accessible work that characterizes reading as a sensual, nearly hedonistic activity. Reading, Barthes charged, is a deliberate, contemplative means of obtaining pleasure and satisfaction, and as such it is far more than mere intellectual process. Peter Brookes, writing in the *New York Times Book Review*, described *The Pleasure of the Text* as a "self-indulgent medition," though he qualified this assessment by acknowledging the work as a "consciously . . . assertive book, Nietzschean in its manner, aiming at effect rather than persuasion."

When *The Pleasure of the Text* appeared in French in 1973 (and in English in 1975), Barthes was recognized as a leading figure in French critical thought. With other intellectuals, ranging from radical psychoanalyst Jacques Lacan to controversial socio-historical theorist Michel Foucault, Barthes enjoyed immense influence in both Europe and the United States. Throughout the remainder of the 1970s, with works such as *Roland Barthes par Roland Barthes* (*Roland Barthes by Roland Barthes*) and *Fragments d'un discours amoureux* (*A Lover's Discourse*), Barthes added to his stature as a provocative, engaging thinker. *A Lover's Discourse* proved a particularly intriguing work, for in it Barthes presented uncharacteristically poignant ruminations on love, its expression, and its articulations. Despite its subject, however, *A Lover's Discourse* is hardly an uplifting work. In it Barthes views love as an exhausting, enslaving emotion, one that often seems masochistic. As John Sturrock wrote in the essay collection *Structuralism and Since*, *A Lover's Discourse* "is a melancholy book to read because the state of being in love is presented by Barthes as a very painful one; but against the pain must be set the lover's perverse pleasure at finding himself trapped in a perfectly intractable situation."

In 1980, only a few years after publishing *A Lover's Discourse*, Barthes was fatally struck by an automobile while crossing a Paris street, and one month later he finally died from massive chest injuries. But with the *Barthes Reader* anthology—edited by Sontag—and several posthumous volumes, Barthes continues to hold high standing in academia as one of his country's most important contemporary thinkers. As Sturrock noted: "One of the lessons he has taught is that we have scant right to call our language our own, because it is a system to which we must surrender much of our individuality whenever we enter it. Whoever speaks or writes is, in his description, no more than 'the great empty envelope' around the words. Barthes, the author, may be only the name on an envelope, but no one in recent years has put the French language to richer, more original, or more intelligent use."

AVOCATIONAL INTERESTS: Reading, playing piano, painting watercolors, watching television.

BIOGRAPHICAL/CRITICAL SOURCES:

BOOKS

Barthes, Roland, *Roland Barthes by Roland Barthes*, translated by Richard Howard, Hill & Wang, 1977.
Contemporary Literary Criticism, Volume 24, Gale, 1983.
LeSage, Laurent, *The French New Criticism: An Introduction and a Sampler*, Pennsylvania State University Press, 1967.
Mauriac, Claude, *The New Literature*, translated by Samuel I. Stone, Braziller, 1959.
Merton, Thomas, *The Literary Essays of Thomas Merton*, New Directions, 1981.
Picard, Raymond, *New Criticism or New Fraud?*, translated by Frank Towne, Washington State University Press, 1969.

Sturrock, John, editor, *Structuralism and Since: From Levi Strauss to Derrida,* Oxford University Press, 1979.

Thody, Philip, *Roland Barthes: A Conservative Estimate,* Humanities Press, 1977.

PERIODICALS

Clio, winter, 1979.
Commentary, January, 1982.
Guardian (London), March 2, 1974.
Gulliver, March, 1973.
Harper's, August, 1980.
Listener, October 12, 1967.
Los Angeles Times, March 27, 1986.
Los Angeles Times Book Review, February 3, 1985, March 8, 1987.
Minnesota Review, fall, 1977.
New Statesmun, April 25, 1980.
Newsweek, December 18, 1978.
New Yorker, November 24, 1975.
New York Times, October 10, 1979.
New York Times Book Review, September 14, 1975, February 4, 1979, June 3, 1979, November 4, 1979, July 24, 1983, December 23, 1984.
Saturday Review, September 2, 1978.
Sewanee Review, summer, 1969.
Times Literary Supplement, September 30, 1965, February 3, 1966, June 15, 1967, September 28, 1967, October 12, 1967, March 24, 1972, August 12, 1983, January 4, 1985, May 2, 1986, July 3, 1987.
Washington Post Book World, October 29, 1978.

OBITUARIES:

PERIODICALS

AB Bookman's Weekly, April 14, 1980.
Chicago Tribune, March 27, 1980.
Los Angeles Times, March 31, 1980.
New York Times, March 27, 1980.
Time, April 7, 1980.
Times (London), March 27, 1980.
Washington Post, March 27, 1980.

*   *   *

BASHEVIS, Isaac
See SINGER, Isaac Bashevis

*   *   *

BASS, Kingsley B., Jr.
See BULLINS, Ed

*   *   *

BASSANI, Giorgio 1916-
(Giacomo Marchi)

PERSONAL: Born April 4, 1916, in Bologna, Italy. *Education:* Graduated from University of Bologna.

ADDRESSES: Home—Via G. B. DeRossi 33, Rome, Italy.

CAREER: Novelist and poet. Accademia Nazionale d'Arte Drammatica, Rome, Italy, instructor in history of theatre, 1957-68; Radio Televisione Italiana, Rome, vice-president, 1964-65.

AWARDS, HONORS: Charles Veillon prize in Italian literature, 1955, for *Gli ultimi anni di Clelia Trotti;* Strega prize, 1956, for *Cinque storie ferraresi;* Viareggio prize, 1962, for *Il giardino dei Finzi-Contini;* Campiello prize, 1969, for *L'airone;* Nelly Sachs prize, 1969; also recipient of Premi Roma.

WRITINGS:

(Under pseudonym Giacomo Marchi) *Una citta di rianura,* [Italy], 1940.
Storie dei poveri amanti e altri versi (poetry), Astrolabio (Rome), 1946.
Te lucis ante (poetry), [Italy], 1947.
Un altra liberta (poetry), [Italy], 1951.
(Author of introduction) *Giovanni Omiccioli,* De Luca (Rome), 1952.
Gli ultimi anni di Clelia Trotti (novella; also see below), Nistri-Lischi (Pisa), 1955.
Cinque storie ferraresi (short stories), Einaudi (Rome), 1956, published as *Dentro le mura,* Mondadori (Milan), 1973, translation by Isabel Quigly published as *A Prospect of Ferrara,* Faber, 1962, translation by William Weaver published as *Five Stories of Ferrara,* Harcourt, 1971.
Gli occhiali d'oro (novel), Einaudi, 1958, 2nd edition, 1962, translation by Quigly published as *The Gold-Rimmed Spectacles,* Atheneum, 1960.
Le storie ferraresi (novellas; includes *Gli ultimi anni di Clelia Trotti*), Einaudi, 1960.
Una notte del '43 (novella), Einaudi, 1960.
(Author of introduction) Mimi Quilici Buzzacchi, *Paesaggio di Spina,* De Luca, 1962.
Il giardino dei Finzi-Contini (novel), Einaudi, 1962, translation by Quigly published as *The Garden of the Finzi-Continis,* Atheneum, 1965.
L'alba ai vetri: Poesie 1942-1950, Einaudi, 1963.
Dietro la porta (novel), Einaudi, 1964, translation by Weaver published as *Behind the Door,* Harcourt, 1972.
Due novelle, Stamperia di Venezia (Venice), 1965.
Le parole preparate, e altri seritti di letteratura, Einaudi, 1966.
L'airone (novel), Mondadori, 1968, translation by Weaver published as *The Heron,* Harcourt, 1970.
Giorgio Bassani: Ansprachen und Dokumente zur Verleihung des Kulturpreises der Stadt Dortmund, Nelly-Sachs-Preis, am 7. Dezember 1969, Stadt- und Landesbibliothek (Dortmund), 1971.
L'odore del fieno (short stories), Mondadori, 1972, translation by Weaver published as *The Smell of Hay,* Harcourt, 1975.
Epitaffio (poetry; also see below), Mondadori, 1974.
Il romanzo di Ferrara, Mondadori, 1974.
In gran segreto (poetry; also see below), Mondadori, 1978.
In rima e senza (poetry), Mondadori, 1982.
Rolls Royce and Other Poems (contains selections from *Epitaffio* and *In gran segreto* in English and Italian), translation by Francesca Valente and others, Aya Press, 1982.
Di la dal cuore, Mondadori, 1984.
Italian Stories, Schocken, 1989.

Editor of journal *Botteghe Oscure* from its founding; editor of *Paragone,* 1953-71.

MEDIA ADAPTATIONS: The Garden of the Finzi-Continis was adapted for film by Vittorio De Sica, c. 1970.

BIOGRAPHICAL/CRITICAL SOURCES:

BOOKS

Contemporary Literary Criticism, Volume 9, Gale, 1978.

BATES, H(erbert) E(rnest) 1905-1974
(Flying Officer X, John Gawsworth)

PERSONAL: Born May 16, 1905, in Rushdon, Northamptonshire, England; died January 29, 1974, in Canterbury, England; son of Albert Ernest and Lucy Elizabeth (Lucas) Bates; married Marjorie Helen Cox, July 18, 1931; children: Ann, Judith, Richard, Jonathan. *Education:* Educated in England.

ADDRESSES: Home—The Granary, Little Chart, Ashford, Kent, England.

CAREER: Writer of novels, short stories, and autobiographies. Worked as reporter for *Northamptonshire Chronicle* and as clerk in leather warehouse in England, until 1926. *Military service:* Royal Air Force, 1941-46; became squadron leader.

MEMBER: Fellow of Royal Society of Literature.

AWARDS, HONORS: Created Commander of the Order of the British Empire, 1973.

WRITINGS:

NOVELS AND NOVELLAS

The Two Sisters, Viking, 1926.
Catherine Foster, Viking, 1929.
The Hessian Prisoner, W. Jackson, 1930.
Charlotte's Row, J. Cape, 1931.
Mr. Esmond's Life, privately printed, 1931.
The Fallow Land, J. Cape, 1932, R. O. Ballou, 1933.
The Poacher, Macmillan, 1935.
A House of Women, Holt, 1936.
Spella Ho, Little, Brown, 1938.
Fair Stood the Wind for France, Little, Brown, 1944.
The Cruise of the Breadwinner, M. Joseph, 1946, Little, Brown, 1947.
The Purple Plain, Little, Brown, 1947.
Dear Life, Little, Brown, 1949.
The Jacaranda Tree, Little, Brown, 1949, abridged version, edited by G. M. Gore Little, Longmans, Green, 1960.
The Scarlet Sword, M. Joseph, 1950, Little, Brown, 1951.
Love for Lydia, M. Joseph, 1952, Penguin, 1956.
The Nature of Love: Three Short Novels, M. Joseph, 1953, Little, Brown, 1954.
The Feast of July, Little, Brown, 1954.
The Sleepless Moon, Little, Brown, 1956.
Dear Life [and] *The Cruise of the Breadwinner,* Transworld Publishers, 1957.
Death of a Huntsman: Four Short Novels (also see below), M. Joseph, 1957, Penguin, 1964.
The Darling Buds of May, Little, Brown, 1958.
A Breath of Fresh Air, Little, Brown, 1959.
An Aspidistra in Babylon: Four Novellas (also see below), M. Joseph, 1960, Penguin, 1964.
The Grapes of Paradise: Eight Novellas (includes *Death of a Huntsman: Four Short Novels* and *An Aspidistra in Babylon: Four Short Novels*), Little, Brown, 1960.
When the Green Woods Laugh, M. Joseph, 1960, Penguin, 1963, published as *Hark, Hark, the Lark!,* Little, Brown, 1961.
The Day of the Tortoise, M. Joseph, 1961.
A Crown of Wild Myrtle, M. Joseph, 1962, Farrar, Straus, 1963.
The Golden Oriole: Five Novellas, Little, Brown, 1962.
Oh! To Be in England, M. Joseph, 1963, Farrar, Straus, 1964.
The Fabulous Mrs. V., M. Joseph, 1964, Penguin, 1970.
A Moment in Time, Farrar, Straus, 1964.
The Distant Hours in Summer, M. Joseph, 1967, Penguin, 1969.
The Wild Cherry Tree, M. Joseph, 1968, Penguin, 1972.

The Triple Echo, M. Joseph, 1970, Penguin, 1972.
Fair Stood the Wind for France, Yours Is the Earth, A Silas Idyll, edited by Geoffrey Halson, Longman, 1971.

SHORT STORIES

The Spring Song [and] *In Spite of That: Two Stories,* privately printed, 1927.
Day's End, and Other Stories, Viking, 1928.
Seven Tales and Alexander, Scholastic Press, 1929, Viking, 1930.
The Black Boxer, Pharos Editions, 1932.
Sally Go Round the Moon, White Owl Press, 1932.
The House With the Apricot, and Two Other Tales, Golden Cockerel, 1933.
The Woman Who Had Imagination, and Other Stories, Macmillan, 1934, reprinted, J. Cape, 1964.
Cut and Come Again: Fourteen Stories, J. Cape, 1935.
Something Short and Sweet, J. Cape, 1937.
The Flying Goat, J. Cape, 1939.
I Am Not Myself, Corvinus Press, 1939.
My Uncle Silas, J. Cape, 1939, Penguin, 1958.
The Beauty of the Dead, and Other Stories, J. Cape, 1940.
Country Tales: Collected Short Stories, J. Cape, 1940.
The Bride Comes to Evensford (also see below), J. Cape, 1943.
The Bride Comes to Evensford, and Other Stories, J. Cape, 1949.
Colonel Julian, and Other Stories, M. Joseph, 1951, Little, Brown, 1952.
The Daffodil Sky, M. Joseph, 1955, Little, Brown, 1956.
Sugar for the Horse, M. Joseph, 1957.
The Watercress Girl, and Other Stories, M. Joseph, 1959, Little, Brown, 1960.
Now Sleeps the Crimson Petal, and Other Stories, M. Joseph, 1961, Penguin, 1962, published as *The Enchantress, and Other Stories,* Little, Brown, 1961.
The Wedding Party, M. Joseph, 1965, Penguin, 1969.
The Four Beauties, M. Joseph, 1968, Penguin, 1972.
A Little of What You Fancy, M. Joseph, 1970, Penguin, 1974.
The Song of the Wren, M. Joseph, 1972, Penguin, 1974.
The Good Corn, and Other Stories, edited by Geoffrey Halson, Longman, 1974.
The Poison Ladies, and Other Stories, A. Wheaton, 1976.

COLLECTIONS

Thirty Tales, J. Cape, 1934.
Thirty-One Selected Tales, J. Cape, 1947.
Selected Short Stories of H. E. Bates, Pocket Books, 1951.
Twenty Tales, J. Cape, 1951.
Selected Stories, Penguin, 1957.
The Best of H. E. Bates, Little, Brown, 1963.
Seven by Five: A Collection of Stories, 1926-1961, M. Joseph, 1963, Penguin, 1972.
H. E. Bates, edited by Alan Cattell, Harrap, 1975.

PLAYS

The Last Bread (one-act), Labour Publishing, 1926.
The Day of Glory (three-act; produced in London, England, 1946), M. Joseph, 1945.

UNDER PSEUDONYM FLYING OFFICER X

The Greatest People in the World, and Other Stories, J. Cape, 1942, published as *There's Something in the Air,* Knopf, 1943.
How Sleep the Brave, and Other Stories, J. Cape, 1943.
The Stories of Flying Officer X, J. Cape, 1952.

OTHER

The Seekers, J. & E. Bumpus, 1926.

The Tree, E. Lahr, 1930.

A Threshing Day, W. & G. Foyle, 1931.

A German Idyll, Golden Cockerel, 1932.

The Story Without an End [and] *The Country Doctor,* White Owl Press, 1932.

The Duet, [London], 1935.

Flowers and Faces, Golden Cockerel, 1935.

Through the Woods: The English Woodland—April to April, Macmillan, 1936.

Down the River, Holt, 1937.

The English Countryside (travel), [England], 1939.

There's Freedom in the Air, Ministry of Information (London), 1939.

The Seasons and the Gardener: A Book for Children, Cambridge University Press, 1940.

The Modern Short Story: A Critical Survey, T. Nelson, 1941.

In the Heart of the Country (also see below), Country Life, 1942.

Country Life, Penguin, 1943.

O! More Than Happy Countryman (also see below), Country Life, 1943, reprint published as *The Happy Countryman,* Salem House, 1987.

The Tinkers of Elstow, [London], 1946.

Otters and Men, National Society for the Abolition of Cruel Sports (London), 1947.

The Country Heart (revised and amended edition of *O! More Than Happy Countryman* and *In the Heart of the Country*), M. Joseph, 1949.

Edward Garnett: A Memoir, M. Parrish, 1950.

Flower Gardening: A Reader's Guide, Cambridge University Press, 1950.

The Country of White Clover, M. Joseph, 1952.

The Face of England, B. T. Batsford, 1952.

Summer in Salandar, Little, Brown, 1957.

Achilles the Donkey (juvenile), F. Watts, 1962.

Achilles and Diana (juvenile), F. Watts, 1963.

Achilles and the Twins (juvenile), F. Watts, 1964.

(Editor) *Six Stories* (includes works by Chekhov, Beerbohm, Joyce, Hemingway, and Bates), Oxford University Press, 1965.

The White Admiral (juvenile), Dobson Books, 1968.

An Autobiography, University of Missouri Press, Volume 1: *The Vanished World,* 1969, Volume 2: *The Blossoming World,* 1971, Volume 3: *The World in Ripeness,* 1972.

A Love of Flowers (autobiography), M. Joseph, 1971.

Dulcima, Penguin, 1971.

A Fountain of Flowers, M. Joseph, 1974.

The Yellow Meads of Asphodel, M. Joseph, 1976, Penguin, 1978.

A Month by the Lake and Other Stories, New Directions, 1987.

A Party for the Girls: Six Stories, New Directions, 1988.

Also author of *Song for December* (poems), 1928, *Christmas, 1930* (poem), 1930, *Holly and Sallow* (poem), 1931, (under name John Gawsworth) *My Beginning,* 1933, and *Pastoral on Paper,* 1956. Author of column, "Country Life," appearing in *Spectator.* Reviewer for magazines, including *Morning Post* and *Spectator.*

MEDIA ADAPTATIONS: Four of Bates' novels, *The Darling Buds of May, Dulcima, The Purple Plain,* and *The Triple Echo,* have been produced as motion pictures, and serialized versions of *Love for Lydia* and his books concerning the Larkin family, including *When the Green Woods Laugh* and *Oh! To Be in England,* were broadcast by the British Broadcasting Corp. (BBC-TV).

SIDELIGHTS: Averaging over one new book each year for a period of more than fifty years, H. E. Bates ranked as one of England's most prolific writers of this century. Often compared to such notables as George Eliot, Thomas Hardy, and D. H. Lawrence, he was regarded for his moving and realistic portrayals of the English countryside. "He was, in no pejorative sense, a prose poet, and his best effects were obtained when his delight in the natural scene, his vivid apprehension of the moods of nature, of the changing seasons and the weather, crystallized into symbols of the states of mind of his characters," expressed one critic for the London *Times.*

The Two Sisters, Bates's first novel, was published when he was twenty. The manuscript greatly impressed Edward Garnett, who immediately recommended it to publisher Jonathan Cape. Bates and Garnett quickly became friends, the latter influencing the former and cultivating the raw talent he saw in the young writer. Bates eventually paid tribute to his long-time mentor in the form of a memoir, written in 1950. So close were the two men, the London *Times* suggested, that "from the very nature of the relation between them, [the book] was as much a piece of autobiography as of biography."

One of Bates's best-known works is *The Poacher.* It is the story of Luke Bishop who, like his father before him, illegally hunts game. Despite the obvious risks involved in their trade, both pursue it diligently until one event shatters everything: Luke's father is killed by the caretaker of the land. When this man is then shot, all evidence points to Luke. Though innocent of the crime, he flees to another county. Under an assumed name, Luke begins life anew as a farmer, a relatively safe and respectable occupation. He marries and becomes a success in his new livelihood, but feels a strong longing for his native soil. Unfortunately, when he returns as an old man, the temptation to fall into his original profession overcomes him. Eager to teach his young grandson the ancient art of his family, Luke is caught while demonstrating the technique and is sent to jail.

"Beautifully and without affectation Mr. Bates has expressed through the story of Luke Bishop's life, his deep feeling for the life of the English countryside, for the changes which have come over it in the last half century and his own nostalgic regret for the order which has passed," summarized Margaret Wallace in her review of the book. Peter Quennell shared Wallace's enthusiasm: "Nothing that [Bates] writes is indistinguished, and there are many passages in *The Poacher* that must be numbered among the most beautiful he has produced."

While serving with the Royal Air Force during the Battle of Britain in World War II, Bates wrote a number of books under the pseudonym Flying Officer X. Drawing from his own experiences, he attempted to portray the courage, stamina, and determination of his fellow men-in-arms. The first of these works was *There's Something in the Air,* a collection of twenty-one short stories. "Here is sheer beauty in writing. This little volume of short pieces will give the reader a clearer conception of the combat's thinking, fighting, living, than anything that has come before. The little tales are gems cut from purest carbon, handed down so that they spit cold fire," praised Meyer Berger. Other critics were not overly impressed; a reviewer for the *Manchester Guardian* wrote, "An unprecedented form of state patronage seems to have set heavily on the author, whose stories are too slickly turned, whose pilots are a thought too heroic (or seems so to Mr. Bates . . .), and one of whose aircraft, at least, is more than a thought too anthropomorphized."

Another of his wartime writings, though not written under a pseudonym, was *A Moment in Time.* In it, Bates concentrated on those not directly involved in the fighting, yet whose lives were just as drastically altered. The central character is the nineteen-year-old Elizabeth. When her home is requisitioned by the military, she and her grandmother are forced to find shelter elsewhere. She returns often, however, and becomes friendly with the pilots. Finding herself in love with one of the fliers, she marries, but her young husband is soon killed in an attack by German bombers. Though devastated emotionally by her loss, Elizabeth is comforted by a neighbor, Tom Hudson, who has secretly admired and loved her.

The book was criticized by Eric Moon in the *Saturday Review* as nothing more than a "sentimental episode from the past" that "does nothing to interpret that past or give it real meaning for the reader of today," but it was praised by others. J. E. Oppenheimer, for one, was moved to proclaim it "poignant, perceptive," and "splendid, satisfying." Oppenheimer added, "It is . . . in character delineation and in the creation of a recognizably realistic setting for the interplay of intense human emotions under great stress that Mr. Bates reaches the heights and merits literary laurels."

Bates's writings have proven their popularity not only in England, but in countries all over the world, as is evidenced by the translations into sixteen languages.

BIOGRAPHICAL/CRITICAL SOURCES:

BOOKS

Contemporary Literary Criticism, Volume 46, Gale 1988.

PERIODICALS

Best Sellers, August 15, 1964.
Chicago Sunday Tribune, October 30, 1960, February 5, 1961.
Fortnightly Quarterly, July, 1936.
Manchester Guardian, October 23, 1942.
Nation, June 19, 1935.
New Statesman and Nation, January 26, 1935, February 5, 1949, November 19, 1955.
New Yorker, January 8, 1971.
New York Herald Tribune Book Review, January 9, 1949, November 20, 1949, October 23, 1960.
New York Herald Tribune Books, September 23, 1963.
New York Times, March 17, 1935, May 16, 1943, January 30, 1949, November 6, 1949, September 19, 1954, September 30, 1962.
New York Times Book Review, October 23, 1960, February 5, 1961, September 30, 1962, August 9, 1964.
San Francisco Chronicle, January 23, 1949.
Saturday Review of Literature, January 8, 1949, November 19, 1949, September 18, 1954, December 29, 1962, August 8, 1964.
Time, October 31, 1960.
Times Literary Supplement, January 22, 1949, October 29, 1954, July 29, 1960, May 25, 1962, September 10, 1964, October 8, 1971, October 13, 1972, February 19, 1988.

OBITUARIES:

PERIODICALS

AB Bookman's Weekly, April 15, 1974.
London Times, January 30, 1974.
Newsweek, February 11, 1974.
New York Times, January 30, 1974.
Time, February 11, 1974.
Washington Post, January 30, 1974.

BAUCHART
See CAMUS, Albert

* * *

BAUM, L(yman) Frank   1856-1919
(Floyd Akers, Laura Bancroft, Louis F. Baum, George Brooks, John Estes Cooke, Captain Hugh Fitzgerald, Suzanne Metcalf, Schuyler Staunton, Edith Van Dyne)

PERSONAL: Born May 15, 1856, in Chittenango, NY; died of complications after a gall-bladder operation, aggravated by chronic heart trouble, May 6, 1919, in Hollywood, CA; son of Benjamin Ward (an oil dealer) and Cynthia (Stanton) Baum; married Maud Gage, November 9, 1882; children: Frank Joslyn, Robert Stanton, Harry Neal, Kenneth Gage. *Education:* Privately tutored at home; also attended Peekskill Military Academy and Syracuse Classical School. *Avocational interests:* Photography, woodworking, gardening.

ADDRESSES: Home—"Ozcot," Hollywood, CA.

CAREER: Playwright, novelist, journalist, author of books for children. Manager of Baum's Opera House, Richburg, NY, 1881-82; worked in family oil business in Syracuse, NY, 1883-88, also raising fancy poultry, and collaborating in the production of a new brand of axle grease ("Baum's Castorine"); operator of a variety store, "Baum's Bazaar," 1888-89, and editor of the newspaper *Saturday Pioneer,* 1889-91, both in Aberdeen, SD; held a variety of positions in Chicago, IL, including newspaper editor for the *Chicago Evening World,* traveling salesman, and crockery buyer, beginning 1891; founded the National Association of Window Trimmers, and edited and published *The Show Window* (a trade magazine), Chicago, 1897-1901; full-time writer, 1901-19.

AWARDS, HONORS: Lewis Carroll Shelf Award, 1968, for *The Wizard of Oz.*

WRITINGS:

"OZ" SERIES

The Wonderful Wizard of Oz, illustrated by William Wallace Denslow, G. M. Hill, 1900, 2nd edition published as *The New Wizard of Oz,* Bobbs-Merrill, 1903, published as *The Wizard of Oz,* Reilly & Lee, 1956, reprinted, Ballantine, 1986.
The Marvelous Land of Oz, Being an Account of the Further Adventures of the Scarecrow and Tin Woodman, illustrated by John R. Neill, Reilly & Britton, 1904, published as *The Land of Oz,* 1904, reprinted, Ballantine, 1985.
Ozma of Oz, illustrated by Neill, Reilly & Britton, 1907, reprinted, Ballantine, 1986.
Dorothy and the Wizard in Oz, illustrated by Neill, Reilly & Britton, 1908, reprinted, Ballantine, 1985.
The Road to Oz, illustrated by Neill, Reilly & Britton, 1909, reprinted, Ballantine, 1984.
The Emerald City of Oz, illustrated by Neill, Reilly & Britton, 1910, reprinted, Ballantine, 1985.
The Patchwork Girl of Oz, illustrated by Neill, Reilly & Britton, 1913, reprinted, Ballantine, 1985.
Tik-Tok of Oz (based in part on Baum's musical "The Tik-Tok Man of Oz"; also see below), illustrated by Neill, Reilly & Britton, 1914, reprinted, Ballantine, 1984.
The Scarecrow of Oz (based in part on Baum's screenplay "His Majesty, the Scarecrow of Oz"; also see below), illustrated by Neill, Reilly & Britton, 1915, reprinted, Ballantine, 1980.

Rinkitink in Oz, illustrated by Neill, Reilly & Britton, 1916, reprinted, Ballantine, 1980.

The Lost Princess of Oz, illustrated by Neill, Reilly & Britton, 1917, reprinted, Ballantine, 1980.

The Tin Woodman of Oz, illustrated by Neill, Reilly & Lee, 1918, reprinted, Ballantine, 1985.

The Magic of Oz, illustrated by Neill, Reilly & Lee, 1919, reprinted, Ballantine, 1981.

Glinda of Oz, illustrated by Neill, Reilly & Lee, 1920, reprinted, Ballantine, 1981.

Baum's "Oz" books, especially the first two volumes of the series, have also appeared in many different editions, with many different illustrators.

"LITTLE WIZARD STORIES" SERIES; ILLUSTRATED BY NEILL

Jack Pumpkinhead and the Sawhorse, Reilly & Britton, 1913.

Little Dorothy and Toto, Reilly & Britton, 1913.

Ozma and the Little Wizard, Reilly & Britton, 1913.

The Cowardly Lion and the Hungry Tiger, Reilly & Britton, 1913.

The Scarecrow and the Tin Woodman, Reilly & Britton, 1913.

Tik-Tok and the Nome King, Reilly & Britton, 1913.

The Little Wizard Stories of Oz (includes the six volumes of the "Little Wizard Stories" series), Reilly & Britton, 1914, reprinted, Schocken, 1985.

OTHER WRITINGS FOR CHILDREN

Mother Goose in Prose, illustrated by Maxfield Parrish, Way & Williams, 1897, reprinted, Outlet Book Co., 1986.

Father Goose: His Book, illustrated by W. W. Denslow, G. M. Hill, 1899.

A New Wonderland, Being the First Account Ever Printed of the Beautiful Valley, and the Wonderful Adventures of Its Inhabitants, illustrated by Frank Ver Beck, R. H. Russell, 1900, revised edition published as *The Surprising Adventures of the Magical Monarch of Mo and His People,* Bobbs-Merrill, 1903, reprinted, Dover, 1968.

The Army Alphabet, illustrated by Harry Kennedy, G. M. Hill, 1900.

The Navy Alphabet, illustrated by Kennedy, G. M. Hill, 1900.

American Fairy Tales, G. M. Hill, 1901, reprinted, Dover, 1978, enlarged edition with additional stories published as *Baum's American Fairy Tales: Stories of Astonishing Adventures of American Boys and Girls with the Fairies of Their Native Land,* Bobbs-Merrill, 1908.

Dot and Tot of Merryland, illustrated by Denslow, G. M. Hill, 1901.

The Master Key: An Electrical Fairy Tale Founded Upon the Mysteries of Electricity and the Optimism of Its Devotees, illustrated by Fanny Y. Cory, Bowen-Merrill, 1901, reprinted, Hyperion Press, 1986.

The Life and Adventures of Santa Claus (also see below), illustrated by Mary Cowles Clark, Bowen-Merrill, 1902, reprinted, New American Library, 1986.

The Enchanted Island of Yew, Whereon Prince Marvel Encountered the High Ki of Twi and Other Surprising People, illustrated by Cory, Bobbs-Merrill, 1903.

The Woggle-Bug Book, illustrated by Ike Morgan, Reilly & Britton, 1905, reprinted, Scholarly Facsimiles, 1978.

Queen Zixi of Ix; or, The Story of the Magic Cloak (originally serialized in *St. Nicholas,* November, 1904-October, 1905; also see below), illustrated by Frederick Richardson, Century, 1905, reprinted, Dover, 1971.

(Under pseudonym Suzanne Metcalf) *Annabel: A Novel for Young Folks,* Reilly & Britton, 1906, 2nd edition, 1912.

John Dough and the Cherub (originally serialized in the Washington *Sunday Star,* October 14-December 30, 1906, and in other papers; also see below), illustrated by Neill, Reilly & Britton, 1906, reprinted, Dover, 1974.

(Under pseudonym Captain Hugh Fitzgerald) *Sam Steele's Adventures on Land and Sea* (also see below), illustrated by Howard Heath, Reilly & Britton, 1906.

(Under pseudonym Captain Hugh Fitzgerald) *Sam Steele's Adventures in Panama* (also see below), Reilly & Britton, 1907.

L. Frank Baum's Juvenile Speaker: Readings and Recitations in Prose and Verse, Humorous and Otherwise, illustrated by Neill and Maginel Wright Enright, Reilly & Britton, 1910, published as *Baum's Own Book for Children: Stories and Verses From the Famous Oz Books, Father Goose: His Book, Etc., Etc., With Many Hitherto Unpublished Selections,* 1911.

The Sea Fairies, illustrated by Neill, Reilly & Britton, 1911, reprinted, Books of Wonder, 1987.

The Daring Twins: A Story for Young Folk, illustrated by Pauline M. Batchelder, Reilly & Britton, 1911.

Sky Island: Being the Further Exciting Adventures of Trot and Cap'n Bill After Their Visit to the Sea Fairies, illustrated by Neill, Reilly & Britton, 1912, reprinted, Books of Wonder, 1988.

Phoebe Daring: A Story for Young Folk, illustrated by Batchelder, Reilly & Britton, 1913.

Jaglon and the Tiger Fairies (originally published in the *Delineator;* also see below), revised and rewritten by Jack Snow, illustrated by Dale Ulrey, Reilly & Lee, 1953.

The Visitors From Oz (based on Baum's newspaper feature "Queer Visitors From the Marvelous Land of Oz," 1904-05), illustrated by Dick Martin, Reilly & Lee, 1960.

Animal Fairy Tales (includes "Jaglon and the Tiger Fairies"; first published in the *Delineator,* January-September, 1905), illustrated by Dick Martin, International Wizard of Oz Club, 1969.

A Kidnapped Santa Claus (first published in the *Delineator,* December, 1904), illustrated by Richard Rosenblum, Bobbs-Merrill, 1969.

"SNUGGLE TALES" SERIES; ILLUSTRATED BY NEILL AND ENRIGHT

Little Bun Rabbit, Reilly & Lee, 1916.

Once Upon a Time, Reilly & Lee, 1916.

The Yellow Hen, Reilly & Lee, 1916.

The Magic Cloak, Reilly & Lee, 1916.

The Ginger-Bread Man, Reilly & Lee, 1917.

Jack Pumpkinhead, Reilly & Lee, 1917.

Oz-Man Tales (includes the first six volumes of the "Snuggle Tales" series), six volumes, Reilly & Lee, 1920.

UNDER PSEUDONYM FLOYD AKERS; "BOY FORTUNE HUNTERS" SERIES

The Boy Fortune Hunters in Alaska (originally published as *Sam Steele's Adventures on Land and Sea* by Captain Hugh Fitzgerald), Reilly & Britton, 1908.

The Boy Fortune Hunters in Egypt, Reilly & Britton, 1908.

The Boy Fortune Hunters in Panama (originally published as *Sam Steele's Adventures in Panama* by Captain Hugh Fitzgerald), Reilly & Britton, 1908.

The Boy Fortune Hunters in China, Reilly & Britton, 1909.

The Boy Fortune Hunters in Yucatan, Reilly & Britton, 1910.

The Boy Fortune Hunters in the South Seas, Reilly & Britton, 1911.

UNDER PSEUDONYM LAURA BANCROFT; "TWINKLE TALES" SERIES; ILLUSTRATED BY ENRIGHT

Bandit Jim Crow, Reilly & Britton, 1906.
Mr. Woodchuck, Reilly & Britton, 1906.
Prairie-Dog Town, Reilly & Britton, 1906.
Prince Mud-Turtle, Reilly & Britton, 1906.
Sugar-Loaf Mountain, Reilly & Britton, 1906.
Twinkle's Enchantment, Reilly & Britton, 1906.
Twinkle and Chubbins: Their Astonishing Adventures in Nature Fairyland (includes the first six volumes of the "Twinkle Tales" series), Reilly & Britton, 1911, reprinted, International Wizard of Oz Club, 1988.
Policeman Bluejay (sequel to *Bandit Jim Crow*), Reilly & Britton, 1907, published as *Babes in Birdland*, 1911, reprinted under name L. Frank Baum, 1917.

UNDER PSEUDONYM EDITH Van DYNE; "AUNT JANE'S NIECES" SERIES

Aunt Jane's Nieces, Reilly & Britton, 1906.
Aunt Jane's Nieces Abroad, Reilly & Britton, 1907.
Aunt Jane's Nieces at Millville, Reilly & Britton, 1908.
Aunt Jane's Nieces at Work, Reilly & Britton, 1909.
Aunt Jane's Nieces in Society, Reilly & Britton, 1910.
Aunt Jane's Nieces and Uncle John, Reilly & Britton, 1911.
Aunt Jane's Nieces on Vacation, Reilly & Britton, 1912.
Aunt Jane's Nieces on the Ranch, Reilly & Britton, 1913.
Aunt Jane's Nieces out West, Reilly & Britton, 1914.
Aunt Jane's Nieces in the Red Cross, Reilly & Britton, 1915.

UNDER PSEUDONYM EDITH Van DYNE

The Flying Girl, illustrated by J. P. Nuyttens, Reilly & Britton, 1911.
The Flying Girl and Her Chum, illustrated by Nuyttens, Reilly & Britton, 1912.
Mary Louise, Reilly & Britton, 1916.
Mary Louise in the Country, Reilly & Britton, 1916.
Mary Louise Solves a Mystery, Reilly & Britton, 1917.
Mary Louise and the Liberty Girls, Reilly & Britton, 1918.

PLAYS

(Under pseudonym Louis F. Baum) "The Maid of Arran" (based on William Black's novel *A Princess of Thule*), first produced in Syracuse, NY, May 15, 1882.
(Under pseudonym Louis F. Baum) "Matches," first produced in Richburg, NY, June, 1882.
(Under pseudonym Louis F. Baum) "Kilmourne; or, O'Connor's Dream," first produced in Syracuse, NY, April, 1888.
"The Wonderful Wizard of Oz" (musical loosely based on Baum's novel; also see below), music by Paul Tietjens, revised version produced under title "The Wizard of Oz" in Chicago, IL, 1902; produced on Broadway, 1903.
(With Emerson Hough) *The Maid of Athens* (fantasy scenario), privately printed, 1903.
(With Mrs. Carter Harrison) *Prince Silverwings* (scenario), A. C. McClurg, 1903.
"The Woggle-Bug" (musical based on *The Marvelous Land of Oz;* also see below), music by Frederick Chapin, first produced in Chicago, 1905.
"The Fairylogue and Radio-Plays" (motion picture and slide presentation; also see below), first produced in Grand Rapids, MI, 1908.

"The Fairy Prince," published in *Entertaining*, December, 1909.
"The Tik-Tok Man of Oz" (musical; also see below), music by Louis F. Gottschalk, first produced in Los Angeles, CA, 1913.
"Stagecraft: The Adventures of a Strictly Moral Man," music by Gottschalk, first produced in Santa Barbara, CA, 1914.
"The Patchwork Girl of Oz" (screenplay), Oz Film Manufacturing Co./Paramount, 1914.
"The Magic Cloak of Oz" (screenplay; loosely based on *Queen Zixi of Ix*), Oz Film Manufacturing Co., 1914.
"The Last Egyptian" (screenplay based on Baum's anonymous novel), Oz Film Manufacturing Co./Alliance Film Co., 1914.
"Violet's Dreams" (four separate screenplays), Oz Film Manufacturing Co., 1914-15.
"His Majesty, the Scarecrow of Oz" (screenplay; released as "The New Wizard of Oz"), Oz Film Manufacturing Co./Alliance Film Co., 1915.
"The Uplift of Lucifer; or, Raising Hell" (also see below), music by Gottschalk, produced in Santa Barbara, 1915.
"The Uplifters' Minstrels," music by Byron Gay, first produced in Del Mar, CA, 1916.
"The Orpheus Road Company," music by Gottschalk, produced at Coronado Beach, CA, 1917.
The Musical Fantasies of L. Frank Baum (includes "The Maid of Athens," "The King of Gee-Whiz," and "The Pipes O' Pan"; also see below), Wizard Press, 1958.
The Uplift of Lucifer (includes "The Uplift of Lucifer; or, Raising Hell," and "The Corrugated Giant"), privately printed, 1963.

Also author of unproduced plays, including (under pseudonym Louis F. Baum) "The Mackrummins," 1882; "The Queen of Killarney," 1885; "King Midas" (comic opera), music by Tietjens, 1901; "The Octopus; or, The Title Trust" (comic opera), music by Tietjens, 1901; "King Jonah XIII" (comic opera), music by Nathanial D. Mann, 1903; (with Isidore Witmark) "The Whatnexters," 1903; "Father Goose," music by Tietjens, 1904; "The Pagan Potentate," music by Tietjens, 1904; "Down Missouri Way," 1907; "Our Mary," 1907; "The Koran of the Prophet," 1909; "The Rainbow's Daughter; or, The Magnet of Love" (based in part on *Ozma of Oz*), 1909; "Ozma of Oz" (based on Baum's book), music by Manuel Klein, 1909; "Peter and Paul" (opera), music by Arthur Pryor, 1909; (with George Scarborough) "The Pipes O' Pan" (musical comedy), music by Tietjens, 1909; "The Girl From Oz," 1909; "The Pea-Green Poodle," 1910; and "The Clock Shop," 1910.

SONGS

(Under pseudonym Louis F. Baum) *Louis F. Baum's Popular Songs as Sung With Immense Success in His Great 5 Act Irish Drama, Maid of Arran*, music by Baum, J. G. Hyde, 1882.
The Songs of Father Goose for the Home, School, and Nursery, music by Alberta N. Hall, G. M. Hill, 1900.
The Wizard of Oz (from the musical), music by Tietjens, M. Witmark & Sons, 1902.
Down among the Marshes: The Alligator Song, music by Baum, M. Witmark & Sons, 1903.
What Did the Woggle-Bug Say?, music by Tietjens, Reilly & Britton, 1904.
The Woggle-Bug (from the musical), music by Chapin, M. Witmark & Sons, 1905.
The Tik-Tok Man of Oz (from the musical), music by Gottschalk, J. H. Remick & Co., 1913.

Susan Doozan, music by Byron Gay, Cooper's Melody Shop, 1920.

The High-Jinks of L. Frank Baum (for "The Uplifters"), Wizard Press, 1959.

OTHER

Baum's Complete Stamp Dealers Directory, Baum, Norris, 1873.

The Book of the Hamburgs: A Brief Treatise Upon the Mating, Rearing and Management of the Different Varieties of Hamburgs, H. H. Stoddard, 1886.

By the Candelabra's Glare: Some Verse, privately printed, 1898, reprinted, Scholarly Facsimiles, 1981.

The Art of Decorating Dry Goods Windows and Interiors, Show Window Publishing, 1900.

(Under pseudonym Schuyler Staunton) *The Fate of a Crown,* Reilly & Britton, 1905.

(Under pseudonym Schuyler Staunton) *Daughters of Destiny,* Reilly & Britton, 1906.

(Author of preface and photographer) Maud Gage Baum, *In Other Lands Than Ours,* privately printed, 1907.

(Under pseudonym John Estes Cooke) *Tamawaca Folks: A Summer Comedy,* Tamawaca Press, 1907.

Father Goose's Year Book: Quaint Quacks and Feathered Shafts for Mature Children, illustrated by Walter J. Enright, Reilly & Britton, 1907.

(Published anonymously) *The Last Egyptian: A Romance of the Nile,* illustrated by Francis P. Wightman, E. Stern, 1908.

Our Landlady (selections from Baum's column in the *Saturday Pioneer* [Aberdeen, S.D.], 1890-91), Friends of the Middle Border, 1941.

Also author of two unpublished novels, *Johnson* and *Molly Oodle.* Contributor of stories and poetry to magazines and newspapers, including *White Elephant, Youth's Companion, Times-Herald* (Chicago), and *St. Nicholas.* Editor and publisher, *Rose Lawn Home Journal* (Chittenango, NY), 1868-71.

MEDIA ADAPTATIONS: "The Wizard of Oz," of interest because it featured Oliver Hardy in his pre-Stan Laurel days as the Tin Woodman, was produced by Chadwick Pictures Corp. in 1925. A "Wizard of Oz" radio show aired on NBC from September, 1933, to April, 1934. The classic film version of "The Wizard of Oz," featuring Judy Garland, Ray Bolger, Bert Lahr, Jack Haley, Margaret Hamilton, and company, was produced by Loew's Inc. in 1939, and the Royal Shakespeare Company staged a production of this version in 1987. On September 18, 1960, the "Shirley Temple Show" presented its own adaptation of *The Land of Oz* on NBC television. Animated cartoon continuations of the *Wizard* include Videocraft's hour-long "Return to Oz," broadcast on NBC in 1964, and Filmation's "Journey Back to Oz," released theatrically in the United States in 1974 (of interest because Judy Garland's daughter Liza Minelli supplied the voice of Dorothy and Margaret Hamilton the voice of Aunt Em). "The Wiz," a musical version of the *Wizard* with an all-black cast, opened on Broadway in 1975; it won the Tony award for best musical of that year, and was made into a motion picture by Universal in 1978. The Australian film "20th Century Oz" was produced by Count Features and released in the United States by Inter Planetary in 1977. Walt Disney Productions filmed "Return to Oz" (loosely based on *The Marvelous Land of Oz* and *Ozma of Oz*) in 1985, and Rankin-Bass produced a puppet-animation "Life and Adventures of Santa Claus," which first aired on CBS, December 17, 1985; "The Dreamer of Oz," an NBC television movie based on Michael Patrick Hearn's Baum biography, starring John Ritter, is scheduled to air in 1990.

SIDELIGHTS: L. Frank Baum, the author of *The Wizard of Oz,* seemed to have been born with the proverbial silver spoon in his mouth. Frank (as he was known to his friends) was born into the wealthy family of Benjamin Ward Baum, a barrel-maker and sawyer who had made a fortune in the Pennsylvania oil fields during the Civil War. Since the young Baum suffered from a weak heart—a defect that forced him to lead a sheltered childhood—he was tutored at home, on the family estate of Roselawn outside the city of Syracuse, New York. An attempt to have him schooled at Peekskill Military Academy failed; young Baum had a seizure that was diagnosed as a heart attack, and the trauma left him with a lifelong distaste for educators and the military in general.

Frank Baum's life exhibited a "boom and bust" cycle, a pattern that began in his youth and lasted for the rest of his life. When he acquired a small printing press in 1870, he showed immediate enthusiasm, producing a small newspaper, *The Rose Lawn Home Journal,* and several other periodicals publishing news on subjects ranging from postage stamps to fancy chicken breeding. Still later, he displayed a passion for the stage, acted for a while with a Shakespearean troupe, and then wrote a five-act Irish melodrama entitled "The Maid of Arran." Financed in part by his father, he took the drama on the road in 1882, even performing it with moderate success in New York City. While still acting in his play he married Maud Gage, the youngest daughter of the noted woman's rights campaigner Matilda Joslyn Gage.

The Baums left the theater in 1883, and Frank opened an oil store and helped found Baum's Castorine Company. It was at this point that bad fortune struck. As a playwright he proved unable to repeat the success of "The Maid of Arran." The company that manufactured his family's lubricant, "Baum's Castorine," suffered financial hardships in the late 1880s. Baum moved west to be near his wife's family, but the store he opened in Aberdeen, South Dakota, closed after only a year (partly because of his liberal credit policies), and the newspaper he edited, the Aberdeen *Saturday Pioneer,* folded early in 1891. He then moved his family from South Dakota to Chicago, where he took a job as a newspaper editor which lasted less than a month. In the mid 1890s he proved moderately successful as a traveling crockery salesman.

The one occupation in which Baum seemed to excel was story telling. In the evenings at home, Baum was in the habit of relating original stories based on Mother Goose rhymes in order to amuse his sons, and his mother-in-law eventually suggested that he should try to sell them. In 1897 the firm of Way & Williams published *Mother Goose in Prose,* Baum's first book for children. The volume sold reasonably well, although the author later admitted that the illustrations by Maxfield Parrish—who became one of America's most popular artists—were more attractive than the text. Baum reflected on his past ineptitude in business in a rueful inscription in a copy of *Mother Goose in Prose* that he presented to his sister. "When I was young," Baum wrote, "I longed to write a great novel that should win me fame. Now that I am getting old my first book is written to amuse children. For, aside from my evident inability to do anything 'great,' I have learned to regard fame as a will-o-the-wisp which, when caught, is not worth the possession; but to please a child is a sweet and lovely thing that warms one's heart and brings its own reward."

"Baum had spent many years feeling his way uncertainly," reported David L. Greene and Dick Martin in *The Oz Scrapbook.* "Now, in his early forties, he had a certain sense of his own future; he would earn his living as a writer." In November of 1897 he started *The Show Window,* a magazine for window dressers that proved very successful and provided Baum with a steady income, as well as allowing him time to write other children's books. Working with W. W. Denslow, an artist acquaintance, Baum produced a volume of children's verses with poster-like illustrations, which he called *Father Goose: His Book.* The book met with much acclaim—although, according to Michael Patrick Hearn in *The Annotated Wizard of Oz,* Baum himself later attributed its popularity to the pictures rather than the verses—and it quickly became the best-selling juvenile picture book of 1899.

Father Goose's success led Baum to complete another story, which he called variously *The Emerald City, From Kansas to Fairyland,* and finally *The Wonderful Wizard of Oz.* It tells of Dorothy Gale's journey from her Kansas prairie home to the land of Oz, the strange friends she makes there, and the adventures they have while trying to send Dorothy home. Published by the George M. Hill Company, a small Chicago press, in September, 1900, the book earned Baum "a special place in the history of children's literature," wrote Hearn in the *Dictionary of Literary Biography,* for its decor as well as its story. "Even today," Hearn continued, "the first edition of *The Wonderful Wizard of Oz* is an impressive piece of bookmaking"; like *Father Goose,* it was lavishly illustrated by Denslow, sporting two dozen color plates and over a hundred textual illustrations.

It was greeted with the same enthusiasm that met *Father Goose;* according to Hearn in *The Annotated Wizard of Oz,* the first printing of ten thousand copies ran out about two weeks after publication, and by January of 1901 the Hill company advertized that it had published around ninety thousand copies of the *Wonderful Wizard.* A contemporary critic, reviewing the book for the *New York Times,* recognized the *Wizard*'s innovations: "The crudeness that was characteristic of the old-time publications . . . would now be enough to cause the modern child to yell with rage and vigor and to instantly reject the offending volume, if not to throw it out of the window. The time when anything was good enough for children has long since passed, and . . . in 'The Wonderful Wizard of Oz' the fact is clearly recognized that the young as well as their elders love novelty. They are pleased with dashes of color and something new in the place of the old, familiar, and winged fairies of Grimm and Andersen."

Critics agree, however, that it is Baum's story rather than Denslow's decorations that continues to interest readers. Although *The Wonderful Wizard* uses some traditional fairy-tale trappings—witches, wizards, and magic—the novel is more remarkable for the changes it introduced into the genre. "Most fairy tales are universal because they occur in distant times and places," Greene and Martin explained. "Baum achieved universality by combining the folk tale with elements familiar to every child—cornfields, things made of tin, circus balloons." Edward Wagenknecht wrote in *Utopia Americana,* "Baum taught American children to look for wonder in the life around them, to realize even smoke and machinery may be transformed into fairy lore if only we have sufficient energy and vision to penetrate to their significance and transform them to our use."

Baum's book broke new ground in other ways as well. "*The Wonderful Wizard of Oz,*" Hearn explained in the *Dictionary of Literary Biography,* "pooh-poohed the old Puritan belief that literature must teach; Baum's book was revolutionary in that it was written 'solely to pleasure children of today.' But . . . the principal reason *The Wonderful Wizard of Oz* survives is that it is an exceptional story." The book, Greene and Martin explained, "was published during a time of populists and progressives and Utopian schemes based on an optimistic view of man that, after two world wars, is attractive today precisely because it is so hard

to accept. In Oz, good motives, ingenuity and trust in oneself always win, although the way to victory is often rough. Oz is a proving ground in which Dorothy and the other child heroes and heroines develop these quintessentially American ideals." Oz itself is a wonderful place, but the characters Dorothy meets there are more wonderful still. "The Scarecrow and the Tin Woodman are among the greatest grotesques in American literature," said Greene and Martin. "They are made human by their very human desires, and Baum supplied many details to render them even more 'real.' "

Although *The Wonderful Wizard of Oz* proved very popular, it was not as financially successful as *Father Goose* had been. However, in 1902 Baum helped adapt the book into a stage musical, which was a smash hit and ran on Broadway for a record 293 performances. The production was graced with many attractive sets and astonishing (for the time) special effects. In order to conform with theatrical tastes of the period, however, Baum and his collaborators had to make some drastic changes in the plot: Dorothy became a teenager, and she was provided with a lover, a poet named Sir Dashemoff Daily, and a pantomime cow named Imogene instead of her little dog Toto. Gag writers turned the comedy team of Fred Stone and David Montgomery, as the Scarecrow and Tin Woodman, into the stars of the show. The prosperity of the stage "Wizard" encouraged many imitations; among the most successful was Victor Herbert's "Babes in Toyland." Herbert went on to feature Montgomery and Stone in his operetta "The Red Mill."

The stage "Wizard" had considerable influence on Baum's future writings as well as the American musical theatre. Although the production proved lucrative, Greene and Martin reported that "expenses and continued financial bad luck offset his income from books and from the play of *The Wizard* to such an extent that in 1903 . . . Baum was insolvent." In 1904, after many requests by children for more adventures of the Scarecrow and Tin Woodman, Baum produced *The Marvelous Land of Oz,* which he dedicated to Montgomery and Stone. Hoping that the new book could be turned into a musical as successful as the *Wizard,* Baum introduced many elements from contemporary theater into his plot, including an army of pretty girls in tight uniforms, another pair of comic grotesques in the form of Jack Pumpkinhead and the Woggle-Bug, and changing the leading boy into a girl at the story's end. The book was very successful; however, when a stage version was produced under the title of "The Woggle-Bug," it failed. Baum was never able to repeat the "Wizard"'s dramatic success, although he continued to put theatrical elements in many of his later Oz books.

Popular demand and financial difficulties forced Baum to return to Oz again and again. In 1908 he had invested in the "Fairylogue and Radio Plays," a combination slide and motion picture presentation about Oz, which, although popular, left him with large debts. In an attempt to save money the Baums moved to Hollywood, California, in 1910. Baum tried to end the Oz series that year with the publication of *The Emerald City of Oz,* but circumstances intervened; in June, 1911, the author declared bankruptcy. In 1913 Baum published *The Patchwork Girl of Oz* and, taking the title of "Royal Historian of Oz," resigned himself to producing a new Oz book each year.

Living in Hollywood, Baum soon became involved in the infant motion picture industry. With some friends, he formed the Oz Film Manufacturing Company and produced several films based on his Oz books and some of his other novels. Although marked by very good special effects, most of the films were not commercially successful, and the company failed in 1915; fortunately,

Baum had not invested his own money in the venture, and escaped the collapse without financial damage. His failing heath, however, curtailed these activities. An operation left him bedridden for the last year of his life, without strength to do much more than answer letters from children. "When the Royal Historian of Oz died on May 6, 1919," declared Allen Eyles in *The World of Oz*, "he was the most celebrated children's author of his time." "The Royal Historian," Eyles concluded, "was going home."

"The Land of Oz was a real place to millions of children and adults, and to many, Baum had seemed a personal friend," said Greene and Martin. "Now Baum was dead; Oz, of course lives on." Reilly & Lee contracted with Ruth Plumly Thompson, a Philadelphia writer, to continue the Oz series after Baum's death, and she wrote nineteen original stories that were as popular as Baum's original fourteen. Oz continues to fascinate readers today; it has inspired authors ranging from Ray Bradbury and Gore Vidal to Erica Jong, and interpretations ranging from the Freudian implications of Dorothy's voyage to a parable on the politics of William Jennings Bryan. A band of Oz enthusiasts formed the International Wizard of Oz Club in 1957, and their journal, the *Baum Bugle*, is an important source of scholarship on Baum and Oz.

BIOGRAPHICAL/CRITICAL SOURCES:

BOOKS

Baum, Frank J., and Russell P. MacFall, *To Please a Child: A Biography of L. Frank Baum, Royal Historian of Oz*, Reilly & Lee, 1961.
Children's Literature Review, Volume 15, Gale, 1988.
Dictionary of Literary Biography, Volume 22: *American Writers for Children, 1900-1960*, Gale, 1983.
Eyles, Allen, *The World of Oz*, HPBooks, 1985.
Ford, Alla T., and Dick Martin, *The Musical Fantasies of L. Frank Baum*, Wizard Press, 1958.
Gardner, Martin, and Russel B. Nye, *The Wizard of Oz and Who He Was*, Michigan State University Press, 1957.
Greene, Douglas G., et al, *Bibliographia Oziana: A Concise Bibliographical Checklist of the Oz Books by L. Frank Baum and His Successors*, International Wizard of Oz Club, 1975, revised and expanded edition, 1988.
Greene, David L., and Dick Martin, *The Oz Scrapbook*, Random House, 1977.
Hearn, Michael Patrick, annotater, *The Annotated Wizard of Oz*, Clarkson N. Potter, 1973.
Hearn, Michael Patrick, editor, *The Wizard of Oz* ("Critical Heritage" series), Schocken, 1983.
Moore, Raylyn, *Wonderful Wizard, Marvelous Land*, Bowling Green University Popular Press, 1974.
Snow, Jack, *Who's Who in Oz*, Reilly & Lee, 1954.
Twentieth-Century Literary Criticism, Volume 7, Gale, 1982.
Wagenknecht, Edward, *Utopia Americana*, University of Washington Book Store, 1929.

PERIODICALS

American Book Collector (special L. Frank Baum issue), December, 1962.
American Heritage, December, 1964.
American Quarterly, spring, 1964.
Baum Bugle, 1957-present.
Bookseller, November 15, 1903.
Georgia Review, fall, 1960.
Journal of Popular Culture, fall, 1973.
New Republic, December 12, 1934.

New York Review of Books, September 29, 1977; October 13, 1977.
New York Times Saturday Review of Books and Art, September 8, 1900.
Portland Telegram, October 22, 1910.
Saturday Review, April 11, 1959.
Times Literary Supplement, March 4, 1969.
Writer's Digest, December, 1952.

OBITUARIES:

PERIODICALS

Seattle Post-Intelligencer, July 13, 1919.

—*Sketch by Kenneth R. Shepherd*

[Sketch reviewed by Michael Patrick Hearn]

*   *   *

BAUM, Louis F.
See BAUM, L(yman) Frank

*   *   *

BAUMBACH, Jonathan   1933-

PERSONAL: Born July 5, 1933; son of Harold M. (an artist) and Ida H. (Zackheim) Baumbach; married Elinor Berkman, September 10, 1956 (divorced, 1967); married Georgia Brown, June 10, 1969; children: (first marriage) David, Nina; (second marriage) Noah, Nicholas. *Education:* Brooklyn College (now of the City University of New York), A.B., 1955; Columbia University, M.F.A., 1956; Stanford University, Ph.D., 1961.

ADDRESSES: Home—320 Stratford Rd., Brooklyn, N.Y. 11218. *Office*— Department of English, Brooklyn College of the City University of New York, Brooklyn, N.Y. 11210.

CAREER: Stanford University, Stanford, Calif., instructor in English, 1958-60; Ohio State University, Columbus, assistant professor of English, 1961-64; New York University, New York, N.Y., assistant professor of English and director of freshman English, 1964-66; Brooklyn College of the City University of New York, Brooklyn, N.Y., associate professor, 1966-70, professor of English, 1970—. Member of board of directors, Teachers and Writers Collaborative, 1966—. Fiction Collective, co-founder, 1974, co-director, 1974-78, currently member of board of directors. Visiting professor, Tufts University, 1970-71, and University of Washington, 1978 and 1983. *Military service:* U.S. Army, 1956-58.

MEMBER: National Society of Film Critics (chairman, 1982-84).

AWARDS, HONORS: Young Writers Award, *New Republic*, 1958; Yaddo fellowship, summers, 1963, 1964, and 1965; National Endowment for the Arts fellowship, 1969; Guggenheim fellowship, 1978; Ingram-Merrill fellowship, 1983.

WRITINGS:

"The One-Eyed Man Is King" (play), first produced at Theater East, New York City, 1956.
The Landscape of Nightmare: Studies in the Contemporary American Novel, New York University Press, 1965.
(Contributor) W. R. Robinson, editor, *Man and the Movies*, Louisiana State University Press, 1967.
(Editor with Arthur Edelstein) *Moderns and Contemporaries: 12 Masters of the Short Story*, Random House, 1968, 2nd edition, 1977.

(Editor) *Writers as Teachers/Teachers as Writers,* Holt, 1970.
(Editor) *Statements: New Fiction from the Fiction Collective,* Braziller, 1975.
(Editor with Peter Spielberg) *Statements 2: New Fiction,* Fiction Collective, 1977.
The Return of Service (story collection), University of Illinois Press, 1979.
The Life and Times of Major Fiction, Fiction Collective, 1987.

Contributor of short stories and articles to *Esquire, Iowa Review, Kenyon Review, Partisan Review, Chicago Review, TriQuarterly, Nation,* and other periodicals. Movie reviewer, *Partisan Review,* 1973-82.

NOVELS

A Man to Conjure With, Random House, 1965.
What Comes Next, Harper, 1968.
Reruns, Fiction Collective, 1974.
Babble, Fiction Collective, 1976.
Chez Charlotte and Emily, Fiction Collective, 1979.
My Father More or Less, Fiction Collective, 1982.

SIDELIGHTS: In his first book, *The Landscape of Nightmare: Studies in the Contemporary American Novel,* experimental writer Jonathan Baumbach examines the works of a number of postwar American novelists. "Baumbach explored each novel," Larry McCaffery of the *Dictionary of Literary Biography* writes, "in terms of how it portrays the nightmarish conditions of contemporary society and how each individual protagonist attempts to carve his own niche, or openly rebels against these conditions." In contrast to the novelists of an earlier generation who expressed the nightmarish quality of society "in terms of social defeats and victories," Bernard McCabe explains in *Commonweal,* the contemporary novelists Baumbach studies express it "in terms of the Self." It is this psychological approach that especially interests Baumbach. The novels he examines, Baumbach clarifies in his study, are concerned with "the confrontation of man with the objectification of his primordial self and his exemplary spiritual passage from innocence to guilt to redemption." Of particular importance to Baumbach, McCaffery reports, is "the way in which [these novels] make manifest the inner worlds and secret lives of their protagonists."

In his own novels, Baumbach also explores "inner worlds and secret lives," but does so through innovative narrative structures. Baumbach's narrative innovations have "placed him in the company of our most serious experimentalists," Jerome Klinkowitz explains in *The Life of Fiction.* The similarities and interrelationships between memories, dreams, our perceptions of the real world, and the images of popular culture are constant concerns in all of Baumbach's fiction. With his first novel, *A Man to Conjure With,* Baumbach "immediately established the shifting terrain of dream, memory, imagination, and public nightmare that his fiction would explore," writes McCaffery. Ironically, it is the most conventional of Baumbach's novels. As Klinkowitz explains, "there is experimentation [in *A Man to Conjure With*], but within traditional bounds; there is nothing unrealistic in the book except the character's dreams, which are clearly identified as such."

The novel concerns Peter Becker, who is trying to restore his marriage after being separated from his wife for many years. By piecing his life back together, Becker also hopes to reestablish a sense of personal identity. Speaking of Becker, Baumbach tells John Graham in *The Writer's Voice: Conversations with Contemporary Writers:* "It's as if all the details will add up to a picture of himself. And then, he can look at himself as he was. He has

the idea, perhaps, that the man he was at twenty is still somewhere there, all the potentiality that was there at twenty and forgotten and lost. To look at himself at twenty is to come back there and start again, to recoup what he's lost."

"Much of the action," writes Klinkowitz, "takes place in Peter [Becker's] dreams, and his character is defined by them." Klinkowitz notes that Baumbach uses dreams in this novel to study the workings of the human imagination and to determine how dreams are expressed in language. Haskel Frankel of the *New York Times Book Review,* although admitting that "there is no question as to the author's talent, sensitivity, control and intelligence," believes *A Man to Conjure With* "adds up to nothing. We are introduced to a man by someone we respect, asked to study the man carefully—and then are never told the point of our studies." S. L. Bellman of *Saturday Review,* however, stresses the importance of the protagonist's dreams. This novel, he writes, "has the character of a weird Freudian nightmare that involves no stage effects or supernaturalism whatever." Also writing in *Saturday Review,* Henry S. Rasnik finds the novel "an ingenious portrait of a schlemiel-Everyman cracking up," while Emile Capouya of *Book Week* believes that "Baumbach writes with great elegance and wit. . . . He is inventive and amusing."

The dreams found in Baumbach's next novel, *What Comes Next,* "are indistinguishable from life," Klinkowitz states, since the protagonist, a college student named Christopher Steiner, is going mad. There is no specific catalyst for his madness. He is simply reacting to his society. "Too much violence in the street. Sex, bombing, suffocation, rape. Too much madness," as Baumbach describes it in the novel. The narrative is structured so as to reflect Steiner's deteriorating state of mind, interweaving his dreams and hallucinations with the real events around him. "Baumbach's short-jabbing prose, skirting the necessary edge of hysteria," writes McCabe, "thrusts the violent city at us. . . . Throughout the novel Baumbach works to dissolve ugly fact into fantasy, fantasy into fact, so that the nightmare and the reality are convincingly one."

C. D. B. Bryan of the *New York Times Book Review* compares Baumbach's handling of *What Comes Next* to the work of Nathanael West. "Baumbach's writing," Bryan states, "like West's, is finely chiseled, keen and tough; his images are violent and garish; his hero, like [West's character] Miss Lonelyhearts, is obsessed by nightmares. . . . [But] Baumbach's value as a writer is that he makes the insanity of his hero seem appallingly sane."

In *Reruns,* Baumbach's narrator is again concerned with reassembling his life into a meaningful pattern. The narrator describes himself as "a hostage to the habit of rerunning the dead past in the cause of waking from the dream." Organized into a series of 33 short chapters, each a "dream-exorcism" as John Ager states in the *Carolina Quarterly,* the book presents the record of a man's life as a month's worth of short films at a cinema. Each chapter, or film, captures a life experience and retells it through dream logic and cinematic language. Some experiences are redone several times in different ways, as if the narrator were attempting to change the past through the power of his imagination. "These 'reruns,'" McCaffery explains, "are nightmarish, frantic, often violent episodes . . . whose characters and events are generated from a wide variety of cultural cliches, fairy tales, stories, and movies. This is a world of terror, loneliness, and absurdity." Irving Malin of the *New Republic* agrees: "Usual routines are destroyed; only explosive energy remains. . . . The confusion, violence, humor, and madness are mixed so quickly that we . . . are overwhelmed."

By using cinematic techniques in *Reruns,* writes Michael Mewshaw in the *New York Times Book Review,* Baumbach attempts to capture in prose "the kind of simultaneous vision a movie or painting can express. He wants to show us objects and characters from mutually exclusive perspectives, to stretch our understanding of time and expand our comprehension of emotions so that contrary feelings will spring from the same experiences." Malin also sees the cinematic presentation as important to the novel's theme. "Baumbach," Malin writes, "asks important questions: does the individual gain self-knowledge by confronting his popular culture? What exactly is the value of dream (fantasy) in creating identity?" In *Reruns,* and the following novels, *Babble* and *Chez Charlotte and Emily,* McCaffery believes, Baumbach explores "the role of the media (especially cinema) in creating societal norms and the individual's notion of self."

The characters and situations of popular culture form an important part of *Babble,* the adventures of a baby-hero. Because the novel is narrated by a 3-year-old, the conventions of fairy tales, comic books, and television are often used to tell the story, because these are the storytelling techniques most familiar to a small child. In this way, McCaffery writes, Baumbach investigates "the process whereby language is discovered and narrative patterns are imposed."

In contrast to Baumbach's previous novels, the distinctions between dream and reality are irrelevant in *Babble* because the baby narrator can make no such distinctions when relating his adventures. Fact, fantasy, and dream are intertwined into "a kind of surreal Bildungsroman," as McCaffery describes the book. Although the novel uses "the episodic form of *Reruns* and the beleaguered protagonists of both earlier novels," Thalia Selz writes in *fiction international,* "a transformation takes place in attitude. *Baby,* whom we seem prepared to label a clown, manages through patience and stratagem, to remain a hero in a dangerous world."

Like *Reruns* and *Babble, Chez Charlotte and Emily* is a fragmented narrative constructed much like a film montage. As Irving Malin writes in the *Hollins Critic,* it is a series of "stories within stories, boxes within boxes. The narrator writes about a couple; the couple write or fantasize about another couple; the third couple in turn have novelistic tendencies." All of the stories thus related are strongly reminiscent of the cinema, partly because the characters restage and reshoot scenes in varying ways, as might be done while making a movie. Other characters have the names of famous movie stars, while certain plot elements have their parallels in old movie scripts. The importance of these cinematic references, McCaffery points out, lies in the characters' ability to use their imaginations to restructure their world. "All these stories," McCaffery states, "are evidently metaphorical reflections of inner tensions, desires, and personality traits. . . . It is . . . through the agency of imagination and metaphor that [the characters] Joshua and Genevieve perpetuate themselves and their relationship, make love and communicate."

In his short story collection *The Return of Service,* Baumbach again uses the materials of popular culture. "Baumbach's stories," writes Terrence Winch of the *Washington Post Book World,* "show the influence of nonsense literature, literary satire and experimental fiction. There is a story about a story, a parody of a detective novel, an essay on a nonexistent, ridiculous novel, [and] a retelling of Hollywood's King Kong myth." Don Skiles of *American Book Review* believes that Baumbach's short stories "reflect the post-modern era, as they try for a form that synchs with a post-television age. . . . *The Return of Service* is a delight, a gratifying book to read, an adventurous, chance-taking

work." Skiles defines Baumbach's concern as "the potential situation, the next curve in the road, the way another party might view the same events . . .; the alternative ways in which a scene may be shot."

"Like many other postmodern writers," McCaffery states, "Baumbach's focus is not so much on the ambiguous, destructive, entropic 'outer world' as it is on the resources of the imagination in coping with this reality. The imagination for Baumbach . . . is instead a realm where man can freely manipulate the components of his experience (which is produced as much by symbols and media-produced substitutions as it is by the so-called real world) into structures of utility, order, and possibly even beauty."

BIOGRAPHICAL/CRITICAL SOURCES:

BOOKS

Baumbach, Jonathan, *The Landscape of Nightmare: Studies in the Contemporary American Novel,* New York University Press, 1965.
Baumbach, *What Comes Next,* Harper, 1968.
Baumbach, *Reruns,* Fiction Collective, 1974.
Contemporary Literary Criticism, Gale, Volume 6, 1976, Volume 23, 1983.
Dictionary of Literary Biography Yearbook: 1980, Gale, 1981.
Graham, John, *The Writer's Voice: Conversations with Contemporary Writers,* Morrow, 1973.
Klinkowitz, Jerome, *The Life of Fiction,* University of Illinois Press, 1977.

PERIODICALS

American Book Review, March/April, 1981.
Book Week, October 3, 1965.
Carolina Quarterly, winter, 1975.
Chicago Review, autumn, 1978.
Contemporary Literature, winter, 1978.
Commonweal, September 24, 1965, December 13,. 1968.
fiction international, No. 6/7, 1976.
Hollins Critic, February, 1980.
Hudson Review, winter, 1976-77.
Kenyon Review, January, 1966.
Nation, December 7, 1974.
New Republic, October 19, 1974.
New York Times Book Review, November 21, 1965, October 13, 1968, October 13, 1974, January 13, 1980, July 27, 1980.
Saturday Review, April 17, 1965, October 26, 1968.
Sewanee Review, July, 1980.
Village Voice, October 31, 1974.
Washington Post Book World, March 30, 1980, May 3, 1982.

*　　*　　*

BEAN, Normal
See BURROUGHS, Edgar Rice

*　　*　　*

BEATTIE, Ann 1947-

PERSONAL: Born September 8, 1947, in Washington, D.C.; daughter of James A. and Charlotte (Crosby) Beattie; married David Gates (a psychiatrist), 1972 (marriage ended); married Lincoln Perry (a painter), 1988. *Education:* American University, B.A., 1969; University of Connecticut, M.A., 1970, further graduate study, 1970-72.

ADDRESSES: Home—Charlottesville, Va. *Agent*—Lynn Nesbit, International Creative Management, 40 West 57th St., New York, N.Y. 10019.

CAREER: Writer. University of Virginia, Charlottesville, visiting writer and lecturer, 1973-77, 1980, 1982; Harvard University, Cambridge, Mass., Briggs-Copeland Lecturer in English, 1977-78.

AWARDS, HONORS: Guggenheim fellowship, 1978; American University Distinguished Alumnae Award, 1980; award of excellence, American Academy and Institute of Arts and Letters, 1980.

WRITINGS:

SHORT STORIES

Distortions, Doubleday, 1976.
Secrets and Surprises, Random House, 1979.
Jacklighting, Metacom Press, 1981.
The Burning House, Random House, 1982.
Where You'll Find Me, and Other Stories, Linden/Simon & Schuster, 1986.

Contributor of numerous short stories to *New Yorker, House and Garden, Ladies' Home Journal, Harper's,* and other magazines.

NOVELS

Chilly Scenes of Winter, Doubleday, 1976.
Falling in Place (novel), Random House, 1980.
Love Always (Book-of-the-Month Club alternate), Random House, 1985.
Picturing Will, Random House, 1990.

OTHER

Spectacles (for children), Workman, 1985.
Alex Katz (nonfiction), Abrams, 1987.
(Editor) *The Best American Short Stories,* Houghton, 1988.

WORK IN PROGRESS: An untitled novel.

SIDELIGHTS: American novelist and short story writer Anne Beattie was a senior at American University when *Mademoiselle* magazine chose her to be its guest editor. The young writer's experiences there helped her to recognize that she did not want a career in journalism, and she began to study literature. Stories she wrote when her classes became boring impressed her professor, who helped her to sell them to small magazines. With this encouragement, she kept writing and eventually sold stories to the *New Yorker* and *Esquire. Chilly Scenes of Winter,* her first novel, became a Book-of-the-Month Club alternate and established her career as a novelist.

Chilly Scenes of Winter is concerned with those people who came of age in the 1960s and find themselves lost and disillusioned in the 1970s. In an interview with Bob Miner published in *Village Voice,* Beattie said: "I was going out of my way in the novel to say something about the '60s having passed. It just seems to me to be an attitude that most of my friends and most of the people I know have. They all feel sort of let down, either by not having involved themselves more in the '60s now that the '70s are so dreadful, or else by having involved themselves to no avail. Most of the people I know are let down—they feel cheated—and these are the people I am writing about." *Yale Review* contributor David Thorburn compliments Beattie on her portrait of the main character, Charles. Thorburn comments, "The hero himself is wonderfully alive: a gentle bewildered man, extravagantly loyal to old friends and to the songs of the sixties, drifting through a final nostalgia for the mythologies of adversary selfhood he ab-

sorbed in college and toward an embarrassed recognition of his hunger for such ordinary adventures as marriage and fatherhood. The unillusioned tenderness that informs Beattie's portrait of her central character is a rare act of intelligence and mimetic art."

Early reviews that cast Beattie as a spokesperson of the '60s generation took a too narrow view, she has often said. She told a writer for the *Los Angeles Times,* "What a lot of writers ignore is that I'm not a sociologist. . . . My test in writing these stories was not, did I get it right about the '60s, but, is it literature?" In subsequent works, she has shown that her subject is human relationships in a world where the erosion of values has resulted in chaos. She has also become known for her distinctive style which does not appeal to all readers, but has been highly praised.

Beattie's style is characterized by simple declarative sentences and an accretion of detail that achieves its effects without adding up to the endings some readers expect. "Beattie understands and dramatizes our formlessness. She is especially the artist of situations, not plots," explains J. D. O'Hara in the *New York Times Book Review. Commentary* contributor John Romano elaborates, "Her sentences are often plain, flat, their grammar exposed like the lighting fixtures in avant-garde furniture boutiques, and the effect is at first wearying. Only later does the sympathetic center of her work betray itself. We may feel misled by the outward reserve, but, again, her willingness to distort when necessary, her passion for the particular, is ultimately an index of her concern for the integrity of things and people in themselves."

Though some regard Beattie's style as an obstacle, other reviewers have found it praiseworthy. *New York Times* critic Anatole Broyard comments: "In spite of a style that virtually eliminates personality, she still manages to haunt the reader with her work. The things her characters say and do are rather like the inexplicable noises very old houses make in the middle of the night. You wake up in alarm when you hear them—what can that be?—then reason asserts itself and you go uneasily back to sleep."

John Updike is another admirer of Beattie's style. "Her details—which include the lyrics of the songs her characters overhear on the radio and the recipes of the rather junky food they eat—calmly accrue," he comments in the *New Yorker.* "Her dialogue trails down the pages with an uncanny fidelity to the low-level heartbreaks behind the banal; her resolutely unmetaphorical style builds around us a maze of familiar truths that nevertheless has something airy, eerie, and in the end lovely about it. Her America is like the America one pieces together from the *National Enquirers* that her characters read—a land of pathetic monstrosities, of pain clothed in cliches, of extraterrestrial trivia. Things happen 'out there,' and their vibes haunt the dreary 'here' we all inhabit."

Regarding her style, Beattie told Miner, "My stories are a lot about chaos and many of the simple flat statements that I bring together are usually non sequiturs or bordering on being non sequiturs—which reinforces the chaos. I write in those flat simple sentences because that's the way I think. I don't mean to do it as a technique." Indeed, her style has more to do with the lives of her characters than with a deliberate attempt to be bland. Physical handicaps, tragic accidents, limited opportunites, emotional paralysis, and anxiety trouble her characters. John Leonard of the *New York Times* remarks that *Falling in Place* "is full of awful thoughts; they jump out at us like foam-rubber rabbits at a laundromat. Miss Beattie, of course, is a master of the unemphatic, the flat utterance, sentences surrounded by silences, voices that come to us in the night as if our heads were shortwave radios, facts that abrade." Her characters, says Leonard, "aren't falling out of grace; they are unacquainted with grace."

In much of Beattie's fiction, as in *Where You'll Find Me,* however, bleak lives are a backdrop for rare moments of compassion and hope. "In all of Beattie's tales," writes *Globe and Mail* contributor Charles Mandel, "her characters are learning to cope with separation, loss, or love. But if not all moments can be greeted with optimism, then at least they may be met with understanding." People drawn by Beattie survive, when they do, on "maintenance doses" of encouragement to carry on, Margaret Atwood remarks in the *New York Times Book Review.* "This, perhaps, is one of the most marvellous things about Beattie's fiction," Mandel concludes. "No matter how much effort is involved in living a life, she seems to be saying, it is ultimately worth living."

Picturing Will, which took five years for Beattie to complete, "takes up once more the lightness and hollowness that go with the narcissism of the '70s and '80s. Liberation from so many outside commands—of religion, duty, guilt, repression—leaves only the body, free of its chains, in a state of weightlessness that is quite the opposite of flying. . . . A world freed of bonds falls apart, and the children fall through the cracks," Richard Eder comments in the *Los Angeles Times.* Will's father and mother divorce when he is still a baby. His mother is affectionate but preoccupied with earning a living as a wedding photographer, an enterprise that turns into a career as an artist. Will's life is a series of encounters with part-time parental figures. Some are caring, but distracted by commitments to their own fulfillment; others make Will the witness to their homosexual affairs. What Will suffers is not their open hostility, but their indifference. Yet Will's story ends with the compassion and hope that readers find in Beattie's other fiction. *Los Angeles Times* writer Josh Getlin relates, "People who at first seem bumbling and ineffective become the real heroes in Will's life."

Beattie's deft handling of this secret and its revelation holds the novel together in the way that action brings coherence to other novels. The narrative is interspersed with sections from an adult's diary, but the reader doesn't learn who wrote these meditations on parenting until Will—by then a parent himself—finds and reads it. Its author was one of the more emotionally distant adults in his life, a caring "parent" Will didn't know he had. " 'Picturing Will' would be admirable for its technique alone; what makes it Beattie's best novel is her new and fearless way with emotional complexity," Laura Shapiro remarks in *Newsweek.* Commenting on her purpose in writing *Picturing Will,* Beattie told D'Arcy Fallon in the *Chicago Tribune,* "It was interesting to put myself in the position of articulating something I do believe, which is: You should be very skeptical about anything you're told."

Several reviewers feel that *Picturing Will* brings together the best elements of the novel format and the style Beattie has developed in her short stories. *Chicago Tribune* reviewer Joseph Coates, for example, relates that in this episodic novel Beattie successfully depicts the "lonely outsider" character that is more readily presented in short stories. This is significant, he says, since the "defined and settled society" usually drawn in novels "is a community that doesn't exist." Coates concludes, "With 'Picturing Will,' and its modulated portraits of a definitive contemporary character type, Beattie becomes a master novelist of our brave new world."

MEDIA ADAPTATIONS: Chilly Scenes of Winter was made into the film *Head Over Heels* and first released in 1979; an edited version was released again in 1982. Also aired in 1982 on PBS's *American Playhouse* series was a dramatised version of "Weekend" (a short story from *Secrets and Surprises*).

BIOGRAPHICAL/CRITICAL SOURCES:

BOOKS

Contemporary Literary Criticism, Gale, Volume 8, 1978, Volume 13, 1980, Volume 18, 1986, Volume 40, 1987.
Contemporary Novelists, St. Martin's, 1986.
Dictionary of Literary Biography Yearbook 1982, Gale, 1983.
McCaffery, Larry, and Gregory, Sinda, *Alive and Writing: Interviews with American Authors of the 1980s,* University of Illinois Press, 1987.

PERIODICALS

Book World, October 3, 1976.
Chicago Tribune, February 5, 1990.
Christian Science Monitor, September 29, 1976.
Commentary, February, 1977.
Hudson Review, spring, 1977, autumn, 1977.
Los Angeles Times, January 18, 1990.
Los Angeles Times Book Review, January 21, 1990.
Ms., December, 1976.
Newsweek, August 23, 1976, January 22, 1990.
New Yorker, November 29, 1976.
New York Times, July 24, 1976, January 3, 1979, January 4, 1990, January 7, 1990.
New York Times Book Review, August 15, 1976, January 14, 1979, June 8, 1980, September 26, 1982.
Partisan Review, Volume 50, number 4, 1983.
Publishers Weekly, September 19, 1986 (interview).
Saturday Review, August 7, 1976.
Tribune Books (Chicago), January 28, 1990.
Village Voice, August 9, 1976.
Washington Post, February 4, 1990.
Washington Post Book World, January 28, 1990.
Yale Review, summer, 1977.

*   *   *

BEAUVOIR, Simone (Lucie Ernestine Marie Bertrand) de 1908-1986

PERSONAL: Born January 9, 1908, in Paris, France; died August 14, 1986, of a respiratory ailment in Paris, France; daughter of Georges Bertrand (an advocate to the Court of Appeal, Paris) and Francoise (Brasseur) de Beauvoir; children: (adopted) Sylvie Le Bon. *Education:* Sorbonne, University of Paris, licencie es lettres and agrege des lettres (philosophy), 1929. *Religion:* Atheist.

ADDRESSES: Home—1 bis rue Schoelcher, 75014 Paris, France.

CAREER: Philosopher, novelist, autobiographer, nonfiction writer, essayist, editor, lecturer, and political activist. Instructor in philosophy at Lycee Montgrand, Marseilles, France, 1931-33, at Lycee Jeanne d'Arc, Rouen, France, 1933-37, at Lycee Moliere and Lycee Camille-See, both Paris, France, 1938-43. Founder and editor, with Jean-Paul Sartre, of *Les Temps modernes,* beginning 1945.

MEMBER: International War Crimes Tribunal, Ligue du Droit des Femmes (president), Choisir.

AWARDS, HONORS: Prix Goncourt, 1954, for *Les Mandarins;* Jerusalem Prize, 1975; Austrian State Prize, 1978; Sonning Prize for European Culture, 1983; LL.D. from Cambridge University.

WRITINGS:

L'Invitee (novel), Gallimard, 1943, reprinted, 1977, translation by Yvonne Moyse and Roger Senhouse published as *She Came to Stay,* Secker & Warburg, 1949, World Publishing, 1954, reprinted, Flamingo, 1984.

Pyrrhus et Cineas (philosophy; also see below), Gallimard, 1944.

Les Bouches inutiles (play in two acts; first performed in Paris), Gallimard, 1945, translation published as *Who Shall Die,* River Press, 1983.

Le Sang des autres (novel), Gallimard, 1946, reprinted, 1982, translation by Moyse and Senhouse published as *The Blood of Others,* Knopf, 1948, reprinted, Pantheon, 1984.

Tous les hommes sont mortel (novel), Gallimard, 1946, reprinted, 1974, translation by Leonard M. Friedman published as *All Men Are Mortal,* World Publishing, 1955.

Pour une morale de l'ambiguite (philosophy; also see below), Gallimard, 1947, reprinted, 1963, translation by Bernard Frechtman published as *The Ethics of Ambiguity,* Philosophical Library, 1948, reprinted, Citadel, 1975.

Pour une morale de l'ambiguite [and] *Pyrrhus et Cineas,* Schoenhof's Foreign Books, 1948.

L'Existentialisme et la sagesse des nations (philosophy; title means "Existentialism and the Wisdom of the Ages"), Nagel, 1948.

L'Amerique au jour le jour (diary), P. Morihien, 1948, translation by Patrick Dudley published as *America Day by Day,* Duckworth, 1952, Grove, 1953.

Le Deuxieme Sexe, two volumes, Gallimard, 1949, translation by H. M. Parshley published as *The Second Sex,* Knopf, 1953, reprinted, Random House, 1974 (Volume 1 published in England as *A History of Sex,* New English Library, 1961, published as *Nature of the Second Sex,* 1963).

The Marquis de Sade (essay; translation of *Faut-il bruler Sade?;* also see below; originally published in *Les Temps modernes*), translation by Annette Michelson Grove, 1953 (published in England as *Must We Burn de Sade?,* Nevill, 1953, reprinted, New English Library, 1972).

Les Mandarins (novel), Gallimard, 1954, reprint published in two volumes, French and European, 1972, translation by Friedman published as *The Mandarins,* World Publishing, 1956, reprinted, Flamingo, 1984.

Privileges (essays; includes *Faut-il bruler Sade?*), Gallimard, 1955.

La Longue Marche: Essai sur la Chine, Gallimard, 1957, translation by Austryn Wainhouse published as *The Long March,* World Publishing, 1958.

Memoires d'une jeune fille rangee (autobiography), Gallimard, 1958, reprinted, 1972, translation by James Kirkup published as *Memoirs of a Dutiful Daughter,* World Publishing, 1959, reprinted, Penguin, 1984.

Brigitte Bardot and the Lolita Syndrome, translated by Frechtman, Reynal, 1960, published with foreword by George Amberg, Arno, 1972.

La Force de l'age (autobiography), Gallimard, 1960, reprinted, 1976, translation by Peter Green published as *The Prime of Life,* World Publishing, 1962.

(With Gisele Halimi) *Djamila Boupacha,* Gallimard, 1962, translation by Green published under same title, Macmillan, 1962.

La Force des choses (autobiography), Gallimard, 1963, reprinted, 1977, translation by Richard Howard published as *The Force of Circumstance,* Putnam, 1965.

Une Mort tres douce (autobiography), Gallimard, 1964, reprinted with English introduction and notes by Ray Davison, Methuen Educational, 1986, translation by Patrick

O'Brian published as *A Very Easy Death,* Putnam, 1966, reprinted, Pantheon, 1985.

(Author of introduction) Charles Perrault, *Bluebeard and Other Fairy Tales of Charles Perrault,* Macmillan, 1964.

(Author of preface) Violette Leduc, *La Batarde,* Gallimard, 1964.

Les Belles Images (novel), Gallimard, 1966, translation by O'Brian published under same title, Putnam, 1968, reprinted with introduction and notes by Blandine Stefanson, Heinemann Educational, 1980.

(Author of preface) Jean-Francois Steiner, *Treblinka,* Simon & Schuster, 1967.

La Femme rompue (three novellas), Gallimard, 1967, translation by O'Brian published as *The Woman Destroyed,* Putnam, 1969, reprinted, Pantheon, 1987.

La Vieillesse (nonfiction), Gallimard, 1970, translation by O'Brian published as *The Coming of Age,* Putnam, 1972 (published in England as *Old Age,* Weidenfeld & Nicolson, 1972).

Tout compte fait (autobiography), Gallimard, 1972, translation by O'Brian published as *All Said and Done,* Putnam, 1974.

Quand prime le spirituel (short stories), Gallimard, 1979, translation by O'Brian published as *When Things of the Spirit Come First: Five Early Tales,* Pantheon, 1982.

Le Ceremonie des adieux: Suivi de entretiens avec Jean-Paul Sartre (reminiscences), Gallimard, 1981, translation published as *Adieux: A Farewell to Sartre,* Pantheon, 1984.

(Contributor with Jean-Paul Sartre; also editor) *Lettres au Castor et a quelques autres,* Gallimard, 1983, Volume 1: *1926-1939,* Volume 2: *1940-1963.*

SIDELIGHTS: At Simone de Beauvoir's funeral on April 19, 1986, flowers from all over the world filled the corner of the Montparnasse cemetery where she was laid to rest next to Jean-Paul Sartre (1905-1980). Banners and cards from the American-based Simone de Beauvoir Society, women's studies groups, women's health centers and centers for battered women, diverse political organizations, and publishing houses attested to the number of lives that the author had touched during her seventy-eight years. Five thousand people, many of them recognizable figures from the political, literary, and film worlds, made their way along the boulevard du Montparnasse past her birthplace, past the cafes where she, Sartre, and their friends had discussed their ideas and written some of their manuscripts, to the cemetery.

Beauvoir was a perceptive witness to the twentieth century, a witness whose works span the period from her early childhood days before World War I to the world of the 1980s. Born in Paris in 1908, in the fourteenth "arrondissement" or district where she continued to live throughout most of her life, Beauvoir was raised by a devoutly Catholic mother from Verdun and an agnostic father, a lawyer who enjoyed participating in amateur theatrical productions. The contrast between the beliefs of the beautiful, timid, provincial Francoise de Beauvoir and those of the debonair Parisian Georges de Beauvoir led the young Simone to assess situations independently, unbiased by the solid parental front presented by the more traditional families of many of her classmates. As family finances dwindled during World War I, Beauvoir observed the uninspiring household chores that fell upon her mother and decided that she herself would never become either a housewife or a mother. She had found such pleasure in teaching her younger sister Helene everything she herself was learning at school that she decided to pursue a teaching career when she grew up.

Beauvoir and her best friend Zaza "Mabille" (Beauvoir often assigned fictional names to friends and family members described in her autobiographical writings) sometimes discussed the relative merits of bringing nine children into the world, as Zaza's mother had done, and of creating books, an infinitely more worthwhile enterprise, the young Beauvoir believed. As the girls matured, Beauvoir observed the degree to which Zaza's mother used her daughter's affection and commitment to Christian obedience to manipulate Zaza's choice of career and mate. When Zaza, tormented by her parents' refusal to grant her permission to marry Maurice Merleau-Ponty, the "Jean Pradelle" of the memoirs, died at twenty-one, Beauvoir felt that her friend had been assassinated by bourgeois morality. Many of Beauvoir's early fictional writings attempted to deal on paper with the emotions stirred by her recollection of the "Mabille" family and of Zaza's death. Only many years later did she learn that Merleau-Ponty, who became a well-known philosopher and writer and remained a close friend of Beauvoir's and Sartre's, was unacceptable to the "Mabilles" because he was an illegitimate child.

Despite her warm memories of going to early morning mass as a little girl with her mother and of drinking hot chocolate on their return, Beauvoir gradually pulled away from the traditional values with which Francoise de Beauvoir hoped to imbue her. She and her sister began to rebel, for example, against the restrictions of the Cours Adeline Desir, the private Catholic school to which they were being sent. Weighing the pleasures of this world against the sacrifices entailed in a belief in an afterlife, the fifteen-year-old Beauvoir opted to concentrate on her life here on earth. Her loss of faith erected a serious barrier to communication with her mother.

Beauvoir was convinced during several years of her adolescence that she was in love with her cousin Jacques Champigneulles ("Jacques Laiguillon" in her memoirs), who introduced her to books by such French authors as Andre Gide, Alain-Fournier, Henry de Montherlant, Jean Cocteau, Paul Claudel, and Paul Valery; these books scandalized Beauvoir's mother, who had carefully pinned together pages of volumes in their home library that she did not want her daughters to read. Jacques Champigneulles, however, seemed unwilling to make a commitment either to Beauvoir or to anything else, and the Beauvoir sisters were totally disillusioned when this bright bohemian opted to marry the wealthy and generously dowried sister of one of his friends.

Because family finances did not allow Georges de Beauvoir to provide dowries, his daughters became unlikely marriage prospects for young middle-class men, and both Simone and Helene were delighted to have this excuse for continuing their studies and pursuing careers. Even as a young girl, Beauvoir had a passion for capturing her life on paper. In the first volume of her autobiography, *Memoires d'une jeune fille rangee* (*Memoirs of a Dutiful Daughter*), she looked back with amusement at her determination, recorded in her adolescent diary, to "tell all"; yet her memoirs, her fiction, her essays, her interviews, and her prefaces do indeed record events, attitudes, customs, and ideas that help define approximately seven decades of the twentieth century.

It was through Rene Maheu, a Sorbonne classmate called "Andre Herbaud" in the memoirs, that Beauvoir first met Jean-Paul Sartre in a study group for which she was to review the works and ideas of German philosopher Gottfried Wilhelm von Leibniz. In Sartre, Beauvoir found the partner of whom she had dreamed as an adolescent. As she remarked in *Memoirs of a Dutiful Daughter,* "Sartre corresponded exactly to the ideal I had set for myself when I was fifteen: he was a soulmate in whom I found, heated to the point of incandescence, all of my passions. With him, I could always share everything." And so she did, for fifty-one years, from the time they became acquainted at the Sorbonne in 1929 until his death on April 15, 1980.

Together Sartre and Beauvoir analyzed their relationship, deciding that they enjoyed an indestructible essential love but that they must leave themselves open to "contingent loves" as well, to expand their range of experience. Although marriage would have enabled them to receive a double teaching assignment instead of being sent off to opposite ends of the country, they were intent upon escaping the obligations that such a "bourgeois" institution would entail. That neither had a particular desire for children was an added reason to avoid marriage. A daring and unconventional arrangement during the early 1930s, their relationship raised consternation in conservative members of Beauvoir's family.

Except for a brief period during World War II, Beauvoir and Sartre never lived together but spent their days writing in their separate quarters and then came together during the evenings to discuss their ideas and to read and criticize one another's manuscripts. As both became well-known figures in the literary world, they found it increasingly difficult to maintain their privacy; as *La Force des choses* (*The Force of Circumstance*) records, they had to alter their routine and avoid certain cafes during the years after the war in order to protect themselves from the prying eyes of the public.

Sartre's autobiography, *Les Mots* (*The Words*), published in 1963, dealt only with the early years of his life. Beauvoir's autobiographical writings provide a much more complete and intimate account of the adult Sartre. In several volumes of reminiscences, Beauvoir described their mutual reluctance to leave their youth behind and become part of the adult world, their struggles to set aside adequate time for writing, the acceptance of their works for publication, their travels, their friendships, their gradually increasing commitment to political involvement; her final autobiographical volume, *Le Ceremonie des adieux: Suivi de entretiens avec Jean-Paul Sartre* (*Adieux: A Farewell to Sartre*), recreates her anguish in witnessing the physical and mental decline of a lifelong companion who had been one of the most brilliant philosophers of the twentieth century.

For Beauvoir, writing was not only a way of preserving life on paper but also a form of catharsis, a means of working out her own problems through fiction. Her early short stories, written between 1935 and 1937 and originally rejected by two publishers, were brought out by Gallimard in 1979. The tales in *Quand prime le spirituel* (*When Things of the Spirit Come First: Five Early Tales*) captured Beauvoir's infatuation with Jacques, the tragedy of Zaza's death, the young philosophy teacher's ambivalence about the impact her ideas and her life-style might have on her impressionable lycee students in Marseille and Rouen, and her sense of excitement as she saw the world opening up before her. Beauvoir identified strongly with her central character Marguerite who, in the final paragraphs of the book, perceives the world as a shiny new penny ready for her to pick up and do with as she wishes. Terry Keefe's *Simone de Beauvoir: A Study of Her Writings* provides a detailed discussion of each of the five stories that make up this collection.

Experimenting with nontraditional relationships, Sartre and Beauvoir had formed a trio with Beauvoir's lycee student Olga Kosakiewicz in 1933. The anguish experienced by Beauvoir as a result of this intimate three-way sharing of lives led to the writing of her first published work, *L'Invitee* (*She Came to Stay*). In this novel, the author relived the hothouse atmosphere generated by the trio, and she chose to destroy the judgmental young intruder, the fictional Xaviere, on paper, but to dedicate her novel to Olga. The real life situation resolved itself less dramatically after Olga became interested in Jacques-Laurent Bost, a former student of Sartre's, and broke away from the trio; the four principals remained lifelong friends, however. In her 1986 study, *Simone de Beauvior,* Judith Okely suggests that *She Came to Stay* reflects not only the Beauvoir-Sartre-Olga trio but also the young Simone's rivalry with her mother for her father's affections.

With World War II Beauvoir's attention shifted from the concerns and crises of her personal life to a broader spectrum of philosophical, moral, and political issues. In the short essay *Pyrrhus et Cineas,* written during a three-week period in 1943, she launched an inquiry into the value of human activity, examining questions of freedom, communication, and the role of the other in the light of the existentialist ideas presented in Sartre's *L'Etre et le neant: Essai d'ontologie phenomenologique* (*Being and Nothingness: Essay on Phenomenological Ontology*). In his 1975 monograph, *Simone de Beauvoir,* Robert Cottrell discusses *Pyrrhus et Cineas* as "a popularization of existentialist thought."

Beauvoir's second novel, *Le Sang des autres* (*The Blood of Others*), focused on the dilemma of dealing with the consequences of one's acts. The liberal Jean Blomart, shaken by the accidental death of a young friend he inspired to participate in a political demonstration, struggles throughout much of the narrative to avoid doing anything that may inadvertently harm another human being, his "search for a saintly purity," as Carol Ascher labels it in *Simone de Beauvoir: A Life of Freedom.* The female protagonist, Helene Bertrand, intent on protecting her own happiness in a world turned upside down by war and the German Occupation, is shaken out of her inertia by the cries of a Jewish mother whose small daughter is being wrenched away from her by the Gestapo. Helene seeks an active and ultimately fatal involvement in terrorist Resistance activities orchestrated by Jean Blomart, who has decided finally that violence is perhaps the only rational response to Hitler's insanity. Infused with the euphoria of Resistance camaraderie, the novel highlights a question that is also central to Sartre's play *Les Mains sales* (*Dirty Hands*)—the relationship between intellectuals and violence.

Moral and ethical issues continued to dominate Beauvoir's works in the 1940s. Caught up in the success of Sartre's play *Les Mouches* (*The Flies*) during the Occupation, she decided that she too would like to write for the theatre. *Les Bouches inutiles* (*Who Shall Die?*), based on a historical incident which took place in the fourteenth century, reprises the main theme of *The Blood of Others,* examining the consequences of a young man's determination to remain pure and blameless by not taking part in the decisions of the town council. The play also protests the assumption that able-bodied young men are the only truly useful citizens in a besieged community. Beauvoir frankly related in her memoirs dramatist Jean Genet's criticism of her theatrical sense, confessing that he sat beside her shaking his head disapprovingly throughout the entire opening night performance. She never again attempted to write for the theatre, although Keefe notes the dramatic potential of her plot and the "spare and sharp" quality of the dialogue in Act I.

One of the most difficult aspects of the war years for Beauvoir and her friends was the often senseless deaths of their contemporaries. In *Simone de Beauvoir: Encounters with Death,* Elaine Marks focuses on the preoccupation with death permeating the writer's works and on what Marks labels her evasions of confrontation with death. For Beauvoir, death was an outrage, a

scandal, and in 1943, she began to write a third novel, *Tous les hommes sont mortel* (*All Are Mortal*), for which she created a hero who has become immortal and who therefore meanders from his thirteenth-century birthplace in Italy on through to the twentieth century. Because Raymond Fosca's alternating attempts to seize political power and to establish peace on earth all result in disappointment and frustration, the reader concludes that immortality would be a curse rather than a blessing, that life's value is derived from sharing experiences with one's contemporaries and from a willingness to take the risks implicit in human mortality. According to *The Force of Circumstance,* this novel was Beauvoir's attempt to deal with her own feelings and anxieties about death. Konrad Bieber, in his 1979 study *Simone de Beauvoir,* senses the presence of "the philosopher behind the novelist" throughout the book yet also notes "long moments of drama, of genuine poignancy, that bring to the fore all that is human."

As Beauvoir's works and Sartre's became better known, the label "existentialist" was regularly attached to them. At first Beauvoir resisted the use of the term, but she and Sartre gradually adopted it and began to try to explain existentialist philosophy to the public. In *Pour une morale de l'ambiguite* (*The Ethics of Ambiguity*), published in 1947, Beauvoir defined existentialism as a philosophy of ambiguity, one which emphasized the tension between living in the present and acting with an eye to one's mortality; she also attempted to answer critics who had accused existentialists of wallowing in absurdity and despair. In the four essays published the following year as *L'Existentialisme et la sagesse des nations* ("Existentialism and the Wisdom of the Ages"), Beauvoir argued for the importance of a philosophical approach to modern life. Here she defended existentialism against accusations of frivolity and gratuitousness and explained that existentialists considered man neither naturally good nor naturally bad: "He is nothing at first; it is up to him to make himself good or bad depending upon whether he assumes his freedom or denies it." Emphasizing the fact that man can be "the sole and sovereign master of his destiny," Beauvoir insisted that existentialist philosophy was essentially optimistic; in *Simone de Beauvoir and the Limits of Commitment,* however, Anne Whitmarsh sees the author's existentialism as "a stern ethical system."

With the end of the war came the opportunity to travel again. Beauvoir spent four months in the United States in 1947, lecturing on college campuses throughout the country about the moral problems facing writers in postwar Europe. She recorded her impressions through journal entries dating from January 25 to May 19, 1947, in *L'Amerique au jour le jour* (*America Day by Day*), which was dedicated to black author Richard Wright and his wife Ellen. Her perceptive eye took in a great variety of detail but saw everything through a lens whose focus was influenced by certain preconceived notions. Keefe finds the value of the book in the record it presents of Beauvoir's "excitement and disappointment at a historical moment when many Europeans knew little about America and were eager to expose themselves to its impact, for better or worse." Consistently critical of capitalist traditions and values, *America Day by Day* can be paired with Beauvoir's account of her 1955 trip to China, *La Longue Marche: Essai sur la Chine* (*The Long March*), in which she euphorically accepts everything in communist China. While praising Beauvoir's ability to evoke settings and glimpses of life in China, Keefe sees *The Long March* as "first and foremost a long, extremely serious attempt to explain the situation of China in 1955-56 and justify the direction in which the new regime [was] guiding the country."

Ready after the war to begin her purely autobiographical works, Beauvoir realized that she first needed to understand the extent to which being born female had influenced the pattern of her life. She therefore spent hours at the Bibliotheque Nationale (National Library) in Paris seeking documentation for each section of the book that was to become the battle cry of feminism in the latter half of the twentieth century. When *Le Deuxieme Sexe* (*The Second Sex*) appeared in 1949, reactions ranged from the horrified gasps of conservative readers to the impassioned gratitude of millions of women who had never before encountered such a frank discussion of their condition. The opening statement of the section on childhood, "One is not born a woman, one becomes one," has become familiar throughout the world, and the book advises women to pursue meaningful careers and to avoid the status of "relative beings" implied, in its author's view, by marriage and motherhood.

Before turning to her memoirs, Beauvoir wrote the novel that won her the prestigious Goncourt Prize. *Les Mandarins* (*The Mandarins*) presents the euphoria of Liberation Day in Paris and the subsequent disillusionment of French intellectuals who had been temporarily convinced that the future was theirs to fashion as they saw fit, but who found themselves gradually dividing into factions as the glow of Resistance companionship and of victory over the Nazis dimmed. Beauvoir always denied that *The Mandarins* was a roman a clef, with Robert Dubreuilh, Henri Perron, and Anne Dubreuilh representing Sartre, Albert Camus, and herself; nonetheless, echoes of the developing rift between Sartre and Camus, of the discussions of staff members of *Les Temps modernes* (the leftist review founded by Sartre, Beauvoir, and their associates), and of the concern of French intellectuals over the revelation of the existence of Soviet work camps are clearly audible throughout the novel. Moreover, Lewis Brogan is certainly a fictionalized portrait of Chicago author Nelson Algren, who became one of Beauvoir's "contingent loves" during her 1947 trip to the States and to whom the novel is dedicated. Whether or not the work is a roman a clef, it is generally regarded, in Ascher's words, as Beauvoir's "richest, most complex, and most beautifully wrought novel."

The first volume of Beauvoir's autobiography appeared in 1958. In *Memoirs of a Dutiful Daughter,* the author chronicled the warmth and affection of the early years of her life, her growing rebellion against bourgeois tradition, her sense of emancipation when she moved from the family apartment on the rue de Rennes to a rented room at her grandmother's. Highlighted in these pages are her close association with her sister—"I felt sorry for only children," she declared, her relationship with Zaza, her infatuation with Jacques. Jean Paul Sartre appears only in the concluding pages of this volume. In *Simone de Beauvoir on Woman,* Jean Leighton focuses on the portrait of Zaza in *Memoirs of a Dutiful Daughter,* finding that she "epitomizes . . . traditional feminine qualities. Next to Simone de Beauvoir she is the most vivid person in the book."

Beauvoir dedicated the second volume of her autobiography, *La Force de l'age* (*The Prime of Life*), to Sartre. The first half of the narrative tells the story of their lives from 1929 to 1939, recounting the exhilarating sense of freedom they experienced as they pooled their money to travel throughout France and to London, Italy, Germany, and Greece. The second half of the book begins in 1939, as the German occupation of France was about to begin, and ends with Liberation Day in Paris in August 1944. These pages provide one of the most vivid accounts of life in France during World War II, as the reader witnesses the lines of people waiting for gas masks, the sirens and descents into metro stations during air raids, and the struggle to find enough food to survive.

These were the years when leftist intellectuals remained in close contact with one another, when Albert Camus, actress Maria Casares, writers Michel Leiris and Raymond Queneau, theatrical director Charles Dullin, and artist Pablo Picasso joined Beauvoir, Sartre, Olga, and Bost in "fiestas" that provided occasional nights of relaxation amidst the bombings and the anticipation of the Allied landing. The emotions of Liberation Day were unforgettable for Beauvoir, who asserted: "No matter what happened afterward, nothing would take those moments away from me; nothing has taken them away; they shine in my past with a brilliance that has never been tarnished."

What did become tarnished, however, were Beauvoir's hopes of participating in the creation of a brave new world, preferably one in which socialism would solve the problems of society. The third volume of autobiography, *The Force of Circumstance,* begins with the Liberation and covers the period from 1944 to early 1963. Despite the success of her many books that were published during those years, despite her extensive travels and increasing political involvement, *The Force of Circumstance* was written with a heavy heart because of the anguish associated with the Algerian war. These were also the years during which Beauvoir began to reflect upon aging and death, began to realize that there were certain activities in which she was engaging for perhaps the last time. The final sentence in the memoir's epilogue has been widely discussed: "I can still see . . . the promises with which I filled my heart when I contemplated that gold mine at my feet, a whole life ahead of me. They have been fulfilled. However, looking back in amazement at that gullible adolescent I once was, I am stupefied to realize to what extent I have been cheated." She felt cheated because the goals she had set for herself did not lead to the sense of fulfillment that she had anticipated; she felt cheated too because all human activity, no matter how successful, leads uncompromisingly to the same impasse, the death of the individual. For Konrad Bieber, *The Force of Circumstance* is "a remarkable monument to the crucial years of the cold war. . . . A whole era, with its ups and downs, its hopes and disillusionments, is seen through the temperament of a highly gifted writer."

1963 was a time of personal crisis for Beauvoir both because of her vision of the state of the modern world and because of the death of her mother. Deeply affected by watching her mother valiantly struggle against cancer, Beauvoir shared with her readers the anxiety of knowing more about her mother's condition than she could reveal to her, the dilemma of how far to authorize heroic medical measures, the pain of helplessly watching a life ebb away. In the moving pages of *Une Mort tres douce* (*A Very Easy Death*), a slender volume dedicated to her sister, the author recaptured the warmth of her childhood relationship with her mother and reactivated her admiration for this woman who had always "lived against herself" yet could still appreciate a ray of sunlight or the song of the birds in the tree outside her hospital window. Looking back at her interaction with her mother, Beauvoir realized the full impact of Francoise de Beauvoir's unhappy childhood, of the unfortunate social restraints that kept her mother from finding a satisfying outlet for the energy and vitality which she had passed on to her daughters but which she had never been able to use appropriately herself. Sartre considered *A Very Easy Death* Beauvoir's best work; Marks, who has commented on its "excruciating lucidity," calls the book the only one of the author's writings "in which the hectic rhythm which she projects on the world is abruptly interrupted and the interruption prolonged."

Tout compte fait (*All Said and Done*), dedicated to Sylvie Le Bon whom Beauvoir later adopted, covers the decade following the publication of *The Force of Circumstance.* Here Beauvoir abandons the chronological treatment of events employed in the earlier volumes of memoirs; instead she devotes one section to speculation about what might have happened *if* she had been born into a different family, she had not met Sartre at the Sorbonne, or had married her cousin Jacques, for example; other sections explore her dreams and provide accounts of her trips to places such as Japan, the U.S.S.R., Israel, and Egypt. After expressing a sense of satisfaction about her ability to communicate the tone of her life to her readers, she leaves it to them to draw whatever conclusions they wish from this particular volume of her autobiography.

Adieux: A Farewell to Sartre, a companion piece to *A Very Easy Death,* records Beauvoir's efforts to cope with the anguish of watching age and illness take their toll on her companion of fifty years. It is dedicated to "those who have loved Sartre, who love him and who will love him." Beauvoir's subsequent publication of Sartre's *Lettres au Castor et a quelques autres* further attempts to share the quality of their relationship with her readers. "Castor" was a nickname invented by her Sorbonne classmate Rene Maheu, who noted the similarity between the name Beauvoir and the English word "beaver" (castor in French) and who considered it an appropriate appellation for the hard-working Beauvoir. The two volumes of Sartre's letters cover a period from 1926 to 1963 and include quite detailed references to his involvements with other women. Some feminist criticism has seen *Adieux,* with its rather graphic account of Sartre's mental and physical decline, as Beauvoir's revenge on her partner for the pain inflicted upon her by his numerous "contingent" affairs. In an essay appearing in *Philosophy and Literature,* Hazel Barnes disagrees, considering these passages "both factual reporting and a tribute" and noting "the profound respect which Sartre and Beauvoir had for each other, something deeper than the obvious affection, companionship and commonality of values, more bedrock than love."

During the mid-1960s Beauvoir had also returned to fiction with a novel, *Les Belles Images.* Dedicated to Claude Lanzmann, one of the younger staff writers for *Les Temps modernes* and a "contingent love" of Beauvoir's from 1952 to 1958, *Les Belles Images* describes a milieu quite alien to Beauvoir, that of the mid-century technocrats. The novel centers on a bright, attractive career woman, comfortably married and the mother of two daughters, who suddenly finds herself caught between two generations as she attempts to help her estranged mother cope with the loss of her wealthy lover and to answer the probing questions of her own ten-year-old daughter about poverty and misery. As she gradually develops sensitivity she has been taught by her mother to restrain, Laurence despairs of ever changing anything in her own life, yet vows in the concluding lines of the novel that she will raise her daughters to express their feelings, to allow themselves to be moved by the plight of undernourished children in Third World countries, of factory workers shackled to uninspiring jobs. Laurence is an incarnation of the contemporary superwoman who attempts to juggle her commitments to her career, her husband, her children, her aging parents, even her lover, until she eventually falls apart under the strain of such responsibilities.

The three stories in the 1967 collection *La Femme rompue* (*The Woman Destroyed*) reflect the degree to which Beauvoir had been listening to the women who wrote and spoke to her about the problems of their more traditional lives. One of the stories, "Age of Discretion," focuses on a recently retired woman professor, author of several books, for whom life seems to lose all meaning when her son abandons academia for a more lucrative

business job and when critics suggest that her latest book merely repeats ideas presented in earlier ones. "Monologue" takes the reader through a New Year's Eve of neurotic ranting by the twice-divorced Murielle, whose possessiveness has driven her sixteen-year-old daughter to suicide and who wants to force her son and her second husband to live with her once again so that she will regain her social status as a wife and mother. The title story highlights the plight of the middle-aged Monique, who abandoned her medical studies in order to marry and have children and who suddenly discovers that her husband is having an affair with a younger and more independent woman. In each case the protagonist has allowed herself to be relegated to the status of a "relative being" dependent upon others for her sense of identity. According to Mary Evans in *Simone de Beauvoir: A Feminist Mandarin,* the setting of both *Les Belles Images* and *The Woman Destroyed* is "the culture in which people become objects, but the objects least able to manipulate their fate are women."

In the late 1960s Beauvoir turned her attention to an important study of old age, a companion piece to *The Second Sex.* She gave her book, published in 1970, the straightforward title *La Vieillesse* ("Old Age"), but the title was euphemistically translated as *The Coming of Age* in the United States. The work focuses upon the generally deplorable existence of most elderly people, and along with a film entitled "Promenades au pays de la vieillesse" ("Wandering through the Pathways of Old Age"), in which Beauvoir appeared, this book defines one of the as yet unresolved dilemmas of the late twentieth century. Bieber sees in *The Coming of Age* an example of Beauvoir's "boundless empathy" and of her understanding of human frailty; Ascher, in contrast, finds it "shocking for its lack of feeling for the special plight of old women" and asserts that for the author the universal is male, at least among the elderly.

Several critics have taken Beauvoir to task for her apparently negative presentation of women and their values. Leighton sees the women of Beauvoir's fiction as "finely etched portraits of various types of femininity [that] personify in a compelling way the pessimistic and anti-feminine bias of *The Second Sex.*" Ascher's personal letter to Beauvoir in the middle of her *Simone de Beauvoir: A Life of Freedom* speaks of "my resistance to accepting your grim view of women's condition." For Evans there is an assumption in Beauvoir's works that "traditionally male activities (the exercise of rationality, independent action, and so on) are in some sense superior, and are instances almost of a higher form of civilization than those concerns—such as child care and the maintenance of daily life—that have traditionally been the preserve of women." Whitmarsh is critical of the author's confining her political commitment to the ethical and the literary rather than extending her activities to the practical aspects of everyday politics. Okely finds that many of Beauvoir's generalizations are based on her limited experience in a small Parisian intellectual circle and do not apply as readily to cultures that are neither western, white, nor middle class.

A substantial number of interviews granted by Beauvoir gave her the opportunity to clarify many of her ideas and to answer her critics. Speaking with Francis Jeanson in an interview published as *Simone de Beauvoir ou l'entreprise de vivre,* she elaborated on her childhood, on her relationship with both her parents, on her conviction that being a woman had never hindered her progress toward the goals she had set for herself. At that particular time (the mid-1960s), she defined feminism as a way of living individually and of fighting collectively and strongly opposed any tendency to consider men as the enemy. Literature, in her opinion, should serve to make people more transparent to one another.

She acknowledged a puritanical strain in herself caused by her early upbringing and spoke with Jeanson about what she labeled her "schizophrenia," a determination to throw herself wholeheartedly into any project she undertook and an accompanying unwillingness to deviate from her original plan even when intervening circumstances made it no longer practical.

Betty Friedan's *It Changed My Life* contains a dialogue with Beauvoir, to whom Friedan looked for answers to the questions raised by the American feminist groups that were forming in the 1970s. In her introduction to this dialogue, Friedan acknowledges her debt to Beauvoir: "I had learned my own existentialism from her. It was *The Second Sex* that introduced me to that approach to reality and political responsibility that . . . led me to whatever original analysis of women's existence I have been able to contribute." When they spoke, however, she and Beauvoir disagreed completely about the viability of motherhood for women seeking their independence and about the possibility of providing salaries for housewives in order to enhance their self-image. In *It Changed My Life,* Friedan expressed disappointment over what she saw in Beauvoir as detachment from the lives of real women, and concluded: "I wish her well. She started me out on a road on which I'll keep moving. . . . There are no gods, no goddesses. . . . We need and can trust no other authority than our own personal truth."

Who was Simone de Beauvoir for others? The newspaper and magazine articles that appeared after her death provide a variety of answers to that question. For many women, she was the person who led the way, who opened up horizons and suggested possibilities of breaking out of the mold society had previously forged for them. The caption on the front page of *Le Nouvel Observateur,* taken from an article by philosophy professor Elisabeth Badinter, proclaimed, "Women, you owe her everything!" According to American feminist Kate Millett, quoted in London's *Observer,* "She had opened a door for us. All of us . . . women everywhere, their lives touched and illumined ever after." In the *New York Times* Gloria Steinem remarked that "More than any other single human being, she's responsible for the current international women's movement," and Betty Friedan labeled her "an authentic heroine in the history of womanhood." Despite her determination never to have children of her own, she became the "symbolic mother" of several generations of women. Josyane Savigneau declared in *Le Monde* that women in responsible positions today are "the descendants of this woman without children . . . who, obstinately, for more than sixty years . . . affirmed that there was nothing wrong with being born a woman."

Most appraisals of Beauvoir's writings focused on *The Second Sex,* called by Philip Wylie in the *New York Times* "one of the few great books of our era." However, Bertrand Poirot-Delpech, who noted in *Le Monde* that Beauvoir was "a much less minor novelist than one might think," described *The Mandarins* as one of the best sources of documentation on the committed intellectuals of the cold war period. Millett pronounced "The Woman Destroyed" "a literary masterpiece" and Beauvoir's books on aging and death great social documents. Michel Contat, writing for *Le Monde,* saw the 1946 novel *All Men Are Mortal* as Beauvoir's most powerful philosophical work, "the most daring, the most scandalous and the most strangely passionate interrogation launched by this great rationalist intellectual against the human condition."

Still other French newspapers highlighted Beauvoir's intelligence and underlined the fact that at twenty-one she was the youngest student ever to receive the "agregation" degree in phi-

losophy. Friends emphasized, however, that her keen mind was accompanied by sincere concern for other people. Jean Cathala noted in *Le Monde* that "her remarkable intelligence was inseparable from her remarkable hearts"; Millett cited her "endless generosity and patience" in giving of herself and her time to others; singer Juliette Greco recalled in *Le Monde* Beauvoir's "generosity, human tenderness and . . . ability to listen." Equally praised in the press was Beauvoir's tireless commitment to causes in which she believed. Contacted by *Le Monde* for his reaction to the author's death, Jack Lang, former Minister of Culture under Francois Mitterrand, described Beauvoir as "a generous human being who never hesitated to defend the cause of the oppressed." Claudine Serre recorded in *Le Monde Aujourd'hui* that to the last days of her life, Beauvoir remained "a free woman opposed to servitude, and nothing ever appeased her anger. . . . Her commitment . . . did not diminish with age."

MEDIA ADAPTATIONS: The Mandarins was adapted for film by Twentieth Century-Fox in 1969; *The Blood of Others* was adapted for film by Home Box Office starring Jodie Foster in 1984.

BIOGRAPHICAL/CRITICAL SOURCES:

BOOKS

Ascher, Carol, *Simone de Beauvoir: A Life of Freedom,* Beacon Press, 1981.

Beauvoir, Simone de, *L'Existentialisme et la sagesse des nations,* Nagel, 1948.

Beauvoir, Simone de, *America Day by Day,* translation by Patrick Dudley, Grove, 1953.

Beauvoir, Simone de, *The Prime of Life,* translation by Peter Green, World Publishing, 1962.

Beauvoir, Simone de, *The Force of Circumstance,* translation by Richard Howard, Putnam, 1965.

Beauvoir, Simone de, *The Second Sex,* translation by H. M. Parshley, Random House, 1974.

Beauvoir, Simone de, *All Said and Done,* translation by Patrick O'Brian, Putnam, 1974.

Beavoir, Simone de, *The Ethics of Ambiguity,* translation by Bernard Frechtman, Citadel, 1975.

Beauvoir, Simone de, *When Things of the Spirit Come First: Five Early Tales,* translation by Patrick O'Brian, Pantheon, 1982.

Beauvoir, Simone de, *Adieux: A Farewell to Sartre,* Pantheon, 1984.

Beauvoir, Simone de, *Memoirs of a Dutiful Daughter,* translation by James Kirkup, Penguin, 1984.

Beauvoir, Simone de, *A Very Easy Death,* translation by Patrick O'Brian, Pantheon, 1985.

Bieber, Konrad, *Simone de Beauvoir,* Twayne, 1979.

Bree, Germaine, *Women Writers in France: Variations on a Theme,* Rutgers University Press, 1973.

Brombert, Victor, *The Intellectual Hero,* Lippincott, 1961.

Brophy, Brigid, *Don't Never Forget: Collected Views and Reviews,* Holt, 1966.

Contemporary Literary Criticism, Gale, Volume 1, 1973, Volume 2, 1974, Volume 4, 1975, Volume 8, 1978, Volume 14, 1980, Volume 31, 1985, Volume 44, 1987, Volume 50, 1988.

Cottrell, Robert D., *Simone de Beauvior,* Ungar, 1975.

Dayan, Josee and Malka Ribowska, *Simone de Beauvoir, un film,* Gallimard, 1979.

Dictionary of Literary Biography, Volume 72: *French Novelists, 1930-1960,* Gale, 1988.

Dictionary of Literary Biography Yearbook: 1986, Gale, 1987.

Evans, Mary, *Simone de Beauvoir: A Feminist Mandarin,* Tavistock, 1985.

Francis, Claude and Fernande Gontier, *Les Ecrits de Simone de Beauvoir,* Gallimard, 1979.

Francis, Claude and Fernande Gontier, *Simone de Beauvoir: A Life . . . A Love Story,* Librairie Academique Perrin, 1985.

Friedan, Betty, *It Changed My Life,* Random House, 1976.

Hatcher, Donald L., *Understanding "The Second Sex,"* P. Lang, 1984.

Jeanson, Francis, *Simone de Beauvoir ou l'entreprise de vivre,* Editions du Seuil, 1966.

Keefe, Terry, *Simone de Beauvoir: A Study of Her Writings,* Barnes, 1983.

Leighton, Jean, *Simone de Beauvoir on Woman,* Associated University Presses, 1975.

Madsen, Axel, *Hearts and Minds: The Common Journey of Simone de Beauvoir and Jean-Paul Sartre,* Morrow, 1977.

Marks, Elaine, *Simone de Beauvior: Encounters with Death,* Rutgers University Press, 1973.

Nedeau, Maurice, *The French Novelist since the War,* Methuen, 1967.

Okely, Judith, *Simone de Beauvoir,* Pantheon, 1986.

Sartre, Jean-Paul, *The Words,* translation by Bernard Fechtman, Braziller, 1964.

Schwarzer, Alice, *After "The Second Sex": Conversations with Simone de Beauvoir,* Pantheon Books, 1984.

Whitmarsh, Anne, *Simone de Beauvoir and the Limits of Commitment,* Cambridge University Press, 1981.

Zephir, Jacques J., *Le Neo-Feminisme de Simone de Beauvoir,* Denoel/Gonthier, 1982.

PERIODICALS

Antioch Review, Volume 31, number 4, 1971-72.
Catholic Forum, October, 1965.
Chicago Tribune Book World, March 20, 1983.
Contemporary French Civilization, spring, 1984.
Dalhousie Review, autumn, 1970.
Feminist Studies, summer, 1979.
Fontaine, October, 1945.
Forum for Modern Languages Studies, April, 1975.
France-Dimanche, April 27, 1986.
French Review, April, 1979.
Globe & Mail (Toronto), April 19, 1986.
Hecate, Volume 7, number 2, 1981.
Journal de la Ligue des Droits de l'Homme, Number 33, 1984.
La Vie en Rose, March 16, 1984.
Le Monde, March 20, 1948, April 16, 1986.
Le Nouvel Observateur, April 18-24, 1986.
L'Express, November 7, 1963.
Los Angeles Times, April 25, 1984.
Nation, June 8, 1958, June 27, 1959, June 14, 1975.
New Statesman, June 6, 1959, January 5, 1968.
Newsweek, June 8, 1959, February 9, 1970.
New Yorker, February 22, 1947.
New York Review of Books, July 20, 1972.
New York Times, June 2, 1974, May 6, 1984, April 15, 1986.
New York Times Book Review, May 18, 1958, June 7, 1959, March 3, 1968, February 23, 1969, July 21, 1974, November 7, 1982.
Paris-Match, April 25, 1986.
Paris Review, spring/summer, 1965.
Philosophy and Literature, Volume 9, number 1, 1985.
Saturday Review, May 22, 1956.
Time, March 20, 1966, May 22, 1972.

Times (London), January 21, 1982, August 12, 1982, May 11, 1984.
Times Literary Supplement, June 5, 1959, May 5, 1966, March 30, 1967, April 4, 1980, December 25, 1981, July 30, 1982, January 21, 1983.
Washington Post Book World, August 18, 1974, May 20, 1984.

OBITUARIES:

PERIODICALS

Figaro, April 20, 1986.
Le Monde Aujourd'hui, April 20-21, 1986.
Newsweek, April 28, 1986.
Observer, April 20, 1986.
Publishers Weekly, May 2, 1986.
Time, April 28, 1986.
Times (London), April 15, 1986.

* * *

BECKETT, Samuel (Barclay) 1906-1989

PERSONAL: Born April 13, 1906, in Foxrock, Dublin, Ireland; died of respiratory failure, December 22, 1989, in Paris, France; son of William Frank (a quantity surveyor) and Mary (an interpreter for the Irish Red Cross; maiden name Roe) Beckett; married Suzanne Dechevaux-Dumesnil (a pianist). *Education:* Attended Portora Royal School, County Fermanagh, Ireland; Trinity College, Dublin, B.A. (French and Italian), 1927, M.A., 1931.

CAREER: Ecole Normale Superieure, Paris, France, lecturer in English, 1928-30; Trinity College, University of Dublin, Dublin, Ireland, lecturer in French, 1930-32 (resigned because "he could not bear the absurdity of teaching to others what he did not know himself"). During the early 1930s he, among others, helped James Joyce, who was then nearly blind, by taking dictation and by copying out parts of *Finnegans Wake.* (Beckett never served as secretary to Joyce as many believe. A. J. Leventhal, writing for Beckett, told *CA* that "there was never any question of a formal position. . . . It's very hard to kill this story.") From 1932 to 1936 Beckett traveled extensively in England and Europe, residing briefly in London and in several European cities. He settled permanently in Paris in 1937. From about 1940 to 1943, Beckett was involved with the French resistance movement and had to hide from the Germans. He spent these years working as a farm hand near Roussillon, an isolated region in southeast France. Since the early 1940s, Beckett has devoted most of his time to writing. *Wartime service:* Storekeeper and interpreter for Irish Red Cross Hospital, St. Lo, France, 1945-46; decorated.

AWARDS, HONORS: Hours Press (Paris) award for the best poem concerning time, 1930, for "Whoroscope"; Italia Prize, 1957, for "All that Fall," and 1959, for "Embers"; *Village Voice* Off-Broadway (Obie) awards for best new play, 1958, for "Endgame," and 1964, for "Play," for distinguished play, 1960, for "Krapp's Last Tape," and for best foreign play, 1962, for "Happy Days"; Litt.D., Trinity College, Dublin, 1959; International Publishers prize, 1961 (shared with Jorge Luis Borges), for all literary work, especially *Molloy, Malone meurt, L'Innommable,* and *Comment c'est.*

WRITINGS:

NOVELS

Murphy (written in English), Routledge & Kegan Paul, 1938, Grove, 1957, French translation by Beckett, Bordas (Paris), 1947.

Molloy (fragment of an earlier version published in *transition,* number 6, 1950, together with an early fragment of *Malone Dies* under collective title, "Two Fragments"; also see below), Editions de Minuit, 1951, English translation by Beckett and Patrick Bowles, Grove, 1955.

Malone meurt, Editions de Minuit, 1951, English translation by Beckett published as *Malone Dies,* Grove, 1956.

Watt (written in English), Olympia Press (Paris), 1953, Grove, 1959, rewritten, and translated into French by the author, Editions de Minuit, 1968.

L'Innommable, Editions de Minuit, 1953, English translation by Beckett published as *The Unnameable,* Grove, 1958.

Three Novels: Molloy, Malone Dies, [and] *The Unnameable,* Grove, 1959.

Comment c'est, Editions de Minuit, 1961, English translation by Beckett published as *How It Is,* Grove, 1964 (excerpts published in *X* [a London magazine], number 1, 1959, and, under title "From an Unabandoned Work," in *Evergreen Review,* September-October, 1960).

Imagination morte imaginez (although only 14 pages long, Beckett called this work a novel), Editions de Minuit, 1965, English translation by Beckett published as *Imagination Dead Imagine,* Calder & Boyars, 1965.

Mercier et Camier, Minuit, 1970, translation by Beckett published as *Mercier and Camier,* Calder & Boyars, 1974, Grove, 1975.

PLAYS

"Le Kid," produced in Dublin, 1931.

En Attendant Godot (first produced in Paris at Theatre de Babylone, January 5, 1953), Editions de Minuit, 1952, English translation by Beckett entitled *Waiting for Godot* (U.S. premiere in Miami Beach, Florida, at Coconut Grove Playhouse, January, 1956; Broadway production at John Golden Theatre, April, 1956), Grove, 1954.

All That Fall (radio play written in English; produced in London for BBC Third Programme, January 13, 1957), Grove, 1957, updated for American radio, 1968-69, French translation by Robert Pinget and Beckett published as *Tous ceux qui tombent,* Editions de Minuit, 1957.

Fin de partie [and] *Acte sans paroles* (both first produced in French on double bill in London at Royal Court Theatre, April 3, 1957), Editions de Minuit, 1957, English translation by Beckett published as *Endgame* [and] *Act Without Words* ("Endgame," a play in one act, produced in New York at Cherry Lane Theatre, 1958; "Act Without Words," a mime for one player, with music by John Beckett, produced in New York at Living Theatre, 1959), Grove, 1958.

From an Abandoned Work (written in English; produced in London for BBC Third Programme, 1957), first published in *Evergreen Review,* Volume 1, number 3, 1957, Faber & Faber, 1958.

Krapp's Last Tape [and] *Embers* (both written in English; "Krapp's Last Tape" first produced in London at Royal Court Theatre, October 28, 1958, then at Provincetown Playhouse, 1960; "Embers" first produced in London for BBC Third Programme, June 24, 1959), Faber & Faber, 1959, published as *Krapp's Last Tape and Other Dramatic Pieces* (also contains "All that Fall," "Act Without Words [I]," and "Act Without Words II" [written in English]), Grove, 1960.

Happy Days (written in English; first produced in New York at Cherry Lane Theatre, September 17, 1961), Grove, 1961, French translation by Beckett published as *Oh les beaux jours,* Editions de Minuit, 1963.

Dramatische Dichtungen (trilingual edition of dramatic works originally published in French; German translations by Elmar Tophoven), Suhrkamp Verlag, 1963-64.

Play and Two Short Pieces for Radio (written in English; contains "Play" [first produced in Ulm, Germany, 1963, then in New York at Cherry Lane Theatre, 1964], "Words and Music" [first published in *Evergreen Review,* November-December, 1962], and "Cascando" [first published in *Dublin Magazine,* October-December, 1936; also see below]), Faber & Faber, 1964.

"Film" (22-minute mime adaptation, by Mariu Karmitz, of "Play"), directed by Alan Schneider for Evergreen Theatres, and starring Buster Keaton, M. K. Productions, 1966.

Comedie et actes divers (contains "Comedie," "Va et vient," "Cascando" [French translation by Beckett of play included in *Play and Two Short Pieces for Radio*], "Paroles et musiques [French translation by Beckett of "Words and Music"], "Dis Joe" [French translation by Beckett of "Eh, Joe?"; also see below], and "Acte sans paroles II" [French translation by Beckett of "Act Without Words II"]; also see below), Editions de Minuit, 1966.

Eh, Joe? and Other Writings (written in English for television; first produced by New York Television Theatre, 1966; also see below), Faber & Faber, 1967.

Come and Go (121-word "dramaticule," first published in French as "Va et vient" in *Comedie et actes divers*), Calder & Boyars, 1967.

Cascando and Other Short Dramatic Pieces, Grove, 1968.

Breath and Other Shorts, Faber, 1971.

Not I, Faber, 1971.

That Time, Faber, 1976.

Footfalls, Faber, 1976.

Ends and Odds: Eight New Dramatic Pieces, Faber, 1977.

Rockaby and Other Short Pieces, Grove, 1981.

Catastrophe et autres dramaticules: Cette fois, Solo, Berceuse, Impromptu d'Ohio, Editions de Minuit, 1982.

Three Occasional Pieces, Faber, 1982.

Collected Shorter Plays, Grove, 1984.

Ohio Impromptu, Catastrophe, and What Where, Grove, 1984.

The Complete Dramatic Works, Faber, 1986.

Also author of "Eleutheria" (French language play), c. 1947. Many of Beckett's works have been adapted for radio and television broadcast.

OTHER

(Contributor) *Our Exagmination round His Factification for Incamination of Work in Progress* (on James Joyce and *Finnegans Wake*), Shakespeare & Co. (Paris), 1929, New Directions, 1939, 2nd edition, 1962.

Whoroscope: Poem on Time (written in English), Hours Press (Paris), 1930.

Proust (criticism, written in English), Chatto & Windus, 1931, Grove, 1957.

More Pricks Than Kicks (ten short stories, written in English), Chatto & Windus, 1934, special edition, Calder & Boyars, 1966.

Echo's Bones and Other Precipitates (poems, written in English), Europa Press (Paris), 1935.

Nouvelles et textes pour rien (fiction; contains "L'Expulse," "Le Calmant," and "La Fin," and thirteen monologues), Editions de Minuit, 1955, translation by Beckett and others published in England as *No's Knife: Collected Shorter Prose, 1947-1965* (also includes "From an Abandoned Work," "Enough," "Imagination Dead Imagine," and "Ping"; also see below), Calder & Boyars, 1967, published as *Stories and Texts for Nothing,* Grove, 1967.

A Samuel Beckett Reader, edited by John Calder, Calder & Boyars, 1967.

(With Georges Duthuit and Jacques Putnam) *Bram van Velde* (criticism of the painter's work), Falaise (Paris), 1958, English translation by Olive Chase and Beckett, Grove, 1960.

Henri Hayden, Waddington Galleries, 1959.

Gedichte (in French and German; contains "Echo's Bones" and 18 poems written between 1937 and 1949; German translations by Eva Hesse), Limes Verlag (Wiesbaden), 1959.

Poems in English, Calder & Boyars, 1961, Grove, 1962.

(With Georges Duthuit) *Proust and Three Dialogues* (criticism), Calder & Boyars, 1965.

Assez, Editions de Minuit, 1966.

Ping, Editions de Minuit, 1966.

Tete-mortes (includes *Imagination morte imaginez, bing, Assez,* and a new novella, *Tete-mortes*), Editions de Minuit, 1967.

Poemes, Editions de Minuit, 1968.

L'Issue, Georges Visat, 1968.

Sans, Editions de Minuit, 1969, translation by Beckett published as *Lessness,* Calder & Boyars, 1971.

Sejour, Georges Richar, 1970.

Premier amour, Editions de Minuit, 1970, translation by Beckett published as *First Love,* Calder & Boyars, 1973.

Le Depeupleur, Editions de Minuit, translation by Beckett published as *The Lost Ones,* Grove, 1972.

The North, Enitharmon Press, 1972.

Abandonne, Georges Visat, 1972.

Au loin un oiseau, Double Elephant Press, 1973.

First Love and Other Shorts, Grove, 1974.

Fizzles, Grove, 1976.

For to End Yet Again and Other Fizzles, Calder, 1976.

I Can't Go On: A Selection from the Works of Samuel Beckett, edited by Richard Seaver, Grove Press, 1976.

All Strange Away, Gotham Book Mart, 1976.

Collected Poems in English and French, Grove, 1977, revised edition published as *Collected Poems 1930-1978,* Calder, 1984.

Four Novellas, Calder, 1977, published as *The Expelled and Other Novellas,* Penguin, 1980.

Six Residua, Calder, 1978.

Company, Grove, 1980.

Mal vu mal dit, Editions de Minuit, 1981, translation by Beckett published as *Ill Seen Ill Said,* Grove, 1982.

Worstward Ho, Grove, 1983.

Disjecta: Miscellaneous Writings and a Dramatic Fragment, edited by Ruby Cohn, Calder, 1983, Grove, 1984.

Collected Shorter Prose 1945-1980, Calder, 1984.

Happy Days: The Production Notebook, edited by James Knowlson, Faber, 1985, Grove, 1986.

Also author of the short story "Premier amour" which was perhaps intended to complete a quartet begun with "L'Expulse," "Le Calmant," and "La Fin." Contributor to *transition, New Review, Evergreen Review, Contempo, Les Temps Modernes, Merlin, Spectrum,* and other periodicals.

SIDELIGHTS: "He wanders among misty bogs turned surreal, he talks to the wee folk of his own bad dreams, he files reports on introspected black visions with a kind of blarney eloquence. Like an actress cradling a doll for her stage baby, his language keens and croons about tales that are not quite there." Melvin Maddocks is talking about Samuel Beckett. "It is neither night nor morning. A man must find himself without the support of groups, or labels, or slogans," writes R. D. Smith. And Beckett, by removing his characters from nearly all recognizable con-

texts, Smith continues, is "engaged in finding or saving" himself. Martin Esslin writes: "What is the essence of the experience of being? asks Beckett. And so he begins to strip away the inessentials. What is the meaning of the phrase 'I am myself'? he asks . . . and is then compelled to try to distinguish between the merely accidental characteristics that make up an individual and the essence of his self." The *Time* reviewer noted: "Some chronicle men on their way up; others tackle men on their way down. Samuel Beckett stalks after men on their way out." Such is the tone of most discussions of Beckett's work. But no reviewer could communicate the unique power of Beckett's writing, his use of "a language in which the emptiness of conventional speech is charged with new emotion." "While [his] lesser colleagues work in rhetoric," writes Smith, Beckett produces poetry. "Well," says Harold Pinter, "I'll buy his goods, hook, line, and sinker, because he leaves no stone unturned and no maggot lonely. He brings forth a body of beauty. His work is beautiful." Leo Bersani, somewhat less politely, writes: "I know of no writer who has come closer than Beckett in his novels to translating the rhythms of defecation into sentence structure." And B. S. Johnson thinks Beckett is "the greatest prose stylist and the most original writer living."

Along with the work of Ionesco, Genet, and Pinter, Beckett's stark plays are said to compose the "Theatre of the Absurd." But to so label Beckett's work is to disqualify one of his own first premises—that, since no human activity has any intrinsic meaning, it is pointless to ascribe traditional or categorical significance to the existence of an object or the performance of a deed. George Wellwarth discusses Beckett's concept of a protean reality: "What all these things—the sameness of human beings and their actions, the vanity of human ambition, the uselessness of thought—amount to is a pessimism deeper than any that has ever been put into words before. Throughout Beckett's work we can find evidence of his conviction that everything is hopeless, meaningless, purposeless, and, above all, agonizing to endure. Beckett's people are leveled off and merged into each other by being all more or less physically disabled—as if this were really the common condition on earth. . . . Beckett is a prophet of negation and sterility. He holds out no hope to humanity, only a picture of unrelieved blackness; and those who profess to see in Beckett signs of a Christian approach or signs of compassion are simply refusing to see what is there." Perhaps Beckett himself states his dilemma most succinctly in *L'Innommable:* "Dans ma vie, puisqu'il faut l'appeler ainsi, il y eut trois choses, l'impossibilite de parler, l'impossibilite de me taire, et la solitude." One must speak; man cannot possibly communicate with his fellows, but the alternative—silence—is irreconcilable with human existence.

Smith and Esslin, however, insist that Beckett does not intend to express unqualified despair, but that, by stripping significance from the world, he is showing us the one way to achieve redemption (although any salvation, according to Beckett's essentially deterministic philosophy, is necessarily only a respite). Smith writes: "Beckett's characters remain at their darkest moments anguished human beings: Beckett, when intellectually at his most pitiless, feels and suffers with them." And Esslin states that Beckett's message "is anything but gloomy or despairing." He writes: "On the contrary: the starkness of [his] reminders of the evanescence of life and the certainty of death, [his] uncompromising rejection of any easy solution or cheap illusion of comfort ultimately has a liberating effect; such is the nature of man that in the very act of facing up to the reality of his condition his dignity is enhanced; we are only defeated by things by which we are taken unawares; what we know and have faced up to we can master." Alec Reid also believes that Beckett's message must be interpreted optimistically. "Beckett's world," he writes, "is one of darkness, of disembodied voices, of ignorance, impotence, and anguish. But even as he insists that he knows nothing, can know nothing, Beckett reminds us of an astronaut, a human surrounded by nothing, walking on nothing. Our spacemen are no cause for despair; no more are Mr. Beckett's explorations." But then, according to *Time* magazine, "Beckett's champions argue that his threnodies in dusky twilight represent the existential metaphor of the human condition, that the thin but unwavering voices of his forlorn characters speak the ultimate statement of affirmation, if only because the merest attempt at communication is itself affirmation."

But in case the reader of Beckett criticism should come to regard this question as the black and white one of "despair" versus "optimism," Richard N. Coe adds new terms to the argument: "To class Beckett himself as the simple incarnation of 'despair' is a drastic oversimplification. To begin with, the concept of 'despair' implies the existence of a related concept 'hope,' and 'hope' implies a certain predictable continuity in time—which continuity Beckett would seriously question. 'Despair,' with all its inherent moral overtones, is a term which is wholly inadequate to describe Beckett's attitude towards the human condition; nor is this condition, in the most current sense of the definition, 'absurd.' It is literally and logically impossible. And in this central concept of 'impossibility,' his thought has most of its origins—as does also his art."

Although John Gassner was not happy with the scholarly complexity of the critical response to Beckett's work (he wrote: "To a parvenu intelligentsia, it would seem that a work of art exists not for its own sake but only for the possibilities of interpreting it"), some critics believe that Beckett's theater is most meaningful when considered within the context of a recognizable literary tradition. Kenneth Allsop writes: "His harsh, desolate, denuded style is entirely and unmistakably his own, but his literary 'form,' the stream-of-consciousness device which most young British writers wouldn't dream of using nowadays for fear of being thought quaint, derives from his years as secretary to James Joyce. That is only a partial explanation. He is in a monolithic way the last of the Left Bank Mohicans of the Twenties; the others of the *avant-garde* died or deserted or prospered, but Beckett was a loyal expatriate." Esslin, J. D. O'Hara, and John Fletcher prefer to align Beckett with the philosophers. "Although Beckett himself is not aware of any such influence," Esslin writes, "his writings might be described as a literary exposition of Sartre's Existentialism." O'Hara sees his work as exponential to the philosophy of Descartes: "In Beckett's world of post-Cartesian dualism, the mind has no connection to the body, its values worth nothing there, and so it cannot logically concern itself with the body's problems." Fletcher concludes that "whatever the truth of the matter, one thing is certain. Beckett has ranged freely among the writings of the philosophers, where he has found confirmation and justification of the metaphysical obsessions that haunt his work: the gulf set between body and mind, the epistemological incertitude. His genius has achieved the transmutation of such speculative problems into art." But, according to Coe, one must keep in mind that "Beckett has renounced his claim to erudition. The main theme of his work is impotence, of mind just as much as of body."

The problem of analyzing and interpreting Beckett's work, on the other hand, has been met with a somewhat surprising amount of scholarship and erudition. But David Hesla's criticism, in which the novels are considered as the expression of Beckett's personal enigma, is equally effective. Hesla notes that

the dilemma which confronts the contemporary writer, according to Beckett, "is constituted . . . by the fact that the writer must take seriously two opposed and apparently irreconcilable claims to his allegiance. On the one hand, he must recognize that the principal fact about modern man's life is that it is a 'mess,' a 'confusion,' a 'chaos.' On the other hand, the writer, as artist, has an obligation to form. But to admit the 'mess' into art is to jeopardize the very nature of art; for the mess 'appears to be the very opposite of form and therefore destructive of the very thing that art holds itself to be.' " Hesla quotes Beckett as saying: "It only means that there will be a new form; and that this form will be of such a type that it admits the chaos and does not try to say that the chaos is really something else. The form and the chaos remain separate. The latter is not reduced to the former. That is why the form itself becomes a preoccupation, because it exists as a problem separate from the material it accommodates. To find a form that accommodates the mess, that is the task of the artist now." Hesla notes that with *Watt* "Beckett has begun a process of removing from his artificial world those tangibles by which the reader usually is able to orient himself in time and space, and those causal relationships amongst the incidents of the plot by which the reader is able to discern the conditions of necessity and probability which—be they never so strained or extraordinary—determine in part the structural coherence and the 'meaning' of the story. . . . In *Watt* he has found the form which permits 'the mess' to enter art without destroying it. He has developed a literary method—the negative way—which is capable of accommodating chaos without reducing it to form. Furthermore, in developing this method he has developed an instrument of greater precision for the explication of a world-view which was only roughly sketched out in *Murphy*. Beckett's work after *Watt* has, in a certain sense, consisted largely in refining and adapting both the manner and the matter of his new art."

Most critics agree that it was with the publication of *Waiting for Godot* that Beckett's prominence was established in the United States. Many, in fact, still consider this play to be his most important work. H. A. Smith calls it "the most comprehensively and profoundly evocative play of the last thirty years," and William R. Mueller and Josephine Jacobsen write: "*Waiting for Godot,* of all of Beckett's dramatic works, expresses most clearly and explicitly the fundamental tension—to wait or not to wait—which is found to a lesser degree in his other writings. The human predicament described in Beckett's first play is that of man living on the Saturday after the Friday of the crucifixion, and not really knowing if all hope is dead or if the next day will bring the new life which has been promised," Allsop found the play's message less ambiguous. He writes: "*Godot* is a hymn to extol the moment when the mind swings off its hinges. . . . Beckett is unconcerned with writing requiems for humanity, for he sees life as polluted and pointless: he merely scrawls its obituary, without bitterness or compassion because he cannot really believe it is worth the words he is wasting." Gassner also found the play to be a straightforward pronouncement, but he did not accept it as a prediction of certain doom. "To all this tohu and bohu about the profundity and difficulty of the play," he wrote, "my reply is simply that there is nothing painfully or exhilaratingly ambiguous about *Waiting for Godot* in the first place. It presents the view that man, the hapless wanderer in the universe, brings his quite wonderful humanity—his human capacity for hope, patience, resilience, and, yes, for love of one's kind, too, as well as his animal nature—to the weird journey of existence. He is lost in the universe and found in his own heart and in the hearts of his fellow men." Bert O. States adds parenthetically: "Convicts and children love it!"

Kenneth Tynan believes that the implications of *Waiting for Godot* are significant not only in themselves, but for all of contemporary theater. He writes: "A special virtue attaches to plays which remind the drama of how much it can do without and still exist. By all known criteria, Beckett's *Waiting for Godot* is a dramatic vacuum. Pity the critic who seeks a chink in its armour, for it is all chink. It has no plot, no climax, no *denouement;* no beginning, no middle, and no end. Unavoidably, it has a situation, and it might be accused of having suspense. . . . *Waiting for Godot* frankly jettisons everything by which we recognise theatre. It arrives at the custom-house, as it were, with no luggage, no passport, and nothing to declare; yet it gets through, as might a pilgrim from Mars. It does this, I believe, by appealing to a definition of drama much more fundamental than any in the books. A play, it asserts and proves, is basically a means of spending two hours in the dark without being bored. . . . It forced me to re-examine the rules which have hitherto governed the drama; and, having done so, to pronounce them not elastic enough."

Some critics found *Endgame* to be an even more powerful expression of Beckett's negativism. Gassner wrote: "Nothing happens in *Endgame* and that nothing is what matters. The author's feeling about nothing also matters, not because it is true or right but because it is a strongly formed attitude, a felt and expressed viewpoint. . . . The yardsticks of dialectical materialism and moralism are equally out in appraising the play. Dialectical materialism could only say that *Endgame* is decadent. Moralism and theology would say that the play is sinful, since nothing damns the soul so much as despair of salvation. Neither yardstick could tell us that this hauntingly powerful work of the imagination is art."

Although critics discuss his plays more frequently than his novels, Beckett himself considers his novels to be his major work. Alec Reid notes: "For Beckett each novel is a journey into the unknown, into an area of utter lawlessness." And the *Times Literary Supplement* reviewer, in his discussion of *Imagination Dead Imagine,* summarizes Beckett's work thus: "[This novel] certainly describes two people in an imaginary situation and it is equally certainly a work of large implications and a desolate, cruel beauty. It might not seem so, however, if it had not been apparent for some time that Mr. Beckett's prose narratives compose a single, long saga of exclusion and heroic relinquishment as well as of the desperate, perhaps unavailing, pursuit of finality." A. I. Leventhal writes: "When Beckett changes to writing his novels in French he leaves behind him much of the humour, grim as it was, in his previous work. He has less interest in making his characters indulge in games to pass the time as in *Waiting for Godot.* They are now concentrating on their *penible* task of dying." Frank Kermode offers this analysis of the novels: "In Beckett's plays the theatrical demand for communicable rhythms and relatively crude satisfactions has had a beneficent effect. But in the novels he yields progressively to the magnetic pull of the primitive, to the desire to achieve, by various forms of decadence and deformation, some Work that eludes the intellect, avoids the spread nets of habitual meaning. Beckett is often allegorical, but he is allegorical in fitful patches, providing illusive toeholds to any reader scrambling for sense." Bersani hasn't discovered the toeholds (and laughs behind his hand at those who have), nor does he think he will, if, as he says, he continues to take Beckett "seriously." Bersani writes: "The most interesting fact about Samuel Beckett's novels is that they are, at their best, almost completely unreadable." Bersani, citing Beckett's expressed desire to fail (to be an artist, for Beckett, is to fail), finds his "extreme attempt to render literature autonomous" to be not only "an ironic reminder of the ultimate dependence of

literature on life," but also a generally suspicious undertaking. "The attempt to eliminate 'occasion' from art," he writes, "is in itself an occasion, and insofar as this attempt is a process of what [Ruby] Cohn has called progressive 'retrenchment,' the process rather than the achievement becomes the subject of Beckett's work."

The fact that most of Beckett's important work was originally written in French is far more than coincidentally significant to his stylistic achievement. Coe explains: "Beckett, in the final analysis, is trying to say what cannot be said; he must be constantly on his guard, therefore, never to yield to the temptation of saying what the words would make him say. Only when language is, as it were, defeated, bound hand and foot; only when it is so rigorously disciplined that each word describes exactly and quasiscientifically the precise concept to which it is related and no other, only then, by the progressive elimination of that which precisely is, is there a remote chance for the human mind to divine the ultimate reality which is not. And this relentless, almost masochistic discipline, which reaches its culmination in *Comment c'est,* Beckett achieves by writing in a language which is not his own—in French." John Barth explains, however, that Beckett's denuded French is yet only another step in his creative process and must not be construed as a total achievement. Barth writes: "Beckett has become virtually mute, musewise, having progressed from marvelously constructed English sentences through terser and terser French ones to the unsyntactical, unpunctuated prose of *Comment c'est* and 'ultimately' to wordless mimes. One might extrapolate a theoretical course for Beckett: language, after all, consists of silence as well as sound, and the mime is still communication . . . but by the language of action. But the language of action consists of rest as well as movement, and so in the context of Beckett's progress immobile, silent figures still aren't altogether ultimate. . . . For Beckett, at this point in his career, to cease to create altogether would be fairly meaningful: his crowning work, his 'last word.' What a convenient corner to paint yourself into!"

Few critics have discussed Beckett's ideas (or the man himself) apart from their manifestation in his work. And Beckett would doubtless have it so. As Robert Wernick writes, "so striking is the personality that emerges from [his] gloomy plays and so striking is the occasionally glimpsed, gaunt pterodactylous face of the real-life Samuel Beckett that many people assume the two are identical. A whole folklore of anecdote has grown up around Beckett, in which he appears as a fanatic solitary, brooding eternally . . . on the black mystery of the human race. . . . It is true that he has built a wall around his country house, but he denies that he built it, as people contend, to shut out the view. It is true he avoids all the trappings of the celebrity life, gives no interviews, attends no cultural congresses. But then, why should he?" Alec Reid met Beckett in New York during the making of "Film" and described him as "a close-knit person, all of a piece." Reid says that Beckett "believes that physical movement conveys at least as much as the words. . . . Once the initial reserve has evaporated Beckett reveals a genius for companionship, a remarkable ability to make those around him feel the better for his presence."

In 1967 the Firehouse Theatre of Minneapolis, directed by Marlow Hotchkiss, performed *Act Without Words I* and *Act Without Words II* simultaneously. Also in 1967, Jack Emery composed and performed an hour-long, one-man program consisting of "a selection of the desperate reveries and furious tirades of half a dozen of Samuel Beckett's dying heroes," including Malone, Hamm, and the Unnameable. The *Punch* reviewer writes: "Many of the passages are fatiguing to follow in the original novels but so conversational are the rhythms of Beckett's language and so eloquently does Mr. Emery speak them (except when he essays a scream) that the effect in a dark, hushed theatre of this grim gallows humour is electrifying. There is more to life than talking of waiting for death, but Beckett has phrases—'Vent the pent!'—that resound in the mind with the urgency of great poetry." Emery's program, which premiered at Arts Theatre, London, was also produced in Glasgow, Edinburgh, and Exeter.

BIOGRAPHICAL/CRITICAL SOURCES:

BOOKS

Allsop, Kenneth, *The Angry Decade,* Copp, 1958.
Armstrong, William A., and others, editors, *Experimental Drama,* G. Bell, 1963.
Beckett at Sixty (a festschrift by twenty-four of his friends), Calder & Boyars, 1967.
Coe, Richard N., *Beckett,* Oliver & Boyd, 1964.
Cohn, Ruby, *Samuel Beckett: The Comic Gamut,* Rutgers University Press, 1962.
Contemporary Literary Criticism, Gale, Volume 1, 1973, Volume 2, 1974, Volume 3, 1975, Volume 4, 1975, Volume 6, 1976, Volume 9, 1978, Volume 10, 1979, Volume 11, 1979, Volume 14, 1980, Volume 18, 1981, Volume 29, 1984.
Dictionary of Literary Biography, Gale, Volume 13: *British Dramatists since World War II,* 1982, Volume 15: *British Novelists, 1930-1959,* 1983.
Esslin, Martin, *The Theatre of the Absurd,* Doubleday-Anchor, 1961.
Fletcher, John, *Samuel Beckett's Art,* Barnes & Noble, 1967.
Gassner, John, *Theatre at the Crossroads,* Holt, 1960.
Guicharnaud, Jacques, and June Beckelman, *Modern French Theatre from Giraudoux to Beckett,* Yale University Press, 1961.
Hoffman, Frederick J., *Samuel Beckett: The Language of Self,* Southern Illinois University Press, 1962.
Kenner, Hugh, *Samuel Beckett,* J. Calder, 1962.
Kermode, Frank, *Puzzles and Epiphanies,* Chilmark, 1962.
Kostelanetz, Richard, editor, *On Contemporary Literature,* Avon, 1954.
Lumley, Frederick, *New Trends in Twentieth-Century Drama,* Oxford University Press, 1967.
Simpson, Alan, *Beckett and Behan and a Theatre in Dublin,* Routledge & Kegan Paul, 1962.
Smith, H. A., and R. D. Smith, contributors, *Contemporary Theatre,* Stratford-upon-Avon Studies 4, edited by John Russell Brown and Bernard Harris, Edward Arnold, 1962.
Tindall, William York, *Samuel Beckett,* Columbia University Press, 1964.
Tynan, Kenneth, *Curtains,* Atheneum, 1961.
Wellwarth, George, *Theatre of Protest and Paradox,* New York University Press, 1964.

PERIODICALS

Atlantic, August, 1967.
Carleton Miscellany, winter, 1967.
Christian Science Monitor, July 27, 1967.
Comparative Literature, winter, 1965.
Critique, spring, 1963, winter, 1964-65.
Esquire, September, 1967.
Hudson Review, spring, 1967.
Kenyon Review, March, 1967.
Life, February 2, 1968.
Listener, August 3, 1967.
Livres de France, January, 1967.
London Magazine, August, 1967.
Manchester Guardian, April 21, 1966.
New Statesman, February 14, 1964, March 25, 1966, July 14, 1967.
New York Review of Books, March 19, 1964, December 7, 1967.
New York Times, July 21, 1964, February 27, 1966, April 19, 1966, July 20, 1967, September 14, 1967.
Observer, July 16, 1967.
Partisan Review, spring, 1966.
Punch, August 2, 1967.
Saturday Review, October 4, 1958.
Time, July 14, 1967.
Times Literary Supplement, December 21, 1962, January 30, 1964, June 30, 1966.
Tri-Quarterly, winter, 1967.
Tulane Drama Review, summer, 1967.
Village Voice, April 6, 1967, July 13, 1967.

OBITUARIES:

PERIODICALS

Chicago Tribune, December 27, 1989.
Los Angeles Times, December 27, 1989.
New York Times, December 27, 1989.

*   *   *

BEHAN, Brendan   1923-1964

PERSONAL: Born February 9, 1923, in Dublin, Ireland; died of alcoholism, jaundice, and diabetes, March 20, 1964; son of Stephen (a house painter, labor leader, and soldier) and Kathleen (Kearney) Behan; married Beatrice ffrench-Salkeld (a painter); children: one daughter. *Education:* Attended Irish Catholic schools. *Religion:* Roman Catholic.

ADDRESSES: Home—London, England.

CAREER: Apprenticed as a house painter, 1937; arrested in Liverpool, England, 1939, convicted of possessing explosives and sent to Borstal (a reform school), 1939-42; arrested and convicted in Dublin, 1942, for revolutionary activities and sentenced to three years in an Irish prison, 1942-45; worked as house painter, seaman, free-lance journalist, and writer, 1945-64.

MEMBER: Fianna Eireann (youth organization), Irish Republican Army (IRA).

WRITINGS:

The Quare Fellow: A Comedy-Drama (three-act play; first produced in Dublin at Pike Theatre, 1954), Grove, 1956.
Borstal Boy, Hutchinson, 1958, Knopf, 1959.
The Hostage (three-act play; first produced in Dublin, 1958), Grove, 1958, third revised edition, Methuen, 1962.
Brendan Behan's Island: An Irish Sketch-Book, Geis, 1962.
Hold Your Hour and Have Another (collected articles), Little, Brown, 1963.
Brendan Behan's New York, Geis, 1964.
The Scarperer, Doubleday, 1964.
The Quare Fellow and The Hostage: Two Plays, Grove, 1964.
Confessions of an Irish Rebel, Hutchinson, 1965, Geis, 1966.
Richard's Cork Leg, edited by Alan Simpson, Grove, 1974.
The Complete Plays, introduction by Simpson, Grove, 1978.
Poems and a Play in Irish (includes "An Giall"), Gallery Books, 1981.
After the Wake, edited by Peter Fallon, O'Brien Press, 1981.

Behan's writings have been translated into Italian, French, and German.

MEDIA ADAPTATIONS: Frank McMahon adapted *Borstal Boy* for the stage; the play won an Antoinette Perry ("Tony") Award and a New York Drama Critics Circle Award as best play of the 1969-70 season. Shay Duffin adapted Behan's works for the play "Shay Duffin Is Brendan Behan: Confessions of an Irish Rebel" in the early 1970s. Both "The Quare Fellow" and "The Hostage" have been made into films.

SIDELIGHTS: Once characterized as "a professional young Irishman," Brendan Behan, in both his life and work, took the role to heart. Even before his early death in 1964 from alcoholism, jaundice, and diabetes, he had become a legend. Stories of his drunken antics and of his youthful "terrorist" activities for the IRA prevailed in the media over mention of his literary creations. His work was often dismissed as the careless outpouring of a sensation-hungry revolutionary without a revolution.

But serious connections have been drawn between the content of Behan's writing, particularly his major plays "The Quare Fellow" and "The Hostage," his politics, and his self-destructive drinking. In his work, as in his life, laughter and the despair of dying are commingled with intoxicating effect. Behan himself once said that he possessed "a sense of humor that would cause me to laugh at a funeral, providing it wasn't my own." About his comedies critic Alfred Kazin stated: "There is the constant suggestion in Behan's work that the laughter which supports despair does not always hide despair. But Behan's is the despair of an authentic predicament, of the actualities of life at the present time." Ted Boyle, in his book *Brendan Behan,* commented: "A good deal of the comedy in Behan's plays portrays the hysteria which overcomes the human being caught in a situation over which he has no control." The criminal about to be hanged in "The Quare Fellow" and the British soldier being held for exchange with a captured IRA member in "The Hostage" are both examples of this comedic circumstance.

Behan's work is also characterized by his talent for realistic dialogue, the gift of his "tape-recorder ear." His later works in fact were taken down on tape, transcribed, and then edited by others. But even in his earlier writing there is the same fidelity to common speech patterns. Kazin commented: "What Behan has done, coming in too late to participate in the Irish literary renaissance, is to identify himself not with the abstract cause of art but with the profane and explosive speech of the streets, the saloons, the prisons."

In 1970 Frank McMahon adapted *Borstal Boy* for the theater. The dramatization, like the book, portrays Behan's early prison years, incorporating the addition of a narrator, the older Behan, who relates the story from downstage. The play conveys, as critic Alan Bunce wrote, "a florid reflection of Behan's adult personality—mellow, tartly philosophical, a mixture of Hibernian ruefulness with lambent humor."

BIOGRAPHICAL/CRITICAL SOURCES:

BOOKS

Atkinson, Brooks, *Tuesdays and Fridays,* Random House, 1963.
Behan, Dominic, *My Brother Brendan,* Frewin, 1965, Simon & Schuster, 1966.
Boyle, Ted E., *Brendan Behan,* Twayne, 1969.
Contemporary Literary Criticism, Gale, Volume 1, 1973, Volume 8, 1978, Volume 11, 1979, Volume 15, 1980.
Dictionary of Literary Biography, Volume 13: *British Dramatists since World War II,* Gale, 1982.
Jeffs, Rae, *Brendan Behan: Man and Showman,* Hutchinson, 1966, World Publishing, 1968.
Kazin, Alfred, *Contemporaries,* Little, Brown, 1959.

Lumley, Frederick, *New Trends in Twentieth-Century Drama,* Oxford University Press, 1967.
McCann, Sean, *The World of Brendan Behan,* Frewin, 1966.
Simpson, Alan, *Beckett and Behan and a Theatre in Dublin,* Routledge & Kegan Paul, 1962.

PERIODICALS

Books Abroad, spring, 1967.
Chicago Tribune, March 12, 1982.
Christian Science Monitor, April 8, 1970.
New York Times, November 4, 1983.
Times (London), October 15, 1986.
Times Literary Supplement, April 22, 1983.
Washington Post Book World, July 4, 1982.

*　　*　　*

BELDONE, Phil "Cheech"
See ELLISON, Harlan

*　　*　　*

BELENO
See AZUELA, Mariano

*　　*　　*

BELL, (Arthur) Clive (Howard)   1881-1964

PERSONAL: Born September 16, 1881, in East Shefford, Bedfordshire, England; died September 18, 1964, in London, England; married Vanessa Stephen; children: Julian. *Education:* Attended Trinity College, Cambridge.

CAREER: Writer, poet, and critic of politics, literature, and art.

AWARDS, HONORS: Chevalier of the Legion of Honor, 1936.

WRITINGS:

Art (criticism and history), Chatto & Windus, 1914, reprinted, Capricorn Books, 1958.
Peace at Once (history), National Labour Press, 1915.
Pot-Boilers (criticism), Chatto & Windus, 1918.
Since Cezanne (criticism), Chatto & Windus, 1922, reprinted, Books for Libraries Press, 1969.
The Legend of Monte della Sibilla; or, Le paradis de la reine Sibille (poem), Hogarth, 1923.
On British Freedom, Chatto & Windus, 1923.
Landmarks in Nineteenth-Century Painting (criticism), Chatto & Windus, 1927, reprinted, Books for Libraries Press, 1967.
Civilization: An Essay (philosophy; also see below), Harcourt, 1928.
Proust (criticism), Hogarth, 1928, Harcourt, 1929, reprinted, Richard West, 1977.
An Account of French Painting (criticism), Chatto & Windus, 1931, reprinted, Richard West, 1979.
Enjoying Pictures: Meditations in the National Gallery and Elsewhere (criticism), Chatto & Windus, 1934.
Old Friends: Personal Recollections (autobiographical; also see below), Chatto & Windus, 1956, Harcourt, 1957.
Civilization and Old Friends, University of Chicago Press, 1973.
Aesthetics and Post-Impressionism: A New Theory of Art, two volumes, Foundation for Classical Reprints, 1985.

Contributor of articles to *New Statesman and Nation.*

SIDELIGHTS: Clive Bell was a member of the "Bloomsbury group" of writers, which included such luminaries as Virginia

Woolf, E. M. Forster, John Maynard Keynes, and Roger Fry. Married to the elder sister of Virginia Woolf, Bell was associated with the informal group of artists by marriage, but also through his literary style. Like many of the group's writers, Bell endeavored to write intellectually and objectively about strong emotions. His treatment of art in this manner established him as a prominent critic and writer. Bell's work was also a major force in obtaining the recognition of modern art. He asserted that form and design were the most important aspects of a work of art. Subject was no longer the focus; instead, the feelings and ideas expressed were emphasized. Bell coined "significant form" as a term of value with which to appraise the purely aesthetic quality of a work of art.

Bell recorded his theory about art in his first book, appropriately entitled *Art*. The volume met with mixed reviews. An *Athenaeum* critic praised *Art* as "the first book, since Ruskin began to publish 'Modern painters' in 1843, that could even conceivably convince a serious-minded person of good judgment that Art is something more than an agreeable ornamentation and seasoning of life." A *New York Times* reviewer disagreed: "It is in this insensitiveness to art of a kind that does not reveal its significance by means of the formulas he has learned that Mr. Bell shows his lack of the deep insight often called tolerance which marks the highest order of mind."

Since Cezanne, another volume of art criticism, received favorable reviews. Burton Rascoe noted: "Bell is honest, he is sincere, and he is a servitor of beauty, a champion of good taste, a valiant defender of culture, and he would not let vanity stand in the way of the universal good. In this book he lends his fine emotional sensibility, his alert intelligence and his happy prose style in the service of beauty, taste and culture."

As a critic of politics and society, Bell was paid similar tribute. Critics praised *On British Freedom* as "a brilliant piece of writing" and "the most spirited, swift, admirably written onslaught" since Shaw's prefaces. *Civilization* was applauded by a *New Statesman* reviewer as "a perfectly clear definition of Civilisation which no one can ignore. It is not only the best and most comprehensible. It is a really brilliant piece of authentic analysis." Bell's plunge into literary criticism with Proust, though, met with less enthusiasm. Edgar Johnson of the *New York Evening Post* panned the volume claiming that "as a contribution either to criticism or art, Mr. Bell's 'Proust' is negligible." On the other hand, a *Times Literary Supplement* critic contended that "Bell is to be congratulated upon having written . . . a most intelligent commentary upon Proust."

Bell's only autobiographical work, *Old Friends*, contains letters and reminiscences about his fellow artists of the Bloomsbury group. David Daiches of the *New York Herald Tribune Book Review* commented that though the book "occasionally irritates by its tone of condescending elegance and its gentlemanly scorn for a younger generation of writers and critics who lack the social advantages possessed by Bloomsbury, it is full of interest for its first-hand account of people, places, and things in a fascinating period of English . . . culture. It will remain an important source in the rapidly growing literature of Bloomsbury."

BIOGRAPHICAL/CRITICAL SOURCES:

PERIODICALS

Atheneum, February 21, 1914.
Atlantic, March, 1957.
Atlantic's Bookshelf, November, 1922.
Bookman, October, 1928.

Boston Transcript, November 17, 1923, October 20, 1928, March 16, 1929.
Christian Science Monitor, February 14, 1957.
Dial, August 19, 1922.
Freeman, October 4, 1922.
Independent, December 8, 1923.
International Journal of Ethics, October, 1928.
London Times Literary Supplement, March 16, 1922.
Nation, September 6, 1922, December 12, 1928, January 2, 1935, March 9, 1957.
Nation and Athenaeum, June 9, 1928, December 8, 1928.
New Republic, August 9, 1922.
New Statesman, June 23, 1923, June 9, 1928, November 24, 1928.
New Statesman and Nation, November 14, 1931, April 21, 1934.
New York Evening Post, February 16, 1929.
New York Herald Tribune, September 30, 1928, September 16, 1934.
New York Herald Tribune Book Review, February 10, 1957.
New York Times, November 15, 1914, October 14, 1923, October 14, 1928, March 24, 1929, March 20, 1932, February 10, 1957.
New York Tribune, June 25, 1922.
Outlook, February 13, 1929.
Saturday Review of Literature, November 24, 1928.
Saturday Review, March 21, 1914, February 16, 1957.
Spectator, July 18, 1914, March 6, 1922, August 18, 1923, December 19, 1931, March 30, 1934.

OBITUARIES:

PERIODICALS

Illustrated London News, September 26, 1964.
New York Times, September 20, 1964.
Spectator, September 25, 1964.
Time, October 2, 1964.

*　　*　　*

BELL, Marvin (Hartley) 1937-

PERSONAL: Born August 3, 1937, in New York, N.Y.; son of Saul and Belle (Spector) Bell; married Mary Mammosser, 1958 (marriage ended); married Dorothy Murphy; children: Nathan Saul, Jason Aaron. *Education:* Alfred University, B.A., 1958; attended Syracuse University, 1958; University of Chicago, M.A., 1961; University of Iowa, M.F.A., 1963.

ADDRESSES: Office—Writers' Workshop, University of Iowa, Iowa City, Iowa 52242.

CAREER: University of Iowa, Writers' Workshop, Iowa City, visiting lecturer, 1965, assistant professor, 1967-69, associate professor, 1969-75, professor of English, 1975—. Visiting lecturer, Oregon State University, 1969, Goddard College, 1972, University of Hawaii, 1981, and University of Washington, 1982; member of faculty, Bread Loaf Writers' Conference, 1973-78 and 1980-82. *Military service:* U.S. Army, 1964-65; first lieutenant.

AWARDS, HONORS: Lamont Award from the Academy of American Poets, 1969, for *A Probable Volume of Dreams;* Bess Hokin Award, *Poetry* (magazine), 1969; Emily Clark Balch Prize, *Virginia Quarterly Review*, 1970; Guggenheim fellowship, 1976; National Endowment for the Arts Fellowship, 1978; Prize, *American Poetry Review*, 1981.

WRITINGS:

POETRY

Poems for Nathan and Saul (pamphlet), Hillsdale Press, 1966.
Things We Dreamt We Died For, Stone Wall Press, 1966.
A Probable Volume of Dreams, Atheneum, 1969.
Woo Havoc (pamphlet), Barn Dream Press, 1971.
The Escape into You, Atheneum, 1971.
Residue of Song, Atheneum, 1974.
Stars Which See, Stars Which Do Not See, Atheneum, 1978.
These Green-Going-to-Yellow, Atheneum, 1981.
(With William Stafford) *Segues: A Correspondence in Poetry,* Godine, 1983.
Drawn by Stones, by Earth, by Things Which Have Been in the Fire, Atheneum, 1984.
New and Selected Poems, Atheneum, 1987.

CONTRIBUTOR TO ANTHOLOGIES

Major Young Poets, edited by Al Lee, World Publishing, 1971.
New Voices in American Poetry, edited by David Allan Evans, Winthrop Publishing, 1973.
Preferences, edited by Richard Howard, Viking, 1974.
American Poetry Anthology, edited by Daniel Halpern, Avon, 1975.
Fifty Poets, edited by Alberta Turner, McKay, 1977.
Contemporary American Poets, edited by Mark Strand, New American Library, 1969.
New Yorker Book of Poems, Viking, 1969.

OTHER

Old Snow Just Melting: Essays and Interviews, University of Michigan Press, 1983.

Writer of column, "Homage to the Runner," for *American Poetry Review,* 1975-78. Editor and publisher, *Statements,* 1959-64; poetry editor, *North American Review,* 1964-69, and *Iowa Review,* 1969-71.

SIDELIGHTS: American poet and critic Marvin Bell "is a poet of the family. He writes of his father, his wives, his sons, and himself in a dynamic interaction of love and loss, accomplishment, and fear of alienation. These are subjects that demand maturity and constant evaluation. A complete reading of Bell's canon shows his ability to understand the durability of the human heart. Equally impressive is his accompanying technical sophistication," comments William M. Robins in the *Dictionary of Literary Biography.* The son of a Jew who immigrated from the Ukraine, Bell writes of distance and reconciliation between people, often touching on his complex relationship to his heritage.

For example, *A Probable Volume of Dreams* opens with a poem addressed to the poet's father, initiating a dialogue that continues throughout Bell's works. "Although Bell is never narrowly confessional, it is important to note just how much the death of the father—his profound absence and presence—helps shape Bell's poetry and create possible worlds. The father: Bell's own dead father, and his growing sense of himself as a father who has sons and who, like him, will someday die," writes Arthur Oberg in *The American Poetry Review.* In addition to this motif, the poems "tell how unlinear life and art are, how 'progress' is a deception of the nineteenth century, how increasingly distant the finishing line for the poet-runner proves to be," Oberg observes. *A Probable Volume of Dreams* won the Lamont Award from the Academy of American Poets in 1969.

Concern with the self and its relationships in the earlier poetry has given way to reflections on the self in relation to nature in later books, such as *Stars Which See, Stars Which Do Not See.* Speaking of this development to Wayne Dodd and Stanley Plumly in an *Ohio Review* interview, Bell said that attention to nature has always been an integral part of his life. He grew up among farmers, so the rural life that so fascinated other writers during the 1960s back-to-nature movement was not Bell's inspiration. His first work came from his interest "in what language could make all by itself. . . . And I was interested in relationships between people. I wrote one whole book of poems-in-series about the relationships between a couple of people, or among several people. But now, for whatever good reasons, I *am* interested in allowing nature to have the place in my poems that it always had in my life," he said.

Bell also said the change in subject matter signalled a change in attitude—personal and cultural. "That is," he said, "contemporary American poetry has been tiresome in its discovery of the individual self, over and over and over, and its discovery of emotions that, indeed, we all have: loneliness, fear, despair, ennui, etcetera. I think it can get tiresome when the discovery of such emotions is more or less all the content there is to a poem. We know these things. . . . So I sort of write poetry nowadays from some other attitudes, I think, that came upon me without my ever really thinking about them. I think, for example, that it's ultimately pleasanter and healthier and better for everyone if one thinks of the self as being very small and very unimportant. . . . And I think, as I may not always have thought, that the only way out of the self is to concentrate on others and on things outside the self."

Bell sometimes refers to this development as an achievement of poetic modesty. He told Dodd and Plumly, "There is a kind of physical reality that we all share a sense of. I mean, we might argue about what reality is, but we all know how to walk across a bridge—instead of walking across the water, for instance. And it seems to me that one definition of modesty in poetry would be a refusal to compromise the physical facts of what it is that is showing up in one's poems," Bell explained.

Speaking of his personal aesthetic, he told the interviewers, "I would like to write poetry which finds salvation in the physical world and the here and now and which defines the soul, if you will, in terms of emotional depth, and that emotional depth in terms of the physical world and the world of human relationships." Regarding style, he added, "I'd like to write a poetry which has little if any insistence about it, as little as possible. I would like to write a poetry which doesn't seem either to buttonhole the reader, or demand too much allegiance, or demand that too much of the world be given up for the special world of the poem."

Reviewers comment that Bell's later poems fulfill these aspirations. G. E. Murray, writing in the *Georgia Review,* declares, "I am impressed by this poet's increasing ability to perceive and praise small wonders. There is life and health in this book, and if sometimes Bell's expression is quiet and reserved, his talent is not. Altogether, *Stars Which See, Stars Which Do Not See* demonstrates an important transitional phase for the poet—a subdued, graceful vein that enables him to 'speak of eyes and seasons' with an intimacy and surehandedness that informs and gratifies. . . . I believe Marvin Bell is on a track of the future—a mature, accessible and personalized venture into the mainstream of contemporary American verse." Of the same book, David St. John writes in *Parnassus,* "Many poets have tried to appropriate into their poems a gritty, tough-talking American character, and to thereby earn for themselves some . . . 'authenticity.'. . . In *Stars Which See, Stars Which Do Not See*, Bell has found within his *own* voice that American voice, and with it the ability to write convincingly about the smallest details of a personal history."

BIOGRAPHICAL/CRITICAL SOURCES:

BOOKS

Contemporary Literary Criticism, Gale, Volume 8, 1978, Volume 31, 1985.
Dictionary of Literary Biography, Volume 5: *American Poets since World War II*, Gale, 1980.
Malkoff, Karl, *Crowell's Handbook of Contemporary American Poetry*, Crowell, 1973.

PERIODICALS

American Poetry Review, May-June, 1976.
Antaeus, spring/summer, 1982.
Antioch Review, spring, 1982.
Chicago Review, Volume 28, number 1, 1976.
Hudson Review, August, 1985.
Iowa Review, winter, 1981.
Missouri Review, summer, 1982.
Nation, February 2, 1970.
New Republic, March 29, 1975.
New York Times Book Review, April 8, 1984, November 11, 1984.
Ohio Review, Volume 17, number 3, 1976.
Parnassus, fall/winter, 1972.
Shenandoah, summer, 1971.
Stand, Volume 13, number 4, 1972.

—Sketch by Marilyn K. Basel

*   *   *

BELL, W. L. D.
    See MENCKEN, H(enry) L(ouis)

*   *   *

BELLAMY, Atwood C.
    See MENCKEN, H(enry) L(ouis)

*   *   *

BELLOW, Saul 1915-

PERSONAL: Born June 10, 1915 (officially recorded as July 10, 1915), in Lachine, Quebec, Canada; came to Chicago at the age of nine; son of Abraham (a Russian emigre and businessman) and Liza (Gordon) Bellow; married Anita Goshkin (a social worker), December 31, 1937 (divorced); married Alexandra Tschacbasov, February 1, 1956 (divorced); married Susan Glassman (a teacher), 1961 (divorced); married Alexandra Ionesco Tuleca (a mathematician), 1974 (divorced); children: (first marriage) Gregory, (second marriage) Adam, (third marriage) Daniel. *Education:* Attended University of Chicago, 1933-35; Northwestern University, B.S. (with honors in sociology and anthropology), 1937; graduate study in anthropology at University of Wisconsin, 1937 (abandoned his studies because "every time I worked on my thesis, it turned out to be a story").

ADDRESSES: Home—Chicago, Ill. *Office*—c/o Committee on Social Thought, University of Chicago, 1126 East 59th St., Chicago, Ill. 60637. *Agent*—Harriet Wasserman Literary Agency, 137 East 36th St., New York, N.Y. 10016.

CAREER: Worked for a time on WPA Writers' Project, writing biographies of authors; Pestalozzi-Froebel Teachers College,

Chicago, Ill., instructor, 1938-42; Encyclopaedia Britannica, Inc., Chicago, member of editorial department of "Great Books" project, 1943-46; University of Minnesota, Minneapolis, member of English department, 1946, assistant professor, 1948-49, associate professor of English, 1954-59; New York University, New York, N.Y., visiting lecturer, 1950-52; Princeton University, Princeton, N.J., creative writing fellow, 1952-53; Bard College, Annandale-on-Hudson, N.Y., faculty member, 1953-54; University of Puerto Rico, Rio Piedras, visiting professor of English, 1961; University of Chicago, Chicago, celebrity in residence, 1962, currently Grunier Distinguished Services Professor, member of Committee on Social Thought, 1962—, chairman, 1970-76. Presented Jefferson Lecture for National Endowment for the Humanities in 1977; has presented Tanner Lectures at Oxford University. Fellow, Academy for Policy Study, 1966; fellow, Brandford College of Yale University. *Wartime service:* Merchant Marine, 1944-45.

MEMBER: Authors League, American Academy of Arts and Letters, PEN, Yaddo Corporation.

AWARDS, HONORS: Short stories included in *Best American Short Stories*, 1944, "Notes of a Dangling Man," and 1950, "Sermon by Doctor Pep"; Guggenheim fellowship in Paris and Rome, 1948; National Institute of Arts and Letters grant, 1952; National Book Award, 1954, for *The Adventures of Augie March*, 1964, for *Herzog*, and 1970, for *Mr. Sammler's Planet;* O. Henry Award, 1956, for "The Gonzaga Manuscripts," and 1980, for "A Silver Dish"; Ford grant, 1959, 1960; Friends of Literature Fiction Award, 1960; James L. Dow Award, 1964; Prix International de Litterature (France; $10,000), 1965, for *Herzog;* Jewish Heritage Award, B'nai B'rith, 1968; Croix de Chevalier (France), 1968; Formentor Prize, 1970; Pulitzer Prize and Nobel Prize for Literature, both 1976, for *Humboldt's Gift;* Gold Medal, American Academy of Arts and Letters, 1977; Emerson-Thoreau Medal, American Academy of Arts and Sciences, 1977; Neil Gunn International fellowship, 1977; Brandeis University Creative Arts Award, 1978; Commander, Legion of Honour (France), 1983; Malaparte Prize for Literature (Italy), 1984; Commander, Order of Arts and Letters (France), 1985; National Medal of Arts, 1988, for "outstanding contributions to the excellence, growth, support and availability of the arts in the United States." D.Litt. from Northwestern University, 1962, and Bard College, 1963; Litt.D. from New York University, 1970, Harvard University, 1972, Yale University, 1972, McGill University, 1973, Brandeis University, 1974, Hebrew Union College, 1976, and Trinity College (Dublin), 1976.

WRITINGS:

NOVELS

Dangling Man, Vanguard, 1944, reprinted, Penguin, 1988.
The Victim, Vanguard, 1947, reprinted, Penguin, 1988.
The Adventures of Augie March (also see below), Viking, 1953, published with introduction by Lionel Trilling, Modern Library, 1965, reprinted, Penguin, 1984.
Seize the Day; With Three Short Stories and a One-Act Play (novella; also contains stories "Father-to-Be," "The Gonzaga Manuscripts," and "Looking for Mr. Green," and play, "The Wrecker"; also see below), Viking, 1956, published singly as *Seize the Day*, 1961, published with introduction by Alfred Kazin, Fawcett, 1968, reprinted, Penguin, 1984.
Henderson the Rain King (also see below), Viking, 1959, reprinted, Penguin, 1984.
Herzog (early drafts published in *Esquire*, July, 1961, and July, 1963, in *Commentary*, July, 1964, and in *Saturday Evening Post*, August 8, 1964; also see below), Viking, 1964, pub-

lished with criticism, edited by Irving Howe, 1976, reprinted, Penguin, 1984.
Mr. Sammler's Planet (originally appeared in a different form in *Atlantic;* also see below), Viking, 1970.
Humboldt's Gift, Viking, 1975.
The Dean's December, Harper, 1982, limited edition with illustrations by Robert Heindel, Franklin Library, 1982.
More Die of Heartbreak, Morrow, 1987.
A Theft (novella; Quality Paperback Book Club dual main selection), Penguin, 1989.
The Bellarosa Connection (novella), Penguin, 1989.

SHORT STORIES

Mosby's Memoirs, and Other Stories (contains "Leaving the Yellow House," "The Old System," "Looking for Mr. Green," "The Gonzaga Manuscripts," "A Father-to-Be," and "Mosby's Memoirs"; also see below), Viking, 1968, reprinted, 1984.
Him with His Foot in His Mouth, and Other Stories (contains "Cousins," "A Silver Dish," "What Kind of Day Did You Have?," "Zetland: By a Character Witness," and "Him with His Foot in His Mouth"), Harper, 1984.

UNCOLLECTED SHORT STORIES

William Phillips and Philip Rahv, editors, *Partisan Reader: Ten Years of Partisan Review, 1934-1944,* (contains "Two Morning Monologues"), introduction by Lionel Trilling, Dial, 1946.
Nelson Algren, editor, *Nelson Algren's Own Book of Lonesome Monsters,* (contains "Address by Gooley MacDowell to the Hasbeens Club of Chicago"), Geis, 1963.
Penny Chapin Hills and L. Rust Hills, editors, *How We Live: Contemporary Life in Contemporary Fiction,* (contains "Herzog Visits Chicago"), Macmillan, 1968.

Other short stories reprinted in more than twenty anthologies.

PLAYS

"Under the Weather" (three one-act comedies: "Orange Souffle," published in *Esquire,* January, 1965, "A Wen," published in *Esquire,* October, 1965, and "Out from Under"), first produced in London, June 7, 1966; produced in Spoleto, Italy, at Festival of Two Worlds, July 14, 1966; produced on Broadway at the Cort Theatre, October 27, 1966.
The Last Analysis, a Play (full-length; first produced on Broadway at the Belasco Theatre, October 1, 1964; acting edition of first version of play printed under original title *Bummidge*), rewritten version published by Viking, 1965.

Also author of play "The Wrecker," *New World Writing 6,* 1954.

OTHER

(Editor with Keith Botsford [first three volumes also with Jack Ludwig]) *The Noble Savage,* five volumes, Meridian, 1961-62.
Recent American Fiction; A Lecture Presented under the Auspices of the Gertrude Clarke Whitall Poetry and Literature Fund, Library of Congress, 1963.
(Editor and author of introduction) *Great Jewish Short Stories,* Dell, 1963, reprinted, 1985.
Acceptance Speech by Saul Bellow, Author of "Herzog," Fiction Winner, National Book Awards, March 9, 1965, privately printed, c. 1965.
The Portable Saul Bellow (contains *Henderson the Rain King* and *Seize the Day,* plus selections from *The Adventures of Augie*

March, Herzog, and *Mr. Sammler's Planet,* and "Leaving the Yellow House," "The Old System," and "Mosby's Memoirs" from *Mosby's Memoirs, and Other Stories*), critical introduction by Gabriel Josipovici, Viking, 1974.
To Jerusalem and Back: A Personal Account (memoirs), Viking, 1976.
Herzog (sound recording of Bellow reading excerpts from novel), Caedmon, 1978.
The Nobel Lecture (first published in *American Scholar,* 1977), Targ Editions, 1979.

Also author of "Deep Readers of the World, Beware!," 1959; *Keynote Address before the Inaugural Session of the XXXIV International P.E.N. Congress, June 13, 1966, at Loeb Student Center,* New York University, 1966; and the Carolyn Benton Cockefair Lecture, "The Novel in a Technological Age," 1973. Contributor to *Partisan Review, Hudson Review, Sewanee Review, New Yorker, New Republic, Nation, New Leader, Saturday Review, Holiday, Reporter, Horizon, Esquire, Commentary, New York Times Book Review,* and other publications. Founder and co-editor of *Noble Savage,* 1960-62. An extensive collection of Bellow's manuscripts, including those from most of the novels, correspondence, and memorabilia, are housed at the Regenstein Library of the University of Chicago. The Humanities Research Center at the University of Texas at Austin holds several manuscripts of *Seize the Day.*

ADAPTATIONS: "The Wrecker" was televised in 1964; a sound recording of the Chicago Radio Theatre presentation of the plays "Orange Souffle" and "The Wrecker" was produced by All-Media Dramatic Workshop, 1978; a television adaptation of *Seize the Day,* featuring Robin Williams and a cameo appearance by Bellow, was broadcast by Public Broadcasting Service, May 1, 1987.

WORK IN PROGRESS: Working on "many things at once."

SIDELIGHTS: Saul Bellow has pursued his career as a writer with a steady commitment to the art of fiction as an indispensable form of knowledge. His canon stands as an eloquent testament to the vital life of the human mind and spirit and to the power of art. "I feel," Bellow explained to Gordon L. Harper in an interview for the *Paris Review,* "that art has something to do with the achievement of stillness in the midst of chaos. A stillness which characterizes prayer, too, and the eye of the storm. I think art has something to do with an arrest of attention in the midst of distraction." Tommy Wilhelm of *Seize the Day* and Artur Sammler of *Mr. Sammler's Planet* offer prayers out of such still centers amid turbulent emotional storms, and Eugene Henderson exclaims in *Henderson the Rain King* that "this is not a sick and hasty ride, helpless, through a dream into oblivion. No, sir! It can be arrested by a thing or two. By art, for instance. The speed is checked, the time is redivided. Measure! That great thought. Mystery." Bellow took Lionel Trilling and Arthur C. Clarke to task in *Harper's* for claiming that scientific truth, a manifestation of man's "maturity," will redeem society through technology "from the childish need for art," including the telling of stories to one another. "Science and technology," Bellow argued, "are not likely to remove this narrative and spellbinding oddity from the soul." But Bellow acknowledged that technology can be distracting to the artist and threatening to his art: "The present age has a certain rationalizing restlessness or cognitive irritability: a participatory delirium that makes the arresting powers of any work intolerable. . . . Technology has weakened certain points of spiritual rest. Wedding guests and ancient mariners both are deafened by the terrific blaring of the technological band."

In his Nobel Prize for Literature acceptance speech, delivered in Stockholm on December 12, 1976, Bellow reaffirmed his conviction that art is more important than science in exploring significant values in twentieth-century human experience. Following Marcel Proust, Bellow explained, "Only art penetrates what pride, passion, intelligence and habit erect on all sides—the seeming realities of this world. There is another reality, the genuine one, which we lose sight of. This other reality is always sending us hints, which, without art, we can't receive. Proust calls these hints our 'true impressions'. . . . The value of literature lies in these intermittent true impressions. . . . What [Joseph] Conrad said was true: art attempts to find in the universe, in matter as well as in the facts of life, what is fundamental, enduring, essential." To Bellow, the novel is "a sort of latter-day lean-to, a hovel in which the spirit takes shelter"; as such, the novel performs the same function that Robert Frost claimed for poetry; it provides "a momentary stay against confusion," and in a world where confusion has become king, momentary stillnesses and humble sanctuaries for the spirit are not insignificant contributions.

The three National Book Awards, the Pulitzer and Nobel Prizes, and the many other honors Bellow has received attest to the high quality he has established as a literary artist. In his essay "Where Do We Go from Here: The Future of Fiction," he has supplied a central standard for the evaluation of the novel: "It becomes art when the views most opposite to the author's own are allowed to exist in full strength. Without this a novel of ideas is mere self-indulgence, and didacticism is simply axe-grinding. The opposites must be free to range themselves against each other, and they must be passionately expressed on both sides. It is for this reason that I say it doesn't matter much what the writer's personal position is, what he wishes to affirm. He may affirm principles we all approve of and write very bad novels." Or as Philip Bummidge says in a Keatsian observation in Bellow's play *The Last Analysis,* "I am convinced that lies are bad art." Giving fair play to the opposition, working through murkiness to clarity, a novel earns its vision. For half a century, Bellow has striven in his work—his art—to give shape and substance to the abstractions by which human beings live. Although individual works have not always risen to his own highest standard, each contributes to a whole that demonstrates a writer deeply engaged with the complexity of human existence and fully committed to his art as a form of understanding; each work thus contributes to the survival of informed intelligence and humanistic culture. His versatility and willingness to take risks have led Bellow to extend his efforts to the short story (*Mosby's Memoirs, and Other Stories* and *Him with His Foot in His Mouth, and Other Stories*), the familiar essay, literary criticism, the drama, and the philosophical-political travelogue (*To Jerusalem and Back: A Personal Account*), but at the core of his art stand the novels.

Bellow's first two novels, *Dangling Man* and *The Victim,* adhere to the standards of traditional novels, a way of paying dues to the literary establishment and the tradition of the well-made novel. With Gordon L. Harper in the *Paris Review* interview, Bellow was explicit about his intent as a novelistic newcomer: "I think when I wrote those early books I was timid. I still felt the incredible effrontery of announcing myself to the world (in part I mean the WASP world) as a writer and an artist. I had to touch a great many bases, demonstrate my abilities, pay my respects to formal requirements. In short, I was afraid to let myself go."

During the composition of *The Adventures of Augie March,* however, Bellow experienced a kind of artistic liberation: "When I began *Augie March,* I took off many of these restraints. I think I took off too many, and went too far, but I was feeling the excitement of discovery." In fact, as Bellow explained to Harvey Breit in *The Writer Observed,* "The great pleasure of the book was that it came easily. All I had to do was to be there with buckets to catch it."

A *Bildungsroman,* or novel of education, and a picaresque quest novel, *The Adventures of Augie March* traces Augie's erratic pursuit of a worthwhile fate. Telling his own story "free style," Augie relives his experiences for the reader from his boyhood in Chicago to his wanderings in Michigan, Mexico, and the African Sea to his maturity as a husband and import businessman in Paris. Augie encounters a Chaucerian pilgrimage of Bellovian characters, and from each Augie learns something about "bitterness in his chosen thing" and thus something about his search for a worthwhile fate. He does not find the fate he imagined, but he does affirm the validity of the search: "Columbus too," says Augie, "thought he was a flop, probably, when they sent him back in chains. Which didn't prove there was no America."

Despite Bellow's admission that he went "too far" and violated formal unity, *Augie March* does have a firm organizing principle, the tension of opposites. Refusing to lead a disappointed life, Augie seeks a worthwhile fate in accordance with what he calls the "axial lines of life," which lead one to "Truth, love, peace, bounty, usefulness, harmony." Augie is a free and optimistic spirit, but Bellow exposes him to characters, ideas, and situations inimical to his freedom and his optimism. The figure Kayo Obermark supplies a name for the negative factors, *moha,* the limitations imposed by the finite and imperfect, "the Bronx cheer of the conditioning forces." Einhorn's and Georgie's handicaps, Simon's monomania and loveless marriage, the superficiality of the Magnuses, the varied victimizations of Jimmy Klein and Mimi Villars, the limited love of Stella, the lost children everywhere—all testify to the power of *moha* and assail the fortress of Augie's dream of happiness on the axial lines of life. But Augie stands firm in his optimism, earning the book's affirmative vision through his awareness of life's dark side and his resilience in the face of it. "It is important to keep in mind," observes Brigitte Scheer-Schaezler in her study *Saul Bellow,* "that Augie's desire for life in the sun is not motivated by a shunning of action or a rejection of consciousness but arises from his knowledge of darkness, the darkness which he says has widened his outlook." "Indeed," says Sarah Blacher Cohen in the *Saul Bellow Journal,* "Augie is the picaresque apostle who, meeting up with errant humanity, eagerly listens to their confessions and generously pardons their sins, even blessing them for their antic trespasses."

To move from the sprawling and affirmative *The Adventures of Augie March* to the compact and brooding *Seize the Day* is to leave the circus for the court. One is colorful, spontaneous, cacophonous, alive; the other is formal, confessional, tense, fatalistic. Whereas Augie defines his humanity through his charm, striving, and compassion, Tommy Wilhelm defines his humanity through his slovenliness, selfishness, and suffering—and, most important, through his desire to be better than he is. A reader is drawn to both figures, a tribute to Bellow's powerful portraiture. The power grows to an extent out of a personal dimension of the novel. "The shrill quality of the marriage relationship between Tommy and his wife," writes Robert Detweiler in *Saul Bellow: A Critical Essay,* "may echo Bellow's own situation at the time. He worked on the story while living in a desert shack in Nevada and waiting out the residency requirements for a divorce." Four times divorced, Bellow inevitably allows his personal anguish to imbue his fiction. Herzog, whose "heart has been shat on," cries out, "*Will never understand what women want. . . . They eat green salad and drink human blood.*" Wilhelm's lonely cries about his wife and his life come "howling like a wolf from the city window."

An anti-hero, Wilhelm has messed up his life. By changing his name (Saul Bellow was born Solomon Bellows), dropping out of school, and failing in business, Tommy has embarrassed and alienated his father, Dr. Adler, a selfish retired physician. Out of his foolish pride, Wilhelm has quit a good job and now can find no other. His mismanagement of his life has led to estrangement from his wife and painful separation from his two boys. In loneliness and desperation, Wilhelm has turned for companionship and advice to a kind of surrogate father, Dr. Tamkin, a quack psychologist, aspiring poet, slick operator in the stock market, and mainline Bellovian reality-instructor. On the titular day depicted in *Seize the Day,* Wilhelm's lifelong miscalculations and bad judgments bring him to his knees. His father and wife turn deaf ears to his appeals for help, Tamkin abandons him after misguiding him into losing his last savings in the stock market, and Tommy ends the day crying unceasingly in a funeral home over the body of a stranger. The final scene is the nadir of Wilhelm's personal failure, the culmination in a symbolic drowning of a sustained pattern of water imagery in the story, and the conclusion of one of Bellow's bleakest but most tightly integrated novels.

"Wilhelm's drowning," notes Keith Opdahl in *The Novels of Saul Bellow: An Introduction,* "is first of all the climax of his day of failure. The water in which he drowns is both the world and his masochistic self which have murdered him." The masochistic self here is what Tamkin termed the "pretender soul"; its death at least opens the way for the emergence of Wilhelm's "true soul," but that redemptive possibility is not realized within the pages of the novel. Clinton W. Trowbridge observes in *Critique: Studies in Modern Fiction* that "the image of the drowning Wilhelm is the controlling one, but because of the book's ironic structure it is an image that functions in two ways. On a first reading, and on each rereading on the surface of our experience, it intensifies sympathy for Wilhelm's condition. Even when Wilhelm is being depicted least sympathetically, when he is most in the wrong, most a slob, we are continually made aware that we are witnessing the strugglings of a drowning man and we want to see him rescued." Writing in Earl Rovit's *Saul Bellow: A Collection of Critical Essays,* M. Gilbert Porter observes that "the unity of effect achieved in *Seize the Day* results from the skillful blending of all the elements of fiction in tightly constructed scenic units functioning very much like poetic images built around a controlling metaphor. Each scene extends the central image of Wilhelm's drowning by embodying a particular aspect of his life that has contributed to the pressure that finally overwhelms him in literal failure and symbolic death and rebirth. Unity is enhanced further by cross references between scenes." In its compactness, unity, and intensity, *Seize the Day* approaches the configuration of poetry.

In *Henderson the Rain King,* Bellow recaptured the spirit of *The Adventures of Augie March* in a spin-off verbal and comic riot of picaresque energy. At age fifty-five, the manic gentile Henderson stands six feet four, weighs two hundred and thirty pounds, has an M.A. from a prestigious eastern university, plus a second wife, seven children, a three-million-dollar estate, and a voice within him crying, "I want, I want, I want," which testifies to both his unhappiness and his aspiration. Although he has most of the things that Madison Avenue equates with human happiness, Henderson feels that a central element is missing from his

life. His vigorous but bumbling quest to discover that element leads him through whimsical pig-farming, gratuitous violence, and antisocial behavior to Africa, where through exotic experiences with African tribes he determines that he can "burst the spirit's sleep" and still the voice within him by serving others as a physician in emulation of his hero Sir Wilfred Grenfill. In the final scene, his dance around the New York-bound plane with the lion cub and the Persian orphan during the refueling stop in symbolic Newfoundland is a rhapsodic celebration of his movement toward community and his confirmed new vision of the possibilities of life over death: "God does not shoot dice with our souls," cries the joyful Henderson, "and therefore grun-tu-molani. . . . I believe there is justice, and that much is promised." According to Walter Clemons and Jack Kroll in a *Newsweek* interview with the author, "Of all his characters, Bellow has said, Henderson, the quixotic seeker of higher truth, is most like himself."

The theme of the novel is a recurrent one in Bellow's fiction: that the world is tough and mysterious, that man is subject to great errors and subsequent pain, but that he yearns for nobility and joy and feels in his deepest soul that such things are possible. The disparity between the exalted aspiration and the flawed self that aspires is, of course, comic. "*Henderson the Rain King* is clearly Bellow's most full-blown comic novel," writes Cohen in *Saul Bellow's Enigmatic Laughter.* "The dreaded nightmare experiences of the earlier realistic novels are transformed into the playful and dreamlike episodes of romance. The comic flaws which the early heroes were often too obtuse to notice are magnified in Henderson, who both flamboyantly exhibits them and exorcises them through his own jocose language."

The ebullience of Henderson is transformed into erudition in his successor, Herzog. "What this country needs," says Herzog, "is a good five-cent synthesis." His frantic attempts to formulate such a synthesis to shore up his disintegrating life is the substance of *Herzog,* Bellow's most well-wrought novel. An older Joseph, a more knowing Henderson, Herzog seeks clarity and justice as a professor of history with a Ph.D. and an impressive professional bibliography. But with the discovery that his wife, Madeleine, and his good friend Gersbach have made him a cuckold and abandoned him to his isolated personal fate, Herzog finds himself lost in the modernist waste land of cynical "reality instructors" and existential nothingness, "down in the mire of post-Renaissance, post-humanistic, post-Cartesian dissolution, next door to the void." Such hostile territory is particularly hard on a sensitive intellectual whose sensibilities are at war with his intellect. With his feelings, he resists the negations of the reality instructors, but the chaotic evidence of his personal life makes an intellectual assent to their conclusions almost irresistible. His final transcendence of their teachings and his own anguish in the pastoral setting of Ludeyville testifies to the power Herzog discovers in simple being and the "law of the heart"; at peace at last, he says, "*I am pretty well satisfied to be, to be just as it is willed, and for as long as I may remain in occupancy.*"

The stress and resolution in *Herzog* is typical of the Bellow canon. "It is this problem," Alfred Kazin says in *Contemporaries,* "first of representing all that a man intends and plans and then of getting him not merely to recognize the countervailing strength of life but to humble himself before it, that is the real situation in all Bellow's novels." Where Kazin sees acceptance and submission, Ihab Hassan, in *Radical Innocence: Studies in the Contemporary American Novel,* sees affirmation in the protagonist as the sequel to his conflict between self and the world: "the movement is from acid defeat to acceptance, and from acceptance to celebration. The querulous and ill-natured hero becomes prodigal and quixotic. In this process something of the dignity that the fictional hero has lost to history is restored to him."

A majority of critics agree, as Harold Bloom observes in the Modern Critical Views collection *Saul Bellow,* that *Herzog* "seems to be Bellow's best and most representative novel." Minority reports have been filed, however. In *Time to Murder and Create,* John W. Aldridge sees the novel "as the Waste Land cliche irrigated and transformed in the Promised Land, while the platitude of Alienation is converted into the even hoarier platitude of Accommodation and Togetherness. For what he finally holds up for our inspection is a new hopeful doctrine of potato love not uncolored by righteous disdain." Richard Poirier, in Rovit's *Saul Bellow: A Collection of Critical Essays,* dismisses the novel as empty rhetoric and its author as intellectually dishonest: "What I call the gap in his novels between their intellectual and historical pretensions, on one side, and the stuff of life as he renders it, on the other, prevents me from believing that he is himself convinced by his snappy contempt for 'the commonplaces of the Waste Land outlook, the cheap mental stimulants of Alienation.'" Such a cavil sounds faint amid the general clamor of praise for *Herzog,* in which Bellow displays his shiniest wares, and whose protagonist seems to represent a culmination of all Bellow's key characters: thinker, victim, sufferer (but a "suffering joker"), quester, struggler, sinner, and, at last, affirmer.

Bellow's seventh novel, *Mr. Sammler's Planet,* is an indignant depiction of contemporary America from the perspective of one of Bellow's most formidable "men thinking," Sammler, Cracow-born Anglophile in his seventies and Jewish survivor of a Nazi pogrom in Poland. His war injuries have left him with a tempered post-grave detachment and vision in only one eye. Thus Sammler sees outward and inward. His good right eye records characters, actions, and events in the world around him. His blind left eye subjects current events to introspective analysis, the historical and philosophical perspective. "The damaged eye seemed to turn in another direction, to be preoccupied separately with different matters." The novel oscillates, then, from action to reflection as Sammler tries to make sense of a planet that seems to be coming unglued. Within that general strategy there are complementary movements from past to present, from public to private, from life to death. Three obliquely related plots provide the structural matrix of the narrative: 1) a Black pickpocket who plies his trade on the Forty-second Street Bus and exposes his penis to Sammler to warn him not to interfere; 2) a book manuscript on space travel and inhabitation of the moon stolen from its author, Dr. Govinda Lal, by Sammler's daughter, Shula; and 3) the slow dying of Dr. Gruner from an aneurysm in his brain. Interspersed are a number of encounters with assorted crazies Sammler must endure.

Bellow told Jane Howard in an interview for *Life* that *Mr. Sammler's Planet* is his own favorite work: "I had a high degree of excitement writing it . . . and finished it in record time. It's my first thoroughly nonapologetic venture into ideas. In *Herzog* . . . and *Henderson the Rain King* I was kidding my way to Jesus, but here I'm baring myself nakedly." The novel and this statement about it marked a shift in proportion in Bellow's art, as abstraction began to overshadow concretion. The change has elicited mixed responses. Robert R. Dutton, in Twayne's *Saul Bellow,* calls the novel "Bellow's highest technical achievement," and Scheer-Schaezler, in support of what she calls "enlarged vision," describes the book as representative of "Bellow's effort to turn the novel into a medium of inquiry. In Bellow's most recent novels, experiences are not so much being undergone as discussed in a probing approach that may well be called essayistic."

In the same vein, Nathan A. Scott, Jr., declares approvingly in *Three American Moralists: Mailer, Bellow, Trilling* that Bellow's "insistently didactic intention has had the effect of making rhetoric itself—rather than action and character—the main source of the essential energies in his fiction. And there is perhaps no other comparable body of work in the literature of the contemporary novel so drenched in ideas and speculations and theories, even commandments."

Other critics, however, have felt that Bellow's expository treatment of ideas in *Mr. Sammler's Planet* vitiates his art. David Galloway writes in *Modern Fiction Studies* that Bellow's emphasis on ideas leads to a failure of imagination, a too easy recourse to stock situations and well-worn character pairings. "The central problem in Bellow's novels," contends Galloway, is that "the imaginative structure fails to provide adequate support for the intellectual structure, so that at crucial moments the author's ideas fail to be organically embodied in character, action, or image." In her review in the *Nation,* Beverly Gross describes the scene at Columbia when Sammler is confronted by a heckler, a mere straw man in her view, as symptomatic of the fundamental flaw in the novel: "When an artist who is no blunderer—and Bellow is a supreme artist—furnishes so false a moment, it is something of a revelation. Bellow has failed to give credibility to the opposition." Benjamin DeMott, writing for *Saturday Review,* finds abstractions vivid in the novel but concretions pale. For example, Sammler's detachment, says DeMott, "attains insufficient substance for the reader, seemingly belonging only to the surface structure of Sammler's mind and story . . . whereas his scorn and vituperation come forth strongly as from the center." Baring himself as ideologist and didact in *Mr. Sammler's Planet,* Bellow ran the risk of violating the principle he set forth in "Where Do We Go from Here" of giving fair play to opposing ideas, but perhaps he did so to counter a movement in fiction, like Hemingway's, that represents ideas but forbids thought. "It shows," Bellow explained in the same essay, "a great skepticism of the strength of art. It makes it appear as though ideas openly expressed would be too much for art to bear."

In *Humboldt's Gift,* Bellow managed to check his growing impulse toward abstraction at the expense of concretion. Like *Herzog, Humboldt's Gift* strikes an aesthetically functional symmetry between idea and image. The novel tells the story of intellectual Chicagoan Charlie Citrine, Pulitzer Prize-winning biographer and dramatist, who approaches the completion of his sixth decade in the company of the nimbus of his deceased poetic mentor, Von Humboldt Fleisher, and the nemesis of his self-appointed materialistic advisor, Rinaldo Cantabile, both manic manipulators. The dead poet speaks to Citrine of his obligation to his creative spirit, art as power. The minor-league Mafioso Cantabile urges capitalistic enterprise, art as profit. Citrine ultimately frees himself from both figures, and at the end walks from the new grave he has provided for Humboldt into an ambivalently emerging spring to begin a meditative life away from the distractions of dissident voices and grotesque behavior.

Charlie's compulsive flights into metaphysical explanations have to contend with the corrective pragmatism of his earthy mistress, Renata: "I prefer to take things as billions of people have throughout history. You work, you get bread, you lose a leg, kiss some fellows, have a baby, you live to be eighty and bug hell out of everybody, or you get hung or drowned. But you don't spend years trying to dope your way out of the human condition. . . . I think when you're dead you're dead, and that's that." Such views lead Renata to abandon the hyperintellectual Citrine and choose an undertaker for a husband, a marriage with death. Charlie resists Renata's reality-instructor text by clinging to a message from the dead poet: "Remember: we are not natural beings but supernatural beings," a spiritual reinforcement of Charlie's natural impulses that represents Humboldt's real gift to his protege.

"The novel therefore explores," says Judie Newman in *Saul Bellow and History,* "different approaches to history and retreats from history: pop history, instant history, history as nightmare, as tragedy, as farce, the retreat into myth or transcendence, or into the eternal present of the crisis mentality. By the novel's various structurings of time, Bellow succeeds in avoiding any one style of approach and thereby liberates the event to be judged in its total context, as it affects its participants, as it is recorded in public records, and as it is inherited, transformed and translated by succeeding generations." Bellow himself says in the *Newsweek* interview, "*Humboldt* is very much a comic book about death," and he sees it as an advance in his own authorial detachment and his function as social historian: "The nice thing about this book, which I was really struggling with in *Herzog,* is that I've really come into a cold air of objectivity about all the people in the book, including Charlie. It really came easily for me to see him as America saw him, and thereby America itself became clearer." Despite Bellow's claim of objectivity, the novel contains several elements of his own personal history—the poker game, for example, and the interest in Steinerian philosophy, which Bellow came to by way of Owen Barfield's *Saving the Appearances.* "Does he mean it?—all this business of the soul and an afterlife, and especially about [Rudolf] Steiner and his anthroposophy [or man-centered religious system]," asks Dutton in his revised *Saul Bellow.* "Yes," he answers, "Bellow does—at least figuratively. As far as Steiner is concerned, he is a figure for an illustration of Bellow's contention, through Charlie, that we must try new ideas, even ideas that are unscientific, and hence, that tend to inhibit us. . . . Charlie triumphs over his inhibitions and is able to go ahead with his irrational studies." Still, several critics have observed that there is a shrugging what-the-hell tone about Charlie's experimental commitment to anthroposophy as well as about his shifty character generally that undermines much of his compulsive philosophizing. The novel plays for laughs—and gets them—but it does so in large measure at the expense of its ostensibly serious purposes.

The humor that dominates *Humboldt's Gift* is conspicuously absent in the ninth novel, *The Dean's December,* in a continuation of the upbeat-downbeat, see-saw pattern of Bellow's fiction. As a journalist turned academic, Dean Albert Corde has accompanied his Romanian-born wife, Minna, to Bucharest to attend her dying mother, Valeria. Isolated in his room or cruising the streets as a "hungry observer" and a "moralist of seeing," Corde observes Bucharest and reflects on Chicago, a city whose "whirling lives" typify the chaotic American reality. The communist and the capitalist cities are grim places of different but related forms of disorder, injustice, repression, and destruction; they are yoked by violence together, for death is everywhere: "I imagine, sometimes," Corde thinks, "that if a film could be made of one's life, every other frame would be death." This macabre mood is sustained throughout the novel even though at the end, after Valeria's death, Corde is comforted briefly by a renewed closeness to his wife that somehow has its counterpart in his closeness to the heavens in the great telescope of the Mount Palomar Observatory. Although he is cold there, he tells his guide, significantly, as they descend, "But I almost mind coming down more"—that is, coming down to earth, where robbery, rape, murder, prejudice, and political injustice mock the human quest for order, beauty, love, and justice. The novel is a dark and brooding ethical statement.

Some of the darkness of *The Dean's December* grew out of Bellow's personal experience. Bellow told William Kennedy in *Esquire* that he wrote the novel "in a year and a half . . . and had no idea it was coming. One of these things that came over me. My wife's mother was dying in Bucharest, and I went with her to give her some support, which in that place one badly needs. The old mother died while we were there." Part of the grimness grew out of actual events, like a sensational Chicago rape case, and out of factual conditions, like the Cabrini Green housing project in Chicago, but most of the pessimism came from Bellow's increasing conviction that the decline of civilization is magnified in American cities. Malcolm Bradbury writes in *The Modern American Novel* that *The Dean's December* "confirms the later Bellow as the novelist of a world which has lost cultural bearings, moved into an age of boredom and terror, violence and indifference, private wealth and public squalor." Bellow himself has been very explicit about his intentions in the novel. He told Matthew C. Roudane in an interview for *Contemporary Literature* that the decaying city has its counterpart in an "inner slum": "What I meant was there is a correspondence between outer and inner, between the brutalized city and the psyche of its citizens. Given their human resources I don't see how people today can experience life at all. Politicians, public figures, professors address 'modern problems' solely in terms of employment. They assume that unemployment causes incoherence, sexual disorders, the abandonment of children, robbery, rape and murder. Plainly, they have no imagination of these evils. They don't even *see* them. And in *The Dean's December* what I did was to say, 'Look!' The first step is to display the facts. But the facts, unless the imagination perceives them, are *not* facts. Perhaps I shouldn't say 'perceives'—I should say 'passionately takes hold.' As an artist does. Mr. Corde, the Dean, passionately takes hold of Chicago and writes his articles like an artist rather than a journalist. . . . It is Corde's conviction that without art, it is impossible to interpret reality, and that the degeneration of art and language leads to the decay of judgment." Ironically, an exchange of styles seems to occur, in effect, between Corde and Bellow, for the passionate intensity that allows Corde's journalism to rise to the status of art—as Bellow describes it here—leads Bellow's prose in the novel as a whole to assume the condition of journalism, the documentary, or, as Roudane observes, "a nonfiction novelistic style," an extension of the essayistic prose that has become more prominent in Bellow's later novels. The result, thematically, is a kind of war correspondent's report on the sobering spectacle of the human race mindlessly consuming its own entrails and indifferent to the art that might save it.

Bellow returns to the comic mode in his tenth novel, *More Die of Heartbreak,* a turgid, almost plotless story of two academics connected less by their blood kinship than by their similarly oblique relations to women and to everyday reality. The narrator is thirty-five-year-old Kenneth Tractenberg, a professor of Russian literature at a university in the Midwest. His beloved uncle, Benn Crader, is an internationally respected botanist whose specialty is Arctic lichens and whose patterns of practical misjudgment make him think of himself as "a phoenix who runs with arsonists." Kenneth, though, admires his uncle for reasons that are not clear. Kenneth's philandering father offers his son a sarcastic but perhaps accurate explanation: "you're one of those continuing-education types and you think Benn still has something to teach you." Although intelligent and ceaselessly introspective, Kenneth and Uncle Benn are curious naifs. Kenneth is at great pains to marry Treckie, the mother of his illegitimate daughter and a woman who rejects him to live with a sadist and travel the flea-market circuits. Uncle Benn marries a spoiled rich girl, Matilda Layamon, whose physician father maneuvers to recover Benn's lost inheritance from crooked Uncle Vilitzer so that Matilda can continue to live a life of pampered ease. Benn escapes both the solicitousness of Kenneth and the machinations of the Layamons, finally, by a Charlie Citrine-like retreat to the North Pole to study lichens.

Although *More Die of Heartbreak* was generally well-received, critical response to the novel has been characterized by qualified praise and reluctantly held reservations. "Kenneth's freeranging mind allows Bellow to put just about everything real and imaginable into this novel," notes Robert Wilson in *USA Today.* "Even so, Kenneth does not seem to me to be among the best of Bellow's characters, nor this among the best of Bellow's comic novels. Kenneth wore me out, especially when his divagations took us so far from the plot that it was barely a memory." Clemons, in *Newsweek,* finds the supporting characters more appealing than the principals: "It's a slight drawback to *More Die of Heartbreak* that the innocents in the foreground, Uncle Benn and Kenneth, are upstaged by their captivating adversaries. . . . Our time with Benn and Kenneth is well spent for the sake of the rascals to whom they introduce us." Rhoda Koenig, reviewing for *New York,* contends that the sympathy implicit in the title is overshadowed by an intelligence that fails to sustain its own weight: "But Bellow's heart seems to be more with the brutal comedy of the doctor than all his sodden mind games with Kenneth and Benn. In *More Die of Heartbreak,* despite the often voiced concern epitomized by the title, it is the mind that is given center stage, and fails to hold it." On the other hand, in the *New York Times Book Review,* William Gaddis judges the return of the wry Bellovian humor an ample trade-off for a makeshift plot: "In *More Die of Heartbreak* we welcome back the calamitous wit of *The Adventures of Augie March* and *Herzog* among people diligently struggling to rearrange one another's lives in their efforts to rescue or simply to define their own. . . . We hear their voices pour from the pages engulfing a plot that is comparatively simple, or would be if left to itself, a possibility this embattled narrator never entertains for a moment." In sum, Bellow's tenth novel has been received as a pleasant but sometimes trying entertainment; it has generated respectful applause but few bravos and no standing ovations.

But Bellow is not greatly affected by critical opinion. In his Cockefair Lecture "The Novel in a Technological Age," delivered in Kansas City in 1973, he observed with typical drollery that "in the sea of literature, there are more ichthyologists than fish." He is not daunted by occasional detractors; he is not inflated by his constant admirers. Defiance of the one or deference to the other would be destructive to his art, and his art is what concerns him. Rovit's comment in his 1967 study *Saul Bellow* that "the seminal image in all of Bellow's fiction is not the image of a man seeking, but that of a man brooding in the midst of his solitude" seems particularly applicable to Bellow himself as he sits alone with his books and his thoughts in the autumn of his life. His thoughts are, as always, of his work and of his world. Despite the charges that his later novels are repetitious and too essayistic, Bellow feels comfortable with his current creative direction. He told David N. Prescott in *Mature Outlook* that his fiction is improving: "Yeah, I think I am getting better. I can think of any number of writers who got better as they got older. Thomas Harding [Hardy] got very good. Ibsen wrote some of his best things when he was older. The painter Titian got really hot when he was in his 80s. Sophocles also wrote some of his very best things in his 80s." And to Clemons, in *Newsweek,* Bellow said, "a writer in his 60s and 70s always has subjects laid aside. Will they be ripe when I'm 90? It's a good reason to hang in there."

BIOGRAPHICAL/CRITICAL SOURCES:

BOOKS

Authors in the News, Volume 2, Gale, 1976.
Aldridge, John W., *Time to Murder and Create,* McKay, 1966.
Bellow, Saul, *Dangling Man,* Vanguard, 1944.
Bellow, Saul, *The Victim,* Vanguard, 1947.
Bellow, Saul, *The Adventures of Augie March,* Viking, 1953.
Bellow, Saul, *Seize the Day,* Viking, 1956.
Bellow, Saul, *Henderson the Rain King,* Viking, 1959.
Bellow, Saul, *Herzog,* Viking, 1964.
Bellow, Saul, *The Last Analysis, a Play,* Viking, 1966.
Bellow, Saul, *Mosby's Memoirs, and Other Stories,* Viking, 1968.
Bellow, Saul, *Mr. Sammler's Planet,* Viking, 1970.
Bellow, Saul, *Humboldt's Gift,* Viking, 1975.
Bellow, Saul, *To Jerusalem and Back: A Personal Account,* Viking, 1976.
Bellow, Saul, *The Nobel Lecture,* Targ Editions, 1979.
Bellow, Saul, *The Dean's December,* Harper, 1982.
Bellow, Saul, *Him with His Foot in His Mouth, and Other Stories,* Harper, 1984.
Bellow, Saul, *More Die of Heartbreak,* Morrow, 1987.
Bestsellers 89, issue 3, 1989.
Bloom, Harold, editor, *Saul Bellow,* Chelsea House, 1986.
Bradbury, Malcolm, *The Modern American Novel,* Oxford University Press, 1983.
Breit, Harvey, *The Writer Observed,* World Publishing, 1956.
Clayton, John J., *Saul Bellow: In Defense of Man,* 2nd edition, Indiana University Press, 1979.
Cohen, Sarah Blacher, *Saul Bellow's Enigmatic Laughter,* University of Illinois Press, 1974.
Concise Dictionary of American Literary Biography: The New Consciousness, 1941-1968, Gale, 1987.
Contemporary Authors Autobiography Series, Gale, Volume 1, 1984.
Contemporary Fiction in America and England, 1950-1970, Gale, 1976.
Contemporary Literary Criticism, Gale, Volume 1, 1973, Volume 2, 1974, Volume 3, 1975, Volume 6, 1976, Volume 8, 1978, Volume 10, 1979, Volume 13, 1980, Volume 15, 1980, Volume 25, 1983, Volume 33, 1985, Volume 34, 1985.
Cronin, Gloria L., and Blaine H. Hall, *Saul Bellow: An Annotated Bibliography,* 2nd edition, Garland Publishing, 1987.
Detweiler, Robert, *Saul Bellow: A Critical Essay,* Eerdmans, 1967.
Dictionary of Literary Biography, Gale, Volume 2: *American Novelists since World War II,* 1978, Volume 28: *Twentieth-Century American Jewish Fiction Writers,* 1984.
Dictionary of Literary Biography Yearbook, 1982, Gale, 1983.
Dutton, Robert R., *Saul Bellow,* Twayne, 1971, revised edition, 1982.
Fuchs, Daniel, *Saul Bellow: Vision and Revision,* Duke University Press, 1984.
Galloway, David D., *The Absurd Hero in American Fiction: Updike, Styron, Bellow, Salinger,* 2md revised edition, University of Texas Press, 1981.
Harper, Howard, *Desperate Faith: A Study of Bellow, Salinger, Mailer, Baldwin, and Updike,* University of North Carolina Press, 1967.
Harris, Mark, *Saul Bellow: Drumlin Woodchuck,* University of Georgia Press, 1980.
Hassan, Ihab, *Radical Innocence: Studies in the Contemporary American Novel,* Harper, 1966.

Howe, Irving, editor, *Saul Bellow: Herzog; Text and Criticism,* Viking, 1976.

Iwayama, Tajiro, editor, *Saul Bellow,* Yamaguchi Shoten (Kyoto, Japan), 1982.

Kazin, Alfred, *Contemporaries,* Little, Brown, 1962.

Kiernan, Robert F., *Saul Bellow,* Continuum, 1989.

Klein, Marcus, *After Alienation: American Novels in Mid-Century,* World Publishing, 1965.

Kulshrestha, Chirantan, *Saul Bellow: The Problem of Affirmation,* Arnold-Heinemann (New Delhi), 1978.

Lercangee, Francine, *Saul Bellow: A Bibliography of Secondary Sources,* Center for American Studies (Brussels), 1977.

Malin, Irving, editor, *Saul Bellow and the Critics,* New York University Press, 1967.

Malin, Irving, *Saul Bellow's Fiction,* Southern Illinois University Press, 1969.

McCadden, Joseph F., *The Flight from Women in the Fiction of Saul Bellow,* University Press of America, 1980.

McConnell, Frank D., *Four Post-War American Novelists: Bellow, Mailer, Barth, and Pynchon,* Chicago University Press, 1977.

Nault, Marianne, *Saul Bellow: His Works and His Critics; An Annotated International Bibliography,* Garland Publishing, 1977.

Newman, Judie, *Saul Bellow and History,* St. Martin's, 1984.

Noreen, Robert G., *Saul Bellow: A Reference Guide,* G. K. Hall, 1978.

Opdahl, Keith, *The Novels of Saul Bellow: An Introduction,* Pennsylvania State University Press, 1967.

Porter, M. Gilbert, *Whence the Power?: The Artistry and Humanity of Saul Bellow,* University of Missouri Press, 1974.

Rodrigues, Eusebio L., *Quest for the Human: An Exploration of Saul Bellow's Fiction,* Bucknell University Press, 1981.

Rovit, Earl, *Saul Bellow,* University of Minnesota Press, 1967.

Rovit, Earl, editor, *Saul Bellow: A Collection of Critical Essays,* Prentice-Hall, 1975.

Scheer-Schaezler, Brigitte, *Saul Bellow,* Ungar, 1972.

Schraepen, Edmond, editor, *Saul Bellow and His Work,* Free University of Brussels, 1978.

Scott, Nathan A., Jr., *Three American Moralists: Mailer, Bellow, Trilling,* University of Notre Dame Press, 1968.

Sokoloff, B. A., and Mark Posner, *Saul Bellow: A Comprehensive Bibliography,* Folcroft Library Editions, 1972.

Tanner, Tony, *Saul Bellow,* Oliver & Boyd, 1965.

Tanner, Tony, *City of Words: American Fiction 1950-1970,* Harper, 1971.

Trachtenberg, Stanley, editor, *Critical Essays on Saul Bellow,* G. K. Hall, 1979.

Wilson, Jonathan, *On Bellow's Planet: Readings from the Dark Side,* Fairleigh Dickinson University Press, 1986.

PERIODICALS

American Literature, Volume 43, number 2, 1971.
Atlantic, January, 1965.
Chicago Review, Volume 23, number 4, 1972.
Chicago Tribune, March 2, 1990.
Contemporary Literature, Volume 25, number 3, 1984.
Critical Quarterly, Volume 15, 1973.
Criticism, Volume 15, number 3, 1973.
Critique: Studies in Modern Fiction, Volume 3, 1960, Volume 7, 1965, Volume 9, 1967, Volume 9, 1968.
Encounter, Volume 24, number 2, 1965, Volume 45, number 5, 1975.
Esquire, February, 1982.
Essays in Literature, Volume 5, 1979.

Forum, Volume 7, 1969, Volume 14, number 1, 1976.
Georgia Review, winter, 1978.
Globe and Mail (Toronto), March 10, 1990.
Harper's, August, 1974.
Hudson Review, Volume 12, 1959.
Journal of American Studies, Volume 7, 1973, Volume 9, 1975, Volume 15, 1981.
Life, April 3, 1970.
Listener, February 13, 1975.
Mature Outlook, Volume 1, number 3, 1984.
Modern Fiction Studies, Volume 12, 1966-67, Volume 17, 1971, Volume 19, 1973, Volume 25, 1979.
Nation, February 9, 1970.
Newsweek, September 1, 1975, June 8, 1987.
New York, June 8, 1987.
New Yorker, September 15, 1975.
New York Times Book Review, February 15, 1959, May 9, 1971, May 24, 1987.
New York Times Magazine, November 21, 1978.
Paris Review, Volume 9, number 36, 1966.
Partisan Review, Volume 26, number 3, 1959.
People, September 8, 1975.
Salmagundi, Volume 30, 1975 (special Bellow issue).
Saturday Review, February 7, 1970.
Saturday Review of Literature, August 22, 1953, September 19, 1953, September 19, 1964.
Saul Bellow Journal, Volume 4, number 1, 1985, Volume 5, numbers 1 and 2, 1986, Volume 6, number 1, 1987.
Saul Bellow Newsletter, Volume 1, number 1, 1981.
Studies in the Literary Imagination, Volume 17, number 2, 1984 (special Bellow issue).
Studies in the Novel, Volume 1, number 3, 1969.
Times Literary Supplement, October 27, 1989.
USA Today, June 5, 1987.
Western Humanities Review, Volume 14, 1960.

*   *   *

BENAVENTE (y MARTINEZ), Jacinto   1866-1954

PERSONAL: Born August 12, 1866, in Madrid, Spain; died July 14, 1954, in Madrid, Spain; son of Mariano Benavente (a pediatrician) and Venancia Martinez. *Education:* Studied law at University of Madrid, 1882-85.

CAREER: Writer. Director of Teatro Espanol, beginning 1920. Actor; founder with Porredon, of a children's theatre, 1909. President of Spanish Theater Commission (advisory body of Central Theater Council), beginning 1936. Lecturer.

MEMBER: Royal Spanish Academy (became honorary member, 1946).

AWARDS, HONORS: Piquer Prize, Royal Spanish Academy, 1912; Nobel Prize in literature, Swedish Academy, 1922; made honorary citizen of New York City, Columbia University and Institute de las Americas, 1923; named "Hijo Predilecto" ("Favorite Son") of Madrid, 1924; Grand Cross of King Alfonso XII (Spain), 1924; Mariano de Cavia Prize for best newspaper article of 1947, 1948.

WRITINGS:

IN ENGLISH TRANSLATION

"El nido ajeno" (three-act play; also see below), first produced in Madrid at Teatro de la Comedia, October 6, 1894, translation published as "Another's Nest" in *Nineteenth Century Spanish Plays,* edited by L. E. Brett, [New York], 1935.

"La gobernadora" (three-act play), first produced in Madrid at Teatro de la Comedia, October 8, 1901, translation by John Garrett Underhill published as *The Governor's Wife: A Comedy in Three Acts,* R. G. Badger (Boston), 1913.

"La noche de sabado" (five-act play), first produced in Madrid at Teatro Espanol, October 26, 1903, translation by Underhill published as *Saturday Night: A Novel for the Stage, in Five Tableaux,* R. G. Badger, 1918, translation by Underhill published under same title with introduction by Underhill, Scribner, 1926.

"No fumadores", first produced in Madrid at Teatro de Lara, March 3, 1904, translation by Underhill published as *No Smoking: A Farce in One Act,* Baker, 1935.

"El encanto de una hora" (one-act dialogue; also see below), first produced in Madrid at Teatro de la Princesa, December 30, 1905, translation by Underhill published as *The Magic of an Hour: A Comedy in One Act,* Baker, 1935.

La sonrisa de Gioconda, 1908, translation by John Armstrong Herman published as *The Smile of Mona Lisa: A Play in One Act,* R. G. Badger, 1915.

El marido de su viuda: Comedia en un acto (first produced in Madrid at Teatro del Principe Alfonso, October 19, 1908), R. Velasco (Madrid), 1908, translation by Underhill published as *His Widow's Husband: A Comedy in One Act,* Baker, 1935.

De cerca: Comedia en un acto (first produced in Madrid at Teatro de Lara, April 10, 1909), Hernando, 1909, translation by Underhill published as *At Close Range: A One-Act Play,* Samuel French, 1936.

El principe que todo lo aprendio en los libros: Comedia en dos actos y siete cuadros (children's fantasy; first produced in Madrid at Teatro del Principe Alfonso, December 20, 1909), Artes Graficas Mateu, 1910, reprinted, Cervantes, 1966, published under title *El principe que todo lo aprendio en los libros,* with notes, exercises, and vocabulary by Aurelio M. Espinosa, World, 1918, translation by Underhill of original Spanish edition published as *The Prince Who Learned Everything out of Books: A Fairy Play in Three Acts and Five Scenes,* R. G. Badger, 1919.

La malquerida (three-act drama), first produced in Madrid at Teatro de la Princesa, December 12, 1913; produced in English translation as "The Passionflower" in New York City, c. 1920), edited with introduction, notes, and vocabulary by Paul T. Manchester, Crofts, 1941, translation by Underhill published as "The Passionflower" in *Twenty-five Modern Plays,* edited by S. M. Tucker and A. S. Downer, 3rd edition, 1953.

Los intereses creados: Comedia de polichinelas en dos actos, tres cuadros y un prologo, (three-act play with prologue; first produced in Madrid at Teatro de Lara, December 9, 1907; produced in English translation as "The Bonds of Interest," in New York City, April 19, 1919; produced in English translation as "The Bias of the World" in London), 4th edition, Nuevo Mundo (Madrid), 1914, reprinted, Fournier, 1950, translation by Underhill published as *The Bonds of Interest,* preface by Underhill, Scribner, 1929, translation by Underhill published as *The Bonds of Interest. Los intereses creados.* (bilingual edition), edited and revised by Hymen Alpern, Ungar, 1967.

La Verdad (dialogue; first produced in Madrid at Teatro de la Comedia), 1915, translation by Underhill published as *The Truth: A Play in One Act,* Baker, 1935.

Plays (contains "His Widow's Husband," "The Bonds of Interest," "The Evil Doers of Good," and "La malquerida"), edited and translated by Underhill, Scribner, 1917.

Plays: Second Series (contains "No Smoking," "Princess Bebe," "The Governor's Wife," and "Autumnal Rose"), edited and translated by Underhill, Scribner, 1919.

"La fuerza bruta" (two-act musical comedy), first produced in Madrid at Teatro de la Zarzuela, 1919, translation by Underhill published as *Brute Force: A Comedy in Two Acts,* Samuel French, 1935.

Plays: Third Series (contains "The Prince Who Learned Everything out of Books," "Saturday Night," "In the Clouds," and "The Truth"), edited and translated by Underhill, Scribner, 1923.

Plays: Fourth Series (contains "The School of Princesses," "A Lady," "The Magic of an Hour," and "Field of Ermine"), edited and translated by Underhill, Scribner, 1924.

(Contributor) Lope de Vega, *Four Plays,* translated by Underhill with a critical essay by Benavente, Scribner, 1936, reprinted, Hyperion Press (Westport, Conn.), 1978.

PUBLISHED PLAYS; IN SPANISH

Teatro fantastico (contains "Comedia italiana" [title means "Italian Comedy"; two scenes], "El criado de Don Juan" [title means "Don Juan's Servant"; also see below], "La senda del amor" [title means "The Path of Love"; one-act comedy for marionettes], "La blancura de Pierrot" [title means "The Whiteness of Pierrot"; one-act pantomine], "Cuento de primavera" [title means "Spring Story"; two-act], "Amor de artista" [title means "Artist's Love"; one-act], "Modernismo" [title means "Modernism"; one-act], and "El encanto de una hora" [title means "The Magic of an Hour"; also see below]), 1892, reprinted, Fortanet (Madrid), 1905.

Los malhechores del bien (two-act; first produced in Madrid at Teatro de Lara, December 1, 1905), edited with introduction, notes and vocabulary by Irving A. Leonard and Robert K. Spaulding, Macmillan, 1933, reprinted, 1961.

Las cigarras hormigas (title means "The Harvest Flies"; three-act; first produced in Madrid at Teatro de la Comedia, December 24, 1905), edited with notes and vocabulary by University of Michigan Sociedad Hispanica, C. W. Graham, 1923.

Los buhos: Comedia en tres actos (title means "The Owls: Three-Act Play"; first produced in Madrid at Teatro de Lara, February 8, 1907), Hernando, 1908.

Hacia la verdad: Escenas de la vida moderna, en tres cuadros (title means "Toward the Truth: Scenes from Modern Life, in Three Scenes"; first produced in Madrid at Teatro del Principe Alfonso, December 23, 1908), Hernando, 1909.

La escuela de las princesas: Comedia en tres actos (title means "The School of Princesses: Play in Three Acts"; first produced in Madrid at Teatro de la Comedia, October 14, 1909), R. Velasco, 1910.

La senorita se aburre: Comedia en un acto, basada en una poesia de Tennyson (title means "The Princess Is Bored: One-Act Play, Based on a Poem by Tennyson"; first produced in Madrid at Teatro del Principe Alfonso, December 1, 1909), R. Velasco, 1910.

La losa de los suenos: Comedia en dos actos (title means "The Graveyard of Dreams: Two-Act Play"; comedy; first produced in Madrid at Teatro de Lara, November 9, 1911), Nuevo Mundo (Madrid), 1911.

El collar de estrellas: Comedia en cuatro actos (title means "The Necklace of Stars: Four-Act Play"; first produced in Madrid at Teatro de la Princesa, March 4, 1915), R. Velasco (Madrid), 1915.

Campo de armino: Comedia en tres actos (title means "Field of Ermine: Three-Act Play"; drama; first produced in Madrid at Teatro de la Princesa, February 14, 1916), R. Velasco and V. H. de Sanz Calleja (Madrid), 1916.

La ciudad alegre y confiada: Comedia en tres cuadros y un prologo, considerados como tres actos (title means "The Joyous and Confident City: Play in Three Scenes and A Prologue, Considered as Three Acts"; sequel to "Los intereses creados"; first produced in Madrid at Teatro de Lara, May 18, 1916), R. Velasco, 1916.

Los cachorros: Comedia en tres actos (three-act; first produced in Madrid at Teatro de la Princesa, March 8, 1918), V. H. de Sanz Calleja, 1918.

La fuerza bruta: Comedia en un acto y dos cuadros (one act; first produced in Madrid at Teatro de Lara, November 19 1908), Hernando, 1909.

Lecciones de buen amor: Comedia en tres actos (title means "Lessons in Good Love: Three-Act Play"; first produced in Madrid at Teatro Espanol, April 2, 1924), Hernando, 1924.

La otra honra: Comedia en tres actos (title means "The Other Honor: Three-Act Play"; first produced in Madrid at Teatro de Lara, September 19, 1924), Hernando, 1924.

La virtud sospechosa: Comedia en tres actos (title means "Suspect Virtue: Three-Act Play"; comedy; first produced in Madrid at Teatro Fontalba, October 20, 1924), Hernando, 1924.

Alfilerazos: Comedia en tres actos (title means "Pinpricks: Comedy in Three Acts"; first produced in Buenos Aires at Teatro Avenida, June 18, 1924; produced in Madrid at Teatro del Centro, October 5, 1925), Hernando, 1925.

Los nuevos yernos: Comedia en tres actos (title means "The New Sons-in-Law: Three-Act Play"; comedy; first produced in Madrid at Teatro Fontalba, October 2, 1925), Hernando, 1925.

La mariposa que volo sobre el mar: Comedia en tres actos (title means "The Butterfly that Flew over the Sea: Three-Act Play"; comedy; first produced in Madrid at Teatro Fontalba, September 22, 1926), Hernando, 1926.

La noche iluminada: Comedia de magia en tres actos (title means "The Illuminated Night: Three-Act Magical Comedy"; first produced in Madrid at Teatro Fontalba, December 22, 1927), Hernando, 1927.

El hijo de Polichinela: Comedia en un prologo y tres actos (comedy; first produced in Madrid at Teatro de Lara, April 16, 1927), Hernando, 1927.

El demonio fue antes angel: Comedia en tres actos (title means "The Devil Used to Be an Angel: Three-Act Play"; comedy; first produced in Madrid at Teatro Calderon, February 18, 1928), Hernando, 1928.

¡No quiero, no quiero!: Comedia en tres actos (title means "I Don't Want To, I Don't Want To: Three-Act Play"; first produced in Madrid at Teatro Fontalba, March 10, 1928), Hernando, 1928.

Pepa Doncel: Comedia en tres actos y dos cuadros (title means "Pepa Doncel: Play in Three Acts and Two Scenes"; first produced in Madrid at Teatro Calderon, November 21, 1928), Hernando, 1928.

Para el cielo y los altares: Drama en tres actos, dividos en trece cuadros, y un epilogo (title means "For Heaven and the Altars: Three-Act Drama, Divided into Thirteen Scenes and an Epilogue"), Hernando, 1928.

Vidas cruzadas: Cinedrama en dos partes, dividida la primera en diez cuadros, y la segunda en tres y un epilogo (title means "Crossed Lives: A Screenplay in Two Parts, the First Di-

vided into Ten Scenes, and the Second into Three and an Epilogue"; first produced in Madrid at Teatro de la Reina Victoria, March 30, 1929), Hernando, 1929.

Los andrajos de la purpura: Drama en cinco actos (title means "Purple Tatters: Drama in Five Acts"; first produced in Madrid at Teatro Munoz Seca, November 6, 1930), Hernando, 1930.

Literatura: Comedia en tres actos (title means "Literature: Play in Three Acts"; first produced in Madrid at Teatro Alcazar, April 4, 1931), Hernando, 1931.

De muy buena familia: Comedia en tres actos (title means "From a Very Good Family: Three-Act Play"; comedy; first produced in Madrid at Teatro Munoz Seca, March 11, 1931), Hernando, 1931.

La melodia del jazz-band: Comedia en un prologo y tres actos (title means "The Jazz Band's Melody: Play with a Prologue and Three Acts"; comedy; first produced in Madrid at Teatro Fontalba, October 30, 1931), Hernando, 1931.

Cuando los hijos de Eva no son los hijos de Adan: Comedia en tres actos (title means "When Eve's Sons Are Not Adam's: Three-Act Play"; based on Margaret Kennedy's novel, *The Constant Nymph*; comedy; first produced in Madrid at Teatro Calderon, November 5, 1931), Hernando, 1931.

Santa Rusia, primera parte de una trilogia (title means "Holy Russia, First Part of a Trilogy"; first produced in Madrid at Teatro Beatriz, October 6, 1932), Imprenta Helenica (Madrid), 1932.

La duquesa gitana: Comedia de magia en cinco actos divididos en diez cuadros (title means "The Gypsy Duchess: Magic Comedy in Five Acts Divided in Ten Scenes"; fist produced in Madrid at Teatro Fontalba, October 28, 1932), Imprenta Helenica, 1932.

La moral del divorcio: Conferencia dialogada, dividida en tres partes (title means "The Moral of Divorce: Lecture in Dialogue, Divided into Three Parts"; first produced in Madrid at Teatro de la Avenida, November 4, 1932), Imprenta Helenica, 1932.

La verdad inventada: Comedia en tres actos (title means "The Invented Truth: Three-Act Play"; comedy; first produced in Madrid at Teatro de Lara, October 27, 1933), Artes Graficas (Madrid), 1933.

El rival de su mujer: Comedia en tres actos (title means "His Wife's Rival: Three-Act Play"; comedy; first produced in Buenos Aires at Teatro Odeon, 1933), Artes Graficas, 1934.

El pan comido en la mano: Comedia en tres actos (title means "Bread Eaten from the Hand: Three-Act Play"; comedy; first produced in Madrid at Teatro Fontalba, January 12, 1934), Artes Graficas, 1934.

Ni al amor ni al mar: Drama en cuatro actos y un epilogo (title means "Neither to Love nor to the Sea: Drama in Four Acts and an Epilogue"; first produced in Madrid at Teatro Espanol, January 19, 1934), Artes Graficas, 1934.

Memorias de un madrileno: Puestas en accion en cinco cuadros (title means "Memories of a Man from Madrid: Performed in Five Scenes"; five-act moving tableaux; first performed in Madrid at Teatro de Lara, November 8, 1934), Artes Graficas, 1934.

La novia de nieve: Comedia en un prologo y tres actos (title means "The Snow Bride: Three-Act Play with a Prologue"; comedy; first produced in Madrid at Teatro Espanol, November 29, 1934), Artes Graficas, 1934.

"No jugueis con esas cosas": Comedia en tres actos (title means " 'Don't Play with Those Things': Three-Act Play"; comedy; first produced in Madrid at Teatro Esclava, January 18, 1935), Artes Graficas, 1935.

Cualquiera lo sabe: Comedia en tres actos (title means "Anyone Knows That: Three-Act Play"; comedy; first produced in Madrid at Teatro de la Comedia, February 13, 1935), Artes Graficas, 1935.

Also author of *La princesa sin corazon* (title means "The Heartless Princess"; one-act horror play), 1908; *¡A ver que hace un hombre!* (title means "Let's See What a Man Does!"), 1909; *Caridad* (title means "Charity"; monologue; first produced in Madrid at Teatro Real, February 3, 1911; one-act), 1918; *¡Si creeras tu que es por mi gusto!* (title means "If You Think I Want It This Way!"; one-act dialogue), 1925; *A las puertas del cielo* (title means "At the Gates of Heaven"; one-act dialogue), 1927; *La culpa es tuya* (title means "It's Your Fault"; three-act comedy; first produced in San Sebastian, Spain, August, 1942, produced in Madrid at Teatro de la Zarzuela, September 17, 1942), 1943; *La enlutada* (title means "The Mourner"; three-act; first produced in Saragossa, Spain at Teatro Principal, October 16, 1942), 1943; *El demonio del teatro* (title means "The Demon of the Theatre"; three-act comedy; first produced in Madrid at Teatro Comico, October 28, 1942), 1943; *Al servicio de su majestad imperial* (title means "In the Service of His Imperial Majesty"; one-act comedy), 1947; *La vida en verso* (title means "Life in Verse"; three-act comedy; first produced in Madrid at Teatro de la Infanta Isabel, November 9, 1951), 1953; *El lebrel del cielo* (title means "The Hound of Heaven"; three-act comedy; based on Francis Thompson's poem of the same title; first produced in Madrid at Teatro Calderon, April 25, 1952), 1953. Plays also published in numerous collections.

PLAY PRODUCTIONS; IN SPANISH

"Gente conocida" (title means "People of Importance"; four-act drama), first produced in Madrid at Teatro de la Comedia, October 21, 1896.

"El marido de la Tellez" (title means "The Tellez Woman's Husband"; one-act), first produced in Madrid at Teatro de Lara, February 13, 1897.

"De alivio" (title means "On Comfort"; one-act monologue), first produced in Madrid at Teatro de la Comedia, February 27, 1897.

"Don Juan" (based on the play by Moliere; five-act), first produced in Madrid at Teatro de la Princesa, October 31, 1897.

"La farandula" (title means "Bombastic Actors"; two-act), produced in Madrid at Teatro de Lara, November 30, 1897.

"La comida de las fieras" (title means "The Wild Beasts' Banquet"; three-act; also see below), first produced in Madrid at Teatro de la Comedia, November 7, 1898.

"Teatro feminista" (title means "Feminist Theatre"; one-act), first produced in Teatro de la Comedia, December 28, 1898.

(Adapter) "Cuento de amor" (title means "Love Story"; based on Shakespeare's "Twelfth Night"; three-act drama), first produced in Madrid at Teatro de la Comedia, March 11, 1899.

"Operacion quirugica" (title means "Surgery"; one-act), first produced in Madrid at Teatro de Lara, May 4, 1899.

"Despedida cruel" (title means "Cruel Farewell"; one-act), first produced in Madrid at Teatro de Lara, December 7, 1899.

"La gata de Angora" (title means "The Angora Cat"; four-act), first produced in Madrid at Teatro de la Comedia, March 31, 1900.

"Viaje de instruccion" (title means "The Journey of Instruction"; one-act musical comedy), first produced in Madrid at Teatro Alhambra, April 6, 1900.

"Por la herida" (title means "Through Affliction"; one-act drama), first produced in Madrid at Teatro de Novedades, July 15, 1900.

"Modas" (title means "Fashions"; one-act farce), first produced in Madrid at Teatro de Lara, January 18, 1901.

"Lo cursi" (title means "Vulgarity"; three-act drama), first produced in Madrid at Teatro de la Comedia, January 19, 1901.

"Sin querer" (title means "In Perfect Innocence"; one-act comic sketch), first produced in Madrid at Teatro de la Comedia, March 3, 1901.

"Sacrificios" (title means "Sacrifices"; three-act drama), first produced in Madrid at Teatro de Novedades, July 19, 1901.

"El primo roman" (three-act), first produced in Saragossa, November 12, 1901.

"Amor de amar" (title means "Love of Loving"; two-act), first produced in Madrid at Teatro de la Comedia, February 24, 1902.

"¡Libertad!" (title means "Liberty!"; three-act; based on a play by Santiago Rusinol y Prats), first produced in Madrid at Teatro de la Comedia, March 17, 1902.

"En tren de los maridos" (title means "In the Husbands' Retinue"; two-act comedy), first produced in Madrid at Teatro de Lara, April 18, 1902.

"Alma triunfante" (title means "Triumphant Soul"; three-act drama), first produced in Madrid at Teatro de la Comedia, December 2, 1902.

"El automovil" (title means "The Automobile"; two-act), first produced in Madrid at Teatro de Lara, December 19, 1902.

"Los favoritos" (title means "The Favorites"; one-act), first produced in Seville, March 20, 1903.

"El hombrecito" (title means "The Manikin"; three-act), first produced in Madrid at Teatro de la Comedia, March 23, 1903.

"Por que se ama" (title means "Why One Loves"; one-act), first produced in Madrid at Teatro Espanol, October 26, 1903.

"Al natural" (title means "No Affectation"; two-act), first produced at Madrid at Teatro de Lara, November 20, 1903.

"La casa de la dicha" (title means "The House of Happiness"; first produced in Barcelona at Teatro Intimo, December 9, 1903.

"El dragon de fuego" (title means "The Fire Dragon"; three-act drama with epilogue), first produced in Madrid at Teatro Espanol, March 16, 1904.

"Rosas de otono" (title means "Autumnal Roses"; three-act drama), first produced in Madrid at Teatro Espanol, April 13, 1905.

"El susto de la condesa" (title means "The Countess's Terror"; one-act dialogue), first produced in Madrid at Teatro Espanol, November 15, 1905.

"Cuento inmoral" (title means "Immoral Story"; one-act monologue), first produced in Madrid at Teatro Espanol, November 15, 1905.

"La sobresalienta" (title means "The Understudy"; one-act lyrical farce), first produced in Madrid at Teatro Espanol, December 23, 1905.

"El encanto de una hora" (title means "The Magic of an Hour"; dialogue), first produced in Madrid at Teatro de la Princesa, December 30, 1905.

"Mas fuerte que el amor" (title means "Stronger than Love"; four-act drama), first produced in Madrid at Teatro Espanol, February 22, 1906.

"La princesa Bebe" (title means "Princess Bebe"; four-act), first produced in Madrid at Teatro Espanol, March 31, 1906.

"El amor asusta" (title means "Love Shocks"; one-act), first produced in Madrid on January 10, 1907.

"Abuela y nieta" (title means "Grandmother and Granddaughter"; one-act dialogue), first produced in Madrid at Teatro de Lara, February 21, 1907.

"La copa encantada" (title means "The Enchanted Cup"; one-act musical comedy), first produced in Madrid at Teatro de la Zarzuela, March 16, 1907.

"Todos somos unos" (title means "All Are One"; one-act lyrical farce), first produced in Madrid at Teatro Esclava, September 21, 1907.

"La historia de Otelo" (title means "The Story of Othello"; one-act), first produced in Madrid at Teatro de Apolo, October 11, 1907.

"Los ojos de los muertos" (title means "The Eyes of the Dead"; three-act drama), first produced in Madrid at Teatro de la Princesa, November 7, 1907.

"Senora Ama" (three-act), first produced in Madrid at Teatro de la Princesa, February 22, 1908.

"De pequenas causas . . ." (title means "From Small Beginnings . . ."; one-act), first produced in Madrid at Teatro de la Princesa, March 14, 1908.

"Por las nubes" (title means "In the Clouds"; two-act; also see below), first produced in Madrid at Teatro de Lara, January 20, 1909.

"El ultimo minue" (title means "The Last Minuet"; one-act comedy), first produced in Madrid at Teatro Benavente, October 23, 1909.

"Ganarse la vida" (title means "Earning a Living"; one-act), first produced in Madrid at Teatro del Principe Alfonso, December 20, 1909.

"El nietecito" (title means "The Little Grandson"; one-act), first produced in Teatro del Principe Alfonso, January 27, 1910.

"El criado de Don Juan" (title means "Don Juan's Servant"; one-act), first produced in Madrid at Teatro Espanol, March 29, 1911.

"La losa de los suenos" (title means "The Graveyard of Dreams"; two-act comedy), first produced in Madrid at Teatro de Lara, November 9, 1911.

"La propia estimacion" (title means "Proper Esteem"; three-act), first produced in Madrid at Teatro de la Comedia, December 22, 1915.

"La mal que nos hacen" (title means "The Evil Done to Us"; three-act), first produced in Madrid at Teatro de la Princesa, March 23, 1917.

"La Inmaculada de los Dolores" (title means "Our Lady of Sorrow"; three-act dramatic novel), first produced in Madrid at Teatro de Lara, April 30, 1918.

"La ley de los hijos" (title means "The Children's Law"; three-act drama), first produced in Madrid at Teatro de la Zarzuela, December 23, 1918.

"Por ser con todos leal, ser para todos traidor" (title means "Loyalty to All Through Treachery to All"; three-act drama), first produced in Madrid at Teatro del Centro, March 5, 1919.

"La vestal de Occidente" (title means "The Vestal of the West"; four-act drama), first produced in Madrid at Teatro de Lara, March 29, 1919.

"La honra de los hombres" (title means "The Honor of Men"; two-act comedy), first produced in Madrid at Teatro de Lara, May 2, 1919.

(Adapter) "El audaz" (five-act drama; based on the novel of the same title by Benito Perez Galdos), first produced in Madrid at Teatro Espanol, December 6, 1919.

"La Cenicienta" (title means "Cinderella"; three-act), first produced in Madrid at Teatro Espanol, December 20, 1919.

"Y va de cuento" (title means "And Once Upon a Time"; four-act fantasy with prologue), first produced in Madrid on December 23, 1919.

"Una senora" (title means "A Lady"; three-act dramatic novel), first produced in Madrid at Teatro del Centro, January 2, 1920.

"Una pobre mujer" (title means "A Poor Woman"; three-act drama), first produced in Madrid at Teatro de la Princesa, April 3, 1920.

"Mas alla de la muerte" (title means "Beyond Death"; three-act drama), first produced in Buenos Aires, August, 1922.

"Por que se quito Juan de la bebida" (title means "Why Juan Quit Drinking"; monologue), first produced in Montevideo, Uruguay at Teatro Soles, August 30, 1922.

"Un par de botas" (title means "A Pair of Boots"; one-act comedy), first produced in Madrid at Teatro de la Princesa, May 24, 1924.

"Nadie sabe lo que quiere; o, El bailarin y el trabajador" (title means "Nobody Knows What He Wants; or, The Dancer and the Laborer"; three-act comedy), first produced in Madrid at Teatro Comico, March 14, 1925.

"El suicidio de Lucerito" (title means "Lucerito's Suicide"; one-act comedy), first produced in Madrid at Teatro Alcazar, July 17, 1925.

"Los amigos del hombre" (title means "Man's Friends"; four-act farce), produced in Madrid at Teatro de la Avenida, November 3, 1930.

"Aves y pajaros" (title means "Birds and Fowl"; two-part), first produced in Madrid at Teatro de Lara, October 20, 1940.

"Lo increible" (title means "The Incredible"; three-act comedy), first produced in Madrid at Teatro de la Comedia, October 25, 1940.

"Abuelo y nieto" (title means "Grandfather and Grandson"; one-act dialogue), produced in San Sebastian, Spain, at Teatro del Principe, August 29, 1941.

"Y amargaba . . ." (title means "And It Was Bitter . . ."; three-act comedy), first produced in Madrid at Teatro de la Zarzuela, November 19, 1941.

"La ultima carta" (title means "The Last Letter"; three-act comedy), first produced in Madrid at Teatro Alcazar, December 9, 1941.

"La honradez de la cerradura" (title means "The Integrity of the Lock"; three-act comedy), first produced in Madrid at Teatro Espanol, April 4, 1942.

"Al fin, mujer" (title means "Finally, Woman"; three-act comedy), first produced in San Sebastian, Spain at Teatro del Principe, September 13, 1942, produced in Madrid at Teatro Alcazar, November 17, 1942.

"¡Hija del alma!" (title means "Daughter of My Soul!"; one-act), first produced in Madrid at Teatro de Lara, September 17, 1942.

"Don Magin, el de las magias" (title means "Don Magin, the Magician"; three-act comedy), first produced in Barcelona at Teatro Barcelona, March 26, 1944, produced in Madrid at Teatro Alcazar, January 12, 1945.

"Los ninos perdidos en la selva" (title means "Children Lost in the Forest": four-act dramatic novel), first produced in Madrid at Teatro de la Infanta Beatriz, April 14, 1944.

"Espejo de grandes" (title means "Mirror of the Great"; one-act), first produced October 12, 1944, produced in Madrid at Teatro de Lara, June 11, 1946.

"Nieve en mayo" (title means "Snow in May"; four-act dramatic poem), first produced in Madrid at Teatro de la Zarzuela, January 19, 1945.

"La ciudad doliente" (title means "The Suffering City"; three-act comedy), first produced in Madrid at Teatro de la Comedia, April 14, 1945.

"Titania" (three-act comedy), first produced in Buenos Aires, September 25, 1945, first produced in Madrid at Teatro Calderon, November 8, 1946.

"La infanzona" (title means "The Noblewoman"; three-act drama), first produced in Buenos Aires, December 6, 1945, produced in Madrid at Teatro Calderon, January 10, 1947.

"Abdicacion" (title means "Abdication"; three-act comedy), first produced in Madrid at Teatro de Lara, March 27, 1948.

"Divorcio de almas" (title means "Divorce of Souls"; three-act comedy), first produced in Madrid at Teatro Fontalba, September 30, 1948.

"Adoracion" (title means "Adoration"; two-act dramatic comedy with prologue), first produced in Madrid at Teatro Comico, December 3, 1948.

"Al amor hay que mandarlo al colegio" (title means "Love Should be Sent to School"; comedy with four episodes), first produced in Madrid at Teatro de Lara, September 29, 1950.

"Su amante esposa" (title means "His Lover-Wife"; three-act comedy), first produced in Madrid at Teatro de la Infanta Isabel, October 20, 1950.

"Tu una vez, y el diablo diez" (title means "You Once, the Devil Ten Times"; three-act comedy), first produced in Valladolid, Spain at Teatro Lope de Vega, October 23, 1950, produced in Madrid at Teatro de la Infanta Isabel, March 27, 1951.

"Mater imperatrix" (three-act dramatic comedy), first produced in Barcelona at Teatro de la Comedia, November 29, 1950, first produced in Madrid at Teatro de la Comedia, January 30, 1951.

"Ha llegado Don Juan" (title means "Don Juan Has Arrived"; two-act comedy with prologue), first produced in Barcelona at Teatro de la Comedia, April 12, 1952.

"Servir" (title means "To Serve"; two-act comedy with interlude), first produced in Madrid at Teatro Maria Guerrero, January 22, 1953.

"El alfiler en la boca" (title means "A Pin in the Mouth"; three-act comedy), first produced in Madrid at Teatro de la Infanta Isabel, February 13, 1953.

"Almas prisioneras" (title means "Imprisoned Souls"; two-act drama with prologue), first produced in Madrid at Teatro Alvarez Quintero, February 26,1953.

"Caperucita asusta al lobo" (title means "Little Red Riding-Hood Frightens the Wolf"; three-act), first produced in Madrid at Teatro de la Infanta Isabel, September 23, 1953.

"Hijos padres de sus padres" (title means "Sons Fathers of their Fathers"; three-act comedy), first produced in Madrid at Teatro de Lara, February 11, 1954.

"El marido de bronce" (three-act comedy), first produced in Madrid at Teatro de la Infanta Isabel, April 23, 1954.

OTHER

Cartas de mujeres (title means "Women's Letters"; fictional letters), 1893, reprinted, Espasa-Calpe, 1965.

Figulinas (sketches), Fortanet, 1898.

(Translator) Alexandre Dumas *pere,* "Mademoiselle de Belle-Isle" (five-act play), first produced in Valladolid, Spain, October 20, 1903.

(Translator) Edward Bulwer-Lytton, "Richelieu" (five-act drama), first produced in Mexico City, March 15, 1904.

(Translator) Emile Augier, "Buena boda" (title means "A Good Marriage"; three-act), first produced in Madrid at Teatro de Sociedad, 1905.

Vilanos (sketches), Fortanet, 1905.

El teatro del pueblo (title means "The People's Theatre"), F. Fe (Madrid), 1909.

(Translator) Paul Hervieu, "El destino manda" (title means "Destiny Commands"; two-act drama; translation of "Le destin est maitre"), first produced in Madrid at Teatro de la Princesa, March 25, 1914.

(Translator) George C. Hazelton and Harry Benrimo, "La tunica amarilla" (title means "The Yellow Tunic"; three-act), first produced in Madrid at Teatro de la Princesa, April 22, 1916.

Los ninos (title means "The Children"; anthology), Hesperia (Madrid), 1917.

"La Mefistofela" (title means "Mephistopheles"; three-act comic operetta), first produced in Madrid at Teatro de la Reina Victoria, April 29, 1918.

Conferencias (title mean "Lectures"), Hernando, 1924.

Pensamientos (title means "Thoughts"), Hernando, 1931.

De sobremesa: Cronicas (title means "After-Dinner Conversation: Chronicles"), F. Fe (Madrid), 1940.

Plan de estudios para una escuela de arte escenico, Aguilar, 1940.

Asi piensan los personajes de Benavente (title means "Benavente's Characters Think Thusly"; excerpts from his writings), edited by Jose Maria Viqueira, Aguilar, 1958.

Recuerdos y olvidos (memorias) (title means "Things Recalled and Forgotten: Memories"), Aguilar, 1959.

Las terceras de ABC (selections of contributions to *ABC*), edited by Adolfo Prego, Prensa Espanola, 1976.

Editor of *El ano germanofilo* (title means "The Germanic Year"; symposium), 1916; also author of unpublished and unproduced play, "El bufon de Hamlet" (title means "The Buffoon of Hamlet"). Also translator of "King Lear" by Shakespeare published as *El rey Lear,* 1911. Weekly columnist, *El Imparcial,* 1908-12. Contributor to *ABC* (Madrid newspaper). Editor, *La Vida Literaria* (magazine).

SIDELIGHTS: Dramatist Jacinto Benavente was the dominant force in Spanish drama during the first third of the twentieth-century. He produced nearly two hundred works for stage and in 1922 was granted the Nobel Prize for literature. Although extremely popular during the early years of his career, many critics noted a decline in Benavente's theatre beginning shortly before he won the highly coveted award. In a *World Literature Today* essay chronicling the Nobel prizes received by Hispanic authors throughout the history of the award, Manuel Duran seemed to summarize modern thought on the playwright when he wrote: "Another prize was squandered in 1922. The laurel went that year to playwright Jacinto Benavente, whose vast production is now mostly obsolete and was already out of phase with modern times when the medallion was conferred." However slighted by today's critics, Benavente's impact on Spanish theatre and the high esteem in which he was held by the theatre-going public and critics of his day cannot be denied.

Son of a well-respected pediatrician (a bust of whom can be found in Madrid's *Buen Retiro* park), Benavente showed an early interest in theatre and as a boy he often wrote short skits to be performed for his young friends. Besides attending plays produced on the stages of Madrid, he read voraciously all the theatre he could find. When as a teenager he learned several foreign languages, he began to read plays by foreign authors, especially those by Shakespeare, in their original languages. Although he studied law for a time, his true career was in the theatre and he soon became an actor with a professional company based in Madrid. (Later in life he stated on numerous occasions that he would have preferred to have been an actor rather than a playwright and often appeared in the cast of his own productions.)

In the late 1880s he began to regularly submit plays to Emilio Mario, a family friend and director of Madrid's famous Teatro de la Comedia. Mario rejected nearly a dozen of the fledgling dramatist's efforts until finally consenting to produce a three-act play entitled "El nido ajeno" ("Another's Nest") in 1894. Although the work was virtually ignored by critics, Benavente's next offering, "Gente conocida" ("People of Importance") won for the playwright an adoring public.

"Gente conocida" introduced to Madrid a type of theatre completely different from that in vogue at the time. Spanish theatre was under the spell of Spain's first Nobel Prize winner, Jose Echegaray (who won the award in 1904), a playwright whose work was characterized by exaggerated melodrama, grandiloquent verses, and artificiality. Although Benavente confessed a deep admiration for the older playwright, his own theatre was in direct contrast to that of Echegaray. "Benavente's theater . . . meant a reaction against the anachronistic, turn-of-the-century Romanticism of Echegaray," wrote Marcelino C. Penuelas in *Jacinto Benavente*. "Against a background of the affected gesture, the hollow voice, the melodramatic, declamatory and solemn tone, the violence of passion and the traditional concept of honor, appear the theater of clever conversation in a confidential, ironic and satirical tone which Benavente succeeded in popularizing."

Critics John Van Horne and Walter Starkie both group Benavente's plays produced from 1894 to 1901 as the author's first period. This phase is marked by what Starkie referred to in *Jacinto Benavente,* his 1924 biography of the author, as "the Toledo blade of satire." In these plays Benavente satirized the decadent upper and middle classes of Madrid and Moraleda, the playwright's fictional version of a provincial town of the countryside surrounding the Spanish capital. Productions of this period include, "La farandula," which compares the empty speech of politicians to the meaningless line of actors; "La comida de las fieras," which explores what happens to a wealthy family when it loses its fortune; and "La gobernadora," which reveals the intrigue behind small town politics.

In these first plays Benavente showed a tendency to imitate several French authors with whose work he was familiar, including Alfred Capus, Mauric Donnay, and Henry Lavedan. All three were playwrights who wrote satirical works about French society. Critics who noted this influence, along with Benavente's obvious rejection of the norm for Spanish theatre of the time established by Echegaray, accused Benavente of not being a true Spanish playwright. "Perhaps without his knowing it, he is more foreign than Spanish," commented Jose Vila Selma in his *Benavente: Fin de siglo* which Penuelas quoted in English translation. Vila Selma continued, "Whatever is new in Benavente's theater is something which singularly sets itself apart from the traditional course." In an essay included in *The Theatre, the Drama, the Girls* George Jean Nathan seemed to side with Vila Selma's assessment when he accused Benavente of copying many of his plays from a variety of Italian, French, German sources.

Benavente's theatre reflected his cosmopolitan life-style: He had traveled extensively through Europe and, because he was fluent in several languages, was familiar with several European literatures. Differing with Vila Selma and Nathan, some critics saw these influences in Benavente's theatre as a reason to praise the playwright for bringing fresh material into the tradition-bound Spanish theatre. "It was he," *Books Abroad* contributor Robert G. Sanchez pointed out, "who brought to the Spanish stage all the currents of the European theater of the first quarter of the century." Julius Brouta, and others, likened Benavente to several

of the best dramatists on the European scene. In comments published in *Drama* Brouta wrote, "Benavente is, in many respects, the Bernard Shaw of Spain. Like Shaw, he is a disciple of Ibsen; like him, an iconoclast, a reformer, a teacher, a preacher, and his dialectics are hardly less efficient or his spirit less brilliant." Elsewhere in the same essay, Brouta noted that Benavente's ironic touch was "similar to that of Anatole France." In a comparison with another European author, *Topic* contributor Alfredo Marquerie found Benavente "had much in common with Oscar Wilde."

While admitting to the European influences in Benavente's theatre, other critics, including Storm Jameson and Starkie, found his work to be firmly rooted in that of the seventeenth-century Spanish playwright Lope de Vega, known as the father of Spanish drama, and who represented the very essence of *lo espanol.* Starkie noted: "Many of [Benavente's] enemies have made it an accusation against him that he introduced foreign ideals which caused the decline of true Spanish art. To those, however, who examine carefully Benavente's drama, it will become plain that foreign influences did not altogether hide the Spanish dramatist who counted back his literary descent to Lope de Vega." In a similar vein, Jameson observed in an essay in his *Modern Drama in Europe,* "The work of Jacinto Benavente is in the highest tradition of the Spanish drama. . . . The creative genius of Lope de Vega informed his vision of reality." "Cosmopolitan as he may be in theories," Van Horne wrote in his introduction to *Tres Comedias: 'Sin querer,' 'De pequenas causas . . .,' 'Los intereses creados,'* "his nature is essentially and intensely Spanish."

Benavente's witty dialogue and fertile imagination won over skeptical actors, critics, and public. The second phase of his career, which in Starkie's estimation covered the years 1901 to 1914, brought the playwright his greatest triumphs. In 1905 he was acclaimed by Madrid's theatrical community with a festival in his honor which concluded with the public reading of a tribute by the great Spanish novelist Benito Perez Galdos. Two plays from this period, "Los intereses creados" ("The Bonds of Interest") and "La malquerida" ("The Passionflower"), were successfully produced in English translation on the New York stage. These plays show Benavente's evolution from the social satire of his first period to a broader scope, including a wide variety of theatrical genres, but often focusing on comedy with a moral tone.

Considered Benavente's masterpiece, "The Bonds of Interest" is a three-act comedy based on the Italian *commedia dell'arte.* This dramatic genre consisted of a improvisational skit performed by actors filling the roles of stock characters, including "the beautiful young lady," her "suitor," "the Doctor," and others. Later versions also included "Polichinelle," who survived to modern times as Punch in Punch and Judy shows, and "Harlequin," known for his unique costume. Benavente's play tells the story of the handsome Leander's attempt to dupe an entire city into thinking he is a wealthy aristocrat traveling incognito. After falling in love with the beautiful Sylvia, daughter of Polichinelle, Leander tells her of his true identity. Meanwhile, Leander's servant, Crispin, who is unaware of his master's confession, contrives to have the whole town and Sylvia turn against Polichinelle. The comedy ends happily with Crispin forced to admit his lies and Sylvia stepping forward to address the audience, declaring that although we are often selfishly ruled by "bonds of interest," the power of love is there to redeem us.

Sylvia's closing statement embodies an important facet of Benavente's view of life as presented in his work: the value of love and tolerance in combating society's evils. In his introduction to

Plays, Benavente's chief translator John Garrett Underhill wrote, "The subject of Jacinto Benavente is the struggle of love against poverty, of obligation against desire, of imputed virtue against the consciousness of sin." Jameson commented on the same aspect of Benavente's work, noting "The other side of the dramatist's passionate indignation is love, love towards the oppressed, the thwarted and the maimed of life. . . . Men are to be pitied, but they are also to be loved. Through the dynamic force of love they will be set free, not from pain, but from despair and the isolation of defeat." "Love stands forth prominently in Benavente as the principle dynamic factor," Brouta concluded.

Many of the plays of Benavente's second period explore the problems of married life. Included in this group is "La Malquerida" ("The Passionflower"), one of the plays individually cited for merit in the Nobel prize presentation address given by the then-chairman of the Nobel Committee of the Swedish Academy, Per Hallstroem. This three-act peasant drama of provincial life focuses on the relationship between Esteban and Acacia, his wife Raimunda's daughter from her first marriage. The play ends tragically with the death of Raimunda at Esteban's hands. Such was the success of the first production of the play in 1913 that Benavente was carried home in triumph by enthusiastic theatre-goers. Sanchez called it "a powerful and fascinating melodrama, a landmark in the modern Spanish theater."

In "La Malquerida," as in many of his plays, Benavente focuses his attention on his female characters. Dubbed a feminist for his portrayals of strong females, he expressed his interest in female characterization in one of his first works, *Cartas de mujeres,* a volume of letters purported to be written by women. "In these letters," Starkie observed, "he tries to plumb the depths of the Spanish woman's soul." Unlike some Spanish dramatists who insisted in their works on the centuries-old concepts of honor and machismo, according to Brouta, Benavente "stoutly espoused the rights of woman, the idea of equality of the sexes, and pointed out the moral obligation which matrimony imposes upon man." He was also fond of poking fun at one of Spain's national heroes, Don Juan, the professional seducer. "Rosas de otono" and "Senora Ama," which each deal with how a woman married to a philandering husband deals with his infidelity, are just two of his works in which his interest in feminine psychology is apparent.

At the beginning of his career, Benavente was seen as a reformer of the Spanish stage and a revealer of the hypocrisy of Spanish society. Because of this revolutionary beginning, Benavente is often included by many critics as a member of Spain's Generation of '98, a loosely knit group of writers who broke with the members of the preceding generation in hopes of avoiding a disaster similar to the one Spain suffered in 1898 when it lost all of its overseas empire. By the time the playwright had entered his third period, starting in 1914, his plays had changed so that characters, and not reform, had became their focus. Speaking of this last phase of Benavente's career Starkie commented, "His heroes and heroines in most cases tend to become mere mechanical symbols of an abstract thought. In many cases also he falls into sentimentality, and mistakes rhetoric for art." He seemed to be writing for that very portion of society that he previously had so bitterly satirized.

When Benavente was awarded the Nobel in 1922, members of the Generation of '98, who previously had held him in high esteem as one of their own, protested vehemently. Penuelas explained that although Benavente had indeed reformed Spanish theatre, at least technically, "he never came to experience the artistic and human anxieties which appeared at the turn of the century in Europe and in Spain with the writers of the Generation of '98." Because of Benavente's failure to continue on the path of revision suggested by his early works, nearly all his plays remain essentially bound to the Spanish society in which they were originally written. As Penuelas concluded: "Although Benavente undoubtedly influenced twentieth-century Spanish writers, the best of his followers oriented their works in other directions and Benavente's theater was soon out of date."

BIOGRAPHICAL/CRITICAL SOURCES:

BOOKS

Benavente, Jacinto, *Plays,* edited and translated by John Garrett Underhill, Scribner, 1917.
Benavente, Jacinto, *Tres comedias: "Sin querer," "De pequenas causas . . .," "Los intereses creados,"* edited by John Van Horne, Heath, 1918.
Jameson, Storm, *Modern Drama in Europe,* Collins, 1920.
Nathan, George Jean, *The Theatre, the Drama, the Girls,* Knopf, 1921.
Noble Prize Library: Asturias, Benavente, Bergson, Helvetica Press, 1971,
Penuelas, Marcelino C., *Jacinto Benavente,* Twayne, 1968.
Starkie, Walter, *Jacinto Benavente,* Oxford University Press, 1924.
Twentieth-Century Literary Criticism, Volume 3, Gale, 1980.
Vila Selma, Jose, *Benavente: Fin de siglo,* Rialp, 1952.

PERIODICALS

Books Abroad, winter, 1955.
Drama, November, 1915.
Topic, spring, 1968.
World Literature Today, spring, 1988.

OBITUARIES:

PERIODICALS

Newsweek, July 26, 1954.
New York Times, July 15, 1954.
Publishers Weekly, August 7, 1954.
Time, July 26, 1954.

—*Sketch by Marian Gonsior*

*   *   *

BENCHLEY, Peter (Bradford) 1940-

PERSONAL: Born May 8, 1940, in New York, N.Y.; son of Nathaniel Goddard (an author) and Marjorie (Bradford) Benchley; married Wendy Wesson, September 19, 1964. *Education:* Harvard University, A.B. (cum laude), 1961. *Agent:* International Creative Management, 40 West 57th St., New York, N.Y. 10019.

CAREER: Novelist. *Washington Post,* Washington, D.C., reporter, 1963; *Newsweek,* New York, N.Y., associate editor, 1964-67; The White House, Washington, D.C., staff assistant to the president, 1967-69; free-lance writer and television news correspondent, beginning 1969. *Military service:* U.S. Marine Corps Reserve, 1962-63.

Member: Coffee House, Spee Club, Hasty Pudding Institute of 1770, Century Association.

WRITINGS:

NOVELS; EXCEPT AS INDICATED

Time and a Ticket (nonfiction), Houghton, 1964.
Jonathan Visits the White House (juvenile), McGraw, 1964.
Jaws (also see below), Doubleday, 1974.
The Deep (also see below), Doubleday, 1976.

The Island (also see below), Doubleday, 1979.
The Girl of the Sea of Cortez, Doubleday, 1982.
Q Clearance, Random House, 1986.
Rummies, Random House, 1989.

SCREENPLAYS

(Co-author) "Jaws" (based on his novel of the same title), Universal, 1975.
(Co-author) "The Deep" (based on his novel of the same title), Columbia, 1977.
"The Island" (based on his novel of the same title), Universal, 1980.

Contributor to *Holiday, New Yorker, Diplomat, Moderator, Vogue, New York Herald-Tribune, New York Times Magazine, National Geographic,* and other periodicals.

SIDELIGHTS: Ever since he began exploring the Atlantic with his father, Peter Benchley has been fascinated by the sea. In 1974, the young writer turned that fascination to profit with a novel that was on the *New York Times* best-seller list for over forty weeks. *Jaws* "put sharks on the map and made him the most successful first novelist in literary history," according to Jennifer Dunning in the *New York Times Book Review.* Since then, all of Benchley's novels have concerned the ocean in one way or another. His first three—*Jaws, The Deep,* and *The Island*—are stories of high adventure in which an unexpected menace lurks in the water; his fourth—*The Girl of the Sea of Cortez*—is less dramatic and more lyrical, a sort of poetic fable with an environmental theme.

Peter Benchley inherited more than just a love of the sea from his father: his literary talents are a family legacy as well. His grandfather was the celebrated humorist Robert Benchley, and his father Nathaniel, also a writer, encouraged his son's interest by offering him, at fifteen, a small salary if he would write every day for a summer. By the time Peter was twenty-one, he had a literary agent from the same institution that represented his dad. Though Peter deemphasizes the role his heritage played in launching his career, Doubleday editor Thomas Congdon became increasingly aware of its importance when he and Benchley were discussing the proposal for *Jaws.* Most of the money in publishing is made by authors with proven track records, while first novels by unknown writers are generally ignored.

But the financial risk of publishing Benchley's first book of adult fiction was mitigated by his famous literary name. "I didn't realize it at the time," Congdon told the *Miami Herald,* "but Benchley did have a track record—his father and his grandfather."

Benchley's proposal also fit the formula of a best-seller. "First, its subject was something-about-which-the-general-public-knows-a-little-but-wants-to-know-more," explains a *Miami Herald* reporter. "Secondly, it conjured up a race memory: the external menace. Such situations as a fire in a skyscraper or a jumbo jet with a dead pilot at the controls. Such appeal to our survival instincts." Not only did *Jaws* catapult to the top of the best-seller lists, it also became an enormously successful motion picture—so successful that it spawned three sequels: "Jaws II," "Jaws 3-D," and "Jaws the Revenge." None of these equaled the original film's intensity. Benchley estimated that the combined revenue from the movie rights, paperback rights, magazine and book club syndications provided him with enough income to write freely for ten years.

Despite its unqualified popularity, *Jaws* drew fire from some critics for what they perceived as weak characterization, contrived sub-plotting, and inappropriate allusions to Herman Melville's classic fish tale, *Moby Dick.* "Benchley claims he wanted to keep this a serious novel, as well as a best-seller, and that was probably his mistake," asserts Michael Rogers in the *Rolling Stone.* "None of the humans are particularly likable or interesting; the shark was easily my favorite character—and one suspects, Benchley's also." Writing in the *New Statesman,* John Sparling concurs: "The characterisation of the humans is fairly rudimentary. . . . The shark, however, is done with exhilarating and alarming skill and every scene in which it appears is imagined at a special pitch of intensity." Other critics, including John Skow, are less appreciative. "Nothing works," writes Skow in *Time,* "not a hokey assignation between [the police chief's] wife and a predatory ichthyologist, and especially not an eat-'em up ending that lacks only Queequeg's coffin to resemble a bathtub version of *Moby Dick.*"

When asked how he felt about having his novel compared to Melville's, Benchley told *Palm Springs Life:* "I'm embarrassed. It isn't that kind of book, really. . . . It's a novel, and I think it's a good one, but it's a story not an allegory. I mean it's nice being a little bit rich and a little bit famous, but dammit, I didn't intend to rank with Melville."

One critic in tune with Benchley's intentions is Gene Lyons. "What one gets from Benchley, and this, I think, is the essence of his commercial genius, is *escape,*" Lyons writes in the *New York Times Book Review.* "Instead of wallowing among the commonplaces of our culture's self-doubt, [his protagonists are] lucky enough to have An Adventure. But for the mundane accidents of fate, it might have been you or me."

Though the plots of Benchley's adventures occasionally strain the limits of credibility, their backgrounds are always carefully researched. In an author's note to *The Island,* his gruesome tale of seventeenth-century style pirates holed up on an island near the Bahamas, Benchley writes that he "consulted scores of books, and while I have endeavored to avoid any resemblance to real characters, I have tried equally hard to be faithful to historical reality." *Chicago Tribune Book World* contributing critic Lloyd Sachs thinks he succeeds: "Benchley has certainly done his homework on pirate lore—his portrait of the murderous but honorable buccaneer Jean-David Nau and his tenth-generation pirates, who are on the brink of extinction, is convincing and entertaining and more than a little affecting. Benchley succeeds in making their plight touching and funny with one small detail: that they have come to prize 6-12 insect repellent more than just about anything."

With the appearance of *The Island*—Benchley's third adventure novel—*Washington Post* reporter Joseph McLellan concluded that Benchley "writes according to a formula. The formula moreover is a simple one: take a lot of salt water and put into it something unexpected and menacing. Anybody can do it, and in the wake of *Jaws,* quite a few have tried. The problem (the writer's problem, not the reader's) is that nobody seems to do it quite as well as Benchley."

Despite a successful track record as an adventure novelist, Benchley abandoned his "formula" when he wrote *The Girl of the Sea of Cortez.* An idyllic tale of a young girl's fascination with the sea and its inhabitants, this book moves much more slowly than Benchley's thrillers—and that's too slowly, some critics say. "This could be a refreshing deviation [from the style of his previous novels], but Benchley doesn't tell a story," notes Lola D. Gillebaard in the *Los Angeles Times Book Review.* "His words describe rather than dramatize. Though his descriptions are often lyrical, this reader yearned for more conflict, more 'and then what happened?'" Writing in the *Washington Post Book*

World, Thomas Gifford expresses a similar view: "When Benchley sticks to the manta ray, the girl, and the memories of her late father . . ., he is often effective, even poignant, moving. But out of water he is quickly beached and gasping his last. The problem is the plot."

Tony Bednarczyk, on the other hand, thinks that "the continual unveiling of thoughts, feelings, discoveries and wonderment about the underwater world," is what makes *The Girl of the Sea of Cortez* a success. Benchley's "book is dedicated to the infinite and mysterious wisdom of Nature," Bednarczyk concludes in *Best Sellers.* "It is not to be missed."

Benchley continued to tackle new genres and subjects with his next work, *Q Clearance,* which he described as "a spy comedy." Set in the post-Reagan era, the novel features Timothy Burnham, a speechwriter or "ventriloquist" for the salty-speaking President Ben Winslow. After Burnham involuntarily gains "Q clearance" because of a promotion, he receives confidential information—which is to be destroyed—concerning nuclear energy. Thereafter Burnham must endure the strong censure of his very liberal wife and children. Calling *Q Clearance* a "prime example of that vanishing literary species, the comic novel," *Los Angeles Times* contributor Elaine Kendall noted that the book's appeal rests in the "merciless sendup of various bureaucrats easily recognizable to anyone who reached the age of reason during the past four administrations."

Kendall also appreciated the humor in Benchley's 1989 novel, *Rummies,* deeming the book "more satirical, less reverent, and far wittier" than many others on the same subject. Dan Wakefield summed up the book's theme in the *Washington Post:* "At its best and most convincing . . . it is about the successful treatment of an Ivy League, up-scale, Eastern intellectual establishment alcoholic." At his family's insistence, Scott Preston, an editor for a large New York publishing house, enters a substance abuse center. There he encounters an assortment of people he considers unlike himself in every way, but he comes to realize that he has more in common with them than he does with anyone else; "Preston is made miserably aware that all differences of education and background vanish in the brotherhood of addiction," Kendall explained in the *Los Angeles Times.* "His evolution from a know-it-all, above-it-all, self-deluding lush to a vulnerable human being . . . is told in moving passages," Wakefield added. When a former glamor/movie star is murdered at the facility, the other patients become involved in solving the crime and working to see justice done; but Wakefield asserted that "the real drama" is still in witnessing Preston change from an out-of-control drinker into a recovered person. In his review of *Rummies* for the *Chicago Tribune,* David E. Jones declared that "Benchley's credentials as a storyteller . . . are only reinforced by this effort, which may be his most ambitious adventure to date."

AVOCATIONAL INTERESTS: Guitar, tennis, sharks, the theater, films.

BIOGRAPHICAL/CRITICAL SOURCES:

BOOKS

Authors in the News, Volume II, Gale, 1976.
Benchley, Peter, *The Island,* Doubleday, 1979.
Contemporary Literary Criticism, Gale, Volume IV, 1975, Volume VIII, 1978.

PERIODICALS

Best Sellers, August, 1982.
Chicago Tribune, November 17, 1989.

Chicago Tribune Book World, May 13, 1979, August 8, 1982, June 8, 1986.
Detroit News, May 6, 1979.
Los Angeles Times, July 4, 1986, November 24, 1989.
Los Angeles Times Book Review, August 22, 1982.
Miami Herald, June 8, 1975.
New Statesman, May 17, 1974, June 22, 1979.
Newsweek, May 10, 1976.
New Yorker, February 18, 1974.
New York Times, January 17, 1974.
New York Times Book Review, February 3, 1974, May 16, 1976, May 13, 1979, July 8, 1979, May 9, 1982, December 17, 1989.
Palm Springs Life, April, 1975.
Rolling Stone, April 11, 1974.
Time, February 4, 1974, July 5, 1982.
Washington Post, September 1, 1978, April 30, 1979, October 19, 1989.
Washington Post Book World, June 13, 1982, June 8, 1986.

* * *

BENJAMIN, Lois
See GOULD, Lois

* * *

BENNETT, Alan   1934-

PERSONAL: Born May 9, 1934, in Leeds, England; son of Walter (a butcher) and Lilian Mary (Peel) Bennett. *Education:* Exeter College, Oxford, B.A. (with honors), 1957. *Religion:* Church of England. *Avocational interests:* Medieval history.

ADDRESSES: Agent—A. D. Peters, 10 Buckingham St., London WC2N 6BU, England.

CAREER: Playwright, screenwriter, and actor on stage and television, 1959—; Oxford University, Magdalen College, Oxford, England, temporary junior lecturer in history, 1960-62. President, North Craven Heritage Trust. *Military service:* Intelligence Corps, 1952-54.

MEMBER: British Actors' Equity Association, Actors' Equity Association, American Federation of Television and Radio Artists.

AWARDS, HONORS: London *Evening Standard* Drama Awards, 1961, for *Beyond the Fringe,* 1968, for *Forty Years On,* 1971, for *Getting On,* and 1985; Antoinette Perry (Tony) Award, and New York Drama Critics Circle Award, both 1963, both for *Beyond the Fringe;* Guild of Television Producers award, 1967, for *On the Margin; Plays & Players* Award for best new play, 1977, for *The Old Country,* and 1986, for *Kafka's Dick;* Broadcasters Press Guild TV Award, 1983, British Academy of Film and Television Arts Writers Award, 1983, and Royal Television Society Award, 1984, all for *An Englishman Abroad.*

WRITINGS:

PLAYS

(With Peter Cook, Jonathan Miller, and Dudley Moore) *Beyond the Fringe* (comedy revue; first produced in Edinburgh, Scotland, 1960; produced on the West End, 1961; produced in New York, 1962), Random House, 1963.
Forty Years On (two-act; first produced in Manchester, England, 1968; produced on the West End, 1968), Faber, 1969.
(With Caryl Brahms and Ned Sherrin) *Sing a Rude Song* (two-act), first produced in London, 1969.

Getting On (two-act; first produced in Brighton, England, 1971; produced on the West End, 1971), Faber, 1972.

Habeas Corpus (two-act; first produced in Oxford, England, 1973; produced on the West End, 1973; produced on Broadway, 1975), Faber, 1973, Samuel French, 1976.

The Old Country (first produced in Oxford, 1977; produced on the West End, 1977), Faber, 1978.

Enjoy (first produced at Richmond Theatre, 1980; produced on the West End, 1980), Faber, 1980.

Office Suite (adaptations of television plays *A Visit From Miss Prothero* and *Doris and Doreen* [also see below], produced in London, 1987), Faber, 1981.

Forty Years On, Getting On, Habeas Corpus, Faber, 1985.

Kafka's Dick (also see below), first produced in London, 1986.

Single Spies (one-act plays), first produced in London, 1988.

TELEPLAYS

On the Margin (television series), British Broadcasting Corp. (BBC-TV), 1966.

A Day Out (also see below), BBC-TV, 1972.

Sunset across the Bay, BBC-TV, 1975.

A Little Outing, BBC-TV, 1978.

A Visit from Miss Prothero, BBC-TV, 1978.

Me, I'm Afraid of Virginia Woolf (also see below), London Weekend Television (LWT), 1978.

Doris and Doreen, LWT, 1978.

The Old Crowd (also see below), LWT, 1979.

One Fine Day (also see below), LWT, 1979.

Afternoon Off (also see below), LWT, 1979.

All Day on the Sands (also see below), LWT, 1979.

The Hedgehog, LWT, 1979.

Objects of Affection (five plays: *Our Winnie, A Woman of No Importance, Rolling Home, Marks,* and *Say Something Happened;* also see below), BBC-TV, 1982.

Intensive Care (also see below), BBC-TV, 1982.

An Englishman Abroad (also see below), BBC-TV, 1982.

Objects of Affection and Other Plays (includes *Intensive Care, A Day Out,* and *An Englishman Abroad*), BBC Publications, 1982.

The Writer in Disguise (includes *Me, I'm Afraid of Virginia Woolf, The Old Crowd, One Fine Day, Afternoon Off,* and *All Day on the Sands*), Faber, 1985.

The Insurance Man (also see below), BBC-TV, 1986.

Talking Heads (BBC-TV, 1987), BBC Publications, 1988.

OTHER

A Private Function (screenplay; Handmade Films, 1984), Faber, 1985.

Two Kafka Plays: Kafka's Dick [and] The Insurance Man, Faber, 1987.

Prick up Your Ears (screenplay; adapted from the biography by John Lahr; Samuel Goldwyn Co., 1987), Faber, 1988.

Also author of radio play, *Uncle Clarence,* 1986. Contributor to periodicals, including London *Times, Listener, Sunday Times,* and *London Review of Books.*

SIDELIGHTS: "Whatever their ostensible subjects, Alan Bennett's plays consistently dramatize man's desire to define himself and his world through teasingly inadequate language, whether conventional adages, women's magazine prose, government jargon, or quotations from the 'Greats,' " Burton Kendle notes in *Contemporary Dramatists.* "The rich parodies that result simultaneously mock and honor this impulse to erect linguistic safeguards in a frightening world." Bennett began his career as an actor, and his collaboration with Dudley Moore, Peter Cook,

and Jonathan Miller, a revue titled *Beyond the Fringe,* became a hit on both sides of the Atlantic. With its New York debut, the play became "the first British equivalent of American-type satire to reach our shores," Richard Brustein comments in the *New Republic,* describing the series of sketches as having "all the qualifications of sick comedy. . . . It roasts all [the] categorical turkeys, it has no firm moral center, it is immoderate, irresponsible, and totally destructive, it affirms no changing world, and—if I may be permitted a . . . judgment of value—it is violently funny." As Matthew Wolf summarizes in the *Chicago Tribune, Beyond the Fringe*'s "anarchic humor helped pave the way for 'Rowan & Martin's Laugh-In' and 'Saturday Night Live' in America and 'Monty Python' in England, despite Bennett's assertion that these latter groups 'take it so much further.' "

His first solo creation, *Forty Years On,* is "a piece dripping with nostalgia for the Edwardian past and undercutting every satiric episode with expressions of affectionate regret," Irving Wardle reports in the London *Times.* Consisting of a play within a play, *Forty Years On* follows the changing of the guard at a boys' boarding school as the headmaster's retirement inspires the performance of a comic revue. A "fragmented, ambiguous, oddly interesting assortment of a play," as *Village Voice* writer Molly Haskell terms it, *Forty Years On* is "what [Bennett] needed to make the transition from revue-sketch writer to playwright," Wardle asserts, serving up a "brand of wry, negative patriotism."

Drama critic J. W. Lambert similarly observes an ambivalent note in Bennett's satire: "Relaxed mockery is [the author's] line and detached affection, rather than any more intense emotion, informs his speculative eye. . . . They make a welcome counterpart to the assorted gobbets of half-baked romanticism which tend to be flung in our faces nowadays." Highlighting the play's satire is the author's flair for language; "as we know from [his previous work], Bennett has a mean ear for cliche and the verbal ingenuity to twist it into appealingly absurd shapes," Benedict Nightingale remarks in the *New Statesman.* In contrast, *New York Times* critic Clive Barnes feels that the satire is "fundamentally . . . cheap and nasty," and faults the play for "pretentiousness and ineptness." Jeremy Kingston, however, praises *Forty Years On* for hitting its satirical targets, writing in *Punch* that Bennett "scores bull's-eyes and inners all down the line." "Ever since [*Beyond the Fringe*] we have been waiting for a full-scale mock-heroic pageant of modern British myth, and Mr. Bennett has now supplied it," Wardle concludes in a *New York Times* review; *Forty Years On* is "a lethally witty series of parodies."

In the 1970s and early 1980s, Bennett wrote over fifteen television scripts, garnering many awards; during this time, he "made the change from satirist to writer of substance without losing a healthy talent for mockery and self-mockery," Andrew Hislop reports in the London *Times.* Despite critical acclaim for his teleplays, however, Bennett wished to return to writing for the stage, "yearning to get away from the naturalism he tends towards in his work for the small screen," Hislop adds. In 1986 Bennett premiered *Kafka's Dick,* a "kind of leisurely vaudeville about the tormented Kafka of litcrit and biographical legend," as *Observer* contributor Michael Ratcliffe describes. Investigating the relationships between biographers and their subjects, *Kafka's Dick* follows the investigations and trials of an insurance salesman who is obsessed with the famous Czech author, and brings in as characters Max Brod, Kafka's friend and literary executor, Kafka's father, and the author himself.

In the London *Times,* Wardle calls the play a "head-on challenge to literary myth," and adds: "There is a great deal more than that, too much in fact, to the play." Other reviewers likewise criticize the work as attempting too much; Ratcliffe observes that the work is "a mordant attack on twentieth-century trivialisation and barbarity by a playwright who cannot resist blunting the force and intensity of his attack by a constant stream of gags." "On the one hand, [Bennett] tilts at what Englishness stifles," Jim Hiley writes in the *Listener,* and yet the playwright himself "refuses to get 'too' serious. He perches fretfully on the fence." Nevertheless, the critic believes that *Kafka's Dick* "provides a rewardingly inventive, provoking, often hilarious night out—a nutritious confection with pins in the cream." And Wardle likewise maintains that while "Bennett has taken more on board than he can deal with . . . there remains, of course, the Bennett dialogue, which is as rich as ever in exquisitely turned domestic banalities and literary give-aways."

"Alan Bennett is not as celebrated or prolific a playwright as his contemporaries Tom Stoppard and Simon Gray, but he ranks right up there with them as a witty and humane observer of England in particular and of mankind in general," Richard Christiansen comments in the *Chicago Tribune.* Bennett presents a similar focus in his first screenplay, *A Private Function,* which Wolf calls "as gently telling a treatment of the British class system as has been seen in years." The film follows a middle-class couple during postwar England as they attempt to ascend the social ladder by providing pork—forbidden by rationing laws—for a society banquet. According to *Chicago Tribune* critic Gene Siskel, "what Bennett has done is simply to throw one solitary wacky element—a pig—into what otherwise would be an entirely credible situation." The result, Siskel continues, is that "everything British is being skewered in a most delightful manner—especially the resentments that one always suspects lurk just beneath the incomparable British politeness." Paul Attanasio, however, believes that the movie doesn't measure up to the previous work of its star, Michael Palin; the critic states in the *Washington Post* that *A Private Function* "misses that touch of madness that Monty Python brought to the same comedic vein." Others, however, find the film a success; "not since the end of the collaboration between Roy and John Boulting . . . and the golden age of the Ealing Studios has there been a stylish English comedy of such high-hearted, self-interested knavery as 'A Private Function,' " claims *New York Times* critic Vincent Canby.

In 1986 Bennett took a more serious turn with *Prick up Your Ears,* a film biography of English playwright Joe Orton, who at age 34 was murdered by his long-time male lover, who then committed suicide. "A bracingly outrageous portrait of the playwright, his free-ranging life and remarkably constricted times," as *Los Angeles Times* film critic Sheila Benson terms it, *Prick up Your Ears* follows Orton's life through a series of flashbacks framed by the investigations of the playwright's biography, John Lahr. As director Stephen Frears told *Chicago Tribune* writer Sid Smith, "Bennett's screenplay is very delicately written, a feast of words and aphorisms and linguistically very precise. We worked hard with the actors to get that precision." Some critics, however, think that the film focuses too much on the details of Orton's life and not enough on his work; Canby comments that the film "goes on to record little more than the facts of the Orton life, [and] the mere existence of the plays." But Benson, while she expresses a similar criticism, commends the film for having "the rhythm and even the insolence of an Orton play, without its dialogue." And Desson Howe echoes previous praises of the author's work, asserting in his *Washington Post* review that "Bennett's screenplay is a case study in irony. He shows the beauty in 'dirtiness,' the humor in human anguish and the art of sarcasm in British culture. . . . Like 'Casablanca,' 'Diva,' 'Clockwork Orange' and countless other quality-cult films,"

Howe concludes, " 'Prick up Your Ears' has an indefinable idiosyncrasy that makes you want to come back for more."

BIOGRAPHICAL/CRITICAL SOURCES:

BOOKS

Contemporary Dramatists, St. James, 1988.
Contemporary Literary Criticism, Gale, Volume 45, 1987.

PERIODICALS

Chicago Tribune, April 12, 1985, April 21, 1985, February 18, 1986, November 16, 1986, May 20, 1987.
Drama, spring, 1969.
Listener, October 2, 1986.
Los Angeles Times, May 1, 1987.
New Republic, December 15, 1962.
New Statesman, November 8, 1968, November 7, 1986.
New York Times, November 5, 1968, July 26, 1969, March 1, 1985, April 17, 1987, May 17, 1987.
Observer, September 28, 1986.
Punch, November 6, 1968.
Times (London), May 4, 1984, September 6, 1986.
Village Voice, January 30, 1969.
Washington Post, April 29, 1985, May 15, 1987, May 16, 1987.

—*Sketch by Diane Telgen*

*   *   *

BENNETT, Elizabeth
See MITCHELL, Margaret (Munnerlyn)

*   *   *

BERGER, Thomas (Louis)   1924-

PERSONAL: Born July 20, 1924, in Cincinnati, Ohio; son of Thomas Charles and Mildred (Bubbe) Berger; married Jeanne Redpath (an artist), June 12, 1950. *Education:* University of Cincinnati, B.A. (honors), 1948; Columbia University, graduate study, 1950-51.

ADDRESSES: Agent—Don Congdon Associates, 156 Fifth Ave., New York, NY 10010.

CAREER: Novelist, short story writer, playwright. Librarian, Rand School of Social Science, 1948-51; staff member, *New York Times Index,* 1951-52; associate editor, *Popular Science Monthly,* 1952-53; film critic, *Esquire,* 1972-73; writer-in-residence, University of Kansas, 1974; Distinguished Visiting Professor, Southampton College, 1975-76; lecturer, Yale University, 1981, 1982; Regents' lecturer, University of California, Davis, 1982. *Military service:* U.S. Army, 1943-46.

MEMBER: Authors Guild, Authors League of America.

AWARDS, HONORS: Dial fellowship, 1962; Western Heritage Award, and Richard and Hinda Rosenthal Award, National Institute of Arts and Letters, both 1965, for *Little Big Man;* Ohioana Book Award, 1982, for *Reinhart's Women;* Pulitzer Prize nomination, 1984, for *The Feud;* Litt.D., Long Island University, 1986; honorary member, Phi Alpha Theta.

WRITINGS:

NOVELS

Crazy in Berlin, Scribner, 1958, Delacorte, 1982.
Reinhart in Love, Scribner, 1962, Delacorte, 1982.
Little Big Man, Dial, 1964, Delacorte, 1979.
Killing Time, Dial, 1967.

Vital Parts, Baron, 1970, Delacorte, 1982.
Regiment of Women, Simon & Schuster, 1973.
Sneaky People, Simon & Schuster, 1975.
Who Is Teddy Villanova?, Delacorte, 1977.
Arthur Rex, Delacorte, 1978.
Neighbors, Delacorte, 1980.
Reinhart's Women, Delacorte, 1981.
The Feud, Delacorte, 1983.
Nowhere, Delacorte, 1985.
Being Invisible, Little, Brown, 1987.
The Houseguest, Little, Brown, 1988.
Changing the Past, Little, Brown, 1989.

OTHER

"Other People" (play) first produced at Berkshire Theatre Festival, 1970.
Granted Wishes (short stories), Lord John Press, 1984.

Also author of "The Burglars," a play published in *New Letters,* fall, 1988. Contributor to numerous magazines, including short stories in *Gentleman's Quarterly, American Review, Penthouse, Playboy, Saturday Evening Post,* and *Harper's.*

MEDIA ADAPTATIONS: The movie version of *Little Big Man,* starring Dustin Hoffman, was released in 1970; the movie version of *The Neighbors,* starring John Belushi, was a Universal Studios release in 1981; and the film version of *The Feud* was released by Castle Hill in 1990.

SIDELIGHTS: "Thomas Berger belongs, with Mark Twain and [H. L.] Mencken and Philip Roth, among our first-rate literary wiseguys," writes John Romano in the *New York Times Book Review.* "Savvy and skeptical, equipped with a natural eloquence and a knack for parody, he has been expertly flinging mud at the more solemn and self-important national myths for more than 20 years." Other critics agree with this assessment of Berger's talent, rating him as one of the leading American satiric novelists. Brom Weber of *Saturday Review* writes that Berger is "one of the most successful satiric observers of the ebb and flow of American life after World War II. His prolificacy promises a continued development of the tragicomic mode of vision." Writing in the *National Review,* Guy Davenport calls Berger "the best satirist in the United States, the most learned scientist of the vulgar, the futile, and the lost, and the most accurate mimic in the trade." In a later *National Review* piece, Davenport elaborates his praise, calling Berger "a comedian whose understanding of humanity is devilishly well informed and splendidly impartial. Nothing is exempt from the splash of his laughter. The result is an amazing universality."

Berger, who often says he writes to celebrate the creative possibilities of language, works with a variety of traditional kinds of fiction. His aim is not to produce parody, satire, or to diagnose social ills, though critics recognize all these features in most of his novels. Critics have especially emphasized the comic social commentary in the books; and in at least two of his novels—*Killing Time* and *Sneaky People*—Berger makes serious comments on modern society. But Berger's forte is the kind of mock-heroism found in his best-known novel, *Little Big Man.* Some critics state that the movie version produced in 1970, which was a box-office success, did not do justice to the novel. Michael Harris opines in the *Washington Post Book World* that "*Little Big Man,* unfortunately obscured by the movie, is nothing less than a masterpiece. American history itself provided Berger with his types—a set of buckskin-fringed waxworks bedizened with legend—and in blowing the myths up to ridiculous proportions he paradoxically succeeded in reclaiming history." Gerald Green,

writing in *Proletarian Writers of the Thirties,* believes that "the glory of *Little Big Man* lies in the way Berger imposes his comic view of life on a deadly accurate portrait of the Old West. . . . It is the truest kind of humor, a humor that derives from real situations and real people. Who can resist Berger's Cheyennes who refer to themselves haughtily as 'The Human Beings?' Or his description of the way an Indian camp smells? Or the Indians' disdain for time, schedules, anything contiguous—a trait which causes them to hate the railroad?"

Although *Little Big Man* was not an immediate success when it was first published in 1964, "its reputation has spread and solidified since then," according to R. V. Cassill of the *New York Times Book Review.* "Now a great many people understand that it was one of the very best novels of the decade and the best novel ever written about the American West. On the strength of this prodigious work alone, the author's reputation can rest secure." *Atlantic's* David Denby believes the book to be "probably as close as sophisticated men can come to a genuine folk version of the Old West. Its central character, Jack Crabb, is not so much a hero as an Everyman—an essentially passive recorder of vivid experience. American history happens to him, runs over him, and fails to break him. . . . Crabb himself is decent, competent, hopeful, and neither outstandingly courageous or weak; life is sordid, absurd, and as Crabb always survives, surprisingly persistent in its ability to make him suffer. . . . Crabb just wants to survive."

Another Berger character who is, more than anything else, a survivor, is Carlo Reinhart, protagonist of *Crazy in Berlin, Reinhart in Love, Vital Parts,* and *Reinhart's Women.* Jib Fowles comments in *New Leader* that both "Reinhart and Crabb were people that Berger obviously liked having around. . . . Reinhart was neither a comedian nor a scapegoat, but he was never far from things comic or painful. . . . Like most of us, Reinhart could not qualify as a hero or anti-hero; he got through, and Berger set it all down in wry and superbly-told accounts." Unlike Crabb, Reinhart lives in the twentieth century and the four books in which he appears take him from his youthful days in World War II (*Crazy in Berlin*) to his middle years in the late 1970s (*Reinhart's Women*). A *Newsweek* reviewer notes that "Berger loves Carlo Reinhart, and he makes us love him, and he does this without resorting to tricks. . . . Reinhart is an unlikely hero: fat, 'bloated with emptiness,' scorned by women and animals, looked through as though he were polluted air, in debt, a voyeur, 'redundant in the logistics of life,' he nonetheless is a splendid man. He is novel, quick to forgive and hope."

The reviewers' opinions on the effectiveness of the Reinhart series and of the individual books differ. Writing in the *National Review,* Davenport believes that the Reinhart saga "stands well against all contenders as the definitive comic portrait of our time." Cassill expresses both the quality and the problems of the series in the *New York Times Book Review:* "There are so very many fine things in all the Reinhart novels and such a heroic unfolding conception that one hates to mention the difficulties of taking them in. Yet, trying to gather Reinhart whole into the mind is like trying to embrace a whale and finding not only that the stretch is terrific but that somehow it isn't quite the same whale when your hands feel their way to the other side of it. . . . Yet, the whole ambiguous carcass is so imposing and looms so enticingly amid the deep waters of the recent past that there is really no choice for the serious reader except to go after it with Ahab's passions. The great thing is that Reinhart and his story are not just Mr. Berger's private whale. They are compounded of our mysterious blessings and curses as well."

Who Is Teddy Villanova? is Berger's exploitation of what the *New York Times*'s John Leonard calls "the pulp detective story, in which, of course, nothing is as it seems and nothing ever makes any sense. The story, moreover, is populated entirely by people who talk like books, usually, but not always, 19th-century books by such Englishmen as Thomas Babington Macaulay and John Ruskin." Writing in the *New York Times Book Review,* Leonard Michaels comments on Berger's style, comparing it to that of S. J. Perelman—"educated, complicated, graceful, silly, destructive in spirit, and brilliant—and it is also something like Mad Comics—densely, sensuously detailed, unpredictable, packed with gags. Beyond all this, it makes an impression of scholarship—that is, Berger seems really to know what he jokes about. This includes not only Hammett and Chandler, but also Racine, Goethe, Ruskin, Elias Canetti, New York and the way its residents behave. . . . His whole novel . . . is like a huge verbal mirror. Its reflections are similar to what we see in much contemporary literature—hilarious and serious at once."

Having exposed the humor of American life from the Old West in *Little Big Man* to the twentieth century in the Reinhart series, Berger turns in *Arthur Rex* to a parody of ancient myth and literature. The *New Republic*'s Garrett Epps calls the book "a massive retelling of the Camelot legend" and says that *Arthur Rex* "may be Berger's most ambitious book, at least in size and literary scale." Commenting in the *New York Times Book Review* on Berger's method in the retelling of this morality tale, John Romano explains that he paints his mythical landscapes "in his droll, relentlessly straight-faced prose, so as to empty them of romance, and let the brutal/crummy facts stare out. His pages swarm with bawdy puns and slapstick and bookish in-jokes; but even at his most absurd, his intrinsic tone is that of a hard-nosed realist who won't let the myths distort his essentially grouchy idea of the way things are."

In *Neighbors,* his tenth novel, Berger returns to the present suburban neighborhood and, according to the *New York Times*'s Christopher Lehmann-Haupt, "parodies all the rituals of neighborliness—the competitiveness, the bonhommie, the striving for civility in the face of what seems to be barbarism—and compresses into a single day a lifetime of over-the-back-fence strife." Paul Gray of *Time* calls *Neighbors* "a tour de force, [Berger's] most successfully sustained comic narrative since *Little Big Man.* . . . Like the best black humor of the 1960s, *Neighbors* offers a version of reality skewed just enough to give paranoia a good name." Berger agrees with Gray's assessment; in a *New York Times Book Review* interview, he told Richard Schickel: "As my tenth novel, begun at the close of my twentieth year as a published novelist, it is appropriately a bizarre celebration of whatever gift I have, the strangest of all my narratives. . . . A poor devil named Earl Keese is tormented by the newcomers in the house next door—who, however, may be essentially better sorts than he. The morality of this work, like that of all my other volumes, will be in doubt until the end of the narrative—and perhaps to the end of eternity, now that I think about it."

Berger said that in *Neighbors* he is paying homage to "[Franz] Kafka, who has always been one of my masters. It was Kafka who taught me that at any moment banality might turn sinister, for existence was not meant to be unfailingly genial." Several reviewers note the debt to Kafka. As Frederick Busch explains in the *Chicago Tribune Book World,* "Kafka has made it clear to us that a middle-class household can breed nightmares *that become true.*" Writing in the *Washington Post,* Joseph McLellan comments that "Berger's debt to Kafka is evident in the slippery way the book's realities keep shifting, the constant confrontation with uncertainty. . . . There is also a trace of Kafka in the way

identities tend to dissolve and shift, and in the constant recurrence of absurdity as a basic plot ingredient. In his exploration of these elements, Berger takes an honorable place in the lineage not only of Kafka but of [master novelists James] Joyce and [Vladimir] Nabokov."

Writing in the *New York Times Book Review,* Thomas Edwards believes that *Neighbors* "raises yet again the embarrassing question of why Thomas Berger isn't more generally recognized as one of the masters of contemporary American fiction." Isa Kapp writes in the *New Republic:* "It is a mystery of literary criticism, that Thomas Berger, one of the most ambitious, versatile, and entertaining of contemporary novelists, is hardly ever mentioned in the company of America's major writers. He is a wit, a fine caricaturist, and his prose crackles with Rabelaisian vitality." Edwards postulates, "No doubt the trouble has something to do with obtuse notions that funny writing can't really be serious, that major talents devote themselves to 'big' subjects and elaborate fictional techniques, that Mr. Berger is too eclectic and unpredictable to be important. . . . But *Neighbors* proves once again that Thomas Berger is one of our most intelligent, witty and independent-minded writers, that he knows, mistrusts and loves the texture of American life and culture as deeply as any novelist alive, and that our failure to read and discuss him is a national disgrace."

In *The Feud,* reports *New York Times Book Review* contributor Anne Tyler, "a gigantic sprawl of disasters [is] triggered by the smallest of events." The owner of a hardware store sees a fire hazard in a customer's unlit cigar; discussion over this perceived threat ends when Reverton, the owner's cousin, forces the customer to apologize at gunpoint. The gun, it turns out, is harmless, but the series of revenges that follow are not; businesses, lives and futures are destroyed before the novel's end. Berger makes the story comic as well as sad; thus, the usual conventions of the feud novel gain new life from Berger, say reviewers. "What makes Thomas Berger's version so fresh is the innocent bewilderment of most of the people involved," Tyler notes. Garrett Epps, writing in the *Washington Post Book World,* concurs: "In presenting this pageant of ignorance, rage, and deceit, Berger is harsh but never cruel. In all their variety, his novels have consistently presented a serious view of humanity as a race utterly spoiled by something that looks a lot like Original Sin. This merciless vision frees Berger somehow to love even his less prepossessing creations."

Critics found *The Feud* remarkable for a number of reasons. As Epps sees it, Berger "taps into" the hidden fire of human hostility "and turns it into something cleansing and safe. That he makes it look easy only adds to the achievement." *New York Times* reviewer Lehmann-Haupt offers, "For all its slapstick comedy and manic plot machinery, what 'The Feud' rather surprisingly adds up to is an ugly portrait of middle America in the 1930's. I can't quite figure out how Mr. Berger has achieved such a realistic mood using such anti-realistic techniques." With similar admiration, *Chicago Tribune Book World* contributor Howard Frank Mosher remarks, "Berger has once again written a novel that spoofs a literary tradition while simultaneously becoming its best contemporary example."

Critical assessments of *Nowhere* and *Being Invisible* generally rate them both as limited successes in comparison to Berger's other novels. A cross between a spy-thriller and an updated *Gulliver's Travels, Nowhere* allows Berger to joke about private eyes while examining human nature, remarks David W. Madden in the *San Francisco Review of Books.* Lehmann-Haupt of the *New York Times* finds it a courageous attempt "to poke fun at every excess of the world from the cold war to racial prejudice," a text troubled by the same kinds of excesses it ridicules. More important to Madden is Berger's "ability of consistently exploring new fictional possibilities" while at the same time returning to characters and themes seen in his earlier novels.

"There is a certain type of scene that no writer does better than Mr. Berger: the depiction of the instant when the most routine social encounter becomes—suddenly and without provocation or warning—pure hell; the simplest exchange of banalities turns sour, then surly, then rancorous, then violent," and accordingly, *Being Invisible* has its "moments of random brutality," writes Francine Prose in the *New York Times Book Review*. The fact that Fred Wagner, the non-hero of *Being Invisible,* can disappear at will gives his story some "marvelous ironies," including Fred's distaste "for the voyeurism, the petty crime, the guilty, secret delights" available to him when he vanishes, Prose relates. In this "fantasy of the white male as victim," as it is described by *Los Angeles Times* reviewer Carolyn See, Fred is "outnumbered by jerks—pushy, stupid, self-satisfied," notes Prose. Fred's blandness beside them becomes a problem for Berger, say reviewers. Fred does not rise beyond "the strictly mundane; no fabulistic soarings are permitted him, no flights, no dizzying privy perspectives on the great world," explains *Times Literary Supplement* reviewer John Clute. However, he points out, "If *Being Invisible* was meant to give modest pleasure and then disappear, it may then be reckoned a success, even in the hour of its passing."

Though *Being Invisible* lacks some of the depth of character achieved in other novels, Fred's world—"one in which total strangers will humiliate you for the fun of it," or kill you for a piece of cheap jewelry—is familiar to Berger fans, Prose adds. Balancing her dissatisfaction with Berger's cartoon-like characters and the disparaging view of female behavior presented in the book, Prose applauds Berger for providing another thought-provoking view of the contemporary world: "As our Government works to persuade us that life is good, that everything is all right, it's an enormous *relief* to hear Mr. Berger's voice sneering, shrill, combative, insisting that life isn't all right or likely to be, that strangers will just as soon kill you as give you the time of day. It is a sign of the times that we feel such affection for Thomas Berger's dogged, cranky courage, and for the denizens of his unwelcoming and chaotic corner of the fictional world."

Many critics feel, as does MacDonald Harris of the *Washington Post Book World*, that Berger excels when observing a quarrel "from the sidelines" in *Neighbors* and *The Feud.* "In *The Houseguest*," says Harris, Berger "takes up the Quarrel again, and treats it in a way that is more complicated, more subtle, and more odd than anything in his previous work." The antagonist, in this case, is a charming visitor who gradually takes control of a well-to-do family's household. At first, his hosts, the Graves family, do not resist, because he serves them as handyman and gourmet cook. But after the outsider steals from them and tricks their daughter into having sex with him, they decide to kill him. He not only survives their violent attacks, but wins a place in the Graves household by providing the amenities which they have grown to expect.

Harris finds *The Houseguest* the most interesting of Berger's novels "because it seems to suggest something more subtle going on under the surface," perhaps an allegorical significance that points to relations between the privileged and underprivileged in America. Since neither class under Berger's gaze behaves admirably, it is clear that "Berger will not take sides," Art Seidenbaum relates in the *Los Angeles Times Book Review*. Seidenbaum calls this a weakness, but other critics find it consistent with the

view of humanity expressed in Berger's other books. In *The Houseguest,* says Harris, Berger remains "ready to strain our credence with . . . the loutish realism of his events. His humor is Rabelaisian: larger than life, improbable and always on the edge of vulgarity; his penchant for stripping off the dirty underwear of life is unrelenting."

BIOGRAPHICAL/CRITICAL SOURCES:

BOOKS

Cohen, Sarah Blacher, editor, *Comic Relief,* University of Illinois Press, 1978.
Contemporary Literary Criticism, Gale, Volume 3, 1975, Volume 5, 1976, Volume 8, 1978, Volume 11, 1979, Volume 18, 1981, Volume 38, 1986.
Dictionary of Literary Biography, Volume 2: *American Novelists since World War II,* Gale, 1978.
Dictionary of Literary Biography Yearbook: 1980, Gale, 1981.
Landon, Brooks, *Thomas Berger,* Twayne, 1989.
Madden, David, editor, *Proletarian Writers of the Thirties,* Southern Illinois University Press, 1968.
Mitchell, Burroughs, *The Education of an Editor,* Doubleday, 1980.
Schulz, Max F., *Black Humor Fiction of the Sixties: A Pluralistic Definition of Man and His World,* Ohio State University Press, 1973.
Thompson, Raymond H., *The Return from Avalon: A Study of Arthurian legend in Modern Fiction,* Greenwood Press, 1985.

PERIODICALS

American Book Review, March-April, 1982.
Antaeus, Number 61, 1988.
Armchair Detective, Number 14, 1981.
Atlantic, March, 1971, September, 1973.
Audience, Volume 2, number 4, 1972.
Best Sellers, November 1, 1964, October 1, 1967, April 15, 1970.
Books and Bookmen, July, 1968.
Book Week, October 25, 1964.
Centennial Review, Number 13, 1969.
Chicago Tribune Book World, April 13, 1980, September 27, 1981, December 18, 1981, May 29, 1983, May 20, 1984, May 19, 1985, June 16, 1985.
Commentary, July, 1970.
Confrontation, spring/summer, 1976.
Detroit News, October 18, 1981.
Globe and Mail (Toronto), July 20, 1985.
Guardian Weekly (Manchester), April 17, 1971.
Harper's, April, 1970.
Hollins Critic, December, 1983.
Life, March 27, 1970.
Listener, July 11, 1974.
Los Angeles Times, May 11, 1987, May 18, 1990.
Los Angeles Times Book Review, November 1, 1981, May 15, 1983, April 3, 1988, September 24, 1989.
Ms., August, 1973.
Nation, August 20, 1977, May 3, 1980, June 11, 1983.
National Review, November 14, 1967, April 21, 1970, October 10, 1975.
New Leader, November 6, 1967, November 12, 1973, May 23, 1977.
New Republic, October 7, 1978, April 26, 1980, May 23, 1983.
Newsweek, April 20, 1970, December 21, 1970.
New Yorker, October 21, 1967.
New York Review of Books, May 26, 1977.

New York Times, September 20, 1967, March 31, 1970, March 18, 1977, April 1, 1980, September 28, 1981, May 2, 1983, April 29, 1985, April 2, 1987, May 4, 1990.

New York Times Book Review, October 11, 1964, September 17, 1967, March 29, 1970, May 13, 1973, April 20, 1975, March 20, 1977, April 17, 1977, November 12, 1978, April 6, 1980, September 27, 1981, June 6, 1982, June 20, 1982, May 8, 1983, April 7, 1985, May 5, 1985, April 2, 1987, April 12, 1987, April 17, 1988, August 27, 1989.

Observer Review, May 5, 1968.

Philological Quarterly, Volume 62, number 1, 1983.

Punch, May 15, 1968.

San Francisco Review of Books, summer, 1985.

Saturday Review, March 21, 1970, July 31, 1973, May-June, 1985.

South Dakota Review, Volume 4, number 2, 1966.

Studies in American Humor, spring, 1983, fall, 1983.

Studies in Medievalism, Volume 2, number 4, 1983.

Time, December 21, 1970, April 7, 1980, October 12, 1981, May 23, 1983, June 17, 1985.

Times (London), January 12, 1984.

Times Literary Supplement, September 3, 1982, February 10, 1984, February 21, 1986, June 17, 1988, July 22, 1988, August 4, 1989, April 27, 1990.

Tribune Books (Chicago), April 12, 1987, November 19, 1989.

Wall Street Journal, February 5, 1979.

Washington Post, April 8, 1970, April 14, 1980, September 14, 1981.

Washington Post Book World, April 20, 1975, September 17, 1978, June 27, 1982, May 15, 1983, August 26, 1984, July 7, 1985, April 19, 1987, April 17, 1988, September 3, 1989.

Western American Literature, Volume 8, numbers 1-2, 1973, Volume 15, number 3, Volume 22, number 4, 1988.

Yale Review, winter, 1981.

*   *   *

BERNE, Eric (Lennard) 1910-1970
(Lennard Gandalac, Ramsbottom Horsely, Peter Pinto, Cyprian St. Cyr)

PERSONAL: Born May 10, 1910, in Montreal, Quebec, Canada; died July 15, 1970, in Monterey, Calif.; became U.S. citizen, 1943; son of David Hillel (a physician) and Sara (Gordon) Berne; twice married (once to Dorothy DeMass, 1949), twice divorced; children: Ellen, Peter, Ricky, Terry; stepchildren: Robert Way, Janice Way (Mrs. Michael Farlinger). *Education:* McGill University, B.A., 1931, M.D. and C.M., 1935; attended Yale Psychiatric Clinic, 1936-38, New York Psychoanalytic Institute, 1941-43, and San Francisco Psychoanalytic Institute, 1947-56.

ADDRESSES: Home—Carmel, Calif.

CAREER: U.S. Army, consultant to Surgeon General, 1951-54; Mount Zion Hospital, San Francisco, Calif., adjunct psychiatrist, 1952-70; Langley Porter Neuropsychiatric Clinic, San Francisco, lecturer, 1960-70; McAuley Clinic, San Francisco, consultant in group therapy, 1962-70. Visiting lecturer, Stanford-Palo Alto Psychiatric Clinic, 1961-63. Diplomate of American Board of Psychiatry and Neurology. Conductor of free seminars for other therapists, San Francisco, 1958-70. *Military service:* U.S. Army, Medical Corps, 1943-46; became major.

MEMBER: American Psychiatric Association (fellow), American Medical Association, American Association for the Advancement of Science, International Transactional Analysis Association (founder; former chairman of board), Indian Psychiatric Society.

WRITINGS:

The Mind in Action, Simon & Schuster, 1947, revised edition published as *Layman's Guide to Psychiatry and Psychoanalysis,* 1957, 3rd edition, 1968.

Transactional Analysis in Psychotherapy: A Systematic Individual and Social Psychiatry, Grove, 1961, reprinted, Ballantine, 1978.

The Structure and Dynamics of Organizations and Groups, Lippincott, 1963.

Games People Play: The Psychology of Human Relationships, Grove, 1964.

Principles of Group Treatment, Oxford University Press, 1966.

The Happy Valley (juvenile), Grove, 1968.

Sex in Human Loving, Simon & Schuster, 1970.

What Do You Say after You Say Hello?: The Psychology of Human Destiny, Grove, 1972.

Transactional Analysis Bulletin, Selected Articles from Volumes 1 through 9, edited by Paul McCormick, TA Press, 1976.

Intuition and Ego States: The Origins of Transactional Analysis, TA Press, 1977.

Hello Sigmund, This Is Eric, edited by L. H. Forman and J. S. Ramsburg, Sheed Andrews, 1978.

Beyond Games and Scripts, edited by Claude M. Steiner and Carmen Kerr, Ballantine, 1978.

Contributor to psychiatric and other journals. Editor of *Transactional Analysis Bulletin,* 1962-70.

WORK IN PROGRESS: A sequel to *Games People Play;* fiction.

SIDELIGHTS: "Life is really very simple," Eric Berne once said. "But if people have to face that fact they get very upset. So they invent religions and pastimes and games. These are the same people who then lament how awful it is that life is complicated. But all complications involve decisions, and a person must assess the probabilities and possibilities, make the best decision and then go down the street whistling."

After listening to his patients relating "games" for some thirty years, Berne decided to gather certain of these breezily-named games into a catalog. At first *Games People Play* was not a success. But three years after its publication, following much word-of-mouth praise, it set a record for remaining on the best-seller list longer than any other nonfictional work in the past ten years and sold over 2,500,000 copies.

Games People Play caused the more staid members of Berne's profession to wince at what they believed to be facile explanations of human interactions. A *Times Literary Supplement* reviewer called the book "little more than psychiatric gimmickry, a parlour game foisted upon the social exchanges common in daily life. . . . By no stretch of the imagination can the book be regarded as a contribution to psychological or psychiatric theory." Other reviewers, such as Ian Jeffries, found the book "fascinating and instructive." Jeffries added: "The question that arises is whether the author has made a real contribution to psychology: and the surprising answer, I think, is that he has. Not only does he offer a thesaurus of social transactions with their explanations and titles, but he does so in a way that makes social learning or training in group psychology quicker and less painful processes. The actual correctness of his scheme is more difficult to judge, but what he says is plausible." In 1967, Berne explained the book's success: "It's the recognition factor—some of us recognize ourselves, some recognize other people."

In many of his writings Berne advanced a theory which he called "transactional analysis," and which one young psychiatrist believes to be "an offshoot of psychoanalysis. It's a useful method of treatment, but it's thoroughly grounded in Freud." Transactions, according to Berne, are "the overt manifestations of social intercourse." Jack Langguth summarized Berne's method of analyzing these transactions: "Where Freud probed forces below the conscious level, Dr. Berne deals chiefly with the three 'different and inconsistent' selves—or ego states—that he believes alternate in speaking for each person. First there is the ego state which 'resembles that of parental figures.' The Parent, at its most benevolent, is the confident self that knows which fork to use, which temptations to resist. At worst, the Parent may crush all joyousness. . . . Second there is the ego state which 'is autonomously directed toward objective appraisal of reality.' This is the Adult. . . . Third, the ego state which 'was fixated in early childhood.'. . . The Child may be charming in its spontaneity or embarrassing in its willful folly." The objective of transactional analysis is to assist the patient in programming his personality in order to allow the proper ego state to function at the proper time. As Berne once put it: "We want to turn frogs into princes. We're not satisfied with making them braver frogs."

MEDIA ADAPTATIONS: A musical comedy version of *Games People Play* was adapted for Broadway production by Cy Feuer and Ernest Martin.

BIOGRAPHICAL/CRITICAL SOURCES:

PERIODICALS

American Journal of Public Health, November, 1963.
American Journal of Sociology, May, 1964.
Life, December 18, 1970.
Newsday, November 28, 1970.
New Statesman, April 29, 1966.
New York Times, July 16, 1970, July 17, 1972.
New York Times Book Review, April, 1967, October 8, 1967, May 11, 1969.
New York Times Magazine, July 17, 1966.
Times Literary Supplement, June 30, 1966.
Tulane Drama Review, summer, 1967.

* * *

BERNHARD, Thomas   1931-1989

PERSONAL: Born September 11, 1931, in Heerland, Holland; grandson of Johannes Freumbichler (a carpenter); emigrated to Austria; died February 12 (exact date unknown), 1989 in Gmunden, Austria, of apparent heart failure. *Education:* Studied music in Vienna and Salzburg.

ADDRESSES: Office—c/o Alfred A. Knopf, Inc., 201 East 50th St., New York, N.Y. 10022.

CAREER: Novelist, dramatist, poet, and journalist. Has worked as a court reporter, critic, and librarian.

AWARDS, HONORS: Bremen Prize, 1965; Austrian State Prize for Literature, 1967; Wildgans Prize, 1968; George Buechner Prize from German Academy of Language and Literature, 1970; Grillparzer Prize, 1971; Seguier Prize, 1974.

WRITINGS:

IN ENGLISH

Vestoerung (novel; title means "Perturbation"), Insel, 1967, translation by Richard Wilson and Clara Wilson published as *Gargoyles,* Knopf, 1970, University of Chicago Press, 1986.
Das Kalkwerk (novel), Suhrkamp, 1970, translation by Sophie Wilkins published as *The Lime Works,* Random House, 1973, University of Chicago Press, 1986.

Die Macht der Gewohnheit: Komoedie (play; also see below; first produced in Salzburg, 1974), Suhrkamp, 1974, translation by Neville Plaice and Stephen Plaice published as *The Force of Habit: A Comedy,* (produced in London, 1976), Heinemann Educational, 1976, text edition published as *Die Salzburger Stucke* (title means "National Theatre Plays: The Force of Habit, a Comedy.")
Der Praesident (title means "The President"), Suhrkamp, 1975, translation by Gitta Honegger published as *The President and Eve of Retirement: Two Plays,* Performing Arts Journal, 1982.
Korrektur (novel), Suhrkamp, 1975, translation by Wilkins published as *Correction,* Knopf, 1979.
Vor dem Ruhestand (play; title means "Before Retirement"; first produced in Bochom, 1980, English version produced as "Eve of Retirement" in Minneapolis, 1982), Suhrkamp, 1979.
Beton (title means "Concrete"), Suhrkamp, 1983, translation by David McLintock published as *Concrete,* Knopf, 1984.
Gathering Evidence: A Memoir, translation by McLintock, Knopf, 1986.
Wittgenstein's Neffe: Eine Freundschaft (autobiographical; title means "Wittgenstein's Nephew: A Friendship"), 1983, translation by McLintock published as *Wittgenstein's Nephew: A Novel,* Knopf, 1989.
Holzfaellen, Suhrkamp, 1984, translation by McLintock published as *The Woodcutters,* Knopf, 1988.

OTHER

Auf der Erde und in der Hoelle (poetry; title means "On Earth and in Hell"), Mueller (Salzburg), 1957.
Unter dem Eisen des Mondes (poetry; title means "Under the Iron of the Moon"), Kipenheuer & Witsch, 1958.
In hora mortis (poetry; title means "In the Hour of Death"), Mueller, 1958.
Die Rosen der Einoede: fuenf Saetze fuer Ballet, Stimmen und Orchester, S. Fischer, 1959.
Frost (novel), Insel, 1963.
Amras (prose), Suhrkamp, 1967.
Prosa, Suhrkamp, 1967.
Ungemach (prose; title means "Trouble"), Suhrkamp, 1968.
Watten: ein Nachlass (prose; title means "Mudflats"), Suhrkamp, 1969.
Ereignisse (title means "Events"), Literarisches Colloquium, 1969.
An der Baumgrenze (novel; title means "At the Timberline"), illustrations by Anton Lehmden, Residenz, 1969.
Ein Fest fuer Boris (play; title means "A Party for Boris"; produced in Hamburg, Germany, 1970), Suhrkamp, 1970.
"Der Berg," published in *Literatur und Kritik,* Number 5, June, 1970.
Gehen, Suhrkamp, 1970.
Midland in Stilfs: Drei Erzaelungen, Suhrkamp, 1970.
Der Italiener (screenplay; title means "The Italian"), Residenz, 1971.
Der Ignorant und der Wahnsinnige (play; first produced in Salzburg, Austria, at Salzburg Festival, 1972; title means "The Ignoramus and the Madman"), Suhrkamp, 1972.
Der Kulterer (screenplay), Residenz, 1974.
Die Jagdgesellschaft (play; title means "The Hunting Party"; first produced in Vienna, 1974), Suhrkamp, 1974.
Die Salzburger Stuecke (also includes *Die Macht der Gewohnheit*), Suhrkamp, 1975.
Die Ursache: Eine Andeutung (autobiographical stories; title means "The Cause"; also see below), Residenz, 1975.

Der Wetterfleck, illustrations by Otto F. Best, Reclam, 1976.

Der Beruehmten (play; title means "The Famous"; first produced at the Burgtheater in Vienna, Austria, 1988), Suhrkamp, 1976.

Der Keller: Eine Entziehung (autobiographical; sequel to *Die Ursache;* title means "The Basement"), Residenz, 1976.

"Heldenplatz" (play; title means "Heroes' Square"), first produced in Vienna, 1976.

Minetti: ein Portrait des Kuenstlers als alter Mann (a play; first produced in Stuttgart, 1976), with photographs by Digne Meller Marcovicz, Suhrkamp, 1977.

Immanuel Kant (a comedy; first produced in Stuttgart, 1978), Suhrkamp, 1978.

Ja, Suhrkamp, 1978.

Der Atem: Eine Entscheidung (autobiographical; sequel to *Der Keller;* title means "The Breath"), Residenz, 1978.

Die Erzaelungen, edited by Ulrich Greiner, Suhrkamp, 1979.

Der Weltverbesserer (play; title means "Worldimprover"; first produced in Bochum, 1980), Suhrkamp, 1979.

Der Stimmenimitator (title means "The Voice-Mime"), Suhrkamp, 1980.

Die Billigesser, Suhrkamp, 1980.

Ueber allen Gipfeln ist Ruh: Ein deutscher Dichtertag um 1980 (play), Suhrkamp, 1981.

Die Kaelt: Eine Isolation (autobiographical; sequel to *Der Atem;* title means "The Cold"), Residenz, 1981.

Am Ziel (play), Suhrkamp, 1981.

Ave Vergil (poems), Suhrkamp, 1981.

Die Untergeher, Suhrkamp, 1983.

Ein Kind (autobiographical; sequel to *Die Kaelt;* title means "A Child"), Residenz, 1983.

Der Schein truegt, Suhrkamp, 1983.

Die Stuecke, 1969-1981, Suhrkamp, 1983.

Der Theatermacher, Suhrkamp, 1984.

Ausloeschung, Suhrkamp, 1986.

Elisabeth II, Suhrkamp, 1987.

Der deutsche Mittagstisch, Suhrkamp, 1988.

Also author of *Die heiligen drei Koenige von St. Vitus* (title means "The Three Wise Men of St. Vitus"), 1955, *Der Schweinehueter* (title means "The Swineherd"), 1956, and *Die Jause* (title means "The Afternoon Snack"), 1965.

SIDELIGHTS: Austrian playwright Thomas Bernhard's pessimistic view of human nature was ever-present in his controversial plays and novels. His works often presented the faults of his culture in a critical light such that he gained a reputation as German literature's most melancholy and bitter writer. Like the works of Mark Twain, Bernhard's later plays were indictments of a culture in decline. His 1984 novel *Holzfaellen* (*The Woodcutters*) was seized by the police because it was thought that it drew an unflattering portrait of a famous Viennese personage. His play "Heldenplatz" ("Heroes' Square"), forthright in its charges that anti-Semitism is widespread in Austria, angered his audiences and the Austrian government, who began to discuss whether or not such work should be censored. Considered by some to be unimportant due to the views he expressed, he was esteemed by others as "one of the greatest writers of the century," notes a writer for the London *Times.*

Many of Bernhard's characters are diseased or disabled. The ringmaster of the circus in *Die Macht der Gewohnheit* (*The Force of Habit*) has a wooden leg; the narrator of *Korrektur* (*Correction*), an idealistic scientist, has a psychotic hatred, and commits suicide. In *Ein Fest fuer Boris,* thirteen legless guests attend a party hosted by a wealthy woman who also has no legs. The woman, misnamed the "Gute" or "Good," is married to Boris,

also legless, who dies while pounding on a drum; because the guests are absorbed in sharing their morbid experiences and dreams with one another, they don't notice the death until the end of the party. "Taken as a whole, the meaning of the play is opaque," wrote a *Books Abroad* reviewer. "Still it communicates messages typical of Thomas Bernhard: life is insufferable, a stifling routine in which human relations are based on mutual hatred and intimidation; social injustice prevails."

Bernhard's novel, *Vestoerung,* translated as *Gargoyles,* revealed Bernhard's belief in the hopelessness of the human condition. In the story, "the patients are the gargoyles of the title and their peculiar arrangements could be well skipped were it not for the brilliance, erudition, and suggestiveness with which Bernhard writes about them," commented a critic in *Antioch Review.* The book was not widely read in the United States, but was very popular in Europe.

Grotesque figures that depict Bernhard's view of human nature appeared often in his other works, as well. The works unanimously stress that man is motivated primarily by madness and disease, noted Martin Esslin in *Modern Drama.* "Life itself is a disease only curable by death. Cripples and madmen merely exhibit, more plainly and therefore perhaps more frankly, what all men suffer from beneath the surface. And even 'genius is a disease,' as the doctor asserts in *The Ignoramus and the Madman,*" Esslin maintained. In *German Life and Letters,* D. A. Craig observed that "the introspective sickness of many of [Bernhard's] characters" indirectly represented the troubles besetting the Austrian people in the wake of two world wars.

Death and disease had always been Bernhard's major concerns. Bernhard's father died just a few years before he himself contracted a lung disease and entered a tuberculosis sanatorium. His mother and grandfather died within the next two years. During these years Bernhard composed his first poems, plays, and short fiction. *Partisan Review* contributor Betty Falkenberg generalized, "all Bernhard's books, all his plays, are really about one thing: death. Death in death, death in life, the futility of all human contact or attempts at understanding, the senselessness of all existence and the cruelty of creating new life, the stupidity of all human beings, the futility of all systems, political or religious, both encompassing as they do the same corruption and stupidity to be found everywhere else." This focus on death paradoxically led his more sensitive characters to an appreciation of the value of commitment; explains Falkenberg, "If there is one thing that can bind people together . . . it can only be the awareness of the total hopelessness of all human endeavor in the light of the fact of death."

Though Bernhard's works express the same themes, they do so by means of a variety of unusual techniques. For example, the novel *Das Kalkwerk* (*The Lime Works*) is narrated by a life-insurance salesman who weaves the story from rumors about a frustrated Austrian writer who has blasted his crippled wife in the head with a shot from her own rifle. "The book is a jungle of meaning, the opposite of simplistic allegory, and a major achievement because of this. . . . *The Lime Works* invites comparison with the run-on novels of Beckett," a *New Republic* reviewer wrote. Ronald De Feo concluded in *National Review* that in this book Bernhard had again demonstrated that he was "one of the most substantive and intense" among German writers.

Bernhard's facility with a variety of techniques brought him the ongoing appreciation of writers and critics. Between 1960 and 1980, he won a number of literary prizes, including the Austrian State Prize for Literature in 1967. American critics valued the masterful style in which he couched his social criticism. Of *The*

Woodcutters, a novel in which the narrator deflates the pretentiousness of local artists, *New York Times Book Review* contributor Mark Anderson commented, "What raises this denunciation of Austria's cultural parochialism above the level of mere satire is Mr. Bernhard's supremely ironic tone of voice and musical sensibility. The narrator's own credibility is constantly undermined by the anxious excessiveness of his attacks, which one gradually comes to see as being aimed as much at himself and his own fear of death as at the guests."

In *The Woodcutters,* a dinner party for artists and intellectuals is the springboard from which the narrator, a vituperative artist largely isolated from the others, berates them in a manner that begins to sound unsound. Part of the attraction for readers is the question of the narrator's reliability as he recounts observations based on thirty years experience with the aristocrats of culture. In this novel, said Coates, Bernhard "comes close to the novelist's ideal of making every gesture meaningful, bathing it in a garish light from the past whose quality of illumination we can never entirely trust." Richard Eder of the *Los Angeles Times* praised the novel's finish, in which the narrator demonstrates that he practices the same kind of pretention that so offends him in the others. Though the reviewer would have liked to see the revelation come sooner, "It is an abrupt reversal, and startlingly effective," he remarked.

Critics also admired Bernhard's mature prose for achieving its effects in the same way that music does. Coates explained that all Bernhard's work shows his training in music. "His books embody such musical values as counterpoint, fugue, leit-motif and harmony, and in at least two of them a play-within-the-novel obliquely reflects on the action." For these reasons and more, *The Woodcutters,* said Martin Seymour-Smith in a *Washington Post Book World* review, is a representative work that can well serve as an "introduction to Bernhard's work as a whole. Apart from perfectly illustrating his shrewdness, disgruntlement and acute awareness, *Woodcutters* is very funny." The novel's success firmly established Bernhard's reputation as a world class novelist to the extent that in the year before his death, some critics regarded the playwright as a candidate for the Nobel Prize.

Bernhard's depiction of the least admirable facets of human nature endeared him to some readers and enraged others. Some critics pointed out that one need not share Bernhard's views to appreciate his mastery of dramatic and novelistic techniques. Speaking of the later plays which had sharpened into "savage aggression against the public itself," Esslin remarked that what makes the playwright's misanthropic works notable is "the artistry with which these impulses are hammered into shape. Bernhard's theatre is essentially a *mannerist* theatre. If his characters are puppets, all the greater the skill with which they perform their intricate dance; if his subject-matter is venom and derision, all the more admirable the perfection of the language in which the venom is spat out, the intricacy of the pattern it creates."

BIOGRAPHICAL/CRITICAL SOURCES:

BOOKS

Arnold, Heinz Ludwig, editor, *Bernhard,* Boorberg, 1974.
Bernhard, Thomas, *Der Ignorant und der Wahnsinnige* (title means "The Ignoramus and the Madman"), Suhrkamp, 1972.
Bernhard, *Die Ursache: Eine Andeutung,* Residenz, 1975.
Bernhard, *Der Keller: Eine Entziehung,* Residenz, 1976.
Bernhard, *Der Atem: Eine Entscheidung,* Residenz, 1978.
Bernhard, *Die Kaelte: Eine Isolation,* Residenz, 1981.
Bernhard, *Ein Kind,* Residenz, 1982.

Bernhard, *Wittgenstein's Neffe: Eine Freundschaft,* Suhrkamp, 1983.
Bernhard, *Gathering Evidence: A Memoir,* translation by David McLintock, Knopf, 1986.
Botond, Anneliese, editor, *Ueber Bernhard,* Suhrkamp, 1970.
Calandra, Denis, *New German Dramatists,* Macmillan, 1983.
Contemporary Literary Criticism, Gale, Volume 3, 1975, Volume 32, 1985.
Dittmar, Jens, *Bernhard Wergeschichte,* Suhrkamp, 1981.
Sorg, Bernard, *Bernhard,* Beck, 1977.

PERIODICALS

Antioch Review, fall, 1970.
Booklist, February 15, 1971, July 15, 1975.
Book World, January 3, 1971.
Chicago Tribune, February 24, 1989.
German Life and Letters, July, 1972.
Globe and Mail (Toronto), August 18, 1984.
Los Angeles Times, January 20, 1988.
Modern Austrian Literature, Number 11, 1978, Number 12, 1979.
Modern Drama, January, 1981.
National Review, February 1, 1974.
New Republic, December, 1973.
New York Times Book Review, July 1, 1984, February 19, 1989.
Partisan Review, Volume 47, number 2, 1980.
Saturday Review, October 31, 1970.
Times Literary Supplement, February 12, 1971, September 29, 1972, February 13, 1976, June 11, 1976.
Tribune Books (Chicago), January 31, 1988.
Washington Post Book World, April 17, 1988, February 19, 1989, March 5, 1989.
World Literature Today, summer, 1977, winter, 1978.

OBITUARIES:

PERIODICALS

Chicago Tribune, February 17, 1989.
Los Angeles Times, February 17, 1989.
New York Times, February 17, 1989.
New York Times Book Review, February 14, 1989.
Times (London), February 17, 1989.
Washington Post, February 21, 1989.

*   *   *

BERRY, Jonas
See ASHBERY, John (Lawrence)

*   *   *

BERRYMAN, John 1914-1972

PERSONAL: Surname originally Smith; name changed upon adoption by mother's second husband, John A. Berryman; born October 25, 1914, in McAlester, Okla.; committed suicide by jumping off a bridge, January 7, 1972, in Minneapolis, Minn.; son of John Allyn (a banker) and Martha (a teacher; maiden name, Little) Smith; married Eileen Mulligan, October 24, 1942 (divorced, 1953); married Ann Levine, 1956 (divorced, 1959); married Kate Donahue, 1961; children: (second marriage) Paul; (third marriage) Martha, Sara. *Education:* Columbia University, A.B., 1936; Clare College, Cambridge, B.A., 1938.

ADDRESSES: Home—33 Arthur Ave. S.E., Minneapolis, Minn. 55414. *Office*— Department of Humanities, University of Minnesota, Minneapolis, Minn.

CAREER: Wayne University (now Wayne State), Detroit, Mich., instructor in English, 1939-40; Harvard University, Cambridge, Mass., instructor, 1940-43; Princeton University, Princeton, N.J., fellow, 1943-44, lecturer in creative writing, 1946-49, Hodder fellow, 1950-51; University of Cincinnati, Cincinnati, Ohio, Elliston Lecturer in Poetry, 1951-52; University of Minnesota, Minneapolis, 1955-72, began as lecturer, became Regents Professor of Humanities. Lecturer at numerous colleges and universities; poet-in-residence, Trinity College, 1967; made U.S. State Department tour to India to read poetry.

MEMBER: National Institute of Arts and Letters, American Academy of Arts and Sciences, Phi Beta Kappa.

AWARDS, HONORS: Kellett fellowship from Columbia University, 1936-38, to study at Clare College; Oldham Shakespeare Scholar, Clare College, 1937; Rockefeller fellow, 1944-46; *Kenyon Review*-Doubleday short story award, 1945, for "The Imaginary Jew"; Shelley Memorial Award, Poetry Society of America, 1949; Levinson Prize, 1950; National Institute of Arts and Letters grant in literature, 1950; Guggenheim fellow, 1952-53 and 1966; *Partisan Review* fellowship, 1957; Harriet Monroe Poetry Award, University of Chicago, 1957; Brandeis University Creative Arts Award, 1959-60; Loines Award, National Institute of Arts and Letters, 1964; Pulitzer Prize, 1965, for *77 Dream Songs;* Academy of American Poets fellowship, 1966; National Endowment for the Arts award, 1967; Emily Clark Balch Award, *Virginia Quarterly Review,* 1968; Bollingen Prize and National Book Award, both 1969, for *His Toy, His Dream, His Rest;* received honorary degrees from Cambridge University and Drake University.

WRITINGS:

POETRY

(Contributor) *Five Young American Poets,* New Directions, 1940.
Poems, New Directions, 1942.
The Dispossessed, Sloane, 1948.
Homage to Mistress Bradstreet, Farrar, Straus, 1956 (published in England as *Homage to Mistress Bradstreet, and Other Poems,* Faber, 1959).
His Thought Made Pockets and the Plane Buckt, C. Fredericks, 1958.
77 Dream Songs, Farrar, Straus, 1964.
Short Poems (includes *The Dispossessed* and *His Thoughts Made Pockets and the Plane Buckt*), Farrar, Straus, 1967.
Berryman's Sonnets, Farrar, Straus, 1967.
I Have Moved to Dublin . . ., Graduates Club (Dublin), 1967.
His Toy, His Dream, His Rest (sequel to *77 Dream Songs*), Farrar, Straus, 1968.
The Dream Songs (includes *77 Dream Songs* and *His Toy, His Dream, His Rest*), Farrar, Straus, 1969.
Love and Fame, Farrar, Straus, 1970, revised edition, 1972.
Delusions, Etc., Farrar, Straus, 1972.
Selected Poems, 1938-1968, Faber, 1972.
Henry's Fate and Other Poems, 1967-1972, edited by John Haffenden, Farrar, Strauss, 1977.
Collected Poems, 1937-1971, edited with introduction by Charles Thornbury, Farrar, Strauss, 1988.

OTHER

Stephen Crane (biography), Sloane, 1950.
(Author of introduction) Mathew Gregory Lewis, *The Monk,* Grove, 1952.
(Editor) Thomas Nash, *Unfortunate Traveller; or, The Life of Jack Wilton,* Putnam, 1960.

(Editor with Ralph Ross and Allen Tate) *The Arts of Reading,* Crowell, 1960.
(Contributor) Howard Nemerov, editor, *Poets on Poetry,* Basic Books, 1966.
Recovery (novel), Farrar, Straus, 1973.
The Freedom of the Poet, Farrar, Straus, 1976.
Stephen Crane: The Red Badge of Courage, Aquila, 1981.
We Dream of Honor: John Berryman's Letters to His Mother, edited by Richard J. Kelly, Norton, 1988.

Contributor to *Southern Review, Kenyon Review, Partisan Review, Nation, New Republic, New Yorker, Accent, Saturday Review, Poetry,* and other periodicals.

WORK IN PROGRESS: A critical biography of Shakespeare, a life of Christ, and a "semi-autobiographical novel."

SIDELIGHTS: Edmund Wilson and Frank Kermode hailed *Homage to Mistress Bradstreet* as the most important work of poetry since T. S. Eliot's *The Waste Land* and *Four Quartets.* Philip Toynbee believes that Berryman and Robert Lowell "have become the most prominent American poets since the recent deaths of Robert Frost, William Carlos Williams, and Theodore Roethke." When *77 Dream Songs* was published, Lowell called it even greater than *Homage to Mistress Bradstreet.* The dream songs "are dazzling even when they befuddle," writes Frederick Seidel. "But Berryman's mature work is always at least dazzling. One takes enormous pleasure just in the expertise. Here are wonderfully intelligent, witty line-breaks that win one's devotion and get memorized like poems. The unmistakable Berryman rhythm, that came into its own in his great *Homage to Mistress Bradstreet,* is less regular and grand now; it calms or swells within a shorter stanza and within a single eighteen-line song. The rhythm is jazzier, odder, more insisted upon and shown off; a syncopation almost." The idiom is entirely his own, "one of the few unmistakable dictions in modern poetry," according to the *Times Literary Supplement.* Always flexible, at times distorted and experimental, it "puns and plays and twists with words in a dreamlike manner reminiscent of Joyce and Cummings, yet quite Berryman's own," writes Louis L. Martz.

M. L. Rosenthal believes that with *77 Dream Songs* Berryman "seriously enters the post-war current of confessional poetry, distinctive for its naked accounts of private suffering, and represented by such poets as Robert Lowell and W. D. Snodgrass. Berryman is the first poet (except Allen Ginsberg, whom he resembles more than he would like to think, perhaps, but whose writing is essentially of a different cast) to pick up Mr. Lowell's cues on so sweeping a scale." However, unlike most confessional poets, Berryman's songs are often surrealistic. Fred Bornhauser writes: "What would be in other poetry the subtle nuance of feeling is here the hush and slush of painful echo drawing nearer. With the impudence of Auden, the boisterous humor of Joyce, the bluntness of Pound, the exoticism of Stevens, the formal freedom of Cummings, and the imaginative flair of Nabokov in his prose, Berryman has composed spontaneous and staggering verses which demand and deserve a like response."

As Seidel observes, "the humor [in *77 Dream Songs*] is wonderful, . . . doing for poetry what William Burroughs, in the Dr. Benway passages of *Naked Lunch,* did for the comic novel." The *Times Literary Supplement* reviewer writes: "The seventy-seven ways of triangulating early twentieth-century existence add up to a complex humility, a vigorous, humorous, vicious and disturbing entertainment, whose degree of moral criticism stems from one rather middle-aged virtue—'one virtue, without which a man can hardly hold his own,' which is 'that a man should always reproach himself. . . .' Mr. Berryman is truly his own 'weary daring man,' 'roiling and babbling & braining.' He has made a tough coherent work, the saga of a de-classed intellectual Prufrock in mid-century."

BIOGRAPHICAL/CRITICAL SOURCES:

BOOKS

Concise Dictionary of American Literary Biography: The New Consciousness: 1941-1968, Gale, 1987.
Contemporary Literary Criticism, Gale, Volume 1, 1973, Volume 2, 1974, Volume 3, 1975, Volume 4, 1975, Volume 13, 1980, Volume 25, 1983.
Dictionary of Literary Biography, Volume 48: *American Poets, 1880-1945, Second Series,* Gale, 1986.
Kelly, R. J., *John Berryman: A Checklist,* Scarecrow, 1972.

PERIODICALS

American Scholar, autumn, 1965.
Atlantic, January, 1965.
Books and Bookmen, January, 1965.
Chelsea, June, 1968.
Encounter, March, 1965.
Life, July 21, 1967.
Minnesota Review, January-April, 1965.
Nation, February 24, 1969.
New Leader, December 2, 1968.
New Statesman, January 15, 1965.
New York Review of Books, June 29, 1967.
New York Times, January 8, 1972.
New York Times Book Review, October 8, 1989.
Poetry, January, 1965.
Reporter, March 25, 1965.
Virginia Quarterly Review, winter, 1965.
Yale Review, winter, 1965, spring, 1969.

* * *

BESTER, Alfred 1913-1987

PERSONAL: Born December 18, 1913, in New York, N.Y.; died in Doylestown, Pa., c. October, 1987; son of James J. (a shoe merchant) and Belle (Silverman) Bester; married Rolly Goulko (an advertising executive), September 16, 1936. *Education:* University of Pennsylvania, B.A., 1935. *Politics:* "Emotional liberal." *Religion:* "Born Jewish but Animist by faith."

ADDRESSES: Home—P.O. Box 202, Ottsville, Pa. 18942. *Agent*—Kirby McCauley, Ltd., 425 Park Ave. S., New York, N.Y. 10016.

CAREER: Free-lance writer in the 1940s and 1950s; editor of several popular magazines from the mid-1950s to the early 1970s, became senior editor of *Holiday* magazine; full-time writer beginning about 1972.

MEMBER: Science Fiction Writers of America.

AWARDS, HONORS: Hugo Award for best novel, Science Fiction Writers of America, 1953, for *The Demolished Man.*

WRITINGS:

Who He? (satirical novel), Dial, 1953 (published in England as *The Rat Race,* Panther, 1959).
The Life and Death of a Satellite (nonfiction), Sidgwick & Jackson, 1967.
(Contributor) Brian W. Aldiss and Harry Harrison, editors, *Hell's Cartographers: Some Personal Histories of Science Fiction Writers* (nonfiction), Harper, 1975.

(Contributor) Andrew Porter, editor, *Experiment Perilous,* Algol Press, 1976.

SCIENCE FICTION

The Demolished Man (novel), Shasta Publications, 1953, new edition, edited by Lester Del Rey, Garland Publishing, 1975.
Tiger! Tiger! (novel), Sidgwick & Jackson, 1955, reprinted, Penguin, 1974, published as *The Stars My Destination,* New American Library, 1957, illustrated edition, edited by H. V. Chaykin, published in two volumes, Baronet, 1979.
Starburst (short stories), New American Library, 1958.
The Dark Side of the Earth (short stories), New American Library, 1964.
An Alfred Bester Omnibus, Sidgwick & Jackson, 1967.
The Computer Connection (novel), Berkley Publishing, 1975 (published in England as *Extro,* Eyre Methuen, 1975).
The Great Short Fiction of Alfred Bester, Berkley Publishing, Volume I: *The Light Fantastic,* 1976, Volume II: *Star Light, Star Bright,* 1976, published in one volume as *Starlight: The Great Short Fiction of Alfred Bester,* 1977.
Golem 100 (novel), Simon & Schuster, 1980.
The Deceivers (novel), Pinnacle Books, 1982.
The Rat Race (novel), Arrow, 1974.

Also author of comic scenarios in the 1940s, including "Superman" and "Batman"; author of radio scripts in the 1940s, including "Charlie Chan" and "The Shadow"; author of television scripts. Author of English libretti for Giuseppe Verdi's "La Traviata" and Modest Petrovich Moussorgsky's "The Fair at Sorochinsk." Contributor to periodicals, including *Holiday, Omni, Show, Venture,* and *Rogue.*

SIDELIGHTS: Although Alfred Bester published relatively little science fiction, wrote William L. Godshalk in the *Dictionary of Literary Biography,* "his impact on the genre has been enormous." He was "a science-fiction writer's writer," Peter Nicholls commented in *Washington Post Book World.* "He has been much admired by the old wave, the hard science men . . . but equally a hero to the young turks of the 1960s new wave, the writers of the left, the people who think that inner space has just as much to do with [science fiction] as outer space."

Bester established his reputation in his earliest science fiction novels *The Demolished Man* and *The Stars My Destination,* works described by Bud Foote in the *Detroit News* as recognized science fiction classics. *The Demolished Man* was Foote's introduction to "the not-yet-christened New Wave," and he points out that it was the first novel to win the newly-created Hugo Award. Bester's *The Stars My Destination* was "said by many people to be the best science fiction novel ever written," T. A. Shippey related in the *Times Literary Supplement.* Bester turned away from science fiction while editing and contributing to *Holiday* magazine, but his reputation remained intact. Nicholls wrote that within the science-fiction genre Bester was "never . . . prolific, merely revolutionary."

Much of Bester's appeal is attributed to his eclecticism. In the opinion of *Village Voice* reviewer Robert Morales, for example, "*The Stars My Destination*—an incredible takeoff on *The Count of Monte Cristo,* and James Joyce pastiche—burlesqued the adventure novel into high art. Both story and novel excel in sheer lunatic excitement." Nicholls called the book's main character "the archetypal Besterman, the 20th-century, pulp equivalent of the malcontent of Jacobean revenge dramas, brooding, sardonic, obsessed and murderous—at once ironic commentator and brutal actor in a dark, amoral world." Bester was "no unconscious myth-maker," Gerald Jonas noted in the *New York Times Book Review.* "He manipulates archetypal themes openly, zestfully, yet with an undertone of self-mockery, as if to let us know that he realizes the absurdity of his enterprise." Godshalk agreed that "his finest work is characterized by a serious playfulness."

The Computer Connection, for instance, was summarized by Godshalk as "a first-person narrative dictated to a diary-computer." In that novel, wrote Jonas, Bester's "premises are so fantastic, his characters are so eccentric, his writing is so breathless that his work must either be swallowed whole, or rejected in its entirety." And, according to Godshalk, the novel *Golem 100,* is an attempt "to explode the parameters of print by combining words, musical scores, and graphics in order to create a new technique of synesthetic visio-narration. The experiment is successful because Bester links new techniques with traditional form."

Bester's writing is distinctive, however, in that it is not "technically oriented science fiction; [Bester's] scientific gadgetry is often not explained, and scientific developments—such as the terraforming of Venus and Mars—are left to the reader's imagination," Godshalk reported. "These are the givens of his fiction, and little is made of them. . . . A more important assumption of his fictive world is that man can develop unusual powers—telepathy, teleportation, and physical immortality—under unusual stress, and that once developed, these powers can be taught to others. . . . Best emphasizes transformation through crisis, evolution through catastrophe."

The author, Godshalk concluded, "has remained constant in his concern with the basics of human passion and personal change. Technically he is an experimenter, and his influence can be charted in the works of such writers as John Brunner, Robert Silverberg, Clifford D. Simak, and Kurt Vonnegut, Jr."

The Demolished Man has been translated into Portuguese; *The Stars My Destination* has been translated into French.

BIOGRAPHICAL/CRITICAL SOURCES:

BOOKS

Clareson, Thomas, editor, *SF: The Other Side of Realism,* Bowling Green University, 1971.
Dictionary of Literary Biography, Volume 8: *Twentieth-Century American Science Fiction Writers,* Gale, 1981.
Platt, Charles, interviewer, *Dream Makers: The Uncommon People Who Write Science Fiction,* Berkeley Publishing, 1980.
Scholes, Robert, and Eric S. Rabkin, editors, *Science Fiction: History, Science, Vision,* Oxford University Press, 1977.
Schweitzer, Darrell, interviewer, *Sf Voices,* TK Graphics, 1976.
Spinrad, Norman, editor, *Modern Science Fiction,* Anchor Press, 1974.
Wendell, Carolyn, *Alfred Bester,* Starmont House, 1982.

PERIODICALS

Detroit News, July 27, 1980.
Extrapolation, May, 1975.
New York Times Book Review, July 20, 1975, September 14, 1980.
Riverside Quarterly, August, 1972.
Times Literary Supplement, December 5, 1975.
Village Voice, May 26, 1980.
Washington Post Book World, May 25, 1980, July 26, 1987.
West Coast Review of Books, September, 1982.

OBITUARIES:

PERIODICALS

Times, October 22, 1987.

*   *   *

BETHLEN, T. D.
   See SILVERBERG, Robert

*   *   *

BETI, Mongo
   See BIYIDI, Alexandre

*   *   *

BETJEMAN, John   1906-1984
   (Epsilon, Richard M. Farren)

PERSONAL: Born August 28, 1906, in Highgate, London, England; died after a long battle with Parkinson's Disease, May 19, 1984, in Trebetherick, Cornwall, England; son of Ernest Edward (a merchant and manufacturer) and Mabel (Dawson) Betjeman; married Penelope Valentine Hester Chetwode, 1932; children: Paul, Candida. *Education:* Attended Marlborough College, Oxford, 1925-27, and Magdalen College, Oxford, 1925-28. *Religion:* Church of England.

ADDRESSES: Home—The Mead, Wantage, Berkshire, England.

CAREER: After leaving school taught cricket and English at a London school; worked as an insurance broker; United Kingdom press attache, Dublin, Ireland, 1941-42; held a post with the British Admiralty, London, 1944; served with British Council, 1944-46. In October, 1972, Queen Elizabeth II appointed him Poet Laureate of England succeeding C. Day Lewis. Member of Royal Fine Arts Commission; governor of Pusey House.

MEMBER: Royal Society of Literature (fellow; Companion of Literature, 1968), Royal Institute of British Architects (honorary associate), American Academy of Arts and Letters (honorary member, 1973), Victorian Society (founder); Athenaeum, Beefsteak Club, Kildare Street Club (Dublin).

AWARDS, HONORS: Heinemann Award, 1948, for *Selected Poems;* Foyle Poetry Prize, 1955, for *A Few Late Chrysanthemums,* and 1959, for *Collected Poems;* Russell Loins Memorial Fund award, 1956; Duff Cooper Prize for *Collected Poems;* Queen's gold medal for poetry, 1960, for *Collected Poems;* Commander, Order of British Empire, 1960; knighted, 1969; D.Litt., University of Reading, University of Birmingham; LL.D., Aberdeen University.

WRITINGS:

VERSE

Mount Zion; or, In Touch with the Infinite, James Press, 1931.
Continual Dew: A Little Book of Bourgeois Verse, J. Murray, 1937.
(Under pseudonym Epsilon) *Sir John Piers,* Westmeath Examiner (Mullingar, Ireland), 1938.
Old Lights for New Chancels: Verses Topographical and Amatory, J. Murray, 1940.
New Bats in Old Belfries: Poems by John Betjeman, J. Murray, 1945.
Slick but Not Streamlined: Poems and Short Pieces, selected and with an introduction by W. H. Auden, Doubleday, 1947.

Selected Poems, compiled with an introduction by John Sparrow, J. Murray, 1948.

St. Katherine's Church, Chiselhampton, Oxfordshire: Verses Turned in Aid of a Public Subscription Towards the Restoration of the Church of St. Katherine, Chiselhampton, [Chiselhampton], 1950.

A Few Late Chrysanthemums: New Poems, J. Murray, 1954, Transatlantic, 1954.

Poems in the Porch, S.P.C.K., 1954.

Collected Poems, compiled and with an introduction by the Earl of Birkenhead, J. Murray, 1958, Houghton, 1959, enlarged edition, J. Murray, 1962, 3rd enlarged edition published as *John Betjeman's Collected Poems,* 1970, Houghton, 1971, 4th edition, J. Murray, 1980.

John Betjeman (selected poems), E. Hulton, 1958.

Poems, Vista Books, 1960.

Summoned by Bells (autobiography in verse), Houghton, 1960, new edition, J. Murray, 1976.

A Ring of Bells, selected with an introduction by Irene Slade, J. Murray, 1962, Houghton, 1963.

High and Low, J. Murray, 1966, Houghton, 1967.

Six Betjeman Songs, music by Mervyn Horder, Duckworth, 1967.

A Nip in the Air, J. Murray, 1975, Norton, 1976.

Betjeman in Miniature: Selected Poems of Sir John Betjeman, Gleniffer Press, 1976.

Metro-land, Warren, 1977.

The Best of Betjeman, selected by John Guest, J. Murray, 1978.

Church Poems, J. Murray, 1981.

Uncollected Poems, J. Murray, 1982.

WORKS ON ARCHITECTURE

Ghastly Good Taste; or, A Depressing Story of the Rise and Fall of English Architecture, Chapman & Hall, 1933, St. Martin's, 1971, reprinted, David & Charles, 1986.

An Oxford University Chest, illustrated by L. Moholy-Nagy and others, J. Miles, 1938.

Antiquarian Prejudice, Hogarth Press, 1939.

Cities and Small Towns ("Britain in Pictures" series), Collins, 1943.

English Cities and Small Towns, Collins, 1943.

First and Last Loves, J. Murray, 1952, Soccer, 1962.

The English Town in the Last Hundred Years (Rede Lecture), Cambridge University Press, 1956.

(Under pseudonym Richard M. Farren) *Ground Plan to Skyline,* Newman Neame, 1960.

The City of London Churches, Pitkin Pictorials, 1965.

Ten Wren Churches, illustrated by R. Beer, Editions Electo, 1970.

A Pictorial History of English Architecture, Macmillan, 1972.

London's Historic Railway Stations, Transatlantic, 1972.

West Country Churches, Society of SS Peter and Paul, 1973.

EDITOR

Shell Guide to Cornwall, Architectural Press, 1934, published as *Cornwall Illustrated,* Architectural Press, 1935, revised edition published as *Cornwall: A Shell Guide,* Faber, 1964.

Cornwall Illustrated in a Series of Views, Architectural Press, 1934.

Devon Shell Guide, Architectural Press, 1936, revised edition, Faber, 1955.

(With Geoffrey Taylor) *English, Scottish, and Welsh Landscape, 1700-c. 1860,* Muller, 1944.

Watergate Children's Classics, Watergate Classics (London), 1947.

(With John Piper) *Murray's Buckinghamshire Architectural Guide,* J. Murray, 1948.

(With Piper) *Murray's Berkshire Architectural Guide,* J. Murray, 1949.

(With Piper) *Shropshire: A Shell Guide,* Faber, 1951.

(With Taylor, and contributor) *English Love Poems,* Faber, 1957.

An American's Guide to English Parish Churches, Including the Isle of Man, McDowell, Obolensky, 1958 (published in England as *Collins Guide to English Parish Churches,* Collins, 1958, revised edition, 1959, subsequent revised editions published as *Collins Pocket Guide to English Parish Churches,* Volume 1: *The North,* Volume 2: *The South,* 1968.

Altar and Pew: Church of England Verses, E. Hulton, 1959.

(With Winnifred Hindley) *A Wealth of Poetry,* Blackwell, 1963.

(And author of introduction) Charles Tennyson Turner, *A Hundred Sonnets,* Hart-Davis, 1960, Dufour, 1961.

(And author of introduction and commentaries) *Victorian and Edwardian London from Old Photographs,* Viking, 1969.

(With David Vaisey) *Victorian and Edwardian Oxford from Old Photographs,* Batsford, 1971.

(With J. S. Gay) *Victorian and Edwardian Brighton from Old Photographs,* Batsford, 1972.

General editor of "Shell Guides" series, Architectural Press, 1934-64.

OTHER

(Author of introduction) Henry J. Newbolt, *Selected Poems,* Nelson, 1940.

Vintage London, Collins, 1942.

John Piper, Penguin, 1944.

(Contributor) Walter James Turner, editor, *A Panorama of Rural England,* Chantecleer Press/Hastings House, 1944.

(Contributor) Turner, editor, *The Englishman's Country,* Collins, 1945.

(Contributor) *Studies in the History of Swindon,* [Swindon], 1950.

The English Scene: A Reader's Guide (includes reading list by L. Russell Muirhead), Cambridge University Press for the National Book League, 1951.

(Contributor) *Gala Day London,* Harvill, 1953.

(Author of introduction) William Purcell, *Onward Christian Soldier,* Longmans, 1957.

(Illustrator) Basil Fulford Lowther Clarke, *English Churches,* London House & Markwell, 1964.

(Contributor) *Moments of Truth* (poetry), privately printed, [London], 1965.

(Contributor) Greater London Council, Historic Buildings Board, *Do You Care About Historic Buildings?,* [London], 1970.

(Contributor) *The Twelfth Man* (in honor of Prince Philip's 50th birthday), Cassell, 1971.

(Contributor) Robin Maugham, *The Barrier,* W. H. Allen, 1973.

A Plea for Holy Trinity Church, Sloan Street, Church Union, 1974.

John Betjeman's Oxford, Oxford University Press, 1980.

Lord Mount Prospect, Tragara Press, 1981.

(Contributor) *Likes and Dislikes: A Private Anthology,* Tragara Press, 1981.

Betjeman's Cornwall, J. Murray, 1984.

Betjeman's London, edited by Pennie Denton, J. Murray, 1988.

Member of staff of *Architectural Review;* film critic for *London Evening Standard;* book reviewer, *Daily Herald* (London); book critic, *Daily Telegraph,* 1952; columnist, *Spectator,* 1954-58.

SIDELIGHTS: John Betjeman, Poet Laureate of England until his death in 1984, has been called a "poet of nostalgia." Jocelyn Brooke wrote in *Ronald Firbank and John Betjeman:* "Modern 'progress' is anathema to him, he loathes 'processed' food, plastics, vita-glass, the Welfare State and (one may infer) democracy, though fortunately for us is still able to laugh at them." His technique is not original, though his sensibility is highly so. He can be "lyrically funny." Brooke continued, "Perhaps he can best be described as a writer who uses the medium of light verse for a serious purpose: not merely as a vehicle for satire or social commentary, but as a means of expressing a peculiar and specialized form of aesthetic emotion, in which nostalgia and humour are about equally blended."

"As his commentators generally observe," Ralph J. Mills pointed out in *Descant,* "John Betjeman is a phenomenon in contemporary English literature, a truly popular poet. The sudden fame won by his *Collected Poems* . . . which sold about 100,000 copies, brought him a wide reputation and made him quickly into a public personality." Betjeman was also admired by such poets and critics as W. H. Auden and Edmund Wilson. Mills said: "Certainly it is very rare in our day to see much accord between distinguished critics and poets on the one hand and the general public on the other; but the very complexity of Betjeman's personality and feelings beneath the skillful though apparently simple surface of his verse probably unites, in whatever different kinds of levels of appreciation, the otherwise remote members of his audience."

Mills called Betjeman a "topographical poet," in the sense that his poems that describe some action or event take place in a particular location, which he describes in great detail. The critic declared that "there is further wide attraction in the fact that his poetry is literal and descriptive rather than symbolic; social rather than private; nostalgic-though balanced by humor and occasional irony, as well as a pervasive lightness of touch; beautifully and precisely evocative of place, period, and the moods they generate. And the manner of his poetry is musically graceful and various in form." Although Betjeman named Eliot, Aldous Huxley, and the Sitwells as influences on his poems, "the clearest and strongest line of descent in his writing," Mills stated, "leads back to 18th and 19th century poets such as Cowper, Crabbe, Tennyson, Dowson, Hardy; the Irish poets Tom Moore and William Allingham; and a host of lesser figures."

An architect as well as a poet, Betjeman was aptly praised by W. H. Auden, in the introduction to *Slick But Not Streamlined,* as a topophile, whose poetry is concerned with actual places, to whom "a branch railroad is as valuable as a Roman wall, a neo-Tudor teashop as interesting as a Gothic cathedral." Auden added: "Topophilia . . . cannot survive at velocities greater than that of a somewhat rusty bicycle. (Hence, Betjeman's obsession with that vehicle.)" Betjeman was passionately involved in projects to preserve buildings of architectural or historical interest. He told Willa Petschek that he was even more interested "in saving groups of buildings of towns that can be ruined by 'a single frightful store that looks like a drive-in movie. The only way to prevent more and more ugly buildings going up,' he has said, 'is to draw people's attention to what's good in all periods.' " Betjeman made numerous appearances on television to promote preservation of his various causes, and became, as Petschek said, "a cherished national cult."

Betjeman championed his causes in his poetry as well; he wrote lovingly of the places of his childhood, and buildings and monuments in danger of destruction. Petschek declared that "Betjeman's approach to architecture (which he values second only to poetry) enabled him to recognize the 'living force' of 19th-century buildings, especially the Victorian Gothic. Partly through his verse and topographical writings, his guidebooks, poetry readings and TV appearances, but also through his warmth and peculiar genius for imparting enthusiasm for everything from rood screens to ladies' legs, he has made the public accept a rapid reversal in taste."

"The detailed recreation of the past in *Summoned by Bells,* as well as in briefer poems," Mills wrote, "is evidence of an almost Proustian memory in Betjeman, who confirms this by saying in the poem that 'Childhood is measured out by sounds and smells/ And sights, before the dark of reason grows.' Indeed, his richest imaginative resources seem to lie in the lost worlds of his childhood and early youth, their emerging interests and passionate attachments; they are restored and transformed in his poems." "But the same past, of course," Mills continued, "harbors the origins of the poet's melancholy, guilt, sense of evil, fear of pain and death, and apparent need for a kind of overmastering love; his authentic religious convictions do not develop, however, until quite a bit later . . . the elements in life which hold profound significance and value for him—except his mature Anglican faith—that is to say, his love for poetry and will to be a poet; his sensitive awareness of landscape; his passion for churches, railways, towns, and architecture: all those materials on which his writing thrives initially appealed to him in his youth." Betjeman says in *Summoned by Bells:* "For myself/I knew as soon as I could read and write/That I must be a poet."

Collected Poems, which brought Betjeman into the limelight, was enthusiastically received by many critics, but not by all of them. T. J. Ross wrote: "Though his ear is as flawless as Tennyson's and his effects sometimes are remarkable, Betjeman creates a world which, unlike the Victorian's, is a miniature." Ross believed that when Betjeman involved the reader completely with his subject "the result [was] poor." Only when he kept the reader at a distance did he bring his work up to the level of "first-rate minor art." Thom Gunn called Betjeman's treatment of the middle class "entirely superficial." A *Times Literary Supplement* reviewer wrote: "Whether or not all Mr. Betjeman's verse is poetry, all his poetry is verse, and in this it is a pleasant change from the shapeless and unarticulated matter . . . offered us by so many of his contemporaries. For Mr. Betjeman is a born versifier, ingenious and endlessly original; his echoes of Tennyson and Crabb, Praed and Father Prout, are never mere *pastiche;* and he is always attentive to the sound of his words, the run of his lines, the shape of his stanzas." Louise Bogan had high praise for Betjeman's work: "Since the early thirties, [he] has been producing light verse in which very close to but not crossing the line of parody, he has revived a whole set of emotional attitudes that can only be called Victorian. . . . His verse forms, elaborately varied, reproduce an entire set of neglected Victorian techniques, which he manipulates with the utmost dexterity and taste. His diction and his observation are delightfully fresh and original. And it is a pleasure to let down our defenses and be swept along by his anapaestic lines, with their bouncing unstressed syllables, and to meet no imperfect or false rhymes in the process; to recognize sentiment so delicately shaded, so sincerely felt, that it becomes immediately acceptable even to our modern sensibilities, grown used to the harsh, the violent, and the horrifying. We often, however, come upon a poem that brings us up short, to experience a melancholy, an irony that is close to Hardy or pathos that is timeless. . . . However light his means, his purpose is never trivial."

"John Betjeman has been described," Petschek wrote, "as looking like a highly intelligent muffin: a small, plump, rumpled man with luminous, soft eyes, a chubby face topped by wisps of white hair and imparting a distinct air of absent-mindedness. He has an eager manner, a kind of old-fashioned courtesy and a sudden, schoolboy laugh which crumples his face like a paper bag." Betjeman once owned a waistcoat which once belonged to Henry James. He told Petschek: "Of course, I only wear it for weddings and funerals." In 1957 Petschek wrote: "[Betjeman's] doll's house study is a jumble of books: old copies of verse, typography and ecclesiology and files of correspondence. The walls are covered with red William Morris wallpaper and pictures by Rossetti, John Piper and Sargent. In the corner a 17th-century clock chimes brassily every quarter hour and the telephone rings continually."

Norman wrote that "after a miserable and pestered home life [Betjeman] found Oxford 'too delightful'; he lounged about in a shantung tie and took lavender-perfumed baths, so much so that C. S. Lewis, his tutor, thought him 'a pretentious playboy.' . . . His great love was the revival of the Gothic style in Victorian architecture. Sometimes, driving a car, he would take both hands from the wheel and yell, 'Phew! Gothic.' " Peter Bull, writing in *The Teddy Bear Book,* told of an afternoon that he and his teddy bear, Theodore, were invited to lunch by Betjeman and Archibald Ormsby-Gore, his "Teddy Bear companion for nearly sixty years," of whom Betjeman spoke in *Summoned by Bells.* Bull discovered that Archibald "had Baptist leanings and disapproved strongly of drinking and smoking. This had led to a certain amount of disagreement with Mr. Betjeman. . . . But the two of them get along rather famously on the whole. . . . Baptist or Protestant, Mr. Ormsby-Gore has tremendous personality—not very surprisingly, I suppose—and he has to keep up with his friend Mr. Betjeman, who is one of the most beloved and revered wits in Britain. . . . In the 1968 Summer Academy Exhibition in London an extraordinary picture by Jann Haworth showed [Betjeman] in triplicate as a teddy bear, his face at different angles surrounded by fur. The work was called 'A Valentine to John Betjeman.' "

Betjeman confided to Norman that "All his life . . . he's felt ruin 'very close'; yet the occasional depressions in his poems must not be interpreted as a desperate man's thought. . . . Betjeman says: 'It's a tone of voice—good old English melancholy, like Hardy, Hood and Tennyson—solid village gloom.' "

MEDIA ADAPTATIONS: Recordings by the author of his own work include "The Poems of John Betjeman: The Golden Treasury of John Betjeman," Spoken Arts; "Poems," Argo; "Summoned by Bells," Argo. Donald Swann has set some of Betjeman's poems to music.

BIOGRAPHICAL/CRITICAL SOURCES:

BOOKS

A Garland for the Laureate: Poems Presented to Sir John Betjeman on His 75th Birthday, Celandine Press, 1981.
Betjeman, John, *Slick But Not Streamlined,* introduction by W. H. Auden, Doubleday, 1947.
Brooke, Jocelyn, *Ronald Firbank and John Betjeman,* Longmans, Green, 1962.
Bull, Peter, *The Teddy Bear Book,* Random House, 1970.
Contemporary Literary Criticism, Gale, Volume 2, 1974, Volume 6, 1976, Volume 10, 1979, Volume 34, 1985, Volume 43, 1987.

Delaney, Frank, *Betjeman Country,* J. Murray, 1983.
Dictionary of Literary Biography, Volume 20: *British Poets, 1914-1945,* Gale, 1983.
Dictionary of Literary Biography Yearbook 1984, Gale, 1985.
Stapleton, Margaret L., *Sir John Betjeman: A Bibliography of Writings by and about Him,* Scarecrow Press, 1974.
Stem, Gladys, *And Did He Stop and Speak to You,* Regnery, 1958.

PERIODICALS

Book World, September 15, 1968.
Books and Bookmen, May, 1967.
Christian Century, February 22, 1961, June 5, 1963.
Commonweal, March 3, 1961.
Descant, spring, 1969.
Listener, January 26, 1967.
London Magazine, March, 1967.
New Statesman, December 3, 1960, January 6, 1961, October 3, 1969.
Newsweek, November 28, 1960.
New Yorker, April 18, 1959, September 2, 1967, May 23, 1970.
New York Herald Tribune Lively Arts, December 4, 1960.
New York Review of Books, May 18, 1967.
New York Times Book Review, September 24, 1967, December 7, 1969.
New York Times Magazine, August 13, 1967.
Poetry Review, summer, 1967.
Punch, April 29, 1970.
Spectator, December 2, 1960, April 18, 1970.
Time, February 2, 1959, December 5, 1960, October 23, 1972, December 4, 1972.
Times (London), May 22, 1984.
Times Literary Supplement, December 12, 1958, November 10, 1966, May 21, 1970.

OBITUARIES:

PERIODICALS

Chicago Tribune, May 21, 1984.
Los Angeles Times, May 21, 1984.
New York Times, May 20, 1984.
Sunday Times (London), May 20, 1984.
Time, May 28, 1984.
Times (London), May 21, 1984.
Washington Post, May 20, 1984.

*   *   *

BETTELHEIM, Bruno   1903-1990

PERSONAL: Born August 28, 1903, in Vienna, Austria; came to United States in 1939, naturalized citizen in 1944; committed suicide after long illness, March 13, 1990, in Silver Springs, Md.; son of Anton and Paula (Seidler) Bettelheim; married Gertrud Weinfeld (a teacher and researcher; died, 1984), May 14, 1941; children: Ruth, Naomi, Eric. *Education:* University of Vienna, Ph.D., 1938. *Politics:* Democrat. *Religion:* Jewish.

ADDRESSES: Home—718 Adelaide Pl., Santa Monica, Calif. 90402 (he moved to a retirement home in Silver Springs, Md., one month before his death).

CAREER: Progressive Education Association, Chicago, Ill., research associate, 1939-41; Rockford College, Rockford, Ill., associate professor of psychology, 1942-44; University of Chicago, Chicago, assistant professor, 1944-47, associate professor, 1947-52, professor of educational psychology, 1952-73, Stella M.

Rowley Distinguished Service Professor of Education, and professor of psychology and psychiatry, 1963-73, head of Sonia Shankman Orthogenic School, 1944-73; writer, 1973-90. Diplomate of American Psychological Association. Fellow of Center for Advanced Studies in the Behavioral Sciences, 1971-72. Former member of Chicago Council for Child Psychology.

MEMBER: American Psychological Association (fellow), American Orthopsychiatric Association (fellow), American Philosophical Association, American Association of University Professors, American Sociological Association, American Academy of Education (founding member), American Academy of Arts and Sciences, Chicago Psychoanalytical Society, Quadrangle Club.

AWARDS, HONORS: D.H.L. from Cornell University; National Book Award and National Book Critics Circle Award, both 1977, both for *The Uses of Enchantment: The Meaning and Importance of Fairy Tales; Los Angeles Times* current interest prize nominee, 1983, for *Freud and Man's Soul.*

WRITINGS:

(With Morris Janowitz) *Dynamics of Prejudice: A Psychological and Sociological Study of Veterans,* Harper, 1950.
Love Is Not Enough: The Treatment of Emotionally Disturbed Children, Free Press, 1950.
Overcoming Prejudice (booklet), Science Research Associates, 1953.
Symbolic Wounds: Puberty Rites and the Envious Male, Free Press, 1954, revised edition, Collier Books, 1962.
Truants from Life: The Rehabilitation of Emotionally Disturbed Children, Free Press, 1955.
The Informed Heart: Autonomy in a Mass Age, Free Press, 1960.
Paul and Mary: Two Case Histories from "Truants from Life," Doubleday-Anchor, 1961.
(With others) *Youth: Change and Challenge* (proceedings of the American Academy of Arts and Sciences), American Academy of Arts and Sciences, 1961.
Dialogues with Mothers, Free Press, 1962.
Child Guidance, a Community Responsibility: An Address, with a Summary of Public Provisions for Child Guidance Services to Michigan Communities, Institute for Community Development and Services, Continuing Education Service, Michigan State University, 1962.
(With Janowitz) *Social Change and Prejudice: Including Dynamics of Prejudice,* Free Press, 1964.
Art: As the Measure of Man, Museum of Modern Art, 1964.
The Empty Fortress: Infantile Autism and the Birth of the Self, Free Press, 1967.
Mental Health in the Slums: Preliminary Draft, Center of Policy Study, University of Chicago, 1968.
The Children of the Dream, Macmillan, 1969, reprinted as *The Children of the Dream: Communal Childrearing and American Education,* Avon, 1970, published in England as *The Children of the Dream: Communal Child-Rearing and Its Implications for Society,* Paladin, 1971.
Food to Nurture the Mind, Children's Foundation (Washington, D.C.), 1970.
Obsolete Youth: Toward a Psychograph of Adolescent Rebellion, San Francisco Press, 1970.
(With others) *Moral Education: Five Lectures,* Harvard University Press, 1970.
A Home for the Heart, Knopf, 1974.
The Uses of Enchantment: The Meaning and Importance of Fairy Tales, Knopf, 1976.

Surviving, and Other Essays, Knopf, 1979, reprinted with a new introduction as *Surviving the Holocaust,* Flamingo, 1986.
(With Karen Zelan) *On Learning to Read: The Child's Fascination with Meaning,* Knopf, 1982.
Freud and Man's Soul, Knopf, 1982.
(With Anne Freedgood) *A Good Enough Parent: A Book on Child-Rearing,* Knopf, 1987.
Freud's Vienna and Other Essays, Knopf, 1990.

Columnist for *Ladies' Home Journal.* Contributor to professional and popular journals, including *New Yorker* and *New York Times Book Review.*

SIDELIGHTS: Bruno Bettelheim was a world authority on the treatment of childhood emotional disorders, especially autism and juvenile psychosis. Himself a survivor of debilitating experiences in concentration camps at Dachau and Buchenwald, Bettelheim brought to his work firsthand knowledge of the acute anxiety engendered by extreme situations; his efforts with mentally ill children reflect his sensitivity to their often-unarticulated fears. Bettelheim's writings have found an audience beyond the psychoanalytic community, as he seeks to explain psychological phenomena without resorting to professional jargon. In books such as *Love Is Not Enough: The Treatment of Emotionally Disturbed Children, Truants from Life: The Rehabilitation of Emotionally Disturbed Children,* and *The Empty Fortress: Infantile Autism and the Birth of the Self,* he described the pioneering efforts of staff at the Sonia Shankman Orthogenic School of the University of Chicago, where he presided from 1944 until 1973. He also wrote two penetrating works on the Nazi death camps, *The Informed Heart: Autonomy in a Mass Age* and *Surviving, and Other Essays,* both of which explore the psychological legacy of the camp experience. After his retirement from the University of Chicago, Bettelheim undertook other projects aimed at specialists and general readers alike. He sounded a call for childhood intellectual stimulation in *The Uses of Enchantment: The Meaning and Importance of Fairy Tales* and *On Learning to Read: The Child's Fascination with Meaning,* and he discussed the implications of mistranslation in *Freud and Man's Soul. Spectator* contributor Anthony Storr believes that Bettelheim's writings bear witness to a "long and fruitful life" celebrating "the fact that the human spirit can sometimes triumph over Hell itself."

New York Times Book Review correspondent Paul Roazen observes that Bettelheim "stands as one of Freud's genuine heirs in our time. Fearlessly independent and yet working within Freud's great discoveries, Bettelheim has sought to think through all of human psychology for himself." To a certain extent, Bettelheim's life paralleled that of the "father of psychoanalysis." Both Bettelheim and Freud grew up in Vienna; both chose to work and live there until Nazi atrocities forced them to go elsewhere. As a young student forty-seven years Freud's junior, Bettelheim was strongly influenced by psychoanalytic theory and was frankly awed by Freud's accomplishments. In a piece for the *New York Times Book Review,* Bettelheim recalled passing the apartment building where Freud lived and worked: "I used to walk on this street, more often than not choosing to use this hilly, unattractive way to get where I was going only because Freud lived there." Having received a Ph.D. in psychology from the University of Vienna in 1938—and having undergone psychoanalysis—Bettelheim set himself on a career dedicated to "a distinctive vein of Freudian orthodoxy, free of the scholasticism that has settled like dust over psychoanalytic literature," according to Joseph Featherstone in *The New Republic.* Like Freud, Bettelheim undertook clinical work that had lasting implications for his writings. Featherstone claims: "In his hands, orthodox concepts are metaphors for real experiences, not abstractions leading bloodless lives of their own."

The Nazis annexed Austria in 1938, just after Bettelheim had finished his degree requirements. Later that same year, Bettelheim, a Jew, was arrested and sent first to Dachau and then to Buchenwald. He endured the camps for one year, and when he was released, be drew upon his harrowing experiences there to form his professional positions. Storr notes that, while incarcerated, Bettelheim "was able to use his psychoanalytic experience and insight to distance himself from the impact of what surrounded him, [and] that made it possible for him to come through. Bettelheim was not only able to survive, but also to make positive use of his experience." In fact, Bettelheim conducted research in the camps and observed the impact of the life-threatening and dehumanizing environment on numerous individuals. After being freed and moving to the United States, he summarized these observations in a landmark article, "Individual and Mass Behavior in Extreme Situations." Ironically, the article, which was the first by a scholar to detail Nazis' methods, was rejected by numerous periodicals until 1943, when it appeared in *The Journal of Abnormal and Social Psychology*. As the death camps were liberated, revealing Bettelheim's assertions and conclusions to be true, his article gained worldwide renown and became required reading for all officers in the United States military service.

Bettelheim's camp experiences are explored in more depth in *The Informed Heart* and *Surviving, and Other Essays*. "Although Bettelheim's contribution to our understanding of psychotic children is important," Storr writes, "it is by his account of the concentration camps that he will be remembered. . . . *The Informed Heart* has long been famous. . . . What he has to say is of such signal importance to our understanding of human nature that it cannot be too often repeated." *New York Review of Books* contributor Charles Rycroft describes *The Informed Heart* as "largely an analysis of what decided whether a person lived or died in a concentration camp. In it [Bettelheim] was concerned not so much with the physical capacity to survive brutality and torture as with the psychological factors determining whether a person will be able to resist demoralization in a setting in which he has ceased to be in any way a free agent a setting, moreover, which is designed to reduce him to a nonentity and, indeed, has no wish that he should go on living." Critics have found much to praise in The Informed Heart. In his *New York Times Book Review* assessment, Franz Alexander remarks: "This is a dignified book, convincing because it is not derived from textbook knowledge, but from insights gained in the laboratory of the author's own life. In it reason and life experiences are closely integrated." *New Statesman* essayist Maurice Richardson contends that the book "gives you the impression of being lit from within by a humanist glow. [Bettelheim's] clinical but by no means cold detachment from the horrors, both factual and social of the camps is moving and impressive."

Almost twenty years separate the publication dates of *The Informed Heart* and *Surviving, and Other Essays*. The latter work represents Bettelheim's retrospective attempts to understand not only the burden of experience he bears, but also the lasting legacy of guilt and commitment borne by all survivors. "The experience had to be confronted," Clara Claiborne Park declares in the *Nation,* "not because it could be denied or left behind . . . but because only by confronting it, not once but over and over again, could meaning be found. The full heroism of that early objectivity [in *The Informed Heart*] can be measured only after reading the later essays." In a *New York Times Book Review* assessment of *Surviving, and Other Essays,* Paul Robinson writes: "Among

Bettelheim's many virtues are intellectual humility, analytic skill and unfailing clarity of expression. He is altogether compelling when he recounts his experiences as a camp inmate and survivor. He's not merely persuasive, but moving when he tells that he was able to retain his identity within the camps because, in his earlier life, he had cultivated the powers of observation and analysis. . . . In his survival, one witnesses the triumph of civilization, of mind, of inner culture against almost impossible odds, and the prospect is exhilarating." *New York Review of Books* essayist Rosemary Dinnage adds that the collection exposes Bettelheim's two great strengths: "his totally realistic acceptance of the satanic in human beings and of the gross disintegrations of personality this can impose on others, and his simultaneous unshaken confidence in order and mutuality and reconstruction." Claiborne Park similarly concludes that in *Surviving, and Other Essays,* "it is finally to the humanity of society that Bettelheim has survived to bear witness."

According to Richard Rhodes in the *Chicago Tribune Book World,* Bettelheim's identity as a psychologist and teacher is closely linked to his identity as a survivor of the Holocaust. Bettelheim's experimental approach at the Orthogenic School "was directly a result of his camp experience," Rhodes states. "He saw at Dachau that a total environment is a far more powerful instrument of personality change than the partial environment of classical psychoanalysis. . . . He realized that camp victims and psychotic children have much in common—that both became what they became by adapting to extreme situations. He designed his school, then, as a total environment that might reverse in the direction of healing and of hope the total environments of extremity that he had experienced and studied. By design and by the sheer force of its director's compassion, the school has salvaged and restored to function children of whom all other agencies had despaired, which for Bettelheim must be a profoundly gratifying experience of humane revenge." Indeed, Elsa First reports in the *New York Review of Books* that Bettelheim was driven "to create a therapeutic environment which in each detail of everyday life would create an existence that he envisioned as the exact opposite of the dehumanization so systematically engineered by the camps." Choosing his staff and even the decor with great care, Bettelheim created "probably the most remarkable mental institution in the country," in the words of a *New Yorker* reviewer. The Orthogenic School, with its humane, deinstitutionalized approach, has had an unprecedented eighty-five per cent cure rate among children thought to be far beyond help.

Love Is Not Enough, Truants from Life, The Empty Fortress, and *A Home for the Heart* all document events at the Orthogenic School and outline Bettelheim's educational and therapeutic philosophy. In *The Empty Fortress,* for instance, Bettelheim advances his theory of autism and reviews the case histories of three autistic children who were patients at the school. Central to Bettelheim's treatment approach is the belief that autistic behavior occurs when a child perceives that none of his acts have any effect on the outside world. Therapy therefore must have as its goal the development of autonomy in the child's social perception. *A Scientific American* reviewer of *The Empty Fortress* finds Bettelheim's strategy in the clinic even more convincing than his theories: "The pragmatic argument of successful therapy is generally powerful in medicine, but the humanity, intelligence, self-sacrifice and endurance of the therapy given by Dr. Bettelheim and his devoted staff seem to outweigh the specific content of any theory." *New Republic* contributor Robert Coles feels that the author is "modest, sensible and unpretentious when he tries to specify the particulars that make for autism."

Bettelheim's 1974 overview of his professional stance, *A Home for the Heart,* also received critical acclaim. Elsa First writes: "Bettelheim's myth of the embattled child served to inspire a powerful amount of goodness within the fortress of his school. His clinical intuitiveness and resourcefulness and the unfailing respect he showed his psychotic children were remarkable. . . . There are many useful lessons to be learned from Bettelheim's retrospective look at his life's work." Elizabeth Janeway expresses a similar view in the *New York Times Book Review:* "Bettelheim combines a capacity for lucid speech with a mind of rare strength and subtlety, as his readers well know. He is a natural parabolist, capable of seeing the universe in a grain of sand and passing the vision on. . . . Those who get most from Bettelheim will be those who read him with eyes open and minds alert to the nuances and vistas of this thought."

During the 1970s and 1980s, Bettelheim focused much of his attention on improving the nurture of healthy children. In *The Children of the Dream: Communal Child-Rearing and American Education* he discussed the ramifications of a childhood spent in an Israeli kibbutz. Both *The Uses of Enchantment* and *On Learning to Read* offer strident calls for reform in American early childhood education through the use of traditional fairy tales and other more stimulating reading matter. Bettelheim believed that fantasy even violent fantasy's necessary for children and that fairy tales often offer healthy outlets for subconscious wishes and anxieties. As Richard Todd notes in an *Atlantic* review of *The Uses of Enchantment,* Bettelheim "makes plain that the [fairy] tales are supple, many-layered things, and that different children may find in the same story quite different, even contradictory, forms of psychic comfort. . . . He is sincere in his urgency about the irreplaceableness of these traditional tales, so many of which are now effectively forgotten, or adulterated into Disneyesque good cheer." *New York Review of Books* essayist Harold Bloom calls *The Uses of Enchantment* "a splendid achievement, brimming with useful ideas, with insights into how young children read and understand, and most of all overflowing with a realistic optimism and with an experienced and therapeutic good will." In his *New York Times Book Review* assessment of *The Uses of Enchantment,* John Updike hails the work as "a charming book about enchantment, a profound book about fairy tales. . . . What is new, and exciting, is the warmth, humane and urgent, with which Bettelheim expounds fairy tales as aids to the child's growth."

In 1982 Bettelheim published his controversial book *Freud and Man's Soul,* a short study of how standard English translations of Freud misrepresent Freud's intentions. Storr explains in the *New Republic:* "[Bettelheim] believes that the effect of the English translation of Freud's ideas was to make them into an abstract intellectual system, something that might be applied to the understanding of others in a cerebral fashion, but that was not easily applicable to the study of one's own unconscious." *Los Angeles Times Book Review* contributor Harvey Mindess further contends that Bettelheim sees the results of these expositional misrepresentations as having produced "an impression of Freud as far more impersonal than he was, and to define psychoanalysis as a medical specialty when its founder intended it to be 'a part of psychology' and an inquiry into the nature of the soul."

Opinions on the validity of Bettelheim's thesis vary widely. *Voice Literary Supplement* reviewer Walter Kendrick asserts that Bettelheim's "desire to make Freud sweet and cuddly has caused him to write a stupid, dangerous little book." Frank Kermode likewise notes in the *New York Times Book Review* that it is "salutary to have instruction in what we have lost [through translation]. But on the evidence here presented, Bettelheim has treated rather harshly a huge labor of translation, carried out with devotion and skill, and has unfairly visited the failings of American psychoanalytic practice on that translation." Storr, on the other hand, finds Bettelheim's concern "to resuscitate Freud as a humanist . . . an understandable aspiration," and in the London *Times,* A. S. Byatt concludes: "We need books like Bettelheim's to keep us alert and supple, to remind us of the complex nature of language and translation, culture and history, the limitations of their power, the power of their limitations."

Both Bettelheim's clinical accomplishments and his body of writing reflect a half century's devotion to improving the human condition. *New York Times* correspondent James Atlas suggests that life itself "has provided Professor Bettelheim with ample opportunities to witness human behavior in all its terrifying variety, and to nurture what is valuable in it while remorselessly condemning what is dangerous." To *Washington Post Book World* critic William McPherson, Bettelheim is "renowned in his field and acclaimed throughout the world" because he is "a survivor who bears witness" not only to the disintegration of the personality but also to the resurgence and resilience of the human spirit. Rosemary Dinnage also contends that Bettelheim's experiences have strengthened, not shaken, his faith in cooperation between individuals. "Bettelheim's achievement," Dinnage concludes, "is that while his professional life has been concerned with the distress of others, he has also been able to teach us through the writings—objective rather than passionate—that are based on his own distresses and endurance. Those experiences are the basis of his special understanding both of the growth and the destruction of what makes a person human."

Close friends of Bettelheim speculate that loneliness—his wife died in 1984 and an ailing body—he had suffered two strokes and congestive heart failure—prompted him to end his life in March, 1990, while in a retirement home in Silver Springs, Maryland.

BIOGRAPHICAL/CRITICAL SOURCES:

BOOKS

Bettelheim, Bruno, *The Informed Heart: Autonomy in a Mass Age,* Free Press, 1960.
Bettelheim, Bruno, *A Home for the Heart,* Knopf, 1974.
Bettelheim, Bruno, *Surviving, and Other Essays,* Knopf, 1979, reprinted with a new introduction as *Surviving the Holocaust,* Flamingo, 1986.

PERIODICALS

America, August 7, 1976.
American Academy of Political and Social Science: Annals, July, 1950, November, 1950, September, 1961.
American Journal of Sociology, May, 1961, July, 1969.
American Political Science Review, June, 1961.
American Sociological Review, August, 1950, October, 1955, June, 1961.
Atlantic, June, 1976.
Book World, April 27, 1969.
Chicago Sunday Tribune, July 16, 1950.
Chicago Tribune Book World, April 29, 1979, February 21, 1982.
Choice, October, 1967, October, 1974, October, 1976.
Christian Century, December 6, 1967, June 23-30, 1976.
Critic, October-December, 1974.
Harper's, June, 1976.
Harvard Educational Review, fall, 1967.
Journal of Home Economics, October, 1955, November, 1962.
Los Angeles Times, October 16, 1983, October 12, 1986, November 12, 1987, January 24, 1990, April 3, 1990.

Los Angeles Times Book Review, January 23, 1983.
Nation, June 24, 1950, July 30, 1955, April 1, 1961, May 12, 1979, February 12, 1983.
National Review, May 10, 1974, August 20, 1976. New Leader, March 31, 1969.
New Republic, May 22, 1961, March 4, 1967, May 24, 1969, April 20, 1974, May 29, 1976, December 31, 1982.
New Statesman, March 17, 1961, September 26, 1969, June 7, 1974.
Newsweek, January 10, 1983.
New Yorker, April 22, 1974, January 25, 1982.
New York Review of Books, May 4, 1967, May 30, 1974, July 15, 1976, April 19, 1979, April 1, 1982.
New York Times, February 12, 1950, September 17, 1950, May 29, 1955, March 24, 1969, August 15, 1979, December 21, 1982, December 27, 1989.
New York Times Book Review, October 8, 1961, February 26, 1967, April 6, 1969, March 17, 1974, May 23, 1976, January 2, 1977, April 29, 1979, January 31, 1982, February 6, 1983, January 21, 1990.
San Francisco Chronicle, March 26, 1950, July 16, 1950.
Saturday Review, July 8, 1961, June 9, 1962, May 17, 1969, May 15, 1976.
Scientific American, July, 1967.
Spectator, October 23, 1976, April 1, 1978, August 11, 1979, March 20, 1982.
Time, May 3, 1976.
Times (London), December 22, 1983.
Times Literary Supplement, October 9, 1969, August 2, 1974, October 1, 1976, July 29, 1983, August 15, 1986.
Tribune Books, December 24, 1989.
Voice Literary Supplement, February, 1983, December, 1985.
Washington Post, December 17, 1989.
Washington Post Book World, June 13, 1976, May 13, 1979, January 3, 1982.

OBITUARIES:

PERIODICALS

Los Angeles Times, March 16, 1990.
New York Times, March 28, 1990.
Washington Post, March 16, 1990.

*   *   *

BIOY CASARES, Adolfo   1914-
(Javier Miranda, Martin Sacastru, pseudonyms; H[onorio] Bustos Domecq, B. Lynch Davis, B. Suarez Lynch, joint pseudonyms)

PERSONAL: Surname appears in some sources as Bioy-Casares; born September 15, 1914, in Buenos Aires, Argentina; son of Adolfo Bioy and Marta Casares; married Silvina Ocampo (a writer), 1940; children: Marta.

ADDRESSES: Home—Posadas 1650, 1112 Buenos Aires, Argentina.

CAREER: Writer.

AWARDS, HONORS: Premio Municipal de la Ciudad de Buenos Aires, 1940, for *La invencion de Morel;* Segundo Premio Nacional de Literatura (Argentina), 1963, for *El lado de la sombra;* Primer Premio Nacional de Literatura (Argentina), 1969, for *El gran serafin;* Gran Premio de Honor, Argentine Society of Writers, 1975; Premio Mondello, 1984, for *Historias fantasticas;* Premio Internacional Literario IILA (Rome), 1986, for *Historias fantasticas* and *Historias de amor.*

WRITINGS:

IN ENGLISH TRANSLATION

La invencion de Morel (novel; also see below), prologue by Jorge Luis Borges, Losada (Buenos Aires), 1940, reprinted, Alianza (Madrid), 1981, translation by Ruth L. C. Simms published with her translation of *La trama celeste* (also see below) as *The Invention of Morel, and Other Stories from "La trama celeste,"* University of Texas Press, 1964, reprinted, 1985.

(Editor with wife, Silvina Ocampo, and Borges, and author of foreword) *Antologia de la literatura fantastica* (title means "Anthology of Fantastic Literature"), Sudamericana (Buenos Aires), 1940, enlarged edition with postscript by Bioy Casares, 1965, translation of revised version published as *The Book of Fantasy,* introduction by Ursula K. Le Guin, Viking, 1988.

(With Borges, under joint pseudonym H. Bustos Domecq) *Seis problemas para don Isidro Parodi* (short stories), Sur (Buenos Aires), 1942, translation by Norman Thomas di Giovanni published under authors' real names as *Six Problems for Don Isidro Parodi,* Dutton, 1983.

El perjurio de la nieve (short stories), Emece, 1945, translation by Simms published as *The Perjury of the Snow,* Vanishing Rotating Triangle (New York), 1964.

Plan de evasion (novel), Emece, 1945, reprinted, 1977, translation by Suzanne J. Levine published as *A Plan for Escape,* Dutton, 1975.

La trama celeste (short stories; title means "The Celestial Plot"), Sur, 1948, reprinted as *La trama celeste y otros relatos,* Centro (Buenos Aires), 1981, translation by Simms published with her translation of *La invencion de Morel* as *The Invention of Morel, and Other Stories from "La trama celeste,"* University of Texas Press, 1964, reprinted, 1985.

El sueno de los heroes (novel), Losada, 1954, reprinted, Alianza, 1976, translation by Diana Thorold published as *The Dream of Heroes,* Dutton, 1988.

(Editor and translator with Borges) *Cuentos breves y extraordinarios: Antologia,* Raigal (Buenos Aires), 1955, revised and enlarged edition, Losada, 1973, translation by Anthony Kerrigan published as *Extraordinary Tales,* Souvenir Press, 1973.

(With Borges) *Cronicas de Bustos Domecq,* Losada, 1967, translation by di Giovanni published as *Chronicles of Bustos Domecq,* Dutton, 1976.

Diario de la guerra del cerdo (novel), Emece, 1969, translation by Gregory Woodruff and Donald A. Yates published as *Diary of the War of the Pig,* McGraw, 1972.

Dormir al sol (novel), Emece, 1973, translation by Levine published as *Asleep in the Sun,* Persea Books, 1975.

La aventura de un fotografo en La Plata (novel), Emece, 1985, translation by Levine published as *Adventures of a Photographer,* Dutton, 1989.

IN SPANISH; SHORT STORIES

(Under pseudonym Martin Sacastru) *Diecisiete disparos contra lo provenir* (title means "Seventeen Shots Against the Future"), Editorial Tor (Buenos Aires), 1933.

Caos, Viau & Zona (Buenos Aires), 1934.

Luis Greve, muerto, Destiempo (Buenos Aires), 1937.

Las visperas de Fausto, La Perdiz (Buenos Aires), 1949.

Historia prodigiosa (title means "Prodigious History"), Obregon (Mexico), 1956, enlarged edition, Emece, 1961.

Guirnalda con amores: Cuentos (title means "A Garland of Love: Stories"), Emece, 1959, reprinted, 1978.

El lado de la sombra (title means "The Shady Side"), Emece, 1962.

El gran serafin, Emece, 1967.

Historias de amor (title means "Love Stories"), Emece, 1972.

Historias fantasticas (title means "Fantastic Stories"), Alianza, 1976.

El heroe de las mujeres, Emece, 1978.

Historias desaforadas, Alianza, 1986.

IN SPANISH; WITH JORGE LUIS BORGES

(Under joint pseudonym H. Bustos Domecq) *Dos fantasias memorables* (short stories), Oportet & Haereses, 1946, reprinted under authors' real names with notes and bibliography by Horacio Jorge Becco, Edicom (Buenos Aires), 1971.

(Under joint pseudonym B. Suarez Lynch) *Un modelo para la muerte* (novel; title means "A Model for Death"), Oportet & Haereses, 1946.

Los orilleros [and] *El paraiso de los creyentes* (screenplays; titles mean "The Hoodlums" and "The Believers' Paradise"; first screenplay produced as an Argentine film, directed by Ricardo Luna, 1975), Losada, 1955, reprinted, 1975.

(And with Hugo Santiago) *Les Autres: Escenario original* (screenplay; produced as a French film directed by Santiago, 1974), C. Bourgois (Paris), 1974.

Nuevos cuentos de Bustos Domecq (short stories), Libreria de la Ciudad, 1977.

IN SPANISH; EDITOR OR COMPILER WITH BORGES

(And with Ocampo) *Antologia poetica argentina* (title means "Anthology of Argentine Poetry"), prologue by Borges, Sudamericana, 1941.

(And translator with Borges) *Los mejores cuentos policiales* (title means "The Best Detective Stories"), Emece, 1943, reprinted, Alianza, 1972.

(And translator with Borges) *Los mejores cuentos policiales: Segunda serie,* Emece, 1951.

(And author of prologue, notes, and glossary with Borges) *Poesia gauchesca* (title means "Gaucho Poetry"), two volumes, Fondo de Cultura Economica, 1955.

Libro del cielo y del infierno (anthology; title means "Book of Heaven and Hell"), Sur, 1960, reprinted, 1975.

Also editor with Borges of series of detective novels, "The Seventh Circle," for Emece, 1943-56.

IN SPANISH; OTHER

Prologo (title means "Prologue"; miscellany), Editorial Biblos (Buenos Aires), 1929.

La nueva tormenta; o, La vida multiple de Juan Ruteno (title means "The New Storm; or, The Multiple Life of Juan Ruteno"; novel), Destiempo, 1935.

La estatua casera (miscellany), Ediciones del Jacaranda (Buenos Aires), 1936.

(With Ocampo) *Los que aman, odian* (title means "Those Who Love, Hate"; novel), Emece, 1946.

Adolfo Bioy Casares (anthology), edited by Ofelia Kovacci, Ediciones Culturales Argentinas, Ministerio de Educacion y Justicia, Direccion General de Cultura, 1963.

La otra aventura (title means "The Other Adventure"; essays), Galerna (Buenos Aires), 1968, reprinted, Emece, 1986.

Adversos milagros: Relatos (anthology), prologue by Enrique Pezzoni, Monte Avila (Caracas), 1969.

Memoria sobre la pampa y los gauchos (title means "Remembrance of the Pampa and the Gauchos"; essay), Sur, 1970, reprinted, Emece, 1986.

(Under pseudonym Javier Miranda) *Breve diccionario del argentino exquisito,* Barros Merino, 1971, enlarged edition with new prologue published under author's real name, Emece, 1978.

Paginas de Adolfo Bioy Casares seleccionadas por el autor (title means "Pages by Adolfo Bioy Casares Selected by the Author"), preface by Alberto Lagunas, Celtia, 1985.

Contributor with Borges, under joint pseudonym B. Lynch Davis, to *Los Anales de Buenos Aires,* 1946-48. Editor with Borges of *Destiempo* (literary magazine), 1936.

SIDELIGHTS: Although in his native Argentina Adolfo Bioy Casares is a respected author of novels and short stories, his fame in the United States is largely due to his collaborative efforts with his more famous countryman, the late Jorge Luis Borges. The two met when Bioy Casares was seventeen, Borges nearly fifteen years his senior. However, Bioy Casares was already a published author and their mutual interest in books filled in whatever gap the difference in age might have meant otherwise. Within a few years of their meeting, they began to write together. Their first joint effort was a commercial pamphlet about yogurt (the Bioy Casares family owned a large dairy ranch and yogurt was one of their products). "That pamphlet was a valuable lesson to me," Bioy Casares recalls in Emir Rodriguez Monegal's *Jorge Luis Borges: A Literary Biography.* "After writing it, I was a different writer, more experienced and skillful. Any collaboration with Borges is the equivalent of years of work."

Rodriguez Monegal quotes Borges as saying that when the two writers worked together on their later fiction "a third man, Honorio Bustos Domecq, emerged and took over." Borges's biographer explains: "Borges and Bioy [Casares] had been replaced by their own creations. A new writer had been born, a writer who ought to be called 'Biorges' because he was neither Borges nor Bioy [Casares], and because he did not stick to one pseudonym." The pseudonym Honorio Bustos Domecq was a combination of the names of two of their great-grandfathers, as were their other pen names, B. Suarez Lynch and B. Lynch Davis. "In a 1964 interview," *Washington Post Book World* contributor Donald A. Yates notes, "Borges offered this insight into the nature of the collaboration. 'We wrote somewhat for each other and since everything happened in a joking mood, the stories turned out so involved, so baroque, that it was difficult to understand them. At first we made jokes, and in the end jokes on jokes. It was a kind of algebraic contest: jokes squared, jokes cubed. . . .' "

At first, the stories and novel which Bioy Casares and Borges wrote together were not very well received in Argentina. When Victoria Ocampo (whose magazine, *Sur,* published the first of the stories in 1942) learned that the Bustos Domecq stories were written by two men, she was appalled that a pseudonymous—and, therefore, frivolous—work had been connected with her serious literary journal. But, eventually, the stories of the Bioy Casares/Borges collaboration attracted the appropriate readers and recognition. As Rodriguez Monegal notes: "The readers [of the original works] did not realize that a joke could be serious, and that irony and parody are among the deadliest forms of criticism. The gap between readers and authors was unbridgeable. Not until Bustos Domecq's first book was reissued a quarter of a century later would it be read by readers who could see its point."

Both *Six Problems for Don Isidro Parodi* and *Chronicles of Bustos Domecq* have been applauded by U.S. reviewers. Some critics delight in the books' humor; others are impressed by the authors' social criticism. In the *New Republic* Clarence Brown refers to *Chronicles of Bustos Domecq*'s "sheer nonsensical hilarity," while in the *Atlantic* Phoebe-Lou Adams calls the same book "hilariously awful and a great creation." In the *Chicago Tribune Book World* Denis Lynn Heyck finds *Six Problems for Don Isidro Parodi* "an extremely funny book. . . . [It] mercilessly exposes Argentine pretentiousness, pseudo-cosmopolitanism, and shallow nativism. . . . And it caricatures those Argentines, and others who live life as if it were bad literature."

In *Six Problems for Don Isidro Parodi,* six people come to Isidro Parodi's jail cell for solutions to their problems. Rodriguez Monegal notices the irony in the "fact that the detective [is] himself in jail (convicted of a murder committed by somebody who had very good connections both with the local authorities and the police.)" Each story is a parody of a particular type of Argentine personality. The first problem, for instance, is proposed by Achilles Molinari, who Yates says represents "the foppish journalist," while the second pokes fun at members of the Argentine Academy of Letters.

Chronicles of Bustos Domecq (published under the authors' real names but purported to be written by Bustos Domecq) is a collection of tongue-in-cheek vignettes of characters from Argentine literary and artistic circles. One piece deals with the poet F. J. C. Loomis, who writes poems containing only one word because of his dislike of metaphors. In *Time* Paul Gray notes that Bustos Domecq explains the poor reception of Loomis's poem "Beret" was due "to the demands it makes on the reader of having to learn French." Other writers or artists Bustos Domecq describes in the short sketches include Adalberto Vilaseco, who repeatedly publishes the same poem, each time with a different title, and artist Antarctic A. Garay, who sets up pieces of junk and invites onlookers to admire the spaces between the numerous items—a concept he calls "concave sculpture."

In these works Bioy Casares and Borges disguise their social criticism with humor. Their complex parodies of the tragically "funny" Argentine society—one in which an author of Borges's stature was "promoted" by the national government from his library post to inspector of chickens and rabbits—deal with false appearances and the acceptance of them as a normal part of Argentine life. They paint a world which Gray describes as "invariably monstrous; [full of] novels and poems that cannot be read, art that cannot be seen, architecture—freed from the 'demands of inhabitability'—that cannot be used." Plot complexity, humor, and the importance of appearances—constants in the work produced by Bioy Casares and Borges—are also found in Bioy Casares's solo efforts.

In Rodriguez Monegal's *Review* essay on Bioy Casares the critic refers to "the almost unbearable complexity of *A Plan for Escape* and the stories of *The Celestial Plot.*" The plots of *The Invention of Morel* and *Asleep in the Sun* are also somewhat complicated. In *The Invention of Morel,* for instance, the narrator is shipwrecked on what he believes to be a deserted island, but soon discovers a group of people on the island with him. After falling in love with one of them, Faustine, he discovers that she and her friends are merely images projected by a machine. Hopelessly in love, he attempts to become part of the film the machine is projecting. *Asleep in the Sun* tells the story of a man named Bordenave who sends his neurotic wife to a clinic only to have her come back "inhabited" by someone else's personality.

Some critics contend that these complex plots add to the humor of Bioy Casares's work. In *Nation,* for example, Richard Kostelanetz calls *The Invention of Morel* "marvelously comic" because of the narrator's repeated attempts to establish a relationship with a woman who does not exist. In the *Bulletin of Hispanic Studies* D. P. Gallagher refers to Bioy Casares's novels and short stories as "comic masterpieces whose fundamental joke is

the gap that separates what his characters know from what is going on." Bordenave's efforts to get his wife out of the clinic are funny because they are rewarded with the return of her body but not of her spirit. This humor, like that in the parodies written with Borges, is a double-edged humor which carries bitterness along with the laughter it inspires.

Toronto *Globe and Mail* contributor Alberto Manguel calls Bioy Casares's work "extraordinary adventures told in a voice that is subtle, interesting and wise." According to Manguel, the reader who discovers Bioy Casares's fiction enters "further into the world of a writer who will, in time, come to be read as one of the wisest interpreters of our unfathomable and bewildering existence." The complex humor of the absurd tales produced by Bioy Casares and Borges, like that of Bioy Casares's solo works, serves to point to a possible better society in which our senses—and our governments—can be trusted to tell us the truth about our world and in which the artist and writer can produce truly meaningful works of artistic expression.

MEDIA ADAPTATIONS: Alain Resnais's film, "Last Year at Marienbad," was based on *A Plan for Escape;* three of the stories in *Six Problems for Don Isidro Parodi* were dramatized for radio broadcast by the British Broadcasting Corporation.

BIOGRAPHICAL/CRITICAL SOURCES:

BOOKS

Contemporary Literary Criticism, Gale, Volume 4, 1975, Volume 8, 1978, Volume 13, 1980.
Rodriguez Monegal, Emir, *Jorge Luis Borges: A Literary Biography,* Dutton, 1978.

PERIODICALS

Atlantic, April, 1976, January, 1979, April, 1981.
Bulletin of Hispanic Studies, July, 1975.
Chicago Tribune Book World, April 19, 1981.
Globe and Mail (Toronto), January 21, 1989.
Nation, October 11, 1965.
New Republic, June 5, 1976.
Review, fall, 1975.
Time, March 29, 1976.
Washington Post Book World, April 19, 1981.

*   *   *

BIRD, C.
  See ELLISON, Harlan

*   *   *

BIRD, Cordwainer
  See ELLISON, Harlan

*   *   *

BIRNEY, (Alfred) Earle 1904-

PERSONAL: Born May 13, 1904, in Calgary, Alberta, Canada; son of William George and Martha (Robertson) Birney; married Esther Bull, April 7, 1937 (divorced, 1977); children: William. *Education:* University of British Columbia, B.A., 1926; University of Toronto, M.A., 1927, Ph.D., 1936; attended University of California, 1927-30, and University of London, 1934-35.

ADDRESSES: Home—R.R. 3, Uxbridge, Ontario, Canada LOC 1KO. *Office*—200 Balliol St., No. 2201, Toronto, Ontario, Canada M4S 1C6.

CAREER: University of Utah, Salt Lake City, instructor, 1930-32, 1933-34; University of Toronto, Toronto, Ontario, Leonard fellow, 1932-33, lecturer, 1936-41, assistant professor of English, 1941-42; Canadian Broadcasting Corp., Montreal, Quebec, supervisor of foreign language shortwave programs to Europe, 1945-46; University of British Columbia, Vancouver, professor of English literature, 1946-63, professor of creative writing, 1963-65; University of Toronto, writer in residence, 1965-67; University of Waterloo, Waterloo, Ontario, writer in residence, 1967-68. Visiting professor, University of Oregon, 1961, and University of California, 1968; writer in residence, University of Western Ontario, 1982-83. Lectured in Japan and India, 1958, U.S. West Coast, 1960, and Latin America, 1962. Contributor of plays, talks, and readings to CBC "Transcanada" radio programs, 1945—; has made frequent appearances on CBC television panels, 1955—. *Military service:* Canadian Army, 1940-45; became major.

MEMBER: Royal Society of Canada (fellow).

AWARDS, HONORS: Governor-General's medal for poetry, 1943, for *David and Other Poems,* and 1946, for *Now Is Time;* Stephen Leacock Medal for Humour, 1949, for *Turvey;* Borestone Mountain prize, 1951; Canadian government fellowship to France, 1953; Lorne Pierce Gold Medal from Royal Society of Canada, 1953; President's Medal for Poetry from University of Western Ontario, 1954; Nuffield fellowship, 1958-59; Canada Council traveling fellowships, 1962-63, 1968, and 1970-71; LL.D., University of Alberta, 1965; Canada Council Medal, 1968; Order of Canada, 1972; Canada Council senior arts fellowship, 1978-80; D.Litt., McGill University, 1979; named Officer of the Order of Canada, 1981; Litt.D., University of Western Ontario, 1981; honorary degree from University of British Columbia, 1987.

WRITINGS:

POEMS

David and Other Poems, Ryerson, 1942.
Now Is Time, Ryerson, 1945.
Strait of Anian, Ryerson, 1948.
Ice Cod Bell or Stone, McClelland & Stewart, 1962.
Near False Creek Mouth, McClelland & Stewart, 1964.
Selected Poems: 1940-1966, McClelland & Stewart, 1966.
Memory No Servant, New Books, 1968.
Poems, McClelland & Stewart, 1969.
Pnomes, Jukollages and Other Stunzas, Gronk Press, 1969.
Rag and Bone Shop, McClelland & Stewart, 1971.
The Bear on the Delhi Road, Chatto & Windus, 1973.
What's So Big about Green?, McClelland & Stewart, 1973.
Collected Poems, two volumes, McClelland & Stewart, 1975.
Alphabeings and Other Seasyours, Pikadilly Press, 1976.
Ghost in the Wheels, McClelland & Stewart, 1977.
Fall by Fury, McClelland & Stewart, 1978.
Copernican Fix, ECW Press, 1985.
One Muddy Hand, McClelland & Stewart, 1986.

Also author of *The Rugging and the Moving Times,* 1976, and *The Mammoth Corridors,* 1980.

EDITOR

Twentieth Century Canadian Poetry (anthology), Ryerson, 1953.
Record of Service of the University of British Columbia in the Second World War, University of British Columbia Press, 1955.
Selected Poems of Malcolm Lowry, City Lights, 1962.

(With Margerie Lowry) Malcolm Lowry, *Lunar Caustic* (novella), Grossman, 1962.

OTHER

Turvey (novel), McClelland & Stewart, 1949, unexpurgated edition, 1976.
Trial of a City (verse play), Ryerson, 1952.
Down the Long Table (novel), McClelland & Stewart, 1955.
The Creative Writer (radio talks), Canadian Broadcasting Corp., 1966.
The Cow Jumped over the Moon: The Writing and Reading of Poetry (literary criticism), Holt, 1972.
The Damnation of Vancouver (verse play), McClelland & Stewart, 1977.
Big Bird in the Bush (short stories and sketches), Valley Editions, 1978.
Spreading Time: Remarks on Canadian Writing, 1926-1979, Vehicule Press, 1980.
Essays on Chaucerian Irony (literary criticism), University of Toronto Press, 1985.
Words on Waves (radio plays), CBC Enterprises, 1985.

Contributor to journals in Canada, the United States, Great Britain, Europe, New Zealand, and Australia. Literary editor, *Canadian Forum,* 1936-40; editor, *Canadian Poetry,* 1946-48; editor in chief, *Prism International,* 1964-65.

WORK IN PROGRESS: Autobiographical material.

SIDELIGHTS: Dubbed "a chronicler of Canada" by Desmond Pacey in his book *Ten Canadian Poets,* Earle Birney is regarded as one of his country's finest poets, if not *the* finest. Fred Cogswell of *Canadian Literature* writes: "Earle Birney, more than any other I poet know, is typical in thought and outlook of the average liberal-minded Canadian. . . . He is rare among our writers in his ability to use forms derived from the whole tradition of poetry to express brilliantly and freshly whatever insight he does have. Moreover, he has an intelligent dedication to his craft that only a professional can possess."

According to W. E. Fredeman of the *British Columbia Library Quarterly,* Birney's poetry can be divided into five major categories: satires, descriptions of war, nature, and love, and poems built on narrative or dramatic situations involving one or more of the other four categories. Due to Birney's extensive travels, his poems frequently become observations of life as seen through the eyes of a traveler (in a geographic as well as a spiritual sense); even his "Canadian" poems are the work of a man who obviously feels very much like a stranger in his own country. A common thread which runs through many of the poems is the theme of man's efforts as a microcosm to come to terms with the macrocosm (society, nature, and so on) within the brief space of a single lifetime. And all of them, claims Fredeman, are "autobiographical and extremely personal." In addition, Fredeman feels that "Birney's poetry is obviously didactic, but rarely in the pejorative sense, for it seldom preaches. [The philosophy it offers the reader is] a broad humanism positing individual involvement and responsibility combined with an insistence on the absolute autonomy of the human will." This will is "expressed with masculine forcefulness in both imagery and diction [which] protects Birney from the snare of sentimental didacticism."

Birney's skill as a satirist, according to most critics, is based on his natural instinct for identifying the ironic and ridiculous aspects of human behavior and, as Derek Stanford of *Books and Bookmen* puts it, on his "nose for the picaresque situation." Much of this satire appears in the form of clever sound and word play (often making use of the idiosyncracies of various dialects or of a particular professional jargon), a field in which Birney is considered an expert. George Woodcock writes in *Queen's Quarterly:* "Birney has always been ready to wear the mask and motley of the clown, in prose and in verse, but he has generally avoided the easy and empty facetiousness of the professional funny man; his comedy . . . is rather of the type—full of verbal quippery and social implication—that we once associated with the Marx Brothers. It is stringent, intelligent, irreverent, and a little irascible." William Walsh of the *Lugano Review,* referring to Birney's humor as "graven-faced and gravelled-voiced," claims that it nonetheless has a buoyancy and balance which sets it apart from ordinary humor. "It has to do with its having nothing abstractly or specifically comic about it. . . . The comic is simply a constituent of the vision and the poetry. It is because he evokes the actual with such presence and authenticity that what is comic in it—and the alert eye can always discern it—strikes one as just and irresistible."

An experimentalist by nature, Birney frequently relies on visual effects (such as a lack of punctuation, unusual spacing, two-tone print, and different type sizes) to add another dimension to his poetry (though his earlier work was written in a conventional manner Birney has since revised it to conform to his new style). However, these attempts generally have not been well-received. Andy Wainwright of *Saturday Night* feels that in Birney's "concrete poems" (poems about buildings written in the shape of buildings, for example) "there is very little depth for the reader to draw on [they] contain the assumption that the linear aspect of poetry is not alive and to make it so one must make pictures with words. But they defeat their own purpose for, in giving his close attention to the word antics, the reader remains firmly rooted to the printed page. . . . Concrete poetry, in Birney's case, is a placing of style before content, and the content suffers as a result." George Bowering of *Canadian Literature* writes: "I still feel that all this is not really the avantgarde. Birney is usually, in these japes, doing something exciting and playful for his own amusement, and that is okay. But the reader is not similarly energized."

Hayden Carruth, commenting in the critical study *Earle Birney,* is somewhat more vehement in his criticism of the poet's visual experiments: "Mr. Birney is insensitive to the actual value of space in the typographical re-presentation of a poem. For what do his spaces accomplish? Exactly what his commas, semicolons, and period accomplished [in the original versions], except that the spaces are harder to read and distractive. . . . The point is that space can be used to do something which cannot be done otherwise, and this is its appropriate use; Mr. Birney seems unaware of it. . . . What [he] has done . . . has no reasonable explanation whatever. It is prosodic fiddle-faddle."

Despite this criticism of Birney's long-standing interest in visual effects, most critics agree that in other respects he is a master of his craft. A reviewer for the *Times Literary Supplement* writes: "Earle Birney is not to be judged as a Canadian poet. In his best work Canada often provides the landscape for his fable or the referents of his argument, but never the limits of his language and imagination. . . . No poet draws upon a richer vocabulary—literary and colloquial, scientific and common. Few poets can handle so wide a range of rhythmic patterns so expressively. Even fewer have Birney's skill in dramatizing an action or anecdote. His ability to capture every level of variety of English speech is at least as rare. Only his ironic humour belongs to many modern poets." Walsh cites Birney's "gift for cut and graven detail, a flowing empathy and a natural rhythm in which the breathing meets the sense to produce an evolving, living line" as one of the poet's chief strengths. He continues his praise by

pointing out that in Birney's poetry there is "a balance or proportion between subject and object, a wholeness and unity in the former recognising the fullness and complexity of the latter. A Birney poem is never—although it is that too—just the evocation of a scene. It always has an intellectual and moral structure. . . . Relaxed, casual and spontaneous [in appearance, it is, in fact,] very cunningly organised."

Commenting on *Selected Poems,* a collection of poetry which virtually spans Birney's entire career, A. J. M. Smith offers this summation of his contributions to Canadian literature: "Earle Birney is one of our major poets, perhaps since the death of E. J. Pratt our leading poet. Certainly he is the only rival of Pratt as the creator of heroic narrative on a bold scale and, unlike Pratt, he has been consistently experimental. He has not always been successful, and he has sometimes aped styles and fashions that are unworthy of his real talents; but without a somewhat boyish spirit of adventure his successes would have been impossible too. The real triumph of *Selected Poems* is that it demonstrates so clearly and forcibly—as does indeed the whole of Birney's career—a unified personality of great charm, wit, strength, and generosity."

As Earle Birney himself comments at the end of his book *The Cow Jumped over the Moon:* "None of us wants merely to live but to affirm life. We all need the therapy of fancy and play, honest emotion, pity, laughter, joy. Especially the joy that comes when the words move someone else from mere living to being Alive, Alive-O!"

Birney's poems have been translated and published in fifteen languages, including French, Spanish, Italian, Greek, Romanian, Hungarian, Russian, Finnish, Dutch, Malayan, Chinese, Japanese and Swahili.

AVOCATIONAL INTERESTS: Travel and sports—formerly mountain climbing, now swimming.

MEDIA ADAPTATIONS: World Records recorded Birney reading sixty of his poems, set to music, in 1982.

BIOGRAPHICAL/CRITICAL SOURCES:

BOOKS

Aichinger, Peter, *Earle Birney,* Twayne, 1979.
Contemporary Literary Criticism, Gale, Volume 1, 1973, Volume 4, 1975, Volume 6, 1976, Volume 11, 1979.
Nesbitt, Bruce, editor, *Earle Birney,* Ryerson, 1974.
Pacey, Desmond, *Ten Canadian Poets,* Ryerson, 1958.

PERIODICALS

Books and Bookmen, November, 1973.
British Columbia Library Quarterly, Number 23, 1960.
Canadian Forum, July, 1971.
Canadian Literature, Number 30, 1966, summer, 1971, summer, 1974.
Lugano Review, Number 1, 1975.
Queen's Quarterly, Number 64, 1958.
Saturday Night, May, 1971.
Times Literary Supplement, October 26, 1973.

*   *   *

BISHOP, Elizabeth   1911-1979

PERSONAL: Born February 8, 1911, in Worcester, Mass; died October 6, 1979, of a cerebral aneurism, in Boston, Mass.; daughter of William Thomas (a builder) and Gertrude (Bulmer) Bishop. *Education:* Vassar College, A.B. (English), 1934.

CAREER: Poet, author of prose, and translator. Library of Congress, Washington, D.C., consultant in poetry, 1949-50, honorary consultant in American Letters, beginning in 1958. Poet in residence, University of Washington, Seattle, 1966; also taught at Harvard University and Massachusetts Institute of Technology.

MEMBER: National Institute of Arts and Letters, Academy of American Poets (chancellor, beginning in 1966).

AWARDS, HONORS: Houghton Mifflin Poetry Award, 1946, for *North & South;* Guggenheim fellowship, 1947; American Academy of Arts and Letters grant, 1951; awarded the first Lucy Martin Donnelly fellowship, Bryn Mawr College, 1951; Shelley Memorial Award, 1952; Academy of American Poets Award, 1955; *Partisan Review* fellowship, 1956; Pulitzer Prize in poetry, 1956, for *Poems: North & South* [and] *A Cold Spring;* Amy Lowell traveling fellowship, 1957; Chapelbrook fellowship, 1962; Academy of American Poets fellowship, 1964; Rockefeller Foundation grant, 1967; Merrill Foundation Award, 1969; National Book Award in poetry, 1970, for *The Complete Poems;* Order Rio Branco (Brazil), 1971; LL.D., Rutgers University and Brown University, both 1972; Harriet Monroe Award for Poetry, 1974; Neustadt International Prize for Literature, 1976; National Book Critics Circle Award in poetry, 1977, for *Geography III.*

WRITINGS:

POETRY

(Contributor) Ann Winslow, editor, *Trial Balances* (anthology of young poets), Macmillan, 1935.
North & South (also see below), Houghton, 1946, reprinted, 1964.
Poems: North & South [and] *A Cold Spring,* Houghton, 1955, abridged edition published as *Poems,* Chatto & Windus, 1956.
Questions of Travel, Farrar, Straus, 1965.
Selected Poems, Chatto & Windus, 1967.
The Ballad of the Burglar of Babylon, Farrar, Straus, 1968.
The Complete Poems, Farrar, Straus, 1969.
Geography III, Farrar, Straus, 1976.
The Complete Poems, 1927-1979, Farrar, Straus, 1983.

Poems anthologized in numerous collections.

OTHER

(Translator from the Portuguese) Alice Brant, *The Diary of "Helena Morley,"* Farrar, Straus, 1957, reprinted, Ecco Press, 1977.
(With the editors of Life) *Brazil,* Time, Inc., 1962.
(Editor with Emanuel Brasil) *An Anthology of Twentieth-Century Brazilian Poetry,* Wesleyan University Press, 1972.
The Collected Prose, edited and introduced by Robert Giroux, Farrar, Straus, 1984.

Also translator, with others, of *Travelling in the Family* by Carlos Drummond. Contributor of poetry and fiction to periodicals, including *Kenyon Review, New Republic, Partisan Review,* and *Poetry.* Co-founder of *Con Spirito,* Vassar College.

SIDELIGHTS: Elizabeth Bishop's refusal to settle for easy answers to life's problems, her handling of both ordinary and exotic topics, her precise yet relaxed technique, and in particular her extraordinary perception all revealed her supreme control over her craft and marked her poetry as major. Bishop's work has had an extraordinary ability to make the most diverse groups of poets—those who normally disagree over themes, techniques,

forms, in short the ideology informing a poem—agree on one point: that she was an artist they could all admire and learn from. As William Meredith put it in his "Invitation to Miss Elizabeth Bishop," reprinted in Lloyd Schwartz and Sybil P. Estess's *Elizabeth Bishop and Her Art:* "[Bishop] will yet civilize and beguile us from our silly schools. The [Charles] Olsons will lie down with the [Richard] Wilburs and the Diane Wakoskis dance quadrilles with the J. V. Cunninghams and the Tooth Mother will suckle the rhymed skunk kittens of [Robert] Lowell."

Only months after Bishop's birth her father died, and her mother suffered a nervous breakdown and never recovered. For her first six years, Bishop lived with her mother's family in Great Village, Nova Scotia, and then moved to the home of her father's parents in Worcester, Massachusetts. The memories of these early traumatic years surface occasionally in poems like "Sestina" or "In the Waiting Room" and the story "In the Village." A lonely child in Great Village and Worcester, a shy orphan with asthma and bronchitis, Bishop found "a much more congenial and sympathetic world for herself in books," according to Anne Stevenson in *Elizabeth Bishop.* In a 1966 *Shenandoah* interview with Ashley Brown, Bishop recollected that while her relatives were not literary, they did own many books, that she started reading poetry when she was eight years old, and that she was also "crazy about fairy tales—Andersen, Grimm, and so on." In "Influences," a memoir published in the *American Poetry Review,* she remembered how old English ballads, nursery rhymes, fairy tales, and riddles affected her as a child and later as a poet. Bishop told Brown during the 1966 interview that when she was thirteen she discovered Walt Whitman; at about the same time, she encountered Emily Dickinson, H. D. (Hilda Doolittle), Joseph Conrad, and Henry James. Soon after she first read some of Gerard Manley Hopkins's poetry, which captivated her. Later at Vassar College she wrote a piece for the *Vassar Review* entitled "Gerard Manley Hopkins: Notes on Timing in His Poetry," and her poem "A Cold Spring," collected in the volume of the same title, begins with an epigraph from Hopkins and is in part a response to Hopkins's perceptions of spring. Bishop also discovered the work of another favorite poet, George Herbert, by the time she was fourteen. Herbert scholar Joseph Summers recalled in the *George Herbert Journal* that when he first met Bishop during the mid-1940s "she knew Herbert's poems better than anyone I had ever met before."

At sixteen, Bishop entered Walnut Hill boarding school in Natick, Massachusetts. Robert Giroux has included the recollection of one of Bishop's schoolmates, Frani Muser, in his introduction to *The Collected Prose:* "When I arrived at the Walnut Hill School in Natick in 1927, I met a most remarkable girl. . . . She had read more widely and deeply than we had. But she carried her learning lightly. She was very funny. She had a big repertory of stories she could tell, not read, and of wonderful songs she could sing, like ballads and sea chanteys. And if some school occasion called for a new song, or a skit, it would appear overnight like magic in her hands. Her name was Elizabeth Bishop. We called her 'Bishop,' spoke of her as 'the Bishop,' and we all knew with no doubt whatsoever that she was a genius." In the interview with Brown, Bishop herself remembered her activities and early work on poetry: "I was on the staff of the literary magazine at school and published some poems there. I had a good Latin teacher and a good English teacher at Walnut Hill. . . . I now wish I'd studied nothing but Latin and Greek in college. In fact I consider myself badly educated. Writing Latin prose and verse is still probably the best possible exercise for a poet."

Bishop began Vassar with the thought of studying music, but as she told Elizabeth Spires in a *Paris Review* interview, the thought of public piano recitals so terrified her that she changed her major to English. Among Bishop's Vassar classmates were some promising writers: "It was a very literary class. Mary McCarthy was a year ahead of me. Eleanor Clark was in my class. And Muriel Rukeyser, for freshman year. We started a magazine you may have heard of, *Con Spirito.* I think I was a junior then. There were six or seven of us—Mary, Eleanor Clark and her older sister, my friends Margaret Miller and Frani Blough, and a couple of others. . . . Most of us had submitted things to the *Vassar Review* and they'd been turned down. It was very old-fashioned then. . . . After [*Con Spirito*'s] third issue the *Vassar Review* came around and a couple of our editors became editors on it and then they published things by us," Bishop told Spires.

The poems "The Flood," "A Word with You," "Hymn to the Virgin," and "Three Sonnets for Eyes" appeared in *Con Spirito,* and "Some Dreams They Forgot," "Valentine," and "Valentine II" were first published in the *Vassar Review;* all of these early works have been collected and reprinted in *The Complete Poems, 1927-1979.* Stevenson has called these poems "exceptionally mature" and technically proficient; Alan Hollinghurst in a 1983 *Poetry Review* article has noted in them "a relished collision of colloquial tone and high formal artifice," finding particularly in "The Flood" an attempt "to create a world free from personalities . . . related to an abiding concern with detachment." Hollinghurst has maintained that this pattern persisted throughout Bishop's work, ultimately forming a body of work "noticeably characterized by its more abstract, questing and, in a way, cerebral poems."

Other readers, however, view "The Flood" in a different relationship to Bishop's canon. Instead of being an early indication of a persistent pattern, the poem, they feel, may present only one segment of a fluctuating tendency to shift between the poles of detachment and involvement, and, in theme, to move increasingly toward the latter position. Robert Lowell sensed that most of the poems in Bishop's first collection *North & South* form a "single symbolic pattern," although one a bit elusive to characterize, as he said in an early *Sewanee Review* assessment; he isolated "two opposing factors," one of which he called "something in motion," and the other "a terminus." More recently, in the *American Poetry Review,* Robert Pinsky has identified what he considers Bishop's great subject: "[The] dual nature of the art [of poetry], its physical reminder of our animal privacy and its formal reminder of our communal dealings. . . . To put the idea a bit differently, her great subject is the contest—or truce, or trade-agreement—between the single human soul on one side and, on the other side, the contingent world of artifacts and other people." And in the 1966 interview with Brown, Bishop herself admitted to the shift between solitary and communal concerns, when she stated that she was "much more interested in social problems and politics now than I was in the '30's."

In many ways poet Marianne Moore was Bishop's mentor. Meeting Bishop while she was still at Vassar, Moore encouraged the younger woman to write, discouraged her from attending medical school, offered editorial and poetic advice during Bishop's early career, and continued a friendship which Bishop recounted with humor and affection both in her poem "Invitation to Miss Marianne Moore," and in her prose piece "Efforts of Affection: A Memoir of Marianne Moore." Throughout their friendship the two poets maintained an active correspondence. They discussed their reading, exchanged books they were eager to have the other read, mailed postcards from exotic places, and sent whimsical little gifts. Bishop solicited Moore's opinions on poems in progress and sometimes mentioned in her letters people or places that later appeared in poems, for instance, the description of a Cuban sitting room that then became part of "Jeronimo's House."

Perhaps because of this friendship and because Moore helped get Bishop's work published in the anthology *Trial Balances,* the introduction of which included Moore's appreciative statements on Bishop, early reviewers continually linked Bishop's poetry with Moore's. They noticed that both poets often described animals and emphasized a visual quality in their work. In a review later collected in *Poetry and the Age,* Randall Jarrell wrote of a poem in *North & South,* "When you read Miss Bishop's 'Florida,' a poem whose first sentence begins, 'The state with the prettiest name,' and whose last sentence begins, 'The alligator, who has five distinct calls: / friendliness, love, mating, war, and warning,' you don't need to be told that the poetry of Marianne Moore was, in the beginning, an appropriately selected foundation for Miss Bishop's work." Less enthusiastically, Louise Bogan noted in a 1946 *New Yorker* review Bishop's "slight addiction to the poetic methods of Marianne Moore."

Aside from continually invoking Moore, whose influence Bishop increasingly questioned as her own reputation grew, most early reviewers voiced respect or praise. Moore herself, in the *Nation,* emphasized Bishop's tasteful poetics, her tactful handling of material, and finally her uninsistent control of tension and emotion. Bogan declared that the poems of *North & South* "strike no attitudes and have not an ounce of superfluous emotional weight, and they combine an unforced ironic humor with a naturalist's accuracy of observation." In *Pleasure Dome: On Reading Modern Poetry,* Lloyd Frankenberg pointed new readers to the very first poem in *North & South,* "The Map," as a reference point from which to begin reading Bishop's poetry. He felt that this work, as well as the rest of the poetry in the collection, possessed a "surface clarity [which] is deceptive. Its effect is so natural, we are hardly aware how much is being described: the map itself, the seacoast it suggests, and a particular way of seeing and relating both. . . . The method is direct, reticent and gracious." Jarrell found Bishop to be morally attractive because in certain of her poems "she understands so well that the wickedness and confusion of the age can explain and extenuate other people's wickedness and confusion, but not, for you, your own," that individual morality "is usually a small, personal, statistical, but heartbreaking or heartwarming affair of omissions and commissions." Lowell praised Bishop's "unrhetorical, cool, and beautifully thought out poems" and labeled her "one of the best craftsmen alive."

A few reviewers did criticize. Oscar Williams declared in the *New Republic* that Bishop had "possibly overeducated herself in what is, or rather was, going on in the best circles, and hasn't trusted enough in her own psyche. She has listened every once in a while to certain cliques which are trying to palm off academic composition as poetic perception." And in a *Partisan Review* assessment of Bishop's *Poems: North & South* [and] *A Cold Spring,* Edward Honig argued that Bishop's poems "arrest one by their brilliant surfaces and transparency. But underneath is a curious rigidity, a disturbing lack of movement and affective life, betraying a sprained and uneasy patience. [The poems] frequently resemble the fish in her most anthologized poem of that name: caught half-dead, the fight knocked out of it, '. . . a grunting weight, battered and venerable and homely,' achieving in the end, a pyrrhic victory by being thrown back into the sea." Like Frankenberg, Honig regarded "The Map" as emblematic of the volume *North & South,* but unlike Frankenberg, he criticized it and then the volume as "a plan for suppressing rather than compressing contours, dimension, tonality, emotion. A slow hard gaze moves behind the deliberately drawn-out ironies."

The poems of *North & South* may indeed prove unsatisfactory in the several ways Honig mentions, yet such shortcomings must be studied, because they reveal an important pattern in Bishop's canon. While the poems surely function to suppress, as Honig suggests, much feeling and movement do exist beneath their surfaces. The poems suppress emotion, not to stifle it, but to transform it into something shaped and artful, something which both contains and embodies change. While Bishop often tended to comfortably deny change, she also knew she needed to accommodate it in order to exist as a person and grow as an artist. Thus she vacillated between the two states throughout her canon.

Bishop's vacillation manifested itself in several ways. She sometimes completely retracted what seemed a decisive judgment, she varied forms and styles, she experimented with tone and diction, and she explored a wide variety of subjects. Inconsistent precisely because it moved back and forth between many different styles ranging from traditional to surreal, *North & South* reflected Bishop's meditation on her own art, her efforts to see what it was, how it affected her, how it would affect her readers. The volume also revealed her questioning how far she should follow already established poetic traditions and how much she should strike out on her own. As a young artist she worried that her comfort with a tradition, with past ideas and forms, might also stifle her own uniqueness. Finding herself breathing what Calvin Bedient has called in a *Parnassus* essay "the awful, sweet ether of tradition," she struggled in her early poetry to find a pure air for nurturing her own style and to change what no longer suited her purpose. *North & South* recorded the beginnings of what would be a life-long effort to merge successfully with a tradition so that her individuality ultimately would shine forth.

North & South was chosen from among 843 manuscripts for the Houghton Mifflin Poetry Award in 1945. In 1949, Bishop was named poetry consultant to the Library of Congress and moved to Washington, D.C. She admitted, however, to both Anne Stevenson and Elizabeth Spires, that she did not enjoy the year: as she told Spires, "There were so many government buildings that looked like Moscow. There was a very nice secretary . . . [who] did most of the work. I'd write something and she'd say, 'Oh, no, that isn't official,' so then she'd rewrite it in gobbledegook. We used to bet on the horses. She and I would sit there reading the Racing Form when poets came to call." Still more awards were forthcoming: the American Academy of Arts and Letters Award in 1950, the Lucy Martin Donnelly Fellowship from Bryn Mawr College in 1951, and the Shelley Memorial Award in 1952.

In 1955 Bishop published *Poems,* which contained both her new volume, *A Cold Spring,* and a reprint of the by then out-of-print *North & South.* In a *Hudson Review* assessment, Anthony Hecht praised Bishop's work generally but regarded the poems in *A Cold Spring* as "not quite up to the level of [Bishop's] earlier work; though it is a little hard to say why. . . . Perhaps it is that . . . [her] attitude . . . is distant . . . and uncommitted." Writing in *Dublin Magazine,* Padraic Fallon, likewise felt that language had "over-awed the person" and that the reader remained unmoved because "in the process of making poetry [Bishop] herself seems to be unmoved." Astutely pointing out that "the rise of the Imagist movement—in England, at least—coincided with the enfranchisement of women," A. Alvarez in the *Kenyon Review* then criticized Bishop for her feminine poetic qualities. Alvarez linked Bishop to Imagism and, like the earlier reviewers of *North & South,* to Marianne Moore's influence. But he ultimately disliked Imagism ("the first full-scale feminist movement in poetry"); he felt Bishop's descriptive powers were overpraised after she wrote *North & South* and considered these powers "little more than an obscure fussiness" conveying a "finicky air" that seemed "improvised and not quite to the point." Alvarez preferred a more masculine style, which he found in "poets like, say, Richard Eberhart, whose language makes you jump to his meaning . . . [and whose] language has a kind of physical complexity."

Ironically, Eberhart himself reviewed Bishop's *Poems* in the *New York Times Book Review,* finding the best poems of *A Cold Spring* to be "as good as anything she has done, but with a difference. The difference is that they seem looser woven, more confessional. . . . [Bishop] has a strong grip on her own realities. She gives the reader a rich world of slow, curious, strong discoveries, uniquely seen and set." Still another poet, Howard Nemerov, writing in *Poetry,* praised Bishop's reluctance to moralize openly and singled out "At the Fishhouses" as the collection's most beautiful poem: "Its slow-paced and intricate visual development seems justly completed by a serious eloquence." Donald Hall in the *New England Quarterly* correctly observed that Bishop's poems show "a desperate hanging on to the object as if in refuge from the self," a crucial tension reiterated by later critics. Declaring that "Elizabeth Bishop is a partisan in the world," Wallace Fowlie in *Commonweal* contended that "the observation and the intuition in [the double sonnet 'The Prodigal'] are equivalent to partisan action in the world." Fowlie also commented on Bishop's language, calling it "even more simple and more unmannered than it was in the early poems. It has become more immediate and more direct . . . more aphoristic, more concise, more energetic . . . more serious, more grave." Yet as Alan Williamson has shown in an essay collected in *Elizabeth Bishop and Her Art,* Bishop tended in the love poems of *A Cold Spring* to distance emotion because feelings such as despair, loneliness, and apprehension were dialectically uncontrollable through reason or, in poetry, through structure. These poems, for him, "betray an immense anxiety about the adjustments between inner and outer worlds" and an obsession with the distance between human beings.

One important tension in Bishop's canon emerged clearly in *A Cold Spring:* the fierce need to settle into absolutes—securities—checked by an equally fierce resistance to this need. Bishop half wished to accept those dogmas, theologies, or poetic schools that had existed as the tradition for many years, but this wish encountered a fierce opponent in her own resistance, stirred mainly by her brutally clear sight. What she saw often rendered tradition unacceptable because, simply, her perceptions offered another story.

Another important tension in *A Cold Spring* occurred between nature and people. In the earlier poems nature was often more closely associated with the mind, with the imagination, than with human interaction, and Bishop frequently used the lure of nature to signify the lure of the mind and the imagination. In "The Imaginary Iceberg," for example, the title object is an ice mountain of the imagination, a mountain that the poet initially prefers to the ship full of companions in travel. But when she favors nature over society, it becomes siren-like, its chief danger an abstract, romantic self-destruction. For Bishop, withdrawal from people thus signified a tragically empty and impoverished life; she foresaw deadly consequences if at any time she employed nature as a means of withdrawal from others rather than as a constant reminder of her moral obligation to maintain and nurture connections with those others, despite the pain involved in such connections.

Although *A Cold Spring* actually contained no clear "resolution" to the split between a self involving nature and people, no one answer for a way to exist, Bishop did hint at what an answer might be. What remained constant through *A Cold Spring* was the tension between the two conditions Bishop had posited as polar opposites. Being a person alive in the world of this volume thus involved in the uneasy trading back and forth between poles; trying to control the mind, yet appreciating its imagination; accepting the past and what it offered, yet growing enough oneself to see clearly; accepting the fact that the life human beings see might be "awful," yet having the courage to face it cheerfully. In 1956, the year after its publication, *Poems: North & South* [and] *A Cold Spring* won the Pulitzer Prize for poetry.

In his book *American Poetry since 1945: A Critical Survey,* Stephen Stepanchev made astute observations about *North & South* and *A Cold Spring* that apply to the rest of Bishop's canon. He declared that Bishop's "At the Fishhouses" "tells brilliantly what Miss Bishop thinks of human knowledge, which is always undermined by time, by change. It is obvious that change is the most disturbing principle of reality for her." Bishop was, for him, "a poet who, early in her career, chose to avoid politics and public issues without, at the same time, abandoning the objective realities that constitute the otherness of the world. She believes in that world, especially when it shocks or baffles her, and she renders it with precision and clarity. By 1955 the interchange between self and scene deepens in her poems, and her love of geography takes her, as tourist and everyman, to many places on many roads."

Although Stepanchev exaggerated Bishop's avoidance of politics and public issues, he was correct about her feelings for change and about geography taking her on many roads, for in late November 1951, Bishop traveled to South America on a cruise. But then, as Ashley Brown described it in a 1977 *Southern Review* essay, "Elizabeth ate some item of fruit . . . that disagreed horribly with her; she was laid up for an extended recovery and her ship sailed on without her. But she had friends in Brazil whom she had known in New York during an earlier period; she liked the country, and she stayed." One poem from *A Cold Spring,* "Arrival at Santos," then was reprinted in her next collection, *Questions of Travel,* where it fit in more exactly with the rest of the poems.

Ten years passed between the publication of *A Cold Spring* and *Questions of Travel,* a period also marked by the appearance of a pictorial history, *Brazil,* which Bishop wrote with the editors of *Life.* Her perception of herself and her world changed recognizably during these years. There she found a culture that contrasted in values and priorities with the North American culture she had known. It is no wonder that the poems in *Questions of Travel* often explored previously unfelt or rediscovered emotions set vibrating by this exotic, emotional culture. She also began to perceive the flaws of her North American culture and to realize that a kind of provincial blindness as emotional paralysis had settled over her.

In the *New Republic,* Frank J. Warnke noted that "*Questions of Travel* is impressively varied in its forms and modes, ranging from the irregular but firmly controlled metrics of many of the Brazilian pieces to such strict forms as the folk ballad . . . and the sestina." Warnke found "the Brazilian half of the book more exciting," but did point out the technical achievement of "Visits to St. Elizabeths," which recounted the poet's responses to Ezra Pound, who had been confined to a mental hospital for his pro-Mussolini broadcasts during World War II. Irvin Ehrenpreis wrote in the *Virginia Quarterly Review* that in this poem, "one

of the masterpieces of this collection, . . . [Bishop's] own presence, on the series of occasions when she saw Pound, is never mentioned; . . . the form is the incremental-refrain structure of 'this is the House that Jack Built.' But by varying or modulating the epithets to reflect with unwavering fidelity the mixture of her feelings toward that great, corrupted poet, she produces a strength of pathos that will make those who read this poem aloud weep."

Remarking, like Howard Moss, on the revolutionary quality of Bishop's verse, Willard Spiegelman in the *Centennial Review* found a "natural hero" in Bishop's work, a hero who "occupies a privileged position which is unattainable by the super—or unnatural—exploits of masculine achievement which the poetry constantly debunks." To illustrate "Bishop's habitual tactic of diminution or undercutting" with which "certain ideas of masculine greatness are filed down or eroded to their essential littleness," Spiegelman cited several poems from this volume, including " 'The Burglar of Babylon' [which] deprives its eponymous hero of his glory by recounting, in childlike ballad quatrains, his life as a petty criminal sought by a whole army of police who finally, and unceremoniously, kill him."

While critics twenty years later would see that Bishop was strongly involved with the world, most contemporary reviewers of *Questions of Travel* missed this characteristic amid the more spectacularly dramatic political movements and poetry of the time. Stepanchev, among others, felt that "public events, political issues, or socioeconomic ideology" did not inspire Bishop and that her poetry left readers unaware of Hitler and World War II: "Unlike many of her Auden-influenced contemporaries, she distrusts history, with its melodramatic blacks and whites, and prefers geography, with its subtle gradations of color."

In 1985 Robert von Hallberg, however, offered another point of view about two of the poems in *Questions of Travel,* "Arrival at Santos," and "Brazil, January 1, 1502." Writing in *American Poetry and Culture, 1945-1980,* von Hallberg declared the latter poem "about the Portuguese colonization of Brazil," in that it focused on the way the Portuguese projected the imaginative structures of a Christian, imperialistic ideology onto the foreign landscape they encountered. He felt that Bishop intended to implicate herself in the actions of the Portuguese by setting up these two poems as "the coordinates of Brazilian history. . . . She comes out of a culture that reaches right back to those Christian imperialists. Horrifying as their actions were . . . she can understand their way of seeing." Von Hallberg also argued that as a poet she sensed the attraction of expansion, and because she did, she became critical; implicating herself, she subtly criticized the expansionist, imperialist position.

Questions of Travel's form openly reflected a point of view hinted at in *North & South* and implied in *A Cold Spring.* The collection's division into two sections, *Brazil* and *Elsewhere,* was more than a convenient sorter for poems about different countries; it reflected the mind organizing the volume. Divisions in all parts of life—between past and present, for instance, or one country and another, even between a person like Bishop and the poor peasants in Brazil—seemed more pronounced than earlier but reflected a lessening of naivete and idealism and, oddly enough, a trust that change, though difficult, was possible. While both of her previous poetry collections also tended to sift into two styles and subject matters, in her third collection, Bishop found a truer metaphor in her Brazilian experience for the apparently unbridgeable gaps she perceived.

Poet Adrienne Rich has said in the *Boston Review* that at first Bishop's exalted reputation "made her less, rather than more available to me. The infrequency of her public appearances and her geographic remoteness—living for many years in Brazil, with a woman as it happened, but we didn't know that—made her an indistinct and problematic life-model for a woman poet." But, "given the times and customs of the 1940s and 1950s Bishop's work now seems . . . remarkably honest and courageous," embodying her need to come to terms "with a personal past, with family and class and race, with her presence as a poet in cities and landscapes where human suffering is not [simply] a metaphor."

Having returned to the United States from Brazil, by 1976 Bishop no longer treated that country in her poetry. The lush, colorful, and sometimes humorous dimensions that Brazil seemed to inspire in her verse therefore disappeared, and *Geography III,* which was published eleven years after *Questions of Travel,* possessed a much more subdued form, tone, and emphasis. While part of *Questions of Travel'*s thematic preoccupation had been the struggle for vision and its ensuing perceptions, *Geography III* seemed to take that vision for granted and to concentrate instead on observing the world with an unfaltering, unclouded eye.

Since *Geography III* was Bishop's fourth book of poetry and followed the premature *The Complete Poems,* which won the National Book Award in 1970, most of her reviewers felt that they now had the perspective to assess *Geography III* in relation to the earlier three books. In *Canto,* J. D. McClatchy, for instance, noted the increasingly autobiographical, intimate quality of the work, an opinion confirmed by Harold Bloom of the *New Republic:* "The poet who gave us meditations like 'The Monument,' 'Roosters,' and 'At the Fishhouses,' comparable to the most memorable poems of [Robert] Frost and [Wallace] Stevens, gives us now work of a curious immediacy, comparable to some of the abrupt lyrics of [Emily] Dickinson, at nearly their most intense. Where the language of personal loss was once barely suggested by Bishop, it now begins to usurp the meditative voice. An oblique power has been displaced by a more direct one, by a controlled pathos all the more deeply moving for having been so long and so nobly postponed."

In *Geography III* Bishop focused her art on what it meant to be human, what people felt living on the earth; the physical world more clearly became a metaphor for her self. While she examined the lives and cares of human beings, the poems sometimes revealed her wondering what those lives and cares had, ultimately, to do with such an apparently impractical activity as creating art, with such an apparently useless craft as poetry. This volume recorded her journey as a geographer of the self and her decisions about art's relevance to life. Loosely outlining a music career, *Geography III* suggested that poetry might ultimately offer knowledge useful in alleviating the pain caused by being human but that it should never become the artist's retreat.

In the villanelle "One Art," perhaps the volume's climax, themes introduced by Bishop elsewhere converged in a perfect lyric indirectly revealing poetry ("Write it!") as one art that could provide some sense of comfort and wholeness in what the collection suggested was a desolate, fragmented, spiritually bankrupt time. But the poems following "One Art" reflected a spirit almost defeated by the world's chaos and cruelty, and Bishop continued musing over her desire to retreat, as in "The End of March" which flirted with her recurring wish to take refuge in a perfect dream house. The final poem, "Five Flights Up," began on a note close to "The End of March," with a mind burdened by consciousness, by time, by the knowledge of what terrible things people can do

to each other, but it concluded with the speaker quietly confronting that world, determined to face what she must.

A consistent moral character thus developed in Bishop's poetry, one that faced up to life's difficulties despite its fervent wish to avoid them and always chose to remain involved with a changing world. The constant struggle between Bishop's Dickinsonian wish to withdraw from the world and her desire to confront the world's sorrows and people was apparent early in Bishop's life—if readers take "In the Waiting Room" as any indication— and it certainly showed up in such early works as "The Imaginary Iceberg" or "The Prodigal." Bishop shied from complete connection with others partly because of her acute lifelong awareness that human beings are always eventually faced with their own solitude. Yet she also realized that being human meant making connections between the self and the world; for in the solitude of old age, what mattered were the pacts people had made with life, the treaties they had managed to negotiate in that war between self and world, and the terrain they had been able to map out to help their friends along their ways.

While known mainly for her poetry, Bishop also published in other genres. Preceding her 1962 text for the pictorial history of Brazil, Bishop's translation, *The Diary of "Helena Morley,"* an account of a young girl's experiences in a nineteenth-century Brazilian mining town, appeared in 1957. In 1972 Bishop coedited with Emanuel Brasil *An Anthology of Twentieth-Century Brazilian Poetry.* In their introduction to this volume, Bishop and Brasil noted the esteem that poets and poetry enjoyed in Brazil, discussed the difficulties of Portuguese versification, and also gave brief highlights of Brazilian poetry—shifts in movements and styles—from the nineteenth century to the time of their volume. Bishop also wrote short stories and memoirs, but these remained uncollected, and many of them unpublished, until the 1984 appearance of *The Collected Prose,* edited by Robert Giroux.

Several of Bishop's best readers have lamented the nature of the criticism treating her work. McClatchy has suggested that because most critics have treated Bishop to "an essentially rhetorical reading" with occasional thematic speculations, their approach is "shortsighted" because "it ignores or distorts or reduces the true power of her work and career." Similarly, in a 1985 *Contemporary Literature* essay, Lee Edelman has noted that many critics "have cited [Bishop's poetry] . . . as exemplary of precise observation and accurate detail, presenting us with an Elizabeth Bishop who seems startingly like some latter-day 'gentle Jane'. . . . Viewing it as a species of moral anecdote, even admirers of Bishop's work have tended to ignore the rigor of her intellect, the range of her allusiveness, the complexity of her tropes." Lynn Keller and Cristanne Miller in a *New England Quarterly* article have observed that the critical tendency to trivialize Bishop's literary contribution represents a failure by many male reviewers to understand that she employed "as a central poetic strategy techniques of indirection available from both literary tradition and women's speech. . . . In [her] work, tools traditionally used by women in speech to control situations without appearing to control, to hide strength while exercising it, complement the more conventional poetic tools that express shades of emotion. . . . Characteristically, in a . . . Bishop poem, subtle manipulations of language create a subtext that contrasts with the direct statement of the poem to reveal a more daring and more intensely personal involvement of the poet with her subject that the surface of the poem suggests or to present a socially disruptive, often feminist, perspective." Moreover, in a *Grand Street* essay, David Kalstone, a longtime friend of Bishop and a major commentator on her work, has persuasively attacked the frequently held assumption that Bishop's work was excessively influenced by Marianne Moore.

Elizabeth Bishop died in 1979, leaving behind an impressive canon of poetry and prose. Among the tributes to Bishop reprinted in *Elizabeth Bishop and Her Art* are those by Richard Wilbur and Frank Bidart. Wilbur recalled, "She attended to her art, but she also attended to other people and to the things of every day. James Merrill put this happily, in a recent reminiscence, when he spoke of her 'life-long impersonation of an ordinary woman.' Well, she was an incomparable poet and a delectable person; we loved her very much." "If the future is smart," Bidart declared, "surely her poems will continue to be read. Great poems don't replace one another; each does something nothing else does. The pathos and intimacy in her work deepened until the very end of her life. On October 6, 1979, we ran out of luck."

AVOCATIONAL INTERESTS: Travel, sailing.

BIOGRAPHICAL/CRITICAL SOURCES:

BOOKS

Bishop, Elizabeth, *The Collected Prose,* edited and introduced by Robert Giroux, Farrar, Straus, 1984.

Boyers, Robert, editor, *Contemporary Poetry in America,* Schocken, 1974.

Brower, Reuben A., editor, *Twentieth Century Literature in Retrospect,* Harvard University Press, 1971.

Contemporary Authors Bibliographical Series, Volume 2: *American Poets,* Gale, 1986.

Contemporary Literary Criticism, Gale, Volume 1, 1973, Volume 4, 1975, Volume 9, 1978, Volume 13, 1980, Volume 15, 1980, Volume 32, 1985.

Dictionary of Literary Biography, Volume 5: *American Poets since World War II,* Gale, 1980.

Engle, Paul, and Joseph Langland, editors, *Poet's Choice,* Dial, 1962.

Frankenberg, Lloyd, *Pleasure Dome: On Reading Modern Poetry,* Houghton, 1949.

Fussell, *Abroad: British Literary Travelling between the Wars,* Oxford University Press, 1980.

Jarrell, Randall, *Poetry and the Age,* Random House, 1953.

Jarrell, Randall, *Third Book of Criticism,* Farrar, Straus, 1969.

Kalstone, David, *Five Temperaments: Elizabeth Bishop, Robert Lowell, James Merrill, Adrienne Rich, John Ashbery,* Oxford University Press, 1977.

MacMahon, Candace, compiler, *Elizabeth Bishop: A Bibliography, 1927-1979,* University Press of Virginia, 1980.

Mazzaro, Jerome, *Postmodern American Poetry,* University of Illinois Press, 1980.

Molesworth, Charles, *The Fierce Embrace: A Study of Contemporary American Poetry,* University of Missouri Press, 1979.

Pinsky, Robert, *The Situation of Poetry,* Princeton University Press, 1976.

Rosenthal, M. L., *The Modern Poets,* Oxford University Press, 1960.

Schwartz, Lloyd, and Sybil P. Estess, editors, *Elizabeth Bishop and Her Art,* University of Michigan Press, 1983.

Stepanchev, Stephen, *American Poetry since 1945: A Critical Survey,* Harper, 1965.

Stevenson, Anne, *Elizabeth Bishop,* Twayne, 1966.

Vendler, Helen, *Part of Nature, Part of Us: Modern American Poets,* Harvard University Press, 1980.

von Hallberg, Robert, *American Poetry and Culture, 1945-1980,* Harvard University Press, 1985.

Winslow, Ann, editor, *Trial Balances,* Macmillan, 1935.

Wylie, Diana E., *Elizabeth Bishop and Howard Nemerov: A Reference Guide,* G. K. Hall, 1983.

PERIODICALS

American Literature, March, 1982, October, 1983.
American Poetry Review, March/April, 1978, January/February, 1980, January/February, 1985.
Antaeus, winter/spring, 1981.
Antioch Review, summer, 1981.
Arizona Quarterly, Volume 32, 1976, winter, 1982.
Atlantic, January, 1966.
Books Abroad, winter, 1967.
Book Week, February 20, 1966.
Book World, April 27, 1969.
Boston Review, April, 1983.
Canadian Poetry, fall/winter, 1980.
Canto, winter, 1977.
Centennial Review, winter, 1978, winter, 1981.
Chicago Review, Volume 18, numbers 3-4, 1966.
Chicago Tribune Book World, April 1, 1984.
Christian Science Monitor, January 6, 1966.
College English, February, 1959.
Commonweal, February 15, 1957.
Contemporary Literature, winter, 1971, fall, 1984, summer, 1985.
Dublin Magazine, January-March, 1957.
Encounter, December, 1983.
Field, fall, 1984.
George Herbert Journal, spring, 1982.
Grand Street, autumn, 1983.
Hollins Critic, February, 1977.
Hudson Review, autumn, 1956.
Iowa Review, winter, 1979.
Kenyon Review, Volume 19, number 2, 1957, Volume 28, number 2, 1966.
Life, July 4, 1969.
Listener, November 30, 1967, June 2, 1983.
London Magazine, March 1968.
London Review of Books, May 7, 1984.
Los Angeles Times Book Review, April 17, 1983, February 19, 1984.
Massachusetts Review, autumn, 1970, autumn, 1982, summer, 1983.
Michigan Quarterly Review, winter, 1977.
Modern Poetry Studies, winter, 1975, spring, 1977, winter, 1977.
Nation, September 28, 1946.
New England Quarterly, June, 1956, December, 1984.
New Leader, December 6, 1965.
New Republic, October 21, 1946, April 9, 1966, February 5, 1977, November 10, 1979, April 4, 1983, March 19, 1984.
New Statesman, April 6, 1984.
Newsweek, January 31, 1977, March 14, 1982, February 13, 1984.
New Yorker, October 5, 1946, October 8, 1955, May 29, 1978.
New York Herald Tribune Book Review, September 4, 1955.
New York Review of Books, October 12, 1967, June 9, 1977.
New York Times, January 22, 1977, February 12, 1983, January 5, 1984.
New York Times Book Review, July 17, 1955, May 5, 1968, January 7, 1973, February 6, 1977, December 3, 1978, February 27, 1983, January 15, 1984.
Observer, April 8, 1984.
Paris Review, summer, 1981.
Parnassus, spring/summer, 1973, fall/winter, 1976, spring/summer, 1977.

Partisan Review, winter, 1956, spring, 1970.

Ploughshares, Volume 2, number 4, 1975, Volume 3, numbers 3 and 4, 1977, Volume 5, number 1, 1979, Volume 6, number 2, 1980.

PN Review, February, 1984.

Poetry, December, 1955, March, 1979.

Poetry Review, June, 1983.

Publishers Weekly, July 7, 1945.

Raritan, summer, 1984.

Salmagundi, summer/fall, 1974.

Saturday Review, January 18, 1958.

Sewanee Review, summer, 1947, spring, 1978.

Shenandoah, Volume 17, number 2, 1966, Volume 33, number 1, 1981-82.

South Atlantic Quarterly, summer, 1983.

South Carolina Review, November, 1977.

Southern Review, autumn, 1977.

Times Literary Supplement, November 23, 1967, March 7, 1980, August 28, 1981, June 3, 1983, April 27, 1984.

Twentieth Century Literature, Volume 11, number 4, 1966, Volume 28, number 4, 1982.

Vanity Fair, June, 1983.

Virginia Quarterly Review, spring, 1966, autumn, 1969, spring, 1984.

Washington Post Book World, February 20, 1983.

World Literature Today, winter, 1977.

Young Readers Review, September, 1968.

OBITUARIES:

PERIODICALS

Chicago Tribune, October 9, 1979.

New York Times, October 8, 1979.

Publishers Weekly, October 22, 1979.

Time, October 22, 1979.

*   *   *

bissett, bill 1939-

PERSONAL: Born November 23, 1939, in Halifax, Nova Scotia, Canada; son of Frederick William and Katherine Hamilton (Covert) Bissett; children: Ooljah. *Education:* Attended Dalhousie University, 1956-57, and University of British Columbia, 1963-65. *Politics:* "equality." *Religion:* "erth air fire n watr."

ADDRESSES: Home—Box 273, 1755 Robson St., Vancouver, British Columbia, Canada V6G 1C9. *Agent*—League of Canadian Poets, 24 Ryerson, Toronto, Ontario, Canada.

CAREER: Poet. Has worked as a record store clerk, library clerk, house painter, ditch digger, gas station attendant, bean picker, disc jockey, construction worker, sign painter, English tutor, fence builder, and hauler. Editor and printer, blewointmentpress, 1964—. Has had one-man art exhibitions at Vancouver Art Gallery, 1972 and 1984, and Western Front Gallery, Vancouver, 1977 and 1979.

MEMBER: League of Canadian Poets, Association of Canadian Publishers, Literary Press Group.

AWARDS, HONORS: Canada Council grants, 1967, 1968, 1972, 1975 and 1977, and travel grants, 1971 and 1977.

WRITINGS:

POETRY

Th jinx ship nd othr trips; pomes-drawings-collage, Very Stone Press, 1966.

we sleep inside each other all, self-illustrated, Ganglia Press, 1966.

Fires in th Tempul, self-illustrated, Very Stone Press, 1967, new edition, Vancouver Art Gallery Publications, 1984.

where is miss florence riddle, Luv Press, 1967.

Lebanon Voices, Weed/Flower Press, 1967.

Of th Land/Divine Service Poems, Weed/Flower Press, 1968.

Awake in th Red Desert!, Talonbooks, 1968.

Killer Whale, See Hear Productions, 1969.

Nobody Owns th Earth, House of Anansi, 1971.

air 6, Air Press, 1971.

Tuff Shit Love Pomes, Bandit/Black Moss Press, 1971.

dragon fly, Weed/Flower Press, 1971.

drifting into war, Talonbooks, 1971.

(With Earle Birney, Judith Copithorne, and Andy Suknaski) *Four Parts Sand: Concrete Poems,* Oberon Press, 1972.

air 10-11-12, Air Press, 1972.

Pass the Food, Release th Spirit Book, Talonbooks, 1973.

Vancouver Mainland Ice and Cold Storage, Writers Forum, 1973.

Medicine my mouths on fire, Oberon Press, 1974.

space travl, Air Press, 1974.

Living with the Vishyun, New Star Books, 1974.

Plutonium Missing, Intermedia, 1976.

An Allusyun to Macbeth, Black Moss Press, 1976.

sailor, Talonbooks, 1978, 2nd edition, 1982.

Beyond Even Faithful Legends, Talonbooks, 1981.

northern birds in color, Talonbooks, 1981.

Seagull on yonge street, Talonbooks, 1983.

Canada Gees Mate for Life, Talonbooks, 1985.

POETRY; PUBLISHED BY BLEWOINTMENTPRESS

what poetiks, 1967.

(th) Gossamer Bed Pan, 1967, new edition, 1974.

Sunday Work?, 1969.

Liberating Skies, 1969.

The Lost Angel Mining Co., 1969.

A Marvellous Experience, 1969.

S th Story I to, 1970.

The Outlaw, 1970.

blew trewz, 1970.

Rush what fukin thery, 1971.

th Ice bag, 1972.

pomes for yoshi, 1972.

th first sufi line, 1973.

what, 1973.

drawings, 1974.

you can eat it at th opening, 1974.

Th fifth sun, 1975.

Image being, 1975.

star-dust, 1975.

Venus, 1975.

th wind up tongue, 1976.

soul arrow, 1979.

sa n th monkey, 1980.

s n his crystal ball, 1981.

Also author of *IBM.*

RECORDINGS

"Awake in th Red Desert," See Hear Productions, 1968.

"Medicine My Mouths on Fire," Oberon, 1976.

"Northern Birds in Color," blewointmentpress, 1982.

"Sonic Horses 1," Underwich Editions, 1984.

OTHER

(Illustrator) Jim Brown, *The Circus in the Boy's Eye*, Very Stone Press, 1966.

Author of television scripts "In search of innocence," 1963, "Strange grey day this," 1964, and "Poets of the 60s," 1967, and of video "Portrait," 1984.

SIDELIGHTS: Employing idiosyncratic spelling and grammar, bill bissett attempts in his poems to recreate the actual way in which language is spoken. His innovative use of typography and margins, and his use of lower-case letters in much of his work, reflects bissett's "idea that relationships such as hierarchy, cause-effect sequences, and linear writings are repressive," as Len Early explains in *Essays on Canadian Writing.*

Several reviewers see a naive quality in bissett's writing. Frank Davey of *Canadian Forum* argues that this naivety has its roots in bissett's basically religious sensibility. The poet's "vision," Davey writes, "is of a transcendent, static world, simple and hard in outline, paralleling our own complex and sordid one just beyond the usual limitations of human perception." The use of a simple, elemental vocabulary and idiosyncratic spelling are bissett's attempts to "write of an unqualified, pure, archetypical, visionary world. . . . [They are] simplifications, meant to indicate a consciousness more attuned to cosmic non-complexity than to earthly convention." Writing in *Canadian Literature,* Al Purdy believes "the very naivete of [bissett's] language and themes, the earnestness and complete personal belief he brings to poems— these make him oddly touching and, I think, worthwhile."

Commenting to *CA,* bissett writes that he is "continuing to xploor vizual n sound writing as well as conversahunal vois writing with accent on/tord picture in th word sound utterance— chants—nd what speech is for—wher it comes from—often without any correct grammar spelling syntax linear meening spelling mor 'phonetik' as sound."

BIOGRAPHICAL/CRITICAL SOURCES:

BOOKS

Contemporary Literary Criticism, Volume XVIII, Gale, 1981.
Dictionary of Literary Biography, Volume 53: *Canadian Writers since 1986,* Gale, 1986.

PERIODICALS

Canadian Forum, July-August, 1972.
Canadian Literature, autumn, 1972, spring, 1973, spring, 1974.
Essays on Canadian Writing, fall, 1976, spring, 1977.
Fiddlehead, spring, 1967.

*   *   *

BIYIDI, Alexandre 1932-
(Mongo Beti, Eza Boto)

PERSONAL: Professionally known as Mongo Beti; born June 30, 1932, in M'Balmayo (one source says Akometam), Cameroon; married; children: three. *Education:* Attended University of Aix-Marseille; received B.A. (with honors) from Sorbonne, University of Paris, M.A., 1966. *Politics:* Marxist.

ADDRESSES: Agent—Helena Strassova, Paris, France.

CAREER: Educator in Lamballe, France; secondary education instructor in classical Greek, Latin, and French literature in Rouen, France. Writer, 1953.

AWARDS, HONORS: Sainte-Beuve Prize, 1948, for *Mission Accomplished,* and 1957, for *King Lazarus.*

WRITINGS:

NOVELS; UNDER PSEUDONYM MONGO BETI, EXCEPT AS NOTED

(Under pseudonym Eza Boto) *Ville cruelle* (title means "Cruel City"), Editions Africaines, 1954.
Le Pauvre Christ de Bomba, Laffont, 1956, translation by Gerald Moore published as *The Poor Christ of Bomba,* Heinemann Educational (London), African Writers Series, 1971.
Mission terminee, Buchet Chastel/Correa, 1957, translation by Peter Green published as *Mission Accomplished,* Macmillan, 1958 (published in England as *Mission to Kala,* Muller, 1958), rewritten by John Davey and published as *Mission to Kala,* Heinemann Educational, African Writers Series, 1964.
Le Roi miracule: Chronique des Essazam, Buchet Chastel/Correa, 1958, English translation published as *King Lazarus,* Muller, 1960, published as *King Lazarus: A Novel,* introduction by O. R. Dathorne, Macmillan/Collier, 1971.
Main basse sur le Cameroun: Autopsie d'une decolonisation (political essay; title means "The Plundering of Cameroon"), F. Maspero, 1972.
Remember Ruben (title in pidgin English), Buchet Chastel, 1973, translation by Moore published under the same title, Three Continents Press, 1980.
Perpetue et l'habitude du malheur, Buchet Chastel, 1974, translation by John Reed and Clive Wake published as *Perpetua and the Habit of Unhappiness,* Heinemann Educational, African Writers Series, 1978.
La Ruine presque cocasse d'un polichinelle: Remember Ruben deux, Harmattan, 1979, translation by Richard Bjornson published as *Lament for an African Pol,* Three Continents Press, 1985.
Les Deux Meres de Guillaume Ismael Dzewatama: Futur Camionneur, Buchet Chastel, 1982.
La Revanche de Guillaume Ismael Dzewatama, Buchet Chastel, 1984.

Founder in 1978 and editor of *Peuples noirs Peuples africains* (tribune of French-speaking black radicals). Contributor during the early 1960s to the anti-colonial journals *Tumultueux Cameroun* and *Revue camerounaise.*

SIDELIGHTS: Born in the Cameroon town of M'Balmayo and educated in French missionary schools and universities, Mongo Beti, as he prefers to be known, centers his novels on the encroachment of Western ideals, education, and religion upon African civilization. In particular, he laments the inability of European administrators and missionaries during the early twentieth century colonial rule to recognize the inherent value of existing African religions and beliefs, as well as the Africans' own inability to withstand European influence. Calling Beti "one of the most elegant and sophisticated of African writers," Eustace Palmer reflected in his book *The Growth of the African Novel* that "taken as a whole [Beti's work] probably gives the most thoroughgoing exposure to the stupidity of the imperialist attempt to devalue traditional education and religion and replace them by an inadequate western educational system and a hypocritical Christian religion."

In his first four novels, written from 1954 to 1958, Beti couches his disdain for European imperialist advances and his own countrymen's gullibility in episodic tales combining comic farce and bitter satire. Thomas Cassirer pointed out in a *L'Esprit Createur* review that each of Beti's anti-imperialist novels features an "African village . . . situated at the meeting point between traditional communal life and a new awareness of imminent change."

When European administrators and missionaries—sometimes well-meaning and sometimes corrupt, but always ignorant—arrive in an untouched African village, misunderstanding and chaos inevitably ensue. Beti emphasizes the absurdity of the misunderstandings, suggesting through satire the harm that befalls both the modern and traditional societies when their people attempt to impose conflicting values on one another.

While a student at Aix, Beti penned his first novel, *Ville cruelle*—which means "Cruel City"—under the pseudonym Eza Boto. He has since repudiated both the name and the novel, which is generally considered weak and melodramatic. Critics have noted, however, that this early effort displays much of the perceptive wit found in his later writings. Set in Tanga, the site of lumber mills and rail yards, the novel details the bewilderment and anger of African workers and their families at this unsolicited imposition of Western industrialization.

In *The Poor Christ of Bomba,* set in the colonial 1930s, comic irony arises when the well-meaning Reverend Father Superior Drumont sets out to convert the inhabitants of a bush village and save them from the greed and temptation that had corrupted Europeans, later to discover that the Africans had only embraced his religion hoping to learn the Europeans' secrets of material success. He also learns that the "sixa," a missionary house where African girls live for several months to learn the duties of a Christian wife, has become an agent not of Christian piety but of venereal disease. "Faced with this horrendous proof that he has unknowingly [perpetrated] the very corruption from which he tried to protect the Africans," Cassirer related, "Father Drumont returns to Europe in despair."

Father Drumont represents the type of missionary Beti treats sympathetically in his novels, according to Cassirer. "They are . . . the only ones who explicitly believe in a universal humanity that transcends barriers of race and culture," he explained. "Yet the missionaries' faith in universal humanity remains purely abstract because their primitivist view of the African leads them to treat him as a pure child of nature with no cultural identity of his own." A. C. Brench further described Beti's missionaries in *The Novelists' Inheritance in French Africa* as "the kind who want to do good for the Africans but, unfortunately for them, start from the premise that all Africans are unable to organize their lives unless helped by Europeans." This well-meaning denial of an inherent African culture and intellect is not only insulting to Africans, Brench suggested, but is harmful to both cultures, as the character Father Drumont learns. "The change that takes place in the Father is one of the most interesting features of the novel," Palmer found. Although not all missionaries are so enlightened during the course of their work, Palmer explained, with each discovery of a failed good intention "the Father seems to be gradually groping his way towards a realization of the validity of traditional life and culture."

The missionary in *King Lazarus,* Father Le Guen, is somewhat more zealous and uncompromising than Father Drumont of *The Poor Christ of Bomba.* Palmer noted, "Thematically, [*King Lazarus*] is similar to the earlier novels since it is also concerned with the exposure of the pretentiousness of an alien cultural and imperialist system which shows little respect for the traditional life and dignity of the people." In the novel, Father Le Guen persuades the polygamous tribal chief of the Essazam to convert to Christianity and give up all but one of his wives. The twenty-two former wives and their families, outraged at the breach of tribal custom as well as at the rudeness of turning the women out of their home, protest to the French colonial authorities. In the confrontation between the civil administration, the missionary, and the tribal chief, Beti exposes the vices of each party. The authorities, attempting to stop Father Le Guen from converting the chief, do not do so out of any respect for the tribal culture but for reasons of political expediency, Palmer pointed out. Father Le Guen believes his firm stand on Christianity and monogamy are for the best, but he ignores such thoughtful and practical considerations as where the now-homeless ex-wives will live. "His zeal might have been partly excused if the conversion to Christianity had made the chief a better man," Palmer maintained. "On the contrary, it seems to liberate the most repulsive impulses in him." Irony and comedy pervade in *King Lazarus* as in Beti's other works, but, according to Palmer, "its prevailing cynicism suggests the bitterness of a man who is probably fed up with most things."

Like *The Poor Christ of Bomba* and *King Lazarus,* Beti's *Mission Accomplished* "is a farce but, at the same time, there is bitterness and sorrow," judged Brench. Set in the 1950s—the last decade of colonial rule in Cameroon—the novel details the shortcomings of the colonial educational system. No whites appear in the novel, but European influence is introduced by the protagonist, Jean-Marie Medza, who returns to his village home after failing his exams at a French secondary school. He is immediately sent to Kala, a bush village, to retrieve the runaway wife of a distant relative. "Initially, he looks upon this mission as a means of parading his superior knowledge," Brench related, and the villagers reward him with food, animals, and the chief's daughter in marriage for the wisdom they believe he is teaching them. "Only later does he realize how inadequate his education and understanding of life really are," Brench remarked. "Jean-Marie appreciates more and more, as his stay lengthens, the positive qualities they have and which he has never been able to acquire." Summarizing Beti's thesis in the novel, Palmer explained that "the formal classical education to which young francophones were exposed was ultimately valueless, since it alienated them from their roots in traditional society, taught them to consider the values of that society inferior to French ones and gave them little preparation for the life they were to lead."

An opponent of the French government in control of his country and, later, of the Yaounde regime in power, Beti left Cameroon before it achieved its independence in 1960. After settling in France, Beti became a teacher and for more than a decade gave up writing. In 1972, however, he composed a lengthy essay entitled *Main basse sur le Cameroun: Autopsie d'une decolonisation* (the title means "The Plundering of Cameroon"), criticizing the Yaounde regime for remaining under the control of the French after the country's formal liberation.

A series of novels soon followed, focusing more on the problems of modern, decolonized Cameroon than on the country during its colonization. Still containing elements of satire, the books assume a documentary-style narrative and approach cynicism more closely than Beti's previous works. In *Remember Ruben, Perpetua and the Habit of Unhappiness,* and *Lament for an African Pol,* Beti depicts the harsh aspects of life under the rule of Baba Toura, a tyrannical president of the United Republic of Cameroon after the country's independence. Wrote Robert P. Smith, Jr., in *World Literature Today,* "Toura's administration, which fosters famine, misery, persecution and corruption in the wake of African independence, is perpetuated by evil characters in the novels against whom heroic protagonists struggle constantly." Heroic inspiration arises from the memory of patriot Ruben Urn Nyobe, leader of political opposition in Cameroon before its independence. Although Ruben himself never appears in the novels, tales of his valiant deeds and lofty ideals motivate oppressed villagers into revolutionary action.

Remember Ruben follows the life of a solitary, young boy renamed Mor-Zamba by the villagers who take him in, and a friend he makes, Abena. When Mor-Zamba is older his neighbors send him to a labor camp to prevent his marriage to the daughter of a prominent villager, and Abena goes after him. The men reunite eighteen years later, Abena having become a revolutionary and a hero, and Mor-Zamba having learned his true origin. Ben Okri of *New Statesman* praised the author's handling of "the relationship between individuals and a complex, clouded situation of emerging national politics," adding that "Beti's depiction of a colony's traumas, confusions and corruptions is vivid and masterly."

Again emphasizing the corruption of national politics through glimpses of the harshness of individual lives, Beti laments the slave-like conditions of the modern woman in contemporary Africa in his *Perpetua and the Habit of Unhappiness.* The novel focuses on the miserable marriage of the main character, Perpetua, to her husband, Edouard; the tender but doomed affair between Perpetua and her lover, Zeyang; and the true friendship between Perpetua and her companion, Anna-Marie. Smith, writing in the *College Language Association Journal,* called the novel "a dramatic indictment of the ill-fated independence in [Beti's] native land dominated by corrupt dictatorial power, as well as a forceful denunciation of the disgraceful status of African women in such regimes." Smith praised Beti's treatment of modern-day Africa, saying the author wrote *Perpetua* "not to criticize the colonial past as was his custom, but to accuse the present period of independence and self-government, and to pave the way to a better future for Africa and Africans."

A novel that "no serious reader of African literature can afford to neglect," advised *Choice*'s N. F. Lazarus, Beti's *Lament for an African Pol* chronicles the activities of Mor-Zamba, who reappears from the novel *Remember Ruben* with two revolutionary friends to organize a resistance "against the despotic rule of a colonially sanctioned chief." According to Smith in *World Literature Today,* "the novel takes on a 'Robin Hood' atmosphere when the three resolute Rubenists set out on their long journey, robbing the rich and giving to the poor, outwitting the oppressors and conveying courage to the oppressed." Affirming that Beti's "storytelling technique remains vibrant and captivating," Smith noted that, as in *Perpetua,* "of particular interest is the author's sympathetic treatment of African women."

Again "studying marriage patterns and the evolving roles of women," Beti's 1982 novel, *Les Deux Meres de Guillaume Ismael Dzewatama: Futur Camionneur,* recounts "a curious love story, full of drama, harmonizing the political and literary," assessed Hal Wylie in a review of the book in *World Literature Today.* Wylie explained that, similar to Beti's other writings, *Les Deux Meres* "focuses on a unique family which nevertheless dramatizes the sad plight of a corrupt, dictatorial country like Beti's own Cameroon." The family in the novel consists of young Guillaume Ismael, his father, and Guillaume's two mothers—the father's first wife and his French mistress, whom he married to resolve a difficult situation. The double marriage solves nothing; instead, it prompts more confusion. Reflected Wylie, "Seeing the tensions from the point of view of the African boy and his good-hearted, idealistic but naive white mother throws into relief the melodrama and pathos of modern Africa and all its ironies."

Commenting on Beti's range of political and social statements and his episodic, satirical method of conveying them, Brench remarked: "Nothing is sacred: prejudices, passions, ideals, purity are all corrupted by Beti's unrelenting laughter and insistence on the physical nature of things. . . . Yet, behind all this there is this inexpressible sadness, as if a great deception had made life bitter and cynical humour was the only relief." Several critics have pointed to a statement about Cameroon made by the character Jean-Marie at the end of *Mission Accomplished,* calling it Beti's lament for the plight of the African people: "The tragedy which our nation is suffering today is that of a man left to his own devices in a world which does not belong to him, which he has not made and does not understand."

MEDIA ADAPTATIONS: Perpetua and the Habit of Unhappiness was adapted by Michael Etherton as a play of the same title; it was first produced in Zaria, Nigeria, in 1981.

BIOGRAPHICAL/CRITICAL SOURCES:

BOOKS

Brench, A. C., *The Novelists' Inheritance in French Africa: Writers from Senegal to Cameroon,* Oxford University Press, 1967.
Contemporary Literary Criticism, Volume 27, Gale, 1984.
Moore, Gerald, *Seven African Writers,* Oxford University Press, 1962.
Palmer, Eustace, *The Growth of the African Novel,* Heinemann Educational, 1979.
The Penguin Companion to Classical, Oriental, and African Literature, McGraw, 1969.

PERIODICALS

Choice, October, 1975, January, 1986.
College Language Association Journal, March, 1976.
Journal of Black Studies, December, 1976.
L'Esprit Createur, autumn, 1970.
Nation, October 11, 1965.
New Statesman, January 30, 1981.
Times Literary Supplement, May 15, 1969, October 29, 1971.
World Literature Today, winter, 1982, winter, 1984.

*   *   *

BLACKWOOD, Caroline 1931-

PERSONAL: Born Lady Caroline Hamilton-Temple-Blackwood, July 16, 1931, in Northern Ireland; daughter of the Marquis and Marchioness of Dufferin and Ava; married Lucien Freud (a painter; divorced); married Israel Citkovitz (a pianist; divorced); married Robert Lowell (a poet), 1972 (died September 12, 1977); children: (with Citkovitz) three daughters (one deceased); (with Lowell) Robert Sheridan.

ADDRESSES: Home—Redcliffe Square, London, England. *Office*—c/o Heinemann Ltd., 10 Upper Grosvenor St., London W1X 9PA, England.

CAREER: Essayist, short-story writer, and novelist.

WRITINGS:

For All That I Found There (short stories and nonfiction), Duckworth, 1973, Braziller, 1974.
The Stepdaughter (novel), Duckworth, 1976, Scribner, 1977.
Great Granny Webster (novel), Duckworth, 1977, Scribner, 1978.
(With Anna Haycraft) *Darling, You Shouldn't Have Gone to So Much Trouble* (cookbook), Cape, 1980.
The Fate of Mary Rose (novel), Summit, 1981.
Goodnight Sweet Ladies (short stories), Heinemann, 1983.
Corrigan (novel), Heinemann, 1984, Viking, 1985.
On the Perimeter (nonfiction), Heinemann, 1984, Penguin, 1985.

In the Pink: Caroline Blackwood on Hunting (nonfiction), Bloomsbury, 1987.

SIDELIGHTS: Well known in England as a novelist and nonfiction writer, Caroline Blackwood evokes unusual praise from a variety of critics. As Priscilla Martin notes in a *Dictionary of Literary Biography* article on the author, "Her material is anguish, dementia, and despair—injuries of all kinds, insanity, rape, murder, internecine marriages, a disastrous face-lift, suicidal isolation. Her distinctive power is to direct an unflinching gaze at the intolerable and convey it in elegant, witty, and dispassionate prose." Such subject matter seems initially unlikely for a woman born Lady Caroline Hamilton-Temple-Blackwood, heiress to an Irish peerage, as well as a descendent of the eighteenth-century dramatist Richard Brinsley Sheridan. "She grew up in the beautiful, crumbling, leaky ancestral mansion, Clandeboye, in County Down, the basis for the white elephant of a stately home in [Blackwood's novel] *Great Granny Webster*," adds Martin. Educated in boarding schools, Blackwood nonetheless learned enough about life to produce a first collection, *For All That I Found There*, that reflects on her youth around Ulster, Northern Ireland, where "the troubles" plagued others. This book "is odd because it's split into three parts: Fiction, Fact, and Ulster," reports *London Magazine* writer Digby Durrant. "But it's not the hopscotch this makes it sound. In fact, this curious dividing . . . is revealing. For the excellent short story writer she is turns into an equally excellent journalist with such smoothness there seems little difference."

With *The Stepdaughter* Blackwood moves into the kind of psychological drama that characterizes the best of her style. The anti-heroine of this first novel has been abandoned by her husband in Manhattan and left with "his grotesquely fat child bloated by rejection and a magnificent apartment with dizzy views through plexiglass," as Duncan Fallowell describes it in a *Spectator* review. There is also a howling infant, the product of their marriage, who is being cared-for by an unhappy *au pair.* The stepmother, known only as "K," fumes constantly and quietly through letters as she plots a way out of her unhappy lot. "Like all [Blackwood's] novels, *The Stepdaughter* can be seen as a modern variation on an established form," notes Martin. "It is a miniature epistolary novel whose arena is . . . the conscience of a threatened and isolated woman." With its "unblinking view of man's selfishness and woman's dependence *The Stepdaughter* is a notable contribution to the women's movement," finds *Encounter* reviewer James Price. "It is also, I should hazard, a philosophical and religious novel. It begins with a cry of pain, which can be seen to be a philosophical position. It ends with a sense of loss, which can be seen to be a religious one. It is an unusual and affecting experience."

The title character of Blackwood's second novel, *Great Granny Webster*, "is enormously wealthy [but] stingy with a vengeance," as Carol Greenberg Felsenthal puts it in *Chicago Tribune Book World*. Granny is "nearly as old-fashioned as she is stingy, but there is absolutely nothing charming or even eccentric about her aversion to modern conveniences," writes Felsenthal, who adds that "no matter what the season, her manor is cold and damp." Since Granny outlives all her friends and enemies, her eventual death is noted only by her great-granddaughter (the book's narrator) and Richards, her "trampled maid," as described by *New York Review of Books* critic Karl Miller. As Granny's history unfolds, it becomes apparent that "the women of the dynasty have been inclined to go mad," Miller offers. The critic goes on to say that in England, where *Great Granny Webster* was first published, "the tale has gone down well [since there] the appetite for the eccentricities and sufferings of the privileged never sleeps.

But there is another reason for its doing well, which has to do with the appetite of its writer. Without being, in any extensive way, artless or careless, it reads like a long and colorful letter, and has the force of an eager unburdening."

Among Blackwood's other novels, *Corrigan* gained favorable notices as a gothic satire in the author's tradition. It centers on the unlikely romance between Devina, a widow wasting away from ennui, and Corrigan, the wheelchair-bound man who rejuvenates her. "Meanwhile, Devina's daughter, Nadine, discovers that she loathes her journalist husband, madly envies her mother, and feels savage ill will toward Corrigan," Laurie Stone observes in a *Village Voice* column. "What Nadine discovers about the mysterious Corrigan and his complex relationship with her mother at the end of her life provides a denouement filled with surprises and irony," *New York Times Book Review* writer Carolyn Gaiser explains. To this reviewer, the author's "sly wit and her affection for her characters brings a glow to these pages, a sunniness that manages to be believable without ever becoming sentimental. [Blackwood] has written a charming tour de force."

Departing from fiction, Blackwood has co-written a cookbook with the arresting title *Darling, You Shouldn't Have Gone to So Much Trouble*, as well as an examination of the British passion for fox hunting and its equally passionate anti-hunting foes. *In the Pink: Caroline Blackwood on Hunting* didn't garner the praise that Blackwood's novels have—"It cannot be said that Lady Caroline knows much about the vast and boring literature on this touchy subject," finds *Spectator* critic Raymond Carr—but the author continues to be cherished in England as a stringent social critic.

BIOGRAPHICAL/CRITICAL SOURCES:

BOOKS

Contemporary Literary Criticism, Gale, Volume 6, 1976, Volume 9, 1978.
Dictionary of Literary Biography, Volume 14: *British Novelists since 1960*, Gale, 1983.

PERIODICALS

Chicago Tribune Book World, September 10, 1978.
Encounter, September, 1976.
London Magazine, October/November, 1974.
Los Angeles Times Book Review, July 28, 1985.
New Statesman, November 30, 1973, June 4, 1976.
New York Review of Books, September 15, 1977, November 9, 1978.
New York Times Book Review, July 26, 1981, July 14, 1985, December 1, 1985.
Spectator, June 5, 1976, September 17, 1977, December 13, 1980, March 7, 1981, October 15, 1983, October 10, 1987.
Times Literary Supplement, April 5, 1974, September 2, 1977, November 14, 1980, February 27, 1981, September 21, 1984, October 19, 1984, September 25, 1987.
Village Voice, June 25, 1985.
Washington Post Book World, June 2, 1974, October 16, 1977, July 10, 1981, June 30, 1985.

*   *   *

BLADE, Alexander
See SILVERBERG, Robert

BLAIR, Eric (Arthur) 1903-1950
(George Orwell)

PERSONAL: Born June 25, 1903, in Motihari, Bengal (now Bihar), India; British citizen born abroad; died of complications from tuberculosis, January 21, 1950, in London, England; buried in All Saints churchyard, Sutton Courtenay, Berkshire, England; son of Richard Walmesley (a colonial civil servant) and Ida Mabel (Limouzin) Blair; married Eileen O'Shaughnessy, June 9, 1936 (died, March 29, 1945); married Sonia Brownell (an editorial assistant), October 13, 1949; children: (adopted) Richard Horatio. *Education:* Graduated from Eton College, 1921. *Politics:* Self-described "Tory anarchist" during early 1930s and "democratic Socialist" beginning in mid-1930s.

CAREER: Writer. Police officer for Indian Imperial Police in Burma, 1922-27; dishwasher in Paris, France, 1929; The Hawthorns (private school), Hayes, Middlesex, England, teacher, 1932-33; Frays College (private school), Uxbridge, England, teacher, 1933; Booklovers' Corner (used book store), London, England, clerk, 1934-36; shopkeeper in Wallington, Herfordshire, England, beginning in 1936; British Broadcasting Corp. (BBC), London, began as assistant, became producer of educational radio programs, 1941-43; *Tribune,* London, literary editor, 1943-45, author of "As I Please" column, 1943-47; *Observer,* London, correspondent in France, Germany, and England, 1945. *Military service:* Militia of Workers' Party of Marxist Unity (POUM), 1937; based in Catalonia, Spain, served on Aragon front during Spanish Civil War; became lieutenant. Local Defence Volunteers (became Home Guard), 1940-43; served in England during World War II; became sergeant.

MEMBER: National Union of Journalists, Freedom Defence Committee (vice-chairman).

WRITINGS:

NOVELS; UNDER PSEUDONYM GEORGE ORWELL

Burmese Days, Harper, 1934.
A Clergyman's Daughter, Gollancz, 1935, Harper, 1936.
Keep the Aspidistra Flying, Gollancz, 1936, Harcourt, 1956.
Coming Up for Air, Gollancz, 1939, Harcourt, 1950.
Animal Farm (Book-of-the-Month Club selection), Secker & Warburg, 1945, Harcourt, 1946.
Nineteen Eighty-Four (Book-of-the-Month Club selection), Harcourt, 1949.
The Penguin Complete Novels of George Orwell (omnibus volume), Penguin, 1983.

NONFICTION; UNDER PSEUDONYM GEORGE ORWELL, EXCEPT AS NOTED

Down and Out in Paris and London, Harper, 1933.
The Road to Wigan Pier, Gollancz, 1937, Harcourt, 1958.
Homage to Catalonia, Secker & Warburg, 1938, Harcourt, 1952.
Inside the Whale, and Other Essays, Gollancz, 1940.
(Contributor) Victor Gollancz, John Strachey, and others, *The Betrayal of the Left: An Examination and Refutation of Communist Policy From October 1939 to January 1941, With Suggestions for an Alternative and an Epilogue on Political Morality,* Gollancz, 1941.
The Lion and the Unicorn: Socialism and the English Genius (essays), Secker & Warburg, 1941.
(Contributor) *Victory, or Vested Interest?,* Routledge, 1942.
James Burnham and the Managerial Revolution, Socialist Book Centre (London), 1946.

Dickens, Dali, and Others (essays), Reynal & Hitchcock, 1946 (published in England as *Critical Essays,* Secker & Warburg, 1946).
The English People, Collins, 1947.
Shooting an Elephant, and Other Essays (includes "A Hanging"), Harcourt, 1950.
Such, Such Were the Joys (essays; includes "Such, Such Were the Joys" and "Why I Write"), Harcourt, 1953 (abridged edition, substituting excerpts from *The Road to Wigan Pier* for "Such, Such Were the Joys," published in England as *England Your England, and Other Essays,* Secker & Warburg, 1953).
The Collected Essays, Journalism, and Letters of George Orwell, edited by wife, Sonia Orwell, and Ian Angus, Volume 1: *An Age Like This,* Volume 2: *My Country Right or Left,* Volume 3: *As I Please,* Volume 4: *In Front of Your Nose,* Harcourt, 1968.
The Penguin Complete Longer Non-Fiction of George Orwell (omnibus volume), Penguin, 1983.
The Penguin Essays of George Orwell, Penguin, 1984.
Orwell: The Lost Writings, edited with an introduction by W. J. West, Arbor House, 1985.
Orwell: The War Broadcasts, edited by W. J. West, Duckworth/British Broadcasting Corp., 1985, also published as *Orwell: The War Commentaries,* Pantheon, 1986.

Contributor, sometimes under name Eric Blair, of numerous articles and reviews to periodicals, including *Adelphi, Contemporary Jewish Record, Horizon, Listener, Manchester Evening News, New English Weekly, New Statesman and Nation,* and *Time and Tide.* Author of "London Letters" column for *Partisan Review,* 1941-46.

OTHER; UNDER PSEUDONYM GEORGE ORWELL

(Editor and author of introduction) E. M. Forster and others, *Talking to India: A Selection of English-Language Broadcasts to India,* Allen & Unwin, 1943.
(Editor with Reginald Reynolds, and author of introduction) *British Pamphleteers,* Volume 1, Wingate, 1948.

Work represented in numerous collections and anthologies, including *The Orwell Reader: Fiction, Essays, Reportage,* Harcourt, 1956.

SIDELIGHTS: "Liberty," wrote Eric Blair under his famous pseudonym of George Orwell, "is telling people what they do not want to hear." Orwell is best known for his novels *Animal Farm* and *Nineteen Eighty-Four,* which warn that the growing power of modern governments—regardless of their ideology—threatens to obliterate such widely held ideals as love of family, tolerance towards others, and the right to make up one's own mind. Convinced that human decency and common sense were the basis of a just society, the author repeatedly found himself in conflict with the ideological mass movements of his time, ranging from capitalism to fascism and communism. Orwell, wrote Laurence Brander, "was an individualist" who confronted "contemporary social and political problems . . . as a man who has done all his thinking for himself." Mistrusting the broad theories of twentieth-century political thinkers, he remained faithful to the truth of his own experience. "These qualities are rare and valuable," Brander declared, "and they are natural sources of his popularity with readers who must learn, like him, to work things out for themselves."

Orwell never wrote an autobiography and in personal conversations he was notably reserved. But as a writer who shunned abstract theory in favor of concrete detail, he gravitated toward the subject matter he knew best: his own life and thoughts. As George Woodcock cautioned, however, "the autobiographical form of [Orwell's] works can be deceptive, if it is taken too literally." At heart, Woodcock suggested, Orwell was a moralist, deeply concerned with the proper conduct of human life. His personal experiences raised ethical questions that he shared with his readers.

"From a very early age . . . I knew that when I grew up I should be a writer," said Orwell in his 1946 essay "Why I Write." Interestingly, Orwell claimed that he first saw writing as a remedy for loneliness. Born in colonial India to a low-level British official, he was sent to England as an infant along with his mother. He was eight and ready for boarding school by the time his father rejoined the family permanently. On the whole Orwell's family seems to have been fairly undemonstrative; his later adulation of family life, Woodcock suggested, may have sprung from feeling emotionally deprived during his youth. If Orwell's family disappointed him, his small hometown of Henley-on-Thames brought compensations. From there he explored the English countryside, fishing, hiking, and learning about animals. Later Orwell appeared to view Henley and its surroundings as symbolic of a calmer, saner world that existed in England before the two world wars. "By retaining one's childhood love of such things as trees, fishes, butterflies, and . . . [even] toads," he wrote, "one makes a peaceful world a little more probable," for if the world is only "steel and concrete . . . human beings will have no outlet for their surplus energy except in hatred and leader worship."

Boarding school was a source of lasting bitterness for Orwell—particularly the English preparatory school, where pre-teenage children were rigorously prepared to enter elite secondary schools and prestigious careers. His experience at St. Cyprian's prep school appears in "Such, Such Were the Joys," an article that Cyril Connolly called the "key to his formation." Judged by this study, St. Cyprian's provided some of Orwell's first glimpses into the misuse of power and the unfairness of England's class-conscious society. "I was in a world where it was *not possible* for me to be good," he wrote of the school's capricious discipline. As a scholarship student, he found that his background in the "lower-upper-middle class"—pursuing upper-class values on a middle-class income—invited the contempt of both his headmaster and his wealthy peers. "In a world where the prime necessities were money, titled relatives, athleticism, tailor-made clothes, neatly-brushed hair, a charming smile, I was no good," the author wrote. "[I knew] that the future was dark. Failure, failure, failure—failure behind me, failure ahead of me—that was by far the deepest conviction that I carried away." Hailed as the most unsparing account of English private schools ever written, "Such, Such Were the Joys" also shows the problem of interpreting Orwell's autobiographical work. Orwell never published this essay and when it appeared after his death, admirers of St. Cyprian's declared it inaccurate. Less partisan observers—including biographer Bernard Crick—note that the author's grim tone, and the insights he claims to have gained as a child, seem too broadly stated to be completely credible. After investigating Orwell's accusations, Crick concluded that while some details had been exaggerated for rhetorical effect, "the school seems to have been a pretty despicable place." Orwell's plight, Crick declared, "was an agony that he never forgot, but he put it to good use to understand the psychology of the poor and oppressed in his early writings and, later on, to champion their causes."

Ironically Orwell was a success by St. Cyprian's standards, going on to Eton College, England's most prestigious secondary school. In its tolerant atmosphere he became rebellious, shunning classwork and team sports in favor of reading or swimming on his own. After graduating in 1921 he had no prospect of entering a major university and showed few regrets. On an apparent whim he volunteered to become a policeman in the Burma branch of the Indian Imperial Police. Five years later he returned to England on medical leave, possibly suffering an early bout of tuberculosis. To the consternation of superiors, he quit without giving an explanation; to the dismay of his parents, he announced he would become a writer, a career in which he had little training or experience. Clearly Burma disturbed Orwell profoundly, although his reticence has kept biographers from knowing many of the personal details. In some of his most admired early writings, however, he alluded to those years with shame and indignation. As he explained in *The Road to Wigan Pier,* "In order to hate imperialism you have got to be part of it." One of Orwell's earliest works is the 1931 essay "A Hanging," which Crick called "the first piece of writing that shows [his] distinctive style and powers." In an observant, plain-spoken, subtly paced narrative the author recalled an execution in the courtyard of a Burmese prison. The condemned man's smallest act—stepping to avoid a puddle—brings Orwell an unsettling awareness that execution means destroying a living consciousness. Once the man is dead, Orwell seems relieved to join the other witnesses in empty-headed chatter. In another celebrated essay, "Shooting an Elephant," the author described his "execution" of an elephant that had briefly run wild and trampled a villager. Though the animal has returned to rationality, Orwell finds that as a colonial policeman he must kill it anyway or lose his authority in the eyes of the Burmese. "When the white man turns tyrant it is his own freedom that he destroys," the author declared. "He wears a mask, and his face grows to fit it."

The constricted life of the white conqueror informs Orwell's first published novel, *Burmese Days* (1934). The main character is John Flory, administrator for a British lumber company in Burma. Flory's skeptical view of colonialism parallels Orwell's own, but at age thirty-five, Flory seems more bitter than Orwell was when he quit Burma in his mid-twenties. As biographer Averil Gardner suggested, Flory can be seen as a portrait of the desperately isolated man Orwell feared he would become if he had stayed. Flory despises English bigotry, but he lacks the moral force to defy the white man's code of political silence or to accept the Burmese as true equals; instead he hopes for a "quite impossible she" who can share his complex discontent. He becomes infatuated with a shallow young Englishwoman, and when he realizes that she cannot accept him on his own terms, he commits suicide. As the story unfolds Orwell offers a detailed portrait of colonial life, including exotic landscapes, smug all-white clubs, and Burmese who variously admire, manipulate, or despise the English. Gardner called *Burmese Days* "an accomplished work of fiction, not only re-creating a Burma the reader knows to have existed, but creating a complex world of characters and relationships that one comes to believe in"—an unusual feat for Orwell, who sometimes failed at description and characterization in his zeal to convey a message. Aside from *Animal Farm* and *Nineteen Eighty-Four,* Gardner concluded, "*Burmese Days* is undoubtedly Orwell's best novel."

Upon returning from Burma, Orwell recalled in *The Road to Wigan Pier,* "I was conscious of an immense weight of guilt that I had got to expiate. I suppose that sounds exaggerated; but if you do for five years a job that you thoroughly disapprove of, you will probably feel the same." He described himself to colleagues as a "Tory anarchist," which seems to mean that he respected traditional ethics but mistrusted any authority that might enforce them. "I now realised that there was no need to go as far as Burma to find tyranny and exploitation," Orwell continued, because the lower classes of Europe were oppressed by poverty just as the Burmese were oppressed by British arms. Unfamiliar with the everyday struggles of the working poor, Orwell was drawn to the more blatant deprivation of tramps and beggars. As writer Jack London had done years before, he dressed as a tramp and explored the London underworld of flophouses and soup kitchens. He also spent nearly two years as a struggling writer in Paris, ending up a penniless dishwasher. These experiences inspired his first published book, *Down and Out in Paris and London* (1933). Autobiographical in form, it is basically a work of social reportage: "Poverty," Orwell declared, "is what I am writing about." At its best *Down and Out* resembles "A Hanging" by mixing social concern with acute observations on human nature. It was praised as a social document by many British and American reviewers, including James Farrell, author of the American realist classic *Studs Lonigan.* But even though Orwell apparently rearranged his account to heighten its dramatic impact, the result remains structurally flawed. The wandering narrative, for example, includes a notoriously overwrought tale of one man's night in a brothel. In "Why I Write," Orwell confessed that he once admired such "purple passages." He needed several years, Crick stressed, to appreciate his strengths.

Orwell's third and fourth books, both novels, reflect his demoralizing struggle to establish himself as a writer. As the 1930s began he had just returned from Paris, having written a series of novels and short stories that he destroyed when they proved unpublishable. His Paris adventure, not yet a book, seemed a fiasco; his savings from Burma were exhausted; and the Great Depression was deepening. For several years he worked reluctantly as a private-school teacher and a bookstore clerk, taking solace in the Anglican religion of his childhood. *A Clergyman's Daughter* and *Keep the Aspidistra Flying* seem to be fictionalized accounts of his frustrations. In each novel, as in *Burmese Days,* an isolated individual tries and fails to transcend his or her social role. *A Clergyman's Daughter* features a passive young woman employed by her father's Anglican church. Struck by amnesia and unable to return home, she begins a journey through English society, picking hops with day laborers and teaching at a repressive private school. Finally she rejoins her parish, having lost her faith but retaining her need for the order provided by a religious life. Gordon Comstock, main character of *Keep the Aspidistra Flying,* hates potted aspidistra vines and every other aspect of his lower-middle-class world. Fleeing the "money-god" that controls his life, he becomes a penniless writer but falls into despair. Rescued by a young woman's love, he resolves to marry and earn a normal living by writing advertisements. Orwell considered these his weakest books, and his admirers generally respect his judgment. Both novels are marred by mechanistic plots: the clergyman's daughter, complained *New Statesman*'s Peter Quennell, is "a literary abstraction to whom things happen." Similarly, Comstock is so dominated by bitterness that his interactions with others seem unconvincing.

"Looking back through my work," Orwell later observed, "I see that it is invariably where I lacked a *political* purpose that I wrote lifeless books." Orwell's writing gained new effectiveness when he found a political focus for his discontent. The high ideals of socialism—economic justice in a democratic society—became a standard by which he judged the world around him. In the mid-1930s, socialist publisher Victor Gollancz commissioned Orwell to write a book on the industrial workers of northern England. There the author gained his first personal contact with the working class—not the outcasts he met as a tramp, but a large segment of society in which hard labor and poverty con-

sumed whole families. His outraged report on the plight of English workers in *The Road to Wigan Pier* displayed his skill as a writer and his new political consciousness. "Orwell has the gift of writing vividly, of creating in the mind's eye a picture of the scene described," said Walter Greenwood in the London *Tribune.* "He takes you down a mine and you crouch with him in the narrow galleries; he shows you miners on their knees shovelling coal over their shoulders, and your muscles begin to ache." "There was such an extraordinary change both in his writing and . . . in his attitude after he'd been to the North and written that book," said magazine publisher Richard Rees. "It was almost as if there'd been a kind of fire smouldering in him all his life which suddenly broke into flame." In the second half of *Wigan Pier*—included against Gollancz's wishes—Orwell defined his personal commitment to socialism. Analyzing his background, he denounced his work in Burma and the middle-class snobbery he learned in childhood. Then, in a notoriously opinionated fashion, he reviewed English socialism with equal frankness. His basic ideas were arguably sound: socialist leaders, fixed on Marxist theories such as class conflict, risked losing the public by seeming narrow-minded and intolerant; to fight the rise of fascism, they should unite the lower and middle classes in a broad crusade for liberty and justice. But as Greenwood noted, the author "has you with him one moment and provoked beyond endurance the next." Socialism, Orwell continued, repelled working people because of its intellectual "cranks," including feminists and advocates of birth control: workers who avoided higher education had more common sense. Such notions were sure to appall many patrons of Gollancz's Left Book Club, and the publisher added an introduction to *Wigan Pier* that chided the author for narrow-mindedness.

Orwell appeared untroubled by the controversy. After years of seeming too poor, homely, or eccentric to attract a wife, he married Eileen O'Shaughnessy and settled happily into life as a village grocer with farm animals in his backyard. He was greatly disturbed, however, by the outbreak of civil war in Spain, where the democratically elected government was menaced by an invading army of fascist rebels. By 1937 he and Eileen were in the Spanish province of Catalonia, where he joined an antifascist militia organized by the Workers' Party of Marxist Unity (POUM) and she worked behind the lines. The couple was drawn into a heartbreaking conflict between personal ideals and power politics, chronicled by Orwell in *Homage to Catalonia.* As the author quickly realized, Spanish leftists had answered the fascist invasion by starting their own revolution behind government lines. Unions and political parties seized businesses—often from fascist sympathizers—in the name of the working class. Leftists dominated the Catalonian capital of Barcelona, where traditional class distinctions, from stylish clothing to formal speech, were now eagerly abolished. Such a spirit extended to the POUM militia, where soldiers argued with their officers and openly debated POUM's political theories. Orwell had mixed feelings about such exuberance: it seemed impractical in wartime, but he considered it fundamental to the classless, democratic society he hoped to see in both Britain and Spain. "[I] had been in contact with something strange and valuable," Orwell wrote, "where hope was more normal than apathy or cynicism, where the word 'comrade' stood for comradeship and not, as in most countries, for humbug. [I] had breathed the air of equality." "Of course," he added, "such a state of affairs could not last."

Soon POUM and other prominent supporters of the Catalonian workers' revolt were suppressed by government police. It has been argued that the government acted from military necessity, but Orwell was appalled to see the Spanish Communists aiding the suppression. He surmised with good reason that they and their Soviet advisers had abandoned the idealistic leftists in a bid to increase their own power. As a writer Orwell was outraged by the ability of Communists to spread lies about POUM, including the widely accepted claim that the group was secretly allied to fascism. He watched helplessly as POUM militiamen, returning from the front lines, were arrested in Barcelona and imprisoned. Recovering from a shot to the throat that he received while on duty, Orwell was lucky to find his wife and escape from Spain alive. As its title suggests, *Homage to Catalonia* was his tribute to the colleagues he left behind. The book was coolly received when it first appeared, for its praise of socialist ideals made it of interest primarily to the Left, yet it criticized leftists for fratricide and susceptibility to propaganda. Years later, when the passions of the 1930s had cooled, the book became known as one of Orwell's finest and a standout among the many narratives of the Spanish Civil War. Literary critics praised his evocation of the "comrades" who befriended him, as well as his vivid but modest account of his time in combat.

Homage to Catalonia marked the emergence of Orwell's mature writing style, which used simple but eloquent prose to convey his concerns for social welfare, individuality, and honesty. "Good prose," he said in "Why I Write," "is like a windowpane." He soon gained a wide audience for his expository writing, which ranged from columns and book reviews to formal essays. Though his articles sometimes display the name-calling that irked readers of *Wigan Pier,* overall they have been lauded for originality, candor, and open-mindedness. Orwell, for instance, pioneered serious writing about popular culture. In "The Art of Donald McGill" he praised the humorous off-color postcards that McGill produced for working-class customers. The cards, he argued, view sex with a healthy openness and remain within the context of marriage and family. Orwell shunned the intricate theories of twentieth-century literary criticism, but his essays on major authors have been praised for their common-sense insight. In "Inside the Whale" he urged writers to show social responsibility, then evaluated the work of Henry Miller, whose *Tropic of Cancer* celebrates the self-indulgent art world of Paris. Miller, Orwell conceded, was a fine writer despite his hedonism because he was true to human experience. Similarly Orwell praised Rudyard Kipling, who he felt had captured such old English virtues as duty and fortitude despite his reactionary politics. When Orwell's essays were collected in four volumes in 1968, prominent writers hailed a major literary event. In *Esquire* Malcolm Muggeridge called the books "a rare treasure for any aspiring writer"; in *Harper's* Irving Howe compared Orwell to William Hazlitt and Samuel Johnson, historic masters of the English essay.

For Orwell and many others, the Spanish Civil War presaged a broader conflict with fascism that would embroil all Europe. He increasingly dreaded the consequences of such a war, concerned that in the name of military necessity many humane ideals—especially the socialist hope of liberty with economic justice—would disappear even without a fascist victory. He advocated pacifism and published a fourth novel, *Coming Up for Air,* that contrasted the menacing world around him with the peace he had known as a child. The book centers on George Bowling, a London salesman plagued by workaday frustrations and by the sense that both fascists and their opponents are filling the world with obsessive hate. During a nostalgic escape to his small hometown, he finds that while his childhood memories are vivid and warm, the town has become ugly and industrialized. Finally he returns home, resolved to face the world's problems as best he can. A few months after the book was published in 1939, World War II began and Orwell swung from pacifism to patriotism. Be-

cause of his tuberculosis and his service in the POUM militia, his attempts to join the war effort were often rebuffed, but eventually he entered the civil defense forces and produced radio programs for the British Broadcasting Corporation (BBC). He wrote the essay *The Lion and the Unicorn* to link socialism to patriotism and English history. Praised for its analysis of English political tradition, the book has also been shunned for its strident nationalism. England "is *your* civilisation, it is *you,*" Orwell told compatriots. "However much you hate it or laugh at it, you will never be happy away from it for any length of time." To foster the English family, he soon urged not only a ban on abortion but a tax on the childless. Orwell's work at the BBC, however, revived his fears about a national mobilization. While preparing cultural talks for broadcast to Asia, he found himself repeatedly compelled to avoid such pressing issues as Asian self-rule and the fate of colonialism. Pleading ill health, he resigned his post and began work on two new novels.

Orwell revived a project that may date back to his time in Spain, in which he hoped to explain his fears for society through a simple story. In particular, at a time when Soviet dictator Joseph Stalin was widely praised for battling Nazi Germany, he wished to separate socialist ideals from Stalin's self-serving distortions of them. "One day," Orwell later recalled, "I saw a little boy . . . driving a huge cart-horse along a narrow path, whipping it whenever it tried to turn. It struck me that if only such animals became aware of their strength we should have no power over them, and that men exploit animals in much the same way as the rich exploit the proletariat." His fantasy became *Animal Farm,* the tale of a barnyard revolt against human masters that parallels the rise and decline of socialism in the Soviet Union. The story opens as animals expel Mr. Jones from his farm and create an "animalist" republic. Most animals have simple dreams of justice, but the pigs are greedy and cunning, and in the end they use "animalist" rhetoric to justify their own tyranny. *Animal Farm* is considered an amazingly successful blend of political satire and childlike fable: Orwell was both a student of Soviet politics and a lover of animals. Completed in 1944, the book remained unpublished for more than a year because British firms, sometimes on government advice, declined to offend the country's Soviet allies. When the small leftist firm of Secker & Warburg printed it, publisher and author suddenly became affluent.

Meanwhile, horrified by government suppression of pacifists (whom he had denounced during his wartime fervor), Orwell became vice-chairman of a civil liberties organization called the Freedom Defence Committee. To show that the wrongs of the Soviet state might occur in any society, he set his next novel in the England of the near future and eventually titled it *Nineteen Eighty-Four*. The book is so grim that some literary critics, noting Orwell's declining health, have surmised that it shows the collapse of his spirit. Arguably, however, it is a summation of themes and ideas from throughout his life and work. In *Nineteen Eighty-Four* the world is divided among three warring superstates, and England is essentially a colony of America—whose people Orwell often accused of enjoying casual brutality. The main character is Winston Smith, who works in London for the Ministry of Truth. In a caricature of Orwell's BBC work and of Spanish Communist propaganda, Winston spends his day rewriting history, employing bits of a new language—Newspeak—designed to make unpatriotic thoughts impossible to express. Like Orwell and Flory in Burma, he is part of a select class of Party members who run the country, and his life is dictated by the need to "wear the mask" of ruler. Among Party members sexuality is strongly discouraged and family life subverted; children inform on their parents. As George Bowling might have feared, hate seems the only human emotion the Party allows: in scheduled two-minute sessions, members rail at Party enemies. Like typical Orwell characters, Winston makes a doomed effort to free himself. He is a frustrated writer like Gordon Comstock, composing an anguished diary that he hides from the surveillance camera in his apartment. He begins an illegal love affair with a fellow Party member, and they briefly escape London's urban decay by trysting in the countryside. They secretly rent a room in a neighborhood of "proles," the working masses, whose daily lives the Party considers unimportant. The proles seem to embody whatever is left of human decency, but they are too poor, ignorant, and passive to appreciate their virtues or their strengths. Soon Winston and his lover are imprisoned and brainwashed, reduced to a childish helplessness Orwell may have made more graphic by recalling his days at St. Cyprian's. Winston's torturer coolly admits the Party's ethic of power for its own sake, depicting the future as "a boot stamping on a human face—for ever."

The very success of *Nineteen Eighty-Four* and *Animal Farm* brought Orwell new troubles, as a new generation of readers—particularly Americans—failed to note his longstanding interest in humane socialism and praised him as a conservative anticommunist. He heightened the impression by using the word "Ingsoc," suggesting a debased English socialism, as the name of the state ideology in *Nineteen Eighty-Four*. Increasingly ill with tuberculosis, Orwell met in his hospital with publisher Fred Warburg and helped compose a press release, which noted that "in the U.S.A. the phrase . . . 'hundred percent Americanism' is suitable and the qualifying adjective is as totalitarian as anyone could wish." The book, they averred, was a warning, not a fatalistic prediction, and they summarized its moral as "*Don't let it happen. It depends on you.*" Meanwhile Orwell faced personal crises. He downplayed his illness, seemingly determined to retain an active life. After Eileen died in 1945 he responded by working harder. Left to care for the couple's adopted son, he appears to have been far more interested than most fathers of his time in the child's welfare. The limited drug therapy available for tuberculosis proved torturous and futile, and in 1950—a few months after his second marriage—he died at the age of forty-six.

Orwell's long struggle for success, his willingness to brave controversy, and his untimely death helped make him a figure of legend. In a famous obituary for *New Statesman,* V. S. Pritchett called him "the wintry conscience of a generation" and "a kind of saint." Soon such accolades were broadened by less discerning observers into a general veneration of Orwell's writings and actions, prompting even well-known admirers such as Woodcock to allude to an "Orwell Industry" or "Cult." Both liberals and conservatives claimed to be his political heirs, while skeptics called him overrated or irrelevant to a changing world. As Orwell himself observed, "saints should always be judged guilty until they are proved innocent." Skeptics justifiably recall that Orwell could be aloof and opinionated as well as warmhearted and tolerant. He never created a consistent system of philosophy, and even seemed to relish human inconsistencies as a force for social moderation. His strengths, accordingly, are difficult to summarize. He may have done the best job himself when he described Charles Dickens, an author whose social concern and faith in human decency he greatly admired. As Crick and others have suggested, the virtues Orwell saw in Dickens were the ones he probably valued in himself. "I see . . . a man who is always fighting against something," Orwell wrote, "but who fights in the open and is not frightened . . . a man who is *generously angry*—in other words . . . a nineteenth-century liberal, a free intelligence, a type hated with equal hatred by all the smelly little

orthodoxies which are now contending for our souls." As long as there are orthodoxies, there will be a need for Orwell.

MEDIA ADAPTATIONS: Animal Farm was adapted for an animated film of the same title, 1955, and by Nelson Slade Bond for a play of the same title, Samuel French, 1964; *Nineteen Eighty-Four* was adapted for films of the same title, 1956 and 1984, and for a play of the same title, Dramatic Publishing, 1963.

AVOCATIONAL INTERESTS: Fishing, carpentry, gardening, raising animals.

BIOGRAPHICAL/CRITICAL SOURCES:

BOOKS

Aldritt, Keith, *The Making of George Orwell,* St. Martin's, 1961.
Atkins, John, *George Orwell: A Literary Study,* Calder & Boyars, 1954.
Bloom, Harold, editor, *Modern Critical Views: George Orwell,* Chelsea House, 1987.
Brander, Laurence, *George Orwell,* Longmans, Green, 1954.
Burgess, Anthony, *1985,* Arrow Books, 1980.
Calder, Jenni, *Chronicles of Conscience: A Study of George Orwell and Arthur Koestler,* Secker & Warburg, 1968.
Connolly, Cyril, *Previous Convictions,* Hamish Hamilton, 1963.
Crick, Bernard, *George Orwell: A Life,* Secker & Warburg, 1980.
Dictionary of Literary Biography, Volume 15: *British Novelists, 1930-1959,* Gale, 1983.
Fyvel, T. R., *George Orwell: A Personal Memoir,* Weidenfeld & Nicolson, 1982.
Gardner, Averil, *George Orwell,* Twayne, 1987.
Hammond, J. R., *A George Orwell Companion,* St. Martin's, 1982.
Hollis, Christopher, *A Study of George Orwell: The Man and His Works,* Hollis & Carter, 1956.
Hynes, Samuel, editor, *Twentieth Century Interpretations of "1984,"* Prentice-Hall, 1971.
Kalechofsky, Roberta, *George Orwell,* Ungar, 1973.
Kubal, David L., *Outside the Whale: George Orwell's Art and Politics,* University of Notre Dame Press, 1972.
Lee, Robert A., *Orwell's Fiction,* University of Notre Dame Press, 1969.
Meyers, Jeffrey, *George Orwell: The Critical Heritage,* Routledge & Kegan Paul, 1975.
Meyers, Jeffrey, *A Reader's Guide to George Orwell,* Rowman & Allanheld, 1984.
Norris, Christopher, editor, *Inside the Myth: Orwell—Views From the Left,* Lawrence & Wishart, 1984.
Orwell, George, *The Road to Wigan Pier,* Harcourt, 1958.
Orwell, George, *The Collected Essays, Journalism, and Letters of George Orwell,* edited by Sonia Orwell and Ian Angus, Harcourt, 1968.
Orwell, George, *Homage to Catalonia,* Harcourt, 1980.
Oxley, B. T., *George Orwell,* Evans Brothers, 1967.
Patai, Daphne, *The Orwell Mystique: A Study in Male Ideology,* University of Massachusetts Press, 1984.
Rees, Richard, *George Orwell: Fugitive From the Camp of Victory,* Secker & Warburg, 1961.
Rodden, John, *The Politics of Literary Reputation: The Making and Claiming of "St. George" Orwell,* Oxford University Press, 1989.
Sandison, Allan, *The Last Man in Europe: An Essay on George Orwell,* Macmillan, 1974.
Slater, Ian, *Orwell: The Road to Airstrip One,* Norton, 1985.
Stansky, Peter and William Abrahams, *The Unknown Orwell,* Constable, 1972.

Stansky, Peter and William Abrahams, *Orwell: The Transformation,* Constable, 1979.

Steinhoff, William, *George Orwell and the Origins of "1984,"* University of Michigan Press, 1975.

Thomas, Hugh, *The Spanish Civil War,* Harper, 1961.

Twentieth-Century Literary Criticism, Gale, Volume 2, 1979, Volume 6, 1982, Volume 15, 1985, Volume 31, 1989.

Voorhees, Richard J., *The Paradox of George Orwell,* Purdue University Studies, 1961.

Williams, Raymond, editor, *George Orwell: A Collection of Critical Essays,* Prentice-Hall, 1974.

Woodcock, George, *The Crystal Spirit: A Study of George Orwell,* new edition, enlarged, Schocken, 1984.

Wykes, David, *A Preface to Orwell,* Longman, 1987.

Zwerdling, Alex, *Orwell and the Left,* Yale University Press, 1974.

PERIODICALS

Atlantic Monthly, September, 1946, March, 1950, November, 1968.

Canadian Forum, December, 1946, February, 1969.

Commentary, June, 1956, January, 1969.

Commonweal, June 18, 1937, September 13, 1946, July 8, 1949, February 3, 1950, June 20, 1952, March 20, 1953, March 23, 1956, January 10, 1969, March 11, 1983, May 20, 1983.

Encounter, December, 1968.

Esquire, March, 1969.

Harper's, January, 1969, January, 1983.

Listener, November 2, 1950, December 12, 1968.

Nation, September 6, 1933, May 25, 1946, September 7, 1946, June 25, 1949, February 4, 1950, December 27, 1952, January 21, 1956, August 30, 1958, February 3, 1969.

New Republic, October 11, 1933, May 6, 1946, September 6, 1946, August 1, 1949, February 20, 1950, December 4, 1950, June 23, 1952, March 16, 1953, November 30, 1968.

New Statesman, March 18, 1933, March 23, 1935, April 25, 1936, May 1, 1937, September 8, 1945, February 16, 1946, June 18, 1949, October 28, 1950, April 20, 1962, October 4, 1968.

Newsweek, October 28, 1968.

New Yorker, May 25, 1946, September 7, 1946, June 18, 1949, January 13, 1951, January 28, 1956, March 29, 1969, March 7, 1983.

New York Review of Books, June 14, 1984.

New York Times Book Review, August 6, 1933, October 28, 1934, August 9, 1936, May 19, 1946, August 25, 1946, June 12, 1949, January 22, 1950, October 29, 1950, May 18, 1952, March 1, 1953, January 28, 1956, October 27, 1968, November 17, 1985.

Observer (London), March 10, 1935, June 12, 1949, January 24, 1954.

Partisan Review, March, 1942, September, 1946, July, 1949, May, 1950.

Saturday Review, May 11, 1946, August 24, 1946, June 11, 1949, February 18, 1950, June 12, 1952, April 25, 1953, January 14, 1956, August 9, 1958, December 28, 1968.

Spectator, March 22, 1935, June 28, 1935, April 24, 1936, August 17, 1945, March 8, 1946.

Time, February 4, 1946, May 20, 1946, June 20, 1949, November 13, 1950, February 6, 1956, August 18, 1958, November 15, 1968, November 28, 1983.

Times Literary Supplement, January 12, 1933, July 18, 1935, May 2, 1936, April 30, 1938, June 17, 1939, April 20, 1940, August 25, 1945, February 23, 1946, June 10, 1949, October
20, 1950, December 4, 1953, October 17, 1968, September 15, 1972, January 3, 1986.

Tribune (London), March 12, 1937.

Washington Post Book World, October 27, 1968.

OBITUARIES:

PERIODICALS

New Statesman, January 28, 1950.
Newsweek, January 30, 1950.
New York Times, January 22, 1950.
Observer (London), January 29, 1950.
Time, January 30, 1950.

—*Sketch by Thomas Kozikowski*

*   *   *

BLAIS, Marie-Claire   1939-

PERSONAL: Born October 5, 1939, in Quebec, Quebec, Canada; daughter of Fernando and Veronique (Nolin) Blais. *Education:* Attended Pensionnat St. Roch in Quebec; studied literature and philosophy at Laval University in Quebec. *Religion:* Catholic.

ADDRESSES: Home—3443 Avenue du Musee, Montreal, Quebec, Canada. *Agent*—Louise Myette, C. P. 851, La Cite, Montreal, Quebec, Canada H2W 2P5.

CAREER: Full-time writer.

MEMBER: P.E.N.

AWARDS, HONORS: Prix de la Langue Francaise from L'Academie Francaise, 1961, for *La Belle bete;* Guggenheim fellowships, 1963 and 1964; Le Prix France-Quebec and Prix Medicis (Paris), both 1966, both for *Une Saison dans la vie d'Emmanuel;* Prix du Gouverneur General du Canada, 1969, for *Les Manuscrits de Pauline Archange;* honorary doctorate from York University (Toronto), 1975; Ordre du Canada, 1975; Prix Belgique, 1976; named honorary professor at Calgary University, 1978; Prix du Gouverneur General du Canada, 1979, for *Le Sourd dans la ville;* Prix Athanase David, 1982; Prix de l'Academie Francaise, 1983.

WRITINGS:

La Belle bete (novel), Institut Litteraire du Quebec, 1959, translation by Merloyd Lawrence published as *Mad Shadows,* Little, Brown, 1961.

Tete Blanche (novel), Institut Litteraire du Quebec, 1960, translation by Charles Fullman under same title, Little, Brown, 1961.

Le Jour est noir (novella), Editions du Jour (Montreal), 1962, translation by Derek Coltman published as *The Day Is Dark* (see below).

Pays voiles (poems), Garneau (Quebec), 1963 (also see below).

Existences (poems), Garneau, 1964 (also see below).

Une Saison dans la vie d'Emmanuel (novel), Editions du Jour, 1965, translation by Coltman published as *A Season in the Life of Emmanuel,* introduction by Edmund Wilson, Farrar, Straus, 1966.

Les Voyageurs sacres (novella), HMH, 1966, translation by Coltman published as *The Three Travelers* (see below).

L'Insoumise (novel), Editions du Jour, 1966, translation by David Lobdell published as *The Fugitive,* Oberon, 1978.

The Day Is Dark [and] The Three Travelers, Farrar, Straus, 1967.

David Sterne (novel), Editions du Jour, 1967, translation by Lobdell under same title, McClelland & Stewart, 1973.

Les Manuscrits de Pauline Archange (novel), Editions du Jour, 1968, translation by Coltman published with translation of *Vivre! Vivre!: La Suite des Manuscrits de Pauline Archange* (see below) as *The Manuscripts of Pauline Archange,* Farrar, Straus, 1970.

Vivre! Vivre!: La Suite des Manuscrits de Pauline Archange (novel), Editions du Jour, 1969.

Les Apparences (novel), Editions du Jour, 1970, translation by Lobdell published as *Durer's Angel,* McClelland & Stewart, 1974.

Le Loup (novel), Editions du Jour, 1972, translation by Sheila Fischman published as *The Wolf,* McClelland & Stewart, 1971.

Un Joualonais sa Joualonie (novel), Editions du Jour, 1973, reprinted as *A coeur joual,* Robert Laffont, 1977; translation by Ralph Manheim published as *St. Lawrence Blues,* Farrar, Straus, 1974.

Une Liaison parisienne (novel), Robert Laffont, 1976, translation by Fischman published as *A Literary Affair,* McClelland & Stewart, 1979.

Le Sourd dans la ville (novel), Stanke, 1979, translation by Carol Dunlop published as *Deaf to the City,* General Publishing, 1979.

Les Nuits de l'underground (novel), Stanke, 1982, translation by Ray Ellenwood published as *Nights of the Underground,* General Publishing, 1982.

Visions d'Anna (novel), Stanke, 1982, translation by Fischman under same title, Lester & Orpen Dennys, 1983.

Pays voiles—Existences, Stanke, 1983.

Also author of *Pierre* (novel), 1984.

PLAYS

L'Execution (two-act; produced in Montreal at Theatre du Rideau Vert, 1967), Editions du Jour, 1968, translation by David Lobdell published as *The Execution,* Talon Books, 1976.

Fievre, Editions du Jour, 1974.

La Nef des sorcieres, Quinze Editeurs, 1976.

L'Ocean murmures, Quinze Editeurs, 1977.

Also author of "La Roulotte aux Poupees" and "Eleanor," both produced in Quebec at Theatre de L'Estoc, and "Sommeil d'Hiver," 1985, and "Fiere," 1985.

SIDELIGHTS: Marie-Claire Blais, according to Edmund Wilson, is "a writer in a class by herself." Although each of her novels is written in a different style and mood, "we know immediately," writes Raymond Rosenthal, "that we are entering a fully imagined world when we start reading any of her books." Wilson wrote that Blais is a "true 'phenomenon'; she may possibly be a genius. At the age of twenty-four, she has produced four remarkable books of a passionate and poetic force that, as far as my reading goes, is not otherwise to be found in French Canadian fiction." That was in 1964; when Wilson read *A Season in the Life of Emmanuel* in 1965, he compared the novel to works by J. M. Synge and William Faulkner.

"*A Season in the Life of Emmanuel* is a particularly Canadian work of art," writes David Stouck, "for the sense of winter and of life's limitations (especially defined by poverty) are nowhere felt more strongly. Yet . . . these physical limitations serve to define the emotional deprivation that is being dramatized. That eroding sense of poverty is never externalized as a social issue, nor is the harshness of the Quebec landscape seen as an existentialist 'condition.' Rather, in the oblique and relentless manner of her writing Miss Blais remains faithful stylistically to the pain-

ful vision of her imagination and in so doing has created both a fully dramatic and genuinely Canadian work of art."

Robertson Davies believes that *The Day Is Dark* and *Three Travelers* are "less substantial than *A Season in the Life of Emmanuel,*" but, he adds, "all the writing of this extraordinary young woman is so individual, so unlike anything else being written on this continent, that admirers of her poetic vision of life may find them even more to their taste." Laurent LeSage says of the two novellas: "Although the basic structures of fiction are still recognizable, they have been weakened and distorted to prevent any illusion of realistic dimension or true-to-life anecdote from distracting us from the author's intention. Without warning the narrative shifts from one character to another, chronology is jumbled, events are sometimes contradictory, and the fancied is never clearly separated from the real. By a series of interior monologues Mlle. Blais works along the lower levels of consciousness, and only rarely does she come to the surface. The world of her revery is the somber, shadowy one of primitive urges and responses. . . . Each [character] obeys a force that resembles a tragic predestination, leading [him] in a lonely quest through life to [his] final destruction." The novellas are actually prose poems, similar in some respects to works by Walter de la Mare. Rosenthal defines the genre as "a piece of prose that should be read more than once, preferably several times. If after reading it in the prescribed fashion," says Rosenthal, "the work assumes depth and color and value it did not have at the first reading, then the author has written a successful prose poem. In a prose poem each word counts and Mlle. Blais generally doesn't waste a syllable."

In his study of Canadian literature, Wilson comments that "these novels of Marie-Claire Blais are the most unrelievedly painful that I remember ever to have read, and one questions . . . the inevitability of so much pain." But Irving Wardle, although he admits that "harshness and squalor are there," sees that, at least in *A Season in the Life of Emmanuel,* these elements "are transformed in the writing into the material of adolescent fantasy. [Blais] has the myth-making faculty, and it is an exciting thing to watch." LeSage writes: "Marie-Claire Blais lets her words pour forth in a rhapsodic torrent. In *Three Travelers* they often form into verses, but everywhere they have the poetic qualities of image and cadence as they create laments and paeans, cries of love, lust, and hate for the wretched characters whose affliction is the sickness of life. The power of her writing is terrific." Wilson explains that "Blais has grown up in this cult, and the idea that man is born to sorrow, the agony of expiation, is at the base of her tragic consciousness. [Her work] is the refinement to a purer kind of poetry than that of the protesting patriots of the desperate cry that arises from the poverty, intellectual and material, the passionate self-punishing piety and the fierce defeated pride of Quebec."

Daniel M. Murtaugh observes that *A Season in the Life of Emmanuel* "has at its center an autobiographical sketch by a consumptive child whose writing is a cry of defiance against the misery of his life and the approach of his death. The manuscripts of a suffering child, a structural detail of that novel, are the sum and substance of its successor. *The Manuscripts of Pauline Archange* takes us through memories of almost unmitigated horror rendered bearable, redeemed even, for us as for the novel's heroine, by the fluid, re-creative medium of her prose. . . . What Pauline remembers does not fall into a conventional plot or lend itself easily to summary. Her life is lived out in the mental and physical squalor of a French Canadian slum, under the tyranny of repressed, frustrated adults who visit their failures in blows upon their consumptive, lamed offspring. To survive is to escape, to rebel, above all, to avoid pity. Pity 'stinks of death,' and only leads to torture and rape of the victims it cannot help. Pauline writes her manuscripts because, as her family tells her, she 'has no heart.' Only at such a cost does she live and speak to us."

Rosenthal emphasizes that Blais has done much to "put Canada on the literary map." He says of her work: "Mlle. Blais leaves out a great deal, almost all the familiar furniture of fiction, and yet her characters have a tenacious life and her themes, though often convoluted and as evanescent as the mist that dominates so much of her imagination, strike home with surprising force." "With *David Sterne*," writes Brian Vintcent, "Mlle. Blais has placed herself firmly and uncompromisingly in the literary tradition of the French moralists leading back through Camus, Genet and Gide to Baudelaire. The book deals in one way or another with many of the themes explored by these writers, and this makes it somewhat derivative. It owes most, perhaps, to the more abstract and less sensational works of Jean Genet, in which the passionate existential wranglings, the rebellion, the life of crime and sensation are so prominent. The confessional and didactic style of the book will also strike echoes in the reader's mind. But *David Sterne* survives and transcends these comparisons. What allows it to do so is the immense compassion and tenderness Mlle. Blais displays for her characters in their whirlwind of struggle and suffering. The hard cold eye she casts on the cruel world of *Mad Shadows* has grown into one full of pity and profound sadness for the fate of men condemned to do battle with themselves."

The *Virginia Quarterly Review* writer concludes: "These are novels to be read slowly and carefully for the unusual insights they present in often difficult but provocative images and sometimes demanding but intriguing technical innovations. This is a serious, talented and deeply effective writer."

BIOGRAPHICAL/CRITICAL SOURCES:

BOOKS

Contemporary Literary Criticism, Gale, Volume 2, 1974, Volume 3, 1975, Volume 6, 1976.
Wilson, Edmund, *O Canada,* Farrar, Straus, 1964.

PERIODICALS

Books Abroad, winter, 1968.
Book Week, June 18, 1967.
Globe and Mail (Toronto), March 30, 1985.
Los Angeles Times, September 18, 1987.
New Statesman, March 31, 1967.
New York Times Book Review, April 30, 1967, September 20, 1987.
Observer, April 2, 1967.
Saturday Review, April 29, 1967.
Times Literary Supplement, March 30, 1967.
Virginia Quarterly Review, autumn, 1967.

*   *   *

BLAKE, Nicholas
See DAY LEWIS, C(ecil)

*   *   *

BLASCO IBANEZ, Vicente   1867-1928

PERSONAL: Born January 29, 1867, in Valencia, Spain; died January 28, 1928, in Menton, France; originally buried in France, reinterred in 1933 in Valencia, Spain; son of Gaspar Blasco Teruel and Ramona Ibanez Martinez; married Maria Blasco del Cacho, November 8, 1891 (died, January, 1925); married Elena Ortuzar Bulnes, October, 1925; children: (first marriage) Mario, Libertad, Julio Cesar, Sigfriedo. *Education:* University of Valencia, licentiate in civil and canonical law, 1888.

ADDRESSES: Home and office—Menton, France.

CAREER: Writer. Secretary to novelist Manuel Fernandez y Gonzalez, Madrid, Spain, beginning 1883. Legislative delegate for six terms; founder of Blasquista party.

AWARDS, HONORS: Honorary degree from George Washington University, Washington, D.C., 1920; Legion d'Honneur (France).

WRITINGS:

NOVELS

¡Viva la republica! (Romeu el guerrillero) (novel in four volumes), Sempere, 1892, Volume 1: *En el crater del volcan,* Volume 2: *La hermosa Liejesa,* Volume 3: *La explosion,* Volume 4: *Guerra sin cuartel.*
Arroz y tartana (also see below), Sempere, 1894, reprinted, Plaza & Janes (Barcelona), 1976, translation by Stuart Edgar Gummon published as *The Three Roses,* Dutton, 1932.
Flor de mayo (includes four stories published in *Cuentos valencianos;* also see below), Sempere, 1896, reprinted, Plaza & Janes, 1978, translation by Arthur Livingston published as *The Mayflower: A Tale of the Valencian Seashore,* Dutton, 1921.
La barraca: Novela (also see below), Sempere, 1898, reprinted, Plaza & Janes, 1977, edited with introduction, notes, and vocabulary by Hayward Keniston, Holt, 1910, translation by Francis Haffkin Snow and Beatrice M. Mekota of original Spanish edition published as *The Cabin,* Knopf, 1917, translation published with a new introduction by John Garrett Underhill, 1938, reprinted, Fertig, 1975.
Entre naranjos (title means "Among the Orange Trees"), Prometeo, 1900, reprinted, Plaza & Janes, 1978, translation by Isaac Goldberg and Arthur Livingston published as *The Torrent,* Dutton, 1921.
Sonnica la cortesana, Sempere, 1901, reprinted, Plaza & Janes, 1978, translation by Frances Douglas published as *Sonnica,* Duffield, 1912.
Canas y barro (also see below), Prometeo, 1902, reprinted, Plaza & Janes, 1978, translation by Issac Goldberg published as *Reeds and Mud,* Dutton, 1928, translation by Lester Beberfall published as *Reeds and Mud,* Branden Press (Boston), 1966.
La catedral (title means "The Cathedral"), Prometeo, 1903, reprinted, Plaza & Janes, 1976, translation by Mrs. W. A. Gillespie published as *The Shadow of the Cathedral,* Constable (London), 1909, Dutton, 1919.
El intruso, Prometeo, 1904, reprinted, Plaza & Janes, 1978, translation by Mrs. W. A. Gillespie published as *The Intruder,* Dutton, 1928.
La voluntad de vivir (title means "The Will to Live"), Prometeo, 1904, reprinted, Planeta (Barcelona), 1953.
La bodega, Sempere, 1905, translation by Goldberg published as *The Fruit of the Vine,* Dutton, 1919.
La horda, Sempere, 1905, translation by Mariano Joaquin Lorente published as *The Mob,* Dutton, 1927.
La maja desnuda (title means "The Nude Maja"), Prometeo, 1906, reprinted, Plaza & Janes, 1977, translation by Hayward Keniston published as *Woman Triumphant,* with an introductory note by the author, Dutton, 1920, translation

by Frances Partridge published as *The Naked Lady,* Elek (London), 1969.

Sangre y arena (also see below), Sempere, 1908, reprinted, Plaza & Janes, 1976, translation by Frances Douglas published as *The Blood of the Arena,* A. C. McClurg (Chicago), 1911, translation by Mrs. W. A. Gillespie published as *Blood and Sand,* Simpkin, Marshall & Co., 1913, Dutton, 1919, published as *The Matador,* Nelson, 1918, edition based on Mrs. Gillespie's translation published as *Blood and Sand: The Life and Loves of a Bullfighter, A New English Version of the Novel,* Dell, 1951, translation by Frances Partridge published as *Blood and Sand,* Ungar, 1958.

Los muertos mandan, Prometeo, 1909, translation by Frances Douglas published as *The Dead Command,* Duffield, 1919, abridged Spanish edition edited by Frederick Augustus Grant Cowper and John Thomas Lister, Harper, 1934.

Luna Benamor (includes "El ultimo leon" and other stories; also see below), Prometeo, 1909, reprinted, Plaza & Janes, 1978, translation by Isaac Goldberg published under same title, J. W. Luce (Boston), 1919.

Los Argonautas: Novela, Prometeo, 1914, reprinted, Plaza & Janes, 1978.

Los cuatro jinetes del Apocalipsis, Prometeo, 1916, reprinted, Plaza & Janes, 1976, translation by Charlotte Brewster Jordan published as *The Four Horsemen of the Apocalypse,* Dutton, 1918, reprinted, 1962.

Mare Nostrum, Prometeo, 1918, reprinted, Plaza & Janes, 1977, translation by Jordan published as *Our Sea,* Dutton, 1919.

Los enemigos de la mujer, Prometeo, 1919, reprinted, Planeta, 1961, translation by Irving Brown published as *The Enemies of Women,* Dutton, 1920.

La tierra de todos (title means "Everyone's Land"), Prometeo, 1921, translation by Leo Ongley published as *The Temptress,* Dutton, 1923.

El paraiso de las mujeres (title means "The Paradise of Women"), Prometeo, 1922, reprinted, Plaza & Janes, 1978.

El comediante Fonseca, Rivadeneyra (Madrid), 1923.

La reina Calafia, Prometeo, 1923, reprinted, Plaza & Janes, 1978, translation published as *Queen Calafia,* Dutton, 1924.

El Papa del mar (also see below), Prometeo, 1925, translation by Arthur Livingston published as *The Pope of the Sea: An Historical Medley,* Dutton, 1927.

A los pies de Venus (los Borgia): Novela (sequel to *El Papa del mar*), Prometeo, 1926, reprinted, Prometeo (Mexico City), 1944, translation by Livingston published as *The Borgias; or, At the Feet of Venus,* Dutton, 1930.

Mademoiselle Norma, [Madrid], 1927.

El conde Garci-Fernandez, reprinted, Cosmopolis, c. 1928.

En busca del Gran Kan (Cristobal Colon) (title means "In Search of the Great Khan [Christopher Columbus]"), Prometeo (Valencia), 1929, reprinted, Plaza & Janes, 1978, translation by Livingston published as *Unknown Lands: The Story of Columbus,* Dutton, 1929.

El caballero de la Virgen (Alonso de Ojeda), Prometeo, 1929, reprinted, Planeta, 1959, translation by Livingston published as *Knight of the Virgin,* Dutton, 1930.

El fantasma de las alas de oro, Prometeo, 1930, translation by Livingston published as *The Phantom with Wings of Gold,* Dutton, 1931.

COLLECTIONS

Fantasias (leyendas y tradiciones) (title means "Fantasies [Legends and Traditions]"; short stories), Prometeo, 1887.

El adios de Schubert (title means "Schubert's Goodbye"; short stories), Prometeo, 1888.

Cuentos valencianos (title means "Valencian Tales"), Prometeo, 1896, reprinted, Plaza & Janes, 1978.

La condenada (cuentos) (title means "The Condemned Woman [Stories]"; includes "En el mar" and other stories), Prometeo, 1900, published as *La condenada y otros cuentos,* Espasa-Calpe, 1960.

The Last Lion and Other Tales (translation of stories included in *Luna Benamor*), Four Seas (Boston), 1919.

El prestamo de la difunta (title means "The Loan of the Dead Woman"; stories; also see below), Prometeo, 1920, edited with introduction, notes, and vocabulary by George Baer Fundenburg and John F. Klein, Century, 1925.

Novelas de la costa azul (title means "Novellas of the Blue Coast"), Prometeo, 1924.

The Old Woman of the Movies, and Other Stories (translation of stories included in *El prestamo de la difunta*), Dutton, 1925.

Obras completas (title means "Complete Works"), eleven volumes, Prometeo, 1925-34, expanded edition published in three volumes, Aguilar, 1946, reprinted, 1964.

Siete cuentos de Vicente Blasco Ibanez, edited with introduction, notes, and vocabulary by Sturgis E. Leavitt, Holt, 1926.

The Mad Virgins, and Other Stories (translation of stories from *El prestamo de la difunta* and other collections), Butterworth, 1926.

Novelas de amor y de muerte (title means "Novellas of Love and Death"), Prometeo, 1927.

La arana negra (title means "The Black Spider"), eleven volumes, Cosmopolis (Madrid), 1928, published in two volumes, A. T. E. (Barcelona), 1975.

Cuentos escogidos (title means "Selected Stories"), edited by J. Bayard Morris, Dent, 1932.

Tres novelas valencianas: Arroz y tartana, La barraca, Canas y barro, Plenitud (Madrid), 1958.

OTHER

Historia de la revolucion espanola (desde la guerra de la independencia a la restauracion en Sagunto) 1808-1874 (title means "History of the Spanish Revolution [from the War of Independence to the Restauration in Sagunto] 1808-1874"), three volumes, Enciclopedia Democratica (Barcelona), 1892, reprinted, Cosmopolis, 1930.

Paris, impresiones de un emigrado (title means "Paris, An Emmigrant's Impressiones"), Prometeo, 1893.

El juez (title means "The Judge"; play), Ripolles, 1894.

En el pais del arte (tres meses en Italia) (travel), Pellicers (Valencia), 1896, reprinted, Plaza & Janes, 1980, translation by Douglas published as *In the Land of Art,* Dutton, 1923.

(Translator from the French and author of preface) Onesime Reclus and J. J. E. Reclus, *Novisima geografia universal,* six volumes, La Novela Ilustrada (Madrid), 1906-07.

Oriente (title means "East"; travel), Prometeo, 1907, reprinted, Plaza & Janes, 1980.

(Translator from the French) Ernesto Laviss and Alfredo Rambaud, *Novisima historia univeral, dirigida a partir del siglo IV,* fifteen volumes, Prometeo, 1908-30.

Argentina y sus grandezas (title means "Argentina and Her Grandeurs"; travel), Espanola Americana (Madrid), 1910.

Historia de la guerra europea de 1914 (title means "History of the European War of 1914"), Prometeo, thirteen volumes, 1914-19.

(Translator from the French) J. C. Mardrus, *El libro de los mil y una noches,* twenty-three volumes, Prometeo, 1915.

The Bull-Fight (Spanish and English text; extract from *Sangre y arena*), translation by C. D. Campbell, Harrap, 1919.

El militarismo mejicano: Estudios publicados en los principales diarios de los Estados Unidos (contains articles originally published in U.S. newspapers), Prometeo, 1920, reprinted, Plaza & Janes, 1979, translation by Jose Padin and Arthur Livingston published as *Mexico in Revolution,* Dutton, 1920.

Vistas sudamericanas (title means "South American Views"; excerpts), edited by Carolina Marcial Dorado, Ginn, 1920.

Una nacion secuestrada (El terror militarista en Espana), J. Dura (Paris), 1924, translation by Leo Ongley published as *Alfonso XIII Unmasked: The Military Terror of Spain,* Dutton, 1924.

Blasco Ibanez: Paisajista (title means "Blasco Ibanez: Landscape Artist"; contains excerpts from his works), edited by Camille Pitollet, Vuibert (Paris), 1924.

La vuelta al mundo de un novelista (memoirs), three volumes, Prometeo, 1924-25, reprinted, Planeta, 1958, translation by Leo Ongley and Arthur Livingston published as *A Novelist's Tour of the World,* Dutton, 1926.

Lo que sera la republica espanola: Al pais y al ejercito (title means "What the Spanish Republic Will Become; To the Country and to the Army"), La Gutenberg (Valencia), 1925.

Por Espana y contra el rey, Excelsior (Paris), 1925.

Estudios literarios (title means "Literary Studies"; essays chiefly on French authors), Prometeo, 1933.

Discursos literarios (title means "Literary Lectures"), Prometeo, 1966.

Cronicas de viaje (title means "Travel Chronicles"), Prometeo, 1967.

Contra la Restauracion: Periodismo politico, 1895-1904 (articles previously published in *El Pueblo*), compiled by P. Smith, Nuestra Cultura (Madrid), 1978.

Founding editor, *El Pueblo* (Valecian newspaper), beginning 1891.

SIDELIGHTS: A novelist, politician, and adventurer who enjoyed worldwide fame during the first part of the twentieth century, Vicente Blasco Ibanez remains a controversial figure in Spanish literature. Blasco Ibanez was a nonconformist committed to political and social action and to the toppling of the Spanish Monarchy that ruled Spain during his lifetime; he pursued these goals both directly as a political activist and indirectly through several of his novels. In his youth his rebellious spirit caused his expulsion from school, and as Ricardo Landeira has pointed out in *The Modern Spanish Novel, 1898-1936,* "this incident of rebelliousness marks the beginning of a chronicled biography that reads like an adventure story worthy of Blasco [Ibanez] the novelist." Repeatedly in his early adulthood he was incarcerated for his outspoken criticism of the government. By the author's own account, his stays in Spanish jails numbered as many as thirty.

No less evident than his nonconformist spirit was Blasco Ibanez's strong literary and journalistic inclination. As a young student, he compiled short stories and news items for circulation among his classmates and wrote an original short story for submission to a literary competition. Blasco Ibanez later founded *El Pueblo,* a liberal newspaper which served as a vehicle for his political ideas and in which he also published short stories and novels in serialized form. Yet throughout his young adult years he compromised his reputation as a writer by moving farther and farther into the realm of political and social activism, a fact that at least partially explains Blasco Ibanez's often unfavorable treatment in Spanish literary histories. In many ways he represented a new literary phenomenon: he shattered the traditional model of the passive intellectual who did not take sides.

Blasco Ibanez's early novels and short stories, all set in his native Valencia, stand as highly original and significant artistic contributions to modern Spanish literature. In his early works, Blasco Ibanez proved himself a natural storyteller and a master of descriptive technique in the Naturalistic and Impressionistic modes. Often referred to as his "Valencian cycle" or "regional works," the novels included in this group are *Arroz y tartana* (*The Three Roses,* 1894), *Flor de mayo* (*The Mayflower,* 1896), *La barraca* (*The Cabin,* 1898), *Entre naranjos* (*The Torrent,* 1900), and *Canas y barro* (*Reeds and Mud,* 1902). Also belonging to this group are such short story collections as *Cuentos valencianos* ("Valencian Tales," 1896) and *La condenada y otros cuentos* ("The Condemned Woman, and Other Stories," 1900).

In these early works Blasco Ibanez treated subjects and settings with which he had had direct contact and revealed an acute understanding of regional social problems. Elements of Naturalism—deterministic themes (such as the human being's subjugation to the natural elements), a focus on the common individual and his struggle for survival in a hostile or uncaring society, and an essential note of pessimism—color these works. But what often separates them from conventional Naturalistic narratives is the quality of the struggle depicted. Blasco Ibanez's characters often take on heroic proportions; they are rarely Naturalism's sickly, feeble men and women, predisposed to failure because of their physical makeup or their heredity.

In his regional works Blasco Ibanez created an artistic canvas that captured the quintessential aspects of the people of Valencia as they lived and worked at the turn of the century. *The Three Roses* portrays the materialistic aspirations of the bourgeoisie; *The Mayflower* and *Reeds and Mud* depict the lives of the people associated with the fishing industry so important to the region; *The Cabin* vividly recreates the hardships of the farmer; and *The Torrent,* which uses the Valencian orange groves as a poetic backdrop, addresses the conflict between materialistic or political aspirations and the desire for purity and beauty.

These novels represent significant contributions to Spanish Naturalism and Realism for several reasons. Blasco Ibanez surpassed many of his contemporaries such as Jose Maria Pereda and Pedro Antonio de Alarcon who, in keeping with the *costumbrista* mode of literature with its focus on customs, types, and characteristic scenes of a particular region, created a rather superficial, romantic image of society. Although Blasco Ibanez did make extensive use of local color and picturesque details, these features never constituted the final objective of his writing. In *Historia social de la literatura espanola,* Carlos Blanco Aguinaga comments on this dimension of Blasco Ibanez's works, stating that "the characteristic Spanish *costumbrista* novel . . . never offers a realistic critical analysis of social conflicts nor a progressive interpretation of those conflicts that one finds in these works of Blasco Ibanez."

The Mayflower illustrates Blasco Ibanez's combining of local color and realistic social analysis. In this novel the *costumbrista* stamp appears in the extensive references to and description of local customs (for example, religious processions and the practice of inaugurating new boats) and in the vision of the fishermen's and fisherwomen's everyday dealings at sea and in the fish market. But the overriding theme of the novel concerns the tremendous danger to which the fishermen must expose themselves and the small compensation they receive from society. In the final episode of the novel, the village witnesses the destruction of a fishing boat during a terrifying storm, and Tia Picores, a wise elder of the town and in many ways a living monument of the region's psychological and spiritual makeup—stoic, proud, hardworking, moral, and peace-loving—conveys Blasco Ibanez's theme. When the boat has finally crashed against the rocks, and hope has faded for a possible sole survivor (a young child who has been equipped with a life preserver and thrown from the ship), Tia Picores turns away to face the city and cries out: "And after this they'll come to the Fishmarket, the harlots, and beat you down, and beat you down! And still they'll say fish comes high, the scullions! And cheap 't would be at fifty, yes, at seventy-five a pound!"

Along with this thematic consideration Blasco Ibanez's early works embody a stylistic feature that also proves original to fiction in the Naturalistic mode: the use of simile and metaphor to create a dramatic tension between the character and his environment. *The Cabin* is exemplary in this respect. In an article appearing in *Hispania,* Douglas Rogers summarizes this technique: "The suggestive power of the similes rings so emphatically throughout the novel that the 'as if' situations are as though converted into effective power, and the sense of a huge, all-controlling destiny, where there once were Greek and Roman Gods, swallows up the smaller intellectual concept of socio-political determinism."

Blasco Ibanez records and dramatically evokes vivid sensations. In so doing, he imbues nature with an often very poetic sense of mystery and power. This quality in Blasco Ibanez's works is often obscured by Naturalistic features, such as determinism and a belief in the destructive power of man's base instincts, which, to be sure, are present in Blasco Ibanez's works. But the poetic quality is just as important since the sea, the earth, and the other natural elements described in the fiction are intrinsically poetic. Nature is a cruel, destructive force; it is also something marvelous and beautiful.

Thematically, the presentation of nature in these terms emphasizes the tragic dimension of the works since the characters are victims of their own courses of action and not mere toys of impersonal, destructive, deterministic forces. Blasco Ibanez's characters are strong-willed and healthy individuals, who in refusing to accept their human limitations and to pay heed to warnings ultimately bring about their own downfall. In *The Mayflower,* for example, the protagonist decides to set sail in the storm, knowing that he is placing himself and his crew in great danger. When he realizes his mistake, he relies upon his abilities as a seaman and makes a desperate but failing attempt to defy the elements.

A variation on this theme appears in one of Blasco Ibanez's most famous short stories, "En el mar" ("At sea"). Here, the protagonist sets out to catch a huge tuna, and when a storm threatens, the character blindly but boldly moves forward, venturing far out into the sea. After a preliminary encounter with the fish, which nearly results in his boat being capsized, a clear warning to the would-be hero, the protagonist is even more determined to catch his prey. He finally succeeds, though at a terrible price: his young son is thrown from the boat during the violent struggle with the fish and is given up for dead. Yet another example of this bold behavior appears in *The Cabin* as a newly arrived farmer decides to cultivate a parcel of land that all the other farmers of the region, joined together in a spirit of solidarity, have sworn to abandon in protest of the unjust treatment and death of the farmer who previously occupied that land. As in the previous narratives, the protagonist is given several warnings but nevertheless persists in his endeavour, even if it means placing his family in great danger. When his cabin is finally burned down, he is forced to leave.

Bernardo Suarez in a *Cuadernos hispanoamericanos* essay states that "nature as it is presented in *The Cabin* . . . is a favorable agent . . . a type of paradise." The notion of paradise helps define man's relationship to nature, a subject that manifests itself repeatedly in Blasco Ibanez's regional novels and short stories. These works artistically convey man as a primitive being exiled from a mythic paradise; providing a chronicle of the social and historical changes that were taking place in Spain at the turn of the century, the regional fiction depicts the lives of individuals caught between present and past, between, on the one hand, the realities of a mechanized economy, government intervention, and a social gospel of "progress" and, on the other, the futile yearning to regain harmony with nature.

In terms of narration, Blasco Ibanez wrote in an objective omniscient mode, often relying on dialogue and indirect discourse to maintain his distance from the work and thereby producing, as Sherman H. Eoff declares in *The Modern Spanish Novel,* "an unusually strong singleness of narrative effect." In adopting the omniscient voice Blasco Ibanez remained faithful to Naturalism, which in theory sought to emulate the laboratory setting of the scientist to insure objectivity and to obtain a "truer" sense of reality. But he rarely made use of Naturalism's encyclopedic descriptive approach, where even the most minute detail is recorded. And in spite of his predominantly objective tone, Blasco Ibanez often playfully interacted with his characters by adding a humorous comment or juxtaposing images that end an ironic quality to his prose. He did not make extensive use of irony, especially as a narrative framework, but it does appear in several novels and short stories; for example, in "El ultimo leon" ("The Last Lion"), a masterful sketch portraying an anachronistic Valencian artisan who champions the cause of tradition (dressing like a legendary lion in a religious procession) in a world which has long since disassociated itself from its noble, legendary past. In such instances the reader encounters compassion, admiration, and humor in the narrator's characterization, but there is no romantic idealization or nostalgic appeal as in the typical *costumbrista* writer.

After the regional works, Blasco Ibanez wrote a series of novels which are commonly referred to as his "thesis cycle." Each of these novels bore a specific ideological orientation and sought to denounce a particular aspect of Spanish society. Much more political than the preceding works, these novels are generally considered artistically inferior to the Valencian cycle. If the early works present a realistic image of society in its many aspects, the thesis cycle addresses specific problems articulated through the struggle of the worker (the proletariat) for economic and political emancipation. *La catedral* (*In the Shadow of the Cathedral,* 1903) seeks to unveil the retrogressive effect of the Catholic Church on the Spaniard; *El intruso* (*The Intruder,* 1904) deals with the problems of the mine workers in northern Spain; *La horda* (*The Mob,* 1905) focuses on the conditions of the inhabitants of Madrid's ghettos; and *La bodega* (*The Fruit of the Vine,* 1905) is an expose of southern Spain's sherry industry, which on the one hand exploits Spanish workers and on the other produces the widely consumed alcohol that ultimately enslaves them by inhibiting their intellectual growth. Other novels can also be loosely classified within this group: *La maja desnuda* (*Woman Triumphant,* 1906) examines the manner in which artistic talent is stifled by capitalistic influences, and *Sangre y arena* (*Blood and Sand,* 1908), the best novel of this group, portrays the bullfighter as a victim of society and tradition. Using as a setting the Balearic Islands, *Los muertos mandan* (*The Dead Command,* 1909) addresses the problem of social barriers and racial prejudices, a theme that reappears in *Luna Benamor* (1909).

Although these works risk being viewed as nothing more than propagandistic documents, they also significantly contribute to modern Spanish literature. Examined in the specific historical context from which they were conceived, they represent an important development in what would later become the contemporary novel of Social Realism. Transitional works, they break with the Naturalistic model by replacing the unique protagonist with the collective protagonist and by discarding the individual focus on a particular scene or situation for a larger historical vision of the worker's universal struggle for equality and justice through socialism. In the novels of the thesis cycle, actual events and social movements are recognizable; for example, the 1892 peasant uprising in southern Spain is incorporated into *The Fruit of the Vine*. One might even say that through his creation of this group of novels Blasco Ibanez could be considered the father of the modern Spanish novel. This opinion is advanced by Raphael Bosch who declares in *La novela espanola del siglo XX* that Blasco Ibanez helped inaugurate "an open novel, attentive to the immediate reality, urgent, common, in opposition to the closed action and the more or less explored characters, all as protagonists, characteristic in the nineteenth century."

The cycle of thesis novels might also be considered important for the light it casts on Blasco Ibanez's relationship with the universally acclaimed group of Spanish writers known as the Generation of 1898, a group to which he technically belonged by virtue of his birthdate. This group included such prominent philosophical and literary figures as Miguel de Unamuno and Pio Baroja, but critics have commonly excluded Blasco Ibanez from this circle on aesthetic grounds: the Generation of 1898 espoused an innovative and experimental style of writing whereas Blasco Ibanez continued to pursue the traditional, realistic manner.

All of these writers, however, including Blasco Ibanez, were deeply concerned with the fate of Spain; they saw the once vast and mighty Spanish empire quickly decline when, defeated by the United States in the Spanish-American War of 1898, it lost its last territorial possessions and whatever remained of its world power. Both Blasco Ibanez and the members of this group wanted to remedy the ills of Spain by introducing national reforms. To this end, Blasco Ibanez proposed the formation of an Academy of Arts and Letters similar to that in France. Initially, the response of the Generation of 1898 was positive, and the Academy was in fact formed, if only in theory. Eduardo Betoret-Paris has observed in an article published in *Hispania* that "not only [was] there a lot in common between the concerns of Blasco [Ibanez] and those of the most distinguished components of the Generation of 1898, but these members also [accepted] Blasco [Ibanez]'s leadership in these enterprises, perhaps because they [knew] that Blasco [Ibanez did] not suffer from the so often referred to *abulia* (apathy)," a common symptom experienced by these writers.

If in his thesis novels Blasco Ibanez was primarily concerned with criticizing contemporary society, in most of his subsequent novels his goal was quite different: he conceived a monumental work of several volumes in which he would present to the world an account of Spain's glorious past, focusing on figures and events that were not well known. This phase of historical vindication might well have represented a desire on Blasco Ibanez's part to balance the negative image of Spain elaborated in his previous novels. On the other hand, the historical framework also allowed him to incorporate his life experiences outside of Spain, especially since many of the themes he treated dealt with voyages, conquest, and discovery. Blasco Ibanez had traveled extensively, giving speeches wherever he went, often about Spain. In many ways he himself was both the Columbus protagonist of *En busca del Gran Kan* (*Unknown Lands: The Story of Columbus,* 1929) and the character Alonso de Ojeda, one of Columbus's ship commanders during his second voyage to the Americas, in *El caballero de la Virgen* (*The Knight of the Virgin,* 1929). Like them, he was engaged in a "mission"; he was spreading Spanish culture throughout the Spanish speaking Americas and the United States as well. Other characters presented in these works are less convincing as historical figures: the Spanish Benedict XIII, Avignon pope during the Church schism in *El papa del mar* (*The Pope of the Sea,* 1925), and the Borgias, also Spanish popes, in *A los pies de Venus (los Borgias)* (*The Borgias; or, At the Feet of Venus,* 1926).

Blasco Ibanez was at the pinnacle of his success during this later period of his life, having a sure platform and an international audience, but this position of renown ultimately proved detrimental to the artistic quality of these works. In most of these writings, his artistry gave way to a formulaic approach to literature in which he wrote to a thesis or endeavored to produce best-sellers. His later books are often marred by incongruous and extraneous elements of romance and intrigue, unrealistic descriptions, and anachronisms. Such works pleased the uncritical reader of commercial fiction but did little to enhance Blasco Ibanez's reputation in literary circles. His early, regional works, however, continue to be held in great esteem by readers throughout the world.

MEDIA ADAPTATIONS: La tierra de todos was adapted for a stage production by L. Linares Becerra, 1927; *Blood and Sand* and *The Four Horsemen of the Apocalypse* were made into films of the same titles starring Rudolph Valentino, produced by Paramount Pictures; *The Four Horsemen of the Apocalypse* was made into a film starring Glenn Ford and Charles Boyer, 1961; four other novels were also made into U.S. films.

BIOGRAPHICAL/CRITICAL SOURCES:

BOOKS

Bell, Aubrey F. G., *Contemporary Spanish Literature,* Knopf, 1925.
Blanco Aguinaga, Carlos, and others, *Historia social de la literatura espanola,* Castalia, 1978.
Bosch, Rafael, *La novela espanola del siglo XX,* Volume 1, Las Americas, 1970.
Cejador y Frauca, Julio, *Historia de la lengua y literatura castellana,* Volume 9, Revista de Archivos, Biliotecas y Museos, 1918.
Day, A. Grove, and Edgar C. Knowlton, *Vicente Blasco Ibanez,* Twayne, 1972.
Eoff, Sherman H., *The Modern Spanish Novel: Comparative Essays Examining the Philosophical Impact of Science on Fiction,* New York University Press, 1961.
Landeira, Ricardo, *The Modern Spanish Novel, 1898-1936,* Twayne, 1985.
Twentieth-Century Literary Criticism, Volume 12, Gale, 1984.

PERIODICALS

Cuadernos hispanoamericanos, May, 1981.
Hispania, Volume 53, number 1, 1969, Volume 53, number 4, 1970.

*   *   *

BLIGHT, Rose
See GREER, Germaine

BLISH, James (Benjamin) 1921-1975
(William Atheling, Jr., Marcus Lyons, Arthur
Merlin, Luke Torley, pseudonyms; Donald Laverty,
John MacDougal, joint pseudonyms)

PERSONAL: Born May 23, 1921, in East Orange, N.J.; died of
cancer, July 30 (one source says 29), 1975, in Henley-on-
Thames, England; son of Asa Rhodes and Dorothea (Sch-
neewind) Blish; married Mildred Virginia Kidd Emden, May 23,
1947 (divorced, 1963); married Judith Ann Lawrence, November 7, 1964; children: (first marriage) Elisabeth, Charles Benjamin. *Education:* Rutgers University, B.Sc., 1942; attended Columbia University, 1945-46.

ADDRESSES: Agent—Robert P. Mills, Ltd., 156 East 52nd St.,
New York, N.Y. 10022.

CAREER: Trade newspaper editor, New York, N.Y., 1947-51;
public relations counsel in New York City and Washington,
D.C., 1951-69; writer. *Military service:* U.S. Army, medical laboratory technician, 1942-44.

MEMBER: Science Fiction Writers of America (vice-president,
1966-68), American Rocket Society, British Interplanetary Society, Society of Authors, James Branch Cabell Society, History
of Science Society, Association of Lunar and Planetary Observers, Authors League, Civil Air Patrol.

AWARDS, HONORS: Hugo Award for best science fiction
novel, 1958, for *A Case of Conscience;* Eighteenth World Science
Fiction Convention Guest of Honor, 1960.

WRITINGS:

Jack of Eagles (science fiction novel), Greenberg, 1952, pub-
lished as *ESPer,* Avon, 1958.
(With Fritz Leiber and Fletcher Pratt) *Witches Three,* Twayne,
1952.
The Warriors of Day (science fiction novel), Galaxy, 1953.
Sword of Xota, Galaxy, 1953.
Earthman, Come Home (science fiction novel; also see below),
Putnam, 1955, reprinted, Hutchinson, 1974.
They Shall Have Stars (science fiction novel; also see below),
Faber, 1956, published as *Year 2018!,* Avon, 1957.
The Seedling Stars (short stories), Gnome, 1957.
The Frozen Year (novel), Ballantine, 1957 (published in England
as *The Fallen Star,* Faber, 1957, reprinted, Hutchinson,
1976).
A Case of Conscience (science fiction novel), Ballantine, 1958, re-
printed, 1987.
VOR (science fiction novel), Avon, 1958.
The Triumph of Time (science fiction novel; also see below),
Avon, 1958 (published in England as *A Clash of Cymbals,*
Faber, 1958).
(With Robert A. W. Lowndes) *The Duplicated Man* (science fic-
tion novel), Avalon, 1959.
Galactic Cluster (short stories), New American Library, 1959.
(With Poul Anderson and Thomas N. Scortia) Leo Margulies,
editor, *Get Out of My Sky,* Fawcett, 1960.
The Star Dwellers (science fiction novel for children), Putnam,
1961.
So Close to Home (short stories), Ballantine, 1961.
(With Virginia Kidd) *Titan's Daughter* (science fiction novel),
Berkley Publishing, 1961.
A Life for the Stars (science fiction novel; also see below), Put-
nam, 1962.
The Night Shapes (novel), Ballantine, 1962.

(Under pseudonym William Atheling, Jr.) *The Issue at Hand:
Studies in Contemporary Magazine Science Fiction,* Advent,
1964, 2nd edition published as *More Issues at Hand: Critical
Studies in Contemporary Science Fiction,* 1970.
Doctor Mirabilis: A Novel, Faber, 1964, revised edition, Dodd,
1971.
Cities in Flight (contains *They Shall Have Stars, A Life for the
Stars, Earthman, Come Home,* and *The Triumph of Time*),
Faber, 1965, Avon, 1966, revised edition, 1970.
Mission to the Heart Stars (science fiction novel for children),
Putnam, 1965.
Best Science Fiction Stories of James Blish, Faber, 1965, revised
edition, 1973, published as *The Testament of Andros,*
Hutchinson, 1977.
(Editor and author of introduction) *New Dreams This Morning,*
Ballantine, 1966.
(With Norman L. Knight) *A Torrent of Faces* (science fiction
novel), Doubleday, 1967.
(Adapter) *Star Trek* (novelizations of scripts from the National
Broadcasting Co. television series; also see below), Bantam,
Volumes 1-11, 1967-75, Volume 12 (with wife, Judith A.
Lawrence), 1977.
Welcome to Mars! (science fiction novel for children), Faber,
1967, Putnam, 1968.
The Vanished Jet (science fiction novel for children), Weybright
& Talley, 1968.
Black Easter; or, Faust Aleph-Null (science fiction novel),
Doubleday, 1968.
(With Robert Silverberg and Roger Zelazny) *Three for Tomor-
row: Three Original Novellas of Science Fiction,* Meredith
Press, 1969.
Anywhen (short stories), Doubleday, 1970, revised edition,
Faber, 1971.
(Editor) *Nebula Award Stories 5,* Doubleday, 1970.
Spock Must Die! (original novel; also see below), Bantam, 1970.
(Editor) *Thirteen O'Clock and Other Zero Hours: The "Cecil
Corwin" Stories of C. M. Kornbluth,* Dell, 1970.
. . . And All the Stars a Stage (science fiction novel), Double-
day, 1971.
The Day After Judgment (science fiction novel), Doubleday,
1971.
The Quincunx of Time (science fiction novel), Dell, 1972.
Midsummer Century (science fiction novel), Doubleday, 1972.
The Star Trek Reader (contains *Star Trek,* Volumes 1-10, Vol-
ume 12, and *Spock Must Die!*), four volumes, Dutton,
1976-78.
The Best of James Blish, edited by Robert A. W. Lowndes, Bal-
lantine, 1979.

Also author of television scripts and motion picture screenplays.
Contributor of short stories, articles, poetry, and criticism, occa-
sionally under pseudonyms, to numerous magazines. Editor,
Vanguard Science Fiction, 1958; co-editor, *Kalki: Studies in
James Branch Cabell,* beginning 1967.

*WORK IN PROGRESS: A History of Witchcraft, Demonology
and Magic;* a study of the semantics of music; *The Sense of
Music;* another science fiction novel.

SIDELIGHTS: Though James Blish was known to many readers
for adapting "Star Trek" television scripts into book form, a
Times Literary Supplement reviewer once referred to him as
"one of the best five or six living writers of science fiction. . . .
His ability to convey without undue emphasis the fundamental
human link that exists between curious forms of man in exotic
surroundings is as faultless as his skill in implying the social and
political changes consequent on technological advance." A *New*

York Herald Tribune Book Review critic wrote: "A rare Martian orchid to James Blish for giving us science fiction in its purest form; the logical extrapolation of present knowledge and probability so that the reader passes without a quiver from the known to the unknown."

Blish made a point of including actual scientific and technological detail in his works, for he felt that it was necessary for a science fiction writer to be as accurate as possible in order to convince the reader of the plausibility of the story. He also, at least after the publication of *A Case of Conscience* in 1958, exhibited a fascination with religious themes, especially Christianity and its struggles with satanic powers as perceived by medieval philosophers.

AVOCATIONAL INTERESTS: Music, astronomy, flying.

BIOGRAPHICAL/CRITICAL SOURCES:

BOOKS

Contemporary Literary Criticism, Volume 14, Gale, 1980.
Dictionary of Literary Biography, Volume 8: *Twentieth-Century American Science Fiction Writers,* Gale, 1981.
Walker, Paul, editor, *Speaking of Science Fiction: The Paul Walker Interviews,* Luna, 1978.

PERIODICALS

Magazine of Fantasy and Science Fiction, April, 1972.
New York Herald Tribune Book Review, April 13, 1952.
Times Literary Supplement, September 21, 1967.
Washington Post Book World, June 27, 1982.
Young Readers' Review, February, 1968.

OBITUARIES:

PERIODICALS

AB Bookman's Weekly, September 8, 1975.
New York Times, July 31, 1975.
Washington Post, August 1, 1975.

*   *   *

BLISS, Reginald
    See WELLS, H(erbert) G(eorge)

*   *   *

BLIXEN, Karen (Christentze Dinesen)   1885-1962
    (Pierre Andrezel, Isak Dinesen, Osccola)

PERSONAL: Born April 17, 1885, in Rungsted, Denmark; died September 7, 1962, of emaciation in Rungsted; daughter of Wilhelm (an army officer and writer under his own name and his Indian name Boganis) and Ingeborg (Westenholz) Dinesen; married Baron Bror Blixen-Finecke (a big-game hunter and writer), January 14, 1914 (divorced, 1921). *Education:* Studied English at Oxford University, 1904; studied painting at Royal Academy in Copenhagen, in Paris, 1910, and in Rome.

ADDRESSES: Home—Rungstedlund, Rungsted Kyst, Denmark.

CAREER: Writer, 1907-62, from 1934 writing in English and translating her own work into Danish. With her husband Baron Blixen, she managed a coffee plantation in British East Africa (now Nairobi, Kenya), 1913-21, then took over the management herself until failing coffee prices forced her to give up the farm in 1931. Commissioned by three Scandinavian newspapers to write a series of twelve articles on wartime Berlin, Paris, and London, 1940.

MEMBER: Danish Academy (founding member), American Academy of Arts and Letters (honorary member), National Institute of Arts and Letters (honorary member), Bayerische Akademie der Schoenen Kuenste (corresponding member), Cosmopolitan Club (New York).

AWARDS, HONORS: Ingenio et Arti Medal from King Frederick IX of Denmark, 1950; The Golden Laurels, 1952; Hans Christian Andersen Prize, 1955; Danish Critics' Prize, 1957; Henri Nathansen Memorial Fund award, 1957.

WRITINGS:

PUBLISHED IN DANISH UNDER NAME KAREN BLIXEN AND IN ENGLISH UNDER PSEUDONYM ISAK DINESEN

Sandhedens Haevn (play; title means "The Revenge of Truth"; first produced at Royal Theatre, Copenhagen, 1936), [Tilskueren], 1926, Gyldendal (Copenhagen), 1960.
Seven Gothic Tales (Book-of-the-Month Club selection), Smith & Haas, 1934, reprinted, Franklin Library, 1978, Danish translation published as *Syv Fantastiske Fortaellinger,* Reitzels, 1935, reprinted, Gyldendal, 1975.
Out of Africa (also see below; Book-of-the-Month Club selection), Putnam (London), 1937, Random House, 1938, reprinted with illustrations, Crown, 1987, Danish translation published as *Den Afrikanske Farm,* Gyldendal, 1937, reprinted, 1977.
Winter's Tales (Book-of-the-Month Club selection), Random House, 1942, reprinted, Books for Libraries, 1971, Danish translation published as *Vinter-Eventyr,* Gyldendal, 1942.
Om revtskrivning 23-24 marts 1938, Gyldendal, 1949.
Farah, Wivel (Copenhagen), 1950.
Daguerreotypier (two radio talks presented January, 1951), Gyldendal, 1951.
Babettes Gaestebud (title means "Babette's Feast"), Fremad (Copenhagen), 1952.
Omkring den Nye Lov om Dyreforsoeg, Politikens Forlag (Copenhagen), 1952.
Kardinalens tredie Historie (title means "The Cardinal's Third Tale"), Gyldendal, 1952.
En Baaltale med 14 Aars Forsinkelse (title means "Bonfire Speech Fourteen Years Delayed"), Berlingske Forlag (Copenhagen), 1953.
Spoegelseshestene, Fremad, 1955.
Last Tales, Random House, 1957, reprinted, 1975, Danish translation published as *Sidste Fortaellinger,* Gyldendal, 1957.
Anecdotes of Destiny (also see below), Random House, 1958, reprinted, 1974, Danish translation published as *Skaebne-Anekdoter,* Gyldendal, 1958, reprinted, 1976.
Skygger paa Graesset, Gyldendal, 1960, published as *Shadows on the Grass* (also see below; Book-of-the-Month Club selection), Random House, 1961.
(Author of introduction) Truman Capote, *Holly* (an edition of *Breakfast at Tiffany's*), Gyldendal, 1960.
(Author of introduction) Olive Schreiner, *The Story of an African Farm,* Limited Editions Club, 1961.
On Mottoes of My Life (originally published in *Proceedings of The American Academy of Arts and Letters and The National Institute of Arts and Letters,* Second Series, Number 10, 1960), Ministry of Foreign Affairs (Copenhagen), 1962.
(Author of introduction) Hans Christian Andersen, *Thumbelina, and Other Stories,* Macmillan, 1962.
Osceola (collection of early stories and poems), Gyldendal, 1962.

(Author of introduction) Basil Davidson, *Det Genfundne Africa,* Gyldendal, 1962.

Ehrengard (also see below), Random House, 1963, Danish translation by Clara Svendsen, Gyldendal, 1963.

Karen Blixen (memorial edition of principal works), Gyldendal, 1964.

Essays, Gyldendal, 1965, expanded edition published as *Mit livs mottoer og andre essays,* 1978.

Efterladte Fortallinger, Gyldendal, 1975.

Carnival: Entertainments and Posthumous Tales, Danish portions translated by P. M. Mitchell and W. D. Paden, University of Chicago Press, 1977.

Breve fra Afrika, Volume I: *1914-1924,* Volume II: *1925-1931,* Gyldendal, 1978, published as *Letters from Africa, 1914-1931,* edited by Frans Lasson and translated by Anne Born, University of Chicago Press, 1981.

Daguerreotypes and Other Essays, Danish portions translated by P. M. Mitchell and W. D. Paden, University of Chicago Press, 1979.

"Det droemmende barn" og andre fortaellinger, Gyldendal, 1979.

Modern aegteskab og andre betragtninger, Gyldendal, 1981, published as *On Modern Marriage: And Other Observations,* St. Martin's, 1986.

Isak Dinesen's Africa: Images of the Wild Continent from the Writer's Life and Words, Sierra Books, 1985.

Samlede essays, Gyldendal, 1985.

Out of Africa [and] *Shadows on the Grass,* Vintage Book, 1985.

Anecdotes of Destiny [and] *Ehrengard,* Vintage Book, 1985.

PUBLISHED UNDER PSEUDONYM PIERRE ANDREZEL

Gengaeldelsens Veje, Danish translation by Clara Svendsen, Gyldendal, 1944, published as *The Angelic Avengers* (Book-of-the-Month Club selection), Random House, 1946, reprinted, University of Chicago Press, 1975.

OTHER

Contributor of short stories, articles, and reviews to *Ladies' Home Journal, Saturday Evening Post, Atlantic, Harper's Bazaar, Vogue, Botteghe Oscure,* and *Heretica.*

SIDELIGHTS: Karen Blixen, better known by her pen name Isak Dinesen, remains one of Denmark's most widely acclaimed modern authors. A prose stylist who wrote skillfully in English as well as in her native Danish, Dinesen composed exotic and archaic tales that set her apart from the literary traditions of her day. Although she was initially snubbed by critics in her native country, Dinesen enjoyed both critical and commercial success in Britain and the United States and was nominated for the Nobel Prize several times during her life. In addition to her considerable literary contributions, Dinesen is perhaps equally well known for her remarkable life, documented in such autobiographical works as *Out of Africa* and *Shadows on the Grass.* As David Lehman notes in *Newsweek:* "She likened herself to Scheherazade—and fully lived up to the name. Danish writer Isak Dinesen led a life as wildly improbable and flamboyantly romantic as her exotic and spellbinding tales."

Tutored at home by a series of governesses, Dinesen showed early artistic promise and as a teenager studied drawing, painting, and languages at a private school in France. In 1903, after a series of comprehensive exams, Dinesen was admitted into the Royal Academy of Fine Arts in Copenhagen. There she developed her affinity for painting, an affinity that was later to be reflected in the rich descriptive style of her writing. According to Judith Thurman's *Isak Dinesen: The Life of a Storyteller,* Dine-

sen later wrote: "[I owe painting] . . . for revealing the nature of reality to me. I have always had difficulty seeing how a landscape looked, if I had not first got the key to it from a great painter. . . . Constable, Gainsborough and Turner showed me England. When I travelled to Holland as a young girl, I understood all the landscape and the cities said because the old Dutch painters did me the kind service of interpreting it." Dinesen dropped out of the Academy several years later and soon thereafter took up writing. Between 1904 and 1908 she wrote the first draft of a puppet play entitled "The Revenge of Truth" as well as a series of tales she called "Likely Stories." Mario Krohn, an art historian Dinesen had met at the Academy, read her work and encouraged Dinesen to take her writing seriously. Krohn also arranged to have some of her stories read by Valdemar Vedel, editor of one of Denmark's most distinguished literary magazines, *Tilskueren.* According to Thurman, Vedel wrote to Krohn that one of Dinesen's tales, "The Hermits," was "so original . . . and so well made that I would like to take it for *Tilskueren.*" He continued, "There is certainly talent in this author." The tale was published in 1907 under the pseudonym Osceola. Two years later Krohn himself became editor of *Tilskueren* and accepted Dinesen's story "The de Cats Family" in 1909.

During these years Dinesen spent much of her time in the company of her upper-class relatives, and she soon found herself deeply but unhappily in love with her second cousin, Hans Blixen-Finecke. The failed love affair had a great impact on Dinesen. According to Thurman she later recalled: "More than anything else, a deep, unrequited love left its mark on my early youth." Extremely depressed, Dinesen left Denmark in 1910 to attend a new art school in Paris. Thurman relates that when Mario Krohn visited Dinesen in Paris and asked her about her literary ambitions she answered that she wanted "all things in life more than to be a writer—travel, dancing, living, the freedom to paint." When she returned to her family estate at Rungstedlund several months later, Dinesen turned to writing as a diversion, revising "The Revenge of Truth" and composing early versions of tales such as "Carnival" and "Peter and Rosa."

A voyage to Rome two years later did little to assuage her depression over her unrequited love, and upon her return Dinesen shocked her family and friends by announcing that she was to marry Hans's twin brother, Bror Blixen. Based on advice from relatives, the engaged couple decided to go to Africa, then thought to be a land of opportunity and excitement for young people with initiative. In 1913 Bror Blixen left for British East Africa and, with capital provided largely by Dinesen's family, purchased a six-thousand-acre coffee plantation outside of Nairobi, Kenya. In January of the following year Dinesen joined the Baron and the two were married on the fourteenth of that month.

Dinesen would not return to writing fiction for many years, but 1914 marks the beginning of her letters to her family and friends, correspondence later compiled and published as *Letters from Africa.* As these letters indicate, the early months in Africa passed well. Dinesen enjoyed living on the plantation and accompanying her husband on safari. She was also taken with her African servants, particularly her cook, Farah, who went on to become Dinesen's friend and confidant. During her time in Africa Dinesen socialized with the upper-class Europeans living there. Many of these aristocrats became models for characters in Dinesen's tales.

Several months after her arrival in Kenya, Dinesen began to suffer from what she believed to be malaria but which later turned out to be a case of syphilis contracted from her husband. To receive treatment, Dinesen returned to Europe. A noted venereologist in Copenhagen arrested the primary syphilis but Dinesen was to suffer the lingering effects of the disease throughout her life.

The next years were difficult ones for Dinesen, both personally and financially. The philandering Baron embarked on extended safaris, ignoring his duties on the farm as well as his wife. Meanwhile, despite her family's continued financial support, the coffee farm was losing large amounts of money. Forced to return to Denmark for treatment of blood poisoning, Dinesen confided her marital problems to her mother and brother Thomas. These problems, combined with the ongoing financial setbacks on the farm, caused Bror's dismissal and Dinesen's appointment as the sole manager of what became known as the Karen Coffee Company. Although her family urged divorce, Dinesen would not comply and agreed only to a separation from the Baron. "I would never demand a divorce or try to push it through against Bror's will. I do not know how anyone can do that unless one is quite frenzied; and even though I have occasionally been angry with Bror or, rather, perhaps, in despair over his behavior, there is far, far too much binding us together from all the years of difficulty we have shared here, for me to be able to take the initiative in putting an end to what, if nothing else, was a most intimate relationship. . . . In any case, it is my heartfelt hope that he will be happy . . . I feel for Bror, and will until I die, the greatest friendship or the deepest tenderness that I am capable of feeling," Dinesen explained in *Letters from Africa*. Eventually the Baron requested and received a divorce.

About this time Dinesen met Denys Finch Hatton, a handsome English pilot and hunter who was to become her companion and lover as well as the first audience for her tales. During Finch Hatton's occasional, and often unannounced, visits, Dinesen would relate to her friend tales she had thought up during his absence. Dinesen liked to think of herself as a modern Scheherazade, weaving imaginative tales to lengthen Finch Hatton's visits.

In 1923, inspired by a debate between her mother and brother concerning sexual morality, Dinesen wrote a long essay entitled "On Modern Marriage and Other Considerations," her first formal writing effort in years. The following year she resubmitted "The Revenge of Truth" to *Tilskueren*. When the work was accepted for publication the following year Dinesen wrote in *Letters from Africa*: "With regard to 'The Revenge of Truth.' I don't want anything in it changed; but I imagine there is little chance of it ever being published. I don't think there is anything blasphemous in it, simply that it is written from an atheist's viewpoint. I believe it would be impossible to write if one gave consideration to who is going to read one's work,—but for that matter I don't think I will be writing anything in the near future."

The mid and late 1920s saw the Karen Coffee Company suffer enormous financial setbacks, and it soon became clear that Dinesen would be forced to sell the farm. To alleviate her anxiety, Dinesen began writing down those fantastic tales she had recounted to Hatton during his stays. She later recalled in *Daguerreotypes and Other Essays*: "During my last months in Africa, as it became clear to me that I could not keep the farm, I had started writing at night, to get my mind off the things which in the daytime it had gone over a hundred times, and on a new track. My squatters on the farm, by then, had got into the habit of coming up to my house and sitting around it for hours in silence, as if just waiting to see how things would develop. I felt their presence there more like a friendly gesture than a reproach, but all the

same of sufficient weight to make it difficult for me to start any undertaking of my own. But they would go away, back to their huts, at nightfall. And I sat there, in the house, alone, or perhaps with Farah, the infallibly loyal, standing motionless in his long white Arab robe with his back to the wall, figures, voices, and colors from far away or from nowhere began to swarm around my paraffin lamp." In such a manner, Dinesen wrote two of her *Seven Gothic Tales*. By 1931 the farm had been auctioned off, and Dinesen was awaiting her return to Denmark. Before she left, she learned that Denys Finch Hatton had been killed when his small plane crashed in Tanganyika. In May of 1931 Dinesen saw Africa for the last time.

Once home at Rungstedlund, Dinesen began to write almost immediately, working in her father's old office. Now, however, her motives were serious. "My home is a lovely place; I might have lived on there from day to day in a kind of sweet idyl; but I could not see any kind of future before me. And I had no money; my dowry, so to say, had gone with the farm. I owed it to the people on whom I was dependent to try to make some kind of existence for myself. Those Gothic Tales began to demand to be written," she later wrote in *Daguerreotypes and Other Essays*. Two years later, at age forty-eight, Dinesen completed her first collection of stories, *Seven Gothic Tales*, but experienced difficulty getting the book into print. Although it was written in English, not many were willing to publish a debut work by an unknown Danish author. Several British publishers rejected the manuscript before Dorothy Canfield Fisher, a friend of Thomas Dinesen and member of the Book-of-the-Month Club selection committee, previewed the book. Impressed with the collection, Fisher sent it to her neighbor, publisher Robert Haas. Haas was equally impressed and published *Seven Gothic Tales* the following year.

An aura of mystery surrounded the book's release. When it offered *Seven Gothic Tales* as a selection in April of 1934, the Book-of-the-Month Club newsletter stated simply, "No clue is available as to the pseudonymic author." Dinesen herself confused matters by preceding her maiden name with a man's first name—Isak, Hebrew for "one who laughs." Dinesen's true identity was not revealed until over fifty thousand copies of *Seven Gothic Tales* were in print. With this collection Dinesen began a long and rewarding relationship with American readers, as five of her books became Book-of-the-Month Club selections.

Although Dinesen later expressed embarrassment over *Seven Gothic Tales*, claiming it was "too elaborate" and had "too much of the author in it," the book was almost universally well received. In a *Saturday Review of Literature* article W. R. Benet praises Dinesen's first collection, calling it "one of the most strangely flavored and subtle volumes of pure creative literature that has appeared in some time, a book of unique atmosphere and scenes indelibly delineated, a book bringing the psychological insight of a Henry James to the material of a Northern Boccaccio, a book of extraordinary fantasy that yet takes us intimately into a vivid variety of human lives." Many critics were intrigued by the mysterious authorship of these seven fantastic tales. Claiming that "no story in the book equals the mystery of the author," Robert Cantwell in his *New Outlook* review of *Seven Gothic Tales* asks, "what modern writer can write such prose and attach so little importance to it?" Similarly, discussing the pseudonymous author in his *Nation* review Mark Van Doren writes: "If as Dorothy Canfield lets fall, the pseudonymous author of these tales is a continental European 'writing in English although that is not native to his pen,' we have here a linguistic triumph for which there is probably no precedent. Barring a few slips from idiom which are so attractive as to seem premeditated, the English of the book is such as I for one have never seen written by a foreigner to the language, and none too often by those in the grammar born. And if, as rumor has it, the author is a Danish woman who never wrote a book before, we have a phenomenon so astonishing as to be incredible.''

In *Seven Gothic Tales* Dinesen introduced stylistic and thematic motifs that are to be found throughout much of her subsequent work. Dinesen derived these motifs largely from two nineteenth-century literary movements—the Gothic and the decadent. As in the novels written in these genres, Dinesen's tales are often characterized by an emphasis on the emotional and spiritual, a nostalgia for the glory of past ages, a predilection for exotic characters, and an overriding sense of mystery, horror, and the supernatural. Writes Eric O. Johannesson in *The World of Isak Dinesen:* "Many of Dinesen's tales are undoubtedly both Gothic and decadent. The spine-chilling tale of terror, with its persecuted women, its ghosts, and its mysterious convents and castles, as well as the cruel tale, with its atmosphere of perversity and artificiality, have served as sources of inspiration for Dinesen." While critics clearly recognize Dinesen's debt to these traditions, several, notably Johannesson and Robert Langbaum, feel that Dinesen goes beyond them. Johannesson claims, "Dinesen's dependence on the Gothic and decadent tradition is evident, but the significant fact concerning this dependence is the manner in which she makes this tradition serve her own vision." Similarly, Langbaum maintains in his book *Isak Dinesen's Art: The Gayety of Vision:* "Isak Dinesen is an important writer because she has understood the tradition behind her and has taken the next step required by that tradition. Like the other, more massive writers of her generation—Rilke, Kafka, Mann, Joyce, Eliot, Yeats, . . .—she takes off from the sense of individuality developed in the course of the nineteenth-century to the point of morbidity, and leads that individuality where it wants to go. She leads it back to a universal principle and a connection with the external world."

Seven Gothic Tales also introduces Dinesen's preoccupation with the principle of interdependence, a principle that becomes further developed in her later volumes of stories. There are interrelationships among individual stories in the volume as well as the existence of stories within stories. Comparing such constructions to "a complex kaleidoscope," Elizabeth Ely Fuller writes in the *New Boston Review:* "Each character and each event works as a little bit of mirror reflecting another character or event, and then turning slightly to catch some other reflection. To reinforce this overall plot structure, Dinesen uses mirror images and similes repeatedly as the characters muse on their own nature and on their relation to others. To any one of them, the story makes no sense, but taken as a whole, the stories, like a piece of music or a minuet, form a complete pattern of movement." The principle of interdependence works on a thematic level in *Seven Gothic Tales* as well, as such disparate concepts as good and evil, comedy and tragedy, and art and life are intricately linked.

In spite of poor health and repeated hospitalizations, Dinesen continued to work on a book of memoirs, entitled *Out of Africa.* An international success simultaneously published in English and Danish, *Out of Africa* "solidified Dinesen's reputation in the United States and Britain," according to Langbaum. Unlike *Seven Gothic Tales,* which was conceived and partially written in Africa, *Out of Africa* was entirely thought of and written after Dinesen's return to Europe. Langbaum sees an interesting reciprocal relationship at work between these first two books. He writes: " 'Seven Gothic Tales' is a great book about Europe, because Isak Dinesen's experience of Africa stands behind it; and Europe stands, in the same way, behind every word of *Out of Af-*

rica. That is why *Out of Africa* (1937) is literature and not just another memoir of an interesting life.''

Considered by many to be the greatest pastoral romance of the twentieth century, *Out of Africa* enjoyed immediate and lasting critical acclaim, particularly from British and American critics. In a *Chicago Tribune* review, Richard Stern calls *Out of Africa* "perhaps the finest book ever written about Africa," claiming that "it casts over landscape, animals, and people the kind of transfixing spell 'Ulysses' casts over Dublin." Katherine Woods, writing in the *New York Times,* praises the book's absence of "sentimentality" and "elaboration" and avers, "Like the Ngong hills—'which are amongst the most beautiful in the world'—this writing is without redundancies, bared to its lines of strength and beauty." Even those critics who find fault with the book's structure commend Dinesen's style. "The tale of increasing tragedy which fills the latter half of the book seems not quite so successful as her earlier chapters," notes Hassoldt Davis in the *Saturday Review of Literature.* "But," he adds, "her book has a solid core of beauty in it, and a style as cadenced, constrained, and graceful as we have today." Similarly, while a reviewer in the *Manchester Guardian* believes "a shrewd editor with a blue pencil could have shortened it by a third and left it a better book," the same critic is quick to add, "Yet, take it for all in all, it is a distinguished piece of work. . . . The profundities of the native mind and the feeling of a semi-personified Africa alike have seldom been rendered with a more sincere sympathy." Hudson Strode seems to capture the sentiments of many critics when he writes in *Books:* "The author casts enchantment over her landscape with the most casual phrases. She rarely comes upon anything straightway. Backward, forward, she goes, a spark here, a flare there, until she has the landscape fairly lit up before you with all its inhabitants and customs in place. The result is a great naturalness."

Many critics feel that, stylistically, *Out of Africa* stands apart from the majority of Dinesen's other work. Writing in *Books West,* Joan Palevsky distinguishes between the "stilted, old-fashioned language" of the story collections and the "perfectly modern English" of *Out of Africa.* Langbaum believes such stylistic differences account for *Out of Africa*'s eventual popularity with Danish audiences: "*Out of Africa* . . . reassured the Danes, who had not liked the decadent, cynical, and perverse quality of *Seven Gothic Tales* that Isak Dinesen had after all a regard for and a knowledge of reality and humanity. The Danish reviewers liked the realism of *Out of Africa* and its humanitarian sensibility, the love she shows in it for animals and simple people.

Letters from Africa, the posthumously published compilation of Dinesen's correspondence with her family and friends, sheds a good deal of light on *Out of Africa.* Begun soon after her arrival to Africa in 1914, these letters provide an interesting subtext, revealing the private, often painful story behind the romantic vision of life presented in the famous memoir. As the letters show, Dinesen endured a number of hardships during her seventeen years in Africa. Lingering bouts of illness, marital problems, increasing loneliness, and financial worries all caused her despair. There is even speculation that Dinesen attempted suicide on at least one occasion during her final years there. Despite their painful revelations, the letters do not deal exclusively with the darker side of Dinesen's Kenyan experience. Throughout the letters, especially the earlier ones, are intermittent periods of happiness, even elation. This is particularly evident in Dinesen's descriptions of her growing attachment to the land of Africa and its people. "Immediately after lunch, Bror and I drove by car to our own farm. It is the most enchanting road you can imagine, like our own Deer Park, and the long blue range of Ngong Hills stretching out beyond it. There are so many flowering trees and shrubs, and a scent rather like bog myrtle, or pine trees, pervades everything. Out here it is not hot at all, the air is so soft and lovely, and one feels so light and free and happy," Dinesen wrote in one of her early entries in *Letters from Africa*.

These letters also offer valuable insights into Dinesen's character. As Carl Bailey notes in his *Village Voice* review, "Karen Blixen's letters were her, sent to stand for herself the way the old potentates used to send emissaries." *Letters from Africa* follows Dinesen's development from naive bride to able plantation manager to financially-ruined-but-unembittered divorcee. Remarks Kathleen Chase in *World Literature Today:* "We see Dinesen unmasked in all her moods and emotions, prejudices and predilections, her thoughts, her periodic nostalgia for Denmark (always flying the Danish flag) and her idyllic relationship with the English safari leader Denys Finch Hatton." Indeed, many of these letters chart Dinesen's increasing romantic feelings for Finch Hatton. As she wrote to her brother Thomas in 1928, "That such a person as Denys does exist,—something I have indeed guessed at before, but hardly dared to believe,—and that I have been lucky enough to meet him in this life and been so close to him,—even though there have been long periods of missing him in between,—compensates for everything else in the world, and other things cease to have any significance." Though Dinesen later experienced difficulty in her relationship with Finch Hatton, most of her letters recall their friendship glowingly.

These letters also reveal a good deal about a more negative aspect of Dinesen's personality, notably her patrician outlook. By her own admission, Dinesen felt an affinity for the aristocracy and a general disdain for all that was bourgeois. In fact, she often called herself "God's little snob." The correspondence in *Letters from Africa* does little to change such a reputation. "Karen Blixen was a terrible snob. Critics have long waxed ingenious in defending her short stories from charges of noblesse oblige; those defenses will be harder to make on the evidence of this collection," claims Carl Bailey in the *Village Voice*. A *New York Times Book Review* contributor admits that *Letters from Africa* often puts Dinesen in a poor light. "Her letters reveal a difficult woman: inconsistent and often cruel in her rejection of family life, emotionally demanding and given to what she herself called 'showing off.' " However, the same reviewer adds, "What saves this collection is her indomitable courage—that willful determination to face misfortune and to see beyond it." Most critics agree with this view and maintain that the overall portrait of Dinesen that emerges from the letters is a positive one. Writes Victoria Glendinning in the *Washington Post Book World:* "It is her will and complete lack of self-pity that make Karen Blixen so sympathetic and save her from the alienating intensity of other solitary searchers such as, for example, Simone Weil. She quotes a definition of true piety as 'loving one's destiny unconditionally.' To be able to do this without losing her resilience was part of Karen Blixen's achievement." Adds Richard Stern in the *Chicago Tribune*, "If these [letters] are not as brilliant as those in her great memoir, there is at least the material for one portrait greater than all the others, that of the great human being behind them all."

Paul Bailey sees a correlation between Dinesen's personal and financial struggles in Africa and her development as a writer. "The stoicism that is everywhere apparent in the intricately detailed stories of Isak Dinesen might well have been born in this, the darkest, period of Karen Blixen's life," writes Bailey in the *Times Literary Supplement*. He adds, "The fascination of this book is not just in the rounded picture it provides of a vanished Africa, vivid though that is, but rather in the way it reveals the tormented landowner developing into the assured literary artist: the confusions of Karen Blixen become the fictional material for the 'one who laughs.' "

With *Winter's Tales* Dinesen broke from the relative realism of *Out of Africa* and returned to the highly imaginative style which characterizes *Seven Gothic Tales*. Although these two collections share a number of similarities, *Winter's Tales* is simpler in style and closer in setting to modern Denmark. These differences, according to Robert Langbaum, account in large part for the popularity of *Winter's Tales* with Danish readers.

Like the *Seven Gothic Tales* before them, these eleven stories met with a good deal of critical acclaim. Edward Weeks, writing in the *Atlantic*, calls the collection "champagne literature—dry, deliciously chilled, fanciful, and faintly amorous." Philip Toynbee, in his *New Statesman and Nation* review, deems the tales "entirely individual," and, noting their "far-off exquisite flavor," compares them to the tales of Hans Christian Andersen and Joseph Conrad. Again, as in her first collection, Dinesen's imaginative style and romantic tendencies drew a great deal of critical attention. Notes Clifton Fadiman in the *New Yorker*, "Suffused with vague aspirations toward some cloudy ideal, with a longing for the impossible, with a brooding delight in magnificent and absurd gestures, with a quality of sleepwalking, they are as far removed from 1943 as anything can well be." The originality of these tales, claims a *Times Literary Supplement* contributor, "proceeds from an astonishing and wholly unexpected sympathy with their powers of romantic phantasmagoria." Some critics, however, find fault with Dinesen's unique writing style. In a *Commonweal* review J. E. Tobin claims, "The characters lack even the vague shape of ghosts; the atmosphere is that of stale perfume; the writing, called quaint by some, is downright awkward." Writes a *Christian Science Monitor* contributor: "The appeal of these new stories lies chiefly in their style, which is distinguished by simplicity and clarity. Their content unfortunately is not so simple nor so clear." The general consensus, however, seems to be one of commendation for both the form and content of *Winter's Tales*. Struthers Brut, writing in the *Saturday Review of Literature*, seems to sum up such a reaction when he maintains: "Often as you read the tales you wonder why you are so interested, so constantly excited, for the tales themselves, all of them symbolic, are not especially exciting in their plots, and the characters are frequently as remote as those in fairy tales, and a great deal of the time you are wandering in a fourth dimension where nothing is clear. But the final effect is unforgettable, just as the moments of reading are unforgettable."

Winter's Tales, Seven Gothic Tales, and *Out of Africa* are generally considered Dinesen's masterpieces. In these first three books, notes Robert Langbaum in his book *Isak Dinesen's Art: The Gayety of Vision*, "she appeared as a fully matured artist and made the reputation she has today." Langbaum also sees a fundamental similarity behind the writing of these volumes. He writes: "Her first three books seem to have been written out of a single motivating force that ends with *Winter's Tales*. In the last books she reworks insights stemming from the experience that lies behind the first three. The experience is of Africa, but of Africa as one side of that antinomy in the modern European soul, which we call romanticism—that antinomy between the modern European and the pre-scientific, pre-industrial past from which he has been cut off, a past rooted in nature and human nature. Isak Dinesen has been able to reinvigorate the romantic tradition because she rediscovered in Africa the validity of all the romantic myths, myths that locate spirit in the elemental—in nature, in the life of primitive people, in instinct and passion, in aristocratic, feudal and tribal societies that have their roots in nature."

Between the publication of *Winter's Tales* (1942) and *Last Tales* (1957) was a fifteen-year hiatus during which Dinesen published only one book—*The Angelic Avengers,* a thriller novel released in 1946 under the pseudonym of Pierre Andrezel. Dinesen was never proud of *The Angelic Avengers* and for many years refused to acknowledge herself as the book's author. Even after such acknowledgment, Dinesen criticized the book, claiming that she wrote it solely for her own amusement as a diversion from the grim realities of Nazi-occupied Denmark. In spite of her disclaimers, the book, a best-seller in Denmark and a Book-of-the-Month Club selection in America, was generally well received.

The primary reason for Dinesen's sparse production between 1942 and 1957 was her continual poor health. Despite a series of corrective operations, Dinesen suffered lingering bouts of illness that greatly hampered her creative output, and she spent much of the 1940s convalescing and occasionally traveling. By 1950 her health had improved, and she delivered a series of broadcasts for Danish radio in which she described her African servant and friend, Farah. These broadcasts foreshadowed some of the material that would later be included in *Shadows on the Grass.* Nineteen-fifty-five marked Dinesen's seventieth birthday, an event that was feted worldwide. In August of that same year a new operation became necessary in which several spinal nerves were severed. Dinesen also underwent an extensive ulcer operation. After the surgery she became an invalid, never again ate normally, and never weighed more than eighty-five pounds. According to Thurman she wrote at the time: "[These] past eight months have been more horrible than I can really describe to others—such continuous, insufferable pains, under which I howled like a wolf, are something one cannot fully comprehend. I feel that I have been in an Underworld. . . . The problem for me now is how I shall manage to come back into the world of human beings. It sometimes feels practically insoluable, though I believe that if I find something to look forward to, it could be possible."

In spite of her poor health and advanced age, Dinesen experienced a great renaissance during the late 1950s and early 1960s. During this period she published three works within a four-year span—*Last Tales* in 1957, *Anecdotes of Destiny* in 1958, and *Shadows on the Grass* in 1961. By now Dinesen was hailed worldwide as a major literary figure and had been nominated for the Nobel Prize several times. When Ernest Hemingway accepted his Nobel Prize in 1954 he said that the award should have been given instead to "that beautiful Danish writer Isak Dinesen."

As in her earlier volumes, the stories in *Last Tales* vary in terms of time and place but seem to deal with many of the same character types and themes, primarily exotic, often aristocratic characters in conflict or in harmony with their destinies. Destiny, more specifically one's control over it, is one of Dinesen's major themes. The characters in Dinesen's stories typically try to come to terms with their lives. In Dinesen's view such a coming to terms involves an acceptance of one's fate as determined by God. As Eric O. Johannesson writes in *The World of Isak Dinesen:* "Dinesen's tales, like the stories in the *Arabian Nights,* proclaim the belief in the all but magic power of the story to provide man with a new vision and a renewed faith in life. Her figures are often Hamlet figures, melancholy men and women who wait for fate to lend them a helping hand, who wait for the storyteller to provide them with a destiny by placing them in a story."

Reviewing *Last Tales* in the *New York Times,* Eudora Welty describes the stories as "austerely objective in their execution, true to her credo of the storyteller's story," and goes on to note that they "are also extremely personal in their point of view, in their great style. They have a vigor which persuades us that vigor perfectly solves the secret of delicacy, for her stories are the essence of delicacy." Although *Last Tales* was her first set of stories in over fifteen years, many critics found that Dinesen had managed to retain her artistic mastery. While admitting that *Last Tales* was "not quite as impressive" as *Seven Gothic Tales,* Charles Rolo nonetheless avers in the *Atlantic* that this collection "is a reminder that Isak Dinesen is one of the finest and most singular artists of our time." In a *Saturday Review* article William Sansom deems Dinesen's method in *Last Tales* "true taletelling" and advises readers: "These stories are strong stuff. Dive beyond the first breakers of a rolling prose—if these distress you—and let the deeper waves take you over like a strong drug: you will be rewarded." Yet some critics were not overly impressed with this collection. Richard Sullivan, writing in the *Chicago Sunday Tribune,* for instance, has mixed feelings about the writing in *Last Tales,* noting that the stories "leave me cold but respectful, unmoved but admiring." Overall, however, the majority of critics side with a *Time* reviewer who writes: "The dozen stories in this new collection may be the literary testament of one of the most skilled but least prolific writers of the 20th century. . . . The characters are large, heroic figures and they are brought to earth with a resounding crash. Such men and women are rare in contemporary fiction; the art to make them live vitally—as Author Dinesen does—is rarer still."

A year after the release of *Last Tales, Anecdotes of Destiny* was published in both the United States and Denmark. A collection of five tales, *Anecdotes of Destiny,* with its preference for exotic locales and predominantly nineteenth-century settings, resembles such earlier works as *Seven Gothic Tales* and *Winter's Tales.* The overall critical reaction to *Anecdotes of Destiny* was somewhat mixed. In his *Manchester Guardian* review of the book W. L. Webb describes *Anecdotes of Destiny* as "a collection of elaborate fairy tales for elderly epicures, very cold, cultured, and romantic, with a faint Yellow Book flavour, and belonging to no world outside of the writer's imagination." But he adds, "One can often admire their jewelled-movement ingenuity without conceding the claims of the faithful to a Larger Significance." Karl Miller, writing in the *Spectator,* maintains that "in the end the trouble is not the values which loom up in the stories and which seem to consist of a preference for wild, wilful gestures to the exclusion of all other human behaviour, but her inability as an artist to sustain these interests in the form she has chosen." Some critics feel that *Anecdotes of Destiny* does not quite measure up to Dinesen's other writing. "If these stories are not quite so weird as the author's earlier ones, they are also not quite so effective, it seems to this reviewer. And occasionally they seem to sprawl somewhat carelessly," remarks Howard Blair in the *San Francisco Chronicle.* V. S. Naipaul in his *New Statesman* review of the book goes even further, averring that "only one anecdote, 'The Immortal Story,' reminds us that this book is by the author of 'Seven Gothic Tales' and 'Out of Africa.' " On the other hand, critics such as R. H. Glauber felt that the stories in *Anecdotes of Destiny* were consistent with Dinesen's previous work. "If they lack something of the complex plotting we had in earlier stories, they have a new feature that more than makes up for it—a sense of fate that hangs over the characters and toward which they rush with dignified haste." Glauber writes in the *New York Herald Tribune Book Review,* "The storytelling is superb. . . . One story in the book, 'Babette's Feast,' surely ranks with the best Dinesen has ever written."

In 1961 *Shadows on the Grass,* a collection of four short essays, was released. It was to be the last of Dinesen's books published during her lifetime. Like *Out of Africa* before it, *Shadows on the Grass* takes as its subject matter Dinesen's years in Africa. While it includes reminiscences about the excitement of hunting lions and the hazards of raising coffee on the equator, the book's main focus is Dinesen's recollections of her African servants.

Despite what W. J. Smith in his *New Republic* review calls the book's "gay and glorious quality," *Shadows on the Grass* was written during a time of great suffering and was often dictated from a hospital bed a few paragraphs at a time. The last of Dinesen's Book-of-the-Month Club selections, *Shadows on the Grass* met with almost universal acclaim. "The four stories in 'Shadows on the Grass' are triumphantly sentimental and gently anecdotal; yet within their miniature frame they have many of the qualities of the finest story-telling," writes William Dunlea in *Commonweal.* Critics particularly laud Dinesen's manner in evoking memories from her past. Claiming the term "reminiscence" is inadequate for what Dinesen does in *Shadows on the Grass,* Phoebe Adams, writing in the *Atlantic,* praises Dinesen's acuteness of perception and "ability to find an undercurrent of wonder in any situation." A *Time* reviewer concurs, claiming: "What the baroness does in this book is scarcely tangible enough to describe. She dips a branch of memory into the pool of the past until it is crystallized with insights, landscapes, literature, and animals that seem as if painted by Henri Rousseau."

In September of 1962, less than a year after the publication of *Shadows on the Grass,* Dinesen finally succumbed to over forty years of illness and died of emaciation at her family estate in Denmark. In keeping with her wishes, Rungstedlund has been preserved as a bird sanctuary, and Dinesen herself is buried there beneath her favorite beech tree. Her legacy has been kept alive by a series of posthumously published works including *Carnival: Entertainments and Posthumous Tales* and, more recently, by a popular Hollywood movie.

That movie, "Out of Africa," is actually a combination of four books—*Out of Africa* and *Letters from Africa* as well as Errol Trzebinski's biography *Silence Will Speak: A Study of the Life of Denys Finch Hatton and His Relationship with Karen Blixen* and *Isak Dinesen: The Life of a Storyteller* by Judith Thurman. The film, starring Robert Redford as Finch Hatton and Meryl Streep as Dinesen, was a commercial as well as critical success, winning a total of seven Oscars, including best picture. The popularity of the film had an immediate and lasting effect on the book-buying public as worldwide sales of Dinesen books increased tenfold in the year following the film's opening. In fact, in March of 1987, *Publishers Weekly* announced that since its 1985 release of the reprint version of *Out of Africa,* Vintage had sold over 653,000 copies of the book, thus making Dinesen a best-selling author almost twenty-five years after her death.

Isak Dinesen always thought of herself as a storyteller rather than a writer. According to Donald Hannah's *"Isak Dinesen" and Karen Blixen: The Mask and the Reality,* Dinesen once wrote: "I belong to an ancient, idle, wild and useless tribe, perhaps I am even one of the last members of it, who, for many thousands of years, in all countries and parts of the world, has, now and again, stayed for a time among hard-working honest people in real life, and sometimes has thus been fortunate enough to create another sort of reality for them, which in some way or another, has satisfied them. I am a storyteller." Dinesen, indeed, led a remarkable life, but it is for her stories that she will be best remembered. Perhaps Eudora Welty puts it best in describing Dinesen's achievement when she writes, "Of a story she made

an essence; of the essence she made an elixir; and of the elixir she began once more to compound the story."

MEDIA ADAPTATIONS: "The Immortal Story" was adapted for film by Orson Welles for Altura in 1968; Irene Worth made a sound recording of "The Old Chevalier" in 1978; "Out of Africa" was filmed, with a screenplay by Kurt Luedtke, by Universal in 1985; Dinesen recorded excerpts from her books for Gyldendal and made two films, consisting of readings, for *Encyclopaedia Britannica;* "Babette's Feast" was filmed by Gabriel Axel in 1988.

BIOGRAPHICAL/CRITICAL SOURCES:

BOOKS

Bjornvig, Thorkild, *The Pact: My Friendship with Isak Dinesen,* Louisiana State University Press, 1974.
Contemporary Literary Criticism, Gale, Volume 10, 1979, Volume 29, 1984.
Dinesen, Isak, *Out of Africa,* Putnam (London), 1937, Random House, 1938, reprinted with illustrations, Crown, 1987, Danish translation published as *Den Afrikanske Farm,* Gyldendal, 1937, reprinted, 1977.
Dinesen, Isak, *Skygger paa Graesset,* Gyldendal, 1960, published as *Shadows on the Grass,* Random House, 1961.
Dinesen, Isak, *Daguerreotypes and Other Essays,* Danish portions translated by P. M. Mitchell and W. D. Paden, University of Chicago Press, 1979.
Breve fra Africa, Volume I: *1914-1924,* Volume II: *1925-1931,* Gyldendal, 1978, published as *Letters from Africa, 1914-1931,* edited by Frans Lasson and translated by Anne Born, University of Chicago Press, 1981.
Dinesen, Thomas, *My Sister, Isak Dinesen,* translated from the Danish by Joan Tate, M. Joseph (London), 1975.
Hannah, Donald, *"Isak Dinesen" and Karen Blixen: The Mask and the Reality,* Putnam, 1971, Random House, 1972.
Henricksen, Liselette, *Isak Dinesen: A Bibliography,* University of Chicago Press, 1977.
Johannesson, Eric O., *The World of Isak Dinesen,* University of Washington Press, 1961.
Langbaum, Robert, *Isak Dinesen's Art: The Gayety of Vision,* University of Chicago Press, 1975.
Migel, Parmenia, *Titania: The Biography of Isak Dinesen,* Random House, 1967.
Svendsen, Clara, editor, *Isak Dinesen: A Memorial,* Random House, 1964.
Svendsen, Clara, editor, *The Life and Destiny of Isak Dinesen,* Random House, 1970.
Thurman, Judith, *Isak Dinesen: The Life of a Storyteller,* St. Martin's, 1982.
Trzebinski, Errol, *Silence Will Speak: A Study of the Life of Denys Finch Hatton and His Relationship with Karen Blixen,* University of Chicago Press, 1977.
Whissen, Thomas R., *Isak Dinesen's Aesthetics,* Kennikat, 1973.

PERIODICALS

American Scholar, autumn, 1963.
Atlantic, June, 1943, January, 1947, December, 1957, November, 1960.
Bookmark, December, 1957.
Books, April 8, 1934, March 6, 1938.
Books and Bookmen, February, 1968.
Books West, Volume 1, number 7, 1977.
Chicago Daily Tribune, April 21, 1934.
Chicago Sunday Tribune, December 8, 1957.
Chicago Tribune, March 30, 1986, January 5, 1987.

Chicago Tribune Book World, September 23, 1979, June 7, 1981.
Christian Science Monitor, June 5, 1943, December 23, 1960, June 13, 1963, February 11, 1980, September 14, 1981.
Commonweal, September 28, 1934, June 18, 1943, January 31, 1947, December 13, 1957.
Harper's, March, 1971.
Hudson Review, spring, 1978, winter, 1981-82.
International Fiction Review, January, 1978.
Library Journal, May 15, 1979.
Los Angeles Times, November 25, 1985, December 8, 1986, January 5, 1987.
Manchester Guardian, December 31, 1937, November 28, 1958.
Nation, April 18, 1934, November 8, 1958, November 5, 1977.
New Boston Review, spring, 1978.
New Outlook, April, 1934.
New Republic, June 7, 1943, January 3, 1961, October 22, 1977.
New Statesman, November 23, 1957, November 1, 1958, October 30, 1981.
New Statesman and Nation, October 20, 1934, April 17, 1943, April 19, 1947.
Newsweek, December 23, 1985.
New Yorker, May 15, 1943, November 9, 1968, December 5, 1977, November 19, 1979, September 7, 1981.
New York Herald Tribune Book Review, June 5, 1947, November 3, 1957, October 12, 1958.
New York Herald Tribune Books, June 16, 1963.
New York Herald Tribune Weekly Book Review, January 5, 1947.
New York Review of Books, May 4, 1978, July 17, 1986.
New York Times, March 6, 1938, January 5, 1947, November 3, 1957, October 12, 1958, December 30, 1985, March 20, 1986.
New York Times Book Review, June 9, 1963, September 20, 1981, December 8, 1985, February 23, 1986, October 16, 1987.
Publishers Weekly, March 13, 1987.
San Francisco Chronicle, October 26, 1958.
Saturday Review, October 6, 1934, November 2, 1957, March 16, 1963, December 10, 1977.
Saturday Review of Literature, April 14, 1934, March 5, 1938, May 15, 1943, January 18, 1947.
Spectator, November 29, 1957, October 17, 1958.
Texas Studies in Literature and Language, winter, 1978.
Time, November 4, 1957, January 6, 1961, September 27, 1968, February 9, 1987.
Times (London), December 3, 1986, March 3, 1988.
Times Literary Supplement, March 13, 1943, January 13, 1978, July 28, 1978, April 4, 1980, September 11, 1981.
Village Voice, September 2, 1981.
Virginia Quarterly Review, autumn, 1968.
Washington Post Book World, August 9, 1981.
World Literature Today, spring, 1979, spring, 1980, spring, 1981, spring, 1982.
Yale Review, summer, 1943.

* * *

BLOUNT, Roy (Alton), Jr. 1941-
(Noah Sanders, C. R. Ways)

PERSONAL: Surname rhymes with "punt"; born October 4, 1941, in Indianapolis, Ind.; son of Roy Alton (a savings and loan executive) and Louise (Floyd) Blount; married Ellen Pearson, September 6, 1964 (divorced March, 1973); married Joan Ackerman, 1976 (separated); children: (first marriage) Ennis Caldwell, John Kirven. *Education:* Vanderbilt University, B.A. (magna cum laude), 1963; Harvard University, M.A., 1964. *Politics:*
"Dated white Southern liberalism, with healthy undertones of redneckery and anarchism; nostalgia for Earl Long." *Religion:* "Lapsed Methodist."

ADDRESSES: Home—Mill River, Mass.; and New York, N.Y.

CAREER: Decatur-DeKalb News, Decatur, Ga., reporter and sports columnist, 1958-59; *Morning Telegraph,* New York City, reporter, summer, 1961; *New Orleans Times-Picayune,* New Orleans, La., reporter, summer, 1963; *Atlanta Journal,* Atlanta, Ga., reporter, editorial writer, and columnist, 1966-68; *Sports Illustrated,* New York City, staff writer, 1968-74, associate editor, 1974-75; free-lance writer, 1975—. Occasional performer for American Humorists' Series, American Place Theatre, 1986, and 1988, and has appeared on "A Prairie Home Companion," "The CBS Morning Show," "The Tonight Show," "The David Letterman Show," "Austin City Limits," "All Things Considered," and many other radio and television programs. Instructor at Georgia State College, 1967-68. Member of usage panel, American Heritage Dictionary. *Military service:* U.S. Army, 1964-66; became first lieutenant.

MEMBER: Phi Beta Kappa.

WRITINGS:

About Three Bricks Shy of a Load, Little, Brown, 1974.
Crackers: This Whole Many-Sided Thing of Jimmy, More Carters, Ominous Little Animals, Sad-Singing Women, My Daddy and Me, Knopf, 1980.
One Fell Soup; or, I'm Just a Bug on the Windshield of Life, Little, Brown, 1982.
What Men Don't Tell Women, Atlantic-Little, Brown, 1984.
Not Exactly What I Had in Mind, Atlantic Monthly Press, 1985.
It Grows on You: A Hair-Raising Survey of Human Plumage, Doubleday, 1986.
"Roy Blount's Happy Hour and a Half" (one-man show), produced Off-Broadway, 1986.
Soupsongs/Webster's Ark (double book of verse), Houghton, 1987.
Now, Where Were We? Getting Back to Basic Truths That We Have Lost Sight of through No Fault of My Own, Villard, 1989.
About Three Bricks Shy . . . And the Load Filled Up, Ballantine, 1989.
First Hubby: A Novel about a Man Who Happens to Be Married to the President of the United States, Villard, 1990.

Also author of two one-act plays produced in Louisville, Ky., 1983 and 1984. Contributor to anthologies, including *The Best of Modern Humor,* 1983, *Laughing Matters,* 1987, *The Norton Book of Light Verse,* 1987, *The Oxford Book of American Light Verse, The Ultimate Baseball Book, Classic Southern Humor,* and *Sudden Fiction.* Columnist, *Atlanta Journal,* 1967-70. Contributor of articles, short stories, poems, crossword puzzles, and drawings, sometimes under pseudonyms Noah Sanders and C. R. Ways, to 92 very different publications, including *Sports Illustrated, New Yorker, Atlantic, New York Times Magazine, Esquire, Playboy, Rolling Stone, GQ, Conde Nast Traveler, Spy,* and *Antaeus.* Contributing editor, *Atlantic,* 1983—.

WORK IN PROGRESS: Lyrics for a musical comedy, "Murder at Elaine's," with book by Nora Ephron.

SIDELIGHTS: Roy Blount, Jr., "is Andy Rooney with a Georgia accent, only funnier," declares Larry L. King in the *Washington Post Book World.* Like Rooney, Blount has entertained the American public not only through his multitudinous magazine publications (his articles have appeared in nearly one hundred different magazines) and his books, but also through other media—he has performed on radio and television shows ranging from Minnesota Public Radio's "A Prairie Home Companion" to NBC's "The David Letterman Show." "The unceasing drip-drip-drip of bizarre images, intricate wordplay, droll asides and crazy ideas disorients the reader," states Patrick F. McManus in the *New York Times Book Review,* "until Mr. Blount finally has him at his mercy." His work has been compared to that of Mark Twain, and his "light touch and sense of bemusement," declares Eric Zorn in the *Chicago Tribune,* "combine with arch intellect to give him the versatility to publish in *Organic Gardening* and *Country Journal* one day and *Harvard Magazine* the next."

Blount's books, says Leslie Bennetts in the *New York Times,* "attest to the breadth of his interests, from 'One Fell Soup, or I'm Just a Bug on the Windshield of Life' (which is also the name of one of the original songs Mr. Blount sings 'unless I'm forcibly deterred') to 'What Men Don't Tell Women' to 'It Grows on You,' a volume about hair." His first book, *About Three Bricks Shy of a Load,* "did for the Pittsburgh Steelers roughly what Sherman did for the South," states Donald Morrison in *Time,* and it "remains the most comic treatise on professional football extinct or extant," reports King. *New York Times Book Review* contributor Robert W. Creamer calls *About Three Bricks Shy of a Load* "a terrific book," and he concludes, "I have never read anything else on pro football, fiction or nonfiction, as good as this."

With his second book, *Crackers: This Whole Many-Sided Thing of Jimmy, More Carters, Ominous Little Animals, Sad-Singing Women, My Daddy and Me,* Blount established his reputation as a humorist. *Crackers* examines the presidency of Jimmy Carter, a Georgian like Blount, and concludes that what the Carter administration needed was a more down-to-earth, redneck, approach to the business of governing the country. "If *Crackers* reveals an overarching thesis, it is that contemporary America, like its president, is too emotionally constrained, too given to artifice, too Northern," explains Morrison. The book was a critical success; Harry Crews, writing in the *Washington Post Book World,* calls *Crackers* "the funniest book I've read in a decade," and labels it "a triumph over subject, proving—if it needed proving again—that there are no dull subjects, only dull writers."

Blount has also achieved success in collections of his magazine articles, including *One Fell Soup; or, I'm Just a Bug on the Windshield of Life, What Men Don't Tell Women, Not Exactly What I Had in Mind, It Grows on You,* and *Now, Where Were We?* Gathered from sources as diverse as *Esquire,* the *New Yorker,* and *Eastern Airlines Pastimes,* the collections prove Blount's "ability to be amusing on a diversity of topics," according to Beaufort Cranford of the *Detroit News.* After all, he asks, "what other source can prove the existence of God by considering the testicle?"

Although some critics—like *Los Angeles Times* contributor Taffy Cannon, who calls Blount's stories "considerably funnier in a bar at midnight than spread at meandering and pointless length across the printed page"—find that Blount's later works aren't as successful as his earlier ones, many others celebrate his collections. "It gives me great pleasure," King declared after reading *One Fell Soup,* "to here officially designate [Blount] . . . a semi-genius at the very least. I have been reading his stuff for years and he seldom fails to break me up." Ron Givens, writing in *Newsweek,* declares, "It's downright refreshing, then, to read somebody who has taste, intelligence, style and, oh, bless you, wit—qualities that Roy Blount Jr. . . . [has] in abundance."

Blount has also attracted attention as a versifier and songwriter. Despite his claims to be "singing impaired," Blount has performed both his stories and his verses in his one-man show, "Roy Blount's Happy Hour and a Half," and on radio programs such as "A Prairie Home Companion." A recent collection of the comic's verse, *Soupsongs/Webster's Ark,* "contains odes to beets, chitlins, barbeque sauce, catfish and grease ('I think that I will never cease/To hold in admiration grease')," explains Bennetts, "along with a 'Song Against Broccoli' that reads in its entirety: 'The neighborhood stores are all out of broccoli,/Loccoli.'" "Blount's verses may resemble Burma Shave's more than Byron's," declares the *Chicago Tribune*'s Jim Spencer, "but they are bodaciously funny."

Critics have tried to define with varying success the sources of Blount's sense of humor. "I can't tell you what makes Roy Blount such a funny writer," confesses *Washington Post Book World* contributor Dennis Drabelle, "—perhaps a dose of comic afflatus administered by the gods." Another contributing factor, suggests Givens, "derives from his off-center perceptions." Kenneth Turan of *Time* calls Blount's work "in the tradition of the great curmudgeons like H. L. Mencken and W. C. Fields." And the comic "is not of the punch-line school of humor writing," declares McManus. "His humor is cumulative in effect, like Chinese water torture. When you can bear it no longer, you collapse into a spasm of mirth, often at a line that taken by itself would provoke no more than a smile."

Roy Blount, Jr., summed up his life for *CA,* saying, "Raised in South by Southern parents. Couldn't play third base well enough so became college journalist. Ridiculed cultural enemies. Boosted integration. Decided to write, teach. Went to Harvard Graduate School. Didn't like it. Went back to journalism. Liked it. Got a column. Ridiculed cultural enemies. Wrote limericks. Boosted integration. Wanted to write for magazines. Took writing job at *Sports Illustrated.* Have seen country, met all kinds of people, heard all different kinds of talk. Like it. Ready now to write a novel that sums it all up."

BIOGRAPHICAL/CRITICAL SOURCES:

BOOKS

Contemporary Literary Criticism, Volume 38, Gale, 1986.

PERIODICALS

Books of the Times, December, 1980.
Chicago Tribune, November 4, 1982, December 24, 1987.
Detroit News, October 17, 1982.
Globe and Mail (Toronto), July 14, 1984.
Los Angeles Times, December 13, 1985.
Newsweek, September 17, 1984.
New York Times, September 27, 1980, November 1, 1982, April 28, 1984, January 25, 1988, January 26, 1988.
New York Times Book Review, December 1, 1974, September 28, 1980, May 13, 1984, November 17, 1985, February 7, 1988, March 26, 1989, April 2, 1989.
Sports Illustrated, February 10, 1969, June 18, 1973, April 15, 1974, August 5, 1974.
Time, October 20, 1980, June 4, 1984.
Times Literary Supplement, June 3, 1983.
Washington Post, June 19, 1984.
Washington Post Book World, September 28, 1980, November 2, 1980, January 23, 1983, October 13, 1985, February 19, 1989.

BLUME, Judy (Sussman) 1938-

PERSONAL: Born February 12, 1938, in Elizabeth, N.J.; daughter of Rudolph (a dentist) and Esther (Rosenfeld) Sussman; married John M. Blume (an attorney), August 15, 1959 (divorced, 1975); married George Cooper (a writer), June 6, 1987; children: (first marriage) Randy Lee (daughter), Lawrence Andrew; (stepdaugher) Amanda. *Education:* New York University, B.A., 1960. *Religion:* Jewish.

ADDRESSES: Home—New York, N.Y.; and northern New Mexico. *Agent*—Harold Ober Associates, Inc., 40 East 49th St., New York, N.Y. 10017.

CAREER: Writer of juvenile and adult fiction. Founder of KIDS Fund, 1981.

MEMBER: Society of Children's Book Writers (member of board), PEN, Authors Guild (member of council), Authors League of America, National Coalition Against Censorship (council of advisors).

AWARDS, HONORS: Are You There God? It's Me, Margaret was chosen one of the best books for children by the *New York Times,* 1970, and has received Nene Award, 1975, Young Hoosier Book Award, 1976, and North Dakota Children's Choice Award, 1979; *Tales of a Fourth Grade Nothing* has received Charlie May Swann Children's Book Award, 1972, Young Readers Choice Award from Pacific Northwest Library Association, Sequoyah Children's Book Award of Oklahoma, both 1975, Massachusetts Children's Book Award, Georgia Children's Book Award, South Carolina Children's Book Award, all 1977, Rhode Island Library Association Award, 1978, North Dakota Children's Choice Award, West Australian Young Readers' Book Award, both 1980, United States Army in Europe Kinderbuch Award, and Great Stone Face Award from the New Hampshire Library Council, both 1981; *Blubber* has received Arizona Young Readers Award, Young Readers Choice Award from Pacific Northwest Library Association, both 1977, and North Dakota Children's Choice Award, 1983; *Otherwise Known as Sheila the Great* has received South Carolina Children's Book Award, 1978; *Superfudge* was selected for Texas Bluebonnet List, 1980, and has received Michigan Young Reader's Award, International Reading Association Children's Choice Award, both 1981, First Buckeye Children's Book Award, Nene Award, Sue Hefley Book Award from Louisiana Association of School Libraries, United States Army in Europe Kinderbuch Award, West Australian Young Readers' Book Award, North Dakota Children's Choice Award, Colorado Children's Book Award, Georgia Children's Book Award, Tennessee Children's Choice Book Award, Utah Children's Book Award, all 1982, Northern Territory Young Readers' Book Award, Young Readers Choice Award from Pacific Northwest Library Association, Garden State Children's Book Award, Iowa Children's Choice Award, Arizona Young Readers' Award, California Young Readers' Medal, and Young Hoosier Book Award, all 1983; *Tiger Eyes* was nominated for an American Book Award, 1983, and has received Dorothy Canfield Fisher Children's Book Award, Buckeye Children's Book Award, and California Young Readers Medal, all 1983.

Golden Archer Award, 1974; Today's Woman Award, 1981; Eleanor Roosevelt Humanitarian Award, Favorite Author—Children's Choice Award, Milner Award, and Jeremiah Ludington Memorial Award, all 1983; Carl Sandburg Freedom to Read Award from Chicago Public Library, 1984; Civil Liberties Award from Atlanta American Civil Liberties Union, and John Rock Award from Center for Population Options, Los Angeles, both 1986; D.H.L., Kean College, 1987; South Australian Youth Media Award for Best Author from South Australian Association for Media Education, 1988.

WRITINGS:

JUVENILE FICTION

The One in the Middle Is the Green Kangaroo, Reilly & Lee, 1969, revised edition, Bradbury, 1981.
Iggie's House, Bradbury, 1970, reprinted, Dell, 1986.
Are You There God? It's Me, Margaret, Bradbury, 1970.
Then Again, Maybe I Won't, Bradbury, 1971, reprinted, Dell, 1986.
Freckle Juice, Four Winds, 1971.
Tales of a Fourth Grade Nothing, Dutton, 1972, reprinted, ABC-Clio, 1987.
Otherwise Known as Sheila the Great (also see below), Dutton, 1972.
It's Not the End of the World, Bradbury, 1972.
Deenie, Bradbury, 1973.
Blubber, Bradbury, 1974.
Starring Sally J. Freedman As Herself, Bradbury, 1977.
Superfudge, Dutton, 1980.
Tiger Eyes, Bradbury, 1981.
The Pain and the Great One, Bradbury, 1984.
The Judy Blume Collection (five-volume boxed set), Dell, 1986.
Just As Long As We're Together, F. Watts, 1987.

OTHER

Forever . . . (young adult), Bradbury, 1975.
Wifey (adult), Putnam, 1977.
The Judy Blume Diary, Dell, 1981.
Smart Women (adult), Putnam, 1984.
Letters to Judy: What Your Kids Wish They Could Tell You (nonfiction), Putnam, 1986.
The Judy Blume Memory Book, Dell, 1988.
(And producer with son, Lawrence Blume) "Otherwise Known As Sheila the Great" (screenplay; adapted from her novel), Barr Films, 1988.

SIDELIGHTS: Judy Blume is one of the most popular authors of young adult novels writing today. *Newsweek* reports that Angeline Moscatt, head librarian of the Children's Room of the New York Library, believes "[Blume] has a way of portraying human foibles in a way kids can relate to. In twenty years, I've never seen such a popular children's author." Blume reflects on the reason for her popularity in a *Publishers Weekly* interview conducted by Sybil Steinberg: "I have a capacity for total recall. That's my talent, if there's a talent involved. I have this gift, this memory, so it's easy to project myself back to certain stages in my life. And I write about what I know is true of kids going through those same stages."

After graduating from an Elizabeth, N.J., high school, Judy Sussman enrolled in New York University with two goals in mind: to find a suitable husband and to obtain a degree in education so she would have a career to fall back on if she ever needed to support herself or her family. In her sophomore year she met and fell in love with a young lawyer, John Blume, and married him in her junior year. A year after graduation her daughter, Randy, was born; a son, Larry, followed two years later.

For several years Blume lived the life of a traditional suburban housewife and mother. She remembers that time as "comfortable and uneventful," but gradually Blume started to feel that something was missing. "Somewhere along the way, my mother's wishes for me—a good husband and good provider—became my way of life," Blume explains to Enid Nemy in the *New York Times*. "I didn't resent it, I only had second thoughts about it later." Looking for a challenge, she began making and selling felt applique banners to decorate children's rooms. Eventually she decided to try writing books for children. Blume would make up stories, composing the text while washing dishes in the evening, and later she would print the manuscript and illustrate it. Blume's early attempts to publish her writing failed. Although she hid in a closet and cried after receiving her first rejection notice, Blume told John Neary of *People:* "I worked myself up to the point where I could get six rejections a week. I would go to bed thinking, 'I'll never get anything published,' and wake up saying, 'I will, too!' "

Deciding she needed professional guidance, Blume enrolled in a course offered by New York University for those interested in learning to write for children. As Blume remarks in Justin Wintle and Emma Fisher's *The Pied Pipers:* "What I did was write like crazy so I had something to turn in every week. My teacher gave me a lot of encouragement. She would write me little notes telling me I would get published one day. . . . I loved it. I even went back. I took the course twice because I didn't want to lose that contact. . . . Before I left the course, after two semesters of basically the same thing, I had sold a couple of stories to magazines, and I had written at least one a version of *The One in the Middle Is the Green Kangaroo,* and finished my first longer book, *Iggie's House.* I wrote that chapter by chapter, week by week, the second semester that I took the course. It was like homework." In 1969, she sold *The One in the Middle Is the Green Kangaroo* to Reilly & Lee, launching what was to become a successful and personally satisfying writing career.

Over the years, Blume's writing has matured and her audience has expanded with each new book. While she at first wrote strictly for younger children, Blume has since published two adult novels and a number of works targeted at adolescents. Although written for different age groups, Blume's books exhibit two similar characteristics: an empathy for the plights and feelings of her characters and a writing style that is humorous and easy to read. In her interview with Steinberg, Blume states: "I hate to categorize books. . . . I wish that older readers would read my books about young people, and I hope that younger readers will grow up to read what I have to say about adult life. I'd like to feel that I write for everybody. I think that my appeal has to do with feelings and with character identification. Things like that don't change from generation to generation. That's what I really know."

Nowhere is Blume's sensitivity and wit more apparent than in her fiction for adolescents, who are undeniably her most loyal and attentive audience. As Naomi Decter observes in *Commentary,* "there is, indeed, scarcely a literate girl of novel-reading age who has not read one or more Blume books." "Judy Blume is a careful observer of the everyday details of children's lives and she has a feel for the little power struggles and shifting alliances of their social relationships," writes R. A. Siegal in *The Lion and the Unicorn.* "Her plots are loose and episodic: they accumulate rather than develop. They are not complicated or demanding." And Walter Clemons remarks in a *Newsweek* review of *Tiger Eyes:* "No wonder teen-agers love Judy Blume's novels: She's very good. . . . Blume's delicate sense of character, eye for social detail and clear access to feelings touches even a hardened older reader. Her intended younger audience gets a first-rate novel written directly to them."

Blume, in turn, enjoys writing for this age group. "When you're 12, you're on the brink of adulthood," Blume tells Joyce May-

nard in the *New York Times Magazine,* "but everything is still in front of you, and you still have the chance to be almost anyone you want. That seemed so appealing to me. I wasn't even 30 when I started writing, but already I didn't feel I had much chance myself."

Many critics have attributed her popularity with adolescent readers to Blume's ability to discuss openly, realistically, and compassionately such subjects as racial prejudice (*Iggie's House*), menstruation (*Are You There God? It's Me, Margaret*), divorce and family breakups (*It's Not the End of the World*), masturbation (*Deenie*), social ostracism (*Blubber*), and first love (*Forever . . .*). "Whether she is writing about female or male sexual awakening, and whatever other adolescent problems, Judy Blume is on target," comments Dorothy M. Broderick in the *New York Times Book Review.* "Her understanding of young people is sympathetic and psychologically sound; her skill engages the reader in human drama without melodrama."

Lavinia Russ writes in a *Publishers Weekly* review of *Are You There God? It's Me, Margaret:* "With sensitivity and humor, Judy Blume has captured the joys, fears and uncertainty that surround a young girl approaching adolescence." Writing about *Blubber,* Zena Sutherland comments in *Bulletin of the Center for Children's Books:* "[Blubber] is a good family story as well as a school story, that [has] good characterization and dialogue, a vigorous first-person writing style, and—Judy Blume demonstrates again—a respectful and perceptive understanding of the anguished concerns of the pre-teen years." And Faith McNulty comments in the *New Yorker:* "I find much in Blume to be thankful for. . . . She writes clean, swift, unadorned prose. She has convinced millions of young people that truth can be found in a book and that reading is fun. At a time that many believe may be the twilight of the written word, those are things to be grateful for."

Most critics agree that Blume achieves this close affinity with her readers through her consistent use of the first-person narrative in her writings. As Siegal explains: "Through this technique she succeeds in establishing intimacy and identification between character and audience. All her books read like diaries or journals and the reader is drawn in by the narrator's self-revelations." Decter also comments on the diary-like quality of Blume's prose. Observes the reviewer: "Given the sophistication of Miss Blume's material, her style is surprisingly simple. She writes for the most part in the first person: her vocabulary, grammar, and syntax are colloquial; her tone, consciously or perhaps not, evokes the awkwardness of a fifth grader's diary."

When asked about her ability to relate to the problems and fears of young people, Blume told Neary. "I knew intuitively what kids wanted to know because I remembered what I wanted to know. I think I write about sexuality because it was uppermost in my mind when I was a kid: the need to know, and not knowing how to find out. My father delivered these little lectures to me, the last one when I was 10, on how babies are made. But questions about what I was feeling, and how my body could feel, I *never* asked my parents." The volume of Blume's fan mail seems to reinforce the fact that she is held in high regard by her readers. Hundreds of letters arrive each week not only praising her books but also asking her for advice or for information. As Blume remarks in *Publishers Weekly,* "I have a wonderful, intimate relationship with kids. It's rare and lovely. They feel that they know me and that I know them."

Some adults, however, take exception to Blume's tendency to avoid resolving her fictional dilemmas in a straightforward fashion. However, the majority of critics believe that it is to Blume's credit that she does not settle all problems for her readers. One such critic, Robert Lipsyte, writes in *Nation:* "Blume explores the feelings of children in a nonjudgmental way. The immediate resolution of a problem is never as important as what the protagonist . . . will learn about herself by confronting her life. The young reader gains from the emotional adventure story both by observing another youngster in a realistic situation and by finding a reference from which to start a discussion with a friend or parent or teacher. For many children, talking about a Blume story is a way to expose their own fears about menstruation or masturbation or death." And Siegal suggests: "It does not seem that Blume's books . . . ought to be discussed and evaluated on the basis of what they teach children about handling specific social or personal problems. Though books of this type may sometimes be useful in giving children a vehicle for recognizing and ventilating their feelings, they are, after all, works of fiction and not self-help manuals."

Even more disturbing to some parents is Blume's treatment of mature issues and her use of frank language. "Menstruation, wet dreams, masturbation, all the things that are whispered about in real school halls are written about" in her books, maintains interviewer Sandy Rovner in the *Washington Post*. In a review of *Are You There God? It's Me, Margaret*, a critic for *Kirkus Reviews* writes that "there's danger in the preoccupation with the physical signs of puberty, [for] the effect is to confirm common anxieties instead of allaying them." And writing in *Book Window* George W. Arthur remarks that while *Are You There God? It's Me, Margaret* is basically "very funny," he feels "there are features of the book which are over-stressed and detract from the author's easy handling of most of the topics she covers."

Other adults defend Blume's choice of subject matter. For example, Natalie Babbitt asserts in the *New York Times Book Review:* "Some parents and librarians have come down hard on Judy Blume for the occasional vulgarities in her stories. Blume's vulgarities, however, exist in real life and are presented in her books with honesty and full acceptance." Remarks Julia Whedon in the *New York Times Book Review:* "Kids read her books with a blushing curiosity once reserved for certain words in the dictionary, parts of the Bible and naughty passages in Hemingway. They know they will find some frank discussion of prurient matters like breasts and menstruation. Some of her readers may also have read [Erica Jong's] *Fear of Flying*, yet they reread *Are You There God? It's Me, Margaret*."

In his review of *Forever . . .* , Blume's story about first love, Nicholas Tucker writes in the *Times Literary Supplement:* "If it is sex that is wanted, there is plenty of it here. . . . Yet even as a fictionalized sex manual, [*Forever . . .*] is nowhere near as explicit as other material available for everyone today, nor is it as erotic as, for example, that 'jolly little story' *Fanny Hill*." In short, concludes Whedon, Blume's "appeal goes beyond sexual frankness; she must be conveying a certain emotional reality that children recognize as true. Portnoy may complain all he wants, but kids will go right on needing reassurance that there is a time of slow awakening, of normal curiosity and confusion about what they are learning and feeling. And this is soft at the core, not hard." And finally *New Yorker* critic McNulty believes that "in a Judy Blume book, realism is everything. True, it has no great depth, but it is extraordinarily convincing. True, she includes unpleasant details—things we all notice but usually don't mention—yet they increase the credibility that is the source of her magnetic power."

Realizing that only a small group is critical of her work and its subject matter, Blume remarked to Maynard in the *New York*

Times Magazine: "What I worry about is that an awful lot of people, looking at my example, have gotten the idea that what sells is teenage sex, and they'll exploit it. I don't believe that sex is why kids like my books. The impression I get, from letter after letter [I receive,] is that a great many kids don't communicate with their parents. They feel alone in the world. Sometimes, reading books that deal with other kids who feel the same things they do, it makes them feel less alone."

Blume feels so strongly about the lack of communication between children and their parents that she established the KIDS Fund in 1981. Financed with royalties from *Letters to Judy: What Your Kids Wish They Could Tell You* and other projects, the fund contributes approximately $45,000 a year to various nonprofit organizations set up to help young people communicate with their parents.

Some of Blume's works are housed in the Kerlan Collection at the University of Minnesota.

MEDIA ADAPTATIONS: Forever . . . was adapted into a television film that aired on CBS-TV, February 6, 1978; *Freckle Juice* was made into an animated film by Barr Films, 1987.

BIOGRAPHICAL/CRITICAL SOURCES:

BOOKS

Children's Literature Review, Gale, Volume 2, 1976, Volume 15, 1988.

Contemporary Literary Criticism, Gale, Volume 12, 1980, Volume 30, 1984.

Dictionary of Literary Biography, Volume 52: *American Writers for Children since 1960: Fiction*, Gale, 1986.

Fisher, Emma and Justin Wintle, *The Pied Pipers*, Paddington Press, 1975.

Gleasner, Diana, *Breakthrough: Women in Writing*, Walker, 1980.

Lee, Betsey, *Judy Blume's Story*, Dillon Press, 1981.

Weidt, Maryann, *Presenting Judy Blume*, Twayne, 1989.

PERIODICALS

Book & Author, March/April, 1984.
Booklist, January 15, 1971, July 1, 1972, January 1, 1975.
Book Window, summer, 1978.
Boston Globe, January 30, 1971.
Bulletin of the Center for Children's Books, February, 1971, July/August, 1972, April, 1974, May, 1975, March, 1976.
Chicago Tribune, September 24, 1978.
Christian Science Monitor, May 14, 1979.
Commentary, March, 1980.
Commonweal, July 4, 1980.
Detroit Free Press, February 26, 1984.
Detroit News Magazine, February 4, 1979.
English Journal, September, 1972, March, 1976.
Junior Bookshelf, February, 1977.
Kirkus Reviews, October 1, 1970, September 1, 1972, April 1, 1977, October 1, 1980.
Library Journal, December 15, 1969, January 16, 1970.
The Lion and the Unicorn, fall, 1978.
Los Angeles Times Book Review, October 5, 1980.
Nation, November 21, 1981.
New Statesman, November 5, 1976, November 14, 1980.
Newsweek, October 9, 1978, December 7, 1981.
New Yorker, December 5, 1983.
New York Times, October 3, 1982.
New York Times Book Review, May 24, 1970, November 8, 1970, December 9, 1970, January 16, 1972, September 3, 1972,

November 3, 1974, December 28, 1975, May 25, 1976, May 1, 1977, November 23, 1980, November 15, 1981.
New York Times Magazine, December 3, 1978, August 23, 1982.
People, October 16, 1978, August 16, 1982, March 19, 1984.
Psychology Today, September, 1974.
Publishers Weekly, January 11, 1971, October 8, 1973, April 17, 1978.
Saturday Review, September 18, 1971.
School Library Journal, December, 1970, May, 1974, November, 1974, May, 1977, January, 1981.
Time, August 23, 1982.
Times Literary Supplement, October 1, 1976, April 7, 1978, November 23, 1979.
Washington Post, November 3, 1981.
Washington Post Book World, August 14, 1977, October 8, 1978, November 9, 1980, September 13, 1981, February 12, 1984.
Writer's Digest, February, 1979.

*   *   *

BLUNDEN, Edmund (Charles) 1896-1974

PERSONAL: Born November 1, 1896, in London, England; died January 20, 1974, near Sudbury, Suffolk, England; son of joint-headmasters of a London school; married Claire Margaret Poynting, 1945; children: four daughters. *Education:* Queen's College, Oxford, M.A. and C.Lit.

ADDRESSES: Home—Long Melford, Suffolk, England.

CAREER: Joined the staff of *The Athenaeum,* 1920, as assistant to Middleton Murry and continued (until 1924) as a regular contributor when *The Athenaeum* was amalgamated with *The Nation,* returned, 1928; Tokyo University, Tokyo, Japan, professor of English, 1924-27; Oxford University, Oxford, England, fellow and tutor in English literature at Merton College, 1931-43, staff member of Senior Training Corps, 1940-44; worked with United Kingdom liaison mission in Tokyo, 1948-50; University of Hong Kong, professor of English, 1953-64; Oxford University Chair of Poetry, 1966-68. *Military service:* Royal Sussex Regiment, 1916-19; served in France and Belgium; Military Cross, 1917.

MEMBER: Royal Society of Literature (fellow), Japan Academy (honorary).

AWARDS, HONORS: Hawthornden Prize, 1922, for *The Shepherd;* Commander, Order of the British Empire, 1951; Queen's Gold Medal for Poetry, 1956; Benson Medal, Royal Society of Literature; Order of the Rising Sun, third class, Japan, 1963; Litt.D., University of Leeds.

WRITINGS:

POETRY

Poems, [Horsham], 1914.
Poems Translated From the French, [Horsham], 1914.
Three Poems, J. Brooker, 1916.
Pastorals: A Book of Verses, E. Macdonald, 1916.
The Barn With Certain Other Poems, Sidgwick & Jackson, 1920, Knopf, 1921.
The Waggoner, and Other Poems, Sidgwick & Jackson, 1920.
The Shepherd, and Other Poems, Knopf, 1922.
To Nature: New Poems, Beaumont Press, 1923.
Edmund Blunden, Benn, 1925.
English Poems, Cobden-Sanderson, 1925, Knopf, 1926.
Masks of Time: A New Collection of Poems Principally Meditative, Beaumont Press, 1925.

(Contributor) Edward Thompson, editor, *The Augustan Books of Modern Poetry,* Benn, 1925, reissued as one part of *Modern Poetry,* L. B. Hill, 1925.
Japanese Garland, Beaumont Press, 1928.
Retreat, Doubleday, Doran, 1928.
Winter Nights: A Reminiscence, Faber & Gwyer, 1928.
Near and Far: New Poems, Cobden-Sanderson, 1929, Harper, 1930.
The Poems of Edmund Blunden, 1914-1930, Cobden-Sanderson, 1930, Harper, 1932.
A Summer's Fancy, Beaumont Press, 1930.
To Themis: Poems on Famous Trials, With Other Pieces, Beaumont Press, 1931.
Halfway House: A Miscellany of New Poems, Cobden-Sanderson, 1932, Macmillan, 1933.
Choice or Chance: New Poems, Cobden-Sanderson, 1934.
Verses: To H. R. H. The Duke of Windsor, Alden Press, 1936.
An Elegy, and Other Poems, Cobden-Sanderson, 1937.
On Several Occasions, by a Fellow of Merton College, Corvinus Press, 1938.
Poems, 1930-1940, Macmillan, 1940.
Shells by a Stream: New Poems, Macmillan, 1944.
After the Bombing, and Other Short Poems, Macmillan, 1949, reprinted, Books for Libraries Press, 1971.
Edmund Blunden (poetry and prose), selection by Kenneth Hopkins, Hart-Davis, 1950, Horizon, 1962, reprinted, Books for Libraries Press, 1970.
Poems of Many Years, Collins, 1957.
A Hong Kong House, Poetry Book Society, 1959 (published in England as *A Hong Kong House: Poems, 1951-1961,* Collins, 1962).
Eleven Poems, Golden Head Press, 1965.
The Midnight Skaters, selection and introduction by C. Day Lewis, Bodley Head, 1968.

PROSE

The Bonadventure: A Random Journal of an Atlantic Holiday, Cobden-Sanderson, 1922, Putnam, 1923.
Christ's Hospital: A Retrospect, Christophers, 1923.
On the Poems of Henry Vaughn: Characteristics and Intimations, With His Principal Latin Poems Carefully Translated Into English Verse, Cobden-Sanderson, 1927, reprinted, Russell, 1969.
Leigh Hunt's "Examiner" Examined, Cobden-Sanderson, 1928, Harper, 1931, reprinted, Archon Books, 1967.
Undertones of War (narrative), Cobden-Sanderson, 1928, Doubleday, Doran, 1929, with new preface by the author, Oxford University Press, 1956, revised edition, Collins, 1965, Harcourt, 1966.
Nature in English Literature, Harcourt, 1929, reprinted, Kennikat, 1970.
De Bello Germanico: A Fragment of Trench History, G. A. Blunden, 1930.
Leigh Hunt and His Circle, Harper, 1930 (published in England as *Leigh Hunt: A Biography,* Cobden-Sanderson, 1930), reprinted as *Leigh Hunt: A Biography,* Archon Books, 1970.
The Somme Battle: Selected Chapters From Undertones of War, Velhagen & Klasing, c. 1930.
In Summer, privately printed for Fytton Armstrong, 1931.
Votive Tablets: Studies Chiefly Appreciative of English Authors and Books, Cobden-Sanderson, 1931, Harper, 1932, reprinted, Books for Libraries Press, 1967.
The Face of England in a Series of Occasional Sketches, Longmans, Green, 1932.

Fall in, Ghosts: An Essay on a Battalion Reunion, White Owl Press, 1932.

Charles Lamb and His Contemporaries, Being the Clark Lectures Delivered at Trinity College, Cambridge, 1932, Cambridge, The University Press, 1933, published as *Charles Lamb and His Contemporaries,* 1937, reprinted, Archon Books, 1967.

(With Sylva Norman) *We'll Shift Our Ground: or, Two on a Tour,* Cobden-Sanderson, 1933.

The Mind's Eye: Essays, J. Cape, 1934, reprinted, Books for Libraries Press, 1967.

Edward Gibbon and His Age, J. W. Arrowsmith, 1935, reprinted, Folcroft, 1974.

Keat's Publisher: A Memoir of John Taylor (1781-1864), J. Cape, 1936.

English Villages, Collins, 1941.

Thomas Hardy, Macmillan, 1941, reprinted, St. Martin's, 1967.

Cricket Country, Collins, 1944.

Shelley: A Life Story, Collins, 1946, Viking, 1947, 2nd edition, Oxford University Press, 1965.

Shakespeare to Hardy, Kenkyusha, 1948, reprinted with corrections, 1949, reprint of 1948 edition, Folcroft, 1969.

Shelley's "Defence of Poetry" and Blunden's Lectures on "Defence," Hokuseido, 1948, reprinted, Folcroft, 1969.

Sons of Light: A Series of Lectures of English Writers, Hosei University Press, 1949, Folcroft, 1969.

Addresses on General Subjects Connected With English Literature, Kenkyusha, 1949, 2nd edition, 1958.

Poetry and Science, and Other Lectures, [Osaka], 1949.

Favorite Studies in English Literature, [Tokyo], 1950.

Influential Books, [Tokyo], 1950.

Reprinted Papers: Partly Concerning Some English Romantic Poets, [Tokyo], 1950, Folcroft Library Editions, 1971.

Chaucer to "B. V.", [Tokyo], 1950, reprinted, Folcroft Library Editions, 1971.

A Wanderer in Japan, [Tokyo], 1950.

John Keats, Longmans, Green, 1950, 2nd revised edition, 1966.

Lectures in English Literature, 2nd edition, Kodokwan, 1952.

The Dede of Pittie (poems and prose), Christ's Hospital, 1953.

Charles Lamb, Longmans, Green, 1954, revised edition, 1964.

War Poets, 1914-1918, Longmans, Green, 1958.

Three Young Poets: Critical Sketches of Byron, Shelley and Keats, Folcroft, 1959.

English Scientists as Men of Letters, Hong Kong University Press, 1961.

John Clare: Beginner's Luck, Bridge Books, 1971.

Also author of *William Crowe, 1745-1829,* Toucan Press.

EDITOR

(With Alan Porter) John Clare, *Poems,* Cobden-Sanderson, 1920.

Christopher Smart, *A Song to David, With Other Poems,* Cobden-Sanderson, 1924.

John Clare, *Madrigals and Chronicles,* Beaumont Press, 1924.

Shelley and Keats as They Struck Their Contemporaries, C. W. Beaumont, 1925, Folcroft Library Editions, 1970, reprint of 1925 edition, Haskell, 1971.

Benjamin Robert Hayden, *Autobiography,* Oxford University Press, 1927.

(Compiler) *A Hundred English Poems From the Fourteenth Century to the Nineteenth,* [Tokyo], 1927, 2nd revised edition, Kenkyusha, 1968.

(Author of introduction and compiler with Cyril Falls, H. M. Tomlinson, R. Wright) *The War, 1914-1918: A Booklist,* The Reader, 1929.

English Poems, revised edition, Duckworth, 1929.

William Collins, *The Poems,* Haslewood Books, 1929.

Great Short Stories of the War: England, France, Germany, America, Eyre & Spottiswoode, 1930.

John Clare, *Sketches in the Life of John Clare,* Cobden-Sanderson, 1931.

Wilfred Owen, *Poems,* Chatto & Windus, 1933, new edition, 1947, New Directions, 1949, author of introduction to amended edition entitled *Collected Poems,* New Directions, 1964.

(Compiler) *Charles Lamb: His Life Recorded by His Contemporaries,* Hogarth Press, 1934.

(With Earl Leslie Griggs) *Coleridge: Studies by Several Hands on the Hundredth Anniversary of His Death,* Constable, 1934, reprinted, Russell, 1970.

Return to Husbandry, J. M. Dent, 1943.

Christopher Smart, *Hymns for the Amusement of Children,* Luttrell Society, 1947.

Francis Carey Slater, *Selected Poems,* Oxford University Press, 1947.

(With others) *The Christ's Hospital Book,* Hamish Hamilton, 1953.

Ivor Gurney, *Poems,* Hutchinson, 1954.

John Keats, *Selected Poems,* Norton, 1955.

Percy Bysshe Shelley, *Poems,* Collins, 1955.

Alfred, Lord Tennyson, *Selected Poems,* Heinemann, 1960.

Thomas Bewick, *A Memoir of Thomas Bewick, Written by Himself, 1822-1828,* Centaur Press, 1961, Southern Illinois University Press, 1962.

(With Bernard Mellor) *Wayside Poems of the Early Eighteenth Century: An Anthology,* Oxford University Press, 1963.

(Author of introduction) William Wordsworth, *The Solitary Song: Poems for Young Readers,* Bodley Head, 1970.

Also author of numerous pamphlets and booklets on literary subjects. Translator of the poetry of Mezzetin and Loret, and of Henry Vaughan's Latin verse. Author of libretto for Gerald Finzi's "An Ode for St. Cecilia's Day," Boosey & Hawkes, 1947. Contributor to *Times Literary Supplement.*

SIDELIGHTS: Margaret Willy has said of Edmund Blunden: "[He is] in direct line of descent from [George] Crabbe and [John] Clare—his roots firmly planted in the sturdy pastoral tradition of English poetry." Another critic, Charles Morgan, noted: "Blunden has within his range both the poetry of observation penetrated and the poetry of the unperceived. In the first respect, he has an affinity with [William] Wordsworth; in the second, with [Samuel] Coleridge." This was not to say, however, that he merely continued a tradition. According to Hugh l'Anson Fausset, Blunden "seldom treads ground which his imagination has not intimately worked, circumscribed as that ground may be. Consequently the tradition which he maintains, he also renews." He "followed no school or fashion," wrote Alec M. Hardie. "The post-war disillusion hit hard at the literary world, old gods apparently had feet of clay, and newness, originality and revolt were the catchwords. To believe [as Blunden did] in the immediate past was [according to many of his contemporaries] to believe in sterility and decadence. Edmund Blunden was [erroneously] labelled a 'Georgian' by many of the rebels." G. S. Fraser added: "With Sassoon, Read and Graves, Blunden is a last important survivor of that generation of first world war poets who passed through and surmounted an ordeal of initiation. . . . [He] is the last surviving poet of the school of Hardy, the last writer of a natively English poetry."

Fausset allowed that the dismissal of Blunden by certain contemporaries was possibly somewhat justified: "The charge brought against him that he has failed to come to grips with contemporary reality and is for that reason inevitably only a minor poet has some truth in it. His very virtues are here his defects. His rootedness in the past and the soil make him impervious to the distractions, the mechanized tensions, the life-and-death struggle of the modern world. He does not stand between two worlds, one dead, one struggling to be born, but in a world of his own, secure and at peace, though tempests rage without or its tranquil air quivers now and then at the thud of distant explosions."

Yet within the limits he had set for himself, Blunden was a notable poet. His subjects include English rural life (for which he is probably best known, though he is no "bucolic escapist," wrote Richard Church) and trench warfare during World War I. He also wrote occasional verse and "personal" poems which Hardie saw as representing "the pilgrimage of a poet often bewildered and in doubt, but rarely in despair, and it is hardly to be wondered at that his imagination and thought have explored more widely the metaphysical realms in ever-increasing persistence. . . . A similar atmosphere pervades his purely imaginative poems; he opens his wings in the clouds of mystery, the kingdom of 'The Ancient Mariner' and 'Christabel.' The riddle of man's power and mind are challenged."

Hardie continued: " 'Blunden's country' cannot be confined. He has found a common link between England and France, England and Japan. Imaginative and poetic reasoning is his country. He seems the legitimate inheritor of the legacy of English literature, and has increased the value of his inheritance, not least by his modesty, tolerance and artistic sincerity."

Blunden was a scholar as well. He was considered to be a leading authority on the English romantic poets, and was responsible for rediscovering John Clare. Hardie wrote: "English literature owes much to him for his biographical discoveries, critical originality and perspicuity; literary periods are now the fuller for his researches."

BIOGRAPHICAL/CRITICAL SOURCES:

BOOKS

Bridges, Robert, *The Dialectical Words in Blunden's Poems,* [Oxford], 1921.
Church, Richard, *Eight for Immortality,* Dent, 1941.
Contemporary Literary Criticism, Gale, Volume 2, 1974, Volume 56, 1989.
Dictionary of Literary Biography, Volume 20: *British Poets, 1914-1945,* Gale, 1983.
Edwards, Oliver, *Talking of Books,* Heinemann, 1957.
Fausset, Hugh I'Anson, *Poets and Pundits,* Yale University Press, 1947.
Hardie, Alec M., *Edmund Blunden,* Longmans, Green, for the British Council, 1958.
Morgan, Charles, *Reflections in a Mirror,* second series, Macmillan, 1947.
Squire, J. C., *Essays on Poetry,* Heinemann, 1923.
Swinnerton, Frank, *The Georgian Scene,* Farrar & Rinehart, 1934.
Williams, Charles, *Poetry at Present,* Clarendon, 1930.

PERIODICALS

English, fall, 1957.
London Magazine, April, 1966.
Poetry, May, 1941.

OBITUARIES:

PERIODICALS

Publishers Weekly, February 18, 1974.

BLY, Robert (Elwood) 1926-

PERSONAL: Born December 23, 1926, in Madison, Minn.; son of Jacob Thomas (a farmer) and Alice (Aws) Bly; married Carolyn McLean, 1955 (divorced, 1979); married Ruth Counsell, 1980; children: Mary, Bridget, Noah Matthew Jacob, Micah John Padma. *Education:* Attended St. Olaf College, 1946-47; Harvard University, A.B., 1950; University of Iowa, M.A., 1956. *Politics:* Democrat. *Religion:* Lutheran.

ADDRESSES: Home—308 First St., Moose Lake, Minn. 55767.

CAREER: Writer. Fifties (became Sixties, Seventies, then Eighties) Press, Madison, Minn., founder, publisher, and editor, 1958—. Conductor of writing workshops; reader. *Military service:* U. S. Navy, 1944-46.

MEMBER: American Academy and Institute of Arts and Letters, Association of Literary Magazines of America (executive committee), American Writers Against the Vietnam War (founder member; co-chairman).

AWARDS, HONORS: Fulbright grant, 1956-57; Amy Lowell travelling fellowship, 1962, for *Silence in the Snowy Fields;* Rockefeller Foundation fellowship, 1967; National Book Award, 1968, for *The Light Around the Body;* nomination for poetry award from *Los Angeles Times,* 1986, for *Selected Poems.*

WRITINGS:

A Broadsheet Against the New York Times Book Review, Sixties Press, 1961.
(With William Duffy and James Wright), *The Lion's Tail and Eyes: Poems Written Out of Laziness and Silence,* Sixties, 1962.
Silence in the Snowy Fields (poetry), Wesleyan University Press, 1962.
The Sea and the Honeycombs (poetry), 1966.
The Light Around the Body (poetry), Harper, 1967.
Chrysanthemums, Ox Head Press, 1967.
Ducks, Ox Head Press, 1967.
(Editor with David Ray) *A Poetry Reading Against the Viet Nam War,* Sixties, 1967.
The Morning Glory: Another Thing That Will Never Be My Friend (prose poems), Kayak Books, 1969, revised, 1970.
(Editor) *Forty Poems Touching Upon Recent History,* Beacon Press, 1970.
The Teeth Mother Naked At Last (poetry), City Light, 1971.
(With William E. Stafford and William Matthews) *Poems for Tennessee,* Tennessee Poetry Press, 1971.
Christmas Eve Service at Midnight at St. Michael's, Sceptre Press, 1972.
Water Under the Earth, Sceptre Press, 1972.
The Dead Seal Near McClure's Beach, Sceptre Press, 1973.
Sleepers Joining Hands (poetry), Harper, 1973.
Jumping Out of Bed (poetry), Barre, 1973.
(With Franz Richter) *Old Man Rubbing His Eyes* (poetry), Unicorn Press, 1975.
The Loon, Ox Head Press, 1977.
This Body Is Made of Camphor and Gopherwood (prose poetry), Harper, 1977.
Leaping Poetry: An Idea With Poems and Translations, Beacon Press, 1978.
Visiting Emily Dickinson's Grave, Red Ozier Press, 1979.
This Tree Will Be Here for a Thousand Years (poetry), Harper, 1979.
Talking All Morning, University of Michigan Press, 1980.
News From the Universe: Poems of Twofold Consciousness, Sierra Books, 1980.

(Editor) *Ten Love Poems,* Alley Press, 1981.

The Man in the Black Coat Turns, Doubleday, 1981.

The Eight Stages of Translation, Rowan Tree, 1982.

Four Ramgaes, Barnwood Press, 1982.

(Editor with Duffy) *The Fifties and the Sixties* (ten volumes), Hobart and William Smith, 1982.

(Editor) *The Winged Life: The Poetic Voice of Henry David Thoreau,* Yolla Bolly, 1986.

Selected Poems, Harper, 1986.

Loving a Woman in Two Worlds, Perennial/Harper, 1987.

Point Reyes Poems, Floating Island, 1989.

TRANSLATOR

Hans Hvass, *Reptiles and Amphibians of the World,* Grosset, 1960.

(With J. Wright) Georg Trakl, *Twenty Poems,* Sixties, 1961.

Selma Lager, *The Story of Gosta Berling,* New American Library, 1962.

(With James Knoefle and Wright) Cesar Vallejo, *Twenty Poems,* Sixties, 1962.

Knut Hamson, *Hunger* (novel), Farrar, Straus, 1967.

(With Christina Paulston) Gunnar Ekeloef, *I Do Best Alone at Night,* Charioteer Press, 1967.

(With Paulston) Ekeloef, *Late Arrival on Earth: Selected Poems,* Rapp & Carroll, 1967.

(With Wright) Pablo Neruda, *Twenty Poems,* Sixties, 1968.

(With others) Yvan Goll, *Selected Poems,* Kayak, 1968.

Issa Kobayashi, *Ten Poems,* privately printed, 1969.

(And editor) Neruda and Vallejo, *Selected Poems,* Beacon Press, 1971.

Kabir, *The Fish in the Sea Is Not Thirsty: Versions of Kabir,* Lillabulero Press, 1971.

Tomas Transtroemer, *Night Vision,* Lillabulero Press, 1971.

Transtroemer, *Twenty Poems,* Seventies Press, 1972.

Rainer Maria Rilke, *Ten Sonnets to Orpheus,* Zephyrus Image, 1972.

Basho, *Basho,* Mudra, 1972.

Federico Garcia Lorca and Juan Ramon Jimenez, *Selected Poems,* Beacon Press, 1973.

Friends, You Drank Some Darkness: Three Swedish Poets—Martinson, Ekeloef, and Transtroemer, Seventies, 1975.

Kabir, *Grass From Two Years,* Ally Press, 1975.

Kabir, *Twenty-eight Poems,* Siddha Yoga Dham, 1975.

Kabir, *Try to Live to See This!,* Ally Press, 1976.

Rilke, *The Voices,* Ally Press, 1977.

Kabir, *The Kabir Book: Forty-Four of the Ecstatic Poems of Kabir,* Beacon Press, 1977.

(And editor) Rilke, *Selected Poems of Rainer Maria Rilke: A Translation From the German, and Commentary,* Harper, 1981.

(With Will Kirkland) Antonio Machado, *Selected Poems and Prose,* White Pine, 1983.

Also translator of such volumes as *Forty Poems of Juan Ramon Jimenez,* 1967, and—with Lewis Hyde—*Twenty Poems of Vincente Alexandre,* 1977.

SIDELIGHTS: In an interview with David Ossman, Bly said that most contemporary American poetry is too old-fashioned. "I think," he said, "that for about 20 or 25 years, American poetry has been out of touch with the current poetry being done in Europe. . . . This is not from a lack of experience so it must be from a lack of a way to approach this experience. My conviction is that poetry in the English and American languages has been tied down too much to the kind of poetry . . . which loses itself in forms and which is too conscious of the English tradi-

tion." At the 1966 Houston Festival of Contemporary Poetry Bly added: "I think it is wrong to approach a poem by studying meter or form. . . . We turn away from content, and take refuge in technique, because we have a fear of content and a fear of experience, everyone shares it."

Bly thinks that, to a certain extent, the so-called Beat poets have successfully countered this "stronghold of Academic poetry." "However," he told Ossman, "[the] poetry itself is old-fashioned. The way [the Beat poets] put together a poem is basically the way a poem was put together in the nineteenth century: making very direct statements and talking directly and specifically about the subject matter. . . . Unless English and American poetry can enter, really, an inward depth, through a kind of surrealism, it will continue to become dryer and dryer."

In his note on the jacket of *Silence in the Snowy Fields,* Bly states that he is "interested in the connection between poetry and simplicity. . . . The fundamental world of poetry is an inward world. We approach it through solitude." He adds that the poems in this volume "move toward that world." Frederick Nordell writes of this collection: "This is no casual rustic versifier but a poet who reaches from his midwestern center to a sophisticated circumference of interest and concern." Nordell noted, however, that Bly is "better at evocative surfaces than ambiguous depths," and a *Virginia Quarterly Review* writer introduced this further reservation: "Seen together, [these poems] reveal weaknesses which were not so apparent when the poems appeared separately. Bly's language is pared down to a bare minimum, and his poems are often repetitions of a series of pastoral scenes with little variation and less imagination. Bald statement is not poetry." But Richard Howard believes that this restriction of language constitutes Bly's achievement: "Robert Bly's success in *Silence in the Snowy Fields* has been to confer upon even the simplest words a weight and consequence as of new things. It is not a difficult or even a structured poetry he writes; Bly is often content with only just enough. . . . But he manages to invest his seasons and spectacles, however dull or even dreary, with so much felt life that the simplest monosyllables speak to him, and to us." The *Times Literary Supplement* reviewer was less kind, and referred to Bly's method as "heavy simplicity." He adds: "For years Mr. Bly has been writing poems so transparent that . . . they tend to go in one eye and out the other. . . . Mr Bly's vocabulary is drab. When he attempts a greater resonance the words fail him." And a favorably disposed critic in the *Chicago Review* noted that "what Bly needs is something to fire him to risk more sustainedly passionate work."

Bly's translations of others' poems make up most of his published work. He explained to Ossman that translation is "the real way that poetry in a given language remains fresh—by receiving stimulation and suggestion constantly from other languages. . . . Americans have felt themselves so powerful and so strong in the world that they really have a kind of superiority complex, even in poetry, toward other nations. We tend not to translate seriously."

BIOGRAPHICAL/CRITICAL SOURCES:

BOOKS

Contemporary Literary Criticism, Gale, Volume 1, 1973, Volume 2, 1974, Volume 5, 1976, Volume 10, 1979, Volume 15, 1980, Volume 38, 1986.

Dictionary of Literary Biography, Volume 5: *American Poets Since World War II,* Gale, 1980.

Ingegard, Friberg, *Moving Inward: A Study of Robert Bly's Poetry,* Acta University Gothoburgensis, 1977.

Lensing, George S., and Ronald Moran, *Four Poets and the Emotive Imagination: Robert Bly, James Wright, Louis Simpson, and William Stafford,* Louisiana State University Press, 1976.

Ossman, David, *The Sullen Art,* Corinth, 1963.

Poems for Young Readers, National Council of Teachers of English, for the Houston Festival of Contemporary Poetry, 1966.

Stepanchev, Stephen, *American Poetry Since 1945: A Critical Survey,* Harper, 1965.

PERIODICALS

American Dialog, winter, 1968-69.
Boundary, spring, 1976.
Chicago Review, Volume 19, Number 2, 1967.
Christian Science Monitor, January 23, 1963.
English Studies, April, 1970.
Iowa Review, summer, 1972, spring, 1973, fall, 1976.
Listener, June 27, 1968.
London, December, 1968.
Los Angeles Times Book Review, May 18, 1980.
Nation, March 25, 1968.
New York Review of Books, June 20, 1968.
New York Times, May 3, 1986.
New York Times Book Review, March 9, 1980, April 26, 1981, February 14, 1982, January 22, 1984, October 13, 1985.
Poetry, June, 1963.
Shenandoah, spring, 1968.
Times Literary Supplement, March 16, 1967, February 20, 1981.
Virginia Quarterly Review, winter, 1963.
Washington Post, October 23, 1980.

*   *   *

BOBETTE
See SIMENON, Georges (Jacques Christian)

*   *   *

BODET, Jaime Torres
See TORRES BODET, Jaime

*   *   *

BOELL, Heinrich (Theodor) 1917-1985

PERSONAL: Born December 21, 1917, in Cologne, Germany (now West Germany); died July 16, 1985, at his home in Huertgen Forest in the Eifel Mountains, near Bonn, West Germany; son of Viktor (a master furniture maker) and Maria (Hermanns) Boell; married Annemarie Cech (a translator), 1942; children: Christoph (died, 1945), Raimund (died, 1982), Rene, Vincent. *Education:* Completed college preparatory school; attended the University of Cologne, 1939. *Religion:* Roman Catholic.

ADDRESSES: Home—An der Nuellheck 19, 5165 Huertgenwald-Grosshau, West Germany.

CAREER: Apprentice to a book dealer in Bonn, Germany, 1938; writer, 1947-85. Guest lecturer of poetics, University of Frankfurt, 1964. *Military service:* German Army, 1939-45; American prisoner of war, 1945.

AWARDS, HONORS: Prize from "Group 47," 1951, for short story "The Black Sheep"; Rene Schickele Prize, 1952; Cultural Prize of German Industry; Southern German Radio Prize and German Critics Prize, both 1953, both for radio play "Moench

and Raeuber"; French Publishers Prize for best foreign novel, *Tribune de Paris,* 1954; Edward von der Heydt Prize from City of Wuppertal, 1958; Grand Art Prize of North Rhine-Westphalia, 1959; Charles Veillon Prize, 1960; Literature Prize of City of Cologne, 1960; Premio d'Isola d'Elba, 1965; Premio Calabria, 1966; George Buechner Prize, German Academy for Language and Poetry, 1967; Nobel Prize for Literature, 1972, for contributions to "a renewal of German literature in the postwar era"; honorary doctorates from Trinity College, University of Dublin, University of Aston, University of Birmingham, and Brunel University, all 1973; Carl von Ossietzky Medal, International League of Human Rights, 1974; first Neil Gunn fellow, Scottish Arts Council, 1974; named honorary member of American Academy of Arts and Letters, and of American National Institute of Art and Literature, both 1974; named honorary citizen of City of Cologne, 1983; honorary title of professor conferred by North Rhine-Westphalia, 1983.

WRITINGS:

FICTION

Der Zug war puenktlich (also see below; novella), F. Middelhauve (Opladen), 1949, reprinted, Deutscher Taschenbuch (Munich), 1973, translation by Richard Graves published as *The Train Was on Time,* Criterion Books, 1956, new translation by Leila Vennewitz, Secker & Warburg, 1973.

Wanderer, kommst du nach Spa (also see below; short stories; includes "Damals in Odessa"), F. Middelhauve, 1950, reprinted, Deutscher Taschenbuch, 1971, translation by Mervyn Savill published as *Traveller, If You Come to Spa,* Arco, 1956, bilingual edition translated and edited by Savill and John Bednall, Max Hueber (Munich), 1956.

Wo warst du, Adam? (also see below; novel), F. Middlehauve, 1951, reprinted, Deutscher Taschenbuch, 1972, translation by Savill published as *Adam, Where Art Thou?,* Criterion Books, 1955, new translation by Vennewitz published as *And Where Were You, Adam?,* McGraw, 1970.

Nicht nur zur Weihnachtszeit (also see below; satire), Frankfurter Verlags-Anstalt (Frankfurt), 1952, expanded edition with other satires published as *Nichtnurzur Weihnachtszeit: Satiren,* Deutscher Taschenbuch, 1966, new edition, Kiepenheuer & Witsch, 1981.

Und sagte kein einziges Wort (also see below; novel), Kiepenheuer & Witsch, 1953, reprinted with epilogue by Gerhard Joop, Ullstein (Frankfurt), 1972, translation by Graves published as *Acquainted with the Night,* Holt, 1954, new translation by Vennewitz published as *And Never Said a Word,* McGraw, 1978.

Haus ohne Hueter (also see below; novel), Kiepenheuer Witsch, 1954, reprinted, 1974, translation by Savill published as *Tomorrow and Yesterday,* Criterion Books, 1957 (published in England as *The Unguarded House,* Arco, 1957).

Das Brot der fruehen Jahre: Erzaehlung (also see below; novella), Kiepenheuer & Witsch, 1955, reprinted, 1980, translation by Savill published as *The Bread of Our Early Years,* Arco, 1957, new translation by Vennewitz published as *The Bread of Those Early Years,* McGraw, 1976.

So ward Abend und Morgen: Erzaehlungen (stories), Verlag der Arche (Zurich), 1955.

Unberechenbare Gaeste: Heitere Erzaehlungen (stories), Verlag der Arche, 1956.

Abenteuer eines Brotbeutels, und andere Geschichten (stories), edited by Richard Plant, Norton, 1957.

Im Tal der donnernden Hufe: Erzaehlung (also see below; novella), Insel-Verlag (Wiesbaden), 1957.

Doktor Murkes gesammeltes Schweigen, und andere Satiren (also see below; satires; includes "Doktor Murkes gesammeltes Schweigen" and "Der Wegwerfer"), Kiepenheuer & Witsch, 1958, reprinted, 1977.

Erzaehlungen (contains *Der Zug war puenktlich* and *Wanderer kommst du nach Spa*), F. Middelhauve, 1958.

Billard um halbzehn (also see below; novel), Kiepenheuer Witsch, 1959, translation by Patrick Bowles published as *Billiards at Half-Past Nine*, Weidenfeld & Nicolson, 1961, McGraw, 1962, new translation by Vennewitz, Avon, 1975.

Der Bahnhof von Zimpren: Erzaehlungen (stories), Peter List (Munich), 1959.

Die Waage der Baleks, und andere Erzaehlungen (stories), Union Verlag (Berlin), 1959.

Der Mann mit den Messern: Erzaehlungen; mit einem autobiographischen Nachwort (stories with an autobiographical epilogue), Reclam (Stuttgart), 1959, reprinted, 1972.

Nicht nur zur Weihnachtszeit [and] *Der Mann mit den Messern,* edited by Dorothea Berger, American Book Company, 1959.

Als der Krieg ausbrach; als der Krieg zu Ende war (also see below), Insel, 1962, published as *Als der Krieg ausbrach: Erzaehlungen,* Deutscher Taschenbuch, 1966.

Ansichten eines Clowns (also see below; novel), Kiepenheuer & Witsch, 1963, translation by Vennewitz published as *The Clown,* McGraw, 1965.

Heinrich Boell, 1947 bis 1951: Der Zug war puenktlich, Wo Warst du, Adam?, und sechsundzwanzig Erzaehlungen (also see below) F. Middelhauve, 1963.

Doktor Murkes gesammeltes Schweigen, and Other Stories, edited by Gertrude Seidmann, introduction by H. M. Waidson, Harrap, 1963.

Entfernung von der Truppe (also see below; novella), Kiepenheuer & Witsch, 1964.

Fuenf Erzaehlungen (also see below; stories), De Roos, 1964.

Absent without Leave: Two Novellas (translation by Vennewitz of *Entfernung von der Truppe* and *Als der Krieg ausbrach; als der Krieg zu Ende war* under the titles "Absent without Leave" and "Enter and Exit"), McGraw, 1965.

Ende einer Dienstfahrt (also see below; novel), Kiepenheuer & Witsch, 1966, translation by Vennewitz published as *The End of a Mission,* McGraw, 1967.

Eighteen Stories (translations by Vennewitz; contains translation of *Im Tal der donnernden Hufe: Erzaehlung* published as "In the Valley of the Thundering Hooves," of "Doktor Murkes gesammeltes Schweigen" published as "Murke's Collected Silences," and of "The Wegwerfer" published as "The Thrower Away"), McGraw, 1966.

Absent without Leave, and Other Stories (translations by Vennewitz), Weidenfeld & Nicholson, 1967.

Und sagte kein einziges Wort [and] *Haus ohne Hueter* [and] *Das Brot der fruehen Jahre,* Kiepenheuer & Witsch, 1969.

Children Are Civilians Too (story translations by Vennewitz; contains translation of *Wanderer, kommst du nach Spa,* which includes "Damals in Odessa" published as "That Time We Were in Odessa," and selected stories from *Heinrich Boell, 1947 bis 1951*), McGraw, 1970.

Adam, and, The Train: Two Novels (translation by Vennewitz of *Wo warst du, Adam?* and *Der Zug war puenktlich*), McGraw, 1970.

Gruppenbild mit Dame (novel), Kiepenheuer & Witsch, 1971, translation by Vennewitz published as *Group Portrait with Lady,* McGraw, 1973.

Die Essenholer, und andere Erzaehlungen (stories), Hirschgraben-Verlag (Frankfurt), 1971.

Fuenf Erzaehlungen (stories), Hyperion-Verlag (Freiburg), 1971.

Billard um halb zehn [and] *Ansichten eines Clowns* [and] *Ende einer Dienstfahrt,* Kiepenheuer & Witsch, 1971.

Erzaehlungen, 1950-1970 (stories), Kiepenheuer & Witsch, 1972.

Erzaehlungen, Grafisk Forlag (Copenhagen), 1973.

Die verlorene Ehre der Katharina Blum; oder, wie Gewalt enstehen und wohin sie fuehren kann (novel with epilogue), Kiepenheuer & Witsch, 1974, translation by Vennewitz published as *The Lost Honor of Katharina Blum: How Violence Develops and Where It Can Lead,* McGraw, 1975.

Mein trauriges Gesicht: Humoresken und Satiren, Phillip Reclam (Leipzig), 1974.

Berichte zur Gesinnungslage der Nation (satire), Kiepenheuer & Witsch, 1975.

Fuersorgliche Belagerung (novel), Kiepenheuer & Witsch, 1979, translation by Vennewitz published as *The Safety Net,* Knopf, 1982.

Du Faehrst zu oft nach Heidelberg (stories), Lamuv (Bornheim-Merten), 1979, published as *Du faehrst zu oft nach Heidelberg und andere Erzaehlungen,* Deutscher Taschenbuch, 1982.

Gesammelte Erzaehlungen (stories), Kiepenheuer & Witsch, 1981.

Das Vermaechtnis (novel originally written in 1948), Lamuv, 1982, translation by Vennewitz published as *A Soldier's Legacy,* Knopf, 1985.

Die Verwundung und andere fruehe Erzaehlungen (stories from 1948-1952), Lamuv, 1983, translation by Vennewitz published as *The Casualty,* Farrar, Straus, 1986.

Der Angriff: Erzaehlungen, 1947-1949 (stories), Kiepenheuer & Witsch, 1983.

Die schwarzen Schafe: Erzaehlungen, 1950-1952 (stories), Kiepenheuer & Witsch, 1983.

Veraenderungen in Staech: Erzaehlungen, 1962-1980 (stories), Kiepenheuer & Witsch, 1984.

Frauen vor Flusslandschaft: Roman in Dialogen und Selbstgespraechen (novel; title means "Women before a River Landscape"), Kiepenheuer & Witsch, 1985.

The Stories of Heinrich Boell (translations by Vennewitz), Random House, 1986.

PLAYS

Die Spurlosen (also see below; radio play), Hans Bredow-Institut (Hamburg), 1957.

Bilanz [and] *Klopfzeichen: Zwei Hoerspiele* (also see below; radio plays; *Bilanz* first produced, 1957; translation of *Klopfzeichen* produced as "The Knocking," British Broadcasting Corp., September, 1967), Reclam, 1961.

Ein Schluck Erde (stage play), Kiepenheuer & Witsch, 1962.

Zum Tee bei Dr. Borsig: Hoerspiele (radio plays), Deutscher Taschenbuch, 1964.

Die Spurlosen: Drei Hoerspiele (radio plays), Insel-Verlag (Leipzig), 1966.

Vier Hoerspiele (radio plays), edited by G. P. Sonnex, Methuen, 1966.

Hausfriedensbruch: Hoerspiel [and] *Aussatz: Schauspiel* (radio play and theatre play, respectively; *Aussatz* first produced at Aachen's City Theatre, October 17, 1970), Kiepenheuer & Witsch, 1969.

(With Dorothee Soelle and Lucas Mariz Boehmer) *Politische Meditationen zu Glueck und Vergeblichkeit* (television plays), Luchterhand (Darmstadt), 1973.

Ein Tag wie sonst: Hoerspiele (radio plays), Deutscher Taschenbuch, 1980.

NONFICTION

Irisches Tagebuch, Kiepenheuer & Witsch, 1957, reprinted, 1972, translation by Vennewitz published as *Irish Journal,* McGraw, 1967, reprinted, Secker & Warburg, 1983.

Brief an einen jungen Katholiken, Kiepenheuer & Witsch, 1961.

Frankfurter Vorlesungen (lectures), Kiepenheuer & Witsch, 1966.

Hierzulande: Aufsaetze (essays), Deutscher Taschenbuch, 1967.

Aufsaetze, Kritiken, Reden (essays, reviews, and speeches), Kiepenheuer & Witsch, 1967.

Neue politische und literarische Schriften (also see below; essays on politics and literature), Kiepenheuer & Witsch, 1973.

Schwierigkeiten mit der Bruederlichkeit: Politische Schriften (selections from *Neue politische und literarische Schriften*), Deutscher Taschenbuch, 1976.

Einmischung erwuenscht (selection of essays and speeches published 1971-1976), Kiepenheuer & Witsch, 1977.

Missing Persons and Other Essays (translations by Vennewitz of selected essays, reviews, and speeches from 1952-1976), McGraw, 1977.

Spuren der Zeitgenossenschaft: Literarische Schriften (selection of literary essays and speeches from 1971-1976), Deutscher Taschenbuch, 1980.

Gefahren von falschen Bruedern: Politische Schriften (selection of political essays and speeches from 1971-1976), Deutscher Taschenbuch, 1980.

Was soll aus dem Jungen bloss werden? Oder Irgendwas mit Buechern (autobiography), Lamuv, 1981, translation by Vennewitz published as *What's to Become of the Boy? Or Something to Do with Books,* Knopf, 1984.

Vermintes Gelaende: Essayistische Schriften 1977-1981 (essays), Kiepenheuer & Witsch, 1982.

Bild, Bonn, Boenisch (political analysis), Lamuv, 1984.

"HEINRICH BOELL WERKE" SERIES; OMNIBUS EDITIONS

Heinrich Boell Werke: Romane und Erzaehlungen 1947-1977 (contains all novels, novellas, and stories from 1947-1977), five volumes, edited by Bernd Balzer, Kiepenheuer & Witsch, 1977.

. . . *Essayistische Schriften und Reden* (contains all essays, reviews, and speeches through 1978), three volumes, edited by Balzer, Kiepenheuer & Witsch, 1979.

. . . *Interviews* (contains all interviews and conversations through 1978), edited by Balzer, Kiepenheuer & Witsch, 1979.

. . . *Hoerspiele, Theaterstuecke, Drehbuecher, Gedichte* (contains all plays for radio, theater, and film through 1978, and poems through 1972), edited by Balzer, Kiepenheuer & Witsch, 1979.

OTHER

Aus unseren Tagen, edited by Gisela Stein, Holt, 1960.

Erzaehlungen, Hoerspiele, Aufsaetze (short stories, radio plays, and essays), Kiepenheuer & Witsch, 1961.

(With others) *Der Rat der Welt-Unweisen,* S. Mohn (Guetersloh), 1965.

(Contributor) Albrecht Beckel, *Mensch, Gesellschaft, Kirche bei Heinrich Boell* (contains "Interview mit mir selbst"), Verlag A. Fromm (Osnabrueck), 1966.

Die Spurlosen, by Heinrich Boell [and] *Philemon und Baukis,* by Leopold Ahlsen, Odyssey Press, 1967.

Gespraech mit dem Zauberer (conversation with Alexander Adrion), Olten, 1968.

Mein trauriges Gesicht: Erzaehlungen und Aufsaetze (stories and essays), Verlag Progress (Moscow), 1968.

Geschichten aus zwoelf Jahren, Suhrkamp, 1969.

Boell fuer Zeitgenossen: Ein kulturgeschichtliches Lesebuch, edited by Ralph Ley, Harper, 1970.

Edition Text [und] *Kritik* (conversation with Heinz Ludwig Arnold), Richard Boorberg (Munich), 1971.

Gedichte (poetry), Literarisches Colloquium (Berlin), 1972.

Heinrich Boell: The Novel Prizewinner Reflects on His Career (sound recording; interview by Edwin Newman), Center for Cassette Studies (North Hollywood, Calif.), c. 1974.

Drei Tage im Maerz (conversations with Christian Linder), Kiepenheuer & Witsch, 1975.

Der Lorbeer ist immer noch bitter: Literarische Schriflen, Deutscher Taschenbuch, 1976.

(With others) *Die Erschiessung des Georg von Rauch,* Wagenbuch (Berlin), 1976.

Querschnitte: Aus Interviews, Aufsaetzen und Reden, edited by Viktor Boell and Renate Matthaei, Kiepenheuer & Witsch, 1977.

(Contributor) J. Davis, P. Broughton, and M. Wood, editors, *Literature, Fiction, Poetry,. Drama* (contains translation by Denver Lindley of *Nicht nur zur Weihnachtszeit* published as "Christmas Every Day"), Scott Foresman, 1977.

Mein Lesebuch, Fischer-Taschenbuch (Frankfurt), 1978.

Eine deutsche Erinnerung (translation from the French by Annette Lallenmand of interview with Rene Wintzen), Kiepenheuer & Witsch, 1979.

Warum haben wir aufeinander geschossen? (conversation with Lew Kopelew), Lamuv, 1981.

Gedichte mit Collagen von Klaus Staeck (poetry), Lamuv, 1975, revised edition with poems through 1980, Deutscher Taschenbuch, 1981.

Antikommunismus in Ost und West (conversations with Kopelew and Heinrich Vormeg), Bund-Verlag (Cologne), 1982.

Ueber Phantasie: Siegfried Lenz, Gespraeche mit Heinrich Boell, Guenter Grass, Walter Kempowski, Pavel Kohout (interview), Hoffmann & Campe, 1982.

Das Heinrich Boell Lesebuch, edited by Viktor Boell, Deutscher Taschenbuch, 1982.

Ein- und Zusprueche: Schriften, Reden und Prosa 1981-1983 (essays, speeches, and prose), Kiepenheuer & Witsch, 1984.

Weil die Stadt so fremd geworden ist (conversation with Vormweg), Lamuv, 1985.

Die Faehigkeit zu trauern: Schriften und Reden, 1983-85, Lamuv, 1986.

Also author of collected work, entitled *Novellen; Erzaehlungen; Heiter-satirische Prosa; Irisches Tagebuch, Aufsaetze,* Buchclub Ex Libris. Also author of text for photography books, including several by Hargeshiemer. Also editor of several books. Contributor to other books, including anthologies. Also translator into German, with wife Annemarie Boell, of novels, stories, and plays, including works by J. D. Salinger, Bernard Malamud, George Bernard Shaw, and O. Henry.

SIDELIGHTS: When German writer Heinrich Boell died on July 16, 1985, the world press frequently repeated the summation that he represented the conscience of his nation. This definition of Boell as a moralist was not a new formulation; it had originated, in fact, with literary critics who derided him as nothing more than a moral trumpeter. But even as the expression took on more positive meaning, Boell particularly disliked the epithet because this purely ethical assessment of his work, he thought, hindered appreciation of his art. Furthermore, Boell believed that a nation whose conscience was found primarily in its writers instead of in its politicians, its religious leaders, or its people was already a lost land.

Nonetheless, since the end of World War II when Boell's writings first began to appear, critics and ordinary readers alike had sensed in his language a powerful moral imperative. Whatever the genre novel, story, satire, play, poem, or essay—the dominant force of the work was always the author's Christian ethics. Boell became one of the most important literary phenomena of the postwar era because his writings, regardless of their subject matter, clearly revealed where he stood as author. He was against war, militarism, and all hypocrisy in politics, religion, and human relations. He excoriated the opportunism of Nazis who became overnight democrats after 1945 and he refused to let Germans forget their recent past. He railed against the Catholic church, of which he was a member, for its cooperation in German rearmament and its role in the restoration of German capitalism. He pointed out repeatedly in the 1950s and 1960s the dangers of the cold war. In the 1960s and 1970s he supported Willy Brandt's *Ostpolitik* (a program to come to terms with West Germany's Communist neighbors); Boell campaigned for Brandt in the 1972 election—as did other writers like Guenter Grass and Siegfried Lenz. In the 1980s his practical idealism led him to support the newly formed Green party, a pro-environmental, anti-nuclear group critical of capitalist policies. He was consistently active in the peace movement throughout the postwar era and in the 1980s demonstrated against the deployment of Pershing II's and cruise missiles on German soil.

The Eastern bloc praised Boell for his anti-militarism and his anti-fascism and lauded him as a model proletarian writer. In all the Eastern European countries he was read and admired. He was a best-selling author in East Germany, Poland, Czechoslovakia, Hungary, and especially in the Soviet Union, where sales of his books totaled roughly three million copies during his lifetime. In the West, Boell's death was reported on the first page of most major newspapers. The *New York Times* quoted the words of his Nobel Prize citation, praising him for his contribution "to the renewal of German literature." In France, *Liberation* gave three full pages to Boell's death, and Monde, comparing him to Albert Camus and Jean-Paul Sartre, praised his morality as an artist, his respect for language, and his responsibility as a writer.

Christian Linder argues correctly in his *Boersenblatt* article that to understand Boell one must understand his youth. Born in the middle of World War I, Boell claimed his earliest memory was of being held in his mother's arms and watching out the family's apartment window while Hindenburg's defeated army marched through Cologne in 1919. By 1923 the inflation caused by Germany's defeat had ravaged the German population worse than the war had done. Boell remembered his father, a master furniture maker, going to the bank to get money in a cart to pay the employees in the family workshop. The money had to be spent immediately because it would be without purchasing power the next day. Boell never forgot the misery brought to his family, friends, and neighbors by the inflation of the 1920s. The stock market crash of 1929 brought the depression and the unemployment of the 1930s, which caused even more suffering. The economic uncertainties of that period also helped fire the flames of hatred in the recently formed National Socialist Party, and Boell witnessed the first Nazi marches through the streets of Cologne and saw how Nazi terror made the once peaceful streets unsafe for ordinary citizens.

Boell's family, like everyone else he knew, lost what financial security they had and with it their faith in an economic-political system that had failed twice in a decade. The fear of social turmoil became part of the psyche of every German. Economic insecurity, the concern for the next meal and a place to stay became the daily worry of a generation. To survive these times when hard work and the occupational skills of Boell's father were not enough, the Boells relied on family solidarity, mutual help, and religious faith for survival.

Although the setting for Boell's stories became Germany after World War II, the formative experiences of these earlier times essentially determined his oeuvre. The security of love, the values of food and drink, the luxury of a cigarette (things often taken for granted in an affluent world, especially in prosperous, modern West Germany) pervade his work. Never far from the surface of Boell's stories is his distrust of prosperity because he knew that wealth could disappear over night and that it was often the enemy of familial cohesiveness and the foe of social unity when it began to divide people into haves and have-nots.

In 1937, when Boell completed his secondary education, he went to Bonn to begin an apprenticeship to a book dealer. But his training was interrupted during the winter of 1938-1939 by induction into the labor service. After completion of this semimilitary obligation, he enrolled briefly as a student at the University of Cologne where he intended to study philology. But before he could really call himself a student, three months before the Second World War started, he was drafted into the army. In the course of the next six years he served as an infantryman on the western front in France and on the eastern front in Russia and in other Eastern European countries as the German army retreated before the Russian forces. During these six years Boell was wounded four times and reached the rank of corporal. Although it was customary for soldiers with his education to be officers, his hatred of the war and army life prevented him from cooperating with the military. At the risk of court-martial and summary execution, he frequently forged papers to see his family or, after his marriage to Annemarie Cech in 1942, to visit his wife in the Rhineland. In April of 1945 Boell was taken prisoner by American troops and interred in Allied POW camps until September of 1945. After his release, he immediately returned to Cologne, which lay eighty percent in ruins, to begin his life as a writer. Having chosen his vocation at the age of seventeen, he had written novels and poems before the war; some of these early works remain in the Boell Archive in Cologne.

The conditions for Boell, as for many Germans, when he returned home were reminiscent of the struggles for food and shelter after World War I; now, however, the problems included not only earning money for rent but finding an apartment still standing, not only buying food but finding food at all, not only paying for heat but finding fuel of any kind. In these first years after the war Boell's wife earned most of the family income as a teacher of English while he took only random jobs; even his reenrollment in the university was merely a strategy to obtain a legal ration card without employment so that he could dedicate the majority of his time to writing.

In these early years, Boell, like other postwar German writers, had to struggle with finding a new German literary language. Under the Nazis German had become polluted by fascist ideology, and the German literary tradition that had served Boell's older contemporaries belonging to the generation of Thomas Mann no longer seemed valid in a post-Auschwitz age. Boell was fortunate in that he found his own style early, one appropriate for his ideas and suitable to the content of his stories. That style can be described as a kind of Hemingwayesque minimalism—simple words in simple sentences—conveying a plainness appropriate to the Germany of 1945, a time when the expression of truth, to be believable again, had to possess the certainty and simplicity of a mathematical statement, like 2 + 2 = 4. The opening lines of any of the stories written before 1950 illustrate the style. "Damals in Odessa" ("That Time We Were in Odessa") starts with seven words: "In Odessa it was very cold then." The story concludes: "It was cold in Odessa, the weather was beautifully clear, and we boarded the plane; and as it rose, we knew suddenly that we would never return, never. . . ." Between the terse opening sentence and the final lines, the story tells of soldiers eating and drinking to forget their fears before going to die. In the history of German literature Boell's sober language has the place accorded a Shaker chair in the history of American furniture.

In 1947 these first stories began to appear in various periodicals. They were collected in 1950 as *Wanderer, kommst du nach Spa* (*Traveller, If You Come to Spa*). In 1983 twenty-two more of these early stories were discovered in the Boell Archive in Cologne and published in the collection *Die Verwundung und andere fruehe Erzaehlungen* (*The Casualty*). Of these early stories the twenty-five in *Traveller, If You Come to Spa* can be found in *Children Are Civilians Too,* while those in *Die Verwundung* have only recently been made available in English. The subject matter of these works is the war and the return of soldiers to a homeland morally impoverished and physically destroyed. Containing none of the heroism and gallantry of popular war literature written during the Weimar Republic, Boell's earliest narratives feature men who die without honor for an inhuman cause. Despite the stark realism of war Boell did not dwell on battle scenes; he more often depicted the boredom of military life and fear of death. In these tales the only haven from despair is love, discovered in momentary encounters between soldiers and women on the periphery of the war.

Two novellas, *Der Zug war puenktlich* (*The Train Was on Time*) and *Das Vermaechtnis* (*A Soldier's Legacy*), and the episodic novel, *Wo warst du, Adam?* (*And Where Were You, Adam?*), represent Boell's longer treatment of the war. While they differ from one another in structure, they, like the shorter works, share a fatalism that death is bigger than life and proclaim a Christian optimism that heavenly consolation is greater than suffering. Thus the war narratives acknowledge that God is still in his heaven, although all is not right with the world.

Boell's epigraph for *And Where Were You, Adam?* (which he took from Antoine de Saint-Exupery's *Flight to Arras*) can stand as a motto for all his war stories from this period: "When I was younger, I took part in real adventures: establishing postal air routes across the Sahara and South America. But war is no true adventure; it is only a substitute for adventure. War is a disease just like typhus." In an essay collected in *The Second World War in Fiction,* Alan Bance claims that this apolitical perspective on the war was typical of German literature in the 1940s and 1950s. He even sees a kind of "realism" in this political vagueness because, as he says, "war is not conducive to clear thinking." In Boell's case the unanalytic response to the war (seeing international conflict as a natural illness) was compounded by his feeling of being a lucky survivor, for only one of four German men in his age group returned from battle. His sense of destiny forced Boell to deal subjectively rather than objectively with the suffering of the Hitler years.

This narrow perspective manifests itself in Boell's simplistic division of characters into two groups: victims and executioners, with the victims often being the Germans themselves. A dichotomous view of World War II is understandable and even accurate for someone who was himself an anti-fascist and a sufferer of twelve years of oppression. Still, the result of the dichotomy is that the war stories cannot reveal truly what the war was about because the limited categories of suffering innocents and brutal henchmen are too unrefined to do the job. This kind of dualism, as Walker Sokel calls it in his *In Sachen Boell* essay, is characteristic of Boell's work in this period but disappears from the later stories as they become more sophisticated in their characterizations. Guenter Wirth's indictment, in *Heinrich Boell,* of the early war stories as "timeless irrationalism" is to the point because certainly war is not like typhus or any other sickness that has biological causes. War is not nature's making; it is made by people who have political and economic interests.

In the stories treating conditions following the war, satire became Boell's main weapon in his chastisement of Germany. Certain of these works, such as *Nicht nur zur Weihnachtszeit* ("Christmas Every Day"), "Dr. Murkes gesammeltes Schweigen" ("Dr. Murke's Collected Silences"), and "Der Wegwerfer" ("The Thrower Away"), have become classics of postwar German literature. A humorous, bizarre fantasy characterizes these satires of developing West German society. In "Christmas Every Day" a tyrannical old aunt demands daily holidays to avoid confronting the guilt of the Hitler years. In "Dr. Murke's Collected Silences" a Ph.D. in psychology, working for a radio station, tries to preserve his sanity by collecting on tape snips of dead air cut from cultural programs. In "The Thrower Away" a fanatical time-study expert makes a place for himself in the business world by systematically destroying junk mail, the surplus production of the advertising industry. Boell's success in this genre, the satirical short story, has led critics such as Erhard Friedrichsmeyer, James Henderson Reid, and Walter Jens to conclude that Boell's acutest artistic sense was his eye for satire. These stories have garnered high critical acclaim because they take to task the shortcomings of all Western democracies even though they are grounded in West German economic and political reality. One recognizes, too, that Boell's satire hits the mark equally as well in the Eastern bloc, where culture is an industry, production often leads to waste, and people avoid confronting the unpleasant past.

Boell's sense of satire is also the high point of many of his novels and raises them in some cases to great literature and in others saves them from the doldrums. For example, in *Ansichten eines Clowns* (*The Clown*), the scene of the penniless clown pantomiming his blindness during the visit of his millionaire industrialist father contains the essence of the novel's political content, and in *Entfernung von der Truppe* ("Absent without Leave"), the narrator's account of his latrine duty in World War II reveals his total alienation from society. In *Ende einer Dienstfahrt* (*End of a Mission*) Boell's choice of a pedantic, objective, understated tone confers on the novel the main feature of its readability; the dry reporting of the events of a trial of a father and son accused of burning an army jeep discloses how the courts and the press keep political protest under control. And Boell's last novel, *Frauen vor Flusslandschaft: Roman in Dialogen und Selbstgespraechen,* published just after his death in 1985, reaches its high point in a long interior monologue by a disenchanted intellectual whose job requires him to write speeches for a corrupt and stupid Christian Democratic minister. Here the monologue summarizes the novel's political intent by revealing the politician's incompetence and moral emptiness as well as the intellectual's sellout of his ideals.

Beginning with the novel *Und sagte kein einziges Wort* (*And Never Said a Word*), Boell developed a new method for dealing with contemporary reality. He began choosing themes, drawing characters, and selecting events tied directly to current developments in Germany. For this reason, his collected works provide a history of the Federal Republic and thereby justify Fritz J. Raddatz's *Zeit* description of the writer as "the Balzac of the Second Republic." Read chronologically, the books treat every significant phase in West German history from the nation's establishment in 1949 to the mid-1980s, including the period of hunger after the war, the restoration of capitalism, the process of rearmament, the achievement of prosperity, the terrorist responses to social and political inequities produced by the economic recovery, and the soul-searching of the 1980s. Treating all these aspects of West German history not as isolated phenomena of the postwar era, but in light of the Hitler years and German history since the turn of the century, Boell's canon not only helped to establish West German literature after the war but also provides a political and social understanding of German development in this century.

In Boell's work ordinary people become objects of social forces, often victims of the decisions of others. In *Die verlorene Ehre der Katharina Blum; oder, wie Gewahlt enstehen und wohin sie fuehren kann* (*The Lost Honor of Katharina Blum: How Violence Develops and Where It Can Lead*), which takes place during four days of carnival in Cologne, Boell showed how an unpolitical, law-abiding young woman could be turned into a vengeful murderer by society's toleration of social injustice. The protagonist, Katharina, becomes a "dangerous" person because she finds herself a victim of character assassination perpetrated by those institutions most responsible for a just democratic society: the press, the police, the law.

The philosophical position implied in Boell's assumption that a person is a product of social forces may be called Marxist, except that it is thoroughly religious, lacks Marxist optimism, and never suggests social change through political organization. Social solutions are not found in Boell's work. Implied, however, is the belief that if people in power practiced more compassion in the execution of their offices, society would be more just. In general, a certain sadness about the human condition prevails in Boell's work, even though a mild optimism flourishes within narrow limits. His protagonists always make important decisions regarding their own lives. They are not completely passive; they do not yield to or accept injustice. Their decisions affirm their individual human dignity and assert a militant humanism. Although their actions may not effect significant social change but merely permit them to live with their consciences, their decisiveness symbolically opposes an unjust world and thereby suggests that social awareness and conscious opposition are the way to a better future. The story of Katharina Blum's vengeance neither recommends nor condones murder, but merely illustrates the simple truth that injustice, when tolerated, is often the cause of social violence.

When the Swedish Academy awarded Boell the Nobel Prize in 1972, it singled out the novel *Gruppenbild mit Dame* (*Group Portrait with Lady*) for special praise, calling that work the summation of Boell's oeuvre. Although the writer continued to publish novels, stories, poems, plays, and essays regularly after 1971, *Group Portrait with Lady* is still regarded as the work that most fully represents the whole of Boell's canon. The book recapitulates his major themes and provides their most masterful formulation.

Boell stated his intention for the novel in an *Akzente* interview with Dieter Wellershoff: "I tried to describe or to write the story of a German woman in her late forties who had taken upon herself the burden of history from 1922-1970." In this story of Leni Gruyten-Pfeiffer, her family, and friends, Boell challenged the norms of West German society with a model of radical socialism and religious humanism. The protagonist Leni synthesizes in her person seeming contradictions. Although she is a simple person, she confounds any attempt at simple explanation. She is a materialist who delights in the senses but also a mystic who penetrates the mystery of the virgin birth, an innocent in her heart and a tramp in the eyes of society, a communist by intuition and an embodiment of the fascist ideal of "the German girl." In her, her Russian lover Boris, and their son Lev, Boell created a holy family that proclaims an undogmatic Christian socialism as a gospel for modern times.

Around Leni are grouped more than 125 characters representing all classes of society and various nations: communists and capitalists, industrialists and proletarians, fascists and anti-fascists, Jews and Moslems, Turks and Germans, rich and poor, saints and sinners the whole spectrum of German society from 1922-1970. To hold the various levels of the story together and to keep Leni in the center of the novel, the work employs two narrative techniques. In the first half of the novel an unnamed narrator scrupulously relates the events of Leni's life. This half of the book consists of the narrator's meticulous research on Leni and his comments on the accuracy and validity of his findings. Leni's story proceeds chronologically from her birth to March 2, 1945, the day in which a nine-hour Allied raid on Cologne effectively brought the war to an end for the people of that city. After this event, midway through the novel, the narrator relinquishes his role as narrator to assume a role as a member of Leni's circle of friends, and to become an actor in the events of the book. At this point various characters tell their life stories from the day of the terrible bombing to 1970. Since these people have contact with Leni their stories also reveal from various perspectives Leni's own life during this twenty-five year period. Again Boell found a structure that allowed him to come to terms with recent German history and postwar developments.

Group Portrait with Lady, is, indeed, the summation of Boell's writing, for it crystalizes the radical message that runs through all of his work since *And Never Said a Word:* Christianity and capitalism are incompatible with each other; their long standing marriage survives only because organized religion continually surrenders its humanistic values to the demands of economics and politics.

MEDIA ADAPTATIONS: "The Lost Honor of Katharina Blum," adapted from Boell's novel of the same title, was released by New World Pictures in 1975.

BIOGRAPHICAL/CRITICAL SOURCES:

BOOKS

Boell, Alfred, *Bilder einer deutschen Familie: Die Boells,* Gustav Luebbe Verlag (Bergisch Gladbach), 1981.
Boell, Heinrich, *Wo warst du, Adam?,* F. Middlehauve, 1951, reprinted Deutscher Taschenbuch, 1972, translation by Savill published as *Adam, Where Art Thou?,* Criterion Books, 1955, new translation by Vennewitz published as *And Where Were You, Adam?,* McGraw, 1970.
Boell, Heinrich, *Children Are Civilians Too* (story translations by Vennewitz), McGraw, 1970.
Boell, Heinrich, *Was soll aus dem Jungen bloss werden? Oder Irgendwas mit Buechern* (autobiography), Lamuv, 1981,

translation by Vennewitz published as *What's to Become of the Boy? Or Something to Do with Books,* Knopf, 1984.

Boell, Rene, Viktor Boell, Reinhold Neven DuMont, Klaus Staeck, and Gerhard Conard, Robert C., *Heinrich Boell,* Twayne, 1981.

Contemporary Literary Criticism, Gale, Volume 2, 1974, Volume 3, 1975, Volume 6, 1976, Volume 11, 1979, Volume 15, 1980, Volume 27, 1984, Volume 39, 1986.

Dictionary of Literary Biography, Volume 69: *Contemporary German Fiction Writers, First Series,* Gale, 1988.

Dictionary of Literary Biography Yearbook: 1985, Gale, 1986.

Edition Text [und] Kritik, Richard Boorberg, 1971.

Friedrichsmeyer, Erhard, *The Major Works of Heinrich Boell: A Critical Commentary,* Monarch Press, 1974.

Friedrichsmeyer, Erhard, *Die satirische Kurzprosa Heinrich Boells,* University of North Carolina Press, 1981.

Gruetzbach, Frank, editor, *Heinrich Boell: Freies Geleit fuer Ulrike Meinhof; ein Artikel und seine Folgen,* Kiepenheuer & Witsch, 1972.

Hoffman, Leopold, *Heinrich Boell: Einfuehrung in Leben und Werk,* 2nd edition, Verlag Edi-Centre (Luxembourg), 1973.

Hoffmann, Gabriele, *Heinrich Boell,* Lamuv, 1986.

Jens, Walter, *Deutsch Literatur der Gegenwart: Themen, Stile, Tendenzen,* 4th edition, Piper (Munich), 1962.

Jurgensen, Manfred, *Boell: Untersuchungen zum Werk,* Francke (Bern), 1975.

Lengning, Werner, editor, *Der Scrifsteller Heinrich Boell: Ein biographisch-bibliographischer Abriss,* Deutscher Taschenbuch, 5th edition, 1977 (previous editions each contain different essay on Boell).

Ley, Ralph, *Boell fuer Zeitgenossen: Ein kulturgeschichtliches Lesebuch,* Harper, 1970.

MacPherson, Enid, *A Student's Guide to Boell,* Heinemann, 1972.

Martin, Werner, compiler, *Heinrich Boell: Eine Bibliographie seiner Werke,* Georg Olms (Hildsheim), 1975.

Reich-Ranicki, Marcel, editor, *In Sachen Boell,* Kiepenheuer & Witsch, 1968, 3rd edition, 1970.

Reid, James Henderson, *Heinrich Boell: Withdrawal and Re-Emergence,* Wolff, 1973.

Schwarz, Wilhelm Johannes, *Der Erzaehler Heinrich Boell: Seine Werke und Gestalten,* 2nd edition, Francke Verlag, 1968.

Schwartz, Wilhelm Johannes, *Heinrich Boell, Teller of Tales: A Study of His Works and Characters,* Ungar, 1969.

Stresau, Hermann, *Heinrich Boell,* Colloquium Verlag (Berlin), 1964.

Wirth, Guenter, *Heinrich Boell: Essayistische Studie ueber religioese und gesellschaftliche Motive im Prosawerk des Dichters,* Union Verlag, 1968.

PERIODICALS

Akzente, Volume 18, 1971.

Boersenblatt, July 23, 1985.

Chicago Tribune Book World, February 7, 1982, July 14, 1985, March 23, 1986.

Germanic Review, summer, 1978, summer, 1984.

German Life and Letters, July, 1959.

German Quarterly, March, 1960, Volume 45, 1972, Volume 50, 1977.

German Tribune, August 5, 1979.

London Review of Books, April 1, 1982, October 23, 1986.

Modern Fiction Studies, autumn, 1975.

Nation, May 3, 1965, October 2, 1967, June 22, 1970, July 30, 1973, February 19, 1977.

New Republic, March 20, 1965, November 27, 1965, November 12, 1966, April 26, 1975, March 3, 1982, October 21, 1985, April 7, 1986.

New Statesman, June 2, 1961, June 25, 1965, March 3, 1967, January 26, 1973, May 11, 1973, October 17, 1975, February 25, 1977, December 9, 1977, September 29, 1978, March 26, 1982, July 29, 1983, March 1, 1985, October 11, 1985, November 21, 1986.

Newsweek, February 8, 1965, September 14, 1970, May 14, 1973, February 22, 1982, October 15, 1984, June 10, 1985.

New Yorker, June 16, 1956, November 20, 1965, October 7, 1967, February 28, 1970, May 19, 1975, August 7, 1978, June 14, 1982, November 12, 1984, April 7, 1986.

New York Review of Books, February 11, 1965, December 29 1966, September 14, 1967, March 26, 1970, November 5, 1970, May 31, 1973, March 18, 1982.

New York Times, January 25, 1965, September 6, 1965, December 31, 1966, August 25, 1967, October 20, 1972, May 9, 1973, May 21, 1975, May 31, 1979, February 5, 1982, October 7, 1984.

New York Times Book Review, January 24, 1965, September 12, 1965, October 16, 1966, August 13, 1967, April 5, 1970, November 5, 1972, May 6, 1973, December 2, 1973, April 27, 1975, January 23, 1977, November 6, 1977, January 8, 1978, May 27, 1979, May 31, 1979, January 31, 1982, February 5, 1982, June 23, 1985, December 29, 1985, February 23, 1986, March 29, 1987, August 23, 1987.

Spiegel, September 2, 1985.

Tagesspiegel, July 22, 1979.

Time, October 21, 1957, January 4, 1963, January 29, 1965, September 24, 1965, March 29, 1968, March 2, 1970, May 28, 1973, February 8, 1982.

Times (London), October 10, 1985, October 16, 1986.

Times Literary Supplement, July 8, 1965, September 8, 1966, November 10, 1966, March 9, 1967, January 4, 1968, August 8, 1968, March 12, 1970, October 8, 1971, January 12, 1973, June 1, 1973, October 11, 1974, October 25, 1974, January 31, 1975, January 30, 1976, February 25, 1977, February 10, 1978, June 30, 1978, March 7, 1980, April 2, 1982, May 7, 1982, August 19, 1983, July 26, 1985, February 14, 1986, May 15, 1987.

Washington Post Book World, May 13, 1973, November 20, 1977, January 24, 1982, November 16, 1984, July 6, 1987.

World Literature Today, summer, 1965, autumn, 1977, summer, 1979, spring, 1980, spring, 1985, spring, 1986.

Zeit, October 9, 1959, August 10, 1971, July 19, 1985, August 2, 1985.

OBITUARIES:

PERIODICALS

Monde (international edition), July 18-24, 1985.

New York Times, July 17, 1985.

Time, July 29, 1985.

Times (London), July 17, 1985.

Washington Post, July 17, 1985, July 28, 1985.

*   *   *

BOGAN, Louise   1897-1970

PERSONAL: Born August 11, 1897, in Livermore Falls, Me.; died February 4, 1970, in New York, N.Y.; daughter of Daniel Joseph and Mary Helen (Shields) Bogan; married Curt Alexander, 1916 (died, 1920); married Raymond Holden (a poet), 1925 (divorced, 1937); children: (first marriage) Mathilde. *Education:* Attended Boston University 1915-16.

ADDRESSES: Home—New York, N.Y.

CAREER: Poet and critic. Free-lance writer in New York City, 1919-25; poetry editor, *New Yorker,* 1931-69. Visiting professor at University of Washington, Seattle, 1948, University of Chicago, 1949, University of Arkansas, 1952, Seminar in American Studies, Salzburg, Austria, 1952, and Brandeis University, Waltham, Massachusetts, 1964-65.

MEMBER: American Academy of Arts and Letters and Academy of American Poets.

AWARDS, HONORS: John Reed Memorial Prize, 1930, and Helen Haire Levinson Memorial Prize, 1937, both from *Poetry;* Guggenheim fellowship, 1933 and 1937; Library of Congress Fellowship in American Letters, 1944; Library of Congress Chair in Poetry, 1945-46; Harriet Monroe Poetry Award, 1948; National Institute of Arts and Letters grant, 1951; Bollingen Prize in Poetry, 1955, for *Collected Poems, 1923-1953;* L.H.D., Western College for Women, 1956; Academy of American Poets fellowship, 1958; Litt.D., Colby College, 1960; Brandeis University Creative Arts Award in Poetry, 1961; National Endowment for the Arts grant, 1967.

WRITINGS:

POETRY

Body of This Death, McBride, 1923.
Dark Summer, Scribner, 1929.
The Sleeping Fury, Scribner, 1937.
Poems and New Poems, Scribner, 1941.
Collected Poems, 1923-1953, Noonday Press, 1954.
The Blue Estuaries: Poems, 1923-1968, Farrar, Straus, 1968.

OTHER

Women, Ward Ritchie, 1929.
Achievement in American Poetry, 1900-1950 (criticism), H. Regnery, 1951.
(Translator) Yvan Goll, *Elegy of Ihpetonga* [and] *Masks of Ashes,* Noonday Press, 1954, reprinted, 1985.
Selected Criticism: Prose, Poetry, Noonday Press, 1955.
(With Archibald MacLeish and Richard Wilbur) *Emily Dickinson: Three Views,* Amherst College Press, 1960, reprinted Norwood Editions, 1977.
(Translator with Elizabeth Mayer) Ernest Juenger, *The Glass Bees,* Noonday Press, 1961.
(Translator) Goll, *The Myth of the Pierced Rock,* Allen Press, 1962.
(Translator with Mayer) Johann Wolfgang von Goethe, *Elective Affinities,* Regnery, 1963.
(Editor and translator with Elizabeth Roget) Jules Renard, *Journal,* Braziller, 1964.
(Editor with William Jay Smith) *The Golden Journey: Poems for Young People,* Reilly & Lee, 1965.
(Author of afterword) Virginia Woolf, *A Writer's Diary, Being Extracts From the Diary of Virginia Woolf,* New American Library, 1968.
A Poet's Alphabet: Reflections on the Literary Art and Vocation, edited by Robert Phelps and Ruth Limmer, McGraw-Hill, 1970.
(Translator with Mayer of verse) Goethe, *The Sorrows of Young Werther, and Novella,* Random House, 1971.
What the Woman Lived: Selected Letters of Louise Bogan, 1920-1970, edited by Ruth Limmer, Harcourt, 1973.

Journey Around My Room: The Autobiography of Bogan, a Mosaic, edited by Limmer, Viking, 1980.

Also author of *Works in the Humanities Published in Great Britain 1939-1946: A Selected List,* 1950. Contributor of verse to *New Republic;* contributor of literary criticism to *New Yorker, Nation, Poetry: A Magazine of Verse,* and *Atlantic Monthly.* Bogan's papers are collected at Amherst College.

SIDELIGHTS: Louise Bogan has been called by some critics the most accomplished woman poet of our time. Her subtle, restrained, intellectual style was greatly influenced by the English metaphysical poets. Many have placed her in the same category with George Herbert, John Donne, and Henry Vaughan. Bogan belonged to a group of brilliant minor poets described by some as the "reactionary generation." Aware of the success of Ezra Pound and T. S. Eliot, Bogan and others chose to follow the traditional English form of expression of the seventeenth century, which included the use of meters. Although she utilized traditional techniques, her poetry is modern, her language immediate and contemporary. Bogan's poetry contains a personal quality derived from personal experience, but it is not private. Her poems, most critics agree, are economical in words and masterpieces of crossed rhythms in which the meter opposes word groupings.

Sleeping Fury was one of the earlier published books of poems by Louise Bogan. The *Springfield Republican* noted that "Miss Bogan's poetry appeals to the comparative few who appreciate delicacy and artistry in verse." *Books* review said Bogan "has achieved a mastery of form rare in the realm of modern poetry. There is creative architecture in even the slightest of her lyrics. Miss Bogan works not as a landscape painter (while her visual imagery is exact, it does not depend on color alone), nor yet as a musician—although in many of her poems, the auditory imagery is superior to the visual: the ear listens, even as the eye sees. Her art is that of a sculpture." A *Nation* critic wrote, "Distinguished is the word one always thinks of in connection with Louise Bogan's poetry. Whatever form she tries, her art is sure, economical, and self-definitive. There is never in her poems a wasted adjective or phrase but always perfect clarity and a consistent mood precisely set down. She can write the completely artless lyric or the very subtle poem worked out through complex imagery."

Reviewing *Poems and New Poems* in *Saturday Review,* William Rose Benet noted, "Her poetry is, and always has been, intensely personal. She has inherited the Celtic magic of language, but has blended it somehow with the tartness of New England." Marianne Moore further observed in *Nation,* "Women are not noted for terseness, but Louise Bogan's art is compactness compacted. Emotion with her, as she has said of certain fiction is 'itself form, the kernel which builds outward form from inward intensity.' She uses a kind of forged rhetoric that nevertheless seems inevitable."

Collected Poems, 1923-1953 was reviewed in the *New York Times* by Richard Eberhart. "Louise Bogan's poems adhere to the center of English with a dark lyrical force," wrote Eberhart. "What she has to say is important. How she says it is pleasing. She is a compulsive poet first, a stylist second. When compulsion and style meet, we have a strong, inimitable Bogan poem." *Saturday Review* commented, "Louise Bogan is mistress of precise images and commands an extensive range of poetic accents and prosodic effects; she is also a musician, whose notes are as crystalline as those of Chopin's Preludes. More than this, one cannot read far in her pages without realizing that at the core of her poetry is mind-stuff which it is fashionable to call metaphysical." These poems are also important because they deal intelligently with the themes of sexual love and bodily decay.

The Blue Estuaries: Poems, 1923-1968 was the final collection of poems published before Louise Bogan's death. The *New York Times* reviewed the book: "Now that we can see the sweep of 45 years work in this collection of over a hundred poems, we can judge what a feat of character it has been. . . . [Her diction] stems from the severest lyrical tradition in English. . . . [Her language is] as supple as it is accurate, dealing with things in their own tones."

With the assistance of William Jay Smith, Louise Bogan compiled an anthology of poems for children. *The Golden Journey: Poems for Young People,* with poems ranging from Shakespeare to Dylan Thomas, was described by James Dickey as possibly "the best general anthology of poems for young people ever compiled. By the poems they present, by their arrangement and timing, the editors subtly hold out the possibility that a child—thought a child—is capable of rising to good poems, and so of becoming, through an encounter which also requires much of him, something more than he was. . . . [This book] could have been selected only by poets as distinguished as these two, and by human beings who realize that to make the wrong concessions to children is injurious to them."

Louise Bogan also wrote a great deal of criticism. *Achievement in American Poetry, 1900-1950* was a brief account of American poetry during the first half of this century. The *Chicago Tribune* described the book as "a delight. Like all Miss Bogan's criticism, this book is full of acute, spirited, and authoritative judgments of writers and works, expressed with grace and wit." The *New York Times* added, "Louise Bogan not only manages to compress a formidable amount of factual information into her small compass but also contrives to do a great deal of satisfactory talking about her facts." The *United States Quarterly Book Review* commented, "Miss Bogan's clarity of style, her ability to compress a great deal of information into a few lucid, interesting phrases, and her severely just appraisal form the chief attractions of this volume."

BIOGRAPHICAL/CRITICAL SOURCES:

BOOKS

Bogan, Louise, *What the Woman Lived: Selected Letters of Louise Bogan, 1920-1970,* edited by Ruth Limmer, Harcourt, 1973.
Contemporary Literary Criticism, Gale, Volume 2, 1974, Volume 39, 1986, Volume 46, 1988.
Dictionary of Literary Biography, Volume 45: *American Poets, 1880-1945,* Gale, 1986.
Frank, Elizabeth, *Louise Bogan: A Portrait,* Knopf, 1985.
Smith, William Jay, *Louise Bogan: A Woman's Words,* Library of Congress, 1971.

PERIODICALS

Books, May 30, 1937.
Chicago Tribune, November 4, 1951.
Nation, April 24, 1937, November 15, 1941.
New York Times, November 25, 1951, May 30, 1954.
New York Times Book Review, November 7, 1965, October 13, 1968.
Saturday Review, April 18, 1937, April 25, 1942, July 3, 1954, February 21, 1970.
United States Quarterly Book Review, March, 1952.

OBITUARIES:

PERIODICALS

Antiquarian Bookman, February 16, 1970.
Newsweek, February 16, 1970.
New Yorker, February 14, 1970.
New York Times, February 5, 1970.
Publishers Weekly, February 23, 1970.
Time, February 16, 1970.
Washington Post, February 6, 1970.

*   *   *

BOLL, Heinrich (Theodor)
    See BOELL, Heinrich (Theodor)

*   *   *

BOLT, Robert (Oxton) 1924-

PERSONAL: Born August 15, 1924, in Sale, Manchester, England; son of Ralph (a shopkeeper) and Leah (a teacher; maiden name, Binnion) Bolt; married Celia Ann Roberts (a painter), November 6, 1949 (divorced, 1967); married Sarah Miles (an actress), 1967; children (first marriage) Sally Simmons, Benedict, Joanna; (second marriage) Thomas. *Education:* University of Manchester, B.A. (honours in history), 1950; University of Exeter, teaching diploma, 1950. *Politics:* Left-wing. *Avocational interests:* Walking and sailing.

ADDRESSES: Agent—Margaret Ramsay, 14a Goodwin's Court, London WC 2, England.

CAREER: Office boy with Sun Life Assurance Office, Manchester, England, 1942; in Devon, 1950-52; Millfield School, Street, Somerset, England, teacher and head of English department, 1952-58. Playwright and film director. *Military service:* Royal Air Force, 1943-44, Royal West African Frontier Force, 1944-46; became lieutenant.

MEMBER: Campaign for Nuclear Disarmament, Association of Cinematography and Television Technicians (president), Writers Guild of Great Britain, The Spares (Somerset; honorary life member).

AWARDS, HONORS: Evening Standard Drama Award, 1957, for *Flowering Cherry;* New York Drama Critics Circle Award, 1962, for *A Man for All Seasons;* British Film Academy Award, and Academy of Motion Picture Arts and Sciences, Academy Award (Oscar) nomination, 1962, both for "Lawrence of Arabia"; Academy of Motion Picture Arts and Sciences, Academy Award, 1966, for "Doctor Zhivago"; New York Film Critics Award for best picture of the year, 1966, Golden Globe Press Award, 1967, and Academy of Motion Picture Arts and Sciences, Academy Award, 1967, all for film, "A Man for All Seasons"; Antoinette Perry (Tony) Award nomination, 1972, for *Vivat! Vivat Regina!;* Commander of British Empire, 1972.

WRITINGS:

PLAYS

"The Last of the Wine" (adaptation of his radio play; also see below), produced in London, 1956.
"The Critic and the Heart," produced in Oxford, England, 1957.
Flowering Cherry (produced in London, 1957, in New York, 1959; also see below), Heinemann, 1958.
A Man for All Seasons (two-act; first draft was broadcast in England, 1954, televised on British Broadcasting Corporation

[BBC-TV], 1957, full-length play produced in London, 1960, in New York, 1961; also see below), Samuel French, 1960, Random House, 1962.

The Tiger and the Horse (three-act; produced in London, 1960; also see below), Heinemann, 1961.

Three Plays (contains *Flowering Cherry, A Man for All Seasons,* and *The Tiger and the Horse*), Heinemann, 1963.

Gentle Jack (produced in London, 1960), Samuel French, 1964, Random House, 1965.

The Thwarting of Baron Bolligrew (two-act children's play; produced in London, 1966), Samuel French, 1966.

"Brother and Sister," produced in Brighton, England, 1967.

Vivat! Vivat Regina! (two-act; first produced in Chichester, England, at the Chichester Theatre, May 20, 1970, produced in Boston at the Shubert Theatre, December 27, 1971), Random House, 1971.

State of Revolution (produced in Birmingham and London, 1977), Samuel French, 1977.

SCREENPLAYS

"Lawrence of Arabia," Columbia, 1962.

"Doctor Zhivago," United Artists, 1966, published as *Doctor Zhivago: The Screenplay,* Random House, 1966.

"A Man for All Seasons" (adaptation of own play), Columbia, 1966.

"Ryan's Daughter," Metro-Goldwyn-Mayer, 1970.

"Lady Caroline Lamb," United Artists, 1972.

The Bounty, Orion, 1984, Jove, 1986.

The Mission, Warner Bros., 1986, Penguin, 1986.

OTHER

Also author of radio plays, including "The Master," 1953, "Fifty Pigs," 1953, "Ladies and Gentlemen," 1954, "The Last of the Wine," 1955, "Mr. Sampson's Sundays," 1955, "The Window," 1958, "The Drunken Sailor," 1958, and "The Banana Tree," 1961. Work included in anthology, *The New Theatre of Europe,* Volume 1, edited by Robert W. Corrigan, Dell, 1962. Contributor to *Esquire, Theatre Arts, Saturday Review,* and other periodicals.

WORK IN PROGRESS: A play on the Russian Revolution.

SIDELIGHTS: Robert Bolt first turned to writing plays when a Nativity play was needed for the school where he was then teaching. He later left teaching to devote all his time to writing. Unlike many of his British contemporaries, he is not a startling innovator but rather, as John Russell Taylor describes him, "a good, traditional playwright." Bolt would, however, like to see drama fictionalized to the point where masks would be worn by the characters.

His portrayal of Thomas More, *A Man for All Seasons,* J. C. Trewin believes is "one of the few contemporary portrait-plays likely to last." Another observer wrote that Bolt "preserves a personal aloofness when it comes to translating life into art. He does not preach; he stands back and relates, creating his own reality in place of an aggressive naturalism." And Walter Kerr praised the play as being "as remarkable in its restraint as in its ultimate fire. . . . What Mr. Bolt has done is to make the human mind shine. The glare is dazzling; the experience exhilarating."

Bolt wrote about his imagery and poetry in a preface to *A Man for All Seasons:* "As a figure for the superhuman context, I took the largest, most alien, least formulated thing I know, the sea and water. The references to ships, rivers, currents, tides, navigation, and so on, are all used for this purpose. Society by contrast fig-

ures as dry land. I set out with no very well formed idea of the kind of play it was to be, except that it was not to be naturalistic. . . . I comfort myself with the thought that it's the nature of imagery to work, in performance at any rate, unconsciously. But if, as I think, a play is more like a poem than a straight narration, still less a demonstration or lecture, then imagery ought to be important. It's perhaps necessary to add that by a poem I mean something tough and precise, not something dreamy." Bolt says he chose More as his protagonist because "a very few people give a tinker's cuss whether or not the sovereign of England is the supreme head of the Church of England insofar as the law of God allows. . . . I wanted an issue which was largely drained of its emotional content now, so that you could see it, as it were, diagramatically. . . . And the second reason why I was attracted to More particularly was that he was a martyr, [though] I am not attracted to martyrs in general. . . . [But] then there dawned the slow realization that More was very good at living as well as able to die. And running these two things in harness, reading more and more about him and thinking about his problem in general, I came very strongly to the conclusion that in a way you can't live properly until you have come to terms with your death."

Bolt's successes have been largely in the area of historical drama. Speaking of *Vivat! Vivat Regina!,* a play about the conflict between Mary, Queen of Scots and Elizabeth I, he said: "I think there is a quite narrow limit to what you may do with the known facts of history. Clearly, you're not writing a history book, but on the other hand, you must be loyal to such facts as are definitely known. Particularly such a salient fact as that these two women, whose lives were so closely intertwined, never in fact effected a meeting! They wanted to meet, but the political circumstances made it either imprudent or disadvantageous for one or the other of them, so it never came off.

"One cannot rewrite history for dramatic effect—not as it happened, but as *should* have happened. If you have a marvelous play in your mind about two queens who eventually meet and have a stand-up barney, fine. But you may not call them Elizabeth and Mary, because we know they didn't meet. . . . Where the facts are not definitely knowable, the playwright is at liberty to read such evidence as is available to him and make up his own mind. But undoubtedly his decision will be colored by his desires as a playwright."

Not only working well with historical subjects, Bolt also uses historical devices, J. W. Lambert said: "Mr. Bolt is what might be called an experimental mainstream dramatist: He effortlessly incorporates the devices of effective staging from any age, including our own, and uses them as what they should be, a means to an end, never allowing them to take charge as ends in themselves. Scene flows easily into scene, scene plays against scene, passing time is covered in a snatch of dialogue, distance is annihilated in an exchange between one side of the stage and the other, naturalism gives way to symbolism, declamation to fantasy—all without the slightest obscurity. Here is real craftsmanship."

Some critics attribute his tremendous success in film to this same traditionalism. Clifford A. Ridly commented that "Bolt's popularity with the Hollywood Establishment should not be too surprising. Hollywood is a conservative place, and *A Man for All Seasons*—like 'Lawrence' and 'Zhivago' before it—is essentially a 'traditional' movie in its values, its conception, its direction." Others see the film success in Bolt's ability to understand the differences between the stage and the screen. Bolt has said "I understand and respect it when a man like Antonioni says that cinema is a visual medium and therefore must make its impact by visual means. I say the less dialogue in a film the better, simply because to see something is more effective than to be told it. But where I differ is that I believe that although absolutely a visual medium, cinema is also a *narrative* medium. It can't help but be simply because it exists over a period of time. I think that the visual people who say they'll make it up hanker after the status of a painter. We have a specific time. An audience sits down at 8 and leaves at 10. There is a need for connection. It need not be like the films David [Lean] and I make—[with] a logical and explicit connection. But one simply cannot juxtapose images and leave it to the imagination of audiences for that connection, or what you wind up with is deadly. When one is responsible for the creation of a film, one is responsible for the necessary connection. There is danger in a film not being explicitly thought out." Bolt commented elsewhere on adapting *A Man for All Seasons:* "Some things had to be sacrificed in order to bring the film in at around two hours. The Common Man, for instance—there's a definite loss there, even though we've given some of his speeches to other characters. . . . There were compensations, of course. We were able to *show* the symbolism of the water, for one thing."

Bolt, says Trewin, is "concerned fiercely with the problems of the individual and his social conscience." Bolt has said: "My first intention in writing this play [*Vivat! Vivat Regina!*] was not to give a history lesson but to create an effective, entertaining, possibly disturbing—and truthful—evening in the theatre. While I hope audiences will find this an exciting narrative, I also hope anyone who thinks about it—or even those who don't—will come away with some slight uneasiness about the nature of power, and about figures who are endowed with power. Both with a certain uneasiness about what they are up to 'on our behalf' and also with a certain pity for the terrifying pressures to which they are subjected."

Theatre Arts notes that he "owes something to such fashionable playwrights of the day as Brecht, Beckett and Tennessee Williams; something but not much. Brecht has taught him now to construct an episodic drama, Beckett and Williams have each contributed to his preoccupation with moral and metaphysical problems. But far more than they, he is a detached writer who separates his creative and intellectual life."

Bolt was jailed briefly in 1961, after participating in a demonstration for nuclear disarmament.

BIOGRAPHICAL/CRITICAL SOURCES:

BOOKS

Armstrong, W. A., and others, editors, *Experimental Drama*, G. Bell, 1963.
Contemporary Literary Criticism, Volume 14, Gale, 1980.
Dictionary of Literary Biography, Volume 13: *British Dramatists since World War II*, Gale, 1982.
Hayman, Ronald, *Robert Bolt*, Heinemann, 1969.

PERIODICALS

Catholic World, September, 1962.
Film-Makers Newsletter, October, 1973.
New York Times, December 13, 1966; December 18, 1966.
Sunday Times (London), November 12, 1972.
Theatre Arts, May, 1963.

*   *   *

BOMBECK, Erma (Louise) 1927-

PERSONAL: Born February 21, 1927, in Dayton, OH; daughter of Cassius Edwin (a laborer) and Erma (Haines) Fiste; married

William Lawrence Bombeck (a school administrator), August 13, 1949; children: Betsy, Andrew, Matthew. *Education:* Attended Ohio University; University of Dayton, B.A., 1949. *Religion:* Roman Catholic.

ADDRESSES: Home—Paradise Valley, AZ. *Agent*—c/o Universal Press Syndicate, 4900 Main St., Kansas City, MO 64112.

CAREER: Author, columnist, humorist, and lecturer. Dayton *Journal Herald*, Dayton, OH, writer, 1949-53; author of weekly column published in *Kettering-Oakwood Times*, 1963-65; author of thrice-weekly column, "At Wit's End," for Dayton *Journal Herald*, 1965, syndicated to sixty-five newspapers by the Newsday Syndicate, 1965-67, and to over nine hundred newspapers by the Field Newspaper Syndicate, beginning 1967; columnist with Pubs.-Hall Syndicate (now North American Syndicate), 1970-85, Los Angeles Times Syndicate, 1985-88, and Universal Press Syndicate, 1988—. Appears twice weekly on "Good Morning America," 1975—. Creator, writer, and executive producer of television series "Maggie," American Broadcasting Co., 1981. Appointed to President's National Advisory Committee for Women, 1978.

MEMBER: American Academy of Humor Columnists, Women in Communication, Sigma Delta Chi.

AWARDS, HONORS: National Headliner Prize from Theta Sigma Phi, 1969; Mark Twain Award for Humor, 1973; numerous honorary doctorates.

WRITINGS:

At Wit's End (collection of columns), Doubleday, 1967.
Just Wait Till You Have Children of Your Own, illustrations by Bil Keane, Doubleday, 1971.
I Lost Everything in the Post-Natal Depression, Doubleday, 1973.
The Grass Is Always Greener over the Septic Tank, McGraw, 1976.
If Life Is a Bowl of Cherries, What Am I Doing in the Pits?, McGraw, 1978.
Aunt Erma's Cope Book: How to Get from Monday to Friday . . . in Twelve Days, McGraw, 1979.
Motherhood: The Second Oldest Profession, McGraw, 1983.
Erma Bombeck Giant Economy Size, Doubleday, 1983.
Laugh Along with Erma Bombeck, Fawcett, 1984.
Four of a Kind: A Treasury of Favorite Works by America's Best-Loved Humorist, McGraw, 1985.
Family: The Ties That Bind . . . and Gag, McGraw, 1987.
I Want to Grow Hair, I Want to Grow up, I Want to Go to Boise: Children Surviving Cancer, Harper, 1989.

Also author of monthly column "Up the Wall" in *Good Housekeeping*, 1969-75. Contributor to *Reader's Digest, Family Circle, Redbook,* and *McCall's.*

MEDIA ADAPTATIONS: Two of Bombeck's lectures have been recorded and released as *The Family That Plays Together Gets on Each Other's Nerves*, Warner Bros. Records, 1977; *The Grass Is Always Greener over the Septic Tank* was produced as a television movie by Columbia Broadcasting Systems, October, 1978.

SIDELIGHTS: Erma Bombeck has made a career of satirizing the various domestic crises confronting the average American household. Called everything from "America's Housewife-at-Large" by *People* to "the female Art Buchwald" by *Time,* Bombeck shares her observations and opinions with millions of followers through her widely syndicated newspaper column "At Wit's End," television appearances, and her bestselling books. Diane Shah reports in *Newsweek* that "Bombeck assumes the role of straight woman in the mad world of suburbia. By rights that role should be a dud, but at a time when being a housewife is widely regarded as practically a social disease, Bombeck has become a pop phenomenon." And Seymour Rothman states in the Toledo *Blade,* "Erma's role in the column is that of a wife and mother who long ago has conceded defeat, but can't find anyone to surrender to."

Bombeck was drawn to the field of journalism at an early age. While attending high school, she worked part time as a copy girl for the Dayton *Journal Herald* and during college was employed as a reporter. After graduating from the University of Dayton with a degree in English, Bombeck became a staff writer for the newspaper, eventually writing feature articles for the women's section. In 1953 Bombeck resigned from her position with the Dayton *Journal Herald* to start a family with her husband, Bill. Twelve years and three children later, Bombeck decided to return to journalism. As she explained in her book *If Life Is a Bowl of Cherries, What Am I Doing in the Pits?:* "I do not feel fulfilled cleaning chrome faucets with a toothbrush. It's my turn." Bombeck approached Ron Ginger, the editor of the *Kettering-Oakwood Times* (a local weekly newspaper), with her idea of writing a humorous column geared toward housewives. Ginger hired Bombeck and set her pay at three dollars per column. Bombeck's column soon became popular and attracted the attention of Glenn Thompson, the editor of the Dayton *Journal Herald.* Thompson offered Bombeck a weekly salary of fifteen dollars to write three columns for his newspaper. Bombeck agreed to the offer. Sensing her potential, Thompson sent a sample of Bombeck's "At Wit's End" columns to the Newsday Syndicate suggesting they might be interested in syndicating the columns nationally. Newsday was impressed and signed Bombeck to a short-term contract. In 1967, with over sixty-five newspapers publishing her columns, Bombeck was offered a long-term contract with the Field Newspaper Syndicate, which she accepted.

Rothman reports that the president of the Field Newspaper Syndicate, Robert G. Cowles, once remarked: "We've been selling Erma as a women's page feature, but we find more and more papers running her in other sections. One has her on the comic page, a number on the feature pages. . . . They found out before we did that she isn't strictly for women." Her seventeen-year partnership with the Field Newspaper Syndicate proved profitable for Bombeck, with over nine hundred newspapers printing her column three times a week. According to a reviewer for *Time,* Bombeck's "enormous appeal contains no surprises. She has, as market researchers say, 'great demographics.' Her writing is aimed primarily at the millions of housewives whose world turns around car pools, P.T.A. meetings and Tupperware parties."

While she writes humorously about the average housewife's plight by using herself and her family as examples, Bombeck does not belittle the woman who chooses to stay at home. As she explains to an interviewer for *People:* "God knows I have laughed at her frustrations. I have dissected her and picked her apart. I have done everything to her you can imagine [over the] years. But she doesn't feel put down by it, she doesn't feel I am making fun of her, she is able to laugh at herself. If I get away with it, it's probably because I am basically one of them." Bombeck further explains to Peggy Rader of the *Akron Beacon Journal:* "My type of humor is almost pure identification. A housewife reads my column and says, 'But that's happened to ME! I know just what she's talking about!' You can't imagine what a great feeling that is for an American housewife. Basically women work alone when they're at home. They think no one is feeling what they are feeling, that no one understands their daily frustrations. But we do; we all do." Shah writes that "Bombeck still

prides herself on being 'just a housewife,' who really still does her own laundry." As Bombeck remarked to Shah, "I spend ninety per cent of my time living scripts and ten per cent writing them."

Lucille G. Crane feels that Bombeck helps her readers laugh at many of their problems. "Bombeck's humor is light, funny," Crane suggests in *Best Sellers.* "Household chores are always easier to do when done on her terms. Enjoyment is the key to her success, and most of her fans wish they could view life and its minor crises through her eyes. Common sense with humor is the Bombeck way." And *New York Times Book Review* critic Robert Lasson believes that women read Bombeck's books and columns because "women who inhabit the real world are told that they can achieve a fairy-tale existence simply by buying a certain vacuum cleaner or changing their brand of coffee. . . . They look around, these women, and something begins to dawn on them, 'Maybe I'm not the only one who isn't a [perfect] wife and mother.' " Bombeck's humor works, Lasson continues, "because it's not just wisecracks or one-liners or gags but marvelously comic insights that grow out of [her] life as organically as fungus forms between the bathroom tiles." Rothman writes that "being funny is a skill, but being funny the way Erma is elevates it to an art. Erma takes a sobering situation and laces it with funny lines to an acceptable philosophic conclusion. The philosophy generally is 'Learn to enjoy frustration.' "

Most of Bombeck's books are extensions of her columns. They are written to the same audience, about the same problems, with the same humor and insight that has endeared her to the readers of her columns. Richard R. Lingeman writes in the *New York Times Book Review* on *If Life Is a Bowl of Cherries, What Am I Doing in the Pits?:* "Her humor is precisely targeted on the large number of housewives in this country who share her experiences. Her style is a bit hectic and slapdash, sounding as though she scrawled the column on the back of a laundry list while stirring the evening's Hamburger Helper. It's the kind of style that is a half beat ahead of her readers, giving them a twitch of recognition and the feeling, 'I might have written that myself.' . . . Her humor is the coping kind—sarcastic shafts at fads and foibles." Although her first three books sold well, *The Grass Is Always Greener over the Septic Tank* sold over half a million copies in hardcover and stayed on the bestseller lists for over ten months. CBS-TV produced the book as a television movie with Carol Burnett and Charles Grodin in the lead roles. Bombeck's following three books, *If Life Is a Bowl of Cherries, What Am I Doing in the Pits?; Aunt Erma's Cope Book: How to Get from Monday to Friday. . . in Twelve Days;* and *Motherhood: The Second Oldest Profession,* also made the bestseller lists.

Bombeck's success may be traced to the affinity between Bombeck and many of the women who read and identify with her writings. As Lingeman observes: "One is left admiring Mrs. Bombeck for giving voice to a segment of the population that is not always heard from, but the trivia of whose lives may be, on the higher scale of things, as significant as anything that takes place in the male or sophisticated or urbane world. There is truth in the best of her humor, as well as sanity." But, as a *Newsweek* writer notes, Bombeck's humor appeals not only to suburban housewives: "Though her sensibility is strictly suburban, Bombeck manages to hit everybody's funny bone. [Once,] she was invited to speak to 3,500 farmers' wives in Kansas City. Fully 9,000 people turned up, and the crowd drew several hundred men as well. [And a] survey by the *Boston Globe* placed Bombeck high on the list of readers' favorites. Even a feminist like syndicated columnist Ellen Goodman admits to being a Bombeck fan." As Jane Holtz Kay states in *Ms.:* "Bombeck is not alone. She is out there where everybody's been headed this last quarter century: she is out there spinning her wheels to the suburbs in the greatest migration in American history. . . . And she is one of the few bards of this place and people."

BIOGRAPHICAL/CRITICAL SOURCES:

BOOKS

Authors in the News, Volume 1, Gale, 1976.
Best Sellers 89, Issue 4, Gale, 1989.
Bombeck, Erma, *If Life Is a Bowl of Cherries, What Am I Doing in the Pits?,* McGraw, 1978.

PERIODICALS

Akron Beacon Journal, May 9, 1975.
Blade (Toledo), February 16, 1975.
Best Sellers, November 15, 1971, September 1, 1973, January, 1977, July, 1978, December, 1979.
Chicago Tribune, October 5, 1989.
Christian Science Monitor, October 8, 1976.
Editor and Publisher, February 13, 1988.
Good Housekeeping, April, 1978.
Kirkus Reviews, April 1, 1978, September 1, 1979.
Library Journal, November 15, 1976, October 15, 1979.
Ms., June, 1977.
Newsweek, January 2, 1978.
New York Times Book Review, October 7, 1973, July 3, 1977, April 30, 1978, November 18, 1979, October 20, 1987.
People, May 22, 1978, May 12, 1980, November 9, 1981, February 13, 1984.
Publishers Weekly, July 19, 1971, June 11, 1973, March 13, 1978, September 10, 1978.
Time, April 13, 1970, May 29, 1978, July 2, 1984.
Tribune Books (Chicago), October 13, 1987, October 5, 1989.
WB, September-October, 1989.

*   *   *

BOND, Edward 1934-

PERSONAL: Born July 18, 1934, in London, England; married Elizabeth Pable, 1971. *Education:* Attended state schools in England until fifteen. *Politics:* Socialist. *Religion:* Atheist.

ADDRESSES: Agent—Margaret Ramsey Ltd., 14A Goodwin's Ct., St. Martin's Lane, London WC2N 4LL, England.

CAREER: Spent early years working in factories and offices; now full-time writer; member of the writers group of the Royal Court Theatre. *Military service:* British Army; served two years with the Infantry.

AWARDS, HONORS: George Devine Award, English Stage Society, 1968, for *Early Morning;* co-recipient, with Peter Barnes, of the John Whiting Playwrights Award, Arts Council, 1969, for *Narrow Road to the Deep North;* Best New Play awards, *Plays and Players,* 1976, for "The Fool," and 1985, for "The War Plays"; D.Lit., Yale University.

WRITINGS:

PLAYS

Saved (first produced on the West Royal Court Theatre, November, 1965; produced in New Haven, Conn., at Yale School of Drama Repertory Theatre, on a triple bill with plays by David Epstein and Anthony Scully, December, 1968; produced Off-Broadway at Chelsea Theater Center, October 28, 1970), Hill & Wang, 1966, Heinemann, 1984.
Early Morning (first produced on the West End at Royal Court Theatre, 1968; produced Off-Broadway at La Mama Exper-

imental Theatre Club, November, 1970), Calder & Boyars, 1968, Hill & Wang, 1969.
Narrow Road to the Deep North (written for the Peoples and Cities Conference in Coventry and first produced there at Belgrade Theatre, June, 1968; produced on the West End at Royal Court Theatre, February 19, 1969; produced in Boston at Charles Playhouse, 1969; produced on Broadway at Vivian Beaumont Theater, January, 1972), Methuen, 1968, Hill & Wang, 1969.
"Black Mass" (also see below), first produced in Sheffield, England, at Sheffield Playhouse, 1970.
The Pope's Wedding and Other Plays (includes "The Pope's Wedding," first produced on the West End at Royal Court Theatre, 1962; "Mr. Dog"; "The King with Golden Eyes"; and "Sharpeville Sequence"), Methuen, 1971.
Lear (first produced on the West End at Royal Court Theatre, September 21, 1971; produced in New Haven at Yale School of Drama Repertory Theatre, April, 1973), Hill & Wang, 1972, student edition with notes and commentary, Methuen, 1983.
The Sea (comedy; also see below; first produced on the West End at Royal Court Theatre, May 22, 1973), Hill & Wang, 1973.
Bingo: Scenes of Money and Death; and Passion (contains "Passion," first produced on the West End at Royal Court Theatre, 1971, produced in New Haven at Yale School of Drama Repertory Theatre, February 1, 1972; and "Bingo" [also see below], produced on the West End at Royal Court Theatre, August, 1974), Methuen, 1974.
Bingo [and] *The Sea,* Hill & Wang, 1975.
The Fool (also see below; first produced in London, 1975), Dramatic Club Publications (Chicago, Ill.), 1978.
(Author of libretto) "We Come to the River" (opera; also see below), music by Hans Werner Henze, (first produced in London at Covent Garden, July, 1976), published as *We Come to the River: Actions for Music,* Schott, 1976.
A-A-America! [and] *Stone* (two plays), Methuen, 1976, revised edition, Heinemann, 1982.
The Fool [and] *We Come to the River* (two plays), Eyre Methuen, 1976.
Plays, Methuen, 1977, published as *Plays One: Saved, Early Morning, The Pope's Wedding,* 1983.
Plays Two (includes "Lear," "The Sea," "Narrow Road to the Deep North," "Black Mass," and "Passion"), Methuen, 1978.
The Woman: Scenes of War and Freedom (first produced in London at National Theatre, 1978), Hill & Wang, 1979.
The Bundle: or, New Narrow Road to the Deep North (first produced in London by Royal Shakespearean Company, 1978; produced at Yale Repertory Theatre, 1979), Heinemann, 1978.
The Worlds, with The Activists Papers (two plays; includes "The Worlds," first produced by Newcastle University Theatre Society, 1979), Methuen, 1980.
(Translator) Frank Wedekind, *Spring Awakening,* Methuen, 1980.
Restoration [and] *The Cat* (includes "Restoration: A Pastoral," a musical, with music by Nick Bicat, first produced in London at the Royal Court Theatre, 1981; and "The Cat," libretto for opera with music by Henze, performed by Stuttgart Opera, 1983), Eyre Methuen, 1982, 2nd edition, Heinemann, 1982.
Summer (also see below; first produced in London at National Theatre, 1982; produced in New York at Manhattan Theatre Club, 1983), Methuen, 1982.
Summer [and] *Fables,* Methuen, 1983.

Derek and Choruses from after the Assassinations, Heinemann, 1984.

The War Plays; Part 1: Red, Black and Ignorant, Part 2: The Tin Can People, Part 3: Great Peace, Methuen, 1985, published in two volumes, Heinemann, 1985.

Human Cannon, Heinemann, 1985.

SCREENPLAYS

"Blow-Up" (based on a short story by Julio Cortazar), Premier Productions, 1969.

(With Clement Biddle-Wood and Mr. Schlondorff) "Michael Kohlhaus" (based on a novella by Heinrich Von Kleist), Columbia, 1969.

"Laughter in the Dark" (based on a novel by Vladimir Nabokov), Lopert, 1969.

"Walkabout" (based on a novel by James Vance Marshall), Twentieth Century-Fox, 1971.

(Author of additional dialogue) "Nicholas and Alexandria" (based on a book by Robert K. Massie), screenplay by James Goldman, Columbia, 1971.

OTHER

Theatre Poems and Songs, edited by Malcolm Hay and Philip Roberts, Methuen, 1978.

(With Douglas Corrance) *Glasgow,* Greene, 1983.

Bond: Poems, 1978 to 1985, Heinemann, 1988.

SIDELIGHTS: "In our decade," writes Marilyn Stasio, "the corruptive side effects of being civilized have intensified . . . boredom into a state of desperation. The result is violence—not raging, or even insane, violence, but pure violence clinically executed out of a kind of dispassionate curiosity." Edward Bond's play "Saved," Stasio believes, "might well be the most important dramatic delineation of the face of an age to emerge from England since John Osborne's *Look Back in Anger.*" For Bond, the violence of our times becomes "an act of examination," says Stasio, "inflicted without malice in order to study its effect—namely feeling, the element of human life most alien to this decade. Survival, even protest . . . Bond insists, is not only recognizing, but, in effect, embracing the existence of this violence. And one must, he says, acknowledge that its emergence was inevitable in this age. This is the substance of this horrible, cruel, and brilliant play which has as its focal point the stoning to death of an infant by some aimless London hoodlums. But this play's real horrors lie in the facility with which the child's family, whose own lives are based on violent relationships, accept the grisly deed as an organic element of their world. To be alive, then, is to feel. To feel *anything.* Thus, inflicting violence becomes an affirmation of life." The violence in "Saved" and "Early Morning" resulted in both plays being banned by the Lord Chamberlain; it was not until the fall of 1968, when official censorship of the English stage was ended, that Bond could even hope to produce his plays without difficulty.

Bond says that the reception of "Saved" outraged him. During an interview with Ronald Bryden, Bond declared: "It didn't knock me out exactly, it surprised me. I was a very simple person. I'd spent a long time learning to write, and do it well. I knew I'd finally done it—written just what I intended; got it right. And suddenly all these people who set themselves up as custodians of art, of artistic opinion, were sounding off in every direction except that. They weren't involved with art at all. . . . But it didn't affect me as a writer. Art is the most private of all activities, and the theatre is the most private of all arts."

John Russell Taylor notes that "in the 'Author's Note' [Bond] wrote for the published text of *Saved* . . . he offers what may

well be the key to most of the difficulties people . . . have often found in his work. 'Like most people,' he says, 'I am a pessimist by experience, but an optimist by nature, and I have no doubt that I shall go on being true to my nature. Experience is depressing, and it would be a mistake to be willing to learn from it.' " Taylor believes that in Bond's early plays "some sort of hope gleams through, if only because some sort of basic goodness survives indestructibly the horrors of experience and steadfastly refuses to learn from them."

Commenting on Bond's career, Bryden states: "Serious critics generally agree that he is the foremost of the new wave of dramatists who followed Osborne and his contemporaries in the 1960s. When his play 'Saved' was staged at the Court in 1965, it was more or less howled down for its violence. . . . But when it was revived in 1969, in repertory with Bond's subsequent plays 'Early Morning' and 'Narrow Road to the Deep North,' recantations poured in and the consensus was that a formidable talent had been savagely misjudged. The conversion of the critics was completed by the arrival of Bond's 'Lear' in 1971."

"Taking Shakespeare's play as a starting point, and perhaps also as an inspiration, Edward Bond has written a modern tragedy in his 'Lear,' " writes R. B. Marriott. "It is Lear in a wildly savage but modern world of power used insanely; of everyone resorting to force, cruelty and repression for the ends of a cause or for personal ends." Marriott continues, "Passion, coming from deep and genuine concern, gives the play its great impact; the fine skill of the playwright makes it a dramatic experience." A *Variety* reviewer, on the other hand, believes that "the play's psychopathy of stupidity and violence is repeated and repeated. There is apostrophized humor, but it's an otherwise unremittingly downbeat piece, of longish (almost three hours) and grueling evening of allegorical drama." Walter Kerr concurs: "There had been no controlling principle to account for the deeds being done, nothing intimately human or narratively necessary to engage us. We were only being invited to watch violence as violence, to accept it as the occasion's *sole* activity. . . . Mr. Bond, whose earlier 'Saved' was a relatively realistic play . . . has here become so obsessed with the idea of violence that he has neglected to give it plausible, or even theatrically coherent, organization."

"The Sea," according to Marriott, "is Edward Bond's best play so far. It is not only larger in scope, at least in human terms, but more deeply affecting and dramatically powerful than any other. . . . [The play] is very moving, full of absorbing things, and has two superb scenes of comedy blended with pathos and horror." Clive Barnes, reviewing "Bingo," writes: "Mr. Bond's new play is about the death of Shakespeare. It is his most direct play since 'Saved,' avoiding both absurdism and symbolism, and dealing with a man at the point of death, literally a man at point of accounting. The man happens to be William Shakespeare, and Mr Bond is artistically honest with the basic facts known of the poet's life and character. But it could almost be any man of feeling, nervously aware of love and hate, and significance and insignificance of worldly goods, coming naked and fearful to that final summing up that is the only thing certain after birth."

Concerning his formal schooling, Bond said that he is glad that his education was "deplorable." "It was marvellous for me. [Schools make] children . . . competitive, aggressive. People are not born violent by nature. Society . . . makes men animals in order to control them. I write because I want to change the structure of society. I think that society as it exists is primitive, dangerous and corrupt—that it destroys people. . . . We've got to get men out of their uniforms, from behind their desks, away from their flagpoles. . . . I've no Utopia, no image of the society I want to see emerge. It would simply be people being themselves, happy in their own way—what could be more natural?"

BIOGRAPHICAL/CRITICAL SOURCES:

BOOKS

Bond, Edward, *Saved,* Hill & Wang, 1966, Heinemann, 1984.
Contemporary Literary Criticism, Gale, Volume 4, 1975, Volume 6, 1976, Volume 13, 1980, Volume 23, 1983.
Coult, Tony, *The Plays of Edward Bond,* Methuen, 1978.
Dictionary of Literary Biography, Volume 13: *British Dramatists since World War II,* Gale, 1982.
Edward Bond: A Companion to the Plays, TQ Publications, 1978.

PERIODICALS

Choice, September, 1967.
Christian Science Monitor, July 6, 1968.
Cue, December 14, 1968.
Listener, April 18, 1968, August 8, 1968, June 18, 1970.
Observer Review, November 9, 1969.
Plays & Players, August, 1970.
Prompt, Number 13, 1969.
Nation, November 16, 1970.
Newsweek, November 9, 1970.
New York, November 9, 1970.
New York Times, November 26, 1970, October 24, 1971, January 7, 1972, April 29, 1973, May 13, 1973, August 19, 1974, August 25, 1974.
Show Business, January 4, 1969.
Stage, October 7, 1971, May 31, 1973.
Time, November 9, 1970, January 17, 1972.
Times (London), July 27, 1985.
Variety, December 18, 1968, January 29, 1969, March 12, 1969, November 18, 1970, October 20, 1971, March 1, 1972, July 4, 1973.
Washington Post, January 24, 1986.

*   *   *

BONNEFOY, Yves   1923-

PERSONAL: Born July 24, 1923, in Tours, France; son of Elie and Helene (Maury) Bonnefoy; married Lucille Vine, 1968; children: one daughter. *Education:* University of Paris, degree in philosophy.

ADDRESSES: Office—College de France, 11 Place Marcelin-Berthelor, 75005 Paris, France.

CAREER: Writer. College de France, Paris, France, professor, 1981—. Has taught literature at various universities, including Brandeis, 1962-64, Johns Hopkins, Princeton, Yale, and Geneva. Co-founder of *L'ephemere* (art and literature journal), 1967.

AWARDS, HONORS: Prix de l' Express, for *Hier regnant desert,* and *L'Improbable,* 1958; Cecil Hemly Award, 1967, for *On the Motion and Immobility of Douve;* Prix des Critiques, 1971; Prix Montaigne, 1978; named honorary fellow, Modern Language Association, 1981; Grand Prix de Loesie, Academie Francaise, 1981; Grand Prix Societe des bens de Lettres, 1987; Bennett Award, *Hudson Review,* 1988.

WRITINGS:

POEMS

Din mouvement et de l'immobilite de Douve, Mercure de France (Paris), 1953, translation by Galway Kinnell published as

On the Motion and Immobility of Douve, Ohio University Press, 1968.
Hier regnant desert (title means "In Yesterday's Desert Realm") Mercure de France, 1958.
Anti-Platon (title means "Against Plato"), Maeght (Paris), 1962.
Pierre ecrite, Mercure de France, 1965, bilingual edition with translation by Susanna Lang published as *Pierre ecrite-Words in Stone,* University of Massachusetts Press, 1976.
Selected Poems, translation by Anthony Rudolf, J. Cape, 1968.
Dans le leurre din seuil (title means "In the Lure of the Threshold"), Mercure de France, 1975.
Poemes, Mercure de France, 1978, translation by Richard Pevear published as *Poems, 1959-1975,* Random House, 1985.
The Origin of Language, G. Nama (New York), 1980.
Things Dying, Things Newborn, translation by Anthony Rudolf, Menard Press, 1986.

CRITICISM

Peintures murales de la France gothique (title means "Mural Paintings of Gothic France"), P. Hartmann (Paris), 1954.
L'Improbable (title means "The Improbable"), Mercure de France, 1959.
La Seconde Simplicite (title means "The Second Simplicity"), Mercure de France, 1961.
Rimbaud par lui-meme, Seuil, 1961, translation by Paul Schmidt published as *Rimbaud,* Harper, 1973.
Miro, La Bibliotheque des arts (Paris), 1964, translation by Judith Landry published as *Miro,* Viking, 1967.
Un revefait a Mantoue (title means "A Dream Dreamt in Mantoue"), Mercure de France, 1967.
La Poesie francaise et le principe d'identite (title means "French Poetry and the Principle of Identity"), Maeght, 1967.
Rome 1630: l'horizon din premier baroque (title means "Rome 1630: Early Baroque and Its Context"). Flammarion, 1970.
L'arrierepays (title means "The Hinterland"), Editions d'Art Albert Skira (Geneva), 1972.
(With Jacques Thuillier) *Garache,* Maeght, 1975.
L'Ordalie (title means "The Ordeal"), Maeght, 1975.
Terre seconde (title means "The Second World"), Association des Amis de Ratilly, 1976.
Rue traversiere (title means "The Cross Street"), Mercure de France, 1977.
Le Nuage rouge (title means "The Red Cloud"), Mercure de France, 1977.
Entretiens sur la poesie, La Baconniere, 1980.
La Presence et l'Image, Mercure de France, 1983.
The Act and the Place of Poetry: Selected Essays, University of Chicago Press, 1989.

TRANSLATOR

Leonora Carrington, *Une chemise de nuit de flanelle,* Les Pas perdus, 1951.
William Shakespeare, *Henri IV, Jules Cesar, Hamlet, Le Conte d'hiver, Venus et Adonis,* [and] *Le Viol de Lucrece* (also see below), Club Francais du Livre, 1957-60.
Shakespeare, *Jules Cesar,* Mercure de France, 1960.
Shakespeare, *Hamlet* (also see below), Mercure de France, 1962.
Shakespeare, *Le Roi Lear* (also see below), Mercure de France, 1965.
Shakespeare, *Romeo et Juliette,* Mercure de France, 1968.
Shakespeare, *Hamlet* [and] *Le Roi Lear,* Gallimard, 1978.
Shakespeare, *Macbeth,* Mercure de France, 1983.

SIDELIGHTS: In a review of Galway Kinnell's translation of *Din mouvement et de l'immobilite de Douve* in *Poetry,* Ralph J. Mills, Jr. pointed out that "by general critical consensus Yves

Bonnefoy is one of the finest poets to emerge in France since World War II." Bonnefoy has been placed in the tradition of Baudelaire, Rimbaud, and Jouve, and has been associated as well with the post-war surrealists. A metaphysical poet, he is distinguished, according to critic Michael Hamburger, by the conviction that "poetry has to do with truth and with salvation."

Bonnefoy's first volume of poetry established his reputation. A sequence of short poems separated into several sections, *Douve* is a difficult work, described by Mills as "reminiscent in part of the hermetic qualities of Mallarme and Valery and others whose technique involves obliquity, spiritual plenitude and vacancy." "Douve" is a female principle, which Bonnefoy himself defined as the relationship between consciousness and nothingness, and she variously represents earth, woman, love, and poetry. The progress of the poem portrays changing moods and metaphysical transformations and sets up dialectics such as mind/spirit, hope/despair, and life/death.

The difficulty of Bonnefoy's poetry arises in part from its remoteness from modern English and American poetry. Hamburger explained: "Its language functions in a radically different way, its movement proceeds in a radically different direction; and above all it assumes an order of pure ideas, or of pure subjectivity, that can be evoked poetically with a minimum of sensuous substantiation." These distinctions are reinforced by what Bonnefoy calls the "semitransparency" of French words, as contrasted with the earthy opaqueness of English. It is his view that the very language in which he writes is fraught with dangers and deficiencies for the poet, against which he must constantly struggle to sustain a "passionate intensity."

Bonnefoy is a respected critic and scholar, as well as a poet, and has written essays on literature, art, and architecture. His translations of Shakespeare are considered to be among the best in French.

BIOGRAPHICAL/CRITICAL SOURCES:

BOOKS

Caws, Mary Anne, *Yves Bonnefoy,* Twayne, 1984.
Contemporary Literary Criticism, Gale, Volume 9, 1978, Volume 15, 1980.
Gavronsky, Serge, *Poems and Texts,* October House, 1969.
Hamburger, Michael, *The Truth of Poetry,* Harcourt, 1970.
Kostelanetz, Richard, editor, *Yale French Studies 21,* 1958.
Naughton, John T., *The Poetics of Yves Bonnefoy,* University of Chicago Press, 1984.
On Contemporary Literature, Avon, 1964.
Thelot, Jerome, *Poetique d'Yves Bonnefoy,* Droz (Geneva), 1983.

PERIODICALS

Poetry, January, 1969, June 1976.
World Literature Today, summer, 1979.

* * *

BONTEMPS, Arna(ud Wendell) 1902-1973

PERSONAL: Born October 13, 1902, in Alexandria, La.; died of a heart attack, June 4, 1973, in Nashville, Tenn.; son of Paul Bismark (a brick mason) and Maria Caroline (a teacher; maiden name, Pembrooke) Bontemps; married Alberta Johnson, August 26, 1926; children: Joan Marie Bontemps Williams, Paul Bismark, Poppy Alberta Bontemps Booker, Camille Ruby Bontemps Graves, Constance Rebecca Bontemps Thomas, Arna Alexander. *Education:* Pacific Union College, B.A., 1923; University of Chicago, M.A., 1943.

ADDRESSES: Home—3506 Geneva Cir., Nashville, Tenn. 37209. *Office*—Fisk University, Nashville, Tenn. 37203.

CAREER: Teacher in New York, N.Y., Huntsville, Ala., and Chicago, Ill., 1923-38; Fisk University, Nashville, Tenn., librarian, 1943-65; University of Illinois at Chicago Circle, professor, 1966-69; Yale University, New Haven, Conn., visiting professor and curator of James Weldon Johnson Collection, 1969; Fisk University, writer in residence, 1970-73. Member of Metropolitan Nashville Board of Education.

MEMBER: National Association for the Advancement of Colored People, P.E.N., American Library Association, Dramatists Guild, Sigma Pi Phi, Omega Psi Phi.

AWARDS, HONORS: Poetry prize from *Crisis* magazine, 1926; Alexander Pushkin poetry prizes, 1926 and 1927; short story prize from *Opportunity,* 1932; Julius Rosenwald fellowships, 1938-39 and 1942-43; Guggenheim fellowship for creative writing, 1949-50; Jane Addams Children's Book Award, 1956, for *Story of the Negro;* Dow Award from Society of Midland Authors, 1967, for *Anyplace But Here;* L.H.D. from Morgan State College, 1969.

WRITINGS:

God Sends Sunday (novel), Harcourt, 1931, reprinted, AMS Press, 1972.
(With Langston Hughes) *Popo and Fifina: Children of Haiti* (juvenile), Macmillan, 1932.
You Can't Pet a Possum, Morrow, 1934.
Black Thunder (historical novel), Macmillan, 1936, reprinted with new introduction by author, Beacon Press, 1968.
Sad Faced Boy (juvenile), Houghton, 1937.
Drums at Dusk (novel), Macmillan, 1939.
(Compiler) *Golden Slippers: An Anthology of Negro Poetry for Young Readers,* Harper, 1941.
(Editor) W. C. Handy, *Father of the Blues: An Autobiography,* Macmillan, 1941, reprinted, Collier, 1970, reprinted, Da Capo Press, 1985.
(With Jack Conroy) *The Fast Sooner Hound* (juvenile), Houghton, 1942.
(With Conroy) *They Seek a City* (history), Doubleday, 1945, revised edition published as *Anyplace But Here,* Hill & Wang, 1966.
We Have Tomorrow (history), Houghton, 1945.
(With Conroy) *Slappy Hooper, the Wonderful Sign Painter* (juvenile), Houghton, 1946.
(With Countee Cullen) "St. Louis Woman" (play; adapted from Bontemps's novel *God Sends Sunday*), first produced on Broadway at Martin Beck Theatre, March 30, 1946; published in *Black Theatre,* edited by Lindsay Patterson, Dodd, 1971.
Story of the Negro, Knopf, 1948, 5th edition, 1969.
(Editor with Hughes) *The Poetry of the Negro: 1746-1949,* Doubleday, 1949, revised edition published as *The Poetry of the Negro: 1746-1970,* 1970.
"Free and Easy" (play), first produced in Amsterdam at Theatre Carre, December 15, 1949.
George Washington Carver, Row, Peterson, 1950.
(With Conroy) *Sam Patch, the High, Wide and Handsome Jumper* (juvenile), Houghton, 1951.
Chariot in the Sky: A Story of the Jubilee Singers (juvenile), Winston, 1951, new edition, Holt, 1971.
The Story of George Washington Carver (juvenile biography), Grosset, 1954.
Lonesome Boy (juvenile), Houghton, 1955.

(Editor with Hughes) *The Book of Negro Folklore,* Dodd, 1958, 2nd edition, 1983.

Frederick Douglass: Slave, Fighter, Freeman, Knopf, 1958.

(Author of introduction) James Weldon Johnson, *The Autobiography of an Ex-Colored Man,* Hill & Wang, 1960.

One Hundred Years of Negro Freedom (history), Dodd, 1961, reprinted, Greenwood Press, 1980.

(Editor) *American Negro Poetry,* Hill & Wang, 1963, revised edition, 1974.

Personals, Paul Bremen, 1963, 2nd edition, 1973.

Famous Negro Athletes (juvenile), Dodd, 1964.

(With Hughes) *I Too Sing America,* Verlag Lamber Lensing, 1964.

(Editor with others) *American Negro Heritage,* Century Schoolbooks Press, 1965.

(Contributor) Herbert Hill, editor, *Anger, and Beyond,* Harper, 1966.

(Compiler and author of introduction) *Great Slave Narratives,* Beacon Press, 1969.

(Author of introduction) Langston Hughes, *Don't You Turn Back: Poems,* Knopf, 1969.

(Compiler) *Hold Fast to Dreams: Poems Old and New,* Follett, 1969.

Mr. Kelso's Lion, Lippincott, 1970.

Free at Last: The Life of Frederick Douglass, Dodd, 1971.

(Editor with others) *Five Black Lives: The Autobiographies of Venture Smith, James Mars, William Grimes, G. W. Offley, and James L. Smith,* Wesleyan University Press, 1971.

Young Booker: Booker T. Washington's Early Days, Dodd, 1972.

The Harlem Renaissance Remembered: Essays Edited with a Commentary by Arna Bontemps, Dodd, 1972.

The Old South: "A Summer Tragedy" and Other Stories of the Thirties, Dodd, 1973.

Arna Bontemps-Langston Hughes Letters, 1925-1967, edited by Charles H. Nichols, Dodd, 1980.

Author of plays "Creole" and "Careless Love." Fiction represented in numerous anthologies, including *Grandma Moses' Story Book,* Random House, 1961. Contributor to periodicals, including *Crisis, Ebony, Harper's,* and *Saturday Review.*

SIDELIGHTS: Arna Bontemps, who was born in Louisiana and raised in California, returned to the South to take the post of librarian at Fisk University and "to write something about the changes I have seen in my lifetime, and about the Negro's awakening and regeneration. That is my theme, and this is where the main action is." For Bontemps, the resolution of American racism should not result in the superimposition of black people on white culture; rather, the "shedding of . . . Negroness is not only impossible but unthinkable. . . . The Southern Negro's link with his past seems to me worth preserving. His greater pride in being himself, I would say, is all to the good, and I think I detect a growing nostalgia for these virtues."

Jonathan Yardley found this nostalgia in Bontemps's book *The Old South.* He commented that the fourteen stories in this book "occupy a territory somewhere between fiction and personal reminiscence. They are low-key, informal and chatty, but possessed of more depth than one initially realizes. Most of them are set in the Depression which was an especially bad time for Southern blacks, yet their mood is neither despairing nor bitter. Rather, Bontemps writes nostalgically about boyhood in the rural South. . . . There are, to be sure, depictions of the terror that could strike the lives of smalltown blacks in the 1930s, but overall the stories convey a genuine love for the South, its people and its land."

In a memorial essay, Virginia Lacy Jones commented on Bontemps's role in American literature. She wrote that his death "marked the end of a brilliant career of an editor, writer, librarian, literary critic, and teacher. He began writing in the early 1920s during the epoch in black literary production known as the Harlem Renaissance, at which time he was closely associated with black poets Langston Hughes, Countee Cullen, James Weldon Johnson, Claude McKay, Sterling Brown, and others, as well as with Charles Johnson, the sociologist, Alain Locke, the prominent cultural historian of the period, and Arthur Schomburg, the famous collector of Negro literature and history. As one of the last survivors of this august group of black writers and artists, he was in constant demand to write and speak. . . . After having produced more than 25 books, . . . Arna Bontemps became a literary critic of considerable stature. His critical insights have been and will continue to be invaluable in the development of understanding and appreciation of black literature and history."

AVOCATIONAL INTERESTS: Literature, theatre, and sports.

BIOGRAPHICAL/CRITICAL SOURCES:

BOOKS

Baker, Houston A., Jr., *Black Literature in America,* McGraw, 1971.

Bone, Robert A., *The Negro Novel in America,* Yale University Press, 1965.

Contemporary Literary Criticism, Gale, Volume 1, 1973, Volume 18, 1981.

Dictionary of Literary Biography, Gale, Volume 48: *American Poets, 1880-1945,* Second Series, 1986, Volume 51: *Afro-American Writers From the Harlem Renaissance to 1940,* 1987.

Nichols, Charles H., editor, *Arna Bontemps-Langston Hughes Letters, 1925-1967,* Dodd, 1980.

PERIODICALS

Black World, September, 1973.
Harper's, April, 1965.
Library Journal, July, 1973.
National Review, September 15, 1972.
Negro Digest, September, 1963, August, 1967.
New Republic, November 4, 1972, January 14, 1974.
New York Times Book Review, December 23, 1973.
Washington Post Book World, September 7, 1969.

*   *   *

BORGES, Jorge Luis   1899-1986
(F[rancisco] Bustos; joint pseudonyms: H[onorio] Bustos Domecq, B. Lynch Davis, B. Suarez Lynch)

PERSONAL: Born August 24, 1899, in Buenos Aires, Argentina; died June 14, 1986, in Geneva, Switzerland, of liver cancer; buried in Plainpalais, Geneva, Switzerland; son of Jorge Guillermo Borges (a lawyer, teacher, and writer) and Leonor Acevedo Suarez (a translator); married Elsa Astete Millan, September 21, 1967 (divorced, 1970); married Maria Kodama, April 26, 1986. *Education:* Attended College Calvin, Geneva, Switzerland, 1914-18.

ADDRESSES: Home—Geneva, Switzerland.

CAREER: Writer. Miguel Cane branch library, Buenos Aires, Argentina, municipal librarian, 1937-46; teacher of English literature at several private institutions and lecturer in Argentina and

Uruguay, 1946-55; National Library, Buenos Aires, director, 1955-73; University of Buenos Aires, Buenos Aires, professor of English and U.S. literature, beginning 1956. Visiting professor or guest lecturer at numerous universities in the United States and throughout the world, including University of Texas, 1961-62, University of Oklahoma, 1969, University of New Hampshire, 1972, and Dickinson College, 1983; Charles Eliot Norton Professor of Poetry, Harvard University, 1967-68.

MEMBER: Argentine Academy of Letters, Argentine Writers Society (president, 1950-53), Modern Language Association of America (honorary fellow, 1961-86), American Association of Teachers of Spanish and Portuguese (honorary fellow, 1965-86).

AWARDS, HONORS: Buenos Aires Municipal Literary Prize, 1928, for *El idioma de los argentinos;* Gran Premio de Honor from Argentine Writers Society, 1945, for *Ficciones, 1935-1944;* Gran Premio Nacional de la Literatura (Argentina), 1957, for *El Aleph;* Prix Formentor from International Congress of Publishers (shared with Samuel Beckett), 1961; Commandeur de l'Ordre des Lettres et des Arts (France), 1962; Ingram Merrill Foundation Award, 1966; Matarazzo Sobrinho Inter-American Literary Prize from Bienal Foundation, 1970; nominated for Neustadt International Prize for Literature, *World Literature Today* and University of Oklahoma, 1970, 1984, and 1986; Jerusalem Prize, 1971; Alfonso Reyes Prize (Mexico), 1973; Gran Cruz del Orden al merito Bernando O'Higgins from Government of Chile, 1976; Gold Medal from French Academy, Order of Merit from Federal Republic of Germany, and Icelandic Falcon Cross, all 1979; Miguel de Cervantes Award (Spain) and Balzan Prize (Italy), both 1980; Ollin Yoliztli Prize (Mexico), 1981; T. S. Eliot Award for Creative Writing from Ingersoll Foundation and Rockford Institute, 1983; Gold Medal of Menendez Pelayo University (Spain), La Gran Cruz de la Orden Alfonso X, el Sabio (Spain), and Legion d'Honneur (France), all 1983; Knight of the British Empire. Recipient of honorary degrees from numerous colleges and universities, including University of Cuyo (Argentina), 1956, University of the Andes (Colombia), 1963, Oxford University, 1970, University of Jerusalem, 1971, Columbia University, 1971, and Michigan State University, 1972.

WRITINGS:

POETRY

Fervor de Buenos Aires (title means "Passion for Buenos Aires"), Serantes (Buenos Aires), 1923, revised edition, Emece, 1969.

Luna de enfrente (title means "Moon across the Way"), Proa (Buenos Aires), 1925.

Cuaderno San Martin (title means "San Martin Copybook"), Proa, 1929.

Poemas, 1923-1943, Losada, 1943, 3rd enlarged edition published as *Obra poetica, 1923-1964,* Emece, 1964, translation published as *Selected Poems, 1923-1967* (bilingual edition; also includes prose), edited, with an introduction and notes, by Norman Thomas di Giovanni, Delacorte, 1972.

Seis poemas escandinavos (title means "Six Scandinavian Poems"), privately printed, 1966.

Siete poemas (title means "Seven Poems"), privately printed, 1967.

El otro, el mismo (title means "The Other, the Same"), Emece, 1969.

Elogio de la sombra, Emece, 1969, translation by di Giovanni published as *In Praise of Darkness* (bilingual edition), Dutton, 1974.

El oro de los tigres (also see below; title means "The Gold of Tigers"), Emece, 1972.

Siete poemas sajones/Seven Saxon Poems, Plain Wrapper Press, 1974.

La rosa profunda (also see below; title means "The Unending Rose"), Emece, 1975.

La moneda de hierro (title means "The Iron Coin"), Emece, 1976.

Historia de la noche (title means "History of Night"), Emece, 1977.

The Gold of Tigers: Selected Later Poems (contains translations of *El oro de los tigres* and *La rosa profunda*), translated by Alastair Reid, Dutton, 1977.

La cifra, Emece, 1981.

Also author of *Los conjurados* (title means "The Conspirators"), 1985.

ESSAYS

Inquisiciones (title means "Inquisitions"), Proa, 1925.

El tamano de mi esperanza (title means "The Measure of My Hope"), Proa, 1926.

El idioma de los argentinos (title means "The Language of the Argentines"), M. Gleizer (Buenos Aires), 1928, 3rd edition (includes three essays by Borges and three by Jose Edmundo Clemente), Emece, 1968.

Figari, privately printed, 1930.

Las Kennigar, Colombo (Buenos Aires), 1933.

Historia de la eternidad (title means "History of Eternity"), Viau y Zona (Buenos Aires), 1936, revised edition published as *Obras completas,* Volume 1, Emece, 1953, reprinted, 1978.

Nueva refutacion del tiempo (title means "New Refutation of Time"), Oportet y Haereses, 1947.

Aspectos de la literatura gauchesca, Numero (Montevideo), 1950.

(With Delia Ingenieros) *Antiguas literaturas germanicas,* Fondo de Cultura Economica (Mexico), 1951, revised edition with Maria Esther Vazquez published as *Literaturas germanicas medievales,* Falbo, 1966, reprinted, Emece, 1978.

Otras inquisiciones, Sur (Buenos Aires), 1952, published as *Obras completas,* Volume 8, Emece, 1960, translation by Ruth L. C. Simms published as *Other Inquisitions, 1937-1952,* University of Texas Press, 1964.

(With Margarita Guerrero) *El "Martin Fierro,"* Columba, 1953, reprinted, Emece, 1979.

(With Bettina Edelberg) *Leopoldo Lugones,* Troquel (Buenos Aires), 1955.

(With Guerrero) *Manual de zoologia fantastica,* Fondo de Cultura Economica, 1957, translation published as *The Imaginary Zoo,* University of California Press, 1969, revised Spanish edition with Guerrero published as *El libro de los seres imaginarios,* Kier (Buenos Aires), 1967, translation and revision by di Giovanni and Borges published as *The Book of Imaginary Beings,* Dutton, 1969.

La poesia gauchesca (title means "Gaucho Poetry"), Centro de Estudios Brasileiros, 1960.

(With Vazquez) *Introduccion a la literatura inglesa,* Columba, 1965, translation by L. Clark Keating and Robert O. Evans published as *An Introduction to English Literature,* University Press of Kentucky, 1974.

(With Esther Zemborain de Torres) *Introduccion a la literatura norteamericana,* Columba, 1967, translation by Keating and Evans published as *An Introduction to American Literature,* University Press of Kentucky, 1971.

(With Alicia Jurado) *¿Que es el budismo?* (title means, "What Is Buddhism?"), Columba, 1976.

Nuevos ensayos dantescos (title means "New Dante Essays,") Espasa-Calpe, 1982.

SHORT STORIES

Historia universal de la infamia, Tor (Buenos Aires), 1935, revised edition published as *Obras completas,* Volume 3, Emece, 1964, translation by di Giovanni published as *A Universal History of Infamy,* Dutton, 1972.

El jardin de senderos que se bifurcan (also see below; title means "Garden of the Forking Paths"), Sur, 1941.

(With Adolfo Bioy Casares, under joint pseudonym H. Bustos Domecq) *Seis problemas para Isidro Parodi,* Sur, 1942, translation by di Giovanni published under authors' real names as *Six Problems for Don Isidro Parodi,* Dutton, 1983.

Ficciones, 1935-1944 (includes *El jardin de senderos que se bifurcan*), Sur, 1944, revised edition published as *Obras completas,* Volume 5, Emece, 1956, reprinted, with English introduction and notes by Gordon Brotherson and Peter Hulme, Harrap, 1976, translation by Anthony Kerrigan and others published as *Ficciones,* edited and with an introduction by Kerrigan, Grove, 1962 (published in England as *Fictions,* John Calder, 1965), reprinted, Limited Editions Club (New York), 1984.

(With Bioy Casares, under joint pseudonym H. Bustos Domecq) *Dos fantasias memorables,* Oportet & Haereses, 1946, reprinted under authors' real names with notes and bibliography by Horacio Jorge Becco, Edicom (Buenos Aires), 1971.

El Aleph, Losada, 1949, revised edition, 1952, published as *Obras completas,* Volume 7, Emece, 1956, translation and revision by di Giovanni in collaboration with Borges published as *The Aleph and Other Stories, 1933-1969,* Dutton, 1970.

(With Luisa Mercedes Levinson) *La hermana de Eloisa* (title means "Eloisa's Sister"), Ene (Buenos Aires), 1955.

(With Bioy Casares) *Cronicas de Bustos Domecq,* Losada, 1967, translation by di Giovanni published as *Chronicles of Bustos Domecq,* Dutton, 1976.

El informe de Brodie, Emece, 1970, translation by di Giovanni in collaboration with Borges published as *Dr. Brodie's Report,* Dutton, 1971.

El matrero, Edicom, 1970.

El congreso, El Archibrazo, 1971, translation by di Giovanni in collaboration with Borges published as *The Congress* (also see below), Enitharmon Press, 1974, translation by Alberto Manguel published as *The Congress of the World,* F. M. Ricci (Milan), 1981.

El libro de arena, Emece, 1975, translation by di Giovanni published with "The Congress" as *The Book of Sand,* Dutton, 1977.

(With Bioy Casares) *Nuevos cuentos de Bustos Domecq,* Libreria de la Cuidad, 1977.

Rosa y azul (contains "La rosa de Paracelso" and "Tigres azules"), Sedmay (Madrid), 1977.

Veinticinco agosto 1983 y otros cuentos de Jorges Luis Borges (includes interview with Borges), Siruela, 1983.

OMNIBUS VOLUMES

La muerte y la brujula (stories; title means "Death and the Compass"), Emece, 1951.

Obras completas, ten volumes, Emece, 1953-67, published as one volume, 1974.

Cuentos (title means "Stories"), Monticello College Press, 1958.

Antologia personal (prose and poetry), Sur, 1961, translation published as *A Personal Anthology,* edited and with foreword by Kerrigan, Grove Press, 1967.

Labyrinths: Selected Stories and Other Writings, edited by Donald A. Yates and James E. Irby, preface by Andre Maurois, New Directions, 1962, augmented edition, 1964, reprinted, Modern Library, 1983.

Nueva antologia personal, Emece, 1968.

Prologos (title means "Prologues"), Torres Aguero (Buenos Aires), 1975.

(With others) *Obras completas en colaboracion* (title means "Complete Works in Collaboration"), Emece, 1979.

Narraciones (stories), edited by Marcos Ricardo Bamatan, Catedra, 1980.

Borges: A Reader (prose and poetry), edited by Emir Rodriguez Monegal and Reid, Dutton, 1981.

Ficcionario: Una antologia de sus textos, edited by Rodriguez Monegal, Fondo de Cultura Economica, 1985.

Textos cautivos: Ensayos y resenas en "El Hogar" (1936-1939) (title means "Captured Texts: Essays and Reviews in 'El Hogar' [1936-1939]"), edited by Rodriguez Monegal and Enrique Sacerio-Gari, Tusquets, 1986.

El aleph borgiano (chiefly book reviews which appeared in journals, 1922-84), edited by Juan Gustavo Cobo Borda and Martha Kovasics de Cubides, Biblioteca Luis-Angel Arango (Bogota), 1987.

Biblioteca personal: Prologos, Alianza, 1988.

OTHER

(Author of afterword) Ildefonso Pereda Valdes, *Antologia de la moderna poesia uruguaya,* El Ateneo (Buenos Aires), 1927.

Evaristo Carriego (biography), M. Gleizer, 1930, revised edition published as *Obras completas,* Volume 4, Emece (Buenos Aires), 1955, translation by di Giovanni published as *Evaristo Carriego: A Book about Old Time Buenos Aires,* Dutton, 1984.

(Translator) Virginia Woolf, *Orlando,* Sur, 1937.

(Editor with Pedro Henriquez Urena) *Antologia clasica de la literatura argentina* (title means "Anthology of Argentine Literature"), Kapelusz (Buenos Aires), 1937.

(Translator and author of prologue) Franz Kafka, *La metamorfosis,* [Buenos Aires], 1938, reprinted, Losada, 1976.

(Editor with Bioy Casares and Silvina Ocampo) *Antologia de la literatura fantastica* (title means "Anthology of Fantastic Literature"), with foreword by Bioy Casares, Sudamericana, 1940, enlarged edition with postscript by Bioy Casares, 1965, translation of revised version published as *The Book of Fantasy,* with introduction by Ursula K. Le Guin, Viking, 1988.

(Author of prologue) Bioy Casares, *La invencion de Morel,* Losada, 1940, reprinted, Alianza, 1981, translation by Simms published as *The Invention of Morel and Other Stories,* University of Texas Press, 1964, reprinted, 1985.

(Editor with Bioy Casares and Ocampo and author of prologue) *Antologia poetica argentina* (title means "Anthology of Argentine Poetry"), Sudamericana, 1941.

(Translator) Henri Michaux, *Un barbaro en Asia,* Sur, 1941.

(Compiler and translator with Bioy Casares) *Los mejores cuentos policiales* (title means "The Best Detective Stories"), Emece, 1943, reprinted, Alianza, 1972.

(Translator and author of prologue) Herman Melville, *Bartleby, el escribiente,* Emece, 1943, reprinted, Marymar (Buenos Aires), 1976.

(Editor with Silvina Bullrich) *El compadrito: Su destino, sus barrios, su musica* (title means "The Buenos Aires Hoodlum: His Destiny, His Neighborhoods, His Music"), Emece, 1945, 2nd edition, Fabril, 1968.

(With Bioy Casares, under joint pseudonym B. Suarez Lynch) *Un modelo para la muerte* (novel; title means "A Model for Death"), Oportet & Haereses, 1946.

(Compiler and translator with Bioy Casares) *Los mejores cuentos policiales: Segunda serie,* Emece, 1951.

(Editor and translator with Bioy Casares) *Cuentos breves y extraordinarios: Antologia,* Raigal (Buenos Aires), 1955, revised and enlarged edition, Losada, 1973, translation by Kerrigan published as *Extraordinary Tales,* Souvenir Press, 1973.

(With Bioy Casares) *Los orilleros* [and] *El paraiso de los creyentes* (screenplays; titles mean "The Hoodlums" and "The Believers' Paradise"; "Los orilleros" produced by Argentine director Ricardo Luna, 1975), Losada, 1955, reprinted, 1975.

(Editor and author of prologue, notes, and glossary with Bioy Casares) *Poesia gauchesca* (title means "Gaucho Poetry"), two volumes, Fondo de Cultura Economica, 1955.

(Translator) William Faulkner, *Las palmeras salvajes,* Sudamericana, 1956.

(Editor with Bioy Casares) *Libro del cielo y del infierno* (anthology; title means "Book of Heaven and Hell"), Sur, 1960, reprinted, 1975.

El hacedor (prose and poetry; Volume 9 of *Obras completas;* title means "The Maker"), Emece, 1960, translation by Mildred Boyer and Harold Morland published as *Dreamtigers,* University of Texas Press, 1964, reprinted, 1985.

(Editor and author of prologue) *Macedonio Fernandez,* Culturales Argentinas, Ministerio de Educacion y Justicia, 1961.

Para las seis cuerdas: Milongas (song lyrics; title means "For the Six Strings: Milongas"), Emece, 1965.

Dialogo con Borges, edited by Victoria Ocampo, Sur, 1969.

(Translator, editor, and author of prologue) Walt Whitman, *Hojas de hierba,* Juarez (Buenos Aires), 1969.

(Compiler and author of prologue) Evaristo Carriego, *Versos,* Universitaria de Buenos Aires, 1972.

Borges on Writing (lectures), edited by di Giovanni, Daniel Halpern, and Frank MacShane, Dutton, 1973.

(With Bioy Casares and Hugo Santiago) *Les Autres: Escenario original* (screenplay; produced in France and directed by Santiago, 1974), C. Bourgois (Paris), 1974.

(Author of prologue) Carlos Zubillaga, *Carlos Gardel,* Jucar (Madrid), 1976.

Cosmogonias (title means "Cosmogonies"), Libreria de la Ciudad, 1976.

Libro de suenos (transcripts of Borges's and others' dreams; title means "Book of Dreams"), Torres Aguero, 1976.

(Author of prologue) Santiago Dabove, *La muerte y su traje,* Calicanto, 1976.

Borges—Imagenes, memorias, dialogos, edited by Vazquez, Monte Avila, 1977.

Adrogue (prose and poetry), privately printed, 1977.

(Editor with Maria Kodama) *Breve antologia anglosajona,* Emece, 1979.

Borges oral (lectures), edited by Martin Mueller, Emece, 1979.

Siete noches (lectures), Fondo de Cultura Economica, 1980, translation by Weinberger published as *Seven Nights,* New Directions, 1984.

(Compiler) Paul Groussac, *Jorge Luis Borges selecciona lo mejor de Paul Groussac,* Fraterna (Buenos Aires), 1981.

(Compiler and author of prologue) Francisco de Quevedo, *Antologia poetica,* Alianza, 1982.

(Compiler and author of introduction) Leopoldo Lugones, *Antologia poetica,* Alianza, 1982.

(Compiler and author of prologue) Pedro Antonio de Alarcon, *El amigo de la muerte,* Siruela (Madrid), 1984.

(With Kodama) *Atlas* (prose and poetry), Sudamericana, 1984, translation by Kerrigan published as *Atlas,* Dutton, 1985.

En voz de Borges (interviews), Offset, 1986.

Libro de dialogos (interviews), edited by Osvaldo Ferrari, Sudamericana, 1986, published as *Dialogos ultimos,* 1987.

Editor with Bioy Casares of series of detective novels, "The Seventh Circle," for Emece, 1943-56. Contributor, under pseudonym F. Bustos, to *Critica* (Buenos Aires), 1933. Contributor, with Bioy Casares under joint pseudonym B. Lynch Davis, to *Los anales de Buenos Aires,* 1946-48. Founding editor of *Prisma* (mural magazine), 1921; founding editor of *Proa* (Buenos Aires literary revue), 1921 and, with Ricardo Guiraldes and Pablo Rojas Paz, 1924-26; literary editor of weekly arts supplement of *Critica,* beginning 1933; editor of biweekly "Foreign Books and Authors" section of *El Hogar* (magazine), 1936-39; co-editor with Bioy Casares of *Destiempo* (literary magazine), 1936; editor of *Los anales de Buenos Aires* (literary journal), 1946-48.

SIDELIGHTS: "Jorge Luis Borges [was] a great writer," noted French author Andre Maurois in his preface to the Argentine poet, essayist, and short story writer's *Labyrinths: Selected Stories and Other Writings,* "who . . . composed only little essays or short narratives. Yet they suffice for us to call him great because of their wonderful intelligence, their wealth of invention, and their tight, almost mathematical style. Argentine by birth and temperament, but nurtured on universal literature, Borges [had] no spiritual homeland."

Borges was nearly unknown in most of the world until 1961 when, in his early sixties, he was awarded the Prix Formentor—the International Publishers Prize—an honor he shared with Irish playwright Samuel Beckett. Before winning the award, according to Gene H. Bell-Villada in *Borges and His Fiction: A Guide to His Mind and Art,* "Borges had been writing in relative obscurity in Buenos Aires, his fiction and poetry read by his compatriots, who were slow in perceiving his worth or even knowing him." The award made Borges internationally famous: a collection of his short stories, *Ficciones,* was simultaneously published in six different countries, and he was invited by the University of Texas to come to the United States to lecture, the first of many international lecture tours.

Borges's international appeal was partly a result of his enormous erudition which is apparent in the multitude of literary allusions from cultures around the globe contained in his writing. "The work of Jorge Luis Borges," Anthony Kerrigan wrote in his introduction to the English translation of *Ficciones,* "is a species of international literary metaphor. He knowledgeably makes a transfer of inherited meanings from Spanish and English, French and German, and sums up a series of analogies, of confrontations, of appositions in other nations' literatures. His Argentinians act out Parisian dramas, his Central European Jews are wise in the ways of the Amazon, his Babylonians are fluent in the paradigms of Babel." In the *National Review* Peter Witonski commented: "Borges' grasp of world literature is one of the fundamental elements of his art."

The familiarity with world literature evident in Borges's work was initiated at an early age, nurtured by a love of reading. His paternal grandmother was English, and, consequently, since she lived with the Borgeses, English and Spanish were spoken in the family home. Jorge Guillermo Borges, Borges's father, had a large library of English and Spanish books in which his son, whose frail constitution made it impossible to participate in more strenuous activities, spent many hours. "If I were asked to name the chief event in my life," Borges stated in "An Autobiographical Essay" that originally appeared in the *New Yorker* and was later included in *The Aleph and Other Stories, 1933-1969,* "I should say my father's library."

Under his grandmother's tutelage, Borges learned to read English before he could read Spanish. Among the first books he read were works in English by Twain, Poe, Longfellow, Stevenson, and Wells. In Borges's autobiographical essay he recalled reading even the great Spanish masterpiece, Cervantes's *Don Quixote,* in English before reading it in Spanish. Borges's father encouraged writing as well as reading: Borges wrote his first story at age seven, and, at nine, saw his Spanish translation of Oscar Wilde's "The Happy Prince" published in a Buenos Aires newspaper. "From the time I was a boy . . . ," Borges noted in his autobiographical essay, "it was tacitly understood that I had to fulfill the literary destiny that circumstances had denied my father. This was something that was taken for granted. . . . I was expected to be a writer."

Borges became a writer whose works were compared to those of many others, Franz Kafka and James Joyce in particular, but whose style was unique. Critics were forced to coin a new word—Borgesian—to capture the magical world invented by the Argentine master. As Jaime Alazraki noted in *Jorge Luis Borges,* "As with Joyce, Kafka, or Faulkner, the name of Borges has become an accepted concept; his creations have generated a dimension that we designate 'Borgesian.'" And, in *Atlantic,* Keith Botsford declared: "Borges is . . . an international phenomenon, . . . a man of letters whose mode of writing and turn of mind are so distinctively his, yet so much a revealed part of our world, that 'Borgesian' has become as commonplace a neologism as the adjectives 'Sartrean' or 'Kafkacsque.'"

Perhaps the most profound consequence of this Borgesian style was the dramatic change it engendered in Latin American literature. "As [Mexican novelist] Carlos Fuentes remarked," according to Bell-Villada in *Nation,* "without Borges the modern Latin American novel simply would not exist." In *Jorge Luis Borges* George R. McMurray explained that "prior to 1950, the vast majority of Latin American novelists relied on traditional realism to depict life in their native lands and convey messages of social protest. Borges not only liberated Latin American literature from documentation but also restored imagination as a major fictional ingredient." Borges's greatest accomplishment, James E. Irby notes in his introductory remarks to *Labyrinths,* was to rise above the regionalism favored by the writers of his time and "to transmute his circumstances into an art as universal as the finest in Europe."

U.S. writers did not escape Borges's influence. "The impact of Borges on the United States writing scene," commented Bell-Villada, "may be almost as great as was his earlier influence on Latin America. The Argentine reawakened for us the possibilities of farfetched fancy, of formal exploration, of parody, intellectuality, and wit." Bell-Villada specifically noted Borges's presence in works by Robert Coover, Donald Barthelme, and John Gardner. Another important novelist, John Barth, confessed Borges's influence in his own novels. The critic concluded that Borges's work paved "the way for numerous literary trends on both American continents, determining the shape of much fiction to come. By rejecting realism and naturalism, he . . . opened up to our Northern writers a virgin field, led them to a wealth of new subjects and procedures."

The foundation of Borges's literary future was laid in 1914 when the Borgeses took an ill-timed trip to Europe. There, the outbreak of World War I stranded them temporarily in Switzerland,

where Borges studied French and Latin in school, taught himself German, and began reading the works of German philosophers and expressionist poets. He was also introduced to the poetry of Walt Whitman in German translation and soon began writing poetry imitative of Whitman's style. "For some time," Rodriguez Monegal wrote in *Borges: A Reader,* "the young man believed Whitman was poetry itself."

After the war the Borgeses settled in Spain for a few years. During this extended stay Borges published reviews, articles, and poetry and became associated with a group of avant-garde poets called Ultraists (named after the magazine, *Ultra,* to which they contributed). Upon Borges's return to Argentina, in 1921, he introduced the tenets of the movement—they believed, for example, in the supremacy of the metaphor—to the Argentine literary scene. His first collection of poems, *Fervor de Buenos Aires,* was written under the spell of this new poetic movement. Although in his autobiographical essay he expressed regret for his "early Ultraist excesses" and in later editions of *Fervor de Buenos Aires* eliminated more than a dozen poems from the text and considerably altered many of the remaining poems, Borges still saw some value in the work. In his autobiographical essay he noted, "I think I have never strayed beyond that book. I feel that all my subsequent writing has only developed themes first taken up there; I feel that all during my lifetime I have been rewriting that one book."

One poem from the volume, "El truco" (a card game), for example, seems to testify to the truth of Borges's statement. In the piece he introduced two themes that appear over and over again in his later writing: circular time and the idea that all people are but one person. "The permutations of the cards," Rodriguez Monegal observed in *Jorge Luis Borges: A Literary Biography,* "although innumerable in limited human experience, are not infinite: given enough time, they will come back again and again. Thus the cardplayers not only are repeating hands that have already come up in the past. In a sense, they are repeating the former players as well: they are the former players."

The decade from 1920 to 1930 was a period of intense activity for Borges. Not only did he publish seven books—four collections of essays and three of poetry—but he also founded three magazines and contributed to nearly a dozen other publications. But although these early works met with some success, it was his work in fiction that would bring him worldwide fame. As McMurray noted, Borges's "highly original short stories—the most important written during the 1940s and early 1950s— . . . made him one of the most widely acclaimed writers of our time."

Illusion is an important part of Borges's fictional world. In *Borges: The Labyrinth Maker,* Ana Maria Barrenechea called it "his resplendent world of shadows." But illusion is present in his manner of writing as well the fictional world he describes. In *World Literature Today,* William Riggan quoted Icelandic author Sigurdur Magnusson's thoughts on this aspect of Borges's work. "With the possible exception of Kafka . . . ," Magnusson stated, "no other writer that I know manages, with such relentless logic, to turn language upon itself to reverse himself time after time with a sentence or a paragraph, and effortlessly, so it seems, come upon surprising yet inevitable conclusions."

Because of Borges's choice of words and the way he used them, the reader is never sure about the possible outcome of the work until he has finished reading it. But, even then, subsequent readings often reveal subtle shades of meaning or entirely new conclusions. In "The South," for example, one cannot be certain if the protagonist, Juan Dahlmann, dies in his hospital bed or in a knife duel. In "The Shape of the Sword" the reader listens to the narrator tell the story of a despicable traitor and only in the last lines of the story does he learn that the narrator is actually talking about himself. The reader cannot even be certain that once he has finished a Borges story that what he read was actually a story. Borges's short narrative "The Approach to al-Mu'tasim," written as a book review of a non-existent book, was originally published in a collection of essays, *Historia de la eternidad.* Even the writer's friends were fooled by the story: Adolfo Bioy Casares, with whom Borges collaborated on many projects, tried to order the book under review from its alleged publisher in London (Borges had used the name of an actual publishing house in the text). Borges didn't acknowledge the hoax until five years later when the story was published in a fiction collection. But the apparent reality of "The Approach to al-Mu'tasim" is not unique to that story. As D. P. Gallagher noted in *Modern Latin American Literature:* "The stories often look real. Borges indeed always deploys illusionists' tricks to make them look so, before demolishing them as fictions. The stories are full of scholarly footnotes, references to real people, precise dates, all sorts of devices designed to give an appearance of reality to extraordinary things. Borges himself appears as a character in several stories and so do some of his friends."

Borges expertly blended the traditional boundaries between fact and fiction and between essay and short story and he was similarly adept at obliterating the border between other genres as well. In a tribute to Borges which appeared in the *New Yorker* after the Argentine's death in 1986, Mexican poet and essayist Octavio Paz wrote: "He cultivated three genres: the essay, the poem, and the short story. The division is arbitrary. His essays read like stories, his stories are poems; and his poems make us think, as though they were essays." In *Review,* Ambrose Gordon, Jr., similarly noted, "His essays are like poems in their almost musical development of themes, his stories are remarkably like his essays, and his poems are often little stories." Borges's "Conjectural Poem," for example, is very much like a short story in that it is an account of the death of one of his ancestors, Francisco Narciso de Laprida. Another poem, "The Golem," is a short narrative relating how Rabbi Low of Prague created an artificial man.

To deal with the problem of actually determining to which genre a prose piece by Borges might belong, Martin S. Stabb proposed in *Jorge Luis Borges* that the usual manner of grouping all of Borges's short fiction as short stories was invalid. Stabb instead divided the Argentine's prose fiction into three categories which took into account Borges's tendency to blur genres: " 'essayistic' fiction," "difficult-to-classify 'intermediate' fiction," and those pieces deemed "conventional short stories." Other reviewers saw a comparable division in Borges's fiction but chose to emphasize the chronological development of his work, noting that his first stories grew out of his essays, his "middle period" stories were more realistic, while his later stories were marked by a return to fantastic themes.

Others commentators on Borges's work chose to avoid classification by genre altogether and concentrated instead on thematic studies. This could be done quite easily for many of Borges's poetic themes, for example, are also found in his work in prose. In *Spanish American Literature: A History* Enrique Anderson-Imbert lists some of the motifs commonly found in Borges's poetry as "time, the meaning of the universe, [and] the personality of man." These same major concerns are found in Borges's essays and fiction as well. When used to examine Borges's short stories, this method recalls Borges's own insistence on exploring fantastic literature based on four key elements. "Borges once claimed that the basic devices of all fantastic literature are only

four in number: the work within the work, the contamination of reality by dream, the voyage in time, and the double," Irby explained. "These are both his essential themes—the problematical nature of the world, of knowledge, of time, of the self—and his essential techniques of construction."

When dealing with a body of work as rich and multifaceted as Borges's, a combination of both interpretive methods seems to impart the most accurate picture of Borges's fiction. Stabb began his study of Borges's "essayistic fiction" with this explanation: "These, and other pieces like them, are often based on readily identified philosophic notions, though many of the personalities used by Borges to make his points are fictional. In none of them is there any real narrative: several are based on invented literary notes describing fictitious authors and their works. It would not be difficult to imagine most of them cast in the form of a traditional essay." In *The Narrow Act: Borges' Art of Illusion,* Ronald J. Christ noted that these characteristics listed by Stamm are very common in Borges. He remarked, "The point of origin for most of Borges' fiction is neither character nor plot, considered in the traditional sense; but instead, a proposition, an idea, a metaphor." Stabb included in this type of fiction the stories "Funes the Memorious," "Pierre Menard, Author of the *Quixote,*" and "Three Versions of Judas." These stories elaborate a multitude of ideas, including the uselessness of unordered knowledge, the impossibility of originality in literature, and the true nature of Jesus.

"Funes the Memorious," listed in Richard Burgin's *Conversations with Jorge Luis Borges* as one of the Argentine's favorite stories, is about Ireneo Funes, a young man who cannot forget anything. His memory is so keen that he is surprised by how different he looks each time he sees himself in a mirror because, unlike the rest of us, he can see the subtle changes that have taken place in his body since the last time he saw his reflection. The story is filled with characteristic Borgesian detail. Funes's memory, for instance, becomes excessive as a result of an accidental fall from a horse. In Borges an accident is a reminder that man is unable to order his existence because the world has a hidden order of its own. Alazraki saw this Borgesian theme as "the tragic contrast between a man who believes himself to be the master and maker of his fate and a text or divine plan in which his fortune has already been written." The deliberately vague quality of the adjectives Borges typically uses in his sparse descriptive passages is also apparent: Funes's features are never clearly distinguished because he lives in a darkened room, he was thrown from his horse on a dark "rainy afternoon," and the horse itself is described as "blue-gray"—neither one color or the other. "This dominant chiaroscuro imagery," commented Bell-Villada, "is further reinforced by Funes's name, a word strongly suggestive of certain Spanish words variously meaning 'funereal,' 'ill-fated,' and 'dark.' " The ambiguity of Borges's descriptions lends a subtle, otherworldly air to this and other examples of his fiction.

Bell-Villada noted another important aspect of the story. When the narrator visits Funes he finds the young man reciting from memory a portion of an actual book, an ancient Roman text entitled *Natural History* written by Pliny, which deals with memory. This is an example of what Bell-Villada called "a typical hall-of-mirrors effect: someone with a perfect memory reciting from memory a passage on memory." According to Bell-Villada "the hall-of-mirrors effect" is comparable to "the work within a work" device mentioned by Borges as essential to fantastic fiction. "Borges is especially renown," Bell-Villada continued, "for his use of . . . the work of art within a work of art. Some of his most celebrated tales ('Pierre Menard,' 'Tlon, Uqbar, Orbis Tertius') deal with nonexistent books and authors. Borges even has a special essay, 'Partial Magic in the *Quixote*,' which deals with a kind of derivative: those works in which a literary character finds himself depicted in a book or a play."

In "Partial Magic in the *Quixote*" (also translated as "Partial Enchantments of the *Quixote*") Borges describes several occasions in world literature when a character reads about himself or sees himself in a play, including episodes from Shakespeare's plays, an epic poem of India, Cervantes's *Don Quixote,* and *The One Thousand and One Nights.* "Why does it disquiet us to know," Borges asked in the essay, "that Don Quixote is a reader of the *Quixote,* and Hamlet is a spectator of *Hamlet?* I believe I have found the answer: those inversions suggest that if the characters in a story can be readers or spectators, then we, their readers, can be fictitious."

With his analysis of this literary device Borges offered his own interpretation of what John Barth referred to in the *Atlantic* as "one of Borges' cardinal themes." Barrenechea explained Borges's technique, noting: "To readers and spectators who consider themselves real beings, these works suggest their possible existence as imaginary entities. In that context lies the key to Borges' work. Relentlessly pursued by a world that is too real and at the same time lacking meaning, he tries to free himself from its obsessions by creating a world of such coherent phantasmagorias that the reader doubts the very reality on which he leans." For example, in one of Borges's variations on "the work within a work," Jaromir Hladik, the protagonist of Borges's story "The Secret Miracle," appears in a footnote to another of Borges's stories, "Three Versions of Judas." The note refers the reader to the *Vindication of Eternity,* a work said to be written by Hladik. In this instance, Borges used a fictional work written by one of his fictional characters to lend an air of erudition to another fictional work about the works of another fictional author.

Borges took "the work within a work" device one step further than any of the examples he spoke of in "Partial Magic in the *Quixote.*" One of his favorite literary allusions was to what he referred to as the six-hundred-and-second night of *A Thousand and One Nights.* On this night, Borges recalled, due to a copyist error, Scheherezade began to tell the Sultan the story of *A Thousand and One Nights* by mistake. Although Borges often referred to this episode, it is just another of his *ficciones,* never having been actually included in the original Arabic text. Thus, each time Borges talks about the episode, he is telling a tale about a fictional character telling a tale about telling a tale. As Barth pointed out, the episode is "a literary illustration of the *regressus in infinitum* [the infinite regression], as are almost all of Borges' principal images and motifs." It is as if two mirrors faced each other on the wall, each endlessly reflecting the reflection of the other.

The effect of referring to a work familiar to his readers in one of his stories and then making up a story about it lends an atmosphere of reality to Borges's fiction. A similar effect is created by the footnotes found in several of Borges's stories such as "Three Versions of Judas" and "Pierre Menard, Author of the *Quixote.*" The use of footnotes is an example of how Borges blended essay and fiction to create his "essayistic fiction." Both stories, just like Borges's "Approach to al-Mu'tasim," were written as book reviews of works written by Borges's fictional authors and, thus, differ sharply in form and content from the traditional short story.

These intrusions of reality on the fictional world are characteristic of Borges's work. He also uses a device, which he calls "the contamination of reality by dream," to produce the same effect

of uneasiness in the reader as "the work within the work" but through directly opposite means. Two examples of stories using this technique are "Tlon, Uqbar, Orbis Tertius" and "The Circular Ruins." The first, which Stabb included in his "difficult-to-classify 'intermediate' fiction," is one of Borges's most discussed works. It tells the story, according to Barrenechea, "of an attempt of a group of men to create a world of their own until, by the sheer weight of concentration, the fantastic creation acquires consistency and some of its objects—a compass, a metallic cone—which are composed of strange matter begin to appear on earth." By the end of the story, the world as we know it is slowly turning into the invented world of Tlon. Stabb called the work "difficult-to-classify" because, he commented, "the excruciating amount of documentary detail (half real, half fictitious) . . . make[s] the piece seem more like an essay" than a short story. There are, in addition, footnotes and a postscript to the story as well as an appearance by Borges himself and references to several other well-known Latin American literary figures, including Borges's friend, Bioy Casares.

"The Circular Ruins," which Stabb considered a "conventional short story," describes a very unconventional situation. (The story is conventional, however, in that there are no footnotes or real people intruding on the fictive nature of the piece.) In the story a man decides to dream about a son until the son becomes real. Later, after the man accomplishes his goal, much to his astonishment, he discovers that he in turn is being dreamt by someone else. "The Circular Ruins" includes several themes seen throughout Borges's work, including man's attempt to establish order in a chaotic universe, the infinite regression, the symbol of the labyrinth, and the idea of all men being one.

The futility of any attempt to order the universe, seen in "Funes the Memorious" and in "The Circular Ruins," is also found in "The Library of Babel" where, according to Alazraki, "Borges presents the world as a library of chaotic books which its librarians cannot read but which they interpret incessantly." The library was one of Borges's favorite images, often repeated in his fiction. In another work, Borges uses the image of a chessboard, however, to elaborate the same theme. In his poem "Chess," he speaks of the king, bishop, and queen who "seek out and begin their armed campaign." But, just as the dreamer dreams a man and causes him to act in a certain way, the campaign is actually being planned by someone other than the members of royalty. "They do not know it is the player's hand," the poem continues, "that dominates and guides their destiny." In the last stanza of the poem Borges uses the same images to suggest the infinite regression: "God moves the player, he in turn, the piece. / But what god beyond God begins the round / of dust and time and sleep and agonies?" Another poem, "The Golem," which tells the story of an artificial man created by a rabbi in Prague, ends in a similar fashion: "At the hour of anguish and vague light, / He would rest his eyes on his Golem. / Who can tell us what God felt, / As he gazed on His rabbi in Prague?" Just as there is a dreamer dreaming a man, and beyond that a dreamer dreaming the dreamer who dreamt the man, then, too, there must be another dreamer beyond that in an infinite succession of dreamers.

The infinite doubling effect inherent in the image of the dreamer who dreams a dreamer and the contrast between a chaotic universe and the order sought by man evoke an image that will be forever linked with Borges's name: the labyrinth. Like the mirror facing the mirror, "the labyrinth is born of duplication," John Sturrock observed in *Paper Tigers: The Ideal Fictions of Jorge Luis Borges,* "of the postulation of an alterative to a given reality, and founded on duplication thereafter." Alazraki concluded: "The labyrinth expresses both sides of the coin: it has an irreversible order if one knows the solution (the gods, God) and it can be at the same time a chaotic maze if the solution constitutes an unattainable secret (men). The labyrinth represents to a greater or less degree the vehicle through which Borges carries his world view to almost all his stories."

The title of the story "The Circular Ruins" suggests a labyrinth. In another story, "The Babylon Lottery," Stabb commented, "an ironically detached narrator depicts life as a labyrinth through which man wanders under the absurd illusion of having understood a chaotic, meaningless world." Labyrinths or references to labyrinths are found in nearly all of Borges's fiction. The labyrinthine form is often present in his poems, too, especially in Borges's early poetry filled with remembrances of wandering the labyrinth-like streets of old Buenos Aires.

In "The Circular Ruins" Borges's returns to another favorite theme: circular time. This theme embraces another device mentioned by Borges as typical of fantastic literature: time travel. Borges's characters, however, do not travel through time in machines; their travel is more on a metaphysical, mythical level. Circular time—a concept also favored by Nietzsche, one of the German philosophers Borges discovered as a boy—is apparent in many of Borges's stories, including "Three Versions of Judas," "The Garden of the Forking Paths," "Tlon, Uqbar, Orbis Tertius," "The Library of Babel," and "The Immortal." It is also found in another of Borges's favorite stories, "Death and the Compass," in which the reader encounters not only a labyrinth but a double as well. Stabb offered the story as a good example of Borges's "conventional short stories."

"Death and the Compass" is a detective story. Erik Lonnrot, the story's detective, commits the fatal error of believing there is an order in the universe that he can understand. When Marcel Yarmolinsky is murdered, Lonnrot refuses to believe it was just an accident; he looks for clues to the murderer's identity in Yarmolinsky's library. Red Scharlach, whose brother Lonnrot had sent to jail, reads about the detective's efforts to solve the murder in the local newspaper and contrives a plot to ambush him. The plan works because Lonnrot, overlooking numerous clues, blindly follows the false trail Scharlach leaves for him.

The final sentences—in which Lonnrot is murdered—change the whole meaning of the narrative, illustrate many of Borges's favorite themes, and crystalize for the reader Borges's thinking on the problem of time. Lonnrot says to Scharlach: " 'I know of one Greek labyrinth which is a single straight line. Along that line so many philosophers have lost themselves that a mere detective might well do so, too. Scharlach, when in some other incarnation you hunt me, pretend to commit (or do commit) a crime at A, then a second crime at B . . . , then a third crime at C. . . . Wait for me afterwards at D. . . . Kill me at D as you now are going to kill me at Triste-le-Roy.' 'The next time I kill you,' said Scharlach, 'I promise you that labyrinth, consisting of a single line which is invisible and unceasing.' He moved back a few steps. Then, very carefully, he fired."

"Death and the Compass" is in many ways a typical detective story, but this last paragraph takes the story far beyond that popular genre. Lonnrot and Scharlach are doubles (Borges gives us a clue in their names: *rot* means red and *scharlach* means scarlet in German) caught in an infinite cycle of pursuing and being pursued. "Their antithetical natures, or inverted mirror images," McMurray observed, "are demonstrated by their roles as detective/criminal and pursuer/pursued roles that become ironically reversed." Rodriguez Monegal concluded: "The concept of the eternal return . . . adds an extra dimension to the story. It changes Scharlach and Lonnrot into characters in a myth: Abel and Cain endlessly performing the killing."

Doubles, which Bell-Villada defined as "any blurring or any seeming multiplication of character identity," are found in many of Borges's works, including "The Waiting," "The Theologians," "The South," "The Shape of the Sword," "Three Versions of Judas," and "Story of the Warrior and the Captive." Borges's explanation of the story "The Theologians" (included in his collection, *The Aleph and Other Stories, 1933-1969*) reveals how a typical Borgesian plot involving doubles works: "In 'The Theologians' you have two enemies," Borges told Burgin in an interview, "and one of them sends the other to the stake. And then they find out somehow they're the same man." In a *Studies in Short Fiction* essay Robert Magliola noticed that "almost every story in *Dr. Brodie's Report* is about two people fixed in some sort of dramatic opposition to each other." In two pieces, "Borges and I" (also translated as "Borges and Myself") and "The Other," Borges appears as a character along with his double. In the former, Borges, the retiring Argentine librarian, contemplates Borges, the world-famous writer. It concludes with one of Borges's most-analyzed sentences: "Which of us is writing this page, I don't know."

Some critics saw Borges's use of the double as an attempt to deal with the duality in his own personality: the struggle between his native Argentine roots and the strong European influence on his writing. They also pointed out what seemed to be an attempt by the author to reconcile through his fiction the reality of his sedentary life of an almost-blind scholar with the longed for adventurous life of his dreams based on that led by his famous ancestors who actively participated in Argentina's wars for independence. This latter tendency is especially evident in "The South," a largely autobiographical story about a library worker who, Bell-Villada noted, like Borges, "is painfully aware of the discordant strains in his ancestry."

The double is also based on what Alazraki called "the pantheistic notion that one man is all men." This suggests, Alazraki observed, "the negation of individual identity, or more exactly, the reduction of all individuals to a general and supreme identity which contains all." Borges developed this theme starting with his very first book. One of its earliest manifestations occurs in Borges's introduction to the 1923 edition of *Fervor de Buenos Aires,* which Norman Thomas di Giovanni quoted in *Selected Poems, 1923-1967.* Borges wrote: "If in the following pages there is some successful verse or other, may the reader forgive me the audacity of having written it before him. We are all one; our inconsequential minds are much alike, and circumstances so influence that it is something of an accident that you are the reader and I am the writer . . . of my verse." Other glimpses of the theme occur in the stories, "Tlon, Uqbar, Orbis Tertius" and "Everything and Nothing." In a footnote to "Tlon, Uqbar, Orbis Tertius" Borges noted: "All men are the same man. All men who repeat a line from Shakespeare *are* William Shakespeare." "Everything and Nothing," which considers the life of a British actor and playwright, also deals with the oneness of all men and recalls Borges's fondness for the image of the infinite number of dreamers from "The Circular Ruins." "Before or after dying" the playwright confronts God saying, "I who have been so many men in vain want to be one and myself." God replies, "Neither am I anyone; I have dreamt the world as you dreamt your work, my Shakespeare, and among the forms in my dream are you, who like myself are many and no one."

The idea that all men are one, which Anderson-Imbert observed calls for the "obliteration of the I," is perhaps Borges's farthest step towards a literature devoid of realism. In this theme we see, according to Christ, "the direction in Borges' stories away from individual psychology toward a universal mythology." This explains why so few of Borges's characters show any psychological development; instead of being interested in his characters as individuals, Borges typically uses them only to further his philosophical beliefs.

All of the characteristics of Borges's work, his blending of genres, confusion of the real and the fictive, his favorite themes and symbols, seem to come together in one of his most quoted passages, the final paragraph of his essay "A New Refutation of Time." While in *Borges: A Reader* Rodriguez Monegal called the essay Borges's "most elaborate attempt to organize a personal system of metaphysics in which he denies time, space, and the individual 'I,' " Alazraki noted that it contains a summation of Borges's belief in "the heroic and tragic condition of man as dream and dreamer."

"Our destiny . . . ," wrote Borges in the essay, "is not horrible because of its unreality; it is horrible because it is irreversible and ironbound. Time is the substance I am made of. Time is a river that carries me away, but I am the river; it is a tiger that mangles me, but I am the tiger; it is a fire that consumes me, but I am the fire. The world, alas, is real; I, alas, am Borges."

MEDIA ADAPTATIONS: "Emma Zunz," a short story, was made into a movie called "Dias de odio" ("Days of Wrath") by Argentine director Leopoldo Torre Nilsson, 1954, a French television movie directed by Alain Magrou, 1969, and a film called "Splits" by U.S. director Leonard Katz, 1978; "Hombre de la esquina rosada," a short story, was made into an Argentine movie of the same title directed by Rene Mugica, 1961; Bernardo Bertolucci based his "La strategia de la ragna" ("The Spider's Stratagem"), a movie made for Italian television, on Borges's short story "El tema del traidor y del heroe," 1970; Hector Olivera, in collaboration with Juan Carlos Onetti, adapted Borges's story "El muerto" for the Argentine movie of the same name, 1975; Borges's short story "La intrusa" was made into a Brazilian film directed by Carlos Hugo Christensen, 1978; three of the stories in *Six Problems for Don Isidro Parodi* were dramatized for radio broadcast by the British Broadcasting Corporation.

BIOGRAPHICAL/CRITICAL SOURCES:

BOOKS

Alazraki, Jaime, *Jorge Luis Borges,* Columbia University Press, 1971.

Anderson-Imbert, Enrique, *Spanish-American Literature: A History,* Volume 2: *1910-1963,* 2nd edition, Wayne State University Press, 1969.

Barrenechea, Ana Maria, *Borges: The Labyrinth Maker,* translated by Robert Lima, New York University Press, 1965.

Bell-Villada, Gene H., *Borges and His Fiction: A Guide to His Mind and Art,* University of North Carolina Press, 1981.

Borges, Jorge Luis, *Ficciones,* translated by Anthony Kerrigan and others, edited and with an introduction by Kerrigan, Grove Press, 1962.

Borges, Jorge Luis, *Labyrinths: Selected Stories and Other Writings,* edited by Donald A. Yates and James E. Irby, New Directions, 1964.

Borges, Jorge Luis, *The Aleph and Other Stories, 1933-1969,* translated and revised by Norman Thomas di Giovanni in collaboration with Borges, Dutton, 1970.

Borges, Jorge Luis, *Selected Poems, 1923-1967,* translated and edited, with an introduction and notes, by Norman Thomas di Giovanni, Delacorte Press, 1972.

Borges, Jorge Luis, *Borges: A Reader,* edited by Emir Rodriguez Monegal and Alastair Reid, Dutton, 1981.

Burgin, Richard, *Conversations with Jorge Luis Borges,* Holt, 1969.

Christ, Ronald J., *The Narrow Act: Borges' Art of Illusion,* New York University Press, 1969.

Contemporary Literary Criticism, Gale, Volume 1, 1973, Volume 2, 1974, Volume 3, 1975, Volume 4, 1975, Volume 6, 1976, Volume 8, 1978, Volume 9, 1978, Volume 10, 1979, Volume 13, 1980, Volume 19, 1981, Volume 44, 1987, Volume 48, 1988.

Dictionary of Literary Biography: Yearbook, 1986, Gale, 1987.

Gallagher, D. P., *Modern Latin American Literature,* Oxford University Press, 1973.

McMurray, George R., *Jorge Luis Borges,* Ungar, 1980.

Rodriguez Monegal, Emir, *Jorge Luis Borges: A Literary Biography,* Dutton, 1978.

Stabb, Martin S., *Jorge Luis Borges,* Twayne, 1970.

PERIODICALS

Atlantic, January, 1967, August, 1967, February, 1972, April, 1981.

Nation, December 29, 1969, August 3, 1970, March 1, 1971, February 21, 1972, October 16, 1972, February 21, 1976.

National Review, March 2, 1973.

Review, spring, 1972, spring, 1975, winter, 1976, January-April, 1981, September-December, 1981.

Studies in Short Fiction, spring, 1974, winter, 1978.

World Literature Today, autumn, 1977, winter, 1984.

Yale Review, October, 1969, autumn, 1974.

OBITUARIES:

PERIODICALS

Detroit News, June 15, 1986, June 22, 1986.

Los Angeles Times, June 15, 1986.

Nation, June 28, 1986.

New Republic, November 3, 1986.

New Yorker, July 7, 1986.

New York Review of Books, August 14, 1986.

New York Times, June 15, 1986.

Publishers Weekly, July 4, 1986.

Time, June 23, 1986.

USA Today, June 16, 1986.

Washington Post, June 15, 1986.

*   *   *

BOTO, Eza
See BIYIDI, Alexandre

*   *   *

BOVA, Ben(jamin William) 1932-

PERSONAL: Born November 8, 1932, in Philadelphia, Pa.; son of Benjamin Pasquale (a tailor) and Giove (Caporiccio) Bova; married Rosa Cucinotta, November 28, 1953 (divorced, 1974); married Barbara Berson Rose, June 28, 1974; children: (first marriage) Michael Francis, Regina Marie. *Education:* Temple University, B.S., 1954. *Religion:* Roman Catholic.

ADDRESSES: Home—32 Gramercy Park S., New York, N.Y. 10003. *Agent*—The Barbara Bova Literary Agency, 32 Gramercy Park S., New York, N.Y. 10003.

CAREER: Upper Darby News, Upper Darby, Pa., editor, 1953-56; Martin Aircraft Co., Baltimore, Md., technical editor on Vanguard project, 1956-58; Massachusetts Institute of Technology, Cambridge, screenwriter for Physical Science Study Committee, 1958-59; Avco-Everett Research Laboratory, Everett, Mass., marketing manager, 1960-71; Conde Nast Publishing Co., New York City, editor of *Analog,* 1971-78; Omni Publications International, New York City, editorial director and vice-president of *Omni,* 1978-82; science and technology consultant, "CBS Morning News" television show. Lecturer at universities and businesses. Science consultant to motion picture and television studios.

MEMBER: National Space Institute, Science Fiction Writers of America, P.E.N. International, American Association for the Advancement of Science, British Interplanetary Society (fellow), Free Space Society (honorary chairman), National Space Club, Nature Conservancy, New York Academy of Sciences, Explorers Club.

AWARDS, HONORS: The Milky Way Galaxy and *The Fourth State of Matter* were named best science books of the year by the American Library Association; Hugo awards, World Science Fiction Convention, 1973-77, and 1979, for best editor; E. E. Smith Memorial Award, New England Science Fiction Society, 1974; named distinguished alumnus, Temple University, 1981; Balrog Award, 1983.

WRITINGS:

SCIENCE FICTION

The Star Conquerors (for children), Winston, 1959.
Star Watchman (for children), Holt, 1964.
The Weathermakers (for children), Holt, 1967.
Out of the Sun (for children), Holt, 1968.
The Dueling Machine (for children), Holt, 1969.
Escape! (for children), Holt, 1970.
Exiled From Earth (for children; first book in trilogy; also see below), Dutton, 1971.
(With George Lucas) *THX 1138* (novelization of screenplay), Paperback Library, 1971.
Flight of Exiles (for children; second book in trilogy; also see below), Dutton, 1972.
As on a Darkling Plain, Walker, 1972.
The Shining Strangers (for children), Walker, 1973.
The Winds of Altair (for children), Dutton, 1973.
When the Sky Burned, Walker, 1973.
Forward in Time (short stories), Walker, 1973.
(With Gordon R. Dickson) *Gremlins, Go Home!,* (for children), St. Martin's, 1974.
End of Exile (for children; third book in trilogy; also see below), Dutton, 1975.
The Starcrossed, Chilton, 1975.
City of Darkness (for children), Scribner, 1976.
Millennium, Random House, 1976.
The Multiple Man, Bobbs-Merrill, 1976.
Colony, Pocket Books, 1978.
Maxwell's Demons (short stories), Baronet, 1978.
Kinsman, Dial, 1979.
The Exiles Trilogy (contains *Exiled From Earth, Flight of Exiles,* and *End of Exile*), Berkley, 1980.
Voyagers, Doubleday, 1981.
Test of Fire, Tor Books, 1982.
Orion, Simon & Schuster, 1984.
Escape Plus Ten (short stories), Tor Books, 1984.
The Kinsman Saga, Tor Books, 1987.
Voyagers II: The Alien Within, Tor Books, 1987.
Welcome to Moon Base, Ballantine, 1987.
Vengeance of Orion, Tor Books, 1988.

The Peacekeepers (for children), Tor Books, 1988.

NONFICTION

The Milky Way Galaxy: Man's Exploration of the Stars, Holt, 1961.
Giants of the Animal World (for children), Whitman Publishing, 1962.
Reptiles Since the World Began (for children), Whitman Publishing, 1964.
The Uses of Space (for children), Holt, 1965.
Magnets and Magnetism (for children), Whitman Publishing, 1966.
In Quest of Quasars: An Introduction to Stars and Starlike Objects (for children), Crowell, 1970.
Planets, Life, and LGM (for children), Addison-Wesley, 1970.
The Fourth State of Matter: Plasma Dynamics and Tomorrow's Technology, St. Martin's, 1971.
The Amazing Laser (for children), Westminster Press, 1972.
The New Astronomies, St. Martin's, 1972.
Starflight and Other Improbabilities (for children), Westminster Press, 1973.
Man Changes the Weather (for children), Addison-Wesley, 1973.
(With Barbara Berson) *Survival Guide for the Suddenly Single,* St. Martin's, 1974.
The Weather Changes Man (for children), Addison-Wesley, 1974.
Workshops in Space (for children), Dutton, 1974.
Through Eyes of Wonder (for children), Addison-Wesley, 1975.
Science: Who Needs It? (for children), Westminster Press, 1975.
Notes to a Science Fiction Writer (for children), Scribner, 1975.
Viewpoint, NESFA Press, 1977.
(With Trudy E. Bell) *Closeup: New Worlds,* St. Martin's, 1977.
The Seeds of Tomorrow (for children), McKay, 1977.
The High Road, Houghton, 1981.
Vision of the Future: The Art of Robert McCall, Abrams, 1982.
Assured Survival: Putting the Star Wars Defense in Perspective, Houghton, 1984.
The Astral Mirror (essays), Tor Books, 1985.
Prometheans, Tor Books, 1986.
Battle Station, Tor Books, 1987.
The Beauty of Light, Wiley, 1988.
(With Sheldon Glashow) *Interactions,* Warner Books, 1988.
Cyberbooks, Tor Books, 1989.

EDITOR

The Many Worlds of SF, Dutton, 1971.
SFWA Hall of Fame, Volume II, Doubleday, 1973.
Analog 9, Doubleday, 1973.
The Analog Science Fact Reader, St. Martin's, 1974.
Analog Annual, Pyramid Publications, 1976.
Analog Yearbook, Baronet, 1978.
Best of Analog, Baronet, 1978.
(With Don Myrus) *The Best of Omni Science Fiction,* Omni Publications International, 1980.
(With Myrus) *The Best of Omni Science Fiction,* four volumes, Omni Publications International, 1980-82.
Best of the Nebulas, St. Martin's, 1989.

SIDELIGHTS: Ben Bova, writes J. D. Brown in the *Dictionary of Literary Biography Yearbook: 1981,* "is a leading spokesman for expanded scientific research and the application of new technologies to solve present and future problems." Bova's science fiction novels are set in the near future and detail the impact of high technology advances in solving the problems of present-day society. In his nonfiction science books, Bova explains the importance of recent scientific discoveries and the social effects these discoveries might have. And as editor of *Omni,* he has presented both science fiction and science fact in a manner meant to enhance the role of technology in the betterment of the human condition.

Brown sees Bova's primary goal in all of his writing and editing to be convincing "the skeptical that proposed [scientific] research programs result in gains in knowledge which ultimately yield enormous practical benefits." Bova's *Workshops in Space,* for example, examines four outer space research stations and explains the beneficial information scientists have learned from using them. In *The Fourth State of Matter,* Bova discusses current scientific research into plasmas which are neither solids, liquids, nor gases—and speculates on their possible uses in the future. A *Choice* reviewer finds the book "Outstanding! Popular treatments of science are difficult to do well and here is a thorough, readable, and reasonably accurate survey of plasmas. [Bova's] treatment of experiments [in the field] is most satisfying."

In his science-fiction novels, Bova dramatizes his interest in scientific solutions to societal problems, particularly the beneficial effects of space exploration on the whole of society. In his novel *Colony,* for example, Bova envisions a near future society in which three groups compete for power on a dangerously overcrowded Earth: a world government, a group of multinational corporations, and an underground terrorist organization. None of these groups has any solution to the pressing problem of overpopulation. "But the novel champions a fourth possibility," writes Brown, "a space vehicle constructed from lunar materials [and] large enough for millions of colonists in space orbit. The argument of the book is that . . . the key to Earth's survival is dispersal of its population throughout the solar system." Edward Wood of *Analog* finds the novel "a fast moving story that gives a very convincing picture of the future."

Speaking of *Colony* to Elton T. Elliott of *Science Fiction Review,* Bova emphasized the importance of space exploration: "One of the points that I am bringing out in . . . *Colony,* is that the [space] colonies, this concept of colonizing the solar system now, is incredibly important for many, many reasons. One of the most important reasons is we will have spread the home grounds of the human race to beyond this one planet. So if we do screw up this planet . . . there will still be a human race surviving elsewhere."

This idea is developed further in *The High Road,* Bova's nonfiction study of space exploration and its effects on Earth society. He states his thesis at the outset of the book: "For humankind to survive the plagues of overpopulation, environmental destruction, and war by the end of the century we must expand into space." The building of permanent orbiting space colonies is especially recommended, as these colonies would be able to construct cheaply a myriad of vital products for the Earth, while relieving the problems of overpopulation by relocating large numbers of people to outer space. Critical reaction to the book has been generally favorable. John Adams of *School Library Journal* judges the book to be "a purposeful and fairly even-minded . . . study of important choices before us." Reuben Benumof of *Science Books and Films* finds it "a vigorous espousal of the benefits of a massive expansion of our present space program [which] will interest anyone who is concerned about alleviating the ills of society." "This is one of the most exciting and positive books to come out in years," Jack Kriwan of *National Review* believes. "It makes a compelling, practical case for America's expansion outward into the space frontier."

"I think that space flight offers perhaps the only opportunity we have," Bova told Elliott, "to solve the problems here on earth. [Few people] became colonists and settled the New World and yet the development of the New World changed the lives of every human being . . . all over the world. Very few human beings will go into space, and yet the things that they do there will change the lives of all the people who remain on earth. It has already changed our lives."

"Bova," Brown concludes, "has consistently pushed beyond formal restrictions and sought new forms to render in human terms the potential meaning and experience of science in the future, a bright, humane future, as opposed to the dark collapse of civilization which Bova regards as inevitable if we refuse to pursue fully all the new avenues of scientific research and technological application."

Bova told *CA:* "The technology developed in space has an immediate and powerful impact on the economy. *The High Road* examines the space effort and what it does for us on a day-to-day level. I've found, not only from my own research but from the work that economists have done, that investment in space has an incredibly beneficial effect on the economy. It lowers the inflation rate, increases productivity, makes real jobs, builds new industries. So it is no coincidence that when we cut the space program in the early 1970s, the economy began to tailspin. As we begin to invest more in space and do more in space, we develop new industries that strengthen our economy.

"I have spent my life with scientists and writers and people in the arts and the technologies, and there are many, many more scientists who understand the Bhagavad Gita and poetry of many languages, who understand and appreciate ballet and opera and the arts in general, than there are so-called humanists who care about or understand the simplest kinds of science. C. P. Snow put it much better. He said, 'If you go to a cocktail party and somebody asks you, "What do you think of Hamlet?" and you say, "I never heard of it," you're regarded as a boor. But if you ask someone at the same cocktail party, "What do you think of the second law of thermodynamics?" he will regard you as a boor for asking such a question.' And to be ignorant of that is to be ignorant of the world.

"I think television covers science the way they cover the circus. You get a story once in a while, but between, when all the really important things are happening, they don't cover it at all. And when it comes to science fiction on television and in the films, they portray a very antiscience attitude. Whether you're talking about 'Star Wars' or 'The Time Bandits,' somehow the scientist always comes out as either the useless, silly, foolish one or as the villain. 'Time Bandits' is a marvelous show, but you'll find that the villain, the Devil, is interested in lasers and computers, while the good guy, God, is interested in flowers and shrubs. This is an attitude that pervades the motion-picture industry. They depend on science and technology; they make millions of dollars out of it. But they always portray the scientist as either an ineffectual fool or a downright villain, cold-blooded and merciless. And that is deathly.

"I think any writer worth his salt is always trying to stretch his muscles and meet new challenges. One of the happiest moments of my life comes when a teacher or librarian or student comes up and says, 'I read such-and-such a book of yours.' There's one book in particular, a children's book called *Escape!* that many librarians have told me about. It was written specifically for kids who don't like to read, and it's been very successful. Not only do I get more mail from that book than any other, but very often when I'm at a convention of librarians, they'll mob me and say,

'Your book has gotten kids to begin reading who have never opened a book before.' And that is a real thrill for me."

BIOGRAPHICAL/CRITICAL SOURCES:

BOOKS

Children's Literature Review, Volume 3, Gale, 1978.
Dictionary of Literary Biography Yearbook, 1981, Gale, 1982.

PERIODICALS

Analog, March, 1979.
Choice, January, 1972.
Christian Science Monitor, November 6, 1969, October 24, 1970.
Economist, September 8, 1973.
Los Angeles Times, November 1, 1988.
Los Angeles Times Book Review, November 1, 1988.
Magazine of Fantasy and Science Fiction, January, 1972, November, 1976, July, 1977.
National Review, May 14, 1982.
New York Times Book Review, November 10, 1974, March 7, 1976, April 11, 1976, September 11, 1988.
Publishers Weekly, November 4, 1988.
School Library Journal, February, 1982.
Science Books and Films, March/April, 1982.
Science Fiction Review, September/October, 1978.
Times Literary Supplement, January 27, 1978.
Washington Post Book World, September 27, 1981.

*   *   *

BOWEN, Elizabeth (Dorothea Cole) 1899-1973

PERSONAL: Born June 7, 1899, in Dublin, Ireland; died February 22, 1973, in London, England; daughter of Henry Charles Cole and Florence Isabella Pomeroy (Colley) Bowen; married Alan Charles Cameron (a professor), August 4, 1923 (died, 1952). *Education:* Studied at Downe House, Downe, Kent, England; attended London County Council School of Art, 1918-19.

CAREER: Writer. *Wartime service:* Worked in a shell-shock hospital near Dublin, Ireland during World War I; worked for Ministry of Information, London, England, serving nights as an air-raid warden, during World War II.

MEMBER: American Academy of Arts and Letters (honorary member), Irish Academy of Letters.

AWARDS, HONORS: Commander, Order of the British Empire, 1948; D.Litt., Trinity College, Dublin, 1949, and Oxford University, 1956; Companion of Literature, Royal Society of Literature, 1965; James Tait Black Memorial Prize, 1970, for *Eva Trout.*

WRITINGS:

NOVELS

The Hotel, Constable, 1927, Dial, 1928.
The Last September, Dial, 1929, new edition with new preface by the author, Knopf, 1952.
Friends and Relations, Dial, 1931.
To the North, Gollancz, 1932, Knopf, 1933.
The House in Paris, Gollancz, 1935, Knopf, 1936.
The Death of the Heart, Gollancz, 1938, Knopf, 1939.
The Heat of the Day (Literary Guild selection), Knopf, 1948.
A World of Love, Knopf, 1955.
The Little Girls, Knopf, 1963.
Eva Trout; or, Changing Scenes, Knopf, 1968.

SHORT STORIES

Encounters (also see below), Boni & Liveright, 1923, new edition, Sidgwick & Jackson, 1949.
Ann Lee's and Other Stories (also see below), Boni & Liveright, 1926, reprinted, Books for Libraries, 1969.
Joining Charles and Other Stories, Dial, 1929.
The Cat Jumps and Other Stories, Gollancz, 1934.
Look at All Those Roses, Knopf, 1941.
The Demon Lover and Other Stories, J. Cape, 1945, published as *Ivy Gripped the Steps and Other Stories,* Knopf, 1946.
Selected Stories, M. Fridberg, 1946.
Early Stories (includes *Encounters* and *Ann Lee's and Other Stories*), Knopf, 1951.
Stories, Knopf, 1959.
A Day in the Dark and Other Stories, J. Cape, 1965.
Irish Stories, Dufour, 1978.
The Collected Stories of Elizabeth Bowen, Knopf, 1981.

OTHER

(Contributor) Charles Davy, editor, *Footnotes to the Film,* Oxford University Press, 1937, reprinted, Arno, 1970.
(Editor) *The Faber Book of Modern Stories,* Faber, 1937.
Bowen's Court (nonfiction), Knopf, 1942, 2nd edition, 1964.
English Novelists, Hastings House, 1942.
Seven Winters (autobiography), Cuala Press (Dublin), 1942, published as *Seven Winters: Memories of a Dublin Childhood* (also see below), Longmans, Green, 1943.
Anthony Trollope: A New Judgement, Oxford University Press, 1946.
(Contributor) John Irwin, compiler, *How I Write My Novels,* Spearman, 1948.
Why Do I Write?: An Exchange of Views between Elizabeth Bowen, Graham Greene, and V. S. Pritchett, Marshall, 1948, Folcroft, 1969.
Collected Impressions (nonfiction), Knopf, 1950.
The Shelbourne Hotel, Knopf, 1951 (published in England as *The Shelbourne: A Centre of Dublin Life for More than a Century,* Harrap, 1951).
(Editor) Katherine Mansfield, *Stories,* Vintage, 1956 (published in England as *34 Short Stories,* Collins, 1957).
(Contributor) Dorothy Wilson, editor, *Family Christmas Book,* Prentice-Hall, 1957.
A Time in Rome (nonfiction), Knopf, 1959.
(Author of introduction) Anthony Trollope, *Doctor Thorne,* Houghton, 1959.
(Author of afterword) Virginia Woolf, *Orlando: A Biography,* New American Library, 1960.
Afterthought: Pieces about Writing (essays and addresses; also see below), Longmans, Green, 1962, Knopf, 1964.
Seven Winters: Memories of a Dublin Childhood and Afterthought: Pieces about Writing, Knopf, 1962.
(Contributor) *These Simple Things,* Simon & Schuster, 1965.
The Good Tiger (juvenile), Knopf, 1965.
Pictures and Conversations (memoirs), Knopf, 1975.
The Mulberry Tree: Writings of Elizabeth Bowen, edited by Hermione Lee, Harcourt, 1987.

Contributor of literary criticism and book reviews to *Tatler* and other journals; author of scripts for British Broadcasting Corp.

SIDELIGHTS: Orville Prescott, in his book *In My Opinion,* called Elizabeth Bowen a "sensitive, fastidious and astute Anglo-Irish woman." She was "a highly conscious artist," wrote Walter Allen in *The Modern Novel,* "who has evolved over the years a prose style that has the elaboration, the richness of texture, the allusiveness of poetry, a prose as carefully wrought, as subtle in its implications, as that of Henry James in his last phase. She has, too, an intense awareness of, and sensitivity to, place and weather, to the living character of houses, for example, and the indefinable yet readily palpable relation set up between them and the people who dwell in them." A *Publishers Weekly* reviewer summarized her reputation, noting that "critics generally consider *The Death of the Heart* her best novel; some call it one of the best English novels of the century."

"When I write, I am re-creating what was created for me," wrote Bowen. "The gladness of vision, in writing, is my own gladness, but not at my own vision." Indeed, "vision and illumination" are key words to much of the criticism of her work. L. A. G. Strong said in *Living Writers:* "First of all, she is an Irish writer—as Irish as Yeats. That means, among other things, that she is very strongly conscious of light." He added: "Everything she sees is seen through an intensely personal prism: thus far she is introverted. The external details are seen with a vivid and accurate eye: in that she is extraverted. . . . She can suggest disquiet, whether moral, physical, or psychic, to a degree unequalled among her contemporaries. She can convey the very texture and perfume of happiness. All these things are the result of a merciless and unfaltering precision of awareness and of expression. All belong to what, for me at least, is the essential quality of her work, illumination."

Much of Bowen's art operates by implication and subtlety. Her characters are largely "cultivated, liberal upper middle-class." Allen wrote: "Her first reputation was as a witty observer of manners, a delicate satirist of social absurdities; but from *To the North* (1932), social comedy, though always there, if sometimes uneasily, has been secondary to a conception of human relations verging upon the tragic. It is as though Henry James has been superimposed upon Jane Austen." Sean O'Faolain noted in *The Vanishing Hero* that the author "has not assumed that the intellect must be abdicated by the modern novelist. She hovers patiently over her subjects. But the prime technical characteristic of her work, as of other modern women writers, such as Virginia Woolf, is that she fills the vacuum which the general disintegration of belief has created in life by the pursuit of sensibility."

Speaking of writing in *Collected Impressions,* Bowen wrote: "Characters pre-exist. They are *found.* They reveal themselves slowly to the novelist's perception—as might fellow-travellers seated opposite one in a very dimly-lit railway carriage. . . . In each of the characters, while he or she is acting, the play and pull of alternatives must be felt. It is in being seen to be capable of alternatives that the character becomes, for the reader, valid." The author added that "a novel must contain at least one *magnetic* character. At least one character capable of keying the reader up, as though he (the reader) were in the presence of someone he is in love with." O'Faolain generalized thus about Bowen's characters: "There is an atmosphere of ancient fable behind all of Miss Bowen's fiction. Her persons are recognizable temperaments rather than composed characters. . . . Her characters are the modern, sophisticated, naturalistic novelist's versions of primitive urges. One feels that if she had lived three hundred and fifty years ago when passions rode freely and fiercely she would have described the dreams that drove Ophelia, Juliet and Desdemona to love and to death."

"Plot," wrote Bowen, "might seem to be a matter of choice. It is not. The particular plot is something the novelist is driven to. It is what is left after the whittling-away of alternatives. . . . Plot is diction. Action of language, language of action. . . . Plot is story. It is also 'a story' in the nursery sense-lie. The novel lies, in saying that something happened that did not. It must, there-

fore, contain uncontradictable truth, to warrant the original lie," the author continued, adding that "plot must further the novel towards its object. What object? The non-poetic statement of a poetic truth. . . . The essence of a poetic truth is that no statement of it can be final. . . . (Much to be learnt from storytelling to children. Much to be learnt from the detective story—especially non-irrelevance). . . . Plot must not cease to move forward. The *actual* speed of the movement must be even. *Apparent* variations in speed are good, necessary, but there must be no actual variations in speed."

Prescott noted that, in her short stories, Bowen "has followed the examples of Chekhov and Katherine Mansfield, concentrating on creation of a mood, insight into character and emotional atmosphere." Bowen, however, felt a certain ambivalence about the short story form which she has practiced since she was twenty. She told Harvey Breit in *The Writer Observed:* "I feel happiest, in the sense of poetic truth, in the short story. Yet if I wrote only short stories, I should feel was shirking. The novel is more of an ethical thing. The short story has the dangers of perfection. Of course, there should be in the novel both the perfections: the sort of architectural proportions and the poetic truth—which are most possible in the short story."

AVOCATIONAL INTERESTS: Music, movies, and detective stories.

BIOGRAPHICAL/CRITICAL SOURCES:

BOOKS

Allen, Walter, *The Modern Novel,* Dutton, 1965.
Bowen, Elizabeth, *Collected Impressions,* Knopf, 1950.
Breit, Harvey, *The Writer Observed,* World Publishing, 1956.
Contemporary Literary Criticism, Gale, Volume 1, 1973, Volume 3, 1975, Volume 6, 1976, Volume 11, 1979, Volume 15, 1980, Volume 22, 1982.
Dictionary of Literary Biography, Volume 15: *British Novelists, 1930-1959,* Gale, 1983.
Glendinning, Victoria, *Elizabeth Bowen,* Knopf, 1977.
O'Faolain, Sean, *The Vanishing Hero,* Little, Brown, 1956.
Phelps, Gilbert, editor, *Living Writers,* Sylvan Press, 1947.
Prescott, Orville, *In My Opinion,* Bobbs-Merrill, 1952.

PERIODICALS

Critique, spring, 1964, spring-summer, 1966.
New Statesman, March 26, 1965, August 6, 1965.
New York Times Book Review, January 26, 1964.
Times Literary Supplement, July 8, 1965.

OBITUARIES:

PERIODICALS

Newsweek, March 5, 1973.
New York Times, February 23, 1973.
Publishers Weekly, March 19, 1973.
Time, March 5, 1973.
Washington Post, February 24, 1973.

*   *   *

BOWLES, Paul (Frederick) 1910-

PERSONAL: Born December 30, 1910, in New York, N.Y.; son of Claude Dietz (a dentist) and Rena (Winnewisser) Bowles; married Jane Auer (a writer) February 21, 1938 (died, 1973). *Education:* Studied music with Aaron Copland in New York and Berlin, 1930-32, and with Virgil Thomson in Paris, 1933-34; also attended School of Design and Liberal Arts, New York, and University of Virginia.

ADDRESSES: Home—2117 Tanger Socco, Tangier, Morocco. *Agent*—William Morris Agency, 1350 Avenue of the Americas, New York, N.Y. 10019.

CAREER: Writer. Composer for stage, and of operas, film scores, ballets, songs, and chamber music; musical works include scores for "The Glass Menagerie," "Love's Old Sweet Song," "My Heart's in the Highlands," "Sweet Bird of Youth," and for the ballets "Pastorelas," "Yankee Clipper," and "Sentimental Colloquy." Visiting professor, San Fernando Valley State College (now California State University, Northridge), 1968.

AWARDS, HONORS: Guggenheim fellowship, 1941; National Institute of Arts and Letters Award in Literature, 1950; Rockefeller grant, 1959; National Endowment for the Arts creative writing fellowship, 1978, and senior fellowship, 1980; American Book Award nomination, 1980, for *Collected Stories of Paul Bowles, 1939-1976.*

WRITINGS:

NOVELS

The Sheltering Sky, New Directions, 1949, reprinted, Ecco Press, 1978.
Let It Come Down, Random House, 1952, reprinted, Black Sparrow Press, 1980.
The Spider's House, Random House, 1955, revised edition, Black Sparrow Press, 1982.
Up Above the World, Simon & Schuster, 1966.

SHORT STORIES

The Delicate Prey, and Other Stories (includes "A Distant Episode"), Random House, 1950, reprinted, Ecco Press, 1972.
A Little Stone: Stories, J. Lehmann, 1950.
The Hours after Noon, Heinemann, 1959.
A Hundred Camels in the Courtyard, City Lights, 1962.
The Time of Friendship, Holt, 1967.
Pages from Cold Point, and Other Stories, P. Owen, 1968.
Three Tales, F. Hallman, 1975.
Things Gone and Things Still Here, Black Sparrow Press, 1977.
Collected Stories of Paul Bowles, 1939-1976, Black Sparrow Press, 1979.
Midnight Mass, and Other Stories, Black Sparrow Press, 1981.
Unwelcome Words, Tombouctou Books, 1988.
Call at Corazon, and Other Stories, P. Owen, 1988.

POETRY

Scenes, Black Sparrow Press, 1968.
The Thicket of Spring: Poems, 1926-1969, Black Sparrow Press, 1972.
Next to Nothing, Starstreams, 1976.
Next to Nothing: Collected Poems, 1926-1977, Black Sparrow Press, 1981.

TRANSLATOR FROM THE MOGHREBI

Driss ben Hamed Charhadi, *A Life Full of Holes,* Grove, 1963.
Mohammed Mrabet, *Love with a Few Hairs,* P. Owen, 1967.
Mrabet, *The Lemon,* P. Owen, 1969.
Mrabet, *M'Hashish,* City Lights, 1969.
Mrabet, *The Boy Who Set the Fire, and Other Stories,* Black Sparrow Press, 1974.
Mrabet, *Hadidan Aharam,* Black Sparrow Press, 1975.
Mrabet, *Harmless Poisons, Blameless Sins,* Black Sparrow Press, 1976.

Mrabet, *Look and Move On,* Black Sparrow Press, 1976.
Mrabet, *The Big Mirror,* Black Sparrow Press, 1977.
Five Eyes, Black Sparrow Press, 1979.
Mrabet, *The Beach Cafe,* Black Sparrow Press, 1980.
Mrabet, *The Chest,* Tombouctou Books, 1983.
Marriage with Papers, Tombouctou Books, 1986.

TRANSLATOR FROM THE FRENCH

Jean-Paul Sartre, *No Exit,* Samuel French, 1946.
Isabelle Eberhardt, *The Oblivion Seekers, and Other Writings,* City Lights, 1975.

Also translator of other works from French.

TRANSLATOR FROM THE ARABIC

Mohamed Choukri, *For Bread Alone,* P. Owen, 1973.
Choukri, *Jean Genet in Tangier,* Ecco Press, 1974.
Choukri, *Tennessee Williams in Tangier,* Cadmus Editions, 1979.

OTHER

(With Luchino Visconti and Tennessee Williams) "Senso" (screenplay), Domenico Forges Davanzati, 1954.
Yallah (travel essays), McDowell, Obolensky, 1957.
Their Heads Are Green and Their Hands Are Blue (travel essays), Random House, 1963 (published in England as *Their Heads Are Green,* P. Owen, 1963).
"Paul Bowles in the Land of the Jumblies" (screenplay), Gary Conklin, 1969.
Without Stopping (autobiography), Putnam, 1972.
Points in Time, Ecco Press, 1982.
(Translator from the Spanish) Rodrigo Rey Rosa, *The Beggar's Knife,* City Lights, 1985.

Also translator of other works from Spanish and Italian.

SIDELIGHTS: Paul Bowles's fiction depicts the frailty of Western rationalism. In the essential Bowles story, American or European travellers visit a civilization that they consider vastly inferior to their own, usually in the North African desert. When they enter that more primitive world, however, their Western values quickly disintegrate. Inevitably, contact with the older culture transforms the traveller's world view; not infrequently, it destroys them. Although he remains best known for his novel *The Sheltering Sky,* Bowles has also distinguished himself as a composer, short story writer, translator, and poet.

Even as a child, Bowles wrote fiction and music; he was sixteen years old when the highly-regarded magazine *transition* published his surrealist poetry. A 1931 trip to Paris really marked the beginning of his adult writing career, however, for it was then that he met and became friends with author Gertrude Stein and her companion, Alice B. Toklas. These two women were to give Bowles important direction concerning his literary efforts. Stein was not fond of surrealism, and her criticism of Bowles's poetry was harsh. In a *Dictionary of Literary Biography* essay, Lawrence D. Stewart quotes her as saying to the young writer, "Now Bravig Imbs, for instance, he's just a very bad poet. . . . But you—you're not a poet at all!"

Stein believed that some time away from Western culture would help Bowles discover his own style. Alice Toklas, who according to Stewart "had a talent for putting people in a proper setting," suggested Morocco. In so doing, she introduced the young author to the place where he would live for most of his life, and which would serve as the setting for the greater part of his fiction. He rented a house in Tangier, sharing it with composer Aaron Copland, who was then serving as Bowles's musical mentor. Although primarily concerned with his composition at this time, Bowles did send to Gertrude Stein some prose passages, which pleased her much more than had his poetry. Stewart quotes a letter to Bowles in which Stein wrote: "I like your story, I like your descriptions, go on with them."

It would be ten years before Bowles would seriously devote himself to writing fiction, however. In the meantime, he returned to New York City; there he was in demand as a composer of theatre music, providing scores for works by such notable playwrights as Tennessee Williams and William Saroyan. One of Bowles's most unusual projects during this period was a ballet choreographed by Spanish artist Salvador Dali. The dance was complicated by costumes featuring floor-length underarm hair, bicyclists riding across the stage, and a large mechanical tortoise which sometimes charged straight for the dancers' feet. "Hisses and catcalls were more or less constant on opening night," recalls Bowles in his *Contemporary Authors Autobiography Series* essay.

It was in 1942 that Bowles again became inspired to write fiction. Watching his wife, Jane Auer, at work on her novel *Two Serious Ladies* "was the thing that detonated the explosion," Stewart quotes Bowles. His stories were soon appearing in such diverse publications as *Harper's Bazaar, View, Mademoiselle,* and *Partisan Review.* When he had collected enough to make up an entire volume, he sent them to a publisher "hoping somehow to bypass the unwritten law which makes it impossible for a writer to publish a book of short stories until after he has published a novel," notes Bowles in *CA Autobiography Series.* He did not succeed in this aim, but after reading his stories, editors at Doubleday were willing to commission a novel. A vivid dream of Morocco convinced Bowles that he must return there to write. Soon he was en route to Fez, and within eight months he had completed *The Sheltering Shy,* a novel so startling that upon receiving the manuscript, Doubleday demanded the return of their advance money, declaring that what Bowles had produced was not a novel.

Subsequently published by New Directions, *The Sheltering Sky* has since been praised as a masterpiece of existential literature. Theodore Solotaroff expresses the opinion of many critics in a *New Republic* article, calling it "one of the most beautifully written novels of the past twenty years and one of the most shattering. Bowles is not the philosopher that Sartre or Camus were, but he is an existentialist to his fingertips, and beside the emotional concreteness of *The Sheltering Sky,* books like *Nausea, The Age of Reason,* or *The Stranger* seem vague, arbitrary, imaginatively barren."

According to Stewart, Bowles himself describes *The Sheltering Sky* as "an adventure story, in which the actual adventures take place on two planes simultaneously: in the actual desert, and in the inner desert of the spirit." The main characters are Port and Kit Moresby, two sophisticated American drifters whose feelings of emptiness are revealed in Port's remark to his wife: "We've never managed, either of us, to get all the way into life." Their wanderings take them to the North African desert. There, writes *Esquire* contributor Tobias Wolff, "in the silent emptiness of desert and sky, the knowledge of their absolute isolation from other people comes upon them so violently that it subverts their belief in their own reality and in the reality of their connection to each other. Doubting that connection is, of course, prelude to betraying it. And betray it they do, in every way." Port falls mortally ill; Kit abandons her dying husband for another man. Eventually, she becomes the mindlessly contented slave of an Arab named Belqassim. Subjugation brings her such peace that when Belqassim loses interest in her, she searches for another captor.

When French colonial authorities finally locate Kit, she has abandoned her identity so completely that she fails even to recognize her own name.

"*The Sheltering Sky* has been called nightmarish; that description lets us off the hook too easily, because it implies a fear of the unreal," believes Wolff. "The power of this novel lies precisely in the reality of what it makes us fear—the sweetness of that voice in each of us that sings the delight of not being responsible. . . . Our failing resistance to . . . attacks on our sense of worth as individuals is the central drama of our time. *The Sheltering Sky* records the struggle with complete fidelity, impassively noting every step in the process of surrender. Like *The Sun Also Rises* and *Under the Volcano,* Bowles's novel enacts a crucial historical moment with such clarity that it has become part of our picture of that moment."

With a critically acclaimed novel to his credit, Bowles was able to publish his collection *The Delicate Prey, and Other Stories.* The stories in this volume, writes Wolff, extend "the perceptions of the novel into even more exotic and disturbing terrain." The title story, for example, delineates a hashish-maddened hunter's murder of three brothers, and the revenge of the slain brothers' tribesmen: after capturing the killer, they bury him up to his neck in sand and abandon him to the elements. In "A Distant Episode," which Tennessee Williams called in *Saturday Review of Literature* "a true masterpiece of short fiction," an American linguistics professor, betrayed by his native guide, is seized by a band of hostile nomads. Mutilated and dressed in a suit of flattened tin cans, the professor is then kept as a hideous pet by the tribesmen, who teach him to dance for their amusement. "The curiosity-seeker has himself become a curiosity, comically and ineffectually armored in the detritus of his own culture," notes Wolff. "The story is a tour de force, an ominous parable of the weakening of the individual will to survive." Solotaroff states that the stories in *The Delicate Prey,* "with their lucid, quiet evocation of mood and motive leading to revelations of scarifying depravity," are so powerful that they make "the nihilism of the early Hemingway seem like a pleasant beery melancholy. . . . These stories . . . make one feel they were written with a razor, so deftly and chillingly do they cut to the bone."

The brutal action that is prevalent in Bowles's stories is in sharp contrast to his cool, detached prose. Stylistically, "he is a classic, master craftsman; precise, incisive, knowing," writes Stephen Koch in *Washington Post Book World.* "There is always some strange mystery lurking in his stories, and there is never a shoddy or lazy line. The result combines the exemplary and the unspeakable in a way that cannot be found anywhere else." Stewart agrees that "Bowles' productions are too finely fashioned ever to be thought ugly—no matter what his subject and materials. His struggle has always been to get further into human consciousness and to explore its manifestations." And Irving Malin writes in *Ontario Review* that although Bowles's fiction frequently depicts some sort of savagery, the author cannot be considered "a sensationalist," for "he does not glory in his painstaking depiction of madness or destruction or mysticism. He believes that life is unpredictably cruel—even to cruel heroes!—and that his accurate, intense art must *contain* the cruelty. His style is thus stripped of prettiness. It is clear, direct, bold."

Bowles's subsequent fiction continued to feature the elements that made *The Sheltering Sky* and *The Delicate Prey* unique: exotic locations, existential concerns, and pristine prose. *Let It Come Down* follows a bank clerk as he flees the desolation of his life in New York City for Tangier, where he experiences a rapid disintegration. In *The Spider's House,* four expatriate Westerners are caught up in the violence of revolution in Fez. *Up Above the World* tells of a jaded American couple traveling across South America. Their entanglement with a stranger leads to their brainwashing and murder. The similarities found in Bowles's works have led some critics to suggest that the author made his strongest statement in his first two books and had failed to develop artistically thereafter. While admiring the author's stylistic mastery, Bernard Bergonzi in the *New York Review of Books* finds "what he does with it very limited and ultimately monotonous. He places his characters before us and then destroys them in an unerring way: it is a remarkable performance, but one expects something more from literature." Francis King concurs in a *Spectator* article that Bowles unfortunately restricts himself to a "constant retreading of the same narrow plot, instead of the exploration of previously untrodden jungle."

Other reviewers maintain that within his self-imposed limits, Bowles demonstrates a versatility and virtuosity that places him at the forefront of American letters. "The novels and stories come at you from every direction, told from the points of view of men, women, Europeans, Arabs, priests, lunatics, murderers, merchants, beggars, animals, and spirits," points out Wolff. "His tales are at once austere, witty, violent, and sensuous. . . . His language has a purity of line, a poise and authority entirely its own, capable of instantly modulating from farce to horror without a ruffle and without giving any signal of delight in itself. In short, Bowles has proven himself, on the evidence of an extraordinary body of writing, to be one of our most serious and authentic literary artists."

Paul Bowles's writing was curtailed when his wife suffered a stroke and, afterwards, a long physical decline. "During the latter years of Jane's illness . . . it was impossible for me to write fiction," he reveals in *CA Autobiography Series*. "The periods which I had to myself were of very short duration: fifteen or twenty minutes, instead of several hours. Frequent interruptions destroyed creative impetus." Discovering that "the act of translating did not suffer in any way from being stopped at short intervals," however, Bowles began what he considers to be some of his most important work. The publication of tales told by his young Arab friends. These tales, often produced when the narrators are under the influence of *kif* (a marijuana-related substance), were tape recorded, transcribed, and translated by Bowles. They illustrate the ways of thought that the American author has come to appreciate during his many years in North Africa.

After Jane Auer's death in 1973, Bowles once again turned to fiction. Some critics indicate that his most recent work may be his most distinguished. Tobias Wolff describes Bowles's 1982 publication, *Points in Time*, as "a nervy, surprising, completely original performance, so original that it can't be referred to any previous category of fiction or nonfiction." The book's structure reflects Bowles's musical training; it is divided into several sections or 'movements.' In this way, the author combines legends, historical anecdotes, description, and passages of popular song to create a portrait of Morocco through the years. It is accomplished with "a centered precision that at times reaches perfection and becomes so memorable, it does damage to the eye and the brain of the reader," says Ben Pleasants in the *Los Angeles Times Book Review*. Tobias Wolff agrees that *Points in Time* is "a brilliant achievement, innovative in form, composed in a language whose every word, every pause feels purposeful and right." Conrad Knickerbocker concludes in a *New York Times* article that among American writers, Bowles continues to stand "in the front rank for the substance of his ideas and for the power

and conviction with which he expresses his own particular vision, which, if hellish, is totally appropriate to the times."

MEDIA ADAPTATIONS: Bowles recorded his short stories "The Delicate Prey" and "A Distant Episode" on an album for Spoken Arts in 1963; his novel *A Hundred Camels in the Courtyard* was recorded for Cadmus Editions in 1981; *The Sheltering Sky* was filmed by director Bernardo Bertolucci in 1990.

BIOGRAPHICAL/CRITICAL SOURCES:

BOOKS

Aldridge, John, *After the Lost Generation,* Noonday, 1951.
Allen, Walter, *The Modern Novel,* Dutton, 1965.
Bainbridge, John, *Another Way of Living: A Gallery of Americans Who Choose to Live in Europe,* Holt, 1968.
Bertens, Hans, *The Fiction of Paul Bowles: The Soul Is the Weariest Part of the Body,* Humanities, 1979.
Bowles, Paul, *Without Stopping,* Putnam, 1972.
Contemporary Authors Autobiography Series, Volume 1, Gale, 1984.
Contemporary Literary Criticism, Gale, Volume 1, 1973, Volume 2, 1974, Volume 19, 1981, Volume 53, 1989.
Dictionary of Literary Biography, Gale, Volume 5: *American Poets since World War II,* 1980, Volume 6: *American Novelists since World War II, Second Series,* 1980.
Sawyer-Laucanno, Christopher, *An Invisible Spectator: A Biography of Paul Bowles,* Weidenfeld & Nicolson, 1989.
Solotaroff, Theodore, *The Red Hot Vacuum, and Other Pieces on the Writing of the Sixties,* Atheneum, 1970.
Steen, Mike, *A Look at Tennessee Williams,* Hawthorn, 1969.
Stewart, Lawrence D., *The Illumination of North Africa,* Southern Illinois University Press, 1974.
Stewart, Lawrence D., *The Mystery and Detection Annual,* Donald Adams, 1973.

PERIODICALS

Books and Bookmen, June, 1968.
Chicago Tribune, August 9, 1988.
Commonweal, March 7, 1952.
Critique, Volume 3, number 1, 1959.
Esquire, May, 1985.
Gargoyle, number 24.
Harper's, October, 1959.
Hollins Critic, April, 1978.
Illustrated London News, January 28, 1967.
Life, July 21, 1967.
Listener, February 2, 1967.
London Magazine, November, 1960, February, 1967, June, 1968.
Los Angeles Times, April 19, 1981.
Los Angeles Times Book Review, September 16, 1984.
Mediterranean Review, winter, 1971.
Nation, September 4, 1967.
National Observer, July 24, 1967.
New England Review, spring, 1980.
New Republic, September 2, 1967, April 22, 1972.
New Statesman, January 27, 1967.
New York Review of Books, November 9, 1967, May 18, 1972.
New York Times, March 12, 1966, March 21, 1972, October 17, 1989.
New York Times Book Review, March 2, 1952, March 9, 1952, August 25, 1963, March 10, 1966, August 6, 1967, April 9, 1972, September 20, 1979.
Ontario Review, spring-summer, 1980.
Partisan Review, winter, 1968.
Punch, February 8, 1967.

Rolling Stone, May 23, 1974.
Saturday Review, December 23, 1950, October 20, 1955.
Spectator, March 20, 1985.
Time, August 4, 1967.
Times (London), August 20, 1981, August 11, 1985.
Times Literary Supplement, September 30, 1949, February 2, 1967, May 9, 1968, October 13, 1972, May 13, 1988.
Voice Literary Supplement, April, 1986.
Washington Post Book World, September 9, 1979, August 2, 1981.

* * *

BOX, Edgar
See VIDAL, Gore

* * *

BOYD, Nancy
See MILLAY, Edna St. Vincent

* * *

BOYLE, Kay 1902-

PERSONAL: Born February 19, 1902, in St. Paul, Minn.; daughter of Howard Peterson and Katherine (Evans) Boyle; married Richard Brault, June 24, 1923 (divorced); married Laurence Vail, April 2, 1931 (divorced, 1943); married Baron Joseph von Franckenstein, February 20, 1943 (died, 1963); children: Sharon Walsh; (second marriage) Apple-Joan, Kathe, Clover; (third marriage) Faith Carson, Ian Savin. *Education:* Studied architecture at Parson's School of Fine and Applied Arts in New York and Ohio Mechanics Institute in Cincinnati, 1917-19; took courses at Columbia University and studied violin at Cincinnati Conservatory of Music. *Politics:* Democrat.

ADDRESSES: Home—41 Yosemite, Oakland, Calif. 94611. *Agent*—Gloria Loomis, Watkins, Loomis Agency, Inc., 150 East 35th St., Suite 530, New York, N.Y. 10016.

CAREER: Writer. Taught night school course in writing, Nyack, N.Y., 1941-43; teacher at Miss Thomas's School in Connecticut during fifties and early sixties; San Francisco State College (now University), San Francisco, Calif., member of English faculty, 1963-79. Member of workshop in the short story, New School for Social Research, 1962; lecturer and writer in residence at various colleges and universities, including Northwestern State University, Spokane, Wash., 1981, and Bowling Green State University, Bowling Green, Ohio, 1986. Fellow at Wesleyan University, Middletown, Conn., 1963, and Radcliffe Institute for Independent Study, 1965.

MEMBER: American Academy and Institute of Arts and Letters (Henry James Chair).

AWARDS, HONORS: Guggenheim fellowships, 1934 and 1961; O. Henry Memorial Award for best short story of the year, 1934, for "The White Horses of Vienna," and 1941, for "Defeat"; D.Litt., Columbia College, 1971, Skidmore College, 1977, and Southern Illinois College, 1982; California Literature Medal Award, 1971, for *Testament for My Students;* National Endowment for the Arts Fellowship, 1980, for "extraordinary contribution to American literature over a lifetime of creative work"; Before Columbus Foundation American Book Award, 1984, for lifetime achievement; Robert Kirsch Award, *Los Angeles Times,* 1986; French-American Foundation Translation prize, 1986, for "distinguished contribution to French and American letters as author and translator"; nominated for *Los Angeles Times* Book Award in poetry, 1986, for *This Is Not a Letter and Other Poems;* Special Award for "Outstanding Literary Achievement," Lannan Foundation, 1989.

WRITINGS:

NOVELS

Plagued by the Nightingale, Cape & Smith, 1931, new edition, Southern Illinois University Press, 1969, reprinted with new introduction by the author, Virago, 1981.
Year before Last, H. Smith, 1932, new edition, Southern Illinois University Press, 1969, reprinted, Penguin, 1986.
Gentlemen, I Address You Privately, Smith & Haas, 1933.
My Next Bride, Harcourt, 1934, reprinted with new introduction by Doris Grumbach, Virago, 1986.
Death of a Man, Harcourt, 1936, reprinted, New Directions, 1989.
Monday Night, Harcourt, 1938, reprinted, P. P. Appel, 1977.
The Crazy Hunter: Three Short Novels (also see below; includes "The Crazy Hunter," "The Bridegroom's Body," and "Big Fiddle"), Harcourt, 1940 (published in England as *The Crazy Hunter and Other Stories,* Faber, 1940), reprinted with introduction by Margaret Atwood, Penguin, 1982.
Primer for Combat, Simon & Schuster, 1942.
Avalanche, Simon & Schuster, 1944.
A Frenchman Must Die, Simon & Schuster, 1946.
1939, Simon & Schuster, 1948.
His Human Majesty, Whittlesey House, 1949.
The Seagull on the Step, Knopf, 1955.
Three Short Novels (includes "The Crazy Hunter," "The Bridegroom's Body," and "Decision"), Beacon, 1958.
Generation without Farewell, Knopf, 1960.
The Underground Woman, Doubleday, 1975.

SHORT STORIES

Short Stories, Black Sun (Paris), 1929.
Wedding Day and Other Stories, Cape & Smith, 1930, reprinted, Books for Libraries Press, 1972.
The First Lover and Other Stories, Random, 1933.
The White Horses of Vienna and Other Stories, Harcourt, 1936.
Thirty Stories, Simon & Schuster, 1946.
The Smoking Mountain: Stories of Post-War Germany, McGraw, 1951.
Nothing Ever Breaks Except the Heart, Doubleday, 1966.
Fifty Stories, Doubleday, 1980.
Life Being the Best and Other Stories, New Directions, 1988.

POETRY

A Statement, Modern Editions Press, 1932.
A Glad Day, New Directions, 1938.
American Citizen: Naturalized in Leadville, Colorado (long poem), Simon & Schuster, 1944.
The Lost Dogs of Phnom Pehn, Two Windows (Berkeley), 1968.
Testament for My Students and Other Poems, Doubleday, 1970.
A Poem for February First 1975, Quercus Press, 1975.
This Is Not a Letter and Other Poems, Sun & Moon, 1985.

JUVENILE

The Youngest Camel, Little, Brown, 1939, revised edition published as *The Youngest Camel: Reconsidered and Rewritten,* Harper, 1959.
Pinky, the Cat Who Liked to Sleep, Crowell-Collier, 1966.
Pinky in Persia, Crowell-Collier, 1968.

NONFICTION

Breaking the Silence: Why a Mother Tells Her Son about the Nazi Era (pamphlet), Institute of Human Relations Press (New York), 1962.

The Long Walk at San Francisco State and Other Essays, Grove, 1970.

(With others) *Four Visions of America,* Capra, 1977.

Words That Must Somehow Be Said: Selected Essays of Kay Boyle, 1927-1984, North Point Press, 1985.

TRANSLATOR FROM THE FRENCH

Joseph Delteil, *Don Juan,* Cape & Smith, 1931.

Rene Crevel, *Mr. Knife Miss Fork,* Black Sun, 1931.

Raymond Radiguet, *Devil in the Flesh,* H. Smith, 1932.

(And author of afterword) Crevel, *Babylon,* North Point Press, 1985.

GHOST WRITER

Gladys Palmer Brooke, *Relations & Complications: Being the Recollections of H. H. the Dayang Muda of Sarawak,* Lane, 1929.

Bettina Bedwell, *Yellow Dusk,* Hurst & Blackett, 1937.

EDITOR

Poems and Sonnets by Ernest Walsh, Harcourt, 1934.

(With former husband Laurence Vail and Nina Conarain) *365 Days,* Harcourt, 1936.

The Autobiography of Emanuel Carnevali, Horizon Press, 1967.

(And contributor of supplementary chapters) Robert McAlmon, *Being Geniuses Together, 1920-1930* (memoirs), Doubleday, 1968, revised edition with new afterword by Boyle, Northpoint Press, 1984.

(With Justine Van Gundy) *Enough of Dying! Voices for Peace,* Laurel, 1972.

OTHER

(Author of foreword) Herbert Kubly, *At Large,* Gollancz, 1963, Doubleday, 1964.

(Author of afterword) McAlmon, *A Hasty Bunch,* Southern Illinois University Press, 1977.

Contributor to anthologies, including numerous volumes of *Best American Short Stories,* edited by Edward O'Brien. On staff of *Broom* magazine, 1922; foreign correspondent in Germany for *New Yorker,* 1946-53. Regular contributor to *Transition, Saturday Evening Post, Harper's,* and *Nation.*

WORK IN PROGRESS: The Irish Women; revised edition of *Gentlemen, I Address You Privately;* a long poem on Samuel Beckett.

SIDELIGHTS: "The older I grow," novelist, short story writer, poet, and essayist Kay Boyle comments in an interview with Kay Mills of the *Los Angeles Times,* "the more I feel that all writers should be more committed to their times and write of their times and of the issues of their times." According to Mills, both Boyle's narrative style and themes reflect the writer's commitment to her times. Boyle's largely autobiographical fiction is her major vehicle for social commentary. Her short stories—which critics such as Robert E. Kroll in *Prairie Schooner* and Theodore L. Gross in *Saturday Review* describe as her best work—illustrate both the writer's noteworthy style and what Gross calls, "her intention to measure [in her fiction] . . . the central issues of our time."

From the publication of Boyle's first volume of short fiction to her anthology of nearly forty years of writing, *Fifty Stories,* her mastery of style has interested critics. When Katherine Anne

Porter examined Boyle's early work in a 1931 review (included in *The Critic as Artist: Essays on Books, 1920-1970*), she noted Boyle's involvement with the experimental Parisian literary monthly, *Transition,* and the journal's effect on Boyle's writing. According to Porter, Boyle's prose "sums up the salient qualities of [those writers who regularly contributed to *Transition*]: a fighting spirit, freshness of feeling, curiosity, the courage of her own attitude and idiom, a violently dedicated search for the meanings and methods of art."

Critical comment on Boyle's style also comes from other sources, including Richard C. Carpenter and Vance Bourjaily. Both compare Boyle's work to that of more well-known writers of the same period. In *Critique: Studies in Modern Fiction,* Carpenter comments: "Like Faulkner or Virginia Woolf or Joyce, Kay Boyle works largely with interior monologue, sometimes with a stream of consciousness, thus setting the internal states of her characters in contrast to the outer world, or complementary to it." In Bourjaily's *New York Times Book Review* essay the critic finds *Fifty Stories* "a wonderful exhibit of . . . techniques and themes [introduced by writers living in Paris in the twenties] in evolution. Among the techniques we have grammatical simplification, rhythmic repetition, the mixing in of vernacular, stream of consciousness, density of impressions, radical imagery and experiments with surrealism that may have originated with Gertrude Stein and James Joyce but became community property of the group."

Like the others members of the American literary set that flourished in Paris during the early years of the twentieth century, Boyle was committed to resisting traditional forms of writing. But, although her writing may have been her first act of defiance against authority, it wasn't her last. During the fifties she fought the accusations and subsequent black-listing brought against her husband, Joseph von Franckenstein, and herself, by Communist-hunters Senator Joseph McCarthy and his fellow investigators. She has continued to speak out against injustice throughout her life no matter how unpopular her views, speaking out in the sixties against the war in Vietnam and in the eighties protesting the U.S. bombing of Libya.

Like the stylistic elements of her fiction, Boyle's most important theme, which *Saturday Review* contributor Carole Cook cites as "the individual's moral responsibility," dates back to some of her earliest writing. For example, in his introduction to *Fifty Stories* David Daiches notes this moral function in particular in Boyle's stories written during World War II. The stories "read as though they have been *lived through* . . . ," he remarks. "But they are far from being merely 'on the spot' reporting, nor are they 'war stories' in the conventional sense. Their object is not to describe either horror or heroism, but to explore the core of human meaning in desperate situations." Earl Rovit finds the same theme in Boyle's stories. He notes in his *Nation* essay, "A steady passionate concern for social justice and an equally unswerving compassion for the poignancies of human suffering are powerful and noble weapons in any artist's arsenal—and to these Kay Boyle can justly lay claim." *Chicago Tribune Book World* contributor Cyra McFadden similarly notes the "strong moral center" illustrated by Boyle's fiction.

Despite general critical approval for Boyle's work, she has never enjoyed wide-spread popularity. *Dictionary of Literary Biography* contributor David V. Koch theorizes that Boyle "has been so busy writing and acting upon her beliefs . . . that she has had little time to cultivate a following. Indeed, seeking literary fame would be contrary to Boyle's beliefs, for she has consistently sought to speak for those who could not speak for themselves."

Boyle's papers and manuscripts are at the Morris Library, Southern Illinois University, Carbondale.

MEDIA ADAPTATIONS: "The Crazy Hunter" was adapted for television by Desilu Productions, 1958; the short story "The Ballet of Central Park" was adapted and filmed as a short subject in 1972; the short story "Maiden, Maiden" was made into a full-length feature film by Highland Films, 1980.

AVOCATIONAL INTERESTS: Riding horses and climbing mountains.

BIOGRAPHICAL/CRITICAL SOURCES:

BOOKS

Boyle, Kay, *Fifty Stories,* introduction by David Daiches, Doubleday, 1980.
Boyle, Kay, *Life Being the Best & Other Stories,* edited and with an introduction by Sandra Whipple Spanier, New Directions, 1988.
Contemporary Authors Autobiography Series, Volume 1, Gale, 1984.
Contemporary Literary Criticism, Gale, Volume 1, 1973, Volume 5, 1976, Volume 19, 1978.
Dictionary of Literary Biography, Gale, Volume 4: *American Writers in Paris, 1920-1939,* 1980, Volume 9: *American Novelists, 1910-1945,* 1981, Volume 48, *American Poets, 1880-1945, Second Series,* 1986.
Madden, Charles F., *Talks with Authors,* Southern Illinois University Press, 1968.
Moore, Harry T., *Age of the Modern and Other Literary Essays,* Southern Illinois University Press, 1971.
Porter, Katherine Anne, *The Critic as Artist: Essays on Books, 1920-1970,* edited by Gilbert A. Harrison, Liveright, 1972.
Spanier, Sandra Whipple, *Kay Boyle: Artist and Activist,* Southern Illinois University Press, 1986.
Wilson, Edmund, *Classics and Commercials: A Literary Chronicle of the Forties,* Farrar, Straus, 1950.
Yalom, Marilyn, editor, *Women Writers of the West Coast,* Capra Press, 1983.

PERIODICALS

Bookman, June, 1932.
Book World, June 9, 1968.
Chicago Tribune Book World, October 12, 1980.
Christian Science Monitor, January 5, 1971, November 10, 1980.
College English, November, 1953.
Critique: Studies in Modern Fiction, winter, 1964-65.
English Journal, November, 1953.
Kenyon Review, spring, 1960.
London Review of Books, April 15, 1982.
Los Angeles Times, December 10, 1980, June 18, 1984, October 12, 1986, September 14, 1989.
Los Angeles Times Book Review, August 4, 1985, September 29, 1985, April 13, 1986.
Ms., August, 1985.
Nation, December 24, 1930, October 24, 1936, June 8, 1970, June 15, 1970, April 26, 1971, June 26, 1972, March 22, 1975, September 27, 1980.
New Republic, April 22, 1931, July 13, 1932, December 13, 1933, October 21, 1936, January 24, 1970, February 8, 1975.
Newsweek, January 25, 1960, January 13, 1975.
New Yorker, January 20, 1975.
New York Herald Tribune Books, November 12, 1933, February 9, 1936, March 10, 1940.

New York Times, November 16, 1930, March 26, 1933, November 12, 1933, October 11, 1936, December 1, 1946, June 21, 1966, September 20, 1989.
New York Times Book Review, July 10, 1966, June 9, 1968, February 2, 1975, September 28, 1980, July 15, 1984, August 25, 1985, September 22, 1985, November 16, 1986, July 3, 1988.
Poetry, November, 1971.
Prairie Schooner, summer, 1963, winter, 1966-67.
Publishers Weekly, October 17, 1980, March 11, 1988.
Saturday Review, March 25, 1933, November 4, 1933, November 30, 1946, April 9, 1949, April 21, 1951, July 16, 1966, January 7, 1978, September, 1980.
Times Literary Supplement, November 30, 1967, April 17, 1981, September 27, 1985.
Washington Post Book World, October 19, 1980, October 5, 1986.
Wilson Library Bulletin, January, 1932.

*   *   *

BOYLE, Mark
See Kienzle, William X(avier)

*   *   *

BRADBURY, Edward P.
See MOORCOCK, Michael (John)

*   *   *

BRADBURY, Malcolm (Stanley) 1932-

PERSONAL: Born September 7, 1932, in Sheffield, England; son of Arthur and Doris (Marshall) Bradbury; married Elizabeth Salt, October, 1959; children: Matthew, Dominic. *Education:* University College, University of Leicester, B.A. (first class honors), 1953; University of London, M.A., 1955; attended University of Manchester, 1956-58, received Ph.D., 1964.

ADDRESSES: Office—School of English and American Studies, University of East Anglia, Norwich, Norfolk NR4 7TJ, England.

CAREER: University of Hull, Hull, England, staff tutor in literature and drama in department of adult education, 1959-61; University of Birmingham, Birmingham, England, lecturer in English language and literature, 1961-65; University of East Anglia, Norwich, England, lecturer, 1965-67, senior lecturer, 1967-69, reader in English, 1969-70, professor of American studies, 1970—. Teaching fellow, Indiana University, 1955-56; junior fellow, Yale University, 1958-59; fellow, Harvard University, 1965-66; visiting professor, University of California, Davis, 1966; visiting fellow, All Souls College, Oxford University, 1969; visiting professor, University of Zurich, 1972; Fanny Hurst Professor of Writing, Washington University, 1982; Davis Professor, University of Queensland, and visiting professor, Griffith University, 1983. Chairman of British Council English Studies Seminar, 1976-84; chairman of judges for Booker-McConnell Prize for Fiction, 1981; director of Radio Broadland (independent radio station).

MEMBER: British Association of American Studies, Society of Authors, P.E.N., Royal Society of Literature (fellow).

AWARDS, HONORS: British Association of American Studies junior fellow in United States, 1958-59; American Council of

Learned Societies fellow, 1965-66; Heinemann Prize, Royal Society of Literature, 1975, for *The History Man;* named among twenty best British writers by Book Marketing Council, 1982; shortlisted for Booker-McConnell Prize for Fiction, 1983, for *Rates of Exchange;* International Emmy Award, 1987, for "Porterhouse Blue"; honorary fellow of Queen Mary College, University of London.

WRITINGS:

Eating People Is Wrong (novel), Secker & Warburg, 1959, Knopf, 1960.

Phogey!; or, How to Have Class in a Classless Society (also see below), Parrish, 1960.

All Dressed Up and Nowhere to Go: The Poor Man's Guide to the Affluent Society (also see below), Parrish, 1962.

Evelyn Waugh (critical study), Oliver & Boyd, 1962.

Stepping Westward (novel), Secker & Warburg, 1965, Houghton, 1966.

(With Allan Rodway) *Two Poets* (verse), Byron Press, 1966.

What Is a Novel?, Edward Arnold, 1969.

The Social Context of Modern English Literature, Schocken, 1971.

Possibilities: Essays on the State of the Novel, Oxford University Press, 1972.

The History Man (novel), Secker & Warburg, 1975, Houghton, 1976.

Who Do You Think You Are?: Stories and Parodies, Secker & Warburg, 1976.

The Outland Dart: American Writers and European Modernism, Oxford University Press, 1978.

Saul Bellow (critical study), Methuen, 1982.

All Dressed Up and Nowhere to Go (contains revised versions of *Phogey!* and *All Dressed Up and Nowhere to Go*), Pavilion, 1982.

Rates of Exchange (novel), Knopf, 1983.

The Modern American Novel, Oxford University Press, 1983.

Why Come to Slaka?, Secker & Warburg, 1986.

Cuts (novel), Harper, 1987.

My Strange Quest for Mensonge, Penguin, 1988.

No, Not Bloomsbury (collected essays), Columbia University Press, 1988.

Unsent Letters: Irreverent Notes from a Literary Life, Penguin, 1988.

The Modern World: Ten Great Writers, Penguin, 1989.

DRAMA

(With David Lodge and James Duckett) "Between These Four Walls" (stage revue), first produced in Birmingham, England, 1963.

(With Lodge, Duckett, and David Turner) "Slap in the Middle" (stage revue), first produced in Birmingham, England, 1965.

(With Chris Bigsby) "The After Dinner Game" (television play), British Broadcasting Corporation (BBC), 1975.

(With Bigsby) "Stones" (television play), BBC, 1976.

"Love on a Gunboat" (television play), BBC, 1977.

"The Enigma" (television play based on a story by John Fowles), BBC, 1980.

"Standing in for Henry" (television play), BBC, 1980.

"Congress" (radio play), BBC, 1981.

The After Dinner Game: Three Plays for Television, Arrow Books, 1982.

"Rates of Exchange" (television series based on own novel), BBC, 1985.

"Blott on the Landscape" (television series adapted from novel by Tom Sharpe), BBC, 1985.

Author, with wife, Elizabeth Bradbury, of radio play "This Sporting Life," 1974-75; "Porterhouse Blue," for television, adapted from work by Tom Sharpe, 1987.

EDITOR

E. M. Forster: A Collection of Critical Essays, Prentice-Hall, 1965.

Mark Twain, *"Pudd'nhead Wilson" and "Those Extraordinary Twins,"* Penguin, 1969.

E. M. Forster, *"A Passage to India": A Casebook*, Macmillan, 1970.

(With David Palmer) *Contemporary Criticism*, Edward Arnold, 1970, St. Martin's, 1971.

(With Eric Mottram and Jean Franco) *The Penguin Companion to American Literature*, McGraw, 1971 (published in England as *The Penguin Companion to Literature*, Volume III: *U.S.A.*, Allen Lane, 1971), published as *The Avenal Companion to English and American Literature*, Avenal Books, 1981.

(With Palmer) *Metaphysical Poetry*, Indiana University Press, 1971.

(With Palmer) *The American Novel and the Nineteen Twenties*, Edward Arnold, 1971.

(With Palmer) *Shakespearian Comedy*, Edward Arnold, 1972.

(With James McFarlane) *Modernism: 1890-1930*, Penguin, 1976.

The Novel Today: Contemporary Writers on Modern Fiction, Rowman & Littlefield, 1977.

(With Palmer) *Decadence and the 1890s*, Edward Arnold, 1979.

(With Palmer) *The Contemporary English Novel*, Edward Arnold, 1979.

(With Palmer) *Contemporary Theatre*, Holmes & Meier, 1979.

(With Howard Temperley) *An Introduction to American Studies*, Longman, 1980.

Stephen Crane, *The Red Badge of Courage* (critical edition), Dent, 1983.

(With Palmer) *Shakespearean Tragedy*, Holmes & Meier, 1984.

The Penguin Book of Modern British Short Stories, Penguin, 1988.

General editor, "Stratford-upon-Avon Studies," Edward Arnold, 1970-81, and "Contemporary Writers," Methuen.

MEDIA ADAPTATIONS: The History Man was adapted as a four-part television series by Christopher Hampton, BBC, 1979.

WORK IN PROGRESS: A History of American Literature, for Methuen; a novella for Century; collected essays for Deutsch; a study of American images of Europe and European images of America.

SIDELIGHTS: Herbert Burke calls Malcolm Bradbury's first novel, *Eating People Is Wrong*, "a novel . . . about how weary academic life is in the English Midlands of the '50s—but this is not a weary novel. Often truly comic, its satire has many barbs and they often draw blood. . . . If seriousness of intent—a sociology of the British establishment of the times as seen through the microcosm of the academy—gets in the way of hearty satire, bawdiness is not lacking." According to Martin Tucker, the author "has written a first novel that is sloppy, structurally flabby, occasionally inane, frequently magnificent and ultimately successful. It is as if [Charles] Dickens and Evelyn Waugh sat down together and said 'Let's write a comic novel in the manner of Kingsley Amis about a man in search of his lost innocence who finds it.' The result is one of the most substantial and dazzling literary feasts this year." Not all reviewers have been so generous in their appraisal of the book, however. Patrick Dennis writes: "While Malcolm Bradbury's first novel is brilliant, witty, sensitive, adult, funny and a lot of other pleasant and desirable things, it is not a good novel. And I know why: Mr. Bradbury has been so busy entertaining himself with his brilliance, wit, etc., that he has quite forgotten about those less gifted people who are expected to buy, read and enjoy his book. . . . While his knaves and fools are elegantly written, his 'sympathetic' characters are so feckless or so grotesque that one has almost no feeling for them." And a *New Yorker* critic finds that "there are no funny situations, and the few comic episodes that occur are much too light, and perhaps also too tired, to stand up against the predominant, tragic predicament that is [the main character's] life . . . and even if this spectacle were more richly decorated than it is with jokes and puns and so on, it would not be good enough. Mr. Bradbury has created a serious and very human character, and has obscured him with jugglers."

Stepping Westward, Bradbury's second novel, also about university life, has been hailed by a *Times Literary Supplement* reviewer as "a *vade mecum* for every youthful or aspiring first visitor to the United States. Every situational joke, every classic encounter is exactly and wittily exploited. The dialogue is often marvellously acute, the tricks of American speech expertly 'bugged.' " On the other hand, however, Rita Estok says that "the school, faculty and students do not ring true; in fact, it is almost a travesty on university life. James Walker, the principal character, never becomes believable and remains unsympathetic throughout the story. *Stepping Westward,* be it a travesty or satire on university life, fails to hit the mark as either." And Bernard McCabe writes: "Within this very funny book Mr. Bradbury proposes a serious novel about freedom and community and friendship's inevitable failures. The result is interesting, but too schematic and analytical to be really successful. The comedy works, though, thanks to Bradbury's artful writing. I leave to some future scholar the precise significance of the recurrent buttocks-motif and ear-motif. . . . [The author's] exaggerated versions of [university life] work by lending a British ear and eye to the oddities of the American scene."

Robert Nye says that Bradbury, in his third novel, *The History Man,* "achieves some charming comic efforts—and not a few cruel ones. Bradbury has a baleful eye for human weakness. He describes with skill and obvious relish. The result is a clever, queer, witty, uncomfortable sort of book—a book whose prose possesses considerable surface brilliance but with a cutting edge concealed beneath." Margaret Drabble calls the book "a small narrative masterpiece," and she feels that "one of the reasons why this novel is so immensely readable is its evocation of physical reality; it may be a book about ideas, but the ideas are embodied in closely observed details. . . . A thoroughly civilized writer, [Bradbury] has written a novel that raises some very serious questions about the nature of civilization without for a moment appearing pretentious or didactic—a fine achievement."

Bradbury's fourth novel, *Rates of Exchange,* was published in 1983 to praise from critics such as *New York Times Book Review* contributor Rachel Billington, who labels it "an astonishing tour de force." The tale of a linguist traveling to a fictive Eastern bloc country, *Rates of Exchange* takes on the subject of language itself and "manages to be funny, gloomy, shrewd and silly all at once," according to Joel Conarroe in the *Washington Post Book World.* Bradbury's inventive use of language—both the locals' fractured English and their native Slakan, a hybrid of several European languages—is a highlight for many reviewers. Notes Anatole Broyard in the *New York Times,* "Bradbury is in such virtuoso form that he can even make you enjoy an entire book in which the majority of the characters speak various degrees of broken English." Although some critics take issue with the book's pacing, characterization, and sometimes uneasy mixture of humor and seriousness, many value its wit and pungent observations on travel. Writes *Los Angeles Times* reviewer Elaine Kendall, "Hilarious and accurate, deepened by the author's concern for subtle political and social factors, 'Rates of Exchange' turns tour de force into an unequivocal compliment, elevating the genre to a major literary category."

Bradbury told *CA:* "As a novelist, I achieved four novels (and a volume of short stories) in twenty-five years. It may seem a slow record, but then I have been a critic, reviewer, and professor of American studies too, as well as a regular writer for television. I believe the writer has a responsibility for literary study, and this belief has gone into my teaching of creative writing and my editorship of series like Methuen Contemporary Writers, where I and my fellow editor Chris Bigsby have sought to show that we live in a major period of literary creation very different from that of the earlier part of the century. I believe in fact we live in a remarkable international age of fiction, and this has affected my own writing. Though I started with provincial themes and in a relatively realistic mode I have grown vastly more international in preoccupation and far more experimental in method. Looking back over my books, they now seem to me to follow the curve of the development of British fiction from the 1950s: from the comic social realism of the postwar period through to a much harsher, more ironic vision which involves the use of fictiveness and fantasy—though always, in my case, with an edge of tragic commentary on the world we live in as this dark century moves to its end. I think I have grown far more exact as a writer, more concerned to deal with major themes, to escape provincial limitations, and to follow the fate of liberal hopes through the many intellectual, moral, and historical challenges it has now to face. As I said in a previous entry for *CA:* 'Serious writing is not an innocent act; it is an act of connection with the major acts of writing achieved by others. It is also . . . a new set of grammars, forms, and styles for the age we live in.'

"My books have been widely translated and are set-texts in schools and universities, and two—*The History Man* and *Rates of Exchange*—have been made into British Broadcasting Corporation television series. This has done a good deal to free me of the unfortunate label of being a 'university novelist,' since my aims are wider. I have myself been considerably influenced by writing for television, and I think the imagery and grammar of film and television has brought home new concepts of presentation and perception to the novel. I have also been influenced by (and perhaps also have influenced) younger writers like Ian McEwan and Clive Sinclair who have been in my creative writing classes at the University of East Anglia. I have fought for a view of the novel in Britain as a serious and experimental form, and I believe it has increasingly become so. I believe in our great need for fiction; in *Rates of Exchange,* set in Eastern Europe, I have tried to relate our awareness of an oppressive modern reality forged by the fictions of politicians and the structures of ideology to our need for true fictions that can challenge them. My basic themes, though, remain the same: the conflict between liberal humanism and the harsh systems and behaviorisms of the modern world, and the tragic implications, which, however, I believe must be expressed in comic form. In an age when the big ideologies grow tired, I think we need the abrasive vision of the writer, and in some of our great contemporaries of the novel, from Saul Bellow to Milan Kundera, I think we find that. So the novel is what gives me hope, and lasting pleasure."

BIOGRAPHICAL/CRITICAL SOURCES:

BOOKS

Bigsby, Christopher, and Heide Ziegler, editors, *The Radical Imagination and the Liberal Tradition: Interviews with English and American Novelists,* Junction Books, 1982.
Contemporary Literary Criticism, Volume 32, Gale, 1985.
Dictionary of Literary Biography, Volume 14: *British Novelists since 1960,* Gale, 1983.

PERIODICALS

Booklist, April 15, 1960.
Books and Bookmen, April, 1983.
Christian Science Monitor, February 18, 1976.
Commonweal, April 22, 1960.
Globe and Mail (Toronto), September 12, 1987, August 20, 1988.
Library Journal, March 1, 1960, June 1, 1966.
Literary Review, October, 1983.
Los Angeles Times, October 21, 1983, December 9, 1988.
Los Angeles Times Book Review, October 18, 1987, September 25, 1988.
National Review, May 2, 1960.
New Statesman, October 31, 1959.
Newsweek, October 24, 1983.
New York Times, April 10, 1960, October 1, 1983, November 7, 1987, January 30, 1989.
New York Times Book Review, February 8, 1976, November 20, 1983, October 18, 1987, September 25, 1988.
New Yorker, July 16, 1960, May 3, 1976.
San Francisco Chronicle, April 26, 1960.
Saturday Review, April 9, 1960, May 21, 1966.
Time, June 3, 1966, November 14, 1983.
Times (London), April 7, 1983, January 14, 1988, May 12, 1988, June 4, 1988.
Times Literary Supplement, November 13, 1959, August 5, 1965, November 7, 1975, September 3, 1982, April 8, 1983, February 22, 1985, October 24, 1986, June 12, 1987, November 12, 1987, May 13, 1988.
Tribune Books (Chicago), August 28, 1988.
Washington Post, October 14, 1987.
Washington Post Book World, November 20, 1983, July 3, 1988.

*   *   *

BRADBURY, Ray (Douglas) 1920-
(Douglas Spaulding, Leonard Spaulding)

PERSONAL: Born August 22, 1920, in Waukegan, Ill.; son of Leonard Spaulding and Esther (Moberg) Bradbury; married Marguerite Susan McClure, September 27, 1947; children: Susan, Ramona, Bettina, Alexandra. *Education:* Attended schools in Waukegan, Ill., and Los Angeles, Calif. *Politics:* Independent. *Religion:* Unitarian Universalist.

ADDRESSES: Home—10265 Cheviot Drive, Los Angeles, Calif. 90064. *Agent*—Don Congdon, 156 Fifth Ave., #625, New York, N.Y. 10010.

CAREER: Newsboy in Los Angeles, Calif., 1940-43; full-time writer, primarily of fantasy and science fiction, 1943—.

MEMBER: Writers Guild of America, Science Fantasy Writers of America.

AWARDS, HONORS: O. Henry Prize, 1947, and 1948; Benjamin Franklin Award for best story of 1953-54 in an American magazine, for "Sun and Shadow" in *The Reporter;* Common-

wealth Club of California gold medal, 1954, for *Fahrenheit 451;* award from National Institute of Arts and Letters, 1954, for contribution to American literature; Boys' Clubs of America Junior Book Award, 1956, for *Switch on the Night;* Golden Eagle Award, 1957, for screenwriting; Academy Award nomination for short film, 1963, for "Icarus Montgolfier Wright"; Mrs. Ann Radcliffe Award, Count Dracula Society, 1965, 1971; Writers Guild Award, 1974; World Fantasy Award, 1977, for life achievement; D.Litt., Whittier College, 1979; Balrog Award, 1979, for best poet; Aviation and Space Writers Award, 1979, for television documentary; Gandalf Award, 1980; Body of Work Award, PEN, 1985; the play version of "The Martian Chronicles" won five Los Angeles Drama Critics Circle Awards.

WRITINGS:

NOVELS

The Martian Chronicles (also see below), Doubleday, 1950, revised edition published in England as *The Silver Locusts,* Hart-Davis, 1951.
Dandelion Wine (also see below), Doubleday, 1957, reprinted, Knopf, 1975.
Something Wicked This Way Comes (also see below), Simon & Schuster, 1962.
Death Is a Lonely Business, Knopf, 1985.
A Graveyard for Lunatics, Knopf, 1990.

STORY COLLECTIONS

Dark Carnival, Arkham, 1947, revised edition, Hamish Hamilton, 1948.
The Illustrated Man, Doubleday, 1951, reprinted, Bantam, 1967, revised edition, Hart-Davis, 1952.
Fahrenheit 451 (contains "Fahrenheit 451" [also see below], "The Playground," and "And the Rock Cried Out"), Ballantine, 1953, reprinted, G. K. Hall, 1988.
The Golden Apples of the Sun (also see below), Doubleday, 1953, reprinted, Greenwood Press, 1971, revised edition, Hart-Davis, 1953.
Fahrenheit 451 (previously published as part of short story collection), Hart-Davis, 1954.
The October Country, Ballantine, 1955, reprinted, Knopf, 1970.
A Medicine for Melancholy (also see below), Doubleday, 1959, revised edition published in England as *The Day It Rained Forever* (also see below), Hart-Davis, 1959.
The Ghoul Keepers, Pyramid Books, 1961.
The Small Assassin, Ace Books, 1962.
The Machineries of Joy, Simon & Schuster, 1964.
The Vintage Bradbury, Vintage Books, 1965.
The Autumn People, Ballantine, 1965.
Tomorrow Midnight, Ballantine, 1966.
Twice Twenty-Two (contains *The Golden Apples of the Sun* and *A Medicine for Melancholy*), Doubleday, 1966.
I Sing the Body Electric!, Knopf, 1969.
(With Robert Bloch) *Bloch and Bradbury: Ten Masterpieces of Science Fiction,* Tower, 1969 (published in England as *Fever Dreams and Other Fantasies,* Sphere, 1970.
(With Bloch) *Whispers from Beyond,* Peacock Press, 1972.
(Selected Stories), Harrap, 1975.
Long after Midnight, Knopf, 1976.
The Best of Bradbury, Bantam, 1976.
To Sing Strange Songs, Wheaton, 1979.
The Stories of Ray Bradbury, Knopf, 1980.
Dinosaur Tales, Bantam, 1983.
A Memory of Murder, Dell, 1984.
The Toynbee Convector, Random House, 1988.

JUVENILES

Switch on the Night, Pantheon, 1955.
R Is for Rocket (story collection), Doubleday, 1962.
S Is for Space (story collection), Doubleday, 1966.
The Halloween Tree, Knopf, 1972.
The April Witch, Creative Education, Inc., 1987.
The Other Foot, Creative Education, Inc., 1987.
The Foghorn (also see below), Creative Education, Inc., 1987.
The Veldt (also see below), Creative Education, Inc., 1987.
Fever Dream, St. Martin's, 1987.

PLAYS

"The Meadow," first produced in Hollywood at the Huntington Hartford Theatre, March, 1960.
"Way in the Middle of the Air," first produced in Hollywood at the Desilu Gower Studios, August, 1962.
The Anthem Sprinters, and Other Antics (includes "The Anthem Sprinters," first produced in Beverly Hills at the Beverly Hills Playhouse, October, 1967), Dial, 1963.
"The World of Ray Bradbury" (three one-acts), first produced in Los Angeles at the Coronet Theater, October, 1964, produced Off-Broadway at Orpheum Theatre, October 8, 1965.
"Leviathan 99" (radio play), British Broadcasting Corp., 1966, first produced in Hollywood at the Stage 9 Theater, November, 1972.
The Day It Rained Forever (one-act), Samuel French, 1966.
The Pedestrian (one-act), Samuel French, 1966.
"Dandelion Wine" (based on his novel of same title; music composed by Billy Goldenberg), first produced at Lincoln Center's Forum Theatre, 1967.
"Christus Apollo" (music composed by Jerry Goldsmith), first produced in Los Angeles at Royce Hall, University of California, December, 1969.
The Wonderful Ice-Cream Suit and Other Plays (contains "The Wonderful Ice-Cream Suit," first produced in Los Angeles at the Coronet Theater, February, 1965, "The Veldt" [based on his story of same title], first produced in London, 1980, and "To the Chicago Abyss"), Bantam, 1972 (published in England as *The Wonderful Ice-Cream Suit and Other Plays for Today, Tomorrow, and Beyond Tomorrow,* Hart-Davis, 1973).
Madrigals for the Space Age (for mixed chorus and narrator, with piano accompaniment; music composed by Lalo Schifrin; first performed in Los Angeles at the Dorothy Chandler Pavilion, January, 1976), Associated Music Publishers, 1972.
Pillar of Fire and Other Plays for Today, Tomorrow, and Beyond Tomorrow (contains "Pillar of Fire," [first produced in Fullerton at the Little Theatre, California State College, December, 1973], "Kaleidoscope," and "The Foghorn" [based on his story of same title], first produced in New York, 1977), Bantam, 1975.
That Ghost, That Bride of Time: Excerpts from a Play-in-Progress, Squires, 1976.
"The Martian Chronicles" (based on his novel of same title), first produced at the Colony Theater in Los Angeles, 1977.
"Fahrenheit 451" (based on his story of same title; musical), first produced at the Colony Theater in Los Angeles, 1979.
A Device Out of Time, Dramatic Publishing, 1986.
"Falling Upward," first produced in Los Angeles at the Melrose Theatre, March, 1988.

FILMS

"It Came from Outer Space," Universal Pictures, 1953.
"The Beast from 20,000 Fathoms" (based on his story, "The Foghorn"), Warner Bros., 1953.
"Moby Dick," Warner Bros., 1956.
(With George C. Johnson) "Icarus Montgolfier Wright," Format Films, 1962.
(Author of narration and creative consultant) "An American Journey," U.S. Government for United States Pavilion at New York World's Fair, 1964.
(Under pseudonym Douglas Spaulding with Ed Weinberger) "Picasso Summer," Warner Bros./Seven Arts, 1972.
"Something Wicked This Way Comes" (based on his novel of same title), Walt Disney, 1983.

Also author of television scripts for "Alfred Hitchcock Presents," "Jane Wyman's Fireside Theatre," "Steve Canyon," "Trouble Shooters," "Twilight Zone," "Alcoa Premiere," and "Curiosity Shop" series. Author of 42 television scripts for "Ray Bradbury Television Theatre," USA Cable Network, 1985-90.

POEMS

Old Ahab's Friend, and Friend to Noah, Speaks His Piece: A Celebration, Roy A. Squires Press, 1971.
When Elephants Last in the Dooryard Bloomed: Celebrations for Almost Any Day in the Year (also see below), Knopf, 1973.
That Son of Richard III: A Birth Announcement, Roy A. Squires Press, 1974.
Where Robot Mice and Robot Men Run Round in Robot Towns (also see below), Knopf, 1977.
Twin Hieroglyphs That Swim the River Dust, Lord John, 1978.
The Bike Repairman, Lord John, 1978.
The Author Considers His Resources, Lord John, 1979.
The Aqueduct, Roy A. Squires Press, 1979.
This Attic Where the Meadow Greens, Lord John, 1979.
The Last Circus, Lord John, 1980.
The Ghosts of Forever (five poems, a story, and an essay), Rizzoli, 1980.
The Haunted Computer and the Android Pope (also see below), Knopf, 1981.
The Complete Poems of Ray Bradbury (contains *Where Robot Mice and Robot Men Run Round in Robot Towns, The Haunted Computer and the Android Pope,* and *When Elephants Last in the Dooryard Bloomed*), Ballantine, 1982.
The Love Affair (a short story and two poems), Lord John, 1983.
Forever and the Earth, limited edition, Croissant & Co., 1984.
Death Has Lost Its Charm for Me, Lord John, 1987.

OTHER

(Editor and contributor) *Timeless Stories for Today and Tomorrow,* Bantam, 1952.
(Editor and contributor) *The Circus of Dr. Lao and Other Improbable Stories,* Bantam, 1956.
(With Lewy Olfson) *Teacher's Guide: Science Fiction,* Bantam, 1968.
Zen and the Art of Writing, Capra Press, 1973.
(With Bruce Murray, Arthur C. Clarke, Walter Sullivan, and Carl Sagan) *Mars and the Mind of Man,* Harper, 1973.
The Mummies of Guanajuato, Abrams, 1978.
Beyond 1984: Remembrance of Things Future, Targ, 1979.
(Author of text) *Los Angeles,* Skyline Press, 1984.
(Author of text) *Orange County,* Skyline Press, 1985.
(Author of text) *The Art of "Playboy,"* Alfred Van der Marck, 1985.

Work is represented in over seven hundred anthologies. Contributor of short stories and articles, sometimes under pseudonyms, to *Playboy, Saturday Review, Weird Tales, Magazine of Fantasy and Science Fiction, Omni, Life,* and other publications.

SIDELIGHTS: Ray Bradbury's science fiction, unlike that of many of his colleagues, de-emphasizes the Buck Rogers-Flash Gordon variety of space hardware and gadgetry in favor of an exploration of the impact of scientific development on human lives. In general, he warns man against becoming too dependent on science and technology at the expense of moral and aesthetic concerns, contending that his stories "are intended as much to instruct how to prevent dooms, as to predict them." Writing in the *Dictionary of Literary Biography,* George Edgar Slusser notes that "to Bradbury, science is the forbidden fruit, destroyer of Eden. . . . In like manner, Bradbury is a fantasist whose fantasies are oddly circumscribed: he writes less about strange things happening to people than about strange imaginings of the human mind. Corresponding, then, to an outer labyrinth of modern technological society is this inner one—fallen beings feeding in isolation on their hopeless dreams."

"If you're too good a scientist, you're not a good writer," Ray Bradbury once told an interviewer. This quote summarizes his unorthodox approach to writing science fiction, an approach which has led some critics to insist that calling him "the world's greatest living science fiction writer" (a phrase which appears on the covers of the paperback editions of his books) does an injustice to the scope of his talent. As Damon Knight observes in his *In Search of Wonder: Critical Essays on Science Fiction:* "The purists are right in saying that [Bradbury] does not write science fiction, and never has." Donald A. Wollheim agrees with Knight's assessment. Writing in *The Universe Makers,* Wollheim states: "Only a very small percentage of Bradbury's works can be classified as science fiction. Although his most 'science-fictional' book, *The Martian Chronicles,* is a classic, its s-f plausibility is slight. . . . It has the form of science fiction but in content there is no effort to implement the factual backgrounds. His Mars bears no relation to the astronomical planet. His stories are stories of people—real and honest and true in their understanding of human nature—but for his purposes the trappings of science fiction are sufficient—mere stage settings. . . . He is outside the field [of science fiction]—a mainstream fantasist of great brilliance, . . . but certainly not 'the world's greatest living science fiction writer.' "

Knight credits Bradbury with a greater range than the science fiction label implies: "His imagery is luminous and penetrating, continually lighting up familiar corners with unexpected words. He never lets an idea go until he has squeezed it dry, and never wastes one. As his talent expands, some of his stories become pointed social commentary; some are surprisingly effective religious tracts, disguised as science fiction; others still are nostalgic vignettes; but under it all is still Bradbury the poet of 20th-century neurosis. Bradbury the isolated spark of consciousness, awake and alone at midnight; Bradbury the grown-up child who still remembers, still believes."

Over the past five decades, Bradbury has managed to create a tremendous amount of work in several genres, including short stories, plays, novels, film scripts, poems, children's books, and nonfiction. He attributes this prolific production to a steady writing routine. "Every single day for 50 years," he tells Aljean Harmetz in the *New York Times,* "if I can get to my typewriter by 9 o'clock, by 10:30 I'm protected against the world." An incredible memory also helps. Bradbury claims total recall of every book he has read and of every film he has seen. This enables him to "cross-pollinate metaphors," as he tells *CA,* from hundreds of sources for his own fiction. He also utilizes a spontaneous writing technique similar to the automatic writing of the surrealists. William F. Touponce in *Extrapolation* quotes Bradbury explaining: "In my early twenties I floundered into a word-association process in which I simply got out of bed each morning, walked to my desk, and put down any word or series of words that happened along in my head." As Touponce relates, Bradbury "advises the aspiring writer to relax and concentrate on the unconscious message. This way of writing shorts out the mind's critical and categorizing activities, allowing the subconscious to speak."

The Martian Chronicles, a lyrical and basically optimistic account of man's colonization of Mars, is widely regarded as Bradbury's most outstanding work. It blends many of his major themes and metaphors, including the conflict between individual and social concerns (that is, freedom versus confinement and conformity) and the idea of space as a frontier wilderness, a place where man sets out on a quasi-religious quest of self-discovery and spiritual renewal. In addition, *The Martian Chronicles* provides the author with an opportunity to explore what he perceives to be the often deadly attraction of the past as opposed to the future and of balance and stability versus change. As in many other Bradbury stories, this idea is expressed in *The Martian Chronicles* via the metaphor of the small, old-fashioned midwestern town ("Green Town, Ill.") which represents peaceful childhood memories of a world that man hesitates to abandon to the passage of time. In his contribution to *Voices for the Future: Essays on Major Science Fiction Writers,* A. James Stupple writes: "Bradbury's point [in *The Martian Chronicles*] is clear: [The Earthmen] met their deaths because of their inability to forget, or at least resist, the past. Thus, the story of this Third Expedition acts as a metaphor for the book as a whole. Again and again the Earthmen make the fatal mistake of trying to recreate an Earth-like past rather than accept the fact that this is Mars—a different, unique new land in which they must be ready to make personal adjustments."

Russell Kirk feels that the greatest strength of *The Martian Chronicles* is its ability to make us look closely at ourselves. In *Enemies of the Permanent Things: Observations of Abnormality in Literature and Politics,* Kirk states: "What gives [*The Martian Chronicles*] their cunning is . . . their portrayal of human nature, in all its baseness and all its promise, against an exquisite stageset. We are shown normality, the permanent things in human nature, by the light of another world; and what we forget about ourselves in the ordinariness of our routine of existence suddenly bursts upon us as a fresh revelation. . . . Bradbury's stories are not an escape from reality; they are windows looking upon enduring reality."

In his essay for *Voices for the Future,* Willis E. McNelly concludes that Bradbury's works, especially *The Martian Chronicles* and the highly-acclaimed *Fahrenheit 451,* prove that "quality writing is possible in [a] much-maligned genre. Bradbury is obviously a careful craftsman, an ardent wordsmith whose attention to the niceties of language and its poetic cadences would have marked him as significant even if he had never written a word about Mars." In short, McNelly continues, Bradbury's "themes . . . place him squarely in the middle of the mainstream of American life and tradition. His eyes are set firmly on the horizon-frontier where dream fathers mission and action mirrors illusion. And if Bradbury's eyes lift from the horizon to the stars, the act is merely an extension of the vision all Americans share. His voice is that of the poet raised against the mechanization of mankind."

In an interview with *Future* magazine, Bradbury admits that poetry does play an important role in his writing. In fact, he notes, "I've found inspiration for many of my short stories in other people's poetry. . . . There have been many times when I've taken a single line of poetry and turned it into a short story. Poetry is an old love of mine, one which is central to my life." Though he is most often called a science fiction writer, Bradbury considers himself to be an "idea writer" instead. "Everything of mine is permeated with my love of ideas—both big and small. It doesn't matter what it is as long as it grabs me and holds me, fascinates me. And then I'll run out and do something about it." Furthermore, he explains, "I write for fun. You can't get too serious. I don't pontificate in my work. I have fun with ideas. I play with them. I approach my craft with enthusiasm and respect. If my work sparks serious thought, fine. But I don't write with that in mind. I'm not a serious person, and I don't like serious people. I don't see myself as a philosopher. That's awfully boring. I want to shun that role. My goal is to entertain myself and others. Hopefully, that will prevent me from taking myself too seriously."

MEDIA ADAPTATIONS: Fahrenheit 451 was filmed by Universal in 1966, and it was adapted as an opera by Georgia Holof and David Mettere and first produced at the Indiana Civic Theater, Fort Wayne, Ind., in November, 1988; *The Illustrated Man* was filmed by Warner Bros. in 1969; the story "The Screaming Woman" was filmed for television in 1972; the story "Murderer" was filmed for television by WGBH-TV in Boston in 1976; *The Martian Chronicles* was filmed as a television mini-series in 1980. Many of Bradbury's works have also been adapted as sound recordings.

AVOCATIONAL INTERESTS: Painting in oil and water colors, collecting Mexican artifacts.

BIOGRAPHICAL/CRITICAL SOURCES:

BOOKS

Authors in the News, Gale, Volume 1, 1976, Volume 2, 1976.
Breit, Harvey, *The Writer Observed,* World Publishing, 1956.
Clareson, Thomas D., editor, *Voices for the Future: Essays on Major Science Fiction Writers,* Volume 1, Bowling Green State University Press, 1976.
Contemporary Literary Criticism, Gale, Volume 1, 1973, Volume 3, 1975, Volume 10, 1979, Volume 15, 1980, Volume 42, 1987.
Dictionary of Literary Biography, Gale, Volume 2: *American Novelists since World War II,* 1978, Volume 8: *Twentieth Century American Science Fiction Writers,* 1981.
Greenberg, Martin H. and Joseph D. Olander, editors, *Ray Bradbury,* Taplinger, 1980.
Johnson, Wayne L., *Ray Bradbury,* Ungar, 1980.
Kirk, Russell, *Enemies of the Permanent Things: Observations of Abnormality in Literature and Politics,* Arlington House, 1969.
Knight, Damon, *In Search of Wonder: Critical Essays on Science Fiction,* 2nd edition, Advent, 1967.
Nolan, William F., *The Ray Bradbury Companion,* Gale, 1974.
Platt, Charles, *Dream Makers: Science Fiction and Fantasy Writers at Work,* Ungar, 1987.
Slusser, George Edgar, *The Bradbury Chronicles,* Borgo, 1977.
Touponce, William F., *Ray Bradbury and the Poetics of Reverie: Fantasy, Science Fiction and the Reader,* UMI Research Press, 1984.
Wollheim, Donald, *The Universe Makers,* Harper, 1971.

PERIODICALS

Extrapolation, fall, 1984.
Future, October, 1978.
National Review, April 4, 1967.
New York Times, April 24, 1983.

New York Times Book Review, August 8, 1951, December 28, 1969, October 29, 1972, October 26, 1980.
Reader's Digest, September, 1986.
Time, March 24, 1975, October 13, 1980.
Washington Post, July 7, 1989.
Writer's Digest, December, 1974, February, 1976.

—*Sketch by Thomas Wiloch*

*   *   *

BRADFORD, Barbara Taylor   1933-

PERSONAL: Born May 10, 1933, in Leeds, Yorkshire, England; came to the United States, 1963; daughter of Winston (an industrial engineer) and Freda (a children's nurse; maiden name Walker) Taylor; married Robert Bradford (a producer), 1963.

CAREER: Yorkshire Evening Post, Yorkshire, England, reporter, 1949-51, women's editor, 1951-53; *Women's Own,* London, England, fashion editor, 1953-54; *London Evening News,* London, columnist, 1955-57; *Woman,* London, features editor, 1962-64; National Design Center, New York, N.Y., editor, 1964-65; *Newsday,* Long Island, N.Y., syndicated columnist, 1966—; writer. Also served as feature writer for *Today* magazine and executive editor of the *London American.*

WRITINGS:

NONFICTION

(Editor) *Children's Stories of the Bible from the Old Testament,* Lion Press, c. 1966.
(Editor) *Children's Stories of Jesus from the New Testament,* Lion Press, c. 1966.
(Editor) Samuel Nisenson, *The Dictionary of One Thousand and One Famous People,* Lion Press, 1966.
A Garland of Children's Verse, Lion Press, 1968.
The Complete Encyclopedia of Homemaking Ideas, Meredith Press, 1968.
How to Be the Perfect Wife: Etiquette to Please Him, Essandess, 1969.
How to Be the Perfect Wife: Entertaining to Please Him, Essandess, 1969.
How to Be the Perfect Wife: Fashions That Please Him, Essandess, c. 1970.
Easy Steps to Successful Decorating, Simon & Schuster, 1971.
How to Solve Your Decorating Problems, Simon & Schuster, 1976.
Decorating Ideas for Casual Living, Simon & Schuster, c. 1977.
Making Space Grow, Simon & Schuster, 1979.
Luxury Designs for Apartment Living, Doubleday, 1981.

FICTION

A Woman of Substance (alternate selection of Doubleday Book Club and Literary Guild), Doubleday, 1979.
Voice of the Heart, Doubleday, 1983.
Hold the Dream (also see below), Doubleday, 1985.
Act of Will, Doubleday, 1986.
To Be the Best, Doubleday, 1988.

OTHER

Also author of "Hold the Dream," a television miniseries adaptation of her novel, 1986. Editor-in-chief, "Guide to Home Decorating Ideas," 1966—.

SIDELIGHTS: Barbara Taylor Bradford has earned a wide readership with her lengthy novels of wealth, intrigue, and love.

Bradford's fiction has sold by the millions in paperback, and two of her books, *A Woman of Substance* and *Hold the Dream,* have been adapted as television miniseries. A former journalist specializing in home decorating, Bradford expresses great satisfaction over the lucrative turn her writing career has taken since 1980. "If anyone asks me whether I like being a popular writer," she told the *New York Times,* "I ask them whether they think I'd rather be an unpopular writer."

Bradford grew up in northern England, an imaginative youngster who had read all the works of Charles Dickens and the Bronte sisters by the time she was twelve. While still a pre-teen she sold her first story, for ten shillings and sixpence, to a British children's magazine. Bradford was determined to become a writer, so at sixteen she abandoned her formal schooling to work as a typist at the *Yorkshire Evening Post.* Within two years she was promoted to editor of the paper's women's page, and two years after that—at the tender age of twenty—she went to London as fashion editor of *Women's Own* magazine. She subsequently worked for a number of London periodicals, including *Today* magazine, the *London Evening News,* and the *London American.*

In 1963 Bradford married and moved to the United States, where she continued her career as a journalist. Through the aegis of *Newsday,* she became author of a syndicated column, "Designing Women," that covered lifestyle and interior decorating topics. Bradford also wrote several books on interior design, including *How To Solve Your Decorating Problems, Decorating Ideas for Casual Living,* and *Luxury Designs for Apartment Living.* As a sideline she began experimenting with fiction; she abandoned four novels before beginning *A Woman of Substance* in the late 1970s.

A Woman of Substance sold an impressive 45,000 copies in hard cover, but it was the paperback edition that broke records. In soft cover, *A Woman of Substance* stayed on the bestseller lists for more than forty weeks; eventually its sales totalled some three million copies. The book begins the saga of Emma Harte, a Yorkshire woman who rises from obscurity to found a retail empire and to enact revenge on the nobleman who seduced and abandoned her. In the *New York Times* Bradford characterized Emma as "a powerful woman who started with nothing but acquired dignity and polish." Bradford added that she strove to make Emma—and her other female characters as well—"tough but not hard."

Hold the Dream and *To Be the Best* continue the chronicle of the Harte family, centering on Emma's shrewd and beautiful granddaughter, Paula McGill O'Neill. Those and Bradford's other bestsellers present "indomitable women who valiantly struggle with adversity, and with their own implacable natures," to quote a *Los Angeles Times Book Review* contributor. Bradford does not consider her works romances, but *Los Angeles Times Book Review* correspondent Judith Moore feels that the author "makes tasteful, intelligent use of the romance genre." Moore continues: "In [Bradford's] hands this maligned category takes on plausibility and a heft more than the book's weight." Moore also suggests that Bradford's characters reveal a 1980s brand of emotional complexity. Her heroes, writes Moore, "reflect the changes in relations between men and women. They encourage women's careers. They cook dinner and clean up the mess. . . . The heroines are also new . . . more autonomous, as motivated by work as by love."

Bradford herself seems highly motivated by the work ethic. Her writing days begin at six in the morning and can last ten to twelve hours—she adapted her novel *Hold the Dream* for television in just five weeks. Bradford told *Writer's Digest* that she derives great satisfaction from the hard work she does for months at a time. "I *need* it," she said. "If I didn't write fiction, they'd take me away in a straitjacket, because I have all this . . . *stuff* going on in my head. I have to get it out . . . . I enjoy writing." Reflecting on her status in the literary community, Bradford told the *New York Times:* "I'm a commercial writer—a storyteller. I suppose I will always write about strong women. I don't mean hard women, though. I mean women of substance."

MEDIA ADAPTATIONS: A Woman of Substance was filmed for television as a six-part miniseries. *Hold the Dream* was filmed for television as a four-hour miniseries.

BIOGRAPHICAL/CRITICAL SOURCES:

PERIODICALS

Atlanta Journal, June 8, 1979.
Columbus Dispatch, July 8, 1979.
Daily Messenger, June 11, 1979.
Detroit News, May 19, 1985.
Globe and Mail (Toronto), November 3, 1984.
Los Angeles Times Book Review, March 20, 1983, August 10, 1986, June 19, 1988.
Naples Daily News, July 29, 1979.
New York Times, November 10, 1981, October 26, 1986.
New York Times Book Review, September 9, 1979, April 24, 1983, June 9, 1985, July 20, 1986, July 31, 1988.
People, June 13, 1983.
St. Louis Post-Dispatch, June 24, 1979.
Washington Post, June 12, 1979, May 17, 1985.
Washington Post Book World, April 3, 1983, July 6, 1986.
Writer, March, 1986.
Writer's Digest, June, 1987.

—*Sketch by Anne Janette Johnson*

* * *

BRADLEY, Marion Zimmer 1930-
(Elfrida Rivers)

PERSONAL: Born June 3, 1930, in Albany, N.Y.; daughter of Leslie (a carpenter) and Evelyn (a historian; maiden name, Conklin) Zimmer; married Robert A. Bradley, October, 1949 (divorced, 1963); married Walter Henry Breen (a numismatist), February, 1964; children: (first marriage) David Robert; (second marriage) Patrick Russell, Moira Evelyn Dorothy. *Education:* Attended New York State College for Teachers (now State University of New York at Albany), 1946-48; Hardin-Simmons College, B.A., 1964; additional study at University of California, Berkeley. *Politics:* None.

ADDRESSES: Home—Berkeley, Calif. *Office*—P.O. Box 245-A, Berkeley, Calif. 94701. *Agent*—Scott Meredith Literary Agency, Inc., 845 Third Ave., New York, N.Y. 10022.

CAREER: Writer and musician; editor, "Marion Zimmer Bradley's Fantasy Magazine."

MEMBER: Authors Guild, Science Fiction Writers of America, Mystery Writers of America, Horror Writers of America, Gay Academic Union, Alpha Chi.

AWARDS, HONORS: Invisible Little Man Award, 1977; Leigh Brackett Memorial Sense of Wonder Award, 1978, for *The Forbidden Tower;* Locus Award for best fantasy novel, 1984, for *The Mists of Avalon.*

WRITINGS:

SCIENCE FICTION/FANTASY

The Door through Space [bound with *Rendezvous on Lost Planet* by A. Bertram Chandler], Ace Books, 1961, reprinted, Arrow, 1979.

Seven from the Stars [bound with *Worlds of the Imperium* by Keith Laumer], Ace Books, 1962.

The Colors of Space, Monarch, 1963, revised edition, Donning, 1988.

Falcons of Narabedla [and] *The Dark Intruder and Other Stories,* Ace Books, 1964.

The Brass Dragon [bound with *Ipomoea* by John Rackham], Ace Books, 1969.

Hunters of the Red Moon, DAW Books, 1973.

The Parting of Arwen (short story), T-K Graphics, 1974.

The Endless Voyage, Ace Books, 1975, expanded edition published as *Endless Universe,* 1979.

The Ruins of Isis, Donning, 1978.

(With brother, Paul Edwin Zimmer) *The Survivors,* DAW Books, 1979.

The House between the Worlds, Doubleday, 1980, revised edition, Del Rey, 1981.

Survey Ship, Ace Books, 1980.

Web of Light (also see below), Donning, 1982.

The Mists of Avalon, Knopf, 1983.

(Editor and contributor) *Greyhaven: An Anthology of Fantasy,* DAW Books, 1983.

Web of Darkness (also see below), Donning, 1983.

The Inheritor, Tor Books, 1984.

(Editor) *Sword and Sorceress* (annual anthology), Volumes 1-5, DAW Books, 1984-88.

Night's Daughter, Ballantine, 1985.

(With Vonda McIntyre) *Lythande* (anthology), DAW Books, 1986.

The Fall of Atlantis (contains *Web of Light* and *Web of Darkness*), Baen Books, 1987.

The Firebrand, Simon & Schuster, 1987.

Warrior Woman, DAW Books, 1988.

"DARKOVER" SCIENCE FICTION SERIES

The Sword of Aldones [and] *The Planet Savers,* Ace Books, 1962, reprinted as *Planet Savers: The Sword of Aldones,* 1984.

The Bloody Sun, Ace Books, 1964, revised edition, 1979.

Star of Danger, Ace Books, 1965, reprinted, 1988.

The Winds of Darkover [bound with *The Anything Tree* by Rackham], Ace Books, 1970, reprinted, 1985.

The World Wreckers, Ace Books, 1971, reprinted, 1988.

Darkover Landfall, DAW Books, 1972.

The Spell Sword, DAW Books, 1974.

The Heritage of Hastur (also see below), DAW Books, 1975.

The Shattered Chain (also see below), DAW Books, 1976.

The Forbidden Tower, DAW Books, 1977.

Stormqueen!, DAW Books, 1978.

(Editor and contributor) *Legends of Hastur and Cassilda,* Thendara House Publications, 1979.

(Editor and contributor) *Tales of the Free Amazons,* Thendara House Publications, 1980.

Two to Conquer, DAW Books, 1980.

(Editor and contributor) *The Keeper's Price and Other Stories,* DAW Books, 1980.

Sharra's Exile (also see below), DAW Books, 1981.

(Editor and contributor) *Sword of Chaos,* DAW Books, 1981.

Children of Hastur (includes *The Heritage of Hastur* and *Sharra's Exile*), Doubleday, 1981.

Hawkmistress!, DAW Books, 1982.

Thendara House (also see below), DAW Books, 1983.

Oath of the Renunciates (includes *The Shattered Chain* and *Thendara House*), Doubleday, 1983.

City of Sorcery, DAW Books, 1984.

(Editor and contributor) *Free Amazons of Darkover,* DAW Books, 1985.

(With the Friends of Darkover) *Red Sun of Darkover,* DAW Books, 1987.

(With the Friends of Darkover) *The Other Side of the Mirror and Other Darkover Stories,* DAW Books, 1987.

(Editor and contributor) *Four Moons of Darkover,* DAW Books, 1988.

OTHER

Songs from Rivendell, privately printed, 1959.

A Complete, Cumulative Checklist of Lesbian, Variant, and Homosexual Fiction, privately printed, 1960.

Castle Terror (novel), Lancer, 1965.

Souvenir of Monique (novel), Ace Books, 1967.

Bluebeard's Daughter (novel), Lancer, 1968.

(Translator) Lope de Vega, *El Villano en su Rincon,* privately printed, 1971.

Dark Satanic (novel), Berkley Publishing, 1972, reprinted, Tor Books, 1988.

In the Steps of the Master (teleplay novelization), Tempo Books, 1973.

Men, Halflings, and Hero Worship (criticism), T-K Graphics, 1973.

The Necessity for Beauty: Robert W. Chamber and the Romantic Tradition (criticism), T-K Graphics, 1974.

The Jewel of Arwen (criticism), T-K Graphics, 1974.

Can Ellen Be Saved? (teleplay novelization), Tempo Books, 1975.

(With Alfred Bester and Norman Spinrad) *Experiment Perilous: Three Essays in Science Fiction,* Algol Press, 1976.

(Contributor) Darrell Schweitzer, editor, *Essays Lovecraftian,* T-K Graphics, 1976.

Drums of Darkness (novel), Ballantine, 1976.

The Catch Trap, Ballantine, 1979.

Also author of novels under undisclosed pseudonyms. Contributor, sometimes under Elfrida Rivers and other pseudonyms, to anthologies and periodicals, including *Magazine of Fantasy and Science Fiction, Amazing Stories,* and *Venture.*

WORK IN PROGRESS: The Forest House, a novel about Eilan, the Druid princess who falsified omens; *The Black Trillium,* a novel, with fellow fantasy writers Andre Norton and Julian May.

SIDELIGHTS: Marion Zimmer Bradley is author of one of the best-loved series in science fiction and fantasy; her "Darkover" novels have not only inspired their own fan magazines, or "fanzines," but also a series of story collections in which other authors set their tales in Bradley's universe. A lost colony rediscovered after centuries of neglect by Earth's "Terran Empire," Darkover has developed its own society and technology, both of which produce internal and external conflicts. Darkover fascinates so many readers because it is a world of many contradictions; not only do the psychic abilities of the natives contrast with the traditional technologies of the empire, but a basically repressive patriarchal society coexists (however uneasily) with groups such as an order of female Renunciates, the "Free Amazons." Consisting of over twenty books and spanning many years of the world's history, "the Darkover novels test various attitudes about the importance of technology, and more important, they study the very nature of human intimacy," claims Rosemarie Arbur in *Twentieth-Century Science Fiction Writers.* The critic explains that "by postulating a Terran Empire the main features of which are advanced technology and bureaucracy, and a Darkover that seems technologically backward and is fiercely individualistic, Bradley sets up a conflict to which there is no 'correct' resolution." The permutations of this basic conflict have provided Bradley with numerous opportunities to explore several themes in various ways.

For example, Susan M. Shwartz observes in *The Feminine Eye: Science Fiction and the Women Who Write It* that one theme in particular provides a foundation for the Darkover novels: "For every gain, there is a risk; choice involves a testing of will and courage." Unlike some fantasy worlds where struggles are easily decided, "on Darkover any attempt at change or progress carries with it the need for pain-filled choice," Shwartz comments. While Bradley provides her characters with ample avenues of action, "in the Darkover books, alternatives are predicated upon two things," the critic outlines: "sincere choice and a willingness to pay the price choice demands." *The Shattered Chain,* for example, "in terms of its structure, plot, characterization, and context within the series, is about all the choices of all women on Darkover and, through them, of all people, male and female, Darkovan and Terran."

The Shattered Chain is one of Bradley's most renowned Darkover novels and, as Arbur describes it in her study *Marion Zimmer Bradley,* "is one of the most thorough and sensitive science-fiction explorations of the variety of options available to a self-actualizing woman; not only does it present us with four strong and different feminine characters who make crucial decisions about their lives but its depth of characterizations permits us to examine in detail the consequences of these decisions." The novel begins as a traditional quest when Lady Rohana, a noblewoman of the ruling class, enlists the aid of a tribe of Free Amazons to rescue a kidnapped kinswoman from a settlement where women are chained to show that they are possessions. But while the rescue is eventually successful, it is only the beginning of a series of conflicts; Rohana's experiences force her to reevaluate her life, and both the daughter of the woman she rescued and a Terran agent who studies the Amazons find themselves examining the limits of their own situations. "As we see in *The Shattered Chain,*" Shwartz concludes, "the payment for taking an oath is the payment for all such choices: pain, with a potential for achievement. In Bradley's other books, too, the price of choice is of great importance."

In coming to this conclusion about the price of choice, Bradley emphasizes two other themes, as Laura Murphy states in the *Dictionary of Literary Biography:* "The first is the reconciliation of conflicting or opposing forces—whether such forces are represented by different cultures or by different facets of a single personality. The second," the critic continues, "closely related to the first, is alienation or exile from a dominant group." While these ideas are featured in Bradley's Darkover series, they also appear in the author's first big mainstream best seller, *The Mists of Avalon.* "Colorfully detailed as a medieval tapestry, *The Mists of Avalon . . .* is probably the most ambitious retelling of the Arthurian legend in the twentieth century," Charlotte Spivack maintains in *Merlin's Daughters: Contemporary Women Writers of Fantasy.* The critic adds that this novel "is much more than a retelling. . . . [It] is a profound revisioning. Imaginatively conceived, intricately structured, and richly peopled, it offers a brilliant reinterpretation of the traditional material from the point of view of the major female characters," such as Arthur's mother Igraine, the Lady of the Lake, Viviane, Arthur's half-

sister, the enchantress Morgaine, and Arthur's wife, Gwenhwyfar.

In addition, Bradley presents the eventual downfall of Arthur's reign as the result of broken promises to the religious leaders of Avalon; while Arthur gained his crown with the aid of Viviane and the Goddess she represents, the influence of Christian priests and Gwenhwyfar lead him to forsake his oath. Thus not only does Bradley present Arthur's story from a different viewpoint, she roots it "in the religious struggle between matriarchal worship of the goddess and the patriarchal institution of Christianity, between what [the author] calls 'the cauldron and the cross,'" describes Spivack. In presenting this conflict, Bradley "memorably depicts the inevitable passing of times and religions by her use of the imagery of different simultaneous worlds, which move out of consciousness as their day ebbs," remarks Maude McDaniel in the *Washington Post.* "Bradley also compares head-on the pre-Christian Druidism of Britain and the Christianity that supplants it, a refreshing change from some modern writers who tend to take refuge at awkward moments in cryptic metaphysics."

Despite this praise for Bradley's fresh approach, McDaniel finds *The Mists of Avalon* too motionless in its treatment of the Arthurian legend: "It all seems strangely static," the critic writes, "set pieces the reader watches rather than enters. Aside from a couple of lackluster jousts, everything is intrigue, jealousy and personal relationships, so that finally we are left with more bawling than brawling." *Science Fiction Review* contributor Darrell Schweitzer concurs, for while he finds *The Mists of Avalon* "certainly an original and quite well-thought-out version," he faults the novel for changes which are "all in the direction of the mundane, the ordinary." The critic explains: "Most of the interesting parts happen offstage. Alas, for whatever reason the women, Morgaine in particular, just aren't that central to the whole story. They aren't present at the crucial moments."

Maureen Quilligan, however, believes that Bradley's emphasis on Morgaine and the other female characters is both effective and appropriate; as she writes in the *New York Times Book Review,* by "looking at the Arthurian legend from the other side, as in one of Morgaine's magic weavings, we see all the interconnecting threads, not merely the artful pattern. . . . 'The Mists of Avalon' rewrites Arthur's story so that we realize it has always also been the story of his sister, the Fairy Queen." By presenting another side, the critic adds, "this, the untold Arthurian story, is no less tragic, but it has gained a mythic coherence; reading it is a deeply moving and at times uncanny experience." "In short," concludes Beverly Deweese in another *Science Fiction Review* article, "Bradley's Arthurian world is intriguingly different. Undoubtedly, the brisk pace, the careful research and the provocative concept will attract and please many readers. . . . [But] overall, *Mists of Avalon* is one of the best and most ambitious of the Arthurian novels, and it should not be missed."

Bradley uses similar themes and approaches in reworking another classic tale: *The Firebrand,* the story of the fall of Troy and of Kassandra, royal daughter of Troy and onetime priestess and Amazon. As the author remarked in an interview with *Publishers Weekly*'s Lisa See, in the story of Troy she saw another instance of male culture overtaking and obscuring female contributions: "During the Dorian invasion, when iron won out over bronze, the female cult died," Bradley explained. "The Minoan and Mycenaean cultures were dead overnight. But you could also look at [that period of history] and say, here were two cultures that should have been ruled by female twins—Helen and

Klytemnestra. And what do you know? When they married Menelaus and Agamemnon, the men took over their cities. I just want to look at what history was really like before the women-haters got hold of it. I want to look at these people like any other people, as though no one had ever written about them before." The result of Bradley's reconstruction, as *New York Times Book Review* contributor Mary Lefkowitz describes it, is that Kassandra "becomes active, even aggressive; she determines the course of history, despite the efforts of her father, her brothers and other brutal male warriors to keep her in her place." "The dust of the war fairly rises off the page," notes a *Publishers Weekly* reviewer, "as Bradley animates this rich history and vivifies the conflicts between a culture that reveres the strength of women and one that makes them mere consorts of powerful men."

Despite this emphasis on female viewpoints in *The Firebrand* and her other fiction, Bradley is not a "feminist" writer. "Though her interest in women's rights is strong," elaborates Murphy, "her works do not reduce to mere polemic." Arbur similarly states that the author "refuses to allow her works to wander into politics unless true concerns of realistic characters bring them there. Her emphasis is on character, not political themes." "Bradley's writing openly with increasing sureness of the human psyche and the human being rendered whole prompted Theodore Sturgeon to call the former [science fiction] fan 'one of the Big ones' currently writing science fiction," Arbur relates in *Twentieth-Century Science Fiction Writers*. "That she has extended her range" beyond science fiction and into "mainstream" fiction, the critic concludes, "suggests that Sturgeon's phrase applies no longer only to the science-fiction writer Marion Zimmer Bradley continues to be, for she has transcended categories."

AVOCATIONAL INTERESTS: "Currently very active in feminist and gay rights," supports Merola, an opera apprentice program.

BIOGRAPHICAL/CRITICAL SOURCES:

BOOKS

Alpers, H. J., editor, *Marion Zimmer Bradley's Darkover,* Corian, 1983.
Arbur, Rosemarie, *Leigh Brackett, Marion Zimmer Bradley, Anne McCaffrey: A Primary and Secondary Bibliography,* G. K. Hall, 1982.
Arbur, Rosemarie, *Marion Zimmer Bradley,* Starmont House, 1985.
Breen, Walter, *The Gemini Problem: A Study of Darkover,* T-K Graphics, 1975.
Breen, Walter, *The Darkover Concordance: A Reader's Guide,* Pennyfarthing Press, 1979.
The Darkover Cookbook, Friends of Darkover, 1977, revised edition, 1979.
Dictionary of Literary Biography, Volume 8: *Twentieth-Century American Science Fiction Writers,* Gale, 1981.
Lane, Daryl, editor, *The Sound of Wonder, Volume 2,* Oryx, 1985.
Magill, Frank, editor, *Survey of Science Fiction Literature,* Volume 1, Salem Press, 1979.
Magill, Frank, editor, *Survey of Modern Fantasy Literature,* Volume 1, Salem Press, 1983.
Paxson, Diana, *Costume and Clothing as a Cultural Index on Darkover,* Friends of Darkover, 1977, revised edition, 1981.
Spivack, Charlotte, *Merlin's Daughters: Contemporary Women of Fantasy,* Greenwood Press, 1987.
Staicar, Tom, editor, *The Feminine Eye: Science Fiction and the Women Who Write It,* Ungar, 1982.
Twentieth-Century Science Fiction Writers, St. James Press, 1986.
Wise, S., *The Darkover Dilemma: Problems of the Darkover Series,* T-K Graphics, 1976.

PERIODICALS

Algol, winter, 1977/1978.
Fantasy Review of Fantasy and Science Fiction, April, 1984.
Los Angeles Times Book Review, February 3, 1983.
Mythlore, spring, 1984.
New York Times Book Review, January 30, 1983, November 29, 1987.
Publishers Weekly, September 11, 1987, October 30, 1987.
San Francisco Examiner, February 27, 1983.
Science Fiction Review, summer, 1983.
Washington Post, January 28, 1983.
West Coast Review of Books, Number 5, 1986.

—*Sketch by Diane Telgen*

* * *

BRAINE, John (Gerard) 1922-1986

PERSONAL: Born April 13, 1922, in Bradford, Yorkshire, England; died of a hemorrhaging ulcer, October 28, 1986, in London, England; son of Fred and Katherine (Henry) Braine; married Helen Patricia Wood, 1955; children: Anthony, Frances, Felicity. *Education:* Leeds School of Librarianship, A.L.A., 1949. *Politics:* Conservative. *Religion:* Roman Catholic.

CAREER: Bingley Public Library, Bingley, England, assistant, 1940-48, chief assistant librarian, 1948-51; librarian at Northumberland County Library, England, 1954-56, and West Riding County Library, England, 1956-57; writer, 1957-86. Member of North Regional Advisory Council, British Broadcasting Corp., 1960-64. *Military service:* Royal Navy, 1942-43.

MEMBER: Arts Theatre Club, Library Association, Authors' Club, Bingley Little Theatre, Bradford Civic Theatre.

WRITINGS:

"The Desert in the Mirror" (play), first produced in Bingley, England, 1951.
Room at the Top (also see below), Houghton, 1957, reprinted, Methuen, 1980.
The Vodi, Eyre & Spottiswoode, 1959, published as *From the Hand of the Hunter,* Houghton, 1960.
Life at the Top (also see below), Houghton, 1962, reprinted, Routledge, Chapman & Hall, 1980.
The Jealous God, Eyre & Spottiswoode, 1964, Houghton, 1965.
The Crying Game, Houghton, 1968.
Stay With Me Till Morning (also see below), Eyre & Spottiswoode, 1970, published as *The View From Tower Hill,* Coward, 1971.
The Queen of a Distant Country (also see below), Methuen, 1972, Coward, 1973.
Writing a Novel, Coward, 1974.
The Pious Agent, Eyre Methuen, 1975, Atheneum, 1976.
Waiting for Sheila (also see below), Eyre Methuen, 1976.
Finger of Fire, Eyre Methuen, 1977.
J. B. Priestley, Weidenfeld & Nicolson, 1978, Barnes & Noble, 1979.
One and Last Love, Eyre Methuen, 1981.
The Two of Us, Methuen, 1984.
These Golden Days, Methuen, 1985.

Contributor to numerous newspapers and periodicals in England and the United States.

FILMSCRIPTS

"Room at the Top," Remus, 1958.

"Life at the Top," Remus, 1965.

"Man at the Top" series, Thames Television, 1970 and 1972.

"Waiting for Sheila" (based on his novel of the same title), Yorkshire Television, 1977.

"Queen of a Distant Country" (based on his novel of the same title), Yorkshire Television, 1978.

"Stay With Me Till Morning" (based on his novel of the same title), Yorkshire Television, 1980.

SIDELIGHTS: With the publication of his first novel, *Room at the Top,* John Braine achieved almost instant literary recognition. The story of a young and ambitious working-class Englishman who eventually joins the urban upper-class that he pretends to disdain, the book drew an overwhelmingly favorable response from both readers and critics. Of the book's theme, Anthony Burgess wrote: "*Room at the Top* was taken by many to be a straight account of achieved ambition. Young man puts boss's daughter in family way and then has it made. But there was much more to the book than that—there was guilt, betrayal of love, the sense that the price of success can be too high and that this, alas, is usually only discovered when success is attained." James W. Lee believed that *Room at the Top* "is a novel which epitomizes its age. Like Ernest Hemingway's *The Sun Also Rises* and F. Scott Fitzgerald's *The Great Gatsby, Room at the Top* probes deeply and tellingly into a central problem of the times. Braine's Joe Lampton is a creation of the postwar British welfare state." Judy Simons, writing in the *Dictionary of Literary Biography,* included Braine with the Angry Young Men of Britain's 1950s, a group of writers who "asserted an ethic of individualism and of rebellious, amoral youth. . . . Braine was in the forefront of the wave of populist writers who, with a contempt for avant-garde fictional devices, rejected notions of artistic elitism and of the refined sensibilities and unique moral position of the writer."

Unfortunately, many of Braine's succeeding novels failed to evoke the same high critical praise as did *Room at the Top.* "Nearly a decade later," wrote John Lahr in his review of *The Crying Game,* "Braine is still scrutinizing English mores with a vicar's scowl, obsessed by evil but unable to fathom it, shocked by the inhumanity of permissiveness without the ability to create characters of human sinew." Felicia Lamport describes *The View From Tower Hill* as a "curiously tepid work" and adds: "Over another signature, *The View From Tower Hill* might have seemed less pallid, but Braine's name triggers expectations of the kind of vitality, power, and urgency that filled his *Room at the Top.* John Braine's bodies are no longer smoldering with life but serenely and prosperously middleaged." Pamela Marsh, in perhaps the harshest assessment of Braine's later work, stated that "John Braine is one of those who have become tagged as a 'one-novel man.' "

According to R. G. G. Price, however, this kind of criticism was unjust: "Early reviews of Mr. Braine took him as more of a highbrow novelist than he ever set out to be and later ones became disgruntled and even hinted at metropolitan corruption of standards. This was unfair. He's no Proust but on the level he aims at he is very good." Moreover, reviews of Braine's later novel, *The Queen of a Distant Country,* indicate a renewed understanding between the author and his critics. "After some dreadful potboiling," wrote a critic for the *Times Literary Supplement* about the book, "John Braine has produced a novel of real unforced style and feeling." Jan B. Gordon allowed that "Braine continues to speak to us with a certain urgency," and that *The Queen of a Distant Country* "talks directly to a civilization which must

now cope with the apathy of a youth which has plugged itself into the system and finds its ideals either co-opted or commercialized."

Critical response was a matter of little importance to Braine. "The people who write the reviews of my books," Simons quoted Braine as saying, "are not the people whom I particularly want to read them, and therefore I'm not interested in what they think." Simons explained that Braine was "defiantly anti-intellectual" and he "consistently maintained his pose of artistic naivete in a literary world that he felt was becoming increasingly elitist and alienated from popular concerns." In similar terms, Alan Warren Friedman in an article for the *Dictionary of Literary Biography* pointed out that Braine was "intensely professional in his attitude toward writing, and contemptuous of the safe and overcivilized academic backgrounds of many of his literary contemporaries, whom he sees as removed from the pressures of modern life and, consequently, limited in the truth they can convey."

In an interview with Kenneth Allsop, Braine said that the novelist's responsibility is "to show his age as it really is. . . . But a writer must be a civilized and tolerant human being, possessing, above all, intellectual integrity. . . . The writer doesn't have to inhabit a rarified moral or intellectual plane, but he must always be, no matter how imperfectly, the conscience of society."

BIOGRAPHICAL/CRITICAL SOURCES:

BOOKS

Allsop, Kenneth, *The Angry Decade,* P. Owen, 1958.

Contemporary Literary Criticism, Gale, Volume 1, 1973, Volume 3, 1975, Volume 41, 1987.

Dictionary of Literary Biography, Volume 15: *British Novelists, 1930-1959,* Gale, 1983.

Dictionary of Literary Biography Yearbook, 1986, Gale, 1987.

Karl, Frederick R., *The Contemporary English Novel,* Farrar, Straus, 1962.

Lee, James W., *John Braine,* Twayne, 1968.

PERIODICALS

Books and Bookmen, April, 1968.

Christian Science Monitor, December 12, 1968.

Commonweal, April 23, 1965, December 14, 1973.

Harper's, April, 1965.

National Observer, November 25, 1968.

Newsweek, April 30, 1973.

New York Times Book Review, April 19, 1959, October 27, 1968, May 27, 1973, May 2, 1976.

Observer (London), February 18, 1979.

Punch, September 4, 1968.

Saturday Review, October 6, 1962, February 27, 1971.

Times Literary Supplement, October 27, 1972, June 20, 1975.

Writer, May, 1972.

OBITUARIES:

PERIODICALS

AB Bookman's Weekly, November 24, 1986.

Chicago Tribune, October 31, 1986.

Los Angeles Times, October 30, 1986.

New York Times, October 30, 1986.

Time, November 10, 1986.

Times (London), October 30, 1986.

Wall Street Journal, October 30, 1986.

Washington Post, October 30, 1986.

BRAUTIGAN, Richard (Gary) 1935-1984

PERSONAL: Born January 30, 1935, in Spokane (some sources say Tacoma), Washington; died of an apparently self-inflicted gunshot wound, September, 1984; son of Bernard F. (a "common laborer") and Lula Mary (a homemaker; maiden name, Keho) Brautigan; married Virginia Dionne Adler, June 8, 1957 (divorced, July 28, 1970); married wife Akiko, 1978 (divorced, 1980); children: (first marriage) Ianthe (daughter).

ADDRESSES: Home—Livingston, Mont. and Bolinas, Calif.

CAREER: Writer. Poet in residence at California Institute of Technology, 1967; instructor at Montana State University, Bozeman, 1982.

AWARDS, HONORS: National Endowment for the Arts grant, 1968.

WRITINGS:

FICTION

A Confederate General From Big Sur (novel), Grove, 1964.
Trout Fishing in America (novel), Four Seasons Foundation, 1967.
In Watermelon Sugar (novel), Four Seasons Foundation, 1967.
Revenge of the Lawn: Stories, 1962-1970, Simon & Schuster, 1971.
The Abortion: An Historical Romance, 1966 (novel), Simon & Schuster, 1971.
The Hawkline Monster: A Gothic Western (novel), Simon & Schuster, 1974.
Willard and His Bowling Trophies: A Perverse Mystery (novel), Simon & Schuster, 1975.
Sombrero Fallout: A Japanese Novel, Simon & Schuster, 1976.
Dreaming of Babylon: A Private Eye Novel, 1942, Delacorte, 1977.
The Tokyo-Montana Press, Delacorte, 1980.

POETRY

The Return of the Rivers, Inferno Press, 1957.
The Galilee Hitch-Hiker, White Rabbit Press, 1958.
Lay the Marble Tea: Twenty-four Poems, Carp Press, 1959.
The Octopus Frontier, Carp Press, 1960.
All Watched Over by Machines of Loving Grace, Communication Co., 1967.
The Pill Versus the Springhill Mine Disaster, Four Seasons Foundation, 1968.
Please Plant This Book (eight poems printed on separate seed packet envelopes), Graham Mackintosh, 1968.
The San Francisco Weather Report, Unicorn Books, 1969.
Rommel Drives on Deep Into Egypt, Delacorte, 1970.
Loading Mercury With a Pitchfork, Simon Schuster Press, 1976.
June 30th, June 30th, Delacorte, 1978.

COLLECTIONS

Trout Fishing in America, The Pill Versus the Springhill Mine Disaster, and In Watermelon Sugar, Delacorte, 1968.

OTHER

Author of story, "Great Golden Telescope," published in *Redbook,* August, 1978. Also author of *I Remember All Those Thousands of Hours in Chicago Area Draft Registers.* Author of recorded phonotape, "Trout Fishing in America," 1973. Co-editor, *Change* (single-issue magazine), 1963.

SIDELIGHTS: Terence Malley observes in his *Richard Brautigan: Writers for the Seventies,* "In general, people who write or talk about Brautigan tend to be either snidely patronizing or vacuously adoring." Certainly Brautigan's work, perhaps due in part to his association with West Coast youth movements, has generated a multitude of critical comment. Robert Novak notes in the *Dictionary of Literary Biography* that "Brautigan is commonly seen as the bridge between the Beat Movement of the 1950s and the youth revolution of the 1960s." A so-called guru of the sixties counterculture, Brautigan wrote of nature, life, and emotion; his unique imagination provided the unusual settings for his themes. Critics frequently compare his work to that of such writers as Thoreau, Hemingway, Barthelme, and Twain. Considered one of the primary writers of the "New Fiction," Brautigan at first experienced difficulty in finding a publisher. Thus, his early work appeared in small presses during the sixties. College audiences of that decade clamored for his "new visions"; *Trout Fishing in America* achieved such popularity that several communes across the country adopted it as their name. In 1969, writer Kurt Vonnegut noticed Brautigan's West Coast success and introduced his work to Delacorte Press, who then reprinted *Trout Fishing in America, In Watermelon Sugar,* and *The Pill Versus the Springhill Mine Disaster.* Delacorte's handling of Brautigan's early work helped expose his writing to readers on a national scale. Considered by most critics to be his best novel, *Trout Fishing in America* (written in 1961 but not published until 1967) established Brautigan as a major force in the mainstream literary scene.

About the body of Brautigan's work, Guy Davenport comments in the *Hudson Review:* "Mr. Brautigan locates his writing on the barricade which the sane mind maintains against spiel and bilge, and here he cavorts with a divine idiocy, thumbing his nose. But he makes clear that at his immediate disposal is a fund of common sense he does not hesitate to bring into play. He is a kind of Thoreau who cannot keep a straight face." Robert Kern presents a more traditional analysis in the *Chicago Review,* asserting, "Brautigan's work in both poetry and prose . . . provides a postmodernist instance of primitive poetics in as pure a form as one could wish and also helps clarify some of the differences between modernism and post-modernism in general." His books mourn the apparent loss of the American Dream, and his characters spend lifetimes searching for an American utopia. *Thoreau Journal Quarterly*'s Brad Hayden explains: "The narrator of Brautigan's novel seeks a pastoral life in nature but does not succeed; his search ends in frustration and disillusionment. En route he comments upon social and personal values in America with an equal sense of despair." Brautigan often linked life and nature in his writing and thus believed one cannot find personal joy within a contaminated environment; he deplored the encroaching pollution of the earth. Critics seem divided as to whether Brautigan's works present a melancholy vision of America, or whether they transcend worldly hardships to offer an ultimately optimistic view of existence. Hayden notes: "Brautigan's final commentary on life in contemporary America is pessimistic to say the least; it's certainly not like Thoreau's commentary in the final stages of *Walden,* which ends optimistically. . . . Yet all is not hopeless in Brautigan's world. Mention is made periodically throughout the book of 'Trout Fishing in America Terrorists'; persons who oppose society and, like Thoreau, live according to the dictates of conscience rather than those of social law." Malley agrees with Hayden's observation, stating, "Although Brautigan is often a very funny writer, he is not finally an optimistic one." In contrast, John Stickney, in a *Life* article, perceives Brautigan's work as generally hopeful: "His message, such as it is, is mild and unprogrammatic, and unfashionably optimistic about human beings—life-affirming rather than life-denying—and involved completely with everyday American experience." Reviewers generally agree that the author's earlier writings present his themes more concisely than his later work; some feel his later work lacks cohesion as well as the perspicacity and precision characteristic of his first efforts. In addition, most critics sharply delineate his prose from his poetry, finding distinct variations in style and quality. Brautigan partially explained the differences in his work, telling Stickney: "I'm not interested in imitating a style or structure I've used before. I'll never write another book like *Trout Fishing in America.* I dismantled that old machine when I finished with it and left the pieces lying around in the backyard to rust in the rain."

Brautigan's prose style inspires numerous comments from critics. Describing him as "a visionary and enthusiast," Stephen Schneck of *Ramparts* claims: "[Brautigan] writes clearly, enunciating each phrase. He is not sloppy, he is not sentimental, he is close to the ground and without intellectual pretensions. He is never profound, but he is often a poet. A literary man of the people: which is to say, he's a gifted hick." Robert Christgau, writing in the *New York Times Book Review,* notes Brautigan's stylistic contributions and echoes Schneck's remarks: "He is a serious writer, certainly, but the mark of his seriousness is in his craft, especially as a stylist; he is without pretensions." An innovative use of language permeated Brautigan's work as he experimented with a variety of highly individual literary techniques. Observes Tony Tanner in his *City of Words: American Fiction 1950-1970:* "He retains the illusion of orthodox syntax and grammar, but the sentences are continually turning off into unexpectedness in ways which pleasantly dissolve our habitual semantic expectations. At the same time, Brautigan is constantly, cunningly, deviating into sense; there is enough linguistic coherence left for us to experience the book as communication, and enough linguistic sport for Brautigan to demonstrate his own freedom from control." Contemporary novelist Tom McGuane also comments on several Brautigan characteristics in the *New York Times Book Review:* "What is important is that Brautigan's outlandish gift is based in traditional narrative virtues. His dialogue is supernaturally exact; his descriptive concision is the perfect carrier for his extraordinary comic perceptions. Moreover, the books possess a springtime moral emptiness; essentially works of language, they offer no bromides for living."

Despite Brautigan's off-beat and fantastic prose, Malley asserts that he "is very much in the American grain." Similarly, *Dictionary of Literary Biography*'s Novak notes of *Trout Fishing in America:* "It has a traditional theme of American novels: the influence of the American frontier and wilderness on the American imagination, its lifestyle, its economics, its ethics, its therapies, its religion, its politics." Kenneth Seib, writing in *Critique: Studies in Modern Fiction,* also observes an attachment to a typically American literary genre: "For all its surface peculiarity, . . . [*Trout Fishing in America*] is centrally located within a major tradition of the American novel—the romance—and is conditioned by Brautigan's concern with the bankrupt ideals of the American past. Its seemingly loose and episodic narrative, its penchant for the marvelous and unusual, its pastoral nostalgia—all of these things give it that sense of 'disconnected and uncontrolled experience' which Richard Chase finds essential to the romance-novel." Agreeing with Seib's remarks, David Lo Vanderwerken comments, also in *Critique: Studies in Modern Fiction,* "In choosing to write the kind of fiction that he does—symbolic, parabolic, fantastic—Brautigan clearly aligns himself with the tradition of American romancers, as opposed to that of the realists."

A concern with nature coupled with often surreal and whimsical plots typifies Brautigan's novels, which combine pastoral imagery with an examination of social disintegration within the contemporary human condition. John Clayton claims in the *New American Review:* "Brautigan's value is in giving us a pastoral vision which can water our spirits as we struggle—the happy knowledge that there is another place to breathe in; his danger, and the danger of the style of youth culture generally, is that we will forget the struggle." Brautigan presents paradoxes within his messages: his characters long for an American Utopia free from pollution and technological innovation, yet they use these very elements to achieve their goals. Conversely, his novels trace the apparent decline of American civilization by using traditional American symbolism and values. In each instance, Brautigan's anti-traditional style emphasizes the importance of the characters' search for, in Novak's words, a "mythical Eden."

Brautigan's characters frequently display similar reactions to similar events. They feel more comfortable in uncomplicated environments, places where "trout fishing" means "fishing for trout." But, as Josephine Hendin remarks in the *New York Times Book Review,* "All Brautigan's characters are fishing . . ., freezing away every psychic ache, or looking for that cold, hard alloy Brautigan calls 'trout steel.' " The simple becomes obtuse, the familiar complex. Pastoral pleasures such as trout fishing emerge as metaphors for social change, for the mutability inherent in technological advancement. Hendin explains, "Brautigan is the prophet of cities built out of ice rather than fire, of an America whose emblem would be no war-god eagle, but an elusive cold fish."

For the more savvy of his characters, however, Brautigan offers a different message, in which survival becomes the key element. Success or failure fade into indistinction as his characters struggle to triumph over a mostly hostile world. As their images of Eden crumble, Brautigan's characters realize that staying alive means readjusting attitudes and priorities. Deep emotion and meaningful relationships serve only to hinder survival; therefore, surface feelings and superficial encounters permeate character interaction. Comments Hendin: "Brautigan's dream world is constituted from watermelon sugar and trout steel, from that mixture of sweetness and detachment that permits you to be kind but never loving, disappointed but never enraged . . . Brautigan makes cutting out your heart the only way to endure, the most beautiful way to protest the fact that life can be an endless down."

Brautigan looked to nature as the one constant of recent times, despite its increasing contamination. In *Trout Fishing in America,* the trout stream, symbolic of the natural beauty and wilderness inherent in America, becomes a reference point for "trout steel," an incomparably tough metal. Perhaps trout steel serves as a metaphor for the durability of nature, yet Brautigan indicates that even nature cannot remain impervious to progress: finally, pieces of a used trout stream are for sale in a junkyard at $6.50 per foot—evidence of nature's ultimate frailty. With the belief that nature should remain untouched, Brautigan exhibits concern at pollution and man-made destruction of natural environments. *Life*'s Stickney notes that Brautigan "was appalled" at the condition of Walden Pond and relates the author's reaction: " 'Where the hell are the trash bins?' [Brautigan] muttered. 'What would Henry David Thoreau think if he could see this place now?' "

Unlike his prose, Brautigan's poetry frequently draws comments of inconsistency from critics. Malley identifies part of this complaint in his *Richard Brautigan:* "In my view, Brautigan's sense of the transforming power of art (of the imagination or the heightened perception) is at the root of one of his chief strengths as a writer—and is also responsible for the unevenness of his work, especially of his poetry." Similar to analyses of his novels, many reviewers find his later poems less brilliant than his earlier attempts. Timothy Daum of *Library Journal* compares Brautigan's first verse efforts to the more recent *Loading Mercury with a Pitchfork,* claiming, "Brautigan's poetic style, previously centered around eclectic insights into how everyday events are transformed into art, is here reduced to quick simulacra of bitter thoughts and cynical visions." In describing *June 30th, June 30th,* Dennis Petticoffer comments, also in *Library Journal,* on the book's irregular balance: "Taken individually, many of these poems do not hold up well. Brautigan himself concedes that the collection is 'uneven.'" Petticoffer concludes that the book "may prove less enticing than Brautigan's earlier works." *The Tokyo-Montana Express* inspired Raymond Carver to write in the *Chicago Tribune Book World* that some of the poems resemble "little astonishments going off in your hands," while others are "so-so, take them or leave them," while still others, "I think too many—are just filling up space." Agreeing with Carver's observation about the book, Barry Yourgrau asserts in the *New York Times Book Review:* "A number of these items strike me as just doodlings falsely promoted from the author's notebooks. Their only function seems to be to make the book fatter on the shelf."

Despite negative comments about his verse, however, many critics admire Brautigan's poetry. At his best, he receives praise for his linguistic precision and imaginative originality. Notes Malley, "Some of Brautigan's best poems, in my opinion, have a quality of fresh, precise observation." The *Georgia Review*'s John Ditsky compares Brautigan's prose and poetry and perceives many similarities: "Richard Brautigan's fiction shares many of the qualities of his poetry—charm, brevity, whimsy, and in many cases a total inability to leave a residue in the consciousness." Michael Rogers claims in the *New York Times Book Review* that "Brautigan's most durable work, in fact, has been his short fiction and verse—shorter pieces containing wit, innovative imagery and unexpected turns of phrase that will almost certainly retain a lasting audience." *Chicago Review*'s Kern identifies qualities of Brautigan's poetic style and categorizes him in a distinct literary genre: "More than anything else, it is probably the flatness and the apparent artlessness of his poetry that are boring and even offensive to some of Brautigan's readers. But it is precisely these elements that constitute what is meant by a primitivist poetics (though Brautigan, admittedly, takes them to a blatant extreme)." About *The Tokyo-Montana Express,* John D. Berry observes in the *Washington Post Book World* that "it is [Brautigan's] unusual descriptions that catch our attention." Michael Mason of the *Times Literary Supplement* sees this book as a culmination of the author's earlier verse attempts and, unlike other critics, praises its consistency: "It may sound odd to say that an author has arrived at a vision which is harmonious with his way of writing after a sequence of no less than eight novels, but it is a claim which can be pressed surprisingly far for Brautigan and *The Tokyo-Montana Express.* . . . The book amounts . . . to a coherent meditation or investigation: united by a vision of things which is melancholy and alienated and which is seeking an assuagement of these feelings."

Dictionary of Literary Biography's Novak describes Brautigan as "a controversial writer because he seems to encourage the self-adoring anti-intellectualism of the young." Few critics would argue that the bulk of Brautigan's work inspires disagreement and controversy. But, according to John Yohalem in the *New York Times Book Review,* Brautigan's work seems to meet with general approval from readers: "Richard Brautigan is a popular writer. He is clever and brief; he touches themes and myths close to the current fantasy without being too difficult or too long to complete and understand at a single sitting. He is witty, likable, even literate—a rare virtue nowadays." *Rolling Stone*'s Gurney Norman concurs with Yohalem's assessment of Brautigan's overall impact: "As a California writer, [Brautigan] stands as a kind of gift from the West Coast to the rest of the nation which, judging from the enormous circulation of his books, is a gift the country willingly accepts."

BIOGRAPHICAL/CRITICAL SOURCES:

BOOKS

Contemporary Literary Criticism, Gale, Volume 1, 1973, Volume 3, 1975, Volume 5, 1976, Volume 9, 1978, Volume 12, 1980, Volume 34, 1985, Volume 42, 1987.
Dictionary of Literary Biography, Gale, Volume 2: *American Novelists since World War II,* 1978, Volume 5: *American Poets since World War II,* 1980.
Dictionary of Literary Biography Yearbook, Gale, *1980,* 1981, *1984,* 1985.
Malley, Terence, *Richard Brautigan: Writers for the Seventies,* Warner Paperback, 1972.
Tanner, Tony, *City of Words: American Fiction 1950-1970,* Harper, 1971.

PERIODICALS

Bulletin of Bibliography, January, 1976.
Chicago Review, Volume XXVII, number 1, 1975.
Chicago Tribune Book World, January 11, 1970, October 26, 1980.
Choice, October, 1976, January, 1977, January, 1978, December, 1978.
Commonweal, September 26, 1969.
Critique: Studies in Modern Fiction, Volume XIII, number 2, 1971, Volume XVI, number 1, 1974.
Encounter, June, 1977.
Georgia Review, fall, 1972.
Harper's, October, 1976.
Hudson Review, Volume XXIII, number 1, 1970, Volume XXVII, number 4, 1974-75.
Library Journal, September 1, 1976, October 1, 1976, February 15, 1978.
Life, August 14, 1970.
London Magazine, February, 1971, August-September, 1971.
Los Angeles Times Book Review, November 9, 1980.
Minnesota Review, Volume X, numbers 3 & 4, 1970.
Modern Fiction Studies, spring, 1973, autumn, 1974.
Modern Occasions, spring, 1972.
New American Review, number 11, 1971.
New Republic, September 20, 1975.
New Statesman, April 4, 1975, May 21, 1976, April 14, 1978.
Newsweek, December 29, 1969, September 9, 1974.
New Yorker, November 21, 1977.
New York Review of Books, April 8, 1965, April 22, 1971.
New York Times, March 30, 1971, November 15, 1971.
New York Times Book Review, February 15, 1970, March 18, 1971, January 16, 1972, December 3, 1972, September 8, 1974, September 14, 1975, October 10, 1976, September 25, 1977, November 2, 1980.
Poetry, April, 1968, March, 1970.
Ramparts, December, 1967.
Rolling Stone, December 9, 1971.
Saturday Review, June 12, 1971, January 10, 1976.
Spectator, April 5, 1975, May 29, 1976, April 22, 1978.
Thoreau Quarterly Journal, July, 1976.

Time, April 5, 1971, November 1, 1971.
Times Literary Supplement, February 2, 1973, April 11, 1975, May 21, 1976, April 1, 1977, April 14, 1978, May 1, 1981.
TriQuarterly, spring, 1970, winter, 1973.
Virginia Quarterly Review, autumn, 1970.
Washington Post Book World, October 19, 1980.
West Coast Review of Books, Volume IV, number 1, 1978.
Western Humanities Review, winter, 1975.

OBITUARIES:

PERIODICALS

Chicago Tribune, October 27, 1984.
Los Angeles Times, October 27, 1984.
Newsweek, November 5, 1984.
New York Times, October 27, 1984.
Time, November 5, 1984.
Times (London), October 27, 1984.
Washington Post, October 27, 1984.

*   *   *

BRECHT, Bertolt   1898-1956

PERSONAL: Born February 10, 1898, in Augsburg, Germany (now West Germany); died of a coronary thrombosis in East Berlin, East Germany, August 14, 1956; son of Berthold Friedrich (a paper mill manager) and Sofie Brezing Brecht; married Marianne Zoff, November 3, 1922 (divorced, 1927); married Helene Weigel, April 10, 1929; children: (first marriage) Hanne Hiob; (second marriage), Stefan, Marie Barbara. *Education:* Attended Munich University, 1917-1921. *Politics:* Marxist. *Religion:* Raised as a Protestant.

CAREER: Playwright, poet, and director. Worked as a dramaturge for the Deutsches Theater during the early 1920s, ending 1925. Founder, Berliner Ensemble. *Wartime service:* Worked as an orderly in an Augsburg hospital, 1918.

AWARDS, HONORS: First prize, *Berliner Illustrierte Zeitung,* 1928, for short story "Die Bestie"; Stalin Freedom Prize, 1955.

WRITINGS:

PLAYS

Baal (also see below), Kiepenheuer (Potsdam), 1922, translated by Eric Bentley as *Baal* in *Baal, A Man's a Man, and The Elephant Calf,* Grove, 1964, reprinted, 1989.
Trommeln in der Nacht: Drama (also see below), Drei Masken (Munich), 1922, edited by Volkmar Sander, Blaisdell, 1969, translated by Anselm Hollo and others as *Drums in the Night* in *Jungle of Cities and Other Plays,* Grove, 1966.
(With Lion Feuchtwanger) *Leben Eduards des Zweiten von England: Nach Marlowe, Histoire* (also see below), Kiepenheuer, 1924, translated by Bentley as *Edward II: A Chronicle Play,* Grove, 1966.
Im Dickicht der Staedte: Der Kampf zweier Maenner in der Riesenstadt Chicago (also see below), Propylaeen (Berlin), 1927, translated by Hollo as *Jungle of Cities* in *Jungle of Cities and Other Plays,* Grove, 1966.
Mann ist Mann: Die Verwandlung des Packers Galy Gay in den Militaerbaracken von Kilkoa im Jahre 1925: Lustspiel (also see below), Propylaeen, 1927, translated by Bentley as *A Man's a Man* in *Baal, A Man's a Man, and The Elephant Calf,* Grove, 1964, reprinted, 1989.
(With Feuchtwanger) *Drei angelsaechsische Stuecke,* Propylaeen-Verlag, 1927.
Aufsteig und Fall der Stadt Mahagonny: Oper in drei Akten (also see below), music by Kurt Weill, Universal-Edition, 1929,

translated by Guy Stern as a brochure entitled *Rise and Fall of the City of Mahagonny* accompanying the recorded version, Columbia, 1959.
Die Dreigroschenoper (based on John Gay's *The Beggar's Opera;* also see below), music by Weill, Universal-Edition, 1929, translated by Bentley and Desmond Vesey as *The Threepenny Opera,* Grove, 1964, reprinted, 1983.
Der Jasager und der Neinsager (first produced in 1930; also see below), Suhrkamp, 1966.
Das Badener Lehrstueck von Einverstaendnis (also see below), first produced in 1930.
Die Massnahme (first produced in 1931; also see below), translated by Carl Mueller as *The Measures Taken* in *The Measures Taken and Other Lehrstuecke,* Methuen, 1977.
Die heilige Johanna der Schlachthoefe: Schauspiel (first produced in 1932; also see below), Kiepenheuer, 1932, translated by Frank Jones as *Saint Joan of the Stockyards,* Indiana University Press, 1969.
Die Mutter (first produced in 1933; also see below), Kiepenheuer, 1933, translated by Lee Baxandall as *The Mother,* Grove, 1965, reprinted, 1989.
Die Rundkoepfe und die Spitzkoepfe (also see below), first produced in 1936, translated by N. Goold-Vershoyle as *Roundheads and Peakheads* in *Jungle of Cities and Other Plays,* Grove, 1966.
Die Ausnahme und die Regel (also see below), first produced in 1937, translated by Bentley as *The Exception and the Rule: A Play in Nine Scenes,* Boston Publishing, 1961.
Die Gewehre der Frau Carrar (first produced in 1937; also see below), Aufbau (Berlin), 1957, translated by George Tabori as *The Guns of Carrar,* Samuel French, 1971.
(With Margarete Steffin) *Das Verhoer des Lukullus: Oper in 12 Bildern* (first produced in 1940; also see below), music by Paul Dessau, Aufbau, 1951.
Furcht und Elend des Dritten Reichs (also see below), Meshdunarodnaja Kniga (Moscow), 1941, Aurora, 1945, translated as *Fear and Misery in the Third Reich,* Mezhdunarodnaya Kniga, 1942, translated by Bentley as *The Private Life of the Master Race,* New Directions, 1944.
Leben des Galilei (first produced in 1943; revised English version with Charles Laughton produced in California, 1947; second revised version produced in 1957), Suhrkamp, 1955, translated by Vesey as *The Life of Galileo,* Methuen, 1960, reprinted, 1986, translated by Laughton as *Galileo,* Grove, 1966.
(With Ruth Berlau) *Der kaukasische Kreidekreis* (first produced in 1949; also see below), Suhrkamp, 1955, translated by Bentley and Maja Apelman as *The Caucasian Chalk Circle* in *Parables for the Theater: Two Plays by Bertolt Brecht,* University of Minnesota Press, 1948, revised edition, Grove, 1961, published separately as *The Caucasian Chalk Circle,* Grove, 1987.
Herr Puntila und sein Knecht: Nach Erzaehlungen der Hella Wuolijoki. Volksstueck in 9 Bildern (first produced in 1950; also see below), Desch (Munich), 1948, reprinted as *Herr Puntila und sein Knecht Matti,* edited by Margaret Mare, Methuen, 1962, translated by Gerhard Nellhaus as *Puntila and His Hired Man,* G. Nellhaus, 1960, translated by John Willett as *Mr. Puntila and His Man Matti,* Methuen, 1977.
Mutter Courage und Ihre Kinder: Eine Chronik aus dem Dreissigjaehrigen Krieg (first produced in 1949; also see below), Suhrkamp, 1949, translated by Bentley as *Mother Courage and Her Children,* Grove, 1949.

Die Verurteilung des Lukullus: Oper (also see below), music by Dessau, Aufbau, 1951, translated by H. R. Hays as *The Trial of Lucullus,* New Directions, 1943.

Der Hofmeister (based on the play by Jacob Michael Reinhold Lenz; also see below), edited by Elizabeth Hauptmann, Suhrkamp, 1951, translated by Pip Broughton as *The Tutor,* Applause Theatre Book Publishers, 1988.

(With Berlau and Steffin) *Der gute Mensch von Sezuan* (first produced in 1953; also see below), music by Dessau, Suhrkamp, 1959, translated by Bentley and Apelman as *The Good Woman of Setzuan* in *Parables for the Theater: Two Plays by Bertolt Brecht,* University of Minnesota Press, 1948, revised edition, Grove, 1961, translated by Willett as *The Good Person of Szechuan,* Methuen, 1965.

Die Geschichte der Simone Marchard, first produced in 1956, translated by Arnold Hinchuffe as *The Visions of Simone Marchard,* [London], c. 1961, translated by Mueller, Grove, 1965.

Die Tage der Kommune (also see below), Suhrkamp, 1957, translated by Leonard J. Lehrman as *The Days of the Commune* in *Dunster Drama Review,* Volume 10, number 2, 1971.

Schweyk im Zweiten Weltkrieg, Suhrkamp, 1959, translated by Peter M. Sandler as *Schweyk in the Second World War,* Brandeis University, 1967.

(With Zuckmayer von Verner Arpe) *Aufruhr und Empoerung,* Sveriges Radio, 1959.

Die sieben Todsuenden der Kleinbuerger, Suhrkamp, 1959.

Drums and Trumpets (translation of Brecht's *Pauken und Trompetten* based on *The Recruiting Officer* by George Farquhar), English version by Rose and Martin Kastner, Trinity College, 1963.

Der aufhaltsame Aufstieg des Arturo Ui (also see below), Suhrkamp, 1965, translated by Tabori as *The Resistable Rise of Auturo Ui: A Gangster Spectacle,* Samuel French, 1971.

Turandot oder Der Kongress der Weisswaescher, Suhrkamp, 1967.

Der Brotladen: Ein Stueckfragment, Suhrkamp, 1967.

(With Dorothy Lane) *Happy End,* music by Weill, Routledge Chapman & Hall, 1983.

POEMS

Taschenpostille: Mit Anleitung, Gesangsnoten und einem Anhange, privately printed, 1926, reprinted, Aufbau, 1958.

Hauspostille: Mit Anleitung, Gesangsnoten und einem Anhang (poems and songs), Propylaeen, 1927, translated by Bentley as *Manual of Piety: A Bilingual Edition,* Grove, 1966.

Lieder, Gedichte, Choere, music by Hanns Eisler, Editions du Carrefour (Paris), 1934.

Svendborger Gedichte; Deutsche Kriegsfibel; Chroniken: Deutsche Satiren fuer den deutschen Freiheitssender, Malik, 1939.

Selected Poems (in German and English), translated and with introduction by Hays, Reynal & Hitchcock, 1947, reprinted, Harcourt, 1975.

Hundert Gedichte, 1918-1950, Aufbau, 1951, reprinted, 1966.

Gedichte, edited by Siegfried Streller, Reclam (Leipzig), 1955.

Gedichte und Lieder, edited by P. Suhrkamp, Suhrkamp, 1956.

Selected Poems, translated by Hays, Grove, 1959.

Ausgewaehlte Gedichte, edited by Siegfried Unseld, Suhrkamp, 1960, reprinted, 1981.

Poems on the Theatre, translated by John Berger and Anna Bostock, Scorpion Press, 1961.

Selected Poems, translated by K. Woelfel, Oxford University Press, 1965.

Liebesgedichte, edited by Hauptmann, Insel Verlag, 1966.

Bertolt Brecht Poems 1913-1956, three volumes, edited by Willett and Manheim, Methuen (London), 1979.

Gedichte fuer Staedtebewohner, edited and with afterword by Franco Buono, Suhrkamp, 1980.

Gedichte aus dem Nachlass, 1913-1956, Suhrkamp, 1982.

COLLECTED WORKS

Versuche, edited by Hauptmann, Volume 1: *Der Flug der Lindberghs; Radiotheorie; Geschichten vom Herrn Keuner; Fatzer, 3,* Kiepenheuer, 1930, Volume 2: *Aufstieg und Fall der Stadt Mahagonny: Ueber die Oper: Aus dem Lesebuch fuer Staedtebewohner: Das Badener Lehrstueck vom Einverstaendnis,* Kiepenheuer, 1930, Volume 3: *Die Dreigroschenoper; Die Beule: Ein Dreigroschenfilm; Der Dreigroschenprozess,* Kiepenheuer, 1931, Volume 4: *Der Jasager und der Neinsager: Schulopern; Die Massnahme: Lehrstueck,* Kiepenheuer, 1931, Volume 5: *Die heilige Johanna der Schlachthoefe: Schauspiel; Geschichten vom Herrn Keuner,* Kiepenheuer, 1932, Volume 6: *Die drei Soldaten: Ein Kinderbuch,* Kiepenheuer, 1932, Volume 7: *Die Mutter; Geschichte aus der Revolution,* Kiepenheuer, 1933, Volume 9: *Mutter Courage und ihre Kinder: Eine Chronik aus dem Dreissigjaehrigen Krieg; Anmerkungen; Fuenf Schwierigkeiten beim Schreiben der Wahrheit,* Suhrkamp, 1949, Volume 10: *Herr Puntila und sein Knecht Matti; Chinesische Gedichte; Dis Ausnahme und die Regel,* Suhrkamp, 1950, Volume 11: *Der Hofmeister; Studien: Neue Technik der Schauspielkunst; Uebungsstuecke fuer Schauspieler; Das Verhoer des Lukullus; Anmerkungen ueber die Oper "Die Verurteilung des Lukullus,"* Suhrkamp, 1951, Volume 12: *Der gute Mensch von Sezuan; Kleines Organon fuer das Theater; Ueber reimlose Lyrik mit unregelmaessigen Rhythmen; Geschichten vom Herrn Keuner,* Suhrkamp, 1953, extra volume: *Die Gewehre der Frau Carrar; Der Augsburger Kreidedreis; Neue Kinderlieder,* Volume 13: *Der kaukasische Kreidekreis; Weite und Vielfalt der realistischen Schreibweise; Buckower Elegien,* Suhrkamp, 1954, Volume 14: *Leben des Galilei; Gedichte aus dem Messingkauf; die Horatier und die Kuratier,* Suhrkamp, 1955, Volume 15: *Die Tage der Kommune; die Dialektik auf dem Theater; Zu "Leben des Galilei"; Drei Reden; Zwei Briefe,* Suhrkamp, 1957, Volumes 5-8: *Die heilige Johanna der Schlachthoefe; Die drei Soldaten; Die Mutter; Die Rundkoepfe und die Spitzkoepfe,* one volume, Suhrkamp, 1959.

Gesammelte Werke, two volumes, Malik, 1938.

Erste Stuecke, two volumes, Suhrkamp, 1953.

Fruehe Stuecke (contains *Baal, Trommeln in der Nacht,* and *Im Dickicht der Stadt*), Deutscher Taschenbuch, 1953.

Stuecke fuer das Theater am Schiffbauerdamm, three volumes, Suhrkamp, 1955-57.

Stuecke, Volume 1: *Baal, Trommeln in der Nacht, Im Dickicht der Staedte,* Volume 2: *Leben Eduards des Zweiten von England, Mann ist Mann,* Volume 3: *Die Dreigroschenoper, Aufstieg und Fall der Stadt Mahagonny, Das Badener Lehrstueck vom Einverstaendnis,* Volume 4: *Die heilige Johanna der Schlachthoefe, Der Jasager und der Neinsager, Die Massnahme,* Aufbau, 1956.

Stuecke aus dem Exil; Die Rundkoepfe und die Spitzkoepfe; Furcht und Elend des Dritten Reiches; Die Gewehre der Frau Carrar; Mutter Courage und ihre Kinder; Das Verhoer des Lukullus; Leben des Galilei; Der gute Mensch von Sezuan; Herr Puntila und sein Knecht Matti; Der aufhaltsame Aufstieg des Arturo Ui; Die Geschichte der Simone Marchard; Schweyk im zweiten Weltkrieg; Der kaukasische Krei-

dekreis; Die Tage der Kommune, five volumes, Suhrkamp, 1957.
Bertolt Brecht (poetry and play selections), edited by Hans Klaehn and Waldemar Sowade, Deutsche Kulturbund, 1958.
Bearbeitungen: Die Antigone des Sophokles; Der Hofmeister; Coriolan; der Prozess der Jeanne d'Arc zu Rouen 1431; Don Juan; Paulsen und Trompeten (*Coriolan* based on Shakespeare's *Coriolanus; Der Prozess der Jeanne d'Arc zu Rouen 1431* based on the version by Anna Segher; *Don Juan* based on the play by Moliere), two volumes, Suhrkamp, 1959.
Plays (contains *The Caucasian Chalk Circle, The Threepenny Opera, The Trial of Lucullus,* and *The Life of Galileo*), Methuen, 1960.
Seven Plays (contains *In the Swamp, A Man's a Man, Saint Joan of the Stockyards, Mother Courage and Her Children, The Life of Galileo, The Good Woman of Setzuan,* and *The Chinese Chalk Circle*), edited and with introduction by Bentley, Grove, 1961.
Die drei Johanna-Stuecke (contains *Die heilige Johanna der Schlachthoefe, Die Geschichte der Simone Marchard,* and *Der Prozess der Jeanne d'Arc zu Rouen 1431*), Fischer Bucherei, 1964.
Geschichten, Volume 1: *Unveroeffentlichte und nicht in Sammlungen enthaltene Geschichten, Eulenspiegelgeschichten,* Volume 2: *Kalendergeschichten, Geschichten vom Herrn Keuner, Fluechtlingsgespraech* (also see below), Suhrkamp, 1965.
The Jewish Wife, and Other Short Plays, translated by Bentley, Grove, 1965.
Einakter: Die Kleinburgerhochzeit, Der Bettler; oder, der tote Hunde, Er treibt einen Teufel aus, Lux in Tenebris, Der Fischzug, Dansen, Was kostet das Eisen?, Suhrkamp, 1966.
Gesammelte Werke, 22 volumes, Suhrkamp, 1967-69, Volumes 1-7: *Stuecke,* translated and edited by Willett and Ralph Manheim as *Collected Plays,* nine volumes, Random House, 1971-73, Volume 8-10: *Gedichte,* translated by Willett and Manheim as *Poems 1913-1956,* Methuen, 1976, Volume 11: *Prosa I,* translated by Willett and Manheim as *Short Stories 1921-1946,* Methuen, 1983, Volumes 15-17: *Schriften zum Theater,* translated by Willett as *Brecht on Theatre,* Hill & Wang, 1964.
Fuenf Lehrstuecke, edited by Keith A. Dickson, Methuen Educational, 1969.
Die Bibel und andere fruehe Einakter, Suhrkamp, 1970.
Lehrstuecke (contains *Der Jasager und der Neinsager, Die Massnahme, Die Ausnahme und die Regel, Die Rundkoepfe und die Spitzkoepfe, Das Badener Lehrstueck von Einverstaendnis*), Rowohlt, 1970.
Werke, five volumes, Aufbau, 1973.
Der Stuecke von Bertolt Brecht in einem Band, Suhrkamp, 1978.

OTHER

Ballade vom armen Stabschef 30: Juni 1934, [Germany], 1934.
Dreigroschenroman (novel), Albert de Lange (Amsterdam), 1934, translated by Vesey and Christopher Lisherwood as *A Penny for the Poor,* R. Hale, 1937, published as *Threepenny Novel,* Grove, 1956, reprinted, Ungar, 1984.
(Translator) M. Andersen-Nexoe, *Die Kindheit: Erinnerungen,* Vereinigung "Kultur und Volk," 1945.
Kalendergeschichten, Mitteldeutscher Verlag, 1948, Norton, 1960, translated by Yvonne Kapp and Michael Hamburger as *Tales from the Calendar,* Methuen, 1961.
Das Zukunftslied: Aufbaulied der FDJ, music by Dessau, Thueringer Volksverlag (Weimar), 1949.

Sinn und Form: Beitraege zur Literatur, Ruetten & Loening, 1949.
Antigonemodell 1948; Die Antigone des Sophokles, nach der Hoelderlinschen Uebertragung fuer die Buehne, bearbeitet, Weiss, 1949, translated by Judith Malina as *Antigone: With Selections from Brecht's Model Book,* Applause Theatre Book, 1989.
(Contributor) Feuchtwanger, *Auswahl,* Greifen (Rudolstadt), 1949.
(Editor with Dessau) *Wir singen zu den Weltfestspielen: Herrnburger Bericht,* Verlag Neues Leben (Berlin), 1951.
Offener Brief an die deutschen Kuenstler und Schriftsteller, [Berlin], 1951.
Die Erziehung der Hirse, Nach dem Bericht von G. Frisch: Der Mann, der das Unmoegliche wahr gemacht hat, Aufbau, 1951.
An meine Landsleute, VEB Offizin Haag-Drugulin (Leipzig), 1951.
(Editor with Berlau, C. Hubalek, and others), *Theaterarbeit: Sechs Auffuehrungen des Berliner Ensembles,* Dresdner Verlag, 1952.
Kriegsfibel, edited by Berlau, Eulenspiegel (Berlin), 1955.
Die Geschaefte des Herrn Julius Caesar: Romanfragment, Aufbau, 1957.
Lieder und Gesaenge, Henschel (Berlin), 1957.
Schriften zum Theater: Ueber eine nicht-aristotelische Dramatik, edited by Unseld, Suhrkamp, 1957.
Geschichten vom Herrn Keuner, Aufbau, 1958.
Brecht: Ein Lesebuch fuer unsere Zeit, edited by Hauptmann and Benno Slupianek, Volksverlag Weimar, 1958.
Bertolt Brecht in Selbstzeugnissen und Bilddokumenten, compiled by Marianne Wolf-Kesting, edited by Paul Raabe, Rowohlt (Hamburg), 1959.
Kleines Organon fuer das Theater: Mit einem "Nachtrag zum Kleinen Organon," Suhrkamp, 1960, translated by Willett as "A Short Organum for the Theatre" in *Brecht on Theatre,* Hill & Wang, 1964.
Fluechtlingsgespraeche, Suhrkamp, 1961.
Helene Weigel, Actress: A Book of Photographs, translated by Berger and Bostock, VEB Edition (Leipzig), 1961.
Gespraech auf der Probe, Sanssouci (Zurich), 1961.
Dialoge aus dem Messingkauf, Suhrkamp, 1964.
Ueber Lyrik, Suhrkamp, 1964.
(Contributor) Samuel Weiss, editor, *Drama in the Modern World* (contains *The Good Woman of Setzuan*), Heath, 1964.
Ein Kinderbuch, illustrated by Elizabeth Shaw, Kinderbuchverlag, c. 1965.
Me-ti; Buch der Wendungen-Fragment, edited by Uwe Johnson, Suhrkamp, 1965.
Ueber Klassiker, edited by Unseld, Insel, 1965.
Ueber Theater, edited by Hecht, Reclam, 1966.
Schriften zur Literatur und Kunst, Suhrkamp, 1967.
Schriften zur Politik und Gesellschaft 1919-1956, Suhrkamp, 1968.
Kuehle Wampe: Protokoll des Films und Materialien, edited by Wolfgang Gersch and Werner Hecht, Suhrkamp, 1969.
Politische Schriften, edited by Hecht, Suhrkamp, 1970.
Ueber den Beruf des Schauspielers, Suhrkamp, 1970.
Ueber experimentelles Theater, edited by Hecht, Suhrkamp, 1970.
Brecht Fibel, edited by Reinhold Grimm and Henry J. Schmidt, Harper, 1970.
Herr Bertolt Brecht sagt, Weismann (Munich), 1970.

Ueber die irdische Liebe und andere gewisse Weltraetsel in Liedern und Balladen, Eulenspiegel Verlag (Berlin), 1971.
Ueber Politik auf dem Theater, edited by Hecht, Suhrkamp, 1971.
Ueber Politik und Kunst, edited by Hecht, Suhrkamp, 1971.
Ueber Realismus, edited by Hecht, Suhrkamp, 1971.
Arbeitsjournal 1938 bis 1955, three volumes, Suhrkamp, 1973.
Der Tui-Roman: Fragment, Suhrkamp, 1973.
Tagebuecher 1920-1922: Autobiographische Aufzeichnungen 1920-1954, edited by Herta Ramthun, Suhrkamp, 1975, translated by Willett as *Diaries 1920-1922,* St. Martin's, 1979.
Brecht in Gespraech, Henschelverlag Kunst und Gesellschaft, 1975.
Und der Haifisch, der hat Zaehne: Die grossen Songs und Kleinen Lieder, Henschelverlag (Berlin), 1977.
Ein gemeiner Kerl: Geschichten, edited by Fritz Hofmann, Aufbau, 1978.
Der Staedtebauer: Geschichten und Anekdoten 1919-1956, edited and with afterword by Hubert Witt, Insel, 1978.
Nordseekrabben, Eulenspiegel, 1979.
Briefe, edited and with commentary by Guenter Glaeser, Suhrkamp, 1981, translated by Willett and Manheim as *Brecht Letters,* Routledge Chapman & Hall, 1989.
Ich leb so gern, Kinderbuchverlag, 1982.
Ueber die bildenden Kuenste, Suhrkamp, 1983.
Kriegsfibel, Eulenspiegel, 1983.
Brecht-Journal, Suhrkamp, 1983.
Fragen an Brecht, Reclam, 1987.

Contributor to periodical *Internationale Literatur: Deutsche Blaetter,* and to other German publications.

MEDIA ADAPTATIONS: Die Dreigroschenoper was adapted as a German film by G. W. Pabst in 1931.

SIDELIGHTS: One of the major playwrights of the twentieth century, Bertolt Brecht was renowned for such works as *The Threepenny Opera, Mother Courage and Her Children, The Life of Galileo,* and *The Caucasian Chalk Circle.* Recognized as one of the main innovators of theatrical technique in modern times, Brecht turned away from conventional dramatic devices in favor of the "epic theater" and the use of the *Verfremdungseffekt* ("estrangement effect"). The purpose of his ground-breaking techniques—distinguished by the use of non-climactic, episodic narrative—was to remind his audiences that what they were seeing was not reality, resulting in a distancing effect that was intended to help them absorb what was being said, rather than what the characters were feeling. His plays are, therefore, didactic, rather than dramatic.

First achieving prominence in 1922 with his play *Trommeln in der Nacht* (*Drums in the Night*), about a soldier who rejects the violent existence of World War I in favor of finding a happy domestic life, the playwright revealed an interest in life's social forces even at the beginning of his career. During the chaotic years of post-World War I Germany, the author turned toward Communism as an answer to the anarchy that surrounded him. Because of his belief in the theories of Marxism, the action in many of his plays is driven by economic and political—rather than psychological or emotional—forces.

Die Dreigroschenoper (*The Threepenny Opera*), based on the eighteenth-century comic opera by John Gay, *The Beggar's Opera,* was a dramatic international success for Brecht, but not for the same reasons that he had intended. Audiences enjoyed the irony of Brecht's dialogue and the catchy jazz music written by Kurt Weill, missing the author's comparisons between capi-

talists and the gangster characters in the play. "If the businessman is identified with the gangster in *The Threepenny Opera,*" noted Robert Brustein in his *The Theatre of Revolt: An Approach to the Modern Drama,* "then he is identified with the warmaker in *Mother Courage.*" In *Mother Courage and Her Children,* a play set during the Thirty Years' War in which a mother unwittingly destroys her family as a result of her attempts to profit from the war, Brecht portrays war as motivated by economics, rather than politics, religion, or nationalism. This play, too, was often misinterpreted by Brecht's audiences, who viewed the protagonist as a tragic human figure, rather than as an example of the folly of capitalism. Modern critics like Brustein have called *Mother Courage* "the culminating work of Brecht's career."

Another well-known Brecht play that also occurs during the Thirty Years' War is *Der kaukasische Kreidekreis* (*The Caucasian Chalk Circle*). The theme of this play, in which a servant girl proves her superior love for her mistress's child over that of its mother, is that "motherhood is based on the bondage created by work and suffering rather than on biological factors," according to *Dictionary of Literary Biography* contributor Siegfried Mews. "In *Der kaukasische Kreidekreis* this new definition of motherhood is expanded to promote a new kind of thinking with regard to property rights." Marxist undertones are also present in Brecht's *Das Leben des Galilei* (*The Life of Galileo*), which is largely concerned with the famous scientist's recantation of his belief in a heliocentric universe when he is faced with the prospect of punishment by the Catholic Church. With this subject, Brecht was able to portray how outside forces often interfere with social progress.

Despite Brecht's faithful allegiance to Marxism and the propagandistic value of the renowned Berliner Ensemble that he founded during his final years in East Berlin, the Communist world was suspicious of Brecht's art. The West, on the other hand, tended to try to ignore the author's political message and praise his artistic achievement. Of Brecht's influence as a political commentator, *Theatre Arts* critic Alan Pryce-Jones wrote: "It has never been recorded that [his plays have] had the least influence on the political thinking of either Right or Left—and influence towards the establishment of a Marxist Europe was their primary aim." "Whether or not Brecht wrote what are all too glibly called 'great' plays," concluded Harold Clurman in a *New York Times Magazine* article, ". . . it is my conviction that his plays are the most important to have been written anywhere" in recent times.

BIOGRAPHICAL/CRITICAL SOURCES:

BOOKS

Abel, Lionel, *Metatheatre: A New View of Dramatic Form,* Hill & Wang, 1963.
Arendt, Hannah, *Men in Dark Times,* Harcourt, 1968.
Barthes, Roland, *Critical Essays,* translated by Richard Howard, Northwestern University Press, 1972.
Bartram, Graham, and Anthony Waine, editors, *Brecht in Perspective,* Longman, 1982.
Bauland, Peter, *The Hooded Eagle: Modern German Drama on the New York Stage,* Syracuse University Press, 1968.
Bentley, Eric, *The Playwright as Thinker: A Study of Drama in Modern Times,* Reynal & Hitchcock, 1946.
Bentley, Eric, *In Search of Theater,* Atheneum, 1953.
Bentley, Eric, *Theatre of War: Comments on 32 Occasions,* Viking, 1972.
Bentley, Eric, *The Brecht Commentaries: 1943-1980,* Grove, 1981.

Block, Haskell M., and Herman Salinger, editors, *The Creative Vision: Modern European Writers on Their Art,* Grove, 1960.

Brustein, Robert, *The Theatre of Revolt: An Approach to the Modern Drama,* Little, Brown, 1964.

Clurman, Harold, *The Naked Image: Observations on the Modern Theatre,* Macmillan, 1966.

Clurman, Harold, *The Divine Pastime: Theatre Essays,* Macmillan, 1974.

Cohn, Ruby, *Currents in Contemporary Drama,* Indiana University Press, 1969.

Cook, Bruce, *Brecht in Exile,* Holt, 1983.

Corrigan, Robert W., *The Theatre in Search of a Fix,* Delacorte, 1973.

Demetz, Peter, editor, *Brecht: A Collection of Critical Essays,* Prentice-Hall, 1962.

Dickson, Keith A., *Towards Utopia: A Study of Brecht,* Clarendon Press, 1978.

Dictionary of Literary Biography, Volume 56: *German Fiction Writers, 1914-1945,* Gale, 1987.

Esslin, Martin, *Brecht, a Choice of Evils: A Critical Study of the Man, His Work and His Opinions,* Eyre & Spottiswoode, 1959.

Esslin, Martin, *Brecht: The Man and His Work,* Doubleday, 1960.

Esslin, Martin, *Bertolt Brecht,* Columbia University Press, 1969.

Ewen, Frederic, *Bertolt Brecht: His Life, His Art, and His Times,* Citadel, 1967.

Gass, William H., *The World within the Word,* Knopf, 1978.

Gassner, John, *The Theatre in Our Times: A Survey of the Men, Materials and Movements in the Modern Theatre,* Crown, 1954.

Gilman, Richard, *The Making of Modern Drama: A Study of Buechner, Ibsen, Strindberg, Chekhov, Pirandello, Brecht, Beckett, Handke,* Farrar, Straus, 1974.

Gray, Ronald D., *Brecht the Dramatist,* Cambridge University Press, 1976.

Greenberg, Clement, *Art and Culture: Critical Essays,* Beacon Press, 1961.

Grossvogel, David I., *Four Playwrights and a Postscript,* Cornell University Press, 1962.

Hill, Claude, *Bertolt Brecht,* Twayne, 1975.

Jones, David Richard, *Great Directors at Work: Stanislavsky, Brecht, Kazan, Brook,* University of California Press, 1986.

Lyons, Charles R., *Bertolt Brecht: The Despair and the Polemic,* Southern Illinois University Press, 1968.

Nathan, George Jean, *The Theatre Book of the Year, 1947-48: A Record and an Interpretation,* Knopf, 1948.

Scott, Nathan A., Jr., *Man in the Modern Theatre,* John Knox, 1965.

Spalek, John M., and Robert F. Bell, *Exile: The Writer's Experience,* University of North Carolina Press, 1982.

Styan, J. L., *Modern Drama in Theory and Practice: Expressionism and Epic Theatre,* Volume 3, Cambridge University Press, 1981.

Szczesny, Gerhard, *The Case against Bertolt Brecht, with Arguments Drawn from His "Life of Galileo,"* translated by Alexander Gode, Ungar, 1969.

Twentieth Century Literary Criticism, Gale, Volume 1, 1978, Volume 6, 1982, Volume 13, 1984, Volume 35, 1990.

Voelker, Klaus, *Brecht: A Biography,* translated by John Nowell, Seabury, 1978.

Weideli, Walter, *The Art of Bertolt Brecht,* translated by Daniel Russell, New York University Press, 1963.

Willett, John, *Brecht in Context: Comparative Approaches,* Methuen, 1984.

Witt, Hubert, editor, *Brecht: As They Knew Him,* translated by John Peet, International Publishers, 1974.

PERIODICALS

Atlantic, January, 1969.

Commonweal, December 19, 1947.

Communications from the International Brecht Society, November, 1984.

Comparative Drama, spring, 1967.

Contemporary Literature, winter, 1970.

Critical Quarterly, summer, 1961.

Drama Review, winter, 1968.

Educational Theatre Journal, March, 1957.

Germanic Review, January, 1966.

Listener, May 6, 1976.

London Review of Books, July 16-August 5, 1981.

Modern Drama, February, 1969.

Modern Language Quarterly, June, 1962; December, 1966.

Nation, May 8, 1967; April 19, 1971; June 7, 1975; May 22, 1976.

New Republic, December 29, 1947.

New Statesman, May 7, 1976.

New Yorker, September 12, 1959.

New York Times Magazine, November 3, 1963.

Oxford Review, Number 2, 1966.

Parnassus: Poetry in Review, spring/summer/fall/winter, 1980.

Theatre Arts, June, 1963.

University of Kansas City Review, October, 1960.

World Review, January, 1951.

Yale Theatre, summer, 1968.

*   *   *

BRENTON, Howard   1942-

PERSONAL: Born December 13, 1942, in Portsmouth, England; son of Donald Henry and Rose Lilian (Lewis) Brenton; married Jane Margaret Fry, January 31, 1970; children: Samuel John. *Education:* St. Catherine's College, Cambridge, B.A. (honors), 1965.

ADDRESSES: Agent—Margaret Ramsey, 14A Goodwin's Court, St. Martin's Lane, London WC2, England.

CAREER: Has worked as stage manager for various repertory companies in England; performed as an actor with Brighton Combination, 1969; Royal Court Theatre, London, England, resident dramatist, 1972—.

AWARDS, HONORS: John Whiting Award, 1970; bursary awards from Arts Council of Great Britain, 1971, for "Christie in Love"; *Evening Standard* award, c. 1976, for "Weapons of Happiness"; London Standard Award, c. 1985, and *Plays and Players* award for best new play, 1985, both for "Pravda."

WRITINGS:

PUBLISHED PLAYS

Revenge (first produced on West End at Royal Court Theatre Upstairs, 1969), Eyre Methuen, 1969.

Christie in Love and Other Plays (includes the one-act plays "Christie in Love," "Heads," and "The Education of Skinny Spew"), Methuen, 1970.

(Co-author) *Lay By* (first produced in Edinburgh, Scotland, 1971), Calder & Boyars, 1972, Riverrun, 1988.

Plays for Public Places (includes the one-act plays "Gum and Goo," "Wesley," and "Scott of the Antarctic; or, What God Didn't See"), Eyre Methuen, 1972.

Hitler Dances (first produced in London at Traverse Theatre
   Workshop, 1972), Methuen, 1982.
Magnificence (first produced on West End at Royal Court The-
   atre, 1973), Methuen, 1973.
(With David Hare) *Brassneck* (first produced in Nottingham,
   England, at Nottingham Playhouse), Methuen, 1974.
The Churchill Play, Methuen, 1974.
Weapons of Happiness (first produced in London), Methuen,
   1976.
Epsom Downs, Methuen, 1977.
Sore Throats and Sonnets of Love and Opposition (includes "Sore
   Throats"), Methuen, 1979.
Plays for the Poor Theatre, Methuen, 1980.
The Romans in Britain, Eyre Methuen, 1980.
Thirteenth Night [and] *A Short Sharp Shock!* (first by Brenton;
   second with Tony Howard), Eyre Methuen, 1981.
(Adapter) Georg Bucchner, *Danton's Death: A New Version*
   (from a translation by Jane Fry), Methuen, 1982.
The Genius (produced in London, 1983), Methuen, 1983.
(With Tunde Ikoli) *Sleeping Policemen,* Heinemann Educa-
   tional, 1984.
Bloody Poetry (produced in London, 1984), Methuen, 1985.
(With Hare) *Pravda* (produced in London, 1985), Methuen,
   1985.
Brenton Plays: One, Heinemann Educational, 1987.

UNPUBLISHED PLAYS

"Ladder of Fools," first produced in Cambridge, England, 1965.
"Winter, Daddykins," first produced in Dublin, Ireland, 1965.
"It's My Criminal," first produced in London, 1966.
"A Sky-Blue Life" (adaptations of stories by Maksim Gorky),
   first produced in London, 1966; revised version produced
   in London at Open Space Theatre, 1971.
"Gargantua," first produced in Brighton, England, 1969.
"Fruit," first produced in London at Royal Court Theatre Up-
   stairs, 1970.
"How Beautiful with Badges," first produced in London at Open
   Space Theatre, 1972.
"Measure for Measure" (adaptation from play of same title by
   William Shakespeare), first produced in Exeter, England,
   1972.
(Co-author) "England's Ireland," first produced in Amsterdam,
   Netherlands, 1972.
(With David Edgar) "A Fart for Europe," first produced in Lon-
   don, 1972.
"The Screens" (adaptation from a play by Jean Genet), first pro-
   duced in Bristol, England, 1973.
(Adapter) Bertolt Brecht, "Conversations in Exile" (from a
   translation by David Dollenmayer), produced in New York
   City, 1987.
"Greenland," produced in London, 1988.

Also author of "Government Property," 1975, "Deeds" (with
Trevor Griffiths, Hare, and Ken Campbell), 1978, "The Thing"
(for children), 1982, and "Iranian Nights" (with Tariq Ali),
1989.

OTHER

Notes from a Psychotic Journal and Other Poems, privately
   printed, 1969.
"Skin Flicker" (screenplay; based on a book by Tony Bicat),
   British Film Institute, 1973.
The Saliva Milkshake, (television play; broadcast 1975), TQ
   Publications, 1977.
Dead Head (television series; broadcast 1986), Heinemann Edu-
   cational, 1987.

Diving for Pearls (novel), Walker, 1989.

Also author of television plays, including "Lushly," 1971, "The
Paradise Run," 1976, and "Desert of Lies," 1984. Translator of
Bertolt Brecht's "Life of Galileo," 1980.

BIOGRAPHICAL/CRITICAL SOURCES:

BOOKS

Contemporary Literary Criticism, Volume 31, Gale, 1985.
Dictionary of Literary Biography, Volume 13: *British Dramatists
   since World War II,* Gale, 1982.

PERIODICALS

Chicago Tribune, January 15, 1989.
Los Angeles Times, April 6, 1984.
New York Times, June 20, 1985, May 29, 1986, January 7, 1987,
   November 3, 1987.
Plays and Players, February, 1972, January, 1986.
Time, June 10, 1985.
Times (London), September 14, 1983, November 7, 1984, May
   4, 1985, April 27, 1988, June 3, 1988.
Times Literary Supplement, June 23-29, 1989

*   *   *

BRESLIN, James   1930-
   (Jimmy Breslin)

PERSONAL: Born October 17, 1930, in Jamaica, N.Y.; son of
James Earl and Frances (a high school teacher and social
worker; maiden name, Curtin) Breslin; married Rosemary Dat-
tolico, December 26, 1954 (died June, 1981); married Ronnie Eldridge (an executive), 1982; children: (first marriage) James and
Kevin (twins), Rosemary, Patrick, Kelly, Christopher; (stepchildren) Daniel, Emily, Lucy. *Education:* Attended Long Island University, 1948-50.

ADDRESSES: Agent—Sterling Lord Agency, 660 Madison
Ave., New York, N.Y. 10021.

CAREER: Worked as a copyboy at the *Long Island Press,* 1948;
sportswriter for several newspapers, including the *New York
Journal-American,* all in New York City, 1950-63; *New York
Herald Tribune* (later *New York World Journal Tribune*), New
York City, began as sportswriter, became columnist, 1963-67;
New York Post, New York City, columnist, 1968-69; author and
free-lance journalist in New York City, 1969—; *New York Daily
News,* New York City, columnist, 1978-88; *Newsday,* Long Is-
land, N.Y., columnist, 1988—. Contributing editor and initiat-
ing writer, *New York* magazine, 1968-71, *New Times* magazine,
1973. Commentator, WABC-TV, 1968-69, WNBC-TV, 1973.
Host of "Jimmy Breslin's People," ABC-TV, 1987. Actor in tele-
vision programs, commercials, and feature film "If Ever I See
You Again." Democratic primary candidate for president of
New York City council, 1969; delegate to Democratic National
Convention, 1972.

MEMBER: Writers Guild of America, Screen Actors Guild,
American Federation of Television and Radio Artists, New
York Boxing Writers Association.

AWARDS, HONORS: Best Sports Stories Award, E. P. Dutton
& Co., 1961, for magazine piece "Racing's Angriest Young
Man"; award for general reporting from Sigma Delta Chi and
Meyer Barger Award from Columbia University, both 1964,
both for article on the death of President John F. Kennedy; New
York Reporters Association Award, 1964; Pulitzer Prize and

George Polk Award, both 1986, both for collected newspaper columns; American Society of Newspaper Editors award, 1988, for commentary-column writing.

WRITINGS:

UNDER NAME JIMMY BRESLIN

Sunny Jim: The Life of America's Most Beloved Horseman, James Fitzsimmons (nonfiction), Doubleday, 1962.

Can't Anybody Here Play This Game? (nonfiction), edited by Dick Schapp, Viking, 1963, reprinted, Penguin, 1982.

The World of Jimmy Breslin (collected articles), annotated by James G. Bellows and Richard C. Wald, Viking, 1967.

The Gang That Couldn't Shoot Straight (novel), Viking, 1969, reprinted, Penguin, 1987.

(With Norman Mailer, Peter Maas, Gloria Steinem, and others) *Running against the Machine: The Mailer-Breslin Campaign* (collected speeches, policy statements, interviews, etc.), edited by Peter Manso, Doubleday, 1970.

World without End, Amen (novel; Book-of-the-Month Club alternate selection) Viking, 1973.

How the Good Guys Finally Won: Notes from an Impeachment Summer (nonfiction), Viking, 1975.

(With Schaap) *.44* (novel), Viking, 1978.

Forsaking All Others (novel), Simon & Schuster, 1982.

The World According to Breslin (collected columns), annotated by Michael J. O'Neill and William Brink, Ticknor & Fields, 1984.

Table Money (novel; Literary Guild selection), Ticknor & Fields, 1986.

He Got Hungry and Forgot His Manners (novel), Ticknor & Fields, 1987.

Contributor to numerous newspapers and magazines, including *Penthouse, Sports Illustrated, Saturday Evening Post, Time,* and *New York.*

SIDELIGHTS: For more than two decades, James ("Jimmy") Breslin has provided the literary voice for a group that for many years had had none—that of New York City's Irish-American working class from the Queens neighborhoods in which Breslin himself grew up. As novelist and columnist for various New York newspapers, Breslin encompasses the "New Journalism" ideals that originated in the 1970s, wherein the writer, far from distancing himself from his subject, instead becomes passionately and personally involved in the story. And so Breslin wrote about politics by throwing himself into the political arena in 1969 by running (unsuccessfully) for president of the New York City council under mayoral candidate Norman Mailer. Their platform: Make New York City America's 51st state. However, in 1977, Breslin became another type of celebrity when accused "Son of Sam" serial murderer David Berkowitz made the columnist the sole recipient of letters sent periodically while officials were combing the city for Berkowitz.

A former sportswriter, Breslin uses the native poetry of the street to make his points. His columns often defend the ordinary man against the bureaucracies of government and industry. Breslin "seems to play by different rules than most reporters, which is probably why it took the Pulitzer committee so long to honor him," notes Jonathan Alter in a 1986 *Newsweek* article published just after the Pulitzer Prize panel finally honored the writer. "For years Breslin's fabled ear for dialogue has struck some colleagues as a bit *too* good, too epigrammatic for the way people really speak between quotation marks," Alter continues. To this charge Breslin responds in the *Newsweek* piece that other reporters "take a cop on the beat and make him sound like he's the under secretary of state. *They're* the ones who make up quotes."

Still, Breslin's dramatic columns once caused a wag to remark, on hearing that the reporter was publishing his first novel, "So what? He's been writing fiction for years." *The Gang That Couldn't Shoot Straight,* the book that marked Breslin's move into fiction, disappointed some critics with what they saw as stereotypical portrayals of comic hoodlums on the make. Thomas Meehan of the *New York Times,* for example, while noting that the book "may be the best first novel written all year by a defeated candidate for President of the City Council," finds the story's humor comes mostly from "mayhem—funny, perhaps, to those capable of getting a laugh out of someone being blown up, garroted, or pitched headfirst off a bridge." Though *New York Times Book Review* critic Christopher Lehmann-Haupt was similarly unimpressed overall with *The Gang That Couldn't Shoot Straight,* he shares Meehan's view that Breslin does touch the book with sharply satirical jabs at New York City. "Indeed, the best parts of the novel (and Breslin addicts should agree) are such throwaway details [as Breslin provides]," adds Meehan, "again, the sort of thing this author does so well in his magazine and newspaper pieces."

Breslin took account of his own background for his next novel, *World without End, Amen,* the tale of a New York cop of Irish background whose racist views and weary existence are challenged when he takes a trip to his mother country and witnesses "The Troubles" ongoing between Catholic and Protestant Irish. "Because [protagonist Dermot Davey's] life is coming apart, the reader might well expect that his visit to the land of his forebears will open up new vistas, not only of social conscience but of meaning, and that the ruined cop will somehow find himself quixotically in the cause of the Irish Republic," writes *Washington Post Book World* reviewer Richard Brown. "This is not the author's intent, however, and except for a moving encounter between father and son in a bar in Derry, . . . the found father is of little significance, and the idea of Ireland as homeland is of even less." In the opinion of *Commentary* critic Dorothy Rabinowitz, "There is no hope for the Dermots and their families, Breslin wishes to teach us—not because they are poor or uncultured or incurious (for so are their kin in Ulster), but because they are political reactionaries. That so much of life's worth should be thought to depend on a certain politics might be thought extraordinary in another time than ours. Yet this is a cornerstone of belief for Breslin, as it is for the sensibility he represents."

Harvey Gardner, writing in the *New York Times Book Review,* finds a split in the quality of *World without End, Amen.* "In a skillful Breslin style the first third of the book draws the picture of Dermot and the cop world he knows. There is a great deal of grim humor, and where humor fails, one sees a satisfaction in showing succinctly the causes of human inadequacy." However, says Gardner, when the action moves to Northern Ireland, the "New York idiom" that Breslin employs "often seems inappropriate. That is something one does not like to say of a writer so much to be valued for his rightness about things on his own turf." A *Times Literary Supplement* reviewer offers a different point of view when he states: "If the story were merely a moral tale of a victor humanized by being made a victim, it would have little to offer but the pleasure afforded by a just come-uppance. Beyond that, though, *World without End, Amen* is memorable for being an account of Northern Ireland by a thuggish but not wholly unfeeling character who cannot work out whether he is a foreigner, or a stranger, or both, or neither. It is a confusion probably shared by half the people in Britain."

The critical success of *World without End, Amen* has helped make Breslin a force to be reckoned with in fictional circles. Two further novels, *Forsaking All Others* and *Table Money,* have caught considerable attention. The former is a reworking of the *Romeo and Juliet* theme involving young lovers trapped by crime and poverty. "Another depiction of an underdog-eat-underdog world," as *Time*'s R. Z. Sheppard puts it, *Forsaking All Others* presents a Puerto Rican lawyer, raised in the slums, who falls for the pampered daughter of a local Mafioso. "Breslin knows the sorry streets of the Bronx. He knows the fear and the quick violence and the hunger that line the curb like children at a parade," states James F. Vesely in a *Detroit News* article. "He understands how people doing small, everyday things can suddenly be in the middle of horrible events." The author "attaches a long and sultry fuse to the plot's ethnic charge," says Sheppard. The critic continues that Breslin "has been accused of many things, though never of wearying his readers. Some, however, may be dissatisfied with the loose connections [among the main characters]. Both story lines meander and end abruptly as if Breslin had run out of anecdotes. But he is a brilliant descriptive journalist and compensates on nearly every page with energetic, often humorous scenes." "This is good, solid work," concludes Vesely. "Not since Piri Thomas' *These Mean Streets* has the plight of the Puerto Rican poor been described so harshly and so well. And for Breslin, this one puts him back on those mean streets where his best writing dwells."

Table Money, a 1986 publication, drew cheers as an insightful look at the lives of working-class "sandhogs," the men who dig the vast tunnels that bring water to New York City. Breslin traces the generations of one family of sandhogs, the Morrisons, back to the first immigrant from Ireland in the nineteenth century. But by 1970, when the novel takes place, the latest Morrison man, Owney, newly returned from Vietnam with a Medal of Honor, becomes plagued by self-doubt when his wife Dolores decides to better their station in life by attending medical school. One writer, George James in the *New York Times Book Review,* expresses surprise that "the blue-collar bard of the Borough of Queens [would write] a strongly feminist novel!" But Breslin's depiction of the strong-willed Dolores, who forges ahead while her husband slips into obscurity, does not surprise her creator. As Breslin tells James, *Table Money* was written during a time in his life when "my wife contracted an illness and I wound up for some time taking care of the house [and six children] and getting closer to a woman than I ever had been before—unfortunately so, in illness. I came out of it with a lot of wreckage in my hands, but I learned from it."

In a *New York Times Book Review* piece on *Table Money,* James Carroll says that "this hero's story, like that of many all-too-American males, becomes the painful story of an alcoholic." The author, Carroll continues, "tells it with an unsparing, almost cruel detachment—sheer truthfulness—that leaves the reader wincing each time Morrison veers into yet another friendly neighborhood bar. But at the same time, in one of this novel's achievements, [Breslin describes] the experience of alcoholism as if from inside it, and the reader is left in the grip of an infinite sorrow." Other critics share Carroll's view that what makes *Table Money* a valuable work is its sense of place and character detail. Breslin "knows how the borough works, how the pride of the people reacts aggressively against condescending Manhattan snobberies, how the stresses of modern life are affecting young people in the strictly old church community of which he writes," as *New York Times* reviewer Richard F. Shepard sees it. And *Newsweek*'s Peter S. Prescott applauds the book's "energy, its muscularity, its thickly textured portrait of a world and a way of life that most people who read books know little of."

Breslin followed *Table Money* with another novel, *He Got Hungry and Forgot His Manners,* but the latter did not receive as much attention, partly because the "deep, bitter, almost Kafkaesque satire," as Lehmann-Haupt calls it in a *New York Times* review, cannot appeal to as wide an audience. *He Got Hungry and Forgot His Manners* is a tall tale involving events surrounding the controversial racial attacks that occurred at Howard Beach, Queens, in 1986. D'Arcy Cosgrove, a priest dispatched by order of the Vatican to the borough following the attacks, believes the incident was sexually motivated. Described in the novel as "a man bristling with celibacy," Cosgrove arrives in Queens accompanied by a seven-foot-tall African cannibal, whose idiosyncratic eating habits accounts for the novel's title. To *Time*'s R. Z. Sheppard, "Cosgrove and his giant sidekick are farcical figures meant to illustrate the failures of both church and state when dealing with morality and poverty. . . . The kinks in New York's welfare bureaucracy are authentic and darkly humorous, but the black characters are not developed beyond their jive. Father D'Arcy's mission is unfocused, his misadventures are a blur, and his conversion from guardian of orthodoxy to radical activist unbelievable, even for farce." Lehmann-Haupt also finds faults in Breslin's style, but adds that "it is easiest to get through such [rough] patches by thinking of the novel as a high-speed animated cartoon."

In his nonwriting life, Breslin has enjoyed a longtime reputation as an iconoclast. Most notably, he has a unique, and personal, style of giving notice to quit: He puts out ads in the *New York Times* and posts signs on his front lawn. For instance, when in 1986 his talk show, "Jimmy Breslin's People," was juggled around the late-night schedule by its network, ABC, then unceremoniously deposited in the undesirable time-slot of 1:30 a.m., Breslin paid for a front-page *Times* ad stating, "ABC Television Network, your services, such as they are, will no longer be required as of 12/20/86," which was the end of his 13-week contract. The *Times* ad was a device Breslin had used before, when he informed the *New York Post*, in 1969, that he intended to give up his column, telling his editor: "Robert J. Allen: You are on your own."

"I'm very rude in the course of business because I got no time," Breslin admits in Alter's *Newsweek* piece, adding, "bombast never hurt anybody." And in the wake of a Pulitzer Prize and other professional kudos, Breslin has developed, in the words of *People* reporter Ken Gross, "a new kind of arrogance, . . . now that the committees and critics agree with what he has been saying for years, namely that he's the best in the business." As Breslin tells Gross, "I waited long enough. Where were they?"

MEDIA ADAPTATIONS: The Gang That Couldn't Shoot Straight was adapted into a feature film.

BIOGRAPHICAL/CRITICAL SOURCES:

BOOKS

Authors in the News, Volume 1, Gale, 1976.
Breslin, Jimmy, *He Got Hungry and Forgot His Manners,* Ticknor & Fields, 1987.
Breslin, Jimmy, *Running against the Machine: The Mailer-Breslin Campaign,* edited by Peter Manso, Doubleday, 1969.
Breslin, Jimmy, *The World According to Breslin,* annotated by Michael J. O'Neill and William Brink, Ticknor & Fields, 1984.

Contemporary Literary Criticism, Gale, Volume 4, 1975, Volume 43, 1987.
Graauer, Neil A., *Wits & Sages,* Johns Hopkins University Press, 1984.

PERIODICALS

Chicago Tribune Book World, October 5, 1986.
Commentary, December, 1975.
Commonweal, August 29, 1975.
Detroit News, August 1, 1982.
Los Angeles Times Book Review, July 25, 1982, May 18, 1986.
New Republic, July 19, 1982.
Newsweek, August 9, 1982, May 12, 1986, May 26, 1986.
New York Times, November 21, 1969, May 19, 1975, May 23, 1978, June 16, 1982, October 26, 1984, May 8, 1986, May 5, 1987, January 11, 1988.
New York Times Book Review, November 30, 1969, August 26, 1973, May 11, 1975, June 20, 1982, May 18, 1986.
People, June 16, 1986, December 15, 1986.
Time, June 12, 1975, June 14, 1982, May 5, 1986, January 4, 1988.
Times Literary Supplement, May 14, 1970, May 3, 1974.
Washington Post Book World, August 12, 1973, July 4, 1982, June 1, 1986.

*   *   *

BRESLIN, Jimmy
   See BRESLIN, James

*   *   *

BRETON, Andre   1896-1966

PERSONAL: Born February 19, 1896, in Tinchebray (Orne), France; died of a heart attack, September 28, 1966; son of Louis (an accountant) and Marguerite (Le Gongues) Breton; married Simone Kahn, September, 1921 (divorced); married Jacqueline Lamba, August, 1934 (divorced); married Elisa Bindhoff, August 20, 1945; children: (second marriage) Aube (Mrs. Yves Elesnet). *Education:* Attended College Chaptal, Paris, 1906-12, Faculte de Medicine, Paris, 1913-15.

ADDRESSES: Home—42 rue Fontaine, Paris 9e, France.

CAREER: Major participant in Dadaist literary movement, 1916-21; contributor to *Phalange, SIC,* and *Nord-Sud,* 1914-19; founder and editor, with Luis Aragon and Philippe Soupault, of the journal *Litterature,* 1919, sole editor, 1922-24; secured interview with Freud after having utilized his methods of psychoanalysis and recorded monologues of patients, 1921; founder of Bureau of Surrealist Research, 1924; editor of *La Revolution Surrealiste,* 1925-29; editor of *Le Surrealisme au Service de la Revolution,* 1930-33; principal director of a literary and art review, *Minotaure,* 1933-39; lecturer on surrealism in Brussels, Prague, and the Canary Islands, 1935; founder, with others, of the Commission of Inquiry into the Moscow Trials, 1936; in Mexico, with Leon Trotsky and Diego Rivera, he established the *Federation Internationale de l'Art Revolutionnaire Independant,* 1938; guest of the Committee of American Aid to Intellectuals in Marseilles, 1940-41; following censorship of some of his works and interrogation by the Vichy government, Breton went to Martinique where he was arrested and confined in a concentration camp; succeeded in coming to the United States, 1941; in New York City, he was founder and editor, with Marcel Duchamp, Max Ernst, and David Hare of the magazine *VVV,*

1942-44; speaker for the "Voice of America," 1942-45; delivered address at Yale University, 1942; studied occultism in the rites of Indian tribes in Arizona, New Mexico, and the West Indies; gave a series of lectures on surrealism in Haiti which precipitated an insurrection there, 1945; returned to France, 1946; adhered to the *Front Humain* movement which became the *Citoyens du Monde,* 1948-49; member of the Committee for the Defence of Garry Davis, 1949; director of the Galerie a l'Etoile Scellee, 1952-54; editor of *Le Surrealisme, Meme,* 1956-57; editor of the surrealist review *La Breche,* 1961-66; organized several exhibitions of surrealism, in London, 1936, Paris, 1938 (fourteen countries represented), 1947, 1958, and 1965, Prague, 1948, New York, 1942 and 1960, and Milan, 1961. *Wartime service:* Medical assistant in army psychiatric centers, 1915-19; medical director of the Ecole de Pilotage at Poitiers, 1939-40.

WRITINGS:

PROSE

Manifeste du surrealisme [et] Poisson-soluble, Editions du Sagittaire, 1924, revised edition augmented with *Lettre aux voyantes,* Simon Kra, 1929.
Les Pas Perdus, N.R.F., 1924, revised edition, Gallimard, 1969.
Legitime defense, Editions Surrealistes, 1926.
Introduction au discours sur le peu de realite, N.R.F. 1927.
Nadja, Gallimard, 1928, revised edition, 1963, translation by Richard Howard published as *Nadja,* Grove, 1960.
Le Surrealisme et la peinture, Gallimard, 1928, revised edition, 1965, translation by Simon W. Taylor published as *Surrealism and Painting,* Macdonald & Co., 1972.
Second manifeste du surrealisme, Simon & Kra, 1930.
Misere de la poesie: "L'Affaire Aragon" devant l'opinion publique, Editions Surrealistes, 1932.
Les Vases communicants, Editions des Cahiers Libres, 1932, reprinted, Gallimard, 1970.
Point du jour, Gallimard, 1934, revised edition, 1970.
Qu'est-ce que le Surrealisme? (text of lecture given in Brussels), R. Henriquez, 1934, translation by David Gascoyne published as *What is Surrealism?,* Faber, 1936.
Du temps que les surrealistes avaient raison, Editions Surrealistes, 1935.
Position politique du surrealisme (collection of Breton's lectures, speeches, and interviews), Editions du Sagittaire, 1935, reprinted, J. J. Pauvert, 1971.
Au lavoir noir, Editions G.L.M., 1936.
L'Amour fou, Gallimard, 1937, reprinted, 1966, translation by Mary Ann Caws published as *Mad Love,* Nebraska University Press, 1988.
Limites non frontiers du surrealisme, N.R.F., 1937.
(Editor and contributor) *Trajectoire du reve,* Editions G.L.M., 1938. (Editor) *Anthologie de l'humour noire,* Editions du Sagittaire, 1940, definitive edition, 1966.
Arcane 17, Brentano's, 1944.
Situation du surrealisme entre les deux guerres (text of lecture given at Yale), Editions de la Revue Fontaine, 1945.
Yves Tanguy (bilingual edition with translation by Bravig Imbs), Pierre Matisse Editions (New York), 1946.
Arcane 17, ente d'Ajours, Editions du Sagittaire, 1947, revised edition augmented with *Andre Breton ou la transparence,* by Michael Beaujour, Plon, 1965.
Les Manifestes du Surrealisme, [suivis de] Prolegomenes a un troisieme manifeste du surrealisme ou non, Editions du Sagittaire, 1947, revised edition augmented with *Du surrealisme en ses oeuvres vives et d'Ephemerides surrealistes,* 1955.
La Lampe dans l'horloge, Robert Marin, 1948.

Flagrant delit: Rimbaud devant la conjuration de l'imposture et du truquage, Thesee, 1949.
(Editor) *Judas, ou Le Vampire surrealiste,* by Ernest de Gengenbach, Les Editions Premieres, 1949.
Entretiens 1913-1952 (text of radio interviews with Breton), Gallimard, 1952, revised edition, 1969.
La Cle des Champs, Editions du Sagittaire, 1953.
Adieu ne plaise (text of speech at the funeral of Francis Picabia, December 4, 1953), Editions P.A.B., 1954.
(Author of text) *Gardenas,* Feigen Gallery, 1961.
(Author of text) *Les Inpires et leurs demeurs* (photographs by Gilles Ehrmann), Editions du Temps, 1962.
(Author of text) *Un Art a l'etat brut: Peintures et sculptures des aborigenes d'Australie,* by Karc Kupka, La Guilde du Livre (Lausanne), 1962.
Manifestes du Surrealisme, definitive edition, J. J. Pauvert, 1962, complete edition, 1972, translation by Richard Seaver and Helen R. Lane published as *Manifestoes of Surrealism,* University of Michigan Press, 1969.
(Author of text) *Pierre Moiliner* (film by Raymond Borde), Le Terrain Vague, 1964.
(Author of text) *L'Ecart absolu,* L'Oeil galerie d'art, 1965.
(Editor) *Le Surrealisme au service de la revolution,* Arno Press, 1968.
Perspective cavaliere, edited by Marguerite Bonnet, Gallimard, 1970.
L'Un dans l'autre, E. Losfeld, 1970.
Communication de Andre-Yves Breton sur l'activite de la 6e Commission depuis 1965, City of Paris, 1971.
(With Paul Eluard) *Sculptures d'Afrique [and]* (with Guillaume Apollinaire) *Sculptures Negres,* Hacker Art Books, 1975.

Also author of *Le Roman francais au XVIIIe siecle,* published by Boivin & Cie.

POETRY AND PROSE POETRY

Mont de piete, Au Sans Pareil, 1919.
(With Philippe Soupault) *Les Champs magnetiques,* Au Sans Pareil, 1920, reprinted, Gallimard, 1971.
Claire de terre, Collection Litterature, 1923, reprinted, Gallimard, 1966.
(With Rene Char and Paul Eluard) *Ralentir travaux,* Editions Surrealistes, 1930, reprinted, J. Corti, 1968.
L'Union libre, [Paris], 1931.
Le Revolver a cheveux blancs, Editions des Cahiers Libres, 1932.
(With others) *Violette Nozieres,* Nicolas Flamel (Brussels), 1933.
L'Air de l'eau, Editions Cahiers d'Art, 1934.
Le Chateau Etoile, Editions Albert Skira, 1937.
Fata Morgana, Editions des Lettres Francaises (Buenos Aires), 1942, translation by Clark Mills published under same title, Black Swan Press, 1969.
Pleine marge, Editions Karl Nierendorf (New York), 1943.
Young Cherry Trees Secured Against Hares: Jeunes cerisiers garantis contreles lievres, bilingual edition with translation by Edouard Roditi, View (New York), 1946, reprinted, University of Michigan Press, 1969.
Ode a Charles Fourier, Editions de la Revue Fontaine, 1947, revised edition with an introduction and notes by Jean Gaulmier, Librairie Klincksieck, 1961, bilingual edition, with translation by Kenneth White, published as *Ode to Charles Fourier,* Cape Goliard Press, 1969.
(With Andre Masson) *Martinique, charmeuse de serpents,* Editions du Sagittaire, 1948, new edition, J. J. Pauvert, 1972.
Poemes, Gallimard, 1948.
Au regard des divinites, Editions Messages, 1949.

Constellations (with 22 gouaches of Joan Miro), Pierre Matisse (New York), 1959.
Le la, Editions P.A.B., 1961.
Signe ascendant, suivi de Fata Morgana, les Etats generaux, Des Epingles tremblantes, Xenophiles, Ode a Charles Fourier, Constellations, Le la, Gallimard, 1968.
Selected Poems, translated by Kenneth White, J. Cape, 1969.

CO-AUTHOR

(With Luis Aragon) *Permettez,* [Paris], 1927.
(With Paul Eluard) *L'Immaculee conception,* Editions Surrealistes, 1930, reprinted, Seghers, 1968.
(With Paul Eluard) *Notes sur la poesie,* Editions G.L.M., 1936.
(With Luis Aragon and Paul Eluard) *Lautremont envers et contre tout,* [Paris], 1937.
(With Jindrich Heisler and Benjamin Peret) *Toyen,* Sokolova (Paris), 1953.
(With Gerard Legrand) *L'Art magique,* Formes et Reflets, 1957.
(With others) *Antonin Artaud, ou, La Sante des poetes,* La tour de feu, 1959.
(With Antoine Adam and R. Etiemble) *L'Affaire Rimbaud,* J. J. Pauvert, 1962.
(With Marcel Duchamp) *Surrealist Intrusion in the Enchanteurs Domain,* Libraire Fischbacker, 1965.
(With others) *Le Groupe, la rupture,* Editions du Seuil, 1970.

CONTRIBUTOR

Herbert Read, editor, *Surrealism,* Faber, 1936, Praeger, 1971.
Ubu enchaine et l'objet aime, Imprimerie de Rocroy, 1937.
La Terre n'est pas une vallee des larmes, Editions "La Boetie," 1945.
Maurice Nadeau, editor, *Documents Surrealistes,* Editions du Seuil, 1948.
Donati, W. N. Dennis, 1949.
Farouche a quatre feuilles, Grasset, 1954.
Robert Lebel, *Sur Marcel Duchamp,* Editions Trianon, 1959, translation by George Heard published as *Marcel Duchamp,* Grove, 1959.
La Poesie dans ses meubles, Officina Undici (Rome), 1964.
Michael Benedikt and George E. Wellwarth, editors and translators, *Modern French Theatre,* Dutton, 1964.

AUTHOR OF INTRODUCTION OR PREFACE

Jean Genbach (Ernst de Gengenbach), *Satan a Paris,* H. Meslin, 1927.
Man Ray: La Photographie n'est pas l'art, Editions G.L.M., 1937.
M. Guggenheim, editor, *Art of This Century,* Art Aid Corporation, 1942.
Benjamin Peret, *La Parole est a Peret,* Editions Surrealistes, 1943.
Francis Picabia, *Choix de poemes,* Editions G.L.M., 1947.
Aime Cesaire, *Cahier d'un retour au pays natal,* Bordas, 1947.
Jacques Vache, *Les Lettres de guerre de Jacques Vache, suivies d'une nouvelle,* K Editeur, 1949.
Maurice Fourre, *A La Nuit du Rose-hotel,* Gallimard, 1950.
Xavier Forneret, *Oeuvres,* Arcanes, 1952.
Achim d'Arnim, *Contes bizarres,* Arcanes, 1953.
Jean Ferry, *Une Etude sur Raymond Roussel,* Arcanes, 1953.
J. Ferry, *Le 81 Mecanicien,* Gallimard, 1953.
Georges Darien, *Le Voleur,* Union general d'editions, 1955.
Oscar Panizza, *Concile d'amour,* J. J. Pauvert, 1960.
Pietre Mabille, *Le Miroir de merveilleux,* Editions de Minuit, 1962.
Jean-Pierre Duprey, *Derriere son double,* Le Soleil Noir, 1964.

Konrad Klapheck, [Paris], 1965.

Charles Maturin, *Melmouth, l'homme errant,* Editions G. P., 1965.

AUTHOR OF INTRODUCTION TO EXHIBITION CATALOGS

La Peinture surrealiste, Galerie Pierre, 1925.

Crise de l'objet, Charles Ratton, 1936.

(With Pau Eluard) *Dictionnaire abrege du surrealisme,* Galerie Beaux-Arts, 1938.

Mexique, Renou et Colle, 1939.

First Papers of Surrealism, Coordinating Council of French Relief Societies, 1942.

Exposition Baya: Derriere le miroir, Galerie Maeght, 1947.

Exposition Toyen, Galerie Denise Rene, 1947.

Jacques Herold, Cahiers d'Art, 1947.

Preliminaires sur matta: Surrealisme et la peinture, Galerie Rene Drouin, 1947.

Seconde Arche, Fontaine, 1947.

Le Surrealisme en 1947, Galerie Maeght, 1947.

Le Cadavre exquis, Galerie Nina Dousset, 1948.

Oceanie, Andree Olive, 1948.

(With Michel Tapie) *Les Statues magiques de Maria,* Galerie Rene Drouin, 1948.

491, Jumelles pour yeux bandes, Galerie Rene Drouin, 1949.

Yves Laloy, La Cour d'Ingres, 1958.

(With Jose Pierre) *Enseignes sournoises,* Galerie Mona Lisa, 1964.

Magritte: Le Sens propre, Galerie Alexandre Iolas, 1964.

OTHER

Oeuvres completes, Gallimard, 1988.

Also author of such works as *Les Malformations congenitales du Poumon,* 1957, and *Perspectives Cavaliere,* Bonnet.

Contributor to many anthologies, including *Petite anthologie poetique du surrealisme,* edited by Georges Hugnet, Editions Jeanne Bucher, 1934; *New Directions in Prose and Poetry: 1940,* New Directions, 1940; *Anthologie du poeme en prose,* edited by Maurice Chapelan, Julliard, 1947; *The Dada Painters and Poets,* edited by Robert Motherwell, Wittenborn, Schultz, 1951; *Mid-Century Anthology of Modern French Poetry from Baudelaire to the Present Day,* edited by C. A. Hackett, Macmillan, 1956; *Le Poeme en prose,* edited by Suzanne Bernard, Libraire Nizet, 1959; *La Poesie surrealiste,* edited by Jean-Louis Bedouin, Editions Seghers, 1964; *Twentieth-Century French Literature to World War II,* edited by Harry T. Moore, Teffer & Simons, 1966.

Contributor to numerous art, literary, political, historical, and other journals worldwide.

SIDELIGHTS: In a statement for *CA,* Andre Breton summarized the scope and purpose of his literary career. "My principle objective," he stated, "has been to promote in art pure psychic automatism 'removed from all control exercised by the reason and disengaged from all esthetic or moral preoccupations' [*Manifeste du surrealisme,* 1924]. My entire life has been devoted to exalting the values of *poetry, love,* and *liberty.* I flatter myself in being one of the very first writers to have denounced the 'Moscow trials.' I have not deviated from that to which committed I myself at the beginning of my career. I have striven, with others, to pursue the struggle that leads to a *recasting of human understanding.* To that end, surrealism was proposed as a means to transform, first and foremost, man's sensibilities. In my opinion, it has not fallen far short of this goal."

The surrealist movement in literature was founded by Breton in the early 1920s and dominated the period between the two wars. It was an outgrowth of the postwar defeatism as well as a reaction against the nihilism of Dada. Breton and his associates audaciously sought to bring about a revolution in man's consciousness, a state of "surreality," the objective of which was "the total liberation of the mind." What was envisaged was an emancipation from reason and logic, thought processes which he believed deaden man's sensitivity. The surrealists decried not so much the absurdity of the world of realities or the deficiencies of man's mind as they did the "limited utilization of the mind and of the objects of experience," writes Anna Balakian. Breton's concern was the intensification of the human experience, the realization of what he called "an ever clearer and at the same time an ever more passionate consciousness of the world perceived by the senses." Only when reason loses its control over the psyche and one approaches the "fantastic," he stated, does "the most profound emotion of the individual have the fullest opportunity to express itself." Once the fetters of rationality are removed, then it is by means of "pure psychic automatism" that "the true functioning of thought" is brought to light.

As an ardent student of the theories and methodology of Freud, Breton sought limitless human potentialities, heretofore untapped, within the realm of dreams and the subconscious. Therefore, at the outset of the surrealistic movement, a systematic investigation of these subliminal forces was conducted. Breton and his colleagues, who included, among others, Philippe Soupault, Paul Eluard, Robert Desnos, and Rene Crevel, experimented daily with writing "automatic texts" in a state of semi-trance, recounting dreams while in hypnotically invoked sleep or when awake, inducing hallucination, and simulating in writing states of mental derangement. The prose poems of Breton and Soupault, *Les Champs magnetiques,* are perhaps the best example of the "automatic texts," writings poured out as rapidly as possible, free from forethought or reconsideration. In *Les Vases communicants* Breton describes the dream and the state of wakefulness as being perpetually interwoven and enriched by one another. Following this experimentation, Breton states that he found within the dream "the principle of the conciliation of opposites." Commenting in 1930 on the past development of surrealism, Breton further stated: "Everything leads to the belief that there exists a certain point in the mind at which life and death, the real and the imaginary, the past and the future, what is communicable and what is incommunicable, the heights and the depths, cease to be perceived as contradictory. It is in vain that one would seek any other motive for surrealist activity than the hope of determining this point" (*Second manifeste du surrealisme,* 1930).

There is, however, less emphasis in the *Second manifeste* on automatic writing and more on the "automatic life" as epitomized in Breton's work *Nadja* (1928). This work is an autobiographical account of his chance meeting with a woman named Nadja who looks fixedly at the surface of her bath water and says, "I am the thought on the bath in the room without mirrors." Life, in Nadja's possession, is magically permeated with sublime and startling coincidences, repeated chance encounters, prescience of objectively insignificant incidents, and spontaneous, poetic reactions to the quotidian as well as to the heart rending. She is the embodiment of Breton's preoccupations with intuitive imagination and *"le hasard objectif,"* objective chance or coincidence which together contribute to the "marvelous" in life.

Breton defined chance as being "the encounter of an external causality and an internal finality, a form of manifestation of the external necessity making its ways in the human unconscious." An individual who can submit himself to the laws of the subconscious is one who then partakes of the "marvelous" because his conscious mind is attuned to both the most fundamental subjective and objective realities. By freeing the imagination, one can conceive of the infinite possibilities of such a harmony. For Breton the imagination accounts for what can be. It is the imaginary, he wrote, that tends to become reality. And frequently in the use of the word "imagination" he denoted intuition. Clairvoyance also was a highly respected phenomena among the surrealists.

It is significant to note that in 1925 in his *Lettre aux voyantes,* published in 1929, Breton stated, "There are people who pretend that the war has taught them something; they are less well off than I who know what the year 1939 is reserving for me." In a sense, surrealism is a form of atheistic mysticism that not only identifies spirit and matter, but challenges man to be his own master, perhaps his own God, by exploiting the resources deep within his mind.

The releasing of these forces had immediate social and political implications, for, as Breton stated in *What is Surrealism?,* the liberation of the mind demands as a primary condition the liberation of man. Consequently, there existed in the period between the two wars an alliance between surrealism and the French Communist Party which sought the political and economic emancipation of man. Like the communists, the surrealists adhered to the philosophy of dialectical materialism. However, this alliance was never complete, for Breton adamantly refused to surrender the freedom and integrity of the writer and artist by subjugating creativity to an ideology. As a result, he expelled from the surrealist group those writers who thus compromised their liberty, broke officially with the Communist Party in 1935, and vociferously protested Stalinist communism. Breton also despised nationalism in any of its forms and strove for a new consciousness of life common to all artists and writers.

For the poet, this passionate dedication to liberty necessitated a liberation from the rules of art. All literary conventions and stylized forms had to be abandoned. Prose achieved a new status in Breton's writings, which was a natural form for automatic writing which demands an "uninterrupted flow of words." His prose, writes Marcel Raymond, "ambles along at a regular pace, fluid and smooth as a piece of pliable wood without knots." His writing is marked by a stream of images consisting of bizarre and illogical metaphors and the juxtaposition of opposites. "Breton called ideas vain and ineffective compared to the force of the sudden unexpected image" and believed that images should "not be directed by thoughts but be conducive to them," writes Anna Balakian. Translation of titles of poems such as "Soluble Fish," "The Whitehaired Revolver," and "Fertile Eyes" set forth the disparity and contradiction inherent in Breton's images. In his tract, *What is Surrealism?,* Breton commented: "He who still refuses to see, for instance, a horse galloping on a tomato should be looked upon as a cretin. A tomato is also a child's balloon—surrealism . . . having suppressed the word 'like'."

What is most frequently revered in Breton's poetry and prose is his treatment of love. Maurice Nadeau remarks that Breton "brought back to poetry the long lost figure of woman as embodiment of magic powers [and as a] creature of grace and promise." Breton unequivocally proclaims the supremacy of love. "Today," he wrote, "it is up to man unhesitatingly to deny everything that can enslave him, and if necessary, to die on a barricade of flowers, if only to give body to a chimera, to woman, and perhaps to her alone, to rescue both that which she brings with her and that which lifts her up.—Silence!—There is no solution outside love." Professor Balakian told *CA* that Breton's writings as well as his personal interviews were marked by the quality of im-

personality. She stated that he refrained from injecting his most subjective self into his poetry and quite deliberately kept his personal life from the eyes of the public. This detachment, as it was explained, contributes to the elements of permanence and universality that are characteristic of his writings which deal with themes such as love and war.

The impact of surrealism on the twentieth century is evident in the novel, poetry, philosophy, painting, photography, the cinema, the theater, and architecture. Surrealism has been described as "one of the most far-reaching attempts at changing not only literature and painting, but psychology, ethics, and man himself" (Peyre, *Yale French Studies,* no. 31.). Eugene Ionesco remarked, "I place Breton on the same level as Einstein, Freud, Jung, and Kafka." Breton himself took account of the effects of the movement when he stated that surrealism "has provoked new states of consciousness and overthrown walls beyond which it was immemorially supposed to be impossible to see; it has modified the sensibility . . . and taken a decisive step towards the unification of the personality, which it found threatened by an ever more profound dissociation." In an interview which took place in 1964, Breton said, "I may live ten more years, but my work is done." Two years later, at the age of seventy, he died from a heart attack.

BIOGRAPHICAL/CRITICAL SOURCES:

BOOKS

Alquie, Ferdinand, *Philosophie du Surrealism,* Flammarion, 1955, translation by Bernard Waldrop published as *Philosophy of Surrealism,* University of Michigan Press, 1965.
Balakian, A. E., *Andre Breton: Magus of Surrealism,* Oxford University Press, 1971.
Balakian, Anna, *The Literary Origins of Surrealism: A New Mysticism in French Poetry,* New York University Press, 1947.
Balakian, Anna, *Surrealism: The Road to the Absolute,* Noonday, 1959.
Breton, Andre, *Poesie et Autre,* edited by Gerard Legrand, Club du Meilleur Livre, 1960.
Browder, Clifford, *Andre Breton: Arbiter of Surrealism,* Librairie Droz (Geneva), 1967.
Caws, M. A., *Surrealism and the Literary Imagination,* Humanities, 1966.
Caws, M. A., *Andre Breton,* Twayne, 1971.
Contemporary Literary Criticism, Gale, Volume 2, 1974, Volume 9, 1978, Volume 15, 1980, Volume 54, 1989.
Crastre, Victor, *Andre Breton,* Arcanes, 1952.
Dictionary of Literary Biography, Volume 65: *French Novelists, 1900-1930,* Gale, 1988.
Fowlie, Wallace, *Age of Surrealism,* Indiana University Press, 1960.
Gascoyne, David, *A Short Survey of Surrealism,* Cogden-Sanderson, 1936.
Homage to Andre Breton, Wittenbom, 1967.
Josephson, Matthew, *Life Among the Surrealists: A Memoir,* Holt, 1962.
Lemaitre, Georges, *From Cubism to Surrealism in French Literature,* Harvard University Press, 1941.
Mauriac, Claude, *Andre Breton,* Editions de Flore, 1949.
Nadeau, Maurice, *Histoire du Surrealisme,* Editions du Seuil, 1946, translation by Richard Howard published as *The History of Surrealism,* Macmillan, 1965.
Raymond, Marcel, *De Baudelaire au Surrealisme,* R. A. Correa, 1933, translation by G.M. published as *From Baudelaire to Surrealism,* Wittenborn, Schultz, 1950.

PERIODICALS

Figaro Litteraire, October 6, 1966.
Le Monde, September 29, 1966.
New York Times, October 9, 1966.
Nouvelles Litteraires, October 6, 1966.
Saturday Review, March 12, 1966, October 29, 1966.
Yale French Studies, Number 31, 1964.

OBITUARIES:

PERIODICALS

New York Times, September 29, 1966.
Time, October 7, 1966.

* * *

BRINK, Andre (Philippus) 1935-

PERSONAL: Born May 29, 1935, in Vrede, South Africa; son of Daniel (a magistrate) and Aletta (a teacher; maiden name, Wolmarans) Brink; married Estelle Naude (divorced); married Salomi Louw (divorced); married Alta Miller (a potter), July 17, 1970; children: Anton, Gustav, Danie, Sonja. *Education:* Potchefstroom University, M.A. (Afrikaans), 1958, M.A. (English), 1959; postgraduate study at Sorbonne, University of Paris, 1959-61; Rhodes University, D.Litt., 1975.

ADDRESSES: Home—Portsbury Rd., Grahamstown, Cape Province 6140, South Africa. *Office*—Department of Afrikaans and Dutch Literature, Rhodes University, Grahamstown, Cape Province 6140, South Africa.

CAREER: Rhodes University, Grahamstown, South Africa, lecturer, 1961-73, senior lecturer, 1974-75, associate professor, 1976-79, professor of Afrikaans and Dutch literature, 1980—. Director of theatrical productions.

MEMBER: South African P.E.N., Afrikaans Writers' Guild (president, 1978-), Society of Netherlandic Literature.

AWARDS, HONORS: Reina Prinsen Geerlings Prize, 1964; Central News Agency award for Afrikaans literature, 1965, for *Ole;* prize for prose translation from South African Academy, 1970, for *Alice Through the Looking Glass;* Central News Agency award for English literature, 1978, for *Rumours of Rain;* Martin Luther King Memorial Prize and Prix Medicis Etranger, both 1980, both for *A Dry White Season;* named chevalier de Legion d'Honneur and officier de l'Ordre des Arts et des Lettres.

WRITINGS:

Lobola vir die lewe (novel; title means "Dowry for Life"), Human & Rousseau, 1962.
Die Ambassadeur (novel), Human & Rousseau, 1963, translation by Andre Brink published as *File on a Diplomat,* Longmans, Green, 1965, revised edition of translation published as *The Ambassador,* Faber, 1985.
Bagasie (three one-act plays), Tafelberg Publishers, 1964.
Ole (travelogue), Human & Rousseau, 1965.
Aspekte van die nuwe prosa (criticism; title means "Aspects of the New Fiction"), Academica, 1967, revised edition, 1975.
Midi (travelogue), Human & Rousseau, 1969.
A Portrait of Woman as a Young Girl (novel), Buren Publishers, 1973.
Kennis van die aand (novel), Buren Publishers, 1973, translation by Brink published as *Looking on Darkness,* W. H. Allen, 1974, Morrow, 1975.
Afrikaners is plesierig (two one-act plays; title means "Afrikaners Make Merry"), Buren Publishers, 1973.

Elders mooiweer en warm (three-act play; title means "Elsewhere Fine and Warm"; first produced in Bloemfontein at Little Theatre, April, 1970), Human & Rousseau, 1974.
Pavane (three-act play; first produced in Cape Town at Hofmeyr Theatre, 1974), Human & Rousseau, 1974.
Aspekte van die nuwe drama (criticism; title means "Aspects of the New Drama"), Academia, 1974.
'n Oomblik in die wind (novel), Taurus, 1975, translation published as *An Instant in the Wind,* W. H. Allen, 1976, Morrow, 1977.
Gerugte van reen (novel), Human & Rousseau, 1978, translation published as *Rumours of Rain,* Morrow, 1978.
'n Droe wit seisoen (novel), Taurus, 1979, translation published as *A Dry White Season,* W. H. Allen, 1979, Morrow, 1980.
Houd-den-Bek (novel; title means "Shut Your Trap"), Taurus, c. 1982, translation published as *A Chain of Voices,* Morrow, 1982.
Miskien nooit, Human and Rousseau, 1982.
Mapmakers: Writing in a State of Siege (essays), Faber, 1983.
Die muur van die pes (novel), Human & Rousseau, 1984, translation published as *The Wall of the Plague,* Summit, 1984.
Loopdoppies, Saayman & Weber, 1984.
Waarom literatuur? (essays), Human & Rousseau, 1985.
Literatuur in die strydperk (essays), Human & Rousseau, 1985.
(Editor with J. M. Coetzee) *A Land Apart: A South African Reader,* Faber, 1986.
States of Emergency, Penguin, 1988, Summit, 1989.

Also translator into Afrikaans of works by other authors, including William Shakespeare, Henry James, Graham Greene, Lewis Carroll, Albert Camus, Marguerite Duras, Georges Simenon, Pavel Kohout, and Cervantes. Author of scenarios for South African films and television series, including "The Settlers." Contributor to books on Afrikaans literature and to periodicals, including *World Literature Today, Asahi Journal,* and *Theatre Quarterly.* Editor of *Standpunte,* 1985—; editor of weekly book page in *Rapport.*

SIDELIGHTS: Andre Brink told *CA:* "My postgraduate study in Paris brought me an explosive awareness of contemporary trends in European literature and resulted in the novel *Lobola vir die lewe,* which has since been termed a breakthrough in the modern Afrikaans novel. I later became involved in the 'Sestiger,' or 'Writers of the Sixties,' movement which brought about a total renewal in Afrikaans fiction by destroying all the existing taboos pertaining to sex, ethics, religion, and politics governing traditional Afrikaans fiction.

"In 1968 I left South Africa to settle in Paris with the exiled poet Breyten Breytenbach, but the nature of the student revolt of that year forced me to reassess my situation as a writer and prompted my return to South Africa in order to accept full responsibility for whatever I wrote, believing that, in a closed society, the writer has a specific social and moral role to fill. This resulted in a more committed form of writing exploring the South African political situation and notably my revulsion of apartheid. My first novel to emerge from this experience was *Kennis van die aand,* which became the first Afrikaans book to be banned by the South African censors. This encouraged me to turn seriously to writing in English in order not to be silenced in my own language. Under the title *Looking on Darkness,* it became an international success, with translations into a dozen languages, including Finnish, Turkish, Japanese, Czechoslovakian, and Russian.

"Since that time I have been writing regularly in both Afrikaans and English, usually preparing a first draft in Afrikaans, followed by a complete rewriting of the novel in English, and a final translation back into Afrikaans. I regard this laborious process as an essential part of exploring my material, using English as an aid to see more clearly and to evaluate more objectively. In *A Chain of Voices,* some of the 'voices' were originally written in Afrikaans and two separate versions were then prepared from this mixed text, in which the different languages prompted differences in point of view and style.

"However close my work is to the realities of South Africa today, the political situation remains a starting point only for my attempts to explore the more abiding themes of human loneliness and man's efforts to reach out and touch someone else. My stated conviction is that literature should never descend to the level of politics; it is rather a matter of elevating and refining politics so as to be worthy of literature.

"America seems to be slowly working its way through racism; whereas in South Africa it is entrenched in the whole system and framework of laws on which society has had its base. It is not just a matter of sentiment, of personal resentment, of tradition and custom, but these negative aspects of society are so firmly rooted in the framework of laws that it is very, very difficult to eradicate. *Looking on Darkness* elicited much comment because it is one of the first Afrikaans novels to confront openly the apartheid system. This account of an illicit love between a 'Cape Coloured' man and a white woman evoked, on the one hand, one of the fiercest polemics in the history of that country's literature and contributed, on the other, to a groundswell of new awareness among white Afrikaners of the common humanity of all people regardless of color. In numerous letters from readers I was told that 'for the first time in my life I now realize that "they" feel and think and react just like "us." ' " In France, where publication of the book coincided with the Soweto riots of 1976, it became something of a handbook on the South African situation and sold over one hundred thousand copies. The same thing happened in other European countries.

"In *An Instant in the Wind* I used essentially the same relationship—a black man and a white woman—but placed it in the midst of the eighteenth century in an attempt to probe the origins of the racial tensions of today. An episode from Australian history in which a shipwrecked woman and a convict return to civilization on foot is here transposed to the Cape Colony with so much verisimilitude that many readers have tried to look up the documentation in the Cape Archives.

"*Rumours of Rain,* set on the eve of the Soweto riots, is placed on a much larger stage. The apartheid mind is demonstrated in the account given by a wealthy businessman of the one weekend in which his whole familiar world collapsed through the conviction of his best friend for terrorism, the revolt of his son, the loss of his mistress, and the sale of his family's farm. In spite of his efforts to rigorously separate all the elements of his life, he becomes the victim of his own paradoxes and faces an apocalypse.

"In comparison with the complex structures of this work, *A Dry White Season* has a deceptively simple plot: a black man dies while being detained by the security police. In all good faith his white friend tries to find out what really happened, and as a result the whole infernal machinery of the State is turned against him. An interesting aspect of this novel is that it was begun almost a year before the death in detention of black-consciousness leader Steve Biko in 1976. In fact, the death of Biko came as such a shock to me that for a long time I couldn't go back to writing. I believe that however outraged or disturbed one may be, a state of inner serenity must be obtained before anything meaningful can emerge in writing.

"In *A Chain of Voices* I have tried to extend and expand my field of vision. Using as a point of departure a slave revolt in the Cape Colony in 1825, I used a series of thirty different narrators to explore the relationships created by a society shaped by the forces of oppression and suffering. The 'separateness' of the voices haunted me; masters and slaves, all tied by the same chains, are totally unable to communicate because their humanity and their individuality are denied by the system they live by. I tried to broaden and deepen the enquiry by relating the voices, in four successive sections, to the elements of earth, water, wind, and fire.

"Since my tastes in literature are catholic, I have never been a disciple of any one school. The most abiding influence on my work, however, has been Albert Camus, notably in his view of man in a state of incessant revolt against the conditions imposed upon him, and reacting creatively to the challenge of meaninglessness. In much of my work this is linked to an element of mysticism derived from the Spanish writers of the seventeenth century. The other most abiding influence on my writing is the study of history. All my work is pervaded with a sense of 'roots,' whether in the collective history of peoples or in the private history of an individual.

"Apart from writing, the theatre is my abiding passion, and since 1969 I have regularly directed plays for professional companies. This, in turn, has stimulated my playwriting, which I often explore as a medium of devastating social satire. In this vein my most notable successes have been a satirical adaptation of Shakespeare's "Comedy of Errors" and the irreverent *Afrikaners is plesierig.* In the latter, Afrikanerdom is represented as a circus tent about to be taken over by a communist proprietor but is instead blown down by the 'winds of change.'

"I have written several scenarios for South African-made films and three television series, all of them based on episodes in South African history."

Brink's subsequent works of fiction continue his examination of South African culture. His 1984 novel *The Wall of the Plague* focuses on a black Capetown woman who must choose between her love for a white South African writer and her faithfulness to her heritage. In *States of Emergency,* published in 1988, a writer's attempt to compose an apolitical love story is marred by the reality of racism, violence, and death.

MEDIA ADAPTATIONS: A Dry White Season was adapted for a film of the same title by Euzhan Palcy and Colin Welland, directed by Palcy, Metro-Goldwyn-Mayer, 1989.

BIOGRAPHICAL/CRITICAL SOURCES:

BOOKS

Contemporary Literary Criticism, Gale, Volume 18, 1981, Volume 36, 1986.

PERIODICALS

Globe and Mail (Toronto), August 20, 1988.
Los Angeles Times, May 18, 1989.
New Statesman, November 17, 1978.
Newsweek, December 2, 1974.
New York Times, February 2, 1984, March 6, 1984.
New York Times Book Review, March 23, 1980, June 13, 1982, March 17, 1985.
Times (London), May 6, 1982.
Washington Post, May 28, 1982, July 13, 1989.
World Literature Today, autumn, 1977, winter 1985, summer, 1986.

BRISCO, P. A.
See MATTHEWS, Patricia (Anne)

*   *   *

BRISCO, Patty
See MATTHEWS, Patricia (Anne)

*   *   *

BRITTAIN, Vera (Mary)   1893(?)-1970

PERSONAL: Born in 1893 (some sources say 1896) in Newcastle, Staffordshire, England; died March 29, 1970; daughter of Thomas Arthur (a paper manufacturer) and Edith Mary (Bervon) Brittain; married George Edward Gordon Catlin (a political scientist and philosopher), June 27, 1925; children: John Edward Jocelyn, Shirley Vivien (Mrs. Bernard Williams). *Education:* Somerville College, Oxford, B.A., 1921, M.A., 1925. *Politics:* Labour Party. *Religion:* Quaker-inclined Anglican.

ADDRESSES: Home—4 Whitehall Ct., London S.W.1, England.

CAREER: Author, journalist, and lecturer. Speaker on seven lecture tours in United States and Canada, 1934-59, other tours in Holland, 1936, Scandinavia, 1945, Germany, 1947, India, 1949-50, 1963, and South Africa, 1960. *Wartime service:* Voluntary Aid Detachment, nurse in London, Malta, and France, 1915-19.

MEMBER: Royal Society of Literature (fellow), Royal Commonwealth Society, International League for Peace and Freedom (vice-president, 1945-70), National Peace Council, (vice-president, 1930-70), Society of Women Writers and Journalists (honorary life member; president, 1965-70), P.E.N., Married Women's Association (president, 1962), National Arts Theatre Club.

AWARDS, HONORS: D.Litt, Mills College, 1950.

WRITINGS:

Verses of a V.A.D., Erskine Macdonald, 1918.
The Dark Tide (novel), Grant Richards, 1923.
Not Without Honour (novel), Grant Richards, 1924.
Women's Work in Modern England, Noel Douglas, 1928.
Halcyon, or the Future of Monogamy, Kegan Paul, 1929.
Testament of Youth (autobiography), Macmillan, 1933, recent edition, Penguin, 1989.
Poems of the War and After, Macmillan, 1934.
Honourable Estate (novel), Macmillan, 1936.
Thrice a Stranger (travel), Macmillan, 1938.
Testament of Friendship (biography), Macmillan, 1940, recent edition, Fontana, 1981.
England's Hour, Macmillan, 1941, recent edition, Futura, 1981.
Humiliation with Honour, Dakers, 1942, Friendship, 1945.
Seed of Chaos, New Vision Publishing, 1944.
(Editor, with husband, George Catlin, and Sheila Hodges) *Above All Nations* (anthology), Gollancz, 1945, Harper, 1949.
Account Rendered (novel), Macmillan, 1945, recent edition, Virago, 1982.
On Becoming a Writer, Hutchinson, 1947, published as *On Being an Author,* Macmillan, 1948.
Born 1925: A Novel of Youth, Macmillan, 1948, recent edition, Virago, 1982.
Valiant Pilgrim, Macmillan, 1950 (published in England as *In the Steps of John Bunyan,* Rich & Cowan, 1950).
The Story of St. Martin's: An Epic of London, St. Martin-in-the-Fields, 1951.

Search after Sunrise: A Traveller's Story, Macmillan, 1951.
Lady into Woman: A History of Women from Victoria to Elizabeth II, Dakers, 1953.
Testament of Experience (autobiography), Macmillan, 1957, recent edition, Fontana, 1980.
(With G. E. W. Sizer) *Long Shadows,* A. Brown, 1958.
The Women at Oxford, Harrap, 1960.
Selected Letters of Winifred Holtby and Vera Brittain, limited edition, A. Brown & Sons, 1960.
The Pictorial History of St. Martin-in-the-Fields, Pitkin Pictorials, 1962.
Pethick-Lawrence: A Portrait, Allen & Unwin, 1963.
The Rebel Passion: A Short History of Some Pioneer Peace-Making, Fellowship Publications, 1964.
Envoy Extraordinary: A Study of Vijaya Lakshmi Pandit and Her Contribution to Modern India, Allen & Unwin, 1965, A. S. Barnes, 1966.
Radclyffe Hall: A Case of Obscenity?, Femina, 1968, A. S. Barnes, 1969.
(Editor with H. S. Reid) Winifred Holtby, *Pavements at Anderby: Tales of 'South Riding' and Other Regions,* Lythway Press, 1974.
Massacre by Bombing, Revisionist Press, 1981.
Chronicle of Youth: The War Diary, 1913-1917, edited by Alan Bishop with Terry Smart, Gollancz, 1981.
(With Winifred Holtby) *Testament of a Generation: The Journalism of Vera Brittain and Winifred Holtby,* edited by Paul Berry and Alan Bishop, Virago, 1985.
Chronicle of Friendship: Diary of the Thirties, 1932-1939, Gollancz, 1986.
Diary 1939-1945: Wartime Chronicle, edited by Alan Bishop and Y. Aleksandra Bennett, Gollancz, 1990.

Contributor to *This Week, Week-end* (Canada), *Author, Books,* and other magazines and newspapers in Great Britain, United States, Canada, and Italy. Chairman emeritus, *Peace News.*

WORK IN PROGRESS: Another biography.

SIDELIGHTS: Vera Brittain once told Mimi Josephson: "I never remember a time when I wasn't certain that I should be an author when I grew up." Her first novel, describing conditions in women's colleges, elicited a storm of protest among Oxford authorities and was banned in Somerville, her own college. The novel, however, was later given extremely favorable reviews.

Another of Brittain's early works, *Testament of Youth,* quickly became a best-seller. "Its impact on campus idealists," wrote Helen Beal Woodward, "was extraordinary. . . . They were . . . impressed by her struggle for a university education, and already converted—or thought they were—to her passionate pacifism." The sequel, *Testament of Experience,* published twenty-four years later, was "truly a remarkable book," said Woodward, "searchingly and sensitively written, the distillate of a life richer than most in love, thought, pain, and achievement. It [was] about as far from a religious do-it-yourself as a book could be, but I think it would be difficult to read it thoughtfully without having, oneself, something of a religious experience." Mimi Josephson wrote that "in the future the two 'Testaments' will be considered not only as a vividly written narrative of one women's life, but as a valuable historical and sociological record giving a true, unbiased picture of the first half of the twentieth century."

Brittain's interest in feminism dated back to her reading of Olive Schreiner's *Women and Labour* at the age of sixteen, reported Josephson. "Brittain very early rebelled against the genteel, useless life of a middle-class provincial 'young lady.' She decided that she wanted to be a useful member of society in her own right; she wanted a university education and, above all, she wanted to write." In all of her work, she was able to combine literary talent and a strong personal and social ideology. Of *Search After Sunrise,* Herbert L. Matthews wrote: "Her calm, sensible, matter-of-fact way of writing does not hide the intensity of her convictions. . . . [She] is impressive because this is such a sensible, honest, careful, unpretentious book, and it is, of course, the work of a keen, trained observer who can set down sights and impressions expertly."

Brittain preferred to work mornings and did all her writing in manuscript. She told Mimi Josephson: "I can't use a typewriter, except for letters. . . . It gets between me and my thought." Josephson commented: "She thinks this is because she has a dislike for mechanical things, even where entertainment is concerned. She does not care for TV, radio or the cinema, but is very fond of the theatre—'I like direct human contact,' she added."

Brittain's travels included forty-seven of the United States; Europe, South Africa, and five Asian countries. She spoke French and German with "reasonable facility."

BIOGRAPHICAL/CRITICAL SOURCES:

BOOKS

Bailey, Hilary, *Vera Brittain,* Penguin, 1987.
Contemporary Literary Criticism, Volume 23, Gale, 1983.

PERIODICALS

Contemporary Review, August, 1963.
John O'London's Weekly, April 30, 1954.
New Republic, October 7, 1957.
New Statesman, February 6, 1960.
New York Times Book Review, March 2, 1952, January 30, 1983.
Saturday Review, August 24, 1957.
Spectator, February 26, 1960.
Times Literary Supplement, March 2, 1990.

OBITUARIES:

PERIODICALS

New York Times, March 30, 1970.
Time, April 13, 1970.
Times (London), March 30, 1970.

*   *   *

BRODSKY, Iosif Alexandrovich 1940-
(Joseph Brodsky)

PERSONAL: Born May 24, 1940, in Leningrad, Soviet Union; son of Alexander I. and Maria M. (Volpert) Brodsky; children: Andrei (son). *Education:* Attended schools in Leningrad, until 1956.

ADDRESSES: Office—Writing Division, School of the Arts, Columbia University, New York, N.Y. 10027; Department of Russian, Mount Holyoke College, South Hadley, Mass. 01075.

CAREER: Poet; worked as stoker, sailor, photographer, geologist's assistant on expedition to Central Asia, coroner's assistant, and farm laborer; exiled by the Soviet government, he left his homeland in June, 1972, for refuge in America; poet-in-residence at University of Michigan, Ann Arbor, beginning 1972; adjunct professor, Columbia University, New York, N.Y.; Mount Holyoke College, South Hadley, Mass., instructor in Russian language department, 1990—.

MEMBER: Bavarian Academy of Sciences (Munich-corresponding member), American Academy of Arts and Sciences, until 1987.

AWARDS, HONORS: D.Litt., Yale University, 1978; Mondello Prize (Italy), 1979; National Book Critics Circle Award nomination, 1980, for *A Part of Speech,* and award, 1986, for *Less Than One: Selected Essays;* MacArthur fellowship, 1981; Guggenheim fellowship; Nobel Prize, 1987.

WRITINGS:

Stikhotvoreniia i poemy (in Russian; title means "Longer and Shorter Poems"), Inter-Language (Washington), 1965.
"Xol 'mi," translated by Jean-Jacques Marie and published in France as *Collines et autres poemes,* Editions de Seuil, 1966.
Ausgewahlte Gedichte (in German), Bechtle Verlag, 1966.
(Under name Joseph Brodsky) *Elegy to John Donne and Other Poems,* selected, translated, and introduced by Nicholas Bethell, Longmans, Green, 1967.
Velka elegie (in Czech), Edice Svedectvi (Paris), 1968.
Ostanovka v pustyne (in Russian; title means "A Halt in the Wilderness"), Chekhov (New York), 1970.
(Under name Joseph Brodsky) *Poems by Joseph Brodsky,* Ardis, 1972.
(Under name Joseph Brodsky) *Selected Poems, Joseph Brodsky,* translated by George L. Kline, Harper, 1973.
(Contributor) *Three Slavic Poets: Joseph Brodsky, Tymoteusz Karpowicz, Djordie Nikoloc,* edited by John Rezek, Elpenor Books, 1975.
(Editor under name Joseph Brodsky with Carl Proffer) *Modern Russian Poets on Poetry: Blok, Mandelstam, Pasternak, Mayakovsky, Gumilev, Tsvetaeva* (nonfiction), Ardis, 1976.
Konets prekrasnoi epokhi: Stikhotvoreniia, 1964-1971 (in Russian; title means "The End of A Wonderful Era: Poems"), Ardis, 1977.
Chast' rechi: Stikhotvoreniia, 1972-1976 (in Russian; title means "A Part of Speech: Poems"), Ardis, 1977, translation published as *A Part of Speech,* Farrar, Straus, 1980.
V Anglii (in Russian; title means "In England"), Ardis, 1977.
Verses on the Winter Campaign 1980, translation by Alan Meyers, Anvil Press (London), 1981.
Rimskie elegii (in Russian; title means "Roman Elegies"), [New York], 1982.
Novye stansy k Avguste: Stikhi k M.B., 1962-1982 (in Russian; title means "New Stanzas to Augusta: Poems to M.B."), Ardis, 1983.
Uraniia: Novaia kniga stikhov (in Russian; title means "Urania: A New Book of Poems"), Ardis, 1984, translation published as *To Urania: Selected Poems, 1965-1985,* Farrar Straus, 1988.
Less than One: Selected Essays, Farrar, Straus, 1984.
Mramor, Ardis, 1984.

Translations of his poems appear in James Scully's *Avenue of the Americas,* University of Massachusetts Press, 1971, and in *New Underground Russian Poets: Poems by Yosif Brodsky [and others].* Poems have been published in anthologies in twelve languages, and in *Russian Review, New York Review of Books, Nouvelle Revue Francaise, Unicorn Journal, Observer Review, Kultura, La Fiera Letteraria, New Yorker, New Leader,* and other journals. He also has done translations of poetry from English and Polish into Russian, and from Russian into Hebrew.

WORK IN PROGRESS: Original poems; translations from English into Russian; an English translation of *Chast' rechi* and a collection of essays, both for Farrar, Straus.

SIDELIGHTS: Inside Russia and out, Nobel Prize winner Joseph Brodsky is considered to be one of the Soviet Union's finest poets, although his work has not yet been published in the U.S.S.R. That and other puzzling aspects of Brodsky's exile have been the subject of wide press coverage since he stopped over in Vienna in June, 1972, en route to the United States. Exile has been difficult for the writer, who was born to middle-class Jewish parents in Leningrad before World War II. In one poem, he describes an exiled writer as one "who survives like a fish in the sand."

In many ways, Brodsky had lived as an exile before leaving his homeland. His father had lost a position of rank in the Russian navy because he was Jewish, and the family lived in poverty. Trying to escape the ever-present images of Lenin, Brodsky quit school and embarked on a self-directed education, reading literary classics and working a variety of unusual jobs, which included assisting a coroner, and a geologist in Central Asia. He learned English and Polish so that he would be able to translate the poems of John Donne and Milosz. His own poetry expressed his independent character with an originality admired by poets such as Anna Akhmatova and condemned by the Russian government.

According to a *Times Literary Supplement* reviewer, Brodsky's poetry "is religious, intimate, depressed, sometimes confused, sometimes martyr-conscious, sometimes elitist in its views, but it does not constitute an attack on Soviet society or ideology unless withdrawal and isolation are deliberately construed as attack: of course they can be, and evidently were." According to *Time,* the poet's expulsion from Russia was "the culmination of an inexplicable secret-police vendetta against him that has been going on for over a decade." Brodsky, who is Jewish, said: "They have simply kicked me out of my country, using the Jewish issue as an excuse." The vendetta first came to a head in a Leningrad trial in 1964, when Brodsky was charged with writing "gibberish" instead of doing honest work; he was sentenced to five years hard labor. Protests from artists and writers helped to secure his release after eighteen months, but his poetry still was banned. Israel invited him to emigrate, and the government encouraged him to go; Brodsky, though, refused, explaining that he did not identify with the Jewish state. Finally, Russian officials insisted that he leave the country. Despite the pressures, Brodsky reportedly wrote to Leonid Brezhnev before leaving Moscow asking for "an opportunity to continue to exist in Russian literature and on Russian soil."

Brodsky's poetry bears the marks of his confrontations with the Russian authorities. "Brodsky is someone who has tasted extremely bitter bread," writes Stephen Spender in *New Statesman,* "and his poetry has the air of being ground out between his teeth. . . . It should not be supposed that he is a liberal, or even a socialist. He deals in unpleasing, hostile truths and is a realist of the least comforting and comfortable kind. Everything nice that you would like him to think, he does not think. But he is utterly truthful, deeply religious, fearless and pure. Loving, as well as hating." Brodsky's "constant theme," relates Philip Howard of the *Times,* "is the contrast between the bleakness of life and the brilliance of language."

Though one might expect Brodsky's poetry to be basically political in nature, this is not the case. "Brodsky's recurrent themes are lyric poets' traditional, indeed timeless concerns—man and nature, love and death, the ineluctability of anguish, the fragility of human achievements and attachments, the preciousness of the privileged moment, the 'unrepeatable.' The tenor of his poetry is not so much apolitical as antipolitical," writes Victor Erlich.

"[His] besetting sin was not 'dissent' in the proper sense of the word, but a total, and on the whole quietly undemonstrative, estrangement from the Soviet ethos."

More than one critic holds the view expressed by Arthur C. Jacobs in *The Jewish Quarterly* that Brodsky is "quite apart from what one thinks of as the main current of Russian verse." A critic in *New Leader* writes: "The noisy rant and attitudinizing rhetoric of public issues are superfluous to Brodsky's moral vision and contradictory to his craft. As with all great lyric poets, Brodsky attends to the immediate, the specific, to what he has internally known and felt, to the lucidities of observation heightened and defined by thought. . . . Poetry of such rare power does not need the sustenance of biography. . . . At the age of thirty-three, he has the unfaltering intellectual authority that poets rarely achieve before middle age."

Though most agree that he is one of the finest living Russian poets, several critics believe that the English translations of his poetry are less impressive. Commenting on George L. Kline's translation of *Selected Poems,* Stephen Spender writes: "These poems are impressive in English, though one is left having to imagine the technical virtuousity of brilliant rhyming [in the originals]. . . . One is never quite allowed to forget that one is reading a second-hand version." F. D. Reeve is somewhat more abrupt: "In *Selected Poems,* the translations and their footnotes seem full of rectitude but lacking poetic rigor. Translating is difficult, I know, and thankless. . . . I think these translations are soupy. . . . How can any of us know who is Joseph Brodsky?" In *A Part of Speech,* Brodsky gathered the work of several translators and made amendments to some of the English versions in an attempt to restore the character of the originals. Brodsky's personal style remains somewhat elusive in that collection due to the subtle effects he achieves in the original Russian, Tom Simmons comments in the *Christian Science Monitor.* Brodsky, he says, "is a poet of dramatic yet delicate vision—a man with a sense of the increasingly obscured loftiness of human life. But under no circumstances is his poetry dully ethereal. His dramatic power cuts both ways: He can portray a luminous moment or a time of seemingly purposeless suffering with equal clarity." Reeve agrees that "Brodsky is an extremely sensitive, alert, skilled, independent, and suggestive poet" whose Russian poems (as distinguished from their English translations) contain "a dignity, a grandeur, and a sadness deeply reflective of Russian culture and of our own world."

Erlich also feels that some of the lines in *Selected Poems* come out "strained or murky," but that Brodsky at his best has "originality, incisiveness, depth and formal mastery which mark a major poet." Czeslaw Milosz feels that Brodsky's background has allowed him to make a vital contribution to literature. Writing in the *New York Review of Books,* Milosz states, "Behind Brodsky's poetry is the experience of political terror, the experience of the debasement of man and the growth of the totalitarian empire. . . . I find it fascinating to read his poems as part of his larger enterprise, which is no less than an attempt to fortify the place of man in a threatening world." This enterprise connects Brodsky to the literary traditions of other times and cultures. Milosz explains, "An intensity that deserves to be called religious combined with a metaphorical denseness makes Brodsky a true descendant of the English metaphysical poets and it is clear he feels an affinity with them." Erlich concludes an analysis of some of Brodsky's major poems by remarking: "The richness and versatility of his gifts, the liveliness and vigor of his intelligence, and his increasingly intimate bond with the Anglo-American literary tradition, augur well for his survival in exile, indeed for his further creative growth."

Brodsky has prospered economically and artistically since taking up residence in the United States, where he has taught at the University of Michigan, has been widely published and translated, and has won several literary grants and prizes, including the Nobel Prize. At first, he was eager to return to Leningrad to see his parents, but he was not allowed to visit them before they died. More recently, he has expressed a change of heart about returning to Russia, which is itself undergoing rapid change. He told David Remnick of the *Washington Post* that those changes "are devoid of autobiographical interest" for him, and that his allegiance is to his language. In the *Detroit News,* Bob McKelvey cites Brodsky's declaration from a letter to Illich, "I belong to the Russian culture. I feel part of it, its component and no change of place can influence the final consequence of this. A language is a much more ancient and inevitable thing than a state. I belong to the Russian language."

BIOGRAPHICAL/CRITICAL SOURCES:

BOOKS

Authors in the News, Volume 1, Gale, 1973.
Brodsky, Joseph, *A Part of Speech,* Farrar, Straus, 1980.
(Under name Joseph Brodsky) *Contemporary Literary Criticism,* Gale, Volume 4, 1975, Volume 6, 1976, Volume 36, 1986, Volume 50, 1988.

PERIODICALS

Antioch Review, winter, 1985.
Choice, April, 1974, September, 1977.
Christian Century, November 11, 1987.
Christian Science Monitor, August 11, 1980.
Detroit Free Press, September 17, 1972, October 23, 1987.
Jewish Quarterly, winter, 1968-69.
Los Angeles Times, October 23, 1987, February 15, 1989.
Nation, October 4, 1980.
New Leader, December 10, 1973, December 14, 1987.
New Statesman, December 14, 1973.
Newsweek, November 2, 1987.
New York Review, August 14, 1980.
New York Review of Books, August 14, 1980, January 21, 1988.
New York Times, October 31, 1987.
New York Times Book Review, November 8, 1987.
Partisan Review, fall, 1974.
Poetry, October, 1975.
Texas Studies in Literature and Language, Number 17, 1975.
Time, June 19, 1972, August 7, 1972, April 7, 1986, November 2, 1987.
Times Literary Supplement, July 20, 1967.
Vogue, February, 1988.
Washington Post, October 23, 1987.
Washington Post Book World, August 24, 1980.

*   *   *

BRODSKY, Joseph
See BRODSKY, Iosif Alexandrovich

*   *   *

BROOK, Peter (Stephen Paul) 1925-

PERSONAL: Born March 21, 1925, in London, England; son of Simon (a chemist) and Ida (a chemist; maiden name, Jansen) Brook; married Natasha Parry (an actress), November 3, 1951; children: one son, one daughter. *Education:* Magdalen College, Oxford, B.A., 1944.

ADDRESSES: Office—International Center of Theatre Research, 9 rue du Cirque, Paris 8, France.

CAREER: Writer. Director of stage productions for Birmingham Repertory Theatre, including "Man and Superman," 1945, and "The Lady From the Sea," 1946; Royal Opera House, including "Boris Godunov," 1947, and "Salome," 1950; Metropolitan Opera, including "Faust," 1953, and "Eugene Onegin," 1957; Royal Shakespeare Co., including "King Lear," 1962, "The Persecution and Assassination of Marat as Performed by the Inmates of the Asylum of Charenton Under the Direction of the Marquis de Sade" (also called "Marat/Sade"), 1964; and Avignon Theater Festival, including "The Mahabharata," 1985. Director of motion pictures for Crown Film Unit, 1945, and "The Beggar's Opera," 1953, "Marat/Sade," 1967, "Tell Me Lies," 1968, "King Lear," 1969, "Meetings With Remarkable Men," 1979, "La Tragedie de Carmen," 1983, and "Mahabharata," 1989. Director of television productions, including "Box for One," 1949, "King Lear," 1953, and "Heaven and Earth," 1957. Founded International Center of Theatre Research, 1970.

MEMBER: Association of Cinematographers and Allied Technicians.

AWARDS, HONORS: Named best director by London Critics' Poll, 1964, and New York Drama Critics' Poll, 1965, and received Antoinette Perry ("Tony") Award for best director from League of New York Theatres and Producers, and Outer Circle Award, both 1965, all for "The Persecution and Assassination of Marat as Performed by the Inmates of the Asylum of Charenton Under the Direction of the Marquis de Sade"; Commander of the Order of the British Empire and Chevalier de l'Ordre des Arts et des Lettres, both 1965; Drama Desk Award for best director, Antoinette Perry Award for best director, and named best director by New York Drama Critics' Poll, all 1970, all for "A Midsummer Night's Dream"; Shakespeare Award from Freiherr von Stein Foundation, 1973; elected to Theater Hall of Fame at Uris Theater, 1983; award from Society of West End Theatre for contribution to American theater, 1983; special Antoinette Perry Award for achievement in lyric theater for "La Tragedie de Carmen"; and other awards.

WRITINGS:

(And director) "U.S." (play), first produced on West End at Aldwych Theatre, October 13, 1966.
The Empty Space (nonfiction), Atheneum, 1968.
Cosmopolitan Tales, Mojave Books, 1980.
(With Marius Constant and Jean-Claude Carriere) "La Tragedie de Carmen" (adapted from the opera by Georges Bizet), produced in New York City at Vivian Beaumont Theater, c. November, 1983.
The Shifting Point: Forty Years of Theatrical Exploration (autobiography), Harper, 1987.

Also author and director of screenplays "Lord of the Flies" (adapted from the novel by William Golding), 1962; "King Lear" (adapted from the play by William Shakespeare), 1971; "Meetings With Remarkable Men," with Jeanne de Salzmann, 1979; "Mahabharata" (based on Indian epic poem), with Carriere, 1989; co-author of "Moderato Cantabile," 1960. Author of "Swann in Love" (screenplay adapted from the Marcel Proust novel *Remembrance of Things Past*), with Carriere and Marie-Helene Estienne, 1984.

SIDELIGHTS: Many theatre critics rank Peter Brook among the most influential figures of the twentieth-century stage. His revolutionary productions of Shakespearean works such as "A

Midsummer Night's Dream" and "King Lear," both of which employed spare settings and offbeat costuming to spark fresh interpretations, revealed Brook's interest in the Absurdist theatre of Samuel Beckett and the political didacticism of Bertolt Brecht. The modern theatre's strength, Brook contended, "lies in making certain little concentrated events in which one can participate—the unique quality of living events that technology makes more and more inaccessible." This twin interest in art and social relevance has endeared Brook to reviewers such as *New York Times*'s Anthony Lewis. "In an increasingly technological world, of huge abstractions, he sees the theater supplying the elements of community and life for which people yearn," wrote Lewis. "It is almost a religious experience."

Brook's initiation to the theatre was fairly auspicious. After graduating from Magdalen College at age twenty, he created brief advertising films for Crown Film Unit. He then involved himself in a production of George Bernard Shaw's "Pygmalion" by the Entertainments National Service Organization. While directing a dress rehearsal, Brook was observed by William Armstrong, a prominent British stage director. Armstrong referred Brook to the Birmingham Repertory Theatre, where the latter made his debut in 1945 as director of Shaw's "Man and Superman." The following year, critics raved about his direction of Shakespeare's "Romeo and Juliet," in which his casting of youthful actors was considered a welcome departure from the stodgy productions that had plagued recent presentations of Shakespeare's work.

Brook scored again with his 1953 production of Gounod's opera "Faust" for the Metropolitan Opera. Rejecting the opera's medieval setting, he placed the action in the nineteenth century and emphasized the customs of that period. "Faust" was therefore more subtly unconventional than Brook's previous efforts. He also directed his first film, "The Beggar's Opera," in 1953. His grasp of cinematic technique was deemed sufficient by most critics, but some complained that scenes were alternately too cinematic and too stage-like. Less successful was Brook's second film, "Moderato Cantabile," an experimental work described by Andrew Sarris as "an exercise in languorous introspection of the Resnais—*Hiroshima Mon Amour* school."

In 1964 Brook implemented improvisation and aspects of Antonin Artaud's "Theatre of Cruelty" in the play "The Persecution and Assassination of Marat as Performed by the Inmates of Charenton Under the Direction of the Marquis de Sade" ("Marat/Sade"). Brook was extremely successful in instilling an obsession with deranged and violent behavior in his actors, and the subsequent performances shocked audiences. "The 'Marat/Sade,' " noted Lewis, "with its unforgettable evocation of the inmates of the Asylum at Charenton, left some in its audience physically ill." Brook repeated his success in 1967 when he directed the film version of the play.

Two other works Brook directed in the 1960s were not as well received. Both the play "U.S." and the motion picture "Tell Me Lies" suffered, according to reviewers, from their contrived attempts at relevance to the Vietnam War. And Sarris complained that "*Tell Me Lies* provides an entirely new set of cinematic conceptions that miscarry in the messiest ways imaginable."

Throughout the 1960s Brook also lectured on drama at universities. In 1968 his comments were collected and published as *The Empty Space*. In the book, Brook divides the theatre into four categories: he calls conventional theatre "deadly," dubs ritualistic works "holy," accessible works "rough," and considers his own style "immediate." The "immediate" approach, according to Gerald Weales, is one "in which the creativity happens at that moment and is shared by performers and audience alike." Weales added that "performers must constantly walk the line between discipline and discovery, avoiding a sealed and finished production, creating the play fresh with each performance."

The Empty Space was generally welcomed by critics as thought-provoking insight into the modern theatre. Weales called it "an exploration." In *Drama*, Edward Argent observed that "it is essential reading for anyone seriously interested in the drama—infuriating to some, baffling maybe, but essential." *New Leader*'s Albert Bermel praised Brook's "tact and eclecticism" and called *The Empty Space* "an absorbing document."

Brook continued directing in the 1970s. His most notable works were the motion pictures "King Lear" and "Meetings With Remarkable Men." *New York Times*'s Vincent Canby called "King Lear" a film "of lovely surprises." He noted, "It's a downhill journey, but one that, by the flash of the lightning that the play provides, illuminates, for a very brief time, the essence of existence without comprehensible moral order, and makes it bearable." John Simon disagreed, contending that "there is almost no poetry at all in the film." He charged that "Brook will do anything for an effect, however nonsensical."

"Meetings With Remarkable Men" was less successful. Brook's biography of Russian mystic G. I. Gurdjieff concentrated on the philosopher's search for enlightenment in the Near East. *Newsweek*'s Jack Kroll complained that Brook's solemn approach overwhelmed the drama. "The ineffable is indeed ineffable," Kroll conceded, "but surely a film on this subject should get under your skin, disrupt your complacency, make you feel the possibility of another kind of inner life." Janet Maslin in the *New York Times* similarly charged, "Watching this handsome, affectless effort feels a little like receiving a series of postcards in the mail, each one beautiful but missing a message on the back." She added, "Certainly 'Meetings With Remarkable Men' is a film that requires supplementary energy, whether it comes from the curiosity, or the prior knowledge that the right audience may provide."

BIOGRAPHICAL/CRITICAL SOURCES:

BOOKS

Sattis, Andrew, *The American Cinema: Directors and Direction, 1929-1968,* Dutton, 1968.

PERIODICALS

Book World, December 29, 1968.
Chicago Tribune, September 26, 1984.
Cue, February 13, 1971.
Drama, spring, 1969.
London, November, 1968.
New Leader, December 2, 1968.
New Statesman, October 18, 1968.
Newsweek, September 3, 1979.
New York, May 26, 1980.
New York Times, October 4, 1955, May 18, 1958, January 15, 1971, December 5, 1971, December 22, 1971, August 5, 1979, May 25, 1980, November 27, 1983, March 22, 1984, July 31, 1985, September 30, 1987, October 19, 1987, November 26, 1987, September 28, 1989, December 26, 1989.
New York Times Book Review, November 17, 1968.
New York Times Magazine, October 4, 1987.
Times (London), April 14, 1988.
Vogue, November 15, 1968.
Washington Post, December 11, 1983, October 5, 1984, November 27, 1989.

BROOKE, Rupert (Chawner) 1887-1915

PERSONAL: Born August 3, 1887, in Rugby, Warwickshire, England; died of blood poisoning, April 23, 1915, near the island of Skyros, Greece; son of William Parker (a secondary school teacher) and Mary Ruth (Cotterill) Brooke. *Education:* King's College, Cambridge, B.A. (with second-class honors), 1909.

CAREER: Writer. Schoolmaster at Rugby School, 1909-10. Traveled to Germany, 1912; traveled to America, 1913, contributing articles to the *Westminster Gazette* and the *New Statesman;* traveled to the South Pacific, 1913-14. *Military service:* Royal Navy Volunteer Reserve, 1914-15; became sub-lieutenant.

AWARDS, HONORS: Fellowship from King's College, Cambridge, c. 1911.

WRITINGS:

Poems, Sidgwick & Jackson, 1911 (also see below).
(Editor with Edward Marsh, and contributor) *Georgian Poetry, 1911-1912* (includes "The Old Vicarage, Grantchester"), Poetry Bookshop, 1912.
Nineteen Fourteen, and Other Poems, Doubleday, 1915 (also see below).
The Collected Poems of Rupert Brooke (includes *Poems* and *Nineteen Fourteen, and Other Poems*), introduction by George Edward Woodberry, John Lane, 1915, reprinted, Dodd, 1980.
Lithuania: A Drama in One Act, Chicago Little Theatre, 1915.
Letters From America (essays first published in *Westminster Gazette* and *New Statesman*), preface by Henry James, Scribner, 1916, reprinted, Beaufort Books, 1988.
John Webster and the Elizabethan Drama (thesis), John Lane, 1916, reprinted, Russell, 1967.
The Collected Poems of Rupert Brooke, edited and with a memoir by Edward Marsh, Sidgwick & Jackson, 1918, revised edition, 1942, reprinted, 1960.
The Poetical Works of Rupert Brooke, edited by Geoffrey Keynes, Faber, 1946, reprinted, 1970.
Democracy and the Arts (nonfiction), Hart-Davis, 1946.
The Prose of Rupert Brooke, edited and introduced by Christopher Hassall, Sidgwick & Jackson, 1956.
The Letters of Rupert Brooke, edited by Geoffrey Keynes, Harcourt, 1968.
Rupert Brooke: A Reappraisal and Selection From His Writings, Some Hitherto Unpublished, edited by Timothy Rogers, Barnes & Noble, 1971.
Letters From Rupert Brooke to His Publisher, 1911-1914, Octagon Books, 1975.

SIDELIGHTS: Few writers have provoked as much excessive praise and scornful condemnation as English poet Rupert Brooke. Handsome, charming, and talented, Brooke was a national hero even before his death in 1915 at the age of twenty-seven. His poetry, with its unabashed patriotism and graceful lyricism, was revered in a country that was yet to feel the devastating effects of two world wars. Brooke's early death only solidified his image as "a golden-haired, blue-eyed English Adonis," as Doris L. Eder notes in the *Dictionary of Literary Biography,* and among those who lauded him after his death were writers Virginia Woolf and Henry James and British statesman Winston Churchill. In the decades after World War I, however, critics reacted against the Brooke legend by calling his verse foolishly naive and sentimental. Despite such extreme opinions, most contemporary observers agree that Brooke—though only a minor poet—occupies a secure place in English literature as a representative of the mood and character of England before World War I.

Brooke's early years were typical of virtually every English boy who was a member of a well-to-do family. He attended a prestigious boarding school—Rugby, where his father was a headmaster—studied Latin and Greek, and began to write poetry. It was taken for granted that Brooke would go on to one of the great English universities, and accordingly he entered Cambridge in 1906.

During his three years at Cambridge, Brooke became a visible figure in English intellectual circles, counting among his acquaintances Virginia Woolf, writer Lytton Strachey, economist John Maynard Keynes and his brother Geoffrey (later to become Brooke's bibliographer), and poet William Butler Yeats. Brooke also continued to write poetry, although his poems from this period are, as Eder comments, "highly derivative, facile literary exercises." In *The Neo-Pagans: Rupert Brooke and the Ordeal of Youth,* Paul Delany gives an example of Brooke's verse from his Cambridge years. Written in 1909, "The Voice," like most of his early poetry, dwells on the themes of love and nature: "Safe in the magic of my woods / I lay, and watched the dying light / . . . The three that I loved, together grew / One, in the hour of knowing, / Night, and the woods, and you." Although his early work is thought to be of little significance, Brooke by this time was considered a serious though unaccomplished poet. In addition, he was an increasingly conspicuous figure in literary circles—a fame fueled without doubt by his charm and good looks.

Between his graduation from Cambridge in 1909 and the start of World War I in 1914, Brooke spent most of his time writing and traveling. His poetry during this period, which still emphasized the themes of love and nature, resembled that of most of the poets of his generation, including D. H. Lawrence, John Drinkwater, and Walter de la Mare. These poets came to be known as Georgian poets (named after England's king at the time); their verse reflects an idealistic preoccupation with rural, youthful motifs. In fact, Brooke and many of his friends enjoyed spending time in the countryside, bathing nude in local streams and sleeping on the ground; such activities earned them the nickname "neo-pagans." Eder points out that "Georgian verse now seems faded and pseudopastoral, a poetry of suburbia written by city dwellers celebrating cozy weekends in flower-wreathed country cottages." At the time, though, such poetry was fashionable and respected, and the first collection of poems by these writers, *Georgian Poetry, 1911-1912,* was extremely successful.

"The Old Vicarage, Grantchester" was Brooke's contribution to *Georgian Poetry,* and it remains one of his most popular poems. Grantchester is a small village near Cambridge where Brooke lived for a time after 1909. Brooke, however, wrote the poem later in a cafe in Germany. The poem's nostalgia for an England far away—"And laughs the immortal river still / Under the mill, under the mill? / . . . Stands the Church clock at ten to three? / And is there honey still for tea?," as quoted by Delany in *The Neo-Pagans*—reflects "patriotism and homesickness at their most endearing," writes Eder. After Brooke's death, Henry James wrote that the poem was "booked for immortality." Christopher Hassall, in his introduction to *The Prose of Rupert Brooke,* offers a perhaps more realistic analysis when he comments that "The Old Vicarage, Grantchester"—though one of Brooke's most personal and original statements—is nonetheless a "lightweight poem."

"The Old Vicarage, Grantchester" was written in mid-1912, one of the most turbulent periods in Brooke's life. According to Delany, Brooke had experienced a sexual crisis—confusion about homosexual impulses and frustration caused by the rejections of a woman with whom he was in love. In early 1912, these tensions culminated in a nervous breakdown. Brooke spent several months in rehabilitation, during which he was not allowed to write poetry. By summer, though, he had recovered enough to travel to Germany, a trip that marked the beginning of almost three years of constant travel. In May of 1913, he traveled to the United States, where he spent four months before sailing to the South Pacific. Of the seven months that Brooke stayed in the Pacific, three were spent in Tahiti, where, as Delany states, he wrote "the best of his poems, and [experienced] probably the most unbroken happiness of his life."

Several of the poems that Brooke wrote during this period are considered to be among his most effective, including "Tiare Tahiti" and "The Great Lover." Delany notes that the first poem's inspiration was a woman called "Taatamata," whom Brooke met and became intimate with in Tahiti. Not surprisingly, the poem is a love poem, a tribute to an exotic land and carefree love: "Hasten, hand in human hand, / Down the dark, the flowered way, / . . . And in the water's soft caress, / Wash the mind of foolishness, / Mamua, until the day." "The Great Lover" is a list "of the hundred and one everyday things that gave [the poet] joy," writes A. C. Ward in *Twentieth-Century Literature: 1901-1950.* "He invested this domestic catalogue with significance and beauty, and turned the commonplace into the strangely new," praises Ward. Similarly, John Lehmann in *Rupert Brooke: His Life and His Legend* remarks on "the precise and vivid images with which in *The Great Lover* [Brooke] enumerates the concrete things that evoke his love in recollection."

Despite the apparent happiness that Brooke found in Tahiti, he decided to return to England in the spring of 1914. Within a few months of his return, World War I began. Like most men of his age and class, Brooke immediately volunteered for service in the war. He joined the Royal Navy Volunteer Reserve; the group's first destination was Antwerp, Belgium, where it stayed through the beginning of 1915. The area around Antwerp was not volatile at this time, though, and the Reserve saw no military action during its entire stay in Belgium. The lull in fighting turned into a fruitful period for Brooke, for it was then that he produced his best-known poetry, the group of five war sonnets titled "Nineteen Fourteen."

Written during late 1914, these sonnets express the hopeful idealism and enthusiasm with which Britain entered the war. In the first sonnet, "Peace," Brooke rejoices in the feeling that the war is a welcome relief to a generation for whom life had been empty and void of meaning. As quoted by Bernard Bergonzi in *Heroes' Twilight: A Study of the Literature of the Great War,* Brooke wrote: "God be thanked Who has matched us with His hour, / And caught our youth, and wakened us from sleeping, / With hand made sure, clear eye, and sharpened power, / To turn, as swimmers into cleanness leaping, / Glad from a world grown old and cold and weary." In the second sonnet, "Safety," Brooke continues to revel in the coming of war by comparing death to a shelter that protects its refugees from the horrors of life.

The third and fourth sonnets are both titled "The Dead," but it is the second of the two that has enjoyed more popularity and more critical acclaim. In this fourth sonnet, Brooke again paints death as a positive, pristine state. For Brooke, death is like an infinite frost that "leaves a white / Unbroken glory, a gathered radiance, / A width, a shining peace, under the night," as quoted by Eder. Finally, Brooke ends the sonnet sequence with "The Soldier," his most famous and most openly patriotic poem. He imagines his own death, but rather than conveying sadness or

fear at such an event, he accepts it as an opportunity to make a noble sacrifice by dying for his country. As quoted by Delany, Brooke wrote: "If I should die, think only this of me, / That there's some corner of a foreign field / That is forever England."

The "Nineteen Fourteen" sonnets were immediately famous. On Easter Sunday in 1915, the dean of St. Paul's Cathedral in London, William Ralph Inge, read aloud "The Soldier." Brooke's death three weeks later insured that his name would always be intertwined with the war sonnets, and with "The Soldier" in particular. As A. C. Ward comments, "The Soldier" "became the one poem inseparably linked with Rupert Brooke's name. It is, for all time, his epitaph—beautiful and tranquil." The events surrounding Brooke's death were a significant factor in the success of "Nineteen Fourteen." In February of 1915, Brooke had been ordered to sail to the Dardanelles—a strait between Europe and Turkey—for the Gallipoli campaign that would begin that spring. During the journey, however, Brooke contracted blood poisoning from an insect bite; he died on April 23 on a ship in the Aegean Sea and was buried in an olive grove on the Greek island of Skyros. Such a death and burial, notes Delany, fueled the myth that the handsome poet had provoked the wrath of angry, jealous gods. "Rupert's death was first reported as caused by sunstroke," writes Delany, "and had not Phoebus Apollo, the golden-haired god of poetry, struck down Marsyas for boasting that he could sing as well as the god?" Furthermore, Brooke died in a part of the world long associated with another famous English poet, George Gordon, Lord Byron. As Delany says, "Now another Cambridge poet, who had loved to swim in Byron's Pool, had shared Byron's fate."

Brooke's death was felt throughout his country; Eder states that "all England mourned the poet-soldier's death." In his tribute to Brooke for the London *Times* as quoted by Delany, Winston Churchill praised Brooke's "classic symmetry of mind and body." "He was all that one would wish England's noblest sons to be," added Churchill, "in days when no sacrifice but the most precious is acceptable." Since the war was still in its early stages, such sentiment could still be cherished. After the staggering number of deaths that the English incurred during the trench warfare of 1916 and 1917, however, such patriotic feeling was viewed—like Brooke's poetry—as foolish and naive. As John Lehmann comments, "What soldier, who had experienced the meaningless horror and foulness of the Western Front stalemate in 1916 and 1917, could think of it as a place to greet 'as swimmers into cleanness leaping' or as a welcome relief 'from a world grown old and cold and weary'?"

A more realistic poetry grew out of the war's latter stages and supplanted Brooke's verse as the most important literary expression of the war. Poets such as Wilfred Owen, Siegfried Sassoon, and Robert Graves captured the terror and tragedy of modern warfare; next to their poetry, Brooke's war sonnets seem "sentimental and unrealistic," notes Lehmann. For several decades after his death Brooke's poetry—though always popular—was dismissed by critics responding both to the consequences of two world wars and to the pessimistic poetry that dominated the age, of which T. S. Eliot's *The Waste Land* is the prime example. But more recent critics, while admitting that Brooke's poetry lacks depth, maintain that his verse does have significance. In *Rupert Brooke: The Man and the Poet,* Robert Brainard Pearsall does not deny the "slightness in mass and idea" of Brooke's work but avers that "all technical criticism droops before the fact that his verse was lyrical, charming, and companionable." Other critics, including Eder and Edward A. McCourt, argue that Brooke's poetry—especially the "Nineteen Fourteen" sequence—is important as a barometer of England between 1910 and 1915. As

Eder states, "Brooke's war sonnets perfectly captured the mood of the moment."

Several observers, both past and present, have speculated as to what Brooke—and his poetry—might have achieved had the poet lived longer. Woolf, who wrote in the *Times Literary Supplement* that Brooke's "poetry was the brilliant by-product of energies not yet turned upon their object," speculated that Brooke might have become prime minister. Lehmann, referring to the legend that continues to surround Brooke—that of the angelic, idealistic, naive young poet—notes that "perhaps, if [Brooke] had survived into 1917 and 1918, he would have dismissed the legend himself more ruthlessly than anyone else." As it is, Brooke left only the legacy of a poetry that reflects his brief, fascinating life. "It is not," writes Timothy Rogers in *Rupert Brooke,* "for flights of fancy or for the deeper philosophic insights that we may read him; rather, for his sensitive response to a short but vivid life."

BIOGRAPHICAL/CRITICAL SOURCES:

BOOKS

Bergonzi, Bernard, *Heroes' Twilight: A Study of the Literature of the Great War,* Constable, 1965.

Brooke, Rupert, *The Prose of Rupert Brooke,* edited and introduced by Christopher Hassall, Sidgwick & Jackson, 1956.

Brooke, Rupert, *The Letters of Rupert Brooke,* edited by Geoffrey Keynes, Harcourt, 1968.

Brooke, Rupert, *Rupert Brooke: A Reappraisal and Selection From His Writings, Some Hitherto Unpublished,* edited by Timothy Rogers, Barnes & Noble, 1971.

Cheason, Denis, *The Cambridgeshire of Rupert Brooke,* privately printed, 1980.

de la Mare, Walter, *Rupert Brooke and the Intellectual Imagination,* Sidgwick & Jackson, 1919.

Delany, Paul, *The Neo-Pagans: Rupert Brooke and the Ordeal of Youth,* Free Press, 1987.

Dictionary of Literary Biography, Volume 19: *British Poets, 1840-1914,* Gale, 1983.

Ford, Boris, editor, *The Modern Age: Volume Seven of the Pelican Guide to English Literature,* 3rd edition, Penguin, 1973.

Hall, Roger and Sandra Martin, editors, *Rupert Brooke in Canada,* PMA Books, 1978.

Hassall, Christopher, *Rupert Brooke: A Biography,* Harcourt, 1964.

Hastings, Michael, *The Handsomest Young Man in England: Rupert Brooke,* Michael Joseph, 1967.

James, Henry, *The Letters of Henry James, Volume II,* edited by Percy Lubbock, Scribner, 1920.

Keynes, Geoffrey, *A Bibliography of Rupert Brooke,* Hart-Davis, 1959.

Lehmann, John, *Rupert Brooke: His Life and His Legend,* Weidenfeld & Nicolson, 1980.

Pearsall, Robert Brainard, *Rupert Brooke: The Man and the Poet,* Humanities Press, 1975.

Stringer, Arthur, *Red Wine of Youth: A Life of Rupert Brooke,* Bobbs-Merrill, 1948.

Twentieth-Century Literary Criticism, Gale, Volume 2, 1979, Volume 7, 1982.

Ward, A. C., *Twentieth-Century Literature: 1901-1950,* 3rd edition, Methuen, 1956.

PERIODICALS

Dalhousie Review, summer, 1944.
New York Times Book Review, November 24, 1968.

Times Literary Supplement, August 8, 1918, July 18, 1968, November 27, 1987.
Voice Literary Supplement, June, 1988.

—*Sketch by Neil R. Schlager*

*   *   *

BROOKE-HAVEN, P.
See WODEHOUSE, P(elham) G(renville)

*   *   *

BROOKNER, Anita 1938-

PERSONAL: Born July 16, 1938, in London, England; daughter of Newson (a company director) and Maude (a singer; maiden name, Schiska) Brookner. *Education:* Received B.A. from King's College, London; received Ph.D. from Courtauld Institute of Art, London.

ADDRESSES: Home—68 Elm Park Gardens, London S.W. 10, England. *Agent*—A. M. Heath, 40 William IV St., London W.C.2, England.

CAREER: University of Reading, Reading, England, visiting lecturer in the history of art, 1959-64; Courtauld Institute of Art, London, England, reader in the history of art, 1964-87; writer. Slade Professor of Art at Cambridge University, 1967-68.

AWARDS, HONORS: Named fellow of the Royal Society of Literature, 1983; received Booker McConnell Prize for fiction from the National Book League, 1984, for the novel *Hotel du lac.*

WRITINGS:

ART HISTORY AND CRITICISM

Watteau, Hamlyn, 1968.
The Genius of the Future: Studies in French Art Criticism, Phaidon, 1971.
Greuze: The Rise and Fall of an Eighteenth-Century Phenomenon, Elek, 1972, Graphic Society, 1974.
Jacques-Louis David: A Personal Interpretation (lecture), Oxford University Press for the British Academy, 1974.
Jacques-Louis David, Chatto & Windus, 1980, Harper, 1981.
(Contributor) Edwin Mullins, editor, *Great Paintings,* St. Martin's, 1981.

Contributor to "The Masters" series, Purnell, 1965-67. Translator of art history publications for Oldbourne Press, 1966.

NOVELS

A Start in Life, J. Cape, 1981, published in the United States as *The Debut,* Linden Press, 1981, Vintage Books, 1985.
Providence, J. Cape, 1982, Pantheon, 1984.
Look at Me, J. Cape, 1983, Pantheon, 1983.
Hotel du lac, J. Cape, 1984, Pantheon, 1984.
Family and Friends, J. Cape, 1985, Pantheon, 1985.
A Misalliance, J. Cape, 1986, Pantheon, 1987.
A Friend From England, J. Cape, 1987, Pantheon, 1988.
Latecomers, Random House, 1988.
Lewis Percy, J. Cape, 1989, Pantheon, 1990.

OTHER

(Editor) *The Stories of Edith Wharton,* Simon & Schuster, 1988.

Contributor of book reviews and articles to periodicals, including the *Times Literary Supplement, Observer, London Sunday*

Times, Writer, London Review of Books, London Standard, Burlington, and *Spectator.*

SIDELIGHTS: Perhaps best known for her novels, including the Booker McConnell Prize-winning *Hotel du lac,* Anita Brookner is an art historian who specializes in French painting from the mid-eighteenth to the mid-nineteenth centuries. Brookner has lectured on art history at the University of London's Courtauld Institute and, in addition to her novels, has written four books on art: *Watteau, The Genius of the Future, Greuze,* and *Jacques-Louis David.* Brookner described these books in a *Saturday Review* interview as "steps in the painful process of self-realization" and termed herself a "speculative" art historian rather than a scholar. Reviewers of her books on art, however, have praised Brookner for her extensive knowledge and explication of her subjects.

A *New York Times Book Review* critic, for instance, while judging the subject to be rather unfruitful, praised Brookner for her "exquisitely scholarly" study of the eighteenth-century French painter Jean-Baptiste Greuze. Concluded the reviewer: "The author's commanding acquaintance with everything and everybody, minor and major, in art, literature, and philosophy of the period [in which Greuze lived]—is staggering, and the grace with which she organizes the minutiae to give them an air of spontaneity even more so."

Of Brookner's book on French painter-politician Jacques-Louis David, who lived from 1748 to 1825, Richard Cobb remarked in the *Times Literary Supplement* that "Anita Brookner's handsome biography is about David as an artist, and is written by an art historian of great sensitivity and understanding." And Celia Betsky, reviewing the book in the *New Republic,* observed that in *Jacques-Louis David* Brookner "provides a superb show of investigative work, a thorough and intelligent probing of the meaning of a man's art."

In *Jacques-Louis David* Brookner focuses mainly on David's life in terms of his art, but his shifts in subject matter and style mirror the political changes in France from the time of the Revolution in 1789, through the Directory and Napoleonic periods, to the restoration of the monarchy in 1815. In Brookner's view, this "immensely sensitive response to historical change is David's most unique and striking feature." She also contends in *Jacques-Louis David* that his ability to adopt new artistic styles and political attitudes signals not merely cunning political survival techniques, but subconscious emotional problems and deep-seated personal resentments, which he could act upon in the name of each succeeding regime. So, Betsky observed, "the political significations long applied to David's work by left and right alike are vehemently gainsaid. Brookner ultimately prefers to see David as a proto-Romantic, a spectacular naif, and an unhappy soul." This is not to say that Brookner overlooks David's flaws. As a *New Yorker* critic remarked, "Brookner admires David's talent, but she is not blind to his shortcomings as an artist or his serious defects as a man." She does, however, attempt to explain these shortcomings and defects, serving as what Betsky described as "a detective of the buried soul." She proposes, for instance, that David, a tense, insecure man living during extremely brutal, politically unstable times, used his art as a release for his violent emotions but also tempered those feelings with an impulse toward perfection and restraint that could account for the static quality of his painting. As Betsky explained, "The apparent motionlessness of David's art, the architectonic and sculptural appearance of even a fold of drapery, merely mask activities in the life that informed the art and, as Brookner emphasizes, the emotions that shaped his character."

In the summer of 1980, Brookner wrote her first novel. Asked how she started writing fiction, Brookner explained in a *Publishers Weekly* interview: "It was most undramatic. . . . I had a long summer vacation in which nothing seemed to be happening, and could have got very sorry for myself and miserable, but it seemed such a waste of time to do that, and I'd always got a lot of nourishment from fiction. I wondered—it occurred to me to see whether I could do it. I didn't think I could. I just wrote a page, the first page, and nobody seemed to think it was wrong. An angel with a flaming sword didn't appear and say, 'You shouldn't be doing this.' So I wrote another page, and another, and at the end of the summer I had a story. That's all I wanted to do—tell a story."

This story, Brookner's first novel, was published in England as *A Start in Life* and in the United States as *The Debut.* It concerns a forty-year-old literary scholar who makes an abortive attempt to break out of the cloistered routine of her life, centered as it is on the literature she studies and the demands of her childish, aging parents. The woman, Ruth Weiss, considers her life "ruined by literature" that has led her to believe that patience and virtue will triumph in the end. Ironically, though she feels betrayed by literature, it is also literature that prompts her to seek real-life fulfillment. A specialist in the works of French novelist Honore de Balzac, Ruth embraces Balzac's opportunistic view of the world and sets out on an adventure; she goes to study in Paris, where she plans a romantic affair. The affair does not materialize, however, and Ruth returns home to care for her dying parents, thus resigning herself to a lonely middle age.

Central to Ruth's reassessment of and attempt to reshape her life are Balzac's female characters, particularly Eugenie Grandet. This character is a virtuous, kind, generous but socially isolated woman whose capacity for love and life is wasted in the midst of the greedy, power-hungry relatives, suitors, and acquaintances who seek her company only for her wealth. The lonely life of the unselfish, unassuming Eugenie serves initially as a warning to Ruth, who seeks to escape such a fate, and finally as a symbol of her own life, sacrificed to the more grasping desires of others. And, as Michele Slung observed in the *Washington Post,* Ruth's "sadness for Eugenie Grandet's wasted life is 'the only permissible grief she allows herself,' " though, Brookner continues in *The Debut,* "beyond the imposed limits it hovered, threatening enormous, unending, and inevitable."

Brookner drew critical praise for the way she interwove her story with the novels of Balzac. Annie Gottlieb, critiquing *The Debut* in the *New York Times Book Review,* remarked, "For those who are at ease in the hyperliterate atmosphere of English novels—and especially those who can also read the occasional French phrases—this is a precise and haunting little performance." Slung, explaining that "what Brookner does is to distill Balzac's [novel series] 'La Comedie Humaine' and spray some of its essence on the story," concluded that "rather than making it forbidding, this academic layering is so skillfully handled by Brookner that it enhances the novel's charms." According to Anne Duchene in her *Times Literary Supplement* review of *A Start in Life,* however, Brookner goes too far in blaming literature "for the festering resentments of filial dutifulness." Still, the critic added, this "hardly matters, given the confidence of the telling." On the whole, concluded Duchene, "Anita Brookner's story deals very directly and tenderly with a narrow but more or less universal seam of experience, that period in which one is disengaging from one's parents. . . . Or, in the case of this heroine, attempting to disengage."

With regard to Brookner's writing in *The Debut,* critics commended her accuracy, sensitivity, and humor. Slung observed that "Brookner's impeccable prose and sly wit make [*The Debut*] a seamless comedy; there's no room for maneuvering, no space in which to project one's ideas of what Ruth should do," and Slung concluded with hopes that Brookner would, like Balzac, proceed with her own "Human Comedy." Duchene remarked that "as well as the arm's length of wit, there is a great deal of precision and perception" in Brookner's rendering of Ruth's story. And Art Seidenbaum, reviewing *The Debut* in the *Los Angeles Times,* concurred, stating: "The art historian who studied portraiture and landscapes also knows the terrain of the heart. Her heroine is almost historic, tethered to responsibility, but her technique is modern, hard-edged and as uneuphemistic as today."

Brookner's second novel, *Providence,* also focuses on an academic. The main character is Kitty Maule, a reserved, elegantly-dressed literature professor who specializes in romanticism at a small but well-funded British college. Raised by her immigrant grandparents, Kitty feels like a foreigner in her native England. She is also in love with her colleague Maurice Bishop, a handsome, clever man with unshakable self-assurance and Catholic faith who remains as distant to Kitty as her desire to become assimilated into British culture.

Like the main character in *The Debut,* Kitty is greatly influenced by the literature she studies. As Galen Strawson explained in the *Times Literary Supplement:* "She works on Romanticism—and seeks to emulate what she finds in it: Romantic-chic, with its Stoic elements, the 'assumption of effortlessness,' 'the dandyism of great endeavor combined with a gracious ease of manner.'" The observations she makes as an instructor on the characters in Benjamin Constant's romantic novel *Adolphe* could also be applied to her own life. But she seemingly ignores some of the darker implications contained in her assessments: "Romantic love can lead to disastrous fidelities. Or ultimately to chastity"; and "It is characteristic of the Romantic to reason endlessly in unbearable situations, and yet remain bound by such situations." Instead, she persists in conducting her life—and her one-sided affair with Maurice—according to what she considers romantic decorum, taking as her motto a remark she makes about the character Adolphe: "Even if the despair is total, the control remains. This is very elegant, very important."

In large part, Kitty's social isolation and loneliness stem from her deep-seated view of herself as a foreigner. Though half-English—her mother was the daughter of French and Russian immigrants, and her father was British—Kitty never knew her father and was raised in the French traditions by her grandparents. She therefore feels like an outsider, and in trying too hard to follow her ideal—romantic in essence—of what it means to be British, she misses the reality. As Strawson explained: "Foreignness is fixed in her, preserved by caution and a sense of not knowing the rules. She sees things that the natural native does not see; but she does not understand the country." Moreover, she represses her more natural, expressive characteristics, which emerge in what Richard Eder, reviewing *Providence* in the *Los Angeles Times,* called "her French moments." In these moments, Eder continued, "Kitty becomes more vivid, and the book's tenuous quality gives way to something more lively and touching." But she "pushes these moments back, and this too is touching," as she attempts to substitute for the satisfactions of vehement emotion and fastidiousness what Brookner describes in *Providence* as "an admiration for carelessness, a more powerful because understated charm." But, concluded Eder: "Kitty never

does get hold of this English charm. It eludes her, and in her pursuit of it, she eludes herself."

Kitty's desire to become acculturated and her romantic ideals and expectations come together in her passion for Maurice Bishop, whom she sees as the epitome of all that she does not have: faith in religion and "Providence," secure pride in his heritage, graceful self-confidence, and unquestioning self-love. Maurice, however, does not reciprocate Kitty's feelings. While she cultivates expectations of love, romance, and marriage with Maurice, he disappoints her at every turn, eventually throwing a party to celebrate Kitty's first public lecture, a party at which she anticipates he will reveal their relationship to the other guests but at which he announces instead that his fiancee is one of Kitty's students.

In response to this announcement, Kitty feels cheated, as though she had been playing the game by the wrong rules. "Quite simply," she reflects, "I lacked the information." Of course, Eder observed, "this lack of information is the point of Anita Brookner's novel, and it does well enough to suggest the character and predicaments of its protagonist." But, the critic noted, "it means that we see the other figures through Kitty's eyes, and since they are cloudy with miscalculation, we can't make much of them ourselves." Maurice, for example, critics generally agreed, serves more as an object for Kitty's emotional projections and as a personification of Kitty's inaccurate, idealistic view of Englishness than as a real character. Strawson observed of Maurice: "Anita Brookner renders this exquisite monster with considerable skill. But his principal fictional function seems to be simply to illuminate the nature and extent of Kitty's misapprehension of England." And Michiko Kakutani observed in the *New York Times:* "Glimpsed almost entirely through Kitty's adoring eyes, Maurice remains an elusive character: while we are told that he is charming and mysteriously alluring, he never really demonstrates these attributes, but rather comes across as a good-looking cipher, on whom Kitty can project her fantasies."

Critics cited other effects produced in *Providence* by a narration of circumstances both almost exclusively in terms of Kitty and through her perspective alone. Joyce Kornblatt, who termed *Providence* a "perfectly observed and quietly witty novel," commented in the *Washington Post:* "Because the novel exists almost entirely inside Kitty Maule's obsessional mind, we do not see her story juxtaposed against any larger society." Moreover, Kornblatt continued, "because she does not venture beyond Kitty's unyielding repression, Anita Brookner only describes, never explores [the] deeper issues of personality and character." As a result, the critic explained, "the book's very strength—the vivid creation of Kitty Maule—becomes its limitation. Still, we must praise this novel for its craft: Each expertly paced scene is brought to life through a fastidious accretion of detail, a fine ear for speech, a narrative diction that is always intelligent and often arresting." Strawson concurred, remarking in particular on Kitty's prolonged passages of self-examination: "These episodes are very well conveyed. And Kitty Maule is finely and richly characterized, with her starting, stalling, over-intellectual sensibility, immune to beauty, and her occasional, almost formal lapses into sentimentality." Kakutani, who deemed Brookner "a highly gifted writer," also noted her "sharp eye for the telling detail" and "a graceful, economical way with words" and pronounced Brookner a "master at creating miniaturist portraits of attenuated lives."

In *Look at Me,* Brookner's third novel, her second to appear in the United States, Brookner portrays the life of Frances Hinton, a young Englishwoman who works as a librarian for a medical institute. As such, she catalogs and files pictures of death and disease culled from throughout history and observes the doctors, researchers, and fellow librarians who people the institute's archives. After work, she returns to the hideously furnished apartment left to her by her deceased mother and writes about what she observes during the day. She is drawn out of her solitary life by Nick Fraser, an attractive young doctor at the institute where Frances works, and his wife, Alix, a glamorous, gregarious woman who initiates relationships for the sake of diversion and casts them off when they cease to amuse her. For a short while, Frances is adopted by the Frasers into their intimate circle, and they invite her for dinners, drinks, even weekend trips. They also set her up with Nick's colleague James, a sensitive, newly divorced man with whom Frances shares a chaste romance. As soon as the two strike out on their own, however, their attempts to retain some privacy concerning their relationship anger Alix, who feels excluded. She loses interest in Frances and pairs James socially with a voluptuous, more outgoing, and less discreet friend. Rejected and enraged, Frances turns to writing as a release and begins working on the novel that will be *Look at Me.*

Critics noted that, like Brookner's other two novels, *The Debut* and *Providence, Look at Me* focuses on loneliness or, more specifically, as a *London Times* reviewer who described Brookner as "the poet of loneliness" explained: "All three novels are minutely observed, elegantly written stories about solitary women, tidy, financially independent, lean women, not young but not old either, full of hope and generosity and not yet fatally disappointed." Julia Epstein, writing in the *Washington Post Book World,* deemed *Look at Me* "simultaneously a tragedy of solitude and loss, and a triumph of the sharp-tongued controlling self." She continued: "Brookner's first novel, *The Debut,* marked off some of this territory, but with a sulkier and more tentative hand. In *Look at Me,* Brookner unveils a portrait of the melancholic woman, 'overpowered by her inability to take the world's measure . . .' as she unveils a narrative voice in full sail." Elaine Kendall likewise asserted in the *Los Angeles Times:* "A powerful emotional undertow surges beneath the tranquil surface of this novel, pulling the reader into unsuspected depths of feeling. Told in the first person, 'Look at Me' is a cry from the heart of a talented young Englishwoman inexplicably stranded on the shoals of life." And Duchene observed in her *Times Literary Supplement* review of *Look at Me:* "Since she came to fiction two novels ago, Anita Brookner has shown herself fascinated by the wilder shores of loneliness, and this third novel is a study in the kind of loneliness that is self-induced and self-destructive."

The root of such self-induced loneliness, according to critics reviewing *Look at Me,* lies in Frances's personality: too passive to express her needs or pursue what she wants effectually, Frances is at the mercy of others with more forceful, outgoing temperaments; she relies on them to include her in their plans and accepts their rejection when they tire of her. Yet, beneath her passive exterior, Frances desires company, pleasure, affection, and attention. As Mary Cantwell noted in the *New York Times Book Review:* "Frances is as incapable of impressing her personality upon a room as she is of turning into the life of the party. Still, she would love to be the latter: 'Look at me, look at me' is her continual, silent plea." Cantwell went on to explain: "Frances is . . . cursed with good manners, the kind that impede appetite. For all her need to be noticed, she is not quite hungry enough." Duchene concurred, stating: "Dutifulness and good manners have . . . made any spontaneity impossible for Frances; though she is, as she constantly reminds us, extremely witty and amusing." Nurtured by Alix and Nick, she temporarily sheds some of her crippling reserve, but when Alix turns on her Frances can-

not sustain her newly-found confidence; she swallows her indignation as Alix interferes in her relationship with James and fails to take action in time to save it. Annie Roston remarked in *Harper's,* "One wonders why Frances must be so maddenly ineffectual and so eerily, frustratingly resigned to her lot." Yet, continued Roston: "She's too likable to be depressing." Other critics, however, differed in their assessment of Frances's appeal. Duchene, for instance, concluded: "The ultimate readjustment, for the reader, is having to realize that Frances, with whom initially we were ready to sympathize, is a very disturbing and distasteful character herself, who has met her match in Alix, and been routed." Kakutani, critiquing *Look at Me* in the *New York Times,* noted that if the Frasers "are guilty of using their friends for entertainment and distraction, Frances, too, is revealed as possessing certain predatory impulses." Cantwell similarly remarked: "It would be an error to see 'Look at Me' simply as a novel about a self-conscious young Englishwoman who becomes a writer on the order of, at a guess, Barbara Pym. Instead, it is a horror story about monsters and their victims told in exceptionally elegant prose. It is a great pleasure to read, especially when one considers that Frances, in becoming a writer, may end up the biggest monster of them all."

Noting that in *Look at Me,* as in her other novels, Brookner admittedly writes about characters who share her solitary, bookish lifestyle as well as many of her personality traits, Roston pointed out that "despite its autobiographical aspects *Look at Me* is saved from dissolving into confessional drivel by its tone of quiet detachment." Kakutani, on the other hand, remarked that though Brookner distances herself from Frances, she remains close enough to convey the depth of her feelings. "A fastidious craftsman, Miss Brookner writes in spare, felicitous prose, using the device of a first-person narrator to balance irony and compassion." Considered by Roston a "remarkably fresh novel" that is "both frustrating and engaging," *Look at Me* was deemed by Epstein "a nearly impossible achievement," a novel about emptiness and vacancy, in which Brookner makes Frances "riveting in her ragged self-knowledge, her ability to look in a mirror, see precisely what others see, and know the image to be false." And *London Times* critic Gay Firth deemed *Look at Me* "a novel sufficiently distinguished to make you blink twice at 'Brookner' on the dust jacket. Blinked at once," Firth concluded, "it might be 'Bronte.' "

Brookner's fourth novel *Hotel du lac,* won the 1984 Booker McConnell Prize, Britain's most prestigious literary award. Noted for its humor as well as its astuteness, *Hotel du lac* centers on the "exile" of a thirty-nine-year-old London woman, Edith Hope, in an off-season Swiss hotel. Edith has been sent off to this hotel by her family and friends to "retrieve her serious and hardworking personality" and to wait for the scandal to die down after jilting her fiance on her wedding day. Instead of doing penance for her transgression, however, she spends her time wryly observing the foibles of her fellow hotel guests, becoming involved in their personal lives, writing letters to her married lover, David, and working on her latest novel—Edith resembles British author Virginia Woolf but writes popular romance novels under the "more thrusting name" of Vanessa Wilde.

Edith's novels, unlike Brookner's, propagate what Edith considers "the most potent myth of all," the romantic notion, represented by Aesop's fable of the tortoise and the hare, that slow and steady wins the race. Or that, as in Edith's novels: "It is the mouselike, unassuming girl who gets the hero, while the scornful temptress with whom he has had a stormy affair retreats baffled from the fray, never to return. The tortoise wins every time." On one level, Edith acknowledges that the myth is false, an attempt to comfort tortoises with the hope of reward. She explains to her agent: "In real life, of course, it is the hare who wins. Every time. Look around you. And in any case it is my contention that Aesop was writing for the tortoise market. Axiomatically. . . . Hares have no time to read. They are too busy winning the game. The propaganda goes all the other way, but only because it is the tortoise who is in need of consolation. Like the meek who are going to inherit the earth." Novelist and critic Anne Tyler remarked of this speech in the *New York Times Book Review:* "Bitter words, yes, but they have a certain humorous twist to them. As does this book, come to think of it. For in its own way *Hotel du lac* itself is a 'Tortoise and the Hare' story, and the tortoise does win—in her own way." According to reviewers of *Hotel du lac,* the character's method of winning is rather ambiguous. Despite her publicly avowed lack of illusion, Edith privately cherishes her romantic ideals and longs, like Brookner's other heroines, for the perfect love to rescue her from loneliness and singlehood. She rejects her first fiance for his dullness and, after an affair with a cynical snobbish hotel guest, makes a discovery about the man that leads her to reject his proposal of marriage as well. She is perhaps less idealistic in her view of the world, or at least more humorously so, than Brookner's other heroines, but she is also less crushed by disappointment, less desperate, and so less willing to compromise her ideals by making an unsuitable marriage. She chooses, rather, to go back to the unmarriageable David.

Hotel du lac is, as are Brookner's three earlier novels, about romance and loneliness in the life of a discreet, educated, literary woman with conventional dreams of love and marriage. More specifically, as John Gross remarked in the *New York Times: Hotel du lac* "is a novel about romance, and reality, and the gap between them and the way the need for romance persists in the full knowledge of that gap." According to *Times Literary Supplement* reviewer Barbara Hardy: "The strength of the story lies in its images of loneliness. The quest for the romantic absolute is lonely, the deprived lover is lonely, Edith's mixture of romantic idealism and awareness is lonely." Gross also noted Brookner's concentration on loneliness in *Hotel du lac* and concluded: "In the abstract, it could easily be made to sound like a study in shades of gray. But that would be to take no account of the writing, which is witty and energetic, or of the storytelling, with its cunningly timed disclosures, or of the piercing accuracy of the book's observations." Furthermore, Hardy asserted: "Deprivation and boredom are the norm [among the characters in *Hotel du lac*], but ending up with rather less than half a loaf is not too bad. Making us feel this is the book's best achievement, more interesting and true than the demonstration of Edith's persistent illusion of monogamous, faithful and unique love." Tyler also commented on the outlook set forth in this novel and distinguished it from that of Brookner's previous novels. "The final mood [of Brookner's novels] has always been bleak, even accusatory—a sort of 'Why me, God' that left the reader slightly alienated," Tyler reported. She continued, "But in *Hotel du lac,* Miss Brookner's most absorbing novel, the heroine is more philosophical from the outset, more self-reliant, more conscious that a solitary life is not, after all, an unmitigated tragedy." Gross concurred, concluding, "In her three earlier novels . . . Brookner staked out a distinctive territory; now she has enlarged its boundaries and made it clear that she is one of the finest novelists of her generation."

In her fifth novel, *Family and Friends,* Brookner further expanded that territory, focusing her attention on an entire family rather than on one individual. This family, the Dorns, moved to London between the World Wars but has retained many of the traditions of its European background, largely due to the influ-

ence that Sofka Dorn, a widow of Jewish-European origin, exercises over her children, Frederick, Alfred, Betty, and Mimi. Two of the children, Frederick and Betty, rebel against tradition and family duties yet attain unexpectedly settled, if vacuous, lives. Frederick, an irresponsible playboy, eventually marries a wealthy heiress and manages her resort hotel, and Betty, who runs away to Paris to become a dancer, ends up as an overweight, poolside-lounging, Hollywood producer's wife. The other two children, Alfred and Mimi, submit to the will of their mother and perpetuate the family traditions. Alfred, a serious young man, sets aside his favored literature and takes over the family business. Mimi, a modest, considerate, and virtuous young woman, suffers a humiliating adolescent heartbreak, then marries a much older man and, after her mother's death, replaces Sofka as the family matriarch.

According to critics, in writing about this family, Brookner has varied her usual "tortoise and the hare" theme by enlarging her cast of main characters and, with this fuller perspective, has qualified its previously absolute definitions of winning and losing. She is also more concerned with relationships other than romances. As Kakutani observed in the *New York Times:* "Now, with her latest novel, *Family and Friends,* Miss Brookner seems to be making a bid to open out her canvas: Her subject is not one waif-like woman, but an entire family; her focus, not simply the consequences of romantic love, but also the effects of the enduring, changing bonds between parents and their children, sisters and their brothers." Jonathan Yardley concurred in the *Washington Post Book World* and remarked: "Admirers of Anita Brookner's four previous novels will be both gratified and startled by *Family and Friends.* Gratified, that is, because Brookner's salient characteristics are once again much in evidence. But startled, too, for without writing a page more than she has in the past, Brookner has nonetheless broadened her territory immensely." According to Frank Kermode, critiquing *Family and Friends* in the *London Review of Books,* "The book gives the story of [the Dorns'] lives, recounting in a newly hectic mode and with notable modifications and triumph of the hare over the tortoise, of the free ones over the disappointed." But, the critic continued, "This time the triumph is hollow and the disappointment far from unmitigated." Concluded Kermode, "In all sorts of ways the texture of this book is richer (it is less an extended nouvelle than a shrunk saga) and a great advance, I think, on *Hotel du lac.*"

Critics noted still another distinction between Brookner's first four novels and *Family and Friends.* While her earlier novels are set in modern times, her fifth novel is set in the past, beginning in the 1930s. Kakutani explained, "Writing in a careful, angled prose, Miss Brookner conjures up the vanished world that a distinguished European family inhabited in London; and she delineates for us, too, the heavy sense of familial duty and social obligation . . . in that unliberated age." Caryn James, writing in the *New York Times Book Review,* observed: "In four previous novels we encounter women whose independence is a mask for stoicism, whose stoicism muffles an impulse to wail 'Poor, lonely me.' So it is a relief that in 'Family and Friends' the author has sent her characters back to the past, where most Anita Brookner people might feel more comfortable." James elaborated this view by commenting: "The Dorns might be ancestors of more familiar Brookner characters; for while the author looks backward, she focuses on the breakdown of the old social code and the forces that have led to her contemporary heroines' oddly dated notions of love and decorum."

One method that Brookner uses to study the past as embodied by the Dorns is examining family photographs, particularly formal wedding pictures. Novelist A. N. Wilson found this technique effective, remarking in his *Times Literary Supplement* review of *Family and Friends,* "Anita Brookner has chosen the medium of photography to help her, and the artifice works well." Kermode noted that *Family and Friends* "starts with a wedding photograph and ends with one, those frozen frames being interrogated and explained by an inquisitive knowing narrator." Brookner's narration, however, departs from these photographs, moving, as Kermode observed, "from static poses to the intricacies of lifelike movement and plot." Kakutani likewise reported that, "using her delicate sense of gesture and detail to give the reader a sense of these characters' daily lives, Miss Brookner swiftly sketches in the changes that will overtake the family." In particular, as Wilson remarked: "The way that the four children respond to [Sofka's] matriarchal tyranny is portrayed with exquisite understatement and a merciless irony which leaves the reader's own affection for Sofka quite unscathed." Moreover, "as the story proceeds," James observed, "each character's loss of innocence makes him or her affecting; and in their disillusionment, the author captures that of a generation and a culture." Yardley, on the other hand, commented, "*Family and Friends* may be in some measure about a family coming apart, but it is also about the loyalties that make it endure." In examining these familial bonds, Yardley concluded, "Brookner has written a novel more expansive and inclusive than any of its four predecessors, and she displays ample reserves of a quality that can only be called kindliness. *Family and Friends* is a fine and heartening book."

In her sixth novel, *A Misalliance,* Brookner once more focuses on a repressed, intellectual woman, a type familiar from the author's earlier novels. Blanche, spurned by her husband of twenty years in favor of a more lively woman named Mousie, spends her time in museums meditating on the two contrasting archetypes of woman she sees in paintings: pleasure-loving nymphs of ancient mythology and dutiful saints who personify emotional martyrdom. In order to create the "misalliance" of the title, Brookner brings together three females who personify these discordant images, as Victoria Glendinning explained in the London *Times.* The doleful Blanche becomes the friend of an "irresponsible" young mother whose "mute and wary child appeals strongly to Blanche"; the three form a sort of love triangle in which two unhappy saints, one middle-aged and one only three years old, are held apart by a nymph. Critics found that the novel maintained Brookner's status as a master of prose. Though wishing the book's characters were more complex, Carole Corbeil in the Toronto *Globe and Mail* praised Brookner for writing "lucidly and stylishly." According to Victoria Glendinning the author is "a major stylist" who writes with "startling grace and confidence." And in a display of satisfaction with Brookner's ideas and her skill at expressing them, Patricia Craig, in her *Times Literary Supplement* review, called *A Misalliance* "a civilized look at contemporary disorder, and a wonderfully poised and pointed examination of the wrong turning."

Brookner's next three works of fiction brought her continued acclaim. *A Friend From England,* for instance, was judged a carefully crafted examination of English sensibilities. *Latecomers,* published in 1988 and ranked by critics among the author's most poignant novels, concerns two men who were orphaned during the Holocaust. While each of the characters attempts to reconcile himself to the past in a different way, both rely heavily on the strength and constancy of familial relationships to establish a place for themselves in the present. The 1989 novel *Lewis Percy,* perhaps less inspired than some of its predecessors, traces an inhibited and unhappily married young man's quest for tranquillity.

Brookner's novels have been written, like *The Debut,* in the summer and written easily with, as Brookner commented in *Saturday Review,* "no drafts, no fetishes, no false starts" as if they had been "encoded in the unconscious." Describing the process of writing as "painful rather than difficult," Brookner elaborated: "You never know what you will learn until you start writing. Then you discover truths you didn't know existed. These books are accidents of the unconscious. It's like dredging, really, seeing if you can keep it going." Furthermore, she told *Publishers Weekly:* "It sounds disingenuous to say this, but when I've written a novel, it's gone, it's left me, it's somebody else's. I never reread them. I can't remember the names of the characters. It's largely a sort of unconscious process. Having said that, I must admit that if it's an unconscious process, then a lot of me must be in them. Yes—aspirations, longings, desires. Sadnesses, too. I don't think I give hostages to fortune in admitting that much."

Critics, however, generally note more explicit similarities between Brookner's life and the lives of her characters. Caroline Moorehead remarked in the London *Times,* "More than most novelists, Anita Brookner seems to invite the suggestion that she is writing not only about herself but about a way of life she knows, understands and does not greatly care for." And Sheila Hale, writing in *Saturday Review,* deemed Brookner "one of the few mature 'narcissistic' novelists to have portrayed her inner life so vividly." Continued Hale: "Of course Anita Brookner's novels are not crudely autobiographical; they are far more devastatingly self-analytical than any straightforward autobiography. Discreet to a fault in her relationships with other people, the woman at their center has revealed herself to her readers with an obsessive honesty that is not rendered less painful by her wit and intelligence."

Asked by Amanda Smith of *Publishers Weekly* whether love is "indeed her subject, as some reviewers have suggested," Brookner responded: "I think that, and something more. . . . How to achieve love, how to be worthy of love, how to conduct love. These are serious matters. It is a messy business. The rules are really crude. The rules are: Who dares, wins. This is bad news for people who don't dare and who see others win. That's the central problem, I think. I think it's the matter nobody gets completely right." Brookner added: "I know about women. . . . I know about their inner lives. I hate the way that certain women get ahead. I'm interested in the reasons for failure. It looks very small the way I write it, but it can concern everybody—everybody is, I should think, beset by worries about how to live their lives properly and yet how to achieve some satisfaction out of them. It's the conflict between the moral sense and the desire to win." Concluded Brookner of her novels: "They've been called very depressing. But anyone who has had unhappy experiences won't find them depressing. It's very unrealistic to find them depressing. Life is depressing if you're frightened of it. The thing is not to be too frightened."

BIOGRAPHICAL/CRITICAL SOURCES:

BOOKS

Brookner, Anita, *Hotel du lac,* Pantheon, 1984.
Contemporary Literary Criticism, Gale, Volume 32, 1985, Volume 34, 1985, Volume 51, 1989.

PERIODICALS

Atlantic Monthly, March, 1985.
Chicago Tribune, March 30, 1989, March 8, 1990.
Globe and Mail (Toronto), November 8, 1986, April 7, 1990.
Harper's, April, 1981, July, 1983.
London Review of Books, September 6, 1984, September 5, 1985.

Los Angeles Times, March 18, 1981, May 3, 1983, February 8, 1984, December 25, 1989.

Los Angeles Times Book Review, March 25, 1990.

Ms., June, 1985.

New Republic, May 30, 1981

New Statesman, May 22, 1981, September 7, 1984.

New Yorker, March 23, 1981, April 9, 1984, February 18, 1985.

New York Review of Books, January 31, 1985.

New York Times, July 4, 1983, February 1, 1984, January 22, 1985, October 12, 1985, February 24, 1989, February 20, 1990, April 6, 1990.

New York Times Book Review, December 3, 1972, March 29, 1981, May 22, 1983, March 18, 1984, February 3, 1985, April 28, 1985, November 10, 1985, March 20, 1988, April 2, 1989, March 11, 1990.

Publishers Weekly, September 6, 1985.

Saturday Review, March/April, 1985, May/June, 1985.

Time, October 28, 1985.

Times (London), March 21, 1983, March 31, 1983, September 6, 1984, October 20, 1984, August 21, 1986.

Times Literary Supplement, November 26, 1971, January 9, 1981, May 29, 1981, May 28, 1982, March 25, 1983, September 14, 1984, April 26, 1985, September 6, 1985, August 29, 1986, August 21, 1987, August 12, 1988, August 25, 1989.

Village Voice. July 5, 1983.

Vogue, February, 1985.

Washington Post, April 28, 1981, March 9, 1984.

Washington Post Book World, July 24, 1983, October 13, 1985, February 28, 1988, February 18, 1990.

*   *   *

BROOKS, Cleanth 1906-

PERSONAL: Born October 16, 1906, in Murray, KY; son of Cleanth (a minister) and Bessie Lee (Witherspoon) Brooks; married Edith Amy Blanchard, September 12, 1934 (died, October, 1986). *Education:* Vanderbilt University, B.A., 1928; Tulane University, M.A., 1929; Oxford University, Rhodes scholar, 1929-32, B.A. (with honors), 1931, B.Litt., 1932. *Politics:* Independent Democrat. *Religion:* Episcopalian.

ADDRESSES: Home—70 Ogden St., New Haven, CT 06511.

CAREER: Louisiana State University, Baton Rouge, 1932-47, began as lecturer, became professor of English, visiting professor, 1970 and 1974; Yale University, New Haven, CT, professor of English, 1947-60, Gray Professor of Rhetoric, 1960-75, professor emeritus, 1975—. Visiting professor of English at University of Texas, summer, 1941, University of Michigan, summer, 1942, University of Chicago, 1945-46, Kenyon School of English, summer, 1948 (fellow, 1948—), University of Southern California, 1953, Breadloaf School of English, 1963, University of South Carolina, 1975, Tulane University, 1976, University of North Carolina, 1977 and 1979, and University of Tennessee, 1978 and 1980; research professor with Bostick Foundation, 1975; Lamar Lecturer, 1984; Jefferson Lecturer, 1985. Member of advisory committee for Boswell Papers, 1950; Library of Congress, fellow, 1953-63, member of council of scholars, 1984-87; American Embassy, London, England, cultural attache, 1964-66; National Humanities Center, fellow, 1980-81.

MEMBER: Modern Language Association of America, American Academy of Arts and Sciences, National Institute of Arts and Letters, American Philosophical Society, American Association of University Professors, Royal Society of Literature, Phi Beta Kappa, Yale Club (New York), Athenaeum, Savile (both London).

AWARDS, HONORS: Guggenheim fellow, 1953 and 1960; senior fellow, National Endowment for the Humanities, 1975; Explicator Award, c. 1980, for *William Faulkner: Toward Yoknapatawpha and Beyond;* D.Litt. from Upsala College, 1963, University of Kentucky, 1963, University of Exeter, 1966, Washington and Lee University, 1968, Tulane University, 1969, University of the South, 1975, and Newberry College, 1979; L.H.D. from University of St. Louis, 1958, Centenary College, 1972, Oglethorpe University, 1976, St. Peter's College, 1978, Lehigh University, 1980, Millsaps College, 1983, University of New Haven, 1984, and University of South Carolina, 1984.

WRITINGS:

EDITOR

(With others) *An Approach to Literature,* Louisiana State University Press, 1936, 5th edition, Prentice-Hall, 1975.

(Editor with Robert Penn Warren, and coauthor) *Understanding Poetry,* Holt, 1938, 4th edition, 1975, transcript of tape recording to accompany 3rd edition entitled *Conversations on the Craft of Poetry: Cleanth Brooks and Robert Penn Warren, with Robert Frost, John Crowe Ransom, Robert Lowell, and Theodore Roethke,* Holt, 1961.

(With Warren) *Understanding Fiction,* F. S. Crofts, 1943, 3rd edition, Prentice-Hall, 1979, abridged edition published as *The Scope of Fiction,* 1960.

(General editor with A. F. Falconer and David Nichol Smith) *The Percy Letters,* 1944-88, volumes 1-6, Louisiana State University Press, volumes 7-9, Yale University Press; editor of Volume 2: *The Correspondence of Thomas Percy and Richard Farmer* and Volume 7: *The Correspondence of Thomas Percy and William Shenstone.*

(With Robert Heilman) *Understanding Drama,* Holt, 1945.

The Poems of John Milton (1645 edition), Harcourt, 1951.

(With Warren) *An Anthology of Stories from the "Southern Review,"* Louisiana State University Press, 1953.

Tragic Themes in Western Literature: Seven Essays by Bernard Knox [and Others], Yale University Press, 1956.

(With Warren and R. W. B. Lewis) *American Literature: The Makers and the Making,* two volumes, St. Martin's, 1973, paperbound edition published in four volumes, 1974.

Southern Review, managing editor with Robert Penn Warren, 1935-41, editor with Warren, 1941-42; member of advisory board, *Kenyon Review,* 1942-60.

OTHER

The Relation of the Alabama-Georgia Dialect to the Provincial Dialects of Great Britain, Louisiana State University Press, 1935.

Modern Poetry and the Tradition, University of North Carolina Press, 1939.

The Well Wrought Urn, Reynal & Hitchcock, 1947, Harcourt, 1956.

(With Warren) *Modern Rhetoric,* Harcourt, 1949, 4th edition, 1979, abridged edition, 1961.

(With Warren) *Fundamentals of Good Writing,* Harcourt, 1950.

(Contributor) *Humanities: An Appraisal,* University of Wisconsin Press, 1950.

(With William Wimsatt) *Literary Criticism: A Short History,* Knopf, 1957.

Metaphor and the Function of Criticism, Institute for Religious and Social Studies, c. 1957.

The Hidden God: Studies in Hemingway, Faulkner, Yeats, Eliot and Warren, Yale University Press, 1963.

William Faulkner: The Yoknapatawpha Country, Yale University Press, 1963.

A Shaping Joy: Studies in the Writer's Craft, Harcourt, 1972.

William Faulkner: Toward Yoknapatawpha and Beyond, Yale University Press, 1978.

(Contributor) Louis D. Dollarhide and Ann J. Abodie, editors, *Eudora Welty: A Form of Thanks,* University Press of Mississippi, 1979.

Cleanth Brooks at the United States Air Force Academy, April 11-12, 1978 (lectures), edited by James A. Grimshaw, Jr., Department of English, U.S. Air Force Academy, 1980.

William Faulkner: First Encounters, Yale University Press, 1983.

The Language of the American South, University of Georgia Press, 1985.

On the Prejudices, Predilections, and Firm Beliefs of William Faulkner, Louisiana State University Press, 1987.

Author of recorded lectures on works by William Faulkner. Contributor of articles and reviews to literary journals.

SIDELIGHTS: Maxwell Geismar introduces Cleanth Brooks as "a brilliant critic of literary technique and rhetoric, particularly in modern verse, and . . . a leading figure in the formalist school of New Critics." Considering Brooks's development as a critic, John Paul Pritchard noted that "Brooks sounded his first note for metaphor as the prime characteristic of poetry in 1935." Pritchard observed that Brooks and Robert Penn Warren, in *Understanding Poetry* (1938), asserted that "the poem . . . must be grasped as a literary object before it can be otherwise considered. . . . A poem proves itself by its effect, and its effect arises not out of the things used but from the poet's use of them. . . . Verse controls words and entices the reader's imagination by its recurrent rhythms to the willing temporary suspension of disbelief."

Central to Brooks's critical position is his contention that a poem cannot be paraphrased without essential loss. Pritchard writes: "In Brooks's eyes the basic critical ill is the tendency to confuse comment on the poem with its essential core. Critics are prone to restate the poem in a prose paraphrase as a step toward elucidating it. Such a procedure, he declares, presumes the paraphrasable part of the poem to be its essential part. But the act splits the poem, which is by nature a whole, into form and content. . . . It totally ignores the poetic function of metaphor and meter."

In a discussion of *The Well Wrought Urn* (1947), Rene Wellek wrote: "Brooks attacks [as] the 'heresy of paraphrase,' all attempts to reduce the poem to its prose content, and he has defended a well defined absolutism: the need of judgement against the flaccid surrender to relativism and historicism. But . . . Brooks has taken special pains to demonstrate that his absolutism of values is not incompatible with a proper regard for history." Speaking of Brooks's critical approach, Wellek notes: "Brooks analyzes poems as structures of opposites, tensions, paradoxes, and ironies with unparalleled skill. Paradox and irony are terms used by him very broadly. Irony is not the opposite of an overt statement, but [according to Brooks] 'a general term for the kind of qualification which the various elements in a context receive from the context.' " In a later discussion of Brooks's approach, Wellek explains: "Irony for Brooks indicates the recognition of incongruities, the ambiguity, the reconciliation of opposites which Brooks finds in all good, that is, complex poetry. Poetry must be ironic in the sense of being able to withstand ironic contemplation."

John Crowe Ransom, a poet and himself a critic, was generally conceded to have christened Brooks and others of similar critical opinion the "New Critics." In 1955 Ransom wrote: "It seems to me that Brooks just now is probably the most forceful and influential critic of poetry that we have. But this does not imply that his authority is universally accepted, for it has turned out even better than that. Where he does not gain assent, he arouses protest and countercriticism. His tone toward other critics is that of an independent, and his tone toward scholars who are occasional critics is cool. This is why a new book by Brooks is a public service."

Ransom goes on to say: "Of course there will be readers who will go all the way with Brooks as if under a spell. I believe the peculiar fascination of his view of poetry is due to its being a kind of modern version of the ancient doctrine of divine inspiration or frenzy. For Brooks, the poem exists in its metaphors. The rest of it he does not particularly remark. He goes straight to the metaphors, thinking it is they which work the miracle that is poetry; and naturally he elects for special notice the most unlikely ones. Hence paradox and irony, of which he is so fond."

In later years, Brooks's critical study extended from the examination of poetry to the study of the novels of William Faulkner. James B. Meriwether wrote of Brooks's *William Faulkner: The Yoknapatawpha Country* (1963): "Brooks's emphasis is literary, not sociological; but his fine synthesis of the major elements in the culture upon which most of Faulkner's best fiction draws is a valuable corrective to studies which have distorted that fiction through a misapprehension of its social and historical background." Meriwether goes on to say that Brooks's book on Faulkner "is one of the best critical studies of any American novelist, and perhaps the most important single critical study yet made of any American novelist of this century."

BIOGRAPHICAL/CRITICAL SOURCES:

BOOKS

Bryher, Jackson R., editor, *Sixteen Modern American Authors,* Norton, 1973.

Contemporary Literary Criticism, Volume 24, Gale, 1983.

Dictionary of Literary Biography, Volume 63: *Modern American Critics, 1920-1955,* Gale, 1988.

Krieger, Murray, *The New Apologists for Poetry,* University of Minnesota Press, 1956.

Poems and Essays, Vintage, 1955.

Pritchard, John Paul, *Criticism in America,* University of Oklahoma Press, 1956.

Simpson, Lewis P., editor, *The Possibilities of Order: Cleanth Brooks and His Work,* Louisiana State University Press, 1975.

Wellek, Rene, *Concepts of Criticism,* Yale University Press, 1963.

Wellek, Rene, *Discriminations,* Yale University Press, 1970.

PERIODICALS

Globe and Mail (Toronto), February 25, 1984.

Los Angeles Times, November 18, 1983.

New York Herald Tribune Books, July 28, 1963.

New York Review of Books, January 9, 1964, May 7, 1987.

New York Times Book Review, December 10, 1972, May 21, 1978, November 13, 1983.

Southern Review, winter, 1974.

Times Literary Supplement, March 30, 1984.

Washington Post, August 31, 1983.

*   *   *

BROOKS, George
   See BAUM, L(yman) Frank

*   *   *

BROOKS, Gwendolyn   1917-

PERSONAL: Born June 7, 1917, in Topeka, Kan.; daughter of David Anderson and Keziah Corinne (Wims) Brooks; married Henry Lowington Blakely, September 17, 1939; children: Henry Lowington, III, Nora. *Education:* Graduate of Wilson Junior College, 1936.

ADDRESSES: Home—7428 South Evans Ave., Chicago, Ill. 60619.

CAREER: Poet and novelist. Publicity director, NAACP Youth Council, Chicago, Ill., 1937-38. Taught poetry at numerous colleges and universities, including Columbia College, Elmhurst College, Northeastern Illinois State College (now Northwestern Illinois University), and University of Wisconsin—Madison, 1969; Distinguished Professor of the Arts, City College of the City University of New York, 1971. Member, Illinois Arts Council.

MEMBER: American Academy of Arts and Letters, National Institute of Arts and Letters, Society of Midland Authors (Chicago).

AWARDS, HONORS: Named one of ten women of the year, *Mademoiselle* magazine, 1945; National Institute of Arts and Letters grant in literature, 1946; American Academy of Arts and Letters award for creative writing, 1946; Guggenheim fellowships, 1946 and 1947; Eunice Tietjens Memorial Prize, *Poetry* magazine, 1949; Pulitzer Prize in poetry, 1950, for *Annie Allen;* Robert F. Ferguson Memorial Award, Friends of Literature, 1964, for *Selected Poems;* Thormod Monsen Literature Award, 1964; Anisfield-Wolf Award, 1968, for *In the Mecca;* named Poet Laureate of Illinois, 1968; Black Academy of Arts and Letters Award, 1971, for outstanding achievement in letters; Shelley Memorial Award, 1976; Poetry Consultant to the Library of Congress, 1985-86; forty-nine honorary degrees from universities and colleges, including Columbia College, 1964, Lake Forest College, 1965, and Brown University, 1974.

WRITINGS:

POETRY

A Street in Bronzeville (also see below), Harper, 1945.
Annie Allen (also see below), Harper, 1949, reprinted, Greenwood Press, 1972.
The Bean Eaters (also see below), Harper, 1960.
In the Time of Detachment, In the Time of Cold, Civil War Centennial Commission of Illinois, 1965.
In the Mecca (also see below), Harper, 1968.
For Illinois 1968: A Sesquicentennial Poem, Harper, 1968.
Riot (also see below), Broadside Press, 1969.
Family Pictures (also see below), Broadside Press, 1970.
Aloneness, Broadside Press, 1971.
Aurora, Broadside Press, 1972.
Beckonings, Broadside Press, 1975.
Primer for Blacks, Black Position Press, 1980.
To Disembark, Third World Press, 1981.
Black Love, Brooks Press, 1982.
Mayor Harold Washington [and] *Chicago, The I Will City,* Brooks Press, 1983.

The Near Johannesburg Bay, and Other Poems, The David Co., 1987.

Also author of *A Catch of Shy Fish,* 1963.

JUVENILE

Bronzeville Boys and Girls (poems), Harper, 1956.
The Tiger Who Wore White Gloves: Or You Are What You Are, Third World Press, 1974, reissued, 1987.

FICTION

Maud Martha (novel; also see below), Harper, 1953, reprinted, The David Co., 1987.
(Contributor) Herbert Hill, editor, *Soon One Morning: New Writing by American Negroes, 1940-1962* (contains the short story "The Life of Lincoln West"), Knopf, 1963, published in England as *Black Voices,* Elek, 1964.
(Contributor) Langston Hughes, editor, *The Best Short Stories by Negro Writers: An Anthology from 1899 to the Present,* Little, Brown, 1967.

COLLECTED WORKS

Selected Poems, Harper, 1963.
The World of Gwendolyn Brooks (contains *A Street in Bronzeville, Annie Allen, Maud Martha, The Bean Eaters,* and *In the Mecca*), Harper, 1971.
Blacks (includes *A Street in Bronzeville, Annie Allen, The Bean Eaters, Maud Martha, A Catch of Shy Fish, Riot, In the Mecca,* and most of *Family Pictures*), The David Co., 1987.

OTHER

(Author of foreword) Langston Hughes, editor, *New Negro Poets USA,* Indiana University Press, 1964.
(With others) *A Portion of that Field: The Centennial of the Burial of Lincoln,* University of Illinois Press, 1967.
(Editor) *A Broadside Treasury,* (poems), Broadside Press, 1971.
(Editor) *Jump Bad: A New Chicago Anthology,* Broadside Press, 1971.
Report from Part One: An Autobiography, Broadside Press, 1972.
(Author of introduction) Arnold Adoff, editor, *The Poetry of Black America: Anthology of the Twentieth Century,* Harper, 1973.
(With Keorapetse Kgositsile, Haki R. Madhubuti, and Dudley Randall) *A Capsule Course in Black Poetry Writing,* Broadside Press, 1975.
Young Poet's Primer (writing manual), Brooks Press, 1981.
Very Young Poets (writing manual), Brooks Press, 1983.

Also author of broadsides *The Wall* and *We Real Cool,* for Broadside Press, and *I See Chicago,* 1964. Contributor of poems and articles to *Ebony, McCall's, Nation, Poetry,* and other periodicals. Contributor of reviews to Chicago *Sun-Times,* Chicago *Daily News,* and *New York Herald Tribune.*

WORK IN PROGRESS: A sequel to *Maud Martha; Winnie,* poems interpreting Winnie Mandela of South Africa.

SIDELIGHTS: In 1950, Gwendolyn Brooks, a highly regarded poet, became the first black author to win the Pulitzer Prize. Her poems from this period, specifically *A Street in Bronzeville* and *Annie Allen,* were "devoted to small, carefully cerebrated, terse portraits of the Black urban poor," Richard K. Barksdale comments in *Modern Black Poets: A Collection of Critical Essays.* Jeanne-Marie A. Miller calls this "city-folk poetry" and describes Brooks's characters as "unheroic black people who fled the land for the city only to discover that there is little difference between the world of the North and the world of the South. One learns from them," Miller continues in the *Journal of Negro Education,* "their dismal joys and their human griefs and pain." Audiences in Chicago, inmates in prisons around the country, and students of all ages have found her poems accessible and relevant. Haki Madhubuti, cited in Jacqueline Trescott's *Washington Post* article on Brooks, points out that Brooks "has, more than any other nationally acclaimed writer, remained in touch with the community she writes about. She lives in the core of Chicago's black community. . . . She is her work." In addition, notes Toni Cade Bambara in the *New York Times Book Review,* Brooks "is known for her technical artistry, having worked her word sorcery in forms as disparate as Italian terza rima and the blues. She has been applauded for revelations of the African experience in America, particularly her sensitive portraits of black women."

Though best known for her poetry, in the 1950s, Brooks published her first novel. *Maud Martha* presents vignettes from a ghetto woman's life in short chapters, says Harry B. Shaw in *Gwendolyn Brooks.* It is "a story of a woman with doubts about herself and where and how she fits into the world. Maud's concern is not so much that she is inferior but that she is perceived as being ugly." Eventually, she takes a stand for her own dignity by turning her back on a patronizing, racist store clerk. "The book is . . . about the triumph of the lowly," comments Shaw. "[Brooks] shows what they go through and exposes the shallowness of the popular, beautiful white people with 'good' hair. One way of looking at the book, then, is as a war with . . . people's concepts of beauty." Its other themes include "the importance of spiritual and physical death," disillusionment with a marriage that amounts to "a step down" in living conditions, and the discovery "that even through disillusionment and spiritual death life will prevail," Shaw maintains. Other reviewers feel that Brooks is more effective when treating the same themes in her poetry, but David Littlejohn, writing in *Black on White: A Critical Survey of Writing by American Negroes,* feels the novel "is a striking human experiment, as exquisitely written . . . as any of Gwendolyn Brook's poetry in verse. . . . It is a powerful, beautiful dagger of a book, as generous as it can possibly be. It teaches more, more quickly, more lastingly, than a thousand pages of protest." In a *Black World* review, Annette Oliver Shands appreciates the way in which *Maud Martha* differs from the works of other early black writers: "Miss Brooks does not specify traits, niceties or assets for members of the Black community to acquire in order to attain their just rights. . . . So, this is not a novel to inspire social advancement on the part of fellow Blacks. Nor does it say *be poor, Black and happy.* The message is to accept the challenge of being human and to assert humanness with urgency."

Although, as Martha Liebrum notes in the *Houston Post,* Brooks "wrote about being black before being black was beautiful," in retrospect her poems have been described as sophisticated, intellectual, and European, or "conditioned" by the established literary tradition. Like her early favorites Emily Dickinson, John Keats, and Percy Bysshe Shelley, Brooks expresses in poetry her love of "the wonders language can achieve," as she told Claudia Tate in an interview for *Black Women Writers at Work.* Barksdale states that by not directly emphasizing any "rhetorical involvement with causes, racial or otherwise," Brooks was merely reflecting "the literary mood of the late 1940's." He suggests that there was little reason for Brooks to confront the problems of racism on a large scale since, in her work, "each character, so neatly and precisely presented, is a racial protest in itself and a symbol of some sharply etched human dilemma."

However, Brooks's later poems show a marked change in tone and content. Just as her first poems reflected the mood of their era, her later works mirror their age by displaying what *National Observer* contributor Bruce Cook calls "an intense awareness of the problems of color and justice." Bambara comments that, at the age of fifty "something happened [to Brooks], a something most certainly in evidence in 'In the Mecca' (1968) and subsequent works—a new movement and energy, intensity, richness, power of statement and a new stripped lean, compressed style. A change of style prompted by a change of mind."

"Though some of her work in the early 1960s had a terse abbreviated style, her conversion to direct political expression happened rapidly after a gathering of black writers at Fisk University in 1967," Trescott reports. Brooks told Tate, "They seemed proud and so committed to their own people. . . . The poets among them felt that black poets should write as blacks, about blacks, and address themselves *to* blacks." If many of her earlier poems had fulfilled this aim, it was not due to conscious intent, she said; but from this time forward, Brooks has thought of herself as an African who has determined not to compromise social comment for the sake of technical proficiency.

Although *In the Mecca* and later works are characterized as tougher and possess what a reviewer for the *Virginia Quarterly Review* describes as "raw power and roughness," critics are quick to indicate that these poems are neither bitter nor vengeful. Instead, according to Cook, they are more "about bitterness" than bitter in themselves. *Dictionary of Literary Biography* essayist Charles Israel suggests that *In the Mecca*'s title poem, for example, shows "a deepening of Brooks's concern with social problems." A mother has lost a small daughter in the block-long ghetto tenement, the Mecca; the long poem traces her steps through the building, revealing her neighbors to be indifferent, or insulated by their own personal obsessions. The mother finds her little girl, who "never learned that black is not beloved," who "Was royalty when poised, / sly, at the A and P's fly-open door," under a Jamaican resident's cot, murdered. The *Virginia Quarterly Review* contributor compares the poem's impact to that of Richard Wright's fiction. R. Baxter Miller, writing in *Black American Poets Between Worlds, 1940-1960,* comments, "*In the Mecca* is a most complex and intriguing book; it seeks to balance the sordid realities of urban life with an imaginative process of reconciliation and redemption." Other poems in the book, occasioned by the death of Malcolm X, or the dedication of a mural of black heroes painted on a Chicago slum building, express the poet's commitment to her people's awareness of themselves as a political as well as a cultural entity.

Her interest in encouraging young blacks to assist and appreciate fledgling black publishing companies led her to leave Harper & Row. In the seventies, she chose Dudley Randall's Broadside Press to publish her poetry (*Riot, Family Pictures, Aloneness, Aurura,* and *Beckonings*) and *Report from Part One,* the first volume of her autobiography. She edited two collections of poetry—*A Broadside Treasury* and *Jump Bad: A New Chicago Anthology*—for the Detroit-based press. The Chicago-based Third World Press, run by Haki R. Madhubuti (formerly Don L. Lee, one of the young poets she had met during the sixties), has also brought two Brooks titles into print. She does not regret having given her support to small publishers who dedicated themselves to the needs of the black community. Brooks was the first writer to read in Broadside's Poet's Theatre Series when it began, and was also the first poet to read in the second opening of the series when the press revived under new ownership in 1988.

Riot, Family Pictures, Beckonings, and other books brought out by black publishers were given brief notice by critics of the literary establishment who "did not wish to encourage Black publishers," said Brooks. Some were disturbed by the political content of these poems. *Riot,* in particular, in which Brooks is the spokesman for the "HEALTHY REBELLION" going on then, as she calls it, was accused of "celebrating violence" by L. L. Shapiro in a *School Library Journal* review. Key poems from these books, later collected in *To Disembark,* call blacks to "work together toward their own REAL emancipation," Brooks indicated. Even so, "the strength here is not in declamation but in [the poet's] genius for psychological insight," claims J. A. Lipari in the *Library Journal.* Addison Gayle points out that the softer poems of this period—the ones asking for stronger interpersonal bonds among black Americans—are no less political: "To espouse and exult in a Black identity, outside the psychic boundaries of white Americans, was to threaten. . . . To advocate and demand love between one Black and another was to begin a new chapter in American history. Taken together, the acknowledgment of a common racial identity among Blacks throughout the world and the suggestion of a love based upon the brotherhood and sisterhood of the oppressed were meant to transform Blacks in America from a minority to a majority, from world victims to, to use Madhubuti's phrase, 'world makers.'"

In the same essay, printed in *Black Women Writers (1950-1980): A Critical Evaluation,* Gayle defends *Riot* and the later books, naming them an important source of inspiration to a rising generation: "It may well be . . . that the function of poetry is not so much to save us from oppression nor from Auschwitz, but to give us the strength to face them, to help us stare down the lynch mob, walk boldly in front of the firing squad. It is just such awareness that the poetry of Gwendolyn Brooks has given us, this that she and those whom she taught/learned from have accomplished for us all. They have told us that for Black Americans there are no havens, that in the eyes of other Americans we are, each and every one of us, rioters. . . . These are dangerous times for Black people. The sensitive Black poet realizes that fact, but far from despairing, picks up his pen, . . . and echoes Gwendolyn Brooks: 'My aim . . . is to write poems that will somehow successfully "call" . . . all black people . . . in gutters, in schools, offices, factories, prisons, the consulate; I wish to teach black people in pulpits, black people in mines, on farms, on thrones.'" Brooks pointed out "a serious error" in this quote; she wants to "reach" people, not "teach" them. She added, "The times for Black people—when*ever* in the clutches of white *manipulation,* have ALWAYS been dangerous." She also advised young poets, "Walking in front of a firing squad is *crazy.* Your effort should be in preventing the *formation* of a firing squad."

The poet's search "for an *expression* relevant to all manner of blacks," as she described her change in focus to Tate, did not alter her mastery of her craft. "While quoting approvingly Ron Karenga's observation that 'the fact that we are black is our ultimate reality,' blackness did not, to her, require simplification of language, symbol, or moral perception," notes C. W. E. Bigsby in *The Second Black Renaissance: Essays in Black Literature.* It did include "the possibility of communicating directly to those in the black community." In the bars and on the street corners were an audience not likely to "go into a bookstore" to buy poetry by anyone, she told George Stavros in a *Contemporary Literature* interview reprinted in *Report from Part One: An Autobiography.* And in the late sixties, Brooks reported, "some of those folks DID" enter bookstores to buy poetry and read it "standing up." To better reach the street audience, Brooks's later poems use more open, less traditional poetic forms and techniques. Pe-

nelope Moffet of the *Los Angeles Times* records the poet's statement that since 1967, she has been "successfully escaping from close rhyme, because it just isn't natural. . . . I've written hundreds . . . of sonnets, and I'll probably never write another one, because I don't feel that this is a sonnet time. It seems to me it's a wild, raw, ragged free verse time." She told Stavros, "I want to write poems that will be non-compromising. I don't want to stop a concern with words doing good jobs, which has always been a concern of mine, but I want to write poems that will be meaningful to those people I described a while ago, things that will touch them." Speaking of later works aimed for that audience, Robert F. Kiernan offers in *American Writing since 1945: A Critical Survey,* "She remains, however, a virtuoso of the lyric and an extraordinary portraitist—probably the finest black poet of the post-Harlem generation."

When *Report from Part One* came out in 1972, some reviewers complained that it did not provide the level of personal detail nor the insight into black literature that they had expected. "They wanted a list of domestic spats," remarked Brooks. Bambara notes that it "is not a sustained dramatic narrative for the nosey, being neither the confessions of a private woman poet or the usual sort of mahogany-desk memoir public personages inflict upon the populace at the first sign of a cardiac. . . . It documents the growth of Gwen Brooks." Other reviewers value it for explaining the poet's new orientation toward her racial heritage and her role as a poet. In a passage she has presented again in later books as a definitive statement, she writes: "I—who have 'gone the gamut' from an almost angry rejection of my dark skin by some of my brainwashed brothers and sisters to a surprised queenhood in the new Black sun—am qualified to enter at least the kindergarten of new consciousness now. New consciousness and trudge-toward-progress. I have hopes for myself. . . . I know now that I am essentially an essential African, in occupancy here because of an indeed 'peculiar' institution. . . . I know that Black fellow-feeling must be the Black man's encyclopedic Primer. I know that the Black-and-white integration concept, which in the mind of some beaming early saint was a dainty spinning dream, has wound down to farce. . . . I know that the Black emphasis must be not *against white* but *FOR Black.* . . . In the Conference-That-Counts, whose date may be 1980 or 2080 (woe betide the Fabric of Man if it is 2080), there will be no looking up nor looking down." In the future, she envisions "the profound and frequent shaking of hands, which in Africa is so important. The shaking of hands in warmth and strength and union."

Brooks put some of the finishing touches on the second volume of her autobiography while serving as Poetry Consultant to the Library of Congress. Brooks was sixty-eight when she became the first black woman to be appointed to the post. Of her many duties there, the most important, in her view, were visits to local schools. "Poetry is life distilled," she told students in a Washington school, Schmich reports. "She urged them to keep journals. She read them a poem about teen suicide. She told them poetry exists where they might not recognize it," such as in John Lennon's song "Eleanor Rigby." Similar visits to colleges, universities, prisons, hospitals, and drug rehabilitation centers characterize her tenure as Poet Laureate of Illinois. In that role, she has sponsored and hosted annual literary awards ceremonies at which she presents prizes paid for "out of [her] own pocket, which, despite her modest means, is of legendary depth," Reginald Gibbons relates in *Tribune Books.* She has honored and encouraged many poets in her state through the Illinois Poets Laureate Awards and Significant Illinois Poets Awards programs.

At one ceremony, says Gibbons, "poetry was, for a time, the vital center of people's lives."

Though her writing is "*to* Blacks," it is "*for* anyone who wants to open the book," she emphasized to Schmich. Brook's objectivity is perhaps the most widely acclaimed feature of her poetry. Janet Overmeyer notes in the *Christian Science Monitor* that Brooks's "particular, outstanding, genius is her unsentimental regard and respect for all human beings. . . . She neither foolishly pities nor condemns—she creates." Overmeyer continues, "From her poet's craft bursts a whole gallery of wholly alive persons, preening, squabbling, loving, weeping; many a novelist cannot do so well in ten times the space." Brooks achieves this effect through a high "degree of artistic control," claims Littlejohn. "The words, lines, and arrangements," he states, "have been worked and worked and worked again into poised exactness: the unexpected apt metaphor, the mock-colloquial asides amid jewelled phrases, the half-ironic repetitions—she knows it all." More importantly, Brooks's objective treatment of issues such as poverty and racism "produces genuine emotional tension," he writes.

This quality also provides her poems with universal appeal. Blyden Jackson states in *Black Poetry in America: Two Essays in Historical Interpretation* that Brooks "is one of those artists of whom it can truthfully be said that things like sex and race, important as they are, . . . appear in her work to be sublimated into insights and revelations of universal application." Although Brooks's characters are primarily black and poor, and live in Northern urban cities, she provides, according to Jackson, through "the close inspection of a limited domain, . . . a view of life in which one may see a microscopic portion of the universe intensely and yet, through that microscopic portion see all truth for the human condition wherever it is." And although the goals and adjustments of black nationalism have been her frequent topics, Houston A. Baker, Jr., says of Brooks in the *CLA Journal,* "The critic (whether black or white) who comes to her work seeking only support for his ideology will be disappointed for, as Etheridge Knight pointed out, she has ever spoken the truth. And truth, one likes to feel, always lies beyond the boundaries of any ideology. Perhaps Miss Brooks' most significant achievement is her endorsement of this point of view. From her hand and fertile imagination have come volumes that transcend the dogma on either side of the American veil." Baker feels that Brooks "represents a singular achievement. Beset by a double consciousness, she has kept herself from being torn asunder by crafting poems that equal the best in the black and white American literary traditions."

Proving the breadth of Brooks's appeal, poets representing a wide variety of "races and . . . poetic camps" gathered at the University of Chicago to celebrate the poet's 70th birthday in 1987, reports Gibbons. Brooks brought them together, he says, "in . . . a moment of good will and cheer." In recognition of her service and achievements, a junior high school in Harvey, Illinois has been named for her. She is also honored at Western Illinois University's Gwendolyn Brooks Center for African-American Literature.

Summing up the poet's accomplishments, Gibbons writes that, beginning with *A Street in Bronzeville,* Brooks has brought national attention to "a part of life that had been grossly neglected by the literary establishment. . . . And because Brooks has been a deeply serious artist . . ., she has created works of special encouragement to black writers and of enduring importance to all readers."

BIOGRAPHICAL/CRITICAL SOURCES:

BOOKS

Authors in the News, Volume 1, Gale, 1976.
Baker, Houston A., Jr., *Singers of Daybreak: Studies in Black American Literature,* Howard University Press, 1974.
Bigsby, C. W. E., editor, *The Black American Writer, Volume II: Poetry and Drama,* Deland, 1969.
Bigsby, C. W. E., *The Second Black Renaissance: Essays in Black Literature,* Greenwood Press, 1980.
Brooks, Gwendolyn, *In the Mecca,* Harper, 1968.
Brooks, Gwendolyn, *Report from Part One: An Anthology,* Broadside Press, 1972.
Brown, Patricia L., Don L. Lee, and Francis Ward, editors, *To Gwen with Love: An Anthology Dedicated to Gwendolyn Brooks,* Johnson Publishing, 1971.
Concise Dictionary of Literary Biography, 1941-1968, Gale, 1985.
Contemporary Literary Criticism, Gale, Volume 1, 1973, Volume 2, 1974, Volume 4, 1975, Volume 5, 1976, Volume 15, 1980, Volume 49, 1988.
Dictionary of Literary Biography, Gale, Volume 5: *American Poets since World War II,* 1980, Volume 75: *Afro-American Writers, 1940-1955,* 1988.
Dembo, L. S. and Pondrom, C. N., editors, *The Contemporary Writer: Interviews with Sixteen Novelists and Poets,* University of Wisconsin Press, 1972.
Drotning, Philip T. and Wesley W. Smith, editors, *Up from the Ghetto,* Cowles, 1970.
Emanuel and Gross, editors, *Dark Symphony: Negro Literature in America,* Free Press, 1968.
Evans, Mari, editor, *Black Women Writers (1950-1980): A Critical Evaluation,* Anchor/Doubleday, 1984.
Gates, Henry Louis, Jr., editor, *Black Literature and Literary Theory,* Methuen, 1984.
Gayle, Addison, editor, *Black Expression,* Weybright & Talley, 1969.
Gibson, Donald B., editor, *Modern Black Poets: A Collection of Critical Essays,* Prentice-Hall, 1973.
Gould, Jean, *Modern American Women Poets,* Dodd, Mead, 1985.
Jackson, Blyden and Louis D. Rubin, Jr., *Black Poetry in America: Two Essays in Historical Interpretation,* Louisiana State University Press, 1974.
Kent, George, *Gwendolyn Brooks: A Life,* University Press of Kentucky, 1988.
Kufrin, Joan, *Uncommon Women,* New Century Publications, 1981.
Littlejohn, David, *Black on White: A Critical Survey of Writing by American Negroes,* Viking, 1966.
Madhubuti, Haki R., *Say that the River Turns: The Impact of Gwendolyn Brooks,* Third World Press, 1987.
Melhem, D. H., *Gwendolyn Brooks: Poetry and the Heroic Voice,* University Press of Kentucky, 1987.
Miller, R. Baxter, *Langston Hughes and Gwendolyn Brooks: A Reference Guide,* Hall, 1978.
Miller, R. Baxter, *Black American Poets between Worlds, 1940-1960,* University of Tennessee Press, 1986.
Mootry, Maria K. and Gary Smith, editors, *A Life Distilled: Gwendolyn Brooks, Her Poetry and Fiction,* University of Illinois Press, 1987.
Newquist, Roy, *Conversations,* Rand McNally, 1967.
Redmond, Eugene B., *Drumvoices: The Mission of Afro-American Poetry,* Doubleday, 1976.
Shaw, Harry F., *Gwendolyn Brooks,* Twayne, 1980.

Tate, Claudia, *Black Women Writers at Work,* Continuum, 1983.

PERIODICALS

Atlantic Monthly, September, 1960.
Best Sellers, April 1, 1973.
Black American Literature Forum, spring, 1977, winter, 1984.
Black Enterprise, June, 1985.
Black Scholar, March, 1981, November, 1984.
Black World, August, 1970, January, 1971, July, 1971, September, 1971, October, 1971, January, 1972, March, 1973, June, 1973, December, 1975.
Book Week, October 27, 1963.
Chicago Tribune, January 14, 1986, June 7, 1987, June 12, 1989.
Christian Science Monitor, September 19, 1968.
CLA Journal, December, 1962, December, 1963, December, 1969, September, 1972, September, 1973, September, 1977, December, 1982.
Contemporary Literature, March 28, 1969, winter, 1970.
Critique, summer, 1984.
Discourse, spring, 1967.
Ebony, July, 1968.
Essence, April, 1971, September, 1984.
Explicator, Volume 58, April, 1976, Volume 36, number 4, summer, 1978.
Houston Post, February 11, 1974.
Journal of Negro Education, winter, 1970.
Library Journal, September 15, 1970.
Los Angeles Times, November 6, 1987.
Los Angeles Times Book Review, September 2, 1984.
Modern Fiction Studies, winter, 1985.
Nation, September, 1962, July 7, 1969.
National Observer, November 9, 1968.
Negro American Literature Forum, fall, 1967, summer, 1974.
Negro Digest, December, 1961, January, 1962, August, 1962, July, 1963, June, 1964, January, 1968.
New Statesman, May 3, 1985.
New Yorker, September 22, 1945, December 17, 1949, October 10, 1953, December 3, 1979.
New York Times, November 4, 1945, October 5, 1953, December 9, 1956, October 6, 1963, March 2, 1969, April 30, 1990.
New York Times Book Review, October 23, 1960, October 6, 1963, March 2, 1969, January 2, 1972, June 4, 1972, December 3, 1972, January 7, 1973, June 10, 1973, December 2, 1973, September 23, 1984, July 5, 1987.
Phylon, Volume XXII, summer, 1961, Volume XXXVII, number 1, March, 1976.
Poetry, Volume 67, December, 1945, Volume 126, 1950, Volume 103, March, 1964.
Publishers Weekly, June 6, 1970.
Ramparts, December, 1968.
Saturday Review, January 19, 1946, September 17, 1949, February 1, 1964.
Saturday Review of Literature, May 20, 1950.
Southern Review, spring, 1965.
Studies in Black Literature, autumn, 1973, spring, 1974, summer, 1974, spring, 1977.
Tribune Books, July 12, 1987.
Virginia Quarterly Review, winter, 1969, winter, 1971.
Washington Post, May 19, 1971, April 19, 1973, March 31, 1987.
Washington Post Book World, November 3, 1968, November 11, 1973.
Women's Review of Books, December, 1984.
World Literature Today, winter, 1985.

BROPHY, Brigid (Antonia) 1929-

PERSONAL: Born June 12, 1929, in London, England; daughter of John (a novelist) and Charis Weare (Grundy) Brophy; married Michael Vincent Levey (director of the National Gallery, London, and author), June 12, 1954; children: Katharine Jane. *Education:* St. Hugh's College, Oxford, 1947-48. *Religion:* Atheist.

ADDRESSES: Home—Flat 3, 185 Old Brompton Rd., London SW5 0AN, England. *Agent*—Giles Gordon, Anthony Sheil Associates, 43 Doughty St., London WC1N 2LF, England.

CAREER: Novelist, essayist, critic, biographer, and dramatist. Shorthand typist for camera firm, London; journalist for *London Magazine;* co-organizer, Writers' Action Group campaign for Public Lending Right, 1972-82. Broadcaster on television and radio in the 1960s and 1970s.

MEMBER: Writers Guild of Great Britain (member of executive council, 1974-78), British Copyright Council (vice-chairperson, 1976-80), Anti-Vivisection Society of Great Britain (vice-president, 1974).

AWARDS, HONORS: Cheltenham Literary Festival first prize for a first novel, 1954, for *Hackenfeller's Ape; London Magazine* prize for prose, 1962, for *Black Ship to Hell;* fellow, Royal Society of Literature, 1973; Tony Godwin Award, 1985.

WRITINGS:

FICTION

The Crown Princess and Other Stories, Viking, 1953.
Hackenfeller's Ape, Hart-Davis, 1953, Random House, 1954, reprinted, Schocken, 1980.
The King of a Rainy Country, Secker & Warburg, 1956, Knopf, 1957.
Flesh, Secker & Warburg, 1962, World, 1963, reprinted, Schocken, 1980.
The Finishing Touch (also see below), Secker & Warburg, 1963, revised edition, GMP, 1987.
The Snow Ball (also see below), Secker & Warburg, 1964, reprinted, Schocken, 1980.
The Finishing Touch [and] *The Snow Ball,* World, 1964.
In Transit: An Heroicycle Novel, Macdonald & Co., 1969, Putnam, 1970.
The Adventures of God in His Search for the Black Girl: A Novel and Some Fables, Macmillan, 1973, Little, Brown, 1974.
Pussy Owl: Superbeast (for children), illustrated by Hilary Hayton, BBC Publications, 1976.
Palace without Chairs: A Baroque Novel, Atheneum, 1978.

NONFICTION

Black Ship to Hell, Harcourt, 1962.
Mozart the Dramatist: A New View of Mozart, His Operas and His Age, Harcourt, 1964.
Don't Never Forget: Collected Views and Reviews, Cape, 1966, Holt, 1967.
(With husband, Michael Levey, and Charles Osborne) *Fifty Works of English and American Literature We Could Do Without,* Rapp & Carroll, 1967, Stein & Day, 1968.
Religious Education in State Schools, Fabian Society, 1967.
Black and White: A Portrait of Aubrey Beardsley, Cape, 1968, Stein & Day, 1969.
The Rights of Animals, Animal Defence and Anti-Vivisection Society, 1969.
The Longford Threat to Freedom, National Secular Society, 1972.

Prancing Novelist: A Defence of Fiction in the Form of a Critical Biography in Praise of Ronald Firbank, Barnes & Noble, 1973.

Beardsley and His World, Harmony Books, 1976.

The Prince and the Wild Geese, pictures by Gregoire Gagarin, St. Martin's, 1983.

A Guide to Public Lending Right, Gower, 1983.

Baroque 'n' Roll and Other Essays, David & Charles, 1987.

Read, Cardinal, 1989.

OTHER

(Author of introduction) Elizabeth Smart, *By Grand Central Station I Sat Down,* Pantheon, 1966.

(Author of introduction) Jane Austen, *Pride and Prejudice,* Pan Books, 1967.

The Burglar (play; first produced in London, 1967), Holt, 1968.

(Author of foreword) M. Hill and M. Lloyd-Jones, *Sex Education: The Erroneous Zone,* National Secular Society, 1970.

(Author of introduction) *Die Zauberfloete* [and] *Die Entfuehrung aus dem Serail* (libretti), translated by L. Salter, Cassell, 1971.

Also author of the radio script "The Waste-Disposal Unit," BBC, 1964. Author of various pamphlets and tracts. Contributor to books, including *Shakespeare Stories,* 1982, and *Dictionary of Literary Biography Yearbook: 1983,* 1984, and to periodicals, including *London Magazine, Short Story Monthly, London Review of Books, Times Literary Supplement,* London *Times, New Statesman, New York Herald Tribune,* and *Texas Quarterly.* Also contributor to psychoanalytic journals.

SIDELIGHTS: English author Brigid Brophy was first introduced to the literary world as the precocious daughter of novelist John Brophy. According to S. J. Newman in the *Dictionary of Literary Biography: British Novelists since 1960,* John Brophy wrote in 1940: "I have a daughter, ten years old, who excels me in everything, even in writing." From ages three to nine, Brigid wrote numerous poetic dramas, inspired by Shakespeare and Sir Walter Scott, and then she stopped writing until the 1950s. She has produced a variety of works, including novels and novellas, essays, criticism, literary biography, various tracts, and additional dramas. And all this from a writer who insists she hates to write: "You know, I don't like to write. I think I actually hate it. You see, it's so difficult. . . . I suffer terribly when I'm writing and I'm absolutely impossible," records Phyllis Meras in the *New York Times Book Review.*

In the words of Newman, "one of the oddest, most brilliant, and most enduring of [the] 1960s symptoms was Brigid Brophy." As a feminist, pacifist, atheist, anti-vivisectionist, and vegetarian, among other things, Brophy had much to speak out on in that turbulent era. She expressed controversial opinions on marriage, the Vietnam War, religious education in schools, sex, and pornography. In response to her outspokenness, Brophy has been labeled many things, including "one of our leading literary shrews" by a *Times Literary Supplement* reviewer: "A lonely, ubiquitous toiler in the weekend graveyards, she has scored some direct hits on massive targets: Kingsley Amis, Henry Miller, Professor Wilson Knight." In turn, Brophy's enthusiasts, coined "brophiles" by *Life* critic Robert Phelps, envision her "the archpriestess of the permissive society, one of the rare and precious human beings who have done something positive, and a saint. Interviewers have been surprised to find a courteous and secluded hostess who claims that she becomes involved in controversies inadvertently," writes Newman. As David Depledge comments in *Books and Bookmen,* "The unfortunate thing about . . . Brophy is that the Gods have cursed her with a facility for being mis-

understood." Depledge believes this misunderstanding may have arisen, in part, from Brophy's many television appearances in the 1960s and 1970s. Brophy admits to being a shy person and Depledge surmises that her shyness and nervousness in front of the cameras "makes her look solemn, and forbiddingly intense. . . . If her tenseness in front of the cameras could be wiped away we might see the mischievousness behind a large number of her dead-pan deliveries." But Brophy also revealed to Depledge that some of the misunderstanding has been self-generated: "I sometimes can't resist the temptation to give fantasy answers to serious questions."

Through the years, critics have found Brophy's writing to be consistently clever and lucid. To Meras, Brophy's distinctions are her "vitriolic pen, penetrating intelligence and neat, sharp critical prose." Newman sees her as a "polymath, pundit and polemicist" and further remarks: "[Brophy] described herself Irishly as the highbrow's lowbrow and her work as a howl for tolerance. In a *Guardian* interview she called herself a most unEnglish writer: 'I am really most interested in intensity. I cannot stand anything that is lukewarm.'" Yet reviewers have sometimes balked at the intensity of Brophy's prose. For example, in a *New Republic* assessment of Brophy's *The Adventures of God in His Search for the Black Girl,* Margaret Walters maintains: "Though she's both inventive and imaginative Brophy has a tendency to try too hard. . . . Determined to mock and shock, she's so unrelentingly the enfant terrible that her flashes of genuine wit get lost. . . . She never misses a chance to throw us off balance, to discomfit and needle us into questioning our prejudices. . . . Bossily she divides us into sheep and goats. If you disagree you're cast into an irrational outer darkness and convicted of being humorless and non-literate."

In her youth, Brophy read the works of George Bernard Shaw, Oscar Wilde, James Joyce, and Ronald Firbank. She learned much about writing from both her novelist father and her mother, a teacher. Brophy studied classics on a Jubilee Scholarship at St. Hugh's College, Oxford, for four terms but was expelled for personal reasons. While working as a shorthand typist in London, she wrote short stories that were eventually published in her collection *The Crown Princess and Other Stories.* A *Times Literary Supplement* reviewer responds to this collection: "Brophy's approach is quite unlike that of her fashionable British contemporaries . . . ; it is more nearly related to that of such tough and sharp American talents as those of Miss Mary McCarthy and Miss Eleanor Clark."

Following *The Crown Princess,* Brophy moved into lengthier fiction and nonfiction works. *Hackenfeller's Ape* was her first novel. According to Brophy, "In my twenty-fifth year, I sat down to write a narrative poem and rose a fortnight later (a fortnight of which I have no memory) having written instead a brief novel called *Hackenfeller's Ape,* which is probably the best I shall ever write and which already displays at its most intense the violently romantic feeling in a precisely classical form to which most of my fiction aspires," records Newman. In this work, a professor of zoology sets an ape free from the London Zoo when he discovers this animal is destined for use in a rocket experiment. In the *Saturday Review,* Joseph Wood Krutch observes that "certainly there is a good deal of originality in [this tale of] a scientist with emotional conflicts who was trying to understand animals, humanity, and possibly even God by observing the behavior of [an ape]." Affected by what she herself saw at the London Zoo, Brophy explains that she "was trying to establish a parallel between shutting people up in prisons and shutting animals up in zoos," notes Newman. *Hackenfeller's Ape* garnered the Cheltenham Literary Festival first prize for a first novel in 1954.

In the early 1960s, Brophy wrote what some reviewers consider her best novels. One of the earliest of these is *Flesh,* a story drawing on the courtship and marriage of two young Jews. The sexually experienced Nancy opens the doors to a new world and, subsequently, a new lifestyle for her introverted husband, Marcus. Yet, to London *Observer* critic Hermione Lee, Marcus is transformed "into an obese, hedonistic aesthete: he becomes the kind of flesh he most admires, that of a Rubens woman. The nasty little tale, very smoothly told, is as much about second-generation North London Jews reacting against parental vulgarity and stuffiness as it is a pastiche of sensual awakening." Newman considers *Flesh* "clinical, but also poetic" and believes Brophy's writing, in this instance, parallels her father's. As for *Saturday Review* contributor Manfred Wolf, he feels the book's subject is too narrow and that there is not enough distance between Brophy and her characters: "*Flesh* would have been a better book if the author had not been so thoroughly taken in by it."

In her 1960s novella *The Finishing Touch,* Brophy presents what she calls a "lesbian fantasy." This novella focuses on an English princess's stay at a finishing school on the French Riviera and the two English lesbians who run it. A number of reviewers detect Ronald Firbank's influence; indeed, Newman records one reviewer's opinion that the book is a posthumous monument to Firbank. Though some critics deem *The Finishing Touch* a depraved work, *Best Sellers* contributor Joseph L. Quinn explains that "what Lionel Trilling said of Nabokov's grisly but beautifully written freak of a novel [*Lolita*] is also true of *The Finishing Touch;* the reader simply cannot work up sufficient indignation. Instead, he remains an amused observer, a sophisticated peeping Tom."

A third novella of this period, *The Snow Ball,* is a comedy of manners perceived by reviewers as Brophy's critique of middle-class morals and hypocrisies. It is a modern-day version of Mozart's opera "Don Giovanni." Martin Tucker explains in the *New York Times Book Review* that in *The Snow Ball* "Brophy offers more than sex and seduction: she offers the commentary of a knowing ironist. Beneath her humor is, if not examination, then at least a stab at the hypocrisies of modern life." According to *New York Review of Books* contributor Eve Auchincloss, "The intellectual jokes [in *The Snow Ball*]—often either banal or irritatingly illegible—take precedence over the interplay of personalities (the people are no more than rather ugly dolls); yet under the surface one senses the beat of a sentimental, vindictive female heart." In Newman's opinion, "There was a lot of uneasy praise from the critics, and even those who disliked the book conceded its effectiveness."

During the time that Brophy was publishing her succession of novels and novellas, she was also broadcasting on radio and television and crafting the critical works for which she has become known. Both *Black Ship to Hell* and *Mozart the Dramatist: A New View of Mozart, His Operas and His Age* are seen as psychoanalytic studies much influenced by Freudian hypotheses. For instance, *New Yorker* contributor Naomi Bliven believes that in *Mozart the Dramatist,* Brophy "applies her own notions of psychoanalysis to the eighteenth century, to the Enlightenment, to Mozart, and to his librettos. She is looking for difficulties. . . . Brophy thinks [Mozart] is not only the greatest opera composer of the eighteenth century (and ever after) but the best expositor, in his operas, of that century's psychosexual problems. These, she believes, matter to us; I am not so certain." In addition, Brophy's *Don't Never Forget: Collected Views and Reviews* attests to

her range and wit on a broad array of topics from animal rights to contemporary writers.

One of Brophy's most controversial critical analyses, the one that induced the *Times Literary Supplement* reviewer to call her "one of our leading literary shrews," is *Fifty Works of English and American Literature We Could Do Without.* In this survey, Brophy, her husband Michael Levey, and Charles Osborne debunk fifty works of fiction which have gained recognition over the years as classics of American and English literature, including *Beowulf, Hamlet, Pilgrim's Progress, The Faerie Queene, Tom Jones,* Gray's *Elegy,* and the accomplishments of T. S. Eliot, William Faulkner, and Gerard Manley Hopkins. The majority of reviewers are equally vehement in their denunciations of Brophy and her co-authors. In his *Encounter* assessment, for instance, Anthony Burgess calls *Fifty Works* a "deplorable little work. . . . I . . . want to express my disquiet that this is what British literary criticism should have come to." Burgess then proposes why the authors published such a "vulgar" book: "One answer, a shameful one, is a hunger for notoriety. Their book, far from being ignored . . . , has had wide newspaper coverage. . . . Like children, they have shown off, and the showing-off has provoked attention." According to Burgess, the authors of *Fifty Works* fail to look at literature in a historic sense. Instead of viewing literature as a continuum over the centuries, Burgess feels Brophy and her collaborators err when addressing the various literary works as isolated forms of entertainment. *Christian Science Monitor* reviewer Alan Levensohn describes the book as "a collection of 50 brief, sneering essays. . . . Their sneering takes many forms, of which the most common is the direct, unsupported insult. . . . Where all else fails, the sneerers resort to amateur Freudianism. . . . The book is not an utter waste. Three of the essays are worth skimming. . . . But the rest is merely relentless, irresponsible invective."

Other critics were not as displeased with *Fifty Works.* A *Saturday Review* writer admires this "poisonously delightful" book, and Edward Weeks concludes in *Atlantic* that "arbitrary and malicious as they are, the trio are protesting against the thoughtless acceptance of 'classics,' established by tradition and perpetuated by the reluctance of teachers and examiners to alter a system which everyone has learned to endure." Finally, a *New York Times Book Review* critic expresses disappointment because the work does not direct enough of its attention to literary giants: "When the authors let fly at bigger game, notably T. S. Eliot, Hemingway and Faulkner, . . . they make one wish they had concentrated on more of these beefy sacred cows."

Brophy's avant-garde work *In Transit: An Heroicycle Novel* was a difficult book for some reviewers to characterize. In Newman's opinion, "though subtitled 'an heroicycle novel,' *In Transit* is less a novel than a cross between a neurotic essay in criticism and a farcical nightmare. . . . The book is best described as an antiantinovel . . . [and] the protagonist . . . is nothing more than a voice." Though some reviewers could not discern a plot, those who did explain that a young girl, Patricia, is waiting at an airport, "a sort of Kennedy Terminal of the psyche," describes Elizabeth Hardwick in *Vogue,* when a sudden amnesia sets in. The girl's identity fades; indeed, she cannot remember her name or her gender. The remainder of the story describes the girl's struggle for personal redefinition. According to Phelps, Brophy's *In Transit* brings to the forefront the concept of the multifaceted individual: "At his innermost center, . . . [a person] is many things, many appetites, all genders. . . . In his soul, he is as polymorphous as the angels. . . . Patricia's breakdown is actually a breakthrough: her tough little ego is fighting for its birthright, and on the last page of *In Transit,* she has died, been reborn, and is about to assume a more spacious selfhood." As for Guy Davenport in the *National Review*, "It is not at all clear just what's going on by way of action." Davenport, like others, finds *In Transit*'s experimental style leads to confusion.

When interviewed by Bolivar Le Franc in *Books and Bookmen*, Brophy remarked that *In Transit* "attempts to be many dimensioned. . . . It is for me rather as if I'd gone on from writing concerti to writing symphony with a big and rather brassy orchestra. . . . It was intended basically to give the reader something which could be read three or four times and still yield something." Brophy, known as a fine punster, utilizes her talent to the utmost in *In Transit*. According to Hardwick, "from the first section . . . to the last . . . everything is in planned disorder, whirling with hallucination, disconnection, puns, fantasy, dreams, phantasmagoria, unexpected wit, and restless allusion. . . . [Brophy] is accompanied on every page by her fellow-traveller and Irishman, James Joyce." Other reviewers detect Joycean similarities as well. In *Books and Bookmen*, V. R. J. Clinton senses Joyce's "anarchy," and Phelps claims that *In Transit* is "robustly, joyously fertilized by James Joyce."

Following *In Transit*, Brophy authored the nearly six-hundred-page *Prancing Novelist: A Defence of Fiction in the Form of a Critical Biography in Praise of Ronald Firbank*. Philippa Pullar remarked in the *Sunday Times*: "Here is Brigid Brophy, whose strength and beauty lies in her lyric brevity, writing a fat and heavy volume about someone whose own strength and beauty also lies in lyric brevity." In this lengthy defense of what most would consider a minor novelist, reviewers sense unjustified admiration and a good deal of self-indulgence. "Inflating him beyond recognition, [Brophy] leaves Firbank a swollen, distorted hulk," offers Michael Rosenthal in the *New York Times Book Review*. "In its willfully perverse view of literary history and literary value, *Prancing Novelist* seems a document more self-serving than anything else, attesting to the uniqueness not of its subject but its author. . . . Those not already committed to Firbank will hardly be encouraged to sample him by the tendentiousness and irresponsibility of much of this book." In a similar vein, *New Republic* critic Lawrence Graver declares that the more Brophy "talks about lyric brevity, reverberating images, eloquent silence, textual spacing and novels that seal themselves in their own autonomy, the more convincing is the conventional wisdom that Firbank's talent is tiny. At times, . . . Brophy seems to glimpse the truth and her frantic language reveals the absurdity of erecting such a monument to a butterfly."

Brophy continued to write both fiction and nonfiction during the 1970s, but she devoted much of her time and energy to the establishment of the British Public Lending Right. With this goal in mind, Brophy and Maureen Duffy formed Writers' Action Group in the early 1970s as a lobbying tool. Brophy's father originated the idea of the Public Lending Right as a means of providing authors a small fee each time their books are on loan from libraries. Though it took a decade of work, in 1979 the Public Lending Right became law in England.

In the early 1980s, tragedy beset Brophy. Following years of good health, Brophy was stricken with multiple sclerosis. In her 1987 book *Baroque 'n' Roll and Other Essays*, Brophy relives the circumstances surrounding the onset and diagnosis of the disease in "A Case-Historical Fragment of Autobiography." As Brophy maintains, the chief "curse" of the disease is that "I must ask constant services of the people I love most closely, of whom I require my three meals a day and constant water and eternal coffee. . . . Sporadically it is, in its manifestations, a disgusting disease. . . . It is an illness accompanied by frustration. . . . It is

an illness that inflicts awareness of loss. . . . All that has happened to me is that I have in part died in advance of the total event." According to John Bayley in the *London Review of Books*, "A Case-Historical Fragment of Autobiography" is the most moving essay in Brophy's *Baroque 'n' Roll* collection: "To observe one's symptoms . . . and one's medical experiences for the benefit of others is a service rarely performed. Brigid Brophy does it with humour and stoicism, and in addition performs the almost impossible feat of thanking her husband and friends for all they have done for her. . . . That is as much a personal triumph as is her always creative criticism." London *Times* critic Peter Ackroyd likewise values the humor and "clarity of judgement" evident in Brophy's personal essay. In addition, he finds her continued argument against vivisection worthy of comment. Brophy "has always been an opponent of vivisection; but now she states that, in the search for the cure of her own disease, 'it is vital that no animal, human or non-human, be tortured or killed.' Under the circumstances this is an eloquent plea; but what is more eloquent still is that, in the course of this autobiographical essay, she has the humility . . . to turn aside from her own sufferings in order to address those of other creatures."

As Ackroyd notes, Brophy has always displayed somewhat of an "anti-autobiographical temperament," thus making *Baroque 'n' Roll* a highly valued departure. Ronald Blythe explains in his *Sunday Telegraph* contribution: "I think that *Baroque 'n' Roll* allows us to view the work of Brigid Brophy in a way not previously possible . . . because she herself has chosen to use the material collected here specifically to illuminate who she is and what she stands for, something she has rather avoided or smudged until now. The result is moving and funny, persnickety and brave, erudite and pleasurable."

Apart from Brophy's autobiographical account, Brophy's essays on the baroque movement, from which the collection gets its title, are also self-revealing. In Bayley's opinion, "the linked essays on baroque which conclude [Brophy's] book are as fascinating as they are informed, and every sentence creates the author, on the one hand, while illuminating the spirit of baroque, on the other. The combination is rare, in every sense, and reveals what all its most devoted clients know by instinct: that art is both communal and personal; that it tells us we are individuals at the same time that it transcends individuality." Indeed, as Kris Kirk maintains in *Gay Times*, it is courage "which has helped [Brophy] give us the gift of this book."

Phelps defines a "brophile" as "one who immoderately loves the tone of voice in the prose of novelist Brophy." A brophile himself, Phelps, writing in a 1970 review, declared Brophy "the best prose writer of her generation (of either gender) in Great Britain today." A manuscript collection of Brophy's work is contained in Lilly Library at Indiana University at Bloomington.

MEDIA ADAPTATIONS: "The Snow Ball" was televised by BBC-TV, April, 1964; "Pussy Owl: Superbeast" was televised by BBC-TV, March, 1976.

BIOGRAPHICAL/CRITICAL SOURCES:

BOOKS

Brophy, Brigid, *Baroque 'n' Roll and Other Essays,* David & Charles, 1987.
Contemporary Authors Autobiography Series, Volume 4, Gale, 1986.
Contemporary Literary Criticism, Gale, Volume 6, 1976, Volume 11, 1979, Volume 29, 1984.
Dick, Kay, *Friends and Friendship,* Sidgwick & Jackson, 1974.

Dictionary of Literary Biography, Volume 14: *British Novelists since 1960,* Gale, 1982.

PERIODICALS

Atlantic, April, 1957, March, 1968.
Best Sellers, July 15, 1964, March 15, 1970.
Books and Bookmen, July, 1967, January, 1969, December, 1969, March, 1974.
Book World, January 25, 1970.
Christian Science Monitor, February 15, 1968, February 14, 1970.
Encounter, August, 1967.
Gay Times, April, 1987.
Guardian, March 20, 1987.
Harper's, March, 1970.
Life, February 13, 1970.
Listener, March 21, 1968, December 6, 1973.
London Review of Books, March 17-31, 1983, March 5, 1987.
National Review, February 10, 1970.
New Republic, June 30, 1973, December 28, 1974.
New Statesman, February 16, 1962, May 26, 1967, April 28, 1978, January 25, 1980.
New Yorker, December 26, 1964.
New York Herald Tribune Book Review, September 27, 1953, February 17, 1957.
New York Review of Books, September 24, 1964.
New York Times, February 27, 1970.
New York Times Book Review, November 29, 1953, July 26, 1964, May 21, 1967, February 25, 1968, July 22, 1973, August 25, 1974, July 16, 1978.
Observer (London), January 13, 1980.
Saturday Review, June 12, 1954, July 27, 1963, February 17, 1968, July 8, 1978.
Spectator, May 6, 1978, February 21, 1987.
Sunday Telegraph, February 15, 1987.
Sunday Times, February 15, 1987.
Time, February 2, 1970.
Times (London), March 10, 1983, February 19, 1987.
Times Literary Supplement, January 23, 1953, February 23, 1962, December 1, 1966, June 1, 1967, October 2, 1969, March 30, 1973, November 23, 1973, April 28, 1978, March 9, 1984, March 13, 1987.
Vogue, March 15, 1970.
Washington Post Book World, August 18, 1974, October 7, 1979.

*   *   *

BROTHER ANTONINUS
See EVERSON, William (Oliver)

*   *   *

BROWN, Dee (Alexander) 1908-

PERSONAL: Born February 28, 1908, in Louisiana; son of Daniel Alexander and Lula (Cranford) Brown; married Sara Baird Stroud, 1934; children: James Mitchell, Linda. *Education:* Attended Arkansas State Teachers College (now University of Central Arkansas); George Washington University, B.L.S., 1937; University of Illinois, M.S., 1952.

ADDRESSES: Home—7 Overlook Dr., Little Rock, Ark. 72207.

CAREER: U.S. Department of Agriculture, Washington, D.C., library assistant, 1934-42; U.S. War Department, Washington, D.C., technical librarian, 1945-48; University of Illinois at Ur-

bana-Champaign, librarian of agriculture, 1948-72, professor, 1962-72. *Military service:* U.S. Army, 1942-45.

MEMBER: Authors Guild, Western Writers of America, Society of American Historians, Beta Phi Mu.

AWARDS, HONORS: Clarence Day Award from American Library Association, 1971, for *The Year of the Century: 1876;* Christophers Award, 1971; Buffalo Award from New York Westerners, 1971, for *Bury My Heart at Wounded Knee;* named Illinoisian of the Year by Illinois News Broadcasters Association, 1972; award for best western for young people from Western Writers of America, 1981, for *Hear That Lonesome Whistle Blow;* Saddleman Award from Western Writers of America, 1984.

WRITINGS:

Wave High the Banner (novel based on life of Davy Crockett), Macrae Smith, 1942.
(With Martin F. Schmitt) *Fighting Indians of the West,* Scribner, 1948.
(With Schmitt) *Trail Driving Days,* Scribner, 1952.
Grierson's Raid, University of Illinois Press, 1954.
(With Schmitt) *The Settlers' West,* Scribner, 1955.
Yellowhorse (novel), Houghton, 1956.
The Gentle Tamers: Women of the Old Wild West, Putnam, 1958.
Cavalry Scout (novel), Permabooks, 1958.
The Bold Cavaliers: Morgan's Second Kentucky Cavalry Raiders, Lippincott, 1959.
They Went Thataway (satirical novel), Putnam, 1960, reprinted as *Pardon My Pandemonium,* August House, 1984.
(Editor) George B. Grinnell, *Pawnee, Blackfoot, and Cheyenne,* Scribner, 1961.
Fort Phil Kearny: An American Saga, Putnam, 1962 (published in England as *The Fetterman Massacre,* Bartie & Jenkins, 1972), reprinted as *The Fetterman Massacre,* University of Nebraska Press, 1984.
The Galvanized Yankees, University of Illinois Press, 1963.
Showdown at Little Big Horn (juvenile), Putnam, 1964.
The Girl from Fort Wicked (novel), Doubleday, 1964.
The Year of the Century: 1876, Scribner, 1966.
Action at Beecher Island, Doubleday, 1967.
Bury My Heart at Wounded Knee: An Indian History of the American West, Holt, 1970, abridged edition for children by Amy Erlich published as *Wounded Knee: An Indian History of the American West,* Holt, 1974.
Andrew Jackson and the Battle of New Orleans, Putnam, 1972.
Tales of the Warrior Ants, Putnam, 1973.
The Westerners, Holt, 1974.
Hear That Lonesome Whistle Blow: Railroads in the West, Holt, 1977.
Teepee Tales of the American Indians, Holt, 1979.
Creek Mary's Blood (novel), Holt, 1980.
The American Spa: Hot Springs, Arkansas, Rose Publishing (Little Rock), 1982.
Killdeer Mountain (novel), Holt, 1983.
A Conspiracy of Knaves (novel), Holt, 1987.
(Contributor) Clarus Backes, editor, *Growing Up West* (tentative title), Knopf, 1989.

Editor of "Rural America" series, Scholarly Resources, 1973. Contributor of articles to periodicals, including *American History Illustrated, Civil War Times,* and *Southern Magazine.* Editor of *Agricultural History,* 1956-58.

SIDELIGHTS: The American West of the nineteenth century figures prominently in the writings of historian and novelist Dee Brown. His bestseller *Bury My Heart at Wounded Knee: An Indian History of the American West,* for example, chronicles the settling of the West during the nineteenth century from the viewpoint of the American Indians. In his novels *Creek Mary's Blood* and *Killdeer Mountain,* Brown dramatizes events and characters from western history, while his many nonfiction works concern such subjects as the building of the railroads, the massacre at Little Big Horn, and women settlers of the old West. In all of his work, Brown has shown a consistent compassion for the American Indians and moral outrage at the injustices they have suffered.

Brown's interest in Indians stems from his childhood in Arkansas where, he told an interviewer for *Publishers Weekly,* "there were quite a few Indians around, people with mixed blood, and at the beginning, I swallowed all the old myths. When I began to travel and meet more Indians I began wondering, Why do people think of them as such villains?" The question spurred Brown to investigate Indians on his own, reading everything he could on their history and culture. This interest led in time to his writing about the American West. Three of his early books, *Fighting Indians of the West, Trail Driving Days,* and *The Settlers' West,* were written with Martin F. Schmitt and were based on historic photographs the two men discovered in the National Archives. Writing their text around these previously unpublished photographs, Brown and Schmitt succeeded in presenting pictorial histories of three great western subjects that had never been seen before.

After writing a score of books about the Old West, Brown embarked upon perhaps his most ambitious and successful historical work, *Bury My Heart at Wounded Knee,* a book that chronicles the settling of the West based on eyewitness reports from the Indians who lived there. Brown's reason for writing the book, explained Peter Farb of the *New York Review of Books,* lie in his belief that "whites have for long had the exclusive use of history and that it is now time to present, with sympathy rather than critically, the red side of the story."

"The Indians," wrote Helen McNeil in her *New Statesman* review of *Bury My Heart,* "knew exactly what was being done to them." Brown uses quotes from the Indians themselves to present their history of the period. The book, according to J. W. Stevenson in *Library Journal,* is "based largely upon primary source material such as treaty council records, pictographic and translated autobiographical accounts of Indian participants in the events, and contemporary newspaper and magazine interviews, [and it is an] extensively researched history." N. Scott Momaday, in his review of the book for the *New York Times Book Review,* agrees with this assessment. *Bury My Heart at Wounded Knee,* he stated, is "a compelling history of the American West, distinguished not because it is an Indian history but because it is so carefully documented and designed." As Brown told an interviewer for *Publishers Weekly,* "I had a document for everything in the book."

The uniquely Indian viewpoint of the book was achieved not only through the extensive use of the Indians' own words, but also by the use of the Indian names for the white historical figures of the period. General Custer, for example, was called "Hard Backsides" by the Indians, and is so referred to in the book. When the names are "consistently used," wrote R. A. Mohl in *Best Sellers,* "these become creative and effective literary devices which force the reader, almost without his knowing it, into the position of the defeated, retreating Indian."

Although *Bury My Heart at Wounded Knee* took him over two years to write in his free time, Brown managed to keep a consistently Indian perspective throughout the whole book. Speaking to Anne Courtmanche-Ellis in the *Wilson Library Bulletin,* Brown explained how he did it: "I would tell myself every night, 'I'm a very, very old Indian, and I'm remembering the past. And I'm looking toward the Atlantic Ocean.' And I always kept that viewpoint every night. That's all I did."

The importance of *Bury My Heart at Wounded Knee* to the field of western history is noted by several reviewers. "Brown," Farb related, "dispels any illusions that may still exist that the Indian wars were civilization's mission or manifest destiny; the Indian wars are shown to be the dirty murders they were. *Bury My Heart* is an extremely ambitious and readable attempt to write a different kind of history of white conquest of the West: from the point of view of the victims, using their words whenever possible." McNeil judged the book to be "a deliberately revisionist history [that tells] the story of the Plains Indians from an amalgamated Indian viewpoint, so that the westward march of the civilized white men, 'like maggots,' according to a Sioux commentator, appears as a barbaric rout of established Indian culture." *Bury My Heart,* Cecil Eby wrote in *Book World,* "will undoubtedly chart the course of other 'revisionist' historical books dealing with the Old West."

Bury My Heart at Wounded Knee became a nationwide bestseller, gaining the number one spot on the country's bestselling books list and selling well over one million copies. But Brown claims the best compliment he ever received for the book came from an old Indian friend who told him: "You didn't write that book. Only an Indian could have written that book! Every time I read a page, I think: That's the way I feel."

In *Hear That Lonesome Whistle Blow,* Brown approached the ruthless settling of the West from a different perspective, writing the history of the building of the western railroads. The book turned out to be an expose of the treacherous dealings of the railroad companies, although Brown claimed, "I didn't start out to write an expose." Union Pacific was so upset with Brown's manuscript that they denied him access to their company library for further research.

Hear That Lonesome Whistle Blow, wrote Margo Jefferson, "is a fast-moving narrative of ambition, greed and conflict that takes in the high-finance railroad moguls, bribing congressmen and future Presidents with lucrative stocks and bonds in exchange for enormous land grants and construction privileges; the waves of Irish and Chinese immigrants building the railroads . . .; the Plains Indians fighting railroad workers to hold onto the land that the government was either cheating them out of or driving them off." Philip French of *New Statesman* agreed but added that "the constant emphasis on shoddy deals serves not merely to qualify almost out of existence the epic nature of the undertaking, but to deny a true complexity to the events and a full humanity to the participants." But Winifred Farrant Bevilacqua, in the *Dictionary of Literary Biography Yearbook: 1980,* described the book as "an engaging reconstruction of the drama surrounding the advent of the iron horse and a case against the railroads."

In his fiction, Brown dramatizes many of the historical themes he presents in his nonfiction, creating stories from the actual historical conditions of the nineteenth century. *Creek Mary's Blood,* for instance, is based on an Indian woman in Georgia who organized an attack on British-held Savannah during the American Revolutionary War. The novel tells her story and that of her descendants as they are pushed farther and farther west by the expanding frontier. Brown told Judy Klemesrud of the *New York*

Times: "I tried to make the historical events as accurate as possible, but I did make some changes for dramatic effect. That's something you never do in nonfiction, and I felt guilty about it."

Despite its fictional liberties, *Creek Mary's Blood* accurately describes Indian life of the nineteenth century while chronicling the lives of one Indian family on their westward trek. Interspersed with their story are chapters about events of the time that affected all Indians. "In this absorbing historical romance," Bevilacqua stated, "Brown skillfully blends fact with fiction but falters in his attempt to confer on his characters an authentic Indian perspective." But Joseph McClellan thought otherwise in the *Washington Post Book:* "Using fictional characters against a carefully researched historical background, [Brown] combines the attractions of both genres. The major incidents of his story are true, but by inventing fictional participants he is able to give the events a human dimension lacking in the historic record."

"The dominant themes of *Creek Mary's Blood,*" explained Mary Anne Norman of the *Lone Star Book Review,* "are the displacement of the Indians and the treachery of the U.S. government in its dealings with the Indians." Through the misfortunes of Creek Mary's family, Brown outlines the fate of all Indians during the course of the nineteenth century. Creek Mary's two husbands, McClellan points out, symbolize the two ways that Indians sought to deal with the white settlers. Her first husband was an English colonist, "who is related thematically to the effort at accommodation and assimilation," McClellan writes. Her second husband was a Cherokee warrior, "a leader of the resistance to white encroachment." "Both ways of coping," McClellan concludes, "ultimately proved futile, and in his novel's epic length Dee Brown has leisure to examine the modes of futility in assimilation and in resistance."

Although concerned with the same themes as his earlier works, Brown's novel *Killdeer Mountain* is a stylistic departure from his previous writings. It is told in a disjointed narrative structure that presents a number of conflicting versions of the same basic story. Reviewing the book for the *Chicago Tribune Book World,* Robert Gish claimed that it is "perhaps [Brown's] most intriguing book to date." Told by a newspaper reporter who is unraveling the true story of Major Charles Rawley, an Indian fighter and military hero, the novel contains the differing accounts of people who knew and worked with him. The reporter's attempts to make sense of the ambiguities and contradictions in the stories, and his efforts to discover the truth concerning the major's heroism and supposed death, turn the novel into a kind of mystery story. "The world we view," Brown stated in the novel, "is a complex mirror that tricks us with false images so that what we believe to have happened . . . may or may not have taken place." "We gradually acquire," wrote Michael A. Schwartz of the *Detroit News,* "a complex tangled web of evidence resting upon a shadow. Brown makes the various guises that Major Rawley assumes seem quite real, and in Rawley's manifestations we discover the ambiguous nature of this country's westward expansion."

The strongest aspect of *Killdeer Mountain,* several critics claim, is Brown's narrative ability, which makes adventurous scenes come alive, while the weakest aspect is his use of dialogue. "Brown's gift for strong narrative," Jonathan Coleman of the *New York Times Book Review* believed, "far outweighs his skill at writing dialogue, which, at times, hurts his novel by trivializing it." In similar terms, C. C. Loomis wrote in the *Washington Post Book World:* "Brown is at his best narrating adventurous episodes within the novel. . . . But most readers want vivid characters in novels as well as vivid narration, and here . . .

Brown has only limited success. . . . [His] dialogue is artificial; it flattens his characters." Brown's narrative strength was best used, Schwartz related, in a scene involving the massacre of Sioux Indians which "shows Brown's mastery as a storyteller and his thorough understanding of these times. . . . It is rendered with such intensity that it becomes a brutally realistic portrait of the Indian wars."

In book after book, Brown has examined the history of the settling of the West and presented the hardships and triumphs of this vast undertaking. He has particularly drawn attention to "the destruction of ancient Indian cultures," Bevilacqua stated, "and investigated other aspects of the toll exacted by the nation's western expansion. He has always been recognized as a tireless researcher and a gifted raconteur who narrates his stories in an informative and entertaining manner."

Brown's books have been published in over twenty languages, including Latvian, Russian, and Icclandic.

BIOGRAPHICAL/CRITICAL SOURCES:

BOOKS

Contemporary Authors Autobiography Series, Volume 6, Gale, 1988.
Contemporary Literary Criticism, Gale, Volume 18, 1981, Volume 47, 1988.
Dictionary of Literary Biography Yearbook: 1980, Gale, 1981.

PERIODICALS

American Historical Review, April, 1955.
American West, March, 1975.
Atlantic Monthly, February, 1971.
Best Sellers, March 1, 1971.
Book World, February 28, 1971.
Catholic World, August, 1971.
Chicago Tribune Book World, March 2, 1980, March 13, 1983.
Christian Century, February 3, 1971.
Christian Science Monitor, June 21, 1977.
Detroit News, July 13, 1983.
Economist, October 2, 1971, September 10, 1977.
Guardian, September 21, 1974.
Journal of American History, November, 1966.
Library Journal, December 15, 1970.
Life, April 2, 1971.
Lone Star Book Review, April, 1980.
Los Angeles Times Book Review, April 3, 1983.
National Review, March 9, 1971.
New Republic, December 14, 1974.
New Statesman, October 1, 1971, September 30, 1977.
Newsweek, February 1, 1971, May 23, 1977, March 28, 1983.
New York, April 7, 1980.
New Yorker, February 13, 1971.
New York Post, April 22, 1971.
New York Review of Books, December 16, 1971.
New York Times, December 3, 1976, April 13, 1980.
New York Times Book Review, May 3, 1942, March 7, 1971, May 15, 1977, April 13, 1980, April 27, 1980, May 25, 1980, April 26, 1981, June 5, 1983.
Pacific Historical Review, November, 1972.
Publishers Weekly, April 19, 1971, March 21, 1980.
Time, February 1, 1971.
Times Literary Supplement, December 16, 1977.
Village Voice, August 5, 1971, June 27, 1977.
Washington Post Book World, March 16, 1980, March 14, 1983.
Wilson Library Bulletin, March, 1978.

BROWN, George Mackay 1921-

PERSONAL: Born October 17, 1921, in Stromness, Orkney Islands, Scotland; son of John and Mary Jane (Mackay) Brown. *Education:* Attended Newbattle Abbey College, 1951-52, 1956; University of Edinburgh, M.A., 1960, graduate study on the poetry of Gerard Manley Hopkins, 1962-64. *Religion:* Catholic.

ADDRESSES: Home—3 Maybum Court, Stromness, Orkney Islands KW16 3DH, Scotland.

CAREER: Poet and author.

MEMBER: Royal Society of Literature (fellow).

AWARDS, HONORS: Arts Council of Great Britain award for poetry, 1965; Society of Authors Travel Award, 1967; Scottish Arts Council Prize and Katherine Mansfield-Menton Prize, both 1969, for *A Time to Keep, and Other Stories;* officer, Order of the British Empire, 1974; LL.D., University of Dundee, 1977; D.Litt., University of Glasgow, 1985; M.A., Open University.

WRITINGS:

NOVELS

Greenvoe: A Novel, Harcourt, 1972.
Magnus: A Novel, Hogarth, 1973.
Time in a Red Coat: A Haunting Parable of War that Echoes Long in the Memory, Chatto & Windus, 1984, Vanguard Press, 1985.

SHORT STORIES

A Calendar of Love, Hogarth, 1967, published as *A Calendar of Love and Other Stories,* Harcourt, 1968.
A Time to Keep, and Other Stories, Hogarth, 1969, Harcourt, 1970.
Hawkfall, and Other Stories, Hogarth, 1974.
The Two Fiddlers: Tales from Orkney (for children), Hogarth, 1974.
The Sun's Net, and Other Stories, Hogarth, 1976.
Pictures in the Cave (for children), Chatto & Windus, 1977.
Witch, and Other Stories, Longman, 1977.
Six Lives of Fankle the Cat (for children), Chatto & Windus, 1980.
Andrina, and Other Stories, Chatto & Windus, 1982.
Christmas Stories, Perpetua Press, 1985.
The Masked Fisherman, and Other Stories, Duval, 1985.
Selected Stories, Vanguard Press, 1986.
The Golden Bird, Vanguard Press, 1987.

PLAYS

"Witch," first produced in Edinburgh, Scotland, 1969.
A Spell for Green Corn (broadcast, 1967; produced in Edinburgh, 1970; adaptation produced at Perth Theatre, March, 1972), Hogarth, 1970.
"The Loom of Light" (also see below), produced in Kirkwall, 1972.
"The Storm Watchers," produced in Edinburgh, 1976.
"The Well" (also see below), produced at St. Magnus Festival, 1981.
"The Voyage of Saint Brandon" (also see below), broadcast, 1984.
Three Plays (contains "The Loom of Light," "The Well," and "The Voyage of Saint Brandon"), Chatto & Windus, 1984.

Also author of "A Celebration for Magnus."

POETRY

The Storm, and Other Poems, Orkney Herald Press, 1954.

Loaves and Fishes, Hogarth, 1959.
The Year of the Whale, Hogarth, 1965.
The Five Voyages of Arnor, K. D. Duval, 1966.
Twelve Poems, Festival Publications, 1968.
Fishermen with Ploughs: A Poem Cycle, Hogarth, 1971.
Lifeboat, and Other Poems, Hogarth, 1971.
Poems New and Selected, Hogarth, 1971, Harcourt, 1973.
(Contributor) Oliver Aston, *Water,* Evans Brothers, 1972.
Winterfold, Chatto & Windus, 1976.
Selected Poems, Hogarth, 1977.
Voyages, Hogarth, 1984.
Christmas Poems, Perpetua Press, 1984.

OTHER

Let's See the Orkney Islands, Thomson, 1948.
Stromness Official Guide, Burrow, 1956.
An Orkney Tapestry (essays), Gollancz, 1969.
Letters from Hamnavoe (selected journalism), Gordon Wright Publishing, 1975.
Edwin Muir: A Brief Memoir, Castlelaw Press, 1975.
From Stone to Thorn, Abingdon, 1975.
George Mackay Brown (sound recording), Claddagh, 1977.
Under Brinkie's Brae (selected journalism), Gordon Wright Publishing, 1979.
Portrait of Orkney, Hogarth, 1981.
Selected Prose, David & Charles, 1989.

Also author of television poem "The Winter Islands," broadcast in 1966; author of several television and radio scripts, including "Orkney Trilogy," "Miss Barraclough," and "Andrina"; author of stage works, "The Loom of Light," 1972, and "The Well," 1981. Also collaborator, with composer Peter Maxwell Davies, of musical works, including an opera, "The Martyrdom of St. Magnus," and a cantata, "Solstice of Light." Brown's manuscripts are collected at the Scottish National Library at University of Edinburgh.

SIDELIGHTS: George Mackay Brown writes of life and nature in his native Orkney Islands. He has written novels, children's stories, essays, and media pieces, although he is best known as a poet. His books often express religious, ritualistic themes, especially relating to Orkney living and his fictional Orkney town, Hamnavoe. Douglas Sealy states in the *Times Literary Supplement,* "Brown's books, with their insistence on the ritual of daily living, on the religious underpinning of our lives, and on the cyclic nature of our existence, are like a richly illuminated book of hours." In an essay in the *Dictionary of Literary Biography,* Thomas J. Start calls Brown "probably the greatest living Scottish writer."

Brown attempts to capture and re-create the reality of his homeland through both his prose and verse. A *Times Literary Supplement* reviewer comments that "Brown is a uniquely observant and skilful chronicler of life in his native Orkneys, past and present." In *Phoenix,* Harold Massingham concurs with the *Times Literary Supplement* observation, noting, "Brown knows where he is and writes with a local and natural authority." Massingham sees the same approach in Brown's poetry: "His local colour, in fact his total effect, is of a mature distillation and blend by an excellent and unmistakable poet patiently subdued by, and to, the demands of his terrain." Reviewing *Voyages* for the *Times Literary Supplement,* Douglas Dunn maintains that "Brown's idealism is retrospective, fictionalizing a place and its meaning through an affectionate exploration of history which he holds up like a cupped treasure in the hands, and as an offering to the residual innocence of his native Orkney Islands."

Brown's work concentrates on traditional values and time-honored ethics. Dunn observes in *Poetry Nation* that "Brown, as a poet of remote island communities and unindustrial, non-urban landscapes, is at odds with the tradition of modern poetry." Dunn continues: "Brown's best poems are . . . full of names and characters, their typical vulnerabilities, and the virtues of the way of life their personalities prove. He celebrates an ideal of community." Sealy also recognizes traditional elements in Brown's poetry, asserting, "Brown, though he acknowledges the contemporary life of the islands intellectually, rejects it emotionally, so that his best poems are always instinct with nostalgia." In a *Times Literary Supplement* review, Dunn remarks upon Brown's traditional qualities in prose as well: "Since *A Calendar of Love* appeared in 1967, Brown has perfected a narrative style of great simplicity, its virtues drawn more from the ancient art of telling tales than from new-fangled methodologies of fiction."

About Brown's efforts in *Andrina, and Other Stories,* Stuart Evans claims in the London *Times* that "this superb teller of tales who, whether he is writing in prose or verse, is always the poet, offers in this book a magical selection." Evans adds, "[The stories'] common strength, apart from George Mackay Brown's exquisite and unerring way with words, is in their humanity." Dunn also applauds Brown's work in the book, stating in the *Times Literary Supplement,* "In writing so controlled, . . . by a poet perfectly at ease with his imagination and a language natural to it, the effect of that apparent collision of old and new can only be fruitful and challenging, as well as, in this case, profoundly enjoyable."

This affinity between Brown's prose and poetry styles has also been noted by Start, who calls Brown "a prose stylist with a poetic vision." Starr finds *Greenvoe,* Brown's novel of an imaginary island town, to be a superb example of Brown's artistry. "It is in *Greenvoe,*" he writes, "that Brown most successfully weaves all of [his recurring themes] into his own seamless garment. . . . *Greenvoe* is . . . the culmination of all of George Mackay Brown's fictional concerns. . . . His novel ranks with *The Great Gatsby, Mrs. Dalloway,* and *The Spire* as among the great prose poems of this century."

Brown doesn't always garner critical praise, however. About *Six Lives of Fankle the Cat,* Charles Causley suggests in the *Times Literary Supplement* that "Brown's relaxed manner and somewhat loosely constructed narrative lack the cutting edge, the dramatic tension, that we have grown to expect from his brilliant creation and re-creation of Orcadian myth and legend, for children and adults." Dunn complains in *Poetry Nation* that "unfortunately, Brown has now put forward a quaintly antithetical notion that there is a certain kind of real life for the good men of the Orkneys, and another kind of life in the cities of the mainland which is so vicious that it brings total punishment." Despite the occasional negative comment, most reviewers admire Brown's work. Evans observes in the *Times* that Brown's "characters greet the imagination with shy or confident assertion, leaving his readers richer for a chuckle or the hint of some sadness shared." Dunn remarks in *Poetry Nation* that in Brown's "best work, he solves all the problems of the poet who wants to be both bucolic, real, hard and northern."

In a brief commentary on his own writing, Brown told *CA:* "Since it seems to me that our civilization will possibly destroy itself before too long, I am interested in the labour and lives of the most primitive people of our civilization, the food-getters (crofters and fishermen) since it is those people living close to the sources of life who are most likely to survive and continue the human story; and since even their lives would be meaningless otherwise, I see religion as an illuminating and stabilising force in the life of a community. Out of these things I make my poems, stories, and plays."

Brown also told *CA* he considers the following "a kind of basic credo": "I believe in dedicated work rather than in 'inspiration'; of course on some days, one writes better than on others. I believe writing to be a craft like carpentry, plumbing, or baking; one does the best one can. Much mischief has been caused by a loose word like 'culture,' which separates the crafts into the higher arts like music, writing, sculpture, and the lowlier workaday arts (those, and the many others like them, that I have mentioned above). In 'culture circles,' there is a tendency to look upon artists as the new priesthood of some esoteric religion. Nonsense—and dangerous nonsense moreover—we are all hewers of wood and drawers of water; only let us do it as thoroughly and joyously as we can."

MEDIA ADAPTATIONS: The Two Fiddlers was adapted as "The Two Fiddlers: Opera in Two Acts" by Peter Maxwell Davies, with the libretto by Davies published by Boosey & Hawkes in 1978; the story "Andrina" of *Andrina, and Other Stories* was made into a television film by Bill Forsyth in 1982.

BIOGRAPHICAL/CRITICAL SOURCES:

BOOKS

Bold, Alan, *George Mackay Brown,* Oliver & Boyd, 1978.
Contemporary Literary Criticism, Volume 5, Gale, 1976.
Dictionary of Literary Biography, Volume 14: *British Novelists since 1960,* Gale, 1983.
Smith, Iain Chrichton, *Iain Chrichton Smith, Norman MacCaig, George Mackay Brown,* Penguin Books, 1972.

PERIODICALS

Hudson Review, Volume 26, number 4, 1973-74.
Listener, April 17, 1967.
Phoenix, winter, 1971.
Poetry Nation, Number 2, 1974.
Times (London), February 13, 1983.
Times Literary Supplement, February 16, 1967, September 28, 1973, February 22, 1980, November 21, 1980, April 10, 1981, April 1, 1983, January 20, 1984.
Washington Post Book World, November 26, 1972.

*   *   *

BROWN, Rita Mae   1944-

PERSONAL: Born November 28, 1944, in Hanover, Pa.; adopted daughter of Ralph (a butcher) and Julia (Buckingham) Brown. *Education:* Attended University of Florida; New York University, B.A., 1968; New York School of Visual Arts, cinematography certificate, 1968; Institute for Policy Studies, Washington, D.C., Ph.D., 1973.

ADDRESSES: Home—Charlottesville, Va. *Agent*—Julian Bach Literary Agency, Inc., 747 Third Ave., New York, N.Y. 10017.

CAREER: Writer. Sterling Publishing, New York, N.Y., photo editor, 1969-70; Federal City College, Washington, D.C., lecturer in sociology, 1970-71; Institute for Policy Studies, Washington, D.C., fellow, 1971-73; Goddard College, Plainfield, Vt., visiting member of faculty in feminist studies, beginning 1973. Member of board of directors of Sagaris, a feminist school.

AWARDS, HONORS: Shared in Writers Guild of America award, 1983, for television special "I Love Liberty."

WRITINGS:

(Translator) *Hrotsvitra: Six Medieval Latin Plays,* New York University Press, 1971.

The Hand That Cradles the Rock (poems), New York University Press, 1971.

Rubyfruit Jungle (novel; also see below), Daughters, Inc., 1973, hardcover edition, Bantam, 1988.

Songs to a Handsome Woman (poems), Diana Press, 1973.

In Her Day (novel), Daughters, Inc., 1976.

A Plain Brown Rapper (essays), Diana Press, 1976.

Six of One (novel), Harper, 1978.

Southern Discomfort (novel), Harper, 1982.

Sudden Death (novel), Bantam, 1983.

High Hearts (novel), Bantam, 1986.

The Poems of Rita Mae Brown, Crossing Press, 1987.

Starting from Scratch: A Different Kind of Writer's Manual (nonfiction), Bantam, 1988.

Bingo (novel), Bantam, 1988.

Also author or co-author of eight screenplays, including "Rubyfruit Jungle" (based on novel of same title) and "Slumber Party Massacre"; contributor to script of television special "I Love Liberty," ABC-TV, 1982.

SIDELIGHTS: With the 1973 publication of her "exuberantly raunchy" autobiographical novel *Rubyfruit Jungle,* Rita Mae Brown joined the ranks of those in the forefront of the feminist and gay rights movements. Described by *Ms.* reviewer Marilyn Webb as "an inspiring, bravado adventure story of a female Huck Finn named Molly Bolt," *Rubyfruit Jungle* was at first rejected by editors at the major New York publishing companies due to what they believed to be its lack of mass-market appeal. Eventually published by the small feminist firm Daughters, Inc., it sold an unexpected 70,000 copies. The book's popularity soon brought it to the attention of Bantam Books, which acquired the rights to *Rubyfruit Jungle* in 1977 and printed an additional 300,000 copies. Total sales of the novel now number more than one million, and in 1988 Bantam released the book for the first time in hardcover form.

As Webb's comment suggests, *Rubyfruit Jungle* is told in a picaresque, Mark Twain-like fashion, an observation shared by *New Boston Review* critic Shelly Temchin Henze. "Imagine, if you will, Tom Sawyer, only smarter; Huckleberry Finn, only foul-mouthed, female, and lesbian, and you have an idea of Molly Bolt," writes Henze. Though some have adopted *Rubyfruit Jungle* as "a symbol of a movement, a sisterly struggle," the critic continues, the plot of the book is basically that of the "classic American success story." Explains Henze: "*Rubyfruit Jungle* is not about revolution, nor even particularly about feminism. It is about standing on your own two feet, creaming the competition, looking out for Number One." The truly original part of the novel, maintains the critic, is Brown's perspective. "While American heroes may occasionally be women, they may not be lesbian. Or if they are, they had better be discreet or at least miserable. Not Molly. She is lusty and lewd and pursues sex with relentless gusto."

Village Voice reviewer Bertha Harris has a few reservations about the authenticity of Brown's portrayal of lesbian life. "Much of Molly's world seems a cardboard stage set lighted to reveal only Molly's virtues and those characteristics which mark her as the 'exceptional' lesbian," remarks Harris. Nevertheless, Harris goes on to state, "it is exactly this quality of *Rubyfruit Jungle* which makes it exemplary (for women) of its kind: an American primitive, whose predecessors have dealt only with male heroes. Although Molly Bolt is not a real woman, she is at least the first real *image* of a heroine in the noble savage, leatherstocking, true-blue bullfighting tradition in this country's literature."

Another *Village Voice* critic, Terry Curtis Fox, views *Rubyfruit Jungle* in a somewhat different light. Like Henze, Fox finds that Brown relies on a well-known theme for her novel; namely, "sensitive member of outside group heads toward American society and lives to tell the tale." Since this portrayal of resilience and triumph in the face of adversity is so familiar and appealing, maintains the reviewer, "you don't have to be gay or female to identify with Molly Bolt—she is one of the outsiders many of us believe ourselves to be." Furthermore, says Fox, Brown "can laugh at herself as well as at others, and make us laugh, too."

Acutely aware of the fact that humor is a quality seldom found in books dealing with homosexual life, Brown attaches special importance to her ability to make readers laugh, regarding it as a means of overcoming offensive stereotypes. "Most lesbians are thought to be ugly, neurotic and self-destructive and I just am not," she explains in a *New York Times* article. "There's no way they can pass me off that way. I'm not passing myself off as gorgeous, and a bastion of sanity, but I'm certainly not like those gay stereotypes of the miserable lesbian, the poor woman who couldn't get a man and eventually commits suicide. . . . I'm funny. Funny people are dangerous. They knock down barriers. It's hard to hate people when they're funny. I try to be like Flip Wilson, who helped a lot of white people understand blacks through humor. One way or another, I'll make 'em laugh, too."

The novel *Six of One* was Brown's second major breakthrough into the mass-market arena. Based once again on the author's own life as well as on the lives of her grandmother, mother, and aunt, *Six of One* (like *Rubyfruit Jungle*) attempts to make its point through ribald humor and an emphasis on the poor and uneducated as sources of practical wisdom. The story chronicles the events in a half-Northern, half-Southern, Pennsylvania-Maryland border town from 1909 to 1980 (focusing on the years between 1911 and 1921) as viewed through the eyes of a colorful assortment of female residents. John Fludas of the *Saturday Review,* noting that *Six of One* is a "bright and worthy successor" to *Rubyfruit Jungle,* writes that Brown "explores the town's cultural psychology like an American Evelyn Waugh, finding dignity and beauty without bypassing the zany and the corrupt. . . . If at times the comedy veers toward slapstick, and if there are spots when the prose just grazes the beauty of the human moment . . ., the novel loses none of its warmth."

Both Eliot Fremont-Smith and Richard Boeth feel that Brown could have done a better job with her material. Commenting in the *Village Voice,* for example, Fremont-Smith admits that *Six of One* "does have a winning cheerfulness," but concludes that "it's mostly just garrulous. . . . As a novel, it doesn't go anywhere; there's no driving edge; and the chatter dissipates. And as a polemical history (the secret and superior dynamics of female relationships), it gives off constant little backfires." *Newsweek* critic Boeth is even less impressed. He states: "It is a major sadness to report that Brown has made her women [in *Six of One*] not only boring but false. . . . Her only verbal tool is the josh—speech that is not quite witty, sly, wry, sardonic, ironic or even, God help us, clever, but only self-consciously breezy. . . . These aren't human beings talking; it's 310 pages of 'Gilligan's Island.' "

Henze also finds fault with Brown's characterization, remarking that the author peoples an otherwise "surprisingly accepting, even celebratory portrait of down-home America" with men and women who exhibit "the simplicity of heroes of a Western."

Continues the critic: "Time progresses, measured off in days and years [in *Six of One*], but the characters do not: the two old biddies at the center of the narrative trade off the same scatological insults at seventy as at six; [another personage] acquires political insight but no emotional depth."

In her *New York Arts Journal* review of *Six of One,* Liz Mednick attributes these characterization problems to Brown's determination "to show how wise, witty, wonderful and cute women really are. Her silent competitor in this game is the masculine standard; her method, systematic oneupmanship. The women in *Six of One* buzz around like furies trying to out-curse, out-class, out-wit, out-smart, out-shout, out-smoke, out-drink, out-read, out-think, out-lech, out-number and outrage every man, dead or alive, in history. Needless to say, ambition frequently leads the author to extremes. . . . As if to insure her success, Brown makes her men as flat as the paper on which they're scrawled. The problem with her men is not even so much that they lack dimension as that they don't quite qualify as male." In short, concludes Mednick, *Six of One* "is less a novel than a wordy costume the author wears to parade herself before her faceless audience. Her heroines are presented not for inspection but as subjects for whom the narrative implicitly demands admiration."

Washington Post Book World reviewer Cynthia Macdonald, on the other hand, cites *Six of One* as evidence of a welcome change in women's literature. She writes: "The vision of women we have usually gotten from women novelists is of pain and struggle or pain and passivity; it is seldom joyous and passionate, and almost never funny. And what humor there was has been of the suffering, self-deprecating New York Jewish stand-up comedian type. *Six of One* by Rita Mae Brown is joyous, passionate and funny. What a pleasure! . . . In spite of its spacious time span, this is no historical novel. . . . [It] clicks between the present and the past neatly and precisely. . . . I believe that Brown uses a kind of revisionist history to support her conviction that what was seen in the first half of the 20th century as the life of women was only what was on the surface, not what was underneath. She opens the seams to give us her vision of what was really there. We are shown not the seamy side of life, but a body ready for anything, especially celebration."

Responding to criticism that women of the early 1900s could not possibly have been as liberated, not to mention as raucous, as they are depicted in the novel, Brown told Leonore Fleischer in a *Washington Post Book World* interview: "I grew up with these two almost mythical figures around me, my mother and my aunt, who didn't give a rat's a— what anybody thought. They'd say anything to anybody, and they did as they damn well pleased. We were so poor, who cares what poor people do? Literature is predominantly written by middle-class people for middle-class people and their lives were real different. As a girl, I never saw a woman knuckle under to a man, or a man to a woman, for that matter. . . . The people closest to me were all very dominating characters. The men weren't weak, but somehow the women . . . were the ones you paid attention to."

Though it, too, focuses on the difficulties straight and gay women face in a hypocritical and judgmental society, Brown's novel *Sudden Death* represents what the author herself terms "a stylistic first for me." Written in an uncharacteristically plain and direct manner, *Sudden Death* examines the "often vicious and cold-blooded" world of professional women's tennis; many readers assume that it more or less chronicles Brown's experiences and observations during her involvement with star player Martina Navratilova. As Brown sees it, however, the book is much more than that: it is the fulfillment of a promise to a dying friend, sportswriter Judy Lacy, who had always wanted to write a novel against the background of women's tennis. Just prior to her death from a brain tumor in 1980, Lacy extracted a reluctant promise from Brown to write such a novel, even though Brown "didn't think sports were a strong enough metaphor for literature." "[Judy] tricked me into writing it," explained the author to Fleischer in a *Publishers Weekly* column. "She knew me well enough to know how I'd feel about my promise, that it would be a deathbed promise. . . . I thought about her all the time I was writing it. It was strange to be using material that you felt belonged to somebody else. It's really Judy's book."

For the most part, critics agree that *Sudden Death* has few of the qualities that make *Rubyfruit Jungle* and *Six of One* so entertaining. In the *Chicago Tribune Book World,* for instance, John Blades notes that despite the inclusion of "intriguing sidelights on how [tennis] has been commercialized and corrupted by sponsors, promoters and greedy players," *Sudden Death* "lacks the wit and vitality that might have made it good, unwholesome fun. Brown seems preoccupied here with extraliterary affairs; less interested in telling a story than in settling old scores."

Anne Chamberlin has a similar reaction to the novel, commenting in the *Washington Post:* "If you thought Nora Ephron's *Heartburn* had cornered the market on true heartbreak, thinly veiled, make room for *Sudden Death.* . . . Don't get mad; get even, as the saying goes, and this novel should bring the score to deuce. It not only chops the stars of women's professional tennis down to size; it tackles the whole pro tennis establishment. . . . Having reduced that tableau to rubble, Brown turns her guns on America's intolerance of lesbians. That's a lot of targets for one bombing run, and all 241 acerbic pages of *Sudden Death* are jammed with as disagreeable a bunch of people doing mean things to each other as you are likely to meet at one time."

"I would like to be able to report without qualification that this novel is a smash, an ace," states *Los Angeles Times Book Review* critic Kay Mills in her article on *Sudden Death.* "But that would be like calling a ball a winner just because you admired the way someone played yesterday." Though Mills does point out that "Brown is devastating to the hype, the fashion shows, [and] the product pimping that now accompany women's tennis," she believes that the protagonist is characterized so flatly "that one is devoid of sympathy for her when a jealous rival seeks to break her."

In short, concludes Elisabeth Jakab in the *New York Times Book Review,* Brown "is not at her best here. The world of tennis does not seem to be congenial terrain for her, and her usually natural and easy style seems cramped. The novel tends to read like the casebook of an anthropologist stranded in the midst of a disappointingly boring tribe. She does what she can, but there's just not that much to work with. In *Sudden Death* we can almost hear the pieces of the plot clanking into their proper slots."

Brown, who says she does not read reviews of her books, is nevertheless aware of the kinds of remarks critics have made about *Sudden Death,* to which she responds: "I don't care; it doesn't matter at all; and anyway, I'm already on the next book. . . . I wrote this because Judy asked me to. . . . I learned a lot, but I can't wait to get back on my own territory." Three years after the publication of *Sudden Death* Brown produced *High Hearts*— "a truly wacko novel," according to the *Los Angeles Times*'s Carolyn See—and two years after that, the novel *Bingo.* While neither book has achieved the popularity and critical respect of *Rubyfruit Jungle,* both have addressed Brown's familiar themes of feminism and relationships—both homosexual and heterosexual—and have satisfied admirers of Brown's glib, often raunchy prose.

Despite her commitment to depicting gay women in a positive light, Brown balks at being labeled a "lesbian writer." In a *Publishers Weekly* interview, she states: "Calling me a lesbian writer is like calling [James] Baldwin a black writer. I say no; he is not: he is a great writer and that is that. I don't understand people who say Baldwin writes about 'the black experience'—as if it is so different from 'the white experience' that the two aren't even parallel. That is so insulting . . . and I really hate it."

In an essay written for the *Publishers Weekly* column "My Say," Brown elaborates on her opposition to the use of such labels. "Classifying fiction by the race, sex or sex preference of the author is a discreet form of censorship," she maintains. "Americans buy books by convicted rapists, murderers and Watergate conspirators because those books are placed on the bestseller shelf, right out in front where people can see them. Yet novels by people who are not safely white or resolutely heterosexual are on the back shelves, out of sight. It's the back of the bus all over again. Is this not a form of censorship? Are we not being told that some novels are more 'American' than others? That some writers are true artists, while the rest of us are 'spokespersons' for our group? What group? A fiction writer owes allegiance to the English language only. With that precious, explosive tool the writer must tell the *emotional* truth. And the truth surely encompasses the fact that we Americans are female and male; white, brown, black, yellow and red; young, old and in-between; rich and poor; straight and gay; smart and stupid. . . . On the page all humans really are created equal. All stories are important. All lives are worthy of concern and description. . . . Incarcerating authors into types is an act of treason against literature and, worse, an assault on the human heart." Therefore, concludes Brown in the *Publishers Weekly* interview, "next time anybody calls me a lesbian writer I'm going to knock their teeth in. I'm a writer and I'm a woman and I'm from the South and I'm alive, and that is that."

BIOGRAPHICAL/CRITICAL SOURCES:

BOOKS

Contemporary Literary Criticism, Gale, Volume 18, 1981, Volume 43, 1987.

PERIODICALS

Best Sellers, February, 1979, May, 1982.
Chicago Tribune Book World, July 4, 1982, July 3, 1983.
Christian Science Monitor, November 22, 1978.
Detroit Free Press, May 15, 1983.
Detroit News, May 8, 1983.
Globe and Mail (Toronto), May 28, 1988, November 5, 1988.
Los Angeles Times, March 10, 1982, April 28, 1986, February 22, 1988, November 10, 1988.
Los Angeles Times Book Review, May 22, 1983, November 27, 1988.
Maclean's, November 13, 1978.
Ms., March, 1974, June, 1974, April, 1977.
Nation, June 19, 1982.
New Boston Review, April-May, 1979.
Newsweek, October 2, 1978.
New York Arts Journal, November-December, 1978.
New York Times, September 26, 1977.
New York Times Book Review, March 21, 1982, June 19, 1983.
People, April 26, 1982.
Publishers Weekly, October 2, 1978, February 18, 1983, July 15, 1983.

Saturday Review, September 30, 1978.
Times Literary Supplement, December 7, 1979.
Village Voice, September 12, 1977, October 9, 1978.
Washington Post, May 31, 1983, October 27, 1988.
Washington Post Book World, October 15, 1978.

*   *   *

BROWN, Sterling Allen   1901-1989

PERSONAL: Born May 1, 1901, in Washington, D.C.; died of leukemia, January 13, 1989, in Takoma Park, Md.; son of Sterling Nelson (a writer and professor of religion at Howard University) and Adelaide Allen Brown; married Daisy Turnbull, September, 1927; children: John L. Dennis. *Education:* Williams College, A.B., 1922; Harvard University, A.M., 1923, graduate study, 1930-31.

ADDRESSES: c/o John L. Dennis, 9704 Saxony Rd., Silver Spring, Md. 20910.

CAREER: Virginia Seminary and College, Lynchburg, Va., English teacher, 1923-26; also worked as a teacher at Lincoln University in Jefferson City, Mo., 1926-28, and at Fisk University, 1928-29; Howard University, Washington, D.C., professor of English, 1929-69. Visiting professor at University of Illinois, University of Minnesota, New York University, New School for Social Research, Sarah Lawrence College, and Vassar College. Editor on Negro Affairs, Federal Writers' Project, 1936-39, and staff member of Carnegie-Myrdal Study of the Negro, 1939.

MEMBER: Phi Beta Kappa.

AWARDS, HONORS: Guggenheim fellowship for creative writing, 1937; honorary doctorates from Howard University, 1971, University of Massachusetts, 1971, Northwestern University, 1973, Williams College and Boston University, both 1974, Brown University and Lewis and Clark College, both 1975, Harvard University, Yale University, University of Maryland, Baltimore County, Lincoln University (Pennsylvania), and University of Pennsylvania; Lenore Marshall Poetry Prize, 1982, for *The Collected Poems of Sterling A. Brown;* named poet laureate of District of Columbia, 1984.

WRITINGS:

POETRY

Southern Road, Harcourt, 1932, revised edition, Beacon Press, 1974.
The Last Ride of Wild Bill, and Eleven Narrative Poems, Broadside Press, 1975.
The Collected Poems of Sterling A. Brown, selected by Michael S. Harper, Harper, 1980.

NONFICTION

Outline for the Study of the Poetry of American Negroes, Harcourt, 1931.
The Negro in American Fiction (also see below), Associates in Negro Folk Education, 1937, Argosy-Antiquarian, 1969.
Negro Poetry and Drama (also see below), Associates in Negro Folk Education, 1937, revised edition, Atheneum, 1969.
(With A. B. Spingarn and Carl Van Vechten) *James Weldon Johnson,* Fisk University Department of Publicity, c. 1941.
(Editor with Arthur P. Davis and Ulysses Lee, and contributor) *The Negro Caravan,* Dryden, 1941, revised edition, Arno, 1970.
Negro Poetry and Drama [and] *The Negro in American Fiction,* Ayer, 1969.

(With George Edmund Haynes) *The Negro Newcomers in Detroit* [and] *The Negro in Washington,* Arno, 1969.

CONTRIBUTOR

Benjamin A. Botkin, editor, *Folk-Say,* University of Oklahoma Press, 1930.

American Stuff: An Anthology of Prose and Verse by Members of the Federal Writers' Project, with Sixteen Prints by the Federal Arts Project, U.S. Government Printing Office, 1937.

Washington City and Capital, U.S. Government Printing Office, 1937.

The Integration of the Negro into American Society, Howard University Press, 1951.

Lillian D. Hornstein, G. D. Percy, and others, editors, *The Reader's Companion to World Literature,* New American Library, 1956.

Langston Hughes and Arna Bontemps, editors, *The Book of Negro Folklore,* Dodd, Mead, 1958.

John Henrik Clarke, editor, *American Negro Short Stories,* Hill & Wang, 1966.

OTHER

Sixteen Poems by Sterling Brown (sound recording), Folkway Records, 1973.

Contributor to *What the Negro Wants,* 1948. Contributor of poetry and articles to anthologies and journals, including *Crisis, Contempo, Nation, New Republic,* and *Journal of Negro Education.* Contributor of column "The Literary Scene: Chronicle and Comment" to *Opportunity,* beginning 1931.

SIDELIGHTS: Sterling Allen Brown has devoted his life to the development of an authentic black folk literature. A poet, critic, and teacher at Howard University for forty years, Brown was one of the first people to identify folklore as a vital component of the black aesthetic and to recognize its validity as a form of artistic expression. He has worked to legitimatize this genre in several ways. As a critic, he has exposed the shortcomings of white literature that stereotypes blacks and demonstrated why black authors are best suited to describe the negro experience. As a poet, he has mined the rich vein of black Southern culture, replacing primitive or sentimental caricatures with authentic folk heroes drawn from Afro-American sources. As a teacher, Brown has encouraged self-confidence among his students, urging them to find their own literary voices and to educate themselves to be an audience worthy of receiving the special gifts of black literature. Overall, Brown's influence in the field of Afro-American literature has been so great that scholar Darwin T. Turner told *Ebony* magazine: "I discovered that all trails led, at some point, to Sterling Brown. His *Negro Caravan* was *the* anthology of Afro-American literature. His unpublished study of Afro-American theater was *the* major work in the field. His study of images of Afro-Americans in American literature was a pioneer work. His essays on folk literature and folklore were preeminent. He was not always the best critic . . . but Brown was and is the literary historian who wrote the Bible for the study of Afro-American literature."

Brown's dedication to his field has been unflinching, but it was not until he was in his late sixties that the author received widespread public acclaim. Before then, he labored in obscurity on the campus of Howard University. His fortune improved in 1968 when the Black Consciousness movement revived an interest in his work. In 1969, two of his most important books of criticism, *Negro Poetry and Drama* and *The Negro in American Fiction,* were reprinted by Argosy; five years later, in 1974, Beacon Press reissued *Southern Road,* his first book of poems. These reprint-

ings stimulated a reconsideration of the author, which culminated in the publication of *The Collected Poems of Sterling A. Brown* in 1980. More than any other single publication, it is this title, which won the 1982 Lenore Marshall Poetry prize, that has brought Brown the widespread recognition that he deserves.

Because he had largely stopped writing poetry by the end of the 1940s, most of *Collected Poems* is comprised of Brown's early verse. Yet the collection is not the work of an apprentice, but rather "reveals Brown as a master and presence indeed . . .," in the view of a *Virginia Quarterly Review* critic. While acknowledging that "his effective range is narrow," the critic calls Brown "a first-rate narrative poet, an eloquent prophet of the folk, and certainly our finest author of Afro-American dialect." *New York Times Book Review* contributor Henry Louis Gates appreciates that in *Collected Poems* "Brown never lapses into bathos or sentimentality. His characters confront catastrophe with all of the irony and stoicism of the blues and of black folklore. What's more, he is able to realize such splendid results in a variety of forms, including the classic and standard blues, the ballad, the sonnet and free verse." Despite Brown's relatively small poetic output, *Washington Post* critic Joseph McClellen believes this collection "is enough to establish the poet as one of our best."

While the book will help insure that Brown is not forgotten, some believe it serves as a painful reminder of a great talent that was stunted because it was ignored. Brown encountered inexplicable resistance to his poetry in the mid-1930s. Even though *Southern Road* had been heralded by critics as the work of a major talent, Brown could not find a publisher for his second volume of poetry. (Titled *No Hiding Place* the work has yet to be published separately though it was included in *Collected Poems.*) Nor was resistance from his publishers the only source of Brown's obscurity. Another part stemmed from Brown's life-long dedication to Howard University. Offered a full-time teaching position at Vassar College in 1945—an offer so extraordinary for a black man at the time that it made national news—Brown politely declined. "I am devoted to Howard," he explained to *Ebony* some twenty-four years later. "These are my people and if I had anything to give they would need it more."

Brown's connection with the university dates back to his birth. He was born in a house that has since become part of the Howard campus. His father, a minister at the Lincoln Congregational Church, was a professor of religion at Howard and a one-time member of the District of Columbia Board of Education. Because of his father's position, young Brown came into contact with some of the most important black leaders of the day. Sociologist and writer W.E.B. DuBois, cultural philosopher and critic Alain Locke, and social historian Kelly Miller were but three of the important personages he came to know while growing up at Howard. Important as these figures were, however, "the person who most encouraged Brown's admiration for literature and the cultural heritage of black people was his mother," according to Joanne V. Gabbin in Volume 51 of the *Dictionary of Literary Biography.*

Adelaide Allen was valedictorian of her graduating class at Fisk University. A poetry lover who read verse aloud, Adelaide introduced her son to the works of Henry Wadsworth Longfellow, Robert Burns, and black poet and family friend Paul Laurence Dunbar. In a 1973 interview with Stephen Jones quoted in Gabbin's article, Brown recalled of his mother: "I remember even now her stopping her sweeping . . . now standing over that broom and reading poetry to me, and she was a good reader, great sense of rhythm." The high school Brown attended further developed his gifts. Dunbar High School (named to honor the poet) was then considered one of the best black schools in the country. Brown had history classes taught by Haley Douglass, Frederick Douglass's grandson, and Neville Thomas, president of the Washington Branch of the NAACP. Among his other teachers were Angelina Weld Grimke and Jessie Redmond Fauset, "artists in their own right," who "taught him a strict sense of academic discipline," according to Gabbin.

After high school, Brown won a scholarship to the predominantly white, ivy league institution, Williams College. There he first began writing poetry. While other young poets his age were imitating T. S. Eliot, Ezra Pound, and other high modernists, Brown was not impressed with their "puzzle poetry." Instead, he turned for his models to the narrative versifiers, poets such as Edwin Arlington Robinson, who captured the tragic drama of ordinary lives, and Robert Frost, who used terse vernacular that sounded like real people talking. At Williams, Brown studied literature with George Dutton, a critical realist who would exert a lasting influence. "Dutton was teaching Joseph Conrad," Brown recalled, as reported in the *New Republic*. "He said Joseph Conrad was being lionized in England . . . [but] Conrad was sitting over in the corner, quiet, not participating. Dutton said he was brooding and probably thinking about his native Poland and the plight of his people. He looked straight at me. I don't know what he meant, but I think he meant, and this is symbolic to me, I think he meant don't get fooled by any lionizing, don't get fooled by being here at Williams with a selective clientele. There is business out there that you have to take care of. Your people, too, are in a plight. I've never forgotten it."

Brown came to believe that one way to help his people was through his writing. "When Carl Sandburg said 'yes' to the American people, I wanted to say 'yes' to my people," Brown recalled in *New Directions: The Howard University Magazine*. In 1923, after receiving his Masters degree from Harvard, Brown embarked on a series of teaching jobs that would help him determine what form that "yes" should assume. He moved south and began to teach among the common people. As an instructor, he gained a reputation as a "red ink man," because he covered his students' papers with corrections. But as a poet, he was learning important lessons from students about black Southern life. Attracted by his openness and easygoing manner, they invited him into their homes to hear worksongs, ballads, and the colorful tales of local lore. He met ex-coalminer Calvin "Big Boy" Davis, who became the inspiration for Brown's "Odyssey of Big Boy" and "Long Gone," as well as singer Luke Johnson, whom he paid a quarter for each song Luke wrote down. As Brown began to amass his own folklore collection, "he realized that worksongs, ballads, blues, and spirituals were, at their best, poetical expressions of Afro-American life," writes Robert O'Meally in the *New Republic*. "And he became increasingly aware of black language as often ironic, understated and double-edged."

At this time many black writers were moving away from using dialect in literature. White abuse of the black idiom had reduced it to a simplistic cliche, which writer James Weldon Johnson believed was capable of only two full stops: humor and pathos. His criticism was largely a reaction against white plantation literature that ridiculed black speech, nonetheless, it was a powerful incentive to negro poets to use traditional English. Against this backdrop, Brown made a decision to explore the potential of folk language. As O'Meally explains, Brown made a commitment "to render black experience as he knew it, using the speech of the people. He would not, because of white stereotyping, avoid phonetical spellings. . . . His goal was not to run from the stereotype but to celebrate the human complexity behind the now grinning, now teary-eyed mask."

In 1929, the same year his father died, Brown returned to Howard University, where he would remain for the rest of his career. Three years later, Harcourt, Brace published *Southern Road,* a first book of poems, drawn primarily from material he had gathered during his travels south. The book was heralded as a breakthrough for black poetry. Alain Locke, one of the chief proponents of what was then called the New Negro Movement, acknowledged the importance of the work in an essay collected in *Negro Anthology.* After explaining that the primary objective of Negro poetry should be "the poetic portrayal of Negro folk-life . . . true in both letter and spirit to the idiom of the folk's own way of feeling and thinking," he declared that with the appearance of *Southern Road,* it could be said "that here for the first time is that much-desired and long-awaited acme attained or brought within actual reach."

James Weldon Johnson was so moved by the work that he provided a glowing introduction in which he reconsidered his earlier objections to black dialect: "Brown's work is not only fine, it is also unique. He began writing just after the Negro poets had generally discarded conventionalized dialect, with its minstrel traditions of Negro life. . . . He infused his poetry with genuine characteristic flavor by adopting as his medium the common, racy, living speech of the Negro in certain phases of real life. For his raw material he dug down into the deep mine of Negro folk poetry." As Sterling Stuckey observes in his introduction to the *Collected Poems,* "it was a remarkable achievement for a young poet: not one of the major reviewers hailed Brown as a poet of promise, as a talented young man awaiting creative maturity; on the contrary, he was regarded as a poet of uncommon sophistication, of demonstrated brilliance whose work had placed him in the front rank of working poets here and elsewhere."

The success of *Southern Road* did not insure Brown's future as a publishing poet. Not only did Harcourt, Brace reject *No Hiding Place* when Brown submitted the manuscript a few years later, they also declined to issue a second printing of *Southern Road,* because they did not think it would be profitable. These decisions had a devastating impact upon Brown's poetic reputation. Because no new poems appeared, many of his admirers assumed he had stopped writing. "That assumption," writes Sterling Stuckey, "together with sadly deficient criticism from some quarters, helped to fix his place in time—as a not very important poet of the past."

Discouraged over the reception of his poems, Brown shifted his energies to other arenas; he continued teaching, but also produced a steady stream of book reviews, essays, and sketches about black life. He argued critically for many of the same goals he had pursued in verse: recognition of a black aesthetic, accurate depiction of the black experience, and the development of a literature worthy of his people's past. One of his most influential forums for dissemination of his ideas was a regular column he wrote for *Opportunity* magazine. There "Brown argued for realism as a mode in literature and against such romantic interpretations of the South as the ones presented in *I'll Take My Stand* (1930), the manifesto of Southern agrarianism produced by contributors to the *Fugitive,* including John Crowe Ransom, Allen Tate, and Robert Penn Warren," writes R.V. Burnette in Volume 63 of the *Dictionary of Literary Biography*. "Although he praised the efforts of white writers like Howard Odum ('he is a poetic craftsman as well as a social observer'), he was relentless in his criticism of popular works that distorted black life and character."

Brown did not limit his writing to periodicals, but also produced several major books on Afro-American studies. His 1938 works,

Negro Poetry and Drama and *The Negro in American Fiction,* are seminal studies of black literary history. The former shows the growth of black artists within the context of American literature and delineates a black aesthetic; the latter examines what has been written about the black man in American fiction since his first appearance in obscure novels of the 1700s. A pioneering work that depicts how the prejudice facing blacks in real life is duplicated in their stereotyped treatment in literature, *The Negro in American Fiction* differs "from the usual academic survey by giving a penetrating analysis of the social factors and attitudes behind the various schools and periods considered," Alain Locke believes, as quoted in Volume 63 of the *Dictionary of Literary Biography.*

In 1941, Brown and two colleagues Arthur P. Davis and Ulysses S. Lee edited *The Negro Caravan,* a book that "defined the field of Afro-American literature as a scholarly and academic discipline," according to *Ebony.* In this anthology, Brown demonstrates how black writers have been influenced by the same literary currents that have shaped the consciousness of all American writers—"puritan didacticism, sentimental humanitarianism, local color, regionalism, realism, naturalism, and experimentalism"—and thus are not exclusively bound by strictures of race. The work has timeless merit, according to Julius Lester, who writes in the introduction to the 1970 revised edition that "it comes as close today as it did in 1941 to being the most important single volume of black writing ever published."

As a writer, Brown's first twelve years at Howard were his most productive. By the mid-1940s, he had completed the major works on which his reputation as an essayist, critic, and poet rests. But even his national reputation as a writer did little to secure his stature in the English department at Howard, where colleagues scoffed at his "lowbrow" interest in jazz and the blues. For decades, Brown paid no mind to this lack of recognition and simply went about his work. When he wanted to give poetry readings, he gave them as a guest lecturer at other campuses. Ultimately his "nonconformity cost him more than he realized," reports Michael Winston in the *Dictionary of Literary Biography,* Volume 51. Shunned by many of Howard's more conservative professors, Brown (who never completed his doctoral degree) began to suffer long periods of depression, sometimes so severe that he required hospitalization. The situation was partially rectified in the late 1960s when students participating in the Black Arts movement demanded that he receive the attention he deserved. In 1971, he was awarded an honorary doctorate from Howard (the first of many he would eventually garner), and several of his most important books were reprinted in the mid-seventies.

In summing up Brown's impact on black literature of the twentieth century, *New Republic* contributor John F. Callahan observes: "It is his achievement to have fulfilled the complex double purpose of writing poetry worthy of a great audience and of helping to shape that diverse, responsive, critical, and inclusive audience through his essays and criticism." Concludes Henry Louis Gates, Jr., in the *New York Times Book Review:* "Such a prolific output in a life that spans the era of Booker T. Washington and the era of Black Power makes him not only the bridge between 19th and 20th-century black literature, but also the last of the great 'race men,' the Afro-American men of letters, a tradition best epitomized by W.E.B. DuBois. A self-styled 'Old Negro,' Sterling Brown is not only the Afro-American Poet Laureate, he is a great poet."

BIOGRAPHICAL/CRITICAL SOURCES:

BOOKS

Brown, Sterling A., Arthur P. Davis and Ulysses Lee, *The Negro Caravan,* Dryden, 1941, revised edition, Arno, 1970.
Brown, Sterling A., *The Collected Poems of Sterling A. Brown,* selected by Michael S. Harper, Harper, 1980.
Contemporary Literary Criticism, Gale, Volume 1, 1973, Volume 23, 1983.
Cunard, Nancy, editor, *Negro Anthology,* Wishart Co., 1934.
Davis, Arthur P., *From the Dark Tower: Afro-American Writers, 1900-1960,* Howard University Press, 1974.
Dictionary of Literary Biography, Gale, Volume 48: *American Poets, 1880-1945,* Second Series, 1986, Volume 51: *Afro-American Writers from the Harlem Renaissance to 1940,* 1987, Volume 63: *Modern American Critics, 1920-1955,* 1988.
Gayle, Addison, Jr., editor, *Black Expression: Essays by and About Black Americans in the Creative Arts,* Weybright & Talley, 1969.
Mangione, Jerre, *The Dream and the Deal: The Federal Writers' Project, 1935-1943,* Little, Brown, 1972.
Wagner, Jean, *Black Poets of the United States: From Paul Laurence Dunbar to Langston Hughes,* translated by Kenneth Douglas, University of Illinois Press, 1973.

PERIODICALS

Black American Literature Forum, spring, 1980.
Callaloo: A Black South Journal of Arts and Letters, February-May, 1982.
Ebony, October, 1976.
Los Angeles Times Book Review, August 3, 1980.
New Directions: The Howard University Magazine, winter, 1974.
New Republic, February 11, 1978, December 20, 1982.
New York Times, May 15, 1932.
New York Times Book Review, November 30, 1969, January 11, 1981.
Studies in the Literary Imagination, fall, 1974.
Village Voice, January 14, 1981.
Virginia Quarterly Review, winter, 1981.
Washington Post, November 16, 1969, May 2, 1979, September 4, 1980, May 12, 1984.

OBITUARIES:

PERIODICALS

Chicago Tribune, January 17, 1989.
Los Angeles Times, January 19, 1989.
New York Times, January 17, 1989.
Washington Post, January 16, 1989.

*   *   *

BROWNMILLER, Susan   1935-

PERSONAL: Born February 15, 1935, in Brooklyn, N.Y. *Education:* Attended Cornell University, 1952-55, and Jefferson School of Social Sciences.

ADDRESSES: Home—61 Jane St., New York, NY 10014.

CAREER: Actress in New York City, 1955-59; *Coronet,* New York City, assistant to managing editor, 1959-60; *Albany Report,* Albany, N.Y., editor, 1961-62; *Newsweek,* New York City, national affairs researcher, 1963-64; *Village Voice,* New York City, staff writer, 1965; National Broadcasting Company (NBC-TV), New York City, reporter, 1965; American Broadcasting Co.

(ABC-TV), New York City, network newswriter, 1966-68; free-lance journalist, 1968-70; writer. Lecturer; organizer of Women Against Pornography.

MEMBER: New York Radical Feminists (co-founder).

AWARDS, HONORS: Grants from Alicia Patterson Foundation and Louis M. Rabinowitz Foundation; *Against Our Will: Men, Women, and Rape* was listed among the outstanding books of the year by the *New York Times Book Review,* 1975; Brownmiller was named one of *Time*'s twelve Women of the Year, 1975.

WRITINGS:

Shirley Chisholm: A Biography (juvenile), Doubleday, 1971.
Against Our Will: Men, Women, and Rape (Book-of-the-Month Club selection), Simon & Schuster, 1975.
Femininity, Simon & Schuster, 1984.
Waverly Place (novel), Grove, 1989.

Contributor of articles to magazines, including *Newsweek, Esquire,* and *New York Times Magazine.*

SIDELIGHTS: Susan Brownmiller was among the first of the politically active feminists in New York City during the 1960s. In 1968 she helped found the New York Radical Feminists, and as a member of that group she took part in a number of protest demonstrations, including a sit-in at the offices of the *Ladies' Home Journal* opposing the magazine's "demeaning" attitude toward women. Her interest in women's rights surfaced in much of her work as a free-lance journalist, and one article she wrote, about Shirley Chisholm, the first black U.S. congresswoman, developed into a biography for young readers. In 1971 Brownmiller helped to organize a "Speak-Out on Rape," and in the process she realized that once again she had the material for a book. She submitted an outline of her idea to Simon & Schuster, they contracted for the book, and Brownmiller began researching the subject of rape. After four years of research and writing, she published *Against Our Will: Men, Women, and Rape.*

Against Our Will explores the history of rape, exploding the myths that, the author says, influence our modern perspective. She traces the political use of rape in war from biblical times through Vietnam, explains the origins of American rape laws, and examines the subjects of interracial rape, homosexual rape, and child molestation. Brownmiller asserts that rape "is nothing more or less than a conscious process of intimidation by which *all men* keep *all women* in a state of fear." Supporting her thesis with facts taken from her extensive research in history, literature, sociology, law, psychoanalysis, mythology, and criminology, Brownmiller argues that rape is not a sexual act but an act of power based on an "anatomical fiat"; it is the result of early man's realization that women could be subjected to "a thoroughly detestable physical conquest from which there could be no retaliation in kind."

Against Our Will was serialized in four magazines and became a best-seller and Book-of-the-Month Club selection, and its nationwide tour made Brownmiller a celebrity. Her appearance on the cover of *Time* as one of the twelve Women of the Year and on television talk shows as a frequent guest confirmed the timeliness of her book. Brownmiller herself remarked, "I saw it as a once-in-a-lifetime subject that had somehow crossed my path," and she expressed gratitude to the women's movement for having given her "a constructive way" to use her rage.

Since Brownmiller's analysis of rape presented a new and controversial viewpoint to an already provocative subject, *Against Our Will* was received with mixed and at times passionate reviews. Editor Carol Eisen Rinzler expressed her regret that Simon &

Schuster, and not she, had published *Against Our Will.* "It is one of the two books I lay awake nights lusting after," she said. Mary Ellen Gale, reviewing for the *New York Times Book Review,* said Brownmiller's book "deserves a place on the shelf next to those rare books about social problems which force us to make connections we have too long evaded, and change the way we feel about what we know." And reviewer Helen E. Schwartz, writing in the *Nation,* indicated the significance *Against Our Will* held for women by relating, "One friend told me that the book was 'so politically important that any criticism you might have of it is secondary.'" Schwartz was also told that if she said anything bad about the book she would be regarded "as an Aunt Thomasina, or whatever the women's movement equivalent is of Uncle Tom."

Described in *Time* as "a kind of *Whole Earth Catalog* of man's inhumanity to women," *Against Our Will* won the applause of male as well as female critics. *Village Voice* critic Eliot Fremont-Smith praised it as "a landmark work in the literature of awareness. . . . Whatever its distorted premises and internal contradictions . . . [it] is a most important, eye-and-mind-opening book." Michael F. McCauley concurred when he said in *Commonweal:* "*Against Our Will* is a poignant, candid, and long overdue analysis of a subject that concerns all. As long as present legal outlooks and cultural mythologies prevail, we are, each one of us, victims of this unspeakable attack on our humanity."

In a review for *Village Voice,* Rinzler said, "It seems evident that 'Against Our Will' will stand up as a major work of history, a classic, if you will," but she also noted that "Brownmiller expects criticism." Indeed, because as Diane Johnson of the *New York Review of Books* observed, "no other subject, it seems, is experienced so differently by men and women as rape. . . . There are really two audiences for [*Against Our Will*], one which will know much of what [Brownmiller] has to say already, and another which is ill-equipped by training or sympathy to understand it at all."

The *National Review*'s M. J. Sobran, Jr., criticized Brownmiller, her book, and her supporters. He excoriated favorable *Village Voice* reviews by Fremont-Smith and Rinzler, labeling Rinzler as "some dizzy feminist," and he ridiculed Brownmiller's scholarship and work as intellectually and stylistically sloppy. "The whole point of her book is the tendentiousness of her research," Sobran declared. "What she is engaged in, really, is not scholarship but henpecking—that conscious process of intimidation by which all women keep all men in terror."

Other critics shared Sobran's contention that Brownmiller's research was biased. *New Leader* critic Ellen Chesler maintained: "While helping to organize a feminist speak-out on rape, Susan Brownmiller made a discovery: Rape could be seen as an extraordinary historical metaphor, a fundamental 'way of looking at male-female relations, at sex, at strength, and at power. Now . . . she has given us a book that jams the facts—against their will—into the Procrustean bed of her original 'moment of revelation.'" In a review for *Commentary,* Michael Novak also complained that Brownmiller's assertions "are surrounded with much rhetoric, a great smokescreen of 'research,' evidence so selective and reasoning so tendentious that to contend against them is to involve oneself in intellectual corruption." Agreeing that "sometimes the book is strident in its tone and one-sided in its presentation," Helene E. Schwartz nevertheless argued that "we should recognize that anger and extremism may be necessary before we can reach the mean of re-education that this book advocates."

In researching and writing *Against Our Will,* Brownmiller was motivated by "a dual sense of purpose," theorized Carol Eisen Rinzler, "a political desire that the book be of value to feminism, and a personal desire to make a lasting contribution to the body of thought." Brownmiller mentions yet another goal in her conclusion to *Against Our Will:* "Fighting back. On a multiplicity of levels, that is the activity we must engage in, together, if we—women—are to redress the imbalance and rid ourselves and men of the ideology of rape. . . . My purpose in this book has been to give rape its history. Now we must deny it a future."

Brownmiller's next book, *Femininity,* is less confrontational in tone than *Against Our Will* but has still provoked mixed reactions. *Femininity* examines the ideal qualities—both physical and emotional—that are generally considered feminine and the lengths women go to conform to those ideals. The controversy arises, Brownmiller told *Detroit News* writer Barbara Hoover, when readers and reviewers "want to know where the blame is—is she blaming men or is she blaming us women? Well," the author explained, "I'm blaming neither. I don't criticize; I just explore the subject."

Brownmiller addresses the subject of child abuse in *Waverly Place,* her first novel. The book is a fictionalized account of the lives of Hedda Nussbaum and her abusive lover, Joel Steinberg, a New York attorney who was accused during the late 1980s of beating to death their illegally adopted daughter. Explaining why she chose to present the story as fiction instead of nonfiction, Brownmiller wrote in her introduction to *Waverly Place:* "I wanted the freedom to invent dialogue, motivations, events, and characters based on my own understanding of battery and abuse, a perspective frequently at variance with the scenarios created by the prosecution or the defense in courts of law." "Brownmiller's effort serves a potentially constructive purpose," assessed reviewer Christopher Lehmann-Haupt in the *New York Times.* "It tries to fill the emotional void created by any incomprehensible human act. It proposes how such a thing could have happened and allows us to participate in the drama of its answer. It offers us an experience of mourning, as well as some reassurance that we ourselves are safe from such disasters. . . . In all these respects," Lehmann-Haupt concluded, "Ms. Brownmiller's novel succeeds very well."

AVOCATIONAL INTERESTS: Travel.

BIOGRAPHICAL/CRITICAL SOURCES:

BOOKS

Brownmiller, Susan, *Against Our Will: Men, Women, and Rape,* Simon & Schuster, 1975.
Brownmiller, *Waverly Place,* Grove, 1989.

PERIODICALS

Commentary, February, 1976.
Commonweal, December 5, 1975.
Detroit News, February 1, 1984.
Nation, November 29, 1975.
National Review, March 5, 1976.
New Leader, January 5, 1976.
New Statesman, December 12, 1975.
New York Review of Books, December 11, 1975.
New York Times, February 2, 1989.
New York Times Book Review, October, 1975, December 28, 1975.
Time, October 13, 1975, January 5, 1976.
Village Voice, October 6, 1975.

BRULLS, Christian
See SIMENON, Georges (Jacques Christian)

*   *   *

BRUNNER, John (Kilian Houston) 1934-
(John Loxmith, Trevor Staines, Keith Woodcott)

PERSONAL: Born September 24, 1934, in Oxfordshire, England; son of Anthony and Felicity (Whittaker) Brunner; married Marjorie Rosamond Sauer, July 12, 1958 (deceased, 1986). *Education:* Attended Cheltenham College, 1948-51.

ADDRESSES: Agent—Mark Hamilton, A.M. Heath & Co., 79 St. Martin's Lane, London WC2N 4AA, England; and William Reiss, John Hawkins & Associates, 71 West 23rd St., New York, N.Y. 10010.

CAREER: Science fiction novelist, songwriter, poet, and freelance writer, 1958—. Abstractor, Industrial Diamond Information Bureau, 1956; editor, Spring Books Ltd., 1956-58. Campaign for Nuclear Disarmament, Hampstead chairman, 1961, member of London regional council, 1962-63, member of national council, 1964-65. Guest novelist in residence, University of Kansas, Lawrence, 1972. Lecturer on science fiction to universities and professional groups in the United States, England, and Italy. *Military service:* Royal Air Force, 1953-55; became pilot officer.

MEMBER: PEN International, European Science Fiction Society (past president), World SF, Science Fiction Writers of America, Authors Guild, Authors League of America, Crime Writers Association, Society of Authors, Science Fiction Foundation (past vice-president), British Science Fiction Association (past chairman), British Film Institute.

AWARDS, HONORS: British Fantasy Award, 1966; Hugo Award, 1968, for *Stand on Zanzibar;* received two British Science Fiction Awards; Prix Apollo; Bronze Porgie Award, *West Coast Review of Books;* Grand Prix du Festival de l'Insolite (France), Cometa d'Argento (twice); Premio Italia; European SF Convention Special Award as Best Western European SF Writer; Clark Ashton Smith Award for fantasy poetry; elected Knight of Mark Twayne (twice).

WRITINGS:

Horses at Home, Spring Books, 1958.
The Brink, Gollancz, 1959.
Echo in the Skull, Ace Books, 1959, expanded version published as *Give Warning to the World,* DAW, 1974.
The Hundredth Millennium, Ace Books, 1959, revised and enlarged edition published as *Catch a Falling Star,* Ace Books, 1968, Ballantine, 1982.
Threshold of Eternity, Ace Books, 1959.
The World Swappers, Ace Books, 1959.
Slavers of Space, Ace Books, 1960.
The Skynappers, Ace Books, 1960.
Sanctuary in the Sky, Ace Books, 1960.
The Atlantic Abomination, Ace Books, 1960, reprinted, 1976.
Meeting at Infinity, Ace Books, 1961.
Secret Agent of Terra, Ace Books, 1962, revised and enlarged edition published as *The Avengers of Carrig,* Dell, 1969.
The Super Barbarians, Ace Books, 1962.
Times without Number, Ace Books, 1962, revised edition, 1969, Ballantine, 1983.
No Future in It, Gollancz, 1962, Doubleday, 1964.
The Dreaming Earth, Pyramid Books, 1963.
The Space Time Juggler, Ace Books, 1963.

The Astronauts Must Not Land, Ace Books, 1963, revised version published as *More Things in Heaven,* Dell, 1973.

The Castaways' World, Ace Books, 1963, revised edition published as *Polymath,* DAW Books, 1978.

Listen! The Stars!, Ace Books, 1963, enlarged version published as *The Stardroppers,* DAW, 1972.

The Rites of Ohe, Ace Books, 1963.

Endless Shadow, Ace Books, 1964, expanded version published as *Manshape,* DAW, 1982.

The Crutch of Memory, Barrie & Rockliff, 1964.

To Conquer Chaos, Ace Books, 1964.

The Whole Man, Ballantine, 1964 (published in England as *Telepathist,* Faber, 1965).

The Squares of the City, Ballantine, 1965.

The Long Result, Faber, 1965, Ballantine, 1981.

No Then, Mayflower, 1965.

Wear the Butchers' Medal, Pocket Books, 1965.

The Altar on Asconel, Ace Books, 1965.

Enigma from Tantalus, Ace Books, 1965.

The Repairmen of Cyclops, Ace Books, 1965.

The Day of the Star Cities, Ace Books, 1965.

Planet of Your Own: Beast of Kohl, Ace Books, 1966.

No Other Gods but Me, Compact Books, 1966.

Out of My Mind, Ballantine, 1967.

Productions of Time, New American Library, 1967.

Quicksand, Doubleday, 1967.

Born under Mars, Ace Books, 1967.

Bedlam Planet, Ace Books, 1968, Ballantine, 1982.

Into the Slave Nebula, Lancer Books, 1968.

Not before Time, New English Library, 1968.

Stand on Zanzibar, Doubleday, 1968, Ballantine, 1988.

Father of Lies, Belmont Books, 1968.

A Plague on Both Your Causes, Hodder & Stoughton, 1969, published in the United States as *Blacklash,* Pyramid Books, 1969.

Black Is the Color, Pyramid Publications, 1969.

Double, Double, Ballantine, 1969.

The Evil That Men Do, Belmont-Tower, 1969.

Timescoop, Dell, 1969.

The Jagged Orbit, Ace Books, 1969.

Good Men Do Nothing, Hodder & Stoughton, 1970.

The Gaudy Shadows, Beagle Books, 1970.

The Devil's Work, Norton, 1970.

Honky in the Woodpile, Constable, 1971.

The Wrong End of Time, Doubleday, 1971.

The Sheep Look Up, Harper, 1972.

Entry to Elsewhen (short stories), DAW Books, 1972.

From This Day Forward, Doubleday, 1972.

The Dramaturges of Yan, Ace Books, 1972, Ballantine, 1982.

Age of Miracles, Ace Books, 1973, revised version published as *The Crucible of Time,* Ballantine, 1984.

The Stone That Never Came Down, Doubleday, 1973.

Web of Everywhere, Bantam, 1974.

The Shockwave Rider, Harper, 1975.

Total Eclipse, Weidenfeld & Nicolson, 1975, DAW Books, 1978.

The Book of John Brunner, DAW, 1976.

(Contributor) *The Craft of Science Fiction,* edited by R. Bretnor, Harper, 1976.

Traveler in Black, Ace Books, 1977.

Interstellar Empire, DAW Books, 1978.

Tomorrow May Even Be Worse, NESFA Press, 1978.

Foreign Constellations (short stories), Everest House, 1979.

The Infinitive of Go, Del Rey Books, 1980.

Players at the Game of People, Ballantine, 1980.

A New Settlement of Old Scores, New England Science Fiction Association, 1983.

The Great Steamboat Race, Ballantine, 1983.

The Tides of Time, Ballantine, 1984.

The Compleat Traveller in Black, Blue Jay Books, 1986.

The Best of John Brunner, edited by Joe Haldemann, 1988.

Children of Thunder, Ballantine, 1989.

Also author of *The Shift Key,* 1987.

UNDER PSEUDONYM KEITH WOODCOTT

I Speak for Earth, Ace Books, 1961.

The Psionic Menace, Ace Books, 1963.

The Ladder in the Sky, Ace Books, 1965.

The Martian Sphinx, Ace Books, 1965.

OTHER

Translator of *The Overlords of War* by Gerard Klein, *Femme Fatale* by Marrianne Leconte, and *Transisters* by Christine Renard; translator of poems by Rilke, George, Ausonius, and others. Stories appear in numerous anthologies including *Sixth Annual of the Year's Best SF, Yet More Penguin Science Fiction, More Adventures on Other Planets, Great Science Fiction Adventures,* and *Alien Worlds.* Also author of film scripts, including "The Terrornauts," Amicus Productions, 1967; author of songs recorded by Pete Seeger and other performing artists. Contributor to many science fiction magazines, and to *Peace News, Aspects, Reason,* and other journals. Contributing editor, *Sanity,* 1964—.

SIDELIGHTS: John Brunner has long been considered one of the more important and successful speculative and extrapolative science fiction writers in the world. In his fiction, Brunner projects many of the current sociological trends, such as environmental problems, into the near-future. John R. Pfeiffer feels that "what is remarkable is Brunner's consistent grace and intelligibility in explaining and abstracting civilization just beyond the threshold of the present."

Edward L. Lamie and Joe De Bolt agree and believe that "in the hands of a superior practitioner, the speculative and extrapolative nature of science fiction makes it an unparalleled tool for exploring the fundamental questions raised by the man-computer relationship and its societal consequences. John Brunner, whose works deal extensively with computers and their human effects, is especially well suited to be the focus of such an analysis. Few authors draw such complete and informed pictures of the computer in our future."

In recent years, Brunner has set his stories in the near-future which many reviewers feel is far more successful than his earlier style of setting his fiction in the far-future. One of these reviewers, William Brown, feels that Brunner is successful because he "does not play runaway games with his images of the future. Almost everything about them is closely related to the present. There is no escape into a Buck Rogers future where amazing new techniques influence behavior or where man has been transformed into a different creature. Brunner's plausible scenarios and characters can be taken seriously."

Discussing the problems of projecting current trends into the near-future, John Brunner told an interviewer for *Writer:* "Naturally, the problem is a tricky one—the moment you set a story even a single generation ahead of your time, you're by definition dealing with people whose prejudices and preferences are no longer the same as ours." William Brown feels Brunner handles this problem of projection well. As he explains: Brunner's "stories are predicated on the basic condition of mankind as it has always been and, as Brunner projects, it always will be. The characters in Brunner's stories are governed by the basic needs, just as characters throughout history have been. They make human choices in the face of their predicaments, and that is what gives the reader such a high degree of catharsis, of pleasure through vicarious identification. Were Brunner to project a new breed of men into a new set of circumstances, the results would be disastrous."

Stand on Zanzibar, winner of the 1968 Hugo Award, is highly regarded by science fiction writers and is often used to represent the genre in college literature courses. Brunner's books play an important role not only in the field of science fiction, but also in the near-future world which they describe. For example, *The Shockwave Rider,* a 1975 work about a man who tampers with computer networks, gained national attention when a computer virus crashed systems around the country in November, 1988. It came to light that Robert Tappan Morris, the originator of the "virus" that was designed as a problem-solving challenge but somehow got out of hand, had been introduced to the subject of computer viruses by Brunner's book. *Los Angeles Times* reporter Paul Dean cites Brunner's comment following his meeting with Morris that for proving the vulnerability of computer-stored data, Morris "has definitely done a service to the public at large." Brunner went on to say that the incident "is an awful warning to the people who have assumed blithely that they can run a modern society on the basis of secretive, computerized information." Computers have a two-fold impact on contemporary life, he explained. While they can make us better informed than people of the past, they can also be used to manipulate information in a way that puts us at great risk. As a result, he warns, "not just life and death of the individual, but life or death of the society is at stake."

BIOGRAPHICAL/CRITICAL SOURCES:

BOOKS

Contemporary Authors Autobiography Series, Volume 8, Gale, 1988.
Contemporary Literary Criticism, Gale, Volume 8, 1978, Volume 10, 1979.
De Bolt, Joseph W., editor, *The Happening Worlds of John Brunner,* Kennikat, 1975.
Platt, Charles, *Dream Makers: The Uncommon People Who Write Science Fiction,* Berkley, 1980.

PERIODICALS

Los Angeles Times, November 9, 1988.
Mother Jones, August, 1976.
New Republic, October 30, 1976.
New York Times Book Review, October 27, 1968.
Writer, December, 1971.
Yale Review, March, 1973.

* * *

BUBER, Martin 1878-1965

PERSONAL: Surname pronounced "*Boo*-ber"; born February 8, 1878, in Vienna, Austria; died June 13, 1965, in Jerusalem, Israel; son of Carl (a farmer) and Elise Buber; married Paula Winkler (a novelist who published under the pseudonym George Mundt (one source says Georg Munkl), 1899 (died, 1958); children: Rafael, Eva Buber Strauss. *Education:* Attended the universities of Vienna, Leipzig, Zurich, and Berlin, 1897-1904; University of Vienna, Ph.D., 1904.

CAREER: Author, editor, scholar, lecturer, and Zionist activist in Austria, Germany, and Switzerland, 1904-23; University of Frankfurt, Frankfurt am Main, Germany, professor of comparative religion, 1923-33; Central Office for Jewish Adult Education, Frankfurt, director, 1933-38: Frankfurter Juedische Lehrhaus (Free Jewish Academy), Frankfurt, director, 1933-38: Hebrew University, Jerusalem, Israel, professor of social philosophy, 1938-51, professor emeritus, beginning in 1951. Institute for Adult Education, Jerusalem, founder and director, 1949-53.

Edited *Die Welt* (Zionist weekly periodical), Berlin, 1901, and *Der Jude* (Zionist monthly periodical), Berlin, 1916-24; co-edited *Die Kreatur* (quarterly religious journal), Berlin, 1926-30.

AWARDS, HONORS: Honorary doctoral degrees from Hebrew Union College, Hebrew University, and the universities of Aberdeen and Paris (Sorbonne); nominated by Hermann Hesse for the Nobel Prize in Literature, 1949; Goethe Prize from the University of Hamburg, 1953, and Peace Prize from the German Book Trade Association, 1955, both recognizing achievement as a writer of prose fiction in German.

WRITINGS:

(Editor) *Juedische Kuenstler,* Juedischer Verlag, 1903.
Die Geschichten des Rabbi Nachman, 1906, translation by Maurice Friedman published as *Tales of Rabbi Nachman,* Horizon, 1968.
(Editor) *Die Gesellschaft: Sammlung sozialpsychologischer Monographien,* Ruetten & Loening, 1906-12.
Die Legende des Baalschem, Ruetten & Loening, 1908, translation by Lucy Cohen published as *Jewish Mysticism and the Legends of Baalshem,* Dent, 1931; translation by Maurice Friedman published as *The Legend of the Baalshem,* Harper, 1955.
Ekstatische Konfessionen, Eugen Diedrichs Verlag, 1909.
Chinesische Geister und Liebesgeschichten, Ruetten & Loening, 1911.
Drei Reden ueber das Judentum, Ruetten & Loening, 1911.
Buberheft: Neue Blaetter, Verlag der Neuen Blaetter, 1913.
Daniel: Gespraeche von der Verwirklichung, Insel Verlag, 1913, translation by Friedman published as *Daniel: Dialogues on Realization,* Holt, 1964.
Kalewala, Georg Mueller, 1914.
Reden und Gleichnisse des Tschuang-Tse, Insel Verlag, 1914.
(Editor) *Die vier Zweige des Mabinogi,* Insel Verlag, 1914.
Die juedische Bewegung: Gesammelte Aufsaetze und Ansprachen, Juedischer Verlag, Volume 1: *1900-1914,* 1916, Volume 2: *1916-1920,* 1921.
Vom Geist des Judentums, Kurt Wolff Verlag, 1916.
Voelker, Staaten und Zion, R. Loewit Verlag, 1917.
Ereignisse und Begegnungen, Insel Verlag, 1917.
Mein Weg zum Chassidismus, Ruetten & Loening, 1918.
Cheruth: Ein Rede ueber Jugend und Religion, R. Loewit Verlag, 1919.
Worte an die Zeit, Dreilander Verlag, Volume 1: *Grundsaetze,* 1919, Volume 2: *Gemeinschaft,* 1919.
Der Heilige Weg, Ruetten & Loening, 1919.
Die Rede, die Lehre, und das Lied, Insel Verlag, 1920.
Der grosse Maggid und seine Nachfolge, Ruetten & Loening, 1922.
Ich and Du, Insel Verlag, 1923, translation by Ronald Gregor Smith published as *I and Thou,* T. & T. Clark, 1937, Scribner, 1957.
Reden ueber das Judentum, Ruetten & Loening, 1923.
Das verborgene Licht, Ruetten & Loening, 1924.
(With Franz Rosenzweig) *Die Schrift,* fifteen volumes, Schocken Verlag, 1925-38, revised edition published in four volumes by Jakob Hegner Verlag, Volume 1: *Die fuenf Buecher der*

Weisung, 1954, Volume 2: *Buecher der Geschichte,* 1958, Volume 3: *Buecher der Kundung,* 1958, Volume 4: *Die Schriftwerke,* 1961.

Des Baal-Schem-Tov Unterweisung im Umgang mit Gott, Jakob Hegner Verlag, 1927.

Die chassidischen Buecher: Gesamtausgabe, Jakob Hegner Verlag, 1928, translation by Olga Marx published as *Tales of the Hasidim,* Schocken, 1948, Volume 1: *The Early Masters,* Volume 2: *The Later Masters.*

(Editor with Ina Britschgi-Schimmer) *Gustav Landauer: Sein Lebensgang in Briefen,* two volumes, Ruetten & Loening, 1929.

Hundert chassidische Geschichten, Schocken Verlag, 1930.

Koenigtum Gottes, Schocken Verlag, 1932, third revised edition, Lambert Schneider Verlag, 1956, translation by Richard Scheimann published as *Kingship of God,* Harper, 1967.

Zwiesprache, Schocken Verlag, 1932, Lambert Schneider Verlag, 1978, translation by Ronald Gregor Smith published as *Between Man and Man,* Macmillan, 1948, new edition translated by Friedman with an afterword by Buber, 1965.

Kampf um Israel: Reden und Schriften, Schocken Verlag, 1933.

Die Troestung Israels, Schocken Verlag, 1933.

Erzaehlungen von Engelm, Geistern und Daemonen, Schocken Verlag, 1934, translation by David Antin and Jerome Rothenberg published as *Tales of Angels, Spirits, and Demons,* Hawk's Well Press, 1958.

Deutung des Chassidismus, Schocken Verlag, 1935, translation by Friedman published as *Hasidism and Modern Man,* Horizon Press, 1958.

Aus Tiefen rufe ich Dich: Dreiundzwanzig Psalmen in der Urschrift mit der Verdeutschung von Martin Bubers, Schocken Verlag, 1936.

Die Frage an den Einzelnen, Schocken Verlag, 1936.

Die Stunde und die Erkenntnis: Reden und Augsaetze, 1933-1935, Schocken Verlag, 1936.

Zion als Ziel und Aufgabe, Schocken Verlag, 1936.

Die Forderang des Geistes und die geschichtliche Wirklichkeit: Antrittsvorlesung gehalten am 25. April 1938 in der Hebraischen Universitaet, Schocken Verlag (Jerusalem), 1938.

Worte an die Jugend, Schocken Verlag, 1938.

(With Judah Magnes) *Two Letters to Gandhi,* Rubin Mass (Jerusalem), 1939.

Ba'yat ha-adam, [Tel-Aviv], 1942-43.

Ha-Ruah veha-metziut, [Tel-Aviv], 1942.

Torat ha-nevi'im, [Tel-Aviv], 1942.

Gog u-Magog, [Jerusalem], 1943, translation from the German manuscript by Ludwig Lewisohn published as *For the Sake of Heaven,* Jewish Publication Society, 1945, Harper, 1953.

Ben 'am le-artso, [Jerusalem], 1944, translation from the German manuscript by Stanley Godman published as *On Zion: The History of an Idea,* Schocken, 1973.

Chassidismus, 1945, translation by Greta Hort published as *Hasidism,* Philosophical Library, 1948.

Be-pardes ha-hasidut, [Tel-Aviv], 1945.

Or ha-ganuz, [Tel-Aviv], 1946, selection translated by Haim Shachter and edited by David Harden published as *From the Treasurehouse of Hassidism: A Selection from 'Or hoganuz' by Martin Buber,* Organizacion Sionista Mundial, [Jerusalem], 1969.

Mamre: Essays in Religion, translation by Greta Hort, Oxford University Press, 1946.

Moses: The Revelation and the Covenant, East West Library, 1946.

Netivot be-utopiyah, [Tel-Aviv], 1947, translation by R. F. C. Hull published as *Paths in Utopia,* Routledge & Kegan Paul, 1949.

(With Judah Magnes) *Arab-Jewish Unity,* Victor Gollancz, 1947.

Dialogisches Leben: Gessamelte philosophische und paedagogische Schriften (includes *Ich and Du, Zwiesprache, Die Frage an den Einzelnen, Ueber das Erzieherische, Das Problem des Menschen*), Gregor Mueller Verlag, 1947.

(With Franz Rosenzweig) *Der Knecht Gottes: Schicksal, Augfage, Trost,* Pulvis Viarum, 1947.

Ten Rungs: Hasidic Sayings, translation from the Hebrew manuscript by Olga Marx, Schocken, 1947.

(Editor with J. L. Magnes and E. Simon) *Towards Union in Palestine: Essays on Zionism and Jewish-Arab Cooperation,* Ihud Association (Jerusalem), 1947, Greenwood, 1972.

Israel and the World: Essays in a Time of Crisis, Schocken, 1948.

Das Problem des Menschen, Lambert Schneider Verlag, 1948.

Der Weg des Menschen: Nach der chassidischen Lehre, [Jerusalem], 1948, Lambert Schneider Verlag, 1960, translation by Friedman published as *The Way of Man According to the Teachings of Hasidism,* Routledge & Kegan Paul, 1950.

The Prophetic Faith, translated from the Hebrew by Carlyle Witton-Davies, Macmillan, 1949.

Die Erzaehlungen der Chassidim, Manesse Verlag, 1950.

Zwei Glaubensweisen, Manesse Verlag, 1950, translation by Norman P. Goldhawk published as *Two Types of Faith,* Macmillan, 1952.

Israel and Palaestina: Zur Geschichte einter Idee, Artemis Verlag, 1950, translation by Stanley Godman published as *Israel and Palestine: The History of an Idea,* Farrar, Straus, 1952, reprinted as *On Zion.*

Urdistanz und Beziehung, Lambert Schneider Verlag, 1951.

At the Turning: Three Addresses on Judaism, Farrar, Straus, 1952.

Bilder von Gut and Boese, Jakob Hegner Verlag, 1952, translation by Michael Bullock published as *Images of Good and Evil,* Routledge & Kegan Paul, 1952.

Die chassidische Botschaft, Lambert Schneider Verlag, 1952.

Right and Wrong: An Interpretation of Some Psalms, translated by Ronald Gregor Smith, S.C.M. Press, 1952.

Zwischen Gesellschaft und Staat, Lambert Schneider Verlag, 1952.

Einsichten: Aus den Schriften gesammelt, Insel Verlag, 1953.

Gottesfinsternis, Manesse Verlag, 1953, translation by Friedman and others published as *Eclipse of God: Studies in the Relation Between Religion and Philosophy,* Harper, 1952.

Good and Evil: Two Interpretations (includes *Right and Wrong* and *Images of Good and Evil*), Scribner, 1953.

Hinweise: Gesammelte Essays, Manesse Verlag, 1953, translation by Friedman published as *Pointing the Way: Collected Essays,* Harper, 1957.

Die Schriften ueber das dialogische Prinzip, Lambert Schneider Verlag, 1954, revised edition, 1973.

Zu einer neuen Verdeutschung der Schrift: Beilage zu dem Werk, Jakob Hegner, 1954.

Der Mensch und sein Gebild, Lambert Schneider Verlag, 1955, translation by Friedman and Ronald Gregor Smith published as *The Knowledge of Man,* Harper, 1965.

Das Sehertum: Anfang und Ausgang, Jakob Hegner, 1955.

Stationen des Glaubens, Insel Verlag, 1956, published in English as *To Hallow This Life,* Harper, 1958.

The Writings of Martin Buber, selected and edited by Will Herberg, World Publishing Co., 1956, New American Library, 1974.

Pirke hasidut, [Jerusalem], 1957.

Schuld und Schuldgefuhle, Lambert Schneider Verlag, 1958.

Be-sod siah, [Jerusalem], 1959.

Te'udah ve-yi'ud, [Jerusalem], 1959.

Begegnung: Autobiographische Fragmente, W. Kohlhammer Verlag, 1960, translation by Friedman published as *Encounter: Autobiographical Fragments,* Open Court, 1972.

The Origin and Meaning of Hasidism, translated by Friedman, Horizon Press, 1960.

(With Nahum Goldmann) *Die Juden in der USSR,* translated from the English manuscript by Wilfried Freiherr von Bredon, Ner-Tamid Verlag, 1961.

Pene adam, [Jerusalem], 1962.

Werke, Koesel Verlag and Lambert Schneider Verlag, Volume 1: *Schriften zur Philosophie,* 1962, Volume 2: *Schriften zur Bibel,* 1964, Volume 3: *Schriften zum Chassidismus,* 1963.

Elija: Ein Mysterienspiel, Lambert Schneider Verlag, 1963, translation published as "Elijah: A Mystery Play" in *Martin Buber and the Theater,* edited by Friedman, Funk & Wagnalls, 1969.

Der Jude und sein Judentum: Gesammelte Aufsaetze und Reden, Joseph Melzer Verlag, 1963.

Nachlese, Lambert Schneider Verlag, 1965.

The Way of Response: Martin Buber, Selections from His Writings, edited by Nahum N. Glatzer, Schocken, 1966.

A Believing Humanism: Gleanings, translated by Friedman, Simon & Schuster, 1967.

On the Bible, edited by Nahum N. Glatzer, Schocken, 1968.

On Judaism (includes translation of lectures from *Reden ueber das Judentum* by Eva Jospe and lectures from *At the Turning*), Schocken, 1968.

Briefwechsel aus sieben Jahrzehnten, Lambert Schneider Verlag, Volume 1: *(1897-1918),* 1972, Volume 2: *(1918-1938),* 1973, Volume 3: *(1938-1965),* 1975.

Meetings, edited and translated by Friedman, Open Court, 1973.

SIDELIGHTS: The Austrian-born Israeli philosopher Martin Buber was one of the major religious existentialist thinkers of the twentieth century. His teaching, a kind of spiritual humanism best expressed in his philosophical masterwork *I and Thou,* has deeply influenced both Jewish and Christian theologians and secular moral philosophers. Buber's life-affirming "philosophy of dialogue" draws on sources as diverse as the anti-religious German philosopher Friedrich Nietzsche and the mystical Hasidic Jewish sect and centers on the proposition that the individual's concrete interaction with others reveals spiritual truth. In addition to his many philosophical works, Buber wrote numerous books on Hasidism and biblical interpretation and produced an acclaimed translation, into German, of the complete Hebrew Bible. Committed to putting his ideas into practice, Buber led a life that enabled him to combine philosophy and career in his roles as educator, Zionist activist, and communitarian socialist.

Martin Buber was born in Vienna in 1878 but grew up in the home of his paternal grandfather, Salomon Buber, in Lemberg, Galicia, then part of the Austro-Hungarian empire and now the city of Lvov in the Soviet Union's Ukrainian Republic. Salomon Buber, a noted Hebrew scholar, thoroughly educated the boy in Jewish culture and religion and introduced him to the mystically inclined Hasidic movement in Galicia, which would later deeply influence Buber's religious philosophy. Buber went on to study philosophy and art history at the universities of Leipzig, Zurich, Berlin, and finally Vienna, where he took his doctoral degree with a dissertation on German mysticism in 1904. As a student, Buber immersed himself in the classic literature of nineteenth-century German idealism and romanticism, and he was profoundly impressed by the existentialist moral philosophy of

Nietzsche, as well as Soren Kierkegaard and Fyodor Dostoyevsky.

While still a student, Buber became active in Theodore Herzl's newly organized Zionist movement, which had the goal of reconstituting a Jewish state in Palestine. From the beginning of his association with the Zionist cause, Buber took the position that the movement could not succeed if it were limited to secular nationalism but that it must entail a spiritual and cultural renewal of world Jewry. Only a return to Judaism's cultural roots, he insisted, could effectively unify Diaspora Jews—those living outside the Holy Land—as a people in the quest for a national homeland and legitimize this goal in the eyes of the rest of the world. Buber urged this viewpoint as editor of the Berlin-based Zionist journal *Die Welt* in 1901, but his ideas were decisively rejected in favor of a purely political movement at the Fifth Zionist Congress held that year.

This defeat prompted Buber to withdraw from active participation in the Zionist movement for a period of several years and to turn his private efforts to achieving the Jewish spiritual renewal he advocated. He began this quest with an intensive study of Hasidism, the joyously communitarian Orthodox movement that had impressed him as a youth in Galicia. To grasp the essence of the Hasidic teaching, Buber turned from the debased and declining present-day Hasidic communities to the writings of the sect's eighteenth-century founder, Baal-Shem-Tov (Israel ben Eliezer) and his great-grandson Nachman ben Simcha. These spiritual leaders stressed the importance of achieving a direct and personal communication with God and of recognizing the divine by "hallowing everyday life" and creating true human community. Hasidism's world-affirming mysticism, which encouraged religious expression through music and dance and judged purity of heart more pleasing to God than learning, emerged partly as a reaction to the legalistic rationalism of rabbinical Judaism, which in turn declared the Hasidic movement heretical. Buber found in Hasidism a spiritual movement capable of rejuvenating the Jewish people, one in which the emphasis on life-enhancing values and the personal encounter with God had certain affinities to the existentialist philosophy that had so impressed him.

Inspired by this discovery, Buber set about the task of collecting and translating into modern German the rich trove of Hasidic literature that was virtually unknown outside of the tiny European Hasidic communities. In Berlin in 1906 he published *The Tales of Rabbi Nachman* and in 1908 *The Legend of the Baal-Shem.* Many other books interpreting and translating the Hasidic teachings followed in later years, including the two-volume *Tales of the Hasidim, The Origin and Meaning of Hasidism, and Hasidism and Modern Man.* Buber also set his only novel, *For the Sake of Heaven,* in an early Russian Hasidic community at the time of the Napoleonic wars and filled the book with Hasidic philosophy. Buber's evocative and stylistically imaginative adaptations of Hasidic tales into the German earned him the Goethe Prize in 1953 and the German Book Trade Association Peace Prize in 1955.

While producing his works on Hasidism in the years before the First World War, Buber also published some collections of mystical writings from other religions, including *Ekstatische Konfessionen,* and delivered influential speeches in several European capitals on the meaning of Jewishness, the most important of which are included in his 1911 work *Drei Reden ueber das Judentum.* At the time, Buber held a rather mystical view of Jewishness that was influenced by the German neo-romantic *volk* movement and located both the unique Jewish spirit and its affinity for the land of Palestine in the racial characteristics or "blood" of the Jewish people. Buber elaborated this view along with his general call for spiritual renewal in *Der Jude,* a widely circulated Zionist journal that he edited from 1916 to 1924. Buber's Zionism was confirmed and strengthened by his conclusion that the eighteenth-century European Hasidic communities had failed to achieve true community because they lacked the legal and territorial independence that would result from national self-determination.

Even as he engaged in these specifically Jewish tasks, Buber was developing a distinctly nonmystical religious philosophy that would appeal to Jews and non-Jews alike and earn him worldwide renown. Buber's emerging "philosophy of dialogue" drew on the Hasidic concerns with "hallowing the everyday" and building a loving spiritual community as well as on the personal commitment and active self-definition central to the existentialist philosophies of Kierkegaard and Nietzsche. Buber planted the seeds of this philosophy in his 1913 book *Daniel,* which counterposed two basic attitudes toward the world: that of "orientation," the objective ordering of the environment for knowledge and use, and that of "realization," the subjective, metaphysical emergence of life's inner meaning.

Buber recast these two basic worldviews in dialogical form in his 1923 philosophical masterwork, *I and Thou.* In this slim but highly influential volume, Buber suggests that the individual confronts the world either as subject-to-object ("I-It") or subject-to-subject ("I-Thou"). The I-It relation objectifies and grasps the world in terms of utilities and is essential to physical survival, while the I-Thou—true relation—involves opening one's full being to meet another spiritual subject. According to Buber, the three types of worldly spiritual subjects with whom one can enter the I-Thou relation are nature, "intelligible forms" or art, and other individuals. Meeting another subject entails meeting oneself because one must surrender one's whole being to the relation: the I of I-Thou, then, is a deeper and richer I than the I of I-It, in which only part of one's being seeks a utility. Whereas objects and the I-It essentially subsist in the past—in terms that have been defined—the I-Thou relation is true presentness: it is open-ended and suspends the movement of time to give a glimpse of eternity. Each particular I-Thou relation is exclusive, since true dialogue is only possible between two subjects at a time, but each radiates universal meaning because it intimates the Eternal Thou, or God.

Buber describes meeting the worldly Thou and meeting God as something of a circular process. Both the love of God and the consciousness of God's love give us the power to love our neighbor: at the same time, meeting our neighbor's Thou helps to reveal God. The Eternal Thou—God—is further intimated by the necessary collapse of every particular I-Thou relation into an I-It relation, which Buber describes as a basic tragedy in the human condition. We are unable to indefinitely sustain our original spiritual relation with a person, a painting, or a landscape, but inevitably begin to analyze it, define it, limit it, and reduce it to an object—in short, we make its Thou into an It and bring it into the world of instrumentalities. The yearning for God is the yearning for the Thou who can never be limited or reduced to an It.

Entering the I-Thou relation, according to Buber, involves both choosing and being chosen; it is paradoxically both an act of grace and a product of one's actions and attitude. Similarly, revelation, or the encounter with the Eternal Thou, cannot be sought as such; one can only prepare for this supreme meeting by engaging in the world with an active love, that is, by seeking to live with one's full being. Each one of us must discover the truth of God in the concrete conditions of our own lives, and fundamentally in our relations with others. "Men do not find God if they stay in the world," Buber remarks in *I and Thou.* "They do not find him if they leave the world. He who goes out with his whole being to meet his Thou, and carries to it all being that is in the world, finds him who cannot be sought." In a later work, *At the Turning,* the philosopher adds, "*You must yourself begin.* Existence will remain meaningless for you if you yourself do not penetrate into it with active love and if you do not in this way discover its meaning for yourself. . . . Meet the world with the fullness of your being, and you shall meet God. . . . If you wish to believe, love."

Buber consequently rejects the traditional religious notion that material and spiritual worlds oppose each other; rather, "there is only the world— which appears to us as twofold in accordance with our twofold attitude." Engaging in the I-It relation, even with people, is necessary for survival, but the morally good individual, says Buber, places greater emphasis on the I-Thou in the overall course of his or her human relations. Evil emerges from the failure to achieve the spiritual self-unification that allows one to live a directed life with one's full being.

"Evil cannot be done with the whole soul; good can only be one with the whole soul," Buber writes in his book *Good and Evil.* Love must see the whole of another being, but hate is "by nature blind," he asserts; only part of one's person hates, and only part of another person can be hated. Evil is accomplished either as a result of simple decisionlessness, allowing oneself to fall passively under the dominance of I-It, or, in its more sinister form, by willful wrong decision, or the deliberate suppression of self-knowledge and spiritual truth in an attempt to create oneself apart from man and God. The good man "stakes his life on his thinking" and lives according to the spiritual truth that is revealed in his concrete interactions with others. Buber stresses that it is not sufficient to mechanically apply moral rules to life's problems; rather, one must confront each moral situation with full creative freedom and openness in the I-Thou dialogue.

Though his dialogical form is unique, Buber's moral thinking has much in common with that of several other modern philosophers in the Judeo-Christian tradition. The I-Thou relation is evocative of Immanuel Kant's "categorical imperative" to treat one's fellow "as an end in himself and never as a means only." Buber's emphasis on dialogue and his assertion that "the fundamental fact of existence is not man, but man-with-man," also closely parallels the thinking of his contemporary, Karl Jaspers, a German religious existentialist who similarly regarded the "loving strife" of true human communication as the opening to transcendence.

The true wellspring of Buber's philosophy, though, is that great dialogue between God and man recorded in the Hebrew Bible. Of Buber's numerous books of biblical interpretation. *Moses* and *The Prophetic Faith* most cogently develop his dialogical themes. A principal goal in these works is to re-establish the basis of true biblical faith, which the author sees as continually threatened by magical, gnostic, and legalistic distortions, both within organized religion and without. In Buber's interpretation, the biblical dialogue is an intensely personal one between "the 'I' of the speaking God and the 'Thou' of the hearing Israel," considered both collectively and individually. The biblical God becomes flesh in order to meet man, and the story of the Bible is basically the chronicle of successive efforts to strengthen, deepen, and more fully personify the dialogue between God and man, which culminates in the promise of the messiah. As Buber sees it, faith in the God of the Bible is not a consoling faith in any superficial sense: on the contrary, God makes an absolute demand on the totality of one's life and being, and shatters all human self-sufficiency and security. Therefore man is under a constant injunction to sustain his part of the dialogue by seeking to interpret and do the will of God in every concrete situation. Because of the difficulties of God's demands and his loving confidence in humankind, men and women meet him in both fear and love—the two attitudes are inextricably merged in divine love.

Buber's deep commitment to the Bible inspired him to initiate a prolonged and fruitful dialogue with the other great biblical religion: Christianity. He helped found the influential religious journal *Die Kreatur* in 1926 and co-edited it for four years with Joseph Wittig, a Catholic, and Viktor von Weizsaecker, a Protestant. In later years, Buber kept up a mutually productive correspondence with the great American Christian existentialist theologians Paul Tillich and Reinhold Niebuhr, the latter of whom acknowledged his specific debt to *I and Thou* for instructing "me and many others on the uniqueness of human selfhood and on the religious dimension of the person." Buber's outstanding work on the relation between Judaism and Christianity is *Two Types of Faith,* published in English in 1952.

In addition to his works of interpretation, Buber's biblical scholarship encompassed the massive project of translating the entire Old Testament from Hebrew into German. The philosopher collaborated with the renowned German Jewish scholar Franz Rosenzweig on this task after the First World War and continued with it on his own after Rosenzweig died in 1929. The fifteen-volume *Die Schrift* was acclaimed for its success in capturing much of the spirit of the Hebrew original lost in previous translations. Rather than adapt the Hebrew to the demands of modern German, Buber managed to twist the German into a form that resembled the ancient text but still remained intelligible.

In keeping with his philosophy, Buber not only wrote about the life of dialogue but pursued it actively as a teacher and educational administrator. As professor of comparative religion at Frankfurt University, he held the only chair of Jewish philosophy at a German university from 1923 until 1933, when the Nazi regime excluded Jews from German educational institutions. For the next five years, Buber directed the Central Office for Jewish Adult Education in Germany and the Frankfurter Juedische Lehrhaus, a free college for Jews. His educational work was credited with helping to spiritually strengthen German Jews at a time of terrible trial for his people. Buber was finally forced to flee Germany in 1938 for Palestine, where he became professor of social philosophy at Hebrew University in Jerusalem. When Israel became an independent state in 1948, the philosopher was appointed director of the Institute for Adult Education in Jerusalem, which trained teachers in the instruction of newly arrived immigrants.

In Palestine, Buber was deeply impressed by the Jewish rural commune movement, which he believed had great potential for helping to realize the full life of the I-Thou dialogue. A "communitarian" socialist since early adulthood, Buber advocates a social philosophy that is closely linked to his religious teaching. In his view, true community emerges out of the I-Thou relationship and must have both a religious foundation, wherein community members are unified in their individual relation with a "divine center," and a socioeconomic foundation, wherein cooperative units maintain the cycle of production and consumption. Buber judged these conditions best realized in the Palestine kibbutzes—small living and working groups—where members could exert

real cooperative control over their conditions of life and bond effectively with one another in the I-Thou relationship while maintaining a healthy degree of individual privacy. These basic social units would in turn associate with one another and with larger socioeconomic units to create an ascending "community of communities" that would ultimately constitute a world society. In his writings on the subject, Buber acknowledges that this decentralized society must develop new and radically different technologies from those already predominant in contemporary urban society and that the optimum balance between local autonomy and centralism will have to be worked out by trial and error in each concrete instance. Buber counterposes this social vision—which bears some affinities to anarchist communitarianism and the contemporary "bioregionalist" movement—to the individualism of modern capitalism and the collectivism of Soviet communism and Western European state socialism. "Individualism understands only a part of man, collectivism understands man only as a part: neither advances to the wholeness of man," the philosopher explains in *Between Man and Man.* "Individualism sees man only in relation to himself, but collectivism does not see man at all; it sees 'society.'" Buber further develops his social views with particular reference to the kibbutz in his 1949 work *Paths in Utopia.*

The example of the kibbutz movement also influenced Buber's later Zionist thinking. Although he never abandoned the mystical view that the Holy Land was uniquely suited to the Jews because of their religious heritage, Buber insisted in the years before the nation of Israel was born that Zionism could only succeed as a form of "Hebrew humanism" that would bring supernatural values into the world. In his 1942 book *Ha-Ruah veha Metziut,* the philosopher contrasts this view "to that Jewish nationalism which regards Israel as a nation like unto other nations, and recognizes no task for Israel save that of preserving and asserting itself. But no nation in the world has this as its only task, for just as an individual who wishes merely to preserve and assert himself leads an unjustified and meaningless existence, so a nation with no other aim deserves to pass away." According to Buber, the specifically Jewish task is to endeavor to realize "the attributes of God revealed to it, justice and love" in concrete life by building the I-Thou relation and examples of true community. Buber decided that fulfilling this task required forming a binational state representing both Jews and Palestinian Arabs, and he collaborated with Hebrew University chancellor Judah Magnes to draft a program advocating the formation of such a state in 1946. After Israel was created a Jewish state two years later, Buber spoke out vigorously to defend the civil and political rights of what had become a largely dispossessed Arab minority in the new country. In a unique gesture that bridged the often bitter divisions between the two peoples in modern Israel, Arab students from Hebrew University placed a wreath on Buber's bier when the great Jewish philosopher died in 1965.

BIOGRAPHICAL/CRITICAL SOURCES:

BOOKS

Arnett, Ronald C., *Communication and Community: Implications of Martin Buber's Dialogue,* Southern Illinois University Press, 1986.

Balthazar, Hans Urs von, *Martin Buber and Christianity,* Harvill, 1958.

Beek, Martinus Adrianus and J. Sperna Weiland, *Martin Buber, Personalist and Prophet,* Newman Press, 1968.

Berkovitz, Eliezer, *A Jewish Critique of the Philosophy of Martin Buber,* Yeshiva University Press, 1962.

Berry, Donald L., *Mutuality: The Vision of Martin Buber,* State University of New York Press, 1985.

Buber, Martin, *The Writings of Martin Buber,* edited by Will Herberg, World Publishing Co., 1956, New American Library, 1974.

Buber, *Meetings,* edited by Maurice Friedman, Open Court, 1973.

Cohen, Arthur A., *Martin Buber,* Hillary House, 1957.

Diamond, Malcolm, *Martin Buber, Jewish Existentialist,* Oxford University Press, 1960.

Edwards, Paul, *Buber and Buberism: A Critical Evaluation,* University of Kansas Press, 1971.

Friedman, Maurice, *Martin Buber: The Life of Dialogue,* Harper, 1960, third edition, University of Chicago Press, 1976.

Friedman, *Martin Buber's Life and Work,* Dutton, Volume 1: *The Early Years, 1878-1923, 1982,* Volume 2: *The Middle Years, 1923-1945,* 1983, Volume 3: *The Later Years, 1945-1965,* 1984.

Friedman, *Martin Buber and the Eternal,* Human Sciences, 1986.

Gordon, Haim and Jochanan Bloch, *Martin Buber: A Centenary Volume,* Ktav Publishing House, 1984.

Hodes, Aubrey, *Martin Buber, an Intimate Portrait,* Viking, 1971.

Kohanski, Alexander S., *Martin Buber's Philosophy of Interhuman Relation,* Associated University Presses, 1982.

Manheim, Werner, *Martin Buber,* Twayne, 1974.

Martin, Bernard, editor, *Great Twentieth-Century Jewish Philosophers: Shestov, Rosenzweig, Buber, With Selections From Their Writings,* Macmillan, 1969.

Moore, Donald J., *Martin Buber, Prophet of Religious Secularism,* Jewish Publication Society of America, 1974.

Oliver, Roy, *Wanderer and the Way: The Hebrew Humanism in the Writings of Martin Buber,* Cornell University Press, 1968.

Schlipp, Paul Arthur and Maurice Friedman, editors, *The Philosophy of Martin Buber,* Open Court, 1967.

Schneider, Grete, *The Hebrew Humanism of Martin Buber,* Wayne State University Press, 1973.

Simon, Akiva Ernst, editor, *Martin Buber, 1878-1978* (library exhibition catalogue), Raphael Haim Hachonen Press (Jerusalem), 1978.

PERIODICALS

Newsweek, April 1, 1957.
New York Times, December 3, 1961.
New York Times Book Review, March 16, 1969.
Times Literary Supplement, December 28, 1973.

OBITUARIES:

PERIODICALS

Commonweal, July 2, 1965.
Newsweek, June 28, 1965.
New York Times, June 14, 1965, June 15, 1965.
Saturday Review, July 24, 1965.
Time, June 25, 1965.

*   *   *

BUCHWALD, Art(hur) 1925-

PERSONAL: Born October 20, 1925, in Mount Vernon, N.Y.; son of Joseph (a curtain manufacturer) and Helen (Kleinberger) Buchwald; married Anne McGarry (a writer; former fashion coordinator for Neiman-Marcus), October 11, 1952; children: Joel, Conchita, Jennifer. *Education:* Attended University of Southern California, 1945-48. *Religion:* Jewish.

ADDRESSES: Office—2000 Pennsylvania Ave., Suite 3804, Washington, D.C. 20006. *Agent*—Sterling Lord Agency, Inc., 660 Madison Ave., New York, N.Y. 10021.

CAREER: New York Herald Tribune, New York, N.Y., columnist for Paris edition, 1949-52; syndicated columnist, 1952—, began with *New York Herald Tribune* Syndicate, currently with *Los Angeles Times* Syndicate. Column published as "Art Buchwald" appears in 550 newspapers worldwide. Frequent lecturer on politics and humor, 1960—. Advisory director, International Social Service. *Military service:* U.S. Marine Corps, 1942-45, with Fourth Marine Air Wing in Pacific; became sergeant.

MEMBER: Overseas Press Club, National Press Club, American Academy and Institute of Arts and Letters, Anglo-American Press Club (Paris).

AWARDS, HONORS: Prix de la Bonne Humeur, 1958, for French translation of *A Gift from the Boys;* L.H.D. from Yale University, 1970; Pulitzer prize, 1982, for commentary.

WRITINGS:

Paris after Dark, Haef, 1950.
Art Buchwald's Paris, Little, 1953.
The Brave Coward, Harper, 1955.
More Caviar, Harper, 1957 (published in England as *I Chose Caviar,* Gollancz, 1957).
A Gift from the Boys (novel), Harper, 1958.
Don't Forget to Write, World Publishing, 1960.
How Much Is That in Dollars?, World Publishing, 1961.
Is It Safe to Drink the Water?, World Publishing, 1962.
I Chose Capitol Punishment, World Publishing, 1963.
. . . And Then I Told the President: The Secret Papers of Art Buchwald, Putnam, 1965.
Son of the Great Society, Putnam, 1966.
Have I Ever Lied to You?, Putnam, 1968.
(Author of introduction and articles) Yasha Beresiner, editor, *The Paper Tiger; or, Words to Hang Yourself By,* with cartoons by Uri Ben-Yehuda, M. Eichenberger, 1968.
The Establishment Is Alive and Well in Washington, Putnam, 1969.
Sheep on the Runway: A Comedy in Two Acts (play; first produced on Broadway at the Helen Hayes Theatre, January 31, 1970; also see below), Samuel French, 1970.
Counting Sheep: The Log and the Complete Play, "Sheep on the Runway," Putnam, 1970.
Oh, to Be a Swinger, Secker & Warburg, 1970.
Getting High in Government Circles, Putnam, 1971.
I Never Danced at the White House, Putnam, 1973.
"I Am Not a Crook," Putnam, 1974.
Washington Is Leaking, Putnam, 1976.
Down the Seine and up the Potomac with Art Buchwald, Putnam, 1977.
The Buchwald Stops Here, Putnam, 1978.
(With wife, Ann Buchwald) *Seems Like Yesterday,* Putnam, 1980.
Laid Back in Washington, Putnam, 1981.
While Reagan Slept, Putnam, 1983.
You Can Fool All of the People All of the Time, Putnam, 1985.
I Think I Don't Remember, Putnam, 1987.
Whose Rose Garden Is It Anyway?, Putnam, 1989.

JUVENILES

The Bollo Caper: A Fable for Children of All Ages, illustrated by
   Julie Brinckloe, Doubleday, 1974.
Irving's Delight: At Last! A Cat Story for the Whole Family!, illus-
   trated by Reynold Ruffins, McKay, 1975.

OTHER

Also author of Art Buchwald's *Secret List to Paris,* 1963. Contributor of numerous humorous essays to magazines.

WORK IN PROGRESS: Another collection of columns.

SIDELIGHTS: For more than three decades Art Buchwald has
been ranked among America's finest writers of humor. His syndicated column, which appears twice weekly in more than five
hundred newspapers worldwide, spoofs the tangled web of national politics and the muddle of modern life. According to
Leonard C. Lewin in the *New York Times Book Review,* Buchwald "may well be the most widely read American political humorist on active duty." His columns, Lewin notes, have "a deceptive simplicity which can be devastating; he is concise, unela-
borate and, incidentally, very funny." Periodically Buchwald
compiles his columns into book form; the resulting works, often
bestsellers, chronicle both political and personal arenas with
tongue-in-cheek satire. *Washington Post Book World* contributor
Vic Sussman writes: "Aside from being entertaining, a collection
of Buchwald's columns forms a unique social history, conveying
the essence and spirit of our times more accurately than any dry
analysis of current events. Buchwald hears with perfect pitch the
babble of cockamamie politicians and bureaucrats, the twaddle
of assorted 'newsmakers,' and the cacophony of our latest fads,
trends and media hype. . . . [He] manages with startling consistency to turn this dross of news into satiric gold. Virtuoso that
he is, he makes the devilish job of writing humor look easy."

Though he resides in Washington, D.C., and has an office near
the White House, Buchwald never socializes or confers with
those in political power. "I feel a pundit like me shouldn't see
people," he told *Time* magazine. "It only confuses me. When
you talk to Senators and Congressmen, you get the impression
they are working, and you know it isn't true." Instead, Buchwald
finds material for his columns by reading three or four major
newspapers every morning, or by watching television news programs. *New York Times Magazine* contributor Thomas Meehan
details the columnist's basic research method: "As he goes
through newspapers and magazines, he frequently clips a story
that he senses might be a taking-off point for one of his columns
and he then either places the clipping in a file folder or more
often simply stuffs it in his shirt pocket. That is the extent of his
research operation." Meehan adds that although Buchwald
often finishes writing his column in less than an hour, he "has
usually been turning over the idea for it in his mind for several
days. In fact, he is obsessed with thinking about ideas and comic
turns of phrase for his columns, and his most characteristic remark when talking with anyone about almost anything is: 'That
could be a column.' "

Whatever his methods, Buchwald has successfully satirized a
succession of presidential administrations, from Eisenhower to
Reagan. Reviewers liken his work to that of some of history's
most notable satirists. Books contributor Al Morgan calls Buchwald "the Breakfast Table Voltaire," and in the *Chicago Tribune
Book World,* former Secretary of State Dean Acheson claims:
"One of the few propositions one can put forward today without
high risk of being proved wrong tomorrow is that Art Buchwald
is probably the greatest satirist in English since [Alexander]
Pope and [Jonathan] Swift. . . . When he holds the mirror to

life, he finds with both Moliere and Shaw the mockery of sense
and reason so well blocked in to begin with that he has only to
add a gay touch of exaggeration and the grotesque to produce
satire." Meehan feels that Buchwald stands alone in his field of
"regularly publishing humor and political satire of consistently
high quality," but the critic suggests that Buchwald would be "in
the front rank even if scores of political satirists were writing
today in our newspapers. . . . As a prose stylist he is no Mark
Twain or H. L. Mencken, nor does he pretend to be. Instead he
is a fairly ordinary writer whose special genius is to see the satirical point that all others might miss." *New York Times Book Review* contributor Gary Blake likewise notes that Buchwald "enlarges small stupidities and hypocrisies until they engulf the
reader, invents confrontations and makes Swiftian proposals
until a small absurdity has triumphed." *Geo* interviewer Andrew
J. Shanley points out that like Twain and Mencken, Buchwald
"is fascinated by the great American system and knows precisely
where its shortcomings and absurdities lie. And like Swift, he
often builds his humor on foundations of anger. Ultimately,
however, Buchwald is unlike anyone else—an American original."

Although Buchwald is today commonly considered "the court
jester of Washington society," to quote Meehan, the witty columnist had a childhood marked by unhappiness and alienation.
He was born on October 20, 1925, in Mount Vernon, New York,
the youngest of four children. Not long after Buchwald was
born, his mother died, and his father, pressed by financial difficulties, was forced to place the children in a series of foster
homes in New York City. For a short period Buchwald even
found himself in the Hebrew Orphan Asylum, after being rejected by various foster families. By the time his father was able
to reassemble the family, Buchwald was sixteen, an indifferent
student, and used to fending for himself. He dropped out of high
school at age seventeen and joined the Marine Corps. According
to a *Time* reporter, the under-aged Buchwald, "told he would
need parental consent, . . . rounded up a drunk who agreed, for
a pint of whisky, to pose as Buchwald *pere.*" The ruse worked,
and Buchwald discovered that he actually enjoyed life in the
armed services. "I felt that the Marines were the only ones I had
ever cared about or who had ever cared about me," he told the
New York Times Magazine. He served in the Pacific theatre from
1942 until 1945 and was discharged with the rank of sergeant.

Late in 1945, Buchwald enrolled at the University of Southern
California even though he did not have a high school diploma.
When the college administration discovered this omission, Buchwald was allowed to stay on as a special student, ineligible for
a degree. He held the position of managing editor of the college
humor magazine, but a *Newsweek* reporter notes that "college
suited him little more than high school." In the spring of 1948,
he received a New York State veteran's bonus check for two hundred fifty dollars, so he quit school and bought a one-way passage to France, arriving in Paris to study French on the G.I. Bill.
According to Meehan, Buchwald never attended classes at the
[Alliance Francaise], however, but instead bribed the attendance
taker to mark him present each day while he used the G.I. Bill
money to live *la vie Boheme* in Montparnasse." To supplement
his income, he landed a job as the Paris stringer for *Variety* magazine. Within three months he had talked his way into the Paris
edition of the *New York Herald Tribune* by offering a sample
nightclub column he proposed to write for that newspaper. He
was offered a weekly salary of twenty-five dollars to review the
Parisian night life.

"Paris after Dark," Buchwald's first column, was expanded to
include restaurants as well as nightclubs, and it appeared four

times per week in the Paris *New York Herald Tribune*. A second column, "Mostly about People," was added in 1951. A year later, a combination of the two columns began to run in stateside editions under the title "Europe's Lighter Side." Soon after changing the title to "Art Buchwald in Paris," the *New York Herald Tribune* syndicated the column to newspapers all over the United States. By 1956, when Buchwald turned thirty-one, his work was showing an evolution of several highly successful comic formulas. Buchwald interviewed American and Continental celebrities such as Grace Kelly, Ingrid Bergman, James Thurber, and Aristotle Onassis, offering their often humorously candid comments to a growing American readership. As a *Newsweek* reporter notes, however, "it was as an offbeat investigator . . . that Buchwald began to hit his real stride." He searched for Turkish baths in Turkey (there were none, he reported), organized an International Food Patrol to monitor the quality of Vienna sausages, and immortalized a fictitious American tourist who vied for the "six minute Louvre" race. Buchwald's tourist swept through the famous museum, viewing the Mona Lisa, the Winged Victory, and the Venus de Milo, in less than four minutes "under perfect conditions, with a smooth floor, excellent lighting, and no wind."

Buchwald first made headlines in 1957 when President Eisenhower visited Paris for treaty conferences. Meehan reports that in his column, Buchwald spoofed the detailed coverage given the press corps each day by the president's press secretary, James Hagerty. Reporters of Buchwald's invention posed questions such as "What time did the President start eating his grapefruit, Jim?" An enraged Hagerty called a special press conference and denounced Buchwald's work as "unadultered rot." Eisenhower, on the other hand, was quite amused by the column and called a quick halt to Hagerty's abuse. Not for the first time, Buchwald had the final say in his column. He replied to Hagerty: "I have been known to write adulterated rot, but never unadulterated rot." The front page coverage of the feud only served to increase Buchwald's popularity.

Buchwald surprised many of his readers and his compatriots in the press when he decided, in 1961, to return to the United States. Meehan writes: "Almost all of his friends advised Buchwald not to make the move, pointing out that while he was probably the most famous American in Paris he'd be simply another face in the crowd in Washington. They suggested, too, that he was risking his professional life, and at a time when his column from Europe was syndicated in 85 papers. He claims not to have had the slightest doubt about his ability to repeat his European success in Washington, and he was right not to have had such doubt, of course his columns from Washington have become vastly more popular and are more satirically biting than anything he wrote from Europe." A *Newsweek* reporter expresses the same opinion: "He had the cushiest newspaper job in Europe—a celebrity interviewing celebrities. . . . But Buchwald tossed over both Paris and status to risk a new career. In going to Washington, rather than New York, he deliberately entered the uncertain field of political humor instead of the old celebrity beat." Assessing Buchwald's level of success after two years in the nation's capital, the reporter affirms: "Since the roly-poly columnist moved, tongue in cheek, to Washington, he has become, quite simply, the funniest U.S. newspaper columnist published today and one of the nation's sharpest political satirists."

Typically, a Buchwald column pokes fun at some aspect of American political or social life, using one of several formulas the author has refined to an imitable degree. Buchwald enjoys turning situations around for satiric effect; for instance, Meehan quotes a 1971 column in which Buchwald claimed: "I can now

reliably report that Vice President Spiro Agnew has no intention of dumping Richard Nixon. . . . A spokesman for the Vice President told me that Agnew was very satisfied with the job his President was doing and that he even intended to give him more responsibilities than any Vice President has ever given his President before." In another of his favorite formats, Buchwald builds his columns around extended conversations, some of which are carried on between himself and an everchanging host of fictitious "specialists," and some of which occur between two or more separate fictional characters. *New York Times* columnist Russell Baker told Meehan: "What most impresses me about Buchwald's writing is his great economy of line, which is especially evident at the beginning of his columns, where he has a genius for setting up complicated premises in a sentence or two." Jeff Greenfield, in a *New York Times Book Review* article, similarly notes: "The remarkable longevity of Buchwald is due to the simplicity of his satirical approach. He has been smart enough to develop a form that is, above all, predictable. Once the comic pretense is set up—stores suspect cash customers in an age of credit, lack of driving is un-American, bureaucrats work hard to avoid working—the column works that premise again and again." According to Robert J. Manning in the *World Journal Tribune*, Buchwald's forte is "the cartoon brought to life, the campus skit or vaudeville blackout raised to a certain This-Is-The-Week-That-Was maturity and social relevance."

Critics praise Buchwald for the consistency of quality that his columns demonstrate. "Perhaps the most impressive thing about Buchwald," contends Meehan, "is simply that he manages year after year to turn out . . . columns of satire . . . and rarely falls below at least a certain level of quality." A *Washington Post Book World* reviewer offers a concurrent assessment: "It is hard enough to write a column, harder still to be funny two or three times a week on demand, and virtually impossible to do it for [more than] a quarter of a century. Buchwald has—and it is an extraordinary accomplishment." *New York Times Book Review* contributor Clifford D. May notes that while not every one of Buchwald's more than five thousand columns has been a gem, "all have had at least a touch of sparkle. Reading them en masse is like listening to a smart-mouthed Greek chorus commenting on the tragi-comic production now playing on the world stage." Some reviewers also accord the columnist respect for the underlying seriousness that fuels his comic work. In the *Washington Post Book World,* Nathaniel Benchley notes: "Trying to write a rational review on a collection of Art Buchwald pieces is like trying to report on a riot in a madhouse; it looks as though most of the characters are crazy, but there's a streak of cold sanity lurking in the background, and you occasionally get the feeling you should be screaming instead of laughing." Sussman feels that Buchwald is "at his best when he's morally outraged at some new hypocrisy or cruelty. Given a clear target, Buchwald forgoes the lightweight humor for bitingly funny and thought-provoking satire." Blake likewise concludes: "One senses that Buchwald is not just milking popular themes, but is sincerely outraged. . . . His crusade sounds most gentle when it is most acerb."

In addition to his numerous collections of columns, Buchwald has authored two children's books as well as a two-act comedy, *Sheep on the Runway,* that appeared on Broadway in 1970. Buchwald succumbed to good-natured pressure when he agreed to write the play; however, the resulting work was a critical and commercial success. In a *New York Times* review, theatre critic Clive Barnes called *Sheep on the Runway* "an always endearing, often very funny play." Set in a fictitious Himalayan nation called Nonomura, the comedy explores a series of bungled U.S. foreign policy moves that reduce the placid monarchy to political chaos. Barnes praises the work for its "gentle but subcutaneously corrosive satire on gunboat politics and the American Way" and adds that Buchwald "sees fun in the grotesque exaggeration of truth—which is, after all, the balloon-pricking business of a satirist." "The play is funniest and strongest when [Buchwald's] characters are blowing up a satirical premise into a comedy balloon of ridiculous though usually recognizable proportions," comments *Christian Science Monitor* reviewer Alan Bunce. Though *Village Voice* critic John Lahr finds *Sheep on the Runway* "surprisingly benign," he nevertheless contends that the work "engages the mind and makes a Broadway audience skeptical of its morning papers. There is a place for Buchwald's talent in the theatre," he concludes.

"Court jesters of old played a role in relieving tensions and maintaining sanity and perspective," writes John Wesley Fuller in the *Christian Science Monitor.* "We need skillful jesters like Art Buchwald today. However tragic, tense—or even humdrum— the daily news, his mercurial wit extracts from it not only laughter, but a balance of common sense and common humanity." Buchwald admits that his humor works as a personal escape valve for frustrations he experiences when confronted by such issues as the arms race, government bureaucracy, drug abuse and inept foreign policy. He told *Geo* magazine that he hopes, through humor, to make a point in a more subtle way. "I can't claim that I've changed anybody's mind," he said, "but it doesn't hurt to have a column the week something's up in Congress because you never know—you might get a vote or two out of it." Though accorded the attention and respect of a national celebrity, Buchwald guards himself against the complacency that sometimes accompanies fame. "What I do is always a challenge," he told *Geo.* "It's not like I broke the home-run record. I have to go to bat [every] week, so I can never relax. Whatever people say about me I accept, but I know I'm only as good as my last column or my last book or whatever I do. I think that anybody who's worth his salt is always walking a tightrope." Buchwald's particular tightrope is one that suits his temperament, as he often agrees during his many lectures and public talks. "Everyone thinks I have one of the best jobs in the world," he is fond of saying. "But, if you look at it objectively and examine it from all sides, I do."

MEDIA ADAPTATIONS: A comedy revue based on Buchwald's European columns was produced in England in 1960.

BIOGRAPHICAL/CRITICAL SOURCES:

BOOKS

Authors in the News, Volume 1, Gale, 1976.
Buchwald, Ann and Art Buchwald, *Seems Like Yesterday,* Putnam, 1980.
Contemporary Literary Criticism, Volume 33, Gale, 1985.
Playboy Interviews, Playboy Press, 1967.

PERIODICALS

Books, November 19, 1961.
Books and Bookmen, August, 1967.
Book World, May 26, 1968, October 5, 1969.
Christian Science Monitor, October 18, 1966, April 16, 1968, *February 6,* 1970, December 20, 1978.
Editor and Publisher, August 17, 1957.
Geo, January, 1984.
Life, March 27, 1970.
Listener, November 26, 1970.
Look, March 13, 1962.
Los Angeles Times, February 8, 1985, November 22, 1988, December 11, 1989, January 9, 1990.

National Observer, February 16, 1970.
New Leader, February 16, 1970.
New Republic, April 22, 1957, October 12, 1974.
New Statesman, October 23, 1970.
Newsweek, February 13, 1956, December 4, 1961, June 7, 1965.
New York, February 16, 1970, September 2, 1970.
New Yorker, February 7, 1970.
New York Herald Tribune Book Review, November 21, 1954, September 7, 1958.
New York Times, August 24, 1969, February 2, 1970, January 9, 1990.
New York Times Book Review, April 19, 1959, September 25, 1960, November 4, 1962, May 2, 1965, October 2, 1966, November 30, 1969, November 11, 1973, September 25, 1977, February 4, 1979, January 3, 1982, October 13, 1985.
New York Times Magazine, January 2, 1972.
People, November 7, 1983.
Philadelphia Bulletin, March 5, 1974.
Publishers Weekly, August 22, 1977.
Punch, January 13, 1971.
Saturday Review, May 8, 1965, October 11, 1969, October 19, 1974.
Time, November 23, 1953, October 3, 1960, June 22, 1962, September 20, 1965, December 15, 1975, April 5, 1976, January 6, 1986.
Times Literary Supplement, November 20, 1970, February 14, 1975.

*   *   *

BUCK, Pearl S(ydenstricker)   1892-1973
(John Sedges)

PERSONAL: Born June 26, 1892, in Hillsboro, W.Va.; died March 6, 1973, in Danby, Vt.; buried on Green Hills Farm, Perkasie, Pa.; daughter of Absalom and Caroline (Stulting) Sydenstricker (both Presbyterian missionaries); married John Lossing Buck (an agriculture instructor), May 13, 1915 (divorced, June 11, 1935); married Richard John Walsh (president of John Day Co., publishers), June 11, 1935 (died May, 1960); children: (first marriage) Carol, Janice (adopted); (second marriage) Richard, John, Edgar, Jean C., Henriette, Theresa, Chieko, Johanna (all adopted). *Education:* Randolph-Macon Woman's College, B.A., 1914; Cornell University, M.A., 1926.

ADDRESSES: Home and office—Pearl S. Buck Foundation, Green Hills Farm, Perkasie, Pa. 18944.

CAREER: Teacher at Randolph-Macon Woman's College, Lynchburg, Va., 1914, University of Nanking, Nanking, China, 1921-31, Southeastern University, Nanking, 1925-27, and Chung Yang University, Nanking, 1928-30; writer. Founder-director, East and West Association, 1941-51; founder, Welcome House, Inc. (adoption agency for Asian-American children), 1949, and Pearl S. Buck Foundation, Inc., 1964. Also active in numerous other child welfare and retarded children's organizations. Member of board of directors, Weather Engineering Corp., 1966.

MEMBER: National Institute of Arts and Letters, American Academy of Arts and Letters, Phi Beta Kappa, Kappa Delta, Cosmopolitan Club (New York).

AWARDS, HONORS: Pulitzer Prize for fiction, 1932, and William Dean Howells Medal for the most distinguished work of American fiction published in the period 1930-35, 1935, both for *The Good Earth;* Nobel Prize for literature, 1938; Women's National Book Association Skinner Award, 1960; Pennsylvania Governor's Award for Excellence, 1968; Philadelphia Club of Advertising Women Award, 1969. Recipient of numerous honorary degrees, including M.A. from Yale University, 1933; D.Litt. from University of West Virginia, 1940, St. Lawrence University, 1942, and Delaware Valley College, 1965; LL.D. from Howard University, 1942, and Muhlenberg College, 1966; L.H.D. from Lincoln University, 1953, Woman's Medical College of Philadelphia, 1954, and Rutgers University, 1969; D.H.L. from University of Pittsburgh, 1960, Bethany College, 1963, and Hahnemann Hospital, 1966; D.Mus. from Combs College of Music, 1962; and H.H.D. from West Virginia State College, 1963. Recipient of more than 300 humanitarian awards, including President's Committee on Employment of Physically Handicapped Citation, 1958, and Big Brothers of America Citation, 1962.

WRITINGS:

FICTION

East Wind: West Wind, John Day, 1930, reprinted, 1967.

The Good Earth (also see below), John Day, 1931, reprinted, Oxford University Press, 1982.

Sons (also see below), John Day, 1932, reprinted, Pocket Books, 1975.

The Young Revolutionist (juvenile), Friendship Press, 1932.

(Translator) Shui-hu Chuan, *All Men Are Brothers,* John Day, 1933, reprinted, 1968.

The First Wife, and Other Stories (also see below), John Day, 1933, reprinted, Methuen, 1963.

The Mother, John Day, 1934, reprinted, 1973.

A House Divided, Reynal & Hitchcock, 1935, reprinted, Pocket Books, 1975.

House of Earth (contains *The Good Earth* and *Sons*), Reynal & Hitchcock, 1935.

This Proud Heart, Reynal & Hitchcock, 1938, reprinted, John Day, 1965.

The Patriot, John Day, 1939.

Stories for Little Children (juvenile), John Day, 1940.

Other Gods: An American Legend, John Day, 1940, reprinted, Severn House, 1976.

Today and Forever: Stories of China (also see below), John Day, 1941.

Dragon Seed, John Day, 1942, reprinted, Pocket Books, 1972.

China Sky, Triangle Books, 1942.

The Chinese Children Next Door (juvenile), John Day, 1942.

The Water-Buffalo Children (juvenile; also see below), John Day, 1943.

Twenty-seven Stories, Sun Dial Press, 1943.

The Promise, John Day, 1943.

The Story of Dragon Seed, John Day, 1944.

The Dragon Fish (juvenile; also see below), John Day, 1944.

(Under pseudonym John Sedges) *The Townsman,* John Day, 1945, reprinted, Pocket Books, 1975, published under name Pearl S. Buck as *The Townsman: A "John Sedges" Novel,* John Day, 1967.

Portrait of a Marriage, John Day, 1945, reprinted, Pocket Books, 1975.

China Flight, Triangle Books, 1945.

Yu Lan: Flying Boy of China (juvenile), John Day, 1945.

Pavilion of Women, 1946, reprinted, Pocket Books, 1978.

Far and Near: Stories of Japan, China, and America, John Day, 1947 (published in England as *Far and Near: Stories of East and West,* Methuen, 1949).

(Under pseudonym John Sedges) *The Angry Wife,* John Day, 1947, reprinted under name Pearl S. Buck, Pocket Books, 1975.

Peony, John Day, 1948, reprinted, Pocket Books, 1978 (published in England as *The Bondmaid,* Methuen, 1949).

The Big Wave (juvenile), John Day, 1948, reprinted, 1973.

(Under pseudonym John Sedges) *The Long Love,* John Day, 1949, reprinted under name Pearl S. Buck, Pocket Books, 1975.

Kinfolk, John Day, 1949, reprinted, Pocket Books, 1978.

One Bright Day (juvenile), John Day, 1950 (published in England as *One Bright Day, and Other Stories for Children,* Methuen, 1952).

God's Men, John Day, 1951, reprinted, Pocket Books, 1978.

The Hidden Flower, John Day, 1952.

(Under pseudonym John Sedges) *Bright Procession,* John Day, 1952.

Come, My Beloved, John Day, 1953, reprinted, Pocket Books, 1975.

(Under pseudonym John Sedges) *Voices in the House,* John Day, 1953, reprinted, White Lion Publishers, 1977.

Johnny Jack and His Beginnings (juvenile; also see below), John Day, 1954.

The Beech Tree (juvenile; also see below), John Day, 1954.

Imperial Woman, John Day, 1956, reprinted, White Lion Publishers, 1977.

Letter From Peking, John Day, 1957, reprinted, Pocket Books, 1975.

Christmas Miniature (juvenile), John Day, 1957 (published in England as *The Christmas Mouse,* Methuen, 1958).

American Triptych: Three "John Sedges" Novels, John Day, 1958.

Command the Morning, John Day, 1959, reprinted, Pocket Books, 1975.

The Christmas Ghost (juvenile), John Day, 1960.

Fourteen Stories, John Day, 1961, reprinted, Pocket Books, 1976 (published in England as *With a Delicate Air, and Other Stories,* Methuen, 1962).

Satan Never Sleeps, Pocket Books, 1962.

Hearts Come Home, and Other Stories, Pocket Books, 1962.

The Living Reed, John Day, 1963, reprinted, Pocket Books, 1979.

Stories of China (contains contents of *The First Wife, and Other Stories* and *Today and Forever*), John Day, 1964.

Escape at Midnight, and Other Stories, Dragonfly Books, 1964.

(Editor) *Fairy Tales of the Orient,* Simon & Schuster, 1965.

Death in the Castle, John Day, 1965.

The Big Fight (juvenile), John Day, 1965.

The Little Fox in the Middle (juvenile), Collier Books, 1966.

The Water-Buffalo Children [and] *The Dragon Fish,* Dell, 1966.

The Time Is Noon, John Day, 1967.

Matthew, Mark, Luke, and John (juvenile), John Day, 1967.

The Beech Tree [and] *Johnny Jack and His Beginnings,* Dell, 1967.

The New Year, John Day, 1968.

The Three Daughters of Madame Liang, John Day, 1969.

The Good Deed, and Other Stories of Asia, Past and Present, John Day, 1969.

Mandala, John Day, 1970.

The Chinese Story Teller, John Day, 1971.

Once Upon a Christmas, John Day, 1972.

The Goddess Abides, 1972.

A Gift for the Children, John Day, 1973.

Mrs. Starling's Problem, John Day, 1973.

All Under Heaven, John Day, 1973.

Words of Love (poetry), John Day, 1974.
The Rainbow, John Day, 1974.
East and West: Stories, John Day, 1975.
Secrets of the Heart: Stories, John Day, 1976.
The Lovers, and Other Stories, John Day, 1977.
Mrs. Stoner and the Sea, and Other Works, Ace Books, 1978.
The Woman Who Was Changed, and Other Stories, Crowell, 1979.
The Old Demon (short stories), Creative Education, 1982.
Little Red (short stories), Creative Education, 1987.

NONFICTION

East and West and the Novel: Sources of the Early Chinese Novel, College of Chinese Studies (Peking), 1932.
Is There a Case for Foreign Missions (pamphlet), North China Language School, 1932.
The Exile (biography of author's mother; also see below), Reynal & Hitchcock, 1936, reprinted, Pocket Books, 1976.
Fighting Angel: Portrait of a Soul (biography of author's father; also see below), Reynal & Hitchcock, 1936, reprinted, Pocket Books, 1976.
The Chinese Novel (lecture), 1939.
Of Men and Women, John Day, 1941, reprinted, 1971.
When the Fun Begins (juvenile), Methuen, 1941.
American Unity and Asia, John Day, 1942, reprinted, Books for Libraries, 1970 (published in England as *Asia and Democracy,* Macmillan, 1943).
Pearl Buck Speaks for Democracy, New York City Common Council for Unity, 1942.
What America Means to Me, John Day, 1943, reprinted, Books for Libraries, 1971.
The Spirit and the Flesh (contains *Fighting Angel* and *The Exile*), John Day, 1944.
(Compiler) *China in Black and White: An Album of Woodcuts,* John Day, 1945.
Tell the People: Mass Education in China, Institute of Pacific Relations, 1945, published as *Tell the People: Talks With James Yen About the Mass Education Movement,* John Day, 1945.
Talk About Russia With Masha Scott, John Day, 1945.
(With Erma von Pustau) *How It Happens: Talk About the German People, 1914-1933,* John Day, 1947.
(With Eslanda Goode Robeson) *American Argument,* John Day, 1949.
The Child Who Never Grew, John Day, 1950.
The Man Who Changed China: The Story of Sun Yat-sen (juvenile), Random House, 1953.
My Several Worlds: A Personal Record, John Day, 1954, reprinted, Pocket Books, 1975.
Friend to Friend: A Candid Exchange Between Pearl S. Buck and Carlos P. Romulo, John Day, 1958.
The Delights of Learning, University of Pittsburgh Press, 1960.
A Bridge for Passing (autobiography), John Day, 1962.
Welcome Child (juvenile), John Day, 1964.
The Joy of Children, John Day, 1964.
(With Gweneth T. Zarfoss) *The Gifts They Bring: Our Debts to the Mentally Retarded,* John Day, 1965.
Children for Adoption, Random House, 1965.
(With others) *My Mother's House,* Appalachia Press, 1966.
The People of Japan, Simon & Schuster, 1966.
(With Theodore F. Harris) *For Spacious Skies: Journal in Dialogue,* John Day, 1966.
To My Daughters, With Love, John Day, 1967.
The Kennedy Women: A Personal Appraisal, Cowles Book Co., 1970.

China as I See It, John Day, 1970.
The Story Bible, Bartholomew House, 1971.
Pearl Buck's America, Bartholomew House, 1971.
Pearl S. Buck's Oriental Cookbook, Simon & Schuster, 1972.
China Past and Present, John Day, 1972.
A Community Success Story: The Founding of the Pearl Buck Center, John Day, 1972.
(Editor) *Pearl Buck's Book of Christmas,* Simon & Schuster, 1974.

PLAYS

"Flight Into China," produced in New York, 1939.
Sun Yat-sen: A Play, Preceded by a Lecture by Dr. Hu-Shih, Universal Distributors, 1944.
"The First Wife," produced in New York, 1945.
"A Desert Incident," produced in New York, 1959.
"Christine," produced in New York, 1960.
"The Guide" (adapted from a novel by N. K. Narayan), produced on Broadway at Lincoln Art Theatre, 1965.

OTHER

Works collected in *A Pearl Buck Reader,* 2 volumes, 1985.

Also author of television drama "The Big Wave," National Broadcasting Co., 1956. Contributor of articles and stories to numerous magazines. Co-editor of *Asia,* 1941-46.

SIDELIGHTS: "One pays the price for being prolific," bestselling author Pearl S. Buck once told an interviewer. "Heaven knows the literary Establishment can't forgive me for it, nor for the fact that my books sell." In retrospect, Buck's assessment of her own career seems to ring true. Despite the fact that she enjoyed world-wide popularity throughout most of her life (at the time of her death, her books had been translated into more languages than any other American writer), critical success eluded her after the prize-winning decade that produced *The Good Earth* and the biographical work *The Spirit and the Flesh.* Suspicious of her tremendously high output and annoyed by her all-too-frequent lapses into didacticism and sentimentality, post-1938 critics regarded her for the most part as a prime example of a "too much, too often" writer.

The only child of Absalom and Caroline Sydenstricker to be born in the United States, Pearl Buck lived in America for only a few months before accompanying her missionary parents on their return to Chinkiang, China. She remained there until reaching the age of seventeen, learning to speak Chinese before English (her parents declined to live in the foreigners' compound in Chinkiang, choosing instead to live among the Chinese) but beginning to read and write in the less difficult English alphabet system. Although her mother encouraged her as a very young child to write something every week, her first direct literary influence was her Chinese nurse, who fascinated her with numerous folk tales of magic and adventure.

Buck's first published works appeared in the *Shanghai Mercury,* an English-language newspaper that had a weekly edition for children; she also wrote for the Randolph-Macon Woman's College paper after returning to the United States for further schooling. In 1927, Buck found herself back in China, this time in Nanking at the time Communists were invading the city with the intention of killing all foreigners. Thanks to the aid of a few loyal friends and servants, Buck and her family managed to escape death by the narrow margin of ten minutes. Her home, however, as well as the manuscript of her first novel, was destroyed in the fire following the raid.

Her second novel, *East Wind: West Wind,* was written in 1925 aboard a ship bound for America. In 1930, after contacting a literary agent she had chosen at random from a handbook, the author received her first taste of success when John Day Co. agreed to publish her work. Ten months after *East Wind: West Wind*'s third printing, *The Good Earth* (which had taken Buck only three months to write) appeared and began an almost two-year stay on the best-seller lists, winning its author a Pulitzer Prize in 1932. This book, along with her 1936 biographies of her parents, *The Exile* and *Fighting Angel,* established Buck's early literary reputation and served as the basis of comparison for all of her later works.

The major goal of Buck's writings throughout her long career was to teach the western world about Asia, especially China, which she naturally knew and loved best. She often described her unique Chinese-American background as one which afforded her the ability to be "mentally bifocal"—that is, she was able to look at two distinctly different cultures and understand and love both of them, each on its own terms. As critic Malcolm Cowley once observed in 1935: "Mrs. Buck has spent so many years in [China], has studied the language so well, has lived on such terms of friendship with the people, that she makes [other writers like] Tretiakov and Malraux seem like tourists dropping ashore from a round-the-world cruise. She has a truly extraordinary gift for presenting the Chinese, not as quaint and illogical, yellow-skinned, exotic devil-dolls, but as human beings merely, animated by motives we can always understand even when the background is strange and topsy-turvy. She seems to know China so well that she no longer judges it even from the standpoint of 'the native Chinese'—whoever he may be—but rather from the standpoint of a particular class, the one that includes the liberal, three-quarters Westernized scholars who deplore the graft and cruelty of the present government but nevertheless keep their heads on their shoulders and hold their noses, and support General Chiang Kaishek because they are afraid of what would happen if he were overthrown."

Phyllis Bentley, commenting during the same period as Cowley, also praised Buck's ability to write knowledgeably of Chinese culture: "Mrs. Buck's chosen scene is modern China. There are parts of that vast country where modern China means the same as ancient China; there are parts where the change of date implies a profound social change. These two Chinas, the old and the new, form the material for Mrs. Buck's art. [An] attempt is made to present China from within, as the Chinese see it. [The] landscape in Mrs. Buck's novels is always presented as seen by familiar eyes. . . . [She] has lived in China so long that she really knows the landscape, and she never once, in all the volumes of her work, forgets it and goes into raptures as over an alien scene. In the same way Mrs. Buck aims to present the Chinese customs as familiar, natural and correct, because so would her characters regard them. [These customs] are all copiously illustrated, but always presented, as it were, unself-consciously, as part of the natural process of living; never by the slightest word or turn of phrase does Mrs. Buck call our attention to the difference of these customs from our own."

Buck was "mentally bifocal" in another sense as well, for her writing style also reflected her dual background. Time and time again critics refer to her "biblical" prose—mellifluous, stately, serious, and lyrical. This was often combined with a narrative style reminiscent of the ancient Chinese saga—straightforward, simple, precise, and concrete—and an emphasis on the role of the novel as a form of entertainment for the common people. Some reviewers have also identified a few key elements that are characteristic of nineteenth-century French Naturalism, such as

the author's documentary approach to her subject matter, her detached and objective narration, her preoccupation with the effects of environment and heredity, and her interest in depicting the lifestyle of members of lower social classes. She also exhibited a typically Chinese respect for tradition and a deep commitment to the family and to what Bentley referred to as "the continuity of life"; that is, "the passing of life on from generation to generation." And even though her characters were almost exclusively Chinese, her stories were designed to have a universal appeal, for she believed very strongly that people the world over, regardless of race, share essentially the same hopes and fears.

The Good Earth is perhaps the best known example of the Pearl Buck's style. Cowley described it as "a parable of the life of man, in his relation to the soil that sustains him. The plot, deliberately commonplace, is given a sort of legendary weight and dignity by being placed in an unfamiliar setting. The biblical style is appropriate to the subject and the characters. If we define a masterpiece as a novel that is living, complete, sustained, but still somewhat limited in its scope as compared with the greatest works of fiction—if we define it as *Wuthering Heights* rather than *War and Peace*—then [*The Good Earth* is a masterpiece]."

Other reviewers were equally impressed. A *New York Times* critic, for example, noted, "In *East Wind: West Wind,* Pearl S. Buck wrote a novel of China which was generally hailed as a very promising first novel. In her second book, *The Good Earth,* she has fulfilled that promise with a brilliance which passes one's most optimistic expectations. Laying aside the question of the locale, *The Good Earth* is an excellent novel. It has style, power, coherence and a pervasive sense of dramatic reality."

A *Books* reviewer claimed that *The Good Earth* depicts "China as it has never before been portrayed in fiction, the China that Chinese live in and as Chinese live. . . . [The story] is, however, much more than China. One need never have lived in China or know anything about the Chinese to understand it or respond to its appeal." A *Spectator* critic also praised its universality: "It is a familiar story; there is not startling psychological observation, though it is complete and whole. We are satisfied of its essential truth; confident, interested, never ruffled: it is a universal story, very well told, honestly, sympathetically, without any self-consciousness whatever. [*The Good Earth*] is a tender and charming book, written in a very personal, but in no way irritating idiom."

Finally, a *Bookman* reviewer observed: "To read this story of Wang Lung is to be slowly and deeply purified; and when the last page is finished it is as if some significant part of one's own days were over. Though I may never see a ricefield, I shall always feel that I have lived for a long time in China. The strange power of a western woman to make an alien civilization seem as casual, as close, as the happenings of the morning is surprising; but it is less amazing than her power to illuminate the destiny of man as it is in all countries and at all times by quietly telling the story of one poor Wang Lung."

Younghill Kang of the *New Republic,* however, did not feel that *The Good Earth* was truly representative of Chinese life. He wrote: "Since Mrs. Buck does not understand the meaning of the Confucian separation of man's kingdom from that of woman, she is like someone trying to write a story of the European Middle Ages without understanding the rudiments of chivalric standards and the institution of Christianity. None of her major descriptions is correct except in minor details. . . . *The Good Earth,* though it has no humor or profound lyric passion, shows good technique and much artistic sincerity. Thus, it is discouraging to find that the novel works toward confusion, not clarification. Its implied comparison between Western and Eastern ways is unjust to the latter."

Sons and *A House Divided* continued the saga of the house of Wang, but neither achieved quite the critical and popular acclaim of *The Good Earth*. Reviewers found *Sons*, for example, to be an adequate enough novel in and of itself, but not as a sequel to a work such as *The Good Earth*. In general, they found it suffered from colorless and unsympathetic characterization and a lack of universality due to its thematic emphasis on warlords and brigands. *A House Divided* was judged to be an even weaker novel; it, too, was criticized for its lack of credible characterization, as well as for its wandering, overburdened plot and an increasingly exaggerated and inappropriate biblical style. For the most part, reviewers felt that neither novel possessed that indefinable "something" that made *The Good Earth* so memorable.

When Pearl Buck won the Nobel Prize for literature in 1938, the judges, though making it clear that the award was for the body of her work, specifically mentioned the biographies of her mother (*The Exile*) and her father (*Fighting Angel*) as particularly outstanding examples of her talent. Commenting on *The Exile*, a *Books* critic wrote: "The events of the story are stirring, but they pale beside the story of the woman and her mastery of circumstance. Restrained, temperate, the book of a novelist who not only loves life but looks at it clear-eyed, *The Exile* is a story of fact as exciting and as moving as any of the fiction in which Pearl Buck has showed life as Carie [her mother] helped her to see it." A *Christian Century* reviewer agreed: "The subject of this story—which is at once a story, a study, a memoir, and a tribute of discerning affection—was evidently a very unusual missionary as well as a very remarkable woman. The book is quite different in style from Mrs. Buck's novels, but is of the same piece of quality and insight."

Several reviewers, however, felt the book lacked the customary universal appeal of a Pearl Buck story, due to its focus on one individual. For example, a *Times Literary Supplement* critic wrote: "This is not a story—however vivid and moving in its detail and its portrait of the martyred Carie—which exhibits Mrs. Buck's peculiar gifts in their finest expression. She . . . suffers from her inability to give free play to her imagination. In her studies of Chinese life she can create for us a type that may or may not be true of any single individual. In *The Exile* she labours to present the whole truth about one particular woman and succeeds only at the cost of artistic verisimilitude."

A *Christian Science Monitor* reviewer expressed a similar sentiment: "In this latest work Mrs. Buck has, to our discomfiture, lost touch with that quality so conspicuous in *The Good Earth*, a flowing style which is thrillingly beautiful in rhythm and cadence. One hears its whisper now too seldom. For *The Exile* is not, like its predecessor, by implication a record of the labor and struggle of all humankind; its scope is narrowed until, in essence at least, it includes only one woman."

Fighting Angel was generally regarded as the better biography of the two, primarily because it contained the quality of universality that *The Exile* lacked. According to Paul A. Doyle, this universal appeal is a result of Buck's "compelling delineation of the nineteenth-century type of crusader—the very essence of rock-ribbed individualism, a fiery zeal. [In short,] Pearl Buck sees her father as a manifestation of a spirit which especially permeated America at a particular time." As a *New York Times* reviewer noted: "In the limpid flowing beauty of Pearl Buck's writing, in the unerring clarity and directness of every word and image and expression, she . . . has drawn a portrait with far more than personal vividness, touched problems as deep as all humanity. And

her incandescent realism lights the very heart of our thought." A *Books* critic felt that "its very difficulty makes this an even finer book than its companion piece. . . . This is the work of maturity—hard-won maturity of heart. A good many layers of soil had to be lived away and written away before this rock could be laid bare. And nobody who has not read the earlier book can know quite what an achievement this one is."

A *Christian Science Monitor* reviewer declared that "with true artistry Mrs. Buck has offered us this portrait of her father. It is an experience to read and ponder this book, for it has the ring of universal truth. One has known just such reformers as was Andy." A *Christian Century* critic admitted that "his daughter's portrayal does not paint out his warts, but it makes him a giant in character and personality, and a giant can carry some warts. No missionary has had a nobler monument."

A *Commonweal* reviewer who enjoyed *The Exile* more than *Fighting Angel* concluded: "If the appeal of *Fighting Angel* is less that of its companion book, *The Exile*, doubtless it is because most of us feel a keener response to the flesh than to the spirit. If the book is less vivid, it is less direct, as its author relies for the most of its material upon relation rather than observation. Although there can be no doubt as to where the major part of [the author's] loyalty lay, she gives a thoroughly admirable and sympathetic account of her father's stalwart faith and indefatigable labors, both in scholarship and evangelism."

In a critical study of Pearl Buck's work, Doyle offers this summation of the author's contributions to literature: "Although she has been virtually ignored by critics for [decades], it may be maintained with much justification that [Buck] has written at least three books of undoubted significance: *The Good Earth* and the biographies of her father and mother." Due to these successes, Doyle continues, "at about the time of the Nobel Award Pearl Buck's writing career certainly seemed to be in the ascent, and to promise further important achievement. After this period, however, Pearl Buck's humanitarian preoccupations seemed to increase. These interests, carried into her fiction, immediately weakened the objectivity of her creation. She began to assert didactic considerations to such an excessive degree that [certain later novels] become propaganda efforts on behalf of China's struggle against Japan. . . . After 1939 she became more facile at constructing her plots, handling dialogue, and in the technical aspects of her craft; but no subsequent significant growth in the artistic features of novel writing occurred in Pearl Buck's work. No experimentation in technique took place, and she made no attempt to penetrate more deeply into character analysis, showed no willingness to seek subtleties of tone or mood, and indicated no interest in using myth or symbolism or other elements characteristic of the modern novel. On this account alone Miss Buck must be neglected by some of the more recent literary critics, . . . [for] her novels do not furnish the layers of meaning and the complexity which modern literary criticism demands. . . . [In addition,] her work has suffered from the inevitable reaction against her best-seller status."

Furthermore, notes Doyle, "another factor in Pearl Buck's loss of prestige in serious literary circles stems from her optimistic, affirmative point of view. She has not lost her faith in progress, and she exalts a Rousseau-Thomas Paine Transcendental type of belief in the innate goodness of most men. . . . [But] judged by her standards—'to please and to amuse,' to relate a captivating story, and to deal with significant problems—Miss Buck must be granted considerable success."

MEDIA ADAPTATIONS: Several of Pearl Buck's novels have been made into motion pictures. *A House Divided* was filmed by

Universal Pictures in 1932; *The Good Earth* and *Dragon Seed* were both filmed by Metro-Goldwyn-Mayer, Inc., the former in 1937 and the latter in 1944; *China Sky* was filmed by RKO General, Inc., in 1945; and *Satan Never Sleeps* was filmed by Twentieth Century-Fox Film Corp. in 1962.

BIOGRAPHICAL/CRITICAL SOURCES:

BOOKS

Authors in the News, Volume 1, Gale, 1976.
Contemporary Literary Criticism, Gale, Volume 7, 1977, Volume 11, 1979, Volume 18, 1981.
Dictionary of Literary Biography, Volume 9: *Amercian Novelists, 1910-1945,* Gale, 1981.

PERIODICALS

Antiquarian Bookman, March 19, 1973.
Atlantic, March, 1937, July, 1969.
Best Sellers, February 1, 1965, April 1, 1968, April 1, 1969, June 1, 1970, November 1, 1970.
Bookman, May, 1931, October, 1932.
Books, March 1, 1931, September 25, 1932, January 20, 1935, February 9, 1936, November 29, 1936.
Chicago Daily Tribune, September 24, 1932.
Chicago Tribune, April 5, 1983.
Christian Century, May 20, 1931, October 5, 1932, March 13, 1935, February 5, 1936, April 7, 1937, December 9, 1970.
Christian Science Monitor, February 7, 1936, December 1, 1936, December 24, 1958, July 10, 1969.
Commonweal, December 11, 1936.
Detroit News, January 16, 1972, November 20, 1979.
Forum, March, 1935.
Nation, May 13, 1931, November 16, 1932, February 6, 1935.
National Observer, April 29, 1968.
New Republic, July 1, 1931, October 26, 1932, January 23, 1935, December 9, 1936.
New Statesman and Nation, May 16, 1931, December 3, 1932.
Newsweek, March 19, 1973.
New York Herald Tribune, January 21, 1935.
New York Times, March 15, 1931, September 25, 1932, January 20, 1935, February 9, 1936, November 29, 1936, September 10, 1969, March 7, 1973, March 10, 1973.
New York Times Book Review, February 23, 1969, March 11, 1979.
Outlook, March 18, 1931.
Publishers Weekly, March 12, 1973.
Saturday Review, March 21, 1931, May 16, 1931, September 24, 1932, November 5, 1932, February 8, 1936, December 5, 1936, March 31, 1956, November 22, 1958, July 12, 1969.
Spectator, May 2, 1931.
Time, July 25, 1969, March 19, 1973.
Times Literary Supplement, October 6, 1932, January 24, 1935, February 15, 1936, October 19, 1967, March 21, 1980.
Washington Post, March 7, 1973, December 22, 1988.

* * *

BUCKLEY, William F(rank), Jr. 1925-

PERSONAL: Born November 24, 1925, in New York, N.Y.; son of William Frank (a lawyer and oilman) and Aloise (Steiner) Buckley; married Patricia Austin Taylor, July 6, 1950; children: Christopher. *Education:* Attended University of Mexico, 1943-44; Yale University, B.A. (with honors), 1950. *Politics:* Republican. *Religion:* Roman Catholic.

ADDRESSES: Office—National Review, 150 East 35th St., New York, N.Y. 10016.

CAREER: Yale University, New Haven, Conn., instructor in Spanish, 1947-51; affiliated with the Central Intelligence Agency (C.I.A.) in Mexico, 1951-52; *American Mercury* (magazine), New York, N.Y., associate editor, 1952; free-lance writer and editor, 1952-55; *National Review* (magazine), New York City, founder, president, and editor-in-chief, 1955—; syndicated columnist, 1962—; host of "Firing Line" weekly television program, 1966—. Conservative Party candidate for mayor of New York City, 1965; member of National Advisory Commission on Information, U.S. Information Agency, 1969-72; public member of the U.S. delegation to the United Nations, 1973. Lecturer, New School for Social Research, 1967-68; Froman Distinguished Professor, Russell Sage College, 1973. Chairman of the board, Starr Broadcasting Group, Inc., 1969-78. *Military service:* U.S. Army, 1944-46; became second lieutenant.

MEMBER: Council on Foreign Relations, Century Association, Mont Pelerin Society, New York Yacht Club, Bohemian Club, Philadelphia Society.

AWARDS, HONORS: Freedom Award, Order of Lafayette, 1966; George Sokolsky Award, American Jewish League against Communism, 1966; Best Columnist of the Year Award, 1967; University of Southern California Distinguished Achievement Award in Journalism, 1968; Liberty Bell Award, New Haven County Bar Association, 1969; Emmy Award, National Academy of Television Arts and Sciences, 1969, for "Firing Line"; Man of the Decade Award, Young Americans for Freedom, 1970; Cleveland Amory Award, *TV Guide,* 1974, for best interviewer/interviewee on television; fellow, Sigma Delta Chi, 1976; Bellarmine Medal, 1977; Americanism Award, Young Republican National Federation, 1979, for contributions to the American principles of freedom, individual liberty, and free enterprise; Carmel Award, American Friends of Haifa University, 1980, for journalism excellence; American Book Award, 1980, for *Stained Glass;* New York University Creative Leadership Award, 1981. Honorary degrees: L.H.D. from Seton Hall University, 1966, Niagara University, 1967, Mount Saint Mary's College, 1969, and University of South Carolina, 1985; LL.D. from St. Peter's College, 1969, Syracuse University, 1969, Ursinus College, 1969, Lehigh University, 1970, Lafayette College, 1972, St. Anselm's College, 1973, St. Bonaventure University, 1974, University of Notre Dame, 1978, New York Law School, 1981, and Colby College, 1985; D.Sc.O. from Curry College, 1970; Litt.D. from St. Vincent College, 1971, Fairleigh Dickinson University, 1973, Alfred University, 1974, College of William and Mary, 1981, William Jewell College, 1982, Albertus Magnus College, 1987, College of St. Thomas, 1987, and Bowling Green State University, 1987.

WRITINGS:

God and Man at Yale: The Superstitions of "Academic Freedom," Regnery, 1951, reprinted, Gateway Editions, 1977.
(With L. Brent Bozell) *McCarthy and His Enemies: The Record and Its Meaning,* Regnery, 1954.
Up from Liberalism, Obolensky, 1959.
Rumbles Left and Right: A Book about Troublesome People and Ideas, Putnam, 1963.
The Unmaking of a Mayor, Viking, 1966.
(Author of introduction) Edgar Smith, *Brief against Death,* Knopf, 1968.
The Jeweler's Eye: A Book of Irresistible Political Reflections, Putnam, 1968.
(Author of introduction) *Will Mrs. Major Go to Hell?: The Collected Work of Aloise Buckley Heath,* Arlington House, 1969.

Quotations from Chairman Bill: The Best of William F. Buckley, Jr., compiled by David Franke, Arlington House, 1970.

The Governor Listeth: A Book of Inspired Political Revelations, Putnam, 1970.

Cruising Speed: A Documentary, Putnam, 1971.

Taiwan: The West Berlin of China, St. John's University Center of Asian Studies, 1971.

Inveighing We Will Go, Putnam, 1972.

Four Reforms: A Guide for the Seventies, Putnam, 1973.

United Nations Journal: A Delegate's Odyssey, Putnam, 1974.

The Assault on the Free Market (lecture), Kansas State University, 1974.

Execution Eve and Other Contemporary Ballads, Putnam, 1975.

Airborne: A Sentimental Journey, Macmillan, 1976.

A Hymnal: The Controversial Arts, Putnam, 1978.

Atlantic High: A Celebration, Doubleday, 1982.

Overdrive: A Personal Documentary, Doubleday, 1983.

Right Reason, Doubleday, 1985.

The Temptation of Wilfred Malachey (juvenile), Workman Publishing, 1985.

Racing through Paradise: A Pacific Passage, Random House, 1987.

On the Firing Line: The Public Life of Our Public Figures, Random House, 1989.

Gratitude, Random House, 1990.

EDITOR

(With others) *The Committee and Its Critics: A Calm Review of the House Committee on Un-American Activities,* Constructive Action, 1963.

Odyssey of a Friend: Whittaker Chambers' Letters to William F. Buckley, Jr., 1954-1961, Putnam, 1970.

Did You Ever See a Dream Walking?: American Conservative Thought in the Twentieth Century, Bobbs-Merrill, 1970.

(With Charles R. Kesler) *Keeping the Tablets: Modern American Conservative Thought,* Harper, 1987.

Also editor, with Stuart W. Little, of *The Buckley-Little Catalogue,* 1984-87.

ESPIONAGE NOVELS

Saving the Queen, Doubleday, 1976.

Stained Glass, Doubleday, 1978, adapted by Buckley as a play, first produced in Louisville, Ky., at the Actors Theater of Louisville, 1989.

Who's on First, Doubleday, 1980.

Marco Polo, If You Can, Doubleday, 1982.

The Story of Henri Tod, Doubleday, 1984.

See You Later, Alligator, Doubleday, 1985.

High Jinx, Doubleday, 1986.

Mongoose, R.I.P., Random House, 1988.

Tucker's Last Stand, Random House, 1990.

CONTRIBUTOR

Ocean Racing, Van Nostrand, 1959.

The Intellectuals, Free Press, 1960.

F. S. Meyer, editor, *What Is Conservatism?,* Holt, 1964.

Dialogues in Americanism, Regnery, 1964.

Edward D. Davis, editor, *The Beatles Book,* Cowles, 1968.

S. Endleman, editor, *Violence in the Streets,* Quadrangle, 1968.

R. Campbell, editor, *Spectrum of Catholic Attitudes,* Bruce Publishing, 1969.

Great Ideas Today Annual, 1970, Encyclopaedia Britannica, 1970.

Fritz Machlup, editor, *Essays on Hayek,* New York University Press, 1976.

OTHER

Also author of "Celestial Navigation," a videocassette. Author of syndicated column "On the Right," 1962—. Contributor to *Esquire, Saturday Review, Harper's, Atlantic, Playboy, New Yorker, New York Times Magazine,* and other publications.

SIDELIGHTS: William F. Buckley, Jr., is one of the most recognized and articulate spokesmen for American conservatives. On his television program "Firing Line," in the pages of *National Review,* the magazine he edits, and through the books and syndicated columns he writes, Buckley argues for individual liberty, the free market, and the traditional moral values of Western culture. His eloquence, wit, and appealing personal style have made him palatable even to many of his political opponents. "The Buckley substance," a writer for *Time* reports, "is forgiven for the Buckley style."

Buckley's writings have been instrumental to the phenomenal growth of the American conservative movement. In the 1950s, when Buckley first appeared on the scene, conservatism was a peripheral presence on the national political spectrum. But in 1980 the conservatives elected Ronald Reagan, a longtime reader of Buckley's *National Review,* as president of the United States. "When the tide of intellectual and political history seemed headed inexorably leftward . . .," Morton Kondracke writes in the *New York Times Book Review,* "Mr. Buckley had the temerity to uphold the cause of Toryism. He and his magazine nurtured the movement . . . and gave it a rallying point and sounding board as it gradually gained the strength and respectability to win the Presidency. Conservatism is far from the dominant intellectual force in the country today, but neither is liberalism. There is now a balance between the movements, a permanent contest, and Mr. Buckley deserves credit for helping make it so."

Buckley first came to public attention in 1951 when he published *God and Man at Yale: The Superstitions of "Academic Freedom,"* an attack against his alma mater, Yale University. The book accuses Yale of fostering values—such as atheism and collectivism—which are anathema to the school's supporters. Further, Buckley claims that Yale stifled the political freedom of its more conservative students. Those students who spoke out against the liberal views of their professors were often ostracized. The book's charges stemmed from Buckley's own experiences while attending Yale, where his views on individualism, the free market, and communism found little support among the liberal academics.

God and Man at Yale raised a storm of controversy as Yale faculty members denounced the charges made against them. Some reviewers joined in the denunciation. McGeorge Bundy, writing in the *Atlantic,* called the book "dishonest in its use of facts, false in its theory, and a discredit to its author." Peter Viereck agreed with Buckley that "more conservatism and traditional morality" were needed at universities and wrote in the *New York Times* that "this important, symptomatic, and widely held book is a necessary counterbalance. However, its Old Guard antithesis to the outworn Marxist thesis is not the liberty security synthesis the future cries for." Frank D. Ashburn of the *Saturday Review of Literature* claimed that *God and Man at Yale* "has the glow and appeal of a fiery cross on a hillside at night. There will undoubtedly be robed figures who gather to it, but the hoods will not be academic. They will cover the face."

But other critics found *God and Man at Yale* to be a serious contribution to the political dialogue. Writing in the *American Mercury,* Max Eastman claimed that the book "is brilliant, sincere, well-informed, keenly reasoned, and exciting to read." Selden Rodman of the *Saturday Review of Literature* called it "an important book, perhaps the most thought-provoking that has appeared in the last decade on the subject of higher education in the United States. . . . That the author happens also to be a conservative, with whose specific religious and economic ideas I find myself not in sympathy, is less important than that he challenges forcefully that brand of 'liberal' materialism which, by making all values 'relative,' honors none." Because of the widespread controversy raised by *God and Man at Yale,* Buckley became well known among the nation's conservatives.

This position as conservative spokesman was vastly strengthened in 1955 when Buckley founded *National Review,* a magazine of conservative opinion. In a statement of purpose published in the magazine's first issue, Buckley states: "The profound crisis of our era is, in essence, the conflict between the Social Engineers, who seek to adjust mankind to conform with scientific utopias, and the disciples of Truth, who defend the organic moral order." At the time of its founding, Richard Brookhiser remarks in *National Review*'s thirtieth anniversary issue, "the forces of conservatism in American thinking were insignificant." But Buckley used the magazine as a rallying point to consolidate the nation's conservatives. He formed a coalition, George H. Nash explains in his *The Conservative Intellectual Movement in America since 1945,* of "New Conservatives, libertarians, and anti-communists." From this core of supporters the *National Review* reached out to a larger audience. Buckley hoped, Nash writes, "to establish a journal which would reach intellectuals." Buckley has said on other occasions that "what we are trying for is the maximum leverage that conservatives can exert."

Although *National Review,* in common with most other magazines of political opinion, has never made a profit (it is subsidized by reader contributions and Buckley's own money), it has become one of the most influential political journals in the country. Nash credits it with a central role in the growth of American conservative thought. "If *National Review* (or something like it) had not been founded," Nash writes, "there would probably have been no interlocking intellectual force on the Right in the 1960's and 1970's. To a very substantial degree, the history of reflective conservatism in America after 1955 is the history of the individuals who collaborated in—or were discovered by—the magazine William F. Buckley, Jr. founded." Gene M. Moore points out in the *Dictionary of Literary Biography Yearbook: 1980* that over the years *National Review* has helped to "launch the careers of such authors and columnists as Renata Adler, Joan Didion, John Leonard, and Garry Wills."

With the growth of the conservative movement, *National Review* now enjoys a circulation of over one hundred thousand. And it can boast of some influential readers as well. President Ronald Reagan, for example, has declared that *National Review* is his favorite magazine. Speaking at the magazine's thirtieth anniversary celebration in 1985—a celebration attended by such notables as Charlton Heston, Tom Selleck, Jack Kemp, and Tom Wolfe—Reagan remarked: "If any of you doubt the impact of *National Review*'s verve and attractiveness, take a look around you this evening. The man standing before you now was a Democrat when he picked up his first issue in a plain brown wrapper; and even now, as an occupant of public housing, he awaits as anxiously as ever his biweekly edition—without the wrapper."

In addition to his writing and editing for the *National Review,* Buckley also writes a syndicated column, "On the Right," which appears in 350 newspapers three times weekly, as well as articles of opinion for various national magazines. Many of these columns and articles have been published in book-length collections. These shorter pieces display Buckley's talent for political

satire. John P. Roche of the *New York Times Book Review,* speaking of Buckley's articles in *Execution Eve and Other Contemporary Ballads,* claims that "no commentator has a surer eye for the contradictions, the hypocrisies, the pretensions of liberal and radical pontiffs . . . even when you wince, reading Buckley is fun." A *Choice* critic, reviewing *A Hymnal: The Controversial Arts,* explains that "Buckley excels in the use of language, the sparkling epigram, and biting sarcasm that penetrates to the heart of a matter." And Steven R. Weisman of the *New York Times Book Review* maintains that "Bill Buckley certainly deserves his reputation as one of the wittiest political satirists writing today."

In other books, Buckley turns from politics to his personal life. *Cruising Speed: A Documentary* is a diary-like account of a typical Buckley week. *Overdrive: A Personal Documentary* follows a similar format. Because of the many activities in which he is typically engaged, and the social opportunities afforded by his political connections and inherited wealth, Buckley's life makes fascinating reading. And he unabashedly shares it with his readers, moving some reviewers to criticize him. Nora Ephron of the *New York Times Book Review,* for example, calls *Overdrive* "an astonishing glimpse of a life of privilege in America today." She complains that "it never seems to cross [Buckley's] mind that any of his remarks might be in poor taste, or his charm finite." And yet Carolyn See of the *Los Angeles Times* believes that the Buckley found in *Overdrive* "is a social butterfly, a gadabout, a mindless snob (or so he would have us believe). . . . Buckley shows us a brittle, acerbic, duty-bound, 'silly,' 'conservative' semi-fudd, with a heart as vast and varicolored and wonderful to watch as a 1930s jukebox."

More universally appreciated are Buckley's sailing books. An avid yachtsman, he chronicles several of his sailing expeditions in *Airborne: A Sentimental Journey, Atlantic High: A Celebration,* and *Racing through Paradise: A Pacific Passage.* These books are as much celebrations of the sailing life as they are the records of particular voyages. Speaking of *Atlantic High,* the account of Buckley's month-long journey from the Virgin Islands to Spain, Morton Hunt of the *New York Times Book Review* calls it "more than an account of that trip, this is a book about a special and precious kind of human experience—the camaraderie of people who join together in a physical enterprise that is, at times, brutally demanding and hazardous and, at other times, idyllically tranquil and beautiful. . . . The shared experience of the sea . . . produces an intimacy and openness that life on shore might need years to achieve. And it is this, more than the experience of the sea itself, that Mr. Buckley is writing about."

When not writing about politics or sailing, Buckley has found time to pen a series of bestselling espionage novels featuring C.I.A. agent Blackford Oakes. The "arch and politically sophisticated" series, as Derrick Murdoch describes the books in the Toronto *Globe and Mail,* is set in the Cold War years of the 1950s and 1960s and takes readers behind the scenes of the major political crises of the time. In doing so, the novels provide Buckley with the opportunity to dramatize some of his ideas concerning East-West relations. As Christopher Lehmann-Haupt of the *New York Times* remarks, "not only can Buckley execute the international thriller as well as nearly anyone working in the genre . . . he threatens to turn this form of fiction into effective propaganda for his ideas."

Saving the Queen, the first of the Blackford Oakes novels, is based in part on Buckley's own experiences in the C.I.A. "The training received by Blackford Oakes is, in exact detail, the training I received," Buckley explains. "In that sense, it's autobiographical." Oakes, a thinly-disguised version of his creator, also shares Buckley's school years at an English public school and at Yale University. The story concerns a leak of classified information at the highest levels of the British government. Oakes is sent to locate the source of the leak and his investigation uncovers a treasonous cousin in the royal family. Robin W. Winks of the *New Republic* finds *Saving the Queen* to be "replete with ambiguity, irony, suspense—all those qualities we associate with [Eric] Ambler, [Graham] Greene, [and John] le Carre." Amnon Kabatchnik of the *Armchair Detective* calls *Saving the Queen* "an entertaining yarn, graced with a literate style, keen knowledge and a twinkling sense of humor [which] injected a touch of sophistication and a flavor of sly irony to the genre of political intrigue."

Buckley's second novel, *Stained Glass,* is set in postwar Germany and revolves around the efforts of both East and West to prevent the reunification of Germany under the popular Count Axel Wintergrin. Both sides fear that a united Germany would be a military threat to the peace of Europe. Oakes penetrates Wintergrin's political organization disguised as an engineer hired to restore a local church. His restoring of broken church windows contrasts ironically with his efforts to keep Germany divided. "This novel is a work of history," Winks maintains, "for it parallels those options that might well have been open to the West [in the 1950s]. . . . *Stained Glass* is closer to the bone than le Carre has ever cut." Jane Larkin Crain of the *Saturday Review* calls it a "first-rate spy story and . . . a disturbing lesson in the unsavory realities of international politics." *Stained Glass* won an American Book Award in 1980.

Later Blackford Oakes novels have concerned the Cuban missile showdown, the launching of Sputnik, and the construction of the Berlin Wall, among other Cold War crises. Buckley recounts these historical events faithfully. Anne Janette Johnson, speaking of *See You Later, Alligator,* which revolves around the Cuban missile crisis, asserts in the *Detroit Free Press* that "history buffs and spy-thriller enthusiasts alike should enjoy this in-depth portrayal of a unique moment in the history of the Western hemisphere." Stefan Kanfer of *Time* acknowledges that "it is to Buckley's credit that within his fiction, actual events are made as urgent and terrifying as they were."

But actual history is only a part of the Blackford Oakes novels. Oakes's missions take place behind the scenes of history. As Michael Malone explains in the *New York Times Book Review,* "Buckley slides his quite fascinatingly imagined, and appallingly conceivable, intrigues into the unknowns surrounding the secret skirmishes between us and them." In several novels Buckley presents the case for an alternative policy from that which was actually followed. "He raises the sort of questions that only the most naive and the most sophisticated political observers would dare to ask," Anatole Broyard remarks in the *New York Times.* "He says, 'What if—' and then proposes something that is as attractive as it is preposterous, something so nearly commonsensical that it throws the entire Western world into pandemonium."

In building his novels around actual events Buckley is obliged to include historical figures in his cast of characters, something he does quite well. Speaking of *See You Later, Alligator,* Murdoch believes that "the telling personal [details] are helping to make the Blackford Oakes series unique in spy fiction." In his review of *The Story of Henri Tod,* Broyard claims that "the best part . . . is [Buckley's] portrait of former President John F. Kennedy. His rendering of Nikita Khrushchev is quite good too, and this tempts me to suggest that Mr. Buckley seems most at home when he projects himself into the minds of heads of state."

Similarly, Elaine Kendall of the *Los Angeles Times Book Review* speculates that Buckley may be evolving into "a psychic historian who can project himself into the most convoluted political minds."

Perhaps Buckley's most influential popular means of spreading the conservative message is his weekly television program, "Firing Line," which reaches several million viewers over the Public Broadcasting System. It is now the thirteenth-longest-running program on either public or commercial television, having been broadcast since 1966, and was the winner of an Emmy Award in 1969. The hour-long show presents debates between Buckley and selected guests from politics or the arts. His guests have ranged from Jorge Luis Borges to Jimmy Carter. "Whether the matter at hand is perfection of the soul or perfection of the state," Michiko Kakutani maintains in the *New York Times,* "exchanges on 'Firing Line' have always been animated by a love of language and a delight in logic."

An articulate and witty television host, Buckley nonetheless upsets some of his guests with his incisive questions. R. Z. Sheppard of *Time* calls him a "TV Torquemada." Describing a typical "Firing Line" show, Phil Garner of the *Atlanta Journal & Constitution* observes that "Buckley's first question, characteristically, sought out the most likely weaknesses in his guests' most cherished positions." Frederick C. Klein compares "the spectacle of William F. Buckley, Jr. spearing a foe" to "the sight of a cat stalking a bird. If you sympathize with the bird, you can still find it possible to admire the grace and ferocity of its pursuer." Buckley explains to Kakutani that many people are anxious to appear on "Firing Line," but that "some people aren't so eager— people with positions not so easily defended in the face of rather relentless scrutiny."

Despite his long involvement in the nation's political life, Buckley has only once sought public office. In 1965 he ran for mayor of New York City in a highly visible, perhaps not-quite-serious campaign. Or maybe, as Buckley explained, it was just that he couldn't work up the "synthetic optimism" his followers expected. When asked, for example, what he would do if elected, Buckley replied: "Demand a recount." Although he lost the election, garnering 13.4% of the vote, Buckley managed to draw public attention to several issues he felt to be of importance, including welfare reform, the New York City traffic problem, and the treatment of criminals. Buckley now considers his political career over. "The only thing that would convince me to run again," he states, "would be a direct order from my Maker, signed in triplicate by each member of the Trinity."

But in 1973 Buckley found himself in government office, this time as a public member of the U.S. delegation to the 28th General Assembly of the United Nations. He was appointed to the post by President Richard Nixon. Although a critic of the U.N. and skeptical of its effectiveness, Buckley took the job. "I saw myself there," Buckley writes of his reasons for accepting the position, "in the center of the great assembly at the U.N. . . . holding the delegates spellbound . . . I would cajole, wheedle, parry, thrust, mesmerize, dismay, seduce, intimidate. The press of the world would rivet its attention on the case the American delegate was making for human rights." But Buckley's dream was not to be. "[If] the Gettysburg Address were to be delivered from the floor of the United Nations," Buckley later told an interviewer, "it would go unnoticed. . . . I soon became aware that the role of oratory was purely ceremonial. No one takes any notice of what is actually said. One listens for the overtones." Buckley has also served as a presidential appointee to the National Advisory Commission on Information, charged with assessing the work of the United States Information Agency. His only other brush with government work came in 1980 when President Reagan, who had just been elected, asked Buckley what position he would like to have in the new administration. "Ventriloquist," said Buckley.

As columnist, television host, novelist, and magazine editor, Buckley is known as "one of the most articulate, provocative, and entertaining spokesmen for American conservatism," as Moore writes. For his role in the development of the modern conservative movement, Buckley "is a man who richly deserves praise," Kondrake believes. "He is generous, erudite, witty and courageous, and he has performed a service to the whole nation, even to those who disagree with him." Writing in the *Los Angeles Times Book Review*, John Haase calls Buckley "witty, erudite, multifaceted, perhaps one of the few great exponents of the English language. He is politically contentious, a 'farceur,' I suspect, but we are willing to forgive all, because mostly Buckley is fun." Summing up Buckley's role in the nation's political life, Moore finds that his "flickering tongue and flashing wit have challenged a generation to remember the old truths while searching for the new, to abhor hypocrisy and to value logic, and to join in the worldwide struggle for human rights and human freedom."

BIOGRAPHICAL/CRITICAL SOURCES:

BOOKS

Buckley, William F., Jr., *The Unmaking of a Mayor*, Viking, 1966.

Buckley, William F., Jr., *Cruising Speed: A Documentary*, Putnam, 1971.

Buckley, William F., Jr., *United Nations Journal: A Delegate's Odyssey*, Putnam, 1974.

Buckley, William F., Jr., *Overdrive: A Personal Documentary*, Doubleday, 1983.

Cain, Edward R., *They'd Rather Be Right: Youth and the Conservative Movement*, Macmillan, 1963.

Contemporary Issues Criticism, Volume 1, Gale, 1982.

Contemporary Literary Criticism, Gale, Volume 7, 1977, Volume 18, 1981, Volume 37, 1986.

Dictionary of Literary Biography Yearbook: 1980, Gale, 1981.

Forster, Arnold and B. R. Epstein, *Danger on the Right*, Random House, 1964.

Judis, John, *William F. Buckley, Jr.: Patron Saint of the Conservatives*, Simon & Schuster, 1988.

Markmann, Charles L., *The Buckleys: A Family Examined*, Morrow, 1973.

Nash, George H., *The Conservative Intellectual Movement in America since 1945*, Basic Books, 1976.

Phelps, Donald, *Covering Ground: Essays for Now*, Croton Press, 1969.

Tuccille, J., *It Usually Begins with Ayn Rand: A Libertarian Odyssey*, Stein & Day, 1972.

PERIODICALS

American Mercury, December, 1951.
Armchair Detective, June, 1976.
Atlanta Journal & Constitution, March 3, 1974.
Atlantic, November, 1951, May, 1954, July, 1968.
Catholic World, November, 1959.
Chicago Tribune, November 8, 1959.
Choice, April, 1979.
Christian Century, July 3, 1968.
Christian Science Monitor, August 29, 1968, August 16, 1978, December 20, 1980, February 24, 1984.

Commentary, April, 1974, November, 1983.
Commonweal, February 15, 1952, May 3, 1963, December 23, 1966, March 1, 1974.
Detroit Free Press, February 24, 1985.
Detroit News, September 19, 1982, August 21, 1983.
Esquire, January, 1961, November, 1966, January, 1968, August, 1969, September, 1969, February, 1972, July, 1976.
Globe and Mail (Toronto), February 18, 1984, April 13, 1985.
Harper's, March, 1967, November, 1971, October, 1983.
Life, September 17, 1965.
Listener, July 3, 1975, March 11, 1976.
Los Angeles Times, August 11, 1983.
Los Angeles Times Book Review, February 7, 1982, September 12, 1982, January 22, 1984, April 7, 1985, March 23, 1986, May 7, 1989.
Mademoiselle, June, 1961.
Modern Age, summer, 1967, summer, 1974.
Nation, October 2, 1972, April 26, 1980.
National Observer, November 29, 1975.
National Review, May 7, 1963, November 15, 1966, July 30, 1968, September 13, 1974, October 24, 1975, December 5, 1975, February 20, 1976, May 13, 1977, June 9, 1978, November 24, 1978, April 4, 1980, January 22, 1982, October 15, 1982, September 2, 1983, February 24, 1984, December 31, 1985.
Negro Digest, April, 1969.
New Leader, January 19, 1976.
New Republic, October 19, 1959, June 10, 1978.
New Statesman, March 12, 1976.
Newsweek, October 17, 1966, March 25, 1968, August 2, 1971, September 30, 1974, January 5, 1976, February 19, 1979.
New Yorker, August 8, 1970, August 21, 1971, August 28, 1971.
New York Review of Books, July 18, 1974, October 13, 1983.
New York Times, November 4, 1951, April 4, 1954, October 6, 1971, April 5, 1978, February 6, 1980, February 25, 1981, December 28, 1981, August 18, 1983, December 21, 1983, February 4, 1985, March 27, 1986, April 5, 1989, May 4, 1989, October 1, 1989.
New York Times Book Review, March 25, 1962, April 28, 1963, October 30, 1966, September 15, 1968, August 2, 1970, September 26, 1971, October 8, 1972, January 13, 1974, September 28, 1975, December 26, 1976, January 11, 1978, May 14, 1978, November 19, 1978, February 17, 1980, March 30, 1980, January 24, 1982, March 7, 1982, September 5, 1982, August 7, 1983, February 5, 1984, March 3, 1985, January 5, 1986, February 9, 1986, April 6, 1986, May 31, 1987, May 28, 1989.
New York Times Magazine, September 5, 1965.
Observer, June 8, 1975.
Playboy, May, 1970.
Progressive, January, 1969.
Publishers Weekly, August 26, 1974.
Punch, July 12, 1978.
Reader's Digest, September, 1971.
Saturday Evening Post, April, 1977.
Saturday Review, April 3, 1954, October 10, 1959, April 27, 1963, August 8, 1970, May 13, 1978, January, 1982.
Saturday Review of Literature, December 15, 1951.
Spectator, June 21, 1975.
Time, October 31, 1960, November 4, 1966, November 3, 1967, August 2, 1971, November 18, 1974, January 5, 1976, December 6, 1976, June 19, 1978, February 19, 1979, February 25, 1980, January 18, 1982, October 25, 1982, December 9, 1985, February 4, 1986, March 31, 1986, June 15, 1987.
Times Literary Supplement, March 12, 1976, July 27, 1984.

Village Voice, February 21, 1974, December 8, 1975.
Wall Street Journal, November 15, 1966, January 31, 1967.
Washington Post, February 12, 1980.
Washington Post Book World, June 30, 1968, January 23, 1972, February 12, 1980, January 10, 1982, September 4, 1983, March 24, 1985, March 9, 1986, May 24, 1987, April 30, 1989.
Worldview, June, 1972.
Yale Review, December, 1959.

*   *   *

BUECHNER, (Carl) Frederick 1926-

PERSONAL: Born July 11, 1926, in New York, N.Y.; son of Carl Frederick and Katherine (Kuhn) Buechner; married Judith Friedrike Merck, April 7, 1956; children: Katherine, Dinah, Sharman. *Education:* Princeton University, A.B., 1948; Union Theological Seminary, B.D., 1958.

ADDRESSES: Home—Rupert, Vt. *Office*—c/o P.O. Box 1160, Pawlet, Vt. 05761. *Agent:* Lucy Kroll Agency, 390 West End Ave., New York, N.Y. 10024.

CAREER: Lawrenceville School, Lawrenceville, N.J., teacher of English, 1948-53; East Harlem Protestant Parish, New York, N.Y., head of employment clinic, 1954-58; ordained minister of the United Presbyterian Church, 1958; Phillips Exeter Academy, Exeter, N.H., chairman of department of religion, 1958-60, school minister, 1960-67; writer, 1967—. Instructor in creative writing, New York University, summers, 1953, 1954. William Belden Nobel Lecturer, Harvard University, 1969; Russell Lecturer, Tufts University, 1971; Lyman Beecher Lecturer, Divinity School, Yale University, 1976; Harris Lecturer, Bangor Seminary, 1979; Zabriskie Lecturer, Virginia Theological Seminary, 1982. Guest preacher and lecturer. Trustee, Barlow School, 1965-71. *Military service:* U.S. Army, 1944-46.

MEMBER: National Council of Churches, Council for Religion in Independent Schools (regional chairman, 1959-63), Foundation for Arts, Religion, and Culture, Presbytery of Northern New England, P.E.N., Authors Guild, Authors League of America, Century Association.

AWARDS, HONORS: O. Henry Memorial Award, 1955, for short story "The Tiger"; Richard and Hinda Rosenthal Award, 1959, for *The Return of Ansel Gibbs;* National Book Award nomination, 1971, for *Lion Country;* Pulitzer Prize nomination, 1980, for *Godric;* D.D. from Virginia Theological Seminary, 1982.

WRITINGS:

NOVELS

A Long Day's Dying, Knopf, 1950.
The Seasons' Difference, Knopf, 1953.
The Return of Ansel Gibbs, Knopf, 1958.
The Final Beast, Atheneum, 1965, reprinted, Harper, 1982.
The Entrance to Porlock, Atheneum, 1970.
Lion Country (also see below), Atheneum, 1971.
Open Heart (also see below), Atheneum, 1972.
Love Feast (also see below), Atheneum, 1974.
Treasure Hunt (also see below), 1977.
The Book of Bebb (contains *Lion Country, Open Heart, Love Feast,* and *Treasure Hunt*), Atheneum, 1979.
Godric, Atheneum, 1980.
Brendan, Atheneum, 1987.

NONFICTION

The Magnificent Defeat (meditations), Seabury, 1966.

The Hungering Dark (meditations), Seabury, 1969.
The Alphabet of Grace (theological and autobiographical essays), Seabury, 1970.
Wishful Thinking: A Theological ABC, Harper, 1973.
The Faces of Jesus, Simon & Schuster, 1974.
Telling the Truth: The Gospel as Tragedy, Comedy, and Fairy Tale, Harper, 1977.
Peculiar Treasures: A Biblical Who's Who, Harper, 1979.
The Sacred Journey (autobiography), Atheneum, 1982.
Now and Then (autobiography), Atheneum, 1983.
A Room Called Remember: Uncollected Pieces, Harper, 1984.
Whistling in the Dark: An ABC Theologized, Harper, 1988.

Short stories have been anthologized in *Prize Stories 1955: The O. Henry Awards,* edited by Paul Engle and Hansford Martin, Doubleday, 1955. Contributor to periodicals, including *Poetry* and *Lawrenceville Literary Magazine.*

SIDELIGHTS: Two years after graduating from Princeton University, Frederick Buechner published his first novel, *A Long Day's Dying.* "[This novel] is a strikingly fine first novel, and it seems entirely safe to say that its publication will introduce a new American novelist of the greatest promise and the greatest talent," declared C. W. Weinberger in the *San Francisco Chronicle.* "In strict accuracy, it is not proper to refer to Mr. Buechner as being a novelist of great promise, for he has already arrived in superlative fashion."

Buechner's *A Long Day's Dying* is generally considered to be an unusually sensitive and insightful study of various relationships. "Buechner has written a perceptive and often astringently witty study of subtle human relationships and delicate tensions," states C. J. Rolo in a review published in *Atlantic,* "a book which continually reaches for the emotional meanings of the moment." And David Daiches writes in the *New York Times* that "this first novel by a young man of twenty-three is a remarkable piece of work. There is a quality of civilized perception here, a sensitive and plastic handling of English prose and an ability to penetrate to the evanescent core of a human situation."

Buechner's second novel, *The Seasons' Difference,* was not greeted with the same degree of enthusiasm as *A Long Day's Dying.* For example, Oliver La Farge points out in *Saturday Review* that "*The Seasons' Difference* starts with promise. Again and again it looks as if the promise were going to be fulfilled. There are moments when it lights up brightly, and one thinks, at last he has hit his stride—but always, somehow, the light goes out again. It is one of those most tantalizing of all things in writing—a near miss." H. L. Roth writes in *Library Journal* that Buechner's "emphasis is less on plot than on the development of atmosphere but even that emphasis seems to get lost in an arty attempt at developing a feeling of mysticism."

However, Tangye Lean finds Buechner's book "brilliant and closely knit both in its rather overloaded descriptive power and its invention." Writing in *Spectator* Lean remarks that "*The Seasons' Difference* may be recommended as one of the most distinguished novels that has recently come out of America." And a critic for *U.S. Quarterly Review* believes that "the arresting quality of this sensitively and elaborately written novel lies in the delineation of its characters, especially the children, and of their interrelations: adult to adult, child to adult, and child to child." Nevertheless, reasons Horace Gregory in the *New York Herald Tribune Book Review,* "Buechner probably needs more time to complete his own vision of the world that is glimpsed in certain descriptive passages of [*The Seasons' Difference*]. The promise of his first book is still awaiting its fulfillment."

Critics were more impressed with Buechner's third novel. "In *The Return of Ansel Gibbs,* Buechner makes a more decisive departure from his earlier manner," Ihab Hassan comments in *Radical Innocence: Studies in the Contemporary American Novel.* "The book is reasonably forthright; its material, though rich in moral ambiguities, is topical rather than mythic, dramatic more than allusive." A reviewer for *Atlantic Monthly* believes that this book "is quite a departure from [Buechner's] two previous novels, which were open to the charge of preciosity. Now the style is less ornate, the plot straightforward." Richard McLaughlin remarks in *Springfield Republican* that Buechner's earlier novels "established him as a writer with a distinguished style but a rather narrow range of interests. In [*The Return of Ansel Gibbs*] he explores, with his usual subtlety and feeling for language and moods, a wider, more public domain."

Writing for *Saturday Review,* A. C. Spectorsky declares that "there is a quality of distinction about Frederick Buechner's [*The Return of Ansel Gibbs*] which might best be compared to the gleam of hand-polished old silver. . . . There is about his work some of the charming cultivation of the best of Marquand, and Cozzens' capacity to make each incident—however casual or trivial in appearance—emerge as meaningful and illuminating."

In 1958, the same year *The Return of Ansel Gibbs* was published, Buechner was ordained a minister of the United Presbyterian Church. For the next several years Buechner performed the duties of school minister at Phillips Exeter Academy while continuing to write his novels. As Elizabeth Janeway explains in the *New York Times:* "Part of Frederick Buechner is a writer of imagination and insight. Part of him is a man with a Christian mission so strong that he decided to enter the Presbyterian ministry. There is no reason why the two shouldn't combine to write excellent and powerful novels."

Not all critics share Janeway's contention that the ministry and the writing of novels is a likely and acceptable combination. A reviewer for *Publishers Weekly* observes that "to a certain number of critics and reviewers . . . there is something disconcerting about a minister who can write a novel . . . containing some vivid sex scenes and a four-letter word or two." Buechner, however, sees no conflict with being a minister and a novelist. He explains in a *Publishers Weekly* interview: "Writing is a kind of ministry." Buechner elaborates further to *CA:* "As a preacher I am trying to do many of the same things I do as a writer. In both I am trying to explore what I believe life is all about, to get people to stop and listen a little to the mystery of their own lives. The process of telling a story is something like religion if only in the sense of suggesting that life itself has a plot and leads to a conclusion that makes some kind of sense."

Buechner's first literary work written after his ordination was *The Final Beast.* Published five years after *The Return of Ansel Gibbs, The Final Beast* displayed a shift in theme that a number of critics, including Gerald Weales, believed would be a preoccupation in future Buechner novels. In the *Reporter,* Weales describes the theme as "the possibility of spiritual rebirth." And a *Choice* reviewer feels this book marks the beginning of Buechner's "concern with religious belief and the religious life." Charles Dollen remarks in *Best Sellers:* "Despite what might sound like heavy drama in the plot, this [book] is a joyous one and its fictional people are searching for, and finding, real happiness. . . . This is a deeply religious book without the slightest hint of [piety] or sentimentalism."

In 1971, Buechner published *Lion Country,* the first book of a tetralogy that also includes *Open Heart, Love Feast,* and *Trea-* *sure Hunt.* Eight years later these four novels were published in one volume entitled *The Book of Bebb.* This tetralogy traces the activities and relationships of Leo Bebb, a former Bible salesman, founder of the Church of Holy Love, Incorporated, and of the Open Heart Church, and president of the Gospel Faith College, a religious diploma mill. Buechner did not originally intend to write a follow-up to *Lion Country.* He explains how the series evolved in his introduction to *The Book of Bebb:* "When I wrote the last sentence of *Lion Country,* I thought I had finished with [the characters in the series] for good but soon found out that they were not finished with me. And so it was with the succeeding volumes, at the end of each of which I rang the curtain down only to find that, after a brief intermission, they'd rung it up again."

With few exceptions critics view the Bebb series to be Buechner's best work. One such reviewer, Christopher Lehmann-Haupt, writes in the *New York Times:* "You smile to think how Frederick Buechner keeps getting better with each new novel, for where he was gently amusing in *Lion Country,* he is funny and profound in *Open Heart.*" While numerous elements have been cited as reasons for the popularity of these four novels, most critics agree that much of the credit belongs to Buechner's presentation of thought-provoking ideas in a witty manner. A reviewer for the *Times Literary Supplement* believes that Buechner maintains "a strange, serene balancing act which blends successfully . . . satirical talent and the moral purpose." And writing in *Publishers Weekly,* a critic notes that the way Buechner "writes is special and engaging—serious, comic, with a kind of reverent irreverence for his people and their lives. [He has an] amused and amusing view." Another reviewer for *Publishers Weekly* holds *Lion Country* up as a perfect example of a "human comedy of complexity and persuasion." And a *Virginia Quarterly Review* writer remarks: "Urbane, arcane, intelligent, low-keyed comedy is rare enough in these parlous times, but [*Lion Country*] is a choice example certain to appeal to a variety of tastes."

Many reviewers have noted that Buechner's comical sense is especially evident in his handling of religious matters. "This may sound like slapstick [to] suggest that although Mr. Buechner takes bows toward religion he is really more interested in laughs," suggests Michael Mewshaw in the *New York Times Book Review,* "but throughout the [tetralogy] he is most serious when he is funny, and he has found an inevitable and instructive confusion between wheat and chaff. As the Bible warns, one can't be cut away without injuring the other." And in a review of *Open Heart,* John Skow observes in *Time:* "It is something of a mystery how Buechner has produced a live, warm, wise comic novel. And yet that is exactly what, in all shifty-eyed innocence, he has done. . . . [He] seems to have found an acceptable way to deal with religious mysteries in fiction."

Many critics agree with Skow that Buechner seems to have mastered a technique for dealing with theological subjects in an entertaining fashion. A reviewer for the *Times Literary Supplement* points out: "The fine lucidity of Mr. Buechner's prose, the pure verve of his humour, the grisly authenticity of his characters and settings make this highly elusive, indeed almost deliquescent brand of Christian Philosophy seem not unpalatable but actually convincing." Lehmann-Haupt writes in the *New York Times* that Buechner's "contrast between the serious and the absurd serves to underline the meaning of both *Love Feast* and the [tetralogy] as a whole: to wit, the message of Jesus Christ may emanate from strange places indeed, but it is the message that matters, not the messenger."

Cynthia Ozick believes that the reason the religious messages seem to fit so well into Buechner's novels is that to the author "sacredness lurks effortlessly (it is pointless to grope after it) nearly everywhere; it singles us out." As Buechner himself writes in *The Hungering Dark:* "There is no place or time so lowly and earthbound but that holiness can be there too. And this means that we are never safe, that there is no place where we can hide from God, no place where we are safe from his power . . . to recreate the human heart because it is . . . just where we least expect him where he comes most fully."

"Life is . . . what Buechner is writing about," says Jonathan Yardley in the *Washington Post Book World.* "Beneath all the antics of Leo Bebb and those who surround him there is a continuing celebration of life and the interrelation of lives. Buechner's people may at first glance seem caricatures, but their robustness is merely humanity magnified." And Thomas Howard remarks in the *New York Times Book Review* that "[Buechner's] vision, then, is that of the poet—the Christian poet. He has articulated what he sees with a freshness and clarity and energy that hails our stultified imaginations."

Another factor that contributes to the success of these novels is Buechner's skill at characterization. "What makes [the Leo Bebb novels] succeed is Buechner's deft placing of all these characters," explains Roger Sale in *Hudson Review,* "keeping them funny or impossible when seen from a distance, then making them briefly very moving when suddenly seen from close up." P. A. Doyle states in *Best Sellers* that Buechner "grasps each figure firmly and forces it to concrete life. A type of Flannery O'Connor vibrant vividness pervades Bebb . . . and the other principals causing them to pop out most fully alive from the novel[s]." And Sale, writing in another issue of *Hudson Review,* singles out Buechner's treatment of the main character, Leo Bebb, and comments: "The word about Bebb is simple—he lights up every page on which he appears, making each one a joy to read and to anticipate, and of all the characters in American literature, only Hemingway's Bill Gorton rivals him in that respect."

Buechner's skillful use of characters does not end with the Bebb series of novels. Numerous reviewers have cited Buechner's following novel, *Godric,* as still another example of how an effective characterization enriches Buechner's novels. In *Godric,* Buechner tells the story of a twelfth-century Anglo-Saxon saint. Francine Cardman illustrates in *Commonweal:* "Peddler, merchant seaman, pilgrim and perhaps pirate, ultimately hermit; roguist, conniving, irascible, repentant, gentle, fierce: Godric is compelling in his struggle for sanctity. Buechner's retelling draws reader/listener into the world of his words, a world and language so strangely and strongly evocative they would seem to be Godric's own." Noel Perrin comments in the *Washington Post Book World* that "the old saint [Godric] is so real that it's hard to remember this is a novel. . . . I can think of only one other book like this: Thomas Mann's *The Holy Sinner.* That's the story, taken from medieval legend, of another carnal saint."

In addition to his novels, Buechner has also written a number of works of nonfiction, including two collections of meditations, several religious studies, and autobiographies. Critics have noted that these books are similar in many ways to Buechner novels. As Edmund Fuller writes in the *New York Times Book Review:* "The same stylistic power, subtlety and originality that have distinguished his novels, from *A Long Day's Dying* to *Open Heart,* lift *Wishful Thinking* far above commonplace religion books nearly to the level of C. S. Lewis's *Screwtape Letters.* An artist is at work here in the vineyard of theology, an able aphorist with

a natural gift for gnomics, a wit with wisdom." Reviewing *The Alphabet of Grace,* Thomas Howard writes in the *New York Times Book Review* that Buechner "takes the common, mundane experiences of daily life and reflects on them. . . . What he does with his material is what the poets do with theirs: he surprises and delights (and—very softly—teaches) us by giving some shape to apparently random experience by uttering it."

"Novelist Buechner writes about as well as anyone we know of, when it comes to Christian themes today," declares a reviewer for *Christian Century.* In an article on *The Alphabet of Grace,* M. M. Shideler observes in another issue of *Christian Century* that "Buechner's style is by turns meditative, narrative and anecdotal. His manner is honest, sensitive and direct." And N. K. Burger observes in the *New York Times Book Review* that in *The Magnificent Defeat* (Buechner's first book of meditations) Buechner "combines high writing skill with a profound understanding of Christian essentials." Tony Stoneburner writes in *Christian Century* that Buechner's collections of meditations "grant relative value to the world, distinguish Christianity and morality, argue the propriety of poetry for discourse about mystery." Commenting on Buechner's second collection, *The Hungering Dark,* Fuller states in the *New York Times Book Review* that "the touches that distinguish [this book] spring from the fact that in addition to Buechner's role as Presbyterian minister and sometime chaplain, . . . he is also one of the better literary talents of his generation. . . . He has artistic as well as pastoral insights into the human soul and also some distinction of style." Reviewing *Telling the Truth: The Gospel as Tragedy, Comedy, and Fairy Tale,* Richard Sistek points out that "this is the kind of book that asks for reflection, creativity, and response. With continually changing times and a church in transition, human experience and creativity are sorely needed to make sense out of change, and move forward with hope. The author has challenged me."

Perhaps nowhere else does the reader achieve a real understanding of Buechner, the author and minister, than in his autobiographies. In his introduction to *The Sacred Journey* Buechner writes: "What I propose to do now is to try listening to my life as a whole, or at least to certain key moments of the first half of my life thus far, for whatever of meaning, of holiness, of God, there may be in it to hear. My assumption is that the story of any one of us is in some measure the story of us all." A *Publishers Weekly* reviewer writes that in *The Sacred Journey,* Buechner "exemplifies his conviction that God speaks to us not just through sounds but 'through events in all their complexity and variety, through the harmonies and disharmonies and counterpoint of all that happens.'"

Reynolds Price remarks in the *New York Times Book Review* that in *The Sacred Journey,* Buechner "isolates and recreates a few powerfully charged incidents ranging from his early childhood to the time of his decision to enter the ministry." "The heart of this book," Julian N. Hart believes, "is a series of encounters for which 'epiphany,' overworked though it may be, is entirely appropriate." Hart writes in the *Washington Post Book World* that "the persistent core metaphor is 'journey'; in his case a life-process defined, not merely punctuated, by revelations of what he comes to acknowledge of divine goodness and power."

Now and Then, Buechner's sequel to *The Sacred Journey,* "picks up where the first book ends, with the author's experience of having his life turned upside down while listening to a George Buttrick sermon," writes Marjorie Casebier McCoy in *Christian Century.* "Part I covers Buechner's years at Union Theological Seminary, where he encountered the theologians and biblical scholars who became his mentors. . . . In Part II Buechner recalls his nine years as a minister and teacher of religion at Phillips Exeter Academy, trying to be an apologist for Christianity against its 'cultured despisers' by presenting the faith 'as appealingly, honestly, relevantly and skillfully as I could.' . . . Part III begins with Buechner's move to Vermont in 1967, chronicles his struggle to minister through full-time writing and speaking, and provides insights into the development of his subsequent novels and nonfiction."

In all of his writings—the collections of meditations, autobiographical studies, as well as fiction—Buechner has proven to many his ability to successfully maintain a literary career that reflects his dual roles as author and minister. Concludes Max L. Autrey in the *Dictionary of Literary Biography Yearbook:* "Early appraisals of Buechner's work have proved accurate. After producing ten novels and volumes of nonfictional writings, he has demonstrated his right to be listed among such contemporary writers as Mailer, Ellison, Updike, and Barth. Although his literary appeal has been primarily to the intelligentsia, he is now widely recognized as a brilliant, inspirational writer and an original voice."

A collection of Buechner's manuscripts has been established at Princeton University.

BIOGRAPHICAL/CRITICAL SOURCES:

BOOKS

Aldridge, John W., *After the Lost Generation,* McGraw, 1951.
Buechner, Frederick, *The Hungering Dark,* Seabury, 1969.
Buechner, *The Alphabet of Grace,* Seabury, 1970.
Buechner, *The Book of Bebb,* Atheneum, 1979.
Buechner, *The Sacred Journey,* Atheneum, 1982.
Buechner, *Now and Then,* Atheneum, 1983.
Contemporary Literary Criticism, Gale, Volume 2, 1974, Volume 4, 1975, Volume 6, 1976, Volume 9, 1978.
Dictionary of Literary Biography Yearbook: 1980, Gale, 1981.
Hassan, Ihab, *Radical Innocence: Studies in the Contemporary American Novel,* Princeton University Press, 1961.

PERIODICALS

America, April 14, 1973, December 14, 1974.
Atlantic Monthly, February, 1950, March, 1958, September, 1979, December, 1980.
Best Sellers, February 1, 1965, March 1, 1971, February, 1978, December, 1980, June, 1982.
Books and Bookmen, March, 1973.
Choice, September, 1971, June, 1978.
Christian Century, February 9, 1966, April 1, 1970, September 19, 1973, October 13, 1982, March 23, 1983.
Commonweal, July, 1971, February 26, 1982.
Hudson Review, winter, 1972-73, winter, 1974-75.
Library Journal, January 1, 1952, April 15, 1979.
National Review, December 20, 1974.
New Republic, January 25, 1975, September 17, 1977.
Newsweek, February 22, 1971, November 10, 1980.
New Yorker, October 21, 1974.
New York Herald Tribune Book Review, January 13, 1952.
New York Review of Books, July 20, 1972.
New York Times, January 8, 1950, February 16, 1958, May 19, 1972, September 25, 1974.
New York Times Book Review, February 20, 1966, March 2, 1969, December 6, 1970, February 14, 1971, June 11, 1972, May 13, 1973, September 22, 1974, October 30, 1977, November 23, 1980, April 11, 1982.

Publishers Weekly, December 28, 1970, March 29, 1971, June 27, 1977, February 12, 1982.
Reporter, September 9, 1965.
San Francisco Chronicle, January 22, 1950.
Saturday Review, January 19, 1952.
Saturday Review of the Society, July 29, 1972.
Saturday Review/World, October 5, 1974.
Spectator, July 25, 1952.
Springfield Republican, May 11, 1958.
Time, April 12, 1971, July 3, 1972.
Times Literary Supplement, December 29, 1972, May 23, 1975, May 12, 1978, June 13, 1981.
U.S. Quarterly Book Review, June, 1952.
Virginia Quarterly Review, summer, 1971, autumn, 1972.
Washington Post Book World, May 28, 1972, November 3, 1974, November 9, 1980, June 6, 1982.

*   *   *

BUERO VALLEJO, Antonio 1916-

PERSONAL: Surname listed in some sources as Buero-Vallejo; born September 29, 1916, in Guadalajara, Spain; son of Francisco Buero (a military engineer) and Cruz Vallejo; married Victoria Rodriguez (an actress), 1959; children: Carlos, Enrique. *Education:* San Fernando School of Fine Arts, Madrid, Spain, 1934-36.

ADDRESSES: Home and office—Calle General Diaz Porlier 36, Madrid 28001, Spain.

CAREER: Playwright, 1949—. Lecturer at universities in the United States, 1966; speaker at Symposium on Spanish Theater, University of North Carolina at Chapel Hill, 1970.

MEMBER: International Committee of the Theatre of the Nations, Hispanic Society of America (corresponding member), American Association of Teachers of Spanish and Portuguese (honorary fellow), Society of Spanish and Spanish-American Studies (honorary fellow), Modern Language Association (honorary fellow), Deutscher Hispanistenverband (honorary fellow), Sociedad General de Autores de Espana, Real Academia Espanola, Ateneo de Madrid (honorary fellow), Circulo de Bellas Artes de Madrid (honorary fellow).

AWARDS, HONORS: Premio Lope de Vega, 1949, for "Historia de una escalera"; Premio Amigos de los Quintero, 1949, for "Las palabras en la arena"; Premio Maria Rolland, 1956, for "Hoy es fiesta," 1958, for "Un sonador para un pueblo," and, 1960, for "Las Meninas"; Premio Nacional de Teatro, 1957, for "Hoy es fiesta," 1958, for "Las cartas boca abajo," 1959, for "Un sonador para un pueblo," and 1980; Premio Marcha de Teatro, 1959, for "Hoy es fiesta"; Premio de la critica de Barcelona, 1960, for "Un sonador para un pueblo"; Premio Larra, 1962, for "El concierto de San Ovidio"; Premio Leopoldo Cano, 1966, 1970, 1972, 1974, and 1976; Medalla de Oro del Espectador y la critica, 1967, 1970, 1974, 1976, 1977, 1981, 1984, and 1986; Premio Mayte and Premio Foro Teatral, both 1974; Medalla de Oro "Gaceta ilustrada," 1976; Officier des Palmes Academiques de France, 1980; Premio Ercilla and Medalla "Valle-Inclan" de la Asociacion de Escritores y Artistas, both 1985; Premio Pablo Iglesias and Premio Miguel de Cervantes, both 1986; Medalla de Oro e Hijo Predilecto de Guadalajara, 1987.

WRITINGS:

IN ENGLISH TRANSLATION

En la ardiente oscuridad: Drama en tres actos (title means "In the Burning Darkness: Three-Act Drama"; first produced in Madrid at Teatro Nacional Maria Guerrero, December 1, 1950; also see below), Alfil (Madrid), 1951, reprinted, Escelicer (Madrid), 1970, critical Spanish edition edited by Wofsy, Scribner, 1954.

La tejedora de suenos: Drama en tres actos (title means "The Dream Weaver: Three-Act Drama"; first produced in Madrid at Teatro Espanol, January 11, 1952; also see below), Alfil, 1952, translation by William I. Oliver published as "The Dreamweaver" in *Masterpieces of the Modern Spanish Theatre,* edited by Robert W. Corrigan, Collier Books, 1967.

Las Meninas: Fantasia velazquena en dos partes (title means "The Ladies-in-Waiting: Velazquen Fantasy in Two Parts"; first produced at Teatro Espanol, December 9, 1960; first published in *Primer Acto,* January, 1961; also see below), Alfil, 1961, critical Spanish edition edited by Juan Rodriguez Castellano, Scribner, 1963, translation by Marion Peter Holt published as *Las Meninas: A Fantasy,* Trinity University Press, 1987.

El concierto de San Ovidio: Parabola en tres actos (title means "The Concert at Saint Ovide: Three-Act Parable"; first produced in Madrid at Teatro Goya, November 16, 1962; first published in *Primer Acto,* December, 1962; also see below), Alfil, 1963, critical Spanish edition edited by Pedro N. Trakas, Scribner, 1965, translation by Farris Anderson of original Spanish version published as *The Concert at Saint Ovide,* Pennsylvania State University Press, 1967, Anderson's translation also published in *The Modern Spanish Stage: Four Plays,* edited by Holt, Hill & Wang, 1970.

El tragaluz: Experimento en dos partes (title means "The Skylight: Two-Part Experiment"; first produced in Madrid at Teatro Bellas Artes, October 7, 1967; first published in *Primer Acto,* November, 1967; also see below), Alfil, 1968, critical Spanish edition edited by Anthony M. Pasquariello and Patricia W. O'Connor, Scribner, 1977, translation by O'Connor of original Spanish version published as "The Basement Window" in *Plays of Protest from the Franco Era,* Sociedad General Espanola de la Libreria (Madrid), 1981.

La doble historia del doctor Valmy: Relato escenico en dos partes (title means "The Double Case-History of Doctor Valmy: Story with Scenes, in Two Parts"; first produced in English translation in Chester, England, at Gateway Theatre, November 22, 1968; first produced in Spanish in Madrid at Teatro Benavente, January 29, 1976; first published in *Artes hispanicas/Hispanic Arts* [bilingual; English translation by Anderson], 1967), edited and annotated by Alfonso M. Gil, Center for Curriculum Development (Philadelphia), 1970, critical Spanish edition edited by William Giuliano, Scribner, 1986.

El sueno de la razon: Fantasia en dos actos (title means "The Sleep of Reason: Two-Act Fantasy"; first produced in Madrid at Teatro de la Reina Victoria, February 6, 1970; also see below), Escelicer, 1970, critical Spanish edition edited by John C. Dowling, Center for Curriculum Development, 1971.

"La fundacion" (title means "The Foundation"; two parts; also see below), first produced in Madrid at Teatro Figaro, January 15, 1974.

Three Plays (contains "The Sleep of Reason," "The Foundation," and "In the Burning Darkness"), translation by Holt, Trinity University Press, 1985.

IN SPANISH; PLAYS

"Las palabras en la arena: Tragedia en un acto" (title means "Words in the Arena: Tragedy in One Act"; also see below), first produced at Teatro Espanol, December 19, 1949.

Historia de una escalera: Drama en tres actos (title means "Story of a Stairway: Three-Act Drama"; first produced at Teatro Espanol, October 14, 1949; also see below), Jose Janes (Barcelona), 1950, critical Spanish edition edited by Jose Sanchez, Scribner, 1955, reprinted, 1971, critical Spanish edition edited by H. Lester and J. A. Zabalbeascoa Bilbao, University of London Press, 1963.

La senal que se espera: Comedia dramatica en tres actos (title means "The Expected Sign: Three-Act Dramatic Comedy"; first produced in Madrid at Teatro de la Infanta Isabel, May 21, 1952), Alfil, 1952.

Casi un cuento de hadas: Una glosa de Perrault, en tres actos (title means "Almost a Fairy Tale: Three-Act Variation on Petrault"; first produced in Madrid at Teatro Alcazar, January 10, 1953), Alfil, 1953, reprinted, Narcea, 1981.

El terror inmovil: Fragmentos de una tragedia irrepresentable (title means "Motionless Terror: Fragments of An Unrepresentable Tragedy"), Alfil, 1954.

Madrugada: Episodio dramatico en dos actos (title means "Daybreak: Two-Act Dramatic Episode"; first produced at Teatro Alcazar, December 9, 1953; also see below), Alfil, 1954, critical Spanish edition edited by Donald W. Bleznick and Martha T. Halsey, Blaisdell (Waltham, Mass.), 1969.

Irene o el tesoro: Fabula en tres actos (title means "Irene; or, The Treasure: Three-Act Fable"; first produced at Teatro Nacional Maria Guerrero, December 14, 1954; also see below), Alfil, 1955.

Aventura en lo gris: Drama en dos actos unidos por un sueno increible (title means "Adventure in Grayness: Drama with Two Acts United by an Incredible Dream"; first published as "Aventura en lo gris: Dos actos grises, unidos por un sueno increible" [subtitle means "Two Gray Acts, United by an Incredible Dream"] in *Teatro: Revista internacional de la escena* [Madrid], January-March, 1954), Puerta del Sol, 1955, revised edition published as *Aventura en lo gris: Dos actos y un sueno* (subtitle means "Two Acts and a Dream"; first produced in Madrid at Teatro Recoletas, October 1, 1963), Alfil, 1964.

Hoy es fiesta: [Tragi]comedia en tres actos (title means "Today Is a Holiday: Three-Act [Tragi]comedy"; first produced at Teatro Nacional Maria Guerrero, September 20, 1956; also see below), Alfil, 1957, reprinted, Alman, 1978, critical Spanish edition edited by J. E. Lyon, Harrap, 1964, Heath, 1966.

Las cartas boca abajo: Tragedia espanola en dos partes, y cuatro cuadros (title means "The Cards Face Down: Spanish Tragedy in Two Parts and Four Scenes"; first produced at Teatro de la Reina Victoria, November 5, 1957; also see below), Alfil, 1958, critical Spanish edition edited by Felix G. Ilarraz, Prentice-Hall, 1967.

Un sonador para un pueblo: Version libre de un episodio historico, en dos partes (title means "A Dreamer for the People: A Version of a Historical Episode, in Two Parts"; first produced at Teatro Espanol, December 18, 1958; also see below), Alfil, 1959, critical Spanish edition edited by Manuela Manzanares de Cirre, Norton, 1966.

Llegada de los dioses (title means "The Gods' Arrival"; first produced in Madrid at Teatro Lara, September 17, 1971; also see below), Aguilar, 1973.

"La detonacion" (two parts; title means "The Detonation"; also see below), first produced at Teatro Bellas Artes, September 20, 1977.

"Jueces en la noche" (two parts; title means "Judges in the Night"; also see below), first produced at Teatro Lara, October 2, 1979.

"Caiman" (two parts; title means "Alligator"; also see below), first produced at Teatro de la Reina Victoria, September 10, 1981.

Dialogo secreto (two parts; title means "Secret Dialogue"; first produced in San Sebastian, Spain, at Teatro Victoria Eugenia, August 6, 1984), Espasa-Calpe, 1985.

Lazaro en el laberinto (two parts; title means "Lazarus in the Labyrinth"; first produced at Teatro Maravillas, December 18, 1986), Espasa-Calpe, 1987.

Also author of unpublished plays "Historia despiada" and "Otro juicio de Salomon," both before 1949, and "Una extranaarmonia," 1957.

OMNIBUS VOLUMES

Historia de una escalera [and] *Las palabras en la arena,* Alfil, 1952, reprinted, Escelicer, 1974.

Teatro, Losada (Buenos Aires), Volume 1: *En la ardiente oscuridad, Madrugada, Hoy es fiesta, Las cartas boca abajo,* 1959, Volume 2: *Historia de una escalera, La tejedora de suenos, Irene o el tesoro, Un sonador para un pueblo,* 1962.

Teatro selecto: Historia de una escalera, Las cartas boca abajo, Un sonador para un pueblo, Las Meninas, El concierto de San Ovidio, edited by Luce Moreau-Anabal, Escelicer, 1966.

Buero Vallejo: Antologia teatral (contains fragments of "Historia de una escalera," "En la ardiente oscuridad," and "Irene o el tesoro"), Coculsa (Madrid), 1966.

Dos dramas de Buero Vallejo: Aventura en lo gris [and] *Las palabras en la arena,* edited by Isabel Magana Schevill, Appleton-Century-Crofts, 1967.

En la ardiente oscuridad [and] *Irene o el tesoro,* Magisterio Espanol (Madrid), 1967.

Teatro: Hoy es fiesta, Las Meninas, [and] *El tragaluz* (includes interviews and critical essays by others), Taurus (Madrid), 1968.

El tragaluz [and] *El sueno de la razon,* Espasa-Calpe, 1970.

El concierto de San Ovidio [and] *El tragaluz,* edited by Ricardo Domenech, Castalia, 1971.

En la ardiente oscuridad [and] *Un sonador para un pueblo,* Espasa-Calpe, 1972.

Historia de una escalera [and] *Llegada de los dioses,* Salvat, 1973.

Historia de una escalera [and] *Las Meninas,* prologue by Domenech, Espasa-Calpe, 1975.

La doble historia del Doctor Valmy [and] *Mito* (also see below), prologue by Francisco Garcia Pavon, Espasa-Calpe, 1976.

La tejedora de suenos [and] *Llegada de los dioses,* edited by Luis Iglesias Feijoo, Catedra, 1976.

La detonacion [and] *Las palabras en la arena,* Espasa-Calpe, 1979.

Jueces en la noche [and] *Hoy es fiesta,* prologue by Feijoo, Espasa-Calpe, 1981.

Caiman [and] *Las cartas boca abajo,* Espasa-Calpe, 1981.

CONTRIBUTOR

Charles Davillier, *Viaje por Espana,* Castilla (Madrid), 1949.

Don Juan y el teatro en Espana: Fotografias de Juan Gyenes, Mundo Hispanico (Madrid), 1955.

Informaciones: Extraordinario teatral del sabado de gloria, [Madrid], 1956.

Guillermo Diaz-Plaja, editor, *El teatro: Enciclopedia del arte escenico,* Noguer (Barcelona), 1958.

Homenaje a Vicente Aleixandre, El Bardo (Barcelona), 1964.

CONTRIBUTOR TO "TEATRO ESPANOL" SERIES; EDITED BY F. C. SAINZ DE ROBLES

Teatro espanol, 1949-1950 (includes "Historia de una escalera"), Aguilar, 1951.

. . . *1950-1951* (includes "En la ardiente oscuridad"), Aguilar, 1952.

. . . *1951-1952* (includes "La tejedora de suenos"), Aguilar, 1953.

. . . *1953-1954* (includes "Madrugada"), Aguilar, 1955.

. . . *1954-1955* (includes "Irene o el tesoro"), Aguilar, 1956.

. . . *1957-1958* (includes "Las cartas boca abajo"), Aguilar, 1959.

. . . *1958-1959* (includes "Un sonador para un pueblo"), Aguilar, 1960.

. . . *1960-1961* (includes "Las Meninas"), Aguilar, 1962.

. . . *1962-1963* (includes "El concierto de San Ovidio"), Aguilar, 1964.

. . . *1967-1968* (includes "El tragaluz"), Aguilar, 1969.

. . . *1969-1970* (includes "El sueno de la razon"), Aguilar, 1971.

. . . *1971-1972* (includes "Llegada de los dioses"), Aguilar, 1973.

. . . *1973-1974* (includes "La fundacion"), Aguilar, 1975.

CONTRIBUTOR TO ANTHOLOGIES

Fernando Diaz-Plaja, editor, *Teatro espanol de hoy: Antologia (1939-1958),* Alfil, 1958, 2nd edition published as *Teatro espanol de hoy: Antologia (1939-1966),* Alfil, 1967.

Antonio Espina, editor, *Las mejores escenas del teatro espanol e hispano-americano,* Aguilar, 1959.

Festival de la literatura espanola contemporanea, Volume 4: *Teatro,* Tawantinsuyu (Lima, Peru), 1960.

Teatro: Buero Vallejo, Delgado Benavente y Aljonso Sastre, Tawantinsuyu, 1960.

Richard E. Chandler and Kessel Schwartz, editors, *A New Anthology of Spanish Literature,* Louisiana State University Press, 1967.

Robert W. Corrigan, editor, *Masterpieces of the Modern Spanish Theatre,* Collier, 1967.

Diego Marin, editor, *Literatura espanola,* Holt, 1968.

Walter T. Pattison and Bleznick, editors, *Representative Spanish Authors,* 3rd edition, Volume 2, Oxford University Press, 1971.

Spanische Stuecke, Henschelverlag (Berlin), 1976.

Anos dificiles, Bruguera, 1977.

TRANSLATOR OF PLAYS

William Shakespeare, *Hamlet: Principe de Dinamarca* (first produced at Teatro Espanol, December 15, 1961), Alfil, 1962.

Bertolt Brecht, *Madre Coraje y sus hijos: Una cronica de la Guerra de los Treinta Anos* (first produced at Teatro Bellas Artes, October 6, 1966), Alfil, 1967.

Also translator of "Vildanden" by Henrik Ibsen, first produced as "El pato silvestre" at Teatro Nacional Maria Guerrero.

OTHER

(Editor with Wofsy) *En la ardente oscuridad,* Macmillan, 1950.

(Author of prologue) Juan B. Devoto and Alberto Sabato, *Un responso para Lazaro,* Almafuerte (Buenos Aires), 1956.

Mito: Libro para una opera (title means "Myth: Book for an Opera"; first published in *Primer Acto,* November-December, 1968), Alfil, 1968.

Tres maestros ante el publico (biographical essays; title means "Three Masters before the Public"), Alianza, 1973.

Also author of screenplays and of sound recording *Me llamo Antonio Buero Vallejo* (title means "My Name is Antonio Buero Vallejo"), Discos Aguilar (Madrid), 1964. Contributor to periodicals, including *Correo Literario, Primer Acto, Revista de Occidente, Pipirijaina, Cuadernos de Agora,* and *Estreno.*

SIDELIGHTS: "The 1949-1950 theatrical season represents a turning point in Spanish drama," writes Martha T. Halsey in *Antonio Buero Vallejo,* "because of the new direction represented by" Buero Vallejo's play "Historia de una escalera" ("Story of a Stairway"). Although this was the Spanish playwright's first produced play, its impact, according to Marion Peter Holt in *The Contemporary Spanish Theater (1949-1972),* was comparable to that of Arthur Miller's "Death of a Salesman," which triumphed on the American stage during the same season. Not only were both plays popular and critical successes during their first theater runs, but they were also ic portrayals of everyday existence in their respective societies.

The effect of Buero Vallejo's play on Spanish drama is described in an Arturo del Hoyo essay which Holt translates (it first appeared in the Spanish literary review *Insula* shortly after "Historia de una escalera" opened). "From the first moments of the performance," del Hoyo notes, "the spectator was aware that *Story of a Stairway,* with its sense of dramatic values, was what had been needed in our theater to help free itself from paralysis, from mediocrity. For since 1939 the Spanish theater had been living among the ruins of the past."

Spanish theater had been living "among the ruins" caused by the bloody Spanish civil war, which devastated the country from 1936 to 1939. Joelyn Ruple's *Antonio Buero Vallejo: The First Fifteen Years* gives a picture of the bleak state of postwar Spanish theater: "During the years immediately following the war the government used the theater and movies for propaganda. There were translations of works from other countries, presentations of the Spanish classics, and some works by contemporary writers, but works censored and in general of limited value."

Strict censorship caused many writers to produce light, inoffensive works rather than risk government reprisals. "The early postwar years," Halsey explains, "had been characterized by a new type of escape theater, termed 'theater of evasion,' which renounced any purposeful interpretation of reality in favor of adventures of a strictly imaginative nature."

However, when Buero Vallejo (who had been studying painting) decided to become a playwright after the war, government censorship and the general evasiveness of Spanish plays of the period were not his most important concerns. He was an ex-prisoner, having been sentenced to death—later commuted to six years imprisonment—for his activities with the Republican (Loyalist) army during the war. But, whereas many writers chose to flee Fascist rule, Buero Vallejo decided instead to remain in Spain and produce plays. While he chose not to overtly attack Spanish authorities in his works, his plays nevertheless subtly protest Spain's repressive society.

Because of Buero Vallejo's technique of veiled criticism, Francis Donahue lists the playwright in *Books Abroad* as the leader of the Spanish "Theater of Commitment." "Spain's Theater of Commitment," Donahue remarks, "is a non-political, political theater, for it makes its impact by indirect means. The antagonist

in the Theater of Commitment is the Establishment. To point out specifically the nature of that antagonist . . . would mean the play would remain unstaged. . . . The cause of the evil conditions remains unspecified, but implied: The Spanish Establishment."

Buero Vallejo's first play, "En la ardiente oscuridad" ("In the Burning Darkness"), is a good example of his theater in general and shows how a playwright of the Theater of Commitment voices criticism in his or her work. According to Halsey the play "contains much of the thematics and symbolism more fully developed in [Buero Vallejo's] later works." Holt concurs, noting, "A consideration of *In the Burning Darkness* . . . is fundamental to an understanding of the playwright's ideas and dramatic techniques."

Although Buero Vallejo may seem to avoid the issue of government oppression in, for example, "In the Burning Darkness" because he writes about a school for the blind, his meaning is subtly revealed. The play tells the story of Ignacio's arrival at the school and how his anger at being blind disrupts the formerly tranquil life of the students. Ruple explains the social protest inherent in the play: "In ['In the Burning Darkness'] we find a philosophical or religious struggle within the protagonist as he pleads to society to look about and see the conditions under which it actually exists, to stop pretending that all is right with the world. . . . He . . . protests a lethargic society which refuses to recognize and reject a dictator." In *The Tragic Stages of Antonio Buero Vallejo,* Robert L. Nicholas agrees that this play, and many of Buero Vallejo's other works, can he viewed in terms of two levels: the surface story and its underlying philosophical truth. "As the play develops," he notes, "it becomes clear that physical blindness is symbolic of spiritual blindness and that a longing for truth, and not physical sight, is the real source of Ignacio's torment."

Many of Buero Vallejo's plays deal with a quest for the truth and the fate of those who look for it in a society blind to its own tragic reality. The seekers of truth in his plays are often "visionaries," according to Holt in his introduction to *Three Plays,* who look "beyond the present reality to a more enlightened future." Ignacio, the blind "trouble-maker" of "In the Burning Darkness," is such a visionary. In three later plays, Buero Vallejo chooses as protagonists figures from Spanish history—the painters Diego de Silva Velazquez and Francisco Jose de Goya, and the writer Mariano Jose de Larra. The three plays in which these historical characters appear—"Las Meninas" ("The Ladies-in-Waiting"), "El sueno de la razon" ("The Sleep of Reason"), and "La detonacion" ("The Detonation"), respectively—deal with, as Halsey comments in *Hispanic Journal,* "the role of the intellectual in a repressive society."

"Las Meninas" takes its name from Velazquez's masterpiece, a 10' x 9' painting of five-year-old Princess Margarita and other members of Philip IV's royal household. The painting has fascinated art critics for centuries because the wonderful portrait of the princess also includes the shadowy images of Spain's king and queen in a background mirror. Buero Vallejo's play explores the political and social implications of the painting, and "the painter," observes Nicholas, ". . . is portrayed as the lonely intellectual who attacks all that is false and unjust in seventeenth-century Spanish society." According to Nicholas, "Las Meninas" "is a . . . plea for justice. More than that, it is a call to responsibility for the intelligentsia. Buero [Vallejo] has pictorially revived a moment in history in order to address and indict his contemporaries. . . . *Las Meninas* is a direct yet subtly conceived attack against censorship."

Nicholas, Halsey, and Ruple comment on the importance of a scene in the play in which Pedro, a half-blind beggar, reacts to Velasquez's preliminary sketch for *Las Meninas.* Ruple translates Pedro's words: "Yes, I think I understand. A serene picture, but containing all the sadness of Spain. Anyone who sees these creatures will understand how irredeemably condemned they are to suffer. They're living ghosts whose truth is death. Whoever sees them in the future will notice it with terror." By implication, Buero Vallejo suggests that under Franco repression Spaniards of the twentieth century are also "irredeemably condemned to suffer."

"El sueno de la razon" takes its name from a late eighteenth-century etching by Goya entitled *El sueno de la razon produce monstruos* ("The Sleep of Reason Produces Monsters"). The etching carries the caption: "Imagination abandoned by reason produces impossible monsters: united with her, she is the mother of the arts and the source of their wonders." The etching is a self-portrait of the artist asleep at his desk while evil-looking winged creatures hover about his head and a large cat-like animal watches him with glowing eyes. The terror depicted in the etching is masterfully portrayed in Buero Vallejo's play, according to critics. Through a variety of techniques he captures the misery of the great artist left totally deaf by illness and under constant threat of harassment or death from the authorities. The playwright uses projections of the "Black Paintings"—strange dark scenes with which Goya covered the interior walls of his country house—to express his emotional turmoil.

Holt refers to a characteristic Buero Vallejo dramatic device introduced in "In the Burning Darkness" and later refined in "The Sleep of Reason." This technique, which the playwright calls "interiorizacion" ("interiorization") appears in the earlier play in a scene that makes Ignacio's blindness startlingly real to the audience. While Ignacio speaks of his horror at being blind, the stage lights begin to dim until the entire theater is completely dark. The darkness lasts through four or five lines of dialogue before the lights are turned on again.

In "The Sleep of Reason" Buero Vallejo forces the audience to experience Goya's deafness: in the latter's presence the actors mouth their lines of dialogue but make no sound. To simulate the artist's inner anguish, amplified heartbeats and the noise of flapping wings fill the theater, but only Goya reacts to them—they are not heard by the other characters. To heighten the drama, the projections of Goya's "Black Paintings" flash across the stage in an ever increasing tempo.

Holt comments: "The momentary dimming of the stage and houselights to a point of absolute darkness in one crucial scene of *In the Burning Darkness* is a far cry from the frequent scenes of silently mouthed dialogue or the visual and aural bombardment of the audience with projections and amplified sounds in *The Sleep of Reason.* . . . The audience is drawn into the mind of a character or into a crucial dramatic situation with intensified personal identification, as the proscenium barrier is bridged and momentarily ceases to exist."

Halsey refers to the techniques of interiorization as "psychic participation." She concludes that through interiorization in both "In the Burning Darkness" and in "The Sleep of Reason," Buero Vallejo produces "a more authentic participation in the reality of the tragedy." According to Halsey the reality in both of these plays "is symbolic, for the blindness portrayed represents . . . man's lack of spiritual vision and the deafness, his alienation or estrangement from his fellow human beings."

The protagonist of Buero Vallejo's "La detonacion" ("The Detonation"), Mariano Jose de Larra, is a visionary similar to the playwright's Ignacio, Velazquez, and Goya. Larra lived during the early 1800s, another period of political struggle in Spain characterized by strict censorship. Just as during Buero Vallejo's time, writers of Larra's era tried to avoid direct confrontation with the authorities by writing comedies. Larra refused to do so, writing instead satirical essays in which he attacked almost every facet of society. In *Hispanic Journal* Halsey calls Larra an "author surrogate." She notes: "Larra stated that to write in Madrid was to weep. Buero [Vallejo] no doubt experienced the same sentiment during the Franco era and initial transition period" after the dictator's death.

In spite of tremendous obstacles, Buero Vallejo achieved success as a playwright from the very beginning of his career. "The Sleep of Reason" is probably his most notable play; after being acclaimed in Madrid it was subsequently produced in a number of European countries. In 1974, it became the first Buero Vallejo play to be produced professionally in the United States. In *The Contemporary Spanish Theater* Holt calls "The Sleep of Reason" "one of the most impressive achievements of [Buero Vallejo's] career" and later adds: "With this play Buero [Vallejo] . . . sustained his right to be included among the major international writers of his day."

In a *Hispania* essay, Patricia W. O'Connor comments that because of Buero Vallejo's position as a highly respected playwright, Spanish censors have given him "relatively few problems" during his long career. But, almost all of his plays underwent at least a few *tachaduras,* or cuts, before they were allowed to be produced. "Aventura en lo gris" ("Adventure in Gray"), for example, although written in 1953, was not performed in Spain until 1963 and then only after extensive revision. The playwright's 1964 work "La doble historia del doctor Valmy" ("The Double Case-History of Doctor Valmy"), which deals with the torture of political prisoners, was not performed in Spain until 1976, after the death of Franco.

Even with the lifting of censorship in the post-Franco era, Buero Vallejo continues to deal with social issues in his plays. He writes about the tragic nature of man in order to hope for a better society. Nicholas observes: "Buero [Vallejo] is no genius—he is not a Goya; he is just an honest, courageous playwright who tries to expose social injustice, and a good, humble man who seeks to understand human suffering. Each is an endless task."

Buero Vallejo told *CA:* "After three years of war and six long years in prison, I had fallen so far behind in my painting studies that I gave them up, and set out to write for the theatre because, naturally, I had also loved the theatre since I was a child. Under Franco's strict censorship this undertaking proved even more difficult, but a set of favorable circumstances permitted me to continue onward. For me and for others, this censorship was a challenge, not just an obstacle, and I wasn't the only one to accept it. Poets, novelists, essayists, and other dramatists tried to convince the Spanish people (and themselves) that, although frequently very painful, a critical and reformative literature was possible in spite of all the environmental and administrative obstacles.

"In regards to the theatre, the official, unwritten watchwords were patriotism, escapism, moralism, and as much laughter as possible. Therefore, one had to do the opposite: tragedy which revealed instead of concealed the fact that one's destiny is a result of human and social factors instead of fate; a denunciation of injustices and frauds, a defense of liberty. And one had, at the same time, to produce serious experiences. Others will say to what extent each of us has attained these goals; perhaps they'll explain it tomorrow when the biases against this literature, which remain very strong, have been dismantled sociologically. I believe undeniably that, between all of us, something, and perhaps even a lot, has been gained. And because of this, our nation also had more support for resistance, hope and clear thinking.

"The Greek tragedians, Shakespeare, Cervantes, Calderon, Unamuno, Ibsen, Pirandello, Brecht have been, among others, my teachers, and their imprint can be observed in my theatre. Although less frequently noted, but perhaps even more important in some of my works, is the presence of Wells and Kafka. As a poet-friend of mine says about himself, I am also a 'child of well-known parents.' My originality, if I have any, is not based on denying them."

MEDIA ADAPTATIONS: "Madrugada" was made into a film.

AVOCATIONAL INTERESTS: Painting.

BIOGRAPHICAL/CRITICAL SOURCES:

BOOKS

Bejel, Emilio F., *Lo moral, lo social y lo metafísico en el teatro de Buero Vallejo,* Florida State University, 1970.
Buero Vallejo, Antonio, *Teatro: Hoy es fiesta, Las Meninas* [and] *El tragaluz,* Taurus, 1968.
Buero Vallejo, Antonio, *Three Plays,* edited and translated by Marion Peter Holt, Trinity University Press, 1985.
Contemporary Literary Criticism, Gale, Volume 15, 1980, Volume 46, 1988.
Corrigan, Robert W., *Masterpieces of the Modern Spanish Theatre,* Collier, 1967.
Domenech, Ricardo, *El teatro de Buero Vallejo,* Gredos, 1973.
Feijoo, Luis Iglesias, *La trayectoria dramatica de Antonio Buero Vallejo,* University of Santiago, 1982.
Halsey, Martha T., *Antonio Buero Vallejo,* Twayne, 1973.
Holt, Marion Peter, *The Modern Spanish Stage: Four Plays,* Hill & Wang, 1970.
Holt, Marion Peter, *The Contemporary Spanish Theater (1949-1972),* Twayne, 1975.
Nicholas, Robert L., *The Tragic Stages of Antonio Buero Vallejo,* Estudios de Hispanofila, 1972.
Ruple, Joelyn, *Antonio Buero Vallejo: The First Fifteen Years,* Eliseo Torres & Sons, 1971.

PERIODICALS

Books Abroad, summer, 1969.
Hispania, March, 1968, September, 1968, December, 1968, May, 1969, September, 1969, December, 1969, September, 1971, December, 1972, May, 1973, September, 1974, September, 1978.
Hispanic Journal, spring, 1984, fall, 1986.
Hispanofila, May, 1970.
Modern Drama, September, 1977.
Modern Language Journal, February, 1972, January, 1973, December, 1978, spring, 1984, fall, 1986.
Revista de estudios hispanicos, November, 1969, May, 1978.

*   *   *

BUKOWSKI, Charles   1920-

PERSONAL: Born August 16, 1920, in Andernach, Germany; brought to the United States, 1922; married Barbara Fry, October, 1955 (divorced); children: Marina Louise. *Education:* Attended Los Angeles City College, 1939-41. *Politics:* None. *Religion:* None.

ADDRESSES: Home—5437-2/5 Carlton Way, Los Angeles, Calif. 90027.

CAREER: Unskilled laborer, beginning 1941, whose positions included dishwasher, truckdriver and loader, mailman, guard, gas station attendant, stock boy, warehouseman, shipping clerk, post office clerk, parking lot attendant, Red Cross orderly, and elevator operator; has worked in dog biscuit factory, slaughterhouse, cake and cookie factory, and has hung posters in New York subways. Former editor of *Harlequin, Laugh Literary,* and *Man the Humping Guns;* columnist ("Notes of a Dirty Old Man"), *Open City* and *Free Press.* Currently "surviving as a professional writer."

AWARDS, HONORS: National Foundation for the Arts grant, 1963; National Endowment for the Arts grant, 1974; Loujon Press Award; Silver Reel Award, San Francisco Festival of the Arts, for documentary film.

WRITINGS:

NOVELS

Post Office, Black Sparrow Press, 1971.
Factotum, Black Sparrow Press, 1975.
Women, Black Sparrow Press, 1978.
Ham on Rye, Black Sparrow Press, 1982.
Horsemeat, Black Sparrow Press, 1982.
Hollywood, Black Sparrow Press, 1989.

SHORT STORIES

Notes of a Dirty Old Man, Essex House, 1969, 2nd edition, 1973.
Erections, Ejaculations, Exhibitions, and General Tales of Ordinary Madness, City Lights, 1972, abridged edition published as *Life and Death in the Charity Ward,* London Magazine Editions, 1974; selections, edited by Gail Ghiarello, published as *Tales of Ordinary Madness* and *The Most Beautiful Woman in Town, and Other Stories,* two volumes, City Lights, 1983.
South of No North: Stories of the Buried Life, Black Sparrow Press, 1973.
Bring Me Your Love, Black Sparrow Press, 1983.
Hot Water Music, Black Sparrow Press, 1983.
There's No Business, Black Sparrow Press, 1984.

POETRY

Flower, Fist, and Bestial Wail, Hearse Press, 1959.
Longshot Poems for Broke Players, 7 Poets Press, 1961.
Run with the Hunted, Midwest Poetry Chap-books, 1962.
Poems and Drawings, EPOS, 1962.
It Catches My Heart in Its Hands: New and Selected Poems, 1955-1963, Loujon Press, 1963.
Grip the Walls, Wormwood Review Press, 1964.
Cold Dogs in the Courtyard, Chicago Literary Times, 1965.
Crucifix in a Deathhand: New Poems, 1963-1965, Loujon Press, 1965.
The Genius of the Crowd, 7 Flowers Press, 1966.
True Story, Black Sparrow Press, 1966.
On Going Out to Get the Mail, Black Sparrow Press, 1966.
To Kiss the Worms Goodnight, Black Sparrow Press, 1966.
The Girls, Black Sparrow Press, 1966.
The Flower Lover, Black Sparrow Press, 1966.
Night's Work, Wormwood Review Press, 1966.
2 by Bukowski, Black Sparrow Press, 1967.
The Curtains Are Waving, Black Sparrow Press, 1967.
At Terror Street and Agony Way, Black Sparrow Press, 1968.
Poems Written before Jumping out of an 8-Story Window, Litmus, 1968.

If We Take . . . , Black Sparrow Press, 1969.
The Days Run Away Like Wild Horses over the Hills, Black Sparrow Press, 1969.
Another Academy, Black Sparrow Press, 1970.
Fire Station, Capricorn Press, 1970.
Mockingbird, Wish Me Luck, Black Sparrow Press, 1972.
Me and Your Sometimes Love Poems, Kisskill Press, 1972.
While the Music Played, Black Sparrow Press, 1973.
Love Poems to Marina, Black Sparrow Press, 1973.
Burning in Water, Drowning in Flame: Selected Poems, 1955-1973, Black Sparrow Press, 1974.
Chilled Green, Alternative Press, c. 1975.
Africa, Paris, Greece, Black Sparrow Press, 1975.
Weather Report, Pomegranate Press, 1975.
Winter, No Mountain, 1975.
Touch Company, bound with *The Last Poem* by Diane Wakoski, Black Sparrow Press, 1975.
Scarlet, Black Sparrow Press, 1976.
Maybe Tomorrow, Black Sparrow Press, 1977.
Love is a Dog from Hell: Poems, 1974-1977, Black Sparrow Press, 1977.
Legs, Hips, and Behind, Wormwood Review Press, 1979.
Play the Piano Drunk Like a Percussion Instrument until the Fingers Begin to Bleed a Bit, Black Sparrow Press, 1979.
A Love Poem, Black Sparrow Press, 1979.
Dangling in the Tournefortia, Black Sparrow Press, 1981.
The Last Generation, Black Sparrow Press, 1982.
Sparks, Black Sparrow Press, 1983.
War All the Time: Poems 1981-1984, Black Sparrow Press, 1984.
The Roominghouse Madrigals: Early Selected Poems, 1946-1966, Black Sparrow Press, 1988.

OTHER

Confessions of a Man Insane Enough to Live with Beasts, Mimeo Press, 1966.
All the Assholes in the World and Mine, Open Skull Press, 1966.
A Bukowski Sampler, edited by Douglas Blazek, Quixote Press, 1969.
(Compiler with Neeli Cherry and Paul Vangelisti) *Anthology of L.A. Poets,* Laugh Literary, 1972.
Art, Black Sparrow Press, 1977.
What They Want, Neville, 1977.
We'll Take Them, Black Sparrow Press, 1978.
You Kissed Lilly, Black Sparrow Press, 1978.
Shakespeare Never Did This, City Lights, 1979.
(With Al Purdy) *The Bukowski/Purdy Letters: A Decade of Dialogue, 1964-1974,* edited by Seamus Cooney, Paget Press (Ontario), 1983.
You Get So Alone at Times That It Just Makes Sense, Black Sparrow Press, 1986.
"Barfly" (screenplay based on Bukowski's life), Cannon Group, 1987 (published as *The Movie "Barfly,"* Black Sparrow Press, 1987).
A Visitor Complains of My Disenfranchise, limited edition, Illuminati, 1987.
Bukowski at Bellevue (video cassette of poetry reading; broadcast on EZTV, West Hollywood, Calif., September 23, 1988), Black Sparrow Press, 1988.
Septuagenarian Stew: Stories and Poems, Black Sparrow Press, 1990.

Also author of *The Copulating Mermaids of Venice, California.* Work represented in anthologies, including *Penguin Modern Poets 13,* 1969, *Six Poets,* 1979, and *Notes from the Underground,* edited by John Bryan. Also wrote one-hour documentary film, produced by KCET, public television Los Angeles.

SIDELIGHTS: Charles Bukowski began writing poetry at the age of 35, but he says he does not consider himself a poet but simply a writer. "To say I'm a poet puts me in the company of versifiers, neon-tasters, fools, clods, and scoundrels masquerading as wise men." He does not like "form" in poetry, calling it "a paycheck for learning to turn the same screw that has held things together." He believes that "life is a spider, we can only dance in the web so long, the thing is gonna get us. . . . I am pretty well hooked-in now, have fallen into some traps, and speak mostly from the bent bone, the flogged spirit. I've had some wild and horrible years and electric and lucky years."

AVOCATIONAL INTERESTS: Horse playing, symphony music.

MEDIA ADAPTATIONS: A film adaptation of *Love Is a Dog from Hell* was produced in 1988; "The Works of Charles Bukowski," based upon more than thirty of his works published by Black Sparrow Press, was staged by California State University in Los Angeles in 1988; "Crazy Love," based on *The Copulating Mermaids of Venice, California,* was filmed in 1989.

BIOGRAPHICAL/CRITICAL SOURCES:

BOOKS

Contemporary Literary Criticism, Gale, Volume 2, 1974, Volume 5, 1976, Volume 41, 1987.
Dictionary of Literary Biography, Volume 5: *American Poets since World War II,* Gale, 1980.
Dorbin, Sanford, *A Bibliography of Charles Bukowski,* Black Sparrow Press, 1969.
Fox, Hugh, *Charles Bukowski: A Critical and Bibliographical Study,* Abyss Publications, 1969.
Sherman, Jory, *Bukowski: Friendship, Fame, and Bestial Myth,* Blue Horse Press, 1982.
Weinberg, Jeffrey, editor, *A Charles Bukowski Checklist,* Water Row Press, 1987.

PERIODICALS

Americas, February, 1964.
Chicago Tribune, July 18, 1989.
Down Here, Volume 1, number 1, 1966.
Globe and Mail (Toronto), January 21, 1984.
Los Angeles Times, March 17, 1983, September 23, 1988.
Los Angeles Times Book Review, October 3, 1982, March 17, 1985, June 4, 1989.
Los Angeles Times Magazine, March 22, 1987, November 3, 1987, November 5, 1987.
Newsweek, October 26, 1987.
New York Times, September 30, 1987.
New York Times Book Review, January 17, 1982, June 11, 1989.
Northwest Review, fall, 1963.
People, November 2, 1987, November 16, 1987.
Review of Contemporary Fiction, fall, 1985 (Bukowski issue).
Times (London), May 28, 1987, August 27, 1987, March 9, 1989, July 8, 1989.
Times Literary Supplement, September 4, 1981, November 12, 1982, December 3, 1982, May 4, 1984, August 11-17, 1989.
Today, April, 1966.
Washington Post, November 20, 1987, June 3, 1988.

*　　*　　*

BULLINS, Ed 1935-
(Kingsley B. Bass, Jr.)

PERSONAL: Born July 2, 1935, in Philadelphia, PA; son of Edward and Bertha Marie (Queen) Bullins; married; wife's name,

Trixie. *Education:* Attended Los Angeles City College and San Francisco State College (now University).

ADDRESSES: Home—2128A Fifth St., Berkeley, CA 94710. *Agent*—Helen Merrill, 435 West 23rd St., No. 1A, New York, NY 10011.

CAREER: Left Philadelphia, PA, for Los Angeles, CA, in 1958, moved to San Francisco, CA, in 1964; cofounder, Black Arts/West; cofounder of the Black Arts Alliance, Black House (Black Panther party headquarters in San Francisco), cultural director until 1967, also serving briefly as Minister of Culture of the Party; joined the New Lafayette Theatre, New York City, in 1967, becoming playwright in residence, 1968, associate director, 1971-73; writers unit coordinator, New York Shakespeare Festival, 1975-82; People's School of Dramatic Arts, San Francisco, play writing teacher, 1983; City College of San Francisco, instructor in dramatic performance, play directing, and play writing, 1984—. Playwright in residence, American Place Theatre, beginning 1973; producing director, Surviving Theatre, beginning 1974; public relations director, Berkeley Black Repertory, 1982; promotion director, Magic Theatre, 1982-83; group sales coordinator, Julian Theatre, 1983; play writing teacher, Bay Area Playwrights Festival, summer, 1983. Also instructor in play writing at numerous colleges and universities, including Hofstra University, New York University, Fordham University, Columbia University, Amherst College, Dartmouth College, Antioch University, and Sonoma State University. *Military service:* U.S. Navy, 1952-55.

MEMBER: Dramatists Guild.

AWARDS, HONORS: American Place Theatre grant, 1967; Vernon Rice Drama Desk Award, 1968, for plays performed at American Place Theatre; four Rockefeller Foundation grants, including 1968, 1970, and 1973; National Endowment for the Arts play writing grant; Obie Award for distinguished play writing, and Black Arts Alliance award, both 1971, for "The Fabulous Miss Marie" and "In New England Winter"; Guggenheim fellowship, 1971 and 1976; grant from Creative Artists Public Service Program, 1973; Obie Award for distinguished play writing and New York Drama Critics Circle Award, both 1975, for "The Taking of Miss Janie"; Litt.D., Columbia College, Chicago, 1976.

WRITINGS:

The Hungered One (collected short fiction), Morrow, 1971.
The Reluctant Rapist (novel), Harper, 1973.

PUBLISHED PLAYS

How Do You Do?: A Nonsense Drama (one-act; first produced as "How Do You Do" in San Francisco at Firehouse Repertory Theatre, August 5, 1965; produced Off-Broadway at La Mama Experimental Theatre Club, February, 1972), Illuminations Press, 1967.
(Editor and contributor) *New Plays from the Black Theatre* (includes "In New England Winter" [one-act; first produced Off-Broadway at New Federal Theatre of Henry Street Playhouse, January 26, 1971]), Bantam, 1969.
Five Plays (includes "Goin' a Buffalo" [three-act; first produced in New York City at American Place Theatre, June 6, 1968], "In the Wine Time" [three-act; first produced at New Lafayette Theatre, December 10, 1968], "A Son Come Home" [one-act; first produced Off-Broadway at American Place Theatre, February 21, 1968; originally published in *Negro Digest,* April, 1968], "The Electronic Nigger" [one-act; first produced at American Place Theatre, February 21,

1968], and "Clara's Ole Man" [one-act; first produced in San Francisco, August 5, 1965; produced at American Place Theatre, February 21, 1968]), Bobbs-Merrill, 1969 (published in England as *The Electronic Nigger, and Other Plays,* Faber, 1970).
"Ya Gonna Let Me Take You Out Tonight, Baby?" (first produced Off-Broadway at Public Theatre, May 17, 1972), published in *Black Arts,* Black Arts Publishing (Detroit), 1969.
"The Gentleman Caller" (one-act; first produced in Brooklyn, NY, with other plays as "A Black Quartet" by Chelsea Theatre Center at Brooklyn Academy of Music, April 25, 1969), published in *A Black Quartet,* New American Library, 1970.
The Duplex: A Black Love Fable in Four Movements (one-act; first produced at New Lafayette Theatre, May 22, 1970; produced at Forum Theatre of Lincoln Center, New York City, March 9, 1972), Morrow, 1971.
The Theme Is Blackness: The Corner, and Other Plays (includes "The Theme Is Blackness" [first produced in San Francisco by San Francisco State College, 1966], "The Corner" [one-act, first produced in Boston by Theatre Company of Boston, 1968; produced Off-Broadway at Public Theatre, June 22, 1972], "Dialect Determinism" [one-act; first produced in San Francisco, August 5, 1965; produced at La Mama Experimental Theatre Club, February 25, 1972], "It Has No Choice" [one-act; first produced in San Francisco by Black Arts/West, spring, 1966; produced at La Mama Experimental Theatre Club, February 25, 1972], "The Helper" [first produced in New York by New Dramatists Workshop, June 1, 1970], "A Minor Scene" [first produced in San Francisco by Black Arts/West, spring, 1966; produced at La Mama Experimental Theatre Club, February 25, 1972], "The Man Who Dug Fish" [first produced by Theatre Company of Boston, June 1, 1970], "Black Commercial #2," "The American Flag Ritual," "State Office Bldg. Curse," "One Minute Commercial," "A Street Play," "Street Sounds" [first produced at La Mama Experimental Theatre Club, October 14, 1970], "A Short Play for a Small Theatre," and "The Play of the Play"), Morrow, 1972.
Four Dynamite Plays (includes: "It Bees Dat Way" [one-act; first produced in London, September 21, 1970; produced in New York at ICA, October, 1970], "Death List" [one-act; first produced in New York by Theatre Black at University of the Streets, October 3, 1970], "The Pig Pen" [one-act; first produced at American Place Theatre, May 20, 1970], and "Night of the Beast" [screenplay]), Morrow, 1972.
(Editor and contributor) *The New Lafayette Theatre Presents; Plays with Aesthetic Comments by Six Black Playwrights: Ed Bullins, J. E. Gaines, Clay Gross, Oyamo, Sonia Sanchez, Richard Wesley,* Anchor Press, 1974.
"The Taking of Miss Janie" (first produced in New York at New Federal Theatre, May 4, 1975), published in *Famous American Plays of the 1970s,* edited by Ted Hoffman, Dell, 1981.

Plays represented in anthologies, including *New American Plays,* Volume III, edited by William M. Hoffman, Hill & Wang, 1970. Also author of "Malcolm: '71 or Publishing Blackness," published in *Black Scholar,* June, 1975.

UNPUBLISHED PLAYS

(With Shirley Tarbell) "The Game of Adam and Eve," first produced in Los Angeles at Playwrights' Theatre, spring, 1966.
(Under pseudonym Kingsley B. Bass, Jr.) "We Righteous Brothers" (adapted from Albert Camus's play *The Just Assassins),*

first produced in New York at New Lafayette Theatre, April 1969.

"A Ritual to Raise the Dead and Foretell the Future," first produced in New York at New Lafayette Theatre, 1970.

"The Devil Catchers," first produced at New Lafayette Theatre, November 27, 1970.

"The Fabulous Miss Marie," first produced at New Lafayette Theatre, March 5, 1971; produced at Mitzi E. Newhouse Theatre of Lincoln Center, May, 1979.

"Next Time . . .," first produced in Bronx, NY, at Bronx Community College, May 8, 1972.

"The Psychic Pretenders (A Black Magic Show)," first produced at New Lafayette Theatre, December, 1972.

"House Party, a Soul Happening," first produced at American Place Theatre, fall, 1973.

"The Mystery of Phillis Wheatley," first produced at New Federal Theatre, February 4, 1976.

"I Am Lucy Terry," first produced at American Place Theatre, February 11, 1976.

"Home Boy," first produced in New York at Perry Street Theatre, September 26, 1976.

"JoAnne!," first produced in New York at Theatre of the Riverside Church, October 7, 1976.

"Storyville," first produced in La Jolla at the Mandeville Theatre, University of California, May, 1977.

"DADDY!," first produced at the New Federal Theatre, June 9, 1977.

"Sepia Star," first produced in New York at Stage 73, August 20, 1977.

"Michael," first produced in New York at New Heritage Repertory Theatre, May, 1978.

"C'mon Back to Heavenly House," first produced in Amherst, MA, at Amherst College Theatre, 1978.

"Leavings," first produced in New York at Syncopation, August, 1980.

"Steve and Velma," first produced in Boston by New African Company, August, 1980.

(Author of book) "I Think It's Gonna Work out Fine" (musical), produced in New York City, 1990.

OTHER

Editor of *Black Theatre,* 1968-73; editor of special black issue of *Drama Review,* summer, 1968. Contributor to *Negro Digest, New York Times,* and other periodicals.

SIDELIGHTS: Ed Bullins is one of the most powerful black voices in contemporary American theater. He began writing plays as a political activist in the mid-1960s and soon emerged as a principal figure in the black arts movement that surfaced in that decade. First as Minister of Culture for California's Black Panther party and then as associate director of Harlem's New Lafayette Theatre, Bullins helped shape a revolutionary "theater of black experience" that took drama to the streets. In over fifty dramatic works, written expressly for and about blacks, Bullins probed the disillusionment and frustration of ghetto life. At the height of his militancy, he advocated cultural separatism between races and outspokenly dismissed white aesthetic standards. Asked by *Race Relations Reporter* contributor Bernard Garnett how he felt about white critics' evaluations of his work, Bullins replied: "It doesn't matter whether they appreciate it. It's not for them." Despite his disinterest, by the late 1960s establishment critics were tracking his work, more often than not praising its lyricism and depth and commending the playwright's ability to transcend narrow politics. As C. W. E. Bigsby points out in *The Second Black Renaissance: Essays in Black Literature,* Bullins "was one of the few black writers of the 1960s who kept a cautious distance from a black drama which defined itself solely in political terms." In the 1970s, Bullins won three Obie Awards for distinguished play writing, a Drama Critics Circle Award, and several prestigious Guggenheim and Rockefeller grants.

Bullins's acceptance into the theatrical mainstream, which accelerated as the black arts movement lost momentum, has presented some difficulty for critics trying to assess the current state of his art. The prolific output of his early years was replaced by a curious silence after 1980. One possible explanation, according to *Black American Literature Forum* contributor Richard G. Scharine, is that Bullins was facing the artistic dilemma that confronts Steve Benson, his most autobiographical protagonist: "As an artist he requires recognition. As a revolutionary he dare not be accepted. But Bullins has been accepted. . . . The real question is whether, severed from his roots and his hate, Bullins can continue to create effectively." In a written response published with the article, Bullins answered the charge: "I was a conscious artist before I was a conscious artist-revolutionary, which has been my salvation and disguise. . . . I do not feel that I am severed from my roots."

Whatever the reasons, productions of Bullins's work were absent from the New York stage for a number of years. There was no indication, however, that the author had stopped writing. Bullins remained at work on his "Twentieth Century Cycle"—a projected series of twenty plays. This dramatic cycle, which features several recurring characters at different times and in different places, is to portray various facets of black life. Bullins's hope, as he explained to Jervis Anderson in a 1973 *New Yorker* interview, is "that the stories will touch the audience in an individual way, with some fresh impressions and some fresh insights into their own lives [and] help them to consider the weight of their experience."

Bullins's desire to express the reality of ordinary black experience reflects the philosophy he developed during his six-year association with the New Lafayette Theatre, a community-based playhouse that was a showpiece of the black arts movement until it closed for lack of funds in 1973. During its halcyon days, the New Lafayette provided a sanctuary wherein the black identity could be nurtured, a crucial goal of Bullins and all the members of that theatrical family. "Our job," former New Lafayette director Robert Macbeth told Anderson, "has always been to show black people who they are, where they are, and what condition they are in. . . . Our function, the healing function of theatre and art, is absolutely vital."

In order to reach his black audience, Bullins has consistently ignored many accepted play writing conventions. "Bullins has never paid much attention to the niceties of formal structure, choosing instead to concentrate on black life as it very likely really is—a continuing succession of encounters and dialogues, major events and non-events, small joys and ever-present sorrows," Catharine Hughes comments in *Plays and Players.* New York theatre critic Clive Barnes calls him "a playwright with his hand on the jugular vein of people. He writes with a conviction and sensitivity, and a wonderful awareness of the way the human animal behaves in his human jungle. . . . Bullins writes so easily and naturally that you watch his plays and you get the impression of overhearing them rather than seeing them."

Part of the authenticity Bullins brings to his dramas may stem from his use of characters drawn from real life. Steve Benson, Cliff Dawson, and Art Garrison are but three of the recurring protagonists who have been closely identified with the author himself. In the early 1970s Steve Benson, who appears in Bullins's novel *The Reluctant Rapist* as well as in "It Has No

Choice," "In New England Winter," and other plays, became so closely associated with his creator that Bullins threatened to eliminate him. "Everybody's got him tagged as me," he told *New York Times* contributor Mel Gussow. "I'm going to kill him off." To a large extent, Steve Benson has disappeared from Bullins's recent dramas, but the link between his art and his life experiences remains a strong one. *Dictionary of Literary Biography* contributor Leslie Sanders explains: "While Bullins frequently warns against turning to his writing for factual details of his life and against identifying him with any single one of his characters, he has never denied the autobiographical quality of his writing. Thus, the tenor, if not the exact substance, of his early years emerges from several of his plays."

Bullins was born and raised in a North Philadelphia ghetto, but was given a middle-class orientation by his mother, a civil servant. He attended a largely white elementary school, where he was an excellent student, and spent his summers vacationing in Maryland farming country. As a junior high student, he was transferred to an inner-city school and joined a gang, the Jet Cobras. During a street fight, he was stabbed in the heart and momentarily lost his life (as does his fictional alter-ego Steve Benson in *The Reluctant Rapist*). The experience, as Bullins explained to *New York Times* contributor Charles M. Young, changed his attitude: "See, when I was young, I was stabbed in a fight. I died. My heart stopped. But I was brought back for a reason. I was gifted with these abilities and I was sent into the world to do what I do because that is the only thing I can do. I write."

Bullins did not immediately recognize his vocation, but spent several years at various jobs. After dropping out of high school, he served in the Navy from 1952 to 1955, where he won a shipboard lightweight boxing championship and started a program of self-education through reading. Not much is known about the years he spent in North Philadelphia after his discharge, but Sanders says "his 1958 departure for Los Angeles quite literally saved his life. When he left Philadelphia, he left behind an unsuccessful marriage and several children." In California, Bullins earned a general equivalency diploma (GED) and started writing. He turned to plays when he realized that the black audience he was trying to reach did not read much fiction and also that he was naturally suited to the dramatic form. But even after moving to San Francisco in 1964, Bullins found little encouragement for his talent. "Nobody would produce my work," he recalled of his early days in the *New Yorker*. "Some people said my language was too obscene, and others said the stuff I was writing was not theatre in the traditional sense." Bullins might have been discouraged had he not chanced upon a production of two plays by LeRoi Jones, "Dutchman" and "The Slave," that reminded him of his own. "I could see that an experienced playwright like Jones was dealing with the same qualities and conditions of black life that moved me," Bullins explained.

Inspired by Jones's example, Bullins and a group of black revolutionaries joined forces to create a militant cultural-political organization called Black House. Among those participating were Huey Newton and Bobby Seale, two young radicals whose politics of revolution would soon coalesce into the Black Panther party. But the alliance between the violent "revolutionary nationalists," such as Seale and Newton, and the more moderate "cultural nationalists," such as Bullins, would be short-lived. As Anderson explains in the *New Yorker:* "The artists were interested solely in the idea of a cultural awakening while the revolutionaries thought, in Bullins' words, that 'culture was a gun.'" Disheartened by the experience, Bullins resigned the post he had been assigned as Black Panther Minister of Culture, severed his ties with the ill-fated Black House, and accepted Robert Mac-

beth's invitation to work at the New Lafayette Theater in New York.

To date, Bullins's association with the New Lafayette Theatre has been one of the most productive creative periods in his life. Between 1967 and 1973 Bullins created and/or produced almost a dozen plays, some of which are still considered his finest work. He also edited the theatre magazine *Black Theatre* and compiled and edited an anthology of six New Lafayette plays. During this time, Bullins was active as a play writing teacher and director as well. Despite Bullins's close ties to the New Lafayette, his plays were also produced Off-Broadway and at other community theaters, notably the American Place Theatre where he became playwright in residence after the New Lafayette's demise.

Bullins's plays of this period share common themes. "Clara's Ole Man," an early drama that established the playwright's reputation in New York during its 1968 production, introduces his concerns. Set in the mid-fifties, it tells the story of twenty-year-old Jack, an upwardly mobile black who goes to the ghetto to visit Clara one afternoon when her "ole man" is at work. Not realizing that Clara's lover is actually Big Girl, a lesbian bully who is home when Jack calls, he gets brutally beaten as a result of his ignorance. Leslie Sanders believes that "in *Clara's Ole Man,* Bullins's greatest work is foreshadowed. Its characters, like those in many of his later plays, emerge from brutal life experiences with tenacity and grace. While their language is often crude, it eloquently expresses their pain and anger, as well as the humor that sustains them." C. W. E. Bigsby believes that "Clara's Ole Man," as well as "Goin' A Buffalo," "In the Wine Time," "In New England Winter," and other plays that Bullins wrote in the mid- to late-1960s project the "sense of a brutalized world. . . . Love devolves into a violent sexuality in which communion becomes simple possession, a struggle for mental and physical dominance. Money is a dominating reality, and alcohol and drugs, like sexuality, the only relief. The tone of the plays is one of desperation and frustration. Individuals are locked together by need, trapped by their own material and biological necessities. Race is only one, and perhaps not even the dominant, reality."

By and large, Bullins's plays of this period have fared well artistically while being criticized, by both black and white critics, for their ideology. Some blacks have objected to what Bigsby calls the "reductive view of human nature" presented in these dramas, along with "their sense of the black ghetto as lacking in any redeeming sense of community or moral values." Other blacks, particularly those who have achieved material success, resent their exclusion from this art form. "I am a young black from a middle-class family and well-educated," reads a letter printed in the *New York Times Magazine* in response to a black arts article. "What sense of self will I ever have if I continue to go to the theatre and movies and never see blacks such as myself in performance?" For the white theater-going community, Bullins's exclusively black drama has raised questions of cultural elitism that seems "to reserve for black art an exclusive and, in some senses, a sacrosanct critical territory," Anderson believes.

Bullins some time ago distanced himself from the critical fray, saying that if he'd listened to what critics have told him, he would have stopped writing long ago. "I don't bother too much what anyone thinks," he told Anderson. "When I sit down in that room by myself, bringing in all that I ever saw, smelled, learned, or checked out, I am the chief determiner of the quality of my work. The only critic that I really trust is me."

BIOGRAPHICAL/CRITICAL SOURCES:

BOOKS

Bigsby, C. W. E., *The Second Black Renaissance: Essays in Black Literature,* Greenwood Press, 1980.
Contemporary Literary Criticism, Gale, Volume 1, 1973, Volume 5, 1976, Volume 7, 1977.
Dictionary of Literary Biography, Gale, Volume 7: *Twentieth-Century American Dramatists,* 1981, Volume 38: *Afro-American Writers after 1955: Dramatists and Prose Writers,* 1985.
Gayle, Addison, editor, *The Black Aesthetic,* Doubleday, 1971.

PERIODICALS

Black American Literature Forum, fall, 1979.
Black Creation, winter, 1973.
Black World, April, 1974.
CLA Journal, June, 1976.
Nation, November 12, 1973, April 5, 1975.
Negro Digest, April, 1969.
Newsweek, May 20, 1968.
New Yorker, June 16, 1973.
New York Times, September 22, 1971, May 18, 1975, June 17, 1977, May 31, 1979, March 17, 1990.
New York Times Book Review, June 20, 1971, September 30, 1973.
New York Times Magazine, September 10, 1972.
Plays and Players, May, 1972, March, 1973.
Race Relations Reporter, February 7, 1972.

* * *

BULTMANN, Rudolf Karl 1884-1976

PERSONAL: Born August 20, 1884, in Wiefelstede, Germany (now West Germany); died July 30, 1976, in Marburg, West Germany; son of Arthur (a parson) and Helene (Stern) Bultmann; married Helene Feldmann, August 6, 1917; children: Antje (Mrs. B. Lemke), Gesine (Mrs. Malte Diesselhorst), Heilke. *Education:* Studied at Universities of Tuebingen, Berlin, Marburg, Lic. theol., 1910. *Religion:* Evangelical.

ADDRESSES: Home—Calvin St. 14, Marburg on the Lahn, West Germany.

CAREER: University of Marburg, Marburg, Germany (now West Germany), instructor in New Testament science, 1912-16; University of Breslau, Breslau, Germany (now Wroclaw, Poland), assistant professor of New Testament science, 1916-20; University of Giessen, Giessen, Germany (now West Germany), professor, 1920-21; University of Marburg, professor, 1921-51, became professor emeritus.

MEMBER: Society of Biblical Literature (honorary), Academies of Oslo, Heidelberg, and Goettingen (corresponding member), Academia Goethena (Sao Paolo, Brazil; corresponding member).

AWARDS, HONORS: D.Theol. from University of Marburg, 1920; D.D. from University of St. Andrews, 1935; D.S.Th. from Syracuse University, 1959; Dr.Phil. from University of Marburg, 1959.

WRITINGS:

Der Stil der paulinischen Predigt und die kynischstoische Diatribe, Vandenhoeck & Ruprecht (Goettingen), 1910.
Die Geschichte der synoptischen Tradition, Vandenhoeck & Ruprecht, 1921, 5th edition, 1961, English translation by John Marsh of the 3rd German edition published as *The History of the Synoptic Tradition,* Harper, 1963.
Jesus, Deutsche Bibliothek (Berlin), 1926, revised edition, Mohr (Tuebingen), 1961, English translation by Louise Pettibone Smith and Erminie Huntress published as *Jesus and the Word,* Scribner, 1934.
Krisis des Glaubens, Krisis der Kirche, Krisis der Religion (lectures delivered at the University of Marburg), A. Toepelmann (Giessen), 1931.
Glauben und Verstehen, Mohr, Volume I, 1933, Volume II, 1954, Volume III, 1960, Volume IV, 1965, English translation by J. C. G. Greig of Volume II published as *Essays: Philosophical and Theological,* Macmillan, 1955.
(Contributor) F. C. Grant, editor and translator, *Form Criticism* (contains "The Study of the Synoptic Gospels"), Willett, 1934, Harper, 1962.
Offenbarung und Heilsgeschehen, A. Lempp (Munich), 1941.
(Contributor) Hans Werner Bartsch, editor, *Kerygma und Mythos: Ein theologisches Gespraech,* two volumes, Reich & Heidrich (Hamburg), 1948-52, English translation by Reginald H. Fuller published as *Kerygma and Myth: A Theological Debate,* S.P.C.K., 1953.
Das Christentum als orientalische und als abendlaendische Religion, F. Truejen (Bremen) 1949.
Das Urchristentum im Rahmen der antiken Religionen, Artemis-Verlag (Zurich), 1949, reprinted, Rowohlt, 1962, English translation by Fuller published as *Primitive Christianity in Its Contemporary Setting,* Meridian, 1956, reprinted, New American Library, 1974.
Theologie des Neuen Testaments, Mohr, 1950, reprinted, 1977, English translation by Kendrick Grobel published as *Theology of the New Testament,* two volumes, Scribner, 1951-55, reprinted as one volume, 1965.
Das Evangelium des Johannes, Vandenhoeck & Ruprecht, 1952.
(With Karl Jaspers) *Die Frage der Entmythologisierung,* R. Piper (Munich), 1954, English translation published as *Myth and Christianity: An Inquiry into the Possibility of Religion without Myth,* Noonday, 1958.
Marburger Predigten, Mohr, 1956, English translation by Harold Knight published as *This World and the Beyond: Marburg Sermons,* Scribner, 1960.
(Editor) *Die Reden des Johannesevangeliums und der Stil der gnostischen Offenbarungsrede,* Vandenhoeck & Ruprecht, 1956.
History and Eschatology (Gifford lectures at University of Edinburgh, 1955), University Press, Edinburgh, 1957, reprinted, Harper, 1962, published as *The Presence of Eternity: History and Eschatology,* Harper, 1957, published as *The Presence of Eternity,* Greenwood, 1975, German version published as *Geschichte und Eschatologie,* Mohr, 1958.
Gnosis (Bible key words), Harper, 1958.
Jesus Christ and Mythology, Scribner, 1958, German version published as *Jesus Christus und die Mythologie: Das Neue Testament im Licht der Bibelkritik,* Furche (Hamburg), 1964.
Das Verhaeltnis der urchristlichen Christusbotschaft zum historischen Jesus, C. Winter (Heidelberg), 1960.
Existence and Faith: Shorter Writings of Rudolf Bultmann, selected, translated, and introduced by Schubert M. Ogden, Meridian, 1960.
Die Erforschung der synoptischen Evangelien, Toepelman (Berlin), 1960.
(With Artur Weiser) *Faith* (Bible key words), translated by Dorothea M. Barton, edited by P. R. Ackroyd, A. & C. Black, 1961.

(With Friedrich Gogarten and Eduard Thurneysen) *Anfaenge der dialektischen Theologie,* C. Kaiser (Munich), 1963.

Exegetische Probleme des zweiten Corintherbriefes, Wissenschaftliche Buchgesellschaft (Darmstadt), 1963.

(With Karl Heinrich Rengstorf) *Hope* (Bible key words), translated by D. M. Barton, edited by Ackroyd, A. & C. Black, 1963.

Der alte und der neue Mensch in der Theologie des Paulus, Wissenschaftliche Buchgesellschaft, 1964, English translation by Keith R. Crim published as *The Old and the New Man in the Letters of Paul,* John Knox, 1967.

(Author of introduction) Adolf von Harnack, *Das Wesen des Christentums,* Siebenstern Taschenbuch Verlag (Munich), 1964.

(With others) *Life and Death* (Bible key words), translated by P. H. Ballard and others, edited by Ackroyd, A. & C. Black, 1965.

(With others) *Translating Theology into the Modern Age,* Volume II, edited by Robert W. Funk and G. Ebeling, Harper Torchbook, 1965.

Beitraege zum Verstaendis der Jenseitigkeit Gottes im Neuen Testament, Wissenschaftliche Buchgesellschaft, 1965.

(With Ebeling) *Theology and Proclamation: A Dialogue with Bultmann,* translated by John Riches, Fortress, 1966.

Die drei Johannesbriefe, Vandenhoeck & Ruprecht, 1967, English translation By R. Philip O'Hara with Lane C. McGaughy and Funk published as *The Johannine Epistles: A Commentary,* Fortress, 1973.

Exegetics, Mohr, 1967.

The Gospel of John: A Commentary, Westminster, 1971.

The Future of Our Religious Past: Essays in Honour of Rudolf Bultmann, S.C.M. Press, 1972.

Rudolf Bultmann, edited with an introduction and notes by E. J. Tinsley, Epworth Press, 1973.

Gesammelte Aufsaetze, Evangelische Verlagsanstalt, 1973.

Der zweite Brief an die Korinther, Vandenhoeck & Ruprecht, 1976, English translation by Wilhelm Linss published as *The Second Letter to the Corinthians,* Augsburg, 1983.

Gedenken an Rudolf Bultmann, Mohr, 1977.

Christ without Myth, translated by S. M. Ogden, Southern Methodist University Press, 1979.

Karl Barth-Rudolf Bultmann Letters 1922-1966, translated and edited by Geoffrey W. Bromiley, Eerdmans, 1981.

(With Karl Jaspers) *Die Frage der Entmythologisierung,* R. Piper (Munich), 1981.

The New Testament and Mythology, and Other Basic Writings, translated and edited by Ogden, Fortress, 1984.

A Translation of the Greek Expressions in the Text of the Gospel of John: A Commentary by Rudolf Bultmann, University Press of America, 1985.

Former editor of *Theologische Rundschau.*

SIDELIGHTS: Rudolf Karl Bultmann, one of Europe's leading theologians, was often included among the ranks of the "crisis theologians," who follow the example set by Karl Barth. Bultmann's principle concern, in the words of a *Times Literary Supplement* contributor, was to "commend what he [regarded] as the essential Christian gospel to people whose mental outlook, moulded by modern influences, is utterly different from that of the first and early Christian centuries, which was mythological and is completely unacceptable to our age." In a *Times Literary Supplement* review of *The History of Synoptic Tradition,* another contributor noted that "Bultmann's work is important because it represents the extreme left wing of historical scepticism. . . . Granted the presuppositions, there is a formidable and ruthless

logic about the process, a massive consistency in the detailed analysis of every phrase of the Greek text." The critic also remarked that British students "will not find the substitution of an existential confrontation for the Christ of Galilee much to their taste—and who can blame them? But it is as well that they should know in their own tongue how formidable the opposition is."

BIOGRAPHICAL/CRITICAL SOURCES:

BOOKS

Kegley, C. W., editor, *The Theology of Rudolf Bultmann,* Harper, 1966.
Macquarrie, John, *Existentialist Theology: A Comparison of Heidegger and Bultmann,* Macmillan, 1955.
Miegge, G., *Gospel and Myth in the Thought of Rudolf Bultmann,* John Knox, 1960.
Owen, H. P., *Revelation and Existence: A Study in the Theology of Rudolf Bultmann,* University of Wales Press, 1957.
Robinson, J. M., *New Quest of the Historical Jesus,* Allenson, 1959.

PERIODICALS

Crozer Quarterly, April, 1952.
Encounter, summer, 1968.
Hibbert Journal, April, 1956, January, 1958.
Times Literary Supplement, August 30, 1957, April 15, 1960, February 27, 1964.

OBITUARIES:

PERIODICALS

New York Times, August 1, 1976.
Time, August 9, 1976.
Washington Post, August 2, 1976.

* * *

BURGESS, Anthony
See WILSON, John (Anthony) Burgess

* * *

BURKE, Kenneth (Duva) 1897-

PERSONAL: Born May 5, 1897, in Pittsburgh, Pa.; son of James Leslie and Lillyan May (Duva) Burke; married Lily Mary Batterham, 1919 (divorced); married Elizabeth Batterham, December 18, 1933; children: (first marriage) Jeanne Elspeth (Mrs. Henry Hart), Eleanor Duva Leacock, Frances Batterham; (second marriage) James Anthony, Kenneth Michael. *Education:* Attended Ohio State University, 1916-17, and Columbia University, 1917-18.

ADDRESSES: *Home and office*—R.D. 2, Andover, N.J. 07821.

CAREER: Laura Spelman Rockefeller Memorial, New York City, researcher, 1926-27; *Dial,* New York City, music critic, other editorial work, 1927-29; Bureau of Social Hygiene, New York City, editorial work, 1928-29; *Nation,* New York City, music critic, 1934-35; New School for Social Research, New York City, lecturer on literary criticism, 1937; University of Chicago, lecturer on literature and literary criticism, 1938 and 1949-50; Bennington College, Bennington, Vt., instructor in theory and practice of literary criticism, 1943-62. Lecturer and/or visiting professor at numerous institutions, including Princeton University, 1949, Kenyon College, 1950, Indiana University

School of Letters, 1953 and 1958, Drew University, 1962-64, Pennsylvania State University, 1963, University of California, Santa Barbara, 1964.

MEMBER: National Institute of Arts and Letters, American Academy of Arts and Sciences.

AWARDS, HONORS: Dial Award for distinguished service to American letters, 1928; Guggenheim fellow, 1935; grants from American Academy of Arts and Letters and National Institute of Arts and Letters, 1946; fellow, Princeton Institute for Advanced Study, 1949; fellow, Center for Advanced Study in the Behavioral Sciences, 1957-58; D. Litt. from Bennington College, 1966; Rockefeller Foundation grant, 1966; Creative Arts Award from Brandeis University, 1967; award from New School for Social Research, 1970; gold medal from National Institute of Arts and Letters, 1975; National Medal for Literature, 1981.

WRITINGS:

The White Oxen, and Other Stories, A. & C. Boni, 1924.

(Translator) Emile Baumann, *Saint Paul,* Harcourt, 1929.

(Translator) Emil Ludwig, *Genius and Character,* J. Cape, 1930, Blue Ribbon Books, 1931.

Counter-Statement (criticism), Harcourt, 1931, 2nd edition, Hermes, 1953.

Towards a Better Life: Being a Series of Epistles, or Declamations, Harcourt, 1932, revised edition, University of California Press, 1966.

Permanence and Change: An Anatomy of Purpose, New Republic, 1935, 2nd revised edition, Bobbs, 1965.

Attitudes Toward History, New Republic, Volume 1: *Acceptance and Rejection: The Curve of History,* 1937, Volume 2: *Analysis of Symbolic Structure,* 1937, revised edition published as one volume, Hermes, 1959.

The Philosophy of Literary Form: Studies in Symbolic Action, Louisiana State University Press, 1941, 2nd revised edition, 1967.

A Grammar of Motives, Prentice-Hall, 1945.

A Rhetoric of Motives, Prentice-Hall, 1950.

(Contributor) Lyman Bryson, editor, *Symbols and Values: An Initial Study,* Harper, 1954.

Books of Moments: Poems, 1915-1954, Hermes, 1955.

The Rhetoric of Religion: Studies in Logology, Beacon, 1961.

A Rhetoric of Motives [and] A Grammar of Motives (also see above), World-Meridian, 1962.

Perspective by Incongruity, edited by Stanley Edgar Hyman and Barbara Karmiller, Indiana University Press, 1964.

Terms for Order, edited by Hyman and Karmiller, Indiana University Press, 1964.

Perspective by Incongruity [and] Terms for Order (selections; also see above), edited by Hyman and Karmiller, Indiana University Press, 1964.

(Translator) Thomas Mann, *Death in Venice,* Knopf, 1965.

Language as Symbolic Action: Essays on Life, Literature, and Method, University of California Press, 1966.

Collected Poems, 1915-1967, University of California Press, 1967.

The Complete White Oxen: Collected Short Fiction, University of California Press, 1968.

Dramatism and Development, Clark University Press, 1972.

(With Julie Kranhold) *Ideas for Environment,* ten volumes, Lear, Siegler, Fearon, 1973-74.

Representing Kenneth Burke, edited by Hayden White and Margaret Brose, Johns Hopkins University Press, 1982.

Contributor of essays, reviews, stories, and poems to periodicals, including *Dial, Kenyon Review, New Republic,* and *Critical Inquiry.*

WORK IN PROGRESS: Symbolic of Motives, the third volume in a series on human relations; a collection of essays.

SIDELIGHTS: Kenneth Burke, whose ideas and writings have provided subject matter for a battery of other writers, labels his vocational and avocational interests "valetudinarian" and adds: "I mean I keep trying to figure out what's wrong with the world, mine enemies and friends, and myself. I tinker shamefacedly at the piano, and make up lame pieces now and then. I fight sporadically to keep the fields around us from becoming too unbearably unsightly. Every now and then something crystallizes into a poem (which I think of as a 'moment'); then I lay aside my work on literary criticism and the philosophy of language until this 'moment' is disposed of.

"One must learn skills (that's the pragmatic angle); one must learn appreciation (that's the aesthetic angle); and one must learn to fear all skills and wonders (that's the ethical angle). Ideally, one should approach all human genius from all three angles. And so it goes, up to the point where (if I may quote a close friend-and-enemy of mine who belatedly but tinkeringly collaborated with an earlier author), 'the rest is rest in silence.' "

Burke's philosophical approach to literature brought him public attention as early as 1925, when he first began to publish the essays which have since placed him among the earliest of the New Critics. And in 1935, when he presented his lecture on "Revolutionary Symbolism in America" to the First Writers' Congress, he became a controversial figure to the communists as well as the capitalists. Although Burke paid little attention to political ideology before 1929, he became a harsh critic of capitalism and its culture after the Depression. But his criticism of capitalism, because of his "ideologically dangerous fondness for paradox," was never wholly acceptable to leftist writers and critics. "A chapter in his Counter-Statement," writes Daniel Aaron, "advocating a kind of revolutionary asceticism, contained a program of action as distasteful to Communists as to capitalists." Aaron continues: "Although the Communists found little of value in Burke's anticapitalist reflections, he continued to speculate publicly on 'the Nature of Art Under Capitalism' and to move slightly closer to the party's position. Capitalism, Burke declared in 1933, was ethically and socially disastrous, because it provided no outlets for men's predatory drives except ruthless competition and war. Under these conditions of competitive capitalism, Burke said, 'Art cannot safely confine itself to merely using the values which arise out of a given social texture and integrating their conflicts, as the soundest, "purist" art will do.' Pure art in these circumstances would become a 'social menace,' a device for 'tolerating the intolerable.' Therefore, art must for the moment, at least, contain 'a large corrective or propaganda element. It must have a definite hortatory function, an element of suasion and/or inducement of the education variety; it must be partially forensic. . . .' Implicit in all of Burke's social and aesthetic theorizing was his belief in the autonomy of the artist and the priority of art over politics. His Communism, if you could call it such, was not deeply or religiously felt; rather, it was a strategy, a tactic, a type of organization."

John Paul Pritchard writes: "Though his philosophical approach to literature is deeply indebted to [T. S.] Eliot, he has consistently used both Freudian and non-Freudian psychology as well as his considerable acquaintance with modern scientific method. Others have been more vociferous and combative, but Burke has earned an established eminence both in and out of the ranks of the New Critics. . . . Burke's few basic principles are far-reaching in their importance and give him a profound influence over recent criticism."

BIOGRAPHICAL/CRITICAL SOURCES:

BOOKS

Aaron, Daniel, *Writers on the Left,* Harcourt, 1961.
Contemporary Literary Criticism, Gale, Volume 2, 1974, Volume 24, 1983.
Dictionary Literary Biography, Gale, Volume 45: *American Poets, 1880-1945, First Series,* 1986, *Modern American Critics, 1920-1955,* 1988.
Fogarty, Daniel S. J., *Roots for a New Rhetoric,* Bureau of Publications, Teachers College, Columbia University, 1959.
Fraiberg, Louis, *Psychoanalysis and American Literary Criticism,* Wayne State University Press, 1960.
Holland, L. Virginia, *Counterpoint: Kenneth Burke and Aristotle's Theories of Rhetoric,* Philosophical Library, 1959.
Hyman, Stanley Edgar, *The Armed Vision: A Study in the Methods of Modern Literary Criticism,* Knopf, 1948.
Knox, George, *Critical Moments: Kenneth Burke's Categories and Critiques,* University of Washington Press, 1957.
Munson, Gorham B., *Destinations: A Canvas of American Literature,* Sears, 1928.
Nichols, Marie H., *Rhetoric and Criticism,* Louisiana State University Press, 1963.
Parkes, Henry Bamford, *The Pragmatic Test: Essays on the History of Ideas,* Colt, 1941.
Pritchard, John Paul, *Criticism in America,* University of Oklahoma Press, 1956.
Rueckert, William H., *Kenneth Burke and the Drama of Human Relations,* University of Minnesota Press, 1963.

*   *   *

BURKE, Ralph
See SILVERBERG, Robert

*   *   *

BURNS, Tex
See L'AMOUR, Louis (Dearborn)

*   *   *

BURROUGHS, Edgar Rice   1875-1950
(Normal Bean, John Tyler McCulloch)

PERSONAL: Born September 1, 1875, in Chicago, Ill.; died March 19, 1950; son of George Tyler (a distiller and battery manufacturer) and Mary Evaline (Zeiger) Burroughs; married Emma Centennia Hulbert, January 1, 1900 (divorced, 1934); married Florence Dearholt, 1935 (divorced, 1942); children: Joan, Hulbert, John Coleman. *Education:* Michigan Military Academy, graduate, 1895.

CAREER: Writer, 1912-50. Michigan Military Academy, Orchard Lake, Mich., instructor and assistant commandant, 1895-96; owner of a stationery store, Pocatello, Id., 1898; associated with American Battery Company, Chicago, Ill., 1899-1903; associated with Sweetser-Burroughs Mining Company in Idaho, 1903-04; Oregon Short Line Railroad Company, Salt Lake City, Ut., railroad policeman, 1904; Sears, Roebuck and Company, Chicago, manager of stenographic department, 1906-08; Burroughs and Dentzer (advertising agency), Chicago, partner,

1908-09; Physicians Co-Operative Association, Chicago, office manager, 1909; State-Burroughs Company (sales firm), Chicago, partner, 1910-11; System Service Bureau, Chicago, manager, 1912-13; mayor, Malibu Beach, Calif., 1933; United Press war correspondent in the Pacific during Second World War. Founder of Edgar Rice Burroughs, Inc. (publishing house), Burroughs-Tarzan Enterprises, and Burroughs-Tarzan Pictures. *Military service:* U.S. Cavalry, 1896-97.

WRITINGS:

NOVELS

Tarzan of the Apes, McClurg, 1914.
The Return of Tarzan, McClurg, 1915.
The Beasts of Tarzan, McClurg, 1916.
The Son of Tarzan, McClurg, 1917.
A Princess of Mars, McClurg, 1917.
The Gods of Mars, McClurg, 1918.
Tarzan and the Jewels of Opar, McClurg, 1918.
The Warlord of Mars, McClurg, 1919.
Thuvia, Maid of Mars, McClurg, 1920.
Tarzan the Terrible, McClurg, 1921.
The Chessmen of Mars, McClurg, 1922.
At the Earth's Core, McClurg, 1922.
Pellucidar, McClurg, 1923.
Tarzan and the Golden Lion, McClurg, 1923.
The Girl from Hollywood, Macaulay, 1923.
Tarzan and the Ant Men, McClurg, 1924.
The Bandit of Hell's Bend, McClurg, 1925.
The War Chief, McClurg, 1927.
The Outlaw of Torn, McClurg, 1927.
Tarzan, Lord of the Jungle, McClurg, 1928.
The Master Mind of Mars, McClurg, 1928.
The Monster Men, McClurg, 1929.
Tarzan and the Lost Empire, Metropolitan, 1929.
Tarzan at the Earth's Core, Metropolitan, 1930.
Tanar of Pellucidar, Metropolitan, 1930.
A Fighting Man of Mars, Metropolitan, 1931.
Tarzan the Invincible, Burroughs, 1931.
Tarzan the Triumphant, Burroughs, 1931.
Jungle Girl, Burroughs, 1932, published as *The Land of Hidden Men,* Ace Books, 1963.
Tarzan and the City of Gold, Burroughs, 1933.
Apache Devil, Burroughs, 1933.
Tarzan and the Lion-Men, Burroughs, 1934.
Pirates of Venus, Burroughs, 1934.
Lost on Venus, Burroughs, 1935.
Tarzan and the Leopard Men, Burroughs, 1935.
Tarzan's Quest, Burroughs, 1936.
Swords of Mars, Burroughs, 1936.
Back to the Stone Age, Burroughs, 1937.
The Oakdale Affair: The Rider, Burroughs, 1937.
Tarzan and the Forbidden City, Burroughs, 1938.
The Lad and the Lion, Burroughs, 1938.
Carson of Venus, Burroughs, 1939.
The Deputy Sheriff of Comanche County, Burroughs, 1940.
Synthetic Men of Mars, Burroughs, 1940.
Land of Terror, Burroughs, 1944.
Escape on Venus, Burroughs, 1946.
Tarzan and the Foreign Legion, Burroughs, 1947.
The People That Time Forgot, Ace Books, 1963.
Tarzan and the Madman, Canaveral Press, 1964.
Beyond the Farthest Star, Ace Books, 1964.
The Girl from Farris's, House of Greystoke, 1965.
The Efficiency Expert, House of Greystoke, 1966.
I Am a Barbarian, Burroughs, 1967.

(Under pseudonym John Tyler McCulloch) *Pirate Blood,* Ace Books, 1970.

STORY COLLECTIONS

Jungle Tales of Tarzan, McClurg, 1919.
Tarzan the Untamed, McClurg, 1920.
The Mucker, McClurg, 1921, (published in England as *The Man without a Soul,* Methuen, 2 volumes, 1921-22).
The Land That Time Forgot, McClurg, 1924.
The Eternal Lover, McClurg, 1925, published as *The Eternal Savage,* Ace Books, 1963.
The Cave Girl, McClurg, 1925.
The Moon Maid, McClurg, 1926, abridged edition published as *The Moon Men,* Canaveral Press, 1962.
The Mad King, McClurg, 1926.
Tarzan the Magnificent, Burroughs, 1939.
Llana of Gathol, Burroughs, 1948.
Beyond Thirty, privately printed, 1955, published as *The Lost Continent,* Ace Books, 1963.
The Man-Eater, privately printed, 1955.
Savage Pellucidar, Canaveral Press, 1963.
Tales of Three Planets, Canaveral Press, 1964.
John Carter of Mars, Canaveral Press, 1964.
Tarzan and the Castaways, Canaveral Press, 1964.
The Wizard of Venus, Ace Books, 1970.

OTHER

The Tarzan Twins (juvenile), Volland, 1927.
Tarzan and the Tarzan Twins, with Jad-Bal-Ja, the Golden Lion (juvenile), Whitman Publishing, 1936.
Official Guide of the Tarzan Clans of America, privately printed, 1939.

Author of column "Laugh It Off," *Honolulu Advertiser,* 1941-42 and 1945. Contributor, sometimes under pseudonym Normal Bean, to *All-Story, Writer's Digest, New York World,* and other publications.

SIDELIGHTS: As the creator of Tarzan, one of the most enduring characters of popular adventure fiction, Edgar Rice Burroughs has earned a lasting place in American literature. Tarzan, the loin-clothed, bare-chested "King of the Jungle," ranks with such fictional characters as Sherlock Holmes and Dracula in sheer name recognition and archetypal power. He has appeared in scores of motion pictures, television programs, comic books, and related media, and he has given birth to many imitators over the years, none of whom have achieved the same level of success. Despite the immense popularity of Tarzan, the character has never been a favorite with librarians, teachers, or literary critics, all of whom relegate the jungle monarch to the realm of cheap pulp adventure. Yet Burroughs's primary goal as a writer, to entertain his readers, was remarkably well satisfied with his Tarzan books. As for why he created Tarzan, Burroughs was always honest about his need for money. "I had a wife and two babies," he once explained.

Burroughs first turned to writing fiction following a series of unsuccessful careers as a railroad policeman, a partner in several businesses, a miner in Idaho, and as a manager for Sears, Roebuck. None of these positions gave him financial security. By 1912 Burroughs, an avid reader of adventure fiction, decided to try writing as a career. His first story, *Under the Moons of Mars,* featured interplanetary adventurer John Carter and sold almost immediately to *All-Story* magazine for $400. It was printed under the pseudonym Normal Bean because Burroughs thought the story of Martian adventure might get him branded crazy if he used his real name. He also wanted to let his readers know

that he was sane, with a "normal bean." His fears were unfounded. Readers demanded more stories of Mars and Burroughs, a success at last, complied. By 1914, Burroughs was earning a reported twenty thousand dollars a year writing for the pulp magazines.

Although his initial success lay with his Mars adventures, Burroughs's most popular character was undoubtedly Tarzan. An instant bestseller from his introduction in the October, 1912, issue of *All-Story,* Tarzan caught the imagination of the American public like few other characters ever had. Orphaned in the African jungle as a baby, Tarzan had been raised by apes and was able to communicate with all of the jungle's animals. His courage, strength, and primitive sense of justice served him well when confronted with treacherous villains, dangerous animals, or wild terrain. His adventures took him to lost cities and into the hollow center of the Earth. By the 1930s Tarzan had made Burroughs wealthy enough to found his own publishing house and motion picture company.

The overwhelming commercial success of the Tarzan books was somewhat dampened by the critical hostility Burroughs received. Critics have been less than kind to Burroughs, labeling his books as little more than crudely written entertainment. Some have even found, just beneath the surface of his fiction, clear signs of fascism, racism, and anti-intellectualism. But as George P. Elliott noted in the *Hudson Review,* Burroughs's "prejudices are so gross that no one bothers to analyze them out or to attack them. . . . They were clear-eyed, well-thewed prejudices arrayed only in a loin cloth; you can take them or leave them, unless *your* big prejudice happens to be anti-prejudice. What matters is the story, which tastes good." Brian Attebury agreed in his *The Fantasy Tradition in American Literature: From Irving to Le Guin:* "Burroughs was neither more nor less than a good storyteller, with as much power—and finesse—as a bulldozer." Writing in *Esquire,* Gore Vidal claimed that, although Burroughs "is innocent of literature," he nonetheless "does have a gift very few writers of any kind possess: he can describe action vividly. . . . Tarzan *in action* is excellent." Michael Orth, denying Burroughs's own claims that he wrote only to provide his readers with entertainment, discovered far more important themes in his books. Burroughs, Orth stated in *Extrapolation,* "wrote stories about the value of an individual in relation to society, the value of progress, the problems and possibilities of advanced technologies, humans' relation to their environment, the proper role of religion, sexual and class politics, and a hundred other typically utopian concerns."

Perhaps the best case for the value of Burroughs's work was presented by Richard A. Lupoff in his *Edgar Rice Burroughs: Master of Adventure.* "When an author," wrote Lupoff, "survives for half a century, not only without the support of the critical or academic community but in the face of these communities' adamant condemnation, it is time to begin asking if a legitimate folk-author has not been here. It is time to start thinking of permanence."

BIOGRAPHICAL/CRITICAL SOURCES:

BOOKS

Day, Bradford M., *Edgar Rice Burroughs Bibliography,* Science Fiction and Fantasy Publications, 1956.
Dictionary of Literary Biography, Volume 8: *Twentieth Century American Science Fiction Writers,* Gale, 1981.
Farmer, Philip Jose, *Tarzan Alive,* Doubleday, 1972.
Fenton, Robert, *Big Swingers: Biography of Edgar Rice Burroughs,* Prentice-Hall, 1967.

Harwood, John, *The Literature of Burroughsiana,* Camille Cazedessus, Jr. [Baton Rouge], 1963.
Heins, Henry Hardy, *A Golden Anniversary Bibliography of Edgar Rice Burroughs,* Donald M. Grant, 1964.
Lupoff, Richard A., *Edgar Rice Burroughs: Master of Adventure,* Canaveral Press, 1965.
Porges, Irwin, *Edgar Rice Burroughs: The Man Who Created Tarzan,* Brigham Young University Press, 1975.
Twentieth-Century Literary Criticism, Gale, Volume 2, 1979, Volume 32, 1989.

PERIODICALS

Esquire, December, 1963.
Hudson Review, autumn, 1959.

*   *   *

BURROUGHS, William S(eward)   1914-
(William Lee, Willy Lee)

PERSONAL: Born February 5, 1914, in St. Louis, Mo.; son of Mortimer P. (a businessman) and Laura (Lee) Burroughs; married Ilse Herzfeld Klapper, 1937 (divorced, 1946); married Joan Vollmer, January 17, 1946 (died September 7, 1951, of an accidental gunshot wound); children: (second marriage) William Seward, Jr. (died March 3, 1981). *Education:* Harvard University, A.B., 1936, graduate study, 1938; attended University of Vienna, 1937, and Mexico City College, 1949-50.

ADDRESSES: Office—William S. Burroughs Communications, P.O. Box 147, Lawrence, Kan. 66044.

CAREER: Writer. Advertising copywriter in New York City, early 1940s; has also worked as bartender, exterminator, and private detective. Actor in motion picture "Drugstore Cowboy," 1989. *Military service:* U.S. Army, 1942.

AWARDS, HONORS: National Institute of Arts and Letters and American Academy, award in literature, 1975, named member, 1983; the Nova Convention, a four-day arts festival held in New York city in 1978, and the Final Academy, held in London in 1982, were organized as tributes to Burroughs.

WRITINGS:

NOVELS

(Under pseudonym William Lee) *Junkie: Confessions of an Unredeemed Drug Addict* (bound with *Narcotic Agent* by Maurice Helbrant), Ace Books, 1953, published separately under name William S. Burroughs, 1964, unexpurgated edition published as *Junky,* Penguin, 1977.
The Naked Lunch (also see below), Olympia Press (Paris), 1959, published as *Naked Lunch,* Grove, 1962.
The Soft Machine (also see below), Olympia Press, 1961, revised edition, Grove, 1966.
The Ticket That Exploded (also see below), Olympia Press, 1962, revised edition, Grove, 1967.
Dead Fingers Talk (contains excerpts from *Naked Lunch, The Soft Machine,* and *The Ticket That Exploded*), Calder/Olympia Press, 1963.
Nova Express (also see below), Grove, 1964.
The Wild Boys: A Book of the Dead (also see below), Grove, 1971, revised edition, Calder, 1979.
Exterminator!, Viking/Seaver, 1973.
Port of Saints, Convent Garden Press (London), 1975, Blue Wind Press, 1979.
Short Novels, Calder, 1978.
Blade Runner: A Movie, Blue Wind Press, 1979.

The Soft Machine, Nova Express, [and] *The Wild Boys,* Grove, 1980.
Cities of the Night, Holt, 1981.
The Place of Dead Roads, Holt, 1984.
Queer, Viking, 1986.
The Western Lands, Viking, 1987.

Also author, with Jack Kerouac, of unpublished novel "And the Hippos Were Boiled in Their Tanks."

OTHER

(With Brion Gysin) *The Exterminator,* Auerhaun Press (San Francisco), 1960.
(With Gysin, Sinclair Beiles, and Gregory Corso) *Minutes to Go* (poems), Two Cities Editions (Paris), 1960, Beach Books, 1968.
(Contributor) Thomas Parkinson, editor, *A Casebook on the Beat,* Crowell, 1961.
(With Allen Ginsberg) *The Yage Letters,* City Lights, 1963.
Takis (exhibition catalog), [New York], 1963.
(Under pseudonym Willy Lee) *Roosevelt after Inauguration,* F— You Press, 1964, published as *Roosevelt after Inauguration, and Other Atrocities,* City Lights, 1979.
Valentine's Day Reading, American Theatre for Poets, 1965.
The White Subway (also see below), Aloes Books, 1965.
Health Bulletin: APO:33: A Metabolic Regulator, F— You Press, 1965, published as *APO:33: A Report on the Synthesis of the Apomorphine Formula,* Beach Books, 1966.
(With Lee Harwood) *Darayt,* Lovebooks, 1965.
(With Claude Pelieu and Carl Weissner) *So Who Owns Death TV?,* Beach Book Texts and Documents, 1967.
They Do Not Always Remember, Delacorte, 1968.
(Author of preface) Jeff Nuttall, *Pig,* Fulcrum Press, 1969.
Ali's Smile, Unicorn Books, 1969.
The Dead Star, Nova Broadcast Press, 1969.
Entretiens avec William Burroughs, Editions Pierre Belfond (Paris), 1969, translation published as *The Job: Interviews with William S. Burroughs,* Grove, 1970, new edition, 1974.
(With Weissner) *The Braille Film,* Nova Broadcast Press, 1970.
(With Gysin) *Third Mind,* Grove, 1970.
The Last Words of Dutch Schultz: A Fiction in the Form of a Film Script, Cape Goliard Press, 1970, Viking Seaver, 1975.
(With Pelieu) *Jack Kerouac* (in French), L'Herne (Paris), 1971.
Electronic Revolution (also see below), Blackmoor Head Press, 1971.
(With Gysin and Ian Somerville) *Brion Gysin Let the Mice In,* Something Else Press, 1973.
Mayfair Academy Series More or Less, Urgency Press Rip-Off, 1973.
The Book of Breathing (also see below), OU Press (Ingatestone, England), 1974, Blue Wind Press, 1975, 2nd edition, 1980.
(With Charles Gatewood) *Sidetripping,* Strawberry Hill, 1975.
(With Eric Mottram) *Snack: Two Tape Transcripts,* Aloes Books, 1975.
Cobblestone Gardens (also see below), Cherry Valley, 1976.
The Retreat Diaries (also see below), City Moon, 1976.
(Author of text) "23 Skidoo," first produced in New York City at the Washington Square Methodist Church, April, 1978.
Naked Scientology, Expanded Media Editions (Bonn), 1978.
Doctor Benway: A Variant Passage from "The Naked Lunch," Bradford Morrow, 1979.
Ah Pook Is Here, and Other Texts: The Book of Breething, Electronic Revolution, Calder, 1979.
Early Routines, Cadmus Editions, 1981.
Letters to Allen Ginsberg, 1953-1957, Full Court Press, 1981.
A William Burroughs Reader, Pan Books, 1982.

(Contributor) Roger Ely, editor, *The Final Academy: Statements of a Kind,* Final Academy, 1982.

The Burroughs File (includes *The White Subway, Cobblestone Gardens,* and *The Retreat Diaries*), City Lights, 1984.

The Adding Machine: Collected Essays, Calder, 1985.

Interzone, Viking, 1989.

Also author, with Pelieu and Weissner, of *Fernseh-Tuberkulose,* 1969, and of films, with Gysin, "Towers Open Fire," 1963, with Antony Balch, "Bill and Tony," 1966, and of "The Cut-Ups." Sound recordings include "Call Me Burroughs," 1965; "William S. Burroughs/John Giorno," 1975; "You're the Man I Want to Share My Money With," 1981; "Nothing Here Now but the Recordings," 1981; and "Revolutions per Minute (The Art Record)," 1982. Also composer of song "Old Lady Sloan," recorded by Mortal Micronotz, 1982. Contributor to "Life Is a Killer," Giorno Poetry Systems.

SIDELIGHTS: A former drug addict turned writer, experimental novelist William S. Burroughs embodies for many observers the artist as outsider and rebel. He has had a tremendous influence as one of the Beat generation of writers, as an avant-garde theorist, and as a counter-culture forerunner. His novel *Junkie: Confessions of an Unredeemed Drug Addict* outlines his life as a morphine addict; *Naked Lunch* successfully overturned America's obscenity laws; his innovative "cut-up" writing technique, his attacks on the control systems enslaving mankind, and his outspoken homosexuality have made him "one of the most controversial and influential writers of the past decades," as Bob Halliday describes him in the *Washington Post Book World.* Henry Allen, writing in the same publication, calls Burroughs "the model of modern man as pariah: eminence grise of the Beat generation, black sheep of the Burroughs adding machine family, junkie, intellectual crank . . ., esoteric novelist . . ., punk saint and grand old man of the seamy underbelly." Robert E. Burkholder admits in the *Dictionary of Literary Biography Yearbook 1981* that Burroughs occupies "a strange cultural position as a major figure of contemporary avant-garde fiction and the so-called Godfather of Punk."

Burroughs comes from a distinguished family. His mother is descended from Civil War leader Robert E. Lee, while his paternal grandfather, for whom Burroughs is named, invented the adding machine and founded the Burroughs Corporation which today manufactures computer equipment. Burroughs has made clear on several occasions that his grandfather sold his share of the company upon retirement and that his family, although of prominent social standing, was not wealthy. He lives entirely on the royalties from his books.

Raised in St. Louis and educated in private schools, Burroughs, Jennie Skerl writes in the *Dictionary of Literary Biography,* was "alienated from a suburban social environment perceived as both boring and hostile. He felt his homosexuality was only part of the reason for his alienation. . . . Timid and solitary, he turned to extensive reading for solace and dreamed of becoming a writer. . . . He early formed a view of the artist as an outlaw and adventurer." In 1936 Burroughs graduated from Harvard University, where he studied English literature. After graduation he tried his hand at several careers. He attended medical school in Vienna with the hope of becoming a doctor; he studied anthropology at Harvard's graduate school; he served in the U.S. Army for several months before being discharged for psychological reasons (he had deliberately cut off the first joint of a finger to impress a friend); and he worked as an advertising copywriter, exterminator, bartender, and private detective. "Burroughs's own

description of his life during the years 1936 to 1944," Skerl recounts, "is one of aimless drifting and boredom."

This aimlessness ended in the mid-1940s when Burroughs was living in New York City. At that time he met several people who were to fundamentally alter the course of his later life. He met and married Joan Vollmer, a widow, in 1946. (Burroughs had previously married a German woman to allow her to legally enter the United States from Nazi Germany. They were divorced in 1946.) Joan introduced him to her friend Jack Kerouac, then a student at Columbia University, who in turn introduced Burroughs to Allen Ginsberg, an aspiring poet. Ginsberg relates in *Jack's Book: An Oral Biography of Jack Kerouac* that he and Kerouac found Burroughs "so interesting and intelligent and worldly wise that he seemed like some sort of intellectual spiritual man of distinction to us." In the same book, Burroughs recalls their initial meeting: "Joan and I were older, and we had done some more reading than they had at the time. I didn't think anything special about it. I recommended a number of books." Burroughs's apartment soon became a gathering place where the three men, later to form the core of the Beat literary movement, shared and discussed their ideas. In 1944 Burroughs also met Herbert Huncke, a drug addict, thief, and male prostitute who introduced him to morphine. Burroughs soon became an addict himself and was to remain one despite several attempts at a cure, until 1957.

Kerouac and Ginsberg's efforts to become writers inspired the older Burroughs to turn to fiction writing. He had made an earlier attempt in the 1930s to write detective stories, but that had ended in failure and Burroughs had not written anything since. He began to write seriously only in the 1940s. As Burroughs tells Charles Platt in *Dream Makers,* Volume 2: *The Uncommon Men and Women Who Write Science Fiction,* "I didn't write anything till I was thirty-five." He explains in *Jack's Book* that Kerouac "had suggested that I write and I wasn't too interested for a long time." He and Kerouac collaborated on a novel in the 1940s entitled "And the Hippos Were Boiled in Their Tanks," a title inspired by a radio broadcast about a fire in the St. Louis zoo.

But Burroughs's writing efforts were soon superseded by his troubles with the law. Because of police pressure in New York, brought on by his morphine addiction and resultant association with the underworld, Burroughs was obliged to move to Texas. When police pressure increased there because he was raising marijuana on his farm, Burroughs moved to Louisiana. After a police raid on his home in Louisiana in early 1949, Burroughs and Joan fled to Mexico to avoid drug and illegal weapons charges. The couple found Mexico to their liking. Morphine could be easily obtained by prescription; and benzedrine, which Joan used, was sold over the counter. For a time Burroughs attended Mexico City College, where he studied architecture, Aztec history, and the Mayan codices.

The Burroughs's stay in Mexico was ended in 1951 with the shooting death of Joan Burroughs. For many years after, stories circulated that Burroughs had killed her in cold blood. In 1984, Burroughs finally explained the incident in "Burroughs," a documentary film made about his life. While living in Mexico, he relates, he and his wife had been arguing frequently. Burroughs had been neglecting her for his homosexual companions. At a drinking party with two visiting Army friends, Joan balanced a glass on her head and dared Burroughs to shoot it off in William Tell style. Burroughs's bullet struck her in the forehead and she died instantly. The authorities ruled her death an accident and Burroughs was released without charges. In *Queer,* a novel written shortly after the accident but not published until 1986, Burroughs dealt indirectly with his wife's death. He states in the book's preface that when he reread the manuscript for publication it had made him feel threatened. It was "painful to an extent I feel it difficult to read, let alone write about. Every word and gesture sets the teeth on edge. The reason for this reluctance becomes clearer as I force myself to look: the book is motivated and formed by an event which is never mentioned, in fact is carefully avoided: the accidental shooting death of my wife."

For several years after his wife's death Burroughs traveled, visiting South America, Morocco, and New York City. He finished his first novel, *Junkie: Confessions of an Unredeemed Drug Addict,* in 1951 while living in Morocco. Ginsberg served as his literary agent, placing the manuscript with the New York paperback publisher Ace Books. The book's subject matter caused Ace to publish an edited version, filled with disclaimers, in a double-book format with Maurice Helbrant's novel *Narcotic Agent* in 1953. Burroughs used the pseudonym William Lee, taken from his mother's maiden name, on the book. The complete, unedited manuscript was finally published under his real name and with the original title, *Junky,* by Penguin in 1977.

Junkie is a "luridly hyperbolic, quasiautobiographical first-person account of the horrors of drug addiction," as Donald Palumbo writes in the *Dictionary of Literary Biography.* Nelson Algren, writing in the *Chicago Tribune Book World* in 1981, finds that *Junkie* was "the first American report on the drug experience and remains the most authentic." In his introduction to the complete edition, Ginsberg cites as *Junkie*'s virtues its "intelligent fact, the clear perception, precise bare language, direct syntax & mind pictures—as well as the enormous sociological grasp, culture-revolutionary attitude toward bureaucracy & law, and the stoic cold-humor'd eye on crime."

Junkie tells the story of William Lee, an "unredeemed" drug addict who becomes involved with the underworld and is forced to travel to avoid the law. Essentially plotless, the novel recounts Lee's withdrawals and cures from four drug addictions and ends with him leaving for the jungles of South America in search of the native drug yage, rumored to give its user telepathic powers. Much of *Junkie* is Burroughs's own life fictionalized in a pulp confessional style. Burroughs's journey to South America was in search of yage; he, too, travelled widely to escape the law; and his own drug experiences parallel those of Lee. As McNally relates, *Junkie* "was a generally straightforward description of [Burroughs's] drug life."

Although this first novel is written in a realistic style not found in Burroughs's subsequent books, it introduces many of the concerns later developed in the more experimental works. "*Junkie*," Skerl explains, "introduces many of Burroughs's continuing themes, characters, images, and settings." Burkholder believes that *Junkie* "is important to an understanding of [Burroughs's] later work. . . . Burroughs's literal description of scenes would eventually be inflated to abstract images, ultimately becoming part of the allegorical war of control in later novels. . . . Later narratives attempt to make the drug experience an archetype for modern man."

Because *Junkie* was a first novel published by a small paperback publisher, it did not receive much critical attention. *Queer,* another book written at this time—concerning a homosexual romance in Mexico City—would not find a publisher until 1986. Burroughs's writing career seemed at a standstill. In 1953 he moved to Tangier, Morocco, where he lived until 1958, writing in seclusion. During this time, Burroughs filled over one thousand pages with fragmentary notes about his travels and drug use and with social satire attacking contemporary society. From

these notes came his next four novels: *Naked Lunch, The Soft Machine, The Ticket That Exploded,* and *Nova Express.*

By 1957 Burroughs's drug addiction was severely restricting his ability to function normally. He recalls in an article for *Evergreen Review:* "I lived in one room in the Native Quarter of Tangier. I had not taken a bath in a year nor changed my clothes or removed them except to stick a needle every hour in the fibrous grey wooden flesh of terminal addiction. . . . I did absolutely nothing. I could look at the end of my shoe for eight hours." When his habit became too expensive, jumping from thirty grains to sixty grains a day and still not enough, Burroughs realized he had to quit. He travelled to London to undergo a new drug rehabilitation treatment developed by Dr. John Yerby Dent. This method involved using apomorphine, a substance produced by boiling morphine in hydrochloric acid. The apomorphine serves as a kind of metabolic regulator to satisfy the addict's craving for drugs without damaging his health. After undergoing Dent's apomorphine treatments, Burroughs was permanently cured of his addiction.

The Naked Lunch, first published in Paris in 1959 and retitled *Naked Lunch* in its American edition of 1962, was assembled from the many notes Burroughs wrote while living in Tangier. Several friends, including Ginsberg, Brion Gysin, Sinclair Beiles, and Alan Ansen, helped Burroughs choose the material to use in the book. Kerouac typed most of the manuscript and provided the book's title, which Burroughs explains in the novel's "Atrophied Preface" as the "frozen moment when everyone sees what is on the end of every fork." *Naked Lunch* is a series of sketches arranged in a random order. Because of the unstructured nature of the book—further enhanced by the random stacking of manuscript pages on a table at his publisher's office which Burroughs held to be as good an ordering of the contents as any—*Naked Lunch* has, Tony Tanner writes in his *City of Words: American Fiction, 1950-1970,* "no narrative continuity, and no sustained point of view; the separate episodes are not interrelated, they coexist in a particular field of force brought together by the mind of Burroughs which then abandons them." Alvin J. Seltzer, in his study *Chaos in the Novel: The Novel in Chaos,* finds that in *Naked Lunch* "all structure is discarded: one can pick up the novel and start his reading anywhere, then go forward, backward or jump around at will. . . . The novel is set up to break down any rational approach to it, any logical system which attempts to reduce a multilevel experience directed toward our central nervous system."

While Burroughs deals only with drug addiction in *Junkie,* in *Naked Lunch* he explores many forms of addiction in human society. As Jerry Bryant writes in *The Open Decision,* "drug addiction is both a literal example of human imprisonment and thought control and a figurative representation of similar forces at work in human society at large." Burroughs argues that mankind is addicted to such things as image, sex, power, language, and government. As he explains in the novel, "there are many forms of addiction, and I think they all obey basic laws." These addictions are used by those in control to subdue the population. William Lee, the protagonist and Burroughs-surrogate of *Junkie,* reappears in *Naked Lunch* as an addict who cures himself only to find that "all of humanity is victimized by some form of addiction. He realizes that the body is a biological trap and that society is run by 'control addicts' who use the needs of the body to satisfy their obsession with power. Thus the terms *addiction* and *junk* . . . are also metaphors for the human condition," Skerl writes.

Because *Naked Lunch* contains graphic sex and violence, no American or English publisher would at first accept it. The book was first published in Paris in 1959. Though there was no American edition of the book until 1962, and the post office would not allow copies of the Paris edition to be mailed to the United States, milder excerpts from the book appeared in American magazines.

The first American edition of *Naked Lunch* appeared in 1962 from Grove Press and was met by a lawsuit in Boston on grounds of obscenity. The subsequent trial brought out Ginsberg, Mailer, and other literary figures to speak on behalf of the novel's redeeming social value, the criteria at the time for acceptable literature. Ginsberg described Burroughs's intentions as "moral . . . defending the good," while Mailer called him a "religious writer" and *Naked Lunch* "a vision of how mankind would act if man was totally divorced from eternity." Burroughs did not appear at the trial, but in an article for *Evergreen Review* he defends "certain passages in the book that have been called pornographic" as being "a tract against Capital Punishment in the manner of Jonathan Swift's Modest Proposal. These sections are intended to reveal capital punishment as the obscene, barbaric and disgusting anachronism that it is." In a landmark decision, a federal court ruled *Naked Lunch* not obscene. As Skerl relates, "*Naked Lunch* was a ground-breaking book in helping to eliminate censorship of the printed word in the United States."

The novel also met with opposition from many members of the literary community. John Wain, in a review for *New Republic,* for example, believes *Naked Lunch* "is of very small significance. It consists of a prolonged scream of hatred and disgust. . . . A book like *Naked Lunch* requires far less talent in the writer, and for that matter less intelligence in the reader than the humblest magazine story or circulating-library novel. From the literary point of view, it is the merest trash, not worth a second glance."

Despite the negative comments and controversy, *Naked Lunch* has received critical praise from most quarters. It was a national best-seller, made Burroughs's literary reputation, and remains his most widely known book. Robert Peters, writing in the *Los Angeles Times Book Review,* calls it "the best American novel of its decade." Jack Kerouac "thought it was wonderful, superseding Genet, De Sade, and Aleister Crowley," according to McNally. Paul Ableman of *Spectator* judges it to be "the most brilliant satire in English since *Gulliver's Travels.*" And Skerl finds *Naked Lunch* "a brilliant work. . . . It significantly contributes to the craft of fiction in subject matter and technique, thus gaining it a permanent place in the history of the novel and the history of the avant-garde."

In his next three novels Burroughs consciously expanded the random structuring used in *Naked Lunch* by introducing the "cut-up" method of composition. The cut-up is derived from the collage of the visual arts, a technique of combining unrelated elements into a new work. Burroughs learned of the cut-up from the experiments of his friend Brion Gysin. Gysin had been cutting newspaper articles into sections and then rearranging the sections at random, while looking away. The resulting juxtapositions of words intrigued Burroughs. He took the method further, cutting texts down the center and placing unrelated halves together to form new sentences. He cut up the works of other writers, his own writings, newspapers, poems, and magazine articles. From the resulting texts he chose fragments and phrases of the most interest and included them in the completed work. Burroughs also developed the fold-in method in which sections of text are folded in half and juxtapositioned to create new works.

Throughout the 1960s he experimented with cut-ups in fiction, film, and tape recordings.

Burroughs tells Platt the importance of the cut-up: "It's closer to the actual facts of perception. . . . I'm talking about how things are actually perceived by the brain." By coming closer to the way the brain perceives information, the cut-up method also frees the author and reader from the traditional constraints of fiction. Cut-ups, according to Burkholder, realize Burroughs's "notion that we need to escape the constraints of Aristotelian logic and the declarative sentence to free ourselves from the false reality and authorial control that traditional fiction has always presented."

The Soft Machine, The Ticket That Exploded, and *Nova Express* are all written in the cut-up method, utilizing the notes Burroughs took in Tangier. Because of this, the novels are not in "straightforward linear form. The reader must piece [the story] together from flashes, obsessive phrases, and incomplete scenes, struggling through disjointed chronology and abrupt changes of narrators, or cryptic cut-ups," Gerard Cordesse writes in *Caliban XII.* The three novels continue the story begun in *Naked Lunch,* forming a tetralogy. The addictions to word, image, power, sex and drugs uncovered by William Lee in *Naked Lunch* are found in the subsequent novels to be the work of the Nova Mob, a group of aliens who control the earth. The Nova Mob takes on the form of viruses to infect mankind with addictions. Through these addictions they have manipulated Earthlings for three thousand years. "Drugs, sex, and power control the body," Skerl explains, "but 'word and image locks' control the mind, that is, conventional patterns of perceiving, thinking, and speaking which determine our interactions with environment and society." Countering the Mob are the Nova Police, who work to regulate man's addictions and use silence and cut-ups to destroy the perception habits enslaving mankind. "The cut-up," Skerl writes, "is a way of exposing word and image controls and thus freeing oneself from them." Bryant sees the Nova Mob as "the symbol of a tyrannical society that flourishes on the destruction of its citizens' independence and integrity. . . . Only those free of the destructive force of the totalitarian state—be it fascist or welfare—can operate as individuals."

The Soft Machine (the title refers to the human brain) outlines the use of control systems throughout human history, tracing the Nova Mob's influence and focusing in particular on the Mayan civilization. The Mayan priesthood maintained social control through the manipulation of their calendar, which was a word and image system forming the basis of the agricultural, social, and religious life of the people. When Lee, an agent of the Nova Police, travels through time to the Mayan civilization, he restructures the calendar and causes the breakdown of the priests' totalitarian system. Vernon finds *The Soft Machine* to be Burroughs's "best use of cut-ups" because he establishes "a dynamic rhythm of cohesion and fragmentation which becomes the experience of the novel."

The Ticket That Exploded takes place in several imaginary settings on other worlds. One of these is the Garden of Delights, where the Nova Police exhibit all the control systems used by the Mob. The city of Minraud, ruled by insect creatures who use "mind tapes" to control individuals and a "reality film" to control the actions of their society, is a Burroughs totalitarian fantasy. The book's cut-up sequences are a means of liberation from totalitarianism. And the final novel of the tetralogy, *Nova Express,* summarizes and condenses the concerns of the previous books while introducing the idea that writing is a powerful tool in resisting control, an idea Burroughs develops in later novels.

The science fiction aspect of the tetralogy becomes dominant in *Nova Express* as giant space battles take place between aliens and Earthlings. The novel ends in a deadlock between the forces of the Nova Mob and Nova Police.

With *The Wild Boys: A Book of the Dead,* published in 1971, and his following books, Burroughs abandoned the extensive cut-ups of his tetralogy in favor of a more conventionally organized narrative. He writes in a popular style and borrows heavily from established commercial genres, suggesting that the elements of popular culture can be used by the writer as tools of liberation. Set in an apocalyptic near-future, *The Wild Boys* presents a group of homosexual hashish smokers who can travel through time and space and who, through their indifference to the images of society, are beyond social control. The story of their ongoing rebellion is told in a series of eighteen related scenes written in the "simple narrative style of popular fiction, especially the pulp fiction [Burroughs] read in his youth," Skerl explains in the *Review of Contemporary Fiction.*

Although there is a change in Burroughs's style in *The Wild Boys,* he is still concerned with personal freedom, the control systems of society, and the efforts to free oneself from social restrictions. These concerns are given a new perspective, however. In *The Wild Boys* "the tide," Cordesse explains, "has turned: language that was the instrument of nova oppression has become a weapon of liberation." As Skerl writes, *The Wild Boys* and the novels that follow it express "more hope for the individual and for change through 'utopian dreams.' " The novel ends with the narrator attempting to break through the time barrier to join the wild boys in the future.

The characters in *The Wild Boys* reappear in *Cities of the Red Night,* a novel interweaving three plot lines set in different times and places. One story follows private detective Clem Snide as he tries to solve a case of ritual murder in the present. Another is set one hundred thousand years in the past where the red virus has broken out in the ancient cities of the Gobi Desert. The primary story is set in the eighteenth century and concerns a group of homosexual pirates who establish a series of libertarian republics in South America and battle the Spanish conquistadors. Each of these narratives is told in the style and language of popular fiction and borrows heavily from the detective, science fiction, and boys' adventure genres.

Critical reaction to *Cities of the Red Night* was divided. Thomas M. Disch, referring to the novel's graphic violence, comments in the *New York Times Book Review* that "opium addicts who are sexually aroused by witnessing and/or enacting garrotings and hangings will find 'Cities' a veritable gallows of delight." Similarly, Peter S. Prescott of *Newsweek* finds that "the inspiration behind [*Cities of the Red Night*] seems retarded: the masturbatory fantasies of a 12-year-old boy who dreams, as boys will, of plague and violent death, of hiding out with his chums in a secret jungle fort and beating up on the adults around him. For a book that seemed to promise some kind of allegory or at least an apocalyptic vision of the world's end, it is a poor dream to come down to."

But other observers were kinder in their assessments of the novel. Perry Meisel, writing in the *New York Times Book Review,* calls *Cities of the Red Night* Burroughs's "best novel," while Steven Shaviro of the *Review of Contemporary Fiction* defines it as a "homoerotic quest romance, in the great American tradition of *Moby Dick.*" John Tytell, in an article for the *American Book Review,* finds that "though not as formally explosive as *Naked Lunch, Cities of the Red Night* is a powerful book and a hauntingly macabre entertainment." Rechy describes the novel as

"Burroughs' masterpiece. In it, the world ends with a bang-and a barely perceived whimper, disguised by the wicked smile of one of the most dazzling magicians of our time."

Speaking of *Cities of the Red Night* in an article for the *New York Times Book Review,* Burroughs explains his intentions: "In 'Cities of the Red Night' I parachute my characters behind enemy lines in time. Their mission is to correct retroactively certain fatal errors at crucial turning points in human history. I am speaking of biological errors that tend to block man's path to his biological and spiritual destiny in space. I postulate a social structure offering maximum variation of small communes, as opposed to the uniformity imposed by industrialization and overpopulation."

Burroughs's next novel, *The Place of Dead Roads,* is set in the 1890s and features a protagonist named William Seward Hall, an author of Westerns under the pen name of Kim Carsons. "Born in St. Louis, largely self-taught (teachers hate him), openly homosexual, fascinated by disease, violence, and extreme, often drug-induced, states of mind, the Kim who gradually takes shape in this novel is, we soon realize, very much a fictional version of Burroughs himself," Jay Tolson writes in the *Washington Post Book World.* This fictionalized Burroughs is, Gerald Nicosia claims in the *Chicago Tribune Book World,* "a classic grotesque and a quintessential American youth. He is a morbid homosexual who performs elaborate rituals of black magic to curse the prigs who condemn him. But he is also sensitive, honest according to his own code, and highly inventive. He wants most of all to be left alone by those who feel the urge to control his life."

To achieve this freedom, Kim forms an outlaw gang called the Wild Fruits and establishes a string of secret bases across the western frontier. The gang wages a guerrilla war against "straight" society in order to create a utopian society where they can live in peace as homosexuals. Nicosia points out that "Burroughs equates the writer with the warrior in that both must outmaneuver mortality—the warrior with his weapons and military expertise, the writer with his ability to 'unwrite' the existing world and replace it with another more congenial to his own nature." To create a new world the writer can only use the memories of his own past—"the place of dead roads"—but he does this "at the peril of becoming trapped by them and repeating his errors, instead of breaking free," Nicosia writes.

As in *The Wild Boys* and *Cities of the Red Night* Burroughs uses a popular narrative style in *The Place of Dead Roads.* Luc Sante of the *New York Review of Books* finds that in *Cities of the Red Night* and *The Place of Dead Roads* Burroughs "has somehow been inspired to emulate the language and themes of such pulp masters as Sax Rohmer, H. P. Lovecraft, Max Brand, and . . . Nick Carter." But Meisel makes clear that "despite a largely naturalistic style and an often conventional mode of storytelling, 'The Place of Dead Roads' slips and slides in time and place—almost unaccountably until one is again reminded that a transpersonal web links everything together."

Like the earlier wild boys, the Wild Fruits travel through time and space, and like the pirates of *Cities of the Red Night,* they battle against alien invaders. The story "loops back and forth," writes David Donnell in the Toronto *Globe & Mail,* "between gay cowboys and social satire, between tech futurism and Mayan altars." The book is structured around a gunfight between Kim Carsons and Mike Chase. The opening scene depicts one version of this gunfight in which both men are shot dead. The novel ends with the same gunfight, but this time only Carsons is killed.

"The first serious gay western," as Donnell describes *The Place of Dead Roads,* is thought by most reviewers to be a highly personal fiction, although there is disagreement as to its ultimate merit. Anatole Broyard of the *New York Times* sees little to praise: "For a celebrated author to publish a novel as poor as 'The Place of Dead Roads' requires a degree of collusion or encouragement on our part. He must have a certain confidence in our credulity, must assume that bad taste is a good bet, that age cannot wither, nor customs stale the appeal of an established reputation." But Nicosia deems the novel "a moving personal saga as well as a record of revolutionary vision," and Tolson believes the book "would be pretty dull fare were it not for the force of Burroughs' genius, his almost terrifying independence, and his refusal to accept any values but his own."

This consistent independence has won Burroughs a loyal readership despite some critical hostility to his style and themes. Two festivals, the Nova Convention in New York in 1978 and the Final Academy in London in 1982, were organized by admirers as tributes to him. These festivals included films, readings, and panels about his work and attracted devotees from the fields of music, literature, and film. As Tolson acknowledges, "I have met a few [of Burroughs's fans] and know that their regard for the man borders on devotion."

Burroughs has been influential in several areas. In literature, he had a tremendous impact on the Beat writers of the 1950s, particularly his friends Ginsberg and Kerouac. George Dordess explains in the *Dictionary of Literary Biography* that both Ginsberg and Kerouac "saw in their older friend a fearless, sardonic experimenter with drugs, sex, and crime, as well as a coolly precise student of those analysts of society's ills, Korzybski, Spengler, and Freud. A good teacher, also, Burroughs willingly passed on his information to his younger friends. He even undertook an informal psychoanalysis of both young men and also served as literary critic." Ginsberg's *Reality Sandwiches,* a book of poems, is directly inspired by *Naked Lunch;* Burroughs appears as a character in several of Kerouac's novels: as Will Dennison in *The Town and the City,* as Old Bull Lee in *On the Road,* as Frank Carmody in *The Subterraneans,* as Bull Hubbard in *Book of Dreams* and *Desolation Angels,* and as Wilson Holmes Hubbard in *Vanity of Duluoz: An Adventurous Education, 1935-46.* Among today's younger experimental writers, too, Burroughs has had a considerable influence. "In their various ways, writers Hunter Thompson, Tom Wolfe and Ken Kesey all are Burroughs' disciples," Larry Kart writes in the *Chicago Tribune Book World.*

But it is possibly outside of literature that Burroughs has enjoyed his greatest following. As a prominent member of the Beat writers, Burroughs helped to inspire the hippie and punk movements of the 1960s and 1970s. His *Junkie* foreshadowed the drug use of the 1960s, and his tetralogy reflected the decade's chaotic rebellion. *Naked Lunch,* Meisel explains, "not only exemplified the Beat subculture out of which Mr. Burroughs emerged; it also prophesied the wider fate of the American sensibility well into the next two decades. By the time the counterculture of the 1960's succeeded the Beats, license had become the law, and Mr. Burroughs had become a principal avatar of the liberationist esthetic he helped create." The publication of *Naked Lunch* effectively ended America's last obscenity laws, opening the way for greater freedom in all the arts and allowing explicit sexual material to be legally published in this country. Burroughs "has had considerably greater cultural impact than the extent of his present readership might indicate," Bruce Cook writes in the *Detroit News.* "It would not be an overstatement to say that he is one of the secret shapers of American culture—such as it is today."

"The master's influence," Kart writes, "also has been felt in the world of rock." The term "heavy metal," a name for a type of rock and roll, comes from *Naked Lunch.* The group Steely Dan borrowed their name from Burroughs's writings. Such groups as the Rolling Stones have written songs about his characters, while David Bowie and Patti Smith admit to using the cut-up method to compose their songs. Burroughs even hit the British record charts with his "Nothing Here but the Recordings," an album containing readings from his work and some cut-up tape recorder experiments. As a *New York Times* writer sums up, "There can be no doubt that Mr. Burroughs has been one of the principal literary influences on rock music." Sante believes that "youth culture since the Sixties has abounded in allusions to his work the way earlier generations drew on Shakespeare or the Bible."

Though his influence in literature and popular culture has been substantial, Burroughs has not yet achieved full academic acceptance. His controversial cut-up method and his graphic writing about drug use and homosexuality have made Burroughs difficult for some observers to evaluate objectively. Seymour Krim of the *Washington Post Book World* points out that one problem with Burroughs's writing is its refusal to fulfill a reader's preconceptions. "Many a decent-minded reader," Krim writes, "is going to give up out of a feeling of bewilderment and impotence because he expects to be spoon-fed in the grand American custom. But Burroughs doesn't make these concessions." As Norman Snider writes in the Toronto *Globe & Mail,* "Burroughs is not the sort of writer whose reputation will ever settle into general and genial acceptance. His work will always have its passionate detractors and ferocious admirers."

Alfred Kazin of the *New York Times Book Review,* while allowing that Burroughs "is indeed a serious man and a considerable writer," nevertheless feels that "his books are not really books, they are compositions that astonish, then pall. They are subjective experiences brought into the world for the hell of it and by the excitement of whatever happens to be present to Burroughs's consciousness when he writes." Sante, too, is of a mixed opinion as to Burroughs's stature. He calls *Naked Lunch* "still his best . . . . it remains a milestone of a kind, going further than any book in plumbing the untouchable aspects of American life." But Sante also believes that Burroughs "shot his wad with this volume."

Part of the resistance to Burroughs's work is perhaps explained by Bruce Cook in his book *The Beat Generation.* Cook gives his opinion that Burroughs "is a very considerable prose artist—intellectually accomplished, technically innovative," and then allows that, if "given different subject matter, [Burroughs] would have enormous appeal to academic critics." Krim sees the subjective nature of Burroughs's work as another possible drawback to its wide acceptance. Burroughs, Krim writes, "gives the very definite impression that he is including us in a private ceremonial obsession over which he has little control. . . . We feel that Burroughs is composing in a trance that removes his work from what we ordinarily think of as 'fiction' or even art. It's as if we had gotten hold of a black ticket to his unconscious, and anyone who makes the trip will see sights and feel feelings that are unique and mind-bending. . . . Totting it all up is of course another, highly subjective story."

But a number of critics praise Burroughs's innovative prose and his exploration of new literary terrain. Harry Marten, for example, writes in the *New York Times Book Review* that Burroughs "has been mixing the satirist's impulse toward invective with the cartoonist's relish for exaggerated gesture, the collage artist's penchant for radical juxtapositions with the slam-bang pace of the carnival barker. In the process, he has mapped a grotesque modern landscape of disintegration whose violence and vulgarity is laced with manic humor." Anthony Burgess, speaking of the tetralogy in his *The Novel Now: A Guide to Contemporary Fiction,* finds Burroughs's style innovative and leading to a "new medium . . . a medium totally fantastic, spaceless, timeless, in which the normal sentence is fractured, the cosmic tries to push its way through bawdry, and the author shakes the reader as a dog shakes a rat." Speaking to the Edinburgh International Writer's Conference, Mailer proclaimed Burroughs as "the only American novelist living today who may conceivably be possessed by genius."

After living abroad for many years Burroughs returned to the United States in 1973, living for a time in New York City and then moving to rural Kansas. In the 1970s he began to give public readings from his work, and has since given over one hundred and fifty readings in the United States, Canada, and in several European countries. He has also read his work on the "Saturday Night Live" television program. "These readings," Burroughs tells *CA,* "are *performances* carefully rehearsed. I am, despite previous disclaimers, an entertainer, in fact a stand-up comic." Through his readings Burroughs's distinctive persona—a gaunt figure dressed impeccably in a dark suit—has become familiar to many of his readers. He possesses a "sad, nasty drawl, a voice that goes well with his face, which has the odd quality of being soft and haggard at the same time, a face that can writhe with tics, then gaze with reptilian stillness," Allen writes. Platt recalls that Burroughs's "complexion is ghostly pale; he peers out into daylight like the caretaker for a mausoleum." Sante likens Burroughs to "the dangerous figure in a worn business outfit who haunts schoolyards and mutters vague fragments about planetary conspiracy."

Speaking of his writing, Burroughs tells *CA* he has been deeply influenced by the authors Denton Welch, Joseph Conrad, Graham Greene, Louis-Ferdinand Celine, Samuel Beckett, Jean Genet, Arthur Rimbaud, and Saint-John Perse. As to his literary intentions, Burroughs explains: "My purpose in writing any book is to do the best job of writing I can do. And that's it."

BIOGRAPHICAL/CRITICAL SOURCES:

BOOKS

Authors in the News, Volume 2, Gale, 1976.

Bartlett, Lee, editor, *The Beats: Essays in Criticism,* McFarland, 1981.

Bowles, Paul, *Without Stopping,* Putnam, 1972.

Bryant, Jerry H., *The Open Decision: The Contemporary American Novel and Its Intellectual Background,* Free Press, 1970.

Burgess, Anthony, *The Novel Now: A Guide to Contemporary Fiction,* Norton, 1967.

Burroughs, William, Jr., *Kentucky Ham,* Dutton, 1973.

Burroughs, William S., *Junky,* Penguin, 1977.

Burroughs, William S., *Cities of the Red Night,* Holt, 1981.

Charters, Ann, *Kerouac: A Biography,* Straight Arrow Books, 1973.

Contemporary Fiction in America and England, 1950-1970, Gale, 1976.

Contemporary Literary Criticism, Gale, Volume 1, 1973, Volume 2, 1974, Volume 5, 1976, Volume 15, 1980, Volume 22, 1982, Volume 42, 1987.

Cook, Bruce, *The Beat Generation,* Scribner, 1971.

Dictionary of Literary Biography, Gale, Volume 2: *American Novelists since World War II,* 1978, Volume 8: *Twentieth Century American Science Fiction Writers,* 1981, Volume 16: *The Beats: Literary Bohemians in Postwar America,* 1983.

Dictionary of Literary Biography Yearbook: 1981, Gale, 1982.

Gifford, Barry and Lawrence Lee, *Jack's Book: An Oral Biography of Jack Kerouac,* St. Martin, 1978.

Goodman, Michael Barry, *William S. Burroughs: An Annotated Bibliography of His Works and Criticism,* Garland Publishing, 1975.

Goodman, Michael Barry, *Contemporary Literary Censorship: The Case History of Burroughs' Naked Lunch,* Scarecrow, 1981.

Harrison, Gilbert A., editor, *The Critic as Artist: Essays on Books, 1920-1970,* Liveright, 1972.

Hassan, Ihab, *The Dismemberment of Orpheus,* Oxford University Press, 1971.

Itinerary 3: Criticism, Bowling Green University, 1977.

Kazin, Alfred, editor, *Writers at Work: The Paris Review Interviews,* Viking, 1967.

Kazin, Alfred, *Bright Book of Life,* Atlantic/Little, Brown, 1973.

Lemaire, Gerard-Georges, *Colloque de Tanger,* Christian Bourgois Editeur, 1976.

Lodge, David, *Modes of Modern Writing,* Cornell University Press, 1977.

Mattram, Eric, *William Burroughs: The Algebra of Need,* Intrepid Press, 1971, new edition, Marion Boyars, 1977.

Maynard, Philippe, *William S. Burroughs,* Seghers, 1975.

McCarthy, Mary, *The Writing on the Wall, and Other Literary Essays,* Harcourt, 1970.

McNally, Dennis, *Desolate Angel: Jack Kerouac, the Beat Generation, and America,* Random House, 1979.

Miles Associates, compilers, *A Descriptive Catalogue of the William S. Burroughs Archive,* Covent Garden Press, 1973.

Morgan, Ted, *Literary Outlaw: The Life and Times of William S. Burroughs,* Holt, 1988.

Nelson, Cary, *The Incarnate Word: Literature and Verbal Space,* University of Illinois Press, 1973.

Odier, Daniel, *The Job: Interviews with William S. Burroughs,* Grove, 1970.

Parkinson, Thomas, editor, *A Casebook on the Beat,* Crowell, 1961.

Pearce, Richard, *Stages of the Clown: Perspectives on Modern Fiction from Dostoevsky to Beckett,* Southern Illinois University Press, 1970.

Platt, Charles, *Dream Makers,* Volume 2: *The Uncommon Men and Women Who Write Science Fiction,* Berkley Publishing, 1983.

Seltzer, Alvin J., *Chaos in the Novel: The Novel in Chaos,* Schocken, 1974.

Tanner, Tony, *City of Words: American Fiction, 1950-1970,* Harper, 1971.

Tytell, John, *Naked Angels: The Lives and Literature of the Beat Generation,* McGraw-Hill, 1976.

Vernon, John, *The Garden and the Map: Schizophrenia in Twentieth Century Literature and Culture,* University of Illinois Press, 1973.

Wilson, Terry and others, *Here to Go: Planet R-101,* ReSearch Publications (San Francisco), 1982.

PERIODICALS

Ambit, Number 27, 1966.

American Book Review, May-June, 1981.

American Scholar, spring, 1965.

Atlantic, December, 1968, April, 1981.

Big Table, summer, 1959.
Calaban XII, Volume XI, number 1, 1975.
Chicago Tribune, June 15, 1984, October 15, 1988.
Chicago Tribune Book World, March 1, 1981, February 9, 1984, June 17, 1984.
Comparative Literature Studies, December, 1978.
Critical Quarterly, autumn, 1966.
Criticism, Number 22, 1980.
Critique, spring, 1963.
Denver Post, June 15, 1975.
Detroit News, March 22, 1981.
Encounter, April, 1963, January, 1967.
Esquire, September, 1971.
Evergreen Review, January-February, 1962, April-May, 1964.
Extrapolation, winter, 1979.
Forum, Number 14, 1976.
Globe & Mail (Toronto), March 10, 1984, February 22, 1986.
Guardian, October 1, 1982.
Harper's, February, 1974.
High Performance Number 4, winter, 1982.
High Times, March, 1979.
Hollins Critic, April, 1977.
Hudson Review, autumn, 1967.
Intrepid, fall/winter, 1969-70.
Iowa Review, spring, 1972.
Journal for the Protection of All Beings, Number 1, 1961.
Journal of Aesthetics and Art Criticism, summer, 1967.
Kulchur, autumn, 1962.
Library Journal, September 1, 1978, November 15, 1980.
Life, November 30, 1959, February 15, 1967.
London Review of Books, April 16-May 6, 1981.
Los Angeles Times, February 10, 1986.
Los Angeles Times Book Review, March 15, 1981, September 19, 1982, July 6, 1986.
Massachusetts Review, Number 8, 1967.
Modern Occasions, winter, 1972.
My Own Mag, August, 1965.
Nation, December 28, 1964, January 25, 1965.
New Republic, August 5, 1967, April 18, 1981.
New Statesman, March 29, 1974, March 27, 1981.
Newsweek, March 9, 1981.
New Worlds, Number 142, 1964.
New Yorker, August 1, 1980.
New York Review of Books, May 10, 1984.
New York Times, December 1, 1978, February 25, 1981, July 22, 1981, February 15, 1984, December 16, 1987.
New York Times Book Review, September 6, 1962, December 12, 1971, June 22, 1975, March 15 1981, February 19, 1984, November 3, 1985, August 17, 1986.
Paris Review, fall, 1965.
Partisan Review, spring, 1963, spring, 1974.
Penthouse, March, 1972.
Re/Search, Number 4/5, 1982.
Review of Contemporary Fiction, Volume 4, number 1, 1984.
Revue des Langues Vivants, Number 42, 1976.
Rolling Stone, May 1, 1972.
Saturday Review, June 27, 1959, January 6, 1979.
Search & Destroy, Number 10, 1978.
Semiotext(e), Volume 4, number 2, 1982.
SF Horizons, Number 2, 1975.
Spectator, July 29, 1960, March 16, 1974, April 4, 1981.
Sphinx, Number 1, 1980.
Style, Number 10, 1976.
Telos, fall, 1972.
Time, November 30, 1962.
Time Out, September 24-30, 1982.
Times (London), April 26, 1984, March 10, 1988.
Times Literary Supplement, December 21, 1979, March 27, 1981, January 24, 1986, March 18, 1988.
Transatlantic Review, winter, 1969-70.
TriQuarterly, spring, 1968.
Twentieth Century Literature, October, 1965, summer, 1978.
Twentieth Century Studies, November, 1969.
unspeakable visions of the individual, Number 4, 1974, Number 5, 1977.
Village Voice Literary Supplement, September, 1982, March, 1984.
Washington Post, February 3, 1984.
Washington Post Book World, March 1, 1981, February 9, 1984, December 29, 1985, December 27, 1987.
West Coast Review, fall, 1969.
World Literature Today, spring, 1981.

* * *

BUSTOS, F(rancisco)
See BORGES, Jorge Luis

* * *

BUSTOS DOMECQ, H(onorio)
See BIOY CASARES, Adolfo and BORGES, Jorge Luis

* * *

BUTLER, Octavia E(stelle)   1947-

PERSONAL: Born June 22, 1947, in Pasadena, Calif.; daughter of Laurice and Octavia M. (Guy) Butler. *Education:* Pasadena City College, A.A., 1968; attended California State University, Los Angeles, 1969.

ADDRESSES: Home—P.O. Box 6604, Los Angeles, Calif. 90055.

CAREER: Free-lance writer, 1970—.

MEMBER: Science Fiction Writers of America.

AWARDS, HONORS: Hugo Award, World Science Fiction Convention, 1984, for short story "Speech Sounds"; Hugo Award, Nebula Award, Science Fiction Writers of America, Locus Award, *Locus* magazine, and award for best novelette, *Science Fiction Chronicle Reader,* all 1985, all for novelette "Bloodchild"; Nebula Award nomination, 1987, for novelette "The Evening and the Morning and the Night."

WRITINGS:

SCIENCE FICTION

Patternmaster, Doubleday, 1976.
Mind of My Mind, Doubleday, 1977.
Survivor, Doubleday, 1978.
Kindred, Doubleday, 1979, 2nd edition, Beacon Press, 1988.
Wild Seed, Doubleday, 1980.
Clay's Ark, St. Martin's, 1984.
Dawn: Xenogenesis, Warner Books, 1987.
Adulthood Rites, Warner Books, 1988.
Imago, Warner Books, 1989.

Contributor to anthologies, including *Clarion,* 1970, and *Chrysalis 4,* 1979; contributor to *Isaac Asimov's Science Fiction Magazine, Future Life, Transmission,* and other publications.

SIDELIGHTS: Concerned with genetic engineering, psionic powers, advanced alien beings, and the nature and proper use of power, Octavia E. Butler's science fiction presents these themes in terms of racial and sexual awareness. "Butler consciously explores the impact of race and sex upon future society," as Frances Smith Foster explains in *Extrapolation*. As one of the few black writers in the science fiction field, and the only black woman, Butler's racial and sexual perspective is unique. This perspective, however, does not limit her fiction or turn it into mere propaganda. "Her stories," Sherley Anne Williams writes in *Ms.*, "aren't overwhelmed by politics, nor are her characters overwhelmed by racism or sexism." Speaking of how Butler's early novels deal with racial questions in particular, John R. Pfeiffer of *Fantasy Review* maintains that "nevertheless, and therefore more remarkably, these are the novels of character that critics so much want to find in science fiction—and which remain so rare. Finally, they are love stories that are mythic, bizarre, exotic and heroic and full of doom and transcendence."

After attending the Clarion Science Fiction Writers' Workshop in 1970, where she studied under some of the field's top writers, Butler began to sell her short stories to science fiction magazines. But she had been writing for many years before Clarion. "I began writing," she comments, "when I was about ten years old for the same reason many people begin reading—to escape loneliness and boredom. I didn't realize then that writing was supposed to be work. It was too much fun. It still is."

Butler's stories have been well received by science fiction fans. In 1985 she won three of the field's top honors—the Nebula Award, the Hugo Award, and the Locus Award—for her novella "Bloodchild," the story of human males on another planet who bear the children of an alien race. "Blood-child," Williams maintains, "explores the paradoxes of power and inequality, and starkly portrays the experience of a class who, like women throughout most of history, are valued chiefly for their reproductive capacities."

It is through her novels, especially those set in the world of the "Patternists," that Butler reaches her largest audience. These novels tell of a society dominated by an elite, specially-bred group of telepaths who are mentally linked together into a hierarchical pattern. Led by a four thousand-year-old alien who survives by killing and then taking over younger bodies, these telepaths seek to create a race of superhumans. The Patternist society is also racked by an alien plague which genetically alters human beings. The novels range over vast reaches of time and space, tracing many hundreds of years of human history from the remote past to the space-faring future.

Among Butler's strengths as a writer is her creation of believable, independent female characters. "Her major characters are black women," Foster explains, and through these characters Butler explores the possibilities for a society open to true sexual equality. In such a society Butler's female characters, "powerful and purposeful in their own right, need not rely upon eroticism to gain their ends," Foster writes. Williams finds that Butler posits "a multiracial society featuring strong women characters."

Critics also praise Butler's controlled, economical prose style. Writing in the *Washington Post Book World*, Elizabeth A. Lynn calls Butler's prose "spare and sure, and even in moments of great tension she never loses control over her pacing or over her sense of story." "Butler," writes Dean R. Lambe of the *Science Fiction Review*, "has a fine hand with lean, well-paced prose."

A novel not set in the Patternist society, Butler's *Kindred* is a work her publisher marketed as mainstream fiction despite its time-travel theme. It concerns Dana, a contemporary black woman who is pulled back in time by her great-great-grandfather, a white plantation owner in the antebellum American South. To insure that he will live to father her great-grandmother, and thus insure her own birth in the twentieth century, Dana is called upon to save the slaveowner's life on several occasions. "Butler makes new and eloquent use of a familiar science-fiction idea, protecting one's own past, to express the tangled interdependency of black and white in the United States," Joanna Russ writes in the *Magazine of Fantasy and Science Fiction*. Williams calls *Kindred* "a startling and engrossing commentary on the complex actuality and continuing heritage of American slavery."

"I began writing science fiction and fantasy," Butler explains, "because both inspire a high level of creativity and offer a great deal of freedom." But she soon found that few science fiction writers exercised this creative freedom. "I remember that when I began reading science fiction," she continues, "I was disappointed at how little this creativity and freedom was used to portray the many racial, ethnic, and class variations. Also, I could not help noticing how few significant women characters there were in science fiction. Fortunately, all of this has been changing over the past few years. I intend my writing to contribute to the change."

Butler enjoys a solid reputation among both readers and critics of science fiction. Although Williams notes that Butler has a "cult status among many black women readers," she also notes that "Butler's work has a scope that commands a wide audience." Speaking of *Kindred* and *Wild Seed*, Pfeiffer argues that with these books Butler "produced two novels of such special excellence that critical appreciation of them will take several years to assemble. To miss them will be to miss unique novels in modern fiction." Margaret Anne O'Connor of the *Dictionary of Literary Biography* simply calls Butler "one of the most promising new writers in America today."

BIOGRAPHICAL/CRITICAL SOURCES:

BOOKS

Contemporary Literary Criticism, Volume 38, Gale, 1986.
Dictionary of Literary Biography, Volume 33: *Afro-American Fiction Writers after 1955,* Gale, 1984.

PERIODICALS

Analog: Science Fiction/Science Fact, January 5, 1981, November, 1984.
Black American Literature Forum, summer, 1984.
Black Scholar, March/April, 1986.
Equal Opportunity Forum Magazine, Number 8, 1980.
Essence, April, 1979.
Extrapolation, spring, 1982.
Fantasy Review, July, 1984.
Janus, winter, 1978-79.
Los Angeles Times, January 30, 1981.
Magazine of Fantasy and Science Fiction, February, 1980, August, 1984.
Ms., March, 1986, June, 1987.
Salaga, 1981.
Science Fiction Review, May, 1984.
Thrust: Science Fiction in Review, summer, 1979.
Washington Post Book World, September 28, 1980, June 28, 1987, July 31, 1988, June 25, 1989.

BUTOR, Michel (Marie Francois) 1926-

PERSONAL: Born September 14, 1926, in Mons-en-Baroeul, France; son of Emile (a railway inspector) and Anne (Brajeux) Butor; married Marie-Josephe Mas, August 22, 1958; children: Cecile, Agnes, Irene, Mathilde. *Education:* Sorbonne, University of Paris, license en philosophie, 1946, diplome d'etudes superieures de philosophie, 1947.

ADDRESSES: Home—Aux Antipodes, chemin de Terra Amata, 23 boulevard Carnot, 06300 Nice, France. *Office*—Faculte des Lettres, University of Geneva, 3 place de l'Universite, 1211 Geneva 4, Switzerland. *Agent*—Georges Borchardt, 136 East 57th St., New York, N.Y., 10022.

CAREER: Teacher of philosophy, Sens, France, 1950; teacher of French in Minya, Egypt, 1950-51, Manchester, England, 1951-53, Salonica, Greece, 1954-55, Geneva, Switzerland, 1956-57; Centre Universitaire de Vincennes, Vincennes, France, associate professor, 1969; University of Nice, Nice, France, associate professor, 1970-73; University of Geneva, Geneva, Switzerland, professor of modern French language and literature, 1975—; writer. Visiting professor of French at several universities in the United States. Advisory editor, Editions Gallimard, Paris, 1958—.

AWARDS, HONORS: Prix Felix Fenelon, 1957, for *L'Emploi du temps;* Prix Theophraste Renaudot, 1957, for *La Modification;* Grand Prix de la Critique Litteraire, Association de Critiques Litteraire, 1960, for *Repertoire;* Ford Foundation grant, 1964; Chevalier de l'Ordre National du Merite; Chevalier des Arts et des Lettres; Docteur es lettres, University of Paris.

WRITINGS:

NOVELS

Passage de Milan, Editions de Minuit, 1954.
L'Emploi du temps, Editions de Minuit, 1956, translation by Jean Stewart published as *Passing Time,* Simon & Schuster, 1960, recent edition, Riverrun, 1980.
La Modification, Editions de Minuit, 1957, translation by Stewart published in America as *Change of Heart,* Simon & Schuster, 1959, published in England as *Second Thoughts,* Faber, 1968, subsequent French edition published as *La Modification* [suivi de] *Le Realisme mythologique de Michel Butor,* the latter by Michel Leiris, Union Generale d'Editions, 1963, French language edition edited by J. Guicharnod published in America by Ginn, 1970.
Degres, Gallimard, 1960, translation by Richard Howard published as *Degrees,* Simon & Schuster, 1961.
6810000 litres d'eau par seconde: Etude stereophonique, Gallimard, 1965, translation by Elinor S. Miller published as *Niagara,* Regnery, 1969.
Portrait de l'artiste en jeune singe, capriccio, Gallimard, 1967.
Passing Time [and] *A Change of Heart: Two Novels,* translated by Stewart, Simon & Schuster, 1969.
Intervalle, Gallimard, 1973.
Matiere de reves, Editions de Minuit, Volume I, same title, 1975, Volume II: *Second sous-sol,* Gallimard, 1976, Volume III: *Troisieme dessous,* Gallimard, 1977, Volume IV: *Quadruple fond,* Gallimard, 1981, Volume V: *Mille et un plis,* Gallimard, 1985.

POEMS

Cycle sur neuf gouaches d'Alexandre Calder (edition consists of 500 copies signed by the artist and the author), La Hune (Paris), 1962.
Illustrations, Gallimard, 1964.

Litanie d'eau (contains ten original engravings by Gregory Masurovsky; edition consists of 105 copies), La Hune, 1964.
(Author of poems) Ruth Francken, *In den Flammen* (watercolors), epigram by Herbert Read, Belser (Stuttgart), 1965.
Comme Shirley (contains drawings by Masurovsky), La Hune, 1966.
Tourmente (contains drawings by Pierre Alechinsky, Bernard Dufour, and Jacques Herold; edition of 130 copies), Fata Morgana (Montpellier), 1968.
Illustrations II, Gallimard, 1969.
L'Oeil des sargasses, illustrated with an original frontispiece by Masurovsky, Editions "Lettera Amorosa," 1972.
Travaux d'approche: Eocene, Miocene, Pliocene, Gallimard, 1972.
L'Oreille de la lune: Voyage en compagnie de Jules Verne, illustrated with engravings by Robert Blanchet, R. Blanchet, 1973.
Illustrations III, Gallimard, 1973.
Illustrations IV, Gallimard, 1976.
Elseneur: Suite dramatique, La Thiele, 1979.
Sept a la demi-douzaine, Lettres de casse, 1982.

NONFICTION

Zanartu (brochure on Enrique Zanartu), Galerie Editions, 1958.
Le Genie de lieu (essays), Volume I: same title, Grasset, 1958, translation by Lydia Davis published as *The Spirit of Mediterranean Places,* Marlboro Press, 1986, Volume II: *Ou,* Gallimard, 1971, Volume III: *Boomerang* (also see below), Gallimard, 1978.
Herold (catalogue for exhibition, May 26-June 16, 1959), Galerie La Cour d'Ingres (Paris), 1959.
Repertoire: Etudes et conferences, 1948-1959 (essays), Editions de Minuit, 1960.
Une histoire extraordinaire: Essai sur un reve de Baudelaire, Gallimard, 1961, translation by Howard published as *Histoire extraordinaire: Essay on a Dream of Baudelaire's,* J. Cape, 1969.
Mobile: Etude pour un representation des Etats-Unis, Gallimard, 1962, translation by Howard published as *Mobile: Study for a Representation of the United States,* Simon & Schuster, 1963.
Description de San Marco, Gallimard, 1963, translation by Barbara Mason published as *Description of San Marco,* York Press, 1983.
Repertoire II: Etudes et conferences, 1959-1963 (essays, addresses, lectures), Editions de Minuit, 1964.
(Contributor) *Open to the World* (essays), Times Literary Supplement, 1964.
(Editor) Michael Eyquem de Montaigne, *Essays,* Union Generale d'Editions, 1964.
Les Oeuvres d'art imaginaires chez Proust (Casal Bequest lecture), Athlone Press (London), 1964.
Bernard Saby (conversation between Butor and Saby; published in conjunction with exhibition at L'Oeil, Galerie d'Art, Paris), Imprimerie Reunies (Lausanne), 1964.
Herold (conversation with Herold; not the same as earlier book), Musee de Poche, 1964.
Essais sur les modernes, Gallimard, 1964.
(Author of text) Bernard Larsson, *Die ganze Stadt Berlin* (photographs), Butor's French translated by Helmut Scheffel, Nannen (Hamburg), 1964.
(Author of text with Harold Rosenberg) Saul Steinberg, *Le Masque* (cartoons; photos by Inge Morath), Maeght, 1966.
(Author of text) *Dialogue des regnes [Cuivres originaux de] Jacques Herold* (original engravings by Herold; edition of

75 copies signed by author and artist), Fequet et Baudier (Paris), 1967.

Paysage de repons [suivi de] *Dialogues des regnes,* Albeuve (Castella), 1968.

La Banlieue de l'aube a l'aurore: Mouvement brownien (contains illustrations by Dufour), Fata Morgana, 1968.

Repertoire III (essays), Editions de Minuit, 1968.

Essais sur "Les Essais" (essays on the essays of Montaigne; contains extracts from *Essays*), Gallimard, 1968.

(With Henri Pousseur) *Votre Faust, fantaisie variable, genre opera* (includes a lecture given by Pousseur and an interview with Pousseur and Butor), Centre d'etudes et de recherches marxistes (Paris), 1968.

Inventory: Essays, edited with an introduction by Howard, Simon & Schuster, 1969.

Essais sur le roman, Gallimard, 1969.

Les Mots dans la peinture, Albert Skira (Geneva), 1969.

La Rose des vents: 32 rhumbs pour Charles Fourier, Gallimard, 1970.

Entretiens avec Georges Charbonnier, Gallimard, 1970.

Dialogue avec 33 variations de Ludwig van Beethoven sur une valse de Diabelli, Gallimard, 1971.

(With Denis Hollier) *Rabelais; ou, C'etait pour rire,* Larousse, 1972.

Les Sept Femmes de Gilbert le Mauvais (autre Heptaedre), Fata Morgana, 1972.

Repertoire IV (critical essays), Editions de Minuit, 1974.

(With Jean Clair and Suzanne Houbart-Wilkin) *Delvaux,* Cosmos (Brussels), 1975, translation published as *Delvaux's Paintings,* Wofsy Fine Arts, 1987.

Tapies, Fondation Marguerite et Aime Maeght (Saint-Paul, France), 1976.

Letters from the Antipodes (a selection from *Boomerang*), translated from the French by Michael Spencer, Ohio University Press, 1981.

Repertoire V, Editions de Minuit, 1982.

(Contributor) *Index des premiers ecrits pedagogiques de J.-J. Rousseau,* Slatkine, 1982.

(With Michel Sicard) *Problemes de l'art contemporain a partir des travaux d'Henri Maccheroni,* C. Bourgois, 1983.

(With Michel Launay) *Resistances: Conversations aux antipodes* (discussion), P.U.F., 1983.

Improvisations sur Flaubert (critical essays), Difference, 1984.

Alechinsky dans le texte, Galilee, 1984.

(With Christian Dotrement) *Cartes et lettres: Correspondance 1966-1979* (correspondance), Galilee, 1986.

Also author of introduction for: James Joyce, *Finnegans Wake,* Gallimard, 1962; William Styron, *La Proie des flammes* (*Set This House on Fire*), Gallimard, 1962; Fyodor Dostoievski, *Le Joueur* (*The Gambler*), Le Livre de Poche, 1963.

TRANSLATOR

(With Lucien Goldmann) Gyorgy Lukacs, *Breve Histoire de la litterature allemande (du XVIIIe siecle a nos jours),* Nagel, 1949.

Aron Gurwitsch, *Theorie du champ de la conscience (The Field of Conscience),* Desclee de Brouwer, 1957.

William Shakespeare, *Tout est bien fini qui finit bien* (translation of *All's Well That Ends Well*), published in *Oeuvres completes,* Volume V, Formes et Reflets, 1959.

Bernardino de Sahagun, *De l'origine des dieux,* Fata Morgana, 1981.

OTHER

Reseau aerien (radio script commissioned by French Broadcasting System; first performed June 16, 1962), Gallimard, 1962.

L'Art de Michel Butor, edited by Claude Book-Senninger and Jack Kolbert, Oxford University Press, 1970.

(With Pierre Barberis and Roland Barthes) *Ecrire, pour quoi? Pour qui?,* P.U.G., 1974.

(With Alechinsky) *La Reve de l'ammonite,* Fata Morgana, 1975.

Tout l'Oeuvre peint de Piet Mondrian, Flammarion, 1976.

(With Alechinsky and Jean-Yves Bosseur) *Materiel pour un Don Juan,* T. Bouchard, 1978.

Envois, Gallimard, 1980.

(With Michel Launay and Henri Maccheroni) *Vanite: Conversation dans les Alpes-Maritimes,* Balland, 1980.

Explorations, Editions de l'Aire, 1981.

(With Chris Marker) *Le Depays,* Herscher, 1982.

Brassee d'avril, Difference, 1982.

(With Pierre Berenger) *Naufrages de l'arche,* published with *Adieu a la galerie de zoologie* by Yves Laissus, Difference, 1982.

Vieira Da Silva: Peintures, Difference, 1983.

Expres, Gallimard, 1983.

Alechinsky: Frontieres et bordures, Galilee (Paris), 1984.

(With Masurovsky) *Dimanche matin,* Instant Perpetuel, 1984.

Loisirs et brouillons, 1964-1984, D. Bedou, 1984.

Herbier lunaire, Difference, 1984.

Avant-gout, Ubacs, 1984.

Improvisations sur Henri Michaux, Fata Morgana, 1985.

(With Stephane Bastin) *La Famille Grabouillage,* D. Bedou, 1985.

(With Herold) *Hors-d'oeuvre,* Instant Perpetuel, 1985.

Chantier, D. Bedou, 1985.

(With Axel Cassel) *Le Scribe,* Spuren, 1985.

L'oeil de Prague: Dialogue avec Charles Baudelaire autour des travaux de Jiri Kolar, suivi de reponses et de Le Prague de Kafka par Jiri Kolar, Difference, 1986.

Avant-gout II, Ubacs, 1987.

Le Retour de Boomerang, Presses Universitaires de France, 1988.

Contributor to numerous publications in France and elsewhere.

SIDELIGHTS: Along with Samuel Beckett, Nathalie Sarraute, and Alain Robbe-Grillet, Butor has been at the vanguard of twentieth-century French literature, engaged in writing what is sometimes referred to by Jean-Paul Sartre's phrase, the "anti-novel," or, the "new novel." The exponents of the new novel, according to Sartre, "make use of the novel in order to challenge the novel, to destroy it before our very eyes while seeming to construct it, to write the novel of a novel unwritten and unwritable." The new novel adds an objective exposition of setting and character, and concentrates on "existence as it is being formed rather than analyzing it after it has happened," Patricia J. Jaeger writes.

For Butor, the novel is an instrument of knowledge, a searching depth-study of personality. He avoids chronological time in favor of "human time" measured in the interior of each character's mind. Jaeger comments: "Butor seems to base most of his books . . . on an examination of the effect of the past, present and future on each other. He is especially aware of the propensity of the human mind to shift its perception of the past in light of new information available only in the present." In addition to juxtaposing several levels of time, he offers no solutions, preferring to focus on the transition of action not on its outcome.

Butor himself sees the novel form as the perfect instrument for combining the two principal interests of his youth, philosophy and poetry. Of Butor's stylistic qualities Laurent Le Sage writes: "Butor's books are like those European museums and galleries he is fond of visiting with his readers, full to the rafters of the most painstaking and minute word-painting, as if there were nothing he could leave out. His descriptions often have a lyrical, even rhapsodical quality." The formation of this style can perhaps be traced to Butor's first encounter with Shelley's poetry at the age of fourteen, when he discovered, he writes, "a lyricism of which the French classics gave me no idea, above all a new sonority, a new way of making words take fire from the rhythm."

Butor has been greatly influenced by Proust. He said once that he had read all of *Remembrance of Things Past* ten times. Henri Peyre writes: "Butor's is the finest mind among those who have undertaken to renovate the novel since 1950—the only one who at times recalls the density and the complex orchestration of the Proustian saga fiction or whose universal intellectual and artistic curiosity grants him a place in the literature of the last third of our century comparable to that of Sartre at mid-century. He received Sartre's blessing and he himself has been generous as well as clear-sighted in praising the avatars of Sartrian thought since 1960." Peyre maintains that until the publication of *Degres* Butor was the "favorite of critics and of philosophers."

Butor has also been influenced by Joyce, whom he greatly admired. The structure of *Passage de Milan*—the entire novel covers twelve hours of time and takes place within an apartment house in Paris, where the residents' lives are regulated by a series of rituals which tend to isolate them from each other rather than bring them closer together—is reminiscent of Joyce's structure in *Ulysses.* A similar structure is used in *L'Emploi du temps.* The novel is in five parts, corresponding to the five months during which the main character keeps a diary. The parts of the novel are each divided into five chapters, for each of the weeks, or portions of weeks in a month. Since Revel does not work on weekends each week has five days. Butor has thus created a schedule for the framework of the book, although he can with his title also be referring to the uses of passing of time. The structure can also be seen in Bleston, the city which Butor creates, and all the details which he carefully sets down. Leon Roudiez states that "Butor is concerned with Bleston not as a city contrasted to the country or the sea, but as a city among cities, as a microcosm of civilization, like Paris in *Passage de Milan.*" The great scope of these first two novels, although they are contained in the framework Butor has provided for them, includes myriad details about the lives of the many people encountered in both books.

La Modification is unlike the first two novels since it "[focuses] on the single action of one individual," as Roudiez says, "clearly circumscribed in time and space, actually and symbolically." Butor uses the second person narrative here very successfully. Roudiez states that the second person "allows for an ambiguous author-reader-character relationship, with the reader oscillating between identification with the prosecuting author, or with the guilty character." The reader is then able to choose, "he is free to act either in good faith or in bad faith." Peyre comments that *La Modification* is "a paradox sustained through two hundred and thirty pages without artificiality or weariness. The stark simplicity of the theme and the unities of time and place, the stillness in the midst of motion, are arresting." Peyre recounts Butor's statement to a *Figaro Litteraire* interviewer: "The narrative absolutely had to be told from the point of view of a character . . . I needed an interior monologue beneath the level of the character himself, with a form between the first and third person. The *vous*

allows me to describe the situation of the character and the manner in which language emerges in him."

Degres has elicited both favorable and unfavorable criticism. Peyre considers the novel a failure, "even as an exercise in the technique of fiction." Harry T. Moore describes the novel as "a microscopic investigation of the life processes themselves, more detailed even than the explorations of Sarraute and Robbe-Grillet, with fewer clues as to what is happening. It is therefore somewhat more difficult to read, but the book remains a fascinating experiment; it deals more thoroughly with space-time concepts than other novels of its school." Roudiez states that *Degres* "is a masterpiece. The initial impetus to the narrative lies in an attempt to recapture the meaning and consciousness of a given hour in the life of a contemporary French lycee, its teachers, and its students, at the beginning of the school year." Roudiez finds that the "architecture" of the novel "is one aspect . . . of which most readers are not aware, and this in itself is an indication of how successfully it has been integrated into the work as a whole." It is divided into three parts, and these are further divided. There are many triangular relationships among characters as well.

Since *Degres* Butor has used his methods of structure and categorization in even more unusual ways. *Mobile* is considered by some to be a novel, but most people would agree that it is not really a novel. Butor's subtitle, "study," in the sense of the French *etude,* is probably the best way to categorize the work. He has used the experience of a trip across the United States for the material of this work, although it is not an actual trip, and many of the facts are not completely accurate. Miller describes the book as "a tiresome montage of disconnected images relieved by catalogues of names, advertising slogans, the prose of road signs." He says that *Mobile* is "a poor imitation of the expressionist techniques." Roudiez would disagree. He says that Butor's "is the phenomenological approach, whereby the book is examined in its attributes as a material object." He finds "a certain amount of virtuosity" in the book. Again, the architecture is not obvious, and Butor has been criticized for this, but a very definite structure is present. Most important for the reader, Roudiez states, "is the manner in which the components have been assembled in order to produce the picture, or 'representation.' Discontinuous accounts of the 1692 Salem trials and of writings by Franklin and Jefferson, newspaper extracts, advertisements, signs, brief statements, names of people, cities, counties, and states form a strange mosaic or, as the text suggests at one point, a patchwork quilt. Naturally, the juxtaposition is not haphazard; as with the states themselves, the basic order is alphabetical (almond through vanilla for ice cream, B.P. through Texaco for gasoline, among others), and a number of complicated modifications are subsequently introduced in order to achieve maximum effect from various confrontations: the procedure is . . . not unrelated to the surrealist image. . . . *Mobile* is a stunning display of colors. A profusion of contrasting tints is found in the flora, the fauna, the human artifacts, and the people themselves."

A resemblance can he seen between *Mobile* and *Description de San Marco,* although the latter is concerned strictly with San Marco, and does not go off in the directions that *Mobile* does. Both of these works have unusual typographical arrangements which help to clarify that which is place. Margins of different sizes are used to differentiate between different elements in the narratives, and in *Mobile* . . . use of italic as well as Roman type is significant. Both books led the way to *Reseau aerien,* which uses the same devices. The book departs from the printed page in the sense that it was written for radio broadcast, and involves not only dialogue but sound as well, which can only be described, and not actually heard, in print. Roudiez writes that "the total impression is one of a choral song of mankind in which unidentified individuals blend their common preoccupations about different things and countries into elemental melodies of love and hate. Trivial concerns, expressed in prosaic fashion, dominate in the early dialogues. Later, as distance, imagination, and dreams affect each traveler, the themes become more basically human; the language waxes lyrical, discursive logic makes way for instinctive association, and ordinary talk is metamorphosed into poetry."

6810000 litres d'eau par seconde is described by Miller as "a story in which Niagara Falls are thunderously dominant. The action, chiefly concerned with newly married couples and older ones nostalgically returning, covers a year, presenting events somewhat in the manner of *Mobile,* with different kinds of type and with speeches intended to be read at different pitches." Butor visited Niagara Falls at different seasons so that he would have more than one set of impressions to write about. He has even written himself in to the book as Quentin, a visiting professor of French. John Sturrock writes: "In its devious and sybilline way, [the book] embodies everything that Butor believes about the function and lofty moral virtues of literature. Making a book for him is an exemplary effort at anamnensis, the model of how we ought all of us to set about salvaging our own past."

Butor as an essayist should not be overlooked. Audrey Foote comments on the essays included in *Inventory:* "Both [Butor's] choice of subjects and his treatment of them reflect a mind of muscular intellectuality, a Huguenot or puritan taste for austerity and economy, and above all an intense need to impose discipline, almost geometric order and unity." Moore comments: "Butor is a critic of pronounced originality, discernment, versatility, wit, and force."

MEDIA ADAPTATIONS: La Modification was filmed by Rene Thevenet-Fono Roma, 1970.

BIOGRAPHICAL/CRITICAL SOURCES:

BOOKS

Albers, R. M., *Michel Butor,* Editions Universitaire, 1964.
Contemporary Literary Criticism, Gale, Volume I, 1973, Volume III, 1975, Volume VIII, 1978, Volume XI, 1979, Volume XV, 1980.
Dictionary of Literary Biography, Volume LXXXIII: *French Novelists Since 1960,* Gale, 1989.
Le Sage, Laurent, *The French New Novel,* Pennsylvania State University Press, 1962.
Lydon, Mary, *Perpetuum Mobile: A Study of the Novels and Aesthetics of Michel Butor,* University of Alberta Press, 1980.
McWilliams, Dean, *The Narrative of Butor: The Writer as Janus,* Ohio University Press, 1978.
Moore, Harry T., *French Literature Since World War II,* Southern Illinois University Press, 1966.
Peyre, Henri, *French Novelists of Today,* Oxford University Press, 1967.
Rahv, Betty T., *From Sartre to the New Novel,* Kennikat Press, 1974.
Roudiez, Leon S., *Michel Butor,* Columbia University Press, 1965.
Spencer, Michael, *Butor,* Twayne, 1974.
Sturrock, John, *The French New Novel: Claude Simon, Michel Butor, Alain Robbe-Grillet,* Oxford University Press, 1969.

PERIODICALS

Book World, February 9, 1969.
Books Abroad, spring, 1968, spring, 1969, spring, 1970, winter, 1971, spring, 1971.
Critique (Paris), February, 1958.
Critique: Studies in Modern Fiction, winter, 1963-64.
French Review, December, 1961, October, 1962.
Kentucky Romance Quarterly, Volume XXXVIII, Number I, 1985.
Les Temps Modernes, April, 1957.
Livres de France, June-July, 1963.
New Statesman, April 7, 1967.
New York Herald Tribune Book Review, August 4, 1963.
New York Review of Books, April 23, 1970.
New York Times Book Review, July 7, 1963, December 28, 1969, August 31, 1986.
Review of Contemporary Fiction, fall, 1985.
Saturday Review, December 18, 1965, August 5, 1967, May 3, 1969.
Times Literary Supplement, March 4, 1965, March 17, 1966, June 22, 1967, April 11, 1968, January 1, 1971, August 6, 1971, August 3, 1973, May 17, 1974, July 18, 1975, October 7, 1977.
Tri-Quarterly Review, winter, 1967.
World Literature Today, autumn, 1977, winter, 1977, winter, 1979, summer, 1981, spring, 1982, autumn, 1983, winter, 1983, spring, 1984, summer, 1984, spring, 1985.
Yale French Studies, summer, 1959.
Yale Review, June, 1959.

*   *   *

BYARS, Betsy (Cromer)   1928-

PERSONAL: Born August 7, 1928, in Charlotte, N.C.; daughter of George Guy and Nan (Rugheimer) Cromer; married Edward Ford Byars (a professor of engineering and writer), June 24, 1950; children: Laurie, Betsy Ann, Nan, Guy. *Education:* Attended Furman University, 1946-48; Queens College, Charlotte, N.C., B.A., 1950.

ADDRESSES: Home—4 Riverpoint, Clemson, S.C. 29631.

CAREER: Writer of books for children.

AWARDS, HONORS: Received American Library Association notable book award for *Trouble River,* 1969, *The Summer of the Swans,* 1970, *The House of Wings,* 1972, and *The Pinballs,* 1977; John Newbery Medal from American Library Association, 1971, for *The Summer of the Swans;* Dorothy Canfield Fisher Memorial Book Award from Vermont State Congress of Parents and Teachers, 1975, for *The Eighteenth Emergency;* Children's Book Award from Child Study Association, 1977, Georgia Children's Book Award, 1979, and Mark Twain Award from Missouri Library Association, William Allen White Award, and California Young Readers Medal Award, all 1980, all for *The Pinballs;* American Book Award, 1981, for *The Night Swimmers;* Tennessee Children's Choice Book Award, 1983, and Sequoyah Children's Book Award, 1984, both for *The Cybil War;* Regina Medal, Catholic Library Association, 1986, "for excellence in the writing of literature for children"; *Cracker Jackson* was selected for *Horn Book Magazine*'s honor list, 1986; William Allen White Award, Maryland Children's Book Award, and South Carolina Children's Book Award, all 1988, all for *Cracker Jackson;* Young Reader's Choice Award, c. 1988, for *The Computer Nut.*

WRITINGS:

FOR CHILDREN

Clementine, Houghton, 1962.
The Dancing Camel, Viking, 1965.
Rama the Gypsy Cat, Viking, 1966.
(Self-illustrated) *The Groober,* Harper, 1967.
The Midnight Fox, Viking, 1968.
Trouble River, Viking, 1969, recent edition, Penguin, 1988.
The Summer of the Swans (Junior Literary Guild selection), Viking, 1970.
Go and Hush the Baby, Viking, 1971.
The House of Wings, Viking, 1972.
The Eighteenth Emergency, Viking, 1973.
The Winged Colt of Casa Mia, Viking, 1973.
After the Goat Man, Viking, 1974.
(Self-illustrated) *The Lace Snail,* Viking, 1975.
The TV Kid, Viking, 1976.
The Pinballs, Harper, 1977.
The Cartoonist, Viking, 1978.
Goodbye, Chicken Little, Harper, 1979.
The Night Swimmers, Delacorte, 1980.
The Cybil War, Viking, 1981.
The Animal, the Vegetable and John D. Jones (Junior Literary Guild selection), Delacorte, 1982.
The Two-Thousand-Pound Goldfish, Harper, 1982.
The Glory Girl, Viking, 1983.
The Computer Nut, Viking, 1984.
Cracker Jackson, Viking, 1985.
The Not-Just-Anybody Family (Junior Literary Guild selection), Delacorte, 1986.
The Blossoms Meet the Vulture Lady, Delacorte, 1986.
The Golly Sisters Go West, Harper, 1986.
The Blossoms and the Green Phantom, Delacorte, 1987.
A Blossom Promise, Delacorte, 1987.
Beans on the Roof, Delacorte, 1988.
The Burning Questions of Bingo Brown, Viking, 1988.
Bingo Brown and the Language of Love, Viking, 1989.

OTHER

Contributor of articles to *Saturday Evening Post, TV Guide, Look,* and other periodicals.

SIDELIGHTS: As author of such award-winning books as *The Summer of the Swans, The Pinballs, The Night Swimmers,* and others, Betsy Byars has established herself as an honest and sensitive writer dealing with young people and some of the troubling issues they must face growing up today. "The hallmark of a Betsy Byars book is its sensitive and subtle telling that echoes the spoken and unspoken thoughts of young people," writes a *New York Times Book Review* critic. "In a succession of psychologically sound stories . . . she has developed her theme: that the extreme inward pain of adolescence lessens as a person reaches outward." And Julia Briggs remarks in the *Times Literary Supplement* that "Byars's forte is the contemporary scene, and within that, the things real kids say and do, and the painful comedy attendant upon the brink of adolescence. She has a sharp eye for behaviour, so that her books are consistently readable."

Although critics knew of and respected her first six books, it was the publication of her seventh book, *The Summer of the Swans,* that quickly brought Byars to the attention of many more reviewers and readers. The recipient of the John Newbery Medal, *The Summer of the Swans* is the story of an awkward adolescent, Sara, and her discovery of self-worth and real happiness. Another major character in Byars's book is Sara's younger brother,

Charlie, who is mentally-impaired and very much dependent on Sara for many of his physical and emotional needs. One night Charlie slips out of the house and disappears into a nearby forest. Frantically Sara searches for Charlie and finally finds not only a safe, but terrified Charlie, but also gains a new and positive sense of herself.

Ethel L. Heins states in the *Horn Book Magazine* that "seldom are the pain of adolescence and the tragedy of mental retardation presented as sensitively and as unpretentiously as in the story of Sara and Charlie. . . . A subtly told story, echoing the spoken and unspoken thought of young people." "*The Summer of the Swans* is a moving and perceptive family story focusing on the relationship of junior high-aged Sara and her younger brother Charlie," comments a reviewer in *Top of the News.* "Throughout this realistic, tender, and sometimes humourous story there is an authentic emotional tension which characterizes the interactions between family and friends. Both Sara and Charlie are realistically portrayed, and the impact of the 'Summer' on Sara's view of herself comes through with unforgettable poignancy. Betsy Byars, a sensitive writer with an ear and heart attuned to the subtleties of growing up, has created a story of extraordinary understanding and warmth."

Barbara H. Baskin and Karen H. Harris explain in their contribution to *Notes from a Different Drummer: A Guide to Juvenile Fiction Portraying the Handicapped* that *The Summer of the Swans* "is essentially a beautifully written story about a sibling's love and responsibility and how mental retardation affects those feelings. The descriptions of behavior are both tender and accurate. [Byars] can describe scenes revealing limitations in ways that reflect reality and avoid maudlin pity."

Many reviewers agree with Baskin and Harris's assessment of Byars's skill in dealing realistically with children and their problems without becoming overly sentimental. And although many of the problems facing children today are complex, reviewers have also admired Byars's ability to analyze these feelings and get to the heart of the issue. For example, Alice Bach remarks in the *New York Times Book Review:* "Byars [is] a dispassionate craftsman, weaving a sturdy homespun tale with the simple words of plain people. She raises thundering questions, but, lacking the egotist's compulsion to provide pat answers, she challenges us to respond to her characters, to react to their situation—to reach toward our own conclusions rather than to swallow the novel passively. And of course she succeeds." And Marilyn Kaye remarks in another edition of the *New York Times Book Review* that "Byars is at her best taking an uncommon situation and treating it to a simple, forthright exploration. *The Two-Thousand-Pound Goldfish* is a provocative and compelling example. Mrs. Byars's straightforward narration lets pure gut feelings come through."

Even though her writing deals with serious issues of great concern to her readers, Byars manages to show the humorous side of many of life's events. In *Children and Books,* Zena Sutherland, Dianne L. Monson, and May Hill Arbuthnot write that "there is in most of Betsy Byars's writing a quiet, understated sense of humor that children quickly recognize and enjoy. More evident, and just as much appreciated, are her compassion and her understanding for the deepest emotions of children." Elaine Moss explains in the *Times Literary Supplement* that "there are many ways in which the author can distance the agonies children endure: humour is Betsy Byars's chosen path." And finally Ann Thwaite remarks in the *Times Literary Supplement* that "Byars has always had a marvellously sure mixture of humour and deep feeling."

In addition to being widely praised for their thoughtful, humorous, yet down-to-earth treatment of distressing situations affecting many of today's youths, Byars's books have also been hailed as having characters with whom readers readily identify. P. L. Gauch points out in the *New York Times Book Review* "in book after book Mrs. Byars has, through her use of metaphor, created unforgettable characters." And Jean Fritz comments in the *New York Times Book Review* that "Byars has always had the capacity to create unique and believable characters."

"There is something uncanny about the way Betsy Byars transcends the book in your hand and gives you living feeling people instead," Jane Langton writes in the *New York Times Book Review:* "In her Newbery-Award-winning *The Summer of the Swans* the identification between reader and young heroine casts so powerful a spell as to seem a kind of magic realism. In her fine . . . book *The Winged Colt of Casa Mia* the word magic occurs to the reader."

Not only do Byars's characters delight her young readers, but these same characters appeal to the adults who read her books. As Fritz remarks in the *New York Times Book Review:* "Whenever I finish a book by Betsy Byars, I have an overwhelming urge to put a star beside the title along with code letters, P. I.—Parents Invited. Indeed, it would be a shame for parents to miss out on Mrs. Byars's books, for no matter how off-beat her characters are, readers (adults and children alike) are bound to identify with them. For Mrs. Byars has uncanny ability to know the secret lives, the outward postures and the exact words her characters would surely use. . . . Betsy Byars drives every nail home and wastes not a one."

MEDIA ADAPTATIONS: The Eighteenth Emergency was made into a television movie entitled "Psst, Hammerman's after You," produced by American Broadcasting Co. (ABC-TV) in 1973; *The Summer of the Swans* was made into a television movie entitled "Sara's Summer of the Swans," produced on ABC-TV in 1974; *The Pinballs* was adapted for television by ABC-TV in 1977; *The Night Swimmers* was made into a television movie entitled "Daddy, I'm Their Mama Now" and produced on the "ABC Afterschool Special" by ABC-TV in 1982; *Trouble River* and *The Winged Colt of Casa Mia* were adapted for television and produced on "Saturday Morning ABC Specials" by ABC-TV.

AVOCATIONAL INTERESTS: Flying (licensed pilot).

BIOGRAPHICAL/CRITICAL SOURCES:

BOOKS

Baskin, Barbara H. and Karen H. Harris, *Notes from a Different Drummer: A Guide to Juvenile Fiction Portraying the Handicapped,* Bowker, 1977.
Children's Literature Review, Volume I, Gale, 1976.
Contemporary Literary Criticism, Volume XXXV, Gale, 1985.
Rees, David, *Painted Desert, Green Shade,* Horn Book, 1984.
Something about the Author Autobiography Series, Volume I, Gale, 1986.
Sutherland, Zena, Dianne L. Monson, and May Hill Arbuthnot, *Children and Books,* 6th edition, Scott, Foresman, 1981.

PERIODICALS

Book Week, October 10, 1965.
Bulletin of the Center for Children's Books, November, 1972, September, 1973, March, 1974, March, 1975, September, 1976, April, 1977.
Children's Book Review, September, 1973, April, 1979.

Christian Science Monitor, November 4, 1965, May 7, 1970, October 3, 1973, November 7, 1973, June 10, 1975, May 3, 1978.
Commonweal, November 22, 1968.
Horn Book Magazine, February, 1971.
Language Arts, October, 1978, September, 1980, October, 1982.
Los Angeles Times Book Review, January 31, 1988.
New York Review of Books, December 14, 1972.
New York Times, December 4, 1979, December 5, 1980, November 30, 1982.
New York Times Book Review, June 14, 1969, February 28, 1971, April 23, 1972, June 4, 1972, November 5, 1972, May 6, 1973, June 10, 1973, August 19, 1973, November 4, 1973, October 13, 1974, November 3, 1974, December 15, 1974, May 2, 1976, October 7, 1979, November 25, 1979, May 4, 1980, July 19, 1981, May 30, 1982, November 28, 1982, January 2, 1983, November 27, 1983, August 4, 1985, June 15, 1986, October 8, 1989.
Observer, September 25, 1977.
Psychology Today, January 10, 1974.
Publishers Weekly, September 16, 1971, April 17, 1978.
Saturday Review, September 18, 1965, November 9, 1968, March 20, 1971, May 20, 1972, November 29, 1975.
Times Literary Supplement, July 2, 1970, July 20, 1970, April 6, 1973, March 29, 1974, April 4, 1975, September 19, 1975, July 16, 1976, October 21, 1977, July 7, 1978, December 14, 1979, July 18, 1980, July 24, 1981, July 23, 1983, November 25, 1983, February 1, 1985, October 11, 1985, June 20, 1986, November 28, 1986, August 21, 1987.
Top of the News, April, 1971.
Washington Post Book World, May 7, 1972, April 10, 1977, May 13, 1979, April 11, 1980, May 10, 1981, July 12, 1981, October 11, 1981, April 11, 1982, October 10, 1982, October 9, 1983, January 13, 1985, May 10, 1987.
Young Readers' Review, January, 1967.

*   *   *

BYATT, A(ntonia) S(usan Drabble)   1936-

PERSONAL: Born August 24, 1936, in Sheffield, England; daughter of John Frederick (a judge) and Kathleen Marie (Bloor) Drabble; married Ian Charles Rayner Byatt (an economist), July 4, 1959 (divorced, 1969); married Peter John Duffy; children: (first marriage) Antonia, Charles (died, 1972); (second marriage) Isabel, Miranda. *Education:* Newnham College, Cambridge, B.A. (first class honors), 1957; graduate study at Bryn Mawr College, 1957-58, and Somerville College, Oxford, 1958-59. *Politics:* "Radical."

ADDRESSES: Home—37 Rusholme Rd., London S.W.15, England.

CAREER: University of London, London, England, staff member in extra-mural department, 1962-71, University College, lecturer, 1972-80, senior lecturer in English, 1981-83, admissions tutor in English, 1980-83; full-time writer, 1983—. Associate of Newnham College, Cambridge, 1977—; fellow of University College, London, 1984—. Part-time lecturer in department of liberal studies, Central School of Art and Design, London, 1965-69; British Council Lecturer in Spain, 1978, India, 1981, and in Germany, Australia, Hong Kong, China, and Korea; George Eliot Centenary Lecturer, 1980. Has done several radio broadcasts and interviews. Member of panel of judges for Booker Prize, 1973, Hawthornden Prize, and David Higham Memorial Prize; member of British Broadcasting Corp. (BBC) Social Effects of Television Advisory Group, 1974-77, member of Communications and Cultural Studies Board of the Council for National Academic Awards, 1978; member of Kingman Committee on the Teaching of English, 1987-88.

MEMBER: Society of Authors (member of committee of management, 1984-88; chairman of committee, 1986-88).

AWARDS, HONORS: English Speaking Union fellowship, 1957-58; fellow of the Royal Society of Literature, 1983; Silver Pen Award for *Still Life;* D. Litt. from University of Bradford, 1987.

WRITINGS:

The Shadow of a Sun (novel), Harcourt, 1964.
Degrees of Freedom: The Novels of Iris Murdoch (literary criticism), Barnes & Noble, 1965.
The Game (novel), Chatto & Windus, 1967, Scribner, 1968.
(Contributor) Isobel Armstrong, editor, *The Major Victorian Poets Reconsidered,* Routledge & Kegan Paul, 1969.
Wordsworth and Coleridge in Their Time (literary criticism), Nelson, 1970, Crane, Russak, 1973, reissued as *Unruly Times,* Hogarth, 1989.
Iris Murdoch, Longman, 1976.
The Virgin in the Garden (first novel in tetralogy), Chatto & Windus, 1978, Knopf, 1979.
(Editor and author of introduction) George Eliot, *The Mill on the Floss,* Penguin, 1979.
(Contributor) Malcolm Bradbury, editor, *The Contemporary English Novel,* Edward Arnold, 1979.
Still Life (second novel in tetralogy), Chatto & Windus, 1986, Scribner, 1987.
Sugar and Other Stories, Scribner, 1987.
(Editor) George Eliot, *Selected Essays, Poems and Other Writings,* Penguin, 1989.
(Editor) Robert Browning, *Dramatic Monologues,* Folio Society, 1990.
Possession: A Romance (novel), Chatto & Windus, 1990.

Author of prefaces to the following novels; published by Virago, except as indicated: Elizabeth Bowen, *The House in Paris,* Penguin, 1976; Grace Paley, *Enormous Changes at the Last Minute,* 1979; Paley, *The Little Disturbances of Man,* 1980; Willa Cather, *My Antonia,* and *A Lost Lady,* 1980, and *My Mortal Enemy, Shadow on the Rock, Death Comes to the Archbishop, O Pioneers!,* and *Lucy Grayheart.*

Also author of dramatized radio documentary on Leo Tolstoy, July, 1978; author of dramatized portraits of George Eliot and Samuel Taylor Coleridge, for the National Portrait Gallery. Regular reviewer for the London *Times* and the *New Statesman;* contributor of reviews to *Encounter, New Review,* and *American Studies.* Member of editorial board of *Encyclopaedia,* Longman-Penguin, 1989.

WORK IN PROGRESS: The third novel of the tetralogy.

SIDELIGHTS: Because of A. S. Byatt's wide experience as a critic, novelist, editor, and lecturer, she "offers in her work an intellectual kaleidoscope of our contemporary world," writes Caryn McTighe Musil in *Dictionary of Literary Biography.* "Her novels, like her life, are dominated by an absorbing, discriminating mind which finds intellectual passions as vibrant and consuming as emotional ones." Musil indicates that Byatt's first novel, *The Shadow of a Sun,* reflects the author's own struggle to combine the role of critic with that of novelist on the one hand and the role of mother with that of visionary on the other. *The Game,* "a piece of technical virtuosity," according to Musil, "is also a taut novel that explores with a courage and determined

honesty greater than [D. H.] Lawrence's the deepest levels of antagonism that come with intimacy. Widely reviewed, especially in Great Britain, *The Game* established Byatt's reputation as an important contemporary novelist, though the book's readership was not extensive."

Byatt's novel *The Virgin in the Garden* is described by *Times Literary Supplement* reviewer Michael Irwin as a "careful, complex novel." The book's action is set in 1953, the year of the coronation of Queen Elizabeth II, and Irwin indicates that "its theme is growing up, coming of age, tasting knowledge." The book "is a highly intellectual operation," points out Iris Murdoch in *New Statesman.* "The characters do a great deal of thinking, and have extremely interesting thoughts which are developed at length." "The novel's central symbol," Musil relates, "is Queen Elizabeth I, a monarch Byatt sees as surviving because she used her mind and thought things out, unlike her rival, Mary, Queen of Scots, who was 'very female and got it wrong.' " In Musil's opinion, the work initiates "the middle phase of [Byatt's] career as a novelist. Much denser [than her previous novels] and dependent on her readers' erudition," *The Virgin in the Garden* "achieves a style that suits Byatt. It blends her acquisitive, intellectual bent with her imaginative compulsion to tell stories," Musil points out. With publication of *The Virgin in the Garden,* maintains Musil, "Byatt has come fully into her own as a fiction writer and has guaranteed her place in literary histories of the future."

Byatt told *CA:* "Perhaps the most important thing to say about my books is that they try to be about the life of the mind as well as of society and the relations between people. I admire—am excited by—intellectual curiosity of any kind (scientific, linguistic, psychological) and also by literature as a complicated, huge, interrelating pattern. I also like recording small observed facts and feelings. I see writing and thinking as a passionate activity, like any other.

"I hope I am a European writer as well as being a local English one. I am at the moment exercised by the problem of communicable detail—can an Italian or a Californian or an Indian take any interest in or appreciate the nuances of an English bus queue? How many readers will have read Milton's *Paradise Lost* or Homer's *The Aeneid?* How many who have not will be annoyed to find them in my books? (This is a reaction I still find puzzling).

"I held a full-time university reading post for eleven years and now feel entirely happy, for the first time in my life, at the prospect of writing full time, thinking things out from beginning to end, and reading for my own purposes. I enjoyed teaching John Donne, Robert Browning, George Eliot, Charles Dickens, Samuel Taylor Coleridge, John Keats, Wallace Stevens, Emily Dickinson, and Henry James. But now reading is even more exciting. The novelist I most love is Marcel Proust. After him Balzac, Dickens, Eliot, Thomas Mann and James, Iris Murdoch, Ford Maddox Ford, and Willa Cather. And Leo Tolstoy and Fyodor Dostoevsky.

"Of course I am a feminist. But I don't want to be required to write to a feminist programme, and I feel uneasy when this seems to be asked of me. I am a bit too old to be a naturally political animal."

BIOGRAPHICAL/CRITICAL SOURCES:

BOOKS

Contemporary Literary Criticism, Volume 19, Gale, 1981.
Dictionary of Literary Biography, Volume 14: *British Novelists Since 1960,* Gale, 1983.

PERIODICALS

Books and Bookmen, January 4, 1979.
Chicago Tribune Book World, January 12, 1986.
Encounter, July, 1968.
Los Angeles Times, November 18, 1985.
Ms., June, 1979.
New Leader, April 23, 1979.
New Statesman, November 3, 1978.
New York Times Book Review, July 26, 1964, March 17, 1968,
    April 1, 1979, November 24, 1985, July 19, 1987.
Times (London), June 6, 1981, April 9, 1987, March 1, 1990.
Times Literary Supplement, January 2, 1964, January 19, 1967,
    November 3, 1978, June 28, 1985, March 2, 1990.
Washington Post, March 16, 1979, November 22, 1985.

C

CABRERA INFANTE, G(uillermo) 1929-
(G. Cain, Guillermo Cain)

PERSONAL: Born April 22, 1929, in Gibara, Cuba; immigrated to London, England, 1966; naturalized British citizen; son of Guillermo Cabrera Lopez (a journalist) and Zoila Infante; married Marta Calvo, August 18, 1953 (divorced, October, 1961); married Miriam Gomez, December 9, 1961; children: (first marriage) Ana, Carola. *Education:* Graduated from University of Havana, Cuba, 1956. *Politics:* "Reactionary on the left." *Religion:* Catholic.

ADDRESSES: Home—53 Gloucester Rd., London SW7, England. *Agent*—Carmen Balcells, Diagonal 580, Barcelona 21, Spain.

CAREER: Writer. School of Journalism, Havana, Cuba, professor of English literature, 1960-61; Government of Cuba, Cuban embassy, Brussels, Belgium, cultural attache, 1962-64, charge d'affaires, 1964-65; scriptwriter for Twentieth-Century Fox and Cupid Productions, 1967-72. Visiting professor, University of Virginia, spring, 1982.

MEMBER: Writers Guild of Great Britain.

AWARDS, HONORS: Asi en la paz como en la guerra was nominated for Prix International de Literature (France), 1962; unpublished manuscript version of *Tres tristes tigres* won Biblioteca Breve Prize (Spain), 1964, and was nominated for Prix Formentor—International Publishers Prize, 1965; Guggenheim fellowship for creative writing, 1970; Prix du Meilleur Livre Etranger (France), 1971, *Tres tristes tigres.*

WRITINGS:

FICTION

Asi en la paz como en la guerra: Cuentos (title means "In Peace as in War: Stories"), Revolucion (Havana), 1960.
Vista del amanecer en el tropico, Seix Barral (Barcelona, Spain), 1965, translation by Suzanne Jill Levine published as *View of Dawn in the Tropics,* Harper, 1978.
Tres tristes tigres (novel), Seix Barral, 1967, translation by Donald Gardner, Levine, and the author published as *Three Trapped Tigers,* Harper, 1971.
La Habana para un infante difunto, Seix Barral, 1979, translation by Levine and the author published as *Infante's Inferno,* Harper, 1984.

FILM CRITICISM

(Under pseudonym G. Cain) *Un oficio del siglo veinte* (title means "A Twentieth-Century Job"; film reviews originally published in magazine *Carteles;* also see below), Revolucion, 1963.
Arcadia todas las noches (title means "Arcadia Every Night"), Seix Barral, 1978.

OTHER

(Editor) *Mensajes de libertad: La Espana rebelde—Ensayos selectos,* Movimiento Universitario Revolucionario (Lima, Peru), 1961.
"Vanishing Point" (screenplay), Twentieth-Century Fox, 1970.
(Translator into Spanish) James Joyce, *Dublineses* (title means "The Dubliners"), Lumen (Barcelona), 1972.
O, Seix Barral, 1975.
Exorcismos del esti(l)o (title means "Summer Exorcisms" and "Exorcising Style"; English, French, and Spanish text), Seix Barral, 1976.
Holy Smoke (nonfiction; English text), Harper, 1986.

Also author of screenplay, "Wonderwall," 1968, and of unfilmed screenplay, "Under the Volcano," based on Malcolm Lowry's novel of the same title. Also translator of stories by Mark Twain, Ambrose Bierce, Sherwood Anderson, Ernest Hemingway, William Faulkner, Dashiell Hammett, J. D. Salinger, Vladimir Nabokov, and others. Work is represented in many anthologies. Contributor to periodicals, including *New Yorker, New Republic, El Pais* (Spain), and *Plural* (Mexico). *Carteles* (Cuban magazine), film reviewer under pseudonymn G. Cain, 1954-60, fiction editor, 1957-60; editor of *Lunes* (weekly literary supplement of Cuban newspaper, *Revolucion*), 1959-61.

WORK IN PROGRESS: Cuerpos divinos (title means "Heavenly Bodies"), a novel about women and writing.

SIDELIGHTS: Talking about his award-winning first novel *Tres tristes tigres,* translated as *Three Trapped Tigers,* Cuban-born writer Guillermo Cabrera Infante tells Rita Guibert in *Seven Voices:* "I would prefer everyone to consider the book solely as a joke lasting about five hundred pages. Latin American literature errs on the side of excessive seriousness, sometimes solemnity. It is like a mask of solemn words, which writers and readers put up with by mutual consent."

In the novel, we hear the voices of a group of friends as they take part in the nightlife of pre-Castro Havana. The friends take turns narrating the story using the colloquial speech of the lower-class inhabitants of that city. Told from so many perspectives using the language of such a small population group, the narrative is not always easy to follow. Elias L. Rivers explains in *Modern Language Notes:* "While some passages are readily accessible to any reader, others are obscured by Cuban vernaculars in phonetic transcription and by word-plays and allusions of many different kinds. A multiplicity of 'voices' engage in narrative, dialogue and soliloquy. [The novel] is a test which fascinates as it eludes and frustrates; the over-all narrative sense is by no-means obvious."

The importance of spoken language in *Three Trapped Tigers* is apparent even in the book's title, which in its English version repeats only the alliteration found in the Spanish title and not the title's actual meaning. Inside the book, the emphasis on sound continues as the characters pun relentlessly. There are so many puns in the book that *New Republic* contributor Gregory Rabassa maintains that in it Cabrera Infante "established himself as the punmaster of Spanish-American literature." Appearing most often are literary puns, including such examples as "Shame's Choice" used to refer to James Joyce, "Scotch Fizzgerald" for Scott Fitzgerald and "Somersault Mom" for Somerset Maugham. In another example, a bongo player—a member of the group of friends whose exploits are followed in the novel—is called "Vincent Bon Gogh."

If the emphasis on spoken rather than written language makes complete understanding of the novel difficult, it has made translating nearly impossible. Comparison of the Spanish, English and French editions of the book prove that readers of each language are not reading the same text. "What Cabrera [Infante] has really done," comments Roger Sale in the *New York Review of Books,* "is to write, presumably with the help of his translators, three similar but different novels." Because of the word play, Sale continues, "quite obviously no translation can work if it attempts word-for-word equivalents."

Playing with words is also an important part of Cabrera Infante's next novel, *Infante's Inferno,* and his nonfiction work, *Holy Smoke.* The latter—Cabrera Infante's first book written originally in English—tells the history of the cigar and describes famous smoking scenes from literature and film. Unlike the nearly universal acclaim received for *Three Trapped Tigers,* critics were unable to reach a consensus on these two works. While some praised Cabrera Infante's continued use of puns as innovative, other had grown tired of the Cuban's verbal contortions.

Commenting on *Infante's Inferno* in the *New York Review of Books* Michael Wood complains that Cabrera Infante's relentless punning "unrepentedly mangles language and hops from one tongue to another like a frog released from the throat. Some of the jokes are . . . terrible. . . . Others are so cumbersome, so fiendishly worked for, that the noise of grinding machinery deafens all the chance of laughter." *New York Review of Books* contributor Josh Rubins has similar problems with *Holy Smoke.* He comments, "In *Holy Smoke* . . . the surfeit of puns seems to arise not from mania . . . , but from mere tic. Or, worse yet, from a computer program."

Other reviewers are not so harsh in their criticism. In Enrique Fernandez's *Voice Literary Supplement* review of *Infante's Inferno,* for example, the critic observes that the novel is written in "an everyday Cuban voice, unaffected, untrammeled [and], authentic." John Gross of the *New York Times* hails Cabrera Infante as a master in the use of language. Commenting on *Holy*

Smoke, he claims: "Conrad and Nabokov apart, no other writer for whom English is a second language can ever have used it with more virtuousity. He is a master of idiomatic echoes and glancing allusions; he keeps up a constant barrage of wordplay, which is often outrageous, but no more outrageous than he intends it to be."

Three Trapped Tigers established Cabrera Infante's reputation as a writer of innovative fiction, a reputation that some critics find justified by his later work. Cabrera Infante once described his literary beginnings to *CA:* "It all began with parody. If it were not for a parody I wrote on a Latin American writer who was later to win the Nobel Prize, I wouldn't have become a professional writer and I wouldn't qualify to be here at all. My parents wanted me to go to University and I would have liked to become a doctor. But somehow that dreadful novel crossed my path. After reading a few pages (I just couldn't stomach it all, of course) and being only seventeen at the time, I said to myself, 'Why, if that's what writing is all about—*anch'io sono scrittore* [I am also a writer]!' To prove I too was a writer I wrote a parody of the pages I had read. It was a dreadfully serious parody and unfortunately the short story I wrote was taken by what was then the most widely-read publication in Latin America, the Cuban magazine, *Bohemia.* They paid me what at the time I considered a fortune and I was hooked: probably hooked by fortune, probably hooked by fame but certainly hooked by writing."

AVOCATIONAL INTERESTS: Birdwatching, old movies.

BIOGRAPHICAL/CRITICAL SOURCES:

BOOKS

Contemporary Literary Criticism, Gale, Volume 5, 1976, Volume 25, 1983, Volume 45, 1987.
Gallagher, David Patrick, *Modern Latin American Literature,* Oxford University Press, 1973.
Guibert, Rita, *Seven Voices,* Knopf, 1973.
Nelson, Ardis L., *Cabrera Infante in the Menippean Tradition,* Juan de la Cuesta (Newark, Delaware), 1983.
Souza, Raymond D., *Major Cuban Novelists: Innovation and Tradition,* University of Missouri Press, 1976.
Tittler, Jonathan, *Narrative Irony in the Contemporary Spanish-American Novel,* Cornell University Press, 1984.

PERIODICALS

Book World, October 3, 1971.
Commonweal, November 12, 1971.
London Review of Books, October 4-17, 1984, February 6, 1986.
Los Angeles Times, June 6, 1984.
Modern Language Notes, March, 1977.
Nation, November 4, 1978.
New Republic, July 9, 1984.
Newsweek, October 25, 1971.
New Yorker, September 19, 1977.
New York Review of Books, December 16, 1971, June 28, 1984, May 8, 1986.
New York Times Book Review, October 17, 1971, May 6, 1984, March 2, 1986.
Observer, September 2, 1984, October 13, 1985, December 21, 1986.
Paris Review, spring, 1983.
Review, January 10, 1972.
Time, January 10, 1972.
Times Literary Supplement, April 18, 1968, October 12, 1984, August 26, 1986.
Village Voice, March 25, 1986.

Voice Literary Supplement, April 18, 1968, October 12, 1984, August 29, 1986.
Washington Post Book World, January 28, 1979, May 27, 1984.
World Literature Today, spring, 1977, summer, 1981.

*   *   *

CADE, Toni
See BAMBARA, Toni Cade

*   *   *

CAIN, G.
See CABRERA INFANTE, G(uillermo)

*   *   *

CAIN, Guillermo
See CABRERA INFANTE, G(uillermo)

*   *   *

CAIN, James M(allahan) 1892-1977

PERSONAL: Born July 1, 1892, in Annapolis, Md.; died October 27, 1977, of a heart attack in University Park, Md.; son of James William (a former president of Washington College) and Rose Cecilia (Mallahan) Cain; married Mary Rebekah Clough, 1920 (divorced); married Elina Sjosted Tyszecka, 1927 (divorced); married Aileen Pringle, 1944 (divorced); married Florence Macbeth Whitwell (an opera singer), 1947 (deceased). *Education:* Washington College, A.B., 1910, A.M., 1917. *Politics:* Democrat.

ADDRESSES: Home—6707 44th Ave., University Park, Hyattsville, Md. 20782.

CAREER: Journalist and writer. *Baltimore American,* Baltimore, Md., staff member, 1917-18; *Baltimore Sun,* Baltimore, reporter, 1919-23; St. John's College, Annapolis, Md., professor of journalism, 1923-24; *New York World,* New York City, editorial writer, 1924-31; *New Yorker,* New York City, managing editor, beginning 1931; screenwriter in Hollywood, Calif., 1932-48. *Military service:* U.S. Army, American Expeditionary Forces, 1918-19; served as editor in chief of *Lorraine Cross,* official newspaper of the 79th Division.

AWARDS, HONORS: Grand Masters Award, Mystery Writers of America, 1970.

WRITINGS:

NOVELS

The Postman Always Rings Twice (also see below), Knopf, 1934, reprinted, Lightyear, 1981.
Serenade (also see below), Knopf, 1937, reprinted AMS Press, 1981.
Mildred Pierce (also see below), Knopf, 1941, reprinted, Lightyear, 1981.
Love's Lovely Counterfeit, Knopf, 1942, reprinted, Vintage Books, 1979.
Double Indemnity (also see below), Avon, 1943, reprinted Random House, 1989.
The Embezzler (also see below), New Avon Library, 1944.
Past All Dishonor (also see below), Knopf, 1946.
The Butterfly (also see below), Knopf, 1947, reprinted, Vintage Books, 1979.
Sinful Woman (also see below), Avon, 1947, reprinted, Creative Arts Books, 1989.

The Moth, Knopf, 1948, abridged edition, New American Library, 1950.
Dishonour, Hale, 1949.
Jealous Woman (also see below), Avon, 1950, reprinted, Creative Arts Books, 1989.
Galatea, Knopf, 1953.
The Root of His Evil, R. Hale, 1954, reprinted, Creative Arts Books, 1989, published as *Shameless,* Avon, 1979.
Mignon, Dial, 1962.
The Magician's Wife, Dial, 1965, reprinted, Carnegie Mellon, 1985.
Rainbow's End, Mason/Charter, 1975.
The Institute, Mason/Charter, 1976.

OMNIBUS EDITIONS

Three of a Kind: Career in C Major, The Embezzler, Double Indemnity ("Career in C Major" originally titled "Two Can Sing," 1938), Knopf, 1943.
Cain Omnibus: The Postman Always Rings Twice, Serenade, Mildred Pierce, World, 1946.
The Embezzler [and] *Double Indemnity,* Triangle Books, 1948.
Jealous Woman [and] *Sinful Woman,* R. Hale, 1955.
Cain x 3: Three Novels (contains *The Postman Always Rings Twice, Mildred Pierce,* and *Double Indemnity;* a Book-of-the-Month selection), introduction by Tom Wolfe, Knopf, 1969.
Three Novels by James M. Cain: Double Indemnity, The Postman Always Rings Twice, Serenade, Bantam, 1973.
Hard Cain (contains *Sinful Woman, Jealous Woman,* and *The Root of His Evil*), introduction by Harlan Ellison, Gregg, 1980.
The Baby in the Icebox, and Other Short Fiction ("The Baby in the Icebox" first published in *American Mercury,* 1933), edited by Roy Hoopes, Holt, 1981.
Career in C Major, and Other Fiction, McGraw, 1986.
Three by Cain: Serenade, Love's Lovely Counterfeit, The Butterfly, McKay, 1989.

OTHER

Our Government (sketches), Knopf, 1930.
"The Postman Always Rings Twice," (play based on his novel of the same title), first produced on Broadway, February 25, 1936.
(Editor) *For Men Only: A Collection of Short Stories,* World, 1944.
The Institute, Dorchester, 1982.
Cloud Nine, Mysterious Press, 1984.
The Enchanted Isle, Mysterious Press, 1986.

Also author of short plays, including, "Hero," "Hemp," "Red, White, and Blue," "Trial by Jury," "Theological Interlude," "Citizenship," "Will of the People," published in *American Mercury,* 1926-29. Author of uncollected stories, including "Dead Man," published in *American Mercury,* 1936, "The Birthday Party," published in *Ladies' Home Journal,* 1936, "The Girl in the Story," published in *Liberty,* 1940, and "Visitor," published in *Esquire,* 1961.

WORK IN PROGRESS: An autobiography.

SIDELIGHTS: When James M. Cain moved to Hollywood to become a screenwriter, he had already run the gamut of writing careers. Behind him lay stints as a newspaper reporter, a professor of journalism at St. John's College, an editorial writer for Walter Lippmann, and the managing editor of the *New Yorker* magazine. And yet none of his efforts had fully taken hold; his career in journalism had been "fragmented and inconclusive," according to Kevin Starr, who reported in *New Republic* that Cain "was on the way to becoming just another hard-drinking Irish-American journalist with baffled aspirations in the direction of literature." And then, in 1934, having been fired by Paramount Pictures and in desperate need of money, the 42-year-old writer published his first novel, *The Postman Always Rings Twice.* Described by Cain biographer Roy Hoopes as "one of those rarest of literary achievements in America: a phenomenal best seller that received the highest acclaim from critics," *Postman* brought Cain "out of obscurity and into the literary limelight where he remained for fourteen years."

After *Postman,* Cain wrote *Double Indemnity, Mildred Pierce,* and *Serenade.* These four books earned him a reputation as a "tough-guy" writer or, as David Madden called him in *James M. Cain,* "the twenty-minute egg" of the "hard-boiled" school. "Cain and other hard-boiled writers," Madden explained in his critical study, "wrote not only about but mainly to the masses, giving violent impetus to their forbidden dreams, dramatizing their darkest temptations and their basic physical drives." His protagonists were the kind of people you read about "almost every day in the newspapers," according to William Rose Benet in *Saturday Review.* "They are chiefly stupid, slightly pathetic, capable of rape, arson, or murder in a sort of dumb, driven way. They have glimmers of decency, passions that overcome them, and are chiefly selfish and morally composed of gelatin while being big, husky brutes to outward view.

Cain resented such categorization. "I don't know what they're talking about—'tough,' 'hard-boiled.' I tried to write as 'people talk,' " he told David Zinsser of *Paris Review.* When asked to describe his work, he said: "I, so far as I can sense the pattern of my mind, write of the wish that comes true, for some reason a terrifying concept, at least to my imagination. I think my stories have some quality of the opening of a forbidden box." What Cain's "forbidden box" contains, according to W. M. Frohock in his *The Novel of Violence in America: 1920-1950,* "invariably turns out to be sex, experienced with perfect animal intensity, sometimes with a little hint of the abnormal or the forbidden about it." Though Cain repeatedly insisted to Zinsser and other interviewers that he took no interest in violence, Frohock argued that "sex, so conceived, is inseparable from violence. Violence is at once associated with the sexual act itself, and made an inevitable accompaniment of anything which tends to frustrate the sexual experience. In addition violence stimulates sexual activity, as in the scene of Nick's murder [in *The Postman Always Rings Twice*]. For Cain, sex and violence are not so much subjects as necessary accessories of the plot." And plot, Frohock continued, is "the essence of the Cain novel."

Chicago Tribune Book World critic David Mamet observed that "the understanding of plot that Cain embraced goes back . . . to Aristotle: Cain discovered the dramatic/tragic plot—discarding narration, exposition, and characterization in favor of event." But unlike the Greek dramas, Cain's books, Frohock argued, do not strike a tragic note "because the violence in them is not endowed with any sort of moral significance. We are aware of his violence not as something which we must accept because it is a part of Man's Fate, but as something for a clever writer to play tricks with." For these reasons, Frohock maintained that "nothing he has ever written has been entirely out of the trash category." But Ross Macdonald, writing in the *New York Times Book Review,* disagreed. Citing Cain's ability to transmute "blood into symbol" as the "stuff of art," he concluded that Cain was "a conscious and deliberate artist" whose novel *The Postman Always Rings Twice* had "moral and symbolic overtones."

James T. Farrell in his *Literature and Morality* expressed still another point of view: "Writers like Cain stand between the work of a serious and tragic character which has been fathered in America by such men as [Theodore] Dreiser and the work derived from the more-or-less forgotten writings of Robert W. Chambers, Gene Stratton-Porter, or Harold Bell Wright. And in this in-between, neither-fish-nor-fowl literary medium, James M. Cain has become the master. He is a literary thrill producer who profits by the reaction against the sentimentality of other years and, at the same time, gains from the prestige of more serious and exploratory writing."

While the argument over the seriousness of Cain's work continues, so too does his popularity. *Cain x 3,* a 1969 reprint of his most popular works, *Postman, Double Indemnity,* and *Mildred Pierce,* found a wide audience, as Macdonald observed. "There is," he said, "a new generation of readers for Cain's stories—*Cain x 3* should make its way into the universities." And Frohock wrote that "in spite of the cheapness which sooner or later finds its way into his novels, an inordinate number of intelligent and fully literate people have read him. He has been translated in many parts of the world, and writers whose stature makes him look stunted have paid him the compliment of imitating him as Albert Camus did, for example, in *The Stranger.*"

In his *Nation* review of *Cain x 3,* Kenneth Lamott explained Cain's continued appeal: "There is the remembered tautness of structure, the absolute control of the well-articulated plot, the cold eye for the essential truth about men and women. The language is spare and clean, only occasionally breaking down into cliche. It is hardly an original observation, but watching Cain at work can still give the reader that particular pleasure that comes from watching a master craftsman, a cabinetmaker fitting a joint, or a potter throwing a pot. I would not go as far as Tom Wolfe, who in his introduction to this book suggests that Norman Mailer might well sit at Cain's feet to learn how to become a real novelist, but the spirit of the suggestion is not without merit."

Despite the success of what Mamet called the "California novels," Cain experienced many bouts of failure in his fiction-writing career. His first effort to write a novel, for example, was a vain attempt as Cain explained to *Paris Review:* "In 1922 when I was still on the *Baltimore Sun,* I took the winter off to go down and work in the mines. I tried to write the Great American Novel, and wrote three of them, none of them any good. I had to come slinking back to work admitting that the Great American Novel hadn't been written."

Six years passed before Cain sold his first piece of fiction—a short story published by H. L. Mencken in the *American Mercury.* Entitled "Pastorale," it was a humorous rendering of a grisly murder, told—according to Hoopes—in the Ring Lardner manner and significant for reasons which he outlined in his *Chicago Tribune Book World* review: "In the first place, Cain now found that he could tell a story in the first person, preferably in the voice of some 'lowlife character,' as his mother called that type. [And in the second,] he also found his favorite theme: Although two people may get away with committing a crime, they cannot live with it." Encouraged by the success of "Pastorale," Cain continued to write short fiction and his name eventually came to the attention of several Hollywood producers who invited him to California. Since he was unhappy in New York, Cain accepted the offer, moving west in 1931. But his efforts at screenwriting were failures and, as Hoopes reported in his introduction to *The Baby in the Icebox, and Other Short Fiction,* "within six months of his arrival in Hollywood, Cain was out of a job in the middle of the Depression, forty years old, and supporting a second wife and her two young children."

Unwilling to return east, Cain took up free-lance writing and, Hoopes reported, "as he drove around in his 1932 Ford roadster, he began to feel more and more that California and its people provided a natural milieu for his writing. And there was one gas station, where he regularly stopped, that provided a spark that would eventually ignite Cain's phenomenal career as a writer of controversial best-sellers. 'Always this bosomy looking thing comes out—commonplace, but sexy, the kind you have ideas about,' he later told an interviewer. 'We always talked while she filled up my tank. One day I read in the paper where a woman who runs a filling station knocked off her husband. Can it be this bosomy thing? I go by and sure enough the place is closed. I inquire. Yes, she's the one—this appetizing but utterly commonplace woman.'

"He began to think: What about a novel in which a woman and a typical California automobile tramp kill the woman's husband to get his gas station and car? Cain and [his wife] Elina discussed the idea for months, but he was still not ready for a long story. At the same time, he only felt comfortable in his writing when he pretended to be someone else, telling his story in the first person, in the manner of Ring Lardner. . . . So Cain put his idea for a novel in the back of his mind and decided to try another short story. The result was 'The Baby in the Icebox,' and like 'Pastorale,'. . . it was written in the first person, Ring Lardner style. But unlike his earlier stories, 'The Baby in the Icebox' was set in the West and had characters who were western in origin. Suddenly Cain found something happening in his fiction." As Cain reported to *Paris Review,* "Out there in California I began writing in the local idiom. Everything broke for me."

Paramount bought the movie rights to "Icebox" and produced the story as "She Made Her Bed," the first in a succession of nine Cain stories and novels that would be adapted to the screen. Meanwhile, in New York, H. L. Mencken had shown "Icebox" to Alfred A. Knopf, a prominent publisher, who liked it so much that he encouraged Cain to try his hand at a novel. Cain did, and just six months later, in June 1933, he had a 159-page manuscript that would eventually become *The Postman Always Rings Twice.*

In an interview with *Paris Review,* Cain discussed the origins of the story: "It was based on the Snyder-Grey case, which was in the papers about then. . . . Grey and this woman Snyder killed her husband for the insurance money. Walter Lippmann went to that trial one day and she brushed by him. . . . Walter said it seemed very odd to be inhaling the perfume or being brushed by the dress of a woman he knew was going to be electrocuted. So the Snyder-Grey case provided the basis. The bit influence in how I wrote *The Postman Always Rings Twice* was this strange guy, Vincent Lawrence, who had more effect on my writing than anyone else. He had a device which he thought was so important—the 'love rack' he called it. . . . What he meant by the 'love rack' was the poetic situation whereby the audience felt the love between the characters. He called this 'the one, the two, and the three.'"

One time, reported Hoopes in the *Washington Post,* "when Lawrence was talking about his 'love rack,' Cain asked: 'Why couldn't the whole thing be a love rack; why such attention to the one episode where they fall in love?' Cain asked why every episode in the story could not be written with a view to its effect on the love story. Lawrence thought that this had possibilities." So Cain wrote a story about Frank Chambers, a young drifter, who wanders into a diner run by a Greek named Nick and his restless wife, Cora, who is disgusted by Nick's "greasiness."

After seeing Cora, Frank agrees to work in the restaurant and they become lovers. Soon Cora convinces Frank to help her murder Nick so that she will inherit his property. Although the first attempt is unsuccessful, their second effort succeeds. But, according to Hoopes, "the murder eventually becomes their love rack, and they are brought to justice when Cora is killed in an automobile accident and Frank is wrongly found guilty of her murder."

The first version of the story was called *Bar-B-Q,* and Knopf turned it down. "At that point," Cain told *Publishers Weekly,* "Lippmann wanted to see the book. He thought he could do something with it. He took it to Macmillan and Macmillan turned it down. Then Lippmann took it back to Knopf and they decided to publish it." But there was one final problem—Knopf did not like the title and wanted it changed. In his *Washington Post* article, Hoopes explained how *Bar-B-Q* was renamed: "Around this time Cain and Lawrence were musing about the agony of sweating out the publication of a first novel and Lawrence told him about sending his first play to a New York producer. Lawrence had been living in Boston then and would go to the window every day to watch for the postman; when he could not stand the waiting, he would go into the back yard, but always listening for the ring. 'And no fooling about that ring. The son-of-a-bitch always rang twice, so you'd know it was the postman.' Lawrence's story reminded Cain of the old Irish tradition that the postman must always ring or in olden days, knock twice. He turned to Lawrence and said, "Vincent, I think I've got my title," Hoopes reported. And Vincent Lawrence's response to Cain's suggestion of *The Postman Always Rings Twice* was "Hey, that is a title. He sure did ring twice for [Frank] Chambers, didn't he?" (Though Chambers did kill Nick, his first attempt was unsuccessful, thus exemplifying how, as Macdonald notes, "everything that happens in this novel happens twice, the first time with a twist [the cat dies instead of the Greek], the second time with a reverse twist.")

Like "Icebox," *Postman* was sold to a movie studio, though it was not filmed for more than ten years. "Mr. Cain's subject matter at the time he wrote was shocking," explained *New York Times* critic John Leonard. "The book was tried for obscenity in Boston, and his own Hollywood did not dare make a movie of it until 10 years after publication, with Lana Turner and John Garfield. And the movie makers dared only after the box-office successes of "Double Indemnity," directed by Billy Wilder, and "Mildred Pierce," for which Joan Crawford won an Academy Award." Though the success of *Postman* got Cain back into the studios as a writer, he was never invited to do the adaptations of his own books. Furthermore, he considered his efforts totally unsuccessful: "I want it understood that I consider I have a record of failure unmatched in Hollywood's history," he told *Publishers Weekly.*

In the early 1940s, Cain attempted to establish an authority headed by what he called "a tough mug," to whom authors would turn over their copyrights. "The authority," explained Leonard, "would have protected authors' rights in courts and legislative halls, represented writers in litigation, negotiated contracts, and lobbied in Washington." While Leonard believed that Cain may have been motivated by the discrepancy between the $12 million that Hollywood made on his books and the $100,000 he received, some of Cain's contemporaries interpreted the project as a "Communist plot" or a "totalitarian attempt to control and manipulate creative talent." Cain's efforts failed.

Shortly afterwards, in 1947, Cain returned to Maryland, where he lived until his death in 1977. "During those twenty-nine years," reported Joe Flaherty in the *New York Times Book Review,* "he wrote nine novels. Three found a publisher; none found a public. Why he left California (he called it El Dorado) and went back to the Eastern Shore is a psychological mystery." In assessing his contribution to modern literature, Madden, writing in his *James M. Cain,* concluded: "Certainly Cain's art, more than anything else, moves even the serious reader to almost complete emotional commitment to the traumatic experiences Cain renders; and this artistic control convinces me that without his finest novels—*The Postman, Serenade, Mildred Pierce,* and *The Butterfly*—the cream of our twentieth-century fiction would be thinner. Straddling realism and expressionism, he often gives us a vivid account of life on the American scene as he has observed and experienced it; and, in his best moments, he provides the finer vibrations afforded by the esthetic experience. Cain takes us through experiences whose special quality is found in no other writer's work."

MEDIA ADAPTATIONS: Two of Cain's short stories have been filmed: "The Baby in the Icebox" was released as "She Made Her Bed," by Paramount in 1934; *Career in C Major* was filmed as "Wife, Husband, Friend," by Twentieth Century Fox in 1938. *The Embezzler* was filmed as "Money and the Woman" by Warner Bros. in 1940; *Double Indemnity* was filmed by Paramount in 1944; *Mildred Pierce* was filmed by Warner Bros. in 1945; *Serenade* was filmed by Warner Bros. in 1956; *Loves' Lovely Counterfeit* was filmed as "Slightly Scarlet" by Benjamin Beaugeus in 1956; *The Root of His Evil* was filmed as "Interlude" by Universal in 1957. In 1938 an authorized version of *The Postman Always Rings Twice* was made in France by Gladiator Films, with the title "Le Dernier Tourant," because Metro-Goldwyn-Mayer, the American owner of the film rights, decided that the film could not be released in the United States. In 1939, G. Musso of Italy released "Obsessione" (a Cocinor-Marcean release of ICI Productions), also based on *The Postman Always Rings Twice.* MGM and Gladiator Films then filed a joint suit against the Italian producers, charging plagiarism. In 1946 the U.S. censorship of the film was lifted and the MGM production was released. Critics agreed, however, that the Italian version was superior to both the American and the French efforts. A Lorimar production of *The Postman Always Rings Twice* was also released in the United States in 1981. In addition, *Postman* was adapted and performed as opera by the Opera Theatre of St. Louis, 1982. *Butterfly* was adapted for the screen by John Goff and Matt Climber and released in 1982.

AVOCATIONAL INTERESTS: Music.

BIOGRAPHICAL/CRITICAL SOURCES:

BOOKS

Authors in the News, Volume 1, Gale, 1976.
Contemporary Literary Criticism, Gale, Volume 3, 1975, Volume 11, 1979, Volume 28, 1984.
Farrell, James T., *Literature and Morality,* Vanguard, 1947.
Frohock, W. M., *The Novel of Violence in America: 1920-1950,* University Press in Dallas, 1950.
Hoopes, Roy, *Cain: The Biography of James M. Cain,* Holt, 1982.
Madden, David, editor, *Tough Guy Writers of the Thirties,* Southern Illinois University Press, 1968,
Madden, David, *James M. Cain,* Twayne, 1970.
Wilson, Edmund, *Classics and Commercials,* Farrar, Straus, 1950.

PERIODICALS

Chicago Tribune Book World, October 4, 1981.

Nation, May 22, 1943, June 16, 1969.
New Republic, October 6, 1941.
New Yorker, January 8, 1966.
New York Times, February 5, 1982, January 26, 1989.
New York Times Book Review, August 8, 1965, March 2, 1969, April 22, 1976, December 13, 1981.
Publishers Weekly, July 24, 1972.
Saturday Review, October 4, 1941, August 14, 1965.
Time, August 27, 1965.
Village Voice, April 8-14, 1981.
Washington Post, January 19, 1969, November 8, 1981.

OBITUARIES:

PERIODICALS

Newsweek, November 7, 1977.
New York Times, October 29, 1977.
Time, November 7, 1977.
Washington Post, October 29, 1977.

*   *   *

CALDER, Nigel (David Ritchie) 1931-

PERSONAL: Born December 2, 1931, in London, England; son of (Peter) Ritchie (Lord Ritchie-Calder; a writer) and Mabel (McKail) Calder; married Elisabeth Palmer (a research assistant and literary agent), May 22, 1954; children: Sarah, Penelope, Simon, Jonathan, Katharine. *Education:* Attended Merchant Taylors' School; Sidney Sussex College, Cambridge, B.A., 1954, M.A., 1957.

ADDRESSES: Home and office—8 The Chase, Furnace Green, Crawley, Sussex, England. *Agent*—Elisabeth Calder, 8 The Chase, Furnace Green, Crawley, Sussex, England.

CAREER: Writer. Mullard Research Laboratories, Redhill, Surrey, England, research physicist, 1954-56; *New Scientist,* London, England, staff writer, 1956-60, science editor, 1960-62, editor, 1962-66. *Military service:* British Army, 1950-51; became lieutenant.

MEMBER: Association of British Science Writers (chairman, 1962-64), Cruising Association (London; vice-president).

AWARDS, HONORS: UNESCO Kalinga Prize for the popularization of science, 1972.

WRITINGS:

Electricity Grows Up, Phoenix House, 1958.
Robots, Roy, 1958.
Radio Astronomy, Roy, 1959, revised edition, Phoenix House, 1964.
(Editor) *The World in 1984,* Penguin, 1964.
The Environment Game, Secker & Warburg, 1967, published as *Eden Was No Garden: An Inquiry Into the Environment of Man,* Holt, 1967.
(Editor) *Unless Peace Comes: A Scientific Forecast of New Weapons,* Viking, 1968.
Technopolis: Social Control of the Uses of Science, MacGibbon & Kee, 1969, Simon & Schuster, 1970.
Violent Universe: An Eyewitness Account of the New Astronomy, BBC Publications, 1969, Viking, 1970.
Living Tomorrow, Penguin, 1970.
The Mind of Man, Viking, 1970.
Restless Earth, Viking, 1972.
The Life Game, BBC Publications, 1973, Viking, 1974.
(Editor) *Nature in the Round,* Weidenfeld & Nicolson, 1973, Viking, 1974.

The Weather Machine: How Our Weather Works and Why It Is Changing, BBC Publications, 1974, Viking, 1975.

The Human Conspiracy, Viking, 1976.

The Key to the Universe, Viking, 1977.

Spaceships of the Mind, Viking, 1978.

Einstein's Universe, Viking, 1979.

Nuclear Nightmares: An Investigation Into Possible Wars, BBC Publications, 1979, Viking, 1980.

The Comet Is Coming!: The Feverish Legacy of Mr. Halley, BBC Publications, 1980, Viking, 1981.

Timescale: An Atlas of the Fourth Dimension Viking, 1984.

1984 and Beyond: Nigel Calder Talks to His Computer About the Future, Viking, 1984.

The English Channel, Penguin, 1986.

(Editor with John Newell) *Future Earth,* Croom Helm, 1989.

Also author of *The Green Machine,* 1986. Author of television documentaries produced by British Broadcasting Corp., some in conjunction with Public Broadcasting System: "Russia: Beneath the Sputniks," 1967; "The World in a Box," 1968; "The Violent Universe," 1969; "The Mind of Man," 1970; "The Restless Earth," 1972; "The Life Game," 1973; "The Weather Machine," 1974; "The Human Conspiracy," 1975; "The Key to the Universe," 1977; "The Whole Universe Show," 1977; "Spaceships of the Mind," 1978; "Einstein's Universe," 1979; "Nuclear Nightmares," 1979; "The Comet Is Coming!," 1981.

Science correspondent for *New Statesman,* 1959-62 and 1966-71. Contributor to science journals in England and the United States.

SIDELIGHTS. Nigel Calder has gained a reputation as a writer of popular works on scientific topics. Calder's books, often published as companion pieces to his television documentaries, cover a wide range of subject matter, including the continental drift, the human mind, and recent discoveries in subatomic physics. In several of his books he speculates on the future and on humanity's place in a changing world.

In *Eden Was No Garden: An Inquiry Into the Environment of Man,* for example, Calder examines the problem of providing food for a rapidly growing earth population. He proposes that large-scale factory food production, not traditional agricultural methods, is the best way to supply food in the future and discusses how new technology would aid the preservation of the environment. R. C. Cowen, in a *Christian Science Monitor* review, says, "Perhaps the book will appeal as a review of today's scientific and technical developments as they bear on man's basic problems." *Library Journal* critic Harold Bloomquist praises Calder's offering of a "full-blown Utopian vision of what the world might be; truthfully, it looks pretty good."

Calder's interest in the future is not limited to earthly matters. His book *Spaceships of the Mind* explores the possibilities of outer space colonization. He includes a study of physicist Gerard O'Neill, who is working on a space superstructure capable of housing its own atmosphere, environment, and populace. "Calder's book is on the borderline between science and fantasy, but no matter," writes Martin Gardner in the *New York Review of Books,* "Calder knows his science, and between discussions of outrageous plans there are solid facts about the universe, and informed speculation about the awesome possibilities that lie ahead as population pressures and energy needs propel us into what O'Neill calls the High Frontier."

Two of Calder's books, *Unless Peace Comes: A Scientific Forecast of New Weapons* and *Nuclear Nightmares: An Investigation Into Possible Wars,* focus on what he perceives to be an immediate

threat to the future of humanity. *Unless Peace Comes,* which Calder edited, contains the thoughts of fifteen scientists from around the world who predict the warfare that may result unless nations can resolve their conflicts peacefully. *Nation* critic John Gliedman finds the book "rather conservative in its approach. No attention is given to the future technology of guerrilla war and counter insurgency. And yet, even with these important omissions, the book illuminates perhaps the greatest of the many ironies of the arms race: that it often feeds upon breakthroughs in civilian fields." In a *New York Times Book Review* article, D. S. Greenberg says that the scientists' contributions "are clearly intended to shock and appall. The intention is achieved, not through raucous prophecy and admonition, but rather through a fairly detached, even-toned recitation of technically attainable possibilities for conducting wars of the next decade, and, equally important, the political tensions that may be created simply because of the existence of unfamiliar and potentially devastating means of warfare."

Calder's concern with atomic warfare is continued in *Nuclear Nightmares.* In this book, the author lists four circumstances—"nightmares"—that might trigger nuclear war: worldwide nuclear arms proliferation, imperfections of command systems, escalation of a conflict in Europe, and the fear of one superpower that the other is about to attempt a disabling first strike. "Calder's particular and enviable talent is for turning abstruse technicalities into everyday language, without damage to the subtlety of the specialists' language," comments John Keegan in *New Republic.* "He demonstrates it once again here and, after reading the book, no layman will be able to take refuge in the comforting belief that he doesn't understand the issues." Keegan continues: "Proliferation is, in the author's view, a problem which the superpowers still could solve between themselves, by forbidding nuclear testing of any sort and making life impossible for states that broke the ban. Inevitably his conclusion has a utopian ring. But what appeal against the apparently inexorable tightening of the nuclear collar around all of our throats has not? At least critics will not be able to accuse him of mere hand-wringing. He knows the facts almost as well as those whose daily round it is to deal with them. He has concrete suggestions to make for setting limits on a trend which no sane person can wish to see continue."

Published during the centenary year of the birth of Albert Einstein, Calder's *Einstein's Universe* interprets the physicist's theories for the nonspecialist reader. However, some critics find the work still too specialized for its intended audience. For instance, *Chicago Tribune Book World* reviewer Guy Murchie notes that while the author "explains all these [theories], and without using academic or technological jargon, not many of us will be able to comprehend how 'all physical processes' are 'governed by the speed of light' or will accept without challenge that 'incest among the gravitons produces the curvature of space.' *Village Voice* critic Eliot Fremont-Smith comments on Calder's simplified approach to Einstein's theory of relativity: "The trouble is that at crucial points it isn't simple at all; it's horrendously complex, convoluted, and contradictory. This makes one fret—not so much over the difficulties of relativity as over the accumulating evidence that, as a layman, one isn't measuring up." According to Edmund Fuller's review in the *Wall Street Journal,* however, the author "is a singularly lucid writer with a gift for the memorable metaphors which, for the general reader, must take the place of the physicist's equations."

Among Calder's other books dealing with natural science are *The Weather Machine: How Our Weather Works and Why It Is Changing* and *The Comet Is Coming!: The Feverish Legacy of*

Mr. Halley. In *The Weather Machine,* the author discusses how changes in climate can affect everything from literature (a particularly wet, gloomy summer influenced Mary Shelley's writing of the gothic classic Frankenstein) to politics (an overly hot summer in 1788 shriveled the grain crops in France, causing bread riots in 1789 and, ultimately, the French Revolution). But, more alarmingly, Calder reports, recent climactic studies indicate a new ice age is imminent—which is "ominous for the human species," as the author puts it. "So, unless [scientists] do something fast," concludes Christopher Lehmann-Haupt in the *New York Times,* "it looks like falling temperatures, severe draught, and woolly mammoths. Thanks to his elegantly diagramed book with its chilly forecast, Mr. Calder has me worrying about the weather for a change."

The phenomenon of Halley's comet is explored in Calder's 1981 book, *The Comet Is Coming!* The comet, which appears once every seventy-six years, has historically induced suicide, human sacrifice, and predictions of Armageddon. "In addition to the army of soothsayers and astrologers who heretofore have interpreted it for us," writes Michael Collins in the *Washington Post Book World,* "Halley is preceded by a first-rate PR man. At T minus five years, Nigel Calder has put together a potpourri of fact and fancy, a fascinating compendium of all we would ask about comets, if we only knew the right questions." Both Collins and *New Republic* reviewer Katha Pollitt note that Calder himself takes a dim view of the fervor caused by the comet; Pollitt remarks that "it's not [the comet's] fault that human beings are superstitious and prone to paranoia," and she praises Calder's "wealth of fascinating comet lore."

Calder has also written on the subject of space and time. *Timescale* covers events which have occurred in the cosmos over the past thirteen billion years, while *1984 and Beyond* offers a reassessment of predictions made in *The World in 1984.*

AVOCATIONAL INTERESTS: Sailing.

BIOGRAPHICAL/CRITICAL SOURCES:

BOOKS

Calder, Nigel, *The Comet Is Coming!: The Feverish Legacy of Mr. Halley,* BBC Publications, 1980, Viking, 1981.
Calder, *Einstein's Universe,* Viking, 1979.
Calder, *The Weather Machine: How Our Weather Works and Why It Is Changing,* BBC Publications, 1974, Viking, 1975.

PERIODICALS

Atlantic, June, 1981.
Chicago Tribune Book World, March 11, 1979.
Christian Science Monitor, June 22, 1967.
Discover, March, 1984.
Library Journal, June 1, 1967.
Listener, April 8, 1976.
Los Angeles Times Book Review, September 21, 1980.
Nation, October 28, 1968.
Natural History, August/September, 1972.
New Republic, January 7, 1978, September 27, 1980, September 23, 1981.
New Statesman, February 29, 1980.
New York Review of Books, September 29, 1977, November 23, 1978.
New York Times, April 17, 1975, March 12, 1979.
New York Times Book Review, July 28, 1968, March 11, 1979, November 23, 1980.
Saturday Review, June 14, 1975.
Scientific American, May, 1971, July, 1972.

Village Voice, March 19, 1979.
Wall Street Journal, March 19, 1979.
Washington Post Book World, March 25, 1979, May 10, 1981, February 2, 1984.

* * *

CALDICOTT, Helen (Mary) 1938-

PERSONAL: Born August 8, 1938, in Melbourne, Victoria, Australia; daughter of Philip (a factory manager) and Mary Mona Enyd (an interior designer; maiden name, Coffey) Broinowski; married William Caldicott (a physician), December 8, 1962; children: Philip, Penny, William, Jr. *Education:* University of Adelaide, received B.S. (surgery), M.B. (medicine), 1961.

ADDRESSES: Home—245 Highland Ave. W., Newton, MA 02165. *Office*—P.O. Box 348, Arlington, MA 02174.

CAREER: Royal Adelaide Hospital, Adelaide, South Australia, Australia, intern, 1961; general practice of medicine in South Australia, 1963-65; Children's Hospital Medical Center, Boston, MA, fellow in nutrition, 1967-68; Adelaide Children's Hospital, Adelaide, intern, 1972, resident, 1973-74, founder and head of cystic fibrosis clinic, 1975-76; Children's Hospital Medical Center, fellow in cystic fibrosis, 1975-76, associate, 1977-80; activist and writer. Harvard University, Medical School, Cambridge, MA, fellow in nutrition, 1966-68, instructor in pediatrics, 1977-80. Appeared in documentary films "Eight Minutes to Midnight: A Portrait of Dr. Helen Caldicott," Physicians for Social Responsibility, 1981, "If You Love This Planet," National Film Board of Canada, 1982, and "In Our Hands," Action for Nuclear Disarmament, 1982; guest on radio and television programs, including "The Merv Griffin Show," "Donahue," "The Today Show," "Good Morning, America," "60 Minutes," and "Nightline."

MEMBER: American Thoracic Society, Royal Australasian College of Physicians, Physicians for Social Responsibility (president, 1978-83; president emeritus, 1983—), Medical Campaign Against Nuclear War (founder), Women's Action for Nuclear Disarmament (founder), Women's Party for Survival (founder).

AWARDS, HONORS: Prize for clinical medicine from British Medical Association, 1960; award from Consumer Action Now, Margaret Mead Award from Environmental Defense Center, Thomas Merton Prize for Peace from Thomas Merton Society, and Humanist of the Year Award from Ethical Society of Boston, all 1980; Gandhi Peace Prize from Promoting Enduring Peace, and SANE Peace Award from SANE Education Fund, both 1981; Humanist of the Year Award from American Association of Humanistic Psychology, and Audubon "A" Award from Massachusetts Audubon Society, both 1982; Woman of the Year Award from Boston College, Peace Award from American Association of University Women, Humanitarian Award from Massachusetts Psychological Association, Elizabeth Blackwell Award from American Medical Women's Association, Abraham L. Sacher Award from Brandeis University, Ansel Adams Award from Second Biennial Fate of the Earth Conference, and Outstanding Writer Award from Massachusetts Bay Association of Writing Programs, all 1984; President's Award from Hofstra University, Integrity Award from John-Roger Foundation, Peace Medal Award from United Nations Association of Australia, and Nobel Peace Prize nomination, all 1985; International Year of Peace Award from Australian Government, 1986; numerous honorary degrees from institutions including Antioch University, Emmanuel College, Russell Sage College, State University of New York at Binghamton, University of Linkoeping (Linkoeping, Sweden), and University of Notre Dame.

WRITINGS:

(With Nancy Herrington and Nahum Stiskin) *Nuclear Madness: What You Can Do!* Autumn Press, 1978, new edition published as *Nuclear Madness: What You Can Do; With a New Chapter on Three Mile Island,* Bantam, 1980.
Missile Envy: The Arms Race and Nuclear War, Morrow, 1984.

SIDELIGHTS: Since her 1971 fight to stop France from testing nuclear weapons over the southern Pacific Ocean, Australian-born physician Helen Caldicott has become "probably the most effective antinuclear speaker" in America, averred Nobel Prize-winning biologist George Wald in a 1979 *Ms.* article. Caldicott's speeches on the health dangers posed by nuclear fallout helped convince many Australians to protest and end the testing; she later led the successful effort to halt uranium mining and exporting in that country also. After moving to the United States in 1977, Caldicott focused much of her energy on protesting against nuclear weapons, pushing for a freeze on the building of such weapons and urging all Americans to become involved in the debate over nuclear technology. In *Nuclear Madness: What You Can Do!,* written with Nancy Herrington and Nahum Stiskin, Caldicott stated: "I believe it imperative that the American public understand that nuclear power generation is neither safe, nor clean, nor cheap; that new initiatives are urgently required if we are to avoid nuclear catastrophe in a world armed to the teeth with atomic weapons; and that these initiatives must begin with awareness, concern, and action on the part of the individual citizen. . . . We must educate ourselves . . . then move powerfully as individuals accepting full responsibility for preserving our planet for our descendants."

Caldicott's own awareness of nuclear hazards stemmed in part from her experiences as a pediatrician. In treating patients stricken with cystic fibrosis and leukemia, she realized that even one radioactive particle could damage a cell or a gene, thus making such genetic diseases and cancers more likely. "I decided that promoting the elimination of nuclear weapons and power was part of practicing . . . real preventive medicine," she told *Ms.* The results of her decision included reviving the antinuclear organization Physicians for Social Responsibility and leaving her medical practice to devote more time to educating the public.

Concern for her children also motivated her to activism. Recounted Caldicott, "When my husband and I decided to have our first child, I had nightmares thinking that the baby would live to see the horrors that I'd read about as a girl." Reading scientific studies of nuclear issues helped solidify her opposition to the technology, showing how weapons tests and routine reactor operation produce substances that affect the entire food chain. Caldicott was particularly troubled to discover that children face the greatest dangers from radiation. Because children are still growing, their cells reproduce quickly; a radiation-damaged cell only reproduces more damaged—cancerous—cells.

From the beginning of her campaign for a nuclear-free world, Caldicott has focused on a personal approach to sharing what she has learned. As a physician and as a parent she addresses church groups, college students, hospital staffs, and labor unions. She reaches many through magazine and newspaper articles, and she speaks on radio and television news programs. Commented Wald in *Ms.,* "She has a gift for making the hard scientific facts meaningful to the public." Using blackboard drawings, Caldicott explains the technological and medical realities, and data collected from government reports and scientific studies fuel her arguments. Yet even while she conveys hard facts, Wald observed, "she doesn't hesitate to raise moral questions or display intense emotions about these matters that are life-threatening in the extreme." To those who criticize her emotional appeal, Caldicott offered her defense in a *Los Angeles Times* article: "This is a very emotional issue. . . . To be unemotional about the end of the world is sick."

Caldicott also spreads her message with her books, which have been deemed useful educational tools. In the *New York Times Book Review* Philip M. Boffey described *Nuclear Madness* as "a primer on the medical hazards of nuclear fission." The critic questioned some of Caldicott's assertions, but he also acknowledged the book's "undeniable strengths," among them clarity, simplicity, a dispassionate tone, and attention to neglected issues. For example, among the issues she discusses is the disposal of radioactive waste; she notes that "even if unbreakable, corrosion-resistant containers could be designed, any storage site on earth would have to be kept under constant surveillance by incorruptible guards, administered by moral politicians living in a stable, warless society, and left undisturbed by earthquakes, natural disasters, or other acts of God for no less than half a million years."

Missile Envy: The Arms Race and Nuclear War analyzes the intricacies of defense strategy and the capabilities of nuclear arsenals worldwide. Caldicott offers several explanations for the U.S.-U.S.S.R. arms race and suggests that human nature must change to prevent the annihilation of mankind. Taylor Branch, writing in the *New York Times Book Review,* faulted Caldicott's diagnosis as superficial and criticized her emotional leaps between denunciations and religious appeals, but the critic judged her arguments regarding specific arms issues convincing. "Caldicott is at her best," Branch reflected, "when she goes into the maw of the doomsday machine itself to describe the missile systems, nuclear warheads and military theories in their deadliest applications." Branch also hailed the author's contention that "the logical consequence of the preparation for nuclear war is nuclear war."

Through her writings and lectures Caldicott "has captured the hearts and minds of people around the world," stated scientist Freeman Dyson in *New Yorker.* "You cannot brush aside her message as the emotional outpouring of a fanatic. She speaks from a solid basis of medical experience." Her work has made countless people aware of the dangers, achieving notable successes in Australia, yet "the world of the warriors [nuclear defense advocates] goes on its way as if Dr. Caldicott didn't exist," asserted Dyson. In December of 1982 Caldicott won a small concession, a lengthy private meeting with U.S. President Ronald Reagan, but she left frustrated because Reagan was "not receptive at all to what I had to say," she recalled in *Missile Envy.* Explained Dyson: "There is prejudice and antipathy on both sides. The military establishment looks on the peace movement as a collection of ignorant people meddling in a business they do not understand, while the peace movement looks on the military establishment as a collection of misguided people protected by bureaucratic formality from all contact with human realities. Both these preconceptions create barriers to understanding." Reflecting on what she has achieved and what remains to be done, Caldicott urged again in *Missile Envy:* "It is time for people to rise to their full moral and spiritual height, to take the world on their shoulders like Atlas. . . . Think how much Americans could achieve by using . . . the democracy they have inherited from their forebears. All it takes is willpower and determination. . . . Think of what we are about to destroy."

BIOGRAPHICAL/CRITICAL SOURCES:

BOOKS

Caldicott, Helen, Nancy Herrington and Nahum Stiskin, *Nuclear Madness: What You Can Do!* Autumn Press, 1978, new edition published as *Nuclear Madness: What You Can Do; With a New Chapter on Three Mile Island,* Bantam, 1980.
Caldicott, Helen, *Missile Envy: The Arms Race and Nuclear War,* Morrow, 1984.
Contemporary Issues Criticism, Volume 2, Gale, 1984.

PERIODICALS

Family Circle, May 18, 1982.
Harper's, March, 1985.
Los Angeles Times, June 27, 1984.
Ms., July, 1979, July, 1984.
New Yorker, February 6, 1984.
New York Times, May 25, 1979, August 18, 1985, June 2, 1986.
New York Times Book Review, August 26, 1979, July 29, 1984.
People, November 30, 1981.

* * *

CALDWELL, Erskine (Preston) 1903-1987

PERSONAL: Born December 17, 1903, in White Oak (some sources say Moreland), GA; died of emphysema and lung cancer, April 11, 1987, in Paradise Valley, AZ; son of Ira Sylvester (a minister) and Caroline Preston (a schoolteacher; maiden name, Bell) Caldwell; married Helen Lannigan, March 3, 1925 (divorced); married Margaret Bourke-White (a photographer), February 27, 1939 (divorced, 1942); married June Johnson, December 21, 1942 (divorced, 1955); married Virginia Moffett Fletcher, January 1, 1957; children: (first marriage) Erskine Preston, Dabney Withers, Janet; (third marriage) Jay Erskine. *Education:* Attended Erskine College, 1920-21, University of Virginia, 1922-26, and University of Pennsylvania, 1924.

ADDRESSES: Agent—McIntosh & Otis, Inc., 475 Fifth Ave., New York, NY 10017.

CAREER: Held various jobs, including mill laborer, cotton picker, cook, waiter, taxicab driver, farmhand, cottonseed shoveler, stonemason's helper, soda jerk, professional football player, bodyguard, stagehand in a burlesque theater, and a hand on a boat running guns to a Central American country in revolt; *Journal,* Atlanta, GA, reporter, 1925; script writer in Hollywood, CA, 1933-34 and 1942-43; newspaper correspondent in Mexico, Spain, Czechoslovakia, Russia, and China, 1938-40; war correspondent in Russia for *Life* Magazine, PM, and Columbia Broadcasting System, Inc., 1941; writer.

MEMBER: American Academy and Institute of Arts and Letters (honorary member), Authors League of America, P.E.N., Phoenix Press Club (life member), San Francisco Press Club (life member).

AWARDS, HONORS: Yale Review Award for fiction, 1933, for short story "Country Full of Swedes."

WRITINGS:

The Bastard (novel; also see below), Heron Press, 1929.
Poor Fool (novel; also see below), Rariora Press, 1930.
American Earth (short story collection), Scribner, 1931, published as *A Swell-Looking Girl,* MacFadden-Bartell, 1965.
Mamma's Little Girl, privately printed, 1932.
Tobacco Road (novel; also see below), Scribner, 1932.
Message for Genevieve, privately printed, 1933.

God's Little Acre (novel), Viking, 1933.
We Are the Living (short story collection), Viking, 1933.
Some American People, R. M. McBride & Co., 1935.
Tenant Farmer, Phalanx Press, 1935.
Journeyman (novel), Viking, 1935.
Kneel to the Rising Sun and Other Stories by Erskine Caldwell, Viking, 1935.
The Sacrilege of Alan Kent (novel; also see below), Falmouth Book House, 1936, reprinted with illustrations by Alexander Calder, Galerie Maeght, 1975.
You Have Seen Their Faces (nonfiction), photographs by Margaret Bourke-White, Viking, 1937.
Southways (short story collection), Viking, 1938.
North of the Danube (nonfiction), photographs by Bourke-White, Viking, 1939.
Trouble in July (novel), Duell, 1940.
Jackpot: The Short Stories of Erskine Caldwell (also see below), Duell, 1940.
Say, Is This the U.S.A.? (nonfiction), photographs by Bourke-White, Duell, 1941.
All Night Long: A Novel of Guerrilla Warfare in Russia, Duell, 1942.
All-out on the Road to Smolensk (nonfiction), Duell, 1942 (published in England as *Moscow under Fire: A Wartime Diary, 1941,* Hutchinson, 1942).
Russia at War (nonfiction), photographs by Bourke-White, Hutchinson, 1942.
Georgia Boy (novel; also see below), Duell, 1943, published as *Georgia Boy and Other Stories,* Avon, 1946.
Twenty-two Great Modern Short Stories from Jackpot, Avon, 1944.
Stories by Erskine Caldwell, Duell, 1944.
Tragic Ground (novel), Duell, 1944.
A Day's Wooing and Other Stories, Grosset, 1944.
The Caldwell Caravan: Novels and Stories by Erskine Caldwell, World Publishing, 1946.
A House in the Uplands (novel), Duell, 1946.
The Sure Hand of God (novel; also see below), Duell, 1947.
Midsummer Passion and Other Stories from Jackpot, Avon, 1948.
This Very Earth (novel), Duell, 1948.
Where the Girls Were Different and Other Stories, Avon, 1948, published as *Where the Girls Were Different,* MacFadden-Bartell, 1965.
Place Called Estherville (novel), Duell, 1949.
Episode in Palmetto (novel), Duell, 1950.
(Editor) Albert Nathaniel Williams, *Rocky Mountain Country,* Duell, 1950.
The Humorous Side of Erskine Caldwell, edited by Robert Cantwell, Duell, 1951.
Call It Experience: The Years of Learning How to Write, Duell, 1951, published as *Call It Experience,* MacFadden-Bartell, 1966.
The Courting of Susie Brown (short story collection), Duell, 1952, (published in England as *The Courting of Susie Brown and Other Stories,* Pan Books, 1958).
A Lamp for Nightfall (novel), Duell, 1952.
Complete Stories, Duell, 1953, published as *The Complete Stories of Erskine Caldwell,* Little, Brown, 1953.
Love and Money (novel), Duell, 1954.
Gretta (novel), Little, Brown, 1955.
Gulf Coast Stories, Little, Brown, 1956.
The Pocket Book of Erskine Caldwell Stories: Thirty-one of the Most Famous Short Stories, Pocket Books, 1957.
Certain Women (short story collection), Little, Brown, 1957.

Molly Cottontail (juvenile), Little, Brown, 1958.

Claudelle Inglish (novel), Little, Brown, 1959 (published in England as *Claudelle,* Heinemann, 1959).

When You Think of Me (short story collection), Little, Brown, 1959.

Three by Caldwell—Tobacco Road, Georgia Boy, The Sure Hand of God: Three Great Novels of the South, Little, Brown, 1960.

Men and Women: Twenty-two Stories, Little, Brown, 1961, published as *Men and Women,* MacFadden-Bartell, 1965.

Jenny by Nature (novel), Farrar, Straus, 1961.

Close to Home (novel), Farrar, Straus, 1962.

The Bastard, Poor Fool [and] *The Sacrilege of Alan Kent,* Bodley Head, 1963.

The Last Night of Summer (novel), Farrar, Straus, 1963.

A Woman in the House, MacFadden-Bartell, 1964.

Around about America (nonfiction), illustrated by wife, Virginia M. Caldwell, Farrar, Straus, 1964.

In Search of Bisco, Farrar, Straus, 1965.

The Deer at Our House (juvenile), Collier, 1966.

In the Shadow of the Steeple (also see below), Heinemann, 1967.

Writing in America, Phaedra Publishers, 1967.

Miss Mamma Aimee (novel), New American Library, 1967.

Summertime Island (novel), World Publishing, 1968.

Deep South: Memory and Observation (nonfiction; Part 1 first published in England as *In the Shadow of the Steeple*), Weybright, 1968.

The Weather Shelter (novel), World Publishing, 1969.

The Earnshaw Neighborhood (novel), World Publishing, 1971.

Annette (novel), New American Library, 1973.

Afternoons in Mid-America: Observations and Impressions (nonfiction), illustrated by V. M. Caldwell, Dodd, 1976.

Stories of Life, North and South, Dodd, 1983.

The Black and White Stories of Erskine Caldwell, edited by Ray McIver, Peachtree Publications, 1984.

With All My Might: An Autobiography, Peachtree Publications, 1987.

Also author of screenplays "A Nation Dances" and "Volcano." Editor, "American Folkways," twenty-five volumes, 1940-55.

A collection of Caldwell's manuscripts is housed in the Baker Library of Dartmouth College, Hanover, NH.

MEDIA ADAPTATIONS: Several of Caldwell's novels have been made into films, including *Tobacco Road,* Twentieth Century-Fox Film Corp., 1941, *God's Little Acre,* United Artists Corp., 1958, and *Claudelle Inglish* (under the title "Claudelle"), Warner Brothers, Inc., 1961. *Tobacco Road* was also adapted for the stage by Jack Kirkland and ran on Broadway for more than seven years.

SIDELIGHTS: As one of America's most banned and censored writers, in addition to being one of its most financially successful, Erskine Caldwell was often "patronized or ignored by academic critics and serious readers," according to James Korges, author of a critical study of the man who has been called "the South's literary bad boy." Korges continued: "Many know of *Tobacco Road* and *God's Little Acre,* but tend to dismiss them as merely popular or salacious novels. Few seem to know the full range of the man's work: his text-picture documentaries, such as the remarkable *North of the Danube;* his charming books for children; his neglected *Georgia Boy,* a book that stands with [William] Faulkner's last work as one of the finest novels of boyhood in American literature; and his short stories, some of which rank with the best of our time. . . . Younger readers dismiss him as a writer of the old pornography, for how tame, demure, almost

tidy seem the passages that were read aloud in courts as evidence of Caldwell's obscenity. . . . Younger critics seem unwilling to read Caldwell with care. . . . That much of [his] work 'grew towards trash' [in the words of Faulkner] does not alter the fact that Caldwell has produced an important body of work in both fiction and nonfiction."

In spite of the fact that, as Korges pointed out, Caldwell was more than just a novelist, his specialty through the years was the depiction of the seamier side of life in the American South—the bigotry, poverty, and misery among small-town "white trash." The son of a Presbyterian minister who made frequent moves from congregation to congregation throughout the South, Caldwell had ample opportunities as a boy to observe the various people and lifestyles of his native region. He often accompanied his father on visits to the homes of his parishioners, for example, and for a time he even drove a country doctor on his rounds. As he once explained to an interviewer: "You learned a lot living in small towns those days before they became smaller versions of the big towns."

Ten of Caldwell's novels—*Tobacco Road, God's Little Acre, Journeyman, Trouble in July, Tragic Ground, A House in the Uplands, The Sure Hand of God, This Very Earth, Place Called Estherville,* and *Episode in Palmetto*—comprise what the author himself referred to as "a cyclorama of Southern life." Unlike Faulkner's mythical Yoknapatawpha County, however, Caldwell's "cyclorama" does not seek to link his characters and events in any kind of overall historical framework; his goal, according to Korges, was to discover "scenes and actions that [embody] themes and types in the present."

Very few, if any, of Caldwell's characters or themes inspire admiration or optimism. His point of view was essentially pessimistic—man is more or less doomed to a life of pain and hurt, subject to the whims of chance and the effects of the actions of others. Virtually everything that happens—whether the results are bad or good—is regarded by Caldwell's characters as a manifestation of the will of God. And though there is room for humor in Caldwell's work, it is of a very bitter variety that only serves to reinforce the author's dark vision of life. One reviewer, W. M. Frohock, saw this type of humor as Caldwell's greatest strength. In his book *The Novel of Violence in America,* Frohock wrote: "There is a special sort of humor in America, native to our earth and deep-rooted in our history. Its material is the man who has been left behind in the rush to develop our frontiers, the man who has stayed in one place, out of and away from the main current of our developing civilization, so largely untouched by what we think of as progress that his folkways and mores seem to us, at their best, quaint and a little exotic—and, at their worst, degenerate. . . . [This type of humor] has been the main source, as well as the great strength, of Erskine Caldwell's novels."

For the most part, Caldwell's characters exhibit the last quality—degeneracy—far more than the former qualities of quaintness and exoticism. This characteristic has inspired much of the negative reaction against his two best-known novels, *Tobacco Road* and *God's Little Acre.* Southerners in particular have found his graphic descriptions of incest, adultery, lynchings, prostitution, lechery, murder, and the excesses of that "old-time religion" to be extremely offensive. Joseph Wood Krutch observed in *The American Drama since 1918: An Informal History:* "[Of] Mr. Caldwell one may see that the rank flavor of his work is as nearly unique as anything in contemporary literature. . . . like [Faulkner] he loves to contemplate the crimes and perversions of degenerate rustics; like both [Ernest Hemingway and Faulkner], his peculiar effects are made possible only by the assumption of an exaggerated detachment from all the ordinary prejudices of either morality or taste and a consequent tendency to present the most violent and repulsive scenes with the elaborate casualness of a careful pseudo-naivete. . . . His starveling remnant of the Georgia poor-white trash is not only beyond all morality and all sense of dignity or shame, it is almost beyond all hope and fear as well. As ramshackle and as decayed as the moldy cabins in which it lives, it is scarcely more than a parody on humanity."

"That [his] material would fall most easily into a tragic or quasi-tragic pattern is obvious enough," continued Krutch. "Caldwell does violence to all our expectations when he treats it as comedy, but he succeeds because he manages to prevent us from feeling at any moment any real kinship with the nominally human creatures of the play. . . . The characters themselves are represented as creatures so nearly subhuman that their actions are almost without human meaning and that one does not feel with them because they themselves obviously feel so little. . . . [But] his race of curiously depraved and yet curiously juicy human grotesques are alive in his plays whether they, or things like them, were ever alive anywhere else or not . . . and no attempts at analysis can deprive them of their life."

Korges agreed that Caldwell's characters are "alive" and that they personify very real human needs and desires. *Tobacco Road,* he proposed, "is about tenacity in the spirits of men and women deserted by God and man. The book is not about tobacco or Georgia, about sexology, or sociology, but is instead a work of literary art about the animal tug toward life that sustains men even in times of deprivation. . . . Life's major vital signs are eating and sexual intercourse, the two motives wittily, grossly, and magnificently rendered [by the author]. . . . The book is also a study in relationships and desertions. Man in this symbolic landscape is frustrated in his relationship to the soil because fertility has deserted the land. The sterile relationship of man to land is paralleled in the sterile [relationships between the main characters]."

Korges also discovered this same theme of sterility in the novel he considered Caldwell's masterpiece, *God's Little Acre.* He questioned its reputation as an " 'expose' of southern mentality or habits," insisting that it is instead "a novel of rich sexuality, sexuality being in this symbolic landscape . . . the one impressive life-sign. Yet just as the farm produces neither cotton nor gold . . ., so no woman in the novel is pregnant, despite all the sexuality. . . . [But] *God's Little Acre* can be read more meaningfully as a novel about dream and reality, power and impotence, the force of life and the force of death. The characters are studies of how single-mindedness of purpose or desire shapes people and compels them to behave in certain ways as economic, sexual, political, or theological agents. Each character . . . is identified by and with his driving motive. . . . Part of the darkness in Caldwell's vision of life . . . is that [their] yearnings are defeated as they are acted out."

The theme of sterility also appears in a more general sense in Caldwell's work. Despite appearances to the contrary, the preservation of family values plays an important part in his novels. In a less "somber" manner than someone like John Steinbeck, for example, Caldwell emphasized the richness of rural family life as opposed to the sterility and brutality of life in the city. Thus, as Korges pointed out, "the emotional poverty of the city folks is set off against the richness of feeling of the impoverished country folk, free from the economic meanness of making good marriages or of charging for sex."

For the most part, critics of the 1930s did not recognize these subliminal shades of meaning in Caldwell's work. Those who were not disgusted by his stories were amused by what they called his "burlesque"-type humor. Commenting on *Tobacco Road,* for example, Horace Gregory of *Books* noted that "Caldwell's humor, like Mark Twain's, has at its source an imagination that stirs the emotions of the reader. The adolescent, almost idiotic gravity of [his] characters produces instantaneous laughter and their sexual adventures are treated with an irreverence that verges upon the robust ribaldry of a burlesque show." A *Forum* critic reported that "Caldwell recites the orgiastic litany calmly and with a serene detachment. Such detachment is not likely to be shared by most readers, who, if they take the book seriously, will probably finish it—if they do finish it—with disgust and a slight retching; but anyone who considers it as subtle burlesque is going to have a fine time."

The *Nation* reviewer, on the other hand, appeared to sense that there was something more to *Tobacco Road* than just entertainment. He wrote: "The notion has gone about that the deliquescent characters, their squalor, their utter placidity, make Caldwell's writing 'primitive'; his sentence structure has made possible the belief that his work is naive; and because the setting is rural and the humors supposedly exaggerated, he is said to resemble Mark Twain and Bret Harte. These false notions have completely obscured what is an original, mature approach to the incongruities existing in a people who ignore the civilization that contains them as completely as the civilization ignores them."

Though *God's Little Acre* also offended some critics, more seemed willing to identify and comment on its literary merits. The *Saturday Review of Literature* critic, after having admitted that it was a novel "that will lift the noses of the sensitive," concluded that it "is nevertheless a beautifully integrated story of the barren Southern farm and the shut Southern mill, and one of the finest studies of the Southern poor white which has ever come into our literature. . . . Mr. Caldwell has caught in poetic quality the debased and futile aspiration of men and women restless in a world of long hungers which must be satisfied quickly, if at all."

The *Forum* reviewer wrote: "There has been considerable genteel ballyhoo in behalf of Erskine Caldwell but this novel is the first thing he has done which seems to this reader to justify in any way the praise the critics have heaped upon him. Despite its faults . . . it is immensely superior to *Tobacco Road* and *American Earth.* This superiority results from the fact that the author has stressed that element in which he is at his best, poor-white rural comedy."

Horace Gregory, commenting once again in *Books,* also agreed that "as a novel *God's Little Acre* has its faults, and there are flaws that in the work of a less gifted writer would be fatal to his progress. . . . But even as it stands I believe the book is an important step in the development of an important young novelist."

After this 1930s "golden age" came a gradual decline in the quality of Caldwell's work, a decline from which many critics believed the author never really recovered. More and more frequently, noted Korges, Caldwell turned to "sensational plotting and trite characterization . . . mixed with a good deal of superficial psychological comment and superficial motivation." Edward Hoagland of the *New York Times Book Review* declared that Caldwell simply "vegetated." He wrote: "The trouble with Caldwell seems to have been that he was finally lackadaisical. The eye that could distill so narrowly, the decent heart that roamed *Tobacco Road,* . . . rather soon stopped looking for new insights. . . . [In his later works] there is no bite or discipline, no old-pro's vigor of craftsmanship. Even his way with dialogue . . . has fallen off to casual indifference."

Walton Beacham of *Nation* acknowledged the value of Caldwell's early contributions, but essentially agreed with Hoagland that the author failed to grow and change with the public's demands for new material: "Not until Caldwell came along as a portrait painter were there clear models of the Southerner, or one type of Southerner, and Caldwell's books became primers, if not prerequisites, for all the other Southern novels read in subsequent years. . . . For at least a decade [his] characters became synonymous with the Southerner, and readers outside the region believed he alone could instruct them in the Southerner's obscure psyche. . . . Sadly, it has been to Caldwell's detriment that he does his journalism so effectively, and so realistically that we believed he was making the sort of myths and metaphors Hemingway had with his journalistic fiction. . . . Having performed the vital service of unlocking fundamental mysteries of the South, Caldwell's photographs became not only unnecessary but annoying. Yes, yes, we said to Caldwell, you've shown us the ugliness and we know too well how it looks. Show us something else. Make the ugliness into something worthwhile which will alleviate our fears. But Caldwell refused, and he outgrew his usefulness, making a nuisance of himself by continuing to show us the obvious, and refusing to create myths which would help set things right again."

Korges, on the other hand, concluded his study of Caldwell on an optimistic note. He wrote: "Caldwell, now in such disrepute among academic critics, will one day be 'discovered,' and his reputation will rest on a few books. . . . Such a selection from the large and uneven body of Caldwell's writing will make clear the strength of his best work in fiction and nonfiction, and will reveal what is now obscured by the very bulk of his output: his is a solid achievement that supports the assertion that he is one of the important writers of our time."

BIOGRAPHICAL/CRITICAL SOURCES:

BOOKS

Allen, Walter, *The Modern Novel,* Dutton, 1965.
Authors in the News, Volume 1, Gale, 1976.
Beach, Joseph Warren, *American Fiction: 1920-1940,* Russell, 1960.
Caldwell, Erskine, *With All My Might: An Autobiography,* Peachtree Publications, 1987.
Contemporary Authors, Autobiography Series, Volume 1, 1984.
Contemporary Literary Criticism, Gale, Volume 1, 1973, Volume 8, 1978, Volume 14, 1980, Volume 50, 1988.
Dictionary of Literary Biography, Gale, Volume 9: *American Novelists, 1910-1945,* 1981, Volume 86: *American Short-Story Writers, 1910-1945, First Series,* 1989.
Frohock, W. M., *The Novel of Violence in America,* revised edition, Southern Methodist University Press, 1957.
Kazin, Alfred, *On Native Grounds,* Reynal, 1942.
Korges, James, *Erskine Caldwell,* University of Minnesota Press, 1969.
Krutch, Joseph Wood, *The American Drama since 1918: An Informal History,* Random House, 1939.
Newquist, Roy, *Counterpoint,* Rand McNally, 1964.

PERIODICALS

Atlantic, July, 1962, November, 1963, May, 1965, October, 1968.
Best Sellers, September 1, 1968, November 15, 1969.
Book Week, May 23, 1943.
Book World, March 24, 1967.
Books and Bookmen, June, 1968.

Books, February 21, 1932, February 5, 1933.
Chicago Daily Tribune, March 4, 1933.
Commonweal, August 21, 1964.
Forum, May, 1932, March, 1933.
Journal and Constitution (Atlanta), May 13, 1973.
Nation, July 6, 1932, October 18, 1933, June 11, 1977.
National Observer, March 25, 1968.
New Republic, March 23, 1932, February 8, 1933, November 6, 1944.
Newsday, October 11, 1969.
New Statesman, March 17, 1961, August 31, 1962.
Newsweek, April 5, 1965.
New Yorker, May 22, 1965.
New York Herald Tribune Book Review, March 30, 1958, April 5, 1959, June 10, 1962.
New York Times, February 5, 1933, April 25, 1943.
New York Times Book Review, February 23, 1958, March 19, 1961, June 17, 1962, April 4, 1965, January 4, 1970, November 14, 1976.
Playboy, May, 1968.
Punch, May 8, 1968.
Saturday Review, May 2, 1959, May 1, 1965.
Saturday Review of Literature, March 5, 1932, February 18, 1933.
Spectator, August 24, 1962.
Springfield Republican, February 15, 1933.
Time, August 25, 1961, June 19, 1964.
Times Literary Supplement, June 26, 1969.

OBITUARIES:

PERIODICALS

Chicago Tribune, April 13, 1987.
Dallas Times Herald, April 13, 1987.
Detroit Free Press, April 13, 1987.
Los Angeles Times, April 13, 1987.
New York Post, April 13, 1987.
New York Times, April 13, 1987.
Time, April 20, 1987.
Washington Post, April 13, 1987.

*   *   *

CALISHER, Hortense 1911-

PERSONAL: Born December 20, 1911, in New York, N.Y.; daughter of Joseph Henry (a manufacturer) and Hedwig (Lichstern) Calisher; married Heaton Bennet Heffelfinger, September 27, 1935 (divorced); married Curtis Arthur Harnack (a novelist), March 27, 1959; children: (first marriage) Bennet Hughes (daughter), Peter Hughes. *Education:* Barnard College, A.B., 1932.

ADDRESSES: Home—205 West 57th St., New York, N.Y. 10019. *Agent*—Candida Donadio & Associates, Inc., 231 West 22nd St., New York, N.Y. 10011.

CAREER: Social worker for Department of Public Welfare, New York, N.Y.; adjunct professor at Barnard College, 1957, Columbia University, 1968-70, and Columbia University School of the Arts, 1972-73. Visiting professor at Brandeis University, 1963-64, City College of the City University of New York, 1970-71, State University of New York at Purchase, 1971-72, Bennington College, 1978, Washington University, St. Louis, Mo., 1979, and Brown University, spring, 1986; Regents Professor, University of California at Irvine, 1975. Visiting lecturer at University of Iowa, 1957 and 1959-60, Stanford University,

1958, Sarah Lawrence College, 1962 and 1967, University of Pennsylvania, 1969, and in West Germany, Yugoslavia, Romania, and Hungary, 1978. Clark Lecturer, Scripps College, 1968.

MEMBER: PEN (president, 1986-87), American Academy and Institute of Arts and Letters (president, 1987-90).

AWARDS, HONORS: Guggenheim fellow, 1951-52 and 1953-54; American Specialist's Grant, U.S. Department of State, 1958, for visiting Southeast Asia; National Council of the Arts award, 1967; Academy of Arts and Letters award, 1967; Litt.D., Skidmore College, 1980, and Grinnell College, 1986; four O. Henry prize story awards; Hurst Fellow, Washington University, 1979; National Book Award nominations for *False Entry,* 1962, *Herself: An Autobiographical Work,* 1973, and *The Collected Stories of Hortense Calisher,* 1976.

WRITINGS:

NOVELS

False Entry, Little, Brown, 1961.
Textures of Life, Little, Brown, 1963.
Journal from Ellipsia, Little, Brown, 1965.
The New Yorkers, Little, Brown, 1969.
Queenie, Arbor House, 1971.
Standard Dreaming, Arbor House, 1972.
Eagle Eye, Arbor House, 1973.
On Keeping Women, Arbor House, 1977.
Mysteries of Motion, Doubleday, 1983.
The Bobby-Soxer, Doubleday, 1986.
Age, Weidenfeld & Nicolson, 1987.

COLLECTIONS

In the Absence of Angels, Little, Brown, 1951.
Tale for the Mirror: A Novella and Other Stories, Little, Brown, 1962.
Extreme Magic: A Novella and Other Stories, Little, Brown, 1964.
The Railway Police [and] *The Last Trolley Ride* (two novellas), Little, Brown, 1966.
The Collected Stories of Hortense Calisher, Arbor House, 1975.
Saratoga, Hot (short stories), Doubleday, 1985.

OTHER

Herself: An Autobiographical Work, Arbor House, 1972.
(Editor, with Shannon Ravenel, and author of introduction) *Best American Short Stories, 1981,* Houghton, 1981.
Kissing Cousins: A Memory, Weidenfeld & Nicolson, 1988.

Work appears in numerous anthologies, including *50 Best American Short Stories, 1915-1965* and *O. Henry Memorial Award Prize Stories.* Contributor of short stories, articles, and reviews to periodicals, including *New York Times, New Yorker, Harper's, Mademoiselle, Ladies' Home Journal, Saturday Evening Post, Gentleman's Quarterly, Kenyon Review,* and *Nation.*

SIDELIGHTS: Hortense Calisher is "among the most literate practitioners of modern American fiction, a stylist wholly committed to the exploitation of language," writes a *Saturday Review* contributor. Calisher's first short stories appeared in the *New Yorker* in the forties, and in the years since then she has steadily alternated her story collections with novels and novellas. In addition, she has written a memoir entitled *Herself* that Robert Kiely in the *New York Times Book Review* considers "primarily and at its best a long meditation on the art of writing fiction in America in the second half of the twentieth century." While the body of Calisher's work has consistently garnered praise, her short stories receive the most acclaim. "Calisher not only is best

at writing short stories, she is one of *the* best," declares Robert Phillips in his *Commonweal* review of *The Collected Stories of Hortense Calisher,* and Calisher's four O. Henry awards seem to support this view.

Reviewers agree that Calisher's sometimes masterful short stories deliver the unexpected. "Calisher has always specialized in astonishment. . . . She excels at jamming shocks into deceptively cool narratives," comments Nora Sayre in the *New York Times Book Review.* For Doris Grumbach, also reviewing in the *New York Times Book Review,* "what happens in [Calisher's] stories is what [Calisher] has defined as 'an apocalypse, served in a very small cup.' Sudden awareness, epiphanies of character are her metier . . . [and] the tea cup is the proper vessel for sudden, small visions into the spirit. In a blaze of light, as startling as Paul's Damascan vision, we see, not a string of events, but a tableau, frozen, static, inevitable—and instructive." Thus, according to Sayre, "a dim, fluttering Southern wallflower becomes a Manhattan Communist, achieving apotheosis and an Order of Stalin, second class, after her accidental death in an explosion; . . . a nighttime scream on 57th Street obsesses and even attracts a widow so lonely that she yearns to hear the scream again; . . . at a posh London dinner table, the women all suddenly remove their blouses;" and a completely bald woman discards her wig while in an intimate embrace with her lover, only to be shunned for her attempt at total honesty.

Calisher's fiction, though varied in tone and theme, is often "sorrowful, for most of her characters suffer from their difference, their isolation, their concern with those terrible needs of the human being which for most of us seem destined never to be fulfilled," offers *New York Times Book Review* critic Gertrude Buckman in her assessment of Calisher's first short story collection, *In the Absence of Angels.* Additionally, Calisher's characters are inclined to reminisce and become nostalgic, and in some way or another they must grapple with failure. In the *Dictionary of Literary Biography,* Carolyn Matalene states that "perhaps the overriding impulse of [Calisher's] literary style is that her characters' carefully nurtured abstractions perpetually clash with realities." Calisher's compelling novella *The Railway Police* manifests this idea. In this novella, Calisher writes of a woman who has been dominated for years by her hereditary baldness; she has even aborted the child in her womb for fear of passing on the defect. After witnessing a vagrant's nonchalant reaction to being thrown off a train by the railway police, the woman, who is never named, attempts to liberate herself from the constraints that have ruled her life. *New York Times Book Review* contributor R. V. Cassill recounts the woman's attempt to marry "a balding gentleman whose anthropological and artistic tastes imply he will accept her ultimate unveiling with joy." Instead, her lover flees, prompting Cassill to label him a representative of "that modern man who yearns for the nudity of the female, but nudity as he has preconceived it, not as the woman in her full hunger for acceptance and revelation knows it must exist." As full of "terror and torment" as Calisher's works sometimes are, Charles Lee states in the *Saturday Review of Literature* that they are "neither without compassion nor, more important, without hope. . . . Calisher seems willing to pin her badly bruised faith on the virtuous potentialities of man." Thus, in *The Railway Police,* "the heroine's baldness, her deformity, is her humanity, and the story asks us to consider what it means to be human," remarks Joan Joffe Hall in the *Saturday Review.*

A substantial amount of Calisher's writing is semiautobiographical, drawing on her heritage as the Jewish daughter of a transplanted Southerner and a German immigrant living a comfortable, middle-class existence in New York. According to Matalene, the sister and brother characters Hester and Joe Elkins (who first appear in *In the Absence of Angels*) are both portraits of Calisher who "grow up and learn about death, about peripheral persons, about female vanity, about the complicity love sometimes requires, and about the burden of parents, whether alive or dead. The Hester stories are, from one point of view, small gems of social history. . . . And, from another point of view, they are quiet and carefully realized fictions of a young woman's growth into loving and remembering and understanding." In addition, Grumbach figures that a third of the stories in *The Collected Stories of Hortense Calisher,* a compilation of Calisher's three previous collections, are about Calisher's own family—"her father, mother, aunts, family hangers-on, servants, her brother. She is best . . . with them because she allows herself to wander among them, an awkward, undervalued, sensitive child among proud, attractive, transplanted, late Victorian Southerners, living out their well-to-do 'comfortable' lives in New York."

Grumbach further labels Calisher the "quintessential New Yorker, entirely comfortable on its streets, in its apartments, lovingly, almost patriotically, wrapping the whole island in the elegant tissue of her words." *Washington Post Book World* commentator Anne Tyler explains that while Calisher's settings are often confined to New York, "sometimes it's New York's Fifth Avenue and sometimes the seedy, leadcolored warehouse district way, way downtown. And at still other times, it's the closed world of those transplants to the city who have managed, somehow, to bring their natural habitats with them intact." Still, at other times Calisher, who calls herself a "city bird," is just at home in the suburbs and small towns or even outer space.

Incorporating Calisher's Jewish heritage, her familiarity with New York, and her understanding of labyrinthine human relationships is her 1969 novel, *The New Yorkers.* In this work judge Simon Mannix returns home from a banquet held in his honor to the noise of a gunshot. His twelve-year-old daughter, Ruth, at the onset of her first menarche, has killed his wife as she lay in the arms of a lover. The remainder of the novel chronicles Mannix's life-transforming attempt to conceal the tragedy, even from Ruth. A reviewer for the *Times Literary Supplement* feels that in *The New Yorkers* Calisher "is out to memorialize an institution even closer to the establishment than the Forsytes—the rich, cultured, philanthropic, New York Jewish family. . . . Her weighty saga is filled with the pain and drama that any family (but in particular such a family, such a race) hides behind its elegant front. . . . Calisher knows how to create the pattern of blood-relationships which tug and strain to keep a family together." Christopher Lehmann-Haupt of the *New York Times* finds that "among [the book's] many themes—which include the relationships of Jews and Gentiles, Jews and Jews, class behavior, parents and children—the predominant one is the polarity between masculinity and femininity. . . . Consider that opening incident again: a girl who has just become a woman kills her mother . . . after having witnessed her fornicating with a strange man. Ruth's act is sexually ambivalent, to say the least. And, sure enough, the climactic chapter of 'The New Yorkers' . . . is Ruth's version of what happened that fatal evening. It is overwhelmingly preoccupied with her search for sexual identity." In the end, on the occasion of Ruth's marriage to a Quaker, "Judge Mannix and his daughter at last manage to put the two halves of their lives together and to affirm both," remarks Matalene.

Apart from its commentary on familial and social relationships, and apart from its treatment of the development of sexual identity, "*The New Yorkers* is a profoundly local novel. Therein lies

its real strength; Calisher knows her chosen city as few others do, and her evocations of it are stunning," claims Matalene. On the other hand, though *New York Times Book Review* contributor John Brooks praises Calisher's insight into human relationships, he feels *The New Yorkers* "is another attempt at the always-elusive, never-quite-achieved Great New York Novel. Certainly this brooding and rather overstuffed Gothic tale isn't that. But it has smaller rewards for the reader with patience."

If there is any one aspect of Calisher's writing on which reviewers disagree, it is her way with language. Some critics find her prose "superlative," "exciting," and "gorgeous," while others describe it as "self-congratulatory," "self-indulgent," and even "pretentious." Jean Martin says in the *Nation* that for Calisher, the telling is all: "In Calisher the art lies in all that she puts into a sentence. From a glittering vocabulary she chooses words that bejewel the tiara of sentence structure." *Saturday Review* critic David Boroff, commenting on Calisher's second short story collection, *Extreme Magic,* likewise considers her "an immaculate stylist, a precisionist of the utmost rigor, and an arresting phrasemaker." Kiely feels her fiction reads like "the kind of language . . . one might expect from a metaphysical poet."

On the other hand, though he admits to a fondness for "a rich, even an overripe prose," *New York Times Book Review* critic Anatole Broyard notes in his assessment of Calisher's novel *On Keeping Women* that "all too often . . . [her] rhetoric seems to me to mire her characters as well as the movement of her book. . . . J. D. Salinger said, sentimentality means loving someone more than God loves them, and I think . . . Calisher may be guilty as charged. Or perhaps it is language that she loves more than God does—it is hard to distinguish people from the prose." Hall makes a similar statement, noting that in the novella *The Last Trolley Ride* "Calisher's style is, at its best, witty and ripe with insights; words melt in her mouth like . . . fritters. But she has such an appetite for language, for seasoning in every sentence, that at its worst her style can become opaque, no medium for discovery and elucidation, a risky idiom for narrating events, dangerous for long fiction." On the whole, says Matalene, "critics are more comfortable with the terse prose of [Calisher's] . . . short story style than with the stylistic exuberances of her novels."

While reviewers inevitably comment on Calisher's literary style, she shuns being labeled a "stylist." "When it begins to be said that I have a style, am a 'stylist,' I chafe. Doesn't this mean I have nothing to say comparable to the way I say it—or else that anything I say will all sound the same?" she questions in *Herself.* Calisher further explains in her memoir that she "hears" her prose before she writes it. According to the author, "this makes for a prose that can always be read, often subtly demands that. Sometimes leading to a rhetoric which, loving its own rhythms, may stray too far from sense, or fall into marvelous accident."

That Calisher may at times use overly fancy prose or self-indulgent language stems from her unwillingness to hide behind her writing. Kiely remarks that "one of the recurring themes of [Calisher's] memoir and one of the distinctions of her art [is] that she does not write on behalf of New Yorkers, Americans, Jews, women, liberals, or, for that matter, writers. She writes on behalf of herself." Though the "invisible novelist" may be the current vogue, "Calisher has never been a writer who masked her thinking self or disappeared into her subject," writes Morris Dickstein in his *New York Times Book Review* article on Calisher's novel *The Bobby-Soxer.* "[Calisher] belongs to a different tradition descending from Henry James, in which the writer's own complex intelligence—his humming eloquence, his subtle knowingness—

becomes essential to his equipment as a storyteller. Far from holding the mirror up to life, this kind of writer diffracts it through the prism of his sensibility, as if to show how many-faceted it is, how much he himself has made it up." And as Matalene observes in her *Dictionary of Literary Biography* essay, "For Calisher, the act of writing and the act of living tend to be congruent, and perhaps this accounts for the deep feeling of sympathy with those ordinary people which her writing conveys. In the conclusion to *Herself* she wrote: 'Perhaps my own process is not so much my own as I thought, nor even one that only artists know—but one that we share with other Americans, other *people.* Less and less do I see any gap—in the process of us all.' "

BIOGRAPHICAL/CRITICAL SOURCES:

BOOKS

Calisher, Hortense, *Herself: An Autobiographical Work,* Arbor House, 1972.
Contemporary Literary Criticism, Gale, Volume 2, 1974, Volume 4, 1975, Volume 8, 1978, Volume 38, 1986.
Dictionary of Literary Biography, Volume 2: *American Novelists since World War II,* Gale, 1978.
Newquist, Roy, *Conversations,* Rand McNally, 1967.

PERIODICALS

Atlantic, October, 1972.
Books, November 4, 1962, April 28, 1963.
Book World, October 1, 1972.
Chicago Tribune, October 6, 1987.
Christian Science Monitor, November 11, 1965, January 18, 1984.
Commonweal, May 7, 1976.
Detroit News, December 25, 1983.
Harper's, March, 1971.
Los Angeles Times, February 25, 1986.
Los Angeles Times Book Review, October 9, 1983, July 21, 1985, December 13, 1987.
Ms., January, 1974.
Nation, November 18, 1961, June 29, 1974.
New Leader, January 19, 1976.
New Republic, November 3, 1973, October 25, 1975.
Newsweek, April 29, 1963, October 16, 1972.
New York Review of Books, June 25, 1964, December 15, 1966.
New York Times, May 12, 1966, April 18, 1969, November 9, 1972, October 13, 1975, November 1, 1977, November 8, 1983.
New York Times Book Review, November 18, 1951, October 29, 1961, May 12, 1963, November 7, 1965, May 22, 1966, April 13, 1969, March 28, 1971, October 1, 1972, November 11, 1973, October 19, 1975, October 23, 1977, November 6, 1983, May 20, 1984, May 26, 1985, March 30, 1986, October 18, 1987, December 18, 1988.
Reporter, November 17, 1966.
Saturday Review, October 27, 1962, May 2, 1964, December 25, 1965, June 18, 1966, April 3, 1971, October 14, 1972, October 18, 1975, July-August, 1985.
Saturday Review of Literature, December 1, 1951.
Time, October 22, 1965, May 16, 1966, May 19, 1969.
Times Literary Supplement, January 15, 1970.
Virginia Quarterly Review, summer, 1969.
Washington Post, December 31, 1983.
Washington Post Book World, March 28, 1971, September 18, 1977, November 6, 1977, June 9, 1985.
Writer's Digest, March, 1969.

CALLAGHAN, Morley Edward   1903-1990

PERSONAL: Born September 22, 1903, in Toronto, Ontario, Canada; son of Thomas and Mary (Dewan) Callaghan; married Loretto Florence Dee, April 16, 1927; children: Michael, Barry. *Education:* St. Michael's College, University of Toronto, B.A., 1925; Osgoode Hall Law School, LL.B., 1928.

ADDRESSES: Home—20 Dale Ave., Toronto, Ontario, Canada.

CAREER: Novelist and short story writer, 1926—. Worked as reporter on *Toronto Daily Star* while in college; stories written during this time found their way, via Ernest Herningway, into Paris literary magazines of that day, including Ezra Pound's *Exile,* and he gave up the idea of practicing law to become a professional writer. Spent a year in Paris, 1928-29, other periods in New York and Pennsylvania, before returning to Toronto, Ontario, to live. Worked during World War II with the Royal Canadian Navy on assignment for the National Film Board, and traveled across Canada as chairman of the radio program "Citizen's Forum."

AWARDS, HONORS: Governor General's Literary Award for fiction (Canada), 1952, for *The Loved and the Lost;* gold medal of Royal achievement of special significance in imaginative literature, 1960; medal of merit, City of Toronto, 1962; LL.D., University of Western Ontario, 1965; Canada Council Molson prize ($15,000), 1970; Royal Bank of Canada award ($50,000) for distinguished work, 1970.

WRITINGS:

NOVELS

Strange Fugitive, Scribner, 1928, Hurtig, 1970.
It's Never Over, Scribner, 1930, reprinted, Macmillan (Toronto), 1972.
No Man's Meat (also see below; novella), Edward W. Titus, At the Sign of the Black Manikin (Paris), 1931.
A Broken Journey, Scribner, 1932, reprinted, Macmillan (Toronto), 1976.
Such Is My Beloved, Scribner, 1934, reissued with an introduction by Malcolm Ross, McClelland & Stewart, 1957.
They Shall Inherit the Earth (also see below), Random House, 1935, reissued with an introduction by F. W. Watt, McClelland & Stewart, 1962.
More Joy in Heaven, Random House, 1937, reissued with an introduction by Hugo McPherson, McClelland & Stewart, 1960.
The Varsity Story, Macmillan, 1948.
Luke Baldwin's Vow (juvenile), Winston, 1948, reprinted, Scholastic Inc., 1974.
The Loved and the Lost, Macmillan, 1951.
The Many Colored Coat, Coward, 1960, original magazine version published as *The Man with the Coat,* Exile Editions, 1988.
A Passion in Rome, Coward, 1961.
A Fine and Private Place, Mason/Charter, 1975.
Close to the Sun Again, Macmillan, 1977.
No Man's Meat and The Enchanted Pimp, Macmillan (Toronto), 1978.
A Time for Judas, Macmillan (Toronto), 1983, St. Martin's, 1984.
Our Lady of the Snows, Macmillan (Toronto), 1985, St. Martin's, 1986.

OTHER

A Native Argosy (short stories), Scribner, 1929, Books for Libraries, 1970.

Now That April's Here, and Other Stories, Random House, 1937.

"Turn Again Home" (play; based on the novel *They Shall Inherit the Earth*), first produced in New York City, 1940, produced under title "Going Home" by the New Play Society, Toronto, 1950.

"To Tell the Truth" (play), first produced by the New Play Society, Toronto, 1949.

Morley Callaghan's Stories, Macmillan, 1959, 2 volume edition, MacGibbon & Kee, 1962.

That Summer in Paris: Memories of Tangled Friendships with Hemingway, Fitzgerald, and Some Others, Coward, 1963.

Stories, Macmillan (Toronto), 1967.

An Autumn Penitent, Macmillan (Toronto), 1973.

The Lost and Found Stories of Morley Callaghan, Lester & Orpen Dennys/Exile Editions, 1985.

Contributor of short stories to *Scribner's, New Yorker, Harper's Bazaar, Maclean's, Esquire, Cosmopolitan, Saturday Evening Post, Yale Review,* and numerous other magazines.

SIDELIGHTS: Edmund Wilson wrote in *0 Canada:* "The Canadian Morley Callaghan, at one time well known in the United States, is today perhaps the most unjustly neglected novelist in the English-speaking world." Wilson noted that "when I talked about Callaghan [in the late 1950s], such people as remembered his existence were likely to think he was dead." Wilson offers several explanations for the fact that Callaghan is virtually unknown outside his native country, the most "striking" reason being "the partial isolation of that country [Canada] from the rest of the cultural world. . . . My further reading of Callaghan's novels has suggested another reason . . . for their relative unpopularity. Almost all of them end in annihilating violence or, more often, in blank unfulfillment. . . . All these endings have their moral point: recognition of personal guilt, loyalty in personal relationships, the nobility of some reckless devotion to a Christian ideal of love which is bound to come to grief in the world. But they are probably too bleak for the ordinary reader. . . . Only a very sober, self-disciplined and 'self-directed' writer could have persisted, from decade to decade, in submitting these parables to the public. They are almost invariably tragic, but their tragedy avoids convulsions and it allows itself no outbreak in tirades."

In *That Summer in Paris* Callaghan documents his experiences as a *Toronto Daily Star* cub reporter and his 1929 trip to Paris, where he became acquainted with and formed opinions on various literary figures, most notably Ernest Hemingway and F. Scott Fitzgerald. William Saroyan said in a review: "Each of the three writers was waging a fight of some kind that the others did not know about, could scarcely guess about, and could not help with. Callaghan's fight seems to have been the easiest—simply to write well and to go on writing well, which he managed to do, which he is still doing, which he does in this book, slight and anecdotal as it is."

Wilson mentioned the universal appeal of Callaghan's work, a quality cited frequently in critical reviews: "The novels of Morley Callaghan do not deal with his native Canada in any editorial or informative way, nor are they aimed at any popular taste, Canadian, 'American' or British. They center on situations of primarily psychological interest that are treated from a moral point of view yet without making moral judgments of any conventional kind." A *Canadian Forum* columnist called *Morley Callaghan's Stories* "one of the few major achievements of Canadian prose,

more powerful than any single Callaghan novel and more worthy of enduring than any single work of his better publicized peers: Anderson, Hemingway and Fitzgerald. Mr. Callaghan does have his limits: he plays no games with time and infinity. Literary innovations leave him cold, the corporational vulture which feeds us all never enters into his fiction. . . . There is one major unreality to which he returns time and time again: emotion. . . . But for his era, when the media, the false prophets, the corporations, did not place so much underbrush between the human being and life (underbrush which the modern writer must deal with), Callaghan created a method that worked extraordinarily well. Never has the urban low bourgeois been dealt with quite so humanely, quite so creatively."

MEDIA ADAPTATIONS: In 1958 Klenman-Davidson Productions filmed *Now That April's Here.*

AVOCATIONAL INTERESTS: Spectator sports.

BIOGRAPHICAL/CRITICAL SOURCES:

BOOKS

Cameron, Donald, *Conversations with Canadian Novelists, Part Two,* Macmillan (Toronto), 1973.

Conron, Brandon, *Morley Callaghan,* Twayne, 1966.

Contemporary Literary Criticism, Gale, Volume 3, 1975, Volume 14, 1980, Volume 41, 1987.

Dictionary of Literary Biography, Volume 68: *Canadian Writers, 1920-1959,* Gale, 1988.

Hoar, Victor, *Morley Callaghan,* Copp, 1969.

Lecker, Robert and Jack David, editors, *The Annotated Bibliography of Canada's Major Authors 5,* ECW Press, 1984.

Morley, Patricia, *Morley Callaghan,* McClelland & Stewart, 1978.

Wilson, Edmund, *O Canada,* Farrar, Straus, 1965.

PERIODICALS

Canadian Forum, March, 1960, February, 1968.

Canadian Literature, summer, 1964.

Dalhousie Review, autumn, 1959.

New Republic, February 9, 1963.

New Yorker, November 26, 1960.

Queen's Quarterly, autumn, 1957.

Tamarack Review, winter, 1962.

* * *

CALVINO, Italo   1923-1985

PERSONAL: Born October 15, 1923, in Santiago de Las Vegas, Cuba; grew up in San Remo, Italy; died following a cerebral hemorrhage, September 19, 1985, in Siena, Italy; son of Mario (a botanist) and Eva (a botanist; maiden name, Mameli) Calvino; married Chichita Singer (a translator), February 19, 1964; children: Giovanna. *Education:* University of Turin, graduated, 1947.

ADDRESSES: Home—Rome, Italy (winters); Castiglione della Pescaia, Siena, Italy (summers). *Agent*—Agenzia Letteraria Internazionale, 41 via Manzoni, 20121 Milan, Italy.

CAREER: Writer. Member of editorial staff of Giulio Einaudi Editore, 1947-83; lecturer. *Military service:* Italian Resistance, 1943-45.

AWARDS, HONORS: Viareggio Prize, 1957; Bagutta Prize, 1959, for *I racconti;* Veillon Prize, 1963; Premio Feltrinelli per la Narrativa, 1972; honorary member of the American Academy and Institute of Arts and Letters, 1975; Oesterreichiches Staatspreis fuer Europaeische Literatur, 1976; *Italian Folktales* was included on the American Library Association's Notable Book List for 1980; Grande Aigle d'Or du Festival du Livre de Nice (France), 1982; Christopher Award, 1982, for *Italian Folktales;* honorary degree from Mt. Holyoke College, 1984; Premio Riccione (Italy), for *Il sentiero dei nidi di ragno.*

WRITINGS:

FICTION

Il sentiero dei nidi di ragno, Einaudi (Turin, Italy), 1947, translation by Archibald Colquhoun published as *The Path to the Nest of Spiders,* Collins, 1956, Beacon Press, 1957, reprinted, Ecco Press, 1976.

Ultimo viene il corvo (short stories; title means "Last Comes the Crow"; also see below), Einaudi, 1949.

Il visconte dimezzato (novel; title means "The Cloven Viscount"; also see below), Einaudi, 1952.

L'entrata en guerra (short stories; title means "Entering the War"), Einaudi, 1954.

Il barone rampante (novel; also see below), Enaudi, 1957, translation by Colquhoun published as *The Baron in the Trees,* Random House, 1959, original Italian text published under original title with introduction, notes, and vocabulary by J. R. Woodhouse, Manchester University Press, 1970.

Il cavaliere inesistente (novel; title means "The Nonexistent Knight"; also see below), Einaudi, 1959.

La giornata d'uno scutatore (novella; title means "The Watcher"; also see below), Einaudi, 1963.

La speculazione edilizia (novella; title means "A Plunge into Real Estate"; also see below), Einaudi, 1963.

Ti con zero (stories), Einaudi, 1967, translation by William Weaver published as *T Zero,* Harcourt, 1969 (published in England as *Time and the Hunter,* J. Cape, 1970).

Le cosmicomiche (stories), Einaudi, translation by Weaver published as *Cosmicomics,* Harcourt, 1968.

La memoria del mondo (stories; title means "Memory of the World"), Einaudi, 1968.

(Contributor) *Tarocchi,* F. M. Ricci (Parma), 1969, translation by Weaver published as *Tarots: The Viscount Pack in Bergamo and New York* (limited edition), F. M. Ricci, 1975.

La citta invisibili (novel), Einaudi, 1972, translation by Weaver published as *Invisible Cities,* Harcourt, 1974.

Il castello dei destini incrociati (includes text originally published in *Tarocchi*), Einaudi, 1973, translation by Weaver published as *The Castle of Crossed Destinies,* Harcourt, 1976.

Marcovaldo ovvero le stagioni in citta, Einaudi, 1973, translation by Weaver published as *Marcovaldo: or, The Seasons in the City,* Harcourt, 1983.

Se una notte d'inverno un viaggiatore (novel), 1979, translation by Weaver published as *If on a winter's night a traveler,* Harcourt, 1981.

Palomar (novel), Einaudi, 1983, translation by Weaver published as *Mr. Palomar,* Harcourt, 1985.

Cosmicomiche vecchie e nuove (title means "Cosmicomics Old and New"), Garzanti, 1984.

Sotto il sole giaguaro (stories), Garzanti, 1986, translation by Weaver published as *Under the Jaguar Sun,* Harcourt, 1988.

OMNIBUS VOLUMES

Adam, One Afternoon and Other Stories (contains translation by Colquhoun and Peggy White of stories in *Ultimo viene il corvo* and "La formica argentina"; also see below), Collins, 1957, reprinted, Secker & Warburg, 1980.

I racconti (title means "Stories"; includes "La nuvola de smog" and "La formica argentina"; also see below), Einaudi, 1958.

I nostri antenati (contains *Il cavaliere inesistente, Il visconte dimezzato,* and *Il barone rampante;* also see below), Einaudi, 1960, reprinted, 1982, translation by Colquhoun with new introduction by the author published as *Our Ancestors,* Secker & Warburg, 1980.

The Nonexistent Knight and The Cloven Viscount: Two Short Novels (contains translation by Colquhoun of *Il visconte dimezzato* and *Il cavaliere inesistente*), Random House, 1962.

La nuvola de smog e La formica argentina (also see below), Einaudi, 1965.

Gli amore dificile (contains stories originally published in *Ultimo viene il corvo* and *I racconti*), Einaudi, 1970, translation by Weaver, Colquhoun, and Wright published as *Difficult Loves,* Harcourt, 1984, translation by Weaver and D. C. Carne-Ross published with their translations of "La nuvola de smog" and *La speculazione edilizia* under same title (also see below), Secker & Warburg.

The Watcher and Other Stories (contains translations by Weaver, Colquhoun, and Wright of *La giornata d'uno scutatore,* "La nuvola de smog," and "La formica argentina"), Harcourt, 1971.

EDITOR OR CO-EDITOR

Cesare Pavese, *La letteratura americana e altri saggi,* Einaudi, 1951.

(And reteller) *Fiabe italiane: Raccolte della tradizione popolare durante gli ultimi cento anni e transcritte in lingua dai vari dialetti,* Einaudi, 1956, translation by Louis Brigante of selections published as *Italian Fables,* Orion Press, 1959, translation by George Martin of complete text published as *Italian Folktales,* Harcourt, 1980.

Pavese, *Poesie edite e inedite,* Einaudi, 1962.

Pavese, *Lettere* (with Lorenzo Mondo and Davide Lajolo), Volume I: *1924-1944,* (sole editor) Volume II: *1945-1950,* Einaudi, 1966.

Vittorini: Progettazione e letteratura, All'insegno del pesce d'oro, 1968.

(And reteller) Ludovico Ariosto, *Orlando furioso,* Einaudi, 1970.

Jakob Ludwig Karl Grimm and Wilhelm Karl Grimm, *Fiabe,* Einaudi, 1970.

L'uccel belverde e altre fiabe italiane, Einaudi, 1972, translation by Sylvia Mulcahy of selections published as *Italian Folk Tales,* Dent (London), 1975.

Il principe granchio e altre fiabe italiane, Einaudi, 1974.

Racconti fantastici dell'Ottocento, Mondadori (Milan), 1983.

Also editor of fiction series "Cento Pagi" for Einaudi.

OTHER

Una pietra sopra: Discorsi di letteratura e societa (essays), Einaudi, 1980, translation by Patrick Creagh published as *The Uses of Literature: Essays,* Harcourt, 1986.

Collezione di sabbia: Emblemi bizzarri e inquietanti del nostro passato e del nostro futuro gli og getti raccontano il mondo (articles), Garzanti, 1984.

The Literature Machine, translation by Creagh, Secker & Warburg, 1987.

Six Memos for the Next Millennium, translation by Creagh, Harvard University Press, 1988.

Co-editor with Elio Vittorini of literary magazine, *Il Menabo,* 1959-66.

SIDELIGHTS: Italian novelist and short story writer Italo Calvino was famous for the monumental collection of Italian fables he edited as well as for the fables he wrote. Commenting in the *New York Times Book Review,* for example, novelist John Gardner called Calvino "one of the world's best fabulists." Although he wrote in what Patchy Wheatley referred to in the *Listener* as a "dazzling variety of fictional styles," his stories and novels were all fables for adults. Gore Vidal noted in a *New York Review of Books* essay that because Calvino both edited and wrote fables he was "someone who reached not only primary school children . . . but, at one time or another, everyone who reads."

Calvino's theory of literature, established very early in his career, dictated his use of the fable. For Calvino, to write any narrative was to write a fable. In *Guide to Contemporary Italian Literature: From Futurism to Neorealism,* Sergio Pacifici quoted a portion of Calvino's 1955 essay "Il midollo del leone" ("The Lion's Marrow") in which the novelist wrote: "The mold of the most ancient fables: the child abandoned in the woods or the knight who must survive encounters with beasts and enchantments remains the irreplaceable scheme of all human stories."

To understand Calvino, therefore, one must first understand the fable. Calvino "portrayed the world around him," Sara Maria Adler noted in *Calvino: The Writer as Fablemaker,* "in the same way it is portrayed in the traditional fable. In all his works, the nature of his narrative coincides with those ingredients which constitute the underlying structure of the genre."

A traditional fable, Adler explained, is told from a child's point of view and usually has a young protagonist. Although not all of Calvino's protagonists or narrators are young, John Gatt-Rutter maintained in the *Journal of European Studies,* "The childlike psychology is characteristic of all [of them], whatever their supposed age." The presence of such a youthful narrator/protagonist in Calvino's work lent a fanciful touch to his fiction because, according to Pacifici, "only a youngster possesses a real sense of enchantment with nature, a sense of tranquility and discovery of the mysteries of life."

Another aspect of the fable is what Adler called "the basic theme of tension between character and environment." A typical tale might have a child lost in the woods, for example. Such tension is also a constant in Calvino's fiction. Adler noted, "No matter what the nature of the author's fantasy may be, in every case his characters are faced with a hostile, challenging environment [over] which they are expected to triumph." In "The Argentine Ant," for instance, a family moves to a house in the country only to find it inhabited by thousands of ants. In a more comic example from *Mr. Palomar,* the title character must decide how to walk by a sunbather who has removed her bathing suit top—without appearing either too interested or too indifferent.

Calvino began his career as a fabulist in the late 1940s while still under the influence of the leading writers of postwar Italy. These authors, who had been kept from writing about the world around them by government censorship, now turned wholeheartedly to their everyday life for themes and action for their narratives. Together they formed the neorealist literary movement and, according to Nicholas A. DeMara in the *Italian Quarterly,* drew "material directly from life and . . . reproduce[d] faithfully real situations through traditional methods."

Conceived in this milieu, Calvino's first novel, *The Path to the Nest of Spiders,* and his short story collections, *Adam, One Afternoon* and *L'entrata in guerra* ("Entering the War"), are all realistic. A *Times Literary Supplement* reviewer noted, for example,

that the narratives were "sometimes based on autobiography, and mainly set against the background of recent Italian history and politics." But even while the three works portrayed the realities of war, Calvino's imagination was the dominant element.

The Italian novelist Cesare Pavese was one of the first to note the appearance of fantasy in Calvino's work. Adler reported that, in a 1947 review of *The Path to the Nest of Spiders,* Pavese praised the book's originality, noting "the shrewdness of Calvino, squirrel of the pen, has been this, to climb upon the plants, more in play than out of fear, and to observe . . . life like a fable of the forest, noisy, multi-colored, [and] 'different'."

Following the standard form of a fable, *The Path to the Nest of Spiders* has a young protagonist, an adolescent boy named Pin. According to critics DeMara and Adler, Calvino's choice of Pin as his protagonist allowed the novelist to add fanciful elements to an otherwise realistic story. "In [*The Path to the Nest of Spiders*]," DeMara stated, "Calvino portray[ed] an essentially realistic world, but through the use of the adolescent figure he [was] frequently able to inject into the work a sense of fantasy." Pin is nearly a child, and he describes his world as many children do, using a combination of real and imaginary elements. A fable-like quality is added to the novel, Adler observed, because "seen through the boy's own eyes . . . [everything] is thus infused with a fanciful and spirited attitude toward life. . . . The countryside may be as lyrical as an animated cartoon, while at other times it may assume the proportions of a nightmare."

Calvino's childlike imagination and sense of playfulness filled his work with fantasy but also served another purpose. According to J. R. Woodhouse in *Italo Calvino: A Reappraisal and Appreciation of the Trilogy,* "Calvino's description of child-like candour is often a very telling way of pointing to an anomaly, a stupidity in society, as well as providing a new and refreshing outlook on often well-worn themes." In this way Calvino added another fable-like dimension to his work, that of moral instruction.

Young people play prominent roles in all three of the novels in Calvino's *Our Ancestors* trilogy: *The Cloven Viscount, The Baron in the Trees,* and *The Nonexistent Knight.* The "tension between character and environment" and the moral intent are also clear in the three works. They demonstrate the reasoning behind JoAnn Cannon's assertion in *Modern Fiction Studies* that "the fantastic in Calvino is not a form of escapism, but is grounded in a persistent sociopolitical concern."

The narrator of *The Baron in the Trees,* for instance, is the younger brother of the twelve-year-old baron of the title who ascends into the trees to avoid eating snail soup. In *Books Abroad,* Pacifici noted that *The Baron in the Trees* stands for man who, by choosing and acting an extraordinarily eccentric role, tries to fulfill a certain aspiration of diversity apparently denied to man in our age." And in his introduction to *Our Ancestors,* Calvino explained the meaning of *The Cloven Viscount,* a narrative about a soldier split in half by a cannonball during a crusade: "Mutilated, incomplete, an enemy to himself is modern man; Marx called him 'alienated,' Freud 'repressed'; a state of ancient harmony is lost, [and] a new state of completeness aspired to."

Calvino's ability to fuse reality and fantasy captured the imagination of critics on both sides of the Atlantic. For example, in the *New York Times Book Review* Alan Cheuse wrote about Calvino's "talent for transforming the mundane into the marvelous," and in the *London Review of Books* Salman Rushdie referred to Calvino's "effortless ability of seeing the miraculous in the quotidian." According to *New York Times* reviewer Anatole Broyard, the books in which Calvino perfected this tendency were three later works: *Cosmicomics, Invisible Cities,* and *If on a winter's night a traveler.* With their juxtaposition of fantasy and reality these books led critics such as John Updike and John Gardner to compare Calvino with two other master storytellers noted for using the same technique in their fiction: Jorge Luis Borges and Gabriel Garcia Marquez.

The stories in *Cosmicomics* as well as most of the stories in *T Zero* and *La memoria del mondo* (*Memory of the World*)—chronicle the adventures of Qfwfq, a strange, chameleon-like creature who was present at the beginning of the universe, the formation of the stars, and the disappearance of the dinosaurs. In a playful scene typical of Calvin—and reminiscent of the comic episodes of Garcia Marquez's *One Hundred Years of Solitude*—Qfwfq describes how time began: According to his story, all the universe was contained in a single point until the day one of the inhabitants of the point, Mrs. Ph(i)Nko, decided to make pasta for everyone. Rushdie explained, "The explosion of the universe outwards . . . is precipitated by the first generous impulse, the first-ever 'true outburst of general love,' when . . . Mrs. Ph(i)Nko cries out: 'Oh, if I only had some room, how I'd love to make some noodles for you boys.'"

Even as his fiction became more and more fantastic in the Qfwfq stories, Calvino continued to maintain the moral and social overtones present in his earlier work. In *Science-Fiction Studies,* Teresa de Lauretis observed that while Calvino's fiction acquired a science-fiction quality during the 1960s and 1970s due to its emphasis on scientific and technological themes, it was still based on specific human concerns. "The works," she commented, "were all highly imaginative, scientifically informed, funny and inspired meditations on one insistent question: What does it mean to be human, to live and die, to reproduce and to create, to desire and to be?"

In a *New Yorker* review Updike made a similar observation about the seriousness underlying Calvino's fantasies. Updike wrote: "Calvino is . . . curious about the human truth as it becomes embedded in its animal, vegetable, historical, and comic contexts; all his investigations spiral in upon the central question of *How shall we live?*"

Invisible Cities was the book which Calvino called his "most finished and perfect" in a *Saturday Review* interview with Alexander Stille. It was also, according to Lorna Sage in the *Observer,* "the book that first brought him large-scale international acclaim."

Invisible Cities relates an imaginary conversation between the thirteenth-century explorer Marco Polo and the emperor Kublai Khan in which Polo describes fifty-five different cities within the emperor's kingdom. Critics applauded the book for the beauty of Calvino's descriptions. In the *New Republic,* for instance, Albert H. Carter III called it "a sensuous delight, a sophisticated literary puzzle," while in the *Chicago Tribune* Constance Markey judged it "a fragile tapestry of mood pieces." Perhaps the most generous praise came from *Times Literary Supplement* contributor Paul Bailey, who observed, "This most beautiful of [Calvino's] books throws up ideas, allusions, and breathtaking imaginative insights on almost every page."

Invisible Cities is another fable with a youthful Marco Polo and a moral to be pondered. Adler explained: "Polo's task is that of teaching the aging Kublai Khan to give a new meaning to his life by challenging the evil forces in his domain and by insuring the safety of whatever is just. . . . [Polo's] observations . . . are a general explanation of the world—a panoramic view where rich and poor, the living and the dead, young and old, are challenged by the complex battles of existence."

In the *Hudson Review,* Dean Flower compared *Invisible Cities* with one of Calvino's later novels, *The Castle of Crossed Destinies,* calling them both "less novels than meditations on the mysteries of fictive structures." This statement could also be applied to Calvino's most experimental novel, *If on a winter's night a traveler. The Castle of Crossed Destinies,* like *The Nonexistent Knight,* is a chivalric tale filled with knights and adventure. *If on a winter's night a traveler,* however, is not only different from Calvino's previous work, it is also marked by a complexity that makes it his least fable-like book.

In *If on a winter's night a traveler,* Calvino parodied modern fictional styles in a complicated novel-within-a-novel format. But even this novel included at least one element of the fable. In *Newsweek* Jim Miller noted that in Calvino's introduction to *Italian Folktales* the novelist wrote, "There must be present [in the . . . tale] the infinite possibilities of mutation, the unifying element in everything: men, beasts, plants, things." While the fable explores mutation in nature, in *If on a winter's night a traveler* Calvino explored the "infinite possibilities of mutation" within the novel.

Calvino's childlike imagination allowed him to leave the tenets of neorealism behind and opened up infinite possibilities for his fiction. He imaginatively used the traditional fable form to write non-traditional fiction. Although he was a fabulist, according to Pacifici in *A Guide to Modern Italian Literature,* Calvino's works were "not . . . flights from reality but [came] from the bitter reality of our twentieth century. They are the means—perhaps the only means left to a writer tired of a photographic obsession with modern life—to re-create a world where people can still be people—that is, where people can still dream and yet understand."

AVOCATIONAL INTERESTS: Movies, especially American ones.

BIOGRAPHICAL/CRITICAL SOURCES:

BOOKS

Adler, Sara Maria, *Calvino: The Writer as Fablemaker,* Ediciones Jose Porrua Turanzas, 1979.
Contemporary Literary Criticism, Gale, Volume V, 1976, Volume VIII, 1978, Volume XI, 1979, Volume XXII, 1982, Volume XXX, 1984, Volume XXXIX, 1986.
Gatt-Rutter, John, *Writers and Politics in Modern Italy,* Holmes & Meier, 1978.
Mandel, Siegfried, editor, *Contemporary European Novelists,* Southern Illinois University Press, 1986.
Pacifici, Sergio, *A Guide to Contemporary Italian Literature: From Futurism to Neorealism,* World, 1962.
Woodhouse, J. R., *Italo Calvino: A Reappraisal and an Appreciation of the Trilogy,* University of Hull, 1968.

PERIODICALS

Atlantic, March, 1977.
Chicago Tribune, November 10, 1985.
Commonweal, November 8, 1957, June 19, 1981.
Globe and Mail (Toronto), July 7, 1984, January 25, 1986, February 4, 1989.
Hudson Review, summer, 1984.
Italian Quarterly, winter, 1971.
Journal of European Studies, December, 1975.
Listener, February 20, 1975, March 17, 1983, September 26, 1985.
London Review of Books, September 30, 1981.

Los Angeles Times Book Review, November 27, 1983, October 6, 1985, October 20, 1985, March 6, 1988, October 30, 1988.

Modern Fiction Studies, spring, 1978.

Nation, February 19, 1977, May 23, 1981, December 29, 1984-January 5, 1985.

New Criterion, December, 1985.

Newsweek, February 14, 1977, November 17, 1980, June 8, 1981, November 28, 1983, October 8, 1984, October 21, 1985.

New Yorker, February 24, 1975, April 18, 1977, February 23, 1981, August 3, 1981, September 10, 1984, October 28, 1985, November 18, 1985.

New York Review of Books, November 21, 1968, January 29, 1970, May 30, 1974, May 12, 1977, June 25, 1981, December 6, 1984, November 21, 1985.

New York Times, October 11, 1959, August 6, 1968, January 13, 1971, May 5, 1981, November 9, 1983, September 25, 1984, November 26, 1984, September 26, 1985.

New York Times Book Review, November 8, 1959, August 5, 1962, August 12, 1968, August 25, 1968, October 12, 1969, February 7, 1971, November 17, 1974, April 10, 1977, October 12, 1980, June 21, 1981, January 22, 1984, October 7, 1984, March 20, 1988, October 23, 1988.

New York Times Magazine, July 10, 1983.

Observer, September 22, 1985.

PMLA, May, 1975.

Saturday Review, December 6, 1959, November 15, 1969, May, 1981, March/April, 1985.

Science-Fiction Studies, March, 1986.

Spectator, February 22, 1975, May 14, 1977, August 15, 1981, September 24, 1983.

Time, January 31, 1977, October 6, 1980, May 25, 1981, October 1, 1984, September 23, 1985.

Times (London), July 9, 1981, September 1, 1983, October 3, 1985.

Times Literary Supplement, April 24, 1959, February 23, 1962, September 8, 1966, April 18, 1968, February 9, 1973, December 14, 1973, February 21, 1975, January 9, 1981, July 10, 1981, September 2, 1983, July 12, 1985, September 26, 1986, August 14, 1987.

Tribune Books (Chicago), October 23, 1988.

Village Voice, December 16, 1981.

Voice Literary Supplement, October, 1986.

Washington Post, January 13, 1984.

Washington Post Book World, April 25, 1971, October 12, 1980, June 7, 1981, November 18, 1984, September 22, 1985, November 16, 1986, March 27, 1988, October 30, 1988.

OBITUARIES:

PERIODICALS

Chicago Tribune, September 21, 1985.

Detroit Free Press, September 20, 1985.

Los Angeles Times, September 21, 1985.

New York Times, September 20, 1985.

Times (London), September 20, 1985.

Washington Post, September 20, 1985.

*   *   *

CAMERON, Eleanor (Frances) 1912-

PERSONAL: Born March 23, 1912, in Winnipeg, Manitoba, Canada; daughter of Henry and Florence Lydia (Vaughan) Butler; married Ian Stuart Cameron (a printer and publisher), June 24, 1934; children: David Gordon. *Education:* Attended University of California, Los Angeles, 1931-33, and Art Center School, Los Angeles, one year.

ADDRESSES: Home—2865 Forest Lodge Rd., Pebble Beach, CA 93953.

CAREER: Public Library, Los Angeles, Calif., clerk, 1930-36; Board of Education Library, Los Angeles, clerk, 1936-42; Foote, Cone & Belding (advertising agency), Los Angeles, research librarian, 1943-44; Honig, Cooper & Harrington (advertising agency), Los Angeles, research librarian, 1956-58; Dan B. Miner Co., Los Angeles, librarian, 1958-59; writer. Member of advisory board, Center for the Study of Children's Literature, Simmons College (Boston), 1977—. Children's literature judge, National Book Awards, 1980. Gertrude Clarke Whittall Lecturer, Library of Congress, 1977.

MEMBER: P.E.N. International, Authors Guild, Authors League of America, Audubon Society, Sierra Club, Wilderness Society, Save-the-Redwoods League.

AWARDS, HONORS: Hawaiian Children's Choice Nene Award, 1960, for *The Wonderful Flight to the Mushroom Planet;* Mystery Writers of America Award, 1964, for *A Spell Is Cast;* California Literature Silver Medal Award from Commonwealth Club of California, 1965, for *A Spell Is Cast,* and 1970, for *The Green and Burning Tree: On the Writing and Enjoyment of Children's Books;* Southern California Council on Literature for Children and Young People Award, 1965, for distinguished contribution to the field of children's literature; *A Room Made of Windows, The Court of the Stone Children, To the Green Mountains, Julia and the Hand of God,* and *That Julia Redfern* are all American Library Association Notable Books; *Boston Globe-Horn Book* Award, 1971, for *A Room Made of Windows;* National Book Award for children's literature, 1974, for *The Court of the Stone Children;* National Book Award runner-up, 1976, for *To the Green Mountains;* Kerlan Award for a body of work, 1985.

WRITINGS:

The Unheard Music (adult novel), Little, Brown, 1950.

The Green and Burning Tree: On the Writing and Enjoyment of Children's Books (critical essays), Atlantic-Little, Brown, 1969.

"MUSHROOM PLANET" SERIES

The Wonderful Flight to the Mushroom Planet (Junior Literary Guild selection), illustrated by Robert Henneberger, Little, Brown, 1954.

Stowaway to the Mushroom Planet (Junior Literary Guild selection), illustrated by Henneberger, Little, Brown, 1956.

Mr. Bass's Planetoid (Junior Literary Guild selection), Little, Brown, 1958.

A Mystery for Mr. Bass, illustrated by Leonard Shortall, Little, Brown, 1960.

Time and Mr. Bass, illustrated by Fred Meise, Little, Brown, 1967.

"JULIA REDFERN" SERIES

A Room Made of Windows, illustrated by Trina Schart Hyman, Little, Brown, 1971.

Julia and the Hand of God (Junior Literary Guild selection), illustrated by Gail Owens, Dutton, 1977.

That Julia Redfern, illustrated by Owens, Dutton, 1982.

Julia's Magic, Dutton, 1984.

The Private Worlds of Julia Redfern, Dutton, 1988.

JUVENILE NOVELS

The Terrible Churnadryne (Junior Literary Guild selection), illustrated by B. Krush and J. Krush, Little, Brown, 1959.

The Mysterious Christmas Shell (sequel to *The Terrible Churnadryne;* Junior Literary Guild selection), illustrated by B. Krush and J. Krush, Little, Brown, 1961.

The Beast with the Magical Horn, illustrated by B. Krush and J. Krush, Little, Brown, 1963.

A Spell Is Cast (Junior Literary Guild selection), illustrated by B. Krush and J. Krush, Little, Brown, 1964.

The Court of the Stone Children (Junior Literary Guild selection), Dutton, 1973.

To the Green Mountains, Dutton, 1975.

Beyond Silence, Dutton, 1980.

CONTRIBUTOR

Paul Heins, editor, *Crosscurrents of Criticism: "Horn Book" Essays, 1968-1969,* Horn Book, 1977.

Prelude: Mini-Seminars on Using Books Creatively, Series 4, Children's Book Council, 1979.

Virginia Haviland, editor, *The Openhearted Audience: Ten Authors Talk about Writing for Children,* Library of Congress, 1980.

Robert Bator, editor, *Signposts to Criticism of Children's Literature,* American Library Association, 1983.

Perry Nodelman and Jill P. May, editors, *Festschrift: A Ten Year Retrospective,* Children's Literature Association, 1983.

Compton Rees, editor, *Children's Literature,* Volume 12, Yale University Press, 1984.

Also contributor to *The First Steps: Best of the Early "Children's Literature Association Quarterly,"* edited by Patricia Dooley, 1984. Contributor to *Horn Book, Wilson Library Bulletin, Children's Literature Association Quarterly,* and other periodicals.

OTHER

Member of editorial board, *Cricket: The Magazine for Children,* 1973—, and *Children's Literature in Education,* 1982—.

The "Mushroom Planet" books have been translated into Spanish; the first book in the series, *The Wonderful Flight to the Mushroom Planet,* has been translated into Japanese and Iranian as well. *The Court of the Stone Children* also has been published in Spanish.

MEDIA ADAPTATIONS: A Room Made of Windows was made into a sound recording by Crane Memorial Library in 1979; *The Court of the Stone Children* is being made into a play.

WORK IN PROGRESS: A second book of critical essays on children's literature.

SIDELIGHTS: Ever since the appearance of Eleanor Cameron's *Wonderful Flight to the Mushroom Planet* in 1954, critics, as well as the general public, have been almost unanimous in their praise of her children's books. One testament to Cameron's writing skill is the long-term popularity of her "Mushroom Planet" series; as recently as 1979 the series's second book, *Stowaway to the Mushroom Planet* (1956), was on the Scholastic Booklist of the one hundred best sellers. The five-book series, which evolved out of Cameron's son's request for a space story with magic in it, focuses on two young boys from earth, David and Tom, who travel to and from the Mushroom Planet Basidium, usually under the tutelage of Basidiumite scientist Mr. Bass. David and Tom perform several heroic feats to protect the Mushroom People and their planet from impinging modernism and various underhanded plots by the evil scientist Prewytt Brumblydge. According to Sue Garness and Grace Sulerud in the *Dictionary of Literary Biography,* "the series appeals to the child's desire to have a place of his own, unknown to adults, where he carries out momentous plans to save the world from destruction or to help others fulfill their destinies."

While Cameron herself admits in *Signposts to Criticism of Children's Literature* that "reviewers called [the 'Mushroom Planet'] stories alternately science fiction and space fantasy," she feels that the point is a moot one. She tends to agree with a friend's interpretation that her writings, in general, fall somewhere in the middle, "between the Red or S[cience] F[iction] end of the spectrum and the works with trolls that are likely to be over in the Violet or Fantasy end. . . . You are playing with and making gentle fun of all space gadgetry, but also you quite soberly present some of the marvelousness and splendor of the universe as revealed by physics and astronomy and their technologies."

For the most part, Cameron's stories for children involve fairly complex space or time fantasies that incorporate elements of humor, suspense, mystery, and the skillful fusion of fictive, historical, and scientific detail. Of Cameron's National Book Award-winning *Court of the Stone Children,* Barbara Wersba writes in the *New York Times Book Review:* "In an age when writers are engulfing children with an almost gratuitous realism, it is exciting to read a story that glances back into the literary shadows of memory, fantasy, and dream." However, Cameron does not create her fantasy worlds at the expense of reality. Regarding Cameron's *Room Made of Windows,* Perry Nodelman writes in the *Children's Literature Association Quarterly* that "to read [the book] is to be convinced that one is reading an autobiography; the book simply *feels* real, like reminiscence rather than like storytelling. . . . Cameron has a double gift; her faith in the magic of self is balanced by a clearheaded knowledge of the world as it actually is. And despite her faith in the healing powers of fantasy, she never lets her characters get away with lies about the world as it actually is."

Unlike some juvenile authors, Cameron avoids "talking down" to her audience; in fact, several of Cameron's books, including *To the Green Mountains, A Room Made of Windows,* and *The Court of the Stone Children,* have been singled out as works which are so thoughtfully constructed that they easily bridge the gap between books written for children and those written for adults. Wersba considers *The Court of the Stone Children* to contain "the kind of writing that one associates with adult novels, and indeed the author has not made a single concession to the conventions of childhood. Her story is complex [and] multi-layered." Patience M. Canham concludes in the *Christian Science Monitor* that Cameron "has the knack of pointing out self-deceptions and other antics of growing up without making them appear either important or 'cute.' And all the while she is imparting ideas about integrity and consideration."

Cameron herself explained to *CA:* "I can't say what started me writing as a child, except that I had been a reading animal from the beginning. By the time I was eleven, the writing process already absorbed me and I knew I wanted to be a writer, an ambition confirmed when my writings were first accepted by the local Berkeley paper when I was twelve. I kept writing through my teens and into my twenties with nothing taken by any publisher until my first novel, *The Unheard Music,* was accepted by Atlantic when I sent it to them on request after the *Atlantic Monthly* rejected a short story. In that book I see now that I wanted to achieve the unfolding of a view of life. It had no plot; I was under the influence of Virginia Woolf, and so a life view, a feeling-tone, was what I had in mind and, to strongly evoke this, the creation of characters the reader could understand and identify with. I have always been much involved with character creation and am bored by novels in which characters have been indifferently felt and therefore indifferently portrayed. I am also drawn by the way a book is written, and therefore I myself have apparently been developing an individual style. I don't try for 'style' as something artificially created, but keep rewriting until I have said exactly what I want to say in just the way I want to say it.

"To begin with, of course, there is place. I have no novel if I have no place, because out of place rise my characters and they make the story move and give it life and meaning and reality. For me it would be hopeless to mechanically construct a plot, for there would be no way in which anything could come alive. Nor could I mechanically construct my characters by drawing up histories and lists of idiosyncrasies and things they must do. Everything grows very slowly over a period of from two to thirty years, during which time I am convinced the unconscious does much of the work.

"I write a book every other year, but I am always working, always thinking, making notes, getting illuminations for my novels from thinking and reading and remembering. When I'm writing a book, I can't always write every day, but I write as long as I can when I'm in the midst of it. The book is *there;* it needs only to find the right tone and rhythm, and that is the difficult part. There is no struggle 'to make the characters come alive' or 'to make the plot work.' The characters present themselves and, through them, if I am convinced of the basic idea that seems to want to be expressed, the story grows naturally. It's up to me to find the fullness and extent of it through words that will reveal it most clearly and satisfyingly.

"Advice for aspiring writers: read the best in any field you want to write in—only the best. But you must have a point of view of your own. If you have no point of view, no convictions about life, no strong sense of self, you will have nothing to say, no base to write from, no ability to develop an individual style."

BIOGRAPHICAL/CRITICAL SOURCES:

BOOKS

Bator, Robert, editor, *Signposts to Criticism of Children's Literature,* American Library Association, 1983.
Children's Literature Review, Volume 1, Gale, 1976.
Dictionary of Literary Biography, Volume 52: *American Writers for Children since 1960: Fiction,* Gale, 1986.
Haviland, Virginia, editor, *The Openhearted Audience: Ten Authors Talk About Writing for Children,* Library of Congress, 1980.
Rees, Compton, editor, *Children's Literature,* Volume 12, Yale University Press, 1984.

PERIODICALS

Best Sellers, May 15, 1971.
Booklist, September 15, 1977.
Book World, May 9, 1971.
Children's Book News, November-December, 1969.
Children's Literature Association Quarterly, winter, 1980, winter, 1981, winter, 1982.
Christian Science Monitor, May 6, 1961.
New York Herald Tribune Book Review, May 14, 1950.
New York Times, November 14, 1954, September 23, 1956.
New York Times Book Review, November 1, 1959, April 25, 1971, May 2, 1971, November 4, 1973, November 9, 1975, March 6, 1983.

Saturday Review, November 13, 1954, September 22, 1956, April 17, 1971.
Saturday Review of Literature, June 25, 1950.

*　　*　　*

CAMPBELL, John W(ood, Jr.)　1910-1971
(Arthur McCann, Don A. Stuart, Karl Van Campen)

PERSONAL: Born June 8, 1910, in Newark, N.J.; died July 11, 1971, in Mountainside, N.J.; son of John W. (a telephone engineer) and Dorothy (Strahorn) Campbell; married Donna Stuart, 1931 (divorced, 1950); married Margaret Winter (a consultant on crewel embroideries), June 15, 1950; children: four. *Education:* Attended Massachusetts Institute of Technology, 1928-31; Duke University, B.Sc., 1933. *Politics:* "May the best man win." *Religion:* Unitarian Universalist.

CAREER: Free-lance writer of science fiction, 1930-37; Conde-Nast Publishing Co., New York, N.Y., 1937-71, editor of *Astounding Stories* (later retitled *Astounding Science Fiction* and *Analog*) 1937-71, and *Unknown* and *Unknown Worlds,* 1939-43. Also worked as a car and gas heater salesman, and in the research departments of Mack Truck, Hoboken Pioneer Instruments, and Carleton Ellis Chemical Co.

AWARDS, HONORS: Hugo Awards for editing, 1953, 1955, 1956, 1957, 1961, 1962, 1964, and 1965; guest of honor at World Science Fiction Conventions in Philadelphia, 1947, San Francisco, 1954, and London, 1957.

WRITINGS:

The Atomic Story (science text), Holt, 1947.
The Mightiest Machine (science fiction novel), Hadley Publishing Co., 1947, reprinted, Ace Books, 1972.
Who Goes There?: Seven Tales of Science Fiction, Shasta, 1948, published in England as *The Thing and Other Stories,* Cherry Tree, 1952.
(Editor) *From Unknown Worlds,* Street & Smith, 1948.
The Incredible Planet (science fiction novel), Fantasy Press, 1949.
The Moon Is Hell! (science fiction novel), Fantasy Press, 1951, reprinted, Ace Books, 1973.
Cloak of Aesir (science fiction short stories), Shasta, 1952.
(Editor) *The Astounding Science Fiction Anthology,* Simon & Schuster, 1952, published in England in 2 volumes as *The First Astounding Science Fiction Anthology* and *The Second Astounding Science Fiction Anthology,* Grayson, 1954, published as *Astounding Tales of Space and Time,* Berkley Publishing, 1957.
The Black Star Passes (science fiction short stories), Fantasy Press, 1953, reprinted, Ace Books, 1972.
Who Goes There? and Other Stories, Dell, 1955.
Islands of Space (science fiction novel), Fantasy Press, 1956.
Invaders from the Infinite (science fiction novel), Gnome Press, 1961.
(Editor) *Prologue to Analog,* Doubleday, 1962.
(Editor) *Analog* (science fiction anthology), 8 volumes, Doubleday, 1963-71.
Collected Editorials from Analog, edited by Harry Harrison, Doubleday, 1966.
The Planeteers (science fiction short stories), Ace Books, 1966.
The Ultimate Weapon (science fiction novel), Ace Books, 1966.
The Best of John W. Campbell (science fiction short stories), Sidgwick & Jackson, 1974.
The Best of John W. Campbell (science fiction short stories), edited by Lester del Rey, Doubleday, 1976.

The Space Beyond (science fiction short stories), Pyramid, 1976.

SIDELIGHTS: John W. Campbell is a legend in the history of science fiction. In his thirty-odd year career as editor of *Astounding Science Fiction*—the major science fiction magazine of the 1940s—he changed the nature of the genre, shifting its focus from the "rockets and rayguns" space opera/adventure that had dominated the field in the 1920s and 1930s to a more humane field, interested in the impact scientific advance might have on humanity. "More clearly than anyone," states Damon Knight in *In Search of Wonder: Essays on Modern Science Fiction,* "Campbell saw that the field was growing up and would only be handicapped by the symbols of its pulpwood infancy; he deliberately built up a readership among practicing scientists and technicians; he made himself the apostle of genuine science in science fiction." He also introduced and nurtured the careers of such giants of the genre as Isaac Asimov, L. Sprague de Camp, Fritz Leiber, L. Ron Hubbard, Robert A. Heinlein, Lester del Rey, Theodore Sturgeon, Poul Anderson, Jack Williamson, and A. E. van Vogt. "Campbell, through these men," declares Theodore Sturgeon in *National Review,* "created a Golden Age of sf."

Campbell began his career in science fiction as a writer. His first story was published in 1930, when he was still in his teens. Campbell's familiarity with scientific hardware helped him master the genre quickly. At that time, explains Russel B. Nye in *The Unembarrassed Muse: The Popular Arts in America,* science fiction "focused on the 'gadget' or 'gimmick,' as one writer called it, which served as the hook on which the narrative hung. It might be a space ship, or a gravitational shift, or a mind-machine, or a time-slip, but whatever it was it was the story's most important element. Characters and plot served chiefly to elucidate the central scientific point; subtlety of motivation or niceties of craftsmanship were of less value than the 'science factor' on which the narrative pivoted. . . . Its aim often seemed to be to convince the public of the beneficial potentials of science as much as to tell a story." Campbell's super-science adventure stories soon rivalled in popularity those of E. E. "Doc" Smith, whose "Skylark" and "Lensman" series helped define space opera on a galactic scale. Under the pseudonym Don A. Stuart, Campbell wrote stories of a quite different nature, in which mood predominated over gadgetry—the publication of one of the Stuart stories, "Twilight," says Sam Moskowitz in *Seekers of Tomorrow: Masters of Science Fiction,* "was to alter the pattern of science-fiction writing." By 1938, Moskowitz declares in *Explorers of the Infinite: Shapers of Science Fiction,* Campbell "was regarded . . . as one of the half-dozen greatest living writers of science fiction."

1938 was also the year in which Campbell was appointed editor of *Astounding,* a position that enabled him to expound his ideas about science fiction; and, says Nye, Campbell "had clear and definite ideas of what he wanted. Instead of concentrating on machines and methodology, he advised writers to emphasize character, style, and the dramatic possibilities of the genre. To him, and to the group of writers he encouraged, science fiction should be not only concerned with scientific and technological change, but with its social and cultural implications as well." "He sought, as in his own writing," states Gerald Conley in the *Dictionary of Literary Biography,* "a balance between the *science* and the *fiction,* through writers who could postulate reasonable scientific advances, in light of current knowledge and then intuit their effects on society and the individual." "The guidelines he created," Conley concludes, "resulted in a quality of science fiction unequalled in the field."

"For SF historians," writes Thomas J. Remington in the *North American Review,* "the association of John Campbell's editorship with *Astounding* stands as *the* event in the 'Golden Age' of science fiction. Campbell's *Astounding* is revered for giving birth to much of the early work of such major SF authors as Robert Heinlein, Theodore Sturgeon, Isaac Asimov, and A. E. van Vogt." Campbell's ideas also inspired his authors; one of his stories formed the basis for Robert A. Heinlein's *Sixth Column,* and Isaac Asimov, says Conley, credits Campbell with the plot of his classic story "Nightfall"—judged by readers one of the best SF stories of all time—and with much of the outline of his original "Foundation" trilogy. Until the 1950s, declares Algis Budrys in the *Magazine of Fantasy and Science Fiction,* "Campbell operated alone upon the hearts and minds of his writers and of his readers, who firmly believed that any newsstand SF not in *Astounding Science Fiction* was a sometimes interesting but always lesser sort of thing."

Campbell's magazine lost its unchallenged leadership position in the 1950s and 1960s with the advent of other quality science fiction publications, including the *Magazine of Fantasy and Science Fiction* and *Galaxy Science Fiction.* As time went on, Campbell's influenced on SF diminished; the 1960s introduced the school of SF known as the New Wave, a subgenre of science fiction that largely concentrated on near-future plots and the social sciences. Campbell himself turned more and more towards esoteric ideas such as L. Ron Hubbard's *Dianetics,* and his magazine, says Conley, "began to turn to the old technological emphasis. Campbell's former fondness for the primacy of scientific idea was perhaps overcoming the successful formula of balance between science and imagination." Yet, Conley states, "if Campbell's influence on science fiction has in fact waned to a degree, it still remains very strong, stronger perhaps than any other in the field." A Martian crater has been named "Campbell" in his honor. However, "the greatest testimony of his place in the history of science fiction," declares Conley, "is surely the title of the Hugo Award for best new writer: the 'John W. Campbell Memorial Award.' "

MEDIA ADAPTATIONS: *Who Goes There?* was adapted as the motion picture "The Thing" (also released as "The Thing from Another World").

AVOCATIONAL INTERESTS: Photography, electronics, working in wood and metal, experiments in extrasensory perception.

BIOGRAPHICAL/CRITICAL SOURCES:

BOOKS

Contemporary Literary Criticism, Volume 32, Gale, 1985.
Dictionary of Literary Biography, Volume 8: *Twentieth-Century American Science Fiction Writers,* Gale, 1981.
Knight, Damon, *In Search of Wonder: Essays on Modern Science Fiction,* Advent, 1967.
Moskowitz, Sam, *Explorers of the Infinite: Shapers of Science Fiction,* World Publishing, 1963.
Moskowitz, Sam, *Seekers of Tomorrow: Masters of Science Fiction,* World Publishing, 1966.
Nye, Russel B., *The Unembarrassed Muse: The Popular Arts in America,* Dial, 1970.

PERIODICALS

Magazine of Fantasy and Science Fiction, December, 1976, March, 1977.
National Review, March 10, 1970.

North American Review, June, 1981.

—*Sketch by Kenneth R. Shepherd*

*   *   *

CAMPBELL, Joseph   1904-1987

PERSONAL: Born March 26, 1904, in New York, N.Y.; died October 30, 1987, in Honolulu, Hawaii; son of Charles William (a hosiery importer and wholesaler) and Josephine (Lynch) Campbell; married Jean Erdman (a dancer and choreographer), May 5, 1938. *Education:* Attended Dartmouth College, 1921-22; Columbia University, A.B., 1925, M.A., 1927, additional graduate study, 1927-28, 1928-29; graduate study at the University of Paris, 1927-28, and the University of Munich, 1928-29.

CAREER: Independent study of mythology, 1929-32; Canterbury School, New Milford, Conn., teacher of French, German, and ancient history, 1932-33; Sarah Lawrence College, Bronxville, N.Y., member of literature department faculty, 1934-72. Lecturer, Foreign Service Institute, U.S. Department of State, 1956-73, and at Columbia University, 1959. President, Creative Film Foundation, 1954-63, and of Foundation for the Open Eye, beginning 1973. Trustee, Bollingen Foundation, 1960-69.

MEMBER: American Folklore Society, American Oriental Society, American Society for the Study of Religion (president, 1972-75), American Academy of Psychotherapists (honorary member), Century Club, New York Athletic Club.

AWARDS, HONORS: Proudfit fellow, 1927-28, 1928-29; grants-in-aid for editing Zimmer volumes, 1946-55; National Institute of Arts and Letters grant in literature, 1949, for *The Hero with a Thousand Faces;* Distinguished Scholar Award, Hofstra University, 1973; D.H.L., Pratt Institute, 1976; Melcher Award for contribution to religious liberalism, 1976, for *The Mythic Image;* National Arts Club medal of honor for literature, 1985; elected to the American Academy of Arts and Letters, 1987.

WRITINGS:

(With Maud Oakes and Jeff King) *Where the Two Come to Their Father: A Navaho War Ceremonial,* Pantheon, 1943.
(With Henry Morton Robinson) *A Skeleton Key to "Finnegans Wake,"* Harcourt, 1944, reprinted, Penguin, 1977.
The Hero with a Thousand Faces, Pantheon, 1949, revised edition, Princeton University Press, 1980.
The Masks of God, Viking, Volume 1: *Primitive Mythology,* 1959, Volume 2: *Oriental Mythology,* 1962, Volume 3: *Occidental Mythology,* 1964, Volume 4: *Creative Mythology,* 1968.
The Flight of the Wild Gander, Viking, 1969.
Myths to Live By, Viking, 1972.
(With M. J. Abadie) *The Mythic Image,* Princeton University Press, 1974.
(With Richard Roberts) *Tarot Revelations,* Alchemy Books, 1980, 2nd edition, Vernal Equinox, 1982.
Historical Atlas of World Mythology, Van der Marck, Volume 1: *The Way of the Animal Powers,* 1983, revised edition published in two parts, Part 1: *Mythologies of the Primitive Hunters and Gatherers,* 1988, Part 2: *Mythology of the Great Hunt,* 1988, Volume 2: *The Way of the Seeded Earth,* Part 1: *The Sacrifice,* 1988.
The Inner Reaches of Outer Space: Metaphor as Myth and as Religion, Van der Marck, 1986.
(With Bill Moyers) *The Power of Myth* (interviews; also see below), Doubleday, 1988.
(With Moyers) "The Power of Myth" (six-part television series), Public Broadcasting Service, 1988.

EDITOR

Heinrich Robert Zimmer, *Myths and Symbols in Indian Art and Civilization,* Pantheon, 1946, reprinted, Princeton University Press, 1971.
Zimmer, *The King and the Corpse: Tales of the Soul's Conquest of Evil,* Pantheon, 1948, reprinted, Princeton University Press, 1971.
Zimmer, *Philosophies of India,* Pantheon, 1951, reprinted, Princeton University Press, 1969.
The Portable Arabian Nights, Viking, 1952.
(General editor) *Papers from the Eranos Yearbooks,* Princeton University Press, Volume 1: *Spirit and Nature,* 1954, Volume 2: *The Mysteries,* 1955, Volume 3: *Man and Time,* 1957, Volume 4: *Spiritual Disciplines,* 1960, Volume 5: *Man and Transformation,* 1964, Volume 6: *The Mystic Vision,* 1969.
Zimmer, *The Art of Indian Asia,* Pantheon, 1955, 2nd edition in two volumes, Princeton University Press, 1960.
Myths, Dreams, and Religion, Dutton, 1970, reprinted, Spring Publications, 1988.
The Portable Jung, Viking, 1972.
Rato K. Losang, *My Life and Times: The Story of a Tibetan Incarnation,* Dutton, 1977.

Also editor of *The Mountainy Singer* by Seosamh MacCathmhaoil, AMS Press. General editor of "Myth and Man" series, Thames & Hudson, 1951-54.

CONTRIBUTOR

The Complete Grimm's Fairy Tales, Pantheon, 1944, reprinted, Random House, 1972.
James Joyce: Two Decades of Criticism, Vanguard, 1948.
Psychoanalysis and Culture, International Universities Press, 1951.
Basic Beliefs, Sheridan, 1959.
Culture in History, Columbia University Press, 1960.
Myth and Mythmaking, Braziller, 1960.
Myths, McGraw, 1974.

Contributor of articles to publications.

WORK IN PROGRESS: Further volumes in the *Historical Atlas of World Mythology.*

SIDELIGHTS: One of the world's leading authorities on mythology and folklore, Joseph Campbell believed that all myth has a common source in the biology of man himself. Mythology is "a production of the human imagination," he told D. J. R. Bruckner of the *New York Times Book Review,* "which is moved by the energies of the organs of the body operating against each other. These are the same in human beings all over the world and this is the basis for the archetypology of myth." Campbell saw the world's myths, religions, and rituals to be humanity's explanations for the essential mystery of creation. "God," Garry Abrams of the *Los Angeles Times* quoted Campbell explaining, "is a metaphor for a mystery that absolutely transcends all categories of human thought. . . . It's as simple as that." Jeffrey Hart of the *National Review* explained that Campbell "sought out the great overarching patterns of human perception that underlie the stories human beings tell about themselves, that inform the works of art they create and the rites they perform." For modern man, Campbell advocated a new mythology, "a modern, planetary myth," he told Chris Goodrich of *Publishers Weekly,* "not one of this group or that group." Campbell's work made him "known among an avid circle of friends and admirers as the Western world's foremost authority on mythology," K. C. Cole wrote in *Newsweek.* Hart called Campbell "a great modern anthropologist, . . . a great modern artist, . . . [and] one of the last survivors of the heroic age of twentieth-century modernism. Like Goethe, whom he worshipped, he combined science and art."

As a young boy in New York City, Campbell was first drawn to mythology by his interest in the American Indians. After a visit to Buffalo Bill's Wild West Show at Madison Square Garden, Campbell invaded his local library and read every book they had about Indian tribes. He spent his spare time touring the American Museum of Natural History with his brother and sister, enthralled by the Indian exhibits there. In school he studied the primitive cultures of the South Pacific and by the time he entered college, Campbell had a wide knowledge of folklore and mythology. Majoring in English and earning a degree in medieval literature, he dropped out of Columbia University's doctoral program when told that mythology was not a fit subject for his thesis. For several years he studied mythology on his own. A stay in California allowed him to accompany a scientific expedition along the Alaskan coast. For a year and a half he lived in a cabin in rural Woodstock, New York, reading scholarly works on mythology, legends, and folklore. In 1932, he was offered a teaching position with his old preparatory school, the Canterbury School, in New Milford, Connecticut. In 1934, he moved to Sarah Lawrence College, where he was to teach literature until 1972.

During his years as a teacher, Campbell produced a massive body of work in the fields of comparative mythology, folklore, and religion. He began during the 1940s by editing the works of the late Heinrich Zimmer, a friend of his who had been a noted Indologist at Columbia University. With Henry Morton Robinson, Campbell also wrote a literary interpretation of James Joyce's novel *Finnegans Wake* in which the story's origins in ancient myth are explained. The book, *A Skeleton Key to "Finnegans Wake,"* is, Andrew Klavan recounted in the *Village Voice,* "still a standard textbook 44 years after its publication."

Campbell's first book as sole author, *The Hero with a Thousand Faces,* took him four years to write. Campbell felt "that the four years he put into *The Hero* were sublime madness, a passage of joyous creativity he has not matched since," Donald Newlove reported in *Esquire. The Hero with a Thousand Faces* attempts to unite the world's mythologies into what Campbell called a "monomyth," the single underlying story which all the myths tell. This story outlines the proper way for man to live. "In Campbell's view," Cole said of the book's thesis, "the myths are not merely entertaining tales, but are allegorical instructions that seek to teach us, as he put it, nothing less than 'how to live a human lifetime under any circumstances.' "

The Hero with a Thousand Faces focuses on the many tales of heroes who overcome great odds to perform impossible tasks. Campbell discerns a consistent pattern in these tales: The hero is called to an adventure which he accepts; he is given charms or magical weapons by a protective figure who is older and wiser; the hero then journeys into an unknown land where he meets demons and undergoes great suffering; the hero triumphs over the menace and is reborn in the process; he then returns to his homeland enriched with new insights that will benefit his people. Campbell saw this story as primarily an inner battle in which the hero undergoes a kind of self-psychotherapy, confronts his own darker side, and gains a greater understanding of himself and his culture in the process.

Early reviewers of *The Hero with a Thousand Faces* were put off by Campbell's almost mystical tone. "It is all presented," complained Max Radin of the *New York Times,* "in the mystical and pseudo-philosophical fog of Jung." H. A. Reinhold of *Common-*

weal found the book to be "full of inconclusive tales [and] vague and shadowy parallels." The *New Yorker* critic judged *The Hero with a Thousand Faces* to be "one of the most fascinating and maddening books of the season." Despite such critical misgivings, the book was awarded a grant-in-literature from the National Institute of Arts and Letters and went on to sell several hundred thousand copies. And Abrams reported that *The Hero with a Thousand Faces* "still sells 10,000 copies a year."

In the four-volume work *The Masks of God,* Campbell surveyed the world's mythology, arguing on behalf of his idea of the monomyth. The first volume, *Primitive Mythology,* begins with the religious ideas of the Bronze Age, when prehistoric men were still hunters and gatherers. At this time, Campbell believed, mankind was stamped with a basic set of religious beliefs, a coda of responses to his questions about the nature of the universe. These beliefs grew from the daily life of early man, a life that consisted of hunting for food, constant migration, and the observance of the cosmos. Because of this experience, peoples throughout the world developed common rituals and beliefs revolving around the hunt, astronomy, and the cycles of nature.

Primitive Mythology, according to Joseph Bram of the *Library Journal,* is "truly thought-provoking and in some ways path breaking and should be welcomed as a real contribution to the ancient science of mythology." But other critics were less sure about the book's importance. S. P. Dunn, in his review for the *American Anthropologist,* claimed that "Campbell has written a stimulating, disturbing, often quite exasperating book." M. E. Opler of the *New York Herald Tribune Book Review* found himself "alternately exhilarated and puzzled. . . . But if Campbell seems sometimes wrong, he is never dull." Philip Rieff of the *American Sociological Review* called *Primitive Mythology* "highly readable, almost too much so. Campbell cannot resist telling a good story. . . . Not all are necessary to his argument." "This work," the *Kirkus Review* contributor commented, "is one of enormous scholarship."

The second volume of *The Masks of God,* entitled *Oriental Mythology,* turns to the East, covering the myths of Egypt, Japan, China, and India. Campbell discusses the particularly Asian ideas of reincarnation and transcendence of the ego, tracing their historical emergence in Eastern culture. Alan Watts, writing of the book for *Saturday Review,* called it "the first time that anyone has put the rich complexities of Asian mythology into a clear historical perspective. . . . What Mr. Campbell is offering here is not so much a mythological encyclopedia as a thoroughly documented discussion of the development of myth and of its function in human cultures. It is a bold, imaginative, deeply stimulating work."

Campbell followed the same historical approach in *Occidental Mythology,* the third volume in the series. Beginning with the prehistoric belief in a mother-goddess, he follows the course of Western religious belief down through the centuries. A strong contrast in attitude is shown between the beliefs of the East and West, a difference that Campbell felt was due to environment. The harsher landscape of the West "challenged man to shape his own destiny," explained Bram, "whereas India and the Far East have always fostered the attitudes of passivity, resignation, and fatalism." Watts, reviewing the book for *New Republic,* thought it to be "the best and richest" volume in the series.

The Masks of God concludes with the volume *Creative Mythology,* in which Campbell shifts his attention from the myths of the past, created by anonymous authors, to those of the present, which have been created by such artists and writers as Dante, James Joyce, and T. S. Eliot. He argues that a new mythology is needed, one that speaks to the entire human race in modern terms, and one that is created by the individual artist from his own life. The book, the *New Yorker* critic summarized, "deals with the modern 'secular' use of myth to express individual experience." Gerald Sykes of the *New York Times Book Review* saw a "major implication" of the book to be that "although we were once given our myths by the group that nurtured us, now we must mine them painfully from the depths of our own experience." Newlove claimed that in *Creative Mythology* Campbell "is out to show the face of God burning away the received masks of culture and to herald the birth within." The *Choice* reviewer called *Creative Mythology* "a landmark in its field," while Bram concluded that it was "a major work of inspired scholarship that no student of mythology will be able to ignore."

In *The Mythic Image* Campbell turned to the origins of myth, arguing that man's unconscious mind, particularly his dreams, formed the basis of all mythology. Through the use of 400 illustrations drawn from all over the world, and ranging from prehistoric cave paintings to the avant-garde works of the present day, he showed how the relationship between myth and dream was evident in mankind's artistic creations. Peter S. Prescott of *Newsweek* described the book as "an iconography of the human spirit." Although he felt that psychologist Carl Jung had raised the same point earlier with his theory of the universal unconscious, Winthrop Sargeant of the *New Yorker* nonetheless believed that the idea "has never before been given such a clear and splendid demonstration" as in *The Mythic Image*. Prescott concluded that the book's premise "is convincing, and elegantly supported by hundreds of excellent reproductions of art."

In 1983 Campbell published the first of a planned six-volume series entitled *Historical Atlas of World Mythology*, a work meant to relate the world's mythological history in a single, all-encompassing narrative. The initial volume, *The Way of the Animal Powers*, covers the beginnings of human culture and examines the early myth of the Great Hunt, a story common to many prehistoric hunting peoples. Combining an authoritative text with an extensive collection of relevant artwork, *The Way of the Animal Powers* is "a beautiful and informative volume by a world-renowned scholar," as C. Robert Nixon commented in *Library Journal*. Wendy O'Flaherty of the *New York Times Book Review* claimed that "no one but Joseph Campbell could conceive of such a scheme or carry it out as boldly as he does in this extraordinary book. . . . It is an exhilarating experience." Hart concluded that *The Way of the Animal Powers* is "one of the great works of our time."

The second volume in the *Historical Atlas of World Mythology*, *The Way of the Seeded Earth*, moves forward in time, focusing on the mythology of the first agricultural communities and contrasting the beliefs of that time with the earlier beliefs of the hunting cultures. As Campbell explained to Goodrich: "In *The Way of the Animal Powers*, . . . people are killing animals all the time; that's where the base of the culture rests. This second book is about women's magic—birth and nourishment. The myth shifts from the male-oriented to the gestation-oriented, and the image is of the plant world." At the time of his death in 1987, Campbell had not yet completed the six volumes of the *Historical Atlas of World Mythology*.

Campbell's last project was a number of interviews with Bill Moyers for a special Public Broadcasting Service television program entitled "The Power of Myth." These interviews were broadcast in 1988 as a six-part series, drawing an audience of some two-and-a-half million people for each episode. A best-selling book based on the television program was also released,

while a video cassette version has sold over 50,000 copies. "The Power of Myth" allows Campbell to range over a host of topics, including the mythology of many cultures, the role of myth in modern society, and the possibilities for myth-making in the future. "Intermittently provocative and ponderous, the conversations are a rambling, serendipitous intellectual journey," explained Clifford Terry of the *Chicago Tribune*. Ironically, because of the program's popularity, Campbell became known to more people after his death than knew him while he was alive. As Cole noted, "Campbell has become something of a legend himself. . . . The hero is dead, but the message lives on."

At the time of his death in late 1987 Campbell had become "one of the world's great scholars and teachers of mythology," Terry reported. His prominence rested as much on his scholarly prowess as on his ability to appeal to a mass audience. As Cole remarked, "Campbell has become the rarest of intellectuals in American life: a serious thinker who has been embraced by the popular culture." Among his most fervent disciples has been filmmaker George Lucas, who credited Campbell with inspiring his movie "Star Wars." "If it hadn't been for him," Lucas told Wolfgang Saxon of the *New York Times*, "it's possible I would still be trying to write 'Star Wars' today." Sir Lauren van der Post, writing in the London *Times*, cited Campbell for his efforts to "rediscover for a deprived world the fundamental mythological pattern of the human spirit. . . . He has done more than any scholar of our time to reconnect modern man to a reality which his mind and spirit were rejecting at great peril to his well-being and sanity." Joseph Coates of the *Chicago Tribune* called Campbell "that rare scholar with something really useful to say about how life should be lived."

MEDIA ADAPTATIONS: "The Power of Myth" television series is available on video cassette from Mystic Fire Video, 1988.

BIOGRAPHICAL/CRITICAL SOURCES:

BOOKS

Bestsellers 89, Issue 2, Gale, 1989.
Campbell, Joseph and Bill Moyers, *The Power of Myth,* Doubleday, 1988.

PERIODICALS

American Anthropologist, December, 1960.
American Sociological Review, December, 1960.
Chicago Tribune, May 23, 1988.
Choice, December, 1968.
Christian Science Monitor, October 9, 1969.
Commentary, December, 1969.
Commonweal, July 8, 1949.
Esquire, September, 1977.
Kirkus Review, August 15, 1959.
Library Journal, September 1, 1959, January 15, 1964, February 15, 1968, January, 1984.
Los Angeles Times, May 27, 1987.
National Review, July 13, 1984.
New Republic, June 27, 1964.
Newsweek, March 31, 1975, November 14, 1988.
New Yorker, May 7, 1949, February 1, 1969, July 21, 1975.
New York Herald Tribune Book Review, November 22, 1959.
New York Times, June 26, 1949, March 22, 1987, November 6, 1989.
New York Times Book Review, May 18, 1969, December 18, 1983.
Publishers Weekly, August 23, 1985.
Saturday Review, June 2, 1962.
Times (London), July 12, 1984.

Village Voice, August 1, 1968, May 24, 1988.

FILMS

"A Hero's Journey: The World of Joseph Campbell," William Free, 1987.

OBITUARIES:

PERIODICALS

Chicago Tribune, November 5, 1987.
Los Angeles Times, November 30, 1987.
National Review, December 4, 1987.
New York Times, November 3, 1987.
Parabola, spring, 1988.
Time, November 16, 1987.
Washington Post, November 4, 1987.

*　　*　　*

CAMUS, Albert 1913-1960
(Bauchart, Albert Mathe; Saetone, a joint pseudonym)

PERSONAL: Name pronounced "Al-*bair* Kah-*mu*"; born November 7, 1913, in Mondovi, Algeria; died January 4, 1960, in an automobile accident; son of Lucien (a farm laborer) and Catherine (a charwoman; maiden name, Sintes) Camus; married Simone Hie, 1933 (divorced); married Francine Faure, 1940; children: (second marriage) Jean (son) and Catherine (twins). *Education:* University of Algiers, diplome d'etudes superieures, 1936. *Religion:* "Atheistic humanist."

ADDRESSES: Home—29 rue Madame, Paris 6eme, France.

CAREER: Novelist, essayist, and playwright. Worked as meteorologist, stockbroker's agent, and civil servant; actor, writer, and producer of stage productions with Theatre du travail (later named Theatre de l'equipe), 1935-38; journalist with Alger-Republican, 1938-40; teacher in Oran, Algeria, 1940-42; journalist in Paris, France, 1942-45; Editions Gallimard, reader, 1943-60, director of Espoir collection; *Combat* (daily newspaper), co-founder, 1945, editor, 1945-47. Staff member of *Paris Soir,* 1938. Founder of Committee to Aid the Victims of Totalitarian States. *Wartime service:* Member of the French resistance movement.

AWARDS, HONORS: Medal of the Liberation; Prix de la critique, 1947, for *La Peste;* Nobel Prize for literature, 1957; Prix algerian du roman.

WRITINGS:

NOVELS

L'Etranger, Gallimard, 1942, translation by Stuart Gilbert published as *The Stranger,* Knopf, 1946, reprinted U.S. edition, Vintage Books, 1972, translation by Matthew Ward published under the same title, Knopf, 1988, (published in England as *The Outsider,* Hamish Hamilton, 1946).
La Peste, Gallimard, 1947, translation by Gilbert published as *The Plague,* Knopf, 1948, reprinted, Vintage Books, 1972.
La Chute, Gallimard, 1956, translation by Justin O'Brien published as *The Fall,* Knopf, 1957.

Also author of unfinished novel *Le Premier Homme* (title means "The First Man").

PLAYS

Le Malentendu [and] *Caligula* (former, three-act, first produced at Theatre des Mathurins, May, 1944; latter, four-act, first produced at Theatre Hebertot in 1945), Gallimard, 1944, translation by Gilbert published as *Caligula* [and] *Cross Purpose* (former produced in New York City, February 10, 1960), New Directions, 1947 (also see below).
L'Etat de siege (first produced in 1948), Gallimard, 1948, translation published as "State of Siege" in *Caligula and Three Other Plays* (also see below).
Les Justes (first produced at Theatre Hebertot, December, 1949), Gallimard, 1950, translation by Elizabeth Sprigge and Philip Warner published as *The Just Assassins,* Microfilm, 1957, published in *Caligula and Three Other Plays* (also see below).
La Devotion a la croix (title means "Devotion to the Cross"; adaptation of the work by Calderon de la Barca), Gallimard, 1953.
Les Esprits (title means "The Wits"; adaptation of the work by Pierre de Larivey), Gallimard, 1953.
Un Cas interessant (title means "An Interesting Case"; adaptation of the work by Dino Buzatti; first produced at Theatre La Bruyere, May, 1955), L'Avant-scene, 1955.
Requiem pour une nonne (adaptation of the novel *Requiem for a Nun,* by William Faulkner; first produced at Theatre des Mathurins, October, 1956), Gallimard, 1956.
Caligula and Three Other Plays (also contains "State of Siege," "Cross Purpose," and "The Just Assassins"), translated by Gilbert, Knopf, 1958.
Les Possedes (adaptation of the novel *The Possessed,* by Fyodor Dostoyevsky; first produced at Theatre Antoine, February, 1955), Gallimard, 1959, translation by O'Brien published as *The Possessed: A Modern Dramatization of Dostoevsky's Novel,* Knopf, 1964.

Also author of unfinished play "Don Juan."

ESSAYS

L'Envers et l'endroit (title means "Inside and Out"), Charlot Alger, 1937. *Le Mythe de Sisyphe,* Gallimard, 1942, translation by O'Brien published as *The Myth of Sisyphus and Other Essays,* Knopf, 1955.
Lettres a un ami allemand, Gallimard, 1945.
Noces (title means "Nuptials"), Charlot Alger, 1945.
L'Existence, Gallimard, 1945.
Le Minotaur; ou, La Halte d'Oran (title means "The Minotaur; or, Stopping at Oran"), Charlot Alger, 1950.
Actuelles I: Chroniques, 1944-1948 (title means "Now I: Chronicles, 1944-1948"), Gallimard, 1950.
L'Homme revolte, Gallimard, 1951, translation by Anthony Bower published as *The Rebel: An Essay on Man in Revolt,* Knopf, 1954, revised edition, 1956.
Actuelles II: Chroniques, 1948-1953 (title means "Now II: Chronicles, 1948-1953"), Gallimard, 1953.
L'Ete (title means "Summer"), Gallimard, 1954.
(With Arthur Koestler) *Reflexions sur la peine capitale* (contains "Reflexions sur la potence," by Koestler, and "Reflexions sur la guillotine," by Camus; translation of latter published separately as *Reflections on the Guillotine;* also see below), Calman-Levy, 1957.
Actuelles III: Chronique algerienne, 1939-1958 (title means "Now III: Algerian Chronicle, 1939-1958"), Gallimard, 1958.
Discours de suede, Gallimard, 1958, translation by O'Brien published as *Speech of Acceptance Upon the Award of the Nobel Prize for Literature, Delivered in Stockholm on the Tenth of December, 1957,* Knopf, 1958.

Reflections on the Guillotine: An Essay on Capital Punishment, translation by Richard Howard, Fridtjof-Karla Publications, 1960.

Neither Victims nor Executioners, translated from the French by Dwight Macdonald, Liberation, 1960.

Resistance, Rebellion, and Death, translated from the French by O'Brien, Knopf, 1961.

Meditations sur le theatre et la vie, P. Alberts, 1961.

Theatre, recrits, nouvelles, Gallimard, 1962.

Essais, Gallimard, 1965.

Lyrical and Critical Essays, edited by Philip Thody, translated from the French by Ellen Conroy Kennedy, Knopf, 1968.

Between Hell and Reason: Essays from the Resistance Newspaper Combat, 1944-1947, translated from the French and edited by Alexandre de Gramont, Wesleyan University Press, in press.

OTHER

L'Exil et le royaume (short stories; contains "Le Renegat," "Jonas," "La Femme adultere," "Les Muets," "L'Hote," and "La Pierre qui pousse"), Gallimard, 1957, translation by O'Brien published as *Exile and the Kingdom,* Hamish Hamilton, 1960.

Carnets: Mai 1935-fevrier 1942, Gallimard, 1962, translation published as *Notebooks: Volume I, 1935-1942,* Knopf, 1963 (published in England as *Carnets: 1935-1942,* Hamish Hamilton, 1963).

Lettre a Bernanos, Minard, 1963.

Carnets: Janvier 1942-mars 1951, Gallimard, 1964, translation by O'Brien published as *Notebooks: 1942-1951,* Modern Library, 1970.

La Mort heureuse, Gallimard, 1971, translation by Jean Sarocchi published as *A Happy Death,* Vintage Books, 1973.

Le Premier Camus, suivi de Ecrits de jeunesse d'Albert Camus, Gallimard, 1973, translation by Kennedy published as *Youthful Writings,* Knopf, 1976.

Fragments d'un Combat: 1938-1940, Alger Republicain, Le Soir Republicain (articles), two volumes, edited by Jacqueline Levi Valensi and Andre Abbou, Gallimard, 1978.

Journaux de voyage, edited by Roger Quillot, Gallimard, 1978, translation by Hugh Levick published as *American Journals,* Paragon House, 1987.

Albert Camus, Jean Grenier: Correspondance: 1932-1960 (letters), edited by Marguerite Dobrenn, Gallimard, 1981.

Carnets: Mars 1951-decembre 1959, Gallimard, 1989.

Author of prefaces to many works. Contributor to *Combat* (under pseudonyms Bauchart and Albert Mathe, and under joint pseudonym Saetone), to *Alger-Republican, Soir-Republican, L'Express,* and many other newspapers and magazines.

COLLECTED WORKS

Oeuvres completes d'Albert Camus, five volumes, Club de l'Honnete Homme, 1983.

SIDELIGHTS: "Above all his contemporaries," declared *Time* magazine, Camus "was the authentic voice of France's war generation." It was he who elucidated the unique problems that troubled his generation, noted Francois Mauriac. Camus, typically pictured in a rumpled trenchcoat with a cigarette dangling from his mouth, his brow furrowed, was also deeply admired by the generation following his own. "He was a moral conscience for thousands of young people in Europe and the United States, as he is still today," William Barnett observed. In response to the international acclaim that seemed to greet him overnight, Camus

asks in *L'Ete* simply, "What else have I done but meditate on an idea I found in the streets of my time?"

Camus did indeed capture in his writings the moral climate of the mid-twentieth century. In the 1940s, values were being challenged as no longer relevant. With the atrocities and feelings of hopelessness brought about by World War II, many people concluded that there is no reason for human existence. But while Camus did most certainly perceive life's absurdity, he did not adopt this point of view. "In the darkest depths of our nihilism," he wrote, "I have sought only for the means to transcend nihilism." *Time* observed that "because Camus articulated despair so eloquently, a generation bred in depression, surrender and occupation chose him its leader in its quest for something to believe in."

In his search to break through the pervading sense of meaninglessness to discover happiness, Camus charted a plan of writing that would eventually encompass at least three cycles. He named each cycle after a figure in mythology, calling the first Sisyphus, the second Prometheus, and the third Nemesis. The novel *The Stranger,* the play *Caligula,* and the essay *The Myth of Sisyphus* together form cycle one, which is concerned with a certain duality in man's nature: the love of life versus the hatred of death.

In *The Stranger,* perhaps Camus's most famous work, the protagonist Meursault takes life for granted until he finds himself awaiting the death penalty for having killed an Arab in a bizarre sequence of events. Meursault is a stranger in life because he does not parrot conventional cant—neither at his mother's funeral nor as the defendant in the courtroom. When his mother dies, for example, he feels little emotion and does not pretend otherwise. Then when his lawyer tries to induce him to respond to judicial questions in the socially acceptable way, Meursault refuses to do so. Those around him are threatened by his candor. He is subsequently sentenced, shunning last of all the chaplain's offer of God. As Maurois put it, "Meursault is saved by that which destroys him," that is, by death.

When *The Stranger* first appeared in print, Jean-Paul Sartre predicted it would become a classic. Often required reading for literature classes, *The Stranger* has been viewed as Camus's only nihilist novel. John Weightman wrote that it is "one of the first modern books—perhaps the very first—in which the Absurdist awareness of the absence of any settled moral truth is worked into all the details of the story." To Henri Peyre, "the romantic condemnation of a bourgeois society whose judges sentence a murder too harshly is a little facile. But the young Camus had thus to begin by setting himself against the world as he found it; before he could discover how to change it or how to rethink it, he had to depict it as unsatisfactory."

In *Caligula,* the concept of the absurd is taken further than in *The Stranger.* The character Caligula is based on Caius Caesare Augustus Germanicus, called Caligula, who became emperor of Rome at the age of twenty-five. A gentle man at the onset of his reign, Caligula gradually evolved into a cruel and heartless ruler who was eventually assassinated. In Camus's portrayal of Caligula, the latter is transformed into a tyrant after the death of his sister-lover Drusilla. It becomes clear to the emperor that "men die and they are unhappy." Like Meursault, Caligula rebels, but his revolt takes a far more extreme form.

Since life is absurd, Caligula reasons, every act is equally senseless. He then proceeds to prove his point by destroying accepted conventions. For instance, he seduces a man's wife, with the man himself as witness, causes a famine, and tortures his subjects indiscriminately. His aim is to educate the self-deluding patricians, noted Germaine Bree. A segment of the oppressed people revolt, which culminates in the assassination of the emperor. Before the end, Caligula laments, "I didn't take the right road, I came out nowhere. My freedom is not the right kind." Robert Jay Lifton called *Caligula* Camus's "most vivid rendition of the absurd survivor, and one of the most important plays ever written about the aberrations of the survivor state."

Sisyphus is another survivor. According to the legend, he is eternally condemned to push a boulder the full height of a mountain only for it to roll back down to the starting point. Sisyphus "is the absurd hero," explains Camus in the essay "The Myth of Sisyphus." "He *is,* as much through his passions as through his torture. His scorn of the gods, his hatred of death, and his passion for life won him that unspeakable penalty in which the whole being is exerted toward accomplishing nothing. This is the price that must be paid for the passions of this world." For Camus, Sisyphus represents all men.

The Fall links the idea of the absurd to Camus's second cycle of writing, Bree pointed out. Written in the first person, as are all of Camus's novels, this particular work can be grouped with the *roman personnels,* observed Rima Drell Reck, as can *The Nephew of Rameau* and *The Rhyme of the Ancient Mariner. The Fall* is a monologue delivered by Jean Baptiste Clemence over a period of five days. Clemence, a one-time lawyer, had abandoned a lucrative practice in Paris. He could no longer in good conscience judge other people without viewing himself as a hypocrite: "Who is to say he is not equally guilty?" he asks himself. Clemence ends up relating his transgressions to all who will listen in a Dutch bar frequented by sailors. "In short," he confesses, "I never bothered with larger concerns except in the intervals between my little flings." His frankness evokes similar disclosures from his listeners, and to Clemence this proves that all men are inherently wicked. Camus describes him as "an empty prophet for a mediocre era." Reck wrote that *The Fall* is "a brilliant representation of the problems of justice and guilt which were Camus's consistent themes."

Revolt is the theme of Prometheus, the mythological hero who represents Camus's second cycle. Camus's version of the parable is against traditional revolution. Prometheus loves man and leads him to battle against the gods, whom Prometheus despises. Eventually, man begins to question his mission, but Prometheus avows his belief in their actions. "Those who doubt will be thrown out into the desert, nailed on a rock, offered as prey to cruel birds. All others shall walk in the dark behind the pensive and solitary master." As Camus puts it, Prometheus has thus become Caesar.

In the novel *The Plague,* the plays *The Just Assassins* and *The State of Siege,* and the essay *The Rebel,* Camus "examines the notion of revolt, as he had already taken and deduced the practical consequences of such a position," observed Bree. Camus's is a metaphysical kind of revolt, referring to "the vision, the questioning, the *protest* which man finds in himself," explained David Anderson. Similarly, Camus writes in *Notebooks* that "the revolutionary spirit lies in man's protest against the human condition."

The Plague is Camus's "most complex and probably his most satisfying work," Philip Thody commented. Moreover, Bree observed that *The Plague* is "within its limits, a great novel, the most disturbing, most moving novel yet to have come out of the chaos of the mid-century." On the other hand, Reck wrote that while the book met with popular acclaim in 1947, she considered it for the contemporary public "a novel whose message is too obvious and whose means are scant."

The story takes place in the Algerian town of Oran, where life is very routine. As the tale progresses, one rat dies, then more rats, then one human, and before long a pestilence has almost imperceptibly ravaged the city. The pain that the plague causes, Maurois pointed out, has at least elicited real feeling from the normally sedate townspeople. The actions of the characters illustrate that the complacent can be moved to take heroic action when faced with an emergency situation. Therefore, there is hope for the human condition, as long as the transition is not forgotten when life returns to normal.

The events are related in the third person by Dr. Rieux, who is not revealed as the narrator until the end of the book. Throughout the story Dr. Rieux fervently strives to aid the plague victims. For him, wrote Bree, "the plague is, in essence, the clear inner awareness of man's accidental and transitory presence on the earth, an awareness that is the source of all metaphysical torment, a torment which in Camus's eyes is one of the characteristics of our time."

The artist Tarrou also combats the disease, alongside his friend Rieux. A sensitive intellectual, Tarrou chronicles in his diary the events taking place in Oran. In one entry he states, "I know with a certain knowledge that each man carries a plague within." The principal difference between Rieux and Tarrou, noted Bree, is that the latter "is trying to purge himself of all evil, trying to transcend his human condition."

The Plague has been viewed as Camus's "most anti-Christian" novel. To Reck, Camus "suggests that faith is questionable, that man's torments are unjustifiable, that religion offers no answers to the travail of quotidian existence." It thus becomes apparent in the narrative that whether there is a God or not, man must take the responsibility for his life into his own hands.

But, to Camus, the plague itself served also as a metaphor for "Fascism, the Nazi era, [and] the occupation of France," wrote Lottman. Irene Finel-Honigman similarly called the story an allegory "of the concentration camps and the prisoner-of-war camps. Oran in this interpretation transcends its definition as a city and becomes a microcosm of a war-torn state."

Although the personification of evil in the symbolic play *The State of Siege* is named "King Plague," and though there are surface similarities to the novel, Camus averred that the play is not an adaptation of *The Plague.* As Bree pointed out, it is instead redolent of *Ubu roi* by Alfred Jarry. When compared to Camus's own works, *The State of Siege* is most similar to *Caligula,* also a "play with death," Bree wrote. "This time, however, death alone does not hold sway, for *L'Etat de siege* also concerns love and life." Diego, the rebel in the play, "stirs up the latent forces of energy and freedom among the inhabitants of Cadiz, awakening the citizens from their lethargy, calling them back to life."

The State of Siege was one of Camus's favorite works, but at its Paris opening the play was a flop. Lottman noted: "With an all-star cast and contributions from . . . notable artists nothing should have gone wrong. But everything did." French author Rene Barjavel's reaction to the production was, "Since I have been going to the theatre, I believe that I have never suffered as much." Camus remarked in the introduction to the English translation of the play that *The State of Siege* "had without effort achieved critical unanimity" and "a complete cutting up."

The Just Assassins (*Les Justes*) was greeted with more opposing reactions. The Communist newspaper *L'Humanite* found the characters unrealistic and the play itself "worse than cold—icy." But *Le Populaire,* a Socialist party publication, reviewed it as "powerful and moving." *The Just Assassins* deals with Russian terrorism in the early 1900s. The plot involves a Socialist group that makes plans to assassinate the Grand Duke. A young poet, Kaliayev, who is totally committed to the cause of the organization, is chosen to throw the bomb that will kill the Duke. Seeing himself as "the avenger of the people," as Bree noted, Kaliayev dies for his actions without regret. But his death raises the question, Is the sacrifice of one person worth the promise of a better future for mankind? Chiarmonte concluded in the *Partisan Review* that "after all is said about the weakness of *Les Justes* as a play, it remains a piece of literary work that commands respect."

Writing *The Rebel*, (*L'Homme revolte*), the last volume in the cycle of Prometheus, was not an easy task for Camus. But he felt it was his responsibility: afterward he could freely devote his time to creating more literature. In his *Notebooks* he states: "For my own part, I should not have written *L'Homme revolte* if in the forties I had not found myself face to face with men whose acts I did not understand. To put it briefly, I did not understand that men could torture others without ever ceasing to look at them."

In *The Rebel*, Camus defines revolt as the "impulse that drives an individual to the defense of a dignity common to all men." He takes the phrase by Descartes, "I think, therefore I am," and turns it into "I revolt, therefore we are." Citing paths of rebellion chosen by numerous figures throughout history, Camus illustrates how each was unsuccessful according to his own definition of revolt. The Marquis de Sade's actions were too calculated, too intellectual; Rimbaud's too individualized. But Camus criticized Hegel's method of rebellion above all, stating that "any revolt which does not recognize that it should transcend nihilism and establish [a] limit is doomed to justify murder and lead to dictatorship," noted Thody.

The Rebel's "structural and rational flaws are glaring," Reck contended, but even so, it sparked more controversy than any other writing by Camus. It is "the only thing written by Camus resembling a political philosophy," said Reck. Probably one of the major conflicts was fostered by Camus's condemnation of Marxism: "End satisfies the means? Is this possible? But what will justify the ends?" Camus further asserted that the Left should oppose Stalinism. This tenet led to an attack of *The Rebel* in *Le Temps moderne* by Francis Jeanson. Camus's friend from Paris's Left Bank, existentialist Jean-Paul Sartre, suggested that Camus respond to the article. Camus did indeed reply, criticizing Sartre's belief that Stalinism should be accepted by the leftists because the majority of the working class had already adopted that philosophy. The result was a much publicized rift between Camus and Sartre. "The break between these two leading French writers touched off literary pyrotechnics vivid even for Paris," wrote the *New York Times*.

Camus never completed the third cycle of his writing to be called Nemesis, concerning measure. At the time of his death, plans for a play entitled "Don Juan" were on the drawing board. Camus had also written about one hundred pages of the rough draft of his epic novel, *The First Man*. Based on the first French settlers in Algeria, the book was to be Camus's *War and Peace*. In addition, Bree gathered from Camus's *Notebooks* that the author was planning a fourth cycle, dealing with compassion and "a certain kind of love."

Not all of Camus's writings fall specifically into the aforementioned categories. In the short story collection *Exile and the Kingdom*, Camus emphasizes "the kingdom of man" in which each hero reaches a new awareness of life, Bree pointed out. Camus also successfully adapted plays, staged others of his own, and wrote a variety of other essays.

The publication of any work by Camus was "eagerly anticipated and greeted in Paris itself," noted Bree. "Discussed, attacked, and defended, it was promptly translated into many languages, and as it crossed national frontiers it was once again attacked, praised, or refuted." But as literature, Rima Drell Reck remarked, Camus's fiction is "conceptionally thin." His novels, for instance, are all essays in fictional form, she said. Camus deliberately chose this medium of expression, though, explained Henri Peyre, to keep his ideas from appearing overly "dry." Reck concluded that "Camus's originality as a novelist lay in his ability to state his insights ambiguously, that is, with the density and complexity of human existence."

The first major writer to emerge from North Africa, Camus was imbued with a "Mediterranean sensibility," wrote Reck, a sensibility that profoundly influenced his writings. Camus saw the Algeria of his youth as a place of perpetual summer. "The sun, the sea, the flowers, the desert, and in contrast, the teeming cities composed his inner, passionately cherished landscape," noted Bree. "At the heart of Camus's sensitivity, imagination and thought, and at the heart of his work, are the beauty of the African coast and the glory of an 'inexhaustible sun.'"

Camus spent the first twenty-seven years of his life in Algiers, Algeria's capital. His family was poor, but because of the sunny Algerian climate, he never felt destitute. He was raised in a second floor apartment—three rooms and a kitchen—in a working-class section of the city. (Later, Camus was to say that he belonged only to the class of mankind.) Besides Camus, the household was made up of his mother, brother, maternal grandmother, and two uncles.

Camus's father, a native Algerian of Alsacian descent, had been killed at the first battle of the Marne when Camus was just a year old. Catherine Sintes Camus, Camus's mother, was of Spanish heritage. Although, unlike her husband, Catherine was illiterate, it has been said that Camus acquired from her a certain Castilian air of nobility, or *pudeur*, as Lottman described it. Because she was partially deaf, and much affected by her husband Lucien's death, Catherine left the rearing of her sons to her own strong-willed mother. That Camus still focused his love on his mother later becomes evident in some of his writings. But, "without general availability of Camus's unfinished novel, *Le Premier Homme* (The First Man), readers will not know the full story of Camus's feelings for this silent, submissive figure who became a more marvelous woman to her son as he grew older," Lottman observed.

Despite the lack of an intellectual atmosphere at home, Camus was nonetheless a superior student at school. An instructor, Louis Germain, recognized potential in the young Camus and encouraged him to excel. Germain lent him books to read, spent extra time with him, and persuaded Camus's autocratic grandmother to permit him to remain in school rather than go to work. He also urged Camus to vie for the scholarship that allowed him to attend high school. In 1957, Camus dedicated his Nobel Prize acceptance speech to this first mentor.

While in his early teens, Camus was an active sports enthusiast. He swam often and was an avid soccer player, serving as goalie for the Racing Universitaire Algerois (RUA). As an adult, he wrote of this experience, "After many years during which I saw many things, what I know most surely about morality and the duty of man I owe to sport and learned in the RUA."

Camus's sports activities came to a halt when, at seventeen, he contracted tuberculosis in his right lung. The disease eventually spread to his left lung as well. With no method yet discovered of removing the tubercle bacilli, Camus was to be afflicted for the remainder of his life, making him a target for depression and flu. At his doctor's recommendation, the seventeen-year-old Camus convalesced at the home of his more affluent Aunt Antoinette and Uncle Acault, a man of "extreme republican and Voltairian persuasion," wrote Philip Thody.

Undaunted by his illness, Camus entered the University of Algiers. There, with Jean Grenier as his new mentor, Camus studied Greek literature, poetry, and philosophy, and discovered the works of Pascal, St. Augustine, Kierkegaard, and Plato. He also belonged to a young intellectual group known as the "North Africa Literary School," which would meet in cafes in the Kasbah to talk over cups of mint tea. Even then Camus had a unique quality about him. Jacques Huergon, a University of Algiers Latin professor, recalled, "He simply loomed up among us as someone whose life was going to be important, who was going to begin, starting at zero and without complacency, the great enterprise of being a man."

In 1936, Camus earned his diplome d'etudes superieures in philosophy, but, because he could not pass the required physical, Camus was prevented from receiving his agregation, the degree that would allow him to teach. He subsequently began a career in journalism, writing first for the *Alger-Republicain*. Meanwhile, Camus became involved in politics and joined the Communist party. As was typical of other leftist students, Camus was "anti-Mussolini, anti-Hitler, anti-Franco, rather vague on facts and enthusiastically in favor of social reform in France," Bree pointed out. Eventually, though, he became disillusioned with the party and broke all ties with it in 1937.

By 1942, Camus had moved to Paris where he became a part of the French resistance movement against German occupation. He was writing *The Plague* and *The Rebel*, while simultaneously working as a reader at the Gallimard publishing company during the day and writing for the underground newspaper *Combat* at night. Jean-Paul Sartre and Simone de Beauvoir were also on the *Combat* staff. So were Andre Malraux and Michel Gallimard (a relative of the publisher), both of whom became Camus's friends. At *Combat*, Camus wrote clandestinely under the names Albert Mathe, Bauchart, and the joint pseudonym Saetone. Despite his precautions, Camus barely escaped being caught by the Nazi gestapo at least once.

The day before Paris's liberation, *Combat* became a full-fledged daily newspaper, with Camus as editor. It had become "one of the best-written newspapers of the French press since the beginning of its existence," contended Jean Daniel. Sartre commented that Camus's editorship of *Combat* was "the admirable coming together of a person, an action, and a work." "He couldn't have known it," observed Lottman, "but the mission he had undertaken was designed to catapult him into instant postwar stardom, he more than anyone else connected with *Combat*." In 1944, Camus left journalism for good to focus entirely on other forms of writing.

Camus became known as an existentialist and a philosopher, but he himself adamantly rejected both labels. In *Actuelles I* he wrote, "I have little liking for the too famous existential philosophy, and to speak frankly, I think its conclusions are false." He further asserted in *Actuelles II*, "I am not a philosopher and never claimed to be one." Instead, he viewed himself as a moralist, by his own definition, "a man with a passion for the human heart."

But even above being a moralist, Camus perceived himself as an artist with a responsibility to mankind. In his Nobel Prize accep-

tance speech, Camus said: "In my eyes, art is not a solitary pleasure. It is a means of moving the greatest number of men by offering them a privileged image of common sufferings and common joys. Thus art forces the artist to isolate himself." Furthermore, the responsibility of the artist is to be aware of and even active in political affairs. Yet this concept is in conflict with the solitude demanded by the actual act of creating art. In Bernard Malamud's opinion, some of Camus's "best writing deals with the relationship between . . . political action and artistic creation."

Camus had just emerged from a long-lived writer's block, full of ideas for future writings, when he died suddenly. On January 4, 1960, Camus was apparently planning on riding the train to Paris from his farmhouse in Loumarin when his friend, Michel Gallimard, traveling with his wife and daughter, offered him a ride. Camus accepted, taking with him the beginnings of *The First Man*. According to *Time* magazine, the Gallimards and Camus were eighty miles outside of Paris when the left rear tire of the Facel Vega blew out. The car spun out of control, hitting one tree, then smashing into another; Camus died upon impact. He was forty-six years old. "News of the death stunned the French literary world of which M. Camus was one of the brightest lights," wrote the *New York Times*. In Francois Mauriac's words, Camus's death was "one of the greatest losses that could have affected French letters at the present time." In general, newspapers commented that it was the absurd death of a man who recognized life as absurd.

BIOGRAPHICAL/CRITICAL SOURCES:

BOOKS

Anderson, David, *The Tragic Protest,* John Knox, 1969.
Bree, Germaine, *Camus,* Rutgers University Press, revised edition, 1964.
Bree, *Camus and Sartre: Crisis and Commitment,* Delacorte, 1972.
Bree and Margaret Otis Guiton, *An Age of Fiction: The French Novel From Gide to Camus,* Rutgers University Press, 1968.
Bree, editor, *Camus: A Collection of Critical Essays,* Prentice-Hall, 1962.
Camus, Albert, *The Stranger,* Knopf, 1946.
Camus, *The Plague,* Knopf, 1948.
Camus, *Actuelles I: Chroniques, 1944-48,* Gallimard, 1950.
Camus, *Actuelles II: Chroniques, 1948-53,* Gallimard, 1953.
Camus, *The Rebel,* Knopf, 1954.
Camus, *The Myth of Sisyphus and Other Essays,* Vintage Books, 1955.
Camus, *The Fall,* Knopf, 1957.
Camus, *Exile and the Kingdom,* Knopf, 1958.
Camus, *Caligula and Three Other Plays,* Knopf, 1958.
Camus, *Actuelles III: Chronique algerienne, 1939-1958,* Gallimard, 1958.
Camus, *Notebooks: 1942-1951,* Modern Library, 1970.
Contemporary Literary Criticism, Gale, Volume 1, 1973, Volume 2, 1974, Volume 4, 1975, Volume 9, 1978, Volume 11, 1979, Volume 32, 1985.
Cruickshank, John, *Albert Camus and the Literature of Revolt,* Galaxy, 1960.
Dictionary of Literary Biography, Volume 72: *French Novelists, 1930-1960,* Gale, 1988.
Hanna, Thomas, *The Thought and Art of Albert Camus,* Regnery, 1958.
Kazin, Alfred, *Contemporaries,* Little, Brown, 1962.
Kellogg, Jean Defrees, *Dark Prophets of Hope: Dostoevsky, Sartre, Camus, Faulkner,* Loyola University Press, 1975.

Lazere, Donald, *The Unique Creation of Albert Camus,* Yale University Press, 1973.

Lebesque, Morvan, *Portrait of Camus,* Herder, 1971.

Lottman, Herbert R., *Albert Camus: A Biography,* Doubleday, 1979.

Maquet, Albert, *Albert Camus: The Invincible Summer,* Humanities Press, 1972.

Mauriac, Claude, *The New Literature,* translated from the French by Samuel I. Stone, Braziller, 1959.

Nadeau, Maurice, *The French Novel Since the War,* translated from the French by A. M. Sheridan-Smith, Methuen, 1967.

O'Brien, Conor Cruise, *Albert Camus of Europe and Africa,* Viking, 1970.

Panichas, George A., editor, *The Politics of Twentieth-Century Novelists,* Hawthorne, 1971.

Parker, Emmet, *Albert Camus: The Artist in the Arena,* University of Wisconsin Press, 1966.

Peyre, Henri, *French Novelists of Today,* Oxford University Press, 1967.

Podhoretz, Norman, *Doings and Undoings,* Farrar, Straus, 1964.

Pollman, Leo, *Sartre and Camus: Literature of Existence,* Ungar, 1970.

Reck, Rima Drell, *Literature and Responsibility: The French Novelist in the Twentieth Century,* Louisiana State University Press, 1969.

Rhein, Philip H., *The Urge to Live: A Comparative Study of Franz Kafka's "Der Prozess" and Albert Camus' "L'Etranger",* University of North Carolina Press, 1964.

Rhein, *Albert Camus,* Twayne, 1969.

Sartre, Jean-Paul, *Situations I,* Gallimard, 1947.

Scott, Nathan A., Jr., editor, *Forms of Extremity in the Modern Novel,* John Knox, 1965.

Thody, Philip, *Albert Camus, 1913-1960,* Macmillan, 1962.

Viallaneix, Paul, *The First Camus: An Introductory Essay and Youthful Writings by Albert Camus,* translated from the French by Ellen Conroy Kennedy, Knopf, 1976.

PERIODICALS

American Poetry Review, January-February, 1973.
Los Angeles Times Book Review, May 29, 1988.
Modern Fiction Studies, summer, 1973, spring, 1978.
New York Review of Books, June 15, 1972.
New York Times, February 3, 1986, April 18, 1988, October 20, 1989.
New York Times Book Review, August 16, 1987.
Renascence, winter, 1976.
Scandinavian Studies, summer, 1976.
Time, March 19, 1979.
Times (London), February 2, 1989, September 1, 1989.
Times Literary Supplement, April 17, 1981.

OBITUARIES:

PERIODICALS

Commonweal, February 12, 1960.
France-Observateur, January 7, 1960.
New Republic, January 18, 1960.
New Statesman, January 9, 1960.
Newsweek, January 18, 1960.
New Yorker, January 16, 1960.
New York Times, January 5, 1960.
Time, January 18, 1960.

CANETTI, Elias 1905-

PERSONAL: Born July 25, 1905, in Russe, Bulgaria; son of Jacques (a businessman) and Mathilde (Arditti) Canetti; married Venetia Taubner-Calderon, February 26, 1934 (died May 1, 1963); married, wife's name Hera; children: (second marriage) Johanna. *Education:* Attended schools in England, Austria, Switzerland, and Germany; University of Vienna, Ph.D., 1929. *Religion:* Jewish.

ADDRESSES: Home—London, England, and Zurich, Switzerland. *Office*—c/o Farrar, Straus & Giroux, 19 Union Sq. West, New York, N.Y. 10003.

CAREER: Writer and lecturer, 1931—.

AWARDS, HONORS: Prix International (Paris), 1949, for *Die Blendung;* Deutscher der Stadt (Vienna), 1966; Deutscher Kritikerpreis (Berlin), 1967; Grosser Oesterreichischer Staatspreis (Vienna), 1968; George Buechner Prize (Darmstadt), 1972; Franz Nabl Prize (Graz), 1975; Nelly Sachs Prize (Dortmund), 1975; Gottfried Keller Preis (Zurich), 1977; Order Pour le merito (Bonn), 1979; Johann Peter Hebel Preis, 1980; Premio Europa Prato (Italy), 1980; Kafka Prize and Nobel Prize for literature, both 1981; Order of Merit, Federal Republic of Germany; D.Litt., University of Manchester; Ph.D., University of Munich.

WRITINGS:

Hochzeit (play; first produced in Braunschweig, West Germany, February 6, 1965), [Berlin], 1932, reprinted, Hanser, 1981, translation by Gitta Honegger published as *The Wedding,* PAJ Publications, 1986.

Die Blendung (novel; title means "The Deception"), H. Reichner, 1935, translation, under the personal supervision of Canetti, by C. V. Wedgwood published as *Auto-da-fe,* J. Cape, 1946, reprinted, Seabury, 1979, published as *The Tower of Babel,* Knopf, 1947.

Fritz Wotruba (criticism), Brueder Rosenbaum, 1955.

Masse und Macht (nonfiction), Claassen, 1960, translation by Carol Stewart published as *Crowds and Power,* Viking, 1962, reprinted, Seabury, 1978.

Welt im Kopf, edited with an introduction by Erich Fried, Stiasny Verlag, 1962.

Komoedie der Eitelkeit (three-part play, written 1933-34; first produced in Braunschweig, November 3, 1965), Hanser, 1964, Sessler (Munich), 1976, translation by Honegger published as *Comedy of Vanity and Life-Terms,* PAJ Publications, 1983.

The Numbered (play; first produced at Oxford Playhouse, Oxford, England, November 5, 1956), published as *Die Befristeten,* Hanser, 1964, published as *The Numbered,* Marion Boyars, 1984.

Dramen (contains *Hochzeit, Komoedie der Eitelkeit,* and *Die Befristeten*), Hanser, 1964.

Aufzeichnungen, 1942-1948 (notebooks), Hanser, 1965.

Die Stimmen von Marrakesch (travel), Hanser, 1968, translation by J. A. Underwood published as *The Voices of Marrakesh: A Record of a Visit,* Seabury, 1978.

Der Andere Prozess, Neue Rundschau, 1968, translation by Christopher Middleton published as *Kafka's Other Trial: The Letters to Felice,* Schocken, 1974.

Macht und Ueberleben: Drei Essays, Literarische Colloquium, 1972.

Die Gespaltene Zukunft: Aufsaetz und Gesppraeche, Hanser, 1972.

Die Provinz des Menschen: Aufzeichnungen 1942-1972, Hanser, 1973, translation by Joachim Neugroschel published as *The Human Province,* Seabury, 1978.

(Author of commentary) Alfred Hrdlicka, *Graphik,* Propylaeen (Berlin), 1973.

Der Ohrenzeuge: 50 Charaktere, Hanser, 1974, translation by Neugroschel published as *Earwitness: Fifty Characters,* Seabury, 1979.

Das Gewissen der Worte: Essays, Hanser, 1975, translation by Neugroschel published as *The Conscience of Words,* Seabury, 1979.

Die Gerettete Zunge: Geschichte einer Jugend (autobiography), Hanser, 1977, translation by Neugroschel published as *The Tongue Set Free: Remembrance of a European Childhood,* Seabury, 1979.

Die Fackel im Ohr: Lebensgeschichte 1921-1931 (autobiography), Hanser, 1980, translation by Neugroschel published as *The Torch in My Ear,* Farrar, Straus, 1982.

Das Augenspiel: Lebensgeschichte 1931-1937 (autobiography), Hanser, 1985, translation by Ralph Manheim published as *The Play of the Eyes,* Farrar, Straus, 1986.

Das Geheimherz der Uhr: Aufzeichnungen, 1973-1985, Hanser, 1987, translation by Joel Agee published as *The Secret Heart of the Clock: Notes, Aphorisms, Fragments, 1973-1985,* Farrar, Straus, 1989.

SIDELIGHTS: Nobel Prize-winner Elias Canetti has achieved a considerable literary reputation primarily on the strength of two works—his 1935 novel *Die Blendung* (published in English as *Auto-da-fe* and *The Tower of Babel*) and his 1960 psychosociological study of crowd behavior, *Masse und Macht* (translated as *Crowds and Power*). These two books established Canetti's position "among the most distinguished writers in contemporary German literature," according to Sidney Rosenfeld in *World Literature Today.* Long admired as a profound thinker in Europe, Canetti was largely overlooked in English-speaking countries until he won the Nobel Prize in 1981. As Susan Sontag notes in the *New York Review of Books,* Canetti's work "has never lacked admirers, and yet aside from scattered reviews he has not been much written about." A recent and aggressive translation program has brought English readers access to most of Canetti's writing, thereby extending his audience beyond the bounds of the literary establishment. Sontag feels that the author's effort "has been to stand apart from other writers and he has succeeded. Shunning the modern means by which a writer gains an audience, he long ago decided that he would, he must, live long enough for his audience to come to him. Canetti is, both literally and by his own ambitions, a writer in exile."

The literal exile to which Sontag alludes began early in Canetti's childhood. Born in Bulgaria to parents whose Jewish forebears were driven from Spain by the Inquisition, Canetti has lived in Austria, Switzerland, Germany, and England. Nazi anti-Semitism compelled him to move to England in 1939, and it was in that country—writing in German—that he composed most of his works. *New Yorker* contributor George Steiner suggests that the "wild hazards" of Canetti's own fate have produced "the stoic force that gives to his writings their compelling edge." Although as Rosenfeld notes, Canetti is a writer "whose sensibilities are keenly attuned to the most critical problems of the modern epoch," Sontag and others credit Canetti with a sophisticated perception of the human psyche that transcends the twentieth century and even the modern age. "Canetti is not Eurocentric—one of his large achievements as a mind," writes Sontag. "Conversant with Chinese as well as with European thought, with Buddhism and Islam as with Christianity, Canetti

enjoys a remarkable freedom from reductive habits of thinking. He seems incapable of using psychological knowledge in a reductive way."

Several essential ideas have intrigued Canetti throughout his working career. His novel *Auto-da-fe* explores one of these, "the destructiveness of paranoia. His great theme is the fascism of the soul, the tendency of the human mind to fortify itself with aggressive power plays," in the words of *Voice Literary Supplement* contributor Gary Giddins. *Chicago Review* essayist Ian Watson contends that in *Auto-da-fe* Canetti uses the minutiae of lunatic delusions to expose "the obsessions and fantasies of everyday life, raised to a new pitch of intensity, where they possess the exaggerated savagery of a cartoon strip." In the *Times Literary Supplement,* Idris Parry comments that Canetti is "a specialist in the observation of fixed ideas. . . . He is fascinated by the delusions of people who live in capsules." Canetti is also associated with a strident rejection of death and an energetic support of life and intellectual growth. Sontag notes: "Canetti insists that death is really unacceptable; unassimilable, because it is what is outside life; unjust, because it limits ambition and insults it." She continues: "Canetti does not justify his yearning for longevity with any appeal to its greater scope for good works. So large is the value of the mind that it alone is used to oppose death."

The theme most closely associated with Canetti, however, is that of the psychology of crowd phenomena, a study that consumed the author for more than thirty years. According to Giddins, Canetti's "fidelity to the study of crowd behavior, . . . surely constitutes one of the most stubborn devotions in contemporary scholarship." In *Crowds and Power,* which he considers his "life's work," Canetti exhaustively explores crowd pathology from historical, psychological, and even biological perspectives, locating its impetus—"the yearning for power—in the very mitosis and cellular colonization from which life derives," to quote Giddins.

Through these and other provocative reflections, Canetti has stimulated his own thought and has offered his readers intense challenges. *Spectator* correspondent Iris Murdoch claims that Canetti's work produces "that rare sense of being 'let out' into an entirely new region of thought. Canetti has done what philosophers ought to do, and what they used to do: he has provided us with new concepts." In *Modern Austrian Literature,* Marion E. Wiley offers similar praise. Wiley writes: "[The] critic accustomed to the desperate confusion reflected in the literature of the later twentieth century may be moved to note that the reflective writing of Canetti is a stimulating and complementary addition to contemporary prose. It is stimulating to share ideas with an author who verbalizes his thoughts with clarity, frequent wit, and appropriate compassion. It is also encouraging to encounter the refutation of inevitability and the advocacy of spirited inquiry. In this respect Canetti is the antipode to the writer who records primarily the spiritual malnutrition of contemporary society and the resulting loss of illusions. Canetti possesses a view of life which impels him to search for alternative approaches to existence."

Much is known about Canetti's early life by virtue of his three autobiographical volumes, translated from the original German as *The Tongue Set Free: Remembrance of a European Childhood, The Torch in My Ear,* and *The Play of the Eyes.* In these works covering the first third of his life, Canetti recounts the many influences on his emotional and intellectual growth—the polyglot culture into which he was born, the demands of his exacting mother, and the inspiration offered by teachers and European literati. Canetti was born in Russe, Bulgaria, a Danube port city where it was common to hear seven or eight languages spoken every day. In his home, his parents addressed him in Ladino, a Spanish dialect of Sephardic exiles; the servants spoke Bulgarian. Additionally, Canetti's parents used German to communicate private thoughts to one another, "and from this association with secrecy the language seemed to him a vehicle of magical incantation," according to Parry. Sontag also notes that Canetti's family example "and the velocity of his childhood all facilitated an avid relation to language." By the time he turned ten, Canetti knew four languages, including the English he learned during a year his family spent in Manchester. It was German, however, that captured his imagination, even though his mother's methods of teaching it were particularly severe. "I was reborn under my mother's influence to the German language, and the spasm of that birth produced the passion tying me to both the language and my mother," Canetti claims in *The Tongue Set Free.* "Without these two, basically one and the same, the further course of my life would have been senseless and incomprehensible."

From 1913 to 1921 Canetti attended school in Vienna and Zurich, pursuing his greatest interests, literature and writing. His father had died and his mother was consumed with concern that a literary bent would cause her son to become "soft." Determined to expose Canetti to harsh reality, she moved him from Zurich to Frankfurt, a city struggling with the ravages of World War I. Canetti finished his secondary schooling there in 1924 and returned to Vienna to study chemistry—at his mother's insistence—even though he was determined to be a writer. Although chemistry held little appeal for him, he obtained a doctorate in the subject from the University of Vienna in 1929. Canetti's college years in Vienna were made more pivotal by his interest in the work of Viennese satirist Karl Kraus, a sensational orator, critic, and author of the journal *Die Fackel* (*The Torch*). *New York Review of Books* contributor S. S. Prawer suggests that Kraus's public readings left a "profound and lasting impression" on the young Canetti. During that period Canetti also met Bertolt Brecht, George Grosz, and Isaac Babel, and he especially enjoyed a productive working relationship with Babel.

In *The Torch in My Ear* Canetti describes the "most crucial day" in his life, July 15, 1927. On that day he was enveloped by and "dissolved" into a crowd of irate workers who burned down Vienna's Palace of Justice in protest over a controversial verdict. In that experience, contends Parry, Canetti "found both theme and image for his life's work. . . . From that moment he resolved to dedicate his energies to the study of crowds and mass phenomena." An idea for fiction also came to Canetti in 1927, according to Parry, but the novel was influenced more by Canetti's impressions of paintings—most notably Rembrandt van Rijn's "Blinding of Samson" and Brueghel's "Triumph of Death"—as well as his fascination with the grotesque and the power of the fixed idea. At the age of twenty-four, Canetti began to write what he thought would be the first of eight novel-length sketches of monomaniac characters—his tale of the "Book Man"'s descent into self-immolation, *Auto-da-fe.*

First published in 1935 as *Die Blendung,* the novel *Auto-da-fe* took on "the monumentality of a classic" almost overnight in Germany, according to Steiner. Its popularity was short-lived, however, because Nazi censors removed it from circulation. After the Second World War, the book slowly began to draw more readers; it was reissued in Germany and an authorized English translation by C. V. Wedgwood appeared in 1946. Modern critics are generous in their praise of the work; some consider it one of the most important novels of the twentieth century. Steiner contends that *Auto-da-fe* "remains a classic study of the violence subtly but steadily present in abstract thought, of the

pathological element in pure scholarship." Calling it "uncompromising and brilliant," *Critique* contributor Mark Sacharoff finds the novel the most "obsessional portrayal of obsessive characters in all of literature. . . . *Auto-da-fe,* long buried by a combination of unfavorable circumstances, has again come to light and now has a chance to be re-evaluated."

In *Harper's,* Jeffrey Burke writes that *Auto-da-fe* "describes the descent into madness of a world-renowned but reclusive sinologist whose scholarly life disintegrates at the hands of three vulgar, brutish characters. . . . It is the professor who dominates the novel. Canetti creates him out of the quirks and compulsions of a strong mind steeped in erudition." Sacharoff suggests that all of the four major characters are "driven from minute to minute by a central preoccupation and by all the speculations which radiate from it. . . . Thus, if we are to speak of Canetti's originality, a good starting-point would be the singularity and unswerving purpose with which he has pursued his characters' warped preoccupations." *Spectator* reviewer Kate O'Brien cites the work for its agonizingly slow detail and its sophisticated method: "With desiccated, pedantic caution, [Canetti] reflects fantasy against fact, merges nightmare with routine, cupidity with fanatical innocence, and so establishes his forces as one great hell. . . . All in a curiously dry writing, where no detail is spared, and while asking the most detached patience for phantasmagoria beyond comparable echo. . . . There is no light. Only vileness enthroned, and reason nobly flying to its own obliteration. A mad, magnificent work which we are not able to endure, which perhaps we are right not to accept, but of which we dare not deny the genius or the justification."

In Steiner's view of *Auto-da-fe,* "the holocaust to come somehow cast its hungry shadow on the entire fable." Parry likewise contends that "the destructive fires of history and the ritual fires of mythology" seem to converge in the novel. Parry adds that in the fate of the central character "we sense both a timeless human declension into death and a contemporary reference to individuality lost in the forest of flags and figures at Nuremburg, that ordered system of savagery." Whether or not the book prefigured the rise of European fascism, its author certainly foresaw the destruction to come in Germany. Canetti left for Paris in 1938 and moved to England in 1939. Nazism and its extreme measures strengthened Canetti's resolve to delve into the psychology of crowds; however, he retained a loyalty to German culture and continued to write in German, attuned, in Sontag's words, to "the higher cosmopolitanism. . . . With this decision, not the one made by most Jewish intellectuals who were refugees from [Adolf] Hitler, Canetti chose to remain unsullied by hatred, a grateful son of German culture who wants to help make it what one can continue to admire. And he has."

Masse und Macht, translated as *Crowds and Power,* is the culmination of more than thirty years' work for Canetti. According to Bruce Cook in the *Washington Post Book World,* the book "astonished the intellectual world—not just with its scholarship, some of it from the most recondite sources, but also with its insights, which are packed into gnomic essays . . . that can be read independently but stand as building blocks of the whole work." Cook adds: "It is a book that is not easily summarized, ranging as it does over the whole of human history to examine every conceivable aspect of mass psychology. . . . Its style, anecdotal and accessible, slyly implies the author's attitude of skepticism toward human institutions and his contempt for the men whom historians hold great. *Crowds and Power* is the nearest thing to a book of wisdom we are likely to get in the 20th century." Murdoch feels that to deal adequately with the work, "one would have to be, like its author, a mixture of historian, sociologist, psychologist, philosopher and poet. One is certainly confronted here with something large and important: an extremely imaginative, original and massively documented theory of the psychology of crowds."

When evaluating *Crowds and Power,* critics stress its unique blend of historical/psychological discourse and poetic anecdotage. In an essay for *Mosaic: A Journal for the Comparative Study of Literature and Ideas,* Dagmar Barnouw suggests that Canetti "does not judge crowds directly . . . from a particularly 'elitist' position, or indirectly like the stoical Freud who finds them frighteningly alien and therefore keeps them at bay. He demonstrates their destructive potential, their deadly interaction with systems of power whose operators know, as Hitler for instance showed very clearly, that the member of a mass society which is, of course, a hierarchically structured group of a great number of individuals, is willing to forget the sting of death . . . if he can rid himself, through temporary immersion in the crowd, of the sting of isolation." Burke notes: "Having made the uncommon choice of so common a fact of life as crowds, [Canetti] then supplies his own definitions, arrives at conclusions, and supports his findings with references from decades of reading in world literature, myth, history, and anthropology. In doing so, he arrives at a level of discourse that is less convincing than it is cerebrally poetic." Despite this objection, Burke claims that *Crowds and Power* "is capable of engaging a willing mind." Murdoch calls the book "marvelously rewarding . . . even if one were to read it without any theoretical interests at all. It is written in a simple, authoritative prose, . . . and it is radiant with imagination and humor. . . . We need and we shall always need the visions of great imaginers and solitary men of genius."

"Since the publication of *Crowds and Power,* Canetti has written several . . . works that encircle the major works like satellites," writes Giddins. "But taken together they also suggest a new and less isolated stage in Canetti's devotion to writing." Canetti's other publications include volumes of essays and aphorisms, plays, criticism, a travelogue, a highly regarded study of a portion of Franz Kafka's letters, and the three volumes of autobiography. Cook feels that as each piece of Canetti's work receives translation, the author "is more clearly defined as the important figure in European literature that he certainly is." Giddins sees a common thread that unites all of Canetti's disparate works. The critic comments: "As novelist, philosopher, and autobiographer, Canetti, the intransigent moral witness, offers no moral codes, utopian dreams, or escape hatches for 'our monstrous century.' The only code to which he adheres absolutely—a writer's code—is to stand in undaunted opposition to his time. . . . At 60, Canetti was essentially a two-book writer. His subsequent work can be read as attempt to integrate the writer into the vision, to demonstrate that 'the representative writer of this age' can personally exemplify the virtues—diligence, disaffection, scholarship, realism—that make grace possible in an insane world."

Canetti eschewed the publicity surrounding his choice as a Nobel Prize recipient, and he continues to live and write far from the public eye. As William Gass observes in *New Republic,* Canetti "has now achieved such fame as to be unknown all over the world. His obscurity is a part of his character, and is a credit to him, for he might be more widely recognized if his thought were sly and riddling, got up in a seductive lingo all its own so as to seem complex and problematic, not simply, plainly, and vertiginously deep." *Spectator* contributor Paul Theroux offers concurrent praise. "Canetti's reputation has been so formidable as to be off-putting;" Theroux contends, "and the less a person like Canetti is read the more grotesque he seems, until at last he becomes merely a terrifying presence. . . . The strange thing is that Canetti sometimes seems so original as to be an invented figure, yet no single mind could have invented this man, unless it were Canetti himself. . . . My feeling is that Canetti has been associated (unfairly) with gloom—long lugubrious tomes written at the Wailing Wall. That is such an unfair impression of a mind so nimble, imaginative and humane." According to Marion E. Wiley, Canetti's reflective prose "attests to the success of his intellectual exploration. In respect to this achievement his prose is a unique contribution to contemporary writing, and his belated reception . . . is a noteworthy entry for a history of German literary reception."

AVOCATIONAL INTERESTS: Canetti gave *CA* the following list: anthropology, history, psychiatry, history of religions, philosophy, sociology, psychology, and the civilizations of Egypt, Sumer, Greece, Rome, Persia, India, China, Japan, Mexico, Maya, Inca. He added: "It is ridiculous to have so many; but they are all equally important to me and have cost me years and decades of study."

BIOGRAPHICAL/CRITICAL SOURCES:

BOOKS

Best, Alan and Hans Wolfschuetz, *Modern Austrian Writing: Literature and Society after 1945,* B & N Imports, 1980.
Canetti, Elias, *Die Gerettete Zunge: Geschichte einer Jugend,* Hanser, 1977, translation by Joachim Neugroschel published as *The Tongue Set Free: Remembrance of a European Childhood,* Seabury, 1979.
Canetti, Elias, *Die Fackel im Ohr: Lebensgeschichte 1921-1931,* Hanser, 1980, translation by Neugroschel published as *The Torch in My Ear,* Farrar, Straus, 1982.
Canetti, Elias, *Das Augenspiel: Lebensgeschichte 1931-1937,* Hanser, 1985, translation by Ralph Manheim published as *The Play of the Eyes,* Farrar, Straus, 1986.
Contemporary Literary Criticism, Gale, Volume 3, 1975, Volume 14, 1980, Volume 25, 1983.
Elias Canetti, R. Boorberg (Stuttgart), 1970.
Hulse, Michael, translator, *Essays in Honor of Elias Canetti,* Farrar, Straus, 1986.
Schultz, Uwe, editor, *Das Tagebuch und der Moderne Autor,* Hanser, 1965.
Sontag, Susan, *Under the Sign of Saturn,* Farrar, Straus, 1980.

PERIODICALS

Books Abroad, autumn, 1965.
Book Week, May 29, 1966.
Canadian Forum, April, 1947.
Chicago Review, May, 1969.
Chicago Tribune Book World, January 6, 1980.
Critique: Studies in Modern Fiction, Volume 14, number 1, 1972.
Globe and Mail (Toronto), October 4, 1986.
Harper's, January, 1980.
Los Angeles Times Book Review, June 6, 1982, October 3, 1982, August 31, 1986.
Manchester Guardian, May 10, 1946.
Modern Austrian Literature, Volume 12, number 2, 1979.
Mosaic: A Journal for the Comparative Study of Literature and Ideas, winter, 1974.
New Republic, November 8, 1982.
Newsweek, October 26, 1981.
New Yorker, May 19, 1980, November 22, 1982.
New York Herald Tribune Book Review, February 23, 1947.
New York Review of Books, September 25, 1980, February 4, 1982, November 4, 1982, July 17, 1986.

New York Times, October 16, 1981, February 27, 1982, March 20, 1982, September 17, 1982, July 1, 1986, August 10, 1986.

New York Times Book Review, April 29, 1979, September 19, 1982.

Publishers Weekly, October 31, 1981.

San Francisco Chronicle, March 9, 1947.

Saturday Review, December, 1978.

Saturday Review of Literature, March 8, 1947.

Spectator, May 24, 1946, September 7, 1962, November 30, 1985, April 19, 1986.

Sunday Times (London), August 15, 1982.

Time, October 26, 1981.

Times (London), February 18, 1982, August 24, 1989.

Times Literary Supplement, July 8, 1965, October 31, 1968, January 15, 1971, January 25, 1974, January 10, 1975, February 28, 1975, December 22, 1975, January 9, 1981, October 23, 1981, July 26, 1985, August 26-September 1, 1988, August 25-31, 1989.

Voice Literary Supplement, March, 1982, October, 1982.

Washington Post, October 16, 1981.

Washington Post Book World, September 26, 1982.

World Literature Today, winter, 1978, spring, 1979, autumn, 1979, spring, 1981, winter, 1985, May 20, 1984.

*   *   *

CANNON, Curt
See HUNTER, Evan

*   *   *

CAPE, Judith
See PAGE, P(atricia) K(athleen)

*   *   *

CAPOTE, Truman   1924-1984

PERSONAL: Original name, Truman Streckfus Persons; name legally changed; born September 30, 1924, in New Orleans, La.; died of liver disease complicated by phlebitis and multiple drug intoxication, August 25, 1984, in Los Angeles, Calif.; son of Archulus Persons (a nonpracticing lawyer) and Lillie Mae (Faulk) Persons Capote; adopted by Joseph G. Capote. *Education:* Attended Trinity School and St. John's Academy, both in New York City, and public schools in Greenwich, Conn.

ADDRESSES: Home—870 United Nations Plaza, New York, N.Y.; also maintained residences in the Hamptons on Long Island, N.Y. and in Verbier, Switzerland.

CAREER: Writer. Worked for *New Yorker* magazine as a newspaper clipper and cartoon cataloger, c. 1943-44; also moonlighted as a filmscript reader and free-lance writer of anecdotes for a digest magazine. Appeared in motion picture "Murder by Death," Columbia, 1976.

MEMBER: National Institute of Arts and Letters.

AWARDS, HONORS: Won first literary prize at age ten in Mobile Press Register contest, for short story "Old Mr. Busybody"; O. Henry Award, Doubleday & Co., 1946, for "Miriam," 1948, for "Shut a Final Door," and 1951; National Institute of Arts and Letters creative writing award, 1959; Edgar Award, Mystery Writers of America, 1966, and National Book Award nomination, 1967, both for *In Cold Blood;* Emmy Award, 1967, for television adaptation "A Christmas Memory."

WRITINGS:

Other Voices, Other Rooms (novel), Random House, 1948, reprinted with an introduction by the author, 1968.

A Tree of Night, and Other Stories (also see below), Random House, 1949.

Local Color (nonfiction sketches), Random House, 1950.

The Grass Harp (novel; also see below), Random House, 1951.

The Grass Harp, and A Tree of Night, and Other Stories, New American Library, 1956.

The Muses Are Heard: An Account (first published in *New Yorker*), Random House, 1956 (published in England as *The Muses Are Heard: An Account of the Porgy and Bess Visit to Leningrad,* Heinemann, 1957).

Breakfast at Tiffany's: A Short Novel and Three Stories, Random House, 1958 (published in England as *Breakfast at Tiffany's,* Hamish Hamilton, 1959).

(Author of commentary) Richard Avedon, *Observations,* Simon & Schuster, 1959.

Selected Writings, introduction by Mark Schorer, Random House, 1963.

In Cold Blood: A True Account of a Multiple Murder and Its Consequences (nonfiction novel; Book-of-the-Month Club selection; first serialized in *New Yorker*), Random House, 1966.

A Christmas Memory (first published in *Mademoiselle,* December, 1956; also see below), Random House, 1966.

The Thanksgiving Visitor (first published in *McCall's;* also see below), Random House, 1968.

The Dogs Bark: Public People and Private Places, Random House, 1973.

Miriam (first published in *Mademoiselle;* also see below), Creative Education, Inc., 1982.

Music for Chameleons: New Writing, Random House, 1983.

One Christmas (first published in *Ladies Home Journal*), Random House, 1983.

Answered Prayers: The Partial Manuscript (first serialized in *Esquire*), edited by Joseph Fox, Random House, 1986, published as *Answered Prayers: The Unfinished Novel,* 1987.

PLAYS

The Grass Harp: A Play (based on his novel of the same title; first produced on Broadway at Martin Beck Theatre, March 27, 1952; produced as a musical on Broadway at Martin Beck Theatre, November, 1971), Random House, 1952.

(With Harold Arlen) *The House of Flowers* (libretto; based on his short story of the same title; first produced on Broadway at Alvin Theatre, December 30, 1954; rewritten version first produced Off-Broadway at Theater de Lys, January 24, 1968), Random House, 1968.

FILMSCRIPTS

(With John Huston) "Beat the Devil," United Artists, 1954.

(With William Archibald and John Mortimer) "The Innocents" (based on Henry James's novel of the same title), Twentieth Century-Fox Film Corp., 1961.

(With Eleanor Perry) "Trilogy" (also see below; adapted from Capote's short stories "Miriam," "Among the Paths to Eden," and "A Christmas Memory"), Allied Artists, 1969.

TELEVISION SCRIPTS

"A Christmas Memory" (based on his book of the same title), American Broadcasting Co. (ABC-TV), December 21, 1966.

"The Thanksgiving Visitor" (based on his book of the same title), American Broadcasting Co. (ABC-TV), November, 1968.

Also author of television play "Among the Paths to Eden" (adapted from his short story of the same title), first produced in 1967, "Laura," 1968, "Behind Prison Walls," 1972, with Tracy Keenan Wynn and Wyatt Cooper, "The Glass House," 1972, and "Crimewatch," 1973.

OTHER

(Author of introduction) *The Collected Works of Jane Bowles,* Farrar, Straus, 1966.
(With E. Perry and Frank Perry) *Trilogy: An Experiment in Multimedia,* Macmillan, 1969.
A Capote Reader, Random House, 1987.

Also author of *Then It All Came Down: Criminal Justice Today Discussed by Police, Criminals, and Correction Officers, With Comments by Truman Capote,* 1976. Contributor to numerous anthologies, including *Five Modern American Short Stories,* edited by Helmut Tischler, M. Diesterweg, 1962. Author of *Esquire* column "Observations," beginning March, 1983. Contributor to national magazines, including *Vogue, Mademoiselle, Ladies Home Journal, Esquire,* and *New Yorker.* Many of Capote's books have been translated into foreign languages, including French, German, Spanish, and Italian.

SIDELIGHTS: A masterful stylist who took great pride in his writing, Truman Capote was also a well-known television personality, openly obsessed with fame. In addition to literary recognition, the flamboyant, Southern-born writer sought social privilege and public celebrity, objectives he achieved in 1948 with the appearance of his first novel, *Other Voices, Other Rooms.* That book—published with a provocative dust-jacket photo of the author that far overshadowed the literary merit of the work—was the start of what Capote later termed "a certain notoriety" that kept step with him over the years. Believing that fame would not affect his art, Capote cultivated an entourage of rich and celebrated friends, observing their foibles with a watchful eye and inspiring confidences he would later betray. By 1959, he had already embarked on *Answered Prayers*—the never-to-be-finished *roman a clef* that precipitated a personal and professional crisis. Then he decided to put it "temporarily" aside while he explored something more serious—"a theme," as he explained to *Newsweek*'s Jack Kroll, "not likely to darken and yellow with time." His idea was to bring "the art of the novelist together with the technique of journalism" to produce a new genre, the nonfiction novel. Over six years in the making, the resulting book was *In Cold Blood: A True Account of a Multiple Murder and Its Consequences,* not only an enormous critical and commercial success, but also a seminal work of new journalism that remains the highlight of Capote's career.

Though the nonfiction novel was his most original contribution to the literary world, Capote also produced conventional writing of top quality. In short stories, plays, straight reportage, television adaptations, and filmscripts, he demonstrated what *Los Angeles Times* contributor Carolyn See called "the uncanny gift of putting a world or a scene together in a few perfect details." Among his other talents were "his patience for fact-collecting, his faithfulness to the true nature of his subject and his consummate gift as a storyteller," according to *New York Times Book Review* contributor Lis Harris. He was, in, the words of David Remnick in the *Washington Post,* "a writer of brilliance, capable of economical, evocative prose. His technique was mature, professional in the best possible sense."

Though his style of writing evolved over the years, falling into what Capote himself considered four different phases, his poetic voice was distinctive right from the start. "Truman had an odd

and personal perspective on experience that only real writers have," poet and novelist James Dickey explained in the *New York Times.* "A lot of writers sweat and labor to acquire that, but Truman Capote had it naturally. He was maybe a little heavy on the Southern gothic side of things, a little bit willfully perverse. . . . But at his best, he had a very great sensitivity and linguistic originality." In the same *New York Times* article, novelist John Knowles expressed a similar view, saying of Capote's voice that "it was like no one else's—precise, clear, sometimes fey, lyrical, witty, graceful."

Capote himself often suggested that his originality was pervasive, influencing not just his writing, but every aspect of his life. "The thing about people like me is that we always knew what we were going to do," Capote told *New York Times Magazine* contributor Anne Taylor Fleming. "Many people spend half their lives not knowing. But I was a very special person, and I had to have a very special life. . . . I would have been successful at whatever I did. But I always knew that I wanted to be a writer and that I wanted to be rich and famous." According to Fleming, "looking at the boy he must have been, the slender, pretty, high-voiced boy . . ., it seems easy to see, too easy maybe, how the kind of fame he coveted would someday become too heavy."

Born Truman Streckfus Persons in New Orleans, Louisiana, Capote had a childhood that, by all accounts, was difficult. His mother, a former Miss Alabama who later committed suicide, considered herself temperamentally unsuited to motherhood and sent him off to be raised by relatives in Monroeville, a small Alabama town. When he was four, his parents ended their marriage in a bitter divorce: his mother went north to New York, his father south to New Orleans, and young Truman became "a spiritual orphan," in Fleming's words. Though he frequently summered with his father, traveling up and down the Mississippi on the family-owned Streckfus Steam Boat Line, the two were never close, and Capote considered him "a bounder and a cad." The Monroeville years were difficult for Capote, comprising a time when he felt "like a turtle on its back. You see," he explained to Fleming, "I was so different from every one, so much more intelligent and sensitive and perceptive. I was having fifty perceptions a minute to everyone else's five. I always felt that nobody was going to understand me, going to understand what I felt about things. I guess that's why I started writing. At least on paper I could put down what I thought."

His closest friends at this time were an elderly cousin, Miss Sook Faulk, whom Fleming describes as "the archetype of the aging innocent, the best of the simple people with an inarticulate wisdom and a childlike capacity for joy and strange imaginings," and a neighboring tomboy, Harper Lee, who helped young Truman type his manuscripts and eventually became an award-winning author herself, writing *To Kill a Mockingbird.* Both personalities appear in Capote's early fiction, his cousin in autobiographical stories, such as "A Christmas Memory," and his friend in his first novel *Other Voices, Other Rooms.*

His mother, meanwhile, had remarried a Cuban-born New York businessman, Joe Capote, and when, after a series of miscarriages, she realized she could have no more children, she sent for Truman. He was nine years old. Legally adopted by his stepfather, the young author attended school in Manhattan, then enrolled at Trinity, and, at thirteen, was sent to live at St. John's Academy, a military boarding school. "I was lonely and very insecure," Capote told *Playboy* interviewer Eric Norden about his schooling. "Who wouldn't be? I was an only child, very sensitive and intelligent, with no sense of being particularly wanted by *anybody.* . . . I wasn't neglected financially; there was always enough money to send me to good schools, and all that. It was just a total *emotional* neglect. I never felt I belonged anywhere. All my family thought there was something wrong with me."

His grades were so low that, over the years, his family began to worry that he might be retarded. But when a special group of WPA researchers came to his school to conduct intelligence tests, Capote received the highest score they had ever seen. "I had the highest intelligence of any child in the United States," Capote told *Washington Post* reporter David Remnick, "an IQ of 215." Nonetheless, he had little use for formal schooling and, though he did graduate from high school (a fact which he obscured for many years), Capote told Norden he was "determined never to set foot inside a college classroom. If I was a writer, fine; if I wasn't, no professor on earth was going to make me one."

In place of formal education, Capote substituted experience, landing a job with the *New Yorker* when he was seventeen. "That job wasn't very glamorous, just clipping newspapers and filing cartoons," Capote told Norden, but it marked the beginning of a long association with the magazine that would serialize his best-known work and, to some extent, shape his writing style. Initially, however, his stories were rejected by the magazine. He made his first big sale shortly after leaving the *New Yorker,* when *Mademoiselle* bought a short story, "Miriam," which later garnered an O. Henry Award. According to *Dictionary of Literary Biography* contributor Craig M. Goad, " 'Miriam' typifies the early Capote manner. It is a story of isolation, dread, and psychological breakdown told in rich, precisely mannered prose. There is little technical or thematic experimentation in 'Miriam' and the other Capote stories that appeared regularly in the postwar years. The shadow of Edgar Allan Poe floats over the surface of these stories, and their chief aim often seems to be only to produce a mild *frisson.*"

"Miriam" caught the attention of Random House editor Robert Linscott, who told Capote that he would be interested in publishing whatever he wanted to write. Capote had already begun work on *Summer Crossing,* "a spare, objective story with a New York setting," according to Capote, who acknowledged in the preface to the 1968 reprint of *Other Voices, Other Rooms* that "in order to complete the book . . . I took courage, quit my job, left New York and settled with relatives in a remote part of Alabama." But, once arrived, Capote began having doubts about his novel. "More and more," he wrote, "*Summer Crossing* seemed to me thin, clever, unfelt." While walking in the woods one afternoon, Capote was seized with a new vision, one inspired by childhood memories. He returned home, "tossed the manuscript of *Summer Crossing* into a bottom bureau drawer, collected several sharp pencils and a fresh pad of yellow lined paper and with pathetic optimism, wrote: *Other Voices, Other Rooms*—a novel by Truman Capote."

The novel took two years to complete and was published in 1948 to mostly favorable reviews. But it was the book's packaging rather than its literary merit that titillated the public's attention, for the dust-jacket photo portrayed the twenty-three-year-old author reclining on a couch, looking "as if he were dreamily contemplating some outrage against conventional morality," according to a report in the *Los Angeles Times.* Because Capote, an open homosexual, had focused on the developing relationship between an effete transvestite and his young male cousin, "readers at the time suspected that Capote may have identified with the book's protagonist and that 'Other Voices, Other Rooms' was a confession of sexual deviation," continued George Ramos and Laurie Becklund in the *Los Angeles Times.* In retrospect, Capote was able to identify the book's many autobiographical ele-

ments—particularly, as he explained in his 1968 preface, the parallels between protagonist Joel Knox's quest for love and his own search for an "essentially imaginary" father—but he did not make the connection at the time. "Rereading it now, I find such self-deception unpardonable," Capote wrote.

What many conservative critics found "unpardonable" was not Capote's self-deception, but rather his aberrant theme. "For all his novel's gifted invention and imagery, the distasteful trappings of its homosexual theme overhang it like Spanish moss," wrote the *Time* contributor. And, writing in the *Nation,* respected literary critic Diana Trilling expressed a similar view: "Even if Mr. Capote were ten or twenty years older than he is, his powers of description and evocation, his ability to bend language to his poetic moods, his ear for dialect and for the varied rhythms of speech would be remarkable. . . . On the other hand, I find myself deeply antipathetic to the whole artistic moral purpose of Mr. Capote's novel. I would freely trade eighty per cent of his technical virtuosity for twenty per cent more value in the uses to which it is put."

Some critics also reacted against the apparent self-consciousness of the writing. "*Other Voices, Other Rooms* is the novel of someone who wanted, with a fixed and single-minded and burning will, to write a novel," wrote Cynthia Ozick in a *New Republic* critique of the twentieth-anniversary edition. "The vision of *Other Voices, Other Rooms* is the vision of capital-A Art—essence freed from existence." What this artistic preoccupation led to, in the eyes of the *Times Literary Supplement* reviewer, was "the temptation to mystify for the sake of mystification." Noted *Saturday Review* contributor Richard McLaughlin: "If he had selected his material more carefully, shown more restraint, and had been less concerned with terrifying us out of our wits, he might have easily made a real and tenderly appealing story out of the experiences of thirteen-year-old Joel Knox and the people he meets during that long and lonely summer of his approaching maturity."

After the publication of *Other Voices, Other Rooms,* Capote moved for a time to Europe, where he traveled widely with novelist Jack Dunphy, "the only man . . . with whom he has ever been in love," according to Fleming in the *New York Times Magazine.* During this ten-year period, which Capote described as the second phase of his development and which ended in 1958, the author experimented with various kinds of writing. There were nonfiction travel essays and portraits (*Local Color, Observations*), short story collections (*A Tree of Night, A Christmas Memory*), adaptations of two earlier fictions into Broadway plays (*The Grass Harp, House of Flowers*), and the scripting of two original films ("Beat the Devil," "The Innocents"). There was also "a great deal of factual reportage, most of it for the *New Yorker,*" Capote recalled in the preface to *Music for Chameleons.* His most memorable assignments included a tongue-in-cheek profile of Marlon Brando and a wry account of a black theatrical troupe's production of "Porgy and Bess" in Russia, later published in book form as *The Muses Are Heard.*

Though Capote's version of the "Porgy and Bess" tour of Russia "didn't quite jibe with the way some other observers of the trip remembered it," according to *Washington Post* reporter Tom Zito, *The Muses Are Heard* was a critical success, which "brilliantly utilized the literary forms of a fiction writer to present factual material." To achieve its effect of "deadpan mockery," the book poked gentle fun at a number of people, leaving "almost everyone touched by Mr. Capote's pen looking a little foolish," according to a review in the *Christian Science Monitor.* But *The Muses Are Heard* had "more to it than entrancing fun," as *Atlan-*

tic contributor C. J. Rolo explained: "While Capote's eye and ear have a radarlike sensitivity to the incongruous and the hilarious, they also dig the significant. What is dingy and nasty in Soviet life is revealed subtly and shrewdly, with a telling selectivity."

That selectivity reflected Capote's approach to his subject. To research his chronicle, he had employed neither tape recorder nor note pad, relying instead upon his photographic memory, which he viewed as the journalist's stock-in-trade. He would write up his impressions at the end of the day, but never during an interview, for he felt note-taking put his subjects on guard. "Taking notes produces the wrong kind of atmosphere," he pointed out to *Newsweek*'s Jack Kroll, explaining how he had trained his memory "by getting a friend to read me the Sears Roebuck catalog. I would have a tape recorder going at the same time. At first I could remember only forty per cent, then after three months sixty per cent. Now I can remember ninety per cent, and who cares about the other ten per cent," he said in 1966.

The Muses Are Heard, which was the first book Capote produced using this method, impressed the *New York Times* reviewer as "a record made by a brilliant writer in a casual, almost flippant manner—but with such freshness, with such light strokes and subtle innuendo, that the book reads like a highly enjoyable, charming story." The technique was so successful that it prompted Capote to envision a new kind of novel—"something on a large scale that would have the credibility of fact, the immediacy of film, the depth and freedom of prose, and the precision of poetry," Capote explained to James Wolcott in the *New York Review of Books.* In his mind, he christened this new genre "the nonfiction novel" and began looking for a suitable theme.

Before Capote found his subject, he published one more conventional novel, *Breakfast at Tiffany's,* later adapted into a popular film starring Audrey Hepburn and George Peppard. The engaging story of Manhattan playgirl Holly Golightly, *Breakfast at Tiffany's* demonstrated a maturity lacking in Capote's early fiction—at least in the opinion of *New Republic* contributor Stanley Kauffmann, who wrote: "It was with *Breakfast at Tiffany's* . . . that . . . Capote began to see enough of life and love to be more interested in his material than himself and to reveal the humor that now seems basic to him." Though Capote conceived of his story as a fiction, he was already drawing heavily from real life incidents, a point not lost on Kauffmann, who observed that "real names might conceivably be affixed to every character in *Breakfast at Tiffany's* and the whole published as a report on Manhattan life in the war years. If this is a restrictive comment, it is not meant to be condemnatory: because from her first appearance Holly leaps to life. Her dialogue has the perfection of pieces of mosaic fitting neatly and unassailably in place. The fey madness and extravagance, character qualities that easily throw fiction off the rails, always seem intrinsic, not contrived. . . . His fiction is strongest, most vital, when it resembles his best non-fiction." In the opinion of the *Times Literary Supplement* critic, the writing in *Breakfast at Tiffany's* "shorn of affection and the too-carefully chosen word," put Capote "in immediate sympathy with his characters" and placed "him at once among the leading American writers of the day."

Capote saw the second phase of his development as a writer come to a close with *Breakfast at Tiffany's,* and, after its publication, he turned his efforts "toward journalism as an art form in itself. I had two reasons," Capote explained in the preface to *Music for Chameleons.* "First, it didn't seem to me that anything truly innovative had occurred in prose writing . . . since the 1920s; second, journalism as an art was almost virgin territory." He began to search in earnest for a suitable subject, experiment-

ing with several different ideas at this time. One project was a Proustian work, according to Baumgold, tentatively entitled *Answered Prayers.* "Capote had the title since the 1950s," wrote Baumgold, and "began in 1958 with notes, a full outline, and an ending." Despite his commitment to the project—which he admittedly envisioned as his masterwork—*Answered Prayers* was "temporarily" shelved when Capote got a brainstorm. "One day," he recalled to Haskel Frankel in the *Saturday Review,* "it suddenly occurred to me that a crime might be an excellent subject to make my big experiment with. . . . Once I had decided on the possibility of a crime . . . I would half-consciously, when looking through the papers, always notice any item that had a reference to a crime."

On November 16, 1959, Capote found what he had been looking for. Briefly noted in a *New York Times* wire story was the multiple murder of a wealthy wheat farmer, his wife, and their two teenage children in a small Kansas town. "Almost instantaneously I thought, well, this is maybe exactly what I want to do, because I don't know anything about that part of the world," Capote told Frankel. "I've never been to Kansas, much less western Kansas. It all seems fresh to me. I'll go without any prejudices. And so I went."

Three days later, Capote arrived in Holcomb, Kansas, accompanied by his childhood friend Harper Lee, who assisted him with the initial research. The town was in the throes of a brutal unsolved slaying, its residents not only traumatized but also deeply suspicious, and the urbane little dandy from New York City was not well received. Capote recalled that it took about a month for his presence to be accepted and that after the killers, Perry Smith and Dick Hickock, were apprehended, people finally began to open up to him. In addition to interviewing the townspeople, murderers, and anyone else even remotely connected to the Clutter case, Capote retraced the killers' flight, journeying south to Miami and Acapulco, renting rooms in the same cheap hotels. He did months of research on the criminal mind and interviewed a number of death row killers, "solely to give me a perspective on these two boys," Capote told George Plimpton in the *New York Times Book Review.* Before he began writing, he had amassed over six thousand pages of notes, explaining, "Eighty per cent of the research I . . . never used. But it gave me such a grounding that I never had any hesitation in my consideration of the subject." All told, the project, which Capote regarded as the third phase of his writing development, consumed almost six years. When it was over, Capote confessed to Frankel, "I would never do it again. . . . If had known what that book was going to cost in every conceivable way, emotionally, I never would have started it, and I really mean that."

Some people attribute Capote's escalating physical and emotional problems to the acute stress he suffered during the project. Fleming reported that this was the period when he "began to take the tranquilizers to which he later became addicted." But, if he paid a high personal price, the financial compensations for *In Cold Blood* were generous, for the story was a commercial success even before it appeared in book form. Serialized in the *New Yorker* in four consecutive issues, *In Cold Blood* boosted the magazine's sales and netted Capote a rumored $70,000 in serialization rights. New American Library paid a reported $700,000 for paperback rights and Columbia Pictures spent almost a million dollars for filming rights. By 1983, according to the *Washington Post, In Cold Blood* had brought the author $2 million in royalties.

The book was also a critical success, described by *New York Times Book Review* contributor Conrad Knickerbocker as "a masterpiece—agonizing, terrible, possessed, proof that the times, so surfeited with disasters, are still capable of tragedy." *In Cold Blood,* according to the *Time* reviewer, "plays a light that illuminates the interior climate of murder with intense fidelity. Capote has invested the victims with a dignity and reality that life hitherto had confined only to the closed circle of their friends, and he has thrust the act of violence itself before the reader as if it were happening before his very eyes." David Remnick deemed certain "passages in it every bit as rhythmically spellbinding as Hemingway's famous opening to 'A Farewell to Arms,' " while F. W. Dupee extolled it as "the best documentary account of an American crime ever written," in the *New York Review of Books.*

Like any experimental literary work, *In Cold Blood* also had its share of detractors. Fellow novelist Norman Mailer, when asked his reaction to Capote's new genre, glibly dismissed it as "a failure of imagination," though as Capote took great pleasure in pointing out, Mailer later employed the same subject and technique in his Pulitzer Prize-winning *The Executioner's Song.* "Now I see that the only prizes Norman wins are for the very same kind of writing," Capote later quipped to the *Washington Post.* "I'm glad I was of some service to him."

Capote, who told Norden that he had "undertaken the most comprehensive and far-reaching experiment to date in the medium of reportage," never doubted the originality of his contribution. But others, like Diana Trilling, were not convinced. "Works of autobiography such as Isak Dinesen's *Out of Africa,* works of history such as Cecil Woodham Smith's *The Reason Why,* works of journalism like James Agee's *Let Us Now Praise Famous Men* are all at least as close to, or far from, proposing a new nonfiction form as Mr. Capote's *In Cold Blood,*" she wrote in the *Partisan Review.* While admitting that "the form is not new or remarkable," the *Times Literary Supplement* reviewer acknowledged that "it is handled here with a narrative skill and delicate sensibility that make this re-telling of a gruesome murder story into a work of art." Capote "did not intend to be merely the novelist-as-journalist, writing diversionary occasional pieces," wrote Conrad Knickerbocker in the *New York Times Book Review.* "In the completer role of novelist-as-journalist-as-artist, he was after a new kind of statement. He wanted the facts to declare a reality that transcended reality."

Capote believed that in order for his nonfiction-novel form to be successful, it must be an objective account in which the author himself did not appear. "Once the narrator does appear," he explained to Plimpton, "he has to appear throughout . . . and the I-I-I intrudes when it really shouldn't." Capote's absence from the story was interpreted as a moral cop-out by some critics, including Cynthia Ozick, who complained that *In Cold Blood* "has excised its chief predicament, the relation of the mind of the observer to the mind of the observed, and therefore it cannot be judged, it escapes interpretation because it flees its own essential deed." Diana Trilling accused Capote of "employing objectivity as a shield for evasion. This is what is resented . . . the sense shared in some dim way by virtually all of Mr. Capote's audience of having been unfairly used in being made to take on the burden of personal involvement pridefully put aside by Mr. Capote himself. An unpleasant critical charge leveled against *In Cold Blood* is that it is itself written in cold blood, exploiting tragedy for personal gain."

No one familiar with Capote's involvement with the Clutter case leveled this charge, for he made his personal commitment clear. "I had to surrender my entire life to this experience," he told Norden. "Try to think what it means to totally immerse yourself in the lives of two men waiting to be hanged, to feel the passage of hours with them, to share every emotion. Short of actually living in a death cell myself, I couldn't have come closer to the experience." Though his sympathies were divided between one of the killers, Perry Smith, and the head of the investigation, Alvin Dewey, Capote worked openly to have the murderers' death sentences commuted. He became physically ill when they were hanged.

Writing in the *Dictionary of Literary Biography,* Craig M. Goad concluded that "the controversy about the nature and literary status of *In Cold Blood* can never be wholly resolved, for it hinges on the definition of art that the individual reader accepts, but there is little doubt that the book creates a vivid portrait of western Kansas and captures the manners and speech of the people who live there. . . . It explores the irony of the fact that the murder of the Clutters, apparently exactly the sort of crime that a prosecuting attorney can describe as being committed 'in cold blood,' was essentially a crime of passion, a brief explosion of repressed rage and hate, while the executions of Hickock and Smith were carried out cold-bloodedly after years of legal wrangling. Finally, and perhaps most importantly, *In Cold Blood* contains the detailed portraits of Hickock and Smith which continue to fascinate not only those with literary interests, but students of criminal psychology as well."

After the book was finished, Capote orchestrated a major promotional campaign, prompting further charges of impropriety, which he answered with one of his quips: "A boy has to hustle his book," he said, according to the *Los Angeles Times.* He took a long vacation from writing and resumed his fast-paced social life, hosting a fancy dress ball for 540 friends in November, 1966. According to Fleming, "Capote worked on the party as if it were a book, laboring over flowers, colors, seating, food—which alone cost $12,000—scrawling details in a notebook in his tiny hand." Many of those closest to the author believed his quest for social acceptance was pathological, compensating for the emotional neglect of his childhood years. "It was harder to do than was the writing for him," Norman Mailer told Julie Baumgold in *New York* magazine. "His talent was his friend. His achievement was his social life."

In 1966, Capote had taken a $750,000 writing advance in the form of stocks and was supposed to resume work on *Answered Prayers,* the nonfiction novel he had named from a quote by Saint Therese: "More tears are shed over answered prayers than unanswered ones." Instead, Capote wrote in the preface to *Music for Chameleons,* "for four years, roughly from 1968 through 1972, I spent most of my time reading and selecting, rewriting and indexing my own letters, other people's letters, my diaries and journals . . . for the years 1943 through 1965." Finally, in 1972, he resumed work on the book, entering what he viewed as the fourth and final cycle of his writing. He wrote the last chapter first, then produced several more chapters in random order. In 1975 and 1976, four chapters were published in *Esquire* magazine.

Capote's reasons for releasing a work in progress remain unclear. Fleming theorized that it was "to jolt himself out of his sadness." Albin Krebs hypothesized that he did it "to keep alive the public's interest in the promised work," while Norman Mailer speculated that it "may have been Capote's deliberate effort to free himself" from the debilitating influence of his cafe society friends. Whatever his reasons, the results, according to Baumgold were "social suicide."

In the work, which Capote likened to a contemporary version of Marcel Proust's *Remembrance of Things Past,* Capote divulged many of the scandalous secrets he had coaxed from his wealthy and powerful friends. "The first excerpt was called 'La Cote Basque,' after the New York restaurant frequented by many of society's more celebrated members," wrote Tom Zito in the *Washington Post.* "Many of the whispered stories and innuendoes he had heard over the years he now had the audacity to print, either factually or thinly veiled. It was as if he was metaphorically recreating what Perry Smith had said in 'In Cold Blood' about the murder of Herbert Clutter: 'I thought he was a very nice gentleman. Softspoken. I thought so right up to the moment I cut his throat.' " The reprisals were swift and immediate. Many of the circles in which he'd traveled now became closed to him. His telephone calls went unreturned. Invitations fell off. Perhaps the most deeply felt repercussion was the loss of his relationship with Babe Paley, once an almost constant companion and friend.

This social crisis was paralleled by a creative crisis that struck Capote around 1977. Dissatisfied with the texture of his writing, Capote reread every word he had ever published and "decided that never, not once in my writing life, had I completely exploded all the energy and esthetic excitements that material contained. Even when it was good," Capote continued in *Music for Chameleons,* "I was never working with more than half, sometimes only a third, of the powers at my command."

In a 1978 television interview with Stanley Siegel, Capote appeared on the air under the influence of drugs and alcohol, confessing that he frequently mixed "them together like some kind of cocktail." Before the segment was cut, Capote attributed his substance abuse problems to "free-floating anxiety," developed as a child: "My mother was a very beautiful girl and only seventeen years old, and she used to lock me in these rooms all the time, and I developed this fantastic anxiety." He also alluded to his artistic problems with *Answered Prayers,* admitting "I'm pretty anxious about this new book of mine . . . really a great sense of anxiety about it."

A legendary fabricator, Capote may well have been exaggerating the hardships of his childhood, at least according to his aunt Marie Rudisill, who told Baumgold that "he might have locked his mother in rooms." Capote's penchant for exaggeration was also confirmed by the late playwright Tennessee Williams, who once told a reporter for the *Washington Post,* "Truman's a mythologist, baby, you know that. That's a polite way of saying he does fabricate. I love him too much to say he's a liar. That's part of his profession." In the case of *Answered Prayers,* however, the writer's block he alluded to was real.

The crux of the problem, as Capote explained in *Music for Chameleons,* was that "by restricting myself to the techniques of whatever form I was working in, I was not using everything I knew about writing—all I'd learned from film scripts, plays, reportage, poetry, the short story, novellas, the novel. A writer ought to have all his colors . . . available on the same palette for mingling. . . . But how?" The solution, he decided after months of contemplation, was to reverse the process of invisibility he'd mastered for *In Cold Blood* and to set himself at "center stage" in his writing. From this vantage point, using dialogue, stage direction, narrative, and a variety of other literary techniques, he would report his tales. This is the approach Capote employed in most of the selections published in his 1980 work, *Music for Chameleons,* the last major book he would write.

A collection of stories and portraits, *Music for Chameleons* has as its centerpiece "Handcarved Coffins"—a 30,000 word "nonfiction account of an American crime." In an interview with *Los Angeles Times* reporter Wayne Warga, Capote attributed his

ability to "get that story at that length" to the innovative techniques he was using. "The entire point of this whole book is stylistic compression. I want everything to be minimal," he explained. But in a *Saturday Review* critique of the work, John Fowles found that "despite [Capote's] claims, the technique is (mercifully) innovatory only in one or two superficial and formal ways; in many more important ones it is a brave step back to older literary virtues. He now writes fiction increasingly near fact, and vice versa. In practice this means that he is very skillfully blending the received techniques of several kinds of writing."

Though *Los Angeles Times Book Review* contributor Thomas Thompson dismissed the book as "fast food coated with snake oil," other reviewers reserved their criticisms for Capote's preface, with its self-conscious posturing about capital-A Art, rather than denouncing the work as a whole. As Anthony Quinton put it in the *London Times,* "Where he is a detached, neutral observer, as in the main item in this collection, there is brilliant force and economy to his writing." Less attractive, "and more conspicuous, is a kind of nervous blustering, only an inch away from self-pity that afflicts Capote when occupied with the topic of his own importance and achievements." Writing in the *Village Voice,* Seymour Krim also addressed this issue, noting: "Not one of these first-person vignettes is boring or without its humane and unexpected charm. And practically all the writing, it is true, is unstudied simplicity at its best, often so light that you can blow it around the room like a tissue-paper airplane. But as far as its living up to the burn-your-bridges trumpet call at the beginning of *Music for Chameleons* . . . , one has to conclude that the ringing peptalk is more important to the author than to the reader."

Like *In Cold Blood, Music for Chameleons* also raised the issue of fact versus fiction. Publicized as a true story, in which names and locations had been changed to protect identities, "Handcarved Coffins" was particularly scrutinized. "The details are so fuzzy and the murders so far-fetched that you begin to wonder whether fact and fiction aren't bubbling together in the same pot," wrote James Wolcott in the *New York Review of Books.* Writing in the *Times Literary Supplement,* David Lodge attributed his skepticism to "the inherent implausibility of the discrete events narrated" as well as "the very literary 'feel' of the whole text." Asked *Time*'s R. Z Sheppard: "How much of this book can be called documentary truth? How much is a masterly synthesis of all the author has learned as a fiction writer, scenarist and journalist? It is impossible to be sure." According to *Washington Post Book World* contributor Noel Perrin, "the proper response is to ignore [Capote's] pronouncements and read his work. D. H. Lawrence's advice, 'Trust the tale and not the teller,' might have been composed with Capote in mind. . . . Trust these tales. They are brilliant renderings of some of the more bizarre aspects of human reality—and if they happen to be literal word-for-word transcriptions, well, no harm in that. Either way, they are superb reading."

Between the appearance of *Music for Chameleons* in 1980 and the author's death in 1984, Capote wrote some magazine pieces and published *One Christmas,* a twenty-one-page short story, packaged as a book. His personal and health problems persisted, but he spoke frequently of the progress he was making on his masterwork *Answered Prayers,* telling *Publishers Weekly* in January, 1984 that he was "finishing my long-lost novel. . . . I hope it will be published in fall 1984." After his death, however, such remarks turned out to have been a smokescreen. Except for the portions published in *Esquire,* no manuscript of *Answered Prayers* was ever found. So convincing had been Capote's fabrications that several obituaries reported that the author was working on his book just hours before his death. Though the exact nature of that prose—whether magazine article, short story, or memoir—has not been determined, consensus is that it does not belong to *Answered Prayers.*

Because Capote had shown bits and pieces of his work in progress to associates and had actually read unpublished passages to friends over the telephone, some people speculate that Capote destroyed what he had written. Baumgold, for instance, alluded to the possibility of whole chapters being "rewritten out of existence in Capote's obsession with getting his work perfect." His editor, Fox, even remembered receiving an additional excerpt, which Capote subsequently took back and never returned. When asked about the content of *Answered Prayers: A Partial Manuscript,* a representative for Random House told *CA,* "We are publishing the excerpts as they appeared in *Esquire* because, as I understand it, there's nothing else that goes with it."

Despite his protestations to the contrary, Capote may never have gotten over his writer's block, and that, in turn, may have contributed to his death, according to Norman Mailer who told Baumgold, "He loved writing so much and had such pride of offering nothing but his best, that when he could no longer deliver, he lost much of his desire to live." Reflecting on Capote's life and work, *Los Angeles Times* contributor Armand S. Deutsch concluded: "The exhausting years of the alcohol and drug battles, the long hospital stays, the illnesses, are behind him. The celebrity, which was such an integral part of him, will soon vanish, but his writing will remain to speak brilliantly and strongly for him."

MEDIA ADAPTATIONS: Capote made a sound recording of his short story "Children on Their Birthdays" for Columbia in the 1950s; *Breakfast at Tiffany's* was filmed by Paramount in 1961; *In Cold Blood* was filmed by Columbia Pictures in 1967; "Handcarved Coffins" was sold to Lester Persky Productions, 1980.

BIOGRAPHICAL/CRITICAL SOURCES:

BOOKS

Capote, Truman, *Other Voices, Other Rooms,* Random House, 1948, reprinted with an introduction by the author, 1968.
Capote, Truman, *Music for Chameleons: New Writing,* Random House, 1983.
Clarke, Gerald, *Capote: A Biography,* Simon & Schuster, 1986.
Contemporary Literary Criticism, Gale, Volume 1, 1973, Volume 3, 1975, Volume 8, 1978, Volume 13, 1980, Volume 14, 1981, Volume 38, 1986.
Dictionary of Literary Biography, Volume 2, *American Novelists Since World War II,* Gale, 1978.
Dictionary of Literary Biography Yearbook: 1980, Gale, 1981.
Hallowell, John, *Between Fact and Fiction: New Journalism and the Nonfiction Novel,* University of North Carolina Press, 1977.
Nance, William L., *The Worlds of Truman Capote,* Stein & Day, 1970.

PERIODICALS

America, January 22, 1966, October 4, 1980.
American Scholar, winter, 1955-56, summer, 1966.
Atlantic, March, 1948, January, 1957, March, 1966.
Book Week, January 16, 1966.
Canadian Forum, March, 1966.
Chicago Tribune, June 5, 1983, July 5, 1987.
Christian Science Monitor, November 8, 1956.
Detroit News, November 27, 1983.
Detroit News Magazine, September 7, 1980.

Harper's, February, 1966.
Listener, March 28, 1968.
Los Angeles Times, August 3, 1980, November 28, 1983, September 2, 1984.
Los Angeles Times Book Review, August 3, 1980.
Nation, February 7, 1966.
New Republic, February 23, 1963, January 22, 1966, January 27, 1973.
New Statesman, August 30, 1963, March 22, 1968.
Newsweek, January 24, 1966.
New York, October 29, 1984, November 26, 1984.
New York Review of Books, February 3, 1966, September 25, 1980.
New York Times, December 2, 1956, January 7, 1980, August 5, 1980, September 10, 1987.
New York Times Book Review, January 18, 1948, February 24, 1952, January 16, 1966, October 28, 1973, August 3, 1980, November 13, 1983.
New York Times Magazine, July 9, 1978, July 16, 1978.
Paris Review, spring-summer, 1957.
Partisan Review, spring, 1966.
Playboy, March, 1968.
Publishers Weekly, January 6, 1984.
Saturday Review, February 14, 1948, February 16, 1963, January 22, 1966, July, 1980.
Spectator, March 18, 1966, March 29, 1968.
Time, January 26, 1948, January 21, 1966, August 4, 1980, September 7, 1987.
Times (London), February 19, 1981.
Times Literary Supplement, October 3, 1948, December 19, 1958, March 17, 1966, August 30, 1974, February 20, 1981.
Village Voice, August 6, 1980.
Washington Post, December 8, 1973, June 6, 1979, June 7, 1979, March 13, 1983, March 31, 1983.
Washington Post Book World, July 27, 1980.

OBITUARIES:

BOOKS

Contemporary Literary Criticism, Volume 34, Gale, 1986.
Dictionary of Literary Biography Yearbook: 1984, Gale, 1985.

PERIODICALS

Chicago Tribune, August 27, 1984.
Los Angeles Times, August 26, 1984.
Newsweek, September 3, 1984.
New York Times, August 27, 1984.
Publishers Weekly, September 7, 1984.
Time, September 3, 1984, September 7, 1988.
Times (London), August 27, 1984.
Washington Post, August 17, 1984.

*   *   *

CARD, Orson Scott 1951-
(Brian Green)

PERSONAL: Born August 24, 1951, in Richland, Wash.; son of Willard Richards (a teacher) and Peggy Jane (a secretary and administrator; maiden name, Park) Card; married Kristine Allen, May 17, 1977; children: Michael Geoffrey, Emily Janice, Charles Benjamin. *Education:* Brigham Young University, B.A. (with distinction), 1975; University of Utah, M.A., 1981. *Politics:* Moderate Democrat. *Religion:* Church of Jesus Christ of Latter-day Saints (Mormon).

ADDRESSES: Home—546 Lindley Rd., Greensboro, N.C. 27410. *Agent*—Barbara Bova, 207 Sedgwick Rd., West Hartford, Conn. 06107.

CAREER: Volunteer Mormon missionary in Brazil, 1971-73; operated repertory theatre in Provo, Utah, 1974-75; Brigham Young University Press, Provo, editor, 1974-76; *Ensign,* Salt Lake City, Utah, assistant editor, 1976-78; free-lance writer and editor, 1978—. Senior editor, Compute! Books, Greensboro, N.C., 1983. Teacher at various universities and writers workshops. Local Democratic precinct election judge and Utah State Democratic Convention delegate.

AWARDS, HONORS: John W. Campbell Award for best new writer of 1977, World Science Fiction Convention, 1978; Hugo Award nominations, World Science Fiction Convention, 1978, 1979, 1980, for short stories, and 1986, for novelette, "Hatrack River"; Nebula Award nominations, Science Fiction Writers of America, 1979, 1980, for short stories; Utah State Institute of Fine Arts prize, 1980, for epic poem "Prentice Alvin and the No-Good Plow"; Hamilton/Brackett Award, 1981, for *Songmaster;* Nebula Award, 1985, Hugo Award, 1986, and Hamilton/Brackett Award, 1986, all for novel *Ender's Game;* Nebula Award, 1986, Hugo Award, 1987, and *Locus* Award, 1987, all for novel *Speaker for the Dead;* World Fantasy Award, 1987, for novelette, "Hatrack River"; Hugo Award, and Locus Award nomination, both 1988, both for novella "Eye for Eye"; Locus Award for best fantasy, Hugo Award nomination, and World Fantasy Award nomination, all 1988, all for novel *Seventh Son.*

WRITINGS:

SCIENCE FICTION/FANTASY

Capitol (collection), Ace Books, 1978.
Hot Sleep, Baronet, 1978.
A Planet Called Treason, St. Martin's, 1979, revised edition, Dell, 1980, new revised edition published as *Treason,* St. Martin's, 1988.
Songmaster, Dial, 1980.
Unaccompanied Sonata and Other Stories, Dial, 1981.
(Editor) *Dragons of Darkness,* Ace Books, 1981.
Hart's Hope, Berkley Publishing, 1982.
The Worthing Chronicle, Ace Books, 1983.
(Editor) *Dragons of Light,* Ace Books, 1983.
Ender's Game (also see below), Tor Books, 1985.
Speaker for the Dead (also see below), Tor Books, 1986.
Ender's Game [and] *Speaker for the Dead,* Tor Books, 1987.
Wyrms, Arbor House, 1987.
(With others) *Free Lancers,* Baen Books, 1987.
Seventh Son (first novel in "The Tales of Alvin Maker" series), St. Martin's, 1987.
Red Prophet (second novel in "The Tales of Alvin Maker" series), Tor Books, 1988.
Prentice Alvin (third novel in "The Tales of Alvin Maker" series), Tor Books, 1989.
Folk of the Fringe (collection), Phantasia Press, 1989.
The Abyss (screenplay novelization), Pocket Books, 1989.

Contributor to numerous anthologies.

PLAYS

"The Apostate," produced in Provo, Utah, 1970.
"In Flight," produced in Provo, 1970.
"Across Five Summers," produced in Provo, 1971.
"Of Gideon," produced in Provo, 1971.
"Stone Tables," produced in Provo at Brigham Young University, 1973.

"A Christmas Carol" (adapted from the story by Charles Dickens), produced in Provo, 1974.
"Father, Mother, Mother, and Mom," produced in Provo, 1974, published in *Sunstone,* 1978.
"Liberty Jail," produced in Provo, 1975.
(Under pseudonym Brian Green) "Rag Mission," published in *Ensign,* July, 1977.

Also author of "Fresh Courage Take," produced in 1978, "Elders and Sisters" (adapted from a work by Gladys Farmer), produced in 1979, and "Wings" (fragment), produced in 1982.

OTHER

Listen, Mom and Dad, Bookcraft, 1978.
Saintspeak: The Mormon Dictionary, Signature Books, 1981.
Ainge, Signature Books, 1982.
A Woman of Destiny (historical novel), Berkley Publishing, 1983, published as *Saints,* Tor Books, 1988.
Characters and Viewpoint, Writers Digest, 1988.

Also author of several hundred audio plays for Living Scriptures; co-author of animated videotapes. Author of regular review columns, "You Got No Friends in This World," *Science Fiction Review,* 1979-86, "Books to Look For," *Fantasy and Science Fiction,* 1987—, and "Gameplay," *Compute!,* 1988—. Contributor of articles and reviews to periodicals, including *Washington Post Book World, Science Fiction Review,* and *Destinies.* Editor, *Short Form,* 1987—.

WORK IN PROGRESS: Alvin Journeyman and *Master Alvin,* Volumes IV and V of "The Tales of Alvin Maker"; *Ender's Children.*

SIDELIGHTS: Since publishing the story that evolved into his award-winning novel *Ender's Game,* Orson Scott Card has become a prominent force in the science fiction and fantasy fields. In 1987, for example, Card became the first writer to win the genre's top awards, the Nebula and the Hugo, for consecutive novels in a continuing series. The first of these two, *Ender's Game,* concerns the training of Ender Wiggin, a six-year-old genius who is the Earth's only hope for victory over invading "bugger" aliens. While this plot appears to be standard science fiction fare, *New York Times Book Review* critic Gerald Jonas observes that "Card has shaped this unpromising material into an affecting novel full of surprises that seem inevitable once they are explained." The difference, assert Jonas and other critics, is in the character of Ender Wiggin, who remains sympathetic despite his acts of violence. A *Kirkus Review* contributor, for example, while noting the plot's inherent weakness, admits that "the long passages focusing on Ender are nearly always enthralling," concluding that *Ender's Game* "is altogether a much more solid, mature, and persuasive effort" than the author's previous work.

Other critics, however, believe that the character of Ender does not overcome the "uninspired notions of Ender's training," as Michael Lassell describes in the *Los Angeles Times Book Review.* While Ender's character is "likable," the critic remarks that he is "utterly unbelievable as a child his age, genius or no." But *Analog Science Fiction/Science Fact* writer Tom Easton suggests that the reader "reserve . . . skepticism of Ender's talent," for the novel "succeeds because of its stress on the value of empathy. . . . The governmental agents who rule young Ender are as guilty of despicable acts, but they are saved by their ability to bleed for the souls they mangle." And Dan K. Moran, who calls *Ender's Game* "the best novel I've read in a long time," adds in the *West Coast Review of Books* that "Ender Wiggin is a unique creation. Orson Scott Card has created a character who deserves to be remembered with the likes of Huckleberry Finn. *Ender's Game* is *that* good."

While *Ender's Game* garnered awards and popularity for Card, its sequel, *Speaker for the Dead,* "is the most powerful work Card has produced," claims Michael R. Collings in *Fantasy Review.* "*Speaker* not only completes *Ender's Game* but transcends it. . . . Read in conjunction with *Ender's Game, Speaker* demonstrates Card's mastery of character, plot, style, theme, and development." Ender Wiggin, now an adult working as a "Speaker for the Dead," travels the galaxy to interpret the lives of the deceased for their families and neighbors; as he travels, he also searches for a home for the eggs of the lone surviving "hive queen" of the race he destroyed as a child. When Ender is called to the colony planet of Lusitania, his visit coincides with the discovery of another intelligent alien race, re-opening the question of co-existence versus survival. "[Card] has woven a constantly escalating storyline which deals with religion, alien/human viewpoints and perspectives on instinctual and cultural levels, the fate of three alien species . . ., and quite possibly the fate of mankind itself," describes *Science Fiction Review* editor Richard E. Geis. "Like *Game, Speaker* deals with issues of evil and empathy, though not in so polarized a way," observes Easton in his review, concluding that "less brash than *Ender's Game, Speaker for the Dead* may be a much better book." In addition, critics find an extra element of complexity in the "Ender" books; *Washington Post Book World* contributor Janrae Frank sees "quasi-religious images and themes" in the conclusions of both novels. Because Card combines these themes with traditional science fiction principles, Collings maintains that the novels "succeed equally as straightforward SF adventure and as allegorical, analogical disquisitions on humanity, morality, salvation, and redemption."

It is this symbolic, metaphorical aspect of Card's work that some critics feel distinguishes and intensifies his writing. "It seemed that whenever Card drifted away from pure sf into the hazier realm of mythmaking, of allegory, he was far more successful," remarks Somtow Sucharitkul in the *Washington Post Book World,* "for his gift lay not in the creation of vividly viable futures but in his ability to feel and transmit a timeless anguish." The critic explains that as Card has de-emphasized elaborate settings in his fiction, he has shown "yet an ever-growing mastery of symbol, form and human emotional processes." In *Wyrms,* for example, a "traditional" quest adventure involving a deposed princess, "there is nothing trite about this book, nothing swollen and contrived," asserts *Los Angeles Times Book Review* contributor Ingrid Rimland. "[*Wyrms*] is many things at once: a parable, a heroic adventure, a philosophical treatise, a finely crafted masterpiece of stylistically honed paragraphs, [and] a careful and smart understatement on the rebellious theme that God might be evil and needs to be slain."

Card continues using symbol and allegory in the "Tales of Alvin Maker" series; the first novel, *Seventh Son,* "begins what may be a significant recasting in fantasy terms of the tall tale in America," describes *Washington Post Book World* reviewer John Clute. Set in a pioneer America where the British Restoration never happened, where the "Crown Colonies" exist alongside the states of Appalachia and New Sweden, and where folk magics such as hexes, dowsers, and torches exist, *Seventh Son* follows the childhood of Alvin Miller, who has enormous magical potential because of his birth as the seventh son of a seventh son. "While this could easily have been another dull tale of the chosen child groomed to be the defender from evil," *Fantasy Review* contributor Martha Soukup believes that Card's use of folk magic and vernacular language, along with strongly realized

characters, creates in *Seventh Son* "more to care about here than an abstract magical battle." Collings similarly notes in the same issue that the novel continues Card's allegorical work, containing a re-working of the life of Joseph Smith, founder of the Mormon Church; nevertheless, comments the critic, Card depicts "this community's people in such a masterly way that their allegorical functioning does not impede our involvement with and deep caring for them. *Seventh Son* is a moving novel." "There is something deeply heart-wrenching about an America come true, even if it is only a dream, a fantasy novel," writes Clute; the critic concludes that "the first volume of *The Tales of Alvin Maker* is sharp and clean and bracing."

"Because we know it is a dream of an America we do not deserve to remember, Orson Scott Card's luminous alternate history of the early 19th century continues to chill as it soothes," Clute explains in a review of *Red Prophet,* the second volume of Alvin's story. The novel traces Alvin's kidnapping by renegade Reds employed by "White Murderer" William Henry Harrison, who wishes to precipitate a massacre of the Shaw-Nee tribe. Alvin is rescued by the Red warrior Ta-Kumsaw, however, and learns of Indian ways even as he attempts to prevent the conflict caused by his supposed capture and murder. While "*Red Prophet* seems initially less ambitious" than its predecessor, covering only one year of time, a *West Coast Review of Books* contributor comments that "in that year, Card creates episodes and images that stun with the power of their emotions." Sue Martin, however, believes that the setting is not enough to overcome the plot, which she describes in the *Los Angeles Times Book Review* as "yet *another* tale of Dark versus Light." The critic states, however, that while Alvin "seems almost Christlike" in his ability to heal and bring people together, the allegory is drawn "without the proselytizing." "*Red Prophet* is the logical and emotional continuation of *Seventh Son,*" maintains the *West Coast Review of Books* writer, "surpassing the earlier volume in power and compassion, in cruelty and love." *Booklist* writer Sally Estes concurs: "Harsher, bleaker, and more mystical than *Seventh Son,*" Card's second volume displays his strong historical background, "keen understanding of religious experience, and, most of all, his mastery of the art of storytelling."

BIOGRAPHICAL/CRITICAL SOURCES:

BOOKS

Contemporary Literary Criticism, Gale, Volume 44, 1987, Volume 47, 1988, Volume 50, 1988.

PERIODICALS

Analog Science Fiction/Science Fact, July, 1983, July, 1985, June, 1986, Mid-December, 1987.
Booklist, December 15, 1985, December 15, 1987.
Fantasy Review, April, 1986, June, 1987, July/August, 1987.
Kirkus Reviews, November 1, 1984.
Los Angeles Times Book Review, September 28, 1980, March 6, 1983, July 22, 1984, February 3, 1985, August 9, 1987, February 14, 1988.
New York Times Book Review, June 16, 1985, October 18, 1987.
Science Fiction and Fantasy Book Review, June, 1983.
Science Fiction Review, August, 1979, February, 1986.
Washington Post Book World, August 24, 1980, January 25, 1981, March 27, 1983, February 23, 1986, August 30, 1987, February 28, 1988.
West Coast Review of Books, March, 1984, July, 1986, Number 2, 1987, Number 4, 1988.

CARDENAL (MARTINEZ), Ernesto 1925-

PERSONAL: Born January 20, 1925, in Granada, Nicaragua; son of Rodolfo and Esmerelda (Martinez) Cardenal. *Education:* Attended University of Mexico, 1944-48, and Columbia University, 1948-49. *Politics:* "Christian-Marxist."

ADDRESSES: Home—Carretera a Masaya Km. 9 1/2, Apt. A-252, Managua, Nicaragua.

CAREER: Ordained Roman Catholic priest, 1965. Poet, and author; formerly Minister of Culture in Nicaragua.

AWARDS, HONORS: Christopher Book Award, 1972, for *The Psalms of Struggle and Liberation;* Premio de la Paz grant, Libreros de la Republica Federal de Alemania, 1980.

WRITINGS:

Ansias lengua de la poesia nueva nicaraguense (poems), [Nicaragua], 1948.
Gethsemani, Ky. (poems), Ecuador 0°0'0", 1960, 2nd edition, with foreword by Thomas Merton, Ediciones La Tertulia (Medellin, Colombia), 1965.
Epigramas: Poemas, Universidad Nacional Autonoma de Mexico, 1961.
Hora 0 (poems), Revista Mexicano de Literatura, 1960.
(Translator and editor at large with Jorge Montoya Toro) *Literatura indigena americana: Antologia,* Editorial Universidad de Antioquia (Medellin), 1964.
(Translator with Jose Coronel Urtecho) *Antologia de la poesia norteamericana,* Aguilar (Madrid), 1963, Alianza (Madrid), 1979.
Oracion por Marilyn Monroe, y otros poemas, Ediciones La Tertulia, 1965, reprinted, Editorial Nueva Nicaragua-Ediciones Monimbo, 1985, translation by Robert Pring-Mill published as *Marilyn Monroe and Other Poems,* Search Press, 1975.
El estrecho dudoso (poems), Ediciones Cultura Hispanica (Madrid), 1966, Editorial Nueva Nicaragua-Ediciones Monimbo, 1985.
Antologia de Ernesto Cardenal (poems), Editora Santiago (Santiago, Chile), 1967.
Poemas de Ernesto Cardenal, Casa de las Americas (Havana), 1967.
Mayapan (poem), Editorial Alemana (Managua, Nicaragua), 1968.
Salmos (poems), Institucion Gran Duque de Alba (Avila, Spain), 1967, Ediciones El Pez y la Serpiente (Managua, Nicaragua), 1975, translation by Emile G. McAnany published as *The Psalms of Struggle and Liberation,* Herder & Herder, 1971, translation from the sixth edition of 1974 by Thomas Blackburn and others published as *Psalms,* Crossroad Publishing, 1981.
Homenaje a los indios americanos (poems), Universidad Nacional Autonoma de Nicaragua, 1969, Laia (Madrid), 1983, translation by Carlos Altschul and Monique Altschul published as *Homage to the American Indians,* Johns Hopkins University Press, 1974.
Vida en el amor (meditations; with foreword by Thomas Merton), Lohle (Buenos Aires), 1970, translation by Kurt Reinhardt published as *To Live is to Love,* Herder & Herder, 1972 (published in England as *Love,* Search Press, 1974), translation by Dinah Livingstone published as *Love,* Crossroad Publishing, 1981.
La hora cero y otros poemas, Ediciones Saturno, 1971, translation by Paul W. Borgeson and Jonathan Cohen published as

Zero Hour and Other Documentary Poems, edited by Donald D. Walsh, New Directions, 1980.
Antologia: Ernesto Cardenal, edited by Pablo Antonio Cuadra, Lohle, 1971, 2nd edition, Universidad Centroamericana, 1975.
Poemas, Editorial Leibres de Sinera, 1971.
Poemas reunidos, 1949-1969, Direccion de Cultura, Universidad de Carabobo, 1972.
(And translator) *Epigramas* (with translations from Catullus and Martial), Lohle, 1972.
En Cuba, Lohle, 1972, translation published as *In Cuba,* New Directions, 1974.
Canto nacional, Siglo Veintiuno (Mexico), 1973.
Oraculo sobre Managua, Lohle, 1973.
(Compiler and author of introduction) *Poesia nicaraguense,* Casa de las Americas, 1973, 4th edition, Editorial Nueva Nicaragua, 1981.
Cardenal en Valencia, Ediciones de la Direccion de Cultura, Universidad de Carabobo (Venezuela), 1974.
El Evangelio en Solentiname (also see below), Ediciones Sigueme, 1975, Editorial Nueva Nicaragua-Ediciones Monimbo, 1983, translation by Donald D. Walsh published as *The Gospel in Solentiname,* Orbis Books, 1976 (published in England as *Love in Practice: The Gospel in Solentiname,* Search Press, 1977), reprinted in four volumes, Orbis Books, 1982.
Poesia escogida, Barral Editores, 1975.
La santidad de la revolucion (title means "The Sanctity of the Revolution"), Ediciones Sigueme, 1976.
Poesia cubana de la revolucion, Extemporaneos, 1976.
Apocalypse, and Other Poems, translation by Thomas Merton, Kenneth Rexroth, Mireya Jaimes-Freyre, and others, New Directions, 1977.
Antologia, Laia (Barcelona, Spain), 1978.
Epigramas, Tusquets (Barcelona), 1978.
Catulo-Marcial en version de Ernesto Cardenal, Laia, 1978.
Canto a un pais que nace, Universidad Autonoma de Puebla, 1978.
In der Nacht Leuchten die Woerter: Gedichte, Aufbau-Verlag, 1979.
Antologia de poesia primitiva, Alianza, 1979.
Nueva antologia poetica, Siglo Veintiuno, 1979.
La paz mundial y la Revolucion de Nicaragua, Ministerio de Cultura, 1981.
Tocar el cielo, Loguez, 1981.
(With Richard Cross) *Nicaraugua: La Guerra de liberacion - der Befreiungskrieg,* Ministerio de Cultura de Nicaragua, c. 1982.
Los campesinos de Solentiname pintan el Evangelio, Monimbo, c.1982.
(Translator from the German) Ursula Schulz, *Tu paz es mi paz,* Editorial Nueva Nicaragua-Ediciones Monimbo, 1982.
(Contributor) *Entrustet Euch!: Fuer Frieden und voelkerverstandigung; Katholiken gegen Faschismus und Krieg* (essays on nuclear disarmament), Roederberg, 1982.
La democratizacion de la cultura, Ministerio de Cultura, 1982.
Nostalgia del futuro: Pintura y buena noticia en Solentiname, Editorial Nueva Nicaragua, 1982.
Evangelio, pueblo, y arte (selections from *El Evangelio en Solentiname*), Loguez, 1983.
Waslala: Poems, translated by Fidel Lopez-Criado and R. A. Kerr, Chase Avenue Press, 1983.
Antologia: Ernesto Cardenal, Editorial Nueva Nicaragua-Ediciones Monimbo, 1983.
Poesia de la nueva Nicaragua, Siglo Veintiuno, 1983.

The Gospel in Art by the Peasants of Solentiname (translated from *Bauern von Solentiname malen des Evangelium*, selections from *El Evangelio en Solentiname*), edited by Philip and Sally Sharper, Orbis Books, 1984.

(Contributor) Teofilo Cabestrero, *Ministros de Dios, ministros del pueblo: Testimonio de tres sacerdotes en el Gobierno Revolucionario de Nicaragua, Ernesto Cardenal, Fernando Cardenal, Miguel d'Escoto*, Ministerio de Cultura, 1985.

Vuelos de Victoria, Visor (Madrid), 1984, Editorial Universitaria, (Leon, Nicaragua), 1987, translation by Marc Zimmerman published as *Flights of Victory: Songs in Celebration of the Nicaraguan Revolution*, Orbis Books, 1985.

Quetzalcoatal, Editorial Nueva Nicaragua-Ediciones Monimbo, 1985.

Nuevo cielo y tierra nueva, Editorial Nueva Nicaragua-Ediciones Monimbo, 1985.

With Walker in Nicaragua and Other Early Poems, 1949-1954, translated by Cohen, Wesleyan University Press, 1985.

(Compiler and author of introduction) *Antologia: Azarias H. Pallais*, Nueva Nicaragua, 1986.

From Nicaragua with Love: Poems 1979-1986, translated by Cohen, City Lights Press, 1986.

Contributor to *Cristianismo y revolucion*, Editorialal 1 Quetzal (Buenos Aires), and *La Batalla de Nicaragua*, Bruguera Mexicana de Ediciones (Mexico).

SIDELIGHTS: Ernesto Cardenal is a major poet of the Spanish language well-known in the United States as a spokesman for justice and self-determination in Latin America. Cardenal, who recognizes that poetry and art are closely tied to politics, used his poetry to protest the encroachments of outsiders in Nicaragua and supported the revolution that overthrew Somoza in 1979. Once the cultural minister of his homeland, Cardenal spends much of his time as "a kind of international ambassador," notes Richard Elman in the *Nation*.

Victor M. Valle, writing in the *Los Angeles Times Calendar*, cites Cardenal's statement, "There has been a great cultural rebirth in Nicaragua since the triumph of the revolution. A saving of all of our culture, that which represents our national identity, especially our folklore." Literacy and poetry workshops established throughout the "nation of poets," as it has been known since the early twentieth century, are well-attended by people whose concerns had been previously unheard. Most workshops are led by government-paid instructors in cultural centers, while others convene in police stations, army barracks, and workplaces such as sugar mills, Valle reports. In these sessions, Romantic and Modern poetry is considered below standard; Cardenal also denigrates socialist realism, which he says "comes from the Stalinist times that required that art be purely political propaganda." The "greatest virtue" of Cardenal's own poems, says a *Times Literary Supplement* reviewer, "is the indirectness of Cardenal's social criticism, which keeps stridency consistently at bay." In addition, says the reviewer, Cardenal's poems "are memorable and important both for their innovations in technique and for their attitudes." In this way they are like the works of Ezra Pound, whose aesthetic standards Cardenal promotes.

Review contributor Isabel Fraire demonstrates that there are many similarities between Cardenal's poetry and Pound's. Like Pound, Cardenal borrows the short, epigrammatic form from the masters of Latin poetry Catullus and Martial, whose works he has translated. Cardenal also borrows the canto form invented by Pound to bring "history into poetry" in a manner that preserves the flavor of the original sources—a technique Pablo Neruda employed with success. Cardenal's use of the canto form

"is much more *cantabile*" than Pound's *Cantos,* says Fraire. "We get passages of a sustained, descriptive lyricism . . . where the intense beauty and harmony of nature or of a certain social order or life style are presented." Pound and Cardenal develop similar themes: "the corrupting effect of moneymaking as the overriding value in a society; the importance of precision and truthfulness in language; the degradation of human values in the world which surrounds us; [and] the search through the past (or, in Cardenal's poetry, in more 'primitive' societies, a kind of contemporary past) for better world-models." Fraire also points out an important difference between the two: "Cardenal is rooted in a wider cultural conscience. Where Pound seems to spring up disconnected from his own contemporary cultural scene and to be working against it, Cardenal is born into a ready-made cultural context and shared political conscience. Cardenal's past is common to all Latin Americans. His present is likewise common to all Latin Americans. He speaks to those who are ready and willing to hear him and are likely to agree on a great many points."

Cardenal's early lyrics express feelings of love, social criticism, political passion, and the quest for a transcendent spiritual life. Following his conversion to Christianity in 1956, Cardenal studied to become a priest in Gethsemani, Kentucky, with Thomas Merton, the scholar, poet, and Trappist monk. While studying with Merton, Cardenal committed himself to the practice of nonviolence. He was not allowed to write secular poetry during this period, but kept notes in a journal that later became the poems in *Gethsemani, Ky.* and the spiritual diary in prose, *Vida en el amor*. Cardenal's stay in Kentucky was troubled by illness; he finished his studies in Cuernevaca, Mexico, where he was ordained in 1965. While there, he wrote *El estrecho dudoso* and other epic poems that discuss Central America's history.

Poems collected in *With Walker in Nicaragua and Other Early Poems, 1949-1954* look at the history of Nicaragua which touches upon the poet's ancestry. During the 1800s, the William Walker expedition from the United States tried to make Nicaragua subservient to the Southern Confederacy. According to legend, a defector from that expedition married into Cardenal's family line. Incorporating details from Ephraim George Squier's chronicles of that period, Cardenal's poem "With Walker in Nicaragua" "is tender toward the invaders without being sentimental," Elman observes. "This is political poetry not because it has a particular rhetorical stance but because it evokes the distant as well as the more recent historical roots of the conflict in Central America," Harris Schiff relates in the *American Book Review*. The poet identifies with a survivor of the ill-fated expedition in order to express the contrast between the violent attitudes of the outsiders and the beauty of the tropical land they hoped to conquer. "The theme of the gringo in a strange land," as Elman puts it, an essentially political topic, is developed frequently in Cardenal's work.

Later poems become increasingly explicit regarding Cardenal's political sympathies. "Zero Hour," for example, is his "single greatest historical poem about gringoism, a patriotic epic of sorts," says Elman. The poem's subject is the assassination of revolutionary leader Cesar Augusto Sandino, who used guerilla tactics against the United States Marines to force them to leave Nicaragua in 1933. "It's a poem of heroic evocation in which the death of a hero is also seen as the rebirth of nationhood: when the hero dies, green herbs rise where he has fallen. It makes innovative use of English and Spanglais and is therefore hard to translate, but . . . it is very much a work of national consciousness and unique poetic expression," Elman relates.

Moving further back in time to reclaim a common heritage for his countrymen, Cardenal recaptures the quality of pre-Columbian life in *Homage to the American Indians*. These descriptions of Mayan, Incan and Nahuatl ways of life present their attractiveness in comparison to the social organization of the present. In these well-crafted and musical poems written at the end of the 1960s, the poet praises "a way of life which celebrates peace above war and spiritual strength above personal wealth. One has a strong sense when reading Cardenal that he is using the American Indian as a vehicle to celebrate those values which are most important to him as a well-educated Trappist monk who has dedicated himself to a life of spiritual retreat," F. Whitney Jones remarks in the *Southern Humanities Review*. That the poems are didactic in no way impedes their effectiveness, say reviewers, who credit the power of the verses to Cardenal's mastery of poetic technique.

The use of Biblical rhetoric and prosody energizes much of Cardenal's poetry. *El estrecho dudoso,* like the Bible, "seeks to convince men that history contains lessons which have a transcendent significance," James J. Alstrum maintains in *Journal of Spanish Studies: Twentieth Century*. Poems in *Salmos,* written in the 1960s, translated and published as *The Psalms of Struggle,* echo the forms and the content of the Old Testament psalms. Cardenal's psalms are updated to speak to the concerns of the oppressed in the twentieth century. "The vocabulary is contemporary but the . . . sheer wonder at the workings of the world, is biblical," Jack Riemer observes in *Commonweal*. "Equally memorable are those Psalms in which Cardenal expresses his horror at the cruelty and the brutality of human life. His anguished outcries over the rapaciousness of the greedy and the viciousness of the dictators are the work of a man who has lived through some of the atrocities of this century."

As the conflict between the Nicaraguan people and the Somoza government escalated, Cardenal became convinced that without violence, the revolution would not succeed. "In 1970 he visited Cuba and experienced what he described as 'a second conversion' which led him to formulate his own philosophy of Christian Marxism. In 1977 the younger Somoza destroyed the community at Solentiname and Cardenal became the field chaplain for the Sandinista National Liberation Front," reports Robert Hass in the *Washington Post Book World*. Poems Cardenal wrote during that "very difficult time in his country"—collected in *Zero Hour and Other Documentary Poems*—are less successful than the earlier and later work, says Hass, since "there is a tendency in them to make of the revolution a symbol that answers all questions." Some reviewers have found the resulting combination of Biblical rhetoric and Marxist revolutionary zeal intimidating. For example, Jascha Kessler, speaking on KUSC-FM radio in Los Angeles, California in 1981, commented, "It is clearly handy to be a trained priest, and to have available for one's poetry the voices of Amos, Isaiah, Hosea and Jeremiah, and to mix prophetic vision with the perspectives of violent revolutionary Marxist ideology. It makes for an incendiary brew indeed. It is not nice; it is not civilized; it is not humane or sceptical or reasonable. But it is all part of the terrible heritage of Central Latin America." Also commenting on *Zero Hour and Other Documentary Poems, American Book Review* contributor Harold Jaffe suggests, "Although the manifest reality of Cardenal's Central America is grim, it's future—which to Cardenal is as 'real' as its present—appears eminently hopeful. Furious or revolted as Cardenal is over this or that dreadful inequity, he never loses hope. His love, his faith in the disadvantaged, his great good humor, his enduring belief that communism and Christ's communion

are at root the same—these extraordinary convictions resound throughout the volume."

"Though Cardenal sees no opposition between Marxism and the radical gospel, neither is he a Moscow-line communist," Mary Anne Rygiel explains in *Southern Humanities Review*. Rygiel cites the poem "Las tortugas" (title means "The Turtles") to demonstrate that Cardenal's reference to "communism" as the order of nature might better be understood as "communalism," a social organization of harmonious interdependence founded on spiritual unity. The poet-priest's social vision stems from his understanding of "the kingdom of God," Lawrence Ferlinghetti notes in *Seven Days in Nicaragua Libre*. "And with [Cardenal's] vision of a primitive Christianity, it was logical for him to add that in his view the Revolution would not have succeeded until there were no more masters and no more slaves. 'The Gospels,' he said, 'foresee a classless society. They foresee also *the withering away of the state*' [Ferlinghetti's emphasis]."

In the 1980s, Pope John Paul II reprimanded Cardenal for promoting a liberation theology that the prelate found divergent from Roman Catholicism. Alstrum notes, however, that *El estrecho dudoso* "reaffirms the Judeo-Christian belief that there is an inexorable progression of historical events which point toward the ultimate consummation of the Divine Word. Cardenal himself views his poetry as merely the medium for his hopeful message of the transformation of the old order into a new and more just society in which the utopian dreams and Christian values of men . . . can finally be realized." Cardenal founded the Christian commune Solentiname on an island in Lake Nicaragua near the Costa Rican border to put that dream into practice.

Some critics feel that the political nature of Cardenal's poetry precludes its appreciation by a sophisticated literary audience. Reviewers responded to the 1966 volume *El estrecho dudoso,* for example, as an attack on the Somoza dynasty while neglecting "the intricate artistry with which Cardenal has intertwined the past and present through myth and history while employing both modern and narrative techniques in his poem," asserts Alstrum. Others point out that Cardenal's work gains importance to the extent that it provides valuable insights into the thinking of his countrymen. Cardenal's poetry, which he read to audiences in the United States during the seventies, was perhaps more informative and accessible than other reports from that region, Kessler concluded in 1981, soon after Nicaraguan revolutionaries ousted the Somoza regime. "It may well be that Cardenal's poems offer us a very clear entrance into the mentality of the men we are facing in the . . . bloody guerilla warfare of Central America," Kessler suggested. More recently, a *New Pages* reviewer comments, "We can learn some contemporary history, [and] discover the feelings and thoughts of the people who were involved in Nicaragua's revolution by reading Cardenal's poems. And once we know what the revolution 'felt' like, we'll be a lot smarter, I believe, than most . . . who . . . make pronouncements about Nicaragua's threat to the free world."

BIOGRAPHICAL/CRITICAL SOURCES:

BOOKS

Bhalla, Alok, *Latin American Writers: A Bibliography with Critical Biographical Introductions,* Envoy Press, 1987.
Brotherston, Gordon, *Latin American Poetry: Origins and Presence,* Cambridge University Press, 1975.
Cardenal, Ernesto, *Zero Hour and Other Documentary Poems,* edited by Donald D. Walsh, New Directions, 1980.
Contemporary Literary Criticism, Volume 31, Gale, 1985.

Ferlinghetti, Lawrence, *Seven Days in Nicaragua Libre,* City Lights Books, 1984.

PERIODICALS

America, November 6, 1976.
American Book Review, summer, 1978, January, 1982, January-February, 1982, September, 1985.
Commonweal, September 17, 1971.
Journal of Spanish Studies: Twentieth Century, spring & fall, 1980.
Los Angeles Times Calendar, January 8, 1984.
Nation, March 30, 1985.
New Leader, May 4, 1981.
New Pages, Volume 10, 1986.
New Republic, October 19, 1974, April 9, 1977.
Parnassus, spring-summer, 1976.
Review, fall, 1976.
Southern Humanities Review, winter, 1976, winter, 1988.
Times Literary Supplement, July 12, 1974, August 6, 1976.
Voice Literary Supplement, September, 1982.
Washington Post Book World, June 23, 1985.
World Literature Today, spring, 1983.

OTHER

Kessler, Jascha, "Ernesto Cardenal: 'Zero Hour and other Documentary Poems' " (radio broadcast), KUSC-FM, Los Angeles, Calif., April 15, 1981.

—*Sketch by Marilyn K. Basel*

*   *   *

CAREY, Peter 1943-

PERSONAL: Born May 7, 1943, in Bacchus Marsh, Victoria, Australia; son of Percival Stanley (an automobile dealer) and Helen Jean (an automobile dealer; maiden name, Warriner) Carey; married Alison Margaret Summers (a theatre director), March 16, 1985; children: Sam Summers Corey. *Education:* Attended Monash University, 1961.

ADDRESSES: Home—Sydney, Australia. *Agent*—Elaine Markson Literary Agency, Inc., 44 Greenwich Ave., New York, N.Y. 10011.

CAREER: Writer. Worked in advertising.

AWARDS, HONORS: New South Wales Premier's Literary Award, 1980, for *War Crimes;* Miles Franklin Award, 1981, and New South Wales Premier's Literary Award and National Book Council Award, both 1982, all for *Bliss;* AWGIE Award and awards for best film and best screenplay from the Australian Film Institute, all 1985, all for "Bliss"; Age Book of the Year and nomination for Booker Prize, both 1985, and Victorian Premier's Literary Award and National Book Council Award, both 1986, all for *Illywhacker;* Booker Prize, 1988, for *Oscar and Lucinda.*

WRITINGS:

The Fat Man in History (short stories; includes "Crabs," "Peeling," "She Wakes," "Life and Death in the South Side Pavilion," "Room No. 5 (Escribo)," "Happy Story," "A Windmill in the West," "Withdrawal," "Report on the Shadow Industry," "Conversation With Unicorns," "American Dreams," and "The Fat Man in History"; also see below), University of Queensland Press, 1974.
War Crimes (short stories; includes "The Journey of a Lifetime," " 'Do You Love Me?' " "The Uses of Williamson Wood,"

"The Last Days of a Famous Mime," "A Schoolboy Prank," "The Chance," "Fragrance of Roses," "The Puzzling Nature of Blue," "Ultra-violet Light," "Kristu-Du," "He Found Her in Late Summer," "Exotic Pleasures," and "War Crimes"; also see below), University of Queensland Press, 1979.
The Fat Man in History, and Other Stories (contains selections from *The Fat Man in History* and *War Crimes,* including "The Fat Man in History," "Peeling," " 'Do You Love Me?' " "The Chance," "The Puzzling Nature of Blue," "Exotic Pleasures," "The Last Days of a Famous Mime," "A Windmill in the West," "American Dreams," and "War Crimes"; also see above), Random House, 1980, reprinted as *Exotic Pleasures,* Picador Books, 1981.
Bliss (novel), University of Queensland Press, 1981, Harper, 1982 (also see below).
Illywhacker (novel), Harper, 1985.
(With Lawrence Ray) *Bliss* (screenplay; adapted from Carey's novel; also see above), Faber, 1986.
Oscar and Lucinda (novel), Harper, 1988.

Work represented in anthologies, including *The Most Beautiful Lies,* Angus & Robertson.

WORK IN PROGRESS: The Tax Inspector, a novel; with Wim Wenders and Solveig Dommartin, "Until the End of the World," a screenplay to be directed by Wenders.

SIDELIGHTS: Peter Carey is an Australian writer who has earned substantial recognition for his quirky, inventive fiction. He published his first short story collection, *The Fat Man in History,* in 1974, and in that volume he presented a matter-of-fact perspective on bizarre and occasionally grotesque subjects. Included in this book are "Conversations With Unicorns," in which the narrator recalls his various encounters with the extraordinary creatures, and "American Dreams," where a clerk succumbs to madness and isolates himself from his community. Upon his death, townspeople discover that in seclusion he constructed a model of their village. More gruesome are "Peeling," in which a character's quirky obsession results in a surreal mutilation, and "Withdrawal," where the protagonist is a necrophile dealer of corpses and severed limbs. Among the more curious figures in this tale is a pig who becomes dependent on narcotics after consuming an addict's excrement.

The publication of *The Fat Man in History* quickly established Carey as an important new figure in Australian literature. One critic, Carl Harrison-Ford, wrote in *Stand* that Carey's first work was "the *succes d'estime* of 1974," and Bruce Bennett declared in *World Literature Written in English* that "Carey's first collection of stories . . . stamps him as the major talent among . . . new writers." Bennett found similarities between Carey's work and that of Kurt Vonnegut and Evelyn Waugh, but he added that "the shaping imagination is Carey's own." For Bennett, Carey was "a true fabulator . . ., one whose inventive, witty fictions both delight and instruct." Similarly, David Gilbey wrote in *Southerly* that *The Fat Man in History* was an "impressive volume," one that "dramatizes some of the dark myths beneath uncertainty and anxiety in contemporary life and does so with deadly, though not humourless, seriousness." Gilbey added that Carey's work was "intricately and surreally resonant and stands out markedly amongst contemporary Australian writing."

Equally unique was *War Crimes,* Carey's second collection of stories. The volume includes such vividly bizarre accounts as "The Chance," where a man vainly attempts to dissuade his lover from entering a lottery in which the major prize is a repulsive body. In the similarly disturbing title piece, a hippie-turned-businessman kills people threatening his profits from frozen food sales. Like the preceding collection, *War Crimes* proved immensely popular in Australia, and it eventually earned Carey the New South Wales Premier's Literary Award in 1979.

Stories from both *The Fat Man in History* and *War Crimes* comprised Carey's third publication, which also bore the title *The Fat Man in History*. This 1980 compilation brought Carey's unusual sensibility to American and British readers, many of whom readily acknowledged him as a unique and masterful storyteller. In his *Times Literary Supplement* review of the compilation, Peter Lewis called Carey an "outstanding writer" and praised his ability to write in a low-key but nonetheless compelling manner. "This naturalizing of the fantastic is probably Carey's most distinctive characteristic," Lewis wrote. "But he is also notable for his supposedly old-fashioned ability to hold the reader's attention." Similarly, *Saturday Review* critic Sandra Katz, who described Carey's work as "somewhere between science fiction and surrealism," declared that "the stories in [*The Fat Man in History*] are as brilliant as they are bizarre."

In 1981 Carey published his first novel, *Bliss*. Like his short stories, *Bliss* is fairly surreal, rendering the bizarre as if it were the norm. The novel's protagonist is Harry Joy, an overworked advertising executive who suffers a near-fatal heart attack. Upon recovering from the heart attack and equally life-threatening open-heart surgery, Joy believes that he is in Hell. He discovers that his wife is compromising him with a close friend and that his seemingly lethargic son is actually a freewheeling drug dealer who forces his sister—Joy's daughter—into committing incest in return for drugs. Joy eventually forsakes his family for Honey Barbara, a worldly nature lover who regularly supports herself as a drug dealer and prostitute. Around the time that he befriends the charge-card accommodating prostitute, Joy also discovers that his advertising company maintains a map indicating cancer density for the area, with accountability traced to the company's clients. Aghast, Joy renounces his work and grows further remote from his family. Eventually, his wife has him committed to a mental institution. There he once again meets Honey Barbara, who has also been incarcerated. Together they escape to her home in a rain forest, where Joy finally finds happiness and fulfillment before meeting an unfortunate demise.

With *Bliss*, Carey gained further acclaim from American and British reviewers. In *British Book News*, Neil Philip referred to *Bliss* as "a rich, rewarding novel: crisply written, daringly conceived, brilliantly achieved," and in the *Washington Post Book World*, Judith Chettle wrote that Carey's novel possessed "all the virtues of a modern fable." For Chettle, Carey was "a writer of power and imagination." Even more impressed was *Spectator* critic Francis King. "In both the breadth of his vision of human life in all its misery and happiness," wrote King, "and in the profundity of his insight into moral dilemmas, Mr. Carey makes the work of most of our 'promising' young and not so young novelists seem tinselly and trivial."

Carey collaborated with director Ray Lawrence on the 1985 film adapted from *Bliss*. By visually rendering the novel's often grotesque and repellant imagery—including cockroaches that wander from a chest wound—the film "Bliss" proved controversial, offending many viewers at the 1985 Cannes Film Festival. But it also won top honors in Australia and developed an enthusiastic following in the United States. Among the film's strongest supporters was *Time*'s Richard Corliss, who commended its "outrage and ecstasy." Finding "Bliss" alternately "extravagant or exasperating," Corliss declared that it "puts nobody to sleep."

In 1985 Carey also published his second novel, *Illywhacker*, a wide-ranging comic work about a 139-year-old trickster and liar, Herbert Badgery. The protagonist's life, which parallels the development of Australia following its independence from England, is full of odd adventures, including stints as a pilot, car salesman, and even snakehandler. His accounts of his escapades, however, are not entirely reliable, and over the course of the novel's six hundred pages Badgery often revels in tomfoolery and goodnatured treachery. But he is hardly the novel's only unusual figure: Molly MaGrath maintains her sanity by periodically shocking herself with an "invigorator belt"; Emma, Badgery's daughter-in-law, lives in a lizard's cage; and an entire village proves gullible enough to cooperate with Badgery in his hastily organized plan to build an Australian airplane. By novel's end, Badgery has recounted many more mad schemes and regaled the reader with recollections of seemingly countless eccentrics.

Illywhacker, like Carey's previous publications, impressed many critics. In *Encounter*, D. J. Taylor called *Illywhacker* "a dazzling and hilarious book" and described the narrative as "a vast, diffuse plot chock-full of luminous characters and incident." Curt Suplee, who reviewed *Illywhacker* in the *Washington Post Book World*, recommended the novel as "huge and hugely rewarding" and added that it was a "rare and valuable" work. And Howard Jacobson, writing in the *New York Times Book Review*, considered *Illywhacker* "a big, garrulous, funny novel, touching, farcical, and passionately bad-tempered." Jacobson also found *Illywhacker* a uniquely Australian work and contended that the experience of reading it was nearly the equivalent of visiting Australia. After noting occasional excesses in the narrative, Jacobson added: "Yet reading *Illywhacker* is not unlike spending a week in the company of the best kind of Australian. The stories keep coming, told with deceptive guilelessness and innocence. The talk is bawdy, the jokes are throwaways and rank, the sex is avid but democratic. Withal there is that haunting nostalgia and desolation that seems to be the immutable condition of the country. If you haven't been to Australia, read *Illywhacker*. It will give you the feeling of it like nothing else I know."

Carey's third novel, *Oscar and Lucinda*, is an extraordinary tale of two compulsive gamblers. The work begins in Victorian England, where the child Oscar endures life under the rigid rule of his intimidating father, a preacher. Later, Oscar breaks from his father and joins the conventional Anglican church, which he serves as a clergyman. Lucinda, meanwhile, has been raised in Australia by her mother, an intellectual who maintains the farm inherited from her late husband. Upon her mother's death, Lucinda inherits funds from the farm's sale. She also becomes owner of a glassworks and consequently devises construction of a glass cathedral. Eventually, Oscar and Lucinda meet on a ship, where Lucinda reveals her own obsession with gambling. Together, Oscar and Lucinda commence an extensive gambling excursion through Australia while simultaneously attempting to spread Christianity throughout the still wild country. When Oscar discovers Lucinda's glass cathedral, he wagers with Lucinda that he can deliver the model to a faraway clergyman whom he mistakenly believes is loved by her. His sea voyage, in which he is accompanied by a memorably colorful crew, constitutes a crisis of faith and self-awareness.

Oscar and Lucinda resulted in still further praise for Carey. Beryl Bainbridge, writing in the *New York Times Book Review*, was particularly impressed with those portions devoted to Oscar's traumatic childhood, though he added that the remaining episodes were "racy with characters, teeming with invention and expressed in superlative language." Bainbridge also declared that Carey shared with Thomas Wolfe "that magnificent vitality, that ebullient delight in character, detail and language that turns a novel into an important book." Even more enthusiastic was *Los Angeles Times* reviewer Carolyn See, who wrote: "There's so much richness here. The sweetness of the star-crossed lovers. The goodness within the stifled English clergyman. The perfect irrationality of human behavior as it plays itself out in minor characters." See contended, "We have a great novelist living on the planet with us, and his name is Peter Carey."

BIOGRAPHICAL/CRITICAL SOURCES:

BOOKS

Contemporary Literary Criticism, Gale, Volume 40, 1986, Volume 55, 1989.

PERIODICALS

British Book News, February, 1981, May, 1982.
Chicago Tribune, February 21, 1986.
Encounter, September-October, 1985.
London Review of Books, April 18, 1985.
Los Angeles Times, October 2, 1980, August 29, 1985, February 21, 1986, June 19, 1988.
New Statesman, October 24, 1980, November 20, 1981, August 19, 1985.
Newsweek, April 19, 1982.
New Yorker, August 23, 1982, November 11, 1985.
New York Times, May 4, 1986.
New York Times Book Review, October 4, 1985, May 29, 1988.
Observer, November 15, 1981, April 14, 1985.
Publishers Weekly, May 31, 1985.
Saturday Review, August, 1980.
Southerly, December, 1977.
Spectator, December 12, 1981.
Stand, Volume 16, number 3, 1975.
Time, March 17, 1986.
Times Literary Supplement, October 31, 1980, November 20, 1981, May 3, 1985.
Voice Literary Supplement, February, 1982.
Washington Post, April 17, 1986.
Washington Post Book World, May 2, 1982, August 18, 1985.
World Literature Written in English, November, 1976.

*　　*　　*

CARR, John Dickson 1906-1977
(Carr Dickson, Carter Dickson)

PERSONAL: Born November 30, 1906, in Uniontown, Pa.; died February 27, 1977, in Greenville, S.C.; son of Wood Nicholas (a U.S. Congressman and the postmaster of Uniontown) and Julia Carr; married Clarice Cleaves, 1931; children: Julia, Bonita, Mary. *Education:* Haverford College, graduate, 1928.

CAREER: Writer, 1930-77. British Broadcasting Corp., London, England, radio script writer during Second World War.

MEMBER: Mystery Writers of America (president, 1949), Baker Street Irregulars; Detection Club (honorary secretary), Savage Club, and Garrick Club (all London).

AWARDS, HONORS: Edgar Allan Poe Award, Mystery Writers of America, 1949, for *The Life of Sir Arthur Conan Doyle,* and 1969; Grand Master Award, Mystery Writers of America, 1962; received two prizes from *Ellery Queen's Mystery Magazine,* one for the story "The Gentleman from Paris."

WRITINGS:

Poison in Jest, Harper, 1932, reprinted, Macmillan, 1985.

(Under pseudonym Carr Dickson) *The Bowstring Murders,* Morrow, 1933.
The Burning Court, Harper, 1937, reprinted, International Polygonics, 1985.
(Under pseudonym Carter Dickson, with John Rhode) *Fatal Descent,* Dodd, Mead, 1939, (published in England as *Drop to His Death,* Heinemann, 1939).
The Emperor's Snuffbox, Harper, 1942, reprinted, Carroll & Graf, 1986.
The Bride of Newgate, Harper, 1950, reprinted, Carroll & Graf, 1986.
The Devil in Velvet, Harper, 1951, reprinted, Carroll & Graf, 1987.
The Nine Wrong Answers, Harper, 1952, reprinted, Carroll & Graf, 1986.
Captain Cut-Throat, Harper, 1955, reprinted, Carroll & Graf, 1988.
Patrick Butler for the Defense, Harper, 1956.
(Under pseudonym Carter Dickson) *Fear Is the Same,* Morrow, 1956.
Fire, Burn!, Harper, 1957, reprinted, Carroll & Graf, 1987.
Scandal at High Chimneys: A Victorian Melodrama, Harper, 1959, reprinted, Carroll & Graf, 1988.
The Witch of the Lowtide: An Edwardian Melodrama, Harper, 1961.
The Demoniacs, Harper, 1962.
Papa La-Bas, Harper, 1968, reprinted, Carroll & Graf, 1989.
The Ghosts' High Noon, Harper, 1969.
Deadly Hall, Harper, 1971, reprinted, Carroll & Graf, 1989.
The Hungry Goblin: A Victorian Detective Novel, Harper, 1972.

"HENRI BENCOLIN" MYSTERY NOVELS

It Walks by Night, Harper, 1930, reprinted, Zebra Books, 1986.
Castle Skull, Harper, 1931, reprinted, Zebra Books, 1987.
The Lost Gallows, Harper, 1931, reprinted, Carroll & Graf, 1986.
The Corpse in the Waxworks, Harper, 1932, reprinted, Macmillan, 1984, (published in England as *The Waxworks Murder,* Hamish Hamilton, 1932).
The Four False Weapons; Being the Return of Bencolin, Harper, 1937, reprinted, 1989.

"DR. GIDEON FELL" MYSTERY NOVELS

Hag's Nook, Harper, 1933, reprinted, International Polygonics, 1985.
The Mad Hatter Mystery, Harper, 1933, reprinted, 1989.
The Blind Barber, Harper, 1934, published as *The Case of the Blind Barber,* Macmillan, 1984.
The Eight of Swords, Harper, 1934, reprinted, Zebra Books, 1986.
Death-Watch, Harper, 1935.
The Three Coffins, Harper, 1935, reprinted, International Polygonics, 1986, (published in England as *The Hollow Man,* Hamish Hamilton, 1935).
The Arabian Nights Murder, Harper, 1936, reprinted, 1989.
To Wake the Dead, Harper, 1938, reprinted, 1989.
The Crooked Hinge, Harper, 1938, reprinted, 1989.
The Problem of the Green Capsule, Harper, 1939, reprinted, International Polygonics, 1986, (published in England as *The Black Spectacles,* Hamish Hamilton, 1939).
The Problem of the Wire Cage, Harper, 1939, reprinted, State Mutual Book, 1982.
The Man Who Could Not Shudder, Harper, 1940.
The Case of the Constant Suicides, Harper, 1941, reprinted, 1989.

Death Turns the Tables, Harper, 1941, reprinted, International Polygonics, 1985, (published in England as *The Seat of the Scornful,* Hamish Hamilton, 1942).

Till Death Do Us Part, Harper, 1944, reprinted, International Polygonics, 1989.

He Who Whispers, Harper, 1946, reprinted, International Polygonics, 1986.

The Sleeping Sphinx, Harper, 1947, reprinted, International Polygonics, 1985.

The Dead Man's Knock, Harper, 1948, reprinted, Zebra Books, 1987.

Below Suspicion, Harper, 1949, reprinted, International Polygonics, 1986.

In Spite of Thunder, Harper, 1960, reprinted, Carroll & Graf, 1987.

The House at Satan's Elbow, Harper, 1965, reprinted, International Polygonics, 1987.

Panic in Box C, Harper, 1966, reprinted, Carroll & Graf, 1987.

Dark of the Moon, Harper, 1967, reprinted, Carroll & Graf, 1987.

STORY COLLECTIONS

(Under pseudonym Carter Dickson) *The Department of Queer Complaints,* Morrow, 1940, published as *Scotland Yard: Department of Queer Complaints,* Dell, 1944.

Dr. Fell, Detective, and Other Stories, Spivak, 1947.

The Third Bullet and Other Stories, Harper, 1954.

(With Adrian Conan Doyle) *The Exploits of Sherlock Holmes,* Random House, 1954.

The Men Who Explained Miracles, Harper, 1963.

The Door to Doom and Other Detections, edited by Douglas C. Greene, Harper, 1980.

NONFICTION

The Murder of Sir Edmund Godfrey, Harper, 1936, reprinted, International Polygonics, 1989.

The Life of Sir Arthur Conan Doyle, Harper, 1949, reprinted, Carroll & Graf, 1987.

(Contributor) Francis M. Nevins, Jr., editor, *The Mystery Writer's Art,* Bowling Green University Popular Press, 1970.

EDITOR

Maiden Murders, Harper, 1952.

Arthur Conan Doyle, *Great Stories,* British Book Centre, 1959.

RADIO SCRIPTS

The Dead Sleep Lightly (collection of radio scripts), edited by Douglas C. Greene, Doubleday, 1983.

Also author of over 75 scripts for "Appointment with Fear," "Suspense," "Cabin B-13," "The Silent Battle," and other radio shows of the 1930s and 1940s.

UNDER PSEUDONYM CARTER DICKSON; "SIR HENRY MERRIVALE" MYSTERY NOVELS

The Plague Court Murders, Morrow, 1934.

The White Priory Murders, Morrow, 1934.

The Red Widow Murders, Morrow, 1935, reprinted, International Polygonics, 1988.

The Unicorn Murders, Morrow, 1935, reprinted, International Polygonics, 1989.

The Magic Lantern Murders, Heinemann, 1936, published as *The Punch and Judy Murders,* Morrow, 1937, reprinted, International Polygonics, 1988.

The Third Bullet, Hodder & Stoughton, 1937.

The Peacock Feather Murders, Morrow, 1937, reprinted, International Polygonics, 1987, (published in England as *The Ten Teacups,* Heinemann, 1937).

Death in Five Boxes, Morrow, 1938, reprinted, Dorchester Publishing, 1977.

The Judas Window, Morrow, 1938, reprinted, International Polygonics, 1987, published as *The Crossbow Murders,* Berkley Publishing, 1964, reprinted, Zebra Books, 1989.

The Reader Is Warned, Morrow, 1939.

And So to Murder, Morrow, 1940, reprinted, Zebra Books, 1988.

Nine—And Death Makes Ten, Morrow, 1940, reprinted, International Polygonics, 1987, published as *Murder in the Atlantic,* World Publishing, 1950, (published in England as *Murder in the Submarine Zone,* Heinemann, 1950).

Seeing Is Believing, Morrow, 1941, published as *Cross of Murder,* World Publishing, 1959.

The Gilded Man, Morrow, 1942, reprinted, International Polygonics, 1988, published as *Death and the Gilded Man,* Pocket Books, 1947.

She Died a Lady, Morrow, 1943, reprinted, Zebra Books, 1987.

He Wouldn't Kill Patience, Morrow, 1944, reprinted, International Polygonics, 1988.

The Curse of the Bronze Lamp, Morrow, 1945, reprinted, Carroll & Graf, 1984, (published in England as *Lord of the Sorcerers,* Heinemann, 1946).

My Late Wives, Morrow, 1946, reprinted, Zebra Books, 1988.

The Skeleton in the Clock, Morrow, 1948, reprinted, Dorchester Publishing, 1977.

A Graveyard to Let, Morrow, 1949, reprinted, Dorchester Publishing, 1978.

Night at the Mocking Widow, Morrow, 1950, reprinted, Zebra Books, 1988.

Behind the Crimson Blind, Morrow, 1952, reprinted, Zebra Books, 1989.

The Cavalier's Cup, Morrow, 1953, reprinted, Zebra Books, 1987.

SIDELIGHTS: As the author of seventy novels, the creator of the historical mystery, the writer of some of radio's finest mystery programs, and the official biographer of Sir Arthur Conan Doyle, John Dickson Carr was one of the mystery field's most esteemed figures. In a tribute to the author in the *Armchair Detective,* R. E. Briney described Carr as "a master of the classic detective story and an unparalleled exponent of the 'locked room' or 'impossible crime' story." In 1962 he was named a Grand Master by the Mystery Writers of America for his many contributions to the genre.

"If there's one thing I can't stand, it's a nice *healthy* murder," Carr once complained to Robert Lewis Taylor of the *New Yorker.* No such murders found their way into Carr's many novels. He specialized in a rather macabre, atmospheric brand of mystery fiction in which there was always a hint of the supernatural. His murders occurred in such exotic locales as opium dens, waxworks, and medieval castles. "His books," Julian Symons wrote in *Mortal Consequences: A History—From the Detective Story to the Crime Novel,* "are full of reference to macabre events and possibilities." Carr had "one of the murkiest imaginations in the entire field of letters," Taylor explained. The critic added that "It is Carr's Halloween mind that sets him apart." Commenting on *The Crooked Hinge,* a *New York Times* reviewer called Carr "an unexcelled master in this field of creepy erudition, swift-moving excitement, and suspense through atmosphere." Speaking of *The Arabian Nights Murders,* the *Manchester Guardian* critic noted that Carr "conveys admirably the atmosphere of mingled farce and terror, and one can always be sure that through the maze of marvels he constructs he will guide his readers by the thread of logic and sound reasoning."

Like other Golden Age mystery writers of the 1930s, Carr was adept at writing an intricate puzzler. The locked room mystery, or "impossible crime" story, was his particular forte. Donald A. Yates, writing in *Armchair Detective,* found that Carr specialized in "making the seemingly impossible possible. . . . His favorite and most entertaining pastime [was] creating and solving one locked room puzzle after another." In *It Walks by Night,* the victim is found beheaded in a room whose only two doors were constantly under observation by police officers. In *The Problem of the Wire Cage,* the victim is found strangled in the middle of a clay tennis court, and only his own footprints lead to the body. One of the finest examples of the locked room mystery, according to George N. Dove in *Clues: A Journal of Detection,* is Carr's *The Three Coffins* (published in England as *The Hollow Man*). Dove called the book "a real masterpiece of complexity." In that novel, Carr even included a "Locked Room Lecture" which Symons called "a splendidly lively and learned discussion of locked-room murders and their possible solutions."

Under his own name, Carr wrote mystery novels featuring Dr. Gideon Fell, a portly, flamboyant figure modeled after G. K. Chesterton. Under the pseudonym Carter Dickson he chronicled the cases of Sir Henry Merrivale, a "buffoon given to profanity, with a lordly sneer," as a writer for the *New York Times* described him. Both detectives are among the mystery genre's most popular characters. Carr's series detectives, according to Briney, "will last as long as the detective itself."

In addition to his mystery novels set in the present day, Carr also pioneered the historical mystery genre—puzzlers set in a meticulously-researched historical setting. The first of these books, *The Bride of Newgate,* was set in the England of the early nineteenth century and dealt with the murder of a leading lord. It was followed by *The Devil in Velvet,* in which a Cambridge professor solves a seventeenth century murder. That book proved to be one of Carr's most popular works, outselling all of his other novels. In *The Hungry Goblin* Carr enjoyed a little twist on his own formula, portraying 19th century British novelist Wilkie Collins as a detective.

During the Second World War, Carr worked for the British Broadcasting Corp. as a writer of propaganda broadcasts about the work of the Resistance movement in occupied Europe. At this time he also originated the popular "Suspense" and "Appointment with Fear" radio series for which he wrote some seventy-five scripts. These scripts were written, Carr once explained, "under the slight difficulty that during the blitz our house was twice demolished while we were inside it." Francis M. Nevins, Jr., in an article for *Armchair Detective,* claimed that Carr's "scripts for 'Suspense' . . . are among the finest mysteries ever written for radio and remain a superb listening experience almost thirty-five years later."

In 1949, Carr was approached by the family of Sir Arthur Conan Doyle to write the official biography of the creator of Sherlock Holmes. Working with family letters, Doyle's notebooks, and what the *New York Times* described as "whole rooms full of personal papers," Carr assembled a "vital and exciting portrait of Sir Arthur," as Elizabeth Johnson of *Commonweal* noted. Writing in the *San Francisco Chronicle,* J. H. Jackson called the biography "a beautiful piece of work. . . . Most will finish the book feeling that they have met an extraordinarily many-sided man, an individual who lived with gusto and vigor the kind of life he believed to be good. . . . Part of this is Doyle himself; part of it is Carr's skill. The combination makes a notable biography."

Carr explained his prolific output as the result of long, hard work. He typically wrote "all day every day, including Sunday, and often far into the night," as Taylor recounted. Carr was once quoted as saying, "I insisted on loafing 18 hours a day at the typewriter ever since I was old enough to know one letter from another." The owner of a vast reference library on such subjects as crime, witchcraft, poison, and murder, he was rarely stuck for an idea. "Plotting," Taylor related, "is easy for Carr—he habitually sees the entire network of human relations as a slough of intrigue—and the blocking out of the separate scenes is perhaps his favorite chore. He hates the actual writing, however, and does it in anguish, emerging from each long session hollow-eyed and spent."

Described by W. Murchison, Jr., of *National Review* as "an unapologetic Tory—an old-fashioned champion of gentility, taste, standards and romance," Carr possessed, according to John Boland of *Books and Bookmen,* an "impeccable style," while his books featured "the faultless construction that we have long come to accept as his trade mark." In his essay for *The Mystery Writer's Art,* Carr defined a mystery novel as "a hoodwinking contest, a duel between author and reader." His formula for a successful mystery? "Merely state your evidence," he advised, "and the reader will mislead himself."

MEDIA ADAPTATIONS: The short story "Death in the Dressing Room" was adapted as an episode in the "Murder Clinic" radio series and first broadcast by the British Broadcasting Corp., September 29, 1942; the short story "Man with a Cloak" was filmed in 1951, "Dangerous Crossing" in 1953, and "Colonel March of Scotland Yard" in 1954; *Fire, Burn!* was adapted for radio by John Keir Cross and first broadcast by the BBC, July 5, 1958; *The Hollow Man* was adapted for radio by Cross and first broadcast by the BBC, January 10, 1959; *The Emperor's Snuffbox* was filmed as "City after Midnight" in 1959; the film rights to the short story "The Gentleman from Paris" were sold.

BIOGRAPHICAL/CRITICAL SOURCES:

BOOKS

Contemporary Literary Criticism, Volume 3, Gale, 1975.
French, Larry L., editor, *Notes for the Curious: A John Dickson Carr Memorial Journal,* Carrian (Chesterfield, Mo.), 1978.
Haycraft, Howard, *Murder for Pleasure: The Life and Times of the Detective Story,* Appleton, 1941.
Hoyt, C. A., editor, *Minor American Novelists,* Southern Illinois University Press, 1970.
Nevins, Francis M., Jr., editor, *The Mystery Writer's Art,* Bowling Green University Popular Press, 1970.
Symons, Julian, *Mortal Consequences: A History—From the Detective Story to the Crime Novel,* Harper, 1972.

PERIODICALS

Armchair Detective, January, 1970, October, 1978, winter, 1979.
Books and Bookmen, December, 1971.
Clues: A Journal of Detection, fall/winter, 1986.
Life, December 29, 1953.
Manchester Guardian, March 6, 1936.
National Review, October 8, 1971.
New Yorker, January 20, 1945, September 8, 1951, September 15, 1951.
New York Times, January 9, 1938, October 16, 1938.
Publishers Weekly, June 27, 1960.

OBITUARIES:

PERIODICALS

Armchair Detective, April, 1977.
Newsweek, March 14, 1977.
New York Times, March 1, 1977.
Time, March 14, 1977.
Washington Post, March 2, 1977.

—*Sketch by Thomas Wiloch*

*   *   *

CARRUTH, Hayden 1921-

PERSONAL: Surname accented on final syllable; born August 3, 1921, in Waterbury, Conn.; son of Gorton Veeder (an editor) and Margery (Barrow) Carruth; married Sara Anderson, March 14, 1943; married Eleanore Ray, November 29, 1952; married Rose Marie Dorn, October 28, 1961; children: (first marriage) Martha Hamilton; (third marriage) David Barrow. *Education:* University of North Carolina, A.B., 1943; University of Chicago, M.A., 1948. *Politics:* Abolitionist.

ADDRESSES: Home—Lewisburg, Pa. *Office*—Department of English, Bucknell University, Lewisburg, Pa. 17837.

CAREER: Poet; free-lance writer and editor. Associate editor, University of Chicago Press, 1951-52; project administrator, Intercultural Publications, Inc., 1952-53. Poet-in-residence, Johnson State College, 1972-74; adjunct professor, University of Vermont, 1975-78; visiting professor, St. Michael's College, Winooskie, Vt.; professor of English, Syracuse University, 1979-85; professor, Bucknell University, 1985—. Owner and operator, Crow's Mark Press, Johnson, Vt. *Military service:* U.S. Army Air Forces, World War II; became staff sergeant; spent two years in Italy.

MEMBER: Johnson Chamber of Commerce.

AWARDS, HONORS: Bess Hokin Prize, 1954, Vachel Lindsay Prize, 1956, Levinson Prize, 1958, and Morton Dauwen Zabel Prize, 1967, all from *Poetry* magazine; Harriet Monroe Poetry Prize, University of Chicago, 1960, for *The Crow and the Heart;* $1500 grant-in-aid for poetry, Brandeis University, 1960; Bollingen Foundation fellowship in criticism, 1962; Helen Bullis Award, University of Washington, 1962; Carl Sandburg Award, *Chicago Daily News,* 1963, for *The Norfolk Poems;* Emily Clark Balch Prize, *Virginia Quarterly Review,* 1964, for *North Winter;* Eunice Tietjens Memorial Prize, 1964; Guggenheim Foundation fellow, 1965 and 1979; National Endowment for the Humanities fellow, 1967; Governor's Medal, State of Vermont, 1974; Shelley Memorial Award, Poetry Society of America, 1978; Lenore Marshall Poetry Prize, 1978, for *Brothers, I Loved You All;* Whiting Writers Award from Whiting Foundation, 1986; senior fellowship from National Endowment for the Arts, c. 1989.

WRITINGS:

POETRY

The Crow and the Heart, 1946-1949, Macmillan, 1959.
Journey to a Known Place (long poem), New Directions, 1961.
The Norfolk Poems: 1 June to 1 September 1961, Prairie Press, 1962.
North Winter, Prairie Press, 1964.
Nothing for Tigers; Poems, 1959-1964, Macmillan, 1965.
Contra Mortem (long poem), Crow's Mark Press, 1967.
(Contributor) *Where Is Vietnam?: American Poets Respond,* Anchor Books, 1967.
For You: Poems, New Directions, 1970.

The Clay Hill Anthology, Prairie Press, 1970.
From Snow and Rock, From Chaos: Poems, 1965-1972, New Directions, 1973.
Dark World, Kayak, 1974.
The Bloomingdale Papers, University of Georgia Press, 1975.
Brothers, I Loved You All, Sheep Meadow Press, 1978.
Almanach du Printemps Vivarois, Nadja, 1979.
The Mythology of Darkness and Light, Tamarack, 1982.
The Sleeping Beauty, Harper, 1983.
If You Call This Cry a Song, Countryman Press, 1983.
Asphalt Georgics, New Directions, 1985.
Lighter Than Air Craft, edited by John Wheatcroft, Press Alley, 1985.
The Selected Poetry of Hayden Carruth, Macmillan, 1986.
Sonnets, Press Alley, 1989.
Tell Me Again How the White Heron Rises and Flies Across the Nacreous River at Twilight Toward the Distant Islands, New Directions, 1989.

Also author of *The Oldest Killed Lake in North America,* 1985, and *Mother,* 1986.

EDITOR

(With James Laughlin) *A New Directions Reader,* New Directions, 1964.
The Voice That Is Great Within Us: American Poetry of the Twentieth Century, Bantam, 1970.
The Bird/Poem Book: Poems on the Wild Birds of North America, McCall, 1970.

OTHER

Appendix A (novel), Macmillan, 1963.
After "The Stranger": Imaginary Dialogues with Camus, Macmillan, 1964.
(Contributor) *The Art of Literary Publishing,* Pushcart Press, 1980.
Working Papers: Selected Essays and Reviews, University of Georgia Press, 1981.
Effluences From the Sacred Caves: More Selected Essays and Reviews, University of Michigan Press, 1984.
Sitting In: Selected Writings on Jazz, Blues, and Related Topics, (includes poetry), University of Iowa Press, 1986.

Contributor to periodicals, including *Poetry, Hudson Review, New Yorker, Partisan Review.* Editor-in-chief, *Poetry,* 1949-50; member of editorial board, *Hudson Review,* 1971—; poetry editor, *Harper's,* 1977-83.

SIDELIGHTS: Though known primarily as a critic and editor, Hayden Carruth is also, according to the *Virginia Quarterly Review,* "a poet who has never received the wide acclaim his work deserves and who is certainly one of the most important poets working in this country today. . . . [He is] technically skilled, lively, never less than completely honest, and as profound and deeply moving as one could ask." Characterized by a calm, tightly controlled, and relatively "plain" language that belies the intensity of feeling behind the words, Carruth's poetry elicits praise from those who admire its wide variety of verse forms and criticism from those who find its precision and restraint too impersonal and academic.

Commenting in his book *Babel to Byzantium,* James Dickey speculates that these opposing views of Carruth's work may result from the occasionally uneven quality of his poetry. In a discussion of *The Crow and the Heart,* for example, Dickey notes "a carefulness which bursts, once or twice or three times, into a kind of frenzied eloquence, a near-hysteria, and in these frightening places sloughing off a set of mannerisms which in the rest of the book seems determined to reduce Carruth to the level of a thousand other poets. . . . [He] is one of the poets (perhaps all poets are some of these poets) who write their best, pushing past limit after limit, only in the grip of recalling some overpowering experience. When he does not have such a subject at hand, Carruth amuses himself by being playfully skillful with internal rhyme, inventing bizarre Sitwellian images, being witty and professionally sharp."

American Poetry Review critic Geoffrey Gardner, who characterizes Carruth as "a poet who has always chosen to make his stand just aside from any of the presently conflicting mainstreams," says that such linguistic playfulness is typical of the poet's early work. He attributes it to Carruth's struggle "to restore equilibrium to the soul [and] clarity to vision, through a passionate command of language," a struggle that gives much of his poetry "a Lear-like words-against-the-storm quality." Continues Gardner: "I won't be the first to say Carruth's early work is cumbered by archaisms, forced inversions, sometimes futile extravagances of vocabulary and a tendency of images and metaphors to reify into a top heavy symbolism. . . . But the courage of [his] poems can't be faulted. From the earliest and against great odds, Carruth made many attempts at many kinds of poems, many forms, contending qualities of diction and texture. . . . If the struggle of contending voices and attitudes often ends in poems that don't quite succeed, it remains that the struggle itself is moving for its truthfulness and intensity. . . . Carruth uniformly refuses to glorify his crazies. They are pain and pain alone. What glory there is—and there are sparks of it everywhere through these early poems—he keeps for the regenerative stirrings against the storm of pain and isolation."

Like many poets, Carruth turns to personal experience for inspiration; however, with the possible exception of *The Bloomingdale Papers* (a long poetic sequence Carruth wrote in the 1950s while confined to a mental hospital for treatment of alcoholism and a nervous breakdown), he does not indulge in the self-obsessed meditations common among some of his peers. Instead, Carruth turns outward, exploring such "universal opposites" as madness (or so-called madness) and sanity or chaos and order. He then tries to balance the negative images—war, loneliness, the destruction of the environment, sadness—with mostly nature-related positive images and activities that communicate a sense of stability—the cycle of the seasons, performing manual labor, contemplating the night sky, observing the serenity of plant and animal life. But, as Gardner points out, "Carruth is not in the least tempted to sentimentality about country life. . . . [He recognizes] that it can be a life of value and nobility in the midst of difficult facts and chaos." Nor is he "abstractly philosophical or cold," according to the critic. "On the contrary," Gardner states, "[his poems] are all poems about very daily affairs: things seen and heard, the loneliness of missing friends absent or dead, the alternations of love for and estrangement from those present, the experiences of a man frequently alone with the non-human which all too often bears the damaging marks of careless human intrusion." Furthermore, he says, "Carruth comes to the politics of all this with a vengeance. . . . [His poems] all bear strong public witness against the wastes and shames of our culture that are destroying human value with a will in a world where values are already hard enough to maintain, in a universe where they are always difficult to discover. Carruth does not express much anger in [his] poems. Yet one feels that an enormous energy of rage has forced them to be."

Concludes Alastair Reid in the *Saturday Review*: "[Carruth's] poems have a sureness to them, a flair and variety. . . . Yet, in

their dedication to finding an equilibrium in an alien and often cruel landscape, Vermont, where the poet has dug himself in, they reflect the moods and struggles of a man never at rest. . . . His work teems with the struggle to live and to make sense, and his poems carve out a kind of grace for us."

Carruth told *CA:* "I have a close but at the same time uncomfortable relationship with the natural world. I've always been most at home in the country probably because I was raised in the country as a boy, and I know something about farming and woodcutting and all the other things that country people know about. That kind of work has been important to me in my personal life and in my writing too. I believe in the values of manual labor and labor that is connected with the earth in some way. But I'm not simply a nature poet. In fact, I consider myself and I consider the whole human race fundamentally alien. By evolving into a state of self-consciousness, we have separated ourselves from the other animals and the plants and from the very earth itself, from the whole universe. So there's a kind of fear and terror involved in living close to nature. My poems, I think, exist in a state of tension between the love of natural beauty and the fear of natural meaninglessness or absurdity.

"I think there are many reasons for poets and artists in general to be depressed these days. . . . They have to do with a lot . . . [of] things that are going on in our civilization. They have to do with the whole evolution of the sociology of literature during the last fifty years. Things have changed; they've turned completely around. I don't know if I can say it briefly but I'll try. When I was young and starting to write poetry seriously and to investigate the resources of modern poetry, as we called it then, we still felt beleaguered; modern poetry was still considered outrageous by most of the people in the publishing business and in the reading audience at large. We still spoke in terms of the true artists and the philistines. We felt that if we could get enough people to read T. S. Eliot and Wallace Stevens and e e cummings and William Carlos Williams and other great poets of that period, then something good would happen in American civilization. We felt a genuine vocation, a calling, to try and make this happen. And we succeeded. Today thousands of people are going to colleges and attending workshops and taking courses in twentieth century literature. Eliot and Stevens are very well known, very well read; and American civilization has sunk steadily, progressively, further and further down until most of the sensible people are in a state of despair. It's pretty obvious that good writing doesn't really have very much impact on social events or national events of any kind. We hope that it has individual impact, that readers here and there are made better in some way by reading our work. But it's a hope; we have no proof."

BIOGRAPHICAL/CRITICAL SOURCES:

BOOKS

Contemporary Literary Criticism, Gale, Volume 4, 1975, Volume 7, 1977, Volume 10, 1979, Volume 18, 1981.
Dickey, James, *Babel to Byzantium,* Farrar, Straus, 1968.
Dictionary of Literary Biography, Volume 5: *American Poets Since World War II,* Gale, 1980.

PERIODICALS

American Poetry Review, May, 1979, January, 1981.
Chicago Tribune Book World, December 26, 1982.
Los Angeles Times Book Review, June 3, 1984.
Nation, February 15, 1965, October 25, 1971.
New York Times, January 3, 1976.

New York Times Book Review, May l2, 1963, April 6, 1975, September 2, 1979, May 23, 1982, August 21, 1983, January 22, 1984, July 14, 1985, May 11, 1986.
Poetry, August, 1963, May, 1974.
Saturday Review, October 27, 1979.
Times Literary Supplement, July 23, 1971.
Virginia Quarterly Review, summer, 1963, summer, 1971, summer, 1979.
Washington Post Book World, January 1, 1984, April 13, 1986.

* * *

CARSON, Rachel Louise 1907-1964

PERSONAL: Born May 27, 1907, in Springfield, Pa.; died of cancer, April 14, 1964, in Silver Spring, Md.; daughter of Robert Warden and Maria Frazier (McLean) Carson. *Education:* Pennsylvania College for Women, A.B., 1929; Johns Hopkins University, A.M., 1932; further graduate study at the Marine Biological Laboratory, Woods Hole, Mass. *Religion:* Presbyterian.

ADDRESSES: Home—Silver Spring, Md.

CAREER: University of Maryland, College Park, member of the zoology staff, 1931-36; U.S. Bureau of Fisheries (now the Fish and Wildlife Service), Washington, D.C., aquatic biologist, beginning, 1936, editor in chief, 1949-52; full-time writer, 1952-64. Instructor at Johns Hopkins University, summers, 1930-36.

MEMBER: American Ornithologists' Union, National Institute of Arts and Letters, Royal Society of Literature (fellow), Audubon Society (director in Washington, D.C.), Society of Women Geographers.

AWARDS, HONORS: Eugene Saxton Memorial fellowship, 1949; George Westinghouse Science Writing Award, 1950; National Book Award, 1951, for *The Sea Around Us;* Guggenheim fellowship, 1951-52; John Burroughs Medal, 1952; Henry G. Bryant Gold Medal, 1952; Page-One Award, 1952; Frances K. Hutchinson Medal, 1952; Silver Jubilee Medal from Limited Editions Club, 1954; book award from National Council of Women in the U.S., 1956; achievement award from American Association of University Women, 1956; Schweitzer Medal from Animal Welfare Institute, 1962; Women's National Book Association Constance Lindsay Skinner Award, 1963; New England Outdoor Writers Association Award, 1963; Conservationist of the Year Award from National Wildlife Federation, 1963; achievement award from Einstein College of Medicine, 1963; Gold Medal from New York Zoological Society; special citations from the Garden Club of America, the Pennsylvania Federation of Women's Clubs, and the Izaak Walton League of America, 1963. D.Sc. from Oberlin College, 1952; D.Litt. from Pennsylvania College for Women, 1952, Drexel Institute of Technology, 1952, and Smith College, 1953.

WRITINGS:

Under the Sea-Wind: A Naturalist's Picture of Ocean Life, illustrated by Howard French, Simon & Schuster, 1941, new edition, Oxford University Press, 1952, reprinted, New American Library, 1978.
Food from the Sea: Fish and Shellfish of New England, U.S. Government Printing Office, 1943.
Food from Home Waters: Fishes of the Middle West, U.S. Department of the Interior, Fish and Wildlife Service, 1943.
Fish and Shellfish of the South Atlantic and Gulf Coasts, U.S. Government Printing Office, 1944.
Fish and Shellfish of the Middle Atlantic Coast, U.S. Government Printing Office, 1945.

The Sea Around Us (also see below), illustrated by Katherine L. Howe, Oxford University Press, 1951, revised edition, Watts, 1966, reprinted, Oxford University Press, 1989.
The Edge of the Sea, illustrated by Bob Hines, Houghton, 1955, reprinted, 1980.
Silent Spring, illustrated by Lois Darling and Louis Darling, Houghton, 1962, limited edition, Limited Editions Club, 1980, 25th anniversary edition, Houghton, 1987.
The Sense of Wonder, Harper, 1965, reprinted, Perennial Library, 1984.
Life Under the Sea (selection from *The Sea Around Us*), Golden Press, 1968.
The Rocky Coast, Macmillan, 1971.
House of Life: Rachel Carson at Work (selections), edited by Paul Brooks, Houghton, 1972.
Silent Spring Revisited, American Chemical Society, 1987.

SIDELIGHTS: Rachel Carson combined her interest in nature and her desire to write into a very successful career. She acquired her love of nature from her mother, who introduced her to the marvels of the outdoors and its creatures. As early as age ten, her writing ability was manifested in contributions to the *St. Nicholas Magazine.*

Under the Sea-Wind, Carson's first book, grew out of an essay entitled "Undersea," which was published in the *Atlantic* in 1937. Reviews of the book, which appeared four years later, included that written by a *Books* reviewer: "Miss Carson's unemotional handling of her subject matter is anything but dull. There is drama in every sentence. She rouses our interest in this ocean world and we want to watch it." A *Scientific Book Club Review* critic observed: "Not since the publication of *Salar the Salmon* has there been a volume so replete with information about sea life as this book by Rachel Carson. . . . In the three parts of the book, Miss Carson employs the device of weaving her story around certain individual creatures, although so many other animal 'personages' appear that a paradoxical sense of orderly confusion is conveyed. Here is the darting, swooping, preying struggle that has been going on for untold centuries. . . . There is poetry here, but no false sentimentality." William Beebe in *Saturday Review of Literature* commented: "The plethora of facts occasionally smothers the smoothness of diction, and distracts the attention from the word picture itself. . . . This is not captious criticism, but an appeal for more simple words, fewer terms of physical and faunal geography, and a greater leisureliness in description."

Miss Carson's second effort, *The Sea Around Us,* required a vast amount of research and two years to write. A *Christian Science Monitor* critic commented, "Rachel Carson has achieved that rare, all but unique phenomenon—a literary work about the sea that is comparable with the best, yet offends neither the natural scientist nor the poet." "Rare indeed," added a contributor to the *Saturday Review of Literature,* "is the individual who can present a comprehensive and well-balanced picture of such a complex entity as the sea in an easy and fluent style and in terms anyone can understand. Rachel Carson is such an individual. Many books have been written on the sea, most of them by scholars with a very detailed knowledge of some aspect of oceanography, but with a limited knowledge of popular presentation. Miss Carson's book is different." Observed a *Nation* reviewer: "Scientifically, *The Sea Around Us* has its shortcomings, but it would be hard to find a style, a sensitivity, a balancing of detail more perfectly suited for the evoking of the sea." Several chapters of the book originally appeared in the *New Yorker* in the summer of 1951, under the title, "Profile of the Sea." A chapter entitled "Birth of an Island" was published earlier in the *Yale Review,* and won for its author the George Westinghouse Foundation Award, given for outstanding scientific writing in a periodical. By October, 1951, sales of the book—338,000 hardcover copies—had carried it to a ninth printing, and to first place on non-fiction best-seller lists. A documentary film of the book was made by RKO, which won an Academy Award for best documentary of feature length in 1952.

"Again author Carson has shown her remarkable talent for catching the breath of science on the still glass of poetry," wrote a *Time* critic about *The Edge of the Sea*. According to a *Christian Science Monitor* contributor, "*The Edge of the Sea* is pitched, perhaps, in a lesser key than was *The Sea Around Us*, if only because the intertidal world is a more limited subject than was the whole sea itself. In her new book, Miss Carson's pen is as poetic as ever and the knowledge she imparts is profound. *The Edge of the Sea* finds a worthy place beside [her] . . . masterpiece of 1951." Added a *Saturday Review* critic: "The book has a notable feature: it appeals both to the mind's eye and to the physical eye. . . . The double impact is much stronger than if the two impressions came separately, and so *The Edge of the Sea* becomes the product of two naturalists working in close cooperation, each one scientifically trained and each an artist, the one with a pen and the other with a pencil [Bob Hines]. Together they take us on a good journey."

Silent Spring was probably Rachel Carson's most influential, as well as most controversial book. The work, which sold over 500,000 hardcover copies, is an indictment of farmers for the use of poisonous chemical fertilizers, and points out the potentially dangerous effects of these on animals, birds, and humans. Called by a *Christian Century* contributor as "a shocking and frightening book," it was further critiqued by the *Christian Science Monitor*, which noted: "Miss Carson has undeniably sketched a one-sided picture. But her distortion is akin to that of the painter who exaggerates to focus attention on essentials. It is not the half-truth of the propagandist." Added a *Saturday Review* contributor: "It is a devastating, heavily documented, relentless attack upon human carelessness, greed, and irresponsibility. . . . If her present book does not possess the beauty of *The Sea Around Us*, it is because she has courageously chosen, at the height of her powers, to educate us upon a sad, an unpleasant, an unbeautiful topic, and one of our own making." Intense public concern created over the book caused President John F. Kennedy to announce a federal investigation into the problem. The report of the President's Science Advisory Committee, issued in May, 1963, agreed with the basic premise of *Silent Spring*, warning against the indiscriminate use of pesticides and urging stricter controls and more research.

Rachel Carson was in the process of finishing *The Sense of Wonder* at the time of her death from cancer in 1964. A *Publishers Weekly* reviewer observed: "The late [Rachel] Carson shares her delight in the miracles of nature, and shows one how to communicate this delight to a child, and how to share his sense of wonder. A treat for sore eyes and weary hearts."

BIOGRAPHICAL/CRITICAL SOURCES:

BOOKS

Anticaglia, Elizabeth, *Twelve American Women*, Nelson-Hall, 1975.
Brooks, Paul, editor, *House of Life: Rachel Carson at Work*, Houghton, 1972.
Coates, Ruth A., *Great American Naturalists*, Lerner, 1974.
Cox, Donald W., *Pioneers of Ecology*, Hammond, 1971.
Elliott, Robert, *Banners of Courage*, Platt, 1972.

Gilfond, Henry, *Heroines of America*, Fleet Press, 1970.
Graham, Frank, Jr., *Since Silent Spring*, Houghton, 1970.
Latham, Jean L., *Rachel Carson Who Loved the Sea*, Garrard, 1973.
St. John, Adela Rogers, *Some Are Born Great*, Doubleday, 1974.
Sterling, Philip, *Sea and Earth: The Life of Rachel Carson*, Crowell, 1970.
Squire, C. B., *Heroes of Conservation*, Fleet Press, 1974.

PERIODICALS

American Forests, July, 1970.
Books, December 14, 1941.
Christian Century, December 19, 1962.
Christian Science Monitor, July 5, 1951, November 10, 1955, September 27, 1962.
Instructor, May, 1968.
Life, October 12, 1962.
Nation, August 4, 1951.
Publishers Weekly, June 19, 1967.
Saturday Review, December 5, 1955, September 29, 1962, May 16, 1964.
Saturday Review of Literature, December 27, 1941, July 7, 1951.
Scientific Book Club Review, October, 1941.
Time, November 7, 1955.

OBITUARIES:

PERIODICALS

Current Biography, June, 1964.
Detroit News, May 28, 1972.
Gleanings, July, 1964.
Illustrated London News, April 25, 1964.
New York Times, April 15, 1964, September 27, 1982, March 10, 1988.
Oil, Paint, and Drug Report, April 20, 1964.
Publishers Weekly, April 27, 1964.

* * *

CARTER, Angela (Olive) 1940-

PERSONAL: Born May 7, 1940, in London, England; daughter of Hugh Alexander (a journalist) and Olive (Farthing) Stalker; married Paul Carter, September 10, 1960 (divorced, 1972). *Education:* University of Bristol, B.A., 1965. *Politics:* Labour Party. *Religion:* None.

ADDRESSES: Agent—Deborah Rogers Ltd., 49 Blenheim Crescent, London W11 2EF, England.

CAREER: Journalist for newspapers in Croyden, Surrey, England, 1958-61; novelist, short-story writer, teacher, and critic. Arts Council fellow in creative writing, University of Sheffield, 1976-78; visiting professor of creative writing, Brown University, Providence, R.I., 1980-81; writer in residence, University of Adelaide, Australia, 1984.

AWARDS, HONORS: John Llewllyn Rhys Memorial Prize, 1968, for *The Magic Toyshop;* Somerset Maugham Award, 1969, for *Several Perceptions;* Cheltenham Festival Literary Award, 1979, for *The Bloody Chamber and Other Stories;* Kurt Maschler Award for children's book, 1982; Kate Greenaway Medal, 1984, for *Sleeping Beauty and Other Favourite Fairy Tales;* James Tait Black Memorial Prize, 1986, for *Nights at the Circus.*

WRITINGS:

Unicorn (poetry collection), Location Press (London), 1966.

The Sadeian Woman and the Ideology of Pornography, Pantheon, 1979 (published in England as *The Sadeian Woman: An Exercise in Cultural History,* Virago, 1979).

(Contributor) *Sex and Sensibility: Stories by Contemporary Women Writers from Nine Countries,* Sidgwick & Jackson, 1981.

NOVELS

Shadow Dance, Heinemann, 1966, published as *Honeybuzzard,* Simon & Schuster, 1967.

The Magic Toyshop (also see below), Heinemann, 1967, Simon & Schuster, 1968.

Several Perceptions, Heinemann, 1968, Simon & Schuster, 1969.

Heroes and Villains, Heinemann, 1969, Simon & Schuster, 1970, reprinted, Penguin, 1988.

Love (also see below), Hart Davis, 1971, reprinted, Penguin, 1988.

The Infernal Desire Machines of Dr. Hoffman, Hart Davis, 1972, published as *The War of Dreams,* Harcourt, 1974.

The Passion of New Eve, Harcourt, 1977.

Nights at the Circus, Chatto & Windus, 1984, Viking, 1985.

Saints and Strangers, Viking, 1986.

STORY COLLECTIONS

Fireworks: Nine Profane Pieces, Quartet Books, 1974, large print edition, ABC-Clio, 1989, published as *Fireworks: Nine Stories in Various Disguises,* Harper, 1981.

The Bloody Chamber and Other Stories, Gollancz, 1979, Harper, 1980.

Black Venus's Tale, Faber-Next, 1980.

Black Venus, Chatto & Windus, 1985.

Artificial Fire (includes *Love*), McClelland & Stewart, 1988.

RADIO SCRIPTS

"Vampirella," 1976.

Come unto These Yellow Sands (first broadcast in 1979), Bloodaxe Books, 1985.

"The Company of Wolves" (based upon a story by Carter), 1980.

"Puss in Boots," 1982.

"A Self-Made Man" (about Ronald Firbank), 1984.

OTHER

Miss Z, the Dark Young Lady (for children), Simon & Schuster, 1970.

The Donkey Prince (for children), Simon & Schuster, 1970.

(Translator) *The Fairy Tales of Charles Perrault,* Gollancz, 1977, Avon, 1979.

Comic and Curious Cats, illustrated by Martin Leman, Crown, 1979.

(With Leslie Carter) *The Music People,* Hamish Hamilton, 1980.

Nothing Sacred: Selected Writings, Virago, 1982.

Moonshadow (for children), Gollancz, 1982.

(Editor) *Sleeping Beauty and Other Favourite Fairy Tales,* Gollancz, 1982, Schocken, 1984.

(With Neil Jordan) "The Company of Wolves" (screenplay), ITC Entertainment, 1985.

(Editor) *Don't Bet on the Prince: Contemporary Feminist Fairy Tales in North America and Europe,* Routledge, Chapman & Hall, 1987.

(Editor) *Wayward Girls and Wicked Women: An Anthology of Subversive Stories,* Penguin, 1989.

"The Magic Toy Shop" (screenplay; based on her novel of same title), Granada Television Production, 1989.

Contributor to *New Society, Vogue, Iowa Review, TriQuarterly,* and other publications.

WORK IN PROGRESS: A collection of journalism and reviews for Virago.

SIDELIGHTS: "Angela Carter," writes Caroline Moorehead of the *Times Literary Supplement,* "is a Gothic writer of allegory and metaphor, myth and symbolism." Carter combines elements from a number of literary genres into a unique style which makes her work "difficult to place," according to Lorna Sage of the *Dictionary of Literary Biography.* James Brockway echoes this appraisal in a review for *Books and Bookmen* in which he defines Carter as "our Lady Edgar Allan Poe. . . . But she is more still. Like all genuine art, hers breaks through the boundaries of one department of art and extends to others. So she is also a female [Waslaw] Nijinsky. . . . She is Aubrey Beardsley. . . . She has also the decadence, the hysteria, and the preciosity of [Joris Karl] Huysmans and [Maurice] Maeterlinck, the doll-like romance of [E.T.A.] Hoffmann. . . . She is also a female [Roman] Polanski. And like all geniuses, she walks the tightrope on one side of which yawns the chasm of madness, on the other the chasm of bathos."

There are four elements in Carter's fiction that critics find recurring in all of her work: A lush, imagistic prose, Gothic themes, violence, and an undercurrent of eroticism. These elements can be found in her first novel, *Shadow Dance,* published in the United States as *Honeybuzzard.* The novel is set in an English junk shop that sells newly fashionable Victorian antiques. The shop is owned by the weak Morris and his vicious partner Honeybuzzard. Honeybuzzard's girlfriend, Ghislaine, is a nymphomaniac whose face Honeybuzzard has mutilated. Sage finds these characters "an ambiguous threesome." Carter "sets a grotesque stage," writes P. L. Sandberg of *Saturday Review,* "and peoples it with characters who are often extravagantly Gothic. . . . She sets up outrageous tensions between her people and suggests many layers of meaning." Morris and Honeybuzzard prowl condemned houses at night, stripping them of items to sell in their shop. Sage believes that "the decay of ordinary possessions into 'antiques' forms a fitting metaphor for the decay of the characters' experience into theater." When Honeybuzzard goes mad and kills Ghislaine, Morris is finally moved to betray him to the police. Edwin Morgan of *New Statesman,* although believing the novel "a little too fashionable" because of its portrayal of the late 1960s London youth culture, nonetheless believes that Carter "shows a decided talent for the grotesque scene, the nightmarish atmosphere, the alarming uncertainties of human relationships." Brockway enjoys the book because it has "an all but unbelievable quality: a *fresh* decadence."

"The fantasy motifs lurking in the background in *Shadow Dance,*" writes Sage, "come into their own in *The Magic Toyshop,*" Carter's second novel. It tells the story of Melanie, a teenaged girl, and her younger brother and sister who, suddenly orphaned, find themselves sent to live with an uncle they have never met. Uncle Philip owns a toyshop where he and his wife, struck dumb on their wedding night, and her two brothers live. The aunt and her brothers are, Sage writes, Uncle Philip's "creatures, as surely as the toys he carves." Gradually, Melanie and the children learn that though Uncle Philip rules the toyshop with dictatorial violence by day, his real passion is the building of a theater of life-sized puppets by night—a theater in which he desires Melanie to play the part of Leda in *Leda and the Swan.* "The plot [of *The Magic Toyshop*]" John Wakeman of the *New York Times Book Review* complains, "is grossly implausible, and seems constantly to be taking directions that surprise the author as much as the reader. . . . And yet the book succeeds, awkwardly but firmly welded together by the heat of its author's imagination. It leaves behind it a flavor, pungent and unsettling, which owes as much to its imperfections as to its virtues." "This story is weird and definitely not for children," admits William McCleary of *Library Journal*. Yet he finds the book "an extraordinary, even brilliant piece of writing."

Carter's third novel, *Several Perceptions,* also set in late 1960s England, tells the story of Joseph Harker, a young man who fails in his suicide attempt and so is forced to reconcile himself with the world. Plagued by hallucinations and macabre images, Harker gradually comes to terms with his life through his interaction with his eccentric neighbors, "a pageantlike array of 'fringe' figures who subsist on 1960s tolerance for impromptu, narcissistic performance," as Sage describes them. It is a nightmarish odyssey which ends with Harker's mock salvation at a Christmas party where "a series of ironic miracles" is staged, Sage writes. "The first three quarters of the book," writes Richard Boston of the *New York Times Book Review*, "gives a powerful account of the horror, the logic and the poetry of the schizophrenic's world. . . . But after [Carter's] early toughmindedness, one had hoped for a more telling denouement than the Spirit of Christmas." The reviewer for the *Times Literary Supplement* believes "it is hard to draw any logical conclusion from Miss Carter's series of images or perceptions. But anyone who has found her previous strange novels . . . sticking uncomfortably in the memory will appreciate that however macabre and sensational the scene is, Miss Carter is not simply an image-maker." Carter won the prestigious Somerset Maugham Award for *Several Perceptions.*

With *Heroes and Villains,* Carter abandoned the settings of her previous novels for the realm of science fiction. Set in a post-World War III world of barbarians and scattered remnants of civilization, the novel is largely a fable about the nature of civilized society. Carter's earlier nightmarish qualities are still present, particularly in the rituals of the barbarians, which allow "fantasies of aggression and possession to blossom into action," Sage writes. Marianne, a young girl in a civilized community, is drawn by fascination to join the barbarians. She "rejects the sterile rationality of [civilization]," writes Boston, "but she is also aware of the monsters that are brought forth [among the barbarians] by the sleep of reason." Brockway finds the novel "too obvious an invention, its hairy and bejewelled young savages too symbolic to be interesting." In contrast to this judgement, the *Times Literary Supplement* critic thinks that the barbarians' "world is richly imagined. . . . The fantasy is made to work through the use of detail and the firmly established individuality of the characters," but the critic finds that "the occasional pretentiousness which creeps into the last part of the book . . . does spoil what is in many ways a remarkably effective novel." Boston judges it "a strange, compelling book" and asserts that Carter "tells her story with considerable skill. Her observation is sharp, and she writes extremely well."

The ironically titled *Love* is again set in Carter's familiar late 1960s England but, as Sage writes, it "is altogether blacker, more erotic, and more lucidly nasty" than her previous novels. The novel details the relationship between Lee, a young teacher, his wife Annabel, a disturbed woman who rarely talks or moves, and Lee's brother Buzz, a voyeur who only experiences the world through photographs. "Mixing the grim, the exotic, the farcical," writes Anita Van Vactor of *Listener,* "Miss Carter traces the growth of a three-way symbiosis, a hermetic mythology decorated by Annabel's suicide attempts." Lee's efforts to escape the relationship by taking a mistress or throwing out his brother are ineffective because of his ultimate devotion to Annabel. "Again [Carter] is concerned," writes the *Times Literary Supplement* reviewer, "with the darker side of sibling affection and the type of

love that consumes. [She] is extremely good at twining the macabre and unlikely with the possible. . . . Carter should add to her reputation by this taut study of strangeness."

Carter returned to an imaginary landscape in *The War of Dreams,* published in England as *The Infernal Desire Machines of Dr. Hoffman.* Using the surrealist goal of manifesting unconscious desires as the basis for her story, she creates Dr. Hoffman, a scientist who discovers "how to set the unconscious free," Sage writes, "and he begins to infiltrate reality with guerrilla images that slide out of mirrors to mingle with the citizenry." When the government bureaucrat Desiderio is beseiged with these hallucinations, he sets off on a quest to find Dr. Hoffman and destroy him. "Along the way," writes William Hjortsberg of the *New York Times Book Review,* "he meets a macabre traveling carnival, an Indian tribe living on river-barges and speaking a kind of birdsong, a troupe of Moroccan acrobats who juggle the dismembered parts of their own bodies, a 'connoisseur of catastrophe,' black African cannibals, Mongolian pirates, a herd of centaurs, and Albertina, Dr. Hoffman's beautiful, Oriental-looking daughter." He also visits a "surreal brothel where android prostitutes enact the transformation of flesh into vegetable, animal, machine," Sage writes. In the end, Desiderio destroys the dream machines of Dr. Hoffman and saves reality. He "chooses the real, chooses contentment rather than ecstasy, reason rather than passion," writes J. D. O'Hara of the *Washington Post Book World.* "So does Carter." Ironically, despite the protagonist's restoration of the real world, *The War of Dreams* marked Carter "more decisively than any of her work up to that point," Sage believes, "as an aggressive anti-realist."

This anti-realist approach is also found in Carter's next novel, *The Passion of New Eve,* a violent sexual odyssey that takes Evelyn, an Englishman who abandons his pregnant girlfriend, from New York to California. Along the way he is captured in the desert by Amazons and surgically transformed into a woman, resides for a time with a Charles Manson-like cult, and finally meets his favorite movie actress, who turns out to be a transvestite. As Peter Ackroyd of *Spectator* writes, it "is a simple story of rape, castration, and apocalypse." Ackroyd particularly believes that Carter's "uneasy tone, perched somewhere between high seriousness and farce, unsettles the narrative as it leaps from one improbability to the next." Unfortunately, he also believes that the "language is so grandiose and verbose it can only transmit fantasies and visions and no novel can survive for long on such a meagre diet."

Sage sees *The Passion of New Eve* as being closely related to the themes presented in Carter's nonfiction book *The Sadeian Woman and the Ideology of Pornography.* This feminist study of pornography argues that the Marquis de Sade created in his pornographic novels truthful portraits of women as they exist in modern society. "In the looking-glass of Sade's misanthropy," Carter writes in the book, "women may see themselves as they have been and it is an uncomfortable sight." In his novels *Justine* and *Juliette,* Sade portrays two kinds of women: the first a passive sex object, the second a dominant tyrant. These, Carter believes, are the only two possibilities for women in an unfree society. What makes Sade unusual as a pornographer, and of special interest to feminists, Carter writes, was his "claiming rights of free sexuality for women, and in installing women as beings of power in his imaginary worlds. This sets him apart from all other pornographers at all times and most other writers of his period."

There are echoes of *The Sadeian Woman* in Carter's collection *Fireworks: Nine Stories in Various Disguises.* Michele Slung of the *Washington Post Book World* writes that "reading *Fireworks,*

I thought of Carter's 'ideology of pornography,' for these tales are nearly all exquisite while at the same time aggressively obscene. Like sinister fruits, they cause us to become addicted to their bizarre flavor." Victoria Glendinning of *New Statesman* finds that the stories "are the result of [Carter's] preoccupation with the imagery of the unconscious. . . . The real world [blossoms] strangely. The tales are full of puppets, mirrors, forests, sequined eyes, shells, flowers and diffuse lust." Although decrying what she sees as the familiarity of Carter's subjects, a familiarity she attributes to Carter's use of archetypal elements, Glendinning concludes: "Angela Carter is a genius of a wordspinner."

Sexual themes are also prevalent in Carter's second story collection, *The Bloody Chamber and Other Stories,* a collection Linda Rolens of the *Los Angeles Times Book Review* describes as "stories with disturbing eroticism" that are composed of "sexuality and violence." "An obsession with sadistic power and masochistic sacrifice pervades *The Bloody Chamber,*" writes Alan Friedman of the *New York Times Book Review.* Retelling old fairy tales in contemporary language, Carter's stories differ from the originals in one important way. "The difference is sex," as Carolyn G. Heilbrun of the *Washington Post Book World* writes. "[Carter] gives women an active part in the stories. In Carter's versions we are delighted to find women who are lusty and clever, animals who are tender and loving, and stories with a narrative pull like Scheherazade's." Susan Kennedy of the *Times Literary Supplement* believes that Carter's stories have "the power, not only to cause us to think again, and deeply, about the mythic sources of our common cultural touchstones, but to plunge us into hackle-raising speculation about aspects of our human/animal nature." "Carter . . . has tried her hand," Rolens states, "at the near impossible and succeeded: She has transformed classic fairy tales into potent adult tales."

Sage finds that although Carter has won several major literary awards, "her preoccupations as a writer—deepened and defined over the years—remain radically at odds with the puritanism and the conventional realism that characterize much British fiction." Moorehead also sees Carter as a unique writer, one whose "imaginary worlds are so original, so bizarre, and so full of talent that they have the clarity of dreams." Carter, who regards the fantasy element of her work as "social satire" or "social realism of the unconscious", explains in a *Publishers Weekly* interview, "I have always felt that one person's fantasy is another person's everyday life. It has its own logic as well. I got more and more into it as I got older, because it's a genre with its own rigorous logic." Describing *Brideshead Revisited,* for instance, as "the purest fantasy," Carter continues: "I have no kind of handle on those characters at all. I haven't been inside a house like that, even gone round to look at it. . . . The whole world of *Brideshead Revisited* is as alien to me as the moon."

BIOGRAPHICAL/CRITICAL SOURCES:

BOOKS

Carter, Angela, *The Sadeian Woman and the Ideology of Pornography,* Pantheon, 1979.
Contemporary Issues Criticism, Volume 1, Gale, 1982.
Contemporary Literary Criticism, Volume 5, Gale, 1976.
Dictionary of Literary Biography, Volume 14: *British Novelists since 1960,* Gale, 1983.

PERIODICALS

Books and Bookmen, February, 1975.
Chicago Tribune, April 22, 1985, September 26, 1986.
Globe and Mail (Toronto), April 20, 1985, March 26, 1988.

Library Journal, February 1, 1968.
Listener, May 20, 1971, September 26, 1974.
Los Angeles Times, April 19, 1985.
Los Angeles Times Book Review, March 16, 1980.
New Review, June/July, 1977.
New Statesman, July 8, 1966, November 14, 1969, August 16, 1974.
New York Times, January 30, 1985, April 19, 1985, July 26, 1989.
New York Times Book Review, February 25, 1968, March 2, 1969, September 13, 1970, September 8, 1974, February 17, 1980, June 14, 1981.
Publishers Weekly, January 4, 1985, June 17, 1986.
Saturday Review, February 18, 1967.
Spectator, March 26, 1977.
Times (London), September 27, 1984, October 10, 1985.
Times Literary Supplement, August 1, 1968, November 20, 1969, June 18, 1971, February 8, 1980, July 4, 1981, December 19, 1986.
Washington Post, December 1, 1989.
Washington Post Book World, August 18, 1974, February 24, 1980, June 28, 1981.

* * *

CARTER, James Earl, Jr. 1924-
(Jimmy Carter)

PERSONAL: Born October 1, 1924, in Archery, Ga.; son of James Earl (a grocer, farm machinery salesman, and politician) and Lillian (a nurse; maiden name, Gordy) Carter; married Rosalynn Smith, July 7, 1946; children: John William, James Earl III, Donnel Jeffery, Amy Lynn. *Education:* Attended Georgia Southwestern College, 1941-42, and Georgia Institute of Technology, 1942-43; U.S. Naval Academy, B.S., 1946; Union College, Schenectady, N.Y., graduate study, 1952. *Politics:* Democrat. *Religion:* Baptist.

ADDRESSES: Home—One Woodland Dr., Plains, Ga. 31780. *Office*—The Carter Center, One Copenhill, Atlanta, Ga. 30307.

CAREER: Farmer, owner, and chief executive of general purpose seed and farm supply firm, 1953-62, 1966-70; State Government, Atlanta, Ga., state senator, 1963-67, governor of Georgia, 1971-75; chairman of Democratic National Committee, 1972-74; United States Government, Washington, D.C., thirty-ninth president of the United States, 1977-81; engaged in farming, diplomacy, public service, and writing, 1981—; Emory University, Atlanta, distinguished professor, 1982—; Carter Center, Atlanta, founder, 1982, chairman of board of trustees, 1986—; Carter-Menhil Human Rights Foundation, Atlanta, president, 1986—.

Member, Sumter County School Board, 1955-62 (chairman, 1960-62), Americus and Sumter County Hospital Authority, 1956-70, Georgia Crop Improvement Association, 1957-63 (president, 1961), and Sumter County Library Board, 1962. President, Plains Development Corp., 1963, and Sumter Redevelopment Corp., 1963; member of executive board, West Central Georgia Planning and Development Commission (now Middle Flint Area Planning and Development Commission), 1964-69 (chairman, 1964). President, Georgia Planning Association, 1968; state chairman, March of Dimes, 1968-70; district governor, Lions Club, 1968-69. Member of board of directors, Habitat for Humanity, 1984-87. Deacon and Sunday School teacher, Baptist Church, Plains, Ga. *Military service:* U.S. Navy, 1947-53; became lieutenant commander.

AWARDS, HONORS: Gold medal from International Institute for Human Rights, 1979; International Mediation Medal from American Arbitration Association, 1979; Harry S. Truman Public Service Award, 1981; Ansel Adams Conservation Award from Wilderness Society, 1982; distinguished service award from Southern Baptist Convention, 1982; Human Rights Award from International League for Human Rights, 1983; Albert Schweitzer Prize for humanitarianism, 1987. Honorary doctorates from Morris Brown College, 1972, University of Notre Dame, 1977, Georgia Institute of Technology and Emory University, both 1979, Weizmann Institute of Science, 1980, Kwansei Gakuim University (Japan) and Georgia Southwestern College, both 1981, Tel Aviv University, 1983, New York Law School, Connecticut State University, and Bates College, all 1985, Centre College and Creighton University, both 1987.

WRITINGS:

UNDER NAME JIMMY CARTER

Why Not the Best? (autobiography), Broadman, 1975.
Addresses of Jimmy Carter, Governor of Georgia, 1971-75, edited by Frank Daniel, Georgia Department of Archives and History, 1975.
"I'll Never Lie to You": Jimmy Carter in His own Words, edited by Robert L. Turner, Ballantine, 1976.
The Wit and Wisdom of Jimmy Carter, edited by Bill Adler, Citadel Press, 1977.
A Government as Good as Its People, Simon & Schuster, 1977.
Carter on the Arts, ACA, 1977.
Letters to the Honorable William Prescott, Gordon Press, 1977.
Jimmy Carter, 1977, two volumes, U.S. Government Printing Office, 1977-78.
The Spiritual Journey of Jimmy Carter, in His Own Words, edited by Wesley G. Pippert, Macmillan, 1978.
Keeping Faith: Memoirs of a President, Bantam, 1983.
Negotiation: The Alternative to Hostility, Mercer University Press, 1984.
The Blood of Abraham: Insights into the Middle East, Houghton, 1985.
(With wife, Rosalynn Carter) *Everything To Gain: Making the Most of the Rest of Your Life,* Random House, 1987.
An Outdoor Journal: Adventures and Reflections, Bantam, 1988.

SIDELIGHTS: Jimmy Carter's singular career has led him from a peanut farm outside Plains, Georgia, to the White House in Washington, D.C., and then back again to Plains. The thirty-ninth president of the United States, Carter took office in 1977 and was defeated by Republican Ronald Reagan in 1981. Since his "retirement," Carter has written a number of books on subjects as varied as Middle East politics and fly fishing; he has also made the news for his participation in humanitarian causes, diplomatic missions, and human rights advocacy.

Most former presidents in the modern era have written memoirs after retiring from politics. Critics feel that what distinguishes Carter's from the rest is his authentic voice. As *Washington Post Book World* correspondent Edwin M. Yoder puts it, "no ghostwriter has haunted this house." Arthur Schlesinger, Jr. describes Carter's style in a *New York Times Book Review* piece. Schlesinger writes: "Carter's tone is direct, colloquial, engaging, often flat but sometimes oddly moving. His faith in work, discipline, education, character recalls an older and better America. He speaks without embarrassment about deeply personal things—trust, truth, the family, love and, when pressed, the Almighty. He rarely goes in for rhetorical pretense or flourish. It is the tone of a plain, homespun American talking seriously to his neighbors or his Sunday School class."

James Earl Carter, Jr. was born and raised in rural Georgia near the tiny town of Plains. His parents were strict Baptists who expected their children to work hard on the farm and in the general store they owned. As a youth Carter showed an aptitude for school work. His love of reading and his Baptist upbringing combined to make him a polite, conscientious student; he graduated at sixteen. After high school Carter attended Georgia Southwestern College and the Georgia Institute of Technology, each for a year. Then he was admitted to the United States Naval Academy at Annapolis. He graduated in the top ten percent of his class in 1946.

Carter expected to spend his whole career in the Navy after his success in Annapolis. In 1951 he was assigned to the nascent nuclear submarine program based in Schenectady, New York. There he was a senior officer on the precommissioning crew of the *Sea Wolf,* the second atomic submarine built in the United States. Carter spent two years studying nuclear physics and supervising the *Sea Wolf.* Then his father died, and he decided to return to Plains to run the family business. The Carter finances were in disarray when he took over, but soon they rebounded when Carter expanded his seed and fertilizer business and opened shelling and warehouse services for his fellow peanut growers. By 1956 Carter was a thriving businessman who was beginning to take steps toward a career in public service.

Carter moved slowly but steadily through the ranks of Georgia Democratic politics. He was somewhat hampered in the late 1950s by his open stand in favor of civil rights legislation for minorities. Carter was elected to the state senate in 1963; he served until 1967, when he was defeated in a primary election for governor. That defeat—once described by Carter as the low point in his life—sparked a "born again" religious experience. With new confidence born of his Christian faith, Carter returned to the political arena. He was elected governor of Georgia in 1970.

The Carter governorship of Georgia saw the employment of women and blacks in record numbers; it was also responsible for streamlining state agencies, opening day care and drug abuse rehabilitation centers, and monitoring the budget on a line-item basis. Concurrent with his governorship, Carter served as the national campaign committee chairman for the Democratic National Committee. In 1974 he announced his intention to run for the presidency of the United States.

Carter and his wife Rosalynn mounted a rigorous campaign for the 1976 nomination, travelling across America and speaking as many as six different places in a day. Carter also released an autobiography, *Why Not the Best?,* that described his youth on the farm, his ideals, and his inspirations. *New Republic* contributor John Seeyle has called *Why Not the Best?* "a classic of its kind, . . . a mixture of the heroic with the pastoral mode that is endemic to the mythic layer of the American identity." Seeyle adds that the work is "essential to an understanding of the meaning of Carter himself, as Jimmy Who? becomes Jimmy What Next?" In the *New York Times Book Review,* William V. Shannon suggests that candidate Carter's autobiography "is a skillful, simply-written blend of personal history, social description and political philosophy that makes fascinating reading." More than one critic has observed that the judicious publication of *Why Not the Best?* helped secure Carter's nomination as the Democratic candidate for president.

The Carter administration took power at a time when scandal had eroded public faith in the presidency. Carter helped to restore the presidential image, but he found himself burdened with rising inflation, high unemployment, and acts of hostility toward Americans abroad, especially in Iran. In the *New York Review of Books,* Nicholas von Hoffman also contends that Carter was "an alien and slightly distasteful figure to the prominent members of his party in Congress," rendering the president "the man running alone, the nude candidate." The last year of his presidency was especially difficult as Carter faced a hostage crisis in Iran that was only resolved the day his successor was sworn in. Still, writes William Shawcross in the *Spectator,* "there was a lot of solid achievement to the Carter years. . . . Carter made human rights for a time a central issue of much of American policy. This commitment, casually derided in drawing rooms of the West, was of immeasurable but immense importance to hundreds of thousands of people all over the world who languished under the neglect which Carter's predecessors and his successor[s] have displayed."

The most noticeable success of the Carter years was the landmark peace treaty between Egypt and Israel, drawn up at Camp David after days of delicate negotiation. A good portion of Carter's 1983 book *Keeping Faith: The Memoirs of a President* deals with the talks that brought an end to the hostilities between Egypt and Israel. That accomplishment helped give Carter "the world's best credentials as a Middle East peacemaker," to quote Stephen S. Rosenfeld in the *Washington Post Book World.* Since leaving the White House, Carter has continued—as a concerned private citizen—to work for peace in that region. In 1985 he published *The Blood of Abraham: Insights into the Middle East,* an account of his interviews with the area's rulers in the 1980s. *Los Angeles Times Book Review* contributor Marvin Seid notes that Carter's views on the Middle East "are shaped by compassion for all those, past and present, who have suffered in this cockpit of religious and nationalistic antagonisms."

Needless to say, Carter and his wife Rosalynn struggled with the sudden transition from public to private life. Both were able, however, to find meaningful goals and projects with which to fill their days. Carter continued his campaign for human rights and founded the Carter Center at Emory University in Atlanta. He also engaged in his favorite outdoor activities, hunting and fishing. In 1987, the two Carters published *Everything To Gain: Making the Most of the Rest of Your Life,* a tandem memoir and self-help book designed for those entering retirement. *New York Times Book Review* correspondent Letty Cottin Pogrebin calls the work "an inspiring account of the creation of a meaningful life—at home and in the larger world—by people who take their principles seriously enough to act on them. Basically, what the Carters decided to do with the rest of their lives was to focus on three personal and political ideals: promoting good health, fulfilling oneself, helping others." The critic concludes: "These are decent human beings. They do good things not because of a photo opportunity but because they believe one person can make a difference."

As a retired president, Carter still wields considerable influence in the political arena. His views are sought on developments in the Middle East, and he has made a number of trips to Central America as an observer. Carter told the *Chicago Tribune:* "Even though I'm out of office, I have access to nearly any leader in the world. I can bring together people who are experts on a specific subject, experts on starvation, on better ways to immunize children, on ways to alleviate human rights suffering. And I can invite political leaders who have the authority to do something about it." Carter offered his personal philosophy in a *Washington Post* profile. "No matter where you live in this nation and no matter what your level of income might be," he said, "you can always find things to do that are productive, helpful to others, challenging, interesting and to some degree adventurous." He concluded: "The second half [of life] can be the best half. And

it can also prove that when you think you are making a sacrifice for the benefit of others, that can turn out to be the greatest advantage and most enjoyable experience of your own life."

BIOGRAPHICAL/CRITICAL SOURCES:

BOOKS

Allen, Gary, *Jimmy Carter—Jimmy Carter,* Seventy Six, 1976.
Carter, Jimmy, *Why Not the Best?,* Broadman, 1975.
Carter, Jimmy, *I'll Never Lie to You: Jimmy Carter in His Own Words,* edited by Robert Turner, Ballantine, 1976.
Carter, Jimmy, *Keeping Faith: Memoirs of a President,* Bantam, 1983.
Slosser, Bob and Howard Norton, *The Miracle of Jimmy Carter,* Logos, 1976.
Wheeler, Leslie, *Jimmy Who?,* Barron's, 1976.

PERIODICALS

Chicago Tribune, March 31, 1985, April 28, 1985, June 12, 1987.
Contemporary Review, September, 1985.
Globe & Mail (Toronto), July 13, 1985.
Harper's, August, 1979.
Los Angeles Times, May 20, 1987, October 14, 1987.
Los Angeles Times Book Review, November 7, 1982, April 7, 1985, August 14, 1988, September 11, 1988.
New Republic, September 11, 1976, June 16, 1979, December 6, 1982.
New Yorker, January 17, 1983, May 20, 1985.
New York Review of Books, August 5, 1976, August 4, 1977, December 16, 1982.
New York Times, June 1, 1982, November 3, 1982, April 18, 1985, December 10, 1985.
New York Times Book Review, June 6, 1976, June 5, 1977, November 7, 1982, April 28, 1985, May 31, 1987, July 3, 1988.
Spectator, January 1, 1983, August 3, 1985.
Time, June 15, 1987.
Times (London), February 6, 1987.
Times Literary Supplement, February 14, 1986.
Village Voice, July 12, 1976.
Washington Post, November 11, 1982, June 2, 1987, June 3, 1987.
Washington Post Book World, October 31, 1982, March 31, 1985, June 5, 1988.

—*Sketch by Anne Janette Johnson*

*　　　*　　　*

CARTER, Jimmy
See CARTER, James Earl, Jr.

*　　　*　　　*

CARTLAND, Barbara (Hamilton) 1901-
(Barbara McCorquodale)

PERSONAL: Born July 9, 1901, in England; daughter of Bertram and Polly (Scobell) Cartland; married Alexander George McCorquodale, 1927 (marriage dissolved, 1933); married Hugh McCorquodale, December 28, 1936 (died December 29, 1963); children: (first marriage) Raine (Countess Spencer); (second marriage) Ian, Glen. *Education:* Attended Malvern Girls' College and Abbey House, Netley Abbey, Hampshire, England. *Politics:* Conservative. *Religion:* Church of England.

ADDRESSES: Home—Camfield Pl., Hatfield, Hertfordshire, England. *Office*—c/o Berkley Publications, Inc., 200 Madison

Ave., New York, NY 10016. *Agent*—Rupert Crew Ltd., King's Mews, Gray's Inn Rd., London WC1N 2JA, England.

CAREER: Writer. Lecturer, historian, political speaker for the Conservative office, and television personality. County councillor for Hertfordshire, nine years; services welfare officer for Bedfordshire, 1941-45; currently chairman of the St. John Council and deputy president of St. John Ambulance Brigade, Hertfordshire, and president of Hertfordshire branch of Royal College of Midwives.

MEMBER: Oxfam (vice-president), National Association of Health (deputy president, 1965; president, 1966).

AWARDS, HONORS: Dame of Grace, St. John of Jerusalem, Certificate of Merit, Eastern Command, 1946; National Home Furnishings Association Woman of the Year Award, 1981; Bishop Wright Air Industry Award for contribution to developing aviation, 1984.

WRITINGS:

NOVELS

Jigsaw, Duckworth, 1925.
Sawdust, Duckworth, 1926.
If the Tree Is Saved, Duckworth, 1929.
For What?, Hutchinson, 1930.
Sweet Punishment, Hutchinson, 1931, Pyramid Publications, 1973.
A Virgin in Mayfair, Hutchinson, 1932, published as *An Innocent in Mayfair,* Pyramid Publications, 1976.
Just off Piccadilly, Hutchinson, 1933, published as *Dance on My Heart,* Pyramid Publications, 1977.
Not Love Alone, Hutchinson, 1933.
A Beggar Wished, Hutchinson, 1934, published as *Rainbow to Heaven,* Pyramid Publications, 1976.
Passionate Attainment, Hutchinson, 1935.
First Class, Lady?, Hutchinson, 1935, published as *Love and Linda,* Pyramid Publications, 1976.
Dangerous Experiment, Hutchinson, 1936, published as *Search for Love,* Greenberg, 1937.
Desperate Defiance, Hutchinson, 1936, Pyramid Publications, 1977.
The Forgotten City (also see below), Hutchinson, 1936.
Saga at Forty, Hutchinson, 1937, published as *Love at Forty,* Pyramid Publications, 1977.
But Never Free, Hutchinson, 1937, published as *The Adventurer,* Pyramid Publications, 1977.
Broken Barriers, Hutchinson, 1938, Pyramid Publications, 1976.
Bitter Winds, Hutchinson, 1938, published as *The Bitter Winds of Love,* Jove, 1978.
The Gods Forget, Hutchinson, 1939, published as *Love in Pity,* Pyramid Publications, 1976.
The Black Panther, Rich & Cowan, 1939, published as *Lost Love,* Pyramid Publications, 1970, reprinted under original title, Hutchinson, 1972.
Stolen Halo, Rich & Cowan, 1940, reprinted, Hutchinson, 1970, published as *The Audacious Adventuress,* Pyramid Publications, 1972, reprinted under original title, 1973.
Now Rough, Now Smooth, Hutchinson, 1941.
Open Wings, a Twenty-Third Novel, Hutchinson, 1942, published as *Open Wings,* Pyramid Publications, 1976.
The Leaping Flame, R. Hale, 1942, Pyramid Publications, 1974.
The Dark Stream, Hutchinson, 1944, published as *This Time It's Love,* Pyramid Publications, 1977.
After the Night, Hutchinson, 1944, published as *Towards the Stars,* 1971, Pyramid Publications, 1975.

Yet She Follows, R. Hale, 1945, published as *A Heart Is Broken,* 1972, Pyramid Publications, 1974.
Escape from Passion, R. Hale, 1945, Pyramid Publications, 1977.
Armour against Love, Hutchinson, 1945, Pyramid Publications, 1974.
Out of Reach, Hutchinson, 1945, reprinted, Hurst & Blackett, 1972.
The Hidden Heart, Hutchinson, 1946, Pyramid Publications, 1970.
Against the Stream, Hutchinson, 1946, Pyramid Publications, 1977.
The Dream Within, Hutchinson, 1947, Pyramid Publications, 1976.
If We Will, Hutchinson, 1947, published as *Where Is Love?,* 1971, Jove, 1978.
Again This Rapture, Hutchinson, 1947, Pyramid Publications, 1977.
No Heart Is Free, Rich & Cowan, 1948, Pyramid Publications, 1975.
A Hazard of Hearts, Rich & Cowan, 1949, Pyramid Publications, 1969.
The Enchanted Moment, Rich & Cowan, 1949, Pyramid Publications, 1976.
A Duel of Hearts, Rich & Cowan, 1949, Pyramid Publications, 1970.
The Knave of Hearts, Rich & Cowan, 1950, Pyramid Publications, 1971.
The Little Pretender, Rich & Cowan, 1950, Pyramid Publications, 1971.
Love Is an Eagle, Rich & Cowan, 1951, Pyramid Publications, 1975.
A Ghost in Monte Carlo, Rich & Cowan, 1951, Pyramid Publications, 1973.
Love Is the Enemy, Rich & Cowan, 1952, Pyramid Publications, 1970.
Cupid Rides Pillion, Hutchinson, 1952, reprinted, Hurst & Blackett, 1969, published as *The Secret Heart,* Pyramid Publications, 1970.
Elizabethan Lover, Hutchinson, 1953, Pyramid Publications, 1971.
Love Me for Ever, Hutchinson, 1954, published as *Love Me Forever,* Pyramid Publications, 1970.
Desire of the Heart, Hutchinson, 1954, Pyramid Publications, 1969.
The Enchanted Waltz, Hutchinson, 1955, Pyramid Publications, 1971.
The Kiss of the Devil, Hutchinson, 1955, Jove, 1981.
The Captive Heart, Hutchinson, 1956, Pyramid Publications, 1970, published as *The Royal Pledge,* 1970.
The Coin of Love, Hutchinson, 1956, Pyramid Publications, 1969.
Sweet Adventure, Hutchinson, 1957, Pyramid Publications, 1970.
Stars in My Heart, Hutchinson, 1957, Pyramid Publications, 1971.
The Golden Gondola, Hutchinson, 1958, Pyramid Publications, 1971.
Love in Hiding, Hutchinson, 1959, Pyramid Publications, 1969.
The Smuggled Heart, Hutchinson, 1959, published as *Debt of Honor,* Pyramid Publications, 1970, reprinted under original title, Jove, 1982.
Love under Fire, Hutchinson, 1960, Pyramid Publications, 1972.
Messenger of Love, Hutchinson, 1961, Pyramid Publications, 1971.

The Wings of Love, Hutchinson, 1962, Pyramid Publications, 1971.

The Hidden Evil, Hutchinson, 1963, Pyramid Publications, 1971.

The Fire of Love, Hutchinson, 1964, Avon, 1970.

The Unpredictable Bride, Hutchinson, 1964, Pyramid Publications, 1969.

Love Holds the Cards, Hutchinson, 1965, Pyramid Publications, 1970.

A Virgin in Paris, Hutchinson, 1966, Pyramid Publications, 1971, published as *An Innocent in Paris,* 1975, reprinted under original title, Jove, 1981.

Love to the Rescue, Hutchinson, 1967, Pyramid Publications, 1970.

Love Is Contraband, Hutchinson, 1968, Pyramid Publications, 1970.

The Enchanting Evil, Hutchinson, 1968, Pyramid Publications, 1969.

The Unknown Heart, Hutchinson, 1969, Pyramid Publications, 1971.

The Innocent Heiress, Pyramid Publications, 1970.

The Reluctant Bride, Hutchinson, 1970, Pyramid Publications, 1972.

The Secret Fear, Hutchinson, 1970, Pyramid Publications, 1971.

The Pretty Horse-Breakers, Hutchinson, 1971, Pyramid Publications, 1975.

The Queen's Messenger, Pyramid Publications, 1971.

Stars in Her Eyes, Pyramid Publications, 1971.

Lost Enchantment, Hutchinson, 1972, Pyramid Publications, 1973.

A Halo for the Devil, Hutchinson, 1972, Pyramid Publications, 1977.

The Irresistible Buck, Hutchinson, 1972, Pyramid Publications, 1975.

The Complacent Wife, Hutchinson, 1972, Jove, 1981.

The Daring Deception, Bantam, 1973.

The Little Adventure, Hutchinson, 1973, Bantam, 1974.

The Wicked Marquis, Hutchinson, 1973, Bantam, 1974.

The Odious Duke, Hutchinson, 1973, Pyramid Publications, 1975.

Journey to Paradise, Bantam, 1974.

No Darkness for Love, Bantam, 1974.

The Bored Bridegroom (also see below), Bantam, 1974.

The Castle of Fear, Bantam, 1974.

The Cruel Count, Pan Books, 1974, Bantam, 1975.

The Dangerous Dandy, Bantam, 1974.

Lessons in Love, Bantam, 1974.

The Penniless Peer, Bantam, 1974.

The Ruthless Rake, Bantam, 1974.

The Glittering Lights, Bantam, 1974.

A Sword to the Heart, Bantam, 1974.

Fire on the Snow, Hutchinson, 1975, Bantam, 1976.

Bewitched, Bantam, 1975.

The Call of the Heart, Bantam, 1975.

The Devil in Love (also see below), Bantam, 1975.

The Flame Is Love, Bantam, 1975.

The Frightened Bride, Bantam, 1975.

The Impetuous Duchess, Bantam, 1975.

The Karma of Love, Bantam, 1975.

Love Is Innocent, Bantam, 1975.

The Magnificent Marriage (also see below), Bantam, 1975.

The Mask of Love, Bantam, 1975.

Shadow of Sin, Bantam, 1975.

The Tears of Love, Bantam, 1975.

A Very Naughty Angel, Bantam, 1975.

As Eagles Fly, Bantam, 1975.

Say Yes, Samantha, Bantam, 1975.

The Elusive Earl, Bantam, 1976.

An Angel in Hell, Bantam, 1976.

An Arrow of Love, Bantam, 1976.

The Blue-eyed Witch, Bantam, 1976.

A Dream from the Night, Bantam, 1976.

The Fragrant Flower, Bantam, 1976.

A Frame of Dreams, Bantam, 1976.

A Gamble with Hearts, Bantam, 1976.

The Golden Illusion, Bantam, 1976.

The Heart Triumphant, Bantam, 1976.

Hungry for Love, Bantam, 1976.

The Husband Hunters, Bantam, 1976.

The Incredible Honeymoon, Bantam, 1976.

A Kiss for the King, Bantam, 1976.

Love in Hiding, Pyramid Publications, 1976.

Moon over Eden, Bantam, 1976.

Never Laugh at Love, Bantam, 1976.

No Time for Love, Bantam, 1976.

Passions in the Sand, Bantam, 1976.

The Proud Princess (also see below), Bantam, 1976.

The Secret of the Glen, Bantam, 1976.

The Slaves of Love, Bantam, 1976.

The Wild Cry of Love, Bantam, 1976.

Conquered by Love, Bantam, 1976.

Love Locked In, Dutton, 1977.

The Mysterious Maid-servant, Bantam, 1977.

The Wild Unwilling Wife, Dutton, 1977.

The Castle Made for Love, Duron Books, 1977.

The Curse of the Clan, Duron Books, 1977.

The Dragon and the Pearl, Duron Books, 1977.

The Hell-cat and the King, Duron Books, 1977.

Look, Listen and Love, Duron Books, 1977.

Love and the Loathsome Leopard, Duron Books, 1977.

The Love Pirate, Duron Books, 1977.

The Marquis Who Hated Women, Duron Books, 1977.

The Naked Battle, Duron Books, 1977.

No Escape from Love, Duron Books, 1977.

The Outrageous Lady, Duron Books, 1977.

Punishment of a Vixen, Duron Books, 1977.

The Saint and the Sinner, Duron Books, 1977.

The Sign of Love, Duron Books, 1977.

The Temptation of Torilla, Duron Books, 1977.

A Touch of Love, Duron Books, 1977.

The Dream and the Glory, Bantam, 1977.

A Duel with Destiny, Bantam, 1977.

Kiss the Moonlight (also see below), Pan Books, 1977.

The Magic of Love, Bantam, 1977.

A Rhapsody of Love, Pan Books, 1977.

The Taming of Lady Lorinda, Bantam, 1977.

Vote for Love, Bantam, 1977.

The Disgraceful Duke, Bantam, 1977.

Love at the Helm, Weidenfeld & Nicolson, 1977, Everest House, 1981.

The Chieftain without a Heart, Dutton, 1978.

A Fugitive from Love, Duron Books, 1978.

The Ghost Who Fell in Love, Dutton, 1978.

Love Leaves at Midnight, Duron Books, 1978.

Love, Lords, and Lady-birds, Dutton, 1978.

The Passion and the Flower, Dutton, 1978.

The Twists and Turns of Love, Duron Books, 1978.

The Irresistible Force, Duron Books, 1978.

The Judgment of Love, Duron Books, 1978.

Lord Ravenscar's Revenge, Duron Books, 1978.

Lovers in Paradise, Duron Books, 1978.
A Princess in Distress, Duron Books, 1978.
The Race for Love, Duron Books, 1978.
A Runaway Star, Duron Books, 1978.
Magic or Mirage?, Duron Books, 1978.
Alone in Paris, Hutchinson, 1978, Duron Books, 1979.
Flowers for the God of Love, Pan Books, 1978, Dutton, 1979.
The Problems of Love, Duron Books, 1978.
The Best of Barbara Cartland (contains *The Proud Princess, The Magnificent Marriage, The Bored Bridegroom, Kiss the Moonlight,* and *The Devil in Love*), Grosset, 1979.
The Drums of Love, Duron Books, 1979.
The Duke and the Preacher's Daughter, Duron Books, 1979.
Imperial Splendor, Dutton, 1979.
Light of the Moon, Duron Books, 1979.
Love in the Clouds, Dutton, 1979.
Love in the Dark, Duron Books, 1979.
The Prince and the Pekingese, Duron Books, 1979.
Love Climbs In, Duron Books, 1979.
The Prisoner of Love, Duron Books, 1979.
A Serpent of Satan, Duron Books, 1979.
The Treasure Is Love, Duron Books, 1979.
The Duchess Disappeared, Duron Books, 1979.
A Nightingale Sang, Duron Books, 1979.
The Dawn of Love, Corgi, 1979, Dutton, 1980.
A Gentleman in Love, Pan Books, 1979, Bantam, 1980.
Only Love, Hutchinson, 1979, Bantam, 1980.
Bride to the King, Corgi, 1979, Dutton, 1980.
Women Have Hearts, Pan Books, 1979, Bantam, 1980.
Terror in the Sun, Bantam, 1979.
Who Can Deny Love?, Bantam, 1979, hardcover edition, Duron Books, 1980.
Love Has His Way, Bantam, 1979, hardcover edition, Duron Books, 1980.
The Explosion of Love, Bantam, 1979.
A Song of Love, Jove, 1980.
Love for Sale, Dutton, 1980.
Lost Laughter, Dutton, 1980.
Free from Fear, Bantam, 1980.
The Goddess and the Gaiety Girl, Bantam, 1980.
Little White Doves of Love, Bantam, 1980.
Ola and the Sea Wolf, Bantam, 1980.
The Perfection of Love, Bantam, 1980.
The Prude and the Prodigal, Bantam, 1980.
Punished with Love, Bantam, 1980.
Heart Is Stolen (published in *Barbara Cartland's World of Romance* magazine), Corgi, 1980.
The Power of the Prince, Bantam, 1980.
Lucifer and the Angel, Bantam, 1980.
Signpost to Love, Bantam, 1980.
From Hell to Heaven, Bantam, 1981.
Pride and the Poor Princess, Bantam, 1981.
Count the Stars, Jove, 1981.
Dollars for the Duke, Bantam, 1981.
Dreams Do Come True, Bantam, 1981.
The Heart of the Clan, Jove, 1981.
In the Arms of Love, Jove, 1981.
Touch a Star, Jove, 1981.
The Kiss of Life, Bantam, 1981.
The Lioness and the Lily, Bantam, 1981.
Love in the Moon, Bantam, 1981.
A Night of Gaiety, Bantam, 1981.
The Waltz of Hearts, Bantam, 1981.
The Wings of Ecstasy, Jove, 1981.
For All Eternity, Jove, 1981.

Afraid, Bantam, 1981.
Love in the Moon, Bantam, 1981.
Enchanted, Bantam, 1981.
Winged Magic, Bantam, 1981.
A Portrait of Love, Bantam, 1981.
The River of Love, Bantam, 1981.
Gift of the Gods, Bantam, 1981.
An Innocent in Russia, Bantam, 1981.
A Shaft of Sunlight, Bantam, 1981.
Pure and Untouched, Bantam, 1981.
Love Wins, Bantam, 1982.
Secret Harbor, Bantam, 1982.
Looking for Love, Bantam, 1982.
The Vibrations of Love, Bantam, 1982.
Lies for Love, Bantam, 1982.
Love Rules, Bantam, 1982.
The Call of the Highlands, Hutchinson, 1982.
Caught by Love, Arrow, 1982.
A King in Love, Everest House, 1982.
Kneel for Mercy, New English Library, 1982.
Love and the Marquis, Pan Books, 1982.
Moments of Love, Pan Books, 1982.
Riding to the Moon, Everest House, 1982.
Diona and a Dalmation, Hutchinson, 1983.
A Duke in Danger, Pan Books, 1983.
Fire in the Blood, Pan Books, 1983.
From Hate to Love, New English Library, 1983.
Gypsy Magic, Pan Books, 1983.
Lights, Laughter, and a Lady, New English Library, 1983.
Love and Lucia, Pan Books, 1983.
Love on the Wind, Pan Books, 1983.
A Marriage Made in Heaven, Corgi, 1983.
A Miracle in Music, Corgi, 1983.
Mission to Monte Carlo, Corgi, 1983.
Tempted to Love, Pan Books, 1983.
Wish for Love, Corgi, 1983.
Barbara Cartland's Princess to the Rescue (juvenile), illustrated by Jane Longmore, F. Watts, 1984.
Bride to a Brigand, New English Library, 1984.
Help from the Heart, Arrow, 1984.
The Island of Love, Pan Books, 1984.
Journey to a Star, Corgi, 1984.
Light of the Gods, Corgi, 1984.
Love Comes West, Pan Books, 1984.
Miracle for a Madonna, Hutchinson, 1984.
Moonlight on the Sphinx, Hutchinson, 1984.
The Peril and the Prince, New English Library, 1984.
Revenge of the Heart, Pan Books, 1984.
Royal Punishment, Severn House, 1984.
The Scots Never Forget, Corgi, 1984.
Theresa and a Tiger, New English Library, 1984.
The Unbreakable Spell, Corgi, 1984.
The Unwanted Wedding, Corgi, 1984.
A Very Unusual Wife, Pan Books, 1984.
White Lilac, Pan Books, 1984.
Alone and Afraid, Pan Books, 1985.
The Devilish Deception, Jove, 1985.
Escape, Jove, 1986.
Look with Love, Pan Books, 1985.
Paradise Found, Jove, 1985.
A Rebel Princess, Corgi, 1985.
Safe at Last, Jove, 1986.
Temptation for a Teacher, Pan Books, 1985.
A Witch's Spell, Corgi, 1985.
An Angel Runs Away, Jove, 1987.

Crowned with Love, Jove, 1986.
The Devil Defeated, Jove, 1986.
A Dream in Spain, Jove, 1986.
The Golden Cage, Jove, 1986.
Haunted, Jove, 1986.
Helga in Hiding, Jove, 1986.
Listen to Love, Jove, 1986.
Love Casts Out Fear, Severn House, 1986, Jove, 1987.
Love Joins the Clans, Pan Books, 1986, Jove, 1987.
The Love Trap, Jove, 1986.
Secret of the Mosque, Pan Books, 1986.
Bewildered in Berlin, Jove, 1987.
Dancing on a Rainbow, Jove, 1987.
The Earl Escapes, Jove, 1987.
Love and Kisses, Jove, 1987.
The Love Puzzle, Jove, 1987.
Forced to Marry, Jove, 1987.
The Love Puzzle, Jove, 1987.
Starlight over Tunis, Jove, 1987.
Wanted—A Wedding Ring, Jove, 1987.
A World of Love, Jove, 1987.
Sapphires in Siam, Jove, 1988.
A Nightingale Sang, State Mutual Book, 1988.

Also author of *Secrets,* 1983, *Love Is a Gamble,* 1985, *Love Is Heaven,* 1985, *Real Love or Fake, The Marquis Wins, Love Is the Key, Love at First Sight, The Secret Princess, Heaven in Hong Kong, Paradise in Penang,* and *A Game for Love.*

"CAMFIELD ROMANCE" SERIES; PUBLISHED BY JOVE

The Poor Governess, 1982.
Winged Victory, 1982.
Lucky in Love, 1982.

NOVELS UNDER NAME BARBARA McCORQUODALE; ALL REPRINTED UNDER NAME BARBARA CARTLAND

Sleeping Swords, R. Hale, 1942.
Love Is Mine, Rich & Cowan, 1952, Pyramid Publications, 1972.
The Passionate Pilgrim, Rich & Cowan, 1952, Pyramid Publications, 1976.
Blue Heather, Rich & Cowan, 1953, Pyramid Publications, 1975.
Wings on My Heart, Rich & Cowan, 1954, Pyramid Publications, 1975.
The Kiss of Paris, Rich & Cowan, 1956, Pyramid Publications, 1972.
The Thief of Love, Jenkins, 1957, Pyramid Publications, 1975.
Love Forbidden, Rich & Cowan, 1957, Pyramid Publications, 1973.
Lights of Love, Jenkins, 1958, Pyramid Publications, 1973.
The Sweet Enchantress, Jenkins, 1958, Pyramid Publications, 1976.
A Kiss of Silk, Jenkins, 1959, Pyramid Publications, 1974.
The Price Is Love, Jenkins, 1960, Pyramid Publications, 1973.
The Run-away Heart, Jenkins, 1961, Pyramid Publications, 1974.
A Light to the Heart, Ward, Lock, 1962, Pyramid Publications, 1973.
Love Is Dangerous, Ward, Lock, 1963, Pyramid Publications, 1976.
Danger by the Nile, Ward, Lock, 1964, Avon, 1975.
Love on the Run, Ward, Lock, 1965, Pyramid Publications, 1973.
Theft of a Heart, Ward, Lock, 1966, Pyramid Publications, 1977.

BIOGRAPHIES

Ronald Cartland (biography of author's brother), preface by Winston Churchill, Collins, 1942, reprinted with introduction by Arthur Bryant, S.P.C.K., 1980.
Bewitching Women, Muller, 1955.
Polly: The Story of My Wonderful Mother, Jenkins, 1956, reprinted, Hutchinson, 1971.
The Outrageous Queen: A Biography of Christina of Sweden, Muller, 1956, Pyramid Publications, 1977.
The Scandalous Life of King Carol, Muller, 1957, reprinted, Corgi, 1974.
The Private Life of Charles II: The Women He Loved, Muller, 1958, reprinted, Corgi, 1974.
The Private Life of Elizabeth, Empress of Austria, Muller, 1959, Pyramid Publications, 1974.
Josephine, Empress of France, Hutchinson, 1961, Pyramid Publications, 1974.
Diane de Poitiers, Hutchinson, 1962.
Metternich: The Passionate Diplomat, Hutchinson, 1964, Pyramid Publications, 1974.

AUTOBIOGRAPHIES

The Isthmus Years: Reminiscences of the Years 1919-1939, Hutchinson, 1943.
The Years of Opportunity: 1939-1945, Hutchinson, 1948.
I Search for Rainbows: 1946-1966, Hutchinson, 1967.
We Danced All Night: 1919-1929, Hutchinson, 1970, Pyramid Publications, 1972.
I Seek the Miraculous, Dutton, 1978.

OTHER NONFICTION

Touch the Stars: A Clue to Happiness, Rider & Co., 1935.
(Editor) Ronald Cartland, *The Common Problem,* Hutchinson, 1943.
You—in the Home, Standard Art Book Co., 1946.
The Fascinating Forties: A Book for the Over-forties, Jenkins, 1954, revised edition, Corgi, 1973.
Marriage for Moderns, Jenkins, 1955.
Be Vivid, Be Vital, Jenkins, 1956.
Love, Life and Sex, Jenkins, 1957, revised edition, Corgi, 1973.
Look Lovely, Be Lovely, Jenkins, 1958.
Vitamins for Vitality, W. & G. Foyle, 1959.
Husbands and Wives, Arthur Barker, 1961, published as *Love and Marriage,* Thorson's, 1971.
Etiquette Handbook, Paul Hamlyn, 1962, revised edition published as *Barbara Cartland's Book of Etiquette,* Hutchinson, 1972.
The Many Facets of Love, W. H. Allen, 1963.
Sex and the Teenager, Muller, 1964.
Living Together, Muller, 1965.
The Pan Book of Charm, Pan Books, 1965.
Woman, the Enigma, Frewin, 1965, Pyramid Publications, 1974.
The Youth Secret, Corgi, 1968, Bantam, 1973.
The Magic of Honey, Corgi, 1970, Pyramid Publications, 1973, revised edition, Corgi, 1977.
Barbara Cartland's Health Food Cookery Book, Hodder & Stoughton, 1972, published as *Barbara Cartland's Health Food Cookery,* Pyramid Publications, 1975.
Barbara Cartland's Book of Beauty and Health, Hodder & Stoughton, 1972.
Men Are Wonderful, Corgi, 1973.
Food for Love, Corgi, 1975.
The Magic of Honey Cookbook, Corgi, 1976.
(With Nigel Gordon) *Recipes for Lovers,* Corgi, 1977, Bantam, 1978.

(Editor) *Barbara Cartland's Book of Useless Information,* foreword by Earl Mountbatten, Bantam, 1977.
Barbara Cartland's Book of Love and Lovers, Ballantine, 1978.
(Editor) *The Light of Love: A Thought for Every Day,* Sheldon Press, 1979, published as *The Light of Love: Lines to Live by Day by Day,* Elsevier/Nelson, 1980.
Romantic Royal Marriages, Beaufort Book Co., 1981.
Barbara Cartland's Etiquette for Love and Romance, Pocket Books, 1984.
Getting Older, Growing Younger, Dodd, 1984.
The Romance of Food, Doubleday, 1984.
Barbara Cartland's Book of Health, Javelin, 1985.

EDITOR; "BARBARA CARTLAND'S LIBRARY OF LOVE" SERIES

Edith Maude Hull, *The Sheik,* Bantam, 1977.
Ethel May Dell, *The Hundredth Chance,* Bantam, 1977.
Dell, *The Knave of Diamonds,* Bantam, 1977.
Dell, *The Way of an Eagle,* Bantam, 1977.
Elinor Glyn, *The Reason Why,* Bantam, 1977.
Ian Hay, *A Safety Match,* Bantam, 1977.
Dell, *The Bars of Iron,* Bantam, 1977.
Glyn, *Man and Maid,* Bantam, 1977.
Glyn, *The Vicissitudes of Evangeline,* Bantam, 1977.
Hull, *The Lion Tamer,* Bantam, 1977.
Hull, *The Sons of the Sheik,* Bantam, 1977.
Glyn, *His Hour,* Bantam, 1977.
Pamela Wynne, *Ashes of Desire,* Bantam, 1978.
Berta Ruck, *His Official Fiancee,* Bantam, 1978.
Dell, *Tetherstones,* Bantam, 1978.
Glyn, *The Sequence,* Bantam, 1978.
Glyn, *The Price of Things,* Bantam, 1978.
Jeffrey Farnol, *The Amateur Gentleman,* Bantam, 1978.
Farnol, *The Broad Highway,* Bantam, 1978.
Gene S. Porter, *Freckles,* Bantam, 1978.
Wynne, *Rainbow in the Spray,* Bantam, 1978.
Glyn, *The Great Moment,* Bantam, 1978.
Glyn, *It,* Bantam, 1978.
Glyn, *Six Days,* Bantam, 1978.
Dell, *Greatheart,* Bantam, 1978.
Vere Lockwood, *Ramazan the Rajah,* Bantam, 1979.
Farnol, *The Money Moon,* Bantam, 1979.
Wynne, *Leave It to Love,* Bantam, 1979.
L. Adams Beck, *The Treasure of Ho* (also see below), Bantam, 1979.
Dell, *The Rocks of Valpre,* Bantam, 1979.
Charles Garvice, *Only a Girl's Love,* Bantam, 1980.
Ruck, *The Bridge of Kisses,* Bantam, 1980.
Lockwood, *Son of the Turk,* Bantam, 1980.
Dell, *The Obstacle Race,* Bantam, 1980.

OTHER

Also author of two plays, "Blood Money," 1925, and, with Bruce Woodhouse, "French Dressing," 1943; author of libretto for radio operetta "The Rose and the Violet," produced in 1942; author of radio play "The Caged Bird: An Episode in the Life of Elizabeth, Empress of Austria," 1957. Has also written for television. Editor of "Barbara Cartland's Library of Ancient Wisdom" series, published by Bantam and Howard & Wyndham, including *The Forgotten City,* by Cartland, *Black Light,* by Talbot Mundy, *Romance of Two Worlds,* by Marie Corelli, and *House of Fulfillment* and *The Treasure of Ho,* both by L. Adams Beck. Author of columns "Here's Health" and "Instant Cookery." Contributor of articles to newspapers and of stories to magazines.

SIDELIGHTS: Known throughout the world as the "Queen of Romance," Barbara Cartland is today's most prolific writer of romantic fiction. With nearly 300 million copies of her novels in print (the *Guinness Book of World Records* lists her as the best-selling author in the world), Cartland, observes *People* magazine, is a veritable "one-woman fantasy factory." Her typical fantasy is quite simple—a chaste and beautiful young woman meets a rich and handsome (but charmingly rakish) man in an exotic place, usually some time during the nineteenth century. They then proceed to fall in love and spend much of their time on the verge of giving in to passion. After overcoming an assortment of obstacles, the still-pure heroine finally marries her ideal and together they allow their emotions free rein at the end of the novel, as in this last line from *Dollars for the Duke:* "Then love carried them on the waves of ecstasy into the starlit sky, and they knew that nothing mattered except that as man and woman they were one now and through all eternity."

Cartland admits her plots are similar, but insists that she has never repeated a situation. "Of course," she explained to an interviewer from the *New Yorker,* "as I always write a story with a virgin heroine, we know the story is always going to be very much the same, because the girl is pure and the man isn't. The man will go to bed with any woman who takes his fancy, so I've got to keep him from going to bed with the heroine until page two hundred, when she has a wedding ring on her finger. I tried writing modern books, but I found it very difficult to create convincing virgins in modern dress, so my stories are always set between approximately 1790 and 1890. As the plots are always similar, I must vary the situations, and I must have exciting and real backgrounds, absolutely authentic. This is the part that interests me most. I love history, and I love research, and I do an enormous amount of it." She also does an enormous amount of traveling, and it is not at all unusual for her to eventually write about some of the many places she has visited: Bali, Singapore, Nepal, Hong Kong, Senegal, Martinique, Guadeloupe, Grenada, and India, to name just a few.

After Cartland does this research, she needs only seven days to complete a novel. Reclining on a chaise lounge in her library, a rug tucked around her feet and her pet Pekingese cuddled next to her, she dictates a chapter a day to a stenographer who arrives promptly at one o'clock and begins to take down Cartland's 10,000-word, two-and-a-quarter-hour-long monologue. "Dictation is why my books sell so well," she told a *Maclean's* interviewer. "When you dictate, you tend to tell your story in nice short little paragraphs. My readers detest long paragraphs." Indeed, her paragraphs are rarely over three lines long, and the lack of subplots in her novels virtually eliminates any complications that could necessitate somewhat lengthier explanations or descriptions. "I keep the story about the hero and heroine solid all the way through," she remarked in *Publishers Weekly.* "There's no time for anything else." Cartland also attributes much of her success to the lack of "pornography" in her novels. "My readers are sick of it," she declared in *Maclean's.* "After all, you can't get more naked than naked and my readers begin to wonder if they're normal when they don't have sex upside down swinging from chandeliers. No, my readers want to read about ladies being made love to gently in the moon light with a frilly nightie on, and that's what I give them." Furthermore, she pointed out in the *New Yorker,* "my books are an escape from the depression and boredom and lack of romance in modern life. And I think I'm the only person who writes what I call straight love—you know, the real Cinderella story—and I think that's the answer. I mean, one has frightfully complicated plots, but they all get unwound in the end and everybody's happy and everything is wonderful. That's what people want."

In addition to its prominent position (above the title and in larger type) on the cover of every one of the books, the Cartland name now adorns a variety of other items. In 1978, for instance, "Barbara Cartland's Album of Love Songs," a recording in which the author was backed by none other than the Royal Philharmonic Orchestra, made its first appearance in the stores. In late 1979, publisher Theodore B. Dolmatch launched *Barbara Cartland's World of Romance,* a monthly magazine featuring a full-length Cartland novel in every issue plus beauty tips, recipes, an astrological column, and profiles with such titles as "Bewitching Women" and "Great Lovers." "Barbara Cartland's Romances," a comic strip based on some of the author's novels, was first offered to newspapers in the United States and abroad by United Features Syndicate in late 1980; a paperback collection of the comics followed a year later.

The spring of 1981 marked the beginning of two more major undertakings bearing the Cartland name, both of which were quite unrelated to publishing: a "Decorating with Love" home furnishings collection, consisting of wallpaper, curtains, table linens, bath accessories, stationery, and other items, all with a pink flowers-and-ribbons design inspired by Cartland's own sketches; and "Barbara Cartland's Romantic Tours," a deluxe seven-day tour of England organized with the typical Cartland reader in mind. As an added attraction, the tour participants lunch with Cartland's daughter and son-in-law, Countess Spencer and Earl Spencer (father of Diana, Princess of Wales), and have tea with the author herself at her country estate. Future Cartland endorsements include a line of perfumes, beauty products, and vitamins.

The novels, however, still reign supreme in the Cartland empire. As Scot Haller of the *Saturday Review* points out, she and other writers of genre fiction have an indisputable talent for satisfying—and reflecting—"the fantasies and desires of vast segments of the book-buying public"; in short, he echoes Cartland's own observation that "that's what people want." Concludes the critic: "For the women who make up 98 percent of Cartland's audience, her novels offer a joy ride through the time tunnel, a travel to an era of seemingly simpler morality and marriages. Although the history lessons differ from title to title, the plots are interchangeable. Her constancy *is* her appeal. Like her chaste heroines, the author is forever faithful to her fans (and her formula). In that regard, she has earned the title frequently bestowed upon her: the High Priestess of Love."

BIOGRAPHICAL/CRITICAL SOURCES:

BOOKS

Cartland, Barbara, *The Isthmus Years: Reminiscences of the Years 1919-1939,* Hutchinson, 1943.
Cartland, Barbara, *The Years of Opportunity: 1939-1945,* Hutchinson, 1948.
Cartland, Barbara, *I Search for Rainbows: 1946-1966,* Hutchinson, 1967.
Cartland, Barbara, *We Danced All Night: 1919-1929,* Hutchinson, 1970, Pyramid Publications, 1972.
Cartland, Barbara, *I Seek the Miraculous,* Dutton, 1978.
Cloud, Henry, *Crusader in Pink,* Everest House, 1980.
Contemporary Authors Autobiography Series, Volume 8, Gale, 1989.
Wyett, Kenneth, *My Key to Life,* Skeffington, 1958.

PERIODICALS

Books, February 21, 1937.
Books and Bookmen, June, 1968, August, 1968, November, 1968, August, 1969, April, 1971.
Dublin Evening Press, July 28, 1976.
Los Angeles Times Book Review, March 25, 1979.
Maclean's, December 11, 1978.
New Statesman, August 4, 1967.
New Yorker, August 9, 1976.
People, May 25, 1981.
Publishers Weekly, June 7, 1976, April 17, 1981.
Punch, August 9, 1967, February 3, 1971.
Saturday Review, March, 1981.
Times Literary Supplement, November 2, 1967.

*   *   *

CARVER, Raymond   1938-1988

PERSONAL: Born May 25, 1938, in Clatskanie, Ore.; died of lung cancer, August 2, 1988, in Port Angeles, Wash.; son of Clevie Raymond (a laborer) and Ella (maiden name, Casey; a homemaker) Carver; married Maryann Burk (a teacher), June 7, 1957 (divorced, October, 1983); children: Christine L., Vance L. *Education:* Humboldt State College (now California State University, Humboldt), A.B., 1963; University of Iowa, further study, 1963-64. *Politics:* Democrat.

ADDRESSES: Home—602 B St., Port Angeles, Wash. 98362. *Agent*—Amanda Urban, International Creative Management, 40 West 57th St., New York, N.Y. 10019.

CAREER: Manual laborer, c. late 1950s-early 1960s; Science Research Associates, Inc., Palo Alto, Calif., editor, 1967-70; University of California, Santa Cruz, lecturer in creative writing, 1971-72; University of California, Berkeley, lecturer in fiction writing, 1972-73; Syracuse University, Syracuse, N.Y., professor of English, 1980-83; writer. Visiting professor of English, Writers Workshop, University of Iowa, 1973-74; visiting distinguished writer, University of Texas at El Paso, 1978-79.

MEMBER: International PEN (member of executive board).

AWARDS, HONORS: National Endowment for the Arts Discovery Award for poetry, 1970; Joseph Henry Jackson Award for fiction, 1971; Wallace Stegner Creative Writing Fellowship, Stanford University, 1972-73; National Book Award nomination in fiction, 1977, for *Will You Please Be Quiet, Please?,* Guggenheim fellowship, 1977-78; National Endowment for the Arts Award in fiction, 1979; Carlos Fuentes Fiction Award, for short story "The Bath"; Mildred and Harold Strauss Living Award, American Academy and Institute of Arts and Letters, 1983; National Book Critics Circle Award nomination in fiction, 1984, and Pulitzer Prize nomination for fiction, 1985, both for *Cathedral;* Levinson Prize for poetry, 1985; National Book Critics Circle Award nomination in fiction, 1988, and Pulitzer Prize nomination for fiction, 1989, both for *Where I'm Calling From.*

WRITINGS:

Near Klamath (poems), Sacramento State College, 1968.
Winter Insomnia (poems), Kayak, 1970.
Put Yourself in My Shoes, Capra, 1974.
Will You Please Be Quiet, Please? (short stories), McGraw, 1976.
At Night the Salmon Move (poems), Capra, 1976.
Furious Seasons (short stories), Capra, 1977.
What We Talk about When We Talk about Love (short stories), Knopf, 1981.
Two Poems, Scarab Press, 1982.

The Pheasant, Metacom, 1982.

Fires: Essays, Poems, Stories, 1966-1982, Capra, 1983.

(Author of foreword) John Gardner, *On Becoming a Novelist,* Harper, 1983.

(Author of introduction) William Kittredge, *We Are Not in This Together,* Greywolf Press, 1984.

Cathedral (short stories), Knopf, 1984.

If It Please You, Lord John, 1984.

Dostoevsky: The Screenplay, Capra, 1985.

The Stories of Raymond Carver, Picador, 1985.

Where Water Comes Together with Other Water (poems), Random House, 1985.

This Water, Ewert, 1985.

Ultramarine (poems), Random House, 1986.

(Editor with Shannon Ravenel) *The Best American Short Stories 1986,* Houghton, 1986.

In a Marine Light (selected poems), Harvill, 1987.

Saints, Random House, 1987.

(Editor with Tom Jenks) *American Short Story Masterpieces,* Delacorte, 1987.

Elephant (short stories), Jungle Garden, 1988.

Where I'm Calling From: New and Selected Stories, Atlantic Monthly Press, 1988.

A New Path to the Waterfall (poems), Atlantic Monthly Press, 1989.

Also author, with Michael Cimino, of script "Purple Lake." Guest editor, *The Best American Short Stories,* 1986. Contributor to anthologies, including *The Best American Short Stories,* 1967, 1982, and 1983, *Short Stories from the Literary Magazines, Best Little Magazine Fiction,* 1970 and 1971, *Prize Stories: The O. Henry Awards,* 1973, 1974, 1975, and 1983, *Pushcart Prize Anthology,* 1976, 1981, 1982, and 1983, *New Voices in American Poetry,* and *The Generation of 2000: Contemporary American Poets.*

Contributor of poems and stories to national periodicals, including *Esquire, New Yorker, Atlantic,* and *Harper's,* and to literary journals, including *Paris Review, Antaeus, Georgia Review, Ohio Review,* and *Poetry.* Editor, *Quarry* (magazine), 1971-72; editor, *Ploughshares,* Volume 9, number 4, 1983.

SIDELIGHTS: Raymond Carver is one of a handful of contemporary short story writers credited with reviving what was once thought of as a dying literary form. His stories mainly take place in his native Pacific Northwest region; they are peopled with the type of lower-middle-class characters the author was familiar with while he was growing up. In a *New York Review of Books* article, Thomas R. Edwards describes Carver's fictional world as a place where "people worry about whether their old cars will start, where unemployment or personal bankruptcy are present dangers, where a good time consists of smoking pot with the neighbors, with a little cream soda and M&M's on the side. . . . Carver's characters are waitresses, mechanics, postmen, high school teachers, factory workers, door-to-door salesmen. [Their surroundings are] not for them a still unspoiled scenic wonderland, but a place where making a living is as hard, and the texture of life as drab, for those without money, as anywhere else."

Carver's own life would seem to parallel that of one of his characters. Born in an Oregon logging town, the author was married and the father of two before he was twenty years old. Also like his characters, Carver worked at a series of lowpaying jobs: he "picked tulips, pumped gas, swept hospital corridors, swabbed toilets, [and] managed an apartment complex," according to Bruce Weber in a *New York Times Magazine* profile of the author. Carver's wife at the time, continues Weber, "worked for the phone company, waited tables, [and] sold a series of book digests door-to-door." Not coincidentally, "of all the writers at work today, Carver may have [had] the most distinct vision of the working class," as Ray Anello observes in a *Newsweek* article. Carver taught creative writing in California and produced two books of poetry before his first book of short stories, *Will You Please Be Quiet, Please?,* was published in 1976.

In introducing readers to his world of the desperation of ordinary people, Carver created tales that are "brief . . . but by no means stark," notes Geoffrey Wolff in his *New York Times Book Review* piece on *Will You Please Be Quiet, Please?* Continues the critic: "They imply complexities of action and motive and they are especially artful in their suggestion of repressed violence. No human blood is shed in any of these stories, yet almost all of them hold a promise of mayhem of some final, awful breaking from confines, and breaking through to liberty." The theme of breaking from confines is central to one of the stories, "Neighbors," in which Bill and Arlene Miller agree to feed their neighbors' cat while the neighbors, the Stones, are on vacation. With access to the Stones' home, the Millers find themselves increasingly taken with their friends' clothes, furniture, and other belongings. Bill and Arlene, in fact, begin to assume the identities of the Stones; "each finds this strangely stimulating, and their sex life prospers, though neither can find anything much to say about it at all," reports Edwards. The end of the story finds the Millers clinging to the Stones' door as their neighbors return, knowing that their rich fantasy life will soon end.

The author's "first book of stories explored a common plight rather than a common subject," notes *New York Times Book Review* critic Michael Wood. "His characters were lost or diminished in their own different ways. The 17 stories in [Carver's third collection, *What We Talk about When We Talk about Love*], make up a more concentrated volume, less a collection than a set of variations on the themes of marriage, infidelity and the disquieting tricks of human affection." "The first few pieces seem thin and perfunctory," Adam Mars-Jones writes in the *Times Literary Supplement,* "and there is a recurring pattern . . . of endings which lurch suddenly sideways, moving off in a direction that seems almost random." Anatole Broyard finds such endings frustrating. In his *New York Times* review of *What We Talk about When We Talk about Love,* Broyard criticizes what he calls "the most flagrant and common imposition in current fiction, to end a story with a sententious ambiguity that leaves the reader holding the bag."

"Perhaps there is a reason for this," says Mars-Jones. "Endings and titles are bound to be a problem for a writer like Carver, since readers and reviewers so habitually use them as keys to interpret everything else in a story. So he must make his endings enigmatic and even mildly surrealist, and his titles for the most part oblique. Sometimes he over-compensates." And *Newsweek*'s Peter S. Prescott feels that all seventeen stories in Carver's third collection "are excellent, and each gives the impression that it could not have been written more forcefully, or in fewer words."

Prescott also notes that the author is concerned "with the collapse of human relationships. Some of his stories take place at the moment things fall apart; others, after the damage has been done, while the shock waves still reverberate. Alcohol and violence are rarely far removed from what happens, but sometimes, in another characteristic maneuver, Carver will nudge the drama that triggers a crisis aside to show that his story has really been about something else all along." "Carver's is not a particularly lyrical prose," says Weber in his *New York Times Magazine* article: "A typical sentence is blunt and uncomplicated, eschewing the ornaments of descriptive adverbs and parenthetical phrases. His rhythms are often repetitive or brusque, as if to suggest the strain of people learning to express newly felt things, fresh emotions. Time passes in agonizingly linear fashion, the chronology of a given scene marked by one fraught and simple gesture after another. Dialogue is usually clipped, and it is studded with commonplace observations of the concrete objects on the table or on the wall rather than the elusive, important issues in the air."

Of Carver's 1984 short fiction collection, *Cathedral,* "it would be hard to imagine a more dispirited assortment of figures," declares David Lehman in a *Newsweek* review. A "note of transcendent indifference, beyond resignation or fatigue, is sounded" in each story, adds Lehman, cautioning, "fun to read they're not." But, the critic stresses, "it's impossible to ignore Carver's immense talent." In *Cathedral,* Carver rewrites the ending of one of his most acclaimed stories from *What We Talk about When We Talk about Love.* The original story, "The Bath," is about a mother who orders a special cake for her eight-year-old son's birthday—but the boy is hit by a car on that day and is rushed to the hospital, where he lingers in a coma. The baker, aware only that the parents haven't picked up their expensive cake, badgers them with endless calls demanding his money. As the story ends, the boy's fate is still unknown, and the desperate parents hear the phone ring again. In *Cathedral,* the author retells this story (now titled "A Small, Good Thing") up to the final phone ring. At this point, ambiguity vanishes; Carver reveals that the boy has died, and the call is from the irate baker. But this time the parents confront the baker with the circumstances, and the apologetic man invites them over to his bakery. There he tells the parents his own sad story of loneliness and despair and feeds them fresh coffee and warm rolls, because "eating is a small, good thing in a time like this."

"In revising 'The Bath' into 'A Small, Good Thing,' Carver has indeed gone into [what he describes as] 'the heart of what the story is about,' and in the process has written an entirely new story—has created, if you will, a completely new world," declares Jonathan Yardley in the *Washington Post Book World.* "The first version is beautifully crafted and admirably concise, but lacking in genuine compassion; the mysterious caller is not so much a human being as a mere voice, malign and characterless. But in the second version that voice becomes a person, one whose own losses are, in different ways, as crippling and heartbreaking as the one suffered by the grieving parents." As Broyard writes in a *New York Times* review of *Cathedral,* "It is typical of Mr. Carver's stories that comfort against adversity is found in incongruous places, that people find improbable solace. The improbable and the homely are [the author's] territory. He works in the bargain basement of the soul." Yardley maintains that " 'The Bath' is a good short story," while " 'A Small; Good Thing' comes breathtakingly close to perfection."

New Republic reviewer Dorothy Wickenden agrees that "A Small, Good Thing" and the story "Cathedral" "are astute, even complex, psychological dramas," but remarks that "a touch of sentimentality, an element previously foreign to Carver's work, has crept into these stories. Perhaps because he doesn't quite trust the sense of hope with which he leaves his characters, the writing at the end becomes self-consciously simple and the scenes of resolution contrived." Yet "compared with his previous two collections of stories," Broyard concludes, "[*Cathedral*] shows an increase in vitality. Like a missionary, Mr. Carver seems to be gradually reclaiming or redeeming his characters."

According to *New York Times Book Review* critic Irving Howe, Carver's stories evoke "strong American literary traditions. For-

mally, they summon remembrances of Hemingway and perhaps Stephen Crane, masters of tightly packed fiction. In subject matter they draw upon the American voice of loneliness and stoicism, the native soul locked in this continent's space. [The author's] characters, like those of many earlier American writers, lack a vocabulary that can release their feelings, so they must express themselves mainly through obscure gesture and berserk display." And Paul Gray, writing about *Cathedral* in *Time,* says that "Carver's art masquerades as accident, scraps of information that might have been overheard at the supermarket checkout or local beer joint. His most memorable people live on the edge: of poverty, alcoholic self-destruction, loneliness. Something in their lives denies them a sense of community. They feel this lack intensely, yet are too wary of intimacy to touch other people, even with language."

Such appraisals of his writing left Carver himself a little wary. He told Weber: "Until I started reading these reviews of my work, praising me, I never felt the people I was writing about were so bad. . . . The waitress, the bus driver, the mechanic, the hotel keeper. God, the country is filled with these people. They're good people. People doing the best they could."

Carver's 1988 short fiction collection *Where I'm Calling From,* released shortly before his death, combines new and previously published stories. The entire volume is colored by Carver's standard themes of alienation, failed relationships, and death, but critics generally considered the newer contributions softer and more rambling than the author's earlier, more intense pieces. *Where I'm Calling From* was nominated for both a Pulitzer Prize and a National Book Critics Circle Award. Selected works by Carver have been translated into at least twenty foreign languages, including Dutch, Arabic, and Japanese.

AVOCATIONAL INTERESTS: Travel.

BIOGRAPHICAL/CRITICAL SOURCES:

BOOKS

Carver, Raymond, *Cathedral,* Knopf, 1984.
Contemporary Literary Criticism, Gale, Volume 22, 1982, Volume 26, 1983, Volume 53, 1989, Volume 55, 1989.
Dictionary of Literary Biography Yearbook, Gale, *1984,* 1985, *1988,* 1989.
Lohafer, Susan, *Coming to Terms with the Short Story,* Louisiana State University Press, 1983.
Weaver, Gordon, editor, *The American Short Story, 1945-1980,* Twayne, 1983.

PERIODICALS

Akros Review, spring, 1984.
Antioch Review, spring, 1984.
Atlantic, June, 1981.
Boston Globe, July 17, 1983.
Canto, Volume 2, number 2, 1978.
Chariton Review, spring, 1984.
Chicago Tribune, October 28, 1986.
Chicago Tribune Book World, October 2, 1983.
Contemporary Literature, winter, 1982.
Detroit News, October 2, 1983.
Eureka Times-Standard (Eureka, Calif.), June 24, 1977.
Georgia Review, fall, 1982.
Globe and Mail (Toronto), November 24, 1984, July 2, 1988.
Harper's Bookletter, April 26, 1976.
Hudson Review, summer, 1976, autumn, 1981, spring, 1984.
Iowa Review, summer, 1979.
London Review of Books, February 2-15, 1984.

Los Angeles Times, May 25, 1988.
Los Angeles Times Book Review, May 24, 1981, October 2, 1983, October 26, 1986, December 28, 1986, January 31, 1988, June 26, 1988.
Nation, July, 1981.
New Republic, April 25, 1981, November 14, 1983.
Newsweek, April 27, 1981, September 5, 1983.
New York, April 20, 1981.
New York Review of Books, November 24, 1983.
New York Times, April 15, 1981, September 5, 1983, May 11, 1988, May 31, 1988.
New York Times Book Review, March 7, 1976, April 26, 1981, February 9, 1986, June 7, 1987, May 15, 1988.
New York Times Magazine, June 24, 1984.
Paris Review, summer, 1983.
People, November 23, 1987.
Philological Quarterly, winter, 1985.
Saturday Review, April, 1981, October, 1983.
Studies in Short Fiction, winter, 1984.
Time, April 6, 1981, September 19, 1983.
Times (London), January 21, 1982, April 17, 1985, May 16, 1985.
Times Literary Supplement, January 22, 1982, February 17, 1984, May 24, 1985, September 15, 1989.
Tribune Books (Chicago), May 8, 1988.
Village Voice, September 18, 1978.
Washington Post Book World, May 3, 1981, September 4, 1983, May 15, 1988.

OBITUARIES:

PERIODICALS

Chicago Tribune, August 3, 1988, August 7, 1988.
Los Angeles Times, August 4, 1988.
New York Times, August 3, 1988.
Times (London), August 4, 1988.
Washington Post, August 4, 1988.

*   *   *

CASARES, Adolfo Bioy
See BIOY CASARES, Adolfo

*   *   *

CASTANEDA, Carlos   1931(?)-

PERSONAL: Author gives birthdate and place as December 25, 1931, in Sao Paulo, Brazil; cites Castaneda as an adopted surname. Immigration records list name as Carlos Cesar Aranha Castaneda, birthdate as December 25, 1925, and place as Cajmarcs, Peru; son of C. N. and Susana (Aranha) Castaneda; came to United States in 1951. Other sources list birthdate from 1925 to late 1930s. *Education:* University of California, Los Angeles, B.A., 1962, M.A., 1964, Ph.D., 1970.

ADDRESSES: Home—308 Westwood Plaza, B101, Los Angeles, Calif. 90024. *Office*—c/o Simon & Schuster, Inc., 1230 Avenue of the Americas, New York, N.Y. 10020. *Agent*—Ned Brown, 407 North Maple Dr., Beverly Hills, Calif. 90210.

CAREER: Anthropologist.

WRITINGS:

The Teachings of Don Juan: A Yaqui Way of Knowledge, University of California Press, 1968.
A Separate Reality: Further Conversations with Don Juan, Simon & Schuster, 1971.

Journey to Ixtlan: The Lessons of Don Juan, Simon & Schuster, 1972.
Tales of Power, Simon & Schuster, 1974.
Trilogy (three volumes), Simon & Schuster, 1974.
Don Juan Quartet (boxed set; includes *The Teachings of Don Juan: A Yaqui Way of Knowledge, A Separate Reality: Further Conversations with Don Juan, Journey to Ixtlan: The Lessons of Don Juan,* and *Tales of Power*), Simon & Schuster, 1975.
The Second Ring of Power, Simon & Schuster, 1977.
The Eagle's Gift, Simon & Schuster, 1981.
The Fire from Within, Simon & Schuster, 1984.
The Power of Silence: Further Lessons of Don Juan, Simon & Schuster, 1987.

SIDELIGHTS: Carlos Castaneda's recorded experiences as an apprentice to Don Juan, a Yaqui Indian *brujo,* or sorcerer, are detailed in his many books, all of which deal with becoming a Yaqui "man of knowledge." According to Castaneda, Don Juan sensed in the younger man "the possibility of a disciple and proceeded to introduce him, by way of rigorous curriculum, into realms of esoteric experience which clash disconcertingly with our prevailing scientific conception of reality," writes *Nation* contributor Theodore Roszak in a review of the author's first book, *The Teachings of Don Juan: A Yaqui Way of Knowledge.* The world through which Don Juan wished to lead Castaneda initially included using hallucinogenic drugs in order to attain certain experiences, although as the books progress, other means are used to reach different levels of consciousness.

A Separate Reality: Further Conversations with Don Juan records Castaneda's subsequent visits with Don Juan and his continuing visits to other phases of the intangible world. *Natural History* contributors William and Claudia Madsen feel the book's strength lies in its presentation of sorcery: "In his haunting story, [Castaneda] draws you into the weird world of witches—a world you will never be able to explain or forget. . . . Castaneda's work is unique because it reveals an inside view of how witchcraft works." However, *New York Times Book Review* contributor William Irwin Thompson thinks that by concentrating on the narrative instead of striving for an anthropological report, Castaneda's style becomes more readable. Throughout his books, the author shows himself as an occasional bungler and reports his teacher's often harsh criticism of his mistakes. Thompson notes this and remarks that Castaneda "can parody himself and mock his own ignorance without ever tilting the balance away from Don Juan toward himself. The tone is . . . perfect for the book."

Journey to Ixtlan: The Lessons of Don Juan concentrates on how a sorcerer becomes a "man of power" through "seeing" instead of using the ordinary means of perception, "looking." In *Book World,* Barry Corbet notes: "*Ixtlan* marks an enormous change in Castaneda. . . . His reporting is warm, human and perceptive. The extraordinary thing is that the book represents very little new teaching from don Juan, but is the result of Castaneda's new ability to discern the best of the earlier teachings. This is a book of rejects, all the field notes he previously considered irrelevant. And it is this material which makes *Ixtlan* such staggeringly beautiful reading. . . . *Journey to Ixtlan* is one of the important statements of our time." A *Times Literary Supplement* contributor, however, feels that Castaneda has drawn too close to his subject, and has "rejected the objective and scientific approach to [his] subject-matter in favour of an extravagant empathy with the human object of [his] studies." While a *Time* contributor, like many other critics, finds Don Juan himself puzzling, he appreciates the *Journey to Ixtlan:* "Indeed, though

[Don Juan] is an enigma wrapped in mystery wrapped in a tortilla, [Castaneda's books are] beautifully lucid. [His] story unfolds with a narrative power unmatched in other anthropological studies. . . . In detail, it is as thoroughly articulated a world as, say, Faulkner's Yoknapatawpha County. In all the books, but especially in *Journey to Ixtlan,* Castaneda makes the reader experience the pressure of mysterious winds and the shiver of leaves at twilight, the hunter's peculiar alertness to sound and smell."

Tales of Power continues with Castaneda's mysterious experiences, although this book centers more on the pupil's dealings with the unseen than with the lessons of his master. Michael Mason, however, writes in the *New Statesman* that Castaneda's ideas may not be as unusual as they seem: "Ideas from European existentialism pervade the book more than Castaneda's admirers might care to recognise," Mason claims. He adds: "*Tales of Power* is not a work of mysticism." Mason also voices an objection to seeing Castaneda as a student of Yaqui spiritism: "The awkwardness arises of how Castaneda can be achieving enlightenment if he is such a spiritual clodhopper." *New York Times Book Review* contributor Elsa First finds the tale more convincing, however: "This is a splendid book, for all that it may seem ungainly, at times ponderous, at others overwrought. . . . [*Tales of Power*] could well be read as a farcical picaresque epic of altered states of consciousness. . . . One of the finest things in [*Tales of Power*], however stylized or fictional it may be, is the convincing portrait of a spiritual teacher working away at his student's tendency to 'indulge' in self-dramatization and self-pity."

Despite the factual presentation of Castaneda's books, many critics have debated whether Don Juan really exists. *New York Times Book Review* Paul Riesman sees them as scholarly works: "Taken together—and they should be read in the order they were written—[Carlos Castaneda's books] form a work which is among the best that the science of anthropology has produced." In another *New York Times Book Review* article, however, Joyce Carol Oates states another view: "I realize that everyone accepts them as anthropological studies, yet they seem to me remarkable works of art, on the Hesse-like theme of a young man's initiation into 'another way' of reality." And Dudley Young, also writing in the *New York Times Book Review,* questions Don Juan's credibility: "Since we are given virtually no information about the Don's credentials as a sorcerer (or indeed about his family or friends) it is very difficult to decide whether his symbology has genuine ethnic roots in Yaqui culture, whether he is just a more or less harmless crank, or whether he was seeking a corrupting kind of power over his disciple. . . . But Mr. Castaneda nowhere considers this possibility." Other reviewers, however, have dismissed the question of Don Juan's origins as irrelevant. According to *Washington Post* contributor Joseph McLellan: "The material in Castaneda's books is probably rooted in some sort of objective or hallucinatory experience—not cynically invented. If he had made it all up, as some observers have suggested, he could surely have produced something more interesting and coherent; something in which he is not seen so constantly as a dimwitted blunderer. Seen in context with other mystical writings, Castaneda's work seems less eccentric and its authenticity seems less dubious. . . . But by the same token, his work becomes less interesting—simply an exotic variant on fairly well-known themes."

Other critics have voiced different objections to Castaneda's writings. Weston LaBarre, in *Seeing Castaneda: Reactions to the "Don Juan" Writings of Carlos Castaneda,* questions the disciple's memory: "The long disquisition of Don Juan and the detailing of each confused emotional reaction of the author, . . . imply

either total recall, novelistic talent, or a tape recorder." And in *Horizon,* Richard de Mille brings up what he considers important inconsistencies: "First, the so-called field reports contradict each other. Carlos meets a certain witch named La Catalina for the first time in 1962 and *again* for the first time in 1965. . . . A second kind of proof arises from absence of convincing detail and presence of implausible detail. . . . A third kind of proof is found in [Don] Juan's teachings, which combine American Indian folklore, oriental mysticism, and European philosophy. Indignantly dismissing such a proof, [Don] Juan's followers declare that enlightened minds think alike in all times and places, but there is more to the proof than similar ideas; there are similar words." But according to Joshua Gilder in his *Saturday Review* article on *The Eagle's Gift:* "It isn't necessary to believe to get swept up in Castaneda's other-worldly narrative; like myth it works a strange and beautiful magic beyond the realm of belief. . . . Sometimes, admittedly, one gets the impression of a con artist simply glorifying in the game—even so, it is a con touched by genius."

BIOGRAPHICAL/CRITICAL SOURCES:

BOOKS

Contemporary Literary Criticism, Volume 12, Gale, 1980.
LaBarre, Weston, *Seeing Castaneda: Reactions to the "Don Juan" Writings of Carlos Castaneda,* edited by Daniel C. Noel, Putnam, 1976.

PERIODICALS

American Anthropologist, Volume 71, number 2, 1969.
Book World, October 22, 1972, November 17, 1974.
Horizon, April, 1979.
Nation, February 10, 1969.
Natural History, June, 1971.
New Statesman, June 27, 1975.
New York Times Book Review, September 29, 1968, February 13, 1972, October 22, 1972, November 26, 1972, October 27, 1974, January 22, 1978.
Psychology Today, December, 1977.
Saturday Review, May, 1981.
Time, November 6, 1972, March 5, 1973.
Times Literary Supplement, June 15, 1973.
Washington Post, December 18, 1987.

—*Sketch by Jani Prescott*

*   *   *

CATHER, Willa
    See CATHER, Willa Sibert

*   *   *

CATHER, Willa Sibert   1873-1947
    (Willa Cather)

PERSONAL: Given name originally Wilella; born December 7, 1873, in Back Creek Valley, Va.; died of a cerebral hemorrhage, April 24, 1947, in New York, N.Y.; daughter of Charles F. (a rancher and insurance salesman) and Mary Virginia (Boak) Cather. *Education:* University of Nebraska, A.B., 1895.

CAREER: Newspaper correspondent in Nebraska, c. 1890-1895; *Daily Leader,* Pittsburgh, Pa., telegraph editor and drama critic, 1897-1901; traveled in Europe, 1902; Allegheny High School, Pittsburgh, teacher of English and Latin and head of English department, 1902-1905; *McClure's*, New York, N.Y., managing editor, 1906-1911; full-time writer, 1911-1947.

MEMBER: American Academy of Arts and Letters.

AWARDS, HONORS: Pulitzer Prize for fiction from Columbia University Graduate School of Journalism, 1922, for *One of Ours;* Howells Medal from the American Academy and Institute of Arts and Letters, 1930, for *Death Comes for the Archbishop;* Prix Femina Americaine, 1932, for distinguished literary accomplishment; Gold Medal of the National Institute of Arts and Letters, 1944; honorary degrees from University of Nebraska, University of Michigan, University of California, and Columbia, Yale, Princeton, and Creighton universities.

WRITINGS:

NOVELS, UNDER NAME WILLA CATHER, EXCEPT AS NOTED

(Under name Willa Sibert Cather) *April Twilights* (poems), Badger, 1903, revised edition published under name Willa Cather, edited by Bernice Slote, University of Nebraska Press, 1968.

(Under name Willa Sibert Cather) *The Troll Garden* (short stories), McClure, Philips, 1905, reprinted with an afterword by Katherine Anne Porter, New American Library, 1961, definitive edition published under name Willa Cather, edited with introduction and notes by James Woodress, University of Nebraska Press, 1983.

(Under name Willa Sibert Cather) *Alexander's Bridge*, Houghton, 1912, published as *Alexander's Bridges*, Heinemann, 1912, revised edition with preface, Houghton, 1922, reprinted under name Willa Cather with introduction by Sharon O'Brien, New American Library, 1988.

(Under name Willa Sibert Cather) *O Pioneers!*, Houghton, 1913, reprinted under name Willa Cather, Thorndike, 1986.

(Under name Willa Sibert Cather) *The Song of the Lark*, Houghton, 1915, reprinted under name Willa Cather, with a new preface by Cather, J. Cape, 1936, revised edition, with introduction by A. S. Byatt, Virago, 1982, reprinted with foreword by Doris Grumbach, Houghton, 1988.

(Under name Willa Sibert Cather) *My Antonia*, illustrations by W. T. Bends, Houghton, 1918, reprinted with introduction by Walter Havighurst, 1949, reprinted, Thorndike, 1986.

Youth and the Bright Medusa (short stories), Knopf, 1920.

One of Ours, Knopf, 1922, reprinted with introduction by Stanley T. Williams, 1926.

A Lost Lady, Knopf, 1923, reprinted, 1969.

The Professor's House, Knopf, 1925, reprinted with introduction by A. S. Byatt, Virago, 1981.

My Mortal Enemy, Knopf, 1926, reprinted with introduction by Byatt, Virago, 1982.

Death Comes for the Archbishop, Knopf, 1927, reprinted with illustrations by Harold Von Schmidt, 1929, reprinted with introduction by Byatt, Virago, 1981.

Shadows on the Rock, Knopf, 1931, reprinted with introduction by Byatt, Virago, 1984.

Obscure Destinies (short stories), Knopf, 1932.

Lucy Gayheart, Knopf, 1935.

Not Under Forty (essays and criticism), Knopf, 1936.

Sapphira and the Slave Girl, Knopf, 1940, reprinted, Vintage Books, 1975.

The Old Beauty and Others (short stories), Knopf, 1948.

COLLECTIONS, UNDER NAME WILLA CATHER

April Twilights and Other Poems, Knopf, 1923, enlarged, 1933, revised edition edited by Slote, University of Nebraska Press, 1962.

The Novels and Stories of Willa Cather, thirteen volumes, Houghton, 1937-1941.

Writings From Willa Cather's Campus Years, edited by James R. Shively, University of Nebraska Press, 1950.

Five Stories (includes article by George N. Kates), Vintage Books, 1956.

Early Stories of Willa Cather, edited by Mildred R. Bennett, Dodd, 1957, reprinted, 1983.

Willa Cather's Collected Short Fiction, 1892-1912, edited by Virginia Faulkner, University of Nebraska Press, 1965, revised, 1970.

The Kingdom of Art: Willa Cather's First Principles and Critical Statements, 1893-1896, edited by Slote, University of Nebraska Press, 1966.

The World and the Parish: Willa Cather's Articles and Reviews, 1893-1902, two volumes, edited by William M. Curtin, University of Nebraska Press, 1970.

Uncle Valentine and Other Stories, edited by Slote, University of Nebraska Press, 1973.

Willa Cather in Person: Interviews, Speeches, and Letters, selected and edited by L. Brent Bohlke, University of Nebraska Press, 1986.

Willa Cather: Twenty-four Stories, selected with introduction by O'Brien, New American Library, 1987.

The Short Stories of Willa Cather, edited by Hermione Lee, Virago, 1989.

OTHER, UNDER NAME WILLA CATHER

(Editor) *The Life of Mary Baker G. Eddy, and the History of Christian Science*, Doubleday, 1909.

(Editor and author of introduction) *The Best Stories of Sarah Orne Jewett*, two volumes, Houghton, 1925.

Willa Cather on Writing, Knopf, 1949, reprinted with foreword by Stephen Tennant, University of Nebraska Press, 1988.

Willa Cather in Europe: Her Own Story of the First Journey, edited with introduction and incidental notes by Kates, Knopf, 1956.

Also author, with Dorothy Canfield, of "The Fear That Walks by Noonday." Contributor of short stories, criticism, and articles to *Home Monthly, Ladies' Home Journal, Nebraska Literary Magazine, Nebraska State Journal, Saturday Evening Post*, and *Smart Set*.

SIDELIGHTS: Willa Sibert Cather is among the most distinguished American women in early twentieth-century fiction. She wrote most of her major works between 1913 and the late 1920s, during an age that encompassed World War I and spanned massive social change and modernization. As related by Louis Auchincloss in *Pioneers and Caretakers*, Cather felt that the world had split in two after 1922 and that she "belonged to the earlier half." Her writings reflect a desire to withdraw from the modern world into the refuge of a stable past.

Critics have compared Cather's balanced, carefully crafted, and evocative prose style to that of other writers, including mentor Sarah Orne Jewett, American novelist Henry James, and French naturalist Gustave Flaubert. Cather strove to preserve the past through her works, depicting the harsh life of pioneering immigrant farmers who settled the prairies of the western United States in such novels as *O Pioneers!* and *My Antonia*. Several other novels and the bulk of her short fiction explore another recurring theme—the complexities of the artistic temperament: Cather often portrayed artists in conflict, wrestling between the sophisticated allure of the East and the freedom and earthy simplicity of the West. According to Frederick J. Hoffman in *The*

Modern Novel in America, "The creative artist is in closest sympathy with what Miss Cather regards as the complete life."

Cather's writings are based largely on her early childhood experiences. Born in the Shenandoah Valley region of Virginia, she moved with her family to Red Cloud, Nebraska, a market town among the state's vast prairie lands, when she was nine years old. Cather grew up among European-born ranchers and farmers. She recognized the harshness of the immigrants' life-style and witnessed the development of their children into an imaginative new generation of Americans with dreams of a life rich in the arts: she would eventually incorporate into her fiction both the stoicism and the ambitions of the body of people with whom she matured.

After graduating from the University of Nebraska in 1895, Cather moved to Pittsburgh, Pennsylvania, where she worked as a journalist, editor, and teacher. In 1906 she accepted a position as editor of *McClure's* magazine in New York City. Having spent more than a decade nurturing her literary aspirations in her spare time, Cather realized by 1911 that she needed to devote more of her time and energy to writing in order to reach her creative potential. That year, at the urging of her friend Jewett, she resigned her post at *McClure's,* forsaking journalism for a career as a full-time writer.

While Cather is known primarily for her novels, her first published work was a volume of poetry titled *April Twilights.* The 1903 collection prefigures the themes of human struggle, unrealized potential, the search for self, and a retreat to the past that would color the author's later fiction, but many critics have agreed that Cather's sentiments are not best expressed in verse. Calling her "one of the few authentic voices among the prose writers of today," Eunice Tietjens, writing in *Poetry,* judged, "Miss Cather is not at heart a poet."

Cather's second publication, a collection of short fiction titled *The Troll Garden,* appeared in 1903. The volume's stories are written in tightly woven, lyrical prose, foreshadowing the graceful and economic style that would become the author's trademark. Each story in *The Troll Garden* features an artist or a character of artistic temperament, and several of the selections are set against the backdrop of a raw prairie. In "The Sculptor's Funeral," an artist's body is brought back to his home on the prairie for burial; yet, even after his death, the village natives fail to appreciate the man's artistic sensibilities. Another story, "The Wagner Matinee," centers on a young man's impressions of his Aunt Georgina, a woman who has led a somber and stifled existence on the plains. Upon attending a concert featuring the music of German composer Richard Wagner, Georgina undergoes a renewal, obtaining from her experience of the music a more enlightened sense of herself. These stories, and others like them, support Hoffman's claim that Cather's "strongest and most bitter criticism of the prairie culture was that it could not understand or abide the artistic soul."

Cather elaborated on the theme of unfulfilled ambitions in the most successful of *The Troll Garden* stories, "Paul's Case." This time, however, the main character is not in conflict with prairie life; rather, Paul, a young dreamer, feels smothered by the static, working-class existence in Pittsburgh. He is drawn to the glamour, excitement, and sophistication of New York. After stealing money from his employer, he travels to the city, takes a room at the Waldorf, and outfits himself with all the amenities of the New York elite. When the money is spent, Paul abandons hope of a brighter future and kills himself. Analyzing the story in *Willa Cather: A Critical Biography,* E. K. Brown asserted, "In the end Paul . . . can't go home again; he has burned his bridges and has no wish to rebuild them." "Paul's Case" is generally regarded as the most striking pronouncement of Cather's belief in the power of the human imagination. The character's impatience, spiritual nihilism, and ultimate despair render him unable to triumph over what Cather portrays as the merely physical constraints of his milieu.

Cather's first novel, *Alexander's Bridge,* was not a critical success. Originally composed while Cather was still an editor at *McClure's* but not published until 1912, the slim book tells of bridge builder Bartley Alexander, a married man in love with a London actress. After deciding to leave his wife for his other love, Alexander is called to inspect a bridge being constructed over the St. Lawrence River. Like Alexander's character, the bridge is flawed; it falls during the inspection, carrying the man to his death. Though critics conceded that it was well constructed, *Alexander's Bridge* was faulted for its overly contrived plot. David Daiches, writing in *Willa Cather: A Critical Introduction,* deemed the work "a mere literary exercise," arguing that in spite of its Jamesian precision and excellent descriptive passages, the novel "nevertheless fails in that the central emotional situations are never fully realized."

Cather expressed little satisfaction with *Alexander's Bridge* and reportedly regarded her next work of fiction, *O Pioneers!,* as her first fully realized novel. The product of two of Cather's earlier short works, *O Pioneers!* focuses on Alexandra Bergson, the strong and determined daughter of a Swedish immigrant. Left to carry on her father's struggle against the harsh prairie lands of the West, the industrious Alexandra fights to keep her family together and sacrifices her youth and beauty to a lifetime of hard labor. While the story ends with Alexandra's eventual success and happiness in her later years with a man worthy of her love, a majority of critics have suggested that the novel gains most of its emotional thrust from a narrative digression involving duplicitous lovers. In this episode Alexandra's youngest brother, Emil, falls in love with Marie Shabata, wife of a gruff and burly Bohemian neighbor. Marie and Emil rendezvous in an orchard; when her husband discovers them together, he kills them both. In a *Bookman* review of *O Pioneers!,* Frederic Taber Cooper called the murder of the lovers "perfect as it is by itself." David Stouck, writing in *Prairie Schooner,* defended Cather's inclusion of the love triangle in the story, stating that "in terms of the novel's epic theme—and it is the epic note which prevails at the end—the death of the lovers is necessary to give Alexandra's story a tragic depth and to allow her old antagonist, nature, to reassert its power. . . . Their death gives Alexandra's life a tragic quality because they represent essentially everything for which she has lived and fought."

Cather's next novel, *The Song of the Lark,* established several stylistic and thematic trends that would dominate her later works. The story turns on Thea Kronborg's rise to fame in the operatic world. The daughter of a Swedish preacher, young and vibrant Thea lives with her family in the small and uninspired town of Moonstone, Colorado. Her affinity for music and fascination with the world of art lead her to study music in Chicago. Following rigorous training in the city, the aspiring soprano retreats to the Southwest for a summer to reflect on the course of her life. Surrounded by the timeless, serene desert—a rich repository of native American artifacts—Thea contemplates the meaning of art. While bathing in a stream below an ancient cliff dwelling, she finds a piece of broken Indian pottery and, in studying it, derives a view of art in general: "The stream and the broken pottery: what was art but an effort to make a sheath, a mould in which to imprison for a moment the shining, elusive element which is life itself?"

The novel ends with Thea's triumph as an opera star. According to Auchincloss, Cather felt in retrospect that *The Song of the Lark* "should have ended with Thea Kronborg's first surmountal of her difficulties, that having escaped to Chicago from the stultification of Moonstone, where a concert or operatic career was inconceivable . . . she should have been left, one foot firmly set on the first rung of her long ladder." Most critics have agreed that the second half of the novel lacks the power of the first. *New Republic* contributor Lawrence Olson echoed the conclusions of several reviewers when he wrote: "Instead of embracing and exploring the fractured consciousness of modern man and reassembling it in a new creative reality . . . [Cather] took refuge in the attractive but unsupported idea that youth is finer than age, or that art is finer than life."

Many critics reviewing *The Song of the Lark* claimed that Thea's personality and emotions are subordinated to her ambitions. Perhaps the most succinct criticism of the character's development came from Auchincloss, who judged that Thea "is too much an artist, too little a woman." In *Willa Cather: The Emerging Voice*, Sharon O'Brien speculated that Cather—a quintessential tomboy in her youth—lacked an innate sense of her "female self" and, therefore, had difficulty portraying women in her fiction. Criticism of Cather's later novels focused not only on the author's perceived failure to create multidimensional female characters, but further suggested that Cather was unable to represent true dramatic relationships in her work. Clifton Fadiman, writing in *Nation*, explained that "Cather's conception of passion is broad. It includes passion for one's work, one's children, one's friends, one's land, one's memories, and for beautiful objects and experiences. But it does not extend, except formally, to sex."

My Antonia, Cather's 1918 novel, is widely regarded among the author's finest works. Reminiscent of the earlier prairie novel *O Pioneers!*, *My Antonia* tells the story of Bohemian immigrant farm girl Antonia Shimerda, a heroic character who has become a literary archetype for the Earth Mother. Narrator Jim Burden, neighbor to the Shimerdas, grows up with Antonia and chronicles her family's struggles to establish themselves on the Nebraska plains. The two characters share a love of the heart which is never expressed physically. Jim goes away to college and studies the classics; Antonia becomes involved with a railroad worker who impregnates and abandons her. The heroine has her baby and eventually finds happiness with a Czechoslovakian farmer named Cuzak. Years later, Jim—now a lawyer in the East—returns to Nebraska to find Antonia physically aged and weary, but exultant in her happy marriage and her many children. In an article for *Literary Review*, T. K. Whipple declared that Antonia's ultimate contentment proves Cather's "world is tragic . . . but not futile."

In *My Antonia*, Cather once again expresses an almost obsessive longing for the past, this time through the character of Antonia's father. Homesick for his native land, Mr. Shimerda despairs and shoots himself. While several critics found Cather's recurring preoccupation with the past destructive, Whipple recognized an element of passion in the theme: "To have cared intensely about anything," the critic concluded, "is not to have lived in vain."

For the four years between 1918 and 1922, Cather published only two works, a volume of short stories titled *Youth and the Bright Medusa* and a novel, *One of Ours*. The *Youth and the Bright Medusa* collection, published in 1920, borrowed largely from stories previously printed in *The Troll Garden*, but also contained several newly anthologized selections, including the critically acclaimed "Coming, Aphrodite!" Four years after the release of *My Antonia*, Cather finally completed her fifth novel,

One of Ours, in 1922. The central character, Claude Wheeler, is a virtuous youth who lives in an increasingly materialistic and prosperous Nebraska. Disillusioned by the deteriorating values of his family, he enlists in the armed forces and dies in battle during World War I. Reviewers felt that Cather's treatment of the Nebraska scenes approached the quality of her best work, but they also alleged that Cather oversimplified the war. Granville Hicks, writing in *English Journal*, called Cather's conception of World War I "romantic and naive," and added, "For Miss Cather, as for Claude, the war provides an escape from apparently insoluble problems." Despite such criticism, *One of Ours* earned the Pulitzer Prize in 1922.

Cather's next novel, *A Lost Lady*, garnered greater praise. Published in 1923, *A Lost Lady* chronicles the death of an era. Following an accident that leaves her once-powerful husband, Captain Forrester, an invalid, Marian Forrester begins a gradual process of moral degeneration. She longs for a life of culture, wealth, and sophistication, an existence which seems unattainable in the face of her husband's condition. Instead of turning her back on the petty bourgeois world of the present, Marian succumbs to its demands, taking refuge in the false comforts of alcohol and sexual abandon. She becomes what Hicks termed "the product of changed times" and a "symbol of the corruption that had overtaken the age."

According to John H. Randall III in *The Landscape and the Looking Glass*, "The deterioration of Mrs. Forrester's character . . . reflects the social disintegration brought about the rising tides of commerce" in post-World War I America. The character is lost "between the pioneer and commercial generations," the critic continued, "unable to act according to the values she holds." Deeming *A Lost Lady* "Cather's most explicit treatment of the passing of the old order" and "the central work of her career," Lionel Trilling, writing in *After the Genteel Tradition*, suggested: "Miss Cather shares the American belief in the tonic moral quality of the pioneer's life; with the passing of the frontier she conceives that a great source of fortitude has been lost."

Perhaps the most powerful expression of Cather's disillusionment with the modern world is her 1925 novel *The Professor's House*. Having earned a prestigious literary prize for his multivolume history of the Spanish in North America, Professor Godfrey St. Peter finds himself weary and uninspired. The completion of the enormous composition leaves him without a focal point for his creative energies. St. Peter's wife sets out to furnish an ostentatious new house with the professor's prize money. Reflecting on the materialistic nature of his family and society at large, St. Peter begins to reminisce about a former student, Tom Outland, who had died in the war. At this point in the story, the narrative breaks to accommodate an account of young Tom's pursuits prior to enrolling at the professor's college, including his discovery of prehistoric cliff dwellings in Colorado and his unsuccessful efforts to secure their preservation. The story then returns to St. Peter, who emerges from a near death experience with a new resolve to go on living.

New Statesman contributor Paul Binding considered *The Professor's House* "one of the 20th century's fictional masterpieces." Alfred Kazin, writing in *On Native Grounds*, agreed, declaring the novel "the most persistently underrated" of Cather's works. He further stated: "The story of Godfrey St. Peter is at once the barest and the most elaborately symbolic version of the story of heroic failure [Cather] told. . . . For St. Peter is at once the archetype of all her characters and the embodiment of her own beliefs."

Cather followed *The Professor's House* with her most inflammatory fiction, *My Mortal Enemy,* about a selfish, embittered, old woman who—looking back on a life lacking monetary prosperity—mourns the day she married for love. The author's next novel, *Death Comes for the Archbishop,* emphasizes the very contentment and tranquillity that was missing in *My Mortal Enemy.* Set in mid-nineteenth-century New Mexico, the episodic story is a fictionalization of the life and achievements of Archbishop Lamy, the territory's first appointed bishop. The novel spans more than four decades in the lives of the archbishop and his vicar, "men of a singular nobility of mind and radiance of personality," commented Binding. The critic proceeded to note an "absence of ambiguity" in the world of the novel: its characters "move through a wild, undisciplined land and lo! the bad are immediately seen in their badness, the good are rewarded, and the middling feel better for contact with such sanctity."

Several critics decried the lack of conflict in *Death Comes for the Archbishop,* implying that Cather's inability to reconcile herself to the modern world forced her to create a haven of beauty and idealism in the past. Kazin asserted that in the novel, the author's characters "no longer had to submit to failure; they lived in a charming and almost antediluvian world of their own. They had withdrawn, as Willa Cather . . . withdrew." Daiches concurred, arguing that "this lively creation of a golden world in which all ideals are realized is . . . fundamentally a 'softer' piece of writing than, say, *My Antonia* with its frustrations counterbalancing successes, or than *The Professor's House,* whose main note is of heroic failure." Despite such criticism, *Death Comes for the Archbishop* earned substantial acclaim for its evocations of the Southwest, and it remains one of Cather's most widely read works.

Shadows on the Rock, published in 1932, marks a further retreat into the past, this time to late-seventeenth-century Quebec. Focusing on one year in the lives of a widowed apothecary and his twelve-year-old daughter, the novel is regarded less for its dramatic action than for its lush descriptive passages and depiction of life along the St. Lawrence River. The book was written at a particularly difficult period in the author's life, following her father's death and the grave illness of her mother. Critics have suggested that Cather—craving stability during trying times—set *Shadows on the Rock* in Quebec because of the city's consistent resistance to change.

Cather's 1932 short story collection *Obscure Destinies* enunciates familiar themes of tradition and retrospection through three stories set in the Midwest. The most famous of these, a selection titled "Old Mrs. Harris," concerns three generations of women in Nebraska. Cather based the characters on her experiences in Red Cloud living with her mother and grandmother. Absorbed in their own lives, the two younger women fail to appreciate Mrs. Harris until after her death. Cather's portrait of isolation and aging was widely praised and, together with "Paul's Case," ranks with her best short fiction.

In 1935 Cather published another novel, *Lucy Gayheart,* which turns on the relationship between young pianist Lucy Gayheart and married baritone Clement Sebastian. Lucy and Clement fall in love, but, following a European summer concert tour, Clement accidentally drowns. After months of remorse and mourning, Lucy vows to resume her career in music; then, while skating on an ice-covered river, she falls through and drowns as well. In an article for *Prairie Schooner,* Paul Comeau theorized that in writing *Lucy Gayheart,* Cather was "not seeking to define the artistic process as she had done previously" but was "reflecting on that process in the distinctly philosophical context of life,

death, and immortality." Comeau continued, "The primary concern then is not to establish the continuing vitality of Lucy Gayheart . . . but to preserve and reflect on her memory."

Although *Lucy Gayheart* sold well, many critics faulted its predictability and oversentimentality. Trilling voiced the opinions of several reviewers, stating that the novel's "characters are unattached to anything save their dreams." Geismar, however, credited Cather with creating "the most complete love relationship" ever to appear in her writings.

Cather's final novel, *Sapphira and the Slave Girl,* was published in 1940. Based on an actual event, the story recounts a young girl's arduous life as a slave during the Civil War. Touching on issues of miscegenation, sexual exploitation, jealousy, and racism, the novel earned praise as a provocative, accomplished work.

In an essay from the 1936 collection *Not Under Forty* titled "The Novel Demeuble," Cather called her approach to the novel "unfurnished": "Out of the teeming, gleaming, stream of the present," she wrote, a novel "must select the eternal material of art." Commenting on the author's lifelong literary achievements, Daiches concluded: "She belongs to no school. . . . The heroic nostalgia that pursued her until the end first changed her from a minor imitator of James to a novelist of fierce originality and individuality, and from the moment she discovered herself with *O Pioneers!* she went her own way with remarkably little notice of her contemporaries. She developed a style both strong and supple, combining forthrightness with sensitivity: she was one of the least showy novelists of her time." Cather died of a massive cerebral hemorrhage on April 24, 1947, in her New York City apartment.

MEDIA ADAPTATIONS: O Pioneers! was adapted for the stage by Darrah Cloud and produced in Boston, Massachusetts, at the Huntington Theater Company, January, 1990.

BIOGRAPHICAL/CRITICAL SOURCES:

BOOKS

Auchincloss, Louis, *Pioneers and Caretakers: A Study of Nine American Women Novelists,* University of Minnesota Press, 1965.

Brown, E. K., *Willa Cather: A Critical Biography,* Knopf, 1953.

Cather, Willa, *The Song of the Lark,* Houghton, 1915.

Cather, Willa, *Not Under Forty,* Knopf, 1936.

Concise Dictionary of American Literary Biography: Realism, Naturalism, and Local Color, 1865-1917, Gale, 1988.

Cowley, Malcolm, editor, *After the Genteel Tradition: American Writers, 1910-1930,* revised edition, Southern Illinois University Press, 1964.

Daiches, David, *Willa Cather: A Critical Introduction,* Cornell University Press, 1951.

Dictionary of Literary Biography, Gale, Volume 9: *American Novelists, 1910-1945,* 1981, Volume 54: *American Poets, 1880-1945, Third Series,* 1987, Volume 78: *American Short Story Writers, 1880-1910,* 1989.

Dictionary of Literary Biography Documentary Series, Volume 1, Gale, 1982.

Edel, Leon, *Willa Cather: The Paradox of Success,* Library of Congress, 1960.

Geismar, Maxwell, *The Last of the Provincials: The American Novel, 1915-1925,* Houghton, 1947.

Hoffman, Frederick J., *The Modern Novel in America, 1900-1950,* Regnery Gateway, 1951.

Kazin, Alfred, *On Native Grounds: An Interpretation of Modern American Prose Literature,* Reynal & Hitchcock, 1942.

O'Brien, Sharon, *Willa Cather: The Emerging Voice,* Oxford University Press, 1987.

Porter, Katherine Anne, *The Collected Essays and Occasional Writings of Katherine Anne Porter,* Delacorte, 1970.

Randall, John H., III, *The Landscape and the Looking Glass: Willa Cather's Search for Meaning,* Houghton, 1960.

Rapin, Rene, *Willa Cather,* McBride, 1930.

Schroeter, James, editor, *Willa Cather and Her Critics,* Cornell University Press, 1967.

Short Story Criticism, Volume 2, Gale, 1989.

Slote, Bernice and Virginia Faulkner, editors, *The Art of Willa Cather,* University of Nebraska Press, 1974.

Stouck, David, *Willa Cather's Imagination,* University of Nebraska Press, 1975.

Twentieth-Century Literary Criticism, Gale, Volume 1, 1978, Volume 11, 1978, Volume 31, 1989.

Wilson, Edmund, *The Shores of Light: A Literary Chronicle of the Twenties and Thirties,* Farrar, Straus, 1952.

PERIODICALS

Bookman, August, 1913.
English Journal, November, 1933.
Literary Review, December 8, 1923.
Mississippi Quarterly, winter, 1981-82.
Nation, July 27, 1921, December 7, 1932.
New Republic, November 27, 1965, July 7, 1973.
New Statesman, August 21, 1981.
New York Times, January 28, 1990.
North American Review, spring, 1924.
Novel: A Forum on Fiction, fall, 1973.
Poetry, July, 1923.
Prairie Schooner, spring, 1972, spring-summer, 1981.
Smart Set, December, 1920.
Times Literary Supplement, November 17, 1989.
Tribune Books, January 4, 1987.

*   *   *

CAULDWELL, Frank
See KING, Francis (Henry)

*   *   *

CAUSLEY, Charles (Stanley)   1917-

PERSONAL: Born August 24, 1917, in Launceston, Cornwall, England; son of Charles Samuel and Laura Jane (Bartlett) Causley. *Education:* Attended Launceston College and Peterborough Training College.

ADDRESSES: Home—2 Cyprus Well, Launceston, Cornwall, England. *Agent*—David Higham Associates Ltd., 5-8 Lower John St., Golden Square, London W1R 4HA, England.

CAREER: Writer; former teacher. Member of Poetry Panel of the Arts Council of Great Britain, 1962-65. *Military service:* Royal Navy, 1940-46.

MEMBER: Royal Society of Literature (fellow, 1958), Poetry Society of Great Britain (vice-president), West County Writers Association (vice-president).

AWARDS, HONORS: Traveling scholarships, Society of Authors, 1954 and 1966; Queen's Gold Medal for Poetry, 1967; Cholmondeley Award for poetry, 1971; D.Litt. from University of Exeter.

WRITINGS:

ALL POEMS EXCEPT AS NOTED

Hands to Dance (short stories), Carroll & Nicholson, 1951, new edition published as *Hands to Dance and Skylark,* Robson Books, 1979.

Farewell, Aggie Weston, Hand & Flower Press, 1951.

Survivor's Leave, Hand & Flower Press, 1953.

Union Street, Hart-Davis, 1957, Houghton, 1958.

The Ballad of Charlotte Dymond (originally published in *Bryanston Miscellany*), privately printed, 1958.

Johnny Alleluia, Hart-Davis, 1961, Dufour, 1962.

(With George Barker and Martin Bell) *Penguin Modern Poets 3,* Penguin, 1962.

Underneath the Water, Macmillan, 1968.

Figure of 8: Narrative Poems, Macmillan, 1969.

Timothy Winters (poem set to music), music by Wallace Southam, Turret Books, 1970.

(With Laurie Lee) *Pergamon Poets X,* compiled by Evan Owen, Pergamon, 1970.

Figgie Hobbin: Poems for Children, Macmillan, 1971, published as *Figgie Hobbin,* Walker & Co., 1973.

The Tail of the Trinosaur, Brockhampton Press, 1973.

Collected Poems, 1951-1975, David Godine, 1975.

The Hill of the Fairy Calf, Hodder & Stoughton, 1976.

Dick Whittington (juvenile), Penguin, 1976.

Here We Go round the Round House, New Broom Press, 1976.

The Animals' Carol, Macmillan, 1978.

The Gift of a Lamb (verse play), Robson Books, 1978.

Three Heads Made of Gold (juvenile), Robson Books, 1978.

The Last King of Cornwall (juvenile), Hodder & Stoughton, 1978.

(Translator) *Twenty-five Poems by Hamdija Demirovic,* Keepsake Press, 1980.

The Ballad of Aucassin and Nicolette (verse play), music by Stephen McNeff, Penguin, 1981.

(Author of introduction) S. Baring-Gould, *Cornwall,* Wildwood House, 1981.

Quack! Said the Billy-Goat (juvenile), Harper, 1986.

Early in the Morning (juvenile), Penguin, 1987.

Secret Destinations, David Godine, 1989.

EDITOR

Peninsula: An Anthology of Verse from the West Country, Macdonald, 1957.

(And author of introduction) *Dawn and Dusk: Poems of Our Time* (juvenile), Brockhampton, 1962, F. Watts, 1963, 2nd edition, Brockhampton, 1972.

(And author of introduction) *Rising Early: Story Poems and Ballads of the 20th Century,* Brockhampton, 1964, published as *Modern Ballads and Story Poems,* F. Watts, 1965.

(And author of introduction) *Modern Folk Ballads,* Studio Vista, 1966.

In the Music I Hear (poems by children), Arc Press, 1970.

(And author of introduction) *Oats and Beans and Barley* (poems by children), Arc Press, 1971.

(And author of introduction) Frances Bellerby, *Selected Poems,* Enitharmon Press, 1971.

The Puffin Book of Magic Verse, Penguin, 1974.

The Puffin Book of Salt-Sea Verse, Penguin, 1978.

The Batsford Book of Story Poems for Children, Batsford, 1979.

The Sun, Dancing (anthology of Christian poetry), Penguin, 1981.

OTHER

Recordings of poems, read by Causley, include: "Authopoetry," Poets Lot Ltd.; "Here Today," "The Jupiter Anthology of 20th Century English Poetry: Part III" (which he also edited), and "The Jupiter Book of Contemporary Ballads," all Jupiter Recordings Ltd.; "The Poet Speaks, Record 8," Argo Record Co. Ltd.; and "Causley Reads Causley," Sentinel. Poems and interviews have been recorded on tape for the British Council. A number of Causley's poems appear in the series "Poetry and Song," Argo, and in settings by folk-singers on a number of long-playing albums.

Contributor to *New Statesman, Spectator, Listener, Encounter, Harper's Bazaar, Ladies' Home Journal, Observer, Sunday Times* (London), *Times Literary Supplement, London Magazine, Twentieth Century, Outposts, Transatlantic Review,* and other periodicals, and to anthologies of verse.

SIDELIGHTS: William Cole of the *Saturday Review* calls poet Charles Causley "a balladeer, a galloping and even galumphing rhythmicist, and a man who believes that the poeticalities of yesteryear can, by pluck and luck, be at once redeemed. Highly colored, highly blithe, his poetry embarks upon a task which is beyond its talents, true though those are, since it is beyond talent: to tap again the age-old sources which have become clogged, cracked, buried."

Several critics have commented on the differences between Causley's use of language and the language of much of contemporary poetry. Richard Pevear of the *Hudson Review* calls attention to "the unusual stringency of [Causley's] language, a violence at times that seems to go beyond what the subject calls for. The speech he hears and makes into poetry is not quite present-day English. In directness of address, in turns of phrase and image, and in a particular quality of imagination, his work reminds me of Scots Gaelic poetry."

In *Poetry Today, 1960-1973,* Anthony Thwaite mentions the apparent simplicity of Causley's poems and comments: "There is in fact a great deal more art in Causley's work than may appear at first sight. . . . A Causley poem is instantly recognizable and always fresh." Pevear believes that "what distinguishes Causley's work is its openness, its unself-consciousness, its disdain of the precious and the overwrought, its crudeness and compression. . . . The solipsism of so much of contemporary writing leaves us unprepared for a poet who takes common life, that is, our life in common, as a reality outside the poem rather than as a pretext for composition."

Causley told *CA:* "*Figure of 8,* a collection of narrative poems, was published as a children's book. I'd hope, though, that the book wouldn't be read by children only—in writing such a book I think one should simply aim at widening the age-range of one's audience, and in the process try and avoid producing poetry and water. . . . In the event, one doesn't think about a possible audience at all when writing: only about the problem of getting the poem on the paper as close as possible to what's in one's head in a vague form. After the poem's written is the time to decide (if ever) what kind of audience it might reach."

Causley has traveled widely from Scapa Flow, off the northern coast of Scotland, to Sydney, Australia, and from Freetown, West Africa, to Rabaul, New Britain; he has visited many countries, including Italy, France, Spain, Poland, and the U.S.S.R. He once said that one of the principal delights of travel was the intense pleasure he experienced on returning to his native Cornwall.

BIOGRAPHICAL/CRITICAL SOURCES:

BOOKS

Contemporary Literary Criticism, Volume 7, Gale, 1977.
Currey, R. N., *Poets of the 1939-1945 War,* published for the British Council and National Book League by Longmans, Green, 1960.
Dictionary of Literary Biography, Volume 27: *Poets of Great Britain and Ireland, 1945-1960,* Gale, 1984.
Jennings, Elizabeth, *Poetry Today,* published for the British Council and National Book League by Longmans, Green, 1961.
Schmidt, Michael, *Fifty Modern British Poets,* Pan Books, 1979.
Thwaite, Anthony, *Poetry Today, 1960-1973,* published for the British Council by Longmans, Green, 1973.

PERIODICALS

Books, January, 1970.
Books and Bookmen, April, 1971.
Hudson Review, summer, 1976.
London Magazine, November, 1968.
Manchester Guardian, January 15, 1965.
New Poetry, Number 45, 1979.
New Statesman, March 22, 1968.
Punch, March 27, 1968.
Saturday Review, February 7, 1976.
Times Educational Supplement, November 17, 1972.
Times Literary Supplement, October 16, 1969.

* * *

CAVALLO, Evelyn
See SPARK, Muriel (Sarah)

* * *

CELA, Camilo Jose   1916-
(Matilde Verdu)

PERSONAL: Surname pronounced *Say*-lah; born May 11, 1916, in Iria Flavia, La Coruna, Spain; son of Camilo (a customs official and part-time writer) and Camila Enmanuela (Trulock Bertorini) Cela; married Maria del Rosario Conde Picavea, March 12, 1944; children: Camilo Jose. *Education:* Attended University of Madrid, 1933-36, and 1939-43.

ADDRESSES: Home—La Bonanova, 07015 Palma de Mallorca, Spain; and Madrid, Spain.

CAREER: Writer; publisher of *Papeles de Son Armadans* (literary monthly), 1956-79. Lecturer in England, France, Latin America, Belgium, Sweden, Italy, and the United States. *Military service:* Served in Spanish Nationalist Army during Spanish Civil War, 1936-39; became corporal.

MEMBER: Real Academia Espanola, Premio Nacional de Literatura, Premio Principe de Asturias, Real Academia Gallega, Hispanic Society of America, American Association of Teachers of Spanish and Portuguese (honorary fellow, 1966—).

AWARDS, HONORS: Premio de la critica, 1955, for *Historias de Venezuela: La Catira;* Spanish National Prize for Literature, 1984, for *Mazurca para dos muertos;* honorary doctorates from Syracuse University, 1964, University of Birmingham, 1976, University of Santiago de Compostela, 1979, University of Palma de Mallorca, 1979, John F. Kennedy University, and Interamericana University; Nobel Prize, 1989.

WRITINGS:

IN ENGLISH TRANSLATION

La familia de Pascual Duarte (novel), Aldecoa (Madrid), 1942, reprinted, Destino (Barcelona), 1982, translation by John Marks published as *Pascual Duarte's Family,* Eyre & Spottiswoode, 1946, translation by Anthony Kerrigan published as *The Family of Pascual Duarte,* Little, Brown, 1964, reprinted, 1990, Spanish/English version by Herma Briffault published as *Pascual Duarte and His Family,* Las Americas Publishing, 1965.

Pabellon de reposo (novel; first published serially in *El Espanol,* March 13 to August 21, 1943), illustrations by Suarez de Arbol, Afrodisio Aguado (Madrid), 1943, reprinted, Destino, 1977, Spanish/English version by Briffault published as *Rest Home,* Las Americas Publishing, 1961.

Las botas de siete leguas: Viaje a la Alcarria, con los versos de su cancionero, cada uno en su debido lugar (travel; also see below), Revista de Occidente, 1948, reprinted, Destino, 1982, published as *Viaje a la Alcarria,* Papeles de Son Armadans, 1958, reprinted, 1976, translation by Frances M. Lopez-Morillos published as *Journey to the Alcarria,* University of Wisconsin Press, 1964, reprinted, Atlantic Monthly Press, 1990.

Caminos inciertos: La colmena (novel), Emece (Buenos Aires), 1951, published as *La colmena,* Noguer (Barcelona), 1955, reprinted, Castalia (Madrid), 1984, translation by I. M. Cohen and Arturo Barea published as *The Hive,* Farrar, Straus, 1953, reprinted, 1990.

Mrs. Caldwell habla con su hijo (novel), Destino, 1953, reprinted, 1979, translation by Jerome S. Bernstein published as *Mrs. Caldwell Speaks to Her Son,* Cornell University Press, 1968.

Also author of *Avila* (travel), 1952, revised edition, 1968, translation by John Forrester published under same title, 1956.

NOVELS

Nuevas andanzas y desventuras de Lazarillo de Tormes, y siete apuntes carpetovetonicos (title means "New Wanderings and Misfortunes of Lazarillo de Tormes"; first published serially in *Juventud,* July 4 to October 18, 1944), La Nave (Madrid), 1944, reprinted, Noguer, 1975.

Santa Balbina 37: Gas en cada piso (novella; title means "Santa Balbina 37, Gas in Every Flat"; also see below), Mirto y Laurel (Melilla, Morocco), 1952, 2nd edition, 1977.

Timoteo, el incomprendido (novella; title means "Misunderstood Timothy"; also see below), Rollan (Madrid), 1952.

Cafe de artistas (novella; also see below), Tecnos (Madrid), 1953.

Historias de Venezuela: La catira (title means "Stories of Venezuela: The Blonde"), illustrations by Ricardo Arenys, Noguer, 1955, published as *La catira,* 1966.

Tobogan de hambrientos (title means "Toboggan of Hungry People"), illustrations by Lorenzo Goni, Noguer, 1962.

Visperas, festividad y octava de San Camilo del ano 1936 en Madrid (title means "Eve, Feast and Octave of San Camilo's Day, 1936, in Madrid"), Alfaguara, 1969, Noguer, 1981.

Oficio de tinieblas 5; o, Novela de tesis escrita para ser cantada por un coro de enfermos (title means "Ministry of Darkness 5; or, Novel with a Thesis Written to Be Sung by a Chorus of Sick People"), Noguer, 1973.

Mazurca para dos muertos (title means "Mazurka for Two Bad People"), Ediciones del Norte (Hanover, N.H.), 1983.

Cristo versus Arizona (title means "Christ versus Arizona"), Seix Barral (Barcelona), 1988.

Also author of *Los cipreses creen en Dios* (title means "The Cypresses Believe in God").

STORIES

Esas nubes que pasan (title means "The Passing Clouds"; also see below), Afrodisio Aguado, 1945, reprinted, Espasa-Calpe (Madrid), 1976.

El bonito crimen del carabinero, y otras invenciones (stories; title means "The Neat Crime of the Carabiniere and Other Tales"; one chapter first published in *Arriba,* April 25, 1946; also see below), Jose Janes (Barcelona), 1947, published as *El bonito crimen del carabinero,* Picazo, 1972.

Baraja de invenciones (title means "Pack of Tales"; also see below), Castalia (Valencia), 1953.

Historias de Espana: Los ciegos, los tontos, illustrations by Manuel Mampaso, Arion (Madrid), 1958, new enlarged edition published in four volumes as *A la pata de palo* (title means "The Man with the Wooden Leg"), illustrations by Goni, Alfaguara, Volume 1: *Historias de Espana* (title means "Stories of Spain"), 1965, Volume 2: *La familia del Heroe; o, Discurso historico de los ultimos restos; ejercicios para una sola mano,* 1965, Volume 3: *El ciudadano Iscariote Reclus* (title means "Citizen Iscariote Reclus"), 1965, Volume 4: *Viaje a U.S.A.* (title means "Trip to the U.S.A."), 1967, published in one volume as *El tacata oxidado: Florilegio de carpetovetonismos y otras lindezas,* Noguer, 1973.

Los viejos amigos, two volumes, illustrations by Jose Maria Prim, Noguer, 1960-61, 3rd edition, 1981.

Gavilla de fabulas sin amor (title means "A Bundle of Loveless Fables"), illustrations by Pablo Picasso, Papeles de Son Armadans (Palma de Mallorca), 1962, reprinted, 1979.

Once cuentos de futbol, illustrations by Pepe, Nacional (Madrid), 1963.

Toreo de salon: Farsa con acompanamiento de clamor y murga, photographs by Oriol Maspons and Julio Ubina, Editorial Lumen (Barcelona), 1963, reprinted, 1984.

Izas, rabizas y colipoterras: Drama con acompanamiento de cachondeo y dolor de corazon, photographs by Juan Colom, Editorial Lumen, 1964, reprinted, 1984.

Nuevas escenas matritenses (title means "New Scenes of Madrid"), seven volumes, photographs by Enrique Palazuela, Alfaguara, 1965-66, published in one volume as *Fotografias al minuto,* Organizacion Sala (Madrid), 1972.

La bandada de palomas (juvenile), illustrations by Jose Correas Flores, Labor, 1969.

Cuentos para leer despues del bano, La Gaya Ciencia (Barcelona), 1974.

Rol de cornudos, Noguer, 1976.

El espejo y otros cuentos, Espasa-Calpe, 1981.

TRAVEL

Del Mino al Bidasoa: Notas de un vagabundaje (title means "From the Mino to the Bidasoa: Notes of a Vagabondage"), Noguer, 1952, reprinted, 1981.

Vagabundo por Castilla (title means "Vagabond in Castile"), Seix Barral, 1955.

Judios, moros y cristianos: Notas de un vagabundaje por Avila, Segovia y sus tierras (title means "Jews, Moors, and Christians: Notes of a Vagabondage through Avila, Segovia, and Their Surroundings"), Destino, 1956, reprinted, 1979.

Primer viaje andaluz: Notas de un vagabundaje por Jaen, Cordoba, Sevilla, Huelva y sus tierras (title means "First Andalusian Trip: Notes on a Vagabondage through Jaen, Cordoba, Seville, Huelva, and Their Surroundings"), illustrations by Jose Hurtuna, Noguer, 1959, reprinted, 1979.

Cuaderno del Guadarrama (title means "Guadarrama Notebook"), illustrations by Eduardo Vicente, Arion, 1959.

Paginas de geografia errabunda (title means "Pages of Wandering Geography"), Alfaguara, 1965.

Viaje al Pirineo de Lerida: Notas de un paseo a pie por el Pallars Sobira, el Valle de Aran y el Condado de Ribagorza, Alfaguara, 1965.

Madrid, illustrations by Juan Esplandiu, Alfaguara, 1966.

Calidoscopio callejero, maritimo y campestre de C.J.C. para el reino y ultramar, Alfaguara, 1966.

La Mancha en el corazon y en los ojos, EDISVEN (Barcelona), 1971.

Balada del vagabundo sin suerte y otros papeles volanderos, Espasa-Calpe, 1973.

Madrid, color y siluta, illustrations by Estrada Vilarrasa, AUSA (Sabadell, Spain), 1985.

Nuevo viaje a la Alcarria, three volumes, Informacion y Revistas (Madrid), 1986.

Also author of *Barcelona,* 1970.

OMNIBUS VOLUMES

El molino de viento, y otras novelas cortas (title means "The Windmill and Other Short Novels"; contains *El molino de viento, Timoteo, el incomprendido* [also see below], *Cafe de artistas* [also see below], and *Santa Balbina 37: Gas en cada piso*), illustrations by Goni, Noguer, 1956, reprinted, 1977.

Mis paginas preferidas (selections), Gredos (Madrid), 1956.

Nuevo retablo de don Cristobita: Invenciones, figuraciones y alucinaciones (stories; contains *Esas nubes que pasan, El bonito crimen del carabinero,* and part of *Baraja de invenciones*), Destino, 1957, reprinted, 1980.

Obra completa (title means "Complete Works"), fourteen volumes, Destino, 1962-83.

Las companias convenientes y otros figimientos y cegueras (stories; title means "Suitable Companions and Other Deceits and Obfuscations"), Destino, 1963, reprinted, 1981.

Cafe de artistas y otros cuentos, Salvat/Alianza, 1969.

Timoteo el incomprendido y otros papeles ibericos, Magisterio Espanol, 1970.

Obras selectas (includes *La familia de Pascual Duarte, Viaje a la Alcarria, La colmena, Mrs. Caldwell habla con su hijo, Iazas, rabizas y colipoterras,* and *El carro de heno; o, El inventor de la guillotina*), Alfaguara, 1971.

Prosa, edited by Jacinto-Luis Guerena with notes and commentaries, Narcea (Madrid), 1974.

Cafe de artistas y otros papeles volanderos, Alce (Madrid), 1978.

Also author of *Antologia,* 1968.

OTHER

Mesa revuelta (essays) Ediciones de los Estudiantes Espanoles, 1945, new and expanded edition (includes text of *Ensuenos y figuraciones*), Taurus (Madrid), 1957.

Pisando la dudosa luz del dia: Poemas de una adolescencia cruel (poems; title means "Treading the Uncertain Light of Day"), Zodiaco (Barcelona), 1945, new corrected and expanded edition, Papales de Son Armadans, 1963.

(Under pseudonym Matilde Verdu) *San Juan de la Cruz,* [Madrid], 1948.

El gallego y su cuadrilla y otros apuntes carpetovetonicos (title means "The Galician and His Troupe and Other Carpeto-Vettonian Notes"), Ricardo Aguilera (Madrid), 1949, 3rd edition corrected and enlarged, Destino, 1967.

Ensuenos y figuraciones, Ediciones G.P., 1954.

La rueda de los ocios (title means "The Wheel of Idle Moments"), Mateu (Barcelona), 1957, reprinted, Alfaguara, 1972.

La obra literaria del pintor Solana: Discurso leido ante la Real Academia Espanola el dia 26 de mayo de 1957 en su recepcion publica por el Excmo. Sr. D. Camilo Jose Cela y contestacion del Excmo. Sr. D. Gregorio Maranon, Papeles de Son Armadans (Madrid), 1957, reprinted, 1972.

Cajon de sastre (articles) Cid (Madrid), 1957, reprinted, Alfaguara, 1970.

Recuerdo de don Pio Baroja (title means "Remembrance of Pio Baroja"), illustrations by Eduardo Vicente, De Andrea (Mexico City), 1958.

La cucana: Memorias (memoirs) Destino, 1959, portion printed as *La rosa,* Destino, 1979.

(Editor) *Homenaje y recuerdo a Gregorio Maranon (1887-1960),* Papeles de Son Armadans, 1961.

Cuatro figuras del 98: Unamuno, Valle Inclan, Baroja, Azorin, y otros retratos ensayos espanoles, Aedos (Barcelona), 1961.

El solitario: Los suenos de Quesada (title means "The Solitary One"), illustrations by Rafael Zabaleta, Papeles de Son Armadans, 1963.

Garito de hospicianos; o, Guirigay de imposturas y bambollas (articles; title means "Poorhouse Inmates; or, Jargon Frauds and Sham"), Noguer, 1963, reprinted, Plaza & Janes, 1986.

(Author of prologue) Tono y Rafael Florez, *Memorias de mi: Novela,* Biblioteca ca Nueva, 1966.

(With Cesareo Rodriguez Aguilera) *Xam* (illustrated art commentary), Daedalus (Palma de Mallorca), 1966.

Diccionario secreto (title means "Secret Dictionary"), Alfaguara, Volume 1, 1968, Volume 2, 1972.

Maria Sabina (dramatic poem; also see below), Papeles de Son Armadans, 1967, 2nd edition bound with *El carro de heno; o, El inventor de la guillotina* (play; also see below), Alfaguara, 1970.

Poesia y cancioneros, [Madrid], 1968.

Homenaje al Bosco, I: El carro de heno; o, El inventor de la guillotina, Papeles de Son Armadans, 1969.

Al servicio de algo, Alfaguara, 1969.

La bola del mundo: Escenas cotidianas, Organizacion Sala (Madrid), 1972.

A vueltas con Espana, Seminarios y Ediciones (Madrid), 1973.

Cristina Mallo (monograph), Theo (Madrid), 1973.

Diccionari manual castella-catala, catala-castella, Bibliograf (Barcelona), 1974.

Enciclopedia de erotismo (title means "Encyclopedia of Eroticism"), D. L. Sedmay (Madrid), 1977.

(Adaptor) Fernando de Rojas, *La Celestina puesta respetuosamente en castellano moderno por Camilo Jose Cela quien anadio muy poco y quito aun menos* (title means "La Celestina Put Respectfully into Modern Castilian by Camilo Jose Cela Who Added a Little and Took Out Even Less"), Destino, 1979.

Los suenos vanos, los angeles curiosos, Argos Vergara (Barcelona), 1979.

Los vasos comunicantes, Bruguera (Barcelona), 1981.

Las companias convenientes y otros figimientos y cegueras, Destino, 1981.

Vuelta de hoja, Destino, 1981.

Album de taller (art commentary), Ambit (Barcelona), 1981.

(Editor and author of prologue) Miguel de Cervantes Saavedra, *El Quijote,* Ediciones Rembrandt (Alicante, Spain), 1981.

El juego de los tres madronos, Destino, 1983.

El asno de Buridan (articles), El Pais (Madrid), 1986.

Also author of *San Camilo,* 1936, reprinted, 1969, *La bandada de palmoas,* 1969, and, with Alfonso Canales, *Cronica del cipote de Archidona* (first published as *La insolita y gloriosa hazana del cipote de Archidona),* 1977. Author of poems "Himno a la muerte" (title means "Hymn to Death"), 1938, and *Dos romances de ciego,* 1966.

SIDELIGHTS: While not widely known in the United States, 1989 Nobel laureate Camilo Jose Cela has played a pivotal role in twentieth-century Spanish literature. Upon awarding the prize to Cela, the Swedish Academy praised the author "for a rich and intensive prose, which with restrained compassion forms a challenging vision of man's vulnerability," relates Sheila Rule for the *New York Times.* In the same article, Rule reports Julio Ortego's statement that "Cela represents the searching for a better literature from the Franco years, through the democratic experiments and into European Spain. At the same time, he remained very Spanish, keeping the cultural traditions of Spanish art and literature in his writing. He didn't follow a European literature, but developed his own style, and so, in his way, symbolized Spain's going through a long period of adjustment." Throughout the Franco regime, Cela suffered from heavy governmental censorship. Many of his books were banned outright or later removed from the shelves: the second edition of *Pascual Duarte* was seized; the censor found it "nauseating," and *The Hive* was initially published in South America. D. W. McPheeters maintains in *Camilo Jose Cela* that, in spite of such opposition, Cela "has always had the courage to express himself frankly, even forthrightly, . . . which has led to problems with an overly squeamish censorship."

Cela's stylistic development has moved from the more traditional *Pascual Duarte* to the innovative fiction of his later novels. McPheeters sees Cela as "dedicated to a constant trying of various forms . . . of fiction in a search for the one that best suits him and . . . what he has to say concerning the human situation. He [is] an outspoken critic of traditional forms of the novel and the restrictions which [some] would impose upon the creative artist." Cela's first novel, *The Family of Pascual Duarte,* has been called the most widely read Spanish novel since *Don Quixote.* It was published in the early 1940s, a time when "the Spanish novel . . . had virtually ceased to exist as a worthy genre," attests McPheeters. "Almost single-handedly, Cela [gave the genre] new life and international significance." Many critics have noted that Cela's national prominence and international fame is a result of the popularity of *The Family of Pascual Duarte* and a later novel, *The Hive.* McPheeters agrees, stating that while *Pascual Duarte,* Cela's first novel, "secured a wide foreign acceptance," *The Hive* "assured his place as one of Europe's outstanding novelists."

Pascual Duarte relates the life of a convicted murderer awaiting execution. It is introduced as a prison letter to an old family friend, but the reader soon becomes immersed in a first-person narrative. Pascual responds to a life of poverty and frustration through killing: his dog, his horse, his wife's lover, and finally, his mother, fall victim to his rage. "A deceptive objectivity masks the presentation of cruel and monstrous scenes, including murder and matricide," *Michigan Quarterly Review* contributor Francis Donahue describes. "In a taut style, with emotion carefully reined, Cela evokes an atmosphere of extreme brutality, one which a nation suffering from the after-effects of a brutal civil war could readily understand and believe." But some reviewers find such intense scenes hinder any identification with the main character. "Pascual Duarte speaks of suffering and ferocity so appalling as to be almost beyond the reach of our sympathy. They stun even more than they horrify," resolves *Saturday Re-*

view contributor Emile Capouya. However, Pierre Courtines in *America* insists that the book is worth the reader's effort: "The dialogues between Cela's leading characters are rapid and dramatic, and his language is rich in imagery that reveals many popular traditions. Cela has combined realism with poetry, and his novel expresses the 'tragic sense of life,' so much a part of the Spanish character."

Some critics, as I. S. Bernstein states in his introduction to *Mrs. Caldwell Speaks to Her Son,* credit Cela with the invention of "tremendismo," a type of fiction which dwells on the darker side of life—the distasteful, the grotesque and the vulgar. Although in his prologue to the Spanish version of *Mrs. Caldwell Speaks to Her Son,* Cela denies this paternity, tremendista elements are abundant in *Pascual Duarte.* As an example of tremendismo, McPheeters translates a portion of the struggle in which Pascual kills his mother: "I was able to bury the blade in her throat. . . . Blood squirted out in a torrent and struck me in the face. It was warm like a belly and tasted the same as the blood of a lamb." Other gruesome incidents fill the pages of the novel; in one scene Pascual's retarded brother's ears are eaten off by a pig. This type of detail—meant to shock the placid reader—is present in a lesser degree or non-existent in some of Cela's novels, but even so, a *Times Literary Supplement* critic calls Cela's works "perversely restricted to a pathology of human decay and loneliness." His *Mazurca para dos muertos,* for example, concludes with a six-page postmortem examination of a cadaver. Even Cela's non-fiction works such as *Enciclopedia de eroticismo* (the title means "Encyclopedia of Eroticism") and *Diccionario secreto,* which contains definitions of vulgar words, are written in defiance of Spain's traditionalist moral code.

The Hive led critics to compare Cela with John Dos Passos, particularly to Dos Passos's novel *Manhattan Transfer,* which characterizes frenetic Manhattan life. Comparisons between the two novels are based on the large number of characters introduced in both works and by the novelists' similarly cinematographic styles. In both novels, the shifting time sequence is similar to the filmmaker's flashback. But while David W. Foster concedes in *Forms in the Work of Camilo Jose Cela* that an analogy can be made between the two techniques, he notes: "Cela's perspective goes much beyond that of the camera in what it is able to record. It is, in effect, all inclusive, omniscient, and omnipresent."

The Hive is frequently seen as Cela's greatest work. In *Books Abroad,* Jacob Ornstein and James Y. Causey note that "Spanish criticism has been almost unanimous in acclaiming this novel as Cela's masterpiece, both for its vigorous simplicity and for the author's artistry in evoking the atmosphere of Madrid during the final days of World War II and the years immediately following." *The Hive*'s publication was typical of Cela's struggle with the censors, as it was banned in Spain and printed in Buenos Aires in 1952; William D. Montalbano reports in the *Los Angeles Times* that Cela autographed copies "a bitter chronicle of a bitter time." *Nation* contributor Maxwell Geismar finds *The Hive* "suffused with anger and bitterness at society in Madrid." The novel portrays the lives of 346 characters during three days in Madrid in the winter of 1943, when the city was facing intense hardship. Although only forty-eight of *The Hive*'s characters play a significant role in the plot, their appearances and disappearances are more important than the story itself. As Foster notes, "[*The Hive*] is one continuous interplay of people. Although chronology is fragmented, the novel is able to develop a world based upon the activities of individuals." And a *Times Literary Supplement* contributor finds that "in spite of the author's literary theories which confuse the reader with an enormous gallery of characters presented in very short passages, *The Hive* is a work of art of great power."

While *The Hive,* as Foster remarks, "has stood as a sort of beacon for Cela's fiction, the one novel to which most critics turn with . . . admiration," Cela has continued producing innovative and award-winning novels. The author "has chosen," Foster points out, "to make his career one of a complete reexamination and reconsideration of the novel as an art form." Foster classifies most of Cela's novels since *Mrs. Caldwell Speaks to Her Son* as experimental. Among the characteristics most prominent in Cela's later work are the decreasing emphasis plot—the sequence of cause and effect is discarded—and an increasing emphasis on artificial patternings of events. Some of his more original novels besides *Mrs. Caldwell* include *Tobogan de hambrientos, Visperas, festividad y octava de San Camilo del ano 1936 en Madrid* (usually referred to as *San Camilo, 1936*), and *Oficio de tinieblas 5.* However, McPheeters believes that these later works may be less accessible to the general reader. He mentions that *Pascual Duarte* and *The Hive* "continue to influence contemporary Spanish writers, but certain innovations in his other works may not gain rapid acceptance."

Mrs. Caldwell contains excerpts from the letters of a mentally disturbed woman to her dead son. McPheeters finds that *Mrs. Caldwell* "is about as much an antinovel as has yet been conceived in Spain." The theme is incest, one ideally suited to Cela's fiction because of its shock value. The form is equally unexpected: although only slightly longer than two hundred pages, it contains two hundred and twelve chapters. There is no connection between the chapters (except for chapters fourteen and sixty) and no reason for ending the novel other than the illegibility of the last of the "Letters from the Royal Hospital for the Insane."

The form and content of *Tobogan de hambrientos, San Camilo, 1936,* and *Oficio de tinieblas 5* are also out of the ordinary. *Oficio de tinieblas,* for example, has no capital letters, while *San Camilo, 1936* has no paragraphs. *Tobogan de hambrientos,* Foster notes, "employs many of the devices of the new novel, especially in its use of pattern and in the rejection of chronology, definable plot, and unified points of view." The book is divided into two hundred units. These two hundred are in turn divided in half and labeled in ascending, then, at the half-way point, in descending numerical order. Each narrative unit presents a new individual or group of individuals and the characters from the first half of the book reappear in the corresponding chapters of the second half.

Except for the epilogue, *San Camilo, 1936* is a young student's continuous stream of consciousness. Again, in content and form the book is far removed from the traditional novel. The book's opening chapter, for instance, includes a list of Madrid's brothels, complete with addresses and names of proprietresses. A *Times Literary Supplement* reviewer remarks on the novel's unusual style: "[Cela] reinforces his . . . contempt for petit-bourgeois credulity by quoting an enormous variety of patent medicine advertisements, [and] making astonishingly free with his sexual and other carnal references, indeed, the language of [the book] is scabrous." While noting Cela's emphasis on "the erotic, obscene and scatological" in *San Camilo, 1936, Hispania* contributor Robert Louis Sheehan also observes the "stylistic innovations" present in the novel, including "the rhythmic reiteration of names, clauses, [and] phrases," the "use of one-paragraph chapters, run-on sentences, and frequent use of commas in place of periods."

Today the name of Camilo Jose Cela is associated with the rebirth of the Spanish novel, and with experimentation in its form and content. *Pascual Duarte* is credited with starting a new school of Spanish literature, while *The Hive* brought a new cinematographic technique to literature, which Margaret E. W. Jones in *The Contemporary Spanish Novel, 1939-1975* believes "suggested new possibilities in [the] elasticity of novelistic form." Jones also confirms the author's sense of exploration, and claims that "Cela has consistently been at the forefront of new movements in the contemporary novel since the 1940s." And Cela himself sums up his feelings on his favorite genre in the dedication to *Journey to the Alcarria*—which Jones quotes—"Anything goes in the novel, as long as it's told with common sense."

MEDIA ADAPTATIONS: The Hive was filmed by director Mario Camus; *The Family of Pascual Duarte* filmed by director Ricardo Franco.

AVOCATIONAL INTERESTS: Collecting wine bottles, stamps, and literary myths.

BIOGRAPHICAL/CRITICAL SOURCES:

BOOKS

Cela, Camilo Jose, *Caminos inciertos: La colmena,* Noguer, 1955.

Cela, Camilo Jose, *Mrs. Caldwell Speaks to Her Son,* translated and with introduction by J. S. Bernstein, Cornell University Press, 1968.

Chandler, Richard E. and Kessel Schwartz, *A New History of Spanish Literature,* Louisiana State University Press, 1961.

Contemporary Authors Autobiography Series, Volume 10, Gale, 1989.

Contemporary Literary Criticism, Gale, Volume 4, 1975, Volume 13, 1980.

Foster, David W., *Forms in the Work of Camilo Jose Cela,* University of Missouri Press, 1967.

Ilie, Paul, *La novelistica de Camilo Jose Cela,* Gredos, 1963.

Jones, Margaret E. W., *The Contemporary Spanish Novel, 1939-1975,* Twayne, 1985.

Kirsner, Robert, *The Novels and Travels of Camilo Jose Cela,* University of North Carolina Press, 1964.

McPheeters, D. W., *Camilo Jose Cela,* Twayne, 1969.

PERIODICALS

America, November 7, 1964.
Books Abroad, spring, 1953, winter, 1971.
Christian Science Monitor, January 14, 1965.
Hispania, March, 1965, March, 1966, September, 1966, September, 1967, May, 1972.
Los Angeles Times, November 2, 1989.
Michigan Quarterly Review, summer, 1969.
Nation, November 14, 1953.
New Statesman, February 19, 1965.
New Yorker, January 30, 1965.
New York Times, October 20, 1989.
New York Times Book Review, May 26, 1968.
Observer, February 14, 1965.
Saturday Review, November 23, 1964.
Spectator, February 19, 1965.
Times Literary Supplement, February 2, 1965, February 25, 1965, May 27, 1965, November 11, 1965, February 12, 1970, April 2, 1970, November 5, 1971, February 11, 1972.
Washington Post, October 20, 1989.
World Literature Today, autumn, 1977, summer, 1982, autumn, 1984.

CELAN, Paul
   See ANTSCHEL, Paul

*   *   *

CELINE, Louis-Ferdinand
   See DESTOUCHES, Louis-Ferdinand(-Auguste)

*   *   *

CENDRARS, Blaise
   See SAUSER-HALL, Frederic

*   *   *

CESAIRE, Aime (Fernand)   1913-

PERSONAL: Born June 25, 1913, in Basse-Pointe, Martinique, West Indies; son of Fernand (a comptroller with the revenue service) and Marie (Hermine) Cesaire; married Suzanne Roussi (a teacher), July 10, 1937; children: Jacques, Jean-Paul, Francis, Ina, Marc, Michelle. *Education:* Attended Ecole Normale Superieure, Paris; Sorbonne, University of Paris, licencie es lettres.

ADDRESSES: Office—Assemblee Nationale, 75007 Paris, France; and La Mairie, 97200 Fort-de-France, Martinique, West Indies.

CAREER: Lycee of Fort-de-France, Martinique, teacher, 1940-45; member of the two French constituent assemblies, 1945-46; mayor of Fort-de-France, 1945; deputy for Martinique in the French National Assembly, 1946. Conseiller general for the fourth canton (district) of Fort-de-France; president of the Parti Progressiste Martiniquais.

MEMBER: Society of African Culture (Paris; president).

AWARDS, HONORS: Aime Cesaire: The Collected Poetry was nominated for the *Los Angeles Times* Book Award, 1984.

WRITINGS:

(With Gaston Monnerville and Leopold Sedar-Senghor) *Commemoration du centenaire de l'abolition de l'esclavage: Discours pronounces a la Sorbonne le 27 avril 1948* (title means "Commemoration of the Centenary of the Abolition of Slavery: Speeches Given at the Sorbonne on April 27, 1948"), Presses Universitaires de France, 1948.
Discours sur le colonialisme, Reclame, 1950, 5th edition, Presence Africaine (Paris), 1970, translation by Joan Pinkham published as *Discourse on Colonialism,* Monthly Review Press, 1972.
Lettre a Maurice Thorez, 3rd edition, Presence Africaine, 1956, translation published as *Letter to Maurice Thorez,* 1957.
Toussaint L'Ouverture: La revolution francaise et le probleme coloniale (title means "Toussaint L'Ouverture: The French Revolution and the Colonial Problem"), Club Francais du Livre, 1960, revised edition, Presence Africaine, 1962.
Ouvres completes (title means "Complete Works"), three volumes, Editions Desormeaux, 1976.
(Contributor) *Studies in French,* William Marsh Rice University, 1977.
Culture and Colonization, University of Yaounde, 1978.

Also author of *Textes,* edited by R. Mercier and M. Battestini, French and European Publications.

POEMS

Les armes miraculeuses (title means "The Miracle Weapons"; also see below), Gallimard, 1946, reprinted, 1970.

Soleil Cou-Coupe (title means "Solar Throat Slashed"), K (Paris), 1948, reprinted (bound with *Antilles a main armee* by Charles Calixte) under title *Poems from Martinique,* Kraus, 1970.
Cahier d'un retour au pays natal, Presence Africaine, 1956, 2nd edition, 1960, translation by Emil Snyders published as *Return to My Native Land,* Presence Africaine, 1968, translation by John Berger and Anna Bostock published under same title, Penguin Books, 1969.
Ferrements (title means "Shackles"; also see below), Editions du Seuil, 1960.
Cadastre (also see below), Editions du Seuil, 1961, translation by Gregson Davis published as *Cadastre,* Third Press, 1972, translation by Snyders and Sanford Upson published under same title, Third Press, 1973.
State of the Union, translation by Clayton Eshleman and Dennis Kelly of selections from *Les armes miraculeuses, Ferrements,* and *Cadastre,* [Bloomington, Ill.], 1966.
Aime Cesaire: The Collected Poetry, translation and with an introduction by Eshleman and Annette Smith, University of California Press, 1983.
Non-Vicious Circle: Twenty Poems, translation by Davis, Stanford University Press, 1985.

Also author of *Corps perdu,* illustrations by Pablo Picasso, 1949, translation by Eshleman and Smith published as *Lost Body,* Braziller; and of *Moi, laminaire.*

PLAYS

Et les chiens se taisaient: Tragedie (title means "And the Dogs Were Silent: A Tragedy"), Presence Africaine, 1956.
La tragedie du roi Christophe, Presence Africaine, 1963, revised edition, 1973, translation by Ralph Manheim published as *The Tragedy of King Christophe,* Grove, 1970.
Une saison au Congo, Editions du Seuil, 1966, translation by Manheim published as *A Season in the Congo* (produced in New York at the Paperback Studio Theatre, July, 1970), Grove, 1969.
Une tempete: d'apres "le tempete" de Shakespeare. Adaptation pour un theatre negre, Editions du Seuil, 1969, translation by Richard Miller published as *A Tempest,* Ubu Repertory, 1986.

OTHER

Editor of *Tropiques,* 1941-45, and of *L'Afrique.*

SIDELIGHTS: Because of his role in creating and promoting negritude, a cultural movement which calls for black people to renounce Western society and adopt the traditional values of black civilization, Aime Cesaire is a prominent figure among blacks in the Third World. A native of the Caribbean island of Martinique, where he has served as mayor of the city of Fort-de-France since 1945, Cesaire also enjoys an international literary reputation for his poems and plays. His 1,000-line poem *Return to My Native Land,* a powerful piece written in extravagant, surreal language and dealing with the reawakening of black racial awareness, is a major work in contemporary French-language literature. Cesaire is, Serge Gavronsky states in the *New York Times Book Review,* "one of the most powerful French poets of this century."

At the age of 18 Cesaire left his native Martinique, at that time a colony of France, to attend school in Paris. The city was the center for a number of political and cultural movements during the 1930s, several of which especially influenced the young Cesaire and his fellow black students. Marxism gave them a revolutionary perspective, while surrealism provided them with a modernist esthetic by which to express themselves. Together with Leon-Goutran Damas and Leopold Sedar Senghor, who later became president of Senegal, Cesaire founded the magazine *L'Etudiant Noir,* in which the ideology of negritude was first developed and explained. "Negritude . . . proclaimed a pride in black culture and, in turning their contemporaries' gaze away from the fascination of things French, these young students began a revolution in attitudes which was to make a profound impact after the war," Clive Wake explains in the *Times Literary Supplement.* The influence of the movement on black writers in Africa and the Caribbean was so pervasive that the term negritude has come to refer to "large areas of black African and Caribbean literature in French, roughly from the 1930s to the 1960s," Christopher Miller writes in the *Washington Post Book World.*

The first use of the word negritude occurred in Cesaire's poem *Return to My Native Land (Cahier d'un retour au pays natal),* first published in the magazine *Volontes* in 1939. In this poem, Cesaire combines an exuberant wordplay, an encyclopedic vocabulary, and daring surreal metaphors with bits of African and Caribbean black history to create an "exorcism . . . of the poet's 'civilized' instincts, his lingering shame at belonging to a country and a race so abject, servile, petty and repressed as is his," Marjorie Perloff writes in the *American Poetry Review.* Gavronsky explains that the poem "is a concerted effort to affirm [Cesaire's] stature in French letters by a sort of poetic one-upmanship but also a determination to create a new language capable of expressing his African heritage." *Return to My Native Land,* Perloff maintains, is "a paratactic catalogue poem that piles up phrase upon phrase, image upon image, in a complex network of repetitions, its thrust is to define the threshold between sleep and waking—the sleep of oppression, the blind acceptance of the status quo, that gives way to rebirth, to a new awareness of what is and may be."

Written as Cesaire himself was leaving Paris to return to Martinique, *Return to My Native Land* reverberates with both personal and racial significance. The poet's definition of his own negritude comes to symbolize the growing self-awareness of all blacks of their cultural heritage. Judith Gleason, writing in the *Negro Digest,* believes that Cesaire's poetry is "grounded in the historical sufferings of a chosen people" and so "his is an angry, authentic vision of the promised land." Jean Paul Sartre, in an article for *The Black American Writer: Poetry and Drama,* writes that "Cesaire's words do not describe negritude, they do not designate it, they do not copy it from the outside like a painter with a model: they create it; they compose it under our very eyes."

Several critics see Cesaire as a writer who embodies the larger struggles of his people in all of his poetry. Hilary Okam of *Yale French Studies,* for example, argues that "Cesaire's poetic idiosyncrasies, especially his search for and use of uncommon vocabulary, are symptomatic of his own mental agony in the search for an exact definition of himself and, by extension, of his people and their common situation and destiny." Okam concludes that "it is clear from [Cesaire's] use of symbols and imagery, that despite years of alienation and acculturation he has continued to live in the concrete reality of his Negro-subjectivity." Writing in the *CLA Journal,* Ruth J. S. Simmons notes that although Cesaire's poetry is personal, he speaks from a perspective shared by many other blacks. "Poetry has been for him," Simmons explains, "an important vehicle of personal growth and self-revelation, [but] it has also been an important expression of the will and personality of a people. . . . [It is] impossible to consider the work of Cesaire outside of the context of the poet's personal vision and definition of his art. He defines his past as Afri-

can, his present as Antillean and his condition as one of having been exploited. . . . To remove Cesaire from this context is to ignore what he was and still is as a man and as a poet."

The concerns found in *Return to My Native Land* ultimately transcend the personal or racial, addressing liberation and self-awareness in universal terms. Gleason calls *Return to My Native Land* "a masterpiece of cultural relevance, every bit as 'important' as 'The Wasteland,' its remarkable virtuosity will ensure its eloquence long after the struggle for human dignity has ceased to be viewed in racial terms." Andre Breton, writing in *What Is Surrealism?: Selected Writings,* also sees larger issues at stake in the poem. "What, in my eyes, renders this protest invaluable," Breton states, "is that it continually transcends the anguish which for a black man is inseparable from the lot of blacks in modern society, and unites with the protest of every poet, artist and thinker worthy of the name . . . to embrace the entire intolerable though amendable condition created for *man* by this society."

Cesaire's poetic language was strongly influenced by the French surrealists of the 1930s, but he uses familiar surrealist poetic techniques in a distinctive manner. Breton claims that Cesaire "is a black man who handles the French language as no white man can handle it today." Alfred Cismaru states in *Renascence* that Cesaire's "separation from Europe makes it possible for him to break with clarity and description, and to become intimate with the fundamental essence of things. Under his powerful, poetic eye, perception knows no limits and pierces appearances without pity. Words emerge and explode like firecrackers, catching the eye and the imagination of the reader. He makes use of the entire dictionary, of artificial and vulgar words, of elegant and forgotten ones, of technical and invented vocabulary, marrying it to Antillean and African syllables, and allowing it to play freely in a sort of flaming folly that is both a challenge and a tenacious attempt at mystification."

The energy of Cesaire's poetic language is seen by some critics as a form of literary violence, with the jarring images and forceful rhythms of the poetry assaulting the reader. Perloff finds that Cesaire's "is a language so violently charged with meaning that each word falls on the ear (or hits the eye) with resounding force." Gleason explains this violence as the expression of an entire race, not just of one man: "Cesaire's is the turbulent poetry of the spiritually dislocated, of the damned. His images strike through the net. . . . Cesaire's is the Black Power of the imagination."

This violent energy is what first drew Cesaire to surrealism. The surrealist artists and writers of the 1930s saw themselves as rebels against a stale and outmoded culture. Their works were meant to revive and express unconscious, suppressed, and forbidden desires. Politically, they aligned themselves with the revolutionary left. As Gavronsky explains, "Cesaire's efforts to forge a verbal medium that would identify him with the opposition to existing political conditions and literary conventions [led him to] the same camp as the Surrealists, who had combined a new poetics that liberated the image from classical restraints with revolutionary politics influenced by Marx and his followers." Cesaire was to remain a surrealist for many years, but he eventually decided that his political concerns would best be served by more realistic forms of writing. "For decades," Karl Keller notes in the *Los Angeles Times Book Review,* "[Cesaire] found the surreal aesthetically revolutionary, but in the face of the torture and the suffering, he has pretty well abandoned it as a luxury."

In the late 1950s Cesaire began to write realistic plays for the theatre, hoping in this way to attract a larger audience to his work. These plays are more explicitly political than his poetry and focus on historical black nationalist leaders of the Third World. *The Tragedy of King Christophe* (*La tragedie du roi Christophe*) is a biographical drama about King Henri Christophe of Haiti, a black leader of that island nation in the early nineteenth century. After fighting in a successful revolution against the French colonists, Christophe assumed power and made himself king. But his cruelty and arbitrary use of power led to a rebellion in turn against his own rule, and Christophe committed suicide. Writing in *Studies in Black Literature*, Henry Cohen calls *The Tragedy of King Christophe* "one of French America's finest literary expressions." *A Season in the Congo* (*Une saison au Congo*) follows the political career of Patrice Lumumba, first president of the Republic of the Congo in Africa. Lumumba's career was also tragic. With the independence of the Congo in 1960, Lumumba became president of the new nation. But the resulting power struggles among black leaders led in 1961 to Lumumba's assassination by his political opponents. The reviewer for *Prairie Schooner* calls *A Season in the Congo* "a passionate and poetic drama." Wake remarks that Cesaire's plays have "greatly widened [his] audience and perhaps tempted them to read the poetry." Gavronsky claims that "in the [1960s, Cesaire] was . . . the leading black dramatist writing in French."

Despite the international acclaim he has received for his poetry and plays, Cesaire is still best known on Martinique for his political career. Since 1945 he has served as mayor of Fort-de-France and as a member of the French National Assembly. For the first decade of his career Cesaire was affiliated with the Communist bloc of the assembly, then moved to the Parti du Regroupement Africain et des Federalistes for a short time, and is now president of the Parti Progressiste Martiniquais, a leftist political organization. Cesaire's often revolutionary rhetoric is in sharp contrast to his usually moderate political actions. He opposes independence for Martinique, for example, and was instrumental in having the island declared an oversea department of France—a status similar to that of Puerto Rico to the United States. And as a chief proponent of negritude, which calls for blacks to reject Western culture, Cesaire nonetheless writes his works in French, not in his native black language of creole.

But what may seem contradictory in Cesaire's life and work is usually seen by critics as the essential tension that makes his voice uniquely important. A. James Arnold, in his *Modernism and Negritude: The Poetry and Poetics of Aime Cesaire*, examines and accepts the tension between Cesaire's European literary sources and his black subject matter and between his modernist sensibility and his black nationalist concerns. Miller explains that "Arnold poses the riddle of Cesaire with admirable clarity" and "effectively defuses . . . either a wholly African or a wholly European Cesaire." This uniting of the European and African is also noted by Clayton Eshleman and Annette Smith in their introduction to *Aime Cesaire: The Collected Poetry*. They describe Cesaire as "a bridge between the twain that, in principle, should never meet, Europe and Africa. . . . It was by borrowing European techniques that he succeeded in expressing his Africanism in its purest form." Similarly, Sartre argues that "in Cesaire, the great surrealist tradition is realized, it takes on its definitive meaning and is destroyed: surrealism—that European movement—is taken from the Europeans by a Black man who turns it against them and gives it vigorously defined function."

It is because of his poetry that Cesaire is primarily known worldwide, while in the Third World he is usually seen as an important black nationalist theoretician. Speaking of his poetry, Gavronsky explains that Cesaire is "among the major French poets of this century." Cismaru believes that Cesaire "is a poet's poet when he stays clear of political questions, a tenacious and violent propagandist when the theme requires it. His place in contemporary French letters . . . is assured in spite of the fact that not many agree with his views on Whites in general, nor with his opinions on Europe, in particular." *Return to My Native Land* has been his most influential work, particularly in the Third World where, Wake notes, "by the 1960s it was widely known and quoted because of its ideological and political significance." To European and American critics, *Return to My Native Land* is seen as a masterpiece of surrealist literature. Cesaire's coining of the term negritude and his continued promotion of a distinctly black culture separate from Western culture has made him especially respected in the emerging black nations. Eshleman and Smith report that "although Cesaire was by no means the sole exponent of negritude, the word is now inseparable from his name, and largely responsible for his prominent position in the Third World."

BIOGRAPHICAL/CRITICAL SOURCES:

BOOKS

Aime Cesaire: Ecrivain Martiniquais, Fernand Nathan, 1967.
Arnold, A. James, *Modernism and Negritude: The Poetry and Poetics of Aime Cesaire*, Harvard University Press, 1981.
Bigsby, C. W. E., editor, *The Black American Writer: Poetry and Drama*, Volume 2, Penguin Books, 1971.
Breton, Andre, *What Is Surrealism?: Selected Writings*, edited by Franklin Rosemont, Monad Press, 1978.
Contemporary Literary Criticism, Gale, Volume 19, 1981, Volume 32, 1985.
Kesteloot, Lilyan, *Aime Cesaire*, P. Seghers, 1962, new edition, 1970.
Leiner, Jacqueline, *Soleil eclate: Melanges offerts a Aime Cesaire a l'occasion de son soixante-dixieme anniversaire par une equipe internationale d'artiste et de chercheurs*, Gunter Narr Verlag (Tubingen), 1985.

PERIODICALS

American Poetry Review, January-February, 1984.
CLA Journal, March, 1976.
Comparative Literature Studies, summer, 1978.
Le Monde, December, 1981.
Los Angeles Times Book Review, December 4, 1983.
Negro Digest, January, 1970.
New York Times Book Review, February 19, 1984.
Prairie Schooner, spring, 1972.
Renascence, winter, 1974.
Studies in Black Literature, winter, 1974.
Times Literary Supplement, July 19, 1985.
Twentieth Century Literature, July, 1972.
Washington Post Book World, February 5, 1984.
Yale French Studies, Number 53, 1976.

*   *   *

CHAMBERS, Jessie
See LAWRENCE, D(avid) H(erbert Richards)

*   *   *

CHANDLER, Raymond (Thornton) 1888-1959

PERSONAL: Born July 23, 1888, in Chicago, Ill.; died March 26, 1959, in La Jolla, Calif.; buried at Mount Hope Cemetery,

San Diego, Calif.; son of Maurice Benjamin and Florence Dart (Thornton) Chandler; married Pearl Cecily (some sources say Eugenia or Eugenie) Hurlburt, 1924 (died, 1954). *Education:* Educated in England, France, and Germany.

ADDRESSES: Home—La Jolla, Calif.

CAREER: The Admiralty, London, England, worker in supplies and accounting departments, 1907; reporter for *Daily Express,* London, and *Western Gazette,* Bristol, England, both 1908-12; worked as menial laborer in St. Louis, Mo., c. 1912; worked at sporting goods company in California; Los Angeles Creamery, Los Angeles, Calif., accountant and bookkeeper, 1912-17; worked at bank in San Francisco, Calif., 1919; *Daily Express,* Los Angeles, reporter, 1919; Dabney Oil Syndicate, Los Angeles, 1922-32, began as bookkeeper, became auditor; writer, 1933-59. *Military service:* Served in Canadian Army, 1917-18, and in Royal Air Force, 1918-19.

MEMBER: Mystery Writers of America (president, 1959).

AWARDS, HONORS: Nomination for Academy Award for best screenplay from Academy of Motion Picture Arts and Sciences, 1944, for "Double Indemnity"; Edgar Allan Poe Award from Mystery Writers of America and nomination for Academy Award for best original screenplay, both 1946, both for "The Blue Dahlia"; Edgar Allan Poe Award from Mystery Writers of America, 1954, for *The Long Goodbye.*

WRITINGS:

The Big Sleep (novel), Knopf, 1939, reprinted, Vintage Books, 1976.
Farewell, My Lovely (novel), Knopf, 1940, reprinted, Vintage Books, 1976.
The High Window (novel), Knopf, 1942, reprinted, Vintage Books, 1976.
The Lady in the Lake (novel), Knopf, 1943, reprinted, Vintage Books, 1976.
Five Murders (short stories), Avon, 1944.
Five Sinister Characters (short stories), Avon, 1945.
Red Wind: A Collection of Short Stories, World, 1946.
Finger Man, and Other Stories, Avon, 1947.
Spanish Blood (short stories), World, 1946.
The Little Sister (novel), Houghton, 1949, reprinted as *Marlowe,* Pocket Books, 1969.
The Simple Art of Murder (includes the stories "Trouble Is My Business" and "Pick-Up on Noon Street," and the essay "The Simple Art of Murder"; also see below), Houghton, 1950, "The Simple Art of Murder" published separately, Pocket Books, 1953.
Trouble Is My Business: Four Stories From "The Simple Art of Murder," Pocket Books, 1951.
Pick-Up on Noon Street (short stories), Pocket Books, 1952.
The Long Good-Bye (novel), Hamish Hamilton, 1953, published as *The Long Goodbye,* Houghton, 1954.
Pearls Are a Nuisance (short stories), Hamish Hamilton, 1953.
Playback (novel), Houghton, 1958.
Raymond Chandler Speaking (letters, criticism, and fiction), edited by Dorothy Gardiner and Kathrine Sorley Walker, Houghton, 1962.
Killer in the Rain (short stories), edited by Philip Durham, Houghton, 1964.
The Smell of Fear (short stories), Hamish Hamilton, 1965.
The Midnight Raymond Chandler (omnibus), edited by Joan Kahn, Houghton, 1971.
Chandler Before Marlowe: Raymond Chandler's Early Prose and Poetry, 1908-1912, edited by Matthew J. Bruccoli, introduc-

tion by Jacques Barzun, University of South Carolina Press, 1973.
The Notebooks of Raymond Chandler, and "English Summer: A Gothic Romance," edited by Frank MacShane, Ecco Press, 1976.
Smart-Aleck Kill (short stories), Penguin, 1976.
The Blue Dahlia (screenplay; released by Paramount, 1946), edited by Bruccoli, Southern Illinois University Press, 1976.
(With James M. Fox) *Raymond Chandler and James M. Fox: Letters,* privately printed, 1979.
Selected Letters of Raymond Chandler, edited by McShane, Columbia University Press, 1981.
Raymond Chandler's Unknown Thriller: The Screenplay of "Playback," Mysterious Press, 1985.
(With Robert B. Parker) *Poodle Springs* (novel), Putnam, 1989.

Works also published in various collections and multi-novel volumes.

Contributor to periodicals, including *Academy, Atlantic Monthly, Black Mask, Detection Fiction Weekly, Detective Story, Dime Detective, Spectator, Unknown,* and *Westminster Gazette.*

OTHER SCREENPLAYS

(With Billy Wilder) "Double Indemnity" (adapted from James M. Cain's novel of the same title), Paramount, 1944.
(With Frank Partos) "And Now Tomorrow" (adapted from Rachel Field's novel of the same title), Paramount, 1944.
(With Hagar Wilde) "The Unseen" (adapted from Ethel Lina White's book *Her Heart in Her Throat*), Paramount, 1945.
(With Czenzi Ormonde) "Strangers on a Train" (adapted from Patricia Highsmith's novel of the same title), Warner Bros., 1951.

SIDELIGHTS: Raymond Chandler has been acclaimed as American literature's finest writer of hard-boiled detective fiction. Despite a romantic nature and genteel tastes, he was drawn to contemporary society's venal underside, and he captured its rough idiom with acuity and imaginative power. His fictional milieu was the mean streets of urban America, a country he described in *Trouble Is My Business* (1951) as "a world gone wrong." He was particularly drawn to southern California, with its image as a modern paradise blighted by corruption, and better than any other writer of his time he captured the area's seamy glamour. For Chandler, the Golden State, bathed in the mystique of the American Dream but vitiated by sham and plunder, symbolized the dark side of success. Indeed his entire fictional canon may be understood as a sustained indictment of a nation obsessed with the pursuit of money and power. As his admirer and literary heir Ross Macdonald declared in his introduction to Matthew J. Bruccoli's *Kenneth Millar/Ross Macdonald: A Checklist,* Chandler was a "slumming angel" who transformed the detective story into a critique of American culture's more base aspects.

Chandler's fiction was propelled by a complex morality, one that biographer Jerry Speir described as an "essential dualism of mind . . . which perpetually balanced an innate romanticism against a very self-conscious cynicism." This dualism was rooted in Chandler's English upbringing. Though born in midwest America, he was transplanted in early youth to England, where he studied the classics and embraced the public school's traditional code of manly virtue through honor and personal sacrifice. At home in his maternal grandmother's household, he was sequestered in what Natasha Spender has described—in an essay collected in editor Miriam Gross's *The World of Raymond Chandler*—as an atmosphere of "high Victorian rectitude," prompting in the adolescent boy both a fussy puritanism and an exaggerated attraction to things masculine and tough.

Perhaps as a consequence of his adolescent confusions, Chandler had little sense of professional direction following his schooling, though he harbored literary ambitions. In his twenties, he worked as a free-lance writer, publishing reviews, poetry, and essays. The poetry, reflecting the more sentimental influences of the era, has been generally dismissed as lofty in subject and mawkish in tone. The essays, however, hint at the wry humor characteristic of Chandler's later works, and behind the elevated Victorian prose of the more atmospheric pieces lurks the same fascination with decadence that surfaced so sharply in Chandler's Los Angeles tales two decades later.

Although realizing his literary aspirations, Chandler soon grew discontented with life in England. "America seemed to call me in some mysterious way," he recalled in a July 1958 letter to English mystery writer Michael Gilbert. Seeking more lucrative prospects, Chandler repatriated to the United States, and he eventually settled in southern California. After a series of false starts he took an executive position with an oil company. Around this time—the mid-1920s—he also married a socially prominent woman who was his elder by eighteen years.

Despite the prosperity and apparent stability that Chandler enjoyed during the next twenty years, he harbored acute inner stresses. In business he vacillated between driving ambition and moral skepticism about money, and in marriage he played both the chivalrous, adulating spouse and the compulsive philanderer. Alcohol, profligacy, and the impending economic catastrophe of the Depression compounded his turmoil, and at the age of forty-four Chandler lost his job. He then decided to fulfill his long-thwarted literary aspirations.

Chandler returned to writing by studying twentieth-century American masters. From Ernest Hemingway he learned a lean prose style and the virtues of masculine ethos, and from Theodore Dreiser and Ring Lardner he took an appreciation for the raw vigor of urban life. Proletarian fiction and Marxist journalism were also influential, for their gritty literary vocabulary proved richly suited to articulating the baneful effects of capitalism. In the pages of *Black Mask* and other pulp magazines, writers like Dashiell Hammett, Erle Stanley Gardner, and Carroll John Daly crafted the hard-boiled genre probing America's criminal domain, and in their works Chandler found the literary materials for his own more complex, more visionary fiction.

Taking inspiration from his precursors in what has come to be called "tough guy" fiction, Chandler published the deftly executed "Blackmailers Don't Shoot" in the December 1933 issue of *Black Mask.* This dark tale of extortion and racketeering contains all the hard-boiled genre's convention: violence, corrupt officials, gangsters and gun molls, and a detective with a fast gun and a code of ethics.

Black Mask was a fitting forum for Chandler and other writers who practiced cynicism while adhering to a romantic ethos. Joseph T. Shaw, chief editor of the magazine, had described its typical reader as "a . . . stalwart, rugged specimen of humanity— hard as nails, swift of hand and foot, clear-eyed, unprovocative but ready to tackle anything that gets in the way." Such readers, Shaw contended, despise "injustice, cowardly underhandedness" and cheer "for the right guy to come out on top." This profile became a model for Chandler's own literary hero: a latter-day knight driven by romantic quests in a seamy world of crime and compromise.

Though inevitably employed as investigators, the heroes of Chandler's tales face challenges beyond mere exercises in discovery. His protagonists are thrown into moral chaos; caught up in webs of deceit, corruption, and bloodshed; and faced with the task of uncovering and overcoming the pervasive wrongdoing. In Chandler's fiction crime is everywhere, and unsavory elements in the law, business, and even the clergy combine to form a criminal society that R. W. Flint described in a *Partisan Review* essay as "a jungle of predatory creatures."

While Chandler's private-eye heroes are essentially the same— grizzled romantics holding to an ideal of gallantry—his actual approach to hard-boiled storytelling underwent some important changes. Increasingly, Chandler's tales of the 1930s came to center on the protagonist's struggle to maintain moral equilibrium, and in his fourth published tale, "Killer in the Rain" (1935), he intensified the hero's alienation and ethical predicament through first-person narration. By adopting and then remodeling devices introduced by Hammett, Chandler presented the hero-as-narrator, a jaded storyteller whose caustic wit and barbed asides illuminate the moral deviations of the criminal world.

In addition Chandler developed his own literary style. More verbally adventurous than Hammett, Chandler produced a narrative pattern blending underworld vernacular with poetic diction. This pattern relied on pungent imagery, including startling similes, for dramatic effect and figurative meaning. As Peter Wolfe wrote in *Something More Than Night: The Case of Raymond Chandler,* Chandler created a darkly lyrical prose that turned his stories into "metaphors of the urban nightmare."

Chandler set most of these "urban nightmares" in Los Angeles, and its portrait is among the most salient feature of his novels. A late comer to southern California, Chandler was at once attracted and repulsed by "its paradox of beauty and tawdriness," as Robert Kirsch asserted in the *Los Angeles Times Book Review.* Chandler knew of California's appeal as a mecca of opportunity—a holdover from the Gold Rush days of easy money—and its image as a pastoral haven. But Los Angeles at mid-century hardly lived up to its advertised allurements, and Chandler was struck by the disparity. Pilgrims to the city found there a sprawling town that had grown explosively and erratically. Irresponsible development, fueled by the discovery of oil in the southern basin in 1892, despoiled the landscape; scandal marred local government; and the movie industry nurtured a subculture of artifice and excess.

Like Gardner and Hammett before him, Chandler drew on the irony of California's status as the Golden State and used the setting to suggest the beguiling and corruptive power of money in American life. Ultimately, Chandler presented a more provocative Los Angeles than had any of his predecessors. In *Nation,* Thomas S. Reck called Chandler "the Los Angeles laureate," adding that "no city lends itself more to metaphor than Los Angeles, and no writer has risen to the implicit challenge better."

In 1939, Chandler vividly depicted Los Angeles in his first novel, *The Big Sleep,* which showed the city as a squalid hotbed of blackmail, gambling, flesh peddling, and drug dealing. The hero is Philip Marlowe, a private detective whose investigation into an apparently routine extortion scheme sucks him into a cycle of progressively more menacing events. In the beginning, Marlowe conceives of his task in relatively simple terms: free the daughter of his employer, the tycoon Sternwood, from extortionists. But like Dante in Hell, Marlowe undertakes a dark and disgusting journey, one that reveals the consequences of ghastly transgressions. The childlike Carmen Sternwood, pampered and indulged from birth, is initially seen as the victim of crime. Marlowe, however, discovers that the Sternwood family's veneer of gentility masks perversion and treachery, and in uncovering the blackmailers he exposes Carmen Sternwood as a murderer. As Peter J. Rabinowitz observed in *Texas Studies in Literature and Language,* "the novel ends not with the soothing conservative affirmation of order, but with something more politically unsettling: . . . a pervasive sense of individual despair, social chaos, and the triumph of evil." Indeed, some critics found *The Big Sleep* so hard-boiled as to make other crime writers seem totally innocuous by comparison.

In Marlowe, the consummate detective, Chandler created his most enduring hero. Like Chandler's earlier heroes, Marlowe is an idealist at heart, and he is embittered by the decadence of contemporary life. He too is cast as a would-be knight, but his chivalry, though admirable to his author, is now seen as "hopelessly anachronistic," according to William H. Marling in his study *Raymond Chandler.* Chandler noted as much in a May, 1959, letter to James Sandoe, a reviewer of detective fiction: "[Marlowe] never gets the girl, never marries, never really has any private life, except insofar as he must eat and sleep and have a place to keep his clothes. . . . He gets nothing but his fee, for which he will if he can protect the innocent, guard the helpless and destroy the wicked, and the fact that he must do this while earning a meagre living in a corrupt world is what makes him stand out."

Throughout *The Big Sleep* and Chandler's subsequent novels, allusions to Marlowe's heroic bravura are pointedly ironic, and he frequently mocks his own gallantry or conceals it behind a caustic wit and tough-guy banter. E. M. Beekman describes the sleuth in the *Massachusetts Review* as "an outsider, a loner, a man who will not fit the pattern" and "must not tow the line." Rootless, friendless, without family bonds, and devoid of personal history, Marlowe is the archetypal modern man, struggling to preserve his integrity in a profligate society of debased values. His self-proclaimed mission—futile but no less implacably pursued—is to cleanse the modern world of its venality.

Determined to remain undefiled by the rapacity that is everywhere around him, Marlowe clings adamantly to his role as a professional. He holds to a pattern of straight dealing with clients and fair compensation for services provided; but honesty is doomed in a culture so acquisitive. As R. W. Lid observed in *Kenyon Review,* Chandler "saw the American psyche as criminally obsessed with the dollar," and he fueled his fiction with this vision of money as pathology. "To hell with the rich," Marlowe says in *The Big Sleep.* "They made me sick."

With *The Big Sleep* Chandler began moving detective fiction away from escapism and mere problem solving. Although he had, at one time, praised the thrillers of Hammett and other pulp writers, he eventually espoused crime novels of greater social criticism. In his essay "The Simple Art of Murder," Chandler lambasted fashionable whodunits as "middling-dull, pooped-out piece[s] of utterly unreal and mechanical fiction," and he advocated the study of crimes rooted in "the seamy side of things"—of murders perpetrated by "the kind of people that commit it for reasons, not just to provide a corpse." Consistent with his conception of America as a slew of capitalist vice, Chandler called for a literature of unsparing realism.

As Chandler's fiction became more complex, it outgrew the short story format. Julian Symonds, in an essay included in Miriam Gross's *The World of Raymond Chandler,* noted: "The pulp magazines had shaped him, but once he had learned the trade they were a restriction. The novels enabled him to burst the bonds and to express the essential Raymond Chandler." After publishing *The Big Sleep* in 1939, Chandler wrote several

more novels featuring Marlowe. In producing these works he mined his own previously published tales, extracting and refashioning plot elements, characters, scenes, and memorable phrasings. Chandler referred to this reworking of material as "cannibalizing"—but this term proved overly modest, for Chandler was able to transform engaging but formula-bound short fiction into novels of compelling power.

Chandler followed *The Big Sleep* with *Farewell, My Lovely* (1940), his personal favorite of the Marlowe novels. This work features all the characteristic Chandler elements and entwines themes of female duplicity, affluent criminality, and police corruption. The story's locale is Bay City, a fictional town—based loosely on Santa Monica—whose resplendent surface belies its corrupt core. As Frank MacShane asserted in *The Life of Raymond Chandler,* "For Chandler, Bay City was a symbol of hypocrisy: he hated the pretense of uprightness in a place virtually owned by a few people with money." Focusing on what Gavin Lambert described in *The Dangerous Edge* as "Chandler's favorite mystery pattern, the secret alliances between wealth and the underworld," *Farewell, My Lovely* concerns a wealthy socialite who commits murder to conceal her lowly show-girl background. Marlowe, seeking to uncover the woman's past, delves into the workings of Bay City law enforcement, which has conspired to guard her secret. He discovers corruption spanning from street police to high-ranking city officials.

The theme of corruption as a massive chain of crime and coverup is reworked in variant fashion in Chandler's subsequent novels. *The High Window* traces the private vices of a high-born Pasadena clan whose misdeeds have recoiled upon them, blighting the entire family and engendering a pattern of violent retribution that destroys them all before ending. *The Lady in the Lake,* reviving *Farewell, My Lovely*'s motif of disguised identity, features an ambitious and amoral social climber who repeatedly sheds aliases as she ensnares others into her ruthless scheme of self-advancement. *The Little Sister,* set in the Hollywood "dream factory," uses the movie industry, with its cynical propagation of illusion and staged sex, to diagnose the deeper social ills that befall a culture smitten with pretense. Philip Marlowe, sentimental but more case-hardened with each new foray into evil, provides the moral and visual sensibility that knits these novels into a cohesive design.

The Long Goodbye (1953), another Marlowe novel, signals some subtle evolutions in Chandler's work. The recurrent story of the woman who schemes her way into high society undergirds this novel, but here the emphasis has shifted from the perfidy of the *femme fatale* to the plight of the men who have been her victims: Roger Wade, a sullen writer drowning in alcohol and self-pity, and Terry Lennox, a self-aggrandizing American with a British background. Both have been viewed by critics as autobiographical portraits of Chandler, for he shared both Wade's acrimonious personality—his writer's angst—and Terry Lennox's British past and flair for self-dramatization. Jerry Speir, in his *Raymond Chandler,* called *The Long Goodbye* Chandler's "most personal novel and his most . . . autobiographical work," and he added that it is Chandler's "boldest attempt to exceed the confines of the detective mystery."

The Long Goodbye also marks a modification in the character of Marlowe, whose tough exterior is here more easily and deeply penetrated, and whose repressed yearnings for both male friendship and romantic love are acted out. Though *The Long Goodbye* reprises the hard-boiled elements that defined Chandler's previous works, some critics complained that its more poignant tone lacked the sparkle of its predecessors. Other critics, however, have admired the novel's sensitive and subtly layered portrait of Marlowe and its more rounded vision of humanity. In *The Black Mask Boys* William F. Nolan expressed the favorable judgment, praising *The Long Goodbye* as Chandler's "finest, most mature writing achievement."

Following the publication of *The Long Goodbye,* Chandler's productivity dissipated markedly. The death of his wife in 1954 after a long illness hurried the decline. Chandler, who had idealized his wife while simultaneously committing repeated infidelities, surrendered increasingly to bouts of guilt and alcoholic depression. His work habits, which had never been stable, degenerated accordingly, and his creativity atrophied.

Playback, published in 1958, represented Chandler's last substantial endeavor. It is a disappointing and relatively uninspired work derived from an unproduced film script. The novel's title calls attention to the recurrent theme of the inescapable past. Marlowe is again faced with an enigmatic woman whose impersonation conceals a string of crimes, but his unraveling of that mystery is overshadowed by an ending that has him accepting a marriage proposal. Most critics share Peter Wolfe's judgment in *Something More Than Night,* where he wrote that *Playback* is "tired and flawed," relying on both cliched plot devices and a banal, unconvincingly romantic resolution.

At the time of his death in 1959, Chandler was at work on a novel in which Marlowe is married and living in Palm Springs. That work, left incomplete by Chandler, was finished by a later crime writer, Robert B. Parker, and published in 1989 as *Poodle Springs.*

Although Chandler will be remembered for his Marlowe novels, he had also proved a successful screenwriter before he began his decline. It is not difficult to understand why Paramount sought out Chandler in 1943 to collaborate with director Billy Wilder on a movie version of James M. Cain's thriller *Double Indemnity.* Cain's grim novel, in which a wife plots with an insurance agent to murder her husband and claim a big payoff, replicates Chandler's own corrupt California world. Chandler's contribution to the film was substantial. Writing most of the film's charged dialogue and restructuring the narrative by layering flashbacks, he produced a deft fusion of the eroticism and danger that characterized the *film noir* genre.

With the success of "Double Indemnity," which earned Chandler an Academy Award nomination, came more film projects. One such project, "Playback," was scrapped in 1947 and emerged later as the novel; the other, "The Blue Dahlia," was completed in 1946 as a vehicle for actor Alan Ladd. Chandler's original story, in which a faithless wife is murdered by a disturbed veteran friend of her husband's, reflected the plot ingenuity and psychological resonance that had been hallmarks of Chandler's best work. But various circumstances, including a hectic production schedule, war-time censorship imposed by the Navy, and Chandler's heavy drinking, resulted in a hurried final script. Though the film proved commercially and critically successful, earning Chandler another Academy Award nomination, it nonetheless served to indicate his growing dissatisfaction with film work. His final filmed script, an adaptation of Patricia Highsmith's thriller *Strangers on a Train,* was disdained by director Alfred Hitchcock, and in the early 1950s Chandler withdrew from Hollywood.

Despite the creative decline and personal dislocation of Chandler's final years, his ample literary legacy was consequential enough to sustain his stature as one of America's most original literary voices. He had demonstrated, better than any other

writer of his day or since, the imaginative possibilities of the detective story, and he had transformed the genre from formulaic puzzlement to cultural inquiry. What was perfunctory violence in the hands of less gifted and less visionary writers was, for Chandler, a kind of poetry of the streets. He invested the regional literature of southern California with evocative power and metaphoric energy, making it stand as an emblem of the latent pathologies of American life. He created enduring images of the dark forces of contemporary experience. Biographer Frank MacShane aptly summarized Chandler's achievement by calling him "a prophet of modern America," one whose vision "has become increasingly fulfilled."

MEDIA ADAPTATIONS: Farewell, My Lovely was filmed as "Murder, My Sweet" with Dick Powell in 1945, and, under its original title, with Robert Mitchum in 1975; *The Big Sleep* was filmed—by director Howard Hawks from an adaptation by William Faulkner, among others—with Humphrey Bogart and Lauren Bacall in 1946, and with Robert Mitchum in 1978; *The Lady in the Lake* was filmed in 1946 by actor-director Robert Montgomery; *The High Window* inspired the 1942 film "Time to Kill" and was filmed as "The Brasher Dubloon" with George Montgomery in 1947; *The Little Sister* was filmed as "Marlowe" with James Garner in 1969; *The Long Goodbye* was filmed—by director Robert Altman—with Elliott Gould in 1973.

BIOGRAPHICAL/CRITICAL SOURCES:

BOOKS

Benstock, Bernard, editor, *Art in Crime Writing: Essays on Detective Fiction,* St. Martin's, 1983.
Bruccoli, Matthew J., *Kenneth Millar/Ross Macdonald: A Checklist,* Gale, 1971.
Bruccoli, Matthew J., *Raymond Chandler: A Descriptive Bibliography,* University of Pittsburgh Press, 1979.
Cawelti, John G., *Adventure, Mystery, and Romance: Formula Stories as Art and Popular Culture,* University of Chicago Press, 1976.
Chandler, Raymond, *The Simple Art of Murder,* Houghton, 1950.
Chandler, Raymond, *Selected Letters of Raymond Chandler,* edited by Frank MacShane, Columbia University Press, 1981.
Dictionary of Literary Biography Documentary Series, Volume 6, Gale, 1989.
Durham, Philip, *Down These Mean Streets a Man Must Go: Raymond Chandler's Knight,* University of North Carolina Press, 1963.
Eames, Hugh, *Sleuths, Inc.,* Lippincott, 1977.
Fine, David, editor, *Los Angeles in Fiction,* University of New Mexico Press, 1984.
Goulart, Ron, editor, *The Hardboiled Dicks: An Anthology and Study of Pulp Detective Fiction,* Pocket Books, 1967.
Gross, Miriam, editor, *The World of Raymond Chandler,* A & W Publishers, 1978.
Hamilton, Cynthia S., *Western and Hard-Boiled Detective Fiction in America: From High Noon to Midnight,* University of Iowa Press, 1987.
Knight, Stephen, *Form and Ideology in Crime Fiction,* Macmillan, 1980.
Lambert, Gavin, *The Dangerous Edge,* Grossman, 1976.
Luhr, William, *Raymond Chandler and Film,* Ungar, 1982.
MacShane, Frank, *The Life of Raymond Chandler,* Dutton, 1976.
Madden, David, *Tough Guy Writers of the Thirties,* Southern Illinois University Press, 1968.
Marling, William H., *Raymond Chandler,* Twayne, 1986.

Maugham, W. Somerset, *The Vagrant Mood*, Doubleday, 1953.

Most, Glenn W., and William W. Stowe, editors, *The Poetics of Murder: Detective Fiction and Literary Theory*, Harcourt, 1983.

Newlin, Keith, *Hardboiled Burlesque: Raymond Chandler's Comic Style*, Brownstone, 1984.

Nolan, William F., *The Black Mask Boys*, Morrow, 1985.

Pendo, Stephen, *Raymond Chandler on Screen: His Novels Into Film*, Scarecrow, 1976.

Porter, Dennis, *The Pursuit of Crime: Art and Ideology in Detective Fiction*, Yale University Press, 1981.

Powell, Lawrence Clark, *California Classics: The Creative Literature of the Golden State*, Ward Ritchie, 1971.

Ruehlmann, William, *Saint With a Gun: The Unlawful American Private Eye*, New York University Press, 1974.

Speir, Jerry, *Raymond Chandler*, Ungar, 1981.

Thorpe, Edward, *Chandlertown: The Los Angeles of Philip Marlowe*, Vermilion, 1983.

Twentieth-Century Literary Criticism, Gale, Volume 1, 1978, Volume 7, 1982.

Wells, Walter, *Tycoons and Locusts: A Regional Look at Hollywood Fiction of the Thirties*, Southern Illinois University Press, 1973.

Wolfe, Peter, *Something More Than Night: The Case of Raymond Chandler*, Bowling Green State University Press, 1985.

PERIODICALS

Antaeus, spring-summer, 1977.
Atlantic Monthly, November, 1945.
Black Mask, April, 1933.
Chicago Tribune, October 12, 1989.
Clues: A Journal of Detection, fall-winter, 1980.
Commentary, February, 1963.
Kenyon Review, spring, 1979.
London Magazine, December, 1959.
Los Angeles Times, October 10, 1988.
Los Angeles Times Book Review, June 27, 1976.
Massachusetts Review, winter, 1973.
Nation, April 23, 1960, September 4, 1960.
New Republic, May 7, 1962.
New Statesman, April 9, 1949.
Newsweek, May 14, 1945, October 31, 1949.
New Yorker, March 11, 1962.
New York Times, May 9, 1946.
New York Times Book Review, September 27, 1949.
New York Times Magazine, December 23, 1973.
Partisan Review, May-June, 1947.
Southern Review, summer, 1970.
Texas Studies in Literature and Language, summer, 1980.
Time, October 3, 1949.
Washington Post, September 11, 1988.

OBITUARIES:

PERIODICALS

New York Times, March 27, 1959.
Times (London), March 28, 1959.

*   *   *

CHAPMAN, Walker
See SILVERBERG, Robert

CHAR, Rene(-Emile) 1907-1988

PERSONAL: Born June 14, 1907, in L'Isle-sur-Sorgue, Vaucluse, France; died, February 19, 1988, in the military hospital Val-de-Grace, Paris, France; buried in L'Isle-sur-Sorgue; son of Emile (an industrialist) and Marie-Therese-Armande (Rouget) Char; married Georgette Goldstein, 1933 (divorced, 1949). *Education:* Baccalaureate degree from Lycee d'Avignon; attended Ecole de Commerce a Marseille, 1925. *Religion:* No religious convictions.

*ADDRESSES:*c/o Editions Gallimard, 5 rue Sebastien Bottin, 75007, Paris, France.

CAREER: Poet. Sojourn in Tunisia, 1924; first went to Paris in 1929, where he met Louis Aragon, Paul Eluard, and Andre Breton; was a companion of the Surrealists, 1930-34, during the second period of the movement; in L'Isle-sur-Sorgue in 1940 the Vichy police searched his home, leading to his denunciation as a communist as a result of his association with Surrealists before the war; between 1940 and 1945, he was regional head of a partisan group in the Alpes-de-Provence for the Armee Secrete, working for the Resistance in France and North Africa, using the name Capitain Alexandre; in 1944, he was wounded by the Germans; a month later he was ordered to Algiers on an advisory mission to Supreme Allied Headquarters. *Military service:* French Artillery, Nimes, 1927-28; served again, 1939-40, in Alsace.

MEMBER: Academie de Baviere (Germany), Modern Language Association of America (honorary fellow).

AWARDS, HONORS: Prix des Critiques, 1966, for *Retour amont. Military*—Chevalier de la Legion d'Honneur; Medaille de la Resistance; Croix de Guerre.

WRITINGS:

Les Cloches sur le coeur, Le Rouge et le noir, 1928.
Arsenal, Meridiens (Nimes), 1929, new edition published as *De la Main a la main,* 1930.
(With Andre Breton and Paul Eluard) *Ralentir travaux,* Editions Surrealistes, 1930, reprinted, J. Corti, 1968.
Le Tombeau des secrets, [Nimes], 1930.
Artine, Editions Surrealistes, 1930, new edition published as *Artine et autres poemes,* Tchou, 1967.
L'Action de la justice est eteinte, Editions Surrealistes, 1931.
Le Marteau sans maitre (also see below), Editions Surrealistes, 1934.
Dependence de l'adieu, G.L.M., 1936.
Moulin premiere (also see below), G.L.M., 1936.
Placard pour un chemin des ecoliers (also see below), G.L.M., 1937.
Dehors la nuit est gouvernee (also see below), G.L.M., 1938.
Seuls demeurent, Gallimard, 1945.
Le Marteau sans maitre [and] *Moulin premier, 1927-1935,* J. Corti, 1945, reprinted, 1963.
Feuillets d'Hypnos (war journal), Gallimard, 1946, translation by Cid Corman published as *Leaves of Hypnos,* Grossman, 1973.
Le Poeme pulverise (also see below), Fontaine, 1947.
Fureur et Mystere, Gallimard, 1948, new edition, 1962.
Fete des arbres et du chasseur, G.L.M., 1948.
Dehors la nuit est gouvernee [and] *Placard pour un chemin des ecoliers,* G.L.M., 1949.
Claire: Theatre de verdure, Gallimard, 1949.
Le Soleil des eaux, etchings by Georges Braque, H. Matarasso, 1949, new edition, Gallimard, 1951.
Les Matinaux, Gallimard, 1950, new edition, 1962.

Art bref [and] *Premieres alluvions,* G.L.M., 1950.
Quatre fascinants: La Minutieuse, S.N. (Paris), 1951.
A une serenite crispee, Gallimard, 1951.
Poemes, wood-cuts by Nicolas de Stael, S.N., 1951.
La Paroi et la prairie, G.L.M., 1952.
Lettera amorosa, Gallimard, 1953, 2nd edition, 1962, lithographs by Braque, E. Engelberts (Geneva), 1963.
Arriere-histoire du "Poeme pulverise" (the 19 texts of *Le Poeme pulverise* with the author's comments on each), lithographs by de Stael, J. Hugues, 1953, 2nd edition, 1972.
Choix de poemes, Brigadas Liricas (Mendoza, Argentina), 1953.
Le Rempart de brindilles, etchings by Wifredo Lam, L. Broder, 1953.
A la sante du serpent, G.L.M., 1954.
Le Deuil des Nevons, etchings by Louis Fernandez, Le Cormier (Brussels), 1954.
Recherche de la base et du sommet [and] *Pauvrete et privilege* (also see below), Gallimard, 1955, new edition, 1965.
Poemes des deux annees, 1953-1954, G.L.M., 1955.
Chanson des etages, P.A.B. (Ales), 1955.
La Bibliotheque est en feu (also see below), etchings by Braque, L. Broder, 1956.
Hypnos Waking (poems and prose), selected and translated by Jackson Mathews, with the collaboration of William Carlos Williams, Richard Wilbur, William Jay Smith, Barbara Howes, W. S. Merwin, and James Wright, Random House, 1956.
Pour nous, Rimbaud, G.L.M., 1956.
En trente-trois morceaux (aphorisms), G.L.M., 1956, reprinted, 1970.
Jeanne qu'on brula verte, illustration by Braque, P.A.B., 1956.
La Bibliotheque est en feu, et autres poemes, G.L.M., 1957.
L'Abominable homme des neiges, Librairie L.D.F. (Cairo), 1957.
L'Une et l'autre, P.A.B., 1957.
De moment en moment, engravings by Joan Miro, P.A.B., 1957.
Les Compagnons dans le jardin, engravings by Zao Wou-Ki, L. Broder, 1957.
Poemes et prose choisis, Gallimard, 1957.
Elisabeth, petite fille, P.A.B., 1958.
Sur la poesie, G.L.M., 1958, new edition, 1967.
Cinq poesies en hommage a Georges Braque, lithographs by Braque, S.N. (Geneva), 1958.
L'Escalier de Flore, engravings by Pablo Picasso, P.A.B., 1958.
La Faux relevee, P.A.B., 1959.
Nous avons (prose poem), engravings by Miro, L. Broder, 1959.
Pourquoi la journee vole, engraving by Picasso, P.A.B., 1960.
Le Rebanque, P.A.B., 1960.
Anthologie, G.L.M., 1960, new edition published as *Anthologie, 1934-1969,* 1970.
Les Dentelles de Montmirail, P.A.B., 1960.
L'Allegresse, engraving by Madeleine Grenier, P.A.B., 1960.
(With Paul Eluard) *Deux poemes,* J. Hugues, 1960.
L'Inclemence lointaine, engravings by Vieira da Silva, P. Beres, 1961.
L'Issue, P.A.B., 1961.
La Montee de la nuit, P.A.B., 1961.
La Parole en archipel, Gallimard, 1962.
Deux Poemes, engraving by da Silva, P.A.B., 1963.
Poemes et prose choisis, Gallimard, 1963.
Impressions anciennes, G.L.M., 1964.
Commune presence, Gallimard, 1964.
L'An 1964, P.A.B., 1964.
L'Age cassant, J. Corti, 1965.
Flux de l'aimant, 2nd edition, G. P. Tarn (Veilhes), 1965.
La Provence, point Omega, [Paris], 1965.

(With Albert Camus) *La Posterite du soleil,* E. Engelberts, 1965.
Retour amont, illustrations by Alberto Giacometti, G.L.M., 1966.
Le Terme epars, Imprimerie Union, 1966.
Trois coups sous les arbres: Theatre saisonnier (collection of six plays), Gallimard, 1967.
Dans la pluie giboyeuse, Gallimard, 1968.
(With Martin Heidegger and others) *L'Endurance de la pensee: Pour Saleur Jean Beaufret,* Plon, 1968.
(With Andre Frenaud and others) *Bazaine,* Maeght, 1968.
Le Chien de coeur, G.L.M., 1969.
L'Effroi, la joie, Au vent d'Arles (Saint-Paul), 1969.
Le Nu perdu, Gallimard, 1971.
La Nuit talismanique, A. Skira (Geneva), 1972.
Picasso sous les ventes Etesiens, French & European, 1973.
Se recontrer paysage avec Joseph Sema, French & European, 1974.
Aromutes Chasseurs, Gallimard, 1975.
Poems of Rene Char, translated with notes by Mary Ann Caws and Jonathan Griffin, Princeton University Press, 1976.
Recherche de la Base et du Sommet, Schoenhof, 1977.
Chants de la Balandrane: Poemes, Gallimard, 1977.
Le Nu perdu et autres poemes, Gallimard, 1978.
Fenetres dormantes et porte sur le toit, Gallimard, 1979.
Oeuvres completes, Gallimard, 1983.
No Seige Is Absolute, translation by Frank Wright, Lost Roads, 1983.

CONTRIBUTOR

Violette nozieres, N. Flamel (Brussels), 1933.
Reves d'encre, J. Corti, 1945.
Les Miroirs profonds, Editions Pierre a Feu, 1947.
Cinq parmi d'autres, Editions de Minuit, 1947.
A Braque, P.A.B., 1955.
Le Ruisseau de ble, P.A.B., 1960.
Poetes, Peintres, Sculpteurs, Maeght, 1960.
Un Jour entier, P.A.B., 1960.
25 octobre 1961, P.A.B., 1961.
13 mai 1962, P.A.B., 1962.
20 avril 1963, P.A.B., 1963.

OTHER

Also translator from the English of Tiggie Ghika's *Le Bleu de l'aile,* Cahiers d'Art, 1948, Theodore Roethke's "Le Reveil," and "Les Orchidees," published in *Preuves,* June, 1959, and (with Tina Jolas) *La Planche de vivre,* poems from the English, Italian, Spanish, and Russian, Gallimard, 1981. Author of numerous prefaces, forewords, introductions, and catalogs, and of Surrealism tracts (1930-34). Also author of numerous pamphlets and leaflets, some decorated with his own engravings. Contributor to *Le Revue Nouvelle, Sagesse, La Revolution Surrealiste, L'Impossible, Cahiers d'Art, Les Lettres Francaises, Les Quatre Vents, Fontaine, Cahiers du Sud, Combat, Mercure de France, Botteghe Oscure, Le Figaro Litteraire, Le Journal des Poetes, Temoins, Carrefour, Action, Realities Secretes, Poetry* (Chicago), *Miscellaneous Man, Western Review, Quarterly Review of Literature, Chelsea, Tiger's Eye, Minnesota Review,* and other publications.

SIDELIGHTS: In 1952 France's most prominent novelist, the late Albert Camus, wrote: "I consider Rene Char to be our greatest living poet, and *Fureur et Mystere* to be the most astonishing product of French poetry since *Les Illuminations* and *Alcools.*" Gabriel Bounoure notes a typical reaction to Char's work: "I remember when I first read Char's poetry I was drawn by its evident greatness, repelled by the asperities, the challenge, and the seismic violence of its inner meaning. . . . Nothing more salutary had appeared since Nietzsche. Cruel and devouring, this work, enclosing us like a single diamond, yet with all the sting of immense spaces of air. Char's universe is the kingdom of the open air." Camus called this poetry "strange and rigorous," emanating from "a poet of all time who speaks for our time in particular."

In the early thirties Char became involved with Surrealism (an artistic style that uses surprising, fantastical imagery), and though he broke with the movement shortly thereafter, the novelty of his imagery and his liberated imagination remain. He is his own master; Camus wrote: "No doubt he did take part in Surrealism, but rather as an ally than as an adherent, and just long enough to discover that he could walk alone with more conviction." Gaetan Picon adds: "Char's work is great, in so far as it both confirms and transcends Surrealism, both fulfills and exposes the poetry of today, inherits the past and opens up the future."

Many of Char's poems are aphoristic—stabbing distillations of language. Emile Snyder writes: "A poem by Rene Char is an act of violence within which serenity awaits the end of violence." The concentrated lucidity he attains is, in Char's words "the wound closest to the sun," and, he might have added, closest to the essence of poetry, so simple that it is most commonly considered difficult. Camus remarked that this poetry "carries daytime and night on the same impulse. . . . And so, when Char's poetry appears to be obscure, it is because a furious condensation of imagery, an intensification of light removes it from that degree of abstract transparency which we all too often demand only because it makes no demands on us."

"A poem," writes Char, "is the fulfillment of a desire which remains desire . . .[,] that instant when beauty, after keeping us waiting a long time, rises out of common things, passes across our radiant field, binds everything that can be bound, lights up everything that needs lighting in our bundle of shadows." His position is one of total involvement and his themes are great and often difficult. Rene Menard observes that "all the poetry of Char seems to me the writing of a presence who wishes himself just, at every instant in his relations with the world. . . . Char does not believe that man or his destiny are absurd. On the contrary, the circumstances of earth, if men would not ruin them by stupidity, blindness, or cruelty, would be a magnificent, an inexhaustible theater for them. . . . Man could be a great 'accompanist' of life. In order to understand and animate that alliance, he has at his disposal Poetry."

Char's concern is with human experience and with beauty amid struggle and chaos. He has said: "Nothing obsesses me but life." And, "In our darkness, there is no one place for beauty. The whole place is for beauty." Ralph J. Mills, Jr., notes Char's concern with the primacy of the poet: "In a world 'faced with the destroyed god,' as he believes, the solitary figure of the poet is transformed into the last priest, the final proprietor of value." Char believes that "to every collapse of the proofs, the poet replies with a salvo of futurity." And, though he calls himself a humanist, the meaning of the poem, James Wright observes, "is not to be found in a prose commentary. It is somehow to be found in the lightning's weeping face."

His language, most frequently compared to fireworks, is "a contained violence," according to Picon, and bears "the tranquil solidity of a mine which the slightest nudge will detonate." He has "surprised the secret of atomic energy in language," identifying "poetry with the word." He seeks in language "cruel tools," and Picon believes this language is lethal, "possessing something of

the feeling of weapons set beneath a glass case." Menard believes it to be a language "unique in present-day Letters. It is neither prose nor poem. . . . Char appears to me the first writer of that future in which, as Being is to be known directly without the cheats of myths and theologies, language will be truly, in the image of Heidegger, 'the house of Being' and will reflect its unity." When obscurity arises in Char's work, it is due, writes Wallace Fowlie in *A Guide to Contemporary French Literature*, to his "seeking essentially to transcribe the subconscious." Beyond this, he seeks to transcribe with beauty, reinstating, writes Picon, "the language which all modern poetry from Rimbaud to Surrealism has constantly tended to disqualify," namely beautiful language. "Char demands not only that language be effective, but that it have beauty."

Char's philosophical master is Heraclitus whom he calls that "vision of a solar eagle" reconciling opposites. Char believes that "the poem is always married to someone," and the technique of his poetry can be expressed in the Heraclitian saying, "The Lord whose oracle is at Delphi neither expresses nor conceals, but indicates." "I am torn," writes Char, "by all the fragments there are." Yet his mind "can polarize the most neutral objects," writes Bounoure. His inspiration is ancient. Camus noted Char's right to "lay claim to the tragic optimism of pre-Socratic Greece. From Empedocles to Nietzsche, a secret had been passed on from summit to summit, an austere and rare tradition which Char has revived after prolonged eclipse. . . . What he has called 'Wisdom, her eyes filled with tears,' is brought to life again, on the very heights of our disasters."

Translations of Char's poems have appeared in Germany, Italy, Spain, South America, Poland, Sweden, U.S.S.R., Yugoslavia, Japan, and other countries.

BIOGRAPHICAL/CRITICAL SOURCES:

BOOKS

Benoit, P. A., *Bibliographie des oeuvres de Rene Char de 1928 a 1963*, Demi-Jour, 1964.
Berger, Pierre, *Rene Char*, Segher, 1951.
Caws, Mary Ann, *The Presence of Rene Char*, Princeton University Press, 1976.
Caws, *Rene Char*, Twayne, 1977.
Contemporary Literary Criticism, Gale, Volume 9, 1981, Volume 11, 1982, Volume 14, 1983, Volume 55, 1989.
Fowlie, Wallace, *A Guide to Contemporary French Literature*, Meridian Books, 1957.
Lawler, James R., *Rene Char, The Myth and the Poetry*, Princeton University Press, 1978.
Mounin, Georges, *Avez-vous la Char?*, Gallimard, 1946.
Piore, Nancy Kline, *Lightning, The Poetry of Rene Char*, Northeastern University Press, Boston, 1981.
Rau, Greta, *Rene Char ou la Poesie accrue*, Corti, 1957.
Rene Char's Poetry, Editions de Luca (Italy), 1956.

PERIODICALS

Chicago Review, autumn, 1961.
The Fifties, third issue, 1959.
L'Arc, Number 22 (special Char issue), 1963.
L'Herne, Number 18 (special Char issue), 1971.
Liberte, July, 1968.
Times Literary Supplement, October 14, 1983.
Western Review, autumn, 1953.
World Literature Today, summer (special Char issue), 1977.

OBITUARIES:

PERIODICALS

Chicago Tribune, February 21, 1988.
Los Angeles Times, February 21, 1988.
New York Times, February 21, 1988.
Times (London), February 22, 1988.

*   *   *

CHARBY, Jay
See ELLISON, Harlan

*   *   *

CHARYN, Jerome   1937-

PERSONAL: Born May 13, 1937, in New York, N.Y.; son of Sam (a furrier) and Fannie (Paley) Charyn; married Marlene Phillips (a writer), January 24, 1965 (divorced). *Education:* Columbia College, B.A. (cum laude), 1959.

ADDRESSES: Home—302 West 12th St., Apt. 10-C, New York, N.Y. 10014. *Office*—Creative Writing Program, Princeton University, Princeton, N.J. 08544. *Agent*—Georges Borchardt, 136 East 57th St., New York, N.Y. 10022.

CAREER: Former recreation leader, Department of Parks, New York, N.Y.; High School of Music and Art, and School of Performing Arts, New York City, English teacher, 1962-64; City College of the City University of New York, New York City, lecturer in English, 1965; Stanford University, Stanford, Calif., assistant professor of English, 1965-68; Herbert Lehman College of the City University of New York, Bronx, N.Y., assistant professor, 1968-72, associate professor, 1972-78, professor of English, 1978-80; Princeton University, Princeton, N.J., visiting professor and lecturer in creative writing, 1980—.

MEMBER: P.E.N. American Center (member of executive board, 1984—), Phi Beta Kappa.

AWARDS, HONORS: Grants from National Endowment for the Arts, 1979 and 1984; Richard and Hinda Rosenthal Foundation Award from American Academy and Institute of Arts and Letters, 1981, for *Darlin' Bill;* Guggenheim grant, 1982.

WRITINGS:

NOVELS, EXCEPT AS NOTED

Once Upon a Droshky, McGraw, 1964.
On the Darkening Green, McGraw, 1965.
The Man Who Grew Younger and Other Stories, Harper, 1967.
Going to Jerusalem, Viking, 1967.
American Scrapbook, Viking, 1969.
Eisenhower, My Eisenhower, Holt, 1971.
The Tar Baby, Holt, 1972.
Blue Eyes (part of *Isaac Quartet* tetralogy; also see below), Simon & Schuster, 1975.
The Education of Patrick Silver (part of *Isaac Quartet* tetralogy; also see below), Arbor House, 1976.
Marilyn the Wild (part of *Isaac Quartet* tetralogy; also see below), Arbor House, 1976.
The Franklin Scare, Arbor House, 1977.
Secret Isaac (part of *Isaac Quartet* tetralogy; also see below), Arbor House, 1978.
The Seventh Babe, Arbor House, 1979.
The Catfish Man: A Conjured Life, Arbor House, 1980.
Darlin' Bill: A Love Story of the Wild West, Arbor House, 1980.
Panna Maria, Arbor House, 1982.

Pinocchio's Nose, Arbor House, 1983.
The Isaac Quartet (contains *Blue Eyes, Marilyn the Wild, The Education of Patrick Silver,* and *Secret Isaac*), Zomba (London), 1984.
War Cries Over Avenue C, Donald I. Fine, 1985.
Metropolis: New York as Myth, Marketplace, and Magical Land (nonfiction), Putnam, 1986.
Paradise Man, Donald I. Fine, 1987.
The Magician's Wife (comic book), Catalan Communications, 1988.
Movieland: Hollywood and the Great American Dream Culture (nonfiction), Putnam, 1989.

Also author of screenplay, "Crayola Detective," 1971. Contributor of short stories to *Commentary, Mademoiselle, Transatlantic Review,* and other publications.

EDITOR

Single Voice: An Anthology of Contemporary Fiction, Macmillan, 1969.
Troubled Vision: An Anthology of Contemporary Short Novels and Passages, Macmillan, 1970.

Founding editor, *Dutton Review,* 1970-72; editor, *Fiction,* 1970-75.

SIDELIGHTS: Jerome Charyn's prose has often been called brilliant, while his novels have been characterized as antirealist, wild, satirical, experimental, and surreal. James Walt of the *Washington Post* calls Charyn "a sophisticated writer" and "extraordinarily gifted."

Charyn's early works are set in New York and primarily tell the stories of Jewish inhabitants of that city. These early works are conventionally organized and written. "Charyn's talent at the outset," writes Albert J. Guerard of *Tri-Quarterly,* "was traditional in a fine uninhibited way: Dickensian, but within a New York Jewish world." Guerard sees Charyn's Dickensian tendency in "the richly loquacious, irrepressible caricatures." Reviewing *The Man Who Grew Younger, and Other Stories* for *Saturday Review,* Samuel I. Bellman discovers "a freshness and yet a face-slapping impact . . . that one won't find in most slick or academic magazines, and it is also this quality of differentness that makes Charyn's collection unusually forceful and artistically successful."

In his first three books—*Once Upon a Droshky, On the Darkening Green,* and *The Man Who Grew Younger*—Charyn used a conventional narrative structure, something Guerard believes "tended to limit rather than encourage Charyn's natural impulse to the fabulous." Although these early works were successful, Charyn did something different in *Going to Jerusalem,* beginning the novel in a conventional manner but slowly transforming it into a more and more fantastic story. What begins as a fairly plausible tour by a chess prodigy becomes a wild odyssey across America. Critical reaction has been mixed. Stephen Wall of the *Observer Review* finds that *Going to Jerusalem* "illustrates the increasing American recourse to fantastical modes," but judges the book "an arbitrary accumulation of irrational incidents." Writing in the *Saturday Review,* Bellman describes the novel as a "wild, zany melange of sketches, revelations, and epistles. . . . Too disorganized for the narrow, conventional taste, this novel calls up moods and responses below the threshold of consciousness." Guerard holds that "*Going to Jerusalem* is a novel full of fictional ideas, rich in Dickensian geniality and comic life, admirable in its effort to achieve a freer form; finally boring."

It was not until *Eisenhower, My Eisenhower* that Charyn left the conventional novel entirely behind him. The book, Guerard writes, is "Charyn's first genuinely antirealist, mythologizing extravaganza and first major effort to reflect the absurd aspects of contemporary urban violence." *Eisenhower, My Eisenhower* is about the Azazians, a race of gypsies living in modern America. They are discriminated against by the Anglos, the dominant group in society, and so engage in urban guerrilla warfare against the Anglos, using a wide variety of absurd disguises and stratagems. Although named in the title, President Eisenhower does not appear as a character in the novel. Critics praised Charyn's humor and intensity but criticized his lack of structure and coherence. "Here," Paul Theroux of the *Washington Post Book World* avows, "is the novel simplified to a freakish cartoon, with enough obscurities and flourishes to pass as serious writing. . . . Charyn's fluency and humor is apparent, but it is entirely a glib surface horror; there is not a coherent thought anywhere." "This comic distortion of contemporary American reality," writes Robert Scholes of *Saturday Review*, "is certainly amusing, and sometimes the satire bites pleasantly." But Scholes finds that "something is lacking in the work of this talented young man. . . . The problem is, in the broadest sense, structural. . . . The ingenuity of the parts is greater than the intelligibility of the whole."

Charyn's subsequent novels have continued in the antirealist vein, violating conventional expectations in narrative structure, characters, and subject matter. Guerard believes that although Charyn's work is experimental, "one discovers certain constants in book after book: the irrepressible comic impulse and the delight in playful inventive language." These elements can be seen in *The Franklin Scare*, for example, a fantasy concerning the presidency of Franklin Roosevelt. Although reference is made to the important events during Roosevelt's administration, the focus of the novel is on Oliver Beebe, a sailor befriended by Roosevelt and given a room in the White House attic. John Leonard of the *New York Times* explains some of the novel's plot this way: "[Beebe] eats Tootsie Rolls and dreams of sleeping with his sister; his sister is actually sleeping with a Spanish Chancellery official on the payroll of the Federal Bureau of Investigation; a Trotskyite poet from Charleston, S.C., plots to assassinate Eleanor Roosevelt with a penknife; the Wild Man of Tangiers, naked in a closet, is hiding from the Secret Service, and the Empress of Bulgaria is dying." Charyn "takes apparently factual details, . . . but he dwells upon them so that they become 'magical' and distorted," Irving Malin observes in his review of the book for the *Hollins Critic*. "Charyn continually stresses the unexpected. . . . His plot refuses to adhere to any 'sane' arrangement. . . . I believe that the world Charyn presents is so *arbitrary*—but deliberately so!—that it is, to use his title-word, 'scary.'" Leonard claims that Charyn "has tamed his prose and makes it perform tricks. It is a New York prose, street-smart, sly and full of lurches, like a series of subway stops on the way to hell." Malin concludes that *The Franklin Scare* is "a wonderfully enjoyable, instructive novel."

Critics point to Charyn's flamboyant characters and stunning prose as other recurring elements in his novels. Charyn, writes LeAnne Schreiber of *Time*, "endows his most grotesque characters with a certain beauty. His kinkiest people—an albino Negro pyromaniac, a senile, one-eyed dishwasher—are the imaginings of a major talent." Melvin Maddocks of the *Christian Science Monitor* thinks that "at their worst, Charyn's characters are eccentrics for eccentricity's sake. At their best, they are imagination-releasing examples of the infinitely varied ways human beings try to fulfill themselves." Speaking of *The Franklin Scare*,

Malin discovers that "by introducing perverse, mad and unreal characters, [Charyn] suggests that 'History,' as we are taught it, is simply another *story*." In *The Catfish Man*, Charyn uses himself as a character. The novel, writes Steven Kosek of the *Chicago Tribune Book World*, is "a humorously idiosyncratic vision of the author's life, not as he remembers it but as he imagines it. . . . The author undergoes a series of physical, sexual, and psychological transformations, rendered as cartoon-like adventures. Together, they comprise a lively, clever, and entertaining story." Charyn's *Pinocchio's Nose* is also autobiographical.

Maddocks describes Charyn's prose as "a special kind of 20th-century whimsy—whistfully fey, in graceful but hard-pressed retreat before history's current brutalities." Emphasizing the energy of Charyn's writing, Malin states that Charyn "uses short sentences which startle us; we are shaken by their bursts of energy and juxtaposition. . . . The sentences are charged; the details move so swiftly and surprisingly that we are unbalanced." Writing in the *New York Times Book Review*, William Plummer states: "Charyn is one of our most consistently daring and interesting writers."

In addition to several novels, Charyn wrote two nonfiction books in the 1980s: *Metropolis: New York as Myth, Marketplace, and Magical Land* and *Movieland: Hollywood and the Great American Dream Culture*. The former is a book of essays about the varied social, cultural, historical, and ethnic aspects of New York City. In the latter, Charyn examines the history of American cinema, pointing out ways in which the movie industry has influenced American culture.

BIOGRAPHICAL/CRITICAL SOURCES:

BOOKS

Contemporary Literary Criticism, Gale, Volume 5, 1976, Volume 8, 1978, Volume 18, 1981.
Dictionary of Literary Biography Yearbook, 1983, Gale, 1984.

PERIODICALS

Atlantic, November, 1977.
Chicago Tribune, May 19, 1985, September 7, 1986.
Chicago Tribune Book World, April 20, 1980, February 8, 1981.
Christian Science Monitor, October 5, 1967, July 24, 1969.
Columbia College Today, winter-spring, 1971.
Commonweal, April 21, 1967, March 26, 1976.
Globe and Mail (Toronto), July 6, 1985.
Hollins Critic, October, 1977.
Hudson Review, summer, 1971.
Library Journal, December 1, 1974.
Life, June 6, 1969.
Los Angeles Times, December 19, 1980, September 24, 1982, July 2, 1986.
Los Angeles Times Book Review, February 7, 1988, June 4, 1989.
Midstream, October, 1969.
New Republic, April 10, 1976.
Newsweek, June 9, 1969.
New York Review of Books, July 22, 1971.
New York Times, June 3, 1969, January 23, 1975, November 19, 1977, June 18, 1979.
New York Times Book Review, September 17, 1967, March 28, 1971, May 2, 1976, September 5, 1976, January 21, 1979, May 6, 1979, April 20, 1980, December 7, 1980, July 16, 1989.
Observer Review, June 30, 1968.
Partisan Review, winter, 1968.
Publishers Weekly, April 26, 1985.
Punch, July 10, 1968.

Rolling Stone, October 18, 1979.
Saturday Review, January 14, 1967, September 9, 1967, August 23, 1969, June 5, 1971.
Time, July 4, 1969, April 19, 1976, October 30, 1978.
Tri-Quarterly, spring, 1974.
Village Voice, April 21, 1980.
Village Voice Literary Supplement, May, 1982.
Virginia Quarterly Review, summer, 1973.
Washington Post, June 21, 1969, December 6, 1980, September 5, 1983, May 3, 1989.
Washington Post Book World, June 6, 1971.

*   *   *

CHAUCER, Daniel
See FORD, Ford Madox

*   *   *

CHEEVER, John 1912-1982

PERSONAL: Born May 27, 1912, in Quincy, Mass.; died June 18, 1982, of cancer; son of Frederick and Mary (Liley) Cheever; married Mary M. Winternitz (a poet and teacher), March 22, 1941; children: Susan, Benjamin Hale, Frederico. *Education:* Attended Thayer Academy. *Religion:* Episcopal.

ADDRESSES: Home—Cedar Lane, Ossining, N.Y. 10562.

CAREER: Novelist and short story writer. Instructor, Barnard College, 1956-57; Ossining (N.Y.) Correctional Facility, 1971-72, and University of Iowa Writers Workshop, 1973; visiting professor of creative writing, Boston University, 1974-75. Member of cultural exchange program to the U.S.S.R., 1964. *Military service:* U.S. Army Signal Corps, 1943-45; became sergeant.

MEMBER: National Institute of Arts and Letters, Century Club (New York).

AWARDS, HONORS: Guggenheim fellowship, 1951; Benjamin Franklin Award, 1955, for "The Five-Forty-Eight"; American Academy of Arts and Letters award in literature, 1956; O. Henry Award, 1956, for "The Country Husband," and 1964, for "The Embarkment for Cythera"; National Book Award in fiction, 1958, for *The Wapshot Chronicle;* Howells Medal, American Academy of Arts and Letters, 1965, for *The Wapshot Scandal;* Editorial Award, *Playboy,* 1969, for "The Yellow Room"; honorary doctorate, Harvard University, 1978; Edward MacDowell Medal, MacDowell Colony, 1979, for outstanding contributions to the arts; Pulitzer Prize in fiction, 1979, National Book Critics Circle Award in fiction, 1979, and American Book Award in fiction, 1981, all for *The Stories of John Cheever;* National Medal for Literature, 1982.

WRITINGS:

NOVELS

The Wapshot Chronicle (also see below), Harper, 1957, reprinted, Franklin Library, 1978.
The Wapshot Scandal (also see below), Harper, 1964, reprinted, 1989.
Bullet Park (Book-of-the-Month Club selection), Knopf, 1969, reprinted, Ballantine, 1987.
Falconer, Knopf, 1977.
The Wapshot Chronicle [and] *The Wapshot Scandal,* Harper, 1979.
Oh, What a Paradise It Seems, Knopf, 1982.

SHORT STORIES

The Way Some People Live: A Book of Stories, Random House, 1943.
The Enormous Radio and Other Stories, Funk, 1953.
(With others) *Stories,* Farrar, Straus, 1956 (published in England as *A Book of Stories,* Gollancz, 1957.
The Housebreaker of Shady Hill and Other Stories, Harper, 1958.
Some People, Places and Things That Will Not Appear in My Next Novel, Harper, 1961.
The Brigadier and the Golf Widow, Harper, 1964.
Homage to Shakespeare, Country Squire Books, 1965.
The World of Apples, Knopf, 1973.
The Day the Pig Fell into the Well (originally published in the *New Yorker,* October 23, 1954), Lord John Press, 1978.
The Stories of John Cheever, Knopf, 1978.
The Leaves, the Lion-Fish and the Bear, Sylvester and Orphanos, 1980.
The Enormous Radio, Creative Education Foundation, 1983.
Angel of the Bridge, Redpath Press, 1987.
Depression Stories by John Cheever: The Apprentice Years, 1931-1945, Academy Chicago, in press.

OTHER

Also author of television scripts, including "Life with Father." Contributor to numerous anthologies, including *O. Henry Prize Stories,* 1941, 1951, 1956, 1964. Contributor to the *New Yorker, Collier's, Story, Yale Review, New Republic, Atlantic,* and other publications.

SIDELIGHTS: John Cheever has come to be considered among the finest American writers of the twentieth century, a master of the short story and a competent novelist. Cheever's long career as a short story writer began at the age of seventeen when he sold his first story to the *New Republic.* He became a regular contributor to the *New Yorker* five years later, a relationship that would last for decades and account for the publication of a majority of his stories. Cheever's short work, at times discounted because it was categorized as *New Yorker* style, earned a wider audience and greater recognition when his collection, *The Stories of John Cheever,* was awarded the Pulitzer Prize in fiction in 1979. The publication of this volume of sixty-one stories, including such titles as "The Enormous Radio," "The Country Husband," "The Chimera," and "The Swimmer," "revived single-handed publishers' and readers' interest in the American short story," according to *Time'*s Paul Gray. Commenting on the author's place in American literature, John Leonard wrote in a 1973 *Atlantic* article, "I happen to believe that John Cheever is our best living writer of short stories: a[n Anton] Chekhov of the exurbs."

Cheever, the novelist, was not as widely praised, but even in this role he has had his champions. In 1977, fellow author John Gardner maintained that "Cheever is one of the few living American novelists who might qualify as true artists. His work ranges from competent to awesome on all the grounds I would count: formal and technical mastery; educated intelligence; what I would call 'artistic sincerity' . . . ; and last, validity." His novels—most notably *The Wapshot Chronicles, Bullet Park,* and *Falconer*—display "a remarkable sensitivity and a grimly humorous assessment of human behavior that capture[s] the anguish of modern man," commented Robert D. Spector in *World Literature Today,* "as much imprisoned by his mind as by the conventions of society."

Cheever was able to draw on the same confined milieu—geographical and social—in creating his five novels and numerous stories. "There is by now a recognizable landscape that can be called Cheever country," Walter Clemons observed in an article in *Newsweek*. It comprises "the rich suburban communities of Westchester and Connecticut," explained Richard Locke in the *New York Times Book Review*, "the towns [the author] calls Shady Hill, St. Botolphs and Bullet Park." In this country, Cheever found the source for his fiction, the lives of upwardly mobile Americans, both urban and suburban, lives lacking purpose and direction. His fictional representation of these lives captures what a *Time* reviewer termed the "social perceptions that seem superficial but somehow manage to reveal (and devastate or exalt) the subjects of his suburban scrutiny." Fashioned from the author's observations and presented in this manner, Cheever's stories have become, in the opinion of Jesse Kornbluth, "a precise dissection of the ascending middle class and the declining American aristocracy."

For the most part, the characters represented in Cheever's short stories and novels are white and Protestant; they are bored with their jobs, trapped in their lifestyles, and out of touch with their families. "Mr. Cheever's account of life in suburbia makes one's soul ache," Guy Davenport remarked in the *National Review*. Added the reviewer: "Here is human energy that once pushed plows and stormed the walls of Jerusalem . . . spent daily in getting up hung over, staggering drugged with tranquilizers to wait for a train to . . . Manhattan. There eight hours are given to the writing of advertisements about halitosis and mouthwash. Then the train back, a cocktail party, and drunk to bed." According to Richard Boeth of *Newsweek,* "what is missing in these people is not the virtue of their forebears . . . but the passion, zest, originality and underlying stoicism that fueled the Wasps' domination of the world for two . . . centuries. Now they're fat and bored and scared and whiny."

Critics have concluded that Cheever is not merely satirizing the upper middle class. According to John W. Aldridge in *Time to Murder and Create: The Contemporary Novel in Crisis,* Cheever "understands just what happens when a man making too much money awakens to the fact that there is nothing left to spend it on except some form of anesthesia against the knowledge that there is nothing left to spend it on." The author's ability to evoke this despair and treat it with compassion and humor is the reason he has been compared to Chekhov. Larry Woiwode explained in the *New York Times Book Review:* "Cheever is as much a master of the short form as Chekhov and should be recognized as such. He shares Chekhov's gentility, ingenuous warmth, humor, universality and all-seeing eye for the absurdities of the world and the foibles and weaknesses of humankind." Writing in *Twentieth Century Literature,* Clinton S. Burhans, Jr. called Cheever "a major chronicler of contemporary absurdity . . . who sees all too clearly into the gap between men's dreams and what they make of them." The critic added that "he sees . . . that men are born more than ever into a world of chance, complexity and ultimate loneliness. . . . Cheever reflects this world in whimsy and fantasy, in irony and extravagance, but never at the cost of his deep compassion for those who must live in it with him."

A recurring theme in Cheever's work is nostalgia, "the particular melancholia induced by long absence from one's country or home," Joan Didion explained in the *New York Times Book Review*. In her estimation, Cheever's characters have "yearned always after some abstraction symbolized by the word 'home,' after 'tenderness,' after 'gentleness,' after remembered houses where the fires were laid and the silver was polished and everything could be 'decent' and 'radiant' and 'clear.' " Even so, Didion added, "Such houses were hard to find in prime condition. To approach one was to hear the quarreling inside. . . . There

was some gap between what these Cheever people searching for home had been led to expect and what they got." What they got, the critic elaborated, was the world of the suburbs, where "jobs and children got lost." As Locke put it, Cheever's character's nostalgia grows out of "their excruciating experience of present incivility, loneliness and moral disarray."

Throughout his tales of despair and nostalgia, Cheever offers an optimistic vision of hope and salvation. His main characters struggle to establish an identity and a set of values "in relation to an essentially meaningless—even absurd—world," Stephen C. Moore commented in the *Western Humanities Review*. Kornbluth found that "Cheever's stories and early novels are not really about people scrapping for social position and money, but about people rising toward grace." In his *Dictionary of Literary Biography* essay, Robert A. Morace came to a similar conclusion. Morace maintained that "while he clearly recognizes those aspects of modern life which might lead to pessimism, his comic vision remains basically optimistic. . . . Many of his characters go down to defeat, usually by their own hand. Those who survive, . . . discover the personal and social virtues of compromise. Having learned of their own and their world's limitations, they can, paradoxically, learn to celebrate the wonder and possibility of life."

Cheever's straightforward language and vivid imagery have been widely praised. Robert Towers of the *New York Times Book Review* called the author "a precisionist of the senses" and explained: "Though his imagery of light has the strongest retinal impact, Cheever's evocation of color and texture and smell is also vivid and persistent. He shares with two very different writers, Lawrence and Faulkner, an extraordinary ability to fix the sensory quality of a particular moment, a particular place, and to make it function not as embellishment but as an essential element in the lives and moods of his characters." Locke commented, "Cheever's largest gift [is] the power to present a sensuous (especially a visual) detail that effortlessly carries intense emotional and symbolic force."

Critics have also been impressed by Cheever's episodic style. In a discussion of the author's first published work, "Expelled," Morace commented: "The opening paragraph lures the reader into a story which, like many of the later works, is a series of sketches rather than a linear narrative. The narrator, who remains detached even while recognizing his own expulsion, focuses on apparently disparate events which, taken together, create a single impression of what life at prep school is like." And in a review of *Bullet Park,* a *Time* critic notes that most of the novel "is composed of Cheever's customary skillful vignettes in which apparent slickness masks real feeling."

Some reviewers did find, however, that although this episodic structure works well in Cheever's short fiction, his novels "flounder under the weight of too many capricious, inspired, zany images," as Joyce Carol Oates remarked in the *Ontario Review*. John Updike once offered a similar appraisal: "In the coining of images and incidents, John Cheever has no peer among contemporary American fiction writers. His short stories dance, skid, twirl, and soar on the strength of his abundant invention; his novels fly apart under its impact." Moreover, Oates contended that though "there are certainly a number of powerful passages in *Falconer,* as in *Bullet Park* and the Wapshot novels, . . . in general the whimsical impulse undercuts and to some extent damages the more serious intentions of the works."

Clemons, among others, drew a different conclusion. He noted that "the accusation that Cheever 'is not a novelist' persists," despite the prestigious awards, such as the Howells Medal and the

National Book Award, his novels have received. Clemons suggested that this lack of reviewer appreciation was due to Cheever's long affiliation with the *New Yorker.* "The recognition of Cheever's [work] has . . . been hindered by its steady appearance in a debonair magazine that is believed to publish something familiarly called 'the *New Yorker* story,' " he wrote, "and we think we know what *that* is." Clemons added: "Randall Jarrell once usefully [defined the novel] as prose fiction of some length that has something wrong with it. What is clearly 'wrong' with Cheever's . . . novels is that they contain separable stretches of exhilarating narrative that might easily have been published as stories. They are loosely knit. But so what?"

Over the years, the critical and popular response to Cheever's work has been decidedly favorable. Although some have argued that his characters are unimportant and peripheral and that the problems and crises experienced by the upper middle class are trivial, others, such as *Time*'s Gray, contended that the "fortunate few [who inhabit Cheever's fiction] are much more significant than critics seeking raw social realism will admit." Gray explained: "Well outside the mainstream, the Cheever people nonetheless reflect it admirably. What they do with themselves is what millions upon millions would do, given enough money and time. And their creator is less interested in his characters as rounded individuals than in the awful, comic and occasionally joyous ways they bungle their opportunities." John Leonard of the *New York Times* found the same merits, concluding that "by writing about any of us, Mr. Cheever writes about all of us, our ethical concerns and our failures of nerve, our experience of the discrepancies and our shred of honor."

Cheever's name is often raised by critics alongside the names of such highly regarded contemporaries as John O'Hara, Saul Bellow, Thomas Pynchon, and Philip Roth. Yet, as Peter S. Prescott noted in a *Newsweek* tribute on the occasion of Cheever's death, "His prose, unmatched in complexity and precision by that of any of his contemporaries . . . is simply beautiful to read, to hear in the inner ear—and it got better all the time." "More precisely than his fellow writers," added Prescott, "he observed and gave voice to the inarticulate agonies that lie just beneath the surface of ordinary lives." In the words of Gray, recorded in a *Time* tribute, Cheever "won fame as a chronicler of mid-century manners, but his deeper subject was always the matter of life and death."

MEDIA ADAPTATIONS: Several of Cheever's short stories have been adapted for motion pictures and television. "The Swimmer" was produced by Columbia in 1968 and PBS-TV broadcast "The Sorrows of Gin," "The Five Forty-Eight," and "O Youth and Beauty!," all in 1979. The film rights to Cheever's novels *The Wapshot Chronicle, The Wapshot Scandal, Bullet Park,* and *Falconer* have been sold.

AVOCATIONAL INTERESTS: Sailing and skiing.

BIOGRAPHICAL/CRITICAL SOURCES:

BOOKS

Aldridge, John W., *Time to Murder and Create: The Contemporary Novel in Crisis,* McKay, 1966.
Bosha, Francis J., *John Cheever: A Reference Guide,* G. K. Hall, 1981.
Cheever, Susan, *Home before Dark,* Houghton, 1984.
Concise Dictionary of American Literary Biography, 1941-1968, Gale, 1987.
Contemporary Authors Bibliographical Series, Volume 1, Gale, 1986.

Contemporary Literary Criticism, Gale, Volume 3, 1975, Volume 7, 1977, Volume 8, 1978, Volume 11, 1979, Volume 15, 1980, Volume 25, 1983.
Dictionary of Literary Biography, Volume 2: *American Novelists since World War II,* Gale, 1978.
Dictionary of Literary Biography Yearbook, Gale, *1980,* 1981, *1982,* 1983.
Donaldson, Scott, editor, *Conversations with John Cheever,* University Press of Mississippi, 1987.
Donaldson, Scott, *John Cheever: A Biography,* Random House, 1988.
Hassan, Ihab, *Radical Innocence,* Princeton University Press, 1961.
Kazin, Alfred, *Bright Book of Life,* Atlantic-Little, Brown, 1973.
Short Story Criticism, Volume 1, Gale, 1988.
Updike, John, *Picked-Up Pieces,* Knopf, 1976.
Waldeland, L., *John Cheever,* G. K. Hall, 1979.

PERIODICALS

Atlantic, May, 1969, June, 1973.
Book Week, January 5, 1964.
Chicago Tribune, February 27, 1989.
Chicago Tribune Magazine, April 22, 1979.
Christian Century, May 21, 1969.
Christian Science Monitor, October 22, 1964.
Commonweal, May 9, 1969.
Critique, spring, 1963.
Detroit News, November 28, 1978.
Life, April 18, 1969.
Manchester Guardian, January 30, 1959.
Ms., April, 1977.
National Review, June 3, 1969.
New Leader, May 26, 1969.
New Republic, May 25, 1953, June 3, 1957, May 15, 1961, January 25, 1964, April 26, 1969.
Newsweek, March 14, 1977, October 30, 1978, June 28, 1982.
New York, April 28, 1969.
New York Herald Tribune Lively Arts, April 30, 1961.
New York Times, March 24, 1965, August 2, 1965, December 18, 1966, April 29, 1969, March 3, 1977, November 7, 1978.
New York Times Book Review, May 10, 1953, September 7, 1958, January 5, 1964, April 27, 1969, May 20, 1973, March 6, 1977, December 3, 1978, January 28, 1979.
New York Times Magazine, October 21, 1979.
Ontario Review, fall/winter, 1977-78.
Ramparts, September, 1969.
San Francisco Chronicle, May 24, 1953, March 25, 1957, April 28, 1961.
Saturday Review, May 27, 1961, April 26, 1969, April 2, 1977.
Time, March 27, 1964, April 25, 1969, February 28, 1977, October 16, 1978, June 28, 1982.
Times Literary Supplement, October 9, 1953, October 18, 1957, August 4, 1961.
Twentieth Century Literature, January, 1969.
Washington Post, April 29, 1969, October 8, 1979.
Washington Post Book World, March 30, 1980.
World Literature Today, autumn, 1977.

* * *

CHESNUTT, Charles W(addell) 1858-1932

PERSONAL: Born June 20, 1858, in Cleveland, Ohio; died November 15, 1932, in Cleveland, Ohio; son of Andrew Jackson (in grocery business) and Ann (one source says Anne) Maria (Sampson) Chesnutt; married Susan Utley Perry (a teacher), June 6,

1878; children: Ethel, Helen Maria, Edwin, Dorothy. *Education:* Educated at schools in Cleveland, Ohio, and Fayetteville, N.C.

ADDRESSES: 9719 Lamont Ave., Cleveland, Ohio.

CAREER: Teacher, lawyer, businessman, and writer. Taught at public schools in Spartanburg, S.C., Charlotte, N.C., and Fayetteville, N.C., 1872-77; New State Normal School, Fayetteville, assistant principal, 1877-80, principal, 1880-83; worked as a reporter for Dow Jones & Co., 1883; *New York Mail and Express,* New York, N.Y., stenographer, reporter, and author of daily column "Wall Street Gossip," 1883; Nickel Plate Railroad Co., Cleveland, Ohio, 1884-89, began as clerk, became stenographer for the firm's legal counsel; admitted to the Bar of Ohio, 1887; private practice of court reporting, beginning in 1890. Active in community affairs and social causes; served on General Committee of National Association for the Advancement of Colored People (NAACP).

AWARDS, HONORS: Spingarn Medal from NAACP, 1928.

WRITINGS:

The Conjure Woman (short stories; contains "The Goophered Grapevine," "Po' Sandy," "Mars Jeems's Nightmare," "The Conjurer's Revenge," "Sis' Becky's Pickaninny," "The Gray Wolf's Ha'nt," and "Hot-Foot Hannibal"), Houghton, 1899, deluxe edition with a foreword by Joel Elias Spingarn, 1929, reprinted, Gregg, 1968, retold for young readers by Ray Anthony Shepard as *Conjure Tales,* with illustrations by John Ross and Clare Romano, Dutton, 1973.

The Wife of His Youth, and Other Stories of the Color Line (short stories; contains "The Wife of His Youth," "Her Virginia Mammy," "The Sheriff's Children," "A Matter of Principle," "Cicely's Dream," "The Passing of Grandison," "Uncle Wellington's Wives," "The Bouquet," and "The Web of Circumstance"), Houghton, 1899, reprinted with illustrations by Clyde O. DeLand, Gregg, 1967.

Frederick Douglass (biography), Small, Maynard, 1899, reprinted, Johnson Reprints, 1970.

The House Behind the Cedars (novel), Houghton, 1900, reprinted, Gregg, 1968, reprinted with an introduction by Darwin Turner, P. F. Collier, 1969.

The Marrow of Tradition (novel), Houghton, 1901, reprinted, Gregg, 1968.

The Colonel's Dream (novel), Doubleday, Page, 1905, reprinted, Gregg, 1968.

Baxter's Procrustes, Rowfant Club (Cleveland, Ohio), 1966.

The Short Fiction of Charles W. Chesnutt, edited with an introduction by Sylvia Lyons Render, Howard University Press, 1974.

Work represented in anthologies.

Contributor to periodicals, including *Alexander's Magazine, Boston Evening Transcript, Family Fiction, Puck, Youth's Companion, Cleveland News and Herald, Atlantic Monthly, Crisis, Overland Monthly, Chicago Ledger, Century, New Haven Register, New York Independent, Outlook,* and *Southern Workman.*

SIDELIGHTS: In her biography, *Charles W. Chesnutt: Pioneer of the Color Line,* Helen M. Chesnutt describes her father as "a pioneer Negro author, the first to exploit in fiction the complex lives of men and women of mixed blood." Similarly, Sylvia Lyons Render writes admiringly in her introduction to *The Short Fiction of Charles W. Chesnutt* of his "extraordinary ability to blend his African and European heritages into distinctly American forms." Because of his fair complexion, Render pointed out,

Chesnutt could have "passed" for white; instead "he chose to remain identified as an Afro-American and sought to remove rather than to avoid various forms of discrimination." Chesnutt also merits recognition as one of the first black American fiction writers to receive serious critical attention and acclaim for portraying blacks realistically and sensitively, shunning condescending characterizations and nostalgia for antebellum days of slavery in the South.

Chesnutt was born in 1858 in Cleveland, Ohio, the son of free Negro parents who had moved from Fayetteville, North Carolina, before the Civil War to escape increasingly severe restrictions on the state's free colored population. In 1866 the family returned to Fayetteville, and Chesnutt's father started a grocery store there. When young Charles wasn't working in the store, he attended the Howard School for blacks, founded by the Freedman's Bureau in 1865. Pressed to help support his family, Chesnutt was forced to end his formal education when he was only fourteen. However, Robert Harris, the school's principal, prevailed upon Charles's father to let his son stay at the school as a pupil-teacher and turn his modest salary over to his father. At sixteen Chesnutt went to Charlotte as a full-time teacher, and in 1877 he returned to Fayetteville as assistant principal of Howard School, becoming its principal upon Harris's death three years later. Concomitantly Chesnutt commenced a vigorous program of reading and study that led to his proficiency in Latin, German, French, mathematics, and stenography. In 1883 Chesnutt resigned his administrative post and struck out alone in search of more lucrative employment in the North. He found a job in New York City as a stenographer and journalist on Wall Street, then later returned to Cleveland, where he worked as a railway clerk.

Chesnutt eventually became a stenographer for the railway company's lawyer, Judge Samuel E. Williamson, in whose office he studied law, and in 1887 he passed the Ohio Bar at the top of his class. Judge Williamson offered to finance a law practice for Chesnutt in Europe, which was less racist than the United States, but Chesnutt declined the offer. He also turned down the invitation of George Washington Cable, a prominent American writer, to become his private secretary.

Instead, in 1890 Chesnutt chose to support his growing family by establishing a court reporting business and devoting his evenings to his longtime avocation, writing fiction. His first stories were generally light in tone and dealt with conventional subjects of appeal to lesser magazines ranging from *Puck* to *Youth's Companion* and to newspaper syndicates such as S. S. McClure's. These early efforts were crowned by *Atlantic Monthly*'s acceptance of his stories "The Goophered Grapevine" in 1887 and "Po' Sandy" in 1888. At Cable's urging he also contributed commentary to the *New York Independent* and other liberal publications, and by 1889 Chesnutt had completed his first novel, eventually published in 1900 as *The House Behind the Cedars.*

Most of the stories Chesnutt produced after 1890, according to Render, "differ in form, tone, and focus from earlier works. The mood is more serious, the humor increasingly subtle and satirical, the irony more apparent, and the action [focused] largely upon Afro-Americans." Furthermore, instead of using contemporary settings, Chesnutt placed his characters in times of slavery or Reconstruction in the Cape Fear River area of Carolina, where he had lived from age eight to age twenty-five. In so doing, he displayed such fidelity to his settings and to the idiosyncrasies of the people of the area—including their folkways, dialects, and superstitions—as to prompt critics to compare his work to that of leading nineteenth-century local colorists Bret Harte and Mark Twain.

Chesnutt's first published volume, *The Conjure Woman*—issued in 1899 by Houghton Mifflin—was a collection of dialect stories told by an old Negro gardener, "Uncle" Julius McAdoo, to his Northern employer. Ostensibly simple tales of metamorphosis, voodoo, and conjuring, they nonetheless illuminate the dynamics of master-slave relationships and the injustices of slavery. One slave-owner, for instance, resorts to conjuring his grapevine to protect his grapes from thieving slaves. That idea misfires when a new slave mistakenly eats one of the "goophered" grapes. Even after he has tried a magic antidote, the unlucky slave has strange tendrils of grapes growing all over his head—grapes that appear every spring and die down in the winter along with his strength and youth, which also wax and wane with the seasons. Yet his owner profits from this, selling the slave in the spring, when he is young and vigorous, and buying him back cheaply in the fall, when he looks about to die. As several critics noted, these stories convey a very different picture of Southern society from that in the Uncle Remus stories of Joel Chandler Harris, in which happy slaves cheerfully tell animal fables about mischievous Brer Rabbit.

In *The Wife of His Youth, and Other Stories of the Color Line,* a second collection of short stories also published in 1899, Chesnutt portrays the dilemma of mulattoes who felt alien in the black community and excluded from the white. Chesnutt satirized the race-conscious Blue Veins of Cleveland—people of Negro descent with skin light enough to show the blueness of their veins—for snubbing their darker-skinned relatives and mimicking middle-class whites. A third 1899 Chesnutt publication was *Frederick Douglass,* a biography of the prominent abolitionist, for the series "Beacon Biographies of Eminent Americans."

In September, 1900, buoyed by the favorable initial reception given *The Conjure Woman, The Wife of His Youth,* and *Frederick Douglass,* Chesnutt closed down his stenography business so that he could write and lecture full time. Financial success, however, did not match critical acclaim and recognition. His first two novels, *The House Behind the Cedars* and *The Marrow of Tradition,* published in 1900 and 1901 respectively, attracted more controversy than sales. Reviewers who had applauded *The Conjure Woman* became disenchanted with Chesnutt when he began to treat taboo themes such as miscegenation and racial hatred. His sympathetic treatment of erotic love in *The House Behind the Cedars* and his pessimism toward the likelihood of racial harmony in *The Marrow of Tradition* outraged critics. Even William Dean Howells, the distinguished American novelist and critic who in 1900 had praised Chesnutt for "sound[ing] a fresh note, boldly, not blatantly" and placed him in the top rank of American short story writers, declared in a 1901 issue of *North American Review* that "at his worst, [Chesnutt] is no worse than the higher average of the ordinary novelists, but he ought always to be very much better, for he began better."

Chesnutt's earnings from the sales of his two novels and from his free-lance journalism and speaking engagements proved inadequate to the financial needs of his family. Consequently in 1902 he reopened the stenography firm he had closed two years earlier. Chesnutt continued writing, however, and in 1905 he published *The Colonel's Dream,* a novel examining the futility of amoral schemes for the economic regeneration of the South. *The Colonel's Dream* received less attention than *The Marrow of Tradition* and garnered even fewer sales. It was to be Chesnutt's last book-length work to appear during his lifetime.

In 1910, five years after the publication of *The Colonel's Dream,* Chesnutt collapsed in his Cleveland office, and he remained unconscious for several days. His recovery was slow, necessitating curtailment of his strenuous schedule of social, public, and professional engagements. In 1920 he suffered an attack of appendicitis followed by peritonitis that left his health permanently impaired.

The 1920s brought some belated recognition to Chesnutt for his literary labors at the turn of the century. In 1928 the NAACP awarded him its Spingarn Medal for his "pioneer work as a literary artist depicting the life and struggles of Americans of Negro descent, and for his long and useful career as scholar, worker, and freeman." And in 1929 Houghton Mifflin reprinted *The Conjure Woman* in a deluxe edition that restored Chesnutt to print thirty years after he had first become an author.

Chesnutt's last published work was an article titled "Post-Bellum—Pre-Harlem" that appeared in *Colophon* a year before his death. In the article Chesnutt reflected on his literary life and on the history of Afro-American writing in general. He summarized his various books and commented on the ambivalence of his publishers toward revealing his racial identity during the early years of his career. He accepted the fact that literary fashion had passed him by, but he proudly noted that Afro-American literature and the attitude of the white literary world had advanced considerably since the days of his earliest publications. Once possibly the only black American to write serious fiction about Negroes, Chesnutt had devoted his art to reorienting his readers toward what he considered the real issues of race in America.

History has at least partially restored Chesnutt's place as one of the most important figures in the early history of black literature in the United States. Critics now acknowledge that Chesnutt helped establish a truly Afro-American literary heritage in the short story and novel, and they credit him with making the broad range of black experience his artistic domain and considering practically everything within it worthy of treatment. Chesnutt is also remembered as a brilliant, gifted man endowed with an indefatigable capacity for hard work and self-discipline and as an ardent crusader for civil rights and equal opportunity. Among the tributes paid Chesnutt at the time of his death was that of American Negro civil rights leader W. E. B. DuBois, who wrote in the January, 1933, *Crisis:* "[Chesnutt] was not a Negro; he was a man. . . . If his white friends could not tolerate colored friends, they need not come to Mr. Chesnutt's home. If colored friends demanded racial segregation and hatred, he had no patience with them. Merit and friendship in his broad and tolerant mind knew no lines of color or race, and all men, good, bad, and indifferent, were simply men."

BIOGRAPHICAL/CRITICAL SOURCES:

BOOKS

Andrews, William L., *The Literary Career of Charles W. Chesnutt,* Louisiana State University Press, 1980.

Bigsby, E. W. E., editor, *The Black American Writer,* Everett/Edwards, 1969.

Bone, Robert A., *The Negro Novel in America,* Yale University Press, 1965.

Brown, Sterling, *The Negro in American Fiction,* Associates in Negro Folk Education, 1937.

Chesnutt, Helen M., *Charles Waddell Chesnutt: Pioneer of the Color Line,* University of North Carolina Press, 1952.

Dictionary of Literary Biography, Gale, Volume 12: *American Realists and Naturalists,* 1982, Volume 50: *Afro-American*

Writers Before the Harlem Renaissance, 1986, Volume 78: *American Short Story Writers, 1880-1910,* 1988.

Ellison, Curtis W. and E. W. Metcalf, Jr., *Charles W. Chesnutt: A Reference Guide,* G. K. Hall, 1977.

Heermance, J. Noel, *Charles W. Chesnutt: America's First Great Black Novelist,* Shoe String, 1974.

Keller, Frances Richardson, *An American Crusade: The Life of Charles Waddell Chesnutt,* Brigham Young University Press, 1978.

Render, Sylvia Lyons, editor, *The Short Fiction of Charles W. Chesnutt,* Howard University Press, 1974.

Twentieth-Century Literary Criticism, Volume 5, Gale, 1981.

PERIODICALS

American Literature, May, 1975.
American Scholar, winter, 1972.
Atlantic Monthly, May, 1900.
Books and Bookmen, December, 1975.
CLA Journal, March, 1972, December, 1974.
Colophon, Volume II, number 5, 1931.
Crisis, January, 1933.
Growing Point, January, 1976.
Kirkus Reviews, September 15, 1973, December 15, 1973.
Kliatt, winter, 1979.
New Republic, March 1, 1975.
New York Times Book Review, November 4, 1973, January 17, 1974.
Observer, December 7, 1975.
Phylon, spring, 1971.
Saturday Review, June 21, 1969, October 25, 1969.
Southern Literary Journal, fall, 1982.
Spectator, March 21, 1969, August 16, 1979.
Times Literary Supplement, December 5, 1975.

* * *

CHESTERTON, G(ilbert) K(eith)   1874-1936

PERSONAL: Born May 28, 1874, in Campden Hill, Kensington, London, England; died of complications resulting from an edematous condition, aggravated by heart and kidney trouble, June 14, 1936, in Beaconsfield, Buckinghamshire, England; son of Edward (a house agent) and Mary Louise (Grosjean) Chesterton; married Francis Blogg, June 28, 1901. *Education:* Attended Colet Court School, London; St. Paul's School, London, 1887-92; Slade School of Art, London, 1893-96. *Religion:* Converted to Roman Catholicism, 1922.

CAREER: Author, social and literary critic, poet and illustrator. Worked for Redway (publisher), 1896, and T. Fisher Unwin, 1896-1902. Leader of the Distributist movement, and president of Distributist League. Lecturer at Notre Dame University, 1930; radio broadcaster during the 1930s.

MEMBER: Royal Society of Literature (fellow), Detection Club (president, 1928-36).

AWARDS, HONORS: Knight Commander with Star, Order of St. Gregory the Great, 1934.

WRITINGS:

NOVELS

The Napoleon of Notting Hill, John Lane/Bodley Head, 1904.
The Man Who Was Thursday: A Nightmare, Dodd, Mead, 1908.
The Ball and the Cross, John Lane, 1909.
Manalive, Nelson, 1912.
The Flying Inn, John Lane, 1914.
The Return of Don Quixote, Dodd, Mead, 1926.

A G. K. Chesterton Omnibus (includes *The Napoleon of Notting Hill, The Man Who Was Thursday,* and *The Flying Inn*), Methuen, 1936.

SHORT STORIES

The Tremendous Adventures of Major Brown, Shurmer Sibthorp, 1903.
The Club of Queer Trades, Harper, 1905.
The Innocence of Father Brown, Cassell, 1911, annotated edition published as *The Annotated Innocence of Father Brown,* edited by Martin Gardner, Oxford University Press, 1987.
The Wisdom of Father Brown, Cassell, 1914.
The Perishing of the Pendragons, Paget, 1914.
The Man Who Knew Too Much and Other Stories, Cassell, 1922, abridged edition published as *The Man Who Knew Too Much,* Harper, 1922.
Tales of the Long Bow, Cassell, 1925, selections published as *The Exclusive Luxury of Enoch Oates* [and] *The Unthinkable Theory of Professor Green,* Dodd, Mead, 1925, and *The Unprecedented Architecture of Commander Blair,* Dodd, Mead, 1925.
The Incredulity of Father Brown, Cassell, 1926.
The Secret of Father Brown, Cassell, 1927.
The Sword of Wood, Elkin Mathews, 1928.
Stories, Harrap, 1928.
The Poet and the Lunatics: Episodes in the Life of Gabriel Gale, Dodd, Mead, 1929.
The Moderate Murderer [and] *The Honest Quack* (also see below), Dodd, Mead, 1929.
The Father Brown Stories, Cassell, 1929, 12th edition, 1974, published as *The Father Brown Omnibus,* Dodd, Mead, 1933, new and revised edition, 1951.
The Ecstatic Thief (also see below), Dodd, Mead, 1930.
Four Faultless Felons (includes *The Moderate Murderer, The Honest Quack, The Ecstatic Thief,* and *The Loyal Traitor*), Dodd, Mead, 1930.
The Scandal of Father Brown, Dodd, Mead, 1935.
The Paradoxes of Mr. Pond, Dodd, Mead, 1937.
The Pocket Book of Father Brown, Pocket Books, 1943.
The Vampire of the Village, privately published, 1947.
Father Brown: Selected Stories, edited and with an introduction by Ronald Knox, Oxford University Press, 1955.
The Amazing Adventures of Father Brown, Dell, 1961.
Father Brown Mystery Stories, selected and edited by Raymond T. Bond, Dodd, Mead, 1962.
G. K. Chesterton: Selected Stories, edited by Kingsley Amis, Faber, 1972.
Daylight and Nightmare: Uncollected Stories and Fables, edited by Marie Smith, Xanadu, 1987.
Thirteen Detectives: Classic Mystery Stories, edited by Marie Smith, Xanadu, 1987.

VERSE

Greybeards at Play: Literature and Art for Old Gentlemen, Rhymes and Sketches (also see below), Johnson, 1900.
The Wild Knight and Other Poems, Richards, 1900, 4th revised edition, Dutton, 1914.
The Ballad of the White Horse, John Lane, 1911.
Poems, John Lane, 1915.
Wine, Water and Song, Methuen, 1915.
A Poem, privately published, 1915.
Old King Cole, privately published, 1920.
The Ballad of St. Barbara and Other Verses, Palmer, 1922.
Poems, Dodd, Mead, 1922.
G. K. Chesterton (collected verse), E. Benn, 1925.

The Queen of Seven Swords, Sheed & Ward, 1926.
The Collected Poems of G. K. Chesterton, Palmer, 1927, Dodd, Mead, 1932, revised edition, Methuen, 1933, Dodd, Mead, 1966.
Gloria in Profundis, Rudge, 1927.
Ubi Ecclesia, Faber, 1929.
Lepanto, Federal Advertising Agency Inc., 1929.
The Grave of Arthur, Faber, 1930.
Graybeards at Play and Other Comic Verse, edited by John Sullivan, Elek, 1974.

LITERARY CRITICISM AND ESSAYS

The Defendant (essays), Johnson, 1901, Dodd, Mead, 1902.
(With J. E. Hodder Williams) *Thomas Carlyle,* Hodder & Stoughton, 1902.
Twelve Types, Humphreys, 1902, enlarged edition published as *Varied Types,* Dodd, Mead, 1908, abridged edition published as *Five Types: A Book of Essays,* Humphreys, 1910, Holt, 1911, new abridged edition published as *Simplicity and Tolstoy,* Humphreys, 1912.
(With W. Robertson Nicoll) *Robert Louis Stevenson,* Pott, 1903.
(With G. H. Perris and Edward Garnett) *Leo Tolstoy,* Pott, 1903.
(With F. G. Kitton) *Charles Dickens,* Pott, 1903.
Robert Browning, Macmillan, 1903.
(With Richard Garnett) *Tennyson,* Hodder & Stoughton, 1903.
(With Lewis Melville) *Thackeray,* Pott, 1903.
G. F. Watts, Dutton, 1904.
Heretics (essays), John Lane, 1905.
Charles Dickens: A Critical Study, Dodd, Mead, 1906, new edition, with a foreword by Alexander Woolcott, published as *Charles Dickens: The Last of the Great Men,* Readers Club Press, 1942.
All Things Considered (essays), John Lane, 1908.
George Bernard Shaw, John Lane/Bodley Head, 1909, revised edition, Devin-Adair, 1950.
Orthodoxy (essays), John Lane/Bodley Head, 1909.
Alarms and Discussions (essays), Methuen, 1910, enlarged edition, Dodd, Mead, 1911.
William Blake, Dutton, 1910.
What's Wrong with the World (essays), Cassell, 1910.
Appreciations and Criticisms of the Works of Charles Dickens, Dutton, 1911.
A Defence of Nonsense and Other Essays, Dodd, Mead, 1911.
The Victorian Age in Literature, Williams & Norgate, 1913.
Utopia of Usurers and Other Essays, Boni & Liveright, 1917.
Charles Dickens Fifty Years After, privately published, 1920.
The Uses of Diversity: A Book of Essays, Methuen, 1920, Dodd, Mead, 1921.
Eugenics and Other Evils (essays), Cassell, 1922.
William Cobbett, Dodd, Mead, 1925.
The Everlasting Man (essays), Dodd, Mead, 1925.
Robert Louis Stevenson, Hodder & Stoughton, 1927, Dodd, Mead, 1928.
Generally Speaking: A Book of Essays, Methuen, 1928.
Essays, Harrap, 1928.
Come to Think of It. . .: A Collection of Essays, Methuen, 1930.
All Is Grist: A Book of Essays, Methuen, 1931, Dodd, Mead, 1932.
Chaucer, Farrar & Rinehart, 1932.
Sidelights on London and Newer York and Other Essays, Sheed & Ward, 1932.
All I Survey: A Book of Essays, Methuen, 1933.
Avowals and Denials: A Book of Essays, Methuen, 1934, Dodd, Mead, 1935.

The Well and the Shallows (essays), Sheed & Ward, 1935.
As I Was Saying: A Book of Essays, Dodd, Mead, 1936.
Essays, edited by John Guest, Collins, 1939.
Selected Essays, edited by Dorothy Collins, Methuen, 1949.
Essays, edited by K. E. Whitehorn, Methuen, 1953.
A Handful of Authors: Essays on Books and Writers, edited by Dorothy Collins, Sheed & Ward, 1953.
The Glass Walking-Stick and Other Essays from the Illustrated London News, 1905-1936, edited by Dorothy Collins, Methuen, 1955.
Lunacy and Letters (essays) edited by Dorothy Collins, Sheed & Ward, 1958.
The Spice of Life and Other Essays, edited by Dorothy Collins, Finlayson, 1964, Dufour, 1966.
Chesterton on Shakespeare, edited by Dorothy Collins, Dufour, 1971.
The Apostle and the Wild Ducks and Other Essays, edited by Dorothy Collins, Elek, 1975.

OTHER

Tremendous Trifles, Dodd, Mead, 1909.
(Editor) *Thackeray* (selections), Bell, 1909.
The Ultimate Lie, privately published, 1910.
(Editor with Alice Meynell) *Samuel Johnson* (selections), Herbert & Daniel, 1911.
A Chesterton Calendar, Kegan Paul, 1911, published as *Wit and Wisdom of G. K. Chesterton,* Dodd, Mead, 1911, published as *Chesterton Day by Day,* Kegan Paul, 1912.
The Future of Religion: Mr. G. K. Chesterton's Reply to Mr. Bernard Shaw, privately published, 1911.
The Conversion of an Anarchist, Paget, 1912.
A Miscellany of Men, Methuen, 1912, enlarged edition, Dodd, Mead, 1912.
Magic: A Fantastic Comedy (play; first produced November 7, 1913, at Little Theatre, London; produced in New York, 1917), Putnam, 1913.
Thoughts from Chesterton, edited by Elsie E. Morton, Harrap, 1913.
The Barbarism of Berlin, Cassell, 1914, published as *The Appetite of Tyranny, Including Letters to an Old Garibaldian,* Dodd, Mead, 1915.
London, photographs by Alvin Langdon Coburn, privately published, 1914.
Prussian versus Belgian Culture, Belgian Relief and Reconstruction Fund, 1914.
Letters to an Old Garibaldian, John Lane, 1915.
The So-Called Belgian Bargain, National War Aims Committee, 1915.
The Crimes of England, Palmer & Hayward, 1915, John Lane, 1916.
Divorce versus Democracy, Society of SS. Peter and Paul, 1916.
Temperance and the Great Alliance, True Temperance Association, 1916.
The G. K. Chesterton Calendar, edited by H. Cecil Palmer, Palmer & Hayward, 1916.
A Shilling for My Thoughts, edited by E. V. Lucas, Methuen, 1916.
A Short History of England, John Lane, 1917.
Lord Kitchener, privately published, 1917.
How to Help Annexation, Hayman Christy & Lilly, 1918.
Irish Impressions, Collins, 1919, John Lane, 1920.
(Editor with Holbrook Jackson and R. Brimley Johnson) Charles Dickens, *The Personal History of David Copperfield,* C. Chivers, 1919.
The Superstition of Divorce, Chatto & Windus, 1920.

The New Jerusalem, Hodder & Stoughton, 1920, Doran, 1921.

What I Saw in America, Hodder & Stoughton, 1922.

Fancies versus Fads, Dodd, Mead, 1923.

St. Francis of Assisi (biography), Hodder & Stoughton, 1923, Doran, 1924.

The End of the Roman Road: A Pageant of Wayfarers, Classic Press, 1924.

The Superstitions of the Sceptic (lecture), Herder, 1925.

A Gleaming Cohort, Being Selections from the Works of G. K. Chesterton, edited by Lucas, Methuen, 1926.

(Editor) *Essays by Divers Hands 6,* Oxford University Press, 1926.

The Outline of Sanity, Sheed & Ward, 1926.

The Catholic Church and Conversion, Macmillan, 1926.

Selected Works, nine volumes, Methuen, 1926.

Social Reform versus Birth Control, Simpkin Marshall, 1927.

The Judgement of Dr. Johnson: A Comedy in Three Acts (play; first produced January 20, 1932, at Arts Theatre Club, London), Sheed & Ward, 1927, Putnam, 1928.

Culture and the Coming Peril (lecture), University of London Press, 1927.

(With George Bernard Shaw) *Do We Agree? A Debate between G. K. Chesterton and Bernard Shaw, with Hilaire Belloc in the Chair,* Mitchell, 1928.

A Chesterton Catholic Anthology, edited by Patrick Braybrooke, Kenedy, 1928.

The Thing, Sheed & Ward, 1929, published as *The Thing: Why I Am a Catholic,* Dodd, Mead, 1930.

G. K. C. as M. C., Being a Collection of Thirty-Seven Introductions, selected and edited by J. P. de Foneska, Methuen, 1929.

The Turkey and the Turk, St. Dominic's Press, 1930.

At the Sign of the World's End, Harvest Press, 1930.

The Resurrection of Rome, Dodd, Mead, 1930.

(With E. Haldeman-Julius) *Is There a Return to Religion?,* Haldeman-Julius, 1931.

(Contributor) *The Floating Admiral,* Hodder & Stoughton, 1931, Doubleday, Doran, 1932.

Christendom in Dublin, Sheed & Ward, 1932.

St. Thomas Aquinas (biography), Sheed & Ward, 1933.

G. K. Chesterton (selected humor), edited by E. V. Knox, Methuen, 1933, published as *Running after One's Hat and Other Whimsies,* McBride, 1933.

(Editor) *G. K.'s* (miscellany from *G. K.'s Weekly*), Rich & Cowan, 1934.

Explaining the English, British Council, 1935.

Stories, Essays, and Poems, Dent, 1935, Dutton, 1957.

Autobiography, Hutchinson, 1936, published as *The Autobiography of G. K. Chesterton,* Sheed & Ward, 1936.

The Man Who Was Chesterton: The Best Essays, Stories, Poems and Other Writings of G. K. Chesterton, compiled and edited by Raymond T. Bond, Dodd, Mead, 1937.

The Coloured Lands, Sheed & Ward, 1938.

The End of the Armistice, compiled by F. J. Sheed, Sheed & Ward, 1940.

(Contributor) Ellery Queen, editor, *To the Queen's Taste,* Little, Brown, 1946.

The Common Man, compiled by F. J. Sheed, Sheed & Ward, 1950.

The Surprise (play; first produced June 5, 1953, at University College Assembly Hall, Hull, England), preface by Dorothy L. Sayers, Sheed & Ward, 1952.

G. K. Chesterton: An Anthology, edited and with an introduction by D. B. Wyndham Lewis, Oxford University Press, 1957.

Essays and Poems, edited by Wilfrid Sheed, Penguin Books, 1958.

Where All Roads Lead, Catholic Truth Society, 1961.

The Man Who Was Orthodox: A Selection from the Uncollected Writings of G. K. Chesterton, edited by A. L. Maycock, Dobson, 1963.

G. K. Chesterton: A Selection from His Non-Fictional Prose, edited by W. H. Auden, Faber, 1970.

G. K.'s Weekly: A Sampler, edited by Lyle W. Dorsett, Loyola University Press, 1986.

Collected Nonsense and Light Verse, edited by Smith, Dodd, Mead, 1987.

As I Was Saying . . .: A Chesterton Reader, edited by Robert Knille, Eerdmans, 1987.

The Essential G. K. Chesterton, edited by P. J. Kavanagh, Oxford University Press, 1987.

Contributor to *Daily News* (London), 1901-13, *Illustrated London News,* 1905-36, and *Daily Herald* (London), 1913-14. Editor, *The Debater* (St. Paul's School publication), 1891-93; co-editor, *Eye Witness,* 1911-12; editor, *New Witness,* 1912-23; editor, *G. K.'s Weekly,* 1925-36. Editor, with H. Jackson and R. B. Johnson, "Readers' Classics" series, 1922. Many of Chesterton's papers are held in the Robert John Bayer Memorial Chesterton Collection, John Carroll University Library, Cleveland, Ohio; other materials are at Columbia University, Marquette University, and the British Library.

SIDELIGHTS: "G. K. Chesterton," declared William B. Furlong in the *Dictionary of Literary Biography,* "was a legend in London literary circles even during his lifetime. George Bernard Shaw called him 'a man of colossal genius,' and as a young man Chesterton was hailed as Fleet Street's reincarnation of Samuel Johnson." Dabbling in genres including journalism, social activism, politics, literary criticism, poetry, drama, and mystery fiction, this huge (over three hundred pounds) genial man dominated British letters during the first decades of the twentieth century. Ian Boyd explained in the *Dictionary of Literary Biography,* "He belonged to that category of writer which used to be called the man of letters, and like the typical man of letters he wrote journalism which included a wide variety of literary forms and literature which possessed many of the characteristics of journalism."

Chesterton, Boyd stated, was "very much in the tradition of the Victorian sage"—a *litterateur* prepared to comment on almost any subject. Thomas M. Leitch asserted in the *Dictionary of Literary Biography* that Chesterton "seemed from his early years to combine the disposition of a determined amateur, the imagination of a fantasist, and the temperament of a gadfly." "His pride in his amateur status," Leitch continued, "as philosopher, historian, and economist; his willingness to debate the most unlikely opponents on the most trivial subjects—gave him a reputation as a heroic crank." He was renowned for his wit, having a special aptitude for the *bon mot;* Furlong reported, "There was the famous telegram to his wife: 'Am in Manchester. Where should I be?' Her rejoinder: 'Home.' Asked on Fleet Street which single book he would want if stranded on a desert island he replied without breaking stride, 'Robertson's Guide to Practical Shipbuilding.' Always though the repartee sparkled best between Shaw and Chesterton. To a rather gaunt Shaw: 'I see there's been a famine in the land.' Reply to a less than gaunt Chesterton: 'Yes, and now I see what caused it.' "

Although best known nowadays for his detective fiction, Chesterton first gained public attention as a journalist and social philosopher. "Like his close friends G. B. Shaw and H. G. Wells,"

Boyd explained, "he preferred the role of teacher and prophet to that of literary man, but unlike them his vision of life was fundamentally Christian and even mystical, and the influence he sought to exercise through his writings was directed toward a social change which would be thoroughly religious." His book *What's Wrong with the World* advocated Distributism, a social philosophy that divided property holders into small communities, trying to foster neighborliness. Chesterton viewed Distributism as a counter to Socialism and Capitalism, ideologies that, he felt, reduced people to inhumane units. Stephen Metcalf, writing in the *Times Literary Supplement,* pointed out that this philosophy, also expounded in the 1904 novel *The Napoleon of Notting Hill,* more accurately reflects modern society's problems than does George Orwell's classic *1984:* "It is not only . . . that Chesterton cared passionately for what ordinary humanity feels and thinks," Metcalf stated. "It is also that he had particular convictions about how one should understand humanity."

Much of Chesterton's work reflected his social concern. Using literary devices such as parable and allegory, he sought to bring about social changes that embodied his religious and political beliefs. Boyd commented on "the close connection between his poetry and his everyday journalism," and concluded, "In this sense, T. S. Eliot's description of Chesterton's poetry as 'first-rate journalistic balladry' turns out to have been particularly perceptive, since it is a reminder about the essential character of all Chesterton's work. In his verse, as in all his writings, his first aim was to comment on the political and social questions of the day." His novels, reported Brian Murray in the *Dictionary of Literary Biography,* "are as frequently called romances, extravaganzas, fantasies, parables, or allegories. For while they are thick with the details of everyday life, Chesterton's hastily written book-length fictions are outlandishly plotted and, in the main, unabashedly didactic."

This didacticism has alienated modern readers from some of Chesterton's fiction. His detective stories, however, remain popular. Chesterton himself was very fond of the detective story: "Virtually all of his fiction," Leitch stated, "contains such typical detective elements as the posing of a riddle and its logical solution; many of his stories have the structure of formal detective stories without the presence of a detective; and in his novel *The Man Who Was Thursday* (1908) detectives appear in wild profusion." The author himself recognized that much of his writing was pedantic and would probably not survive him. "Chesterton assumed that he would never be considered a novelist of enormous importance," asserted Murray; "that, as a writer of fiction, he would always remain best known for the long series of Father Brown stories he began with *The Innocence of Father Brown* in 1911—stories he sometimes tossed off in a day or two."

Loosely based upon Chesterton's friend, the Roman Catholic priest John O'Connor, Father Brown "drops typical Chestertonian quips as he solves ghastly transgressions not with Holmes-sharp logic but by 'getting inside' the criminal mind," according to Murray. Rather than using deductive methods to discover the perpetrator of a crime, Father Brown—whom Chesterton depicted in his *Autobiography* as "shabby and shapeless [in appearance], his face round and expressionless, his manners clumsy"—bases his conclusions on his knowledge of human nature. This knowledge is drawn in part from his experience in the confessional box, but also from his recognition of his own capacity for evil. "The little priest could see," stated Ronald Knox in his introduction to *Father Brown: Selected Stories,* "not as a psychologist, but as a moralist, into the dark places of the human heart; could guess, therefore, at what point envy, or fear, or resentment would pass the bounds of the normal, and the cords of

convention would snap, so that a man was hurried into crime." "To Father Brown," wrote Eric Routley in *The Puritan Pleasures of the Detective Story: A Personal Monograph,* "any criminal is a good man gone wrong. He is not an evil man who has cut himself off from the comprehension or sympathy of those who labour to be good."

Father Brown remains, in the minds of most readers, Chesterton's greatest creation, although his contribution to the art of mystery writing is also recognized. "If Chesterton had not created Father Brown," Leitch declared, "his detective fiction would rarely be read today, but his place in the historical development of the genre would still be secure." "Long before he published his last Father Brown stories," the contributor continued, "Chesterton was widely regarded as the father of the modern English detective story. When Anthony Berkeley founded the Detection Club in 1928, it was Chesterton, not Conan Doyle [creator of Sherlock Holmes], who became its first president and served in this capacity until his death." In addition, Leitch asserted, Chesterton "was the first habitual writer of detective stories . . . to insist on the conceptual unity of the form, a criterion he expounded at length in several essays on the subject."

Under the influence of Chesterton's Father Brown, the mystery story became less a portrait of the detective's personality, and more a puzzle that the detective and the reader could both solve. "Chesterton's determination to provide his audience with all the clues available to his detectives," stated Leitch, "has been so widely imitated as to become the defining characteristic of the formal or golden age period (roughly 1920-1940) in detective fiction. . . . Modern readers, for whom the term *whodunit* has become synonymous with *detective story,* forget that the concealment of the criminal's identity as the central mystery of the story is a relatively modern convention." He continued, "Chesterton's Father Brown stories, many of which present murder puzzles in which the murderer's identity constitutes the climactic revelation, are the most orthodox of his stories in the context of the succeeding golden age, whose conventions they so largely established." In the end, H. R. F. Keating (himself a prominent mystery writer) concluded in *Twentieth-Century Crime and Mystery Writers,* "Chesterton's fame rests on the priest with 'the harmless, human name of Brown' and it will endure."

BIOGRAPHICAL/CRITICAL SOURCES:

BOOKS

Barker, Dudley, *G. K. Chesterton: A Biography,* Stein & Day, 1973.

Belloc, Hilaire, *The Place of Gilbert Chesterton in English Letters,* Sheed & Ward, 1940.

Bogaerts, Anthony Mattheus Adrianus, *Chesterton and the Victorian Age,* Rozenbeek en Venemans, 1940.

Boyd, Ian, *The Novels of G. K. Chesterton: A Study in Art and Propaganda,* Barnes & Noble, 1975.

Canovan, Margaret, *G. K. Chesterton: Radical Populist,* Harcourt, 1977.

Carol, Sister M., *G. K. Chesterton: The Dynamic Classicist,* Morilal Banarsidass, 1971.

Chesterton, Cecil, *Gilbert K. Chesterton: A Criticism,* John Lane, 1909.

Chesterton, G. K., *Autobiography,* Hutchinson, 1936, published as *The Autobiography of G. K. Chesterton,* Sheed & Ward, 1936.

Clemens, Cyril, *Chesterton as Seen by His Contemporaries,* Mark Twain Society, 1939.

Clipper, Lawrence J., *G. K. Chesterton,* Twayne, 1974.

Coates, John, *Chesterton and the Edwardian Cultural Crisis,* Hull University Press, 1984.

Conlon, D. J., editor, *G. K. Chesterton: A Half Century of Views,* Oxford University Press, 1987.

Dale, Alzina Stone, *The Outline of Sanity: A Life of G. K. Chesterton,* Eerdmans, 1982.

Dictionary of Literary Biography, Gale, Volume 10: *Modern British Dramatists, 1900-1945,* 1982, Volume 19: *British Poets, 1880-1914,* 1983, Volume 34: *British Novelists, 1890-1929: Traditionalists,* 1985, Volume 70: *British Mystery Writers, 1860-1919,* 1988.

Hollis, Christopher, *The Mind of Chesterton,* Hollis & Carter, 1970.

Hunter, Lynette, *G. K. Chesterton: Explorations in Allegory,* St. Martin's, 1979.

Kenner, Hugh, *Paradox in Chesterton,* Sheed & Ward, 1947.

Knox, Ronald, editor and author of introduction, *Father Brown: Selected Stories* by G. K. Chesterton, Oxford University Press, 1955.

O'Connor, John, *Father Brown on Chesterton,* Muller/Burns, Oates, 1937.

Rauch, Rufus William, *A Chesterton Celebration,* Notre Dame University Press, 1983.

Routley, Eric, *The Puritan Pleasures of the Detective Story: A Personal Monograph,* Gollancz, 1972.

Short Story Criticism, Volume 1, Gale, 1988.

Sprug, Joseph W., editor, *An Index to G. K. Chesterton,* Catholic University of America Press, 1966.

Sullivan, John, *G. K. Chesterton: A Bibliography,* University of London Press, 1958.

Sullivan, John, *Chesterton Continued: A Bibliographic Supplement,* University of London Press, 1968.

Titterton, W. R., *G. K. Chesterton: A Portrait,* Organ, 1936.

Twentieth-Century Crime and Mystery Writers, 2nd edition, St. James Press/St. Martin's, 1985.

Twentieth-Century Literary Criticism, Volume 6, Gale, 1982.

Ward, Maisie, *Gilbert Keith Chesterton,* Sheed & Ward, 1943.

PERIODICALS

Chesterton Review, fall/winter, 1974—.

Times Literary Supplement, December 25-31, 1987.

—Sketch by Kenneth R. Shepherd

*   *   *

CH'IEN Chung-shu   1910-
(Qian Zhongshu)

PERSONAL: Born November 21, 1910, in Wuhsi, Kiangsu, China; married Yang Jiang (a writer), 1935; children: Qian Yuan. *Education:* Attended Qinghua University, 1929-33; Oxford University, B.Litt., 1937; further study in Paris, France, 1937-38.

ADDRESSES: Office—c/o Chinese Academy of Social Sciences, 5 Jianguomen Nei Da Jie 5 Hao, Beijing, People's Republic of China.

CAREER: Writer, 1932—. Teacher at various schools in China, including Guanghua University, Shanghai, 1933-1935; Southwest Associated University, Yunnan (now Kun-ming), 1938-39; Lantian Normal College, Baoqing, Hunan, 1939-41; Aurora Women's College, Shanghai, 1941-45; National Jinan University, Shanghai, 1946-1948; and Qinghua University, Peking, 1949-52; senior fellow of the Institute of Chinese Literature of the Chinese Academy of Social Sciences, 1952—.

MEMBER: Chinese Academy of Social Sciences (vice-president, 1982—).

WRITINGS:

UNDER NAME CH'IEN CHUNG-SHU

Xie zai rensheng bianshang (essays; title means "Written on the Margin of Life"), [Shanghai], 1941.

Ren, Shou, Gui (short stories; title means "Humans, Beasts, and Ghosts"; contains "God's Dream," "The Cat," "Inspiration," and "Souvenir"), Kaiming (Shanghai), 1946.

Wei cheng (novel), Chenguang (Shanghai), 1947, reprinted, Renmin Wenxue (Peking), 1980, translation by Jeanne Kelly and Nathan K. Mao published as *Fortress Besieged,* Indiana University Press, 1979.

Tan yi lu (essays; title means "On Poetry and Poetics"), Kaiming (Shanghai), 1948, revised edition, Zhonghua (Peking), 1984.

Song shi xuan zhu (title means "Annotated Anthology of Song Poetry"), Renmin Wenxue (Peking), 1958, revised, 1979.

Jiu wen sipian (title means "Four Old Essays"), Guji (Shanghai), 1979.

Guanzhui pian (title means "Partial Views on Ideas and Letters"), four volumes, Zhonghua (Peking), 1979-80.

Qizhui ji (title means "Seven Essays: A Miscellany"), Guji, 1985.

Works have also been published under name variation Qian Zhongshu. Also author of an essay on Chinese literature, included in *Chinese Year Book,* 1944-45. Works represented in anthologies, such as *Modern Chinese Stories and Novellas, 1919-1949.*

Editor of *Philobiblon.* Contributor of reviews and literary criticism to periodicals, including *T'ien Hsia Monthly, Wenxue Yanjiu,* and *Renditions.*

SIDELIGHTS: Though largely unknown in the West, Ch'ien Chung-shu is one of China's most distinguished literary figures. The author of numerous essays, a significant body of literary criticism, and several short stories, he is probably best known for *Fortress Besieged,* his only novel. Originally published in Shanghai as *Wei cheng* in 1947, the controversial satire did not appear in English translation until more than thirty years later. The novel is now regarded as one of the greatest Chinese literary works of the twentieth century.

Ch'ien was born into a scholarly family that fostered an appreciation of culture and the arts. A gifted student, Ch'ien soon established himself as an outspoken member of the Chinese intelligentsia, publishing his first articles of literary criticism by the age of twenty. His early reviews of works by Chinese writers Zhou Zuoren, Cao Baohua, and Shen Qiwu argue for a break from the traditional forms of Chinese literature and an infusion of renewed passion into modern writings. According to Theodore Huters in *Qian Zhongshu,* the author's criticism is pervaded by "ambivalence," that contrasts "the need for Chinese literature to break new ground" with "the complaisance toward and sense of continuity with tradition."

Ch'ien wrote only a small body of short fiction. Huters contended that these works are marked by "a pronounced thinness of texture" and reflect the difficulty the author faced in shifting from the expository style of the essay to the narrative voice of fiction. Four of Ch'ien's stories were collected in the 1946 volume *Ren, Shou, Gui* ("Humans, Beasts, and Ghosts"). One story, "God's Dream," chronicles the creation of humans and their subsequent degeneration into a virtueless species. Faulted for its contrived and digressive nature and limited plot and character development, the story was nevertheless praised for its strong images and original ideas. "Inspiration," another story in the collection, employs complex word plays in a satire of literary culture, but several critics were again disappointed by the stilted evolution of plot and character.

The other two stories in *Ren, Shou, Gui* received a more enthusiastic critical reception. "Souvenir," about the ramifications of a woman's affair with her husband's cousin, and "The Cat," a chronicle of jealousy and revenge between husband and wife, both achieve "more control over the various elements of fiction . . ., [making] real progress toward the harmonization of narrative devices that [would] reach fruition in *Fortress Besieged,*" noted Huters.

Fortress Besieged takes its title from a French proverb: "Marriage is like a fortress besieged; those who are outside want to get in; those who are inside want to get out." Set mainly in Japanese-occupied China from 1937 to 1939, the satirically comical novel centers on a weak-willed protagonist, Fang Hongjian, returning to Shanghai by boat following a four-year stay in Europe. Fang had traveled to the continent to obtain a doctorate but, devoting little time to his studies, he eventually runs low on money. Having procured a fraudulent degree, he boards a boat to Shanghai and becomes embroiled in a love triangle: after a brief affair and rejection, Fang misleads another woman into believing he loves her. He eventually marries a third woman, but the match proves unsuitable and soon dissolves. *Fortress Besieged* was lauded for its wry wit, penetrating insights into human nature, and provocative use of language. Angela Jung Palanduri, writing in the *Journal of Asian Studies,* declared that the novel's "rich verbal texture . . . makes this prose narrative border on poetry."

In his preface to *Fortress Besieged,* Ch'ien implies that Fang is the satirical embodiment of all westernized pseudointellectuals, a segment of the Chinese population for which the author holds little regard. An evocation of the moral and cultural dissolution of a society from within, the novel is generally regarded as a testament to the futile human pursuit of the unattainable and, noted Francis B. Randall in *National Review,* "the desperate peril and likely fall of the great Chinese culture that once was." In an article for *World Literature Today,* Robert E. Hegel commented on the novel's power: "It's wit aside, *Fortress Besieged* is a disturbing book, leaving the reader exposed in the existential isolation that remains when both laughter and tears finally subside. Certainly this is one of the finest works of contemporary Chinese fiction."

Fortress Besieged is Ch'ien's only lengthy work of fiction. The Chinese civil war and the spread of communism in the years following the novel's original 1947 publication served to stifle reactionary writing in China. Ch'ien chose to abandon fiction writing, publishing essays—including the 1948 collection *Tan yi lu,* a notable volume concerning traditional poetry—and his annotated anthology of Song dynasty poetry during the late 1940s and 1950s. He withdrew from the literary scene in the 1960s but re-emerged after a change in China's political regime in 1978. The next year Ch'ien toured the United States as a delegate of the Chinese Academy of Social Sciences. *Guanzhui pian,* a four-volume examination of classic Chinese works, was composed by Ch'ien during his silence and published in Peking between 1979 and 1980. While acknowledging Ch'ien's contribution to Chinese literature and criticism, David Hawkes, writing in the *Times Literary Supplement,* lamented that the country's "most intellectually distinguished" twentieth-century writer did not follow his masterful novel *Fortress Besieged* with another work

of fiction: "So brilliant a beginning if it had been made almost anywhere else in the world would almost certainly have been followed by other equally brilliant and more mature successors."

BIOGRAPHICAL/CRITICAL SOURCES:

BOOKS

Ch'ien Chung-shu, *Fortress Besieged,* translated by Jeanne Kelly and Nathan K. Mao, Indiana University Press, 1979.
Contemporary Literary Criticism, Volume 22, Gale, 1982.
Huters, Theodore, *Qian Zhongshu,* Twayne, 1982.

PERIODICALS

Journal of Asian Studies, November, 1980.
National Review, June 13, 1980.
Spectator, July 12, 1980.
Times Literary Supplement, June 27, 1980.
World Literature Today, autumn, 1980.

*　　*　　*

CHILDRESS, Alice 1920-

PERSONAL: Surname is pronounced "*Chil*-dress"; born October 12, 1920, in Charleston, S.C.; married second husband, Nathan Woodard (a musician), July 17, 1957; children: (first marriage) Jean (Mrs. Richard Lee). *Education:* Attended public schools in New York, N.Y.

ADDRESSES: Home—New York, N.Y. *Office*—Beacon Press, 25 Beacon St., Boston, Mass. 02108. *Agent*—Flora Roberts, Inc., 157 West 57th St., Penthouse A, New York, N.Y. 10019.

CAREER: Playwright, novelist, actress, and director. Began career in theatre as an actress, with her first appearance in "On Strivers Row," 1940; actress and director with American Negro Theatre, New York, N.Y., for eleven years; played in "Natural Man," 1941, "Anna Lucasta," 1944, and her own play "Florence" (which she also directed), 1949; has also performed on Broadway and television. Lecturer at universities and schools; member of panel discussions and conferences on Black American theatre at numerous institutions, including New School for Social Research, 1965, and Fisk University, 1966; visiting scholar at Radcliffe Institute for Independent Study (now Mary Ingraham Bunting Institute), Cambridge, Mass., 1966-68. Member of governing board of Frances Delafield Hospital.

MEMBER: PEN, Dramatists Guild (member of council), American Federation of Television and Radio Artists, Writers Guild of America East (member of council), Harlem Writers Guild.

AWARDS, HONORS: Obie Award for best original Off-Broadway play, *Village Voice,* 1956, for "Trouble in Mind"; John Golden Fund for Playwrights grant, 1957; Rockefeller grant, 1967; *A Hero Ain't Nothin' but a Sandwich* was named one of the Outstanding Books of the Year by *New York Times Book Review,* 1973, and a Best Young Adult Book of 1975 by American Library Association; Woodward School Book Award, 1974, Jane Addams Children's Book Honor Award for young adult novel, 1974, National Book Award nomination, 1974, and Lewis Carroll Shelf Award, University of Wisconsin, 1975, all for *A Hero Ain't Nothin' but a Sandwich;* named honorary citizen of Atlanta, Ga., 1975, for opening of "Wedding Band"; Sojourner Truth Award, National Association of Negro Business and Professional Women's Clubs, 1975; Virgin Islands film festival award for best screenplay, 1977, for "A Hero Ain't Nothin' but a Sandwich"; first Paul Robeson Award for Outstanding Contributions to the Performing Arts, Black Filmmakers Hall of Fame,

1977, for "A Hero Ain't Nothin' but a Sandwich"; "Alice Childress Week" officially observed in Charleston and Columbia, S.C., 1977, to celebrate opening of "Sea Island Song"; *Rainbow Jordan* was named one of the "Best Books" by *School Library Journal,* 1981, one of the Outstanding Books of the Year by *New York Times,* 1982, and a notable children's trade book in social studies by National Council for the Social Studies and Children's Book Council, 1982; honorable mention, Coretta Scott King Award, 1982, for *Rainbow Jordan.*

WRITINGS:

Like One of the Family: Conversations from a Domestic's Life, Independence Publishers, 1956, reprinted with an introduction by Trudier Harris, Beacon Press, 1986.
(Editor) *Black Scenes* (collection of scenes from plays written by Afro-Americans about the Black experience), Doubleday, 1971.
A Hero Ain't Nothin' but a Sandwich (novel; also see below), Coward, 1973.
A Short Walk (novel), Coward, 1979.
Rainbow Jordan (novel), Coward, 1981.
Many Closets, Coward, 1987.
Those Other People, Putnam, 1989.

PLAYS

"Florence" (one-act), first produced in New York City at American Negro Theatre, directed by and starring Childress, 1949.
"Just a Little Simple" (based on Langston Hughes's short story collection *Simple Speaks His Mind*), first produced in New York City at Club Baron Theatre, September, 1950.
"Gold through the Trees," first produced at Club Baron Theatre, 1952.
"Trouble in Mind," first produced Off-Broadway at Greenwich Mews Theatre, directed by Childress, November 3, 1955, revised version published in *Black Theatre: A Twentieth-Century Collection of the Work of Its Best Playwrights,* edited by Lindsay Patterson, Dodd, 1971.
Wedding Band: A Love/Hate Story in Black and White (first produced in Ann Arbor, Mich., at University of Michigan, December 7, 1966; produced Off-Broadway at New York Shakespeare Festival Theatre, directed by Childress and Joseph Papp, September 26, 1972; also see below), Samuel French, 1973.
"String" (one-act; based on Guy de Maupassant's story "A Piece of String"; also see below), first produced Off-Broadway at St. Mark's Playhouse, March 25, 1969.
"Mojo: A Black Love Story" (one-act; also see below), produced in New York City at New Heritage Theatre, November, 1970.
Mojo [and] *String,* Dramatists Play Service, 1971.
When the Rattlesnake Sounds: A Play (juvenile), illustrated by Charles Lilly, Coward, 1975.
Let's Hear It for the Queen: A Play (juvenile), Coward, 1976.
"Sea Island Song," produced in Charleston, S.C., 1977, produced as "Gullah" in Amherst, Mass., at University of Massachusetts—Amherst, 1984.
"Moms: A Praise Play for a Black Comedienne" (based on the life of Jackie "Moms" Mabley), music and lyrics by Childress and her husband, Nathan Woodard, first produced by Green Plays at Art Awareness, 1986, produced Off-Broadway at Hudson Guild Theatre, February 4, 1987.

Also author of "Martin Luther King at Montgomery, Alabama," music by Woodard, 1969, "A Man Bearing a Pitcher," 1969, "The African Garden," music by Woodard, 1971, and

"Vashti's Magic Mirror"; author of "The Freedom Drum," music by Woodard, produced as "Young Man Martin Luther King" by Performing Arts Repertory Theatre (on tour), 1969-71.

SCREENPLAYS

Wine in the Wilderness: A Comedy-Drama (first produced in Boston by WGBH-TV, March 4, 1969), Dramatists Play Service, 1969.
"Wedding Band" (based on her play of the same title), American Broadcasting Companies (ABC-TV), 1973.
"A Hero Ain't Nothin' but a Sandwich" (based on her novel of the same title), New World Pictures, 1978.
"String" (based on her play of the same title), Public Broadcasting Service (PBS-TV), 1979.

CONTRIBUTOR

Langston Hughes, editor, *The Best Short Stories by Negro Writers: An Anthology from 1899 to the Present,* Little, Brown, 1967.
Plays to Remember (includes "The World on a Hill"), Macmillan, 1968.
Stanley Richards, editor, *The Best Short Plays of 1972,* Chilton, 1972.
The Young American Basic Reading Program, Lyons & Carnaham, 1972.
Success in Reading, Silver Burdette, 1972.
Richards, editor, *Best Short Plays of the World Theatre, 1968-1973,* Crown, 1973.
Patterson, editor, *Anthology of the Afro-American in the Theatre: A Critical Approach,* Publishers Agency, 1978.
R. Baxter Miller, editor, *Black American Literature and Humanism,* University of Kentucky Press, 1981.
Mari Evans, editor, *Black Women Writers (1950-1980): A Critical Evaluation,* Doubleday-Anchor, 1984.

Also contributor to *Keeping the Faith,* edited by Pat Exum.

OTHER

Author of "Here's Mildred" column in *Baltimore Afro-American,* 1956-58. Contributor of plays, articles, and reviews to *Masses and Mainstream, Black World, Freedomways, Essence, Negro Digest, New York Times,* and other publications.

SIDELIGHTS: Alice Childress's work is noted for its frank treatment of racial issues, its compassionate yet discerning characterizations, and its universal appeal. Because her books and plays often deal with such controversial subjects as miscegenation and teenage drug addiction, her work has been banned in certain locations. She recalls that some affiliate stations refused to carry the nationally televised broadcasts of "Wedding Band" and "Wine in the Wilderness," and in the case of the latter play, the entire state of Alabama banned the telecast. Childress notes in addition that as late as 1973 the novel *A Hero Ain't Nothin' but a Sandwich* "was the first book banned in a Savannah, Georgia school library since *Catcher in the Rye,* which the same school banned in the fifties." Despite such regional resistance, Childress has won praise and respect for writings that a *Variety* reviewer terms "powerful and poetic."

A talented writer and performer in several media, Childress began her career in the theater, initially as an actress and later as a director and playwright. Although "theater histories make only passing mention of her, . . . she was in the forefront of important developments in that medium," writes *Dictionary of Literary Biography* contributor Trudier Harris. Rosemary Curb points out in another *Dictionary of Literary Biography* article that Childress's 1952 drama "Gold Through the Trees" was "the first play by a black woman professionally produced on the American stage." Moreover, Curb adds, "As a result of successful performances of [her 1950s plays 'Just a Little Simple' and 'Gold Through the Trees'], Childress initiated Harlem's first all-union Off-Broadway contracts recognizing the Actors Equity Association and the Harlem Stage Hand Local."

Partly because of her pioneering efforts, Childress is considered a crusader by many. But she is also known as "a writer who resists compromise," says Doris E. Abramson in *Negro Playwrights in the American Theatre: 1925-1959.* "She tries to write about [black] problems as honestly as she can." The problems Childress addresses most often are racism and its effects. Her "Trouble in Mind," for example, is a play within a play that focuses on the anger and frustration experienced by a troupe of black actors as they try to perform stereotyped roles in a play that has been written, produced, and directed by whites. As Sally R. Sommer explains in the *Village Voice,* "The plot is about an emerging rebellion begun as the heroine, Wiletta, refuses to enact a namby-Mammy, either in the play or for her director." In the *New York Times,* Arthur Gelb states that Childress "has some witty and penetrating things to say about the dearth of roles for [black] actors in the contemporary theatre, the cutthroat competition for these parts and the fact that [black] actors often find themselves playing stereotyped roles in which they cannot bring themselves to believe." And of "Wedding Band," a play about an interracial relationship that takes place in South Carolina during World War I, Clive Barnes writes in the *New York Times,* "Childress very carefully suggests the stirrings of black consciousness, as well as the strength of white bigotry."

Critics Sommer and the *New York Times*'s Richard Eder find that Childress's treatment of the themes and issues in "Trouble in Mind" and "Wedding Band" gives these plays a timeless quality. "Writing in 1955, . . . Alice Childress used the concentric circles of the play-within-the-play to examine the multiple roles blacks enact in order to survive," Sommer remarks. She finds that viewing "Trouble in Mind" years later enables one to see "its double cutting edge: It predicts not only the course of social history but the course of black playwriting." Eder states: "The question [in 'Wedding Band'] is whether race is a category of humanity or a division of it. The question is old by now, and was in 1965, [when the play was written,] but it takes the freshness of new life in the marvelous characters that Miss Childress has created to ask it."

The strength and insight of Childress's characterizations have been widely commented upon; critics contend that the characters who populate her plays and novels are believable and memorable. Eder praises the "rich and lively characterization" of "Wedding Band." Similarly impressed, Harold Clurman writes in the *Nation* that "there is an honest pathos in the telling of this simple story, and some humorous and touching thumbnail sketches reveal knowledge and understanding of the people dealt with." In the novel *A Short Walk,* Childress chronicles the life of a fictitious black woman, Cora James, from her birth in 1900 to her death in the middle of the century, illustrating, as *Washington Post* critic Joseph McLellan describes it, "a transitional generation in black American society." McLellan notes that the story "wanders considerably" and that "the reader is left with no firm conclusion that can be put into a neat sentence or two." What is more important, he asserts, is that "the wandering has been through some interesting scenery, and instead of a conclusion the reader has come to know a human being—complex, struggling valiantly and totally believable." And of Childress's novel about teenage heroin addiction, *A Hero Ain't Nothin' but*

a Sandwich, the *Lion and the Unicorn*'s Miguel Oritz states, "The portrait of whites is more realistic in this book, more compassionate, and at the same time, because it is believable, more scathing."

Some criticism has been leveled at what such reviewers as Abramson and Edith Oliver believe to be Childress's tendency to speechify, especially in her plays. "A reader of the script is very much aware of the author pulling strings, putting her own words into a number of mouths," Abramson says of "Trouble in Mind." According to Oliver in the *New Yorker,* "The first act [of 'Wedding Band'] is splendid, but after that we hit a few jarring notes, when the characters seem to be speaking as much for the benefit of us eavesdroppers out front . . . as for the benefit of one another."

For the most part, however, Childress's work has been acclaimed for its honesty, insight, and compassion. In his review of *A Hero Ain't Nothin' but a Sandwich,* Oritz writes: "The book conveys very strongly the message that we are all human, even when we are acting in ways that we are somewhat ashamed of. The structure of the book grows out of the personalities of the characters, and the author makes us aware of how much the economic and social circumstances dictate a character's actions." Loften Mitchell concludes in *Crisis:* "Childress writes with a sharp, satiric touch. Character seems to interest her more than plot. Her characterizations are piercing, her observations devastating."

Alice Childress commented: "Books, plays, tele-plays, motion picture scenarios, etc., I seem caught up in a fragmentation of writing skills. But an idea comes to me in a certain form and, if it stays with me, must be written out or put in outline form before I can move on to the next event. I sometimes wonder about writing in different forms; could it be that women are used to dealing with the bits and pieces of life and do not feel as [compelled to specialize]? The play form is the one most familiar to me and so influences all of my writing—I think in scenes.

"My young years were very old in feeling, I was shut out of so much for so long. [I] soon began to embrace the low-profile as a way of life, which helped me to develop as a writer. Quiet living is restful when one's writing is labeled 'controversial.'

"Happily, I managed to save a bit of my youth for spending in these later years. Oh yes, there are other things to be saved [besides] money. If we hang on to that part within that was once childhood, I believe we enter into a new time dimension and every day becomes another lifetime in itself. This gift of understanding is often given to those who constantly battle against the negatives of life with determination."

BIOGRAPHICAL/CRITICAL SOURCES:

BOOKS

Abramson, Doris E., *Negro Playwrights in the American Theatre, 1925-1959,* Columbia University Press, 1969.

Betsko, Kathleen, and Rachel Koenig, *Interviews with Contemporary Women Playwrights,* Beech Tree Books, 1987.

Children's Literature Review, Volume 14, Gale, 1988.

Contemporary Literary Criticism, Gale, Volume 12, 1980, Volume 15, 1980.

Dictionary of Literary Biography, Gale, Volume 7: *Twentieth-Century American Dramatists,* 1981, Volume 38: *Afro-American Writers after 1955: Dramatists and Prose Writers,* 1985.

Donelson, Kenneth L., and Alleen Pace Nilson, *Literature for Today's Young Adults,* Scott, Foresman, 1980, 2nd edition, 1985.

Evans, Mari, editor, *Black Women Writers (1950-1980): A Critical Evaluation,* Doubleday-Anchor, 1984.

Hatch, James V., *Black Theater, U.S.A.: Forty-five Plays by Black Americans,* Free Press, 1974.

Mitchell, Loften, editor, *Voices of the Black Theatre,* James White, 1975.

Street, Douglas, editor, *Children's Novels and the Movies,* Ungar, 1983.

PERIODICALS

Crisis, April, 1965.
Freedomways, Volume 14, number 1, 1974.
Interracial Books for Children Bulletin, Volume 12, numbers 7-8, 1981.
Lion and the Unicorn, fall, 1978.
Los Angeles Times, November 13, 1978, February 25, 1983.
Los Angeles Times Book Review, July 25, 1982.
Ms., December, 1979.
Nation, November 13, 1972.
Negro Digest, April, 1967, January, 1968.
Newsweek, August 31, 1987.
New Yorker, November 4, 1972, November 19, 1979.
New York Times, November 5, 1955, February 2, 1969, April 2, 1969, October 27, 1972, November 5, 1972, February 3, 1978, January 11, 1979, January 23, 1987, February 10, 1987, March 6, 1987, August 18, 1987, October 22, 1987.
New York Times Book Review, November 4, 1973, November 11, 1979, April 25, 1981.
Show Business, April 12, 1969.
Variety, December 20, 1972. Village Voice, January 15, 1979.
Washington Post, May 18, 1971, December 28, 1979.

*   *   *

CHOMSKY, (Avram) Noam 1928-

PERSONAL: Born December 7, 1928, in Philadelphia, Pa.; son of William (a Hebrew scholar) and Elsie (Simonofsky) Chomsky; married Carol Schatz (a linguist and specialist in educational technology), December 24, 1949; children: Aviva, Diane, Harry Alan. *Education:* University of Pennsylvania, B.A., 1949, M.A., 1951, Ph.D., 1955. *Politics:* Libertarian socialist.

ADDRESSES: Home—15 Suzanne Rd., Lexington, Mass. 02173. *Office*—Department of Linguistics and Philosophy, Massachusetts Institute of Technology, Room 20D-219, 77 Massachusetts Ave., Cambridge, Mass. 02139.

CAREER: Massachusetts Institute of Technology, Cambridge, assistant professor, 1955-58, associate professor, 1958-62, professor, 1962-65, Ferrari P. Ward Professor of Modern Languages and Linguistics, 1966-76, Institute Professor, 1976—. Visiting professor of linguistics, Columbia University, 1957-58, University of California, Los Angeles, 1966, University of California, Berkeley, 1966-67, and Syracuse University, 1982. Member, Institute of Advanced Study, Princeton University, 1958-59. John Locke lecturer, Oxford University, 1969; Bertrand Russell Memorial Lecturer, Cambridge University, 1971; Nehru Memorial Lecturer, University of New Delhi, 1972; Huizinga Lecturer, University of Leiden, 1977; Woodbridge Lecturer, Columbia University, 1978; Kant Lecturer, Stanford University, 1979.

MEMBER: National Academy of Sciences, American Academy of Arts and Sciences, Linguistic Society of America, American Philosophical Association, American Association for the Advancement of Science, British Academy (corresponding fellow), British Psychological Society (honorary member), Deutsche Akademie der Naturforscher Leopoldina, Utrecht Society of Arts and Sciences.

AWARDS, HONORS: Junior fellow, Harvard Society of Fellows, 1951-55; research fellow at Harvard Cognitive Studies Center, 1964-67; named one of the "makers of the twentieth century" by the London *Times,* 1970; Guggenheim fellowship, 1971-72; distinguished scientific contribution from American Psychological Association, 1984; Gustavus Myers Center Award, 1986 and 1988; George Orwell Award, National Council of Teachers of English, 1987; Kyoto Prize in Basic Sciences, 1988. Honorary degrees include D.H.L. from University of Chicago, 1967, Loyola University of Chicago and Swarthmore College, 1970, Bard College, 1971, University of Massachusetts, 1973, and University of Pennsylvania, 1984; and D.Litt. from University of London, 1967, Delhi University, 1972, Visva-Bharati University (West Bengal), 1980.

WRITINGS:

Syntactic Structures, Mouton & Co., 1957, reprinted, 1978.
Current Issues in Linguistic Theory, Mouton & Co., 1964.
Aspects of the Theory of Syntax, M.I.T. Press, 1965, reprinted, 1986.
Cartesian Linguistics: A Chapter in the History of Rationalist Thought, Harper, 1966.
Topics in the Theory of Generative Grammar, Mouton & Co., 1966, reprinted, 1978.
(With Morris Halle) *Sound Patterns of English,* Harper, 1968.
Language and Mind, Harcourt, 1968, enlarged edition, 1972.
American Power and the New Mandarins, Pantheon, 1969.
At War with Asia, Pantheon, 1970.
Problems of Knowledge and Freedom: The Russell Lectures, Pantheon, 1971.
(With George A. Miller) *Analyse formelle des langues naturelles,* Mouton & Co., 1971.
Studies on Semantics in Generative Grammar, Mouton & Co., 1972.
(Editor with Howard Zinn) *The Pentagon Papers, Volume 5: Critical Essays,* Beacon Press, 1972.
(With Edward Herman) *Counterrevolutionary Violence,* Warner Modular, Inc., 1974.
Peace in the Middle East?, Pantheon, 1975.
The Logical Structure of Linguistic Theory, Plenum, 1975.
Reflections on Language, Pantheon, 1975.
Essays on Form and Interpretation, North-Holland, 1977.
Dialogues avec Mitsou Ronat, Flammarion, 1977, translation published as *Language and Responsibility,* Pantheon, 1979.
Human Rights and American Foreign Policy, Spokesman, 1978.
(With Herman) *The Political Economy of Human Rights,* South End, 1979, Volume I: *The Washington Connection and Third World Fascism,* Volume II: *After the Cataclysm: Postwar Indochina and the Construction of Imperial Ideology.*
Rules and Representations, Columbia University Press, 1980.
Language and Learning: The Debate between Jean Piaget and Noam Chomsky, edited by Massimo Piattelli-Palmarini, Harvard University Press, 1980.
Lectures on Government and Binding, Foris, 1981.
Radical Priorities, Black Rose Books, 1981.
Towards a New Cold War: Essays on the Current Crisis and How We Got There, Pantheon, 1982.
Noam Chomsky on the Generative Enterprise: A Discussion with Riny Huybregts and Henk van Riemsdijk, Foris, 1982.
(With Jonathan Steele and John Gittings) *Superpowers in Collision: The Cold War Now,* Penguin Books, 1982.
Some Concepts and Consequences of the Theory of Government and Binding, M.I.T. Press, 1982.

The Fateful Triangle: The United States, Israel, and the Palestinians, South End, 1983.

Turning the Tide: U.S. Intervention in Central America and the Struggle for Peace, South End, 1985.

Barriers, M.I.T. Press, 1986.

Knowledge of Language: Its Nature, Origins, and Use, Praeger, 1986.

Pirates and Emperors: International Terrorism in the Real World, Claremont, 1986.

On Power and Ideology: The Managua Lectures, South End, 1987.

The Chomsky Reader, edited by James Peck, Pantheon, 1987.

Language and Problems of Knowledge: The Managua Lectures, M.I.T. Press, 1987.

Language in a Psychological Setting, Sophia University (Tokyo), 1987.

Generative Grammar: Its Basis, Development, and Prospects, Kyoto University of Foreign Studies, 1988.

The Culture of Terrorism, South End, 1988.

(With Edward S. Herman) *Manufacturing Consent: The Political Economy of the Mass Media,* Pantheon, 1988.

Necessary Illusions: Thought Control in a Democratic Society, South End, 1989.

Language and Politics, edited by Carlos P. Otero, Black Rose Books, 1989.

Contributor of numerous articles to scholarly and general periodicals.

SIDELIGHTS: "Judged in terms of the power, range, novelty and influence of his thought, Noam Chomsky is arguably the most important intellectual alive today," writes Paul Robinson in the *New York Times Book Review.* Chomsky, a professor of linguistics at the Massachusetts Institute of Technology, has attracted worldwide attention with his ground-breaking research into the nature of human language and communication. As the founder of the "Chomskyan Revolution," the scholar has become the center of a debate that transcends formal linguistics to embrace psychology, philosophy, and even genetics. *New York Times Magazine* contributor Daniel Yergin maintains that Chomsky's "formulation of 'transformational grammar' has been acclaimed as one of the major achievements of the century. Where others heard only a Babel of fragments, he found a linguistic order. His work has been compared to the unraveling of the genetic code of the DNA molecule." Yergin further contends that Chomsky's discoveries have had an impact "on everything from the way children are taught foreign languages to what it means when we say that we are human." Chomsky is also an impassioned critic of American foreign policy, especially as it affects ordinary citizens of Third World nations. Many of his books since 1969 concern themselves with "the perfidy of American influence overseas," to quote *Atlantic* essayist James Fallows. In *America,* Kenneth J. Gavin finds a unifying strain in all of Chomsky's various writings. The author's goal, says Gavin, is "to highlight principles of human knowledge and indicate the priority of these principles in the reconstruction of a society. His efforts leave us with more than enough to think about."

Chomsky was born in Philadelphia on December 7, 1928. His father was a Hebrew scholar of considerable repute, so even as a youngster Chomsky "picked up a body of informal knowledge about the structure and history of the Semitic languages," according to David Cohen in *Psychologists on Psychology.* While still in high school Chomsky proofread the manuscript of his father's edition of a medieval Hebrew grammar. Yergin notes: "This backdoor introduction to 'historical linguistics' had considerable impact in the future; it helped fuel his later conviction

that the explanation of how language worked, rather than categories and description, was the business of linguistic study." The young Chomsky was more interested in politics than grammar, however. He was especially passionate about the rebirth of a Jewish culture and society in what later became the state of Israel, and for a time he entertained the idea of moving there. In 1945 he enrolled at the University of Pennsylvania, where he came under the influence of Zellig Harris, a noted professor of linguistics. John Lyons observes in *Noam Chomsky* that it was the student's "sympathies with Harris's political views that led him to work as an undergraduate in linguistics. There is a sense, therefore, in which politics brought him into linguistics."

The school of linguistics in which Chomsky took his collegiate training held as its goal the formal and autonomous description of languages without wide reference to the meaning—or semantics—of utterances. Lyons elaborates: "Semantic considerations were strictly subordinated to the task of identifying the units of phonology and syntax and were not involved at all in the specification of the rules or principles governing their permissible combinations. This part of the grammar was to be a purely *formal* study, independent of semantics." Chomsky questioned this approach in his early work in generative grammar as a student at the University of Pennsylvania and broke with it more radically while in the Harvard Society of Fellows from 1951. There he was immersed in new developments in mathematical logic, the abstract theory of thinking machines, and the latest psychological and philosophical debates. These ideas led him to develop further his earlier work on generative grammar and to ask "precise and formal questions about linguistics and language," to quote Justin Leiber in his work *Noam Chomsky: A Philosophical Overview.* Leiber adds: "His results led him to criticize and discard the prevailing views in linguistics."

What Chomsky began to develop in the 1950s was a mathematically precise description of some of human language's most striking features. Yergin contends that the scholar was "particularly fascinated by 'generative systems'—the procedures by which a mathematician, starting with postulates and utilizing principles and inferences, can generate an infinite number of proofs. He thought that perhaps language was 'generated' from a few principles as well." Yergin claims that this line of reasoning led Chomsky to another salient question, namely: *"How is it possible that, if language is only a learned habit, one can be continually creative and innovative in its use?"* This question—and its explication—would provide a novel and compelling critique of two established fields, traditional structural linguistics and behavioral psychology. Leiber concludes that Chomsky's new theory "explained many features of language that were beyond structuralist linguistics and placed the specific data, and many lower-level generalizations, of the structuralists within a richer theory."

Many of Chomsky's novel ideas saw print in his first book, *Syntactic Structures,* published in 1957. Yergin calls the work "the pale blue book . . . which heralded the Chomskyan Revolution." He adds that the volume "demonstrated that important facts about language could not be explained by either structural linguistics or by computer theory, which was then becoming fashionable in the field. In 'Syntactic Structures,' Chomsky departed from his mentors in stressing the importance of explaining creativity in language and introduces his own transformational grammar as a more 'powerful' explanation of how we make sentences." Webster Schott offers a similar assessment in the *Washington Post Book World.* In *Syntactic Structures,* writes Schott, "Chomsky [presents] and [seems] to demonstrate the proposition that every human being has an innate ability to acquire language, and this ability to learn language is called into use when one hears, at the right age, language for the first time. He also [offers] a concept—it came to be known as 'generative' or 'transformational-generative' grammar—which [has] made it possible to predict ('generate') the sentence combinations in a language and to describe their structure." Lyons states that the short and relatively nontechnical *Syntactic Structures* "revolutionized the scientific study of language."

The proofs Chomsky uses for his theories are complex, but his conclusions are readily accessible. Robinson observes that, put as simply as possible, Chomsky's view holds that "the ability to speak and understand a language cannot be explained in purely empirical terms—that is, purely by induction. When we 'learn' a language, he says, we are able to formulate and understand all sorts of sentences that we've never heard before. What we 'know,' therefore, must be something deeper—a grammar—that makes an infinite variety of sentences possible. Chomsky believes that the capacity to master grammatical structures is innate: It is genetically determined, a product of the evolutionary process, just as the organic structures of our bodies are." A strict "stimulus-response" mechanism cannot adequately account for the way young children master language during the first four years of life; the child, to quote Cohen, "learns . . . to extract the more complex rules of grammar needed for speech." Leiber explains that for Chomsky, then, the primary interest of the linguist should be with specifying the "device of some sort" that *generates* an infinite variety of grammatically-correct sentences. "This device will specify what is somehow 'internalized' in the competent speaker-hearer of the language," Leiber writes. "Though the most usual label for Chomsky's general sort of linguistics is 'transformational-generative linguistics,' the most crucial word is 'generative'—as opposed to 'taxonomical'—since the primary concern is with the 'principles and processes by which sentences are constructed in particular languages,' not with the identification and classification of items found in the surface end product of these principles and processes."

One of the mechanisms Chomsky proposes for sentence generation is the "deep structure-surface structure" scenario. According to Yergin, the surface structure " 'faces out' on the world and, by certain phonological rules, is converted into the sounds we hear; it corresponds to the parsing of sentences which we all learned from our indefatigable junior high English teachers. The deep structure 'faces inward' toward the hazy region of conceptualization, is more abstract and related to meaning. It expresses the basic logical relations between nouns and verbs." Transformational grammar therefore "consists of a limited series of rules, expressed in mathematical notation, which transform deep structures into well-formed surface structures. The transformational grammar thus relates meaning and sound." Cohen discusses the applications of this concept. "Chomsky has analysed the necessary constituents of the deep structure and the transformations through which this deep structure is turned into the surface structure we recognize and use as sentences. He has, of course, extended his theory from this point into the implications for our knowledge of man that comes from the fact that our knowledge of language is based upon this deep structure, a structure that we cannot guess or divine just from speaking, and upon the necessary transformations."

Chomsky has argued that all natural human languages possess deep and surface structures and cycles of transformations between them. In the *Nation,* Gilbert Harman writes: "These built-in aspects of grammar will be parts of the grammar of every language. They are, in other words, aspects of 'universal grammar.' We must therefore suppose that people have a specific faculty of language, a kind of 'mental organ' which develops in the appropriate way, given appropriate experience, yielding a knowledge of whatever language is spoken in their community." John Sturrock elaborates in the *New York Times Book Review:* "Chomskyism starts with grammar and finishes in genetics. Drill deep enough into the structure of our sentences, he maintains, and you will come to those ultimate abstractions with which we were born, the grammar of any given language being originally determined by the fairly restricted grammatical possibilities programmed in the brain. . . . DNA sets up to master a syntax, the accident of birth determines which one." Needless to say, not everyone agrees with Chomsky's view. *Psychology Today* contributor Howard Gardner calls the human being in Chomsky's formulation "a totally preprogrammed computer, one that needs merely to be plugged into the appropriate outlet." Lyons, conversely, states that Chomsky "was surely right to challenge 'the belief that the mind must be simpler in its structure than any known physical organ and that the most primitive of assumptions must be adequate to explain whatever phenomena can be observed.' "

Obviously, Chomsky's theory has as much to do with psychology and philosophy as it does with linguistics. For instance, the very premises of the scholar's work have made him one of the most devastating critics of behaviorism, the view that suggests all human responses are learned through conditioning. Sturrock notes: "Chomsky's case is that . . . that fanatical core known as behaviorism, has a theory of learning, all rote and Pavlovian reinforcement, which is deficient and, in the end, degrading. . . . [Behaviorists], given their sinister theory of learning, must be proponents of the view that human nature is not nature at all, but a social product conditioned from outside. Chomsky finds hope and a decisive guarantee of intellectual freedom in the cognitive structures which sit incorruptibly in the fastness of our brains." Chomsky's work reinforces the philosophical tradition of "rationalism," the contention that the mind, or "reason," contributes to human knowledge beyond what is gained by experience. He is opposed by the "empiricists," who claim that all knowledge derives from external stimuli, including language. In the *Nation,* Edward Marcotte declares: "What started as purely linguistic research . . . has led, through involvement in political causes and an identification with an older philosophic tradition, to no less than an attempt to formulate an overall theory of man. The roots of this are manifest in the linguistic theory. . . . The discovery of cognitive structures common to the human race but only to humans (species specific), leads quite easily to thinking of unalienable human attributes." Leiber concludes: "Mind is the software of human psychology, and thought is individuated as instances of the mind's operations. The behaviorist is seen to be insisting . . . on a very minimal sort of software; the rationalist is out to show that much more powerful and abstract, perhaps in good measure innate, software has to be involved. One can feel unhappy with Chomsky's particular way of putting, or productively narrowing, the issue, but it is not an unreasonable viewpoint. Chomsky has an interesting and important sense of *know* at hand. He is looking at men in a way that has an established and well-defined sense when applied to thinking devices."

While establishing his academic reputation, Chomsky continued to be concerned about the direction of American politics and ideology. His moral indignation rose in the 1960s until he became "one of the most articulate spokesmen of the resistance against the Vietnam war," to quote Jan G. Deutsche in the *New York Times Book Review.* Chomsky attacked the war in articles, in books, and from the podium; in the process he became better known for his political views than for his linguistic scholarship. In a *New York Times* piece written during that era, Thomas Lask observes: "Unlike many others, even those who oppose the war, Noam Chomsky can't stand it and his hatred of what we are doing there and his shame, as well as his loathing for the men who defend and give it countenance are tangible enough to touch." *Nation* essayist Brian Morton finds "nothing exotic about his critique of the U.S. role in Vietnam: He attempted no analysis of arcane economic or political structures. All he did was evaluate our government's actions by the same standards that we apply when we evaluate the actions of other governments."

Chomsky's first book-length work on Vietnam, *American Power and the New Mandarins,* offers "a searing criticism of the system of values and decision-making that drove the United States to the jungles of Southeast Asia," according to Michael R. Beschloss in the *Washington Post Book World.* The book's strongest vitriol is directed toward those so-called "New Mandarins"—the technocrats, bureaucrats, and university-trained scholars who defend America's right to dominate the globe. Deutsch states that Chomsky's concern "is not simply that social scientists have participated widely in designing and executing war-related projects. What he finds disturbing are the consequences of access to power by intellectuals; the difficulties involved in retaining a critical stance toward a society that makes the reward of power available as well as the need to be 'constructive,' the recognition as problems of only those difficulties that are soluble by the means at hand." Inevitably, Chomsky's volume has drawn scathing criticism from those who oppose his views and high praise from those who agree with him. *Chicago Tribune Book World* reviewer Arthur Schlesinger, Jr., claims: "Judging by *American Power and the New Mandarins,* one can only conclude that Chomsky's idea of the responsibility of an intellectual is to forswear reasoned analysis, indulge in moralistic declamation, fabricate evidence when necessary and shout always at the top of one's voice. It need hardly be said that, should the intellectual community follow the Chomsky example, it would betray its own traditions and hasten society along the road to unreason and disaster." In the *Nation,* Robert Sklar feels otherwise about the work. The critic contends: "The importance of *American Power and the New Mandarins* lies in its power to free our minds from old perspectives, to stimulate new efforts at historical, political and social thought."

Subsequent Chomsky books on American foreign policy have explored other political hotbeds around the world, drawing the conclusion that U.S. interests in human rights, justice, and morality are inevitably subordinated to big business profit-taking. As Beschloss notes, Chomsky's "is a portrait of corporate executives manipulating foreign policy for profit motives, of Third World peoples devastated for drifting away from the American 'grand area' of influence; of hand-maiden journalists, politicians, and intellectuals shrouding the darker realities of American statecraft under platitudes about idealism and goodwill with an eye toward their flow of rewards from the Establishment." *Times Literary Supplement* correspondent Charles Townshend observes that Chomsky "sees a 'totalitarian mentality' arising out of the mainstream American belief in the fundamental righteousness and benevolence of the United States, the sanctity and nobility of its aims. The publicly tolerated 'spectrum of discussion' of these aims is narrow." Chomsky himself transcends that narrow spectrum, adducing "example after example to illuminate how American policies have led knowingly to large scale human suffering," to quote Beschloss. In the *New York Times Book Review,* Sheldon S. Wolin suggests that the author "is relentless in tracking down official lies and exposing hypocrisy and moral indifference in the high places. . . . Yet the passion of Chomsky's in-

dictment is always controlled, and while he is harsh toward his opponents, he is never unfair or arrogant."

Other critics have been less sanguine about Chomsky's political views; in fact, some have actually labeled him a pariah and attempted to discredit him on a number of grounds. "It has been Chomsky's singular fate to have been banished to the margins of political debate," writes Steve Wasserman in the *Los Angeles Times Book Review.* "His opinions have been deemed so kooky—and his personality so cranky—that his writings no longer appear in the forums . . . in which he was once so welcome." Wolin offers one dissenting view: "Chomsky's political writings are curiously untheoretical, which is surprising in a writer renowned for his contributions to linguistic theory. His apparent assumption is that politics is not a theoretical subject. . . . One gets the impression from reading Chomsky that if it were not urgently necessary to expose lies, immorality and the abuse of power, politics would have no serious claim upon the theoretical mind." *New York Times Book Review* contributor Paul Robinson notes that in Chomsky's case, "the popular or accessible [political] works often seem to belie the intellectual powers unambiguously established in the professional works. . . . Indeed, one might argue that the discrepancy is more extreme in his work than in that of any other important intellectual." Morton feels that the attacks on Chomsky's historical/political scholarship—and more recently the tendency to ignore his work—have affected his level of stridency. The critic observes, for instance, that "his later tone is that of a man who doesn't expect anything to change. . . . Chomsky is savagely indignant because the values he cherishes are being strangled. But increasingly, the reasons for his indignation—the values he cherishes—are hard to see in his work. Only the indignation is clear."

Chomsky has his champions, however. Leiber, for one, finds an overriding commitment to freedom in the author's work—"the freedom of the individual to produce and create as he will without the goad of external force, economic competition for survival, or legal and economic restraint on social, intellectual, or artistic experiment; and the freedom of ethnic and national groups to work out their own destinies without the intervention of one or another Big Brother." "From his earliest writings to his latest, Chomsky has looked with astonishment at what the powerful do to the powerless," Morton declares. "He has never let his sense of outrage become dulled. If his voice has grown hoarse over twenty years, who can blame him? And who can feel superior? No one has given himself more deeply to the struggle against the horrors of our time. His hoarseness is a better thing than our suavity." Deutsch writes: "The most convincing indication of the extent to which Chomsky's wide ranging indictment of United States society and policy must be taken seriously is that a man possessed of these sensibilities should have felt compelled to undertake it." Morton offers a compelling conclusion. "Americans are no longer convinced that our government has the right to destroy any country it wants to," the essayist states. "And to the extent that this is true, Chomsky, along with others like him, deserves much of the credit. He did his job well."

In 1970, the London *Times* named Chomsky one of the thousand "makers of the twentieth century." According to Yergin, his theory "remains the foundation of linguistics today," and "his vision of a complex universe within the mind, governed by myriad rules and prohibitions and yet infinite in its creative potential, opens up vistas possibly as important as Einstein's theories." Yergin adds: "The impact of Chomsky's work may not be felt for years. . . . Yet this beginning has revolutionized the study of language and has redirected and redefined the broad inquiry into intelligence and how it works." Robinson calls the scholar's work "a prolonged celebration of the enormous gulf that separates man from the rest of nature. He seems overwhelmed by the intellectual powers that man contains within himself. Certainly nobody ever stated the case for those powers more emphatically, nor exemplified them more impressively in his own work. Reading Chomsky on linguistics, one repeatedly has the impression of attending to one of the more powerful thinkers who ever lived."

Chomsky has also earned a place in history for his political writings. According to Christopher Lehmann-Haupt in the *New York Times,* Chomsky "continues to challenge our assumptions long after other critics have gone to bed. He has become the foremost gadfly of our national conscience." *New Statesman* correspondent Francis Hope praises Chomsky for "a proud defensive independence, a good plain writer's hatred of expert mystification, a doctrine of resistance which runs against the melioristic and participatory current of most contemporary intellectual life." Hope concludes: "Such men are dangerous; the lack of them is disastrous."

BIOGRAPHICAL/CRITICAL SOURCES:

BOOKS

Cohen, David, *Psychologists on Psychology,* Taplinger, 1977.
Contemporary Issues Criticism, Volume 1, Gale, 1982.
Greene, Judith, *Psycholinguistics: Chomsky and Psychology,* Penguin Books, 1972.
Harman, Gilbert, editor, *On Noam Chomsky: Critical Essays,* Anchor Press, 1974.
Kim-Renaud, Young-Key, *Studies in Korean Linguistics,* Hanshin Publishing, 1986.
Leiber, Justin, *Noam Chomsky: A Philosophical Overview,* Twayne, 1975.
Lyons, John, *Noam Chomsky,* 2nd edition, Penguin Books, 1977.
Mehta, Ved, *John Is Easy to Please,* Farrar, Straus, 1971.
Osiatynski, Wiktor, *Contrasts: Soviet and American Thinkers Discuss the Future,* Macmillan, 1984.
Rieber, Robert W., editor, *Dialogues on the Psychology of Language and Thought: Conversations with Noam Chomsky, Charles Osgood, Jean Piaget, Ulric Neisser, and Marcel Kinsbourne,* Plenum, 1983.
Sampson, Geoffrey, *Liberty and Language,* Oxford University Press, 1979.
Thinkers of the Twentieth Century, Gale, 1983.

PERIODICALS

America, December 11, 1971.
Atlantic, July, 1973, February, 1982.
Book World, March 23, 1969.
Christian Century, July 23, 1969.
Christian Science Monitor, April 3, 1969, May 14, 1970.
Chronicle of Higher Education, May 12, 1982.
Commentary, May, 1969.
Dissent, January-February, 1970.
Economist, November 29, 1969.
Globe and Mail (Toronto), June 16, 1984, July 5, 1986.
Harvard Education Review, winter, 1969.
Horizon, spring, 1971.
International Affairs, January, 1971.
Los Angeles Times Book Review, December 27, 1981, June 8, 1986, August 30, 1987.
Maclean's, August 18, 1980.
Nation, September 9, 1968, March 24, 1969, May 17, 1971, May 8, 1976, March 31, 1979, February 16, 1980, December 22, 1984, December 26, 1987-January 2, 1988, May 7, 1988.

National Review, June 17, 1969.
New Republic, April 19, 1969, October 26, 1974, March 13, 1976, February 17, 1979, September 6-13, 1980, March 24, 1982, March 23, 1987.
New Statesman, November 28, 1969, August 17, 1979, April 25, 1980, July 17, 1981, August 14, 1981, September 11, 1981, January 21, 1983.
Newsweek, March 24, 1969.
New Yorker, November 11, 1969, May 8, 1971.
New York Review of Books, August 9, 1973, January 23, 1975, November 11, 1976, October 23, 1980.
New York Times, March 18, 1969, August 2, 1973, February 5, 1979, March 8, 1982.
New York Times Book Review, March 16, 1969, January 17, 1971, January 9, 1972, September 30, 1973, October 6, 1974, February 15, 1976, February 25, 1979, October 19, 1980, March 21, 1982, April 13, 1986.
New York Times Magazine, May 6, 1968, December 3, 1972.
Progressive, December, 1982.
Psychology Today, July, 1979.
Saturday Review, May 31, 1969.
Science and Society, spring, 1970.
Sewanee Review, winter, 1977.
Times Literary Supplement, March 27, 1969, March 31, 1972, December 21, 1973, December 12, 1975, September 10, 1976, November 21, 1980, February 27, 1981, July 23, 1982, July 15-21, 1988.
Village Voice, June 18, 1980, June 23, 1980, July 13, 1982.
Virginia Quarterly Review, summer, 1969.
Washington Post Book World, March 11, 1979, March 7, 1982, February 21, 1988.

*   *   *

CHRISTIE, Agatha (Mary Clarissa) 1890-1976
(Agatha Christie Mallowan, Mary Westmacott)

PERSONAL: Born September 15, 1890, in Torquay, Devon, England; died January 12, 1976, in Wallingford, England; daughter of Frederick Alvah and Clarissa Miller; married Archibald Christie (a colonel in Royal Air Corps), December 24, 1914 (divorced, 1928; died, 1962); married Max Edgar Lucien Mallowan (an archaeologist), September 11, 1930 (died, 1978); children: (first marriage) Rosalind. *Education:* Tutored at home by her mother until age 16; later studied singing and piano in Paris.

CAREER: Writer. During World War I, served as Voluntary Aid Detachment (V.A.D.) nurse in a Red Cross Hospital, Torquay, South Devon, England; after divorce in 1928, traveled for several years; after marriage to Max Mallowan, 1930, helped him with tabulations and photography at his excavations in Iraq and Syria; during World War II, worked in dispensary for University College Hospital, London, England; during postwar 1940s, helped her husband with excavation of Assyrian ruins.

MEMBER: Royal Society of Literature (fellow), Detection Club (president).

AWARDS, HONORS: Grand Master Award, Mystery Writers of America, 1954; New York Drama Critics' Circle Award, 1955, for "Witness for the Prosecution"; Commander of the British Empire, 1956; D.Litt., University of Exeter, 1961; Dame Commander, Order of the British Empire, 1971.

WRITINGS:

MYSTERY NOVELS

The Secret Adversary, Dodd, 1922, reprinted, Bantam, 1970.

The Man in the Brown Suit, Dodd, 1924.
The Secret of Chimneys, Dodd, 1925, reprinted, Dell, 1978.
The Seven Dials Mystery, Dodd, 1929, reprinted, Bantam, 1976.
The Murder at Hazelmoor, Dodd, 1931 (published in England as *The Sittaford Mystery,* Collins, 1931).
Why Didn't They Ask Evans?, Collins, 1934, reprinted, Dodd, 1968, published as *The Boomerang Clue,* Dodd, 1935, reprinted, G. K. Hall, 1988.
Easy to Kill, Dodd, 1939 (published in England as *Murder Is Easy,* Collins, 1939), reprinted, Pocket Books, 1984.
Ten Little Niggers (also see below), Collins, 1939, reprinted, 1977, published as *And Then There Were None,* Dodd, 1940, published as *Ten Little Indians,* Pocket Books, 1965, reprinted, Dodd, 1978.
N or M?: A New Mystery, Dodd, 1941, reprinted, 1974.
Death Comes as the End, Dodd, 1944.
Towards Zero (also see below), Dodd, 1944, reprinted, 1974.
Remembered Death, Dodd, 1945, reprinted, Pocket Books, 1975 (published in England as *Sparkling Cyanide,* Collins, 1945).
The Crooked House, Dodd, 1949.
They Came to Baghdad, Dodd, 1951, reprinted, Berkley, 1989.
Destination Unknown, Collins, 1954, reprinted, 1978, published as *So Many Steps to Death,* Dodd, 1955.
Ordeal by Innocence, Collins, 1958, Dodd, 1959.
The Pale Horse, Collins, 1961, Dodd, 1962, reprinted, Pocket Books, 1976.
Endless Night, Collins, 1967, Dodd, 1968.
By the Pricking of My Thumbs, Dodd, 1968.
Passenger to Frankfurt, Dodd, 1970.
Postern of Fate, Dodd, 1973.
Murder on Board, Dodd, 1974.

NOVELS FEATURING HERCULE POIROT

The Mysterious Affair at Styles, Lane, 1920, Dodd, 1927, Bantam, 1983.
The Murder on the Links, Dodd, 1923, reprinted, Triad Panther, 1978.
The Murder of Roger Ackroyd, Dodd, 1926, reprinted, Pocket Books, 1983.
The Big Four, Dodd, 1927.
The Mystery of the Blue Train, Dodd, 1928, reprinted, 1973.
Peril at End House, Dodd, 1932, reprinted, Pocket Books, 1982.
Thirteen at Dinner, Dodd, 1933 (published in England as *Lord Edgware Dies,* Collins, 1933, reprinted, 1977).
Murder in Three Acts, Dodd, 1934, reprinted, Popular Library, 1977 (published in England as *Three Act Tragedy,* Collins, 1935).
Murder on the Calais Coach, Dodd, 1934 (published in England as *Murder on the Orient Express,* Collins, 1934, reprinted, Pocket Books, 1976).
Death in the Air, Dodd, 1935 (published in England as *Death in the Clouds,* Collins, 1935), reprinted, Berkley, 1987.
The A.B.C. Murders, Dodd, 1936, reprinted, Pocket Books, 1976, published as *The Alphabet Murders,* Pocket Books, 1966.
Cards on the Table, Collins, 1936, Dodd, 1937.
Murder in Mesopotamia, Dodd, 1936, reprinted, Dell, 1976.
Poirot Loses a Client, Dodd, 1937 (published in England as *Dumb Witness,* Collins, 1937), reprinted, Berkley, 1985.
Death on the Nile (also see below), Collins, 1937, Dodd, 1938.
Appointment With Death (also see below), Dodd, 1938, reprinted, Berkley, 1988.
Hercule Poirot's Christmas, Collins, 1938, reprinted, 1977, published as *Murder for Christmas,* Dodd, 1939, published as *A Holiday for Murder,* Avon, 1947.

One, Two, Buckle My Shoe, Collins, 1940, published as *The Patriotic Murders,* Dodd, 1941, published as *An Overdose of Death,* Dell, 1953, reprinted as *The Patriotic Murders,* edited by Roger Cooper, Berkley, 1988.
Sad Cypress, Dodd, 1940, reprinted, Dell, 1970.
Evil Under the Sun, Dodd, 1941, reprinted, Pocket Books, 1985.
Murder in Retrospect, Dodd, 1942 (published in England as *Five Little Pigs* [also see below], Collins, 1942).
The Hollow (also see below), Dodd, 1946, published as *Murder After Hours,* Dell, 1954, reprinted, 1978.
There Is a Tide . . ., Dodd, 1948, reprinted, Dell, 1970 (published in England as *Taken at the Flood,* Collins, 1948).
Mrs. McGinty's Dead, Dodd, 1952.
Funerals Are Fatal, Dodd, 1953 (published in England as *After the Funeral,* Collins, 1953; published as *Murder at the Gallop,* Fontana, 1963), reprinted, Pocket Books, 1987.
Hickory, Dickory, Death, Dodd, 1955 (published in England as *Hickory, Dickory, Dock,* Collins, 1955), reprinted, Pocket Books, 1988.
Dead Man's Folly, Dodd, 1956, reprinted, Pocket Books, 1984.
Cat Among the Pigeons, Collins, 1959, Dodd, 1960, reprinted, Pocket Books, 1985.
The Clocks, Collins, 1963, Dodd, 1964.
Third Girl, Collins, 1966, Dodd, 1967.
Hallowe'en Party, Dodd, 1969.
Elephants Can Remember, Dodd, 1972.
Curtain: Hercule Poirot's Last Case, Dodd, 1975.

Hercule Poirot novels also published in various omnibus volumes (see below).

NOVELS FEATURING MISS JANE MARPLE

The Murder at the Vicarage, Dodd, 1930, reprinted, Berkley, 1984.
The Body in the Library, Dodd, 1942, reprinted, Pocket Books, 1983.
The Moving Finger, Dodd, 1942, reprinted, Berkley, 1986.
A Murder Is Announced, Dodd, 1950, reprinted, Pocket Books, 1985.
Murder With Mirrors, Dodd, 1952, reprinted, Pocket Books, 1976 (published in England as *They Do It With Mirrors,* Collins, 1952).
A Pocket Full of Rye, Collins, 1953, Dodd, 1954, reprinted, Pocket Books, 1986.
What Mrs. McGillicudy Saw!, Dodd, 1957, reprinted, Pocket Books, 1976 (published in England as *4:50 From Paddington,* Collins, 1957), published as *Murder She Said,* Pocket Books, 1961.
The Mirror Crack'd From Side to Side, Collins, 1962, published as *The Mirror Crack'd,* Dodd, 1963.
A Caribbean Mystery, Collins, 1964, Dodd, 1965, reprinted, Pocket Books, 1976.
At Bertram's Hotel, Collins, 1965, Dodd, 1966, revised edition, Pocket Books, 1984.
Nemesis, Dodd, 1971.
Sleeping Murder, Dodd, 1976.

Miss Jane Marple novels also published in various omnibus volumes (see below).

SHORT STORY COLLECTIONS

Poirot Investigates, Lane, 1924, Dodd, 1925, reprinted, Bantam, 1983.
Partners in Crime, Dodd, 1929 (abridged edition published in England as *The Sunningdale Mystery,* Collins, 1933).

The Under Dog, and Other Stories, Readers Library, 1929, reprinted, Dell, 1978.

The Mysterious Mr. Quin, Dodd, 1930, reprinted, Dell, 1976.

The Thirteen Problems, Collins, 1932, published as *The Tuesday Club Murders,* Dodd, 1933, reprinted, Dell, 1967, abridged edition published as *The Mystery of the Blue Geraniums, and Other Tuesday Club Murders,* Bantam, 1940.

The Hound of Death, and Other Stories, Odhams Press, 1933.

Mr. Parker Pyne, Detective, Dodd, 1934 (published in England as *Parker Pyne Investigates,* Collins, 1934), reprinted, Berkley, 1986.

The Listerdale Mystery, and Other Stories, Collins, 1934.

Dead Man's Mirror, and Other Stories, Dodd, 1937 (published in England as *Murder in the News, and Other Stories,* Collins, 1937).

The Regatta Mystery, and Other Stories, Dodd, 1939, reprinted, Berkley, 1987.

The Mystery of the Baghdad Chest, Bantam, 1943.

The Mystery of the Crime in Cabin 66, Bantam, 1943 (published in England as *The Crime in Cabin 66,* Vallencey, 1944).

Poirot and the Regatta Mystery, Bantam, 1943.

Poirot on Holiday, Todd, 1943.

Problem at Pollensa Bay [and] Christmas Adventure, Todd, 1943.

The Veiled Lady [and] The Mystery of the Baghdad Chest, Todd, 1944.

Poirot Knows the Murderer, Todd, 1946.

Poirot Lends a Hand, Todd, 1946.

The Labours of Hercules: New Adventures in Crime by Hercule Poirot, Dodd, 1947 (published in England as *Labours of Hercules: Short Stories,* Collins, 1947).

Witness for the Prosecution, and Other Stories, Dell, 1949, reprinted, 1978, published as *Three Blind Mice, and Other Stories,* Dodd, 1950, reprinted, Dell, 1980.

The Adventures of the Christmas Pudding, and Selection of Entrees, Collins, 1960.

Double Sin, and Other Stories, Dodd, 1961, reprinted, Berkley, 1987.

13 for Luck!: A Selection of Mystery Stories for Young Readers, Dodd, 1961.

Surprise! Surprise!: A Collection of Mystery Stories With Unexpected Endings, Dodd, 1965.

(Under name Agatha Christie Mallowan) *Star Over Bethlehem, and Other Stories,* Dodd, 1965.

13 Clues for Miss Marple, Dodd, 1966.

Selected Stories, Progress Publishers (Moscow), 1969.

The Underdog, and Other Stories, Dell, 1969.

The Golden Ball, and Other Stories, Dodd, 1971.

Poirot's Early Cases, Dodd, 1974.

Miss Marple's Final Cases, and Others, Collins, 1979.

Miss Marple, the Complete Short Stories, Berkley, 1986.

Short stories also collected in various other volumes.

OMNIBUS VOLUMES

Agatha Christie Omnibus (contains *The Mysterious Affair at Styles, The Murder on the Links,* and *Poirot Investigates*), Lane, 1931.

The Agatha Christie Omnibus of Crime (contains *The Sittaford Mystery, The Seven Dials Mystery, The Mystery of the Blue Train,* and *The Murder of Roger Ackroyd*), Collins, 1932.

Hercule Poirot, Master Detective (contains *The Murder of Roger Ackroyd, Murder on the Calais Coach,* and *Thirteen at Dinner*), Dodd, 1936, published as *Three Christie Crimes,* Grosset, 1937.

Two Detective Stories in One Volume: The Mysterious Affair at Styles [and] The Murder on the Links, Dodd, 1940.

Triple Threat: Exploits of Three Famous Detectives, Hercule Poirot, Harley Quin and Tuppence (contains *Poirot Investigates, The Mysterious Mr. Quin,* and *Partners in Crime*), Dodd, 1943.

Crime Reader (contains selections from *Poirot Investigates, The Mysterious Mr. Quin,* and *Partners in Crime*), World, 1944.

Perilous Journeys of Hercule Poirot (contains *The Mystery of the Blue Train, Death on the Nile,* and *Murder in Mesopotamia*), Dodd, 1954.

Surprise Ending by Hercule Poirot (contains *The A.B.C. Murders, Murder in Three Acts,* and *Cards on the Table*), Dodd, 1956.

Christie Classics (contains *The Murder of Roger Ackroyd, And Then There Were None, Witness for the Prosecution, Philomel Cottage,* and *Three Blind Mice*), Dodd, 1957.

Murder Preferred (contains *The Patriotic Murders, A Murder Is Announced,* and *Murder in Retrospect*), Dodd, 1960.

Make Mine Murder! (contains *Appointment With Death, Peril at End House,* and *Sad Cypress*), Dodd, 1962.

A Holiday for Murder, Bantam, 1962.

Murder International (contains *So Many Steps to Death, Death Comes as the End,* and *Evil Under the Sun*), Dodd, 1965.

Murder in Our Midst (contains *The Body in the Library, Murder at the Vicarage,* and *The Moving Finger*), Dodd, 1967.

Spies Among Us (contains *They Came to Baghdad, N or M?: A New Mystery,* and *Murder in Mesopotamia*), Dodd, 1968.

The Nursery Rhyme Murders (contains *A Pocket Full of Rye; Hickory, Dickory, Death;* and *The Crooked House*), Dodd, 1970.

Murder-Go-Round (contains *Thirteen at Dinner, The A.B.C. Murders,* and *Funerals Are Fatal*), Dodd, 1972.

Murder on Board (contains *Death in the Air, The Mystery of the Blue Train,* and *What Mrs. McGillicudy Saw!*), Dodd, 1974.

Agatha Christie, Best Loved Sleuth (contains *The Moving Finger, Murder in Three Acts, Murder on the Links,* and *There Is a Tide*), Berkley, 1988.

Agatha Christie: Murder by the Box (includes *The Secret of Chimneys, The Man in the Brown Suit,* and *Partners in Crime*), Berkley, 1988.

Works also published in numerous other omnibus volumes.

PLAYS

Black Coffee (first produced on the West End at St. Martin's Theatre, 1931), Baker, 1934.

Ten Little Niggers (based on novel of the same title; first produced in London at Wimbledon Theatre, 1943; produced on Broadway at Broadhurst Theatre, 1944), Samuel French (London), 1944, published as *Ten Little Indians,* Samuel French (New York), 1946.

Appointment With Death (based on the novel of the same title; first produced on the West End at Piccadilly Theatre, 1945; also see below), Samuel French, 1945.

"Little Horizon" (based on the novel *Death on the Nile;* first produced in London at Wimbledon Theatre, 1945), revised version entitled *Murder on the Nile* (first produced on the West End at Ambassadors Theatre, 1946; produced on Broadway at Plymouth Theatre, 1946), Samuel French, 1948.

The Hollow (based on the novel of the same title; first produced on the West End at Fortune Theatre, 1951; produced in Princeton, N.J., 1952; produced in New York, 1978), Samuel French, 1952.

The Mousetrap (based on the radio script "Three Blind Mice"; first produced on the West End at Ambassadors Theatre, November 25, 1952; produced Off-Broadway at Maidman Playhouse, 1960), Samuel French, 1954.

Witness for the Prosecution (based on the short story of the same title; first produced in London, 1953; produced in New York, 1954), Samuel French, 1954.

Spider's Web (first produced on the West End at Savoy Theatre, 1954; produced in New York, 1974), Samuel French, 1957.

(With Gerald Verner) *Towards Zero* (based on the novel of the same title; first produced in London, 1956; produced on Broadway at the St. James Theatre, 1956), Dramatists Play Service, 1957.

The Unexpected Guest (first produced on the West End at Duchess Theatre, 1958), Samuel French, 1958.

Verdict (first produced on the West End at Strand Theatre, 1958), Samuel French, 1958.

Go Back for Murder (based on the novel *Five Little Pigs;* first produced on the West End at Duchess Theatre, 1960), Samuel French, 1960.

Rule of Three (contains "Afternoon at the Sea-side" [first produced in London, 1962], "The Patient" [first produced in New York, 1978], and "The Rats" [first produced in New York, 1974]), Samuel French, 1963.

"Fiddlers Three," first produced in Southsea at Kings Theatre, June 7, 1971; produced in London, 1972.

Akhnaton (first produced under title "Akhnaton and Nefertiti" in New York, 1979), Dodd, 1973.

The Mousetrap, and Other Plays (contains "Witness for the Prosecution," "Ten Little Indians," "Appointment With Death," "The Hollow," "Towards Zero," "Verdict," and "Go Back for Murder"), with introduction by Ira Levin, Dodd, 1978.

NOVELS UNDER PSEUDONYM MARY WESTMACOTT

Giants' Bread, Doubleday, 1930.

Unfinished Portrait, Doubleday, 1934, reprinted, Arbor House, 1972.

Absent in the Spring, Farrar & Rinehart, 1944.

The Rose and the Yew Tree, Rinehart, 1948.

A Daughter's a Daughter, Heinemann, 1952.

The Burden, Heinemann, 1956.

OTHER

The Road of Dreams (poems), Bles, 1925.

Come, Tell Me How You Live (autobiographical travel book), Dodd, 1946.

Poems, Dodd, 1973.

(Editor with others) *The Times of London Anthology of Detective Stories,* John Day, 1973.

An Autobiography, Dodd, 1977.

SIDELIGHTS: "Oh, I'm an incredible sausage machine," the late mystery writer Agatha Christie once jokingly claimed, speaking of her prolific output of novels, stories, and plays. Christie's many works sold a phenomenal 400 million copies—a record topped only by the Bible and William Shakespeare—and were translated into 103 languages. Her play "The Mousetrap," originally written as a birthday gift for Queen Mary, is the longest running play in theatrical history. These staggering statistics testify to the enduring popularity of Christie's work.

"I don't enjoy writing detective stories," Christie once told an interviewer. "I enjoy thinking of a detective story, planning it, but when the time comes to write it, it is like going to work every day, like having a job." Christie only began writing on a dare from her sister, who challenged her to "write a good detective story." Christie wrote one, *The Mysterious Affair at Styles,* and in 1920 it was published by the English firm of Lane. Although the book only sold some two thousand copies and earned Chris-

tie seventy dollars, the publication encouraged her to continue writing mysteries. Throughout the 1920s she wrote them steadily, building a loyal following among mystery aficionados for her unfailingly clever plots.

It wasn't until the publication of *The Murder of Roger Ackroyd* in 1926 that Christie's talent for deceptive mystery plotting caught the attention of the general reading public. The sheer audacity of the novel's plot resolution—the murderer is revealed as a character traditionally above suspicion in mystery novels—outraged, surprised, and delighted readers everywhere. "*The Murder of Roger Ackroyd,*" wrote the *New York Times* reviewer, "cannot be too highly praised for its clean-cut construction, its unusually plausible explanation at the end, and its ability to stimulate the analytical faculties of the reader." "The secret [of this novel] is more than usually original and ingenious," the *Nation* reviewer thought, "and is a device which no other writer could have employed without mishap." William Rose Benet of *Saturday Review* recommended that *The Murder of Roger Ackroyd* "should go on the shelf with the books of first rank in its field. The detective story pure and simple has as definite limitations of form as the sonnet in poetry. Within these limitations, with admirable structured art, Miss Christie has genuinely achieved." Writing in *Murder for Pleasure: The Life and Times of the Detective Story,* Howard Haycraft judged the book "a tour de force in every sense of the word and one of the true classics of the literature."

The Murder of Roger Ackroyd proved to be the first in a long string of superlative and highly original mystery novels that made Christie's name synonymous with the mystery story. Such books as *The A.B.C. Murders, Ten Little Indians,* and *Murder on the Orient Express* have been especially singled out by critics as among the best of Christie's work and, indeed, among the finest novels to have been written in the mystery genre. "These books," Anthony Lejeune of *Spectator* believed, "are famous because each of them turns on a piece of misdirection and a solution which, in their day, were startlingly innovatory."

The best of Christie's novels are intricate puzzles presented in such a way as to misdirect the reader's attention away from the most important clues. The solution of the puzzle is invariably startling, although entirely logical and consistent with the rest of the story. "Agatha Christie at her best," Francis Wyndham of the *Times Literary Supplement* stated, "writes animated algebra. She dares us to solve a basic equation buried beneath a proliferation of irrelevancies. By the last page, everything should have been eliminated except for the motive and identity of the murderer; the elaborate working-out, apparently too complicated to grasp, is suddenly reduced to satisfactory simplicity. The effect is one of comfortable catharsis."

"As the genre's undisputed queen of the maze," a *Time* critic wrote, "Christie laid her tantalizing plots so precisely and dropped her false leads so cunningly that few—if any—readers could guess the identity of the villain." Reviewing *The A.B.C. Murders* for *Spectator,* Nicholas Blake expressed a quite common response to a Christie mystery: "One can only chalk up yet another defeat at [Christie's] hands and admit sadly that she has led one up the garden path with her usual blend of duplicity and fairness." Speaking of *Ten Little Indians,* Ralph Partridge of *New Statesman* gave a similar appraisal: "Apart from one little dubious proceeding there is no cheating; the reader is just bamboozled in a straightforward way from first to last. To show her utter superiority over our deductive faculty, from time to time Mrs. Christie even allows us to know what every character present is thinking and still we can't guess!"

Christie's ability to construct a baffling puzzle was, Emma Lathen wrote in *Agatha Christie: First Lady of Crime,* the strongest aspect of her writing. "Friend and foe alike," Lathen stated, "bow to the queen of the puzzle. Every Christie plot resolution had been hailed as a masterpiece of sleight-of-hand; she herself as a virtuoso of subterfuge." Julian Symons echoed this judgment in his contribution to *Agatha Christie: First Lady of Crime:* "Agatha Christie's claim to supremacy among the classical detective story writers of her time rests on her originality in constructing puzzles. This was her supreme skill. . . . Although the detective story is ephemeral literature, the puzzle which it embodies has a permanent appeal. . . . If her work survives it will be because she was the supreme mistress of a magical skill that is a permanent, although often secret, concern of humanity: the construction and the solution of puzzles."

Over the fifty years of Christie's writing career, other factors have been suggested for the phenomenal popularity of her books. Lejeune cited three primary factors: "The texture of her writing; a texture smooth and homely as cream, . . . the ability to buttonhole a reader, to make (as Raymond Chandler put it) 'each page throw the hook for the next,' . . . [and] the quality of cosiness." A *Times Literary Supplement* reviewer offered the view that Christie "never excluded any characters from possible revelation as murderers, not the sweet young girl, the charming youth, the wise old man, not even the dear old lady."

Another important factor in Christie's popularity must lie in her ability to create charming and enduring detective characters. Undoubtedly her most popular detective has been Hercule Poirot, an eccentric and amusingly pompous Belgian detective who Christie described in *The Mysterious Affair at Styles* as "an extraordinary-looking little man. He was hardly more than five feet, four inches, but carried himself with great dignity. His head was exactly the shape of an egg. His moustache was very still and military. The neatness of his attire was almost incredible. I believe a speck of dust would have caused him more pain than a bullet wound."

According to David J. Grossvogel in *Mystery and Its Fictions: From Oedipus to Agatha Christie,* Christie "was aware of the faintly ridiculous figure cut by Poirot when she baptized him. She named him after a vegetable—the leek (*poireau,* which also means a wart, in French)—to which she opposed the (barely) Christian name Hercule, in such a way that each name would cast ridicule on the other." Grossvogel saw this bit of absurdity as essential to Poirot's success as a character. He believed that, in order to maintain the tension in a mystery story, there must be some doubt as to the detective's ability to solve the crime. Because Poirot is often "patronizingly dismissed" by other characters, his eventual solution of the crime is that much more entertaining. "Part of the artificial surprise of the detective story," Grossvogel observed, "is contained within the detective who triumphs, as he brings the action to a close, even over his own shortcomings."

"Few fictional sleuths," wrote Howard Haycraft, "can surpass the amazing little Belgian—with his waxed moustache and egg-shaped head, his inflated confidence in the infallibility of his 'little grey cells,' his murderous attacks on the English language—either for individuality or ingenuity." "Poirot," Lejeune explained, "like a survivor from an almost extinct race of giants, is one of the last of the Great Detectives: and the mention of his name should be enough to remind us of how much pleasure Agatha Christie gave millions of people over the past fifty years."

Poirot's illustrious career came to an end in *Curtain: Hercule Poirot's Last Case,* published shortly before Christie's death.

Written just after World War II and secreted in a bank vault, the book was originally intended to be posthumously published, but Christie decided to enjoy the ending of Poirot's career herself and published the book early. "Curtain," wrote Peter Prescott of *Newsweek,* "is one of Christie's most ingenious stories, a tour de force in which the lady who had bent all the rules of the genre before bends them yet again." John Heideury of *Commonweal* expressed the usual bafflement when confronted with a Christie mystery: "On page 35 I had guessed the identity of the murderer, by the next page knew the victim, and on page 112 deduced the motive. (On page 41 I had changed my mind and reversed murderer and victim, but on page 69 returned steadfast to my original position.) . . . I was wrong on all counts at book's end."

Christie's own favorite among her detectives was Miss Jane Marple, a spinster who lives in a small town in the English countryside. "Both Poirot and Miss Marple," wrote Ralph Tyler in *Saturday Review,* "are made a little bit absurd, so that we do not begrudge them their astuteness." In *Agatha Christie: First Lady of Crime,* Julian Symons gave Christie's own views of her two famous detectives: "Miss Marple, she said, was more fun [than Poirot], and like many aunts and grandmothers was 'a splendid natural detective when it comes to observing human nature.' " In contrast to Poirot, a professional detective who attributes his successes to the use of his "little grey cells," Miss Marple is an amateur crime solver who often "owes her success," Margot Peters and Agate Nesaule Krouse wrote in *Southwest Review,* "to intuition and nosiness. Operating on the theory that human nature is universal, she ferrets out the criminal by his resemblance to someone she has known in her native village of St. Mary Mead, since her knowledge of life extends little farther."

Despite what they see as Christie's sexist portrayal of female characters, Peters and Krouse concluded that "Christie is not as sexist" as some other female mystery writers. Miss Marple, for example, is "self-sufficient, possessing a zest for life depending in no way on a man's support or approval." Some observers compared Miss Marple to Christie herself, but Christie rejected the idea. "I don't have Jane Marple's guilty-till-proven-innocent attitude," she said. "But, like Jane, I don't accept surface appearances."

While her mystery novels featuring Hercule Poirot and Miss Marple have enjoyed tremendous success and established Christie as the most widely-read mystery writer of all time, her relatively small output of plays has set equally impressive records. She is the only playwright to have had three plays running simultaneously on London's West End while another of her plays was running on Broadway. Christie's "The Mousetrap" holds the singular distinction of being the longest-running play in theatrical history. It has been translated into 22 languages, performed in 41 countries, and seen by an estimated four million people. Despite the success of the work, Christie received no royalties for it. She gave the rights to her 9-year-old grandson when the play first opened in 1952. The grandson, it is estimated, has since earned well over three million dollars from his grandmother's gift.

Any evaluation of Christie's career must take into account the enormous influence she had on the mystery genre. Lejeune pointed out that the secret to Christie's success lies "partly in her plots. . . . If they seem hackneyed or contrived now or even too easily guessable, that is precisely because they left so permanent an impression on the detective story genre." "I strongly suspect," Anthony Boucher declared, "that future scholars of the simon-pure detective novel will hold that its greatest practitioner . . . has been Agatha Christie."

Upon Christie's death in 1976, Max Lowenthal of the *New York Times* offered this summary of her work: "Dame Agatha's forte was supremely adroit plotting and sharp, believable characterization (even the names she used usually rang true). Her style and rhetoric were not remarkable; her writing was almost invariably sound and workmanlike, without pretense or flourish. Her characters were likely to be of the middle-middle class or upper-middle class, and there were certain archetypes, such as the crass American or the stuffy retired army officer now in his anecdotage. However familiar all this might be, the reader would turn the pages mesmerized as unexpected twist piled on unexpected twist until, in the end, he was taken by surprise. There was simply no outguessing Poirot or Miss Marple—or Agatha Christie."

MEDIA ADAPTATIONS: The Murder of Roger Ackroyd was adapted for the stage by Michael Morton and first produced under the title "Alibi" on the West End at Prince of Wales Theatre in 1928; the short story "Philomel Cottage" was adapted for the stage by Frank Vosper and first produced under the title "Love From a Stranger" on the West End at Wyndham's Theatre in 1936; *Peril at End House* was adapted for the stage by Arnold Ridley and first produced on the West End at the Vaudeville Theatre in 1940; *Murder at the Vicarage* was adapted for the stage by Moie Charles and Barbara Toy and first produced in London at the Playhouse Theatre in 1949; *Towards Zero* was adapted for the stage by Gerald Verner and first produced on Broadway at the St. James Theatre in 1956. The short story "Philomel Cottage" was filmed under the title "Love From a Stranger" by United Artists in 1937, and by Eagle Lion in 1947; *And Then There Were None* was filmed by Twentieth Century-Fox in 1945; *Witness for the Prosecution* was filmed for theatrical release by United Artists in 1957 and for television by Columbia Broadcasting System in 1982; *The Spider's Web* was filmed by United Artists in 1960; *Murder She Said* was filmed by Metro-Goldwyn-Mayer in 1962; *Murder at the Gallop* was filmed by Metro-Goldwyn-Mayer in 1963; *Mrs. McGinty's Dead* was filmed under the title "Murder Most Foul" by Metro-Goldwyn-Mayer in 1965; *Ten Little Indians* was filmed by Associated British & Pathe Film in 1965; *The Alphabet Murders* was filmed by Metro-Goldwyn-Mayer in 1967; *Endless Night* was filmed by British Lion Films in 1971; *Murder on the Orient Express* was filmed by EMI in 1974; *Death on the Nile* was filmed by Paramount in 1978; *The Mirror Crack'd* was filmed by EMI in 1980; *The Seven Dials Mystery* and *Why Didn't They Ask Evans?* were filmed by London Weekend Television in 1980; *Evil Under the Sun* was filmed by Universal in 1982. "Murder Ahoy," filmed by Metro-Goldwyn-Mayer in 1964, features the character Miss Jane Marple in a story not written by Christie.

BIOGRAPHICAL/CRITICAL SOURCES:

BOOKS

Authors in the News, Gale, Volume 1, 1976, Volume 2, 1976.
Bargainnier, Earl F., *The Gentle Art of Murder: The Detective Fiction of Agatha Christie,* Bowling Green University Press, 1981.
Barnard, Robert, *A Talent to Deceive: An Appreciation of Agatha Christie,* Dodd, 1980.
Behre, F., *Agatha Christie's Writings,* Adler, 1967.
Contemporary Literary Criticism, Gale, Volume 1, 1973, Volume 6, 1976, Volume 8, 1978, Volume 12, 1980, Volume 39, 1986, Volume 48, 1988.
Christie, Agatha, *Come, Tell Me How You Live,* Dodd, 1946.
Christie, Agatha, *An Autobiography,* Dodd, 1977.
Dictionary of Literary Biography, Gale, Volume 13: *British Dramatists Since World War II,* Gale, 1982, Volume 77: *British Mystery Writers, 1920-1939,* 1989.
Feinman, Jeffrey, *The Mysterious World of Agatha Christie,* Award Books, 1975.
Gregg, Hubert, *Agatha Christie and All That Mousetrap,* William Kimber (London), 1981.
Grossvogel, David I., *Mystery and Its Fictions: From Oedipus to Agatha Christie,* Johns Hopkins University Press, 1979.
Haycraft, Howard, *Murder for Pleasure: The Life and Times of the Detective Story,* Biblo & Tannen, 1969.
Keating, H. R. F., editor, *Agatha Christie: First Lady of Crime,* Holt, 1977.
Mallowan, Max, *Mallowan's Memoirs,* Dodd, 1977.
Morgan, Janet, *Agatha Christie: A Biography,* J. Cape, 1984.
Ramsey, Gordon C., *Agatha Christie: Mistress of Mystery,* Dodd, 1967.
Riley, Dick, and Pam McAllister, editors, *The Bedside, Bathtub, and Armchair Companion to Agatha Christie,* Ungar, 1979.
Robyns, Gwen, *The Mystery of Agatha Christie,* Doubleday, 1978.
Symons, Julian, *Mortal Consequences: A History—From the Detective Story to the Crime Novel,* Harper, 1972.
Symons, Julian, and Tom Adams, *Agatha Christie: The Art of Her Crimes, the Paintings of Tom Adams,* Everest House, 1982.
Toye, Randall, *The Agatha Christie Who's Who,* Holt, 1980.
Wynn, Nancy Blue, *An Agatha Christie Chronology,* Ace Books, 1976.

PERIODICALS

Armchair Detective, April, 1978, summer, 1981.
Christian Science Monitor, December 20, 1967.
Commonweal, February 13, 1976.
Detroit News, November 13, 1977.
Harvard Magazine, October, 1975.
Life, December 1, 1967.
Milwaukee Journal, February 1, 1976.
Nation, July 3, 1926.
New Republic, July 31, 1976.
New Statesman, May 10, 1930, December 18, 1937, November 18, 1939.
Newsweek, October 6, 1975.
New Yorker, October 14, 1944, January 30, 1978.
New York Herald Tribune Book Review, March 4, 1934.
New York Review of Books, December 21, 1978.
New York Times, July 18, 1926, November 10, 1977.
New York Times Book Review, March 25, 1923, April 20, 1924, September 22, 1929, February 25, 1940, September 25, 1966, March 17, 1968.
Pittsburgh Press, March 28, 1976.
Saturday Review, July 24, 1926, October 4, 1975.
Seattle Post-Intelligencer, December 23, 1973.
Southwest Review, spring, 1974.
Spectator, May 31, 1930, February 14, 1936, September 19, 1970.
Times Literary Supplement, April 3, 1924, June 10, 1926, December 2, 1965, September 26, 1975.

OBITUARIES:

PERIODICALS

AB Bookman's Weekly, April 5, 1976.
Bookseller, January 17, 1976.
Detroit Free Press, January 14, 1976.
Newsweek, January 26, 1976.
New York Times, January 13, 1976.

Publishers Weekly, January 19, 1976.
School Library Journal, February, 1976.
Time, January 26, 1976.
Washington Post, January 13, 1976.

*   *   *

CHUBB, Elmer
See MASTERS, Edgar Lee

*   *   *

CHURCHILL, Caryl 1938-

PERSONAL: Born September 3, 1938, in London, England; married David Harter (a barrister), 1961; children: three sons. *Education:* Lady Margaret Hall, Oxford, B.A., 1960.

ADDRESSES: 12 Thornhill Square, London N.1, England. *Agent*—Margaret Ramsay Ltd., 14A Goodwin's Court, London WC2N 4LL, England.

CAREER: Writer. Royal Court Theater, London, England, resident dramatist, 1974-75, tutor for Young Writers' Group.

AWARDS, HONORS: Richard Hillary Memorial Prize, 1961; Obie Award, 1982-83, and runner-up for Susan Smith Blackburn Prize, 1983, both for "Top Girls"; Susan Smith Blackburn Prize, 1984, for "Fen"; Olivier Award for best play of the season and *London Evening Standard* award for best comedy, both 1987, for "Serious Money"; *Time Out* award, 1987.

WRITINGS:

PUBLISHED PLAYS

"The Ants," (radio play; broadcast in 1962), in *Penguin New English Dramatists Twelve,* Penguin, 1968.
Owners (first produced in London at Royal Court Theater Upstairs, November 22, 1972; produced in New York, 1973; also see below), Eyre Methuen, 1973.
Light Shining in Buckinghamshire (first produced in Edinburgh, Scotland, at Traverse Theater, July, 1976; also see below), Pluto Press, 1978.
Vinegar Tom (first produced in Hull, England, at Hull Arts Centre, September 7, 1976; also see below), TQ Publications, 1978.
Traps (first produced in London at Royal Court Theater Upstairs, January 27, 1977; produced in New York at Remains Theater, March, 1983; also see below), Pluto Press, 1978.
Cloud Nine (first produced in London at Royal Court Theater, March 29, 1979; produced Off-Broadway at Lucille Lortel's Theater de Lys, May 18, 1981; also see below), Pluto Press, 1979.
Top Girls (first produced in London at Royal Court Theater, 1982; produced Off-Broadway at Public Theater, December 28, 1982), Samuel French, 1982, fully revised edition, Methuen, 1984.
Fen (first produced in London at Almeida Theater, March, 1983; produced Off-Broadway at Public Theater, May, 1983; also see below), Methuen, 1983, published as *Fen: A Drama,* Samuel French, 1984.
Softcops (also see below), Methuen, 1984.
Churchill: Plays One (includes "Owners," "Light Shining in Buckinghamshire," "Vinegar Tom," "Traps," and "Cloud Nine"), Methuen, 1985.
Softcops; and Fen, Methuen, 1986.
(With David Lan) *A Mouthful of Birds* (first produced in London at Royal Court Theater, November, 1986), Heinemann Educational, 1987.

Serious Money (first produced in London at Royal Court Theater, March, 1987; produced Off-Broadway at Public Theater, December 3, 1987; produced on Broadway at Royale Theater, January 18, 1988), Heinemann Educational, 1987.

UNPUBLISHED PLAYS

"Downstairs," first produced in Oxford, England, 1958; produced in London, 1959.
"Having a Wonderful Time," first produced in London, 1960.
"Easy Death," first produced in Oxford, 1962.
"Schreber's Nervous Illness," first broadcast on radio, 1972; first produced in London at King's Head Lunchtime Theater, December 6, 1972.
"Perfect Happiness," first broadcast on radio, 1973; produced in London at Soho Poly Lunchtime Theater, March 10, 1974.
"Objections to Sex and Violence," first produced in London at Royal Court Theater, January 2, 1975.
"Moving Clocks Go Slow," first produced in London at Royal Court Theater Upstairs, June 2, 1975.
(With David Bradford, Bryony Lavery, and Michelene Wandor) "Floorshow," first produced in London at North London Poly Theater, October, 1977.
"Three More Sleepless Nights," first produced in London at Soho Poly Theater, June 10, 1980.
(With Geraldine Pilgrim, Pete Brooks, and John Ashford) "Midday Sun," produced in London, 1984.
"Ice Cream" (one-act; also see below), produced in London at Royal Court Theater, 1989.
"Ice Cream with Hot Fudge" (one-acts; contains "Ice Cream" and "Hot Fudge"), first produced in New York at Public Theater, May 1, 1990.

Also author of television plays, including "The Judge's Wife," 1972, "Turkish Delight," 1974, "The After Dinner Joke," 1978, "The Legion Hall Bombing," 1978, and "Crimes," 1981. Author of radio plays, such as "Lovesick," 1967, "Identical Twins," 1968, "Abortive," 1971, "Not, Not, Not, Not, Not Enough Oxygen," 1971, and "Henry's Past," 1972.

SIDELIGHTS: Applauded by *Los Angeles Times* critic Clarke Taylor for "bringing vitality as well as a flamboyant theatricality to playwriting," Caryl Churchill is a strikingly promising figure in the world of contemporary drama. In fact, she is among the most widely performed and published of female British dramatists today, and her popularity extends to New York as well. According to Robert Asahina in the *Hudson Review,* "Churchill belongs to the loose coalition of vaguely Marxist playwrights in England who emerged in the mid-seventies from the radical theater movement called The Fringe, which arose during the late sixties in reaction against the psychologistic tradition that had dominated the British stage since the appearance of [John] Osborne and [Harold] Pinter." As a "vaguely Marxist playwright," Churchill confidently voices socialist and feminist opinions, but at the same time, says Dan Sullivan in the *Los Angeles Times,* she "has the kind of mind that deals with big issues lightly, not to demean them, but to remind us that issues and answers are abstractions—the spirit comes first." Reviewing for the *New Statesman,* Benedict Nightingale remarked in 1982: "We can no longer patronise women playwrights as peripheral. I think Caryl Churchill is well on the way to being a major talent." And, indeed, by 1983 Churchill had three hits running in New York at the same time.

Churchill began her literary career in the sixties writing radio plays like "The Ants" and "Identical Twins," which are recognized for their leftist orientation. Although she initially received critical attention in the mid-seventies for her two stage plays

"Objections to Sex and Violence" and "Light Shining in Buckinghamshire," "Cloud Nine" was her first theatrical triumph and, in particular, her "ticket to success in the United States. . . . The play opened Off-Broadway in New York at the Theatre de Lys in May 1981 to positive reviews, enthusiastic audiences, and a long run," notes Erica Beth Weintraub in the *Dictionary of Literary Biography*. In 1983, Sullivan called "Cloud Nine" "the freshest and most original show of the theater season—of several seasons," while *Los Angeles Times* commentator Sylvie Drake had to ask: "What, indeed, hath . . . Churchill wrought? A sexual comedy? A feminist tract? A satire on sexual politics? A paean to androgyny? A dream play? A reality play? 'Cloud Nine' has been called all of those and, in one way or another, it is each of them. Its . . . success Off Broadway . . . indicates there's something in it for everyone."

For reviewers, much of "Cloud Nine"'s appeal stems from its experimental technique. Frank Rich notes in the *New York Times* that in this play about "sexual confusion[,] . . . not only does [Churchill] examine a cornucopia of sexual permutations—from heterosexual adultery right up to bisexual incest—but she does so with a wild array of dramatic styles and tricks." Whereas Act I is set in British colonial Africa of 1880, Act II takes place in present-day London, and those characters reappearing in Act II have aged a mere twenty-five years rather than the expected hundred. "As if this weren't mad enough, the seven actors change roles for Act II—and don't necessarily play characters of their own age or gender," offers Rich. "Betty, the sweet little wife, is played by a man," notes Richard Christensen in the *Chicago Tribune*. "Edward, the son and heir, is played by a girl. And Joshua, the black servant, is played by a white man." *Washington Post* reviewer David Richards finds that "the cross-casting reinforces the play's point that within every creature lurk a number of conflicting sexual identities. Just as the characters find themselves taking on new roles over the years, so do the actors." And as for Churchill's odd chronological technique, Sullivan feels in one way "we can defend Churchill's device as a symbolic statement of how slow the emotional growth rate of the human race is, as compared to the fast flip of cultural fashion."

"Churchill [in 'Cloud Nine'] obviously prefers the sexual freedom of the 1980s to the sexual repression of the Victorians," says Sullivan. "To find one's pleasure, she seems to say, is to begin to find one's essence—and, like angels, each of us is a separate creation." Along the same lines, *New York Post* contributor Clive Barnes applauds Churchill's nonjudgmental attitude and her belief that all human relationships, "if genuine, have their validity." However, while Barnes believes "Cloud Nine" is "fundamentally a play about love relationships to which the fading Empire merely provides the backcloth," Sullivan says it is more—"[Its] deepest topic isn't sex, but power: the husband's over the wife, the home country's over the colony . . ., the parent's over the child."

Reviewers of "Cloud Nine" applaud the play's originality, intelligence, and capacity for throwing theatrical convention by the wayside, but some consider it disorganized and some cannot quite make it out. While Sullivan believes "Cloud Nine" "isn't for those who think that there's too much talk about sex in the theater these days," he says it "left me on cloud nine." Asahina, in turn, views "Cloud Nine" as "a rather old-fashioned satire, because there is very little at stake. No one today would defend the racist and sexist attitudes of Victorian colonials; the only problem facing a contemporary playwright is coming up with clever new ways of savaging those old beliefs, and Churchill certainly succeeds in doing so." While Barnes believes "Cloud Nine" is far from perfect, he concludes that this "zany play . . .

has something to say to us today about kindness, affection, perversion and most of all, love."

A few years after "Cloud Nine"'s favorable reception, "Top Girls" garnered as much attention. "['Cloud Nine' and 'Top Girls'] taken together, show that [Churchill] has evolved into a playwright of genuine audacity and assurance, able to use her considerable wit and intelligence in ways at once unusual, resonant and dramatically riveting," remarks Nightingale. "As with 'Cloud Nine,' " writes Sullivan in another *Los Angeles Times* review, "['Top Girls'] makes its own rules, not to be willful, but to throw an unexpected light on its subject—the question of where women are going, now that they are free."

"Simply put[,] . . . 'Top Girls' is a blistering yet sympathetic look at women who achieve success by adopting the worst dog-eat-dog traits of self-made men," states Rich. The protagonist of the play is Marlene, who has just been promoted to managing director of Top Girls Employment Agency. She appears to be the embodiment of success but, adds Rich in a second review of "Top Girls," "when we watch Marlene's chillingly antiseptic agency in action, we quickly see that it is designed to coach its female clients into adopting . . . the steely selfishness and aggression that ostensibly propel one forward in the Darwinist business world. Marlene's own emotional and sexual life is as barren as Lady Macbeth's. . . . She's even abandoned her illegitimate and dull-witted daughter . . ., leaving her sister to raise the girl as her own child instead." According to Sullivan, "Top Girls" is Churchill's indictment of a capitalist system that produces such individuals.

"Top Girls" "discards the very notion of rules and simply blooms," states Sullivan in his first *Los Angeles Times* review of the play. Additionally, *Chicago Tribune* critic Sid Smith feels "Top Girls" "sometimes soars to sociological heights" and is "strong evidence of Churchill's audacity and imagination," but he also believes it is "overwritten and occasionally too gimmicky" and calls the play a "flawed gem." While Rich views "Top Girls" as "almost always fascinating," he says "some of the play's slippage . . . occur[s] . . . when . . . Churchill's experiments run on self-indulgently," an aspect which other reviewers also sense. Although Rich further considers "Top Girls"'s message "far more simplistic and obvious than the fervent pansexuality of 'Cloud Nine,' " he goes on in a later review to pronounce it "one of the few plays [of the 1983] season that allow[ed] its audience to watch a truly original theatrical mind at work."

Churchill's "Fen" is a "dark, richly textured play that New York [took] to its heart," notes Jennifer Dunning in the *New York Times*. "Fen" evolved out of Churchill's association with London's Joint Stock Theater Group, a changing corps of actors and playwrights committed to the creation of experimental drama. Several actor-members of the Joint Stock group, which is considered the finest "fringe" company in Britain, immersed themselves into a farm community in the Fens of England for two weeks. According to Dunning, the actors lived with, worked with, and listened to the Fen inhabitants, and thereby "learned about lives that were hard and narrow, circumscribed by community and religious tradition, [by] tight-fisted landowners and avaricious land-buying conglomerates." After Joint Stock's preliminary research, Churchill went off on a nine-week stint to write a play incorporating the troupe's many discoveries. Her resultant drama received the 1984 Susan Smith Blackburn Prize, an award given "to a woman who deserves recognition for having written a work of outstanding quality for the English-speaking theater."

As with Churchill's other successful plays, "Fen" relies on innovative techniques that appeal to both critics and the public. The play's six actors, for example, portray twenty-two characters of differing ages in what Rich labels in a 1984 *New York Times* review "associatively linked vignettes whose pungent language and frequently eerie events sweep us into an exotic world. Some pieces of the mosaic are journalistic, didactic or historical. . . . Other scenes are hallucinatory. . . . But most of the time, . . . Churchill focuses on the quotidian rituals of work and family—and it's these fiercely etched passages that are the most haunting."

The laboring women of "Fen" are "the less privileged sisters [whom] . . . top girls [like Marlene] leave behind," says Rich in an earlier review of "Fen." "These sad serfs . . . can only ameliorate their misery in self-destructive ways: by drinking in a pub or gossiping or taking Valium or betraying one another or going mad." Though "Fen" is obviously not the humor-laden piece "Top Girls" is, Rich believes Churchill has drawn the characters in both plays as "helpless, exploited victims of a dehumanizing capitalistic system." And, as Nightingale sees it in the *New York Times,* "neither in the Middle West nor anywhere else in America will you find people quite so paralyzed by class and tradition, so stuck in the roles that birth and geography have thrust upon them, as . . . Churchill's villagers. . . . But what makes the play doubly, trebly alien is that . . . Churchill, while mourning their fatalism, is a sort of fatalist herself. The feeling runs through the play that as long as the economic system is what it is these people will be what they are." In contrast, Nightingale in his *New Statesman* review finds that Churchill's "distaste for the economic and social status quo doesn't mean she's relentlessly deterministic." Rich suggests that because there is no redemption in "Fen," because the very characters who act to resurrect their lives end up in the mire, or dead, as is the case with one of the angst-ridden protagonists who insists her extramarital lover kill her, Churchill is convinced that the only way to win in a capitalist society is to adopt the "selfish, ruthless traits" of top girls like Marlene. But Churchill herself voiced a more optimistic opinion in Taylor's 1983 review: "I very much believe in the possibilities of openness and change and of giving up authoritarianism . . ., which includes giving up Empire."

" 'Fen,' " writes Rich, "is dour, difficult and, unlike either 'Top Girls' or 'Cloud [Nine],' never coy about its rather stridently doctrinaire socialism: it's the most stylistically consistent of . . . Churchill's plays and at times the most off-putting. It is also yet another confirmation that its author possesses one of the boldest theatrical imaginations to emerge in [the 1980s]." However, *Los Angeles Times* staff writer Sylvie Drake labels "Fen" a disappointment "full of the hackneyed puritanical neuroses of the white Anglo-Saxon Protestant." Similarly, in *New York* magazine John Simon calls it an "unsuccessful work," mainly because he feels Churchill is "trying to do too much and . . . with far too little" and because he finds there is confusion of characters. Nevertheless, Nightingale concludes in the *New York Times* that although "Fen" is not Churchill's finest play, "it confirms her status as a writer of rare intelligence, sympathy and scope, as complete as any the English-speaking stage can currently offer."

BIOGRAPHICAL/CRITICAL SOURCES:

BOOKS

Contemporary Literary Criticism, Gale, Volume 31, 1985, Volume 55, 1989.
Dictionary of Literary Biography, Volume 13: *British Dramatists since World War II,* Gale, 1982.

PERIODICALS

Chicago Tribune, March 4, 1983, March 11, 1983, April 8, 1986.
Cue, May 26, 1973.
Drama, spring, 1975.
Hudson Review, winter, 1981-82.
Los Angeles Times, May 6, 1983, May 10, 1983, May 29, 1983, June 12, 1983, June 21, 1983, June 27, 1983, April 14, 1984, October 4, 1984, November 9, 1984, November 15, 1984.
New Statesman, September 10, 1982, February 25, 1983, January 27, 1984.
New York, June 13, 1983.
New York Post, May 19, 1981, May 31, 1983.
New York Times, May 21, 1981, August 8, 1982, December 29, 1982, January 6, 1983, February 25, 1983, March 13, 1983, March 17, 1983, May 31, 1983, March 5, 1984, March 25, 1984, November 22, 1987, December 4, 1987, January 3, 1988, January 28, 1988, April 29, 1990, May 4, 1990.
Plays and Players, March, 1975, February, 1977, November, 1982.
Times (London), January 3, 1975, June 12, 1980, September 10, 1980, February 10, 1983, February 18, 1983, August 2, 1983, January 12, 1984, November 29, 1986, March 30, 1987.
Times Literary Supplement, September 24, 1982.
Washington Post, April 6, 1984, December 9, 1987.

*   *   *

CHURCHILL, Winston (Leonard Spencer)   1874-1965

PERSONAL: Born November 30, 1874, at Blenheim Palace, Oxfordshire, England; died of a cerebral thrombosis, January 24, 1965, in London, England; son of Lord Randolph Henry Spencer (a politician) and Jennie (Jerome) Churchill; married Clementine Ogilvy Hozier, September, 1908; children: Randolph, Sarah, Diana, Mary, and another daughter (died in infancy). *Education:* Royal Military Academy at Sandhurst, received degree, 1894.

CAREER: Soldier, statesman, historian, journalist. Correspondent for the *London Daily Telegraph* and *Morning Post* covering the South African Boer War, 1899; member of British Parliament from Oldham, beginning 1900; undersecretary for the colonies, 1905-08; member of Parliament from Northwest Manchester, 1906-08, from Dundee, 1908-18; president of the board of trade, 1908-10; home secretary, 1910-11; first lord of the admiralty, 1911-15; minister of munitions, 1916-18; secretary of state for war and for air, 1918-21; secretary of state for air and colonies, 1921-22; painter and writer, 1922-24; member of parliament from Epping, 1922-45; chancellor of the exchequer, 1924-29; writer, 1929-39; first lord of the admiralty, 1939-40; prime minister of Great Britain, 1940-45; member of Parliament from Woodford, 1945-65, leader of opposition in Parliament, 1945-51; prime minister, 1951-55; minister of defense, beginning 1951. Lord rector at University of Edinburgh, 1929-31; chancellor of Bristol University, 1930; lord warden of the Cinque Ports, beginning 1941. *Military service:* Royal Army, 1895-99, served in Cuba, India, and the Sudan; commanded Sixth Royal Scots Fusiliers as lieutenant-colonel, 1916.

AWARDS, HONORS: Albert Gold Medal of the Royal Society, 1945; Order of Merit, 1946; elected Royal Academician Extraordinary, 1948; Grotius Medal (Netherlands), 1949; London *Times* literary award, 1949; created Knight of the Garter by Queen Elizabeth II, 1953; Nobel Prize for literature, 1953; Williamsburg Award, 1955; Charlemagne Prize (West Germany),

1956; made honorary U.S. citizen by act of Congress, 1963; recipient of numerous others awards, including more than eighteen honorary degrees from British and foreign universities.

WRITINGS:

The Story of the Malakand Field Force: An Episode of Frontier War (also see below), Longmans, Green, 1898, reprinted, Norton, 1989.

The River War: An Historical Account of the Reconquest of the Soudan (also see below), two volumes, Longmans, Green, 1899, revised single-volume edition, 1902, reprinted, New English Library, 1973.

Ian Hamilton's March; Together with Extracts from the Diary of Lieutenant H. Frankland (also see below), Longmans, Green, 1900.

London to Ladysmith via Pretoria (also see below), Longmans, Green, 1900.

Savrola: A Tale of the Revolution in Laurania (novel), Longmans, Green, 1900, reprinted, Chivers, 1973.

Lord Randolph Churchill, two volumes, Macmillan, 1906, new edition, Odhams Press, 1952.

My African Journey, Hodder & Stoughton, 1908, reprinted, Norton, 1989.

The World Crisis, Scribner, Volume I: *1911-1914,* 1923, Volume II: *1915,* 1923, Volumes III and IV: *1916-1918,* 1927, Volume V: *The Aftermath,* 1929, Volume VI: *The Unknown War: The Eastern Front,* 1931, revised and abridged edition of original four volumes, 1931.

A Roving Commission: My Early Life, Scribner, 1930, (published in England as *My Early Life: A Roving Commission,* Butterworth, 1930), reprinted under original British title, Scribner, 1987.

Amid These Storms: Thoughts and Adventures, Scribner, 1932, published as *Thoughts and Adventures,* Macmillan, 1942, reprinted under original title, Books for Libraries, 1972.

Marlborough: His Life and Times, six volumes, Scribner, 1933-38, abridged edition published as *Marlborough and His Times,* 1968.

Great Contemporaries, Putnam, 1937, revised edition, Butterworth, 1938, reprinted, University of Chicago Press, 1973.

Ten Chapters, 1942 to 1945, Hutchinson, 1945.

The Second World War, Houghton, Volume I: *The Gathering Storm,* 1948, Volume II: *Their Finest Hour,* 1949, Volume III: *The Grand Alliance,* 1950, Volume IV: *The Hinge of Fate,* 1951, Volume V: *Closing the Ring,* 1951, Volume VI: *Triumph and Tragedy,* 1954, six-volume set reprinted, 1986, abridged edition of original six volumes, with epilogue, 1959, published as *Memoirs of the Second World War,* Bonanza Books, 1978.

A History of the English-speaking Peoples, Dodd, Volume I: *The Birth of Britain to 1485,* 1956, Volume II: *The New World, 1485-1688,* 1956, Volume III: *The Age of Revolution, 1688-1815,* 1957, Volume IV: *The Great Democracies, 1815-1901,* 1958 (published as *The American Civil War,* 1961, reprinted, Crown, 1985), four-volume set reprinted, 1983, abridged edition of original four volumes published as *The Island Race,* Dodd, 1964.

SPEECHES

Mr. Broderick's Army, A. L. Humphreys, 1903, reprinted, Churchilliana, 1977.

For Free Trade, A. L. Humphreys, 1906, reprinted, Churchilliana, 1977.

Liberalism and the Social Problem, Hodder & Stoughton, 1909, reprinted, Haskell House, 1973.

The People's Rights, Hodder & Stoughton, 1910, reprinted, J. Cape, 1970, Taplinger, 1971.

India: Speeches and an Introduction, Butterworth, 1931.

While England Slept: A Survey of World Affairs 1932-1938, Putnam, 1938, reprinted, Irvington, 1982 (published in England as *Arms and the Covenant,* Harrap, 1938).

Step by Step: 1936-1939, Putnam, 1939, reprinted, Books for Libraries, 1971.

Blood, Sweat, and Tears, Putnam, 1941 (published in England as *Into Battle,* Cassell, 1941), published as *Churchill in His Own Words: Years of Greatness; Memorable Speeches of the Man of the Century,* Capricorn Books, 1966.

Broadcast Addresses to the People of Great Britain, Italy, Poland, Russia, and the United States, Ransohoffs, 1941.

The Unrelenting Struggle, Little, Brown, 1942, reprinted, Books for Libraries, 1971.

The End of the Beginning, Little, Brown, 1943, reprinted, Books for Libraries, 1972.

Winston Churchill, Prime Minister: A Selection from Speeches Made by Winston Churchill during the Four Years That Britain Has Been at War, British Information Services, 1943.

Onwards to Victory, Little, Brown, 1944.

The Dawn of Liberation, Little, Brown, 1945.

Victory, Little, Brown, 1946.

Winston Churchill's Secret Session Speeches, Simon & Schuster, 1946 (published in England as *Secret Session Speeches,* Cassell, 1946).

The Sinews of Peace: Post-War Speeches, Houghton, 1948.

Europe Unite: Speeches 1947 and 1948, Houghton, 1950.

War Speeches, Cassell, 1951-52, Houghton, 1953.

In the Balance: Speeches 1949 and 1950, Houghton, 1952.

Stemming the Tide: Speeches 1951 and 1952, Cassell, 1953, Houghton, 1954.

The Unwritten Alliance: Speeches 1953 to 1959, Cassell, 1963.

COLLECTIONS

Maxims and Reflections, Eyre & Spottiswoode, 1948, Houghton, 1949, revised and enlarged edition published as *Sir Winston Churchill: A Self-Portrait,* Eyre & Spottiswoode, 1954.

A Churchill Reader: The Wit and Wisdom of Sir Winston Churchill, Houghton, 1954.

The Wisdom of Sir Winston Churchill (selections from speeches, 1900-55), Allen & Unwin, 1956.

The Eloquence of Winston Churchill, New American Library, 1957.

Great War Speeches, Transworld, 1959.

Frontiers and Wars (contains abridged editions of *The Story of the Malakand Field Force, The River War, Ian Hamilton's March,* and *London to Ladysmith via Pretoria*), Harcourt, 1962.

A Churchill Anthology (selected writings and speeches), Odhams, 1962.

First Journey, Heinemann, 1964, Random House, 1965.

The Churchill Wit, Coward, 1965.

Great Destiny: Sixty Years of the Memorable Events in the Life of the Man of the Century, Recounted in His Own Incomparable Words, Putnam, 1965, published as *Churchill in His Own Words: Years of Adventure, Memorable Events in the Life of the Man of the Century,* Capricorn Books, 1966.

The Wit of Sir Winston, Frewin, 1965.

Churchill on Men and Events (selections from *Thoughts and Adventures* and *Great Contemporaries*), Ginn, 1965.

Irrepressible Churchill: A Treasury of Winston Churchill's Wit, World Publishing, 1966.

Never Give In! The Challenging Words of Winston Churchill, introduction by Dwight D. Eisenhower, Hallmark, 1967.

Heroes of History (selections from *A History of the English-speaking Peoples* and other works), Dodd, 1968.

The Roar of the Lion, Wingate, 1969.

Winston Churchill on America and Britain: A Selection of His Thoughts on America and Britain, foreword by wife, Lady Churchill, Walker, 1970.

If I Live My Life Again, W. H. Allen, 1974.

Immortal Jester: A Treasury of the Great Good Humor of Sir Winston Churchill, 1874-1965, Frewin, 1974.

Young Winston's Wars: The Original Dispatches of Winston S. Churchill, War Correspondent, 1897-1900, Cooper, 1972, Viking, 1973.

Winston S. Churchill: His Complete Speeches, 1897-1963, eight volumes, Chelsea House, 1974.

The Collected Works of Winston Churchill, a centenary limited edition, Library of Imperial History, Volume I: *My Early Life; My African Journey,* 1973, Volume II: *The Story of the Malakand Field Force,* 1974, Volume III: *The River War,* 1974, Volume IV: *The Boer War; London to Ladysmith via Pretoria; Ian Hamilton's March,* 1974 (*The Boer War* reprinted by Norton, 1989), Volume V: *Savrola,* 1974, Volume VI: *Lord Randolph Churchill,* 1974, Volume VII: *Mr. Broderick's Army and Other Early Speeches* (includes *For Free Trade, Liberalism and the Social Problem, The People's Rights,* and *India*), 1974, Volumes VIII-XII: *The World Crisis,* 1974, Volume XIII: *Thoughts and Adventures,* 1974, Volumes XIV-XV: *Marlborough: His Life and Times,* 1974, Volume XVI: *Great Contemporaries,* 1974, Volume XVII: *Arms and the Covenant,* 1975, Volume XVIII: *Step by Step, 1936-1939,* 1975, Volumes XIX-XXI: *The War Speeches,* 1975, Volumes XXII-XXVII: *The Second World War,* 1975, Volumes XXVIII-XXX: *Post-War Speeches,* 1975, Volumes XXXI-XXXIV: *A History of the English-speaking Peoples,* 1976.

OTHER

Painting as a Pastime, Whittlesey House, 1950.

(With others) *The Eagle Book of Adventure Stories,* Hulton, 1950.

Churchill: His Paintings, foreword by Lady Churchill, World Publishing, 1967.

(With John Glubb) *Great Issues 71: A Forum on Important Questions Facing the American Public,* Troy State University, 1972.

Memories and Adventures, Weidenfeld, 1989.

Also author of *Coniston,* 1906, reprinted by Irvington, 1972.

SIDELIGHTS: Winston Churchill led an impressive life. His parliamentary career spanned the reigns of six monarchs, from Queen Victoria to her great-great-granddaughter, Elizabeth II. His early military service included hand-to-hand combat in the Sudan, and he lived to see the use of atomic weapons as a means to end World War II.

The world recognized Churchill in many guises. He was most familiar as a diplomat in his homburg hat and bowtie flashing the V-for-Victory sign with his index and middle fingers; but he was also a weekend artisan, building garden walls at his home at Chartwell, as well as an accomplished painter. His paintings were regularly exhibited at the Royal Academy, which held a one-man retrospective of his work in 1958.

Evaluating Churchill's contribution, both as a historian and a world leader, John Kenneth Galbraith noted the enormous importance of his "fearsome certainty that he was completely right." But Galbraith added that "the greater element in Churchill's power was his use of language as a weapon." Not only could Churchill amass and organize huge quantities of information; he could also communicate it with an air of excitement and vitality. This in turn depended, Galbraith believed, "on inventive, if often extravagant and sometimes reckless, use of adjective and metaphor . . . [and] on the power, resource, and flow of the language itself."

Churchill's speeches during World War II are an example of this power. As A. J. P. Taylor said: "Great Britain was never so free from political controversy as during World War II. . . . This unity rested on a partnership between Churchill and the Britain people. His speeches, a mixture of old-fashioned rhetoric and homespun humor, struck the right note and made him uniquely popular. . . . There have been many great British leaders. There has only been one whom everyone recognized as the embodiment of the national will."

"His eloquence," Manfred Weidhorn pointed out, "rallied the free world in the face of mortal perils," and his words and phrases—like "blood, toil, tears, and sweat" or "the iron curtain"—have assumed a permanent place in our language and culture. His humor and wit, amply recorded in a number of collections, were mischievous and ribald, consistent with the aplomb demonstrated in his formal addresses. An example is his frequently quoted retort to Lady Astor who had told him, "If I were to marry you, I'd feed you poison." Churchill's response: "And if I were your husband, I'd take it."

That Churchill was both a writer and a fighter, a historian and a statesman, makes his contribution all the more remarkable. Henry Steele Commager explained: "There was no division, and certainly no conflict, between the two activities—the making and the writing of history. . . . For Churchill wrote history in order to mold it and, so we sometimes suspect, he made history in order to write it." This means, in Weidhorn's words, that "Churchill ranks with the very few men—Thucydides, Caesar, Clarendon—who have been ambidextrous in this way, who have achieved political and literary prominence, combined dynamism of word and deed."

Churchill's military career began almost immediately upon his graduation with honors from Sandhurst, the West Point of Great Britain. In March, 1895, he was appointed to the Fourth (Queen's Own) Hussars as a sub-lieutenant, assigned to duty at the Aldershop camp in Hampshire. After attachment as an "observer" to an anti-insurrectionary Spanish force in Cuba, he served in Bangalore, India. His next assignments included the Tirah Expeditionary Force in 1898 and the Nile Expeditionary Force, where he participated in the famous cavalry charge at Omdurman.

Churchill also saw battle as a journalist. In 1897, as a war correspondent for the *London Daily Telegraph,* he joined General Sir Benden Blood's expedition against the Pathams in the area of the Malakand Pass. In a similar capacity for the *London Morning Post,* he went to South Africa after the outbreak of the Boer War; there, on November 15, 1899, he was taken prisoner by Louis Botha, who later became the first prime minister of the Union of South Africa and a close friend of Sir Winston's. Churchill's subsequent dramatic escape from a Pretoria prison, which brought him immediate world fame, is detailed in his autobiography, *A Roving Commission.*

Churchill followed his great escape with a lecture tour of the United States, and thus helped finance the start of his political career. It began with an unsuccessful stand as a Conservative in a by-election in Oldham, Lancashire, in 1898; he ran again for the position, successfully, in 1900. Over the next three years, however, he found himself in disagreement with his party, particularly over the high tariff policy of Joseph Chamberlain. Therefore, in 1904 he "crossed the aisle" in the House of Commons and affiliated himself with the free-trade Liberals. His first election as a Liberal occurred in Northwest Manchester in 1906. Cabinet positions followed, first under-secretary for the colonies, then privy councillor. Upon the rise of Herbert Henry Asquith to prime minister in 1908, Churchill became president of the board of trade and home secretary. In these last two positions Churchill sponsored such progressive legislation as the establishment of the British Labor Exchanges, old age pensions, and health and unemployment insurance.

In 1911 Churchill became first lord of the admiralty, readying the British fleet for war with Germany. By the start of World War I in 1914, the Royal Navy was so well prepared, having changed over from coal to oil-fueled vessels, that it quickly confined the German fleet to its home ports. The Germans refrained from an all-out naval confrontation, relying instead upon the submarine. Churchill's other major accomplishment at this time was the establishment of the Royal Air Force, first called the Royal Flying Corps. But after encountering loud criticism for the British landings on Gallipoli (the Dardanelles campaign), which resulted in heavy casualties, Churchill was demoted. He resigned his office in 1916 to go to the front as a lieutenant-colonel in command of the Sixth Royal Fusiliers. Nevertheless, he was soon recalled by Prime Minister Lloyd George to become minister of munitions.

After World War I Churchill introduced a number of military reforms as secretary of state for war and for air (1918-21). As secretary for the colonies (1921-22), he worked toward the establishment of new Arab states, toward a Jewish homeland in the Middle East, and toward an Irish free state. At this time Churchill was growing increasingly anti-socialist, setting himself at odds with the pro-labor segment of the Liberal party. His use of British troops to suppress the Bolshevist regime in the Soviet Union lost him the favor of Lloyd George, who appointed Sir Robert Horne chancellor of the exchequer over Churchill. But in 1924 Churchill rejoined the Conservatives and was immediately named chancellor of the exchequer.

Churchill was out of office during the 1930s until the outbreak of World War II. Then, as a result of public pressure, he was reappointed first lord of the admiralty in September, 1939. Upon the resignation of Neville Chamberlain in May, 1940, Churchill became prime minister, a position he held almost unchallenged till the end of the war. In his first speech as prime minister in the House of Commons, after the fall of France to the Nazis, he made clear Britain's uncompromising ambition: "You ask, what is our aim? I can answer in one word: Victory—victory at all costs, victory in spite of all terror; victory, however long and hard the road maybe."

From the start, Churchill insisted on Hitler's unconditional surrender—negotiated peace or compromise never entered into his policy. What changed was his application of policy. Initially, before the United States entered the war and when most of Europe was under Nazi domination, Churchill planned for Britain to fight alone. His two main strategies at this time were to bomb Germany and to concentrate forces in the Mediterranean and the Middle East. Of the bombing plan, he once wrote: "There is one thing that will bring Hitler down, and that is an absolutely devastating, exterminating attack by very heavy bombers from this

country upon the Nazi homeland." Both these strategies were continued when the United States entered the war following the Japanese attack on Pearl Harbor. The first act of Allied cooperation was the landing in North Africa, followed by the invasion of Italy.

Churchill knew that he needed American aid—first economic, then military. He set himself to securing what he called the Grand Alliance, an Anglo-American partnership that eventually proved "closer than any alliance in modern history." The Alliance was strengthened at a meeting at sea in August, 1941, when Churchill and President Franklin D. Roosevelt drew up a joint declaration known as the Atlantic Charter. Many subsequent sessions to discuss Allied strategy took place, and some of the more famous (like that at Yalta in November, 1945) included the Soviet leader Joseph Stalin.

Two features of the close Anglo-American relations had lasting ramifications for Great Britain. The first was the Lend Lease Act, which had been passed by the U.S. Congress on January 10, 1941. Originally an agreement extending from the United States to China and countries of the British Empire, it provided for the transfer of war supplies to nations considered vital to the defense of the United States. In the House of Commons, Churchill called the bill "the most unsordid act in the history of any nation." Lend-Lease had expanded to include most of the Allied nations when President Harry S Truman called for an end to the program in 1945. In exchange for Lend-Lease, Britain made sacrifices. Taylor explained: "The American financial authorities stripped Great Britain of her gold reserves and her overseas investments. . . . British exports were restricted, American officials supervised and checked all British foreign trade and American exporters moved ruthlessly into overseas markets that had hitherto been British." After the war, imperial preference and controlled exchanges were abolished; and London ceased to be an independent financial center.

The other issue was Churchill's relations with Soviet Russia. Both Britain and the United States embraced the Soviets as their only powerful ally on the European continent, despite differences in political ideology. As Taylor pointed out, "Russia was fighting Germany and so giving the British a breathing space." In the face of geographic obstacles, Britain and America sent Russia what aid they could. Furthermore, Churchill established "relations of personal intimacy with Stalin . . . more than any other man could have done; with Churchill, Stalin became a human being."

Neither Churchill nor Roosevelt nor the Soviets themselves, however, expected the Germans to be defeated on the Russian front. When the Russians won—in fact, marching into Berlin ahead of the Americans and the British—Churchill had to face the reality of a great Communist power controlling part of Europe. His proposal was a division of Europe into spheres of interest: Eastern Europe to the Soviets, Western Europe to Britain and America. The iron curtain, as Churchill dubbed it, had fallen.

Nevertheless, questions of economic stability or Communist threat were put aside during the war. As John Maynard Keynes said: "We threw good housekeeping to the wind. But we saved ourselves and we helped to save the world." It wasn't until Germany surrendered that the British people reexamined their devotion to Churchill and support of his policies. But with peace in the offing, the country began to clamor for an election. Held in July, 1945, it resulted in a Labor party victory, and Churchill was replaced as prime minister by Clement Atlee at the Potsdam conference.

Six years as leader of His Majesty's Loyal Opposition followed, during which time he warned Western democracies to stand firm against the Soviet Union and support the United Nations. In 1951 he was returned to the premiership, where he continued to support such Western federations as the North Atlantic Treaty Organization (NATO) and the Council of Europe (CE). At the same time he was cautious on the domestic front, preserving such socialist measures as the National Health Act and nationalization of the railroads and the Bank of England. Churchill retired from public life in 1955, turning over his office to Anthony Eden.

Churchill's career as a historian coincided with his military and political roles. But while his military education was formal, his historical training was self-acquired. When he went into battle, he also immersed himself in historical study. In later life he recalled: "All through the long, glittering, middle hours of the Indian day, from when we quitted stables till when the evening shadows proclaimed the hour of Polo, I devoured Gibbon." He also read Macaulay, Lecky, and Hallam, as well as the philosophy of Plato and Aristotle. The influence of Darwin, too, can be seen in his belief that life is a struggle in which the fit and the courageous are most likely to survive.

Churchill's sense of the glory of England remained with him all his life. Four times in two centuries, England had saved Europe from tyrants: Louis XIV, Napoleon, Kaiser Wilhelm II, and Hitler. As Churchill saw it, "this island race" was on the side not only of progress and enlightenment but of liberty and justice as well. Commager observed: "He never forgot it was the English tongue that was heard in Chicago and Vancouver, Johannesburg and Sydney, or that it was English law that was pronounced in Washington and Ottawa, Canberra and New Delhi, and English parliamentary governments that flourished in scores of nations on every continent."

Churchill incorporated his belief in England into a philosophy that has been equated with both eighteenth-century and Victorian thought. He saw history as a question of morality, a struggle between right and wrong, between freedom and tyranny. Its purpose was to teach by example, especially by the examples of great leaders and by the examples of war. Such a historical perspective has lead some critics to label Churchill a romantic.

Churchill's specialty was probably military history. "He learned of wars by fighting in them," Commager noted, and it was a subject central to most of his writings. He covered wars that ranged from India, Cuba, and the Sudan to South Africa, Western Europe, and eventually the entire globe. He observed them as a cavalryman and a journalist, then as the lord of the admiralty and the supreme commander of the Allied forces. He was, Commager said, "in all likelihood, the greatest of military historians who wrote in English." Even his least characteristic book, the autobiographical novel *Savrola,* is "a testament to Churchill's early sophistication in military and political matters," wrote Manfred Weidhorn.

Churchill's early military experience resulted in several volumes, notably those published collectively as *Frontiers and Wars.* His journalism, which at the time provided a needed source of income, has also been collected as *Young Winston's Wars.* But his first major literary undertaking began in 1902 when the family trustees gave him his father's papers. The project was, according to Weidhorn, "not only an homage to the father never fully known or confronted on equal terms and a revelation to the world of the greatness of the prematurely dead statesman . . . but also a discovery of and dedication to the father's values, a study of a political program handed down from one generation to the next within the same family." Commager described the two-volume *Life of Lord Randolph Churchill* as "judicious, comprehensive, and mature, penetrating not only to the realities of politics in those turbulent years, but to the realities of character."

Churchill worked on his other biography, *Marlborough,* for five years. Of this study he wrote: "It is my hope to recall this great shade from the past, and not only invest him with the panoply, but make him living and ultimate to modern eyes. I hope to show that he was not only the foremost of English soldiers, but in the first rank among the statesmen of our history; not only that he was a Titan . . . but that he was a virtuous and benevolent being, eminently serviceable to his age and country, capable of drawing harmony and design from chaos." Commager remarked: "Rarely in the history of historical writing have author and subject seemed so made for each other as were Churchill and the Duke of Marlborough."

In *The World Crisis,* Churchill presented himself as a participant in history. Lord Balfour called it "Winston's brilliant autobiography disguised as a history of the universe." It outlines his career against a background of international affairs, and it records not only the events of World War II, but also of the years preceding it. While such critics as Robert R. James considered these six volumes among Churchill's best, Weidhorn felt the balance between history and memoir was not successfully maintained: "Uneven, at times naive, bombastic, dated, it is, finally, a personal account, an 'entertainment,' a piece of storytelling or fine journalism that often masquerades as a formal analytic history."

The Second World War was also autobiographical, but to Weidhorn it was more successful than *The World Crisis.* It is "the usual Churchillian melange of autobiography, apologia, general history, and selected documents; of impersonal autobiography and personal history. But it is much more unified because Churchill was in a central position continuously and could observe events from a higher vantage point." As a result, continued Weidhorn, it benefits from a dramatic narrative flow as well as convincing evocation of setting, mood, and character.

In Churchill's later years, *The Second World War* and *History of the English-speaking Peoples* were outsold only by the Bible. *History of the English-speaking Peoples,* his last major work, was written for the most part in the late 1930s, but not published until 1956. It chronicles the rise of the British Empire and the English-speaking world, but it is also a vehicle for Churchill's ideas about politics, history, and tradition. "As Churchill saw it, the welfare of mankind was inextricably bound up with that of the English-speaking peoples," Commager explained. "It was, above all else, the English character which had lighted up the corridors of time." "The impact Churchill had on the lives of his contemporaries will never be forgotten. When he died he was acclaimed a citizen of the world and given a state funeral in St. Paul's Cathedral, an honor previously bestowed "on only two other men of war—Admiral Lord Nelson, victor at Trafalgar, and the Duke of Wellington, victor at Waterloo." Such were his honors because, as Taylor noted, to men of the time "he was the savior of his country, the first Englishman to be so hailed since King Alfred the Great."

AVOCATIONAL INTERESTS: Painting, gardening.

BIOGRAPHICAL/CRITICAL SOURCES:

BOOKS

Alberg, Victor Lincoln, *Winston Churchill,* Twayne, 1973.
Ashley, Maurice, *Churchill as Historian,* Scribner, 1968.
Bardens, Dennis, *Churchill in Parliament,* Barnes, 1969.

Broad, Lewis, *Winston Churchill: A Biography,* two volumes, Greenwood, 1972. Brockway, T. B., editor, *Language and Politics,* D. C. Heath, 1965.

Churchill, Randolph Spencer, and Martin Gilbert, *Winston S. Churchill,* eight volumes, Heinemann, 1967-88.

Churchill, Sarah, *Thread in the Tapestry,* Dodd, 1967.

Churchill by His Contemporaries, Hodder & Stoughton, 1965.

Churchill Centenary, 1874-1974: The Greatest Man in Living Memory, Associated Newspapers Group, 1974.

Connell, John, *Winston Churchill,* Longmans, Green, 1956.

de Mendelssohn, Peter, *The Age of Churchill,* Knopf, 1961.

Gardner, Brian, *Churchill in His Time: A Study in a Reputation, 1939-1945,* Methuen, 1968.

Gilbert, Martin, editor, *Churchill,* Prentice-Hall, 1967.

Jacobs, William Jay, *Churchill,* Benziger, 1976.

Lowenheim, Francis L., and others, editors, *Roosevelt and Churchill, Their Secret Wartime Correspondence,* Saturday Review Press, 1975.

Macmillan, Harold, *Past Masters,* Harper, 1975.

Mason, David, *Churchill,* Ballantine, 1972.

Payne, Pierre Stephen Robert, *Great Man: A Portrait of Winston Churchill,* Coward, 1974.

Peckenham, Elizabeth Harman, *Winston Churchill: A Pictorial Life Story,* Rand McNally, 1974.

Pelling, Henry, *Winston Churchill,* Dutton, 1974.

Schoenfeld, Maxwell Philip, *Sir Winston Churchill: His Life and Times,* Dryden, 1973.

Stansky, Peter, editor, *Churchill: A Profile,* Hill and Wang, 1973.

Tames, Richard, *Sir Winston Churchill: An Illustrated Life of Sir Winston Churchill, 1874-1965,* Shire, 1974.

Taylor, A.J.P., and others, *Churchill Revised: A Critical Assessment,* Dial, 1969.

Weidhorn, Manfred, *Sword and Pen: A Survey of the Writings of Sir Winston Churchill,* University of New Mexico Press, 1974.

Whatney, John Basil, *Churchills: Portrait of a Great Family,* Gordon Cremonesi, 1977.

Wilson, Harold, *Prime Minister on Prime Ministers,* Summit, 1977.

Wolff, Michael, *Winston Churchill,* Heron, 1970.

PERIODICALS

American Heritage, December, 1962, October, 1972, December, 1973.

American Historical Review, July, 1927, July, 1949, October, 1956.

American Mercury, October, 1949.

Atlantic Monthly, July, 1948, September, 1949, January, 1951.

Encounter, April, 1977.

Esquire, June, 1961, October 24, 1978.

Harper's, December, 1954, September, 1975.

History Today, January, 1975.

Intellect, November, 1974.

Life, March 14, 1948, June 21, 1948, April 4, 1955.

Nation, May 6, 1950, March 19, 1956, December 1, 1956, July 5, 1958, September 21, 1974.

Newsweek, January 21, 1946, January 28, 1946, March 18, 1946, March 25, 1946, April 8, 1946, August 26, 1946, April 8, 1946, August 18, 1947, October 31, 1947, June 21, 1948, April 4, 1949, March 6, 1950, May 4, 1953, October 20, 1953, December 6, 1954, March 4, 1957, May 13, 1957, March 17, 1958, May 5, 1958, September 8, 1958, February 16, 1959, March 24, 1961, September 3, 1962, April 22, 1963, May 18, 1970, May 15, 1973, November 18, 1974, November 13, 1978.

New York Times, March 6, 1927, March 17, 1929, November 20, 1930, November 29, 1931, December 4, 1932, November 12, 1933, March 17, 1935, March 28, 1937, November 14, 1937, October 9, 1938, October 23, 1938, September 3, 1939, April 13, 1941, October 25, 1942, August 22, 1943, July 23, 1944, August 5, 1945, August 25, 1946, June 20, 1948, March,, 13, 1949, April 3, 1949, June 12, 1949, February 12, 1950, April 23, 1950, June 11, 1950, November 26, 1950, November 25, 1951, November 29, 1953, April 15, 1956, August 22, 1956, November 25, 1956, February 22, 1959.

New York Times Book Review, March 20, 1955, November 24, 1974.

New York Times Magazine, February 9, 1947, November 21, 1948, January 2, 1949, November 2, 1949, November 26, 1950, October 14, 1951, November 11, 1951, January 4, 1953, October 25, 1953, November 28, 1954, April 1, 1956, January 19, 1958, February 16, 1958, November 1, 1964, October 5, 1969, April 28, 1974.

Saturday Review, March 16, 1929, October 31, 1953, November 28, 1953, December 4, 1954, April 21, 1956, February 6, 1965, May 18, 1968.

Saturday Review of Literature, April 30, 1927, June 19, 1948, March 4, 1950, November 25, 1950.

Speech, April, 1972.

Time, January 21, 1946, March 18, 1946, April 1, 1946, June 10, 1946, May 19, 1947, December 20, 1948, May 10, 1948, January 2, 1950, November 5, 1951, December 15, 1952, February 1, 1954, June 21, 1954, December 13, 1954, March 28, 1955, June 10, 1958, July 6, 1962, December 4, 1964, February 25, 1966, April 22, 1966, May 6, 1966, November 24, .1967, May 31, 1968.

Times Literary Supplement, March 3, 1927, October 23, 1950, November 5, 1931, October 12, 1933, October 9, 1937, June 25, 1938, July 1, 1939, October 3, 1942, July 31, 1943, July 1, 1944, July 27, 1946, September 28, 1946, August 14, 1948, July 1, 1949, July 21, 1950, April 27, 1956, November 30, 1956, October 26, 1967, September 15, 1972.

OBITUARIES:

PERIODICALS

America, January 30, 1965.

Atlantic, March, 1965.

Commonweal, February 19, 1965.

Life, January 29, 1965.

National Review, February 9, 1965.

New Statesman, January 29, 1965.

Newsweek, February 1, 1965.

New York Times, January 24, 1965.

Time, January 29, 1965.

U.S. News and World Report, February 1, 1965.

*   *   *

CIARDI, John (Anthony) 1916-1986
(John Anthony)

PERSONAL: Surname pronounced *Char*-dee; born June 24, 1916, in Boston, Mass.; died of a heart attack, March 30, 1986, in Edison, N.J.; son of Carminantonia (an insurance agent) and Concetta (De Benedictus) Ciardi; married Myra Judith Hostetter, July 28, 1946; children: Myra Judith, John Lyle Pritchett, Benn Anthony. *Education:* Attended Bates College, 1934-36; Tufts College (now University), A.B. (magna cum laude), 1938; University of Michigan, M.A., 1939. *Politics:* Democrat.

ADDRESSES: Home—359 Middlesex Ave., Metuchen, N.J. 08840; and 725 Windsor Lane, Key West, Fla. 33040.

CAREER: Poet and critic. University of Kansas City, Kansas City, Mo., instructor in English, 1940-42, 1946; Harvard University, Cambridge, Mass., Briggs-Copeland Instructor in English, 1946-48, Briggs-Copeland Assistant Professor of English, 1948-53; Rutgers University, New Brunswick, N.J., lecturer, 1953-54, associate professor, 1954-56, professor of English, 1956-61; *Saturday Review,* New York, N.Y., poetry editor, 1956-72. Bread Loaf Writers' Conference, lecturer beginning 1947, director, 1955-72; lecturer in American poetry, Salzburg Seminar in American Studies, 1951. Editor with Twayne Publishers, 1949; served as a judge in Children's Literature Section of National Book Awards, 1969. Host of "Accent," a weekly educational program presented by Columbia Broadcasting System-Television, 1961-62. Has given public poetry readings. *Military service:* U.S. Army Air Forces, 1942-45; served as gunner on B-29 in air offensive against Japan; became technical sergeant; received Air Medal with Oak Leaf Cluster.

MEMBER: American Academy of Arts and Sciences (fellow), National Institute of Arts and Letters (fellow), National College English Association (director, 1955-57; president, 1958-59), Northeast College English Association (past president), Phi Beta Kappa.

AWARDS, HONORS: Avery Hopwood Award for poetry, University of Michigan, 1939; Oscar Blumenthal Prize, 1943; Eunice Tietjens Award, 1945; Levinson Prize, 1946; Golden Rose trophy of New England Poetry Club, 1948; Fund for the Advancement of Education grant, 1952; Harriet Monroe Memorial Prize, 1955; Prix de Rome, American Academy of Arts and Letters, 1956-57; Litt.D., Tufts University, 1960; Junior Book Award, Boys' Clubs of America, 1962, for *The Man Who Sang the Sillies;* D.Hum., Wayne State University, 1963, and Keane College of New Jersey, 1976; LL.D., Ursinus College, 1964; L.H.D., Kalamazoo College, 1964, Bates College, 1970, Washington University, 1971, and Ohio Wesleyan University, 1971.

WRITINGS:

POETRY

Homeward to America, Holt, 1940.
Other Skies, Atlantic Monthly Press, 1947.
Live Another Day: Poems, Twayne, 1949.
As If: Poems New and Selected, Rutgers University Press, 1955.
I Marry You: A Sheaf of Love Poems, Rutgers University Press, 1958.
Thirty-Nine Poems, Rutgers University Press, 1959.
In the Stoneworks, Rutgers University Press, 1961.
In Fact, Rutgers University Press, 1962.
Person to Person, Rutgers University Press, 1964.
This Strangest Everything, Rutgers University Press, 1966.
An Alphabestiary, Lippincott, 1967.
A Genesis, Touchstone Publishers (New York), 1967.
The Achievement of John Ciardi: A Comprehensive Selection of his Poems with a Critical Introduction (poetry textbook), edited by Miller Williams, Scott, Foresman, 1969.
Lives of X (autobiographical poetry), Rutgers University Press, 1971.
The Little That Is All, Rutgers University Press, 1974.
For Instance, Norton, 1979.
Selected Poems, University of Arkansas Press, 1984.
The Birds of Pompeii, University of Arkansas Press, 1985.
Echoes: Poems Left Behind, University of Arkansas Press, 1989.

Poems of Love and Marriage, University of Arkansas Press, 1989.

JUVENILES

The Reason for the Pelican (poetry), Lippincott, 1959.
Scrappy the Pup (poetry), Lippincott, 1960.
The Man Who Sang the Sillies (poetry), Lippincott, 1961.
I Met a Man (poetry), Houghton, 1961.
You Read to Me, I'll Read to You (poetry), Lippincott, 1962.
The Wish-Tree (fiction), Crowell-Collier, 1962.
John J. Plenty and Fiddler Dan: A New Fable of the Grasshopper and the Ant (poetry), Lippincott, 1963.
You Know Who (poetry), Lippincott, 1964.
The King Who Saved Himself from Being Saved (poetry), Lippincott, 1965.
The Monster Den; or, Look What Happened at My House—and to It (poetry), Lippincott, 1966.
Someone Could Win a Polar Bear (poetry), Lippincott, 1970.
Fast and Slow: Poems for Advanced Children and Beginning Parents (poetry), Houghton, 1975.
Doodle Soup, Houghton, 1986.

TRANSLATOR

Dante Alighieri, *The Inferno* (poetry; also see below), Rutgers University Press, 1954.
Dante, *The Purgatorio* (poetry; also see below), New American Library, 1961.
Dante, *The Paradiso* (poetry; also see below), New American Library, 1970.
The Divine Comedy (includes *The Inferno, The Purgatorio,* and *The Paradiso*), Norton, 1977.

RECORDINGS

"About Eskimos and Other Poems" (cassette phonotape), Spoken Arts, 1974.
"What Do You Know about Poetry?: An Introduction to Poetry for Children" (cassette phonotape), Spoken Arts, 1974.
"What Is a Poem?: A Discussion of How Poems Are Made" (phonodisc), Spoken Arts, 1974.
"Why Noah Praised the Whale and Other Poems" (cassette phonotape), Spoken Arts, 1974.

OTHER

(Editor) *Mid-Century American Poets,* Twayne, 1950.
(Author of introduction) Fritz Leiber and others, *Witches Three* (prose), Twayne, 1952.
(Contributor) William White, *John Ciardi: A Bibliography,* Wayne State University Press, 1959.
(Editor and contributor) *How Does a Poem Mean?* (prose), Houghton, 1960, 2nd edition (with Miller Williams), 1975.
Dialogue with an Audience (collection of *Saturday Review* essays), Lippincott, 1963.
(Editor with James M. Reid and Laurence Perrine) *Poetry: A Closer Look* (prose), Harcourt, 1963.
(Contributor) A. L. Bader, editor, *To the Young Writer* (prose), University of Michigan Press, 1965.
(Contributor) *Dante Alighieri: Three Lectures* (prose), Library of Congress, 1965.
(Author of introduction) John A. Holmes, *The Selected Poems,* Beacon Press, 1965.
(With Joseph B. Roberts) *On Poetry and the Poetic Process* (prose), Troy State University Press, 1971.
Manner of Speaking (selected *Saturday Review* columns), Rutgers University Press, 1972.
(With Isaac Asimov) *Limericks, Too Gross,* Norton, 1978.

A Browser's Dictionary and Native's Guide to the Unknown American Language, Harper, 1980.

(With Laurence Urdang and Frederick Dickerson) *Plain English in a Complex Society,* Poynter Center, Indiana University, 1980.

(With Asimov) *A Grossery of Limericks,* Norton, 1981.

A Second Browser's Dictionary and Native's Guide to the Unknown American Language, Harper, 1983.

Good Words to You: An All-New Browser's Dictionary and Native's Guide to the Unknown American Language, Harper, 1987.

The Complete Browser's Dictionary: The Best of John Ciardi's Two Browser's Dictionaries in a Single Compendium of Curious Expressions and Intriguing Facts, Harper, 1988.

Saipan: The War Diary of John Ciardi, University of Arkansas Press, 1988.

The Hopeful Trout and Other Limericks, Houghton, 1989.

Also contributor of short story, under name John Anthony, to science fiction anthology *A Decade of Fantasy and Science Fiction: Out of This World Masterworks by Masterminds of the Near and the Far Out.* Contributor of articles and essays to periodicals. Contributing editor, *Saturday Review,* 1955—, and *World Magazine,* 1970-72.

WORK IN PROGRESS: Additional volumes of *A Browser's Dictionary;* a book of juvenile poems; a book of "senile" poems.

SIDELIGHTS: To millions of Americans, the late John Ciardi was "Mr. Poet, the one who has written, talked, taught, edited, translated, anthologized, criticized, and propelled poetry into a popular, lively art," according to Peter Comer of the *Chicago Tribune.* Although recognized primarily as a poet and critic, Ciardi's literary endeavors encompassed a vast range of material. From juvenile nonsense poetry to scholarly verse translations, Ciardi made an impact upon the general public. His poetry received popular approval while his academic research attracted critical kudos. Driven by his love of words and language, John Ciardi provided lively and frequently controversial offerings to the literary scene.

The son of Italian immigrants, Ciardi, at age three, lost his father in an automobile accident. Ciardi recalls a peaceful youth, enlivened by the addition of Irish and Italian families to the neighborhood. His tranquil life developed into a series of bruises and black eyes as the neighborhood children clashed frequently. Perhaps due to his heritage, Ciardi's interest in Italian literature has resulted in translations of Dante's *Inferno* that many authorities consider classics.

Once a denizen of the English faculties at Harvard and Rutgers, Ciardi, in 1961, broke with formalized education in favor of pursuing his own literary endeavors full-time. He remained a part of the academic community through countless lectures and poetry readings each year, in addition to numerous appearances on educational television. Influenced by his favorite teacher at Tufts University, poet John Holmes, Ciardi decided early in his college career to devote time to writing verse. He turned to composing juvenile poetry as a means of playing and reading with his own children. His juvenile selections have been enormously successful, especially *I Met a Man.* Ciardi's position as a poetry critic with *Saturday Review* developed from his own verse publications, but he told Comer that "it was a hobby job," adding, "I think at most it earned me $4,000 a year."

Ciardi was strongly in favor of exposing poetry to mass audiences. Aware of the linguistic and allusive complexities inherent in "good" verse and acknowledging the public's general aversion to poems, he consciously attempted to address the average reader through much of his work. While not sacrificing his message for popularity and renown, Ciardi nevertheless gained a large public following. While critics acclaimed the intellectual elements in his work, the reading public derived equal meaning and relevance from his poetry. In his preface to *Dialogue with an Audience,* Ciardi expressed the hope that some readers "can be brought to a more than merely general interest in poetry."

Ciardi's work has inspired both praise and criticism from reviewers. Edward Cifelli writes in the *CEA Critic:* "Ciardi's verse is intensely personal, introspective, and self-revealing. His poems reflect the quiet considerations of a thoughtful, sensitive man. They are not white-hot representations of emotion: Ciardi more often thinks about passion. His diction is less emotionally charged than it is intricately patterned. Frequently passion emerges in Ciardi 'imagery' only after it has been filtered through the poet's sense of the ironic or comic." Cifelli also believes that "[Ciardi] focuses with remarkable clarity on the elements upon which one builds a theme into a poem," adding, "The theme that exemplifies the great diversity of Ciardi's talent is poetry itself." In the *Dictionary of Literary Biography,* Alice Smith Haynes analyzes the totality of the poet's verse and its connected relativity: "Just as [Ciardi] maintains that Dante must be experienced as a whole, so his poetry, more than that of most poets, must be seen as an interrelated body of parts." In the *Chicago Tribune,* Reed Whittemore, also a poet and essayist, observes: "If [Ciardi's] poetry has any persistent theme, it is probably that human nonsense and folly are persistent. He is a cynic all right. . . . But he is not all cynic. The positive feelings do slop pleasantly through." Corner illustrates Ciardi's literary success: "John Ciardi long has been the rare American who could walk into a bank, declare his occupation as 'poet,' and emerge with a mortgage."

Ciardi's verse often breaks with contemporary poetic tendencies. Whittemore writes that current poetry "has gone off to make a kind of fin-de-siecle career of mental lapses, to put bright images in odd places on mostly empty pages, and to plow up acres and acres of private sensibility"; Whittemore states that since Ciardi has not "lapsed" into this new set of poetic criteria, his recent work has become somewhat "unfashionable." John W. Hughes of the *Saturday Review* also finds limitations in twentieth-century verse, but unlike Whittemore, feels Ciardi's reputation survives the shift in poetic direction: "Ciardi follows Wordsworth and Frost in molding the blank verse to the flowing immediacy of his remembrances, and in so doing explodes some of the mind-forged manacles that shackle modern poetry." Ciardi himself, in the *Writer,* alluded to changing poetry values and their effect on his appeal. He commented: "Too many poets today, especially the activist poets, think that the only prerequisite [to writing good poetry] is the excitation of their own ignorance. I become unpopular with them. . . . The very fact that I would suggest [that a poet needs training] makes me a reactionary, warloving, establishment racist out to oppress the poor. I have no answer. Just goodbye."

As a critic, Ciardi frequently provoked controversy with his frank and often candidly honest reviews. Known for promoting poetry, he nonetheless never shied away from denigrating what he considers unworthy verse. The first major disturbance surrounding his assessment of poetry stemmed from his unfavorable *Saturday Review* article about Anne Morrow Lindbergh's *The Unicorn.* Such forthright criticism in 1957 shocked readers and prompted voluminous mail protest. Ciardi defended his position in later issues of the magazine, arguing that a critic's role is to examine the work itself, not the popularity of the artist. He also maintained that the primary responsibility of good poetry lies to itself, and that the publishing arena should not serve simply to enhance any particular individual's reputation. Ciardi's fresh approach to criticism set the mood for later evaluative standards not yet accepted in the late 1950s.

Ciardi held firm convictions regarding the process of self-evaluation of one's work. In the *Writer,* he asserted that unsuccessful poems reveal information which may prove valuable to future achievement: "I learned that the rate at which one recognizes his own badness is the rate at which he grows as a writer." Ciardi did not deny the sentiment behind failed verse; he simply defined the writer's abortive attempt to identify and describe the experience: "When a bad writer thinks he has caught the miracle, or some piece of it, his wrong impression is invariably due to the fact that he *felt* a poem but did not manage to *write* one. The miracle stayed inside his head. . . . He has *lived* a poem; he has not *made* one." Further, Ciardi advocated "ruthless" examination of one's work, claiming: "The wastebasket is a prime resource. . . . It forces me to recognize what I have done badly."

About the creative process itself, Ciardi argued in the *Writer* that "it isn't easy to make a poem," adding: "It is better than easy: it is joyously, consumingly difficult. As it is difficult, too, though without joy, to face one's failures." Noting that the creation of successful verse requires definite skill, he wrote: "I insist that a poet needs at least as much training as does a concert pianist. More, I think, but that is already too much for the ignorantly excited." Believing that "the minimum requirement for a good poem is a miracle," he explained: "The poem must somehow turn out better than anyone—the poet included—had any right to expect. No matter how small the miracle, the hope of it is my one reason for writing." He also felt the poem's strength will lead the writer unerringly: "The poet cannot know where he is going: he must take his direction from the poem itself."

Despite his love of the humble literary life, Ciardi did not snub financial gain. In the *Writer,* he indicated that although his writing "has been a love affair, not a sales campaign," he cherished the "bonuses—grants, prizes, even a small, slow rain of checks," commenting: "How could I fail to rejoice in that overflow of good? I wish it to every writer, and wish him my sense of joy in it." Stating that "I have never known of anyone who turned to poetry in the expectation of becoming rich by it," he cited his own satisfaction as "total payment." Ciardi nevertheless "kept his fingers in . . . many literary pies," in Corner's words. Corner noted that the poet was fond of saying, "I am my broker's keeper."

Eschewing quick, financially-rewarding pieces in favor of a multitude of more demanding projects, Ciardi had no patience with glibly mawkish poets. In spite of, or perhaps because of, his popularity with the public, Ciardi ascertained that his work met his own rigorous approval before publishing even a stanza of verse. Describing Rod McKuen and Edgar Guest as "writers whose remouthing of sentiments catches some tawdry emotional impulse in commercial quantities," he thought that such poets "believe seriously in the inanities they write." Ciardi explained, "I doubt that they have sold out to the dollar sign: more tragically, they have sold out to themselves."

One of Ciardi's late passions emerged in his conversation with Corner: "I'm not a complicated man, and I don't have any gripping internal problems. But I get interested in things. Words have become a happy obsession." His linguistic research culminated in a multi-volume work, *The Browser's Dictionary.* In the first volume, Ciardi indulged his interest in etymology, word der-

ivations, and linguistic development throughout the entries. Concentrating on precision, the tome reflected Ciardi's commitment to bringing the intricacies of language closer to the reading public.

Reassessing his writing career, John Ciardi told Corner that perhaps his first works exhibit indiscriminate editing: "Early on I was offered more chances to publish than was really good for me, and I lacked the character to say no. . . . I need to go back over everything and take only the ones that stay memorable for me, probably less than half I've published. And I'd like to signalize that the other ones are fakes. . . . I denounce them. . . . I did not write them." Despite his concern over quality, Ciardi remained immersed in literary pursuits. His opinion in the *Writer* that "what passes as our poetry has too largely been taken over by loud illiterates and by officiously important editors" belies his constant quest for self-improvement. He wrote "as an alcoholic drinks, compulsively." This "tough-guy poet, the art's Edward C. Robinson, with his feelings leaking out unexpectedly in the midst of flat, machine-gun commentary," in Whittemore's words, explained to Corner: "I find I like what I do . . . and enjoy working at the things I enjoy. To me that's a description of blessedness." Perhaps to ensure the perpetuation of his poetic dominion even in death, John Ciardi created his own epitaph: "Here, time concurring (and it does);/Lies Ciardi. If no kingdom come,/A kingdom was. Such as it was/This one beside it is a slum."

AVOCATIONAL INTERESTS: "Indifferent golf and neglected gardening."

BIOGRAPHICAL/CRITICAL SOURCES:

BOOKS

Ciardi, John, *Lives of X,* Rutgers University Press, 1971.
Contemporary Literary Criticism, Gale, Volume 10, 1979, Volume 40, 1986, Volume 44, 1987.
Dictionary of Literary Biography, Volume 5: *American Poets since World War II,* Gale, 1980.
Dictionary of Literary Biography Yearbook: 1986, Gale, 1987.
Hopkins, Lee Bennett, *Books Are by People,* Citation Press, 1969.
John Ciardi, Twayne, 1980.
White, William, *John Ciardi: A Bibliography,* Wayne State University Press, 1959.

PERIODICALS

America, July 27, 1957.
Book Week, September 29, 1963, November 1, 1964, November 8, 1970, September 24, 1972, September 28, 1980.
Booklist, December 1, 1972, February 1, 1975, October 15, 1979, July 15, 1980.
CEA Critic, November, 1973.
Chicago Review, autumn-winter, 1956, summer, 1957.
Chicago Tribune, December 16, 1979, September 8, 1980.
Choice, October, 1967, February, 1972, February, 1975, June, 1979.
Christian Science Monitor, December 24, 1964, May 7, 1975, October 23, 1978, January 2, 1980.
Contemporary Literature, winter, 1968.
Critic, December, 1963-January, 1964.
Detroit Free Press, February 28, 1964.
Explicator, December, 1968, May, 1970.
Nation, September 13, 1958.
National Observer, November 30, 1970.
New York Times Book Review, April 16, 1950, July 4, 1954, August 3, 1958, November 11, 1962, May 12, 1963, November

10, 1963, October 4, 1964, November 1, 1964, November 8, 1970, May 4, 1975, November 16, 1975, August 17, 1980.

New York Herald Tribune, November 11, 1962, August 11, 1963.

Poetry, September, 1940, May, 1948, July, 1956, October, 1958, December, 1962, July, 1963, December, 1967, July, 1975.

Prairie Schooner, winter, 1972-73.

Saturday Review, January 28, 1956, November 10, 1962, March 23, 1963, December 14, 1963, June 3, 1967, February 6, 1971, May 22, 1971, November 27, 1971. May 31, 1975.

Time, February 18, 1957, February 26, 1979.

University of Kansas City Review, autumn, 1949.

Virginia Quarterly Review, winter, 1964, spring, 1965.

Wall Street Journal, May 28, 1971.

Writer, March, 1964, August, 1976, June, 1980.

Yale Review, March, 1956.

OBITUARIES:

PERIODICALS

Chicago Tribune, April 3, 1986.
Detroit News, April 2, 1986.
Milwaukee Sentinel, April 1, 1986.
Newsweek, April 14, 1986.
New York Times, April 2, 1986.
Time, April 14, 1986.
Washington Post, April 2, 1986.
Woodbridge News Tribune (Woodbridge, N.J.), September 25, 1986.

* * *

CIXOUS, Helene 1937-

PERSONAL: Surname is pronounced "Siksu"; born June 5, 1937, in Oran, Algeria; daughter of Georges (a physician) and Eva (a midwife; maiden name, Klein) Cixous; married, 1955 (divorced, 1964); children: Anne Berger, Pierre-Francois Berger. *Education:* Received Agregation d'Anglais, 1959, and Docteur es Lettres, 1968. *Religion:* Jewish.

ADDRESSES: Home—38 bis, avenue Rene Coty, 75014 Paris, France. *Office*—Universite de Paris VIII, 2 rue de la Liberte, 93526 St. Denis, France.

CAREER: University of Bordeaux, Bordeaux, France, assistante, 1962-65; University of Paris (Sorbonne), Paris, France, maitre assistante, 1965-67; University of Paris X (Nanterre), Nanterre, France, maitre de conference, 1967-68; University of Paris VIII (Vincennes at St. Denis), St. Denis, France, helped found the university's experimental branch at St. Denis, 1968, professor of English literature, 1968—, founder and director of Centre de Recherches en Etudes Feminines, 1974—. Visiting professor and lecturer at several universities, including Columbia University, Cornell University, Dartmouth College, New York University, State University of New York at Binghampton and Buffalo, University of Wisconsin—Madison, Yale University, and universities in Austria, Canada, Denmark, England, and Spain.

AWARDS, HONORS: Prix Medici, 1969, for *Dedans.*

WRITINGS:

Le Prenom de Dieu (stories), Grasset et Fasquelle, 1967.
L'Exil de James Joyce; ou, L'Art du remplacement (doctoral thesis), Grasset et Fasquelle, 1968, translation by Sally A. J. Purcell published as *The Exile of James Joyce,* D. Lewis (New York), 1972.

Dedans (novel), Grasset et Fasquelle, 1969, translation by Carol Barko published as *Inside,* Schocken, 1986.
(Co-editor and co-author with Pierre Dommergues and Marianne Debouzy) *Les Etats-Unis d'aujourd'hui,* Colin, 1969.
Le Troisieme Corps (novel), Grasset et Fasquelle, 1970.
Les Commencements (novel), Grasset et Fasquelle, 1970.
Un Vrai Jardin (poetic short story), L'Herne, 1971.
Neutre (novel), Grasset et Fasquelle, 1972.
Portrait du soleil (novel), Denoel, 1973.
Tombe (novel), Seuil, 1973.
Prenoms de personne (essays), Seuil, 1974.
(With Catherine Clement) *La Jeune Nee* (essay), Union Generale d'Editions, 1975, translation by Betsy Wing published as *The Newly Born Woman,* with introduction by Sandra M. Gilbert, University of Minnesota Press, 1986.
Un K. incomprehensible: Pierre Goldman, Bourgois, 1975.
Revolutions pour plus d'un Faust (novel), Seuil, 1975.
Souffles (fiction), Femmes, 1975.
La (fiction), Gallimard, 1976.
Partie, Femmes, 1976.
Angst (fiction), Femmes, 1977, translation by Jo Levy published as *Angst,* Riverrun Press, 1985.
(With Madeleine Gagnon and Annie Leclerc) *La Venue a l'ecriture* (essay), Union Generale d'Editions, c. 1977.
Le Nom d'Oedipe: Chant du corps interdit (libretto), music by Andre Boucourechliev, Femmes, 1978.
Preparatifs de noces au dela de l'abime, Femmes, 1978.
Ananke, Femmes, c. 1979.
Vivre l'orange/To Live the Orange (fiction; bilingual edition), English translation by Ann Liddle and Sarah Cornell, Femmes, 1979.
Illa (fiction), Femmes, 1980.
With; ou, L'Art de l'innocence (fiction), Femmes, 1981.
Limonade tout etait si infini (fiction), Femmes, 1982.
Le Livre de Promethea (fiction), Gallimard, 1983, translation by Betsy Wing published by University of Nebraska Press, in press.
(With Madeleine Chapsal and Sonia Rykiel) Daniele Flis, editor, *Rykiel,* illustrations by Pascale Ogee, Herscher, c. 1985.
La Bataille d'Arcachon (tale), Trois, 1986.
Entre l'ecriture (essays) Femmes, c. 1986, translation by Deborah W. Carpenter, Sarah Cornell, and Suzan Sellers published by Femmes, 1988.

Author of manifesto "Le Rire de la Meduse" (title means "The Laugh of the Medusa"). Co-founder of *Revue de Theorie et d'Analyse Litteraire: Poetique* in 1969.

Work represented in anthologies, including *New French Feminisms,* edited by Elaine Marks and Isabelle de Courtivron, University of Massachusetts Press, 1980, and *The Future of Literary Theory,* edited by Ralph Cohen, 1987. Contributor to periodicals, including *Boundary, L'Herne, Le Monde, New Literary History, Poetique,* and *Signs.*

PLAYS

La Pupille, Gallimard, 1972.
Portrait de Dora, Femmes, 1976, translation by Anita Barros published as *Benmussa Directs: Portrait of Dora* [and] *The Singular Life of Albert Nobbs* (the latter adapted by Simone Benmussa from George Moore's short story "Albert Nobbs," and translation from the French by Barbara Wright), Riverrun Press, 1979.
"La Prise de l'Ecole de Madhubai," first produced at L'Avant-Scene Theatre, 1984.

"L'Histoire terrible mais inachevee de Norodom Sihanouk, Roi du Cambodge," first produced at Theatre du Soleil, 1985.
"L'Indiade; ou, L'Inde de mes reves," first produced at Theatre du Soleil, September, 1987.

SIDELIGHTS: Helene Cixous, a professor at the University of Paris and a founder and director of one of France's few centers for women's studies, was the winner of the 1969 Prix Medici for her first novel, *Dedans,* translated in 1986 as *Inside. La Jeune Nee,* which she wrote in 1976 with Catherine Clement and which was translated ten years later as *The Newly Born Woman,* was deemed a "ground-breaking feminist tract" by the *New York Times Book Review.* Cixous also received wide acclaim for her doctoral thesis, published in 1968 as *L'Exil de James Joyce; ou, L'Art de remplacement* and translated in 1972 as *The Exile of James Joyce.* Although she supports and writes women's literature, Cixous does not consider herself a feminist because of the political and masculine overtones she finds in the term. She is, however, one of the best known and most influential advocates of *ecriture feminine,* or feminine writing—a form that she stresses may include works by both male and female writers. "This writing is dedicated to exploding the binary oppositions on which Western thinking rests," explained Marianne Hirsch in the *New York Times Book Review,* "which relegate woman to the side of silence, of otherness."

Cixous, like other French feminist writers, emphasizes "the place of 'woman' in language and the question of a feminine relation to language that [has] relatively little currency within Anglophone feminist thought," explained translator Annette Kuhn in *Signs.* This concern is of particular importance to the French because their language, unlike English, is based upon distinctly "masculine" and "feminine" words and images. Many of Cixous's writings attempt to negate the male/female distinction through puns and word manipulations. For this reason, Kuhn wrote, "it is very difficult for translation to do full justice to Cixous's writing, which is actually organized around a pervasive play with, and subversion of, linguistic signifiers."

The English translation of Cixous's award-winning first novel, *Dedans,* was published as *Inside* in 1986, seventeen years after the original French edition appeared. The highly metaphoric work is commonly regarded as an autobiography, although the author did not introduce the book as such. The main character, like Cixous, was born of a North African Jewish father and a German Jewish mother and was raised in Algeria. The novel depicts the daughter's intense love for her father and the grief she suffers when he dies young, as Cixous's father had. "It dwells on a sense of enclosure and entrapment," Marianne Hirsch described. "The nameless narrator . . . is inside a family romance where her father is God, the owner of all the words, and where her German-speaking mother offers no access to knowledge." After her father dies, the daughter imagines his death ceaselessly, trying to understand it. Finally, related Hirsch, "she gains the means to write from [her father's] overwhelming bodily closeness and from his empowering mental gifts in life."

Some feminists have decried the importance of the father's role in *Inside* as defeating the purpose of feminism, and a *Kirkus Review* critic deemed the "densely compact philosophical narrative" simply "intellectual passion from the school of radical French narrative, by turns brilliant and boring." Hirsch, however, offered high praise for the "series of reflections on identity, death and writing." The reviewer noted that *Inside* was timely as well as poignant, calling it a "moving and disturbing experimental work written at the moment of emergence of feminist consciousness—both for the author herself and for a broader in-

tellectual and political movement whose important representative she would become."

Cixous maintains her "special and elusive style" in *Angst,* according to Lorna Sage in the *Observer.* The novel, first published in 1977, was translated into English in 1985. "The writing is dense, direct, often lurid with metaphor" as it records a woman's reflections on her life and her attempt to create mental order out of the chaos she finds, wrote Sage. Nicole Irving in *Times Literary Supplement* praised Cixous's innovative prose style as well as the "loving" translation by Jo Levy, despite calling much of the book "incomprehensible": "[Cixous's] text has a rhythmic pattern, moving from obscurity to relative clarity, from the bodily (erotic and otherwise) to the sometimes punning metaphysical, from violence to calm and occasional tenderness, and at the end, 'she' [the main character] reaches a wholeness." As Sage observed: "The writing is alive even at its oddest."

Most of Cixous's other works, like *Inside* and *Angst,* forsake a traditional literary plot in favor of a speculative or philosophical inner narrative. The works therefore contain elements of fiction, discourse, and poetry. "The categories are relative and deceptive," noted Judith Morganroth Schneider in *World Literature Today,* "for her texts . . . resolutely resist classification." Marianne Hirsch explained that the ambiguity arises because Cixous's "fiction is always based on literary, philosophical and psychoanalytic readings and her theory is written in a personal voice and metaphorical style." Schneider characterized Cixous's 1976 work, *La,* as "fiction and theory posing the question of the feminine text and the feminine unconscious." The reviewer commented that, in *La,* "rules of syntax, grammar, logic are incessantly, violently, exuberantly broken," expressing Cixous's interpretation of feminine writing, which Schneider described as "a passionate outpouring, indifferent to censorship, sensual, bisexually erotic, moving impetuously through disintegration and reintegration of language."

Like Hirsch and Schneider, Olga Prjevalinskaya Ferrer observed in her *World Literature Today* review of *Partie* that "Helene Cixous's works most certainly voice a protest against the very strict rules of French intellectual thought and its expression through speech and writing." Perhaps as a protest against even the traditional appearance of books, Ferrer speculated, Cixous presented the work as a wide book divided into two sections, each upside-down in relation to the other, with pages meeting in the middle of the volume. Commenting on the difficulty of classifying *Partie* in terms of genre, Ferrer stated: "Though [Cixous's] writings are, most of the time, poetic, her originality and freedom have surpassed any poetic thought, any poetic trends." The author's freedom of expression, the reviewer asserted, provides *Partie* "an enchanting depth."

The same freedom of thought and expression grants a "definite charm" to *Illa,* judged Ferrer in a later review. "From the first lines of *Illa,*" the reviewer appraised, "we are fully immersed in a lyrical world of feminine self-awareness." The book—whose title is a Latin feminine pronoun and adjective—discusses the relationship between the various roles women fulfill in their lives. "Every passage, every syntagma, shows psycho-poetic mastery, creative uniqueness," lauded Ferrer. "No matter how unexpected Cixous's wording might seem, the reader feels at ease and allows himself to be carried away by the current of her suggestive prose, as by the rhythm of a musical composition."

With; ou, L'Art de l'innocence is likewise about woman's multiplicity. "Cixous's sinuous prose poem is a conversation between various aspects of her person," explained Rosette C. Lamont in *World Literature Today.* Although the author's various selves are disparate, Lamont observed, "the many voices of Cixous's novel-poem blend into a single interrogation about freedom, a multilingual existence in *l'ecriture* and the mystery of being woman."

Most of Cixous's critics, while echoing Judith Morganroth Schneider's assertion of being both "exhilarated and exasperated" by the author's unorthodox writing technique, praised Cixous's innovative theories of feminism and her unique manner of expressing them. "In her theoretical feminist writings, Cixous has called for a new language as the precondition of a new reality," observed Nicole Irving. The new language and syntax easily give rise to confusion and misinterpretation, but as Olga Prjevalinskaya Ferrer noted: "Despite the ambivalences and flagrant contradictions, truth and authentic logic always prevail." Rosette C. Lamont concluded in *World Literature Today:* "Helene Cixous is not moved by modest ambition; she would like to decipher the universe. Love of Woman, of women, of stars, words, languages, language allows her to rise from her finitude."

BIOGRAPHICAL/CRITICAL SOURCES:

BOOKS

Conley, Verena Andermatt, *Writing the Feminine,* University of Nebraska Press, 1984.
Gelfland, Elissa and Virginia Hules, editors, *French Feminist Criticism: Women, Language, and Literature,* Garland Publishing, 1985.
Marks, Elaine and Isabelle de Courtivron, editors, *New French Feminisms,* University of Massachusetts Press, 1980.
Moi, Toril, *Sexual/Textual Politics: Feminist Literary Theory,* Methuen, 1985.
Stambolian, George and Elaine Marks, editors, *Homosexuality and French Literature,* Cornell University Press, 1979.

PERIODICALS

Contemporary Literature, summer, 1983.
Kirkus Reviews, September 1, 1986.
Liberation, December 22, 1982, December 30, 1983.
Le Monde, July 28, 1977.
New York Times Book Review, February 11, 1973, August 24, 1986, December 7, 1986.
Observer, January 12, 1986.
Signs, autumn, 1981.
Substance, Volume 10, number 3, 1981.
Times Literary Supplement, April 24, 1969, February 12, 1971, March 21, 1986.
Women's Review, May, 1985.
World Literature Today, winter, 1977, spring, 1977, summer, 1977, spring, 1981, summer, 1982, winter, 1984.

*　　　*　　　*

CLANCY, Thomas L., Jr. 1947-
(Tom Clancy)

PERSONAL: Born in 1947 in Baltimore, Md.; son of a mail carrier and a credit employee; married Wanda Thomas (an insurance agency manager) in August, 1969; children: Michelle, Christine, Tom, Kathleen. *Education:* Graduated from Loyola College, Baltimore, Md., 1969. *Politics:* Conservative. *Religion:* Roman Catholic.

ADDRESSES: P.O. Box 800, Huntingtown, Md. 20639-0800.

CAREER: Insurance agent in Baltimore, Md., and Hartford, Conn., until 1973; O. F. Bowen Agency (insurance company), Owings, Md., agent, beginning in 1973, owner, beginning in 1980; writer.

WRITINGS:

NOVELS; UNDER NAME TOM CLANCY

The Hunt for Red October, Naval Institute Press, 1984.
Red Storm Rising, Putnam, 1986.
Patriot Games, Putnam, 1987.
The Cardinal of the Kremlin, Putnam, 1988.
Clear and Present Danger, Putnam, 1989.

WORK IN PROGRESS: Three novels, including *Without Remorse.*

SIDELIGHTS: Known for hugely successful, detailed novels about espionage, the military, and advanced military technology, Tom Clancy was proclaimed "king of the techno-thriller" by Patrick Anderson in the *New York Times Magazine.* Since the 1984 publication of his first novel, the acclaimed *Hunt for Red October,* all of his books have become best-sellers. Popular with armed forces personnel as well as the public, they have garnered praise from such prominent figures as former President Ronald Reagan and Secretary of Defense Caspar Weinberger. Clancy's work has also received more negative attention from officials who found his extrapolations from declassified information uncomfortably close to the top-secret reality and from reviewers who criticized his characterizations and too-perfect weaponry. Still, sales in the millions and constant best-seller status attest to his continued popularity as "novelist laureate of the military-industrial complex," as Ross Thomas described him in the *Washington Post Book World.*

The Hunt for Red October, which describes the race between U.S. and Soviet forces to get their hands on a defecting Russian submarine captain and his state-of-the-art vessel, marked a number of firsts. It was a first novel for both its author and its publisher, Naval Institute Press, whose catalogue had previously consisted of scholarly and strategic works and the occasional collection of short stories or poems about the sea. It was the first best-seller for both parties as well, and it became the first of Clancy's books to be made into a motion picture. Conceived before the author, an insurance agent, had ever set foot on a submarine, it is "a tremendously enjoyable and gripping novel of naval derring-do," according to *Washington Post Book World* critic Reid Beddow. The book contains descriptions of high-tech military hardware so advanced that former Navy Secretary John Lehman, quoted in *Time,* joked that he "would have had [Clancy] court-martialed: the book revealed that much that had been classified about antisubmarine warfare. Of course, nobody for a moment suspected him of getting access to classified information." The details were actually based on unclassified books and naval documents, Clancy's interviews with submariners, and his own educated guesses, the author asserts. Admitting that "neither characterization nor dialogue are strong weapons in Clancy's literary arsenal," Richard Setlowe in the *Los Angeles Times Book Review* nonetheless expressed an opinion shared by other reviewers: "At his best, Clancy has a terrific talent for taking the arcana of U.S. and Soviet submarine warfare, the subtleties of sonar and the techno-babble of nuclear power plants and transforming them into taut drama."

In Clancy's second novel, *Red Storm Rising,* U.S.-Soviet conflict escalates to a non-nuclear World War III. Crippled by a Moslem terrorist attack on a major Siberian oil refinery, the Soviet Union plots to defeat the countries in the North Atlantic Treaty Organization (NATO) so that it can dominate oil-rich Arab nations unhindered. The novel covers military action on land and in the air as well as on submarines; its complicated narrative prompted *Chicago Tribune Book World* reviewer Douglas Balz to note that Clancy's "skill with the plot . . . is his real strength." Balz and other critics faulted Clancy's characterization, although in the *New York Times Book Review* Robert Lekachman deemed the problem irrelevant to the book's merits as a "rattling good yarn" with "lots of action" and the "comforting certainty that our side will win." John Keegan, writing in the *Washington Post Book World,* called *Red Storm Rising* "a brilliant military fantasy—and far too close to reality for comfort."

Patriot Games, Clancy's third book, tells how former Marine officer Jack Ryan, a key figure in *The Hunt for Red October,* places himself between a particularly fanatical branch of the Irish Republican Army and the British royal family. Several reviewers criticized it for lack of credibility, lags in the action, simplistic moral lines, and, again, poor characterization, conceding nevertheless that it should appeal to fans of the earlier books. Anderson voiced another perspective: " 'Patriot Games' is a powerful piece of popular fiction; its plot, if implausible, is irresistible, and its emotions are universal." Pointing out Clancy's authentic detail, powerful suspense, and relevance to current history, James Idema suggested in a *Tribune Books* review that "most readers [will] find the story preposterous yet thoroughly enjoyable."

Ryan appears again in *The Cardinal of the Kremlin,* which returns to the theme of conflict between the United States and the Soviet Union. In this episode, regarded by critics such as Lekachman as "by far the best of the Jack Ryan series" to date, Clancy focuses on the controversial laser-satellite "strategic defense systems" also known as "Star Wars." According to Lekachman: "The adventure . . . is of high quality. And while [Clancy's] prose is no better than workmanlike . . ., the unmasking of the title's secret agent, the Cardinal, is as sophisticated an exercise in the craft of espionage as I have yet to encounter." Remarked *Fortune* contributor Andrew Ferguson, Clancy "aims not only to entertain but also to let his readers in on the 'inside story,' meanwhile discussing with relish the strategic and technological issues of war and peace." Concluded Ferguson, "It is refreshing to find a member of the literati who is willing to deal with [defense policy] in a manner more sophisticated than signing the latest disarmament petition in the New York *Times.*"

In *Clear and Present Danger* Ryan, in league with the Central Intelligence Agency (CIA), joins the fight against the powerful South American organizations that supply illegal drugs to the U.S. market. After the director of the Federal Bureau of Investigation (FBI) is murdered on a trip to Colombia, the fight becomes a covert war, with foot soldiers and fighter planes unleashed on virtually any target suspected of drug involvement. Reviewing the novel in the *Wall Street Journal,* former Assistant Secretary of State Elliott Abrams wrote, "What helps to make 'Clear and Present Danger' such compelling reading is a fairly sophisticated view of Latin politics combined with Mr. Clancy's patented, tautly shaped scenes, fleshed out with colorful technical data and tough talk." Abrams commended Clancy's awareness of the ethical dilemmas that complicate such covert military operations. Some reviewers echoed earlier criticisms of Clancy's characterizations, his focus on technology, and his prose style, but, noted Evan Thomas in *Newsweek,* "it doesn't really matter if his characters are two dimensional and his machines are too perfect. He whirls them through a half dozen converging subplots until they collide in a satisfyingly slam-bang finale." Thomas called the book "Clancy's best thriller since his first" and "a surprisingly successful cautionary tale."

Unprecedented knowledge of military technology, plots of rousing adventure and taut suspense, and themes that address current international concerns have combined to make Clancy "one of the most popular authors in the country," in the estimation of *Washington Post Book World* writer David Streitfeld. He is so well liked by military personnel, in particular, that he has been invited to military bases and given tours of ships; reported Evan Thomas in *Newsweek,* "Bluntly put, the Navy realized that Clancy was good for business." Some critics even credit the author with helping to banish the negative opinion of the military that arose after the United States's controversial involvement in the Vietnam War. As for criticism of his work, Clancy admitted in a *Washington Post* article: "I'm not that good a writer. I do a good action scene. I handle technology well. I like to think that I do a fair—fairer—job of representing the kind of people we have in the Navy . . . portraying them the way they really are. Beyond that, I'll try to . . . improve what needs improving." The secrets of his success as an entertainer, concluded Anderson, are "a genius for big, compelling plots, a passion for research, a natural narrative gift, a solid prose style, a hyperactive . . . imagination and a blissfully uncomplicated view of human nature and international affairs."

MEDIA ADAPTATIONS: The Hunt for Red October was adapted as a film for Paramount, directed by John McTiernan and starring Sean Connery and Alec Baldwin, 1990.

BIOGRAPHICAL/CRITICAL SOURCES:

BOOKS

Bestsellers 89, Issue 1, Gale, 1989.
Bestsellers 90, Issue 1, Gale, 1990.
Contemporary Literary Criticism, Volume 45, Gale, 1987.

PERIODICALS

Chicago Tribune Book World, September 7, 1986.
Detroit News, January 20, 1985.
Fortune, July 18, 1988.
Globe and Mail (Toronto), September 2, 1989.
Los Angeles Times, July 16, 1989.
Los Angeles Times Book Review, December 9, 1984, July 26, 1987.
Newsweek, August 17, 1987, August 8, 1988, August 21, 1989.
New York Times, July 17, 1986, August 12, 1986, February 25, 1990, March 1, 1990.
New York Times Book Review, July 27, 1986, August 2, 1987, July 31, 1988, August 13, 1989.
New York Times Magazine, May 1, 1988.
People, September 8, 1986, September 12, 1988.
Publishers Weekly, August 8, 1986, July 1, 1988.
Time, March 4, 1985, August 11, 1986, August 24, 1987, July 25, 1988, August 21, 1989, March 5, 1990, March 12, 1990.
Tribune Books, July 5, 1987.
Wall Street Journal, August 16, 1989.
Washington Post, January 29, 1985, March 17, 1989, March 2, 1990.
Washington Post Book World, October 21, 1984, July 27, 1986, May 14, 1989, August 13, 1989.
Writer's Digest, October, 1987.

*　　*　　*

CLANCY, Tom
   See CLANCY, Thomas L., Jr.

CLARK, Kenneth (Mackenzie) 1903-1983

PERSONAL: Born July 13, 1903, in London, England; died after a short illness, May 21, 1983, in Hythe, England; son of Kenneth Mackenzie (an industrial tycoon) and Margaret Alice (McArthur) Clark; married Elizabeth Martin, 1927 (died, 1976); married Nolwen de Janze-Rice, 1977; children: Alan, Rolin, Colette. *Education:* Trinity College, Oxford, received A.B., M.A., Ph.D.

CAREER: Worked with Bernard Berenson in England, Italy, and France, 1926-28; Ashmolean Museum, Oxford, England, keeper of department of fine art, 1931-33; National Gallery, London, England, director, 1934-45; surveyor of king's pictures, Hampton Court, Buckingham Palace, and Windsor Palace, England, 1934-44; U.K. Ministry of Information, controller of home publicity and director of films division, 1939-41; Oxford University, Oxford, Slade Professor of Fine Arts, 1946-50 and 1961-62; University of York, Heslington, York, England, chancellor, beginning in 1969. Chairman of Arts Council of Great Britain, 1953-60, and Independent Television Authority, 1954-57.

MEMBER: British Academy (fellow), Royal College of Art (fellow), National Art Collection Fund, Contemporary Art Society, Covent Garden Opera Trust, Victoria and Albert Museum (member of advisory council). Committee member of numerous organizations, including National Theatre Board, Conseil Artistique des Musees Nationaux, and Art Collection Fund. Honorary member of organizations, including Royal Scottish Academy, Swedish Academy, American Academy of Arts and Letters, Commendatore della Corona d'Italia, Commendatore al Ordine de Merito, Florentine Academy, American Institute of Architects, fellow of the Royal Institute of British Architects.

AWARDS, HONORS: Created Knight Commander of the Bath, 1938; knighted by Queen Elizabeth II, 1953; Serena Medal from British Academy for Italian Studies, 1955; Companion of Honor, 1959; fellow at University of Oxford, 1968; created Baron of Saltwood (life peerage), 1969; U.S. National Gallery of Art Award for distinguished services, 1970, for "Civilisation"; named Companion of Literature by Royal Society of Literature, 1974; Order of Merit, 1976; gold medal from New York University; commander of French Legion of Honor; Knight of the Lion of Finland. Honorary degrees from more than ten universities and colleges.

WRITINGS:

The Gothic Revival: An Essay in the History of Taste, Constable, 1929.
(With David Lindsay) *A Commemorative Catalogue of the Exhibition of Italian Art,* [London], 1931.
A Catalogue of the Drawings of Leonardo da Vinci in the Collection of His Majesty the King, at Windsor Castle, three volumes, Macmillan, 1935, 2nd edition, Phaidon Press, 1968-69.
Leonardo da Vinci: An Account of His Development as an Artist, Macmillan, 1939, 2nd edition, Cambridge University Press, 1952.
(Editor) *The Penguin Modern Painters,* Penguin, 1943.
Landscape into Art, John Murray, 1949, Penguin, 1956, revised and enlarged edition, Harper, 1979.
(Author of introduction) *Paintings of Graham Bell,* Lund Humphries, 1947.
Landscape Painting, Scribner, 1950.
Piero della Francesca, Phaidon Press, 1951.

Moments of Vision, Oxford University Press, 1954, variant edition, John Murray, 1975.
Selected Drawings from Windsor Castle: Leonardo da Vinci, three volumes, Phaidon Press, 1955.
The Nude: A Study in Ideal Form, Pantheon Books, 1956, Penguin, 1960.
Looking at Pictures, Holt, 1960.
(Author of introduction and notes) Walter H. Pater, *The Renaissance: Studies in Art and Poetry,* Collins, 1961.
Sidney Nolan, Thames & Hudson, 1961.
Provincialism, Oxford University Press, 1963.
(Author of introduction) Douglas Cooper, editor, *Great Private Collections,* Macmillan, 1963.
(Editor) *Ruskin Today* (anthology), John Murray, 1964.
Rembrandt and the Italian Renaissance, John Murray, 1966.
(Editor) R. M. Slyth, *Guides to the Published Work of Art Historians,* Bournemouth, 1968.
"Civilisation" (television series; also see below), British Broadcasting Corp. (BBC), 1969.
Civilisation: A Personal View, John Murray, 1969, Harper, 1970, 2nd edition, John Murray, 1971.
The Artist Grows Old, Cambridge University Press, 1972.
Studies in the History of the Renaissance, Fontana, 1973.
Blake and Visionary Art, University of Glasgow, 1973.
"Romantic versus Classic Art" (television series; also see below), BBC, 1973.
The Romantic Rebellion: Romantic versus Classic Art, John Murray, 1973.
Another Part of the Wood: A Self-Portrait, John Murray, 1974, Harper, 1975.
(Editor) *Henry Moore Drawings,* Thames & Hudson, 1974.
Concept of Universal Man, Ditchley Foundation, 1976.
The Drawings by Sandro Botticelli for Dante's "Divine Comedy": After the Originals in the Berlin Museums and the Vatican, Thames & Hudson, 1976.
Animals and Men: Their Relationship as Reflected in Western Art from Prehistory to the Present Day, Thames & Hudson, 1977.
The Other Half: A Self-Portrait, John Murray, 1977.
An Introduction to Rembrandt, John Murray, 1978.
The Best of Aubrey Beardsley, John Murray, 1979.
Happiness, University of Birmingham, 1979.
Feminine Beauty, Rizzoli, 1980.
(With David Finn) *The Florence Baptistry Doors,* Thames & Hudson, 1980.
What Is a Masterpiece?, Thames & Hudson, 1981.
Moments of Vision and Other Essays, Harper, 1982.

Also author of *A Failure of Nerve,* 1967.

SIDELIGHTS: Sir Kenneth Clark, English art authority and historian, has been called a "Renaissance grandee," the "picture of patrician grace," and the "quintessential English gentleman." Heir to a vast fortune amassed by his tycoon father, he described his parents as belonging "to a section of society known as the 'idle rich,' and although, in that golden age, many people were richer, there can be few who were idler. . . . They were two of the most irresponsible people I have ever known." His father, though he encouraged young Kenneth in his passion for art, spent his days with drink, and his mother, whose harsh indifference left him frequently in the care of servants who mistreated him, revealed to him early the cruel injustices of life. "Kenneth Clark was left in no doubt," stated John Russell, "that life has its vicissitudes. He developed two lines of defense: a lifelong passion for works of art and a highly developed sense for the ridiculous."

After completing his studies at Oxford University, Clark journeyed to Florence with renowned art authority Bernard Berenson to work on a revision of the latter's *Florentine Drawings.* Upon returning to England, Clark published his first book, *The Gothic Revival,* at the age of twenty-six. A year later he was named keeper of the fine art department of the Ashmolean Museum at Oxford, and by the time he reached thirty, he was appointed to the prestigious post of director of London's National Gallery, the youngest ever so honored.

The following years saw Clark's career moving rapidly in several different directions. So successful were his endeavors that he himself dubbed the years from 1932 to 1939 the "Clark Boom." But even in the midst of such meteoric rise, he never lost sight of his goal to bring art to the masses. With the advent of World War II, when all the art works of the National Gallery had to be moved to Wales for protection from German bombers, he brought back a different work each month and presented lunchtime concerts in the abandoned Gallery to lift the morale of his fellow countrymen and women.

One of Clark's major projects was the undertaking of a television series on art and culture for the British Broadcasting Corp. In discussing the enterprise with one of the directors, the word "civilisation" was mentioned. "I had no clear idea what he meant, but I thought it was preferable to barbarism and fancied that this was the moment to say so," recalled Clark in the foreword to *Civilisation.* He went on to express that he "would like to think that these programmes have done two things: they have made people feel that they are part of a great human achievement, and be proud of it; and they have made them feel humble in thinking of the great men and women of the past. Also, I like to think that they are entertaining." While the televised version of "Civilisation" was praised highly, the book version, for some, was disappointing. Oswell Blakeston felt that the "idea of presenting a selection of crucial civilising episodes from the Fall of the Roman Empire to the present day was a serious one—for TV; but when a book raises such profound issues as the nature of civilisation, it needs backbone, an all-over philosophy which is fully reasoned and unclouded. . . . I'm not impressed with the book as book, which is another way of saying that I'm not impressed with the trivialisation of the TV medium."

While there are critics who have condemned Clark as a fraud who attempts to be an expert on everything from Gothic architecture to Renaissance music to classical painting, Clark himself protested: "I've never tried to be an expert on all of those things. If you like to say I'm a popularizer, I have no objection. My main aim has been to make things understandable to people." Regarding the success of Clark's intention, Nigel Nicolson declared, "He is our greatest communicator, a scholar with the boldness to believe that whatever is intelligible to him can be made intelligible to people with little learning, a popularizer who never surrendered his integrity, who talked up, never down, who has a historical perspective in both directions, who has provided three generations with a set of scales on which to weigh the past and present achievement, never pontifical, always lucid, always enthusiastic, believing that people, anybody, can be brought to care for what he most cares for himself."

The Romantic Rebellion was another book derived from a televised series, though not so well received as was "Civilisation." "On the whole," claimed Ruth Berenson, "it offers the neophyte a well written, if incomplete, introduction to some of the great artists of the late eighteenth and nineteenth centuries. For readers with more than a passing acquaintance with the subject, however, Lord Clark hasn't much new to say—though he does say

it very well indeed." Comprised of essays on thirteen artists of the classic and romantic periods, Clark presented *The Romantic Rebellion* as a broad survey of the age. " 'The Romantic Rebellion,' " assessed Peter Conrad, "is remarkable in dealing not only in great confident arcs of generalisation about cultural history but in those small, unique apprehensions of detail which are Kenneth Clark's signature."

In *Animals and Men,* Clark took the reader on a "delightful romp" through the animal kingdom as depicted by the Lascaux cave drawings of pre-literate man and into the abstract world of Pablo Picasso. The book was written at the urgings of Fleur Cowles, the international trustee of the World Wildlife Fund (which, incidentally, receives a percentage of the royalties). Howard Fox related that Clark "pursues his thesis that a dual relationship of love and worship, enmity and fear, has persisted between men and animals since prehistory." Jan Morris, however, suggested that it is an "irony that a book professing to examine the immemorial relationship between man and beast should disregard the very territories where they have come closest to understanding one another." Fox disagreed, stating that "it is very much to Clark's credit that in his brevity he piques the reader's curiosity rather than lays it to rest. For lovers of animals and art, the book is a delight; for those who like one but not the other, the book could provide just enough substance for a second look."

Clark's two autobiographies, *Another Part of the Wood* and *The Other Half,* have received contrasting reviews. The latter, for example, has been deemed by Christopher Booker "one of the most unconsciously self-revealing books ever written," but was also referred to by Rene Kuhn Bryant as one that details a life "without revealing more than the merest minimum of the man who has written it." Clark's style of writing is another aspect that invites opposing opinions. Robert Melville flatly stated that part of the fascination is "his attempt to find a style in which to present himself to the general reader as an ordinary chap who happens to be a wealthy aesthete, and one of the most sensitive and stylish writers we have ever had. He makes a glorious hash of it. His false modesty is excruciating." On the other hand, Bryant asserted that "Clark marries substance with style, links wit to criticism, and demonstrates yet again his extraordinary ability to convey complex conceptions to a diverse and random audience with clarity and concision."

Another Part of the Wood, which recalls Clark's life until his late thirties, confirms that he was "brought face to face at a very early age with the fragility and instability of our human lot," observed John Russell. Though he was the product of a wealthy family and had tremendous success in his career, Clark himself conceded that he learned from playwright Henrik Ibsen "how full of cruel surprises life can be, how mixed are all motives, how under each layer of deception lies a still deeper layer of self-deception." He saw his life as one long string of good luck and felt somewhat awed by it all: "How my small talents came to arouse this kind of mass hysteria I shall never understand." In fact, he admitted to being almost bullied by his own phenomenal rise and reputation as the foremost authority on art and culture, and revealed that he was afflicted by "that subtle corruption that attacks almost everyone when he can no longer be contradicted or prevented from doing things, and when everyone except a few old friends kow-tows him."

BIOGRAPHICAL/CRITICAL SOURCES:

BOOKS

Clark, Kenneth, *Civilisation,* John Murray, 1969, Harper, 1970, 2nd edition, John Murray, 1971.
Clark, Kenneth, *Another Part of the Wood: A Self-Portrait,* John Murray, 1974, Harper, 1975.
Clark, Kenneth, *The Other Half: A Self-Portrait,* John Murray, 1977.

PERIODICALS

Books and Bookmen, September, 1971.
Chicago Tribune Book World, December 7, 1980.
Los Angeles Times Book Review, June 27, 1982.
National Review, April 26, 1974.
New Statesman, November 30, 1973, October 11, 1974.
New York Times, September 17, 1976, May 29, 1978, April 14, 1982.
New York Times Book Review, March 30, 1975, July 2, 1978, November 29, 1980.
Saturday Review, August 28, 1971.
Spectator, November 12, 1977.
Times Literary Supplement, November 14, 1980.
Washington Post, May 17, 1978.
Washington Post Book World, November 13, 1977, May 11, 1980, November 30, 1980.

OBITUARIES:

PERIODICALS

Chicago Tribune, May 23, 1983.
Los Angeles Times, May 22, 1983.
Newsweek, May 30, 1983.
New York Times, May 22, 1983.
Publishers Weekly, June 3, 1983.
Time, June 6, 1983.
Times (London), May 23, 1983.

*   *   *

CLARK, Mary Higgins 1929-

PERSONAL: Born December 24, 1929, in New York, N.Y.; daughter of Luke Joseph (a restaurant owner) and Nora C. (a buyer; maiden name, Durkin) Higgins; married Warren F. Clark (an airline executive), December 26, 1949 (died September 26, 1964); married Raymond Charles Ploetz (an attorney), August 8, 1978 (marriage annulled); children: Marilyn, Warren, David, Carol, Patricia. *Education:* Attended Villa Maria Academy, Ward Secretarial School, and New York University; Fordham University, B.A. (summa cum laude), 1979. *Politics:* Republican. *Religion:* Roman Catholic.

ADDRESSES: Home—2508 Cleveland Ave., Washington Township, N.J. 07675; and 200 Central Park S., New York, N.Y. 10019. *Agent*—Eugene H. Winick, McIntosh & Otis, Inc., 475 Fifth Ave., New York, N.Y. 10017.

CAREER: Writer. Remington Rand, New York City, advertising assistant, 1946; stewardess for Pan American Airlines, 1949-50; radio scriptwriter and producer for Robert G. Jennings, 1965-70; Aerial Communications, New York City, vice-president, partner, creative director, and producer of radio programming, 1970-80; David J. Clark Enterprises, New York City, chairman of the board and creative director, 1980—. Chairman, International Crime Writers Congress, 1988.

MEMBER: Mystery Writers of America (president, 1987; member of board of directors), Authors Guild, Authors League of America, American Academy of Arts and Sciences, American Society of Journalists and Authors, American Irish Historical Society (member of executive council).

AWARDS, HONORS: New Jersey Author Award, 1969, for *Aspire to the Heavens,* 1977, for *Where Are the Children?,* and 1978, for *A Stranger Is Watching;* Grand Prix de Litterature Policiere (France), 1980; honorary doctorate, Villanova University, 1983.

WRITINGS:

Aspire to the Heavens: A Biography of George Washington, Meredith Press, 1969.
Where Are the Children?, Simon & Schuster, 1975.
A Stranger Is Watching, Simon & Schuster, 1978.
(Contributor) *I, Witness,* Times Books, 1978.
The Cradle Will Fall (Literary Guild selection), Simon & Schuster, 1980.
A Cry in the Night, Simon & Schuster, 1982.
Stillwatch, Simon & Schuster, 1984.
(With Thomas Chastain and others) *Murder in Manhattan,* Morrow, 1986.
Weep No More, My Lady, Simon & Schuster, 1987.
(Editor) *Murder on the Aisle: The 1987 Mystery Writers of America Anthology,* Simon & Schuster, 1987.
While My Pretty One Sleeps, Simon & Schuster, 1989.
The Anastasia Syndrome and Other Stories, Simon & Schuster, 1989.

Work anthologized in *The Best "Saturday Evening Post" Stories,* 1962. Also author of syndicated radio dramas. Contributor of stories to periodicals, including *Saturday Evening Post, Redbook, McCall's,* and *Family Circle.*

WORK IN PROGRESS: Loves Music, Loves to Dance, a mystery for Simon & Schuster.

SIDELIGHTS: When Mary Higgins Clark was widowed after fifteen years of marriage, she was suddenly faced with supporting her five children alone. Writing had long been a hobby, so she went to work creating short stories for women's magazines and scripts for radio programs. "Each [script] was four minutes long," she told Herbert Mitgang in the *New York Times Book Review.* "In that time you had to tell a story and leave room for two messages from the sponsor. It taught me to write tightly." Clark's writing skill gradually developed into a masterly method of storytelling, and her stories involving terror found in the lives of ordinary people have become best-sellers and earned millions of dollars—in 1989, the author signed a contract with Simon & Schuster for $11.4 million, the largest ever between a writer and publisher.

Clark showed she could sustain her writing beyond the length of short stories and radio scripts with *Aspire to the Heavens,* a biography of George Washington. But with a printing of only 1700 copies, her first book was not a commercial success. "The bookstores thought it was a prayer book and put it in the religion section," she told Jean M. White in the *Washington Post.* Clark now terms this work a "collector's item."

Success came with her first novel, *Where Are the Children?*—a best-seller in 1975, earning over one hundred thousand dollars in paperback royalties. She followed that with another thriller called *A Stranger Is Watching,* which earned more than one million dollars in paperback rights and was filmed by Metro-Goldwyn-Mayer in 1982. For Clark, this meant financial security. "The [money] changed my life in the nicest way," she told Bina Bernard in *People.* "It took all the choking sensation out of paying for the kids' schools."

Clark has been equally successful with her more recent suspense novels—*The Cradle Will Fall, A Cry in the Night, Stillwatch, Weep No More, My Lady,* and *While My Pretty One Sleeps*—partly because of hard work and perseverance. She is a dedicated worker who gets up at 5 a.m. several times a week to write once she becomes involved in a book. "You don't put off writing," she explains to White. "I wrote one short story that sold to *Redbook* while waiting in the dentist's office for the orthodontist to do one of my children's teeth."

But the key to Clark's popularity, according to several critics, is her technique. White maintains that Clark "is a master storyteller who builds her taut suspense in a limited time frame," noting that *Where Are the Children?* takes place in one day and *A Stranger Is Watching* in three. Carolyn Banks, moreover, points out in the *Washington Post* that there is a kind of "Mary Higgins Clark formula" that readers both expect and enjoy: "There are no ambiguities in any Clark book. We know whom and what to root for, and we do. Similarly, we boo and hiss or gasp when the author wants us to. Clark is a master manipulator."

Clark's style is to write about "terror lurking beneath the surface of everyday life," observes White. "[She] writes about ordinary people suddenly caught up in frightening situations as they ride a bus or vacuum the living room." Clark explains in the *Washington Post:* "I write for the mainstream. I write about nice people not looking for trouble. They find evil in their own car, home, everyday life." In her more recent works, however, Clark "specializes in murderous tales played out against glamorous backgrounds and featuring what you would have to call the world of elegant women," Louise Bernikow states in *Cosmopolitan. Weep No More My Lady,* for example, is set at a posh California spa, and *While My Pretty One Sleeps* deals with the world of Manhattan high fashion.

Although Clark wants to provide her readers with entertainment and romance, she told *CA:* "I feel a good suspense novel can and should hold a mirror up to society and make a social comment." Clark also told Bernard: "I would like to get across a sense of values. I like nice, strong, people confronting the forces of evil and vanquishing them."

MEDIA ADAPTATIONS: A Stranger Is Watching was filmed by Metro-Goldwyn-Mayer in 1982; *The Cradle Will Fall* was shown on CBS as a "Movie of the Week" in 1984; *A Cry in the Night* was filmed by Rosten productions in 1985; *Where Are the Children?* was filmed by Columbia in 1986; *Stillwatch* was broadcast on CBS in 1987; Ellipse, a French production company, is producing *Weep No More My Lady, A Cry in the Night* (which will star Clark's daughter Carol) and two stories from *The Anastasia Syndrome.*

AVOCATIONAL INTERESTS: Traveling, skiing, tennis, playing piano.

BIOGRAPHICAL/CRITICAL SOURCES:

BOOKS

Bestsellers 89, Issue 4, Gale, 1989.

PERIODICALS

Best Sellers, December, 1984.
Chicago Tribune, September 20, 1987, July 31, 1989.
Chicago Tribune Book World, June 8, 1980.
Cosmopolitan, May, 1989.
Newsweek, June 30, 1980.
New Yorker, August 4, 1980.
New York Times, January 22, 1982, December 6, 1989.

New York Times Book Review, May 14, 1978, November 14, 1982.
People, March 6, 1978.
Publishers Weekly, May 19, 1989.
Washington Post, May 19, 1980, July 17, 1980, October 18, 1982, August 10, 1987.

* * *

CLARKE, Arthur C(harles) 1917-
(E. G. O'Brien, Charles Willis)

PERSONAL: Born December 16, 1917, in Minehead, Somersetshire, England; son of Charles Wright (a farmer) and Nora (Willis) Clarke; married Marilyn Mayfield, 1953 (divorced, 1964). *Education:* King's College, University of London, B.Sc. (first class honors), 1948.

ADDRESSES: Home—25, Barnes Pl., Colombo 7, Sri Lanka. *Agent*—Scott Meredith Literary Agency, Inc., 845 Third Ave., New York, N.Y. 10022; and David Higham Associates, 5-8 Lower John St., Golden Square, London W1R 4HA, England.

CAREER: British Civil Service, His Majesty's Exchequer and Audit Department, London, England, auditor, 1936-41; Institution of Electrical Engineers, *Science Abstracts,* London, assistant editor, 1949-50; free-lance writer, 1951—. Underwater explorer and photographer, in partnership with Mike Wilson, on Great Barrier Reef of Australia and coast of Sri Lanka, 1954-64. Has appeared on television and radio numerous times, including as commentator with Walter Cronkite on Apollo missions, CBS-TV, 1968-70, and as host of television series "Arthur C. Clarke's Mysterious World," 1980, and "Arthur C. Clarke's World of Strange Powers," 1984. Acted role of Leonard Woolf in Lester James Peries's film "Beddagama" (based on Woolf's *The Village in the Jungle*), 1979.

Director of Rocket Publishing Co., United Kingdom, and Underwater Safaris, Sri Lanka; founder and patron, Arthur C. Clarke Centre for Modern Technologies, Sri Lanka, 1984—. Chancellor of University of Moratuwa, Sri Lanka, 1979—; Vikram Sarabhai Professor, Physical Research Laboratory, Ahmedabad, India, 1980; trustee, Institute of Integral Education, Sri Lanka. Fellow, Franklin Institute, 1971, King's College, 1977, Institute of Robotics, Carnegie-Mellon University, 1981. Lecturer, touring United States and Britain, 1957-74. Board member of National Space Institute, United States, Space Generation Foundation, United States, International Astronomical Union (Search for ExtraTerrestrial Intelligence) Commission 51, International Space University, Institute of Fundamental Studies, Sri Lanka, and Planetary Society, United States. Chairman, Second International Astronautics Congress, London, 1951; moderator, "Space Flight Report to the Nation," New York, 1961. *Military Service:* Royal Air Force, radar instructor, 1941-46; became flight lieutenant.

MEMBER: International Academy of Astronautics (honorary fellow), International Science Writers Association, International Council for Integrative Studies, World Academy of Art and Science (academician), British Interplanetary Society (honorary fellow; chairman, 1946-47, 1950-53), Royal Astronomical Society (fellow), British Astronomical Association, Association of British Science Writers (life member), British Science Fiction Association (patron), Royal Society of Arts (fellow), Society of Authors (council member), American Institute of Aeronautics and Astronautics (honorary fellow), American Astronautical Society (honorary fellow), American Association for the Advancement of Science, National Academy of Engineering (United States; foreign associate), Science Fiction Writers of America, Science Fiction Foundation, H. G. Wells Society (honorary vice president), Third World Academy of Sciences (associate fellow), Sri Lanka Astronomical Society (patron), Institute of Engineers (Sri Lanka; honorary fellow), Sri Lanka Animal Welfare Association (patron), British Sub-Aqua Club.

AWARDS, HONORS: International Fantasy Award, 1952, for *The Exploration of Space;* Hugo Award, World Science Fiction Convention, 1956, for "The Star"; Kalinga Prize, UNESCO, 1961, for science writing; Junior Book Award, Boy's Club of America, 1961; Stuart Ballantine Gold Medal, Franklin Institute, 1963, for originating concept of communications satellites; Robert Ball Award, Aviation-Space Writers Association, 1965, for best aerospace reporting of the year in any medium; Westinghouse Science Writing Award, American Association for the Advancement of Science, 1969; Second International Film Festival special award, and Academy Award nomination for best screenplay with Stanley Kubrick, Academy of Motion Picture Arts and Sciences, both 1969, both for "2001: A Space Odyssey"; *Playboy* editorial award, 1971, 1982; D.Sc., Beaver College, 1971, and University of Moratuwa, 1979; Nebula Award, Science Fiction Writers of America, 1972, for "A Meeting with Medusa"; Nebula Award, 1973, Hugo Award, 1974, John W. Campbell Memorial Award, Science Fiction Research Association, 1974, and Jupiter Award, Instructors of Science Fiction in Higher Education, 1974, all for *Rendezvous with Rama;* Aerospace Communications Award, American Institute of Aeronautics and Astronautics, 1974; Bradford Washburn Award, Boston Museum of Science, 1977, for "contributions to the public understanding of science"; GALAXY Award, 1979; Nebula and Hugo Awards, both 1980, both for *The Fountains of Paradise;* special Emmy Award for engineering, National Academy of Television Arts and Sciences, 1981, for contributions to satellite broadcasting; "Lensman" Award, 1982; Marconi International Fellowship, 1982; Centennial Medal, Institute of Electrical and Electronics Engineers, 1984; E. M. Emme Astronautical Literature Award, American Astronautical Society, 1984; Grand Master Award, Science Fiction Writers of America, 1986; Vidya Jyothi Medal (Presidential Science Award), 1986; Charles A. Lindbergh Award, 1987; named to Society of Satellite Professionals Hall of Fame, 1987; named to Aerospace Hall of Fame, 1988; D.Litt., University of Bath, 1988.

WRITINGS:

NONFICTION

Interplanetary Flight: An Introduction to Astronautics, Temple, 1950, Harper, 1951, 2nd edition, 1960.
The Exploration of Space (U.S. Book-of-the-Month Club selection), Harper, 1951, revised edition, Pocket Books, 1979.
The Young Traveller in Space, Phoenix, 1953, published as *Going into Space,* Harper, 1954, revised edition (with Robert Silverberg) published as *Into Space: A Young Person's Guide to Space,* Harper, 1971.
The Exploration of the Moon, Harper, 1954.
The Coast of Coral, Harper, 1956.
The Reefs of Taprobane: Underwater Adventures around Ceylon, Harper, 1957.
The Scottie Book of Space Travel, Transworld Publishers, 1957.
The Making of a Moon: The Story of the Earth Satellite Program, Harper, 1957, revised edition, 1958.
Voice across the Sea, Harper, 1958, revised edition, 1974.
(With Mike Wilson) *Boy beneath the Sea,* Harper, 1958.

The Challenge of the Spaceship: Previews of Tomorrow's World, Harper, 1959.
(With Wilson) *The First Five Fathoms: A Guide to Underwater Adventure,* Harper, 1960.
The Challenge of the Sea, Holt, 1960.
(With Wilson) *Indian Ocean Adventure,* Harper, 1961.
Profiles of the Future: An Inquiry into the Limits of the Possible, Harper, 1962, revised edition, Holt, 1984.
The Treasure of the Great Reef, Harper, 1964, new edition, Ballantine, 1974.
(With Wilson) *Indian Ocean Treasure,* Harper, 1964.
(With the editors of *Life*) *Man and Space,* Time-Life, 1964.
Voices from the Sky: Previews of the Coming Space Age, Harper, 1965.
(Editor) *The Coming of the Space Age: Famous Accounts of Man's Probing of the Universe,* Meredith, 1967.
The Promise of Space, Harper, 1968.
(With Neil Armstrong, Michael Collins, Edwin E. Aldrin, Jr., Gene Farmer, and Dora Jane Hamblin) *First on the Moon,* Little, Brown, 1970.
Report on Planet Three and Other Speculations, Harper, 1972.
(With Chesley Bonestell) *Beyond Jupiter,* Little, Brown, 1972.
(With others) *Mars and the Mind of Man,* Harper, 1973.
The View from Serendip (autobiography), Random House, 1977.
"Arthur C. Clarke's Mysterious World" (also see below; television series), Yorkshire Television, 1980.
(With Simon Welfare and John Fairley) *Arthur C. Clarke's Mysterious World* (based on the television series), A & W Publishers, 1980.
Ascent to Orbit, a Scientific Autobiography: The Technical Writings of Arthur C. Clarke, Wiley, 1984.
1984: Spring—A Choice of Futures, Del Rey, 1984.
(With Welfare and Fairley) *Arthur C. Clarke's World of Strange Powers* (also see below; based on the television series of same title), Putnam, 1984.
(With Peter Hyams) *The Odyssey File,* Fawcett, 1985.
Arthur C. Clarke's July 20, 2019: Life in the 21st Century, Macmillan, 1986.
Arthur C. Clarke's Chronicles of the Strange and Mysterious, edited by Welfare and Fairley, Collins, 1987.
Astounding Days: A Science Fictional Autobiography, Bantam, 1989.

FICTION

The Sands of Mars, Sidgwick & Jackson, 1951, Gnome Press, 1952.
Prelude to Space, World Editions, 1951, published as *Master of Space,* Lancer Books, 1961, published as *The Space Dreamers,* 1969.
Islands in the Sky, Winston, 1952, new edition, Penguin Books, 1972.
Childhood's End, Ballantine, 1953.
Against the Fall of Night (also see below), Gnome Press, 1953.
Expedition to Earth (short stories), Ballantine, 1953.
Earthlight, Ballantine, 1955.
Reach for Tomorrow (short stories), Ballantine, 1956.
The City and the Stars (based on novel *Against the Fall of Night*), Harcourt, 1956.
The Deep Range, Harcourt, 1957.
Tales from the White Hart, Ballantine, 1957.
The Other Side of the Sky (short stories), Harcourt, 1958.
Across the Sea of Stars (anthology), Harcourt, 1959.
A Fall of Moondust, Harcourt, 1961, abridged edition, University of London Press, 1964.
From the Oceans, from the Stars (anthology), Harcourt, 1962.

Tales of Ten Worlds (short stories), Harcourt, 1962.

Dolphin Island: A Story of the People of the Sea, Holt, 1963.

Glide Path, Harcourt, 1963.

Prelude to Mars (anthology), Harcourt, 1965.

An Arthur C. Clarke Omnibus (three novels), Sidgwick & Jackson, 1965.

(Editor) *Time Probe: The Science in Science Fiction,* Dial, 1966.

The Nine Billion Names of God (short stories), Harcourt, 1967.

A Second Arthur C. Clarke Omnibus (three novels), Sidgwick & Jackson, 1968.

(With Stanley Kubrick) "2001: A Space Odyssey" (screenplay; also see below), Metro-Goldwyn-Mayer, 1968.

2001: A Space Odyssey (based on the screenplay), New American Library, 1968, published with new afterward, 1982.

The Lion of Comarre; and, Against the Fall of Night, Harcourt, 1968.

The Lost Worlds of 2001, New American Library, 1972.

The Wind from the Sun (short stories), Harcourt, 1972.

(Editor) *Three for Tomorrow,* Sphere Books, 1972.

Of Time and Stars: The Worlds of Arthur C. Clarke (short stories), Gollancz, 1972.

Rendezvous with Rama, Harcourt, 1973, adapted edition, Oxford University Press, 1979.

The Best of Arthur C. Clarke, edited by Angus Wells, Sidgwick & Jackson, 1973, published as two volumes, Volume 1: *1937-1955,* Volume 2: *1956-1972,* 1977.

Imperial Earth: A Fantasy of Love and Discord, Gollancz, 1975, Harcourt, 1976.

Four Great Science Fiction Novels, Gollancz, 1978.

The Fountains of Paradise, Harcourt, 1979.

(Editor with George Proctor) *The Science Fiction Hall of Fame,* Volume 3: *The Nebula Winners,* Avon, 1982.

2010: Odyssey Two, Del Rey, 1982.

The Sentinel: Masterworks of Science Fiction and Fantasy (short stories), Berkley Publishing, 1983.

Selected Works, Heinemann, 1985.

The Songs of Distant Earth, Del Rey, 1986.

2061: Odyssey Three, Del Rey, 1988.

(With Gentry Lee) *Cradle,* Warner Books, 1988.

A Meeting with Medusa (bound with *Green Mars* by Kim Stanley Robinson), Tor Books, 1988.

(With Lee) *Rama II,* Bantam, 1989.

The Ghost from Grand Banks, Bantam, 1990.

OTHER

Opus 700, Gollancz, 1990.

Also author of television series "Arthur C. Clarke's World of Strange Powers" and a movie treatment based on *Cradle.* Author of afterwords for "Arthur C. Clarke's Venus Prime Series." Clarke has made several sound recordings of his works for Caedmon. Contributor of over six hundred articles and short stories, occasionally under pseudonyms E. G. O'Brien and Charles Willis, to numerous magazines, including *Harper's, Playboy, New York Times Magazine, Vogue, Holiday,* and *Horizon.*

Clarke's works have been translated into Polish, Russian, French, German, Spanish, Serbo-Croatian, Greek, Hebrew, Dutch, and over twenty other languages.

WORK IN PROGRESS: Afterwords for "Arthur C. Clarke's Venus Prime Series," Volumes 3-6; *Rama III* and *Rama IV,* with Gentry Lee, for Bantam; *Tales from Planet Earth; Arthur C. Clarke's Century of Mysteries,* with John Fairley and Simon Welfare, for Collins; editing *Project Solar Sail* for the World Space Foundation; consulting on television scripts for a series adaptation of *A Fall of Moondust.*

SIDELIGHTS: Renowned not only for his science fiction, which has earned him the title of Grand Master from the Science Fiction Writers of America, Arthur C. Clarke also has a reputation for first-rate scientific and technical writing. Perhaps best known in this field for "Extraterrestrial Relays," the 1945 article in which he first proposed the idea of communications satellites, Clarke has also published works on such diverse topics as underwater diving, space exploration, and scientific extrapolation. Nevertheless, it is Clarke's science fiction which has secured him his reputation, with such novels as *Childhood's End* and *Rendezvous with Rama* acknowledged as classics in their field. In addition, his story "The Nine Billion Names of God" was named to the science fiction "Hall of Fame," while the movie "2001: A Space Odyssey," written with director Stanley Kubrick, has been called the most important science fiction film ever made.

Often dealing with themes of exploration and discovery, Clarke's fiction almost always conveys to the reader a sense of wonder about the universe. Some critics, seeing the author's detailed descriptions of possible futures, have accused Clarke of ignoring the human element for the sake of science in his work. But while the development of scientific ideas and speculations plays a large role in Clarke's narratives, "what distinguishes Clarke's fictions from the usually more ephemeral examples of science fiction is his vision," asserts Eric S. Rabkin in his study *Arthur C. Clarke.* This vision, writes Rabkin, is "a humane and open and fundamentally optimistic view of humankind and its potential in a universe which dwarfs us in physical size but which we may hope some day to match in spirit."

Born in 1917 in an English seaside town, Clarke first discovered science fiction at the age of 12, when he encountered the pulp magazine *Amazing Stories.* The encounter soon became an "addiction," as Clarke describes in the *New York Times Book Review:* "During my lunch hour away from school I used to haunt the local Woolworths in search of my fix, which cost threepence a shot, roughly a quarter today." The young Clarke then began nurturing his love for the genre on the books of such English writers as H. G. Wells and Olaf Stapledon. He started writing his own stories for a school magazine while in his teens, but was unable to continue his schooling for lack of funds. He consequently secured a civil service job as an auditor, which left him plenty of free time to pursue his "hobby." Alone in London, Clarke joined an association of several science fiction and space enthusiasts, and as he relates in *The View from Serendip,* "my life was dominated by the infant British Interplanetary Society, of which I was treasurer and general propagandist." As part of his involvement with the BIS, Clarke wrote several scientific articles on the feasibility of space travel for the organization's journal; the BIS also gained him contacts with several science fiction editors and writers, which led to the publication of some of his short stories.

In 1941, although his auditor's position was still a reserved occupation, Clarke engaged in "what was probably the single most decisive act of my entire life," as he describes in *Ascent to Orbit: The Technical Writings of Arthur C. Clarke;* he voluntarily enlisted in the Royal Air Force. En route to becoming a radar instructor in a new system called Ground Controlled Approach, Clarke taught himself mathematical and electronics theory. After World War II ended, Clarke entered college and obtained a degree in physics as well as pure and applied mathematics; after graduation he spent two years as an assistant editor for a technical journal. But with publication of the novel *Childhood's End* (1953) and *The Exploration of Space,* which in 1952 was the first science book ever chosen as a Book-of-the-Month Club selection, Clarke began earning enough money to pursue writing full-time.

The Exploration of Space, besides allowing Clarke to leave his job, also broke ground in explaining scientific ideas to a popular audience. As H. H. Holmes describes in the *New York Herald Tribune Book Review,* in "the realm of speculative factual writing . . . Mr. Clarke's new book will serve as the most important yet in its field. Not that it says much that is new," explains Holmes, but because "it is precisely calculated to bring our present knowledge of space travel before a whole new public." What enables the book to reach such an audience is a "charm and magnetism" that is due to "Clarke's ability to reduce complex subjects to simple language and his steadfast avoidance of fantasy as a substitute for factual narration," observes Roy Gibbons in the *Chicago Sunday Tribune.* In contrast, F. L. Whipple writes in a 1952 *Saturday Review* article that the author's "imagination sometimes overwhelms his good resolve, causing him to stray from the narrow path of scientific probability." But Clarke himself "reminds us that in the history of scientific prediction, the wildest flights of fancy have fallen short of subsequent realities," observes Charles J. Rolo in the *Atlantic.* While its overall result might seem fantastic, *The Exploration of Space* is "an exceptionally lucid job of scientific exposition for the layman," concludes Rolo.

Clarke applied the same speculative techniques to other areas in the 1962 book *Profiles of the Future: An Inquiry into the Limits of the Possible.* The author "has a thorough grounding in science, and, in addition has a nimble and most receptive mind," states Isaac Asimov in the *New York Times Book Review.* "Nothing reasonable frightens him simply because it seems fantastic, and equally important—nothing foolish attracts him simply because it seems fantastic." As his previous books have been, *Profiles of the Future* "is highly entertaining reading," remarks R. C. Cowen in the *Christian Science Monitor.* "It also is informative, for the author is careful to adhere to the yardstick of natural laws that set the bounds of the possible." The critic concludes that Clarke "thus helps a layman to learn the difference between rational speculation and . . . wholly baseless imaginings." Asimov concurs, writing that "this book offers all of us a chance to raise our eyes from the ground and to contemplate the scenery ahead. It is marvelous scenery indeed, and there could scarcely be a better guide to its landmarks than Arthur Clarke."

Although most speculative science texts are soon outdated, Clarke's work has withstood years of technical progress. In *The Promise of Space,* published in 1968 to "replace" *The Exploration of Space,* Clarke "is able to show the manner in which many of his predictions have been fulfilled," notes a *Times Literary Supplement* contributor. But rather than simply cataloging recent discoveries, Clarke's work incorporates them into new ideas: "All through the book Clarke not only recounts what has been done during the last two decades," describes Willy Ley in the *New York Times Book Review,* "but has his eye on both the immediate results and the future." Similarly, *Science* contributor Eugene M. Emme asserts that the book contains "the best available summary of scientific and imaginative theory regarding space potentials. . . . Collectively they offer a most persuasive rationale." A 1984 revision of *Profiles of the Future* also withstands years of advancement: "Testing the limits of technological progress," observes David N. Samuelson in the *Los Angeles Times Book Review,* "it has remained remarkably current since its 1962 book publication." Gregory Benford, who calls Clarke "a vindicated sage in his own time," theorizes in the *Washington Post Book World* that while "books on futurology date notoriously, this one has not, principally because Clarke was unafraid of being adventurous." And *New York Times Book Review* writer

Gerald Jonas offers this reason for Clarke's success: "What makes Clarke such an effective popularizer of science is that, without bobbling a decimal point or fudging a complex concept, he gives voice to the romantic side of scientific inquiry."

Although much of Clarke's early fiction reinforced the idea that space travel was an eventuality, *Childhood's End,* his first successful novel, is "Clarke's only work—fiction or nonfiction—in which 'The stars are not for Man,' " suggests Thomas D. Clareson in *Voices for the Future.* The novel relates the appearance of the Overlords, a race of devil-shaped aliens who have come to guide Earth to peace and prosperity. Beginning by eliminating all individual governments and thus ending war, the Overlords use their superior technology to solve the problems of poverty, hunger, and oppression. The cost of this utopia is that most scientific research is set aside as unnecessary, and the exploration of space is forbidden. The motives of the Overlords become clear as the youngest generation of humans develops extrasensory powers; the children of Earth are to join the Overmind, a collective galactic "spirit" that transcends physical form. The need for science, technology, and space is eliminated with humanity's maturation, and the Earth itself is destroyed as her children join the Overmind.

Some critics view *Childhood's End* as the first manifestation of the theme of spiritual evolution that appears throughout Clarke's fiction. John Huntington, writing in the critical anthology *Arthur C. Clarke,* believes the novel to be Clarke's solution to one of the problems posed by technological progress: how can spiritual development keep pace with scientific development when by making man comfortable, science often takes away man's curiosity and drive. *Childhood's End* solves the problem with a stage of "transcendent evolution," and Huntington proposes that "it is its elegant solution to the problem of progress that has rightly earned *Childhood's End* that 'classic' status it now enjoys." Donald A. Wollheim, however, considers this solution a negative one; writing in *The Universe Makers* he comments that the work "has always seemed to me to be a novel of despair. Others may see it as offering hope, but this tampering with humanity always struck me as being synthetic." But other critics reaffirm the novel as hopeful: *Childhood's End* "becomes a magnificently desperate attempt to continue to hope for a future for the race in the face of mounting evidence to the contrary," writes John Hollow in *Against the Night, the Stars: The Science Fiction of Arthur C. Clarke.* Written in 1953 in the midst of the Cold War, "it becomes, in fact, a sometimes brilliant attempt to turn the contrary evidence to the positive," adds Hollow. "It becomes nothing less than an effort to make positive the destruction of the race."

For all its uplifting themes, some critics still fault the novel as imperfect. David N. Samuelson, for example, notes in the anthology *Arthur C. Clarke* that "the literate reader, especially, may be put off by an imbalance between abstract theme and concrete illustration, by a persistent banality of style, in short, by what may seem a curious inattention to the means by which the author communicates his vision." Holmes, reviewing Clarke's book in the *New York Herald Tribune,* calls *Childhood's End* "at once his least successful and most promising [work]." The critic elaborates by remarking that the basic ideas are "fascinating, but the awkward imbalance between the vast major plot and a series of small-scale subplots makes for a diffuse and distracting novel." Nevertheless, the novel "has a way of lingering in the imagination that suggests it may in time, and defiance of all criticism, find a place in the supreme pantheon of [science fiction] beside such works as [Mary Shelley's] *Frankenstein* and [H. G. Wells's] *The Time Machine,* " observes Thomas M. Disch in the *Times*

Literary Supplement. And *Science Fiction Review* writer Gene DeWeese declares, thirty years after its publication, that *Childhood's End* "in my opinion [is] the best SF novel ever written."

Perhaps Clarke's best known work, *2001: A Space Odyssey* was the result of four years work on both the film version and the subsequent novel. The collaboration between Clarke and director Stanley Kubrick began when the filmmaker sought a suitable basis for making the "proverbial good science fiction movie," as he has frequently described it. The two finally settled upon Clarke's 1951 short story "The Sentinel," and developed it "not [into] a script, which in [Kubrick's] view does not contain enough of the visual and emotional information necessary for filming, but a prose version, rather like a novel," relates Michel Ciment in *Focus on the Science Fiction Film.* The result "was of more help to him in creating the right atmosphere because it was more generous in its descriptions," adds Ciment.

The film and the novel have the same basic premise: a large black monolith has been sent to Earth to encourage the development of Man. First shown assisting in the "dawn of man" four million years ago, a monolith is next uncovered on the moon, and upon its unveiling sends a strong radio signal toward the outer planets. As a result the spaceship *Discovery,* operated by the intelligent computer HAL 9000, is sent in the direction of the signal to investigate. However, while the human crew is kept ignorant of the ship's true assignment, the HAL 9000 begins to eliminate what it sees as obstacles in the way of the mission—including all of the crew. First captain Dave Bowman manages to survive, however, and upon his arrival at a moon of Saturn (Jupiter in the film) encounters yet a third monolith which precipitates a journey through the infinite, "into a world where time and space are relative in ways beyond Einstein," describes Penelope Gilliatt in the *New Yorker.* Bowman is transformed during this journey, and subsequently arrives at a higher plane of evolution as the Star Child. "In the final transfiguration," notes Tim Hunter in *Film Heritage,* "director Kubrick and co-author Arthur Clarke . . . suggest that evolutionary progress may in fact be cyclical, perhaps in the shape of a helix formation." The critic explains: "Man progresses to a certain point in evolution, then begins again from scratch on a higher level."

Because of the film's complexity and length, of which less than one-third was dedicated to dialogue, the early reviews of "2001" were mixed. Although "2001" was a landmark in the use of special visual effects, many critics found that the abundance of detail overwhelms the plot and character. "Very quickly we see that the gadgets are there for themselves, not for use in an artwork," comments the *New Republic*'s Stanley Kauffmann. By de-emphasizing the human aspects, says Kauffmann, the result is "a film that is so dull, it even dulls our interest in the technical ingenuity for the sake of which Kubrick has allowed it to become dull." Similarly, Joseph Gelmis of *Newsday* states that "because its characters are standardized, bland, depersonalized near-automatons who have surrendered their humanity to the computers, the film is antidramatic and thus self-defeating. It moves at a slow, smug pace." But "after seeing *2001: A Space Odyssey* a second time," Gelmis asserts his conviction that "it is a masterwork. . . . This awesome film is light-years ahead of any science fiction you have ever seen." The critic explains that upon a second screening, he understands it is the "dullness" of the characters and conversation "that makes the symbolic rebirth of this automaton Everyman of the 21st century so profoundly stirring and such a joyous reaffirmation of life." Gilliatt concurs, contending that Clarke and Kubrick "have found a powerful idea to impel space conquerors whom puny times have robbed of much curiosity. The hunt for the remnant of a civilization . . .

turns the shots of emptied, comic, ludicrously dehumanized men into something more poignant." Later reviews of the film acknowledge its brilliance; a 1984 *New York Times* article by Vincent Canby calls it a "witty, mind-bending science fiction classic" that is "forever separate . . . from all [films] that came before and all that have come after."

"Clarke's *2001: A Space Odyssey* was an extraordinary development in fiction, a novel written in collaboration with the director who was simultaneously filming it," writes Colin Greenland of the *Times Literary Supplement.* Clarke himself explains in the epilogue to the 1982 edition of *2001* that during the project he "often had the strange experience of revising the manuscript *after* viewing rushes based upon an earlier version of the story—a stimulating but rather expensive way of writing a novel." Because the book appeared three months after the movie's premiere, it was inevitable that critics would draw comparisons between the two. *New Statesman* contributor Brenda Maddox finds the book lacking beside the movie; the novel "has all the faults of the film and none of its virtues." The critic elaborates: "The characters still have the subtlety of comic-strip men and, lacking the film's spectacular visual gimmickry . . . the story must propel itself with little gusts of scientific explanation." In contrast, Eliot Fremont-Smith asserts in the *New York Times* that "the immense and moving fantasy-idea of '2001' . . . is an idea that can be *dramatically* envisioned only in the free oscillations of the delicately cued and stretched mind." The critic adds that the film "is too direct for this, its wonders too unsubtle and, for all their majesty, too confining." And where the movie may have been obscure, "all of it becomes clear and convincing in the novel. It is indeed an odyssey, this story, this exhilarating and rather chilling science fiction fantasy." Nevertheless, in comparing the visual genius of the film with the clarity of the book, Clarke himself admits in *Focus on the Science Fiction Film* that both versions "did something that the other couldn't have done."

2001 has also been compared to Clarke's other work and has received similar criticisms, such as the accusation that the novel concentrates on science at the expense of story. A *Times Literary Supplement* reviewer, for example, comments that "too often the whole affair collapses into the science-popularization for which Mr. Clarke is well known." But Rabkin, while acknowledging the technical elements of the novel, believes that *2001* blends these elements into a "mature amalgamation" with Clarke's "spiritual commitment to a homocentric and optimistic vision. In many ways," concludes Rabkin, "the book may be his culminating artistic achievement." And *New Yorker* contributor Jeremy Bernstein similarly considers *2001* "one of [Clarke's] best, full of poetry, scientific imagination, and typical wry Clarke wit." Claiming that the author's work transcends the typical science fiction novel, the critic writes that "the Clarke genre is something else again. By standing the universe on its head, he makes us see the ordinary universe in a different light." Summarizing Clarke's work with *2001* in a 1983 article, Jonas declares that " '2001' is not just another science-fiction novel or movie. It is a science-fiction milestone—one of the best novels in the genre and undoubtedly the best s.f. movie ever made."

"Although it lacks some of the metaphysical fireworks and haunting visionary poetry of [his earlier work]," Clarke's *Rendezvous with Rama* is nevertheless "essentially an expression of wonder in the presence of Mystery," comments a *Virginia Quarterly Review* contributor. Written in 1973, the novel is the only work to win all four major awards of its genre; Disch calls it "probably [Clarke's] most considerable work of art." The book follows the appearance of an asteroid-like object which is hurtling directly towards the inner solar system—and which turns out to be a cylindrical, obviously unnatural artifact. An Earth ship is dispatched to the object, labeled "Rama," and a team led by commander Bill Norton enters to investigate. The exploration of the many mysterious aspects of Rama is interrupted by several distractions—including the emergence of what appears to be generated life forms and the arrival of a nuclear warhead sent by paranoid colonists from nearby Mercury. The study of Rama is concluded safely, however, although Norton's team has not gathered enough information to discern a purpose to the craft. Seemingly indifferent to a meeting with intelligent life, Rama then exits the solar system and continues its journey. "This is story-telling of the highest order," notes Theodore Sturgeon in the *New York Times Book Review.* "There are perpetual surprise, constant evocation of the sense of wonder, and occasions of the most breathless suspense."

Because the emphasis of the novel is on the exploration of Rama, "Mr. Clarke, according to his custom, is benignly indifferent to the niceties of characterization," writes *New York Times* contributor John Leonard. Melody Hardy similarly observes in *Best Sellers* that the book "is almost totally devoid of human interest," although she does admit that "it does possess the enticing characteristics of science fiction at its best." Sturgeon suggests, however, that this lack of characterization may be an asset, for "unbothered by human subtleties one may gaze cleareyed at the horizonless reach of the man's mind, its command of naked Euclidean spectacle." Hardy also grants that "perhaps Clarke's disinterest in characterization results from this view that the universe is indifferent to man." Rabkin calls the book's resolution, where man is ignored by an extra-solar intelligence, a "unique repudiation of his homocentrism," an idea common to science fiction that man is important or unique to the universe. "But having done that," continues Rabkin, Clarke creates "a novel not only of science but of a science dramatized, humanized. In the exploration of Rama, we readers feel the challenge of discovery and the exhilaration of using our minds, of encountering the new." Concludes the critic: "That is one reason why the book, although it defies homocentrism, seems to uplift us. . . . *Rendezvous with Rama* is Arthur C. Clarke's most mature exploration of his constant theme of the meaning for mankind of science." Clarke collaborated with Gentry Lee in *Rendezvous with Rama*'s sequel, *Rama II*—which describes the arrival of another spacecraft similar to the original Rama—and has plans for two more sequels in the future.

Although classic works such as *Childhood's End* and *Rendezvous with Rama* focus on the effects of extraterrestrial visitation, Clarke's next two works concentrate more on the achievements of humanity. *Imperial Earth: A Fantasy of Love and Discord,* which takes place in the quincentennial year of 2276, most directly "shows Clarke at the height of his [extrapolative] powers," remarks Jonas. The novel includes demonstrations of outer planet mining operations, cloning, and spaceship propulsion systems, all woven into the story of Titan native Duncan Makenzie's visit to Earth. Duncan's trip serves many purposes; ostensibly it is to deliver an address at the quincenntenial celebration, but it is also to investigate political and scientific intrigues, as well as to procure, through cloning, an heir for the sterile Duncan. Through Duncan's eyes "Clarke not only supplies us with a fair number of technological wonders," observes Mark Rose in the *New Republic,* but the author also "makes much of such human matters as the political and psychological isolation of a distant colonial world such as Titan." Nevertheless, "one problem with the full-blown novel of extrapolation is that the author may neglect plot and character," states Jonas. But while he notes

some of these faults, *National Review* contributor Steve Ownbey calls *Imperial Earth* "a book nobody should miss. It's an utterly delightful tale, suspenseful and moving, full of unexpected chuckles and stunning surprises." And Rose comments that the novel is "a literary performance conducted with genuine intelligence and grace."

Clarke's Hugo and Nebula-winning *The Fountains of Paradise* is even more technical in its basic premise: the construction of an orbital "space elevator" designed to make escaping the Earth's gravity a simple process. Based on actual scientific treatises, Clarke once again develops his idea "with sufficient technical detail to lend plausibility" says Jonas, "and the more plausible it sounds, the more stupendous it becomes." The novel also concerns Vannevar Morgan, the engineer obsessed with realizing the creation of his space elevator. Providing a "curious backdrop" to Morgan's enterprise is "a highly advanced galactic civilization [which] has already communicated with the human race through a robot probe," summarizes Jonas. In addition, Morgan's story is paralleled by the account of Prince Kalidasa, who two thousand years earlier challenged the gods by attempting to build a garden tower into heaven—on Taprobane, the same island that Morgan wants for his elevator. But while critics commend this parallel, they fault Clarke for not sustaining it: "the direct interweaving of Kalidasa's story should have extended throughout the entire work rather than petering out," comments Paul Granahan in *Best Sellers.* Similarly, *New Republic* contributor Tim Myers criticizes Clarke for ending the parallel: "The Indian king, the only character with nobility, is taken from us. We are left with Morgan, a pathetic egotist who is also hopelessly stereotyped."

In contrast to these criticisms, Algis Budrys praises the author for combining two themes that have marked Clarke's work: mysticism and technology. In the *Magazine of Fantasy and Science Fiction,* Budrys comments that *The Fountains of Paradise* "is the first instance in which all the author's demonstrated capabilities have melded. Not *perfectly,* mind you . . . but more than well enough to constitute a crucial event in Clarke's career, and thus in SF." And Steve Brown expresses the opinion in *Science Fiction Review* that "Clarke's prose hasn't been this good in years, effortless, stripped to the bone, and clear as mylar." Continues the critic: "The Tower is much more impressive than Rama, (or [Larry] Niven's Ringworld, for that matter) because it seems so *real,* something that could, and should, actually be done. . . . [Clarke's] total control of his material illuminates every corner of the landscape, in deft little brushstrokes." "As I read I kept pushing myself further and further back in my chair, squealing with vertigo," recounts *New Statesman* contributor Kingsley Amis. "This is not Arthur Clarke's best novel, . . . [but] it's delightfully written, always interesting, and at times almost unbearably exciting."

Although for several years Clarke (and others) insisted that a sequel to *2001* would be impossible, in 1982 Clarke published *2010: Odyssey Two.* Incorporating elements of both the film and novel versions, as well as new information from the Voyager probes of Jupiter, in *2010* "Clarke sensibly steps back down to our level to tell the story of a combined Russian and American expedition to salvage Bowman's deserted ship, the Discovery, and find out what happened," relates Greenland. Although the expedition finds the remains of the ship and repairs the HAL 9000, the purpose of the black monolith mystifies them. While some critics find this an adequate approach to a sequel, others criticize Clarke for even attempting to follow up a "classic." De-Weese believes a large problem is that *2010* "is not so much a sequel to the original book, which was in many ways superior to the movie, but a sequel to and an explanation of the movie. Unfortunately, many of these explanations already existed [in the novel of *2001*]." *Washington Post Book World* contributor Michael Bishop similarly notes a tendency to over-explain: "Ponderous expository dialogue alternates with straightforward expository passages in which [protagonist] Heywood Floyd . . . or the author himself lectures the reader." And Jonas complains that *2010* "violates the mystery [of the original] at every turn."

In addition, observers comment on a lack of emphasis on character; Jonas writes that Clarke "fails to make [the characters] any more interesting as people than they were the first time around." The emotional level seems to be overly subdued, remarks Greenland; Clarke "can't handle any of the real turbulence of human intercourse." But while noting similar flaws in the novel's characterization, Bishop admits that in *2010* "Clarke has striven heroically to outfit his characters with recognizable longings, prejudices, and fears." And Hollow believes that emotional detachment is an important theme of the novel, suggesting that in *2010* "the natural process of maturity—and perhaps of evolution—is away from such fatal attractions."

Despite the various criticisms, *2010* still "has its share of that same sense of wonder, which means that it is one of the dozen or so most enjoyable SF books of the year," says DeWeese. "Clarke deftly blends discovery, philosophy, and a newly acquired sense of play," states *Time* contributor Peter Stoler, creating a work that will "entertain" readers. Cary Neeper presents a similar assessment in the *Christian Science Monitor,* noting that "Clarke's story drives on to an exciting finish in which the mix of fantasy and fact leaves the reader well satisfied with a book masterfully written." And in contrast to the criticisms of the sequel's worthiness, Bud Foote claims in the *Detroit News* that with "the book's penultimate triumph [of] a new, awesome and terrifying world transformation," Clarke has created "a fine book." The critic concludes that *2010* "is better than the original book, and it illuminates and completes the original movie. It is so good, in fact, that even Clarke couldn't write a sequel to it."

Despite this assertion and Clarke's own remarks to the *Washington Post*'s Curt Suplee that "if I ever do write 'Odyssey III'—allowing for the fact that my energies are declining—it won't be before the year 2001," 1988 brought *2061: Odyssey Three,* the next chapter in the saga of the black monolith. 2061 is the year of the next appearance of Halley's comet; *Odyssey Three* follows Heywood Floyd on a survey of the object. While en route, the survey party is redirected to rescue a ship that has crashed on the Jovian moon of Europa—the one celestial object the monoliths have warned humans against visiting. Some critics have been skeptical of a second sequel, such as the *Time* reviewer who finds that "the mix of imagination and anachronism is wearing as thin as the oxygen layer on Mars." Although Jonas also observes that "Mr. Clarke's heart is obviously not in the obligatory action scenes that advance the plot," he concedes that the author "remains a master at describing the wonders of the universe in sentences that combine a respect for scientific accuracy with an often startling lyricism." Clarke "is not to be measured by the same standards we apply to a mundane plot-smith," asserts David Brin in the *Los Angeles Times.* "He is, after all, the poet laureate of the Space Age. He is at his best making the reader feel, along with Heywood Floyd," continues Brin, "how fine it might be to stand upon an ancient comet, out under the stars, knowing that it is those dreams that finally come true that are the best dreams of all." And a *Kirkus Reviews* writer claims that *2061* is "the all-round best *Odyssey* so far. Indeed Clarke, with an absorbing blend of scientific extrapolation and events that

generate their own tension, has returned to something like vintage form."

Between the publication of the two *Odyssey* sequels Clarke finished *The Songs of Distant Earth,* an elaborate revision and extension of a short story first published in 1958. The novel takes place on the ocean world of Thalassa, where the few habitable islands there have been populated by descendants of an Earth "seedship," sent to perpetuate humanity even after the nova explosion of the Earth's sun. The Thalassan society is a type of utopia, for superstition, prejudice, and extreme violence no longer exist; the robots who raised the first generations eliminated all religion and art which might encourage these elements. The Thalassans are seemingly content with their world when the starship *Magellan* lands, bringing with it the last survivors of (and witnesses to) the Earth's destruction. Although the ship is not permitted to colonize a world that has already been settled, the idyllic setting tempts the crew to a possible mutiny. Further complicating the situation is the emergence of a marine life form that appears to be intelligent, creating a possible conflict on two different fronts.

Although this dilemma "makes for an interesting novel," *Science Fiction Review* contributor Richard E. Geis still faults Clarke's plot as improbable, decrying the lack of individual conflict. Echoing previous criticisms, Geis comments that the "characters are uncomplicated, non-neurotic, with only minor problems to be solved. . . . Clarke has written a story of plausible high-tech future science and peopled it with implausible, idealized, 'nice' humans." In contrast, Dan K. Moran of the *West Coast Review of Books* believes that "how Clarke deals with the mutiny is interesting; and his characters come alive throughout." Nevertheless, the critic finds that "the great flaw is the lack of sense-of-wonder. Nothing herein is really new, neither science nor Clarke's synthesis," concludes Moran.

Countering the criticism that the novel lacks conflict, Jonas suggests that "the drama that interests Mr. Clarke is played out on a much larger canvas. It concerns the lures and limitations of knowledge, the destiny of mankind and the fate of the universe. . . . He knows what few philosophers (or poets, for that matter) know—prolixity only diminishes big themes." "It is ultimately not Clarke's ambitious imagination, or his skilful depiction of the joys of reason, that characterizes *The Songs of Distant Earth,*" observes Greenland, "but rather the pathos of his vision of humanity, burdened by knowledge and loss, exiled from innocence and tranquility, forever searching the stars for the face of God." Jonas similarly notes that "the key to [Clarke's] achievement is to be found not in his utopian fantasies but in his poetic evocation of human dignity in the face of death." Concludes the critic: "This is not a poetry that relies on fresh language or fresh insights; it is a poetry of perspective, of attitude; it invites us to forget our petty problems in the contemplation of a mortality so immense as to mimic immortality in scale." "*The Songs of Distant Earth,* in other words, repeats the question that *Childhood's End, 2001,* and *2010* were meant to answer," declares Hollow. The resolution or "discovery that our species is a part of some near-divine plan [does not] really answer the central difficulty, that each of us will one day have to stop voyaging into the future."

This question or "grand theme" that runs throughout Clarke's fiction "can be stated only in the form of a paradox," suggests Jonas: "Man is most himself when he strives greatly, when he challenges the very laws of the universe; yet man is small and the universe is large, and anything he creates must, in the long run, be dwarfed by the works of others." The science in Clarke's fiction provides a good backdrop for this theme; Benford writes that Clarke "prefers a pure, dispassionate statement of facts and relationships, yet the result is not cold. Instead, he achieves a rendering of the scientific esthetic, with its respect for the universal qualities of intelligence, its tenacity and curiosity. His fiction neglects conflict and the broad spectrum of emotion, which gives it a curiously refreshing honesty." Although Clarke's fiction "may appear to be about science, appear to be about numbers, appear to be about ideas," Rabkin feels that "in fact at bottom whatever Clarke writes is about people and that means it is about the human spirit."

"Science fiction is often called escapism—always in a negative sense," Clarke told Alice K. Turner in a *Publishers Weekly* interview. "Of course it's not true. Science fiction is virtually the only kind of writing that's dealing with real problems and possibilities; it's a concerned fiction." Clarke added that "we know so much more now that we don't have to waste time on the petty things of the past. We can use the enormous technological advances in our work. Vision is wider now, and interest has never been deeper." Although he has been involved with the genre for over half a century, Clarke believes that "today's readers of science fiction are indeed fortunate; this really is the genre's Gold Age," the author writes in a 1983 *New York Times Book Review* article. Nevertheless, Clarke has not greatly changed his style and themes throughout his career. "I guess I'm just an old conservative," the author told Charles Platt in *Dream Makers: The Uncommon Men and Women Who Write Science Fiction*. "Although, really, if I have stayed true to the original form of my writing that's simply because I have a constant commitment to science." Clarke also remarked to Platt that he is proud of retaining the "sense of wonder" in his writing: "I regard it as something of an achievement not to have become cynical. . . . I do remain an optimist, especially in my fiction, because I hope it may operate as a self-fulfilling prophecy." This dedication to the idealism of science is reflected in a 1966 interview with *New York Times Magazine* contributor Godfrey Smith: referring to the consequences of the space race, Clarke commented that "of the many lessons to be drawn from this slice of recent history, the one that I wish to emphasize is this. Anything that is theoretically possible will be achieved in practice, no matter what the technical difficulties, if it is desired greatly enough."

MEDIA ADAPTATIONS: 2010: Odyssey Two was filmed in 1984 by Metro-Goldwyn-Mayer (Clarke has a cameo in the film); the short story "The Star" was adapted for an episode of "The New Twilight Zone" by CBS-TV in 1985. The following works have been optioned for movies: *Childhood's End,* by Universal; *The Songs of Distant Earth,* by Michael Phillips; *The Fountains of Paradise,* by Robert Swarthe; and *Cradle,* by Peter Guber.

AVOCATIONAL INTERESTS: "Observing the equatorial skies with a fourteen-inch telescope," table-tennis, scuba diving, and "playing with his Rhodesian Ridgeback and his six computers."

BIOGRAPHICAL/CRITICAL SOURCES:

BOOKS

Agel, Jerome, editor, *The Making of Kubrick's 2001,* New American Library, 1970.

Clareson, Thomas D., editor, *Voices for the Future: Essays on Major SF Writers,* Bowling Green University Press, 1976.

Clarke, Arthur C., *2001: A Space Odyssey,* New American Library, 1968, published with new afterword, 1982.

Clarke, Arthur C., *The View from Serendip,* Random House, 1977.

Clarke, Arthur C., *Ascent to Orbit, a Technical Autobiography: The Technical Writings of Arthur C. Clarke,* Wiley, 1984.

Clarke, Arthur C., *Astounding Days,* Bantam, 1989.

Contemporary Literary Criticism, Gale, Volume 1, 1973, Volume 4, 1975, Volume 13, 1980, Volume 16, 1981, Volume 18, 1981, Volume 35, 1985.

Hollow, John, *Against the Night, the Stars: The Science Fiction of Arthur C. Clarke,* Harcourt, 1983, expanded edition, Ohio University Press, 1987.

Johnson, William, editor, *Focus on the Science Fiction Film,* Prentice-Hall, 1972.

Olander, Joseph D., and Martin Harry Greenburg, editors, *Arthur C. Clarke,* Taplinger, 1977.

Platt, Charles, *Dream Makers: The Uncommon Men and Women Who Write Science Fiction,* Volume 2, Berkley Publishing, 1983.

Rabkin, Eric S., *Arthur C. Clarke,* Starmont House, 1979.

Samuelson, David N., *Arthur C. Clarke: A Primary and Secondary Bibliography,* G. K. Hall, 1984.

Slusser, George Edgar, *The Space Odysseys of Arthur C. Clarke,* Borgo Press, 1978.

Wollheim, Donald A., *The Universe Makers,* Harper, 1971.

PERIODICALS

Atlantic, July, 1952.

Best Sellers, October 1, 1973, May, 1979.

Chicago Sunday Tribune, July 13, 1952.

Christian Science Monitor, February 26, 1963, December 3, 1982.

Detroit News, November 28, 1982.

Kirkus Reviews, November 1, 1987.

Los Angeles Times, December 1, 1982.

Los Angeles Times Book Review, December 19, 1982, March 4, 1984, December 6, 1987.

Magazine of Fantasy and Science Fiction, September, 1979.

National Review, May 14, 1976.

New Republic, May 4, 1968, March 20, 1976, March 24, 1979.

Newsday, April 4, 1968, April 20, 1968.

New Statesman, December 20, 1968, January 26, 1979.

New Yorker, April 24, 1965, May 27, 1967, April 13, 1968, September 21, 1968, August 9, 1969, December 13, 1982, December 20, 1982.

New York Herald Tribune Book Review, July 13, 1952, August 10, 1952, August 23, 1953.

New York Times, May 29, 1968, July 5, 1968, August 22, 1973, February 26, 1985.

New York Times Book Review, March 14, 1954, April 14, 1963, August 25, 1968, September 23, 1973, January 18, 1976, October 30, 1977, March 18, 1979, January 23, 1983, March 6, 1983, May 11, 1986, December 20, 1987, December 31, 1989.

New York Times Magazine, March 6, 1966.

Omni, March, 1979.

Playboy, July, 1986.

Publishers Weekly, September 10, 1973, June 14, 1976.

Saturday Review, July 5, 1952, April 20, 1968.

Science, August 30, 1968.

Science Fiction Review, March/April, 1979, August, 1981, February, 1983, May, 1984, summer, 1986.

Time, July 19, 1968, November 15, 1982, January 11, 1988.

Times Literary Supplement, July 15, 1968, January 2, 1969, December 5, 1975, June 16, 1978, January 21, 1983, October 31, 1986.

Virginia Quarterly Review, winter, 1974.

Washington Post, February 16, 1982, November 16, 1982.

Washington Post Book World, December 26, 1982, March 25, 1984, December 31, 1989.
West Coast Review of Books, Number 1, 1986.

* * *

CLAVELL, James (duMaresq) 1925-

PERSONAL: Born October 10, 1925, in Australia; came to the United States, 1953; naturalized, 1963; son of Richard Charles (a captain in the British Royal Navy) and Eileen Clavell; married April Stride, February 20, 1951; children: Michaela, Holly. *Education:* Attended University of Birmingham, 1946-47. *Avocational interests:* Sailing, flying helicopters.

ADDRESSES: Agent—Foreign Rights, Inc., 400 East 58th St., #17D, New York, N.Y. 10022.

CAREER: Worked as a carpenter, 1953; screenwriter, director, and producer, 1954—, director of television programs, 1958—, novelist, 1962—. *Military service:* Served as captain with the Royal Artillery, 1940-46.

MEMBER: Writers Guild, Authors League of America, Producers Guild, Dramatists Guild, Directors Guild.

AWARDS, HONORS: Writers Guild Best Screenplay Award, 1964, for "The Great Escape"; honorary doctorates from the University of Maryland and the University of Bradford.

WRITINGS:

NOVELS

King Rat, Little, Brown, 1962, reprinted as *James Clavell's "King Rat,"* Delacorte, 1983.
Tai-Pan: A Novel of Hong Kong, Atheneum, 1966, reprinted, Delacorte, 1983.
Shogun: A Novel of Japan, Atheneum, 1975.
Noble House: A Novel of Contemporary Hong Kong, Delacorte, 1981.
The Children's Story, Delacorte, 1981.
James Clavell's "Whirlwind," William Morrow, 1986.
James Clavell's "Thrump-o-moto" (juvenile), illustrated by George Sharp, Delacorte, 1986.

SCREENPLAYS

"The Fly," Twentieth Century-Fox, 1958.
"Watusi," Metro-Goldwyn-Mayer, 1959.
(Also producer and director) "Five Gates to Hell," Twentieth Century-Fox, 1959.
"Walk Like a Dragon," Paramount, 1960.
"The Great Escape," United Artists, 1963.
"633 Squadron," United Artists, 1964.
"The Satan Bug," United Artists, 1965.
"Where's Jack?," Paramount, 1968.
(Also producer and director) "To Sir with Love," Columbia, 1969.
(Also producer and director) "The Last Valley," ABC Pictures, 1969.

OTHER

"Countdown to Armageddon: E—mc 2" (play), first produced in Vancouver, British Columbia, by Vancouver Playhouse Theatre, November, 1966.
(Author of introduction) *The Making of James Clavell's "Shogun,"* Dell, 1980.
(Editor and author of foreword) Sun Tzu, *The Art of War,* Hodder & Stoughton, 1981, Delacorte, 1983.

Also author of poetry ("published and paid, by God").

MEDIA ADAPTATIONS: Movies—"King Rat" was produced by Columbia, 1965; "Tai-Pan" was produced by DeLaurentiis Entertainment Group, 1986. *Television*—"Shogun" was produced as a miniseries in 1980 (Clavell was executive producer); "The Children's Story" was produced as a Mobile Showcase special in 1982; *Noble House* was produced as a miniseries entitled "James Clavell's 'Noble House' " in 1988; a miniseries based on *King Rat* and one based on *Whirlwind* are planned. *Theatre*—*Shogun* was produced for the stage at the Kennedy Center in Washington, D.C., and on Broadway at the Marriott Marquis Center in 1990.

WORK IN PROGRESS: A sequel to *Whirlwind.*

SIDELIGHTS: James Clavell, who calls himself an "old-fashioned storyteller," is one of the twentieth century's most widely read novelists. His sagas of the Far East—*Tai-Pan: A Novel of Hong Kong, Shogun: A Novel of Japan,* and *Noble House: A Novel of Contemporary Hong Kong*—have each sold millions of copies and dominated bestseller lists for months, while his Iran-based adventure, *James Clavell's "Whirlwind,"* commanded a record-setting $5,000,000 advance from its publisher. An industry insider told the *Los Angeles Times* that Clavell is "one of the very few writers . . . whose names have marquee value. Clavell's name on the cover sells enormous quantities of books." The reason for Clavell's popularity is quite simple. As James Vesely notes in the *Detroit News,* the author "always does one thing right: he is never boring." Indeed, Clavell combines action, intrigue, cultural conflicts, and romance to produce "event-packed books with the addictive appeal of popcorn," to quote *Detroit News* correspondent Helen Dudar. Although critics agree that Clavell's blockbusters never aspire to literary greatness, they also concur that his works possess the sort of research and detail rarely found in so-called "popular novels." In the *National Review,* Terry Teachout calls Clavell a "first-rate novelist of the second rank," the kind of writer "who provides genuinely stimulating literary entertainment without insulting the sensibilities."

Washington Post contributor Cynthia Gorney describes the main theme of Clavell's novels; namely, "the enormous gulf between Asian and Occidental views of the world." Against exotic backgrounds, the books explore the powerful human obsession with waging war, cornering power, or forming giant corporations. International espionage, skulduggery, and forbidden romance often round out the picture. "Each of [Clavell's] novels involves an enormous amount of research and enough plot for a dozen books," writes Ann Marie Cunningham in the *Los Angeles Times.* "All describe strategic thinking during wartime: Teams of tough British boys try to extract themselves from tight spots, . . . often in parts of the former empire." According to Webster Schott in the *New York Times Book Review,* Clavell is "neither literary psychoanalyst nor philosophizing intellectual. He reports the world as he sees people—in terms of power, control, strength. . . . He writes in the oldest and grandest tradition that fiction knows." Likewise, *Chicago Tribune* correspondent Harrison E. Salisbury claims that the author "gives you your money's worth if you like suspense, blood, thunder, romance, intrigue, lust, greed, dirty work—you name it—and pages. He is a generous man." Clavell has "sprayed his prose in machine-gun fashion, strafing targets the size of billboards," notes Paul King in *Maclean's.* "Still, he has learned the art of structuring convoluted plots that would have dazzled even Dickens. Above all, with lengthy tales of gut wrenching suspense, Clavell has mastered the technique of keeping readers turning pages until dawn."

"The people I write about are mostly doers," Clavell told the *Washington Post.* "They're not people who sit on their tails in New York, who are concerned about their place in life or should they get a divorce." His epics, he told *Publishers Weekly,* concern "ordinary people placed in extraordinary circumstances and exposed to danger. They have to do something to extract themselves from this situation, and what you have, then, are heroics and a good read." In the *New York Times Magazine,* Paul Bernstein compares Clavell's characters to those of Charles Dickens. "Dickens's big-hearted orphans become Clavell's larger-than-life men of action," writes Bernstein, "Dickens's hard-hearted villains, Clavell's hard-hearted business or political adversaries. The social commentary of Dickens becomes in Clavell cross-cultural education and reactionary political warnings." Schott admits in the *Washington Post Book World* that some of Clavell's characters are romantic stereotypes. The critic adds, however, that "others are troubled outsiders, wondering who they are and what their lives mean. Some of his villains and contemporary courtesans have distant cousins in Marvel Comics. But others are men and women painfully compromised into evil because they do not know how to fight evil without becoming it." Elsewhere in the same review, Schott offers further praise for Clavell: "The riches of his imagination and the reach of his authority are only the start. James Clavell tells his stories so well . . . that it's possible to miss the tough-minded intelligence at work. . . . Clavell knows people and what motivates them. He understands systems and how they work and fail. He remembers history and sees what technology has wrought. . . . James Clavell does more than entertain. He transports us into worlds we've not known, stimulating, educating, questioning almost simultaneously."

Clavell's life has been almost as eventful as one of his books. He was born in Australia in 1924, the son of a British Royal Navy captain who traveled to ports all over the world. As a child, Clavell relished the swashbuckling sea tales—most of them fictional—recounted by his father and grandfather, both career military men. A career in the service seemed a natural choice for Clavell, too, and after his secondary schooling was completed, he joined the Royal Artillery in 1940. A year later, he was sent to fight in the Far East and was wounded by machine-gun fire in the jungles of Malaysia. For several months he hid in a Malay village, but he was eventually captured by the Japanese and sent to the notorious Changi prison near Singapore. The conditions at Changi were so severe that only 10,000 of its 150,000 inmates survived incarceration—and Clavell was there three and a half years. He told the *Guardian:* "Changi was a school for survivors. It gave me a strength most people don't have. I have an awareness of life others lack. Changi was my university. . . . Those who were supposed to survive didn't." The experience invested Clavell with some of the same verve that characterizes his fictional protagonists. Calling Changi "the rock" on which he put his life, he said: "So long as I remember Changi, I know I'm living forty borrowed lifetimes."

Released from captivity after the war, Clavell returned to Great Britain to continue his military career. A motorcycle accident left him lame in one leg, however, and he was discharged in 1946. He attended Birmingham University briefly, considering law or engineering as a profession, but when he began to visit movie sets with his future wife—an aspiring actress—he became fascinated with directing and writing for films. He entered the movie industry on the ground floor as a distributor, gradually moving into production work. In 1953 he and his wife emigrated to the United States, where, after a period of television production in New York, they moved to Hollywood. There Clavell bluffed his way into a screenwriting contract ("They liked my accent, I suppose," he told the *Washington Post*) and set to work in the field that would bring him his first success. His first produced screenplay, "The Fly," was based on a science fiction story about an atomic scientist whose experiments cause an exchange of heads with a housefly. The movie made $4,000,000 profit in two years and has since become a classic genre film in its own right and the source of several sequels and remakes. Clavell won a Writers Guild Best Screenplay Award for the 1963 film "The Great Escape," also a box-office success. The author is best remembered, though, for the films he produced, directed, *and* wrote—most notably the 1969 hit "To Sir with Love." Made with a budget of $625,000, the movie about a black teacher's efforts to mold a class of tough British delinquents grossed $15,000,000. Both Clavell and star Sidney Poitier had contracted for percentages of the profits, so the project proved lucrative indeed.

A Hollywood screenwriters' strike brought a fortuitous change to Clavell's career in 1960. Simultaneously sidelined from his regular employment and haunted by returning memories of Changi, he began to work on a novel about his prison experiences. The process of writing unbottled many suppressed emotions; in twelve weeks he had completed the first draft of *King Rat.* Set in Changi, the novel follows the fortunes of an English prisoner of war and his ruthless American comrade in their struggles to survive the brutal conditions. *New York Times Book Review* contributor Martin Levin notes: "All personal relationships [in the work] pale beside the impersonal, soul-disintegrating evil of Changi itself which Mr. Clavell, himself a Japanese P.O.W. for three years, renders with stunning authority." Some critics have maintained that the book loses some impact because it is aimed at the popular audience, but Paul King calls it the work of "a sensitive craftsman." A *New York Herald Tribune Books* reviewer concludes that *King Rat* is "at once fascinating in narrative detail, penetrating in observation of human nature under survival stress, and provoking in its analysis of right and wrong." In the *Christian Science Monitor,* R. R. Bruun also observes that by virtue of his careful plotting, "Mr. Clavell manages to keep the tension wound up to the snapping point through much of the book." *King Rat* was a bestseller, and it was also adapted for film in 1965.

Clavell was still primarily a screenwriter when he penned *Tai-Pan,* a sweeping fictional account of the founding of Hong Kong. A historical novel set in 1841, the story recounts the adventures of Dirk Struan, first tai-pan (merchant overlord) of the Noble House trading company. Struan builds his empire on the nearly deserted peninsula of Hong Kong, convinced that a British colony there would provide a power base for the growing empire. *New York Times* reviewer Orville Prescott claims that in *Tai-Pan,* Clavell "holds attention with a relentless grip. 'Tai-Pan' frequently is crude. It is grossly exaggerated much of the time. But seldom does a novel appear so stuffed with imaginative invention, so packed with melodramatic action, so gaudy and flamboyant with blood and sin, treachery and conspiracy, sex and murder." A *Time* critic calls the work "a belly-gutting, god-rotting typhoon of a book" and adds: "Its narrative pace is numbing, its style deafening, its language penny dreadful. . . . It isn't art and it isn't truth. But its very energy and scope command the eye." *Tai-Pan* has certainly commanded the eyes of many readers. Since its publication in 1966, and its forty-four-week stay on the bestseller lists, it has sold more than two million copies. It too has been made into a motion picture that was released in 1986.

According to Gorney, Clavell's best-known novel, *Shogun,* had an inauspicious beginning in the author's mind. She writes:

"James Clavell, his imagination awash with plans for the modern-day Asian chronicle that was to be his third novel, picked up one of his 9-year-old daughter's school books one afternoon in London, and came upon an intriguing bit of history." He read the following sentence from the text: "In 1600, an Englishman went to Japan and became a Samurai." Fascinated by that possibility, Clavell began to read everything he could find about medieval Japan and Will Adams, the historical figure in question. The research led Clavell into the story of *Shogun,* but it also gave him a new understanding of the culture that had kept him in captivity during the Second World War. "I started reading about Japan's history and characteristics," he told the *New York Times,* "and then the way the Japanese treated me and my brothers became clearer to me." After a year of research in the British Museum and several visits to Japan, Clavell created the tale of John Blackthorne, an Elizabethan sailor cast upon the shores of Japan during a period of internal conflict between rival warlords. Spanning all the elements of seventeenth-century Japanese society, the adventure recounts Blackthorne's transformation from a European "barbarian" into a trusted adviser to the powerful Shogun Toranaga.

Most critics have praised *Shogun* for its historical detail as well as for its riveting plot. "Clavell offers a wide-ranging view of feudal Japan at a time of crisis," states Bruce Cook in the *Washington Post Book World.* Elsewhere Cook notes: "Scene after scene is given, conversation after conversation reported, with the point not merely of advancing the narrative (which does somehow grind inexorably forward), but also of imparting to us the peculiar flavor of life in feudal Japan and the unique code of conduct (*bushido*) which dominated life there and then." Other reviewers have cited the story itself as the source of *Shogun*'s appeal. Gorney calls it "one of those books that blots up vacations and imperils marriages, because it simply will not let the reader go," and *Library Journal* contributor Mitsu Yamamoto deems it "a wonderful churning brew of adventure, intrigue, love, philosophy, and history." "Clavell has a gift," contends Schott in the *New York Times Book Review.* "It may be something that cannot be taught or earned. He breathes narrative. It's almost impossible not to continue to read 'Shogun' once having opened it. The imagination is possessed by Blackthorne, Toranaga and medieval Japan. Clavell creates a world: people, customs, settings, needs and desires all become so enveloping that you forget who and where you are."

Praise has also been forthcoming for *Noble House,* Clavell's 1981 bestseller. *Washington Post* correspondent Sandy Rovner notes that the novel about financial power struggles in modern Hong Kong is "1,207 pages long, 2 1/2 inches (not counting covers) thick and 3 pounds and 13 ounces to drag around because you can't put it down." Henry S. Hayward offers a similar opinion in the *Christian Science Monitor.* "James Clavell is a master yarn-spinner and an expert on detail," Hayward writes. "Indeed, one sometimes feels overwhelmed with the masses of information and wishes a firmer editing pencil had been applied. But the author, nevertheless, is in a class with James Michener and Robert Elegant in his ability to handle a massive cast and hold your attention through the intricacies of a 1,200 page plot." Teachout notes that one "races through *Noble House* like a fire engine, torn between savoring each tasty bit of local color and wanting to find out as soon as possible what new outrage [the hero] will put down next." In the *New York Times Book Review,* Schott concludes that the novel "isn't primarily about any particular story or character or set of characters. It's about a condition that's a place, Hong Kong. Mr. Clavell perceives that city to be a unique setting for extremes of greed and vengefulness, international intrigue and silky romance." Commenting on Clavell's plotting, *New York Times* columnist Christopher Lehmann-Haupt observes: "Curiously enough, its staggering complexity is one of the things that the novel has going for it. Not only is 'Noble House' as long as life, it's also as rich with possibilities. . . . There are so many irons in the fire that almost anything can plausibly happen."

Clavell's successes with his novels have not been limited to the sales of books. As Teachout notes, "even non-readers have gotten pleasure out of his lucrative knack for telling an appealing story." Through movies and miniseries television dramas, Clavell's works have reached audiences estimated in the hundreds of millions. The best known of these efforts are "King Rat," a film produced in 1965, "Shogun," which aired on television in 1980, "Tai-Pan," a 1986 movie, and "James Clavell's 'Noble House,'" a 1988 miniseries. Clavell, who has served as executive producer for the "Shogun" and "Noble House" miniseries, expresses great approval for the use of his work in that medium. "Television keeps you current, and so do movies," he told *Publishers Weekly.* "People are seeing your name regularly enough that they remember you. . . . In a way, it makes me almost a brand name."

The publishing industry seems to concur that Clavell's name alone is quite appealing to book buyers. An auction of his 1986 novel *Whirlwind* brought Clavell an unprecedented $5,000,000 advance from the William Morrow Company, which had based its bid on a preview of only 10 percent of the manuscript. Morrow also ordered a first printing of 950,000 hardcover copies, another unprecedented move. Set in Iran during the hectic weeks after the overthrow of the Shah, *Whirlwind* charts the activities of a group of helicopter pilots trying to move their precious machinery out of the country before the government can seize it. Dorothy Allison describes the work as "1147 pages of violence, passion, cutthroat business, religious obsession, and martyrdom—exactly what his readers expect and want along with their exotic settings." Although the book has received mixed reviews, it was also a bestseller; a miniseries based on it has been planned.

In various interviews, Clavell has discussed both his aims as a writer and his methods of putting a book together. He told the *Los Angeles Times* that when he starts a novel, he doesn't have a detailed plan in his mind. "I look at storytelling in picture form," he said. "I watch the story happen, and I describe what I see. When you write a screenplay, you write only what you can photograph and what you can hear. As a result, my books have no fat, no purple prose, and they're very visual." Writing a lengthy novel, he told the *Washington Post,* "is pertinacity, you know, grim determination. And a marvelous selfishness to finish, to exclude everything. I begrudge the time spent away from my novel. . . . I've got this need to finish, to find the last page." Clavell said in the *National Review* that his basic goal is entertainment—for himself as well as his readers. "I'm not a novelist, I'm a storyteller," he contended. "I'm not a literary figure at all. I work very hard and try to do the best I can; and I try and write for myself, thinking that what I like, other people may like. My attitude is perhaps more romantic than psychiatric. I've never been trained as a writer, either. I stumbled into it in a funny way; I do not know how it works; and I'm petrified that it will vanish as easily as it came!" Clavell concluded his remarks in the *National Review* with comments about why he keeps writing: "My concern is with the people who read my books for pleasure; hopefully, I can entertain them; hopefully, I can pass on a little information which I find interesting. And hopefully—perhaps—I can be a bridge between East and West."

BIOGRAPHICAL/CRITICAL SOURCES:

BOOKS

Contemporary Literary Criticism, Gale, Volume 6, 1976, Volume 25, 1983.
The Making of James Clavell's "Shogun," Dell, 1980.

PERIODICALS

Best Sellers, July 15, 1966, October, 1981.
Chicago Tribune, April 12, 1981, February 18, 1982, November 21, 1986.
Christian Science Monitor, August 9, 1962, June 24, 1981.
Detroit News, May 3, 1981.
Globe and Mail (Toronto), January 4, 1986.
Guardian, October 4, 1975.
Los Angeles Times, November 7, 1986, December 11, 1986.
Maclean's, May 11, 1981, November 24, 1986.
National Review, November 12, 1982.
New Republic, July 4, 1981.
New Statesman, November 21, 1975.
Newsweek, November 10, 1986.
New York Herald Tribune Books, August 5, 1962.
New York Review of Books, September 18, 1975, December 18, 1986.
New York Times, May 4, 1966, April 28, 1981, May 17, 1981, February 18, 1982, December 28, 1985, January 7, 1986, January 11, 1986, November 1, 1986, November 7, 1986, November 17, 1986.
New York Times Book Review, August 12, 1962, May 22, 1966, June 22, 1975, May 3, 1981.
New York Times Magazine, September 13, 1981.
Publishers Weekly. October 24, 1986.
Saturday Review, August 11, 1962.
Time, June 17, 1966, July 7, 1975, July 6, 1981.
Times Literary Supplement, December 5, 1986, December 26, 1986.
Village Voice, September 2, 1981, December 16, 1986.
Washington Post, February 4, 1979, May 5, 1981, November 11, 1986.
Washington Post Book World, July 13, 1975, October 26, 1986, December 7, 1986.

*   *   *

CLEARY, Beverly (Atlee Bunn) 1916-

PERSONAL: Born in 1916, in McMinnville, Ore.; daughter of Chester Lloyd and Mable (Atlee) Bunn; married Clarence T. Cleary, 1940; children: Marianne Elisabeth, Malcolm James (twins). *Education:* University of California, Berkeley, B.A., 1938; University of Washington, Seattle, B.A. in Librarianship, 1939.

ADDRESSES: Home—California. *Office*—c/o William Morrow & Co., 105 Madison Ave., New York, N.Y. 10016.

CAREER: Public Library, Yakima, Wash., children's librarian, 1939-40; U.S. Army Hospital, Oakland, Calif., post librarian, 1942-45; writer for young people, 1950—.

MEMBER: Authors Guild, Authors League of America.

AWARDS, HONORS: Young Readers' Choice Award from Pacific Northwest Library Association, 1957, for *Henry and Ribsy,* 1960, for *Henry and the Paper Route,* 1968, for *The Mouse and the Motorcycle,* 1971, for *Ramona the Pest,* and 1980, for *Ramona and Her Father;* Dorothy Canfield Fisher Memorial Children's Book Award, 1958, for *Fifteen,* 1961, for *Ribsy,* and 1985,

for *Dear Mr. Henshaw;* Notable Book citation from American Library Association, 1961, for *Jean and Johnny,* 1966, for *The Mouse and the Motorcycle,* 1978, for *Ramona and Her Father,* and 1984, for *Dear Mr. Henshaw;* South Central Iowa Association of Classroom Teachers' Youth Award, 1968, for *The Mouse and the Motorcycle;* Nene Award from Hawaii Association of School Librarians and Hawaii Library Association, 1968, for *Ribsy,* 1969, for *The Mouse and the Motorcycle,* 1971, for *Ramona the Pest,* 1972, for *Runaway Ralph,* and 1980, for *Ramona and Her Father;* William Allen White Award from Kansas Association of School Libraries and Kansas Teachers' Association, 1968, for *The Mouse and the Motorcycle,* and 1975, for *Socks.*

Georgia Children's Book Award from College of Education of University of Georgia, 1970, Sequoyah Children's Book Award from Oklahoma Library Association, 1971, and Massachusetts Children's Book Award nomination, 1977, all for *Ramona the Pest;* New England Round Table of Children's Librarians Honor Book Award, 1972, for *Henry Huggins,* and 1973, for *The Mouse and the Motorcycle;* Sue Hefley Award from Louisiana Association of School Librarians, 1972, and Surrey School Book Award from Surrey School District, 1974, both for *The Mouse and the Motorcycle;* Charlie Mae Simon Award from Arkansas Elementary School Council, 1973, for *Runaway Ralph,* and 1984, for *Ramona Quimby, Age 8;* Distinguished Alumna Award from University of Washington, 1975; Laura Ingalls Wilder Award from American Library Association, 1975, for substantial and lasting contributions to children's literature; Golden Archer Award from University of Wisconsin, 1977, for *Socks* and *Ramona the Brave;* Children's Choice Election Award, second place, 1978; *Ramona and Her Father* appeared on *Horn Book*'s honor list, 1978; Mark Twain Award from Missouri Library Association and Missouri Association of School Librarians, 1978, for *Ramona the Brave;* Newbery Honor Book Award from American Library Association and Boston Globe-*Horn Book* Honor Award, both 1978, for *Ramona and Her Father.*

International Board on Books for Young People Honor Book Award, Tennessee Children's Book Award from Tennessee Library Association, Utah Children's Book Award of Children's Library Association of Utah, and Garden State Award of New Jersey Library Association, all 1980 for *Ramona and Her Father;* Regina Medal from Catholic Library Association, 1980, for "continued distinguished contributions to literature"; Land of Enchantment (New Mexico) Children's Award and Texas Bluebonnet Award, both 1981, for *Ramona and Her Father;* American Book Award, 1981, for *Ramona and Her Mother; Ramona Quimby, Age 8* was included on *School Library Journal*'s "Best Books 1981" list; de Grummond Award from University of Mississippi and Medallion from University of Southern Mississippi, both 1982, for distinguished contributions to children's literature; *Ralph S. Mouse* was included on *School Library Journal*'s "Best Books 1982" list; Newbery Honor Book Award, American Library Association and American Book Award nomination, both 1982, for *Ramona Quimby, Age 8;* Garden State Children's Choice Award from New Jersey Library Association, 1982, for *Ramona and Her Mother,* 1984, for *Ramona Quimby, Age 8,* and 1985, for *Ralph S. Mouse.*

Dear Mr. Henshaw was included on *School Library Journal*'s "Best Books of 1983" list, was named a *New York Times* Notable Book of 1983, and appeared on *Horn Book*'s honor list, 1984; California Association of Teachers of English Award and Golden Kite Award from Society of Children's Book Writers, both 1983, for *Ralph S. Mouse;* Christopher Award, 1983, for *Dear Mr. Henshaw;* Charles Near Simon Award from Arkansas Elementary School Council, Michigan Young Readers Award, and

Buckeye Children's Book Award, all 1984, for *Ramona Quimby, Age 8;* Iowa Children's Choice Award from Iowa Educational Media Association, 1984, for *Ralph S. Mouse,* Newbery Medal from American Library Association and Commonwealth Silver Medal from Commonwealth Club of California, both 1984, for *Dear Mr. Henshaw;* Buckeye Children's Book Award, 1985, for *Ramona and Her Mother; Everychild* citation for children's books, 1985.

WRITINGS:

Henry Huggins, Morrow, 1950.
Ellen Tebbits, Morrow, 1951, reprinted, 1989.
Henry and Beezus, Morrow, 1952, reprinted, 1989.
Otis Spofford, Morrow, 1953, reprinted, 1989.
Henry and Ribsy, Morrow, 1954, reprinted, 1989.
Beezus and Ramona, Morrow, 1955, reprinted, 1989.
Fifteen, Morrow, 1956.
Henry and the Paper Route, Morrow, 1957.
The Luckiest Girl, Morrow, 1958.
Jean and Johnny, Morrow, 1959.
The Real Hole (pre-school), Morrow, 1960, revised edition, 1986.
Hullabaloo ABC (pre-school) Parnassus, 1960.
Two Dog Biscuits (preschool), Morrow, 1961, revised edition, 1986.
Emily's Runaway Imagination, Morrow, 1961, reprinted, 1989.
Henry and the Clubhouse, Morrow, 1962.
Sister of the Bride, Morrow, 1963.
Ribsy, Morrow, 1964.
The Mouse and the Motorcycle, Morrow, 1965.
Mitch and Amy, Morrow, 1967.
Ramona the Pest (also see below), Morrow, 1968.
Runaway Ralph, Morrow, 1970.
Socks, Morrow, 1973.
The Sausage at the End of the Nose (play), Children's Book Council, 1974.
Ramona the Brave, Morrow, 1975.
Ramona and Her Father (also see below), Morrow, 1977.
Ramona and Her Mother (also see below), Morrow, 1979.
Ramona Quimby, Age 8 (also see below), Morrow, 1981.
Ralph S. Mouse, Morrow, 1982.
Dear Mr. Henshaw, Morrow, 1983.
Cutting Up with Ramona!, Dell, 1983.
Ramona Forever (also see below), Morrow, 1984.
The Ramona Quimby Diary, Morrow, 1984.
Lucky Chuck, Morrow, 1984.
Beezus and Ramona Diary, Morrow, 1986.
The Growing-Up Feet, Morrow, 1987.
Janet's Thingamajigs, Morrow, 1987.
A Girl from Yamhill: A Memoir, Morrow, 1988.
Ramona Quimby: The Making of a Television Film, Dell, 1988.
Meet Ramona Quimby (includes *Ramona and Her Father, Ramona and Her Mother, Ramona Forever, Ramona Quimby, Age 8,* and *Ramona the Pest*), Dell, 1989.

Also author of *Ramona and her Friends* and *Leave it to Beaver.* Contributor of an adult short story to *Women's Day.*

SIDELIGHTS: Beverly Cleary's humorous, realistic portrayal of American children's lives has made her a favorite of young readers and their parents for over thirty years. Books were important to Cleary from an early age; her mother established the first lending library in the small town where the author was born. "It was in this dingy room filled with shabby leather-covered chairs and smelling of stale cigar smoke that I made the most magic of dis-

coveries," she recalls in *Top of the News.* "There were books for children!"

Cleary looked eagerly forward to school and learning to read. Once there, however, she found herself stifled by the rigid teaching methods of that time. "We had no bright beckoning book with such words as 'fun,' 'adventure,' or 'horizon' to tempt us on. . . . Our primer looked grim," she remembers in a *Horn Book* article. "Its olive-green cover with its austere black lettering bore the symbol of a beacon light, presumably to guide us and to warn us of the dangers that lay within. . . . The first grade was soon sorted into three reading groups: Bluebirds, Redbirds, and Blackbirds. I was a Blackbird, the only girl Blackbird among the boy Blackbirds who had to sit in the row by the blackboard. . . . To be a Blackbird was to be disgraced. I wanted to read, but somehow I could not. I wept at home while my puzzled mother tried to drill me on the dreaded word charts."

Under the guidance of a better teacher in the second grade, Cleary learned "to plod through [the] reader a step or two ahead of disgrace" and eventually regained her original enthusiasm for books. She found, however, that the books available were ultimately unsatisfying, for they bore no relation to the life she knew as a middle-class child in Portland, Oregon. Instead, they were about "wealthy English children who had nannies and pony carts or books about poor children whose problems were solved by a long-lost rich relative turning up in the last chapter," she explained in a speech reprinted in *Horn Book.* "I had had enough. . . . I wanted to read funny stories about the sort of children I knew and decided that someday when I grew up I would write them."

Cleary did just that, setting most of her books on or around Klickitat Street, a real street near her childhood home. The children in her books face situations common in real children's lives—finding a stray dog, forgetting to deliver newspapers, the horror of having to kiss in a school play. They discover that adults are not always fair; they misbehave. Cleary recalled in a speech reprinted in *Catholic Library World* that "*Otis Spofford* was considered controversial when it was published in 1953, and some school libraries did not buy it because Otis threw spitballs and did not repent."

Perhaps the most endearing and popular of Beverly Cleary's characters is Ramona Quimby, a spunky little girl who has been making fairly regular appearances in her books since the Henry Huggins stories of the 1950s. It was not until 1968, however, with the publication of *Ramona the Pest,* that Ramona had a book to herself. Critics as well as readers responded enthusiastically to this expansion of Ramona's character, and each successive book has been met with almost unqualified praise. A critic in *Young Readers' Review* comments: "As in all her books about the boys and girls of Klickitat Street, Mrs. Cleary invests [*Ramona the Pest*] with charm, humor, and complete honesty. There are some adults who can remember many incidents from their early childhood; there are few who can remember how they felt about things and why; there are fewer who can communicate these feelings. And fewer still who can retain the humorous aspects. Mrs. Cleary is one of those rare ones. . . . Even boys and girls who dislike stories about children younger than themselves enjoy the incidents in which Ramona makes a pest of herself. . . . Ramona has never been funnier and has never been so sympathetic a character. . . . As usual, this is standard Cleary first rate entertainment." Polly Goodwin of *Book World* calls Ramona "a wonderfully real little girl trying hard to express herself, to understand and be understood in a bewildering world."

The sequel to *Ramona the Pest,* entitled *Ramona the Brave,* was equally well received. A reviewer in the *Bulletin of the Center for Children's Books* writes that it is "diverting [and] written with the ebullient humor and sympathy that distinguish Cleary's stories. Ramona is as convincing a first-grader as a fictional character can be." *Growing Point* calls it "straight domestic writing at its liveliest and most skilful."

Cleary told *CA* that in the books about Ramona she is writing about a "child's relationship with adults." This is evident in *Ramona and Her Father,* in which Mr. Quimby loses his job and begins to smoke too much, prompting Ramona to start a ferocious no-smoking campaign in order to save her father's life. A critic in *Booklist* writes: "With her uncanny gift for pinpointing the thoughts and feelings of children right down to their own phraseology—while honoring the boundaries of clean, simple writing—the author catches a family situation that puts strain on each of its members, despite their intrinsic strength and invincible humor. . . . [The resulting story is] true, warm-hearted, and funny." A reviewer in *Growing Point* notes that "the humorous tone of these neatly particularised domestic situations is never flippant, and behind it a picture is built up of a stable and sensible American family, in which that wayward individualist Ramona is able to develop in happy security." *Times Literary Supplement* contributor Peter Hunt further praises Cleary for her skill in pulling off "the difficult trick of keeping to a second-grader's viewpoint without being condescending or 'cute.' "

Katherine Paterson analyzes Cleary's brand of humor in a *Washington Post Book World* article. "When I was young there were two kinds of funny—funny ha-ha and funny peculiar," she writes. "A lot of funny ha-ha things happen in Cleary's books, but her real specialty is another kind of funny, which is a cross between funny ha-ha and funny ahhh. Cleary has the rare gift of being able to reveal us to ourselves while still keeping an arm around our shoulder. We laugh (ha ha) to recognize that funny, peculiar little self we were and are and then laugh (ahhh) with relief that we've been understood at last. . . . Cleary is loved because she can describe simply the complex feelings of a child. But even more, Cleary is able to sketch clearly with a few perfect strokes the inexplicable adult world as seen through a child's eyes."

Publication of *Dear Mr. Henshaw* in 1983 marked Cleary's response to many letters asking for a book about a child of divorce. In this book, Leigh Botts's letters to his favorite author reveal his loneliness and confusion following his parents' separation. While the typical Cleary humor is still present, *Dear Mr. Henshaw* represents a change in style and tone for Cleary; it is the author's most serious work. She remarked in a speech reprinted in *Horn Book:* "When I wrote *Dear Mr. Henshaw,* I did not expect every reader to like Leigh as much as Ramona. Although I am deeply touched that my books have reached two generations of children, popularity has never been my goal. If it had been, I would have written *Ramona Solves the Mystery of the Haunted House and Finds a Baby Brother* or something like *Henry and Beezus Play Doctor,* instead of a book about the feelings of a lonely child of divorce."

Critics and children alike responded enthusiastically to Cleary's efforts. Natalie Babbitt declares in the *New York Times Book Review:* "Beverly Cleary has written many very good books over the years. This one is the best. It is a first-rate, poignant story. . . . There is so much in it, all presented so simply, that it's hard to find a way to do it justice. Mrs. Cleary knows the voice of children. Dialogue has always been one of the strongest parts of her work. And here, where all is dialogue, that strength can shine alone and be doubly impressive. . . . What a lovely, well-crafted, three-dimensional work this is. And how reassuring . . . to see that a 27th book can be so fresh and strong. Lots of adjectives here; she deserves them all."

MEDIA ADAPTATIONS: Pied Piper produced recordings and filmstrips of *Henry and the Clubhouse,* 1962, and *Ribsy,* 1964. Miller-Brody produced recordings, some with accompanying filmstrips, of *Ramona and Her Father,* 1979, *Beezus and Ramona,* 1980, Henry Huggins, 1980, *Henry and Ribsy,* 1980, *Ramona and Her Mother,* 1980, *Ramona the Brave,* 1980, *Ramona Quimby, Age 8,* 1981, *Henry and Beezus,* 1981, *Ralph S. Mouse,* 1983, and *Dear Mr. Henshaw,* 1984. A ten-part series based on the "Ramona" books is being produced by Public Broadcasting Service; a two-part series based on *The Mouse and the Motorcycle* is being produced by Churchill Films for American Broadcasting Companies, Inc. (ABC-TV); television programs based on the "Henry Huggins" books have appeared in Japan, Sweden, and Denmark.

AVOCATIONAL INTERESTS: Travel, needlework.

BIOGRAPHICAL/CRITICAL SOURCES:

BOOKS

Arbuthnot, May Hill, *Children and Books,* 3rd edition, Scott, Foresman, 1964.
Books for Children, 1960-65, American Library Association, 1966.
Carlsen, R. Robert, *Books and the Teen-Age Reader,* Harper, 1967.
Chambers, Mary, editor, *The Signal Review I: A Selective Guide to Children's Literature,* Thimble Press, 1983.
The Children's Bookshelf, Child Study Association of America, 1965.
Children's Literature Review, Gale, Volume 2, 1976, Volume 8, 1985.
Cullinan, Bernice E., and others, *Literature and the Child,* Harcourt, 1981.
Dictionary of Literary Biography, Volume 52: *American Writers for Children since 1960: Fiction,* Gale, 1986.
Dreyer, Sharon Spredemann, *The Bookfinder: A Guide to Children's Literature about the Needs and Problems of Youth Aged 2-15,* American Guidance Service, 1977.
Eakin, Mary K., *Good Books for Children: A Selection of Outstanding Children's Books Published, 1950-65,* University of Chicago Press, 1966.
Egoff, Sheila A., *Thursday's Child: Trends and Patterns in Contemporary Children's Literature,* American Library Association, 1981.
Hopkins, Lee Bennett, *More Books by More People,* Citation Press, 1974.
Huck, Charlotte S., and Doris Young Kuhn, *Children's Literature in the Elementary School,* 2nd edition, Holt, 1968.
Rees, David, *The Marble in the Water: Essays on Contemporary Writers of Fiction for Children and Young Adults,* Horn Book, 1980.
Sadker, Myra Pollack, and David Miller Sadker, *Now upon a Time: A Contemporary View of Children's Literature,* Harper, 1977.
Sarrick, Nancy, *A Teacher's Guide to Children's Books,* Merrill, 1966.
Sebesta, Sam Keaton, and William J. Iverson, *Literature for Thursday's Child,* Science Research Associates, 1975.
Sutherland, Zena, and others, *Children and Books,* 6th edition, Scott, Foresman, 1981.

Townsend, John Rowe, *Written for Children: An Outline of English-Language Literature,* Horn Book, 1981.

PERIODICALS

Atlantic, December, 1953, December, 1964.
Booklist, September 1, 1953, September 1, 1954, October 1, 1977, May 1, 1979, September 1, 1981, September 1, 1983, September 1, 1984.
Book Window, spring, 1981.
Book World, September 8, 1968.
Bulletin of the Center for Children's Books, September, 1959, September, 1961, October, 1963, May, 1967, July, 1975, December, 1977, June, 1979, September, 1982, May, 1984, September, 1984.
Catholic Library World, February, 1980, July-August, 1981.
Children's Book Review, spring, 1975.
Christian Science Monitor, September 6, 1951, November 27, 1957, November 15, 1962, October 15, 1979, May 14, 1982, June 6, 1983.
Detroit News, August 10, 1983.
Early Years, August-September, 1982.
Elementary English, November, 1967.
Growing Point, March, 1963, January, 1976, September, 1978, July, 1980, January, 1983, May, 1983.
Horn Book, December, 1951, December 1959, October, 1962, October, 1963, December, 1964, June, 1969, August, 1970, August, 1975, December, 1977, October, 1982, December, 1982, October, 1983, August, 1984, September, 1984.
Language Arts, January, 1979.
Library Journal, September 15, 1950, October 15, 1952, September 15, 1957, September 15, 1962.
New York Herald Tribune Book Review, October 14, 1951, October 12, 1952, September 27, 1953, November 6, 1955, November 18, 1956, November 1959.
New York Times Book Review, September 14, 1952, October 4, 1953, September 26, 1954, September 16, 1956, October 9, 1960, December 26, 1965, October 14, 1979, November 1, 1981, October 23, 1983, November 11, 1984, November 10, 1985.
Oklahoma Librarian, July, 1971.
Pacific Northwest Library Association Quarterly, April, 1961.
Pacific Sun Literary Quarterly, May 14, 1975.
Publishers Weekly, August 4, 1951, August 15, 1953, July 10, 1954, August 13, 1955, September 1961, April 3, 1967, April 15, 1968, May 14, 1970, March 31, 1975, February 23, 1976, October 1, 1977, July 30, 1979, July 10, 1981, March 2, 1984.
St. Louis Globe-Democrat, February 13, 1984.
Saturday Review, November 17, 1956, October 28, 1961, March 18, 1967, May 9, 1970.
Saturday Review of Literature, November 1950, November 10, 1951.
School Librarian, June, 1974, June, 1981.
Signal, January, 1981.
Southeastern Librarian, fall, 1968.
Times Literary Supplement, July 7, 1978, July 2, 1980, January 13, 1984, November 20, 1984, February 1985.
Top of the News, December, 1957, April, 1975, winter, 1977.
Washington Post, May 31, 1983, January 10, 1984.
Washington Post Book World, October 9, 1977, July 12, 1981, September 12, 1982, August 14, 1983, September 9, 1984.
Wilson Library Bulletin, October, 1961.
Writers Digest, January, 1983.
Young Readers' Review, November, 1965, February, 1966, May, 1968.

OTHER

"Meet the Newbery Author: Beverly Cleary" (filmstrip), Random House/Miller Brody.

*   *   *

CLEESE, John (Marwood) 1939-
(Monty Python, a joint pseudonym)

PERSONAL: Born October 27, 1939, in Weston-super-Mare, Somerset, England; son of Reginald (in insurance sales) and Muriel (an acrobat; maiden name, Cross) Cleese; married Connie Booth (an actress and writer), February 20, 1968 (divorced, 1978); married Barbara Trentham (a director, actress, and artist), February 15, 1981 (separated); children: (first marriage) Cynthia; (second marriage) Camilla. *Education:* Downing College, Cambridge, M.A., 1963. *Politics:* Social-Democrat Liberal.

ADDRESSES: c/o Video Arts Ltd., 68 Oxford St., London W1, England.; c/o David Wilkinson, 6-8 Haymarket St., London SW1, England.

CAREER: Writer and member with Graham Chapman, Terry Gilliam, Eric Idle, Terry Jones, and Michael Palin of comedy team collectively known as Monty Python, 1969-82. Writer for and performer, with others, in television series "The Frost Report," 1966-67, "At Last the 1948 Show," 1966-67, "Monty Python's Flying Circus," 1969-73, and "Fawlty Towers," 1975-79. Actor in stage productions, including "Footlights Revue" (later "Cambridge Circus"), 1963, and "Half a Sixpence," 1965.

Actor in motion pictures, including "Interlude," 1968, "The Rise and Rise of Michael Rimmer," 1970, "The Magic Christian," 1970, "The Statue," 1971, "And Now for Something Completely Different," 1971, "Monty Python and the Holy Grail," 1975, "Monty Python's Life of Brian," 1977, "The Secret Policeman's Ball," 1979, "True Bandits," 1981, "The Great Muppet Caper," 1981, "The Secret Policeman's Other Ball," 1982, "Monty Python Live at the Hollywood Bowl," 1982, "Monty Python's The Meaning of Life," 1983, "Yellowbeard," 1983, "Privates on Parade," 1983, "Silverado," 1985, "Clockwise," 1986, and "A Fish Called Wanda," 1988. Appeared in British Broadcasting Corporation (BBC-TV) production "Taming of the Shrew," 1980. Video Arts Ltd., London, England, founder and producer of and actor in business training films, 1972—. Creator of commercial advertisements for various companies.

AWARDS, HONORS: LL.D., St. Andrews University, 1971; Queen's Award for Exports, 1982, for Video Arts commercial series created for American radio broadcast; co-winner of Golden Palm, Cannes Film Festival, 1983, for "Monty Python's The Meaning of Life"; Academy Award (Oscar) nomination for best original screenplay, Academy of Motion Pictures and Sciences, 1988, for "A Fish Called Wanda."

WRITINGS:

(With Jack Hobbs and Joe McGrath) *The Strange Case of the End of Civilisation As We Know It,* Star Books, 1970.
(With Connie Booth) *Fawlty Towers,* Futura, Volume I, 1977, Volume II, 1979.
(With Robin Skynner) *Families and How To Survive Them* (nonfiction), cartoons by Bud Handelman, Methuen (London), 1983.
The Golden Skits of Wing-Commander Muriel Volestrangler, FHRS and Bar, Methuen (London), 1984.

A Fish Called Wanda (screenplay; based on original story authored with Charles Crichton), Metro-Goldwyn-Mayer, 1988, Applause Theatre Book Publishers, 1988.

(With Booth) *The Complete Fawlty Towers,* Pantheon, 1989.

CONTRIBUTOR TO MONTY PYTHON BOOKS

Monty Python's Big Red Book, edited by Eric Idle, Methuen, 1972, Warner Books, 1975 (also see below).

The Brand New Monty Python Bok, illustrated by Terry Gilliam, under pseudonym Jerry Gillian, and Peter Brooks, edited by Idle, Methuen, 1973, also published as *The Brand New Monty Python Paperbok,* Methuen, 1974 (also see below).

Monty Python and the Holy Grail, Methuen, 1977, also published as *Monty Python's Second Film: A First Draft,* Methuen, 1977 (also see below).

Monty Python's Life of Brian (of Nazareth) [and] *Montypythonscrapbook* (the former adapted from motion picture with the same title [also see below]), Grosset, 1979.

The Complete Works of Shakespeare and Monty Python (contains *Monty Python's Big Red Book* and *The Brand New Monty Python Paperbok*), Eyre Methuen, 1981.

CONTRIBUTOR TO MONTY PYTHON SCREENPLAYS

"And Now for Something Completely Different," Columbia Pictures, 1972.

"Pythons in Deutschland" (television movie), Batavia Atelier, c. 1972.

"Monty Python and the Holy Grail," Cinema 5, 1975.

"Monty Python's Life of Brian," Warner Bros., 1979.

"Monty Python Live at the Hollywood Bowl," Handmade Films/Columbia Pictures, 1982.

"Monty Python's The Meaning of Life," Universal Pictures, 1983.

TELEVISION SCRIPTS

(Contributor) "The Frost Report" (comedy series), British Broadcasting Corp. (BBC-TV), 1966-67.

(Contributor) "Monty Python's Flying Circus" (comedy series), BBC-TV, 1969-73, broadcast in the United States by Public Broadcasting Service (PBS-TV).

Also author, with Booth, of "Fawlty Towers" (comedy series), broadcast in the United States by PBS-TV. Contributor to "At Last the 1948 Show," 1966-67.

RECORDINGS

(With Tim Brooke-Taylor, David Frost, and others) *The Frost Report on Britain,* Starline, 1966.

(With Booth) *Fawlty Towers,* BBC Records, 1979.

(With Booth) *Fawlty Towers/Second Sitting,* BBC Records, 1981.

(With Booth) *Fawlty Towers/At Your Service,* BBC Records, 1982.

CONTRIBUTOR TO MONTY PYTHON RECORDINGS

Monty Python's Flying Circus, BBC Records, 1969.

Another Monty Python Record, Charisma, 1970.

Monty Python's Previous Record, Charisma, 1972.

Monty Python's Matching Tie and Handkerchief, Charisma, 1974, Arista, 1975.

Monty Python Live at Drury Lane, Charisma, 1974.

The Album of the Soundtrack of the Trailer of the Film Monty Python and the Holy Grail, Arista, 1975.

Monty Python Live at City Center, Arista, 1976.

Monty Python's Instant Record Collection, Charisma, 1977.

Monty Python's Life of Brian (original soundtrack recording; includes dialogue and songs "Brian" and "Always Look on the Bright Side of Life"), Warner Bros., 1979.

Monty Python's Contractual Obligation Album, Arista, 1980.

Monty Python's The Meaning of Life (original soundtrack recording; includes dialogue and songs "Every Sperm Is Sacred" and "The Galaxy Song"), CBS Records, 1983.

OTHER

Also contributor to screenplays, including "The Rise and Rise of Michael Rimmer" and "The Magic Christian," both 1970.

Also creator of commercial advertisements for radio and television and of fifty business training films, including "Meeting, Bloody Meetings," "The Secretary and Her Boss," "The Balance Sheet Barrier," and "Time Management Delegation."

WORK IN PROGRESS: Life and How to Survive It, a second book with Robin Skynner.

SIDELIGHTS: "Pythons—they have a singular genius for making nonsensical fun of all who are pompous, pretentious, humorless, or boring, or who take themselves too seriously," wrote Tom Meehan in a *New York Times Magazine* article featuring the British comedy team Monty Python, of which John Cleese was a member from 1969 to 1974. In characterizing Cleese and his more memorable roles as a performer in the team's popular comedy series "Monty Python's Flying Circus," a writer for the *New Yorker* remarked that the actor-comedian "is rather dangerous-looking" and "excels at invective. His moments of triumph, which are legion, and include his portrayals of a high official in the Ministry of Silly Walks, of an Army sergeant teaching recruits how to defend themselves against someone armed with a piece of fresh fruit, and of a refreshment seller hawking albatross ('Stormy petrel on a stick!')."

Cleese's comedy career began in the mid-1960s while he was studying law at Cambridge University. Although he eventually earned his degree, he preferred a job with the British Broadcasting Corporation (BBC) to a legal career. As a cast member of the "Footlights Revue" he appeared on London's West End and subsequently on Broadway when the show became the "Cambridge Circus." Returning to England, he became a writer and performer for the weekly comedy program "The Frost Report" and later, "At Last the 1948 Show." After landing a number of minor acting roles in such motion pictures as "Interlude," "The Rise and Rise of Michael Rimmer," and "The Magic Christian," Cleese pooled his talents with those of fellow comedians Graham Chapman, Terry Jones, Eric Idle, Michael Palin, and cartoonist Terry Gilliam to produce the British Broadcasting Corporation comedy series "Monty Python's Flying Circus."

From its introduction in 1969, the off-beat show ran for five years as Great Britain's highest-rated television program, with a viewing audience of approximately ten million. For their United States debut, the Pythons put together several of their most popular skits to make the 1972 feature film "And Now For Something Completely Different," but it was not until 1974 that "Flying Circus" came to American television via the Public Broadcasting Service (PBS). The show soon became what *Newsweek*'s Harry F. Waters hailed as "the most improbably successful program in the history of American public television." In describing the Python's popularity—a phenomenon Waters labeled "Pythonmania"—Meehan suggested that "part of [the group's] infinite charm is that they're willing to try almost anything and to lampoon just about anyone." The critic further remarked that watching the half-hour program "is a bit like making a dizzying journey through a surreal fun house. Mixing filmed sketches that rarely last longer than a minute or two with bizarre pieces of animation, the program leaps wildly about in time and place. A sketch may begin in rural 17th-century England, for instance, and a moment later its characters are browsing in a modern-day London pornographic bookshop."

In 1974, the same year "Flying Circus" was first broadcast in the United States, Cleese left the group and the Pythons stopped filming new shows. Cleese went on to collaborate with his first wife, actress Connie Booth, in writing for the BBC comedy series "Fawlty Towers," in which Cleese starred as the muddled and moody innkeeper, Basil Fawlty. Although no longer an active member of the Python team, he also helped create Monty Python books and recordings, as well as several full-length movies, most notably "Monty Python and the Holy Grail," "Monty Python's Life of Brian," and "Monty Python's The Meaning of Life."

Deemed "a marvelously particular kind of lunatic endeavor" by *New York Times* critic Vincent Canby, "Monty Python and the Holy Grail" is a comic reworking of the legend of King Arthur. In the Python version of the search for the grail, Arthur and his knights find themselves in a variety of ludicrous situations, including a battle where the king's adversaries hurl muddied animal carcasses at the grail seekers from atop a castle wall. The knights never find the grail; instead, their adventures end abruptly with a scene in which modern-day policemen place King Arthur's men under arrest. "The whole film," noted Penelope Gilliatt in the *New Yorker,* "which is often recklessly funny and sometimes a matter of comic genius, is a triumph of errancy and muddle."

Cleese's next filmmaking efforts with the Python troupe resulted in "Monty Python's Life of Brian," a parody of such Hollywood biblical productions as "The Greatest Story Ever Told" and "King of Kings." Characterized by Canby as "the foulest-spoken biblical epic ever made, as well as the best-humored," "Life of Brian" centers on the misadventures of Brian Cohen of Nazareth, beginning with the day he is born: He shares his birthday with the infant Jesus and is momentarily mistaken for the Christchild by three men bearing gifts. Most of his life is spent dodging his followers, who claim Brian as their messiah.

The film immediately sparked controversy among religious groups, who condemned it as blasphemy. "This is no gentle spoof, no good-natured satire of cherished beliefs," admitted *Time* reviewer Richard Schickel. "The Python's assault on religion is as intense as their attack on romantic chivalry in 'Monty Python and the Holy Grail.' " Nevertheless, *Chicago Tribune* critic Gene Siskel found "Life of Brian" a "gentle but very funny parody" whose "humor is light and very clever," and David Ansen wrote in his *Newsweek* review that "though the pious will blanch, Pythonmaniacs should find this film a treasure trove of unborn-again humor." Stanley Kauffmann expressed a similar opinion, writing in the *New Republic,* "Even when I wasn't laughing, I was happy, which to me is a sign of really good comedy."

In much the same way they produced "Flying Circus" and "Completely Different," the Pythons presented their next film, "Monty Python's The Meaning of Life," as a series of sketches representing the phases of human life. In one of the first scenes, titled "Growth and Learning," Cleese plays a schoolmaster who conducts a sex education class before a group of inattentive schoolboys, using his wife as a visual aid. In another skit, Cleese appears as a headwaiter who caters to Mr. Creosote, an enormous patron who, after ordering two servings of everything on the menu, spends the meal alternately gorging himself and vomiting. The Pythons also take aim at the Catholic religion in a fully choreographed musical number, "Every Sperm Is Sacred." "As the Pythons run the gamut of life, they do so with a great deal of frank language and specificity about what are sometimes called private parts," Sheila Benson observed in the *Los Angeles Times,* adding that "those either violently for or against this sort of thing are hereby warned, so they can make their plans accordingly." *New York Times*'s Canby found "Meaning of Life" "sometimes hilarious and colossally rude but, as often as it evokes laughs, it overwhelms them by the majesty of its production and special effects." Siskel called the film "fresh and original and delightfully offensive. What more can you ask of a comedy?"

While Cleese's career during his association with the Pythons appeared to be one of lucrative fun and games, the comedian nevertheless suffered frequently from tension and depression. In an effort to cope with such problems, Cleese entered into group therapy for more than three years during the mid-1970s. He found the experience "the most interesting of his adult life," according to *London Times* writer Paul Nathanson, and in 1981 collaborated with his psychotherapist, Robin Skynner, to write *Families and How to Survive Them.* Presented in dialogue format—with Cleese posing questions and Skynner providing answers—the 1983 book covers "problems of marriage, babies, toddlers, children, and family relationships as well as authority and teenagers," Nathanson summarized. Reviewing the book in the *Times Literary Supplement,* Anthony Clare described its approach as one of common sense but that "the problem . . . is that many readers will reach the same conclusions as Cleese and Skynner without undergoing the rigours of finishing the book." Still, Clare noted that "there is much to chew on between Cleese's jokes, Skynner's aphorisms and [illustrator] Bud Handleman's uneven cartoons, as long as prospective readers don't expect too substantial a meal."

Among Cleese's other projects—independent of the Pythons—has been producing business training films as owner and president of his London-based company, Video Arts Ltd. Distributed to such corporations as Gulf Oil, IBM, and Hilton Hotels, the films parody problems of everyday business life and feature Cleese "invariably depicted blundering through one managerial situation after another," remarked a writer for *People.* Cleese has also created and appeared in a number of advertisements for products throughout the world.

Cleese returned to the big screen in 1988 with the film "A Fish Called Wanda," for which he also penned the screenplay. The film received a nomination for an Academy Award in that category. In the comedy Cleese portrays Archie Leach, a genteel British barrister who defends the leader of a jewel heist. After the successful holdup, each of the accomplices turns against the other; greed is "at the heart of the plot," as Charlie Champlin observed in the *Los Angeles Times.* The thieves include Wanda (played by Jamie Lee Curtis), her secret, decidedly stupid, and maniacal lover Otto (Kevin Kline), and their stuttering, animal-loving friend, Ken (Michael Palin). Wanda and Otto tip off the police, betraying the leader, George (who mistakenly believes Wanda is in love with him), not knowing that George had hidden the jewels. In the guise of an admiring law student, the seductive Wanda lures Archie into an affair in the hope that he can tell her the jewels' whereabouts. A bold, sexy American, Wanda is a "gust of fresh air" to the repressed lawyer, whose professional and family life is lackluster, commented Sheila Benson in the *Los Angeles Times.* The movie "pretends to be a caper movie about a smooth London jewel heist and its infinitely complex aftermath," Benson added. "Actually," Benson continued, "it's a smart farce about ingrained cultural differences, playing the clenched respectability of the Brits against the heavy spontaneity—some might call it vulgarity—of the Yanks." Dave Kehr of the *Chicago Tribune* wrote that "the movie's basic joke holds that the overbearing, unselfconscious Americans will do anything and say anything (and usually as loudly as possible), while the timorous British are nearly too polite to breathe."

While Wanda is endearing herself to Leach (and infuriating the jealous Otto), Ken tries to dispose of the only witness to the crime—an old lady who owns three lapdogs. To his anguish, Ken inadvertently kills one dog after another in his assassination attempts on the lady, who finally collapses from a heart attack when the last dog dies. Ken is the only other person who knows the location of the jewels, and when Otto discovers this, he tries to torture Ken into telling by eating his pet fish, named after Wanda. Otto meets his end at the hands of Ken, and after Leach's wife discovers his infidelity and announces that she wants a divorce, Leach and Wanda board a plane and take off with the loot.

The fish-eating scene, and the comic treatment of Ken's stuttering, drew criticism from animal rights groups and the National Stuttering Project, respectively. The filmmakers answered protests by saying that the fish was merely gelatin, and that Ken's character was not meant to typify or ridicule stutterers. Reviewers also faulted the film for its nervous, frantic pace. *Washington Post*'s Rita Kempley, on the other hand, calling the film "dark and strange, even sadistic" praised it as "guilty fun with the unsettling feel of 'Something Wild' and 'After Hours,' male fantasies in which kinky women lure uptight fish out of the water. . . . 'Wanda' is a Harlequin romance for men, a breakthrough for Britain and a deftly directed and wonderfully acted sex farce for consenting adults."

Cleese told *CA:* "I've enjoyed my years in the world of jokes but now that Video Arts has given me financial independence, I intend to spend more time exploring other fields. Whether they will lead eventually to films or television programs, I'm not sure. The second book with Robin Skynner looks like a fascinating start on this fallow period."

BIOGRAPHICAL/CRITICAL SOURCES:

BOOKS

Contemporary Literary Criticism, Volume 21, Gale, 1982.
Hewison, Robert, *Monty Python: The Case Against,* Methuen, 1981.
Hewison, Robert, *Footlights!,* Methuen, 1983.
Perry, George, *The Life of Python,* Pavilion Books, 1983.
Wilmut, Roger, *From Fringe to Flying Circus,* Methuen, 1980.

PERIODICALS

Chicago Tribune, September 21, 1979, April 1, 1983, July 29, 1988.
Chicago Tribune-Arts, November 2, 1986.
Los Angeles Times, March 31, 1983, July 15, 1988, August 4, 1988.
New Republic, September 23, 1972, May 24, 1975, September 22, 1979, April 18, 1983.
Newsweek, September 3, 1979, July 12, 1982, April 4, 1983.
New Yorker, August 26, 1972, May 5, 1975, May 12, 1975, August 27, 1979.
New York Times, April 28, 1975, April 16, 1976, August 17, 1979, March 31, 1983.
New York Times Magazine, April 18, 1976, December 25, 1988.
People, August 22, 1982, September 26, 1983.
Time, May 26, 1975, September 17, 1979, March 28, 1983.
Times (London), June 10, 1983, September 28, 1983.

Times Literary Supplement, November 11, 1983.
Washington Post, July 29, 1988, July 31, 1988, September 13, 1988.

*   *   *

CLERK, N. W.
See LEWIS, C(live) S(taples)

*   *   *

CLIFTON, (Thelma) Lucille   1936-

PERSONAL: Born June 27, 1936, in Depew, N.Y.; daughter of Samuel Louis, Sr. (a laborer) and Thelma (a laborer; maiden name, Moore) Sayles; married Fred James Clifton (an educator, writer, and artist), May 10, 1958 (died November 10, 1984); children: Sidney, Fredrica, Channing, Gillian, Graham, Alexia. *Education:* Attended Howard University, 1953-55, and Fredonia State Teachers College (now State University of New York College at Fredonia), 1955.

ADDRESSES: Agent—Marilyn Marlow, Curtis Brown Ltd., 10 Astor Pl., New York, N.Y. 10003.

CAREER: New York State Division of Employment, Buffalo, claims clerk, 1958-60; U.S. Office of Education, Washington, D.C., literature assistant for CAREL (Central Atlantic Regional Educational Laboratory), 1969-71; Coppin State College, Baltimore, Md., poet in residence, 1971-74; writer. Visiting writer, Columbia University School of the Arts; Jerry Moore Visiting Writer, George Washington University, 1982-83; University of California, Santa Cruz, professor of literature and creative writing, 1985—. Trustee, Enoch Pratt Free Library, Baltimore.

MEMBER: International PEN, Authors Guild, Authors League of America.

AWARDS, HONORS: Discovery Award, New York YW-YMHA Poetry Center, 1969; *Good Times: Poems* cited as one of the year's ten best books by the *New York Times,* 1969; National Endowment for the Arts awards, 1970 and 1972; Poet Laureate of the State of Maryland, 1979-82; Juniper Prize, 1980; Coretta Scott King Award, 1984, for *Everett Anderson's Goodbye;* honorary degrees from University of Maryland and Towson State University.

WRITINGS:

ADULTS

Good Times: Poems, Random House, 1969.
Good News about the Earth: New Poems, Random House, 1972.
An Ordinary Woman (poetry), Random House, 1974.
Generations: A Memoir (prose), Random House, 1976.
Two-Headed Woman (poetry), University of Massachusetts Press, 1980.
Good Woman: Poems and a Memoir, 1969-1980, Boa Editions, 1987.
Next: New Poems, Boa Editions, 1987.

JUVENILES

The Black BCs (alphabet poems), Dutton, 1970.
Good, Says Jerome, illustrations by Stephanie Douglas, Dutton, 1973.
All Us Come Cross the Water, pictures by John Steptoe, Holt, 1973.
Don't You Remember?, illustrations by Evaline Ness, Dutton, 1973.
The Boy Who Didn't Believe in Spring, pictures by Brinton Turkle, Dutton, 1973.

The Times They Used to Be, illustrations by Susan Jeschke, Holt, 1974.

My Brother Fine with Me, illustrations by Moneta Barnett, Holt, 1975.

Three Wishes, illustrations by Douglas, Viking, 1976.

Amifika, illustrations by Thomas DiGrazia, Dutton, 1977.

The Lucky Stone, illustrations by Dale Payson, Delacorte, 1979.

My Friend Jacob, illustrations by DiGrazia, Dutton, 1980.

Sonora Beautiful, illustrations by Michael Garland, Dutton, 1981.

"EVERETT ANDERSON" SERIES; JUVENILE

Some of the Days of Everett Anderson, Holt, 1970.

Everett Anderson's Christmas Coming, illustrations by Ness, Holt, 1971.

Everett Anderson's Year, illustrations by Ann Grifalconi, Holt, 1974.

Everett Anderson's Friend, illustrations by Grifalconi, Holt, 1976.

Everett Anderson's 1 2 3, illustrations by Grifalconi, Holt, 1977.

Everett Anderson's Nine Month Long, illustrations by Grifalconi, Holt, 1978.

Everett Anderson's Goodbye, illustrations by Grifalconi, Holt, 1983.

OTHER

(Contributor) Marlo Thomas and others, *Free to Be . . . You and Me,* McGraw-Hill, 1974.

(Contributor) Langston Hughes and Arna Bontemps, *Poetry of the Negro, 1746-1970,* Doubleday, 1970.

Also contributor to *Free to Be a Family,* 1987, *Norton Anthology of Literature by Women, Coming into the Light,* and *Stealing the Language.* Contributor of fiction to *Negro Digest, Redbook, House and Garden,* and *Atlantic.* Contributor of nonfiction to *Ms.* and *Essence.*

SIDELIGHTS: Lucille Clifton "began composing and writing stories at an early age and has been much encouraged by an ever-growing reading audience and a fine critical reputation," writes Wallace R. Peppers in a *Dictionary of Literary Biography* essay. "In many ways her themes are traditional: she writes of her family because she is greatly interested in making sense of their lives and relationships; she writes of adversity and success in the ghetto community; and she writes of her role as a poet." Clifton's work emphasizes endurance and strength through adversity. Ronald Baughman suggests in his *Dictionary of Literary Biography* essay that "Clifton's pride in being black and in being a woman helps her transform difficult circumstances into a qualified affirmation about the black urban world she portrays." Writing in Mari Evans's *Black Women Writers (1950-1980): A Critical Evaluation,* Haki Madhubuti (formerly Don L. Lee) states: "She is a writer of complexity, and she makes her readers work and think. Her poetry has a quiet force without being pushy or alien. Whether she is cutting through family relationships, surviving American racial attitudes, or just simply renewing love ties, she puts something heavy on your mind. The great majority of her published poetry is significant. At the base of her work is concern for the Black family, especially the destruction of its youth. Her eye is for the uniqueness of our people, always concentrating on the small strengths that have allowed us to survive the horrors of Western life."

Clifton's first volume of poetry, *Good Times: Poems,* which was cited by the *New York Times* as one of 1969's ten best books, is described by Peppers as a "varied collection of character sketches written with third person narrative voices." Baughman notes that "these poems attain power not only through their subject matter but also through their careful techniques; among Clifton's most successful poetic devices . . . are the precise evocative images that give substance to her rhetorical statements and a frequent duality of vision that lends complexity to her portraits of place and character." Calling the book's title "ironic," Baughman indicates, "Although the urban ghetto can, through its many hardships, create figures who are tough enough to survive and triumph, the overriding concern of this book is with the horrors of the location, with the human carnage that results from such problems as poverty, unemployment, substandard housing, and inadequate education." Baughman recognizes that although "these portraits of human devastation reflect the trying circumstances of life in the ghetto . . . the writer also records some joy in her world, however strained and limited that joy might be." Madhubuti thinks that although this is her first book of poetry, it "cannot be looked upon as simply a 'first effort.' The work is unusually compacted and memory-evoking." As Johari Amini (formerly Jewel C. Latimore) suggests in *Black World,* "The poetry is filled with the sensations of coming up black with the kind of love that keeps you from dying in desperation."

In Clifton's second volume of poetry, *Good News about the Earth: New Poems,* "the elusive good times seem more attainable," remarks Baughman, who summarizes the three sections into which the book is divided: the first section "focuses on the sterility and destruction of 'white ways,' newly perceived through the social upheavals of the early 1970s"; the second section "presents a series of homages to black leaders of the late 1960s and early 1970s"; and the third section "deals with biblical characters powerfully rendered in terms of the black experience." Harriet Jackson Scarupa notes in *Ms.* that after having read what Clifton says about blackness and black pride, some critics "have concluded that Clifton hates whites. [Clifton] considers this a misreading. When she equates whiteness with death, blackness with life, she says: 'What I'm talking about is a certain kind of white arrogance—and not all white people have it—that is not good. I think airs of superiority are very dangerous. I believe in justice. I try not to be about hatred.' " Writing in *Poetry,* Ralph J. Mills, Jr., says that Clifton's poetic scope transcends the black experience "to embrace the entire world, human and non-human, in the deep affirmation she makes in the teeth of negative evidence. She is a master of her style, with its spare, elliptical, idiomatic, rhythmical speech, and of prophetic warning in the same language." Angela Jackson, who thinks that it "is a book written in wisdom," concludes in *Black World* that "Clifton and *Good News about the Earth* will make you shake yo head. Ain't nothing else to say."

An Ordinary Woman, Clifton's third collection of poems, "abandons many of the broad racial issues examined in the two preceding books and focuses instead on the narrower but equally complex issues of the writer's roles as woman and poet," says Baughman. Peppers notes that "the poems take as their theme a historical, social, and spiritual assessment of the current generation in the genealogical line" of Clifton's great great-grandmother who had been taken from her home in Dahomey, West Africa, and brought to America in slavery in 1830. Peppers notes that by taking an ordinary experience and personalizing it, "Clifton has elevated the experience into a public confession" which may be shared, and "it is this shared sense of situation, an easy identification between speaker and reader, that heightens the notion of ordinariness and gives . . . the collection an added dimension." Helen Vendler writes in the *New York Times Book Review* that "Clifton recalls for us those bare places we have all waited as 'ordinary women,' with no choices but yes or no, no art, no grace, no words, no reprieve." "Written in the same ironic, yet cautiously optimistic spirit as her earlier published work," observes Peppers, the book is "lively, full of vigor, passion, and an all-consuming honesty."

In *Generations: A Memoir,* "it is as if [Clifton] were showing us a cherished family album and telling us the story about each person which seemed to sum him or her up best," says a *New Yorker* contributor. Calling the book an "eloquent eulogy of [Clifton's] parents," Reynolds Price writes in the *New York Times Book Review* that "as with most elegists, her purpose is perpetuation and celebration, not judgment. There is no attempt to see either parent whole; no attempt at the recovery of history not witnessed by or told to the author. There is no sustained chronological narrative. Instead, clusters of brief anecdote gather round two poles, the deaths of father and mother." Price, however, believes that *Generations* stands "worthily" among the other modern elegies that assert that "we may survive, some lively few, if we've troubled to *be* alive and loved." However, a contributor to *Virginia Quarterly Review* thinks that the book is "more than an elegy or a personal memoir. It is an attempt on the part of one woman to retrieve and lyrically to celebrate, her Afro-American heritage."

"Clifton is a poet of a literary tradition which includes such varied poets as Walt Whitman, Emily Dickinson, and Gwendolyn Brooks, who have inspired and informed her work," writes Audrey T. McCluskey in Evans's *Black Women Writers (1950-1980).* McCluskey finds that "Clifton's belief in her ability (and ours) to make things better and her belief in the concept of personal responsibility pervade her work. These views are especially pronounced in her books for children." Clifton's books for children are characterized by a positive view of black heritage and an urban setting peopled by nontraditional families. Critics recognize that although her works speak directly to a specific audience, they reveal the concerns of all children. In a *Language Arts* interview with Rudine Sims, Clifton was asked where she gets her ideas for stories: "Well, I had six kids in seven years, and when you have a lot of children, you tend to attract children, and you see so many kids, you get ideas from that. And I have such a good memory from my own childhood, my own time. I have great respect for young people; I like them enormously."

Clifton's books for children are designed to help them understand their world. *My Friend Jacob,* for instance, is a story "in which a black child speaks with affection and patience of his friendship with a white adolescent neighbor . . . who is retarded," writes Zena Sutherland in *Bulletin of the Center for Children's Books.* "Jacob is Sam's 'very very best friend' and all of his best qualities are appreciated by Sam, just as all of his limitations are accepted. . . . It is strong in the simplicity and warmth with which a handicapped person is loved rather than pitied, enjoyed rather than tolerated." Critics find that Clifton's characters and their relationships are accurately and positively drawn. Ismat Abdal-Haqq notes in *Interracial Books for Children Bulletin* that "the two boys have a strong relationship filled with trust and affection. The author depicts this relationship and their everyday adventures in a way that is unmarred by the mawkish sentimentality that often characterizes tales of the mentally disabled." And a contributor to *Reading Teacher* states that "in a matter-of-fact, low-keyed style, we discover how [Sam and Jacob] help one another grow and understand the world."

Clifton's children's books also facilitate an understanding of black heritage specifically, which in turn fosters an important link with the past generally. *All Us Come Cross the Water,* for example, "in a very straight-forward way . . . shows the rela-

tionship of Africa to Blacks in the U.S. without getting into a heavy rap about 'Pan-Africanism,' " states Judy Richardson in the *Journal of Negro Education,* adding that Clifton "seems able to get inside a little boy's head, and knows how to represent that on paper." An awareness of one's origins figures also in *The Times They Used to Be.* Called a "short and impeccable vignette—laced with idiom and humor of rural Black folk," by Rosalind K. Goddard in *School Library Journal,* it is further described by Lee A. Daniels in the *Washington Post* as a "story in which a young girl catches her first glimpse of the new technological era in a hardware store window, and learns of death and life." "Most books that awaken adult nostalgia are not as appealing to young readers," says Sutherland in *Bulletin of the Center for Children's Books,* "but this brief story has enough warmth and vitality and humor for any reader."

In addition to quickening an awareness of black heritage, Clifton's books for children frequently include an element of fantasy as well. Writing about *Three Wishes,* in which a young girl finds a lucky penny on New Year's Day and makes three wishes upon it, Christopher Lehmann-Haupt in the *New York Times Book Review* calls it "an urbanized version of the traditional tale in which the first wish reveals the power of the magic object . . . the second wish is a mistake, and the third undoes the second." Lehmann-Haupt adds that "too few children's books for blacks justify their ethnicity, but this one is a winning blend of black English and bright illustration." And *The Lucky Stone,* in which a lucky stone provides good fortune for all of its owners, is described by Ruth K. MacDonald in *School Library Journal* as: "Four short stories about four generations of Black women and their dealings with a lucky stone. . . . Clifton uses as a frame device a grandmother telling the history of the stone to her granddaughter; by the end, the granddaughter has inherited the stone herself." A contributor to *Interracial Books for Children Bulletin* states that "the concept of past and present is usually hard for children to grasp but this book puts the passing of time in a perspective that children can understand. . . . This book contains information on various aspects of Black culture—slavery, religion and extended family—all conveyed in a way that is both positive and accurate." Michele Slung writes in the *Washington Post Book World* that the book "is at once talisman and anthology: over the years it has gathered unto it story after story, episodes indicating its power, both as a charm and as a unit of oral tradition. Clifton has a knack for projecting strong positive values without seeming too goody-goody; her poet's ear is one fact in this, her sense of humor another."

While Clifton's books for children emphasize an understanding of the past, they also focus on the present. Her series of books about Everett Anderson, for instance, explore the experiences of a young child's world in flux. Writing in *Language Arts* about *Everett Anderson's 1 2 3,* in which a young boy's mother considers remarriage, Ruth M. Stein notes that "previous books contained wistful references to Everett Anderson's absent daddy; the latest one tells how the worried little boy gradually became reconciled to the idea of a new father joining the family." And writing about *Everett Anderson's Nine Month Long,* which concerns the anticipated birth of the family's newest member, a contributor to *Interracial Books for Children Bulletin* considers that "this book, written in wonderful poetic style . . . projects a warm, loving, understanding and supportive family." Joan W. Blos, who feels that "the establishment of an active, effective, and supportive male figure is an important part of this story," adds in *School Library Journal,* "So is its tacit acknowledgement that, for the younger child, a mother's pregnancy means disturbing changes now as well as a sibling later." However, just as the birth of a sibling can cause upheaval in a child's world, so, too, can death. In *Everett Anderson's Goodbye,* Everett has difficulty coping with the death of his father; he "misses his Daddy, as he moves through the five stages of grief: denial, anger, bargaining, depression and acceptance," writes a *Washington Post Book World* contributor.

Barbara Walker writes in *Interracial Books for Children Bulletin* that "Clifton is a gifted poet with the greater gift of being able to write poetry for children." Clifton indicates to Sims that she doesn't think of it as poetry especially for children, though. "It seems to me that if you write poetry for children, you have to keep too many things in mind other than the poem. So I'm just writing a poem." *Some of the Days of Everett Anderson* is a book of nine poems, about which Marjorie Lewis observes in *School Library Journal,* "Some of the days of six-year-old 'ebony Everett Anderson' are happy; some lonely—but all of them are special, reflecting the author's own pride in being black." In the *New York Times Book Review,* Hoyt W. Fuller thinks that Clifton has "a profoundly simple way of saying all that is important to say, and we know that the struggle is worth it, that the all-important battle of image is being won, and that the future of all those beautiful black children out there need not be twisted and broken." *Everett Anderson's Christmas Coming* concerns Christmas preparations in which "each of the five days before Everett's Christmas is described by a verse," says Anita Silvey in the *Horn Book,* observing that "the overall richness of Everett's experiences dominates the text." Jane O'Reilly suggests in the *New York Times Book Review* that "Everett Anderson, black and boyish, is glimpsed, rather than explained through poems about him." *Everett Anderson's Year* celebrates "a year in the life of a city child . . . in appealing verses," says Beryl Robinson in *Horn Book,* adding that "mischief, fun, gaiety, and poignancy are a part of his days as the year progresses. The portrayals of child and mother are lively and solid, executed with both strength and tenderness."

Language is important in Clifton's writing. In answer to Sim's question about the presence of both black and white children in her work, Clifton responds specifically about *Sonora Beautiful,* which is about the insecurities and dissatisfaction of an adolescent girl and which has only white characters: "In this book, I *heard* the characters as white. I have a tendency to *hear* the language of the characters, and then I know something about who the people are." However, regarding objections to the black vernacular she often uses, Clifton tells Sims: "I do not write out of weakness. That is to say, I do not write the language I write because I don't know any other. . . . But I have a certain integrity about my art, and in *my* art you have to be honest and you have to have people talking the way they really talk. So all of my books are not in the same language." Asked by Sims whether or not she feels any special pressures or special opportunities as a black author, Clifton responds: "I do feel a responsibility. . . . First, I'm going to write books that tend to celebrate life. I'm about that. And I wish to have children see people like themselves in books. . . . I also take seriously the responsibility of not lying. . . . I'm not going to say that life is wretched if circumstance is wretched, because that's not true. So I take that responsibility, but it's a responsibility to the truth, and to my art as much as anything. I owe everybody that. . . . It's the truth as I see it, and that's what my responsibility is."

"Browsing through a volume of Lucille Clifton's poems or reading one of her children's books to my son," says Scarupa, "always makes me feel good: good to be black, good to be a woman, good to be alive." "I am excited about her work because she reflects me; she tells my story in a way and with an eloquence that

is beyond my ability," concurs Madhubuti, who concludes: "To be original, relevant, and revolutionary in the mouth of fire is the mark of a dangerous person. Lucille Clifton is a poet of *mean* talent who has not let her gifts separate her from the work at hand. She is a teacher and an example. To read her is to give birth to bright seasons." Clifton, herself, has commented on her role as a poet in *Black Women Writers (1950-1980):* "I am interested in trying to render big ideas in a simple way . . . in being understood not admired. I wish to celebrate and not to be celebrated (though a little celebration is a lot of fun). I am a woman and I write from that experience. I am a Black woman and I write from that experience. I do not feel inhibited or bound by what I am." She adds: "Sometimes I think that the most anger comes from ones who were late in discovering that when the world said nigger it meant them too. I grew up knowing that the world meant me too but that was the world's insanity and not mine. I have been treated in publishing very much like other poets are treated, that is, not really very well. I continue to write since my life as a human only includes my life as a poet, it doesn't depend on it."

BIOGRAPHICAL/CRITICAL SOURCES:

BOOKS

Beckles, Frances N., *20 Black Women,* Gateway Press, 1978.
Black Writers, Gale, 1989.
Children's Literature Review, Volume V, Gale, 1983.
Contemporary Literary Criticism, Volume IX, Gale, 1981.
Dictionary of Literary Biography, Gale, Volume V: *American Poets since World War II,* 1980, Volume XLI: *Afro-American Poets since 1955,* 1985.
Dreyer, Sharon Spredemann, *The Bookfinder: A Guide to Children's Literature about the Needs and Problems of Youth Aged 2-15,* Volume I, American Guidance Service, 1977.
Evans, Mari, editor, *Black Women Writers (1950-1980): A Critical Evaluation,* Doubleday-Anchor, 1984.

PERIODICALS

America, May 1, 1976.
Black Scholar, March, 1981.
Black World, July, 1970, February, 1973.
Book World, March 8, 1970, November 8, 1970, November 11, 1973, November 10, 1974, December 8, 1974, December 11, 1977, September 14, 1980, July 20, 1986, May 10, 1987.
Bulletin of the Center for Children's Books, March, 1971, November, 1974, March, 1976, September, 1980.
Horn Book, December, 1971, August, 1973, February, 1975, December, 1975, October, 1977.
Interracial Books for Children Bulletin, Volume V, numbers 7 and 8, 1975, Volume VII, number 1, 1976, Volume VIII, number 1, 1977, Volume X, number 5, 1979, Volume XI, numbers 1 and 2, 1980, Volume XII, number 2, 1981.
Journal of Negro Education, summer, 1974.
Journal of Reading, February, 1977, December, 1986.
Kirkus Reviews, April 15, 1970, October 1, 1970, December 15, 1974, April 15, 1976, February 15, 1982.
Language Arts, January, 1978, February 2, 1982.
Ms., October, 1976.
New Yorker, April 5, 1976.
New York Times, December 20, 1976.
New York Times Book Review, September 6, 1970, December 6, 1970, December 5, 1971, November 4, 1973, April 6, 1975, March 14, 1976, May 15, 1977.
Poetry, May, 1973.
Reading Teacher, October, 1978, March, 1981.
Redbook, November, 1969.

Saturday Review, December 11, 1971, August 12, 1972, December 4, 1973.
School Library Journal, May, 1970, December, 1970, September, 1974, December, 1977, February, 1979, March, 1980.
Tribune Books, August 30, 1987.
Virginia Quarterly Review, fall, 1976.
Voice of Youth Advocates, April, 1982.
Washington Post, November 10, 1974, August 9, 1979.
Washington Post Book World, February 10, 1980.
Western Humanities Review, summer, 1970.

* * *

CLINTON, Dirk
See SILVERBERG, Robert

* * *

CLUTHA, Janet Paterson Frame 1924-
(Janet Frame)

PERSONAL: Original name Janet Paterson Frame; surname legally changed; born August 28, 1924, in Dunedin, New Zealand; daughter of George Samuel (a train engineer) and Lottie Clarice (Godfrey) Frame. *Education:* Attended Dunedin Teachers Training College and Otago University.

ADDRESSES: Home—276 Glenfield Rd., Auckland 10, New Zealand. *Agent*—Brandt & Brandt, 101 Park Ave., New York, N.Y. 10017.

CAREER: Writer.

AWARDS, HONORS: Hubert Church Memorial Awards, for *The Lagoon, Scented Gardens for the Blind, A State of Siege,* and *Intensive Care;* Literary Fund award, New Zealand, for *Owls Do Cry;* New Zealand Scholarship in Letters, 1964; Robert Burns fellowship, 1965, and H.D.L., 1978, both from Otago University; Menton fellowship, 1974; Wattie Book of the Year from the Book Publishers Association of New Zealand, 1984, for *To the Island,* and 1986, for *The Envoy from Mirror City;* Commonwealth Writers Prize, 1989, for *The Carpathians.*

WRITINGS:

ALL UNDER NAME JANET FRAME

NOVELS

Owls Do Cry, Pegasus Press, 1957, Braziller, 1960.
Faces in the Water, Braziller, 1961.
The Edge of the Alphabet, Braziller, 1962.
Scented Gardens for the Blind, Pegasus Press, 1963, Braziller, 1964.
The Adaptable Man, Braziller, 1965.
A State of Siege, Braziller, 1966.
The Rainbirds, W. H. Allen, 1968, published as *Yellow Flowers in the Antipodean Room,* Braziller, 1969.
Intensive Care, Braziller, 1970.
Daughter Buffalo, Braziller, 1972.
Living in the Maniototo, Braziller, 1979.
The Carpathians, Braziller, 1988.

SHORT STORIES

The Lagoon: Stories, Pegasus Press, 1951, revised edition published as *The Lagoon and Other Stories,* 1961.
The Reservoir: Stories and Sketches [and] *Snowman, Snowman: Fables and Fantasies,* two volumes, Braziller, 1963.
The Reservoir and Other Stories, Pegasus Press, 1966.

OTHER

The Pocket Mirror (poems), Braziller, 1967.
Mona Minim and the Smell of the Sun (juvenile), Braziller, 1969.
To the Island, Braziller, 1983.
An Angel at My Table (autobiography), Braziller, 1984.
The Envoy from Mirror City (autobiography), Braziller, 1985.

Contributor of short stories to *New Yorker* and *Harper's Bazaar.*

SIDELIGHTS: Janet Frame's writing, generally characterized by a dark and pessimistic tone, reflects her own history of mental breakdown and hospitalization. However, Frame proves her versatility with her vivid geographic descriptions of her native New Zealand and her occasional optimism. James Burns calls Frame "New Zealand's brightest light in the literary scene" and further comments that her "achievement in the short story and novel would appear to be based on personal experience in the field of mental illness." Indeed, her novel *Faces in the Water* was written, according to Burns, when "a doctor suggested that as an exercise in therapy she write the story of her experiences in mental hospitals." Joyce Carol Oates thought it "her best book, for here Miss Frame dealt with the fluid boundary between sanity and madness, the watery depths of madness in which the normal 'see' their own faces. If they recoil in horror, is it not because they are themselves partly mad?"

Thomas L. Vince finds *Intensive Care* "morbid, dense, dreary, incoherent and impossible to decipher." This chronicle of two families living in Waipori, New Zealand includes several tragic elements: an obese daughter working for the Bruised Baby Society; a son-in-law whose love affair with a teenager ends in the murder of the girl and her parents and the man's suicide; and a futuristic era in which societal problems are met by a computer marking people for death. Arthur Edelstein writes that the novel "is bewildering yet powerful, an experience in which it cannot be determined how many layers of dream one has descended into, in which the characters dreaming seem themselves to be dreamed, as though all were the fevered conjurings of a patient in one of the novel's 'Recovery Units.'" Julian Moynahan calls the book "careless with respect to the moral issues the lives of its principal characters fitfully reflect" and thought that this novel would not add to Frame's popularity. A critic for *Time* writes that *Intensive Care* continues Frame's preoccupation with history as "a hereditary malignancy that engulfs the present and dooms the future to madness, loneliness and death."

In *A State of Siege,* the protagonist Malfred Signal retires to an isolated island after years of nursing her ailing mother. While on the island she endures a night of terror and dies. David Hayman comments: "*A State of Siege* is another of Janet Frame's exercises in false perspectives, an attempt to telescope the impressions and attitudes of a wasted life." Anne Francis finds that "the theme of this highly introspective novel, that of self-appraisal, is well sustained. Malfred's life has no dramatic highlights, but the reader is swept along by the author's compassion for her subject." A *Times Literary Supplement* reviewer comments that Frame offered "a moving portrait of loneliness and middle age." The tension resulting from the natural and human factors helped make the book a successful movie produced with the assistance of the New Zealand Film Commission; the film won a Golden Globe Award.

With *Daughter Buffalo,* Frame appears to leave her preoccupation with insanity and the insane and turns to death as her subject matter. "In this astounding novel," Roger Baker writes, "Janet Frame tackles death in full frontal manner. . . . While extraordinary the novel is thoughtful, serious and intelligent in every phrase and every pause." Barbara Harte comments that Frame's "technique in *Daughter Buffalo* is virtually a novel within a novel, or a dual novel, and within this perilous framework, anathema to the insensitive amateur, she has succeeded admirably." Josephine Hendin also finds this novel an admirable success. "She writes with a lyrical brilliance, with a genius for the narrowest, the darkest corners of human need," Hendin comments. "But she writes with a beauty that confers a morbid grandeur, that makes poetry of the particular, the private, the enclosed. And she has written a novel as gleaming as pure, black, shattered glass." Alice Van Buren recommends the novel to "anyone with a plain healthy interest in death, or in language, or in Janet Frame."

Frequently, critics applaud Frame's grasp of New Zealand geography. Reviewing *Yellow Flowers in the Antipodean Room* Muriel Haynes comments on "the sweep and sharpness of her observations of this part of the world she knows so thoroughly. No detail escapes her regarding the endless perversity by which nature's beneficence, its unifying religious presence, has been corrupted through a cult of Philistine pleasure seeking and chauvinism." Kathleen Nott remarks that Frame possesses "insight, wit, compassion and remarkable control of the underlying symbolic and mythical themes which never destroy the surface, the bright, clean, modern, rather suburban welfare New Zealand. . . . She can pile up the imagery."

In her volume of poetry *Pocket Mirror*, Frame again displays her knowledge of her native New Zealand and writes with unusual optimism. In a letter to James Burns dated September, 1965, Frame writes: "My poetry (if it can be called by such a grand name) is more private, more like a diary, and often it is in condensed form a statement of what may appear later as a story or novel." Frame's best poems, according to John Press, are those in which she is "intent on language, not feeling." Press also comments that her "imagery, sensibility and emotional reactions to landscapes, paintings and human predicaments are abundant and generous." Stephen Stepanchev characterizes Frame as "a poet of place" and writes that her poems "evoke the sights, sounds and smells of a terrain unfamiliar to most of her American readers: Dunedin, New Zealand." He concludes: "It is clear that Janet Frame is a poet with eyes that see and an imagination that discovers apt resemblances among the scattered data of reality. These powers are put at the service of her native land, for as she says, 'It is places that will not perish.' "

MEDIA ADAPTATIONS: A State of Siege was adapted for a film of the same title, directed by Costa-Gavras, released by Cinema 5, 1973.

BIOGRAPHICAL/CRITICAL SOURCES:

BOOKS

Contemporary Literary Criticism, Gale, Volume II, 1974, Volume III, 1975, Volume VI, 1976, Volume XXVI, 1983.
Hyman, Stanley Edgar, *Standards: A Chronicle of Books for Our Time,* Horizon Press, 1966.

PERIODICALS

Best Sellers, June 15, 1970, October 1, 1972.
Books Abroad, spring, 1967, summer, 1967.
Books and Bookmen, June, 1967, July, 1973.
Harvard Advocate, winter, 1973.
New Leader, August 14, 1967.
New Republic, May 31, 1975.
New Yorker, September 30, 1972.
New York Review, February 27, 1969.

New York Times, February 3, 1969.
New York Times Book Review, February 9, 1969, May 3, 1970, August 27, 1972, September 16, 1979, January 22, 1989.
Observer Review, October 13, 1968.
Punch, February 7, 1968.
Saturday Review, April 19, 1969.
Southern Review, Volume IX, number 3, summer, 1973.
Time, March 21, 1969, May 18, 1970.
Times Literary Supplement, October 21, 1965, April 27, 1967, February 15, 1968, January 26, 1973.
Washington Post Book World, August 26, 1979.

* * *

COCTEAU, Jean (Maurice Eugene Clement) 1889-1963

PERSONAL: Born July 5, 1889, in Maisons-Laffitte (Seine-et-Oise), France; died October 11, 1963; son of Georges (a lawyer) and Eugenie (Lecomte) Cocteau. *Education:* Studied at Lycee Condorcet, Paris; attended private classes.

CAREER: Poet, playwright, novelist, essayist, painter, and director; became an early celebrity after a reading of his first poems at the Theatre Femina, Paris, France, 1916; founded the review, *Scheherazade,* with Maurice Rostand and others; met Diaghilev, 1912, and wrote his first scenario for ballet, "Le Dieu Bleu"; during World War I, went to Rheims as a civilian ambulance driver, and later to Belgium where he joined a group of marine-riflemen, until it was discovered that his presence was unauthorized; served for a while with an auxiliary corps in Paris; founded Editions de la Sirene with Blaise Cendrars, 1918; contributor on the arts to *Paris-Midi,* March to August, 1919; in 1936, made a trip around the world in eighty days, after a wager with *France-Soir;* wrote a regular series for *Ce Soir,* 1937-38; produced his first cartoon for a tapestry, commissioned by Gobelins, 1948; visited the United States in late 1948; presented the film "Le Testament d'Orphee" in Warsaw, Poland, 1960.

MEMBER: Academie Francaise, Academie Royale de Belgique, Academie Mallarme, American Academy, German Academy (Berlin), Academie de Jazz (president), Academie du Disque, Association France-Hongrie, National Institute of Arts and Letters (New York; honorary member).

AWARDS, HONORS: Prix Louions-Delluc, 1946; Grand Prix de la Critique Internationale, 1950; Grand Prix du Film Avant-garde, 1950, for *Orphee;* D.Litt., Oxford University, 1956; Commandeur de la Legion d'Honneur, 1961.

WRITINGS:

POETRY

La Lampe d'Aladin, Societe d'Editions, 1909.
Le Prince frivole, Mercure de France, 1910.
La Danse de Sophocle, Mercure de France, 1912.
Le Cap de Bonne-Esperance, Editions de la Sirene, 1919.
L'Ode a Picasso, Francois Bernouard, 1919.
(With Andre Lhote) *Escales,* Editions de la Sirene, 1920.
Poesies: 1917-20, Editions de la Sirene, 1920.
Vocabulaire, Editions de la Sirene, 1922.
Plain-Chant, Stock, 1923.
Poesie, 1916-23, Gallimard, 1924.
La Rose de Francois, Francois Bernouard, 1924.
Cri ecrit, Imprimerie de Montane (Montpellier), 1925.
Pierre Mutilee, Editions des Cahiers Libres, 1925.
L'Ange heurtebise, Stock, 1925.

Opera: Oeuvres poetiques 1925-27, Stock, 1927, revised edition, 1959, published as *Oeuvres poetiques: 1925-27,* Dutilleul, 1959.

Morceaux choisis, Gallimard, 1932, published as *Poemes,* H. Kaeser (Lausanne), 1945.

Mythologie (poems written on lithographic stones; contains 10 original lithographs by Giorgio di Chirico), Editions de Quatre-Chemins, 1934.

Allegories, Gallimard, 1941.

Leone, Nouvelle Revue Francaise, 1945, translation by Alan Neame published as *Leoun,* [London], 1960.

La Crucifixion, Morihien, 1946.

Le Chiffre sept, Seghers, 1952.

Appogiatures (with a portrait of Cocteau by Modigliani), Editions du Rocher (Monaco), 1953.

Dentelle d'eternite, Seghers, 1953.

Clair-Obscur, Editions du Rocher, 1954.

Poemes: 1916-55, Gallimard, 1956.

(Contributor) Paul Eluard, *Corps memorabiles,* Seghers, 1958.

De la Brouille, Editions Dynamo (Liege), 1960.

Ceremonial espagnol du Phoenix [suivi de] *La Partie d'echecs,* Gallimard, 1961.

Le Requiem, Gallimard, 1962.

Faire-Part (ninety-one previously unpublished poems), foreword by Jean Marais and Claude-Michel Cluny, Librairie Saint-Germain des Pres, 1968.

NOVELS

Le Potomak, Societe Litteraire de France, 1919, definitive edition, Stock, 1924.

(Self-illustrated) *Le Grand ecart,* Stock, 1923, reprinted, 1970, translation by Lewis Galantiere published as *The Grand Ecart,* Putnam, 1925, translation by Dorothy Williams published as *The Miscreant,* P. Owen, 1958.

Thomas l'imposteur, Nouvelle Revue Francaise, 1923, revised edition, edited by Bernard Garniez, Macmillan, 1964, translation and introduction by Galantiere published as *Thomas the Impostor,* Appleton, 1925, translation by Williams published as *The Impostor,* Noonday Press, 1957.

Les Enfants terribles, Grasset, 1929, reprinted, 1963, revised edition, edited by Jacques Hardre, Blaisdell, 1969, translation by Samuel Putnam published as *Enfants Terribles,* Harcourt, 1930, translation by Rosamund Lehmann published in England as *The Children of the Game,* Harvill, 1955, same translation published as *The Holy Terrors* (not the same as translation of *Les Monstres sacres,* below), New Directions, 1957.

La Fin du Potomak, Gallimard, 1940.

Deux travestis (contains lithographs by Cocteau), Fournier, 1947.

PLAYS

Les Maries de la tour Eiffel, Nouvelle Revue Francaise, 1924, translation by Dudley Fitts published as "The Eiffel Tower Wedding Party," in *The Infernal Machine, and Other Plays,* New Directions, 1963, translation by Michael Benedikt published as "The Wedding on the Eiffel Tower," in *Modern French Plays,* Faber, 1964.

Orphee, Stock, 1927, translation by Carl Wildman published as *Orphee: A Tragedy in One Act* (first produced in New York at Living Theatre as "Orpheus," September 30, 1954), Oxford University Press, 1933, translation by John Savacool published as *Orphee,* New Directions, 1963.

Antigone, Nouvelle Revue Francaise, 1928, translation by Wildman published in *Four Plays,* MacGibbon & Kee, 1961.

La Voix humaine (first produced in Paris at Comedie Francaise, February 17, 1930), Stock, 1930, translation by Wildman published as *The Human Voice,* Vision Press, 1951 (produced in New York, 1980).

La Machine infernale, Grasset, 1934, reprinted, Livre de Poche, 1974, published in England in French, under the original title, with an introduction and notes by W. M. Landers, Harrap, 1957, translation and introduction by Wildman published as *The Infernal Machine,* Oxford University Press, 1936, translation by Albert Bermel published as *The Infernal Machine,* New Directions, 1963.

Les Chevaliers de la table ronde, Gallimard, 1937, reprinted, 1966, translation by W. H. Auden published as *The Knights of the Round Table,* New Directions, 1963.

Les Parents terribles, Gallimard, 1938, reprinted, 1972, revised edition, edited by R. K. Totton, Methuen, 1972, translation by Charles Frank published as *Intimate Relations,* MacGibbon & Kee, 1962.

Les Monstres sacres, Gallimard, 1940, translation by Edward O. Marsh published as *The Holy Terrors,* MacGibbon & Kee, 1962.

La Machine a ecrire, Gallimard, 1941, translation by Ronald Duncan published as *The Typewriter,* Dobson, 1957.

Renaud et Armide, Gallimard, 1943.

L'Aigle a deux tetes, Gallimard, 1946, reprinted, 1973, translation by Duncan published as *The Eagle Has Two Heads,* Funk, 1948, translation by Wildman published as *The Eagle with Two Heads,* MacGibbon & Kee, 1962.

(Adaptor) Tennessee Williams, *Un Tramway nomme desir* (first produced in Paris at Theatre Edouard VII, October, 1949), Bordas, 1949.

Bacchus, Gallimard, 1952, translation by Mary C. Hoeck published as *Bacchus: A Play,* New Directions, 1963.

(Translator and adaptor) Jerome Kilty, *Cher menteur* (first produced in Paris at Theatre de l'Athenee, October 4, 1960), Paris-Theatre, 1960.

L'Impromptu du Palais-Royal, Gallimard, 1962.

Also author of "Parade," 1917, and "Le Boeuf sur le toit," 1920.

OPERA

Oedipus rex: Opera-oratorio en deux actes d'apres Sophocle, Boosey & Hawkes, 1949.

FILMS; SCENARIST AND ADAPTOR

(And director) *Le Sang d'un poete* (produced, 1930), scenario, with photographs, published by Editions du Rocher, 1948, augmented edition, 1957, translation by Lily Pons published as *Blood of a Poet,* Bodley Press, 1949.

"La Comedie du bonheur," produced, 1940.

"Le Baron fantome" (appeared also as actor), produced, 1942.

(And co-director with Jean Delannoy) *L'Eternel retour* (scenario and photographs; produced, 1943), Nouvelles Editions Francaises, 1948.

"Les Dames du Bois du Boulogne," produced, 1944.

(And director) *La Belle et la bete* (based on a fairy tale by Mme. Leprince de Beaumont; produced, 1945), Editions du Rocher, 1958, bilingual edition, New York University Press, 1970.

Ruy Blas (adaptation of the play by Victor Hugo; produced, 1947), Editions du Rocher, 1947.

"La Voix humaine" (adaptation of his one act play), produced, 1947.

(And director) "L'Aigle a deux tetes" (adaptation of his play), produced, 1947.

"Noces de sable," produced 1948.

(And director) *Les Parents terribles* (adaptation of his play; scenario and photographs; produced, 1948), Le Monde Illustre, 1949, translation and adaptation by Charles Frank produced under title "Intimate Relations" (also known as "Disobedient"), 1952.

"Les Enfants terribles" (adaptation of his novel), produced, 1948.

(And director) *Orphee* (scenario and photographs; speaks a few lines as "author"; produced, 1949), Andre Bonne, 1951.

(And director) "Santo Sospiro" (short film), produced, 1951.

"Ce Siecle a cinquante ans" (short film), produced, 1952.

"La Coronna nagra," produced, 1952.

(And director) "Le Rouge est mis" (short film), produced, 1952.

(And director) *Le Testament d'Orphee* (produced, 1959), Editions du Rocher, 1959.

NONFICTION

Le Coq et l'arlequin (notes on music, with a portrait of Cocteau by Picasso), Editions de la Sirene, 1918, translation by Rollo H. Myers published as *Cock and Harlequin: Notes Concerning Music,* Egoist Press (London), 1921.

Dans le ciel de la patrie, Societe Spad, 1918.

Le Secret professionnel, Stock, 1922.

Dessins, Stock, 1923, translation published as *Drawings,* Dover, 1972.

Picasso, Stock, 1923.

Lettre a Jacques Maritain, Stock, 1926 (selected excerpts in English included in *Journals,* 1956; also see below), published as *Lettre a Maritain: Reponse a Jean Cocteau* (including response by Maritain), Stock, 1964.

Le Rappel a l'ordre, Stock, 1926, translation by Myers published as *A Call to Order,* Faber & Gwyer, 1926, reprinted, Haskell House, 1974.

Romeo et Juliette: Pretexte a mise en scene d'apres le drame de William Shakespeare, Se Vend au Sans Pareil, 1926.

Le Mystere laic (an essay on indirect study), Editions de Quatre Chemins, 1928, published as *Essai de critique indirecte: Le mystere laic-Des beaux arts consideres comme un assassinat,* introduction by Bernard Grasset, Grasset, 1932.

(Self illustrated) *Opium: Journal d'une desintoxication,* Stock, 1930, reprinted, 1972, translation by Ernest Boyd published as *Opium: The Diary of an Addict* (contains twenty-seven illustrations by Cocteau), Longmans, Green, 1932, translation by Margaret Crosland and Sinclair Road published as *Opium: The Diary of a Cure,* P. Owen, 1957, revised edition, 1968, Grove, 1958.

Le Livre blanc, Editions du Signe, 1930, reprinted, B. Laville, 1970, published as *The White Paper,* Olympia Press (Paris), 1957, Macaulay, 1958, translation with an introduction by Crosland, containing woodcuts by Cocteau, published as *Le Livre blanc,* P. Owen, 1969.

(Self-illustrated) *Portraits-Souvenir, 1900-1914,* Grasset, 1935, translation by Crosland published as *Paris Album, 1900-1914,* W. H. Allen, 1956.

(Contributor) Gea Augsbourg, *La Vie de Darius Milhaud,* Correa, 1935.

60 dessins pour "Les Enfants terribles", Grasset, 1935.

Mon premier voyage: Tour du monde en 80 jours, Gallimard, 1936, translation by Stuart Gilbert published as *Round the World Again in Eighty Days,* G. Routledge, 1937, translation by W. J. Strachan published as *My Journey Round the World,* P. Owen, 1958.

Dessins en marge du texte des "Chevaliers de la table ronde," Gallimard, 1941.

Le Greco, Le Divan, 1943.

Portrait de Mounet-Sully (contains sixteen drawings by Cocteau), F. Bernouard (Paris), 1945.

La Belle et la bete: Journal d'un film, Janin, 1946, translation by Ronald Duncan published as *Diary of a Film,* Roy, 1950, revised edition published as *Beauty and the Beast: Diary of a Film,* Dover, 1972.

Poesie critique (poetry criticism), edited by Henri Parisot, Editions des Quatre Vents, 1946, published in two volumes, Gallimard, 1959.

(With Paul Claudel, Paul Eluard, and Stephane Mallarme) *De la musique encore et toujours!,* preface by Paul Valery, Editions du Tambourinaire, 1946.

La Difficulte d'etre, P. Morihien, 1947, translation by Elizabeth Sprigge published as *The Difficulty of Being,* introduction by Ned Rorem, P. Owen, 1966, Coward, 1967.

Le Foyer des artistes, Plon, 1947.

L'Eternel retour, Nouvelles Editions Francaises, 1947.

Art and Faith: Letters between Jacques Maritain and Jean Cocteau, Philosophical Library, 1948.

(Self-illustrated) *Drole de menage,* P. Morihien, 1948.

Lettre aux Americains, Grasset, 1949.

(Editor) *Almanach du theatre et du cinema,* Editions de Flore, 1949.

Maalesh: Journal d'une tournee de theatre, Gallimard, 1949, translation by Mary C. Hoeck published as *Maalesh: Theatrical Tour in the Middle East,* P. Owen, 1956.

(Editor) *Choix de lettres de Max Jacob a Jean Cocteau: 1919-1944,* P. Morihien, 1949.

Dufy, Flammarion, 1950.

(With Andre Bazin) *Orson Welles,* Chavane, 1950.

Modigliani, F. Hazin (Paris), 1950.

(With others) *Portrait de famille,* Fini, 1950.

Jean Marais, Calmann-Levy, 1951, reprinted, 1975.

Entretiens autour de cinematographe, recueillis par Andre Fraigneau, A. Bonne, 1951, translation by Vera Traill published as *Cocteau on Film: A Conversation Recorded by Andre Fraigneau,* Roy, 1954, reprinted, Dover, 1972.

Journal d'un inconnu, Grasset, 1952, translation by Alec Brown published as *The Hand of a Stranger,* Elek Books (London), 1956, Horizon, 1959.

Reines de la France, Grasset, 1952.

(With Julien Green) *Gide vivant* (includes commentary by Cocteau and excerpts from the diary of Green), Amiot-Dumont, 1952.

Carte blanche (prose sketches with drawings, watercolors and photographs by Cocteau), Mermod (Lausanne), 1953.

(With others) *Prestige de la danse,* Clamart, 1953.

Discours de reception de M. Jean Cocteau a l'Academie francaise et reponse de M. Andre Maurois, Gallimard, 1955.

Look to the Glory of Your Firm and the Excellence of Your Merchandise, for If You Deem These Good, Your Welfare Becomes the Welfare of All, translated by Lewis Galantiere, Draeger (Montrouge), c.1955.

Aux confins de la Chine, Edition Caracteres, 1955.

Colette: Discours de reception a l'Academie Royale de Belgique, Grasset, 1955 (extracts in English published in *My Contemporaries,* 1967; also see below).

Lettre sur la poesie, Dutilleul, 1955.

Le Dragon des mers, Georges Guillot, 1955.

(Contributor) *Marbre et decoration,* Federation Marbriere de France, c.1955. *Journals* (contains sixteen drawings by Cocteau), edited and translated with an introduction by Wallace Fowlie, Criterion Books, 1956.

Adieu a Mistinguett, Editions Dynamo, 1956.

Art et sport, Savonnet (Limoges), 1956.

Impression: Arts de la rue, Editions Dynamo, 1956.

(Author of introduction and notes) Jean Dauven, compiler, *Jean Cocteau chez les sirens: Une experience de linguistic sur le discours de reception a l'Academie francaise de M. Jean Cocteau* (illustrations by Picasso), Editions du Rocher, 1956.

Temoignage (with portrait and engraving by Picasso), P. Bertrand, 1956.

Le Discours de Strasbourg, Societe Messine d'Editions et d'Impressions (Metz), 1956.

Le Discours d'Oxford, Gallimard, 1956, translation by Jean Stewart published as "Poetry and Invisibility," in *London Magazine,* January, 1957.

(With Louis Aragon) *Entretiens sur le Musee de Dresde,* Cercle d'Art, 1957, translation published as *Conversations on the Dresden Gallery,* Holmes, 1983.

Erik Satie, Editions Dynamo, 1957.

La Chapelle Saint Pierre, Villefranche sur Mer, Editions du Rocher, 1957.

La Corrida du premier mai, Grasset, 1957.

Comme un miel noir (in French and English), L'Ecole Estienne, 1958.

(With Roloff Beny and others) *Merveilles de la Mediterranee,* Arthaud, 1958.

Paraprosodies precedees de 7 dialogues, Editions Du Rocher, 1958.

(Contributor) G. Coanet, *De bas en haut,* La Societe Messine d'Editions et d'Impressions (Metz), 1958.

La Salle des mariages, Hotel de ville de Menton, Editions du Rocher, 1958.

La Canne blanche, Editions Estienne, 1959.

Gondole des morts, All'Insegne del Pesce d'Oro (Milan), 1959.

Guide a l'usage des visiteurs de la Chapelle Saint Blaise des Simples, Editions du Rocher, 1960, reprinted, 1975.

De la brouille, Editions Dynamo, 1960.

Notes sur "Le Testament d'Orphee," Editions Dynamo, 1960.

(Editor) *Amedeo Modigilani: Quinze dessins,* Leda, 1960.

Decentralisation, [Paris], 1961.

Du Serieux, [Paris], 1961.

(With others) *Insania pingens,* Ciba (Basle), 1961, published as *Petits maitres de la folies,* Clairfontaines (Lausanne), 1961.

Le Cordon ombilical, Plon, 1962.

Picasso: 1916-1961 (with twenty-four original lithographs by Picasso), Editions du Rocher, 1962.

Discours a l'Academie royale de langue et de litterature francaises, Editions Dynamo, 1962.

Hommage, Editions Dynamo, 1962.

Interview par Jean Breton (preceded by two poems by Cocteau, "Malediction au laurier," and "Hommage a Igor Stravinsky"), [Paris], 1963.

Adieu d'Antonio Ordonez, Editions Forces Vives, 1963.

(Contributor) *La Comtesse de Noailles,* Librairie Academique Perrin, 1963.

(Contributor) *Exposition les peintres temoins de leur temps* (catalog), Musee Galliera (Paris), 1963.

(Contributor) *Toros muertos,* Editions Forces Vives, 1963.

La Mesangere, De Tartas, 1963.

Jean Cocteau: Entretien avec Roger Stephane (interview), J. Tallandier, 1964.

(Contributor) *Exposition Lucien Clergue* (catalog), Le Musee (Luneville), 1964.

Entretien avec Andre Fraigneau (interview), preface by Pierre de Boisdeffre, Union Generale d'Editions, 1965.

Pegase, Nouveau Cercle Parisien du Livre, 1965.

My Contemporaries, translated, edited, and introduced by Crosland, P. Owen, 1967, Chilton, 1968.

Entre Radiguet et Picasso, Editions Hermann, 1967.

Professional Secrets: The Autobiography of Jean Cocteau (not related to 1922 book), translated by Richard Howard, edited by Robert Phelps, Farrar, Straus, 1970.

Lettres a Andre Gide avec quelques reponses d'Andre Gide, La Table Ronde, 1970.

(With Raymond Radiguet) *Paul et Virginie,* Edition Speciale, 1973.

Lettres a Milorad, Editions Saint-Germain-des-Pres, 1975.

Also author of an unpublished ballet scenario, "Le Dieu bleu," 1912.

OMNIBUS VOLUMES

Call to Order (contains *Cock and Harlequin, Professional Secrets,* and other critical essays), translated by Rollo H. Myers, Holt, 1923, reprinted, Haskell House, 1974.

Oedipe Roi [and] *Romeo et Julliette,* Plon, 1928.

Jean Cocteau (contains a study of Roger Lannes, poems, and a bibliography), Seghers, 1945, revised edition, 1969.

Oeuvres completes, 10 volumes, Marguerat, 1947-50.

Theatre, 2 volumes, Gallimard, 1948, augmented edition, 2 volumes, Grasset, 1957.

Poemes (contains *Leone, Allegories, La Crucifixion,* and "Neige"), Gallimard, 1948.

Theatre de Poche, P. Morihien, 1949, published as *Nouveau theatre de poche,* Editions du Rocher, 1960.

Anthologie poetique de Jean Cocteau, Le Club Francais du Livre, 1951.

Venise images par Ferruccio Leiss [and] *L'Autre face de Venise par Jean Cocteau,* D. Guarnati (Milan), 1953.

Le Grand ecart [and] *La Voix humaine,* Club des Editeurs, 1957.

Impression [with] *Arts de la rue* [and] *Eloge de l'imprimerie,* Editions Dynamo, 1957.

Ceremonial espagnal du phenix [with] *La Partie d'eches,* Gallimard, 1961.

Cocteau par Lui-meme, edited by Andre Fraigneau, Editions du Seuil, 1957.

Five Plays (contains "Orphee," "Antigone," "Intimate Relations," "The Holy Terrors," "The Eagle with Two Heads"), Hill & Wang, 1961.

Orpheus, Oedipus Rex, [and] *The Infernal Machine,* translated with a foreword and introductory essay by Wildman, Oxford University Press, 1962.

Four Plays (contains "Antigone," "Intimate Relations," "The Holy Terrors," "The Eagle with Two Heads"), MacGibbon Kee, 1962.

Les Enfants terribles [and] *Les Parents terribles,* Club des Librairies de France, 1962.

Special Cocteau: Les Maries de la Tour Eiffel [and] *Les Chevaliers de la table ronde,* [Paris], 1966.

Opera [with] *Le Discours du grand sommeil,* preface by Jacques Brosse, Gallimard, 1967.

The Infernal Machine, and Other Plays, New Directions, 1967.

Opera [with] *Plain-Chant,* Livre de Poche, 1967.

Le Cap de Bonne Esperance [with] *Discours du grand sommeil,* Gallimard, 1967.

Pages choisies, edited by Robert Prat, Hachette, 1967.

Opera [with] *Des mots, De mon style,* Tchou, 1967.

Two Screenplays: The Blood of a Poet [and] *The Testament of Orpheus,* translated by Carol Martin-Sperry, Orion Press, 1968.

Screenplays and Other Writings on the Cinema (contains "Blood of a Poet," "Beauty and the Beast," "Testament of Orpheus"), Orion Press, 1968.

White Paper [with] *The Naked Beast at Heaven's Gate,* the latter by P. Angelique, Greenleaf Classics, 1968.

Three Screenplays: L'Eternal retour, Orphee, La Belle et la bete, translated by Carol Martin-Sperry, Orion Press, 1968.

Cocteau's World (anthology), translated and edited by Margaret Crosland, P. Owen, 1971, Dodd, 1973.

Du cinematographie (collected works), edited by Andre Bernard and Claude Gauteur, P. Belfond, 1973.

Entretiens sur le cinematographie, edited by Bernard and Gauteur, P. Belfond, 1973.

Mon Premier voyage, Des beaux-arts consideres comme un assassinat, Lettre a Maritan, Vialetay, 1973.

Orphee: Extraits de la tragedie d'Orphee ainsi que des films Orphee et Le Testament d'Orphee, Bordas, 1973.

Poesie de journalism, 1935-1938, P. Belfond, 1973.

Also published *Paraprosodies* [precedees de] *Sept dialogues avec le Seigneur qui est en nous,* Editions du Rocher.

SIDELIGHTS: Wallace Fowlie has said of Jean Cocteau, "Variousness is the clue to his genius." Listing some of his many achievements, Fowlie reported: "When Cocteau played the drums in a jazz band, he helped launch the fashion of jazz. His first film, 'Le Sang d'un poete,' initiated a use of the *merveilleux* in cinema art that is still being copied. . . . With *Antigone* and *Orphee,* in which he played Angel Heurtebise in the Pitoeff production, he rejuvenated the theatre of antiquity. . . . He was also among the very first to call attention to the art of Picasso and the art of Louis Armstrong." A *National Observer* writer suggests that, "of the artistic generation whose daring gave birth to Twentieth Century Art, Cocteau came closest to being a Renaissance man."

His versatility, however, caused some damage to his reputation as a serious artist. Henri Peyre wrote, "It became customary to be entertained by Cocteau's chameleon-like metamorphoses and to treat him considerably as a 'juggler.' " But he went on to point out that: "The illusionist in Cocteau . . . was the outward mask which he liked to offer to the public in self-defence." According to Fowlie, the serious purposes behind his work emerged when he was awarded high academic honors: "It became apparent that the long career had not been motivated by the ambition to amuse, that . . . Cocteau was an indefatigable worker, a man believing that a supernatural force always directed the natural forces, . . . whose seeming facility was his method of work."

Cocteau was born into a social milieu whose members, according to Elizabeth Sprigge and Jean-Jacques Kihm, "led an enchanted existence, in which the arts were recognised as an essential part of good living." As a child he formed a lifelong passion for the theatre, which he described many times as, "the fever of crimson and gold." Fowlie reported: "The atmosphere of the theatre became a world for him. . . . Every detail of a theatre production fascinated him, from the luminously painted backdrop to the women selling caramels in the intermission." Writing of Cocteau's own work in the theater, Peyre contended that *"La Machine infernale* remains the best modernization of the Oedipus story in our generation."

Cocteau has also been especially highly praised for his films. Andre Fraigneau gave this assessment of the screen version of "Orphee": "Like a poem, a great novel, or a sequence in music, [it] can and calls out to be seen and heard again. There is no example of cinema in which the decline of the genre is contradicted with greater force." In this film, Cocteau's concern with unusual effects was given full play; Sprigge and Kihm noted that he "was able to indulge his obsession with mirrors to the full." They continued: "He greatly enjoyed both the real mirrors and the ingenious semblance of mirrors: frames framing a void, the construction of twin rooms and twin objects, which if you were quick enough you could see not to be perfectly inverted, Maria Casares playing back to back with her double, Jean Marais disappearing through a void, which in the next shot was filled with a mirror." When considering such effects, Fowlie pointed out that "it is well to remember Cocteau's statement that he is not a maker of films in the ordinary sense. He calls himself a poet using the camera as a vehicle for the projection of dreams."

Summing up the whole of Cocteau's achievement, Fowlie gave him a high place in the French critical tradition: "All of Cocteau's work can justifiably be called a 'poetry of criticism,' because in it he gives himself over without effort to the delight of judging, to the enjoyment of a game of ideas which forms the basis of criticism. Cocteau is one of those French writers—novelists, poets, dramatists—who are critics, and among the finest that France has produced, critics not only in their critical essays but also in their creative works."

Cocteau is buried at Milly-la-Foret, in the garden of the chapel Saint-Blaise-des Simples, which he designed himself.

MEDIA ADAPTATIONS: There are several recordings of Cocteau's works in French; *Opium: Journal of a Cure* has been dramatized by Roc Brynner and produced in Dublin and London, 1969, and in New York, 1970.

BIOGRAPHICAL/CRITICAL SOURCES:

BOOKS

Brown, Frederick, *An Impersonation of Angels: A Biography of Jean Cocteau,* Viking, 1968.

Cocteau, Jean, *Professional Secrets: The Autobiography of Jean Cocteau,* translated by Richard Howard, edited by Robert Phelps, Farrar, Straus, 1970.

Contemporary Literary Criticism, Gale, Volume 1, 1973, Volume 8, 1978, Volume 15, 1980, Volume 16, 1981, Volume 43, 1987.

Crosland, Margaret, *Jean Cocteau,* Knopf, 1956.

Dictionary of Literary Biography, Volume 65: *French Novelists, 1900-1930,* Gale, 1988.

Fowlie, Wallace, editor and translator, *The Journals of Jean Cocteau,* Criterion, 1956.

Fowlie, *Jean Cocteau: The History of a Poet's Age,* Indiana University Press, 1966.

Fraigneau, Andre, *Jean Cocteau: Entretiens autour du cinematographe,* Andre Bonne, 1951, translation by Vera Traill published as *Cocteau on the Film: A Conversation Recorded by Andre Fraigneau,* Dobson, 1954.

Fraigneau, Andre, *Cocteau par lui-meme,* Editions du Seuil, 1957, translation by Donald Lehmkuhl published as *Cocteau,* Grove, 1961.

Fraigneau, Andre, *Jean Cocteau: Entretiens a la radio,* preface by Pierre de Boisdeffre, Union Generale d'Editions, 1965.

Gilson, Rene, *Jean Cocteau* (on his film work), Seghers, 1964, Crown, 1969.

Knapp, Bettina L., *Jean Cocteau,* Twayne, 1970.

Lannes, Roger, *Jean Cocteau,* Seghers, 1945.

Sprigge, Elizabeth and Jean-Jacques Kihm, *Jean Cocteau: The Man and the Mirror,* Gollancz, 1968.

Steegmullen, Francis, *Cocteau,* Little, Brown, 1970.

PERIODICALS

Adam, Number 300, 1965.

American Imago, summer, 1976.

Chicago Tribune, May 17, 1988, July 2, 1989.

Choice, November, 1973.
Commentary, April, 1971.
Commonweal, November 17, 1967.
Empreintes (Brussels), May, June, July, 1950.
La Table Ronde, October, 1955.
London Magazine, March, 1967.
Los Angeles Times, February 12, 1989.
National Observer, June 12, 1967.
New Yorker, September 27, 1969.
New York Times, May 13, 1984, April 17, 1988, September 22, 1989.
New York Times Book Review, December 25, 1966.
Times (London), November 28, 1984, April 4, 1985, April 2, 1987.
Times Literary Supplement, October 6-12, 1989.

* * *

COETZEE, J(ohn) M(ichael) 1940-

PERSONAL: Born February 9, 1940, in South Africa; son of a sheep farmer; children: Nicholas, Gisela. *Education:* University of Cape Town, M.A., 1963; University of Texas, Ph.D., 1969.

ADDRESSES: Home—P.O. Box 92, Rondebosch 7700, South Africa. *Agent*—Peter Lampack, 551 Fifth Ave., New York, N.Y. 10017.

CAREER: International Business Machines (IBM), London, England, applications programmer, 1962-63; International Computers, Bracknell, England, systems programmer, 1964-65; State University of New York at Buffalo, assistant professor of English, 1968-71; University of Cape Town, Cape Town, South Africa, lecturer in English, 1972-82, professor of general literature, 1983—. Butler Professor of English, State University of New York at Buffalo, 1984; Hinkley Professor of English, Johns Hopkins University, 1986.

MEMBER: International Comparative Literature Association, Modern Language Association of America.

AWARDS, HONORS: CNA Literary Award, 1977, for *In the Heart of the Country;* CNA Literary Award, James Tait Black Prize, and Geoffrey Faber Award, all 1980, all for *Waiting for the Barbarians;* CNA Literary Award, Booker-McConnell Prize, and Prix Femina Etranger, all 1984, all for *Life & Times of Michael K;* Jerusalem Prize for the Freedom of the Individual in Society, 1987.

WRITINGS:

Dusklands (two novellas), Ravan Press (Johannesburg), 1974, Penguin Books, 1985.
(Translator) Marcellus Emants, *A Posthumous Confession,* Twayne, 1976.
From the Heart of the Country (novel), Harper, 1977 (published in England as *In the Heart of the Country,* Secker & Warburg, 1977), reprinted as *In the Heart of the Country,* Penguin Books, 1982.
Waiting for the Barbarians (novel), Secker & Warburg, 1980, Penguin Books, 1982.
Life & Times of Michael K (novel), Secker & Warburg, 1983, Viking, 1984.
(Translator) Wilma Stockenstroem, *The Expedition to the Baobab Tree,* Faber, 1983.
(Editor with Andre Brink) *A Land Apart: A Contemporary South African Reader,* Viking, 1987.
Foe (novel), Viking, 1987.
White Writing: On the Culture of Letters in South Africa (essays), Yale University Press, 1988.

SIDELIGHTS: J. M. Coetzee is a South African scholar and writer whose work has found a substantial audience outside his native country. Coetzee's symbolic and allegorical fiction explores the psychopathology of the oppressor and the victim, a theme inspired by the author's long residence in the land of apartheid. According to Peter Lewis in the *Times Literary Supplement,* what Coetzee is interested in is "the abuse of power, the state's need for victims and enemies, and the predicament of the liberal conscience, not only in their South African manifestations." Indeed, many critics feel that Coetzee's works reveal not only South Africa's agony but also the plight of any nation that uses law and force to control segments of the population. "Mr. Coetzee's subdued yet urgent lament is for the sadness of a South Africa that has made dependents and parasites and prisoners of its own children, black and white," writes Cynthia Ozick in the *New York Times Book Review.* ". . . He discloses, in the language of imagination, the lumbering hoaxes and self-deceptions of stupidity. His theme is the wild and merciless power of inanity."

"Of all the writers of recent eminence, . . . J. M. Coetzee embodies, as do few of his contemporaries, the idea that fiction should serve social and political uses," claims Bruce Allen in the *Christian Science Monitor.* Coetzee's message is both timely and humane—namely, that empire-building poses devastating consequences for common folk. As Denis Donoghue puts it in the *New York Times Book Review,* Coetzee's fiction implies "that every colonial society is caught between a past so seemingly changeless that it may be conceived beyond time and history, and a present moment entirely given over to power, empire, history and the systems that further those interests." The prevailing sense is of ultimate malaise, of the extinguishing of the self from daily exposure to brutality and privation. Coetzee's vision may have universal applications, writes Nadine Gordimer in the *New York Review of Books,* but "the presentation of the truth and meaning of what white has done to black stands out on every page, celebrating its writer's superb, unafraid creative energy as it does." Gordimer concludes that Coetzee "has won (or lost?) his inner struggle and now writes, from among the smell of weary flesh, [works] of the closest and deepest engagement with . . . victimized people."

Coetzee is more than a mere propagandist, however. Lewis contends that his South African citizenship notwithstanding, the author "is too intelligent a novelist to cater for moralistic voyeurs. This does not mean that he avoids the social and political crises edging his country towards catastrophe. But he chooses not to handle such themes in the direct, realistic way that writers of older generations, such as Alan Paton, preferred to employ. Instead, Coetzee has developed a symbolic and even allegorical mode of fiction—not to escape the living nightmare of South Africa but to define the psychopathological underlying the sociological, and in doing so to locate the archetypal in the particular." Gornick maintains that the felt reality in Coetzee's work "is the remoteness and the peculiar silence: as of an unholy quiet at the center. . . . J. M. Coetzee's novels, at their best, remind one of the South African silence. They enrich a body of work that is, finally, a testament to the irreducible in human life." To quote Richard Eder in the *Los Angeles Times Book Review,* the author "is from South Africa, where alienation is not a choice but a necessity; and as such, instills a transcendent vitality in its highly crafted distortions. . . . Though there may be something odd and mannered about [his] parables, our reaction is not 'These are strange stories,' but rather, 'Life is a strange place.' "

Coetzee was born and raised in Cape Town, South Africa, and is of Afrikaner descent. His childhood was spent in Cape Town and in more than a dozen small farming villages on the nearby plain known as the karroo. From an early age he was exposed to several languages: his parents spoke English and Afrikaans, as did his teachers, and he learned both tongues as well as Dutch, German, and French. In college at the University of Cape Town, Coetzee majored in mathematics. He began his working life as a computer programmer in Great Britain, but after several years he decided to return to school. This he did in the United States at the University of Texas, where he earned a Ph.D. in linguistics. Ian Glenn, a colleague from the University of Cape Town, claims in the *Washington Post* that Coetzee is "a rare phenomenon, a writer-scholar," adding: "Even if he hadn't had a career as a novelist he would have had a very considerable one as an academic. . . . He's combined three or four [disciplines]—linguistics, translation, literary criticism and creative writing. . . . It's a remarkable spectrum, and that's what makes him interesting."

After teaching for several years in the United States, Coetzee returned to South Africa in 1971. He took a professorship at the University of Cape Town, and only then did he begin to produce creative writing. His first work, *Dusklands,* was published when he was thirty-four. *Dusklands* contains two novellas, the first concerning the Vietnam War and the second concerning colonization of South Africa in the previous century. *Times Literary Supplement* reviewer Roger Owen calls the book "a kind of diptych, carefully hinged and aligned, and of a texture so glassy and mirror-like that each story throws light on the other. . . . Overall the book is rich, inventive, and full of energy. The prose is varied and flexible, responsive to many changes of mood and pace." *Books Abroad* contributor Ursula A. Barnett praises Coetzee's skill "in writing convincingly in the first person of characters whose ideas are often repugnant to him," and concludes that *Dusklands* traces "the guilt of the white man to its base" and further explores "the guilt and duty of the individual in the Western World."

Coetzee followed *Dusklands* with a novel, *In the Heart of the Country* (first published in America as *From the Heart of the Country*). Written in diary form, the work tells the story of an aging spinster's descent into madness on an isolated sheep farm in the karroo. In what may or may not be delusions, the narrator describes murdering her father as he sleeps with his black mistress and disposing of the corpse in a porcupine den. She then recounts her increasingly difficult relations with the black woman and her husband, the farm's overseer. *New York Times* correspondent Christopher Lehmann-Haupt declares that with *In the Heart of the Country,* Coetzee has "succeeded in creating a tragic fable of colonialism that [surpasses] the boundaries of his native South Africa and [makes] universal the agony of its conscience-stricken European protagonist."

In the Heart of the Country earned significant critical praise both within South Africa and beyond its borders, winning the CNA Literary Award in 1977. *Encounter* contributor Tom Paulin describes the work as "an intellectual lyric which sings the absence of history, the electric lull before history breaks, rather than a chronicle of a frustrated woman's life—on the level of individual psychology the story is unconvincing but as a piece of cultural psychoanalysis and diagnosis, it's glitteringly precise. It tells of a society turned to stone and of terrible retributions to come." In the *Village Voice,* Vivian Gornick observes that the novel "captures and reflects an essence of South African writing. . . . These mad doings on an empty plain where nothing stirs and the most ordinary human sympathies are long dead, their skeletons swarming with flesh-eating insects—all this accumulates into a penetrating atmosphere, oppressive and peculiarly South Afri-

can." According to Barend J. Toerien in *World Literature Today,* the book's basic theme "is a spiritual search for God, for a reaching out beyond the restrictions imposed by Calvinism; but above all it is a search for the self." The critic concludes: "I can hardly recall a work more steeped in the authentic and historical South African situation. Over it all hangs a brooding intensity, intermixed with a crazy humor."

Waiting for the Barbarians, first published in 1980, is probably Coetzee's best known novel. The clearly allegorical tale is set in an isolated outpost on the edge of a great Empire. In a first-person account, the village's magistrate describes the horrors that occur when agents of the Empire's defense forces perceive a threat from the barbarians who live in the uncharted deserts beyond the village. *Waiting for the Barbarians,* writes Jon Pareles in the *Voice Literary Supplement,* "is about the links between invaders, colonizers, and torturers—beyond the clear connections of history and metaphor to the murky emotional ones. . . . Coetzee tells his desolate parable with a minimum of self-righteousness. Details—desert storms, crowds turning mean—are measured and resonant; Coetzee rises to eloquence, yet refuses good guy/bad guy melodrama." *Chicago Tribune Book World* correspondent James Idema notes that the book "is about conscience and responsibility; about how by not taking action against evils we see all too clearly around us we not only acquiesce in them but are in complicity with those who created them. When we stay comfortably aloof from human wretchedness, we promote and perpetuate even as we denounce the political arrangements that brought it about. This uncompromisingly bleak message comes across in a story of profound beauty, clarity and eloquence, which even at its most melodramatic holds to a biblical nobility."

Waiting for the Barbarians won a number of prestigious prizes, including the James Tait Black Memorial Award. In America, where it first appeared as part of the Penguin Books reprint series, the novel earned accolades from critics. *Los Angeles Times Book Review* contributor Doris Grumbach, for example, calls *Waiting for the Barbarians* "a work of art. . . . The novel weaves dreams, fantasies, cruel events, terrible events and philosophical ruminations into a disturbing and moving tapestry. . . . The remarkable thing about this novel is that in spite of the strong layer of moral lesson, the characters are vivid and visible to the reading eye." Idema deems the book "all the more powerful for its vagueness of place and time. What its author has done, and with stunning effect, is to reveal to us the most familiar subject of all—ourselves. . . . We needn't be either barbaric or supremely civilized to be discomfited in very direct ways by [Coetzee's] argument that we share wickedness with the rest of the human family." Idema concludes that the work is "a spare, introspective masterpiece, dense with the ironies and contradictions of what we call unbearable truths. It deserves a large audience."

Ordeal, survival, and freedom are also the controlling themes of *Life & Times of Michael K,* first published in America in 1984. Coetzee's fourth work of fiction explores the travails of a simple, mildly handicapped man buffeted nearly to death by his country's curfews, detainment camps, and civil war. Michael K and his ill mother seek to escape from the riots and shortages in Cape Town by returning to the farm community where the mother spent her youth. En route to the village, Michael K's mother dies, leaving him stranded among a vague military campaign in the hinterland. In the *Washington Post Book World,* Jonathan Yardley notes that the novel is about "the unquenchable human urge for 'the thrill of being free' as it finds expression in the life of a good and innocent man; it is therefore also a novel about the ways in which the state attempts to suppress that urge through the camps it constructs and the wars it wages." London *Times* correspondent Andrew Sinclair writes: "Never does Coetzee refer to skin colour nor to politics, only to the fundamentals of living at all in the bleak and ravaged land. He describes universals, and, in his particular and unfortunate country, cries out from dignity and from woe."

"One reads 'Life & Times of Michael K' with an absorption bordering on compulsion," claims Lehmann-Haupt. "The deadpan tone of the narrative creates a vacuum that sucks you along, and as you get more involved you grow to identify with the stoic hero as the ultimate 'escape artist' in a world of violent and brutal contention." Gordimer notes that with *Life & Times of Michael K* Coetzee "has written a marvelous work that leaves nothing unsaid—and could not be better said—about what human beings do to fellow human beings in South Africa. . . . Beyond all creeds and moralities, this work of art asserts, there is only one: to keep the earth alive, and only one salvation, the survival that comes from her." *Life & Times of Michael K* won the Booker-McConnell Award, England's top literary prize, in 1984. "What makes [this] story so powerful is the corresponding purity of Coetzee's fiction, which refuses to be assimilated into any of the easy formulas available to an author who chooses human freedom as his subject," writes Michael F. Harper in the *Los Angeles Times Book Review.* Harper further states that the novel reveals a "clean, spare prose serving the human purposes of a fine sensibility. Michael K's story is a fable, and in the hands of a lesser writer it could easily have dwindled into a vacuous allegorical tract. But Coetzee emulates his hero—a simple gardener—by keeping his nose close to the earth, earning his reader's assent to his argument by grounding it in a narrative full of closely observed, finely etched concrete detail." As *Maclean's* contributor Mark Abley puts it, *Life & Times of Michael K* "begins as a study of an apparently ordinary man; it develops into a portrait of an exceptional human being, written with unusual power and beauty."

In his novel *Foe,* published in 1987, Coetzee recasts the well-known tale of Robinson Crusoe, using the story of the shipwrecked mariner as a meditation on the obligations of art to pursue truth and reality. The heroine, Susan Barton, offers her experiences of survival on a deserted island to an English writer named Foe. When the financially-strapped Foe fictionalizes her rather mundane tale, Susan protests—and subsequently becomes perplexed by the confusion of fable and reality in her life in London. In his *Washington Post Book World* review, Russell Banks calls *Foe* "a small miracle of a book," adding that the work is "a profoundly intelligent meditation on the nature of language and art, and a witty commentary on one of the most influential works in Western literature. . . . *Foe* is a deeply moving personal testament concerning the most painful political and cultural issue of our century." *New York Times* columnist Michiko Kakutani concludes that, in *Foe,* "the operative forces are not so much history or politics as art and imagination—how can one individual's story be apprehended and translated through language by another?" The critic comments that the novel is "a finely honed testament to its author's intelligence, imagination and skill."

In 1987 Coetzee was awarded the Jerusalem Prize for the Freedom of the Individual in Society. Accepting his award in Jerusalem, Coetzee called on his nation's government to dismantle the apartheid system that legislates rigid racial segregation. Reflecting on the fiction being produced in his homeland, Coetzee said: "South African literature is a literature in bondage. It is a less than fully human literature. It is exactly the kind of literature

you would expect people to write from prison." Coetzee warned that the "deformed and stunted relations between human beings" engendered by apartheid could only lead to "a deformed and stunted inner life"—exactly the conundrum his own fiction explores so passionately.

Yardley observes that Coetzee's work is more than mere political cant. As the critic puts it, "the suspected ulterior motives of those who come to praise [Coetzee] must not be permitted to cloud his own quite genuine literary accomplishments, the ardent sincerity of his views or the courage he displays in writing so devastatingly about his country's inhuman government." Ozick too speaks to the author's literary contribution, to the force his writing gives to his arguments. "Mr. Coetzee is a writer of clarifying inventiveness and translucent conviction," Ozick states. "Both are given voice gradually, seepingly, as if time itself were a character in the [narratives]. . . . Mr. Coetzee's landscapes of suffering are defined by the little-by-little art of moral disclosure. . . . At the same time they defy the vice of abstraction; they are engrossed in the minute and the concrete. It would be possible, following Mr. Coetzee's dazzling precise illuminations, to learn how to sow, or use a pump, or make a house of earth. The grain of his sentences is flat and austere, but also so purifying to the senses that one comes away feeling that one's eye has been sharpened, one's hearing vivified, not only for the bright proliferations of nature, but for human unexpectedness." Gordimer offers her praise of Coetzee in more succinct terms. The author, she concludes, has "an imagination that soars like a lark and sees from up there like an eagle."

MEDIA ADAPTATIONS: An adaptation of *In the Heart of the Country* was filmed as "Dust," by ICA (Great Britain), 1986.

BIOGRAPHICAL/CRITICAL SOURCES:

BOOKS

Contemporary Literary Criticism, Gale, Volume 23, 1983, Volume 33, 1985.

PERIODICALS

Africa Today, third quarter, 1980.
America, September 25, 1982.
Books Abroad, spring, 1976.
Books in Canada, August/September, 1982.
British Book News, April, 1981.
Chicago Tribune Book World, April 25, 1982, January 22, 1984.
Christian Science Monitor, December 12, 1983.
Encounter, October, 1977, January, 1984.
Globe & Mail (Toronto), August 30, 1986.
Listener, August 18, 1977.
Los Angeles Times Book Review, May 23, 1982, January 15, 1984, February 22, 1987.
Maclean's, January 30, 1984.
New Republic, December 19, 1983.
Newsweek, May 31, 1982, January 2, 1984, February 23, 1987.
New York, April 26, 1982.
New Yorker, July 12, 1982.
New York Review of Books, December 2, 1982, February 2, 1984.
New York Times, December 6, 1983, February 11, 1987, April 11, 1987.
New York Times Book Review, April 18, 1982, December 11, 1983, February 22, 1987.
Spectator, December 13, 1980, September 20, 1986.
Time, March 23, 1987.
Times (London), September 29, 1983, September 11, 1986, May 28, 1988.

Times Literary Supplement, July 22, 1977, November 7, 1980, January 14, 1983, September 30, 1983, September 23, 1988.
Village Voice, March 20, 1984.
Voice Literary Supplement, April, 1982.
Washington Post, October 29, 1983.
Washington Post Book World, May 2, 1982, December 11, 1983, March 8, 1987.
World Literature Today, spring, 1978, summer, 1978, autumn, 1981.
World Literature Written in English, spring, 1980.

*   *   *

COFFEY, Brian
See KOONTZ, Dean R(ay)

*   *   *

COHEN, Leonard (Norman) 1934-

PERSONAL: Born September 21, 1934, in Montreal, Quebec, Canada; son of Nathan B. and Marsha (Klinitsky) Cohen; children: Adam, Lorca. *Education:* McGill University, B.A., 1955; graduate study, Columbia University.

ADDRESSES: Home—Montreal, Quebec, Canada; and Greece. *Office*—c/o McClelland & Stewart, 25 Hollinger Rd., Toronto, Ont., Canada M4B 3G2.

CAREER: Poet, novelist, singer, and composer. Formerly associated with Stranger Music, Inc., New York, N.Y.; has given concerts in the United States, Canada, and Europe. Has appeared on television, including in documentary film "The Song of Leonard Cohen," 1980, and series "Miami Vice."

AWARDS, HONORS: McGill Literary Award, 1956; Canada Council grant, 1960-61; Quebec Literary Award, 1964; LL.B., Dalhousie University, 1971; Canadian Authors Association Literary Award for poetry, 1985, for *Book of Mercy;* Crystal Globe Award, Columbia Records, for sales of five million albums.

WRITINGS:

POETRY

Let Us Compare Mythologies, Contact Press, 1956.
The Spice Box of Earth, McClelland & Stewart (Toronto), 1961, Viking, 1965.
Flowers for Hitler, McClelland & Stewart, 1964.
Parasites of Heaven, McClelland & Stewart, 1966.
Selected Poems, 1955-1968, Viking, 1968.
The Energy of Slaves, McClelland & Stewart, 1972, Viking, 1973.
(With Jurgen Jaensch) *Credo,* Garuda Verlag, 1977.
Death of a Lady's Man (includes journal entries), McClelland & Stewart, 1978, Viking, 1979.
Book of Mercy, Random House, 1984.

RECORDINGS

Songs of Leonard Cohen, Columbia, 1968.
Songs from a Room, Columbia, 1969.
Songs of Love and Hate, Columbia, 1971.
Leonard Cohen: Live Songs, Columbia, 1973.
New Skin for the Old Ceremony, Columbia, 1974.
Death of a Lady's Man, Warner Brothers, 1977.
Recent Songs, Columbia, 1979.
Various Positions, Columbia, 1984.
I'm Your Man, Columbia, 1988.

OTHER

The Favorite Game (novel), Viking, 1963.

Beautiful Losers (novel), Viking, 1966.
Songs of Leonard Cohen, Macmillan, 1969.
"The New Step" (play), produced in London, 1972.
"Sisters of Mercy: A Journey into the Words and Music of Leonard Cohen" (play), produced at Niagara-on-the-Lake, Ontario, and in New York, 1973.

Also author of video production, "I Am a Hotel." Contributor of poetry to many anthologies, including *The Penguin Book of Canadian Verse,* edited by Ralph Gastafson, Penguin, 1967, and *Five Canadian Poets,* edited by Eli Mandel, Holt-Rinehart (Toronto), 1970, and to magazines.

Cohen's work has been translated into Hebrew, Spanish, and French.

WORK IN PROGRESS: Editing a collection of his poems.

SIDELIGHTS: Leonard Cohen gained international popularity as a coffeehouse singer with his songs of love and protest in the 1960s and 1970s. "His image is a touchstone . . . for an entire student generation," a *Times Literary Supplement* reviewer wrote in a 1970 article. "As poet, novelist and, above all, as a composer/lyricist/singer, . . . he embodies the dreams of many young people." His work has continued to appeal to students, and today, state Pamela Andriotakis and Richard Bulahan in *People,* his followers "often are teenagers, the children of his early admirers."

Cohen began his career as a poet. His first collection, *Let Us Compare Mythologies,* won the 1956 McGill Literary Award, the prize for which was a plane ticket to the city of Cohen's choice. He elected to travel to Jerusalem but stopped in London, where friends encouraged him to discipline his writing. With their support, he remained in England and completed the first draft of a novel, *The Favorite Game,* in eight months. In 1960 Cohen moved to the Greek island of Hydra, which was his home for the next six years. During that time he published three books of poetry and two novels. He also wrote songs but made no attempt to sell them.

Critics received his first books favorably. Samuel I. Bellman, commenting on *The Favorite Game* in *Congress Bi-Weekly,* states: "[F. Scott] Fitzgerald is most strongly evoked here. . . . With the compassion of Philip Roth in *Letting Go* (1962), an intricate study of parent-child relationships, Cohen has given his itinerant, fatuous and self-alienated young poet a moment of greatness." Calvin Bedient in the *New York Times Book Review* credits Cohen's early poems as showing "a splashy imaginative energy that, combined with a hard attitude and frequent candor, [makes] them challenging." And a *Times Literary Supplement* reviewer, writing of Cohen's second novel, *Beautiful Losers,* remarks: "Like the early work of another all-embracing nonstylist, Thomas Wolfe, it has the fascination of its untamed energy."

Cohen's early work received critical acclaim, but, the author told Tom Chaffin in *Canadian Forum,* "I really couldn't meet any of my own bills." That situation was unexpectedly remedied in 1966 when, while visiting New York, Cohen was introduced to singer Judy Collins. She asked to hear his songs and was so impressed by them that she recorded several of them on her next album. They were hits, and soon other singers were eager to record Cohen's works. "Suzanne," "Sisters of Mercy," "The Story of Abraham and Isaac," and "Stories of the Street" were all successes for various recording artists. In 1968, Cohen decided to cut his own album, although he told Chaffin: "Sometimes I think my voice is very bad. I can almost make myself cry with it very early in the morning." As Chaffin describes it, "While Cohen's fluid, opulently lyric guitar work is of studio musician calibre, his voice is deep, untrained, often off-pitch, sometimes unmercifully rasping—and somehow the perfect foil for his soft Debussy-like melodies." The public liked his first album, *Songs of Leonard Cohen,* and subsequent records also sold well. Concert tours were faithfully attended, and the Canadian poet had taken a major step toward becoming what Andriotakis and Bulahan call an "undisputed cult figure."

Cohen's fame as a recording artist caused some literary critics to examine his later poetry in relation to his popular songs. David Lehman in *Poetry,* for example, writes: "The real tension in Cohen's work is due . . . to a clash between poetry and the elements of songwriting which Cohen superimposes on it." "His poems have a randomness which betrays the lack of any sustained vision," a *Times Literary Supplement* reviewer observes. "They are, in short, the poems of a songwriter who is able to convince a semi-literate public that his talent goes deeper simply because his lyrics possess an apparent concern with deeper issues and avoid the more honest banalities of 'moon/June.' " James Healy's *Prairie Schooner* review also suggests that Cohen's real talent lies in songwriting, not poetry: "*The Energy of Slaves* (Viking Press) is a painful disappointment. . . . Cohen's music is his best weapon and maybe he will come to realize this."

Leslie Fielder, however, maintains in *Running Man* that this sharp division between pop artist and literary artist is unrealistic and unnecessary. Today's poet, the critic proposes, works in "the new post-Modernist world in which the old distinctions between low and high art, mass culture and *belles-lettres* have lapsed completely." Reviewing *Death of a Lady's Man* in *Saturday Night,* Eli Mandel claims that Cohen's work defies categorization and calls the book "wildly energetic, threatening to fly apart in any one of the thousand directions to which it is attracted, a witty, moving, despairing book, lyrical, dramatic, musical, endlessly entertaining, often boring, even terribly self-centered—further revelations of a mind and personality that will continue to baffle our best critics and to entrance and offend an audience he cultivates and seduces." Cohen himself "reacts caustically to critics who have suggested that his recent celebrity has blunted his powers on the printed page," writes Chaffin. "He also rejects the notion of any tension between his roles as a solitary poet and public performer." Of his simple style, Cohen told Chaffin, "I like austerity. . . . I like it as a style."

In Mandel's opinion, Cohen's work has a "magical luminosity" that accounts for his great success and popularity. "Cohen's method is without doubt surrealistic, what Robert Bly recently called 'leaping poetry,' the sudden alteration that occurs when something more than mere association develops in the poetic connection. It's enough to take you by the heart and shake you as if you were in a great windstorm or encountering for the first time one of those huge ships of imagination that Fellini or Rilke saw. Or, to use Bly's example, it's as if the poet suddenly leapt from one brain to another. . . . Cohen is capable of those great leaps of imagination; that is why he remains one of [Canada's] best, most loved poets."

BIOGRAPHICAL/CRITICAL SOURCES:

BOOKS

Contemporary Literary Criticism, Gale, Volume 3, 1975, Volume 38, 1986.
Dictionary of Literary Biography, Volume 38: *Canadian Writers, First Series,* Gale, 1986.
Gnarowski, Michael, *Leonard Cohen: The Artist and His Critics,* McGraw, 1976.
Ondaatje, Michael, *Leonard Cohen,* McClelland & Stewart, 1970.
Sylvestre, Guy, and others, editors, *Canadian Writers,* revised edition, Ryerson, 1966.

PERIODICALS

Beloit Poetry Journal, winter, 1968-69.
Canadian Forum, July, 1967, September, 1970, August-September, 1983.
Canadian Literature, winter, 1965.
Congress Bi-Weekly, December 20, 1963.
Globe and Mail (Toronto), April 21, 1984.
Jewish Quarterly, autumn, 1972.
Life, June 28, 1968.
Los Angeles Times, July 13, 1988.
McCall's, January, 1969.
National Observer, September 9, 1968.
New Leader, May 23, 1966.
New York Review of Books, April 28, 1966.
New York Times, April 4, 1966.
New York Times Book Review, May 8, 1966, February 18, 1973.
People, January 14, 1980.
Poetry, December, 1973.
Prairie Schooner, summer, 1973.
Running Man, July-August, 1969.
Saturday Night, February, 1968, November, 1978.
Time, September 13, 1968.
Times Literary Supplement, April 23, 1970, September 18, 1970, January 5, 1973.
Washington Post, July 20, 1988, October 30, 1988.

*   *   *

COLEGATE, Isabel   1931-

PERSONAL: Born September 10, 1931, in Lincolnshire, England; daughter of Sir Arthur Colegate (a member of Parliament) and Lady Colegate Worsley; married Michael Briggs (director of an engineering firm), September 12, 1953; children: Emily, Barnaby, Joshua. *Education:* Attended boarding schools in Shropshire and Norfolk, England.

ADDRESSES: Home—Midford Castle, Bath, Somerset BA2 7BU, England. *Agent*—A. D. Peters Ltd., 10 Buckingham St., London WC2N 6BU, England.

CAREER: Novelist, short story writer, and critic.

AWARDS, HONORS: W. H. Smith Literary Award, 1981, for *The Shooting Party.*

WRITINGS:

The Blackmailer (also see below), Anthony Blond, 1958.
A Man of Power (also see below), Anthony Blond, 1960.
The Great Occasion (also see below), Anthony Blond, 1962.
Statues in a Garden, Bodley Head, 1964, Knopf, 1966, Penguin, 1983.
Orlando King (first novel in trilogy; also see below), Bodley Head, 1968, Knopf, 1969.
Orlando at the Brazen Threshold (second novel in trilogy; also see below), Bodley Head, 1971.
Agatha (third novel in trilogy; also see below), Bodley Head, 1973.
News from the City of the Sun, Hamish Hamilton, 1979.
The Shooting Party, Hamish Hamilton, 1980, Viking, 1981.
Three Novels: The Blackmailer, A Man of Power, and The Great Occasion, Blond & Briggs, 1983, Viking, 1984.

The Orlando Trilogy (includes *Orlando King, Orlando at the Brazen Threshold,* and *Agatha*), Penguin, 1984.
A Glimpse of Sion's Glory, Viking, 1985.
Deceits of Time, Viking, 1988.

Statues in a Garden has been translated into Spanish. Contributor of book reviews to magazines and newspapers, including *Spectator, Times Literary Supplement,* and *Washington Post.* Contributor to literary journals.

WORK IN PROGRESS: Another novel.

SIDELIGHTS: Isabel Colegate has gained respect both in the United States and in her native England as an elegant stylist whose novels depict the lives of individuals shaped by the mores and ideals of twentieth-century British society. Her books, full of precise and detailed description, deeply perceived characters, and a carefully controlled tone, offer evocative and accurate portrayals of history along with acute social commentary. Colegate displays a particular talent for describing the British upper class of the period prior to the outbreak of World War I and the permanent transformations in society that occurred afterwards. Her novels explore the various facades erected before the upper classes, discovering "the fatal flaws in a superficially attractive way of life and in character," according to Rosemary Herbert in *Publishers Weekly.* By looking beneath the veneer of society, Colegate succeeds in exposing the fundamental natures of its individuals and as Alice Digilio observes in the *Washington Post,* "class lays bare the most basic elements of their characters—pride, envy, anger, ambition, avarice, even sexual passion."

Overall, Colegate's metier is an ability to effectively evoke meaning from whatever twentieth-century historical period about which she chooses to write. Her novels often employ historical settings that are marked by political or social turmoil which accentuate the individual struggles of her characters; moreover, her adherence to historical accuracy provides a certain balance to their portrayal. Ariel Swartley in the *Voice Literary Supplement* detects an objectiveness in Colegate's approach, writing, "[she] is able to reproduce her characters' muddle of impulse, rationalization, and unexamined assumptions, while seeming to plead their case for them. . . . And when those characters are isolated by history, her observations seem similarly removed, as trapped under glass as they are. . . . She accords her villains the same sympathetic interest as her heroines; she is as attentive to their ideas and explanations of themselves as to the swamp of emotions that lie below."

Colegate gained the attention of American readers in 1981 with her award-winning book *The Shooting Party,* yet her critical reputation in England had been solid since the publication of three early novels: *The Blackmailer, A Man of Power,* and *The Great Occasion.* Published in the United States in 1984 as a one-volume collection entitled *Three Novels,* these early works are connected by "the standard British sardonic blend of love and power and class," as Dorothy Wickenden notes in *New Republic,* but they are nonetheless "remarkable . . . for their verve and versatility." Wickenden further states that they "are the work of a young writer . . . with an unfaltering voice, a distinctive comic sensibility, and a sure moral vision." *The Blackmailer,* Colegate's first novel, is about "a young lawyer and novice blackmailer who is deluded in his belief that he can worm his way into the higher reaches of society by his own cleverness," according to Wickenden, yet he becomes "no match for the subtle evils of his social superiors." At the same time, however, Sarah Turvey observes in the *Dictionary of Literary Biography* that Colegate shows the upper class "in retreat before forces it cannot understand," a theme of new social order replacing the established social order,

which is further explored in Colegate's later novels. A character in *The Blackmailer* comments, "The world's changed. People have no sense of values, no decency, they're all out for what they can get. Our sort of people get pushed aside by all the lies and ingratitude."

The struggle of individuals attempting to achieve or maintain desired positions within society likewise marks *A Man of Power* and *The Great Occasion.* Regarding *A Man of Power,* Susan Slocum Hinerfield notes in the *Los Angeles Times Book Review* that Lewis Ogden, an industrialist who is "the man of power," feels that "Society" is "missing from his life" and that "the aristocracy aligns with all that is sterling, lasting, and good." "What Lewis wants, perhaps," Hinerfield continues, "is to join the gentlemen in their effortless assumption of superiority, to be privy to ancient secrets, to see into the heart of England." Lewis's efforts to attain such a status, however, have serious consequences for those around him, and in the end, Lewis sees that "beneath the veneer of Society are cruelty, opportunism, barbarism, heartlessness, secrets he does not want to know," as Hinerfield observes. In *The Great Occasion,* a group of five sisters attempt "to create futures for themselves in a changing society which no longer provides women with the constricting security of a preordained position," Turvey notes. "The satisfactions of [the book]," writes Digilio, "are not unlike those of Jane Austin's novels—a circumscribed world, a prescribed social code to be either flouted or adhered to and a fine collection of independent characters." "In many ways," Turvey observes, "the five Dodson daughters provide prototypes for many of Colegate's later women."

In a preface to the one-volume edition of the three novels, Colegate remarked that "these three seem to me now to be the ones I wrote instinctively and without difficulty; this makes me remember them with indulgence and feel pleased to see them in print again." Wendy Lesser, writing in the *Hudson Review,* finds such a tone "self-deprecating" and maintains that these first novels "are not mere outpourings, but the skilled work of a talented young writer who definitely had something to say." Wickenden concurs, stating that "unlike her clumsy heroes and her youthful heroines, [Colegate] . . . intuitively understands all about the 'hateful little sounds' that social creatures make as they scrabble after the unattainable." Digilio sees *Three Novels* as the novelist's apprenticeship. "These early novels," she writes, "when [Colegate] . . . was learning her craft, show a substantial talent. . . . Here is a social commentator, satirist and keen observer, juggling the imperatives of storytelling, learning to make all the elements mesh."

Colegate's next novel, *Statues in a Garden,* marks a turning point in the direction of her writing. Colegate explains in her *CA* interview, "with *Statues in a Garden,* I was starting to look backwards. . . . I saw that it was possible to write about a time other than my own but still within living memory, and reach something which people who had been alive at that time recognized as being truthful." Turvey calls *Statues in a Garden* "the most experimental novel of the corpus . . . [and] also Colegate's most tentative book, both in terms of narrative technique and in its effort to engage with a nexus of history, myth, and fiction concepts which are to be taken up again and again in her later work." Colegate's intent is touched upon towards the beginning of the novel as she writes, "we are not trying to recapture an age as it was or to write history: we are trying to remember the background for a private fable. A private background for a private fable." Turvey, however, detects "a strange tension between this claim and the choice of a particularly portentous moment in history for the setting of the novel, recreated with a specificity and precision that indicate extensive historical research."

The novel takes place in 1914 before the onset of World War I and traces the tragedy that befalls the upper-class family of Sir Alymer Weston upon the disclosure of a love affair involving his wife and nephew, who is also his adopted son. Colegate's choice of the historically important and much written-about years before World War I as the time period to place a story which, in the words of a *Times Literary Supplement* critic, "could have happened at any time," was considered a bold move by some reviewers. "[While] no responsible literary adviser could have recommended such a theme . . .," notes the *Times Literary Supplement* critic, "[Colegate] is so well-informed that the background falls effortlessly into place, and the period is evoked with none of the staginess that undoes so many period novels." "[The] story," continues the reviewer, ". . . certainly lost nothing by being set in that particular July."

The historical period of pre-World War I England accentuates the drama of *Statues in a Garden* as it unfolds. Frank Littler notes in the *New York Times Book Review* that, "chapter by chapter—because the story is beautifully graduated—it becomes clear that just as the nation at large fails to discern the beckoning holocaust, this essentially decent statesman [Weston] has no inkling of the personal tragedy that is closing in on him." He further states that "the sexual explosion, when it comes, would be shocking in any zeitgeist"; however, the backdrop of Edwardian society adds an intensity which, "in the golden age of top-hatted statesmen and their osprey-feathered ladies[,] . . . is appalling in its brutality." Colegate's recurring theme of a new order replacing the established order is likewise realized in the sexual act itself which, as Turvey points out, "flouts not only the ideal of graciousness which the society upholds, but the 'incestuousness' of the act also threatens the foundations of the family structures on which the society is actually based." Turvey calls *Statues in a Garden* "a troubled and fascinating novel, and a watershed in Colegate's development."

The four novels that follow *Statues in a Garden* similarly rely upon accurate historical detail to add layers of meaning to the main story, yet Colegate does not return to a pre-World War I setting until *The Shooting Party.* The Orlando Trilogy, comprised of three separately published novels entitled *Orlando King, Orlando at the Brazen Threshold,* and *Agatha,* follows the rise and fall of a successful politician, Orlando King, and the life of his daughter, Agatha. Set in the years between 1930 and 1956, "the personal drama [of the trilogy]," comments Turvey, "is played out against a background of punctuating historical events: the rise of Hitler and Moseley; the Munich accord; World War II; and finally the Suez Canal crisis and the Hungarian uprising." "The trilogy is also," Turvey notes, "clearly structured around a reenactment of the Oedipus myth, producing close parallels of event and character." The epiphany experienced by Orlando as his tragedy unfolds is, according to a *Times Literary Supplement* reviewer, "the realization that his world, so seductively easy to conquer, . . . [has] nothing but guilt to offer in return."

Aileen Pippett in the *New York Times Book Review* observes that the character of Orlando, who is intended to parallel the classical Oedipus, "is never described, only the effect he has on others, without his caring one way or another, for the point about him is that he is a creature from another world, with the attributes of a mythic hero. . . . He simply appears and cuts a swathe through every life he contacts." Turvey states that an "awareness" exists in the trilogy of "the seemingly contradictory claims

of the individual and of the historical forces beyond the grasp of the individual." As a result, "the meshing of history and myth produces an uneasy alliance which declares its uncertainty through the ambivalence of the narrative tone." "The novels," Turvey adds, "attempt to work through some of the questions which are raised by *Statues in a Garden.*"

Colegate's next novel, *News from the City of the Sun,* spans the years between 1930 and the early 1970s and traces the history of a Utopian community founded in an abbey by three brothers. Again, Colegate uses historical detail as a backdrop to help define her characters. In turn, as Turvey notes, "the social and political changes which occur . . . are registered by the nature of the people who arrive at the community: from the unemployed miners in the Depression years to the hippies of the 1960s and the female revolutionaries of the early 1970s." Peter Kemp in the *Listener* notes that in this novel, "the incongruous and the unpredictable feature prominently." "The result," he continues, "is an ironic and occasionally painful comedy about the odd interaction between human nature, life's surprises, and Utopian ideals." Colegate explains in her *CA* interview that *News from the City of the Sun* was a new experience for her, "something [she] hadn't done before in terms of the period of time covered, the numbers of characters, the fact that there was not really a plot so much as a theme."

In her next novel, *The Shooting Party,* Colegate returns to the time period before World War I for the setting of a story which, in the words of John Naughton in the *Listener,* "is a stunning picture of the British upper classes at the pinnacle of their evolution." Winner of the W. H. Smith Literary Award in 1981, *The Shooting Party* has become Colegate's most acclaimed novel. Charles Champlin writes in the *Los Angeles Times,* "*The Shooting Party* is not only about events in England in 1913, it might somehow have in the best sense come forward from the literature of 1913, a lost manuscript by a fine author, let us say, published at last after being found beneath some linens in the ancestral armoire."

The Shooting Party presages the demise of the British upper classes in the social upheaval following World War I. The story of a shooting party at an elite country estate which ends with an accidental killing, the novel serves as "a metaphor for the workings of polite society, just as it might serve as a metaphor for the movement of Europe toward war," notes Linda Barett Osborne in the *Washington Post.* "At each level there are disturbing forces underlying the civilized order." Thus, as the weekend closes with an accidental shooting and death, so the era in which the story takes place ends with the first shots of the war. King writes that Colegate "invests the beauty of the Oxfordshire estate in autumn with a grave, poetic melancholy. The same melancholy seems, like an autumnal mist, to cling about [the] characters even at their most buoyant and boisterous as they play childish hide-and-seek, consume lavish meals, or carry on their intrigues with each other. The leaves are already falling; and this privileged order is about to fall, too."

The impact of *The Shooting Party* stems not only from its story, but also from its style. Osborne writes that the novel "unfolds like an album of sepia photographs, its people recognizable yet muted, set in formal clothing and poses that bespeak the manners and attitudes of another age." A *Virginia Quarterly Review* critic states that Colegate "has an eye and an ear for a time and place she can never have seen or heard, . . . [and] she wraps up the reader in her own time warp." "Colegate explores this world," comments Jack Beatty in the *New Republic,* "with affection and distance, recording its grace as well as its cruelty, setting it off now from this point of view and now from that in order to see it whole, and finally making it both meaningful and moving."

The critical and popular success of *The Shooting Party* seems not to have exerted a great influence on the direction of Colegate's next book, *A Glimpse of Sion's Glory*. A collection of three novellas—including a story that approaches science fiction—the book displays Colegate's gifts as social commentator while exploring the often destructive effects that humans bear upon one another, a theme often expressed in Colegate's work. The stories are not as dependent upon historical setting as her other works, however. Swartley writes that the stories in *A Glimpse of Sion's Glory* "examine the past and even the future, but are firmly grounded in the present." "Where once," Swartley elaborates, "Colegate energetically placed her characters in the perspective of history or tragedy, [in *Sion's Glory*] she allows them to create that perspective for themselves." Colegate, nonetheless, maintains in the book what Anne Bernays in the *New York Times Book Review* describes as her "supreme gift . . . to recreate dramatically and in breathtaking prose the ambiguous, troublesome flow of life."

The stories are, for the most part, thematically independent of one another. As Toby Fitton in the *Times Literary Supplement* comments, "they are loosely connected by the theme of how particular moments of revelation—anthropological, intellectual and artistic-sexual—affect the very varied characters, but there is wisely no forced attempt at linkage." Richard Eder in the *Los Angeles Times* finds, however, that "the glimpse of glory in the title piece . . . refers to the portion of radiance, a kind of ritual overdrive, that may seize people for a time, before it is extinguished in the grittiness of everyday human needs."

The title story tells of an ambassador's wife from a conventional and proper background who receives a confessional and affectionate letter from a free-spirited former Oxford acquaintance, which raises some difficult questions concerning the choices she has made in life. In "The Girl Who Lived among Artists," Colegate describes the effects of an attractive young bohemian girl on her circle of friends and lovers, while the third piece in the collection, "Distant Cousins," is about the discovery of a separate human species which is accidentally destroyed after exposure to Western scientists. According to Fitton, "Distant Cousins" suggests how this "genetically different intellectual race might have offered possibilities of Redemption to mere humankind." Regarding the stories as a whole, King in the *Spectator* finds a common theme "in the way in which each of the leading characters searches for something—some knowledge, some love, some faith—beyond day-to-day experience." "This search," he continues, "baffled but always persistent, gives a pathos to the book at even its lightest moments."

Because of the praise *The Shooting Party* earned as a masterful evocation of England's Edwardian and prewar years, critical reaction to the different direction taken with *A Glimpse of Sion's Glory* was mixed. However, as Colegate mentions in her *Publishers Weekly* interview with Herbert, she is "not interested in doing what . . . [she's] done before." Jonathan Keates adds in the *Observer* that, " 'The Shooting Party' has encouraged a somewhat misleading view of Isabel Colegate . . . celebrating what are vaguely referred to as 'bygone values.' " As the corpus of Colegate's work demonstrates, she is more apt to portray the classes for what they actually are or were, without imparting any particular judgement. "In a perfect marriage of content and style," writes Hinerfeld, "[Colegate] inquires into the nature of human transactions . . . with a certain coolness, a detachment." Andrew Sinclair, in a London *Times* article, concurs with such

a characterization, concluding that Colegate possesses "an understanding of all sorts of people and the social differences necessary to them, so that the war between the classes is replaced by a truce observed without malice, irony, or guilt."

MEDIA ADAPTATIONS: A film, "The Shooting Party," 1985, starring James Mason and Sir John Gielgud, was adapted from Colegate's novel of the same title and produced by Geoff Reeve Films in Great Britain.

BIOGRAPHICAL/CRITICAL SOURCES:

BOOKS

Contemporary Literary Criticism, Volume 36, Gale, 1986.
Dictionary of Literary Biography, Volume 14: *British Novelists since 1960,* Gale, 1983.

PERIODICALS

Atlantic, April, 1981.
Best Sellers, May 1, 1969.
Books and Bookmen, October, 1979.
Books of the Times, August, 1981.
Boston Review, February, 1986.
British Book News, May, 1982.
Contemporary Review, January, 1974.
Harper's, April, 1966, May, 1969.
Hudson Review, autumn, 1984.
Library Journal, April 1, 1966.
Listener, August 27, 1964, October 25, 1973, August 2, 1979, September 4, 1980, May 30, 1985.
London Review of Books, July 18, 1985.
Los Angeles Times, May 29, 1981.
Los Angeles Times Book Review, May 27, 1984, November 27, 1985, December 25, 1988.
New Republic, April 18, 1981, May 28, 1984.
New Statesman, May 4, 1962, August 21, 1964, September 20, 1968, July 13, 1979, September 12, 1980, June 7, 1985.
New Yorker, July 9, 1966, May 10, 1969, May 25, 1981, May 7, 1984, December 16, 1985.
New York Times, May 16, 1981, December 10, 1988.
New York Times Book Review, March 20, 1966, May 25, 1969, July 11, 1982, August 15, 1982, September 9, 1984, November 17, 1985, December 11, 1988.
Observer, May 23, 1971, September 7, 1980, June 9, 1985.
Publishers Weekly, December 13, 1985.
Punch, September 18, 1968.
Saturday Review, May, 1981.
Spectator, January 29, 1960, July 21, 1979, September 13, 1980, June 8, 1985.
Time, July 6, 1981.
Times (London), February 18, 1980, February 12, 1981, January 26, 1985, February 6, 1985, June 6, 1985.
Times Literary Supplement, October 28, 1964, September 19, 1968, May 20, 1971, October 5, 1973, December 14, 1979, September 12, 1980, April 26, 1985, June 21, 1985, September 2, 1988.
Voice Literary Supplement, December, 1985.
Virginia Quarterly Review, autumn, 1966, autumn, 1981.
Washington Post, July 13, 1981, April 17, 1984.
Washington Post Book World, January 12, 1986, November 13, 1988.

*   *   *

COLEMAN, Emmett
See REED, Ishmael

COLETTE, (Sidonie-Gabrielle) 1873-1954
(Willy, Colette Willy)

PERSONAL: Born January 28, 1873, in Burgundy, France; died August 3, 1954, in Paris, France; daughter of Jules and Sidonie Colette; married Henry Gauthier-Villars (music critic, journalist, and novelist), 1893 (separated, 1906; divorced, 1910); married Baron Henri de Jouvenel des Ursins (politician and editor), December 19, 1912 (divorced, c. 1925); married Maurice Goudeket, April, 1935; children: (second marriage) Colette de Jouvenel ("Bel-Gazou").

CAREER: Novelist and short story writer; music hall dancer and mime, 1906-11; columnist for *Le Matin,* beginning in 1911.

AWARDS, HONORS: Elected to Royal Belgian Academy and Goncourt Academy (president); grand officer of the Legion of Honor; received state funeral, France's highest posthumous honor.

WRITINGS:

(Under pseudonym Willy) *Claudine a l'ecole,* Ollendorff, 1900, translation by Janet Flanner published as *Claudine at School,* Gollancz, 1930, also translated by H. Mirande, A. & C. Boni, 1930.

(Under pseudonym Willy) *Claudine a Paris,* Mercure de France, 1901, published as *Claudine amoureuse,* Ollendorff, 1902, translation by James Whitall published as *Young Lady of Paris,* A. & C. Boni, 1931.

(Under pseudonym Willy) *Claudine en menage,* Mercure de France, 1902, translation by Frederick A. Blossom published as *The Indulgent Husband,* Farrar & Rinehart, 1935.

(Under pseudonym Willy) *Claudine s'en va: Journal d'Annie,* Ollendorff, 1903, translation by Blossom published as *The Innocent Wife,* Farrar & Rinehart, 1935, translation by Antonia White published as *Claudine and Annie,* Secker & Warburg, 1962.

(Under pseudonym Willy), *Minne,* Ollendorff, 1904, revised and published with *Les Egarements de Minne* (also see below) as *L'Ingenue libertine,* under name Colette Willy, 1909 (also see below).

(Under name Colette Wiley) *Dialogues de betes,* Mercure de France, 1904, enlarged edition published as *Douze Dialogues de betes,* 1930 (also see below).

(Under pseudonym Willy) *Les Egarements de Minne,* Ollendorff, 1905, revised and published with *Minne* as *L'Igenue libertine,* under name Colette Willy, 1909 (also see below).

(Under name Colette Willy) *La Retraite sentimentale,* Mercure de France, 1907, translation by Margaret Crosland published as *Retreat From Love,* Indiana University Press, 1974.

(Under name Colette Willy) *Les Vrilles de la vigne* (title means "The Tendrils of the Vine"), Editions de la Vie Parisienne, 1908.

(Under name Colette Willy) *L'Igenue libertine* (contains *Minne* and *Les Egarements de Minne*), Ollendorff, 1909, translation by Rosemary Carr Benet published as *The Gentle Libertine,* Farrar & Rinehart, 1931.

(Under name Colette Willy) *La Vagabonde,* Ollendorff, 1910 (also see below), translation by Charlotte Remfry-Kidd published as *Renee la vagabonde,* Doubleday, 1931, translation by Enid McLeod published as *The Vagabond,* Secker & Warburg, 1954.

L'Envers du music-hall, Flammarion, 1913, translation by Anne-Marie Callimachi published as *Music-Hall Sidelights* with Helen Beauclerk's translation of *Mes Apprentissages* (also

see below), Secker & Warburg, 1957, reprinted with Raymond Postgate's translation of *Mitsou* (also see below), Farrar, 1958.

L'Entrave, Librairie des Lettres, 1913, translation by Viola Gerard Garvin published as *Recaptured,* Gollancz, 1931, Doubleday, 1932, translation by White published as *The Shackle,* Secker & Warburg, 1964, reprinted as *The Captive,* Penguin, 1970.

Prrou, Poucette et quelques autres, Librairie des Lettres, 1913.

La Paix chez les betes, Georges Cres, 1916 (also see below).

Les Heures longues, 1914-1917, Fayard, 1917.

Les Enfants dans les ruines, Editions de la Maison du Livre, 1917.

Dans la foule, Georges Cres, 1918.

Mitsou; ou, Comment l'esprit vient aux filles (includes *En Camarades, piece en deux actes*), Fayard, 1919, reprinted, 1984, translation by Jane Terry published as *Mitsou; or, How Girls Grow Wise,* A. & C. Boni, 1930.

La Chambre eclairee, Edouard Joseph, 1920.

Cheri, Fayard, 1920 (also see below), translation by Flanner published under same title, A. & C. Boni, 1930.

La Maison de Claudine, Ferenczi, 1922, revised, 1930, translation by McLeod and Una Vicenzo Troubridge published as *My Mother's House* (also see below) with McLeod's translation of *Sido* (also see below), Farrar, 1953.

Le Voyage egoiste, Editions d'Art Edouard Pelletan, 1922.

(With Leopold Marchand) *Cheri, comedie en quatre actes* (adapted from Colette's novel), Librairie Theatrale, 1922.

La Vagabonde (four-act comedy adapted from Colette's novel of the same title; first produced in Paris at the Theatre de la Renaissance), Impr. de l'Illustration, 1923.

Le Ble en herbe, Flammarion, 1923, translation by Ida Zeitlin published as *The Ripening,* Farrar, 1932, translation by Roger Senhouse published as *Ripening Seed,* Secker & Warburg, 1955, Farrar, 1956.

Reverie du nouvel an, Stock, 1923.

La Femme cachee, Flammarion, 1924, translation by Crosland published as *The Other Woman,* Owen, 1971.

Aventures quotidiennes, Flammarion, 1924.

Quatre Saisons, Philippe Ortiz, 1925.

L'Enfant et les sortileges, Durand, 1925.

La Fin de Cheri, Flammarion, 1926, translation published as *The Last of Cheri,* Putnam, 1932.

La Naissance du jour, Flammarion, 1928, reprinted, 1984, translation by Benet published as *A Lesson in Love,* Farrar, 1932, reprinted as *Morning Glory,* Gollancz, 1932, translation by McLeod published as *Break of Day,* Farrar, 1961.

Renee Vivien, Edouard Champion, 1928.

La Seconde, Ferenczi, 1929, translation by Garvin published as *The Other One,* Cosmopolitan Book Corp., 1931, translation reprinted as *Fanny and Jane,* Gollancz, 1931.

Sido; ou, Les Pointes cardinaux, Editions Kra, 1929, revised, Ferenczi, 1930, translation by McLeod published as *Sido* with McLeod and Troubridge's translation of *La Maison de Claudine,* Farrar, 1953.

Histoires pour Bel-Gazou, Stock, 1930.

Prisons et paradis, Ferenczi, 1932, revised, 1935, reprinted, Fayard, 1986.

Ces Plaisirs, Ferenczi, 1932, reprinted as *Le Pur et l'impur,* Armes de France, 1941, translation by Edith Dally published as *The Pure and the Impure,* Ferrar, 1933, translation also published as *These Pleasures,* White Owl, 1934.

La Chatte, Grasset, 1933, translation by Morris Bentinck published as *Saha the Cat,* Farrar, 1936.

Duo, Ferenczi, 1934, translation by Blossom published under same title, Farrar, 1935.

La Jumelle noire, four volumes, Ferenczi, 1934-38.

Discours de reception a l'Academie Royale de Langue et de Litterature Francaises de Belgique, Grasset, 1936.

Mes Apprentissages: Ce que Claudine n'a pas dit, Ferenczi, 1936, translation by Helen Beauclerk published as *My Apprenticeships* with Callimachi's translation of *L'Envers du music-hall,* Secker & Warburg, 1957.

Bella-Vista, Ferenczi, 1937, reprinted, Fayard, 1986.

Le Toutounier, Ferenczi, 1939.

Chambre d'hotel, Fayard, 1940, translation by Patrick Leigh Fermor published as *Chance Acquaintances* with his translation of *Julie de Carneilhan* (also see below), Secker & Warburg, 1952, and with his translations of *Gigi* (also see below) and *Julie de Carneilhan,* Farrar, 1952.

Mes Cahiers, Armes de France, 1941.

Journal a rebours, Fayard, 1941, translation by David Le Vay published with his translation of *Paris de ma fenetre* (also see below) as *Looking Backwards* (also see below).

Julie de Carneilhan, Fayard, 1941, translation by Fermor published with *Chambre d'hotel,* Secker & Warburg, 1952, and with *Gigi* and *Chambre d'hotel,* Farrar, 1952.

De ma fenetre, Armes de France, 1942, enlarged edition published as *Paris de ma fenetre,* translation by Le Vay published with his translation of *Journal a rebours* as *Looking Backwards* (also see below).

De la patte a l'aile, Correa, 1943.

Flore et Pomone, Galerie Charpentier, 1943.

Nudite, Mappemonde, 1943.

Le Kepi, Fayard, 1943.

Broderie ancienne, Editions du Rocher, 1944.

Gigi et autres nouvelles, La Guilde du Livre, 1944 (also see below), translation by Fermor of title story published with his translations of *Julie de Carneilhan* and *Chambre d'hotel,* Farrar, 1952.

Trois . . . six . . . neuf, Correa, 1944.

Belles Saisons, Galerie Charpentier, 1945.

L'Etoile vesper, Milieu du Monde, 1946, translation by Le Vay published as *The Evening Star,* Owen, 1973, Bobbs-Merrill, 1974.

Pour un herbier, Mermod, 1948, translation by Senhouse published as *For a Flower Album,* McKay, 1959.

Trait pour trait, Fleuron, 1949.

Journal intermittent, Fleuron, 1949 (also see below).

Le Fanal bleu, Ferenczi, 1949, translation by Senhouse published as *The Blue Lantern,* Farrar, 1963.

La Fleur de l'age, Fleuron, 1949.

En Pays connu, Manuel Bruker, 1949.

Chats de Colette, A. Michel, 1950.

(With Anita Loos) *Gigi* (play; adapted from Colette's novel of the same title), France-Illustration, 1954.

Creatures Great and Small: Creature Conversations; Other Creatures; Creature Comforts (includes *Dialogues de betes* and *La Paix chez les betes*), translated by McLeod, Farrar, 1957.

Paysages et portraits, Flammarion, 1958.

Notes marocaines, Mermod, 1958.

The Stories of Colette, translated by White, Secker & Warburg, 1958, published as *The Tender Shoot and Other Stories,* Farrar, 1959.

Decouvertes, Mermod, 1961.

Earthly Paradise: An Autobiography Drawn From Her Lifelong Writings, edited by Robert Phelps, translated by Beauclerk and others, Farrar, 1966.

Contes des mille et un matins, Flammarion, 1970, translation by Le Vay and Crosland published as *The Thousand and One Mornings,* Bobbs-Merrill, 1973.

Places (includes *Journal intermittent*), translated by Le Vay, Owen, 1970, Bobbs-Merrill, 1971.

Journey for Myself: Selfish Memories, translated by Le Vay, Owen, 1971.

Looking Backwards (contains Le Vay's translations of *De ma fenetre* and *Journal a rebours*), Indiana University Press, 1975.

CORRESPONDENCE

Lettres a Helene Picard, Flammarion, 1958 (also see below).

Lettres a Marguerite Moreno, Flammarion, 1959 (also see below).

Lettres de la vagabonde, Flammarion, 1961 (also see below).

Lettres au petit corsaire, Flammarion, 1963 (also see below).

Lettres a ses pairs, Flammarion, 1973 (also see below).

Letters From Colette (contains excerpts from *Lettres a Helene Picard, Lettres a Marguerite Moreno, Lettres de la vagabonde, Lettres au petit corsaire,* and *Lettres a ses pairs*), translated by Phelps, Farrar, 1980.

COLLECTED WORKS

Oeuvres completes, fifteen volumes, compiled with an introduction by Colette and Maurice Goudeket, Flammarion, 1948-50, enlarged edition published as *Oeuvres completes de Colette,* sixteen volumes, with illustrations and previously unpublished pieces, Editions du Club de l'Honnete Homme, 1973-76.

The Collected Stories of Colette, edited with an introduction by Phelps, translated by Matthew Ward, Farrar, 1983.

Colette: Oeuvres, edited by Claude Pichois, Gallimard, 1984-86.

SIDELIGHTS: Sidonie-Gabrielle Colette, better known as Colette, was an important figure in early twentieth-century French literature. Her impressive series of novels, stories, plays, and newspaper articles include chronicles of backstage life in turn-of-the-century music halls, novels of love and betrayal from the early 1900s through World War II, and nostalgic reminiscences of her childhood. All of Colette's works are marked by sensitive descriptions of nature, sexual frankness, and a flair for the theatrical. Robert Cottrell noted in an essay collected in *Women, the Arts, and the 1920s in Paris and New York* that Colette's 1920 novel *Cheri,* "firmly established her reputation in France as a popular novelist" and as one of the best women writers of her day. Elected to Belgium's Royal Academy of French Language and Literature in 1935, Colette was the first woman to serve as president of France's prestigious literary jury, the Goncourt Academy, and the first woman to attain the rank of Grand Officer of the Legion of Honor.

While not overtly treating or advancing the feminist movements of the late nineteenth or twentieth centuries, Colette's varied works of fiction allow for both coquetry and independence, as well as fidelity and sexual adventure among women. "We suspect that something new in women's writing begins with Colette," wrote Erica Mendelson Eisinger and Mari Ward McCarty in their introduction to *Colette: The Woman, The Writer.* "The androcentric [male-centered] optic is displaced," they continued, and "a new subject appears: the woman who desires." Some critics have complained, however, that Colette's male characters appear wooden, one-dimensional, and far less interesting than her women. Nevertheless, as Marcelle Biolley-Godino argued in *L'Homme-objet chez Colette,* it is precisely by this reversal of the traditional novelistic point of view, by this objectification of the male under the dominant gaze of the desiring female, that Colette strikes a new chord in the French novel. Quoted in Joanna Richardson's *Colette,* French critic Gaeton Picon agreed: "If Colette has seduced and fascinated so many readers," he asserted, "it goes without saying that it is [because] this experience of love, which men never cease to describe, is written as they cannot ever write it. It is written for the first time with this precision, this determination, by the other partner, the mysterious partner who is so often silent."

Colette would most likely have remained silent, as she herself recognized, without the partnership of her first husband. In 1893, a country girl barely twenty years of age, Colette married the socially prominent journalist and music critic Henry Gauthier-Villars, better known in Parisian circles simply as "Willy." Fourteen years her senior, Willy dominated his young wife and introduced her to Parisian high life. In her 1936 work *Mes Apprentissages* (translated as *My Apprenticeships*), Colette recalls her thirteen years as Madame Colette Willy: "It is true that, at first, ridden by youth and ignorance, I had known intoxication—a guilty rapture, an atrocious, impure, adolescent impulse. There are many scarcely nubile girls who dream of becoming the show, the plaything, the licentious masterpiece of some middle-aged man. It is an ugly dream that is punished by its fulfillment. . . . So I was punished, quickly and thoroughly." Willy was not only openly unfaithful to his wife, but he apparently exploited the talent for literature he discovered in her.

Ostensibly a prolific novelist and journalist, Willy operated on the simple principle of signing his name to works actually penned by others. It was perhaps only a matter of time before Willy brought his wife into his underground workshop of ghost writers. In the late 1890s, as Colette told the story in *My Apprenticeships,* Willy asked her to write a memoir of her school years in the Burgundian town of Saint-Sauveur. However, he judged the finished manuscript worthless and consigned it to a desk drawer. Some two years later, Willy rediscovered it, swore roundly at his lack of foresight, and set his wife to work spicing up the manuscript that he now recognized as having commercial potential. In *My Apprenticeships,* Colette recalled—in Willy's words—just what the book needed to be salable: " 'Couldn't you add a little spice to these—er—childish affairs?' M. Willy said to me. 'A tender and over intimate affection, for instance. . . . And rather more playfulness. . . . D'you see what I mean?' " The fruit of this uneven collaboration between husband and wife, *Claudine a l'ecole* (translated as *Claudine at School*) was published in 1900. It bore only Willy's signature.

The book was an immediate success, and thus Colette, who would protest all her life that she had no writer's "vocation," became a novelist. She produced, one after another, the sequels to *Claudine at School* that Willy also claimed as his own: *Claudine a Paris* (title means "Claudine in Paris") in 1901, *Claudine en menage* (title means "Claudine Married") in 1902, *Claudine s'en va* (later translated as *Claudine and Annie*) in 1903. The series turned Willy and Colette into indisputable Parisian celebrities.

Looking back on the beginnings of her career, again in *My Apprenticeships,* Colette proclaimed herself in turn amused, severe, and rueful with regard to the "Claudines." She was already a harsh judge of her own efforts. "I did not think very highly of my first book," she commented, "or of its three sequels. Time has not changed my opinion, and my judgment on all the *Claudines* is still severe. . . . I do not like to rediscover, glancing through these very old books, the suppleness of mood that understood so well what was required of it, the submission to every hint and the already deft manner of avoiding difficulties." She

was particularly upset that Willy had contrived to sell to their publisher all the rights to the "Claudines," thus depriving her of a potential source of income after their divorce in 1910. "I had dutifully set my signature beside my husband's on the two contracts. I shall never forgive myself for having done so. The renunciation was indeed the most unpardonable act that fear ever made me commit," Colette admitted in the introduction to her *Oeuvres completes* (*Complete Works*).

Despite her later repudiation of them, the "Claudine" novels reveal Colette's mastery of the basic craft of narrative fiction. Her character descriptions are consistent, her dialogues are lively and individualized, and her plots are well structured, if somewhat predictable. More importantly, the "Claudine" cycle is evidence of how rapidly the author—supposedly without vocation—developed an authoritative narrative voice.

The most obviously autobiographical of the cycle, the first Claudine is, according to several critics, overly coy. The young and flippant narrator is based on the stereotype of an innocently perverse schoolgirl. Thus *Claudine at School* creates an uncomfortable complicity between the reader and the disingenuous first-person narrator, alluding to the various hetero- and homosexual mischief at her village school, while maintaining the image of an innocent schoolgirl. As Claudine's experiences in the successive novels coincide more closely with Colette's adult perspectives, the narrative voice gradually sheds this uncomfortable cuteness and becomes more maturely self-reflective. Still speaking in the first person, the Claudine of *Claudine a Paris* begins to use stories about erotic experience as both a defense and a lure in the war between the sexes. And, confused by the insistence with which her new husband pushes her into a lesbian affair, the Claudine of *Claudine en menage* limits her narration to only those circumstances and interpretations that logically fall to her limited point of view; her innocence is here legimately attributable to her youth and naivete.

Finally, *Claudine and Annie* marks the end of Colette's apprenticeship in narrative voice. Here Claudine, though still a rough double of Colette herself, is at last presented in the third person by a new narrator, the newlywed Annie. Gradually liberating herself from her authoritarian husband, Annie represents a split within the original Claudine character and is therefore a freer fictionalization of Colette herself. Annie is the first in a long series of Colettean women to opt for lives on their own without benefit of marriage. Having discovered her husband's infidelity, Annie bravely files for divorce, accepting in advance both the solitude and the dangerous sexual allure to which she thus condemns herself: "I shall be the woman travelling alone," she predicts, "who intrigues a hotel dining-room for a week, with whom schoolboys on holiday and arthritics in spas suddenly fall violently in love. . . . I shall be the solitary diner, whose pallor provides scandal with an excuse for inventing all kinds of drama . . . the lady in black, or the lady in blue, whose melancholy reserve frustrates and repulses the compatriot she meets on her travels. . . . The one who is murdered one night in a hotel bedroom and whose body is found outraged and bleeding. . . ."

The 1907 novel *La Retraite sentimentale* (translated as *Retreat From Love*), was published shortly after Colette and Willy separated. The last of the Claudine novels, it ends the cycle with both an indictment and a panegyric of marriage. In contrast with both Colette and Annie, Claudine finally obtains her independence through widowhood and is given over to a peaceful retirement with her dog, her cats, and her tender memories in the tranquil confines of her childhood home: "We'll leave the door open so that the night may enter, with its scent of invisible gardenia—

and the bat which will hang upside down from the muslin curtains—and he too who does not leave me, who watches over the rest of my life, and for whom I keep my eyelids open, without sleeping, in order to see him more clearly. . . ."

The signature "Colette Willy" first appeared on the 1904 *Dialogues de betes,* written while Colette was still married to and living with Willy. The work is a collection of short dialogues featuring the bull terrier Toby-Chien and the angora cat Kiki-la-Doucette. In *Colette Free and Fettered,* Michele Sarde speculated that Willy allowed Colette to sign her own name to these short writings, since he judged them to be women's pieces and of scant commercial value compared to the "Claudines." He was apparently unimpressed with this aspect of his wife's talent; as Colette recalled in *My Apprenticeships,* he remarked that he hadn't known he had married "the last of the lyric poets." In the preface to *Dialogues de betes,* however, as reprinted in Colette's *Complete Works,* the Belgian Symbolist poet Francis Jammes lavishly praised both Colette's bourgeois domestic sense and her poetic gifts: "It pleased Mme. Colette Willy," he wrote "to concentrate in two charming little animals all the fragrance of the gardens, all the freshness of the prairies, all the heat of the departmental road, all the emotions of man. . . ." In addition, critics have indicated that *Dialogues* is significant for its precise characterizations of its animal protagonists and its tender-comic evocations of human foibles through the personalities attributed to the animals. Colette surrounded herself with pets throughout her life; this intense love of animals would continue to be a hallmark of her fictional world as well, reaching its apogee perhaps in the short novel from 1933, *La Chatte,* in which a newlywed husband's preference for his cat and his wife's jealousy over this preference break up their marriage just three months after the wedding.

The short novel *Minne,* published the same year as *Dialogue de betes,* was cast in the mold of the "Claudines." The work depicts a young girl's obsession with the mysterious leader of a band of delinquents; their petty criminal exploits in the no-man's-land of the Paris fortifications stimulate Minne's romantic imagination and lead her on a nightmarish odyssey through the nighttime city. Colette recounted in a later preface to the work that she had hoped to publish *Minne* under her own name, and so "it was necessary, to keep away from it a [husband's] greediness that usually addressed itself to works the size of a novel, that my story should be kept rather brief." But Willy again foresaw the success of his wife's literary endeavors and published *Minne* under his name. A sequel to the work, which appeared in 1905 as *Les Egarements de Minne* ("Minne's Misconduct"), was again signed "Willy."

Les Egarements de Minne tells a tale of male sexual ineptitude. Now married to her sincere if plodding cousin Antoine, Minne embarks on a long course of adulteries in search of an elusive sexual fulfillment that she finally discovers, mostly by accident, in the arms of her own husband. In 1909 Colette joined the two *Minnes* into a single novel, *L'Ingenue libertine* (translated as *The Gentile Libertine*), which she signed "Colette Willy." She reportedly complained nevertheless that the combined edition neither convinced her of the worth of "Minne's Misconduct" nor, "reconciled" her to her beginnings as a novelist. Critics generally rank the two "Minne" volumes among Colette's lesser works. While Minne as an adolescent has a distinct right to her sexual fantasies and Colette's implicit justification of female adultery on the basis of sexual dissatisfaction was audacious for her time, these aspects of the novel do not blend into a seamless whole. Nor is the conclusion—that Minne's experience of sexual fulfillment in Antoine's arms resolves their previous difficulties and

bonds them together for life—as convincing to a modern reader as it might have been for Colette's audience in 1905.

Colette's first divorce forced her to tap her own resources for her financial and professional survival. In an essay collected in *Colette: The Woman, The Writer,* Janet Whatley described how the ability to survive reversals of romantic or domestic fortune is a trait uniquely ascribed to the female characters in Colette's work. "Most of Colette's heroines place a certain value on unhappiness," Whatley observed; "They do not wallow in it: they use it as a source of energy. To be unhappy is to make one's own acquaintance." The 1908 collection of reflective pieces *Les Vrilles de la vigne* ("The Tendrils of the Vine") shows how quickly Colette arrived at this parallel of unhappiness and self-knowledge. Certain of the short narrative pieces in the work suggest the genteel retreat of the disabused ex-wife into a countryside solitude shared only with her dog, her cat, and the selected women friends who remain in discreet relations with the "disgraced" divorcee. In reality, however, Colette's postdivorce period was much more public than this, much noisier and more scandalous. She was openly cohabitating with a new mentor, the well-known lesbian Missy de Belbeuf, the Marquise de Morny; their love scene in the pantomime "Reve d'Egypte" ("Egyptian Dream") performed at the Moulin Rouge in January 1903 had created a city-wide scandal. De Belbeuf is widely considered to be the tender lover celebrated in *Les Vrilles de la vigne.*

Colette's bisexuality, of which her affair with de Belbeuf was perhaps the most flagrant example, contributed to her reputation for sensuality, if not questionable morality. (Her works figured on Rome's *Index of Forbidden Books,* and her two divorces would ultimately deny her the Catholic rites of burial.) Sarde maintained that the affair with de Belbeuf (lasting from about 1906 until 1911) was a direct consequence of Colette's disastrous first marriage. "Ten years older than Colette, the Marquise had played the part usually taken by a male lover in the Willy-Colette separation. Colette was fundamentally monogamous, and Willy had hurt her so cruelly that she had conceived an enormous distrust for the entire male gender," Sarde declared. In spite of this, however, critics have indicated that Colette's writings implicitly acknowledge the importance of the male in ratifying a female's self-worth.

Another major cycle of Colette's narrative works deals with her career between 1906 and 1911 as a music-hall dancer and mime. The 1913 *L'Envers du music-hall (Music-Hall Sidelights)* and *Mitsou* (1919), as well as her earlier work *La Vagabonde (The Vagabond,* 1910) have as their setting the behind-the-scenes world of the traveling song, dance, pantomime, and animal acts that made up the popular French theatre of the music hall and the cafe-concert during the first decades of the twentieth century. *The Vagabond* and *Mitsou* are both novels of rejection. In the former, protagonist Renee turns down a marriage proposal, fearing that acceptance will cost her her freedom. In the latter, set during the First World War, music-hall performer Mitsou falls in love by correspondence with the young man who signs himself the "Blue Lieutenant" after the color of his uniform. Their first night together, however, proves disastrous and Mitsou's new lover feigns an early end to his leave in order to break their next date. Mitsou responds with the distinctive wisdom of Colette's heroines, writing to her lieutenant, "You say: 'Madame, I am charmed to be with you. I must just slip out to get some cigarettes; I won't be a minute,' and you leave her there for the rest of her life."

Sarde has traced connections between the decisions of these two music-hall heroines and those that determined Colette's own relationships with men in the period following her first divorce. Around 1910 she received an offer of marriage from department store heir Auguste Heriot but, according to Sarde, "countered her friends' attempts at her [marital] rehabilitation with a stubborn and active resistance . . . reflected in *La Vagabonde.*" *Mitsou* might also be read as a reflection of this continuing fear of commitment, of this suspicion that however strong the initial attraction between the couple, faithfulness on the part of the male is pure fantasy. By the time *Mitsou* appeared in 1919, however, Colette had already accepted her own return to domesticity. In December 1912 she married her second husband, the Baron Henri de Jouvenel des Ursins, an up-and-coming French political figure who was also one of the chief editors of the Paris daily *Le Matin,* for which Colette had been writing a weekly column since December 1911. In July 1913, at forty years of age, she gave birth to her only child, Colette de Jouvenel, nicknamed as Colette herself had been as a child, "Bel-Gazou."

In *L'Entrave* (translated as *The Shackle*), the 1916 sequel to *The Vagabond,* Renee allows herself to be seduced by the much younger Jean, with whom she has little in common beyond their physical attraction. Jean betrays her, and the ending of the novel thus casts Jean, rather than Renee, in the privileged role of wanderer: "It seems to me," Renee concludes, "as I watch him launch out enthusiastically into life, that he has changed places with me; that he is the eager vagabond and that I am the one who gazes after him, anchored forever." If this exchange of female for male independence appears strikingly unfair, Colette herself expressed considerable dissatisfaction with the conclusion to *L'Entrave.* In *L'Etoile vesper* (*The Evening Star,* 1936) she recalled that, interrupted by the birth of her daughter, the novel, "did not recover from the blows inflicted by the feeble and triumphant creature. Consider, hypothetical readers, consider the scamped ending, the inadequate corridor through which I desired my diminished heroes to pass. Consider the fine but empty tone of an ending in which they do not believe, and the modal chord, as a musician might say, so hurriedly sounded. . . . I have, since, tried to rewrite the ending of *L'Entrave.* I have not succeeded."

Colette's shorter pieces from 1911 to 1924 appear in collections published between 1916 and 1924 (available in translation in *Creatures Great and Small* and *Journey for Myself: Selfish Memories*). In these short pieces, often produced under newspaper deadline, she proved equally at ease describing the cozy retreat of a corner by the hearth or observing the tumult of a political meeting. The beauties of nature, the change of seasons, the wisdom of animals, and the comfort of home are all favorite themes. Into these pieces she poured her receptivity to what Joan Hinde Stewart, writing in *Colette,* called the "fleeting encounters [that] enriched her as woman and as writer," as well as her professional discipline. Both of these strains are apparent in Colette's later comments about her art in *Journal a rebours,* published in 1941. Colette here recalled that, blissfully free of the compulsion to write, her early years taught her to experience without afterthought the living world around her. "My childhood, my free and solitary adolescence," she wrote, "both preserved from the cares of self-expression, were both uniquely occupied with directing their subtle antennae towards whatever contemplates and listens to itself, probes itself and breathes. . . ." Once embarked upon her career, she embraced it wholeheartedly, recording the scenes around her even during the confusion of the exodus from Paris in the wake of the June 1940 German victory during World War II. "Every spectacle," she commented in *Journal a rebours,* "elicits the same obligation, which is perhaps only a temptation: to write, to depict."

Colette's marriage to Henri de Jouvenel ended in divorce in 1925. The union had foundered on two crises in particular: Jouvenel's affair with the Rumanian princess Marthe Bibesco begun in 1923, and Colette's affair with the adolescent Bertrand de Jouvenel, Henri's second oldest son by his former lover Isabelle de Comminges, and thus Colette's stepson. Colette's situation at the end of this second marriage, however, was far better assured than it had been at the end of her first: touring as an actress and lecturer, writing drama criticism in addition to her stories and novels, she was now an established artist in her own right.

Prior to her divorce, Colette completed the 1920 novel *Cheri,* a vehicle for two of her most memorable characters. In this story the aging courtesan Lea de Lonval discovers to what depths of devotion and renunciation she has been inspired by her love for the much younger Cheri, the spoiled and remarkably beautiful son of her friend Charlotte Peloux. Although Colette paints a compelling portrait of Lea as a woman coming to terms with her age, it was the character of Cheri himself, an indisputably dominant male, god-like and childishly selfish in his need for love and admiration, that guaranteed the novel's success. In *The Evening Star,* Colette recalled with amusement the question a young journalist still saw fit to ask her twenty-five years after the novel's publication: "Madame, did Cheri . . . did Cheri ever exist?" She assured her readers that he had, but not in flesh and blood: "I could not wholeheartedly affirm that the Cheri . . . of my novel resembled anyone," she continued. "But I should lie if I said that he resembled no one. But that everyone should model Cheri in their own fashion, isn't that just what I wanted?" Colette made no secret of the just pride she took in *Cheri:* "For the first time in my life," she wrote in *The Evening Star,* "I felt morally certain of having written a novel for which I needed neither blush nor doubt, a novel whose appearance massed partisans and critics round it. . . . I know where my best work as a writer is to be found."

In *La Maison de Claudine* (*My Mother's House,* 1922) Colette turned her considerable scenic talents—the ability to evoke in a few brief pages a precise atmosphere, a moral lesson, or a psychological insight—to the service of her nostalgia for her childhood home—indeed, for the entire lost world of childhood. But Colette's most vivid example of nostalgic writing is the 1929 memoir *Sido.* In the joint preface to *Sido* and *My Mother's House* in her *Complete Works,* Colette credited her mother, Sidonie Colette, known as Sido, with both the happiness of her childhood and the wisdom of her adult years: "As a child I was poor and happy, like many children who need neither money nor comfort to achieve an active sort of happiness. But my felicity knew another and less commonplace secret: the presence of her who, instead of receding far from me through the gates of death, has revealed herself more vividly to me as I grow older."

Sylvie Romanowski has suggested in an essay appearing in *Colette: The Woman, The Writer* that Sido stands out from the rest of Colette's women by her mythic dimension. "[It] is only with respect to Sido," Romanowski noted, "that Colette brings any metaphysical or religious dimensions into her writings. . . . [Sido's] superior understanding of nature and people does not come from some mysterious or magical power, but from her instincts, her intuitive participation in nature, her reverent respect towards the holiness of all life." In Colette's memoir, Sido appears as a type of primordial Earth Mother; it is she who teaches her daughter to read and respect nature, who raises her children to value individuality over convention, and who approaches her own aging with a serenity unmatched by any of Colette's other heroines. While admitting the possibility that Sido may thus be "idealized from childhood perceptions that persist into adult memory," Romanowski nevertheless concluded that Sido "remains a woman of flesh and blood with her own shortcomings and idiosyncrasies that make her a very concrete person on a par with other women in Colette's writings. Both an ideal figure and real person, Sido is the least ambiguous woman among [Colette's principal female types]."

Colette's other major works from the 1920s include *Le Ble en herbe* (1923; translated as *Ripening Seed*) and *La Naissance du jour* (1928; translated as *Morning Glory*). Both works feature young men caught between two generations of women. In *Ripening Seed,* an adolescent assumes he possesses the great mysteries of life once he has been seduced by the mature Madame Dalleray. With his fifteen-year-old childhood friend Vinca, however, he discovers sex as a natural experience that fulfills the woman but leaves the man strangely empty, since it is he, not Vinca, who mourns what has been lost the morning after their night together. In the poetically rambling *Morning Glory,* the narrator describes a long night's conversation in which she discourages the attentions of her young neighbor Valere Vial. Joan Hinde Stewart, writing in her *Colette,* called *Morning Glory* Colette's "most complicated work, . . . a self-portrait of extraordinary density and ambiguity."

Colette's style has been praised as precise, evocative and sensual. Her letter to writer Marguerite Moreno critiquing a passage from Moreno's memoirs suggests what Colette valued in her own writing. "Do you understand that . . . not one word either *shows* or *makes us hear* those you are talking about?" she chides Moreno, advising her to transpose her account of a dinner party into dialogue. "No narration, good Lord!" Colette continues. "Touches and scattered colors, and no need to conclude. . . . Stick in a decor, and guests, and even some dishes, otherwise it doesn't work!" She concludes with an admonition that she herself took to heart in her own writing. "And try, dear heart," she tells Moreno, "not to show us that it bugs you to write." Criticism indicates that for Colette, a finished literary work had to be seamless; the effort of the writing and rewriting had to disappear beneath the apparent naturalness and inevitability of the final version. She summed up her opinion in a letter to Moreno, writing: "I loathe grandiloquent endings."

As a theme of Colette's work, homosexuality is but one part of the overriding attention she gives to the senses in all their pleasures and pitfalls; one may just as easily accuse her of indiscretion for her rhapsodic descriptions of nature as for her descriptions of sexual experience. The work most explicitly devoted to homosexuality, the 1932 *Le Pur et l'impur* (*The Pure and the Impure,* originally entitled *Ces Plaisirs [These Pleasures]*), is in fact a curious memoir describing people she had known or known of, including Missy de Belbeuf (appearing in the guise of the virile La Chevaliere); the lesbian poet and suicide Renee Vivien; and the couple known as the Ladies of Llangollen, celebrated for their lifelong devotion to each other. In an essay collected in *Colette: The Woman, The Writer,* Ann Cothran and Diane Griffin Crowder referred to *The Pure and the Impure* as a "remarkable literary achievement by virtue of both form and content"; they further contended that the imagery of the work functions to blur conventional notions of gender, sexuality, and morality, concluding that "purity for [Colette] is sensory, not cognitive or rational." Calling *The Pure and the Impure* Colette's "most awkward and resistant text," Jacob Stockinger, in his essay from *Colette: The Woman, The Writer,* defined her integrative view of sexuality that refuses to stereotype and that, in her work as in her personal life, "form[ed] a continuum in which she moved freely from male to female lovers and back again. . . . In Colette's world," Stockinger concluded, "once lesbians escape both

male domination and masculine masquerading, a welcome confrontation with femaleness inevitably occurs. Her lesbians are not exiles from the woman's condition but insiders who carry crucial lessons for their sisters."

In 1935 Colette married her third and last husband, Maurice Goudeket, who was sixteen years her junior. The two had been a couple since 1925, and her later writings refer to Goudeket as her best friend and companion. He undertook in 1939 the first edition of Colette's *Complete Works* and nursed her faithfully through her long bout with arthritis that set in following a fracture of her fibula in September 1931 and that by the end of her life had almost completely immobilized her. Goudeket, a Jew, was arrested in December of 1941 and detained in a prison camp outside of Paris for two months. The anguish Colette experienced during Goudeket's imprisonment fills her postwar work *The Evening Star,* while instilling a sense of sisterhood among women who have known a similar anguish: "We [women] know how to laugh, and very well," concludes one section of the work. "But just a word, the mention of a date, an anecdote, and there reappears fleetingly on our faces the old expression of the women you were—destitute, hunted, partnerless. . . . If one of you here should be called to the telephone, she stops laughing, she coughs as if something had gone down the wrong way, she says in a feeble little voice: Oh dear, what can they want of me? She, no more than I, likes the doorbell, the clock striking, loud speakers, sirens. A whole family of sonorities has become hateful to us, since. . . ."

The novella *Gigi* is probably Colette's best known postwar work, partially because of its successful screen adaptation. *Gigi* tells the story of a young girl who is destined for a career as modern-day a courtesan, but who opts instead for a love match, which has a double-edged verve to it. Colette once again builds a love story around a disproportioned couple (Gaston is considerably older than Gigi and enjoys much higher social status) and attributes a precocious, prematurely disillusioned wisdom to her adolescent heroine. Certain, as are all of Colette's women, that Gaston will eventually betray her, Gigi confesses her love for him as the lesser of two evils: she would, she tells him in Colette's parody of the romantic happy ending, rather be unhappy with him than unhappy without him.

Some observers have noted that many of Colette's later works of fiction and nonfiction can seem rambling and anecdotal; these writings lack the incisiveness, clean pacing, and crisp insight of her earlier works. The author's various journals and memoirs—the 1942 *De ma fenetre* and the 1949 *Journal intermittent,* in addition to *The Evening Star* and *The Blue Lantern,*—are, by her own admission, less chronological accounts of her life or philosophical reflections on her experiences than they are scattered collections of anecdotes, observations, character portraits, reminiscences, and comments. "I do not possess the knack of writing a proper journal," she declared at the beginning of *The Blue Lantern.* "The art of selection, of noting things of mark, retaining the unusual while discarding the commonplace, has never been mine, since most of the time I am stimulated and quickened by the ordinary." The increasing immobility imposed upon her by her arthritis is a dominant theme of *The Blue Lantern.* Its title refers to the blue shade of the lamp in her window by which, confined to her sofa-bed, she continued to write. Colette died in Paris on August 3, 1954; her funeral on August 7 was the first state funeral accorded to a woman in France.

MEDIA ADAPTATIONS: Claudine at School was adapted for stage; *Cheri* was adapted for both stage and film; *Gigi* was adapted for an Academy Award-winning film of the same title by Alan Jay Lerner, directed by Vincente Minnelli, Metro-Goldwyn-Mayer, 1958.

BIOGRAPHICAL/CRITICAL SOURCES:

BOOKS

Biolley-Godino, Marcelle, *L'Homme-objet chez Colette,* Klinck-sieck, 1972.

Colette (under pseudonym Willy), *Minne,* Ollendorff, 1904.

Colette, *Mitsou,* translated by Jane Terry, A. & C. Boni, 1930.

Colette (under name Colette Willy), *The Gentile Libertine,* translated by Rosemary Carr Benet, Farrar, 1931.

Colette, *Oeuvres completes,* fifteen volumes, introduction by Colette and Maurice Goudeket, Flammarion, 1948-50.

Colette, *My Mother's House* [and] *Sido,* translation of the former by Enid McLeod and Una Vicenzo Troubridge and the latter by McLeod, Farrar, 1953.

Colette (under name Colette Willy), *The Vagabond,* translated by McLeod, Secker & Warburg, 1954.

Colette, *My Apprenticeships,* translated by Helen Beauclerk, Secker & Warburg, 1957.

Colette, *Creatures Great and Small: Creature Conversations; Other Creatures; Creature Comforts,* translated by McLeod, Farrar, 1957.

Colette, *Lettres a Marguerite Moreno,* Flammarion, 1959.

Colette (under pseudonym Willy), *Claudine and Annie,* translated by Antonia White, Secker & Warburg, 1962.

Colette, *The Blue Lantern,* translated by Roger Senhouse, Farrar, 1963.

Colette, *The Shackle,* translated by White, Secker & Warburg, 1964.

Colette, *The Evening Star,* translated by David Le Vay, Bobbs-Merrill, 1974.

Colette, *Earthly Paradise: An Autobiography Drawn From Her Lifetime Writings,* edited by Robert Phelps, Farrar, 1966.

Colette (under name Colette Willy), *Retreat From Love,* translated by Margaret Crosland, Indiana University Press, 1974.

Colette, *Looking Backwards,* translated by Le Vay, Indiana University Press, 1975.

Cottrell, Robert D., *Colette,* Ungar, 1974.

Crosland, Margaret, *Colette—The Difficulty of Loving: A Biography,* Dell, 1973.

Dictionary of Literary Biography, Volume 65: *French Novelists, 1930-1960,* Gale, 1988.

Eisinger, Erica Mendelson and Mari Ward McCarty, editors, *Colette: The Woman, the Writer,* Pennsylvania State University Press, 1981.

Perry, R. and M. W. Brownley, editors, *Mothering the Mind: Twelve Studies of Writers and Their Silent Partners,* Holmes & Meier, 1984.

Richardson, Joanna, *Colette,* F. Watts, 1984.

Sarde, Michele, *Colette Free and Fettered,* translated by R. Miller, Morrow, 1980.

Stewart, Joan Hinde, *Colette,* Twayne, 1983.

Twentieth-Century Literary Criticism, Gale, Volume 1, 1978, Volume 5, 1981, Volume 16, 1985.

Wheeler, K. W. and V. L. Lussier, editors, *Women, the Arts, and the 1920s in Paris and New York,* Transaction Books, 1982.

PERIODICALS

Centerpoint: A Journal of Interdisciplinary Studies, fall-spring, 1981.

Contemporary Literature, summer, 1983.

Modern Language Studies, spring, 1981, summer, 1983.

New Republic, September 6, 1954.

Times Literary Supplement, August 22, 1968.

* * *

COLLINS, Hunt
   See HUNTER, Evan

* * *

COLUM, Padraic   1881-1972

PERSONAL: Born December 8, 1881, in Longford, Ireland; came to the United States in 1914; died of a stroke, January 12, 1972, in Enfield, Conn.; son of Padraic (a warehouse master) and Susanna (MacCormack) Colum; married Mary Gunning Maguire (a writer), 1912 (died, 1957). *Education:* Educated at local schools. *Religion:* Catholic.

CAREER: Playwright, essayist, novelist, poet, and author of books for children; worked briefly for a railroad; became full-time writer in Dublin, Ireland, 1901; was a founder of the Irish National Theatre (later known as the Abbey), and co-founder and editor for a time of the *Irish Review.* Visited Hawaii, 1923, at the request of its legislature to reshape the island's traditional stories.

MEMBER: Irish Academy of Literature, American Academy of Arts and Letters, Poetry Society of America (president, 1938-39).

AWARDS, HONORS: Runner-up for the Newbery Medal, 1922, for *The Golden Fleece and the Heroes Who Lived Before Achilles,* 1926, for *The Voyagers, Being Legends and Romances of Atlantic Discovery,* and 1934, for *The Big Tree of Bunlahy: Stories of My Own Countryside;* American Academy of Poets Award, 1952; Gregory Medal of the Irish Academy of Letters, 1953; Regina Medal, 1961; Boston Arts Festival Poet (citation), 1961; Georgetown University 175th Anniversary Medal of Honor, 1964; Litt.D., Columbia University, 1958, and Trinity College, Dublin, 1958.

WRITINGS:

CHILDREN'S STORIES

A Boy in Eirinn, Dutton, 1913, revised edition, Dutton, 1929.

The King of Ireland's Son, Holt, 1916, 3rd edition, Floris Books, 1978.

(Editor) Jonathan Swift, *Gulliver's Travels* (an abridged edition for children), Macmillan, 1917, reprinted, 1964.

The Adventures of Odysseus [and] *The Tale of Troy,* Macmillan, 1918, published as *The Children's Homer: The Adventures of Odysseus* [and] *The Tale of Troy,* 1962.

The Boy Who Knew What the Birds Said, Macmillan, 1918.

The Girl Who Sat by the Ashes, Macmillan, 1919, revised edition, 1968.

The Children of Odin: The Book of Northern Myths, Macmillan, 1920, reprinted, 1984.

The Boy Apprenticed to an Enchanter, Macmillan, 1920, reprinted, 1966.

The Golden Fleece and the Heroes Who Lived Before Achilles, Macmillan, 1921, reprinted, 1962.

The Children Who Followed the Piper, Macmillan, 1922.

(Editor) *A Thousand and One Nights: Tales of Wonder and Magnificence,* Macmillan, 1923.

The Six Who Were Left on a Shoe, Macmillan, 1923, reprinted, McGraw-Hill, 1968.

The Peep-Show Man, Macmillan, 1924.

The Island of the Mighty, Being the Hero Stories of Celtic Britain Retold from The Mabinogion, Macmillan, 1924.

Tales and Legends of Hawaii, Yale University Press, Volume 1: *At the Gateways of the Day*, 1924, Volume 2: *The Bright Islands*, 1925, published as *Legends of Hawaii*, 1937.

The Forge in the Forest, Macmillan, 1925.

The Voyagers, Being Legends and Romances of Atlantic Discovery, Macmillan, 1925.

The Fountain of Youth: Stories to Be Told, Macmillan, 1927, excerpts published separately as *Story Telling New and Old*, Macmillan, 1968.

Three Men: A Tale, Matthews & Marrot, 1930.

The Big Tree of Bunlahy: Stories of My Own Countryside, Macmillan, 1933.

The White Sparrow, Macmillan, 1933, reprinted, McGraw-Hill, 1972, published as *Sparrow Alone*, Blackie, 1975.

Where the Winds Never Blew and the Cocks Never Crew, Macmillan, 1940.

The Frenzied Prince, Being Heroic Stories of Ancient Ireland, McKay, 1943.

(Editor) *The Arabian Nights: Tales of Wonder and Magnificence*, Macmillan, 1953.

The Stone of Victory and Other Tales, McGraw-Hill, 1966.

POEMS

Heather Ale: A Book of Verse, [Dublin], 1907.

Wild Earth: A Book of Verse, Maunsel (Dublin), 1907.

Wild Earth and Other Poems, Holt, 1916.

(Editor with Thomas P. MacDonagh and Edward J. O'Brien) *Poems of the Irish Revolutionary Brotherhood*, Small, Maynard, 1916, reprinted, Longwood Publishing, 1978.

Dramatic Legends and Other Poems, Macmillan, 1922.

(Editor) *An Anthology of Irish Verse*, Boni & Liveright, 1922, reissued, Liveright, 1972.

The Way of the Cross: Devotions on the Progress of Our Lord Jesus Christ from the Judgement Hall to Calvary, Seymour, 1926.

Creatures, Macmillan, 1927.

Old Pastures, Macmillan, 1930.

Poems, Macmillan, 1932, revised edition published as *Collected Poems*, Devin-Adair, 1953.

The Story of Lowry Maen, Macmillan, 1937.

Flower Pieces: New Poems, Orwell Press (Dublin), 1938.

The Jackdaw, Gayfield Press (Dublin), 1939.

Ten Poems, Dolmen Press (Dublin), 1952.

The Vegetable Kingdom, Indiana University Press, 1954.

Garland Sunday, privately printed, 1958.

Irish Elegies, Dolmen Press, 1958, revised edition, 1961.

The Poet's Circuits: Collected Poems of Ireland, Oxford University Press, 1960, centenary edition, Humanities Press, 1981.

(Editor) *The Poems of Samuel Ferguson*, Dufour, 1963.

(Editor) *Roofs of Gold: Poems to Read Aloud*, Macmillan, 1964.

Images of Departure, Dolmen Press, 1969.

Selected Poems of Padraic Colum, edited by Sanford Sternlicht, Syracuse University Press, 1989.

PLAYS

The Children of Lir [and] *Brian Boru*, published in *Irish Independent*, 1902.

The Kingdom of the Young (produced in 1902), published in *United Irishman*, 1903.

The Foleys [and] *Eoghan's Wife*, published in *United Irishman*, 1903.

The Saxon Shillin' (produced in Dublin, 1903), published in *Lost Plays of the Irish Renaissance*, edited by Robert Hogan and James Kilroy, Proscenium Press, 1970.

A Fiddler's House (produced in Dublin, 1903, under title "Broken Soil"; three-act; also see below), Maunsel, 1907.

The Land (produced in Dublin and London, 1905; three-act; also see below), Maunsel, 1905.

The Miracle of the Corn: A Miracle Play (produced in Dublin, 1908, and London, 1910), Theatre Arts, 1925.

Thomas Muskerry (three-act; also see below) Maunsel, 1910.

"The Destruction of the Hostel," produced in Dublin, 1910.

The Desert (produced in Dublin under title "Mogu the Wanderer," 1937; three-act), Devereux Newth, 1912, published as *Mogu the Wanderer; or, The Desert: A Fantastic Comedy*, Little, Brown, 1917.

The Betrayal (produced in Manchester, 1913, and in Pittsburgh, 1914), published in *One-Act Plays of To-Day 4*, edited by J. W. Marriott, Harrap, 1928.

Three Plays: The Fiddler's House, The Land, Thomas Muskerry, Little, Brown, 1916, reprinted, Dufour, 1963.

(With F. E. Washburn-Freund) "The Grasshopper" (adaption of a play by Count Keyserling), produced in New York, 1917.

Balloon (produced in Ogunquit, Maine), Macmillan, 1929.

"The Show-Booth" (adaptation of a play by Alexander Blok), produced in Dublin, 1948.

(With wife, Mary Colum) *Moytura: A Play for Dancers*, Oxford University Press, 1963.

"The Challengers: Monasterboice, Glendalough, Cloughoughter," produced in Dublin, 1966.

(With Basil Blackwell) "The Road 'round Ireland" (adaptation of the work by Colum; also see below), produced in Norwalk, Conn., 1967; produced in New York under title "Carricknabauna," 1967.

Selected Plays of Padraic Colum, edited by Sanford Sternlicht, Syracuse University Press, 1989.

OTHER

Studies (miscellany), Maunsel, 1907.

My Irish Year (autobiography), J. Pott, 1912.

(Editor) *Oliver Goldsmith*, Browne, 1913.

(With others) *The Irish Rebellion of 1916 and Its Martyrs: Erin's Tragic Easter*, edited by Maurice Joy, Devin Adair, 1916.

(Editor) *Broad-Sheet Ballads, Being a Collection of Irish Popular Songs*, Maunsel, 1913.

Castle Conquer (novel), Macmillan, 1923.

The Road 'round Ireland, Macmillan, 1926.

(Contributor) *Book of Modern Catholic Prose*, edited by Theodore Maynard, Holt, 1928.

(With others) *James Stephens*, Macmillan, 1928, published as *On James Stephens*, R. West, 1977.

Orpheus: Myths of the World, Macmillan, 1930, published as *Myths of the World*, Grosset & Dunlap, 1976.

Cross Roads in Ireland, Macmillan, 1930.

Ella Young: An Appreciation, Longman, 1931.

A Half-Day's Ride; or, Estates in Corsica (essays), Macmillan, 1932, reprinted, Books for Libraries, 1969.

The Legend of Saint Columba, Macmillan, 1935.

(Editor) *A Treasury of Irish Folklore: The Stories, Traditions, Legends, Humor, Wisdom, Ballads, and Songs of the Irish People*, Crown Publishers, 1954, reprinted, 1967.

The Flying Swans (novel), Crown Publishers, 1957, reprinted, A. Figgis (Dublin), 1969.

(With M. Colum) *Our Friend James Joyce*, Doubleday, 1958.

Ourselves Alone! The Story of Arthur Griffith and the Origin of the Irish Free State, Crown Publishers, 1959 (published in Ireland as *Arthur Griffith,* Browne & Nolan, 1959).
(Editor with Margaret Freeman Cabell) *Between Friends: Letters of James Branch Cabell and Others,* Harcourt, 1962.
Selected Short Stories of Padraic Colum, Syracuse University Press, 1985.

The largest number of Colum's papers are in the Berg Collection of the New York Public Library. Others are held at the library of the State University of New York at Binghamton.

SIDELIGHTS: As a young boy, Padraic Colum lived with his grandmother, where he would find himself being entertained by a storyteller narrating legends and reciting songs and poetry. These early childhood experiences would later influence the author's own writings. By the time he was twenty years old, Colum had received recognition as both a poet and playwright. His name was soon associated with William Butler Yeats, Lady Gregory, John Millington Synge, A. E. (George W. Russell), and others who made literary contributions to the period known as the Irish Renaissance. Although he was co-founder of the Irish National Theatre (later known as the Abbey), and author of its first successful play, *The Land,* Colum eventually cut his connections with the theatre over disagreement with the drama company policy.

The Irish-American author began writing children's books after he came to the United States in 1914. According to a *New York Times* article, Colum credited his popularity with children to his belief that one should not talk down to them. The author philosophized, "If children are to will out of the imagination, and create out of the will, we must see to it that their imaginations are not clipped or made trivial."

Colum was very devoted to his wife, Mary. Together they wrote the book, *Our Friend James Joyce.* A critic for the *Chicago Sunday Tribune* reviewed the book as being "the outcome of their [the Colums] warm affection for Joyce, an affection that is all the warmer for being far from blind." Colum's respect for Joyce as a friend and peer made him a dedicated member of the James Joyce Society.

Although never quite reaching the prominence of some of his contemporaries, many of the author's poems have been set to music and have become familiar Irish folksongs. In a *New York Times* article, Colum was quoted as saying, "Poems are made to be said. They are for our voices, not just for our eyes."

BIOGRAPHICAL/CRITICAL SOURCES:

Benet, Laura, *Famous Storytellers for Young People,* Dodd, 1968.

Bowen, Zack R., *Padraic Colum: A Biographical Critical Introduction,* Southern Illinois University Press, 1970.

Catholic Literary Revival, Bruce Publishers, 1935.

Contemporary Drama of Ireland, Little, Brown, 1917.

Contemporary Literary Criticism, Volume 28, Gale, 1984.

Dictionary of Literary Biography, Volume 19: *British Poets, 1880-1914,* Gale, 1983.

Farrar, John C., editor, *Literary Spotlight,* Doran, 1924.

Robinson, Lennox, editor, *Irish Theatre,* Macmillan, 1939.

Tendencies of Modern English Drama, Scribner, 1923.

PERIODICALS

Catholic Library World, December, 1960.

Chicago Sunday Tribune, August 24, 1958.
Times Literary Supplement, April 2, 1982, October 10, 1986.

OBITUARIES:

PERIODICALS

Commonwealth, February 11, 1972.
Detroit News, January 12, 1972.
Newsweek, January 24, 1972.
New York Times, January 12, 1972.
Publishers Weekly, February 21, 1972.
Time, January 24, 1972.
Washington Post, January 13, 1972.

*   *   *

COLVIN, James
See MOORCOCK, Michael (John)

*   *   *

COLWIN, Laurie   1944-

PERSONAL: Born in 1944 in New York, N.Y.; daughter of Peter Barnett Colwin (an executive and director of United Jewish Appeal); married Juris Jurjevics (a publisher and proprietor of Soho Press); children: Rosa. *Education:* Attended Bard College and Columbia School of General Studies.

ADDRESSES: c/o Alfred A. Knopf, Inc., 201 East 50th St., New York, N.Y. 10022.

CAREER: Member of publishing house editorial staff, Pantheon, Viking, Putnam, and Dutton, all in New York City; also worked for literary agents, Sanford Greenburger and Candida Donadio; writer. Professor of writing, 1985-86. Volunteer worker, Coalition for the Homeless, and Antonio Olivieri Shelter for Homeless Women.

WRITINGS:

Passion and Affect (short stories), Viking, 1974 (published in England as *Dangerous French Mistress and Other Stories,* Chatto & Windus, 1975).
Shine on, Bright and Dangerous Object (novel), Viking, 1975.
Happy All the Time (novel), Knopf, 1978.
The Lone Pilgrim (short stories), Knopf, 1981.
Family Happiness (novel), Knopf, 1982.
Another Marvelous Thing (short stories), Knopf, 1986.
Home Cooking: A Writer in the Kitchen (short pieces), Knopf, 1988.
Goodbye without Leaving, Poseidon Press, 1990.

SIDELIGHTS: "Happiness is an interesting topic," Laurie Colwin told Madalynne Reuter in a *Publishers Weekly* interview. Colwin explores the many facets of happiness in her novels and short story collections, which usually focus upon the comfortable bourgeoisie of her native New York City. In her portrayals of life among the upper classes, Colwin is often compared to John Updike and John Cheever. But while she shares with these authors an interest in the emotions of urbane types, a distinctive Colwin theme is "privacy, with its dangers and its attractiveness," according to William Spiegelman in a *Dictionary of Literary Biography* article. "Only privacy allows for the sanctity and integrity of the individual; and whether it is disrupted by the unknown or the goofy, usually in the form of love, it is the central gift to which her characters aspire or cling."

The author is noted for the light touch she brings to her characters' conflicts, especially the romantic ones. In her critically acclaimed collection *The Lone Pilgrim,* for example, Colwin has characters who "are exceptionally appealing, fun to have around," as *Chicago Tribune Book World* critic Alice Adams sees it. "Typically a Colwin heroine has a good, slightly offbeat job (that is to say, nothing to do with banks or computers or merchandising). . . . She also has interesting sidelines," such as the title character of *The Lone Pilgrim,* an illustrator of children's books, who practices being a "perfect houseguest" on the side.

"The real joy, however, what really makes you smile as you read along is Colwin's reflections [on romance]," states Adams. "Friends' love affairs, unless they are saggingly repetitive, are often fun to hear about, but how much more so if the friend has managed to overlay his or her adventures with serious, wise, and original reflections, so that you are not only amused but enlightened, elevated even. . . . These stories of Laurie Colwin's could be viewed as reflections or meditations on the nature of love, especially romantic love, her true subject."

Another Marvelous Thing, a collection of related short stories, continues the author's exploration of love and happiness. The pieces chronicle the adulterous affair of economists Frank and Josephine ("Billy"). While both find the affair exotic and exciting, Frank and Billy also realize that their respective spouses are too perfect for them to leave. "It is the adulterers who are incompatible, an irony at once deliciously comic and far too tidy," Melvin Maddocks says in *Time.* After the affair breaks off, Billy finds herself pregnant, and she declares that Frank had been her "child substitute" and when Billy gives birth to a son she replaces "metaphor with life," according to Maddocks.

In a *New York Times* review of *Another Marvelous Thing,* Michiko Kakutani finds fault with some of the early stories, pointing out that Colwin "never reveals the full subtext that must inform [the dialogue]. She never lets the reader in on the characters' real feelings, never sets their affair in any context with their inner lives or their lives at home." In the later stories, however, the situations have "more ballast and weight," says Kakutani, adding that in these tales the author "uses her elegant, delicately colored prose to explore the effects of a relationship on an individual psyche, instead of simply using it to embroider pretty, but merely decorative, patterns on her old subjects of happiness and love." To *Los Angeles Times* reviewer Richard Eder, *Another Marvelous Thing* "is tender without sentimentality, witty without posturing, clear-minded without cynicism and winning without being winsome. It has acute and alluring things to say about the fog between the sexes; and in its idiosyncratic way, it manages to be a feminist book that is fond of women."

Colwin's novels reflect the themes in her short stories. *Happy All the Time* relates how a pair of upper-class cousins, Guido and Vincent, court and marry women who at first seem unlikely future wives: Holly Sturgis, a mysteriously perfect creature who leaves Guido bemused and entranced, and Misty Berkowitz, whose apprehension and skepticism gradually soften. As John Romano remarks in the *New York Times Book Review,* "It's a lovely book. . . . The people in it are nice and better than nice. Laurie Colwin writes a sentence of porcelain-like clarity, to use an adjective she favors. Her book has the elegance called Mozartian—pretty themes, memorable melodies. The four people in it are a kind of quartet, a counterpoint of character-types, and their effect is harmony." Moreover, "the [eventual] successful depiction of happiness is rare enough to qualify Colwin's novel as daring experimental fiction," maintains *Newsweek*'s Walter Clemons. Clemons considers the book a "canny Manhattan pastorale," which "strikes me as at least as much fun to read as [Jane

Austen's] 'Sense and Sensibility.' I recommend it highly: it is sweet, sharply funny and altogether unusual."

The central figure in Colwin's third novel, *Family Happiness,* is Polly Demarest, a Manhattanite who at first seems to lead the ideal life: successful husband, two children, impressive home and no material worries. But behind the domestic facade Polly is facing a crisis of identity that culminates in a secret affair with an artist named Lincoln Bennett. "It is a measure of the complexity of this novel that although what could be described (much too glibly) as Polly's 'liberation' is its central subject, and though its treatment of her emotional awakening is thoroughly positive, Colwin offers no sermons and no easy answers," writes *Washington Post Book World* critic Jonathan Yardley.

Colwin's prose "contributes to the swift development of Polly's situation that of a woman torn between her sense of family obligation and a wildly fulfilling love affair," reports Christopher Lehmann-Haupt. In his *New York Times* article, Lehmann-Haupt also sees some problems with *Family Happiness,* "chief among them a tendency of the story to dwell too long and insistently on Polly's troubles with her family . . . [caused by repetition and the author's] occasional tendency to tell rather than show, to announce instead of dramatize." And while *Times Literary Supplement* reviewer Victoria Rothschild notes that "where the novel falls short is in its central confrontations: neither [Lincoln] nor Henry the husband has enough substance to become more than agreeably perfect," the critic also feels that "the strength of *Family Happiness* lies in its asides, in the comic caricatures of minor figures in Polly's life, and the light, incidental satire that results from their exchanges."

The novel was more enthusiastically received by Yardley, who concludes his review by asking, "What more could a sensible reader want than what Laurie Colwin offers in *Family Happiness?* Okay: it's not *Anna Karenina.* . . . But comparisons will get you nowhere. There is much to be said for novels . . . that deliver more than they seem to promise. *Family Happiness* is one of these: a wonderful surprise for which I find myself enormously grateful." As *Newsweek* critic Gene Lyons comments, "Only a novelist with Laurie Colwin's conciseness, ear for dialogue and talent for creating a vivid world of minor characters could make so familiar a story as consistently amusing and ultimately surprising as this one."

BIOGRAPHICAL/CRITICAL SOURCES:

BOOKS

Contemporary Literary Criticism, Gale, Volume 5, 1976, Volume 13, 1980, Volume 23, 1983.
Dictionary of Literary Biography Yearbook: 1980, Gale, 1981.

PERIODICALS

Atlantic, October, 1978.
Carolina Quarterly, spring, 1974.
Chicago Tribune Book World, March 1, 1981.
Harper's, April, 1979, September, 1982.
Los Angeles Times, February 17, 1981, March 26, 1986.
Ms., October, 1978.
Nation, November 20, 1982.
New England Review, winter, 1978.
New Republic, April 27, 1974.
Newsweek, October 9, 1978, September 27, 1982.
New York Times, January 24, 1974, March 4, 1981, September 16, 1982, March 26, 1986, May 4, 1990.
New York Times Book Review, November 19, 1978, January 25, 1981, September 19, 1981, April 3, 1986.

Publishers Weekly, September 10, 1982.
Saturday Review, October 14, 1978.
Sewanee Review, fall, 1974.
Time, March 9, 1981, April 21, 1986.
Times Literary Supplement, September 5, 1975, August 7, 1981, May 6, 1983.
Village Voice, August 4, 1975, October 9, 1978.
Washington Post, November 13, 1988.
Washington Post Book World, February 22, 1981, September 12, 1982, March 23, 1986, April 29, 1990.

*   *   *

COMMAGER, Henry Steele 1902-

PERSONAL: Born October 25, 1902, in Pittsburgh, Pa.; son of James Williams and Anna Elizabeth (Dan) Commager; married Evan Carroll, July 3, 1928; married Mary E. Powlesland, July 14, 1979; children: (first marriage) Henry Steele (deceased), Nellie Thomas McColl, Elisabeth Carroll. *Education:* University of Chicago, Ph.B., 1923, M.A., 1924, Ph.D., 1928; attended University of Copenhagen; Cambridge University, M.A.; Oxford University, M.A. *Politics:* Independent Democrat.

ADDRESSES: Home—405 South Pleasant St., Amherst, Mass. 01002. *Office*—Department of history, Amherst College, Amherst, Mass. 01002.

CAREER: New York University, New York, N.Y., instructor in history, 1926-29, assistant professor, 1929-30, associate professor, 1930-31, professor, 1931-38; Columbia University, New York, N.Y., professor of American history, 1939-56, adjunct professor, 1956-59, Speranza Lecturer, 1960; Amherst College, Amherst, Mass., Smith Professor of History, 1956-72, Simpson Lecturer, 1972-. Pitt Professor of American History, Cambridge University, 1941, 1947-48; Bacon Lecturer, Boston University, 1943; Richards Lecturer, University of Virginia, 1944; Harmsworth Professor of American History, Oxford University, 1952-53; Gottesman Lecturer, Uppsala University, 1953; Ziskind Professor, Brandeis University, 1955; Commonwealth Lecturer, University of London, 1963; Harris Lecturer, Northwestern University, 1964; Patton Lecturer, Indiana University, 1977. Visiting professor or lecturer at several universities in the United States and abroad. Member of War Department Commission on History of the War; travelled to Britain for War Department, Office of War Information, summer, 1943, and to France and Belgium, 1945. *Military service:* Served with U.S. Army Information and Education Division, 1945.

MEMBER: American Academy of Arts and Letters, American Scandinavian Society (fellow), American Antiquarian Society, Massachusetts Historical Society, Phi Beta Kappa, Century Association, St. Botolph's (Boston), Athenaeum Club (London).

AWARDS, HONORS: Herbert B. Adams Award of the American Historical Association, 1929; special award from Hillman Foundation, 1954, for *Freedom, Loyalty, Dissent,* Guggenheim fellowship, 1960-61; Gold Medal Award for history from American Academy and Institute of Arts and Letters, 1972; Sarah Josepha Hale Award, 1973; decorated Knight, Order of Dannebrog. Honorary degrees from numerous colleges and universities.

WRITINGS:

The Literature of the Pioneer West, [Saint Paul], 1927.
(With Samuel Eliot Morison) *The Growth of the American Republic,* Oxford University Press, 1931, 7th edition, 1980, ab-

breviated and newly revised edition published as *A Concise History of the American Republic,* 1977.
Our Nation's Development, Harper, 1934.
Theodore Parker, Little, Brown, 1936, reissued with a new introduction, Beacon Press, 1960.
(With Allan Nevins) *America: The Story of a Free People,* Little, Brown, 1942, Oxford University Press, 1976, reissued in paperback as *The Pocket History of the United States,* Pocket Books, 1943, revised edition, 1982.
Majority Rule and Minority Rights, Oxford University Press, 1943.
(With Nevins) *A Short History of the United States,* Modern Library, 1945, 6th edition, Knopf, 1976.
The American Mind: An Interpretation of American Thought and Character Since the 1880's, Yale University Press, 1950.
(With others) *Civil Liberties under Attack,* University of Pennsylvania Press, 1951.
(Contributor) Courtlandt Canby, editor, *The World of History,* New American Library, 1954.
(With Geoffrey Brunn) *Europe and America since 1492,* Houghton, 1954.
Freedom, Loyalty, Dissent, Oxford University Press, 1954.
Federal Centralization and the Press, University of Minnesota, 1956.
(Contributor) *Conference on the American High School,* University of Chicago Press, 1958.
(With Robert W. McEwen and Brand Blanshard) *Education in a Free Society,* University of Pittsburgh Press, 1961.
The Nature and the Study of History, C. E. Merrill, 1965.
The Role of Scholarship in an Age of Science, Laramie, 1965.
Freedom and Order: A Commentary on the American Political Scene, Braziller, 1966.
The Study of History, C. E. Merrill, 1966.
(With Elmo Giordonetti) *Was America a Mistake?: An Eighteenth Century Controversy,* Harper, 1967.
The Search for a Usable Past, and Other Essays in Historiography, Knopf, 1967.
(With Richard B. Morris) *Colonies in Transition,* Harper, 1968.
The Commonwealth of Learning, Harper, 1968.
The Defeat of America: Presidential Power and the National Character, Simon & Schuster, 1974.
Britain through American Eyes, McGraw, 1974.
Jefferson, Nationalism, and the Enlightenment, Braziller, 1974.
The Empire of Reason: How Europe Imagined and America Realized the Enlightenment, Doubleday, 1977.
(Author of text) *Mort Kuenstler's 50 Epic Paintings of America,* Abbeville Press, 1979.
(With Raymond H. Muessig) *The Study and Teaching of History,* Merrill, 1980.
(Author of introduction) *The Civil War Almanac,* Facts on File, 1983.
(Author of introduction) *Of America East and West: From the Writings of Paul Horgan,* Farrar, Straus, 1984.

EDITOR

Documents of American History (Volume 1, to 1898; Volume 2, from 1865), F. S. Crofts, 1934, 10th edition, Prentice-Hall, 1988.
(With Nevins) *The Heritage of America,* Little, Brown, 1939, revised and enlarged edition, 1949.
(And author of historical narrative) *The Story of the Second World War,* Little, Brown, 1945.
(And author of introduction and notes) *America in Perspective: The United States through Foreign Eyes,* Random House 1947, abridged edition, New American Library, 1959.

Alexis de Tocqueville, *Democracy in America,* translated by Henry Reeve, Oxford University Press, 1947.

Selections from The Federalist, Appleton, 1949.

(With others) *Years of the Modern: An American Appraisal,* Longmans, Green, 1949.

The Blue and the Gray: The Story of the Civil War as Told by Participants, two volumes, Bobbs-Merrill, 1950, reprinted, Fairfax Press, 1982.

William Dean Howells, *Selected Writings,* Random House 1950.

(And author of commentary) *Living Ideas in America,* Harper, 1951, enlarged edition, 1967.

(With Morris) *The Spirit of Seventy-Six: The Story of the American Revolution as Told by the Participants,* two volumes, Bobbs-Merrill, 1958, bicentennial edition, Harper, 1975, reprinted, Bonanza Books, 1983.

Official Atlas of the Civil War, Yoseloff, 1958.

Living Documents of American History, [Washington], 1960.

The Era of Reform, 1830-1860, Van Nostrand, 1960, reprinted, Krieger, 1982.

Theodore Parker: An Anthology, Beacon Press, 1960.

James Bryce, *Reflections on American Institutions: Selections from The American Commonwealth,* Fawcett, 1961.

Immigration and American History: Essays in Honor of Theodore C. Blegen, University of Minnesota Press, 1961.

Chester Bowles, *The Conscience of a Liberal,* Harper, 1962.

Winston Churchill, *History of the English-Speaking Peoples* (one volume of a four volume series), Bantam, 1963.

Noah Webster's American Spelling Book, Teachers College Press, 1963.

The Defeat of the Confederacy: A Documentary Survey, Van Nostrand, 1964.

Fifty Basic Civil War Documents, Van Nostrand, 1965, reprinted, Krieger, 1982.

(Consulting editor) *Encyclopedia of American History,* Harper, 1965.

Lester Ward and the Welfare State, Bobbs-Merrill, 1966.

The Struggle for Racial Equality: A Documentary Record, Harper, 1967.

Churchill, *Marlborough: His Life and Times,* Scribner, 1968.

(And author of introduction and commentary) *Britain through American Eyes,* Bodley Head, 1974.

(With others) *The West: An Illustrated History,* Promotory Press, 1976.

Edward M. Kennedy, *Our Day and Generation: The Words of Edward M. Kennedy,* Simon & Schuster, 1979.

(With others) *Illustrated History of the American Civil War,* Orbis, 1979.

Also editor with Morris of the "New American Nation" series, published by Harper; editor-in-chief of *The American Destiny: An Illustrated Bicentennial History of the United States,* twenty volumes, published by Danbury Press.

JUVENILES

(With Eugene Campbell Barker) *Our Nation,* Row, Peterson, 1941.

(Editor) *St. Nicholas Anthology,* Random House, 1948.

(Editor) *Second St. Nicholas Anthology,* Random House, 1950.

America's Robert E. Lee, Houghton, 1951.

Chestnut Squirrel, Houghton, 1952.

The First Book of American History, illustrated by Leonard Everett Fisher, F. Watts, 1957.

The Great Declaration, Bobbs-Merrill, 1958.

A Picture History of the United States of America, F. Watts, 1958.

The Great Proclamation, Bobbs-Merrill, 1960, reprinted, 1977.

The Great Constitution, Bobbs-Merrill, 1961.

Crusaders for Freedom, Doubleday, 1962.

OTHER

Contributor of essays to scholarly and popular journals, including *Book Week, New York Times Book Review, New Republic, Saturday Review, New York Review of Books,* and *American Scholar.*

WORK IN PROGRESS: Editing "The Rise of the American Nation," a projected fifty-volume series.

SIDELIGHTS: Henry Steele Commager has been one of America's preeminent historians for more than half a century. His writings include textbooks for children and college students, edited compilations of historical source material, original studies of the nature of American democracy, and biographies of prominent Americans. As Lawrence Wells Cobb explains in the *Dictionary of Literary Biography,* Commager "has devoted his energies to making it easier for scholars and lay readers both to 'get at' the sources of the American historical record and to understand their heritage more fully. He has undertaken these tasks so that his readers might become more informed and responsible participants in the great experiment launched in the eighteenth century to make a free, democratic, and bountiful society a reality on the North American continent." *New Republic* contributor Alexander R. Butler calls Commager "one of America's most distinguished historians," a scholar whose "excellent reputation" stems from his "simple, straightforward, and assertive" style. Behind that style lies serious conviction, however. Butler notes that Commager is "convinced that the reader can learn from history" and profit from the lessons of the usable past. Cobb likewise observes that in his writings the historian demands "that Americans live responsibly and prove worthy of their heritage." His sprightly style, his eye for the illuminating vignette, his catholic knowledge, and his optimistic perspective have served him well in bringing his insights to generations of readers."

Commager's best known book is *The Growth of the American Republic,* a title he co-authored with Samuel Eliot Morison. First published in 1931, the work is still in print and is still used as a standard text in undergraduate history courses. According to *New York Times Book Review* correspondent Esmond Wright, the "limpidly clear style and the easy marshaling of arguments . . . have made 'The Growth of the American Republic' one of the most unusual and certainly one of the most readable of textbooks." Commager's other books for lay readers include a 1941 title *Our Nation* for high school students, and a 1942 popular study *America: The Story of a Free People,* co-authored by Allan Nevins. Commager's aim, in Cobb's words, has been "always to provide the facts within the matrix of an unobtrusive liberal interpretation and to provoke thought on the part of the reader." As early as 1934 Commager also began the editing duties for which he has become well known; his *Documents of American History* collects in two volumes the important primary sources on the creation and development of the United States. Cobb calls the work "the best single-volume source book in its field." Throughout the following forty years Commager continued to publish anthologies of historical source material; his efforts have produced, among others, *The Blue and the Gray: The Story of the Civil War as Told by Participants, The Era of Reform, 1830-1860,* and *The Struggle for Racial Equality: A Documentary History.* Cobb claims that such collections are "intended to put the words and ideas that shaped America within easy reach of both the generalist and interested layman." In the *New York Herald Tribune Book Review,* Bernard DeVoto contends that these books provide "a way of experiencing the nation's most tremendous experience. No one can read [them] without being impelled to think searchingly about the American people, the American nation, the American past and future."

As a scholar Commager has sought to define the strengths of democracy. Cobb suggests that the historian's theses "always revolved around Jeffersonian liberalism: give the public the maximum amount of information and the people can be trusted to make the right decisions in the long run." Such a view stresses the importance of education as well as the necessity for free speech and dissent, so Commager became one of the strongest opponents of the 1950s' communist-fearing conformity. His comment in the 1951 volume *Civil Liberties under Attack* has since become famous: "The great danger that threatens us is neither heterodox thought nor orthodox thought, but the absence of thought." Commager continued to argue for the preservation of free speech and inquiry as the Vietnam War escalated in the 1960s. According to Cobb, the historian "reminded visitors, distressed to see all the unrest in America, . . . that the idealism of the 1960s was a reassertion, not a repudiation, of our Revolutionary ideals of liberty and equality." Since then, in such essentially optimistic books as *Jefferson, Nationalism, and the Enlightenment* and *The Empire of Reason: How Europe Imagined and America Realized the Enlightenment*, Commager has maintained that America is an ongoing experiment in the practical implementation of philosophy; the nation's continued strength depends on its forging a link with the ideals of the founding generation. As Cobb puts it, history is "definitely a usable past for citizens of the United States, and this history [is] also a living proof to all the people of the world that such 'good things' as continental self-government and socio-economic mobility [are] possible."

Commager's commitment to educating the public has not led him to adopt the pose of a judge. Rather, he offers readers a spectrum of facts which they can judge themselves. Critics such as *New York Times* columnist Herbert Mitgang note, however, that Commager's very enthusiasm for history and the "crystalline clarity of the writing" he produces cause "explosions in the reader's mind." Mitgang concludes: "Here is history to be pondered and cherished." Cobb sees Commager as an author who has "kindled a love for the spectacle of history and personality in thousands of young minds" through his juvenile literature and his many source books. *Atlantic* contributor C. J. Rolo also contends that Commager's value as a writer "is that he combines an exhilarating enthusiasm for his subject with a keenly critical viewpoint and an absence of cant that is becoming increasingly rare." Amherst College's Simpson Lecturer is continuing to edit and compile historical texts that reveal both the benefits and the challenges of democratic government. In the *New York Times Book Review*, Arthur Schlesinger, Jr. concludes that in Henry Steele Commager, "learning and reason are at the service of a mind whose understanding of democracy gains brilliance and power from a passion for democratic freedom."

BIOGRAPHICAL/CRITICAL SOURCES:

BOOKS

Civil Liberties under Attack, University of Pennsylvania Press, 1951.
Dictionary of Literary Biography, Volume 17: *Twentieth Century American Historians*, Gale, 1983.
Garraty, John, *Interpreting American History: Conversations with Historians*, Macmillan, 1970.
Hyman, Harold M. and Leonard W. Levy, editors, *Freedom and Reform: Essays in Honor of Henry Steele Commager*, Harper, 1967.

PERIODICALS

Atlantic, May, 1950.
Christian Century, July 5, 1950, October 24, 1962.
Christian Science Monitor, April 6, 1936, March 18, 1950.
Commonweal, May 5, 1950.
Nation, April 22, 1950, December 23, 1950.
New Republic, April 24, 1950, May 24, 1954, May 20, 1967, December 21, 1974.
New Statesman, June 2, 1967.
Newsweek, November 15, 1948.
New York Herald Tribune Book Review, March 12, 1950, November 19, 1950, May 30, 1954.
New York Times, March 12, 1950, November 12, 1950, June 7, 1977.
New York Times Book Review, March 12, 1950, October 23, 1966, June 25, 1967, November 26, 1967, August 14, 1977, November 4, 1979, April 8, 1984.
San Francisco Chronicle, March 24, 1950, November 26, 1950.
Saturday Review, March 11, 1950, December 2, 1950, May 1, 1954, January 28, 1967, May 14, 1977.
Survey, April, 1950.
Time, December 11, 1950.
Times Literary Supplement, November 17, 1950, July 23, 1954, September 27, 1974, August 4, 1978.
Yale Review, summer, 1950.

* * *

COMMONER, Barry 1917-

PERSONAL: Born May 28, 1917, in New York, N.Y.; son of Isidore (a tailor) and Goldie (Yarmolinsky) Commoner; married Gloria C. Gordon (a psychologist), December 1, 1946; children: Lucy Alison, Fredric Gordon. *Education:* Columbia University, A.B., 1937; Harvard University, M.A., 1938, Ph.D., 1941. *Religion:* Humanist.

ADDRESSES: Office—Queens College Center for the Biology of Natural Systems, Flushing, N.Y. 11367.

CAREER: Queens College (now of the City University of New York), Flushing, N.Y., instructor in biology, 1940-42; *Science Illustrated* magazine, New York, N.Y., associate editor, 1946-47; Washington University, St. Louis, Mo., associate professor, 1947-53, professor of plant physiology, 1953-76; chairman of department of botany, 1965-69, director of Center for the Biology of Natural Systems, 1965-81, professor of environmental science, 1976-81; Queens College, Flushing, director of Center for the Biology of Natural Systems, 1981—, professor of earth and environmental science, 1981-87, professor emeritus, 1987—. Visiting professor of community health at Albert Einstein College of Medicine, 1981-87. St. Louis Committee for Environmental Information (formerly St. Louis Committee for Nuclear Information), co-founder, member of board of directors, 1958—, vice-president, 1958-65, president, 1965-66; Scientists Institute for Public Information, member of board of directors, 1963—, chairman, 1969—; member of board of directors, Universities National Anti-War Fund; member of board of consulting experts, Rachel Carson Trust for Living Environment, 1967—; member of advisory board or council, University of Oklahoma Law Center Committee, 1967-70, U.S. Department of the Interior study group on sonic boom, 1967-68, Office of Education council on environmental education, 1971—, Coalition Health Communities, 1975, U.S. Department of Commerce secretary's advisory council, 1976, New York State Commission on Science and Technology, 1981—, Commission for Responsible Genetics,

1983—, and Vietnam Veterans of America Foundation council on dioxin, 1985—. Trustee of Institute for Environmental Education. Citizens Party candidate for president of United States, 1980. *Military service:* U.S. Naval Reserve, 1942-54; served in Naval Air Force and as liaison officer with Senate Committee on Military Affairs; became lieutenant.

MEMBER: American Association for the Advancement of Science (fellow; member of board of directors, 1967—), American Institute of Biological Sciences (member of governing board, 1965-67), Society of General Physiologists (member of council, 1961), American Society of Plant Physiologists, American Society of Biological Chemists, American Association of University Professors, National Parks Association (member of board of directors, 1968—), American Chemical Society, American School Health Association, Ecological Society of America, Federation of American Scientists, British Soil Association (honorary life vice-president, 1968—), Sigma Xi, Phi Beta Kappa.

AWARDS, HONORS: Newcomb Cleveland Prize from American Association for the Advancement of Science, 1953; LL.D. from University of California, 1967, and Grinnell College, 1981; First International Humanist Award from International Humanist and Ethical Union, 1970; Phi Beta Kappa Award, 1972, and International Prize for Safeguarding the Environment from the City of Cervia, Italy, 1973, both for *The Closing Circle;* commander in the Order of the Merit (Italy), 1977; Premio Iglesias (Sardinia, Italy), 1978, for *The Poverty of Power,* and 1982, for *The Politics of Energy;* American Institute of Architects Medal, 1979; D.Sc. from Hahnemann Medical College, 1963, Clark University, 1967, Grinnell College, 1968, Lehigh University, 1969, Williams College, 1970, Ripon College, 1971, Colgate University, 1972, Cleveland State University, 1980, and St. Lawrence University, 1988.

WRITINGS:

Science and Survival, Viking, 1966.
(With others) *Balance and Biosphere: A Radio Symposium on the Environmental Crisis,* Canadian Broadcasting Corp., 1971.
The Closing Circle: Nature, Man, and Technology, Knopf, 1971 (published in England as *The Closing Circle: Confronting the Environmental Crisis,* Cape, 1972), 2nd edition, Bantam, 1974.
(Contributor) *Electric Power Consumption and Human Welfare: The Social Consequences of the Environmental Effects of Electric Power Use,* Washington University, 1972.
(Editor) Virginia Brodine, *Air Pollution,* Harcourt, 1973.
(With others) *The Effect of Recent Energy Price Increases on Field Crop Production Costs,* Center for the Biology of Natural Systems, Washington University, 1974.
(Editor) Julian McCaull and Janice Crossland, *Water Pollution,* Harcourt, 1974.
(Editor with Howard Boksenbaum and Michael Corr) *Energy and Human Welfare,* Volume 1: *The Social Costs of Power Production,* Volume 2: *Alternative Technologies for Power Production,* Volume 3: *Human Welfare: The End Use for Power,* Macmillan Information, 1976.
The Poverty of Power: Energy and the Economic Crisis, Random House, 1976.
Energy (essays from *New Yorker*), New Yorker, 1976.
Reliability of Bacterial Mutagenesis Techniques to Distinguish Carcinogenic and Noncarcinogenic Chemicals, Environmental Protection Agency, 1976.
The Politics of Energy, Knopf, 1979.
Making Peace With the Planet, Pantheon, 1990.

OTHER

Power to the Person (sound recording), Big Sur Recordings, 1971.
The Destruction of Our Environment (sound recording), Pacifica Tape Library, 1972.
The Human Meaning of the Environmental Crisis (sound recording), Big Sur Recordings, 1973.
The Environment and the Energy Crisis (sound recording), Encyclopedia Americana/CBS News Audio Resource Library, 1973.
Freedom and the Environment (sound recording), Pennsylvania State Library, 1976.

Contributor of more than two hundred articles to journals in his field. Member of editorial board, *International Review of Cytology,* 1957-65, *Problems of Virology,* 1956-60, *American Naturalist,* 1959-63, *Theoretical Biology,* 1960-64, *Science Year,* 1967-72, *World Book Encyclopedia,* 1968-73, *Environmental Pollution,* 1969-79, *National Wildlife,* 1970—, and *Environment Magazine,* 1977—; honorary member of editorial advisory board, *Chemosphere,* 1972—; member of board of sponsors, *In These Times,* 1976—.

WORK IN PROGRESS: Research on the origins and significance of the environmental and energy crises, and other technical studies.

SIDELIGHTS: In a review of Barry Commoner's *Closing Circle,* Christopher Lehmann-Haupt wrote: "Dr. Commoner's is not a Doomsday book at all. . . . Dr. Commoner presents as lucid a description of ecology and its laws as I have yet come across. In between, he illustrates how those laws have been broken with disastrous consequences. . . . He weighs the impacts on the environment of our population explosion and in particular our shockingly high per capita consumption of natural resources."

Commoner explains, "Human beings have broken out of the circle of life, driven not by biological need, but by the social organization which they have devised to 'conquer' nature; means of gaining wealth that are governed by requirements conflicting with those which govern nature. The end result is the environmental crisis, a crisis of survival. Once more, to survive, we must close the circle. We must learn how to restore to nature the wealth that we borrow from it."

BIOGRAPHICAL/CRITICAL SOURCES:

BOOKS

Chisholm, Anne, *Philosophers of the Earth,* Dutton, 1972.
Contemporary Literary Criticism, Volume 1, Gale, 1982.

PERIODICALS

Los Angeles Times, May 2, 1990.
Nation, September 22, 1979.
New Republic, November 6, 1971, August 18, 1979.
Newsweek, November 1, 1971, December 27, 1971, May 31, 1976.
New York Review of Books, August 5, 1976.
New York Times, April 22, 1970, January 15, 1988.
New York Times Book Review, November 6, 1966, October 17, 1971, May 23, 1976, June 5, 1977, July 29, 1979, April 22, 1990.
Saturday Review, May 15, 1976, September 1, 1979.
Spectator, January 22, 1977.
Time, February 2, 1970, May 31, 1976.
Village Voice, May 3, 1976.
Washington Post Book World, October 10, 1971, May 9, 1976, December 12, 1976, June 24, 1979.

COMPTON-BURNETT, I(vy) 1884(?)-1969

PERSONAL: Born c. June 5, 1884, in Middlesex, England; died August 27, 1969, in London, England; daughter of James (a doctor) and Katharine (Rees) Compton-Burnett. *Education:* University of London, Royal Holloway College, B.A., 1907.

ADDRESSES: Home—5 Braemar Mansions, Cornwall Gardens, London, England. *Agent*—Curtis Brown Ltd., 1 Craven Hill, London W2 3EP, England.

CAREER: Novelist.

AWARDS, HONORS: Founders Scholarship, Royal Holloway College, 1906; Commander of the Order of the British Empire, 1951; James Tait Black Memorial Prize, 1956, for *Mother and Son;* D.Litt., University of Leeds, 1960; Dame Commander of the Order of the British Empire, 1967.

WRITINGS:

Dolores, Blackwood, 1911, reprinted, 1971.
Pastors and Masters, Heath Cranton, 1925, reprinted, International Publications Service, 1967.
Brothers and Sisters, Harcourt, 1930, reprinted, Gollancz, 1961.
Men and Wives, Harcourt, 1931, reprinted, Gollancz, 1966.
More Women Than Men, Heinemann, 1933, reprinted, International Publications Service, 1971.
A House and Its Head, Heinemann, 1935, reprinted, Gollancz, 1966.
Daughters and Sons, Gollancz, 1937, reprinted, International Publications Service, 1974.
A Family and a Fortune, Gollancz, 1939, reprinted, Simon & Schuster, 1965.
Parents and Children, Gollancz, 1941, reprinted, Penguin, 1986.
Elders and Betters, Gollancz, 1944, reprinted, 1977.
Manservant and Maidservant, Gollancz, 1947, reprinted, 1969, published as *Bullivant and the Lambs,* Knopf, 1948.
Two Worlds and Their Ways, Knopf, 1949, reprinted, Gollancz, 1964.
Darkness and Day, Knopf, 1951, reprinted, International Publications Service, 1974.
The Present and the Past, Messner, 1954, reprinted, Penguin, 1986.
Mother and Son, Messner, 1955, reprinted, 1977.
A Father and His Fate, Messner, 1958.
A Heritage and Its History, Simon & Schuster, 1960.
The Mighty and Their Fall, Simon & Schuster, 1962.
A God and His Gifts, Gollancz, 1963, Simon & Schuster, 1964.
The Last and the First, Knopf, 1971.
Collected Works, nineteen volumes, Gollancz, 1972.

SIDELIGHTS: British novelist Ivy Compton-Burnett wrote of the upper-class, seemingly genteel world that existed in England before the First World War, a world Edward Sackville-West once compared to that of "Jane Austen, of George Eliot, of Mrs. Gaskell. But with this difference—that the plots which involve that outwardly quiet and orderly world are violent and dramatic in the extreme."

Choosing to regard Victorian and Edwardian family life as a model of civilization as a whole, Compton-Burnett explored the "swamp of discontent, mixed motives, and deception" that exist just below the surface of normal social behavior, according to Frederick R. Karl. Family members snipe at and tyrannize each other while maintaining an appropriate veneer of politeness and wit. Her plots, in which lost objects, suppressed wills, overheard conversations, and concealed identities figure prominently, are of only secondary concern; the real focus is the manner in which

relatives proceed to destroy themselves when faced with the sudden emergence of certain skeletons from the family closet—among them such "universal sins" as murder, incest, adultery, suicide, and theft.

Despite the limited social and chronological context of her novels, Compton-Burnett managed to convey the sense of "a timeless present," observed critic Blake Nevius. A. C. Ward attributed her contemporary appeal to the fact that she combined "a Victorian stuffiness of atmosphere and a Victorian appetite for melodrama with a twentieth-century ruthlessness in stripping off conventional veils of pretence in order to expose make-believers, hypocrites, and petty tyrants naked to their souls." Like the author's plots, however, these assorted "make-believers, hypocrites, and petty tyrants" vary little from book to book; Compton-Burnett's women, for example, are nearly always domineering and evil, her men are either overly effete or obsessed with power, and her children and young adults are lonely and pitiably mistreated. Yet it would be incorrect, insisted Robert Liddell, to label them as mere "types": "They are in fact very subtly differentiated. They are limited on the whole to certain broad categories, because the plot is to deal with certain kinds of happenings. Since the happenings come out of the people, that entails certain kinds of people." At any rate, noted Pamela Hansford Johnson, all of them "exemplify the real horror of human frailty. . . . [They live in] a world where everyone says what he thinks and where deadly words are spoken. Her people are Mr. and Mrs. Darling gone sour."

"Deadly spoken words," in fact, provide the main narrative thrust of Compton-Burnett' novels, for each one consists of approximately ninety-five percent conversation. Though each character is described in detail at the time of his or her first appearance, after that there are few, if any, references to physical traits; landscapes, houses, and rooms are not described at all. Because these brief and infrequent passages serve as little more than stage directions, many critics maintained that her novels had more in common with plays than they did with other novels. But as Nevius pointed out, in Compton-Burnett's case the dialogue "is made to bear a greater burden than in either the drama or the conventional novel. It has usurped almost completely the functions of exposition, narrative and description."

Another burden Compton-Burnett forced her dialogue to bear was the highly stylized tone of her characters' speech. Deliberately artificial, bland, and sententious, it requires the reader to concentrate fully on what is being said and who is saying it. Explained Julian Mitchell of *Plays and Players:* "The conversations are so full of nuance and subtlety that it takes a new reader several chapters to get the hang of them, and sometimes he gives up in despair. There is no internalisation, no 'he thought' and 'she wondered,' to help him understand what's going on or what the characters' motives are. . . . And, greatest difficulty of all, the characters seem at first reading, and sometimes at second, all to talk alike. This is an illusion: once one's ear is trained to Compton-Burnett one can hear that everyone speaks quite differently and individually."

Ruth Blackman of the *Christian Science Monitor* agreed that straightening out who said what in a Compton-Burnett novel can be exasperating at times, but she emphasized that making the effort to keep track is the only way a reader can become familiar with each character. Wrote Blackman: "[Compton-Burnett] works very little from the interior of a character. Once she has placed him in his family relationship, and sketched in his outward aspect, she leaves him to reveal himself through conversation. And what conversation! Brilliant, incisive, subtle, ironic (and, the unenchanted might say, endless), it is absolutely plausible but like nothing ever heard."

In the eyes of several critics, including Arnold Kettle, both humor and dramatic tension in Compton-Burnett's novels originate in the contrast the author set up "between what is actually said [in the dialogues] and what is expressed but only thought and the consequent ruthlessness in the exposure of the underlying issues and implications of a scene." In short, Compton-Burnett's technique was to devise a situation in which there is a marked difference between appearance and reality, then examine that difference with a wit, said Kettle, that "is not a matter of superficial smartness or a cunning ornamentation of style. It springs from deep in her observation of life, from her critical consideration of the standards and values of the society she is presenting." But because of what those acidic observations implied about human nature, some readers and critics found her type of wit more "frightening" than funny. Quite often, wrote Milton Crane in the *Saturday Review,* the cumulative effect of such grim irony is one of "an ultimately distressing, though unfailingly interesting, exercise in savage comedy." Commented an *Outlook* critic, "Not everybody can stand to be dashed with ice water."

Malcolm Bradbury, though, felt that Compton-Burnett's books "were, and remain, ambiguous. One could see in them a kind of essential artlessness, or else a very high kind of artistic management, a precision of control both moral and technical of the most eminent sort. One could read them as an elegant camp game played with life, or as a harsh and cruel, almost a tragic, vision of experience. And one could find them either basically reassuring novels, nostalgic under the wit and malice, or else profoundly disturbing works."

Johnson agreed with this assessment. Compton-Burnett, she concluded, "is not to be mildly liked or disliked. She is a writer to be left alone, or else to be made into an addiction. . . . Yet readers who come to know her fascination will discern one startling fact; that this piercingly wise, discreet, mannered Victoriana conceals abysses of the human personality."

As the author herself once commented: "My writing does not seem to me 'stylised.' I do not feel that I have any real or organic knowledge of life later than about 1910—should not write of later times with enough grasp or confidence. . . . I think that actual life supplies a writer with characters less than is thought. . . . As regards plots, I find real life no help at all. Real life seems to have no plots. And as I think a plot desirable and almost necessary I have this extra grudge against life. But I do think there are signs that strange things happen, though they do not emerge."

Compton-Burnett's style was parodied by Richard Mallett in *Literary Upshots,* J. Cape, 1951. *A Heritage and Its History* and *A Family and a Fortune* have been dramatized by Julian Mitchell.

BIOGRAPHICAL/CRITICAL SOURCES:

BOOKS

Allen, Walter, *The Modern Novel,* Dutton, 1965.
Baldanza, Frank, *Ivy Compton-Burnett,* Twayne, 1964.
Burkhart, Charles, *I. Compton-Burnett,* Gollancz, 1965.
Contemporary Literary Criticism, Gale, Volume 1, 1973, Volume 3, 1975, Volume 10, 1979, Volume 15, 1980, Volume 34, 1985.
Dick, Kay, *Ivy and Stevie: Ivy Compton-Burnett and Stevie Smith—Conversations and Reflections,* Duckworth, 1971.
Dictionary of Literary Biography, Volume 36: *British Novelists, 1890-1929: Modernists,* Gale, 1985.
Greig, Cicely, *Ivy Compton-Burnett: A Memoir,* Gamestone Press, 1972. Grylls, R. Glynn, *I. Compton-Burnett,* Longman, 1971.
Hansford Johnson, Peter, *I. Compton-Burnett,* Longmans, Green, 1951.
Karl, Frederick R., *A Reader's Guide to the Contemporary English Novel,* Farrar, Strauss, 1962.
Kettle, Arnold, *An Introduction to the English Novel,* Volume 2, Hutchinson, 1960.
Liddell, Robert, *A Treatise on the Novel,* J. Cape, 1947, reprinted, University of Chicago Press, 1969.
McCarthy, Mary, *The Writing on the Wall and Other Essays,* Harcourt, 1970.
Nevius, Blake, *Ivy Compton-Burnett,* Columbia University Press, 1970.
Prescott, Orville, *In My Opinion,* Bobbs-Merrill, 1952.
Sackville-West, Edward, *Inclinations,* Scribner, 1949.
Sackville-West, Edward, *Living Writers,* Sylvan Press, 1947.
Sprigge, Elizabeth, *Life of Ivy Compton-Burnett,* Braziller, 1973.
Spurling, Hilary, *Ivy When Young: The Early Life of I. Compton-Burnett, 1884-1919,* Gollancz, 1974.

PERIODICALS

Atlantic, June, 1949, March, 1962, March, 1964.
Books, April 24, 1938.
Book Week, February 2, 1964.
Boston Transcript, December 4, 1929.
Chicago Sunday Tribune, February 25, 1962.
Christian Science Monitor, September 7, 1929, June 16, 1949, January 28, 1960.
Commonweal, November 13, 1953, April 17, 1964.
Encounter, July, 1973.
English Studies, Number 1, 1970.
Guardian, September 18, 1959, September 22, 1961.
Hudson Review, winter, 1971-72.
Manchester Guardian, March 16, 1937, June 17, 1949, March 27, 1953, February 8, 1955, August 20, 1957.
Nation, April 30, 1955.
New Republic, June 14, 1948, April 1, 1955, March 4, 1957.
New Statesman, June 1, 1929, August 10, 1957, September 19, 1959, September 22, 1961, December 6, 1963.
New Statesman and Nation, April 11, 1931, March 20, 1937, April 28, 1951, April 4, 1953, March 5, 1955.
Newsweek, April 23, 1973.
New Yorker, June 19, 1948, June 11, 1949, March 24, 1951, January 19, 1957, May 5, 1962, May 2, 1964.
New York Evening Post, November 23, 1929.
New York Herald Tribune Book Review, October 18, 1953, March 20, 1955, February 3, 1957, March 30, 1958, February 7, 1960, March 11, 1962.
New York Herald Tribune Books, November 10, 1929, March 11, 1962.
New York Herald Tribune Weekly Book Review, June 13, 1948, June 5, 1949.
New York Times, October 6, 1929, May 3, 1931, April 24, 1938, June 20, 1948, June 5, 1949, March 18, 1951, October 4, 1953, March 20, 1955, November 18, 1956, March 23, 1958, May 20, 1965.
New York Times Book Review, January 31, 1960, February 11, 1962, February 2, 1964, August 15, 1971.
Outlook, April 29, 1931.
Partisan Review, winter, 1965.
Plays and Players, April, 1975.

San Francisco Chronicle, March 24, 1951.
Saturday Review, March 26, 1955, March 2, 1957, April 19, 1958, February 10, 1962, February 1, 1964, February 20, 1965.
Saturday Review of Literature, November 30, 1929, July 25, 1931, April 23, 1938, June 26, 1948, June 4, 1949.
Spectator, March 19, 1937, March 7, 1947, June 24, 1949, February 18, 1955, August 16, 1957, September 18, 1959, September 22, 1961.
Springfield Republican, May 22, 1938, January 31, 1960.
Time, April 4, 1955, January 28, 1957, February 15, 1960, March 2, 1962, August 16, 1971.
Times Literary Supplement, April 10, 1937, March 22, 1947, June 17, 1949, April 20, 1951, February 11, 1955, August 16, 1957, September 18, 1959, September 22, 1961, November 21, 1963, November 11, 1965, February 5, 1971.

OBITUARIES:

PERIODICALS

New York Times, August 28, 1969.
Observer Review, September 7, 1969.
Spectator, September 6, 1969.
Times (London), August 28, 1969.

*   *   *

CONDON, Richard (Thomas) 1915-

PERSONAL: Born March 18, 1915, in New York, N.Y.; son of Richard Aloysius and Martha Irene (Pickering) Condon; married Evelyn Hunt, January 14, 1938; children: Deborah Evelyn Weldon, Wendy Ann Jackson. *Education:* Attended schools in New York.

ADDRESSES: Home—3436 Asbury, Dallas, Tex. 75205. *Agent*—Harold Matson, 276 Fifth Ave., New York, N.Y. 10001.

CAREER: Publicist in New York City and Hollywood, Calif., for Walt Disney Productions, 1936-41, Twentieth Century-Fox Film Corp., 1941-45, Richard Condon, Inc., 1945-48, and Paramount Pictures Corp., 1948-53, and in Europe and Great Britain for United Artists Corp., 1953-57; novelist. Producer, with Jose Ferrer, of Broadway shows "Twentieth Century" and "Stalag 17," 1951-52.

MEMBER: International Confederation of Book Actors (honorary life president), Dramatists Guild, Authors Guild, Authors League of America.

AWARDS, HONORS: Decorated chevalier La Confrerie du Tastevin, 1968, commanderie du Bontemps, 1969, and chevalier Chaine des Rotisseurs, 1976; Academy Award nomination, Writers Guild of America award, and Bafta Award from British Academy of Film and Television Sciences, all 1986, all for screenplay "Prizzi's Honor."

WRITINGS:

NOVELS

The Oldest Confession, Appleton-Century-Crofts, 1958.
The Manchurian Candidate, McGraw, 1959.
Some Angry Angel: A Mid-Century Faerie Tale, McGraw, 1960.
A Talent for Loving; or, The Great Cowboy Race, McGraw, 1961.
An Infinity of Mirrors, Random House, 1964.
Any God Will Do, Random House, 1965.
The Ecstasy Business, Dial, 1967.
Mile High, Dial, 1968.
The Vertical Smile, Dial, 1971.
Arigato, Dial, 1972.

Winter Kills, Dial, 1974.
The Star Spangled Crunch, Bantam, 1974.
Money Is Love, Dial, 1975.
The Whisper of the Axe, Dial, 1976.
The Abandoned Woman: A Tragedy of Manners, Dial, 1977.
Bandicoot, Dial, 1978.
Death of a Politician, Richard Marek, 1978.
The Entwining, Richard Marek, 1980.
Prizzi's Honor (second novel in trilogy; also see below), Coward, McCann & Geoghegan, 1982.
A Trembling upon Rome, Putnam, 1983.
Prizzi's Family (first novel in trilogy), Putnam, 1986.
Prizzi's Glory (third novel in trilogy), Dutton, 1988.
Emperor of America, Simon & Schuster, 1990.

OTHER

"Men of Distinction" (play), produced on Broadway, 1953.
And Then We Moved to Rossenarra; or, The Art of Emigrating, Dial, 1973.
(With daughter, Wendy Jackson) *The Mexican Stove: What to Put on It and in It,* Doubleday, 1973, reprinted as *Ole Mole! Great Recipes in the Classic Mexican Tradition,* Taylor Publishing, 1988.
(With Janet Roach) "Prizzi's Honor" (screenplay; adapted from his novel), Twentieth Century-Fox, 1985.

Also author of screenplay, "The Summer Music." Contributor to *Holiday, Nation, Vogue, Harper's, Gourmet, Esquire, Travel and Leisure,* and *Sunday Times Magazine.* Condon's novels have been published in twenty-two languages and in braille.

WORK IN PROGRESS: Get out of My Dream, a novel; screenplays based on *Arigato* and *Bandicoot.*

SIDELIGHTS: Since he began writing at age forty-two following a successful career as a movie publicist, novelist Richard Condon "has proved original, prolific, and profitable, possibly in that order," writes *Los Angeles Times* arts editor Charles Champlin. Condon's reputation as a writer of what Richard Lingeman describes in the *New York Times* as "cynical, hip political thrillers that contain [a unique] extravagance of invention" was secured with his first two novels, *The Oldest Confession* and *The Manchurian Candidate.* Condon's body of work includes over twenty novels, two nonfiction books, a handful of plays and screenplays, and numerous articles on his twin passions, food and travel. This output has netted him an income of about two and a half million dollars, which Condon told *Publishers Weekly* interviewer John F. Baker "sounds like a lot, but it's only about what someone in middle management would have made over the same period in salary. The difference—and it's an important one—is that I've lived wherever I wanted to, and I didn't have to drive to the office everyday."

Condon has taken full advantage of his freedom as a writer. Although he now resides in the United States, for nineteen years Condon and his family lived in countries such as France, Spain, Switzerland, and Ireland. Condon's focus in his novels however, usually reflects his concerns about American society, particularly the United States government. Condon commented to Herbert Mitgang in the *New York Times:* "Every book I've ever written has been about abuse of power. I feel very strongly about that. I'd like people to know how deeply their politicians are wronging them."

Condon's preoccupation with examining abuses of power has made him into a cult figure of sorts to readers who share his convictions. *New York Times Book Review* contributor Leo Braudy describes Condon's writing as "paranoid surrealism," fiction that draws "equally on the facts of national life and the cliches of popular fiction to create a world where technology, politics and history [have] run wild and the only possible humanism [is] gallows humor." Other novelists who have written in this genre include Joseph Heller, William Burroughs, Norman Mailer, Thomas Berger, Ken Kesey, and Thomas Pynchon. Braudy declares that Condon is "one of the most distinguished members of this group and through the controlled corrosiveness of his two great early novels—'The Manchurian Candidate' (1959) and 'Some Angry Angel' (1960)—has some claim to being a founder."

As Braudy indicates, Condon's novels are entertaining, despite their underlying seriousness. This assessment is compatible with Condon's personal goals as a writer, which he discusses in a *People* magazine interview with Anne Maier. "I have never written for any other reason than to earn a living. This is certainly true of other writers, but some poor souls get mightily confused with art. I am a public entertainer who sees his first duty as the need to entertain himself." Most reviewers share Condon's candid view of his writing. A *New York Times Book Review* contributor, for example, writes: "Despite the cult that has grown up around Condon, he is not really a great novelist, and certainly makes no pretensions about the value of his work. But as a practitioner of the fiction of information, no one else comes close to him." Since Condon's novels entertainingly mirror the concerns of readers, they fulfill what *Washington Post Book World* contributor Roderick MacLeish describes as the primary obligations of the thriller novel: "To tell a good story and to reflect the fears and fantasies of [the author's] time." Condon, in MacLeish's estimation, "is one of the living masters of [this] genre."

Most of the material for Condon's personal blend of reality and bizarre invention—called "mythologized fact" by one reviewer—has come from "the dirty linen closets of politics and money," according to a *New York Review of Books* critic. "His view—it might be called Condon's Law—is that when you don't know the whole truth, the worst you can imagine is bound to be close. . . . [He] isn't an analyst but an exploiter of our need to believe the worst. He does it skillfully, but his books would be less fun than they are if one didn't suspect that he believes the worst too, that his pictures of a world of fools eternally at the mercy of knaves are also pictures of what, with anger and disgust, he takes to be the case."

The "mythologized fact" of Condon's second novel, *The Manchurian Candidate,* "touched a nerve that made America jump," according to a *Newsweek* reviewer. Published in 1959, *The Manchurian Candidate* remains Condon's most highly acclaimed novel, one that critics frequently cite as a basis of comparison to his later works. The title of the book refers to the main character, Raymond Shaw, a soldier who becomes a prisoner of war in Korea and is unknowingly brainwashed into committing crimes for his former captors *after* he returns to the United States. Commenting on this novel as well as on Condon's first novel, *The Oldest Confession, New Yorker* critic Whitney Baillett writes that they both "are brilliant, highly individualistic, and hopelessly unfashionable demonstrations of how to write stylishly, tell fascinating stories, assemble plots that suggest the peerless mazes of Wilkie Collins, be very funny, make acute social observations, and ram home digestible morals. They demonstrate, in short, a good many of the things that were expected of the novel before the creative-writing courses got its practitioners brooding in their mirrors." A *Chicago Sunday Tribune* reviewer describes *The Manchurian Candidate* as "a novel of today, crammed with suspense, humor, horror, satire, sex, and intrigue. . . . Fitting all [the] sidelines of the plot into a whole was a monumental writ-

ing task, and few authors could have succeeded as admirably as Condon. The result is an exciting, brilliantly told story, peopled with characters symbolic of our times."

Although other reviewers express similarly enthusiastic opinions about the novel, they distinguish carefully between Condon's novel and literature. A *New Statesman* critic, for example, comments that *The Manchurian Candidate* is "so well written, and so ingeniously constructed, that [it] command[s] the highest admiration without ever being considered, or even asking to be considered, as 'literature.' " A *New York Herald Tribune Book Review* critic calls the novel "a smooth and palatable pousse-cafe of political satire, psychological speculation, pleasantly risque antics a la Thorne Smith, and espionage maneuvering. . . . The basic assumptions of the plot do not withstand close examination. Happily, however, such examination is not necessary: this is a diversion, and a good one." After recommending a place for it on a "Ten Best Bad Novels" list—"books whose artistic flaws are mountainous but whose merits, like Loreleis on the rocks above, keep on luring readers"—a *Time* reviewer notes: "The book carries a superstructure of plot that would capsize Hawaii, and badly insufficient philosophical ballast. Yet Condon distributes his sour, malicious humor with such vigor and impartiality that the novel is certain to be read and enjoyed."

Although Condon followed *The Manchurian Candidate* with several relatively successful novels, some reviewers were disappointed by his post-1964 efforts. A few became increasingly annoyed by Condon's mania for trivia and for what they perceived to be thinly veiled didacticism masquerading as satire. Others cited his lack of restraint as a major problem, claiming that it led him to portray scenes that are in bad taste or far too exaggerated to be anywhere near believable. In a review of *The Ecstasy Business,* for example, a *Christian Century* reviewer writes: "Condon's fans will find all the old razzmatazz here—the gimmicky language . . . and a cast of larger-than life zanies. . . . [But] like Condon's fourth novel, *A Talent for Loving,* this, his seventh, is a pointlessly funny 'entertainment,' a white rather than a black comedy. . . . [*The Ecstasy Business*] is an immoral waste of Condon's talent. Most damning of all: even the humor rests on shaky topical sands; the next generation will need scholarly footnotes to know why they should have laughed at Condon's parting shot."

Reviews of *An Infinity of Mirrors* (1964), and *The Vertical Smile* (1971) revealed similarly disillusioned opinions. In a review of *The Vertical Smile,* a *Time* critic declares: "Since the foaming manias of [his first two novels], Condon's fine, random wrath has aged until it is nothing more than irritability. Once he could have picked up the Republican and Democratic parties by their tails and swung them around his head like a couple of dead cats. . . . Now he can't manage it." Reed Whittemore speculates in the *New Republic:* "My guess is that Condon has had it with the genre itself, and this is his way of moving on—to what and where I wouldn't know. A large talent in limbo." Reviewing *An Infinity of Mirrors* in *Newsweek,* the critic concludes: "Condon, who seems to be equipped to write sound, pertinent, appealing stories in the almost vacant territory between the literary drive-ins of Robbins and Wallace and the transcendental realm of pure literature, has suffered here, one hopes, a temporary setback."

Critics' hopes for Condon's recovery were realized with the publication of his 1974 novel *Winter Kills.* Condon's most enthusiastically received novel since *The Manchurian Candidate, Winter Kills* closely parallels the lives of members of the Kennedy family. The main character, Nick Thirkield, is the half brother of John F. Kennedy analogue Tim Kegan, a young, liberal Irish president who is assassinated by a lone maniac. The assassin is caught and charged with the murder, but when Thirkield learns that another man may also have been involved, he has the case reopened.

Several reviewers found themselves pleasantly surprised by *Winter Kills.* Leo Braudy, for example, comments that *Winter Kills* is "a triumph of satire and knowledge, with a delicacy of style and a command of tone that puts Condon once again into the first rank of American novelists." Braudy explains, " 'Winter Kills' succeeds so brilliantly because the Kennedy assassination furnished Condon with a familiar mythic landscape through which his Gulliver-like hero can wander, simultaneously prey to Lilliputian politics, Brobdingnagian physicality, Laputan science, and Houyhnhnm moralism." Christopher Lehmann-Haupt expresses a like opinion in the *New York Times.* "By the time I reached the end of the novel's incredibly complex plot and had followed Nick Thirkield through the many blind alleys and trapdoors that eventually bring him face to face with the person behind his brother's assassination, I was a Richard Condon fan once more."

Extrapolation contributor Joe Sanders once observed: "In Condon's novels, politics determines the shape of society, but politics is not a voluntary, cooperative activity, entered into for some common end; it is a device by which a few clever people manipulate many others to gain their selfish ends." Sanders's comment is particularly relevant to *Winter Kills,* for the novel's conclusion reveals that the person responsible for arranging Kegan's assassination is none other than his own father, a likeness of Joseph Kennedy. Discussing the similarities between his novel and historical events, Condon told *Washington Post* reporter Joseph McLellan: "It doesn't really matter who killed Kennedy or who killed Abe Lincoln—they're dead. What matters is that the manipulators are so powerful they can have someone like that killed because he's bad for business."

Time reviewer John Skow, however, finds Condon's paranoia simplistic. He writes, "Condon has unraveled. The world's villainy simply does not work so simply. To pretend that it does is mindless mischief." Braudy, on the other hand, describes *Winter Kills* as "a paranoid novel that does not leave us trapped inside its world, but functions instead as a liberation, exposing through the gentler orders of fiction the way we have been programmed to believe anything in print." A *Spectator* contributor comments that Condon's ending, intended to surprise the reader, is really quite traditional. "The novel falls apart into scraps of received phraseology and it is so bound by the conventional laws of fiction that the conventionally surprising ending can be guessed a third of the way through—on the antique, statistical principle of bad crime fiction that the guilty party is always the one who is least suspected." And while Lehmann-Haupt also expresses disappointment because he "caught on too early what the ultimate outcome would be," he finds the novel's conclusion satisfying. He writes: "It may not be true that America is run by a small, conspiring oligarchy. It may not be true that things happen in the White House at the whim of movie stars and labor leaders, of courtesans and generals. But the possibilities are no longer inconceivable."

Condon's novel *Prizzi's Honor* deals with a similarly sensitive milieu: organized crime. Although this setting has been exploited by several other authors, notably Mario Puzo, reviewers believe that Condon's novel offers a fresh outlook. Champlin observes in the *Los Angeles Times Book Review:* "Condon, once again accepting the perceived reality as police leaks, newspaper exposes and Puzo have given it to us—complete with Sicilian litany of *consiglieri, capiregimes, sottocapos, soldati,* and a godfather with a lethal wheeze and a mind Machiavelli might envy—steps over it to present an outrageous and original love story." *New York Times Book Review* editor Robert Asahina notes: "Richard Condon is not Mario Puzo; suspense, not the family saga, is his forte. And he winds the mainspring of the plot so tight that the surprise ending will knock your reading glasses off. Yet 'Prizzi's Honor' is also a sendup of the prevailing sentimental picture of the underworld. To Mr. Condon, there is honor among these thieves but it is precisely in the name of *omerta* that the *fratellanza* has been willing to 'cheat, corrupt, scam, and murder anybody who stands between them and a buck.' "

The novel's love interest involves Charley Partanna, a gourmet cook, compulsive house cleaner, and hit man for the Prizzi family, and Irene Walker, a tax consultant and free-lance killer for hire. "It is something of a challenge to a novelist to create a love interest in a story that pairs two ruthless murderers," observes *Times Literary Supplement* critic Alan Bold. "Irene is presented as a colder fish than Charley—she has risen to the top of her profession on account of her ability to murder without remorse. She is as sound a psychopath as Charley. Condon suggests, however, that such creatures are capable of a great passion and Charley, for one, is sure that his love is the real thing." *New York Times* reviewer Susan Bolotin likewise comments on the originality of this pairing: "If boy-meets-girl/boy-gets-girl love stories seem poisonously tiresome to you, Richard Condon's boisterous new novel may prove the perfect antidote. It's true that 'Prizzi's Honor' starts off with a familiar melody . . . , but the book soon turns into a fugue with variations so intricate that the genre may never recover."

Despite opposition from Charley's father, Charley and Irene are wed. Condon takes the couple through a convoluted plot that includes "a kidnapping, international financial intrigue, a gangland war, police on the take, the power struggle within the family, contract killings, [and] lots of jolly sex," writes Bolotin. According to several reviewers, Condon's exploration of the seamier side of organized crime is distressing. *Best Sellers* contributor Tony Bednarczyk writes: "There is solid storytelling, but the subject raises disturbing questions about morals, and-or the lack thereof. It is a fast-paced, very readable story, but one feels a bit guilty for being interested in what comes next." A *Washington Post Book World* reviewer finds it unrealistic for Condon to expect readers to care about his psychopathic characters simply because he gives them "a few homey attributes." The reviewer adds that Charley's cooking and cleaning compulsions are "supposed to endear him to us, despite the fact that he goes for the slow kill, described in lavish detail. We're to laugh while his wife [Irene], plotting kidnapping and murder, at the same time dazzles as a hostess."

While *Time* critic Michael Demarest also believes that *Prizzi's Honor,* "like most of [Condon's] books, comes sometimes too close to the truth for comfort," he nevertheless concludes: "Condon's stylish prose and rich comedic gift once again spice a moral sensibility that has animated 16 novels since *The Manchurian Candidate* appeared in 1962. If wit and irony could somehow neutralize villainy, the novelist would make a fine FBI director." Other reviewers express similarly laudatory views. Champlin writes: "Condon is once again the storytelling satirist with a sharp eye and a high velocity typewriter. 'Prizzi's Honor' may not be his best work but it ranks well up in the canon." Concludes Asahina: "Twenty years after 'The Manchurian Candidate,' it's nice to know that Mr. Condon is still up to his sly tricks. In his case, at least, it's a pleasure that—as he tells us an old Sicilian proverb has it—'The less things change, the more they remain the same.' "

Prizzi's Honor was also made into a successful film of the same title, with Jack Nicholson and Kathleen Turner playing the roles of Charley Partanna and Irene Walker. Using a script by Condon and Janet Roach, the project was initiated and eventually directed by John Huston, who was attracted to the material by "that wonderful hyperbole and extravagance mixed with grandeur that Richard [Condon] has in all his best books—I thought this one epitomized that," he told *New York Times* reporter Janet Maslin. Huston added that he was also drawn to the book's "outstandingly jaundiced view of American enterprise and the ethics of the business world."

Huston and movie critics alike believe that "Prizzi's Honor" is faithful to the novel, a feat they attribute to Condon and Roach's skillfully adapted screenplay. Huston commented to Maslin: " 'Prizzi's Honor'. . . has the same quality as the book—it walks a very narrow tightrope, it can turn funny and then turn serious. This, I hope, is the unique quality of the picture: the ability to be not just one thing." *New York Times* critic Vincent Canby notes: "Admirers of Mr. Condon may be glad to know that great chunks of the original Condon dialogue are as alive on screen as on the page." Paul Attanasio similarly observes in the *Washington Post* that "Richard Condon has nicely adapted the screenplay (along with Janet Roach) by cutting and splicing his own novel—it's a cornucopia of quirks, homely maxims, bits of mob jargon and odd arcana about everything from interior decorating to hormonal secretions. Condon and Roach have an acute feel for the elaborate rhythms of Brooklynese; and they succeed elegantly at making the lives of the hoodlums seem completely normal, at making murder as routine as taking out the garbage."

"Prizzi's Honor" received unequivocal praise from many reviewers; some described the film as the year's finest. Canby writes: " 'Prizzi's Honor' delivers a kind of high most commonly associated with controlled substances, or with works of art of liberating imagination. From start to finish, this exhilarating adaptation of Richard Condon's phantasmagorical and witty novel—set inside the world of the Mafia—ascends, plunges and races around hairpin curves, only to shoot up again and dive over another precipice." *Chicago Tribune* reviewer Gene Siskel describes "Prizzi's Honor" as "a classic piece of moviemaking," and *Los Angeles Times* film critic Sheila Benson notes, "To say the film is the treasure of the year would be to bad-mouth it in this disastrous season. 'Prizzi's Honor' would be the vastly original centerpiece of a great year." Benson concludes: "In its dangerous mix of love and murder, Huston is traversing terrain that he (and certainly 'The Manchurian Candidate' author Condon) blazed decades ago. This '80s-version denouement may distress the squeamish, but it's right in keeping with Prizzi honor."

MEDIA ADAPTATIONS: United Artists filmed *The Oldest Confession* in 1961 as "The Happy Thieves" and *The Manchurian Candidate* in 1962; *Winter Kills* was filmed by Avco Embassy Pictures in 1979; *A Talent for Loving* was adapted for film.

BIOGRAPHICAL/CRITICAL SOURCES:

BOOKS

Bestsellers 90, Issue 3, Gale, 1990.
Condon, Richard, *Death of a Politician,* Richard Marek, 1978.
Contemporary Authors Autobiography Series, Volume 1, Gale, 1984.
Contemporary Literary Criticism, Gale, Volume 4, 1975, Volume 6, 1976, Volume 8, 1978, Volume 10, 1979, Volume 45, 1987.

Newquist, Roy, *Conversations,* Volume 1, Rand McNally, 1967.

PERIODICALS

Best Sellers, September 15, 1964, September 1, 1969, June, 1982, December, 1986.
Chicago Sunday Tribune, March 1, 1958, May 31, 1959.
Chicago Tribune, June 14, 1985.
Chicago Tribune Book World, June 6, 1982.
Christian Century, September 16, 1964, February 21, 1968, October 1, 1969.
Extrapolation, summer, 1984.
Harper's, September, 1977, May, 1983.
Los Angeles Times, February 19, 1983, June 14, 1985, August 16, 1987.
Los Angeles Times Book Review, April 25, 1982.
New Republic, October 16, 1971.
New Statesman, November 8, 1968, October 10, 1969, September 5, 1975, August 13, 1976.
Newsweek, September 14, 1964, June 9, 1975.
New Yorker, June 21, 1958, May 30, 1959, April 2, 1960, July 22, 1961, August 25, 1975, December 11, 1978.
New York Herald Tribune Book Review, June 1, 1958, June 28, 1959, May 1, 1960.
New York Review of Books, February 8, 1979.
New York Times, June 22, 1958, April 26, 1959, May 24, 1974, May 21, 1976, April 20, 1982, June 9, 1985, June 14, 1985, October 29, 1986.
New York Times Book Review, March 20, 1960, July 23, 1961, September 13, 1964, October 29, 1967, August 31, 1969, October 10, 1971, May 26, 1974, May 25, 1975, May 23, 1976, April 18, 1982, September 4, 1983, September 28, 1986.
New York Times Magazine, September 2, 1979.
People, December 8, 1986.
Publishers Weekly, June 24, 1983.
Spectator, April 22, 1972, September 21, 1974.
Time, July 6, 1959, July 21, 1961, March 22, 1968, September 5, 1969, October 4, 1971, June 24, 1974, June 2, 1975, May 17, 1982, June 10, 1985, September 22, 1986.
Times (London), October 25, 1985, January 15, 1987.
Times Literary Supplement, October 5, 1967, October 16, 1969, April 28, 1972, September 20, 1974, June 11, 1982.
Washington Post, November 10, 1978, May 10, 1979, September 13, 1980.
Washington Post Book World, May 30, 1976, April 4, 1982, June 14, 1985, August 24, 1986.

*   *   *

CONNELL, Evan S(helby), Jr. 1924-

PERSONAL: Born August 17, 1924, in Kansas City, Mo.; son of Evan Shelby (a surgeon) and Elton (Williamson) Connell. *Education:* Attended Dartmouth College, 1941-43; University of Kansas, A.B., 1947; graduate study at Stanford University, 1947-48, Columbia University, 1948-49, and San Francisco State College (now University).

ADDRESSES: Home—487 Sherwood Dr., Sausalito, Calif. 94965. *Agent*—Elizabeth McKee, 22 East 40th St., New York, N.Y. 10016.

CAREER: Writer. *Military service:* U.S. Navy, pilot, 1943-45; served as flight instructor.

AWARDS, HONORS: Eugene F. Saxton fellow, 1953; Guggenheim fellow, 1963; Rockefeller Foundation grant, 1967; nomination for award for general nonfiction from National Book Critics Circle, 1984, for *Son of the Morning Star: Custer and the Little Bighorn.*

WRITINGS:

The Anatomy Lesson, and Other Stories, Viking, 1957.
Mrs. Bridge (novel), Viking, 1959.
The Patriot (novel), Viking, 1960.
(Editor) Jerry Stoll, *I Am a Lover,* Angel Island Publications, 1961.
Notes From a Bottle Found on the Beach at Carmel (epic poem), Viking, 1963.
At the Crossroads: Stories, Simon & Schuster, 1965.
The Diary of a Rapist (novel), Simon & Schuster, 1966.
Mr. Bridge (novel), Knopf, 1969.
(Editor) *Woman by Three,* Pacific Coast Publishers, 1969.
Points for a Compass Rose (epic poem), Knopf, 1973.
The Connoisseur (novel), Knopf, 1974.
Double Honeymoon (novel), Putnam, 1976.
A Long Desire (nonfiction), Holt, 1979.
The White Lantern (nonfiction), Holt, 1980.
St. Augustine's Pigeon (stories), North Point Press, 1980.
Son of the Morning Star: Custer and the Little Bighorn (nonfiction), North Point Press, 1984.

Contributor of short stories to periodicals, including *Carolina Quarterly, Paris Review,* and *Esquire.* Editor of *Contact* (literary magazine), 1959-65.

SIDELIGHTS: The works of Evan S. Connell, Jr., have been widely reviewed and highly praised. The critical acclaim began with his first collection, *The Anatomy Lesson, and Other Stories.* At the time of the book's publication in 1957, Anne Chamberlain wrote that "with a virtuoso's dexterity [Connell] explores theme and treatment, subject matter and attack, darting from the precious and the esoteric to almost legendary folk tales, laid in his native Midwest and in distant corners of America. This is a many-faceted writer." Siegfried Mandel called him a "craftsman who can evoke, sustain and dignify the 'small' tragedy that is often hidden from view." And William Hogan said that the stories in *The Anatomy Lesson* are "well-observed, well-worked slices of life that exhibit craftsmanship, discipline and maturity. Connell is obviously a serious writer of promise and I look forward with great expectations to the publication of his first novel."

That first novel, *Mrs. Bridge,* published in 1959, is probably Connell's best-known work as well as the one to which his subsequent books are most often compared. In it the author tells the story of India Bridge, an upper-class midwestern woman, wife of a lawyer, mother of three children, who comes to personify Connell's concept of the idle rich: She is easily confused; she is bored with her leisure-class existence; and she is dominated by materialism and the need to be "socially correct." India Bridge, according to some critics, may be the most fully developed character in any post-World War II American novel. Anne Chamberlain says that Connell has achieved "a triumph of ironic characterization. In his heroine, who appears at first meeting the acme of mediocrity, he manages to create an interesting, a pathetically comic, a tragically lonely figure. . . . It is sad, somewhat terrifying to reflect upon the numberless Mrs. Bridges trotting befuddledly through this urgent age." Dorothy Nyen finds that "Mr. Connell has been most successful in his dissection of one life of quiet desperation which stands for many such lives." Hollis Summers calls the author "a skilled pointillist. Rarely does he fail to place his dot of character in the proper place. The novel, for all its fragility, is sturdy. Although the heroine does

not realize her moments' significances, the reader does understand—and cares."

In the decade following the publication of *Mrs. Bridge,* Connell published two more novels, *The Patriot* and *The Diary of a Rapist,* one book-length poem, *Notes From a Bottle Found on the Beach at Carmel,* and a collection of short stories, *At the Crossroads;* most of these were generously accepted by reviewers. He then returned to the Bridge family for his fourth novel, *Mr. Bridge,* which tells the story from the husband's point of view. A *Playboy* critic calls the book "a brilliant dissection of the quintessential small-town WASP—performed under the light of high art, with irony, insight, and a bleak pity." Webster Schott writes: "Had Sinclair Lewis possessed compassion equal to his anger, discipline to complement his energy, he might have written *Mr. Bridge.* Evan Connell looks at his world straight. No artifice. But with full awareness of the quiet comedy, tenderness and tight-lipped waste. This job need not be done again. *Mr. Bridge* is a tour de force of contemporary American realism, a beautiful work of fiction." One or two reviewers feel that the novel doesn't quite live up to Connell's work in *Mrs. Bridge;* some believe that the characterization is somewhat weaker in the newer book. However, as John Gross explains: "If *Mr. Bridge* is a less engaging work than its predecessor, it is chiefly because Walter Bridge himself has little of his wife's pathos. Where she was vulnerable in her innocence, funny and touching in her hapless cultural aspirations, he is rigid, efficient, proud of knowing his own mind. Not an especially likable man; but then Mr. Connell's purpose in writing about him is not to draw up a brief for the defense, but simply to restore a cliche-figure to humanity."

It is interesting to note that reviewer Charles Thomas Samuels disagrees with the majority; he feels that Connell's work prior to *Mr. Bridge* was, for the most part, unappealing in subject matter and character; and he dismisses as unsophisticated those critics who found merit in the earlier books. Samuels says that "everything Connell writes is competent, but none of his previous books is enough like another to persuade us that we must grant his subjects and dwell on his style. *Mrs. Bridge* is written in colorless prose, but *Rapist* recalls Celine. In his stories Connell moves from porno-baroque (in the Muhlbach tales from *At the Crossroads*) to arch *New Yorker.*" Samuels also finds Connell lacking as a storyteller. He cites Roth and Bellow as writers who, although equally deficient in this area, are able to "find cunning facades for their jerry-built structures (through Portnoy's psychoanalysis or Herzog's letters), whereas Connell is ingenuous in disguising his inability to construct a tale. *Mrs. Bridge* is written in a series of very short chapters (some paragraph-long) that simply slice up the heroine's life, while *The Diary* employs the oldest and least convincing plot evasion known to literature. Evan Connell, then, is a novelist who can't construct stories about uninteresting or remote people told in characterless prose." Having levelled these criticisms, however, Samuels goes on to explain why he chose to call attention to Connell's work: "Because in everything he writes, he is admirably serious and painstaking and because, like a character actor who disappears into his role, Connell always has the potential for turning imitation into insight. All he needed was a good part, which he has found in *Mr. Bridge.*"

In response to interviewer Lawrence Bensky's question about his lack of commercial success, Connell admitted that his writing had, thus far, been an "economic uncertainty" but noted that "the most important thing for me is what I'm working on. New York and the publishing world seem very distant and very hard to comprehend at this distance." When asked for his critical opinion of modern American literature, Connell told Bensky: "I seldom like anything I read; most contemporary fiction is so bad. I look through things in bookstores, read the first few pages, and I see what the writer is getting at. Usually it's like looking through a piece of pipe—there's nothing at the other end. There are two or three books a year that people call masterpieces [a word that is used not infrequently in reviews of his own work]. I wait a few years, and if they're still around, I might read them." Connell said that he has observed an ongoing trend toward romanticism in this country, and "what I've tried to do as a writer is get behind this romanticism and into people's fantasies—and show them as they are."

Aside from his novels, Connell's most notable work is *Son of the Morning Star*, his account of the Battle of the Little Bighorn, where Sioux Indian Sitting Bull's warriors overwhelmed General George Custer's band of American troops. A reviewer for the *Detroit News* praised *Son of the Morning Star* as "astonishingly good, the stuff of which classics are made."

BIOGRAPHICAL/CRITICAL SOURCES:

BOOKS

Contemporary Literary Criticism, Gale, Volume 4, 1975, Volume 6, 1976, Volume 45, 1987.
Dictionary of Literary Biography, Volume 2: *American Novelists since World War II,* Gale, 1978.
Dictionary of Literary Biography Yearbook: 1981, Gale, 1982.

PERIODICALS

Best Sellers, April 15, 1969, June 15, 1973.
Catholic World, March, 1959.
Christian Science Monitor, May 22, 1969.
Commonweal, February 13, 1959, August 23, 1963.
Detroit News, March 10, 1985.
Harper's, January, 1974.
Kenyon Review, September, 1966.
Kirkus Reviews, March 1, 1957, July 15, 1960.
Library Journal, April 15, 1957, January 1, 1959, September 1, 1960, March 15, 1973, August, 1974.
Life, April 25, 1969.
Nation, June 15, 1963, June 30, 1969.
National Review, February 28, 1975.
New Republic, June 7, 1969.
New Statesman, February 13, 1960.
Newsweek, May 12, 1969.
New Yorker, October 14, 1974.
New York Herald Tribune Book Review, May 26, 1957, January 18, 1959, September 25, 1960, May 26, 1963.
New York Review, April 24, 1969.
New York Review of Books, June 23, 1966, May 17, 1973, November 28, 1974.
New York Times, May 19, 1957, February 1, 1959, April 23, 1969, February 13, 1985.
New York Times Book Review, September 25, 1960, April 20, 1969, April 29, 1973, September 1, 1974, May 23, 1976, June 24, 1979, July 20, 1980.
Playboy, June, 1969.
San Francisco Chronicle, May 28, 1957, January 19, 1959, September 19, 1960.
Saturday Review, May 18, 1957, January 31, 1959, September 24, 1960, July 17, 1965, May 3, 1969, April 17, 1976.
Time, May 27, 1957, January 19, 1959, June 20, 1969, September 2, 1974, June 21, 1976.
Virginia Quarterly Review, autumn, 1965, summer, 1969.
Washington Post, July 17, 1979.

Washington Post Book World, April 20, 1969, May 27, 1973, September 1, 1974, July 13, 1980.
Wisconsin Studies in Contemporary Literature, summer, 1967.

*   *   *

CONNOLLY, Cyril (Vernon)   1903-1974 (Palinurus)

PERSONAL: Born September 10, 1903, in Coventry, England; died November 26, 1974; son of Matthew (an army major) and Muriel (Vernon) Connolly; married Deirdre Craig, 1959; children: one son, one daughter. *Education:* Attended Balliol College, Oxford.

CAREER: Writer for the *New Statesman* and other periodicals, 1927-74; *Horizon,* London, England, founder, editor, and writer, 1939-50; *Observer,* London, literary editor, 1942-43; weekly contributor to the *Sunday Times,* 1951-74.

MEMBER: Royal Society of Literature (fellow), White's, Pratt's, Beefsteak Clubs.

AWARDS, HONORS: Chevalier de la Legion d'Honneur; Brackenbury scholar; D.Litt., Trinity College, Dublin; Companion of Honour, L'Academie Francaise; knighted; Commander of the Order of the British Empire, 1972.

WRITINGS:

The Rock Pool (fiction), Scribner, 1936.
Enemies of Promise, Routledge & Kegan Paul, 1938, Little, Brown, 1939, revised edition, Macmillan, 1948.
(Editor) *Horizon Stories,* Faber, 1943, Vanguard, 1946.
(Translator) Jean Bruller (writing under pseudonym Vercors), *Silence of the Sea,* Macmillan, 1944 (published in England as *Put Out the Light,* Macmillan, 1944).
(Under pseudonym Palinurus) *The Unquiet Grave: A Word Cycle,* Horizon (London), 1944, Harper, 1945, revised edition, Hamish Hamilton, 1945.
The Condemned Playground (essays), Routledge & Kegan Paul, 1945, Macmillan, 1946.
The Missing Diplomats, Queen Anne Press, 1952.
Ideas and Places, Harper, 1953.
The Golden Horizon, Weidenfeld & Nicolson, 1953, University Books, 1955.
(Editor and author of introduction) *Great English Short Novels,* Dial, 1953.
(With Jerome Zerbe) *Les Pavillons: French Pavilions of the Eighteenth Century,* Macmillan, 1962.
Previous Convictions: Selected Writings of a Decade, Harper, 1963.
The Modern Movement: 100 Key Books from England, France, and America, Deutsch, 1965, Atheneum, 1966.
(Translator with Simon W. Taylor) Alfred Jarry, *The Ubu Plays* (contains *Ubu Rex, Ubu Cuckolded,* and *Ubu Enchained*), Grove, 1969.
The Evening Colonnade, Harcourt, 1975.
The Selected Essays of Cyril Connolly, edited by Peter Quennell, Persea Books, 1984.

Contributor of article to *Art and Literature.*

SIDELIGHTS: Cyril Connolly related his "Georgian boyhood" in Eton College in the last part of his formidable work *Enemies of Promise.* He believed that he was a spoiled child who suffered all the miseries of the English public school caste system while managing to acquire an excellent education. With a sharp tongue he wasn't afraid to use, he was at times a critic of the literary world, at times a self-critic. Remembering a "very nasty review" he had written on Ernest Hemingway's *Green Hills of Africa,* Connolly remarked that "the first time I met Hemingway I was introduced to him, just after I had reviewed this book, in Sylvia Beach's bookshop in Paris. When he realised who I was, he turned to Sylvia Beach and he said: 'This is a very bad moment for both of us.' That, I think, is a lovely remark: you see, he forgave me, because I was minding terribly the tactlessness of being introduced to him after writing this review, and he showed that he minded the review. We had dinner together and we became great friends, because after all I had liked his earlier books and said so."

The *New Yorker* critic found *Enemies of Promise* to be "a collection of searching and idea-packed literary essays, precisely noting the temper of current writing and pointing out the pitfalls that beset the beginning or the successful author." To Geoffrey Grigson, the complete book was most interesting, sociologically, "as a specimen [and] as a piece from the war between the ninety per cent art-gentlemen and his gentility. It is good to see conscience at work in an art-gentleman." James Stern reflected that "had I a son, whether destined for Eton, Dalton or the dogs, I would place a copy of *Enemies of Promise* in his hands at an early age. For this book is an education, a warning, an encouragement, a preparation for the literary life."

In 1968, responding to questions about the whole of his own "literary life" and the things which influenced it, Connolly told interviewer Richard Kershaw that his own family "would have liked me most of all, I think, to go into the Foreign Office; failing that, they'd have liked me to take some kind of nice job, like a clerk in the House of Commons, or perhaps the Lords, or anything but the thing that I did do—which was to waste a lot of time and be very extravagant and get so into debt that I spent years trying to get out of it."

Kershaw queried Connolly if involvement in politics had prevented him from doing writing he ought to have done, to which Connolly replied: "I would say only myself has prevented me doing the writing I ought to have done. A writer ought to have politics, but when it comes to the executive side of politics, standing for Parliament, speaking at a lot of meetings, being on committees, writing a lot of pamphlets, unless you're that kind of writer it must be bad for you. A writer has a vintage product which is him. He produces his little *vin ordinaire* called Chateau Connolly or whatever it is. Well, that wine results from his personality being kept in a certain condition, a certain temperature, a certain soil; and if you take him too far away from that, he becomes indistinguishable from other products of the new political soil. The Spanish war produced its best work from writers who were not involved in the running of the war but who made private sorties into it." Connolly attested, "I could never do more than write for some political cause. But I was political. So were Auden and Spender and Isherwood, of the people I knew who were slightly younger than me, and many people of my own age. But for us, the Spanish war was the crux of everything, and it was such a disaster to our hopes: it was so awful to see the side we were convinced was right totally defeated, with the democracies looking on, either sadly or cheering. It made one feel nothing could be done by politics. You had to give up all that side. And then go back into the ivory tower."

To the Virginia Woolf idea that it is essential for a writer to have a room of his own and a private income, Connolly responded: "Well, I think the room of one's own—don't forget, half of one's life one is married and hasn't got a room of one's own, unless you have a large study of your own—is a great help. There is no doubt that one's best thoughts come reading at night when you have gone to bed. If you can't read half the night your tank doesn't fill up for the next day. And a private income is very, very good too, if it isn't too big or too small. [T. S.] Eliot had a tiny income, which was no good to him. When he was offered to leave the bank where he worked, in return for a fixed income of 250 pounds a year subscribed by his admirers, he refused to leave: 'With that income I would still have to work for my living. I would do just as much journalism as if I didn't have an income at all. I'd rather stay in the bank.' Which he did for another few years. . . . A good writer rises above everything and it's an alibi to say: 'I can't write, I haven't got a room of my own . . .' 'I can't write, I haven't got a private income . . .' 'I can't write, I'm a journalist,' and so on. Those are all alibis. But I have seen in my contemporaries a great many who could have been much better if it hadn't been for two or three things: social climbing, drink and unhappy love affairs, due to flaws in themselves which made their love affairs go on for too long, or become too unhappy. All novelists," Connolly reflected, "have got to be social animals, I think. You can't write a novel if you don't go to parties. And even poets have got to take a lot of their material from daily life or from things they do."

Kershaw asked Connolly if he thought psychoanalyst Sigmund Freud, political philosopher Karl Marx, politicians, and great mass movements had destroyed the ability to be a writer in the sense that Connolly wished to be thirty or forty years ago, when he had started. Connolly answered: "Each has made it harder. Freud has made it very much harder. For a critic Freud is invaluable as a tool to help you to understand other writers and the processes derived from their childhood. But in yourself Freud is a blocker: the moment you know enough Freud you know your own motives. Take, for instance, condemnation. Part of a critic's professional talent is his ability to abuse other people, especially if he can do it with moral indignation. Well, when you read Freud, who says, 'Whatever you blame you wish to do yourself,' you cannot blame in the same way. . . . I think nowadays [that the 'enemies of promise' are] the pressure of instant success, the enormous sums to be made by one book and the pathetically small ones to be made by the other ninety-nine. And, of course, the general visual impact of the television world—that is very bad for the writer, who has based himself for 2,000 years on the idea of the private person writing in his lavatory for someone who is going to read him in their lavatory. The totally private life of the writer," Connolly observed, "has become economically impossible. The cottage in the country where the Georgian poet did his own cooking and wrote his imitation Elizabethan sonnets—all that has become rather ridiculous. You couldn't live like that now. You'd get nothing but a lot of brown envelopes from the Income Tax." Connolly felt strongly "that all human beings are sentenced to death and that as the sentence will never be commuted, we are all entitled to the amenities of the condemned cell."

BIOGRAPHICAL/CRITICAL SOURCES:

BOOKS

Enright, D. J., *Conspirators and Poets,* Dufour, 1966.
Martin, Kingsley, editor, *New Statesman Profiles,* Phoenix House, 1958.

PERIODICALS

Boston Transcript, October 10, 1936.
Encounter, February, 1964.
Listener, April 11, 1968.
Manchester Guardian, December 13, 1938.

New Republic, July 15, 1946, January 31, 1948.
New Statesman and Nation, May 30, 1953.
New Yorker, April 8, 1939, October 27, 1945.
New York Herald Tribune Weekly Book Review, February 27, 1949.
New York Times Book Review, October 11, 1936, October 7, 1945.
Spectator, November 12, 1938.
Time, March 25, 1966.

*   *   *

CONRAD, Joseph   1857-1924

PERSONAL: Birth-given name Jozef Teodor Konrad Nalecz Korzeniowski; name legally changed; born December 3, 1857, in Berdiczew, Podolia, Russia (now Poland); naturalized British citizen, 1886; died of a heart attack, August 3, 1924, in Bishopsbourne, Kent, England; buried in Canterbury, England; son of Apollo Nalecz (a poet, writer, and political activist) and Ewa (Bobrowski) Korzeniowski; married Jessie George, March 24, 1896; children: Alfred Borys, John Alexander. *Education:* Studied at schools in Poland and under tutors in Europe. *Religion:* Roman Catholic.

CAREER: Joined French Merchant Marine, 1874, sailed to Martinique and to West Indies as apprentice and then steward, 1875; British Merchant Service, 1878-94, traveled to Africa, Australia, India, Indonesia, and the Orient; full-time writer, 1894-1924.

MEMBER: Athenaeum Club.

WRITINGS:

FICTION

Almayer's Folly: A Story of an Eastern River (novel), Macmillan, 1895, published as *Almayer's Folly,* Doubleday, Page, 1921, reprinted, Penquin, 1976.
An Outcast of the Islands (novel), D. Appleton, 1896, reprinted, Penguin, 1975.
The Children of the Sea: A Tale of the Forecastle (novel), Dodd, Mead, 1897 (published in England as *The Nigger of the "Narcissus": A Tale of the Sea,* Heinemann, 1898), published with new preface by Conrad as *The Nigger of the "Narcissus": A Tale of the Forecastle,* Doubleday, Page, 1914, published under English title, Doubleday, Page, 1926, reprinted under title *The Nigger of the "Narcissus,"* Doubleday, Doran, 1938, recent edition, Norton, 1979.
Tales of Unrest (stories; includes "The Idiots," "An Outpost of Progress," and "The Lagoon"), Scribner, 1898, reprinted, Penguin, 1977.
Lord Jim: A Romance (novel), Doubleday, McClure, 1900 (published in England as *Lord Jim: A Tale,* W. Blackwood, 1900), published under English title, Doubleday, Page, 1927, published as *Lord Jim,* introduction by J. Donald Adams, Modern Library, 1931, enlarged edition, F. Watts, 1966, recent edition, Oxford University Press, 1983.
(With Ford Madox Heuffer [later Ford Madox Ford]) *The Inheritors: An Extravagant Story* (novel), McClure, Phillips, 1901, reprinted with introduction by Elaine L. Kleiner, Gregg Press, 1976.
"Youth: A Narrative," and Two Other Stories (contains "Youth, A Narrative," "Heart of Darkness" [also see below], and "The End of the Tether"), W. Blackwood, 1902, published as *"Youth" and Two Other Stories,* McClure, Phillips, 1903, reprinted with introduction by Morton Dauwen Zabel,

Doubleday, 1959, recent edition published as *"Youth," "Heart of Darkness," and "The End of the Tether,"* Oxford University Press, 1984.
Typhoon, illustrations by Maurice Grieffenhagen, Putnam, 1902 (also see below).
Typhoon, and Other Stories (includes "To-Morrow" [also see below] and "Falk"), Heinemann, 1903, Doubleday, Page, 1926.
(With Ford) *Romance* (novel), Smith, Elder, 1903, McClure, Phillips, 1904, reprinted with afterword by Arthur Mizener, New American Library, 1968.
Nostromo: A Tale of the Seabord (novel), Harper & Brothers, 1904, recent edition, Oxford University Press, 1984.
The Secret Agent: A Simple Tale (novel), Harper & Brothers, 1907, recent edition, Viking, 1985 (also see below).
The Point of Honor: A Military Tale, illustrations by Dan Sayre Broesbeck, McClure, 1908.
"Falk," "Amy Foster," "To-Morrow": Three Stories by Joseph Conrad, McClure, Phillips, 1908.
A Set of Six (stories), Methuen, 1908, Doubleday, Page, 1915.
Under Western Eyes (novel), Harper & Brothers, 1911, recent edition, Viking, 1985.
'Twixt Land and Sea (stories; includes "The Secret Sharer" [also see below], "A Smile of Fortune," and "Freya of the Seven Isles"), Hodder & Stoughton, 1912, reprinted, Penguin, 1978.
Chance: A Tale in Two Parts (novel), Doubleday, Page, 1913, reprinted, 1957, recent edition, Hogarth Press, 1984.
Victory: An Island Tale (novel), Doubleday, Page, 1915, reprinted, Penguin, 1966.
Within the Tides: Tales (includes "Because of the Dollars" [also see below] and "The Planter of Malata"), Dent, 1915, Doubleday, Page, 1916, reprinted, Penguin, 1978.
The Shadow Line: A Confession (novel), Doubleday, Page, 1917, recent edition, Oxford University Press, 1985.
The Arrow of Gold: A Story Between Two Notes (novel), Doubleday, Page, 1919, reprinted, Norton, 1968.
The Rescue: A Romance of the Shallows (novel), Doubleday, Page, 1920, reprinted, Norton, 1968.
The Rover (novella), Doubleday, Page, 1923, reprinted, T. Nelson, 1964.
(With Heuffer) *The Nature of a Crime,* Doubleday, Page, 1924.
Suspense: A Napoleonic Novel (unfinished), Doubleday, Page, 1925.
Tales of Hearsay, preface by R. B. Cunninghame Graham, Doubleday, Page, 1925.
The Sisters (unfinished), introduction by Ford, C. Gaige, 1928.
"Heart of Darkness" and "The Secret Sharer," introduction by Albert J. Guerard, New American Library, 1950.

Stories and novels also in other multi-titled volumes.

PLAYS

One Day More: A Play in One Act (adaptation of Conrad's story "To-Morrow"; first performed June 25, 1905), Clement Shorter, 1917, Doubleday, Page, 1920 (also see below).
The Secret Agent: A Drama in Four Acts (adaptation of Conrad's novel of the same title), H. J. Goulden, 1921 (also see below).
Laughing Anne: A Play (adaptation of Conrad's story "Because of the Dollars"), Morland Press, 1923 (also see below).
Laughing Anne [and] *One Day More,* introduction by John Galsworthy, J. Castle, 1924, Doubleday, Page, 1925.
Three Plays: Laughing Anne, One Day More, [and] *The Secret Agent,* Methuen, 1934.

CORRESPONDENCE

Lettres Francaises, introduction and notes by Georges Jean-Aubry, Gallimard, 1920.

Joseph Conrad's Letters to His Wife, Bookman's Journal, 1927.

Letters From Joseph Conrad, 1895-1924, edited with introduction and notes by Edward Garnett, Bobbs-Merrill, 1928.

Conrad to a Friend: One Hundred Fifty Selected Letters From Joseph Conrad to Richard Curle, edited with introduction and notes by Richard Curle, Bobbs-Merrill, 1928.

Letters of Joseph Conrad to Marguerite Poradowska, 1890-1920, translated from the French and edited with introduction and notes by John A. Gee and Paul J. Sturm, Yale University Press, 1940.

Joseph Conrad: Letters to William Blackwood and David S. Meldrum, edited by William Blackburn, Duke University Press, 1958.

Conrad's Polish Background: Letters to and From Polish Friends, translated by Halina Carroll, edited by Zdzislaw Najder, Oxford University Press, 1964.

Joseph Conrad and Warrington Dawson: The Record of a Friendship, edited by Dale B. J. Randall, Duke University Press, 1968.

Joseph Conrad's Letters to Cunninghame Graham, edited by C. T. Watts, Cambridge University Press, 1969.

The Collected Letters of Joseph Conrad, edited by Frederick R. Karl and Laurence Davies, Cambridge University Press, Volume I: *1861-1897,* 1983, Volume II: *1898-1902,* 1988.

OTHER

The Mirror of the Sea: Memories and Impressions (autobiographical essays), Harper & Brothers, 1906, reprinted, Marlboro Press, 1988 (also see below).

A Personal Record (autobiography), Harper & Brothers, 1912, reprinted, Marlboro Press, 1988 (published in England as *Some Reminiscences,* Eveleigh Nash, 1912; also see below).

Notes on Life and Letters (essays), Doubleday, Page, 1921, reprinted, Books for Libraries Press, 1972.

Notes on My Books, Doubleday, Page, 1921.

(Contributor) *Hugh Walpole: Appreciations,* Doran, 1923.

(Contributor) Charles Kenneth Scott-Moncrief, editor, *Marcel Proust: An English Tribute,* Chatto & Windus, 1923.

Last Essays (includes "Geography and Some Explorers"), introduction by Richard Curle, Doubleday, Page, 1926, reprinted, Books for Libraries Press, 1970.

Joseph Conrad's Diary of His Journey up the Valley of the Congo in 1890, Strangeways, 1926 (also see below).

Joseph Conrad's Prefaces to His Works, introduction by Edward Garnett, Dent, 1937.

Joseph Conrad on Fiction, edited by Walter F. Wright, University of Nebraska Press, 1964.

Congo Diary and Other Uncollected Pieces, edited by Najder, Doubleday, 1978.

The Mirror of the Sea [and] *A Personal Record,* Oxford University Press, 1988.

Contributor to periodicals, including *Oxford and Cambridge Review,* London *Times, Fortnightly Review,* and the *Daily Mail.*

OMNIBUS VOLUMES

Wisdom and Beauty From Conrad, selected and arranged by M. Harriet M. Capes, Melrose, 1915, Doubleday, 1922, reprinted, Haskell House, 1976.

The Shorter Tales of Joseph Conrad, Doubleday, 1924, reprinted, Books for Libraries Press, 1970.

The Complete Short Stories of Joseph Conrad, Hutchinson, 1933.

The Famous Stories of Joseph Conrad, Doubleday, 1938.

A Conrad Argosy, Doubleday, 1942.

The Portable Conrad, edited with introduction and notes by Zabel, Viking, 1947, reprinted, Penguin, 1976.

Tales of Land and Sea, illustrated by Richard M. Powers, introduction by William McFee, Hanover House, 1953.

Tales of the East and West, edited with introduction by Zabel, Doubleday, 1958.

Tales of Heroes and History, edited by Zabel, Doubleday, 1960.

Tales of the East, edited with introduction by Zabel, Doubleday, 1961.

Great Short Works of Joseph Conrad, Harper, 1967.

Stories and Tales of Joseph Conrad, Funk & Wagnalls, 1968.

Sea Stories, Granada, 1984.

Stories and novels also published together in other collections; works widely represented in anthologies.

COLLECTED WORKS

The Works of Joseph Conrad, twenty-one volumes, Dent, 1923-38, reprinted and enlarged, twenty-six volumes, 1946-55.

The Collected Works of Joseph Conrad, twenty-one volumes, Doubleday, 1925.

SIDELIGHTS: Joseph Conrad was a British novelist and short story writer whose major works appeared between 1895 and 1924. Conrad's work marks a shift from the novel as popular entertainment to the novel as high art, an art as carefully crafted as poetry. His experiments in fictional form and narrative prepared the way for the technical innovations of novelists Virginia Woolf, William Faulkner, and John Fowles; his characteristic themes of alienation and thwarted heroism and his preoccupation with individuals in remote places have had continuing impact on writers throughout this century.

Conrad was born in Russian-occupied Poland on December 3, 1857. Although Poland had been a major power in central Europe from the fourteenth through seventeenth centuries, the country had been partitioned into German, Austrian, and Russian sectors, and, by the time of Conrad's birth, only Warsaw remained under Polish control. The Poles fought partition and occupation, particularly Russian occupation, with patriotic and religious fervor. Conrad's family on both sides had a history of commitment to the cause of a free Poland; his parents, Apollo and Ewa Korzeniowski, were active in the insurrection of 1863. The Russian authorities sentenced the family to exile in Vologda, Russia, then, after two years, to Chernikhov in the Ukraine. When Conrad was five, his mother died from illness worsened by the privations of their exile. Ewa's death plunged Apollo into depression and illness, despite his having gained permission to return to Warsaw. When he died in May of 1869, he was given a public funeral befitting a hero.

Conrad, twelve years old, was put in the care of his mother's younger brother, Tadeusz Bobrowski, a lawyer. Conrad remained under Tadeusz's care until the age of seventeen, when, after two years of importuning his uncle, he was allowed to attend a maritime school in Marseilles. Conrad's four years in Marseilles have received considerable scrutiny because of evidence of his attempted suicide. Conrad himself told his son and friends that he had been shot in the chest during a duel. But Bobrowski, who went to his nephew's rescue, seems plainly to say in a letter to a friend that Conrad had tried to kill himself, as Zdzislaw Najder in *Joseph Conrad: A Chronicle* and Frederick R. Karl in *Joseph Conrad: The Three Lives* point out. Biographers speculate that the suicide attempt may have been the result of debts, a foiled love relationship, or disappointed expectations. When Conrad reovered from his injury, he fulfilled his ambition to sail on an English ship, the *Mavis,* bound for Constantinople.

Conrad spent the next fifteen years on English ships, where he was known among sailors as "Polish Joe." Conrad rose steadily in his profession, passing the required examinations for second mate in 1880, first mate in 1883, and then, on his second try, captain in 1886, the same year he became a naturalized British citizen. In 1890 Conrad accepted a job as commander of a Congo River steamboat owned by a Belgian firm. Once in Africa, he saw extreme examples of imperialistic exploitation, which he described in "Geography and Some Explorers" (included in the collection *Last Essays*) as "the vilest scramble for loot that ever disfigured the history of human conscience and geographical exploration." When he arrived at the town of Kinshasa after a thirty-six-day overland trek, he found his command had been sunk, but he was given another steamboat and ordered to proceed immediately up the Congo River to rescue Georges Antoine Klein, a valuable company agent who had taken ill. On the return trip the agent died, and Conrad was stalled in Kinshasa, perhaps, as some have theorized, because he did not get on with his superiors. After months fighting fever and dysentery, he returned to Europe, his health wrecked.

During the next five years, Conrad spent less time at sea and committed himself to the life of a writer. In 1894 his guardian, Bobrowski, died. A year later, Conrad published his first novel, *Almayer's Folly: A Story of an Eastern River,* and dedicated it to his uncle. His second novel, *An Outcast of the Islands,* derived in plot and theme from the first, followed quickly in 1898, a productivity stimulated, perhaps, by Conrad's marriage in 1896 to Jessie George, with whom he had two sons, Borys and John. During his long career as author of English fiction, Conrad wrote three works with Ford Madox Ford, more than a dozen novels, twenty-nine short stories and novellas, two books of essays, two memoirs, and three plays. Conrad died on August 3, 1924. He was buried at the cemetery of St. Thomas Catholic Church in Canterbury, where his tombstone bears a passage from sixteenth-century British poet Edmund Spenser's *The Faerie Queene:* "Sleepe after toyle, port after stormie seas, / Ease after warre, death after life does greatly please."

Critics have divided Conrad's canon into three phases. The first phase includes the works from *Almayer's Folly* through *Typhoon* (1903). Based squarely on Conrad's experiences in Eastern seas, the early work earned him a reputation as a teller of sea stories. In the middle phase, from *Nostromo* (1904) to *Under Western Eyes* (1911), autobiographical elements are either vastly transformed or subordinated to political themes. The late work, from *Chance* (1913) to the posthumous *Suspense* (1925), is less coherent as a body than the early or middle work, and it is usually set apart simply on the basis of its alleged inferiority to Conrad's previous writings.

Much of the fiction in Conrad's early phase arose from his experiences as mate on the trading vessel *Vidar,* on which he sailed from Singapore on several voyages throughout the Malay Archipelago beginning in 1887. The works based on Conrad's life on the *Vidar* include his first novel, *Almayer's Folly,* many short stories, and four other novels: *An Outcast of the Islands, Lord Jim, Victory,* and *The Rescue.* Recognized for its experiments in narrative technique, evocation of place, characterization, and profound exploration of alienation, *Almayer's Folly* is considered a remarkable first novel.

Almayer's Folly centers on Kaspar Almayer, a Dutch trader at the port of Sambir, holding what had been a very profitable post until Arabs found their way through the thirty miles of the Pantai River channels to the town. Almayer dreams of returning, with his beloved half-caste daughter Nina, to the native land that he has never seen. A third major figure in the tale, Dain Waris, is a Malay chieftain from Bali, sent out by his father, the Rajah, to secure gunpowder to fight the Dutch. The fourth actor is Tom Lingard, an aging British trader-adventurer. All intensely isolated, these figures are bound together in a "community of hopes and fears." Almayer's hope is riches and escape from the swamps of Sambir (he had married Lingard's adopted Sulu daughter to secure Lingard's fortune). Lingard's hope is to discover a mountain of gold in the Bornean interior, for which project he loses the wealth Almayer had expected. Dain lives to defeat the Dutch and, unknown to Almayer, to carry off his daughter. Lingard disappears into Europe, trying to raise financial backing for his expeditions into the interior. Almayer loses his daughter and all his hopes, which are symbolized by his "folly," a large house he had begun building in better days; he finally turns to opium to forget. Dain and Nina gain one another, but Nina, though in love with Dain, admits to her father before she departs, "No two human beings understand each other. They can understand but their own voices."

In addition to introducing the typical Conradian theme of alienation, *Almayer's Folly* also displays several techniques that would become characteristic of Conrad's fiction, including experimentation with narrative flashbacks and flashforwards and with the juxtaposition of points of view. The novel's evocation of place is authentic, as are all its minor characters. The work was well received by critics; an anonymous reviewer for *Bookman* termed it "a remarkable novel where wild nature and strange humanity [are] powerfully portrayed." Conrad's second work, *An Outcast of the Islands* (1896), which recounts how the Arabs traveled up the Pantai and ruined Lingard's monopoly, received even better press than *Almayer's Folly.* Both novels, however, are considered minor works.

After he had finished *An Outcast of the Islands,* Conrad wrote three short stories ("The Idiots," "The Lagoon," "An Outpost of Progress"), and then began *The Nigger of the "Narcissus"* (1898; originally published as *The Children of the Sea,* 1897). Whereas the earlier novels and tales are derivative, solidly in a tradition of what Conrad called in the work's preface stories of the "white man in the tropics," *The Nigger of the "Narcissus"* transcends and transforms the sea tale as told by such nineteenth-century writers as James Fenimore Cooper, Frederick Marryat, Richard Henry Dana, and Herman Melville. Conrad combined his intimate understanding of life at sea with his vision of "the truth of life," which he also explains in the novel's preface. "Truth," he wrote, is "what is enduring and essential," yet it is also an "appeal of one temperament to all the other innumerable temperaments." Both absolute and changing, truth is "the stress and passion within the core of each convincing moment"; it is "the feeling of unavoidable solidarity . . . which binds men to each other and all mankind to the visible world." Thus, in Conrad's view, art is an intimation of solidarity forged despite each person's individual loneliness.

Conrad's notion of loneliness is profoundly expressed in *The Nigger of the "Narcissus."* Ship and sea bind the ship's crew together physically, but each crew member understands only his own voice. The common seamen of the "Narcissus" are for a time bound all the more by the sad, mysterious figure of the black man, James Wait, who "waits" for death and is so frightened of it that he feigns illness. The men take sides with him against the officers when the captain confines Wait to a cabin as punishment for his shamming. This confinement is actually an act of compassion on the captain's part, for he sees that Wait is truly ill. But the order leads to a mutinous moment when the worst of the crew, a scruffy cockney named Donkin, hurls a belaying pin at the captain. The crew is rendered incompetent, divided by its fascination with Wait. Thirty hours of a violent storm restore a sense of solidarity on the ship, but only temporarily. When Wait finally dies, the narrator (an unnamed member of the crew) understands that the bond holding the crew together has been as false as Wait's initial pretense.

Another work based on Conrad's life as a sailor, "Heart of Darkness" (1899 in serial form), is the first of three great works produced by Conrad between 1897 and 1902. The novella is a fictional version of Conrad's Congo experience. An indictment of European imperialism, the work takes much of its descriptive material from a diary Conrad kept during his service in the African interior. The story is told by Marlow, who narrates the events of his journey up the Congo to four companions on a boat on London's Thames River. In the employ of the Belgian government, Marlow is charged with finding and relieving Kurtz, one of Belgium's most profitable ivory traders. Through Marlow's narration, Conrad exposes the brutal exploitation and destruction wreaked by the Belgians on the African country and its people and satirizes such bourgeois European ideals as the work ethic, efficiency, faith, home and family, community, progress, self-restraint, and the processes of law. Small incidents in each stage of Marlow's journey dramatize the corruption of these ideals: a French man-of-war firing into the bush like a toy ship at a continent; black workers left to die in a grove; and an accountant who keeps his books "in apple-pie order" despite the groans of a man dying nearby.

Marlow first learns about Kurtz from several other employees at the central trading station. Kurtz is variously praised as a "first-class agent," a "very remarkable person," and "an emissary of pity, science, progress, and devil knows what else." Marlow overhears the manager describing Kurtz as a Christian soldier who preached that "each station should be like a beacon on the road towards better things, a centre for trade, of course, but also for humanizing, improving, instructing." Marlow consequently fixes his hopes upon Kurtz's fabled integrity, but instead of a beacon, Marlow finds a dying man driven insane by his own greedy and murderous behavior.

"Heart of Darkness" appeared first in book form with two other complementary tales—"Youth," in which Conrad introduces Marlow, and "The End of the Tether." The author once described the three works as tales of youth, middle age, and old age. Neither of the other two stories is as respected as "Heart of Darkness," but both are powerful. "Youth" is centered on a simple but gripping and funny incident taking place on the ship *Judea.* "The End of the Tether," in contrast, is the most pessimistic of Conrad's early works, its protagonist an old, blind captain who commits suicide.

Lord Jim (1900), perhaps Conrad's greatest novel and certainly his best known, is also narrated by Marlow. The first four chapters are told by an anonymous narrator who relates the early life and career of the titular figure. After the initial chapters, the narrative presents Marlow watching the proceedings of a maritime Board of Inquiry, which is probing the conduct of the captain and officers of the *Patna.* Believing the ship to be sinking, the crew had abandoned the ship and left the eight hundred pilgrims on board to drown. Jim is one of the deserters, and Marlow befriends him. Jim, who never admits guilt, appeals deeply to Marlow as the embodiment of hopeful youth. After the court pronounces Jim's guilt, Marlow obtains several jobs for Jim, each

one ending when his involvement in the *Patna* affair is revealed. Finally Marlow seeks the advice of an old trader and explorer, Stein, who gives Jim charge of a remote but prosperous trading post, Patusan.

There Jim rises to a place of honor. The natives call him "Tuan Jim"—Lord Jim. But Jim fails again with the arrival of the renegade, Gentleman Brown. An escaped convict, Brown intends to ravage the village, but he and his men are trapped by the villagers, who have united under Jim's leadership. Brown, however, makes an instinctive and devastating reference to Jim's past, asking him if he agrees that when "it came to saving one's own life in the dark, one didn't care who else went—three, thirty, three hundred people." Jim lets Brown and his men have an open road back to sea, but the white trader whom Jim has supplanted shows Brown how to ambush a contingent of men led by Jim's best friend, Dain Maroola. When his friend is murdered by Brown, Jim presents himself to Dain's father to be shot.

Using chronological juxtapositions, sudden and rapid jumps in time, and incidents placed within incidents, Conrad designed *Lord Jim* to sustain pervasive ironies and ambiguities. Thus the telling of the tale is just as much the subject of *Lord Jim* as are heroism, courage, self-understanding, or the impingement of European ideals upon native peoples. The novel's unresolved ambiguities still fascinate readers.

Typhoon (1902), the last work of Conrad's early period, focuses on the responses of officers to a natural and human crisis. The natural crisis is a typhoon; the human crisis is occasioned by the cargo, a load of coolies returning home with their wages of several years kept in small wooden chests. During the gale, the chests smash and the coolies start a free-for-all. Captain MacWhirr sends in an officer to quell the riot, then devises a way to distribute the cash among the laborers. *Typhoon* is considered Conrad's best piece of direct, idiomatic prose. In contrast to *Lord Jim* and "Heart of Darkness," it has a simple, linear narrative structure, each of its five chapters marking off a distinct segment of the tale.

While Conrad's early work typed him as a writer of the sea, the major works of his middle period—*Nostromo* (1904), *The Secret Agent* (1907), and *Under Western Eyes* (1911)—turn resolutely away from the sea to cities and to the development of political themes that had been implicit but secondary in the early work. Among Conrad scholars, the first two of these novels are rated very highly, and the last also has devoted admirers. But these novels diverged from Conrad's earlier concerns, eliciting criticism from some of his contemporaries. British novelist D. H. Lawrence, for example, thought *Under Western Eyes* incomprehensible and boring, although he liked Conrad's previous works very much. *Nostromo* received negatived reviews, except in American newspapers; fourteen years after its publication, Virginia Woolf, in the *Times Literary Supplement,* called the novel a "rare and magnificent wreck." The judgment would be echoed forty years later by Albert J. Guerard in *Conrad the Novelist;* for him, *Nostromo* was "a great but radically defective novel." Not until the 1960s were *Nostromo, The Secret Agent,* and *Under Western Eyes* accorded the esteem they now have among Conrad scholars. Among critics in general, *The Secret Agent* is greatly admired for the ferocity of its plot and the sustained irony of its tone.

Nostromo is a critique of materialism. Set in Sulaco, a town in the imaginary South American country of Costaguana, the novel illustrates the impact of material interests on individuals and communities. The central characters, Charles Gould and Nostromo, are both aliens in a strange land. Gould is the descendant of two generations of Englishmen settled in Costaguana, Nostromo an Italian sailor come ashore to try his luck. Utilizing new technology, Gould reopens the silver mines that had ruined his father, joining forces with the railway and the steamship company to become the dominant force in the political and economic life of Costaguana. Nostromo rises from laborer to foreman of the dock workers of the steamship company. The central event in the tale is a revolution led by a general of native Indian descent. The courage and resolution of Gould and Nostromo defeat the rebels, but both men's values, critics have argued, have become slightly tainted.

A plot summary of *Nostromo* looks clearer and simpler than it is. It too is rendered subtle by narrative juxtapositions, but those are of less moment than the vivid stories of the novel's secondary characters, who suffer with Gould and Nostromo in Costaguana. Referring to the narrative methods of *Nostromo*, Guerard claims that Conrad's techniques are "an important step in that deformalization of the novel which will attract the twentieth century's greatest talents." Yet at the same time, *Nostromo* seems a nineteenth-century novel, Dickensian in its wealth of character and incident. It looks as much backward to Dickens's *Bleak House* as forward to William Faulkner's *The Sound and the Fury.*

The Secret Agent is a more austere, ironic fiction. Set in London, the novel uses as its central incident the death of an idiot boy named Stevie. Stevie's brother-in-law, Verloc, is a triple agent—working for the police, for the anarchists, and for an unnamed central European power; he uses the code name Agent Delta. As a cover Verloc sells cheap stationery and petty pornography; in this way he has lived for several years, happily married to Stevie's sister, Winnie. But his European paymaster suddenly demands real action from him—a bombing—in order to stir up popular resentment against the anarchists and thus abolish the haven England provides for them. Verloc is outraged at this intrusion into his placid, bourgeois existence, but he has no choice. He obtains the bomb and gives it to Stevie to carry. On the way to the target the boy trips over a root and is blown to bits. When Winnie learns how her brother died, she stabs Verloc, runs off with an anarchist, and commits suicide on the crossing to France.

The final work of Conrad's political phase, *Under Western Eyes,* is set in Russia and Geneva. Protagonist Razumov, a student who is the illegitimate and unacknowledged son of a Russian official, is implicated in an assassination. He turns over one assassin to the authorities and is sent off to Geneva to act as a double agent, since the revolutionaries believe him to have been an accomplice of the real assassin, Victor Haldin. In Geneva he meets Haldin's sister, falls in love with her, confesses his guilt, and, deafened by a revolutionary who is also a double agent, is run over and maimed for life. The tale's narrator is an English professor of languages who lives in Geneva. His sustained incomprehension of events is interpreted as a study of the differences between the traditions of autocracy and democracy.

The work of Conrad's third and last period is much less thematically unified than the work of the earlier phases. Marlow appears again in the 1913 novel *Chance* and tells the tale of Flora DeBarral, daughter of a ruined financier, and her lover, Captain Anthony. *Victory* (1915) relates the story of another pair of lovers, Axel Heyst and Lena. The first novel ends happily for the lovers; the second, set in the East of *Lord Jim,* ends with Lena's death from a gun shot and Heyst's suicide. In 1920, Conrad published a novel that he had begun in 1897 as a sequel to *Almayer's Folly* and *An Outcast of the Islands.* Originally titled "The Rescuer," *The Rescue* portrays Lingard's love for a married woman, Edith

Travers, a love that destroys his plans to help a native friend regain his land.

All of the work in Conrad's third phase looks, in part, to the past. In 1919 Conrad looked back even farther, to his days in Marseilles, for material for *The Arrow of Gold,* in which love is found and lost amid intrigue, duels, and gunrunning. Conrad set his last two novels, *The Rover* (1923) and the incomplete *Suspense* (1925), during the Napoleonic Wars. He had wanted to write an historical novel for many years, a desire that was perhaps an outgrowth of his lifelong preoccupation with the individual's relationship to history. In *The Rover* Conrad creates an optimistic tale, with an elderly seaman as its protagonist.

Although the claim is rarely made that any one of these last works is the equal of *Lord Jim* or *Nostromo,* critical debate about the intrinsic merits of *Chance, Victory,* and *The Rescue* has been intense. Thomas Moser's *Joseph Conrad: Achievement and Decline* focuses the debate about the later works. Moser put the issue in uncompromising terms: for him, the work after "The Secret Sharer" (1912) shows "the degeneration of Conrad's prose style." *Victory* is "utterly inferior" to *Nostromo,* the critic declared. Moser blames the falling off on Conrad's turning to "love stories, the intended meanings of which ran counter to the deepest impulses of his being." "Love"—that is, female sexuality—was for Conrad the "uncongenial subject," Moser contended. John Palmer, however, in *Joseph Conrad's Fiction: A Study in Literary Growth,* argued that Moser and others ignored or misread the subtle and complex ironies in *Chance, Victory,* and *The Rescue.* The later works, for Palmer, must be seen as ironic allegories in which Conrad grows both in thought and in technical virtuosity. But there is, nonetheless, a consensus that Conrad's greatest achievements in fiction came between 1897 and 1907, in such works as *The Nigger of the "Narcissus," * "Heart of Darkness," *Lord Jim,* and *The Secret Agent,* in which he experimented with innovative narrative techniques in order to explore the mysterious, elemental passions of human existence.

MEDIA ADAPTATIONS: Lord Jim was released as a movie starring Peter O'Toole by Columbia in 1965; Conrad's short story "The Secret Sharer" was adapted into a one-act play of the same title by C. R. Wobbe in 1969; the award-winning 1979 United Artists film "Apocalypse Now," starring Marlon Brando and Martin Sheen, is an adaptation of Conrad's "Heart of Darkness."

BIOGRAPHICAL/CRITICAL SOURCES:

BOOKS

Conrad, Joseph, *Almayer's Folly,* Macmillan, 1895.
Conrad, Joseph, *"Heart of Darkness" and "The Secret Sharer," * New American Library, 1950.
Conrad, Joseph, *Last Essays,* Doubleday, 1926.
Conrad, Joseph, *Lord Jim,* Modern Library, 1931.
Conrad, Joseph, *The Nigger of the "Narcissus," * Doubleday, 1938.
Conrad, Joseph, *A Personal Record,* Doubleday, 1925.
Dictionary of Literary Biography, Gale, Volume 10, *Modern British Dramatists, 1940-1945,* Volume 34, *British Novelists, 1890-1920: Traditionalists,* 1985.
Ford, Ford Madox, *Joseph Conrad: A Personal Remembrance,* Little, Brown, 1924.
Gillon, Adam, *Joseph Conrad,* Twayne, 1982.
Guerard, Albert J., *Conrad the Novelist,* Harvard University Press, 1958.
Jean-Aubry, Georges, *Joseph Conrad, Life and Letters,* Heinemann, 1927.

Karl, Frederick R., *Joseph Conrad: The Three Lives,* Farrar, Straus, 1979.

Moser, Thomas C., *Joseph Conrad: Achievement and Decline,* Harvard University Press, 1958.

Murfin, Ross C., editor, *Conrad Revisited: Essays for the Eighties,* University of Alabama Press, 1985.

Najder, Zdzislaw, editor, *Conrad's Polish Background: Letters to and From Polish Friends,* translated by Halina Carroll, Oxford University Press, 1964.

Najder, Zdzislaw, *Joseph Conrad: A Chronicle,* Rutgers University Press, 1983.

Palmer, John, *Joseph Conrad's Fiction: A Study in Literary Growth,* Cornell University Press, 1968.

Sherry, Norman, *Conrad: The Critical Heritage,* Routledge and Kegan Paul, 1973.

Twentieth-Century Literary Criticism, Gale, Volume 1, 1978, Volume 6, 1982, Volume 13, 1984, Volume 25, 1988.

PERIODICALS

Bookman, May, 1896.
New York Times Book Review, January 25, 1987.
Times Literary Supplement, March 15, 1918.

* * *

CONRAN, Shirley (Ida) 1932-

PERSONAL: Born September 21, 1932, in London, England; daughter of W. Thirlby (a pilot) and Ida (Wakelin) Pearce; married Terence Conran (a furniture company president), 1955 (marriage ended, 1962); married John Stephenson; children: Sebastian Orby, Jasper Alexander Thirlby. *Education:* Attended Southern College of Art, Portsmouth, England.

ADDRESSES: Home—502 Le Bahia, 29 Ave. Princess Grace, Monte Carlo, Monaco; 19 Regent's Park Terr., London NW1 7ED, England. *Office*—c/o Coutts Bank, 14 Lombard St., London EC4, England. *Agent*—Morton Janklow Associates, 598 Madison Ave., New York, N.Y. 10022.

CAREER: Conran Fabrics Ltd., London, England, founder, co-owner, and fabric designer, 1957-62; member, selection committee, Design Center, 1961-69; *Daily Mail,* London, began as design consultant and part-time writer, 1969, became full-time design writer; "Life and Style" editor, *Over 21,* 1972-74. Solo exhibition of paintings at Architectural Association; judge for British Council of Industrial Design, 1961-69; judge for Duke of Edinburgh's design-of-the-year award; adviser to British jewelry industry.

WRITINGS:

Superwoman: Everywoman's Book of Household Management, Sidgwick & Jackson, Volume I, 1975, Volume II, 1977, published in the United States in one volume as *Superwoman,* illustrated by Jan Mitchener, Crown, 1978.
Superwoman Yearbook: A Home Notebook, Including the Superwoman Diary for 1977 and Patric Walker's Guide to Your Future in the Stars, Sidgwick & Jackson, 1976.
Superwoman Yearbook: A Home Notebook, Including the Superwoman Diary for 1978 and Patric Walker's Guide to Your Future in the Stars, Sidgwick & Jackson, 1977.
Superwoman Two, Sidgwick & Jackson, 1977, published as *Superwoman in Action,* Penguin, 1979.
(With Elizabeth Sidney) *Futures: How to Survive Life after Thirty,* Sidgwick & Jackson, 1979, revised edition published as *Futurewoman: How to Survive Life,* Penguin, 1981.

Lace: A Novel, Simon & Schuster, 1982.
The Magic Garden, Macdonald, 1983.
Lace II (sequel to *Lace: A Novel*), Penguin, 1985.
The Legend, Simon & Schuster, 1985.
Savages, Simon & Schuster, 1987.

Also author of *Printed Textile Design for Studio Publication,* 1975, and *Forever Superwoman,* Penguin. Past member of editorial staff of *Observer.*

WORK IN PROGRESS: Down with Superwoman!, a sequel to the original.

SIDELIGHTS: Shirley Conran's *Lace,* set in glamorous capitals the world over, "was tailor-made to be a hit, from its conception to its cover—replete with satin sheets, lingerie, champagne glasses and caviar," writes Rudy Maxa in the *Washington Post.* Sold to Simon & Schuster for $750,000 in 1982, *Lace* earned the equivalent in foreign and dramatic rights before the book had even hit the market, notes Maxa. Despite the popular success of this best-selling novel, *Lace* has received mixed reviews from critics, several of whom believe the book is not as good as some of its predecessors in the genre. "The problem with [*Lace*]," suggests Eden Ross Lipson in the *New York Times Book Review,* ". . . is that it should have been terrific. Heaven knows it is cut from Rona Jaffe's plot model and tailored with the ruffles of Judith Krantz. But it is only O.K. junk fiction." According to *Washington Post* critic Jonathan Yardley, "Conran is familiar with the ingredients of the schlock novel of the 1980s and she is not in the least embarrassed about heaving them all into the pot, especially those having to do with sexual versions and perversions." At the same time, Yardley stresses that Conran knows the secret to success in the genre. "As such enterprises go," writes Yardley, "[*Lace*] is a reasonably professional piece of work. By comparison with Susann and Krantz, . . . Conran is a competent writer, even if that is a somewhat limited compliment." And "what matters," Yardley continues, "are the . . . glimpses she provides into the inaccessible, mysterious, hopelessly alluring world of global glamor."

When asked by London *Times* reviewer John Mortimer about the prevalence of sexual scenes in *Lace,* Conran explained: "I wrote them because I wanted to show that D. H. Lawrence got it *wrong,* and Hemingway got it *wrong.* They didn't understand how women feel." Conran further commented to Mortimer that "about 30 per cent of the readers [of *Lace*] may be men who read it to find out about women." *Los Angeles Times Book Review* contributor Kristiana Gregory believes Conran's "viewpoint of female sexuality helps explain her popularity."

Conran told *CA* that she hopes her books improve life for women. Offering advice to other writers, Conran said, "Be truthful to yourself, always plan what you intend to do before you do it, and pick a good editor."

MEDIA ADAPTATIONS: Lace was made into a six-hour miniseries and first broadcast by ABC-TV in 1984; *Lace II* was also made into a miniseries.

AVOCATIONAL INTERESTS: Reading, skiing, long-distance swimming, yoga, collecting houses and antique glass.

BIOGRAPHICAL/CRITICAL SOURCES:

BOOKS

Mortimer, John Clifford, *In Character,* Penguin, 1984.

PERIODICALS

Globe and Mail (Toronto), September 5, 1987.

Los Angeles Times Book Review, March 31, 1985, September 6, 1987.
New York Times Book Review, October 3, 1982.
Times (London), August 22, 1982.
Tribune Books (Chicago), September 6, 1987.
Washington Post, August 4, 1982, September 8, 1982.
Washington Post Book World, September 6, 1987.

* * *

CONROY, Pat 1945-

PERSONAL: Born October 26, 1945, in Atlanta, Ga.; son of Don (a military officer) and Peg (Peek) Conroy; married Barbara Bolling, 1969 (divorced, 1977); married Lenore Gurewitz, March 21, 1981; children: (first marriage) Megan; Jessica, Melissa (stepdaughters); (second marriage) Susannah; Gregory, Emily (stepchildren). *Education:* Citadel, B.A., 1967.

ADDRESSES: Office—1069 Juniper St. N.E., Atlanta, Ga. 30309. *Agent*—Julian Bach Literary Agency, 747 Third Ave., New York, N.Y. 10017.

CAREER: Writer. Worked as schoolteacher in Daufuski, S.C., 1969.

AWARDS, HONORS: Anisfield-Wolf Award, Cleveland Foundation, 1972, for *The Water Is Wide; The Lords of Discipline* was nominated for the Robert Kennedy Book Award, Robert F. Kennedy Memorial, 1981.

WRITINGS:

The Boo, McClure, 1970.
The Water Is Wide, Houghton, 1972.
The Great Santini, Houghton, 1976.
The Lords of Discipline, Houghton, 1980.
The Prince of Tides, Houghton, 1986.

MEDIA ADAPTATIONS: The film "Conrack," based on *The Water Is Wide,* was produced by Twentieth-Century Fox in 1974; the musical "Conrack" was adapted for the stage by Granville Burgess, and was first produced Off-Off Broadway at AMAS Repertory Theater, November, 1987; "The Great Santini" was produced by Warner Brothers in 1979; "The Lords of Discipline" was produced by Paramount in 1983.

SIDELIGHTS: Best-selling novelist Pat Conroy has worked some of his bitterest experiences into stories that present ironic, often jarring, yet humorous views of life and relationships in the contemporary South. Garry Abrams in the *Los Angeles Times* reports that "Misfortune has been good to novelist Pat Conroy. It gave him a family of disciplinarians, misfits, eccentrics, liars and loudmouths. It gave him a Southern childhood in which the bizarre competed with the merely strange. It gave him a military school education apparently imported from Sparta by way of Prussia. It gave him a divorce and a breakdown followed by intensive therapy. It gave him everything he needed to write best sellers, make millions and live in Rome." Brigitte Weeks touches on Conroy's appeal in the *Washington Post.* "With his feet set firmly on his native earth, Conroy is, above all, a storyteller. His tales are full of the exaggeration and wild humor of stories told around a camp fire."

While his most recent works are fictional, critics frequently consider Conroy's novels autobiographical. Conroy's father was a Marine Corps pilot from Chicago who believed in strong discipline; his mother was an outwardly yielding Southerner who actually ran the household. "When he [Conroy's father] returned home from work my sister would yell, 'Godzilla's home' and the

seven children would melt into whatever house we happened to be living in at the time. He was no match for my mother's byzantine and remarkable powers of intrigue. Neither were her children. It took me 30 years to realize that I had grown up in my mother's house and not my father's," Conroy is quoted in the *Book-of-the-Month Club News.* Still, critics frequently mention the ambivalent father-son relationships that appear in his novels. Gail Godwin in the *New York Times Book Review* describes Conroy's work: "The Southern-boy protagonists of Pat Conroy's fiction have twin obsessions—oppressive fathers or father figures, and the South. Against both they fight furiously for selfhood and independence, yet they never manage to secede from their seductive entrappers. Some fatal combination of nostalgia and loyalty holds them back; they remain ambivalent sons of their families and their region, alternately railing against, then shamelessly romanticizing, the myths and strictures that imprison them."

Conroy's first work to receive national attention was openly autobiographical. After graduation, Conroy taught English in public high schools, but unsatisfied, he looked for a new challenge. When a desired position in the Peace Corps did not surface, he took a job teaching nearly illiterate black children on Daufuskie Island, a small, isolated area off the South Carolina coast. But he was not prepared for his new students. They did not know the name of their country, that they lived on the Atlantic Ocean, or that the world was round. On the other hand, Conroy found his pupils expected him to know how to set a trap, skin a muskrat, and plant okra. Conroy came to enjoy his unusual class, but eventually his unorthodox teaching methods and disregard for the authorities turned numerous school officials against him and cost him his job. As a way of coping with his fury at the dismissal, Conroy wrote *The Water Is Wide,* an account of his experiences. As he told Ted Mahar for the *Oregonian,* "When you get fired like that, you have to do something. I couldn't get a job with the charges the school board leveled against me." The process of writing did more than cool him down however; he also gained a new perspective on his reasons for choosing Daufuskie (Yamacraw Island in the book) and on his own responses to racism. Anatole Broyard describes Conroy in the *New York Times Book Review* as "a former redneck and self-proclaimed racist, [who] brought to Yamacraw the supererogatory fervor of the recently converted." In *The Water Is Wide,* Conroy agrees: "At this time of my life a black man could probably have handed me a bucket of cow p—, commanded me to drink it in order that I might rid my soul of the stench of racism, and I would only have asked for a straw. . . . It dawned on me that I came to Yamacraw for a fallacious reason: I needed to be cleansed, born again, resurrected by good works and suffering, purified of the dark cankers that grew like toadstools in my past."

After the successful publication of *The Water is Wide,* Conroy began writing full-time. Although his following book, *The Great Santini,* was a novel, many critics think it represents his adolescence. An article in the *Virginia Quarterly Review* states that "The dialogue, anecdotes, and family atmosphere are pure Marine and probably autobiographical." Conroy did draw heavily on his family background to write the story of a tough Marine, Bull Meecham, his long-suffering wife, Lillian, and the eldest son Ben, who is striving for independence outside his father's control. Robert E. Burkholder writes in *Critique: Studies in Modern Fiction,* that *The Great Santini* "is a curious blend of lurid reality and fantastic comedy, which deals with approximately one year in the life of Ben Meecham and his family. It is primarily a novel of initiation, but central to the concept of Ben's initiation into manhood and to the meaning of the whole novel is the idea that individual myths must be stripped away from Ben and the other major characters before Ben can approach reality with objectivity and maturity." Part of Ben's growing up involves rejecting the image of his father's infallibility. In one scene, Ben finally beats his father at a game of basketball. As the game ends, he tells him: "Do you know, Dad, that not one of us here has ever beaten you in a single game? Not checkers, not dominoes, not softball, nothing."

According to Robert M. Willingham in the *Dictionary of Literary Biography,* after his defeat, "Bull does not outwardly change. He still blusters, curses, flashes toughness and resoluteness, but his family has become more to him than before. When Colonel Meecham's plane crashes and he is killed, one learns that the crash was unavoidable, but Bull's death was not: 'Am commencing starbord turn to avoid populated area. Will attempt to punch out when wings are level. Wish me luck. Over.' The priority was to avoid populated areas, 'where people lived and slept, where families slept. Families like my family, wives like my wife, sons like my sons, daughters like my daughters.' He never punched out."

Bull Meecham is modeled on Conroy's father, Colonel Donald Conroy, who "would make John Wayne look like a pansy," as Conroy told Bill McDonald for the South Carolina *State.* Conroy reports that his father initially disliked *The Great Santini.* The author said to *Chicago Tribune* contributor Peer Gorner that "Dad could only read the book halfway through before throwing it across the room. Then people started telling him he actually was lovable. Now, he signs Christmas cards 'The Great Santini,' and goes around talking about childrearing and how we need to have more discipline in the home—a sort of Nazi Dr. Spock." The movie created from the novel helped to change the Colonel's attitude. "The Great Santini" starred Robert Duvall, and the Colonel liked the way "his" character came across. In a *Washington Post* interview, Conroy related an incident of one-upmanship that seems borrowed from the book. "He (the Colonel) came to the opening of 'The Great Santini' movie here in Washington. I introduced the film to the audience, and in the course of my remarks I pointed out why he had chosen the military as a career. It was, of course, something that occurred to him on the day when he discovered that his body temperature and his IQ were the same number. Then, when it was his turn to talk, all he said was, 'I want to say that my body temperature has always been 160 degrees.' People laughed harder. So you see, I still can't beat him." Conroy's father, however, says it is important to remember that *The Great Santini* is fiction. Willingham adds, "Colonel Conroy offers these comments: 'Pat embellished everything. Where's the truth in all these incidents? There is a moment of truth. Where it is, I suspect only Pat and I recognize.' "

Another period of Conroy's life appeared in his next book, *The Lords of Discipline.* According to his father's wishes, Conroy attended the Citadel, South Carolina's venerable military academy. "Quirky, eccentric, and unforgettable," Conroy describes the academy in the preface to *The Boo,* his first book, which gave a nostalgic look at the Citadel and its Commander of Cadets during the 1960s. But Willingham describes the Citadel in another way: "It is also an anachronism of the 1960s with a general disregard for the existence of the outside world." *The Lords of Discipline* paints an even bleaker picture of its fictionalized institution, the Carolina Military Institute. This school, says Frank Rose in the *Washington Post Book World,* "combines some of the more quaint and murderous aspects of the Citadel, West Point, and Virginia Military Institute."

The Lords of Discipline concerns Will, the narrator, and his three roommates. Will is a senior cadet assigned to watch over the Institute's first black student. The novel's tension lies in the conflict between group loyalty and personal responsibility. Will eventually discovers the Ten, "a secret mafia whose existence has long been rumored but never proven, a silent and malevolent force dedicated . . . to maintain the purity of the Institute—racial purity included," comments Rose. He continues, "What Conroy has achieved is twofold; his book is at once a suspense-ridden duel between conflicting ideals of manhood and a paean to brother love that ends in betrayal and death. Out of the shards of broken friendship a blunted triumph emerges, and it is here, when the duel is won, that the reader finally comprehends the terrible price that any form of manhood can exact."

According to its author, *The Lords of Discipline* describes the love between men. "I wrote it because I wanted to tell about how little women understand about men," he said in a *Washington Post* article. "The one cultural fact of life about military schools is that they are men living with men. And they love each other. The love between these men is shown only in obscure ways, which have to be learned by them. The four roommates who go through this book are very different from each other, but they have a powerful code. They have ways to prove their love to each other, and they're part of the rites of passage." And contradicting an old myth, Conroy adds, "There is no homosexuality under these conditions. If you smile, they'll kill you. You can imagine what would happen to a homosexual."

While *The Lords of Discipline* portrays deep friendships, it also contains a theme common to many of Conroy's books: the coexistence of love and brutality. "This book . . . makes 'The Lord of the Flies' sound like 'The Sound of Music,' " writes Christian Williams in the *Washington Post.* A *Chicago Tribune Book World* reviewer warns, "Conroy's chilling depictions of hazing are for strong stomachs only." And George Cohen in a later Chicago *Tribune Books* article describes the novel's pull for readers: "It is our attraction to violence—observed from the safest of places—together with our admiration for the rebel who beats the system, and Conroy's imposing ability as a storyteller that make the novel engrossing."

Conroy's wildest tale is *The Prince of Tides,* which follows Tom Wingo, an unemployed high school English teacher and football coach on a journey from coastal South Carolina to New York City to help his twin sister Savannah. Savannah, a well-known poet, is recovering from a nervous breakdown and suicide attempt. In an attempt to help Savannah's psychiatrist understand her patient, Tom relates the Wingo family's bizarre history. Despite the horrors the Wingos have suffered, including several rapes and the death of their brother, a sense of optimism prevails. Writes Judy Bass in Chicago *Tribune Books,* "Pat Conroy has fashioned a brilliant novel that ultimately affirms life, hope and the belief that one's future need not be contaminated by a monstrous past. In addition, Conroy . . . deals with the most prostrating crises in human experience—death of a loved one, parental brutality, injustice, insanity—without lapsing into pedantry or oppressive gloom."

The Price of Tide's style drew more attention than that of Conroy's other books. Some critics felt the novel was overblown: Richard Eder in the *Los Angeles Times Book Review* claims that "Inflation is the order of the day. The characters do too much, feel too much, suffer too much, eat too much, signify too much, and above all, talk too much. And, as with the classical American tomato, quantity is at the expense of quality." Godwin says that while "the ambition, invention and sheer irony in this book are admirable . . . many readers will be put off by the turgid, high-flown rhetoric that the author must have decided would best match his grandiose designs. And as the bizarre, hyperbolic episodes of Wingo family life mount up, other readers are likely to feel they are being bombarded by whoppers told by an over-wrought boy eager to impress or shock." But more critics have appreciated what *Detroit News* contributor Ruth Pollack Coughlin calls "spectacular, lyrical prose with a bitter sense of humor." The novel is long, says Weeks, "monstrously long, yet a pleasure to read, flawed yet stuffed to the endpapers with lyricism, melodrama, anguish and plain old suspense. Given all that, one can brush aside its lapses like troublesome flies."

Conroy's family judged the novel more harshly than did the reviewers. Although his mother is the inspiration for shrimper's wife Lila Wingo, she died before he finished the novel and never saw it. Conroy's sister, who did see the book, was offended. As Conroy told Rick Groen for the Toronto *Globe and Mail,* "Yes, my sister is also a poet in New York who has also had serious breakdowns. We were very close, but she has not spoken to me . . . since the book. I'm saddened, but when you write autobiography, this is one of the consequences. They're allowed to be mad at you. They have the right." This, however, was not the first time a family member reacted negatively to one of Conroy's books. *The Great Santini* infuriated his Chicago relatives: "My grandmother and grandfather told me they never wanted to see me or my children again," Conroy told Sam Staggs for *Publishers Weekly.* Conroy's Southern relatives have also responded to the sex scenes and "immodest" language in his books. Staggs relates, "After *The Lords of Discipline* was published, Conroy's Aunt Helen telephoned him and said, 'Pat, I hope someday you'll write a book a Christian can read.' 'How far did you get?' her nephew asked. 'Page four, and I declare, I've never been so embarrassed.' "

But Hollywood has given Conroy's novels a warm reception. *The Great Santini* wasn't his only book to become a movie. *The Water Is Wide* was made into "Conrack," starring Jon Voight, and later became a musical also entitled "Conrack." *The Lords of Discipline* kept the same title as a film and featured David Keith. Conroy himself wrote a screenplay for *The Prince of Tides,* learning a lesson about Hollywood in the process. When producers offered him $100,000 to write the screenplay, he took it happily. They liked his work, but then decided to send it to an experienced Hollywood rewrite man who received $500,000 for the job.

When Staggs asked why Conroy's books "make such entertaining movies," the author replied, "I always figure it's because I'm incredibly shallow. I write a straight story line, and I guess that's what they need. The dialogue also seems to be serviceable in a Hollywood way. But most important, I do the thing that Southerners do naturally—I tell stories. I always try to make sure there's a good story going on in my books." Conroy further explained his method of writing to Gorner: "When I'm writing, I have no idea where I'm going. People get married, and I didn't realize they were engaged. People die in these novels and I'm surprised. They take on this little subterranean life of their own. They reveal secrets to me even as I'm doing it. Maybe this is a dangerous way to work, but for me it becomes the pleasure of writing. . . . Critics call me a popular novelist, but writing popular novels isn't what urges me on. If I could write like Faulkner or Thomas Wolfe, I surely would. I'd much rather write like them than like me. Each book has been more ambitious. I'm trying to be more courageous."

BIOGRAPHICAL/CRITICAL SOURCES:

BOOKS

Authors in the News, Volume I, Gale, 1976.
Contemporary Literary Criticism, Volume XXX, Gale, 1984.
Dictionary of Literary Biography, Volume VI: *American Novelists since World War II, Second Series,* Gale, 1980.

PERIODICALS

Book-of-the-Month Club News, December, 1986.
Chicago Tribune, November 25, 1986.
Chicago Tribune Book World, October 19, 1980, September 14, 1986, October 19, 1986.
Cincinnati Enquirer, March 25, 1974.
Critique: Studies in Modern Fiction, Vol. XXI, no. 1, 1979.
Detroit News, October 12, 1986, December 20, 1987.
Globe and Mail (Toronto), February 28, 1987, November 28, 1987.
Los Angeles Times, February 19, 1983, October 12, 1986, October 19, 1986, December 12, 1986.
Los Angeles Times Book Review, October 19, 1986.
New York Times, January 10, 1987.
New York Times Book Review, July 13, 1972, September 24, 1972, December 7, 1980, October 12, 1986.
Oregonian, April 28, 1974.
Publishers Weekly, May 15, 1972, September 5, 1986.
State (Columbia, South Carolina), March 31, 1974.
Time, October 13, 1986.
Tribune Books (Chicago), September 14, 1986, October 19, 1986.
Virginia Quarterly Review, autumn, 1976.
Washington Post, October 23, 1980.
Washington Post Book World, October 19, 1980, October 12, 1986.

*   *   *

CONYBEARE, Charles Augustus
   See ELIOT, T(homas) S(tearns)

*   *   *

COOK, Roy
   See SILVERBERG, Robert

*   *   *

COOKE, John Estes
   See BAUM, L(yman) Frank

*   *   *

COOKE, M. E.
   See CREASEY, John

*   *   *

COOKE, Margaret
   See CREASEY, John

*   *   *

COOKSON, Catherine (McMullen) 1906-
   (Catherine Marchant)

PERSONAL: Born June 20, 1906, in Tyne Dock, South Shields, England; mother's name, Catherine Fawcett; married Thomas H. Cookson (a schoolmaster), June 1, 1940.

ADDRESSES: Home—Bristol Lodge, Langley on Tyne, Northumberland, England. *Agent*—Anthony Sheil Associates Ltd., 43 Doughty St., London WC1N 2LF, England.

CAREER: Writer. Lecturer for women's groups and other organizations.

MEMBER: Society of Authors, PEN (England), Authors Guild (U.S.A.), Authors League of America, Women's Press Club (London).

AWARDS, HONORS: Winifred Holtby Award for best regional novel from Royal Society of Literature, 1968, for *The Round Tower;* Order of the British Empire, 1985; recipient of Freedom of the County Borough of South Shields in recognition of her services to the city.

WRITINGS:

Kate Hannigan, Macdonald & Co., 1950, reprinted, Macdonald & Jane's, 1979.

Fifteen Streets (also see below), Macdonald & Co., 1952, reprinted, Corgi Books, 1979.

Colour Blind, Macdonald & Co., 1953, reprinted, Macdonald & Jane's, 1975, published as *Color Blind,* New American Library, 1977.

Maggie Rowan, Macdonald & Co., 1954, New American Library, 1975.

Rooney, Macdonald & Co., 1957, reprinted, Macdonald & Jane's, 1974.

The Menagerie, Macdonald & Co., 1958, reprinted, Macdonald & Janc's, 1974.

Slinky Jane, Macdonald & Co., 1959, reprinted, Macdonald & Jane's, 1979.

Fenwick Houses, Macdonald & Co., 1960, reprinted, Macdonald & Jane's, 1979.

The Garment, Macdonald & Co., 1962, New American Library, 1974.

The Blind Miller (also see below), Macdonald & Co., 1963, reprinted, Heinemann, 1979.

Hannah Massey, Macdonald & Co., 1964, New American Library, 1973.

The Long Corridor, Macdonald & Co., 1965, New American Library, 1976.

The Unbaited Trap, Macdonald & Co., 1966, New American Library, 1974.

Katie Mulholland, Macdonald & Co., 1967, reprinted, Macdonald & Jane's, 1980.

The Round Tower (also see below), Macdonald & Co., 1968, New American Library, 1975.

The Nice Bloke, Macdonald & Co., 1969, published as *The Husband,* New American Library, 1976.

Our Kate: An Autobiography, Macdonald & Co., 1969, Bobbs-Merrill, 1971, published as *Our Kate: Catherine Cookson—Her Personal Story,* Macdonald & Jane's, 1974.

The Glass Virgin, Macdonald & Co., 1970, Bantam, 1981.

The Invitation, Macdonald & Co., 1970, New American Library, 1974.

The Dwelling Place, Macdonald & Jane's, 1971.

Fanny McBride, Corgi Books, 1971, reprinted, Macdonald & Jane's, 1980.

Feathers in the Fire (also see below), Macdonald & Co., 1971, Bobbs-Merrill, 1972.

Pure as the Lily, Macdonald & Co., 1972, Bobbs-Merrill, 1973.

The Invisible Cord (also see below), Dutton, 1975.

The Gambling Man (also see below), Morrow, 1975.

The Tide of Life, Morrow, 1976.

The Girl (also see below), Morrow, 1977.

The Cinder Path (also see below), Morrow, 1978.

Tilly Trotter, Heinemann, 1978, published as *Tilly,* Morrow, 1980.

Selected Works, Heinemann/Octopus, Volume 1 (contains *Fifteen Streets, The Blind Miller, The Round Tower, Feathers in the Fire,* and *A Grand Man* [also see below]), 1978, Volume 2 (contains *The Mallen Streak* [also see below], *The Invisible Cord, The Gambling Man, The Girl,* and *The Cinder Path*), 1980.

The Man Who Cried, Morrow, 1979.

Tilly Wed, Morrow, 1981 (published in England as *Tilly Trotter Wed,* Heinemann, 1981).

Tilly Alone, Morrow, 1982 (published in England as *Tilly Widowed,* Heinemann, 1982).

The Whip, Summit Books, 1982.

Hamilton (comic), Heinemann, 1983.

The Black Velvet Gown, Summit Books, 1984.

Goodbye Hamilton, Heinemann, 1984.

The Bannaman Legacy, Summit Books, 1985 (published in England as *A Dinner of Herbs,* Heinemann, 1985).

Harold, Heinemann, 1985.

The Moth, Summit Books, 1986.

Bill Bailey, Heinemann, 1986.

Catherine Cookson Country, Heinemann, 1986.

The Parson's Daughter, Summit Books, 1987.

The Harrogate Secret, Summit Books, 1988.

Bailey Chronicles, Summit Books, 1989.

Spaniard's Gift, Summit Books, 1989.

Thornman Inheritance, Summit Books, 1989.

"MARY ANN" SERIES

A Grand Man, Macdonald & Co., 1954, Macmillan, 1955, reprinted, Morrow, 1975.

The Lord and Mary Ann, Macdonald & Co., 1956, reprinted, Macdonald & Jane's, 1974, Morrow, 1975.

The Devil and Mary Ann, Macdonald & Co., 1958, Morrow, 1976.

Love and Mary Ann, Macdonald & Co., 1961, Morrow, 1976.

Life and Mary Ann, Macdonald & Co., 1962, Morrow, 1977.

Marriage and Mary Ann, Macdonald & Co., 1964, Morrow, 1978.

Mary Ann's Angels, Macdonald & Co., 1965, Morrow, 1978.

Mary Ann and Bill, Macdonald & Co., 1966, Morrow, 1979.

Mary Ann Omnibus (contains all novels in "Mary Ann" series), Macdonald & Jane's, 1981.

"MALLEN NOVELS" TRILOGY

The Mallen Streak (also see below), Heinemann, 1973.

The Mallen Girl (also see below), Heinemann, 1974.

The Mallen Lot, Dutton, 1974 (published in England as *The Mallen Litter* [also see below], Heinemann, 1974).

The Mallen Novels (contains *The Mallen Streak, The Mallen Girl,* and *The Mallen Litter*), Heinemann, 1979.

JUVENILE NOVELS

Matty Doolin, Macdonald & Co., 1965, New American Library, 1976.

Joe and the Gladiator, Macdonald & Co., 1968.

The Nipper, Bobbs-Merrill, 1970.

Blue Baccy, Macdonald & Jane's, 1972, Bobbs-Merrill, 1973.

Our John Willie, Morrow, 1974.

Mrs. Flanagan's Trumpet, Macdonald & Jane's, 1977, Lothrop, 1980.

Go Tell It to Mrs. Golightly, Macdonald & Jane's, 1977, Lothrop, 1980.

Lanky Jones, Lothrop, 1981.

UNDER PSEUDONYM CATHERINE MARCHANT

Heritage of Folly, Macdonald & Co., 1963, reprinted, Macdonald & Jane's, 1980.
The Fen Tiger, Macdonald & Co., 1963, Morrow, 1979.
House of Men, Macdonald & Co., 1964, Macdonald & Jane's, 1980.
Evil at Roger's Cross, Lancer Books, 1965, revised edition published as *The Iron Facade,* Heinemann, 1976, Morrow, 1980.
Miss Martha Mary Crawford, Heinemann, 1975, Morrow, 1976.
The Slow Awakening, Heinemann, 1976, Morrow, 1977.

SIDELIGHTS: Catherine Cookson is a prolific British author with a large following. Her family sagas, for which she is most noted, are read in some thirty countries, and in the early 1980s she was commemorated by Corgi Books for exceeding the 27 million mark in paperback sales alone. According to Anne Duchene in the *Times Literary Supplement,* "these days there are never fewer than fifty Cookson titles in print in English at any time; they are translated into fifteen languages; and new books are still readily produced." In a London *Times* interview with Caroline Moorehead, Cookson emphasizes that she never has trouble coming up with ideas for her historical novels: "I've always been a jabberer. I just talked. I see everything in images. The plot sort of unfolds. Even the dialogue. In the morning, it's all there to put down." The fact that readers easily identify with Cookson's characters is part of the reason her works have sold so well. As Duchene observes: "[Cookson] writes stories in which her readers can gratefully recognize experiences and emotions of their own—heightened, to be sure, by greater comedy or greater violence than their own lives normally vouchsafe, but based on all their own affections, furies, aspirations and reactions."

BIOGRAPHICAL/CRITICAL SOURCES:

BOOKS

Cookson, Catherine, *Our Kate: An Autobiography,* Macdonald & Co., 1969, Bobbs-Merrill, 1971, published as *Our Kate: Catherine Cookson—Her Personal Story,* Macdonald & Jane's, 1974.

PERIODICALS

Catholic World, June, 1955.
New York Times, January 7, 1955.
New York Times Book Review, October 20, 1974.
Times (London), August 15, 1983.
Times Literary Supplement, January 7, 1955, June 19, 1969, July 24, 1981.

*   *   *

COOPER, Henry St. John
See CREASEY, John

*   *   *

COOVER, Robert (Lowell) 1932-

PERSONAL: Born February 4, 1932, in Charles City, Iowa; son of Grant Marion and Maxine (Sweet) Coover; married Maria del Pilar Sans-Mallafre, June 3, 1959; children: Diana Nin, Sara Chapin, Roderick Luis. *Education:* Attended Southern Illinois University at Carbondale, 1949-51; Indiana University at Bloomington, B.A. 1953; University of Chicago, M.A., 1965.

ADDRESSES: Home—Providence, R.I. *Agent*—Georges Borchardt, Inc., 136 East 57th St., New York, N.Y. 10022.

CAREER: Writer of fiction and poetry. Instructor, Bard College, Annandale-on-Hudson, N.Y., 1966-67, University of Iowa, Iowa City, 1967-69, Princeton University, Princeton, N.J., 1972-73, Columbia University, New York, N.Y., 1972, Virginia Military Institute, Lexington, 1976, Brandeis University, Waltham, Mass., 1981, and Brown University, Providence, R.I., 1981—. Organized conference on literature, "Unspeakable Practices: A Three-Day Celebration of Iconoclastic American Fiction," Brown University, 1988. Producer and director of film "On a Confrontation in Iowa City," 1969. *Military service:* U.S. Naval Reserve, 1953-57; became lieutenant.

MEMBER: American Academy of Arts and Letters (1987—).

AWARDS, HONORS: William Faulkner Award for best first novel, 1966, for *The Origin of the Brunists;* Rockefeller Foundation grant, 1969; Guggenheim fellowships, 1971 and 1974; citation in fiction from Brandeis University, 1971; Academy of Arts and Letters award, 1975; National Book Award nomination, 1977, for *The Public Burning;* National Endowment for the Humanities Award, 1985; Rea Award (short story), Dungannon Foundation, 1987, for *A Night at the Movies.*

WRITINGS:

The Origin of the Brunists (novel; also see below), Putnam, 1966.
The Universal Baseball Association, Inc., J. Henry Waugh, Prop. (novel), Random House, 1968.
Pricksongs & Descants (collected short fiction), Dutton, 1969.
(Editor with Kent Dixon) *The Stone Wall Book of Short Fiction,* Stone Wall Press, 1973.
(Editor, with Elliott Anderson) *Minute Stories,* Braziller, 1976.
The Public Burning (novel), Viking, 1977.
The Hair O' the Chine, Bruccoli-Clark, 1979.
A Political Fable, Viking, 1980.
After Lazarus: A Filmscript, Bruccoli-Clark, 1980.
Charlie in the House of Rue, Penmaen, 1980.
The Convention, Lord John, 1981.
Spanking the Maid, Grove, 1982.
In Bed One Night and Other Brief Encounters, Burning Deck, 1983.
Gerald's Party: A Novel, Simon & Schuster, 1985.
(With Brian Swann) *The Plot of the Mice and Other Stories, Including Aesop's Forest,* Capra Press, 1986.
A Night at the Movies or You Must Remember This (short stories), Simon & Schuster, 1987.
Whatever Happened to Gloomy Gus of the Chicago Bears?, Linden Press, 1987.

PLAYS

A Theological Position (contains "A Theological Position" and "Rip Awake" [both produced in Los Angeles, Calif., 1975], "The Kid," [produced Off-Broadway, American Place Theatre, November 17, 1972], "Love Scene," [produced in Paris as "Scene d'amour," 1973, produced in New York City, 1974]), Dutton, 1972.

Work represented in many anthologies, including *New American Review 4,* New American Library, 1968, *New American Review 14,* Simon & Schuster, 1972, and *American Review,* Bantam, 1974. Contributor of short stories, poems, essays, and translations to numerous periodicals, including *Evergreen Review, Cavalier, Esquire, Tri-Quarterly, Harper's, Antioch Review, Quar-*

terly Review of Literature, Playboy, and *Fiddlehead.* Fiction editor, *Iowa Review,* 1974-77.

WORK IN PROGRESS: "Several narratives, short and long, in various media."

SIDELIGHTS: Robert Coover's work has generated much attention, especially among college audiences and critics, who contend that Coover, by mixing the actual with illusion, creates another, alternative world. Amazing, fantastic, and magic are among the words used to describe the effect of his fiction. *Time*'s Paul Gray notes that Coover has won a "reputation as an avant-gardist who can do with reality what a magician does with a pack of cards: Shuffle the familiar into unexpected patterns." Coover begins his novels with ordinary subjects and events, then introduces elements of fantasy and fear which, left unhindered, grow to equal, if not surpass, what is real within the situation. Michael Mason of the *Times Literary Supplement* believes that Coover structures his novels around the idea of "an American superstition giving rise to its appropriate imaginary apocalypse."

The Origin of the Brunists, Coover's first and most conventional novel, chronicles the rise and fall of a fictitious religious cult. This cult arises when the sole survivor of a mining disaster, Giovanni Bruno, claims to have been visited by the Virgin Mary and rescued via divine intervention. As the cult grows in numbers and hysteria, it is exploited and inflamed by the local newspaper editor until the situation reaches what Philip Callow of *Books and Bookmen* terms "apocalyptic proportions." Although some critics, such as Callow, find the novel's conclusion disappointing and anticlimactic, others, such as the *New Statesman*'s Miles Burrows, describe the book as being "a major work in the sense that it is long, dense, and alive to a degree that makes life outside the covers almost pallid."

In a *New Republic* review of Coover's second novel, *The Universal Baseball Association, Inc.,* Richard Gilman writes, "What this novel summons to action is our sense . . . of the possible substitution of one world for another, of the way reality implies alternatives." The book's protagonist, Henry Waugh, is bored with his job and his life. To alleviate his boredom, Waugh creates, within his imagination, an entire baseball league, complete with statistics and team and player names and histories. Plays, players, and fates are determined by dice, and Waugh, according to Gilman, presides "over this world of chance with a creator's calm dignity." When the dice rule that a favored player must die during a game, both Waugh's imaginary and real worlds fall apart. Waugh could, of course, choose to ignore the dice's decision, but to do so would be in violation of "the necessary laws that hold the cosmos together," a *Time* reviewer explains. At the novel's end, Waugh disappears from the story, leaving his players to fashion their own existence, myths, and rituals. The *National Observer*'s Clifford A. Ridley comments: "[This] is a novel about continuity, about order, about reason, about God, and about the relationships between them. Which is to say that it is a parable of human existence, but do not feel put off by that; for it is a parable couched in such head-long, original prose and set down in a microcosmos of such consistent fascination that it is far too busy entertaining to stop and instruct." Red Smith, however, disagrees. In a *Book World* review, Smith remarks: "A little fantasy goes a long way, though, and after an imaginary beanball kills an imaginary player the author never finds the strike zone again. It all becomes a smothering bore." Ronald Sukenick of the *New York Review* shares Smith's assessment of the novel's second-half: "Baseball has already been made to carry a heavy cargo in this book but now it gets heavier. With the plausibility of the actual game lost, the philosophical freight

begins to take over. Mythy echoes and allusions fall thick as snow."

Pricksongs & Descants, Coover's collection of short fiction pieces, has been widely praised. Coover's experimental forms and techniques produce "extreme verbal magic," according to Christopher Lehmann-Haupt of the *New York Times.* "Nothing in Mr. Coover's writing is quite what it seems to be," the critic continues. "In the pattern of the leaves there is always the smile of the Cheshire Cat." And Marni Jackson in *Critique* explains: "An innocent situation develops a dozen sinister possibilities, sprouting in the readers imagination while they are suspended, open-ended, on the page. . . . Every disturbing twist the story might take is explored; all of them could have happened, or none. . . . Like a good conjurer, even when you recognize his gimmicks, the illusion continues to work."

Reaction to *The Public Burning,* Coover's "factional" account of the conviction and execution in 1953 of alleged spies Julius and Ethel Rosenberg, has been mixed. A satire on the mood and mentality of the nation at the time of the execution, the novel loosely combines fact and fiction. Coover sets the site of the Rosenbergs' electrocutions in Times Square, adds surrealistic parodies of various personalities and events of the era, and provides then Vice-President Richard Nixon as the narrator-commentator. Most critics admire Coover's effort but criticize the book for being excessive and undisciplined. Piers Brendon of *Books and Bookmen* describes the novel as a "literary photomontage" and "a paean of American self-hatred, a torrid indictment of the morally bankrupt society where for so long Nixon was the one." Lehmann-Haupt, in a later *New York Times* review, states that he was "shocked and amazed" by the book; he explains: "*The Public Burning* is an astonishing spectacle. It does not invite us to participate. . . . It merely allows us to watch, somewhat warily, as its author performs."

In the *New York Times Book Review,* Thomas R. Edwards notes that "horror and anger are the governing feelings in *The Public Burning.*" He comments: "As a work of literary art, *The Public Burning* suffers from excess. . . . But all vigorous satire is simplistic and excessive, and this book is an extraordinary act of moral passion." Brendon was similarly impressed by the novel's scope and also aware of its ultimate shortcomings: "*The Public Burning* is an ambitious failure. It is a huge, sprawling, brilliant, original exercise in literary photo-montage. It combines fact and fiction, comedy and terror, surrealism and satire, travesty and tragedy. [But it] is too overblown, too undisciplined, too crude, too lurid."

Overall, most critics agree that Coover is among the more notable new writers of the past two decades. Noting Coover's experimental approach to fictional forms and his originality and versatility as a prose stylist, they frequently compare his work to that of John Barth's, Donald Barthelme's, and Thomas Pynchon's. In his review of *Pricksongs & Descants,* Lehmann-Haupt calls Coover "among the best we now have writing." And Joyce Carol Oates comments in the *Southern Review:* "Coover . . . exists blatantly and brilliantly in his fiction as an authorial consciousness. . . . He will remind readers of William Gass, of John Barth, of Samuel Beckett. He is as surprising as any of these writers, and as funny as Donald Barthelme; both crude and intellectual, predictable and alarming, he gives the impression of thoroughly enjoying his craft."

MEDIA ADAPTATIONS: Film rights to "The Baby Sitter," a story from *Pricksongs & Descants,* have been sold.

BIOGRAPHICAL/CRITICAL SOURCES:

BOOKS

Anderson, R., *Robert Coover,* Twayne, 1981.
Contemporary Literary Criticism, Gale, Volume 3, 1975, Volume 7, 1977, Volume 15, 1980, Volume 32, 1985, Volume 46, 1988.
Dictionary of Literary Biography, Volume 2: *American Novelists since World War II,* Gale, 1978.
Dictionary of Literary Biography Yearbook, 1981, Gale, 1982.
Gass, William, *Fiction and the Figures of Life,* Knopf, 1971.
Gordon, L. G., *Robert Coover,* Southern Illinois University Press, 1983.
McCaffery, L., *The Metafictional Muse,* University of Pittsburgh Press, 1982.
McKeon, Z. Karl, *Novels and Arguments,* University of Chicago, 1982.
Schulz, Max, *Black Humor Fiction of the 1960s,* Ohio University Press, 1973.

PERIODICALS

Atlantic, November, 1977.
Atlantic Journal & Constitution, March 1, 1987.
Books and Bookmen, May, 1967, August, 1978.
Book World, July 7, 1968, November 2, 1969.
Critique, Volume 11, number 3, 1969.
Cue, November 25, 1972.
Esquire, December, 1970.
Hollins Critic, April, 1970.
Los Angeles Times, February 6, 1987.
Los Angeles Times Book Review, October 25, 1987.
Nation, December 8, 1969.
National Observer, July 29, 1968.
New Republic, August, 17, 1967.
New Statesman, April 14, 1967, June 16, 1978.
Newsweek, December 1, 1969.
New York Review, March 13, 1969.
New York Times, June 13, 1968, October 22, 1969, November 18, 1972, September 7, 1977, December 19, 1985, January 7, 1987, August 22, 1987.
New York Times Book Review, July 7, 1968, August 14, 1977, June 27, 1982, February 1, 1987, September 27, 1987.
Publishers Weekly, December 26, 1986.
Saturday Review, August 31, 1968.
Time, June 28, 1968, August 8, 1977.
Times (London), February 5, 1987.
Times Literary Supplement, June 16, 1978, February 13, 1987.
Tribune Books, August 16, 1987.
Village Voice, July 30, 1970.
Washington Post Book World, May 11, 1982, March 1, 1987.

*   *   *

CORMIER, Robert (Edmund) 1925-
(John Fitch IV)

PERSONAL: Born January 17, 1925, in Leominster, Mass.; son of Lucien Joseph (a factory worker) and Irma (Collins) Cormier; married Constance B. Senay, November 6, 1948; children: Roberta S., Peter J., Christine J., Renee E. *Education:* Attended Fitchburg State College, one year.

ADDRESSES: Home—1177 Main St., Leominster, Mass. 01453.

CAREER: Radio WTAG, Worcester, Mass., writer, 1946-48; *Telegram & Gazette,* Worcester, reporter, 1948-55; *Fitchburg Sentinel,* Fitchburg, Mass., reporter, 1955-59, wire editor, 1959-66, became associate editor, 1966; free-lance writer, 1978—. Writing consultant to the *Telegram & Gazette.*

MEMBER: L'Union St. Jean Baptiste d'Amerique.

AWARDS, HONORS: Best human interest story of the year, Associated Press in New England, 1959 and 1973; best newspaper column, K. R. Thomson Newspapers, Inc., 1974; "Outstanding Book of the Year" awards, New York Times, 1974, for *The Chocolate War,* 1977, for *I Am the Cheese,* and 1979, for *After the First Death;* "Best Book for Young Adults" citations, American Library Association, 1974, for *The Chocolate War,* 1977, for *I Am the Cheese,* 1979, for *After the First Death,* and 1983, for *The Bumblebee Flies Anyway;* Maxi Award, Media and Methods, 1976; Doctor of Letters, Fitchburg State College, 1977; Woodward School Annual Book Award, 1978, for *I Am the Cheese;* Lewis Carroll Shelf Award, 1979, for *The Chocolate War;* "Notable Children's Trade Book in the Field of Social Studies" citation, National Council for Social Studies and Children's Book Council, 1980, for *Eight Plus One;* Assembly on Literature for Adolescents (ALAN) Award, National Council of Teachers of English, 1982; "Best of the Best Books, 1970-1983" citations, American Library Association, for *The Chocolate War, I Am the Cheese,* and *After the First Death;* "Best Books of 1983" citation, School Library Journal, for *The Bumblebee Flies Anyway;* "Honor List" citation, *Horn Book,* 1986, for *Beyond the Chocolate War.*

WRITINGS:

FICTION

Now and at the Hour, (novel), Coward, 1960.
A Little Raw on Monday Mornings (novel), Sheed, 1963.
Take Me Where the Good Times Are (novel), Macmillan, 1965.
The Chocolate War (novel), Pantheon, 1974, with teacher's guide by Lou Willett Stanek, Dell, 1975.
I Am the Cheese (novel), Pantheon, 1977, with teacher's guide by Stanek, Dell, 1978.
After the First Death (novel), Pantheon, 1979.
Eight Plus One (short stories), Pantheon, 1980.
The Bumblebee Flies Anyway (novel), Pantheon, 1983.
Beyond the Chocolate War (novel), Knopf, 1985.
Fade, Delacorte, 1988.

Also author of *The Rumple Country* and *In the Midst of Winter,* both unpublished novels.

CONTRIBUTOR

Betsy Hearne and Marilyn Kay, editors, *Celebrating Children's Books: Essays in Honor of Zena Sutherland,* Lothrop, 1981.
Sixteen: Short Stories by Outstanding Writers for Young Adults, Delacorte, 1984.
Mark I. West, editor, *Trust Your Children: Voices against Censorship in Children's Literature,* Neal-Schuman, 1987.

OTHER

Fitchburg Sentinel, author of book review column, "The Sentinel Bookman," 1964-78, and of human interest column under pseudonym John Fitch IV, 1969-78; also author of monthly human interest column, "1177 Main Street," for *St. Anthony Messenger,* 1972-82. Contributor of articles and short stories to periodicals, including *Catholic Library World, McCall's, Redbook, Saturday Evening Post, Sign,* and *Woman's Day.*

WORK IN PROGRESS: Another novel.

SIDELIGHTS: With his 1974 novel *The Chocolate War* and the string of acclaimed works that followed, Robert Cormier has secured a position as one of today's foremost authors writing for adolescents. Tony Schwartz in *Newsweek* calls Cormier young adult literature's "best-selling heavyweight writer, an equivalent to Saul Bellow or William Styron." Cormier's much-discussed—and, in some circles, controversial—novels explore themes uncommon to young adult fiction, such as the relationship between good and evil, the struggle of individuals with institutions, and the abuse of power and authority. His novels involve teenage protagonists faced with difficult, uncompromising situations: Jerry Renault in *The Chocolate War,* brutalized by an entire school for his decision to boycott a fund-raising campaign; Ben in *After the First Death,* betrayed by his own father in order to protect a secret government project; and Kate, also in *After the First Death,* killed by a terrorist to whom she had expressed compassion and understanding. "Cormier seems to believe that teenagers are more idealistic today than in years past," writes Joe Stines in the *Dictionary of Literary Biography,* "and he affords them respect and responsibility in his writing while simultaneously awakening them to the harsh realities of life in contemporary America." While some reviewers and educators have criticized Cormier's work for portraying too bleak a view of reality for adolescents—his work has been nearly banned from some school libraries—a larger number recognize the value and contribution of his fiction to the corpus of young adult literature. W. Geiger Ellis in the *ALAN Review* praises Cormier for characters that have "stepped boldly and independently into the world of adolescent literature where most characters finally got their first bra, reached a decision about having intercourse, chose to have an abortion or a baby, kicked a drug habit or adjusted to a single-parent home. . . . It took the good sense of [Cormier] to have a larger view and see the much greater problems that young people face."

Cormier has commented on how he finds the trials that face adolescents both meaningful and inspiring. "An adult is in charge of his own life, while teen-agers face . . . tests every day and yet they're held down," he told Merri Rosenberg in the *New York Times Book Review.* "They don't have the freedom that adults have. . . . Kids that age want to be independent and free, and they think they are, but they're the most conformist group in the world. . . . It's a wonderfully dramatic time to write about." Cormier's understanding of adolescent issues and his ability to communicate to adolescents is evident in the large number who have been compelled to either write or call Cormier directly with questions or comments about his books. Cormier has found that his young readers are generally untroubled by the messages of his novels. "They don't get upset," he told Rosenberg, "They might say to me, 'Gee I wish Jerry Renault . . . hadn't lost in the end,' but they're not upset about the world I portray because they're in that world every day and they know it's war, psychological war. I seldom get a young person taking me to task for being too brutal." Cormier maintains that he writes novels with young adults as characters, and not young adult novels, although he acknowledges the fact that adolescents are his most avid readers. "I've aimed for the intelligent reader," he told *CA,* "and have often found that that reader is fourteen years old." Questioned about the possible role models he may be providing teenagers, Cormier told Anita Silvey in *Horn Book Magazine,* "I'm not worrying about corrupting youth. I'm worrying about writing realistically and truthfully to affect the reader. . . . What I worry about is good taste and getting my message across by whatever means I can."

Cormier had three moderately successful "adult" novels to his credit—*Now and at the Hour, A Little Raw on Monday Mornings,* and *Take Me Where the Good Times Are,* in addition to numerous short stories—yet Stines notes that the best-selling and critically acclaimed *The Chocolate War* has emerged as the "cornerstone of his writing career." Extending from a personal experience in which Cormier's son refused to sell chocolates for a high school fund-raiser, *The Chocolate War,* according to Theodore Weesner in the *New York Times Book Review,* is "a story with a highly serious message not only about the usurpation and misuse of power but about power's inevitable staying." In the novel, Jerry Renault, a perplexed freshman at a Catholic boys school, is caught in a power play between Archie Costello, leader of the school's gang-like secret society, and Brother Leon, the school's headmaster and organizer of the fund-raiser. The headmaster secretly enlists the gang to help sell the chocolates; at the same time Archie, the leader, challenges Jerry to boycott the sale for ten days. Jerry complies; however, when the ten days are over, he decides (for reasons he's not sure of) to continue the boycott. When Jerry's stand begins to catch on with other students, the fund-raiser is threatened. Archie proceeds to focus the gang's activities on ensuring the success of the chocolate sale. Under their influence, which includes blackmail and physical force, sales increase dramatically and the fund-raiser becomes very popular. Jerry, however, continues to hold out and becomes the scorn of the school. In the novel's final scene, Archie rigs a fight in which Jerry is nearly beaten to death by the gang leader's subordinates. "Do I dare disturb the universe?" the motto Jerry has posted in his locker—takes on special meaning. "Worse than the physical and official brutality is Jerry's moral breakdown," observes Hazel Rochman in the *New York Times Book Review.* "He discovers his own pleasure in violence, and in his defeat whispers to the friend who betrayed him: 'play ball. . . . Don't disturb the universe.' "

The Chocolate War created a sensation among critics, the majority of whom found its messages both powerful and disturbing. A number of reviewers focused on the fine line drawn between good and evil. "*The Chocolate War . . .* is a tour de force, and a tour de force of realism," writes Peter Hunt in the *Times Literary Supplement.* "With a pace and terror reminiscent of [Arthur Miller's] *The Crucible,* we see growing up as the realization that the world is rotten; that good and evil are barely distinguishable—both show weakness, fear, and selfishness." Margery Fisher echoes this view, stating in *Growing Point* that *The Chocolate War* "ends in doubt—one might say in an inglorious draw. Presumably [Cormier] was not evading an ending but honestly intended to suggest that no decision between Good and Evil was really possible." The novel also makes a strong case against complacency, however. "Cormier underscores the fact that good guys do not always win," writes Stines, "[and] indicts those who remain indifferent in the face of evil or wrongdoing, pointing out that anyone who takes the risk of challenging evil can be destroyed both physically and psychologically." Patricia Campbell concurs, pointing out in her book *Presenting Robert Cormier* that *The Chocolate War* stresses the importance of standing up for one's convictions and supporting those who take initiative. "Only by making that gesture can we hold on to our humanity, even when defeat is inevitable. . . . When the agents of evil are other human beings, perhaps good can win if enough people have the courage to take a stand together."

The Chocolate War also addresses the pressures and dangers of conformity. In *The Marble in the Water: Essays on Contemporary Writers of Fiction for Children and Young Adults,* David Rees notes that "on the surface . . . [the novel] is about power,

power structures, corruption—about how absolute power corrupts absolutely. But, more subtly, beneath the surface, it is about compromise and the choice between hunting with the pack or searching for strength as an individual: about the toughness needed in the struggle to be a successful outsider. . . . The desire to be accepted is a major weakness which can easily be exploited by the wicked." Weesner finds that the novel's message regarding conformity and power offers a potentially important learning tool. "Presenting as it does a philosophical plateau between childhood and adulthood, [*The Chocolate War*] seems an ideal study for the high school classroom. The characters . . . are accurate and touch close enough to raise questions of identification, questions of one's location within an arena of power, and also provide some hard recognition of the functions of power within a society."

Although *The Chocolate War* received extensive praise from numerous critics and garnered a number of literary awards, some reviewers questioned the book's suitability for young audiences. Comments range from labeling the novel "not appropriate for young people because it presents a distorted view of reality and because it lacks hope" (Norma Bagnell, *Top of the News*) to "there is no place on the shelves of a children's library for such a delight in the destruction of innocence" (*Junior Bookshelf*). The book was nearly banned from some school libraries on the basis that its themes were disturbing and inappropriate for young readers. "The book always triumphed, but even when you won, you lost," Cormier told Laurel Graeber in a *Publishers Weekly* profile. "They'd say, 'Well, okay, but we'll put a mark on it indicating there's special permission needed to read it, or we'll put it in a special section.' And the narrowness of the victories always bother me—a three-to-two committee vote isn't any resounding triumph. And I'm just a minor part of it all, when you consider the great books that are being attacked."

Response to negative criticism of *The Chocolate War* was both extensive and direct. Betty Carter and Karen Harris write in *Top of the News* that "Robert Cormier does not leave his readers without hope, but he does deliver a warning: they may not plead innocence, ignorance, or prior commitments when the threat of tyranny confronts them. He does not imply that resistance is easy, but he insists it is mandatory." Commenting in *Signal*, Pelorus responds to those critics who claim that the realism in the novel is too attractive and that the ending is hopeless: "I would argue, and I fancy Cormier would too, that the real point of his book is to cause young readers to see the result of certain kinds of behavior and to opt not for the hopeless end that the logically worked-out image presents, but just for the opposite." In *American Libraries*, Richard Peck called *The Chocolate War* "surely the most uncompromising novel ever directed to the '12 and up reader'—and very likely the most necessary. It depicts the mass psychology behind the looming menace of the gangs that have never been more omnipotent than now. . . . Anyone banning this book for its locker-room-realistic language is committing a crime against the young."

Cormier's next novel, *I Am the Cheese,* is one of psychological suspense and deception, "a horrifying tale of government corruption, espionage, and counter espionage told by an innocent young victim," writes S. L. Kennerly in *School Library Journal*. The victim is fourteen-year-old Adam Farmer, the son of a man with a hidden past: a government witness living under a false identity. One part of the book is told by Adam; another part, running concurrently, is a series of taped conversations between Adam and a psychiatrist pretending to help him, but really a government agent trying to determine what he knows. Bit by bit, Adam discovers (as does the reader) that no one around him is

what they seem and neither is he. Rather, notes Newgate Callendar in the *New York Times Book Review,* Adam is "indeed the cheese—the bait around which the rats gather. Little he can do about it, except react the way God and Freud have provided. The ending is grim indeed." Anne Scott MacLeod in *Children's Literature in Education* describes *I Am the Cheese* as Cormier's "most Kafka-esque" novel, writing that "the narrative technique, combined with a nearly overwhelming sense of loneliness, helplessness, and hopelessness give . . . a surreal quality. . . . It is as though [Adam] were alone in a computer room where every machine is programmed to cancel him out."

Several critics commented on similarities between *I Am the Cheese* and *The Chocolate War*. Paul Heins of *Horn Book* believes that in both books, "Mr. Cormier is actually writing about human integrity; and in the course of doing so, he cogently uncovers the lacerations that evil often inflicts upon the innocent." Lance Salway of the *Times Literary Supplement* states that the theme dominating the two novels is one "of innocence and morality destroyed by the ruthless ambition of the masters of a corrupt society." He also notes, however, that *I Am the Cheese* extends into more disturbing territory. "The hero is an unwilling, uncomprehending and truly innocent victim of a greater, more hideous conspiracy; the corrupt society is our own, and the innocent victim must be completely destroyed in order to sustain it." Rees echoes this aspect: "There is little obvious compromise in *I Am the Cheese,* for political power and corruption are not illustrated in this book through the world of school life, but by the power of the government itself, and Cormier's message here is much more bleak: that the stand of one or two individuals against the whole apparatus of government is hopeless."

A number of reviewers singled out the structure and writing technique of *I Am the Cheese* as important to its impact. "The genius of the novel is that it is both a logical puzzle and exciting thriller, that it engenders detachment and involvement at the same time," writes Perry Nodelman in *Children's Literature in Education.* "Cormier achieves that paradoxical combination by focusing our attention on the past—making us think about what might have happened, as mysteries do—while at the same time keeping us ignorant of the present that mysterious past led to." Adam's bike ride through the New England countryside—the significance of which the reader gradually realizes—exemplifies this technique. "As in dreams real emotions are translated into fantasy people and events," writes Campbell, "so as the bike ride progresses Adam's hidden awareness of the menace all around him begins to come to the forefront of his mind and take on personification, shape, and form." This effect ultimately accentuates the novel's message. "The book is more than just a good thriller," notes Salway. "Cormier has written a chilling study of a mind on the verge of disintegration, and presented us with a view of our society that is too dire to contemplate." Charles Michener, in a 1977 issue of *Newsweek,* proclaimed *I Am the Cheese* "simply one of the best novels written for any age group this year," adding that "Cormier's style is swift and sure; his sense of place and people is . . . colorful . . . ; his denouement is truly shattering, explosive with paranoia and compassion."

Cormier's next novel, *After the First Death,* is another psychological thriller which further explores the themes of fear, betrayal, and the abuses of power, while charting new territory. An account of terrorists hijacking a busload of schoolchildren in Massachusetts, *After the First Death* moves deeply into the minds of three teenage protagonists: Miro, one of the terrorist hijackers, Kate, the driver of the bus, and Ben, son of an Army general in negotiation with the terrorists. Amelia M. Bell in the *ALAN Review* notes a similarity among these three characters in that their "lives are irrevocably changed by events beyond their control," and that they share a "quest for the knowledge and experience that mark the closing of the gap between childhood and adulthood." However, Dominic Hibberd observes in the *Times Literary Supplement* that this knowledge and experience develop in "a bleak world, in which understanding is corrupted into manipulation and love into destruction." As in other Cormier novels, an adult world is implicated. Ellis writes that "the adults in whose orbits [the young adults] move . . . have their own desperate needs, and no matter what side they are on and no matter how fervently they believe that they act only to create a world fit for their children, it is their children that they sacrifice to the process." Barbara F. Harrison echoes both these points in *Horn Book Magazine:* "On one level the book is about the nature of individual and collective identity. On another, it is about the victimization of innocence."

MacLeod calls these first three young adult novels of Cormier "at bottom, political." Accordingly, Cormier is distinguished as a novelist for adolescents in that he "is far more interested in the systems by which a society operates than he is in individuals. His novels center on the interplay between individuals and their context, between the needs and demands of the system and the needs and rights of individuals—in other words, on the political context in which his characters, like all of us, must live." In line with the two previous novels, *After the First Death* "shows privileged position and privileged information used to manipulate the weak and the unwary," MacLeod continues; it is particularly similar to *I Am the Cheese* in that "the discussion of political evil is cast in fiercely contemporary terms, and the shadow of statism stretches long over the narrative." Cormier likewise presents a warning in *After the First Death* "that political innocence is a dangerous quality, that it can be a kind of collaboration with evil, that innocence is often acquiescence through moral neutrality in the abuse of power by the powerful, and in the sacrifice of the individual to the political organization." Campbell clarifies the roots of this struggle. "The 'enemy' . . . is not necessarily evil. The unifying characteristic in all these manifestations of the concept can be neatly pinned down with the word 'implacable'. . . . What fascinates Cormier, the eternal question that draws him back again and again, is 'How can we confront the utterly Implacable and still remain human?' His emotion centers on the individual made powerless, cut off from all recourse."

Cormier's sequel, *Beyond the Chocolate War,* together with these first three young adult novels, "form a tetralogy of political statement and are undoubtedly Cormier's mature masterpieces," writes Campbell. The four are connected by "the brilliant and complex structure, the intricate wordplay and subtlety of thought, and above all the power and conviction of theme [that] are unequaled by anything of his that came before or has yet come after." *Beyond the Chocolate War* was largely written at the urgings of numerous readers who pressed Cormier for knowledge of the original characters' fates, something in which Cormier was also interested. While reviewers detect the presence of traditional Cormier themes in the sequel, some have remarked that the novel focuses on character development at the expense of thematic development. Rochman comments that *Beyond the Chocolate War* is "not as starkly dramatic as its predecessor," noting that "it relies too much on . . . explication, and there is less action and more emphasis on the internal lives of many characters." Roger Sutton concurs, writing in the *School Library Journal* that "Cormier continues his exploration into good and evil . . . [yet] intensifies and explicates what was powerfully implicit in the first book. While the sequel can be read independently, [new] readers . . . may be puzzled by what is essentially

a string of thematic reverberations." Nonetheless, Sarah Hayes maintains in the *Times Literary Supplement* that Cormier "excels in his juxtaposition of the horrific and the ordinary; of the sinister and the explicable." As in his other novels, Cormier is interested in "the flashpoint at which violence can suddenly erupt, and as suddenly turn tragedy into farce."

Cormier's 1983 novel, *The Bumblebee Flies Anyway,* is distinct from his other young adult writings. "Balancing on the fine line between realism and fantasy, [the novel] finds joy and even triumph in the grimmest circumstances," writes John Knowles in the *New York Times Book Review. The Bumblebee Flies Anyway* takes place in the "Complex," an experimental hospital for the incurably ill, where the resident patients have volunteered to be subjects for testing drugs that may help cure people in the future. One of the patients, Barney, comes up with the idea of providing his friend Mazzo, another patient, the thrill of a lifetime. Barney leads a group of the residents on a project that involves disassembling a wooden mock-up sports car from a neighboring junkyard and reassembling it into a vehicle that will fly them into space. "The last ride of this car," remarks Knowles, "is to be apocalyptic, a defiance of gravity, just as the flight of the bumblebee, aerodynamically implausible, seems to be." There is an implication that a suicide pact is being made among the friends; however, the broader implication is, as Campbell notes, the realization of "free choice" outside "the terrible, implacable fact of impending death," and that "suicide is irreconcilable with an act of faith." Barney's building of the car represents the attainment of "that humanizing gesture against the Implacable that is so central in Cormier's cosmos." The action of the story is played out in an almost dreamlike state that mixes hope with tragedy. Zena Sutherland remarks in *Bulletin of the Center for Children's Books* that "it moves, with relentless inevitability . . . to the requiem of hopeless despair that, for each patient, still holds some passion for an affirmative act of life."

Despite its serious and grim subject matter, *The Bumblebee Flies Anyway* impressed reviewers with its resilience. Anthony Horowitz writes in the *Times Literary Supplement* that although "[the novel] raises some profound questions about medical ethics, about manipulation and about the attitudes to death of the dying and those closest to them[,] . . . even more enduring . . . are the final images of the book where, despite everything, a mood of magnificent optimism prevails, soaring from the terrible mundanity of pain and suffering to the inspiring and poetic victory of the unbroken human spirit." Similarly, Knowles detects a sense of triumph in the book's ending: "Into the doomed, compartmentalized, infected world of the Complex there comes a kind of hope, of a flight defying the laws of the universe, of 'breaking through the grayness and the loneliness . . . out into the stars and the planets and beyond.'"

Fantasy also plays a role in Cormier's 1988 novel, *Fade.* In the first half of the novel, narrator Paul Moreaux recounts the summer of 1938, when as a youth he discovers that he has inherited a bizarre family trait: the power to make himself invisible. *Washington Post* reviewer S. P. Somtow notes that "this ability, at first a curiosity, becomes a terrifying obsession as Paul begins to see more and more of the shadowy side of human nature." While spying on his older relatives, he witnesses shocking sexual episodes that destroy his innocence. And during another invisible adventure he kills a local villain, after which he is determined never again to use his mysterious ability. The novel then shifts into the present. Paul has become a famous writer but has died recently, leaving behind a manuscript that details his power to fade and his attempts to track down a nephew that has inherited the trait. Angry and unhappy, the nephew uses his power in destructive ways; "the novel's climax deals with Paul's efforts to save [his nephew] from the darkness within," notes Somtow.

As with Cormier's other books, some critics found the material in *Fade* too disturbing for young readers. Writing in the *Los Angeles Times Book Review*, Kristiana Gregory comments that "there are passages that will make some parents jump from their seats" and adds that " 'Fade' is not for kids." Other reviewers viewed the book in a different light. *Times Literary Supplement* contributor Sam Swope, for instance, agrees that in *Fade* the "melancholy alienation [evident in Cormier's other novels] reaches its most . . . violent conclusion." Nevertheless, Swope avers that "the elegiac prose is the best Cormier has written" and calls *Fade* "a fascinating, unforgettable book." Similarly, Somtow writes that " 'Fade' is an indisputably powerful book. It deals uncompromisingly with dark subjects. . . . It's not a comforting book, and it tells truths that many would rather not face, but it tells them with compassion and grace."

Reflecting on what is most important to him as a writer, Cormier has stated that expressing both the truth and the emotional content of his artistic vision are utmost, a commitment that many reviewers feel contributes to making Cormier's work unique within the scope of young adult literature. "[The] novels of Robert Cormier have consistently transcended the limitations of the genre," writes Geraldine DeLuca in the *Lion and the Unicorn*. "He has avoided the thin characterizations and glib language that are so familiar . . . perhaps because he is faithful to his own vision, writing more truly for himself than many other writers." In an interview with Paul Janezco of *English Journal*, Cormier talks about the particular importance that emotions play: "[An] emotion sparks my impulse to write and I find myself at the typewriter trying to get the emotion and its impact down on paper. . . . The thing I'm trying to do is communicate with the reader—communicate the emotion I want him to feel. I sacrifice everything to do that. I want to hit the reader with whatever emotion I want to portray, or whatever action will make it vivid." In the *Proceedings of the Eighth Annual Conference of the Children's Literature Association*, Millicent Lenz describes Cormier as a "romantic ironist" and states that he is "to be thanked for his unflinching artistic presentation of evil, for by it we may rediscover the vision of the good." Lenz cites lines from a passage in *After the First Death* describing the character Kate: "She caught her breath, pondering a new thought: the possibility that hope comes out of hopelessness and that the opposites of things carry the seeds of birth—love out of hate, good out of evil. Didn't flowers grow out of dirt?"

MEDIA ADAPTATIONS: "The Chocolate War," "I Am the Cheese," and "After the First Death," were all released as records and cassettes by Miller Brody in 1982; "I Am the Cheese," was adapted into a film and released in 1983 by the Almi Group, starring Robert Wagner, Hope Lange, Robert Macnaughton, and featuring Cormier in the role of Mr. Hertz; "The Chocolate War" was adapted into a film and released in 1988 by the Management Company Entertainment Group, starring John Glover, Ilan Mitchell-Smith, and Wally Ward.

BIOGRAPHICAL/CRITICAL SOURCES:

BOOKS

Campbell, Patricia J., *Presenting Robert Cormier*, Twayne, 1985.
Children's Literature Review, Volume 12, Gale, 1987.
Concise Dictionary of American Literary Biography: Broadening Views, 1968-1988, Gale, 1989.
Contemporary Literary Criticism, Gale, Volume 12, 1980, Volume 30, 1984.
Cormier, Robert, *The Chocolate War*, Pantheon, 1974.
Cormier, Robert, *After the First Death*, Pantheon, 1979.
Cormier, Robert, *Eight Plus One*, Pantheon, 1980.
Cormier, Robert, *The Bumblebee Flies Anyway*, Pantheon, 1983.
Dictionary of Literary Biography, Volume 52: *American Writers for Children since 1960: Fiction*, Gale, 1986.
Inglis, Fred, *The Promise of Happiness: Value and Meaning in Children's Fiction*, Cambridge University Press, 1981.
Rees, David, *The Marble in the Water: Essays on Contemporary Writers of Fiction for Children and Young Adults*, Horn Book, 1980.

PERIODICALS

ALAN Review, fall, 1981, winter, 1985.
America, May 15, 1965.
American Libraries, October, 1974.
Atlantic, September, 1960.
Best Sellers, October 1, 1963, April 15, 1974, November, 1980.
Booklist, July 1, 1974, September 15, 1980, September 1, 1983, March 15, 1985.
Books for Keeps, September, 1985.
Boston Globe Magazine, November 16, 1980.
Bulletin of the Center for Children's Books, December, 1980, September, 1983.
Catholic World, December, 1960.
Children's Literature Association Quarterly, spring, 1986.
Children's Literature in Education, summer, 1981, summer, 1983.
Christian Science Monitor, June 1, 1979, May 20, 1980.
Commonweal, July 2, 1965.
English Journal, September, 1975, September, 1977.
Fitchburg Sentinel, August 2, 1960.
Growing Point, July, 1975.
Horn Book, August, 1977, April, 1979.
Horn Book Magazine, December, 1983, March-April, 1985, July-August, 1985.
Junior Bookshelf June, 1975, August, 1979, December, 1985.
Kirkus Reviews, June 1, 1960.
Leominster Daily Enterprise, July 28, 1960.
Lion and the Unicorn, fall, 1978, winter, 1979-80.
Los Angeles Times, November 23, 1988.
Los Angeles Times Book Review, March 26, 1989.
Manchester Guardian, June 22, 1979.
Media and Methods, May-June, 1978.
Newsweek, December 19, 1977, July 16, 1979.
New York Herald Tribune Book Review, July 31, 1960.
New York Times, November 11, 1983.
New York Times Book Review, April 25, 1965, May 5, 1974, May 1, 1977, April 29, 1979, November 9, 1980, November 13, 1983, May 5, 1985.
Proceedings of the Eighth Annual Conference of the Children's Literature Association, March, 1981.
Publishers Weekly, October 7, 1983, July 24, 1987.
School Library Journal, May, 1977, March, 1979, September, 1980, November, 1982, April, 1985.
Signal, September, 1975.
Time, August 1, 1960.
Times (London), November 14, 1985.
Times Educational Supplement, November 18, 1977, January 13, 1984.
Times Literary Supplement, April 4, 1975, December 2, 1977, December 14, 1979, November 25, 1983, November 29, 1985, November 25, 1988.
Top of the News, spring, 1980, winter, 1980.
Voice of Youth Advocates, December, 1980.

Washington Post, December 24, 1988.
Washington Post Book World, May 13, 1979, November 6, 1983, June 9, 1985.
World of Children's Books, fall, 1977.

*   *   *

CORNWELL, David (John Moore) 1931-
(John le Carre)

PERSONAL: Born October 19, 1931, in Poole, Dorsetshire, England; son of Ronald Thomas Archibald and Olive (Glassy) Cornwell; married Alison Ann Veronica Sharp, 1954 (divorced, 1971); married Valerie Jane Eustace, 1972; children: (first marriage) Simon, Stephen, Timothy; (second marriage) Nicholas. *Education:* Attended Bern University, 1948-49; Lincoln College, Oxford, B.A. (with honours), 1956.

ADDRESSES: Agent—Bruce Hunter, David Higham Ltd., 5-8 Lower John St., W1R 4HA, England.

CAREER: Writer. Eton College, Buckinghamshire, England, tutor, 1956-58; British Foreign Office, second secretary in Bonn, West Germany, 1960-63, consul in Hamburg, West Germany, 1963-64.

AWARDS, HONORS: British Crime Novel Award, 1963; Somerset Maugham Award, 1964; Edgar Allan Poe Award, Mystery Writers of America, 1965; Gold Dagger, Crime Writers Association, 1978; Black Memorial Award, 1978; Grand Master Award, Mystery Writers of America, 1986; Diamond Dagger, Crime Writers Association, 1988.

WRITINGS:

Call for the Dead (also see below), Gollancz, 1960, Walker, 1962, published as *The Deadly Affair,* Penguin, 1966.
A Murder of Quality (also see below), Gollancz, 1962, Walker, 1963.
The Spy Who Came In from the Cold, Coward, 1963.
The Incongruous Spy: Two Novels of Suspense (contains *Call for the Dead* and *A Murder of Quality*), Walker, 1964.
The Looking Glass War, Coward, 1965.
"Dare I Weep, Dare I Mourn" (screenplay), produced on "Stage 66" by American Broadcasting Corp., 1966.
A Small Town in Germany, Coward, 1968.
(Author of introduction) Bruce Page, Phillip Knightley, and David Leitch, *The Philby Conspiracy,* Doubleday, 1968.
The Naive and Sentimental Lover, Knopf, 1971.
Tinker, Tailor, Soldier, Spy (also see below), Knopf, 1977.
Smiley's People (also see below), Knopf, 1980.
The Quest for Karla (contains *Tinker, Tailor, Soldier, Spy, The Honourable Schoolboy,* and *Smiley's People*), Knopf, 1982.
The Little Drummer Girl, Knopf, 1983.
A Perfect Spy, Knopf, 1986.
The Russia House, Knopf, 1989.

SIDELIGHTS: The novels of David Cornwell, written under the pseudonym John le Carre, depict the clandestine world of Cold War espionage as a morally ambiguous realm where treachery, deceit, fear, and betrayal are the norm. The atmosphere in a le Carre novel, writes a reviewer for the *Times Literary Supplement,* is one of "grubby realism and moral squalor, the frazzled, fatigued sensitivity of decent men obliged to betray or kill others no worse than themselves." Le Carre uses his fiction to dramatize what he sees as the moral bankruptcy of the Cold War. In an open letter published in *Encounter,* le Carre writes: "There is no victory and no virtue in the Cold War, only a condition of

human illness and a political misery." Leonard Downie, Jr., quotes le Carre in a *Washington Post* article as saying, "We are in the process of doing things in defense of our society which may very well produce a society which is not worth defending." It is this paradox, and the moral ambiguity which accompanies it, that informs le Carre's espionage novels and makes them, many critics believe, among the finest works of their genre. Le Carre's novels are believed by some critics to have raised the entire espionage genre to a more respectable and serious level of literature. "The espionage novel," writes Joseph McClellan in the *Washington Post Book World,* for example, "has become a characteristic expression of our time . . . and John le Carre is one of the handful of writers who have made it so." "More than any other writer," George Grella states in the *New Republic,* "[le Carre] has established the spy as an appropriate figure and espionage as an appropriate activity for our time, providing both symbol and metaphor to explain contemporary history."

Le Carre began writing espionage fiction in the early 1960s while working as a diplomat with the British Foreign Office in London. He had earlier worked for an undisclosed length of time with the British Secret Service, and there is some speculation among reviewers that le Carre's work as a diplomat was also espionage-related, a speculation le Carre dismisses as untrue. Nevertheless, his novels reveal an intimate knowledge of the workings of the British government's espionage bureaucracy. "Le Carre's contribution to the fiction of espionage," writes Anthony Burgess in the *New York Times Book Review,* "has its roots in the truth of how a spy system works. . . . The people who run Intelligence totally lack glamour, their service is short of money, [and] they are up against the crassness of politicians. Their men in the field are frightened, make blunders, grow sick of a trade in which the opposed sides too often seem to interpenetrate and wear the same face." Geoffrey Stokes, writing in the *Village Voice,* goes so far as to claim that in le Carre's novels, "bureaucracy [is] transformed into poetry." Because of his diplomatic position when he first began writing, Cornwell was not permitted to publish anything under his real name, and so the pseudonym John le Carre was born. "Le Carre" is French for "the square." "I've told so many lies about where I got the name from," Downie quotes le Carre as explaining, "but I really don't remember. The one time I did the celebrity circuit in America, I was reduced to inventing the fiction that I'd been riding on a bus to the foreign office and abstracted the name from a shoeshop. But that was simply because I couldn't convince anybody it came from nowhere."

Although the source for his pseudonym is now forgotten, the initial inspiration for le Carre's fiction is easily found. It comes from the sensational disclosures in the 1950s that several high-ranking members of the British Secret Service and Foreign Office were actually Soviet agents. These deep-penetration agents, called "moles," had infiltrated the British espionage establishment during the Second World War and had, over a period of years, risen to extremely sensitive positions. Of the several spies discovered, the most highly placed was Kim Philby, a man generally acknowledged to be the greatest traitor in British history. Philby had been in charge of British counter intelligence against the Soviet Union while secretly working for the Soviets, and was responsible for betraying hundreds of British agents to their deaths. These real-life espionage revelations caught the interest of the British reading public and such books as Ian Fleming's "James Bond" spy series became best-sellers. Le Carre, too, because of his own intelligence work, was intrigued and disturbed by the discovery of traitors in the British Secret Service. Grella states that le Carre has an "obsession with the relationship between love and betrayal" and has consistently explored this theme in all of his fiction.

Le Carre wrote his first two novels, *Call for the Dead* and *A Murder of Quality,* while working for the Foreign Office, first in London and then in Bonn, West Germany. At that time, the German capital was a center for intelligence operations. "You couldn't have been [in Germany] at that period," le Carre tells Miriam Gross of the *Chicago Tribune Magazine,* "without being aware of the shadow of an enormous intelligence apparatus." Le Carre introduced George Smiley, an intelligence agent featured in many of his later novels, in *Call for the Dead.* Smiley is an "improbable spy master," writes Richard W. Noland in *Clues: A Journal of Detection.* "[He is] short, fat, quiet and wears 'really bad clothes, which hung about his squat frame like skin on a shrunken toad,' " Noland quotes from *Call for the Dead.* Though physically unimposing, Smiley is a brilliant espionage agent who has served in the British Secret Service for more than thirty years. In *Call for the Dead,* Smiley investigates the suicide of a Foreign Office clerk who had just been given a security clearance, while in *A Murder of Quality* he tracks down the murderer of a schoolmaster's wife.

It wasn't until the publication of *The Spy Who Came In from the Cold* in 1963 that le Carre's work attracted widespread critical and popular acclaim. An immediate world-wide best-seller (the book has sold over twenty million copies since it first appeared), *Spy* enabled le Carre to leave his position with the Foreign Office to write full time. He tells Nicholas Wapshott of the London *Times:* "I had said to my accountant, if my assets reach 20,000 pounds, would you let me know? . . . When he told me I had reached that amount, with *The Spy Who Came In from the Cold,* it was a great relief. . . . I gave in my resignation." The novel tells the story of Alec Leamas, a fifty-year old British intelligence agent who wishes to retire from active duty and "come in from the cold," as he describes it. He is persuaded to take on one last assignment before leaving the Secret Service: a pretended defection behind the Iron Curtain to give false information to the East Germans implicating one of their high-ranking intelligence officers as a British agent. It is thought that the officer will then be imprisoned, thereby removing him from effective espionage work against the British. Leamas's real mission, and the treachery of his superiors, only gradually becomes clear to him as the plot unfolds.

Le Carre's pessimism about East-West relations is clearly evident in *Spy,* where both sides in the Cold War conflict are depicted as amoral and murderous. "The bureaucracies of East and West," writes Noland, describing the situation as related in *Spy,* "wage the Cold War by one simple rule—operational convenience. . . . In the name of operational convenience and alliances of expediency, any and all human values—including love and life itself—are expendable." In *Spy,* writes a *Times Literary Supplement* critic, le Carre puts forth the ideas that "the spy is generally a weak man, the tool of bureaucrats who are neither scrupulous nor particularly efficient, and that there is nothing to choose between 'us' and 'them' in an ethical sense." This is underlined when Leamas and his girlfriend are pitted against the intelligence agencies of both Britain and East Germany, "the two apparently opposed organizations on one side and helpless human beings . . . on the other," as Julian Symons writes in *Mortal Consequences: A History from the Detective Story to the Crime Novel.* Symons believes that *Spy* is the best of le Carre's novels because in *Spy* "the story is most bitterly and clearly told, the lesson of human degradation involved in spying most faithfully read."

Many of the qualities in le Carre's writing that are most praised by critics were first displayed in *Spy.* One of these is an authenticity and realism not usually found in espionage fiction. "Here is a book," Anthony Boucher writes in the *New York Times Book Review,* "a light year removed from the sometimes entertaining trivia which have (in the guise of spy novels) cluttered the publishers' lists." A reviewer for the *Times Literary Supplement* believes that, in *Spy,* "the technicalities of [spy] network organization carry a stamp of authenticity seldom found in stories of this nature," although the critic decries the "basically sensational" subject matter.

To make his work seem as authentic as possible, le Carre introduces a number of slang terms peculiar to the espionage underworld. Words like "mole," borrowed from the Soviet KGB, and "circus," a nickname for the British Secret Service, are used throughout *Spy.* Some of these terms are actual espionage jargon, but many were invented by le Carre himself. "I thought it very important," le Carre tells Gross, "to give the reader the illusion of entering the secret world, and to that end I invented jargon that would be graphic and at the same time mysterious. Some people find it irritating. I rather like it." Le Carre, Downie reports, "borrowed 'mole' from the KGB and is pleased that it has quickly become part of the real spy language of the West."

Graham Greene sets the tone for most critical commentary about *The Spy Who Came In from the Cold* when he calls it, as K. G. Jackson of *Harper* quotes Greene, "the best spy novel I have ever read." D. B. Hughes of *Book Week* also praises *Spy* as "a beautifully written, understated and immensely perilous story. . . . Only rarely does a book of this quality appear—an inspired work and one in which the author's own inner excitement kindles the page." Several critics feel that with this novel le Carre transcends the espionage genre entirely, writing not category fiction but literature. Noland finds, for example, that with *The Spy Who Came In from the Cold* le Carre's "spy fiction became something more than most conventional spy fiction. It became, in fact, a political statement about the moral confusion and bankruptcy of the Cold War." Boucher also sees something more to le Carre's novel. "The author develops his story superbly," he writes, "both as a compelling and dazzlingly plotted thriller, and as a substantial and penetrating novel of our time. [Le Carre is one of] the small rank of [espionage] writers who can create a novel of significance, while losing none of the excitement of the tale of sheer adventure."

This high critical praise has continued with each succeeding espionage novel le Carre has published. *The Looking Glass War,* for example, is described by Hughes as "a superb spy story, unflawed, a bitter, cruel, dispassionate—yet passionate—study of an unimportant piece of espionage and the unimportant little men who are involved in it." A group of British agents mount an operation into East Germany that is doomed to failure under present political conditions, a fact which the agents refuse to see. Symons argues in *New Review* that in both *Spy* and *The Looking Glass War,* betrayal is the primary theme. In the first, an agent is betrayed to further the career of a more highly placed agent. In the second, an entire operation is abandoned and the people involved in it are left to die. It is possible, Symons writes, "to see espionage activities as brave and patriotic . . ., and yet to view them also as basically disgusting, outrages to the human personality. From such a point of view these two books seem to say an ultimate word about the nature of spying."

Le Carre draws heavily upon his time at the British Foreign Office in writing *A Small Town in Germany,* a novel set in Bonn, West Germany. The novel relates the story of a British diplomat who disappears with very sensitive documents which may damage Britain's chances of joining the Common Market. Speaking of the novel in a *Nation* review, John Gliedman states that le Carre "has long been a master of the essential machinery of the spy and detective novel. He has also shown himself to be a sensitive observer of character and manner, within the limits of the genre. But nothing which has come before quite prepares us for the literary distinction of this effort—the quality of its prose, the complexity of its construction, the cunning of some of its dialogue. . . . It represents something of a breakthrough in the use of the spy genre for serious purposes. *A Small Town in Germany* is that rarest of all things in contemporary fiction—good art which is also popular art." Robert Ostermann, writing in *National Observer,* agrees that *A Small Town in Germany* is better than le Carre's previous fiction. He calls it "broader in scope and more confidently crafted; tuned with exquisite fineness to the sliding nuances of its characters; shot through with the physical presence of Bonn, . . . and conveyed in a tough, precise prose that matches the novel's mordant tone down to the smallest metaphor."

Tinker, Tailor, Soldier, Spy, le Carre's next espionage novel, begins a loosely connected trilogy in which George Smiley is pitted against the Russian master spy "Karla." Writing in *Newsweek,* Alexis Gelber and Edward Behr report that "with *Tinker, Tailor* and Smiley, [le Carre] hit his stride." *Tinker, Tailor* is a fictionalized treatment of the Kim Philby spy case in which Smiley goes after a Soviet mole in British intelligence, a mole placed and directed by Karla. The novel's structure "derives from the action of Smiley's search," writes Noland. "[Smiley] must pursue his man through the maze of official documents." Knowing that the mole must be a highly placed agent, Smiley goes back through the records of intelligence operations, seeking a pattern of failure which might be attributed to the machinations of a particular agent. His investigation finally becomes, Noland believes, "a moral search . . . a quest for some kind of truth about England."

As in previous novels, le Carre examines the ramifications of betrayal, but this time in greater depth than he had previously attempted. The mole Smiley uncovers has not only betrayed his country and friends but has seduced Smiley's wife as well. The critic for the *Times Literary Supplement* sees a "moral dilemma" at the center of the book: "Smiley gets his man. In doing so he removes from another man his last illusions about friendship, loyalty and love, and he himself is left drained in much the same way. It is a sombre and tragic theme, memorably presented." Similarly, Richard Locke writes in the *New York Times Book Review* of the "interlocking themes of sexual and political betrayal" to be found in *Tinker, Tailor.* Writing in *Clues: A Journal of Detection,* Holly Beth King sees a deeper significance to the novel's title, which is derived from a children's nursery rhyme. King sees a "whole intricately woven set of relationships between adults and children, between innocence and disillusionment, between loyalty and betrayal that gives the novel's title a deeper resonance."

Although the complexity of *Tinker, Tailor* is praised by many critics, Pearl K. Bell writes in *New Leader* that "it is myopic and unjust to link le Carre with high art." Bell believes that a more correct evaluation of le Carre would see him as "a master craftsman of ingeniously plotted suspense, weaving astoundingly intricate fantasies of discovery, stealth, surprise, duplicity, and final exposure." Similarly, Locke finds that "le Carre belongs to the select company of such spy and detective story writers as Arthur Conan Doyle and Graham Greene in England and Dashiell Hammett, James M. Cain, Raymond Chandler, and Ross Macdonald in America. There are those who read crime and espio-

nage books for the plot and those who read them for the atmosphere . . . le Carre's books . . . offer plenty for both kinds of readers." Bell concludes that le Carre is "unarguably the most brilliantly imaginative practitioner of the [espionage] genre today." Writing in *Newsweek,* Peter S. Prescott defines what sets le Carre's espionage fiction apart from many other works in the genre. "Le Carre's work is above all plausible," he writes, "rooted not in extravagant fantasies of the cold war but in the realities of the bureaucratic rivalry summoned up through vapors of nostalgia and bitterness, in understated pessimism, in images of attenuation and grinding down." In *Tinker, Tailor,* Stokes argues, "Smiley is merely the protagonist; bureaucracy itself is the hero. . . . Without the structure bureaucracy imposes on the random accumulation of facts that assail us on a daily basis, there is indeed only 'perpetual chaos.'"

Smiley's running battle with the Soviet spy master Karla continues in *The Honourable Schoolboy,* a novel set in Hong Kong, where British intelligence is investigating a prosperous businessman who seems to be working for the Soviets. Several critics point out a similarity between le Carre's novel and Joseph Conrad's novel *Lord Jim.* The character Jerry Westerby, a British intelligence officer and friend of Smiley, is very similar to Conrad's character Jim. "Le Carre," Noland states, "obviously has Conrad's romantic protagonist in mind in his portrait of Westerby and in many of the events of the story." This "huge and hugely engrossing new thriller . . . ," writes David Ansen in *Newsweek,* "keeps opening out, like a Conrad adventure, into ever-widening pools of moral and emotional complexity."

Again concerned with one of Karla's moles, this one working inside Communist China, *The Honourable Schoolboy* traces Smiley's diligent efforts to discover and capture the agent for the West. As in previous novels, *Schoolboy* depicts an agent, this time Westerby, who is at odds with the amorality of espionage work and who, because of his belief in human values, loses his life in the course of an espionage operation. "The point, surely," writes Noland, "is that such romantic heroism is not very useful in the world of Cold War espionage." "It is difficult not to overpraise [*The Honourable Schoolboy*]," Mollie Panter-Downes writes in her *New Yorker* review. Although believing the novel too long, the plot "essentially thin," and le Carre's "fondness for stylistic mocking" embarrassing, Panter-Downes nonetheless praises *The Honourable Schoolboy.* "It has a compelling pace," she states, "a depth beyond its genre, a feeling for even the least of its characters, a horrifying vision of the doomed and embattled Southeast Asian left in the wake of the Vietnam War, and a dozen set pieces—following, fleeing, interrogating—that are awesomely fine."

Not all critics are as impressed with the novel. Louis Finger, writing in the *New Statesman,* believes that "the things that are wrong with le Carre, at the level of seriousness he no doubt feels he's aimed for here, totally debilitate the book's appeal as a run-of-the-mill espionage yarn." Responding to critics who classify le Carre's work as literature, Clive James of the *New York Review of Books* states that "raising le Carre to the plane of literature has helped rob him of his more enviable role as a popular writer who could take you unawares."

Le Carre brings his trilogy to a close with *Smiley's People,* the last confrontation between George Smiley and the Soviet master spy Karla. No longer content to thwart Karla's agents, Smiley works in this novel to force Karla himself to defect to the West. This operation is done off the record because the British Secret Service, due to political pressure, cannot engage in an offensive intelligence operation. It becomes instead a personal mission involving the retired Smiley and the friends and espionage contacts he has gathered over the years. "Smiley and his people," Noland states, "carry it out by personal choice and commitment, not for the British (or American) establishment. The whole operation is a victory for personal human loyalty and skill."

Despite the success of the operation, there is an ambiguity about it which brings into question the morality of espionage. "Smiley and his people are fighting for decency," writes Michael Wood in the *New York Times Book Review,* "but there is more blood on their hands than they or anyone else care to contemplate." Julian Moynihan clarifies this in *New Republic.* "We know," Moynihan writes, "that Smiley has ruined many lives, some innocent, in his tenacious pursuit of Karla; . . . and we just don't believe that the dirty tricks of one side are OK because they were ordered up by a decent little English guy with a disarming name." "If this is the end of the Smiley stories . . . ," writes Joseph McClellan in the *Washington Post Book World,* "it is an appropriately ambiguous conclusion to a series that has dealt splendidly in ambiguities from the beginning."

"In *Smiley's People,*" Tom Buckley states in *Quest/80,* "le Carre has done what no sensible person would have thought possible. He has written a novel at least as good as, and in some respects better than, his masterpiece, *The Spy Who Came In from the Cold.*" Jonathan Yardley agrees in an article for the *Washington Post,* calling it "the best of the le Carre's novels." Yardley goes on to evaluate le Carre's achievement as a writer by stating that he "has produced a body of work that is notable for technical brilliance, depth, and consistency of themes, and absolute verisimilitude."

In *The Little Drummer Girl,* le Carre turns to a different world arena for his setting—the Middle East refugee camps of the Palestinians. "It is as if Mr. le Carre," writes Anatole Broyard of the *New York Times,* "has had enough of British politics, as if he feels that neither Britain nor the Soviet Union is at the hot center of things anymore." Le Carre had originally planned to write a Smiley story set in the Middle East but could not find a convincing plot for his character. Because the espionage activity in this novel is of an active and open variety, unusual for le Carre, there is a great deal more action in *Drummer Girl* than is usual for a le Carre novel. There is also a female protagonist, le Carre's first, who is recruited by the Israelis to infiltrate a Palestinian terrorist group and set up its leader for assassination. "The Israelis triumph in the novel," William F. Buckley, Jr., writes in *National Review,* "even as they do in life. But Mr. le Carre is careful to even up the moral odds. . . . He permits the Palestinian point to be made with rare and convincing eloquence." Writing in *Esquire,* Martin Cruz Smith gives the opinion that *The Little Drummer Girl* is "the most balanced novel about Jews and Arabs, outrage for outrage and tear for tear, I've read." "Without condoning terrorism," Gelber and Behr write, "the book makes the reasons for it understandable—perhaps the first popular novel to do so."

Because of this insistence upon looking at both sides in the Middle East conflict as having valid reasons for waging war, le Carre succeeds, many critics believe, in presenting the situation in its complexity. It is through the character of Charlie, an actress recruited by the Israelis for the mission, that le Carre presents the arguments of both the Arabs and Jews. Charlie is first converted to the Israeli position by Israeli Intelligence and then, in order to play the part of a Palestinian sympathizer convincingly, she is indoctrinated in the Palestinian position. "In the course of the story," Hope Hale Davis states in the *New Leader,* "we have a chance, with Charlie, to become passionately partisan on one side and then the other, and also—with less risk to the psyche than Charlie suffers—both sides at once." According to Mark Abley, writing in *Maclean's,* le Carre "is resigned to the fact that neither side will be pleased by his controversial new novel." This is because le Carre portrays both sides as amoral killers, much the way he portrays both sides in the Cold War. Le Carre tells *Newsweek:* "There was no way of telling the story attractively unless one accepted certain premises—that terrible things were being done to the Jews. I began with the traditional Jewish hero looking for a Palestinian 'baddie.' Once into the narrative, the reader, I believed, would be prepared to consider more ambiguous moral preoccupations."

Some reviewers, however, see le Carre as an apologist for the Palestine Liberation Organization (PLO) and *The Little Drummer Girl* as lacking the moral ambiguity that characterizes his earlier books. "Here, one might have thought, is an ideal subject for moral ambiguity," David Pryce-Jones writes in the *New Republic.* "Le Carre finds it clear-cut. To him, the Palestinians are good, the Israelis bad." In their review of the book for *Chronicles of Culture,* Rael Jean Isaac and Erich Isaac acknowledge that le Carre does introduce the kind of moral ambiguities and correspondences between adversaries that he uses in other novels, "but these suggestions of ambiguity and correspondence are deceptive, for le Carre sets Israel up as the villain of this novel. . . . Le Carre employs meretricious techniques to make Israel appear guilty of the vicious practices that the PLO has made famous."

Speaking of the relationship between his life and writings to Fred Hauptfuhrer of *People,* le Carre reveals: "If I write knowledgeably about gothic conspiracies, it's because I had knowledge of them from earliest childhood." In several published interviews, le Carre has spoken of his personal life and how the business dealings and political ambitions of his father colored his own views of the world. Because his father often found himself in legal or financial trouble due to his sometimes questionable business deals, the family found itself, le Carre tells Gross, "often living in the style of millionaire paupers. . . . And so we arrived in educated, middle-class society feeling almost like spies, knowing that we had no social hinterland, that we had a great deal to conceal and a lot of pretending to do." In an interview with Melvyn Bragg in the *New York Times Book Review,* le Carre states: "From early on, I was extremely secretive and began to think that I was, so to speak, born into occupied territory." He tells *Newsweek* that "there is a correlation, I suppose, between the secret life of my father and the secret life I entered at a formative age." Le Carre fictionalized his relationship with his father in the 1986 novel, *A Perfect Spy.*

"As for my own writing," le Carre tells Gross, "the real fun is the fun of finding that you've enchanted people, enchanted them in the sense that you've admitted them to a world they didn't know about. And also that you've given them a great deal of relief, in a strange way, because they've discovered a bit of life interpreted for them in ways that, after all, they find they understand."

MEDIA ADAPTATIONS: The Spy Who Came In from the Cold was filmed by Paramount in 1965; *Call for the Dead* was filmed as "The Deadly Affair" by Columbia in 1967; *The Looking Glass War* was filmed by Columbia in 1970; *Tinker, Tailor, Soldier, Spy* was filmed for television by the British Broadcasting Corp. in 1980; *Smiley's People* was filmed for television by the British Broadcasting Corp. in 1982; *The Little Drummer Girl* was filmed by Warner Brothers; *A Perfect Spy* was a seven-hour BBC-TV series and was shown on public television's "Masterpiece Theatre" in the United States; a film version of *The Russia House,* written by Tom Stoppard, directed by Fred Schepisi, and starring Sean Connery and Michelle Pfeiffer, is scheduled for release in 1990.

BIOGRAPHICAL/CRITICAL SOURCES:

BOOKS

Bestsellers 89, Issue 4, Gale, 1989.
Contemporary Literary Criticism, Gale, Volume 3, 1975, Volume 5, 1976, Volume 9, 1978, Volume 15, 1980, Volume 28, 1984.
Dictionary of Literary Biography, Volume 87: *British Mystery and Thriller Writers since 1940, First Series,* Gale, 1989.
Harper, Ralph, *The World of the Thriller,* Press of Case Western University, 1969.
Palmer, Jerry, *Thrillers: Genesis and Structure of a Popular Genre,* St. Martin's, 1979.
Symons, Julian, *Mortal Consequences: A History from the Detective Story to the Crime Novel,* Harper, 1972.

PERIODICALS

Armchair Detective, spring, 1980.
Book Week, January 26, 1964.
Chicago Tribune, June 19, 1989.
Chicago Tribune Book World, March 6, 1983.
Chicago Tribune Magazine, March 23, 1980.
Christian Science Monitor, January 14, 1980.
Chronicles of Culture, August, 1983.
Clues: A Journal of Detection, fall/winter, 1980, fall/winter, 1982.
Commentary, June, 1983.
Detroit News, August 29, 1982.
Esquire, April, 1983.
Globe and Mail (Toronto), June 10, 1989.
Harper, January, 1964, November, 1965, December, 1968.
Life, February 28, 1964.
Listener, July 4, 1974.
Los Angeles Times, May 31, 1989, October 16, 1989.
Los Angeles Times Book Review, June 18, 1989.
Maclean's, March 7, 1983.
Nation, December 30, 1968.
National Observer, October 28, 1968.
National Review, March 13, 1983.
New Leader, June 24, 1974, March 7, 1983.
New Republic, July 31, 1976, January 19, 1980, April 18, 1983.
New Review, July, 1974.
New Statesman, July 12, 1974, September 23, 1977.
Newsweek, October 28, 1968, June 17, 1974, September 26, 1977, March 7, 1983, June 5, 1989.
New York, December 24, 1979, October 25, 1982.
New Yorker, October 3, 1977.
New York Review of Books, October 27, 1977, February 7, 1980, April 14, 1983.
New York Times, January 28, 1969, September 22, 1977, February 25, 1983.
New York Times Book Review, January 12, 1964, June 5, 1965, March 11, 1966, January 27, 1967, June 30, 1974, September 25, 1977, January 6, 1980, March 13, 1983, May 21, 1989.
New York Times Magazine, September 8, 1974.
People, August 19, 1974.
Publishers Weekly, September 19, 1977.
Quest/80, January, 1980.
Salmagundi, summer, 1970.
Saturday Review, July 24, 1965.

Spectator, July 6, 1974.
Time, January 17, 1964, May 29, 1964, September 29, 1980.
Times (London), September 6, 1982, June 24, 1989.
Times Literary Supplement, September 13, 1963, June 24, 1965, September 24, 1971, July 19, 1974, September 9, 1977, August 4, 1989.
Tribune Books (Chicago), May 21, 1989.
Village Voice, October 24, 1977, January 14, 1980.
Washington Post, September 29, 1980, November 29, 1982, May 25, 1989, October 14, 1989.
Washington Post Book World, December 8, 1974, December 23, 1979, June 4, 1989.

*   *   *

CORSO, (Nunzio) Gregory   1930-

PERSONAL: Born March 26, 1930, in New York, N.Y.; son of Fortunato Samuel and Michelina (Colonni) Corso; married Sally November (now a teacher), May 7, 1963 (divorced); married Belle Carpenter, 1968; children: (first marriage) Mirandia; (second marriage) Cybelle Nuncia, Max-Orphe. *Education:* Attended grammar school. *Politics:* "Individualism and freedom." *Religion:* "God."

ADDRESSES: Home—100 Sullivan St., New York, NY.

CAREER: Prison inmate, 1947-50; manual laborer in New York City, 1950-51; employee of *Los Angeles Examiner,* Los Angeles, Calif., 1951-52; merchant seaman on Norwegian vessels, 1952-53. After his merchant marine experience and before leaving the United States in 1959 for extensive travel, Corso attracted widespread attention in a series of poetry readings in the East and Midwest. Since returning to the United States, Corso has devoted himself to writing. Appeared in Peter Whitehead's film, "Wholly Communion," and in Andy Warhol's "Couch," the latter in 1965.

AWARDS, HONORS: Longview Award for poem, "Marriage"; $1,000 award from the Poetry Foundation; Jean Stein Award for Poetry from American Academy and Institute of Arts and Letters, 1986.

WRITINGS:

The Vestal Lady on Brattle, and Other Poems, R. Brukenfeld (Cambridge, Mass.), 1955.
"This Hung-Up Age" (play) produced at Harvard University, 1955.
Bomb (poem; broadside), [San Francisco], 1958.
Gasoline (poems), introduction by Allen Ginsberg, City Lights, 1958.
(With Henk Marsman) *A Pulp Magazine for the Dead Generation: Poems,* Dead Language, 1959.
(With William S. Burroughs, Brion Gysin, and Sinclair Beiles) *Minutes to Go,* Two Cities Editions (Paris, France), 1960.
Happy Birthday of Death (poems), New Directions, 1960.
(Editor with Walter Hollerer) *Junge Amerikanische Lyrik* (anthology), Carl Hansen Verlag, 1961.
The American Express (novel), Olympia Press, 1961.
(With Anselm Hollo and Tom Raworth) *The Minicab War,* Matrix Press, 1961.
Find It So Hard to Write the How Why & What . . . , Paterson Society, 1961.
Long Live Man (poems), New Directions, 1962.
Selected Poems, Eyre & Spottiswoode, 1962.
(With Lawrence Ferlinghetti and Allen Ginsberg) *Penguin Modern Poets 5,* Penguin, 1963.
The Mutation of the Spirit: A Shuffle Poem, Death Press, 1964.

There Is Yet Time to Run Back Through Life and Expiate All That's Been Sadly Done (poems), New Directions, 1965.

(Contributor) Paris Leary and Robert Kelly, editors, *A Controversy of Poets,* Doubleday Anchor, 1965.

(With Jay Socin) "Happy Death" (screenplay), 1965.

The Geometric Poem: A Long Experimental Poem, Composite of Many Lines and Angles Selective, [Milan, Italy], 1966.

(Contributor) Bob Booker and George Foster, editors, *Pardon Me, Sir, But Is My Eye Hurting Your Elbow?* (screenplays), Bernard Geis, 1967.

10 Times a Poem: Collected at Random From 2 Suitcases Filled With Poems—the Gathering of 5 Years, Poets Press, 1967.

Elegiac Feelings American, New Directions, 1970.

Gregory Corso, Phoenix Book Shop, 1971.

Ankh, Phoenix Book Shop, 1971.

Egyptian Cross, Phoenix Book Shop, 1971.

The Night Last Night Was at Its Nightest . . . , Phoenix Book Shop, 1972.

Earth Egg, Unmuzzled Ox, 1974.

Way Out: A Poem in Discord (play), Bardo Matrix (Kathmandu, Nepal), 1974.

The Japanese Notebook Ox, Unmuzzled Ox, 1974.

Collected Plays, City Lights, 1980.

Writings From Ox, edited by Michael Andre, Unmuzzled Ox, 1981.

Herald of the Autochthonic Spirit, New Directions, 1981.

Contributor to periodicals, including *Evergreen Review* and *Litterair Paspoort.*

SIDELIGHTS: Gregory Corso is a key member of the Beats, a group of convention-breaking writers who are generally credited with sparking much of the social and political change that transformed America in the 1960s. But as Corso makes clear in his poem "Columbia U Poesy Reading—1975" in *Herald of the Autochthonic Spirit,* the Beats were essentially revolutionaries of the *spirit.* Corso's work is an unbroken testament to the belief that revolution is a matter of obedience to one's own poetic self and private music rather than to any movement, political or otherwise.

Among the Beats, Corso is closest to Allen Ginsberg as a writer. They met in a Greenwich Village bar in 1950 when Corso was working on his first poems. Until then he had read only traditional poetry, and Ginsberg introduced him to contemporary, experimental work. The result was crucial, and within a few years Corso was writing in long Whitmanesque lines similar to those Ginsberg had developed in his own work. The surreal word combinations that began to appear in Ginsberg's work about the same time may in turn suggest Corso's reciprocal influence.

Corso's work is a special example of the poetics of voice, for unlike many poets he never abandoned completely his interest in older conventions of rhyme, meter, and stanzaic pattern. He trained himself in an immense range of poetries from German Romanticism to seventeenth-century lyricism and from the Babylonian epic *Gilgamesh* to Walt Whitman's *Leaves of Grass.* Even when Beat Generation writers with whom he was associated, particularly Ginsberg and Jack Kerouac, were talking about poetry as immediate expression or utterance, Corso continued to consider his own works as crafted objects.

In spite of Corso's great respect for traditional poetics, however, most of his work owes more to the extemporaneous phrasings of jazz than to conventional metrics, and he can move within the same poem from formal modes to improvisatory structures. In the work of another poet that kind of transition might be jarring, but Corso is able to accomplish it without making it seem unnat-

ural or discordant. In an interview with Gavin Selerie for *Riverside Interviews,* Corso said, "My music is built in—it's already natural. I don't play with the meter." In other words, if the metric is to be regular or traditional, it must arise naturally from the poet's voice; it is never, in any case, consciously chosen.

Corso's vocabulary is as eclectic as his sense of form, borrowing as freely from words heard in the street as from the archaic diction of seventeenth-century English poetry. As he told Michael Andre, for three years before he was twenty he worked with one of the standard dictionaries and "got that whole book in me, all the obsolete and archaic words. And through that I knew that I was in love with language and vocabulary, because the words and the way they looked to me, the way they sounded, and what they meant, how they were defined and all that, I tried to revive them, and I did."

Although Corso uses traditional forms and archaic diction, he does it entirely in his own way. Whatever his sources, whether English Romanticism or modern jazz, he is always the streetwise poet or what Bruce Cook in *The Beat Generation* calls "an urchin Shelley." To evoke past traditions with irony or greater sophistication would destroy much that is essential to Corso's voice. Gaiser suggested that in his poems he adopts "the mask of the sophisticated child whose every display of mad spontaneity and bizarre perception is consciously and effectively designed"—as if he is in some way deceiving his audience. But the poems at their best are controlled by an authentic, distinctive, and enormously effective voice that can range from sentimental affection and pathos to exuberance and dadaist irreverence toward almost anything except poetry itself.

Corso primarily was self-educated as a poet. His childhood was spent largely in orphanages and foster homes, and he never attended school beyond the sixth grade. When he was twelve, he was held as a material witness in a trial and spent several months in prison where, as he wrote in a biographical sketch for *The New American Poetry,* the other prisoners "abused me terribly, and I was indeed like an angel then because when they stole my food and beat me up and threw pee in my cell, I . . . would come out and tell them my beautiful dream about a floating girl who landed before a deep pit and just stared." He later spent three months under observation at Bellevue Hospital.

When Corso was sixteen, he was sent to jail for three years for theft. There he read widely in the classics, including Fyodor Dostoevsky, Stendahl, Percy Bysshe Shelley, Thomas Chatterton, and Christopher Marlowe. Corso was particularly drawn to Shelley, although perhaps less for his poetry than for the example he set as a poet dedicated to his art. After his release from prison in 1950, Corso worked as a laborer, a newspaper reporter in Los Angeles, and a sailor on a boat to Africa and South America.

In 1954 Corso moved to Boston, where several important poets, including Edward Marshall and John Wieners, were experimenting with the poetics of voice. But the center for Corso's life there was not "the School of Boston," as these poets were called, but Harvard and particularly the Harvard library, where he spent his days reading the great works of poetry. His first published poems appeared in the *Harvard Advocate* in 1954, and his play, "In This Hung-Up Age" (concerning a group of Americans who, after their bus breaks down midway across the continent, are trampled by buffalo), was performed by students at the university the following year.

Harvard and Radcliffe students also underwrote the expenses of Corso's first book, *The Vestal Lady on Brattle, and Other Poems,* the work of a young man fascinated with poetry but as yet without a complete sense of his own voice. The poems here are largely apprentice work heavily indebted to Corso's reading, yet from time to time, as in "This Is America," they break out with the kind of ecstatic, transcendent energy that characterizes most of his better-known poems. They also use jazz rhythms (notably in "Requiem for 'Bird' Parker, Musician," the strongest poem in the book), cadences of spoken English, and hipster jargon.

Reviewing the book for *Poetry,* Reuel Denney asked whether "a small group jargon" such as bop language would "sound interesting" to those who were not part of that culture. Corso, he concluded, "cannot balance the richness of the bebop group jargon . . . with the clarity he needs to make his work meaningful to a wider-than-clique audience." However, within a few years, that "small group jargon" became, of course, a national idiom.

Corso moved to San Francisco in 1956, too late to participate in the famous reading at the Six Gallery, at which Ginsberg read "Howl" and which, since it was widely noted in newspapers and popular magazines, is conventionally cited as the first major public event in the rise of the Beat movement. Corso was soon identified as one of the major figures of the movement, however, and that celebrity or notoriety undoubtedly contributed much to the fame of his poetry in the late 1950s and early 1960s. With Ginsberg, he also co-authored "The Literary Revolution in America" (published in *Litterair Paspoort*), an article in which they declared that America now had poets who "have taken it upon themselves, with angelic clarions in hand, to announce their discontent, their demands, their hope, their final wondrous unimaginable dream."

From 1957 to 1958, Corso lived in Paris, where, he told Michael Andre, "things burst and opened, and I said, 'I will just let the lines go. . . .' " Poems that resulted were published in *Gasoline,* his first major book. *Gasoline* also contains poems written while Corso was traveling with Ginsberg in Mexico, and Ginsberg's influence is evident in much of the work. Here Whitman's long poetic line has become Corso's much as it had become Ginsberg's, and the diction is occasionally reminiscent of Ginsberg as well. "Ode to Coit Tower," for example, echoes "In the Baggage Room at Greyhound," on which Ginsberg recently had been working, and "Sun" utilizes structural devices and incantatory effects used in "Howl." But however influential Ginsberg may have been, Corso always maintained his own distinctive voice. In an essay collected in *The Beats: Essays in Criticism,* Geoffrey Thurley summarized some of the principal characteristics that differentiate Corso from Ginsberg: "Where Ginsberg is all expression and voice, Corso is calm and quick, whimsical often, witty rather than humourous, semantically swift rather than prophetically incantatory."

The influence of bop is far more evident in *Gasoline* than in *The Vestal Lady on Brattle.* In his introduction, Ginsberg quotes Corso as saying that his poems were written the way Charlie Parker and Miles Davis played music. He would start with standard diction and rhythm but then be "intentionally distracted diversed [sic] into my own sound." The result is an intricate linguistic pattern involving extremely subtle modulations of sound and rhythm. "For Corso," Neeli Cherkovski wrote in *Whitman's Wild Children: Profiles of Ten Contemporary American Poets,* "poetry is at its best when it can create a totally unexpected expression," and many of these linguistic fusions suggest the pleasure in invention for its own sake. As Gullea pointed out, however, Corso's word play often leads to images which are "surreal in that they assert a reality higher than the one perceived by the ordinary person, who is too concerned with meaning, which is

a process of compartmentalizing the things of this world. In 'Birthplace Revisited,' for example, facing a man wielding a knife, the speaker 'pump[s] him full of lost watches.' The whole thrust of Corso's use of such images is to shatter these compartments, to unify everything in the cosmos by juxtaposing disparate elements in the melting pot of the poet's imagination."

In the 1960s, though Beats such as Ginsberg and Kerouac became cult figures for the counterculture, Corso was generally overlooked. He taught for a while at the University of New York at Buffalo, but his appointment was terminated when he refused to sign a loyalty oath required of all university employees by the state of New York. Then in 1969, Kerouac died, and Corso responded with "Elegiac Feelings American," a major poem that became the title work in the collection published the following year. Corso had never been as politically motivated a poet as Ginsberg, but "Elegiac Feelings American" is a profound statement of his frustration at the apparent collapse of the revolution of the spirit that he and other Beat writers had once thought would alter America irrevocably. But the promise is not gone absolutely, and if America, as the poem contends, destroyed Kerouac, there are still those who followed him: "the children of flowers."

Corso shaped his poems from 1970 to 1974 into a book that he planned to call *Who Am I—Who I Am,* but the manuscript was stolen, and there were no other copies. Aside from chapbooks and a few miscellaneous publications, he did not issue other work until 1981 when *Herald of the Autochthonic Spirit* appeared. Shorter than any of his major books since *Gasoline,* it contains some excellent poems, many of them written in clipped, almost prosaic lines more reminiscent of William Carlos Williams than of Whitman. "Return" deals with barren times in which there had been no poems but also asserts that the poet can now write again and that "the past [is] my future." The new poems, however, are generally more subdued than the earlier ones, though there are delightful surreal flights, as in "The Whole Mess . . . Almost," in which the poet cleans his apartment of Truth, God, Beauty, Death, and essentially everything but Humor.

By the early 1980s, when Corso's *Herald of the Autochthonic Spirit* was published, language-centered writing, in which the conventions of language themselves become the subjects of poems, had long since surpassed the poetics of voice as the center of attention for many younger poets working outside academic traditions. Thus the book was not widely reviewed, even though it contains some of Corso's best work. But if the voice that shaped these poems is often quieter than it had been a generation before, it nonetheless continues to affirm Kenneth Rexroth's characterization of Corso as "a real wildman." "At his worst," Rexroth added, "he is an amusing literary curiosity; at his best, his poems are metaphysical hotfoots and poetic cannon crackers."

BIOGRAPHICAL/CRITICAL SOURCES:

BOOKS

Allen, Donald M., editor, *The New American Poetry,* Grove Press, 1960.

Allen, and Warren Tallman, *The Poetics of the New American Poetry,* Grove Press, 1973.

Bartlett, Lee, *The Beats: Essays in Criticism,* McFarland, 1981.

Chassman, Neil A., editor, *Poets of the Cities: New York and San Francisco, 1950-1965,* Dutton, 1974.

Cherkovski, Neeli, *Whitman's Wild Children: Profiles of Ten Contemporary American Poets,* Lapis Press, 1988.

Contemporary Literary Criticism, Gale, Volume 1, 1973, Volume 11, 1979.

Cook, Bruce, *The Beat Generation,* Scribner, 1971.

Corso, Gregory, *Gasoline,* introduction by Allen Ginsberg, City Lights, 1958.

Dictionary of Literary Biography, Gale, Volume 5: *American Poets Since World War II,* 1980, Volume 16: *The Beats: Literary Bohemianism in Postwar America,* 1983.

Gifford, Barry, and Lawrence Lee, *Jack's Book: An Oral Biography of Jack Kerouac,* St. Martin's, 1978.

Knight, Arthur, and Kit Knight, editors, *The Beat Vision: A Primary Sourcebook,* Paragon House, 1987.

Leary, Paris, and Robert Kelly, editors, *A Controversy of Poets,* Doubleday Anchor, 1965.

Nemerov, Howard, editor, *Poets on Poetry,* Basic Books, 1966.

Parkinson, Thomas, editor, *A Casebook on the Beat,* Crowell, 1961.

Rexroth, Kenneth, *Assays,* New Directions, 1961.

Selerie, Gavin, *Riverside Interviews 3: Gregory Corso,* Binnacle Press, 1982.

Tytell, John, *Naked Angels: The Lives and Literature of the Beat Generation,* McGraw, 1976.

Wilson, Robert A., *A Bibliography of Works by Gregory Corso, 1954-1965,* Phoenix Book Shop, 1966.

PERIODICALS

Hudson Review, spring, 1963.

Kenyon Review, spring, 1963.

North Dakota Quarterly, spring, 1982.

Partisan Review, fall, 1960.

Poetry, October, 1956.

Thoth, winter, 1971.

Unmuzzled Ox, winter, 1981.

* * *

CORTAZAR, Julio   1914-1984
(Julio Denis)

PERSONAL: Born August 26, 1914, in Brussels, Belgium; held dual citizenship in Argentina and (beginning 1981) France; died of a heart attack February 12, 1984, in Paris, France; son of Julio Jose and Maria Herminia (Descotte) Cortazar; married former spouse Aurora Bernardez, August 23, 1953. *Education:* Received degrees in teaching and public translating; attended Buenos Aires University.

CAREER: Writer. High school teacher in Bolivar and Chivilcoy, both in Argentina, 1937-44; teacher of French literature, University of Cuyo, Mendoza, Argentina, 1944-45; manager, Argentine Publishing Association (Camara Argentina del Libro), Buenos Aires, Argentina, 1946-48; public translator in Argentina, 1948-51; free-lance translator for UNESCO, Paris, France, 1952-84. Member of jury, Casa de las Americas Award.

AWARDS, HONORS: Prix Medicis, 1974, for *Libro de Manuel;* Ruben Dario Order of Cultural Independence awarded by Government of Nicaragua, 1983.

WRITINGS:

FICTION

Bestiario (stories; title means "Bestiary"; also see below), Sudamericana (Buenos Aires), 1951, reprinted, 1983.

Final del juego (stories; also see below), Los Presentes (Mexico), 1956, expanded edition, Sudamericana, 1964, reprinted, 1983.

Las armas secretas (stories; title means "The Secret Weapons"; also see below), Sudamericana, 1959, reprinted, Catedra (Madrid), 1983.

Los premios (novel), Sudamericana, 1960, reprinted, Ediciones B, 1987, translation by Elaine Kerrigan published as *The Winners,* Pantheon, 1965, reprinted, 1984.

Historias de cronopios y de famas, Minotauro (Buenos Aires), 1962, reprinted, Alfaguara, 1984, translation by Paul Blackburn published as *Cronopios and Famas,* Pantheon, 1969.

Rayuela (novel), Sudamericana, 1963, reprinted, 1984, translation by Gregory Rabassa published as *Hopscotch,* Pantheon, 1966, reprinted, 1987.

Cuentos (collection), Casa de las Americas (Havana), 1964.

Todos los fuegos el fuego (stories), Sudamericana, 1966, reprinted, 1981, translation by Suzanne Jill Levine published as *All Fires the Fire, and Other Stories,* Pantheon, 1973, reprinted, 1988.

La vuelta al dia en ochenta mundos (essays, poetry, and stories), Siglo Veintiuno (Mexico), 1967, reprinted, 1984, translation by Thomas Christensen published as *Around the Day in Eighty Worlds,* North Point Press, 1986.

El perseguidor y otros cuentos (stories), Centro Editor para America Latina (Buenos Aires), 1967, reprinted, Bruguera, 1983.

End of the Game, and Other Stories, translated by Blackburn (includes stories from *Final del juego, Bestiario,* and *Las armas secretas*), Pantheon, 1967, published as *Blow-Up, and Other Stories,* Collier, 1968, reprinted, Pantheon, 1985.

Ceremonias (collection), Seix Barral, 1968, reprinted, 1983.

62: Modelo para armar (novel), Sudamericana, 1968, translation by Rabassa published as *62: A Model Kit,* Pantheon, 1972.

Ultimo round (essays, poetry, and stories; title means "Last Round"), Siglo Veintiuno, 1969, reprinted, 1984.

Relatos (collection), Sudamericana, 1970.

La isla a mediodia y otros relatos (contains twelve previously published stories), Salvat, 1971.

Libro de Manuel (novel), Sudamericana, 1973, translation by Rabassa published as *A Manual for Manuel,* Pantheon, 1978.

Octaedro (stories; title means "Octahedron"; also see below), Sudamericana, 1974.

Antologia (collection), La Libreria, 1975.

Fantomas contra los vampiros multinacionales (title means "Fantomas Takes on the Multinational Vampires"), Excelsior (Mexico), 1975.

Los relatos (collection), four volumes, Alianza, 1976-1985.

Alguien que anda por ahi y otros relatos (stories), Alfaguara (Madrid), 1977, translation by Rabassa published as *A Change of Light, and Other Stories* (includes *Octaedro;* also see below), Knopf, 1980.

Territorios, Siglo Veintiuno, 1978.

Un tal Lucas, Alfaguara, 1979, translation by Rabassa published as *A Certain Lucas,* Knopf, 1984.

Queremos tanto a Glenda, Alfaguara, 1980, translation by Rabassa published as *We Love Glenda So Much, and Other Tales* (also see below), Knopf, 1983.

Deshoras (short stories), Alfaguara, 1982.

We Love Glenda So Much [and] *A Change of Light,* Vintage, 1984.

TRANSLATOR

Alfred Stern, *Filosofia de la risa y del llanto,* Iman (Buenos Aires), 1950.

Lord Houghton, *Vida y cartas de John Keats,* Iman, 1955.

Marguerite Yourcenar, *Memorias de Adriano,* Sudamericana, 1955.

Edgar Allan Poe, *Obras en prosa,* two volumes, Revista de Occidente, 1956.

Poe, *Cuentos,* Editorial Nacional de Cuba, 1963.

Poe, *Aventuras de Arthur Gordon Pym,* Instituto del Libro (Havana), 1968.

Poe, *Eureka,* Alianza (Madrid), 1972.

Daniel Defoe, *Robinson Crusoe,* Bruguera, 1981.

Also translator of works by G. K. Chesterton, Andre Gide, and Jean Giono, published in Argentina between 1948 and 1951.

OTHER

(Under pseudonym Julio Denis) *Presencia* (poems; title means "Presence"), El Bibliofilo (Buenos Aires), 1938.

Los reyes (play; title means "The Monarchs"), Gulab y Aldabahor (Buenos Aires), 1949, reprinted, Alfaguara, 1982.

(Contributor) *Buenos Aires de la fundacion a la angustia,* Ediciones de la Flor (Buenos Aires), 1967.

(With others) *Cuba por argentinos,* Merlin (Buenos Aires), 1968.

Buenos Aires, Buenos Aires (includes French and English translations), Sudamericana, 1968.

Viaje alrededor de una mesa (title means "Trip around a Table"), Cuadernos de Rayuela (Buenos Aires), 1970.

(With Oscar Collazos and Mario Vargas Llosa) *Literatura en la revolucion y revolucion en la literatura,* Siglo Veintiuno, 1970.

(Contributor) *Literatura y arte nuevo en Cuba,* Estela (Barcelona), 1971.

Pameos y meopas (poetry), Editorial Libre de Sivera (Barcelona), 1971.

Prosa del observatorio, Lumen (Barcelona), 1972.

La casilla de los Morelli (essays), edited by Jose Julio Ortega, Tusquets, 1973.

Convergencias, divergencias, incidencias, edited by Ortega, Tusquets, 1973.

(Author of text) *Humanario,* La Azotea (Buenos Aires), 1976.

(Author of text) *Paris: Ritmos de una ciudad,* Edhasa (Barcelona), 1981.

Paris: The Essence of an Image, Norton, 1981.

(With Carol Dunlop) *Los autonautas de la cosmopista,* Muchnik (Buenos Aires), 1983.

Nicaragua tan violentamente dulce (essays), Nueva Nicaragua, 1983.

Argentina: Anos de almabradas culturales (essays), edited by Saul Yurkievich, Muchnik, 1984.

Nada a pehuajo: Un acto; Adios, Robinson (plays), Katun, 1984.

Salvo el crepusculo (poems), Nueva Imagen, 1984.

Textos politicos, Plaza y Janes, 1985.

Divertimento, Sudamericana/Planeta, 1986.

El examen, Sudamericana/Planeta, 1986.

Nicaraguan Sketches, Norton, 1989.

Contributor to numerous periodicals, including *Revista Iberoamericana, Cuadernos Hispanoamericanos, Books Abroad,* and *Casa de las Americas.*

SIDELIGHTS: Argentine author Julio Cortazar was "one of the world's greatest writers," according to novelist Stephen Dobyns. "His range of styles," Dobyns wrote in the *Washington Post Book World,* "his ability to paint a scene, his humor, his endlessly peculiar mind makes many of his stories wonderful. His novel *Hopscotch* is considered one of the best novels written by a South American."

A popular as well as a critical success, *Hopscotch* not only established Cortazar's reputation as a novelist of international merit but also, according to David W. Foster in *Currents in the Contemporary Argentine Novel,* prompted wider acceptance in the United States of novels written by other Latin Americans. For this reason many critics, such as Jaime Alazraki in *The Final Island,* viewed the book as "a turning point for Latin American literature." A *Times Literary Supplement* reviewer, for example, called *Hopscotch* "the first great novel of Spanish America."

Still other critics, including novelists Jose Donoso and C. D. B. Bryan, saw the novel in the context of world literature. Donoso, in his *The Boom in Spanish American Literature: A Personal History,* claimed that *Hopscotch* "humanized the novel." Cortazar was a writer, Donoso continued, "who [dared] to be discursive and whose pages [were] sprinkled with names of musicians, painters, art galleries, . . . movie directors[, and] all this had an undisguised place within his novel, something which I would never have dared to presume to be right for the Latin American novel, since it was fine for [German novelist] Thomas Mann but not for us." In the *New York Times Book Review,* Bryan stated: "I think *Hopscotch* is the most magnificent book I have ever read. No novel has so satisfactorily and completely and beautifully explored man's compulsion to explore life, to search for its meaning, to challenge its mysteries. Nor has any novel in recent memory lavished such love and attention upon the full spectrum of the writer's craft."

Cortazar attempted to perfect his craft by constant experimentation. In his longer fiction he pursued, as Leo Bersani observed in the *New York Times Book Review,* both "subversion and renewal of novelistic form." This subversion and renewal was of such importance to Cortazar that often the form of his novels overshadowed the action that they described. Through the form of his fiction Cortazar invited the reader to participate in the writer's craft and to share in the creation of the novel.

Hopscotch is one such novel. In *Into the Mainstream: Conversations with Latin-America Writers,* Luis Harss and Barbara Dohmann wrote that *Hopscotch* "is the first Latin American novel which takes itself as its own central topic or, in other words, is essentially about the writing of itself. It lives in constant metamorphoses, as an unfinished process that invents itself as it goes, involving the reader in such a way to make him part of the creative impulse." Thus, *Hopscotch* begins with a "Table of Instructions" that tells the reader that there are at least two ways to read the novel. The first is reading chapters one to fifty-six in numerical order. When the reader finishes chapter fifty-six he can, according to the instructions, stop reading and "ignore what follows [nearly one hundred more short chapters] with a clean conscience." The other way of reading suggested by the instructions is to start with chapter seventy-two and then skip from chapter to chapter (hence, the title of the book), following the sequence indicated at the end of each chapter by a number which tells the reader which chapter is next. Read the second way, the reader finds that chapter 131 refers him to chapter fifty-eight, and chapter fifty-eight to chapter 131, so that he is confronted with a novel that has no end. With his "Table of Instructions" Cortazar forces the reader to write the novel while he is reading it.

Cortazar's other experimental works include *62: A Model Kit* (considered a sequel to *Hopscotch*), *A Manual for Manuel, Ultimo round* ("Last Round"), and *Fantomas contra los vampiros multinacionales* ("Fantomas Takes on the Multinational Vampires"). *62: A Model Kit* is based on chapter sixty-two of *Hopscotch* in which a character, Morelli, expresses his desire to write a new type of novel. "If I were to write this book," Morelli states, "standard behavior would be inexplicable by means of current instrumental psychology. Everything would be a kind of disquiet, a continuous uprooting, a territory where psychological causality would yield disconcertedly."

In *62: A Model Kit* Cortazar attempted to put these ideas into action. Time and space have no meaning in the novel: although it takes place in Paris, London, and Vienna, the characters move and interact as if they are in one single space. The characters themselves are sketchily presented in fragments that must be assembled by the readers; chapters are replaced by short scenes separated by blank spaces on the pages of the novel. Cortazar noted in the book's introduction that once again the reader must help create the novel: "The reader's option, his personal montage of the elements in the tale, will in each case be the book he has chosen to read."

A Manual for Manuel continues in the experimental vein. Megan Marshall described the book in *New Republic* as "a novel that merges story and history, a supposed scrapbook of news clippings, journal entries, diagrams, transcripts of conversations, and much more." The book, about the kidnapping of a Latin American diplomat by a group of guerillas in Paris, is told from the double perspective of an unnamed member of the group, who takes notes on the plans for the kidnapping, and a nonmember of the group, Andres, who reads the notes. Periodically, these two narrations are interrupted by the inclusion of English-, French-, and Spanish-language texts reproduced in the pages of the novel. These texts, actual articles collected by Cortazar from various sources, form part of a scrapbook being assembled for Manuel, the child of two of the members of the group. On one page, for example, Cortazar reprinted a statistical table originally published in 1969 by the U.S. Department of Defense that shows how many Latin Americans have received military training in the United States. The reader reads about the compilation of the scrapbook for Manuel, while at the same time reading the scrapbook and reacting to the historical truth it contains.

Other such experimentation is found in *Ultimo round,* a collection of essays, stories, and poetry. William L. Siemens noted in the *International Fiction Review* that this book, like *Hopscotch* and *62: A Model Kit,* "is a good example of audience-participation art." In *Ultimo round,* he declared, "it is impossible for the reader to proceed in a conventional manner. Upon opening the book the reader notes that there are two sets of pages within the binding, and he must immediately decide which of them to read first, and even whether he will go through by reading the top and then the bottom of page one, and so on."

Cortazar's brief narrative *Fantomas contra los vampiros multinacionales* is yet another experiment with new forms of fiction. It presents, in comic book form, the story of a "superhero," Fantomas, who gathers together "the greatest contemporary writers" to fight the destructive powers of the multinational corporations. Chilean Octavio Paz, Italian Alberto Moravia, and American Susan Sontag, along with Cortazar himself, appear as characters in the comic book. Although short, the work embodies several constants in Cortazar's fiction: the comic (the comic book form itself), the interplay of fantasy and reality (the appearance of historical figures in a fictional work), and a commitment to social activism (the portrayal of the writer as a politically involved individual). These three elements, together with Cortazar's experiments with the novelistic form, are the basic components of his fiction.

Cortazar explained how these elements function together in his essay "Algunos aspectos del cuento" ("Some Aspects of the Story"), which Alazraki quoted in *The Final Island.* His work,

Cortazar claimed, was "an alternative to that false realism which assumed that everything can be neatly described as was upheld by the philosophic and scientific optimism of the eighteenth century, that is, within a world ruled more or less harmoniously by a system of laws, of principles, of causal relations, of well defined psychologies, of well mapped geographies. . . . In my case, the suspicion of another order, more secret and less communicable [was one of the principles guiding] my personal search for a literature beyond overly naive forms of realism." Whatever the method, whether new narrative forms, unexpected humor, incursions into fantasy, or pleas for a more humane society, Cortazar strove to shake the reader out of traditional ways of thinking and seeing the world and to replace them with new and more viable models. Dobyn explained in the *Washington Post Book World,* "Cortazar wants to jolt people out of their self-complacency, to make them doubt their own definition of the world."

Cortazar's last full-length work of fiction, *A Certain Lucas,* for example, "is a kind of sampler of narrative ideas, a playful anthology of form, including everything from parables to parodies, folk tales to metafictions," as Robert Coover describes it in the *New York Times Book Review.* Including chapters with such titles as "Lucas, His Shopping," "Lucas, His Battles with the Hydra," and "Lucas, His Pianists," the book "builds a portrait, montage-like, through a succession of short sketches (humorous set-pieces, really) full of outrageous inventions, leaping and dream-like associations and funny turns of phrase," states *Los Angeles Times Book Review* critic Charles Champlin. "Lucas is not Cortazar," Dobyns suggests in the *Washington Post Book World,* "but occasionally he seems to stand for him and so the book takes on an autobiographical quality as we read about Lucas' friends, his struggles with himself, his dreams, his tastes, his view of writing." The result, writes Champlin, might appear to be "no more than a series of extravagant jokes, [and] it would be an exceptional passing entertainment but no more than that. Yet under the cover of raillery, self-indicting foolishness and extremely tall tales," the critic continues, "Cortazar is discovered to be a thoughtful, deep-feeling man, impassioned, sentimental, angry, complicated, a philosopher exploring appearances vs. realities is the way of philosophers ever." "What we see in Lucas and in much of Cortazar's work is a fierce love of this earth, despite the awfulness, and a fierce respect for life's ridiculousness," concludes Dobyns. "And in the midst of this ridiculousness, Cortazar dances . . . and that dance comforts and eases our own course through the world."

This ridiculousness, or humor, in Cortazar's work often derived from what a *Time* reviewer referred to as the author's "ability to present common objects from strange perspectives as if he had just invented them." Cortazar, declared Tom Bishop in *Saturday Review,* was "an intellectual humorist. . . . [He had] a rare gift for isolating the absurd in everyday life [and] for depicting the foibles in human behavior with an unerring thrust that [was] satiric yet compassionate."

Hopscotch is filled with humorous elements, some of which Saul Yurkievich listed in *The Final Island.* He included "references to the ridiculous, . . . recourse to the outlandish, . . . absurd associations, . . . juxtaposition of the majestic with the popular or vulgar," as well as "puns, . . . [and] polyglot insults." *New York Times* writer John Leonard called absurdity "obligatory" in a work by Cortazar and gave examples of the absurd found in *A Manual for Manuel,* such as "a turquoise penguin [is] flown by jet to Argentina; the stealing of 9,000 wigs . . . and obsessive puns." In an interview with Evelyn Picon Garfield, quoted in *Books Abroad,* Cortazar called *Cronopios and Famas* his "most playful book." It is, he continued, "really a game, a very fascinating game, lots of fun, almost like a tennis match."

This book of short, story-like narratives deals with two groups of creatures described by Arthur Curley in *Library Journal* as the "warm life-loving cronopios and practical, conventional famas . . . imaginary but typical personages between whom communication is usually impossible and always ridiculous." One portion of the book, called "The Instruction Manual," contains detailed explanations of various everyday activities, including how to climb stairs, how to wind a clock, and how to cry. In order to cry correctly, the author suggested thinking of a duck covered with ants. With these satiric instructions Cortazar, according to Paul West in *Book World*, "cleanses the doors of perception and mounts a subtle, bland assault on the mental rigidities we hold most dear." By forcing us to think about everyday occurrences in a new way, Cortazar, Malva E. Filer noted in *Books Abroad*, "expresses his rebellion against objects and persons that make up our everyday life and the mechanical ways by which we relate to them." Filer continued: "In Cortazar's fictional world [a] routine life is the great scandal against which every individual must rebel with all his strength. And if he is not willing to do so, extraordinary elements are usually summoned to force him out of this despicable and abject comfort."

These "extraordinary elements" enter into the lives of Cortazar's characters in the form of fantastic episodes which interrupt their otherwise normal existences. Alexander Coleman observed in *Cinco maestros: Cuentos modernos de Hispanoamerica* ("Five Masters: Modern Spanish-American Stories"): "Cortazar's stories start in a disarmingly conversational way, with plenty of local touches. But something always seems to go awry just when we least expect it." "Axolotl," a short story described by novelist Joyce Carol Oates in the *New York Times Book Review* as her favorite Cortazar tale, begins innocently: a man describes his trips to the Parisian botanical gardens to watch a certain type of salamander called an axolotl. But the serenity ends when the narrator admits, "Now I am an axolotl." In another story, a woman has a dream about a beggar who lives in Budapest (a city the woman has never visited). The woman ends up actually going to Budapest where she finds herself walking across a bridge as the beggar woman from her dream approaches from the opposite side. The two women embrace in the middle of the bridge and the first woman is transformed into the beggar woman—she can feel the snow seeping through the holes in her shoes—while she sees her former self walk away. In yet another story, a motorcyclist is involved in a minor traffic accident and suddenly finds himself thrown back in time where he becomes the victim of an Aztec ritual sacrifice. Daniel Stern noted in *Nation* that with these stories and others like them "it is as if Cortazar is showing us that it is essential for us to reimagine the reality in which we live and which we can no longer take for granted."

Although during the last years of his life Cortazar was so involved with political activism that Jason Weiss described him in the *Los Angeles Times* as a writer with hardly any time to write, the Argentine had early in his career been criticized "for his apparent indifference to the brutish situation" of his fellow Latin Americans, according to Leonard. Evidence of his growing political preoccupation is found in his later stories and novels. Leonard observed, for instance, that *A Manual for Manuel* "is a primer on the necessity of revolutionary action," and William Kennedy in the *Washington Post Book World* noted that the newspaper clippings included in the novel "touch[ed] the open nerve of political oppression in Latin America." Many of the narratives in *A Change of Light, and Other Stories* are also politically oriented. Oates described the impact of one story in the *New York Times Book Review*. In "Apocalypse at Solentiname," a photographer develops his vacation photographs of happy, smiling people only to discover pictures of people being tortured. Oates commented, "The narrator . . . contemplates in despair the impotence of art to deal with in any significant way, the 'life of permanent uncertainty . . . [in] almost all of Latin America, a life surrounded by fear and death.' "

Cortazar's fictional world, according to Alazraki in *The Final Island*, "represents a challenge to culture." This challenge is embedded in the author's belief in a reality that reaches beyond our everyday existence. Alazraki noted that Cortazar once declared, "Our daily reality masks a second reality which is neither mysterious nor theological, but profoundly human. Yet, due to a long series of mistakes, it has remained concealed under a reality prefabricated by many centuries of culture, a culture in which there are great achievements but also profound aberrations, profound distortions." Bryan further explained these ideas in the *New York Times Book Review*: Cortazar's "surrealistic treatment of the most pedestrian acts suggest[ed] that one way to combat alienation is to return to the original receptiveness of childhood, to recapture this original innocence, by returning to the concept of life as a game."

Cortazar confronted his reader with unexpected forms, with humor, fantasy, and unseemly reality in order to challenge him to live a more meaningful life. He summarized his theory of fiction (and of life) in an essay, "The Present State of Fiction in Latin America," which appeared in *Books Abroad*. The Argentine concluded: "The fantastic is something that one must never say good-bye to lightly. The man of the future . . . will have to find the bases of a reality which is truly his and, at the same time, maintain the capacity of dreaming and playing which I have tried to show you . . . , since it is through those doors that the Other, the fantastic dimension, and the unexpected will always slip, as will all that will save us from that obedient robot into which so many technocrats would like to convert us and which we will not accept—ever."

MEDIA ADAPTATIONS: The story "Las babas del diablo," from the collection *Las armas secretas* was the basis for Michaelangelo Antonioni's 1966 film "Blow Up."

AVOCATIONAL INTERESTS: Jazz, movies.

BIOGRAPHICAL/CRITICAL SOURCES:

BOOKS

Alazraki, Jaime and Ivar Ivask, editors, *The Final Island: The Fiction of Julio Cortazar*, University of Oklahoma Press, 1978.

Boldy, Steven, *The Novels of Cortazar*, Cambridge University Press, 1980.

Coleman, Alexander, editor, *Cinco maestros: Cuentos modernos de Hispanoamerica*, Harcourt, Brace & World, 1969.

Contemporary Literary Criticism, Gale, Volume 2, 1974, Volume 3, 1975, Volume 5, 1976, Volume 10, 1979, Volume 13, 1980, Volume 15, 1980, Volume 33, 1985, Volume 34, 1985.

Donoso, Jose, *Historia personal del "boom,"* Anagrama (Barcelona), 1972, translation by Gregory Kolovakos published as *The Boom in Spanish American Literature: A Personal History*, Columbia University Press, 1977.

Foster, David W., *Currents in the Contemporary Argentine Novel*, University of Missouri Press, 1975.

Garfield, Evelyn Picon, *Julio Cortazar*, Ungar, 1975.

Garfield, Evelyn Picon, *Cortazar por Cortazar* (interviews), Universidad Veracruzana, 1981.

Giacoman, Helmy F., editor, *Homenaje a Julio Cortazar,* Anaya, 1972.

Harss, Luis and Barbara Dohmann, *Into the Mainstream: Conversations with Latin-American Writers,* Harper, 1967.

Prego, Omar, *La fascinacion de las palabras* (interviews), Muchnik, 1985.

Vasquez Amaral, Jose, *The Contemporary Latin American Narrative,* Las Americas, 1970.

PERIODICALS

America, April 17, 1965, July 9, 1966, December 22, 1973.
Atlantic, June, 1969, October, 1973.
Books Abroad, fall, 1965, winter, 1968, summer, 1969, winter, 1970, summer, 1976.
Book World, August 17, 1969.
Casa de las Americas, numbers 15-16, 1962.
Chicago Tribune, September 24, 1978.
Chicago Tribune Book World, November 16, 1980, May 8, 1983.
Christian Science Monitor, August 15, 1967, July 3, 1969, December 4, 1978.
Commentary, October, 1966.
El Pais, April 19, 1981.
Hispania, December, 1973.
Hudson Review, spring, 1974.
International Fiction Review, January, 1974, January, 1975.
Library Journal, July, 1967, September, 1969, September 15, 1980.
Listener, December 20, 1979.
Los Angeles Times, August 28, 1983.
Los Angeles Times Book Review, December 28, 1980, June 12, 1983, May 27, 1984.
Nation, September 18, 1967.
National Review, July 25, 1967.
New Republic, April 23, 1966, July 15, 1967, October 21, 1978, October 25, 1980.
New Yorker, May 18, 1965, February 25, 1974.
New York Review of Books, March 25, 1965, April 28, 1966, April 19, 1973, October 12, 1978.
New York Times, November 13, 1978, March 24, 1983.
New York Times Book Review, March 21, 1965, April 10, 1966, June 15, 1969, November 26, 1972, September 9, 1973, November 19, 1978, November 9, 1980, March 4, 1984, May 20, 1984.
Novel: A Forum on Fiction, fall, 1967.
Review of Contemporary Fiction (special Cortazar issue), fall, 1983.
Revista Iberoamericana, July-December, 1973.
Saturday Review, March 27, 1965, April 9, 1966, July 22, 1967, September 27, 1969.
Time, April 29, 1966, June 13, 1969, October 1, 1973.
Times Literary Supplement, October 12, 1973, December 7, 1979.
Virginia Quarterly Review, spring, 1973.
Washington Post Book World, November 18, 1973, November 5, 1978, November 23, 1980, May 1, 1983, June 24, 1984.
World Literature Today, winter, 1977, winter, 1980.

OBITUARIES:

PERIODICALS

Chicago Tribune, February 14, 1984.
Globe and Mail (Toronto), February 18, 1984.
Los Angeles Times, February 14, 1984.
New York Times, February 13, 1984.
Times (London), February 14, 1984.
Voice Literary Supplement, March, 1984.

Washington Post, February 13, 1984.

* * *

COURTNEY, Robert
See ELLISON, Harlan

* * *

COUSINS, Norman 1915-

PERSONAL: Born June 24, 1915, in Union Hill, N.J.; son of Samuel and Sara Barry (Miller) Cousins; married Ellen Kopf, June 23, 1939; children: Andrea, Amy Loveman, Candis Hitzig, Sara Kit. *Education:* Attended Teachers College, Columbia University.

ADDRESSES: Home—2644 Eden Pl., Beverly Hills, Calif. 90201. *Office*—Department of Psychiatry and Biobehavioral Sciences, 2859 Slichter Hall, University of California, Los Angeles, Calif. 90024.

CAREER: New York Evening Post, New York City, educational editor, 1934-35; *Current History,* New York City, 1935-40, began as book critic, became literary editor and managing editor; *Saturday Review of Literature* (now *Saturday Review*), New York City, executive editor, 1940-42, editor, 1942-71; *World,* New York City, editor, 1972-73; *Saturday Review/World,* New York City, editor, 1973-74; *Saturday Review,* New York City, editor, 1975-78; University of California, Los Angeles, currently professor of medical humanities and affiliated with Brain Research Institute. McCall's Corp., New York City, vice-president and director, beginning 1961.

Office of War Information, Overseas Bureau, member of editorial board, 1943-45; co-chairman of national campaign board of 1943 Victory Book Campaign. U. S. Government diplomat and lecturer in India, Pakistan, and Ceylon, 1951; Japan-America exchange lecturer, Japan, 1953. Chairman of board of directors of National Educational Television, 1969-70; member of Commission to Study Organized Peace; member of board of directors of Freedom House and Willkie Memorial Foundation; member of board of directors of Columbia University Conference on Science, Philosophy, and Religion. Chairman of Connecticut Fact Finding Commission on Education, 1948-52; founder and president of United World Federalists, 1952-54, honorary president, 1954-56; co-chairman of National Committee for a Sane Nuclear Policy, 1957-63.

MEMBER: American Council of Learned Societies (member-at-large), National Planning Association, National Academy of Sciences (member of committee on international relations), United Nations Association (director of U.S. Division), World Association of World Federalists, Council on Foreign Relations, National Press Club, Overseas Press Club (member of board of governors), P.E.N. (vice-president of American Center, 1952-55), Century Club, Coffee House (New York).

AWARDS, HONORS: Thomas Jefferson Award for the Advancement of Democracy in Journalism, 1948; Tuition Plan award for outstanding service to American education, 1951; Benjamin Franklin citation in magazine journalism, 1956; Wayne State University award for national service to education, 1958; New York State Citizens Education Commission award, 1959; John Dewey Award for Education, 1959; New York State Citizens Education Community award, 1959; Eleanor Roosevelt Peace award, 1963; Publius award, United World Federalists, 1964; Overseas Press Club award, 1965; Distinguished Citizen award, Connecticut Bar Association, 1965; New York Academy of Public Education award, 1966; Family of Man award, 1968; Annual award, Aquinas College, 1968; national magazine award, Association of Deans of Journalism Schools, 1969.

Peace medal, United Nations, 1971; Sarah Josepha Hale award, 1971; Carr Van Anda award for contributions to journalism, Ohio State University, 1971; Gold medal for literature, National Arts Club, 1972; Journalism Honor award, University of Missouri School of Journalism, 1972; Irita Van Doren book award, 1972; award for service to the environment, Government of Canada, 1972; Henry Johnson Fisher award as magazine publisher of the year, Magazine Publishers Association, 1971; Human Resources award, 1977; Convocation medal, American College of Cardiology, 1978; Author of the Year award, American Society of Journalists and Authors, 1981; American Book Award nomination in paperback nonfiction, 1982, for *Anatomy of an Illness as Perceived by the Patient.*

Also recipient of nearly fifty honorary doctorate degrees, including: Litt.D., American University, 1948, and Elmira College, Ripon College, Wilmington College, and University of Vermont, all 1957, and Western Michigan University; L.H.D., Boston University and Colby College, both 1953, Denison University, 1954, and Colgate University, 1958; L.L.D., Washington and Jefferson College, 1956, and Syracuse University and Albright College, both 1957; Ed.D., Rhode Island College of Education, 1958.

WRITINGS:

The Good Inheritance: The Democratic Chance, Coward, 1942.
(Editor) *A Treasury of Democracy,* Coward 1942.
Modern Man Is Obsolete, Viking, 1945.
(Editor with William Rose Benet) *An Anthology of the Poetry of Liberty,* Modern Library, 1945.
(Editor) *Writing for Love or Money: Thirty-Five Essays Reprinted from the Saturday Review of Literature,* Longmans, Green, 1949, reprinted, Books for Libraries Press, 1970.
(Contributor) John W. Chase, editor, *Years of the Modern,* Longmans, Green, 1949.
(With Jawaharlal Nehru) *Talks with Nehru,* Day, 1951.
Who Speaks for Man?, Macmillan, 1953.
Amy Loveman, 1881-1955, A Eulogy (pamphlet), Overbrook Press, 1956.
The Religious Beliefs of the Founding Fathers, 1958.
(Editor) *In God We Trust,* Harper, 1958.
(Editor) Francis March, *Thesaurus Dictionary,* Doubleday, 1958.
The Rejection of Nothingness (pamphlet), Pacific School of Religion, 1959.
Dr. Schweitzer of Lambarene, Harper, 1960, reprinted, Greenwood Press, 1973.
In Place of Folly, Harper, 1961, revised edition, Washington Square Press, 1962.
Can Cultures Co-Exist? (symposium), Ministry of Scientific Research & Cultural Affairs (New Delhi), 1963.
(With others) *". . . Therefore Choose Life, That Thou Mayest Live, Thou and Thy Seed,"* Center for the Study of Democratic Institutions, 1965.
(Editor) *Profiles of Nehru: America Remembers a World Leader,* Indian Book Co., 1966.
(Editor) *Great American Essays,* Dell, 1967.
Present Tense: An American Editors Odyssey, McGraw, 1967.
(With others) *Issues: 1968,* University Press of Kansas, 1968.
Profiles of Gandhi: America Remembers a World Leader, Indian Book Co., 1969.

The Improbable Triumvirate: John F. Kennedy, Pope Paul, Nikita Khruschev: An Asterisk to the History of a Hopeful Year, 1962-1963, Norton, 1972.
The Celebration of Life: A Dialogue on Immortality and Infinity, Harper, 1974.
The Quest for Immortality, Harper, 1974.
(Editor with Mary L. Dimond) *Memoirs of a Man: Grenville Clark,* Norton, 1975.
Anatomy of an Illness as Perceived by the Patient: Reflections on Healing and Regeneration, G. K. Hall, 1979, published as *Anatomy of an Illness as Perceived by the Patient,* Bantam, 1981.
Reflections on Healing and Regeneration, G. K. Hall, 1980.
Human Options: An Autobiographical Notebook, Norton, 1981.
The Physician in Literature, Saunders, 1981.
Healing and Belief, Mosaic Press, 1982.
The Healing Heart: Antidotes to Panic and Helplessness, Norton, 1983.
The Trial of Dr. Mesmer: A Play, Norton, 1984.
Albert Schweitzer's Mission: Healing and Peace, Norton, 1985.
The Human Adventure: A Camera Chronicle, Saybrook, 1986.
The Pathology of Power, Norton, 1987.
(Editor) *The Republic of Reason: The Personal Philosophies of the Founding Fathers,* Harper, 1988.
(Author of commentary) *Jason Sitwell's Book of Spoofs,* Dutton, 1989.
Head First: The Biology of Hope, Dutton, 1989.

Also author of *The Last Defense in a Nuclear Age,* 1960. Also featured in sound recording "Betting One's Life on the Future of Print," Development Digest, 1973. Editor *U. S. A.,* 1943-45; member of board of editors, *Encyclopaedia Britannica;* editorial supervisor, *March's Dictionary-Thesaurus,* 1980.

SIDELIGHTS: "I get a kick out of challenging the odds," Norman Cousins tells *Publishers Weekly* interviewer Lisa See. His life and career have given him ample opportunity to do just that. As longtime editor of *Saturday Review,* Cousins bolstered that magazine's circulation to 650,000. He has also served as a diplomat during three presidential administrations, become a professor of medical humanities, and produced numerous books on political and social issues. In the process, Cousins fended off a life-threatening disease and a massive coronary, both times using his own regimen of nutritional and emotional support systems as opposed to traditional methods of treatment (and he chronicles his experiences in two books, *Anatomy of an Illness as Perceived by the Patient: Reflections on Healing and Regeneration* and *The Healing Heart: Antidotes to Panic and Helplessness*). "Cousins has led a wonderful, if strangely related, series of overlapping lives," comments See. "He is a complex meshing of science and letters. He is serious and silly, intellectual and maniacal."

Cousins is often described as the man who laughed his way to health, a simplified explanation of the controversial healing method the author/editor employed when he was diagnosed in the mid-1960s as having ankylosing spondylitis. The degenerative disease causes the breakdown of collagen, the fiberous tissue that binds together the body's cells. Almost completely paralyzed, given only a few months to live, Cousins ordered himself checked out of the hospital where he had spent weeks undergoing tests. He moved into a hotel room and began taking extremely high doses of vitamin C, counting on the ascorbic acid to oxygenate his bloodstream, counteracting the effects of the illness. At the same time, intent on maintaining a positive mental outlook, Cousins exposed himself to equally high doses of humor—old "Candid Camera" tapes, Marx Brothers movies, and books by P. G. Wodehouse, Robert Benchley, and James

Thurber. This unusual regimen started to work: "I made the joyous discovery that ten minutes of genuine belly laughter had an anesthetic effect and would give me at least two hours of pain-free sleep," writes Cousins in *Anatomy of an Illness.* Slowly, the patient regained use of his limbs. As his condition steadily improved over the following months, Cousins resumed his busy life, eventually returning to work full-time at the *Saturday Review.*

As Cousins notes in his book, "the will to live is not a theoretical abstraction, but a physiologic reality with therapeutic characteristics." While not denying that the right attitude can certainly help a patient through his illness, some of his critics have questioned the nature of Cousins's ailment and the healing methods he now swears by. In a *Commentary* article Florence A. Ruderman takes exception to the author's case history as related in *Anatomy of an Illness.* Ruderman emphasizes that she does believe the " 'positive emotions' play a role in health. But the 'positive emotions' that are a force in maintaining life, well-being, resistance to disease, or recuperative or regenerative capacity, are those that stem from deep, relatively constant levels of one's psychological nature, one's inner being. They are affected by long-term circumstances of life and by major life events."

The critic also asks if Cousins's treatment can be adapted by the general public—and if it should be at all. "Should *all* patients have the same rights and freedom that Cousins had?," she writes. "If not, why is it inspiring that such rights and deference were accorded to Cousins? Under what circumstances should doctors allow patients to choose their own drugs, invent their own routines and regimens—in effect, direct their doctors? . . . How was it possible for so many doctors to greet [the author's] account with enthusiasm, and ignore every substantive and ethical issue in it?" Responding to Ruderman's charge, Cousins says in the *Publishers Weekly* article that "she didn't see the medical reports and didn't interview the doctors." Another criticism, he adds, "in the *Mt. Sinai Journal of Medicine,* . . . said that I might have had a nominal remission. That may be right, but the doctors didn't think so at the time."

Others find more to recommend in *Anatomy of an Illness.* Daphne Abeel suggests in *New Republic* that Cousins's story "is a tribute to what may be achieved by the individual. It is not a brief for self-cure in any and all circumstances, as he is quick to point out. And it must be said that not every patient will possess Cousins's unusual curiosity and knowledge about medicine. Still, his example of gumption and faith will offer hope to many." And *Washington Post* critic Richard Restak calls the book "an entertaining and instructive example of an inspired participation on the part of a patient in his own treatment."

In December, 1980, some fifteen years after winning his bout with ankylosing spondylitis, Cousins suffered a near-fatal heart attack while on a teaching assignment in California. Again faced with the challenge of restoring his health, Cousins responded by telling his doctors at the UCLA Intensive Care unit that they were "looking at what is probably the darndest healing machine that has ever been wheeled into the hospital," according to Joel Elkes's *Saturday Review* article on *The Healing Heart.* "As before," Elkes continues, "Cousins makes his body a personal laboratory and befriends the society within his skin. He refuses morphine; he asks for a change in the visiting routine to ensure rest. Gradually he improves."

One major obstacle Cousins faced in his recovery was the treadmill test, designed to chart the progress of his heart rate. The patient was "scared stiff at *being* exercised, at an accelerating pace, on a moving band over which he had no control," explains Elkes. "He tries to suppress his fear, but fails and has to stop. He tries

again and cannot manage." Realizing his fear was the factor in slowing his progress, Cousins adopted a more relaxed life style, changing his diet and avoiding stressful situations. "As his health improves, Cousins repeats the treadmill examination," Fred Rosenfelt reports in the *Los Angeles Times.* "This time, he controls the machine while listening to classical music and comedy tapes. His test is better."

In publishing these findings in *The Healing Heart,* Cousins again met with mixed reaction. Rosenfelt, for instance, while acknowledging that the author's "opinion of the salutary effects of positive emotion is widely accepted," nevertheless wonders "how many patients have the fortitude to disagree with their physicians and follow an alternative recovery program after a major heart attack? Furthermore, if a large number of individuals do so, how many will improve or worsen?" Elkes, on the other hand, argues that *The Healing Heart* is not a medical textbook, but a study of "awareness, listening, trust, choice, and intention, and about the intelligent use of a benevolent, centering will. It is about communication and partnership between the healer and the healed. It addresses as complementary the art of medicine and the science of medicine, the person and the institution, and freedom of choice and professional responsibility. [The book] affirms hope and belief as biologically constructive forces: not as blind faith, but as belief guided by knowledge and tempered by reason. It asserts that the quality of a person's life is the sum of the quality of his days."

Despite his bouts with near-fatal ailments, Cousins has remained an active literary force. His most popular book of the late 1980s is almost certainly *Head First,* a further elucidation of his beliefs and concerns regarding medicine and doctor-patient relations. Another key work, 1987's *The Pathology of Power,* addresses the issue of world peace. Wray Herbert, writing in the *Washington Post Book World,* hailed this volume as "an important and disturbing document."

Cousins's books have been translated into several languages.

MEDIA ADAPTATIONS: Anatomy of an Illness as Perceived by the Patient: Reflections on Healing and Regeneration was adapted into a television movie for Columbia Broadcasting System. Titled "Anatomy of an Illness," the film starred Ed Asner as Cousins and was broadcast on May 15, 1984.

BIOGRAPHICAL/CRITICAL SOURCES:

BOOKS

Cousins, Norman, *Present Tense: An American Editor's Odyssey,* McGraw, 1967.
Cousins, Norman, *Anatomy of an Illness as Perceived by the Patient: Reflections on Healing and Regeneration,* G. K. Hall, 1979, published as *Anatomy of an Illness as Perceived by the Patient,* Bantam, 1981.
Cousins, Norman, *Human Options: An Autobiographical Notebook,* Norton, 1981.
Cousins, Norman, *The Healing Heart: Antidotes to Panic and Helplessness,* Norton, 1983.

PERIODICALS

Chicago Tribune, December 26, 1979.
Commentary, May, 1980.
Detroit News, June 22, 1980.
Esquire, February, 1980.
Los Angeles Times, September 29, 1983.
Los Angeles Times Book Review, December 13, 1981, October 24, 1982, December 3, 1989.
National Review, April 30, 1982, December 9, 1983.

New Republic, September 29, 1979.
New Statesman, October 3, 1980.
New York Times, June 22, 1972, September 15, 1979, May 8, 1984, May 15, 1984.
New York Times Book Review, January 1, 1984.
People, June 1, 1979.
Publishers Weekly, September 23, 1983.
Saturday Review, September-October, 1983.
Time, August 30, 1982.
Times Literary Supplement, March 30, 1984.
Washington Post, October 9, 1979, November 9, 1981.
Washington Post Book World, April 12, 1987, November 5, 1989.

*   *   *

COUSTEAU, Jacques-Yves 1910-

PERSONAL: Born June 11, 1910, in St. Andre-de-Cubzac, France; son of Daniel P. (a lawyer) and Elizabeth (Duranthon) Cousteau; married Simone Melchior, July 12, 1937; children: Jean-Michel, Philippe (died June 28, 1979). *Education:* French Naval Academy, graduate, 1933.

ADDRESSES: Cousteau Society, 777 Third Ave., New York, N.Y. 10017; 930 West 21st St., Norfolk, Va. 23517; Fondation Cousteau, 25 Avenue Wagram, 75017 Paris, France; and Musec Oceanographique, Avenue Saint-Martin, Monacoville, Monaco.

CAREER: Undersea explorer, photographer, inventor, environmentalist, film producer, and writer. Entered French Navy in 1930; became interested in diving in 1936; began working on underwater breathing apparatus and, with Emile Gagnan, developed the Aqua-lung in 1942; founder and head, with Philippe Taillez, of Groupe d'Etudes et Recherches Sous-Marines (Undersea Research Group) of French Navy, 1946-56; Campagnes Oceanographiques Francaises, Marseilles, France, founder, president, and chairman, beginning in 1950; Centre d'Etudes Marines Advancecs, Marseilles, founder, president, and chairman, beginning in 1952; Institute Oceanographique et Musee (Oceanographic Institute and Museum), Monaco, director, beginning in 1957; US Divers Co., Santa Ana, Calif., chairman, beginning in 1957; The Cousteau Society, New York, N.Y., founder, president and chairman, beginning in 1973.

After World War II founded various marketing, manufacturing, engineering, and research organizations that were incorporated as Cousteau Group in 1973; director of Conshelf Saturation Dive program, beginning in 1962; general secretary of International Commission for the Scientific Exploration of the Mediterranean, beginning in 1966; chairman of Eurocean, 1971-76. Inventor of numerous undersea devices, including diving saucers, the Bathygraf cinecamera, deepsea camera sleds, and mini-submarines. Leader of oceanographic research expeditions throughout the world in cooperation with many research institutes, broadcasting companies, and universities, including National Geographic Society, French National Research Center, National Aeronautics and Space Administration, National Film Board of Canada, Public Broadcasting System, Turner Broadcasting System, and Texas A & M University. *Military service:* French Navy, 1930-57; resigned with rank of lieutenant commander; member of French underground during World War II; received Croix de Guerre with palm, Merite Agricole, Merite Maritime; named officier des Arts et Lettres, Commander, Legion of Honor.

MEMBER: National Academy of Sciences (United States).

AWARDS, HONORS: Gold Medal, National Geographic Society, 1961; Bradford Prize, Boston Museum Of Science, 1965; Potts Medal, Franklin Institute, 1970; D.Sc., Brandeis University, 1970, University of California, Berkeley, 1970, Rensselaer Polytechnical Institute, 1977, Harvard University, 1979, University of Gent (Belgium), 1983; Gold Medal, Grand Prix d'Oceanographie Albert Ier, 1971; Grande Medaille d'Or (Gold Medal), Societe d'Encouragement au Progres, 1973; New England Aquarium award, 1973; Prix de la Couronne d'Or, 1973; Pollenadella Bravura award, 1974; special prize of Cervia (Italy), 1976; Manley Bendell Prize, 1976; International Environment Prize, United Nations, 1977; Jean Sainteny Prize, 1980; Europe Prize, Kiwanis International, 1980; Neptune Award, 1982; Lindbergh Award, 1982; Bruno H. Schubert Foundation prize, 1983; Gold Medal, New York Zoological Society; named Commandeur du Merite Sportif; Presidential Medal of Freedom, 1985; Founder's Award, International Council of National Academy of Arts and Sciences, 1987; National Geographic Society Centennial Award, 1988; inducted into Acadamie Francaise, 1989.

Film awards: Cannes Film Festival award, 1946, for "Epaves"; Grand Prix, Gold Palm, Cannes Film Festival, 1956, for "Le Monde du Silence"; Academy of Motion Picture Arts and Sciences (Oscar) awards, 1957, for "The Silent World," 1959, for "The Golden Fish," and 1965, for "World Without Sun"; National Academy of Television Arts and Sciences (Emmy) awards, 1969, for "The Desert Whales," 1970, for "The Tragedy of the Red Salmon," 1971, for "Lagoon of Lost Ships," "The Dragons of Galapagos," "Secrets of Sunken Caves," and "The Unsinkable Sea Otter!," 1972, for "A Sound of Dolphins," 1974, for "Beneath the Frozen World," and more than forty-five additional Emmy nominations; Chris Bronze Plaque award, 1977, for "The Power Game."

WRITINGS:

ILLUSTRATED WITH OWN PHOTOGRAPHY

(With Philippe Taillez and Frederic Dumas) *Par dix-huit metres de fond: Histoire d'un film* (title means "Sixty Feet Down: The Story of a Film"), Durel, 1946.
La Plongee en schaphandre (title means "SCUBA Diving"), Elzevir, 1950.
(With Dumas) *The Silent World* (Reader's Digest Book Club selection; Book-of-the-Month Club selection), Harper, 1953, reissued, Lyons & Burford, 1987.
(With Jacques Bourcart) *La Mer* (title means "The Sea"), Larousse, 1953.
(Contributor) John Oliver LaGorce, editor, *Book of Fishes,* National Geographic Society, 1958.
(Editor with James Dugan) *Captain Cousteau's Underwater Treasury,* Harper, 1959.
(With Dugan) *The Living Sea,* Harper, 1963, reissued, Lyons & Burford, 1988.
(Compiler) *Bibliographie de la sismique marine* (title means "Bibliography of Marine Seismology"), Oceanographic Institute (Monaco), 1964.
Le Monde sans soleil, Hachette, 1964, English-language version edited by Dugan, published as *World Without Sun,* Harper, 1965.
(Contributor) Nicholas Dent, editor, *The Sea* (eight volumes), M. Cavendish, 1974.
(With Yves Paccalet) *Saumons, castors et loutres,* Flammarion, 1978.
(With Paccalet) *Le surprises de la mer,* Flammarion, 1980.
A Bill of Rights for Future Generations, Myrin Institute, 1980.
(With Henri Jacquier) *Francais, on a vole ta mer,* Laffont, 1981.
(With Paccalet) *A la recherche de l'Atlantide,* Flammarion, 1981.

The Cousteau Almanac: An Inventory of Life on Our Water Planet, Doubleday, 1981 (published in England as *Almanac of the Environment,* Doubleday, 1981).

(With M. Richards) *Jacques Cousteau's Amazon Journey,* Abrams, 1984.

(With James Cribb) *Marine Life of the Caribbean,* Skyline Press, 1984.

(With Paccalet) *Jacques Cousteau: Whales,* Abrams, 1988.

"UNDERSEA DISCOVERY" SERIES; PUBLISHED BY DOUBLEDAY, EXCEPT AS NOTED

(With son, Philippe Cousteau) *Les Requins,* Flammarion, 1970, translation by Francis Price published as *The Shark: Splendid Savage of the Sea,* 1970.

(With Philippe Diole) *Un Tresor englouti,* Flammarion, 1971, translation by J. F. Bernard published as *Diving for Sunken Treasure,* 1971.

La Vie et mort des coraux, Flammarion, 1971, translation by Bernard published as *Life and Death in a Coral Sea,* 1971.

(With Diole) *Nos Amies les baleines,* Flammarion, 1972, translation by Bernard published as *The Whale: Mighty Monarch of the Sea,* 1972.

(With Diole) *Pieuvres: La Fin d'un malentendu,* Flammarion, 1973, translation by Bernard published as *Octopus and Squid: The Soft Intelligence,* 1973.

(With Diole) *Trois Aventures de la Calypso,* Flammarion, 1973, translation by Bernard published as *Three Adventures: Galapagos, Titicaca, the Blue Holes,* 1973 (published in England as *Galapagos, Titicaca, the Blue Holes: Three Adventures,* Cassell, 1973).

(With Diole) *Compagnons de plongee,* Flammarion, 1974 translation by Bernard published as *Diving Companions: Sea Lion, Elephant Seal, Walrus,* 1974.

(With Diole) *Les Dauphins et la liberte,* Flammarion, 1975, translation by Bernard published as *Dolphins,* 1975.

"THE OCEAN WORLD" ENCYCLOPEDIA SERIES; PUBLISHED BY WORLD PUBLISHING, EXCEPT AS NOTED

Oasis in Space, 1972 (also see below).
The Act of Life, 1972 (also see below).
Quest for Food, 1973 (also see below).
Window in the Sea, 1973 (also see below).
The Art of Motion, 1973, revised edition, Danbury, 1975 (also see below).
Attack and Defense, 1973, revised edition, Danbury, 1975 (also see below).
Invisible Messages, 1973, revised edition, Danbury, 1975 (also see below).
Instinct and Intelligence, 1973 (also see below).
Pharaohs of the Sea, 1973 (also see below).
Mammals in the Sea, 1973 (also see below).
Provinces of the Sea, 1973 (also see below).
Man Re-enters the Sea, 1974 (also see below).
A Sea of Legends: Inspiration from the Sea, 1973 (also see below).
The Adventure of Life, 1973, revised edition, Danbury, 1975 (also see below).
Outer and Inner Space, 1974 (also see below).
The White Caps, 1974 (also see below).
Riches of the Sea, 1974, revised edition, Danbury, 1975 (also see below).
Challenges of the Sea, 1973 (also see below).
The Sea in Danger, 1974 (also see below).
Guide to the Sea and Index, 1974 (also see below).
The Ocean World (one-volume condensation of first twenty books of "The Ocean World" series), Abrams, 1979.

Cousteau's Calypso, Abrams, 1983.

FILMS

Author of "The Silent World," 1956, "The Golden Fish," 1959, "World Without Sun," 1964, and "Voyage to the Edge of the World," 1975. Producer of twenty short documentaries, 1942-56.

"THE UNDERSEA WORLD OF JACQUES COUSTEAU" TELEVISION SERIES, PRODUCED BY AMERICAN BROADCASTING SYSTEM

"Sharks," 1968.
"The Savage World of the Coral Jungle," 1968.
"Search in the Deep," 1968.
"Whales," 1968.
"The Unexpected Voyage of Pepito and Cristobal," 1969.
"Sunken Treasure," 1969.
"The Legend of Lake Titicaca," 1969.
"The Desert Whales," 1969.
"The Night of the Squid," 1970.
"The Return of the Sea Elephant," 1970.
"Those Incredible Diving Machines," 1970.
"The Water Planet," 1970.
"Lagoon of Lost Ships," 1971.
"The Dragons of Galapagos," 1971.
"Secrets of the Sunken Caves," 1971.
"The Unsinkable Sea Otter!," 1971.
"Octopus, Octopus," 1971.
"The Forgotten Mermaids," 1972.
"A Sound of Dolphins," 1972.
"The Smile of the Walrus," 1972.
"500 Million Years Beneath the Sea," 1973.
"Hippo!," 1973.
"The Singing Whale," 1973.
"South to Fire and Ice," 1973.
"The Flight of Penguins," 1974.
"Beneath the Frozen World," 1974.
"Blizzard at Hope Bay," 1974.
"Life at the End of the World," 1974.
"Beavers of the North Country," 1975.
"The Coral Divers of Corsica," 1975.
"The Sleeping Sharks of Yucatan," 1975.
"The Sea Birds of Isabela," 1975.
"Mysteries of the Hidden Reefs," 1976.
"The Fish That Swallowed Jonah," 1976.
"The Incredible March of the Spiny Lobsters," 1976.

"OASIS IN SPACE" TELEVISION SERIES

"What Price Progress?," 1977.
"Grain of Conscience," 1977.
"Troubled Waters," 1977.
"Population Time Bomb," 1977.
"The Power Game," 1977.
"Visions of Tomorrow," 1977.

"THE COUSTEAU ODYSSEY" TELEVISION SERIES

"Calypso's Search for the Britannic," 1977.
"Diving for Roman Plunder," 1978.
"Calypso's Search for Atlantis: Part I," 1978.
"Calypso's Search for Atlantis: Part II," 1978.
"Blind Prophets of Easter Island," 1978.
"Time Bomb at Fifty Fathoms," 1979.
"Mediterranean: Cradle or Coffin?," 1979.
"The Nile: Part I," 1979.
"The Nile: Part II," 1979.

"Lost Relics of the Sea," 1980.
"Clipperton: The Island Time Forgot," 1981.
"Warm Blooded Sea," 1981.

"THE COUSTEAU AMAZON" TELEVISION SERIES

"Journey to a Thousand Rivers," 1984.
"The New El Dorado: Invaders and Exiles," 1984.
"River of the Future," 1984.
"Snowstorm in the Jungle," 1985.

OTHER TELEVISION WORKS

Author of "The World of Jacques-Yves Cousteau," Columbia Broadcasting System, 1966, "Cries from the Deep," 1982, "St. Lawrence: Stairway to the Sea," 1982, "The Reluctant Ally," 1985, "The Friendly Foe," 1985, "Jacques Cousteau: The First Seventy-Five Years," 1985, "Riders of the Wind," 1986, and "Island of Peace," 1988.

Also author of twenty programs of "Rediscovery of the World" series, for Turner Broadcasting System, beginning in 1986.

SIDELIGHTS: French marine explorer Jacques-Yves Cousteau is a familiar figure to most Americans, thanks to frequent national television broadcasts of the films he has made to record the expeditions of his ship, *Calypso.* Millions of viewers have enjoyed these vicarious visits to a mysterious land they will probably never experience personally—the world of undersea life. In the minds of many, Cousteau is perpetually underwater, revealing new wonders, or commanding operations from Calypso's deck, wearing his familiar red cap. It is true that a full third of each year is spent aboard his ship, but Captain Cousteau also plays less-visible roles as inventor, businessman, and conservationist. All of these ventures grew from his ongoing fascination with the territory he was among the first to explore. In his book *The Silent World,* Cousteau recounts his first vision of undersea life and the effect it had on him: "One Sunday morning in 1936 at Le Mourillon, near Toulon, I waded into the Mediterranean and looked into it through Fernez goggles. I was a regular Navy gunner, a good swimmer interested only in perfecting my crawl style. The sea was merely a salty obstacle that burned my eyes. I was astounded by what I saw in the shallow shingle at Le Mourillon, rocks covered with green, brown and silver forests of algae and fishes unknown to me, swimming in crystalline water. Standing up to breathe I saw a trolley car, people, electric-light poles. I put my eyes under again and civilization vanished with one last bow. I was in a jungle never seen by those who floated on the opaque roof. Sometimes we are lucky enough to know that our lives have been changed, to discard the old, embrace the new, and run headlong down an immutable course. It happened to me at Le Mourillon on that summer's day, when my eyes were opened on the sea."

Cousteau was eager to see more of this new world. But in 1936 methods of undersea exploration were quite limited. The young Navy gunner quickly mastered skin diving, but a skin diver can remain submerged only for as long as he can hold his breath. The only alternative, helmet diving, allows greater time underwater, but the helmet diver is tethered to a ship by his umbilici, weighed down by ponderous boots, and has his head encased in a heavy copper helmet. He is "a cripple in an alien land," according to Cousteau. Determined to overcome such limitations, he and a friend, Emile Gagnan, began designing the Aqua-lung, or self-contained underwater breathing apparatus (SCUBA). If successful, the Aqua-lung would allow a man to swim as freely as the fish and remain submerged for more than an hour. In 1943 Cousteau made his first dive with the experimental equipment. To his delight, he enjoyed perfect freedom of movement. Loops,

somersaults, and barrel rolls were all performed on that first dive by the elated inventor; he and his companions in the project soon dubbed themselves "menfish." In time, the Aqua-lung completely revolutionized undersea exploration.

Salvaging vessels torpedoed in World War II, discovering the remains of a treasure-laden argosy sunk about 80 B.C., and observing the actions of the unpredictable shark were among Cousteau's early projects utilizing the Aqua-lung. Recording these exploits on film was a prime objective, one that led to several breakthroughs in underwater photography. In time, as his ventures became more complicated and wide-ranging, Cousteau outfitted a ship to suit his unique needs—the *Calypso,* formerly an American mine sweeper. To date, *Calypso* and its crew have cruised from the Arctic to the Antarctic, up the Amazon and Mississippi rivers, into the Great Lakes, and along every coastline but Asia's, exploring the life of these waterways. New equipment and techniques are constantly being developed to enhance *Calypso*'s capabilities; much of it is eventually adapted for commercial use. Cousteau's sheer enjoyment of the *Calypso* expeditions is the force behind this pioneering work. "In the beginning," he told C. Gregory Jensen in the *Los Angeles Times,* "it was all a wonder. I was investigating an unknown world—not unknown scientifically, but unknown visually. Naturally I was fascinated by it. It was like giving a child an inexhaustible new toy. It was the same with inventions. It is fun to play with toys."

When Cousteau began to document his experiences in books and films, the general public shared his fascination and wonder. His works became popular successes, as well as being highly praised by reviewers. The author's enthusiasm and fluid writing style are often cited as key elements in his books. Reviewing his first widely-read volume *The Silent World* in the *New York Herald Tribune Book Review,* Rachel Carson states, "Captain Cousteau succeeds admirably in giving his readers a sense of personal participation in these explorations of a strange world. We feel that we know what a diver sees, feels, and thinks as he descends into the blue twilight of the sea. . . . This is a book that leads us on, page by page, and when the end is reached we are likely to begin again at Page 1." "Captain Cousteau, unlike many writers about the deep, has not marred his stories with supercharged prose," notes Gilbert Klingel in the *New York Times Book Review.* "[He] has placed the thrill of ocean investigation within the reach of nearly everyone." "He is unfailingly interesting," writes Desmond Young in the *New York Times Book Review.* "His descriptions gracefully combine literary style and scientific nomenclature. . . . Most of us must be content to see all these submarine marvels vicariously. Thanks to Captain Cousteau, we can do so, with immense pleasure, in this entrancing book." And in a *Christian Science Monitor* article, Robert C. Cowen declares, "Reading Jacques-Yves Cousteau's captivating new book [*The Living Sea*], I had a strong impulse to hand in this review and immediately take off to find *Calypso.*"

Cousteau's work has drawn criticism from some members of the academic community, who consider it inaccurate and unscientific. Cowen challenges this judgement: "Some academic oceanographers have found it fashionable to discount his exploits. But the years of effort that have been compressed into the pages of [*The Living Sea*] speak for themselves of the great contribution Captain Cousteau has made to oceanographic science. He would himself lay no claim to being a scientific expert. Yet from the aqua lung to his most recent innovation of the diving saucer, he has done as much if not more than any other contemporary marine explorer to open the way to a new opportunity for undersea research." In an interview with C. Gregory Jensen in the *Los Angeles Times,* Cousteau said simply, "I have one asset, the only one I have, built over fifty years of dedication . . . credibility. I have never tried to falsify data. People know that I am reliable."

Over the years, Cousteau has witnessed a steady deterioration in the quality of the oceans. Society's abuse, including toxic chemical dumping, overfishing, and the destruction of fragile marine habitats, has had grave consequences for the vitality of the sea. The situation is very serious, according to Cousteau. In an article appearing in *National Geographic* magazine, he writes, "In the more than half a century I have dedicated to the sea, I have had moments of despair." However, he continues, "Fundamentally I remain an optimist. If I were not, I should pack my instruments, dock my vessel, and head inland." His optimism led him to create in 1973 the Cousteau Society, a nonprofit environmentalist organization funded in part by royalties from the explorer's books and films. The goal of the Cousteau Society, its founder told Jensen, is to promote "good management of our home, which is the planet."

Perhaps surprisingly, marine pollution is not the primary target of the organization. Cousteau explained to Jensen, "What is the use of trying to manage the planet if there is to be no planet to manage, if it is all to be vaporized? So the problem of nuclear war becomes No. 1. It must, must be prevented." The society's second priority: finding new ways to aid the impoverished Third World. "The mass of human beings is probably less well off than the mass of animals," Cousteau declared to Jensen. "For me this is a paradox. Man is the lord of creation, and two-thirds of us live in total poverty. Now our organizations are in the process of defining a doctrine that we call Ecotech—combining economics, ecology and technology, which too often fight with one another." Research is also under way concerning aquaculture, or sea farming. "We want to take a poor, over-crowded, undernourished island. With our biomass project, using sea algae, we will make that island not only self-sufficient but make it an exporter of energy and food within five years. Then we can turn that blueprint over to international organizations to use elsewhere." After addressing the problems of nuclear war and world hunger, the Cousteau Society turns its energies directly to environmental issues. The *Calypso*'s captain has personally testified before the U.S. Congress in cases involving the welfare of the seas.

While Cousteau remains active in documenting the activities of the undersea world, he emphasizes that the greatest challenge to him is to help in the solution of some of the vast problems that are facing humankind. He told Jensen, "It sounds pretentious to say it, but I have a pathetic compassion for the human condition. I am no longer able to enjoy fully my own life because I cannot stop thinking of those who have nothing." In *National Geographic,* Cousteau writes that we must attain a greater awareness of global unity if we are to survive: "All animals, including man, share the same basic motivations: territory, food, reproduction, competition among species. The key word to describe life is, therefore, unity. . . . Space exploration has brought us the most precious gift of all, a global consciousness. However fragmented the world, however intense the national rivalries, it is an inexorable fact that we become more interdependent every day. I believe that national sovereignties will shrink in the face of universal interdependence. The sea, the great unifier, is man's only hope. Now, as never before, the old phrase has a literal meaning: We are all in the same boat. That boat is the spaceship earth, a blue jewel glowing in the night of space, radiant and shining with the fluid of life—the all-encompassing sea."

BIOGRAPHICAL/CRITICAL SOURCES:

BOOKS

Canning, John, editor, *100 Great Adventures,* Taplinger, 1969.
Contemporary Literary Criticism, Volume XXX, Gale, 1984.
Cousteau, Jacques-Yves and Frederic Dumas, *The Silent World,* Harper, 1953.
Dugan, James, *Undersea Explorer: The Story of Captain Cousteau* (juvenile), Harper, 1957.
Dunaway, Philip and George De Kay, editors, *Turning Point,* Random House, 1958.
Elliot, Robert, *Banners of Courage* (juvenile), Platt & Munk, 1972.
Guberlet, Muriel, *Explorers of the Sea,* Ronald, 1964.
Olney, Ross R., *Men against the Sea,* Grosset, 1969.
Shannon, Terry, *Saucer in the Sea* (juvenile), Golden Gate, 1965.
Wagner, Frederick, *Famous Underwater Adventurers,* Dodd, 1962.
Westman, P., *Jacques Cousteau: Free Flight Undersea,* Dillon, 1980.

PERIODICALS

The American Way, August, 1974.
Best Sellers, November 15, 1970, December 1, 1971.
Christian Science Monitor, April 25, 1963.
Cosmopolitan, January, 1960.
Detroit Free Press, December 16, 1973, May 26, 1976.
Holiday, September, 1955.
L'Express, August 4-10, 1969.
Life, November 27, 1950.
Los Angeles Times, May 10, 1984.
National Geographic, December, 1981.
Nature, January 12, 1957.
New Scientist, July 21, 1977.
New Yorker, November 7, 1970.
New York Herald Tribune, April 28, 1963.
New York Herald Tribune Book Review, February 8, 1953, February 22, 1953.
New York Times Book Review, February 8, 1953, February 22, 1953, April 28, 1963, December 5, 1971, January 13, 1980, December 2, 1984.
New York Times Magazine, April 21, 1963.
Parade Magazine, March 16, 1975.
People, September 15, 1975.
Pittsburgh Press, March 2, 1975.
Saturday Review, July 10, 1976.
Science Illustrated, December, 1948.
Time, March 28, 1960.
Times Literary Supplement, November 6, 1970, August 20, 1971, March 3, 1972.
Washington Post, March 15, 1987, March 22, 1987, December 4, 1988, September 21, 1989.

[Sketch verified by Karen G. Brazeau, assistant to Jacques-Yves Cousteau]

*　　*　　*

COWARD, Noel (Peirce) 1899-1973
(Hernia Whittlebot)

PERSONAL: Some sources spell middle name "Pierce"; born December 16, 1899, in Teddington-on-Thames, Middlesex, England; died March 26, 1973; son of Arthur Sabin (a clerk in a music publishing house and piano salesman) and Violet Agnes (Veitch) Coward. *Education:* Attended Chapel Royal School,

Clapham; drama instruction at Miss Italia Conti's Academy, Liverpool; privately educated.

ADDRESSES: Home—Les Avants, sur Montreux, Switzerland.

CAREER: Playwright, author, composer, songwriter, actor, singer, director, producer, and nightclub entertainer. Actor in plays, including, "The Goldfish," "The Great Name," and "Where the Rainbow Ends," 1911; "Hannele," "War in the Air," "A Little Fowl Play," and "Peter Pan," 1913; "Charley's Aunt," "The Light Blues," and "The Happy Family," 1916; "The Saving Grace," 1917; "Scandal," 1918; "The Knight of the Burning Pestle," 1919; "Polly With a Past," 1921; "The Constant Nymph," 1926; "The Second Man," 1928; "Journey's End," c. 1930; and "The Apple Cart," 1953. Narrator of "Carnival of Animals," Carnegie Hall (New York), 1956. Actor in films, including "Hearts of the World," 1918; "The Scoundrel," 1935; "Around the World in 80 Days," 1956; "Our Man in Havana" and "Surprise Package," 1960; "Paris When It Sizzles," 1964; "Bunny Lake Is Missing," 1965; and "Boom!" and "The Italian Job," 1968. Producer of the films "Blithe Spirit," 1945, and "This Happy Breed," 1946. President of Actors' Orphanage, 1934-56. *Military service:* British Army, Artists' Rifles, 1918; entertained troops during World War II.

MEMBER: Royal Society of Literature (fellow).

AWARDS, HONORS: New York Drama Critics Circle award for best foreign play, 1942, for *Blithe Spirit;* special Academy Award ("Oscar") for outstanding production achievement from Academy of Motion Picture Arts and Sciences, 1942, for "In Which We Serve;" special Antoinette Perry Award ("Tony"), 1970; D.Litt. from University of Sussex, 1972.

WRITINGS:

PUBLISHED PLAYS

"*I'll Leave It to You*" (first produced in London at New Theatre, 1920), French, 1920.

The Young Idea (first produced in London at Savoy Theatre, 1923), French, 1924.

The Rat Trap, Benn, 1924.

The Vortex (first produced in London at Everyman Theatre, 1924; director, with Basil Dean, of Broadway production at Henry Miller's Theater, 1925), Harper, 1925.

Fallen Angels (first produced in London at Globe Theatre, 1925; produced in New York at Playhouse, 1956), Benn, 1925, French (New York), 1958.

Hay Fever (first produced in London at Ambassador's Theatre, 1925; produced in New York at Maxine Elliot's Theatre, 1925), Harper, 1925, revised edition, French, 1927, with an introduction by author, Heinemann, 1965.

Easy Virtue (first produced in London at St. Martin's Theatre, 1926), Benn, 1926.

This Was a Man (first produced in London), Harper, 1926.

The Marquise (first produced in London at Criterion Theatre, 1927; produced in New York at Biltmore Theatre, 1927), Benn, 1927.

Home Chat (first produced in London at Duke of York's Theatre, 1927), M. Secker, 1927.

Sirocco (first produced in London at Daly's Theatre, 1927), M. Secker, 1927.

(And composer and lyricist) *Charles B. Cochran's Revue* (first produced in London at London Pavilion, 1931), Chappell, 1928.

(And director) *Bitter Sweet* (operetta; first produced in London at His Majesty's Theatre, 1929; Broadway production di-

rected by Coward at Times Square Theatre, 1931), Heinemann, 1930, Doubleday, 1931.

Post-Mortem, Doubleday, 1931.

(And director) *Cavalcade* (first produced in London at Drury Lane Theatre, 1931), Heinemann, 1932, Doubleday, 1933.

(And producer with Alfred Lunt and Lynn Fontanne) *Design for Living* (first produced in New York at Ethel Barrymore Theatre, 1933), Doubleday, 1933.

Conversation Piece (first produced in London at His Majesty's Theatre, 1934; Broadway production directed by Coward at 44th Street Theatre, 1934), Doubleday, 1934.

(And director) *Point Valaine* (first produced in New York at Ethel Barrymore Theater, 1935), Doubleday, 1935.

(And director) *Tonight at 8:30* (series of plays consisting of "The Astonished Heart," "Family Album," "Fumed Oak," "Hands Across the Sea," "Red Peppers," "Shadow Play," "Still Life," "Ways and Means," and "We Were Dancing"; first six plays originally produced in London at Phoenix Theatre, 1936; entire series produced in New York at National Theater, 1936), Doubleday, 1936 (also see below).

The Astonished Heart (part of "Tonight at 8:30" series; also see above), French, 1938.

Family Album (part of "Tonight at 8:30" series; also see above), French, 1938.

Fumed Oak (part of "Tonight at 8:30" series; also see above), French, 1938.

Hands Across the Sea (part of "Tonight at 8:30" series; also see above), French, 1938.

Red Peppers (musical interlude; part of "Tonight at 8:30" series; also see above), French, 1938.

Shadow Play (musical; part of "Tonight at 8:30" series; also see above), French, 1938.

Still Life (part of "Tonight at 8:30" series; also see above), French, 1938.

We Were Dancing (part of "Tonight at 8:30" series; also see above), French, 1938.

(And composer and lyricist) *Operette* (first produced in London at His Majesty's Theatre, 1938), Heinemann, 1938.

(And composer) *This Year of Grace* (revue; first produced in New York at Selwyn Theater, 1928), published in *Second Play Parade,* Heinemann, 1939 (also see below).

(And composer and lyricist) *Words and Music* (revue; first production directed and conducted by Coward in London at Adelphi Theatre, 1932), published in *Second Play Parade,* Heinemann, 1939 (also see below).

Blithe Spirit (first produced in London at Piccadilly Theatre, 1941; produced in New York at Morosco Theater, 1941), Doubleday, 1941.

(And director) *Relative Values* (first produced in London at Savoy Theatre, 1951), Heinemann, 1942.

(And director) *Present Laughter* (first produced in England, 1942; produced in London at Haymarket Theatre, 1943; produced in Paris at Theatre Edouard VII, 1948, with title "Joyeux Chagrins"), Heinemann, 1943, Doubleday, 1947.

(And director) *This Happy Breed* (first produced in London at Haymarket Theater, 1943), Heinemann, 1943, Doubleday, 1947.

Peace in Our Time, Heinemann, 1947, Doubleday, 1948.

(And director) *Quadrille* (first produced in London at Phoenix Theatre, 1952; produced in New York at Coronet Theater, 1954), Heinemann, 1952, Doubleday, 1955.

(And composer and lyricist) *After the Ball* (operetta based on Oscar Wilde's *Lady Windermere's Fan;* first produced in London at Globe Theatre, 1954), Chappell, 1954.

South Sea Bubble (first produced in London at Lyric Theatre, 1956), Heinemann, 1956.

(And director with John Gielgud) *Nude With Violin* (first produced in New York at Belasco Theater, 1957), Heinemann, 1957, Doubleday, 1958, revised acting edition, French, 1958.

Look After Lulu (based on Georges Feydeau's *Occupe-toi d'Amelie;* first produced in London at Royal Court Theatre, 1959; produced in New York at Henry Miller's Theatre, 1959), Heinemann, 1959.

Waiting in the Wings (first produced in London at Duke of York's Theatre, 1960), Heinemann, 1960, Doubleday, 1961.

(And composer, lyricist, and director) *Sail Away* (libretto; first produced in New York at Broadhurst Theater, 1961), Bonard Productions, 1961.

Suite in Three Keys (includes "A Song at Twilight," "Shadows of the Evening," and "Come Into the Garden, Maud"; first produced in London at Queens Theatre, 1966), Heinemann, 1966, Doubleday, 1967.

Shadows of the Evening, French, 1967 (also see above).

Come Into the Garden, Maud, French, 1967 (also see above).

A Song at Twilight, French, 1967 (also see above).

Private Lives (first produced in London at Phoenix Theatre, 1930), Doubleday, 1968.

UNPUBLISHED PLAYS

(And composer and lyricist with Ronald Jeans) "London Calling," first produced in London at Duke of York's Theatre, 1923.

(With others) "Charlot's Revue," first produced in London at Prince of Wales Theatre, 1924.

(And composer with others) "On With the Dance" (revue), first produced in London, 1925.

"Biography," first produced in London at Globe Theatre, 1934.

(Composer and lyricist) "Set to Music" (revue), first production directed by Coward in New York at Music Box, 1939.

"Sigh No More" (revue), first produced in London at Piccadilly Theatre, 1945.

(And director) "Pacific 1860" (musical), first produced in London at Drury Lane Theatre, 1946.

(And director) "Ace of Clubs" (musical), first produced in London at Cambridge Theatre, 1950.

(And director) "Island Fling," first produced in 1951.

(Author of scenario and score) "London Morning" (ballet), 1959.

(Composer and lyricist) "The Girl Who Came to Supper" (based on *The Sleeping Prince,* by Terence M. Rattigan), first produced in New York at Broadway Theater, 1963.

(And director) "High Spirits" (musical adaptation of Coward's *Blithe Spirit*), first produced in New York at Alvin Theater, 1964.

(Contributor of material) "Carol Channing With 10 Stout-Hearted Men" (revue), first produced in London at Drury Lane Theatre, 1970.

OMNIBUS VOLUMES

Three Plays: The Rat Trap, The Vortex [and] *Fallen Angels* (also contains Coward's reply to his critics), Benn, 1925.

The Plays of Noel Coward, first series (contains "Sirocco," "Home Chat," and "The Queen Was in the Parlour"), Doubleday, 1928.

Bitter Sweet, and Other Plays (contains "Bitter Sweet," "Easy Virtue," and Hay Fever"), notes by W. Somerset Maugham, Doubleday, 1929.

Collected Sketches and Lyrics, Hutchinson, 1931, Doubleday, 1932.

Play Parade (contains "Design for Living," "Cavalcade," "Private Lives," "Bitter Sweet," "Post-Mortem," "The Vortex," and "Hay Fever"), Doubleday, 1933, revised edition, Heinemann, 1949.

Tonight at 8:30, three volumes, Doubleday, 1936.

Second Play Parade (contains "This Year of Grace" "Words and Music" "Operette," and "Conversation Piece"), Heinemann, 1939, 2nd edition published as *Play Parade, Volume II,* with addition of "Fallen Angels" and "Easy Virtue," 1950.

Curtain Calls (includes "Tonight at 8:30," "Ways and Means," "Still Life," "Family Album," "Conversation Piece," "Easy Virtue," "Point Valaine," and "This Was a Man"), Doubleday, 1940.

Play Parade, Volume III (contains "The Queen Was in the Parlour," "I'll Leave It to You," "The Young Idea," "Sirocco," "The Rat Trap," "This Was a Man," "Home Chat," and "The Marquise"), Heinemann. 1950.

Play Parade, Volume IV (contains "Tonight at 8:30," "Present Laughter," and "This Happy Breed"), Heinemann, 1952.

Play Parade, Volume V, Heinemann, 1958.

Play Parade, Volume VI, Heinemann, 1962.

Three Plays by Noel Coward: Blithe Spirit, Hay Fever, [and] *Private Lives,* with an introduction by Edward Albee, Dell, 1965.

FILMS

(Author of dialogue and lyrics) "Bitter Sweet," United Artists, 1933.

(And producer, actor, composer, and co-director) "In Which We Serve," United Artists, 1942.

(And producer) "Brief Encounter" (adaptation of *Still Life* and *Fumed Oak*), Universal, 1946 (screenplay published in *Three British Screen Plays,* edited by Roger Manvell, Methuen, 1950).

(Contributor and actor) "The Astonished Heart," Universal, 1950.

Also contributor of material to "Meet Me Tonight," a film adaptation of *Tonight at 8:30,* 1952; and to "Together With Music," a television play produced by Ford Star Jubilee, CBS-TV, 1955.

FICTION

To Step Aside (seven short stories), Doubleday, 1939.

Star Quality (six short stories), Doubleday, 1951.

Short Stories, Short Plays, and Songs, Dell, 1955.

Pomp and Circumstance (novel), Doubleday, 1960.

Collected Short Stories, Heinemann, 1962, new edition published as *The Collected Short Stories of Noel Coward,* 1969.

Seven Stories, Doubleday, 1963.

Pretty Polly Barlow, and Other Stories, Heinemann, 1964, published as *Pretty Polly, and Other Stories,* Doubleday, 1965.

Bon Voyage and Other Stories, Heinemann, 1967, published as *Bon Voyage,* Doubleday, 1968.

The Collected Stories of Noel Coward, Dutton, 1983.

OTHER

(Compiler) *Terribly Intimate Portraits,* Boni & Liveright, 1922.

A Withered Nosegay (imaginary biographies), Christophers, 1922.

(Under pseudonym Hernia Whittlebot; real name cited as editor) *Chelsea Buns* (poems), Hutchinson, 1925.

(Editor) *Spangled Unicorn* (anthology), Hutchinson, 1932, Doubleday, 1933.

Present Indicative (autobiography), Doubleday, 1937 (also see below).

Australia Visited, 1940 (broadcast series), Heinemann, 1941.

Middle East Diary, Doubleday, 1944.

Noel Coward Song Book, Simon & Schuster, 1953.

Future Indefinite (autobiography; sequel to *Present Indicative*), Doubleday, 1954 (also see below).

(Editor) Frederick Thomas Bason, *Last Bassoon,* Parrish, 1960.

(Translator) J. Dramese, *Les Folies du Music-hall,* Blond, 1962.

The Lyrics of Noel Coward, Heinemann, 1965, Doubleday, 1967.

Not Yet the Dodo and Other Verses, Heinemann, 1967, Doubleday, 1968.

Dick Richards, compiler, *The Wit of Noel Coward,* Frewin, 1968.

(Author of introduction) Michael Arlen, *The London Venture,* Cassell, 1968.

(Author of foreword) Raymond Mander and Joe Mitchenson, *Musical Comedy: A Story in Pictures,* P. Davies, 1969, Taplinger, 1970.

(Author of text) John Hadfield, editor, *A Last Encore* (pictures), Little, Brown, 1973.

Collected Verse of Noel Coward, edited by Graham Payn and Martin Tickner, Routledge, Chapman & Hall, 1985.

Autobiography, Volume I: *Present Indicative,* Volume II: *Past Conditional,* Volume III: *Future Indicative,* Methuen, 1986.

(Author of introduction) *The Penguin Complete Saki,* Penguin, 1988.

SIDELIGHTS: Coward's "music has been played by innumerable dance orchestras," writes Frank Swinnerton in *The Georgian Literary Scene.* "His plays have been booed (Coward facing the boos with every appearance of dignity) and extolled. He has been billed, in the cinemas of England, as the greatest living dramatist. He has been inaccurately reported as marooned upon a desert island; plays of his have been banned by the censor in England; he has written prefaces (and they have been printed) in italics. He knows all the smart people, and he neither drinks nor stays up late. He is liked wherever he goes; and might at any time, if it has not happened already, be mobbed by those outrageous harpies who molest actors and actresses at stage doors in London. His plays are denied wit by the dramatic critics, and yet in their way are wittier than most other smart plays except those by Frederick Lonsdale.

"It would appear that exception has been taken to some of Coward's work on the ground that it directly encourages immorality. That is very strange. His plays are among the most moral plays ever written. He has been one of the most successful playwrights of modern times, and he has had much applause.

"Why should he be banned? The answer is, according to Coward, that the Middle Classes impose the weight of their 'massed illiteracy' upon the theatre. He says: 'I do resent very deeply, on my own behalf and on behalf of those young writers who are sincerely attempting to mirror contemporary life honestly and truthfully . . . that this weight of bourgeois ignorance and false sentimentality should not only be allowed to force those in authority to crush down rising talent for the sole reason that its outlook doesn't quite conform with the moral traditions of twenty-five years ago, but that it should be encouraged in every possible way by the press.'

"It is his object to mirror contemporary life. Not all contemporary life, but a section of it. And the part he mirrors is a part given to promiscuity, drunkenness, drugging, and fighting. . . . The only trouble is that these plays about neurotics do not quite satisfy us that neuroticism is a completely valuable theme; or

that (assuming it to be a valuable theme) Coward has seen it more than superficially. The plays are written with much verve, and many lively sallies adorn them. The chit-chat they contain is insulting, irreverent, cheeky, and full of surprise. They are less good when Coward is serious; for then he gropes a little in the profundities, and his long theatrical experience does him an ill turn by making him specious. Therefore his lighter plays, or the lighter moments in his less frivolous plays, are best. . . . His wit, though it is not of the most subtle and distinguished kind, is fresh and amusing."

As an actor, Coward was both praised and panned. John Weightman, reviewing the 1966 production of "Suite in Three Keys," in which Coward played, wrote: "[Coward] had a way of getting up from his seat and moving jerkily about the stage or fiddling with the drinks tray that said quite clearly: 'I must vary things here with a bit of business.' More than once he appeared so bored with his lines he couldn't even remember them, and the clear, feminine voice of the prompter rang through the hush. And the pace! He lobbed the witticisms into the audience and waited for the crash of Philistine mirth. It usually occurred, but with the disjointed automatism of canned applause. . . . In short, Mr. Coward was a sad disappointment to me."

Others believe Coward's subtle style of "non-acting" was both polished and natural. Of his own work, Coward told Michael Macowan: "Acting is not a state of being; it is giving an impression of feeling. . . . I believe that all acting is a question of control, the control of the actor of himself, and through himself of the audience." Coward said that he preferred playing someone else's work to his own; he added: "I always forget when I'm playing in my own plays that I am the author. Not at rehearsals, when I'm after the others, but when I'm actually doing it."

Coward had little admiration for the contemporary English and American theaters, which, for him, were characterized by sloppy acting, lack of flair, and bad plays. He saw this development as the result of modern disrespect for the sanctity of the theater (he always rehearsed in a freshly pressed suit, regardless of his role, and abhorred the blue jeans and old sweaters that he saw at the rehearsals of new plays). He told Macowan: "In the old days, before the war, in the 'twenties and the 'thirties, whenever I was about to do a new production in England I always used to go to New York for a fortnight and go to every single play, because the tempo and the wonderful speed and vitality of the American theatre was then far superior to the English. Since the war, the American theatre has deteriorated, I think, enormously; in England the standard is immensely high among young actors. But owing to the dearth of light-comedy playwrights it is rather fashionable now to say the day of the well-made play is over. That is nonsense. What they mean is that many of the playwrights don't know enough about it to construct a play properly. But in the last few years in the English theatre I think too much emphasis has been placed on the lower orders of life, so that it is now considered out of the question for a duchess to suffer labour pains—just wouldn't be possible because she has a big income. That has made a slight bias, so that all the young people have lost a certain style that we had in the old days." He did, however, respect Harold Pinter, whose contemporary plays have elicited much critical acclaim: "Oh, [Pinter is] an absolutely meticulous director," he told Macowan. "Every pause is professionally timed and the net result is, think, remarkable. I think he is a very extraordinary writer and also a remarkable theatre man."

As he told Albin Krebs, Coward had the following advice for playwrights: "Consider the public. Treat it with tact and courtesy. It will accept much from you if you are clever enough to win it to your side. Never fear it nor despise it. Coax it, charm it, interest it, stimulate it, shock it now and then if you must, make it laugh, make it cry, but above all, dear pioneers . . . never, never, never bore the living hell out of it."

By reputation Coward was a sophisticated and urbane playboy, as trim and dapper at sixty-seven as he was in the 1920s. "The legend of my playboyishness," he told Harvey Breit, "has lasted into my vintage. If the legend were true, how could I have managed to get anything done?" Breit asked Coward how he did manage. "I get up at 6," Coward replied. "I start work at 7 and work four and a half hours, and I *still* get to the beach before lunch. The thing is to have time, and peace." Coward worked fast and did little rewriting. "With a play I go straight on until I'm finished," he told Breit. "I do it straight on the typewriter. It was five days for *Blithe Spirit*. No, no changes. It was all complete. Maybe a few typographical errors. The quicker I write my plays, the better they are. I know this is a dangerous fact for would-be writers."

Although Coward had many critics, his success as a writer and performer and his devotion to the theater have long been firmly established. Jere Real feels that "inherent in Coward's work is a perceptive comic sense of the foibles of the human condition that transcends both the topical and the intellectual." And Brendan Gill once asserted, "Coward is the greatest of English theatrical figures in the multifariousness of his gifts." As T. E. Kalem notes, Coward "was never cool about the theater. . . . It was his cross, his sword, and his crown. He served it with undeviating grace, wit and loyalty."

MEDIA ADAPTATIONS: Several revues were based on excerpts from Coward's works, including: "And Now Noel Coward," retitled "Noel Coward's Sweet Potato," both produced in New York, 1968; "Cowardy Custard," produced in New York, 1972, published as *Cowardy Custard: The World of Noel Coward*, Heinemann, 1973; and "Oh Coward!" produced in New York, 1972, published as *Oh Coward! A Musical Comedy Revue*, Doubleday, 1974. The musical "Mr. and Mrs.," an adaptation of *Still Life* and *Fumed Oak*, was produced in London, 1968.

Numerous film adaptations have been made of Coward's work, including: "Private Lives," Metro-Goldwyn-Mayer, 1931; "Design for Living," Paramount, 1933; "We Were Dancing" (based in part on *Tonight at 8:30*), Metro-Goldwyn-Mayer, 1942; "A Matter of Innocence" (based on short story "Pretty Polly"), Universal, 1967; and "Heart of a Woman" (adaptation of *Cavalcade*).

Coward was the subject of a television special, "David Frost Presents Noel Coward," in 1969. He also recorded a reading titled "Noel and Gertie" from *Private Lives* for Odeon.

BIOGRAPHICAL/CRITICAL SOURCES:

BOOKS

Breit, Harvey, *The Writer Observed*, World Publishing, 1956.
Contemporary Literary Criticism, Gale, Volume 1, 1973, Volume 9, 1978, Volume 29, 1984, Volume 51, 1989.
Coward, Noel, *Present Indicative*, Doubleday, 1937.
Coward, Noel, *Future Indefinite*, Doubleday, 1954.
Dictionary of Literary Biography, Volume 10: *Modern British Dramatists, 1900-1945*, Gale, 1982.
Morley, Sheridan, *Talent to Amuse: A Biography of Noel Coward*, Doubleday, 1969.
Swinnerton, Frank, *The Georgian Literary Scene*, Dent, 1938, revised edition, 1951.

PERIODICALS

Chicago Tribune Book World, December 11, 1983.
Encounter, July, 1966.
Listener, April 7, 1966.
Los Angeles Times Book Review, September 29, 1985.
New York Times Book Review, December 18, 1983.
Times (London), May 1, 1986.
Times Literary Supplement, March 25, 1983, May 9, 1986.

* * *

COWLEY, Malcolm 1898-1989

PERSONAL: Born August 24, 1898, in Belsano, Pa.; died of a heart attack, March 27 (one source says March 28), 1989, in New Milford, Conn.; son of William (a homeopathic physician) and Josephine (Hutmacher) Cowley; married Marguerite Frances Baird, August, 1919 (divorced, June, 1932); married Muriel Maurer, June 18, 1932; children: Robert William. *Education:* Harvard University, B.A. (cum laude), 1920; Universite de Montpellier, diplome, 1922. *Politics:* Democrat.

ADDRESSES: Home and office—Church Rd., Sherman, Conn. 06784.

CAREER: Writer, editor, lecturer. Worked for Sweet's Architectural Service, New York City; free-lance writer and translator, 1925-29; *New Republic*, New York City, literary editor, 1929-40; Office of Facts and Figures, Washington, D.C., member of staff, 1942; Viking Press, New York City, literary adviser, 1948-85. Visiting professor, University of Washington, 1950, Stanford University, 1956, 1959, 1960-61, and 1965, University of Michigan, 1957, University of California, 1962, Cornell University, 1964, Hollins College, 1968 and 1970, University of Minnesota, 1971, and University of Warwick, 1973. Helped organize first American Writers Congress in 1935, and was active in League of American Writers which grew out of the Congress; director of Corporation of Yaddo. Chairman of zoning board, Sherman, Conn., 1945-68. *Wartime service:* American Field Service, 1917; served in France. U.S. Army, artillery officers' training school, 1918.

MEMBER: National Institute of Arts and Letters (president, 1956-59 and 1962-65), American Academy of Arts and Letters (chancellor, 1967-76), Club des Bibliophages, Phi Beta Kappa, Century Association and Harvard Club (both New York).

AWARDS, HONORS: Levinson Prize, 1928, and Harriet Monroe Memorial Prize, 1939, both for verse published in *Poetry*; National Institute of Arts and Letters grant in literature, 1946; National Endowment for the Arts grant, 1967; Signet Society Medal, 1976; Hubbell Medal for service to the study of American letters, 1979; National Institute Gold Medal, 1981; Who's Who in America Achievement Award, 1984; Elmer Holmes Bobst Award for Arts and Letters, New York University, 1985, for literary criticism. Litt.D. from Franklin and Marshall College, 1961, Colby College, 1962, University of Warwick, 1975, University of New Haven, 1976, Monmouth College, 1978, and Indiana University of Pennsylvania, 1985.

WRITINGS:

PUBLISHED BY VIKING EXCEPT AS INDICATED

Exile's Return (literary history of the 1920s), Norton, 1934, revised edition, Viking, 1951, reprinted, 1983.
The Literary Situation (literary history), 1954.
(With Daniel Pratt Mannix) *Black Cargoes: A History of the Atlantic Slave Trade, 1518-1865*, 1962.
The Faulkner-Cowley File, 1966.

Think Back on Us: A Contemporary Chronicle of the 1930s (literary history), edited and with an introduction by Henry Dan Piper, Southern Illinois University Press, 1969.

A Many-Windowed House: Collected Essays on American Writers and American Writing, Southern Illinois University Press, 1970.

(With Howard Hugo) *The Lesson of the Masters* (criticism), Scribner, 1971.

A Second Flowering: Works and Days of the Lost Generation (literary history), 1973.

And I Worked at the Writer's Trade (memoirs), 1978.

The Dream of the Golden Mountains: Remembering the 1930s (memoirs), 1980.

The View from Eighty (essay), 1980.

The Flower and the Leaf (selected essays), edited by Donald W. Faulkner, Viking, 1985.

Unshaken Friend (profile of Maxwell Perkins), Roberts Rinehart, 1986.

POETRY

Blue Juniata, Cape & Smith, 1929.
The Dry Season, New Directions, 1941.
Blue Juniata: Collected Poems, Viking, 1968.
Blue Juniata: A Life, Viking, 1985.

EDITOR

Brantz Mayer, *Adventures of an African Slaver: Being a True Account of the Life of Captain Theodore Canot,* Garden City, 1928.

After the Genteel Tradition: American Writers since 1910, Norton, 1937, revised edition, Southern Illinois University Press, 1964.

(With Bernard Smith) *Books That Changed Our Minds,* Doubleday, 1940.

The Portable Hemingway, Viking, 1944.

(With Hannah Josephson) *Aragon: Poet of the French Resistance,* Duell, Sloan & Pearce, 1945 (published in England as *Aragon: Poet of Resurgent France,* Pilot Press, 1946).

The Portable Faulkner, Viking, 1946, revised edition, 1966.

The Portable Hawthorne, Viking, 1948, revised edition, 1969.

The Complete Poetry and Prose of Walt Whitman, Pellegrini, 1948, published as *The Works of Walt Whitman,* Funk, 1968.

Stories by F. Scott Fitzgerald, Scribner, 1951.

Fitzgerald, *Tender Is the Night,* Scribner, 1951.

(With Edmund Wilson) *Three Novels by F. Scott Fitzgerald,* Scribner, 1953.

Great Tales of the Deep South, Lion Press, 1955.

Writers at Work: The "Paris Review" Interviews, Viking, 1958.

Walt Whitman, *Leaves of Grass: The First (1855) Edition,* Viking, 1959.

Sherwood Anderson, *Winesburg, Ohio,* Viking, 1960.

(With son, Robert Cowley) *Fitzgerald and the Jazz Age,* Scribner, 1966.

TRANSLATOR FROM THE FRENCH

Pierre MacOrlan, *On Board the Morning Star,* A. & C. Boni, 1924.

Joseph Delteil, *Joan of Arc,* Minton, 1926.

Paul Valery, *Variety,* Harcourt, 1927.

Marthe Lucie Bibesco, *Catherine-Paris,* Harcourt, 1928.

Bibesco, *The Green Parrot,* Harcourt, 1929.

Maurice Barres, *The Sacred Hill,* Macaulay, 1929.

Raymond Radiguet, *The Count's Ball,* Norton, 1929.

Andre Gide, *Imaginary Interviews,* Knopf, 1944.

(With James R. Lawler) Valery, *Leonardo, Poe, Mallarme,* Princeton University Press, 1972.

Associate editor, *Broom,* 1928, and *Secession;* associate editor and book critic, *New Republic,* 1929-44.

SIDELIGHTS: In 1934 Malcolm Cowley published an autobiographical literary history, *Exile's Return,* and established himself as an important writer. In 1965 the editor of *Literary Times* wrote, "Malcolm Cowley is, next to Edmund Wilson, the finest literary historian and critic . . . in America today."

In the early 1930s, Cowley's name was frequently associated with the political left. But, as Murray Kempton notes, "even then, Cowley's was a commitment primarily literary. He remained a spectator and he confessed in 1934 that, as 'a petty bourgeois critic,' he was debarred from complete involvement." Daniel Aaron adds: "Few writers identified with the left during this period managed better than Cowley did to remain on speaking terms with literary acquaintances to the right and left of him." Aaron believes that it was Cowley's intention, in advocating leftist principles, to "mediate between the 'art as a weapon' school of literary judgment and ivory-tower subjectivism," and he believed that Communist ideology proposed an environment in which the artist could function most effectively. Kempton outlines his argument: "Malcolm Cowley [was not a Communist, but he] believed that the young writer was wise to be one and could give him better reasons than he could give himself. . . . The revolution could give a man, Cowley indicated, the gift of prophecy. 'It gives the sense of human life, not as a medley of accidents, but as a connected and continuous process. . . . It gives the values, the unified interpretation without which one can neither write good history nor good tragedy.' Cowley was not one of the committed and he was there mainly as an ornament. He confessed himself unable by condition and vestiges of class heritage to contest for the glories of this vision; they belonged to the young and the plebeian." Cowley thought that the revolution provided a "new source of strength" for the writer who could derive inspiration from the potential greatness of a rising class. Kempton continues: "For Cowley and his friends social rebellion was a new turn and the passion they brought to it seems more rhetorical now than they knew then. Cowley was the most articulate historian of their highly complicated state of mind, and his *Exile's Return . . .* is their best testament."

Reviewers frequently note that Cowley's most important achievement as a critic has been his treatment of William Faulkner's fiction. The *Literary Times* editor writes: "Probably more than any single person, Cowley is responsible for the entrenchment of . . . Faulkner as a major American writer with his brilliant introduction and presentation of *The Portable Faulkner* in 1946."

But Cowley is most often recognized as a literary historian, and his *Exile's Return,* if not the definitive chronicle of the 1920s, is certainly one of the most widely read. When the book was first published, Isabel Paterson of *Books* called it "touching, interesting, amusing; it reveals a likable soul and, therefore, should appeal to a much wider audience than the literary group with which it is concerned." In a *New York Post* review, Herschel Brickell stated that "the writing in the book is a good deal better than the thinking," but went on to say that it was "undeniably an important contribution to American literary history of our times." And J. D. Adams of the *New York Times* wrote: "As the sincere attempt of a writer of our time to explain himself and his generation, to trace the flux of ideas and other influences to which he was subjected during his formative years, Mr. Cowley's book is a valuable document. It should interest the literary historian of the future no less than it must interest Mr. Cowley's contemporaries, however hard some of them may find it to grant him all his premises and to agree with all his deductions from them." When *Exile's Return* was revised in 1951, the new edition sparked further critical commentary. Lloyd Morris, in a *New York Herald Tribune Book Review* article, called it "the most vivacious of all accounts of literary life during the fabulous 1920s" and said that the book "offers an intimate realistic portrait of the era that produced a renaissance in American fiction and poetry." J. W. Krutch of the *Saturday Review of Literature* noted that "Mr. Cowley's estimate of his most successful elder contemporaries, including Joyce, Eliot, and Proust, is cool and on the whole rather remarkably far this side of idolatry. But these evaluations do not seem unjust, and his picture of life on the Left Bank and in Greenwich Village is highly colored without being exaggerated."

Another literary history for which Cowley has received considerable praise is *A Second Flowering,* a book dealing with eight literary figures: Fitzgerald, Hemingway, Dos Passos, Cummings, Wilder, Faulkner, Wolfe, and Hart Crane. William Styron, in a *New York Times Book Review* article, writes: "It is testimony to Cowley's gifts both as a critic and a literary chronicler that the angle of vision seems new; that is, not only are his insights into these writers' works almost consistently arresting, but so are his portraits of the men themselves. . . . Cowley can be as rough and relentless as an old mill-wheel in his judgments, whether it be upon some odious personal quality, such as Hemingway's unregenerate and infantile competitiveness, or on a matter of literature. Either way, the critic cuts close to the bone." P. S. Prescott of *Newsweek* agrees that the essays in this book are "a skillful blend of criticism and biography" and adds that the pieces "on the individual writers, all of whom have been overobserved and overanalyzed, remain fresh and perceptive." Prescott concludes, "Cowley's book, I think, may be—and may remain—the best brief introduction to the generation."

Writing in the *Sewanee Review,* Lewis P. Simpson expresses his opinion that *A Second Flowering* "represents a part of a long struggle on Cowley's part to redeem the American writer from his condition of alienation. It would be misleading to say that this struggle has dominated Cowley's wide-ranging work as a literary critic. It is hardly too much to say that it provides a strong unifying theme in his complex and varied achievement. But in the same breath we must observe that it is a struggle Cowley has never intended to win. When we add to his criticism Cowley's small but important body of poetry, we see running through the whole range of his work as a twentieth-century poet, critic, and literary and cultural historian a basic motive of alienation. As both a creator and an interpreter of the literature of the lost generation, Cowley is a contributor to one of its leading aspects: a myth or a legend of creativity which is definable as a poetics of exile. He apprehended first the American writer's exile from childhood, second his exile from society, and finally his exile from what may be termed the sense of being in the wholeness of the self. The first two revelations are stated in Cowley's best-known book, *Exile's Return;* the third—of which the first two are stages—is nowhere, so far as I know, set down explicitly by Cowley. It does not lend itself to overstatement. Implied in the first edition of *Exile's Return,* it is significantly modified or even repudiated in the second, a reversal which carries over strikingly in a remarkable essay entitled 'A Natural History of the American Writer.' But on the other hand its implication is strong in three of Cowley's most significant essays, those on Frost, Hawthorne, and Whitman. Its major appearance may be discerned in *Blue Juniata: Collected Poems.*"

In an interview with Allen Geller, Cowley compared contemporary literature to the work produced in the twenties and thirties. "I think there is a very interesting group of writers today," he said, mentioning Saul Bellow and John Cheever among those he considered most important. "[Literary taste] has become more sophisticated. Whether it's better or not is always the question, but it has more knowledge, more points of reference." He added, "The great change from the 1930s is that nobody any longer believes in his duty or ability to any extent or in any manner whatever to reshape or alter conditions."

In a *Southern Review* interview with Diane U. Eisenberg, Cowley commented on the state of free-lance writing today in comparison to when he began working: "The trade of free lance is harder today. I don't think there are so many free-lance fiction writers. There are not many magazines that publish their work. As late as the 1920s and 1930s there were dozens of magazines that published short stories and paid for them. The *Saturday Evening Post* paid Scott Fitzgerald $4000 per story a while in the early thirties. On that, Fitzgerald could live like a spendthrift prince. And I think there were others who were paid up to $5000 by the *Post* at that time. That doesn't exist now; there's one magazine that pays well for stories and that is the *New Yorker.* I don't think there's another one. Many magazines pay well for articles and so most free lancers you meet today are article writers, not fiction writers. On the other hand, at the popular top of the profession it is novelist fiction writers who hit the jackpot."

Eisenberg asked, "Are you satisfied with what you've accomplished?" In reply, Cowley said: "No! Distinctly dissatisfied! It goes back to a long and bad error that I made during my twenties. That is, partly influenced by French friends, I decided, 'Well, I just have to keep at this thing honestly and if I make any great success in my twenties or thirties I'm not going to keep at it honestly,' so I actually tried not to make a success. I was the anticareerist at that time for myself. And a part of the result was that I didn't drive myself to write some big work that was really expected of me. I had chances, too, but I didn't drive myself to finish it. And the fact that I didn't drive myself hard enough in my twenties is the big error I made. I should have been looking much more at the big overall pattern . . . keeping at producing bigger books."

In his final statement to Eisenberg, Cowley concluded: "The writer's trade is a laborious, tedious but lovely occupation of putting words into patterns. I love that trade, profession, vocation. And that is something that persists over time."

Four years before his death, Cowley told *CA:* "I take pride in the fact that most of my books have been published since I was seventy years old. Before 1970 my work did not attract much critical or biographical attention. Since then, it has attracted too much, in my judgment, and I couldn't begin to draw up a list of secondary sources.

"I had to retire from writing for publication about the time of my 87th birthday, in 1983. Additional books to be prepared from my papers include selected letters to and from Kenneth Burke—seventy years of correspondence mostly on literary matters, a unique collection.

"My papers are at the Newberry Library in Chicago, where they are open to scholars. No secrets. Everything hangs out on the line. Another extensive collection is that of Mrs. Wayne B. Nuzum in Boulder, Colorado. Papers concerning Hart Crane, William Faulkner, and Edmund Wilson are housed at Yale University. Too damned many papers. Not enough remaining time."

AVOCATIONAL INTERESTS: Gardening, pine trees.

BIOGRAPHICAL/CRITICAL SOURCES:

BOOKS

Aaron, Daniel, *Writers on the Left,* Harcourt, 1961.
Breit, Harvey, *The Writer Observed,* World Publishing, 1956.
Contemporary Literary Criticism, Volume 39, Gale, 1986.
Dictionary of Literary Biography, Gale, Volume 4: *American Writers in Paris, 1920-1939,* 1980, Volume 48: *American Poets, 1880-1945, Second Series,* 1986.
Eisenberg, Diane U., *Malcolm Cowley: A Checklist of His Writings, 1915-1973,* Southern Illinois University Press, 1975.
Kempf, James M., *The Early Career of Malcolm Cowley,* Louisiana State University Press, 1985.
Kempton, Murray, *Part of Our Time,* Simon & Schuster, 1955.
Nemerov, Howard, *Poetry and Fiction: Essays,* Princeton University Press, 1963.
Rahv, Philip, editor, *Discovery of Europe,* Houghton, 1947.
Rexroth, Kenneth, *Assays,* New Directions, 1961.
Simpson, Lewis P., *The Brazen Face of History,* 1980.
Writers at Work, Volume 7, Viking, 1986.
Young, Thomas Daniel, *Conversations With Malcolm Cowley,* University Press of Mississippi, 1986.

PERIODICALS

Bookman, October, 1930.
Booklist, June 15, 1951.
Books, May 27, 1934.
Canadian Forum, January, 1968.
Chicago Tribune, March 3, 1985.
Choice, September, 1973.
Globe and Mail (Toronto), June 15, 1985.
Literary Times, April, 1965.
Los Angeles Times, September 7, 1980, August 4, 1985.
Nation, July 4, 1934, June 5, 1967.
New Republic, March 11, 1967.
New Yorker, June 30, 1951, June 23, 1973.
New York Herald Tribune Book Review, May 28, 1934, June 24, 1951, October 7, 1951.
New York Post, June 2, 1934.
New York Times, May 27, 1934, June 10, 1951, February 13, 1962, August 17, 1977, April 28, 1978, March 26, 1980, October 1, 1980, December 11, 1985.
New York Times Book Review, July 8, 1951, February 12, 1967, November 17, 1968, May 6, 1973.
Saturday Review, March 11, 1967.
Saturday Review of Literature, January 16, 1934, June 30, 1951.
Sewanee Review, spring, 1976.
Southern Review, spring, 1977.
Washington Post Book World, September 7, 1980, January 20, 1985, January 26, 1986.

OBITUARIES:

PERIODICALS

Chicago Tribune, March 29, 1989.
Los Angeles Times, March 29, 1989.
New York Times, March 29, 1989.
Times (London), March 30, 1989.

*   *   *

COX, William Trevor 1928-
(William Trevor)

PERSONAL: Born May 24, 1928, in Mitchelstown, County Cork, Ireland; son of James William (a banker) and Gertrude (Davison) Cox; married Jane Ryan, August 26, 1952; children: Patrick, Dominic. *Education:* Attended St. Columba's College, Dublin, Ireland, 1942-46; Trinity College, Dublin, B.A., 1950. *Politics:* "A liberal."

ADDRESSES: Home—Stentwood House, Dunkeswell, Honiton, Devonshire, England. *Agent*—Literistic Ltd., 32 West 40th St., No. 5F, New York, N.Y. 10018; and A. D. Peters & Company Ltd., 5th Floor, The Chambers, Chelsea Harbour, London SW10, England.

CAREER: History teacher in Armagh, Northern Ireland, 1950-52; art teacher in Rugby, England, 1952-56, and in Taunton, England, 1956-60; advertising copywriter in London, England, 1960-65; writer, 1965—.

MEMBER: Irish Academy of Letters.

AWARDS, HONORS: Winner of Irish section, "Unknown Political Prisoner" sculpture competition, 1953; second prize, *Transatlantic Review* short story competition, 1964; Hawthornden Prize, 1965; Society of Authors' traveling scholarship, 1972; Allied Irish Bank Prize for literature, 1978; Whitbread Prize for fiction, 1978, for *The Children of Dynmouth;* Benson Medal, Royal Society of Literature, 1978; Commander, Order of the British Empire, 1979; Giles Cooper award for radio play, 1980, for "Beyond the Pale," and 1982, for "Autumn Sunshine"; Whitbread Prize for best novel, 1983, for *Fools of Fortune;* D.Litt. from University of Exeter, 1984; Hon.D.Lit. from University of Belfast, 1989.

WRITINGS:

UNDER NAME WILLIAM TREVOR

A Standard of Behavior, Hutchinson, 1958.
The Old Boys, Viking, 1964.
The Boarding-House, Viking, 1965.
The Love Department, Bodley Head, 1966, Viking, 1967.
The Day We Got Drunk on Cake, and Other Stories, Bodley Head, 1967, Viking, 1968.
Mrs. Eckdorf in O'Neill's Hotel, Bodley Head, 1969, Viking, 1970.
The Old Boys (play; adapted from his novel; first produced on the West End at Mermaid Theatre, July 29, 1971), Davis-Poynter, 1971.
Miss Gomez and the Brethren, Bodley Head, 1971.
The Ballroom of Romance, and Other Stories, Viking, 1972.
"Going Home" (one-act play), first produced in London at King's Head Islington, February 29, 1972.
Elizabeth Alone, Viking, 1973.
Angels at the Ritz and Other Stories, Viking, 1975.
The Children of Dynmouth, Bodley Head, 1976, Viking, 1977.
Lovers of Their Time, Viking, 1979.
Other People's Worlds, Bodley Head, 1980, Viking, 1981.
"Scenes from an Album" (play), first produced in Dublin at the Abbey Theatre, 1981.
Beyond the Pale and Other Stories, Bodley Head, 1981, Viking, 1982.
Fools of Fortune, Viking, 1983.
A Writer's Ireland: Landscape in Literature, Viking, 1984.
The News from Ireland and Other Stories, Viking, 1986.
Nights at the Alexandra, Harper, 1987.
The Silence in the Garden, Viking, 1988.
(Editor) *The Oxford Book of Irish Short Stories,* Oxford University Press, 1989.
Family Sins and Other Stories, Viking, 1989.

Stories anthologized in: *Voices 2,* edited by Michael Ratcliffe, M. Joseph, 1964; *Winter's Tales 14,* edited by Kevin Crossley-Holland, Macmillan, 1968; *Splinters: A New Anthology of Modern Macabre Fiction,* edited by Alex Hamilton, Hutchinson, 1968, Walker & Co., 1969; *The Bedside Guardian,* edited by W. L. Webb, Collins, 1969; *The Seventh Ghost Book,* edited by Rosemary Timperley, Barrie & Jenkins, 1972; *Modern Irish Short Stories,* edited by David Marcus, Sphere, 1972; *The Eighth Ghost Book,* edited by Timperley, Barrie & Jenkins, 1973; *Winter's Tales from Ireland 2,* edited by Kevin Casey, Macmillan, 1973; *Modern Irish Love Stories,* edited by Marcus, Sphere, 1974; *The Bodley Head Book of Longer Short Stories,* edited by James Michie, Bodley Head, 1974; *A Book of Contemporary Nightmares,* edited by Giles Gordon, M. Joseph, 1977; *Best for Winter,* edited by A. D. Maclean, Macmillan, 1979; *The Bodley Head Book of Irish Short Stories,* edited by Marcus, Bodley Head, 1980.

Contributor of short stories to *Transatlantic Review, London Magazine, Town, Queen, Nova, Encounter, Times* (London), *Irish Press, Penguin Modern Stories, Listener, Argosy, Redbook, Atlantic, Observer, New Yorker, Spectator, Antaeus, Antioch Review,* and other periodicals. Author of television and radio plays for British Broadcasting Corp. and ITV, including "The Old Boys," "O Fat White Woman," and "The Grass Widows."

MEDIA ADAPTATIONS: Fools of Fortune was adapted into a film directed by Pat O'Connor and released c. 1990.

SIDELIGHTS: William Trevor Cox, better known as William Trevor, is an Irish-born short story writer, novelist, and playwright who has also adapted many of his short stories for production by the British Broadcasting Corporation. A resident of Devon, England, Trevor draws heavily upon Irish/Anglo manners and attitudes in his development of characters and themes. Trevor molds his characters with an empathy born of common experience, and critics often note the believability this lends to his characterizations. British short story writer and critic V. S. Pritchett, who feels that Trevor "is one of the finest short story writers at present writing in the Anglo-Irish modes," comments in a review of *Lovers of Their Time* for the *New York Review of Books* that Trevor's characters "live by an obscure dignity and pride. . . . [Trevor's] art is to show they have their part in an exceptional destiny and even in a history beyond the private." Although Trevor often presents moral messages through his characters, Pritchett declares that Trevor "truthfully allows life to present itself without preaching." In the same vein, Frank Tuohy, reviewing *Other People's Worlds* for the *Times Literary Supplement,* writes that "without being overtly moralistic, [Trevor] holds certain assumptions about the nature of human beings, and these assumptions form the rules of the game."

Trevor's characters are plagued with problems both of circumstance, particularly class, and of their own making. *New Statesman* critic Zahir Jamal notes that "Trevor's open, persevering sympathies go out to the unrecognised characters of time: ordinary lives shaped through silt and scythe and then forsaken or betrayed by failures of not-so-common understanding." In addition to their problems, writes Julia O'Faolain in a review of *Lovers of Their Time* for the *Washington Post Book World,* Trevor's characters are unified by a shared penchant for nostalgia: "Looking back is a thing which characters in all these stories do. The book's title is ironic, for few of them care for the present. Some suffer from it; others retreat into folly or fantasy, but the author himself confronts it with a cold, Prufrockian eye."

Several other critics also note Trevor's interest in the memories of his characters. Victoria Glendinning of the *New York Times Book Review* quotes from one of the stories in *Lovers of Their Time* to illustrate the point: " 'There are casualties in wars thousands of miles from where the fighting is'. . . . Thus the unseemly past troubles the complacent present." In Glendinning's view, "this distancing technique . . . is very classical; it is like Racine and Corneille in 17th-century French drama, in which no one does anything on stage but talk, and messengers hurtle in and out with news of battles, disasters, murders and suicides that determine the plot but are never seen by the audience and actors." Anatole Broyard of the *New York Times,* however, feels that the nostalgic element of characterization is overworked. "Too many of Trevor's characters are haunted by the past," he writes. "After a while, when I grew tired of them, they reminded me of the sort of people who sentimentalize in attics. Although nothing demands deftness so much as nostalgia, Mr. Trevor is sometimes content just to shamble around it." In Broyard's opinion, Trevor "writes best of people caught between yes and no, people who live in a poetic limbo, unable to resist or realize their daydreams." Tom Paulin addresses the issue of nostalgia in his review of *Lovers of Their Time* for *Encounter.* Although he praises Trevor for writing with "the most accurate sympathy," he finds the atmosphere in Trevor's stories "oddly dated," with Trevor "settl[ing] for a decent, tolerant, middle-brow obviousness, a kind of synthetic mustiness."

Ironically, the "impartial economy" that is "one of the most remarkable features of [Trevor's] writing" to Paulin is a symptom of technical weakness to Victoria Glendinning. "William Trevor is a professional craftsman," she writes, "and occasionally in his professionalism he sets up his characters a little glibly, economy of expression becoming economy of invention: 'Mr. Gregar was a stout man and his wife was exceedingly thin.' " Approaching the question from another vantage point, Broyard conjectures that appreciation of Trevor's so-called economy may depend on acculturated values: "Sometimes, in British fiction, it is hard to distinguish between subtlety and lack of substance, just as in certain kinds of American writing, energy is often mistaken for significance, and momentum for development." Lawrence Graver of the *New Republic* agrees with Paulin that Trevor's spareness is intentional and successful. Commenting on another work, he notes that the writing in *The Old Boys* "registers sharp impressions through fastidious understatement."

Trevor's humor, like his characterizations, is subtle; it is also dark, and yet many critics find its dry wit appealing. Lawrence Graver describes Trevor as "one of the most accomplished of those British writers who see life as a 'farce in a vale of tears.' " Graver sees Trevor's novel *The Old Boys* as a "morbid comedy of manners, gaiety mixed with dread in exact proportions." Frank Tuohy of the *Times Literary Supplement* suggests that humor plays a role in easing the reader into the appropriate willing suspension of disbelief: "*Other People's Worlds* is a work of the blackest humour, but far from depressing in effect. Perhaps this is because Trevor's skill goes beyond observation. He has an extraordinary gift for inventing small significant incidents. Only when one closes the book . . . must certain doubts arise about the world which has been examined."

AVOCATIONAL INTERESTS: Eating, drinking, friends, traveling, gardening, walking; prefers listening to talking.

BIOGRAPHICAL/CRITICAL SOURCES:

BOOKS

Contemporary Literary Criticism, Gale, Volume 7, 1977, Volume 9, 1978, Volume 14, 1980, Volume 25, 1983.
Dictionary of Literary Biography, Volume 14: *British Novelists since 1960,* Gale, 1983.

PERIODICALS

Atlantic Monthly, August, 1986.
Books and Bookmen, July, 1967.
Chicago Tribune, November 13, 1987, September 30, 1988.
Chicago Tribune Book World, July 29, 1979, March 15, 1981, February 14, 1982, October 30, 1983.
Christian Science Monitor, February 26, 1970.
Encounter, January, 1979.
Globe and Mail (Toronto), December 31, 1983, October 24, 1987, September 17, 1988.
London Magazine, August, 1968.
Los Angeles Times, October 2, 1983, September 29, 1988.
Los Angeles Times Book Review, January 11, 1981, March 11, 1984, May 4, 1986, August 6, 1989.
New Republic, February 4, 1967.
New Statesman, October 15, 1971, July 9, 1976, September 22, 1978.
Newsweek, June 14, 1976, February 22, 1982, October 10, 1983.
New Yorker, July 12, 1976.
New York Review of Books, April 19, 1979, March 19, 1981.
New York Times, September 31, 1972, March 31, 1979, January 17, 1981, February 3, 1982, September 26, 1983, May 14, 1986, August 27, 1988, May 11, 1990.
New York Times Book Review, February 11, 1968, July 11, 1976, April 8, 1979, February 1, 1981, February 21, 1982, October 2, 1983, June 8, 1986, October 9, 1988.
Plays and Players, September, 1971.
Spectator, October 11, 1969, May 13, 1972.
Stage, March 9, 1972.
Time, January 26, 1970, October 10, 1983.
Times (London), October 15, 1981, April 28, 1983, March 20, 1986.
Times Literary Supplement, October 26, 1973, June 20, 1980, October 16, 1981, April 29, 1983, August 31, 1984, April 11, 1986, November 5, 1987, June 10, 1988, January 26, 1990.
Tribune Books (Chicago), September 10, 1989.
Vogue, February 1, 1968.
Washington Post Book World, April 8, 1979, February 1, 1981, February 21, 1982, September 25, 1983, March 4, 1984, May 25, 1986, August 28, 1988.

*   *   *

COZZENS, James Gould 1903-1978

PERSONAL: Born August 19, 1903, in Chicago, Ill.; died August 9, 1978, of pneumonia following treatment for cancer of the spine, in Stuart, Fla.; cremated; son of Henry William and Bertha (Wood) Cozzens; married Sylvia Bernice Baumgarten (a literary agent), December 31, 1927 (died January 30, 1978). *Education:* Graduate of Kent (Conn.) School, 1922; attended Harvard University, 1922-24.

ADDRESSES: Office—c/o Harcourt Brace Jovanovich, 750 Third Ave., New York, N.Y. 10017.

CAREER: Writer. Taught children of American engineers in Tuinucu, Cuba, 1925-26; spent one year in Europe as a traveling tutor, 1926-27; librarian at the New York Athletic Club, 1927; worked in advertising, 1928; associate editor of *Fortune* magazine, 1938; farmer. *Military service:* U.S. Army Air Forces, 1942-45; became major.

MEMBER: National Institute of Arts and Letters.

AWARDS, HONORS: O. Henry Award, Doubleday & Co., 1931, for short story "A Farewell to Cuba," and 1936, for short story "Total Stranger"; Pulitzer Prize, 1949, for *Guard of Honor;* Litt.D., Harvard University, 1952; William Dean Howells Medal, American Academy of Arts and Letters, 1960, for *By Love Possessed.*

WRITINGS:

NOVELS

Confusion, B. J. Brimmer, 1924.
Michael Scarlett, A & C Boni, 1925.
Cock Pit, Morrow, 1928.
The Son of Perdition, Morrow, 1929, reprinted, AMS Press, 1989.
S.S. San Pedro (Book-of-the-Month Club selection; also see below), Harcourt, 1931, reprinted, 1967.
The Last Adam (Book-of-the-Month Club selection), Harcourt, 1933, reprinted, Carroll & Graf, 1986 (original edition published in England as *A Cure of Flesh,* Longmans, Green, 1934, reprinted, 1958).
Castaway (also see below), Random House, 1934, reprinted, Harcourt, 1967.
Men and Brethren, Harcourt, 1936, reprinted, 1957.
Ask Me Tomorrow, Harcourt, 1940, published as *Ask Me Tomorrow; or, The Pleasant Comedy of Young Fortunas,* Harcourt, 1969.
The Just and the Unjust (Book-of-the-Month Club selection), Harcourt, 1942, reprinted, 1965.
Guard of Honor, Harcourt, 1948, reprinted, 1983.
S.S. San Pedro [and] *Castaway,* Modern Library, 1956.
By Love Possessed (Book-of-the-Month Club selection; *Reader's Digest* condensed book selection), Harcourt, 1957.
Morning Noon and Night, Harcourt, 1968.

OTHER

(Contributor) Burton Rascoe, editor, *Morrow's Almanack for the Year of Our Lord 1929,* Morrow, 1928.
(Contributor) Thayer Hobson, editor, *Morrow's Almanack Every-Day Book for 1930,* Morrow, 1929.
Children and Others (stories), Harcourt, 1964.
(Author of introduction) James B. Meriwether, *James Gould Cozzens: A Checklist,* Gale, 1972.
A Flower in Her Hair, Bruccoli Clark, 1974.
A Rope for Dr. Webster (essay), Bruccoli Clark, 1976.
Matthew J. Bruccoli, editor, *Just Representations: A James Gould Cozzens Reader,* Southern Illinois University Press, 1978.
Bruccoli, editor, *A Time of War: Air Force Diaries and Pentagon Memos, 1943-1945,* Bruccoli Clark, 1984.
Bruccoli, editor, *Selected Notebooks, 1960-1967,* Bruccoli Clark, 1984.

Contributor of short stories, poems, and essays to periodicals, including the *Atlantic, Pictorial Review, Saturday Evening Post, Collier's, Redbook, Kent Quarterly, Bookman, Town & Country, Harvard Advocate,* and *Woman's Home Companion.* Some of Cozzens's novels have been translated into foreign languages, including Burmese, Italian, German, Portuguese, and Japanese. Cozzens's manuscripts and papers are located at the Princeton University Library.

WORK IN PROGRESS: A Skyborn Music and *The Wind the Rain,* both novels.

SIDELIGHTS: Throughout his life James Gould Cozzens dedicated himself to the task of writing honestly. In a diary entry dated January 13, 1922, when he was eighteen, he wrote: "The start made on my novel, to be called tentatively 'Confusion,' was not altogether satisfactory. I am not able to explain why, but I know that the work was not distinguished and I must insist on its being that, I must deliberately set out for that goal." Later, in a letter to his mother, he declared: "I start to see that the whole problem of honesty in writing is insoluble—the most you can do is get at truth through the classic casuistry. You cannot tell what was so, for stating the facts would give the reader a 'false impression.' For a 'true impression' you must say what is calculated to create it, not always, nor indeed very often, what was in fact the case" (March 23, 1937). Finally, in a notebook entry on November 12, 1967, Cozzens stated, "What I want to do is present stuff in the form of true experience, the happenings of living life as I have found them to happen." Despite—or perhaps because of—his efforts to provide intelligent readers with what English poet John Milton described as a "new acquist of true experience," Cozzens remains the least read and least regarded major American novelist.

After publishing four novels for which he received little money or critical recognition, Cozzens gained his first writing success with *S. S. San Pedro,* a novel based on the real-life sinking of the *Vestris* in a November gale with heavy loss of life. Only 133 pages long, *S.S. San Pedro,* the first novel in which Cozzens consistently maintained an objective tone and a detached point of view, was selected as a September 1931 choice by the Book-of-the-Month Club. As Bruccoli notes in *James Gould Cozzens: A Life Apart:* "The process of rewriting the novel through successive versions had brought control over his material and style. Having published four self-indulgent novels, he moved at twenty-eight into his unembellished middle style." Increasingly concerned with structure, Cozzens regarded *S.S. San Pedro* as his first mature work, though it is flawed by the obviously symbolic use of Dr. Percival, a grotesque figure, to prefigure death. After he experimented with allegory again in *Castaway* Cozzens then permanently abandoned it.

While working on *S.S. San Pedro* in 1929 and 1930, Cozzens resumed writing commercial short stories to improve his plotting and earn money. He explained to his mother on August 23, 1929: "As you know, this business of technique has been obsessing me all summer. . . . To learn to write and write decently is simply a much longer and harder thing than is generally admitted." On June 21, 1930, the *Saturday Evening Post* published "Someday You'll Be Sorry," the first of five stories about the Durham School and its headmaster, Dr. Holt. Cozzens soon began a novel situated in a small Connecticut town. "This setting," he wrote in an inscribed copy of *The Last Adam,* "is imagined to be Kent, Connecticut, with a green like New Milford's along US 7 as it passes through Kent." Published in 1933, *The Last Adam* was Cozzens's most successful work to date, containing the qualities that distinguish his best novels. Not only does it scrutinize a profession through its central character, Dr. Bull, but it weaves cause and effect together in a dispassionate, objective style. The protagonist, moreover, acknowledges human limitations and acts within them. Harry John Mooney, in his critical work *James Gould Cozzens: Novelist of Intellect,* declares: "What *The Last Adam* revealed, above all else, was the rapidly developing direction of James Gould Cozzens himself."

The principal subject of the novel is the community of New Winton—its tight structure and the interrelations of its people. Cozzens, however, had not yet invested his central character with those traits generally belonging to his professional men. Barely competent and decidedly unconcerned about his patients, Dr. Bull's neglect is partly responsible for a typhoid epidemic; yet he nevertheless possesses an elemental force: "Something unkillable. Something here when the first men walked erect; here now.

The last man would twitch with it when the earth expired. A good greedy vitality, surely the very vitality of the world and the flesh; it survived all blunders and injuries." Unlike Dr. Bull, however, the professionals in Cozzens's later novels believe firmly in responsibility and adherence to duty. Near the end of *The Last Adam,* Cozzens quotes from Milton's *Samson Agonistes:* "His servants he, with new acquist / Of true experience from this great event / With peace and consolation both dismissed, / And calm of mind." As Bruccoli notes in *James Gould Cozzens: A Life Apart,* " 'New acquist of true experience' would become his test of literature: the presentation of convincing characters in convincing action, unimpaired by sentimental theories about human nature, to provide the reader with an undistorted recognition of behavior."

Early in 1933 the Cozzenses moved to Carrs Farm, three miles outside Lambertville, New Jersey. The move gave Cozzens a feeling of "extraordinary repose" and permitted him to garden extensively. The sixth revision of *Castaway* was completed in May. An experimental work with open-ended meanings, the novel, Cozzens explained in a letter to Bruccoli dated February 22, 1976, "was a semi-symbolic, semi-allegoric fictional demonstration of the proposition that the principle of living adds up to self-killing." Mooney declares that "the central philosophical argument of the novel seems to suggest that man operating outside the social body and therefore forced to turn inward upon himself can in the end only destroy himself, since he is thus compelled to recognize his own fundamental self. The novel displays not only Cozzens's belief in the disorder readily manifested when the individual is removed from the social stricture but also, by implication, Cozzens's respect for imposed order."

Castaway opens with the protagonist, Mr. Lecky, emerging into the vast material abundance of a department store. Inexplicably, his watch has stopped, and though the store is unpopulated, he becomes almost incapacitated by unnamed fears and begins stalking his Doppelganger, or ghostly counterpart. Cozzens provides no reason for the situation or any account of the outside world, and the principle action in the novel may occur within Mr. Lecky's consciousness, though the work does not employ stream-of-consciousness techniques. In the English edition, which preceded the Random House edition by more than a month, a Longmans editor did give a partial explanation of the situation: "Alone in a vast Department Store, the sole survivor of a catastrophe that has destroyed New York, Mr. Lecky finds himself a commonplace Robinson Crusoe, cut off from his kind amidst the fantastic plenty of the twentieth century. There is everything to sustain life in abundance, and nothing to fear—except . . ." Cozzens himself had also provided clues in the text that explained the catastrophe, but these were deleted for the Random House edition because he believed they engaged the reader in irrelevant speculation. Critics generally misread the book, some believing it a fable about Depression America.

Cozzens wrote his mother on April 29, 1934: "I have got surer and surer that the poor and wretched are, nine cases in ten, what their capacities entitle them to be. . . . I think any reasonable person will agree that it has been again and again proved in this country that anyone who has the wit to get it can have everything there is—you don't need birth, or money, or education to start with and Lord God how much more equal can you make equality," Cozzens's antidemocratic inclinations—particularly his suggestion that those endowed with breeding, superior education, and inherent disposition ought to order their communities—begin to manifest themselves in *Castaway.* Indeed, the novel reads as a study in the impoverishment of those less endowed individuals. Mr. Lecky has no survival skills, despite the store's abundance, and he becomes the victim of his own inadequacies. Intelligent enough only to recognize that he is not enjoying complete gratification from the material wealth about him, he does not know how to make any of it his own. Paralyzed by indecision and lacking self-reliance, Mr. Lecky embodies a mediocrity of intelligence and sensibility that renders him incapable of realistically viewing his world. Beginning with his next novel, *Men and Brethren,* Cozzens depicted an American aristocracy in which ability and a sense of duty were primarily discerned in those who possessed the advantages of family and position.

Men and Brethren constitutes the first novel in which Cozzens fully portrayed the concept of duty that characterizes his major fiction. Ernest Cudlipp, an Episcopalian minister, struggles with himself and the truth of appearances. As Louis Coxe observes in his 1955 *American Literature* essay, Cudlipp and such men as Colonel Ross in *Guard of Honor* "have worked out for themselves a mode of action and a standard of conduct by which they judge others and by which we as readers may judge them." Recognizing the burden placed upon him, the duty that makes him an early model of the Cozzens hero, Cudlipp explains to an adulterous woman whose abortion he has arranged, "This is the answer. A great obligation has been laid upon me to do or be whatever good thing I have learned I ought to be, or know I can do. I can't excuse myself from it. I dare not bury it or throw it away." The Cozzens hero is a man aware of requirements, a man of intelligence, determination, education, and analytical skills, who, because of his position and his ability to fulfill the duties of that position, helps hold society together.

Men and Brethren achieves a tight structure that enforces both the simultaneity of action and the complexity of causes. In *The Last Adam* Cozzens had depicted tangential events, but the time scheme was loose and the novel lacked a central intelligence. Limited to parts of only two days, *Men and Brethren* achieves unity because events in the novel are seen from Cudlipp's point of view. As Bruccoli notes in his critical biography, "The third-person narrative provides the impression of standing with the author behind Cudlipp and observing everything from Cudlipp's perspective, thereby providing the effect of detachment combined with close participation." The novel ends with Cudlipp's recitation of St. Matthew's parable of the talents: "For the kingdom of heaven is as a man traveling into a far country, who called his own servants and delivered unto them his goods." Depicting the faithful, good servant, Cozzens achieved a convincing portrait of a priest, despite his personal antipathy to religious people. Writing to his mother on July 23, 1935, he complained that the book was "a little thin probably because if I got right down to it I find it hard to conceive of a professional Christian who isn't a fool, or a knave."

Cozzens devoted himself primarily to short stories in 1936 as he studied possible subjects for another novel. Between 1934 and 1938 he published twelve stories, writing them now only for money because he regarded the form as too confining. "Total Stranger," published in the *Saturday Evening Post,* was awarded the O. Henry Prize for the best story of 1936. Only partly playful, Cozzens wrote his mother on December 4 that he considered it "a piece of damned impertinence for anyone to try to give me a prize. . . . I don't doubt that fundamentally the reason I prefer to live as nearly like a recluse as possible is that subconsciously I know that people, the world, never would and never will greet my entrances into it with the reverent applause required for my pleasure and if cannot have that I will not, in effect, play." Feeling it degrading to sell himself, Cozzens withdrew from literary life—though not from writing—while still in his early thirties.

In March 1937 Cozzens began work on what would become his ninth novel, *Ask Me Tomorrow.* "My conception," he wrote on March 2, "in so far as I ever have one for a book, was one of mild distaste for a series of scenes and events viewed in retrospect—the parts that were perhaps pleasant at the time becoming by passage of years rather fatuous and sad; the parts that were unpleasant becoming rather fatuous and sad too." His concern continued to be with honesty in writing: "The truth is always too complicated and usually too implausible. It has to be simplified and suggested and the most you can hope for is to present selected material in such a way that an intelligent reader will be conscious of the not-expressed and inexpressible real truth—or at least, and more often, not too conscious of a falseness" (March 17, 1939). Cozzens's most autobiographical novel, *Ask Me Tomorrow* attempts to explain the prideful behavior of Francis Ellery, a writer in reduced circumstances working in Europe as a traveling tutor. Early in the book, Ellery thinks: "The hard fact was, circumstances rarely misled, and appearances were always full of truth. . . . People who are poor, while they may be estimable and virtuous, confess in the fact of poverty an incapacity for mastering their environment; and what excuse or justification their incapacity may have interests only themselves." At the end of the novel, Ellery realizes the insignificance of his place in the world. He reflects: "To or about the course of events you could say what you liked; but events never stopped to argue with you."

In an *American Scholar* essay, John William Ward declares: "To act in the full awareness of the conditions within which he must act is, for Cozzens, the dignity of man." Critics note that Ellery finally achieves a certain worthiness because he glimpses the interlocking simultaneity of events, but *Ask Me Tomorrow* lacks the narrative scope to permit adequate development of an epiphany. Despite the fact that the novel is the one on which he labored the longest and which he felt came nearest to fulfilling his intentions, its critical reception disappointed Cozzens. Even the favorable reviews were unenthusiastic.

In June 1940 Cozzens granted Robert Van Gelder of the *New York Times Book Review* an interview—his first since 1932 and his last until 1957. Having long believed that the publication of *Confusion* at a young age confirmed his natural faults, Cozzens declared that "it is taking all of my effort now, in my mid-thirties, to wipe out those faults, to really learn to write." He planned to spend the summer in court collecting material for a new novel "about a lawyer who must make a choice between an ideal and what might be called a selfish, practical consideration." His mother urged him to make his fiction more pleasing to readers by presenting more attractive characters, a deficiency critics had noted. In a letter dated February 7, 1941, he responded: "Yes, I very well know about the importance of sentimentality, . . . but the truth is, I fail because of an inability to write that sort of stuff convincingly."

Completed in March 1942, *The Just and the Unjust* covers three days of a murder trial. Judge Coates's concluding instruction to his son Abner, the assistant district attorney, echoes Ernest Cudlipp's position in *Men and Brethren* and states the familiar Cozzens directive. One should employ his talents, do his job, fulfill his responsibilities: "The world gets up in the morning and is fed and goes to work, and in the evening it comes home and is fed again and perhaps has a little amusement and goes to sleep. To make that possible, so much has to be done by so many people that, on the face of it, it is impossible. Well, every day we have to do it; and every day, come hell, come high water, we're going to have to go on doing it as well as we can."

Like *Men and Brethren, The Just and the Unjust* is structured around a multiplicity of events that affect the protagonist during a short time period. Cozzens weaves expository flashbacks to support the present time sequence and to suggest the complexity of concurrent actions; the method is one he would employ again in *Guard of Honor*. As Bruccoli observes in *James Gould Cozzens: A Life Apart:* "His major novel—more than those of any other American writer—simulate the chain of cause and effect (but in Cozzens it is frequently perceived as effect and cause) that determine behavior." Cozzens also depicts the mental processes of his characters while maintaining the objectivity of the third.person perspective, a method that reinforces what Coxe refers to as "the double vision of modern man, the central paradox of action and contemplation, of understanding and conduct, of the ironic view and the heroic efficacy."

Cozzens considered a political novel, but Pearl Harbor temporarily ended his fiction writing. Assigned to the Training Literature Section of the Training Aids Directorate, a part of the Army Air Forces School of Applied Tactics, Cozzens wrote manuals and special reports. Replying to a questionnaire from Twentieth Century Authors in 1942, he wrote in part: "My social preference is to be left alone, and people have always seemed willing, even eager, to gratify my inclination. I am more or less illiberal, and strongly antipathetic to all political and artistic movements." Bruccoli theorizes in his Cozzens biography that "his rare public statements combined self-directed irony with role-playing as a defensive tactic, demonstrating his indifference to popularity by insulating himself from the tastes and fashions of the time." Owing largely to Cozzens himself, the public viewed him as cranky and outdated.

On October 6, 1942, while stationed in Washington, D.C., Cozzens began keeping a detailed, typed diary that not only chronicled his daily service activities but also described the hundreds of people he met. Eventually, his assignment provided him access to almost all reports from every theater of the war, and though he had not yet begun planning an air force novel, Cozzens recognized the value of his experiences. When discharged, he had compiled 380 single-spaced pages of diaries that—supplemented by his Pentagon memos—formed a useful historical record. While preparing certain of his notes, Cozzens found the idea for *Guard of Honor*. In a letter to his English editor, he wrote: "What I wanted to write about here, the essence of the thing to be said, the point of it all, what I felt to be the important meaning of this particular human experience, was its immensity and immense complexity. . . . I wanted to show the real (as now saw it) meaning of the whole business, the peculiar effects of the interaction of innumerable individuals functioning in ways at once determined by and determining the functioning of innumerable others—all in the common and in every case nearly helpless involvement in what had ceased to be just an 'organization' . . . and became if not an organism with life and purposes of its own, at least an entity, like a crowd." Pleading the Army's side, the novel won the Pulitzer Prize in 1949.

Tightly plotted, *Guard of Honor* covers seventy-two hours at Ocanara Air Base, Florida, in September 1943. The third-person omniscient narrator—recognizably Cozzens himself—is not so much seeking solutions as he is identifying the limitations inhibiting human conduct. The novel's actual subject is not General Beal's crisis—the challenge to segregated clubs by black pilots—but the overwhelming complexity of the U.S. Army Air Forces. Both Colonel Ross, who provides the perspective of the professional officer, and Captain Hicks, who represents the viewpoint of the civilian drafted to be a soldier, come to realize the intricate chain of cause and effect that, together with the operation of good and bad luck, restricts human action. In his *New York Herald Tribune* review, Mark Shorer identified the theme as "power, the hierarchy of power, and the responsibility of power," for, as Colonel Ross thinks: "Downheartedness was no man's part. A man must stand up and do the best he can with what there is. If the thing he labored to uncover now seemed in danger of stultifying him, could a rational being find nothing to do? If mind failed you, seeing no pattern; and heart failed you, seeing no point, the stout, stubborn will must be up and doing. A pattern should be found; a point should be imposed. Was that too much? It was not." Despite Cozzens's ability to treat a profession with convincing familiarity, however, critics continued to complain that his characters lacked emotion. Brendan Gill in the *New Yorker* claimed that *Guard of Honor* failed to achieve great novel status because of "an absence of deep feeling, of a fastidious shying-off on the part of the novelist, of an inconspicuous but nagging failure to commit himself beyond irony." Cozzens called such critics "sentimentalists." Other critics such as Chester E. Eisinger in *Fiction of the Forties* protested that Cozzens's realism constituted a deficiency in imagination. "He is a writer who says all he knows, and who expects that to be enough. . . . No ultimate mystery, never to be plumbed, throws its shadow upon his word." He continued: "Cozzens not only defends the status quo against attack, but he is eager to assert his approval of its essential character." In response, Cozzens declared to *CA:* "I don't defend anything; I don't eagerly assert anything."

In January 1949, Cozzens began *By Love Possessed,* a novel, he wrote his mother on April 3, that meant "to say something about the cardinal human need to do what you want to, at any cost to yourself or other people; and however indirectly or circuitously, however unreasonably or unwisely, which is what I think is meant by love or being possessed by it." Although he predicted that the novel would appear in 1952, Cozzens found that the complexity of his artistic method and the standards he set for himself had made writing more difficult, and the book was not published until 1957. On February 1, 1951, he described his method as "taking things that appear simple and reducing them to their essential complexity." *By Love Possessed* centers on forty-nine hours in the life of Arthur Winner, a lawyer involved in a complex of problems resulting from the many varieties of love altruism; marital, parental, and filial affection; lust; religion; and friendship. The son of a "man of reason," Arthur Winner regards passions as subverting order, and he believes that though no one is immune from them, the reasoning man controls his emotions. He discovers, however, that reason itself is limited. His partner, Julius Penrose, echoes Fulke Greville: "Passion and reason, self-division's cause!"

Bruccoli observes in his biography that "Cozzens conveys his understanding of life through the contrapuntal structure of his fiction. Meaning is enforced by organization as well as by style." In *By Love Possessed* Judge Dealey thinks: "Whatever happens, happens because a lot of other things have happened already. When it gets to where you come in—well, it's bound to be pretty late in the day." Attempting to solve fiction's problem of representing the passage of time and synchronizing simultaneous events, Cozzens elaborately extended his use of flashbacks to depict more than fifty years of the past within forty-nine hours of the present. Behavior in the novel, then, becomes deterministic, owing to hereditary and environmental factors, but Cozzens contends that luck is also a factor. In 1976 he declared in *Who's Who in America,* "The longer I watch men and life, the surer I get that success whenever more than minor comes of luck alone. By comparison, no principles, ideas, goals and standards of conduct matter much in an achieving of it." However, Cozzens felt that no one could afford complacency.

Cozzens's style was becoming a concern of the critics, for he refused to make concessions to inattentive or ignorant readers. *By Love Possessed* contains long, complex sentences, with inverted syntax and heavy subordination, as well as parenthetical constructions and elaborate quotations; reviewers called it "baroque." However, Cozzens aimed at a precision of statement, and his unfamiliar words, inverted word order, and double negatives (for example, "not unlikely" instead of "likely") sought to present the truth of experience. The "complications" in certain paragraphs, he wrote Charles Phillips on May 22, 1958, "were indeed a studied attempt to so reproduce or simulate the process of thought that the reader would go through it instead of just hearing about it." Abandoning the inflated, romantic wordiness of his early novels and the unadorned style of the 1930s and 1940s, Cozzens adopted a qualifying and meditative style that critics consistently attacked.

Against Bernice's advice, Cozzens consented to an interview with *Time*. Entitled "The Hermit of Lambertville," the cover story of September 2, 1957, sold thousands of copies of *By Love Possessed;* but because Cozzens did not exercise his option of checking the piece for accuracy, factual errors and misrepresentations in the article resulted in readers viewing Cozzens as an arrogant crank. Initial reviews of the novel, however, were overwhelmingly favorable, until a critical reevaluation directly attacked the book's style and eventually accused Cozzens of anti-Catholic and anti-Semitic feelings. Dwight Macdonald's *Commentary* review charged Cozzens with "the unforgivable novelistic sin: he is unaware of the nature of his characters." Cozzens, in turn, wrote to Macdonald: "I see that you don't understand prose structure very well; that shades of meaning in words are, like irony, altogether lost on you; and that your imperceptiveness is, for an educated adult, quite remarkable." In a notebook entry dated November 28, 1964, Cozzens dismissed the racism charges as "crap": "I know I wouldn't be anti-anybody by category or class for the bad (not good) reason that this would involve by definition some subscribing to or standing on principle; and I really have no principles. I don't give a hoot in hell about the race, color, religion of individuals. All I go by is whether find this one agreeable—or, in short: if he be not bad to me, what care I how bad he be?"

The Cozzenses sold Carrs Farm and moved to "Shadowbrook" outside Williamstown, Massachusetts, in the fall of 1958. Between 1960 and 1965 he filled ten notebooks, in addition to diary entries, an act owing largely to his increasing inability to write fiction that met his requirements. Still directing his career, Bernice proposed a volume of Cozzens's short stories. She may or may not have known that the six years of silence since *By Love Possessed* had generated literary gossip that Macdonald's article had crushed her husband and that he had become an alcoholic. Containing seventeen stories, *Children and Others* appeared in July 1964, while Cozzens continued his attempts on his next novel.

After a series of false starts, Cozzens shifted the new work, *Morning Noon and Night,* to the first person, which, he wrote in his notebook on November 20, 1964, "seemed to release me at once." The novel opens with Henry Dodd Worthington making a statement of fact: "I have been young and now am old." The remainder of the book constitutes the narrator's attempt to depict what exactly his life has been and what, if anything, he has learned from it: "What is this life? Who am I; what is this 'I' in me." Worthington's narrative—a meditative memoir—is carried along principally by a process of association of ideas, for the simultaneity of events precludes any final unified understanding. The seemingly unstructured account provides the means not only by which Worthington examines himself and the roles he has played but also the way through which he relates the truths he has learned. The process of narration corresponds with what Worthington believes is the nature of memory—"Give it liberty, and order be damned"-and the inconsistencies inherent in memory's operation. Cozzens in *Morning Noon and Night* thus produced a narrative style that supported the matter of the novel.

Because the form of *Morning Noon and Night* was dense, Cozzens warned his publisher against expecting sales comparable to those for *By Love Possessed.* "I'm trying to see if I can, through a fictional pattern meant to make them readable, lay out observations of mine on human behavior and the human condition using material taken directly or indirectly from my personal experience. I write in the hope that what recount may for some people (and much fear 'some' can't possibly mean 100,000) relate itself rewardingly to their own experience and observation. . . . About fiction-writing my only thought is that writers write whatever they are able to write in whatever way they are able to write it."

Morning Noon and Night offers a perspective different from Cozzens's other novels. Previously, his characters—from Ernest Cudlipp through Arthur Winner—had insisted that the rational individual work within the limitations of the system or society of which he was a part. Colonel Ross in *Guard of Honor* maintains that "a pattern should be found; a point should be imposed" on the disorder characteristic of life. Worthington, however, the epitome of management acumen, sees only the pervasiveness of good or bad luck, though he believes the struggle for achievement is valuable in itself. The novel ends: "A calling or twittering of skylarks or other birds has ceased; the immense silence settles, and the child must soon be taken away to bed. Yes; good night, good night. Good night, any surviving dear old Carian guests. Good night, ladies. Good night, all." Such a closing motif can be viewed as Cozzens's valedictory. As Bruccoli observes in *James Gould Cozzens: A Life Apart:* "Although he expected to continue writing for publication the novel is virtually an inventory of things Cozzens valued (the Puritan ethic, ability, intelligence, reason, the lessons of experience) and depreciated (self-indulgent emotion, youth, the liberal establishment, the literary life)."

An important word in the novel is "inappetency," which depicts Worthington's—and Cozzens's—loss of the appetite for living. In May 1911 Cozzens blacked out while driving. The ensuing wreck, he wrote his friend and publisher William Jovanovich in a July 24 letter, resulted in "a terrific if not testable beating which would plague me for weeks, and indeed now see probably for months and maybe forever . . . the incident seems pretty much to put a period to life up here." Cozzens reflected in a later letter to Jovanovich, "I really died in that car and this is someone posing as me" (April 9, 1972). The Cozzenses sold "Shadowbrook" and, after disposing of his book and record collections, moved to Stuart, Florida. By the end of 1974, Cozzens had stopped writing, telling his publisher that "these days I find myself stultified by seeing I simply have nothing to say to or for contemporary Making-It Literary Establishment, or to satisfy current Intellectual Elite Criticism. . . . In clear fact work of mine's all out of season." He resumed keeping detailed diaries, which chronicled his disrelish for life and which depicted his interest in suicide: "Since there's nothing here I enjoy, want, feel interest in, or can look forward to but more silly annoyances and unbecoming behavior on my part what the hell is that 12 gauge pump gun in my closet for if not to blow the top of my head and make these odds at even. Real trouble: those who have wisely done it I find I rather despise?" (March 4, 1975).

After a long illness, Bernice died on January 30, 1978. On June 22, Cozzens was hospitalized and operated on for cancer of the spine. He remained in the hospital for six weeks while receiving cobalt treatments. Ten days before his seventy-fifth birthday, Cozzens died. His remains were immediately cremated. In presenting his fiction as a "form of true experience," Cozzens had addressed subjects and employed artistic techniques the extent of which have yet to be fully appreciated. By showing the intelligent reader "the happenings of living life," Cozzens also portrayed himself and the manner of artist he was.

MEDIA ADAPTATIONS: The Last Adam was made into a motion picture entitled "Doctor Bull," 1933, starring Will Rogers; *By Love Possessed* was made into a motion picture by United Artists, 1961, starring Efrem Zimbalist, Jr., and Lana Turner.

BIOGRAPHICAL/CRITICAL SOURCES:

BOOKS

Blackmur, Richard P., *The Expanse of Greatness,* Peter Smith, 1958.

Bracher, Frederick, *The Novels of James Gould Cozzens,* Harcourt, 1959.

Bruccoli, Matthew J., editor, *Just Representations: A James Gould Cozzens Reader,* Southern Illinois University, 1978.

Bruccoli, Matthew J., editor, *James Gould Cozzens: New Acquist of True Experience,* Southern Illinois University Press, 1979.

Bruccoli, Matthew, J., *James Gould Cozzens: A Descriptive Bibliography,* University of Pittsburgh Press, 1981.

Bruccoli, Matthew J., *James Gould Cozzens: A Life Apart,* Harcourt, 1983.

Contemporary Literary Criticism, Gale, Volume I, 1973, Volume IV, 1975, Volume XI, 1979.

Cozzens, James Gould, *Confusion,* B. J. Brimmer, 1924.

Cozzens, James Gould, *Michael Scarlett,* A & C Boni, 1925.

Cozzens, James Gould, *Cock Pit,* Morrow, 1928.

Cozzens, James Gould, *The Son of Perdition,* Morrow, 1929.

Cozzens, James Gould, *S.S. San Pedro,* Harcourt, 1931, reprinted, 1967.

Cozzens, James Gould, *The Last Adam,* Harcourt, 1933, reprinted, Carroll & Graf, 1986.

Cozzens, James Gould, *Castaway,* Random House, 1934, reprinted, Harcourt, 1957.

Cozzens, James Gould, *Men and Brethren,* Harcourt, 1936, reprinted, 1957.

Cozzens, James Gould, *Ask Me Tomorrow,* Harcourt, 1940, published as *Ask Me Tomorrow; or, The Pleasant Comedy of Young Fortunas,* Harcourt, 1969.

Cozzens, James Gould, *The Just and the Unjust,* Harcourt, 1942, reprinted, 1983.

Cozzens, James Gould, *Guard of Honor,* Harcourt, 1948, reprinted, 1983.

Cozzens, James Gould, *By Love Possessed,* Harcourt, 1957.

Cozzens, James Gould, *Morning Noon and Night,* Harcourt, 1968.

Davies, Horton, *A Mirror of the Ministry in Modern Novels,* Oxford University Press, 1959.

Dictionary of Literary Biography, Volume IX: *American Novelists, 1910-1945,* Gale, 1981.

Dictionary of Literary Biography Documentary Series, Volume II, Gale, 1982.

Dictionary of Literary Biography Yearbook: 1984, Gale, 1985.

Eisinger, Chester E., *Fiction of the Forties,* University of Chicago Press, 1963.

French, Warren, *The Forties: Fiction, Poetry, Drama,* Everett/Edwards, 1969.

Gardiner, Harold C., *Fifty Years of the American Novel: 1900-1950,* Scribner, 1951.

Geismar, Maxwell, *American Moderns from Rebellion to Conformity,* Hill & Wang, 1958.

Hicks, Granville, *James Gould Cozzens,* University of Minnesota Press, 1966.

Kunitz, Stanley J., and Howard Haycraft, editors, *Twentieth Century Authors,* Wilson, 1942.

Madden Daniel, editor, *Proletarian Writers of the Thirties,* Southern Illinois University Press, 1968.

Maxwell, D. E. S., *Cozzens,* Oliver & Boyd, 1964.

Maxwell, D. E. S. *American Fiction: The Intellectual Background,* Columbia University Press, 1963.

Michel, Pierre, *James Gould Cozzens: An Annotated Checklist,* Kent State University Press, 1971.

Michel, Pierre, *James Gould Cozzens,* Twayne, 1974.

Miller, Wayne Charles, *An Armed America: Its Face in Fiction,* New York University Press, 1970.

Millgate, Michael, *American Social Fiction: James to Cozzens,* Barnes & Noble, 1964.

Mizener, Arthur, *The Sense of Life in the Modern Novel,* Houghton, 1964.

Mizener, Arthur, *Twelve Great American Novels,* New American Library, 1967.

Mooney, Harry John, Jr., *James Gould Cozzens: Novelist of Intellect,* University of Pittsburgh Press, 1963.

Nemerov, Howard, *Poetry and Fiction: Essays,* Rutgers University Press, 1963.

Noble, David W., *The Eternal Adam and the New World Garden: The Central Myth in the American Novel since 1830,* Braziller, 1968.

Prescott, Orville, *In My Opinion,* Bobbs-Merrill, 1952.

Stuckey, W. J., *The Pulitzer Prize Novels: A Critical Backward Look,* University of Oklahoma Press, 1966.

Walcutt, Charles Child, *Man's Changing Mask: Modes and Methods of Characterization in Fiction,* University of Minnesota Press, 1966.

Whitbread, Thomas, *Seven Contemporary Authors,* University of Texas Press, 1966.

PERIODICALS

America, October 5, 1957.

American Literature, May, 1955.

American Scholar, winter, 1957-58, spring, 1958.

Antioch Review, summer, 1958.

Arizona Quarterly, summer, 1960, winter, 1962.

Atlantic, March, 1920, August, 1964, September, 1968.

Best Sellers, April 1, 1969, September 1, 1969.

Book-of-the-Month Club News, December, 1932.

Book Week, August 2, 1964.

Book World, September 8, 1968.

Catholic World, November, 1957.

Christian Science Monitor, September 19, 1968.

College English, January, 1950, January, 1956, April, 1958.

Commentary, January, 1958, September, 1968, September, 1983.

Commonweal, January, 1958, April 4, 1958.

Critical Quarterly, spring, 1962.

Critique: Studies in Modern Fiction, winter, 1958.

Daily Princetonian, June 2, 1925.

English Journal, January, 1950.

Harper's, February, 1949, September, 1957, October, 1968.

House and Garden, September, 1957.
Hudson Review, winter, 1957-58.
Kenyon Review, November, 1966.
Life, August 30, 1968.
Los Angeles Times Book Review, August 26, 1984.
Nation, January 15, 1936, November 2, 1957, September 9, 1968.
National Review, November 1, 1968.
New Leader, October 3, 1983.
New Mexico Quarterly Review, winter, 1949, winter, 1951.
New Republic, January 20, 1957, September 16, 1957, June 9, 1958.
Newsweek, April 28, 1958, August 26, 1968.
New Yorker, October 9, 1948, August 24, 1957, February 8, 1958, November 2, 1968.
New York Evening Post, September 29, 1928.
New York Herald Tribune, January 8, 1933, October 10, 1948, August 25, 1957.
New York Times, April 27, 1924, November 15, 1925, July 22, 1942, August 25, 1957, August 9, 1959, August 20, 1968, July 30, 1978.
New York Times Book Review, June 23, 1940, August 25, 1957, August 9, 1959, August 2, 1964, August 25, 1968, July 3, 1983.
Observer Review, January 29, 1969.
Pacific Spectator, winter, 1951, summer, 1955.
Perspectives USA, winter, 1954.
Princeton University Library Chronicle, autumn, 1957.
Reporter, October 3, 1957, September 10, 1964.
Saturday Review, August 24, 1957, August 8, 1959.
Shenandoah, winter, 1959.
Spectator, December 26, 1958, May 21, 1965, February 21, 1969.
Spectrum, spring-summer, 1960.
Texas Studies in Literature and Language, spring, 1959.
Time, September 2, 1957, August 8, 1968.
Tomorrow, May, 1947.
Twentieth-Century Literature, July, 1960.
Virginia Quarterly Review, winter, 1969.
Vogue, November 15, 1957.
Washington Post Book World, July 25, 1982.
Western Humanities Review, autumn, 1965.

OBITUARIES:

PERIODICALS

Newsweek, August 28, 1978.
Publishers Weekly, September 4, 1978.
Time, August 28, 1978.
Washington Post, August 19, 1978.

*   *   *

CRAIG, A. A.
See ANDERSON, Poul (William)

*   *   *

CRANE, (Harold) Hart 1899-1932

PERSONAL: Born July 21, 1899, in Garrettsville, Ohio; committed suicide, April 27 (some sources say April 26), 1932, in the Gulf of Mexico; son of Clarance A. (a storeowner and manufacturer) and Grace Edna (Hart) Crane. *Education:* Attended public schools in Cleveland, Ohio.

ADDRESSES: Home—Chagrin Falls, Ohio.

CAREER: Writer. Worked as mechanic bench hand and shipyard laborer in Ohio in mid-1910s; newspaper reporter for Cleve-land *Plain Dealer* in Cleveland, Ohio, 1919; advertising manager for *Little Review* in New York City, 1919; shipping clerk for Rheinthal and Newman in New York City, 1919; advertising copywriter for various firms in Cleveland and New York City in 1920s; in sales in New York City in mid-1920s.

AWARDS, HONORS: Helen Waire Levinson Prize, 1930; Guggenheim fellow, 1931-32.

WRITINGS:

White Buildings (poetry), foreword by Allen Tate, Boni & Live-right, 1926, reprinted, Liveright, 1972.
The Bridge (poetry), Black Sun Press, 1930, Liveright, 1930, reprinted, 1970.
The Collected Poems of Hart Crane, edited by Waldo Frank, Liveright, 1933.
Voyages: Six Poems From White Buildings, illustrations by Leon-ard Baskin, Museum of Modern Art, 1957.
The Complete Poems and Selected Letters and Prose of Hart Crane, edited by Brom Weber, Doubleday/Anchor, 1966.
Twenty-one Letters From Hart Crane to George Bryan, edited by Joseph Katz, Hugh C. Atkinson, and Richard A. Ploch, Ohio State University Press, 1968.
Robber Rocks: Letters and Memories of Hart Crane, 1923-1932, edited by Susan Jenkins Brown, Wesleyan University Press, 1969.
Ten Unpublished Poems, Gotham Book Mart, 1972.
(With others) *The Letters of Hart Crane and His Family,* edited by Thomas S. W. Lewis, Columbia University Press, 1974.
(With Yvor Winters) *Hart Crane and Yvor Winters: Their Liter-ary Correspondence,* edited by Thomas Parkinson, University of California Press, 1978.
The Poems of Hart Crane, edited by Marc Simon, Liveright, 1986.

Work represented in numerous anthologies, including *The New Pocket Anthology of American Verse* and *The Norton Anthology of Modern Poetry.*

Contributor to periodicals, including *Bruno's Weekly, Modern School, Modernist, Pagan,* and *S4N.*

SIDELIGHTS: Hart Crane is a legendary figure among Ameri-can poets. In his personal life he showed little self-esteem, in-dulging in great and frequent bouts of alcohol abuse and homo-sexual promiscuity. In his art, however, he showed surprising optimism. Critics have contended that for Crane, misery and de-spair were redeemed through the apprehension of beauty, and in some of his greatest verses he articulated his own quest for re-demption. He also believed strongly in the peculiarly naive American Romanticism extending back through Walt Whitman to Ralph Waldo Emerson, and in his most ambitious work, *The Bridge,* Crane sought nothing less than an expression of the American experience in its entirety. His failure in this attempt, as many critics noted, was rather to be expected. His effort, how-ever, not only impressed many of those same critics but prompted a few of them to see Crane as a pivotal figure in Ameri-can literature, and he has since come to be regarded as both the quintessential Romantic artist and the embodiment of those ex-treme characteristics—hope and despair, redemption and dam-nation—that seemed to preoccupy many writers in his time. As Allen Tate wrote in *Essays of Four Decades,* "Crane was one of those men whom every age seems to select as the spokesman of its spiritual life; they give the age away."

Crane was born in Garrettsville, Ohio, in 1899 of bourgeois par-ents—his father was a businessman who produced chocolates, and his mother was an emotionally unstable woman known for her beauty. Crane's relationship with his mother was stifling in its intensity. His parents fought regularly, and his mother succeeded in engaging his sympathies against his father. In addition, his mother used him as an often inappropriate confidant in complaining about the sex act and her real and imagined health problems. During his mother's bouts of hypochondria, Crane often spent an inordinate amount of time in her company, comforting and consoling her. This unusual intimacy proved overwhelmingly distressful to Crane, but even in adulthood he often remained incapable of freeing himself from his mother's considerable control.

As a result of real and imagined problems, Crane's mother suffered a nervous collapse in 1908, and while she recuperated, he moved to his grandmother's home in Cleveland. There he spent most of his formative years and showed his first enthusiasm for poetry. His grandmother's library was extensive, featuring editions of complete works by poets such as Victorian Robert Browning and Americans Ralph Waldo Emerson and Walt Whitman, both of whom became major influences in Crane's poetry. During his mid-teens Crane continued to read extensively, broadening his interests to include such writers as philosopher Plato, novelist Honore de Balzac, and Romantic poet Percy Bysshe Shelley. Crane's formal education, however, was continually undermined by family problems necessitating prolonged absences from school. Finally, in 1916, he left Cleveland without graduating and moved to New York City to attend Columbia University, which he hoped to enter upon passing an entrance examination.

Once in New York City, however, Crane abandoned any pretence of acquiring a college education and began vigorously pursuing a literary career. Through a painter he knew earlier from Cleveland, Crane met other writers and gained exposure to various art movements and ideas. Reading the works of French Symbolists Charles Baudelaire and Arthur Rimbaud and contemporary Irishmen William Butler Yeats and James Joyce, writing, and socializing with other artists—and aspiring artists—left Crane little time or energy for work. Instead of seeking regular employment, he relied on his parents to provide financial support. Their continual squabbling, however, sometimes resulted in unfortunate delays of his funds, and so Crane occasionally sold advertising for the publication *Little Review,* which promoted the work of modernists such as Joyce and T. S. Eliot.

Crane also associated with a far different periodical, *Seven Arts,* which devoted itself to traditional American literature extending from Nathaniel Hawthorne and Walt Whitman to Sherwood Anderson and Robert Frost. Both *Seven Arts* and *Little Review* exerted considerable influence on the impressionable Crane, and in his own poetry he would seek to reconcile the two magazines' disparate philosophies. At this time—around 1917—Crane was already producing publishable verse. Some of these works appeared in the local journal *Pagan.* Relatively short, Crane's poems from this period reveal his interests in both tradition and experimentation, merging a rhyming structure with jarringly contemporary imagery. These early poems, though admired by some critics, were never held highly by Crane, and he never reprinted them in his lifetime.

Initially, Crane found New York City invigorating and even inspiring. Although he abused alcohol and consistently indulged his sexual proclivity for sailors, he still managed to work diligently on his poetry. But his parents divorced in 1917, and afterwards his mother arrived—with her mother—to stay in his one-bedroom apartment. Bedridden from emotional exhaustion, Crane's mother demanded his near constant attention. His problems mounted when his father, increasingly prosperous in the chocolate business, nonetheless threatened to withhold further funds until Crane found a job. To escape the pressures of family life, Crane attempted to enlist in the Army, only to be rejected as a minor. He then left New York City for Cleveland and found work in a munitions plant for the duration of World War I.

After the war, Crane stayed in Cleveland and found work as a reporter for the Cleveland *Plain Dealer.* He held that job only briefly, however, before returning to New York City to work once again for the *Little Review.* In mid-1919 his father used his influence in obtaining a position for his son as a shipping clerk. But Crane stayed at that job for only a few months before moving back to Ohio to work for his father's own company. Their relationship, though, was hardly congenial, for Crane's father professed little understanding of his son's lifestyle, and Crane, in turn, accorded little compassion for his father, despite the latter's trying marriage and divorce. Complicating matters further was the presence of Crane's mother, with whom Crane had begun living after she returned to Cleveland. Tensions finally exploded in the spring of 1921 when Crane's father criticized the son's maternal ties, whereupon Crane apparently announced that he would no longer associate with his father. As biographer John Unterecker noted in *Voyager: A Life of Hart Crane:* "[Crane's father] . . . turned white with rage, shouting that if Hart didn't apologize he would be disinherited. Hart climaxed the scene by screaming curses on his father and his father's money." The two men did not speak to each for the next two years.

Upon leaving his father's company, Crane stayed briefly in Cleveland working for advertising companies. He then found similar work in New York City, but moving there hardly solved his ongoing personal problems. His mother continued to ply his sympathies by mail, regaling him with accounts of her emotional and physical troubles. Crane sought solace in sex but inevitably found heartbreak, for his infatuations with other men, including many sailors, went largely unreciprocated. Curiously, his fluctuating emotional state—which ranged from manic euphoria to dire depression, both exacerbated by alcohol abuse—led him to distort his childhood memories into fond recollections, though he managed to resist his mother's constant pleas to return to her home in Cleveland.

By 1922 Crane had already written many of the poems that would comprise his first collection, *White Buildings.* Among the most important of these verses is "Chaplinesque," which he produced after viewing the great comic Charlie Chaplin's film "The Kid." In this poem Chaplin's chief character—a fun-loving, mischievous tramp—represents the poet, whose own pursuit may be perceived as trivial but is nonetheless profound. For Crane, the film character's optimism and sensitivity bears similarities to poets' own outlooks toward adversity, and the tramp's apparent disregard for his own persecution is indication of his innocence: "We will sidestep, and to the final smirk / Dally the doom of that inevitable thumb / That slowly chafes its puckered index toward us, / Facing the dull squint with what innocence / And what surprise!"

In "Lachrymae Christi," another major poem from this period, Crane expresses a more profound sympathy for the poet, whose suffering inevitably leads to redemption. Here, through mysterious imagery and symbolism, Crane portrays nature, specifically as it is renewed in springtime, as a reflection of the poet's own rejuvenation: "Lean long from sable, slender boughs, / Unstanched and luminous. And as the nights / Strike from Thee perfect spheres, / Lift up in lilac-emerald breath the grail / Of earth again— / Thy face / From charred and riven stakes, O / Dionysus, Thy / Unmangled smile." In his volume *Hart Crane,* Vincent Quinn noted that "the birthpangs of spring, and the anguish of the poet are presented as analogous instances of torment" and added, "From this gathering of pain, a chorus of triumph emerges."

Aside from "Chaplinesque" and "Lachrymae Christi," the most impressive poem Crane produced before 1924 was probably "For the Marriage of Faustus and Helen," a relatively expansive work reveling in the optimism that Crane believed prevalent throughout America at the time—the early 1920s. With this poem, he reinforces his own optimism by setting the marriage in contemporary times: Faustus rides a streetcar, and Helen appears at a jazz club. Here Faustus represents the poet seeking ideal beauty, and Helen embodies that beauty. In the poem's concluding section, Helen's beauty encompasses the triumph of the times too, and Crane calls for recognition of the age as one in which the poetic imagination surpasses the despair of recent events, notably World War I: "Distinctly praise the years, whose volatile / Blamed bleeding hands extend and thresh the height / The imagination spans beyond despair, / Outpacing bargain, vocable and prayer."

Unfortunately, the optimism expressed in such poems as "For the Marriage of Faustus and Helen" was hardly indicative of Crane's emotional state at the time. Soon after completing the aforementioned poem in the spring of 1923, Crane moved back to New York City and found work at another advertising agency. Not surprisingly, he once again found the job tedious and unrewarding. Adding to his displeasure was the unwelcome tumult and cacophony of city occurrences—automobile traffic, street vendors, and endless waves of marching pedestrians—that corrupted his concentration and stifled his imagination. By autumn Crane feared that his anxiety would soon lead to a nervous breakdown and so fled the city for nearby Woodstock. There he reveled in the relative tranquility of the rural environment and enjoyed the company of a few close friends.

Once revived, Crane traveled back to New York City. Soon afterwards he fell in love with a sailor, Emil Opffer, and their relationship—one of intense sexual passion and occasional turbulence—inspired "Voyages," a poetic sequence in praise of love. In *Hart Crane,* Quinn described this poem as "a celebration of the transforming power of love" and added that the work's "metaphor is the sea, and its movement is from the lover's dedication to a human and therefore changeable lover to a beloved beyond time and change." Here the sea represents love in all its shifting complexity from calm to storm, and love, in turn, serves as the salvation of us all: "Bind us in time, O Season clear, and awe. / O minstrel galleons of Carib fire, / Bequeath us to no earthly shore until / Is answered in the vortex of our grave / The seal's wide spindrift gaze toward paradise." With its dazzling poeticism and mysteriously inspiring perspective, this poem is often hailed as Crane's greatest achievement. R. W. B. Lewis, for instance, wrote in *The Poetry of Hart Crane* that the poem was Crane's "lyrical masterpiece."

By the time he finished "Voyages" in 1924, Crane had already commenced the first drafts of his ambitious poem *The Bridge,* which he intended, at least in part, as an uplifting alternative to T. S. Eliot's bleak masterwork, *The Waste Land.* With this long poem, which eventually comprised fifteen sections and sixty pages, Crane sought to provide a panorama of what he called "the American experience." Adopting the Brooklyn Bridge as the poem's sustaining symbol, Crane celebrates, in often hopelessly obscure imagery, various peoples and places—from explorer Christopher Columbus and the legendary Rip Van Win-

kle to the contemporary New England landscape and the East River tunnel. The bridge, in turn, serves as the structure uniting, and representing, all that is America. In addition, it functions as the embodiment of uniquely American optimism and serves as a source of inspiration and patriotic devotion: "O Sleepless as the river under thee, / Vaulting the sea, the prairies' dreaming sod, / Unto us lowliest sometime sweep, descend / And of the curveship lend a myth to God."

In 1926, while Crane worked on *The Bridge,* his verse collection *White Buildings* was published. This work earned him substantial respect as an imposing stylist, one whose lyricism and imagery recalled the French Romantics Baudelaire and Rimbaud. But it prompted speculation that Crane was an imprecise and confused artist, one who sometimes settled for sound instead of sense. Edmund Wilson, for instance, wrote in *New Republic* that "though [Crane] can sometimes move us, the emotion is oddly vague." For Wilson, whose essay was later reprinted in *The Shores of Light,* Crane possessed "a style that is strikingly original—almost something like a great style, if there could be such a thing as a great style which was . . . not . . . applied to any subject at all."

Crane, for his part, responded to similar charges from *Poetry* editor Harriet Monroe by claiming, in an appropriately confused manner, that his poetry is consistent with the *illogicality* of the genre. "It all comes to the recognition," he declared, "that emotional dynamics are not to be confused with any absolute order of rationalized definitions; ergo, in poetry the *rationale* of metaphor belongs to another order of experience than science, and is not to be limited by a scientific and arbitrary code or relationships either in verbal inflections or concepts."

By the time that *White Buildings* appeared in print, Crane's intense relationship with sailor Emil Opffer had already faded. Crane returned to his former ways, enjoying promiscuity, abusing alcohol, and alternating from obnoxious euphoria to disturbing depression. Constant conflict with his mother further aggravated his already unstable demeanor, as did the death of his grandmother in 1928. More positively, Crane realized a reconciliation with his father around that time, but the parent's death soon afterward only served to plunge the poet once more into depression.

With his inheritance, Crane fled his manipulative mother and traveled to Europe. There he associated with prominent figures in Paris's American expatriate community, notably publisher and poet Harry Crosby, who murdered his mistress and killed himself the following year. Crane wrote little in Europe, indulging instead in alcohol and carousing. When he returned to the United States he wallowed further in excessive drinking and sexual relations. Furthermore, his self-confidence was shaken by the disappointing reception accorded *The Bridge* by critics, many of whom expressed respect for his effort but dissatisfaction with his achievement. But even critics that deemed Crane's work a failure readily expressed respect for his creative undertaking. William Rose Benet, for instance, declared in the *Saturday Review of Literature* that Crane had "failed in creating what might have been a truly great poem." But Benet nonetheless deemed *The Bridge* "fascinating" and declared that it "reveals potencies in the author that may make his next work even more remarkable."

Crane, however, had entered a creative slump from which he would not recover. Perhaps sensing a decline in his literary skills, he applied for a Guggenheim fellowship with intentions of studying European culture and the American poetic sensibility. After obtaining the fellowship, though, Crane traveled to Mexico and continued his self-destructive behavior. At this time he also experienced a heterosexual romance—presumably his only one—with Peggy Baird, who was then married to prominent literary figure Malcolm Cowley. During this time Crane wrote only infrequently, producing largely inferior work that only confirmed his own fear that his talent had declined significantly. Finally, in 1932, his despair turned all-consuming, and on April 27, while traveling by ship with Baird, Crane killed himself by leaping into the Gulf of Mexico.

In the years since his death, Crane has earned recognition as an ambitious and accomplished—if not entirely successful—poet, one whose goals vastly exceeded his capabilities (and, probably, anyone else's) but whose talent nonetheless enabled him to explore the limits of self-expression both provocatively and profoundly. Allen Tate, writing in his *Essays of Four Decades,* assessed Crane's artistic achievement as an admirable, but unavoidable, failure. Tate noted that Crane, like the earlier Romantics, attempted the overwhelming imposition of his own will in his poetry, and in so doing reached the point at which his will, and thus his art, became self-reflexive, and thus self-destructive. "By attempting an extreme solution to the romantic problem," Tate contended, "Crane proved that it cannot be solved."

Other critics have tended to share Tate's general assessment of Crane as a flawed but nonetheless invaluable poet. R. P. Blackmur, in his essay collection *The Double Agent,* acknowledged Crane's shortcomings and accepted that in reading Crane "we must make allowances for him." But Blackmur also wrote: "Merely because Crane is imperfect in his kind is no reason to give him up; there is no plethora of perfection, and the imperfect beauty, like life, retains its fascination. And there is about him, too—such were his gifts for the hearts of words, such the vitality of his intelligence—the distraught but exciting splendour of a great failure." Likewise laudatory was poet Brother Antonius, who wrote in *Commonweal* that Crane, despite his failings, achieved much as an artist. "Crane . . . was woefully deficient in the stabilizing apprehension of the concrete," Antonius conceded. But he added that through this deficiency Crane "purchased a kind of heroic redemption, in that he was enabled to register most vividly reality as he did apprehend it . . ., and hence make of his death that sacrifice by which an age enables those whom it destroys to accomplish what we others need to know."

BIOGRAPHICAL/CRITICAL SOURCES:

BOOKS

Blackmur, R. P., *The Double Agent: Essays in Craft and Elucidation,* Arrow Editions, 1935.

Butterfield, R. W., *The Broken Arch: A Study of Hart Crane,* Oliver & Boyd, 1969.

Clark, David R., editor, *The Merrill Studies in "The Bridge,"* Merrill, 1970.

Clark, David R., editor, *Critical Essays on Hart Crane,* G. K. Hall, 1982.

Combs, Robert, *Vision of the Voyage: Hart Crane and the Psychology of Romanticism,* Memphis State University Press, 1978.

Cowley, Malcolm, *Exile's Return: A Literary Odyssey of the 1920's,* Viking, 1951.

Crane, Hart, *The Collected Poems of Hart Crane,* edited by Waldo Frank, Liveright, 1933.

Dembo, L. S., *Hart Crane's Sanskrit Charge: A Study of The Bridge,* Cornell University Press, 1960.

Dictionary of Literary Biography, Gale, Volume 4: *American Writers in Paris, 1920-1939,* 1980, Volume 48: *American Poets, 1880-1945, Second Series,* 1986.

Frank, Waldo, *In the American Jungle: 1925-1936,* Farrar & Rinehart, 1937.

Hanley, Alfred, *Hart Crane's Holy Vision: "White Buildings,"* Duquesne University Press, 1981.

Hazo, Samuel, *Hart Crane: An Introduction and Interpretation,* Barnes & Noble, 1963.

Horton, Philip, *Hart Crane: The Life of an American Poet,* Norton, 1937.

Leibowitz, Herbert A., *Hart Crane: An Introduction to the Poetry,* Columbia University Press, 1968.

Lewis, R. W. B., *The Poetry of Hart Crane: A Critical Study,* Princeton University Press, 1967.

Munson, Gorham B., *Destinations: A Canvass of American Literature Since 1900,* J. H. Sears, 1928.

Nilsen, Helge Normann, *Hart Crane's Divided Vision: An Analysis of The Bridge,* Universitetssforlaget (Oslo, Norway), 1980.

Paul, Sherman, *Hart's "Bridge,"* University of Illinois Press, 1972.

Perry, Robert L., *The Shared Vision of Waldo Frank and Hart Crane,* University of Nebraska Press, 1966.

Quinn, Vincent G., *Hart Crane,* Twayne, 1963.

Schwartz, Joseph, *Hart Crane: A Reference Guide,* G. K. Hall, 1983.

Spears, Monroe K., *Hart Crane,* University of Minneapolis Press, 1965.

Sugg, Richard P., *Hart Crane's "The Bridge": A Description of Its Life,* University of Alabama Press, 1976.

Tate, Allen, *Essays of Four Decades,* Swallow Press, 1968.

Trachtenbert, Alan, editor, *Hart Crane: A Collection of Critical Essays,* Prentice-Hall, 1982.

Twentieth-Century Literary Criticism, Gale, Volume 2, 1979, Volume 5, 1981.

Unterecker, John, *Voyager: A Life of Hart Crane,* Farrar, Strauss, 1969.

Uroff, M. D., *Hart Crane: The Patterns of His Poetry,* University of Illinois Press, 1974.

Weber, Brom, *Hart Crane: A Biographical and Critical Study,* Bodley Press, 1948.

Wilson, Edmund, *The Shores of Light: A Literary Chronicle of the Twenties and Thirties,* Farrar, Straus, 1952.

PERIODICALS

American Literature, March, 1967, March, 1968.

Arizona Quarterly, spring, 1964.

Commonweal, October 26, 1962.

Critical Inquiry, autumn, 1975.

New Republic, March 16, 1927, May 11, 1927, August 31, 1953.

Papers on Language and Literature, summer, 1980.

PMLA, March, 1951, January, 1981.

Poetry, October, 1926.

Prairie Schooner, summer, 1974.

Saturday Review of Literature, July 5, 1930.

Sewanee Review, January-March, 1950, July-September, 1965.

Southern Review, July, 1975.

Twentieth Century Literature, October, 1967.

University of Kansas Review, winter, 1949.

Wisconsin Studies in Contemporary Literature, spring-summer, 1962.

CREASEY, John 1908-1973

(Gordon Ashe, M. E. Cooke, Margaret Cooke, Henry St. John Cooper, Credo, Norman Deane, Elise Fecamps, Robert Caine Frazer, Patrick Gill, Michael Halliday, Brian Hope, Colin Hughes, Kyle Hunt, Abel Mann, Peter Manton, J. J. Marric, James Marsden, Richard Martin, Rodney Mattheson, Anthony Morton, Ken Ranger, William K. Reilly, Tex Riley, Jeremy York; Charles Hogarth, a joint pseudonym)

PERSONAL: Born September 17, 1908, in Southfields, Surrey, England; died June 9, 1973, of congestive heart failure, in Bodenham, Salisbury, England; buried in Bodenham churchyard; son of Joseph (a cabinet maker and coach builder) and Ruth (Creasey) Creasey; married Margaret Elizabeth Cooke, 1935 (divorced, 1939); married (Evelyn) Jean Fudge, February 16, 1941 (divorced, 1970); married Jeanne Williams (a writer), October, 1970 (divorced, 1973); married Diana Hamilton Farrell, May, 1973; children: (first marriage) Colin John; (second marriage) Martin John, Richard John. *Education:* Attended London elementary and secondary schools. *Politics:* Liberal.

CAREER: Writer. Held various clerical jobs, London, England, 1926-35. Publisher, Jay Books, 1957-59; director of Robert Sommerville Ltd. (literary agency) and of Salisbury Arts Theatre. Member of governing body of Liberal Party, 1945-50; Liberal Party candidate for Parliament, 1950; founder of All Party Alliance Movement, 1967; All Party Alliance Movement candidate for Parliament, 1967-68. Chairman of fund-raising committees for famine relief and refugee organizations, including National Savings Movement, United Europe, and Oxford Committee for Famine Relief.

MEMBER: Crime Writers Association (co-founder; chairman, 1953-57), Mystery Writers of America (chairman, 1966-67), Western Writers of America, Authors' League, Society of Authors (London), P.E.N., National Liberal Club, Paternosters (chairman, 1967), Rotary International, Westerners Club (Tucson, Arizona), Royal Automobile Club (London).

AWARDS, HONORS: Member, Order of the British Empire (M.B.E.), 1946; Mystery Writers of America, Edgar Allan Poe Award, 1962, for *Gideon's Fire,* and Grand Master Award, 1969, for outstanding contributions to the mystery novel genre.

WRITINGS:

Seven Times Seven (mystery novel), Melrose, 1932, reprinted, Arrow Books, 1970.
Men, Maids, and Murder (mystery novel), Melrose, 1933, reprinted, Arrow Books, 1972.
Four of the Best (collection), Hodder & Stoughton, 1955.
(Editor and contributor) *Mystery Bedside Book,* six volumes, Hodder & Stoughton, 1960-65.
The Mountain of the Blind (mystery novel), Hodder & Stoughton, 1960.
The Foothills of Fear (mystery novel), Hodder & Stoughton, 1961.
(Editor) *Crimes across the Sea* (anthology), Harper, 1964.
The Masters of Bow Street (mystery novel), Hodder & Stoughton, 1972, Simon & Schuster, 1974.

JUVENILE FICTION

The Men Who Died Laughing, Thompson, 1935.
The Killer Squad, George Newnes, 1936.
Blazing the Air Trail, Low, 1936.

The Jungle Flight Mystery, Low, 1936.
The Mystery Plane, Low, 1936.
Murder by Magic, Amalgamated Press, 1937.
The Mysterious Mr. Rocco, Mellifont Press, 1937.
The S.O.S. Flight, Low, 1937.
The Secret Aeroplane Mystery, Low, 1937.
The Treasure Flight, Low, 1937.
The Air Marauders, Low, 1937.
The Black Biplane, Low, 1937.
The Mystery Flight, Low, 1937.
The Double Motive, Mellifont Press, 1938.
The Doublecross of Death, Mellifont, 1938.
The Missing Hoard, Mellifont Press, 1938.
Mystery of Manby House, Northern News Syndicate, 1938.
The Fighting Flyers, Low, 1938.
The Flying Stowaways, Low, 1938.
The Miracle 'Plane, Low, 1938.
Dixon Hawke: Secret Agent, Thompson, 1939.
Documents of Death, Mellifont Press, 1939.
The Hidden Hoard, Mellifont Press, 1939.
The Blue Flyer, Mellifont Press, 1939.
The Jumper, Northern News Syndicate, 1939.
The Mystery of Blackmoor Prison, Mellifont Press, 1939.
The Sacred Eye, Thompson, 1939.
Mottled Death, Thompson, 1939.
Peril by Air, George Newnes, 1939.
The Flying Turk, Low, 1939.
The Ship of Death, Thompson, 1939.
The Monarch of the Skies, Low, 1939.
Dazzle—Air Ace No. One, George Newnes, 1940.
Five Missing Men, George Newnes, 1940.
The Poison Gas Robberies, Mellifont Press, 1940.
The Cinema Crimes, T. A. & E. Pemberton, 1945.
The Missing Monoplane, Low, 1947.

NONFICTION

(Ghost writer) *Jimmy Wilde: Fighting Was My Business,* M. Joseph, 1938.
(Compiler and editor) *Action Stations!: An Account of the H.M.S. Dorsetshire and Her Earlier Namesakes,* John Long, 1942.
(With Walter Hutchinson) *The Printer's Devil: The History of a Printer's Charity,* Hutchinson, 1943.
Heroes of the Air: A Tribute to the Courage, Sacrifice and Skill of the Men of the R.A.F., Dorset "Wings for Victory" Campaign Committee, 1943.
(With John Lock) *Log of a Merchant Airman,* Stanley Paul, 1943.
(Under pseudonym Credo) *Man in Danger,* Hutchinson, 1948.
(With Jean Creasey) *Round the World in 465 Days,* R. Hale, 1953.
Round the Table: The First Twenty-Five Years of the English Goodwill Association, National Association of Round Tables of Great Britain and Ireland, 1953.
(With Jean Creasey and sons, Martin and Richard Creasey) *Let's Look at America,* R. Hale, 1956.
They Didn't Mean to Kill: The Real Story of Road Accidents, Their Cause, Costs and Cure, Hodder & Stoughton, 1960.
(With Jean, M., and R. Creasey) *Optimists in Africa,* Howard Timmins (Capetown), 1963.
African Holiday, illustrations and captions by M. Creasey, Howard Timmins, 1963.
Good, God and Man: An Outline of the Philosophy of Self-ism, illustrations by M. Creasey, Hodder & Stoughton, 1968, Walker & Co., 1971.

Evolution to Democracy, Hodder & Stoughton, 1969, revised edition, White Lion, 1972.

"DEPARTMENT Z" MYSTERIES

The Death Miser, Melrose, 1933.

Redhead, Hurst & Blackett, 1933, revised edition, Arrow Books, 1971.

First Came a Murder, Melrose, 1934, revised edition, John Long, 1969, McKay, 1972.

Death round the Corner, Melrose, 1935, revised edition, Popular Library, 1970.

The Mark of the Crescent, Melrose, 1935, revised edition, John Long, 1970, Popular Library, 1972.

Thunder in Europe, Melrose, 1936, reprinted, Arrow Books, 1968, revised edition, John Long, 1970, Popular Library, 1972.

The Terror Trap, Melrose, 1936, revised edition, Arrow Books, 1969, Popular Library, 1972.

Carriers of Death, Melrose, 1937, revised edition, Popular Library, 1968.

Days of Danger, Melrose, 1937, reprinted, Arrow Books, 1968, revised edition, John Long, 1970, Popular Library, 1972.

Death Stands By, John Long, 1938, revised edition, Arrow Books, 1966, Popular Library, 1972.

Menace!, John Long, 1938, revised edition, Popular Library, 1971.

Murder Must Wait, Melrose, 1939, revised edition, John Long, 1969, Popular Library, 1972.

Panic!, John Long, 1939, reprinted, Arrow Books, 1969, Popular Library, 1972.

Death by Night, John Long, 1940, revised edition, Arrow Books, 1970, Popular Library, 1972.

The Island of Peril, John Long, 1940, reprinted, Arrow Books, 1968, revised edition, John Long, 1970, Popular Library, 1976.

Sabotage, John Long, 1941, revised edition, Arrow Books, 1971, Popular Library, 1976.

Go away Death, John Long, 1941, revised edition, 1969, Popular Library, 1976.

The Day of Disaster, John Long, 1942, reprinted, Arrow Books, 1968, revised edition, John Long, 1969.

Prepare for Action, Stanley Paul, 1942, revised edition, Arrow Books, 1966, Popular Library, 1975.

No Darker Crime, Stanley Paul, 1943, reprinted, Arrow Books, 1969, Popular Library, 1976.

Dark Peril, Stanley Paul, 1944, revised edition, John Long, 1969, Popular Library, 1975.

The Peril Ahead, Stanley Paul, 1946, revised edition, John Long, 1969, Popular Library, 1974.

The League of Dark Men, Stanley Paul, 1947, revised edition, John Long, 1968, Popular Library, 1975.

The Department of Death, Evans Brothers, 1949, Popular Library, 1979.

The Enemy Within, Evans Brothers, 1950, Popular Library, 1977.

Dead or Alive, Evans Brothers, 1951, reprinted, Arrow Books, 1969, Popular Library, 1974.

A Kind of a Prisoner, Hodder & Stoughton, 1956, reprinted, Arrow Books, 1972, Popular Library, 1975.

The Black Spiders, Hodder & Stoughton, 1957, reprinted, Arrow Books, 1972, Popular Library, 1975.

"SEXTON BLAKE" MYSTERIES

The Case of the Murdered Financier, Amalgamated Press, 1937.

The Great Air Swindle, Amalgamated Press, 1939.

The Man From Fleet Street, Amalgamated Press, 1940.

The Case of the Mad Inventor, Amalgamated Press, 1942.

Private Carter's Crime, Amalgamated Press, 1943.

"THE TOFF" MYSTERIES

Introducing the Toff, John Long, 1938, revised edition, 1954.

The Toff Goes On, John Long, 1939, revised edition, 1955.

. . . Steps Out, John Long, 1939, revised edition, 1955.

Here Comes. . . , John Long, 1940, Walker & Co., 1967, revised edition, Sphere Books, 1969.

. . . Breaks In, John Long, 1940, revised edition, 1955.

Salute the Toff, John Long, 1941, Walker & Co., 1971.

. . . Proceeds, John Long, 1941, Walker & Co., 1968.

. . . Goes to Market, John Long, 1942, Walker & Co 1967.

. . . Is Back, John Long, 1942, revised edition, Corgi Books, 1971, Walker & Co., 1974.

. . . Among Millions, John Long, 1943, revised edition, Panther Books, 1964, Walker & Co., 1976.

Accuse . . . , John Long, 1943, revised edition, Corgi Books, 1972, Walker & Co., 1975.

. . . and the Curate, John Long, 1944, Walker & Co., 1969 (published in England as *. . . and the Deadly Parson,* Lancer Books, 1970).

. . . and the Great Illusion, John Long, 1944, Walker & Co. 1967.

Feathers for . . . , John Long, 1945, revised edition, Hodder & Stoughton, 1964, Walker & Co., 1970.

. . . and the Lady, John Long, 1946, reprinted, Sphere Books, 1970, Walker & Co., 1975.

. . . on Ice, John Long, 1946, revised edition, Corgi Books, 1976, published as *Poison for . . . ,* Pyramid Publications, 1976.

Hammer . . . , John Long, 1947, reprinted, Corgi Books, 1975.

. . . in Town, John Long, 1948, reprinted, Sphere Books, 1969, revised edition, Walker & Co., 1977.

. . . Takes Shares, John Long, 1948, revised edition, Corgi Books, 1971, Walker & Co., 1972.

. . . and Old Harry, John Long, 1949, revised edition, Hodder & Stoughton, 1964, Walker & Co., 1970.

. . . on Board, Evans Brothers, 1949, revised edition, Corgi Books, 1971, Walker & Co., 1973.

Fool . . . , Evans Brothers, 1950, Walker & Co., 1966.

Kill . . . , Evans Brothers, 1950, Walker & Co., 1966, revised edition, Corgi Books, 1972.

A Knife for . . . , Evans Brothers, 1951, Pyramid Publica-tions, 1964, revised edition, Corgi Books, 1971.

. . . Goes Gay, Evans Brothers, 1951, published as *A Mask for . . . ,* Walker & Co., 1966.

Hunt . . . , Evans Brothers, 1952, Walker & Co., 1969, revised edition, Corgi Books, 1972.

Call . . . , Hodder & Stoughton, 1953, Walker & Co., 1969.

. . . Down Under, Hodder & Stoughton, 1953, Walker & Co., 1969 (published in England as *Break . . . ,* Lancer Books, 1970).

Murder out of the Past, and Under-Cover Man (short stories), Barrington Gray, 1953.

. . . at Butlin's, Hodder & Stoughton, 1954, reprinted, Corgi Books, 1974, Walker & Co., 1976.

. . . on the Trail, Everybody's Books, c. 1954.

. . . at the Fair, Hodder & Stoughton, 1954, Walker & Co., 1968.

A Six for . . . , Hodder & Stoughton, 1955, Walker & Co., 1969 (published in England as *A Score for . . . ,* Lancer Books, 1972).

. . . and the Deep Blue Sea, Hodder & Stoughton, 1955, Walker & Co., 1967.

Make-Up for . . . , Hodder & Stoughton, 1956, Walker & Co., 1967 (published in England as *Kiss . . . ,* Lancer Books, 1971).

. . . in New York, Hodder & Stoughton, 1956, Pyramid Publications, 1964.

Model for . . . , Hodder & Stoughton, 1957, Pyramid Publications, 1965.

. . . on Fire, Hodder & Stoughton, 1957, Walker & Co., 1966.

. . . and the Stolen Tresses, Hodder & Stoughton, 1958, Walker & Co., 1965.

. . . on the Farm, Hodder & Stoughton, 1958, Walker & Co., 1964, published as *Terror for . . . ,* Pyramid Publications, 1965.

Double for . . . , Hodder & Stoughton, 1959, Walker & Co., 1965.

. . . and the Runaway Bride, Hodder & Stoughton, 1959, Walker & Co., 1964, reprinted, Severn House, 1980.

A Rocket for . . . , Hodder & Stoughton, 1960, Pyramid Publications, 1964, reprinted, Severn House, 1980.

. . . and the Kidnapped Child, Hodder & Stoughton, 1960, Walker & Co., 1965.

Follow . . . , Hodder,& Stoughton, 1961, Walker & Co., 1967.

. . . and the Teds, Hodder & Stoughton, 1961, published as *. . . and the Toughs,* Walker & Co., 1968.

A Doll for . . . . Hodder & Stoughton, 1963, Walker & Co., 1965.

Leave It to . . . , Hodder & Stoughton, 1963, Pyramid Publication 1965.

. . . and the Spider, Hodder & Stoughton, 1965, Walker & Co., 1966.

. . . in Wax, Walker & Co., 1966.

A Bundle for . . . , Hodder & Stoughton, 1967, Walker & Co., 1968.

Stars for . . . , Walker & Co., 1968.

. . . and the Golden Boy, Walker & Co., 1969.

. . . and the Fallen Angels, Walker & Co., 1970.

Vote for . . . , Walker & Co., 1971.

. . . and the Trip-Trip-Triplets, Walker & Co., 1972.

. . . and the Terrified Taximan, Walker & Co., 1973.

. . . and the Sleepy Cowboy, Hodder & Stoughton, 1977.

"ROGER WEST" MYSTERIES

Inspector West Takes Charge, Stanley Paul, 1942, revised edition, Pan Books, 1963, Scribner, 1972.

. . . Leaves Town, Stanley Paul, 1943, published as *Go Away Murder,* Lancer Books, 1972.

. . . at Home, Stanley Paul, 1944, reprinted, Coronet Books, 1972, Scribner, 1973.

. . . Regrets, Stanley Paul, 1945, revised edition, Hodder & Stoughton, 1965.

Holiday for Inspector West, Stanley Paul, 1946, reprinted, Coronet Books, 1974.

Battle for . . . , Stanley Paul, 1948.

Triumph for . . . , Stanley Paul, 1948, published as *The Case against Paul Raeburn,* Harper, 1958.

. . Kicks Off, Stanley Paul, 1949, reprinted, Coronet Books, 1971, published as *Sport for . . . ,* Lancer Books, 1971.

. . . Alone, Evans Brothers, 1950, reprinted, Lythway Press, 1972, Scribner, 1975.

. . . Cries Wolf, Evans Brothers, 1950, reprinted, Lythway Press, 1973, published as *The Creepers,* Harper, 1952.

A Case for Evans Brothers, 1951, reprinted, Lythway Press, 1973, published as *Figure in the Dusk,* Harper, 1952.

Puzzle for . . . , Evans Brothers, 1951, reprinted, Lythway Press, 1972, published as *The Dissemblers,* Scribner, 1967.

. . . at Bay, Evans Brothers, 1952, published as *The Blind Spot,* Harper, 1954, published as *The Case of the Acid Throwers,* Avon, 1960.

A Gun for . . . , Hodder & Stoughton, 1953, reprinted, Ulverscroft Large Print Books, 1972, published as *Give a Man a Gun,* Harper, 1954.

Send . . . , Hodder & Stoughton, 1953, revised edition, Coronet Books, 1972, Scribner, 1976, published as *Send Superintendent West,* Pan Books, 1965.

A Beauty for . . . , Hodder & Stoughton, 1954, reprinted, 1972, published as *The Beauty Queen Killer,* Harper, 1956, published as *So Young, So Cold, So Fair,* Dell, 1958.

. . . Makes Haste, Hodder & Stoughton, 1955, published as *The Gelignite Gang,* Harper, 1956, published as *Night of the Watchman,* Berkley Publishing.

Two for . . . , Hodder & Stoughton, 1955, reprinted, Pan Books, 1969, published as *Murder: One, Two, Three,* Scribner, 1960, published as *Murder Tips the Scales,* Berkley Publishing, 1962.

Parcels for . . . , Hodder & Stoughton, 1956, reprinted, 1971, published as *Death of a Postman,* Harper, 1957.

A Prince for . . . , Hodder & Stoughton, 1956, published as *Death of an Assassin,* Scribner, 1960.

Accident for . . . , Hodder & Stoughton, 1957, reprinted, 1972, published as *Hit and Run,* Scribner, 1959.

Find . . . , Hodder & Stoughton, 1957, reprinted, Lythway Press, 1977, published as *The Trouble at Saxby's,* Harper, 1959, published as *Doorway to Death,* Berkley Publishing, 1961.

Murder, London—New York, Hodder & Stoughton, 1958, Scribner, 1961, reprinted, Hutchinson, 1976.

Strike for Death, Hodder & Stoughton, 1958, published as *The Killing Strike,* Scribner, 1961.

Death of a Racehorse, Hodder & Stoughton, 1959, Scribner, 1962.

The Case of the Innocent Victims, Hodder & Stoughton, 1959, Scribner, 1966.

Murder on the Line, Hodder & Stoughton, 1960, Scribner, 1963.

Death in Cold Print, Hodder & Stoughton, 1961, Scribner, 1962.

The Scene of the Crime, Hodder & Stoughton, 1961, Scribner, 1963.

Policeman's Dread, Hodder & Stoughton, 1962, Scribner, 1964.

Hang the Little Man, Scribner, 1963.

Look Three Ways at Murder, Hodder & Stoughton, 1964, Scribner, 1965. *Murder, London—Australia,* Scribner, 1965.

Murder, London—South Africa, Scribner, 1966.

The Executioners, Scribner, 1967.

So Young to Burn, Scribner, 1968.

Murder, London—Miami, Scribner. 1969.

A Part for a Policeman, Scribner, 1970.

Alibi, Scribner, 1971 (published in England as *Alibi for . . . ,* Coronet Books, 1973).

A Splinter of Glass, Scribner, 1972.

The Theft of Magna Carta, Scribner, 1973.

The Extortioners, Hodder & Stoughton, 1974, Scribner, 1975.

A Sharp Rise in Crime, Scribner, 1978.

"DR. PALFREY" MYSTERIES

Traitors' Doom, John Long, 1942, reprinted, 1968, Walker & Co., 1970.

The Valley of Fear, John Long, 1943, published as *The Perilous Country,* 1949, revised edition, Arrow Books, 1966, Walker & Co., 1973.

The Legion of the Lost, John Long, 1943, Steven Daye, 1944, revised edition, John Long, 1968, Walker & Co., 1974.

Dangerous Quest, John Long, 1944, revised edition, Arrow Books, 1965, Walker & Co., 1974.

Death in the Rising Sun, John Long, 1945, revised edition, 1970, Walker & Co., 1976.

The Hounds of Vengeance, John Long, 1945, revised edition, 1969.

Shadow of Doom, John Long, 1946, revised edition, 1970.

The House of Bears, John Long, 1946, revised edition, 1962, Walker & Co., 1975.

Dark Harvest, John Long, 1947, revised edition, Arrow Books, 1962, Walker & Co., 1977.

The Wings of Peace, John Long, 1948, revised edition, 1969, Walker & Co., 1978.

Sons of Satan, John Long, 1948, revised edition, 1972.

The Dawn of Darkness, John Long, 1949.

The League of Light, Evans Brothers, 1949, revised edition, 1969.

The Man Who Shook the World, Evans Brothers, 1950, revised edition, John Long, 1972.

The Prophet of Fire, Evans Brothers, 1951, Walker & Co., 1978.

The Children of Hate, Evans Brothers, 1952, published as *The Children of Despair,* Jay Books, 1958, revised edition, John Long, 1970, published as *The Killers of Innocence,* Walker & Co., 1971.

The Touch of Death, Hodder & Stoughton, 1954, Walker & Co., 1968.

The Mists of Fear, Hodder & Stoughton, 1955, reprinted, Hodder Paperbacks, 1970, Walker & Co., 1977.

The Flood, Hodder & Stoughton, 1956, Walker & Co., 1969.

The Plague of Silence, Hodder & Stoughton, 1958, Walker & Co., 1968.

The Drought, Hodder & Stoughton, 1959, Walker & Co., 1967 (published in England as *Dry Spell,* New English Library, 1967).

The Terror: The Return of Dr. Palfrey, Hodder & Stoughton, 1963, Walker & Co., 1966.

The Depths, Hodder & Stoughton, 1963, Walker & Co., 1966.

The Sleep, Hodder & Stoughton, 1964, Walker & Co., 1968.

The Inferno, Hodder & Stoughton, 1965, Walker & Co., 1968.

The Famine, Hodder & Stoughton, 1967, Walker & Co., 1968.

The Blight, Walker & Co., 1968.

The Oasis, Hodder & Stoughton, 1969, Walker & Co., 1970.

The Smog, Hodder & Stoughton, 1970, Walker & Co., 1971.

The Unbegotten, Hodder & Stoughton, 1971, Walker & Co., 1972.

The Insulators, Hodder & Stoughton, 1972, Walker & Co., 1973.

The Voiceless Ones, Hodder & Stoughton, 1973, Walker & Co., 1974.

The Thunder-Maker, Walker & Co., 1976.

The Whirlwind, Hodder & Stoughton, 1979.

PLAYS

Gideon's Fear (adaptation of his novel *Gideon's Week* [see below under pseudonym J. J. Marric]; first produced in Salisbury, England, 1960), Evans Brothers, 1967.

"Strike for Death," first produced in Salisbury, 1960.

The Toff: A Comedy Thriller in Three Acts, Evans Brothers, 1963.

"Hear Nothing, Say All," first produced in Salisbury, 1964.

MYSTERIES UNDER PSEUDONYM GORDON ASHE

Who Was the Jester?, George Newnes, 1940, published as *The Masked Gunman: The Man Who Stayed Alive,* John Long, 1955, reprinted, Corgi Books, 1975.

No Need to Die, John Long, 1956, reprinted, Corgi Books, 1975.

"PATRICK DAWLISH" MYSTERIES UNDER ASHE PSEUDONYM

The Speaker, John Long, 1939, reprinted, Transworld (London), 1966, published as *The Croaker,* Holt, 1972.

Death on Demand, John Long, 1939, reprinted, Transworld (London), 1967.

Terror by Day, John Long, 1940.

The Secret Murder, John Long 1940, revised edition, Corgi Books, 1972.

'Ware Danger!, John Long, 1941, reprinted Corgi Books, 1972.

Murder Most Foul, John Long, 1942, revised edition, Corgi Books, 1973.

There Goes Death, John Long, 1942, revised edition, Corgi Books, 1973.

Death in High Places, John Long, 1942, revised edition, Corgi Books, 1973.

Death in Flames, John Long, 1943, revised edition, Corgi Books, 1973.

Two Men Missing, John Long, 1943, revised edition, Corgi Books, 1971.

Rogues Rampant, John Long, 1944, revised edition, Corgi Books, 1973.

Death on the Move, John Long, 1945, reprinted, Corgi Books, 1969.

Invitation to Adventure, John Long, 1945, reprinted, Corgi Books, 1969.

Here Is Danger, John Long, 1946, reprinted, Corgi Books, 1970.

Give Me Murder, John Long, 1947, reprinted, Corgi Books, 1966.

Murder Too Late, John Long, 1947, reprinted, Corgi Books, 1968.

Engagement with Death, John Long, 1948, reprinted, Corgi Books, 1970.

Dark Mystery, John Long, 1948, reprinted, Corgi Books, 1971.

A Puzzle in Pearls, John Long, 1949, revised edition, Corgi Books, 1971.

Kill or Be Killed, Evans Brothers, 1950, reprinted, Lythway Press, 1973.

The Dark Circle, Evans Brothers, 1950, reprinted, Corgi Books, 1969.

Murder with Mushrooms, Evans Brothers, 1950, revised edition, Corgi Books, 1971, Holt, 1974.

Death in Diamonds, Evans Brothers, 1951, reprinted, Corgi Books, 1968.

Missing or Dead, Evans Brothers, 1951.

Death in a Hurry, Evans Brothers, 1952.

The Long Search, John Long, 1953, reprinted, Corgi Books, 1974, published as *Drop Dead,* Ace Books, 1954.

Sleepy Death, John Long, 1953.

Double for Death, John Long, 1954, Holt, 1969.

Death in the Trees, John Long, 1954, reprinted, Corgi Books, 1975, published as *You've Bet Your Life,* Ace Books, 1957.

The Kidnapped Child, John Long, 1955, Holt, 1971, published as *The Snatch,* Corgi Books, 1965.

Day of Fear, John Long, 1956, Holt, 1978.

Wait for Death, John Long, 1957, Holt, 1972.

Come Home to Death, John Long, 1958, published as *The Pack of Lies,* Doubleday, 1959.

Elope to Death, John Long, 1959, Holt, 1977.

The Man Who Laughed at Murder, Doubleday, 1960 (published in England as *Don't Let Him Kill,* 1960, reprinted, Corgi Books, 1975).

"CRIME HATERS" MYSTERIES (CONTINUATION OF "DAWLISH" MYSTERIES) UNDER ASHE PSEUDONYM

The Crime Haters, Doubleday, 1960.
Rogue's Ransom, Doubleday, 1961.
Death from Below, John Long, 1963, Holt, 1968.
The Big Call, John Long, 1964, Holt, 1975.
A Promise of Diamonds, Dodd, 1964.
A Taste of Treasure, Holt, 1966.
A Clutch of Coppers, John Long, 1967, Holt, 1969.
A Shadow of Death, John Long, 1968, Holt, 1976.
A Scream of Murder, John Long, 1969, Holt, 1970.
A Nest of Traitors, John Long, 1970, Holt, 1971.
A Rabble of Rebels, Holt, 1972.
A Life for a Death, Holt, 1973.
A Herald of Doom, John Long, 1974, Holt, 1975.
A Blast of Trumpets, Holt, 1975.
A Plague of Demons, John Long, 1976, Holt, 1977.

MYSTERIES UNDER PSEUDONYM M. E. COOKE; PUBLISHED BY MELLIFONT PRESS, EXCEPT AS NOTED

Fire of Death, Fiction House, 1934.
The Black Heart, Gramor Publications, 1935.
The Casino Mystery, 1935.
The Crime Gang, 1935.
The Death Drive, 1935.
Number One's Last Crime, Fiction House, 1935.
The Stolen Formula Mystery, 1935.
The Big Radium Mystery, 1936.
The Day of Terror, 1936.
The Dummy Robberies, 1936.
No One's Last Crime, Fiction House, 1936.
The Hypnotic Demon, Fiction House, 1936.
The Moat Farm Mystery, Fiction House, 1936.
The Secret Fortune, Fiction House, 1936.
The Successful Alibi, 1936.
The Hadfield Mystery, 1937.
The Moving Eye, 1937.
The Raven, Fiction House, 1937.
The Mountain Terror, 1938.
For Her Sister's Sake, Fiction House, 1938.
The Verrall Street Affair, George Newnes, 1940.

ROMANCE NOVELS UNDER PSEUDONYM MARGARET COOKE; PUBLISHED BY FICTION HOUSE, EXCEPT AS NOTED

For Love's Sake, Northern News Syndicate, 1934.
Troubled Journey, 1936.
False Love or True?, Northern News Syndicate, 1937.
Fate's Playthings, 1938.
Web of Destiny, 1938.
Whose Lover?, 1938.
A Mannequin's Romance, 1938.
Love Calls Twice, Northern News Syndicate, 1938.
The Road to Happiness, 1938.
The Turn of Fate, 1939.
Love Triumphant, 1939.
Love Comes Back, 1939.
Crossroads of Love, Mellifont Press, 1939.
Love's Journey, 1940.

ROMANCE NOVELS UNDER PSEUDONYM HENRY ST. JOHN COOPER; PUBLISHED BY LOW

Chains of Love, 1937.
Love's Pilgrimage, 1937.
The Tangled Legacy, 1938.
The Greater Desire, 1938.
Love's Ordeal, 1939.
The Lost Lover, 1940.

MYSTERIES UNDER PSEUDONYM NORMAN DEANE

Play for Murder, Hurst & Blackett, 1946, revised edition, Arrow Books, 1975.
The Silent House, Hurst & Blackett, 1947, revised edition, Arrow Books, 1973.
Why Murder?, Hurst & Blackett, 1948, revised edition, Arrow Books, 1975.
Intent to Murder, Hurst & Blackett, 1948, revised edition, Arrow Books, 1973.
The Man I Didn't Kill, Hurst & Blackett, 1950, reprint published under pseudonym Michael Halliday (see below), revised edition, Arrow Books, 1972.
No Hurry to Kill, Hurst & Blackett, 1950, revised edition, Arrow Books, 1973.
Double for Murder, Hurst & Blackett, 1951, revised edition, Arrow Books, 1972.
Golden Death, Hurst & Blackett, 1952.
Look at Murder, Hurst & Blackett, 1952, revised edition, Arrow Books, 1974.
Murder Ahead, Hurst & Blackett, 1953, revised edition, Arrow Books, 1974.
Death in the Spanish Sun, Hurst & Blackett, 1954, reprint published under name Michael Halliday (see below).
Incense of Death, Hurst & Blackett, 1954, reprinted, New English Library, 1969.

"BRUCE MURDOCH" MYSTERIES UNDER DEANE PSEUDONYM

Secret Errand, Hurst & Blackett, 1939, revised edition published under author's own name, New English Library, 1968, McKay, 1974.
Dangerous Journey, Hurst & Blackett, 1939, revised edition published under author's own name, Arrow Books, 1971, McKay, 1974.
Unknown Mission, Hurst & Blackett, 1940, revised edition, McKay, 1972.
The Withered Man, Hurst & Blackett, 1940, revised edition published under author's own name, Arrow Books, 1971.
I Am the Withered Man, Hurst & Blackett, revised edition published under author's own name, Arrow Books, 1971, McKay, 1973.
Where Is the Withered Man?, Hurst & Blackett, 1942, revised edition, McKay, 1972.

"LIBERATOR" MYSTERIES UNDER DEANE PSEUDONYM

Return to Adventure, Hurst & Blackett, 1943, revised edition, John Long, 1974.
Gateway to Escape, Hurst & Blackett, 1944, revised edition, Arrow Books, 1973.
Come Home to Crime, Hurst & Blackett, 1945, revised edition, John Long, 1974.

ROMANCE NOVELS UNDER PSEUDONYM ELISE FECAMPS; PUBLISHED BY FICTION HOUSE

Love of Hate, 1936.
Love's Triumph, 1936.

True Love, 1937.

"MARK KIRBY" MYSTERIES UNDER PSEUDONYM ROBERT CAINE FRAZER; PUBLISHED BY POCKET BOOKS, EXCEPT AS NOTED

Mark Kirby Solves a Murder, 1959 (published in England as *R.I.S.C.,* Collins, 1962, reprinted as *The Timid Tycoon,* Fontana Books, 1966).
. . . and the Secret Syndicate, 1960 (published in England as *The Secret Syndicate,* Collins, 1963).
. . . and the Miami Mob, 1960 (published in England as *The Miami Mob* with *Mark Kirby Stands Alone,* Collins, 1965).
The Hollywood Hoax, 1961.
. . . Stands Alone, 1962 (published in England as *. . . and the Manhattan Murders,* Fontana Books, 1966).
. . . Takes a Risk, 1962.

JUVENILE FICTION UNDER PSEUDONYM PATRICK GILL; PUBLISHED BY MELLIFONT PRESS

The Fighting Footballers, 1937.
The Laughing Lightweight, 1937.
The Battle for the Cup, 1939.
The Fighting Tramp, 1939.
The Mystery of the Centre-Forward, 1939.
The 10,000 Trophy Race, 1939.
The Secret Supercharger, 1940.

MYSTERIES UNDER PSEUDONYM MICHAEL HALLIDAY

Four Find Danger, Cassell, 1937.
Three for Adventure, Cassell, 1937, revised edition, Corgi Books, 1976.
Two Meet Trouble, Cassell, 1938, reprinted, Corgi Books, 1975.
Murder Comes Home, Stanley Paul, 1940.
Heir to Murder, Stanley Paul, 1940.
Murder by the Way, Stanley Paul, 1941, reprinted, Lythway Press, 1973.
Who Saw Him Die?, Stanley Paul, 1941.
Foul Play Suspected, Stanley Paul, 1942.
Who Died at the Grange?, Stanley Paul, 1942.
Five to Kill, Stanley Paul, 1943.
Murder at Kings's Kitchen, Stanley Paul, 1943, reprinted, Lythway Press, 1972.
Who Said Murder?, Stanley Paul, 1944.
No Crime More Cruel, Stanley Paul, 1944.
Crime with Many Voices, Stanley Paul, 1945.
Murder Makes Murder, Stanley Paul, 1946.
Mastery Motive, Stanley Paul, 1947, revised edition published under pseudonym Jeremy York in "Superintendent Folly" series (see below).
Lend a Hand to Murder, Stanley Paul, 1947, reprinted, Lythway Press, 1973.
First a Murder, Stanley Paul, 1948, revised edition published under pseudonym Jeremy York in "Superintendent Folly" series (see below).
No End to Danger, Stanley Paul, 1948, reprinted, Lythway Press, 1972.
Who Killed Rebecca?, Stanley Paul, 1949.
The Dying Witnesses, Evans Brothers, 1949, reprinted, Lythway Press, 1973.
Dine with Murder, Evans Brothers, 1950.
Murder Week-End, Evans Brothers, 1951, reprinted, Lythway Press, 1974.
Quarrel with Murder, Evans Brothers, 1951, revised edition, Corgi Books, 1975.
Murder at End House, Hodder & Stoughton, 1955,

Murder Assured, Hodder & Stoughton, 1958.
Hate to Kill, Hodder & Stoughton, 1962.
The Guilt of Innocence, Hodder & Stoughton, 1964.
The Man I Didn't Kill, Hodder & Stoughton, 1961.
Death in the Spanish Sun, reprinted, Mayflower Dell, 1968.

MYSTERIES UNDER HALLIDAY PSEUDONYM (PUBLISHED IN UNITED STATES UNDER PSEUDONYM JEREMY YORK)

Death out of Darkness, Hodder & Stoughton, 1954, World Publishing, 1971.
Out of the Shadows, Hodder & Stoughton, 1954, World Publishing, 1971.
Cat and Mouse, Hodder & Stoughton, 1955, reprinted, White Lion, 1974, published as *Hilda, Take Heed,* Scribner, 1957.
Death of a Stranger, Hodder & Stoughton, 1957, reprinted, White Lion, 1972, published as *Come Here and Die,* Scribner, 1959.
Runaway, Hodder & Stoughton, 1957, World Publishing, 1971.
Missing from Home, Hodder & Stoughton, 1959, published as *Missing,* Scribner, 1960.
Thicker than Water, Hodder & Stoughton, 1959, Doubleday, 1962.
Go ahead with Murder, Hodder & Stoughton, published as *Two for the Money,* Doubleday, 1962.
How Many to Kill?, Hodder & Stoughton, 1960, published as *The Girl with the Leopard Skin Bag,* Scribner, 1961.
The Edge of Terror, Hodder & Stoughton, 1961, Macmillan, 1963.
The Man I Killed, Hodder & Stoughton, 1961, Macmillan, 1963.
The Quiet Fear, Hodder & Stoughton, 1963, Macmillan, 1968.

"FAME BROTHERS" MYSTERIES UNDER HALLIDAY PSEUDONYM

Take a Body, Evans Brothers, 1951, revised edition, Hodder & Stoughton, 1964, World Publishing, 1972.
Lame Dog Murders, Evans Brothers, 1952, World Publishing, 1972.
Murder in the Stars, Hodder & Stoughton, 1953, World Publishing, 1973.
Man on the Run, Hodder & Stoughton, 1953, World Publishing, 1972.

"DR. EMMANUEL CELLINI" MYSTERIES UNDER HALLIDAY PSEUDONYM (PUBLISHED IN UNITED STATES UNDER PSEUDONYM KYLE HUNT)

Cunning as a Fox, Hodder & Stoughton, 1965, Macmillan, 1965.
Wicked as the Devil, Hodder & Stoughton, 1966, Macmillan, 1966.
Slick as a Serpent, Hodder & Stoughton, 1967, Macmillan, 1967.
Cruel as a Cat, Hodder & Stoughton, 1971.
Too Good to Be True, Hodder & Stoughton, 1969, Macmillan, 1969.
A Period of Evil, Hodder & Stoughton, 1970, World Publishing, 1971.
As Lonely as the Damned, Hodder & Stoughton, 1971, World Publishing, 1972.
As Empty as Hate, Hodder & Stoughton, 1972, World Publishing, 1972.
As Merry as Hell, Hodder & Stoughton, 1973, Stein & Day, 1974.
This Man Did I Kill?, Hodder & Stoughton, 1974, Stein & Day, 1974.
The Man Who Was Not Himself, Hodder & Stoughton, 1976, Stein & Day, 1976.

OTHER MYSTERIES UNDER HUNT PSEUDONYM

Kill Once, Kill Twice, Simon & Schuster, 1956.
Kill a Wicked Man, Simon & Schuster, 1957.
Kill My Love, Simon & Schuster, 1958, reprinted, White Lion, 1973.
To Kill a Killer, Random House, 1960.

MYSTERIES UNDER PSEUDONYM BRIAN HOPE

Four Motives for Murder, George Newnes, 1938.

MYSTERIES UNDER PSEUDONYM COLIN HUGHES

Triple Murder, George Newnes, 1940, (also published as *What Dark Motive?*).

MYSTERIES UNDER PSEUDONYM ABEL MANN

Danger Woman, Pocket Books, 1966.

MYSTERIES UNDER PSEUDONYM PETER MANTON; PUBLISHED BY WRIGHT & BROWN, EXCEPT AS NOTED

The Grey Vale School Mystery (juvenile fiction), Low, 1937.
Stand by for Danger, 1937.
The Circle of Justice, 1938, revised edition, New English Library, 1959.
Three Days' Terror, 1938, reprinted, New English Library, 1969.
The Crime Syndicate, 1939, revised edition, New English Library, 1969.
Death Looks On, 1939.
Murder in the Highlands, 1939, reprinted, Lythway Press, 1973.
The Midget Marvel (juvenile fiction), Mellifont Press, 1940.
Policeman's Triumph, 1949.
Thief in the Night, 1950, reprinted, Lythway Press, 1973.
No Escape from Murder, 1953.
The Crooked Killer, 1954.
The Charity Murders, 1954.

"GIDEON" MYSTERIES UNDER PSEUDONYM J. J. MARRIC; PUBLISHED BY HARPER, EXCEPT AS NOTED

Gideon's Day, 1955, reprinted, Popular Library, 1979, published as *Gideon of Scotland Yard,* Berkeley Publishing, 1958.
Gideon's Week, reprinted, F. A. Thorpe, 1970.
. . . *Night,* 1957, reprinted, Popular Library, 1978.
. . . *Month,* 1958, reprinted, F. A. Thorpe, 1975.
. . . *Staff,* 1959, reprinted, Coronet Books, 1975.
. . . *Risk,* 1960.
. . . *Fire,* 1961.
. . . *March,* 1962, reprinted, Popular Library, 1977.
. . . *Ride,* 1963, reprinted, Popular Library, 1979.
Gideon at Work, 1964 (published in England as *The Gideon Omnibus,* Hodder & Stoughton, 1964.
. . . *Vote,* 1964.
. . . *Lot,* 1964, reprinted, Popular Library, 1979.
. . . *Badge,* 1966.
. . . *Wrath,* 1967.
. . . *River,* 1968.
. . . *Power,* 1969.
. . . *Sport,* 1970.
. . . *Art,* 1971.
. . . *Men,* 1972.
. . . *Press,* 1973.
London Omnibus, Hodder & Stoughton, 1973.
. . . *Fog,* 1974.
. . . *Drive,* 1976.

JUVENILE FICTION UNDER PSEUDONYM JAMES MARSDEN

Ned Cartwright—Middleweight Champion, Mellifont Press, 1935.

UNDER PSEUDONYM RICHARD MARTIN

Keys to Crime (mystery), William Earl & Co., 1947, reprinted, Lythway Press, 1973.
Vote for Murder (mystery). William Earl & Co. 1948, reprinted, Lythway Press, 1973.
Adrian and Jonathon, Hodder & Stoughton, 1954, reprinted, Lythway Press, 1972.

MYSTERIES UNDER PSEUDONYM ANTHONY MORTON; PUBLISHED BY LOW

Mr. Quentin Investigates, 1943, reprinted, Lythway Press, 1973.
Introducing Mr. Brandon, 1944, reprinted, Lythway Press, 1973.

"BARON" MYSTERIES UNDER MORTON PSEUDONYM

The Man in the Blue Mask, Lippincott, 1937 (published in England as *Meet the Baron,* Harrap, 1937, reprinted, Corgi Books, 1971.
The Return of Blue Mask, Lippincott, 1937 (published in England as *The Baron Returns,* Harrap, 1937, reprinted, Corgi Books, 1974).
Salute Blue Masks!, Lippincott, 1938 (published in England as *The Baron Again,* Low, 1938, reprinted, Corgi Books, 1969).
Blue Mask at Bay, Lippincott, 1938 (published in England as *The Baron at Bay,* Low, 1938).
Alias Blue Mask, Lippincott, 1939 (published in England as *Alias the Baron,* Low, 1939, reprinted, Transworld [London], 1966).
Challenge Blue Mask!, Lippincott, 1939 (published in England as *The Baron at Large,* Low, 1939), revised edition published as *The Baron at Large,* Corgi Books, 1972, Walker & Co., 1975.
Blue Mask Strikes Again, Lippincott, 1940 (published in England as *Versus the Baron,* Low, 1940, reprinted, Lythway Press, 1972).
Blue Mask Victorious, Lippincott, 1940 (published in England as *Call for the Baron,* Low, 1940, reprinted, Corgi Books, 1973), revised edition published as *Call for the Baron,* Walker & Co., 1976.
The Baron Comes Back, Low, 1943, reprinted, Corgi Books, 1973.
A Case for the Baron, Low, 1945, Duell, Sloan & Pearce, 1949, reprinted, Corgi Books, 1968.
Reward for the Baron, Low, 1945, reprinted, Corgi Books, 1970.
Career for the Baron, Low, 1946, Duell, Sloan & Pearce, 1950, reprinted, Lythway Press, 1974.
The Baron and the Beggar, Low, 1947, Duell, Sloan & Pearce, 1950, reprinted, Corgi Books, 1974.
Blame the Baron, Low, 1948, Duell, Sloan & Pearce, 1951.
A Rope for the Baron, 1948, Duell, Sloan & Pearce, 1949, reprinted, Corgi Books, 1975.
Books for the Baron, Low, 1949, Duell, Sloan & Pearce, 1952.
Cry for the Baron, Low, 1950, Walker & Co., 1970.
Trap . . . , Low, 1950, Walker & Co., 1971.
Attack . . . , Low, 1951, revised edition, Corgi Books, 1972.
Shadow . . . , Low, 1951, reprinted, Lythway Press, 1976.
Warn . . . , Low, 1952.
The Baron Goes East, Low, 1953, reprinted, White Lion, 1973.
. . . *in France,* Hodder & Stoughton, 1953, reprinted, Hodder Paperbacks, 1970, Walker & Co., 1976.

Danger for . . ., Hodder & Stoughton, 1953, reprinted, Hodder Paperbacks, 1971, Walker & Co., 1974.

. . . Goes Fast, Hodder & Stoughton, 1954, Walker & Co., 1972.

Nest-Egg for . . ., Hodder & Stoughton, 1954, reprinted, Hodder Paperbacks, 1972, published as *Deaf, Dumb, and Blonde*, Doubleday, 1961.

Help from . . ., Hodder & Stoughton, 1955, reprinted, White Lion, 1973, Walker & Co., 1977.

Hide . . ., Hodder & Stoughton, 1956, Walker & Co., 1978.

Frame . . ., Hodder & Stoughton, 1957, reprinted, White Lion, 1976, published as *The Double Frame*, Doubleday, 1961.

Red Eye for . . ., Hodder & Stoughton, 1958, published as *Blood Red*, Doubleday, 1960.

Black for . . ., Hodder & Stoughton, 1959, reprinted, Coronet Books, 1974, published as *If Anything Happens to Hester*, Doubleday, 1962.

Salute for . . ., Hodder & Stoughton, 1960, Walker & Co., 1973.

A Branch for . . ., Hodder & Stoughton, 1961, published as *Branches Out*, Scribner, 1967.

Bad for . . ., Hodder & Stoughton, 1962, published as *. . . and the Stolen Legacy*, Scribner, 1967.

A Sword for . . ., Hodder & Stoughton, 1963, published as *. . . and the Mogul Swords*, Scribner, 1966.

. . . on Board, Hodder & Stoughton, 1964, Walker & Co., 1968.

. . . and the Chinese Puzzle, Hodder & Stoughton, 1965, Scribner, 1966.

Sport for . . ., Hodder & Stoughton, 1966, Walker & Co., 1969.

Affair for . . ., Hodder & Stoughton, 1967, Walker & Co 1968.

. . . and the Missing Old Masters, Hodder & Stoughton, 1968, Walker & Co., 1969.

. . . and the Unfinished Portrait, Hodder & Stoughton, 1969, Walker & Co., 1970.

Last Laugh for . . ., Hodder & Stoughton, 1970, Walker & Co., 1971.

. . . Goes A-Buying, Hodder & Stoughton, 1971, Walker & Co.,1972.

. . . and the Arrogant Artist, Hodder & Stoughton, 1972, Walker & Co., 1973.

Burgle . . ., Hodder & Stoughton, 1973, Walker & Co., 1974.

. . . , King-Maker, Walker & Co., 1975.

Love for . . ., Hodder & Stoughton, 1979.

WESTERNS UNDER PSEUDONYM KEN RANGER

One-Shot Marriott, Low, 1938.
Roaring Guns, Low, 1939.

WESTERNS UNDER PSEUDONYM WILLIAM K. REILLY

Range War, Stanley Paul, 1939.
Two Gun Texan, Stanley Paul, 1939;
Gun Feud, Stanley Paul, 1940.
Stolen Range, Stanley Paul, 1940.
War on Lazy-K, Stanley Paul, 1941, Phoenix Press, 1946.
Outlaw's Vengeance, Stanley Paul, 1941.
Guns over Blue Lake, Jenkins, 1942.
Riders of Dry Gulch, Jenkins, 1943.
Long John Rides the Range, Jenkins, 1944.
Miracle Range, Jenkins, 1945.
The Secret of the Range, Jenkins, 1946.
Outlaw Guns, William Earl & Co., 1949.
Range Vengeance, Ward, Lock, 1953.

WESTERNS UNDER PSEUDONYM TEX RILEY; PUBLISHED BY WRIGHT & BROWN, EXCEPT AS NOTED

Two-Gun Girl, 1938.
Gun-Smoke Range, 1938.

Gunshot Mesa, 1939.
The Shootin' Sheriff, 1940.
Rustler's Range, 1940.
Masked Riders, 1940.
Death Canyon, 1941, reprinted, Lythway Press, 1974.
Guns on the Range, 1942.
Range Justice, 1943.
Outlaw Hollow, 1944.
Hidden Range, William Earl & Co., 1946.
Forgotten Range, William Earl & Co., 1947.
Trigger Justice, William Earl & Co., 1948.
Lynch Hollow, William Earl & Co., 1949.

MYSTERIES UNDER PSEUDONYM JEREMY YORK

By Persons Unknown, Bles, 1941, reprinted, Lythway Press, 1972.

Murder Unseen, Bles, 1943.

No Alibi, Melrose, 1943, reprinted, Lythway Press, 1972.

Murder in the Family, Melrose, 1944, revised edition published in "Superintendent Folly" series (see below).

Yesterday's Murder, Melrose, 1945.

Wilful Murder, McNaughton, 1946.

Death to My Killer, Melrose, 1950, Macmillan, 1966.

Sentence of Death, Melrose, 1950, Macmillan, 1964.

Voyage with Murder, Melrose, 1952, reprinted, Lythway Press, 1975.

Safari with Fear, Melrose, 1953, reprinted, Lythway Press, 1974.

So Soon to Die, Stanley Paul, 1955, Scribner, 1957.

Seeds of Murder, Stanley Paul, 1956, Scribner, 1958.

Sight of Death, Stanley Paul, 1956, Scribner, 1958.

My Brother's Killer, John Long, 1958, Scribner, 1959.

Hide and Kill, John Long, 1959, Scribner, 1960.

To Kill or to Die, John Long, 1960, Macmillan, 1966, published as *To Kill or Die*, Panther Books, 1965.

"SUPERINTENDENT FOLLY" MYSTERIES UNDER YORK PSEUDONYM

Find the Body, Melrose, 1945, revised edition, Macmillan, 1967.

Murder Came Late, Melrose, 1946, revised edition, Macmillan, 1969.

Let's Kill Uncle Lionel, Melrose, 1947, revised edition, Corgi Books, 1973, McKay, 1976.

Run Away to Murder, Melrose, 1947, Macmillan, 1970.

Close the Door on Murder, Melrose, 1948, revised edition, Corgi Books, 1971, McKay, 1973.

The Gallows Are Waiting, Melrose, 1949, revised edition, Corgi Books, 1972, McKay, 1973.

First a Murder, revised edition, Corgi Books, 1970, McKay, 1972.

Mystery Motive, revised edition, Corgi Books, 1970, published in United States under author's own name, McKay, 1974.

Murder in the Family, revised edition, McKay, 1976.

MYSTERIES, WITH IAN BOWEN, UNDER JOINT PSEUDONYM CHARLES HOGARTH

Murder on Largo Island, Selwyn & Blount, 1944.

OTHER

Also author of juvenile fiction *One Glorious Term* and *The Captain of the Fifth*, published by Low in 1930s; *The Fear of Felix Corder, John Brand: Fugitive*, and *The Night of Dread*, published by Fleetway Press; and *Dazzle and the Red Bomber*, published by George Newnes. Also author, under pseudonym Rodney Mattheson, of *The Dark Shadow* and *The House of Ferrars*, both published by Fiction House. Contributor to numerous magazines, including *Ellery Queen's Mystery Magazine* and *Armchair Detective*. Editor of *John Creasey Mystery Magazine,* 1956-65.

SIDELIGHTS: "If such a man were created in a novel, no one could possibly believe in him. In real life he is almost unbelievable; it is hardly surprising that his English publishers call him 'a legend in his own lifetime.' " John Creasey thus summarized his career in an autobiographical article which he wrote in the third person for *Armchair Detective.*

Creasey had reason to speak in superlatives; a retelling of his life actually sounds like a not-too-believable work of fiction. Facts concerning his literary output are astonishing: The author of nearly six hundred books, Creasey was the world's most prolific writer of crime fiction in English. He once estimated that between three and four thousand different editions of his books had appeared in a total of twenty-six languages. At the time of his death nearly sixty million copies of his books had been sold worldwide.

Creasey's popular success allowed him to live a life as colorful as that of one of his characters. He lived in a forty-two room manor, virtually commuted between England and the United States, traveled twice around the world, married four times, started his own political party, ran for the British Parliament several times, and owned a Rolls-Royce marked with the symbol of his "Toff" character—a monocled gentleman sporting a top hat.

His success, while based on reader acceptance of his novels, was largely a product of his own determination. For example, although Creasey began submitting articles for publication when only ten, by age seventeen he had also collected an amazing total of 743 rejection slips from publishers. Although he had his first novel published by the time he was twenty-seven, it was actually the tenth he had written, and during the same period of time he had been fired from twenty-five jobs—often for writing on his employer's time. But Creasey did not believe in defeat. *Armchair Detective* editor Allen J. Hubin once wrote: "I was greatly struck with [Creasey's] confidence and determination. 743 rejection slips without a sale! the imagination boggles. . . . But as John says, 'It was never a question of "if," it was only a question of "when." ' "

This determined attitude remained with Creasey throughout his life; he did not accept setbacks, he fought them. When told by many acquaintances that he would "never be able to sell" in the United States, Creasey responded by personally visiting nineteen U.S. publishers and editors in an attempt to discover the reason for lack of positive reader response to the previous U.S. editions of his books. Unsatisfied with the various explanations he received, he developed his own theory. Unlike their British counterparts, American readers of crime novels, he believed, needed a protagonist with whom they could more readily identify. He purposely set out to change his style, making his novels more acceptable to the American audience.

In 1951, Creasey spent six months in the United States attempting to convince American companies to accept his books for publication. Again, he received rejection slips—sixty-eight—but finally obtained a contract from Harper to publish *Inspector West Cries Wolf* (appearing under the U.S. title *The Creepers*). As in the past, Creasey's persistence led to success. The novel was well received in the United States, and the entire collection of Inspector West books became one of his most popular series among U.S. readers.

Although the "Inspector West" series was also one of Creasey's own favorites, his "Gideon" books, written under the pseud-

onym J. J. Marric, most favorably impressed reviewers. Under this pseudonym, according to a *London Times* article, "[Creasey] received far better reviews than he was accustomed to get under his own name." In the *Detroit News,* for example, Richard Werry noted, "Marric's characters have real personal problems which make them more substantial than the papier-mache stereotypes common in most mystery fiction." Julian Symons also commented on the high quality of Marric's writing. In *Mortal Consequences* Symons wrote: "Creasey's Gideon books, written as J. J. Marric, are his best work. . . . His stories are notable for the ingenuity of the ideas with which he overflows." The *New York Times Book Review*'s Anthony Boucher added: "[Creasey's 'Gideon' books] are marked by the technically dazzling handling of a large number of plots in small compass. . . . All of the Creasey avatars are skilled at telling an exciting story; Marric, in addition, can *write.*"

Not all reviewers, however, had such high regard for Creasey's work. A *New York Times* writer observed: "Mr. Creasey had his detractors among professional critics, some of whom described his writings as undistinguished." Critics, believing that quick production diminished the quality of his writing, belittled Creasey for his rapid rate of publication. A *New York Times Book Review* writer, for example, described Creasey as "a sort of homicide computer—punch a button and out comes a book." Lewis Nichols, also writing in the *New York Times Book Review,* saw Creasey more as a business concern than as an author and referred to him as "Syndicate C."

Creasey, later in life, was able to shrug off such criticism. In *Writer,* he once jokingly called himself "a hackneyed old professional . . . suspected . . . by so many to have invented the computer first and Creasey and pen-names later." Early in his career, however, a critic who accused him of being more interested in quickly-completed than well-written prose caused Creasey to reevaluate his writing method. Claiming in a *Newsweek* article, "I need to write with speed or it's no good," Creasey had attempted to write two books a week, with one day off between for playing cricket. After realizing the truth behind the critic's comments, Creasey decided to slow his pace to a pattern consistently followed until his death.

He began to take greater care in the production of his books. Each was written in longhand first, then scrutinized and revised five or six times before going to the publisher—often up to twelve months after being originally written. Creasey also began the practice of revising his earlier novels to make them more contemporary as well as to polish his style. He had a staff of readers instructed "tear to bits" each of the novels due to be revised. Using these critical reports, Creasey made the necessary revisions and then had the book retyped and reread by other assistants. Some books were so extensively rewritten that the original detective was completely replaced by another character.

At times, revision also meant that a novel would appear under a different Creasey pseudonym than the one under which it had originally appeared. While several of his early pen names were chosen for him by his publishers, others, like J. J. Marric, originated with Creasey. J. J. Marric was chosen deliberately for the "Gideon" series; the name derived from the initials of the given names of Creasey and his second wife, Jean, combined with the first syllables of the given names of their two sons: *Mar*tin and *Rich*ard. Creasey once gave the reason for both his use of pseudonyms and his enormous number of books in *Newsweek.* He explained: "When I began writing, I discovered that the only way to make a living at the craft was to publish more than two books a year. Since, at that time, no publishers wanted to print more than two books a year from one author, I just changed names; then, too, different pen names permit me to write in different tones."

No matter which pseudonym was used, there was always a "special stamp" of a Creasey book, according to Hubin in the *New York Times Book Review.* These distinguishing characteristics, as Hubin saw them, were "uncluttered plotting, and emphasis . . . on the basic goodness of most people involved." Newgate Callendar referred to "the Creasey formula" in a *New York Times Book Review* article. In Callendar's analysis, a typical Creasey novel had "a fairly rat-tat-tat style—short sentences, lots of padding, emphasis on plot gimmicks, [and] very little in the way of characterization." William Vivian Butler had yet another enumeration of Creasey literary characteristics. He listed the following points in a *Spectator* review: "The driving narrative, the subtly understated heroics, the simple humanity, the strident small-l liberalism, the all-embracing love of London—and, above all, the dogged vulnerable heroes."

Creasey devoted the last year of his life to the production of a novel telling the history of London's Metropolitan Police. "He meant this . . . to be," according to the London *Times,* "a vindication of his claim to be a serious writer." Creasey's avid readers never doubted this claim. A London *Times* writer noted, "His business, he believed, was to sell books and to entertain." Creasey accomplished both these aims. As reviewer Butler stated in *Spectator,* "[His career was an] incredible forty-year, six hundred book feast . . . [for] his fans."

MEDIA ADAPTATIONS: John Creasey's books have been adapted for two British television series, "Gideon" and "The Baron." A number of his novels have also been adapted for films, including "Salute the Toff," 1951, and "Hammer the Toff," 1952, by Butcher; "Gideon's Day," by Columbia Production Ltd., 1958; and "Cat and Mouse," by Eros, 1958.

BIOGRAPHICAL/CRITICAL SOURCES:

BOOKS

Contemporary Literary Criticism, Volume 11, Gale, 1979.
Creasey, John, and Robert E. Briney, *John Creasey—Fact or Fiction? A Candid Commentary in Third Person, With a Bibliography,* Armchair Detective Press, 1978, revised edition, 1969.
Dictionary of Literary Biography, Volume 77: *British Mystery Writers, 1920-1939,* Gale, 1989.
Symons, Julian, *Mortal Consequences: A History—From the Detective Story to the Crime Novel,* Harper, 1972.

PERIODICALS

Armchair Detective, October, 1968.
Detroit News, November 28, 1971, June 4, 1972.
Life, April 27, 1962.
Newsday, December 12, 1970.
Newsweek, February 2, 1958.
New York Times, July 22, 1972.
New York Times Book Review, November 28, 1958, January 22, 1961, March 18, 1962, July 28, 1968, September 1, 1968, November 3, 1968, January 19, 1969, June 1, 1969, April 11, 1976.
Publishers Weekly, February 8, 1965.
Spectator, March 22, 1975.
Times Literary Supplement, September 18, 1969, January 22, 1970, October 22, 1971.
Variety, June 10, 1970.
Writer, September, 1972.

OBITUARIES:

PERIODICALS

AB Bookman's Weekly, October 1, 1973.
New York Times, June 10, 1973.
Times (London), June 11, 1973.
Publishers Weekly, June 18, 1973.
Newsweek, June 25, 1973.

*   *   *

CREDO
See CREASEY, John

*   *   *

CREELEY, Robert (White) 1926-

PERSONAL: Born May 21, 1926, in Arlington, Mass.; son of Oscar Slade (a physician) and Genevieve (Jules) Creeley; married Ann McKinnon, 1946 (divorced, 1955); married Bobbie Louise Hawkins, January 27, 1957 (divorced, 1976); married Penelope Highton, 1977; children: (first marriage) David, Thomas, Charlotte; (second marriage) Kirsten (stepdaughter), Leslie (stepdaughter; deceased), Sarah, Katherine; (third marriage) William, Hannah. *Education:* Attended Harvard University, 1943-44 and 1945-46; Black Mountain College, B.A., 1955; University of New Mexico, M.A., 1960.

ADDRESSES: Office—Department of English, State University of New York, Buffalo, NY 14260.

CAREER: Poet, novelist, short story writer, essayist, and editor. Divers Press, Palma, Mallorca, Spain, founder and publisher, 1950-54; Black Mountain College, Black Mountain, N.C., instructor in English, 1954-55; instructor at school for young boys, Albuquerque, N.M., beginning 1956; University of New Mexico, Albuquerque, instructor in English, 1961-62; University of British Columbia, Vancouver, instructor in English, 1962-63; University of New Mexico, lecturer in English, 1963-65; State University of New York at Buffalo, visiting professor, 1965-66, professor of English, 1967—, David Gray Professor of Poetry and Letters, 1978—. Bicentennial chair of American studies at University of Helsinki, Finland, 1988. Participated in numerous poetry readings and writers' conferences. With American Field Service, India and Burma, 1945-46.

MEMBER: American Academy and Institute of Arts and Letters.

AWARDS, HONORS: Levinson Prize, 1960, for group of ten poems published in *Poetry;* D. H. Lawrence fellowship (for summer writing), University of New Mexico, 1960; National Book Award nomination, 1962, for *For Love;* Leviton-Blumenthal Prize, 1964, for group of thirteen poems published in *Poetry;* Guggenheim fellowship in poetry, 1964-65 and 1971; Rockefeller Foundation grant, 1966; Union League Civic and Arts Foundation Prize, 1967; Shelley Award, 1981, and Frost Medal, 1987, both from Poetry Society of America; National Endowment for the Arts grant, 1982; Deutsche Auftauschdienst Programme (DADD) providing residency in Berlin, 1983 and 1987; Leone d'Oro Premio Speziale, Venice, 1985; Walt Whitman citation of merit, 1989; named New York State Poet, 1989.

WRITINGS:

POETRY

Le Fou, Golden Goose Press, 1952.
The Kind of Act Of, Divers Press (Palma, Mallorca, Spain), 1953.

The Immoral Proposition, Jonathan Williams, 1953.

A Snarling Garland of Xmas Verse (published anonymously), Divers Press, 1954.

All That Is Lovely in Men, Jonathan Williams, 1955.

(With others) *Ferrin and Others,* Gerhardt (Germany), 1955.

If You, Porpoise Bookshop, 1956.

The Whip, Migrant Books, 1957.

A Form of Women, Jargon Books, 1959.

For Love: Poems 1950-1960, Scribner, 1962.

Distance, Terrence Williams, 1964.

Two Poems, Oyez, 1964.

Hi There!, Finial Press, 1965.

Words (eight poems), Perishable Press, 1965.

Poems 1950-1965, Calder & Boyars, 1966.

About Women, Gemini, 1966.

For Joel, Perishable Press, 1966.

A Sight, Cape Coliard Press, 1967.

Words (eighty-four poems), Scribner, 1967.

Robert Creeley Reads (with recording), Turret Books, 1967.

The Finger, Black Sparrow Press, 1968, enlarged edition published as *The Finger Poems, 1966-1969,* Calder & Boyars, 1970.

5 Numbers (five poems), Poets Press, 1968, published as *Numbers* (text in English and German), translation by Klaus Reichert, Galerie Schmela (Dusseldorf, Germany), 1968.

The Charm: Early and Collected Poems, Perishable Press, 1968, expanded edition published as *The Charm,* Four Seasons Foundation, 1969.

Divisions and Other Early Poems, Perishable Press, 1968.

Pieces (fourteen poems), Black Sparrow Press, 1968.

The Boy (poem poster), Gallery Upstairs Press, 1968.

Mazatlan: Sea, Poets Press, 1969.

Pieces (seventy-two poems), Scribner, 1969.

Hero, Indianakatz, 1969.

A Wall, Bouwerie Editions, 1969.

For Betsy and Tom, Alternative Press, 1970.

For Benny and Sabrina, Samuel Charters, 1970.

America, Press of the Black Flag, 1970.

Christmas: May 10, 1970, Lockwood Memorial Library, State University of New York at Buffalo, 1970.

St. Martin's, Black Sparrow Press, 1971.

1-2-3-4-5-6-7-8-9-0, drawings by Arthur Okamura, Shambala, 1971.

Sea, Cranium Press, 1971.

For the Graduation, Cranium Press, 1971.

Change, Hermes Free Press, 1972.

One Day after Another, Alternative Press, 1972.

For My Mother: Genevieve Jules Creeley, 8 April 1887-7 October 1972 (limited edition), Sceptre Press, 1973.

His Idea, Coach House Press, 1973.

Kitchen, Wine Press, 1973.

Sitting Here, University of Connecticut Library, 1974.

Thirty Things, Black Sparrow Press, 1974.

Backwards, Sceptre Press, 1975.

Hello, Hawk Press, 1976, expanded edition published as *Hello: A Journal, February 29-May 3, 1976,* New Directions, 1978.

Away, Black Sparrow Press, 1976.

Presences (also see below), Scribner, 1976.

Selected Poems, Scribner, 1976.

Myself, Sceptre Press, 1977.

Later, Toothpaste, 1978, expanded edition, New Directions, 1979.

The Collected Poems of Robert Creeley, 1945-1975, University of California Press, 1982.

Echoes, Toothpaste, 1982.

Mirrors, New Directions, 1983.

Memories, Pig Press, 1984.

Memory Gardens, New Directions, 1986.

The Company, Burning Deck, 1988.

EDITOR

Charles Olson, *Mayan Letters,* Divers Press, 1953, Grossman, 1968.

(With Donald M. Allen, and contributor) *New American Story,* Grove, 1965.

(And author of introduction) Olson, *Selected Writings,* New Directions, 1966.

(With Allen, and contributor) *The New Writing in the U.S.A.,* Penguin, 1967.

Whitman, Penguin, 1973.

(And contributor) *The Essential Burns,* Ecco Press, 1989.

OTHER

The Gold Diggers (short stories), Divers Press, 1954, expanded edition published as *The Gold Diggers and Other Stories,* J. Calder, 1965, reprinted, Marion Boyars, 1980.

The Island (novel), Scribner, 1963, reprinted, Marion Boyars, 1980.

An American Sense (essay), Sigma Press, 1965.

A Quick Graph: Collected Notes and Essays, edited by Donald M. Allen, Four Seasons Foundation, 1970.

Notebook, Bouwerie Editions, 1972.

Listen (play; produced in London, 1972), Black Sparrow Press, 1972.

A Sense of Measure (essays), Calder & Boyars, 1972.

A Day Book (poems and prose; also see below), Scribner, 1972.

Inside Out (lecture), Black Sparrow Press, 1973.

Contexts of Poetry: Interviews 1961-1971, Four Seasons Foundation, 1973.

The Creative (lecture), Black Sparrow Press, 1973.

Mabel: A Story, and Other Prose (includes *A Day Book* and *Presences*), Calder & Boyars, 1976.

Was That a Real Poem and Other Essays, Four Seasons Foundation, 1979.

Charles Olson and Robert Creeley: The Complete Correspondence, eight volumes, edited by George Butterick, Black Sparrow Press, 1980-87.

Collected Prose, Marion Boyars, 1984, corrected edition, University of California Press, c. 1987.

Collected Essays, University of California Press, 1989.

Work represented in numerous anthologies, including *The New American Poetry: 1945-1960,* edited by Allen, Grove, 1960; *A Controversy of Poets,* edited by Paris Leary and Robert Kelly, Doubleday, 1965; *Norton Anthology of Modern Poetry,* edited by Richard Ellmann and Robert O'Clair, Norton, 1973; and *The New Oxford Book of American Verse,* edited by Ellmann, Oxford University Press, 1976. Contributor to literary periodicals, including *Paris Review, Nation, Black Mountain Review, Origin, Yugen,* and *Big Table.* Founder and editor, *Black Mountain Review,* 1954-57.

SIDELIGHTS: Once known primarily for his association with the group called the "Black Mountain Poets," Robert Creeley has become an important and influential literary figure in his own right. Creeley first began to develop his writing talents while attending Holderness School in Plymouth, New Hampshire, on a scholarship. His articles and stories appeared regularly in the school's literary magazine, and in his senior year he became its editor in chief. Creeley was admitted to Harvard in 1943, but his academic life was disrupted when he served as an ambulance driver for the American Field Service in 1944 and 1945.

Creeley returned to Harvard after the war and became associated with the literary crowd there, a group that included writers John Hawkes, Mitchell Goodman, and Kenneth Koch. He began corresponding with Cid Corman and Charles Olson, two poets who were to have a substantial influence on the direction of his future work. Excited especially by Olson's ideas about literature, Creeley began to develop a distinctive poetic style.

Throughout the 1950s he was associated with the "Black Mountain Poets," a group of writers including Denise Levertov, Ed Dorn, Fielding Dawson, and others who had some connection with Black Mountain College, an experimental, communal college in North Carolina that was a haven for many innovative writers and artists of the period. Creeley edited the *Black Mountain Review* and developed a close and lasting relationship with Olson, who was the rector of the college. The two engaged in a lengthy, intensive correspondence about literary matters that has been collected and published as *Charles Olson and Robert Creeley: The Complete Correspondence.* Olson and Creeley together developed the concept of "projective verse," a kind of poetry that abandoned traditional forms in favor of a freely constructed verse that took shape as the process of composing it was underway. Olson called this process "composition by field," and his famous essay on the subject, "Projective Verse," was as important for the poets of the emerging generation of the 1950s as T. S. Eliot's "Tradition and the Individual Talent" was to the poets of the previous generation. Olson credited Creeley with formulating one of the basic principles of this new poetry: the idea that "form is never more than an extension of content."

According to Cynthia Edelberg in *Robert Creeley's Poetry: A Critical Introduction,* another important influence on Creeley's work at this time was Paul Valery, whose book *Monsieur Teste* "was Creeley's bible from the late forties until he rejected it in the sixties." In this work Valery contends that the most significant subject for any writer is the operation of his own mind and its interaction with the world. Creeley's emphasis on charting his impressions of an immediate experience may well have been derived from his reading of Valery. But it was shaped as well by the poetic climate of the 1950s and early 1960s, which made the "chronicle of the moment" a characteristic poetic form, from the *Lunch Poems* of Frank O'Hara to the Whitmanesque catalogs of Allen Ginsberg and the harrowing confessional exposes of Sylvia Plath and Robert Lowell.

Creeley was a leader in the generational shift that veered away from history and tradition as primary poetic sources and gave new prominence to the ongoing experiences of an individual's life. Because of this emphasis, the major events of his life loom large in his literary work. Creeley's marriage to Ann McKinnon ended in divorce in 1955. The breakup of that relationship is chronicled in fictional form in his only novel, *The Island,* which drew upon his experiences on the island of Mallorca, off the coast of Spain, where he lived with Ann and their three children in 1953 and 1954. After the divorce Creeley returned to Black Mountain College for a brief time before moving west to make a new life. He was in San Francisco during the flowering of the "San Francisco Poetry Renaissance" and became associated for a time with the writers of the Beat Generation: Allen Ginsberg, Jack Kerouac, Michael McClure, and others. His work appeared in the influential "beat" anthology, *The New American Poetry: 1945-1960,* edited by Donald Allen.

In 1956 Creeley accepted a teaching position at a boys' school in Albuquerque, New Mexico, where he met his second wife,

Bobbie Louise Hawkins. Bobbie and her two daughters from a previous marriage, Kirsten and Leslie, formed his new family; two additional daughters, Sarah and Katherine, were born in the late 1950s. The Creeleys spent two winters in Guatemala before returning to Albuquerque where he received an M.A. degree. In 1961 his stepdaughter Leslie was killed in an accident. This event is the subject of one of his most moving poems, "For Leslie."

Though Creeley published poetry and fiction throughout the 1950s and 1960s and had even established his own imprint, the Divers Press, in 1952, his work did not receive important national recognition until Scribner published his first major collection, *For Love: Poems 1950-1960,* in 1962. This book collected work that he had been issuing in small editions and little magazines during the previous decade.

At this point in Creeley's career, his distinctive poetic voice gathered large numbers of followers and imitators. It was a voice that conveyed, as William Spanos declared in *Boundary*'s Creeley issue, "a music from the edge" that epitomized the poetry revolution of the period. Along with Allen Ginsberg, Lawrence Ferlinghetti, Paul Blackburn, Gary Snyder, and other poets who were intent on linking poetry and performance, Creeley awakened a sense of new rhythmical possibilities for the spoken word. The unforgettable sound of his voice reading poetry typified Olson's famous dictum that poetry needed to put into itself "the breathing of the man who writes." Creeley's mentors were Ezra Pound, William Carlos Williams, Louis Zukofsky, and Olson, and the odd, off-center sound of his work when he reads it aloud is an amalgam of those influences. As he writes, in *A Sense of Measure,* "Williams showed me early on that rhythm was a very subtle experience, and that words might share equivalent duration even though 'formally' they seemed in no way to do so. Pound said, 'LISTEN to the sound that it makes,' and Olson . . . made it evident that we could only go 'By ear.' Finally, there was and is the fact of, what it was one had to say—in Louis Zukofsky's sense, 'Out of deep need'. . .!"

The very first poem in *For Love,* "Hart Crane," with its unorthodox, Williams-like line breaks, its nearly hidden internal rhymes, its subtle assonance and sibilance, announces the Creeley style: "He had been stuttering, by the edge / of the street, one foot still / on the sidewalk, and the other / in the gutter . . . / like a bird, say, wired to flight, the / wings, pinned to their motion, stuffed." That style can be defined by an intense concentration on the sounds and rhythms of language as well as the placement of the words on the page. This intensity produces a kind of minimal poetry, which seeks to extract the bare linguistic bones from ongoing life experiences. In his introduction to *The New Writing in the U.S.A.,* Creeley cites approvingly Herman Melville's definition of "visible truth"—"the apprehension of the absolute condition of present things"—and supplements it with William Burroughs's famous statement from *Naked Lunch* about the writer's task: "There is only one thing a writer can write about: what is in front of his senses at the moment of writing. . . . I am a recording instrument . . . I do not presume to impose 'story' 'plot' 'continuity'."

Applying Burroughs's assertion to poetry meant not imposing on the work lyricism, metaphor, paradox, irony, closure, or any other conventional elements of poetry. Creeley's most memorable early poems nearly always adopted this antipoetic stance toward both language and experience. They avoided traditional poetic devices in favor of a keen attentiveness to experience and to the ways in which a writer struggles to articulate consciousness. Characteristically, the reader is plunged into the middle of an ongoing occurrence by means of a snatch of conversation, or more usually, by an internal monologue that recreates the feeling of a fleeting moment, a sudden awareness, or a traumatic event. The poems are built around Creeley's perception of the event and the "visible truth" he garners from it. That is, he seems to be searching constantly for an absolute truth in a fleeting moment. This pattern is true of almost all of the most frequently anthologized poems, such as "I Know a Man" ("As I said to my / friend, because I am always talking—John, I / said . . ."), "The Whip" ("I spent a night turning in bed, / my love was a feather, / a flat / sleeping thing . . ."), "The Warning" ("For love—I would / split open your head and put / a candle in / behind the eyes"), and "A Wicker Basket" ("Comes the time when it's later / and onto your table the headwaiter / puts the bill . . .").

Creeley sharpened and developed this style throughout the 1960s and 1970s in a series of books that seemed almost designed to exemplify the principles of projective verse and the ideas about poetry he proposed in a number of critical essays and talks. A poem called "Waiting" from *Words,* Creeley's second major collection, characterizes the problems a writer encounters transforming experience into poetry. His typical stance, described in this poem, is that of a poet struggling to bring a poem into being with no resources other than the heightened attention he brings to the task. He "pushes behind the words," giving his emotions and experiences the formal contours that embody their meaning. Creeley's fear is that the words will quit coming: "What if it all stops. / Then silence / is as silence was / again."

For Creeley, without the words that emanate from experience, life seems "a dull space of hanging actions"; the relations between things become severed and a sense of utter formlessness prevails. By discovering the appropriate form for the transitory emotional states he *needs* to write about, Creeley has always *used* poetry to take stock of both the world around him and the state of his being at any particular moment. In addition, he has always tried to write about his experiences without the stale viewpoint of habitual thought. As he puts it in a poem called "The Mountains in the Desert": "Tonight let me go / at last out of whatever / mind I thought to have, / and all the habits of it." These lines are not a longing for insanity but rather a call for a clarity of vision unencumbered by preconceptions. It is Creeley's version of the advice Ezra Pound gave to all creative artists, "Make it New."

In *Pieces, A Day Book, Thirty Things,* and *Hello: A Journal, February 29-May 3, 1976,* books published between 1968 and 1978, Creeley attempted to break down the concept of a "single poem" by offering his readers sequential, associated fragments of poems with indeterminate beginnings and endings. All of these works are energized by the same heightened attention to the present that characterizes Creeley's earlier work; but in *Hello,* a book written as journal entries over a five-week period while Creeley traveled in the Orient and South Pacific, he speculates on the possibility of using memory rather than the present as a poetic source. The poetry remains stubbornly rooted in the present despite the insistent intrusion of memories, both recent and long past.

Many of the poems in *Hello* refer to the last days of Creeley's relationship with his second wife, Bobbie. That marriage ended in divorce in 1976, the same year he met Penelope Highton, his third wife, while traveling in New Zealand. In this sense, the book may be described in much the same terms as Sherman Paul in his book *The Lost America of Love* describes *For Love,* "Poems of two marriages, the breakup of one, the beginning of another." For all of Creeley's experimentation, he has always been in some ways an exceedingly domestic poet; his mother, children, wives,

and close friends are the subjects of his best work. Because Creeley's second marriage lasted nearly twenty years, the sense of a major chunk of his life drifting away from him is very strong in *Hello.* Creeley here conveys the traumatic emotional state that almost always accompanies the breakup of long-term relationships. En route to Perth, he writes: "Sitting here in limbo, there are / people walking through my head." In Singapore he remarks on his tenuous hold on things: "Getting fainter, in the world, / fearing something's fading, / deadened, tentative responses— / go hours without eating, / scared without someone to be / with me. These empty days." Although *Hello* is superficially a record of Creeley's travels, the poems are not really about the countries he has visited, but rather about the landscape of mind he has brought with him.

It is not until Creeley's next major collection, *Later,* published in 1979, that the poetry seems to shift into a new phase characterized by a greater emphasis on memory, a new sense of life's discrete phases, and an intense preoccupation with aging. In "Myself," the first poem in *Later,* he writes: "I want, if older, / still to know / why, human, men / and women are / so torn, so lost / why hopes cannot / find a better world / than this." This futile but deeply human quest captures the spirit of Creeley's later work. It embodies a commonly shared realization: one becomes older but still knows very little about essential aspects of life, particularly the mysteries of human relationships. And as Alan Williamson observes in his *New York Times Book Review* assessment of *Later,* "In general, the stronger the note of elegiac bafflement and rage (the past utterly gone, the compensating wisdom not forthcoming), the better the writing."

In one of several poems in *Later* called "For Pen"—the title echoing his vocation as well as referring more apparently to the nickname of his third wife, Penelope—Creeley finds little difference between the desires of youth and age, except that age conspires with physical decline to make a mockery of desire. Ultimately, the speaker seems to come to terms with the inevitability of aging. This tone of resigned acceptance characterizes many of the poems in *Later.* These are in fact "later" poems, that phase of Creeley's life and career has arrived. He realizes, in "After," that "I'll not write again / things a young man / thinks, not the words / of that feeling." But there are other words he can and does make poetry of—the words of present feelings that both incorporate and reflect upon the past. These words are the "measure" of a life—what one is and has been capable of. "Measure is my testament," Creeley writes in *A Sense of Measure.* "What uses me is what I use and in that complex measure is the issue. I cannot cut down trees with my bare hand, which is measure of both tree and hand. In that way I feel that poetry, in the very subtlety of its relation to image and rhythm, offers an intensely various record of such things. It is equally one of them." Creeley continues to adhere to this testament in *Later,* where the poems seem to be a part of his continuing effort to discover the measure of things—the worth of any of life's singular episodes to the whole of that life.

This effort culminates in the ten-part title poem, "Later," written over a period of ten days in September of 1977. The poem presents a kaleidoscopic view of various times and events important to Creeley's life, beginning with an evocation of lost youth. Youth, in later life, can only become a palpable part of the present through the evocative power of memory. Another section of the poem comments on how certain empirical sensations are repositories of memory. A taste, a smell, a touch, can evoke a lost world: "sudden / smell of burning / leaves makes / place in time / these days / (these days) / passing, / common / to one / and all." The parenthetical "these days" refers to the days of the past encapsulated in the present through the recollection of certain images and physical sensations. "Later" continues to present a flood of childhood memories: a lost childhood dog that Creeley fantasizes running into again after all these years; memories of his mother and friends and neighbors; sights and sounds of his early days all evoked and made a part of the poetry he is composing in an attic room in Buffalo, September, 1977: "There's more always here / than just me, in this room, / this attic, apartment, / this house, this world, / can't escape."

The poem's final lines reveal the most affirmative and optimistic aspects of Creeley's later work: "the wonder of life is / that *it is* at all, / this sticky sentimental / warm enclosure, / feels at place in the physical / with others, / lets mind wander / to wondering thought, / then lets go of itself, / finds a home / on earth." This acceptance of things as they are is tempered in the later work by a nostalgia for things as they were. One feels, in *Later,* a longing for the excitement and turmoil of the Black Mountain-Beat Generation days when poetry seemed much more central to American life and culture than it does in the technology-dominated society of the later twentieth century.

In the work produced after the material included in his *Collected Poems, 1945-1975* there is an increasing tendency to derive poetry from what the English Romantic poet William Wordsworth called "emotion recollected in tranquility." It is a poetry that remembers and reflects and seems much less tied to the exigencies of the present than the earlier work. In *Mirrors,* published in 1984, the commitment to identifying and reconstructing those moments from the past that have most shaped his life deepens. The collection bears an epigraph from Francis Bacon: "In Mirrours, there is the like / Angle of Incidence, from the Object / to the Glasse, and from the Glasse / to the Eye." Poetry, in this sense, is the mirror which deflects the memory of past experience into our awareness in the present. Creeley reaches into early childhood in a poem called "Memory 1930" to illuminate the moment he learned of his father's death at a time when he was obviously too young to comprehend the impact it would have on his entire life. Here he presents it as a major fissure in his early life, viewed from an "angle of incidence" over fifty years later. He creates a picture of himself as a child, witnessing what appears as a surreal scene: "I sit, intent, fat / the youngest of the suddenly / disjunct family, whose father is / being then driven in an ambulance / across the lawn, in the snow, to die." The slowness of the final line with its two pauses causes the image of the departing ambulance to appear as if in slow motion. It is as if Creeley, who has written about the death of his father more obliquely in earlier work, can now bring that momentous event clearly into focus so that he observes the impact it had on his young self, who sits intently observing its occurrence. The older Creeley watches the young Creeley watching his father being driven away in an ambulance to die.

This poem and others in *Mirrors* are attempts at recovering those pieces of the past that best reflect Creeley's life. Although memory is the source of many of these poems, Creeley is after an evocation of the experience itself, not merely its memory. But in language, experience can be recreated only through the reflective medium of words. The poems here give us pieces of the mirror, the whole of which contains an image of Creeley's life. In poem after poem are echoes of Ezra Pound's "*dove sta memora,*" that major theme of lost memories in the *Pisan Cantos,* a poem Pound wrote at age sixty, determined to perpetuate the things that meant most to him. "What thou lovest well remains," he wrote in that poem's most famous lines, "the rest is dross, / What thou lov'st well shall not be reft from thee / What thou lov'st well is thy true heritage." And "Pull down thy vanity, it is not man /

Made courage, or made order, or made grace." Creeley concludes a poem called "Song" with a similar sentiment: "All vanity, all mind flies / but love remains, love, nor dies / even without me. Never dies."

Mirrors reveals how much a part of our characters memories become with each passing year, so that as we age we accumulate the mannerisms of our parents and reexperience past situations. In "Mother's Voice," Creeley not only hears his mother's voice, but makes it a part of his own: "In these few years / since her death I hear / mother's voice say / under my own, I won't / want any more of that. / My cheekbones resonate / with her emphasis." This theme of the present incorporating the past is most literal in "Prospect," one of the most memorable poems in *Mirrors.* It is an atypical Creeley poem because it utilizes conventional elements of poetry—symbolism, metaphor, and imagery—in a surprisingly traditional manner. In fact, the poem has a remarkably unique resonance because Creeley's physical description of nature conveys both present and past psychological states. It takes no deep looking into the poem to see the landscape as emblematic of the state of Creeley's later life, invigorated by a new marriage and the birth of a new child, his son William. The poem concludes with the reflections awakened by a contemplation of the landscape: "It is thoughtful, provokes here / quiet reflections, settles the self / down to waiting now apart / from time, which is done, / this green space, faintly painful." The final phrase surprises, coming at the end of an otherwise tranquil and nearly celebratory poem. It reminds the reader that although embarking on a new life can create the illusion that it is possible to exist in an Edenic landscape apart from time, in reality the past remains an integral part of the present. "Faintly painful," with its echoing first syllable rhyme, is exactly right to convey the contrary feelings of both relief and regret that the poem ultimately leaves the reader with—relief that the thoughtfulness the landscape provokes is not more painful, regret that there is any pain at all.

But pain has been one of the most constant elements in Creeley's work, and this later poetry continues to search for words to express it with sensitivity and exactness and without the sometimes maudlin excesses of "confessional" verse. Though these poems are more rooted in memory than the earlier work, Creeley remains committed to the poetic task of getting things exactly right. This has been the task of his writing throughout his career, and as readers look into the "mirror" of Creeley's work, they can see not only his aging, but their own.

BIOGRAPHICAL/CRITICAL SOURCES:

BOOKS

Allen, Donald, editor, *The New American Poetry: 1945-1960,* Grove, 1960.

Allen, editor, *Robert Creeley, Contexts of Poetry: Interviews, 1961-1971,* Four Seasons Foundation, 1973.

Allen and Warren Tallman, editors, *The Poetics of the New American Poetry,* Grove, 1973.

Butterick, George F., editor, *Charles Olson and Robert Creeley: The Complete Correspondence,* Black Sparrow Press, 1980.

Contemporary Authors, Autobiography Series, Volume 10, Gale, 1989.

Contemporary Literary Criticism, Gale, Volume 1, 1973, Volume 2, 1974, Volume 4, 1975, Volume 8, 1978, Volume 11, 1979, Volume 15, 1980, Volume 36, 1986.

Corman, Cid, editor, *The Gist of Origin,* Viking, 1975.

Creeley, Robert, *For Love: Poems 1950-1960,* Scribner, 1962.

Creeley, *Words,* Perishable Press, 1965.

Creeley, *A Sense of Measure,* Calder & Boyars, 1972.

Creeley, *Hello,* Hawk Press, 1976, expanded edition published as *Hello: A Journal, February 29-May 3, 1976,* New Directions, 1978.

Creeley, *Later,* Toothpaste, 1978, expanded edition, New Directions, 1979.

Creeley, *Was That a Real Poem and Other Essays,* edited by Allen, Four Seasons Foundation, 1979.

Creeley, *The Collected Poems of Robert Creeley, 1945-1975,* University of California Press, 1982.

Creeley, *Mirrors,* New Directions, 1983.

Creeley and Allen, editors, *New American Story,* Grove, 1965.

Creeley and Allen, editors, *The New Writing in the U.S.A.,* Penguin, 1967.

Dictionary of Literary Biography, Gale, Volume 5: *American Poets since World War II,* 1980, Volume 16: *The Beats: Literary Bohemians in Postwar America,* 1983.

Edelberg, Cynthia Dubin, *Robert Creeley's Poetry: A Critical Introduction,* University of New Mexico Press, 1978.

Ford, Arthur L., *Robert Creeley,* Twayne, 1978.

Novik, Mary, *Robert Creeley: An Inventory, 1945-1970,* Kent State University Press, 1973.

Olson, Charles, *Mayan Letters,* edited by Creeley, Divers Press, 1953, Grossman, 1968.

Olson, *The Human Universe,* Auerhan, 1965.

Paul, Sherman, *The Lost America of Love,* Louisiana State University Press, 1981.

Sheffler, Ronald Anthony, *The Development of Robert Creeley's Poetry,* University of Massachusetts, 1971.

Wilson, John, editor, *Robert Creeley's Life and Work: A Sense of Increment,* University of Michigan Press, 1987.

PERIODICALS

American Book Review, May/June, 1984.
American Poetry Review, November/December, 1976.
Atlantic, November, 1962, February, 1968, October, 1977.
Books Abroad, autumn, 1967.
Book Week, June 4, 1967.
Boundary 2, spring, 1975, spring and fall (special two-volume issue on Creeley), 1978.
Cambridge Quarterly, summer, 1969.
Canadian Forum, August, 1967, September, 1970.
Christian Science Monitor, October 9, 1969.
Commonweal, December 10, 1965.
Contemporary Literature, spring, 1972.
Critique, spring, 1964.
Encounter, February, 1969.
Fifties, Volume 2, 1959.
Harper's, August, 1967, September, 1983.
Hudson Review, summer, 1963, summer, 1967, spring, 1970, summer, 1977.
Iowa Review, spring, 1982.
Kenyon Review, spring, 1970.
Kulchur, Number 3, 1961.
Library Journal, September 1, 1979.
Listener, March 23, 1967.
London Magazine, June/July, 1973.
Los Angeles Times Book Review, April 17, 1983, October 30, 1983, March 4, 1984, June 24, 1984.
Minnesota Review, Volume 8, number 2, 1968, Volume 9, number 1, 1969.
Modern Poetry Studies, winter, 1977.
Nation, August 25, 1962.
National Observer, October 30, 1967.
National Review, November 19, 1960.
New Leader, October 27, 1969.

New Republic, October 11, 1969, December 18, 1976.
New Statesman, August 6, 1965, March 10, 1987.
New York Review of Books, January 20, 1966, August 1, 1968.
New York Times, June 27, 1967.
New York Times Book Review, November 4, 1962, September 22, 1963, November 19, 1967, October 27, 1968, January 7, 1973, May 1, 1977, March 9, 1980, August 7, 1983, June 24, 1984, September 23, 1984.
Observer (London), September 6, 1970.
Open Letter, winter, 1976-77.
Paris Review, fall, 1968.
Parnassus, fall/winter, 1984.
Partisan Review, summer, 1968.
Poetry, March, 1954, May, 1958, September, 1958, March, 1963, April, 1964, August, 1966, January, 1968, March, 1968, August, 1968, May, 1970, December, 1970, September, 1984.
Publishers Weekly, March 18, 1968.
Sagetreib, Volume 1, number 3, 1982, Volume 3, number 2, 1984.
Saturday Review, August 4, 1962, December 11, 1965, June 3, 1967.
Sewanee Review, winter, 1961.
Southwest Review, winter, 1964.
Time, July 12, 1971.
Times Literary Supplement, March 16, 1967, August 7, 1970, November 12, 1970, December 11, 1970, May 20, 1977, May 30, 1980, February 20, 1981, November 4, 1983.
Village Voice, October 22, 1958, December 10, 1979, November 25, 1981.
Virginia Quarterly Review, summer, 1968, winter, 1972, spring, 1973.
Western Humanities Review, spring, 1970.
World Literature Today, autumn, 1984.
Yale Review, October, 1962, December, 1969, spring, 1970.

*   *   *

CREWS, Harry (Eugene) 1935-

PERSONAL: Born June 6, 1935, in Alma, Ga.; son of Ray (a farmer) and Myrtice (Haselden) Crews; married Sally Thornton Ellis, January 24, 1960 (divorced); children: Patrick Scott (deceased), Byron Jason. *Education:* University of Florida, B.A., 1960, M.S.Ed., 1962.

ADDRESSES: Home—1800 Northwest 8th Ave., Gainesville, Fla. 32601.

CAREER: Writer. Broward Junior College, Ft. Lauderdale, Fla., teacher of English, 1962-68; University of Florida, Gainesville, associate professor, 1968-74, professor of English, 1974-88. *Military service:* U.S. Marine Corps, 1953-56; became sergeant.

WRITINGS:

NOVELS

The Gospel Singer, Morrow, 1968.
Naked in Garden Hills, Morrow, 1969.
This Thing Don't Lead to Heaven, Morrow, 1970.
Karate Is a Thing of the Spirit, Morrow, 1971.
Car, Morrow, 1972.
The Hawk Is Dying, Knopf, 1973.
The Gypsy's Curse, Knopf, 1974.
A Feast of Snakes, Atheneum, 1976.
All We Need of Hell, Harper, 1987.
The Knockout Artist, Harper, 1988.

SHORT STORIES

The Enthusiast, Palaemon Press, 1981.
Two, Lord John, 1984.

Contributor of stories to *Florida Quarterly* and *Craft and Vision.*

OTHER

A Childhood: The Biography of a Place (autobiography), Harper, 1978.
Blood and Grits (nonfiction), Harper, 1979.
Florida Frenzy (essays and stories), University Presses of Florida, 1982.

Author of column "Grits" for *Esquire.* Contributor to *Sewanee Review, Georgia Review,* and *Playboy.*

WORK IN PROGRESS: A novel titled *Body,* about female bodybuilding; a play.

SIDELIGHTS: Reading novelist Harry Crews, Allen Shepherd maintains in the *Dictionary of Literary Biography,* "is not something one wants to do too much of at a single sitting; the intensity of his vision is unsettling." This vision is both comic and tragic, nostalgic and grotesque, and is focused on the American South where Crews was raised and still lives. His characters, often physically deformed or strangely obsessed, are grotesques in the southern gothic tradition, and his stories are violent and extreme. Michael Mewshaw, writing in the *Nation,* explains that Crews "has taken a cast of the misfit and malformed—freaks, side-show performers, psychopaths, cripples, midgets and catatonics—and yoked it to plots which are even more improbable than his characters." Frank W. Shelton of the *Southern Literary Journal* defines the world of Crews's fiction as "mysterious, violent and dangerous" and calls his vision "a lonely and extremely sad one." But Mewshaw does not find Crews's vision essentially sad. He finds that Crews is "beset by existential nausea but, like any normal American, is not blind to the humor of it all. Bleak, mordant, appalling, Harry Crews can also be hilarious." Vivian Mercier of the *World* echoes this idea, remarking that "reading Crews is a bit like undergoing major surgery with laughing gas." Crews has been most widely praised for six of his novels: *The Gospel Singer, Naked in Garden Hills, Karate Is a Thing of the Spirit, Car, The Hawk Is Dying,* and *A Feast of Snakes.* His autobiography, *A Childhood: The Biography of a Place,* which provides insights into the origins of his fiction, has also garnered critical appreciation.

Crews first began to create stories as a boy in rural Georgia during the Depression. Living in an area where, he claims in *A Childhood,* "there wasn't enough cash money . . . to close up a dead man's eyes," Crews and his friends found a wonderland in the Sears, Roebuck mail order catalog. The boys called the catalog their dreambook because the models seemed unnaturally perfect to them, and the merchandise was far beyond their reach. While poring over the catalog pictures, Crews entertained his friends by spinning stories about the models and products. "I had decided that all the people in the catalog were related," he explains in *A Childhood,* "not necessarily blood kin but knew one another. . . . And it was out of this knowledge that I first began to make up stories."

After serving four years in the U.S. Marines, which he joined at the age of seventeen, Crews went to the University of Florida, where he was inspired by writer-in-residence Andrew Lyle to begin writing seriously. Crews studied Graham Greene's novel *The End of the Affair* while learning to write. He tells Steve Oney in the *New York Times Book Review* that he picked the book apart to see "how in the hell you do it." Crews reduced the novel

to numbers: how many characters, how many scenes, how many rooms, and so on. Then he wrote a novel following that formula exactly. "It was the bad novel I knew it would be," Crews remembers. "But by doing it I learned more about writing fiction and writing a novel . . . than I had from any class."

Crews writes of his native Georgia in *The Gospel Singer,* his first published novel. A popular traveling evangelist, the Gospel Singer appears in his hometown of Enigma during a concert tour. His local sweetheart has recently been murdered and, it is suspected, raped by a black man. The Singer is trailed into town by the Freak Fair, a sideshow of human oddities—including the show's owner, a man with an oversized foot—working the crowds attracted by the Singer's revival meetings. When the accused murderer is threatened with lynching, the Gospel Singer tries to save him by revealing that the murdered woman was not in fact a violated virgin but "the biggest whore who ever walked in Enigma," as Shepherd writes. In the resulting chaos the townspeople lynch both men.

Response to *The Gospel Singer* was generally favorable. Though Walter Sullivan of *Sewanee Review* finds the book has "all the hallmarks of a first novel: it is energetic but uneven, competent but clumsy, not finally satisfactory but memorable nonetheless," he believes that "Crews has a good eye, an excellent ear for voices, and a fine dramatic sense." Martin Levin of the *New York Times Book Review* thinks *The Gospel Singer* "has a nice wild flavor and a dash of Grand Guignol strong enough to meet the severe standards of Southern decadence." And Guy Davenport of *National Review* calls the novel "a frenetic sideshow of Georgia poor white trash and their Hochkultur."

Crews followed *The Gospel Singer* with *Naked in Garden Hills,* a book Jean Stafford of the *New York Times Book Review* believes "lives up to and beyond the shining promise of . . . 'The Gospel Singer.' It is southern Gothic at its best, a Hieronymus Bosch landscape in Dixie inhabited by monstrous, darling pets." The novel revolves around the almost helpless Mayhugh Aaron, known as the Fat Man because of his six-hundred-pound frame, and his valet John Henry Williams, a tiny black man who takes care of him. Fat Man owns most of Garden Hills, a town where the local phosphate mine is the only source of employment. When the mine is exhausted and closed, the town faces financial collapse. To avoid ruin, Dolly Ferguson opens a nightclub with go-go dancers and a sideshow to attract the tourist trade. She wants Fat Man as her star sideshow exhibit, but he refuses. As his employees, including Williams the valet, are one by one hired away by Dolly, and as his financial situation deteriorates, the Fat Man is reduced to a humiliated and helpless figure. He is finally forced to join the sideshow. "Bleeding, beaten by the mob of tourists, naked, and drooling, he crawls to his waiting cage and is lifted high in the light," Shepherd recounts.

Writing in the *New York Times Book Review,* Jonathan Yardley finds *Naked in Garden Hills* "a convincing grotesque of a rotting American landscape and its decadent inhabitants." Shelton believes the novel "treats religion in an almost allegorical way." He cites the novel's title as a reference to the Garden of Eden, sees Jack O'Boylan, the out-of-state mine owner, as a God figure, and pictures Dolly Ferguson as a kind of savior meant to restore the town. But the novel's ending, in which "everyone is consumed by Dolly's voracious appetite for success," shows that "man's desire to find meaning in his life leads to degradation, exploitation and the denial of love," Shelton writes.

A religious dimension can also be found in *Karate Is a Thing of the Spirit.* In this novel Crews writes of an outlaw karate class that meets on a Florida beach and is barred from tournament competition because of its deadly reputation. John Kaimon wanders into this circle and becomes a member, undergoing the rigorous training under the hot sun. The star member of the class, brown belt Gaye Nell Odell, becomes pregnant, possibly by Kaimon, and at novel's end the couple drive out of town together. Shelton finds both Kaimon and Odell searching for something—something they both find in the discipline of karate. The training, Shelton argues, "is an almost religious ritual through which people attempt to link and fulfill body and spirit." John Deck of the *New York Times Book Review* observes that, after a slow start, "the novel takes off, in the manner of a fire storm, rushing at amazing speed, eating up the oxygen, scorching everything it touches."

In *Car* Crews examines another physical discipline, this one far less common than karate. Herman Mack, whose family is in the auto junkyard business, decides it is his destiny to eat an automobile, four ounces at a time each day. His daily ingestion of the cut-up auto is broadcast on national television as a sports event. At first pleased with his instant notoriety, Herman falls in love with a prostitute and ends by abandoning his spectacle before it is finished. Yardley calls the ending "mere sentimentality" and a "flabby resolution," but also believes the novel "a marvelous idea" and "exceedingly funny, indeed painfully so." The reviewer for the *Times Literary Supplement* finds the novel "a satire on two alleged vices of the American people: an extravagant fondness for motor-cars, and a taste for ghoulish spectacle." Christopher Lehmann-Haupt of the *New York Times* also sees larger implications in the story, concluding that *Car* "may very well be the best metaphor yet made up about America's passionate love affair with the automobile."

A character's obsession also dominates Crews's novel *The Hawk Is Dying*. George Gattling becomes obsessed with training a wild hawk, an obsession that estranges him from his family and friends. But his efforts eventually reach fruition when "the hawk has finally been 'manned,' and flies free to kill and return again to Gattling's hand," resulting in "one moment of absolute value—and hence absolute beauty," as the critic for the *Times Literary Supplement* explains. The story is told in "comic-horrific scenes," the critic remarks. Mercier also finds this odd mix in the novel, writing that "beauty and pity and terror coexist with satire and grotesque humor." Similarly, Phoebe Adams of *Atlantic* calls *The Hawk is Dying* "a bizarre mixture of tragedy and farce." But she goes on to say that, though "the events of this novel are hardly realistic . . ., the book becomes immensely convincing because the underlying pattern of desperation over wasted time and neglected abilities is real and recognizable."

Crews examines a town's obsession with rattlesnakes in *A Feast of Snakes*. He fictionalizes a unique yearly custom in Mystic, Georgia, where the townspeople hold a Rattlesnake Roundup at which they crown a rattlesnake queen, hold a snake fight, and even dine on rattlesnake. The novel follows local resident Joe Lon Mackey, who is unhappily married, illiterate, and bitter abut his life. Crews shows the pressures which drive Mackey to go on a murderous rampage at the snake roundup.

The gruesome events leading up to this final outburst of violence are seen by many critics to be expertly handled by Crews. "Crews," Paul D. Zimmerman writes in *Newsweek*, "has an ugly knack for making the most sordid sequences amusing, for evoking an absolutely venomous atmosphere, unredeemed by charity or hope. Few writers could pull off the sort of finale that has mad-eyed red-necks rushing in sudden bursts across a snake-scattered, bonfire-bright field, their loins enflamed by the local beauty contestants, their blood racing with whisky, their hearts

ready for violence. Crews does." The critic for the *New Yorker* judges Crews to be "a writer of extraordinary power. Joe Lon is a monster, but we are forced to accept him as human, and even as sympathetic. Mr. Crews' story makes us gag, but he holds us, in awe and admiration, to the sickening end."

Crews's nonfiction book *A Childhood* gives some insight into the sources of his fiction. In this book Crews recounts the first six years of his life. It was a period, he claims, when "what has been most significant in my life had all taken place." Crews's father died when he was two years old. His mother remarried his uncle, a man she later left because of his violent rages. Crews had a bout with polio, which paralyzed his legs for a time and forced him to hobble on the floor. A fall into a tub of scalding water, used for removing the skin off slaughtered hogs, removed the first layer of skin on most of Crews's body. "The skin on the top of the wrist and the back of my hand, along with the fingernails," he remembers in the book, "all just turned loose and slid on down to the ground." Crews recalls the poverty of this period for the *New York Times Book Review:* "None of the kids I played with ate very well—bless their hearts. We kind of came up on a steady diet of biscuits made with lard and water, no milk. Hardly ate any meat whatsoever. We ate clay to make up for mineral deficiency. I know it sounds kind of pitiful. I didn't think it was pitiful then, don't now. It's just the way it was." Roy Blount, Jr., comments in the *Chicago Tribune Book World*, "If any writer as accomplished as Crews has ever come through so much and from so far behind I would like for somebody to write in and tell me."

The book's subtitle, *The Biography of a Place*, refers to rural Georgia's Bacon County, where Crews's family lived on a series of tenant farms. Despite the hardships of his childhood, Crews presents the people of his home county in a warm, honest, and unapologetic manner. He tells of the faith healers who tried to cure his polio; of the old black nurse who threatened him with her hexing powers; and of the family friend who robbed their smokehouse on the night Crews's father died. As Crews recounts, "It was a world in which survival depended on raw courage, a courage born out of desperation and sustained by a lack of alternatives." Robert Sherrill of the *New York Times Book Review* admits: "It's easy to despise poor folks. 'A Childhood' makes it more difficult. It raises almost to a level of heroism these people who seem of a different century."

Critical reaction to *A Childhood* was generally positive, with several critics citing Crews's restraint in recounting his life. Mewshaw, for example, finds that throughout the book Crews "maintains a precarious balance between sentiment and sensation, memory and madness, and manages to convince the reader of two mutually exclusive imperatives which have shaped his life—the desire to escape Bacon County and the constant ineluctable need to go back, if only in memory." The *New Yorker* critic writes that Crews remembers his childhood with "a sense of grateful escape and shattering loss which have the confusing certainty of truth." Allen Lacy of *Chronicle Review* calls *A Childhood* "a book of great emotional power, fashioned out of often savage stuff by a superb craftsman who possesses both a comic eye and a tragic sense of life."

Assessing Crews's career, Clarence Petersen in the *Chicago Tribune Book World* sees autobiography as a primary component in all of his fiction. Petersen writes that Crews's "writing is informed by an unimaginably brutal and grotesque childhood and by a deep love of language, literature, nature, blood sports and his own kind of people—namely rural, Southern, harddrinking, honest-measure hell-raisers." Shaun O'Connell also believes that

Crews draws heavily upon his own life experiences for his fiction, maintaining in an article for the *New Boston Review* that his books "simultaneously incorporate and transcend his personal history. . . . Crews has concocted elaborate metaphors, images more sustainingly inventive than most metafictionists, tropes which subsume his past, conceits which widen our sense of the possible as they make the magical and the freakish more plausible."

Crews's own explanation of how he writes stresses the spontaneous nature of his work and places little emphasis on his subject matter. Speaking to Al Burt of the *Miami Herald,* Crews reveals how he begins a novel: "I start with a place and somebody and then I just try to know the story. . . . I don't give a rat's ass where the novel's going." When writing *Naked in Garden Hills,* for example, he began with the first line in the book and the idea for the Fat Man character and began to write. Crews claims that the story itself is not important. "The important thing is the writer whose perceptions all of this is being filtered through. The writer's vision of the world," he tells Burt. "It doesn't matter what he writes about."

But some observers judge Crews's stories to be excessive. "His harshest critics claim that Crews always pushes things too far—to the point where his characters turn into caricatures and his plots become cartoons," Mewshaw explains. One such critic is Sarah Blackburn of the *New York Times Book Review,* who describes *The Hawk Is Dying* as "a festival of mangled animals, tortured sexuality and innocence betrayed." James Atlas in *Time* calls Crews "a Southern gothic novelist who often makes William Faulkner look pastoral by comparison." Crews's novel *A Feast of Snakes* was even banned in the Republic of South Africa.

Admirers of Crews, however, cite his ability to transform unusual or extreme subjects into credible, moving stories. Doris Grumbach, writing in *Saturday Review,* admits that Crews's novels possess a "bizarre, mad, violent, and tragic quality," but believes that Crews "has a sympathy for maimed and deformed characters, a love of strange situations, and the talent to make it all, somehow, entirely believable." Shepherd, speaking of *Car, The Hawk Is Dying,* and *A Feast of Snakes* in an article for *Critique: Studies in Modern Fiction,* argues that Crews displays "in these strangely powerful outlandish, excessive, grotesquely alive novels a gift at once formidable frightening." Crews is also praised for his humor. Davenport declares him "a comic novelist of magnificent gifts," while George Cohen of the *Chicago Tribune Book World* calls Crews "one of the most perceptive and amusing writers around." Grumbach concludes her assessment by calling Crews "one of the most consistently interesting novelists now writing" and a "storytelling master."

Despite the widespread attention Crews earned from writing novels, he took an eleven-year respite from the genre, during which time he produced the nonfiction *Blood and Grits* and an essay and story collection titled *Florida Frenzy.* The author resumed writing longer works of fiction in late 1980s, producing the novels *All We Need of Hell* and *The Knockout Artist.* Like his books from previous decades, the works have been acclaimed for their gritty Southern flavor and offbeat characters. *All We Need of Hell* concerns Duffy Deeter, an overly driven attorney who constantly seeks to prove his manliness. When his wife throws him out of the house, Duffy commences a spree of exercise and drinking, a session that ends when a former enemy teaches Duffy the virtues of love, friendship, and forgiveness.

"If 'All We Need of Hell' ran according to Harry Crews's earlier fictional form," remarks Christopher Lehmann-Haupt in the *New York Times,* "Duffy's misadventures would lead him to

some bizarre or even ghoulish fate." Noting, though, that "something new has been added" to Crews's fiction, the reviewer laments that "there is something decidedly forced and even sentimental about [the story's positive] turn of events. . . . We come away from the novel regarding it as a distinctly lesser effort." Beaufort Cranford writing in the *Detroit News* was similarly disappointed, commenting that "we readers of Crews suddenly find ourselves on alarmingly cheerful ground. . . . [The ending to] *All We Need of Hell* is a . . . shock, much like a sudden infusion of sugar." Despite complaints that Crews has softened his fiction, Lehmann-Haupt concludes that "we can't help forgiving him for it. There's still such a vividness to his characters. There's still such ease to his prose. . . . [And] he still has the power to make us smile and even laugh out loud."

Crews followed *All We Need of Hell* with *The Knockout Artist* in 1988. The story focuses on Eugene Biggs, a promising young boxer whose career ends after he develops a glass jaw and is rendered incapable of further fighting. To survive, Eugene earns money by staging shows wherein he knocks himself out. Humiliated by his own exploits and burdened by an assortment of unusual friends, Eugene finally decides to break the destructive pattern of his life and becomes a boxing trainer.

Like in *All We Need of Hell, The Knockout Artist*'s ending disappointed some reviewers. Lehmann-Haupt, for example, writes: "When Eugene Biggs makes up his mind to stop knocking himself out and to walk away from all the losers who are dragging him down, it has the effect of turning his hell into a comic book, where the colors are brighter than the world's and the people are less than real." Don Robertson in the *Washington Post Book World,* though, disagrees, declaring that "at the book's conclusion . . ., Eugene Biggs has been, in effect, a Hemingway hero, and he's responded heroically with that quality Hemingway so famously called grace under pressure." Summing up his opinion of *The Knockout Artist* while making reference to Crews's previous fiction, Robertson concludes: "It's masterful, and it's moving, and it's quite funny at times . . ., and here's hoping Harry Crews prevails and flourishes and gives us more karate and snakes and grits and blood and hell and all the rest of that stuff. Hooray for him, and hooray for this mean little masterpiece he's wound up and so skillfully thrown in the world's astonished collective face."

BIOGRAPHICAL/CRITICAL SOURCES:

BOOKS

Authors in the News, Volume I, Gale, 1976.
Contemporary Literary Criticism, Gale, Volume VI, 1976, Volume XXIII, 1983, Volume ILIX, 1988.
Crews, Harry, *A Childhood: The Biography of a Place,* Harper, 1978.
Dictionary of Literary Biography, Volume VI: *American Novelists since World War II, Second Series,* Gale, 1980.
Jeffrey, David K., editor, *A Grit's Triumph: Essays on the Works of Harry Crews,* Associated Faculty Press, 1983.

PERIODICALS

America, December 23, 1978.
Atlantic, April, 1973.
Chicago Tribune Book World, October 29, 1978, March 11, 1979, July 18, 1982, July 31, 1983.
Chronicle Review, April 16, 1979.
Contemporary Review, April, 1977.
Critique: Studies in Modern Fiction, September, 1978.
Detroit News, February 1, 1987.
Los Angeles Times Book Review, May 3, 1987, May 22, 1988.

Maclean's, March 26, 1979.
Miami Herald, June 30, 1974.
Nation, February 3, 1979.
National Review, April 21, 1970.
New Boston Review, February-March, 1979.
New Republic, March 31, 1973.
Newsweek, August 2, 1976.
New Yorker, July 15, 1974, July 26, 1976, November 6, 1978.
New York Times, March 2, 1972, March 21, 1973, April 30, 1974, July 12, 1976, December 11, 1978, February 6, 1979, January 12, 1987, February 19, 1987, April 18, 1988.
New York Times Book Review, February 18, 1968, April 13, 1969, April 26, 1970, April 25, 1971, February 27, 1972, March 25, 1973, March 10, 1974, June 2, 1974, June 23, 1974, September 12, 1976, December 24, 1978, March 25, 1979, February 1, 1987, May 1, 1988.
People, June 8, 1987.
Prairie Schooner, spring, 1974.
Publishers Weekly, April 15, 1988.
Saturday Review, November 11, 1978.
Sewanee Review, winter, 1969.
Shenandoah, summer, 1974.
Southern Literary Journal, spring 1980.
Spectator, January 22, 1977.
Time, September 13, 1976, October 23, 1978, March 5, 1979.
Times Literary Supplement, February 2, 1973, January 11, 1974, January 24, 1975, January 21, 1977, December 7, 1979.
Village Voice, October 30, 1978.
Washington Post, March 29, 1979.
Washington Post Book World, April 15, 1973, July 24, 1983, May 1, 1988.
World, April 24, 1973.

*   *   *

CRICHTON, (John) Michael 1942-
(Jeffery Hudson, John Lange; Michael Douglas, a joint pseudonym)

PERSONAL: Surname is pronounced "Cry-ton"; born October 23, 1942, in Chicago, Ill.; son of John Henderson (a corporate president) and Zula (Miller) Crichton; married Joan Radam, January 1, 1965 (divorced, 1970); married Kathy St. Johns, 1978 (divorced, 1980). *Education:* Harvard University, A.B. (summa cum laude), 1964, M.D., 1969.

ADDRESSES: Office—2049 Century Park E. 4000, Los Angeles, Calif. 90067.

CAREER: Salk Institute for Biological Studies, La Jolla, Calif., post-doctoral fellow, 1969-70; full-time writer of books and films; director of films and television movies, including a Movie of the Week, "Pursuit" (based on his novel *Binary*), American Broadcasting Co., 1972, "Westworld," Metro-Goldwyn-Mayer, 1973, "Coma," United Artists, 1978, "The Great Train Robbery," United Artists, 1979, "Looker," Warner Bros., 1981, and "Runaway," Tri-Star Pictures, 1984.

MEMBER: Mystery Writers Guild of America West, Authors Guild, Authors League of America, Academy of Motion Picture Arts and Sciences, Director's Guild of America, P.E.N., Aesculaepian Society, Phi Beta Kappa.

AWARDS, HONORS: Edgar Award of the Mystery Writers of America, 1968, for *A Case of Need,* and 1979, for film "The Great Train Robbery"; Association of American Medical Writers writer of the year award, 1970, for *Five Patients: The Hospital Explained.*

WRITINGS:

The Andromeda Strain (novel; Book-of-the-Month Club and Literary Guild selection), Knopf, 1969.
Five Patients: The Hospital Explained (nonfiction; Doubleday Book Club selection), Knopf, 1970.
(With brother Douglas Crichton, under joint pseudonym Michael Douglas) *Dealing: Or, the Berkeley-to-Boston Forty-Brick Lost-Bag Blues,* Knopf, 1971.
The Terminal Man (novel; Book-of-the-Month Club selection), Knopf, 1972.
Westworld (also see below), Bantam, 1974.
The Great Train Robbery (also see below; Book-of-the-Month Club and Reader's Digest selection), Knopf, 1975.
Eaters of the Dead: The Manuscript of Ibn Fadlan, Relating His Experiences with the Northmen in A.D. 922, Knopf, 1976.
Jasper Johns (nonfiction), Abrams, 1977.
Congo, Knopf, 1980.
Electronic Life: How to Think about Computers (nonfiction), Knopf, 1983.
Sphere, Knopf, 1987.
Travels, Knopf, 1988.
Jurassic Park, Knopf, 1990.

SCREENPLAYS

"Westworld" (based on his novel of the same title), Metro-Goldwyn-Mayer, 1973.
"Coma" (based on a novel of the same title by Robin Cook), United Artists, 1977.
"The Great Train Robbery" (based on his novel of the same title), United Artists, 1978.
"Looker," Warner Bros., 1981.
"Runaway," Tri-Star Pictures, 1984.

UNDER PSEUDONYM JOHN LANGE, EXCEPT AS INDICATED

Odds On, New American Library, 1966.
Scratch One, New American Library, 1967.
(Under pseudonym Jeffery Hudson) *A Case of Need,* New American Library, 1968.
Easy Go, New American Library, 1968, published as *The Last Tomb,* Bantam, 1974.
Zero Cool, New American Library, 1969.
The Venom Business, New American Library, 1969.
Drug of Choice, New American Library, 1970.
Grave Descend, New American Library, 1970.
Binary, Knopf, 1971.

SIDELIGHTS: From his pseudonymous potboilers to his best-selling novels, from his popular films to his critically acclaimed nonfiction studies, Michael Crichton has found success in virtually every field into which he has ventured. Best known for his suspense-filled novels *The Andromeda Strain* and *The Terminal Man* and as the writer-director of such like-minded movies as "Looker" and "Coma," Crichton has an "approach to writing [that] is consistent from work to work," according to Robert L. Sims in his *Dictionary of Literary Biography* article about the writer. "He fully exploits the techniques available to the omniscient author, controlling every facet of his plots, which are constructed as suspensefully as [an Alfred] Hitchcock film."

In fact, famed film director Hitchcock was a major influence on the young Crichton. "I'd always wanted to direct movies," he tells Ned Smith of *American Way.* "My first hero was Alfred Hitchcock—I knew who [he] was long before I knew who Charles Dickens was. I guess one of the reasons I identify with him now is that it seems to me we get a lot of the same criticism." Some of that criticism focuses on the fact that Crichton's heroes, like Hitchcock's, "are one-dimensional figures whose psychological makeups are determined by the particular drama in which they are involved," as Sims explains. "By and large, [Crichton's] characters tend to be exceptional people (scientists, psychiatrists, doctors, etc.) possessing specialized skills, who find themselves in extraordinary situations. [The author] often uses flashbacks to develop his characters. Although his plots are more memorable than his characters, the success of his fiction depends on human fallibility."

A Harvard University-trained doctor and scientist, Crichton infuses his fiction with highly-detailed jargon, sometimes fabricating language and fact. Such is the case with *The Great Train Robbery,* an adventure set in Victorian England. The author remarks to Smith that, while the research for his novel was extensive, "many times I'd make something up, and then, just by accident, later discover it was true. [But] I don't worry about people taking it as true. Basically, I think the feeling, the tone, is accurate." As for his use of slang in the novel, "a lot of it's real, but a lot of it isn't. The English publishers went over the manuscript very carefully with an eye to weeding out Americanisms, but it's a very 'outsiders' book, which was intentional too. I didn't live in eighteen fifty-five; I'm not English. [*The Great Train Robbery* is] about how much you really know, a game of trying to be true to what you can know, and trying to give the impression you weren't making up very much, when you were, in fact, making up everything." This exegis can almost serve as a summary of Crichton's body of fiction. As Sims comments, the author "prefaces his novels with scientific, medical, and historical introductions and adds minidigressions which establish verisimilitude and promote suspension of disbelief in his readers." Crichton also likes writing around established forms: *The Terminal Man* is his acknowledged revision of Mary Shelley's gothic classic *Frankenstein;* a 1976 work, *Eaters of the Dead: The Manuscript of Ibn Fadlan, Relating His Experiences with the Northmen in A.D. 922,* has clear ties to *Beowulf.*

And with *Congo,* the author created a tale reminiscent of *King Solomon's Mines.* The novel centers on a trek through darkest Africa undertaken by a band of corporate-sponsored diamond hunters who are searching for "the big prize: a mother lode of industrial blue diamonds—type IIb boron-coated—which when developed would render nuclear energy and weapons obsolete," as Christopher Schemering relates in a *Washington Post* review. Accompanying scientists Karen Ross and Peter Elliot and bush guide Charles Munro is Amy, a gorilla who communicates with humans by using sign language. "Having set up his premise, the action comes fast at regular intervals, with each new vicissitude—kidnapping, machine-gun fire, unfriendly Pygmies, killer monkeys, cannibals, volcanoes, missile attacks and tsetse flies—bumping into the next with such impatient impertinence that one suspects Crichton can't wait for the next disaster," Schemering states.

Don Strachan, reviewing the novel for the *Los Angeles Times,* is one of several critics who find that, "as is too often the case in sci-fi thrillers, [Congo's] machines are more exciting than its people. Munro, jungle guide extraordinaire, enjoys a dramatic buildup before he appears, but once onstage, he shows nary a sign of individuality. [Karen Ross] is inhumanly ruthless. Peter Elliot exists only as the scientist studying Amy the gorilla, [and Amy,] oddly, is the one character with human dimensions. She may have a child's vocabulary (620 words) but she has a child's vulnerability as well, a trait made more endearing by the cold-bloodedness of 'Congo's' human world." However, adds Strachan, "I don't want to leave the impression that [the novel] isn't an enjoyable trek. Crichton chooses ingenious, imaginative and

speculative approaches to issues that move us on very deep levels. He may not be a literary force, but as a storyteller he's at once informative and entertaining."

Even before *Congo* was published, its author had already sold the film rights to his book. As a screenwriter and director, Crichton "is in increasing demand" in Hollywood, according to *People* magazine's Andrea Chambers, "even though he has yet to direct any but his own screenplays." Comparing his early career in medicine to that of his one in films, Crichton adds: "I think what I'm doing is socially useful. People need the mirrors of experience they find in books and movies. They want to feel they're not alone. People undervalue movie directors and overvalue doctors. One is as good as another." With the exception of "The Great Train Robbery," which Crichton directed as an old-fashioned action-adventure film, all of his movies have explored the far reaches of science, from grisly medical experimentation ("Coma") to androids run amok ("Westworld"). In the process these films often evoke high-tech terrors reminiscent of *The Andromeda Strain* and *The Terminal Man,* both of which were adapted for the screen by other writers.

But the author's real message in these scientific suspense tales, according to Sims, is that, "for the immediate future at least, technological innovations offer the same possibilities and limitations as their human creators." Indeed, Crichton the nonfiction writer is interested in informing his readers about what wonders the new technology can offer. In this vein he produced *Electronic Life: How to Think about Computers,* a layman's guide to hard-and-software usage. The author "insists that the greatest challenge of his book was in attempting to coax readers out of their anxieties about using computers," says Richard Kay in *Publishers Weekly.* "There are so many people who react viscerally when they see a computer," Crichton observes to Kay. "They see a machine with green letters and they simply back away. Of course, they're reacting emotionally. You don't have to use a computer in your life if you don't want to, but it's unfortunate when people decide not to use computers because of fear."

The author seeks to quell this fear by using direct, straightforward information mixed with a good deal of confidence-inspiring prose. "You're a general, not a private," he writes in the introduction to *Electronic Life.* "In fact, there are no privates. Step to the mirror and salute yourself—then go and carry out your own orders." Remarks a *Time* reviewer: "The book's great value is common sense. It recommends that no computer should be bought on the promise of what will be available next week or next month, because such promises are seldom kept. And the author gently reproves old computer hands irritated by the latest category of social bore, the newly minted fanatic." *Los Angeles Times Book Review* critic Richard O'Reilly notes that Crichton "also has some good insights on the relationship of science and society, praising the irrational side of existence in a way you might not expect from a person so enmeshed in science. Computers are 'most easily used to create models that fit the scientific world view,' Crichton writes, which is fine 'so long as the power of the machines does not seduce us into allowing the machines to define reality for us.' "

In 1988, Crichton published *Sphere,* a novel about the oceanic excavation of an alien spacecraft believed to have landed on earth three centuries ago. The author's 1989 book *Travels* is an autobiographical travelogue, chronicling both his worldwide journeys and his spiritual growth.

"Crichton says he has 'never, ever been sorry' he gave up medicine" to pursue his other careers, notes Connie Lauerman in the *Chicago Tribune.* "He once said he was 'a pottering amateur,' not dedicated enough to practice medicine." The writer-director himself comments to Lauerman: "Most of the doctors I know will come to the point where they will be asking themselves, 'How important is what I'm doing; am I really helping people?' An awful lot of the people they see, they can't help. Many physicians have misgivings about what they're doing, though the public doesn't perceive that. I think even with books and movies I remember Orson Welles once said you get to a point in your life where you wonder if this is a fit occupation for a grown man. I don't know if asking the question is a function of who you are, that some people will ask that question because that's the kind of person they are and some people will never ask that question."

Crichton told *CA:* "I think there is [always] energy available to do what interests you—that's the easiest thing to do. The hardest thing to do is what doesn't interest you; that's when you have to drag yourself out of bed in the morning. So actually I'm assisted by the degree to which I can get up and say, well, I'll just do whatever I want to do."

MEDIA ADAPTATIONS: The Andromeda Strain was adapted into a film by Universal in 1971; *Binary* was adapted into a television movie entitled "Pursuit," for American Broadcasting Co. in 1972; *A Case of Need* was adapted into the film "The Carey Treatment," for Metro-Goldwyn Mayer (MGM) in 1973; *The Terminal Man* was adapted into a film for MGM in 1974; *Congo* has been optioned for filming.

AVOCATIONAL INTERESTS: Art, tennis, scuba diving.

BIOGRAPHICAL/CRITICAL SOURCES:

BOOKS

Contemporary Literary Criticism, Gale, Volume 2, 1974, Volume 6, 1976, Volume 54, 1989.
Crichton, Michael, *Electronic Life: How to Think about Computers,* Knopf, 1983.
Dictionary of Literary Biography Yearbook: 1981, Gale, 1982.

PERIODICALS

American Way, September, 1975.
Best Sellers, August 15, 1968.
Chicago Tribune, February 12, 1979, October 10, 1983, June 24, 1987, April 17, 1988.
Commonweal, August 8, 1969.
Detroit News, December 28, 1980.
Harper's, August, 1969.
Life, May 30, 1969, June 19, 1970.
Los Angeles Times, December 28, 1980.
Los Angeles Times Book Review, September 4, 1983, July 12, 1987, April 24, 1988.
Nation, June 15, 1970, November 26, 1977.
Newsweek, June 26, 1969, June 8, 1970, May 8, 1972, June 23, 1975.
New Yorker, October 5, 1968.
New York Times, February 9, 1969, May 30, 1969, June 10, 1975, February 2, 1978, October 30, 1981, September 16, 1983.
New York Times Book Review, August 18, 1968, August 2, 1970, April 30, 1972, June 22, 1975, April 25, 1976, December 7, 1980, February 1, 1981, July 12, 1987, June 26, 1988.
People, February 18, 1981.
Publishers Weekly, July 15, 1983.
Saturday Review, June 28, 1969, August 30, 1969.
Time, June 6, 1969, May 8, 1972, July 14, 1975, October 24, 1983.
Times Literary Supplement, October 16, 1969, July 17, 1981, October 21, 1988.

Washington Post, November 24, 1980.
Washington Post Book World, June 14, 1987.

*   *   *

CROVES, Hal
    See TRAVEN, B.

*   *   *

CULLEN, Countee   1903-1946

PERSONAL: Birth-given name Countee LeRoy Porter; first name pronounced "Coun-tay"; born May 30, 1903, in Louisville, Ky. (some sources say New York City, or Baltimore, Md.); died of uremic poisoning, January 9, 1946, in New York City; buried in Woodlawn Cemetery, New York City; married Nina Yolande DuBois, April 9, 1928 (divorced, 1930); married Ida Mae Roberson, September 27, 1940. *Education:* New York University, B.A., 1925; Harvard University, M.A., 1926.

CAREER: Poet, columnist, editor, novelist, playwright, children's writer, and educator. Assistant editor and author of monthly column "The Dark Tower" for *Opportunity: Journal of Negro Life,* 1926-28; traveled back and forth between France and the United States, 1928-34; Frederick Douglass Junior High School, New York City, teacher of English, French, and creative writing, 1934-45.

MEMBER: New York Civic Club, Phi Beta Kappa, Alpha Delta Phi.

AWARDS, HONORS: Witter Bynner Prize for poetry for "Poems," John Reed Memorial Prize from Poetry magazine for "Threnody for a Brown Girl," Amy Spingarn Award from *Crisis* magazine for "Two Moods of Love," and second prize winner in Palm Poetry Contest for "Wisdom Cometh With the Years," all 1925; second prize winner in *Crisis* Poetry Contest, 1926, for "Thoughts in a Zoo"; Harmon Foundation Literary Award from National Association for the Advancement of Colored People (NAACP), 1927, for "distinguished achievement in literature by a Negro"; Guggenheim Foundation fellowship, France, 1928-30.

WRITINGS:

POETRY

Color (includes "Heritage," "Atlantic City Waiter," "Near White," "To a Brown Boy," "For a Lady I Know," "Yet Do I Marvel," "Incident," "The Shroud of Color," "Oh, for a Little While Be Kind," "Brown Boy to Brown Girl," and "Pagan Prayer"), Harper, 1925, reprinted, Arno Press, 1969.
Copper Sun (includes "If Love Be Staunch," "The Love Tree," "Nocturne," "Threnody for a Brown Girl," and "To Lovers of Earth: Fair Warning"), decorations by Charles Cullen, Harper, 1927.
(Editor) *Caroling Dusk: An Anthology of Verse by Negro Poets,* decorations by Aaron Douglas, Harper, 1927, reprinted, 1974.
The Black Christ, and Other Poems (includes "The Black Christ," "Song of Praise," "Works to My Love," "In the Midst of Life," "Self Criticism," "To Certain Critics," and "The Wish"), decorations by Charles Cullen, Harper, 1929, reprinted, University Microfilms, 1973.
The Medea, and Some Poems (includes translation of Euripides' play *Medea,* "Scottsboro, Too, Is Worth Its Song," "Me-

dusa," "The Cat," "Only the Polished Skeleton," "Sleep," "After a Visit," and "To France"), Harper, 1935.

On These I Stand: An Anthology of the Best Poems of Countee Cullen (includes "Dear Friends and Gentle Hearts," "Christus natus est," and some previously unpublished poems), Harper, 1947.

OTHER

The Ballad of the Brown Girl: An Old Ballad Retold, illustrations and decorations by Charles Cullen, Harper, 1927.

(Author of introduction) Frank Ankenbrand and Isaac Benjamin, *The House of Vanity,* Leibman Press, 1928.

One Way to Heaven (novel), Harper, 1932, reprinted, AMS Press, 1975 (also see below).

(Contributor) Fred J. Ringel, editor, *America as Americans See It,* Harcourt, 1932.

The Lost Zoo (a Rhyme for the Young, but Not Too Young), illustrations by Charles Sebree, Harper, 1940, new edition, with illustrations by Joseph Low, Follett, 1969.

My Lives and How I Lost Them (juvenile; autobiography of fictional character Christopher Cat), drawings by Robert Reid Macguire, Harper, 1942, new edition, with illustrations by Rainey Bennett, Follett, 1971.

(With Owen Dodson) "The Third Fourth of July" (one-act play), published in *Theatre Arts,* 1946.

(With Arna Bontemps) "St. Louis Woman" (musical adaptation of Bontemps's novel *God Sends Sunday;* first produced at Martin Beck Theater in New York City, March 30, 1946), published in *Black Theatre,* edited by Lindsay Patterson, Dodd, 1971.

Also author of unpublished plays, including "Let the Day Perish" (with Waters Turpin), "The Spirit of Peace," and "Heaven's My Home" (an adaptation, with Harry Hamilton, of Cullen's novel, *One Way to Heaven*), and of book reviews.

Contributor to *Crisis, Phylon, Bookman, Harper's, American Mercury, Century, Nation, Poetry,* and other periodicals.

SIDELIGHTS: Countee Cullen was perhaps the most representative voice of the Harlem Renaissance. His life story is essentially a tale of youthful exuberance and talent of a star that flashed across the Afro-American firmament and then sank toward the horizon. When his paternal grandmother and guardian died in 1918, the fifteen-year-old Countee LeRoy Porter was taken into the home of the Reverend Frederick A. Cullen, the pastor of Salem Methodist Episcopal Church, Harlem's largest congregation. There the young Countee entered the approximate center of black politics and culture in the United States and acquired both the name and awareness of the influential clergyman who was later elected president of the Harlem chapter of the National Association for the Advancement of Colored People (NAACP).

In view of America's racial climate during the 1920s, Harlem was scarcely a serene place, but it was an enormously stimulating milieu for Afro-American intellectuals. The high hopes of the black community for acceptance and equality had turned to disillusionment at the end of World War I, when returning black soldiers all too often experienced unemployment and were otherwise mistreated. Resentment pulsated through black urban centers like Harlem, which had burgeoned during the war as black workers migrated there to fill jobs temporarily vacated by the diversion of white laborers into the military. For the first time in Afro-American history, a black urban consciousness conducive to the flowering of the arts was developing. From Harlem, the largest of the new, densely populated black urban communities

in which Cullen was listening and learning burst forth an outpouring of Afro-American arts known as the Harlem Renaissance.

While Cullen's informal education was shaped by his exposure to black ideas and yearnings, his formal education derived from almost totally white influences. This dichotomy heavily influenced his creative work and his criticism, particularly because he did extremely well at the white-dominated institutions he attended and won the approbation of white academia. In high school Cullen earned academic honors that in turn garnered him the posts of vice-president of his class and editor of the school newspaper, as well as prizes for poetry and oratory. His glory continued at New York University, where he obtained first or second prizes in a number of poetry contests, including the national Witter Bynner Contests for undergraduate poetry and contests sponsored by *Poetry* magazine. Harvard University's Irving Babbitt publicly lauded Cullen's "The Ballad of the Brown Girl," and in 1925, which proved a bumper year for the young man's harvest of literary prizes, Cullen graduated from New York University, was accepted into Harvard's masters program, and published his first volume of poetry, *Color.*

During the next four years Cullen reached his zenith. A celebrated young man about Harlem, he had in print by 1929 several books of his own poems and a collection of poetry he edited, *Caroling Dusk,* written by other Afro-Americans. His letters from Harvard to his Harlem friend Harold Jackman exuded self-satisfaction and sometimes the snide intolerance of the *enfant terrible.* The climax of those heady years may have come in 1928. That year Cullen was awarded a Guggenheim fellowship to write poetry in France, and he married Nina Yolande DuBois, the daughter of W. E. B. DuBois, a man who for decades was the acknowledged leader of the Afro-American intellectual community. Few social events in Harlem rivaled the magnitude of the latter event, and much of Harlem joined in the festivities that marked the joining of the Cullen and DuBois lineages, two of its most notable families.

Because of Cullen's success in both black and white cultures, and because of his romantic temperament, he formulated an aesthetic that embraced both cultures. He came to believe that art transcended race and that it could be used as a vehicle to minimize the distance between black and white peoples. When he chose as his models poet John Keats and to a lesser extent A. E. Housman, he did so not consciously to curry favor with white America but for four logical reasons: First, though there had been Afro-American poets, there was not yet an Afro-American poetic tradition—in any meaningful sense of the term—to draw upon. Second, the English poetic tradition was the one that was available to him—the one that had been taught to him in schools he attended. Third, he felt challenged to demonstrate that a black poet could excel within that traditional framework. And fourth, he felt absolutely free to choose as exemplars any poets in the world with whom he sensed a temperamental affinity (and he certainly had that affinity with Housman and, especially, Keats). In addition, he shared their romantic self-involvement; he had an ego that was sensitive to the slightest tremors and that needed expression to remain whole, and like Keats he had to believe in human perfectibility.

In poems such as "Heritage" and "Atlantic City Waiter," Cullen reflects the urge to reclaim African arts—a phenomenon called "Negritude" that was one of the motifs of the Harlem Renaissance. The cornerstone of his aesthetic, however, was the call for black-American poets to work conservatively, as he did, within English conventions. In his 1927 foreword to *Caroling Dusk,*

Cullen observed that "since theirs is . . . the heritage of the English language, their work will not present any serious aberration from poetic tendencies of their times." Braving the wrath of less moderate peers, he further stated that "negro poets, dependent as they are on the English language, may have more to gain from the rich background of English and American poetry than from any nebulous atavistic yearnings toward an African inheritance." Even the subtitle of the collection, *An Anthology of Verse by Negro Poets,* reflects his belief in the essential oneness of art; it implies no distinction between white poetry and black poetry, and it assumes there is only poetry, which in the case of *Caroling Dusk* is simply composed by Afro-American writers.

His dedication to oneness led Cullen to be cautious of any black writer's work that threatened to erect rather than pull down barricades between the races. Thus, in a February, 1926, "Dark Tower" column in which Cullen reviewed Langston Hughes's *The Weary Blues,* Cullen pressed Hughes not to be a "racial artist" and to omit jazz rhythms from his poems. In a later column he prodded black writers to censor themselves by avoiding "some things, some truths of Negro life and thought . . . that all Negroes know, but take no pride in." For Cullen, showcasing unpleasant realities would "but strengthen the bitterness of our enemies" and thereby weaken the bridge of art between blacks and whites.

Such warnings, however, did not prevent the critic Cullen from praising black artists whenever he found their work meritorious, even when it was overtly racial. In another of his "Dark Tower" columns, he complimented Amy Spingarn's *Pride and Humility,* for example, even though he thought its "clearest notes" were to be heard "in those poems which have a racial framework." Since his primary criterion for judging a work was always aesthetic, Cullen applauded any poetry that appealed to him, without regard to the color of the writer. He had good things to say about Edna St. Vincent Millay, E. A. Robinson, and Robert Frost, but he was less favorable toward such avant garde poets as Amy Lowell, in whose work he found little "for the hungry heart to feed upon." Generally, three principles informed his criticism: First, he tended to be more attracted to romantic rather than unromantic poetry. Second, he was conservative in his tastes and therefore put off by experimentation such as that of Amy Lowell. Third, although he put special effort into trying to further the interests of black artists, he was governed by a keen sense of impartiality and a commitment to bringing the races into closer harmony.

A paradox exists, however, between Cullen's philosophy and writing. While he argued that racial poetry was a detriment to the color-blindness he craved, he was at the same time so affronted by the racial injustice in America that his own best verse—indeed most of his verse—gave voice to racial protest. In fact, the title of Cullen's 1925 collection, *Color,* was not chosen unintentionally, nor did Cullen include sections with that same title in later volumes by accident. Both early and late in his career he was, in spite of himself, largely a racial poet. This is evident throughout Cullen's works from the *Color* pieces and the introduction of racial violence into his 1927 work *The Ballad of the Brown Girl* to the poems that he selected for the posthumously published *On These I Stand,* of which substantially more than half are racial poems.

Of the six identifiable racial themes in Cullen's poetry, the first is Negritude, or Pan-African impulse, a pervasive element of the 1920s international black literary movement that scholar Arthur P. Davis in a 1953 *Phylon* essay called "the alien-and-exile theme." Specific examples of this motif in Cullen's poetry in-

clude his attribution of descent from African kings to the girl featured in *The Ballad of the Brown Girl* as well as the submerged pride exhibited by the waiter in the poem "Atlantic City Waiter" whose graceful movement resulted from "Ten thousand years on jungle clues." Probably the best-known illustration of the Pan-African impulse in Cullen's poetry is found in "Heritage," where the narrator realizes that although he must suppress his African heritage, he cannot ultimately surrender his black heart and mind to white civilization. "Heritage," like most of the Negritude poems of the Harlem Renaissance and like political expression such as Marcus Garvey's popular back-to-Africa movement, powerfully suggests the duality of the black psyche—the simultaneous allegiance to America and rage at her racial inequities.

Four similar themes recur in Cullen's poems, expressing other forms of racial bias. These include a kind of black chauvinism that prevailed at the time and that Cullen portrayed in both *The Ballad of the Brown Girl* and *The Black Christ,* when in those works he judged that the passion of blacks was better than that of whites. Likewise, the poem "Near White" exemplifies the author's admonition against miscegenation, and in "To a Brown Boy" Cullen propounds a racially motivated affinity toward death as a preferred escape from racial frustration and outrage. Another poem, "For a Lady I Know," presents a satirical view of whites obliviously mistreating their black counterparts as it depicts blacks in heaven doing their "celestial chores" so that upper-class whites can remain in their heavenly beds.

Using a sixth motif, Cullen exhibits a direct expression of irrepressible anger at racial unfairness. His outcry is more muted than that of some other Harlem Renaissance poets—Hughes, for example, and Claude McKay—but that is a matter of Cullen's innate and learned gentility. Those who overlook Cullen's strong indictment of racism in American society miss the main thrust of his work. His poetry throbs with anger as in "Incident" when he recalls his personal response to being called "nigger" on a Baltimore bus, or in the selection "Yet Do I Marvel," in which Cullen identifies what he regards as God's most astonishing miscue that he could "make a poet black, and bid him sing!" In addition to his own personal experiences, Cullen also focuses on public events. For instance, in "Scottsboro, Too, Is Worth Its Song," he upbraids American poets, who had championed the cause of white anarchists in the controversial Sacco-Vanzetti trials, for not defending the nine black youths indicted on charges of raping two white girls in a freight car passing through Scottsboro, Alabama, in 1931.

In *The Book of American Negro Poetry,* author James Weldon Johnson explained with acute sympathy Cullen's compulsion to write poetry that seems to fly in the face of his declarations against poetry of race. Johnson wrote: "Strangely, it is because Cullen revolts against . . . racial limitations—technical and spiritual—that the best of his poetry is motivated by race. He is always seeking to free himself and his art from these bonds. He never entirely escapes, but from the very fret and chafe he brings forth poetry that contains the quintessence of race consciousness."

Cullen, then, was a forceful but genteel protest poet; yet, he was much more. He was also consistent in his intention to write good traditional poetry for the social purpose of showing what common sense should have told white Americans but what they still demanded be proven to them—that blacks *could* write poetry and write it as well as anyone. To that end, much of Cullen's poetry deals with such universal subjects as faith and doubt, love, and mortality.

On the subject of religion, Cullen waywardly progressed from uncertainty to Christian acceptance. Early on he was given to irony and even defiance in moments of youthful skepticism. In "Heritage," for example, he observes that a black Christ could command his faith better than the white one. When he was twenty-four, he provided a third-person description of himself in which he commented that his "chief problem has been that of reconciling a Christian upbringing with a pagan inclination. His life so far has not convinced him that the problem is insoluble." But before very long, his grandmother Porter's influence and that of the Cullen rectory won out. Outrage over racial injustice notwithstanding, he had fairly well controlled the "pagan inclination" in favor of Christian orthodoxy by 1929, when he published *The Black Christ, and Other Poems.* In the opening of the book's narrative title poem, the protagonist sings of embracing God in spite of certain earthly obstacles that he summarizes as "my country's shame." The speaker's brother has been beaten to death by a white lynch mob for an innocent relationship with a white woman; the narrator's resentment toward a savior who allows such evil to occur is overcome by his mother's proclamation of her unshakable faith, and any residue of doubt disappears when the murdered brother is resurrected. At the end the family is left to prosper in its piety. Furthermore, among the few previously unpublished poems that Cullen selected for inclusion in the posthumously published collection *On These I Stand* is one that confirms his continuing religious commitment as a way to cope with the injustices and disappointments of his life. Written during World War I, "Christus natus est" asserts that amid all the tragedy of war "The manger still / Outshines the throne" and that "Christ must and will / Come to his own."

To understand Cullen's treatment of love it is necessary first to examine the effete—weak or effeminate—quality of many of his love poems. David Levering Lewis, in *When Harlem Was in Vogue,* asserted that "impotence and death run through [Cullen's] poetry like dark threads, entangling his most affirmative lines." In general, Cullen's love poetry is clearly characterized not only by misgivings about women but also by a distrust of the emotion of heterosexual love. His "Medusa" and "The Cat," both contained in *The Medea, and Some Poems,* illustrate this vision of male-female relationships. In Cullen's version of the ancient myth, it is not the hideousness of Medusa that blinds the men who gaze upon her, but rather her beauty. So great is the destructive power of the attractive female that the narrator in "The Cat" imagines in the animal "A woman with thine eyes, satanic beast / Profound and cold as scythes to mow me down." Male lovers, on the other hand are often portrayed as sickly with apprehension that a relationship is about to be ended either by a fickle partner or by death. In "If Love Be Staunch," for example, the speaker warns that love lasts no longer than "water stays in a sieve" and in "The Love Tree" Cullen portrays love as a crucifixion whereby future lovers may realize that "'Twas break of heart that made the love tree grow." What Lewis identified in Cullen's love poems as a "corroding suspicion of life cursed from birth" may have resulted from Cullen's alleged homosexuality.

Cullen's treatment of death in his writing was shaped by his early encounters with the deaths of his parents, brother, and grandmother, as well as by a premonition of his own premature demise. Running through his poems are a sense of the brevity of life and a romantic craving for the surcease of death. In "Nocturne" and "Works to My Love," death is readily accepted as a natural element of life. "Threnody for a Brown Girl" and "In the Midst of Life" portray even warmer feelings towards death as a welcome escape. And in poems such as "Only the Polished Skeleton" death is gratefully anticipated to bring relief from ra-cial oppression: A stripped skeleton has no race; it can but "measure the worth of all it so despised." Looking forward to death, Cullen meanwhile accepted sleep as an effective surrogate. In the poem "Sleep" he portrays slumber as "lovelier" and "kinder" than any alternative. It is both a feline killer and gentle nourisher that suckles the sleeper: "though the suck be short 'tis good." In April, 1943, less than three years before he died of uremic poisoning, Cullen related in "Dear Friends and Gentle Hearts" that "blessedly this breath departs."

After 1929 Cullen's production of verse dropped off dramatically. It was limited to his translation of Euripides' play *Medea,* which appeared along with some new poems in his 1935 collection *The Medea, and Some Poems* and later with half a dozen previously unpublished pieces that were included in his posthumously published collection, *On These I Stand.* A complexity of reasons contributed to the dimming of his poetic star. The Harlem Renaissance required a white audience to sustain it, and as whites became preoccupied with their own tenuous situation during the Great Depression, they lost interest in the Afro-American arts. Also, Cullen's idealism about building a bridge of poetry between the races had been sorely tested by the time the 1920s ended. Moreover, he seemed affected by legitimate doubts concerning his growth as a poet. In "Self Criticism" he reflected whether he would go on singing a "failing note still vainly clinging / To the throat of the stricken swan."

While his supporters continued to defend him on racial rather than literary grounds, his detractors gradually increased in numbers with the publication of each successive collection of his poetry. Harry Alan Potamkin, in a 1927 *New Republic* review of *Copper Sun,* found that Cullen had not really progressed since *Color* and that the poet had "capitalized on the fact of race." The reviewer concluded, in fact, that Cullen's poetry "begins and ends with a epithet skill." With the appearance of *The Black Christ, and Other Poems* in 1929, *Nation's* Granville Hicks joined the chorus of critics expressing reservations and remarked that "in general, Mr. Cullen's talents do not seem to be developing as one might wish."

For a combination of causes, then, beginning in the early 1930s Cullen largely curtailed his poetic output and channeled his creative energy into other genres. He wrote a novel, *One Way to Heaven,* published in 1932, but its poor critical reception made it his only novel. The book reveals a flair for satire in its secondary plot, which centers around the Harlem salon of the irrepressible hostess Constancia Brandon; one particularly effective episode features a white intellectual bigot who is invited to read his tract, "The Menace of the Negro to Our American Civilization," to an audience of mainly black intellectuals. The novel itself, however, suffers from a fatal structural flaw. Cullen never successfully integrated the secondary plot—a takeoff on his own experience in Harlem intellectual circles—with the major story line, a melodrama in which itinerant con man Sam Lucas undergoes a fake religious conversion to edge his way into a Harlem congregation; marries and then cheats on his sweet young wife; and finally, on his death bed undergoes a change of heart. The characters in the main plot are generally based on stereotypes common in black-American folklore—the fast-talking trickster and the sagacious saintly old aunt, for example. Although Cullen displays some compassion toward them and a good deal of good-natured wit in dealing with the satirical figures, the two plots never adequately come together. As Rudolph Fisher said in a *New York Herald Tribune* review of *One Way to Heaven,* it was as if Cullen were "exhibiting a lovely pastel and cartoon on the same frame."

When thirty-one-year-old Cullen turned to teaching in 1934, he was determined to find some way other than literature to contribute to social change, but he did not abandon writing entirely. In 1935 he published his version of *Medea* (with the speeches and choral passages curiously attenuated) and collaborated with Harry Hamilton on "Heaven's My Home," a dramatic adaptation of *One Way to Heaven*. The play, which was never published, is actually more contrived than Cullen's novel, but unlike the original work, "Heaven's My Home" manages to integrate the two plots by introducing a sexual relationship between the protagonists Lucas and Brandon.

Toward the end of his life, in the 1940s, Cullen was relatively successful as a dramatist. With another collaborator, Owen Dodson, he worked on several projects, including "The Third Fourth of July," a one-act play printed in *Theatre Arts* in August, 1946. During this period Cullen rejected a professorship at Fisk University and instead remained in New York to work with Arna Bontemps on a dramatic version of her novel *God Sends Sunday*. Cullen, who suggested the adaptation, made this endeavor the center of his life, but the enterprise caused him much grief. By 1945 the play had become the musical "St. Louis Woman," and celebrated performer Lena Horne was expected to star in its Broadway and Hollywood productions. Then disaster struck. Walter White of the National Association for the Advancement of Colored People (NAACP) argued that the play, set in the black ghetto of St. Louis and featuring lower-class and seedy characters, was demeaning to blacks. Cullen was blamed for revealing the seamy side of black life, the very thing he had warned other black writers not to do. Many of Cullen's friends refused to defend him; some joined the attack, which was patently unjust. Admittedly, greed and criminality figure in the play, which focuses on the struggle between overbearing salon keeper-gambler Bigelow Brown and diminutive jockey Lil Augie for the affections of Della Greene, a hard-nosed and soft-hearted beauty.

But as Cullen argued, the play really deals with human virtues—honor, love, decency, and loyalty. The controversy rounding it wore on, however, until 1946. In March of that year, "St. Louis Woman" finally premiered on Broadway, featuring songs by Johnny Mercer and Harold Arlen such as "Come Rain, Come Shine" and making singer Pearl Bailey a star. Unfortunately, Cullen had died almost three months earlier and was to be remembered primarily for the poems he had written in his twenties when he was one of Harlem's brightest luminaries.

The limitations of Cullen's poetry such as its archaic and imitative ring, its occasional verbosity, and its tendency to sacrifice sense for conventional prosody restricted his literary status to that of a minor poet with a real lyrical gift. But he was not guilty of the obsequious acceptance of white values for which 1960s black power poets such as Don Lee were to dismiss him. Cullen never compromised his integrity as a black man to gain advantage for himself. His primary goal was to bring America closer to racial harmony through his own art and that of his peers and ultimately to achieve complete and colorblind artistic freedom. As he defiantly proclaimed in "To Certain Critics" (published in *The Black Christ*), though some might call him a traitor to blacks, his program was too universal to be contained: "Never shall the clan / Confine my singing to its ways / Beyond the ways of man."

Probably more than any other writer of the Harlem Renaissance, Cullen carried out the intentions of black American intellectual leaders such as W. E. B. DuBois and James Weldon Johnson. These men had nothing but the highest praise for Cullen, for he was brilliantly practicing what they advocated, and he came close to embodying Alain Locke's "New Negro." "In a time," DuBois wrote in a 1928 *Crisis* essay, "when it is vogue to make much of the Negro's aptitude for clownishness or to depict him objectively as a serio-comic figure, it is a fine and praiseworthy act for Mr. Cullen to show through the interpretation of his own subjectivity the inner workings of the Negro soul and mind." Johnson was pleased with Cullen's decision not to recognize "any limitation to 'racial' themes and forms." In Cullen's wish not to be "a negro poet," Johnson insisted, the writer was "not only within his right: he is right." As these authorities attest, to read Countee Cullen's work is to hear a voice as representative of the Harlem Renaissance as it is possible to find.

BIOGRAPHICAL/CRITICAL SOURCES:

BOOKS

Baker, Houston A., Jr., *A Many-Colored Coat of Dreams: The Poetry of Countee Cullen*, Broadside Press, 1974.

Bone, Robert, *The Negro Novel in America*, Yale University Press, 1965.

Bronz, Stephen H., *Roots of Racial Consciousness; The 1920s: Three Harlem Renaissance Authors*, Libra, 1964.

Davis, Arthur P., *From the Dark Tower: Afro-American Writers, 1900-1960*, Howard University Press, 1974.

Dictionary of Literary Biography, Gale, Volume 4: *American Writers in Paris: 1920-1939*, 1980, Volume 48: *American Poets: 1880-1945, Second Series*, 1986, Volume 51: *Afro-American Writers from the Harlem Renaissance to 1940*, 1987.

Ferguson, Blanche E., *Countee Cullen and the Negro Renaissance*, Dodd, 1966.

Huggins, Nathan Irvin, *Harlem Renaissance*, Oxford, 1971.

Johnson, James Weldon, *The Book of American Negro Poetry*, Harcourt, 1922, revised edition, 1931, Harbrace, 1959.

Johnson, *Black Manhattan*, Knopf, 1930.

Lee, Don L., *Dynamite Voices I: Black Voices of the 1960s*, Broadside Press, 1971.

Littlejohn, David, *Black on White: A Critical Survey of Writing by American Negroes*, Viking, 1966.

Lewis, David Levering, *When Harlem Was in Vogue*, Knopf, 1981.

Locke, Alain, *Four Negro Poets*, Albert & Charles Boni, 1925.

Locke, *The New Negro, An Interpretation*, Albert & Charles Boni, 1925.

Margolies, Edward, *Native Sons: A Critical Study of Twentieth-Century Negro American Authors*, Lippincott, 1968.

Perry, Margaret, *A Bio-Bibliography of Countee P. Cullen, 1903-1946*, Greenwood, 1971.

Redding, J. Saunders, *To Make a Poet Black*, University of North Carolina Press, 1939.

Rosenblatt, Roger, *Black Fiction*, Harvard University Press, 1974.

Shucard, Alan, *Countee Cullen*, Twayne, 1984.

Singh, Amritjit, *The Novels of the Harlem Renaissance: Twelve Black Authors, 1923-1933*, Pennsylvania State University Press, 1976.

Twentieth-Century Literary Criticism, Volume 4, Gale, 1981.

Wagner, Jean, *Black Poets of the United States: From Paul Laurence Dunbar to Langston Hughes*, University of Illinois Press, 1973.

PERIODICALS

Atlantic Monthly, No. 79, March, 1947.
College Language Association Journal, No. 13, 1970.
Crisis, No. 35, June, 1928.

Critique, No. 11, 1969.
Nation, March 12, 1930.
New Republic, No. 52, 1927.
New York Herald Tribune of Books, February 28, 1932.
Phylon, No. 14, 1953.

*   *   *

CUMMINGS, E(dward) E(stlin) 1894-1962

PERSONAL: Born October 14, 1894, in Cambridge, Mass.; died September 3, 1962, in North Conway, N.H.; buried in Forest Hills Cemetery, Boston, Mass.; son of Edward (a professor of sociology and political science and a Unitarian minister) and Rebecca Haswell (Clarke) Cummings; married Elaine Orr Thayer, March 19, 1924 (divorced, 1925); married Anne Minnerly Barton, May 1, 1929 (divorced, 1932); married (common law) Marion Morehouse, 1934; children: (first marriage) Nancy. *Education:* Harvard University, A.B. (magna cum laude), 1915, M.A., 1916.

CAREER: Poet, painter, novelist, and playwright. Charles Eliot Norton Professor of Poetry, Harvard University, 1952-53. One-man exhibitions at American British Art Centre, 1949, and Rochester Memorial Gallery, 1959. *Wartime service:* Served as an ambulance driver with the Norton-Harjes Ambulance Service in France, 1917; detained on suspicion of treason and held in a French internment camp, 1917; U.S. Army, private, 1918-1919.

MEMBER: National Academy of Arts and Letters.

AWARDS, HONORS: Dial (magazine) Award, 1925, for distinguished service to American letters; Guggenheim fellowship, 1933 and 1951; Levinson Prize, *Poetry* (magazine), 1939; Shelley Memorial Award, Poetry Society of America, 1945; Academy of American Poets fellowship, 1950; Harriet Monroe Poetry Award, 1950; Eunice Teitjens Memorial Prize, *Poetry,* 1952; National Book Award special citation, 1955, for *Poems, 1923-1954;* Festival Poet, Boston Arts Festival, 1957; Bollingen Prize in Poetry, Yale University, 1958; Oscar Blumenthal Prize, *Poetry,* 1962.

WRITINGS:

POEMS

(Contributor) *Eight Harvard Poets,* L. J. Gomme, 1917.
Tulips and Chimneys (also see below), T. Seltzer, 1923, enlarged edition, Golden Eagle Press, 1937.
Puella Mia, Golden Eagle Press, 1923.
XLI Poems, Dial, 1925.
& (also see below), privately printed, 1925.
is 5, Boni & Liveright, 1926, reprinted, Liveright, 1985.
Christmas Tree, American Book Bindery, 1928.
W(ViVa), Liveright, 1931, reprinted, 1979.
(Contributor) Peter Neagoe, editor, *Americans Abroad: An Anthology,* Servire, 1932.
No Thanks, Golden Eagle Press, 1935, reprinted, Liveright, 1978.
1/20, Roger Roughton, 1936.
Collected Poems, Harcourt, 1938.
50 Poems, Duell, Sloan & Pearce, 1940.
1 x 1, Holt, 1944.
Xaipe: Seventy-One Poems, Oxford University Press, 1950, reprinted, Liveright, 1979.
Poems, 1923-1954, Harcourt, 1954.
95 Poems, Harcourt, 1958.
100 Selected Poems, Grove, 1958.
Selected Poems, 1923-1958, Faber, 1960.
73 Poems, Harcourt, 1963.

A Selection of Poems, Harcourt, 1965.
Complete Poems, 1923-1962, two volumes, MacGibbon & Kee, 1968, revised edition published in one volume as *Complete Poems, 1913-1962,* Harcourt, 1972.
Poems, 1905-1962, edited by Firmage, Marchim Press, 1973.
Tulips & Chimneys: The Original 1922 Manuscript with the 35 Additional Poems from &, edited by Firmage, Liveright, 1976.
(Contributor) Nancy Cummings De Forzet, *Charon's Daughter: A Passion of Identity,* Liveright, 1977.
Love Is Most Mad and Moonly, Addison-Wesley, 1978.
(Chaire), Liveright, 1979.
Complete Poems, 1910-1962, Granada, 1982.
Hist Whist and Other Poems for Children, edited by Firmage, Liveright, 1983.
Etcetera: The Unpublished Poems of E. E. Cummings, edited by Firmage and Richard S. Kennedy, Liveright, 1984.
In Just-Spring, Little, Brown, 1988.

OTHER

The Enormous Room, Boni & Liveright, 1922, revised edition, Liveright, 1978.
Him (three-act play; first produced in New York at the Provincetown Playhouse, April 18, 1928), Boni & Liveright, 1927, new edition, Liveright, 1970.
[No title] (collection of stories), Covici Friede, 1930.
CIOPW (artwork), Covici Friede, 1931.
Eimi (travel diary), Covici Friede, 1933, 4th edition, Grove, 1958.
(Translator) Louis Aragon, *The Red Front,* Contempo, 1933.
Tom (ballet based on *Uncle Tom's Cabin* by Harriet Beecher Stowe), Arrow Editions, 1935.
Anthropos: The Future of Art, Golden Eagle Press, 1944, reprinted, Norwood, 1978.
Santa Claus: A Morality (play), Holt, 1946.
i: six nonlectures, Harvard University Press, 1953.
E. E. Cummings: A Miscellany, Argophile Press, 1958, revised edition edited by George Firmage, October Press, 1965.
(With wife, Marion Morehouse) *Adventures in Value,* Harcourt, 1962.
Fairy Tales, Harcourt, 1965.
Three Plays and a Ballet, edited by Firmage, October House, 1967.
Selected Letters of E. E. Cummings, edited by F. W. Dupee and George Stade, Harcourt, 1969.
"E. E. Cummings Reads His Collected Poetry, 1943-1958" (recording), Caedmon, 1977.
Little Tree (juvenile), Crown, 1987.

SIDELIGHTS: "Among the most innovative of twentieth-century poets," according to Jenny Penberthy in the *Dictionary of Literary Biography,* E. E. Cummings experimented with poetic form and language to create a distinct personal style. A Cummings poem is spare and precise, employing a few key words eccentrically placed on the page. Some of these words were invented by Cummings, often by combining two common words into a new synthesis. He also revised grammatical and linguistic rules to suit his own purposes, using such words as "if," "am," and "because" as nouns, for example, or assigning his own private meanings to words. Despite their nontraditional form, Cummings' poems came to be popular with many readers. "No one else," Randall Jarrell claimed in his *The Third Book of Criticism,* "has ever made avant-garde, experimental poems so attractive to the general and the special reader." By the time of his death in 1962 Cummings held a prominent position in twentieth-century poetry. John Logan in *Modern American Poetry: Essays in Criticism* called him "one of the greatest lyric poets in our language." Stanley Edgar Hyman wrote in *Standards: A Chronicle of Books for Our Time:* "Cummings has written at least a dozen poems that seem to me matchless. Three are among the great love poems of our time or any time." Malcolm Cowley admitted in the *Yale Review* that Cummings "suffers from comparison with those [poets] who built on a larger scale—Eliot, Aiken, Crane, Auden among others—but still he is unsurpassed in his special field, one of the masters."

Cummings decided to become a poet when he was still a child. Between the ages of eight and twenty-two, he wrote a poem a day, exploring many traditional poetic forms. By the time he was in Harvard in 1916, modern poetry had caught his interest. He began to write avant-garde poems in which conventional punctuation and syntax were ignored in favor of a dynamic use of language. Cummings also experimented with poems as visual objects on the page. These early efforts were included in *Eight Harvard Poets,* a collection of poems by members of the Harvard Poetry Society.

After graduating from Harvard, Cummings spent a month working for a mail order book dealer. He left the job because of the tedium. In April of 1917, with the First World War raging in Europe and the United States not yet involved, he volunteered for the Norton-Harjes Ambulance Service in France. Ambulance work was a popular choice with those who, like Cummings, considered themselves to be pacifists. He was soon stationed on the French-German border with fellow American William Slater Brown, and the two young men became fast friends. To relieve the boredom of their assignment, they inserted veiled and provocative comments into their letters back home, trying to outwit and baffle the French censors. They also befriended soldiers in nearby units. Such activities led in September of 1917 to their being held on suspicion of treason and sent to an internment camp in Normandy for questioning. Cummings and Brown were housed in a large, one-room holding area along with other suspicious foreigners. Only outraged protests from his father finally secured Cummings' release in December of 1917; Brown was not released until April of the following year. In July of 1918, with the United States entering the war, Cummings was drafted into the U.S. Army and spent some six months at a training camp in Massachusetts.

Upon leaving the army in January of 1919, Cummings resumed his affair with Elaine Thayer, the wife of his friend Schofield Thayer. Thayer knew and approved of the relationship. In December of 1919 Elaine gave birth to Cummings' daughter, Nancy, and Thayer gave the child his name. Cummings was not to marry Elaine until 1924, after she and Thayer divorced. He adopted Nancy at this time; she was not to know that Cummings was her real father until 1948. This first marriage did not last long. Two months after their wedding, Elaine left for Europe to settle her late sister's estate. She met another man during the Atlantic crossing and fell in love with him. She divorced Cummings in 1925.

The early twenties were an extremely productive time for Cummings. In 1922 he published his first book, *The Enormous Room,* a fictionalized account of his French captivity. Critical reaction was overwhelmingly positive, although Cummings' account of his imprisonment was oddly cheerful in tone and freewheeling in style. He depicted his internment camp stay as a period of inner growth. As David E. Smith wrote in *Twentieth Century Literature, The Enormous Room*'s emphasis "is upon what the initiate has learned from his journey. In this instance, the maimed hero can never again regard the outer world (i.e., 'civili-

zation') without irony. But the spiritual lesson he learned from his sojourn with a community of brothers will be repeated in his subsequent writings both as an ironical dismissal of the values of his contemporary world, and as a sensitive, almost mystical celebration of the quality of Christian love." John Dos Passos, in a review of the book for *Dial,* claimed that "in a style infinitely swift and crisply flexible, an individual not ashamed of his loves and hates, great or trivial, has expressed a bit of the underside of History with indelible vividness." Writing of the book in 1938, John Peale Bishop claimed in the *Southern Review:* "*The Enormous Room* has the effect of making all but a very few comparable books that came out of the War look shoddy and worn."

Cummings' first collection of poems, *Tulips and Chimneys,* appeared in 1923. His eccentric use of grammar and punctuation are evident in the volume, though many of the poems are written in conventional language. "The language of *Tulips and Chimneys,* . . . like the imagery, the verse forms, the subject matter, and the thought, is sometimes good, sometimes bad," wrote Robert E. Maurer in the *Bucknell Review.* "But the book is so obviously the work of a talented young man who is striking off in new directions, groping for original and yet precise expression, experimenting in public, that it seems uncharitable to dwell too long on its shortcomings."

The original manuscript for *Tulips and Chimneys* was cut down by the publisher. These deleted poems were published in 1925 as *&,* so titled because Cummings wanted the original book to be titled *Tulips & Chimneys* but was overruled. Another collection quickly followed: *XLI Poems,* also in 1925. In a review of *XLI Poems* for *Nation,* Mark Van Doren defined Cummings as a poet with "a richly sensuous mind; his verse is distinguished by fluidity and weight; he is equipped to range lustily and long among the major passions." At the end of 1925 *Dial* magazine chose Cummings for their annual award of $2,000, a sum equalling a full year's income for the writer. The following year a new collection, *Is 5,* was published, for which Cummings wrote an introduction meant to explain his approach to poetry. In the introduction he argued forcefully for poetry as a "process" rather than a "product."

It was with these collections of the 1920s that Cummings established his reputation as an avant-garde poet conducting daring experiments with language. Speaking of these language experiments, M. L. Rosenthal wrote in *The Modern Poets: A Critical Introduction:* "The chief effect of Cummings' jugglery with syntax, grammar, and diction was to blow open otherwise trite and bathetic motifs through a dynamic rediscovery of the energies sealed up in conventional usage. . . . He succeeded masterfully in splitting the atom of the cute commonplace." "Cummings," Richard P. Blackmur wrote in *The Double Agent: Essays in Craft and Elucidation,* "has a fine talent for using familiar, even almost dead words, in such a context as to make them suddenly impervious to every ordinary sense; they become unable to speak, but with a great air of being bursting with something very important and precise to say." Bethany K. Dumas wrote in her *E. E. Cummings: A Remembrance of Miracles* that "more important than the specific devices used by Cummings is the use to which he puts the devices. That is a complex matter; irregular spacing . . . allows both amplification and retardation. Further, spacing of key words allows puns which would otherwise be impossible. Some devices, such as the use of lowercase letters at the beginnings of lines . . . allow a kind of distortion that often reenforces that of the syntax. . . . All these devices have the effect of jarring the reader, of forcing him to examine experience with fresh eyes." S. I. Hayakawa also remarked on this quality in Cummings' poetry. "No modern poet to my knowledge,"

Hayakawa wrote in *Poetry,* "has such a clear, childlike perception as E. E. Cummings—a way of coming smack against things with unaffected delight and wonder. This candor . . . results in breath-takingly clean vision." Norman Friedman explained in his *E. E. Cummings: The Growth of a Writer* that Cummings' innovations "are best understood as various ways of stripping the film of familiarity from language in order to strip the film of familiarity from the world. Transform the word, he seems to have felt, and you are on the way to transforming the world."

Other critics focused on the subjects of Cummings' poetry. Though his poetic language was uniquely his own, Cummings' poems were unusual because they unabashedly focused on such traditional and somewhat passe poetic themes as love, childhood, and flowers. What Cummings did with such subjects, according to Stephen E. Whicher in *Twelve American Poets,* was, "by verbal ingenuity, without the irony with which another modern poet would treat such a topic, create a sophisticated modern facsimile of the 'naive' lyricism of Campion or Blake." This resulted in what Whicher termed "the renewal of the cliche." Penberthy detected in Cummings a "nineteenth-century romantic reverence for natural order over man-made order, for intuition and imagination over routine-grounded perception. His exalted vision of life and love is served well by his linguistic agility. He was an unabashed lyricist, a modern cavalier love poet. But alongside his lyrical celebrations of nature, love, and the imagination are his satirical denouncements of tawdry, defiling, flat-footed, urban and political life—open terrain for invective and verbal inventiveness."

This satirical aspect to Cummings' work drew both praise and criticism. His attacks on the mass mind, conventional patterns of thought, and society's restrictions on free expression, were born of his strong commitment to the individual. In the "nonlectures" he delivered at Harvard University Cummings explained his position: "So far as I am concerned, poetry and every other art was, is, and forever will be strictly and distinctly a question of individuality." As Penberthy noted, Cummings' consistent attitude in all of his work was "condemning mankind while idealizing the individual." "Cummings' lifelong belief," Bernard Dekle stated in *Profiles of Modern American Authors,* "was a simple faith in the miracle of man's individuality. Much of his literary effort was directed against what he considered the principal enemies of this individuality—mass thought, group conformity, and commercialism." For this reason, Cummings satirized what he called "mostpeople," that is, the herd mentality found in modern society. "At heart," Logan explained, "the quarrels of Cummings are a resistance to the small minds of every kind, political, scientific, philosophical, and literary, who insist on limiting the real and the true to what they think they know or can respond to. As a preventive to this kind of limitation, Cummings is directly opposed to letting us rest in what we believe we know; and this is the key to the rhetorical function of his famous language."

Cummings was also ranked among the best love poets of his time. "Love always was . . . Cummings' chief subject of interest," Friedman wrote in his *E. E. Cummings: The Art of His Poetry.* "The traditional lyric situation, representing the lover speaking of love to his lady, has been given in our time a special flavor and emphasis by Cummings. Not only the lover and his lady, but love itself—its quality, its value, its feel, its meaning—is a subject of continuing concern to our speaker." Love was, in Cummings' poems, equated to such other concepts as joy and growth, a relationship which "had its source," wrote Robert E. Wegner in *The Poetry and Prose of E. E. Cummings,* "in Cummings' experience as a child; he grew up in an aura of love. . . .

Love is the propelling force behind a great body of his poetry." Friedman noted that Cummings was "in the habit of associating love, as a subject, with the landscape, the seasons, the times of day, and with time and death—as poets have always done in the past."

Cummings' early love poems were frankly erotic and were meant to shock the Puritanical sensibilities of the 1920s. Penberthy noted that the poet's first wife, Elaine, inspired "scores of Cummings's best erotic poems." But, as Wegner wrote, "In time he came to see love and the dignity of the human being as inseparable." Maurer also commented on this change in Cummings' outlook; there was, Maurer wrote, a "fundamental change of attitude which manifested itself in his growing reverence and dedication to lasting love." Hyatt H. Waggoner, writing in *American Poets from the Puritans to the Present,* noted that "the love poems are generally, after the 1920s, religious in tone and implication, and the religious poems very often take off from the clue provided by a pair of lovers, so that often the two subjects are hardly, if at all, separable." Rushworth M. Kidder also noted this development in the love poems, and he traced the evolution of Cummings' thoughts on the subject. Writing in his *E. E. Cummings: An Introduction to the Poetry,* Kidder reported that in the early poems, love is depicted as "an echo of popularly romantic notions, and it grows in early volumes to a sometimes amorphous phenomenon seasoned by a not entirely unselfish lust. By [his] last poems, however, it has come to be a purified and radiant idea, unentangled with flesh and worlds, the agent of the highest transcendence. It is not far, as poem after poem has hinted, from the Christian conception of love as God." Waggoner concluded that Cummings "wrote some of the finest celebrations of sexual love and of the religious experience of awe and natural piety produced in our century, precisely at a time when it was most unfashionable to write such poems."

In addition to his poetry, Cummings was also known for his play, *Him,* and for the travel diary, *Eimi. Him* consisted of a sequence of skits drawing from burlesque, the circus, and the avant-garde, and jumping quickly from tragedy to grotesque comedy. The male character is named Him; the female character is Me. "The play begins," Harold Clurman wrote in *Nation,* "as a series of feverish images of a girl undergoing anaesthesia during an abortion. She is 'me,' who thinks of her lover as 'him.'" In the program to the play, staged at the Provincetown Playhouse, Cummings provided a warning to the audience: "Relax and give the play a chance to strut its stuff—relax, stop wondering what it's all 'about'—like many strange and familiar things, Life included, this Play isn't 'about,' it simply is. Don't try to enjoy it, let it try to enjoy you. DON'T TRY TO UNDERSTAND IT, LET IT TRY TO UNDERSTAND YOU." Clurman believed that "the play's purest element is contained in duos of love. They are the most sensitive and touching in American playwriting. Their intimacy and passion, conveyed in an odd exquisiteness of writing, are implied rather than declared. We realize that no matter how much 'him' wishes to express his closeness to 'me,' he is frustrated not only by the fullness of his feeling but by his inability to credit his emotion in a world as obscenely chaotic as the one in which he is lost."

In 1931 Cummings traveled to the Soviet Union. Like many other writers and artists of the time, he was hopeful that the communist revolution had created a better society. After a short time in the country, however, it became clear to Cummings that the Soviet Union was a dictatorship in which the individual was severely regimented by the state. His diary of the visit, in which he bitterly attacked the Soviet regime for its dehumanizing policies, was published in 1933 as *Eimi,* the Greek word for "I am."

In it, he described the Soviet Union as an "uncircus of noncreatures." Lenin's tomb, in which the late dictator's preserved body is on display, especially revolted Cummings and inspired him to create the most impassioned writing in the book. "The style which Cummings began in poetry," Bishop wrote, "reaches its most complete development in the prose of *Eimi*. Indeed, one might almost say that, without knowing it, Cummings had been acquiring a certain skill over the years, in order that, when occasion arose, he might set down in words the full horror of Lenin's tomb." In tracing the course of his thirty-five day trip through the Soviet Union, Cummings made frequent allusion to Dante's *Inferno* and its story of a descent into Hell, equating the two journeys. It is only after crossing back into Europe at book's end that "it is once more possible for [Cummings] to assume the full responsibility of being a man . . . ," Bishop wrote. "Now he knows there is but one freedom . . . , the freedom of the will, responsive and responsible, and that from it all other freedoms take their course." Kidder called *Eimi* "a report of the grim inhumanities of the Soviet system, of repression, apathy, priggishness, kitsch, and enervating suspicion." For some time after publication of *Eimi*, Kidder reported, Cummings had a difficult time getting his poetry published. The overwhelmingly left-wing publishers of the time refused to accept his work. Cummings had to resort to self-publishing several volumes of his work during the later 1930s.

In 1952, Cummings was invited to give the Charles Eliot Norton lectures in poetry at Harvard University. His lectures, later published as *i: six nonlectures*, were highly personal accounts of his life and work, "autobiographical rambles," as Penberthy described them. The first two lectures reminisce about his childhood and parents; the third lecture tells of his schooldays at Harvard, his years in New York, and his stay in Paris during the 1920s. The last three lectures present his own ideas about writing. In his conclusion to the lecture series Cummings summed up his thoughts with these words, quoting his own poetry where appropriate: "I am someone who proudly and humbly affirms that love is the mystery-of-mysteries, and that nothing measurable matters 'a very good God damn'; that 'an artist, a man, a failure' is no mere whenfully accreting mechanism, but a givingly eternal complexity—neither some soulless and heartless ultrapredatory infra-animal nor any understandingly knowing and believing and thinking automaton, but a naturally and miraculously whole human being—a feelingly illimitable individual; whose only happiness is to transcend himself, whose every agony is to grow."

Critics of Cummings' work were divided into two camps as to the importance of his career. His detractors called his failure to develop as a writer a major weakness; Cummings' work changed little from the 1920s to the 1950s. Others saw him as merely clever but with little lasting value beyond a few technical innovations. Still others questioned the ideas in his poetry, or seeming lack of them. George Stade in the *New York Times Book Review* claimed that "intellectually speaking, Cummings was a case of arrested development. He was a brilliant 20-year-old, but he remained merely precocious to the end of his life. That may be one source of his appeal." James G. Southworth, writing in *Some Modern American Poets*, argued that Cummings "is too much out of the stream of life for his work to have significance." Southworth went on to say that "the reader must not mistake Mr. Cummings for an intellectual poet."

But Cummings' supporters acclaimed his achievement. In a 1959 essay reprinted in his collection *Babel to Byzantium*, James Dickey proclaimed: "I think that Cummings is a daringly original poet, with more vitality and more sheer, uncompromising talent than any other living American writer." Although admitting that Cummings' work was not faultless, Dickey stated that he felt "ashamed and even a little guilty in picking out flaws" in the poems, a process he likened to calling attention to "the aesthetic defects in a rose. It is better to say what must finally be said about Cummings: that he has helped to give life to the language." In similar terms, Rosenthal explained that "Cummings's great forte is the manipulation of traditional forms and attitudes in an original way. In his best work he has the swift sureness of ear and idiom of a Catullus, and the same way of bringing together a racy colloquialism and the richer tones of high poetic style." Maurer believed that Cummings' best work exhibited "a new and delightful sense of linguistic invention, precise and vigorous." Penberthy concluded that "Cummings's achievement deserves acclaim. He established the poem as a visual object . . .; he revealed, by his x-ray probings, the faceted possibilities of the single word; and like such prose writers as Vladimir Nabokov and Tom Stoppard, he promoted sheer playfulness with language. Despite a growing abundance of second-rate imitations, his poems continue to amuse, delight, and provoke."

BIOGRAPHICAL/CRITICAL SOURCES:

BOOKS

Baum, S. V., editor, *EETI: E. E. Cummings and the Critics*, Michigan State University Press, 1962.

Blackmur, Richard P., *The Double Agent: Essays in Craft and Elucidation*, Arrow Editions, 1935.

Contemporary Literary Criticism, Gale, Volume 1, 1973, Volume 3, 1975, Volume 8, 1978, Volume 12, 1980, Volume 15, 1980.

Cummings, E. E., *The Enormous Room*, Boni & Liveright, 1922, revised edition, Liveright, 1978.

Cummings, E. E., *Is 5*, Boni & Liveright, 1926, reprinted, Liveright, 1985.

Cummings, E. E., *Eimi*, Covici Friede, 1933, 4th edition, Grove, 1958.

Cummings, E. E., *i: six nonlectures*, Harvard University Press, 1953.

Cummings, E. E., *Selected Letters of E. E. Cummings*, edited by F. W. Dupee and George Stade, Harcourt, 1969.

Dekle, Bernard, *Profiles of Modern American Authors*, Tuttle, 1969.

Deutsch, Babette, *Poetry in Our Time*, Doubleday, 1963.

Dickey, James, *Babel to Byzantium*, Farrar, 1968.

Dictionary of Literary Biography, Gale, Volume 4: *American Writers in Paris, 1920-1939*, 1980, Volume 48: *American Poets, 1880-1945*, second series, 1986.

Dumas, Bethany K., *E. E. Cummings: A Remembrance of Miracles*, Barnes & Noble, 1974.

Fairley, Irene, *E. E. Cummings & Ungrammar: A Study of Syntactic Deviance in His Poems*, Windmill Press, 1975.

Firmage, George J., *E. E. Cummings: A Bibliography*, Wesleyan University Press, 1960.

Friedman, Norman, *E. E. Cummings: The Art of His Poetry*, Johns Hopkins University Press, 1960.

Friedman, Norman, *E. E. Cummings: The Growth of a Writer*, Southern Illinois University Press, 1964.

Friedman, Norman, *E. E. Cummings: A Collection of Critical Essays*, Prentice-Hall, 1972.

Hoffman, Frederick J., *The Twenties: American Writing in the Postwar Decade*, revised edition, Collier, 1962.

Hyman, Stanley Edgar, *Standards: A Chronicle of Books for Our Time*, Horizon, 1966.

Jarrell, Randall, *The Third Book of Criticism*, Farrar, 1969.

Kennedy, Richard S., *Dreams in the Mirror: A Biography of E. E. Cummings,* Liveright, 1980.

Kidder, Rushworth M., *E. E. Cummings: An Introduction to the Poetry,* Columbia University Press, 1979.

Marks, Barry, *E. E. Cummings,* Twayne, 1963.

Mazzaro, Jerome, editor, *Modern American Poetry: Essays in Criticism,* McKay, 1970.

Norman, Charles, *E. E. Cummings: The Magic-Maker,* revised edition, Duell, Sloan & Pearce, 1964.

Rosenthal, M. L., *The Modern Poets: A Critical Introduction,* Oxford University Press, 1960.

Rotella, Guy L., *E. E. Cummings: A Reference Guide,* G. K. Hall, 1979.

Southworth, James G., *Some Modern American Poets,* Basil Blackwell, 1950.

Triem, Eve, *E. E. Cummings,* University of Minnesota Press, 1969.

Waggoner, Hyatt H., *American Poets from the Puritans to the Present,* Houghton, 1968.

Wegner, Robert E., *The Poetry and Prose of E. E. Cummings,* Harcourt, 1965.

Whicher, Stephen E. and Lars Ahnebrink, editors, *Twelve American Poets,* Almquist & Wiksell, 1959.

PERIODICALS

Bucknell Review, May, 1955.

Contemporary Literature, autumn, 1976.

Dial, July, 1922.

Georgia Review, summer, 1978.

Journal of Modern Literature, April, 1979 (special Cummings issue).

Nation, July 8, 1925, May 11, 1974.

New York Times Book Review, July 22, 1973.

Poetry, August, 1933, August, 1938.

Southern Review, summer, 1938, summer, 1941.

Twentieth Century Literature, July, 1965.

Wake, spring, 1976 (special Cummings issue).

Yale Review, spring, 1973.

OBITUARIES:

PERIODICALS

New York Times, September 4, 1962.

—*Sketch by Thomas Wiloch*

*   *   *

CURTIS, Price
See ELLISON, Harlan

D

D. P.
See WELLS, H(erbert) G(eorge)

*   *   *

DAHL, Roald 1916-

PERSONAL: Given name is pronounced "Roo-aal"; born September 13, 1916, in Llandaff, South Wales; son of Harald (a shipbroker, painter, and horticulturist) and Sofie (Hesselberg) Dahl; married Patricia Neal (an actress), July 2, 1953 (divorced, 1983); married Felicity Ann Crosland, 1983; children: (first marriage) Olivia (deceased), Tessa, Theo, Ophelia, Lucy. *Education:* Graduate of British public schools, 1932.

ADDRESSES: Home—Gipsy House, Great Missenden, Buckinghamshire HP16 0PB, England. *Agent*—Watkins Loomis Agency, 150 East 35th St., New York, N.Y. 10016.

CAREER: Shell Oil Co., London, England, member of eastern staff, 1933-37, member of staff in Dar-es-Salaam, Tanzania, 1937-39; writer. *Military service:* Royal Air Force, fighter pilot, 1939-45; became wing commander.

AWARDS, HONORS: Edgar Award, Mystery Writers of America, 1954, 1959, and 1980; Whitbread Award, 1983, for *The Witches;* World Fantasy Convention Lifetime Achievement Award, and Federation of Children's Book Groups Award, both 1983.

WRITINGS:

Sometime Never: A Fable for Supermen (novel), Scribner, 1948.
My Uncle Oswald (novel), M. Joseph, 1979, Knopf, 1980.
Going Solo (autobiography), Farrar, Straus, 1986.
Rhyme Stew (comic verse), Viking Kestrel, 1989.

FOR JUVENILES

The Gremlins, Random House, 1943.
James and the Giant Peach (also see below), Knopf, 1961.
Charlie and the Chocolate Factory (also see below), Knopf, 1964, revised edition, 1973.
The Magic Finger, Harper, 1966.
Fantastic Mr. Fox (also see below), Knopf, 1970.
Charlie and The Great Glass Elevator: The Further Adventures of Charlie Bucket and Willy Wonka, Chocolate-Maker Extraordinary, Knopf, 1972.

Danny: The Champion of the World, Knopf, 1975 (collected with *James and the Giant Peach* and *Fantastic Mr. Fox,* Bantam, 1983).
The Enormous Crocodile, Knopf, 1976.
The Wonderful Story of Henry Sugar and Six More, Knopf, 1977.
Complete Adventures of Charlie and Mr. Willy Wonka, Allen & Unwin, 1978.
The Twits, J. Cape, 1980, Knopf, 1981.
George's Marvellous Medicine, J. Cape, 1981.
Roald Dahl's Revolting Rhymes, Knopf, 1982.
The BFG, Farrar, Straus, 1982.
Dirty Beasts, Farrar, Straus, 1983.
The Witches, Farrar, Straus, 1984.
Boy: Tales of Childhood, Farrar, Straus, 1984.
The Giraffe and Pelly and Me, Farrar, Straus, 1985.
Matilda, Viking Kestrel, 1989.

SHORT STORY COLLECTIONS

Over to You: Ten Stories of Flyers and Flying, Reynal, 1946.
Someone Like You (Book-of-the-Month Club alternate selection; also see below), Knopf, 1953, revised edition, M. Joseph, 1961.
Kiss, Kiss (also see below), Knopf, 1960.
Twenty-Nine Kisses (contains contents of *Someone Like You* and *Kiss, Kiss*), M. Joseph, 1969.
Selected Stories, Random House, 1970.
Switch Bitch, Knopf, 1974.
The Best of Roald Dahl, Random House, 1978.
Tales of the Unexpected, Vintage, 1979.
Taste and Other Tales, Longman, 1979.
More Tales of the Unexpected, Penguin, 1980.
Roald Dahl's Book of Ghost Stories, Farrar, Straus, 1983.
The Roald Dahl Omnibus, Hippocrene Books, 1987.
Ah, Sweet Mystery of Life, Viking Kestrel, 1989.

SCREENPLAYS

"You Only Live Twice," United Artists, 1967.
(With Ken Hughes) "Chitty Chitty Bang Bang," United Artists, 1968.
"The Night-digger" (based on "Nest in a Falling Tree," by Joy Crowley), Metro-Goldwyn-Mayer, 1970.
"Willy Wonka and the Chocolate Factory" (based on *Charlie and the Chocolate Factory*), Paramount, 1971.

Also author of screenplays "Oh Death, Where Is Thy Sting-a Ling-a-Ling?," United Artists, and "The Lightning Bug" and "The Road Builder."

OTHER

Author of stage play "The Honeys," produced in New York, N.Y., 1955. Contributor to anthologies and to periodicals including *Harper's, Atlantic, Esquire,* and *Saturday Evening Post.*

SIDELIGHTS: "Roald Dahl is certainly one of the more difficult authors to categorise, not only because he writes for all ages from infancy upwards, but also because his work reflects several contrasting moods and a willingness to experiment with literary methods," observes Alasdair Campbell in an issue of *School Librarian.* Other critics have no problem pegging Dahl as engagingly cynical, as purposely outrageous, as rampantly hilarious. Best known for his children's books, the Welsh native began writing after leaving the RAF where, as a fighter pilot, he had crashed a plane "at 200 mph, bashing his head off the reflector sight and flattening his nose," as *Times* writer Peter Lennon relates. "Having until then produced only dogged schoolboy letters, [Dahl's] first letter home from hospital was brilliant. He was a writer. A squashed one, but a writer."

Soon afterward Dahl began publishing short stories, poems and novels, most with a bizarre bent to them, at least one provoking a great deal of controversy. This was the 1964 novel *Charlie and the Chocolate Factory.* Perhaps Dahl's best known work, this morality tale finds young Charlie Bucket one of five lucky children chosen to tour the legendary top-secret chocolate factory belonging to the reclusive Willy Wonka. The controversy began when critics and readers took umbrage with the author's depiction of a group of characters called the Oompa-Loompas, who work in the factory. Described by Dahl in the story as a tribe of "miniature pygmies" from "the very deepest and darkest part of the African jungle where no white man has ever been before," the Oompa-Loompas are also depicted as unthinking, unfeeling creatures who live only to serve. "It seems to me that the West has been treated to 'dark Africa' too many times and that it is racism to perpetuate the myth and image of darkness," notes Lois Kalb Bouchard in an article printed in the volume *The Black American in Books for Children: Readings in Racism.* "The children who find the golden admission tickets are never designated white in words, but the Oompa-Loompas are designated Black, and the illustrations show white children . . . ," concludes Bouchard. "I suspect, also, that in our cultural context of racism, the small size of the Black characters becomes a symbol of their implied inadequacies."

But racism isn't the book's only shortcoming, according to Myra Pollack Sadker and David Miller Sadker in their study *Now upon a Time: A Contemporary View of Children's Literature.* "Were there greater sensitivity to mistreatment and misrepresentation of the elderly, [the novel] would have received criticism as an 'ageist' book as well," they write. "At the book's conclusion Charlie arrives home in triumph in a glass elevator piloted by Willy Wonka himself. When the bedridden grandparents learn that they are to live out the rest of their days in the chocolate factory, they refuse to go and scream that they would rather die in their beds. Willy Wonka and Charlie, taking no notice whatsoever of their protests and screams, simply push the old people, beds and all, into the glass elevator. The message with which we close the book is that the needs and desires and opinions of old people are totally irrelevant and inconsequential."

Not every critic objected to *Charlie and the Chocolate Factory.* *New York Times Book Review* writer Aileen Pippen called the book "a Dickensian delight, and [the factory], with its laughing, singing, tiny Oompa-Loompa workers, is sheer joy." And according to J. S. Jenkins in *Children's Book News,* "Roald Dahl has a rare and rich gift. . . . Children laugh and gasp at his splendid fantasies—the waterfalls of chocolate, the everlasting gobstoppers, the chewing-gum machines. All words and sounds are grist to his mill, and the mixture of elan and nicety with which he uses them gives a zest to his writing which is all too seldom found in children's books." Nevertheless, in a revised edition of *Charlie and the Chocolate Factory,* released in 1973 to coincide with a movie-musical version of the story, the Oompa-Loompas are rewritten as raceless gnomes who serve as a Greek chorus as well as factory workers.

Dahl brought out a sequel, *Charlie and the Great Glass Elevator: The Further Adventures of Charlie Bucket and Willy Wonka, Chocolate-Maker Extraordinary,* in 1972. In a *New York Times Book Review* article, Julia Whedon notes that this work features all of the original *Charlie* cast with new supporting players, including "a President of the United States whose Nanny is Vice President (and still pushes him around). He poses knock-knock jokes to other heads of state when he's playing around with his red telephone and has a childish Cabinet (the Chief Spy wears a false mustache, the Chief Financial Adviser 'balances' the budget—on the top of his head). In short, like the first 'Charlie,' this one strikes me as a very easy fantasy, not very intensively developed. It's almost funny, almost suspenseful, only coyly screwball."

More recently, the author has begun to produce autobiographical stories. In *Boy: Tales of Childhood,* a 1985 release, Dahl "explains in the introduction that he is not writing a boring history of his life, but about those things—comic, painful, unpleasant— that he has never been able to forget," according to *New York Times Book Review* critic Hazel Rochman. "There were vacations in Norway [Dahl's parentage is Norwegian], feasts and mischief in his close, large, wealthy and almost entirely female family. . . . But from age of 9 to 18 he endured the harsh rigor of select English boys' boarding schools, where, as in Dickens's novels of childhood, grotesque adults wielded savage power over the helpless and innocent students." In his memoirs, Rochman concludes, Dahl "is in quiet control, chatting to his readers, explaining a few historical differences, illustrating each incident with scraps of his weekly letters home. . . . The tension between this casual commonsense tone and the lurking demonic terror gives these tales their power."

Dahl followed *Boy* with *Going Solo,* which chronicles the author's tour of duty in the RAF, and spares no detail in relating the horrors of war. "He is a natural story-teller," says *Times Literary Supplement* critic of Dahl, "and *Going Solo* describes without either false modesty or conceit some remarkable exploits. If this book were fiction . . . one might suspect that the writer was laying it on a bit, but one trusts Dahl from the outset." In *Time* reviewer R. Z. Sheppard's view, Dahl "tells of his wartime adventures with an ordinariness of tone that contrasts with the ghastliness of his experiences. This, of course, is the preferred method for a successful horror story. *Going Solo* is much more: a brief, masterly remembrance of the gifts of youth and good luck."

The author has long acknowledged his bizarre reputation as a children's fantasist, but admits he cannot directly trace the beginnings of these tendencies. "I don't know where my ideas come from," Dahl tells Lennon in the *Times* interview. "Perhaps my Norwegian background is an influence. Plots just wander into my head. They are like dreams, one is terrified of losing them.

Once I stopped the car and got out and wrote a word or two on the dust of the [trunk] lid so I wouldn't forget an idea."

MEDIA ADAPTATIONS: Charlie and the Chocolate Factory was adapted for the stage by Richard R. George, and published by Penguin Books in 1983.

BIOGRAPHICAL/CRITICAL SOURCES:

BOOKS

Children's Literature Review, Volume 7, Gale, 1984.
Contemporary Literary Criticism, Gale, Volume 1, 1973, Volume 6, 1976, Volume 18, 1981.
Dahl, Roald, *Charlie and the Chocolate Factory,* Knopf, 1964, revised edition, 1973.
Dahl, Roald, *Boy: Tales of Childhood,* Farrar, Straus, 1985.
Dahl, Roald, *Going Solo,* Farrar, Straus, 1986.
McCann, Donnarae, and Gloria Woodard, editors, *The Black American in Books for Children: Readings in Racism,* Scarecrow, 1972.
Sadker, Mara Pollak, and David Miller Sadker, *Now upon a Time: A Contemporary View of Children's Literature,* Harper, 1977.

PERIODICALS

Chicago Tribune, October 21, 1986.
Chicago Tribune Book World, August 10, 1980, May 17, 1981.
Children's Book News, March-April, 1968.
Children's Literature in Education, summer, 1976.
Horn Book, December, 1972, February, 1973, April, 1973, June, 1973.
New Republic, October 19, 1974, April 19, 1980.
New York Review of Books, December 17, 1970, December 14, 1972.
New York Times Book Review, October 25, 1964, September 17, 1972, October 26, 1975, March 29, 1981, January 9, 1983, January 20, 1985, October 12, 1986, January 15, 1989.
Saturday Review, March 10, 1973.
School Librarian, June, 1981.
Times (London), December 22, 1983.
Times Literary Supplement, June 15, 1973, December 5, 1975, July 23, 1982, November 30, 1984, September 12, 1986.
Washington Post, October 8, 1986.
Washington Post Book World, November 13, 1978, May 8, 1983, January 13, 1985.

—*Sketch by Susan Salter*

*   *   *

DAHLBERG, Edward   1900-1977

PERSONAL: Born July 22, 1900, in Boston, Mass.; died February 27, 1977, in Santa Barbara, Calif.; son of Saul Gottdank (a barber) and Elizabeth Dahlberg (a hairdresser); married Fanya Fass, 1926 (divorced); married Winifred Sheehan Moore, 1942; married Rlene LaFleur Howell, 1950; married Julia Lawlor, June 13, 1967; children: (second marriage) Geoffrey, Joel. *Education:* Attended University of California, Berkeley, 1921-23; Columbia University, B.S., 1925.

CAREER: Writer. Teacher at James Madison High School and Thomas Jefferson High School, New York City, 1925-26; New York University, New York City, visiting lecturer in Graduate School, 1950, 1961, lecturer in School of General Education, 1961-62; University of Missouri at Kansas City, Carolyn Benton Cockefair Professor, 1964-65, professor of language and litera-

ture, beginning 1966. Visiting professor at Columbia University, 1968. *Military service:* U.S. Army, private.

MEMBER: National Institute of Arts and Letters.

AWARDS, HONORS: Attended McDowell Colony, 1930; National Institute of Arts and Letters grant, 1961; Rockefeller Foundation grant, 1965, 1966; Ariadne Foundation grant, 1970; Cultural Council Foundation award, 1971; National Foundation on Arts and Humanities award; Longview Foundation grant; CAPS grant; National Endowment for the Arts grant.

WRITINGS:

Bottom Dogs (also see below; novel), with introduction by D. H. Lawrence, Putnam (London), 1929, Simon & Schuster, 1930, reprinted, AMS Press, 1976.
From Flushing to Calvary (also see below; novel), Harcourt, 1932.
Kentucky Blue Grass Henry Smith (prose poem), White Horse Press (Cleveland), 1932.
Those Who Perish (also see below; novel), John Day, 1934, reprinted, AMS Press, 1977.
(Author of introduction) Kenneth Fearing, *Poems,* Dynamo (New York), 1936.
Do These Bones Live (criticism), Harcourt, 1941, revised edition published in England as *Sing O Barren,* Routledge, 1947, 2nd revised edition published as *Can These Bones Live,* New Directions, 1960.
The Flea of Sodom (essays), New Directions, 1950.
The Sorrows of Priapus (also see below; philosophy), New Directions, 1957.
Moby Dick: An Hamitic Dream, Fairleigh Dickinson University, 1960.
(With Herbert Read) *Truth Is More Sacred* (critical exchange on modern literature), Horizon, 1961.
Alms for Oblivion (essays), University of Minnesota Press, 1964.
Because I Was Flesh (autobiography), New Directions, 1964.
Reasons of the Heart (aphorisms), Horizon, 1965.
Cipango's Hinder Door (poems), University of Texas Press, 1966.
The Leafless American, and Other Writings, edited by Harold Billings, Roger Beacham, 1967.
The Edward Dahlberg Reader, edited by Paul Carroll, New Directions, 1967.
Epitaphs of Our Times: The Letters of Edward Dahlberg, edited by Edwin Seaver, Braziller, 1967.
The Carnal Myth: A Look into Classical Sensuality (also see below), Weybright, 1968.
The Confessions of Edward Dahlberg, Braziller, 1971.
(Compiler and contributor) *The Gold of Ophir: Travels, Myths and Legends in the New World,* Dutton, 1972.
The Sorrows of Priapus: Consisting of The Sorrows of Priapus and The Carnal Myth, Harcourt, 1973.
The Olive of Minerva; or, The Comedy of a Cuckold, Crowell, 1976.
Bottom Dogs, From Flushing to Calvary, Those Who Perish, and Hitherto Unpublished and Uncollected Works, Crowell, 1976.

CONTRIBUTOR

Henry Hart, editor, *American Writers' Congress,* International Publishers, 1935.
Martha Foley and David Burnett, editors, *Best American Short Stories, 1961-1962,* Houghton, 1962.
Stanley Burnshaw, editor, *Varieties of Literary Experience,* New York University Press, 1962.
Louis Filler, editor, *The Anxious Years,* Putnam, 1963.

Also contributor to volumes of *New Directions in Prose and Poetry,* edited by James Laughlin, New Directions.

OTHER

Contributor of short stories, reviews, essays, and articles to *Nation, New Republic, New York Times, Holiday, Poetry, This Quarter, Twentieth Century, Massachusetts Review, New York Review of Books, New York Times Book Review,* and other publications.

WORK IN PROGRESS: At the time of his death in 1977 Dahlberg was reported to have been working on two books: *Rightness Is All* and *Jesus, Man or Apocrypha.*

SIDELIGHTS: Throughout his long and varied literary career, Edward Dahlberg was a puzzle to many American critics. His distinctive, eccentric, and often archaic style caused the literary establishment to either dismiss his work or to praise him as a genius. As Edmund White explained in the *New Republic,* "Dahlberg continues to be one of the most unaccountable forces in American letters, a phenomenon that every critic seeks, in one way or another, either to justify or dismiss." Why Dahlberg chose to write in such a singular manner was also a puzzle to critics. "Even critics who are theoretically quite opposed to examining a man's work as a pendant to his life find themselves worrying over how Dahlberg *got to be this way,*" as White wrote. Dahlberg was also adept at shedding labels that confined his talents. His early books earned him the title of "proletarian novelist," but he later gained critical recognition for his poetry, which was rich in allusion, while his work as an essayist, philosopher and literary critic earned him yet further accolades. Perhaps his most widely respected work is an autobiography, *Because I Was Flesh.* X. J. Kennedy, writing in the *New York Times Book Review,* called Dahlberg "a rare figure among American writers: a man of letters in the European sense, a versatile performer in more than one genre."

Perhaps the overriding feature of Dahlberg's work, particularly during the 1960s, was his stance as a sophisticated outsider who berated the culture of his day, as a curmudgeon who hurled invective at those whom he thought his inferiors. This attitude did not endear him to many readers. He "is not," Robert M. Adams admitted in the *New York Review of Books,* "an easy writer to like. . . . He is given to vociferous protests about his own genuineness and authenticity; and to make it the more exemplary, he vigorously denigrates almost all his contemporaries and most of his predecessors." Arno Karlen of the *New York Times Book Review* compared Dahlberg to the poet John Donne, "the poet-preacher whose bitterness and warmth were also those of a sensual man alive to regret, whose life's lessons were also burned into his bones, making him somber and sardonic, witty and kind with sensual pessimism. Sometimes Dahlberg sours into misogynous rant, which is ungenerous and thus unbecoming; just as his diction may become labored, so his pessimism may become a truculent pose."

To fashion the raw experience of life into art, Dahlberg employed myth, "which, in his best work, functions as a way of giving depth, perspective, and perhaps order" to life, according to Adams. Raymond Rosenthal, writing in the *Nation,* called Dahlberg "a lone searcher for the true myths of human destiny in our violent, barren, raddled land." Dahlberg himself explained his use of myth in these words: "Until he is connected with the fens, the ravines, the stars, [man] is more solitary than any beast. Man is a god, and kin to men, when he is a river, a mountain, a horse, a moon. . . . The American legend is the mesa and the bison; it is the myth of a tragic terrain stalked by banished men." In

his article for the *Dictionary of Literary Biography,* Larry R. Smith quoted Dahlberg as saying: "As for myself, I'm a medievalist, a horse and buggy American, a barbarian, anything, that can bring me back to the communal song of labor, sky, star, field, love."

Much of Dahlberg's fiction was drawn from his troubled childhood. Dahlberg was born illegitimately at a charity hospital in Boston in 1900. His mother was Elizabeth Dahlberg, married and the mother of three other children, and his father was Elizabeth's lover, a Jewish barber named Saul Gottdank. Following Dahlberg's birth, the couple took him and moved to Dallas, Texas. Once there, Gottdank stole Elizabeth's money, left town, and abandoned her. Later reconciliations in Memphis and New Orleans ended with similar betrayals. Elizabeth wandered about the South and Midwest for several years before settling in Kansas City, where she opened a hair salon. But the family's troubles continued. Despite the successful business, Elizabeth was to lose her money to a string of opportunistic men. One of these men suggested that she send Edward to an orphanage so he would not be exposed to the immorality of the Kansas City streets. She did so in 1912, and Edward entered the Jewish Orphan Asylum in Cleveland. With his admission to the orphanage, Smith remarked, "life turned from harsh to grim" for the young boy. Children at the orphanage were called by their numbers instead of their names; the windows in the building were barred; and the boredom and brutality of the place caused Dahlberg to suppress his emotions.

Upon reaching legal age in 1917, Dahlberg left the orphanage and served a brief stint as a Western Union messenger in Cleveland before making his way back to Kansas City and his mother. In the next few years Dahlberg was to work in the stockyards as a drover and serve in the U.S. Army as a private. He also wandered about the American West as a hobo, working as a dishwasher, cook, and day laborer to pay his way. In 1919 he made his home at the Los Angeles YMCA. It was there he met Max Lewis, an older, self-educated man who taught Dahlberg to appreciate such writers as Friedrich Nietzsche, Samuel Butler, and Ralph Waldo Emerson. Dahlberg developed an interest in learning, and Lewis encouraged him to attend college. In 1921 Dahlberg enrolled at the University of California at Berkeley, where he majored in philosophy and anthropology. He transferred to Columbia University in 1923 to finish his degree. Upon graduation in 1925, Dahlberg taught at James Madison and Thomas Jefferson high schools in New York City.

After marrying Fanya Fass, the daughter of a Cleveland industrialist, in 1926, Dahlberg and his new wife moved to Europe. The couple divorced soon after arriving. For a time Dahlberg was a part of the expatriate group of American writers living in Paris. He became friends with Hart Crane, Robert McAlmon, and Richard Aldington. While living in Brussels in 1928, he completed his first novel, *Bottom Dogs,* based on his childhood experiences at the orphanage and as a hobo traveling in the American West. The novel was marked by Dahlberg's use of coarse slang and his often graphic descriptions of down-and-out workers, farmers, and wanderers. It was published in England in 1929 and in the United States in 1930.

In his introduction to *Bottom Dogs,* D. H. Lawrence praised Dahlberg as a naturalist writer who successfully recreated the psychological mind-set of society's underclass. The novel's style, Lawrence wrote, "seems to me excellent, fitting the matter. It is sheer bottom-dog style, the bottom-dog mind expressing itself direct, almost as if it barked. That directness, that unsentimental and non-dramatised thoroughness of setting down the under-dog mind surpasses anything I know. I don't want to read any more books like this. But I am glad to have read this one, just to know what is the last word in repulsive consciousness, consciousness in a state of repulsion."

Several critics agreed with Lawrence, finding that *Bottom Dogs* accurately reflected the language and life of the lowest levels of society. Herbert Leibowitz of the *American Scholar* judged the novel's language to be "bare of mythical adornments, a flat morose voice moving over the terrain of memory, never straying from its tone of inert defeat, as the hero, Lorry Lewis, wanders across America. There is no connection among characters, just a drab amnesia, the stylistic counterpart of the Great Depression." Walter Allen, writing in his *The Modern Novel,* maintained that *Bottom Dogs* "communicates hopelessness, the hopelessness of the . . . lives of the bottom dogs, men and women who can sink no lower in the social and economic system."

For writing of society's underclass in the language of the streets, Dahlberg became immensely influential. Other writers adopted the approach, which came to be known during the 1930s as social realism or proletarian writing. In his book *Proletarian Writers of the Thirties,* Jules Chametsky described Dahlberg as a pioneer of proletarian writing: "Dahlberg's language of disgust, his imagery of rot and decay—and most importantly—his pioneering exploration of the bottom-dog milieux of flophouses, hobo jungles, and freight cars certainly places him in the vanguard of that school." J. D. O'Hara in the *New York Times Book Review* credited Dahlberg with having spawned the proletarian school of writing, but "those writers who had seized on his 'Bottom Dogs' style worked it to death in the service of Communism."

In his next two novels, *From Flushing to Calvary* and *Those Who Perish,* Dahlberg continued to write of his early life, garnering a reputation as one of the decade's leading proletarian novelists. Writing in the *Massachusetts Review,* Frank MacShane called these early books "socially committed. . . . More deeply, they were fed by [Dahlberg's] own anger at injustice. They were written in a colloquial style suited, as was thought, to the proletariat." Dahlberg's political inclinations moved him to work with other leftist writers of the 1930s. He helped to organize the communist-dominated American Writers' Congress of 1935, where he delivered a paper entitled "Fascism and Writers." By the late 1930s, however, his novels, although critically accepted, "showed no artistic growth, so Dahlberg, who meanwhile had fallen out with the Communists and who had genuine literary ambitions, ceased writing and began to read," according to MacShane. Dahlberg later repudiated his early novels as "mediocre manipulations of his childhood and young manhood, disfigured by self-pity," as Leibowitz explained. He also referred to the books as "dunghill fiction."

For many years Dahlberg wrote no new fiction, instead devoting his time to an intense study of literature. In this study he rejected most of the authors and books of the twentieth century, preferring such earlier writers as Shakespeare, Cervantes, Melville, Poe, Dickinson, and especially Thoreau. His readings of their works resulted in a writing style drastically different from his proletarian approach of the 1930s. He left behind the "linguistic void and gibbering of robots that he says marked much of the fiction and discourse of the thirties," Leibowitz stated.

Dahlberg's new style, first presented in the essay collection *Do These Bones Live* (later published as *Can These Bones Live*), is rich in biblical cadence, allusions, and aphoristic pronouncements. It is, White maintained, "a new language, an amalgam of 17th-century prose, moralizing in the style of La Rochefoucauld and queer classical learning. The effect of this language is in turn unintelligible, beautiful and ludicrous." Brom Weber in the *Saturday Review* claimed that "Dahlberg's baroque exuberance marks a return to the florid style of Melville and, beyond him in time, of Puritans Cotton Mather and Nathaniel Ward, whose fervid prose, like that of Dahlberg, is rich in rare and archaic diction, allusions to and quotations from more ancient savants, paradoxes, contradictions, factual errors, misinterpretations, impatience with contemporaries, and powerful self-assertiveness."

Do These Bones Live, "a brilliant and profound survey of American literature," as Allen Tate called it in the *Sewanee Review,* also introduced Dahlberg's support for a mythical kind of writing meant to endow ordinary life with greater significance. As John Wain wrote in the *New York Review of Books,* Dahlberg's later work "was largely concerned to transmogrify experience into myth: to give to everyday episodes that range of implication which animates the great anonymous world-explaining stories of mankind." Accordingly, Dahlberg criticized such earlier American writers as Whitman and Poe, citing the limitations of their work in comparison to such writers as Dante, who had used myth more effectively. He also condemned modernist writing, especially the works of Eliot and Pound. *Do These Bones Live,* Weber explained, "is the literary and cultural criticism of an impassioned lyric poet."

During the 1940s and 1950s, Dahlberg published little new work. Then, beginning in the early 1960s, he entered a period of production that was surprising for a middle-aged writer, publishing an average of one new book every year. Perhaps the most important of these later works was the autobiography *Because I Was Flesh,* a book in which Dahlberg came to terms with the circumstances of his early life and, in particular, with his mixed feelings about his mother. Adams described *Because I Was Flesh* as "Dahlberg's extended tribute to his mother" as well as the author's "one sustained achievement."

Critics praised Dahlberg for successfully transforming the story of his life into a form of myth. *Because I Was Flesh,* according to Wain, "succeeds in the tremendous undertaking of mythologizing modern America, as thoroughly as Joyce mythologized Dublin." Smith explained that "the book is a synthesis of Dahlberg's pithy epigrams, his concise realistic detail, and his passages of philosophical reverie. It fuses myth and reality in a flowing style that encompasses emotion, thought, and humor." MacShane noted that in *Because I Was Flesh* the "bare narrative was given substance by the rich prose in which it was written—a prose that incorporated literary, historical and mythical references so as to give the story greater resonance than was possible when accepting the limitations of colloquial English. The danger of the method is that it can be artificially literary and therefore pretentious; but *Because I Was Flesh* is grounded in observed reality." Leibowitz concluded: "*Because I Was Flesh* is a masterpiece of Oedipal obsession, a poetic memoir of primal sunderings and rages."

Although he had been writing poetry for many years, it was only during the 1960s that Dahlberg published his work in book form. *Cipango's Hinder Door* and *The Leafless American, and Other Writings* present thirty of his poems, most of them mythologizing American history as well as Dahlberg's own personal past. Cipango is the name of the mythical Asian land which Columbus believed he had discovered when he landed in the New World, Kennedy explained in his review of *Cipango's Hinder Door.* Thus, "Dahlberg's theme is the discovery of a new world—the rediscovery, to be exact [and] the rediscovery of America is another name for a discovery of himself," Kennedy concluded.

"Dahlberg's poetry," Smith observed, "can be described as epigrammatic, lyric, densely mythical in reference . . ., rhythmic, intense, and progressing in associative or lyrical leaps." Donald W. Baker of *Poetry* claimed that "the best of his work, alive with incantatory rhythms and a prophetic tone, generates the power of psalm and prayer."

Much of Dahlberg's later reputation was colored by his often acrid commentary on contemporary literature and society. O'Hara labeled these comments as being "consistently hostile, vituperative, personally insulting and wrong." Several critics compared Dahlberg to biblical figures like Ishmael and Jeremiah who spoke out against the sinful ways of their time. Benjamin T. Spencer, in an article for *Twentieth Century Literature,* credited Dahlberg with "the stance of an Old Testament prophet" and a "self-appointed mission to cleanse the Augean stables of literature." Saul Maloff remarked in *Commonweal* that "the jeremiad is his characteristic tone. . . . Dahlberg is a crank in a peculiarly American grain, a solitary who sets himself intransigently against all contemporary literary conventions and traditions, and rails against the mainstream and all its tributaries as they churn unheeding past."

His controversial criticism focused on what Dahlberg saw as contemporary literature's lack of morals, and on the limitations of a rational and scientific worldview. White summarized Dahlberg's "moral analysis" as a belief "that sexuality is permanently at war with man's higher aspirations and must be disciplined; that human companionship is a great good, though difficult to find and keep; that instinct is often more trustworthy than reason; that accumulating wisdom, however, is honorable, if vain practice; that each person's character is so inflexible it cannot be significantly improved; that the machine age is an abomination; and that life is tragic." Rosenthal explained that Dahlberg's "cause, his importance, lie in his ingrained suspicion of the rationalistic, scientific heritage which has imprisoned intellect in our time. He knows, instinctively . . . that above reason and the soul or spirit stands . . . the good of the intellect, the light of wisdom which is a perpetual source of interpretation and transformation. Dahlberg instinctively knows that the method of this form of intellect is the explanation of myths, the presentation of symbols, the search for ancient wisdom."

Because of the singular nature of his vision and the sometimes scathing words he had for his contemporaries, Dahlberg's literary standing is still undecided. Dahlberg, Tate believed, "like Thoreau whom he admires more than any other nineteenth-century American, eludes his contemporaries; he may have to wait for understanding until the historians of ideas of the next generation can place him historically. For we have at present neither literary nor historical standards which can guide us into Mr. Dahlberg's books written since *Bottom Dogs.*" Smith called him "a rare American poet of mythography as well as lyric personal verse. His extraordinary prose style is at times of erudite obscurism, and at [other times] personal and poetic. . . . In Edward Dahlberg the writing is the man, and there is much in the experience of that life to make his work tragically, comically, even beautifully unique." August Derleth described Dahlberg as being "as much a genius as anyone of whom I can think, past or present." He credited Dahlberg's sheer talent as the cause of critical resistance to his work: "The world is seldom ready to extend genius a helping hand, but only to salute genius when he who possessed it is safely underground." Writing in the *New York Times Book Review* about his career as a writer, Dahlberg once claimed: "I never put together a shoal of vowels and consonants for mammon or for that other whore, fame. I propose to go along as I always have done, sowing dragon's teeth when nec-

essary, and seeding affections in the souls of my unknown readers if I can."

BIOGRAPHICAL/CRITICAL SOURCES:

BOOKS

Allen, Walter, *The Modern Novel,* Dutton, 1964.
Billings, Harold, editor, *Edward Dahlberg: American Ishmael of Letters,* Roger Beacham, 1968.
Billings, Harold, *A Bibliography of Edward Dahlberg,* University of Texas Press, 1971.
Contemporary Literary Criticism, Gale, Volume 1, 1973, Volume 7, 1977, Volume 14, 1980.
Dahlberg, Edward, *Bottom Dogs,* Putnam, 1929, Simon & Schuster, 1930.
Dahlberg, Edward, *Because I Was Flesh,* New Directions, 1964.
Dahlberg, Edward, *Confessions of Edward Dahlberg,* Braziller, 1971.
DeFanti, Charles, *The Wages of Expectation: A Biography of Edward Dahlberg,* New York University Press, 1978.
Dictionary of Literary Biography, Volume 48: *American Poets, 1880-1945, Second Series,* Gale, 1986.
Madden, Donald, editor, *Proletarian Writers of the Thirties,* Southern Illinois University Press, 1968.
Moramarco, Fred, *Edward Dahlberg,* Twayne, 1972.
Williams, Jonathan, editor, *Edward Dahlberg: A Tribute,* David Lewis, 1971.
Wilson, Edmund, *The Shores of Light,* Farrar, Straus, 1952.

PERIODICALS

American Scholar, summer, 1975.
Atlantic, March, 1971.
Book World, June 2, 1968, July 21, 1968, February 16, 1969.
Christian Science Monitor, April 13, 1967.
Commonweal, February 19, 1971.
Contemporary Literature, spring, 1977.
Massachusetts Review, spring, 1964, spring, 1978.
Nation, November 11, 1968.
National Review, September 19, 1967.
New Republic, August 3, 1968, February 6, 1971.
Newsweek, January 23, 1967.
New York Review of Books, August 24, 1967, January 2, 1969.
New York Times Book Review, December 19, 1965, June 19, 1966, January 15, 1967, March 5, 1967, August 18, 1968, April 18, 1976.
Poetry, March, 1967.
Saturday Review, March 6, 1971.
Sewanee Review, spring, 1961.
Southern Review, spring, 1965, summer, 1967.
Twentieth Century Literature, December, 1975.
Western Humanities Review, summer, 1966.

OBITUARIES:

PERIODICALS

New York Times, February 28, 1977.
Publishers Weekly, March 21, 1977.
Time, March 14, 1977.
Washington Post, March 2, 1977.

—*Sketch by Thomas Wiloch*

DAILEY, Janet (Ann) 1944-

PERSONAL: Born May 21, 1944, in Storm Lake, Iowa; daughter of Boyd (a farmer) and Louise Haradon; married William Dailey; stepchildren: two. *Religion:* Methodist.

ADDRESSES: Home—Branson, Mo. *Office*—Janbill Ltd., Star Route 4, Box 2197, Branson, Mo. 65616.

CAREER: Worked as a secretary in Nebraska and Iowa, 1962-74; writer, 1974—.

AWARDS, HONORS: Romance Writers of America, Golden Heart Award, 1981, Golden Pen Award, 1987.

WRITINGS:

No Quarter Asked, Harlequin, 1976.
Boss Man from Ogallala, Harlequin, 1976.
Savage Land, Harlequin, 1976.
Land of Enchantment, Harlequin, 1976.
Fire and Ice, Harlequin, 1976.
The Homeplace, Harlequin, 1976.
After the Storm, Harlequin, 1976.
Dangerous Masquerade, Harlequin, 1977.
Night of the Cotillion, Harlequin, 1977.
Valley of the Vapors, Harlequin, 1977.
Fiesta San Antonio, Harlequin, 1977.
Show Me, Harlequin, 1977.
Bluegrass King, Harlequin, 1977.
A Lyon's Share, Harlequin, 1977.
The Widow and the Wastrel, Harlequin, 1977.
The Ivory Cane, Harlequin, 1978.
The Indy Man, Harlequin, 1978.
Darling Jenny, Harlequin, 1978.
Reilly's Woman, Harlequin, 1978.
To Tell the Truth, Harlequin, 1978.
Sonora Sundown, Harlequin, 1978.
Big Sky Country, Harlequin, 1978.
Something Extra, Harlequin, 1978.
Master Fiddler, Harlequin, 1978.
Beware of the Stranger, Harlequin, 1978.
Giant of Mesabi, Harlequin, 1978.
The Matchmakers, Harlequin, 1978.
For Bitter or Worse, Harlequin, 1979.
Green Mountain Man, Harlequin, 1979.
Six White Horses, Harlequin, 1979.
Summer Mahogany, Harlequin, 1979.
The Bride of the Delta Queen, Harlequin, 1979.
Touch the Wind, Pocket Books, 1979.
Tidewater Lover, Harlequin, 1979.
Strange Bedfellow, Harlequin, 1979.
Low Country Liar, Harlequin, 1979.
Sweet Promise, Harlequin, 1979.
For Mike's Sake, Harlequin, 1979.
Sentimental Journey, Harlequin, 1979.
A Land Called Deseret, Harlequin, 1979.
Kona Winds, Harlequin, 1980.
That Boston Man, Harlequin, 1980.
The Rogue, Pocket Books, 1980.
Bed of Grass, Harlequin, 1980.
The Thawing of Mara, Harlequin, 1980.
The Mating Season, Harlequin, 1980.
Lord of the High Lonesome, Harlequin, 1980.
Southern Nights, Harlequin, 1980.
Ride the Thunder, Pocket Books, 1980.
Enemy in Camp, Harlequin, 1980.
Difficult Decision, Harlequin, 1980.

Heart of Stone, Harlequin, 1980.
One of the Boys, Harlequin, 1980.
Night Way, Pocket Books, 1981.
Wild and Wonderful, Harlequin, 1981.
A Tradition of Pride, Harlequin, 1981.
The Traveling Kind, Harlequin, 1981.
The Hostage Bride, Silhouette Books, 1981.
Dakota Dreamin', Harlequin, 1981.
This Calder Sky (Doubleday Book Club selection), Pocket Books, 1981.
The Lancaster Men, Silhouette Books, 1981.
For the Love of God, Silhouette Books, 1981.
Northern Magic, Harlequin, 1982.
With A Little Luck, Harlequin, 1982.
Terms of Surrender, Silhouette Books, 1982.
That Carolina Summer, Harlequin, 1982.
This Calder Range (Doubleday Book Club selection), Pocket Books, 1982.
Wildcatter's Woman, Silhouette Books, 1982.
Foxfire Light, Silhouette Books, 1982.
The Second Time, Silhouette Books, 1982.
Mistletoe and Holly, Silhouette Books, 1982.
Stands a Calder Man, Pocket Books, 1983.
Separate Cabins, Silhouette Books, 1983.
Western Man, Silhouette Books, 1983.
Calder Born, Calder Bred (Doubleday Book Club selection), Pocket Books, 1983.
Best Way to Lose, Silhouette Books, 1983.
Leftover Love, Silhouette Books, 1984.
Silver Wings, Santiago Blue (Doubleday Book Club selection and Literary Guild selection), Poseidon, 1984.
The Pride of Hannah Wade (Doubleday Book Club selection), Pocket Books, 1985.
The Glory Game (Doubleday Book Club selection and Literary Guild selection), Poseidon, 1985.
The Great Alone, Poseidon, 1986.
Heiress (Doubleday Book Club and Literary Guild selection), Little, Brown, 1987.
Rivals (Literary Guild selection), Little, Brown, 1989.

Also author of a screenplay based on her novel *Foxfire Light,* 1983; composer of lyrics for country western songs. Author and publisher of *Janet Dailey Newsletter.*

SIDELIGHTS: With over eighty novels to her credit, romance writer Janet Dailey is currently the fifth best-selling author in the world, just behind Harold Robbins, Barbara Cartland, Irving Wallace, and Louis L'Amour. In the little more than ten years that she has been writing, Dailey has seen her books sell well over 100 million copies in nineteen languages.

A voracious reader as a child, Dailey knew as a teenager that she wanted to be a writer. After high school, however, she left her hometown to work as a secretary for an Omaha construction company owned by Bill Dailey, whom she later married. After years of helping run the business, Bill made Janet a partner. In 1974, they decided to sell the company. The couple then set off to journey across America in a travel trailer.

Deciding that she could write better romance novels than the ones she had been reading to occupy her free time, Dailey, with her husband's encouragement, started to work on her first romance novel. "I kept saying to Bill that this is the kind of book I'd like to write," she remarked in *Forbes.* "He got tired of hearing that in a hurry and told me to write the book, not just talk about it." Upon its completion, the novel was immediately accepted for publication by Toronto's Harlequin Books, becoming the first of more than fifty Dailey titles brought out by the Canadian firm; for years she was the only American romance writer Harlequin published.

One reason for Dailey's enormous literary output in such a brief period is her strict writing schedule. Six mornings a week, with only an occasional day off for promotional engagements or other business obligations, she writes from eleven to fifteen pages of manuscript. Calling herself a "workaholic," Dailey explained in *Working Woman* the motivation behind maintaining such a work schedule: "I get so involved that if weren't sitting down at the typewriter, the story would just be going around in my head all the time anyway; once you start that first page, your life starts to revolve around the book."

According to Eliot Fremont-Smith in the *Voice Literary Supplement,* "Dailey writes two kinds of novels—15O-pagers and 350-pagers—though 18O-pagers and 24O-pagers have at least been experimented with. . . . The 15Os take her nine days to complete, the 35Os between 30 and 45 days." As she declared to Linda Witt of *People,* "working two years on a novel would drive me up the wall."

This dedication to her writing, coupled with her respect for her craft, seems to be a major attraction for Dailey's multitude of readers. "My romance readers are like me," she once stated in the *New York Times Book Review.* "They are work-oriented women who are under a great deal of stress. They are very involved . . . and they need an escape." Furthermore, the author continued, "I'm not identified with Hollywood decadence. I still have too much dirt between my toes; wear Levi's rather than Calvin Klein's. My readers know that I'm a Midwestern girl and that I hold to Midwestern values."

Even though Dailey's books are extremely popular with readers, they have generally not been well reviewed or treated very seriously by critics. Many point to the never-changing themes of romance novels, to the predictable plots, and to the similarity of characters as reasons why they virtually ignore this genre. *People's* Margot Dougherty describes Dailey's novels as "escapist literature, smooth and shallow." The author answers this charge in *Redbook:* "It's true that they're called escape novels, but they won't work unless there's an element of reality too. I show a genuine conflict between the hero and heroine. Real or imagined, the conflict exists and they can't wish it away. The characters cope with it, find a way to resolve it, and that resolution involves change—it brings them closer together. We can all recognize that kind of pattern from our own relationships, even if the setting is idealistic and escape-oriented."

When Joseph Parisi of the *Chicago Tribune* asked Bill Dailey to explain why he felt critics tended to ignore his wife's books, he remarked: "We've talked to critics before, and they can't see any value in this [type of literature]. And, of course, our comment back is we're not trying to write the Great American Novel. We're pleasing ourselves. We got 22 million readers in this country and 53 million around the world. We couldn't care less, really. It's nice to be on the *New York Times* [bestsellers list], and we are. But if you've got 22 million readers who love the books and they can associate with Janet, that beats hell out of a dozen critics." Added Janet Dailey in *Working Woman:* "I often respond to critics with the cliche that Bob Hope isn't going to win any awards for acting, in the same way that I'm never going to win a Pulitzer. But look at the entertainment we give."

Dailey's husband serves as her manager as well as her partner in their joint business firm, Janbill Ltd. In the writing area, Bill Dailey handles all of the research—supplying his wife with the details that make her novels as authentic as possible—helps edit her manuscripts, and organizes her schedule. As he explained to Alice Turner of *Redbook:* "I went to Jan and laid out a plan for doing these stories. She would do the writing, and I would manage her career and take care of all the research and the business. We would be a team. And that's the way we've done it." Agreeing, Janet Dailey remarked to Witt: "Bill and I are a team. You can't be Rodgers and Hammerstein when you are only Rodgers."

Janet and Bill Dailey are also involved in a variety of other ventures. Their companies include such enterprises as a television production company, a restaurant/lounge, a music publishing company, and several country music theaters. But their biggest project to date is their theme park and resort complex called Wildwood, U.S.A., located in their hometown of Branson, Missouri.

Dailey and her books generate so much interest among her readers that she and her husband began publishing the *Janet Dailey Newsletter.* With over 53,000 subscribers, the quarterly keeps Dailey's fans up-to-date on her writing, answers their questions, and informs them about her professional and personal activities.

When Dailey was asked what it is about her books that triggers such interest and loyalty, she told Joseph Parisi of the *Chicago Tribune:* "The first thing is story. The second thing is traditional values. And by that I'm talking about loyalty, fidelity, honesty in relationships. . . . It's also touching on feelings. . . . A writer must write it so the reader will feel it, to the point where he hurts and cries and he laughs and he feels the warmth in it."

In addition to her numerous romance novels, Dailey has also written books that the *Saturday Review* describes as "part modern romance, part modern western, and part modern gothic." Among these novels are her four volume multigenerational saga on the Calder family and the book *Silver Wings, Santiago Blue,* which Dailey describes in *Working Woman* as "fiction, but with a nonfictional theme."

In 1984 she published her last strictly romance-type novel, saying in *Publishers Weekly,* "I quit writing category romances with the publication of *Leftover Love,* . . . I was—and am—moving on as a writer." Explaining herself further in the *Chicago Tribune,* Dailey noted that she is going to concentrate on "more historical or general fiction. But I'm going to stay with the strong love theme: . . . Pick up any best seller and you'll find it there."

One of the reviewers who has taken a serious look at Dailey's books is Eliot Fremont-Smith. Writing in a *Voice Literary Supplement* review of *Calder Born, Calder Bred,* Fremont-Smith states that Dailey's "books are about courage and grit. They are not escapes from a world that is drab, but invitations to a world that is, though conflicted, exciting, wonderful, and eventually fulfilling for those with right values and an understanding of what this thing called 'man' is. The idea is to partake, participate. The message is, you can do it, with the books as a demo. The function is to release innate bravery."

MEDIA ADAPTATIONS: The film rights to Dailey's Calder series have been purchased for production as a television miniseries.

AVOCATIONAL INTERESTS: Travel.

BIOGRAPHICAL/CRITICAL SOURCES:

BOOKS

Falk, Kathryn, *Love's Leading Ladies,* Pinnacle Books, 1982.

PERIODICALS

Booklist, March 1, 1982, December 15, 1982, September 1, 1983.
Chicago Tribune, June 12, 1983, July 13, 1986.
Cosmopolitan, September, 1984.
Detroit News, July 21, 1985.
Forbes, March 6, 1978.
Inside Books, December, 1988.
Kirkus Reviews, February 15, 1982, July 15, 1983.
Ladies Home Journal, May, 1985.
Library Journal, August, 1984.
Los Angeles Times, September 7, 1984.
Los Angeles Times Book Review, December 19, 1982, December 16, 1983.
New York Times Book Review, August 3, 1980, August 16, 1981, August 26, 1984, March 17, 1985.
People, July 13, 1981, September 17, 1984, March 18, 1985.
Publishers Weekly, April 2, 1979, November 28, 1980, June 12, 1981, February 26, 1982, November 26, 1982, August 24, 1984.
Redbook, June, 1983.
Saturday Review, March, 1981.
Voice Literary Supplement, October, 1983.
Washington Post Book World, March 3, 1985.
Working Woman, March, 1984.

*   *   *

DALE, George E.
See ASIMOV, Isaac

*   *   *

DALY, Mary 1928-

PERSONAL: Born October 16, 1928, in Schenectady, N.Y.; daughter of Frank X. (a salesman) and Anna Catherine (Morse) Daly. *Education:* College of St. Rose, B.A., 1950; Catholic University of America, M.A., 1952,; St. Mary's College, Notre Dame, Ind., Ph.D., 1954; University of Fribourg, S.T.D., 1963, Ph.D., 1965.

ADDRESSES: Home—55A Norwood Ave., Newton Centre, Mass. 02159. *Office*—Department of Theology, Boston College, Chestnut Hill, Mass. 02167. *Agent*—Charlotte Raymond, 23 Waldron Ct., Marblehead, Mass. 01945.

CAREER: Cardinal Cushing College, Brookline, Mass., teacher of philosophy and theology, 1954-59; Junior Year Abroad programs, Fribourg, Switzerland, teacher of philosophy and theology, 1959-66; Boston College, Chestnut Hill, Mass., assistant professor, 1966-69, associate professor of theology, 1969—. Visiting lecturer in English, St. Mary's College, 1952-54.

MEMBER: American Catholic Philosophical Association, American Academy of Religion, American Academy of Political and Social Science, American Association of University Professors, National Organization for Women, Society for the Scientific Study of Religion.

WRITINGS:

Natural Knowledge of God in the Philosophy of Jacques Maritain, Catholic Book Agency (Rome), 1966.
The Church and the Second Sex, Harper, 1968, with a new Feminist Postchristian introduction by the author, 1975, revised edition, Beacon Press, 1985.
(Contributor) William Jerry Boney and Lawrence E. Molumby, editors, *The New Catholic Day: Catholic Theologians of the Renewal,* John Knox, 1968.

(Contributor) William J. Wilson, editor, *Demands for Christian Renewal,* Maryknoll Publications, 1968.
Beyond God the Father: Toward a Philosophy of Women's Liberation, Beacon Press, 1973, 2nd revised edition, 1985.
Gyn/Ecology: The Metaethics of Radical Feminism, Beacon Press, 1978.
Pure Lust: Elemental Feminist Philosophy, Beacon Press, 1984.
(With Jane Caputi) *Websters' First New Intergalactic Wickedary of the English Language,* Beacon Press, 1987.

Contributor to numerous anthologies, including *Sisterhood Is Powerful,* edited by Robin Morgan, Random House, 1970, and *Voices of the New Feminism,* edited by Mary Lou Thompson, Beacon Press, 1970. Contributor to *Dictionary of the History of Ideas;* contributor of articles and reviews to *Commonweal, National Catholic Reporter, Quest, Social Policy,* and other journals.

SIDELIGHTS: Theologian Mary Daly's work has evolved from criticism of the anti-feminist stance of the Catholic Church—in *The Church and the Second Sex*—to later books of more universal scope, centering on the misogynistic tendencies of society and how to deal with them. Religion is a cornerstone of society, however, and remains the starting point for Daly's theories. She maintains that all religions are patriarchal and thus explains the patriarchal attitudes of the modern world. "All [religions] . . . ," she writes in *Gyn/Ecology: The Metaethics of Radical Feminism,* "are erected as parts of the male's shelter against anomie. And the symbolic message of all the sects of the religion which is patriarchy is this: Women are the dreaded anomie. Consequently, women are the objects of male terror, the projected personifications of 'The Enemy.' "

As the scope of Daly's books widened from a religious to a societal focus so did her interest in what *New York Times Book Review* contributor Demaris Wehr describes as "the role of language in the transformation of consciousness," a theme which Wehr finds throughout Daly's work. In Wehr's review of *Pure Lust: Elemental Feminist Philosphy* the critic notes that, while in *The Church and the Second Sex* Daly focuses on "antifeminism in language" and in *Beyond God the Father* suggests that new non-sexist words need to be created, in *Gyn/Ecology* and *Pure Lust* the Daly offers the reader a new feminist vocabulary. In both of the later books Daly takes derogatory terms for women, such as shrew, hag, or crone, and uses them as words of praise, capitalizing them to emphasize the importance of the women to which they refer. Her *Websters' First New Intergalactic Wickedary of the English Language,* a collaborative effort with Jane Caputi, is a glossary of these old words with new definitions as well as the many new words created by Daly. Commenting on the feminist's vocabulary, Wehr notes, "Whether it is invigorating or arduous to read [these new words] (they are all Very Big) depends on varying factors, such as how alert the reader is at the time. But the point is, new words challenge us to think different thoughts in different ways. This is exciting."

In his *Spectator* review of *Pure Lust* David Sexton elaborates more fully on Daly's unique use of language to express her beliefs. "Daly herself," he observes, "attempts to write a language that is free of unwanted associations—a form of alliterative thought chant, decorated with typographical freaks. Words are given arbitrary new histories—('we are not surprised to hear that *dream* is said to be etymologically related to the Latvian word (dunduris) meaning gadfly, wasp. For Metamorphosing women sting and provoke each other to Change'). . . . Daly's prose is in fact thrillingly horrid; it reads like Carlyle under the influence of *Finnegans Wake.*" In Sara Maitland's *New Statesman* review of the same volume, the critic expresses similar doubts about

Daly's style but also praises her work, "Daly is probably the most important Radical Feminist thinker around; she is also a writer of flamboyant brilliance—despite the fact that her addiction to alliteration is wearing, she has an unmatched depth of passion, imagination and pure verbal wit."

Other critics suggest that Daly's use of language may obscure her message, thus diluting her substantial contribution to feminist theory. In a *Ms.* essay devoted to Daly's work, noted feminist Lindsy Van Gelder complains about the difficulty of reading *Gyn/Ecology.* Van Gelder comments: "The first Passage, some 100 pages long, abounds with lengthy quotations from Merriam-Webster, forays into Greek and Latin derivations, invented words . . ., and endless puns. . . . The section may seem tiresome to women who have already thought through the limitations of patriarchal language and tiring to those who have not." Helen McNeil also finds fault with the same volume: "Throughout *Gyn/Ecology,* words are punned upon, slashed apart and stitched together, and broken down into polemic etymologies. . . . Unfortunately Daly's verbal play often obfuscates her argument, forcing even what she would call a Revolting Hag Searcher, like this reviewer, to struggle just to make basic sense of passages which as often as not are about the most gross and hideous persecutions of women. Having suffered these outrages, must we now kill ourselves *reading* about them too?" But, while Van Gelder sees little in the work to praise, McNeil calls it "an important book for its fierceness as much as for its facts."

Summarizing her views for *CA,* Daly once wrote: "My fundamental interest is the women's revolution, which I see as the radical source of possibility for other forms of liberation from oppressive structures. I am interested precisely in the spiritual dimension of women's liberation, in its transforming potential in relation to religious consciousness and the forms in which this consciousness expresses itself. This is not 'one area' of theology; rather, it challenges the whole patriarchal religion."

BIOGRAPHICAL/CRITICAL SOURCES:

BOOKS

Contemporary Issues Criticism, Volume 1, Gale, 1982.
Daly, Mary, *Gyn/Ecology: The Metaethics of Radical Feminism,* Beacon Press, 1978.

PERIODICALS

Ms., February, 1979.
New Statesman, April 4, 1980, January 18, 1985.
New York Times Book Review, July 22, 1984.
Spectator, February 23, 1985.

* * *

DANIELS, Brett
   See ADLER, Renata

* * *

DANNAY, Frederic 1905-1982
   (Daniel Nathan; Barnaby Ross and Ellery Queen, joint pseudonyms)

PERSONAL: Name originally Daniel Nathan; name legally changed; born October 20, 1905, in Brooklyn, N.Y.; died after a brief illness, September 3, 1982, in White Plains, N.Y.; son of Meyer H. and Dora (Walerstein) Nathan; married Mary Beck (deceased); married Hilda Wiesenthal (died, 1972); married

Rose Koppel; children: (first marriage) Douglas, Richard; (second marriage) Stephen (deceased).

CAREER: After what he called a "patchwork" of jobs, Dannay worked in advertising, becoming a copywriter, art director, and account executive for various advertising agencies; he was also a typographic consultant. He left advertising just after publication of the first Ellery Queen novel in 1929. He later became a full-time writer and editor. From 1933 to 1934 he made lecture tours with Manfred B. Lee; from 1958 to 1959, he was visiting professor at the University of Texas at Austin.

MEMBER: Mystery Writers of America (co-founder and past co-president, with Manfred B. Lee), Crime Writers' Association (London), Baker Street Irregulars.

AWARDS, HONORS: Mystery Writers of America, Edgar Allan Poe Annual Award, 1945, for best radio program, 1947, for outstanding contribution in the field of the mystery short story, 1949, to *Ellery Queen's Mystery Magazine,* for outstanding contribution in the field of the mystery short story, Special Book Award, 1951, Grand Master Award, 1960; Pocket Books, Silver Gertrude (signifying membership in Million Copy Club), Gold Gertrude (signifying membership in Five Million Copy Club); American Red Cross citation for outstanding national service, 1945; National War Fund citation for meritorious service, 1945; Youth Oscar Award, Youth United, 1949, as distinguished ex-Brooklynite; *TV Guide* Gold Medal Award, 1950, to the Ellery Queen TV series as "Mystery Show of the Year"; Ellery Queen ranked third in Gallup Poll of Best Mystery Writers of All Time, 1950; Ellery Queen was ranked, in an international poll of experts, among the ten best active mystery writers, 1951; *True* magazine citation to Ellery Queen TV series, 1952; Edgar Allan Poe Ring, Mystery Writers of Japan, 1956; Grand Prix de Litterature Policiere, 1978, for *And On the Eighth Day;* honorary doctorate, Carroll College, 1979; many awards during 1979 for the fiftieth anniversary of *The Roman Hat Mystery,* the first Ellery Queen book.

WRITINGS:

NOVELS; WITH MANFRED B. LEE, UNDER JOINT PSEUDONYM ELLERY QUEEN

The Roman Hat Mystery, Stokes, 1929, reprinted, Mysterious Press, 1979.
The French Powder Mystery, Stokes, 1930, reissued, Buccaneer Books, 1976.
The Dutch Shoe Mystery, Stokes, 1931, reissued, Buccaneer Books, 1976.
The Greek Coffin Mystery, Stokes, 1932, reissued, Buccaneer Books, 1976.
The Egyptian Cross Mystery, Stokes, 1932, reissued, Buccaneer Books, 1976.
The American Gun Mystery, Stokes, 1933, reissued, Ballantine, 1979.
The Siamese Twin Mystery, Stokes, 1933, reissued, Buccaneer Books, 1980.
The Chinese Orange Mystery, Stokes, 1934, reissued, Buccaneer Books, 1976.
The Spanish Cape Mystery, Stokes, 1935, reissued, Buccaneer Books, 1976.
Halfway House, Stokes, 1936.
The Door Between, Stokes, 1937.
The Devil to Pay, Stokes, 1938.
The Four of Hearts, Stokes, 1938.
The Dragon's Teeth, Stokes, 1939.
Calamity Town, Little, Brown, 1942.

There Was an Old Woman, Little, Brown, 1943.
The Murderer Is a Fox, Little, Brown, 1945.
Ten Days' Wonder, Little, Brown, 1948.
Cat of Many Tails, Little, Brown, 1949, reissued, International Polygonics, 1988.
Double, Double, Little, Brown, 1950.
The Origin of Evil, Little, Brown, 1951.
The King Is Dead, Little, Brown, 1952.
The Scarlet Letters, Little, Brown, 1953.
The Glass Village, Little, Brown, 1954.
Inspector Queen's Own Case, Simon & Schuster, 1956.
The Finishing Stroke, Simon & Schuster, 1958, reissued, Carrol & Graf, 1988.
The Player on the Other Side, Random House, 1963.
And On the Eighth Day, Random House, 1964, reissued, Ballantine, 1976.
The Fourth Side of the Triangle, Random House, 1965, reissued, Ballantine, 1975.
A Study in Terror, Lancer Books, 1966.
Face to Face, New American Library, 1967.
The House of Brass, New American Library, 1968.
Cop Out, World Publishing, 1969.
The Last Woman in His Life, World Publishing, 1970.
A Fine and Private Place, World Publishing, 1971.

SHORT STORY COLLECTIONS; WITH MANFRED B. LEE, UNDER JOINT PSEUDONYM ELLERY QUEEN

The Adventures of Ellery Queen, Stokes, 1934.
The New Adventures of Ellery Queen, Stokes, 1940.
The Case Book of Ellery Queen, Bestseller, 1945.
Calendar of Crime, Little, Brown, 1952.
Q.B.I.: Queen's Bureau of Investigation, Little, Brown, 1955.
Queens Full, Random House, 1965.
Q.E.D.: Queen's Experiments in Detection, New American Library, 1968.
The Detective Short Story: A Bibliography, Biblo & Tannen, 1969.

OMNIBUS VOLUMES

The Ellery Queen Omnibus (contains *The French Powder Mystery, The Dutch Shoe Mystery,* and *The Greek Coffin Mystery,*) Gollancz, 1934.
The Ellery Queen Omnibus (contains *The Roman Hot Mystery, The French Powder Mystery,* and *The Egyptian Cross Mystery*), Grosset, 1936.
Ellery Queen's Big Book (contains *The Siamese Twin Mystery* and *The Greek Coffin Mystery*), Grosset, 1938.
Ellery Queen's Adventure Omnibus (contains *The Adventures of Ellery Queen* and *The New Adventures of Ellery Queen*), Grosset, 1941.
Ellery Queen's Parade (contains *The Greek Coffin Mystery* and *The Siamese Twin Mystery*), World Publishing, 1944.
The Case Book of Ellery Queen (contains *The Adventures of Ellery Queen* and *The New Adventures of Ellery Queen*), Gollancz, 1949.
The Wrightsville Murders (contains *Calamity Town, The Murderer Is a Fox,* and *Ten Days' Wonder*), Little, Brown, 1956.
The Hollywood Murders (contains *The Devil to Pay, The Four of Hearts,* and *The Origin of Evil*), Lippincott, 1957.
The New York Murders (contains *Cat of Many Tails, The Scarlet Letters,* and *The American Gun Mystery*), Little, Brown, 1958.
The XYZ Murders (contains *The Tragedy of X, The Tragedy of Y,* and *The Tragedy of Z; also see below*), Lippincott, 1961.

The Bizarre Murders (contains *The Siamese Twin Mystery, The Chinese Orange Mystery,* and *The Spanish Cape Mystery*) Lippincott, 1962.

NONFICTION ABOUT THE MYSTERY GENRE; WITH MANFRED B. LEE, UNDER JOINT PSEUDONYM ELLERY QUEEN

The Detective Short Story: A Bibliography, Little, Brown, 1942, reprinted, Biblo & Tannen, 1969.
Queen's Quorum: A History of the Detective-Crime Short Story, Little, Brown, 1951, new edition, Biblo & Tannen, 1969.
In the Queen's Parlor, and Other Leaves from the Editor's Notebook (criticism), Simon & Schuster, 1957, reprinted, Biblo & Tannen, 1969.

NONFICTION ABOUT TRUE CRIME; WITH MANFRED B. LEE, UNDER JOINT PSEUDONYM ELLERY QUEEN

Ellery Queen's International Case Book, Dell, 1964.
The Woman in the Case, Bantam, 1966 (published in England as *Deadlier than the Male,* Transworld Publishers, 1966).

EDITOR OF ANTHOLOGIES; WITH MANFRED B. LEE UNTIL 1971, SOLE EDITOR AFTER 1971; UNDER PSEUDONYM ELLERY QUEEN

Challenge to the Reader, Stokes, 1938.
101 Years' Entertainment: The Great Detective Stories, 1841-1941, Little, Brown, 1941.
Sporting Blood: The Great Sports Detective Stories, Little, Brown, 1942 (published in England as *Sporting Detective Stories,* Faber, 1946).
The Female of the Species: The Great Women Detectives and Criminals, Little, Brown, 1943 (published in England as *Ladies in Crime: A Collection of Detective Stories by English and American Writers,* Faber, 1947).
The Misadventures of Sherlock Holmes, Little, Brown, 1944.
Best Stories from Ellery Queen's Mystery Magazine, Detective Book Club, 1944.
Rogues' Gallery: The Great Criminals of Modern Fiction, Little, Brown, 1945.
To the Queen's Taste: The First Supplement to 101 Years' Entertainment, Little, Brown, 1946.
Murder by Experts, Ziff-Davis Publications, 1947.
20th Century Detective Stories, World Publishing, 1948, 2nd edition, Pocket Books, 1964.
The Literature of Crime: Stories by World-Famous Authors, Little, Brown, 1950, published as *Ellery Queen's Book of Mystery Stories,* Pan, 1957.
Ellery Queen's 12, Dell, 1964.
Ellery Queen's Lethal Black Book, Dell, 1965.
Poetic Justice: 23 Stories of Crime, Mystery, and Detection by World-Famous Poets from Geoffrey Chaucer to Dylan Thomas, New American Library, 1967.
Minimysteries: 70 Short-Stories of Crime, Mystery, and Detection, World Publishing, 1969.
Ellery Queen's Murder—in Spades, Pyramid, 1969.
Ellery Queen's Shoot the Works, Pyramid, 1969.
Ellery Queen's Mystery Jackpot, Pyramid, 1970.
The Golden 13: 13 First Prize Winners from Ellery Queen's Mystery Magazine, World Publishing, 1971.
Ellery Queen's Best Bets, Pyramid, 1972.
Ellery Queen's Japanese Golden Dozen: The Detective Story World in Japan, Tuttle, 1978.

EDITOR OF "MYSTERY ANNUAL ANTHOLOGY" SERIES; WITH MANFRED B. LEE UNTIL 1971, SOLE EDITOR AFTER 1971; UNDER PSEUDONYM ELLERY QUEEN

The Queen's Awards, 1946, Little, Brown, 1946.
The Queen's Awards, 1947, Little, Brown, 1947.
The Queen's Awards, 1948, Little, Brown, 1948.
The Queen's Awards, 1949, Little, Brown, 1949.
The Queen's Awards, Fifth Series, Little, Brown, 1950.
The Queen's Awards, Sixth Series, Little, Brown, 1951.
The Queen's Awards, Seventh Series, Little, Brown, 1952.
The Queen's Awards, Eighth Series, Little, Brown, 1953.
Ellery Queen's Awards, Ninth Series, Little, Brown, 1954.
Ellery Queen's Awards, Tenth Series, Little, Brown, 1955.
Ellery Queen's Awards, Eleventh Series, Simon & Schuster, 1956.
Ellery Queen's Awards, Twelfth Series, Simon & Schuster, 1957.
Ellery Queen's Awards, Thirteenth Annual, Random House, 1958 (published in England as *Ellery Queen's Choice: Thirteenth Series,* Collins, 1960).
Ellery Queen's Awards, 14th Mystery Annual, Random House, 1960 (published in England as *Ellery Queen's Choice: Fourteenth Series,* Collins, 1961).
Ellery Queen's Awards, 15th Mystery Annual, Random House, 1960.
Ellery Queen's Awards, 16th Mystery Annual, Random House, 1961.
To Be Read before Midnight, Random House, 1962.
Ellery Queen's Mystery Mix No. 18, Random House, 1963.
Ellery Queen's Double Dozen, Random House, 1964 (published in England as *Ellery Queen's 19th Mystery Annual,* Gollancz, 1965).
Ellery Queen's 20th Anniversary Annual, Random House, 1965.
Ellery Queen's Crime Carousel, New American Library, 1966.
Ellery Queen's All-Star Line-up, New American Library, 1967.
Ellery Queen's Mystery Parade, New American Library, 1968.
Ellery Queen's Murder Menu, World Publishing 1969.
Ellery Queen's Grand Slam, World Publishing, 1970.
Ellery Queen's Headliners, World Publishing, 1971.
Ellery Queen's Mystery Bag, World Publishing, 1972.
Ellery Queen's Crookbook, Random House, 1974.
Ellery Queen's Murdercade, Random House, 1975.
Ellery Queen's Crime Wave, Putnam, 1976.
Ellery Queen's Searches and Seizures, Dial, 1977.
Ellery Queen's a Multitude of Sins, Davis Publications (New York), 1978.
Ellery Queen's The Scenes of the Crime, Davis Publications, 1979.
Ellery Queen's Circumstantial Evidence, Davis Publications, 1980.

Also editor of *Ellery Queen's Masks of Mystery, Ellery Queen's Secrets of Mystery, Ellery Queen's The Golden Thirteen, Ellery Queen's Veils of Mystery,* and *Ellery Queen's Wings of Mystery.*

OTHER SERIES

Editor of "Ellery Queen's Anthology" series, with Manfred B. Lee until 1971, sole editor after 1971, under pseudonym Ellery Queen, published in magazine format by Davis Publications, beginning in 1959.

Editor of "Masterpieces of Mystery" series, under pseudonym Ellery Queen, published by Meredith Corp., 1976-79.

EDITOR OF SHORT STORY COLLECTIONS; UNDER PSEUDONYM ELLERY QUEEN

Dashiell Hammett, *The Adventures of Sam Spade and Other Stories,* Bestseller, 1944, published as *They Can Only Hang You Once and Other Stories,* Mercury, 1949.
Hammett, *The Continental Op,* Bestseller, 1945.
Hammett, *The Return of the Continental Op,* Jonathan, 1945.
Hammett, *Hammett Homicides,* Bestseller, 1946.
Hammett, *Dead Yellow Women,* Jonathan, 1947.
Stuart Palmer, *The Riddles of Hildegarde Withers,* Jonathan, 1947.
John Dickson Carr, *Dr. Fell, Detective, and Other Stories,* Mercury, 1947.
Roy Vickers, *The Department of Dead Ends,* Bestseller, 1947.
Margery Allingham, *The Case Book of Mr. Campion,* Mercury, 1947.
O. Henry, *Cops and Robbers,* Bestseller, 1948.
Hammett, *Nightmare Town,* Mercury, 1948.
Palmer, *The Monkey Murder and Other Stories,* Bestseller, 1950.
Hammett, *The Creeping Siamese,* Jonathan, 1950.
Hammett, *Women in the Dark,* Jonathan, 1952.
Hammett, *A Man Named Thin and Other Stories,* Mercury, 1962.
Erle Stanley Gardner, *The Case of the Murderer's Bride and Other Stories,* Davis Publications, 1969.
Lawrence Treat, *P As in Police,* Davis Publications, 1970.
Edward D. Hoch, *The Spy and the Thief,* Davis Publications, 1971.
Michael Gilbert, *Amateur in Violence,* Davis Publications, 1973.
Stanley Ellin, *Kindly Dig Your Grave and Other Wicked Stories,* Davis Publications, 1975.
Julian Symons, *How to Trap a Crook and Twelve Other Mysteries,* Davis Publications, 1977.
Gardner, *The Amazing Adventures of Lester Leith,* Davis Publications, 1980.

NOVELS; WITH MANFRED B. LEE, UNDER JOINT PSEUDONYM BARNABY ROSS

The Tragedy of X, Viking, 1932, reissued under pseudonym Ellery Queen, Stokes, 1940, reissued, International Polygonics, 1986.
The Tragedy of Y, Viking, 1932, reissued under pseudonym Ellery Queen, Stokes, 1941, reissued, International Polygonics, 1987.
The Tragedy of Z, Viking, 1933, reissued under pseudonym Ellery Queen, Little, Brown, 1942, reissued, International Polygonics, 1987.
Drury Lane's Last Case, Viking, 1933, reissued under pseudonym Ellery Queen, Little, Brown, 1946, reissued, International Polygonics, 1987.

OTHER

(Under name Daniel Nathan) *The Golden Summer* (autobiographical novel), Little, Brown, 1953.
Ellery Queen's Prime Crimes, Book Sales Inc., 1988.
The Best of Ellery Queen, State Mutual Book, 1989.
(With others) *Six of the Best: Short Novels by Masters of Mystery,* Carroll & Graf, 1989.

Author with Manfred B. Lee under joint pseudonym Ellery Queen of radio scripts for "The Adventures of Ellery Queen" radio show, 1938-49, and of short stories and articles for numerous magazines including *Cosmopolitan, Playboy, Argosy, Saturday Evening Past, Today's Family* and *Redbook.* Editor with Manfred B. Lee under joint pseudonym Ellery Queen of *Mystery*

League, 1933-34, and *Ellery Queen's Mystery Magazine,* 1941-71, sole editor, beginning in 1971.

SIDELIGHTS: Ellery Queen, the joint pseudonym of the late Frederic Dannay and cousin, Manfred B. Lee, continues to be a prominent figure in the detective/mystery genre as author, anthologist, and founder of *Ellery Queen's Mystery Magazine.* "Few writers," Allen J. Hubin notes, "have made as great an impact on 20th century American detective fiction as Ellery Queen."

Ellery Queen was created in 1929 when Dannay and Lee wrote a mystery novel for a writing contest. They used the name Ellery Queen for the novel's protagonist, a clever young detective, as well as for their own pseudonym, reasoning that the public would more easily remember the name if it were used twice. Their novel, *The Roman Hat Mystery,* won the contest, and the firm of Frederick A. Stokes later accepted it for publication. It sold well, and what Francis M. Nevins, Jr., calls "the most successful collaboration in the history of prose fiction" was on its way.

The Queen novels of the 1930s are complex, logically-solved puzzles containing, as Julian Symons notes, "a relentlessly analytical treatment of every possible clue and argument. Judged as exercises in rational deduction," he continues, "these are certainly among the best detective stories ever written." Although praising the deductive complexity of the stories, some critics found these early mysteries too cold, favoring intellectual passions over emotional ones.

Queen's novels published after this time have had a variety of goals, concerning themselves less strictly with the mystery than did the earlier books. *The Glass Village,* for instance, is a political statement against the McCarthy witch hunts of the fifties. *Calamity Town* carefully delineates the varied customs and inhabitants of a small town. Other novels, like *Ten Days' Wonder,* create what Francis M. Nevins, Jr., calls "a private, topsy-turvy, Alice-in-Wonderland otherworld" in which the mystery is unraveled.

In addition to being successful novelists, Dannay and Lee also earned acclaim for their mystery anthologies. In more than one hundred anthologies, they gathered together not only the best of contemporary mystery fiction (most of which is taken from *Ellery Queen's Mystery Magazine*) but hard-to-find classics of the genre as well. These anthologies have popularized the mystery field while preserving in print historically important examples of the form. Anthony Boucher writes that "much though we may admire Queen the writer, it is Queen the editor who is unquestionably immortal."

Another aspect of the Ellery Queen popularity lies in *Ellery Queen's Mystery Magazine,* a hugely successful mystery publication that Dannay and Lee founded in 1941 and that has continued publication since Dannay's death in 1982. During a time when many popular fiction magazines have gone out of business, forcing mystery writers to abandon the short story in favor of the novel, *Ellery Queen's* has published and encouraged short mystery fiction. It has done much to keep the mystery and crime short story alive. "It is not too much to say," Julian Symons writes, "that the continuation of the crime short story as we know it, like its development during the past twenty years, seems largely dependent upon *Ellery Queen's Mystery Magazine.*"

About his writing, Dannay once told *CA:* "I've written three critical works on the [mystery] field (one a bibliography, one a history and critical estimate, and one a book of essays and opinions), and have come to this decision: no more 'invasions' of the

critics' and historians' provinces until I hang up my gloves as a writer and editor in the field."

Dannay revealed in the 1960s that his original name was Daniel Nathan. About his present name he told *CA:* "Frederic was chosen because of my deep affection for Chopin—Chopin's first name was Frederic, so spelled. Dannay [consists of] the first half of my real first name, Daniel, plus nay, the phonetic spelling of first half of my real last name, Nathan."

Queen books have sold millions of copies in numerous hardcover and paperback editions in America and abroad.

AVOCATIONAL INTERESTS: Book and stamp collecting.

MEDIA ADAPTATIONS: A radio series and several television series have been based on the character; several Queen novels have been made into movies.

BIOGRAPHICAL/CRITICAL SOURCES:

BOOKS

Barzun, Jacques and Wendell Hertig Taylor, *A Catalogue of Crime,* Harper, 1971.
Boucher, Anthony, *Ellery Queen: A Double Profile* (pamphlet), Little, Brown, 1951.
Contemporary Literary Criticism, Gale, Volume III, 1975, Volume XI, 1979.
Haycraft, Howard, *Murder for Pleasure: The Life and Times of the Detective Story,* Appleton-Century, 1941.
Mott, Frank Luther, *Golden Multitudes,* Macmillan, 1947.
Nevins, Francis M., Jr., *Royal Bloodline: Ellery Queen, Author and Detective,* Bowling Green University Press, 1973.
Richmond, John and Abril Lamarque, *Brooklyn, U.S.A.,* Creative Age Press, 1946.
A Silver Anniversary Tribute to Ellery Queen from Authors, Critics, Editors, and Famous Fans (pamphlet), Little, Brown, 1954.
Symons, Julian, *Mortal Consequences: A History from the Detective Story to the Crime Novel,* Harper, 1972.
Thomson, Henry Douglas, *Masters of Mystery: A Study of the Detective Story,* Collins, 1931.

PERIODICALS

The Armchair Detective, January, 1970, October, 1972.
Book World, August 18, 1974.
Coronet, December, 1942.
Detroit News, April 26, 1979.
The Ellery Queen Review (magazine for collectors of Ellery Queen books), 1968-71.
Life, November 22, 1943.
London Sunday Express, December 13, 1970.
Look, April 21, 1970.
MD, December, 1967.
New Republic, November 26, 1977.
Newsweek, June 26, 1939.
New Yorker, March 16, 1940.
New York Times, November 15, 1940, February 22, 1969, April 5, 1971.
New York Times Book Review, February 26, 1961, October 8, 1967, December 1, 1968.
Observer, October 5, 1975.
People, March 5, 1979.
Publishers Weekly, October 10, 1936, November 20, 1943, March 10, 1969.
Spectator, January 1, 1977.
Time, October 23, 1939.
Times Literary Supplement, November 12, 1976.

Wilson Library Bulletin, April, 1942.

OBITUARIES:

PERIODICALS

AB Bookman's Weekly, October 4, 1982.
Los Angeles Times, September 5, 1982.
Newsweek, September 20, 1982.
New York Times, September 5, 1982.
Publishers Weekly, September 24, 1982.
Time, September 20, 1982.
Times (London), September 6, 1982.
Washington Post, September 5, 1982.

*   *   *

d'ANTIBES, Germain
See SIMENON, Georges (Jacques Christian)

*   *   *

DARIO, Ruben   1867-1916

PERSONAL: Name originally Felix Ruben Garcia y Sarmiento; born January 18, 1867, in Metapa, Nicaragua; died February 6, 1916, in Leon, Nicaragua; married Rafaela Contrera, 1890 (died, 1892); married Francisca Sanchez; children: two sons (one from each marriage). *Education:* Attended a Jesuit school.

CAREER: Writer and poet. Began work as a journalist for newspapers in Santiago and Valparaiso, Chile, and Buenos Aires, Argentina, c. 1881. Became correspondent for *La Nacion,* Buenos Aires, and other Latin American papers in Latin America; Paris, France; and Madrid, Spain. Founder, with Gilberto Freyre, of *Revista de America,* 1896. Also served in various diplomatic and representative posts for Colombia and Nicaragua.

WRITINGS:

Primeras notas (title means "First Notes"), Tipografia Nacional, 1888.
Azul (poetry and short prose; title means "Blue"), [Chile], 1888, reprinted, Espasa-Calpe (Madrid), 1984 (also see below).
Los raros (literary biography and critical essays; title means "The Rare Ones"), 1893, reprinted, Universidad Autonoma Metropolitana (Mexico), 1985 (also see below).
Prosas profanas (title means "Profane Prose"), 1896, reprinted, introduction and notes by Ignacio M. Zuleta, Castalia (Madrid), 1983 (also see below).
Castelar, B. R. Serra (Madrid), 1899.
Espana contemporanea (title means "Contemporary Spain"), Garnier (Paris), 1901, reprinted, Lumen, 1987 (also see below).
Cantos de vida y esperanza, Los cisnes, y otros poemas (title means "Songs of Life and Hope, The Swans, and Other Poems"), [Madrid], 1905, reprinted, Nacional (Mexico), 1957 (also see below).
El canto errante (poetry; title means "The Wandering Song"), M. Perez Villavicencio (Madrid), 1907, reprinted, Espasa-Calpe, 1965 (also see below).
El viaje a Nicaragua; e, Intermezzo tropical (travel writings), Biblioteca "Ateneo" (Madrid), 1909, reprinted, Ministerio de Cultura, 1982 (also see below).
Poema del otono y otros poemas (title means "Poem of Autumn and Other Poems"), Biblioteca "Ateneo," 1910, Espasa-Calpe, 1973 (also see below).
Muy antiguo y muy moderno (poetry; title means "Very Old and Very Modern"), Biblioteca Corona (Madrid), 1915.

El mundo de los suenos: Prosas postumas (title means "The World of Dreams: Posthumous Prose"), Libreria de la Viuda de Pueyo (Madrid), 1917.
Sol del domingo (title means "Sunday Sun"), Sucesores de Hernando (Madrid), 1917.
Alfonso XIII y sus primeras notas (addresses, essays, lectures and biographical text; title means "Alfonso the Thirteenth and His Principal Notes"), R. Dario Sanchez (Madrid), 1921.
Baladas y canciones (title means "Ballads and Songs"), prologue by Andres Gonzalez-Blanco, Biblioteca Ruben Dario Hijo (Madrid), 1923.
Sonetos (title means "Sonnets"), Biblioteca Ruben Dario (Madrid), 1929.
En busca del alba (poetry; title means "In Search of Dawn"), Aristides Quillet (Buenos Aires), 1941.
Brumas y luces (poetry; title means "Fogs and Lights"), Ediciones Argentinas "S.I.A.," 1943.
Wakonda: Poemas, Guillermo Kraft (Buenos Aires), 1944.
"El ruisenor azul": Poemas ineditos y poemas olvidados (title means "The Blue Nightingale: Unpublished and Forgotten Poems"), prologue by Alberto Ghiraldo, Talleres Graficos Casa Nacional del Nino, c. 1945.
Quince poesias (title means "Fifteen Poems"), illustrated by Mallol Suazo, Argos (Barcelona), 1946.
Cerebros y corazones (biographical sketches; title means "Minds and Hearts"), Nova (Buenos Aires), 1948.
La amargura de la Patagonia (novella; title means "The Grief of Patagonia"), Nova (Buenos Aires), 1950.
El manto de Nangasasu (novella; title means "The Cloak of Nangasasu"), S.A.C.D.I.C., 1958.
El sapo de oro (novella; title means "The Golden Toad"), G. Kraft (Buenos Aires), 1962.

Also author of *Epistolas y poemas* (title means "Epistles and Poems"), 1885; *Abrojos* (poetry; title means "Thorns"), 1887; *Canto epico a las glorias de Chile* (poetry; title means "Epic Song to the Glories of Chile"), 1887; *Emelina* (novel), with Eduardo Poirier, 1887; *Las rosas andinas: Rimas y contra-rimas* (title means "Andean Roses: Rhymes and Counter-Rhymes"), with Ruben Rubi, 1888; *Rimas* (title means "Poems"), 1888; *Peregrinaciones* (travel writings; title means "Journeys"), 1901 (also see below); *Oda a Mitre* (poetry; title means "Ode to Mitre"), 1906 (also see below); *Canto a la Argentina y otros poemas* (title means "Song to Argentina and Other Poems"), c. 1910 (also see below); *Historia de mis libros* (title means "The Story of My Books"), 1912; *Caras y caretas* (title means "Faces and Masks"), 1912; *Vida de Ruben Dario, escrita por el mismo* (title means "The Life of Ruben Dario, Written By Himself"), 1916; *Edelmira* (fiction), edited by Francisco Contreras, c. 1926; and *El hombre de oro* (title means "The Golden Man"), Zig-Zag.

Fiction and verse also published in numerous anthologies and collections.

IN ENGLISH

Eleven Poems, introduction by Pedro Henriquez Urena, translation by Thomas Walsh and Salomon de la Selva, Putnam, 1916, revised edition published as *Eleven Poems of Ruben Dario: Bilingual Edition,* Gordon, 1977.
Selected Poems of Ruben Dario, introduction by Octavio Paz, translated by Lysander Kemp, University of Texas Press, 1965, reprinted, 1988.

COLLECTIONS

Obras completas (title means "Complete Works"), twenty-two volumes, edited by author's son, Ruben Dario Sanchez, illustrations by Enrique Ochoa, Mundo Latino (Madrid), Volume 1: *La caravana pasa* (poetry; title means "The Caravan Passes"), prologue by Ghiraldo, 1917; Volume 2: *Prosas profanas,* 1917; Volume 3: *Tierras solares* (travel writings; title means "Lands of the Sun"), 1917; Volume 4: *Azul,* 1917; Volume 5: *Parisiana,* 1917; Volume 6: *Los raros,* 1918; Volume 7: *Cantos de vida y esperanza, Los cisnes, y otros poemas,* 1920; Volume 8: *Letras* (addresses, essays, lectures), 1918; Volume 9: *Canto a la Argentina, Oda a Mitre, y otros poemas,* 1918; Volume 10: *Opiniones,* 1918; Volume 11: *Poema del otono y otros poemas,* 1918; Volume 12: *Peregrinaciones,* 1918; Volume 13: *Prosas politicas: Las republicas americanas* (title means "Political Prose: The American Republics"), 1918; Volume 14: *Cuentos y cronicas* (title means "Stories and Chronicles"), 1918; Volume 15: *Autobiografia,* 1918; Volume 16: *El canto errante,* 1918; Volume 17: *El viaje a Nicaragua, e historia de mis libros* (title means "The Trip to Nicaragua and the Story of My Books"), 1919; Volume 18: *Todo al vuelo* (title means "All On the Fly"), 1919; Volume 19: *Espana contemporanea,* 1919; Volume 20: *Prosa dispersa* (title means "Random Prose"), 1919; Volume 21: *Lira postuma* (title means "Posthumous Verse"), 1919; Volume 22: *Cabezas: Pensadores y artistas, politicos* (biographical essays; title means "Heads: Thinkers, Artists, Politicians"), 1919.

Obras poeticas completas (title means "Complete Poetic Works"), twenty-one volumes, edited by Ghiraldo and Gonzalez-Blanco, [Madrid], 1923-29, new edition edited by A. Mendez Plancarte, [Madrid], 1952.

Cuentos completos (title means "Complete Stories"), edited with notes by Ernesto Mejia Sanchez, preliminary study by Raimundo Lida, Fondo de Cultura Economica (Mexico), 1950, reprinted, 1983.

Poesias completas (title means "Complete Poems"), two volumes, edited by Alfonso Mendez Plancarte, 1952, revised edition edited by Antonio Oliver Belmas, 1967.

Several volumes of Dario's *Obras completas* were reissued separately during the 1980s. Works collected in other volumes, including *Obra poetica* (title means "Poetic Works"), four volumes, 1914-1916; *Textos socio-politicos,* [Managua], 1980; *Poesias escogidas,* 1982; and *Cuentos fantasticos,* Alianza (Madrid), 1982.

SIDELIGHTS: Nicaraguan writer Ruben Dario ranks among the most esteemed and enduring figures in South American literature. A journalist, critic, poet and author of short stories, he is credited with both founding and leading the *modernista* literary movement, which ended a period of creative latency among Spanish-language writers. Dario is probably best remembered for his innovative poetry, noted for its blending of experimental rhymes and meters with elements of French and Italian culture, classical literature, and mythology.

A bright and inquisitive child, Dario displayed a propensity for poetry while he was still quite young. His aunt, who raised him after the separation of his parents, nurtured his literary aspirations, and his early interest in journalism led to his association with members of the European and South American intelligentsia. By the turn of the twentieth century, Dario had taken his place among the literary and cultural elite and, as a foreign correspondent and diplomat, had become a symbol of a new bohemianism in Latin America. Stephen Kinzer, writing in the *New York Times,* summarized the author's career as that of a "vagabond poet who . . . influence[d] Latin American and Spanish literature forever and dazzle[d] Europe as no provincial ever had."

Though generally dismissed by critics as an uninspired and predictable contribution to the romance genre, *Emelina*—one of Dario's earliest writings and his only novel—offers a glimpse at the artistry that the poet would perfect in his 1888 volume *Azul* ("Blue"), a work that revolutionized Spanish letters. The poetry and short prose in *Azul* marks a deliberate break with the conventions of Romanticism, a bold experimentation with line and metre construction, and an introduction to Dario's celebration of literature as an *alcazar interior* ("tower of ivory"), a dreamlike shelter dedicated to pure art. Another collection, *Prosas profanas* ("Profane Prose"), first published in 1896, is a masterful, melodic display of the poet's fascination with Symbolism. The 1905 volume *Cantos de vida y esperanza* ("Songs of Life and Hope"), however, reveals a change in Dario's orientation as an artist—a move away from the idealistic "ivory tower" toward the global concerns of political and humanistic unity and nationalism among Hispanics. In *Studies in Spanish-American Literature,* Isaac Goldberg asserted: "*Cantos de vida y esperanza* is the keystone of Dario's poetical arch. It most exemplifies the man that wrote it; it most reveals his dual nature, his inner sincerity, his complete psychology; it is the artist at maturity."

Dario remains largely unknown among English-speaking readers, mainly because of the difficulty in translating his poetry while preserving the unique rhythms and linguistic nuances that the works possess in their original form. However, two volumes of the author's poems are available in English, and several critics have noted that the universality of Dario's themes precludes the problem of accessibility. Commenting on Dario's widespread appeal, Goldberg rated the poet among "the consecrated few who belong to no nation because they belong to all." And S. Griswold Morley, writing in *Dial,* concluded: "What cannot be denied is that Dario, single-handed, initiated a movement in Spain that affects today nearly every branch of literary art; that he renovated the technique of both poetry and prose; that he made his own many diverse styles; and that his verse is often so inevitable as to touch the finality of art."

BIOGRAPHICAL/CRITICAL SOURCES:

BOOKS

Dario, Ruben, *Eleven Poems of Ruben Dario,* introduction by Pedro Henriquez Urena, translated by Thomas Walsh and Salomon de la Selva, Putnam, 1916.

Dario, Ruben, *Selected Poems of Ruben Dario,* introduction by Octavio Paz, translated by Lysander Kemp, University of Texas Press, 1965.

Ellis, Keith, *Critical Approaches to Ruben Dario,* University of Toronto Press, 1974.

Fiore, Dolores Ackel, *Ruben Dario in Search of Inspiration: Greco-Roman Mythology in His Stories and Poetry,* Las Americas Publishing Co., 1963.

Fitzmaurice-Kelly, James, *Some Masters of Spanish Verse,* Oxford University Press, 1924.

Goldberg, Isaac, *Studies in Spanish-American Literature,* Brentano's, 1920.

Peers, E. Allison, *A Critical Anthology of Spanish Verse,* University of California Press, 1949.

Twentieth-Century Literary Criticism, Volume 4, Gale, 1981.

Watland, Charles D., *Poet-Errant: A Biography of Ruben Dario,* Philosophical Library, 1965.

PERIODICALS

Dial, June 14, 1917.
Hispania, March, 1919, May, 1966.
Latin American Literary Review, spring, 1973.

New York Times, January 18, 1987.
Poetry, July, 1916.

*   *   *

DAVIE, Donald (Alfred) 1922-

PERSONAL: Born July 17, 1922, in Barnsley, Yorkshire, England; son of George Clarke and Alice (Sugden) Davie; married Doreen John, January 13, 1945; children: Richard Mark, Diana Margaret, Patrick George. *Education:* St. Catharine's College, Cambridge, B.A., 1947, M.A., 1949, Ph.D., 1951. *Religion:* Episcopalian.

ADDRESSES: Home—4 High St., Silverton, Exeter EX5 4JB, England.

CAREER: Trinity College, Dublin, Ireland, lecturer, 1950-54, fellow, 1954-57; Cambridge University, Gonville and Caius College, Cambridge, England, lecturer in English and fellow, 1959-64; University of Essex, Colchester, England, professor of literature and dean of comparative studies, 1964-68; Stanford University, Stanford, Calif., professor of English, 1968-78; Vanderbilt University, Nashville, Tenn., Andrew Mellon Professor of Humanities, 1978-88. Visiting professor, University of California, Santa Barbara, 1957-58; Bing Professor of English and American Literature University of Southern California, 1968-69. British Council lecturer, Budapest, 1961; Elliston Lecturer, University of Cincinnati, 1963; lecturer in English, Cambridge University. *Military service:* Royal Navy, 1941-46; became sub-lieutenant.

MEMBER: London Library, Savile Club (London).

AWARDS, HONORS: Honorary fellow, St. Catharine's College, 1973; Guggenheim fellow, 1973; fellow, American Academy of Arts and Sciences, 1973; D.Litt., University of Southern California, 1978; honorary fellow, Trinity College, Dublin, 1978; Fellow of the British Academy, 1986.

WRITINGS:

POETRY

Brides of Reason, Fantasy Press, 1955.
A Winter Talent and Other Poems, Routledge & Kegan Paul, 1957.
The Forests of Lithuania (adapted from a poem by Adam Mickiewicz; Poetry Book Society selection), Marvell Press, 1960.
New and Selected Poems, Wesleyan University Press, 1961.
A Sequence for Francis Parkman, Marvell Press, 1962.
Events and Wisdoms: Poems 1957-1963, Routledge & Kegan Paul, 1964, Wesleyan University Press, 1965.
Poems, Turret Books, 1969.
Essex Poems: 1963-1967, Routledge & Kegan Paul, 1969.
Six Epistles to Eva Hesse, London Magazine Editions, 1970.
Collected Poems: 1950-1970, Oxford University Press, 1972.
Orpheus, Poem-of-the-Month Club, 1974.
The Shires: Poems (also see below), Routledge & Kegan Paul, 1974, Oxford University Press, 1975.
In the Stopping Train and Other Poems, Carcanet, 1977.
Three for Water-Music [and] *The Shires,* Carcanet, 1981.
Collected Poems, 1970-1983, University of Notre Dame Press, 1982.
Selected Poems, Carcanet, 1985.
To Scorch or Freeze: Poems about the Sacred, University of Chicago Press, 1988.
Under Briggflatts, Carcanet, 1989.

CRITICISM

Purity of Diction in English Verse, Chatto & Windus, 1952, Oxford University Press, 1953, reprinted, Schocken, 1967.
Articulate Energy: An Inquiry into the Syntax of English Poetry, Routledge & Kegan Paul, 1955, Harcourt, 1958, reprinted, Reprint Services, 1988.
The Heyday of Sir Walter Scott, Barnes & Noble, 1961.
The Language of Science and the Language of Literature, 1700-1740, Sheed, 1963.
Ezra Pound: Poet as Sculptor, Oxford University Press 1964, new edition, Viking, 1976.
Thomas Hardy and British Poetry, Oxford University Press, 1972.
The Augustan Lyric, Barnes & Noble, 1974.
The Poet in the Imaginary Museum: Essays of Two Decades, edited by Barry Alpert, Persea Books, 1977.
A Gathered Church: The Literature of the English Dissenting Interest, 1700-1930, Oxford University Press, 1978.
Trying to Explain, University of Michigan Press, 1979.
Kenneth Allott and the Thirties, University of Liverpool Press, 1980.
(With Robert Stevenson) *English Hymnology in the Eighteenth Century: Papers Read at a Clark Library Seminar, 5 March 1977,* William Andrews Clark Memorial Library, University of California, Los Angeles, 1980.
Dissentient Voice, University of Notre Dame Press, 1982.
Czeslaw Milosz and the Insufficiency of Lyric, University of Tennessee Press, 1986.

EDITOR

The Late Augustans: Longer Poems of the Later Eighteenth Century, Macmillan, 1958.
Poems: Poetry Supplement, Poetry Book Society, 1960.
Poetics Poetyka, Panstwowe Wydawn (Warsaw), 1961.
William Wordsworth, *Selected Poems of Wordsworth,* Harrap, 1962.
Russian Literature and Modern English Fiction: A Collection of Critical Essays, University of Chicago Press, 1965.
(With Angela Livingstone) *Pasternak,* Macmillan, 1969.
The New Oxford Book of Christian Verse, Oxford University Press, 1982.

TRANSLATOR

(Also author of commentary) Boris Pasternak, *The Poems of Doctor Zhivago,* Barnes Noble, 1965.

OTHER

Donald Davie Reading at Stanford (recording), Stanford Program for Recording in Sound, 1974.
(Author of introduction) Elizabeth Daryush, *Collected Poems,* Carcanet, 1976.
(Author of introduction) Yvor Winters, *Collected Poems of Yvor Winters,* Carcanet, 1978, Swallow Press, 1980.
These the Companions: Recollections (memoirs), Cambridge University Press, 1982.

Contributor of poetry and critical essays to anthologies and books. Contributor to periodicals, including *New Republic, Yale Review, PN Review,* and *Times Literary Supplement.* Member of editorial board, *Poetics,* Mouton, 1963.

SIDELIGHTS: The author of highly respected poetry and literary criticism, British writer and scholar Donald Davie is a literary traditionalist interested in the "purity of language." As Davie explains in his *Purity of Diction,* "[The poet] is responsible to the community in which he writes for purifying and correcting the spoken language." This objective is expressed in Davie's poetry by a careful concern for, and an attempt to enlighten the reader in, the proper use of language. Subtle differences between similar-meaning words, for instance, are carefully distinguished by their contrasting use in a Davie poem. This practice, Davie states, "purifies the spoken tongue, for it makes the reader alive to nice meanings." Davie is also interested in a "pure" use of metaphors. "If the poet who coins new metaphors *enlarges* the language," he writes, "the poet who enlivens dead metaphors can be said to *purify* the language." By using a familiar metaphor in a new way, Davie believes the poet can give it renewed life. "Davie's object," George Dekker points out, "[is] to draw attention to the cultural power these 'dead' metaphors of dead cultures still have to control our living processes of thought and feeling." Emily Grosholz in the *Hudson Review* calls Davie "one of the master-workers of our language."

Davie's poetry is frequently theoretical in nature, and he is often described by critics as an "academic" poet. As a result, his poetry is sometimes criticized for its formality and lack of emotion. Nonetheless, reviewers find Davie's poetry distinctly compelling. Regarding *Collected Poems, 1970-1983,* John Lucas notes in the *New Statesman* that "if poems were made solely of ideas there would be few more interesting poets than Donald Davie. For his seriousness about ideas is never in doubt: he ponders questions, argues with himself and others, and it seems inevitable that, reading him, you want to argue back. . . . Davie is very readable, perhaps because his literary, donnish qualities compel him to take the reader seriously, so that although you often feel talked at you never feel talked down to."

Davie is as well known for his criticism as he is his poetry. As with his poetry, his criticism often focuses on purity of language. He especially notes with concern the tendency of modern poetry to abandon or disregard syntax. Noting the relationship between "law in language and law in conduct," Davie writes that "one could almost say . . . that to dislocate syntax in poetry is to threaten the rule of law in the civilized community." He asserts that "systems of syntax are part of the heritable property of past civilization, and to hold firm to them is to be traditional in the best and most important sense." Regarding *The Poet in the Imaginary Museum: Essays of Two Decades,* D. E. Richardson notes in the *Sewanee Review* that "like the early modernists whom he admires, Davie wishes the poet to keep his head in a confusing world by embracing the old role of the artist as artificer or maker, rather than secular prophet, thinker, or creator of alternative worlds. . . . Davie thinks of the poet as working somehow like other artists, and he resorts readily to analogies between poetry and other arts, especially music, sculpture, and architecture."

BIOGRAPHICAL/CRITICAL SOURCES:

BOOKS

Contemporary Authors Autobiography Series, Volume 3, Gale, 1986.
Contemporary Literary Criticism, Gale, Volume 5, 1976, Volume 8, 1978, Volume 10, 1979, Volume 31, 1985.
Dictionary of Literary Biography, Volume 27: *Poets of Great Britain and Ireland, 1945-1960,* Gale, 1984.
O'Connor, William Van, *The New University Wits and the End of Modernism,* Southern Illinois University Press, 1963.

PERIODICALS

Agenda, autumn-winter, 1970, summer, 1976.
Best Sellers, September, 1976.
Booklist, March 15, 1976.

Book World, March 7, 1976.
Harper's, July, 1976.
Hudson Review, spring, 1967, summer, 1973, winter, 1973-74, autumn, 1983.
London Magazine, December, 1969, November, 1970.
New Republic, October 2, 1976, November 27, 1976, October 22, 1977.
New Statesman, September 25, 1970, December 1, 1972, March 23, 1973, October 18, 1974, August 5, 1983.
New Yorker, August 16, 1976.
New York Review of Books, May 27, 1976.
New York Times Book Review, February 6, 1966, January 7, 1973, March 26, 1978, April 11, 1982, November 21, 1982, October 7, 1984.
Parnassus: Poetry in Review, fall-winter, 1974.
Poetry, May, 1962, August, 1973, January, 1976.
Poetry Nation, Number 3, 1974.
Review, December, 1964.
Sewanee Review, October, 1977, October, 1978.
South Atlantic Quarterly, summer, 1974.
Southwest Review, autumn, 1975.
Times (London), August 4, 1983.
Times Literary Supplement, November 27, 1970, December 22, 1972, July 13, 1973, October 4, 1974, May 16, 1980, November 27, 1981, January 8, 1982, October 8, 1982, March 16, 1984, January 21, 1986, April 7-13, 1989, June 17, 1989, November 24-30, 1989.
Virginia Quarterly Review, spring, 1973.
Western Humanities Review, winter, 1965, summer, 1974.
Yale Review, June, 1977.

*   *   *

DAVIES, (William) Robertson   1913-
(Samuel Marchbanks)

PERSONAL: Born August 28, 1913, in Thamesville, Ontario, Canada; son of William Rupert (a publisher) and Florence Sheppard (McKay) Davies; married Brenda Matthews, February 2, 1940; children: Miranda, Jennifer (Mrs. C. T. Surridge), Rosamund (Mrs. John Cunnington). *Education:* Attended Upper Canada College, Toronto, and Queen's University at Kingston; Balliol College, Oxford, B.Litt., 1938.

ADDRESSES: Home—40 Oaklands Ave., Suite 303, Toronto, Ontario, Canada M4V 2Z3. *Office*—Massey College, University of Toronto, 4 Devonshire Pl., Toronto, Ontario, Canada M5S 2E1. *Agent*—Curtis Brown Ltd., 10 Astor Pl., New York, N.Y. 10003.

CAREER: Old Vic Company, London, England, teacher and actor, 1938-40; *Saturday Night,* Toronto, Ontario, literary editor, 1940-42; *Examiner,* Peterborough, Ontario, editor and publisher, 1942-62; University of Toronto, Toronto, professor of English, 1960-81, master of Massey College, 1962-81, emeritus professor and master, 1981—. Senator, Stratford Shakespeare Festival, Stratford, Ontario.

MEMBER: Royal Society of Canada (fellow), Playwrights Union of Canada, Royal Society of Literature (fellow), American Academy and Institute of Arts and Letters (honorary member), Authors Guild, Authors League of America, Dramatists Guild, Writers' Union (Canada), P.E.N. International.

AWARDS, HONORS: Louis Jouvet Prize for directing, Dominion Drama Festival, 1949; Stephen Leacock Medal for Humour, 1954, for *Leaven of Malice;* LL.D., University of Alberta, 1957,

Queen's University, 1962, University of Manitoba, 1972, University of Calgary, 1975, and University of Toronto, 1981; D.Litt., McMaster University, 1959, University of Windsor, 1971, York University, 1973, Mount Allison University, 1973, Memorial University of Newfoundland, 1974, University of Western Ontario, 1974, McGill University, 1974, Trent University, 1974, University of Lethbridge, 1981, University of Waterloo, 1981, University of British Columbia, 1983, and University of Santa Clara, 1985; Lorne Pierce Medal, Royal Society of Canada, 1961; D.C.L., Bishop's University, 1967; Companion of the Order of Canada, 1972; Governor General's Award for fiction, 1973, for *The Manticore;* D.Hum. Litt., University of Rochester, 1983; honorary fellow of Balliol College, Oxford, 1986, and Trinity College, University of Toronto, 1987; City of Toronto Book Award, 1986; Canadian Authors Association Literary Award for Fiction, 1986, for *What's Bred in the Bone; What's Bred in the Bone* was shortlisted for Booker Prize, 1986; Banff Centre School of Fine Arts National Award, 1986; Lifetime Achievement Award from Toronto Arts Awards, 1986; Gold Medal of Honor for Literature from National Arts Club (New York), 1987; World Fantasy Convention Award for *High Spirits.*

WRITINGS:

THE "SALTERTON TRILOGY"; NOVELS

Tempest-Tost (also see below), Clarke, Irwin, 1951, Rinehart, 1952, reprinted, Penguin, 1980.
Leaven of Malice (also see below), Clarke, Irwin, 1954, Scribner, 1955, reprinted, Penguin, 1980.
A Mixture of Frailties (also see below), Scribner, 1958, reprinted, Penguin, 1980.
The Salterton Trilogy (contains *Tempest-Tost, Leaven of Malice,* and *A Mixture of Frailties*), Penguin, 1986.

THE "DEPTFORD TRILOGY"; NOVELS

Fifth Business (also see below), Viking, 1970.
The Manticore (also see below), Viking, 1972.
World of Wonders (also see below), Macmillan (Toronto), 1975, Viking, 1976.
The Deptford Trilogy (contains *Fifth Business, The Manticore,* and *World of Wonders*), Penguin, 1985.

THE "CORNISH TRILOGY"; NOVELS

The Rebel Angels, Viking, 1982.
What's Bred in the Bone, Viking, 1985.
The Lyre of Orpheus, Viking, 1988.

OTHER FICTION

High Spirits (stories), Viking, 1983.

NONFICTION

Shakespeare's Boy Actors, Dent, 1939, Russell, 1964.
Shakespeare for Young Players: A Junior Course, Clarke, Irwin, 1942.
The Diary of Samuel Marchbanks (collection of newspaper pieces originally published under pseudonym Samuel Marchbanks; also see below), Clarke, Irwin, 1947.
The Table Talk of Samuel Marchbanks (collection of newspaper pieces originally published under pseudonym Samuel Marchbanks; also see below), Clarke, Irwin, 1949.
(With Tyrone Guthrie and Grant Macdonald) *Renown at Stratford: A Record of the Shakespearean Festival in Canada,* Clarke, Irwin, 1953, new edition, 1971.
(With Guthrie and Macdonald) *Twice Have the Trumpets Sounded: A Record of the Stratford Shakespearean Festival in Canada,* Clarke, Irwin, 1954.

(With Guthrie, Boyd Neal, and Tanya Moiseiwitsch) *Thrice the Brinded Cat Hath Mew'd: A Record of the Stratford Shakespearean Festival in Canada,* Clarke, Irwin, 1955.
A Voice from the Attic, Knopf, 1960 (published in England as *The Personal Art: Reading to Good Purpose,* Secker & Warburg, 1961, reprinted, Darby Books, 1983).
Le Jeu de centenaire, Comission du Centenaire, c. 1967.
Samuel Marchbanks' Almanack (collection of newspaper pieces originally published under pseudonym Samuel Marchbanks; also see below), McClelland & Stewart, 1967.
The Heart of a Merry Christmas, Macmillan (Toronto), 1970.
Stephen Leacock, McClelland & Stewart, 1970.
(Editor and author of introduction) *Feast of Stephen: An Anthology of Some of the Less Familiar Writings of Stephen Leacock,* McClelland & Stewart, 1970.
(With Michael R. Booth, Richard Southern, Frederick Marker, and Lise-Lone Marker) *The Revels History of Drama in English,* Volume 6: *1750-1880,* Methuen, 1975.
One Half of Robertson Davies: Provocative Pronouncements on a Wide Range of Topics, Macmillan (Toronto), 1977, published as *One Half of Robertson Davies,* Viking, 1978.
The Enthusiasms of Robertson Davies, edited by Judith Skelton Grant, McClelland & Stewart, 1979.
(Contributor) Robert G. Lawrence and Samuel L. Macey, editors, *Studies in Robertson Davies' Deptford Trilogy,* English Literary Studies, University of Victoria, 1980.
The Well-Tempered Critic: One Man's View of Theatre and Letters in Canada, edited by Grant, McClelland & Stewart, 1981.
The Mirror of Nature (lectures), University of Toronto Press, 1983.
The Papers of Samuel Marchbanks (contains portions of *The Diary of Samuel Marchbanks, The Table Talk of Samuel Marchbanks,* and *Samuel Marchbanks' Almanack*), Irwin Publishing, 1985, Viking, 1986.

PLAYS

Fortune, My Foe (first produced in Kingston, Ontario, by the International Players, 1948), Clarke, Irwin, 1949.
Eros at Breakfast and Other Plays (contains "Eros at Breakfast" [first produced in Montreal, Quebec, at the Montreal Repertory Theatre, 1948], "Overlaid" [first produced in Peterborough, Ontario, at Peterborough Little Theatre, 1947], "The Voice of the People" [also see below; first produced in Montreal at the Montreal Repertory Theatre, 1948], "At the Gates of the Righteous" [first produced in Peterborough at the Peterborough Little Theatre, 1948], and "Hope Deferred" [first produced in Montreal at the Montreal Repertory Theatre, 1948]), with introduction by Tyrone Guthrie, Clarke, Irwin, 1949, revised edition published as *Four Favorite Plays,* 1968.
At My Heart's Core (first produced in Peterborough at the Peterborough Little Theatre, 1950), Clarke, Irwin, 1952.
A Masque of Aesop (first produced in Toronto, Ontario, at Upper Canada College, May, 1952), Clarke, Irwin, 1952.
A Jig for the Gypsy (first produced in Toronto at the Crest Theatre, 1954), Clarke, Irwin, 1955.
Love and Libel (based on *Leaven of Malice;* first produced in Toronto at the Royal Alexandra Theatre, November, 1960; first produced on Broadway at the Martin Beck Theatre, December, 1960), Studio Duplicating Service, 1960.
A Masque of Mr. Punch (first produced in Toronto at Upper Canada College, 1962), Oxford University Press, 1963.
The Voice of the People, Book Society of Canada, 1968.

Hunting Stuart and Other Plays (contains "Hunting Stuart" [first produced in Toronto at the Crest Theatre, 1955], "King Phoenix" [first produced in Peterborough, 1950], and "General Confession"), New Press, 1972.

"Brothers in the Black Art," first produced on Canadian Broadcasting Corporation, 1974.

Question Time (first produced in Toronto at the St. Lawrence Center, 1975), Macmillan, 1975.

"Pontiac and the Green Man," first produced in Toronto at the Macmillan Theatre, 1977.

SIDELIGHTS: The "Deptford Trilogy"—consisting of the novels *Fifth Business, The Manticore,* and *World of Wonders*—has brought Robertson Davies to international attention as one of Canada's leading men of letters. "These novels," Claude Bissell writes in *Canadian Literature,* "comprise the major piece of prose fiction in Canadian literature—in scope, in the constant interplay of wit and intelligence, in the persistent attempt to find a pattern in this[, as Davies states in the trilogy,] 'life of marvels, cruel circumstances, obscenities, and commonplaces.' "

The trilogy traces the lives of three Canadian men from the small town of Deptford, Ontario, who are bound together by a single tragic event from their childhood. At the age of ten, Dunstan Ramsay and Percy "Boy" Staunton are throwing snowballs at one another. Staunton throws a snowball at Ramsay which contains a rock. Ramsay ducks. The snowball strikes Mrs. Mary Dempster in the head, causing her to give birth prematurely to a son, Paul Dempster, and to have a mental breakdown that ends in her permanent hospitalization. Each novel of the trilogy revolves around this tragedy and deals primarily with one of the three men involved: *Fifth Business* with Dunstan Ramsay, who becomes a teacher; *The Manticore* with Boy Staunton, a politician; and *World of Wonders* with Paul Dempster, a stage magician. "*Fifth Business* provides the brickwork," John Alwyne writes in the *New Statesman,* "the two later volumes, the lath and plaster. But what a magnificent building is the result. [The trilogy] bears comparison with any fiction of the last decade."

Davies did not intend to write a trilogy when he first began *Fifth Business.* His initial story idea prompted him to write the novel, he tells *Time* (Canada), "but found almost as soon as had finished it that wasn't all wanted to say." So Davies wrote *The Manticore* to tell more of his story. Reviewers then asked "to hear about the magician who appeared in the other two novels," Davies explains, "and I thought 'Well, I know a lot about magicians' and I wrote the third book."

Despite the unplanned development of the trilogy, it has garnered extensive critical praise and each volume has been an international bestseller. The first volume, *Fifth Business,* is, Sam Solecki maintains in *Canadian Forum,* "Davies' masterpiece and . . . among the handful of Canadian novels that count." In the form of an autobiographical letter written by Dunstan Ramsay upon his retirement, the novel delineates the course of Ramsay's life and how it was shaped by the pivotal snowball incident. Because he avoided being hit, and thereby caused Mrs. Dempster's injury, Ramsay has lived his life suffering under a tremendous guilt. This guilt inspired an interest in hagiology, the study of saints, and Ramsay becomes in later years the foremost Protestant authority on the lives of the saints. "All the lore on saints and myth," Judith Skelton Giant states in *Book Forum,* "is firmly connected to the central character, reflecting his interests, showing how he thinks, influencing his life, and playing a part in his interpretation of events." It is in terms of hagiology that Ramsay eventually comes to a realization about himself. His autobiographical letter finally "leads Ramsay to comprehension of

his own nature—which is not saintly," John Skow reports in *Time.*

Much of this same story is reexamined in *The Manticore,* the second novel of the trilogy, which takes place after the mysterious death of prominent Canadian politician Boy Staunton. Staunton has been found drowned in his car at the bottom of Lake Ontario, a rock in his mouth. Investigation proves the rock to be the same one that Staunton threw at Mrs. Dempster some sixty years before. Ramsay, obsessed with the incident, had saved it. But how Staunton died, and why he had the rock in his mouth, is unknown. During a performance by the magician Magnus Eisengrim (Paul Dempster's stage name), a floating brass head is featured that answers questions from the audience. Staunton's son David asks the head an explosive question, "Who killed Boy Staunton?" In the tumult caused by his outburst, David runs from the theater. His breakdown and subsequent Jungian psychoanalysis in Switzerland make up the rest of the novel. During his analysis, David comes to terms with his late father's career. "The blend of masterly characterization, cunning plot, shifting point of view, and uncommon detail, all fixed in the clearest, most literate prose, is superbly achieved," writes Pat Barclay in *Canadian Literature.*

The life story of Paul Dempster is told in *World of Wonders,* the final volume of the trilogy. As a young boy, Dempster is kidnapped by a homosexual stage magician while visiting a travelling carnival. Dempster stays with the carnival as it makes its way across Canada, intent on becoming a magician himself by learning the secrets of the man who abducted him. While learning the trade, Dempster works inside a mechanical fortune-telling gypsy, operating the gears that make it seem lifelike. When the carnival breaks up, Dempster heads for Europe where he finds work as a double for a popular stage actor. With his knowledge of magic and the stage manner he has acquired from the theater people he knows, Dempster strikes out on his own as a magician, becoming one of the most successful acts on the continent. *World of Wonders,* Michael Mewshaw states in the *New York Times Book Review,* is "a novel of stunning verbal energy and intelligence." L. J. Davis of *New Republic* believes the novel's "situation is shamelessly contrived, and the language fairly reeks of the footlights (to say nothing of, yes, brimstone)." Furthermore, Davis contends that *World of Wonders* "isn't so much a novel as it is a brilliant act whose strength lies in the complexity of its symbolism and the perfection of its artifice." It is, Davis judges, "a splendid conclusion" to the trilogy.

In each of these novels the lead character undergoes a psychological transformation. Dunstan Ramsay finds the key to himself in the study of saints and myth, using these archetypes for greater self-understanding. David Staunton relies on Jungian psychoanalysis to help him in discovering his true nature and in coming to terms with his father's disreputable life and mysterious death. Paul Dempster learns from his work as a magician and his life in the theater about reality and illusion, gaining insight into his own personality. The three novels are, Bissell explains, "essentially parts of a whole: three parallel pilgrimages." Grant, too, sees the essential search in which the three characters are engaged. She believes they explore different aspects of nature, however. "Dunstan moves toward God and Boy toward the Devil," Grant writes, "[while Dempster] experiences both." This experience of both good and evil, Grant believes, allows those dark aspects of the mind to be exposed and confronted. "Not everything that has been labeled Evil proves to be so," Grant states, "nor all that has been repressed ought to remain so. And the genuinely evil and justifiably banished are weaker if faced and understood." Grant believes that "together with the vigorous, lively and eccentric narrators of the [Deptford] trilogy, these moral, . . . mythic and psychological ideas have given these books a place among the dozen significant works of fiction published in Canada during the seventies." Peter S. Prescott, writing in *Newsweek,* sees the revelations of the three characters in similar terms. Davies, he writes, "means to recharge the world with a wonder it has lost, to re-create through the intervention of saints and miracles, psychoanalysts and sleight-of-hand a proper sense of awe at life's mystery and a recognition of the price that must be paid for initiation into that mystery."

The recurring theme of self-discovery follows the pattern established by psychologist Carl Jung, although Davies does not adhere strictly to Jungian psychology. He has explored a number of models for "complete human identity," Patricia Monk writes in her *The Smaller Infinity: The Jungian Self in the Novels of Robertson Davies,* and though he has a "deep and long-lasting affinity with Jung, . . . Davies eventually moves beyond his affinity . . . to a more impartial assessment of Jungianism as simply one way of looking at the universe, one myth among a number of others." Still, in common with the Jungian belief in archetypal influence on the human mind, Davies presents in his fiction characters who "discover the meaning of their lives," Roger Sale writes in the *New York Review of Books,* "by discovering the ways those lives conform to ancient patterns." Peter Baltensperger, writing in *Canadian Literature,* sees this as a consistent theme in all of Davies's fiction, not only in the "Deptford Trilogy." This theme Baltensperger defines as "the conquest of one's Self in the inner struggle and the knowledge of oneself as fully human."

Commenting to *CA,* Davies clarifies the primary concern in all of his work. "The theme which lies at the root of all my novels is the isolation of the human spirit," he explains. "I have not attempted to deal with it in a gloomy fashion but rather to demonstrate that what my characters do that might be called really significant is done on their own volition and usually contrary to what is expected of them. This theme is worked out in terms of characters who are trying to escape from early influences and find their own place in the world but who are reluctant to do so in a way that will bring pain and disappointment to others."

Many critics label Davies a traditionalist who is a bit old-fashioned in his approach to writing. I. M. Owen of *Saturday Night,* for example, places Davies "curiously apart from the main stream of contemporary fiction." A critic for the *Washington Post Book World* characterizes Davies as "a true novelist writing imagined stories, wonderful stories full of magic and incandescence, thought and literary art," something the critic does not find in other contemporary fiction. Davies is known as a moralist who believes in a tangible good and evil, a fine storyteller who consciously uses theatrical melodrama to enliven his plots, and a master of a wide variety of genres and styles.

Davies's strong moral sense is evident in the "Deptford Trilogy" where, Mewshaw finds, "no action is without consequences." This unflinching explication of his characters' behavior makes for "a constant, lively judging and damning of characters," as the writer for *Time* (Canada) reports. "The habit of stern judgment is missing from most modern discourse," he continues, "which tends charitably or fearfully to find excuses. But it is abundantly present in Davies's novels." These judgments are rooted in Davies's belief, Jean Strouse of *Newsweek* quotes him as saying, that "sin is the great unacknowledged element in modern life." It is sin which Davies explores in his novels, setting his characters to "grapple with magic, madness, mysticism, Gnosti-

cism, miracles, freaks, saints, devils, Jung, Freud, God, mythic beasts, guilt, dominion and human nature."

Since he has written a number of plays, been a teacher and actor with the Old Vic Company, and served on the board of the Stratford Shakespeare Festival for many years, it is not surprising to find that Davies employs theatrical elements in his novels. He uses theatricality to move his story along at a quicker pace. In *World of Wonders,* a *Time* critic states, the characters "are brilliant talkers, but when they natter on too long, the highly theatrical author causes a grotesque face to appear at a window, drops someone through a trap door or stages a preposterous recognition scene." These melodramatic touches come naturally to Davies who, Davis remarks, "is a player in love with the play, and the kind of play he loves is melodrama." In his collection of lectures entitled *The Mirror of Nature,* Davies makes his case on behalf of melodrama and attempts, as Alberto Manguel writes in the Toronto *Globe & Mail,* "to save melodrama's lost honor." Davies argues in this book that "theatre is a coarse art. . . . It appeals immediately to primary, not secondary elements in human nature." Melodrama's emphasis on creating an emotional response in its audience, Davies continues, is true to theatre's fundamental purpose. Manguel concludes that Davies "succeeds" in justifying his own use of melodrama.

The range of Davies's abilities is reflected not only in the variety of genres in which he has written but in his ability to move "easily from the bawdiest humor to the loftiest abstraction, charging every character and idea with power and fascination," as Mewshaw states. Davies's work in the "Deptford Trilogy," Strouse maintains, encompasses such divergent elements as "mystery, grotesquerie, desolation and psychological sagacity." Walter E. Swayze of *Canadian Forum* notes that although Davies has written in a "diversity of styles . . . direct expression and bold colour have been constant features." Admitting that Davies is a "fine writer—deft, resourceful, diverse and . . . very funny," John Kenneth Galbraith nonetheless writes in the *New York Times Book Review* that Davies's greatest strength is "his imagination."

Calling Davies "a compellingly inventive storyteller" who has garnered an "affectionate following," James Idema of the *Chicago Tribune Book World* explains the appeal of his fiction. It lies in "his way of placing ordinary humans in the midst of extraordinary events, of bringing innocent, resolutely straight characters into contact with bonafide exotics," Idema believes. "The 'real world' interests [Davies] only as a starting point. Enigma, myth, illusion and magic are the stuff of his elegant stories." Similarly, William Kennedy observes in the *New York Times Book Review* that Davies "conveys a sense of real life lived in a fully imagined if sometimes mythical and magical world." Comparing the role of the novelist with that of the magician, because both "mean us to believe in what never happened and to this end use many conjuror's tricks," Prescott defines Davies as one writer "who takes seriously his magician's role." In doing so, Davies has become "one of the most gifted and accomplished literary entertainers now writing in English," as a writer for *Time* remarks. In a speech given at the University of Windsor and quoted by *Time* (Canada), Davies observes that "though it is always an unwise thing to say too loudly—because you never know who may be listening—I am a happy man."

BIOGRAPHICAL/CRITICAL SOURCES:

BOOKS

Anthony, Geraldine, editor, *Stage Voices: 12 Canadian Playwrights Talk about Their Lives and Work,* Doubleday, 1978.

Bestsellers 89, Issue 2, Gale, 1989.

Buitenhuis, Elspeth, *Robertson Davies,* Forum House Publishing, 1972.

Cameron, Donald, *Conversations with Canadian Novelists,* Part 1, Macmillan, 1973.

Contemporary Literary Criticism, Gale, Volume 2, 1974, Volume 7, 1977, Volume 13, 1980, Volume 25, 1983, Volume 42, 1987.

Davies, Robertson, *Fifth Business,* Viking, 1970.

Davies, Robertson, *The Manticore,* Viking, 1972.

Davies, Robertson, *World of Wonders,* Macmillan (Toronto), 1975, Viking, 1976.

Davies, Robertson, *The Mirror of Nature,* University of Toronto Press, 1983.

Dictionary of Literary Biography, Volume 68: *Canadian Writers, 1920-1959, First Series,* Gale, 1988.

Grant, Judith Skelton, *Robertson Davies,* McClelland & Stewart, 1978.

Heath, Jeffrey M., editor, *Profiles in Canadian Literature #2,* Dundum Press, 1980.

Jones, Joseph, and Johanna Jones, *Canadian Fiction,* Twayne, 1981.

King, Bruce, *The New English Literatures: Cultural Nationalism in a Changing World,* St. Martin's Press, 1980.

Klinck, Carl F., editor, *Literary History of Canada,* University of Toronto Press, 2nd edition, 1976.

Lawrence, Robert G., and Samuel L. Macey, editors, *Studies in Robertson Davies' Deptford Trilogy,* English Literary Studies, University of Victoria, 1980.

Monk, Patricia, *The Smaller Infinity: The Jungian Self in the Novels of Robertson Davies,* University of Toronto Press, 1982.

Moore, Mavor, *Four Canadian Playwrights,* Holt, 1973.

Morley, Patricia, *Robertson Davies,* Gage Educational Publishing, 1977.

New, William H., editor, *Dramatists in Canada: Selected Essays,* University of British Columbia Press, 1972.

Stone-Blackburn, Susan, *Robertson Davies: Playwright,* University of British Columbia Press, 1985.

Stouck, David, *Major Canadian Authors: A Critical Introduction,* University of Nebraska Press, 1984.

PERIODICALS

America, December 16, 1972.

Book Forum, Volume 4, number 1, 1978.

Books in Canada, November, 1985, August, 1988.

Book World, December 13, 1970.

Canadian Forum, June, 1950, December, 1975, October, 1977, December-January, 1981-82.

Canadian Literature, spring, 1960, winter, 1961, spring, 1973, winter, 1974, winter, 1976.

Canadian Review, fall, 1976.

Chicago Tribune, July 26, 1986.

Chicago Tribune Book World, January 31, 1982.

Dalhousie Review, autumn, 1981.

Detroit Free Press, January 22, 1989, February 6, 1989.

Essays on Canadian Writing, spring, 1987.

Financial Post, January 19, 1963.

Globe & Mail (Toronto), March 5, 1977, January 7, 1984, September 10, 1988, September 17, 1988.

Journal of Canadian Fiction, winter, 1972, winter, 1982.

Journal of Canadian Studies, February, 1977.

Library Quarterly, April, 1969.

Listener, April 15, 1971.

Los Angeles Times, January 29, 1982.

Los Angeles Times Book Review, December 1, 1985, January 29, 1989, January 30, 1989.

Maclean's, March 15, 1952, September, 1972, November 18, 1985, October 19, 1987, September 12, 1988.

Nation, April 24, 1982.

New Republic, March 13, 1976, April 15, 1978, March 10, 1982, December 30, 1985.

New Statesman, April 20, 1973, April 4, 1980, October 14, 1988.

Newsweek, January 18, 1971, March 22, 1976, February 8, 1982.

New Yorker, January 27, 1986.

New York Review of Books, February 8, 1973, February 27, 1986.

New York Times, February 8, 1982, November 6, 1985, December 28, 1988, December 29, 1988.

New York Times Book Review, December 20, 1970, November 19, 1972, April 25, 1976, February 14, 1982, December 15, 1985, January 8, 1989.

Observer (London), October 2, 1988.

Quill & Quire, August, 1988.

Rolling Stone, December 1, 1977.

San Francisco Review of Books, spring, 1987.

Saturday Night, April 26, 1947, December 13, 1947, February 14, 1953, November, 1967, October, 1985.

Saturday Review, December 26, 1970, April 3, 1976.

Spectator, August 21, 1982, October 8, 1988.

Tamarack Review, autumn, 1958.

Time, January 11, 1971, May 17, 1976, December 26, 1988.

Time (Canada), November 3, 1975.

Times Literary Supplement, March 26, 1982, February 28, 1986, October 16, 1987, September 23, 1988.

Tribune Books, December 25, 1988.

University of Toronto Quarterly, Number 21, 1952.

Washington Post, January 11, 1989.

Washington Post Book World, May 30, 1976, February 7, 1982, October 30, 1983, November 17, 1985, July 20, 1986, June 5, 1988, December 18, 1988.

*   *   *

DAVIS, B. Lynch
    See BIOY CASARES, Adolfo and BORGES, Jorge Luis

*   *   *

DAVISON, Lawrence H.
    See LAWRENCE, D(avid) H(erbert Richards)

*   *   *

DAY LEWIS, C(ecil)   1904-1972
(Nicholas Blake)

PERSONAL: Born April 27, 1904, in Ballintubber, Ireland; died May 22, 1972; son of F. C. (a minister) and Kathleen Blake (Squires; a collateral descendant of Oliver Goldsmith) Day Lewis; married Constance Mary King, 1928 (divorced, 1951); married Jill Angela Henriette Balcon, April 27, 1951; children: (first marriage) Sean Francis, Nicholas Charles; (second marriage) Lydia Tamasin, Daniel Michael. *Education:* Attended Wadham College, Oxford.

ADDRESSES: Home—6 Crooms Hill, Greenwich, London SE 10, England. *Office*—Chatto & Windus Ltd., 40 William IV St., London WC2, England.

CAREER: Assistant master at Summerfields, Oxford, England, 1927-28, at Larchfield, Helensburgh, Scotland, 1928-30, and at

Cheltenham College, England, 1930-35; editor with Ministry of Information, 1941-46; Trinity College, Cambridge, England, Clark Lecturer, 1946; Oxford University, Oxford, England, professor of poetry, 1951-56; Harvard University, Cambridge, Mass., Charles Eliot Norton Professor of Poetry, 1964-65. Appointed Poet Laureate of Britain by Queen Elizabeth II, 1968. Member of Arts Council, 1962-72; member of board of directors, Chatto & Windus Ltd. (publishers).

MEMBER: Royal Society of Literature (fellow; vice president, 1958-72), Royal Society of Arts (fellow), American Academy of Arts and Letters (honorary member), Athenaeum.

AWARDS, HONORS: Companion, Order of British Empire, 1950; D.Litt., University of Exeter, 1965, University of Hull, 1970; Litt.D., Trinity College, Dublin, 1968.

WRITINGS:

Beechen Vigil, and Other Poems, Fortune Press, 1925.
Country Comets (poetry), 1928.
Transitional Poem, Hogarth, 1929.
From Feathers to Iron (poetry), Hogarth, 1932.
Dick Willoughby (juvenile fiction), Basil Blackwell, 1933, Random House, 1938.
The Magnetic Mountain (poetry), Hogarth, 1933.
A Hope for Poetry (criticism), Basil Blackwell, 1934, reprinted with a postscript, Folcroft, 1969.
Collected Poems, 1929-1933, Hogarth, 1935, 2nd edition, 1945.
Collected Poems, 1929-1933 [and] *A Hope For Poetry,* Random House, 1935.
Revolution in Writing (commentary), Hogarth, 1935, reprinted, Folcroft, 1969.
A Time to Dance, and Other Poems, Hogarth, 1935.
We're Not Going to Do Nothing (commentary), Left Review, 1936, reprinted, Folcroft, 1970.
The Friendly Tree (novel), J. Cape, 1936, Harper, 1937.
Noah and the Waters (modern morality play), Hogarth, 1936.
A Time to Dance; Noah and the Waters, [and] *Revolution in Writing,* Random House, 1936.
(With L. S. Stebbing) *Imagination and Thinking,* Life and Leisure, 1936.
Starting Point (novel), J. Cape, 1937, Harper, 1938.
Overtures to Death, and Other Poems, J. Cape, 1938.
Child of Misfortune (novel), J. Cape, 1939.
Poems in Wartime, J. Cape, 1940.
Selected Poems, Hogarth, 1940, revised edition, Penguin, 1969.
Word Over All (poetry), J. Cape, 1943, Transatlantic, 1944.
Poetry for You: A Book for Boys and Girls on the Enjoyment of Poetry (juvenile), Basil Blackwell, 1944, Oxford University Press (New York), 1947, reissued, Soccer, 1966.
Short is the Time: Poems, 1936-1943 (previously published as *Overtures to Death and Word Over All*), Oxford University Press (New York), 1945.
The Poetic Image (criticism), Oxford University Press, 1947.
Enjoying Poetry, Cambridge University Press for National Book League, 1947, reprinted, Folcroft, 1970.
The Colloquial Element in English Poetry (criticism), Literary and Philosophical Society of Newcastle-upon-Tyne, 1947.
Collected Poems, 1929-1936, Hogarth, 1948.
Poems, 1943-1947, Oxford University Press, 1948.
The Otterbury Incident (juvenile; adaptation of the French film "Nous le gosses," released in England as "Us Kids"), Putnam, 1948, reissued, 1963.
The Poet's Task (criticism), Clarendon Press, 1951, reprinted, Folcroft, 1970.
The Grand Manner (criticism), University of Nottingham, 1952.

An Italian Visit (narrative poem), Harper, 1953.
The Lyrical Poetry of Thomas Hardy (criticism), Oxford University Press, 1953, Folcroft Editions, 1970.
Collected Poems, J. Cape, 1954, published as *Collected Poems, 1954,* 1970, reprinted, 1988.
Christmas Eve, Faber, 1954.
Notable Images of Virtue: Emily Bronte, George Meredith, W. B. Yeats, Ryerson, 1954, reprinted, Folcroft, 1969.
Pegasus, and Other Poems, J. Cape, 1957, Harper, 1958.
The Poet's Way of Knowledge, Cambridge University Press, 1957.
The Newborn: D. M. B., 29th April, 1957 (poetry), Favil Press of Kensington, 1957.
The Buried Day (autobiography), Harper, 1960.
English Lyric Poems, 1500-1900, Appleton, 1961 (published in England as *A Book of English Lyrics,* Chatto & Windus, 1961).
The Gate, and Other Poems, J. Cape, 1962.
Requiem for the Living (poetry), Harper, 1964.
On Not Saying Anything (poetry), privately printed, 1964.
The Lyric Impulse (Charles Eliot Norton lectures), Harvard University Press, 1965.
(With R. A. Scott-James) *Thomas Hardy* (criticism), Longman, 1965.
The Room, and Other Poems, J. Cape, 1965.
A Marriage Song for Albert and Barbara (poetry), privately printed, 1965.
Selected Poems, Harper, 1967, revised edition, Penguin, 1969.
Selections from His Poetry [by] *C. Day Lewis* (also published as *C. Day Lewis: Selections from His Poetry*), edited by Patric Dickinson, Chatto & Windus, 1967.
The Abbey That Refused to Die: A Poem, Ballintubber Abbey, 1967.
A Need for Poetry?, University of Hull, 1968.
The Whispering Roots, and Other Poems, Harper, 1970 (published in England as *The Whispering Roots,* J. Cape, 1970).
Going My Way, [London], 1970.
The Poems of C. Day Lewis, edited by Ian Parson, J. Cape, 1970.
On Translating Poetry: A Lecture, Abbey Press, 1970.

DETECTIVE NOVELS; UNDER PSEUDONYM NICHOLAS BLAKE

A Question of Proof, Harper, 1935, reissued, Collins, 1969.
Shell of Death, Harper, 1936 (published in England as *Thou Shell of Death,* Collins, 1936, reissued, 1971).
There's Trouble Brewing, Harper, 1937.
The Beast Must Die, Harper, 1938.
The Smiler With the Knife, Harper, 1939, reissued, Collins, 1972.
The Summer Camp Mystery, Harper, 1940 (published in England as *Malice in Wonderland,* Collins, 1940; American paperback edition published as *Malice with Murder*).
The Corpse in the Snowman, Harper, 1941 (published in England as *The Case of the Abominable Snowman,* Collins, 1941).
Minute for Murder, Harper, 1947.
Head of a Traveler, Harper, 1949.
The Dreadful Hollow, Harper, 1953.
The Whisper in the Gloom, Harper, 1954.
A Tangled Web, Harper, 1956, reissued, Chivers, 1973.
End of Chapter, Harper, 1957.
A Penknife in My Heart, Collins, 1958, Harper, 1959.
The Widow's Cruise, Harper, 1959.
The Worm of Death, Harper, 1961.
The Deadly Joker, Collins, 1963.
The Sad Variety, Harper, 1964.

The Morning after Death, Collins, 1966.
The Nicholas Blake Omnibus, Collins, 1966.
The Private Wound, Harper, 1968.

EDITOR

(With W. H. Auden) *Oxford Poetry,* Basil Blackwell, 1927-32.
The Mind in Chains: Socialism and the Cultural Revolution, Muller Ltd., 1937, reprinted, Folcroft 1972.
(With John Lehmann, T. A. Jackson Fox, and Ralph Winston) *Ralph Fox: Writer in Arms,* International Publishers, 1937.
(With Charles Fenby) *Anatomy of Oxford: An Anthology,* J. Cape, 1938.
(With L. A. G. Strong) *An Anthology of Modern Verse, 1920-1940* (also published as *A New Anthology of Modern Verse, 1920-1940*), Methuen, 1941, reissued, 1963.
The Echoing Green: An Anthology of Verse, three volumes, Basil Blackwell, 1941-43, reissued, 1960-63.
(With others) *Orion,* Nicholson & Watson, Volume II, 1945, Volume III, 1946.
(And author of introduction) Francis T. Palgrave, *The Golden Treasury of the Best Songs and Lyrical Poems in the English Language,* Collins, 1954.
(With John Lehmann) *The Chatto Book of Modern Poetry, 1915-1955,* Chatto & Windus, 1956, reprinted, Greenwood Press, 1978.
Charles Dickens, *The Mystery of Edwin Drood,* Collins, 1956.
(With Kathleen Nott and Thomas Blackburn) *New Poems 1957,* M. Joseph, 1957.
(And author of introduction and notes) Wilfred Owen, *Collected Poems,* amended edition, New Directions, 1954.
(And author of introduction) Edmund Charles Blunden, *The Midnight Skaters: Poems for Young Readers,* Bodley Head, 1968.
The Poems of Robert Browning, Limited Editions Club (Cambridge), 1969, Heritage Press, 1971.
A Choice of Keats's Verse, Faber, 1971.
George Crabbe, *Crabbe,* Penguin, 1973.

TRANSLATOR

Virgil, *Georgics,* J. Cape, 1940.
Paul Valery, *Le Cimetiere marin,* Secker & Warburg, 1947.
Virgil, *Aeneid,* Oxford University Press, 1952, Doubleday Anchor, 1953.
Virgil, *Eclogues,* J. Cape, 1963.
The Eclogues and Georgics of Virgil, Doubleday Anchor, 1964 (published in England as *The Eclogues: Georgics and Aeneid,* Oxford University Press, 1966).
(With Matyas Sarkozi) Erzsi Gazdas, *The Tomtit in the Rain: Traditional Hungarian Rhymes,* Chatto & Windus, 1971.

AUTHOR OF INTRODUCTION

Selected Poems of Robert Frost, J. Cape, 1936.
Julius Lipton, *Poems of Strife,* Lawrence, 1936.
Collected Poems of Lilian Bowes Lyon, Dutton, 1948.
George Meredith, *Modern Love,* Hart-Davis, 1948.

SIDELIGHTS: When C. Day Lewis was appointed Poet Laureate of Great Britain, a reviewer in the *Beloit Poetry Journal* commented: "If one may judge by his past performance, it is an honor that he will till with a good deal more distinction than most of his predecessors. As this volume [*Selected Poems*] quickly demonstrates, he is a poet of superb range. Three themes seem to recur over the years: an admiration for all that is truly heroic, a feeling for the ephemeral quality of life, and a quest for pure and true identity. But there are other themes, too—lighter,

less cerebral. But everything he writes is touched with a sense of the truly poetic. He is a major figure."

This regard has not always been shared by critics, nor have his poems been considered of uniformly high quality. Philip Booth offered an explanation: "To look to these poems for the verbal energy of Ted Hughes or the imagistic precision of Philip Larkin is to miss the personal perspective which characterizes this collection [*Selected Poems*]. . . . Day Lewis is not everyone's cup of tea, especially in an America where stronger, colder, and more bitter drinks are now more fashionable. But to ask these poems to be other than they are would be to deny the very civilization to which they are native; the collection is a wholly honorable brew."

Day Lewis's own history provides other clues to his diversity. The late Poet Laureate was once a poet of revolution, inextricably linked with the avant-garde Oxford poets of the 1930s, W. H. Auden, Stephen Spender, and Louis MacNeice. His poems of that period were mostly parodies, and considered highly imitative. Brian Jones wrote that it was not until 1943 that Day Lewis published verse "which gives the authentic shock of originality. . . . Since then, Day Lewis has continued in this much more personal vein . . . which seems to arise genuinely from his own personality. And it is clear from his 'Thirties verse that he could not at that time find a satisfactory voice because he knew only too well what it naturally was—a late Romantic's, words which it was a disgrace to utter at that time. And so he hid it, became a mimic, or at best used his true voice when he was pretending it was somebody else's, as in his parodies."

His prose, on the other hand, was always highly regarded, from his early political essays, to his quite successful "Nicholas Blake" novels, which he began as pot-boilers. "From most of the news stories about the appointment of Cecil Day Lewis as Poet Laureate of Great Britain," noted Anthony Boucher, "you would gather that he is one of those lyric dons who dash off an occasional detective story in their lighter moments. In fact the poet is . . . a hardworking professional in crime, who . . . is also one of England's two or three leading reviewers of crime fiction. Blake's stature among mystery novelists is at least as high as that of Day Lewis among poets; he has excelled both in the straight detective puzzle and in the broader study of crime and character, as well as in happy blends of the two methods."

Often classified as a Georgian, Day Lewis was a skilled craftsman, excelling at highly disciplined traditional verse forms, at his best in meditative poems. "I always wished to be lucid," he once commented, and his best poems are noted for lucidity, simplicity, and quiet lyricism. "He is a quiet writer," observed John Wain, "with a preference for ordered syntax and regular form, who likes to brood rather than to exclaim." He called himself a member of the "derriere garde," and, according to Peter Gellatly, "derided his 'too meticulous words,' and disclaimed for his works that 'divine incontinence' which he considers an essential element in good poetry. He obviously admires the roistering, Dylan-like figure but cannot emulate him. Wild singing is not for Day Lewis. On the other hand, his temperateness and steadiness of outlook sometimes invest his poems with a glossy perfection that is rarely seen elsewhere."

As Poet Laureate—a position paying somewhat more than $230 per year—he turned out official verse not noted for literary distinction. Yet he could still write in another vein; his last collection elicited this reassurance from Derek Stattford: "it is good to see Mr. Day Lewis in such a fine and charming fettle. . . . Those . . . who may have feared this poet would be throttled by his chain of office can breathe a deep sigh of relief and get down to enjoying *The Whispering Roots.*"

BIOGRAPHICAL/CRITICAL SOURCES:

BOOKS

Contemporary Literary Criticism, Gale, Volume 1, 1973, Volume 6, 1976, Volume 10, 1979.
Dictionary of Literary Biography, Gale, Volume 15: *British Novelists, 1930-1959,* 1983, Volume 20: *British Poets, 1914-1945,* 1983, Volume 77: *British Mystery Writers, 1920-1939,* 1988.
Dyment, Clifford, *C. Day Lewis,* Longmans, Green, for the British Council, 1955.
Handley-Taylor, Geoffrey and Timothy d'Arch Smith, *C. Day Lewis, The Poet Laureate: A Bibliography,* St. James Press, 1968.

PERIODICALS

New Republic, March 28, 1964.
New Statesman, June 14, 1958.
New York Review of Books, June 25, 1964.
New York Times Book Review, June 22, 1958.
Poetry, August, 1958.
Times Literary Supplement, March 6, 1959.
Washington Post Book World, June 21, 1981.

*   *   *

DEANE, Norman
    See CREASEY, John

*   *   *

de BEAUVOIR, Simone (Lucie Ernestine Marie Bertrand)
    See BEAUVOIR, Simone (Lucie Ernestine Marie Bertrand) de

*   *   *

de BONO, Edward   1933-

PERSONAL: Born May 19, 1933, in Malta; son of Joseph Edward (a physician) and Josephine (Bums) de Bono; married Josephine Hall-White, 1971; children: two sons. *Education:* Royal University of Malta, B.Sc., 1953, M.D., 1955; Oxford University, M.A., 1957, D.Phil., 1961; Cambridge University, Ph.D. 1963. *Avocational interests:* Polo, canoeing (paddled 112 miles from Oxford to London non-stop while at Oxford University), and games design.

ADDRESSES: Home—11 Warkworth St., Cambridge, England. *Office*— Cambridge University, Cambridge, England. *Agent*—Michael Homiman, A. P. Watt, 26-28 Bedford Row, London WC1R 4HL, England.

CAREER: Oxford University, Oxford, England, research assistant, 1957-60, lecturer, 1960-61; University of London, London, England, lecturer, 1961-63; Cambridge University, Cambridge, England, assistant director of research, 1963—. Research associate, Harvard University, Cambridge, Mass., 1965-66. Lecturer to industry and education groups on research cognitive processes. Inventor; designer of the L-game. Honorary director and founding member of Cognitive Research Trust.

MEMBER: Medical Research Society.

AWARDS, HONORS: Rhodes scholar.

WRITINGS:

The Use of Lateral Thinking, J. Cape, 1967, published as *New Think: The Use of Lateral Thinking in the Generation of Ideas,* Basic Books, 1968.
The Five-Day Course in Thinking, Basic Books, 1967.
The Mechanism of Mind, Simon & Schuster, 1969.
Lateral Thinking: Creativity Step by Step, Harper, 1970 (published in England as *Lateral Thinking: A Textbook of Creativity,* Ward, Lock, 1970).
The Dog Exercising Machine, J. Cape, 1970, Simon & Schuster, 1971.
(Editor) *Technology Today,* Routledge & Kegan Paul, 1971.
Lateral Thinking for Management: A Handbook of Creativity, American Management Association, 1971.
Practical Thinking: Four Ways to Be Right, Five Ways to Be Wrong, Five Ways to Understand, J. Cape, 1971.
Children Solve Problems, Penguin, 1972, Harper, 1974.
About Think, J. Cape, 1972.
PO: A Device for Successful Thinking, Simon & Schuster, 1972 (published in England as *PO: Beyond Yes and No,* Penguin, 1973).
(Editor) *Eureka: A History of Inventions,* Holt, 1974.
Teaching Thinking, Maurice Temple Smith, 1976.
The Greatest Thinkers, Putnam, 1976.
Wordpower: An Illustrated Dictionary of Vital Words, Harper, 1977.
Opportunities: A Handbook of Business Opportunity Search, Associated Business Programmes (London), 1978.
The Happiness Purpose, Maurice Temple Smith, 1978.
Future Positive, Maurice Temple Smith, 1980.
"The Greatest Thinkers" (television series), thirteen parts, WDR (Germany), 1980.
Atlas of Management Thinking, Maurice Temple Smith, 1981.
de Bono's Course in Thinking, BBC Publications, 1982.
"de Bono's Thinking Course" (television series), ten parts, British Broadcasting Corporation, 1982.
Tactics: The Art and Science of Success, Little, Brown, 1984.
Six Thinking Hats: An Essential Approach to Business Management from the Creator of Lateral Thinking, Little, Brown, 1986.
Letters to Thinkers: Further Thoughts on Lateral Thinking, State Mutual Book, 1987.

Also author of *Masterthinker's Handbook* and *Conflicts: A Better Way to Resolve Them,* for International Center for Creative Thinking. Writer of television items, and of feature stories for *Sunday Mirror, Telegraph Magazine, Nova, Oz, Mind Alive, Science Journal, Sunday Times, Fashion,* and *Honey.* Contributor of articles to professional journals.

BIOGRAPHICAL/CRITICAL SOURCES:

PERIODICALS

Chicago Tribune, February 24, 1985.
Realites (France), August, 1967.
Realites (United States), November, 1967.
Times Literary Supplement, August 9, 1985.

*   *   *

de FILIPPO, Eduardo   1900-1984

PERSONAL: Name listed in one source as originally Eduardo Pasarelli; born May 24, 1900, in Naples, Italy; died of kidney failure, October 31 (some sources say November 1), 1984, in Rome, Italy; son of Eduardo Scarpetta (a writer and actor) and

Luisa de Filippo; married Dorothy Pennington (marriage ended); married Thea Prandi (an actress), 1954 (died, 1961); married Isabella Quarantotti (a stage designer), 1977; children: one son, one daughter (died, 1960).

ADDRESSES: Home—Via Aquileia 14/16, Rome, Italy.

CAREER: Writer; director of radio productions, stage works—including operas—and motion pictures; actor. Worked as actor, utility worker, and writer in L. Carini's theatre company, 1913; actor and writer (under various pseudonyms) in Molinari Company, 1929-31; co-founded Il Teatro Umoristico ("Company of the Humorous Theatre"), 1932; founded La Scarpettiana and Il Teatro di Eduardo. Lecturer at University of Rome in early 1980s.

AWARDS, HONORS: Premio Internazionale per il Teatro from Accademia dei Lincei, 1972; award for best play from London *Evening Standard,* 1972, for "Saturday, Sunday, Monday"; Premio Internazionale from the Teatro Luigi Pirandello, 1975; honorary doctorate from the University of Birmingham, 1977.

WRITINGS:

POETRY

La poesie di Eduardo, Einaudi, 1975.

Also author of *Il paese di Pulcinella* (title means "The Home of Pulcinella"), 1951, and *O Canisto,* 1971.

PLAYS

Sik Sik, l'artefice magico (one-act; title means "Sik-Sik, the Magic Draftsman"), [Italy], 1932.
(With G. Riva) "La speranza ha trovato un alloggio" (three-act; title means "Hope Has Found a Lodging"), first produced in Milan at Teatro Olimpia, April 15, 1936.
Uno coi capelli bianchi (three-act; title means "Someone With White Hair"), [Italy], 1938.
La parte di Amleto (one-act; title means "Hamlet's Part"), [Italy], 1940.
Non ti pago! (three-act; title means "I Won't Pay You"), [Italy], 1941, reprinted, Einaudi, 1966.
(With A. Curcio and R. De Angelis) "La fortuna con l'effe maiuscola" (three-act; title means "Fortune With a Capital F"), produced in Turin at Teatro Alfieri, March 24, 1942.
Io, l'erede (three-act; title means "I, the Heir"), [Italy], 1942, reprinted, Einaudi, 1976.
Questi fantasmi! (three-act; title means "These Ghosts!"; first produced in Rome at Teatro Eliseo, January 12, 1946), [Italy], 1946, reprinted, Einaudi, 1972, translation by Marguerita Carra and Louise H. Warner produced as "Neapolitan Ghosts" in New Haven at Yale Repertory Theatre, 1986.
Filumena marturano (three-act; first produced in Naples, November 7, 1946), [Italy], 1947, reprinted, Einaudi, 1975, translation by Keith Waterhouse and Willis Hall published as *Filumena,* Samuel French, 1978.
"San Carlino 1947" (one-act), first produced in Milan at the Mediolanum, April 8, 1947.
Le bugie con le gambe lunghe (three-act; first produced in Rome at Teatro Eliseo, January 14, 1948), [Italy], 1948, translation produced as "Lies With Long Legs," 1957.
Le voci di dentro (three-act; title means "Voices From Within"; first produced in Milan at Teatro Nuovo, December 11, 1948), [Italy], 1949, reprinted, Einaudi, 1971, translation by N. F. Simpson produced as "Inner Voices" in London at the Lyttelton Theatre, 1983.

Napoli Milionaria (three-act; first produced in 1945; translation produced as "Naples Millionaire" in London, 1972), Einaudi, 1950, reprinted, 1974.
La grande magica (three-act; title means "The Big Magic"; first produced in Naples at Teatro Mercadante, December 14, 1949), [Italy], 1950, translation by Carlo Ardito produced as "Grand Magic" in New York City at the Manhattan Theatre Club, 1979.
La paura numero uno (three-act; title means "Fear Number One"; first produced in Venice at Teatro la Fenice, July 29, 1950), [Italy], 1951.
"Il successo del giorno" (one-act; title means "The Outcome of the Day"), first produced in Rome at Ridotto del Teatro Eliseo, May 9, 1952.
I morti non fanno paura (one-act; title means "The Dead Are Harmless"; first produced in Rome at Ridotto del Teatro Eliseo, May 9, 1952), [Italy], 1956.
Amicizia (one-act; title means "Friendship"; first produced in Rome at Ridotto del Teatro Eliseo, May 9, 1952), [Italy], 1956.
Mia famiglia (three-act; title means "My Family"; first produced in Perugia at Teatro Morlacchi, January 16, 1955; produced in Rome at Ridotto del Teatro Eliseo, January 18, 1955), Einaudi, 1956.
Bene mio e core mio (three-act; title means "My Darling and My Love"; first produced in Rome at Ridotto del Teatro Eliseo, November 11, 1955), [Italy], 1956.
De pretore Vincenzo (first produced in Genoa at Teatro Politeama, December 3, 1961), Einaudi, 1957.
Uomo e galantuomo (three-act; title means "Man and Gentleman"; first produced in 1933), Einaudi, 1966.
Ogni ano punto e da capo, Einaudi, 1971.
Il contratto, Einaudi, 1971.
Il monumento, Einaudi, 1971.
"Natale in casa Cupiello" (title means "Christmas at the Cupiellos"; first produced in 1931), Einaudi, 1972.
Il sindaco del Rione Sanita (first produced in 1960), Einaudi, 1972.
Gli esami non finiscono mai, Einaudi, 1973.
Ditegli sempre: si (first produced in 1931), Einaudi, 1974.
Sabato, Demenica e Lunedi (three-act; first produced in Rome at Teatro Quirino, November 6, 1959), Einaudi, 1974, translation by Waterhouse and Hall published as *Saturday, Sunday, Monday,* Heinemann, 1974.
Three Plays (contains translations of *Il sindaco del Rione Sanita, La grande magica,* and *Filumena marturano*), translated by Carlo Ardito, Hamilton, 1976.

Also author of "I farmacia de turno" (one-act; title means "Pharmacy Open on Alternate Sundays"), 1920; "Ho fatto il guaio? Riparero" (three-act; title means "I Did Wrong? I'll Fix Things"), 1926; (with brother, Peppino de Filippo) "Prova generale" (one-act; title means "Final Dress Rehearsal"), 1929; "L'opera dei pupi" (title means "Puppet Play"), 1931; "L'ultimo bottone" (one-act; title means "The Last Button"), 1931; "E s'e 'nfucato o' sole" (title means "The Sun's Caught Fire"), 1932; (with C. Mauro) "Cento di questi giorni" (title means "A Hundred of Such Days"), 1932; "La voce del padrone" (one-act; title means "His Master's Voice"), 1932; "Quei figuri di trent'anni fa" (one-act; title means "Those Faces of Thirty Years Ago"), 1932; "Addio Nico!" (one-act; title means "Goodbye, Nico!"), 1932; "Gennariello" (one-act), 1932; "Tre mesi dopo" (one-act; title means "Three Months Later"), 1932; "Chi e cchiu felice'e me!" (two-act; title means "Who's Happier Than I Am?"), 1932; "Requie all'anima sua" (one-act; title means "Peace to Him"), 1932; "Ditegli sempre si" (two-act; title means "Always Tell

Him Yes"), 1932; (with M. Scarpetta) "Parlate al portiere" (one-act; title means "Speak to the Porter"), 1932; "Una bella trovata" (one-act; title means "A Fine Expedient"), 1932; "Cuoco cuoco della mala cucina" (one-act; title means "Cook, Cook of the Bad Kitchen"), 1932; "Il the delle cinque" (one-act; title means "Five O'Clock Tea"), 1932; "Il dono di Natale" (one-act; title means "Christmas Gift"), 1934; "Sentiteci ad ogni costo" (one-act; title means "Listen at All Costs"), 1935; "Quinto, piano, ti saluto!" (one-act; title means "Goodbye, Fifth Floor!"), 1935; "L'abito nuovo" (three act; adapted from a piece by Luigi Pirandello; title means "The New Clothes"), 1937; "Pericolosamente" (one-act; title means "Dangerously"), 1938; "In licenza" (title means "On Leave"), 1941; "Occhiali neri" (title means "Dark Glasses"), 1945; "Pulcinella in cerca sella sua fortuna per Napoli," 1958; "Il figlio die Pulcinella," 1962; and "Pippino Givello" 1964.

Plays published in various multi-work volumes, including *Cantata dei giorni pari* (title means "Cantata for Early Days").

SCREENPLAYS

(With Alberto Moravia and Cesare Zavattini) "Ieri, oggi e domani," Champion-Concordia, 1963, released in the United States as "Yesterday, Today, and Tomorrow," Embassy, 1964.

(With Renato Castellani, Antonio Guerra, Leo Benvenuto, and Piero de Barnardi) "Matrimonio all'italiana" (adapted from de Filippo's play "Filumena marturano"; also see above), [Italy], 1964, released in the United States as "Marriage Italian Style," Embassy, 1964.

(And director) "Shoot Loud, Louder . . . I Don't Understand" (adapted from de Filippo's play "Le voci di dentro"; also see above), Embassy, 1967.

Also author of "Sono stato io!" (title means "I Did It!"), 1937; author of film released in the United States as "Scarred" (adapted from a story by Salvatore di Ciagomo), Sasolaro Films, 1951; author—with P. Tellini and A. Majuri—and director of film released in the United States as "Side Street Story," Joseph Burstyn, 1954.

SIDELIGHTS: Eduardo de Filippo is among Italy's most distinguished contemporary playwrights. He entered the theatre while still an adolescent, performing with siblings in his father's troupe, then moving to comedic and musical companies. By 1930, de Filippo had collaborated—frequently under pseudonyms—on numerous skits and one-act farces. Around this time he re-teamed with family members and began performing his own works in Naples. He also commenced his film career, appearing in the 1932 production "Tre uomini in frak" (title means "Three Men in Tails"). Five years later he made his screenwriting debut with "Sono stato io!" (title means "I Did It!"). During World War II de Filippo worked only sporadically, but once peace was restored he resumed his varied careers, and throughout the remainder of the 1940s he produced what are usually considered his greatest works.

Among de Filippo's first important works from this period is "Naples Millionaire," a realistic drama about a family's involvement in the Italian black market. He followed this work with "Questi fantasmi" (produced as "Neopolitan Ghosts"), a 1946 comedy in which a husband mistakes his wife's ever-present lover for a ghost. This play, while enjoying sufficient acclaim in Italy, has apparently suffered—along with other de Filippo works—in English translation. A 1986 production, for instance, was reviewed by the *New York Times*'s Mel Gussow as "a single farcical joke stretched to three acts." Gussow conceded, however, that "there has been difficulty in commuicating [de Filippo's] humor to an English-speaking audience, especially in the United States."

In 1946 the prolific de Filippo also wrote "Filumena marturano" (produced as "Filumena"), in which a former prostitute obtains financial stability for her three offspring by successfully conning her lover—who is already engaged to a younger woman—into marriage. As with other de Filippo works, "Filumena marturano" enjoys substantial acclaim in Italy but has proved relatively unimpressive in English translation. *Washington Post* James Larner, assessing a 1980 Baltimore performance, speculated that "there may be elements of 'Filumena' that are simply not exportable." He added: "This is a play that needs to be acted tempestuously, with noise and pace and Latin fervor. But instead of crackling like fireworks, [this production] merely smokes and sputters."

With plays such as "Filumena" de Filippo confirmed his reputation, at least in Italy, as a leading farceur. He continued his success with "Le voci di dentro" (produced as "Inner Voices"), in which a man mistakes for reality his dream in which a friend is murdered by neighbors. After learning of his folly, the dreamer is visited by the falsely accused neighbors, who accuse each other of plotting the crime.

Shifting reality is also the premise of "La grande magica" (produced as "Grand Magic"), de Filippo's complex 1949 comedy about infidelity and faith. In this play an adultress cuckolds her husband after vanishing as part of a magic show. When she fails to return, her husband is given a small box from which she can be produced if he trusts in her fidelity. Four years pass before the untrusting husband, convinced by the magician that only a few minutes have elapsed, decides to open the box. But before he has opened it, his wife reappears. The husband, however, prefers to believe that she is still inside the box.

Like other de Filippo plays, "Grand Magic" enjoys greater recognition in Italy than in the United States. *New York Times* critic Richard Eder, reviewing a 1979 production, noted that "it aspires to more sweep than it can swing." Eder dismissed the production as "pretty close to disaster" and expressed particular dissatisfaction with Carlo Ardito's translation, decrying it as "almost unsayable." Eder added that the production "leaves the quality of the original quite obscured."

De Filippo continued writing plays in the 1960s and '70s. With English-speaking audiences, he enjoyed perhaps his greatest success in the 1970s with "Saturday, Sunday, Monday," a translated production of his "Sabato, Demenica e Lunedi." But even this work, well-received in London, ran only briefly on Broadway.

It is probably as a screenwriter that de Filippo received his greatest recognition in the United States. Italian sex comedies were particularly prevalent among foreign films shown in America during the 1960s. Among de Filippo's contributions to the genre are such films released in the United States as "Marriage Italian Style," featuring Sophia Loren and Marcello Mastroianni, and "Shoot Loud, Louder . . . I Don't Understand," pairing Raquel Welch and Mastroianni. Such films depended more on the sex appeal of their performers than on the logic of their narratives, however, and thus are hardly indicative of de Filippo's talents.

De Filippo died at age eighty-four in Rome. Though less than well-known in the United States, he still enjoys immense status in his native Italy, with some critics ranking him second only to Luigi Pirandello, with whom de Filippo had, incidently, once worked. Some reviewers have also seen de Filippo's influence in the works of later Italian playwrights, notably Dario Fo. And it is not just as a playwright that de Filippo is respected in Italy: he has published well-received volumes of verse and prose, and he has developed such a following as an actor—on both stage and screen—that he is readily identified by just his first name. He continued acting into his eightieth year, leaving the stage after a performance in one of Pirandello's plays. It was only as an actor, apparently, that de Filippo expressed any qualms regarding his rich and varied career. "My one regret was that I never did Moliere or Shakespeare," he told Caroline Moorehead in a 1983 London *Times.* "I would have liked to have done Hamlet."

MEDIA ADAPTATIONS: "Filumena marturano" was filmed prior to the 1964 version involving de Filippo; "Questi fantasmi!" was adapted as a film released in the United States as "Ghosts Italian Style" in 1969.

BIOGRAPHICAL/CRITICAL SOURCES:

BOOKS

Daubeny, Peter, *My World of Theatre,* J. Cape, 1971.

PERIODICALS

New York Times, October 27, 1951, June 24, 1954, September 21, 1967, January 23, 1969, January 8, 1979, February 11, 1980, November 5, 1986.
Times (London), June 24, 1983.
Washington Post, January 10, 1980.

OBITUARIES:

PERIODICALS

Chicago Tribune, November 2, 1984.
New York Times, November 2, 1984.
Times (London), November 2, 1984.
Washington Post, November 3, 1984.

—*Sketch by Les Stone*

*   *   *

DEIGHTON, Len
    See DEIGHTON, Leonard Cyril

*   *   *

DEIGHTON, Leonard Cyril   1929-
    (Len Deighton)

PERSONAL: Born February 18, 1929, in Marylebone, London, England; married Shirley Thompson (an illustrator), 1960. *Education:* Attended St. Martin's School of Art, London, three years; Royal College of Art, graduate.

ADDRESSES: Office—25 Newman St., London W.1, England.

CAREER: Author. Worked as a railway lengthman, an assistant pastry cook at the Royal Festival Hall, 1951, a manager of a gown factory in Aldgate, England, a waiter in Piccadilly, an advertising man in London and New York City, a teacher in Brittany, a co-proprietor of a glossy magazine, and as a magazine artist and news photographer; steward, British Overseas Airways Corporation (BOAC), 1956-57; producer of films, including "Only When I Larf," based on his novel of the same title, 1969.

WRITINGS:

UNDER NAME LEN DEIGHTON

Only When I Larf (novel), M. Joseph, 1968, published as *Only When I Laugh,* Mysterious Press, 1987.

"Oh, What a Lovely War!" (screenplay), Paramount, 1969.
Bomber: Events Relating to the Last Flight of an R.A.F. Bomber Over Germany on the Night of June 31, 1943 (novel), Harper, 1970.
Declarations of War (story collection), J. Cape, 1971, published as *Eleven Declarations of War,* Harcourt, 1975.
Close-Up (novel), Atheneum, 1972.
SS-GB: Nazi-Occupied Britain, 1941 (novel), J. Cape, 1978, Knopf, 1979.
Goodbye, Mickey Mouse (novel; Book-of-the-Month Club selection), Knopf, 1982.
Winter: A Novel of a Berlin Family (Book-of-the-Month Club alternate selection), Knopf, 1988.

Also author of television scripts "Long Past Glory," 1963, and "It Must Have Been Two Other Fellows," 1977. Also author of weekly comic strip on cooking, *Observer,* 1962—.

ESPIONAGE NOVELS; UNDER NAME LEN DEIGHTON

The Ipcress File, Fawcett, 1962, reprinted, Ballantine, 1982.
Horse Under Water (Literary Guild selection), J. Cape, 1963, Putnam, 1967.
Funeral in Berlin, J. Cape, 1964, Putnam, 1965.
The Billion Dollar Brain, Putnam, 1966.
An Expensive Place to Die, Putnam, 1967.
Spy Story, Harcourt, 1974.
Yesterday's Spy, Harcourt, 1975.
Twinkle, Twinkle, Little Spy, J. Cape, 1976, published as *Catch a Falling Spy,* Harcourt, 1976.
XPD, Knopf, 1981.
Berlin Game, Knopf, 1983.
Mexico Set (Literary Guild selection), Knopf, 1985.
London Match, Knopf, 1985.
Spy Hook (Book-of-the-Month Club selection), Knopf, 1988.
Spy Line, Knopf, 1989.
Spy Sinker, Harper, 1990.

NONFICTION; UNDER NAME LEN DEIGHTON

(Editor) *Drinks-man-ship: Town's Album of Fine Wines and High Spirits,* Haymarket Press, 1964.
Ou est le garlic; or, Len Deighton's French Cookbook, Penguin, 1965, revised edition published as *Basic French Cooking,* J. Cape, 1979.
Action Cookbook: Len Deighton's Guide to Eating, J. Cape, 1965.
Len Deighton's Cookstrip Cook Book, Bernard Geis Associates, 1966.
(Editor with Michael Rand and Howard Loxton) *The Assassination of President Kennedy,* J. Cape, 1967.
(Editor and contributor) *Len Deighton's London Dossier,* J. Cape, 1967.
Len Deighton's Continental Dossier: A Collection of Cultural, Culinary, Historical, Spooky, Grim and Preposterous Fact, compiled by Victor and Margaret Pettitt, M. Joseph, 1968.
Fighter: The True Story of the Battle of Britain, J. Cape, 1977, Knopf, 1978.
(With Peter Mayle) *How to Be a Pregnant Father,* Lyle Stuart, 1977.
(With Arnold Schwartzman) *Airshipwreck,* J. Cape, 1978, Holt, 1979.
(With Simon Goodenough) *Tactical Genius in Battle,* Phaidon Press, 1979.
Blitzkrieg: From the Rise of Hitler to the Fall of Dunkirk, Coward, 1980.
Battle of Britain, Coward, 1980.

WORK IN PROGRESS: Spy Sinker, the third and final novel in Deighton's second trilogy about the adventures of British intelligence agent Bernard Samson.

SIDELIGHTS: With his early novels, especially *The Ipcress File* and *Funeral in Berlin,* Len Deighton established himself as one of the mainstays of modern espionage fiction. He is often ranked—along with Graham Greene, John le Carre, and Ian Fleming—among the foremost writers in the field. Deighton shows a painstaking attention to accuracy in depicting espionage activities, and in his early novels this realism was combined with a light ironic touch that set his work apart. Deighton, David Quammen remarks in the *New York Times Book Review,* is "a talented, droll and original spy novelist."

Deighton's early novels are written in an elliptical style that emphasizes the mysterious nature of the espionage activities portrayed. They feature a nameless British intelligence officer who is quite different from the usual fictional spy. This officer is a reluctant spy, cynical, and full of wisecracks. Unlike many other British agents, he is also, Julian Symons states in *Mortal Consequences: A History—From the Detective Story to the Crime Novel,* "a working-class boy from Brunley, opposed to all authority, who dislikes or distrusts anybody outside his own class. He is set down in a world of terrifying complexity, in which nobody is ever what he seems." "The creation of this slightly anarchic, wise-cracking, working-class hero," T. J. Binyon writes in the *Times Literary Supplement,* "was Deighton's most original contribution to the spy thriller. And this, taken together with his characteristic highly elliptical expositional manner, with his fascination with the technical nuts and bolts of espionage, and with a gift for vivid, startling description, make the first seven [of Deighton's spy] stories classics of the genre." Peter S. Prescott of *Newsweek,* speaking of the early novels featuring Deighton's nameless hero, finds that the style, marked by "oblique narration, nervous laughter and ironic detachment, . . . effectively transformed [Deighton's] spy stories into comedies of manners."

Deighton's elliptical style in these early books is clipped and episodic, deliberately omitting vital explanations of what his characters are discussing or thinking. This style, Robin W. Winks writes in the *New Republic,* makes Deighton's "plots seem more complex than they are. . . . Because very little is stated explicitly, sequences appear to begin in mid-passage, and only through observation of the action does one come to understand either the motives of the villains, or the thought processes of the heroes." In these novels, Winks concludes, "Deighton had patented a style in which every third paragraph appeared to have been left out." Although this style confuses some readers—Prescott claims that Deighton's "specialty has always been a nearly incoherent plot"—Pearl K. Bell finds it well suited to the subject matter of Deighton's novels. Writing in *New Leader,* Bell states that Deighton's "obsessive reliance on the blurred and intangible, on loaded pauses and mysteriously disjointed dialogue, did convey the shadowy meanness of the spy's world, with its elusive loyalties, camouflaged identities and weary brutality."

Deighton was an immediate success with his first novel, *The Ipcress File,* a book that the late Anthony Boucher of the *New York Times Book Review* admits "caused quite a stir among both critics and customers in England." Introducing Deighton's nameless protagonist in an adventure that takes him to a nuclear testing site on a Pacific atoll, to the Middle East, and behind the Iron Curtain, the book continues to be popular for its combination of a serious espionage plot with a parody of the genre. As Richard Locke observes in the *New York Times Book Review, The Ipcress*

File possesses "a Kennedy-cool amorality . . ., a cross of Hammett and cold war lingo."

Critics praise the book's gritty evocation of intelligence work, ironic narrative, and comic touches. Boucher calls it "a sharply written, ironic and realistic tale of modern spy activities." Deighton's humor attracts the most attention from John B. Cullen of *Best Sellers,* who claims that in *The Ipcress File* "Deighton writes with a tongue-in-cheek attitude. . . . No one is spared the needle of subtle ridicule, but the author still tells a plausible story which holds your attention throughout." However, for Robert Donald Spectar of the *New York Herald Tribune Book Review* Deighton's humor ruins the espionage story. "Deighton," Spectar writes, "has combined picaresque satire, parody, and suspense and produced a hybrid more humorous than thrilling." But this opinion is disputed by G. W. Stonier in the *New Statesman.* Comparing Deighton with James Bond creator Ian Fleming, Stonier finds Deighton to be "a good deal more expert and twice the writer" and believes "there has been no brighter arrival on the shady scene since Graham Greene." Even in 1979, some seventeen years after the book's initial publication, Julian Symons of the *New York Times Book Review* was moved to call *The Ipcress File* "a dazzling performance. The verve and energy, the rattle of wit in the dialogue, the side-of-the-mouth comments, the evident pleasure taken in cocking a snook at the British spy story's upper-middle-class tradition—all these, together with the teasing convolutions of the plot, made it clear that a writer of remarkable talent in this field had appeared."

Deighton's reputation as an espionage writer was enhanced by *Funeral in Berlin,* a story revolving around an attempt to smuggle a defecting East German biologist out of Berlin. With the assistance of a high-ranking Russian agent, former Nazi intelligence officers, and a free-lance operator of doubtful allegiance, Deighton's unnamed hero arranges the details of the defection. The many plot twists, and Deighton's enigmatic presentation of his story, prompt Stephen Hugh-Jones of *New Statesman* to admit, "I spent most of the book wondering what the devil was going on." Boucher finds the mysterious goings-on to be handled well. "The double and triple crosses involved," Boucher writes, "are beautifully worked out." Published at the same time as John le Carre's classic espionage tale *The Spy Who Came in From the Cold,* a novel also set in Germany's divided city, *Funeral in Berlin* compares favorably with its competitor. Boucher calls its plot "very nearly as complex and nicely calculated," while Charles Poore of the *New York Times* maintains it is "even better" than le Carre's book. It is, Poore concludes, "a ferociously cool fable of the current struggle between East and West." Andy East of *Armchair Detective* claims that *Funeral in Berlin* "has endured as Deighton's most celebrated novel."

Since these early novels, Deighton's style has evolved, becoming more expansive and less oblique. His "approach has grown more sophisticated," Mark Schorr relates in the *Los Angeles Times Book Review.* "His more recent writings offer a deft balance of fact, scene-setting and the who-can-we-trust paranoia that makes spy novels engrossing." Peter Elstob of *Books and Bookmen* elaborates on the change. Deighton "develops with each new book," Elstob believes. "He could have gone on repeating the formula of *The Ipcress File* with undoubted success, but instead he tried for more subtlety, for more convincing, more substantial characters."

Of his later espionage novels, perhaps his most important work has been the trilogy comprised of *Berlin Game, Mexico Set,* and *London Match.* Here, Deighton spins a long story of moles (agents working within an enemy intelligence organization), defection, and betrayal that also comments on his own writing career, the espionage genre, and the cold war between East and West that has inspired such fiction. Derrick Murdoch of the Toronto *Globe and Mail* calls the trilogy "Deighton's most ambitious project; the conventional spy-story turned inside-out."

The first novel of the trilogy, *Berlin Game,* opens with two agents waiting near the Berlin Wall for a defector to cross over from East Berlin. "How long have we been sitting here?" asks Bernie Samson, British agent and the protagonist of the trilogy. "Nearly a quarter of a century," his companion replies. With that exchange Deighton underlines the familiarity of this scene in espionage fiction, in his own early work and in the work of others, while commenting on the continuing relevance of the Berlin Wall as a symbol of East-West conflict, notes Anthony Olcott in the *Washington Post Book World*. Deighton, Olcott argues, "is not only aware of this familiarity, it is his subject. . . . Berlin and the Wall remain as much the embodiment of East-West rivalry as ever. . . . To read *Berlin Game* is to shrug off 25 years of acclimatization to the Cold War, and to recall what espionage fiction is about in the first place."

In *Berlin Game,* Samson works to uncover a Soviet agent secretly working at the highest levels of British intelligence. This, too, is a standard plot in spy fiction, inspired by the real-life case of Soviet spy Kim Philby. But, as the *New Yorker* critic points out, "Deighton, as always, makes the familiar twists and turns of spy errantry new again, partly by his grip of narrative, partly by his grasp of character, and partly by his easy, sardonic tone." Prescott claims that the novel does not display the wit of Deighton's earlier works, but the book overcomes its faults because of Deighton's overall skill as a storyteller. "Each scene in this story," Prescott writes, "is so adroitly realized that it creates its own suspense. Samson, the people who work for him, his wife, even the twits who have some reason to be working for Moscow, are interesting characters; what they say to each other is convincing. Besides, the book is full of Berlin lore: we can easily believe that Samson did grow up there and thinks of it as home." In like terms, Christopher Lehmann-Haupt of the *New York Times* holds that in *Berlin Game* "the immediate scene is always brilliantly clear, thanks mostly to Mr. Deighton's intimate familiarity with the Berlin landscape. Every building and street seems to have resonance for him, which he imparts to the reader." Olcott judges *Berlin Game* to be "among Deighton's best books" because "his Berlin, his characters, the smallest details of his narrative are so sharp." Olcott concludes that it is "a book to strip away the age-withered, custom-staled betrayals of all that quarter century of novels, perhaps even of history, and once again make painful, real, alive, the meaning of treason."

Mexico Set continues the story begun in *Berlin Game.* In the first book, Samson uncovers the spy in British intelligence—his own wife—and she defects to East Germany. To redeem himself in the eyes of his superiors, who now harbor understandable doubts about his own loyalty, Samson works in *Mexico Set* to convince a Russian KGB agent to defect. But the agent may only be a plant meant to further discredit Samson and destroy his credibility. If Samson cannot convince him to defect, his superiors may assume that he is secretly working for the Russians himself. But the Russian may defect only to provide British intelligence with "proof" of Samson's treason. As in *Berlin Game,* Deighton relates this novel back to the origins of the cold war and, "just when you've forgotten what the Cold War was all about, Len Deighton takes you right back to the [Berlin] Wall and rubs your nose on it," as Chuck Moss writes in the *Detroit News.*

Samson's efforts to persuade the Russian agent to defect take him from London to Mexico, Paris, and Berlin. "Every mile along the way," Noel Behn writes in the *Chicago Tribune,* "objectives seem to alter, friends and enemies become indistinguishable, perils increase, people disappear, people die." Behn finds it is Deighton's characters that make the story believable: "They strut forward one after the other—amusing, beguiling, arousing, deceiving, threatening—making us look in the wrong direction when it most behooves the prestidigitator's purpose." Ross Thomas also sees Deighton's characters as an essential ingredient in the novel's success. Writing in the *Washington Post Book World,* Thomas reports that Deighton "serves up fascinating glimpses of such types as the nearly senile head of British intelligence; a KGB major with a passion for Sherlock Holmes; and Samson's boyhood friend and Jewish orphan, Werner Volkmann," all of whom Thomas finds to be "convincing characters." Thomas concludes that *Mexico Set* is "one of [Deighton's] better efforts," while Behn calls the novel "a pure tale, told by an author at the height of his power."

In the final novel of the trilogy, *London Match,* the Russian agent has defected to the British. But Samson must now decide whether the defector is telling the truth when he insists that a high-ranking member of British intelligence is a Russian mole. The situation grows more complicated when the suspected mole, one of Samson's superiors, comes to Samson for help in clearing his name. *London Match* "is the most complex novel of the trilogy," Julius Lester writes in the *New York Times Book Review.*

But Lester finds *London Match*'s complexity to be a liability. He thinks "the feeling it conveys of being trapped in a maze of distorting mirrors is almost a cliche in spy novels now." Similarly, Gene Lyons of *Newsweek* calls *London Match* "not the most original spy story ever told." In his review of the book for the *Washington Post Book World,* J. I. M. Stewart criticizes Deighton's characterization. He states that "the characters, although liable to bore a little during their frequently over-extended verbal fencings, are tenaciously true to themselves even if not quite to human nature."

But even critics with reservations about some of the novel's qualities find aspects of the book to praise. Stewart lauds Deighton's ability to recreate the settings of his story. "The places, whether urban or rural, can be described only as triumphs alike of painstaking observation and striking descriptive power," Stewart writes. Lester finds this strength, too, calling "the best character" in the book "the city of Berlin. It is a living presence, and in some of the descriptions one can almost hear the stones breathing."

More favorable critics point to Deighton's handling of characters as one of the book's best features. Schorr, for example, believes that "Deighton gives a skilled and believable portrait of Samson. . . . Samson maintains his professional cool, but there is a sense that emotions are repressed, and not nonexistent, as with too many other spy heroes." Margaret Cannon of the Toronto *Globe and Mail* has nothing but praise for *London Match.* She calls the trilogy "some of [Deighton's] best work," and *London Match* "a brilliant climax to the story."

Deighton continues Samson's adventures in the 1988 *Spy Hook,* the first story in a second trilogy about the British intelligence agent. In this thriller, Samson is charged with accounting for the disappearance of millions in Secret Service funds. At first, he suspects his ex-wife—who defected in the earlier *Berlin Game*—as the thief, but later Samson learns that his superiors have begun to suspect him for the crime. *Spy Hook* was chosen as a Book-of-the-Month Club selection and became a best-seller. Critical reception of the work was generally favorable, with reviewers praising the book's carefully developed and intricate plot, detailed settings, and suspenseful atmosphere. A number of reviewers, however, reacted negatively to the book's ending, which they feel is too ambiguous. "Deighton's craftsmanship—his taut action and his insightful study of complex characters under pressure—is very much in place here, but many . . . unanswered questions raised in *Spy Hook* remain just that at the novel's conclusion," states Don G. Campbell, for example, in the *Los Angeles Times Book Review*. Several critics, though, share Margaret Cannon's Toronto *Globe and Mail* assessment of *Spy Hook* as matching Deighton's previous achievements in the espionage genre. The novel, she writes, "promises to be even better than its terrific predecessors and proves that Deighton, the old spymaster, is still in top form." In 1989, Deighton followed *Spy Hook* with the trilogy's second installment, *Spy Line,* with the third and concluding book, *Spy Sinker,* to follow.

Although Deighton is best known for his espionage fiction, he has also written best-selling novels outside the espionage field, as well as books of military history. These other novels and books of history are usually concerned with the events and figures of the World War II. Among the most successful of his novels have been *SS-GB: Nazi-Occupied Britain, 1941* and *Goodbye, Mickey Mouse. Fighter: The True Story of the Battle of Britain* has earned Deighton praise as a writer of military history. Deighton's writing in other fields has shown him, Symons writes, to be "determined not to stay within the conventional pattern of the spy story or thriller."

SS-GB takes place in an alternative history of World War II, a history in which England lost the crucial Battle of Britain and Nazi Germany conquered the country. The story takes place after the conquest when Scotland Yard superintendent Douglas Archer investigates a murder and finds that the trail leads to the upper echelons of the Nazi party. An underground plot to rescue the king of England, who is being held prisoner in the Tower of London, and the ongoing efforts of the Nazis to develop the atom bomb also complicate Archer's problems. "As is usual with Mr. Deighton," John Leonard writes in *Books of the Times,* "there are as many twists as there are betrayals."

Deighton's ability to fully render what a Nazi-occupied Britain would be like is the most widely-noted strength of the book. "The atmosphere of occupied England," Michael Demarest writes in his review of *SS-GB* for *Newsweek,* "is limned in eerie detail. . . . In fact, Deighton's ungreened isle frequently seems even more realistic than the authentic backgrounds of his previous novels." "What especially distinguishes 'SS-GB,' " Leonard believes, "is its gritty atmosphere, the shadows of defeat on every page. Yes, we think, this is what martial law would feel like; this is the way the Germans would have behaved; this is how rationing and the black market and curfews and detention camps would work; this is the contempt for ourselves that we would experience."

Although Michael Howard of the *Times Literary Supplement* agrees that "there can be little doubt that this is much the way things would have turned out if the Germans had won the war in 1940," he nonetheless concludes that "on this level of imaginative creation Mr. Deighton is so good that the second level, the plot itself, seems by comparison unnecessarily silly and confused." This criticism of the novel's plot is shared by Paul Ableman of the *Spectator,* who complains: "From about Page 100, the subversive thought kept surfacing: what is the point of this kind of historical 'might have been'? . . . I fear [the novel] ultimately

lost its hold on me. We could have been given the same yarn set in occupied France."

But Symons and many other reviewers judge *SS-GB* a successful and imaginative novel. It is, Symons writes, "a triumphant success. It is Mr. Deighton's best book, one that blends his expertise in the spy field with his interest in military and political history to produce an absorbingly exciting spy story that is also a fascinating exercise in might-have-been speculation." And Demarest concludes his review by predicting that *SS-GB* "is on its way to becoming a worldwide classic of the 'What If?' genre."

Goodbye, Mickey Mouse, another Deighton novel about World War II, concerns a group of American pilots in England who run fighter protection for the bombers making daylight runs over Germany. It is described by Thomas Gifford of the *Washington Post Book World* as "satisfying on every imaginable level, but truly astonishing in its recreation of a time and place through minute detail." Equally high praise comes from Peter Andrews, who writes in his review for the *New York Times Book Review:* "Deighton's latest World War II adventure novel is such a plain, old-fashioned, good book about combat pilots who make war and fall in love that it defies a complicated examination. . . . 'Goodbye, Mickey Mouse' is high adventure of the best sort but always solidly true to life."

Not all reviewers were so enthusiastic, but even those with reservations about the novel's ultimate quality were impressed with the way Deighton presented the scenes of aerial combat. "As long as he keeps his propellers turning," Prescott allows in his *Newsweek* review, "Deighton's book lives. He understands the camaraderie of pilots and to a lesser degree the politics of combat. . . . It's a pity that his people, like his prose, are built from plywood." Similarly, the reviewer for *Harper's* reports that "the book is oddly anemic—except on the subject of fighter planes. Deighton's obsession with planes makes the combat sequences lurid and exciting. If only the rest of the book were too."

While sharing the belief that Deighton writes extremely well about aerial combat, Lehmann-Haupt sees a more serious side to the novel which, for him, raises it "above the merely entertaining." Deighton, Lehmann-Haupt writes, "has an almost uncanny ability to make war action in the air come visually alive. . . . But what is most intriguing about 'Goodbye, Mickey Mouse' is that it explores a profound but little noticed aspect of war—namely, the necessity it creates for parents to send their children off to death." The book's title, the last words of a dying pilot to his friend, Lieutenant Morse, nicknamed Mickey Mouse, are "also an expression of farewell to childhood and its trivialities, as well as what a father or mother might say to a departing son," Lehmann-Haupt concludes. Gifford, too, interprets the novel on a more serious level. Speaking of the generation who fought in the Second World War, many of whom are "approaching the time when they will one by one pass into our history," Gifford finds Deighton's novel a tribute to that generation and its monumental fight. "Some of them," Gifford writes, "are fittingly memorialized in Deighton's hugely assured novel."

The crucial Battle of Britain, which figures prominently in *SS-GB,* and the air battles of that period, which appear in *Goodbye, Mickey Mouse,* are further explored in the nonfiction *Fighter,* a history of the Royal Air Force defense of England during the Battle of Britain. A highly acclaimed popular account of what Noble Frankland of the *Times Literary Supplement* calls "among the handful of decisive battles in British history," *Fighter* "is the best, most dispassionate story of the battle I have read," Drew Middleton states in the *New York Times Book Review,* "and I say that even though the book destroyed many of my illusions and, indeed, attacks the validity of some of what I wrote as an eyewitness of the air battle 38 years ago."

The Battle of Britain took place over several months of 1940. After overrunning France, the Nazi leadership focused their attention on softening up England for an invasion. They launched extensive bombing raids against the British Isles, attacking the city of London, air bases, factories, and seaports. The Royal Air Force, vastly outnumbered by their opponents, bravely fought the Germans to a standstill which resulted in the proposed invasion being delayed and ultimately canceled. Or so most historians relate the story.

Deighton dispels some of the myths about the Battle of Britain still widely believed by most historians. He shows, for example, that a major reason for the failure of the German offensive was the decision to shift the main attack from British airfields to the city of London. The Nazis hoped that bombing the civilian population would cause Britain to sue for peace. But leaving the airfields alone only allowed the Royal Air Force to launch their fighter planes against the German bombers. And when bomber losses rose too high, the Nazi invasion plans were called off.

Other insights into the Battle of Britain include the facts "that British anti-aircraft fire was ineffective, that some R.A.F. ground personnel fled under fire, that the Admiralty provoked costly skirmishes. . . . The book resounds with exploded myths," Leonard Bushkoff writes in the *Washington Post Book World.* Deighton also shows that British estimates of German losses were far higher than they actually were, while British losses were reported to be less serious than was actually the case. But Bushkoff sees the importance of these revelations to be inconsequential. "Is debunking sufficient to carry a book that essentially is a rehash of earlier works?" he asks. Frankland admits that Deighton is sometimes "prone to get his technicalities wrong," but finds that "the Battle of Britain after all is a very difficult subject. No two people seem quite to agree about when it began, when it ended, what were its turning points or why they occurred. . . . Len Deighton cuts through this fog incisively and utterly correctly." In his article for the *Saturday Review,* George H. Reeves reports that "there is a profusion of detail in *Fighter* . . . that will delight the military history specialist, and Deighton's well-paced narrative and techniques of deft characterization will also hold the attention of the general reader." He believes that Deighton "has turned his hand with commendable results to the writing of military history."

In all of his writing, whether fiction or nonfiction, Deighton shows a concern for an accurate and detailed presentation of the facts. He has included appendices in several novels to explain to his readers such espionage esoterica as the structure of foreign intelligence organizations and the effects of various poisons. Howard claims that Deighton "takes enormous, almost obsessional care to get the background to his books exactly right."

Part of Deighton's research involves extensive travel throughout the world; he is reported to have contacts in cities as far-flung as Anchorage and Casablanca. These research trips have sometimes proven dangerous. Hugh Moffett notes that Deighton was once "hauled into police barracks in Czechoslovakia when he neglected to renew his visa." And Russian soldiers once took him into custody in East Berlin. For *Bomber: Events Relating to the Last Flight of an R.A.F. Bomber Over Germany on the Night of June 31, 1943,* Deighton made three trips to Germany and spent several years in research, gathering some half million words in notes. Research for the books *Fighter* and *Blitzkreig: From the Rise of Hitler to the Fall of Dunkirk* took nearly nine years. But these efforts have paid off. MacLeish believes that in a Deighton novel, "the atmospherics ring forever true. Deighton seems to know the places he writes about." Speaking of *XPD,* Les Whitten of the *Washington Post Book World* finds that "the research on exotic guns, cars, poisons, trains, wall safes, foliage is shining and satisfying evidence of the hard work Deighton has done to make his background genuine and informative."

Deighton turns to historical fiction in his 1987 book *Winter: A Novel of a Berlin Family.* The story of a well-to-do German family led by a banker and war financier, *Winter* depicts how cultural and historical factors influence the attitudes of his two sons, one of whom joins the murderous Nazi party, while the other moves to the United States and marries a Jewish woman. The mixed criticism for *Winter* revolves around Deighton's sympathetic portrayals of his Nazi characters and around the novel's wide historical scope, which some reviewers feel is inadequately represented, mainly through dialogue rather than plot.

Deighton's position as one of the most prominent of contemporary espionage writers is secure. Cannon describes him as "one of the finest living writers of espionage novels." Schorr relates that it was Rudyard Kipling who "first called espionage the 'Great Game,' and no one is more adept at providing a fictional play-by-play than Len Deighton." Writing in *Whodunit?: A Guide to Crime, Suspense and Spy Fiction* about his life as a writer, Deighton reveals: "I have no formal training and have evolved a muddled sort of system by trial and error. . . . My own writing is characterized by an agonizing reappraisal of everything I write so that I have to work seven days a week. . . . The most difficult lesson to learn is that thousands and thousands of words must go into the waste paper basket." Summing up his feelings about being a best-selling author, Deighton concludes, "It's not such a bad job after all; except for sitting here at this damned typewriter."

MEDIA ADAPTATIONS: The Ipcress File was filmed by Universal in 1965, *Funeral in Berlin* by Paramount in 1966, *The Billion Dollar Brain* by United Artists in 1967, and *Only When I Larf* by Paramount in 1969; *Spy Story* was filmed in 1976; film rights to *An Expensive Place to Die* have been sold. Deighton's nameless British spy hero was given the name Harry Palmer in the film adaptations of his adventures.

BIOGRAPHICAL/CRITICAL SOURCES:

BOOKS

Bestsellers 89, Issue 2, Gale, 1989.
Contemporary Literary Criticism, Gale, Volume 4, 1975, Volume 7, 1977, Volume 22, 1982, Volume 46, 1988.
Keating, H. R. F., editor, *Whodunit?: A Guide to Crime, Suspense and Spy Fiction,* Van Nostrand, 1982.
Symons, Julian, *Mortal Consequences: A History—From the Detective Story to the Crime Novel,* Harper, 1972.

PERIODICALS

Armchair Detective, winter, 1986.
Best Sellers, November 15, 1963, January 1, 1968.
Books and Bookmen, September, 1967, December, 1971.
Books of the Times, February, 1979, August, 1981.
British Book News, December, 1980.
Chicago Tribune, February 24, 1985, December 27, 1987.
Chicago Tribune Book World, March 18, 1979, January 19, 1986.
Detroit News, February 3, 1985, February 9, 1986.
Globe and Mail (Toronto), December 1, 1984, December 14, 1985.
Harper's, November, 1982.
Life, March 25, 1966.

London Review of Books, March 19-April 1, 1981.
Los Angeles Times, November 26, 1982, March 23, 1987.
Los Angeles Times Book Review, March 17, 1985, February 16, 1986, November 22, 1987.
New Leader, January 19, 1976.
New Republic, December 13, 1975.
New Statesman, December 7, 1962, September 8, 1964, May 12, 1967, June 18, 1976, August 25, 1978.
Newsweek, January 18, 1965, January 31, 1966, June 26, 1972, October 14, 1974, February 19, 1979, December 27, 1982, December 19, 1983, February 11, 1985, January 13, 1986.
New Yorker, February 3, 1968, May 7, 1979, February 6, 1984.
New York Herald Tribune Book Review, November 17, 1963.
New York Times, January 12, 1965, October 17, 1970, October 16, 1976, September 20, 1977, May 13, 1981, June 21, 1981, December 7, 1982, December 12, 1983, December 21, 1987.
New York Times Book Review, November 10, 1963, January 17, 1965, May 21, 1967, January 14, 1968, October 4, 1970, April 13, 1975, July 9, 1978, February 25, 1979, May 3, 1981, November 14, 1982, January 8, 1984, March 10, 1985, December 1, 1985, January 10, 1988, December 25, 1988.
Playboy, May, 1966.
Saturday Review, January 30, 1965, June 10, 1978.
Spectator, September 24, 1977, September 2, 1978, April 18, 1981.
Time, March 12, 1979, April 27, 1981, January 13, 1986, December 28, 1987, December 5, 1988.
Times Literary Supplement, February 8, 1963, June 1, 1967, June 22, 1967, September 25, 1970, June 16, 1972, May 3, 1974, October 28, 1977, September 15, 1978, March 13, 1981, October 21, 1983.
Tribune Books (Chicago), January 1, 1989, January 8, 1989.
Village Voice, February 19, 1979.
Wall Street Journal, May 21, 1980.
Washington Post, October 9, 1970, December 13, 1988, December 12, 1989.
Washington Post Book World, September 29, 1974, June 4, 1978, March 20, 1979, April 14, 1981, November 7, 1982, January 8, 1984, January 27, 1985, December 15, 1985, December 20, 1987.

* * *

DELANEY, Franey
See O'HARA, John (Henry)

* * *

DELANEY, Shelagh 1939-

PERSONAL: First name is pronounced *She*-la; born November 25, 1939, in Salford, Lancashire, England; daughter of Joseph (a bus inspector) and Elsie Delaney; children: one daughter. *Education:* Attended Broughton Secondary School.

ADDRESSES: Home— London, England. *Agent—*Tessa Sayle, 11 Jubilee Place, London, SW3 3TE, England.

CAREER: Writer. Has worked as a salesperson, milk depot clerk, and usherette; former photography assistant, Metro-Vickers, London, England.

AWARDS, HONORS: Charles Henry Foyle New Play Award, 1958, New York Drama Critics Award, 1961, and Arts Council bursary, all for *A Taste of Honey;* British Film Academy Award, 1961, Robert Flaherty Award, both for screenplay of "A Taste of Honey"; Encyclopedia Britannica award, 1963; Writers Guild

Award for best screenplay, 1968, for "Charlie Bubbles"; Prix Film Jeuness-Etranger, 1985, for "Dance with a Stranger"; Fellow of the Royal Society of Literature, 1985.

WRITINGS:

A Taste of Honey (play; first produced in Stratford, England, at Theatre Royal, May 27, 1958; produced on Broadway at Lyceum Theatre, October 4, 1960; screenplay adaptation, with Tony Richardson, produced by Continental Film Corp., 1962.), Grove, 1959.
The Lion in Love (play; first produced in Coventry, England, at the Belgrade Theatre, September 5, 1960; produced in New York City at One Sheridan Square, April 25, 1963), Grove, 1961.
Sweetly Sings the Donkey (short stories), Putnam, 1963.
"Charlie Bubbles" (screenplay), Memorial Enterprises/ Universal Films, 1968.
"Did Your Nanny Come from Bergen?" (television play), British Broadcasting Corp. (BBC-TV), 1970.
"The Raging Moon" (screenplay), Associated British Films, 1970.
"St. Martin's Summer" (television play), London Weekend Television, 1974.
The House That Jack Built (play; first produced as a television series by BBC-TV, 1977; produced Off-Off-Broadway at the Cubiculo Theater, 1979), Duckworth, 1977.
"Find Me First" (television play), BBC-TV, 1979.
"So Does the Nightingale" (radio play), BBC Radio, 1980.
"Don't Worry about Matilda" (radio play), BBC Radio, 1981.
"Rape" (television play), Granada Television, 1981.
Writing Woman, Schocken, 1984.
"Dance with a Stranger" (screenplay), Samuel Goldwyn Co., 1985.

Also author of screenplay, "The White Bus," 1966. Contributor of articles to *New York Times Magazine, Saturday Evening Post, Cosmopolitan,* and *Evergreen Review.*

SIDELIGHTS: In 1958, 18-year-old Shelagh Delaney made her successful debut as a playwright with a work she had written in only two weeks, "A Taste of Honey." Winning the New York Drama Critics Award and, in its film version, a British Film Academy Award, "A Taste of Honey" portrays the seamy side of life in an industrial northern England town. With its realistic setting and characters, use of slang, and inclusion of black and homosexual characters, the play initially caused Delaney to be grouped with other playwrights of the 1950s, like John Osborne, who were known collectively as the "Angry Young Men." Her involvement in anti-nuclear demonstrations with the Committee of 100, which led to her and Osborne's arrest in London's Trafalgar Square on September 17, 1961, reinforced the social protester label. However, as Susan Whitehead points out in a *Dictionary of Literary Biography* entry, Delaney is different from writers like Osborne "because she knew what to be angry about. But anger of any kind is not an emotion which underlies her writing. Instead, Delaney has created characters . . ., who, while struggling against each other, ultimately accept their lives."

The playwright wrote "A Taste of Honey" partly as a reaction to plays like Terence Rattigan's "Variation on a Theme," and partly because she wanted to "write as people talk. . . . I had strong ideas about what I wanted to see in the theater," Delaney says in the *Dictionary of Literary Biography.* The play concerns a mother and daughter who cannot relate to each other, a typical avant guarde theme of alienation. The daughter has an affair with a black sailor and is helped through pregnancy by a young homosexual. "These are people living hand-to-mouth and making a bad meal of it," describes Walter Kerr in the *New York Herald Tribune*. But despite the bleak situation, "it is a gutsy play, full of rowdy impertinence and genuinely comic indignation," claims *New York* magazine contributor John Simon. Unlike other plays of the time, the character of Jo in "A Taste of Honey" does not "rail savagely and ineffectually against the others—authority, the Establishment, fate," remarks John Russell Taylor in his book *The Angry Theatre: New British Drama*. Instead, as *Encounter* reviewer Colin MacInnes says, the play "gives a final overwhelming impression of good health—of a feeling for life that is positive, sensible, and generous." Simon concludes that "A Taste of Honey" is "honest rather than stagy, forthright rather than would-be-symbolic—in short, pungently, poignantly, unself-consciously human."

Delaney's next play, "The Lion in Love," was neither commercially nor critically successful. Therefore, remarks Taylor, "a number of commentators were quite ready to write ["A Taste of Honey"] off as a freak success." Whitehead maintains that although "The Lion in Love" is not as strong a play as its predecessor, it "bears witness to Delaney's development as a writer, being more dramatically complex than *A Taste of Honey*." The story involves an English working class couple named Frank and Kit, who are trapped in an unhappy marriage. Despite being an unhappy story, Edith Oliver comments in the *New Yorker* that "there is more ebullience in it . . . than in many comedies I can think of." Taylor is also encouraged by the increase in scope in "The Lion in Love," remarking that "it has more characters, a more diffuse action, and the central character is now a mature woman, instead of a girl just emerging from childhood," as in "A Taste of Honey."

After her initial success in writing for the stage, Delaney did not write for the theater again until 1979, when she adapted her script for the 1977 BBC television series "The House That Jack Built" for an Off-Off-Broadway production. Her writing during this interim was mostly directed toward television and radio, except for her short story collection *Sweetly Sings the Donkey*. But after she had written several more plays for radio and television, film producer Roger Randall-Cutler asked her in 1985 to write a film script about the real-life story of Ruth Ellis, the last woman in England to be convicted and executed for murder.

Delaney had some misgivings about the project, though. "It wasn't my style," she reflects in an article she wrote for the *New York Times*. "It was too difficult. And it was dangerous. After all, Ruth Ellis was real and hitherto I had only dealt, professionally, at least, with fragments of my imagination." In a review of "Dance with a Stranger," *Washington Post*'s Paul Attanasio notes that the author's reservations about the dangers of this subject were not unfounded. Since the conclusion of the film is inevitable, says Attanasio, "it's not exactly the kind of movie that will have you grabbing onto your armrests." Nevertheless, *New York Times* critic Vincent Canby believes that " 'Dance With a Stranger' is a startling and involving melodrama about the sort of banal crime that obsessed [French filmmaker Francois] Truffaut." And in a later *New York Times* article, Canby explains that "the film is fascinating not because it works in sentimental ways to lead us into some sort of identification with Ruth Ellis," but because the film "successfully locate[s] the humanity of this woman."

It is Delaney's ability to portray the humanity of her characters that adds an important dimension to her realistic approach. "Delaney seems to write from an urge to communicate direct experience rather than from any sociopathic standpoint," comments Whitehead. In the stories in *Sweetly Sings the Donkey*, for exam-

ple, *Best Sellers* contributor Sister M. Gregory feels that the author's pessimistic viewpoint and realistic style are "mitigated by her respect for the dignity of the human personality, her uncompromising honesty and her wry humor." The author also has a "natural sense of theatre" which Gregory perceives even in the playwright's short stories. Oliver similarly calls Shelagh Delaney "a natural playwright if ever there was one. She is able to give the audience . . . not only a sense of the diversity of the life she depicts but a feeling of being part of it."

BIOGRAPHICAL/CRITICAL SOURCES:

BOOKS

Armstrong, W. A., editor, *Experimental Drama*, G. Bell, 1963.
Contemporary Literary Criticism, Volume 29, Gale, 1984.
Dictionary of Literary Biography, Volume 13: *British Dramatists since World War II*, Gale, 1982.
Taylor, John Russell, *The Angry Theater: New British Drama*, Hill & Wang, 1969.
Welwarth, George, *Theater of Protest and Paradox*, New York University Press, 1964.

PERIODICALS

Best Sellers, September 1, 1963.
Encounter, April, 1959.
New York, May 11, 1981.
New Yorker, May 4, 1963.
New York Herald Tribune, October 10, 1960.
New York Times, August 4, 1985, August 9, 1985, August 18, 1985.
Times (London), September 13, 1960.
Washington Post, August 21, 1985.

*　　*　　*

DELANY, Samuel R(ay, Jr.) 1942-

PERSONAL: Born April 1, 1942, in New York, NY; son of Samuel R. (a funeral director) and Margaret Carey (a library clerk; maiden name, Boyd) Delany; married Marilyn Hacker (a poet), August 24, 1961 (divorced, 1980); children: Iva Alyxander. *Education:* Attended City College (now of the City University of New York), 1960 and 1962-63.

ADDRESSES: Agent—Henry Morrison, Inc., Box 235, Bedford Hills, NY 10507.

CAREER: Writer. Butler Professor of English, State University of New York at Buffalo, 1975; senior fellow at the Center for Twentieth Century Studies, University of Wisconsin—Milwaukee, 1977; senior fellow at the Society for the Humanities, Cornell University, 1987; professor of comparative literature, University of Massachusetts—Amherst, 1988.

AWARDS, HONORS: Science Fiction Writers of America, Nebula Awards for best novel in 1966 for *Babel-17* and in 1967 for *The Einstein Intersection*, for best short story in 1967 for "Aye and Gomorrah," and for best novelette in 1969 for "Time Considered as a Helix of Semi-Precious Stones"; Hugo Award for best short story, Science Fiction Convention, 1970, for "Time Considered as a Helix of Semi-Precious Stones"; American Book Award nomination, 1980, for *Tales of Neveryon;* Pilgrim Award, Science Fiction Research Association, 1985.

WRITINGS:

SCIENCE FICTION

The Jewels of Aptor (abridged edition bound with *Second Ending* by James White), Ace Books, 1962, hardcover edition, Gollancz, 1968, complete edition published with an introduction by Don Hausdorff, Gregg Press, 1976.

Captives of the Flame (first novel in trilogy; bound with *The Psionic Menace* by Keith Woodcott), Ace Books, 1963, revised edition published under author's original title *Out of the Dead City* (also see below), Sphere Books, 1968.

The Towers of Toron (second novel in trilogy; also see below; bound with *The Lunar Eye* by Robert Moore Williams), Ace Books, 1964.

City of a Thousand Suns (third novel in trilogy; also see below), Ace Books, 1965.

The Ballad of Beta-2 (also see below; bound with *Alpha Yes, Terra No!* by Emil Petaja), Ace Books, 1965, hardcover edition published with an introduction by David G. Hartwell, Gregg Press, 1977.

Empire Star (also see below; bound with *The Three Lords of Imeten* by Tom Purdom), Ace Books, 1966, hardcover edition published with an introduction by Hartwell, Gregg Press, 1977.

Babel-17, Ace Books, 1966, hardcover edition, Gollancz, 1967, published with an introduction by Robert Scholes, 1976.

The Einstein Intersection, slightly abridged edition, Ace Books, 1967, hardcover edition, Gollancz, 1968, complete edition, Ace Books, 1972.

Nova, Doubleday, 1968.

The Fall of the Towers (trilogy; contains *Out of the Dead City, The Towers of Toron,* and *City of a Thousand Suns*), Ace Books, 1970, hardcover edition published with introduction by Joseph Milicia, Gregg Press, 1977.

Driftglass: Ten Tales of Speculative Fiction, Doubleday, 1971.

The Tides of Lust, Lancer Books, 1973.

Dhalgren, Bantam, 1975, hardcover edition published with introduction by Jean Mark Gawron, Gregg Press, 1978.

The Ballad of Beta-2 [and] *Empire Star,* Ace Books, 1975.

Triton, Bantam, 1976.

Empire: A Visual Novel, illustrations by Howard V. Chaykin, Berkley Books, 1978.

Distant Stars, Bantam, 1981.

Stars in My Pocket Like Grains of Sand, Bantam, 1984.

The Complete Nebula Award-Winning Fiction, Bantam, 1986.

The Star Pits (bound with *Tango Charlie and Foxtrot Romeo* by John Varley), Tor Books, 1989.

"RETURN TO NEVERYON" SERIES; SWORD AND SORCERY NOVELS

Tales of Neveryon, Bantam, 1979.

Neveryona; or, The Tale of Signs and Cities, Bantam, 1983.

Flight from Neveryon, Bantam, 1985.

The Bridge of Lost Desire, Arbor House, 1987.

OTHER

The Jewel-Hinged Jaw: Notes on the Language of Science Fiction, Dragon Press, 1977, revised edition, Berkley Publishing, 1978.

The American Shore: Meditations on a Tale of Science Fiction by Thomas M. Disch—"Angouleme" (criticism), Dragon Press, 1978.

Heavenly Breakfast: An Essay on the Winter of Love (memoir), Bantam, 1979.

Starboard Wine: More Notes on the Language of Science Fiction, Dragon Press, 1984.

The Motion of Light in Water: Sex and Science Fiction Writing in the East Village, 1957-1965, Arbor House, 1988.

Wagner/Artaud: A Play of Nineteenth and Twentieth Century Critical Fictions, Ansatz Press, 1988.

Straits of Messina (essays), Serconia Press, 1988.

Also author of scripts, director, and editor for two short films, "Tiresias," 1970, and "The Orchid," 1971; author of two scripts for the "Wonder Woman Comic Series," 1972, and of the radio play "The Star Pit," based on his short story of the same title. Editor, *Quark,* 1970-71.

SIDELIGHTS: "Samuel R. Delany is one of today's most innovative and imaginative writers of science-fiction," comments Jane Branham Weedman in her study of the author, *Samuel R. Delany.* In his science fiction, which includes over fifteen novels and two collections of short stories, the author "has explored what happens when alien world views intersect, collide, or mesh," writes Greg Tate in the *Voice Literary Supplement.* Delany first appeared on the science fiction horizon in the early 1960s, and in the decade that followed he established himself as one of the stars of the genre. Like many of his contemporaries who entered science fiction in the 1960s, he is less concerned with the conventions of the genre, more interested in science fiction as literature, literature which offers a wide range of artistic opportunities. As a result, maintains Weedman, "Delany's works are excellent examples of modern science-fiction as it has developed from the earlier and more limited science-fiction tradition, especially because of his manipulation of cultural theories, his detailed futuristic or alternate settings, and his stylistic innovations."

"One is drawn into Delany's stories because they have a complexity," observes Sandra Y. Govan in the *Black American Literature Forum,* "an acute consciousness of language, structure, and form; a dexterous ability to weave together mythology and anthropology, linguistic theory and cultural history, gestalt psychology and sociology as well as philosophy, structuralism, and the adventure story." At the center of the complex web of personal, cultural, artistic, and intellectual concerns that provides the framework for all of his work is Delany's examination of how language and myth influence reality. "According to [the author]," writes Govan in the *Dictionary of Literary Biography,* "language identifies or negates the self. It is self-reflective; it shapes perceptions." By shaping perceptions, language in turn has the capacity to shape reality. Myths can exercise much the same power. In his science fiction, Delany "creates new myths, or inversions of old ones, by which his protagonists measure themselves and their societies against the traditional myths that Delany includes," Weedman observes. In this way, as Peter S. Alterman comments in the *Dictionary of Literary Biography,* the author confronts "the question of the extent to which myths and archetypes create reality."

In societies in which language and myth are recognized as determinants of reality, the artist—one who works in language and myth—plays a crucial part. For this reason, the protagonist of a Delany novel is often an artist of some sort. "The role which Delany defines for the artist is to observe, record, transmit, and question paradigms in society," explains Weedman. But Delany's artists do more than chronicle and critique the societies of which they are a part. His artists are always among those at the margin of society; they are outcasts and often criminals. "The criminal and the artist both operate outside the normal standards of society," observes Alterman, "according to their own self-centered value systems." The artist/ criminal goes beyond observation and commentary. His actions at the margin push society's values to their limits and beyond, providing the experimentation necessary to prepare for eventual change.

Delany entered the world of science fiction in 1962 with the publication of his novel *The Jewels of Aptor.* Over the next six years, he published eight more, including *Babel-17, The Einstein Intersection,* and *Nova,* his first printed originally in hardcover. Douglas Barbour, writing in *Science Fiction Writers,* describes these early novels as "colorful, exciting, entertaining, and intellectually provocative to a degree not found in most genre science fiction." Barbour adds that although they do adhere to science fiction conventions, they "begin the exploration of those literary obsessions that define [Delany's] oeuvre: problems of communication and community; new kinds of sexual/love/family relationships; the artist as social outsider . . .; cultural interactions and the exploration of human social possibilities these allow; archetypal and mythic structures in the imagination."

With the publication of *Babel-17* in 1966, Delany began to gain recognition in the science fiction world. The novel, which earned its author his first Nebula Award, is a story of galactic warfare between the forces of the Alliance, which includes the Earth, and the forces of the Invaders. The poet Rydra Wong is enlisted by Alliance intelligence to decipher communications intercepted from its enemy. When she discovers that these dispatches contain not a code but rather an unknown language, her quest becomes one of learning this mysterious tongue labeled *Babel-17.* While leading an interstellar mission in search of clues, Rydra gains insights into the nature of language and, in the process, discovers the unique character of the enigmatic new language of the Invaders.

Babel-17 itself becomes an exploration of language and its ability to structure experience. A central image in the novel, as George Edgar Slusser points out in his study *The Delany Intersection: Samuel R. Delany Considered as a Writer of Semi-Precious Words,* is that of "the web and its weaver or breaker." The web, continues Slusser, "stands, simultaneously, for unity and isolation, interconnectedness and entanglement." And, as Peter Alterman points out in *Science-Fiction Studies,* "the web is an image of the effect of language on the mind and of the mind as shaper of reality." Weedman elaborates in her essay on the novel: "The language one learns necessarily constrains and structures what it is that one says." In its ability to connect and constrain is the power of the language/web. "Language . . . has a direct effect on how one thinks," explains Weedman, "since the structure of the language influences the processes by which one formulates ideas." At the center of the language as web "is one who joins and cuts—the artist-hero," comments Slusser. And, in *Babel-17,* the poet Rydra Wong demonstrates that only she is able to master this new language weapon and turn it against its creators.

Delany followed *Babel-17* with another Nebula winner, *The Einstein Intersection.* This novel represents a "move from a consideration of the relationship among language, thought, action and time to an analytic and imaginative investigation of the patterns of myths and archetypes and their interaction with the conscious mind," writes Alterman. Slusser sees this development in themes as part of a logical progression: "[Myths] too are seen essentially as language constructs: verbal scenarios for human action sanctioned by tradition or authority." Comparing this novel to *Babel-17,* he adds that "Delany's sense of the language act, in this novel, has a broader social valence."

The Einstein Intersection relates the story of a strange race of beings that occupies a post-apocalyptic Earth. This race assumes the traditions—economic, political, and religious—of the extinct humans in an attempt to make sense of the remnant world in which they find themselves. "While they try to live by the myths of man," writes Barbour in *Foundation,* "they cannot create a viable culture of their own. . . . Their more profound hope is

to recognize that they do not have to live out the old myths at all, that the 'difference' they seek to hide or dissemble is the key to their cultural and racial salvation."

"Difference is a key word in this novel," Weedman explains, "for it designates the importance of the individual and his ability to make choices, on the basis of being different from others, which affect his life, thus enabling him to question the paradigms of his society." The artist is the embodiment of this difference and in *The Einstein Intersection* the artist is Lobey, a musician. The power of Lobey's music is its ability to create order, to destroy the old myths and usher in the new. At its core, then, "*The Einstein Intersection* is . . . a novel about experiments in culture," Weedman comments.

Delany's next novel, *Nova,* "stands as the summation of [his] career up to that time," writes Barbour in *Science Fiction Writers: Critical Studies of the Major Authors from the Early Nineteenth Century to the Present Day.* "Packing his story full of color and incident, violent action and tender introspective moments, he has created one of the grandest space operas ever written." In this novel, Delany presents a galaxy divided into three camps, all embroiled in a bitter conflict caused by a shortage of the fuel illyrion on which they all depend. In chronicling one group's quest for a new source of the fuel, the author examines, according to Weedman, "how technology changes the world and philosophies for world survival. Delany also explores conflicts between and within societies, as well as the problems created by people's different perceptions and different reality models."

"In developing this tale," notes Slusser, "Delany has inverted the traditional epic relationship, in which the human subject (the quest) dominates the 'form.' Here instead is a 'subjunctive epic.' Men do not struggle against an inhuman system so much as inside an unhuman one." The system inside which these societies struggle is economic; the goal of the quester, who is driven by selfishness, is a commodity. Whether the commodity is abundant or scarce, as Jeanne Murray Walker points out in *Extrapolation,* this "is a world where groups are out of alignment, off balance, where some suffer while others prosper, where the object of exchange is used to divide rather than to unite." Walker concludes in her essay that "by ordering the action of *Nova* in the quest pattern, but assuming a value system quite different from that assumed by medieval romance writers, Delany shows that neither pattern nor action operate as they once did. Both fail." Even so, as she continues, "individuals must continue to quest. Through their quests they find meaning for themselves."

After the publication of *Nova,* Delany turned his creative urges to forms other than the novel, writing a number of short stories, editing four quarterlies of speculative fiction, and dabbling in such diverse media as film and comic books. Also at this time, he engaged himself in conceiving, writing, and polishing what would become his longest, most complex, and most controversial novel, *Dhalgren*—a work that would earn him national recognition. On its shifting surface, this novel represents the experience of a nameless amnesiac, an artist/criminal, during the period of time he spends in a temporally and spatially isolated city scarred by destruction and decay. As Alterman relates in the *Dictionary of Literary Biography,* "it begins with the genesis of a protagonist, one so unformed that he has no name, no identity, the quest for which is the novel's central theme." The critic goes on to explain that "at the end Kid has a name and a life, both of which are the novel itself; he is a persona whose experience in *Dhalgren* defines him."

Dhalgren's length and complexity provide a significant challenge to readers, but as Gerald Jonas observes in the *New York Times*

Book Review, "the most important fact about Delany's novel . . . is that nothing in it is clear. Nothing is meant to be clear." He adds: "An event may be described two or three times, and each recounting is slightly disconcertingly different from the one before." What is more, continues the reviewer, "the nameless narrator experiences time discontinuously; whole days seem to be excised from his memory." According to Weedman, "Delany creates disorientation in *Dhalgren* to explore the problems which occur when reality models differ from reality." And in Jonas's estimation, "If the book can be said to be *about* anything, it is about nothing less than the nature of reality."

"*Dhalgren* has drawn more widely divergent critical response than any other Delany novel," comments Govan in her *Dictionary of Literary Biography* essay. "Some reviewers deny that it is science fiction, while others praise it for its daring and experimental form." For instance, *Magazine of Fantasy and Science Fiction* book reviewer Algis Budrys contends that "this book is not science fiction, or science fantasy, but allegorical quasi-fantasy on the [James Gould] Cozzens model. Thus, although it demonstrates the breadth of Delany's education, and many of its passages are excellent prose, it presents no new literary inventions." In his *Science Fiction Writers* essay, Barbour describes the same novel as "the very stuff of science fiction but lacking the usual structural emblems of the genre." "One thing is certain," offers Jonas, " 'Dhalgren' is not a conventional novel, whether considered in terms of S.F. or the mainstream."

Following the exhaustive involvement with Kid necessary to complete *Dhalgren,* Delany chose to do a novel in which he distanced himself from his protagonist, giving him a chance to look at the relationship between an individual and his society in a new light. "I wanted to do a psychological analysis of someone with whom you're just not in sympathy, someone whom you watch making all the wrong choices, even though his plight itself is sympathetic," Delany explained in an interview with Larry McCaffery and Sinda Gregory published in their book *Alive and Writing: Interviews with American Authors of the 1980s.* The novel is *Triton;* its main character is Bron.

"*Triton* is set in a sort of sexual utopia, where every form of sexual behavior is accepted, and sex-change operations (not to mention 'refixations,' to alter sexual preference) are common," observes Michael Goodwin in *Mother Jones.* In this world of freedom lives Bron, whom Govan describes in *Black American Literature Forum* as "a narrow-minded, isolated man, so self-serving that he is incapable of reaching outside himself to love another or even understand another despite his best intentions." In an attempt to solve his problems, he undergoes a sex-change operation, but finds no happiness. "Bron is finally trapped in total social and psychological stasis, lost in isolation beyond any help her society can offer its citizens," comments Barbour in *Science Fiction Writers.*

In this novel, once again Delany creates an exotic new world, having values and conventions that differ from ours. In exploring this fictional world, he can set up a critique of our present-day society. In *Triton,* he casts a critical eye, as Weedman points out, on "sexual persecution against women, ambisexuals, and homosexuals." She concludes that the work is "on the necessity of knowing one's self despite sexual identification, knowing one's sexual identity is not one's total identity."

In the 1980s, Delany continued to experiment in his fiction writing. In his "Neveryon" series, which includes *Tales of Neveryon, Neveryona; or, The Tale of Signs and Cities, Flight from Neveryon,* and *The Bridge of Lost Desire,* he chooses a different setting. "Instead of being set in some imagined future, [they] are set

in some magical, distant past, just as civilization is being created," observes McCaffery in a *Science-Fiction Studies* interview of Delany. Their focus, suggests Gregory in the same interview, is "power—all kinds of power: sexual, economic, even racial power via the issue of slavery."

Throughout these tales of a world of dragons, treasures, and fabulous cities Delany weaves the story of Gorgik, a slave who rises to power and abolishes slavery. In one story, the novel-length "Tale of Plagues and Carnivals," he shifts in time from his primitive world to present-day New York and back to examine the devastating effects of a disease such as acquired immune deficiency syndrom (AIDS). And, in the appendices that accompany each of these books, he reflects on the creative process itself. Of the four, it is *Neveryona,* the story of Pryn—a girl who flees her mountain home on a journey of discovery—that has received the most attention from reviewers. *Science Fiction and Fantasy Book Review* contributor Michael R. Collings calls it "a stirring fable of adventure and education, of heroic action and even more heroic normality in a world where survival itself is constantly threatened." Faren C. Miller finds the book groundbreaking; she writes in *Locus:* "Combining differing perspectives with extraordinary talent for the *details* of a world—its smells, its shadows, workaday furnishings, and playful frills—Delany has produced a sourcebook for a new generation of fantasy writers." The book also "presents a new manifestation of Delany's continuing concern for language and the magic of fiction, whereby words become symbols for other, larger things," Collings observes.

In *Stars in My Pocket Like Grains of Sand,* Delany returns to distant worlds of the future. The book is "a densely textured, intricately worked out novelistic structure which delights and astonishes even as it forces a confrontation with a wide range of thought-provoking issues," writes McCaffery in *Fantasy Review.* Included are "an examination of interstellar politics among thousands of far flung worlds, a love story, a meandering essay on the variety of human relationships and the inexplicability of sexual attractiveness, and a hypnotic crash-course on a fascinating body of literature which does not yet exist," notes H. J. Kirchhoff in the Toronto *Globe and Mail.*

Beneath the surface features, as Jonas suggests in the *New York Times Book Review,* the reader can discover the fullness of this Delany novel. The reviewer writes: "To unpack the layers of meaning in seemingly offhand remarks or exchanges of social pleasantries, the reader must be alert to small shifts in emphasis, repeated phrases or gestures that assume new significance in new contexts, patterns of behavior that only become apparent when the author supplies a crucial piece of information at just the proper moment." Here in the words and gestures of the characters and the subtle way in which the author fashions his work is the fundamental concern of the novel. "I take the most basic subject here to be the nature of information itself," McCaffery explains, "the way it is processed, stored and decoded symbolically, the way it is distorted by the present and the past, the way it has become a commodity . . . the way that the play of textualities defines our perception of the universe."

"This is an astonishing new Delany," according to Somtow Sucharitkul in the *Washington Post Book World,* "more richly textured, smoother, more colorful than ever before." Jonas commends the novel because of the interaction it encourages with the reader. "Sentence by sentence, phrase by phrase, it invites the reader to collaborate in the process of creation, in a way that few novels do," writes the reviewer. "The reader who accepts this invitation has an extraordinarily satisfying experience in store for him/her." "*Stars in My Pocket Like Grains of Sand* . . . confirms that [Delany] is American SF's most consistently brilliant and inventive writer," McCaffery claims.

Critics often comment on Delany's use of fiction as a forum to call for greater acceptance of women's rights and gay rights; yet, as Govan maintains in her *Dictionary of Literary Biography* contribution, "a recurring motif frequently overlooked in Delany's fiction is his subtle emphasis on race. Black and mixed-blood characters cross the spectrum of his speculative futures, both as a testimony to a future Delany believes will change to reflect human diversity honestly and as a commentary on the racial politics of the present."

In novels such as *Babel-17,* Delany demonstrates how language can be used to rob the black man of his identity. "White culture exerts a great influence because it can force stereotypic definitions on the black person," writes Weedman. She adds that "if the black person capitulates to the definition imposed on him by a force outside of his culture, then he is in danger of losing his identity." In his other novels, Govan points out, "Delany utilizes existing negative racial mythologies about blacks, but, in all his works, he twists the commonplace images and stereotypes to his own ends." In using his fiction to promote awareness of the race issue, he and other black writers like him "have mastered the dominant culture's language and turned it against its formulators in protest," writes Weedman.

"Delany is not only a gifted writer," claims Barbour in his *Foundation* article, "he is one of the most articulate theorists of sf to have emerged from the ranks of its writers." In such critical works as *The Jewel-Hinged Jaw, The American Shore,* and *Starboard Wine,* "he has done much to open up critical discussion of sf as a genre, forcefully arguing its great potential as art," adds the reviewer. In his nonfiction, Delany offers a functional description of science fiction and contrasts it with other genres such as naturalistic fiction and fantasy. He also attempts to expand "the domain of his chosen genre by claiming it the modern mode of fiction *par excellence,*" comments Slusser, "the one most suited to deal with the complexities of paradox and probability, chaos, irrationality, and the need for logic and order."

Samuel R. Delany is not a simple man: a black man in a white society, a writer who suffers from dyslexia, an artist who is also a critic. His race, lifestyle, chosen profession, and chosen genre keep him far from the mainstream. "His own term 'multiplex' probably best describes his work (attitudes, ideas, themes, craftsmanship, all their inter-relations, as well as his relation as artist, to them all)," Barbour suggests. And, adds the reviewer, "His great perseverance in continually developing his craft and never resting on his past achievements is revealed in the steady growth in [his] artistry." In Weedman's estimation, "Few writers approach the lyricism, the command of language, the powerful combination of style and content that distinguishes Delany's works. More importantly," she concludes, "few writers, whether in science fiction or mundane fiction, so successfully create works which make us question ourselves, our actions, our beliefs, and our society as Delany has helped us do."

BIOGRAPHICAL/CRITICAL SOURCES:

BOOKS

Bleiler, E. F., editor, *Science Fiction Writers: Critical Studies of the Major Authors from the Early Nineteenth Century to the Present Day,* Scribner, 1982.
Contemporary Literary Criticism, Gale, Volume 8, 1978, Volume 14, 1980, Volume 38, 1986.
Delany, Samuel R., *The Jewel-Hinged Jaw: Notes on the Language of Science Fiction,* Dragon Press, 1977, revised edition, Berkley Publishing, 1978.
Delany, Samuel R., *Heavenly Breakfast: An Essay on the Winter of Love,* Bantam, 1979.
Delany, Samuel R., *The Motion of Light in Water: Sex and Science Fiction Writing in the East Village, 1957-1965,* Arbor House, 1988.
Dictionary of Literary Biography, Gale, Volume 8: *Twentieth-Century American Science Fiction Writers,* 1981, Volume 33: *Afro-American Fiction Writers after 1955,* 1984.
McCaffery, Larry, and Sinda Gregory, editors, *Alive and Writing: Interviews with American Authors of the 1980s,* University of Illinois Press, 1987.
Peplow, Michael W., and Robert S. Bravard, *Samuel R. Delany: A Primary and Secondary Bibliography, 1962-1979,* G. K. Hall, 1980.
Platt, Charles, editor, *Dream Makers: The Uncommon People Who Write Science Fiction,* Berkley Books, 1980.
Slusser, George Edgar, *The Delany Intersection: Samuel R. Delany Considered as a Writer of Semi-Precious Words,* Borgo, 1977.
Weedman, Jane Branham, *Samuel R. Delany,* Starmont House, 1982.

PERIODICALS

Analog Science Fiction/Science Fact, April, 1985.
Black American Literature Forum, summer, 1984.
Commonweal, December 5, 1975.
Extrapolation, fall, 1982.
Fantasy Review, December, 1984.
Foundation, March, 1975.
Globe and Mail (Toronto), February 9, 1985.
Locus, summer, 1983.
Los Angeles Times Book Review, March 13, 1988.
Magazine of Fantasy and Science Fiction, November, 1975, June, 1980.
Mother Jones, August, 1976.
New York Times Book Review, February 16, 1975, March 28, 1976, October 28, 1979, February 10, 1985.
Publishers Weekly, January 29, 1988.
Science Fiction and Fantasy Book Review, July/August, 1983.
Science Fiction Chronicle, November, 1987.
Science-Fiction Studies, Volume 4, number 11, 1977, Volume 14, number 2, 1987.
Voice Literary Supplement, February, 1985.
Washington Post Book World, January 27, 1985.

*   *   *

DELAPORTE, Theophile
See GREEN, Julien (Hartridge)

*   *   *

DELIBES, Miguel
See DELIBES SETIEN, Miguel

*   *   *

DELIBES SETIEN, Miguel   1920-
(Miguel Delibes)

PERSONAL: Born October 17, 1920, in Valladolid, Spain; son of Adolfo (a professor) and Maria (Setien) Delibes; married Angeles de Castro Ruiz, April 23, 1946 (died November, 1974); children: Miguel, Angeles, German, Elisa, Juan, Adolfo, Camino. *Education:* Hermanos Doctrina Cristiana, Bachillerato; Universidad de Valladolid, Doctor en Derecho (law), 1944; attended Escuela Altos Estudios Mercantiles, and Escuela Periodismo. *Religion:* Roman Catholic.

ADDRESSES: Home—Dos de Mayo 10, Valladolid, Spain. *Agent*—Ediciones Destino, Consejo de Ciento 425, Barcelona 9, Spain.

CAREER: Novelist and writer. Teacher of mercantile law, University de Valladolid, Valladolid, Spain. Director, El Norte de Castilla, Valladolid. Visiting professor, University of Maryland, 1964. *Military service:* Spanish Navy, 1938-39.

MEMBER: Real Academia Espanola, Hispanic Society.

AWARDS, HONORS: Nadal Prize, 1947, for *La sombra del cipres es alargada;* Ministry of Information Cervantes Prize (Spanish national prize for literature), 1955, for *Diario de un cazador;* Critics Prize (Spain), 1963; Asturias Prize, 1982.

WRITINGS:

UNDER NAME MIGUEL DELIBES; NOVELS, EXCEPT AS INDICATED

La sombra del cipres es alagarda (also see below; title means "The Cypress's Shadow is Long"), Ediciones Destino, 1948, reprinted, 1979.

Aun es de dia, Ediciones Destino, 1949, 2nd edition, 1962, reprinted, 1982.

El camino (also see below; title means "The Road"), Ediciones Destino, 1950, reprinted, 1984, self-illustrated edition, Holt, 1960, translation by Brita Haycraft published as *The Path,* John Day, 1961.

Mi idolatrado hijo Sisi (also see below), Ediciones Destino, 1953, reprinted, 1980.

El loco (novella; also see below), Editorial Tecnos, 1953.

La partida (fiction; includes "La Partida," "El refugio," "Una peseta para el tranvia," "El manguero," "El campeonato," "El traslado," "El primer pitillo," "La contradiccion," "En una noche asi," and "La conferencia"), L. de Caralt, 1954, 2nd edition, Alianza Editorial, 1969, reprinted, 1982.

Diario de un cazador, Ediciones Destino, 1955, reprinted, 1980.

Siestas con viento sur (novellas; includes "La mortaja," "El loco," "Los nogales," and "Los railes"), Ediciones Destino, 1957, 2nd edition, 1967.

Diario de un emigrante, Ediciones Destino, 1958, reprinted, 1977.

La hoja roja, Ediciones Destino, 1959, 3rd edition, 1975.

Las ratas, Ediciones Destino, 1962, 7th edition, 1971, Harrap, 1969.

Obra completa (includes "Prologo," "La sombra de cipres es alargada," "El camino," and "Mi idolatrado hijo Sisi"), Part 1, Ediciones Destino, 1964.

Cinco horas con Mario, Ediciones Destino, 1966, 9th edition, 1975, translation by Frances M. Lopez-Morillas published as *Five Hours with Mario,* Columbia University Press, 1989.

La Mortaja (novellas; also see above; includes "La mortaja," "El amor propio de Juanito Osuna," "El patio de vecindad," "El sol," "La fe," "El conejo," "La perra," and "Navidad sin ambiente"), Alianza Editorial, 1969, 2nd edition, 1974.

Parabola del naufrago, Ediciones Destino, 1969, 3rd edition, 1971, translation by Lopez-Morillas published as *The Hedge,* Columbia University Press, 1983.

(With others) *La sombra del cipres es alargada [por] Miguel Delibes. Sobre las piedras grises [por] Sebastian Juan Arbo. Las*

ultimas horas [por] Jose Suarez Carreno, Ediciones Destino, 1970.

Mi mundo y el mundo: Seleccion antologica de obras del autor, para ninos de 11 a 14 anos, Minon, 1970.

Smoke on the Ground, translation by Alfred Johnson, Doubleday, 1972.

El principe destronado, Ediciones Destino, 1973, reprinted, 1982.

Las guerras de nuestros antepasados, Ediciones Destino, 1974, 5th edition, 1979.

El disputado voto del senor Cayo, Ediciones Destino, 1978.

Los santos inocentes, Planeta, 1981.

Tres pajaros de cuenta, Minon, 1982.

Cartas de amor de un sexagenario voluptuoso, Ediciones Destino, 1983.

El tesoro, Ediciones Destino, 1985.

377A, madera de heroe, Ediciones Destino, 1987.

NONFICTION

Un novelista descubre America, Editora Nacional, 1956.

La barberia: Portada de Coll, G. P. Ediciones , 1957.

Castilla, Editorial Lumen, 1960, published as *Viejas historias de Castilla la Vieja,* Ediciones Destino, 1964, 3rd edition, 1974, Alianza Editorial, 1982.

Por esos mundos: Sudamerica con escala en las Canarias, Ediciones Destino, 1971, 2nd edition, 1972.

La caza de la perdiz roja, Editorial Lumen, 1963, 2nd edition, 1975.

Europa: Parada y fonda, Ediciones Cid, 1963, reprinted, Plaza & Janes, 1981.

El libro de la caza menor, Ediciones Destino, 1964, 3rd edition, 1973.

USA y yo, Ediciones Destino, 1966, Odyssey, 1970.

Vivir al dia (also see below), Ediciones Destino, 1968, 2nd edition, 1975.

(Contributor) Susanne Filkau, editor, *Historias de la guerra civil,* Edition Langewiesche-Brandt, 1968.

La primavera de Praga, Alianza Editorial, 1968.

Con la escopeta al hombro (also see below), Ediciones Destino, 1970, 2nd edition, 1971.

Un ano de mi vida (also see below), Ediciones Destino, 1972.

La caza en Espana, Alianza Editorial, 1972.

Castilla en mi obra, Editorial Magistero Espanol, 1972.

S.O.S.: El sentido del progreso desde mi obra, Ediciones Destino, 1975.

Aventuras, venturas, y desventuras de un cazador a rabo, Ediciones Destino, 1976.

Mis amigas las truchas, Ediciones Destino, 1977.

Castilla, lo castellano y los castellanos, Editorial Planeta, 1979.

El desputado voto del senor Cayo, Ediciones Destino, 1980.

Las perdices del domingo, 2nd edition, Ediciones Destino, 1981.

Dos viajes en automovil: Suecia y Paises Bajos, Plaza & Janes, 1982.

El otro futbol, Ediciones Destino, 1982.

La censura de prensa en los anos 40, y otros ensayos, Ambito, 1985.

Castilla habla, Ediciones Destino, 1986.

OTHER

Cesar Alonso de los Rios, *Conversaciones con Delibes,* Emesa (Madrid), 1971.

Javier Goni, *Cinco horas con Miguel Delibes,* Anjana, 1985.

Also author of another volume of *Obra completa,* which includes "Vivir al dia," "Con la escopeta al hombro," and "Un ano de mi vida," for Ediciones Destino. Author of television plays *Tier-*

ras de Valladolid, 1966, *La mortaja,* and *Castilla, esta es mi tierra,* 1983.

SIDELIGHTS: Miguel Delibes Setien is considered one of Spain's most important novelists; his work is distinguished by its stark realism, rural subject matter, and well-developed characters. Ronald Schwartz explains in *Spain's New Wave Novelists: 1950-1974,* "Delibes has been always considered a major novelist whose career is constantly developing, growing in quantity and quality, and becoming more prestigious because of his consistent use of Realism and his attachment to rural themes, which display a variety of character types. . . . Critics acknowledge his skepticism, pessimism, reactionary vision of nature, his love for the man of instinct, of nature in contrast to a 'civilized' product, in short, his negative view of progress and 'civilization,' his black humor and cold intellectualism."

A recurrent theme in fiction by Delibes is the message that technological and social changes brought about during the twentieth century have resulted in the alienation and repression of the individual. As they find their places in the world of business, many of his characters feel isolated. This is perhaps best seen in *The Hedge,* a novel in which a sensitive clerk degenerates into a fearful person who will do almost anything—even resort to violence—to maintain his sense of material security. At first, "Jacinto is scared of losing his job, of having children and having to raise them to be either victims or executioners in a pitiless society," Toby Talbot relates in the *New York Times Book Review.* Sent by an authoritarian official to be rehabilitated after questioning the difference between zero and the letter "O" in the documents he transcribes, Jacinto notices that a thick hedge separates him from the rest of the world. The hedge depicts "the encroachment of an Orwellian state," Talbot explains, and Jacinto's degeneration shows that the end result of the encroachment is "the dehumanization of man, victimized by his own progress, specialization and conformity. And along with it comes the disintegration of thought and language," two activities eventually dominated and regulated by the state.

Five Hours with Mario, a novel regarded as a masterpiece by some critics, also shows the human fight for liberty and dignity against oppressive forces. The narrator Carmen's husband has just died and we listen as she critically reviews their life together. Reduced to poverty for daring to confront the repressive authorities, her husband had failed to improve her material standard of living. While berating him, she exhibits her own failure to live up to her stated ideals. Delibes thus criticizes many aspects of traditional and modern life in Spain. In addition, the novel "addresses lost words, last words and listening—important issues in a country that is now free to examine its conscience and its recent history," *New York Times Book Review* critic Arthur J. Sabatini comments.

The realism and themes of nature in Delibes Setien's work have been widely praised. Schwartz believes that the author demonstrates "an enormous capacity to capture within his writings the essence of nature by means of his starkly Realist style." In the *New York Times Book Review,* Martin Levin constrasts the "charming and nostalgic" view of nature rendered by "Anglo-Saxon novels" to the harsh atmosphere of *Smoke on the Ground.* "The land is wretchedly poor," he writes, "the climate is harsh, and the atmosphere has a haunting, 19th-century bleakness, although it is set in the age of moon missions." Schwartz believes that with the "harmonious" combination of "humor, tenderness, nature and tragedy" evident in Delibes Setien's later work, he is "reviving the theme of nature as a literary element indispensable to the human condition and portraying this harmony through his extremely personal style."

MEDIA ADAPTATIONS: Some of Delibes Setien's works have been adapted for Spanish television. Feature-length film adaptations of his work include "Retrato de familia," based on his novel *Mi idolatrado hijo Sisi,* filmed in 1975, "La guerra de papa," produced in 1978, and based on the novel *El principe destronada,* and "The Holy Innocents," directed by Mario Camus. *Cinco horas con Mario* has also been filmed.

BIOGRAPHICAL/CRITICAL SOURCES:

BOOKS

Alonso de los Rios, Cesar, *Conversaciones con Delibes,* Emesa (Madrid), 1971.
Contemporary Literary Criticism, Gale, Volume 8, 1978, Volume 18, 1981.
Diaz, Janet W., *Delibes,* Twayne, 1971.
Estudios sobre Delibes, Universidad Complutense, 1983.
Gullon, Agnes, *La novela experimental de Delibes,* Taurus, 1981.
Schwartz, Ronald, *Spain's New Wave Novelists: 1950-1974,* Scarecrow Press, 1976.
Umbral, Francisco, *Delibes,* Emesa, 1970.

PERIODICALS

Antioch Review, June, 1973.
Booklist, February 15, 1971.
Hispania, December 1971, December, 1972, March, 1974, May, 1974, May, 1976.
New York Times Book Review, August 20, 1972, December 11, 1983, January 22, 1989.
Times Literary Supplement, April 20, 1967, June 11, 1970.
World Literature Today, summer, 1977.

* * *

DeLILLO, Don 1936-

PERSONAL: Born November 20, 1936, in New York, N.Y.; married wife, Barbara (a bank worker and harpsichordist). *Education:* Graduated from Fordham University, 1958.

ADDRESSES: Agent—Wallace & Sheil, 177 East 70th St., New York, N.Y. 10021.

CAREER: Writer.

MEMBER: American Academy and Institute of Arts and Letters.

AWARDS, HONORS: Guggenheim fellowship, 1979; American Academy and Institute of Arts and Letters Award in Literature, 1984; *White Noise* won an American Book Award in fiction and was nominated for a National Book Critics Circle Award, both 1985; *Libra* was nominated for a National Book Award in fiction and a National Book Critics Circle Award, both 1989; *Libra* was awarded the first International Fiction Prize from the *Irish Times* and Aer Lingus, 1989.

WRITINGS:

NOVELS

Americana, Houghton, 1971.
End Zone, Houghton, 1972.
Great Jones Street, Houghton, 1973.
Ratner's Star, Knopf, 1976.
Players, Knopf, distributed by Random House, 1977.
Running Dog, Knopf, 1978.
The Names, Knopf, distributed by Random House, 1982.

White Noise, Viking, 1985.
Libra (Book-of-the-Month Club selection), Viking, 1988.

PLAYS

"The Day Room," first produced in Cambridge, Mass., by the American Repertory Theater, April, 1986.

Also author of "The Engineer of Moonlight."

CONTRIBUTOR

Baxter Hathaway, editor, *Stories from Epoch,* Cornell University Press, 1966.
Gordon Lish, editor, *The Secret Life of Our Times,* Doubleday, 1973.
Jack Hicks, editor, *Cutting Edges,* Holt, 1973.
William O'Rourke, editor, *On the Job,* Random House, 1977.
L. Rust Hills, editor, *Great Esquire Fiction,* Viking, 1983.

Contributor of short stories to periodicals, including *New Yorker, Esquire, Sports Illustrated,* and *Atlantic.*

SIDELIGHTS: With each of his novels Don DeLillo has enhanced his literary reputation and gained a wider audience for his carefully crafted prose. He first attracted critical attention in the early 1970s when he published two ambitious and elusive novels about games: *End Zone,* an existential comedy which parlays football into a metaphor for thermonuclear war, and *Ratner's Star,* a surrealistic science fiction that is structurally akin to the mathematical formulas it employs. The verbal precision, dazzling intelligence, and sharp wit of these books made DeLillo a critical favorite, "but without bestseller sales figures or a dependable cult following, he has become something of a reviewer's writer," according to R. Z. Sheppard in *Time.* But thanks largely to the impact of *White Noise* and his first best-seller *Libra,* his name has become more widely known. A major literary event when it was published, *White Noise* received front page *New York Times Book Review* coverage and garnered the American Book Award in fiction in 1985. "In fact," writes *Chicago Tribune Book World* contributor John W. Aldridge, "with this, his eighth novel, DeLillo has won the right not only to be ranked with [Thomas] Pynchon and [William] Gaddis but recognized as having surpassed them in brilliance, versatility, and breadth of imagination. DeLillo shares with them, but in a degree greater than theirs, that rarest of creative gifts, the ability to identify and describe, as if from the perspective of another galaxy, the exact look and feel of contemporary reality." DeLillo's next novel, *Libra,* is an account of the life of Lee Harvey Oswald, John F. Kennedy's assassin. A stunning success—*Libra* was nominated for the National Book Award and won the newly inaugurated International Fiction Prize from the *Irish Times*—Walter Clemons in *Newsweek* called it "an overwhelming novel".

DeLillo has written about football and science, political conspiracies, pornographic crime rings, urban terrorists, cult murderers, chemical accidents, and other modern-day concerns. His subjects vary from novel to novel, but all of his books document the disintegration of order in contemporary society and the attendant rise of paranoia everywhere. "There is a sense in much modern life that almost anything, perhaps especially anything horrid, that might be imagined will turn up as a logical and unforeseen consequence of earlier social trends," notes Roz Kaveney in the *Times Literary Supplement.* "DeLillo takes this and builds round it a gentle fiction dominated by the appropriate lack of surprise, even by bland resignation." In her *New York Review of Books* essay, Diane Johnson portrays DeLillo as a kind of twentieth-century Charles Dickens, using noxious elements of modern life the way Dickens used dustheaps, to "embody the moral defects of the society that produces them." She speculates in a *New York Times Book Review* critique that DeLillo's novels "have been much praised but not so much read, perhaps because they deal with deeply shocking things about America that people would rather not face."

Another reason his works are not better known has to do with the low profile that DeLillo consciously maintains. He does not make television appearances, give lectures, participate in promotional campaigns, or otherwise plug his books. Only with reluctance does he grant interviews, as Thomas LeClair learned when he tracked the elusive author down in Greece. "When I managed to get to Athens in September of 1979, and not long after I met him, he handed me a business card engraved with his name and 'I don't want to talk about it,'" LeClair writes in the introduction to his *Contemporary Literature* interview. Once they began taping, LeClair realized that "Don DeLillo's elusiveness comes naturally, necessarily, from his concern with what he quotes Hermann Broch as calling 'the word beyond speech.'"

DeLillo's obsession with language links him to other members of literature's experimental school. "Like his contemporaries, William Gass, Robert Coover, and John Barth, he may be termed a 'metafictionist'," writes Michael Oriard in *Critique: Studies in Modern Fiction.* "Like these writers, he is strongly aware of the nature of language and makes language itself, and the process of using language, his themes." In his interview with LeClair, DeLillo suggests that after writing *End Zone* he realized "that language was a subject as well as an instrument in my work." Later, he elaborated: "What writing means to me is trying to make interesting, clear, beautiful language. Working at sentences and rhythms is probably the most satisfying thing I do as a writer. I think after a while a writer can begin to know himself through his language. He sees someone or something reflected back at him from these constructions. Over the years it's possible for a writer to shape himself as a human being through the language he uses. I think written language, fiction, goes that deep."

In his novels DeLillo makes no attempt to demystify the writing process; on the contrary, some of his books seem purposefully arcane. Oriard compares these works to "jigsaw puzzles assembled on a card table that is bumped—the pieces are all there but they do not seem to fit neatly together." DeLillo himself, in a widely quoted passage from *Ratner's Star,* has written: "There's a whole class of writers who don't want their books to be read. This to some extent explains their crazed prose. To express what is expressible isn't why you write if you're in this class of writers. To be understood is faintly embarrassing. What you want to express is the violence of your desire not to be read. The friction of audiences is what drives writers crazy. These people are going to read what you write. The more they understand, the crazier you get. You can't let them know what you're writing about. Once they know, you're finished."

DeLillo stops short of identifying himself as that species of writer, but he did tell LeClair that he has felt "some of the pull of crazed prose. There's an element of contempt for meanings. You want to write outside the usual framework. You want to dare readers to make a commitment you know they can't make. That's part of it. There's also the sense of drowning in information and in the mass awareness of things. Everybody seems to know everything. Subjects surface and are totally exhausted in a matter of days. . . . The writer is driven by his conviction that some truths aren't arrived at so easily, that life is still full of mystery, that it might be better for you, dear reader, if you went back to the living section of your newspaper because this is the dying section and you don't really want to be here. This writer is working against the age and so he feels some satisfaction at not being widely read. He is diminished by an audience."

DeLillo's antisocial sentiments may have frightened off readers, but they have not fazed critics. Rising to his challenge of commitment, they have lavished attention on his publications, offering thoughtful interpretations of his complex work. Those who have studied the body of his writing recognize recurring themes, which darken and turn more ominous as the work evolves. "From *Americana* to *End Zone* to *Great Jones Street* to *Ratner's Star* DeLillo traces a single search for the source of life's meaning," explains Oriard. "By the end of *Ratner's Star,* the quest has been literally turned inside out, the path from chaos to knowledge becomes a Moebius strip that brings the seeker back to chaos."

The quest in DeLillo's first novel, *Americana,* involves a disillusioned television executive's search for a national identity. Abandoning his job, producer David Bell embarks on a cross-country odyssey to "nail down the gas-driven, motel-housed American soul," *Village Voice* contributor Albert Mobilio explains. Even in this early work, DeLillo's obsession with language dominates the narrative: his first-person narrator describes his quest as a "literary venture," using images that compare the western landscape to linguistic patterns on a page. "For years I had been held fast by the great unwinding mystery of this deep sink of land, the thick paragraphs and imposing photos, the gallop of panting adjectives, prairie truth and the clean kills of eagles," says Bell. *Americana,* like most first novels, was not widely reviewed, but it did attract favorable notice from some established New York critics, who expressed enthusiasm for DeLillo's remarkable verbal gifts. "It is a familiar story by now, flawed in the telling," notes *New York Times* contributor Christopher Lehmann-Haupt in a representative review. "But the language soars and dips, and it imparts a great deal." *New York Times Book Review* contributor Thomas R. Edwards deems it "a savagely funny portrait of middle-class anomie in a bad time," but also notes that the book was "too long and visibly ambitious, and too much like too many other recent novels, to seem as good as it should have."

Edwards finds DeLillo's second novel—in which the quest for meaning is transferred from the American roadside to the sports arena—a more successful venture. "In 'End Zone,' " writes Edwards, "DeLillo finds in college football a more original and efficient vehicle for his sense of things now." This episodic, largely plotless novel focuses on the final attempt college athlete Gary Harkness makes to prove himself as a football player in a small west Texas school. Gary, who spends his free time playing war games, is attracted to carefully structured systems of ordered violence that afford opportunities for complete control. Edwards speculates that "Gary's involvement with [football] is a version of his horrified fascination with the vocabulary, theory and technology of modern war." Out on the playing field, Gary wins all but one of his football games, but "it's a season of losses all the same," Edwards concludes, for not only do minor characters suffer setbacks and tragedies but Gary "ends up in the infirmary with a mysterious brain-fever being fed through plastic tubes."

Gary's hunger strike has been interpreted as a final existential attempt to exert control. "He's paring things down. He is struggling, trying to face something he felt had to be faced," DeLillo told LeClair. Thus the "end zone" of this novel becomes a symbolic setting that represents "not only the goal of the running back in a football game, but the human condition at the outer extremity of existence, a place where the world is on the verge of disintegration, and the characters teeter between genius and

madness," Oriard believes. "In this region of end zones that DeLillo describes, characters struggle for order and meaning as their world moves inexorably towards chaos. DeLillo's men and women fight the natural law of entropy, while human violence hastens its inevitable consequences."

Notwithstanding its grim overtones and ambiguous ending, *End Zone* is not unremittingly pessimistic, according to reviewers who see a measure of hope reflected in the characters' portrayals. "The absurd Texas football players of 'End Zone', infected as they were with racism and the worship of technocracy, were also weirdly capable of love, and DeLillo depicted them as salvageable—human and struggling victims of their time and place," writes *New York Times Book Review* contributor Sara Blackburn. *Dictionary of Literary Biography* contributor Frank Day offers a similar view: "Gary [and his friends] Anatole and Myna are memorable people. One cares about them. They hang on, they keep control, and they even triumph in small ways with wit, courage, and resourcefulness."

The next American milieu DeLillo tackled was the world of rock stars and the drug culture in the novel *Great Jones Street.* Walter Clemons's assessment of the novel as an "in-between book" is representative of critical opinion, and while critics realized that DeLillo was extending himself as a writer, they weren't completely satisfied with the result. "The rock stars, drug dealers and hangers-on that populate 'Great Jones Street' are so totally freaked out, so slickly devoted to destruction and evil, so obsessed with manipulating and acquiring that they're beyond redemption," writes *New York Times Book Review* contributor Sara Blackburn, who deems the work "more of a sour, admirably written lecture than a novel, a book that is always puffing to keep up with the power and intensity of its subject."

DeLillo turned to the genre of science fiction for his fourth book, *Ratner's Star,* a pivotal work about a fourteen-year-old mathematical genius and Nobel laureate, Billy Twillig. "There is no easy way to describe *Ratner's Star,* a cheerfully apocalyptic novel," writes Amanda Heller in the *Atlantic.* "Imagine *Alice in Wonderland* set at the Princeton Institute for Advanced Studies." A reviewer for the *New Yorker* finds it "a whimsical, surrealistic excursion into the modern scientific mind." *New York Times Book Review* contributor George Stade describes it as "not only interesting, but funny (in a nervous kind of way). From it comes an unambiguous signal that DeLillo has arrived, bearing many gifts. He is smart, observant, fluent, a brilliant mimic and an ingenious architect."

Modeled after Lewis Carroll's *Alice in Wonderland,* DeLillo's novel is comprised of two sections, "Adventures" and "Reflections," that mimic the structural divisions of Carroll's book. "The comic, episodic discontinuous style of the book's first half is reflected in reverse in its symmetrically opposite second part," writes G. M. Knoll in *America.* He continues, "All that has been asserted or hypothesized about the signals from Ratner's Star is here denied. Billy's assignment is now to assist in the development of a language to answer the star's message rather than decipher the meaning of the signals." DeLillo's goal in this venture, according to *Time*'s Paul Gray, "is to show how the codification of phenomena as practiced by scientists leads to absurdity and madness." In his interview with LeClair, however, DeLillo says that his primary intention was "to produce a book that would be naked structure. The structure would be the book."

This emphasis on composition results in a deemphasis on plot and character that is representative of all DeLillo's books. Stade traces the historical development of this style, which he calls "Menippean satire," and proclaims it "the right form . . . for fiction writers who have little interest in fitting together rounded characters, social relations and sequential plots—or who see little evidence of them in experience. It is the right form when experience seems to consist of discontinuous selves, collapsing institutions and arrested developments, which is how it seems to seem right now to our best fiction writers." Others, however, lament the superficial characterization that often results. Gray, for instance, finds the protagonists of *Ratner's Star* reduced to "cartoon characters," while a *New Yorker* reviewer dismisses them as "caricaturish." Concludes Knoll, "without consistently developed characters in action, this brilliant, truly amazing, but finally frustrating book rings a bit hollow."

Ratner's Star marks a turning point in DeLillo's fiction, say critics who note a shift in the pacing and tone of subsequent books. "Since *Ratner's Star,* the apogee or nadir of his mirror-game experiments, DeLillo has opened his fiction to the possibilities of more extroverted action," observes *New Republic* contributor Robert Towers. "The speeded-up pace in both *Players* and *Running Dog* seems to me all to the good." Accompanying this accelerated narrative, however, is a noticeable change in the kinds of people DeLillo is writing about. Hardened by exposure to modern society, cynical in their views of life, these characters "are not sustained by the illusion that answers to cosmic questions can be found," Oriard believes. Nor are their self-serving quests particularly admirable, according to *Dictionary of Literary Biography* contributor Frank Day, who maintains that readers may have a hard time sympathizing with protagonists whose lives are "parables of betrayal and degeneration. The frail, confused youths of the early novels are here displaced by characters influenced by popular espionage fiction."

In *Players* DeLillo employs a prologue—a sophisticated bit of pure fiction in which the characters are temporarily suspended outside the apparatus of the story—to introduce his themes. Before the narrative starts, DeLillo collects his as-yet-unnamed protagonists on an empty airplane, seating them in the lounge to watch a grisly film. "The Movie," as this prelude is called, depicts an unsuspecting band of Sunday golfers being attacked and murdered by marauding hippies, who splatter the scenic green landscape with blood. Without earphones the passengers can't hear the dialogue, so the pianist improvises silent-movie music to accompany the scene. "The passengers laugh, cheer, clap," notes *New York Times Book Review* contributor Diane Johnson. "It is the terrorists whom they applaud." When the movie ends, the lights come up and the passengers, now identified as protagonists Lyle and Pammy Wynant and friends, step off the plane and into the story—a tale of terrorists, murder, and wasted lives.

A hip New York couple, Pammy and Lyle are bored to distraction by each other and their jobs. She's a promotional writer at the Grief Management Council, an organization that "served the community in its efforts to understand and assimilate grief." He's a stockbroker on Wall Street, who spends his free time parked in front of the TV set, flipping channels, not in hopes of finding a good program but because "he simply enjoyed jerking the dial into fresh image burns." The emptiness of their lives is reflected in their shallow banter, as this exchange over a broken appliance: " 'How come no dishwasher?' 'I want these glasses to know what it feels like to be washed by human hands,' she said. 'I don't want them to grow up thinking everything's done the easy way, by machine, with impersonal detergent.' 'It's broken again?' 'You call.' 'You, for once.' "

The breakdown of the dishwasher precipitates the breakdown of their marriage. Pammy moves out, heading off to Maine with a pair of homosexual lovers, one of whom will become her lover

and commit suicide. She will return home. Lyle takes up with a mindless secretary who is linked to a terrorist group responsible for murdering a man on the Stock Exchange floor. Intrigued by the glamour of revolutionary violence, Lyle joins forces with the terrorists, but also covers himself by informing on their activities to law enforcement agencies. "The end," notes John Updike in the *New Yorker,* "finds him in a motel in Canada, having double-crossed everybody but on excellent terms, it seems, with himself." Both he and Pammy have become players in the game.

Noting that DeLillo is that rare kind of novelist who looks "grandly at the whole state of things," Johnson postulates that "since Freud, we've been used to the way novelists normally present a character: looks normal, is secretly strange and individual. In the first of many inversions of appearance and reality that structure the book, Pammy and Lyle look interesting and seem to do interesting things, but do not interest themselves. The richness is only superficial. . . . Pammy and Lyle have no history; they are without pasts, were never children, come from nowhere. They worry that they have become too complex to experience things directly and acutely, but the opposite is true. They are being reduced by contemporary reality to numb simplicity, lassitude." For people like Lyle and Pammy who daily combat chaos, "it's a relief to become a player, in any game," writes Johnson, "for there, where chance operates only within calculable limits, you can grasp the pattern. Terrorist action is not so much an example of lawlessness as a comment on the rules, an aspect of the structure itself."

Because *Players*'s characters are "zombies," *New York Times* reviewer John Leonard postulates that they aren't worth caring about. "What remains for us to care about, then, is wit, intelligence, and language," he says, adding that DeLillo "has developed a prose style that amounts to incantation. It is full of stops and magic, an abrupt keening, here and there glissando, crazy syllogisms, rogue puns. It thumps, winks, foreshortens, slides." *National Review* contributor Zane Kotker also considers the characters uncompelling, but finds himself moved by "the totality of the book: *Players* hovers in the mind, echoing, waiting to be more fully understood, to be realized from yet another angled reflector." Updike deems DeLillo "original, versatile, and, in his disdain of last year's emotional guarantees, fastidious. He brings to human phenomena the dispassionate mathematics and spatial subtleties of particle physics. Into our technology-riddled daily lives he reads the sinister ambiguities, the floating ugliness of America's recent history. . . . But the very intensity of Mr. DeLillo's wish, in this novel, to say something new about the matter has evaporated the matter, leaving behind an exquisite ash-skeleton of elliptic dialogue and spindly motivation."

DeLillo followed *Players* with two psychological thrillers, *Running Dog* and *The Names,* the latter of which was praised for its improved characterization. But it was with *White Noise* that DeLillo first impressed critics with his rendition of fully realized characters in a minimalist prose style. Noting that with each book DeLillo becomes increasingly elliptical, *Village Voice* contributor Albert Mobilio observes that "the distillation is matched by a more subtle and convincing treatment of his characters' inner lives. This broadened emotional vocabulary charges *White Noise* with a resonance and credibility that makes it difficult to ignore. Critics who have argued that his work is too clever and overly intellectual should take notice: DeLillo's dark vision is now hard-earned. It strikes at both heart and head."

A novel about technology and death, *White Noise* unfolds as the first-person narrative of Jack Gladney, chairman of the department of Hitler studies at a small liberal arts school, College-on-the-Hill. Gladney lives with his fourth wife Babette—an ample, disheveled woman who teaches an adult education class in posture and reads to the blind—and their four children from previous marriages, Wilder, Steffie, Denise, and Heinrich. Life seems full for the Gladneys, but early on, Jack confesses that he and Babette are obsessed with a troubling question: "Who will die first?" Even as they debate it, small signs of trouble begin to surface: the children are evacuated from grade school because of an unidentified toxin in the atmosphere, and Babette can't remember facts or incidents because she's secretly taking medication that impairs her memory. One clear winter day, a major chemical spill jeopardizes the whole city. Everyone is forced to evacuate and, on his way to the shelter Jack stops to get gas, inadvertently exposing himself to the "airborne toxic event." Informed that "anything that puts you in contact with actual emissions means we have a situation," Jack becomes convinced that he is dying. (As proof, his computerized health profile spews out "bracketed numbers with pulsing stars.") When Jack discovers that Babette's medication (which she has committed adultery to obtain) is an experimental substance said to combat fear of death, he vows to find more of the substance for himself. His quest to obtain the illicit drug at any cost forms the closing chapters of the novel.

Newsweek's Walter Clemons writes that *White Noise* should win DeLillo "wide recognition, till now only flickeringly granted as one of the best American novelists. Comic and touching, ingenious and weird, 'White Noise' looks, at first, reassuringly like an example of a familiar genre, the campus novel." But, he goes on to say, the novel "tunes us in on frequencies we haven't heard in other accounts of how we live now. Occult supermarket tabloids are joined with TV disaster footage as household staples providing nourishment and febrile attractions. Fleeting appearances or phone calls from the Gladneys' previous spouses give us the start of surprise we experience when we learn that couples we know have a previous family we haven't heard about." Also commenting on DeLillo's depiction of domestic scenes is Jay McInerney, who writes in the *New Republic* that "DeLillo's portrait of this postnuclear family is one of the simpler pleasures of this novel. Gladney's oldest, Heinrich, is a sullen and precocious fourteen-year-old who plays chess by mail with a convicted murderer and keeps his father off balance with sophistic deconstructions of conventional wisdom, and bulletins from the frontiers of high school chemistry. Denise, eleven, is engaged in a constant campaign to root out her mother's faults, particularly short-term memory loss, and to instruct her stepsister, Steffie, in the cruel ways of the world. Wilder, the baby, is the holy innocent, the preverbal totem figure who gives the family a precious and fragile sense of identity." Bert Testa hypothesizes in the Toronto *Globe and Mail* that "*White Noise* plays off the familiar and the disturbing without ever tipping into the merely grotesque. When DeLillo constantly returns to Jack's quotidian family life, he means his readers to enter a firmly drawn circle that not even a little toxic apocalypse can break."

One of the few dissenting opinions on the success of *White Noise* is offered by *Washington Post Book World* reviewer Jonathan Yardley. Acknowledging that DeLillo is "a prodigiously gifted writer," Yardley then admonishes the author for squandering his efforts on "fiction as political tract. This is what makes DeLillo so irritating and frustrating," Yardley continues, "he's a writer of stupendous talents, yet he wastes those talents on monotonously apocalyptic novels the essential business of which is to retail the shopworn campus ideology of the '60s and '70s. . . . He's a pamphleteer, not a novelist." In direct contrast to those who find the Gladney family poignant and beautifully rendered,

Yardley dismisses them as puppets, lacking "genuine humanity" and existing solely to parrot DeLillo's ideas. "DeLillo can *write*," concludes Yardley. "But that's not enough. Until he has something to say that comes from the heart rather than the evening news, his novels will fall short of his talents."

Addressing her *New York Review of Books* essay directly to Yardley's objections, Diane Johnson defends DeLillo's political themes: "Is topicality only transmogrified into art with the passage of time? Without a willingness to engage the problems of the world around him, we would not have the novels of Dickens, just as, without an acid tone and interest in abstraction we would not have the novels of Voltaire. . . . Besides, there is the special pleasure afforded by the extraordinary language, the coherence of the imagery, saturated with chemicals and whiteness and themes of poisons and shopping, the nice balance of humor and poignance, solemn nonsense and real questions." Echoing these sentiments, Jay McInerney concludes: "*White Noise* is a stunning performance from one of our finest and most intelligent novelists. . . . At his best, DeLillo masterfully orchestrates the idioms of pop culture, science, computer technology, advertising, politics, semiotics, espionage, and about thirty other specialized vocabularies. . . . *White Noise* is one of his most accessible novels. Access and interface with it immediately."

"The world of *Libra* is not the modern or technological brilliant world that characters in my other novels try to confront," De-Lillo explained his 1988 fiction offering to the *New York Times*'s Herbert Mitgang. "This is a different kind of novel, a terminus of human feelings. It takes place at the far end of the map." In *Libra* DeLillo mixes fact with fiction in a discussion of the events that led to the assassination of President John F. Kennedy on November 22, 1963, in Dallas, Texas. He dispels the myth that Kennedy was shot by a lone gunman, Lee Harvey Oswald, by uncovering information supporting a conspiracy theory, acknowledged by some historians. DeLillo spent three years researching and writing about Oswald's life, tracing his career as a Marxist in the American military and his consequent defection to the Soviet Union and return to the United States. DeLillo surmises that in America a coterie of underworld and government figures—enemies of Kennedy—recruited Oswald as a scapegoat for an assassination attempt that should have been botched.

"At what point exactly does fact drift over into fiction?" Anne Tyler asked in her *New York Times Book Review* critique of *Libra*. "The book is so seamlessly written that perhaps not even those people who own . . . copies of the Warren report could say for certain." Richard Eder in the *Los Angeles Times Book Review* agreed, noting that in the novel "DeLillo disassembles his plots with the finest of jigsaw cuts, scrambles their order and has us reassemble them. As the assorted characters go about their missions, we discern them more by intuition than by perception. The chronology goes back and forth, disorienting us. We do not so much follow what is going on as infiltrate it." Robert Dunn observed in *Mother Jones* that in his study of the president's assassin DeLillo "has found a story beyond imagination, one whose significance is indisputable and ongoing . . . and he carefully hews to known facts and approaches all events with respect, even awe. By giving Oswald and the forces he represents full body, DeLillo has written his best novel."

BIOGRAPHICAL/CRITICAL SOURCES:

BOOKS

Bestsellers 89, Issue 1, Gale, 1989.

Contemporary Literary Criticism, Gale, Volume 8, 1978, Volume 10, 1979, Volume 13, 1980, Volume 27, 1984, Volume 39, 1986, Volume 54, 1989.

DeLillo, Don, *Americana,* Houghton, 1971.

DeLillo, Don, *Players,* Knopf, distributed by Random House, 1977.

DeLillo, Don, *White Noise,* Viking, 1985.

Dictionary of Literary Biography, Volume 6: *American Novelists Since World War II, Second Series,* Gale, 1980.

PERIODICALS

America, August 7, 1976, July 6-13, 1985.

Antioch Review, spring, 1972, winter, 1983.

Atlantic, August, 1976, February, 1985.

Chicago Tribune Book World, November 7, 1982, January 3, 1985, July 31, 1988.

Contemporary Literature, winter, 1982.

Critique: Studies in Modern Fiction, Volume 20, number 1, 1978.

Detroit News, February 24, 1985.

Globe and Mail (Toronto), March 9, 1985, August 27, 1988.

Harper's, September, 1977, December, 1982.

Los Angeles Times, July 29, 1984, August 12, 1988.

Los Angeles Time s Book Review, November 7, 1982, January 13, 1985, July 31, 1988.

Maclean's, August 29, 1988.

Mother Jones, September, 1988.

Nation, September 17, 1977, October 18, 1980, December 11, 1982, February 2, 1985, September 19, 1988.

National Review, October 28, 1977.

New Republic, October 7, 1978, November 22, 1982, February 4, 1985.

Newsweek, June 7, 1976, August 29, 1977, October 25, 1982, January 21, 1985, August 15, 1988.

New Yorker, July 12, 1976, March 27, 1978, September 18, 1978, April 4, 1983.

New York Review of Books, June 29, 1972, December 16, 1982, March 14, 1985, August 18, 1988.

New York Times, May 6, 1971, March 22, 1972, April 16, 1973, May 27, 1976, August 11, 1977, September 16, 1980, October 12, 1982, January 7, 1985, December 20, 1987, December 21, 1987, July 19, 1988, May 18, 1989, September 24, 1989.

New York Times Book Review, May 30, 1971, April 9, 1972, April 22, 1973, June 20, 1976, September 4, 1977, November 12, 1978, October 10, 1982, January 13, 1985, July 24, 1988.

Partisan Review, Number 3, 1979.

Publishers Weekly, August 19, 1988.

Saturday Review, September 3, 1977, September 16, 1978.

Time, June 7, 1976, November 8, 1982, January 21, 1985, August 1, 1988.

Times (London), January 23, 1986.

Times Literary Supplement, September 14, 1973, December 9, 1983, January 17, 1986.

USA Today, January 11, 1985.

Village Voice, April 30, 1985.

Voice Literary Supplement, December, 1981, November, 1982.

Washington Post, August 24, 1988, May 11, 1989.

Washington Post Book World, April 16, 1972, April 15, 1973, June 13, 1976, August 21, 1977, October 15, 1978, October 10, 1982, January 13, 1985, July 31, 1988.

DELORIA, Vine (Victor), Jr. 1933-

PERSONAL: Born March 26, 1933, in Martin, S.D.; son of Vine (a clergyman) and Barbara (Eastburn) Deloria; married Barbara Jeanne Nystrom, June 14, 1958; children: Philip, Daniel, Jeanne. *Education:* Iowa State University, B.S., 1958; Lutheran School of Theology, Rock Island, Ill., M.Th., 1963; University of Colorado, J.D., 1970. *Politics:* Republican. *Religion:* "Seven Day Absentist."

ADDRESSES: Home—Tucson, Ariz. 85710. *Office*—Department of Political Science, University of Arizona, Tucson, Ariz. 85721.

CAREER: United Scholarship Service, Denver, Colo., staff associate, 1963-64; National Congress of American Indians, Washington, D.C., executive director, 1964-67; Institute for the Development of Indian Law, Golden, Colo., chairman, 1970-76; University of Arizona, Tucson, professor of political science, 1978—, chairman of American Indian studies, 1979-82. Lecturer at Western Washington State College (now University), 1970-72, and University of California, Los Angeles, 1972-74. Member, Board of Inquiry on Hunger and Malnutrition in the United States, 1967-68, executive council of Episcopal Church, 1969-70, and National Office for Rights of the Indigent. Consultant to U.S. Senate Select Committee on Aging. *Military service:* U.S. Marine Corps Reserve, 1954-56.

MEMBER: Amnesty International, American Bar Association, American Judicature Society, Authors Guild, Authors League of America, Advocates for the Arts, American Indian Resource Association (vice chairman, 1973-75), Colorado Authors League.

AWARDS, HONORS: Anisfield-Wolf Award, 1970, for *Custer Died for Your Sins;* D.H.Litt., Augustana College, 1971; Indian Achievement Award from Indian Council Fire, 1972; D.H.L., Scholastica College, 1976, and Hamline University, 1979; Distinguished Alumni Award, Iowa State University, 1977, and University of Colorado School of Law, 1985.

WRITINGS:

Custer Died for Your Sins: An Indian Manifesto, Macmillan, 1969.

We Talk, You Listen: New Tribes, New Turf, Macmillan, 1970.

(Compiler) *Of Utmost Good Faith,* Straight Arrow Books, 1971.

God Is Red, Grosset, 1973.

Behind the Trail of Broken Treaties: An Indian Declaration of Independence, Delacorte, 1974.

The Indian Affair, Friendship, 1974.

Indians of the Pacific Northwest, Doubleday, 1977.

The Metaphysics of Modern Existence, Harper, 1979.

(With Clifford Lytle) *American Indians, American Justice,* University of Texas Press, 1983.

(With Lytle) *The Nations Within: The Past and Future of American Indian Sovereignty,* Pantheon, 1984.

EDITOR

(And author of introduction) Jennings Cooper Wise, *The Red Man in the New World Drama,* Macmillan, 1971.

(With Sandra L. Cadwalader) *The Aggressions of Civilization: Federal Indian Policy Since the 1880s,* Temple University Press, 1984.

A Sender of Words: Essays in Memory of John G. Neihardt, Howe Brothers, 1984.

American Indian Policy in the Twentieth Century, University of Oklahoma Press, 1984.

WORK IN PROGRESS: Research on Indian legends concerning the creation of mountains, rivers, and other natural phenomena; research on Indian treaties, social problems, and political history.

SIDELIGHTS: "Among his people Vine Deloria, Jr., has achieved a status somewhat similar to that of Sitting Bull's leadership of the Sioux tribes a century ago," writes Dee Brown in the *New York Times Book Review.* A Standing Rock Sioux lawyer and educator, Deloria is perhaps the most prominent spokesman in the country for native American nationalism. Brought to public attention in 1969 with the publication of his first book, *Custer Died for Your Sins: An Indian Manifesto,* Deloria, says Douglas N. Mount of *Publishers Weekly,* "wants to be the red man's Ralph Nader." To that end, he has, in addition to having served as executive director of the National Congress of American Indians and chairman of the Institute for the Development of Indian Law, written several books which serve as legal and historical sourcebooks as well as sharply defined statements of Indian nationalism.

Custer Died for Your Sins: An Indian Manifesto is both a scathing indictment of white America's treatment of Indians and an articulation of the goal of Indian activists: an existence that is culturally but not economically separate. J. A. Phillips of *Best Sellers* notes that if this book "is indicative of Deloria's methods, he's more interested in results than in being tactful. Nauseated by the traditional Indian image, he asserts the worth if not the dignity of the redman and blasts the political, social, and religious forces that perpetuate the Little Big Horn and wigwam stereotyping of his people." A *Time* critic writes that what Deloria really wants to talk about, aside from the origins of scalping and the differences between Black and Indian nationalism, is something "few white Americans know anything about—termination and tribalism." Termination is a U.S. Government policy designed to cut federal aid to Indians, close down reservations, and blend all remaining Indians into the American economic and cultural mainstream. The *Time* critic says that in Deloria's opinion, "the termination policy, which implies integration of Indians, is a loser's game."

Deloria sees tribalism—whereby peoplehood, land, and religion form a single covenantal relationship that gives each community unique character—as the key to the whole Indian struggle, but adds that it may also be the Indians' greatest liability. In an interview with Mount, he describes tribalism as "a way of life, a way of thinking, . . . a great tradition which is timeless, which has nothing to do with the sequence of events. This creates a wonderful relaxing atmosphere, a tremendous sense of invulnerability." But he cautions that it also fosters the impression that the white man will just go away and leave the Indian alone.

Tribalism is also the subject of Deloria's second book, *We Talk, You Listen: New Tribes, New Turf.* Examining what he considers to be the deteriorating core of contemporary technological society, Deloria attacks the corporate patterns of American life, advocates a return to tribal social organization, and describes the tribal characteristics he perceives in American minority groups. Cecil Eby of *Book World* writes that in this book, as well as in *Custer Died for Your Sins,* Deloria "describes the thrust of the Red-Power movement without anointing himself as its oracle or its official spokesman. . . . [He] brings into focus the moods and habitat of the contemporary Indian as seen by a Standing Rock Sioux, not by a research anthropologist or a jobber in the basketry trades. He peels away layers of tinsel and feathers heaped upon the Indian by misinformed whites . . . and he reveals an uncanny ability for impaling them on the fine points of

their own illogic." However, N. Scott Momaday, writing in the *New York Review of Books,* considers Deloria's portrayal of the contemporary Indian weak: "Deloria is a thoughtful man, and he is articulate as well; but [*Custer Died for Your Sins* and *We Talk, You Listen*] are disappointing in one respect: they tell us very little about Indians, after all. In neither book is there any real evocation of that spirit and mentality which distinguishes the Indian as a man and as a race. This seems all the more regrettable in view of the fact that he really knows something about the subject by virtue of blood as well as experience."

In *God Is Red,* Deloria, the son of an Indian Episcopalian clergyman and himself seminary-trained, not only attempts to evoke that spirit and mentality which is unique to the Indian but argues that its theological basis in tribal religions seems to be "more at home in the modern world than Christian ideas and Western man's traditional concepts." Asserting that Christianity inculcates and justifies imperialism, rootlessness, and ecocide, Deloria maintains that America can survive only if there is a revolution in theological concepts. Peter Mayer says in *Best Sellers* that "Deloria could have made his point—that Indian religious practices are far more in accord with the necessities of contemporary life than are Christian—without dredging up the many failures of the sons of the Church upon the earth. . . . But read the book; I found it hard to put down."

Serving as an Indian treaties expert, Deloria was the first witness for the defense in the Wounded Knee trial of 1974, held in St. Paul, Minnesota. His book *Behind the Trail of Broken Treaties* "is not only the best account yet written of events leading to Wounded Knee 1973," writes Dee Brown in the *New York Times Book Review,* but "it is also a compelling argument for a reopening of the treaty-making procedure between Indian tribes and the U.S. Government." L. A. Howard of *Best Sellers* echoes Brown's assessment: "Step by step, argument by argument, [Deloria] refutes those who would label treaty-making as an implausible way at best for the United States to conduct its relations with the American Indians. L. E. Oliva of *Library Journal* notes that Deloria does not consider this proposal "as a panacea but simply as a necessary first step" to insure the survival of Indian tribes, their lands, and their ways of life. What Deloria hopes for is a new treaty relationship which will give Indian tribes the status of quasi-international independence, with the United States acting as protector.

BIOGRAPHICAL/CRITICAL SOURCES:

BOOKS

Contemporary Literary Criticism, Volume XXI, Gale, 1982.
Deloria, Vine, Jr., *Custer Died for Your Sins: An Indian Manifesto,* Macmillan, 1969.
Deloria, Vine, Jr., *God Is Red,* Grosset, 1973.
Gridley, Marian E., *Contemporary American Indian Leaders,* Dodd, 1972.
Gridley, Marian E., editor, *Indians of Today,* I.C.F.P., 1971.

PERIODICALS

America, March 16, 1974, May 22, 1976.
American Anthropologist, Volume LXXIII, number 4, 1971, Volume LXXVII, number 1, 1975.
American Political Science Review, December, 1976.
Best Sellers, October 15, 1969, November 15, 1973, September 1, 1974.
Booklist, September 1, 1977.
Book World, October 4, 1970.
Choice, December, 1974, April, 1975.
Christian Century, February 18, 1970.

Christian Science Monitor, February, 26, 1970, January 2, 1974.
Commonweal, February 6, 1970.
Harper's, November, 1970.
Mademoiselle, April, 1971.
Nation, January 26, 1970, February 9, 1974.
New Yorker, October 24, 1970.
New York Review of Books, April 8, 1971.
New York Times Book Review, November 9, 1969, September 13, 1970, November 24, 1974.
Pacific Historical Review, November, 1970.
Publishers Weekly, December 1, 1969.
Saturday Review, October 4, 1969.
School Library Journal, April, 1977.
Time, October 10, 1969.

*   *   *

del REY, Lester 1915-

(John Alvarez, Cameron Hall, Marion Henry, Wade Kaempfert, Henry Marion, Philip St. John, Erik van Lhin, Kenneth Wright; joint pseudonyms: Philip James, Edson McCann, Charles Satterfield)

PERSONAL: Name originally Ramon Felipe San Juan Mario Silvo Enrico Alvarez del Rey; born June 2, 1915, in Clydesdale, Minn.; son of Franc (a carpenter and farmer) and Jane (Sidway) del Rey; married Evelyn Harrison (marriage ended); married fourth wife, Judy-Lynn Benjamin (a writer and science fiction editor), March 21, 1971. *Education:* Attended George Washington University, 1931-33. *Politics:* Independent.

ADDRESSES: Home—310 East 46th St., New York, N.Y. 10017. *Agent*—Scott Meredith Literary Agency, 845 Third Ave., New York, N.Y. 10022.

CAREER: Writer and editor. Fantasy editor, Ballantine books, beginning in 1975. Teacher of fantasy fiction at New York University, 1972-73. Author's agent, Scott Meredith Literary Agency, 1947-50. Sheet metal worker, McDonnell Aircraft Corp., 1942-44.

MEMBER: Authors Guild, Authors League of America, Society of Illustrators, Trap Door Spiders Club.

AWARDS, HONORS: Boy's Clubs of America science fiction award, 1953, for *Marooned on Mars;* guest of honor, World Science Fiction Convention, 1967.

WRITINGS:

. . . And Some Were Human, Prime Press, 1948, abridged edition, Ballantine, 1961.
It's Your Atomic Age: An Exploration in Simple Everyday Terms of the Meaning of Atomic Energy to the Average Person, Abelard Press, 1951.
(Editor and author of introduction with Cecile Matschat and Carl Cramer) *The Year after Tomorrow: An Anthology of Science Fiction Stories,* Winston, 1954.
(With Frederik Pohl under pseudonym Edson McCann) *Preferred Risk,* Simon & Schuster, 1955.
Nerves, Ballantine, 1956, revised edition, 1976.
(Under pseudonym Erik van Lhin) *Police Your Planet,* Avalon, 1956, enlarged edition published under name Lester del Rey with Erik van Lhin, Ballantine, 1975.
Robots and Changelings: Eleven Science Fiction Stories, Ballantine, 1957.
Day of the Giants, Avalon, 1959.
(Author of introduction) Hans Santesson, editor, *The Fantastic Universe Omnibus,* Prentice-Hall, 1960.

The Mysterious Earth, Chilton, 1960.
The Mysterious Sea, Chilton, 1961.
The Eleventh Commandment, Regency Books, 1962, revised edition, Ballantine, 1970.
Two Complete Novels: The Sky Is Falling [and] *Badge of Infamy,* Galaxy, 1963, reissued as *The Sky Is Falling* [and] *Badge of Infamy,* Ace, 1973.
The Mysterious Sky, Chilton, 1964.
Mortals and Monsters: Twelve Science Fiction Stories, Ballantine, 1965.
(With Paul Fairman) *The Scheme of Things,* Belmont, 1966.
Pstalemate, Putnam, 1971, reissued, Ballantine, 1986.
(Author of introduction) Robert Silverberg, editor, *The Day the Sun Stood Still,* Thomas Nelson, 1972.
(Editor) *Best Science Fiction Stories of the Year,* Volumes I-V, Dutton, 1972-76.
Gods and Golems, Five Short Novels of Science Fiction, Ballantine, 1973.
(Editor and author of introduction with Isaac Asimov) *John W. Campbell Anthology,* Doubleday, 1973.
(Editor and author of introduction) *The Best of Frederik Pohl,* Doubleday, 1975.
(Editor and author of introduction) *The Best of C. L. Moore,* Ballantine, 1975.
(Editor and author of introduction) *Fantastic Science Fiction Art,* Ballantine, 1975.
Early del Rey, Doubleday, 1975.
(Editor and author of introduction) *The Best of John W. Campbell,* Doubleday, 1976.
(Author of introduction) *The Best of Robert Bloch,* Ballantine, 1977.
(Author of introduction) *The Fantastic Art of Boris Vallejo,* Ballantine, 1978.
The Best of Lester del Rey, Ballantine, 1978.
(With Raymond F. Jones) *Weeping May Tarry,* Pinnacle Books, 1978.
(Editor) *The Best of Hal Clement,* Ballantine, 1979.
The World of Science Fiction: 1926-1976, Garland, 1980.

Also editor of science fiction books published by Garland Publishing, including *New Lands* and *Wild Talents* by Charles Fort, *In Caverns Below* by Stanton A. Coblentz, *Shot into Infinity* by Otto W. Gail, *Destination Infinity* by Henry Kuttner, *Skylark Duquesne* by Edward E. Smith, and *The Brain Machine* and *Venus Equilateral* by George O. Smith, all 1975.

FOR CHILDREN

A Pirate Flag for Monterey, Winston, 1952.
Marooned on Mars, Winston, 1952.
(Under pseudonym Philip St. John) *Rocket Jockey,* Winston, 1952, reissued, Ballantine, 1982 (published in England as *Rocket Pilot,* Hutchinson, 1955).
Attack from Atlantis, Winston, 1953, reissued, Ballantine, 1982.
(Under pseudonym Erik van Lhin) *Battle on Mercury,* Winston, 1953.
(Under pseudonym Kenneth Wright) *The Mysterious Planet,* Winston, 1953, reissued under name Lester del Rey, Ballantine, 1982.
Step to the Stars, Winston, 1954.
(Under pseudonym Philip St. John) *Rockets to Nowhere,* Winston, 1954.
Mission to the Moon, Winston, 1956.
Rockets through Space: The Story of Man's Preparations to Explore the Universe, Winston, 1957, revised edition, 1960.
The Cave of Spears, Knopf, 1957.
Space Flight, Golden Press, 1959.

Moon of Mutiny, Holt, 1961, reissued, Ballantine, 1982.
Rocks and What They Tell Us, Whitman, 1961.
Outpost of Jupiter, Holt, 1963, reissued, Ballantine, 1982.
(With Fairman) *Rocket from Infinity,* Holt, 1966.
(With Fairman) *The Infinite Worlds of Maybe,* Holt, 1966.

OTHER

Also author of plot outlines for novels ghostwritten by Paul Fairman and published under name Lester del Rey, including *Siege Perilous,* Lancer, 1966, published as *The Man without a Planet,* Lancer, 1970, *Runaway Robot* (for children), Westminster, 1965, *Tunnel through Time* (for children), Westminster, 1966, and *Prisoners of Space* (for children), Westminster, 1966.

Contributor of short fiction, sometimes under pseudonyms John Alvarez, Marion Henry, Philip James, Wade Kaempfert, and Henry Marion, to periodicals, including *Galaxy, Analog, Amazing Stories, Fantastic Universe,* and *Fantasy and Science Fiction.* Editor of science fiction magazines, 1952-74, including *Science Fiction Adventures,* under pseudonym Philip St. John, 1952-53, *Fantasy Fiction,* 1953 (one issue appeared under pseudonym Cameron Hall), *Rocket Stories,* under pseudonym Wade Kaempfert, 1953, and *Worlds of Fantasy,* 1968-70; *Galaxy* and *If* magazines, managing editor, 1968-69, feature editor, 1969-74.

SIDELIGHTS: "If there is a finer short story craftsman in all of [science fiction than Lester del Rey], show him to me," challenges Algis Budrys in the *Magazine of Fantasy and Science Fiction.* "Don't show me the hosts of more widely admired ones, or the more popular ones, or the more ideologically accepted ones of the moment. Never mind the ones who write more elegant words. Just show me the one who knows more about communicating with the reader, and the handful of those who have endured longer than he." As one of the pioneer writers and editors of science fiction, Lester del Rey can claim a "unique place in the colorful history" of the genre, writes Greta Eisner in *Dictionary of Literary Biography.* According to Eisner, del Rey has "been instrumental in guiding the fortunes of science fiction from the vagaries of the early pulp-magazine market to the respectability of the prestigious del Rey imprint [Ballantine Books's science fiction and fantasy imprint]."

One of del Rey's most common themes is that of the relationship between man and his creations. In "Helen O'Loy," a variation on the Pygmalion story, a man creates a beautiful female robot and marries her. As he ages, she also does so artificially, to preserve the illusion of her humanity. Although she could have immortality, when her creator dies, she burns out all her circuits. Though labelling this resolution somewhat sentimental, Eisner states that it "in no way detracts from the fundamental question the story raises. . . . What can we hope for by uniting ourselves with the appearance of things as we would have them, instead of committing ourselves to the mysterious, ever-changing, and palpable reality which often eludes us?"

She continues: "Del Rey is preoccupied with the precarious relationship between man and his creations. Often in these tales survival hinges on the sensitivity, vision, and common sense with which man, moral and mutable, handles the inorganic creatures produced by his fertile brain. The struggle between man as maker-creator and man as destroyer is a struggle for the survival of man himself—and for his humanity. This theme, effectively tapping into a primary anxiety of our age, becomes the axis of del Rey's fiction." Eisner criticizes some of del Rey's work—particularly his juvenile novels—as suffering from thin characterization. However, Budrys disagrees, writing, "When [del Rey]

thinks of a character, he thinks that person through to the last electron."

Eisner concludes: "At his best, del Rey is a sensitive and articulate spokesman for humanistic values in a world no longer able to discern properly what constitutes the uniquely human and thus no longer willing to cherish and preserve it. Del Rey balances cynicism and optimism: man, he seems to say, carries within him the seeds of his own destruction and the means of his own salvation. In the balance is all of civilization, and del Rey skillfully charts for his readers some of the crucial distance between the struggle and the promise."

Del Rey told *CA:* "I do believe that science fiction or fantasy must entertain and must have beginning, middle and end; that stories are read for the plot and re-read for the characterization—if there is any; and that science, when used, should be accurate, and consistency and logic be observed. My knowledge of science is not formal, but is sufficient to discuss (and edit) the work of qualified scientists. I've written books on nuclear physics, rocketry, geology, oceanography, and astronomy. My best knowledge is in physics, mathematics, and electronics.

"So far as I can determine, my writing was not strongly influenced by any single science fiction writer. My reading background was always catholic, from Shakespeare (long before I ever saw a play or found that the works were supposed to be Great Literature) and Gibbon to Burroughs and Merritt. If anything influenced me, probably the Bible (as literature—at least in part) and the whole range of better pulp fiction made the strongest impression on me.

"I do *not* believe in ESP (or psi), flying saucers, Bermuda triangles, the need for relevance in science fiction (beyond the universals that exist beyond current fads), or the insignificance of man."

AVOCATIONAL INTERESTS: Cabinet making, baseball, football, hockey, cooking, typewriters, hi-fi equipment, and music (especially classical, but "even some oriental and real hillbilly-western music, and real jazz").

BIOGRAPHICAL/CRITICAL SOURCES:

BOOKS

Dictionary of Literary Biography, Volume VIII: *Twentieth-Century American Science Fiction Writers,* Gale, 1981.
Moskowitz, Sam, *Seekers of Tomorrow,* Hyperion Press, 1974.

PERIODICALS

Choice, June, 1980.
Magazine of Fantasy and Science Fiction, March, 1979.
Times (London), April 14, 1983.
Times Literary Supplement, February 2, 1973.
Washington Post Book World, December 23, 1979.

*   *   *

de MAN, Paul (Adolph Michel)   1919-1983

PERSONAL: Born December 6, 1919, in Antwerp, Belgium; immigrated to United States, 1947; died of cancer, December 21, 1983, in New Haven, Conn.; son of Robert (a manufacturer of X-ray equipment) and Magdalena (de Brey) de Man; married Anaide Baraghian, 1943 (marriage ended); married Patricia Kelley, 1950; children: (first marriage) Hendrik, Robert, Marc; (second marriage) Patricia, Michael. *Education:* University of Brussels, Candidature, 1942; Harvard University, M.A., 1958, Ph.D., 1960.

ADDRESSES: Home—Woodbridge, Conn.

CAREER: Le Soir (daily newspaper), Brussels, Belgium, writer, 1940-42; worked as a translator and in publishing business in Brussels and Antwerp, Belgium, 1942-47; affiliated with faculty of University of Zurich, Zurich, Switzerland; Bard College, Annandale-on-Hudson, N.Y., teacher of French literature, 1949-51; Berlitz School, Boston, Mass., French teacher, beginning in 1951; Harvard University, Cambridge, Mass., lecturer, c. 1955-60; Cornell University, Ithaca, N.Y., teacher, 1960-67; Johns Hopkins University, Baltimore, Md., professor of humanistic studies, 1967-70; Yale University, New Haven, Conn., 1970-83, became Sterling Professor of Humanities and chairman of department of comparative literature.

WRITINGS:

(Translator) Paul Alverdes, *Le Double Visage,* Editions de la Toison d'Or (Brussels), 1942.

(Translator) Filip de Pillecyn, *Le Soldat Johan,* Editions de la Toison d'Or, 1942.

(Translator) Albert Erich Brinckmann, *Esprit des nations,* Editions de la Toison d'Or, 1943.

(Translator) Herman Melville, *Moby Dick,* Helicon, Kipdorp (Antwerp), 1945.

(Editor and translator) Gustave Flaubert, *Madame Bovary: Backgrounds and Sources; Essays in Criticism,* Norton, 1965.

Field of Comparative Literature: Analysis of Needs, [Ithaca, N.Y.], 1967.

Blindness and Insight: Essays in the Rhetoric of Contemporary Criticism, Oxford University Press, 1971, 2nd edition, revised, with introduction by Wlad Godzich, University of Minnesota Press, 1983.

(Editor) Ranier Maria Rilke, *Oeuvres,* Editions du Seuil, 1972.

Allegories of Reading: Figural Language in Rousseau, Nietzsche, Rilke, and Proust, Yale University Press, 1979.

(With Harold Bloom, Jacques Derrida, Geoffrey H. Hartman, and J. Hillis Miller) *Deconstruction and Criticism,* Seabury Press, 1979.

The Rhetoric of Romanticism, Columbia University Press, 1984.

The Resistance to Theory, foreword by Wlad Godzich, University of Minnesota Press, 1986.

Aesthetic Ideology, edited by Andrzej Warminski, University of Minnesota Press, 1988.

Fugitive Writings, edited by Lindsay Waters, University of Minnesota Press, 1988.

Wartime Journalism, 1939-1943, University of Nebraska Press, 1988.

Critical Writings, 1953-1978, introduction by Lindsay Waters, University of Minnesota Press, 1988.

Also author of foreword to Carol Jacobs's *The Dissimulating Harmony,* 1978. Contributor to American, Flemish, and French periodicals, including *Critical Inquiry, Critique, Het Vlaamsche Land, Les Cahiers du libre examen, Monde nouveau, Preuves,* and *Revue internationale de philosophie.*

SIDELIGHTS: "Venerated as a teacher and scholar, [Paul de Man] was the originator of a controversial theory of language that some say may place him among the greatest thinkers of his age," a *New York Times* reporter professed. De Man and French philosopher Jacques Derrida revolutionized literary criticism in America by devising deconstructionism, a theory that emphasizes the uncertainty of meaning caused by the imprecision of language. But after de Man's death in 1983 his work was clouded in controversy when a student compiling a bibliography of his works uncovered numerous articles that he had written for a pro-

Nazi and anti-Semitic newspaper, *Le Soir,* in his native Belgium between 1940 and 1942.

Born in Antwerp and graduated from the University of Brussels, de Man immigrated to the United States following World War II and took his master's degree and doctorate at Harvard University. He subsequently taught at Cornell and Johns Hopkins universities before settling at Yale University in 1970, where he stayed until his death in 1983. His presence at Yale, as well as the presence of other outstanding deconstructive critics including J. Hillis Miller and Geoffrey Hartman, brought great prestige to the school, which subsequently became known as the seat of deconstructive theory in the United States.

During his second year at Yale de Man published *Blindness and Insight: Essays in the Rhetoric of Contemporary Criticism,* a collection of articles that previously appeared in journals during de Man's tenure at Harvard and Cornell. Revised in 1983 with five additional essays, *Blindness and Insight* is considered by scholars to be the best introduction to de Man's early academic work. The volume includes such essays as "Criticism and Crisis," "Literary History and Literary Modernity," and an English translation of de Man's 1956 article "Impasse de la critique formaliste," which introduced French readers to New Criticism, an Anglo-American literary theory that was considered radical at the time. The New Critics maintained that a text's meaning could be discovered by reconciling its ambiguities and contradictions, disregarding the influences of an author's psychology, biography, culture, and politics on the text's meaning.

"To write critically about critics," de Man wrote in *Blindness and Insight,* "becomes a way to reflect on the paradoxical effectiveness of a blinded vision that has to be rectified by means of insights that it unwittingly provides," Jonathan Culler quoted the author in the *Dictionary of Literary Biography.* In *Blindness and Insight* de Man explains the principle behind a deconstructive reading: a scholar, when closely reading a text, can uncover many of the author's unstated philosophical, cultural, and linguistic assumptions by exposing contradictions that appear in the language of a text. In turn, a subsequent critic can discover the hidden assumptions in that scholar's analysis. Thus deconstruction posits the radical notion that the meaning of the text resides as much in the act of interpretation as in the words of the text itself.

Blindness and Insight contains deconstructive readings of texts such as "Heidegger's Exegesis of Holderlin," in which de Man critiques German philosopher Martin Heidegger's study of works by German poet Friedrich Holderlin. Also included is an essay on Hungarian Marxist philosopher and critic Gyorgy Lukacs's reading of French novelist Gustave Flaubert's *Education sentimentale,* as well as what many consider de Man's most influential work, an analysis of Derrida's criticism of writings by French author Jean-Jacques Rousseau. Articles such as these by de Man and other deconstructive scholars often brought scorn upon the new school of criticism; its detractors, such as *New York Review of Books* contributor Denis Donoghue, discounted the system as "mainly a commentary written in the margin of other philosophical and literary texts." Nonetheless, Culler attests, with *Blindness and Insight* scholars began reading literary criticism with the kind of attention that was only given previously to literary and philosophical works.

Allegories of Reading: Figural Language in Rousseau, Nietzsche, Rilke, and Proust, de Man's second collection of essays, consists of works published in journals during the 1970s. A volume of dense and difficult close readings of works by French and German writers, it contains analyses of Rousseau's novel *La Nou-*

velle Heloise and *Discourse on the Origin of Language,* Friedrich Nietzsche's philosophical treatise *The Birth of Tragedy,* many of Ranier Maria Rilke's poems, and Marcel Proust's epic novel *Remembrance of Things Past.* In *Allegories of Reading* de Man pays extremely close attention to the use of language in these works, dissecting allegories and metaphors to answer the questions "precisely whether a literary text is *about* that which it describes, represents, or states," Anthony Thorlby cited de Man in the *Times Literary Supplement,* or "whether *all* language is about language."

The main assertion of *Allegories of Reading* (and of deconstructive theory) is that language cannot be taken literally. Because all language is metaphorical, where one set of signs are only substitutions for another, there is no reconcilability or oneness between a word and the idea of the specific object. Robert Alter in *New Republic* explained that deconstruction professes "the relation between word and referent, signifier and signified, is inevitably an arbitrary and conventional one. . . . [W]hat appears to be literal is necessarily metaphorical; what is proffered as reality is in fact fiction." Thus when language uses metaphors to be most authoritative it undermines its own intent by clearly revealing its fictive nature. Furthermore, when studying a literary text the reader cannot reconcile the difference between the opposing literal and the figurative meanings of the work, thus the text is considered "unreadable."

Yet, if de Man's theory is true, *Allegories of Reading* itself—relying on written language—is an unreadable text, according to *Washington Post Book World* contributor Julia Epstein. She observed that in the work "de Man presents a system of figurative language and literary structure. Then, as systematically, he unravels his own system." Indeed, de Man admits that his own theory is disputable. In *Allegories of Reading,* cited by Thorlby, he writes: "A text . . . although it presents itself legitimately as a demystification of literary rhetoric remains entirely literary, rhetorical, and deceptive itself."

A major complaint of deconstructionism's critics is that the theory attacks language's ability to represent reality. Thorlby remarked, "de Man is knowingly condescending towards anyone who . . . enjoys 'a literal or thematic reading that takes the value assertions of the text at their word.' " Epstein, another detractor, stated: "Where other interpreters look for referential meaning, substance, values, truth . . . deconstructors see the traditional quest for meaning as a naive search for the nonexistent." Deconstructionist Culler admits that "De Man's writing grants great authority to texts—a power of illumination which is a power of disruption—but little authority to meaning. . . . His works celebrate great literary and philosophical texts for their insightful undoings of the meanings that usually pass for their value." Thus a work must be read "as though it referred primarily to itself," Thorlby explained de Man's process.

Mark Edmundson, in a *Harper's* article titled "A Will to Cultural Power," echoed Thorlby and Epstein's concerns, stating that "one result of [deconstructive] reading is to place in doubt the myth of the author as a shaping deity. To the deconstructor the author appears to be more a relay point for language than its sovereign authority." Likewise, Denis Donoghue, in a *New York Review of Books* critique of *Deconstruction and Criticism,* a 1979 offering de Man wrote with Harold Bloom, Derrida, Hartman, and Miller, asserts that de Man, in his deconstructive reading of Percy Bysshe Shelley's "The Triumph of Life," denies the poet any active role in the writing process, ascribing to language and grammar what is normally ascribed to the author. Donoghue opined, "If [deconstruction] were to prevail, it would

surround with anxiety and misgiving not only the reading of poems but the negotiation of every major theme in Western literature and philosophy."

The first volume of de Man's essays collected after the author's death in 1983 was published the following year. *The Rhetoric of Romanticism,* compiled from articles written after 1956 and two never before issued, is considered an indispensable tool by scholars of romanticism. In this strictly linguistic approach to romantic and postromantic themes de Man studies the course toward greater concreteness in poetic diction (especially when writing of nature), the shift from the use of allegorical to symbolic language, and the development of the study of the union of imagination and nature. He writes on individual romantics, including Rousseau, William Wordsworth, Shelley, William Butler Yeats, and Holderlin, and examines the general relationship among German, French, and English trends in romanticism. Culler reflected that *The Rhetoric of Romanticism* was extremely influential; it forced literary critics to reassess the place of European romantic writings in the canon of world literature.

Three other collections of de Man's academic essays have been published posthumously. Both *The Resistance to Theory,* consisting of six recent essays focusing on contemporary literary criticism, and *Aesthetic Ideology,* featuring essays on German philosophers Immanuel Kant and Georg Hegel and German writer Friedrich von Schiller, explore the incompatibility of a linguistically oriented and an aesthetic approach to literature. *Fugitive Writings,* also published in 1988, is a group of essays on literary criticism de Man wrote during the 1950s for the French periodicals *Critique* and *Monde nouveau.*

In December, 1987, the *New York Times* revealed that from 1940 until 1942 de Man, under his own name, wrote more than one hundred articles for *Le Soir,* a pro-Nazi and strongly anti-Semitic daily newspaper in his native Belgium, then occupied by the German army. A Belgian graduate student, Ortwin de Graef, came across these essays and book and music reviews when compiling a list of de Man's works. The uncovering of de Man's writings for *Le Soir*—which have been collected in *Wartime Journalism, 1939-1943*—shocked many who knew de Man, for his colleagues considered him an unbiased and affable man. These articles "seem so at odds with the sense of the person I knew later on," reflected Neil Hertz, one of de Man's friends, quoted in the *New York Times.* Shochana Felman, a student of de Man's at Yale, added that she thought he was "almost entirely without prejudice," claiming de Man "took an ethical stance in all his daily life." Peter Brooks, with whom de Man worked at Yale, in a letter to the editor of the *New York Times,* claimed that he and many of de Man's friends and colleagues "wish to testify that [de Man's] life and character, as we knew them, suggested a complete repudiation of the hateful things he wrote in a sordid time."

Many scholars agree that in only one of the articles, "Jews in Contemporary Literature," does de Man take an overtly anti-Semitic stance. In the piece he states that Jews "pollute" modern fiction and that their influence in modern letters is negligible. However, some of de Man's detractors detect anti-Semitic sentiments in his other articles, including reviews of works by Austrian writer Franz Kafka and French historian Daniel Halevy. The revelation increased the existing controversy surrounding deconstruction theory, which the *New York Times* reporter alleged "always reflects the biases of its users." But Hartman, writing in the *New Republic,* rebutted the *New York Times* article, stating that de Man's "position is the very opposite of an idealism that confuses intellect and action, ideology and political praxis." De Man, Hartman asserted, stressed "the non-identity of these realms."

BIOGRAPHICAL/CRITICAL SOURCES:

BOOKS

Contemporary Literary Criticism, Volume 55, Gale, 1989.
Derrida, Jacques, *Memoires: Lectures for Paul de Man,* translated by Cecile Lindsay, Jonathan Culler, and Eduardo Cadava, Columbia University Press, 1986.
Dictionary of Literary Biography, Volume 67: *Modern American Critics Since 1955,* Gale, 1988.
Eagleton, Terry, *Literary Theory: An Introduction,* University of Minnesota Press, 1983.
Responses, University of Nebraska Press, 1989.

PERIODICALS

Critical Inquiry, spring, 1982, summer, 1986.
Harper's, July, 1988.
Insight, January 23, 1989.
Nation, January 9, 1988, April 9, 1988.
New Republic, April 25, 1983, July 7, 1986, March 7, 1988.
Newsweek, February 15, 1988.
New York Review of Books, June 12, 1980.
New York Times, December 1, 1987, August 28, 1988, October 2, 1988, January 25, 1989.
Times Literary Supplement, February 29, 1980, January 17, 1986, November 6, 1987.
Village Voice Literary Supplement, April, 1988.
Washington Post Book World, February 24, 1980.

OBITUARIES:

PERIODICALS

New York Times, December 31, 1983.

*   *   *

DEMIJOHN, Thom
   See DISCH, Thomas M(ichael)

*   *   *

de MONTHERLANT, Henry (Milon)
   See MONTHERLANT, Henry (Milon) de

*   *   *

DENIS, Julio
   See CORTAZAR, Julio

*   *   *

DENMARK, Harrison
   See ZELAZNY, Roger (Joseph)

*   *   *

DENNIS, Nigel (Forbes) 1912-

PERSONAL: Born January 16, 1912, in Surrey, England; son of Michael Frederic Beauchamp (a lieutenant colonel, British Army) and Louise (Bosanquet) Dennis; married first wife, Marie Madeleine Massias (marriage ended); married second wife, Beatrice Matthew, September 13, 1959; children: Frederica Forbes, Michelle (Mrs. John Herbert). *Education:* Educated at an En-

glish preparatory school, followed by Plumtree School in Southern Rhodesia, and Odenwaldschule in Germany. *Religion:* None.

ADDRESSES: Home—Malta. *Agent*—A. M. Heath & Co., 40-42 William IV St., London WC2N 4DD, England.

CAREER: National Board of Review of Motion Pictures, New York City, secretary, 1935-36; *New Republic,* New York City, assistant editor and book review editor, 1937-38; book reviewer for *Time* in New York City, 1940-49, and in London, England, 1949-59; *Encounter* (magazine), London, drama critic, 1960-63, co-editor, 1967-70; *Sunday Telegraph,* London, book reviewer, 1961—.

MEMBER: Royal Society of Literature (fellow), Casino Maltese (Malta).

AWARDS, HONORS: Houghton Mifflin-Eyre & Spottiswoode Prize, 1950, for *A Sea Change;* Royal Society of Literature award, 1965, for *Jonathan Swift: A Short Character;* Heinemann Award, 1966, for nonfiction.

WRITINGS:

A Sea Change (novel), Houghton, 1949 (published in England as *Boys and Girls Come Out to Play,* Eyre & Spottiswoode, 1949).
Cards of Identity (novel), Vanguard, 1955.
Two Plays and a Preface: Cards of Identity and The Making of Moo ("Cards of Identity" is based on novel of same title, first produced on West End at Royal Court Theatre, July, 1956; "The Making of Moo" first produced at Royal Court Theatre, 1957), Weidenfeld & Nicolson, 1958, Vanguard, 1959.
Dramatic Essays, Weidenfeld & Nicolson, 1962.
August for the People (produced on West End at Royal Court Theatre and at Edinburgh Festival, 1962), Samuel French (London), 1962.
Jonathan Swift: A Short Character (biography), Macmillan, 1964.
A House in Order (novel), Vanguard, 1966.
Exotics: Poems of the Mediterranean and Middle East, Weidenfeld & Nicolson, 1970, Vanguard, 1971.
An Essay on Malta, illustrations by Osbert Lancaster, J. Murray, 1972.
"Swansong for Seven Voices" (radio play), British Broadcasting Corporation (BBC), 1985.

SIDELIGHTS: George Wellwarth writes: "Perhaps the reason for [Nigel] Dennis's excellence is that he is an unabashedly intellectual dramatist. At the same time his plays are vastly entertaining and first-rate theater. They do not, however, resemble the average Broadway or West End play. They are not, like commercial dramas, built around a situation into which some references to serious plays have been injected. Dennis's plays, like Shaw's, are built around a serious moral or intellectual problem, and the situation of the play grows out of the problem (that is to say, created solely for the purpose of theatrically illustrating the problem)." A *Times Literary Supplement* reviewer comments that Dennis's novel, *A House in Order,* resembles a Samuel Beckett play. Dennis himself has written, in *Dramatic Essays,* about the plays of Beckett and Eugene Ionesco, and in *A House in Order* has created a character and situation, although in novel rather than play form, very much like those of Beckett and Ionesco. In *Dramatic Essays* he states: "We know immediately that neither Mr. Beckett's nor Mr. Ionesco's images intend to follow a course that exists in real life; we are to watch them move only in parallel to reality, throwing its light upon it but never imitating it except when imitation enhances unreality."

Dennis rebuts the theory of T. S. Eliot and Jean-Paul Sartre that commitment is the main essential of human existence, arguing that the nature of commitment is of far greater importance. The *Times Literary Supplement* reviewer describes *A House in Order,* in which the main character is dedicated to the rearing of plants, as "an allegory on the position of the artist in society." A *Hudson Review* critic writes: "*A House in Order* is beautifully written, in a prose of tense lucidity; it is brief and spare, and it never takes its eye off the target."

Wellwarth says of *Two Plays and a Preface,* "The two plays are preceded by a long and brilliantly written essay that further strengthens Dennis's right to be looked upon as a worthy, direct-line descendant of Shaw." "The Making of Moo," subtitled "A History of Religion in Three Acts," is Dennis's expression of his atheistic beliefs. "Cards of Identity" illustrates Dennis's thesis that modern psychology "exists to provide people with new identities, to replace the inadequate ones they have made for themselves." "For Dennis personal consciousness is not a sign of mental aberration, and his play is a protest against the pressing-iron technique of modern psychiatry. . . . In [him] the English-speaking intellectual drama has found a new representative. . . . [The plays] are superbly written . . . with an innate and instinctive sense of theater. They, together with the brilliantly witty preface . . . [constitute] the best that British drama has produced since the death of Shaw."

In 1934 Nigel Dennis came to New York for a "short visit" which lasted fifteen years. He has a special interest in Italy, the Persian Gulf, and Malta, where he lives.

BIOGRAPHICAL/CRITICAL SOURCES:

BOOKS

Contemporary Fiction in America and England, 1950-1970, Gale, 1976.
Contemporary Literary Criticism, Volume 8, Gale, 1978.
Dictionary of Literary Biography, Gale, Volume 13: *British Dramatists since World War II,* 1982, Volume 15: *British Novelists, 1930-1959,* 1983.
Wellwarth, George, *Theatre of Protest and Paradox,* New York University Press, 1964.

PERIODICALS

Hudson Review, spring, 1967.
New Republic, August 29, 1960.
New York Times Book Review, December 13, 1964.
Time, January 15, 1965.
Times Literary Supplement, October 27, 1966.

*   *   *

de ROUTISIE, Albert
    See ARAGON, Louis

*   *   *

DERSONNES, Jacques
    See SIMENON, Georges (Jacques Christian)

*   *   *

DESAI, Anita   1937-

PERSONAL: Born June 24, 1937, in Mussoorie, India; daughter of D. N. (a businessman) and Toni (Nime) Mazumdar; married Ashvin Desai (an executive), December 13, 1958; children:

Rahul, Tani, Arjun, Kiran. *Education:* Delhi University, B.A., 1957.

*ADDRESSES:*c/o Heinemann Ltd., 10 Upper Grosvenor St., London W1X 9PA, England.

CAREER: Writer. Member of Advisory Board for English, Sahitya Akademi, New Delhi, India, 1972—.

MEMBER: Royal Society of Literature (fellow).

AWARDS, HONORS: Winifred Holtby Prize, Royal Society of Literature, 1978; Sahitya Academy award, 1979; *Guardian* award for children's book, 1982.

WRITINGS:

Cry, The Peacock (novel), P. Owen, 1963.
Voices in the City (novel), P. Owen, 1965.
Bye-Bye, Blackbird (novel), Hind Pocket Books, 1968.
The Peacock Garden (juvenile), India Book House, 1974.
Where Shall We Go This Summer? (novel), Vikas Publishing House, 1975.
Cat on a Houseboat (juvenile), Orient Longmans, 1976.
Fire on the Mountain (novel), Harper, 1977.
Games at Twilight and Other Stories, Heinemann, 1978, Harper, 1980.
Clear Light of Day (novel), Harper, 1980.
The Village by the Sea (juvenile), Heinemann, 1982.
In Custody (novel), Heinemann, 1984, Harper, 1985.
Baumgartner's Bombay (novel), Knopf, 1989.

Contributor of short stories to periodicals, including *Thought, Envoy, Writers Workshop, Quest, Indian Literature, Illustrated Weekly of India, Fesmina,* and *Harper's Bazaar.*

WORK IN PROGRESS: An untitled novel.

SIDELIGHTS: Indian writer Anita Desai focuses her novels upon the personal struggles of her Indian characters to cope with the problems of contemporary life. In this way, she manages to portray the cultural and social changes that her native country has undergone since the departure of the British. One of Desai's major themes is the relationships between family members, and especially the emotional tribulations of women whose independence is suppressed by Indian society. For example, her first novel, *Cry, the Peacock,* concerns a woman who has found it impossible to assert her individuality; the theme of the despairing woman is also explored in Desai's *Where Shall We Go This Summer?* Other novels explore life in urban India (*Voices in the City*), the clash between eastern and western cultures (*Bye-Bye, Blackbird*), and the differences between the generations (*Fire on the Mountain*).

Desai is frequently praised by critics for her ability to capture the local color of her country and the ways in which eastern and western cultures have blended together there, a skill that has become more developed with each successive novel. A large part of this skill is due to her use of imagery, one of the most important devices in Desai's novels. Because of this emphasis on imagery, Desai is referred to by such reviewers as *World Literature Today* contributor Madhusudan Prasad as an "imagist-novelist. . . . [Her use of imagery is] a remarkable quality of her craft that she has carefully maintained in all her later fiction" since *Cry, the Peacock.* Employing this imagery to suggest rather than overtly explain her themes, Desai's plots sometimes appear deceptively simple; but, as Anthony Thwaite points out in *New Republic,* "she is such a consummate artist that she [is able to suggest], beyond the confines of the plot and the machinations of her characters, the immensities that lie beyond them—the immensities of India."

BIOGRAPHICAL/CRITICAL SOURCES:

BOOKS

Bellioppa, Meena, *The Fiction of Anita Desai,* Writers Workshop, 1971.
Contemporary Literary Criticism, Gale, Volume 19, 1981, Volume 37, 1986.
Mukheijee, Meenakshi, *The Twice-Born Fiction,* Arnold Heinemann, 1972.
Srinivasa Iyengar, K. R., *Indian Writing in English,* Asia Publishing House, 1962.
Verghese, Paul, *Indian Writing in English,* Asia Publishing House, 1970.

PERIODICALS

Chicago Tribune, September 1, 1985.
Chicago Tribune Book World, August 23, 1981.
Globe and Mail (Toronto), August 20, 1988.
Los Angeles Times, July 31, 1980.
Los Angeles Times Book Review, March 3, 1985. April 9, 1989.
New Republic, March 18, 1985.
New York Times, November 24, 1980, February 22, 1985, March 14, 1989.
New York Times Book Review, November 20 1977, June 22, 1980, November 23, 1980, April 9, 1989.
Time, July 1, 1985.
Times (London), September 4, 1980.
Times Literary Supplement, September 5, 1980, September 7, 1984, October 19, 1984, July 15, 1988.
Tribune Books (Chicago), March 5, 1989.
Washington Post Book World, January 11, 1981, October 7, 1984, March 31, 1985, February 26, 1989.
World Literature Today, summer, 1984.

* * *

de SAINT ROMAN, Arnaud
See ARAGON, Louis

* * *

DESTOUCHES, Louis-Ferdinand(-Auguste) 1894-1961
(Louis-Ferdinand Celine)

PERSONAL: Born May 27, 1894, in Courbevoie, France; died of a stroke, July 1, 1961, in Paris, France; son of Ferdinand-Auguste Destouches (an insurance executive) and Marguerite-Louise-Celine Guilloux (a businesswoman); married Suzanne Nebout (a barmaid), 1915 (marriage ended, 1916); married Edith Follet, August, 1919 (divorced, 1926); married Lucette Almanzor (a dancer), February, 1943; children: (second marriage) Colette. *Education:* University of Rennes, baccalaureat degree, 1919; University of Paris, medical degree, 1924.

CAREER: Writer and medical doctor. Worked in passport office of French Consulate in London, England, 1915-16; agent with a French lumber company in Africa, 1916-17; worked for Rockefeller Foundation as a health lecturer in Brittany, 1917-20; in private medical practice, Rennes, France, 1924-25; worked as a doctor with the League of Nations, 1925-28, traveling in the United States, Canada, Cuba, Africa, and Switzerland; in private medical practice, Paris, France, 1928-31; doctor with municipal clinic, Clichy, France, 1931-38; volunteer doctor on French naval vessel, 1939; doctor with municipal clinic, Satrouville, France, 1940-41; doctor-in-charge at municipal clinic, Bezons, France, 1942; left France, 1944, and traveled through Germany to Denmark as a collaborationist, 1945, and imprisoned for fourteen months; lived in Koersor, Denmark, 1947-51; received French government amnesty, 1950; returned to France to practice medicine in the town of Meudon. *Military service:* French Army, 1912-15, served in the cavalry; became sergeant; wounded in action; mentioned in dispatches; received Medaille Militaire.

AWARDS, HONORS: Theophraste Renaudot Prize, 1933, for *Voyage au bout de la nuit.*

WRITINGS:

La Vie et l'oeuvre de Philippe-Ignace Semmelweis (doctoral thesis; also see below), Francis Simon (Rennes), 1924, reprinted, Gallimard, 1952.
La Quinine en therapeutique, Doin (Paris), 1925.

UNDER PSEUDONYM LOUIS-FERDINAND CELINE; IN ENGLISH

Voyage au bout de la nuit, Denoel, 1932, reprinted, Gallimard, 1972, translation by J. P. Marks published as *Journey to the End of the Night,* Little, Brown, 1934, reprinted, New Directions, 1983.
Mort a credit, Denoel, 1936, reprinted, Gallimard, 1969, translation by Marks published as *Death on the Installment Plan,* Little, Brown, 1938, new translation by Ralph Manheim, New Directions, 1966.
Mea culpa, suivi de la vie et l'ouvre de Philippe-Ignace Semmelweis (also see below), Denoel, 1937, translation by Robert A. Parker published as *Mea Culpa and the Life and Work of Semmelweis,* Little, Brown, 1937.
Guignol's Band, Denoel, 1941, Gallimard, 1967, translation by B. Frechtman and J. T. Nile published under same title, New Directions, 1954.
Entretiens avec le professeur Y, Gallimard, 1955, bilingual English/French edition with translation by Luce Stanford published as *Conversations with Professor Y,* University Press of New England, 1986.
D'un chateau a l'autre, Gallimard, 1957, translation by Manheim published as *Castle to Castle,* Delacorte, 1968, reprinted, Carroll & Graf, 1987.
Nord, Gallimard, 1960, translation by Manheim published as *North,* Delacorte, 1972.
Rigodon, Gallimard, 1969, translation by Manheim published as *Rigadoon,* Delacorte, 1974.

UNDER PSEUDONYM LOUIS-FERDINAND CELINE; OTHER

L'Eglise (five-act play), Denoel, 1933.
Secrets dans l'ile, Gallimard, 1936.
Hommage a Zola, Denoel, 1936.
Van Bagaden, Denoel, 1937.
Bagatelles pour un massacre, Denoel, 1937.
L'Ecole des cadavres, Denoel, 1938.
Les Beaux Draps, Nouvelles editions francaises, 1941.
Preface pour Bezons a travers les ages, Denoel, 1944.
A l'agite du bocal, P. L. de Tartas, 1948.
Foudres et fleches, C. de Jonquieres, 1949.
Casse-pipe, F. Chambriand, 1949, reprinted (bound with *Carnet du Cuirassier Destouches*), Gallimard, 1975.
Scandale aux abysses, F. Chambriand, 1950.
Feerie pour un autre fois, Gallimard, 1952, reprinted, 1977.
Normance, Gallimard, 1954.

Ballet sans personne, sans musique, sans rien, Gallimard, 1959.

La Naissance d'une fee (ballet), Gallimard, 1959.

Voyou Paul, Pauvre Virginie, Gallimard, 1959.

Vive l'amnestie Monsieur, Editions Dynamo, 1963.

Le Pont de Londres, Gallimard, 1964.

Oeuvres de Louis-Ferdinand Celine, Balland, five volumes, 1966-69.

Romans, edited by Henri Godard, two volumes, Gallimard, 1973-74, revised one-volume edition, 1981.

Semmelweis et autres ecrits medicaux, edited by Jean-Pierre Dauphin and H. Godard, Gallimard, 1977.

Lettres et premiers ecrits d'Afrique (1916-1917), Gallimard, 1977.

Progres, Mercure de France, 1978.

Oeuvres de Celine, edited by Frederic Vitoux, nine volumes, Club de l'Honnete Homme, 1981—.

Lettres a Albert Paraz (1947-1957), Gallimard, 1981.

Chansons, Flute de Pan, 1981.

Arletty, jeune fille dauphinoise, Flute de Pan, 1983.

Lettres a son avocat: 118 lettres inedites a Maitre Albert Naud, Flute de Pan, 1984.

Maudits soupirs pour une autre fois, Gallimard, 1986.

Also author of *Lettres a des amies,* 1980.

SIDELIGHTS: Louis-Ferdinand Celine was among the most distinguished and influential writers of the twentieth century. His five most successful novels—*Journey to the End of the Night, Death on the Installment Plan, Castle to Castle, North,* and *Rigadoon*—introduced a scabrous, hallucinatory approach to fiction that has influenced the work of many writers throughout the world. John Fraser, writing in *Wisconsin Studies in Contemporary Literature,* called Celine "the only genius in French literature since Proust." And yet, for many years Celine faced massive opposition to his work. He was, as David Hayman wrote in his study *Louis-Ferdinand Celine,* "one of the least recognized writers of his generation." The primary reasons for Celine's long obscurity lie in his outspoken political beliefs and the abrasive nature of his literary work. "Celine's harsh style and sordid perspective, his reputation as a collaborationist, his anti-Semitism and racism are largely to blame for this neglect," Hayman contended. Richard Seaver, writing in *Saturday Review,* explained that "political considerations . . . too long deprived Celine of his due." It was not until the 1960s that the literary community began to accept Celine as a major figure and to evaluate his work in unbiased terms.

Celine's controversial novels are marked by misanthropic narrators, free-wheeling invective, ferocious humor, and squalid settings ranging from the jungles of Africa to the factories of Detroit. His unrestrained language is a unique amalgam of French slang, profanity, street grammar, and near-delirium. His episodic plots are rendered in burlesque fashion and are laced with an acidic satire. His work has often been compared to that of such earlier writers as Rimbaud, Baudelaire, and Jarry. Bettina Knapp described Celine's linguistic landscape in her study *Celine: Man of Hate:* "Huge verbal frescoes loom forth, horrendous-looking giants trample about, paraplegics, paralytics, gnomes, bloodied remnants hover over the narrations; scenes of dismemberment, insanity, murder, disease parade before the readers' eyes in all of their sublime and hideous grandeur." Maurice Nadeau, writing in his *The French Novel since the War,* claimed that Celine possessed "a living, colourful language of flesh and blood which translates emotion and feeling in direct terms. . . . It brings literary expression back to life." Hayman thought that Celine's books were "packed with exclamations of anguish and anger unsurpassed in the literature of any language or any century."

Celine began his career as a writer only after serving in the First World War and spending several years as a medical doctor. His military service began in 1912 when, in apparent reaction to an argument with his family, he enlisted in the French cavalry. When war broke out, Celine's unit saw heavy fighting on the German front. While stationed near the town of Ypres in October of 1914, Celine "volunteered for a dangerous front-line mission in Flanders, carried it out successfully, but was gravely wounded on the way back to base," as Merlin Thomas explained in his study *Louis-Ferdinand Celine.* His battlefield exploits earned him a medal for heroic conduct under fire, and he was featured on the cover of the popular weekly magazine *L'Illustre National.* In January of 1915, Celine underwent surgery on his injured arm, was given a three-month convalescent leave, and later that year was judged unfit for further combat duty and released from his military obligation. His right arm was to remain partially paralyzed for the rest of his life.

Celine worked with the passport office of the French Consulate in London, England, during 1915 and 1916. During this time he married a French woman who was also working in London. Because their marriage was never recorded with the French Consulate, it was never legally recognized under French law. When, in 1916, Celine abandoned his wife and left England, it was as if the marriage had never taken place. He spent a year working for a French lumber company in Africa, then returned to France and took a position with the Rockefeller Foundation. On behalf of the foundation, he toured the French province of Brittany, giving lectures on tuberculosis. At the same time he studied medicine at the University of Rennes, where he received a degree in 1919. He married again that same year. After earning a medical degree in 1924, Celine entered private medical practice and settled in Rennes with his wife and young daughter. But conventional married life did not appeal to him. By 1925, he was working for the League of Nations and traveling throughout Europe and North America on their behalf, while his wife and child were left behind. He never again returned to them. By the late 1920s, Celine was back in France, practicing medicine near Paris. He took a position with a municipal clinic in 1931, where he worked almost exclusively with the poor. From then until the end of his life, Celine practiced medicine only among the needy, despite the financial hardships that choice entailed. He argued that he could not in good conscience make money from the suffering of others.

Celine turned to literature while working as a doctor among the poor. He had already published several works on medicine, including his doctoral thesis on the life and work of Philippe-Ignace Semmelweis, before attempting to write fiction. He said on several occasions that his motivation to write a novel came from his belief that he could make enough money from writing to buy himself a decent apartment. The salary he made from his medical work was too modest to allow him this luxury; few of his patients were able to pay even the small amounts he charged for his services.

His first work, a novel entitled *Journey to the End of the Night* (originally *Voyage au bout de le nuit*), took him five years to write. Inspired in part by the success of Eugene Dabit's novel *Hotel du Nord,* which concerned the French underclass Celine knew from his medical work, *Journey to the End of the Night* also focused on the urban poor, drawing from Celine's experiences as a doctor. When it was finally completed in 1932, the one-thousand-page manuscript was sent off to two French publishing houses, Gallimard and Denoel. Gallimard found the book too controversial and suggested that its author might need to finance its publication himself. But Robert Denoel, a new publisher who had brought out several other controversial manuscripts, accepted Celine's novel. In an ultimately unsuccessful effort to separate his medical career from his literary one, the author published the work under the pseudonym Louis-Ferdinand Celine while continuing to practice medicine under his given name of Louis-Ferdinand Destouches.

Journey to the End of the Night is told in the first person by Bardamu, a character who closely resembles Celine himself and whose life in the military during the First World War, in medical school after the war, and as a married doctor among the poor strongly parallels that of the author. Bardamu fights in the army during the First World War and is wounded in much the same manner as Celine himself was wounded. After the war, he travels around the world, visiting many of the same places Celine visited during his work with the League of Nations. Finally, he becomes a doctor and works among the poor. "The subject of the book in the most general sense," Thomas explained, "could be said to be Bardamu's voyage of discovery through life, . . . until through the practice of medicine he comes to understand the futility of so much of human existence and recognize the significance of death."

The novel is composed, according to Irving Howe in his book *A World More Attractive: A View of Modern Literature and Politics,* "as a series of loosely-related episodes, a string of surrealist burlesques, fables of horror and manic extravaganzas, each following upon the other with energy and speed." Some of the incidents are taken from Celine's experiences as a doctor and are little changed. Others use actual experience as a starting point for Celine's acerbic and cynical commentary on life and humanity. Writing in the *New York Times,* Anatole Broyard claimed that "in his first and best book, 'Journey to the End of the Night,' Celine had hardly a good word for anybody, yet you felt that he was in closer touch with the human race, with people in the depths of their souls, than any other author in this century. And though 'Journey' was distilled out of disgust, the aftertaste was not sour—as it so often is with modern French novels—but bittersweet. His disgust was a kind of curdled love."

Journey to the End of the Night was phenomenally popular throughout Europe. Critics of both political extremes hailed it. Leon Daudet of the reactionary newspaper *L'Action Francaise* fought unsuccessfully to have Celine awarded the prestigious Prix Goncourt. Soviet revolutionary Leon Trotsky praised Celine in the highest of terms. Celine, he wrote in the *Atlantic Monthly,* "walked into great literature as other men walk into their own homes." Mavis Gallant, speaking of the book in the *New York Times Book Review,* explained that "Celine's dark nihilism, his use of street language, the undertow of mystery and death that tugs at the novel from start to finish were wildly attractive to both Left and Right; both could read into it a prophecy about collapse, the end of shoddy democracy, the death of sickened Europe." The reading public made *Journey to the End of the Night* a best-seller. "Celine's cynicism and denunciations seemed to speak for everyone," Allen Thiher wrote in *Celine: The Novel as Delirium.* "[His] popular, obscene language was like a violent gust of fresh air breaking into the literary climate." And attacks against the book's alleged obscenity merely provoked more interest and increased sales. "It was an immediate, enormous success," Thomas wrote, "and Celine found himself famous overnight and pretty prosperous very soon."

He followed this initial success with *Death on the Installment Plan* (originally *Mort a Credit*), a novel which takes the premises of the first book to their logical extremes. "An even grizzlier testimony than *Journey to the End of the Night,*" as Howe believed, "Celine's second novel is written in a fitful and exuberant prose, and its tone is one of joyous loathing. . . . The misanthropy of the earlier novel ripens into outright paranoia; but with such bubbling energy, such a bilious and sizzling rhetoric, such a manic insistence upon dredging up the last recollection of filth! *Death on the Installment Plan* is a prolonged recital of cheating, venality and betrayal."

Featuring a narrator named Ferdinand, *Death on the Installment Plan* largely fictionalizes much of Celine's childhood, transforming it into a horrific and tragicomic story. Thiher stated that *Death on the Installment Plan* "presents a vision of a world in which delirious, comic automatons blindly act out their obsessions with predictably cataclysmic results." Fraser maintained that in this book, Celine "has rendered with a Shakespearean energy and vividness the horrors of an existence in which the 'everyday' bears in upon one monstrously, and one doesn't have even the normal amount of unconsciously assimilated mental procedures, let alone consciously shared theories and value-systems, for ordering it and making it intellectually endurable." Hayman described *Death on the Installment Plan* as "a cruel, a brutal, an explosive book, a Gargantuan burst of hilarity released from the pit. But the rage, hysteria, and hallucination are all controlled and masterfully timed."

In both of these novels, Celine employed a misanthropic, first-person narrator, a device he was to continue in his later works. In an article for the *National Review,* Guy Davenport described Celine's typical narrator: "Reading Celine is the same as falling in with a mad old man of glittering and feverish eye whom, he will shout in your face, the world has treated unfairly. He rambles, borders on an inspired inarticulateness, repeats himself, spits, insults, rolls shoelace-loosening obscenities on his tongue, and damns everything in sight except his wife, his cat Brebert, and himself. He is a thoroughly unsavory old cooter, and he meant to be."

These narrators recount their stories in a language that is highly charged with venom, cynicism, disgust, and black humor. Their speech is part poetry and part obscenity, possessing what Gillian Tindall of the *New Statesman* called a "genteel crudeness." "It is not slang, as such, that informs almost every sentence of his long works," Tindall explained, "but a subtler and all-pervading coarseness, a lace-matted vulgarity as domestically familiar and unmistakable as human smells. There is no word for this voice, for no one else has written in it, but it is for this that Celine is read, appreciated and remembered." Douglas Johnson of the *Spectator* compared Celine's own conversation to that of his characters. "Celine would talk violently and contemptuously," Johnson wrote. "He sensed disaster everywhere; he saw unhappiness, disease and death; he denounced conspiracy, wickedness and hypocrisy. He had a gift for telling stories and a weakness for telling those which were impossible. . . . And his writing is like that."

These first two novels established Celine as a prominent writer of the 1930s. But this reputation was tarnished by his increasingly political work. This political phase began in 1936, when Celine was obliged to visit the Soviet Union. Soviet law forbade the export of literary royalties to writers who lived outside the country. Soviet law, too, required writers to spend their royalties only in the Soviet Union. To obtain and use the money he had made from the Russian editions of his novels, Celine went to Moscow.

His visit to the Soviet Union was at first enjoyable. Like many other writers and intellectuals of the time, Celine believed that the Soviets were creating a viable alternative society to the capitalist West. But after a short time in the country, he realized how wrong he had been. He found the country to be a police state where the oppression of the masses was even worse than that found in the West. And the Soviet communists were as materialistic as the bourgeoisie that Celine despised. Outraged, he began to speak out against them. Upon his return to France, he published *Mea Culpa,* a book denouncing the Soviet system, and declared himself to be "an avowed enemy of all Communists," as O'Connell reported.

This break with the French political left was detrimental to Celine's literary reputation; many of the critical journals of the 1930s sympathized with the communists. But Celine's reputation was hurt most by his next three books. In these works, he turned his attention from the communists to the Jews, whom he accused of conspiring to start another world war. In *Bagatelles pour un massacre* ("Trifles for a Massacre" in English), published in 1937, Celine spoke of a Jewish plot to involve the gentiles of Europe in a major war, the "massacre" of the book's title. He argued that both communism and capitalism were materialistic systems invented by Jews, while war was the means by which the Jews weakened their enemies. O'Connell believed that the book's contentions were not coherently argued, and that "this work rambles on and winds around itself, spilling forth hatred, venom, lies, and distortions as it goes."

Celine's second book about the Jews, *L'Ecole des cadavres* ("School for Cadavers" in English), appeared in 1938 and reiterated his earlier statements about the coming Jewish war, while underlining what Celine called his basically pacifistic reasons for writing about it. He ends the book with a call for a military and political alliance between France and Nazi Germany as a way to keep the peace in Europe. In *Les Beaux Draps* ("A Nice Mess" in English), published in 1941 while Paris was already occupied by the German military, Celine attacks the French bourgeoisie. He sees this class as being primarily Jewish, decidedly materialistic, and a menace to the French gentile population. He proposes a reorganization of society to abolish the class system and replace it with a form of National Socialism, similar to that established in Hitler's Germany. Speaking of the anti-Semitic books, Broyard noted that they were "murderous, inflammatory, impossible to imagine coming from France's greatest living novelist. To despise everyone is all right—it is not uncommon among French intellectuals—but to narrow it down to the Jews is something else. Especially on the eve of World War II."

Explanations for why Celine wrote these three books vary according to whether the commentator is sympathetic or hostile to the author. Kinder critics attribute his motivations to genuine pacifistic feelings and argue that his anti-Semitism was a simple mistake. Others see psychological reasons for Celine's dislike of Jews, declaring in some cases that he may have been mad or a paranoiac. They point to the vitriol of his novels as a sign of Celine's mental instability. Whatever his reasons for writing these books—and to his credit, Celine refused in later life to allow them to be reprinted—it is undoubtedly true that he spent the war years in occupied France and by all accounts was on friendly, although not close, terms with the Nazis. As Broyard noted in the *New York Times Book Review,* "the relation between [Celine's] genius as a novelist and his anti-Semitism has never been satisfactorily explained."

At war's end, Celine's life was in danger. He was denounced as a collaborationist over BBC radio. The French Resistance marked him for execution and began to send death threats to his house. When France fell to the Allied forces in 1944, Celine and his third wife fled first to Germany and then to Denmark, a country where he had banked a considerable amount of his royalties. The apartment he left behind in Paris was ransacked by the French Resistance, and many of his papers and manuscripts were destroyed.

But even in Denmark Celine was not safe. On Christmas eve of 1945, he was arrested by the Danish authorities. Although the French government wanted to extradite him for trial as a collaborationist, the Danes refused. Instead, they imprisoned him for some fourteen months. He was only released in 1947 because of his failing health. Celine remained in Denmark until receiving an official amnesty from the French government in 1950. At that time, a French court cleared him of any wrongdoing during the war. He spent the remaining years of his life as a doctor in the French town of Meudon.

Celine's postwar career was crippled by his earlier political pronouncements, and he was often the target of political attack. In 1945, Jean-Paul Sartre accused Celine of having been paid by the Nazis to write on their behalf. Celine answered him in a book entitled *A l'agite du bocal,* defending his political beliefs and denying that he had been paid to express them. Other leftist spokesmen charged him with having advocated the extermination of the Jews, of having worked with the Gestapo, and of having gotten off far too lightly for his crimes. George Grant, writing in *Queen's Quarterly,* explained that "the French Left were baying for [Celine's] blood." Nadeau argued that "when Celine spoke of the 'witch-hunt' he was subjected to; when, before his return to France, he complained of being a 'scape-goat,' he was not far from the truth."

Celine also had trouble finding a publisher upon his return to France. Robert Denoel had been assassinated in 1945, and the publishing house that bore his name was accused of collaboration with the Nazis. It was not allowed to operate until finally cleared of the charge in 1947. Several of Celine's books appeared from smaller publishers, but they received little critical attention. As O'Connell remarked, "the silence and critical indifference that often follow the death of a major author appeared to be taking place while Celine was still alive and writing."

It was not until the publication of *Castle to Castle* (originally *D'un chateau l'autre*) in 1957 that Celine began once more to attract serious critical attention. He had used a misanthropic, first-person narrator in his earlier fiction. But in *Castle to Castle* he began to openly cast himself as the misanthrope, and the stories he narrated occupy the blurred realm between fiction and autobiography. He thereby satirized his own efforts as a writer while poking fun at the monstrous image his political enemies had given him.

Castle to Castle recounts the problems that Celine had experienced since war's end. It begins with the author at home, explaining that he is only writing this book because his publisher demands that he write it to justify the advance he has been paid. "He is forever counting the number of pages completed, piling them up seemingly against his will, but knowing all the time that Gallimard will accept nothing less," O'Connell explained. After some seventy pages of grumbling about his relationship with his publisher, Celine settles into a recounting of his war years in France and of his sufferings after the war at a German castle where members of the French occupation government took refuge.

"The reader," John Weightman said in the *New York Review of Books,* "has to surrender himself to an impressionistic, paranoiac monologue, in which more often than not the sentences are left unfinished, the transitions from one idea to the next are not explained, and many of Celine's contemporaries are referred to elliptically and derisively under transparent nicknames." Writing in *Critique: Studies in Modern Fiction,* Haminda Bosmajian called *Castle to Castle* "a novel where the lines between fictional reality and the reality of fiction remain fluid, a novel which reveals with disconcerting honesty not only the human condition of Celine, but also that of ourselves."

Celine followed much the same approach in the novel *North* (originally *Nord*). "Once again," Lee T. Lemon wrote in *Prairie Schooner,* "Celine is the protagonist of his own novel." In this book he traces his travels across Germany and into Denmark at war's end. The book, as a critic for the *Times Literary Supplement* remarked, "does not record the convulsions of the Reich in collapse but recreates them." Thomas found the novel to be a successful blend of humor and danger. "Taking us through a whole series of events and adventures," he wrote, "the book leaves an overall impression of a vividly recollected nightmare. . . . Celine's 'hallucinatory' manner is much in evidence, but never sustained over long sections . . ., and with it there goes a sharp sense of humour and a savage awareness of man's cruelty to man. If the circumstances were not so miserable and depressing, *Nord* would undoubtedly be a very funny book indeed; as it is there are many passages where the sense of absurdity is stronger than the sense of menace and danger, and Celine succeeds in controlling the balance with consummate skill." Hayman claimed that *North* showed Celine to be "at the height of his technical powers" and "is filled with brilliant technical turns, unified but rich in detail and incident, abounding in dramatic sequences, comic tension, irony, and surprise."

Celine concludes the story of his wartime adventures in *Rigadoon,* a book which recounts the trials he suffered in Denmark. It was the last book he was to write. On the very day he completed the manuscript, Celine suffered a stroke and passed away. Grant described the desperate escape across war-torn Europe with which these three final novels are concerned. "The journey," Grant recounted, "takes place while the Russian armies get closer and closer, and while the American and British bombers flatten and reflatten the cities. Roosevelt's unconditional surrender is in full swing. Europe is being demolished by the two great continental empires with the help of the British. Celine's chronicle is of the collapse of that Europe and is laid before us with prodigality." Grant concluded that Celine's final trilogy "is one of the great masterpieces of western art and the greatest literary masterpiece of this era."

By the time of his death in 1961, Celine had reclaimed a place in contemporary French literature. His later novels had won him renewed critical respect, while his early books still commanded a wide and appreciative audience. But he was perhaps more widely known for his pervasive influence on a host of other writers. He is, according to Rima Drell Reck in her *Literature and Responsibility: The French Novelist in the Twentieth Century,* "the strongest subterranean force in the novel today." Among those he is credited with having influenced are Sartre (whose novel *Nausea* was dedicated to Celine), Henry Miller, Albert Camus, Samuel Beckett, Alain Robbe-Grillet, Michel Butor, William Burroughs, Thomas Pynchon, Gunter Grass, and Joseph Heller. Much of this influence was due to Celine's shattering of accepted approaches to the novel through his wild, personal, and aggressively nihilistic style. He created new possibilities for what the novel could be, possibilities which other writers

explored. Erika Ostrovsky, writing in her *Celine and His Vision,* outlined what she saw as the author's literary impact. "Essentially," she wrote, "it consists of the creation of a new tone, a literary ambience which pervades an entire sector of modern letters and exceeds the limits of national boundaries or personal orientation and background."

Despite his influence, Celine is still denigrated by some critics. Davenport claimed that Celine's "significance remains to be seen. He was an angry old man talking, talking. It will take a critic more patient than most of us to sift through his ravings and decide if there is anything in it." Even more dubious of Celine's achievement is Henri Peyre who, in his book *French Novelists of Today,* criticized "the monotony of Celine's inspiration, the artificiality of his language and the 'pompierisme' of his tawdry sentimentality." Paul West wrote in *Book World* that "your mature reader dismisses Celine as a barfing werewolf (antihumanist, antihuman, self-obsessed, crypto-war-criminal, etc.)" And some critics still cannot evaluate Celine's literary efforts objectively because of his outspoken political beliefs, anti-Semitism, and racism.

But many critics find great value in his work, claiming that Celine is among the leading figures in the literature of the extreme. Stephen Day, writing in *Queen's Quarterly,* explained: "Observed as a whole, Celine's work is a journey through the events of the twentieth century with its wars, chaos and apprehension. And a great part of Celine's urge to write is the desire to achieve a mode of expression capable of relating them." Milton Hindus argued in an article for *MOSAIC: A Journal for the Comparative Study of Literature and Ideas* that Celine "has long seemed to me one of the masters of the novel of the twentieth century. . . . His picaresque tales of various underworlds bare the scabrous backside of our civilization." Thiher maintained that "Celine's work stands as a monument to . . . dissonance, rage, and madness." Weightman claimed that "there can be no doubt about the historical importance of Louis-Ferdinand Celine in the literature of anarchistic revolt. He was the first great foul-mouthed rhapsodist of the 20th century to proclaim a satanic vision of a godless world, rolling helplessly through space and infested with crawling millions of suffering, diseased, sex-obsessed, maniacal human beings." In similar terms, Hayman concluded that Celine "is the black magician of hilarity and rage, the perverse mirror of twentieth-century energy—a force so dynamic and diverse that it leads inevitably to overproduction and suicide. His vision supplements in our time that of Kafka, Beckett, or Grass, putting a real gun in the hand of the metaphorical fool, substituting explosion for restraint. He stands next to Proust as the painter of a moribund society, next to Joyce as a liberator of language. He is unmatched as a comic genius, the father of verbal slapstick."

In judging Celine's ultimate worth as a writer, critics point to several aspects of his work which they believe will last. Thiher concluded that, despite the extreme nature of his writings, it is Celine's ultimately liberating energy that will endure. "The Celinian novel," Thiher wrote, "is one of the most naked revelations of the tormented self in modern literature. . . . Language mimics madness and destruction in Celine. [But] it also mimics a riotous joy, the joy of shouting down all the misery and injustice with which life can crush a man. It is this exuberance that will not allow us to abandon Celine." Thomas argued that Celine's extreme literary vision, because of its basic honesty in reflecting the nature of our time, would last longer than those of other twentieth century writers. Celine was, Thomas wrote, "a witness of our century, of one of the most violent and troublous periods in human history. . . . The testimony this witness gives is bleak and even frightening for the most part, but by no means exclusively so. It may well be that future generations will regard it as a reasonable picture of an age. . . . They will perhaps find it more rewarding than that of most of his contemporaries." Writing in the *Dictionary of Literary Biography,* O'Connell claimed that "in Celine's work a whole civilization is judged deficient, as is perhaps even mankind itself. Such an accusatory image remains popular, generation after generation; despite tremendous social changes in Europe and the rest of the world, present readers can find in Celine outbursts of sarcasm and anger against individuals and institutions that seem timely today."

BIOGRAPHICAL/CRITICAL SOURCES:

BOOKS

Bardeche, Maurice, *Louis-Ferdinand Celine,* Table Ronde, 1986.
Bree, Germaine and Margaret Guiton, *The French Novel from Gide to Camus,* Harcourt, 1962.
Contemporary Literary Criticism, Gale, Volume 1, 1973, Volume 3, 1975, Volume 4, 1975, Volume 7, 1977, Volume 9, 1978, Volume 15, 1980, Volume 47, 1988.
Dauphin, Jean-Pierre and Jacques Boudillet, *Album Celine,* Gallimard, 1977.
Dictionary of Literary Biography, Volume 72: *French Novelists, 1930-1960,* Gale, 1988.
Flynn, James and C. K. Mertz, *Understanding Celine,* Genitron, 1984.
Gibault, Francois, *Celine,* three volumes, Mercure de France, 1977-85.
Hanrez, Marc, *Celine,* Gallimard, 1961.
Hayman, David, *Louis-Ferdinand Celine,* Columbia University Press, 1965.
Hindus, Milton, *The Crippled Giant: A Bizarre Adventure in Contemporary Letters,* Boar's Head Books, 1950.
Howe, Irving, *A World More Attractive: A View of Modern Literature and Politics,* Horizon Press, 1963.
Knapp, Bettina L., *Celine: Man of Hate,* University of Alabama Press, 1974.
Luce, Stanford L. and William K. Buckley, *A Half Century of Celine: An Annotated Bibliography, 1932-1982,* Garland, 1983.
Mahe, Henri, *La Brinquebale avec Celine: Cent lettres inedites,* La Table Ronde, 1969.
Matthews, J. H., *The Inner Dream: Celine as Novelist,* Syracuse University Press, 1978.
McCarthy, Patrick, *Celine: A Critical Biography,* Allen Lane, 1975.
Morand, Jacqueline, *Les Idees politiques de Louis-Ferdinand Celine,* Pichon et Durand-Auzias, 1972.
Nadeau, Maurice, *The French Novel since the War,* Grove, 1969.
O'Connell, David, *Louis-Ferdinand Celine,* Twayne, 1976.
Ostrowsky, Erika, *Celine and His Vision,* New York University Press, 1967.
Ostrowsky, Erika, *Voyeur Voyant: A Portrait of Louis-Ferdinand Celine,* Random House, 1971.
Peyre, Henri, *French Novelists of Today,* Oxford University Press, 1967.
Poulet, Robert, *Mon ami Bardamu: Entretiens familiers avec L.-F. Celine,* Plon, 1971.
Queriere, Yves de la, *Celine et les mots,* University of Kentucky Press, 1973.
Reck, Rima Drell, *Literature and Responsibility: The French Novelist in the Twentieth Century,* Louisiana State University Press, 1969.
Richard, J.-P., *La Nausee de Celine,* Scolies Fata Morgana, 1973.
Roux, Dominique de, *La Mort de L.-F. Celine,* Christian Bourgeois, 1966.
Thiher, Allen, *Celine: The Novel as Delirium,* Rutgers University Press, 1972.
Vandromme, Paul, *Louis-Ferdinand Celine,* Editions Universitaires, 1963.
Vitoux, F., *Louis-Ferdinand Celine: Misere et parole,* Gallimard, 1973.

PERIODICALS

Atlantic Monthly, October, 1935.
Book World, January 30, 1972.
Canadian Review of Comparative Literature, winter, 1981.
Critique: Studies in Modern Fiction, Volume XIV, number 1, 1972.
L'Herne, Number 3, 1963.
L'Illustre National, December 28, 1914.
Modern Fiction Studies, spring, 1970.
MOSAIC: A Journal for the Comparative Study of Literature and Ideas, spring, 1973, spring, 1975.
Nation, May 2, 1934.
National Review, March 31, 1972.
New Statesman, July 11, 1975.
New York Review of Books, June 5, 1969.
New York Times, April 22, 1934, January 12, 1972.
New York Times Book Review, July 18, 1976, August 31, 1986, February 1, 1987.
Queen's Quarterly, autumn, 1983, spring, 1987.
Saturday Review, February 5, 1972, August 7, 1976.
Saturday Review of Literature, April 28, 1934.
Spectator, June 29, 1934, July 5, 1975.
Times Literary Supplement, September 1, 1972, June 6, 1986.
Western Humanities Review, autumn, 1967.
Wisconsin Studies in Contemporary Literature, Volume 8, number 1, 1967.
World Literature Today, autumn, 1986.

*   *   *

De VRIES, Peter   1910-

PERSONAL: Born February 27, 1910, in Chicago, Ill.; son of Joost (a furniture warehouse owner) and Henrietta (Eldersveld) De Vries; married Katinka Loeser (a writer), October 16, 1943; children: Jan, Peter Jon, Emily, Derek. *Education:* Calvin College, A.B., 1931; Northwestern University, summer student, 1931. *Politics:* Democrat.

ADDRESSES: Home—170 Cross Highway, Westport, Conn. 06880. *Office*—New Yorker, 25 West 43rd St., New York, N.Y. 10036.

CAREER: Editor of community newspapers, Chicago, Ill., 1931; worked as operator of candy-vending machines, taffy apple peddler, and radio actor, 1931-38; free-lance writer, 1931—; *Poetry* magazine, associate editor, 1938-42, co-editor, 1942-44; *New Yorker* magazine, member of editorial staff, 1944—.

MEMBER: American Academy and Institute of Arts and Letters.

AWARDS, HONORS: American Academy and Institute of Arts and Letters grant, 1946; D.H.L. from University of Bridgeport, 1968.

WRITINGS:

But Who Wakes the Bugler?, Houghton, 1940.
The Handsome Heart, Coward, 1943.
Angels Can't Do Better, Coward, 1944.

No But I Saw the Movie (stories), Little, Brown, 1952.
The Tunnel of Love (Atlantic Book Club selection; also see below), Little, Brown, 1954.
Comfort Me with Apples, Little, Brown, 1956.
(With Joseph Fields) *The Tunnel of Love* (dramatization of the novel; produced on Broadway by Theatre Guild, 1957), Little, Brown, 1957.
The Mackerel Plaza, Little, Brown, 1958.
The Tents of Wickedness (sequel to *Comfort Me with Apples;* Book-of-the-Month Club selection), Little, Brown, 1959.
Through the Fields of Clover, Little, Brown, 1961.
The Blood of the Lamb, Little, Brown, 1962.
Reuben, Reuben, Little, Brown, 1964.
Let Me Count the Ways, Little, Brown, 1965.
The Vale of Laughter, Little, Brown, 1967.
The Cat's Pajamas [and] *Witch's Milk,* Little, Brown, 1968.
Mrs. Wallop, Little, Brown, 1970.
Into Your Tent I'll Creep, Little, Brown, 1971.
Without a Stitch in Time (stories), Little, Brown, 1972.
Forever Panting, Little, Brown, 1973.
The Glory of the Hummingbird, Little, Brown, 1974.
I Hear American Swinging, Little, Brown, 1976.
Madder Music, Little, Brown, 1977.
Consenting Adults; or, The Duchess Will Be Furious, Little, Brown, 1980.
Sauce for the Goose, Little, Brown, 1981.
Slouching towards Kalamazoo, Little, Brown, 1983.
The Prick of Noon, Little, Brown, 1985.
Peckham's Marbles, Putnam, 1986.

SIDELIGHTS: Peter De Vries is a prolific fiction writer whose droll satire and imaginative wordplay have won him a devoted readership. He has frequently contributed short stories to *New Yorker* magazine, where he became a staff member in 1944, and he has written more than twenty novels since his first appeared in 1940. "Something of a national humorist laureate," according to *Publishers Weekly* interviewer Sybil S. Steinberg, De Vries typically mocks American social classes, religion (the author was raised in a strict Calvinist tradition), education, and sex.

The plots of De Vries's books are often considered merely loose devices for showcasing the author's poignant social observations and copious witticisms. *Consenting Adults; or, The Duchess Will Be Furious,* for example, features a young man from a working-class background who seeks to advance his position by attending college. He suffers a nervous breakdown after studying nihilist philosophy and, after documenting his collapse for the departments of English and psychology, receives a B+ for the experience. To alleviate his fears of nonexistence, wrote Christopher Cerf in the *New York Times Book Review,* the protagonist resolves to indulge exclusively in "the pleasures of the flesh," which then constitute most of the novel. Because of the lack of a compelling plot, Cerf observed, readers will likely find the book easy to set down. "But they will almost surely pick it up again," he added, "refreshed and ready to enjoy more magic from one of the true masters of humorous style the past half-century has produced."

De Vries's more recent novels, including *The Prick of Noon* and *Peckham's Marbles,* have proved no less satisfying. *The Prick of Noon,* whose title is quoted from Shakespeare's *Romeo and Juliet,* concerns a pornographer who markets his films as educational ("sexucational") guides and sells them to the social elite. This book "ranks among [De Vries's] better books," judged John Gross in his *New York Times* review, "and it is a measure of its success, and of his comic gift, that the potential sleaziness of his theme is kept wholly at bay." *Peckham's Marbles*—about a pro-

fessor who fails as a teacher, author, and lover, and is advised "to have his marbles examined"—was described by Ralph C. Wood in the *Christian Century* as "the usual De Vriesian fare—outrageously punning, inside-out, upside down." But unlike many of De Vries's amusing but relatively "forgettable" books, Wood added, "*Peckham's Marbles* is truly memorable." In an essay published in *American Humor: An Interdisciplinary Newsletter,* T. Jeff Evans offered an inclusive view of De Vries's fiction. "Taken together," Evans wrote, "the novels of Peter De Vries form a fascinating investigation into the mores of America over the last thirty years. . . . There is a purposeful confluence . . . between idea and form in De Vries' work," the reviewer elaborated, "a deft union of language, style, wit, and theme that creates an enduring comic vision of the way we live."

MEDIA ADAPTATIONS: The Tunnel of Love was filmed by Metro-Goldwyn-Mayer in 1958; the first section of *Reuben, Reuben* was adapted by Herman Shumlin as a play titled "Spofford" and produced on Broadway at the ANTA Theatre, December 12, 1967; *Let Me Count the Ways* was adapted by Freeman and Karl Tunberg as a motion picture titled "How Do I Love Thee?," ABC Pictures Corp., 1970; *Witch's Milk* was adapted by Julius J. Epstein as a motion picture titled "Pete 'n' Tillie," Universal, 1972; the second section of *Reuben, Reuben* was adapted as a motion picture of the same title, Taft, 1983.

BIOGRAPHICAL/CRITICAL SOURCES:

BOOKS

Bowden, J. H., *Peter De Vries,* Twayne, 1983.
Contemporary Literary Criticism, Gale, Volume 1, 1973, Volume 2, 1974, Volume 3, 1975, Volume 7, 1977, Volume 10, 1979, Volume 28, 1984, Volume 46, 1988.
Dictionary of Literary Biography, Volume 6: *American Novelists since World War II, Second Series,* Gale, 1980.
Dictionary of Literary Biography Yearbook: 1982, Gale, 1983.
Jellema, Roderick, *Peter De Vries: A Critical Essay,* Eerdmans, 1966.

PERIODICALS

American Humor: An Interdisciplinary Newsletter, fall, 1980.
Catholic World, April, 1962.
Christian Century, December 24, 1986.
Commonweal, February 10, 1961.
Harper's, September, 1965.
Life, August 6, 1965.
New York Times, January 27, 1969.
New York Times Book Review, August 17, 1980, August 14, 1983, April 5, 1985.
Newsweek, February 17, 1964.
Publishers Weekly, October 16, 1981.
San Francisco Chronicle, March 9, 1958.
Saturday Review, March 24, 1962.

*   *   *

DEXTER, Pete 1943-

PERSONAL: Born in 1943, in Pontiac, Mich.; previously married and divorced; married second wife, Dian; children: (second marriage) Casey. *Education:* Received degree from University of South Dakota, 1970. *Avocational interests:* Boxing.

ADDRESSES: Home—1170 Markham Way, Sacramento, Calif. 95818. *Office*—Sacramento Bee, 21st and Q Streets, Box 15779, Sacramento, Calif. 95852. *Agent*—Esther Newberg, International Creative Management, 40 West 57th St., New York, N.Y. 10019.

CAREER: West Palm Beach Post, Palm Beach, Fla., reporter, 1971-72; *Philadelphia Daily News,* Philadelphia, Pa., columnist, 1972-84; *Sacramento Bee,* Sacramento, Calif., columnist, 1985—; novelist. Worked as a truck driver, gas station attendant, mail sorter, construction laborer, and salesman.

AWARDS, HONORS: National Endowment for the Arts grant to write poetry; National Book Award, and National Book Critics Circle Award nomination, both 1988, both for *Paris Trout.*

WRITINGS:

God's Pocket (novel), Random House, 1984.
Deadwood (novel), Random House, 1986.
Paris Trout (novel), Random House, 1988.

Contributor to periodicals, including *Esquire, Sports Illustrated,* and *Playboy.*

WORK IN PROGRESS: Screenplays for *Deadwood* and *Paris Trout;* a novel.

SIDELIGHTS: National Book Award-winning author Pete Dexter is noted for his novels that mix violence with humor, display his sharp ear for dialogue and eye for local color, and contain well-rounded and often eccentric characters. An outspoken journalist with the *Philadelphia Daily News* for twelve years and with the *Sacramento Bee* since 1985, Dexter turned to writing fiction after nearly being beaten to death by readers who were infuriated by one of his *Daily News* columns. Thus no stranger to brutality, he focuses in his novels on how communities react to violence and murder. Dexter's first book, *God's Pocket,* turns on the death of an abrasive white construction worker in Philadelphia; *Deadwood* relates the assassination of legendary outlaw "Wild Bill" Hickok in a western gold-rush town; and *Paris Trout* explores the aftermath of the shooting of an innocent black girl in Georgia.

Born in Michigan and raised in Georgia and South Dakota, Dexter graduated from the University of South Dakota in 1970 after attending for eight years (he would quit when the weather got cold). He secured a job as a reporter with the *West Palm Beach Post* but left after two years ("I wasn't the best writer there," he explained in the *New York Times Book Review*). He then worked at a gas station with another former *Post* reporter but quit ("I wasn't even the best writer in the gas station") to join the *Philadelphia Daily News* in 1972. A decade later he was badly beaten in a barroom brawl by baseball-bat and tire-iron wielding denizens of a Philadelphia neighborhood who were angered by a column he had written about a drug-related murder that happened there. Dexter survived with a broken back and hip and an altered sense of taste from the blows to his head. Forced to give up his favorite pastime, drinking (beer, according to Dexter, now tastes like battery acid), he devoted his spare time to writing. The result was three critically acclaimed novels.

Dexter's first work, *God's Pocket,* was published in 1984. It begins with what Julius Lester in *New York Times Book Review* called an "auspicious comic opening": "Leon Hubbard died ten minutes into lunch break on the first Monday in May, on the construction site of the new one-story trauma wing at Holy Redeemer Hospital in South Philadelphia. One way or the other, he was going to lose the job." Drug-addict bricklayer Leon prompted his own demise when he threatened a black co-worker named Lucien with a straight razor; Lucien consequently bashed Leon in the back of the head with a lead pipe. Glad to be rid of the troublemaker, the other workers and the foreman told the

police it was an accidental death. This "random incident," according to Paul Gray in *Time,* turns "into a picaresque romp" when Leon's devoted mother Jeanie and her second husband Mickey, who is constantly trying to prove his devotion to her, believe otherwise. At the grieving mother's request, Mickey must tap his underground connections to find out who killed Leon.

Reviewers of *God's Pocket* commended Dexter for his masterful control of comic situations, fluent prose, and idiomatic dialogue. Gray also appreciated the novel's "impressive ballast of local color," noting that the rough working-class Philadelphia neighborhood called God's Pocket "seems all too real: narrow houses, streets, lives; a place where the Hollywood Bar, the social hub of the area, does 'half its business before noon.' " Some critics, however, criticized *God's Pocket* for being too ambitious. Gray, for instance, complained that Dexter "piles on more complications and coincidences than his novel ought to carry" and added that there are too many characters and subplots. Mickey, for example, in addition to having to please Jeanie by identifying Leon's murderer, must raise six thousand dollars to bury him in a mahogany casket. But because he cannot pay the undertaker for the funeral due to his losing efforts at the racetrack, Mickey is forced to drive Leon's embalmed corpse around in his refrigerated meat truck, which he uses to sell stolen meat for his two-bit mobster boss. For another subplot Dexter created Richard Shellburn, an alcoholic Philadelphia newspaper columnist who is also suspicious of Leon's mysterious demise. Shellburn is later beaten to death by the threatened residents of God's Pocket.

Dexter's second novel, *Deadwood,* focuses on the death of American folk hero James Butler "Wild Bill" Hickok. In the novel Hickok, his longtime partner "Colorado" Charley Utter, and follower Malcolm Nash escort a wagon train of prostitutes to the Dakota gold rush town of Deadwood in 1876. Hickok, once renowned as the best pistol shot in the West, is now an aging Wild West show performer who drinks to overcome the pain of syphilis. About a third of the way into *Deadwood* he is shot to death by a hired killer while playing poker in a saloon. "The rest of this hilarious and rousing novel," according to Dennis Drabelle in *Book World,* concerns itself with how "the other characters cope with [Hickok's] transformation from living to dead legend."

New York Times Book Review contributor Ron Hansen remarked that after his hero's death Dexter fills the pages of the novel with "some intriguingly extravagant minor characters." Populating Dexter's town of Deadwood are China Doll, a prostitute seeking revenge on Utter for burning the corpse of her brother; her pimp, Al Swearingen, who brutally rapes Nash; "Calamity" Jane Cannery, who claims that she is the widow of Hickok; and trapeze artist Agnes Lake, Hickok's true widow, who befriends Cannery. "All of them become threads in the tapestry of Deadwood," Drabelle noted, "and the town itself becomes the protagonist."

Critics praised *Deadwood* for its local color, shrewd characterization, and deftly handled bawdy situations. " 'Deadwood' is unpredictable, hyperbolic and, page after page, uproarious," Hansen attested. "[It is] a joshing book written in high spirits and a raw appreciation for the past." "The writing is engagingly colloquial without being silly, and well suited to the multiple character points of view," *Village Voice* contributor M. George Stevenson assessed. "And the book *is* very funny and filled with wry observations about the surfaces of frontier life." "With its stylish humor and convincing demonstration of how the fables of the Wild West originated," Drabelle concluded, "*Deadwood* may well be the best Western ever written."

Dexter received the National Book Award and was shortlisted for the National Book Critics Circle Award for his third book, *Paris Trout*. Set in the 1950s in the town of Cotton Point, Georgia, the novel concerns the amoral Paris Trout, a white hardware store owner and loanshark to the black community who is nonetheless locally respected. When a young black man, Henry Ray Boxer, refuses to make payments on a car he bought from Trout after it was hit by a truck, Trout and a crony barge into the man's home to collect on the loan. Not finding him there, Trout shoots Boxer's mother in the back and kills a fourteen-year old girl who lives with the family.

Reluctantly, the authorities arrest, try, and sentence Trout to three years hard labor. Convinced of his right to collect on a debt and determined not to do time for what he does not consider a crime, Trout bribes his way out of going to prison. In the aftermath he grows increasingly demented and becomes, in the words of *Los Angeles Times Book Review* contributor Richard Eder, "a primal evil, all will and no humanity." "Before it is over," *Book World* contributor Judith Paterson noted, "[Trout's] unyielding conviction that everything he does is right has thrown the whole town off its moral center and exposed the link between Trout's depravity and the town's silent endorsement of all kinds of inhumanities—including racism, sexism and economic exploitation."

"If 'Paris Trout' is about a community hamstrung by its accommodations," Eder continued, "it is also, at every moment, about the individuals caught in the accommodation. Dexter portrays them with marvelous sharpness." An increasingly paranoid Trout sleeps with a sheet of lead under his bed to shield himself from assassination and is convinced that his wife Hanna is trying to poison him. Hanna, a stoical schoolteacher who married Trout later in life to escape spinsterhood, is psychologically and sexually brutalized by him throughout their marriage. She consequently has an affair with Trout's gentleman defense lawyer, Harry Seagraves, who represented Trout out of social obligation but abandoned him after the trial. Hanna also hires local attorney Carl Bonner to represent her in divorce proceedings against her husband. "Perfectly offsetting graphic horror and comedy," Dean Faulkner Wells assessed in *Chicago Tribune Book World*, "Dexter brings all these characters together in an explosive conclusion."

"With a touch of the mastery that graces the best fiction about the South," Pete Axthelm observed in his *Newsweek* review of *Paris Trout*, "Dexter has conjured up characters stroked broadly, voices that ring true—and vignettes crafted in miniature in a way that haunts." Numerous critics mentioned similarities between Dexter and various Southern writers, claiming that his dark humor is reminiscent of the works of Flannery O'Connor and that his use of violence is Faulknerian. Dexter is quick to mention, though, that he is not a "Southern" writer (*Paris Trout* is his only book set in the South), but he is grateful for the praise. George Melly in *New Statesman and Society*, in fact, found differences between William Faulkner and Dexter. He noted that although *Paris Trout* is set in Faulkner's South, "it is free of Faulkner's convoluted style. The prose is taut, the feeling for time and place exact."

Dexter also denied the claim of some reviewers that *Paris Trout* symbolizes "racism, class war and inhumanity in the pre-civil-rights-era South," according to Glenn Collins of the *New York Times*. The author told the journalist that the events of *Paris Trout* "could have happened anywhere. The South has no lock on violence. In fact, South *Philadelphia* is more violent than the South." Deborah Mason in the *New York Times Book Review* commended Dexter for this insight, noting that "at a time when virulent racial incidents can no longer be conveniently fenced off in small Southern towns, Mr. Dexter's great accomplishment is to remind us, with lucidity and stinging frankness, the lengths to which we will go to deny our own racism and to reassure ourselves that we are innocent." Eder agreed. "The monstrousness, even of the decent people, hangs over the entire book," he confessed. "It is one of the elements that make 'Paris Trout' a masterpiece, complex and breath-taking."

BIOGRAPHICAL/CRITICAL SOURCES:

BOOKS

Bestsellers 89, Issue 2, Gale, 1989.
Contemporary Literary Criticism, Gale, Volume 34, 1985, Volume 55, 1989.
Dexter, Pete, *God's Pocket,* Random House, 1984.
Dexter, Pete, *Paris Trout,* Random House, 1988.

PERIODICALS

Chicago Tribune Book World, April 6, 1986, August 7, 1988.
Los Angeles Times, December 1, 1988.
Los Angeles Times Book Review, July 24, 1988.
Nation, March 10, 1984.
New Statesman and Society, October 7, 1988.
New York Times, December 5, 1988.
New York Times Book Review, February 19, 1984, April 20, 1986, July 24, 1988.
Sports Illustrated, February 23, 1987.
Time, April 2, 1984.
Village Voice, June 17, 1986.
Washington Post, November 28, 1988.
Washington Post Book World, June 1, 1986, July 10, 1988, November 30, 1988.

—*Sketch by Carol Lynn DeKane*

* * *

DIAMANO, Silmang
   See SENGHOR, Leopold Sedar

* * *

di BASSETTO, Corno
   See SHAW, George Bernard

* * *

DICK, Philip K(indred)   1928-1982
(Richard Phillips)

PERSONAL: Born December 16, 1928, in Chicago, Ill.; died of heart failure following a stroke, March 2, 1982, in Santa Ana, Calif.; son of Joseph Edgar (a government employee) and Dorothy (Kindred) Dick; married wife Jeannette, 1949 (divorced); married wife Kleo, 1951 (divorced); married wife Ann, 1958 (divorced); married wife Nancy, April 18, 1967 (divorced); married Tessa Busby, April 18, 1973 (divorced); children: (third marriage) Laura; (fourth marriage) Isolde; (fifth marriage) Christopher. *Education:* Attended University of California, Berkeley, 1950. *Politics:* "Antiwar, pro-life." *Religion:* Episcopalian.

CAREER: Writer. Hosted classical music program on KSMO Radio, 1947; worked in a record store, 1948-52; occasional lecturer at California State University, Fullerton; active in drug rehabilitation and anti-abortion work.

MEMBER: Science Fiction Writers of America, Animal Protection Institute.

AWARDS, HONORS: Hugo Award, World Science Fiction Convention, 1962, for *The Man in the High Castle;* John W. Campbell Memorial Award, 1974, for *Flow My Tears, the Policeman Said;* guest of honor, Science Fiction Festival, Metz, France, 1978; the Philip K. Dick Memorial Award has been created by Norwescon, an annual science fiction convention in Seattle, Wash.

WRITINGS:

SCIENCE FICTION NOVELS

Solar Lottery (bound with *The Big Jump* by Leigh Brackett), Ace Books, 1955, reprinted separately, Gregg, 1976 (published separately in England as *World of Chance,* Rich & Cowan, 1956).

The World Jones Made (bound with *Agent of the Unknown* by Margaret St. Clair), Ace Books, 1956, reprinted, Bart Books, 1988.

The Man Who Japed (bound with *The Space-Born* by E. C. Tubb), Ace Books, 1956.

Eye in the Sky, Ace Books, 1957, reprinted, G. K. Hall, 1979.

The Cosmic Puppets (bound with *Sargasso of Space* by Andrew North), Ace Books, 1957, reprinted separately, Berkley Publishing, 1983.

Time Out of Joint, Lippincott, 1959, reprinted, Bluejay Books, 1984.

Dr. Futurity, (also see below; bound with *Slavers of Space* by John Brunner), Ace Books, 1960, reprinted (bound with *The Unteleported Man* by Dick), 1972, reprinted separately, Berkley Publishing, 1984.

Vulcan's Hammer (bound with *The Skynappers* by Brunner), Ace Books, 1960.

The Man in the High Castle, Putnam, 1962, reprinted, Berkley Publishing, 1984.

The Game-Players of Titan, Ace Books, 1963.

Martian Time-Slip, Ballantine, 1964, reprinted, 1981.

The Penultimate Truth, Belmont-Tower, 1964, reprinted, Bluejay Books, 1984.

The Simulacra, Ace Books, 1964.

Clans of the Alphane Moon, Ace Books, 1964, reprinted, Bluejay Books, 1984.

Dr. Bloodmoney; or, How We Got Along after the Bomb, Ace Books, 1965, reprinted, Bluejay Books, 1984.

The Three Stigmata of Palmer Eldritch, Doubleday, 1965, reprinted, DAW Books, 1984.

Now Wait for Last Year, Doubleday, 1966, reprinted, DAW Books, 1981.

The Crack in Space (also see below), Ace Books, 1966.

The Unteleported Man (also see below; bound with *The Mind Monsters* by Howard L. Cory), Ace Books, 1966, reprinted (bound with *Dr. Futurity* by Dick), 1972, reprinted separately, Berkley Publishing, 1983.

(With Ray Nelson) *The Ganymede Takeover,* Ace Books, 1967.

Counter-Clock World, Berkley Publishing, 1967.

The Zap Gun, Pyramid Publications, 1967, reprinted, Bluejay Books, 1985.

Do Androids Dream of Electric Sheep?, Doubleday, 1968, published as *Blade Runner,* Ballantine, 1982.

Ubik (also see below), Doubleday, 1969.

Galactic Pot-Healer, Doubleday, 1969.

A Philip K. Dick Omnibus (contains *The Crack in Space, The Unteleported Man,* and *Dr. Futurity*), Sidgwick & Jackson, 1970.

A Maze of Death, Doubleday, 1970.

Our Friends from Frolix 8, Ace Books, 1970.

We Can Build You, DAW Books, 1972.

Flow My Tears, the Policeman Said, Doubleday, 1974.

(With Roger Zelazny) *Deus Irae,* Doubleday, 1976.

A Scanner Darkly, Doubleday, 1977.

VALIS, Bantam, 1981.

The Divine Invasion, Pocket Books, 1981.

The Transmigration of Timothy Archer, Pocket Books, 1982.

Puttering about in a Small Land, Academy Chicago, 1985.

Radio Free Albemuth, Arbor House, 1985.

Humpty Dumpty in Oakland, Gollancz, 1986.

Mary and the Giant, Arbor House, 1987.

Nick and the Glimmung, Gollancz, 1988.

The Broken Bubble, Arbor House, 1988.

STORY COLLECTIONS

A Handful of Darkness, Rich & Cowan, 1955, reprinted, Gregg, 1978.

The Variable Man and Other Stories, Ace Books, 1957.

The Preserving Machine and Other Stories, Ace Books, 1969.

The Book of Philip K. Dick, DAW Books, 1973 (published in England as *The Turning Wheel and Other Stories,* Coronet, 1977).

The Best of Philip K. Dick, Ballantine, 1977.

The Golden Man, Berkley Publishing, 1980.

Robots, Androids, and Mechanical Oddities: The Science Fiction of Philip K. Dick, edited by Patricia Warrick and Martin H. Greenberg, Southern Illinois University Press, 1984.

Lies, Inc., Gollancz, 1984.

I Hope I Shall Arrive Soon, Doubleday, 1985.

The Collected Stories of Philip K. Dick, 5 volumes, Underwood/Miller, 1987.

CONTRIBUTOR

August Derleth, editor, *Time to Come,* Farrar, Straus, 1954.

Frederik Pohl, editor, *Star Science Fiction Stories #3,* Ballantine, 1955.

Anthony Boucher, editor, *A Treasury of Great Science Fiction,* Volume I, Doubleday, 1959.

Harlan Ellison, editor, *Dangerous Visions: 33 Original Stories,* Doubleday, 1967.

Edward L. Ferman and Barry N. Malzberg, editors, *Final Stage,* Charterhouse, 1974.

Willis E. McNelly, editor, *Science Fiction: The Academic Awakening,* College English Association, 1974.

Bruce Gillespie, editor, *Philip K. Dick: Electric Shepherd,* Norstrilia Press (Melbourne), 1975.

Peter Nicholls, editor, *Science Fiction at Large,* Gollancz, 1976, Harper, 1977.

OTHER

Confessions of a Crap Artist, Jack Isidore (of Seville, Calif): A Chronicle of Verified Scientific Fact, 1945-1959 (novel), Entwhistle Books, 1975.

A Letter from Philip K. Dick (pamphlet), Philip K. Dick Society, 1983.

The Man Whose Teeth Were Exactly Alike (novel), Mark Ziesing, 1984.

In Milton Lumky Territory (novel), Ultramarine, 1984.

Ubik: The Screenplay (based on novel of same title), Corroboree, 1985.

The Dark-Haired Girl, Mark Ziesing, 1989.

Also author of radio scripts for the Mutual Broadcasting System. Contributor of more than 100 stories, some under pseudonym Richard Phillips, to *Magazine of Fantasy and Science Fiction, Galaxy, Amazing Science Fiction Stories,* and other magazines.

SIDELIGHTS: The central problem in much of the late Philip K. Dick's science fiction is how to distinguish the real from the unreal. He once told *CA:* "My major preoccupation is the question, 'What is reality?' " In novel after novel, Dick's characters find that their familiar world is in fact an illusion, either self-created or imposed on them by others. Dick "liked to begin a novel," Patricia Warrick wrote in *Science-Fiction Studies,* "with a commonplace world and then have his characters fall through the floor of this normal world into a strange new reality." Drug-induced hallucinations, robots and androids, mystical visions, paranoic delusions, and alternate or artificial worlds are the stuff of which Dick's flexible universe is made. "All of his work," Charles Platt wrote in *Dream Makers: The Uncommon People Who Write Science Fiction,* "starts with the basic assumption that there cannot be one, single, objective reality. Everything is a matter of perception. The ground is liable to shift under your feet. A protagonist may find himself living out another person's dream, or he may enter a drug-induced state that actually makes better sense than the real world, or he may cross into a different universe completely."

Despite the mutable and often dangerous nature of Dick's fictional worlds, his characters retain at least a faint hope for the future, and manage to survive and comfort one another. Dick's characters are usually ordinary people—repairmen, homemakers, students, salesmen—caught up in overwhelming situations that call into question their basic beliefs about themselves and their world. In *The Three Stigmata of Palmer Eldritch,* powerful drugs create such believable hallucinations that users find it difficult to know when the hallucination has ended and the real world has returned. A character in *Time Out of Joint* discovers that he does not really live in a mid-twentieth-century American town as he had believed. He lives in an artificial replica of an American town built by a government of the future for its own purposes. In *Eye in the Sky,* eight people at a research facility are pushed by a freak accident into a state of consciousness where each one's subjective reality becomes real for the entire group for a time. They experience worlds where the ideas of a religious cult member, a communist, a puritan, and a paranoid are literally true. The ability of Dick's characters to survive these situations, preserving their sanity and humanity in the process, is what Dick celebrated. His novels presented a "world where ordinary people do the best they can against death-driven, malevolent forces," Tom Whalen wrote in the *American Book Review.*

In many books Dick stressed the importance of emotion, "which in his view made men human," Steven Kosek wrote in the *Chicago Tribune Book World.* In *Now Wait for Last Year,* it is the ability to feel for others that distinguishes the aliens from the Earthlings, while in *Do Androids Dream of Electric Sheep?,* a similar ability separates the androids from human beings. This emphasis on human emotions is usually contrasted with the technological environment in which Dick's characters find themselves. The typical Dick novel is set in a technologically advanced, near-future America which is falling apart in some way. Caught in the accelerating chaos, his characters need all of their humanity to survive. "There are no heroics in Dick's books," Ursula K. LeGuin wrote in *New Republic,* "but there are heroes. One is reminded of [Charles] Dickens: what counts is the honesty, constancy, kindness and patience of ordinary people."

Dick had, John Clute maintained in the *Washington Post Book World,* a "self-lacerating, feverish, deeply argued refusal to believe that the diseased prison of a world we all live in could possibly be the 'real' world." As Dick himself explained it in his introduction to the story collection *The Golden Man:* "I want to write about people I love, and put them into a fictional world spun out of my own mind, not the world we actually have, because the world we actually have does not meet my standards." In the afterword to that same collection, Dick explained why he chose to write science fiction: "SF is a field of rebellion: against accepted ideas, institutions, against all that is. In my writing I even question the universe; wonder out loud if it is real, and wonder out loud if all of us are real."

This questioning of reality was often accomplished through the use of "two basic narrative situations. . . .," Patrick G. Hogan, Jr., wrote in the *Dictionary of Literary Biography.* "One favorite plot device is that of alternate universes or parallel worlds. . . . [Dick] is also fascinated by what he characteristically calls simulacra, devices ranging from merely complex mechanical and electronic constructs to androids, and by the paradoxes created by their relationships to organic life, especially that of human beings." Many critics consider the best of Dick's novels about alternate universes to be *The Man in the High Castle, The Three Stigmata of Palmer Eldritch,* and *Flow My Tears, the Policeman Said. Do Androids Dream of Electric Sheep?* is probably his best known novel about simulacra.

The Man in the High Castle, winner of the 1962 Hugo Award and generally considered Dick's best novel, is set in a world in which America lost the Second World War. The nation has been divided in two and occupied by the Germans and Japanese. Most of the novel takes place on the Japanese-occupied West Coast and revolves around a group of Americans who are trying to cope with their status as subject people. Concerned primarily with creating a believable alternate society, the novel reveals in the process "how easily this nation would have surrendered its own culture under a Japanese occupation and how compatible American fears, prejudices, and desires were with Nazism," as Hogan remarked. The novel's "man in the high castle" is the author of an underground best-selling book about an alternate world where America won the war. "I did seven years of research for *The Man in the High Castle,*" Dick said in an interview for the *Missouri Review.* "I had prime-source material at the Berkeley-Cal library right from the gestapo's mouth—stuff that had been seized after World War II. . . . That's . . . why I've never written a sequel to it: it's too horrible, too awful. I started several times to write a sequel, but I [would have] had to go back and read about Nazis again, so I couldn't do it." Dick used the I Ching, an ancient Chinese divining system, to plot *The Man in the High Castle.* At each critical juncture in the narrative, Dick consulted the I Ching to determine the proper course of the plot.

The alternate universes in *The Three Stigmata of Palmer Eldritch* are created by powerful hallucinogenic drugs. The novel is set in the near-future when the increasing heat of the sun is making life on Earth impossible. The United Nations is forcing people to immigrate to Mars, an inhospitable desert waste where colonists must live in underground hovels. Because of the boredom of colony life, a drug-induced fantasy world has been devised which uses small dolls and miniature settings. When a colonist takes the drug Can-D, he becomes one of the dolls and lives for a brief time in an Earth-like setting. The manufacturer of the dolls and settings—a company named Perky Pat Layouts, after the female doll—also sells Can-D. When Palmer Eldritch returns from a deep-space exploration, he brings with him a supply of the new and more powerful drug Chew-Z. Eldritch has also acquired three "stigmata"—an artificial metallic arm, enormous steel teeth, and artificial eyes. His Chew-Z is cheaper and longer-lasting than Can-D and he soon is selling it to the Martian colonists. But Chew-Z doesn't seem to wear off. The user is moved into a world that seems like his own but with the important difference that Palmer Eldritch has god-like powers. Bruce Gillespie, writing in *Philip K. Dick: Electric Shepherd,* called *Palmer Eldritch* "one of the few masterpieces of recent science fiction."

Dick received the John W. Campbell Memorial Award for *Flow My Tears, the Policeman Said,* a near-future novel in which popular television talk show host Jason Taverner wakes up one morning in a world where he is unknown. No record even exists of his having been born, an awkward situation in the records-conscious police state that Taverner's California has become. The explanation for this impossibility is that Taverner is living within the drug hallucination of Alys Buckper, and in that hallucination there is no place for him. The powerful drug, able to impose Alys's hallucination on reality itself, eventually kills her, and Taverner is set free. "Dick skillfully explores the psychological ramifications of this nightmare," Gerald Jonas commented in the *New York Times Book Review,* "but he is even more interested in the reaction of a ruthlessly efficient computerized police state to the existence of a man, who, according to the computers, should not exist."

Do Androids Dream of Electric Sheep? is Dick's most celebrated novel about simulacra, mechanical objects which simulate life. In this novel Dick posits a world in which androids are so highly developed that it is only by the most rigid testing that one can distinguish them from human beings. The key difference is the quality of empathy which humans have for other living things. When some androids escape from a work colony and make their way to Earth, bounty hunter Rick Deckard must find them. But Deckard gradually comes to feel compassion for the androids, realizing that the tests he gives measure only a subtle difference between androids and humans. In contrast to this officially-sanctioned tracking and killing of androids, this near-future society accepts artificial animals of all kinds—everything from sheep to spiders. With most real animals extinct, replicas are fashionable to own. One of the rarest animals is the toad, and when Deckard discovers one in the desert he believes he has made an important find. But even in the desert there are no real animals. Deckard notices a small control panel in the toad's abdomen. Nonetheless, he takes the toad home and cares for him. His wife, touched by his concern for the "creature," buys some electric flies for the toad to eat. "Against this bizarre background of pervasive fakery," Philip Strick wrote in *Sight and Sound,* "the erosion of authentic humanity by undetectable android imitations has all the plausibility of a new and lethal plague whereby evolution would become substitution and nobody would notice the difference." Writing in *Philip K. Dick,* Patricia S. Warrick called *Do Androids Dream of Electric Sheep?* "one of Dick's finest novels," citing its "complexity of structure and idea." *Androids* was loosely adapted as the film "Blade Runner" in 1982.

Several critics have commented on the structure of Dick's fiction, pointing out that many novels end inconclusively and are often filled with deliberate paradoxes and inconsistencies. Angus Taylor, writing in his *Philip K. Dick and the Umbrella of Light,* explained that Dick "undermines the plot in its superficial aspect by throwing roadblocks in the way of the smooth succession of events, and asks us to divert our attention, to search out and accept the poetic core of the work; he tries to focus our attention on the plot as a 'net' for catching something strange and otherworldly." In similar terms, Roger Zelazny noted in *Philip K. Dick: Electric Shepherd* that "the subjective response, when a Philip Dick book has been finished and put aside is that, upon reflection, it does not seem so much that one holds the memory of a story; rather, it is the after effects of a poem rich in metaphor that seem to remain." Writing in *Extrapolation,* Mary Kay Bray saw Dick's novels as using a "mandalic" structure. "The key to

mandalic structure," Bray wrote, "is that it radiates from a center and must suggest that center in all its patterns and images. In point of view and details of landscape and character, Dick's novels manage just that." Also writing in *Extrapolation,* Warrick argued that in Dick's novels, he creates a "bi-polar construction" of reality. This construction presents both sides of a question simultaneously, expecting a synthesis from the reader. This synthesis results in the reader seeing "from opposite directions simultaneously. He is rewarded with a fleeting epiphany—Dick's vision of 'process reality,'" Warrick wrote. "Ultimately, however, one intuits, not analyzes, Dick's meaning."

In writing several novels, Dick drew upon his own life experiences. *A Scanner Darkly,* for example, is dedicated to a list of Dick's friends who died or suffered permanent health damage because of drugs. The novel concerns undercover narcotics agent Bob Arctor, who is assigned to investigate himself. His superiors are unaware of his undercover identity and Arctor cannot afford to reveal it. He investigates himself to avoid suspicion. While conducting the investigation, however, Arctor is taking the drug Substance D. The drug splits his personality until he no longer recognizes himself in surveillance videotapes. Arctor's condition worsens until he is finally put into a drug rehabilitation program. "The novel," Patrick Parrinder wrote in the *Times Literary Supplement,* "is a frightening allegory of the process of drug abuse, in which some of the alternative realities experienced are revealed as the hallucinations of terminal addicts." "Drug misuse is not a disease," Dick wrote in an author's note to the novel, "it is a decision, like the decision to step out in front of a moving car." Dick himself suffered pancreatic damage from his involvement with drugs. His use of amphetamines resulted in the high blood pressure which eventually ended in his fatal stroke. Dick told Platt that he had "regarded drugs as dangerous and potentially lethal, but had a cat's curiosity. It was my interest in the human mind that made me curious. . . . These were essentially religious strivings that were appearing in me."

This interest in religion crystallized in 1974 in a mystical experience which changed the course of Dick's career. "I experienced an invasion of my mind," Dick explained to Platt, "by a transcendentally rational mind, as if I had been insane all my life and suddenly had become sane." For several months, this presence took over Dick's mind and directed his actions. He claimed that it straightened out his health and finances and put his business affairs in order. Despite numerous efforts to rationalize the experience, Dick was unable to come to any conclusions about it. In *VALIS, The Divine Invasion,* and *The Transmigration of Timothy Archer,* Dick wrote of theological paradoxes and seekers after truth, exploring various religious concepts for possible answers. Dick realized the disturbing appearance of his claims. In *VALIS,* he questioned his own sanity through two characters who are aspects of himself. Horselover Fat is a half-mad mystic who hears God's voice in his head. The other character, Phil Dick, is a writer who tries to understand Horselover, although he regards him in a bemused manner. It is revealed in the course of the novel that Horselover is actually a psychological projection of Phil. He has been created as a way to deal with the death of Phil's loved ones, to act as a shield against accepting those deaths. With this revelation, Clute observed, "we begin to see the artfulness in the way Dick has chosen to handle (like a magician, or a writer) material too nutty to accept, too admonitory to forget, too haunting to abandon." After asking the question "Was Phil Dick sane?," Peter Nicholls wrote in *Science Fiction Review* that "the question has no absolute answer. . . . Phil thought that God had reached into his mind. To this day I am not sure whether he meant this literally or metaphorically."

At his best, Dick is generally regarded as one of the finest science fiction writers of his time. Nicholls believed him to be "one of the greatest science fiction writers in history, and one of this century's most important writers in any field." He was, Whalen maintained, "one of America's best writers. . . . He was a great science fiction writer, so much so, that one is reluctant to apply the SF label, with its undeserved stigma, to his writing." Similarly, Clute held that Dick was the "greatest of science fiction writers—though he's by no means the best writer of science fiction" to clarify that what Dick wrote was concerned with the human condition, not with the technological progress of the future. Kosek believed Dick had a "very intense and morally significant vision of life" which he made evident in "a long string of compelling, idiosyncratic novels . . ., most of which embodied a single urgent message: Things are not what they seem to be." In her evaluation of Dick's work, LeGuin stressed that it was easy to misinterpret him. A reader "may put the book down believing that he's read a clever sci-fi thriller and nothing more," LeGuin wrote. "The fact that what Dick is entertaining us about is reality and madness, time and death, sin and salvation—this has escaped most readers and critics. Nobody notices; nobody notices that we have our own homegrown [Jorge Luis] Borges, and have had him for 30 years."

A number of original novels and stories by Dick have been published posthumously.

MEDIA ADAPTATIONS: Do Androids Dream of Electric Sheep? was filmed as "Blade Runner" by Warner Brothers in 1982. Film rights for the stories "We Can Remember It for You Wholesale" and "Second Variety" have been sold. *Ubik* has been optioned for a film adaptation.

BIOGRAPHICAL/CRITICAL SOURCES:

BOOKS

Aldiss, Brian W., *The Shape of Future Things,* Faber, 1970.
Aldiss, Brian W., *The Billion Year Spree,* Doubleday, 1973.
Contemporary Literary Criticism, Gale, Volume X, 1979, Volume XXX, 1984.
Dick, Philip K., *A Scanner Darkly,* Doubleday, 1977.
Dick, Philip K., *The Golden Man,* Berkley Publishing, 1980.
Dick, Philip K., *A Letter from Philip K. Dick,* Philip K. Dick Society, 1983.
Dictionary of Literary Biography, Volume VIII: *Twentieth Century American Science-Fiction Writers,* two volumes Gale, 1981.
Gillespie, Bruce, editor, *Philip K. Dick: Electric Shepherd,* Norstrilia Press (Melbourne), 1975.
Greenberg, Martin Harry and Joseph D. Olander, editors, *Philip K. Dick,* Taplinger, 1983.
Ketterer, David, *New Worlds for Old: The Apocalyptic Imagination, Science Fiction, and American Literature,* Indiana University Press, 1974.
Knight, Damon, *In Search of Wonder,* Advent Publishers, 2nd edition, 1967.
Levack, Daniel J. H. and Steven Owen Godersky, *PKD: A Philip K. Dick Bibliography,* Underwood/Miller, 1981.
Moskowitz, Sam, *Seekers of Tomorrow,* Ballantine, 1967.
Mullen, R. D. and Darko Suvin, editors, *Science-Fiction Studies: Selected Articles on Science Fiction, 1973-1975,* Gregg, 1976.
Nicholls, Peter, editor, *Science Fiction at Large,* Harper, 1976.
Parrinder, Peter, *Science Fiction: A Critical Guide,* Longman, 1979.
Platt, Charles, *Dream Makers: The Uncommon People Who Write Science Fiction,* Berkley Publishing, 1980.
Reilly, Robert, editor, *The Transcendent Adventure,* Greenwood Press, 1983.
Rickman, Gregg, *Philip K. Dick: In His Own Words,* Fragments, 1984.
Scholes, Robert and Eric S. Rabkin, *Science Fiction: History, Science, Vision,* Oxford University Press, 1977.
Spinrad, Norman, *Modern Science Fiction,* Doubleday, 1974.
Taylor, Angus, *Philip K. Dick and the Umbrella of Light,* T-K Graphics, 1975.
Tolley, Michael and Kirpal Singh, editors, *The Stellar Gauge,* [Carlton, Australia], 1981.
Wolfe, Gary K., editor, *Science Fiction Dialogues,* Academy Chicago, 1982.

PERIODICALS

American Book Review, January, 1984.
Best Sellers, November, 1976, May, 1977.
Chicago Tribune Book World, July 4, 1982, February 16, 1986.
Extrapolation, summer, 1979, summer, 1980, summer, 1983.
Fantasy Review, October, 1984.
Listener, May 29, 1975.
Los Angeles Times Book Review, September 6, 1981.
Magazine of Fantasy and Science Fiction, June, 1963, August, 1968, January, 1975, August, 1978, July, 1980.
Missouri Review, Volume VII, number 2, 1984.
New Republic, October 30, 1976, November 26, 1977.
New Statesman, December 17, 1976, December 16, 1977.
New Worlds, March, 1966, May, 1969.
New York Times Book Review, July 20, 1975, December 1, 1985, January 12, 1986.
Observer, December 8, 1974.
Philip K. Dick Society Newsletter, 1983—.
Science Fiction Review, Volume V, number 2, 1976, Volume V, number 4, 1976, February, 1977, summer, 1983, November, 1983.
Science-Fiction Studies, March, 1975, July, 1980, July, 1983, March, 1984.
Sight and Sound, summer, 1982.
Spectator, November 19, 1977.
Times Literary Supplement, June 12, 1969, July 8, 1977, January 27, 1978, January 17, 1986, February 7, 1986, February 6, 1987, September 30, 1988, December 8, 1989.
Vertex, February, 1974.
Village Literary Supplement, August, 1982.
Washington Post Book World, February 22, 1981, May 23, 1982, June 30, 1985, May 25, 1986, August 2, 1987.

OBITUARIES:

PERIODICALS

Chicago Tribune, March 4, 1982.
Fantasy Newsletter, April/May, 1982.
Los Angeles Times, March 8, 1982.
Newsweek, March 15, 1982.
New York Times, March 3, 1982.
Publishers Weekly, March 19, 1982.
Science-Fiction Studies, July, 1982.
Time, March 15, 1982.
Times (London), March 15, 1982.
Washington Post, March 4, 1982.

*   *   *

DICKEY, James (Lafayette) 1923-

PERSONAL: Born February 2, 1923, in Atlanta, Ga.; son of Eugene (a lawyer) and Maibelle (Swift) Dickey; married Maxine

Syerson, November 4, 1948 (died October 28, 1976); married Deborah Dodson, December 30, 1976; children: (first marriage) Christopher Swift, Keven Webster; (second marriage) Bronwen Elaine. *Education:* Attended Clemson College (now University), 1942; Vanderbilt University, B.A. (magna cum laude), 1949, M.A., 1950.

ADDRESSES: Home—4620 Lelia's Court, Lake Katherine, Columbia, S.C. 29206. *Office*—Department of English, University of South Carolina, Columbia, S.C. 29208.

CAREER: Poet, novelist, and essayist. Instructor in English at Rice Institute (now Rice University), Houston, Tex., 1950 and 1952-54, and University of Florida, Gainesville, 1955-56; worked in advertising, 1956-60, first as copywriter for McCann-Erickson, New York, N.Y., then as official for Liller, Neal, Battle & Lindsey and Burke Dowling Adams, both in Atlanta, Ga. Poet-in-residence at Reed College, Portland, Ore., 1963-64; San Fernando Valley State College (now California State University, Northridge), Northridge, Calif., 1964-65; University of Wisconsin—Madison, 1966; University of Wisconsin—Milwaukee, 1967; and Washington University, St. Louis, Mo., 1968. Georgia Institute of Technology, Atlanta, Franklin Distinguished Professor of English, 1968; University of South Carolina, Columbia, professor of English and poet-in-residence, 1969. Library of Congress, consultant in poetry, 1966-68, honorary consultant in American Letters, 1968-71. *Military service:* U.S. Army Air Forces, World War II, flew 100 combat missions in 418th Night Fighter Squadron. U.S. Air Force, served in Korean War; awarded Air Medal.

MEMBER: American Academy of Arts and Sciences, American Academy of Arts and Letters, National Institute of Arts and Letters, Phi Beta Kappa.

AWARDS, HONORS: Sewanee Review poetry fellowship, 1954-55; Union League Civic and Arts Foundation Prize, 1958, Vachel Lindsay Prize, 1959, and Levinson Prize, 1982, all from *Poetry* magazine; Guggenheim fellowship, 1961-62; National Book Award for poetry and Melville Cane Award of Poetry Society of America, both 1966, for *Buckdancer's Choice;* National Institute of Arts and Letters grant, 1966; Medicis prize for best foreign book of the year (Paris), 1971, for *Deliverance;* invited to read poem "The Strength of Fields" at Inauguration of President Jimmy Carter, 1977; New York Quarterly Poetry Day Award, 1977; invited to read poem "For a Time and Place" at second inauguration of Richard Riley, governor of South Carolina, 1983.

WRITINGS:

POETRY

Into the Stone, and Other Poems, Scribner, 1960.
Drowning with Others (also see below), Wesleyan University Press, 1962.
Helmets (also see below), Wesleyan University Press, 1964.
Two Poems of the Air, Centicore Press (Portland), 1964.
Buckdancer's Choice, Wesleyan University Press, 1965.
Poems, 1957-1967 (selections issued as miniature edition prior to publication), Wesleyan University Press, 1968.
The Eye-Beaters, Blood, Victory, Madness, Buckhead, and Mercy, Doubleday, 1970.
(Adaptor with others of English versions) Evgenii Evtushenko, *Stolen Apples: Poetry,* Doubleday, 1971.
Exchanges, Bruccoli Clark, 1971.
The Zodiac (long poem; based on Hendrik Marsman's poem of the same title), Doubleday and Bruccoli Clark, 1976.

The Strength of Fields (poem; also see below), Bruccoli Clark, 1977.
Tucky the Hunter (juvenile), Crown, 1978.
The Strength of Fields (collection; title poem previously published separately), Doubleday, 1979.
Head Deep in Strange Sounds: Improvisations from the UnEnglish, Palaemon Press, 1979.
Scion, Deerfield Press, 1980.
The Early Motion: "Drowning with Others" and "Helmets," Wesleyan University Press, 1981.
Falling, May Day Sermon, and Other Poems, Wesleyan University Press, 1981.
The Eagle's Mile, Bruccoli Clark, 1981.
Puella, Doubleday, 1982.
Vaermland, Palaemon Press, 1982.
False Youth: Four Seasons, Pressworks, 1983.
The Central Motion, Wesleyan University Press, 1983.
(With Sharon Anglin Kuhne) *Intervisions: Poems and Photographs,* Visualternatives, 1983.
Veteran Birth: The Gadfly Poems, 1947-1949, Palaemon Press, 1983.
Bronwen, The Traw, and the Shape Shifter, Harcourt, 1986.
Of Prisons and Ideas, Harcourt, 1987.
Summons, Bruccoli Clark, 1988.

Poems represented in many anthologies, including: *Contemporary American Poetry,* edited by Donald Hall, Penguin, 1962; *American Poetry since 1945,* edited by Stephen Stepanchev, Harper, 1965; *The New Modern Poets,* edited by M. L. Rosenthal, Macmillan, 1967; *Where Is Viet Nam?: American Poets Respond,* edited by Walter Lowenfels, Doubleday, 1967; *Poems of Our Moment: Contemporary Poets of the English Language,* edited by John Hollander, Pegasus, 1968; *The Norton Anthology of Poetry,* revised shorter edition, edited by Alexander W. Allison, Herbert Barrows, Caesar R. Blake, Arthur J. Carr, Arthur M. Eastman, and Hubert M. English, Jr., Norton, 1975; *The Norton Introduction to Literature,* second edition, edited by Carl E. Bain, Jerome Beaty, and J. Paul Hunter, Norton, 1977; *The Norton Anthology of American Literature,* Volume 2, edited by Ronald Gottesman, Laurence B. Holland, William H. Pritchard, and David Kalstone, Norton, 1979.

PROSE

The Suspect in Poetry (criticism), Sixties Press, 1964.
A Private Brinksmanship (lecture given at Pitzer College, June 6, 1965), Castle Press (Pasadena), 1965.
Spinning the Crystal Ball: Some Guesses at the Future of American Poetry (lecture given at Library of Congress, April 24, 1967), Library of Congress, 1967.
Metaphor as Pure Adventure (lecture given at Library of Congress, December 4, 1967), Library of Congress, 1968.
Babel to Byzantium: Poets and Poetry Now (criticism), Farrar, Straus, 1968.
(Author of introduction) Paul Carroll, editor, *New American Poets,* Follett, 1968.
Deliverance (novel; Literary Guild selection; excerpt entitled "Two Days in September" published in *Atlantic,* February, 1970; also see below), Houghton, 1970.
Self-Interviews (informal monologues; excerpt entitled "The Poet Tries to Make a Kind of Order" published in *Mademoiselle,* September, 1970), recorded and edited by Barbara Reiss and James Reiss, Doubleday, 1970.
Sorties: Journals and New Essays, Doubleday, 1971.
(With Hubert Shuptrine) *Jericho: The South Beheld* (Book-of-the-Month Club alternate selection), Oxmoor, 1974.

(With Marvin Hayes) *God's Images: The Bible, a New Vision,* Oxmoor, 1977.

The Enemy from Eden, Lord John Press, 1978.

In Pursuit of the Grey Soul, Bruccoli Clark, 1978.

(Author of afterword) Thomas Boyd, *Through Wheat,* Southern Illinois University Press, 1978.

(Author of foreword) Richard Eberhart, *Of Poetry and Poets,* University of Illinois Press, 1979.

(Author of introduction) Samuel Clemens, *The Adventures of Tom Sawyer* [and] *The Adventures of Huckleberry Finn,* New American Library, 1979.

The Water Bug's Mittens (Ezra Pound Lecture at University of Idaho), Bruccoli Clark, 1980.

(Author of foreword) *Dictionary of Literary Biography,* Volume 5: *American Poets since World War II,* Gale, 1980.

The Starry Place between the Antlers: Why I Live in South Carolina, Bruccoli Clark, 1981.

Night Hurdling (also contains three poems), Bruccoli Clark, 1983.

(Author of introduction) *From the Green Horseshoe: Poems by James Dickey's Students,* University of South Carolina Press, 1987.

Alnilam, Doubleday, 1987.

Wayfarer, Oxmoor, 1988.

SCREENPLAYS

Deliverance (based on Dickey's novel of the same title; produced by Warner Bros., 1972), Southern Illinois University Press, 1982.

"The Call of the Wild" (based on the novel by Jack London), produced by National Broadcasting Co. (NBC-TV), 1976.

Also author of "To Gene Bullard" and "The Sentence."

CONTRIBUTOR

Louis D. Rubin, Jr., and Robert D. Jacobs, editors, *Modern Southern Literature in Its Cultural Setting,* Doubleday, 1961.

Morton Dauwen Zabel, editor, *Selected Poems of Edwin Arlington Robinson,* Macmillan, 1965.

Howard Nemerov, editor, *Poets on Poetry,* Basic Books, 1966.

Oscar Williams, editor, *Master Poems of the English Language,* Trident Press, 1966.

Teaching in America, Fifth Annual Conference of the National Committee for Support of the Public Schools, 1967.

Robert M. Hutchins and Mortimer J. Adler, editors-in-chief, *The Great Ideas of Today: 1968,* Encyclopaedia Britannica, 1968.

Pages: The World of Books, Writers, and Writing, Volume 1, Gale, 1976.

Conversations with Writers, Volume 1, Gale, 1977.

Contributor of poems, essays, articles, and reviews to more than thirty periodicals, including *Atlantic, Harper's, Hudson Review, Nation, New Yorker, Paris Review, Poetry, Sewanee Review, Times Literary Supplement,* and *Virginia Quarterly Review.*

WORK IN PROGRESS: Crux, a sequel to *Alnilam;* books of poetry.

SIDELIGHTS: James Dickey is regarded as a major American poet because of his unique vision and style. "It is clear," says Joyce Carol Oates in her *New Heaven, New Earth,* "that Dickey desires to take on 'his' own personal history as an analogue to or a microscopic exploration of twentieth-century American history, which is one of the reasons he is so important a poet." Winner of both the 1966 National Book Award and the Melville

Cane Award for *Buckdancer's Choice,* Dickey has been called an expansional poet, not only because the voices in his work loom large enough to address or represent facets of the American experience, but also because his violent imagery and eccentric style exceed the bounds of more traditional norms, often producing a quality he describes as "country surrealism." One of Dickey's principal themes, usually expressed through a direct confrontation between or a surreal juxtaposition of the world of nature and the world of civilized man, is the need to intensify life by maintaining contact with the primitive impulses, sensations, and ways of seeing suppressed by modern society. It is a theme made explicit in his internationally bestselling novel *Deliverance* and is one given much attention in critical reviews. Through his poetry and prose, Dickey has come to be known as a shaman of our culture, for as Joan Bobbitt writes in *Concerning Poetry,* he "sees civilization as so far removed from nature, its primal antecedent, that only [grotesque] aberrations can aptly depict their relationship and, as he implies, possibly restore them to harmony and order."

Although he started writing poetry in 1947 at the age of twenty-four, Dickey did not become a full-time poet until thirteen years later. After earning a master's degree in 1950, he taught and lectured for six years at several colleges but decided to forsake academic life for the advertising business when some of his poems were construed to be obscene. "I thought if my chosen profession, teaching, was going to fall out to be that sort of situation," he says in *Conversations with Writers,* "I'd rather go for the buck and make some damn dough in the market place. I had the confidence of Lucifer in myself by that time, and I was beginning to appear all over the place in the *Hudson Review, Partisan* [*Review*], *Sewanee* [*Review*], *Kenyon* [*Review*], and so on. I figured that the kind of thing that an advertising writer would be able to write, I could do with the little finger of the left hand, and they were getting paid good dough for it. I happened to have been right."

Dickey got a job with McCann-Erickson, the biggest ad agency in New York at the time, and wrote jingles for its Coca-Cola account. Later, he went to Liller, Neal, Battle & Lindsey in Atlanta, Ga., for twice the salary, working on potato chips and fertilizer accounts, and then jumped agencies again for still another increase, becoming an executive with Burke Dowling Adams, where his primary concern was the Delta Airlines account. Robert W. Hill reports in *Dictionary of Literary Biography* that by the late 1950s, Dickey was earning enough to have a secure future in the business. But after his first book, *Into the Stone, and Other Poems,* was published in 1960, Dickey left advertising to devote all his time to poetry. "There could have been no more unpromising enterprise or means of earning a livelihood than that of being an American poet," he admits in *Conversations with Writers.* "It's different now. They're still having a relatively rocky road, but it ain't like it was when I used to give readings sometimes for maybe ten or fifteen dollars, where there would be five people in the audiences three of them relatives."

Dickey's emotional attachment to his craft—obviously large enough to lead him to abandon a lucrative career in advertising—surfaced early in his writing career. "I came to poetry with no particular qualifications," he recounts in *Poets on Poetry.* "I had begun to suspect, however, that there is a poet—or a kind of poet—buried in every human being like Ariel in his tree, and that the people whom we are pleased to call poets are only those who have felt the need and contrived the means to release this spirit from its prison. As soon as I began writing I knew that I had the need, but that the means were not immediately forthcoming. I knew nothing whatever of poetic technique, of metrics, prosody, stanzaic construction, and to a certain extent I still consider those things as secondary to something else which I can only define, using one of the words I most despised in my younger days, as the spirit of poetry: the individually imaginative or visionary quality."

In seeking the means to liberate his poetic spirit, Dickey concentrated at first on rhythms, on anapests and iambs. "Although I didn't care for rhyme and the 'packaged' quality which it gives even the best poems," he says in *Poets on Poetry,* "I did care very much for meter, or at least rhythm." With his prize-winning collection, *Buckdancer's Choice,* he began using the split line and free verse forms that have come to be associated with his work. But perhaps the most recognizable feature of his stylistic development has been his ambitious experimentation with language and form—inverted or odd syntax, horizontal spaces within lines, spread-eagled and ode-like shaped poems. Dickey's poems, writes Paul Zweig in the *New York Times Book Review,* "are like richly modulated hollers; a sort of rough, American-style bel canto advertising its freedom from the constraints of ordinary language. Dickey's style is so personal, his rhythms so willfully eccentric, that the poems seem to swell up and overflow like that oldest of American art forms, the boast."

According to David Kalstone in another *New York Times Book Review* article, Dickey's "achievement has been to press the limit of language and, in his criticism, to point up the strengths of other writers who do: Hart Crane, [D. H.] Lawrence, [Theodore] Roethke." L. M. Rosenberg expresses a similar sentiment in the *Chicago Tribune Book World.* Claiming that for "sheer beauty and passion we have no greater spokesman, nor do we have any poet more powerfully, naturally musical [than Dickey]," Rosenberg maintains that Dickey's "experiments with language and form are the experiments of a man who understands that one of the strangest things about poetry is the way it looks on the page: It just isn't normal. The question of how to move the reader's eye along the page, particularly as it makes an unnatural jump from line to line . . ., how to slow the reader down or speed him up, how to give words back their original, almost totemic power-that's something any poet thinks a lot about, and it's something Dickey works with almost obsessively.

Dickey's stylistic endeavors, however, only partially explain why he is, in the minds of several critics, the most frequently discussed American poet of his generation. As noted above, in *Poets on Poetry* he admits that he considers style subordinate to the spirit of poetry, the "individually imaginative" vision of the poet, and, according to William Meredith in the *New York Times Book Review,* he consequently looks "for shapes and rhythms that correspond exactly to the kind of testimony his poems have always been. When he is testifying to an experience that declares its shape and meaning eloquently—'The Shark's Parlor' and 'Falling' are examples of this—the poems have form in [Ezra] Pound's phrase, as a tree has form." But in addition to the unity of form and content, there is in Dickey's poetry, as well as his criticism, says William Heyen in the *Southern Review,* "an emphasis on the humanism, or the morality or larger concerns of poetry. There's the idea that what the poet has to reach for is not necessarily affirmation, but, yes, a kind of affirming of values."

A primary thematic concern of Dickey's, one served well by his vigorous style, is the need "to get back wholeness of being, to respond full-heartedly and full-bodiedly to experience," observes Anatole Broyard of the *New York Times.* In *Poets on Poetry,* Dickey recalls that the subject matter of his early poems came from the principal incidents of his life, "those times when I felt most strongly and was most aware of the intense reality of the objects and people I moved among. If I were to arrange my own poems in some such scheme, chronologizing them, they would form a sort of story of this kind, leading from childhood in the north of Georgia through high school with its athletics and wild motorcycle riding, through a beginning attempt at education in an agricultural college, through World War II and the Korean War as a flyer in a night-fighter squadron, through another beginning at college, this time completed, through various attempts at a valid love affair culminating in the single successful one known as 'marriage,' through two children, several deaths in the family, travels, reflections, and so on."

Despite the many allusions to his own life, Dickey "is able to assimilate and report the experiences of others and himself, coming to that kind of peculiarly Dickeyesque fusion of selves so powerfully worked in 'Drinking from a Helmet,' 'Slave Quarters,' and 'The Firebombing,' " claims Robert W. Hill. "This aesthetic viewpoint, with the speaker self-consciously observing, knowing that he has a perspective that is momentary and unique, that the time and the place are special, that the voice of the visionary observer is the only one to deal with the striking matter before him, emphasizes Dickey's dedication to art, to the exploration of the creative process, especially with regard to the use of narrative voice under special, extreme conditions."

Extreme conditions permeate Dickey's work. "To make a radical simplification," writes Monroe K. Spears in *Dionysus and the City,* "the central impulse of Dickey's poetry may be said to be that of identifying with human or other creatures in moments of ultimate confrontation, of violence and truth. A good example is [the poem] 'Falling,' which imagines the thoughts and feelings of an airline stewardess, accidentally swept through an emergency door, as she falls thousands of feet to her death" in a field in Kansas. Alive as she hurtles through space, she strips and imagines making love "in a furious, death-defying motion toward fertile farms and sensuous people who must in their blood understand even such a strange, naked ritual," explains Robert W. Hill. "Hers is a dance all the way to death; she makes a poem of her last life and a fertility prayer of her last breath: 'AH, GOD—.' "

Many of Dickey's poems explore moments of being as known by horses, dogs, deer, bees, boars, and other inhabitants of nonhuman worlds. In "The Sheep Child," for example, a creature half child and half sheep (the result of boys coupling with sheep) speaks out from a jar of formaldehyde. The poem "attains very nearly the power of mythic utterance," maintains Hill, for the sheep child "shows its magnified view of the truth of two worlds," the fusion of man and nature, with an "eternal, unyielding vision." In Hill's opinion, "The Sheep Child" is "the most radical expression of Dickey's sense of transcendence in fusing man and nature to achieve 'imperishable vision,' " but it is not the only such expression.

"Everywhere in [Dickey's] body of writing in-touchness with 'the other forms of life' stands forth as a primary value," asserts Benjamin DeMott in *Saturday Review.* "The strength of this body of poetry lies in its feeling for the generative power at the core of existence. A first-rate Dickey poem breathes the energy of the world, and testifies to the poet's capacity for rising out of tranced dailiness—habitual, half-lived life—into a more intense physicality, a burly appetitive wanting-ness of being. To read him is, for an instant, to share that capacity. The sense of expended effort, of imagination under pressure, is vivid as the man drives himself to speak from levels of creaturehood wholly different from his own. And the palpableness of this near-physical effort rouses in the reader new alertness to human possibility. In the act of grasping energy or violence from within, mastering it, embodying it in verbal rhythms, the poet presses the neglected natural nerve in humanness."

Along with DeMott, critics generally agree that by pressing "the neglected natural nerve in humanness" through shockingly bizarre or surreal images, Dickey seeks to depict man's proper relationship with nature. "It is rarely or never so simple as this," cautions Howard Nemerov in *Reflexions on Poetry and Poetics,* "yet the intention seems often enough this, a feeling one's way down the chain of being, a becoming the voice which shall make dumb things respond, sometimes to their hurt or deaths, a sensing of alien modes of experience, mostly in darkness or in an unfamiliar light; reason accepting its animality; a poetry whose transcendences come of its reconciliations. Salvation is this: apprehending the continuousness of forms, the flowing of one energy through everything." "Dickey makes it clear," suggests Joan Bobbitt, "that what seems to be unnatural is only so because of its context in a civilized world, and that these deviations actually possess a vitality which modern man has lost."

In an interview with William Heyen in the *Southern Review,* Dickey comments on the necessity for man to make some sort of connection with animal life: "I remember a quotation from D. H. Lawrence to the effect that we are in the process of losing the cosmos. We dominate it, but in a sense we've lost it or we're losing it. It's the sense of being part of what Lovejoy called 'the great chain of being.' Randall Jarrell, one of my favorite critics and poets, was a great punster, and he said that we have substituted for the great chain of being 'the great chain of buying,' which is, maybe, something that's diametrically opposed, and will be the ruination of everything."

Dickey has been widely praised for having what Herbert Leibowitz in the *New York Times Book Review* calls "a shrewd and troubled knowledge of the 'primal powers' " of nature, as well as "a dramatic skill in presenting the endless beauty of instinct, the feel of icy undertows and warm shallows, the bloodlettings which are a regular part of nature's law." But because a Dickey poem centers on "moments of ultimate confrontation" as Spears says, and because that confrontation often seems to involve a conflict with the norms of civilized society, Dickey has been criticized for what some see as an inherent preoccupation with violence that leads to a castigation of modern society. Paul Zweig, for example, maintains that Dickey's "imagination rides the edge of violence," and James Aronson claims in the *Antioch Review* that this characteristic has given Dickey a reputation as "a kind of primitive savage" who extols the virtues of uncivilized life.

Although Dickey's images are often primitive and animistic, many reviewers consider it a mistake to see him as a spokesman for a return to savagery. Joyce Carol Oates writes that Dickey, "so disturbing to many of us, must be seen in a larger context, as a kind of 'shaman,' a man necessarily at war with his civilization because that civilization will not, cannot, understand what he is saying." A writer in the *Virginia Quarterly Review* observes that at the heart of Dickey's work lies a "desperate insistence that every human experience, however painful or ugly, be viewed as a possible occasion for the renewal of life, [and] with Dickey any renewal inevitably requires struggle."

According to Robert W. Hill and James Aronson, a typical case of misinterpretation involves "The Firebombing," the first poem in *Buckdancer's Choice.* In part a result of Dickey's own experiences in the air force as a fighter-pilot, the poem presents a speaker who, in a momentary flashback, recalls that twenty years ago he was dropping 300-gallon tanks filled with napalm and gasoline on neighborhoods much like his own. Aronson reports that some readers believe the poem portrays the "joy of destroying" experienced by men at war, or even suggests that destruction itself is natural, when actually the poem expresses the complex emotion of "guilt at the inability to feel guilt." Hill concurs: "The moral indignation that might flood so readily for artists and thinkers flows less surely and less fleetingly for one whose life has depended upon a certain screening out of moral subtleties in times of actual combat. The 'luxury' of moral pangs seems to come upon the fighter-pilot in 'The Firebombing' only after his war is over, his safety and his family's restored to allow the contemplation of distant and not-to-be-altered acts of horrible proportion."

Noting the characteristic power of Dickey's vision and the intensity of his language, Joyce Carol Oates calls "The Firebombing" the central poem of his work. "It is," she writes, "unforgettable, and seems to me an important achievement in our contemporary literature, a masterpiece that could only have been written by an American, and only by Dickey. Having shown us so convincingly in his poetry how natural, how inevitable, is man's love for all things, Dickey now shows us what happens when man is forced to destroy, forced to step down into history and be an American ('and proud of it'). In so doing he enters a tragic dimension in which few poets indeed have operated. Could Whitman's affirmation hold out if he were forced to affirm not just the violence of others, but his own?"

Critics generally see in Dickey's internationally best-selling novel *Deliverance* a thematic continuity with his poetry. A novel about how decent men kill, it is also about the bringing forth, through confrontation, of those qualities in a man that usually lie buried. Simply put, *Deliverance* is the story of four Atlanta suburbanites on a back-to-nature canoe trip that turns into a terrifying test of survival. Dickey, who has made a number of canoe and bow-hunting trips in the wilds of northern Georgia, told Walter Clemons in the *New York Times Book Review* that much of the story was suggested by incidents that had happened to him or that he had heard about through friends. All those experiences, according to Dickey, share the feeling of excitement and fear that "comes from being in an unprotected situation where the safeties of law and what we call civilization don't apply, they just don't. A snake can bite you and you can die before you could get treatment. There are men in those remote parts that'd just as soon kill you as look at you. And you could turn into a counter-monster yourself, doing whatever you felt compelled to do to survive."

"In writing *Deliverance,*" says the *New York Times*'s Christopher Lehmann-Haupt, "Dickey obviously made up his mind to tell a story, and on the theory that a story is an entertaining lie, he has produced a double-clutching whopper." Three ill-prepared businessmen join Lewis Medlock, an avid sportsman who constantly lectures about the purity of nature and the corruption of civilization, on a weekend escape from the banality of suburban living. Canoeing down a wild and difficult stretch of the Cahulawassee River, the men experience only the natural hazards of the river on the first day. Their idyllic sense of community with nature and of masculine camaraderie is shattered on the second, however, when two members of the party, resting from the unaccustomed strain, are surprised by two malicious strangers coming out of the woods. Ed Gentry, the novel's narrator, is tied to a tree while Bobby Trippe is held at gunpoint and sexually assaulted by one of the mountain men. Before the attack can go much further, Lewis catches up, kills one of the assailants by shooting an arrow into his back—thereby partially avenging the homosexual rape—and scares off the other. Fearing a trial conducted by city-hating hicks, the canoeists decide to bury the body and continue on down the river. But after Drew, the sole member of the party to advocate informing the authorities, accidentally drowns, and Lewis suffers a broken leg, Ed must kill the other assailant who is gunning them from the cliffs above the Cahulawassee.

Critical reactions to *Deliverance* help explain its popular success. "The story is absorbing," writes Evan S. Connell, Jr. in the *New York Times Book Review,* "even when you are not quite persuaded Dickey has told the truth. He is effective and he is deft, with the fine hand of an archer." Lehmann-Haupt gives the book similar praise, stating that Dickey "has succeeded in hammering out a comparatively lean prose style (for a man in the habit of loading words with meaning) and built the elements of his yarn into its structure. And except for one blind lead and an irritating logical discrepancy, he has built well. Best of all, he has made a monument to tall stories."

Though Christopher Ricks, critiquing the novel in the *New York Review of Books,* believes *Deliverance* is "too patently the concoction of a situation in which it will be morally permissible— nay, essential—to kill men with a bow and arrow," Charles Thomas Samuels points out in the *New Republic* that Dickey "himself seems aware of the harshness of his substructure and the absurdity of some of his details," and overcomes these deficiencies through his stylistic maneuvers: "Such is Dickey's linguistic virtuosity that he totally realizes an improbable plot. How a man acts when shot by an arrow, what it feels like to scale a cliff or to capsize, the ironic psychology of fear: these things are conveyed with remarkable descriptive writing. His publishers are right to call *Deliverance* a tour de force."

Much more than a violent adventure tale, *Deliverance* is a novel of initiation that, according to William Stephenson in the *Georgia Review,* "has the potential of becoming a classic." As a result of their experience, Lewis and Ed come to a realization of the natural savagery of man in nature, says C. Hines Edwards in *Critique.* "In three days they have retraced the course of human development and have found in the natural state not the romantic ideal of beauty in nature coupled with brotherhood among men but beauty in nature coupled with the necessity to kill men, coolly and in the course of things." In line with this view, Charles Thomas Samuels and other critics note that *Deliverance* alludes to Joseph Conrad's *Heart of Darkness.*

Richard Finholt suggests in *American Visionary Fiction* that there are other literary allusions: "Ed Gentry, the quintessential contemporary American, a soft and overweight suburbanite, finds himself nonetheless [among the chosen] of Lewis. If this is not exactly the honor of being chosen by Odysseus to man the voyage to Ithaca, it is at least as good as being asked by [Hemingway] himself to join him on the 'tragic adventure' of fishing the swamp on the big two-hearted river. And since Lewis's river happens to flow through just such a dreaded underworld, his weekend canoe trip takes on an epical significance demanding an American-bred heroism that is at least Hemingwayesque, if not Homeric." Finholt considers the novel a return to a time when "the final difference between meaning and meaninglessness was the hero's ability, versus his inability, to act when the necessary time came. This is the nature of Ed's discovery after undergoing an initiation rite into heroism on the death climb up the cliff."

Consistent with this interpretation of *Deliverance* as epic, a *Times Literary Supplement* reviewer claims Lewis and Ed "are not horrified by what has happened, they are renewed by it; it was, once it became inevitable, indispensable to them. This shockingly credible insight is the central point of the book, and

James Dickey reveals it with an appropriate and rewarding subtlety."

Donald W. Markos, discussing the novel in the *Southern Review,* observes that while the book "is in an obvious sense a celebration of an anachronistic concept of manhood," it is more complex than that. "It does not propose that all men embark on canoe trips or undergo a regimen of weight lifting and archery in order to salvage their manhood. An interesting conversation between Medlock and the narrator prior to the outing reveals that masculine prowess is not the primary norm of the book." Joyce Carol Oates echoes this sentiment, noting that *Deliverance* is "about our deep, instinctive needs to get back to nature, to establish some kind of rapport with primitive energies; but it is also about the need of some men to do violence, to be delivered out of their banal lives by a violence so irreparable that it can never be confessed." Oates calls the book "a fantasy of a highly civilized and affluent society, which imagines physical violence to be transforming in a mystical—and therefore permanent—sense, a society in which rites of initiation no longer exist. . . . Dickey's work is significant in its expression of the savagery that always threatens to become an ideal, when faith in human values is difficult to come by or when a culture cannot accommodate man's most basic instincts."

Edward Doughtie concludes in the *Southwest Review* that through *Deliverance,* "Dickey shows art to be a necessary mediator between nature—both the exterior nature of woods and rivers and the interior nature of man's drives and dreams—and modern urban 'civilized' life. Both the natural world and the civilized world have their virtues, beauties, dangers, and horrors. The positive elements of nature can be stifled by civilization; but without civilization the darker, destructive natural forces may get out of hand. Art is a product of civilization, and a civilizing force, yet for Dickey genuine art never loses touch with the primitive: in short, art embraces both Dionysus and Apollo."

Deliverance represents only one of Dickey's ventures outside the realm of poetry. He not only adapted the novel for the screen but also appeared in the box-office smash as the redneck Sheriff Bullard, whom the canoeists face at the end of their journey. In addition to criticism, Dickey has published a retelling of several biblical stories, *God's Images: The Bible, a New Vision,* as well as *Jericho: The South Beheld,* an exploration of "the rich prose language and sensual impressions of the American South, which Dickey has publicly championed," writes Robert W. Hill. "Like Whitman or Twain," says Michael Dirda in the *Washington Post Book World,* "Dickey seems in a characteristic American tradition, ever ready to light out for new territories."

Dickey reportedly spent more than thirty years working on his lengthy World War II novel *Alnilam,* which was published in 1987. Named for the central star in the belt of the constellation Orion, *Alnilam* concerns the recently blinded Frank Cahill's search for the son he has never met. Cahill slowly discovers that his son, an extraordinary pilot thought to have been killed in an aircraft training accident, had been the leader of a mysterious, dictatorial military training cult known as Alnilam. The novel received mixed reviews, with most critics comparing it unfavorably to the powerful *Deliverance.* As Erling Friis-Baastad put it in the Toronto *Globe and Mail, Alnilam* "is an awkward and overworked book, but the touch of a master poet can still be experienced periodically throughout . . . at least by those who can endure the uphill read."

Despite his excursions into other genres, Dickey's main concern "will always be poetry," he admits in the *New York Times.* "In poetry you have the utmost concentration of meaning in the shortest space." In a 1981 *Writer's Yearbook* interview, Dickey elaborates on his devotion to verse: "Poetry is, I think, the highest medium that mankind has ever come up with. It's language itself, which is a miraculous medium which makes everything else that man has ever done possible."

Dickey told *CA:* "I'm the same way about novels as I am about anything I write. I build them very slowly. I work on the principle that the first fifty ways I try to write a novel or a critical piece or a poem or a movie are going to be wrong. But you get a direction in some way or other. Keep drafting and redrafting and something emerges eventually. If the subject is intense, if you are intense about it, something will come. In my case, at least, the final work is nothing like what I started out with; generally I don't have a very good idea at first. But something begins to form in some unforeseen, perhaps unforeseeable, shape. It's like creating something out of nothing—creation ex nihilo, which is said to be impossible. God must have done it, I guess, but nobody else can—except poets."

BIOGRAPHICAL/CRITICAL SOURCES:

BOOKS

Authors in the News, Volumes 1-2, Gale, 1976.

Boyars, Robert, editor, *Contemporary Poetry in America,* Schocken, 1974.

Calhoun, Richard J., editor, *James Dickey: The Expansive Imagination,* Everett/Edwards, 1973.

Carroll, Paul, *The Poem in Its Skin,* Follett, 1968.

Contemporary Literary Criticism, Gale, Volume 1, 1973, Volume 2, 1974, Volume 4, 1975, Volume 7, 1977, Volume 10, 1979, Volume 15, 1980, Volume 47, 1988.

Conversations with Writers, Volume 1, Gale, 1977.

De La Fuente, Patricia, editor, *James Dickey: Splintered Sunlight,* School of Humanities, Pan American University, 1979.

Dickey, James, *Self-Interviews,* recorded and edited by Barbara Reiss and James Reiss, Doubleday, 1970.

Dictionary of Literary Biography, Gale, Volume 5: *American Poets since World War II,* 1980, *Yearbook: 1982,* 1983, *Documentary Series,* Volume 7, 1989.

Elledge, J., *James Dickey,* Scarecrow, 1979.

Finholt, Richard, *American Visionary Fiction: Mad Metaphysics as Salvation Psychology,* Kennikat, 1978.

Garrett, George, editor, *The Writer's Voice: Conversations with Contemporary Writers,* Morrow, 1973.

Glancy, Eileen, *James Dickey: The Critic as Poet* (annotated bibliography with introductory essay), Whitston Publishing, 1971.

Hill, Robert and Calhoun, *James Dickey,* Twayne, 1983.

Howard, Richard, *Alone with America: Essays on the Art of Poetry in the United States since 1950,* Atheneum, 1969.

Lieberman, Laurence, editor, *The Achievement of James Dickey,* Scott, Foresman, 1968.

Lieberman, Laurence, *Unassigned Frequencies: American Poetry in Review, 1964-77,* University of Illinois, 1978.

Nemerov, Howard, editor, *Poets on Poetry,* Basic Books, 1966.

Nemerov, Howard, *Reflexions on Poetry and Poetics,* Rutgers University Press, 1972.

Oates, Joyce Carol, *New Heaven, New Earth: The Visionary Experience in Literature,* Vanguard, 1974.

Pages: The World of Books, Writers, and Writing, Volume 1, Gale, 1976.

Rosenthal, M. L., *The New Poets: American and British Poetry since World War II,* Oxford University Press, 1967.

Shaw, Robert B., editor, *American Poetry since 1960: Some Critical Perspectives,* Carcanet, 1973.

Spears, Monroe K., *Dionysus and the City: Modernism in Twentieth-Century Poetry,* Oxford University Press, 1970.

Stepanchev, Stephen, *American Poetry since 1945,* Harper, 1965.

Vernon, John, *The Garden and the Map: Schizophrenia in Twentieth-Century Literature and Culture,* University of Illinois Press, 1973.

Walsh, Chad, *Today's Poets,* Scribner, 1964.

Weigl, Bruce, and Terry Hummer, editors, *James Dickey: The Imagination of Glory,* University of Illinois Press, 1984.

PERIODICALS

Agenda, winter-spring, 1977.

Antioch Review, fall-winter, 1970-71.

Atlantic, October, 1967, November, 1968, December, 1974, February, 1980.

Best Sellers, April 1, 1970.

Book List, July 15, 1971.

Chicago Review, November 1, 1966.

Chicago Tribune, May 10, 1987.

Chicago Tribune Book World, January 27, 1980.

Christian Science Monitor, December 3, 1964, November 12, 1970, February 20, 1980.

Commonweal, December 1, 1967, February 19, 1971, September 29, 1972, December 3, 1976.

Concerning Poetry, spring, 1978.

Contemporary Literature, summer, 1975.

Critic, May, 1970.

Critique, Volume 15, number 2, 1973.

Esquire, December, 1970.

Georgia Review, spring, 1968, summer, 1969, spring, 1974, summer, 1978.

Globe and Mail (Toronto), August 15, 1987.

Hudson Review, autumn, 1967, autumn, 1968.

Life, July 22, 1966.

Literary News, May-June, 1967.

Los Angeles Times, May 19, 1968, February 26, 1980, July 9, 1987.

Los Angeles Times Book Review, June 27, 1982.

Mademoiselle, September, 1970, August, 1972.

Milwaukee Journal, March 20, 1966.

Modern Fiction Studies, summer, 1975.

Nation, June 20, 1966, April 24, 1967, March 23, 1970, April 6, 1970.

New Leader, May 22, 1967, May 20, 1968.

New Republic, September 9, 1967, June 29, 1968, April 18, 1970, December 5, 1970, August 5, 1972, November 30, 1974, November 20, 1976, January 5, 1980, January 12, 1980.

New Statesman, September 11, 1970.

Newsweek, March 30, 1970, August 7, 1972, December 6, 1976, January 31, 1977.

New Yorker, May 2, 1970, August 5, 1972.

New York Review of Books, April 23, 1970.

New York Times, March 16, 1966, September 10, 1966, March 27, 1970, December 17, 1971, July 31, 1972, August 20, 1972, January 22, 1977, June 1, 1987.

New York Times Book Review, January 3, 1965, February 6, 1966, April 23, 1967, March 22, 1970, June 7, 1970, November 8, 1970, December 6, 1970, January 23, 1972, February 9, 1975, November 14, 1976, December 18, 1977, July 15, 1979, January 6, 1980, June 3, 1984, March 8, 1987, June 21, 1987.

Paris Review, spring, 1976.

Partisan Review, summer, 1966.

Playboy, May, 1971.
Poetry, October, 1966, March, 1968, July, 1971.
Publishers Weekly, May 29, 1987.
Salmagundi, spring-summer, 1973.
Saturday Review, May 6, 1967, March 11, 1970, March 28, 1970.
Saturday Review of Science, August 5, 1972.
Sewanee Review, winter, 1963, summer, 1966, spring, 1969.
Sixties, winter, 1964, spring, 1967.
Southern Review, winter, 1971, summer, 1971, winter, 1973, spring, 1973.
Southwest Review, spring, 1979.
Time, December 13, 1968, April 20, 1970, August 7, 1972, June 29, 1987.
Times Literary Supplement, October 29, 1964, May 18, 1967, September 11, 1970, May 21, 1971.
Triquarterly, winter, 1968.
Virginia Quarterly Review, autumn, 1968, winter, 1971.
Washington Post, May 24, 1987.
Washington Post Book World, June 30, 1968, March 15, 1970, December 6, 1970, April 25, 1971, November 21, 1976, December 30, 1979.
Yale Review, October, 1962, December, 1967, winter, 1968, October, 1970.

FILMS

"Lord Let Me Dic But Not Die Out: James Dickey, Poet," Encyclopaedia Britannica, 1970.

* * *

DICKSON, Carr
    See CARR, John Dickson

* * *

DICKSON, Carter
    See CARR, John Dickson

* * *

DIDION, Joan   1934-

PERSONAL: Born December 5, 1934, in Sacramento, Calif.; daughter of Frank Reese and Eduene (Jerrett) Didion; married John Gregory Dunne (a writer), January 30, 1964; children: Quintana Roo (daughter). *Education:* University of California, Berkeley, B.A., 1956.

ADDRESSES: Home—Los Angeles, Calif. *Agent*—Lois Wallace, The Wallace Literary Agency, 177 East 70th St., New York, N.Y. 10021.

CAREER: Writer. *Vogue,* New York, N.Y., 1956-63, began as promotional copywriter, became associate feature editor. Visiting regents lecturer in English, University of California, Berkeley, 1975.

AWARDS, HONORS: First prize, *Vogue*'s Prix de Paris, 1956; Bread Loaf fellowship in fiction, 1963; National Book Award nomination in fiction, 1971, for *Play It as It Lays;* Morton Dauwen Zabel Award, National Institute of Arts and Letters, 1978; National Book Critics Circle Prize nomination in nonfiction, 1980, and American Book Award nomination in nonfiction, 1981, both for *The White Album; Los Angeles Times* Book Prize nomination in fiction, 1984, for *Democracy.*

WRITINGS:

Run River (novel), Obolensky, 1963.

Slouching Towards Bethlehem (essays), Farrar, Straus, 1968.
Play It as It Lays (novel; also see below), Farrar, Straus, 1970.
A Book of Common Prayer (novel), Simon & Schuster, 1977.
The White Album (essays), Simon & Schuster, 1979.
Salvador (nonfiction), Simon & Schuster, 1983.
Democracy (novel), Simon & Schuster, 1984.
Miami (nonfiction), Simon & Schuster, 1987.

SCREENPLAYS; WITH HUSBAND, JOHN GREGORY DUNNE

"Panic in Needle Park" (based on a James Mills book of the same title), Twentieth Century-Fox, 1971.
"Play It as It Lays" (based on Didion's book of the same title), Universal, 1972.
(And others) "A Star Is Born," Warner Bros., 1976.
"True Confessions" (based on Dunne's novel of the same title), United Artists, 1981.

OTHER

Author of column, with Dunne, "Points West," *Saturday Evening Post,* 1967-69, and "The Coast," *Esquire,* 1976-77; former columnist, *Life.* Contributor of short stories, articles, and reviews to numerous magazines, including *Vogue, Saturday Evening Post, Holiday, Harper's Bazaar, New Yorker, New York Review of Books,* and the *New York Times Book Review.* Former contributing editor, *National Review.*

SIDELIGHTS: An elegant prose stylist and one of the most celebrated of the new journalists, Joan Didion possesses a distinct literary voice, widely praised for its precision and control. She is, by her own admission, a non-intellectual writer, more concerned with images than ideas and renowned for her use of the telling detail. In addition to being "a gifted reporter," Didion, according to *New York Times Magazine* contributor Michiko Kakutani, "is also a prescient witness, finding in her own experiences parallels of the times. The voice is always precise, the tone unsentimental, the view unabashedly subjective. She takes things personally." For years, Didion's favorite subject was her native California, a state that seemed to supply ample evidence of the disorder in society, confirming her suspicion that "things fall apart; the center cannot hold," to quote the poet W. B. Yeats as Didion does. Though her theme has not changed, in recent years she has broadened her perspective, turning to the troubled countries of Central America and Southeast Asia for new material.

Didion's work is characterized by her obsession with perfection. "I'm not much interested in spontaneity," she admitted to Digby Diehl of the *Los Angeles Times.* "What concerns me is total control." In addition to writing novels and essays, Didion sometimes collaborates on screenplays with her husband, the novelist John Gregory Dunne. These projects provide considerable income and the chance to work closely with other artists but Didion finds them restrictive, like being "copilot on an airplane," to use her husband's words. In a *New York Review of Books* article, Dunne writes that a screenwriter must "cede to the director certain essential writer's function—space, mood, style, point-of-view, rhythm, texture," and Didion has acknowledged that this is her opinion, too.

In her quest for controlled perfection, Didion revises her writing repeatedly, working and reworking the exact placement of important details. *Newsweek*'s Peter S. Prescott says she is "able to condense into a paragraph what others would take three pages to expound. Unerringly, she seizes the exact phrase that not only describes but comments on a scene." According to *New York Times* reviewer John Leonard, "nobody writes better English prose than Joan Didion. Try to rearrange one of her sentences, and you've realized that the sentence was inevitable, a hologram."

Didion's emphasis on image and detail reflects her perceptual orientation. She has often said that she is not the least bit intellectual and in a lecture she delivered at her alma mater she explained the way her mind works: "During the years I was an undergraduate at Berkeley, I . . . kept trying to find that part of my mind that could deal in abstracts. But my mind kept veering inexorably back like some kind of boomerang I was stuck with—to the specific, to the tangible, to what was generally considered by everyone I knew, the peripheral. I would try to think about the Great Dialectic and would find myself thinking instead about how the light was falling through the window in an apartment I had on the North Side. How it was hitting the floor."

In many of her novels, Didion's starting point has been an image not unlike a shaft of light, a scene that has "a shimmer around the edges" and that she builds her story around. "For my first novel, 'Run River,' it was a detailed picture of a man and a woman in a house on the Sacramento River," she told Diehl in the *Los Angeles Times.* "For 'Play It as It Lays,' it was a starlet being paged at the Riviera Hotel in Las Vegas at one o'clock in the morning. For 'A Book of Common Prayer,' it was the picture of an American woman in an airport coffee shop in Central America. I find that when I explore these pictures, they each contain the essential story for the novels they generated."

Though she often builds a whole book around a single "picture," Didion's writing can seem fragmented, her chapters short and disjointed, her images unexplored. "Everything depends on the selection and placement of details," notes *Newsweek's* Walter Clemons, who calls it "a perilous method. At her worse Didion sounds supercilious, an uncommitted connoisseur of fragments, a severe snob."

Didion knows her concerns are not the standard ones and in one of her better-known essays, "In the Islands," she describes herself as "a woman who for some time now has felt radically separated from most of the ideas that seem to interest other people." Though she once listed herself a "republican," she has long since abandoned such allegiances, telling *New York Times Book Review* contributor Sara Davidson, "I never had faith that the answers to human problems lay in anything that could be called political. I thought the answers, if there were answers, lay someplace in man's soul." In 1972, she wrote a piece called "The Women's Movement," dismissing feminism as a "curious historical anomaly" which had been trivialized by people who did not understand its Marxist roots. Feminists were not amused. In a long and highly critical *Nation* essay Barbara Grizzuti Harrison attacks Didion's attitude as a pose. "What interests me more than her trivial and trivializing essay on women's liberation is that she sometimes expresses notions that would not be at all alien to the staunchest of feminists: 'Women don't ever win. Because winners have to believe they can affect the dice.' If that is not a tacit admission that women are relatively powerless, what is? Still, for Didion to have any sympathy with anyone who aligns herself with any cause, any movement is too much to hope for. Like Grace in *A Book of Common Prayer,* she is *de afuera*—the outsider: 'I have been *de afuera* all my life.' I think she wears that singularity like a badge. *I am different* translates into *I am superior.*"

"I have a theatrical temperament," Didion explained to Kakutani. "I'm not interested in the middle road—maybe because everyone's on it. Rationality, reasonableness bewilder me. I think it comes out of being a 'daughter of the Golden West.' A lot of the stories I was brought up on had to do with extreme actions—

leaving everything behind, crossing the trackless wastes, and in those stories the people who stayed behind and had their settled ways—those people were not the people who got the prize. The prize was California."

Born to a family that settled in the Sacramento Valley in the 1800s, Didion hails from a long line of pioneers. Her great-great-great grandmother, Nancy Hardin Cornwall, was originally a member of the 1846 Donner party, but she avoided the disaster that befell that group (trapped in a mountain pass by an early blizzard, they resorted to cannibalism to stay alive) by splitting off from them early to head north through Oregon. Cornwall's own forebears had followed the frontier westward, and this pioneer heritage has exerted a strong influence on Didion, ingraining her with what Kakutani calls "a kind of hard-boiled individualism" or, as Didion puts it, an "ineptness at tolerating the complexities of postindustrial life."

Though her home life was stable, Didion was a skittish child, frightened of everything from atom bombs to rattlesnakes and convinced that the bridge over the Sacramento River would collapse if she ventured there. To redirect her daughter's energies, Didion's mother gave her a notebook and suggested that she "stop whining" and start writing. Her first story, written at age five, concerns a woman who imagines she is freezing to death in the Arctic, only to awaken and discover that she is burning in the desert sun.

During Didion's grade school years, World War II erupted, and the family followed her father from one Army base to another for the duration of the war. Afterwards, the Didions returned to Sacramento, but the experience left its mark on Joan, who turned increasingly to books instead of people for company. By the time she was a teenager, she was recopying passages from Ernest Hemingway and Joseph Conrad to find out the way sentences were put together.

After high school, Didion enrolled at the University of California at Berkeley, where she majored in English literature and published her first short story in *Occident,* a campus magazine. In her senior year, 1955, she entered *Vogue's* Prix de Paris contest with an article on William Wilson Wurster, the father of the San Francisco style of architecture. It won first prize. In lieu of a trip to France, Didion accepted a cash award and a job at *Vogue's* New York office, where she remained for eight years, rising from promotional copywriter to associate feature editor. During this period, she met John Gregory Dunne and, after several years of friendship, they married, becoming not just matrimonial partners but literary collaborators as well.

While she was still at *Vogue,* Didion began writing her first novel, *Run River* (published to what she calls "deafening disinterest"). The book's long descriptive passages about the Sacramento landscape were Didion's way of dealing with her homesickness. In 1964, she gave in to her longing and moved back to the West Coast with Dunne, determined to earn a living as a freelance reporter. Working together on a series of magazine columns about California for the *Saturday Evening Post,* the couple earned a meager $7,000 in their first year of what Diehl facetiously calls "the Good Life in Los Angeles." But their writing did attract widespread attention, and when Didion's columns were collected and published in a separate volume called *Slouching Towards Bethlehem,* her reputation as an essayist soared.

The book takes its theme from Yeats's poem "The Second Coming," which reads: "Things fall apart; the center cannot hold;/ Mere anarchy is loosed upon the world." For Didion those words sum up the chaos of the sixties, a chaos so far reaching that it affected her ability to perform. Convinced "that writing was an irrelevant act, that the world as I had understood it no longer existed," Didion, as she states in the book's preface, realized, "If I was to work again, at all, it would be necessary for me to come to terms with disorder." She went to Haight Ashbury to explore the hippie movement and out of that experience came the title essay, "Slouching Towards Bethlehem."

Many critics praise it highly. Dan Wakefield, for instance, expresses hope in the *New York Times Book Review* that the collection will be recognized "not as a better or worse example of what some people call 'mere journalism,' but as a rich display of some of the best prose written today." Writing in the *Christian Science Monitor,* Melvin Maddocks suggests, "Her melancholy voice is that of a last survivor dictating a superbly written wreckage report onto a tape she doubts will ever be played." And while *Best Sellers* reviewer T. O'Hara argues that "the devotion she gives to America-the-uprooted-the-lunatic-and-the-alienated is sullied by an inability to modulate, to achieve a respectable distance," several others applaud her subjectivity. "Nobody captured the slack-jawed Haight Ashbury hippies any better," states *Saturday Review* contributor Martin Kasindorf. Or, as Wakefield puts it, Didion's "personality does not self-indulgently intrude itself on her subjects, it informs and illuminates them."

In 1970, Didion published *Play It as It Lays,* a best-selling novel that received a National Book Award nomination and, at the same time, created enormous controversy with its apparently nihilistic theme. The portrait of a woman on what *New York Times Book Review* contributor Lore Segal calls a "downward path to wisdom," *Play It as It Lays* tells the story of Maria Wyeth's struggle to find meaning in a meaningless world. "The setting is the desert; the cast, the careless hedonists of Hollywood; the emotional climate, bleak as the surroundings," Kakutani reports in the *New York Times Magazine.* Composed of eighty-four brief chapters, some less than a page in length, the book possesses a cinematic quality and such technical precision that Richard Shickel remarks in *Harper's* that it is "a rather cold and calculated fiction—more a problem in human geometry . . . than a novel that truly lives."

"The trouble with this book is the nothing *inside* Maria," according to Lore Segal, who adds that the "book feels as if it were written out of an insufficient impulse by a writer who doesn't know what else to do with all that talent and skill." *New York Review of Books* critic D. A. N. Jones finds himself unmoved: "Although she seems to be in hell, and although every event is charged with misery, *Play It as It Lays* cannot be honestly called depressing. The neat, cinematic construction, the harsh wit of the mean, soulless dialogue stimulate a certain exhilaration, as when we appreciate a harmonious and well-proportioned painting of some cruelly martyred saint in whom we do not believe."

John Leonard in the *New York Times,* on the other hand, expresses a different view: "While the result is not exactly pleasant, it seems to me just about perfect according to its own austere terms," he writes in his review of the novel. "So long as novels are permitted to be about visions, to explore situations, to see truths beyond individual manipulation, then Miss Didion need not equip Maria with a Roto-Rooter or a dose of ideological uplift. The courage to say 'Why not?' to Nothingness is more than enough."

A Book of Common Prayer, Didion's third novel, continues her theme of social disintegration with the story of Charlotte Douglas, a Californian "immaculate of history, innocent of politics." Until her daughter Marin abandoned home and family to join a group of terrorists, Charlotte was a typically naive American,

one who "understood that something was always going on in the world but believed that it would turn out all right," according to the story's narrator, Grace Strasser-Mendana. When things fall apart, Charlotte takes refuge in Boca Grande, a fictitious Central American country embroiled in its own domestic conflicts. There she idles away her days at the airport coffee shop, futilely waiting for her daughter to surface and eventually losing her life in a military coup.

In the interview with Davidson, Didion discussed the texture she was trying to achieve in the novel: "I wrote it down on the map of Central America. 'Surface like a rainbow slick, shifting, fall, thrown away, iridescent.' I wanted to do a deceptive surface that appeared to be one thing and turned color as you looked through it." Didion originally got the story idea during a 1973 trip to Cartagena, Colombia, when her plane stopped over in the Panama airport for an hour. "My experience of that airport was very vivid, super-real," Didion told Diehl in the *Saturday Review.* "I could see the opening scene of a woman having a contretemps with a waitress in the coffee shop about boiling her water twenty minutes for a cup of tea. I started to think about what she was doing there and the novel began to unfold."

Because Charlotte's story is told by Grace, an American expatriate and long-time Boca Grande resident, the book presented several technical problems. "The narrator was not present during most of the events she's telling you about. And her only source is a woman incapable of seeing the truth," Didion explained to Diehl. In her *New York Times Book Review* article, Joyce Carol Oates speculates that Didion employs this technique because Grace "allows Joan Didion a free play of her own speculative intelligence that would have been impossible had the story been told by Charlotte. The device of an uninvolved narrator is a tricky one, since a number of private details must be presented as if they were within the range of the narrator's experience. But it is a measure of Didion's skill as a novelist that one never questions [Grace's] near omniscience in recalling Charlotte's story."

"Grace appears to debunk Charlotte, to expose her pathetic delusions, but the tenderness she brings to bear on the case serves to redeem the other woman—until she becomes an instance of a sort of gallant particularity for which no science can ever account," writes Frederick Raphael in the *Saturday Review.* Christopher Lehmann-Haupt, on the other hand, maintains in the *New York Times* that Didion "simply asks too much of Charlotte, and overburdened as she is by the pitiless cruelty of the narrator's vision, she collapses under the strain."

Margot Hentoff believes that the book would have more impact if Didion had accurately interpreted "the actual state of the union. We are not dead souls," she writes in the *Village Voice,* "the edge of the abyss was not even close, and we Americans have fallen from grace and lost our innocence so many times that by now the supply of both seems inexhaustible. Let me say that I think Joan Didion is one of our very best writers." She continues, "Didion writes more movingly of time and loss than any other writer of my generation. In her essays. Not in the novels. She has the capacity, I think, to be the Chekhov of our time, but her novels do not come alive because they are insufficiently distanced from her own anxiety—too relentlessly ironic in tone, too emotionally controlled, as if the form itself were the bars of a cell."

After *A Book of Common Prayer,* Didion published *The White Album,* a second collection of magazine essays, similar in tone to *Slouching Towards Bethlehem,* but wider in scope, more tentative and less absolute. "I don't have as many answers as I did when I wrote 'Slouching,'" Didion explained to Kakutani. She called the book *The White Album* in consideration of a famous Beatles album that captured for her the disturbing ambience of the sixties. "I am talking here about a time when I began to doubt the premises of all the stories I had ever told myself," Didion writes in the title essay. "This period began around 1966 and continued until 1971. During this time," says Didion, "all I knew was what I saw: flash pictures in variable sequence, images with no 'meaning' beyond their temporary arrangement, not a movie but a cutting-room experience."

Diagnosed at this time as "fundamentally pessimistic, fatalistic, and depressive," Didion includes not only such personal data as her psychiatric profile, but also public news about incidents, including the Charles Manson murders and Robert Kennedy's death. "At times, it seems Didion's own fear and malaise run parallel like train tracks to those of the era," observes Hillary Johnson in the *Christian Science Monitor. New York Times Book Review* contributor Robert Towers calls her title essay "the best short piece (37 pages) on the late 1960's that I have yet read," attributing its success in large part to "the use to which personal neurosis has been put. Joan Didion makes no bones about the seriousness of the neurosis, but she gives the impression of having refined it to the point where it vibrates in exquisite attunement to the larger craziness of the world. It is her nerve-frayed awareness of the gap between the supposedly meaningful 'script' by which we try to live and the absurdities by which we are bombarded that has brought her vision to its preternaturally sharp focus and has helped make her the extraordinary reporter she is."

In her later work, Didion has broadened her perspective while retaining her subjective approach. "I had certain questions about California," she explained to Martin Kasindorf in the *Saturday Review*. "I didn't answer the questions. But I got tired of asking them. I would like to ask some other questions, I think." Among those questions was one about the differences between the United States and its southern neighbors. First surfacing in *A Book of Common Prayer* with its fictitious Central American setting, this question is journalistically addressed in *Salvador,* a nonfiction book. Based on Didion's experiences and written with the assistance of her husband's notes, *Salvador* chronicles the two weeks that Didion and Dunne spent in the war-torn country of El Salvador in June, 1982. "Alternately detached and compassionate, this slim essay is many things at once," observes Carolyn Forche in the *Chicago Tribune Book World:* "a sidelong reflection on the limits of the now-old new journalism; a tourist guide manque; a surrealist docu-drama; a withering indictment of American foreign policy; and a poetic exploration in fear." What the book is not is a panacea—*Salvador* neither offers solutions nor supports any political regime.

While the book has been highly acclaimed for its literary merits, *Salvador* has been criticized on other grounds. *Newsweek* critic Gene Lyon, for example, allows that "Didion gets exactly right both the ghastliness and the pointlessness of the current killing frenzy in El Salvador" but then suggests that "ghastliness and pointlessness are Didion's invariable themes wherever she goes. Most readers will not get very far in this very short book without wondering whether she visited that sad and tortured place less to report than to validate the Didion world view." Others question Didion's credentials as a historian: "Let me get this straight," writes one reader in a letter to the *Los Angeles Times.* "Joan Didion spends two weeks in El Salvador and suddenly becomes a bigger expert on this country than anyone who has previously covered it? How can this be?" And Leonel Gomez Videz, former deputy director of the Agrarian Reform Institute in El Salvador, faults the book for mystifying a subject that desper-

ately needs to be understood. "What she provides is a horrific description of atrocity: 'The dead and pieces of the dead turn up in El Salvador everywhere, every day, as taken for granted as in a nightmare, or a horror movie,' " he writes, quoting *Salvador* in the *New Republic.* "What point is Didion making? Such lurid details make for compelling prose, but in the absence of any analysis of why such murders occur, they seem at best to bolster her thesis of mindless terror and at worst to suggest a penchant for gratuitous special effects."

Juan M. Vasquez, on the other hand, defends Didion's approach. "Didion's book is not for the seekers of solutions, those who would feed the contents of El Salvador into a computer and expect a tidy answer to emerge—pressed, neat, ready for consumption," he writes in the *Los Angeles Times Book Review.* "It is, rather, for those who can subscribe to the foolishness of such notions and who can appreciate that the way some people live—the way some countries live—is not always believable, but it is all too crushingly real." Moreover, Forche maintains that "Didion achieves in this slender volume what she seldom does in her fiction: a consummate political artwork. For the otherwise powerless artist, the tenacious pursuit of reality and the past, in countries where both are constantly thrown into doubt, constitutes the most meaningful act of defiance."

One year after *Salvador* was published, Didion brought out *Democracy,* an enigmatic novel over six years in the making, which features Joan Didion, the author, in a central role. Begun, she writes in the novel, "at a time in my life when I lacked certainty, lacked even that minimum level of ego which all writers recognize as essential to the writing of novels," the book was to have been the story of a family of American colonialists whose interests were firmly entrenched in the Pacific when Hawaii was still a territory. She tells us she abandoned this story because she "lost nerve." But one of the family members continued to haunt her. That was Inez Christian, the daughter, whose fate became entwined for a time with the fate of the nation and whose story Didion ultimately tells.

In the spring of 1975—at the time the United States completed its evacuation of Vietnam and Cambodia—Inez's father is arrested for a double murder with political and racial overtones. "The Christians and their in-laws are the emblems of a misplaced confidence," according to John Lownsbrough in the Toronto *Globe and Mail,* "the flotsam and jetsam of a Manifest Destiny no longer so manifest. Their disintegration as a family in the spring of 1975 . . . is paralleled by the fall of Saigon a bit later that year and the effective disintegration of the American expansionist dream in all its ethnocentric optimism." Somehow, her family's tragedy enables Inez to break free of her marriage to a self-serving politician and escape to Malaysia with Jack Lovett, a free-lance C.I.A. agent and the man she has always loved. Though he dies abruptly, Inez holds onto her freedom, choosing to remain in Kuala Lumpur where she works among the Vietnamese refugees.

The story is gradually revealed in a series of short imagistic chapters that segue back and forth through time, reminding *New York Times Book Review* contributor Mary McCarthy of "a jigsaw puzzle that is slowly being put together with a continual shuffling and re-examination of pieces still on the edges or heaped in the middle of the design." The confusion is heightened by Didion's curious mixing of fact and fiction. She says, for instance, that she first met Inez Christian in 1960 when they were both working for *Vogue.* Didion's employment is an easily verified matter of record, but those who go searching for substantiation of Inez's career come up with a blank. To Mary McCarthy this "raises the question 'What are we supposed to believe here?' . . . What is a live fact—Joan Didion—doing in a work of fiction?"

Some critics argue that the author's presence is intrusive and narcissistic, attracting unnecessary attention to itself. But *New York Times* reviewer Christopher Lehmann-Haupt maintains it "is actually not a bad strategy on Miss Didion's part—this thrust and parry with the reader, this breaking into the narrative with remarks such as . . . 'Let the reader be introduced to Joan Didion, upon whose character and doings much will depend of whatever interest these pages may have.' It creates the illusion that journalism instead of fiction is going on in the pages of 'Democracy,' and this is good because Miss Didion has always been more sure-footed as a reporter."

New York Review of Books critic Thomas R. Edwards believes *Democracy* "finally earns its complexity of form. It is indeed 'a hard story to tell' and the presence in it of 'Joan Didion' trying to tell it is an essential part of its subject. Throughout one senses the author struggling with the moral difficulty that makes the story hard to tell—how to stop claiming what Inez finally relinquishes, 'the American exemption' from having to recognize that history records not the victory of personal wills over reality . . . but the 'undertow of having and not having, the convulsions of a world largely unaffected by the individual efforts of anyone in it.'" At the story's end, "when the retreat from Vietnam is finished and Inez is alone in Kuala Lumpur, a penitent working with the refugees democracy has created, we feel that along with the novelist and her characters, we too have learned something about the importance of memory," writes Peter Collier in the *Chicago Tribune Book World.* "We also note that Didion, who has earlier compared the writer to the aerialist, is still on the high wire, a little shaky perhaps, but in no real danger of falling."

BIOGRAPHICAL/CRITICAL SOURCES:

BOOKS

Authors in the News, Volume 1, Gale, 1976.
Contemporary Literary Criticism, Gale, Volume 1, 1973, Volume 3, 1975, Volume 8, 1978, Volume 14, 1980.
Dictionary of Literary Biography, Volume 2: *American Novelists since World War II,* Gale, 1978.
Dictionary of Literary Biography Yearbook: 1981, Gale, 1982.
Didion, Joan, *Slouching Towards Bethlehem,* Farrar, Straus, 1968.
Didion, Joan, *A Book of Common Prayer,* Simon & Schuster, 1977.
Didion, Joan, *The White Album,* Simon & Schuster, 1979.
Didion, Joan, *Democracy,* Simon & Schuster, 1984.
Friedman, Ellen G., editor, *Joan Didion: Essays and Conversations,* Ontario Review Press, 1984.
Kazin, Alfred, *Bright Book of Life: American Novelists and Storytellers from Hemingway to Mailer,* Little, Brown, 1973.
Winchell, Mark Royden, *Joan Didion,* Twayne, 1980.

PERIODICALS

Atlantic, April, 1977.
Best Sellers, June 1, 1968, August 1, 1970.
Book World, July 28, 1968.
Chicago Tribune, June 12, 1979, March 13, 1988.
Chicago Tribune Book World, July 1, 1979, April 3, 1983, April 15, 1984, July 14, 1985.
Chicago Tribune Magazine, May 2, 1982.
Christian Science Monitor, May 16, 1968, September 24, 1970, July 9, 1979.
Commonweal, November 29, 1968.

Detroit News, August 12, 1979.
Globe and Mail (Toronto), April 28, 1984.
Harper's, August, 1970, December, 1971.
Harvard Advocate, winter, 1973.
Los Angeles Times, May 9, 1971, July 4, 1976, May 9, 1988, February 1, 1987.
Los Angeles Times Book Review, March 20, 1983, September 27, 1987.
Miami Herald, December 2, 1973.
Ms., February, 1977.
Nation, September 26, 1979.
National Review, June 4, 1968, August 25, 1970, October 12, 1979.
New Republic, June 6, 1983.
Newsweek, August 3, 1970, December 21, 1970, March 21, 1977, June 25, 1979, March 28, 1983, April 16, 1984.
New Yorker, June 20, 1977, April 18, 1983.
New York Magazine, February 15, 1971, June 13, 1979.
New York Review of Books, October 22, 1970, May 10, 1984.
New York Times, July 21, 1970, October 30, 1972, March 21, 1977, June 5, 1979, March 11, 1983, April 6, 1984, September 14, 1984, September 28, 1987, February 23, 1989.
New York Times Book Review, July 21, 1968, August 9, 1970, April 13, 1977, June 17, 1979, March 13, 1983, April 22, 1984, October 25, 1987.
New York Times Magazine, June 10, 1979, February 8, 1987.
San Francisco Review of Books, May, 1977.
Saturday Review, August 15, 1970, March 5, 1977, September 15, 1979, April, 1982.
Sewanee Review, fall, 1977.
Time, August 10, 1970, March 28, 1977, August 20, 1979, April 4, 1983, May 7, 1984, September 28, 1987.
Times (London), July 8, 1989.
Times Literary Supplement, February 12, 1970, March 12, 1971, July 8, 1977, November 30, 1979, June 24, 1983, March 18-24, 1988.
Tribune Books (Chicago), October 4, 1987.
Village Voice, February 28, 1977, June 25, 1979.
Washington Post, April 8, 1983.
Washington Post Book World, June 17, 1979, March 13, 1983, April 15, 1984, October 4, 1987.

*   *   *

DILLARD, Annie 1945-

PERSONAL: Born April 30, 1945, in Pittsburgh, Pa.; daughter of Frank and Pam (Lambert) Doak; married Gary Clevidence (an anthropologist), April 12, 1980 (marriage ended); married Robert D. Richardson, Jr. (an author), c. 1988; children: Cody Rose. *Education:* Hollins College, B.A., 1967, M.A., 1968.

ADDRESSES: Agent—Blanche Gregory, 2 Tudor City Place, New York, N.Y. 10017.

CAREER: Writer. Western Washington University, Bellingham, scholar-in-residence, 1975-79; Wesleyan University, Middletown, Conn., distinguished visiting professor, beginning in 1979, full adjunct professor, beginning in 1983, writer in residence, beginning in 1987. Member of board of advisers, Ossabaw Island Project; board member, Western States Arts Foundation; member of U.S. cultural delegation to China, spring, 1982.

MEMBER: International P.E.N., Authors Guild, Poetry Society of America, National Citizens for Public Libraries, New York Public Library National Literary Committee, Phi Beta Kappa.

AWARDS, HONORS: Pulitzer Prize for general nonfiction, 1974, for *Pilgrim at Tinker Creek;* New York Press Club Award for Excellence, 1975; Washington State Governor's Award for Literature, 1978; grants from National Endowment for the Arts, 1980-81, and Guggenheim Foundation, 1985-86; *Los Angeles Times* Book Prize nomination, 1982, for *Living by Fiction;* honorary degree from Boston College, 1986; National Book Critics Circle award nomination, 1987, for *An American Childhood;* Appalachian Gold Medallion, University of Charleston, 1989; St. Botolph's Club Foundation Award, Boston, 1989.

WRITINGS:

Tickets for a Prayer Wheel (poems), University of Missouri Press, 1974.
Pilgrim at Tinker Creek, Harper's Magazine Press, 1974 (also see below).
Holy the Firm, Harper, 1978 (also see below).
The Weasel, limited edition, Rara Avis Press, 1981.
Living By Fiction, Harper, 1982 (also see below).
Teaching a Stone to Talk: Expeditions and Encounters, Harper, 1982 (also see below).
Encounters With Chinese Writers, Wesleyan University Press, 1984.
An American Childhood, Harper, 1987 (also see below).
(With Russell Baker and others) *Inventing the Truth: The Art and Craft of Memoir,* edited by William Zinsser, Houghton, 1987.
(Editor with Robert Atwan) *The Best American Essays, 1988,* Ticknor & Fields, 1988.
The Annie Dillard Library (contains *Living by Fiction, An American Childhood, Holy the Firm, Pilgrim at Tinker Creek,* and *Teaching a Stone to Talk*), Harper, 1989.
The Writing Life, Harper, 1989.

Works have been widely anthologized. Columnist, *Living Wilderness,* 1973-75. Contributor of fiction, essays, and poetry to *Atlantic Monthly, Prose, American Scholar, Poetry, Chicago Review, Antaeus, Sports Illustrated, Esquire,* and many other periodicals. Contributing editor, *Harper's,* 1974-81 and 1983-85.

WORK IN PROGRESS: Essays for periodicals; a book.

SIDELIGHTS: Few young writers know the pleasure of having their first published prose receive widespread critical acclaim. Fewer still are awarded a major literary prize for this same work. Annie Dillard's *Pilgrim at Tinker Creek,* however, inspired several favorable comparisons with no less than Thoreau's *Walden* and also won a Pulitzer Prize in 1974.

Describing herself as "a poet and a walker with a background in theology and a penchant for quirky facts," Dillard reveals early in the book her intention to present "what Thoreau called 'a meteorological journal of the mind' "; that is, a detailed account of a period of solitude spent in communion with nature and in deep meditation. As a *Commentary* critic observes, *Pilgrim at Tinker Creek* belongs "squarely in the American tradition of essayistic narratives in which one person, unencumbered by *idees recues,* stripped of conventional prejudices, tries to 'front the essential facts,' to make sense of the universe starting from degree zero."

Continues the critic: "One of the most pleasing traits of the book is the graceful harmony between scrutiny of real phenomena and the reflections to which that gives rise. Anecdotes of animal behavior become so effortlessly enlarged into symbols by the deepened insight of meditation. Like a true transcendentalist, Miss Dillard understands her task to be that of full alertness, of making herself a conscious receptacle of all impressions. She is a connoisseur of spirit, who knows that seeing, if intense enough, becomes vision."

Furthermore, states the critic, Dillard's meditations appear even more attractive to the reader due to the beauty of her language, "which is scrupulously precise, unpretentiously lyrical, and sometimes charged with power of concentrated perception. Most of the natural lore which she chooses to relate is fascinating enough in itself, and Miss Dillard has a good eye for its most dramatic elements. . . . She has the rare ability to recreate the emotional tone of experience without abandoning accuracy or specificity of detail."

Eleanor B. Wymard of *Commonweal* sees strains of existentialism rather than transcendentalism in *Pilgrim at Tinker Creek.* After pointing out that Dillard is firmly convinced that "beauty and violence are equal parts of the mystery of creation," she notes: "As her narrative develops, [the author] grows comfortable with ambiguity, accepting the senseless ways of nature while scrupulously describing it. Fidelity to horrible detail makes her celebration of life startling, for her style is so careful of the minute that her theme, in comparison, borders on the irrational. How can one be a believer while portraying honestly the chaotic ways of nature? . . . Dillard is exploring, in truth, not merely the woodland of Tinker Creek, but, more profoundly, what it means to be a believer in God. . . . By insisting that human beings have the visionary capacity to see both the beauty and the violence of the world with new eyes, Dillard is different from the traditional Transcendentalist. Although the 'anchor-hold' at Tinker Creek reminds one inevitably of Walden Pond, Dillard is closer to Melville than to Thoreau. Her awareness of both light and darkness is profound. . . . [She] witnesses to the existential condition as nature reveals it, begging us to see it with her, for freedom to Annie Dillard lies in acute awareness of the terms of life. She does not intend her hermitage at Tinker Creek to stand as a political statement nor to inspire ethical behavior or social reform. If she has a mission, it is purely that of the Christian artist: to offer new insight into human existence. For Annie Dillard, it is significant to feel nature profoundly, for then she is close to asking the ultimate question about being, and, for her, to do this is everything."

Melvin Maddocks of *Time* observes in his review of *Pilgrim at Tinker Creek* that "at first she seems to fit into a pattern as predictable as a wildlife calendar, this Annie Dillard, . . . who looks out of her cottage window on nature and, sure enough, starting right on schedule with January, records the seasons as they come and go at Tinker Creek in Virginia. . . . [But] reader, beware of this deceptive girl. . . . Here is no gentle romantic twirling a buttercup, no graceful inscriber of 365 inspirational prose poems. . . . To an age hooked on novelty, variety and pluralism, her message is as clear as William Blake's: 'See a world in a grain of sand'—if you dare. Allying herself to leeched turtles, she sums up herself and perhaps her species thus: 'I am a frayed and nibbled survivor in a fallen world.' But what she has done is bear witness to her mystery as no leeched turtle (and few living writers) could—in a remarkable psalm of terror and celebration."

Several reviewers, though they admit that *Pilgrim at Tinker Creek* has its virtues, also find certain aspects of it silly or annoying. Charles Deemer of the *New Leader,* for example, claims that "if Annie Dillard had not spelled out what she was up to in this book, I don't think I would have guessed. . . . Her observations are typically described in overstatement reaching toward hysteria, and the lessons she would impart are at best sophomoric, at worst pompous twaddle. Still, there is enough fun and good will in *Pilgrim at Tinker Creek* that I cannot dismiss it altogether. . . . I must confess that I, too, enjoy moments beside creek and pond, and I, too, have seen and thought things which have changed my life. But if Annie Dillard wants to change lives, she had better talk sense or breath spiritual fire. . . . She only demonstrates once again how terribly self-centered the species can be, with respect both to its place in nature and to its place among fellow humans. Call this book a meteorological journal of an egomaniac. . . . There is not one genuine ecological concern voiced in the entire book. The focus is on the silly notion that insects and plants should behave like people. . . . But Dillard isn't really so naive. Her style simply gets away from her."

Muriel Haynes of *Ms.* is somewhat more charitable in her assessment of *Pilgrim at Tinker Creek.* Calling it "a passionate vision [that] will console many," she writes: "[Dillard's] style slides in and out of the colloquial and the everyday to the reverential and the celebratory. Her imaginative flights have the special beauty of surprise. . . . No one could fail to find her facts enthralling. She has read and quotes or paraphrases scores of writings about natural phenomena, marvelous tales told by travelers to regions hidden from most of us. Her own experiences are less exotic but meticulously graphic. She writes with appreciation and respect for all living creatures." Nevertheless, Haynes concludes, "Dillard is susceptible to fits of rapture. From time to time her prose reaches a school-girlish pitch. At moments of ecstasy she tends to become overwrought; reeling, staggering, gasping for death, she surrenders to self-dramatization. Yet in control she can soar with words of moving purity."

Eudora Welty, commenting in the *New York Times Book Review,* feels that "a reader's heart must go out to a young writer with a sense of wonder so fearless and unbridled. . . . There is ambition about [Dillard's] book that I like, one that is deeper than the ambition to declare wonder aloud. It is the ambition to feel. This is a guess. But if this is what she has at heart, I am not quite sure that in writing this book she wholly accomplished it." After quoting a particularly confusing paragraph, for example, Welty states, "I honestly do not know what she is talking about at such times. The only thing I could swear to is that the writing here leaves something to be desired." Furthermore, continues Welty, "[the] author is given to changing style or shifting moods with disconcerting frequency and abruptness. . . . You might be reading letters home from camp, where the moment before you might have thought you were deep in the Book of Leviticus."

In a somewhat different vein, the critic questions the advisability of making the book so self-oriented. She remarks: "Annie Dillard is the only person in her book, substantially the only one in her world; I recall no outside human speech coming to break the long soliloquy of the author. Speaking of the universe very often, she is yet self-surrounded, and, beyond that, book-surrounded. Her own book might have taken in more of human life without losing a bit of the wonder she was after. Might it not have gained more?"

Despite these faults, however, Welty concludes that the book has merit. "Is the Pilgrim on her right road?," she asks. "That depends on what the Pilgrim's destination is. But how much better, in any case, to wonder than not to wonder, to dance with astonishment and go spinning in praise, than not to know enough to dance or praise at all; to be blessed with more imagination than you might know at the given moment what to do with than to be cursed with too little to give you—and other people—any trouble."

On the other hand, Hayden Carruth, writing in the *Virginia Quarterly Review,* says *Pilgrim at Tinker Creek* is a "dangerous" and "subversive" book due to its obvious affection for nostalgia. He writes: "In many respects Annie Dillard's book . . . is so ingratiating that even readers who find themselves in fundamental disagreement with it may take pleasure from it, a good deal of pleasure. . . . [She] has done what many would like but few are able to do. She has organized her life, there in her primarily natural habitat, so that she has plenty of time to spend not only in the field but in the library and laboratory as well. . . . And she uses her knowledge well. . . . Inevitably, however, she does more than this: she asks what it all means. . . . Out of these quandaries Annie Dillard always contrives to emerge with a statement of spiritual affirmation, a statement which is, moreover, though expressive of her own sensibility, conventional in substance. . . . In essence her view in plain old-fashioned optimistic American transcendentalism, ornamented though it may be with examples from quantum physics and biochemistry. . . . [She also] devotes many pages to what can only be called rhapsody, evocation in words of her own epiphanies. Unfortunately, much of this writing is confused, exaggerated, sentimental, and unconvincing. . . . [Furthermore,] Annie Dillard's book is a work done in 'the deep affection of nostalgia' (her words) for an abstract past, with little reference to life on this planet at this moment, its hazards and misdirections, and to this extent it is a dangerous book, literally a subversive book, in spite of its attractions. To my mind the view of man and nature held by any honest farmer . . . is historically more relevant and humanly far more responsible than the atavistic and essentially passive, not to say evasive, view held by Annie Dillard."

America's Mike Major does not subscribe to this view of Dillard and her work. Commenting on her writing in general, he notes: "Dillard brings to her work an artist's eye, a scientist's curiosity, a metaphysician's mind, all woven together in what might be called, essentially, a theologian's quest. . . . [She] is not so much an aging hippie doing her own precious little thing, or even a detached, observing scientist, as an intellectual sculptress, painstakingly constructing a huge, objective scaffolding capable of encompassing ultimate meanings, a penetrating vision into the realities of nature, man and God. Unambitious the woman is not. . . . [Her] nonfiction reads like poetry because, in fact, it is. Her forging together of these two disparate forms was accomplished not without some travail. . . . The reason for her extraordinary efforts lies in her passion to charge her prose with such inner cohesiveness that it fulfills the function of poetry. She constructs her nonfiction as carefully as a sonnet. . . . [But] more than artist, scientist, thinker or even theologian, Dillard is primarily a mystic, bruising her soul against the Absolute."

Dillard explained to Major that "people want to make you into a cult figure because of what they fancy to be your life style, when the truth is your life is literature. You're writing consciously, off of hundreds of index cards, often distorting the literal truth to achieve an artistic one. It's all hard, conscious, terribly frustrating work! But this never occurs to people. They think it happens in a dream, that you just sit on a tree stump and take dictation from some little chipmunk! . . . If you're going to think or write seriously, you have to be intelligent. You have to keep learning or die on your feet." Recalling the grueling ordeal of working on *Pilgrim at Tinker Creek*—an eight-month, seven-days-a-week, fifteen-to-sixteen-hour-a-day project, accomplished not in the great outdoors, but in a library study carrel—Dillard concludes, "I rarely write, I hate to write."

In the years following the publication of *Pilgrim at Tinker Creek,* Dillard penned a number of other acclaimed books, including a short narrative titled *Holy the Firm; Living by Fiction,* a volume of literary criticism; an essay collection titled *Teaching a Stone to Talk; Encounters With Chinese Writers,* Dillard's account of her experience as a member of a U.S. cultural delegation that traveled to China in 1982; *An American Childhood,* a memoir about growing up in Pittsburgh; and *The Writing Life,* a narrative consisting of metaphors about the process of writing.

BIOGRAPHICAL/CRITICAL SOURCES:

BOOKS

Contemporary Literary Criticism, Volume IX, Gale 1978.
Dictionary of Literary Biography Yearbook: 1980, Gale, 1981.

PERIODICALS

America, April 20, 1974, February 11, 1978, May 6, 1978.
Best Sellers, December, 1977.
Chicago Tribune, October 1, 1987.
Chicago Tribune Book World, September 12, 1982, November 21, 1982.
Commentary, October, 1974.
Commonweal, October 24, 1975, February 3, 1978.
Detroit News, October 31, 1982.
Globe and Mail (Toronto), November 28, 1987.
Los Angeles Times, April 27, 1982, November 19, 1982.
Los Angeles Times Book Review, November 18, 1984, September 20, 1987.
Ms., August, 1974.
New Leader, June 24, 1974.
New Republic, April 6, 1974.
New York Times, September 21, 1977, March 12, 1982, November 25, 1982.
New York Times Book Review, March 24, 1974, May 9, 1982, November 28, 1982, September 23, 1984, September 27, 1987, September 17, 1989.
People, October 19, 1987.
Publishers Weekly, September 1, 1989.
Time, March 18, 1974, October 10, 1977.
Tribune Books (Chicago), September 13, 1987, December 18, 1988, August 27, 1989.
Virginia Quarterly Review, autumn, 1974.
Washington Post, October 28, 1987.
Washington Post Book World, October 16, 1977, April 4, 1982, January 2, 1983, September 9, 1984, September 6, 1987, September 24, 1989.

*　　*　　*

DINESEN, Isak
See BLIXEN, Karen (Christentze Dinesen)

*　　*　　*

DIOP, Birago (Ismael) 1906-1989
(Max, d'Alain Provist)

PERSONAL: Some sources spell middle name "Ismail"; born December 11, 1906, in Ouakam (some sources say Dakar), Senegal; died November 25, 1989, in Dakar, Senegal; son of Ismael (a master mason) and Sokhna (Diawara) Diop; married Marie-Louise Pradere (an accountant), 1934 (deceased); children: Renee, Andree. *Education:* Received doctorate from Ecole Nationale Veterinaire de Toulouse, 1933; attended Institut de Medecine Veterinaire Exotique, c. 1934, and Ecole Francaise des Cuirs et Peaux.

ADDRESSES: B.P. No. 5018, Dakar, Senegal.

CAREER: Head of government cattle inspection service in Senegal and French Sudan (now Mali), c. 1934-42; employed at Institut de Medecine Veterinaire Exotique in Paris, France, 1942-44; interim head of zoological technical services in Ivory Coast,

1946; head of zoological technical services in Upper Volta (now Burkina Faso), 1947-50, in Mauritania, 1950-54, and in Senegal, 1955; administrator for Societe de la Radio-diffusion d'Outre-Mer (broadcasting company), 1957; ambassador from Senegal to Tunisia during early 1960s; veterinarian in private practice in Dakar, Senegal, beginning c. 1964. Vice-president of Confederation Internationale des Societes d'Auteurs et Compositeurs, 1982; president of reading board of Nouvelles Editions Africaines (publisher); official of Institut des Hautes Etudes de Defense Nationale (French national defense institute). *Military service:* Nurse in military hospital in St.-Louis, Senegal, 1928-29.

MEMBER: Association des Ecrivains du Senegal (president), Bureau Senegalais des Droits d'Auteur (president of administrative council), Societe des Gens de Lettres de France, Pen-Club, Rotary-Club de Dakar, Anemon.

AWARDS, HONORS: Grand Prix Litteraire de l'Afrique-Occidentale Francaise, for *Les Contes d'Amadou Koumba;* Grand Prix Litteraire de l'Afrique Noire from Association des Ecrivains d'Expression Francaise de la Mer et de l'Outre Mer (now Association des Ecrivains de Langue Francaise), 1964, for *Contes et lavanes.* Officier de la Legion d'Honneur; commandeur des Palmes Academiques; chevalier de l'Etoile Noire; chevalier du Merite Agricole; chevalier des Arts et des Lettres; grand-croix de l'Ordre National Senegalais; grand officier de l'Ordre de la Republique Tunisienne; grand officier de l'Ordre National Ivoirien.

WRITINGS:

SHORT STORIES

Les Contes d'Amadou Koumba (includes "Maman-Caiman," "Les Mamelles," and "Sarzan"), Fasquelle, 1947, reprinted, Presence Africaine, 1978.
Les Nouveaux Contes d'Amadou Koumba (title means "The New Tales of Amadou Koumba"; includes "L'Os de Mor Lam"), preface by Leopold Sedar Senghor, Presence Africaine, 1958.
Contes et lavanes (title means "Tales and Commentaries"), Presence Africaine, 1963.
Tales of Amadou Koumba (collection; includes "A Judgment"), translation and introduction by Dorothy S. Blair, Oxford University Press, 1966.
Contes choisis (collection), edited with an introduction by Joyce A. Hutchinson, Cambridge University Press, 1967.
Contes d'Awa, illustrations by A. Diallo, Nouvelles Editions Africaines, 1977.
Mother Crocodile—Maman-Caiman, translation and adaptation by Rosa Guy, illustrations by John Steptoe, Delacorte Press, 1981.

PLAYS; ADAPTED FROM HIS SHORT STORIES

"Sarzan," performed in Dakar, Senegal, 1955.
L'Os de Mor Lam (performed at Theatre National Daniel Sorano, Senegal, 1967-68), Nouvelles Editions Africaines, 1977.

Also adapted "Maman-Caiman" and "Les Mamelles."

OTHER

Leurres et lueurs (poems; title means "Lures and Lights"; includes "Viatique"), Presence Africaine, 1960.
Birago Diop, ecrivain senegalais (collection), commentary by Roger Mercier and M. and S. Battestini, F. Nathan, 1964.
Memoires (autobiography), Presence Africaine, Volume 1: *La Plume raboutee* (title means "The Piecemeal Pen"), 1978,

Volume 2: *A Rebrousse-temps* (title means "Against the Grain of Time"), 1982, Volume 3: *A Rebrousse-gens: Epissures, entrelacs, et reliefs,* 1985.

Work represented in anthologies, including *Anthologie de la nouvelle poesie negre et malagache de langue francaise,* edited by Leopold Sedar Senghor, Presses Universitaires de France, 1948; *A Book of African Verse,* Heinemann, 1964; and *An Anthology of African and Malagasy Poetry in French,* Oxford University Press, 1965.

Contributor to periodicals, including *L'Echo des etudiants* (sometimes under pseudonyms Max and d'Alain Provist), *L'Etudiant noir,* and *Presence africaine.*

SIDELIGHTS: Birago Diop was an author and poet best known for short stories inspired by the folktales of West Africa. Born and raised in Senegal, formerly a French colony, Diop wrote in French, although some of his works have been translated into English and other languages. As a young man Diop left Senegal for France, where he studied veterinary science at the Ecole Nationale Veterinaire in Toulouse. After receiving his doctorate in 1933 he went to Paris, where he encountered a community of black writers from the French colonial empire that included Aime Cesaire of Martinique and Leopold Sedar Senghor of Senegal. Senghor and Cesaire led the Negritude movement, which rejected the assimilation of black colonial peoples into French culture, asserting instead the value of the black heritage. Inspired by the movement, Diop wrote poems such as "Viatique," a vivid portrayal of the initiation ceremony of an African tribe. His work appeared in two of Senghor's groundbreaking efforts at publishing Franco-African authors: the journal *L'Etudiant noir* and the book *Anthologie de la nouvelle poesie negre et malagache de langue francaise.*

Later in the 1930s Diop returned to French West Africa, and in his work as a government veterinarian he traveled widely throughout the region, sometimes into remote areas of the interior. He turned from poetry to the short story, "the most traditional form of African literature," as Joyce A. Hutchinson observed in her introduction to *Contes choisis.* For centuries African literature was primarily spoken, and storytellers such as the *griots* of West Africa found the short story a convenient form in which to provide moral lessons or to discuss the human condition. When Diop published his first collection of stories, *Les Contes d'Amadou Koumba,* he said they were drawn verbatim from a *griot* named Amadou whom he had met during his travels. In a later interview for *Le Soleil,* however, he acknowledged that Amadou was a composite of many storytellers he had encountered, including members of his own family.

In fact many commentators, including Senghor, have suggested that Diop's stories succeed on the printed page because they are a skillful combination of African oral tradition and the author's own considerable talent as a writer. Diop "uses tradition, of which he is proud," Hutchinson wrote in 1967, "but he does not insist in an unintelligent fashion on tradition for tradition's sake. He resuscitates the spirit and the style of the traditional *conte* [tale] in beautiful French, without losing all the qualities which were in the vernacular version."

Diop's tales have often been praised for their varied and skillful observations on human nature. In "L'Os de Mor Lam," for instance, a selfish man prefers to be buried alive rather than share his supper with a neighbor. The author often drew upon traditional animal tales, which put human foibles on display by endowing animals with exaggerated forms of human characteristics. In one African story cycle, which Diop used extensively, a physically strong but foolish hyena is repeatedly bested by a hare who relies on intelligence rather than strength.

Reviewers generally note that Diop preferred laughter to melodrama in his stories, and in *The African Experience in Literature and Ideology* Abiola Irele stressed the "gentle" quality of Diop's humor. But other commentators agreed with Dorothy S. Blair, who in her foreword to *Tales of Amadou Koumba* held that some stories contain a sharper element of social satire. "Sarzan," for example, describes the comeuppance of an African villager who returns from service in the French Army and tries to impose French culture on his people. And in "A Judgment," according to John Field of *Books and Bookmen,* a couple with marital problems must endure first the "pompous legalism" of the village elders and then the "arbitrary and callous" judgment of a Muslim lord.

In adapting the oral folktale to a written form, Diop strove to maintain the spontaneity of human speech, and to do so he interspersed his prose with dialogue, songs, and poems—all part of the African storyteller's technique, as Hutchinson noted. "Diop's use of dialogue is masterly," she remarked. "He uses the whole range of human emotional expression: shouts, cries, tears, so vividly that one can without difficulty imagine and supply the accompanying gestures and the intonation of the voice." Accordingly, Diop adapted several of his stories for the stage, including "Sarzan" and "L'Os de Mor Lam." Writing in *World Literature Today,* Eileen Julien praised Diop's adaptation of "L'Os" for "depict[ing] in a warm and colorful style the manners of an African village," including "gatherings, prayers, communal rites and . . . ubiquitous, compelling chatter." "All of these," she averred, "are the matter of which theatre is made."

Diop's adaptations of the folktale have made him one of Africa's most widely read authors, and he received numerous awards and distinctions. His first volume of tales promptly won the Grand Prix Litteraire de l'Afrique-Occidentale Francaise; for Diop's second volume, Senghor, who had become one of Senegal's most prominent writers and political leaders, wrote a laudatory preface. After Senghor led Senegal to independence in 1960 he sought Diop as the country's first ambassador to Tunisia. Between 1978 and 1985 Diop produced three highly detailed volumes of memoirs, including his account of the early days of the Negritude movement in Paris. Summarizing Diop's literary achievement, Hutchinson praised the author for showing that short stories in the traditional African style are "not just children's tales, not just sociological or even historical material, but a work of art, part of Africa's cultural heritage."

BIOGRAPHICAL/CRITICAL SOURCES:

BOOKS

Diop, Birago, *Les Nouveaux Contes d'Amadou Koumba,* preface by Leopold Sedar Senghor, Presence Africaine, 1958.
Diop, Birago, *Tales of Amadou Koumba,* translation and introduction by Dorothy S. Blair, Oxford University Press, 1966.
Diop, Birago, *Contes choisis,* edited with an introduction by Joyce A. Hutchinson, Cambridge University Press, 1967.
Diop, Birago, *Memoires,* three volumes, Presence Africaine, 1978-1985.
Irele, Abiola, *The African Experience in Literature and Ideology,* Heinemann, 1981.

PERIODICALS

Books and Bookmen, October, 1986.
Le Soleil, December 11, 1976.
World Literature Today, winter, 1979, autumn, 1986.

OBITUARIES:

PERIODICALS

New York Times, November 29, 1989.

* * *

DISCH, Thomas M(ichael) 1940-
(Tom Disch, Leonie Hargrave; Thom Demijohn and Cassandra Knye, joint pseudonyms)

PERSONAL: Born February 2, 1940, in Des Moines, Iowa; son of Felix Henry and Helen (Gilbertson) Disch. *Education:* Attended New York University, 1959-62.

ADDRESSES: Agent—Barney Karpfinger, 18 East 48th St., New York, N.Y. 10017.

CAREER: Free-lance writer, 1964——. Lecturer at universities.

MEMBER: P.E.N., Writers Guild East, National Book Critics Circle.

AWARDS, HONORS: O. Henry Prize, 1975, for story "Getting into Death," and 1979, for story "Xmas"; John W. Campbell Memorial Award, 1980, for *On Wings of Song;* British Science Fiction Award, 1981, and Locus Award, 1982, both for story "The Brave Little Toaster."

WRITINGS:

NOVELS

The Genocides, Berkley Publishing, 1965.
Mankind under the Leash (also see below), Ace Books, 1966 (published in England as *The Puppies of Terra,* Panther Books, 1978).
(With John Sladek under joint pseudonym Cassandra Knye) *The House That Fear Built,* Paperback Library, 1966.
Echo Round His Bones, Berkley Publishing, 1967.
(With Sladek under joint pseudonym Thom Demijohn) *Black Alice,* Doubleday, 1968, reprinted, Carroll & Graf, 1989.
Camp Concentration, Hart-Davis, 1968, Doubleday, 1969.
The Prisoner, Ace Books, 1969.
334, MacGibbon & Kee, 1972, Avon, 1974.
(Under pseudonym Leonie Hargrave) *Clara Reeve,* Knopf, 1975.
On Wings of Song, St. Martin's, 1979.
Triplicity (omnibus volume), Doubleday, 1980.
(With Charles Naylor) *Neighboring Lives,* Scribner, 1981.
The Businessman: A Tale of Terror, Harper, 1984.
Amnesia (computer-interactive novel), Electronic Arts, 1985.

STORY COLLECTIONS

One Hundred and Two H-Bombs and Other Science Fiction Stories (also see below), Compact Books, 1966, revised edition published as *One Hundred and Two H-Bombs,* Berkley Publishing, 1969 (published in England as *White Fang Goes Dingo and Other Funny S. F. Stories,* Arrow Books, 1971).
Under Compulsion, Hart-Davis, 1968, published as *Fun with Your New Head,* Doubleday, 1969.
Getting into Death: The Best Short Stories of Thomas M. Disch, Hart-Davis, 1973, revised edition, Knopf, 1976.
The Early Science Fiction Stories of Thomas M. Disch (contains *Mankind under the Leash* and *One Hundred and Two H-Bombs and Other Science Fiction Stories*), Gregg, 1977.
Fundamental Disch, Bantam, 1980.
The Man Who Had No Idea, Bantam, 1982.

POETRY

(With Marilyn Hacker and Charles Platt) *Highway Sandwiches,* privately printed, 1970.
The Right Way to Figure Plumbing, Basilisk Press, 1972.
ABCDEFG HIJKLM NPOQRST UVWXYZ, Anvil Press Poetry, 1981.
Orders of the Retina, Toothpaste Press, 1982.
Burn This, Hutchinson, 1982.
Here I Am, There You Are, Where Were We, Hutchinson, 1984.
(Under name Tom Disch) *Yes Let's: New and Selected Poems,* Johns Hopkins University Press, 1989.

EDITOR

(Ghost editor with Robert Arthur) *Alfred Hitchcock Presents: Stories That Scared Even Me,* Random House, 1967.
The Ruins of Earth: An Anthology of Stories of the Immediate Future, Putnam, 1971.
Bad Moon Rising: An Anthology of Political Foreboding, Harper, 1975.
The New Improved Sun: An Anthology of Utopian Science Fiction, Harper, 1975.
(With Naylor) *New Constellations: An Anthology of Tomorrow's Mythologies,* Harper, 1976.
(With Naylor) *Strangeness: A Collection of Curious Tales,* Scribner, 1977.
Richard Lupoff, *Stroka Prospekt,* Toothpaste Press, 1982.

OTHER

(Librettist) "The Fall of the House of Usher" (opera), first produced in New York, N.Y., by the Bel Canto Opera Company, 1979.
(Librettist) "Frankenstein" (opera), first produced in Greenvale, N.Y., at the C. W. Post Center of Long Island University, 1982.
Ringtime (short story), Toothpaste Press, 1983.
Torturing Mr. Amberwell (short story), Cheap Street, 1985.
The Brave Little Toaster (juvenile), Doubleday, 1986.
The Brave Little Toaster Goes to Mars (juvenile), Doubleday, 1988.
The Silver Pillow: A Tale of Witchcraft, Mark Ziesing, 1988.

Work appears in anthologies. Contributor to *Transatlantic Review, Playboy, Harper's,* and other periodicals. Regular reviewer for *Times Literary Supplement* and *Washington Post Book World.*

SIDELIGHTS: An author of science fiction, poetry, historical novels, opera librettos, and computer-interactive fiction, Thomas M. Disch has been cited as "one of the most remarkably multi-talented writers around" by a reviewer for the *Washington Post Book World.* Noting the diversity of Disch's work, Charles Platt writes in *Dream Makers: The Uncommon People Who Write Science Fiction* that "he has traveled widely, through almost every genre and technique. And in each field [Disch] has made himself at home, never ill-at-ease or out-of-place, writing with the same implacable control and elegant manners."

Disch began his career by writing science fiction, where his unique vision—"dark, disturbing, and skeptical," as Erich S. Rupprecht calls it in the *Dictionary of Literary Biography*—made his work stand out from the rest of the genre. His first novel, *The Genocides,* concerns an alien invasion of Earth. But it differs from other such invasion novels in that the aliens win, and all human beings are exterminated. The invasion is carried out by sowing the Earth with the seeds of gigantic plants that disrupt their surroundings as they grow, eventually crowding out all other forms of life. When a few human survivors try to fight back, they are easily destroyed by the mechanical robots who tend the plants. The aliens themselves are never seen, make no attempt to contact the humans, and seem unaware of or indifferent to the destruction they have caused. When they kill the last of the humans, it is similar to the killing of insects in a farm field and just as impersonal. "The novel succeeds on several counts," Rupprecht states. "One source of its power is the utter absurdity of the humans' situation. Like characters in a Kafka novel, they are absolutely bewildered by events outside their control. . . . The novel is also powerful in the way that it forces the reader to alter his perspective, to reexamine what it means to be human." Speaking to Platt, Disch explains that he found the conventional alien invasion story, in which the humans overcome great odds to win, unsatisfying. "Let's be honest," Disch states, "the real interest in this kind of story is to see some devastating cataclysm *wipe mankind out.* There's a grandeur in that idea that all the other people threw away and trivialized. My point was simply to write a book where you don't spoil that beauty and pleasure at the end."

Camp Concentration, another early Disch novel and one of his best known, is equally uncompromising in its approach. It is set at a secret prison camp run by the U.S. Army where selected prisoners are being treated with a new drug that increases their intelligence. Unfortunately, this drug also causes the prisoners' early deaths. The novel is in the form of a diary kept by one of the prisoners. The diary's style grows more complex as the narrative develops, reflecting the prisoner's increasing intelligence. According to Robert Scholes and Eric S. Rabkin in *Science Fiction: History, Science, Vision,* the novel "combines considerable technical resources in the management of the narrative . . . with a probing inquiry into human values." Rupprecht draws a parallel between *Camp Concentration* and *The Genocides.* In both novels, he argues, the characters must survive inescapable situations. Disch's continuing theme, Rupprecht summarizes, is "charting his characters' attempts to keep themselves intact in a world which grows increasingly hostile, irrational, inhuman."

This theme is also found in *334,* a novel set in a New York City housing project of the future. Divided into six loosely related sections, the novel presents the daily lives of residents of the building, which is located at 334 East Eleventh Street. The characters live in boredom and poverty; their city is rundown and dirty. The world of the novel, Scholes and Rabkin believe, "is not radically different from ours in many respects but deeply troubling for reasons that apply to the present New York as well. Above all, the aimlessness and purposelessness of the lives chronicled is affecting." In his analysis of the book, Rupprecht also notes the similarity between the novel's setting and the world of the present. He finds *334* to be "a slightly distorted mirror image of contemporary life." Although the *Washington Post Book World* reviewer judges the setting to be "an interesting, plausible and unpleasant near-future world where urban life is even more constricted than now," he nonetheless believes that "survival and aspiration remain possible." Rupprecht praises *334* as Disch's "most brilliant and disturbing work. . . . One can think of few writers—of science fiction or other genres—who could convey a similar sense of emptiness, of yearning, of ruin with this power and grace. . . . Like all great writers, Disch forces his readers to see the reality of their lives in a way that is fresh, startling disturbing, and moving." Speaking of *Camp Concentration* and *334,* David Lehman of the *Times Literary Supplement* states that these two novels "seem to transcend their genre without betraying it; they manage to break down the barriers separating science

fiction from 'literature,' and they do so by shrewdly manipulating the conventions of the former."

On Wings of Song, winner of the John W. Campbell Memorial Award, has also been praised for its ability to transcend its science fiction trappings to work as literature. As Joanna Russ comments in the *Magazine of Fantasy and Science Fiction,* "Science-fiction writers and readers often talk about uniting science fiction with the mainstream; Disch has done it [in *On Wings of Song*], by pushing the possibilities of science fiction to the limit." The novel depicts a future America where the coastal cities are decadent and decrepit, and the rest of the country is run by smothering corporate bureaucracies. In this society it is possible to "fly" in one's spirit body by singing with the proper amount of honest feeling. When Daniel Weinrab and his wife Boadicea attempt to fly, Boadicea is successful, leaving her physical body behind in a comatose state, but Daniel fails. The rest of the novel traces his efforts to rejoin his wife.

There is a strong satirical element in *On Wings of Song* that moves Russ to call it "an ominous attack on the morals and good customs of Middle America" and Hermione Lee of the *Observer* to compare it with Nathanael West's *A Cool Million.* But John Calvin Batchelor of the *Village Voice* believes that with *On Wings of Song* "Disch achieves a blend of the conflicting mix in his oeuvre—the rebellion, silliness, despair, survival, aesthetics—to produce a novel that may be read both as a condemnation of Amerika and as an affirmation of America, of its innovative citizenry."

In *Neighboring Lives,* Disch turns from science fiction to the historical novel, teaming with Charles Naylor to write a fictional account of nineteenth-century Chelsea, a section of London where many famous artists and writers lived at the time. It is, Elaine Kendall writes in the *Los Angeles Times,* "a sort of group biography." Based on letters and journals of the principal characters, *Neighboring Lives* interweaves the life histories of such people as Thomas Carlyle, John Stuart Mill, Gabriel Rossetti, John Ruskin, Lewis Carroll, and Frederick Chopin. "This is not pageantry—peak moments in the lives of the great—but montage of small, telling events that quietly evoke the spirit of time and place," Laura Geringer writes in *Saturday Review.* Chopin demonstrates to Mrs. Carlyle that her piano is out of tune; Lewis Carroll ponders over a title for his children's book about a young girl named Alice; Algernon Charles Swinburne takes George Meredith's son to look at boats on the Thames. "There is no story here, no gathering force, none of the momentum we expect of a 'novel,' " Cynthia King writes in the *Detroit News.* "But that word on the cover allows this probing of minds of people long dead, this invention of actions and motives and conversations." Disch and Naylor, Jean Strouse writes in *Newsweek,* "have given vivid fictional life to a wide range of mid-century characters [in *Neighboring Lives*]." Although Strouse admits that the authors "have taken poetic license with time and fact" to write their novel, they "have clearly also done their homework and have delivered a period Chelsea refined and enhanced by fiction."

With *The Businessman: A Tale of Terror,* Disch explores the genre of horror fiction in a satirical, ironic manner. Businessman Bob Glandier murders his wife, Giselle, but she returns to haunt him. A monstrous spirit, Bob and Giselle's offspring, also haunts him. Meanwhile, the ghost of poet John Berryman is forced to haunt Minneapolis by a nineteenth-century poet who controls limbo. And heaven turns out to be equipped with television sets on which celestial residents can watch reruns of their own lives. The novel, Stephen Dobyns writes in the *Washington Post,* "draws from a number of strange tales ranging from 'The Exorcist' to 'The Frog Prince' and one could scarcely credit any of it if Disch weren't an excellent writer." Glandier has denied "the possibility of a spiritual realm that can make itself wondrously felt in the here and now," David Lehman writes in *Newsweek.* " 'The Businessman' is a hymn to this possibility." It is a possibility, however, that Disch handles in an ironic manner. He writes in the novel: "The source of grace—let us be honest and call it God—is also an ironist and a dweller in paradoxes." Although Glandier eventually dies as punishment for the murder he has committed, John Clute writes in the *Times Literary Supplement,* "the outcome is arbitrary. At the heart of the book there is a cruel vertigo of godlessness." This distressing tone moves Marion Zimmer Bradley to write in the *New York Times Book Review:* "It is all very elegantly satirical: none of these horrors really induce pity or terror. There's a lot of literary trivia and a lot of clever literary allusions concealed in the book, but there is no impulse to suspend disbelief."

Such negative reaction to Disch's work, Clute explains, is often due to the fact that Disch is "an ironist in a culture which tends to treat irony as suspect, frivolous, metropolitan." Fred Pfeil of the *San Francisco Review of Books* takes exception to Bradley's comment. Bradley "got one thing right," Pfeil concedes. "As a standard Stephen-King-style horror novel, *The Businessman* is all screwed up." Pfeil believes the novel combines the banal with the horrifying to create the true feeling of contemporary society. It is, Pfeil argues, both realistic and fantastic. "A realistic novel," he writes, "*because* a fantastic one; because in a fully consumerized society all the landscape is always already commodified, sloganized, in effect possessed. It is then the formal machinery of the horror novel that comes to seem slightly silly in *The Businessman,* the images of sheerest dailiness that smack of fear." Clute judges *The Businessman* to be "a *tour de force* of polished, distanced, sly narrative art."

The variety found in Disch's novels also extends to his short stories, where he has explored a number of different genres. As Disch tells Platt: "Part of my notion of a proper ambition is that one should excel at a wide range of tasks." "Getting into Death," a short story about Gothic novelist Cassandra Knye searching among her fictional characters for help in accepting her imminent death, won Disch an O. Henry prize in 1975. (Disch and John Sladek had used the joint pseudonym Cassandra Knye in writing the Gothic novel *The House That Fear Built* in 1966.) The collection *Getting into Death: The Best Short Stories of Thomas M. Disch* exhibits a sampling of the many styles Disch has employed in his short fiction. "At times [in this collection] he sounds like a soft-spoken contributor to The New Yorker," Edmund White maintains in the *New York Times Book Review,* "at others like Jerzy Kosinski, and at still others like Jules Feiffer." "The Asian Shore," a story in which an American in Turkey gradually transforms into a Turk, is called by a reviewer for the *Times Literary Supplement* "this collection's single solid achievement." Reviewing the same collection, Paul Gray states in *Time* that "it is one thing to cerebrate; to narrate is quite another. . . . Thomas M. Disch can do both." Citing the fantastic nature of many of the collection's stories, Gray points out that "fantasy makes many adults nervous. . . . Disch shows that an unfettered imagination need not be childish or frivolous. His stories show just how serious fancies can be." Writing in the *Los Angeles Times Book Review* about the collection *The Man Who Had No Idea,* Don Strachen echoes this assessment of Disch's short stories. He "reminds us," Strachen believes, "what the fantasy short story can do. His prose twists and turns down cerebral corridors; his situations entertain hosts of human quandaries simultaneously." Speaking of the stories "The Asian Shore" and

"Bodies," both collected in *Fundamental Disch,* William Boyd of the *Times Literary Supplement* describes them as "superb examples of modern short fiction."

"The distinctive qualities of Disch's prose fiction—wit, invention, and the gift of gab—are the virtues of his verse as well," Lehman writes in the *Times Literary Supplement.* "Disch has, in addition to a highly developed nose for the new, an excellent ear and a clever tongue." Disch's poetry ranges over a wide variety of forms. He writes free verse, light verse, odes, sonnets, and ballads. But whatever the form, Disch's poetry is a "lucid and accessible art," as Blake Morrison calls it in the *Times Literary Supplement.* Unlike some modern poets, Disch is concerned with being understood. This concern is evident in several of his poems, often addressed to particular poets, in which he distances himself "from prevailing fashions," as Morrison explains.

Gavin Ewart of the *Times Literary Supplement* likens Disch as a poet to "John Updike, John Fuller or X. J. Kennedy . . . somebody, that is, who is not afraid to write what used to be called Light Verse, somebody with a games-playing mind and an interest in the shapes of poems, somebody, too, who is very accomplished at writing them." Disch's interest in games-playing is reflected in Judith Moffet's comment in the *Washington Post Book World* that he displays "an interest in a dazzling surface rather than substance. . . . Disch's delight in his own dexterity is infectious at first. Before long, though, one begins to doubt whether he takes himself seriously enough." Ewart disagrees. In his review of *ABCDEFG HIJKLM NPOQRST UVWXYZ,* Ewart finds that Disch has written "serious poems of great merit." Morrison maintains that Disch is "never less than enjoyable and accomplished." And, reviewing Disch's 1989 poetry collection *Yes, Let's,* Howard Frank Mosher admires Disch's works "characterized by a refreshing combination of blunt (but good-humored) honesty, and wit." The reviewer decided that the author is "not only a gifted and technically versatile poet . . ., but a poet eminently of and for our times."

In most evaluations of his work, Disch is praised for his great imagination. In science fiction, Lehman writes in *Newsweek,* Disch enjoys a reputation as "the strongest—and surely the most fiercely literary—of the genre's recent practitioners. . . . His flights of fancy, fueled by never-failing powers of invention, succeed in raising ordinary life to mythic status." In speaking to Platt, Disch emphasizes that fiction, whether fantastic or not, needs to address life in a realistic manner. "I'm not saying that every writer has to be a realist," Disch explains, "but in terms of the ethical sensibility brought to bear in a work of imagination, there has to be some complex moral understanding of the world. In the art I like, I require irony, for instance, or simply some sense that the writer isn't telling egregious lies about the lives we lead."

BIOGRAPHICAL/CRITICAL SOURCES:

BOOKS

Contemporary Literary Criticism, Volume VII, Gale, 1977, Volume XXXVI, 1986.

Delany, Samuel R., *The Jewel-Hinged Jaw: Notes on the Language of Science Fiction,* Dragon (Elizabethtown, N.Y.), 1977.

Delany, Samuel R., *The American Shore: Meditations on a Tale of Science Fiction by Thomas M. Disch,* Dragon, 1978.

Dictionary of Literary Biography, Volume VIII: *Twentieth-Century American Science-Fiction Writers,* Gale, 1981.

Disch, Thomas M., *The Businessman: A Tale of Terror,* Harper, 1984.

Platt, Charles, *Dream Makers: The Uncommon People Who Write Science Fiction,* Berkley Publishing, 1980.

Scholes, Robert and Eric S. Rabkin, *Science Fiction: History, Science, Vision,* Oxford University Press, 1977.

PERIODICALS

American Book Review, July-August, 1985.

Chicago Tribune Book World, March 22, 1981, September 25, 1988.

Detroit Free Press, January 20, 1987.

Detroit News, April 19, 1981.

Los Angeles Times, February 3, 1981.

Los Angeles Times Book Review, November 21, 1982, July 13, 1984, August 13, 1989.

Magazine of Fantasy and Science Fiction, February, 1980.

Minnesota Review, fall, 1984.

New Statesman, June 22, 1979, May 22, 1981, July 13, 1984.

Newsweek, March 9, 1981, July 2, 1984.

New York Times Book Review, July 27, 1975, March 21, 1976, October 28, 1979, March 22, 1981, August 26, 1984, April 20, 1986.

Observer, June 24, 1979.

San Francisco Review of Books, November-December, 1984.

Saturday Review, February, 1981.

Time, July 28, 1975, February 9, 1976, July 9, 1984.

Times Literary Supplement, February 15, 1974, May 15, 1981, June 12, 1981, June 19, 1981, August 27, 1982, May 25, 1984, September 15, 1989.

Village Voice, August 27-September 2, 1980.

Virginia Quarterly Review, summer, 1976.

Washington Post, July 3, 1984.

Washington Post Book World, November 23, 1980, March 1, 1981, July 26, 1981, October 31, 1982, March 13, 1983, April 13, 1986, August 6, 1989.

*   *   *

DISCH, Tom
See DISCH, Thomas M(ichael)

*   *   *

d'ISLY, Georges
See SIMENON, Georges (Jacques Christian)

*   *   *

DOCTOROW, E(dgar) L(aurence)   1931-

PERSONAL: Born January 6, 1931, in New York, NY; son of David R. (a music store proprietor) and Rose (a pianist; maiden name, Levine) Doctorow; married Helen Esther Setzer (a writer), August 20, 1954; children: Jenny, Caroline, Richard. *Education:* Kenyon College, A.B. (with honors), 1952; Columbia University, graduate study, 1952-53.

ADDRESSES: Home—New Rochelle, NY; and c/o Random House Publishers, 201 East 50th St., New York, NY 10022.

CAREER: Script reader, Columbia Pictures Industries, Inc., New York City; New American Library, New York City, senior editor, 1959-64; Dial Press, New York City, editor-in-chief, 1964-69, vice president, 1968-69; University of California, Irvine, writer in residence, 1969-70; Sarah Lawrence College, Bronxville, NY, member of faculty, 1971-78; New York University, New York City, professor of English, 1982—. Creative writ-

ing fellow, Yale School of Drama, 1974-75; visiting professor, University of Utah, 1975; visiting senior fellow, Princeton University, 1980-81. *Military service:* U.S. Army, Signal Corps, 1953-55.

MEMBER: American Academy and Institute of Arts and Letters, Authors Guild (director), PEN (director), Writers Guild of America, East, Century Association.

AWARDS, HONORS: National Book Award nomination, 1972, for *The Book of Daniel;* Guggenheim fellowship, 1973; Creative Artists Service fellow, 1973-74; National Book Critics Circle Award and Arts and Letters award, 1976, both for *Ragtime;* L.H.D., Kenyon College, 1976; Litt.D., Hobart and William Smith Colleges, 1979; American Book Award, 1986, for *World's Fair.*

WRITINGS:

NOVELS

Welcome to Hard Times, Simon & Schuster, 1960, reprinted, Fawcett, 1988 (published in England as *Bad Man from Bodie,* Deutsch, 1961).

Big as Life, Simon & Schuster, 1966.

The Book of Daniel (also see below), Random House, 1971, reprinted, Fawcett, 1987.

Ragtime (Book-of-the-Month Club selection), Random House, 1975.

Loon Lake, Random House, 1980.

World's Fair, Random House, 1985.

Billy Bathgate (Book-of-the-Month Club main selection), Random House, 1989.

OTHER

(Contributor) Theodore Solotaroff, editor, *New American Review 2,* New American Library, 1968.

Drinks before Dinner (play; first produced Off-Broadway at Public Theater, November 22, 1978), Random House, 1979.

American Anthem, photographs by Jean-Claude Suares, Stewart, Tabori, 1982.

Daniel (screenplay; based on author's *The Book of Daniel*), Paramount Pictures, 1983.

Lives of the Poets: Six Stories and a Novella, Random House, 1984.

MEDIA ADAPTATIONS: In 1967, Metro-Goldwyn-Mayer produced a movie version of *Welcome to Hard Times,* which starred Henry Fonda. Doctorow, who had nothing to do with the film adaptation, has referred to it as the second worst movie ever made. Unlike with *Welcome to Hard Times,* he was involved, at least for a time, with the film version of *Ragtime,* which was released in 1981. Dino De Laurentiis hired Robert Altman to direct the film, and after scrapping someone else's screenplay, Altman convinced Doctorow to write one. De Laurentiis eventually fired Altman, and then Doctorow's script was rejected for being too long. Milos Forman eventually took over the directing, and playwright Michael Weller wrote the screenplay; it starred James Cagney in his last screen performance. However, Doctorow did write the screenplay for *Daniel,* the film adaptation of *The Book of Daniel,* which was produced by Paramount Pictures in 1983 and starred Timothy Hutton.

SIDELIGHTS: E. L. Doctorow is a highly regarded novelist and playwright known for his serious philosophical probings, the subtlety and variety of his prose style, and his unusual use of historical figures in fictional works. Doctorow's first novel, *Welcome to Hard Times,* was inspired, he told Jonathan Yardley of the *Miami Herald,* by his job as a reader for Columbia Pictures, where he "was accursed to read things that were submitted to this company and write synopses of them." "I had to suffer one lousy Western after another," continued Doctorow, "and it occurred to me that I could lie about the West in a much more interesting way than any of these people were lying. I wrote a short story, and it subsequently became the first chapter of that novel." The resulting book, unlike many Westerns, is concerned with grave issues. As Wirt Williams notes in the *New York Times Book Review,* the novel addresses "one of the favorite problems of philosophers: the relationship of man and evil. . . . Perhaps the primary theme of the novel is that evil can only be resisted psychically: when the rational controls that order man's existence slacken, destruction comes. [Joseph] Conrad said it best in *Heart of Darkness,* but Mr. Doctorow has said it impressively. His book is taut and dramatic, exciting and successfully symbolic." Similarly, Kevin Stan, writing in the *New Republic,* remarks: "*Welcome to Hard Times*. . . is a superb piece of fiction: lean and mean, and thematically significant. . . . He takes the thin, somewhat sordid and incipiently depressing materials of the Great Plains experience and fashions them into a myth of good and evil. . . . He does it marvelously, with economy and with great narrative power."

After writing a Western of sorts, Doctorow turned to another form not usually heralded by critics: science-fiction. In *Big as Life,* two naked human giants materialize in New York harbor. The novel examines the ways in which its characters deal with a seemingly impending catastrophe. Like *Hard Times, Big as Life* enjoyed much critical approval. A *Choice* reviewer, for example, comments that "Doctorow's dead pan manner . . . turns from satire to tenderness and human concern. A performance closer to James Purdy than to [George] Orwell or [Aldous] Huxley, but in a minor key." In spite of reviewers' praise, however, *Big as Life,* like *Welcome to Hard Times,* was not a large commercial success.

The Book of Daniel, Doctorow's third book, involves yet another traditional form, the historical novel. It is a fictional account based on the relationship between Julius and Ethel Rosenberg and their children. The Rosenbergs were Communists who were convicted of and executed for conspiracy to commit treason. Many feel that they were victims of the sometimes hysterical anti-communist fever of the 1950s. As with *Welcome to Hard Times* and *Big as Life,* Doctorow has modified the traditional form to suit his purposes. The work is not an examination of the guilt or innocence of the Rosenbergs, but as David Emblidge observes in *Southwest Review,* a look at the central character Daniel's psychology, his attempts to deal with the trauma he suffered from his parents' death. Thus many critics argue that the book, unlike typical historical novels, is largely independent of historical fact. Jane Richmond, writing in *Partisan Review,* believes that "if Julius and Ethel Rosenberg had never existed, the book would be just as good as it is." In like manner, Stanley Kauffmann, in the *New Republic,* remarks: "I haven't looked up the facts of the Rosenberg case; it would be offensive to the quality of this novel to check it against those facts."

Many critics were very impressed with the achievement of *The Book of Daniel.* Kauffmann terms it "the political novel of our age, the best American work of its kind that I know since Lionel Trilling's *The Middle of the Journey.*" P. S. Prescott of *Newsweek* adds that *The Book of Daniel* "is a purgative book, angry and more deeply felt than all but a few contemporary American novels, a novel about defeat, impotent rage, the passing of the burden of suffering through generations. . . . There is no question here of our suspending disbelief, but rather how when we have finished, we may regain stability." And Richmond calls it "a bril-

liant achievement and the best contemporary novel I've read since reading Frederick Exley's *A Fan's Notes.* . . . It is a book of infinite detail and tender attention to the edges of life as well as to its dead center."

In *Ragtime,* Doctorow forays deeper into historical territory. The novel interweaves the lives of an upper-middle-class WASP family, a poor immigrant family, and the family of a black ragtime musician with historical figures such as I. P. Morgan, Harry Houdini, Henry Ford, and Emma Goldman. Particularly intriguing to readers is that Doctorow shows famous people involved in unusual, sometimes ludicrous, situations. In the *Washington Post Book World,* Raymond Sokolov notes that "Doctorow turns history into myth and myth into history. . . . [He] continually teases our suspicion of literary artifice with apparently true historical description. . . . On the one hand, the 'fact' tugs one toward taking the episode as history. On the other, the doubt that lingers makes one want to take the narrative as an invention." Sokolov argues that Doctorow "teases" the reader in order to make him try "to sort out what the author is doing. That is, we find ourselves paying Doctorow the most important tribute. We watch to see what he is doing."

Newsweek's Walter Clemons also finds himself teased by *Ragtime*'s historical episodes: "The very fact that the book stirs one to parlor-game research is amusing evidence that Doctorow has already won the game: I found myself looking up details because I wanted them to be true." In addition, George Stade, in the *New York Times Book Review,* expresses a belief similar to Sokolov's. "In this excellent novel," Stade writes, "silhouettes and rags not only make fiction out of history but also reveal the fictions out of which history is made. It incorporates the fictions and realities of the era of ragtime while it rags our fictions about it. It is an anti-nostalgic novel that incorporates our nostalgia about its subject."

David Emblidge, however, provides a more somber view of Doctorow's use of history. He contends that there is a motif common to *Welcome to Hard Times, The Book of Daniel,* and *Ragtime:* "This motif is the idea of history as a repetitive process, almost a cyclical one, in which man is an unwilling, unknowing pawn, easily seduced into a belief in 'progress.'" Doctorow intertwines historical figures and fictional characters to mock a romantic theory of history. "Again the point of view," Emblidge continues, "in political terms, is that history . . . is far from progressive evolution toward peace among men. *Ragtime* is an indictment of the recurrent malignancies of spirit beneath the period's chimerical technological progress and social harmony." Emblidge even finds that ragtime music, which superimposes melodic improvisation on "fundamental repetition," "becomes symbolic of the historical process: endless recurrence under a distracting facade of individualistic variation."

Not all critics admire Doctorow's manipulation of history. In *Books and Bookmen,* Paul Levy maintains that *Ragtime* "falsifies history. Freud, Jung, Emma Goldman, Henry Ford, Pierpont Morgan, Stanford White and Harry Houdini simply did not perpetrate the grotesqueries they are made to commit in its pages. That is all. There is no problem. The characters in *Ragtime* that bear those famous names are not historical personages; they are merely pawns in Doctorow's particularly dotty and tasteless game of chess." On the other hand, Doctorow denies the need for historical accuracy. In a *Publishers Weekly* interview he suggests that the figures represent "images of that time" and are used "because they carried for me the right overtones of the time." And when asked if some of the incidents actually occurred, Doctorow declined to answer directly: "What's real and what isn't? I used to know but I've forgotten. Let's just say that *Ragtime* is a mingling of fact and invention—a novelist's revenge on an age that celebrates nonfiction."

Ragtime's political content also generates debate. Several reviewers believe that *Ragtime* presents a simplistic leftist viewpoint. Hilton Kramer of *Commentary,* for instance, contends that "the villains in *Ragtime,* drawn with all the subtlety of a William Gropper cartoon, are all representatives of money, the middle class, and white ethnic prejudice. . . . *Ragtime* is a political romance. . . . The major fictional characters . . . are all ideological inventions, designed to serve the purposes of a political fable." Similarly, Jeffrey Hart, writing in the *National Review,* objects that Doctorow judges his revolutionary and minority characters much less harshly than the middle and upper-class WASP figures, which results in "what can be called left-wing pastoral," a form of sentimentality.

In spite of some protest on political and historical grounds, *Ragtime* garnered copious praise. "*Ragtime,*" Eliot Fremont-Smith of the *Village Voice* comments, "is simply splendid. . . . It's a bag of riches, totally lucid and accessible, full of surprises, epiphanies, little time-bombs that alter one's view of things, and enormous fun to read." Walter Clemons finds that "*Ragtime* is as exhilarating as a deep breath of pure oxygen." In the *New Republic,* Doris Grumbach remarks that "*Ragtime* is a model of a novel: compact because it is perfectly controlled, spare, because a loose end would have detracted from the shape it has, completely absorbing, because once in, there is no possible way out except through the last page." Kauffmann, in a *Saturday Review* critique, adds that "*Ragtime* is a unique and beautiful work of art about American destiny, built of fact and logical fantasy, governed by music heard and sensed, responsive to cinema both as method and historical datum, shaken by a continental pulse."

The prose style of *Ragtime* is especially hailed. Yet at least a few readers denigrate *Ragtime*'s writing. In the *Village Voice,* Greil Marcus calls it "all surface." And Jonathan Raban, writing in *Encounter,* feels that *Ragtime* "is chock-a-block with glittering, unexamined conceits . . . , little firecrackers that glow with suggestive, but finally fraudulent brilliance, because they can be pursued no further than the sentences which encapsulate them." In contrast, Grumbach notes: "My enthusiasm for [*Ragtime*] is based primarily on the quality of the prose, an ingenious representation in words and sentences of Scott Joplin's rag rhythms." "Like ragtime," remarks R. Z. Sheppard of *Time,* "Doctorow's book is a native American fugue, rhythmic, melodic and stately. . . . Its lyric tone, fluid structure and vigorous rhythms give it a musical quality that explanation mutes." Moreover, Kauffmann, in *Saturday Review,* finds that the book is written "exquisitely. . . . The 'ragtime' effect is fundamentally to capture a change in the rhythm of American life, a change to the impelling beat of a new century."

That many reviewers focus on the power of *Ragtime*'s prose, that some describe it as "completely absorbing" and "totally lucid and accessible" would be no surprise to Doctorow. For as he explains to John F. Baker in the *Publishers Weekly* interview, in writing *Ragtime* he "was very deliberately concentrating on the narrative element. I wanted a really relentless narrative, full of ongoing energy. I wanted to recover that really marvelous tool for a novelist, the sense of motion." Furthermore, Doctorow told Jonathan Yardley: "I don't think a writer can ignore seventy years of optical technology. . . . You can't ignore the fact that children grow up now and see a commercial which in thirty seconds or a minute has five or eight scenes and tells a whole story. . . . People understand things very rapidly today, and I

really want to keep one step ahead of them." Doctorow also remarks to Yardley that "in a certain sense [*Ragtime*] was an act of exploration, to find out what it itself was about. I did that with *Daniel,* too. [In] the first two books I was very calculating, and I think that was a mistake. I learned to trust the act of writing and not to impose the degree of control that could kill whatever might happen."

In *Loon Lake,* Doctorow continues to experiment with prose style and to evoke yet another period in American history, the Depression. The novel's plot revolves around the various relationships between an industrial tycoon, his famous aviatrix-wife, gangsters and their entourage, an alcoholic poet, and Joe, a young drifter who stumbles onto the tycoon's opulent residence in the Adirondacks. The novel works on several levels with "concentrically expanding ripples of implication," according to Robert Towers in the *New York Times Book Review.* For the most part, however, it is Doctorow's portrait of the American dream versus the American reality which forms the novel's core. As Christopher Lehmann-Haupt of the *New York Times* explains, "[*Loon Lake*] is a complex and haunting meditation on modern American history."

Time's Paul Gray believes that "Doctorow is . . . playing a variation on an old theme: The American dream, set to the music of an American nightmare, the Depression." Lehmann-Haupt infers a similar correlation and elaborates: "This novel could easily have been subtitled *An American Tragedy Revisited. . . . Loon Lake* contains [several] parallels to, as well as ironic comments on, the themes of [Theodore] Dreiser's story. . . . Had Dreiser lived to witness the disruptions of post-World War II American society—and had he possessed Mr. Doctorow's narrative dexterity—he might have written something like *Loon Lake.*"

Doctorow's extraordinary narrative style has generated much critical comment. "The written surface of *Loon Lake* is ruffled and choppy," Gray remarks. "Swatches of poetry are jumbled together with passages of computerese and snippets of mysteriously disembodied conversation. Narration switches suddenly from first to third person, or vice versa, and it is not always clear just who is telling what." A reviewer for the *Chicago Tribune* finds such "stylistic tricks" annoyingly distractive. "We balk at the frequent overwriting, and the clumsy run-on sentences," he reports. "We can see that Doctorow is trying to convey rootlessness and social unrest through an insouciant free play of language and syntax . . . ; the problem is that these eccentricities draw disproportionate attention to themselves, away from the characters and their concerns."

Doctorow, seemingly in anticipation of such criticism, defends his unconventional narrative approach in a *New York Times Book Review* interview with Victor S. Navasky: "[In *Loon Lake*] you don't know who's talking so that's one more convention out the window. That gives me pleasure, and I think it might give pleasure to readers, too. Don't underestimate them. People are smart, and they are not strangers to discontinuity. There's an immense amount of energy attached to breaking up your narrative and leaping into different voices, times, skins, and making the book happen and then letting the reader take care of himself."

While reviewers note certain structural flaws in *Loon Lake,* they praise the novel's overall literary significance and indicate that it is something of a milestone in Doctorow's career. "*Loon Lake* is not as elegantly formed as *Ragtime,*" Stade comments in *Nation,* ". . . but it is even more ambitious particularly in its mixture of styles and in its reach for significance." Gray echoes this assessment when he writes: "Doctorow may try to do too much in *Loon Lake*. . . . But the author's skill at historical reconstruction, so evident in *Ragtime*, remains impressive here; the novel's fragments and edgy, nervous rhythms call up an age of clashing anxiety. *Loon Lake* tantalizes long after it is ended." Moreover, Stade finds that *Loon Lake* contains "a tone, a mood, an atmosphere, a texture, a poetry, a felt and meditated vision of how things go with us" that is only hinted at in Doctorow's four previous novels. And the *Chicago Tribune* reviewer, despite his earlier criticism, concludes: "*Loon Lake* is highly interesting—for its relationship among the other novels . . . in Doctorow's developing portrayal of modern America; for its echoes of and associations with other fiction . . . ; for its maverick theorizing about capitalism vs. socialism vs. individuality; and its intrinsic picturesqueness and dramatic power. At its best, this straining, challenging book becomes an unpleasantly accurate synthesis of the American experience; a fractious, swaggering song of ourselves."

Doctorow's play, *Drinks before Dinner*, seems to have been created through an analogous act of exploration. In *Nation*, he states that the play "originated not in an idea or a character or a story but in a sense of heightened language, a way of talking. It was not until I had the sound of it in my ear that I thought about saying something. The language preceded the intention. . . . The process of making something up is best experienced as fortuitous, unplanned, exploratory. You write to find out what it is you're writing." In composing *Drinks before Dinner*, Doctorow worked from sound to words to characters. Does this "flawed" method of composition show a "defective understanding of what theater is supposed to do?" wonders Doctorow. His answer: "I suspect so. Especially if we are talking of the American theater, in which the presentation of the psychologized ego is so central as to be an article of faith. And that is the point. The idea of character as we normally celebrate it on the American stage is what this play seems to question."

Doctorow's experiment garners a mixed response from drama critics. In *Village Voice*, Michael Feingold observes that in *Drinks before Dinner* Doctorow "has tried to do something incomparably more ambitious than any new American play has done in years—he has tried to put the whole case against civilization in a nutshell." According to Feingold, the intent is defeated by a "schizoid" plot and "flat, prosy, and empty" writing. "I salute his desire to say something gigantic," Feingold concludes; "how I wish he had found a way to say it fully, genuinely, and dramatically." Richard Eder of the *New York Times* responds more positively: "Mr. Doctorow's turns of thought can be odd, witty and occasionally quite remarkable. His theme—that the world is blindly destroying itself and not worrying about it—is hardly original, but certainly worth saying. And he finds thoughtful and striking ways of saying it, even though eventually the play becomes an endless epigram, a butterfly that turns into a centipede." "Still, a play of ideas is rare enough nowadays," Eder observes, "and Mr. Doctorow's are sharp enough to supplement intellectual suspense when the dramatic suspense bogs down."

Doctorow's more recent books, *World's Fair* and *Billy Bathgate*, are both set in 1930s-era New York and have received wide critical acclaim. *World's Fair*, considered by many reviewers to be autobiographical in nature, relates a boy's experiences in New York City during the depression and ends with his visit to the 1939 World's Fair. Although *World's Fair* received an American Book Award, many critics view the author's next novel, *Billy Bathgate*, to be an even greater achievement. The story of 15-year-old Billy Behan's initiation into the world of organized crime is a "grand entertainment that is also a triumphant work

of art," according to *Washington Post Book World* contributor Pete Hamill. A number of reviewers especially appreciated Doctorow's ability to avoid cliched characters: "Even the various gangsters [in *Billy Bathgate*] are multidimensional," Anne Tyler remarked with pleasure in the *New York Times Book Review*. The completion of *Billy Bathgate* was also a milestone for its author. Discussing *Billy Bathgate* in the *Washington Post*, Doctorow revealed that he felt he had been "liberated by it to a certain extent. . . . Certain themes and preoccupations, that leitmotif that I've been working with for several years. I think now I can write anything. The possibilities are limitless. I've somehow been set free by this book."

BIOGRAPHICAL/CRITICAL SOURCES:

BOOKS

Authors in the News, Volume 2, Gale, 1976.
Bestsellers 89, Issue 3, Gale, 1989.
Concise Dictionary of American Literary Biography: Broadening Views, 1968-1988, Gale, 1989.
Contemporary Literary Criticism, Gale, Volume 6, 1976, Volume 11, 1979, Volume 15, 1980, Volume 18, 1981, Volume 37, 1986, Volume 44, 1987.
Dictionary of Literary Biography, Volume 2: *American Novelists since World War II*, 1978, Volume 28: *Twentieth-Century American-Jewish Fiction Writers*, 1984.
Dictionary of Literary Biography Yearbook: 1980, Gale, 1981.
Johnson, Diane, *Terrorists and Novelists*, Knopf, 1982.
Levine, Paul, *E. L. Doctorow*, Methuen, 1985.
Trenner, Richard, editor, *E. L. Doctorow: Essays and Conversations*, Ontario Review Press, 1983.

PERIODICALS

American Literature, March, 1978.
American Scholar, winter, 1975/1976.
Atlantic Monthly, September, 1980.
Best Sellers, June 1, 1966, August 15, 1971.
Books and Bookmen, June, 1976.
Chicago Tribune, September 28, 1980.
Choice, November, 1966.
Commentary, October, 1975, March, 1986.
Detroit Free Press, February 19, 1989.
Detroit News, November 10, 1985.
Drama, January, 1980.
Encounter, February, 1976.
Globe and Mail (Toronto), March 11, 1989.
Hudson Review, summer, 1986.
Journal of Popular Culture, fall, 1979.
London Magazine, February, 1986.
Los Angeles Times Book Review, November 24, 1985, March 5, 1989.
Manchester Guardian, February 23, 1986.
Miami Herald, December 21, 1975.
Midstream, December, 1975.
Midwest Quarterly, autumn, 1983.
Modern Fiction Studies, summer, 1976.
Nation, June 2, 1979, September 27, 1980, November 17, 1984, November 30, 1985.
National Review, August 15, 1975, March 14, 1986.
New Leader, December 16-30, 1985.
New Republic, June 5, 1971, July 5, 1975, September 6, 1975, September 20, 1980, December 3, 1984.
Newsweek, June 7, 1971, July 14, 1975, November 4, 1985.
New York, September 29, 1980, November 25, 1985.
New Yorker, December 9, 1985.
New York Herald Tribune, January 22, 1961.

New York Review of Books, August 7, 1975, December 19, 1985.

New York Times, August 4, 1978, November 24, 1978, September 12, 1980, November 6, 1984, October 31, 1985, February 9, 1989.

New York Times Book Review, September 25, 1960, July 4, 1971, July 6, 1975, September 28, 1980, December 6, 1984, November 10, 1985, February 26, 1989.

Partisan Review, fall, 1972.

People, March 20, 1989.

Progressive, March, 1986.

Publishers Weekly, June 30, 1975.

Saturday Review, July 17, 1971, July 26, 1975, September, 1980.

South Atlantic Quarterly, winter, 1982.

Southwest Review, autumn, 1977.

Springfield Republican, September 18, 1960.

Time, July 14, 1975, September 22, 1980, December 18, 1985.

Times Literary Supplement, February 14, 1986.

Village Voice, July 7, 1975, August 4, 1975, December 4, 1978, November 26, 1985.

Wall Street Journal, February 7, 1986.

Washington Post Book World, July 13, 1975, September 28, 1980, November 11, 1984, November 17, 1985, February 19, 1989.

*   *   *

DOMECQ, H(onorio) Bustos
See BIOY CASARES, Adolfo and BORGES, Jorge Luis

*   *   *

DOMINI, Rey
See LORDE, Audre (Geraldine)

*   *   *

DOMINIQUE
See PROUST, (Valentin-Louis-George-Eugene-)Marcel

*   *   *

DONLEAVY, J(ames) P(atrick) 1926-

PERSONAL: Born April 23, 1926, in Brooklyn, N.Y.; became Irish citizen, 1967; married Valerie Heron (divorced); married Mary Wilson Price, 1970; children: (first marriage) Philip, Karen; (second marriage) Rebecca Wallis, Rory. *Education:* Attended Trinity College, Dublin.

ADDRESSES: Home and office—Levington Park, Mullingar, County Westmeath, Ireland.

CAREER: Writer and playwright. Founder with son Philip Donleavy and producer Robert Mitchell of De Alfonce Tennis Association for the Promotion of the Superlative Game of Eccentric Champions. *Military service:* U.S. Navy, served in World War II.

AWARDS, HONORS: Most Promising Playwright Award, *Evening Standard,* 1960, for *Fairy Tales of New York;* Brandeis University Creative Arts Award, 1961-62, for two plays, *The Ginger Man* and *Fairy Tales of New York;* citation from National Institute and American Academy of Arts and Letters, 1975.

WRITINGS:

FICTION

The Ginger Man (novel; also see below), Olympia Press (Paris), 1955, published with introduction by Arland Ussher, Spearman (London), 1956, Obolensky, 1958, complete and unexpurgated edition, Delacorte, 1965, published with illustrations by Graham McCallum, Edito-Service, 1973, published as limited edition with illustrations by Skip Liepke, Franklin Library, 1978.

A Singular Man (novel), Little, Brown, 1963.

Meet My Maker the Mad Molecule (short stories; also see below), Little, Brown, 1964, reprinted, Penguin, 1981.

The Saddest Summer of Samuel S (novel; also see below), Delacorte/Seymour Lawrence, 1966.

The Beastly Beatitudes of Balthazar B (novel), Delacorte/Seymour Lawrence, 1968.

The Onion Eaters (novel), Delacorte, 1971, reprinted, Penguin in association with Eyre and Spottiswoode, 1986.

A Fairy Tale of New York (novel; also see below), Delacorte/Seymour Lawrence, 1973.

The Destinies of Darcy Dancer, Gentleman (novel), illustrations by Jim Campbell, Delacorte/Seymour Lawrence, 1977, published as limited edition, Franklin Library, 1977.

Schultz (novel), Delacorte/Seymour Lawrence, 1979.

Meet My Maker the Mad Molecule [and] *The Saddest Summer of Samuel S,* Dell, 1979.

Leila: Further in the Destinies of Darcy Dancer, Gentleman (novel; sequel to *The Destinies of Darcy Dancer, Gentleman*), Delacorte/Seymour Lawrence, 1983, published as limited edition with "A Special Message for the First Edition from J. P. Donleavy," Franklin Library, 1983 (published in England as *Leila: Further in the Life and Destinies of Darcy Dancer, Gentleman,* Allen Lane, 1983).

Are You Listening Rabbi Loew? (novel; sequel to *Schultz*), Viking, 1987.

A Singular Country (novel), Penguin, 1990.

PLAYS

The Ginger Man (adaptation of his novel of same title; first produced at Fortune Theatre, London, September 15, 1959; produced at Gaiety Theatre, Dublin, October 26, 1959; produced on Broadway at Orpheum Theatre, November 21, 1963; contains introduction "What They Did in Dublin"; also see below), Random House, 1961 (published in England as *What They Did in Dublin with The Ginger Man,* MacGibbon and Kee, 1961; also see below).

Fairy Tales of New York (based upon his novel *A Fairy Tale of New York;* first produced at Comedy Theatre, London, January 24, 1961; also see below), Random House, 1961.

A Singular Man (first produced at Comedy Theatre, October 21, 1964; produced at Westport County Playhouse, Connecticut, September 4, 1967; also see below), Bodley Head, 1964.

The Plays of J. P. Donleavy; with a Preface by the Author (contains *What They Did in Dublin with The Ginger Man, The Ginger Man, Fairy Tales of New York, A Singular Man, The Saddest Summer of Samuel S*), photographs of productions by Lewis Morley, Delacorte/Seymour Lawrence, 1973.

"The Beastly Beatitudes of Balthazar B" (adaptation of his novel of same title; first produced in London, 1981).

Also author of radio play, *Helen,* 1956.

OTHER

The Unexpurgated Code: A Complete Manual of Survival and Manners, illustrations by the author, Delacorte/Seymour Lawrence, 1975.
De Alfonce Tennis: The Superlative Game of Eccentric Champions, Its History, Accoutrements, Rules, Conduct, and Regimen, Dutton/Seymour Lawrence, 1984.
J. P. Donleavy's Ireland: In All Her Sins and in Some of Her Graces, Viking, 1986 (published in England as *Ireland: In All Her Sins and in Some of Her Graces,* M. Joseph, 1986).

Contributor of short fiction and essays to *Atlantic, Playboy, Queen* (London), *Saturday Evening Post,* and *Saturday Review.*

WORK IN PROGRESS: *The History of The Ginger Man; The Unexpurgated Code of Foxhunting;* the third volume of *The Destinies of Darcy Dancer, Gentleman;* screenplay for film adaptation of *The Ginger Man.*

SIDELIGHTS: "If there is an archetypal post-World War II American writer-in-exile it may well be James Patrick Donleavy," writes William E. Grant in a *Dictionary of Literary Biography* essay. The son of Irish immigrant parents, Donleavy renounced the America of their dreams for an Ireland of his own, and became a citizen when Ireland granted tax-free status to its authors. Although literary success came several years after the publication of his stylistically innovative first novel, *The Ginger Man,* Donleavy is now internationally recognized for having written what many consider a modern classic. Referring to the "sense of exile and alienation that seems to haunt his life as well as his work," Grant observes that "even achieving the literary success he thought America would deny him has not lessened his alienation from his country, though it has enhanced the style in which he expresses his exile status." Donleavy now writes at his expansive two-hundred-year-old manor situated on nearly two hundred acres in County Westmeath. "He's a sort of born-again Irishman who enthusiastically embraces the life of a man of letters and leisure, adopting not only an Irish country estate but also the appropriate deportment and brogue," says Peter Ross in the *Detroit News.* "He also happens to be one of the funniest and most audacious writers around."

Donleavy's decision to emigrate, although precipitated by difficulty finding a publisher for his first novel, appears to have been the result of a slowly evolving dissatisfaction with what he refers to in his *Atlantic* essay, "An Expatriate Looks at America," as "a country corrosive of the spirit." Donleavy explains: "Each time I go to these United States I start anew trying to figure them out. After two weeks I decide that like anywhere, greed, lust and envy make them work. But in America it is big greed, big lust, big envy." Although Donleavy remembers his childhood in the Bronx as peaceful, New York City became an increasingly threatening presence, and the omnipresent violence made him fearful of death there. He recalls in the *Atlantic* that "something in one's bowels was saying no to this land. Where my childhood friends were growing up, just as their parents did, to be trapped trembling and terrified in a nightmare." Skeptical of America's treatment of its artists as well, Donleavy felt at the outset of his career that he stood little chance of achieving literary success in a land he describes in the *Atlantic* as a place "where your media mesmerized brain shuts off when the media does." He adds, "And if I stayed they would, without even trying, or knowing, kill me."

Donleavy was resolved to achieve recognition and relates in a *Paris Review* interview with Molly McKaughan: "I realized that the only way you could ever tackle the world was to write some-thing that no one could hold off, a book that would go everywhere, into everyone's hands. And I decided then to write a novel which would shake the world. I shook my fist and said I would do it." That novel, *The Ginger Man,* is set in post-World War II Dublin and details the hedonistic existence of Sebastian Dangerfield who, according to Alfred Rushton in the Toronto *Globe and Mail,* gave "moral turpitude a new lease on life." Donleavy began crafting the novel while still a student in Dublin but returned to New York to complete and publish it. He indicates in the *Paris Review* that Scribners, to whom he first took the manuscript, thought it was one of the best ever brought to them; its content, however, prevented them from publishing it. Forty-five publishers rejected the novel because they "thought it was a dirty book—scatological, unreadable, obscene," Donleavy tells David Remnick in the *Washington Post.* "My life literally depended on getting this book into print, and when I couldn't, it just drove me out of America."

In the *Paris Review,* Donleavy recalls his reluctance to edit *The Ginger Man* into acceptability: "I had a sense that the book held itself together on the basis of these scatological parts. That its life was in these parts. And I was quite aware that cutting them would be severely damaging to it." Brendan Behan, the legendary Irish playwright and patriot with whom Donleavy became friends during his Dublin days, suggested sending the manuscript to the Olympia Press in Paris, where it eventually was accepted. Following its publication as part of an overtly pornographic series, however, a lengthy legal battle ensued in which Donleavy emerged as the owner of the publishing house. Despite "the potential for literary damage, publication by Olympia Press had the generally salutary effect of establishing the unexpurgated edition of *The Ginger Man* as an underground classic before complete editions became available," notes Grant. In order to ensure the novel's publication in England, though, and to get it recognized and reviewed, Donleavy agreed to certain cuts, stating in the *Paris Review:* "It was an act of pure practicality. If someone wanted to read the unexpurgated edition, they could buy it in Paris. I had published it as I had written it, so it wasn't wrong, then, to publish it to establish my reputation."

Although Donleavy's reputation had to endure both court battles and censors, his experience as a litigant proved invaluable in negotiating subsequent contracts with publishers. "He's very courtly, but he's a very sharp businessman," comments Donleavy's longtime publisher Seymour Lawrence, according to Samuel Allis in the *Washington Post.* "He does all of his negotiating and, unlike most authors, he understands copyrights. He drives a hard bargain, but he's the most professional author I've ever known."

Critics were unsure at first how to categorize Donleavy and his *The Ginger Man.* Grant observes that the critical establishment "debated whether Donleavy belonged with Britain's Angry Young Men, America's black humorists, or France's existentialists." In his *Doings and Undoings,* Norman Podhoretz calls *The Ginger Man* "fundamentally a book without hope." Similarly, in his *Radical Innocence: Studies in the Contemporary American Novel,* Ihab Hassan considers the novel to be "full of gusto, seething with life, but its energy may be the energy of negation, and its vitality has a nasty edge." The nihilism in *The Ginger Man* "refers us to the postwar, existential era," states Hassan. "Traditional values are not in the process of dying, they have ceased entirely to operate, and their stark absence leaves men to shift for themselves as best they can." The "freshness" of the characterization of Sebastian Dangerfield was one of the most critically acclaimed aspects of the novel, notes Grant, who adds that some critics recognized that the character "existed almost totally outside any system of ideas."

Despite the commercial success of Donleavy's subsequent work, the critics generally consider his reputation to rest solely on *The Ginger Man.* "So far as most critics and reviewers are concerned, the later works have been but pale shadows of the first brilliant success, and the publication of each succeeding novel has seen a decline in critical attention," writes Grant. Some critics believe that Donleavy has run out of ideas, that he is refurbishing old material, reworking or resurrecting earlier work. For instance, in a *Harper's* review of *The Destinies of Darcy Dancer, Gentleman,* Michael Malone compares a Donleavy book to Guinness stout: "It's distinctive, it's carbonated, it's brimmed with what Hazlitt called 'gusto,' and those who like it can drink it forever. The ingredients never change." Donleavy pays attention to the critics only in a "fairly superficial way" because, as he says in the *Paris Review,* "A writer must always be aware that he has to be a supreme critic. . . . And only his judgement matters." Allis indicates, however, that Donleavy "displays something close to hostility toward academics and the people who review his books and plays," and that he discourages academic interest in his work because he says, "I never want [to] get that self-conscious of my literary position." Grant suggests that "though none individually rivals the first masterpiece, several of these later works deserve wider attention than they have had from the American reading public and critical establishment alike."

Critics point to several characteristics of the bleak but bawdy *The Ginger Man* that surface in Donleavy's later work: Beneath the bawdy humor lies an inherent despondency, with licentiousness masking the more profound search for love; and bizarre, eccentric characters, around whom his books revolve, tend to be alienated, victimized by life, and weakened by impending death. "The novels range from variations of the humorous—slapstick, scatological, sardonic—to the sentimental in an idiosyncratic style that conveys the pressure of time on language," writes Thomas LeClair in *Contemporary Literature.* "But such features of Donleavy's work are finally extensions of and returns to death, the test of man's mettle in landscapes made pale by death's presence."

An awareness of death figures significantly in Donleavy's work, and the question Donleavy's heroes "answer in their own, progressively inefficacious ways," writes LeClair in *Twentieth Century Literature,* is, "How does a man weakened by an awareness of death survive in a world experienced as magical with malevolence?" LeClair observes that "to evade his consciousness of mortality, Sebastian Dangerfield . . . lives a hedonistic life in the present and dreams of relaxed ease for the future"; and the rich and reclusive George Smith of Donleavy's *A Singular Man,* who is absorbed with the idea of death and even builds his own mausoleum, "separates himself from the world in a parody of Howard Hughes' and John Paul Getty's attempts to avoid the disease of life." LeClair notes in *Critique: Studies in Modern Fiction* that "the heroes of *The Saddest Summer of Samuel S, The Beastly Beatitudes of Balthazar B,* and *The Onion Eaters* all attempt to overcome their fear of their own death or their sadness about the death of others through love."

According to Grant, the theme of love and loss is also important in much of Donleavy's work. Concerning *The Saddest Summer of Samuel S,* about an eminent literary figure in the United States who undergoes psychoanalysis in Vienna in order to live a more conventional life, Grant writes: "Longing for a love he has never had and cannot find because in spite of his need he cannot give, Samuel S is the victim of a life that cannot be lived over and a

destiny that cannot be changed." The character, observes Grant, is withdrawn and "trapped in a life-in-death state of mind with neither belief nor passion to motivate him." Similarly, in *The Beastly Beatitudes of Balthazar B,* a novel that details the lonely life of a wealthy young man whose marriage collapses, the hero is "separated from those he loves . . . and seeks completion by loving others, a simple but impossible quest," says Shaun O'Connell in the *Nation.* Robert Scholes observes in the *Saturday Review* that although this "shy and gentle" character seeks love, "it proves elusive, even harder to keep than to find." And O'Connell sees in Donleavy "the joy of the artist who can embody his vision, however bleak, the self-certainty of the writer who can so eloquently move his hero to name his pain."

However, writing in *Book World* about Donleavy's *The Destinies of Darcy Dancer, Gentleman,* a novel in which a young aristocrat is thwarted in several of his attempts at love, Curt Suplee suggests that "Donleavy does not write novels so much as Oedipal fairy tales: semirealistic fables in which the same patterns are obsessively reenacted. Invariably, a young man finds himself trapped in a society dominated by hostile father figures and devoid of the uncritical comfort afforded by mothers. . . . Every time the young man attempts to assert his ego in this world, he fails or is beaten, and flees to succour—either to the manic medium of alcohol or the overt mother-surrogates who provide sex and self-esteem, for a while." O'Connell finds, though, that Donleavy's characters "press the possibilities of life with high style and win many tactical victories of great hilarity . . . before they are defeated," and he believes that "Donleavy's vision of sadness seems earned, won by a search of all the possible routes toward happiness."

Focusing on the bawdiness in Donleavy's work, critics sometimes fault it for what they consider to be gratuitously lewd language and a reliance upon sexual slapstick. A *Times Literary Supplement* reviewer of *The Onion Eaters,* for instance, states that "the scenes of violence and the sexual encounters suggest an attitude to the human body and its functions, weaknesses and pleasures, which is anything but tender, compassionate, or celebratory." The novel is about a young and handsome character named Clayton Claw Clever Clementine, who in addition to being somewhat freakishly over-endowed sexually, has inherited an Irish manor and must confront what a *New Statesman* contributor refers to as a "bizarre collection of servants and . . . an ever-growing crew of sex-obsessed weirdies." Guy Davenport finds in the *National Review* that "Donleavy is uninterruptedly bawdy, yet his obscenity is so grand and so open, that it rises above giving offense into a realm of its own, unchallenged and wild." Critics also recognize, however, that Donleavy's humor belies an inherent sadness. "Donleavy writes sad and lonely books," says R. Z. Sheppard in a *Time* review of *The Onion Eaters.* Sheppard finds that Donleavy's fictional worlds are "closed worlds, their boundaries no more distant than the most prominent erectile tissue. Alone, without context or meaning, the flesh is all." Sheppard suggests that the absence of meaning in the novel as well as its "animal warmth, at once grotesque and touching," is perhaps Donleavy's way of asserting that "this warmth is the only thing about which we can be certain."

Writing in *Newsweek* about Donleavy's nonfictional *The Unexpurgated Code: A Complete Manual of Survival and Manners,* Arthur Cooper describes Donleavy's humor: "Like Mel Brooks, he knows that bad taste is merely a joke that doesn't get a laugh. And like Brooks, Donleavy's demonic humor is utterly democratic, thrusting the needle into everyone regardless of race, creed, color, or ability to control one's bowels." Referring to the book as "a collection of bilious and often funny rules for living,"

Melvin Maddocks observes in *Time* that "between the lines, Donleavy's diatribes manage to say more." Maddocks believes that Donleavy's "visions of grace, chivalry and order" reveal the author as "an inverted romantic, profoundly sad beneath his disguise because he and the world are no better than they happen to be." Similarly, in a *Midwest Quarterly* assessment of *The Unexpurgated Code,* Charles G. Masinton suggests that "Donleavy normally proceeds by means of instinct, inspiration, and intuition—the tools of a romantic artist. He aims to produce belly laughs and . . . a sympathetic response to his chief characters; he does not set out to impose order and rationality on experience. And instead of elevated language (which he often parodies quite effectively), he records with great skill an earthy vernacular full of both comic and lyric possibilities." While Grant believes that Donleavy's "characteristic tone of pessimism, melancholia, alienation, and human failure . . . suggest Jonathan Swift's misanthropic humor," he also finds it reminiscent of Mark Twain's later work, "which combines pessimism and humor in an elegiac, melancholic, and misanthropic voice."

In assessing Donleavy's fiction, notes Lask, "critics keep citing his first book . . . some saying that nothing after it has equaled that first effort, and objecting to his language, which has a syntax of its own, without connectives or prepositions, shifting tense at will." Stylistically innovative, *The Ginger Man* employs not only a shifting point of view (from first to third person) so that Dangerfield becomes both observer and observed but, according to Grant, it "relies on rapidly moving, nearly staccato sentence fragments which capture brilliantly the chaotic and fragmented qualities of Dangerfield's world." Donleavy explains that the language is "designed to reflect the way the mind works," says Lask in a *New York Times* review of *Schultz,* a novel about the exploits of an American producer of vulgar plays in London. In the *Paris Review,* Donleavy offers a more detailed explanation: "You're trying to get what you've written on your page into a reader's mind as quickly as possible, and to keep them seeing it. That is why I use the short, truncated telegraphic sentences. They are the most efficient use of language, and I think the brain puts words together the way I do."

Some critics think Donleavy has become a "prisoner of style," says Paul Abelman in the *Spectator,* that "he has never escaped from the prose techniques which he invented for his fine first novel." Abelman believes that "the style of the later books is not really that of *The Ginger Man* at all but simply one that employs superficial aspects of it and neglects the lyrical essence." Unlike *The Ginger Man,* says Abelman, the other books are "monster prose poems founded on the most plodding, leaden metrical foot known to the English language [the spondee—two stressed syllables regularly repeated]." Abelman, though, considers Donleavy "possibly the greatest lyrical humorist to emerge since the war," and adds that he "has that to his credit which few living writers can claim: a modern classic." Although Donleavy indicates to Thomas Lask in the *New York Times* that he's as "delighted" with *The Ginger Man* as when he first wrote it, he feels that his subsequent books keep *The Ginger Man* alive. Commenting to Remnick that he does not feel *The Ginger Man* represents his "best work," Donleavy states, "When I pick it up and read it now critically as a piece of writing, in technical terms, it doesn't compare to later books." Acknowledging in the *Paris Review* that his subsequent writing has not provided the pleasure that *The Ginger Man* did, Donleavy says: "I don't think you ever have that again. When an author's recognized, all that leaves him, because that's what he's needed to force himself to go through the terrible agony of being unknown and being able to

face the world and the fact that it's a giant, vast place where nearly every man is saying: Dear God, hear my tiny voice."

Grant believes that "Donleavy remains essentially the exile who once wrote of America, 'there it goes, a runaway horse, with no one in control.' " Donleavy recalls in his *Atlantic* essay, that "each time you arrive anew in America, you find how small you are and how dismally you impress against the giantness and power of this country where you are so obviously, and with millions like yourself, so totally fatally expendable." Grant notes that this vision is often expressed in Donleavy's portrayal of the United States as a nightmare. In *A Fairy Tale of New York,* for instance, the wife of the Brooklyn-born, Bronx-raised, and Europe-educated Cornelius Christian dies on their way to New York; and without money or friends, Christian is taken advantage of by everyone. "Affection, loathing, nostalgia and fear are the main components of the attitude he brings to bear upon his native place," writes Julian Moynahan in the *Washington Post Book World,* adding that "hidden away in the book for those who can find it is a good deal of personal revelation, a good deal of alembicated and metamorphosed autobiography." As D. Keith Mano states in the *New York Times Book Review,* the book is "about social impotence and despair. Valleys of humiliation, sloughs of despond." The story focuses on the brutality of New York City; and Christian, who lacks the funds to move, sees emigration as the only answer to his liberation. "Yet Donleavy's thunderous, superb humor has the efficacy of grace," says Mano. "It heals and conquers and ratifies." And a *Times Literary Supplement* contributor, who remarks that "few writers know how to enjoy verbal promiscuity like . . . Donleavy," considers that "it is largely because of the confidence of the style, too, that you come out of the welter of failure and misery feeling good—nastiness is inevitably laced with hilarity and sentiment in his telling it."

Moving to Ireland changed his life "utterly," he says in the *Paris Review.* "It also romanticized the United States for me so that it became a subject for me as a writer." However, in the *Atlantic,* Donleavy speaks about the indelibility of his American beginnings: "As far away as you may go, or as foreign as your life can ever become, there is something that always stays stained American in you." About living among the Irish, however, Donleavy remarks in a *Publishers Weekly* interview: "Literally, everywhere you go here, they're half nuts. It's very tough to discover real insanity, because the whole race is like that, and, indeed, this is the place to come if you're not right in the head." John Kelly writes in the *Times Literary Supplement* that "during a disconsolate return to his native America," Donleavy discovered that "Ireland is a state of mind" and his recent *J. P. Donleavy's Ireland: In All Her Sins and Some of Her Graces* "attempts a description of that state of mind." Donleavy recreates autobiographically his first exposure to the postwar Dublin that, says Kelly, provided the "raw material" for "Donleavy's mythmaking imagination." In a Toronto *Globe and Mail* review of the book, Rushton thinks that "Donleavy belongs to the people he describes, and acknowledges their kinship by giving them their full due." As Kevin E. Gallagher comments in the *Los Angeles Times Book Review,* it is "a love story that, I think never ends for anyone who cares, like this, about a place."

Although Donleavy's *The Ginger Man* remains the standard by which the entirety of his work is measured, his writing has generated the full spectrum of critical response. Ken Lawless in an *Antioch Review* of *The Destinies of Darcy Dancer, Gentleman,* for example, writes that "no literary artist working in English today is better than J. P. Donleavy, and few merit comparison with him." On the other hand, in the *New York Times Book Review,*

Geoffrey Wolff reacts to similar critical assessments of Donleavy's work with: "Nonsense. He is an Irish tenor who sets his blarney to short songs that are sometimes as soft as velvet or good stout, sometimes plangent, elliptical and coarse." However, Grant suggests that "at the very least, he represents the example of a writer who goes very much his own way, eschewing both the popular success of the best-sellers and the literary acclaim of the academic establishment. At best, a case can be made for a few of his novels as primary expressions within the black humorist tradition of modern literature. Certainly he is a foremost American exponent of the Kafkaesque vision of the modern world, and his better works strongly express that sense of universal absurdity at which we can only laugh."

"After all my years of struggle, it makes me realize that in my own way I have conquered America, totally silently, totally from underground and from within and that television or being interviewed doesn't matter," Donleavy relates in the *Paris Review*. In his *Saturday Review* essay, "The Author and His Image," Donleavy ponders the complexities of an author's image in its various aspects from obscurity through success, and concludes: "But you know no matter what you do the world will always finally turn its face away. Back into all its own troubled lives. . . . Forgetting what you wanted them to see. Silent with what you wanted them to say. And empty with what you wanted them to feel. Except somewhere you know there will be a voice. At least once asking, Hey what happened to that guy, did he die, you know the one, who wrote that book, can't remember his name but he was famous as hell. That was the author. And that was his image."

BIOGRAPHICAL/CRITICAL SOURCES·

BOOKS

Authors in the News, Volume 2, Gale, 1976.
Contemporary Fiction in America and England, 1950-1970, Gale, 1976.
Contemporary Literary Criticism, Gale, Volume 1, 1973, Volume 4, 1975, Volume 6, 1976, Volume 10, 1979, Volume 45, 1987.
Dictionary of Literary Biography, Volume 6: *American Novelists since World War II*, Gale, 1980.
Donleavy, J. P., *The Ginger Man*, Olympia Press, 1955, published with introduction by Arland Ussher, Spearman, 1956, Obolensky, 1958, complete and unexpurgated edition, Delacorte, 1965, published with illustrations by Graham McCallum, Edito-Service, 1973, published as limited edition with illustrations by Skip Liepke, Franklin Library, 1978.
Donleavy, J. P., *J. P. Donleavy's Ireland: In All Her Sins and in Some of Her Graces*, Viking, 1986.
Hassan, Ihab, *Radical Innocence: Studies in the Contemporary American Novel*, Princeton University Press, 1961.
Masinton, Charles G., *J. P. Donleavy: The Style of His Sadness and Humor*, Popular Press, 1975.
Podhoretz, Norman, *Doings and Undoings*, Farrar, Straus, 1964.
Sharma, R. K., *Isolation and Protest: A Case Study of J. P. Donleavy's Fiction*, Ajanta (New Delhi), 1983.

PERIODICALS

America, May 3, 1969, May 10, 1980.
Antioch Review, winter, 1978, winter, 1980.
Architectural Digest, November, 1986.
Atlantic, December, 1968, December, 1976, December, 1977, June, 1979.
Books, November, 1987.

Chicago Tribune, May 25, 1958, May 19, 1985.
Chicago Tribune Book World, October 28, 1979.
Commonweal, August 15, 1958, December 2, 1966, March 7, 1969.
Contemporary Literature, Volume 12, number 3, 1971.
Critique: Studies in Modern Fiction, Volume 9, number 2, 1976, Volume 12, number 3, 1971, Volume 17, number 1, 1975.
Detroit News, October 2, 1983, June 9, 1985.
Economist, November 10, 1973.
Globe and Mail (Toronto), October 13, 1984, January 17, 1987, April 18, 1987, November 19, 1988.
Harper's, December, 1977.
Listener, May 11, 1978, October 29, 1987.
Los Angeles Times, October 28, 1983.
Los Angeles Times Book Review, October 7, 1979, May 5, 1985, November 16, 1986, November 13, 1988.
Michigan Academician, winter, 1974, summer, 1976.
Midcontinent American Studies Journal, spring, 1967.
Midwest Quarterly, winter, 1977.
Nation, May 24, 1958, December 14, 1963, January 20, 1969.
National Review, October 18, 1971.
New Leader, December 19, 1977.
New Republic, December 14, 1963, March 1, 1969, July 24, 1971, December 15, 1979.
New Statesman, April 17, 1964, February 7, 1969, July 16, 1971, May 12, 1978, March 28, 1980, October 14, 1983.
Newsweek, November 11, 1963, March 21, 1966, November 18, 1968, September 15, 1975.
New Yorker, October 25, 1958, May 16, 1964, October 15, 1966, October 8, 1973, December 19, 1977.
New York Herald Tribune Book Review, May 11, 1958.
New York Review of Books, January 2, 1969.
New York Times, May 11, 1958, November 16, 1979, April 17, 1987, October 12, 1988.
New York Times Book Review, November 24, 1963, November 7, 1965, December 5, 1965, March 20, 1966, December 29, 1968, September 5, 1971, September 23, 1973, November 6, 1977, October 7, 1979, October 26, 1980, October 11, 1983, October 30, 1983, April 28, 1985, November 27, 1988.
Observer (London), November 8, 1987.
Paris Review, fall, 1975.
Publishers Weekly, October 31, 1986.
Punch, October 21, 1987.
Saturday Review, May 10, 1958, November 23, 1963, November 23, 1968, November 12, 1977, January 20,1979.
Spectator, September 22, 1973, May 13, 1978, April 12, 1980, December 8, 1984, July 19, 1986.
Studies in Contemporary Satire, Number 1, 1975.
Time, March 18, 1966, December 6, 1968, July 5, 1971, October 29, 1973, September 22, 1975, November 14, 1977, October 15, 1979.
Times (London), October 13, 1983, July 17, 1986, October 29, 1987.
Times Literary Supplement, April 30, 1964, May 6, 1965, May 5, 1967, March 20, 1969, July 23, 1971, September 7, 1973, May 12, 1978, April 4, 1980, October 28, 1983, November 16, 1984, December 19, 1986.
Tribune Books, January 25, 1987, October 2, 1988.
Twentieth Century Literature, January, 1968, July, 1972.
Village Voice, September 17, 1979.
Washington Post, October 30, 1979, February 24, 1985, September 29, 1988.
Washington Post Book World, September 30, 1973, November 13, 1977.

World Literature Today, summer, 1978, summer, 1980, spring, 1984.
Yale Review, October, 1966.

*   *   *

DONOSO (YANEZ), Jose 1924-

PERSONAL: Born October 5, 1924, in Santiago, Chile; son of Jose Donoso (a physician) and Alicia Yanez; married Maria del Pilar Serrano (a translator), 1961. *Education:* Attended University of Chile, beginning in 1947; Princeton University, A.B., 1951.

ADDRESSES: Home—Santiago, Chile.

CAREER: Writer, journalist, and translator. Shepherd in southern Chile, 1945-46; dockhand in Buenos Aires, Argentina, c. 1946; Kent School, Santiago, Chile, English teacher, c. 1953; Catholic University of Chile, Santiago, professor of conversational English, beginning in 1954; worked in Buenos Aires, 1958-60; *Ercilla* (weekly newsmagazine), Santiago, journalist with assignments in Europe, beginning in 1960, editor and literary critic, beginning in 1962; University of Chile, Santiago, lecturer at school of journalism, beginning in 1962; *Siempre* (periodical), Mexico City, Mexico, literary critic, 1965; University of Iowa, Dubuque, teacher of writing and modern Spanish American literature at Writers' Workshop, 1965-67; Colorado State University, Fort Collins, teacher, 1969.

AWARDS, HONORS: Santiago Municipal Short Story Prize, 1955, for *Veraneo y otros cuentos;* Chile-Italia Prize for journalism, 1960; William Faulkner Foundation Prize, 1962, for *Coronacion;* Guggenheim awards, 1968 and 1973; Critics Award for best novel in Spanish, 1979, for *Casa de campo.*

WRITINGS:

Veraneo y otros cuentos (title means "Summertime and Other Stories"), privately printed (Santiago, Chile), 1955.
Dos cuentos (title means "Two Stories"), Guardia Vieja, 1956.
Coronacion (novel), Nascimento, 1957, Seix Barral, 1981, translation by Jocasta Goodwin published as *Coronation,* Knopf, 1965.
El charleston (short stories; title means "The Charleston"), Nascimento, 1960.
Los mejores cuentos de Jose Donoso (short stories; title means "The Best Stories of Jose Donoso"), Zig-Zag, 1965.
Este domingo (novel), Zig-Zag, 1965, translation by Lorraine O'Grady Freeman published as *This Sunday,* Knopf, 1967.
El lugar sin limites (novella; title means "The Place Without Limits"), J. Moritz (Mexico), 1966; translation by Suzanne Jill Levine and Hallie D. Taylor published as *Hell Has No Limits* in *Triple Cross,* Dutton, 1972.
(Editor with William A. Henkin and others) *The Tri-Quarterly Anthology of Contemporary Latin American Literature,* Dutton, 1969.
El obsceno parajo de la noche (novel), Seix Barral, 1970, translation by Hardie St. Martin and Leonard Mades published as *The Obscene Bird of Night,* Knopf, 1973.
Cuentos (title means "Stories"), Seix Barral, 1971, translation by Andree Conrad published as *Charleston and Other Stories,* David Godine, 1977.
Historia personal del "boom" (memoir), Anagrama (Barcelona), 1972, translation by Gregory Kolovakos published as *The Boom in Spanish American Literature: A Personal History,* Columbia University Press, 1977.

Tres novelitas burguesas (title means "Three Bourgeois Novellas"), Seix Barral, 1973, translation by Andree Conrad published as *Sacred Families: Three Novellas,* Knopf, 1977.
Casa de campo (novel), Seix Barral, 1978, translation by David Pritchard and Suzanne Jill Levine published as *A House in the Country,* Knopf, 1984.
El jardin de al lado (novel; title means "The Garden Next Door"), Seix Barral, 1981.
La misteriosa desparicion de la Marquesita de Loria (novel; title means "The Mysterious Disappearance of the Young Marchioness of Loria"), Seix Barral, 1981.
Poemas de un novelista (poems), Ganymedes (Santiago), 1981.
Cuatro para Delfina (novellas; title means "Four for Delfina"), Seix Barral, 1982.
La desesperanza (novel; title means "Despair"), Seix Barral, 1986, translation by Alfred MacAdam published as *Curfew,* Weidenfeld & Nicolson, 1988.
(Contributor) Doris Meyer, editor, *Lives on the Line: The Testimony of Contemporary Latin American Authors,* University of California Press, 1988.

Translator into Spanish of numerous works, including *The Life of Sir Arthur Conan Doyle* by John Dickson Carr and *Last Tales* by Isak Dinesen, and, with wife, Maria del Pilar Serrano, of *The Scarlet Letter* by Nathaniel Hawthorne and *Les Personnages* by Françoise Malet-Joris. Contributor of articles and short stories to periodicals, including *Americas, mss.* (Princeton University), and *Review.*

WORK IN PROGRESS: A work set in the coal-mining community of Chile, excerpted in *Review,* January-June, 1988, under the title "The Fish in the Window."

SIDELIGHTS: "I fear simplification more than anything," said Chilean novelist Jose Donoso in *Partisan Review.* Donoso's novels, noted for their complexity and insistent pessimism, seem to embody his observation that life, society, and writing are each an "adventure into [a] mad, dark thing." Donoso has often been ranked among the finest Latin American authors of the twentieth century; he has been hailed as a master by Mexican novelist Carlos Fuentes and Spanish filmmaker Luis Bunuel, two of his most renowned contemporaries. "He is an extraordinarily sophisticated writer," wrote *Newsweek*'s Walter Clemons, "in perfect control of time dissolves, contradictory voices, gritty realism and hallucinatory fugues."

Observers suggest that Donoso's concern with the complexity of life is particularly appropriate to the situation in his homeland. Chile, which appeared to be a moderate, stable democracy for most of the twentieth century, erupted in violent political conflict in the 1970s. The country lurched abruptly from the Marxist government of Salvador Allende to the brutal conservative dictatorship of General Augusto Pinochet. From the time his first novels appeared in the 1950s, Donoso was praised for his sense of the strained relations between rich and poor that underlay Chilean society. The author is reluctant, however, to be viewed as a social commentator: he seems determined, in both his life and his work, to avoid the didacticism he has seen in politics. "Ideologies and cosmogonies are alien to me," he stated in *Lives on the Line.* "Their life is too short and they are too soon proved wrong, their place immediately taken by another explanation of the world." Accordingly, as Donoso observed in *Review,* "I'm not interested in the novels of ideas. . . . If I write a novel, it won't be to express an idea I saw in an essay."

Writers of the Chilean left, Donoso suggested, have repeatedly challenged his political standoffishness; sometimes, he observed in *Nation,* he has been "denounced . . . as decadent bourgeois."

But Donoso's many admirers suggest that his pessimistic outlook, even his refusal to offer a solution to the problems that he surveys in his work, reflects an acute awareness of the breadth and depth of human suffering. As Z. Nelly Martinez explained in *Books Abroad:* "Beyond the social reality and its multiple stratification, Donoso probes into life's duality of good and evil, order and chaos, life and death, and examines man's inability to reconcile both sides of existence. Therein lies the tragedy; for, despite man's effort to build an illusion of order, life's anarchy eventually overcomes him." In much of the author's work, as Martinez observed, "madness, abdication to chaos, becomes the only alternative." Against such all-encompassing pain, Donoso seems to offer hope primarily in the form of intellectual understanding. "Kicking people in the shins gets you nowhere," he said in the *New York Times Book Review.* "Understanding gets you much farther."

Donoso was born into a family that kept a tenuous foothold in Chile's respectable upper middle class. His father "was a young physician more addicted to horse racing and to playing cards than to his profession," the author recalled in *Review.* His mother, who "somehow coped," came from "the ne'er-do-well branch of a *nouveau riche* family." The father used family connections to get a newspaper job, but he was fired; thereafter he became house physician to three decrepit great-aunts whose fortunes he hoped to inherit. When the aunts died, the Donosos inherited nothing. But soon they were sheltering other relatives, including an irresponsible uncle and Donoso's grandmother, who lived with the family for ten years while slowly succumbing to insanity. "The gradual process of [my grandmother's] deterioration, intertwined with lightning flashes of memory and family lore . . . is one of the episodes that has most marked my life," Donoso declared, "not because I loved this old woman but because her madness brought the ironies of family life and the horrors of aging and dying so cruelly into focus." He became a high-school truant and then a dropout, associating with bums and spending a year as a shepherd in the remote grasslands of southern Chile. In his early twenties he returned home and resumed his education, rejecting the traditional careers open to "an upper middle-class boy" by becoming an undergraduate English major.

Donoso describes his literary development in the memoir *Historia personal del "boom" (The Boom in Spanish American Literature: A Personal History).* The book introduces readers to one of the most renowned periods in Spanish American Literature—the "Boom," a flowering of literary activity during the 1960s—by showing its relationship to Donoso's own life. As an aspiring author in the 1950s, Donoso relates in his memoir, he shared with other young writers throughout Latin America the sense of being "asphyxiated" by the provincial cultural environment of his native land. Great authors of the past such as Mexico's Manuel Azuela, who saw the novel as a practical way to discuss contemporary social problems, seemed to members of Donoso's generation like "statues in a park." The earnest, simple style that such "grandfathers" had made popular seemed to rob the novel of creativity and expressiveness. The region's publishers, too poor to take risks on new talent, preferred to reprint literary classics and popular foreign works; accordingly, Donoso and his peers had difficulty getting published, often had to sell copies of their books on their own, and found it difficult to obtain each others' work in print. For role models, Donoso declares, writers of his generation looked beyond the Hispanic world. Some authors he mentions, including William Faulkner and Henry James, were subtle stylists who experimented with the conventions of the novel, showing, for instance, how a character's point of view could affect their perception of reality. Others, including

Franz Kafka and Albert Camus, were critics of human nature who seemed to have little hope of reform: their works showed isolated individuals grappling with an uncaring and fundamentally absurd society. By the late 1950s and early 1960s, Donoso began to see such innovative writing in novels by his peers, notably Cuba's Alejo Carpentier and Mexico's Carlos Fuentes. Such works, Donoso recalls, were "a spur to my envy, to my need to emulate," and they confirmed his sense that "the baroque, the distorted, the excessive could all increase the possibilities of the novel."

In his first novel, *Coronacion (Coronation)*, Donoso combined traditional realism with the more complex personal vision that would emerge in his later works. The book's main character is an affluent old woman who lives with her servants in a mansion; her vivid delusions and curses frighten her grandson, a repressed middle-aged bachelor. The old woman, Donoso admitted, is a portrait of his insane grandmother, and some relatives were indignant at the resemblance. Reviewers in Chile praised *Coronation* as a realistic depiction of that country's society, especially, recalled Donoso in *The Boom,* "the decadence of the upper class." Wishing to transcend realism, Donoso found such praise frustrating. The resolution of the novel, he suggested, was designed to challenge traditional literary style. The book's climax largely abandons the restraints of realism by dwelling on madness and the grotesque. The old woman, costumed and crowned by her maids during a drunken prank, dies convinced she has already gone to heaven. The grandson, confronting his mortality and his unfulfilling life, concludes that God himself must have been mad to create such a world and then follows his grandmother into insanity. *Coronation* brought Donoso an international reputation and won the 1962 William Faulkner Foundation Prize, established in Faulkner's will to encourage the translation of outstanding Latin American fiction into English.

Donoso's second novel, *Este domingo (This Sunday)*, with its themes of upper-class decay and incipient chaos, has often been likened to *Coronation.* Many reviewers considered the later work a significant advance for Donoso, showing greater subtlety, impact, and stylistic sophistication. "As Donoso sees it," wrote Alexander Coleman in the *New York Times Book Review,* "the rich are different because they cannot live without the underworld of the poor to exploit and command." Don Alvaro is an affluent, middle-aged professional who has grown up weak and ineffective, but has kept a sense of virility by making a chambermaid his mistress. His wife Chepa, who has an obsessive need to minister to others, becomes the domineering patroness to a paroled murderer still drawn toward a life of crime. The novel's climax occurs when Chepa, unhappy with the parolee's conduct, seeks him out in the slum where he lives; she is hounded by poor neighborhood children and collapses on a trash heap. Throughout the book Donoso experiments with differing points of view, showing parts of the story through the eyes of its obsessive participants, and part through the eyes of a young relative of Alvaro, too naive to understand the underlying brutality of the world around him. Noting Donoso's "cool and biting intelligence," Coleman praised the author's "perfect balance between compulsion and control as he exorcises his infernally driven characters."

Donoso delved much further into obsession and fantasy with his novella *El lugar sin limites (Hell Has No Limits)*, written at about the same time as *This Sunday.* The work is set in an isolated small town owned by Don Alejo, a powerful, all-knowing, selfish aristocrat whom many reviewers saw as the satirical embodiment of an unfeeling God. The main character is Manuela, whose delusions about being a lithe, young female dancer are lavishly echoed by the story's narration; in fact, however, Manuela is an aging male transvestite who works as a dancer in his daughter's bordello and uses fantasy to transcend his absurd existence. The story culminates in violence when Pancho, a virile male truckdriver attracted to Manuela, lashes out against his own underlying homosexuality by savagely assaulting the transvestite. Biographer George McMurray considered *Hell Has No Limits* a powerful comment on the futility of human aspirations, so pessimistic as to approach nihilism. The author's intentions, McMurray explained, "are to undermine traditional values, reveal the bankruptcy of reason, and jar the reader onto new levels of awareness by exposing the other side of reality." McMurray found the story one of Donoso's most accomplished works.

During the 1960s Donoso moved beyond the intellectual confines of Chile to become part of a growing international community of Latin American writers—major figures of the Boom—who knew each other as friends and colleagues and shared moral support, ideas, and interesting books. At a 1962 conference of such writers he became close friends with Carlos Fuentes; after attending another conference in Mexico two years later, Donoso began more than a dozen years of voluntary exile from his homeland. He wrote *Hell Has No Limits* while renting a house from Fuentes in Mexico, taught for two years at the University of Iowa's prestigious Writers Workshop, then settled in Spain. Meanwhile he went through numerous drafts of a novel far more lengthy, intricate, and allusive than his previous efforts. Its title came from a letter that young Henry James received from his father Henry Sr., warning about life's underlying chaos. "Life is no farce," the letter advised: "the natural inheritance of everyone who is capable of spiritual life is an unsubdued forest where the wolf howls and the obscene bird of night chatters."

When *El obsceno parajo de la noche* (*The Obscene Bird of Night*) finally emerged in 1970, reviewers found it both masterful and indescribable—"How do you review a dream?" asked Wolfgang Luchtig in *Books Abroad.* The novel is narrated by Humberto, an unsuccessful writer who becomes the retainer to a decaying aristocratic family and the tutor of their only son and heir. The child, monstrously deformed, is seen by his father as an emblem of chaos and is surrounded by freaks so that he will seem "normal." Eventually Humberto apparently flees to one of the family's charitable ventures—a decrepit convent that houses some of society's castoff women, ranging from the elderly to young orphans. Throughout the novel past and present are confusingly intermingled, and characters undergo bizarre transformations, sometimes melting into one another. Humberto appears as a deaf-mute servant in the convent; is apparently transformed into a baby by the old women, who often seem to be witches; and is finally sealed in a bundle of rags and thrown onto a fire, where he turns to ashes as the book ends.

Observers such as McMurray suggest that the novel should not be viewed as a "story" in the conventional sense, but as an outpouring of the deranged mind of its narrator, Humberto. According to such a view, Humberto is a schizophrenic, driven mad, perhaps, by his lack of success; his narration is disordered because he freely mixes reality with his fantasies, fears, and resentments of the world. Humberto's many transformations reflect his disintegrating personality, as he picks up and discards various identities in an effort to define himself; his bizarre demise, in which he is cut off from the world and then destroyed, represents the madman's final withdrawal from reality. In *Review* Donoso said that while the narrator is hardly autobiographical in a literal sense, "he is the autobiography of my fears, of my fantasies"; interestingly, the author finished his book while recovering from an episode of near-madness, brought on by a traumatic ulcer operation and the administration of pain-killing

drugs. "Basically I don't know what my novel is about," Donoso also observed. "It's something that has happened to me rather than something I've written." "Donoso does not offer us . . . a novel simply to read," explained *Review*'s John J. Hassett, "but one to experience in which we are continuously called upon to give the text some order by discovering its unities and its repetitions." Many commentators ranked *The Obscene Bird of Night* among the best novels of the Boom era, which ended in the early 1970s; Donoso was favorably compared with Gabriel Garcia Marquez, a Boom author who eventually won the Nobel Prize.

Until the 1980s Donoso continued to reside primarily in Spain. After he finished *The Obscene Bird of Night,* his writing began to change: his style became less hallucinatory and his narratives were less concerned with the Chilean aristocracy. Some of his work was set in Spain, including *Tres novelitas burguesas* (*Sacred Families*), novellas that portray that country's upper middle class with a blend of fantasy and social satire, and *El jardin de al lado* ("The Garden Next Door"), which features a novelist-in-exile who is haunted by his past. Throughout his years in Spain, Donoso reported in *Lives on the Line,* he found it impossible to cut his emotional ties to Chile. He did not feel nostalgia, he continued, but rather "the *guilt of absence*" or the "guilt of not being connected with action." His dilemma was heightened because he remained abroad by choice while Pinochet established his dictatorship. "All of us who lived abroad during that period who didn't have to," he explained in *Vogue,* "have a terrible feeling of guilt" because "we didn't share in the history of Chile during a very important time."

In the mid-1970s Donoso resolved to discuss Chile's turmoil in a novel, which became *Casa de campo* (*A House in the Country*). Aware that he was cut off from the daily life of Chileans—including the way they spoke—he wrote about them indirectly, creating what reviewers called a political allegory. Once more Donoso set his book in an aristocratic household. When the estate's owners leave on an excursion, their children (perhaps representing the middle class) and exploited Indians from the surrounding area (perhaps the working class) take over and wreak havoc. They are led by an aristocratic uncle (Salvador Allende?) who may be insane or may be the victim of injustice at the hands of his relatives. When the owners return, they use servants to ruthlessly re-establish order and then proclaim—despite all the bitterness they have engendered—that nothing has changed since they first left. Though some reviewers faulted the novel for being too intellectual and emotionally detached, others found it highly relevant and involving. "The combination of literary grace, political urgency and a fierce and untethered imagination," wrote Charles Champlin in the *Los Angeles Times Book Review,* "give Donoso and 'A House in the Country' the power of an aimed projectile."

By the mid-1980s Donoso had resettled in Chile, and in 1986 he produced a more direct study of life under Pinochet in the novel *La desesperanza* (*Curfew*). Though the book describes both Pinochet's torturers and the dispossessed poor, its principal focus is the country's well-educated, dispirited political left. The two main characters—a onetime revolutionary and a political folksinger who fled to Paris—share deep feelings of guilt because they were not punished as much by the regime as were other leftists. Their old comrades, meanwhile, seem paralyzed by infighting, didacticism, and bitterness. The book was highly praised by prominent American critics and, notably, by Jacobo Timerman, an Argentine journalist respected worldwide as an eloquent victim of political oppression. "Donoso is a moderate who has written a revolutionary novel," Timerman observed in *Vogue;* in *New Yorker* he wrote that "it is a relief, finally, to read a work of Chilean literature in which none of the characters are above history or appear to dominate it." *Curfew,* reviewers suggested, displays the deep personal flaws of leftists and rightists alike: by avoiding simple conclusions, the novel makes plain that Chile abounds in uncertainty and despair. In contrast to its reception abroad, *Curfew* was viewed rather coolly by many Chilean intellectuals. "The book doesn't flag-wave" or "present an alternative," Donoso explained in *Vogue,* and "people would respect me much more if it did." However, he observed, "I'm not a crusader. I'm not a hero. I'm just a man who is very hurt, and who wants change."

BIOGRAPHICAL/CRITICAL SOURCES:

BOOKS

Contemporary Literary Criticism, Gale, Volume 4, 1975, Volume 8, 1978, Volume 11, 1979, Volume 32, 1985.
Donoso, Jose, *The Boom in Spanish American Literature: A Personal History,* Columbia University Press, 1977.
Forster, Merlin H., editor, *Tradition and Renewal: Essays on Twentieth-Century Latin American Literature and Culture,* University of Illinois Press, 1975.
MacAdam, Alfred J., *Modern Latin American Narratives: The Dreams of Reason,* University of Chicago Press, 1977.
McMurray, George R., *Jose Donoso,* Twayne, 1979.
Meyer, Doris, editor, *Lives on the Line: The Testimony of Contemporary Latin American Authors,* University of California Press, 1988.
Schwartz, Ronald, *Nomads, Exiles, and Emigres: The Rebirth of the Latin American Narrative, 1960-80,* Scarecrow Press, 1980.

PERIODICALS

Americas, June 9, 1984, November/December, 1987.
Book Forum, summer, 1977.
Books Abroad, winter, 1968, winter, 1972, spring, 1972, spring, 1975.
Christian Science Monitor, June 27, 1973, June 2, 1988.
Commonweal, September 21, 1973, May 18, 1984.
Contemporary Literature, Volume 28, number 4, 1987.
Essays in Literature, spring, 1975.
Hispania, May, 1972.
Hudson Review, winter, 1978, winter, 1989.
Journal of Spanish Studies: Twentieth Century, winter, 1973.
Los Angeles Times Book Review, February 5, 1984, May 15, 1988.
Modern Fiction Studies, winter, 1978.
Nation, March 11, 1968, June 11, 1973, February 11, 1978.
New Leader, October 1, 1973.
New Statesman, June 18, 1965, March 1, 1974.
Newsweek, June 4, 1973.
New Yorker, June 16, 1973, April 30, 1984, November 2, 1987, June 13, 1988.
New York Review of Books, April 19, 1973, December 13, 1973, August 4, 1977, July 18, 1985.
New York Times Book Review, March 14, 1965, November 26, 1967, December 24, 1972, June 17, 1973, June 26, 1977, February 26, 1984, May 29, 1988.
Partisan Review, fall, 1974, number 1, 1982, number 2, 1986.
PMLA, January, 1978.
Punch, April 18, 1984.
Review, fall, 1973, January-May, 1984.
Revista de Estudios Hispanicos, January, 1975.
Saturday Review, March 13, 1965, December 9, 1967, January 23, 1971, July 9, 1977.
Spectator, June 18, 1965.

Studies in Short Fiction, winter, 1971.
Symposium, summer, 1976.
Time, April 23, 1965, July 30, 1973, June 27, 1977, February 20, 1984.
Times Literary Supplement, July 1, 1965, October 12, 1967, February 22, 1968, July 2, 1971, February 10, 1978, April 6, 1984.
Village Voice, March 27, 1984.
Vogue, May, 1988.
Washington Post Book World, May 27, 1973, August 14, 1977, February 26, 1984, May 22, 1988.
World Literature Today, autumn, 1977, spring, 1981, summer, 1982, winter, 1983.

—*Sketch by Thomas Kozikowski*

*   *   *

DOOLITTLE, Hilda   1886-1961
(H. D.; John Helforth, a pseudonym)

PERSONAL: Born September 19, 1886, in Bethlehem, Pa.; died of a heart attack, September 27, 1961, in Zurich, Switzerland; daughter of Charles Leander (a professor of mathematics and astronomy) and Helen Eugeneia (Woole) Doolittle; married Richard Aldington (a writer), October, 1913 (separated, 1919; divorced, 1938); children: Perdita (Mrs. John Schaffner). *Education:* Attended Bryn Mawr College, 1900-06.

CAREER: Poet, playwright, novelist, and translator. Literary editor of the *Egoist,* 1916-17; contributing editor of *Close-Up* (cinema journal), 1927-31. Actress with Paul Robeson in film "Borderline," c. 1930.

AWARDS, HONORS: Guarantors Prize from *Poetry,* 1915; Levinson Prize, 1938, and Harriet Monroe Memorial Prize, 1958, both for poetry published in *Poetry;* Brandeis University Creative Arts Medal, 1959, for lifetime of distinguished achievement; Award of Merit Medal for poetry from National Institute and American Academy of Arts and Letters, 1960.

WRITINGS:

UNDER INITIALS H. D.

Sea Garden (poems), Constable, 1916, reprinted, St. Martin's, 1975.
(Translator) *Choruses From the Iphigenia in Aulis by Euripides,* Clerk's Private Press, 1916.
The Tribute and Circe: Two Poems, Clerk's Private Press, 1917.
Hymen (poems), Holt, 1921.
Heliodora and Other Poems, Houghton, 1924.
Collected Poems of H. D., Boni & Liveright, 1925.
H. D. (poems), edited by Hugh Mearns, Simon & Schuster, 1926.
Palimpsest (novel), Houghton, 1926, revised edition, Southern Illinois University Press, 1968.
Hippolytus Temporizes: A Play in Three Acts, Houghton, 1927, revised, 1985.
Hedylus (novel), Houghton, 1928, revised edition, 1980.
Red Roses for Bronze (poems), Random House, 1929, reprinted, AMS Press, 1970.
Borderline—A Pool Film with Paul Robeson, Mercury, 1930.
Kora and Ka (novel), Darantiere (Dijon, France), 1934, Bios, 1978.
The Usual Star (poems), Darantiere, 1934.
The Hedgehog (children's fiction), Brendin, 1936.
(Translator) Euripides, *Ion* (play), Houghton, 1937, revised, 1985.
What Do I Love? (poems), Brendin, 1944.

The Walls Do Not Fall (poems; also see below), Oxford University Press, 1944.

Tribute to the Angels (poems; also see below), Oxford University Press, 1945.

The Flowering of the Rod (poems; also see below), Oxford University Press, 1946.

By Avon River (poetry and prose), Macmillan, 1949, revised edition, 1986.

Tribute to Freud, with Unpublished Letters to Freud by the Author, Pantheon, 1956, enlarged edition, McGraw, 1975, 2nd edition published as *Tribute to Freud: Writing on the Wall,* New Directions, 1984.

Selected Poems, Grove, 1957.

Bid Me to Live: A Madrigal (novel), Grove, 1960, revised edition, 1983.

Helen in Egypt (poem), Grove, 1961.

Two Poems (originally published in *Life and Letters Today,* 1937), Arif, 1971.

Temple of the Sun, Arif, 1972.

Hermetic Definition, New Directions, 1972.

Trilogy: The Walls Do Not Fall, Tribute to the Angels, The Flowering of the Rod, New Directions, 1973.

The Poet and the Dancer (originally published in *Life and Letters Today,* December, 1935), Five Trees Press, 1975.

(Contributor) Eric Walter White, *Images of H. D.,* Enitharmon, 1976.

End to Torment: A Memoir of Ezra Pound, edited by Norman Holmes Pearson and Michael King, New Directions, 1979.

HERmione, New Directions, 1981, published as *Her,* Virago, 1984.

The Gift (memoir), New Directions, 1982.

Collected Poems 1912-1944, edited by Louis L. Martz, New Directions, 1983.

Notes on Thought and Vision and The Wise Sappho, City Lights Books, 1983.

Priest and A Dead Priestess Speaks (two poems), Copper Canyon Press, 1983.

Selected Poems, edited by Louis L. Martz, Carcanet Press, 1989.

OTHER

(Under pseudonym John Helforth) *Nights,* Darantiere, 1935.

Work represented in anthologies, including *Des Imagistes: An Anthology,* edited by Ezra Pound, A. & C. Boni, 1914; *Some Imagist Poets: An Anthology,* edited by Amy Lowell, Houghton, 1915-17; *Contact Collection of Contemporary Writers,* edited by Robert McAlmon, Contact Editions, 1925. Contributor to *Poetry* and other periodicals. Translator of Euripides's *Hippolytus,* 1919. Collections of H. D.'s papers are housed at the Beinecke Library, Yale University.

SIDELIGHTS: As one of the founders of Imagism, Hilda Doolittle (known as H. D.) became known as much for her poetry as for her association with the group's distinguished writers. Yet her own stark and concrete poetry typified the demands of Imagism as set forth by Ezra Pound and a core of other avant-garde poets. By the mid-1920's, however, after a series of personal crises and the passing of the Imagist years, H. D. sought a more secluded life in Switzerland. But the events of her time—her psychoanalysis with Sigmund Freud, World War II, her advancing age and growing Christian faith—continued to be reflected in her writing. Although in many ways she wrote more productively and diversely than ever before, the influence she held early in her career has not been forgotten: H. D. remains known to many as "the perfect Imagist."

Clearly the most influential figure in H. D.'s early years was Ezra Pound. The two met when H. D. was fifteen, he sixteen, reported Melody Zajdel, and for a while were engaged—until H. D.'s father broke up the relationship. But they continued to share their love of literature, classical as well as modern, with Pound encouraging H. D. by bringing her "armfuls of books to read." Pound also introduced her to a close friend, William Carlos Williams. Pound, Williams, H. D., and her Bryn Mawr classmate, Marianne Moore, as undergraduates, were sharing the literary theories that would lead each of them to play a distinct role in changing the course of American poetry. As F. D. Reeve marvelled: "Young college poets who, in necessary protest, seek new voices must look back in wonder at the constellate quadruplet at Pennsylvania and Bryn Mawr in the early 1900's . . . and be awed by the energy, flamboyance, talent, and revolutionary zeal of those undergraduates."

In 1906 H. D. left Bryn Mawr because of poor health. She continued to study on her own, though, and began to write seriously for the first time. When Pound left the United States for Europe in 1908, publishing his first book in Venice and joining the literary circles in London, H. D. stayed behind, contributing poems, stories, and articles to a variety of newspapers and small journals.

H. D. fell under Pound's influence again in 1911. She had left on a summer vacation to Europe, where she eventually settled permanently, and met Pound in London. There she was introduced to many of his literary friends, among them Ford Maddox Ford, William Butler Yeats, F. S. Flint, and Richard Aldington. But Pound, at first, remained most influential: "I had never heard of *verse libre,*" H. D. recalled, "till I was 'discovered' by Ezra Pound. . . . I did a few poems that I don't think Ezra liked . . ., but later he was beautiful about my first authentic verses, . . . and sent my poems in for me to Miss Monroe [Harriet Monroe, editor of *Poetry* in Chicago]. He signed them for me 'H. D., Imagiste.' "

H. D., Pound, Flint, and Aldington formed the core of what became known as the Imagist movement. Living in Europe and publishing in the United States through *Poetry,* the group shaped the course of modern poetry. They abandoned the formalities of the poetry of the time as they set forth their Imagist tenets, calling for an economical verse in the language of common speech, composed "in sequence of the musical phrase, not in sequence of a metronome." The Imagists "were the innovators of poetic form," Horace Gregory pointed out, "and not those who wrote for the sake of merely seeming 'new' or experimental." But to many readers, the new poetry was scandalous. According to Reeve, the Imagists "made *Poetry* the subject of newspaper editorials and indignant letters; they had made poetry news."

Though H. D. wrote in the Imagist mode throughout much of her career, the movement itself was short-lived. Pound, who by some accounts invented the school solely to bring attention to H. D.'s work, drifted away from the movement's center and was replaced by Amy Lowell. (Disgusted with Lowell's influence in the group, Pound then dubbed the school "Amygism.") When the last *Some Imagist Poets* anthology was published in 1917, it was accompanied with an explanation that its contributors could better establish their own direction as writers independent of the Imagist label. H. D. herself would later place the movement that had given her a name in a lowered perspective. "I don't know that labels matter very much," she once said. "One writes the kind of poetry one likes. Other people put labels on it. Imagism was something that was important for poets learning their craft early in this century. But after learning his craft, the poet will find his true direction."

The highlight of H. D.'s personal life during these years was her relationship with fellow Imagist Richard Aldington. The two married in 1913, bonded by what Zajdel called a "mutual interest in classical literature, a mutual contempt of middle-class hypocrisy, and a mutual dedication to careers in poetry." They appeared to those around them as happy—Lowell thought them "a perfectly charming young couple"—but that joy was interrupted by World War I. Aldington went into service in 1916 while H. D. assumed his post as literary editor of the *Egoist.* Upon his return, however, their relationship began to deteriorate, leaving H. D. alone to endure a most difficult period of her life.

In addition to her marital problems, H. D. faced other serious personal crises at this time. In 1918 her brother was killed in action in France. Later that year, in poor health and pregnant for the second time (her first pregnancy had ended in miscarriage), H. D. separated from Aldington. Her daughter Perdita was born in 1919; but also in that year H. D.'s father died. H. D.'s despondency was broken only with the help of a new friend, Winnifred Ellerman, known pseudonymously as Bryher.

H. D.'s relationship with Bryher was the "single bright spot" of the time, reported Zajdel. Bryher stabilized her friend during her emotional crises, and offered H. D. encouragement as a writer as well. The two had met after Bryher had sent H. D. a letter praising *Sea Garden,* and Bryher continued to compliment H. D.'s work: she called *Hymen* "a beacon to those who, in a destructive age, believe in life." H. D., in turn, provided Bryher the encouragement she needed to pursue her own writing; she eventually became a successful novelist. Between 1919 and 1923 the two also traveled extensively, to Greece, Egypt, and America, spending most of their time in London between travels. H. D. finally settled in Switzerland in 1924.

By that time, the publication of *Hymen* and *Heliodora* had given H. D.'s poetry a significant platform from which to be judged. Readers praised her work for its economy of language and its precision, but also detected hints of emotion uncharacteristic of much Imagist work. "H. D. is that unique thing, an imagist poet with passion as well as pattern," wrote Mark Van Doren. "She goes on carving her Greek world out of pure, white rock, inlaying it all the while with Mediterranean purple and the hues of wind-flowers infinitely alive." Whether she chose as her subjects symbols from the Hellenic world or objects taken from nature, she fused her abilities to create and to control. As Willard Thorp wrote of the second part of the poem "Garden," H. D. displayed "perfectly in thirteen lines the oppressiveness of fructifying summer heat." Thorp also admired H. D.'s poetry for capturing its subjects "much as Cezanne's painting of still life does."

The publication of *Collected Poems* in 1925 is considered a watershed in H. D.'s career. The book helped establish H. D.'s reputation by bringing into one volume all of her poems and translations. To William Carlos Williams, *Collected Poems* presented H. D.'s work together "as a clear story. There is an extraordinary vista of a strong rise, beginning with youth and extending over a long period of a woman's growth and blossoming and further rise from that flower into a world beyond it, that should be to every American a source of strengthening pride." But at the same time, as Vincent Quinn' biography of the poet suggested, the book has done H. D. one particular disservice: "the title suggests the end rather than the beginning of her career."

Aside from the publication of *Collected Poems,* the mid-1920's marked several other shifts in H. D.'s career. During this time

she abandoned the active literary life of the expatriate circles and moved to Switzerland. Though she did travel some and lived in London during World War II, Switzerland remained her "permanent" home. Also during the 1920's H. D. changed the focus of her writing, broadening into some different types of poetry as well as into drama and fiction.

Though H. D. impressed some readers with her first two books of fiction, critics at the same time found them lacking. Her three-story collection, *Palimpsest,* "is a repository for the themes H. D. would explore throughout the rest of her career," declared Zajdel. Specifically, H. D. was concerned with the artist's search for identity and the role of the artist in society. In H. D.'s second work of fiction, *Hedylus,* she explored a mother-son relationship. Praise for these works centered around her "exquisite" prose and the beauty of her presentation. Reservations about them, on the other hand, pointed to their difficult and exclusive nature. Babette Deutsch, for example, said *Palimpsest* is a book "for poets and patient intellectuals." She added, however, that "to dismiss it as caviar would be to emphasize its delicacy at the expense of its indubitable strength."

During the 1930's H. D. published little while living privately in Switzerland. A major influence on her in this time was the psychoanalysis she submitted to under the guidance of Sigmund Freud. Feeling the need "to dig down and dig out, root out my personal weeds, strengthen my purpose, reaffirm my beliefs, canalize my energies," H. D. first sought Freud's help in 1933 and visited him again a year later. She published her recollections of the experience in her 1956 book, *Tribute to Freud.* "Essentially," said Quinn, "the work is a self-portrait brought into focus by her confrontation with Freud." Freud helped H. D. to understand her dreams, Quinn reported, but the two differed in their beliefs in immortality. As H. D. herself wrote, Freud's argument was that a "belief in the soul's survival, in a life after death . . . was the last and greatest phantasy." H. D., in comparison, longed "for the Absolute," said Quinn. "She clung to the faith that the shortcomings of time would be overcome in eternity."

H. D. regained some attention as a poet with the release of the separate volumes of the "war trilogy" in the mid-1940's. Her most recent major publication before that, *Red Roses for Bronze* (1929), had been noted for some stylistic innovations but had also, according to Zajdel, "marked the end of H. D.'s popularity with the public." And while the trilogy did not bring her immediate fame, it was evidence of a renewed creative vigor. "The genesis of *Trilogy* lies in the catalytic effects on H. D. of living in war-time London," said Peter Scupham. "Her sense of living at a turning point in time led her to these meditations on the nature of the poet's role, the correspondences between Christian belief and the Egyptian pantheon, the presences of the spiritual world and the healing and unifying visions of reconciliation."

In *The Walls Do Not Fall,* the first volume of the trilogy, H. D. asserted her idealism—her belief in man's union with God—in the face of war, reported Quinn. *Tribute to the Angels* follows that same theme, focusing on the conflict between faith and war. With her faith firmly established, H. D. then sought in *Flowering of the Rod,* a mystical vision, "a transcendental union with God." This section of the trilogy has been criticized for being too mystical; but, as Quinn noted, "although the reader may be dismayed by H. D.'s theology, his sympathy is almost certain to be aroused by the candor and intensity of her quest for a religious experience."

Corresponding with the power of H. D.'s vision was an equally strong poetic presentation. "There are in these poems the same qualities found in the verse written more than a decade earlier," remarked Donald Barlow Stauffer: "precision of image and word, directness of statement, but with a sureness and evenness of tone that show how firmly she was in control of the world she had chosen to re-create."

After the war, H. D. returned to Switzerland, where she wrote her third major work of fiction, *Bid Me to Live*. The novel is her *roman a clef* about life in London in the 1920's. "I am Julia," H. D. told *Newsweek*'s Lionel Durand upon the novel's release in 1960, "and all the others are real people." Specifically, those others include D. H. Lawrence, his wife, and Aldington. In the novel Julia's marriage dissolves and she becomes involved in a Platonic relationship with another man. When that man withdraws from her, her solution, said Zajdel, "is a dedication to her life as an artist and an affirmation of her identity as a creator and poet."

The theme of artist as hero is prevalent throughout H. D.'s work. Her use of the theme in *Bid Me to Live* was criticized by Quinn, however, who called Julia an "optimistic fatalist." But as C. H. Sisson noted, H. D. "lived obscurely with the illusion—which is not entirely an illusion—that if the artist gets on with his art all will be well."

H. D. offered a different sort of optimism in her last major poetic work, *Helen in Egypt*. A book-length mixture of poetry and prose in three parts, Helen is the author's recreation of the Helen-Achilles myth. Her theme, said Quinn, "is stark and transcendental: the perfect love that she and Achilles seek is to be found in death: 'the dart of Love/is the dart of Death.' " Horace Gregory reinforced this notion when he said "her overlying theme . . . is one of rebirth and resurrection." *Helen in Egypt* is also important as a representative display of the themes and techniques H. D. employed throughout her career. Emily Stipes Watts as well as other critics agreed that "Helen in Egypt is the climax of H. D.'s career both intellectually and poetically."

Though few would argue about H. D.'s importance as an influence on modern poetry, many are still unconvinced of the lasting merits of her work. Readers have been deterred from much of her writing because of the preciousness of her language, the abundance of mythology, the limited world of her focus. And though she did broaden her subject range after World War II, as Quinn noted, she did so at the expense of the clarity and conciseness that had been her trademark. Still, her technical achievements, her poignant portrayals of her personal struggles, and the beauty of her work have all earned a significant amount of praise. As Sisson pointed out, the prospective reader of H. D. might be a little surprised to find that "H. D. offers more than the formal virtues which are usually allowed to her work, and that . . . work abundantly repays the not very strenuous labor of reading it."

To many, H. D. will be remembered as "a poets' poet." "To be 'a poets' poet,' " said Gregory, "has few tangible rewards, for this means that the poet who holds that title must often wait upon the future for true recognition." For the time being, however, H. D.'s achievement has been measured in comparison with the "major poets of the twentieth century," asserted Hyatt H. Waggoner, "or at least with those in some sort of second category, like [Conrad] Aiken or [Archibald] MacLeish or [John Crowe] Ransom." And in the process of gaining her stature, "the notes she made in her journey, in her poems, compose one of the really distinguished bodies of work of this century."

BIOGRAPHICAL/CRITICAL SOURCES:

BOOKS

Aldington, Richard, *Life for Life's Sake: A Book of Reminiscences*, Viking, 1941.

Bryher, *The Heart to Artemis: A Writer's Memoirs*, Harcourt, 1962.

Coffman, Stanley K., *Imagism: A Chapter for the History of Modern Poetry*, University of Oklahoma Press, 1950.

Contemporary Literary Criticism, Gale, Volume 3, 1975, Volume 8, 1978, Volume 14, 1980, Volume 31, 1985, Volume 34, 1985.

Dictionary of Literary Biography, Gale, Volume 4: *American Writers in Paris*, 1920-39, 1980, Volume 45: *American Poets, 1880-1945*, 1986.

Ellmann, Richard, and Robert O'Clair, editors, *The Norton Anthology of Modern Poetry*, Norton, 1973.

Foster, Damon S., *Amy Lowell*, Houghton, 1935.

Gregory, Horace, and Marya Zaturenska, *A History of American Poetry: 1900-1940*, Harcourt, 1942.

Guest, Barbara, *Herself Defined: The Poet H. D. and Her World*, Daoubleday, 1984.

H. D., *Helen in Egypt*, introduction by Horace Gregory, New Directions, 1974.

Holland, Norman N., *Poems in Persons: An Introduction to the Psychoanalysis of Literature*, Norton, 1973.

Hughes, Glenn, *Imagism and the Imagists*, Humanities Press, 1931.

Lawrence, D. H., *A Composite Biography*, three volumes, University of Wisconsin Press, 1957-59.

Perkins, David, *A History of Modern Poetry: From the 1890's to the High Modernist Mode*, Harvard University Press, 1976.

Quinn, Vincent, *Hilda Doolittle (H. D.)*, Twayne, 1967.

Robinson, Janice S., *H. D.: The Life and Work of an American Poet*, Houghton, 1982.

Stauffer, Donald Barlow, *A Short History of American Poetry*, Dutton, 1974.

Swann, Thomas Burnett, *The Classical World of H. D.*, University of Nebraska Press, 1962.

Waggoner, Hyatt H., *American Poets From the Puritans to the Present*, Houghton, 1968.

Watts, Emily Stipes, *The Poetry of American Women from 1632 to 1945*, University of Texas Press, 1977.

White, Eric Walter, *Images of H. D.*, Enitharmon, 1976.

PERIODICALS

Agenda, autumn, 1974.

Best Sellers, February 15, 1974, June, 1975.

Books, February 14, 1932.

Christian Science Monitor, October 26, 1961.

College English, March, 1975.

Commonweal, April 18, 1958.

Contemporary Literature, autumn, 1969, spring, 1978.

Essays in Criticism, July, 1977.

Literary Review, May 23, 1925, November 27, 1926.

Mississippi Quarterly, fall, 1962.

Nation, April 26, 1922, November 12, 1924, August 19, 1925, October 8, 1973.

New Republic, January 2, 1929, February 16, 1974.

Newsweek, May 2, 1960.

New York Herald Tribune Book Review, November 28, 1926, June 12, 1960.

New York Times, August 31, 1924, November 21, 1926, November 18, 1928, January 31, 1932, July 31, 1949, September 22, 1957.

New York Times Book Review, May 1, 1960, December 24, 1961.
Poetry, March, 1922, November, 1932, April. 1947, January, 1958, June, 1962, June, 1974.
Poetry Nation, number 4, 1975.
Saturday Review, May 28, 1960.
Saturday Review of Literature, January 1, 1927, December 22, 1928, December 29, 1945, February 22, 1947, August 20, 1949.
Sewanee Review, spring, 1948.
Spectator, February 25, 1922, December 31, 1931.
Times Literary Supplement, July 3, 1924, July 27, 1946, March 23, 1973, March 15, 1974.
Triquarterly, spring, 1968.
Weekly Book Review, October 1, 1944.

OBITUARIES:

PERIODICALS

Newsweek, October 9, 1961.
New York Times, September 29, 1961.
Publishers Weekly, October 23, 1961.
Time, October 6, 1961.

*   *   *

DORSAN, Luc
See SIMENON, Georges (Jacques Christian)

*   *   *

DORSANGE, Jean
See SIMENON, Georges (Jacques Christian)

*   *   *

DOS PASSOS, John (Roderigo)   1896-1970

PERSONAL: Born January 14, 1896, in Chicago, Ill.; died, apparently of a heart attack, September 28, 1970, in Baltimore,. Md.; buried in Westmoreland Co., Va.; son of John Randolph Dos Passos (an attorney) and Lucy Addison Sprigg Madison; married Katherine F. Smith, August 21, 1929 (died, 1947); married Elizabeth Hamlin Holdridge, August 6, 1949; children: (second marriage) Lucy Hamlin. *Education:* Harvard University, B.A. (cum laude), 1916. *Politics:* Began left-wing, shifting to conservative in his later years.

ADDRESSES: Home—Westmoreland, Va. *Agent*—Brandt & Brandt Literary Agents, 1501 Broadway, New York, N.Y. 10036.

CAREER: Volunteered for ambulance duty in France with Norton-Harjes Ambulance Unit, 1917, in Italy with Red Cross, 1918, and with U.S. Army Medical Corps, 1918-19; traveled to Near East with Near East Relief, 1921; *New Masses,* founder, 1926, executive board member, beginning 1926; correspondent in Central America, 1932; correspondent for *Life* magazine in the Pacific, 1945, and in South America, 1948. Treasurer, National Committee for Defense of Political Prisoners, 1932.

MEMBER: American Academy of Arts and Letters, American Academy of Arts and Sciences, Authors League, Virginia Committee on Constitutional Government.

AWARDS, HONORS: Guggenheim fellowships, 1939, 1940, 1942; National Institute of Arts and Letters Gold Medal Award for fiction, 1957; Antonio Feltrinelli Prize from Italian Academia Nazionale dei Lincei, 1967, for innovation in narrative.

WRITINGS:

(Contributor) *Eight Harvard Poets,* Laurence J. Gomme, 1917.
One Man's Initiation—1917, Allen & Unwin, 1919, Doran, 1920, published as *First Encounter,* Philosophical Library, 1945, unexpurgated edition published with new introduction, Cornell University Press, 1969.
Three Soldiers, Doran, 1921, reprinted, Houghton, 1964.
Rosinante to the Road Again, Doran, 1922.
A Pushcart at the Curb, Doran, 1922.
Streets of Night, Doran, 1923.
Manhattan Transfer, Harper, 1925, reprinted, Bentley, 1980.
Orient Express, Harper, 1927, reprinted, Octagon, 1976.
Facing the Chair: Story of the Americanization of Two Foreign-born Workmen, Sacco-Vanzetti Defense Committee (Boston), 1927, reprinted, DaCapo Press, 1970.
The 42nd Parallel (first book in "U.S.A." trilogy; also see below), Harcourt, 1930, reprinted, New American Library, 1969.
1919 (second book in "U.S.A." trilogy; also see below), Harcourt, 1932, reprinted, New American Library, 1969.
Culture and the Crisis: An Open Letter to the Writers, Artists, Teachers, Physicians, Engineers, Scientists, and Other Professional Workers of America, League of Professional Groups for Foster & Ford (New York), 1932.
In All Countries, Harcourt, 1934.
The Big Money (third book in "U.S.A." trilogy; also see below), Harcourt, 1936, reprinted, New American Library, 1966.
(Contributor) Henry Hart, editor, *American Writers Conference,* International Publishers, 1935.
The Villages Are the Heart of Spain, Esquire-Coronet, 1937.
Journeys between Wars, Harcourt, 1938, reprinted, Octagon, 1980.
U.S.A. (trilogy; contains *The 42nd Parallel, 1919,* and *The Big Money*), Harcourt, 1938.
Adventures of a Young Man (first book in "District of Columbia" trilogy; also see below), Houghton, 1939, reprinted, Queens House, 1977.
The Living Thoughts of Tom Paine, Presented by John Dos Passos, Longmans, Green, 1940, reprinted, Fawcett, 1964.
The Ground We Stand On, Harcourt, 1941, reprinted, Kraus Reprints, 1970.
(Contributor) Herman Ould, editor, *Writers in Freedom,* Hutchinson, 1942.
Number One (second book in "District of Columbia" trilogy; also see below), Houghton, 1943, reprinted, Queens House, 1977.
State of the Nation, Houghton, 1944, reprinted, Greenwood Press, 1973.
Tour of Duty, Houghton, 1946, reprinted, Greenwood Press, 1974.
The Grand Design (third book in "District of Columbia" trilogy; also see below), Houghton, 1949, reprinted, Queens House, 1977.
The Prospect Before Us, Houghton, 1950, reprinted, Greenwood Press, 1973.
Life's Picture History of World War II, Time Inc., 1950.
Chosen Country, Houghton, 1951.
District of Columbia (trilogy; contains *Adventures of a Young Man, Number One,* and *The Grand Design*), Houghton, 1952.
The Head and Heart of Thomas Jefferson, Doubleday, 1954.
Most Likely to Succeed, Prentice-Hall, 1954.
The Theme Is Freedom, Dodd, 1956, reprinted, Arno, 1971.
The Men Who Made the Nation, Doubleday, 1957.

(Contributor) *Essays on Individuality,* University of Pennsylvania Press, 1958.

The Great Days, Sagamore, 1958.

Prospects of a Golden Age, Prentice-Hall, 1959.

Midcentury: A Contemporary Chronicle, Houghton, 1961.

Mr. Wilson's War, Doubleday, 1962.

Brazil on the Move (travel), Doubleday, 1963.

Occasions and Protests (essays, 1936-1964), Regnery, 1964.

Thomas Jefferson: The Making of a President, Houghton, 1964.

(Contributor) Allan Nevins, editor, *Lincoln and the Gettysberg Address,* University of Illinois Press, 1964.

The Shackles of Power: Three Jeffersonian Decades, 1801-1826, Doubleday, 1966.

The World in a Glass: A View of Our Century Selected from the Novels of John Dos Passos, Houghton, 1966.

The Best Times: An Informal Memoir, New American Library, 1966.

The Portugal Story: Three Centuries of Exploration and Discovery, Doubleday, 1969.

Easter Island: Island of Enigmas, Doubleday, 1971.

The Fourteenth Chronicle: Letters and Diaries of John Dos Passos, edited by Townsend Ludington, Gambit, 1973.

Century's Ebb: The Thirteenth Chronicle, Gambit, 1975.

Promise of U.S.A.: John Dos Passos' Thumbnail Biographies, edited by Edgar Stanton, Hwong Publishing, 1975.

PLAYS

The Garbage Man (produced, 1926; also see below), Harper, 1926.

Airways, Inc. (also see below), Macaulay, 1928.

Three Plays: The Garbage Man, Airways, Inc., Fortune Heights (produced in U.S.S.R., 1933), Harcourt, 1934.

(With Paul Shyre) *U.S.A.: A Dramatic Revue,* Samuel French, 1963.

OTHER

Translator from the French, and illustrator, of B. Cendrar's *Panama.* Contributor to *Nation, New Republic, New Masses, Common Sense, Esquire, Partisan Review, National Review,* and other periodicals.

An extensive collection of manuscripts and other working materials is housed at the Alderman Library of the University of Virginia.

SIDELIGHTS: Jean-Paul Sartre once called John Dos Passos "the best novelist of our time." Nevertheless, Gore Vidal noted that although he was "admired extravagantly in the '20's and '30's, Dos Passos was largely ignored in the '40's and '50's, his new works passed over either in silence or else noted with that ritual sadness we reserve for those whose promise to art has not been kept."

Reviews of his earlier works reflect the expectations that Dos Passos raised in the literary world. Sinclair Lewis heralded *Manhattan Transfer* as "a novel of the very first importance; a book which the idle reader can devour yet which the literary analyst must take as possibly inaugurating, at long last, the vast and blazing dawn we have awaited. It may be the foundation of a whole new school of novel-writing. Dos Passos may be, more than Dreiser, Cather, Hergesheimer, Cabell, or Anderson the father of humanized and living fiction . . . not merely for America but for the world! . . . I regard *Manhattan Transfer* as more important in every way than anything by Gertrude Stein or Marcel Proust or even the great white boar, Mr. Joyce's Ulysses." Mary Ross wrote of *1919:* "Mr. Dos Passos's writing is always distinguished by a remarkable sensuous perception, but more than

that, he has a directness, independence and poignancy of thought and emotion that seems to me unexcelled in current fiction. . . . *1919* will disturb or offend some of its readers. Their recoil will be in itself a mark of its force. No novel with which I am familiar seems to me to have surpassed it in power, range, and beauty."

After the completion of the *U.S.A.* trilogy, Theodore Spencer declared: "No one concerned with the health of the novel as a living form can fail to . . . regard his achievement with respect. He writes from a wise and comprehending point of view; his construction is firm; his narrative is swift, realistic, and interesting. There are few novelists in this country today whose craftsmanship is as secure, and whose sense of American life as understanding and awake." However, Alfred Kazin noted that while *U.S.A.* became an epic, "it is a history of defeat. There are no flags for the spirit in it, and no victory save the mind's silent victory that integrity can acknowledge to itself. It is one of the saddest books ever written by an American." Even so, Kazin added, "what Waldo Frank said of Mencken is particularly relevant to Dos Passos: he brings energy to despair."

Viewed from the perspective of thirty years later, Peter Meinke's review of *The Fourteenth Chronicle* found Dos Passos "to be in that main American tradition beginning with Whitman that seeks to grasp the American experience by accumulation of detail, by great width and scope, by swallowing America whole, as it were, rather than carving out deep chunks from certain sections as his friends Hemingway, Fitzgerald, Faulkner and Cummings did. . . . While the book is ultimately sad, with the elderly out-of-step writer exclaiming that 'the rank idiocy of the younger generation is more than I can swallow' the main impression one gets from reading it is that of a decent and generous man of boundless enthusiasm and energy." D. J. Stewart's review of *Occasions and Protests* noted the "startling emphasis on vision, on seeing clear, rounded, individual shapes of things provides a kind of touchstone wherewith to reread and better understand what these pieces are about. For they are essentially the reactions to life of a man who uses his eyes intensely and voraciously, one who lives with and through his vision." Dos Passos sees things with the coolness and the clarity of the camera's eye, which accounts for one of his most frequently-mentioned faults: his two-dimensional vision tends to create types, defeating the creation of characters with any true individuality.

Don Gifford offered a possible explanation for these types: "At its core, Dos Passos's 'settled theory' is bitterly anti-intellectual—it postulates a 'natural man' who shares 'certain simple realities which are universal to all men.' " Walter Allen, however, believed that Dos Passos did not become a reactionary in his later years, but that "he [continued] to attack, in the name of individual freedom, power that he [believed had] become monolithic. He remains essentially an anarchist." A *Time* reviewer grants that "politics helped to undermine [Dos Passos's] reputation." Nevertheless, "the most consistent theme in his life was a vaguely anarchic impulse, a craving for individuality which no ideology could permanently satisfy."

According to Gifford, Dos Passos explained his philosophy in *Occasions and Protests*—that "personal freedom and individual liberty constitute the highest good, and that this good is under attack by evil in the form of institutional authority in mass society (big government, big labor, big business, etc.) and in the form of 'the prescriptions of doctrine' (Communism, liberalism, conformism, etc.)." However, this philosophy does not produce an optimistic view of his characters. Edmund Wilson asserted many years ago that Dos Passos's "disapproval of capitalistic society becomes distaste for all the human beings who compose it." This same view was expressed in 1939 by Alfred Kazin, who wrote: "For Dos Passos irony itself has become the supreme style; the cold, methodical ferocity of his prose, with its light, bitter thrust, its extraordinary pliability and ease, becomes a cackling solemnity. [*Adventures of a Young Man*] really trembles with an internal disgust. Dos Passos has always disliked most of his characters, but here his characteristic repugnance and exasperation yield to pure hatred."

The effects of these emotions were examined by Sartre. "Dos Passos' hate, despair, and lofty contempt are real," he commented. "But that is precisely why his world is not real; it is a created object. I know of none—not even Faulkner's or Kafka's—in which the art is greater or better hidden. I know of none that is more precious, more touching or closer to us. This is because he takes his material from our world. And yet, there is no stranger or more distant world. Dos Passos has invented only one thing, an art of story-telling. But that is enough to create a universe." A reviewer for *Christian Century* detailed the disintegration of such a universe when he wrote: "Great was the fall of novelist Dos Passos from the ideological summit he had assumed in the leftist movements of the 1930's. His style, his provocativeness, his sense of the current—none of these has left him. But he has become a rather weary and repetitive recaller of an American past most of which never existed." Maxwell Geismar continues the discussion, commenting that "the decline of Dos Passos's work is another tragedy in contemporary letters. But if the trouble with the later Hemingway or the later Faulkner is that they are not really serious any more, perhaps the trouble with Dos Passos is that he has become much too serious."

R. A. Fraser lamented that, in *Occasions and Protests*, "nothing is left of the Dos Passos style but his habit of omitting the hyphen. His prose could once—perhaps will again—slap life into the cheeks of the most commonplace landscape, the most banal event; here . . . it's rouge that's being applied, slowly, laboriously and inaccurately. Even his ear has betrayed him." John Gross wrote in his review of *Midcentury,* "All one can do for the sake of the man who once wrote *Manhattan Transfer* and *The Big Money* is look the other way." H. M. Robinson seems similarly inclined. He recalled: "Time was, when the publication of a novel by John Dos Passos called for the lighting of bonfires on promontories. But no triumphant flare will greet the appearance of his latest work. . . . Kindly reviewers may regard the book as a temporary lapse of energy. . . . But Mr. Dos Passos deserves something more constructive than mercy. . . . The weakness of *The Grand Design* proceeds not so much from the waning of Mr. Dos Passos's creative powers—though there is a marked decline here—as from the exhaustion of the genre in which he is working." "Yet," Vidal noted, "there is something about Dos Passos which makes a fellow writer unexpectedly protective, partly out of compassion for the man himself, and partly because the fate of Dos Passos is a chilling reminder of those condemned to write for life that this is the way it almost always is in a society which, to put it tactfully, has no great interest in the development of writers, a process too slow for the American temperament. As a result our literature is rich with sprinters but significantly short of milers."

"Decline is probably a merely conventional way to characterize the shift in Dos Passos's approach to interpreting American life," Herbert Gold commented. "He was more consistent than we realized. His first radical work is animated by boyish bitterness and anger—combined with the youthful ambition to make a literary mark. The later conservative or right-wing work is animated by aging bitterness and anger—combined with the older man's desire to take a few revenges on a time that has passed him

by. What remains constant, and of constant value in a writer who never quite achieved his ambitions, is a passion that might be derived from both the paltriest and the deepest of sources: the sense of his unique self." To this, Granville Hicks conceded that "Dos Passos cannot now reach the height he reached in *U.S.A.* but *Midcentury* shows how much there is that he can still do well. . . . And, tired and hopeless as he may be, Dos Passos is still a man of solid integrity, saying exactly what he thinks."

Examination of the decline in Dos Passos's popularity yields several conjectures as to what went wrong. Vance Bourjaily claimed: "Dos Passos, through the years, has become a better and better writer; but the appeal of his point of view has grown narrower and narrower. For a work of literature at its best, is a creation; and *The Grand Design,* with its caricatures and its atmosphere of intangible bias, is merely an interpretation." Early in Dos Passos's career Henry Hazlitt foresaw such difficulties. "Mr. Dos Passos is a writer of extraordinary talent," he wrote in his review of *The 42nd Parallel.* "He knows American critics, he knows a great deal about life, he has a shrewd insight into men and women. . . . But it leaves one wondering whether [his] present method is not more a handicap than a help to him. This kaleidoscopic shaking of the fragments of several novels into one no longer has the attraction of novelty, and its other advantages are not always clear." In 1961, John Wrenn demonstrated the validity of Hazlitt's misgivings. He explained: "Dos Passos has been admired for characteristics which today, with a perspective of twenty years, appear to be superficial: for his success in the novel of protest; for his brilliant technical innovations in such a work as *U.S.A.;* for his contemporaneity—his grasp of the problems and events of the time as they related to individual characters in his fiction. When the novel of protest became all too familiar, the innovations of *U.S.A.* no longer new, and the events of his major novels no longer current ones, even his best work seemed to become no longer relevant."

One of Dos Passos' loyal admirers, James T. Farrell, wrote in 1958: "John Dos Passos writes with great ease and he is technically inventive. . . . From *Three Soldiers* to *The Great Days,* we can see in Dos Passos the effort of one man of talent and sensibility to take hold of this changing play of forces in our life." But Wrenn observed that contemporary Americans were no longer his audience, principally because he had been stereotyped as "rebel of the twenties, ex-communist, political novelist, disillusioned social critic," and writers so labeled were out of fashion. Robie Macaulay felt that much of Dos Passos' work was "bound to taste rather stale to this generation, a spectacle not current enough to be news and not quite old enough to be history. . . . But, given enough distance, Dos Passos will have his day again. How he will be read in another time is hard to say. . . . I should say that it will be less as a social interpreter than as a primitive portraitist of American lives during a certain time." To this Thomas Lask added: "Dos Passos may become known as the author of one book, but in its range and reach, in its willingness to meet head on the possibilities of American life, it is large enough to be considered a life's work."

Arthur Mizener noted that, in spite of his faults, "Dos Passos is the only major American novelist of the twentieth century who has had the desire and the power to surround the lives of his characters with what Lionel Trilling once called 'the buzz of history'—the actual, homely, everyday sounds of current events and politics, of social ambitions and the struggle for money, of small pleasures and trivial corruptions, amidst which we all live. He has given us a major aspect of our experience that has hardly been touched by any other novelist of our time." Kazin echoed these sentiments when he wrote: "It is often assumed that Dos

Passos was a 'left-wing' novelist in the Thirties who, like other novelists of the period, turned conservative and thus changed and lost his creative identity. . . . But [*U.S.A.*] is not simply a 'left-wing' novel, and its technical inventiveness and freshness of style are typical of the Twenties rather than the Thirties. In any event, Dos Passos has always been so detached from all group thinking that it is impossible to understand his development as a novelist by identifying him with the radical novelists of the Thirties. He began earlier. . . . In all periods he has followed his own perky, obstinately independent course. . . . It is not his values but the loss by many educated people of a belief in 'history' that has caused Dos Passos's relative isolation in recent years. Alone among his literary cronies, Dos Passos managed to add this idea of history as the great operative force to their enthusiasm for radical technique, the language of Joyce, and 'the religion of the world.' "

AVOCATIONAL INTERESTS: Travel, sailing, canoeing, gardening, painting watercolors.

BIOGRAPHICAL/CRITICAL SOURCES:

BOOKS

Allen, Walter, *The Modern Novel in Britain and the United States,* Dutton, 1965.
Beach, Joseph Warren, *American Fiction: 1920-1940,* Russell & Russell, 1960.
Becker, George J., *John Dos Passos,* Ungar, 1974.
Belkind, Allen, editor, *Dos Passos, the Critics, and the Writer's Intention,* Southern Illinois University Press, 1972.
Brantley, John, *The Fiction of John Dos Passos,* San Antonio College, 1964.
Commager, Henry Steele, *The American Mind,* Yale University Press, 1950.
Concise Dictionary of American Literary Biography: The Age of Maturity, 1921-1941, Gale, 1989.
Contemporary Literary Criticism, Gale, Volume 1, 1973, Volume 4, 1975, Volume 7, 1978, Volume 11, 1979, Volume 15, 1980, Volume 25, 1983, Volume 34, 1985.
Cowley, Malcolm, *Exile's Return,* revised edition, Viking, 1951.
Cowley, *Second Flowering,* Viking, 1973.
Dictionary of Literary Biography, Gale, Volume 4: *American Writers in Paris, 1920-1939,* 1980, Volume 9: *American Novelists, 1910-1945,* 1981.
Dictionary of Literary Biography Documentary Series, Volume 1, Gale, 1982.
Dos Passos, John, *Fourteenth Chronicle: Letters and Diaries,* edited by Townsend Ludington, Deutsch, 1974.
Eastman, Mark, and others, *John Dos Passos: An Appreciation,* Prentice-Hall, 1954.
Eisinger, Chester E., *Fiction of the Forties,* University of Chicago Press, 1963.
Fruhock, W. M., *The Novel of Violence in America: 1920-1950,* University Press in Dallas, 1950.
Geismar, Maxwell, *Writers in Crisis,* Houghton, 1942.
Geismar, *American Moderns: From Rebellion to Conformity,* Hill & Wang, 1958.
Hook, Andrew, editor, *Dos Passos: A Collection of Critical Essays,* Prentice-Hall, 1974.
Kazin, Alfred, *Native Grounds,* Reynal, 1942.
Knox, G. A., and H. M. Stahl, *Dos Passos and the Revolting Playwrights,* Folcroft, 1976.
Landsberg, Melvin, *Dos Passos' Path to U.S.A.: A Political Biography, 1912-1936,* Colorado Associated University Press, 1972.
Longstreet, Stephen, *We All Went to Paris,* Macmillan, 1972.

Ludington, Townsend, *John Dos Passos: A Twentieth Century Odyssey,* Dutton, 1980.
Mizener, Arthur, *Twelve Great American Novels,* New American Library, 1967.
Potter, Jack, *A Bibliography of John Dos Passos,* Normandie House, 1950.
Rogers, Francis M., *The Portuguese Heritage of John Dos Passos,* Portuguese Continental Union of the U.S.A., 1976.
Sartre, Jean-Paul, *Literary and Philosophical Essays,* Rider, 1955.
Wilson, Edmund, *The Triple Thinkers,* revised edition, Oxford University Press, 1948.
Wilson, *The Shores of Light,* Farrar, Straus, 1952.
Wrenn, John H., *John Dos Passos,* Twayne, 1961.

PERIODICALS

Atlantic, October, 1936, April, 1943, March, 1961.
Atlantic Bookshelf, June 30, 1930.
Bookmen, December, 1922.
Books, March 13, 1932, April 29, 1934, July 1, 1934, June 4, 1939.
Book Week, March 28, 1965.
Catholic World, February, 1949.
Christian Century, November 28, 1962, November 4, 1964.
Christian Science Monitor, March 2, 1961.
Commonweal, June 2, 1939, March 5, 1943, January 28, 1949, October 8, 1954.
Esquire, May, 1961.
Forum, September, 1936.
Living Age, September, 1939.
Nation, November 15, 1922, March 12, 1930, June 3, 1939, April 14, 1956.
Nation and Athenaeum, November 1, 1930.
National Review, December 1, 1964, October 20, 1970.
New Leader, March 15, 1965.
New Republic, June 14, 1939, September 1, 1941, July 24, 1944, September 2, 1946, September 27, 1954, April 28, 1958.
New Statesman, October 27, 1961.
New Statesman and Nation, June 11, 1932.
Newsweek, October 12, 1970.
New Yorker, June 3, 1939, August 24, 1946, March 18, 1961.
New York Herald Tribune Books, December 2, 1962.
New York Herald Tribune Lively Arts, February 26, 1961.
New York Herald Tribune Weekly Book Review, January 2, 1949.
New York Times, May 6, 1934, May 20, 1934, August 31, 1941, July 23, 1944, September 29, 1970.
New York Times Book Review, December 20, 1959, December 25, 1960, April 7, 1963, January 10, 1965.
Paris Review, spring, 1969.
Review of Reviews, September, 1936.
Social Education, April, 1965.
South Atlantic Quarterly, spring, 1966.
Statesman, March 1, 1968.
San Francisco Chronicle, January 9, 1949, February 26, 1961.
Saturday Review, December 12, 1959, February 25, 1961, March 15, 1969.
Saturday Review of Literature, December 5, 1925, May 5, 1934, September 2, 1944, January 8, 1949.
Saturday Review/World, September 11, 1973.
Spectator, September 27, 1930.
Springfield Republican, March 13, 1932.
Time, September 27, 1954, March 3, 1961, October 12, 1970.
Times Literary Supplement, June 17, 1939, October 27, 1950, January 28, 1965.
Twentieth Century Literature, October, 1967.

Washington Post Book World, October 28, 1973.
Yale Review, summer, 1943.

*   *   *

DOSSAGE, Jean
   See SIMENON, Georges (Jacques Christian)

*   *   *

DOUGLAS, Michael
   See CRICHTON, (John) Michael

*   *   *

DOYLE, Arthur Conan   1859-1930

PERSONAL: Born May 22, 1859, in Edinburgh, Scotland; died of a heart attack, July 7 (one source says July 6), 1930, in Crowborough, Sussex, England; buried at Windlesham, Crowborough, Sussex, England; son of Charles Altamont (a civil servant and artist) and Mary (Foley) Doyle; married Louise Hawkins, August 6, 1885 (died, 1906); married Jean Leckie, September 18, 1907; children: (first marriage) Mary Louise, Kingsley; (second marriage) Denis, Adrian Malcolm, Lena Jean. *Education:* Edinburgh University, B.M., 1881, M.D., 1885.

ADDRESSES: Home—Windlesham, Crowborough, Sussex, England.

CAREER: Assistant to physician in Birmingham, England, 1879; ship's surgeon on whaling voyage to Arctic, 1880; ship's surgeon on voyage to west coast of Africa, 1881-82; physician in Southsea, Portsmouth, England, 1882-90; ophthalmologist in London, England, 1891; writer. Lectured on spiritualism in Europe, Australia, the United States, and Canada, 1917-25, South Africa, 1928, and Sweden, 1929. *Wartime service:* Served during the Boer War as chief surgeon of a field hospital in Bloemfontein, South Africa, 1900.

AWARDS, HONORS: Knighted, 1902.

WRITINGS:

SHERLOCK HOLMES DETECTIVE FICTION

A Study in Scarlet (novel; first published in *Beeton's Christmas Annual,* November, 1887), illustrations by father, Charles Doyle, Ward, Lock, 1888, Lippincott, 1890, introduction by Hugh Greene, Doubleday, 1977.
The Sign of Four (novel; first published in *Lippincott's Monthly* magazine, February, 1890), Blackett, 1890, Collier, 1891, introduction by Graham Greene, Doubleday, 1977, published as *The Sign of the Four,* Conkey, 1900, illustrations by Frank Bolle, Lion Books, c. 1973, published as *The Sign of the Four; or, The Problem of the Sholtos,* introduction by P. G. Wodehouse, Ballantine, c. 1975.
The Adventures of Sherlock Holmes (short stories), illustrations by Paget, Newnes, 1892, Harper, 1892, reprinted with new introduction, A & W Visual Library, 1975.
The Memoirs of Sherlock Holmes (short stories), illustrations by Sidney Paget, Newnes, 1893, illustrations by W. H. Hyde and Paget, Harper, 1894, reprinted with new introduction by Leslie Fielder, Schocken, 1976.
The Hound of the Baskervilles (novel; serialized in *Strand* magazine, 1901-02), illustrations by Paget, Newnes, 1902, McClure, Phillips, 1902, foreword and afterword by John Fowles, Doubleday, 1977.
The Return of Sherlock Holmes (short stories), illustrations by Paget, Newnes, 1905, McClure, Phillips, 1905, reprinted

with new introduction by Samuel Rosenberg, Schocken, 1975.
The Valley of Fear (novel; serialized in *Strand* magazine, 1914-1915), Smith, Elder, 1915, Berkley Books, 1982, published as *The Valley of Fear: A Sherlock Holmes Novel,* illustrations by Arthur I. Keller, Doran, 1915.
His Last Bow: Some Reminiscences of Sherlock Holmes (short stories), J. Murray, 1917, reprinted with introduction by Julian Symons, J. Murray, 1974, published as *His Last Bow: A Reminiscence of Sherlock Holmes,* Doran, 1917.
The Case-Book of Sherlock Holmes (short stories), J. Murray, 1927, Doran, 1927, reprinted with introduction by C. P. Snow, J. Murray, 1974.
The Annotated Sherlock Holmes: The Four Novels and the Fifty-six Short Stories Complete, edited with introduction, notes, and bibliography by William S. Baring-Gould, illustrations by Charles Doyle and others, C. N. Potter, 1967, reissued, 1986.
The Uncollected Sherlock Holmes (short stories), compiled by Richard Lancelyn Green, Penguin Books, 1983.

NOVELS

The Mystery of Cloomber, Ward & Downey, 1889, Munro, 1895, reprinted, illustrations by Paul M. McCall, afterword by Jack Tracy, Gaslight, 1980.
The Firm of Girdlestone (semiautobiographical), Chatto & Windus, 1890, Lovell, 1890, reprinted, illustrations by McCall, afterword by Jack Tracy, Gaslight, 1980.
The Doings of Raffles Haw (serialized in *Answers,* 1891-92), Lovell, Coryell, 1891, Cassell, 1892, reprinted, illustrations by McCall, embellishments by James B. Campbell, afterword by John Bennett Shaw, Gaslight, 1981.
Beyond the City, George Newnes, 1892, illustrations by Pamela Mattix, afterword by Howard Lachtman, Gaslight, 1982.
The Parasite, Constable, 1894, published as *The Parasite: A Story,* illustrations by Howard Pyle, Harper, 1895.
The Stark Munro Letters: Being a Series of Sixteen Letters Written by J. Stark Munro, M.B., to his Friend and Former Fellow-Student, Herbert Swanborough, of Lowell, Massachusetts, During the Years 1881-1884 (autobiographical), Longmans, Green, 1895, Appleton, 1895, reprinted, Gaslight, 1982.
Rodney Stone, illustrations by Paget, Smith, Elder, 1896, Appleton, 1896, reprinted, J. Murray, 1963.
The Tragedy of the Korosko, illustrations by Paget, Smith, Elder, 1898, reprinted, Gaslight, 1983, published as *A Desert Drama: Being the Tragedy of the Korosko,* Lippincott, 1898.
A Duet with an Occasional Chorus, Richards, 1899, Appleton, 1899, reprinted, Gaslight, 1985.
The Lost World, Hodder & Stoughton, 1912, Doran, 1912, reprinted, Berkley Publishing, 1965.
The Poison Belt, illustrations by Harry Rountree, Hodder & Stoughton, 1913, Doran, 1913, introduction by John Dickson Carr, epilogue by Harlow Shapley, Berkley Publishing, 1966.
The Land of Mist, Hutchinson, 1925, Doran, 1926.

HISTORICAL NOVELS

Micah Clarke: His Statement as Made to His Three Grandchildren, Joseph, Gervas, and Reuben, During the Hard Winter of 1734, Longmans, Green, 1889, Harper, 1889, edited by Virginia Kirkus, illustrations by Henry C. Pitz, Harper, 1929.
The White Company (serialized in *Cornhill* magazine, 1891), Smith, Elder, 1891, Lovell, 1891, Burt, c. 1982.

The Refugees: A Tale of Two Continents (serialized in *Harper's Monthly* magazine, 1893), Longmans, Green, 1893, illustrations by T. De Thulstrup, Harper, 1893, J. Murray, 1960.

The Great Shadow (first published in *Arrowsmith's Christmas Annual*, 1892), Arrowsmith, 1893, Harper, 1893, reprinted, 1920.

Uncle Bernac: A Memory of the Empire, illustrations by Robert Sauber, Smith, Elder, 1897, Appleton, 1897, illustrations by John Mackay, J. Murray, 1968.

Sir Nigel (sequel to *The White Company;* serialized in *Strand* magazine, 1905-06), illustrations by Arthur Twidle, Smith, Elder, 1906, illustrations by the Kinneys, McClure, Phillips, 1906, Hart Publishing, 1976.

Sir Arthur Conan Doyle: The Historical Romances, two volumes, New Orchard England, 1986.

SHORT STORIES

Mysteries and Adventures, Scott, 1890, published as *The Gully of Bluemansdyke and Other Stories*, Scott, 1892, published as *My Friend the The Captain of the Polestar and Other Tales*, Longmans, Green, 1890, Munro, 1894, reprinted, Books for Libraries Press, 1970.

Murderer and Other Mysteries and Adventures, Lovell, Coryell, 1893, reprinted, Books for Libraries Press, 1971.

(With Campbell Rae Brown) *An Actor's Duel* [and] *The Winning Shot* (the former by Brown, the latter by Doyle), Dicks, 1894.

Round the Red Lamp: Being Facts and Fancies of Medical Life (horror), Methuen, 1894, Appleton, 1894, reprinted, Books for Libraries Press, 1969.

The Surgeon of Gaster Fell (also see below), Ivers, 1895.

The Exploits of Brigadier Gerard (adventure), illustrations by W. B. Wollen, Newnes, 1896, Appleton, 1896, reprinted, J. Murray, 1976.

The Green Flag and Other Stories of War and Sport, Smith, Elder, 1900, McClure, Phillips, 1900, reprinted, Books for Libraries Press, 1969.

Adventures of Gerard, illustrations by W. B. Wollen, Newnes, 1903, McClure, Phillips, 1903, reprinted with introduction by Elizabeth Longford, J. Murray, 1976.

Round the Fire Stories, Smith, Elder, 1908, McClure, 1908.

One Crowded Hour (also see below), Paget, 1911.

The Last Galley: Impressions and Tales, illustrations by N. C. Wyeth and Rountree, Smith, Elder, 1911, Doubleday, Page, 1911, reprinted, J. Murray, 1931.

Danger! And Other Stories, J. Murray, 1918, Doran, 1919 (see above).

Tales of the Ring and Camp, J. Murray, 1922, published as *The Croxley Master and Other Tales of the Ring and Camp*, Doran, 1925.

Tales of Terror and Mystery, Murray, 1922; published as *The Black Doctor and Other Tales of Terror and Mystery*, Doran, 1925, reprinted, Buccaneer Books, 1982.

Tales of Twilight and the Unseen, J. Murray, 1922, published as *The Great Keinplatz Experiment and Other Tales of Twilight and the Unseen*, Doran, 1925.

Tales of Adventure and Medical Life, J. Murray, 1922, published as *The Man from Archangel and Other Tales of Adventure*, Doran, 1925, reprinted, Books for Libraries Press, 1969.

Tales of Long Ago, J. Murray, 1922, published as *The Last of the Legions and Other Tales of Long Ago*, Doran, 1925.

The Three of Them: A Reminiscence, J. Murray, 1923.

The Macarot Deep and Other Stories, J. Murray, 1929, Doubleday, Doran, 1929.

Complete Professor Challenger Stories, Transatlantic, 1952.

Uncollected Stories: The Unknown Conan Doyle, compiled with an introduction by John Michael Gibson and Richard Lancelyn Green, Secker & Warburg, 1982.

Conan Doyle Stories, Hippocrene Books, 1985.

PLAYS

(With J. M. Barrie) *Jane Annie; or, The Good Conduct Prize* (comic opera; first produced in London at Savoy Theatre, May 13, 1893), Chappell, 1893.

"Foreign Policy" (one-act; based on own short story "A Question of Diplomacy"), first produced in London at Terry's Theatre, June 3, 1893.

Waterloo (one-act; based on own short story "A Straggler of '15"; first produced as "A Story of Waterloo" in Bristol, England, at Prince's Theatre, September 21, 1894), Samuel French, 1907.

"Halves" (prologue and three acts; based on story of same title by James Payn), first produced in Aberdeen, Scotland, at Her Majesty's Theatre, April 10, 1899.

(With William Gillette) *Sherlock Holmes* (four-act; based on Doyle's short story "The Strange Case of Miss Faulkner; first produced in London at Duke of York's Theatre, June 12, 1899; produced in Buffalo, N.Y., at Star Theatre, October 23, 1899; produced Off-Broadway at Garrick Theatre, November 6, 1899), Samuel French, 1922.

A Duet (A Duologue) (one-act comedy; based on own novel *A Duet with an Occasional Chorus;* first produced in London at Steinway Hall, October 27, 1902), Samuel French, 1903.

"Brigadier Gerard" (four-act comedy), first produced in London at Imperial Theatre, March 3, 1906; produced in New York City at Savoy Theatre, November 5, 1906.

"The Fires of Fate" (four-act; based on own novel *The Tragedy of the Korosko*), first produced in Liverpool, England, at Shakespeare Theatre, June 11, 1909; produced in New York City at Liberty Theatre, December 28, 1909.

"The House of Temperley," first produced in London at Adelphi Theatre, February 11, 1910.

"A Pot of Caviare" (one-act; based on own short story of same title), first produced in London at Adelphi Theatre, April 19, 1910.

The Speckled Band: An Adventure of Sherlock Holmes (three-act; based on own short story "The Adventure of the Speckled Band"; first produced in London at Adelphi Theatre, June 4, 1910; produced Off-Broadway at Garrick Theatre, November 21, 1910; produced on the West End at *Strand* Theatre, February 6, 1911), Samuel French 1912.

The Crown Diamond (one-act; first produced in Bristol, England, at the Hippodrome, May 2, 1921), privately printed, 1958.

It's Time Something Happened (one-act), Appleton, 1925.

Exile: A Drama of Christmas Eve (one-act), Appleton, 1925.

Also author of "Angels of Darkness" (three-act), "Sir Charles Tregellis," "Admiral Denver," "The Stonor Case," "The Lift," and "Mrs. Thompson" (based on the novel of the same title by W. B. Maxwell).

WORKS ON SPIRITUALISM

The New Revelation, Hodder & Stoughton, 1918, Doran, 1918.

The Vital Message, Hodder & Stoughton, 1919, Doran, 1919.

Spiritualism and Rationalism, Hodder & Stoughton, 1920.

The Wanderings of a Spiritualist, Hodder & Stoughton, 1921, Doran, 1921.

The Evidence for Fairies, Doran, 1921.

Fairies Photographed, Doran, 1921.

The Coming of the Fairies, Hodder & Stoughton, 1922, Doran, 1922, reprinted, Weiser, 1972.

(With others) *The Case for Spirit Photography,* preface by Fred Barlow, Hutchinson, 1922, Doran, 1923.

Our American Adventure, Hodder & Stoughton, 1923, Doran, 1923.

(Compiler) *The Spiritualists' Reader,* Two Worlds, 1924.

Our Second American Adventure, Hodder & Stoughton, 1924, Little, Brown, 1924.

(Contributor) James Marchant, editor, *Survival,* Putnam, 1924, Doyle's contribution published separately as *Psychic Experiences,* Putnam, 1925.

The History of Spiritualism, two volumes, Cassell, 1926, Doran, 1926, reprinted, Arno Press, 1975.

Pheneas Speaks: Direct Spirit Communications in the Family Circle, Psychic Press, 1927, Doran, 1927.

Our African Winter, J. Murray, 1929.

The Roman Catholic Church: A Rejoinder, Psychic Press, 1929.

The Edge of the Unknown (essays), J. Murray, 1930, Putnam, 1930, reprinted, Berkley Publishing, 1968.

OTHER

Songs of Action (poetry; also see below), Smith, Elder, 1898, Doubleday & McClure, 1898.

The Great Boer War, Smith, Elder, 1900, McClure, Phillips, 1900, reprinted, Struik, 1976.

The War in South Africa: Its Cause and Conduct, Smith, Elder, 1902, McClure, Phillips, 1902.

The Story of Mr. George Edalji, privately printed, 1907, published as *The Case of Mr. George Edalji,* Blake, 1907.

Through the Magic Door (criticism), illustrations by W. Russell Flint, Smith, Elder, 1907, McClure, 1908, Doubleday, Page, 1925.

The Crime of the Congo, Hutchinson, 1909, Doubleday, Page, 1909.

Songs of the Road (poetry; also see below), Smith, Elder, 1911, Doubleday, Page, 1911.

The Case of Oscar Slater, Hodder & Stoughton, 1912.

Great Britain and the Next War, Small, Maynard, 1914.

To Arms!, preface by F. E. Smith, Hodder & Stoughton, 1914.

The German War (essays), Hodder & Stoughton, 1914.

Western Wanderings, Doran, 1915.

A Visit to Three Fronts: June, 1916, Hodder & Stoughton, 1916, published as *A Visit to Three Fronts: Glimpses of the British, Italian, and French Lines,* Doran, 1916.

The Origin and Outbreak of the War, Doran, 1916.

The British Campaign in France and Flanders, six volumes, Hodder & Stoughton, 1916-20, Doran, 1916-20, enlarged edition published as *The British Campaigns in Europe, 1914-1919,* Bles, 1928.

The Guards Came Through and Other Poems (also see below), J. Murray, 1919, Doran, 1920.

The Poems of Arthur Conan Doyle: Collected Edition (contains *Songs of Action, Songs of the Road,* and *The Guards Came Through and Other Poems*), J. Murray, 1922.

Memories and Adventures (autobiography), Hodder & Stoughton, 1924, Little, Brown, 1924, reprinted, Darby, 1983.

Strange Studies From Life: Containing Three Hitherto Uncollected Tales Based on the Annals of True Crime, additional material by Philip Trevor, edited with an introduction by Peter Ruber, Candlelight Press, 1963.

Essays on Photography: The Unknown Conan Doyle, compiled with an introduction by John Michael Gibson and Richard Lancelyn Green, Secker & Warburg, 1982.

Letters to the Press, edited by and R. L. Green, University of Iowa Press, 1986.

Contributor of works such as "The Truth About Sherlock Holmes" in a variety of genres to many magazines and newspapers, including *Strand, Chambers's Journal, Harper's, Blackwood's, Saturday Evening Post, McClure's, London Society, Cornhill, Lippincott's, Boston Herald, Philadelphia Inquirer, St. Louis Post-Dispatch,* and *New York Times.* Translator from the French of *The Mystery of Joan of Arc* by Leon Denis, J. Murray, 1924, Dutton, 1925.

SIDELIGHTS: Sir Arthur Conan Doyle was not a great writer, but he created one of the most famous characters in the history of fiction. Indeed, the name of Sherlock Holmes is synonymous with detective; and the deerstalker cap and calabash pipe suggest Holmes to people all over the world, even to those who have never read any of the four novels and fifty-six short stories Doyle wrote about him. Yet those kinds of cap and pipe are not mentioned and the phrase "Elementary, my dear Watson" is never uttered in any of the sixty tales. Many who are familiar with Sherlock Holmes have never heard of Arthur Conan Doyle; to countless others, Doyle is known only as the author of the Holmes stories.

What is true today was also very largely true during Doyle's lifetime, and this fact did not make him happy. He felt that he had better things to offer the world of literature than a series of detective stories; in particular, he thought that his greatest achievements in fiction were his historical novels. Outside the realm of fiction, he believed that his most important writings were those in which he attempted to prove the truth of spiritualism and communication with the dead, a cause to which he devoted the last eleven years of his life. Doyle was so afraid that Holmes would distract his own and his readers' attention from what he considered his more important work that he killed the detective in one story, only to be forced by public demand to resurrect him later.

Although Doyle was not a great writer who communicated profound truths about the human condition, he was a good writer, with four principal areas of strength. First, his style was vigorous, clear, and readable. In fact, as he himself declared in a 1923 *Collier's* essay, "The Truth About Sherlock Holmes," his style might have been too clear: "I cultivate a simple style and avoid long words so far as possible, and it may be that this surface of ease has sometimes caused the reader to underrate the amount of real research which lies in all my historical novels." As one of his biographers, Ronald Pearsall, put it in *Conan Doyle: A Biographical Solution:* "Doyle's style hardly altered for forty years. He sat down and wrote, unworried by the hesitations and concern for literary propriety that make 'artistic' novelists of his time (such as George Moore) almost unreadable. He was never brainwashed by 'fine writing.' " Judging by the almost complete absence of revisions in his extant manuscripts, this style was as easy for him to write as it is to read.

Second, Doyle was able, through concise, sensuous description, to evoke atmosphere and a sense of place. Even today, tourists who visit London for the first time after reading the Sherlock Holmes stories often experience a feeling of familiarity, as though they had been there before. In the most famous of the Holmes novels, *The Hound of the Baskervilles* (1902), the eeriness of the moors is vividly conveyed, and in certain passages of Doyle's historical novels, the reader is almost thrust bodily into the clang and crash of medieval hand-to-hand combat.

Third, Doyle could create memorable characters who, though not realistically drawn, are endowed with such striking personalities that they seem more real than many actual people. This believability applies not only to Sherlock Holmes, to whom mail, bearing his fictitious address, 221B Baker Street, London, is still sent, but applies also to such other Doyle heroes as Brigadier Etienne Gerard, Professor George Edward Challenger, and Sir Nigel Loring. At the same time, however, many of the minor characters in Doyle's fiction are not well defined or seem to be mere stock types: the innocent young woman, the unregenerate villain, the loyal companion, the stolid but bumbling Scotland Yard official.

Fourth, and perhaps most important, Doyle was a master storyteller. Even his weaker fictional efforts hold the reader's interest; when his plots are hackneyed and contain no real surprises which is sometimes the case, even though Doyle prided himself on his ability to devise ingenious plots-the reader is carried along by the sheer power of the storyteller's art. In fact, this talent, like his lucid style, produced repercussions that were unwanted by Doyle: his historical novels, which he intended as authentic recreations of life in earlier periods and which were supposed to educate Englishmen in the history of their country, were treated by reviewers only as exciting adventure yarns.

Doyle was a professional writer, in the most complete sense of that term. After he gave up the practice of medicine in 1891, he lived and supported a large family on the income from his writing alone. By the 1920's he was the most highly paid writer in the world, commanding ten shillings a word. Market considerations occasionally entered into his decisions about what to write—especially in regard to the Sherlock Holmes stories, for which he was offered so much money that he was virtually forced to write them. But for the most part, he wrote what he wanted to write, and his choice was usually in harmony with what the public in Britain and America wanted to read. Most of his works appeared first in magazines and then in book form so that he was paid twice for each. His short stories were published in magazines and then collected in books; his novels were usually serialized in periodicals before appearing between hard covers. Doyle was also a professional author in the sense that he wrote almost constantly: on trains, in cabs, while posing for photographs, while carrying on a conversation at a party. According to his biographers, in his younger days, he could write without being distracted by one of his daughters crawling across his desk or even tearing up his manuscripts; later, he spent long hours behind a closed study door through which his children knew better than to try to enter. He kept diaries and notebooks, and most of his experiences and travels sooner or later provided material for published articles and books.

Doyle was also a professional in that he wrote in virtually every form and genre: detective stories, historical novels, science fiction, horror stories, domestic comedy, sports stories, poetry, and plays; he even collaborated on an operetta—one of his few failures. A significant portion of his writing was nonfiction, to which he brought the same stylistic and storytelling skills that made his fiction so popular. He was knighted not, as many people suppose, for writing the Sherlock Holmes stories, but for his pamphlet defending British actions in South Africa during the Boer War of 1899 to 1902. He also wrote histories of that war and of World War I, articles on military preparedness, literary criticism, histories and defenses of spiritualism, and vindications of men unjustly convicted of crimes.

In spite of his prodigious literary output, Doyle was by no means a retiring, closeted intellectual. He was a man of action, large in stature—six feet two inches tall, two hundred ten pounds in his prime—and an all-around athlete, proficient in rugby, boxing, and cricket; Doyle, his biographers claim, introduced the sport of skiing into Switzerland. Too old to fight in the Boer War, he served as a surgeon with a privately financed hospital near the front in South Africa. During World War I, he organized a volunteer rifle company—the forerunner of the modern Home Guard—and toured the front lines to gather material for his history of the conflict.

Doyle was a true man of his time: until his obsession with spiritualism began to make him look somewhat foolish, he was regarded on both sides of the Atlantic as the very symbol of British probity, stolidity, and common sense. He shared the prejudices of his time and place in his unswerving support of the British Empire, his steadfast opposition to women's suffrage, his unquestioning acceptance of the class system, and his hostility to labor unions and Mormons. On the other hand, he was a man behind his time in that he believed in and guided his behavior by a knightly code of honor. But he was also ahead of his time: he kept abreast of scientific discoveries, and he wrote articles and stories predicting the advent of such phenomena as television and submarine warfare.

Doyle started out as a doctor rather than a writer. While attending Edinburgh University in the late 1870s, he met Dr. Joseph Bell, a surgeon who was able to deduce his patients' occupations and other information from observing their appearance; Bell became the model for Sherlock Holmes, as professor of physiology William Rutherford did for another Doyle character, Professor Challenger. To help pay for his education, Doyle worked during vacations as an assistant to various doctors. The nephew of one of these physicians told Doyle that his letters were so vivid he ought to try to write something to sell. This encouragement launched Doyle's professional writing career. His first story was rejected, but the second, "The Mystery of Sasassa Valley," appeared anonymously in *Chambers's Journal* in 1879. It is the tale of three young adventurers in South Africa who investigate a native superstition about a demon with a glowing red eye and discover a huge diamond. Another story, "The American's Tale," written in imitation of Bret Harte, was published in the Christmas, 1880, issue of *London Society*.

Doyle indulged his taste for real-life adventure by signing on as a ship's surgeon on a seven-month Arctic whaling and sealing expedition in 1880; as Pearsall comments, "his whaler types crop up time and time again in his stories, sometimes dressed up in army uniform." After receiving his Bachelor of Medicine degree in 1881, he sailed to Africa as a surgeon on a freighter. On his return, he wrote an account of the voyage for the *British Journal of Photography* and submitted short stories for publication in *London Society* and *Blackwood's*.

In 1886 Doyle decided to try his hand at a detective novel. He said later that all the detective fiction he had read was unsatisfactory because the solution of the mystery was made to depend on chance or on some flash of intuition by the detective; Doyle, as he declared in "The Truth about Sherlock Holmes," wanted to try to "reduce this fascinating but unorganized business to something nearer to an exact science." Influenced by Poe's Dupin stories, the Lecoq novels of Emile Gaboriau, and Sergeant Cuff in Wilkie Collins's *The Moonstone* (1868), Doyle began work on a novel he called "A Tangled Skein." His notes reveal that his detective protagonist was originally to be called "Sherrinford Holmes" and the narrator "Ormond Sacker"; but these names were quickly replaced by "Sherlock Holmes" and "John H. Watson, M.D.," and the title of the novel became *A Study in Scarlet*.

Doyle wrote the novel in three weeks during March and April, 1886, and sent it to the *Cornhill;* the editor, James Payn, liked but rejected it because it was too long to publish in one issue and too short to serialize. The novel was accepted by Ward, Lock for publication in their *Beeton's Christmas Annual* for 1887, more than a year away. They paid Doyle twenty-five pounds for the complete rights to the story—the only money he ever received for it. When *A Study in Scarlet* appeared, it caused no great stir; but the 1887 edition of *Beeton's Christmas Annual* sold out—it is now one of the rarest and most valuable publications in the world—and the novel received complimentary reviews in minor journals and newspapers. Ward, Lock republished it in book form in 1888 with six illustrations by Doyle's father, who had been in an asylum suffering from alcoholism since 1879.

In July 1887, Doyle started work on the first of his historical novels, *Micah Clarke,* dealing with the Duke of Monmouth's rebellion against his father, Charles II, in the seventeenth century. According to John Dickson Carr in *The Life of Sir Arthur Conan Doyle,* "The power of Micah Clarke, aside from its best action scenes—the bloodhounds on Salisbury Plain, the brush with the King's Dragoons, the fight in Wells Cathedral, the blinding battlepiece at Sedgemoor—still lies in its characterization: that other imagination, the use of homely detail, by which each character grows into life before ever a shot is fired in war." Charles Higham points out in *The Adventures of Conan Doyle: The Life of the Creator of Sherlock Holmes,* that "the descriptions of war have a remarkable intensity, being alive with the author's love of battle"—at this time Doyle had never experienced a real war—but says that "the book suffers from deliberately antiquated 'period' diction in the dialogue and some of the descriptive material." Like many of Doyle's fictional works, the novel is narrated in the first person in this case by Micah, a supporter of Monmouth. Doyle later claimed to have spent two years in research and five months in writing the book.

Micah Clarke received enthusiastic reviews when it was published in February, 1889, and Doyle immediately began work on another historical novel, *The White Company,* set in the fourteenth century. Between researching and writing *The White Company,* Doyle received an offer from the American editor of *Lippincott's* magazine, which was published in both Philadelphia and London, for another Sherlock Holmes story. The proposal was made at a dinner in London that was also attended by Oscar Wilde; out of this meeting came both Doyle's *The Sign of Four* and Wilde's *The Picture of Dorian Gray* (1891). *The Sign of Four*—published in the United States as *The Sign of the Four*—is set in 1888 and involves an Indian treasure, a one-legged man, a vicious Pygmy with a deadly blowgun, a character closely modeled on Oscar Wilde, and a chase down the Thames River in a motor launch. *The Sign of Four* appeared complete in one issue of *Lippincott's* and also in book form in 1890. It was well received, particularly in America, but the sensational popularity of Sherlock Holmes was yet to come.

After writing *The Sign of Four,* Doyle went back to *The White Company.* The novel follows the adventures in England, France, and Spain of the knight Sir Nigel Loring, his squire Alleyne Edricson, Edricson's friend John of Hordle, and the bowman Samkin Aylward. As Higham says, it is "somewhat dated today" but is "vigorously told and scrupulously accurate." Doyle felt that the novel illuminated the national traditions of England and revealed for the first time the significance of the rise of the longbowman. He was disturbed that critics regarded it simply as a rousing adventure story. *The White Company* was serialized in the *Cornhill* before appearing in book form in 1891, and went through numerous editions.

In 1891, Doyle set himself up as an eye specialist in London, though he never attracted a single patient. Instead, he contributed a humorous story about a phonograph, "The Voice of Science," to the March, 1891, issue of a new illustrated monthly, the *Strand.* Doyle soon realized that a series of stories with a continuing central character could build reader loyalty for the magazine; since he had already created Sherlock Holmes, he quickly wrote six short stories featuring Holmes. When the first of these, "A Scandal in Bohemia," appeared in the July, 1891, issue of the *Strand,* the phenomenal popularity of Sherlock Holmes began. Doyle received thirty-five pounds for each story.

The stories were illustrated by Sidney Paget, whom the editors had hired by mistake, thinking that they were getting his better-known brother Walter. Sidney Paget did as much as Doyle to establish the image of Sherlock Holmes that stands today. He made Holmes handsomer than Doyle's original conception; he also introduced the deerstalker cap, which actually appears in the illustrations for only eight of the thirty-eight stories for which Paget provided art work before his death in 1908; in the rest of the pictures Holmes wears various types of headgear, including toppers, felt hats, bowlers, homburgs, and even a straw boater; Doyle himself gives his detective a "close-fitting cloth cap" in one story and an "ear-flapped traveling cap" in another.

After the first few Holmes stories had appeared in the *Strand,* Doyle found himself nationally famous. He therefore decided to give up medicine, take up residence in the suburbs, and live entirely by his pen. When the editors of the *Strand* asked for more Holmes stories beyond the original six, Doyle, who had other projects in mind, set a price for the work that he was sure would be rejected. Instead, his demand for fifty pounds per story was immediately accepted. He dashed off six more stories at the rate of about two per week, then turned to another historical novel, *The Refugees,* which was serialized and then published in book form in 1893. Doyle was never very happy with the novel, though Carr says that "the adventure-scenes in the great forests have never been surpassed for sheer vividness and power of action. They have diabolical reality, as though painted Indian-faces really did look through a suburban window." But even Carr admits that "it is an uneven book," and Pearsall says that "readers of the *Strand* and posterity did not give, and have not given, a button for the epoch of Louis XIV and the boring misadventures of the Huguenots as laid out, in all their detail, in *The Refugees.*" In the same period Doyle wrote his first dramatic work: a one-act play based on his short story "A Straggler of '15," which had appeared in *Harper's Weekly* in March, 1891. He sent the play to actor and theatre manager Henry Irving, who changed the title to "A Story of Waterloo" and performed it successfully on tour in 1894 and at his Lyceum Theatre in London in 1896.

The first twelve Holmes stories were collected as *The Adventures of Sherlock Holmes,* and the *Strand* asked for more. Hoping to quiet the editors' requests, Doyle demanded what he considered an outrageous amount, £1,000 for another dozen stories. Again, the editors accepted. While working on these stories, the incredibly productive Doyle wrote a novel about suburban life, *Beyond the City,* and another historical novel, *The Great Shadow.* Higham calls the latter work "tedious," though Carr says that the description of the Battle of Waterloo at the end "rings in the ears and stifles the nostrils with gun smoke." Doyle also helped his friend James Barrie, who had fallen ill, complete an operetta, *Jane Annie; or, The Good Conduct Prize,* which was a resounding failure when it was performed at the Savoy Theatre in May, 1893.

In the fall of 1893, Doyle's wife, Louise, was diagnosed as having tuberculosis and given only months to live; in fact, she survived for thirteen years. Burdened with concern for his wife, tired of inventing new plots for the Holmes stories, and convinced that his detective was consuming the time and attention due his "better" work, Doyle killed Holmes in "The Final Problem," the last of the twelve stories he had promised the *Strand.* In this story, set in April, 1891 Holmes and Watson are pursued to Switzerland by the arch-criminal Professor James Moriarty, whose gang has been destroyed through Holmes's efforts. Watson returns to the brink of the Reichenbach Falls, after having been called away on a ruse, to find a note from Holmes and evidence that he and Moriarty have struggled and then fallen over the precipice to their deaths. When the story appeared in the *Strand* in December, 1893, twenty thousand readers canceled their subscriptions, businessmen dressed in mourning, and Doyle received letters addressing him as "You Brute." Unremorseful, Doyle collected the second twelve Holmes stories as *The Memoirs of Sherlock Holmes* and wrote *The Stark Munro Letters,* an autobiographical novel, based on Doyle's experiences with Dr. Budd, that contains some of his best comedy but ends when the protagonist and his wife are killed in a railroad accident.

Doyle then wrote the first series of Brigadier Gerard stories for the *Strand.* Gerard was based on the real-life French General Baron de Marbot, whose memoirs Doyle had read in 1892. The two series of stories, collected as *The Exploits of Brigadier Gerard* and *Adventures of Gerard,* form in Carr's judgment "the finest picture he ever did of the Napoleonic campaigns. And the reason is this: that he saw it through the eyes of a Frenchman." Gerard's "naive boasting, his complacence, his firm conviction that every woman is in love with him, all blind the reader with mirth. Above everything, his serene good nature never fails. He curls his side-whiskers, gives his mustache the Marengo twist, and rides living out of the page." The stories are exciting and frequently hilarious—sometimes with a grim humor, as characters are run through with swords or decapitated—and Gerard is one of Doyle's most memorable creations.

In 1897 Doyle wrote a play about Sherlock Holmes, which he sent to actor Beerbohm Tree. When Tree wanted the part of Holmes rewritten to suit himself, Doyle refused. His agent then sent the manuscript to a New York impresario, who gave it to American actor William Gillette. Gillette rewrote the play as a melodrama based on several of Doyle's stories, and Doyle's original manuscript has been lost. According to Carr and Higham, Gillette cabled Doyle, "May I marry Holmes?" Doyle replied, "You may marry him or murder him or do whatever you like with him." Gillette did not write into the play a marriage for Holmes, although—equally out of character for the reasoning machine Doyle had created—Gillette's Holmes did fall in love.

In the spring of 1898 Doyle began a new series of stories for the *Strand* which were collected as *Round the Fire Stories.* One of these, "The Lost Special," in which a train vanishes without a trace between stations, is, according to Carr, "by far his finest mystery (as distinguished from detective) story." In the fall, he wrote *A Duet with an Occasional Chorus,* a warm, gentle, humorous look at the ordinary life of a middle-class suburban couple. The book was always one of his favorites; he refused to allow it to be serialized, because he thought serialization would ruin it. Though H. G. Wells and Algernon Charles Swinburne admired it, the novel was too great a departure from what the public and critics expected from Doyle, and it was not successful.

When fighting broke out in South Africa between the governing British colonists and the Dutch-descended settlers known as the Boers, Doyle was too old at forty-one to enlist as a soldier. He instead served for three months in 1900 as a doctor in a private military hospital in Bloemfontein, South Africa. On his return to England he wrote *The Great Boer War,* an accurate and impartial history of the conflict up to that time. The book was and is highly respected; but its final chapter advocating the modernization of the British army—an argument he had earlier presented in the *Cornhill*—predictably earned him the scorn of the military establishment. However, all of the reforms he proposed were subsequently adopted. Later, angered by charges that the British committed atrocities during the Boer War, Doyle wrote in one week a sixty-thousand-word pamphlet in rebuttal. Published in January, 1902, *The War in South Africa: Its Cause and Conduct* was sold for sixpence per copy in Britain; thousands of translations were given away in France, Russia, Germany, and other countries. All profits from the sale of the book were donated to charity. For producing this propaganda triumph, Doyle was knighted on August 9, 1902.

In March, 1901, Doyle went on a golfing holiday with Fletcher Robinson, who told him the legend of a ghostly hound from Robinson's native Dartmoor, in Devonshire. After a trip to Dartmoor with Robinson, Doyle began writing what he called "a real creeper" of a novel based on the legend. Almost as an afterthought, he decided to use Sherlock Holmes in the novel, titled *The Hound of the Baskervilles;* but he was careful to set the story in 1899, before Holmes's death in the Reichenbach Falls. According to Carr, *The Hound of the Baskervilles* "is the only tale, long or short, in which the story dominates Holmes rather than Holmes dominating the story; what captures the reader is less the Victorian detective than the Gothic romance."

While *The Hound of the Baskervilles* was being serialized in the *Strand,* Gillette's play, *Sherlock Holmes,* which had already been a hit in the United States, opened in London with equal success. Gillette went on to make a career of portraying Holmes, which he did until he was an elderly man. It was he who was responsible for the popular conception of the detective puffing on a curved-stem pipe, which he adopted because it was easy for him to use on stage; over the years, cartoonists exaggerated the pipe into the monstrous calabash. In fact, the only pipes mentioned in the Doyle stories are a brier, a long-stemmed cherrywood, and an oily black clay.

In 1903 *McClure's* magazine in New York offered Doyle $5,000 per story if he would bring Sherlock Holmes back to life, and the *Strand* offered more than half that amount for the British rights. Persuaded by these astronomical sums, Doyle agreed. In "The Empty House," Holmes reappears in London and tells the shocked Watson that his knowledge of the Japanese martial art of baritsu enabled him to slip through Moriarty's grasp and that the evil professor had plunged into the Reichenbach Falls alone. For reasons that, upon close examination, do not make a great deal of sense, Holmes decided to fake his own death and disappear. He has returned in "The Empty House" to apprehend Moriarty's last remaining henchman, Colonel Sebastian Moran, "the most dangerous man in London." The story is set in April, 1894, meaning that Holmes had been away for three years; in actual time, it had been ten years since he had last shown himself in "The Final Problem."

The appearance of "The Empty House" in the *Strand* in October, 1903, created a sensation. Along with twelve more stories, which ran in the magazine until December 1904, it was collected in *The Return of Sherlock Holmes.* Holmes was as popular as ever, though some critics have contended that the stories written after what is known as "the Great Hiatus" are generally not up to the standard of the earlier ones. Doyle was aware of this opinion, and although he disagreed with it, he enjoyed reporting as he did in "The Truth About Sherlock Holmes"—the words of the Cornish boatman who said to him: "I think, sir, when Holmes fell over that cliff, he may not have killed himself, but all the same he was never quite the same man afterwards." Stephen Knight notes, in *Form and Ideology in Crime Fiction,* that some of the changes in the later Holmes stories correspond to changes in Doyle's own situation: "The older Doyle was a much more prosperous and prestigious man, and the later Sherlock Holmes becomes more respectable. . . . Holmes gives up cocaine, goes for healthy walks, gets on better with the police and is much less barbed towards Watson." Some of the stories Doyle wrote after reintroducing Holmes are set in the period after Holmes's return; others are purportedly records of cases that occurred before his disappearance.

Doyle very quickly wrote the tales that make up *The Return of Sherlock Holmes,* then turned to another historical novel. After a year of research and a year of writing, *Sir Nigel* began to run in the *Strand* in December, 1905. The book is what would now be called a "prequel" to *The White Company* and begins with Nigel Loring as a young man setting out to do three great deeds in order to be worthy of his lady. Doyle always considered the two novels about the fourteenth century to be his greatest work; but *Sir Nigel,* like its predecessor, was praised merely as an exciting adventure tale.

Inspired by learning of the discovery near his home in Sussex of fossilized dinosaur footprints, Doyle in the fall and winter of 1911 wrote *The Lost World,* the story of four adventurers who find living prehistoric animals and people on an isolated mesa in Brazil. The young, naive journalist-narrator Edward Malone; the thin, sardonic, pipe-puffing Professor Summerlee; the dashing hunter Lord John Roxton; and above all, the squat, powerful, bellowing sarcastic genius Professor George Edward Challenger are all vividly and memorably drawn characters. The story presents scenes of high comedy, as when Malone tries to pass himself off as a scientist on his first meeting with Challenger but is trapped by the professor's pseudo-scientific doubletalk, and scenes of high adventure on the mesa. Furthermore, Doyle's descriptions of the pterodactyls and dinosaurs are scientifically accurate. At the end of 1912, Doyle produced another novel about Professor Challenger and his three friends. In *The Poison Belt,* the earth passes through a poisonous zone in the "ether," and everyone in the world except the four heroes—who are supplied with oxygen in an airtight room—appears to have died. In the end, what seemed to be death turns out to have been suspended animation.

Doyle had completed by April, 1914, his final full-length Sherlock Holmes novel, *The Valley of Fear,* a locked-room murder mystery. As in *A Study in Scarlet,* a long central section, told in the third person, details the events in the past that led up to the crime; this section is set in the Pennsylvania coal fields and involves a terrorist labor organization, the "Scowrers," based on the real-life Molly Maguires. Though the interpolated section is a fine adventure story in itself, some critics have objected to the obvious anti-labor bias displayed by Doyle here. The first part of the novel, in which the murder is solved by Holmes, has been called by Carr—himself a writer of mystery novels—"a very nearly perfect piece of detective-story writing" and "our clearest example of Conan Doyle's contribution to the detective story." According to Carr, Doyle "invented the enigmatic clue, . . . the trick by which the detective—while giving you perfectly fair opportunity to guess—makes you wonder what in sanity's name he is talking about." Pearsall, on the other hand, points out that al-

though the murder takes place in a moated manor house, "there is something lacking in atmosphere. . . . Darkest Sussex was different from the darkest Devon of *The Hound of the Baskervilles.* . . . The action is restricted to the manor house, with the actors moving around, occasionally displaying emotion, searching a room or making pregnant remarks. . . . There is no need for Watson's trusty revolver." Pearsall concluded that the novel's "killer in a yellow coat riding a bicycle" is far from menacing. The story, set in the period before Holmes's disappearance at the Reichenbach Falls, gives Professor Moriarty a backstage role.

Doyle's response to the outbreak of World War I was characteristic: he both took direct action forming a volunteer rifle company in his area and visiting the front and wrote about it in articles, lectures, and several books, including the six-volume *The British Campaign in France and Flanders.* He brought Holmes into the war in "His Last Bow," in which the sixty-year-old detective comes out of retirement—he has been keeping bees on the Sussex Downs since 1903—to capture a German spy. (While working undercover, Holmes uses the alias "Altamont," Doyle's father's middle name.) The story was written in 1917 but is set just before the outbreak of the war in August, 1914. It was made the title piece in a collection of stories that had been appearing in the *Strand* at long intervals since 1908.

Sherlock Holmes' stories continued to appear at irregular intervals over the years, and in 1927 the last twelve of them were collected as *The Case-Book of Sherlock Holmes.* In the book's preface Doyle announced his intention to write no more of the stories: "I fear that Mr. Sherlock Holmes may become like one of those popular tenors who, having outlived their time, are still tempted to make repeated farewell bows to their indulgent audiences. This must cease and he must go the way of all flesh, material or imaginary." To stop writing the Holmes narratives had also been Doyle's intention when he wrote "The Final Problem" in 1893, but thirty-four years later he held to his resolution.

Exhausted from his travels and suffering from heart disease, Doyle died on July 7, 1930. The historical novels of which he was so proud are rarely read, but enjoyment is still derived from the Brigadier Gerard stories and *The Lost World.* The latter was made into a still well-regarded silent film in 1925 and has been the inspiration for other science-fiction films, including the classic "King Kong." But above all, of course, Doyle is known for the Sherlock Holmes novels and short stories. These have remained continually in print and have been translated into at least fifty-six languages. The characters of Holmes and Watson have been depicted in plays, motion pictures, radio and television programs, a musical comedy, a ballet, cartoons, and comic strips; and the instantly recognizable figure of Holmes has been used in advertisements for all sorts of products. Holmes is referred to in such literary works as James Joyce's *Finnegan's Wake;* poet T. S. Eliot's "Macavity: The Mystery Cat" is obviously based on Professor Moriarty; and the dialogue between Becket and the Second Tempter in Eliot's blank-verse play *Murder in the Cathedral* was consciously based on the Musgrave Ritual in Doyle's 1893 story of that name.

Perhaps the most remarkable aspect of the Holmes phenomenon is the tongue-in-cheek pseudo-scholarship that has grown up around the stories. The practitioners of this elaborate game—who call themselves Sherlockians or, in Britain, Holmesians—are educated, usually professional people. Adopting the pretense that Holmes really existed, that the stories are actual case reports written by Watson (or in two instances by Holmes himself), and that Doyle was merely Watson's literary agent, they study the sixty tales—called "the Canon"—to develop theories about un-recorded parts of the characters' lives and to try to explain away the main inconsistencies Doyle carelessly introduced into the stories. Among the questions that have been discussed are exact chronology of the cases, which university Holmes attended, the number of times Watson was married, the location of Watson's war wound or wounds (in *A Study in Scarlet* it is clearly in his shoulder; in *The Sign of Four* it is just as clearly in his leg), and why Watson's wife calls him "James" in "The Adventure of the Engineer's Thumb" when it was established in *A Study in Scarlet* that his name was John. Another perennial problem has been the exact location of Holmes's house in Baker Street, since the ad-dress 221B did not exist in the nineteenth century. Each theory is based on some hint in the stories—no matter how slender—and is buttressed with argument and evidence, including re-search in Victorian and Edwardian newspapers and almanacs. This tradition began in 1911 with Ronald Knox's paper "Studies in the Literature of Sherlock Holmes" and has been carried on in countless articles and books since then. In his two massive bibliographies, Ronald De Waal lists 4,457 such items through 1979. Some Sherlockians also try their hands at writing pas-tiches, or imitation Sherlock Holmes stories, copying the style of the originals as closely as possible. Some book-length pas-tiches, such as Nicholas Meyer's *The Seven-Per-Cent Solution*, have been commercially successful.

Beginning with the 1933 founding in New York of the Baker Street Irregulars (named for the street urchins who assist Holmes in three of the stories), Sherlockians have been organized in clubs in at least thirteen countries, including Australia, Burma, Denmark, Germany, Holland, New Zealand, Venezuela, Sweden, and Japan. In the United States, the clubs are known as "scion societies" and take their names from titles of the sto-ries, from cases alluded to by Watson but never recorded, or from something somehow connected with the stories: for exam-ple, the Greek Interpreters of East Lansing, Michigan; the Hounds of the Baskervilles of Chicago; the Naval Treaty of St. Louis; and the Red-Headed League of Westtown, Pennsylvania. These societies tend to come into and disappear from existence, but as of 1980 about two hundred of them were organized in the United States. In addition, two periodicals are devoted entirely to Sherlockian scholarship: the *Baker Street Journal*, published by the Baker Street Irregulars, and the *Sherlock Holmes Journal*, published by the Sherlock Holmes Society of London.

The Sherlock Holmes stories have also been the subject of analy-sis more serious than the playful pseudo-scholarship of the Sher-lockians. Stephen Knight, wruting in *Form and Ideology in Crime Fiction*, for example, has looked at them from a sociologi-cal perspective and has concluded that the stories became popu-lar because they gave fictional form to the world view, the hopes, and the fears of the late-Victorian middle-class readers of the *Strand*. According to Knight, Holmes represented the power of individualistic, scientific rationality to impose order on an in-creasingly chaotic world. In some of the stories Knight has also found symbolism personal to Doyle: in "The Man With the Twisted Lip," for instance, a respectable reporter discovers that he can earn more money for his family by disguising himself as a deformed beggar; the reporter's situation, Knight believes, rep-resents Doyle's recognition that he had prostituted his own liter-ary talent by writing the Holmes stories strictly for money. Doyle himself, as well as his most famous character, continues to be an object of fascination. In 1983, John Hathaway Winslow and Alfred Meyer, in a *Science 83* article, proposed the theory that Doyle was the perpetrator of the famous Piltdown Man

hoax in 1912. His motive was ostensibly to get revenge on the scientists who scoffed at his beloved spiritualism.

Yet although his "serious" fiction has not attracted the attention he desired, Doyle's creation of Sherlock Holmes has insured his immortality as a writer. No other character in the history of fic-tion has ever inspired such devotion and enthusiasm, and this fact must stand as a tribute to Doyle's talent. The Holmes stories were written carelessly, hastily, and almost always purely for money; but the unstudied and spontaneous nature of the narra-tives allowed Doyle's creative abilities to be exemplified more fully than did the historical novels for which he prepared so care-fully and on which he labored so arduously.

MEDIA ADAPTATIONS: Many of Doyle's works have been adapted for film, including *A Study in Scarlet, The Adventures of Sherlock Holmes, The Hound of the Baskervilles, His Last Bow, The Firm of Girdlestone*, and *The Exploits of Brigadier Ge-rard*. Doyle's writings have also been adapted for plays, televi-sion broadcasts, and filmstrips.

BIOGRAPHICAL/CRITICAL SOURCES:

BOOKS

Baring-Gould, William S., *Sherlock Holmes of Baker Street: A Life of the World's First Consulting Detective*, C. N. Potter, 1962.

Blackbeard, Bill, *Sherlock Holmes in America*, Abrams, 1981.

Brend, Gavin, *My Dear Holmes: A Study in Sherlock*, Allen & Unwin, 1951.

Brown, Ivor, *Conan Doyle: A Biography of the Creator of Sher-lock Holmes*, Hamilton, 1972.

Butters, Roger, *First Person Singular: A Review of the Life and Work of Sherlock Holmes, the World's First Consulting De-tective*, Vantage, 1984.

Carr, John Dickson, *The Life of Sir Arthur Conan Doyle*, Har-per, 1949.

Cawelti, John G., *Adventure, Mystery, and Romance: Formula Stories as Art and Popular Culture*, University of Chicago Press, 1976.

Cox, Dan R., *Arthur Conan Doyle*, Ungar, 1985.

Dakin, D. Martin, *A Sherlock Holmes Commentary*, Drake, 1972.

De Waal, Ronald Burt, *The World Bibliography of Sherlock Holmes and Dr. Watson*, Bramhall House, 1974.

De Waal, *The International Sherlock Holmes: A Companion to the World Bibliography of Sherlock Holmes and Dr. Watson*, Archon Books, 1980.

Dictionary of Literary Biography, Gale, Volume 18: *Victorian Novelists*, 1983, Volume 70: *British Mystery Writers, 1860-1919*, 1988.

Doyle, Adrian Conan, *The True Conan Doyle*, J. Murray, 1945.

Doyle, Sir Arthur Conan, *My Memories and Adventures*, Little, Brown, 1924, reprinted, Darby, 1983.

Dudley-Edwards, Owen, *The Quest for Sherlock Holmes: A Bio-graphical Study of Arthur Conan Doyle*, B & N Imports, 1983.

Eyles, Allen, *Sherlock Holmes: A Centenary Celebration*, Har-per, 1987.

Haining, Peter, editor, *The Sherlock Holmes Scrapbook*, New English Library, 1973.

Haining, editor, *A Sherlock Holmes Compendium*, Castle, 1980.

Haining, editor, *The Final Adventures of Sherlock Holmes*, Cas-tle, 1981.

Hall, Trevor H., *Sherlock Holmes: Ten Literary Studies*, Duck-worth, 1969.

Hall, *The Late Mr. Sherlock Holmes and Other Literary Studies,* Duckworth, 1971.

Hall, *Sherlock Holmes and His Creator,* St. Martin's, 1977, reprinted, 1983.

Hardwick, Michael and Mollie Hardwick, *The Man Who Was Sherlock Holmes,* J. Murray, 1964.

Hardwick, Michael and Mollie Hardwick, *The Sherlock Holmes Companion,* Bramhall House, 1977.

Harrison, Michael, *In the Footsteps of Sherlock Holmes,* Cassell, 1958.

Harrison, *The World of Sherlock Holmes,* Muller, 1973.

Higham, Charles, *The Adventures of Conan Doyle: The Life of the Creator of Sherlock Holmes,* Norton, 1976.

Holroyd, James Edward, editor, *Seventeen Steps to 221B: A Collection of Sherlockian Pieces by English Writers,* Allen & Unwin, 1967.

Keating, H. D. F., *Sherlock Holmes: The Man and His World,* Thames & Hudson, 1979.

Klinefelter, Walter, *The Origins of Sherlock Holmes,* Gaslight, 1983.

Knight, Stephen, *Form and Ideology in Crime Fiction,* Indiana University Press, 1980.

Lachtman, Howard, *Sherlock Slept Here: A Brief History of the Singular Adventures of Sir Arthur Conan Doyle in America, with Some Observations upon the Exploits of Mr. Sherlock Holmes,* Capra, 1985.

Lamond, John, *Arthur Conan Doyle: A Memoir,* J. Murray, 1931.

Morley, Christopher, editor, *Sherlock Holmes and Dr. Watson: A Textbook of Friendship,* Harcourt, 1944.

Pearsall, Ronald, Conan Doyle: A Biographical Solution, St. Martin's, 1977.

Pearson, Hesketh, *Conan Doyle: His Life and Art,* Methuen, 1943, reprinted, Taplinger, 1977.

Pointer, Michael, *The Public Life of Sherlock Holmes,* David & Charles, 1975.

Pointer, *The Sherlock Holmes File,* C. N. Potter, 1976.

Rodin, A. E. and Jack D. Key, *Medical Casebook of Doctor Arthur Conan Doyle: From Practitioner to Sherlock Holmes and Beyond,* Krieger, 1984.

Rosenberg, Samuel, *Naked Is the Best Disguise: The Death and Resurrection of Sherlock Holmes,* Bobbs-Merrill, 1974.

Sayers, Dorothy L., *Unpopular Opinions,* Gollancz, 1946.

Shreffler, Philip A., editor, *The Baker Street Reader: Cornerstone Writings About Sherlock Holmes,* Greenwood Press, 1984.

Starrett, Vincent, editor, *221B: Studies in Sherlock Holmes,* Macmillan, 1940.

Starrett, Vincent, *The Private Life of Sherlock Holmes,* University of Chicago Press, 1906, reprinted, Haskell House, 1971.

Tracy, Jack, *The Encyclopedia Sherlockiana,* Doubleday, 1977.

Van Liere, Edward J., *A Doctor Enjoys Sherlock Holmes,* Vantage, 1959.

PERIODICALS

American Scholar, autumn, 1968.

Blue Book, July, 1912, May, 1953.

Bookman, December, 1892, February, 1901, July, 1901, May, 1902, August, 1903, November, 1912, July, 1914, July, 1922, October, 1927, August, 1929.

Collier's, August 15, 1908, December 29, 1923.

Harper's, May, 1948.

Hudson Review, winter, 1949.

Les Nouvelles Litteraires (Paris), September 12, 1925.

Living Age, March 22, 1919, November 28, 1925.

Los Angeles Times, January 14, 1987, January 18, 1987.

Medical Times, July, 1971.

Modern Fiction Studies, spring, 1969.

New England Journal of Medicine, October 1, 1953.

Newsweek, August 24, 1959, November 18, 1974.

New Yorker, February 17, 1945.

New York Review of Books, August 17, 1978.

New York Times, March 9, 1952, January 17, 1987.

New York Times Book Review, April 2, 1944, January 21, 1968.

Pacific Quarterly, January, 1978.

Paris Match, August 8, 1959.

Playboy, December, 1966, January, 1975.

Punch, June 20, 1951.

Quarterly Review, July, 1904.

Reader, August, 1905.

San Francisco Review of Books, December, 1976, February, 1977, March, 1977.

Saturday Review, April 27, 1968.

Saturday Review of Literature, July 19, 1930, August 2, 1930, April 29, 1939, February 17, 1940.

Science 83, September, 1983.

Sports Illustrated, March 19, 1973.

Strand, August, 1892, September, 1930, August, 1943.

Texas Quarterly, summer, 1968.

Twentieth Century (London), May, 1901.

West Coast Review of Books, April, 1975.

Woman's Home Companion, November, 1930.

*   *   *

DOYLE, John
   See GRAVES, Robert (von Ranke)

*   *   *

Dr. A
   See ASIMOV, Isaac

*   *   *

DRABBLE, Margaret   1939-

PERSONAL: Born June 5, 1939, in Sheffield, England; daughter of John Frederick (a judge) and Kathleen Marie (Bloor) Drabble; married Clive Walter Swift (an actor with Royal Shakespeare Company), June, 1960 (divorced, 1975); married Michael Holroyd (an author and biographer), 1982; children: (first marriage) Adam Richard George, Rebecca Margaret, Joseph. *Education:* Newnham College, Cambridge, B.A. (first class honors), 1960.

ADDRESSES: Agent—A. D. Peters & Co. Ltd., 10 Buckingham St., London WC2N 6BU, England.

CAREER: Novelist, playwright, biographer, critic, editor, and short story writer. Member of Royal Shakespeare Company, one year.

MEMBER: National Book League (deputy chairperson, 1978-80; chairperson, 1980-82).

AWARDS, HONORS: John Llewelyn Rhys Memorial Award, 1966, for *The Millstone;* James Tait Black Memorial Book Prize, 1968, for *Jerusalem the Golden;* Book of the Year Award from *Yorkshire Post,* 1972, for *The Needle's Eye;* E. M. Forster Award from National Institute and American Academy of Arts and Letters, 1973; D.Litt. from University of Sheffield, 1976, University of Manchester, 1987, University of Keele, 1988, University of Bradford, 1988; *The Middle Ground* was named a notable book of 1980 by the American Library Association, 1981.

WRITINGS:

NOVELS

A Summer Bird-Cage, Weidenfeld & Nicolson, 1963, Morrow, 1964.

The Garrick Year, Weidenfeld & Nicolson, 1964, Morrow, 1965.

The Millstone, Weidenfeld & Nicolson, 1965, Morrow, 1966, published with new introduction by Drabble and editorial material compiled by Michael Marland, Longman, 1970, published as *Thank You All Very Much* (also see below), New American Library, 1973.

Jerusalem the Golden, Morrow, 1967.

The Waterfall, Knopf, 1969.

The Needle's Eye, Knopf, 1972.

The Realms of Gold, Knopf, 1975.

The Ice Age, Knopf, 1977.

The Middle Ground, Knopf, 1980.

The Radiant Way (first novel in a trilogy), Knopf, 1987.

A Natural Curiosity (second novel in a trilogy), Viking, 1989.

OTHER

Wordsworth (criticism), Evans Brothers, 1966, Arco, 1969.

"Thank You All Very Much" (screenplay; based on Drabble's novel, *The Millstone*), Columbia, 1969, released in England as "A Touch of Class," 1969.

(Editor with B. S. Johnson) *London Consequences* (group novel), Greater London Arts Association, 1972.

Arnold Bennett (biography), Knopf, 1974.

(Editor) Jane Austen, *Lady Susan, the Watsons and Sanditon,* Penguin, 1975.

(Editor) *The Genius of Thomas Hardy,* Knopf, 1976.

For Queen and Country: Britain in the Victorian Age, Deutsch, 1978, published as *For Queen and Country: Victorian England,* Houghton, 1979.

A Writer's Britain: Landscape and Literature, photographs by Jorge Lewinski, Knopf, 1979.

(General editor) *The Oxford Companion to English Literature,* 5th edition, Oxford University Press, 1985.

(Editor with Jenny Stringer) *The Concise Oxford Companion to English Literature,* Oxford University Press, 1987.

Also author of play, "Bird of Paradise," produced in London, 1969. Writer of dialogue, "Isadora," Universal, 1968, and of story for "A Roman Marriage," Winkast Productions. Author of television play, "Laura," produced by Granada Television, 1964. Contributor to numerous anthologies. Contributor to British literary journals, and to *Punch* and *Vogue.*

WORK IN PROGRESS: The third novel in her recent trilogy.

SIDELIGHTS: On the strength of her first three novels, *A Summer Bird-Cage* (1962), *The Garrick Year* (1964), and *The Millstone* (1965), Margaret Drabble made her reputation in the early 1960s as the preeminent novelist of the modern woman. Her first three protagonists share the attributes of what Drabble calls "the high-powered girls": they are all young, attractive, talented, and smart.

Two of them, Sarah Bennett of *A Summer Bird-Cage* and Rosamund Stacey of *The Millstone,* are, like Drabble herself, Oxbridge graduates. Sarah has given up the notion of going on to get a higher degree because "you can't be a sexy don," and she has spent a year rather aimlessly looking for something to do that is worthy of her talents and education. In the course of the novel, she considers her options, partly represented by her beautiful sister Louise, who has sacrificed any ambition she had to marry a rich, fussy, rather sexless man, and partly by her Oxford

friends, most of whom are working at dull jobs in London and falling short of their ambitions almost as badly as Louise is. In the end, Sarah is preparing to marry her long-time Oxford boyfriend, though she insists that she will "marry a don" as opposed to becoming "a don's wife." Rosamund, a Cambridge graduate, is more determined and less conventional. Not only does she earn her doctorate in English literature during the course of the novel, but she also becomes pregnant, has the baby on her own, and discovers the profound experience of mother-love at the same time.

At twenty-six, somewhat older than the other two characters and the mother of two small children, Emma Evans of *The Garrick Year* experiences more "adult" problems. Having just been offered a chance to escape from the domestic routine for part of the day by reading the news on television, she finds that she must move her family from London to Hereford, where her actor husband has a year's engagement with a provincial theatre company. There she tries to escape the even more intense boredom by having an affair with her husband's director. Like Rosamund, Emma finds that motherhood is the dominant factor in her life and that both she and her husband are bound to their marriage by that most important factor, the children.

Charles Burkhardt has remarked, "I do not believe anyone has written as intensely and movingly of pregnancy, childbirth, and young motherhood as Drabble, in her early novels, has." What makes her treatment of motherhood so important is the intense examination she gives it, the recognition that it is worthy of attention because it is the most significant event at that moment in the lives of the women she writes about, and by extension at some point in most of the lives of the women who in large part make up her readership. As Pamela Bromberg has noted, "Maternal love is, throughout Drabble, an agent of salvation both because she sees it as 'an image of unselfish love' and because it represents the fulfillment of biological destiny. Drabble understands and enjoys, as perhaps few other late twentieth century women writers do, the profound experience of rightness that many women find in their generativity."

Drabble's approach is compelling in its realism, however, because she does not blink at the extreme ambivalence her characters feel toward motherhood and the enforced domesticity accompanying it. Gail Cunningham has remarked that Drabble "seems to offer two main kinds of thematic focus, one through literary references . . . and the other through children; they reflect, in fact, the two extremes of the typical Margaret Drabble heroine, the brains and breasts dichotomy." As Valerie Myer has put it in *Margaret Drabble: Puritanism and Permissiveness,* "The woman undergraduate's interest is divided between her academic work and her feminine destiny, which at the university stage appears as though it will take the conventional social forms. The conflict is between the duty of the self-imposed task and instinct." The early Drabble heroine is constantly fighting the two opposing forces of ambition—the need to do something in the world, "the greater gifts, greater duty to society line," as she describes it in *A Summer Bird-Cage*—and the social and biological urge to get married and/or have babies.

Drabble's treatment of this most basic feminist dichotomy embodies an ambivalence that is reflected in feminist reaction to her work. Nancy Hardin has written in *Contemporary Literature* that "Drabble's novels are studies of human nature with the emphasis on feminine nature. That is not to say she is a feminist writer; she is too private a person and is not one who fits well into organizations or women's liberation groups." In one interview, Drabble said, "The women's movement is a phenomenon that got started after I got started, so I don't really see where I fit into it," and in another she remarked, "In some of my books I've tried to avoid writing as a woman because it does create its own narrowness." In some ways, a later novel, *The Middle Ground* (1980) is a critique of the women's movement. Its heroine, Kate Armstrong, has made her career writing journalistic pieces on women's issues. At forty-one, Kate confesses that she is "tired of women," and she makes disparaging references to well-known feminist documents such as Marilyn French's novel *The Women's Room.* Kate's views would seem to be in keeping with Drabble's statement in an interview that she is "not at all keen on the feminist view that there's a male conspiracy to put women down. I don't think that's true. Society is organized so that these collisions and disasters take place, which they have notably. There's no use pretending that marriage is in a good state or that the relations between the sexes are happy at the moment. It's no good blaming patriarchy or men for this. Both sexes are at fault."

Nonetheless, as Virginia Beards has pointed out in *Critique,* Drabble's novels show her sense of women's alienation from the system: "Bungled and achieved female self-definition is her consistent theme; her women might set out to pay homage to patriarchy's dearest forms but en route their increasing awareness of the absurdity of their sexual, social, and economic positions results in their befuddlement and defeat within the system. Only occasionally and in a limited sense do her women manage to infiltrate intellectually or economically the masculine milieu." Beards finds a positive quality in Drabble's having channeled her resistance to strict feminist doctrine into art: "She evidently lacks the idealism that active feminist politics demands while her awareness of human inequities needs no heightening through consciousness raising sessions. The conversion of the sexual protest into novels is what makes her interesting. The choices of artist over activist and imitation over frontal attack allow a subtlety and sensitivity that politics frequently precludes."

Not all feminists are as amenable to Drabble's chosen position, however. Elizabeth Fox-Genovese has severely criticized Drabble's treatment of women. She suggests in *Partisan Review* that *The Ice Age* (1977) "ends chillingly with a simple and total condemnation of female experience" and that "it has rendered explicitly the increasingly harsh repudiation of female being that has emerged through her rapid succession of novels." "Taken as a group," Fox-Genovese contends, "Drabble's women offer a picture of predatory narcissism, their occasional victimhood and suffering being, as Drabble acknowledges, no more than another way of getting what they want."

A middle ground is taken by Ellen Cronan Rose, who acknowledges that "what Drabble seems to find difficult, if not impossible, is giving her whole-hearted support to female characters who are radically feminist in their critique of patriarchy" and that "Drabble has done more than imagine what men must feel and believe and value; she has to some extent endorsed it." Rose finds Drabble's ambivalent treatment appropriate to some extent, however, for it reflects the ambivalence of the women she writes about and who form her readership. "Drabble seems not so much ordinary as exemplary. . . . For the women who constitute the bulk of her readership, her novels embody their own deep-seated ambivalence about feminism, with its exhilatory vision and its terrifying challenge."

The two novels that followed these early treatments of women, *Jerusalem the Golden* (1967) and *The Waterfall* (1969), represent a considerable development for Drabble as a novelist. Rose contends that *Jerusalem the Golden* is Drabble's "first wholly real-

ized novel, economical in its construction, finely precise in its characterization of the heroine. In later novels she will be more profound; never will she be more completely in control of her material than in this relatively early work."

Burkhardt has observed that Drabble's "efforts to liberate herself from the solipsistic constitute . . . the direction she's taken," and this drive is nowhere more evident than in *Jerusalem the Golden*'s determined expansion of subject beyond the individual to the social, familial, and physical environment. Clara Maugham is not an upper-middle-class Oxbridge type, but a working class girl from the north of England who has won for herself a scholarship to the University of London. Drabble's study of this "high-powered girl" and her eager pursuit of "the social joys" in her version of "Jerusalem the Golden," upperclass London, is also a study of Clara's working-class origins and values in confrontation with the world of the Denhams, the artistic and aristocratic family that provides her with her role-model Clelia and her lover Gabriel.

The Waterfall returns to the solipsistic protagonist, but treats her in a much more self-conscious way. The most "experimental" of Drabble's novels, *The Waterfall* has as its primary stylistic characteristic a divided narrative point of view. The first half of the book is in the third person, narrated from the point of view of the protagonist Jane Gray, a young woman on the verge of agoraphobia. She is the mother of a small child, and her husband has left her during the sixth month of her second pregnancy. The novel opens with the birth of her second child and her falling in love with her cousin's husband and continues with Jane's experience of the ensuing affair, which is presented as the highest and most consuming of passions. In the middle of the novel, however, Jane breaks out in the first person, exclaiming, "Lies, lies, it's all lies. A pack of lies. . . . What have I tried to describe? A passion, a love, an unreal life, a life in limbo, without anxiety, guilt, corpses." The two voices then alternate, the third-person narrator creating an intense and unreal story of passionate love and the first-person narrator training an objective, almost cynical eye on the novel's events and characters. In one sense, this split expresses a division that runs throughout Drabble's fiction, between a romantic yearning for coherence through love and a realistic skepticism prompted by the awareness of conflict and incoherence.

Critics have been divided both on the nature of the split in point of view and on its success. Writing in *Journal of Narrative Technique,* Caryn Fuoroli maintains that it results from Drabble's "inability to control narration" and that the novel fails because the technique keeps her from realizing "the full potential of her material." Myer, on the other hand, has written that *The Waterfall* is Drabble's "neatest exposition of her central concern, and paradoxically the most conclusive in its dramatized recognition that there is no true solution to the conflict between instinct and morality." Rose believes that the novel works because its point of view is a dramatization of the conflict of the woman artist: "She has divided herself into Jane, the woman (whose experience is liquid), and Jane Gray, the artist (who gives form, order, and shapeliness to that experience)." Rose contends in *Contemporary Literature* that this is the fundamental truth the novel succeeds in expressing: "In order to be whole (and wholly a woman), Drabble suggests, a woman must reconcile these divisions. And if a woman writer is to articulate this experience of what it is to be a woman, she must devise a form, as Drabble has done in *The Waterfall,* which amalgamates feminine fluidity and masculine shapeliness."

Drabble's use of passionate love, in the form of an obsessive dependence on Jane's lover James, as the force that makes unity out of this fundamental division has also been controversial. Joan Korenman has complained in *Critique* that, while "Jane is the first of Drabble's protagonists to enjoy sex," she fails "to make Jane's salvation through sexual passion compelling or convincing, let alone attractive. Jane remains almost pathologically helpless and cloyingly dependent on James." Drabble essentially agrees with this criticism. In one interview she called *The Waterfall* a "neurotic book," and in another she said, "*The Waterfall* is a wicked book, you see. . . . I can only respect the attack by people who say that you should not put into people's heads the idea that one can be saved from fairly pathological conditions by loving a man. People say that's not how I approach my life. There's no guidance in that for me. And that's true."

Jerusalem the Golden's broader canvas and *The Waterfall*'s self-conscious narration were perhaps necessary first steps toward Drabble's full development in the mid-1970s. Her two biggest novels, *The Needle's Eye* (1972) and *The Realms of Gold* (1975), were written during this period, and together they represent her finest and fullest exploration of substantial themes: *The Needle's Eye* of personal morality and *The Realms of Gold* of the possibilities for individual achievement despite limitations beyond the individual's physical, social, familiar, psychological, and spiritual control. Myer contends that Drabble's "continuing theme is a reconsideration and reevaluation of the English puritan tradition. She has recognized that this strain, though popularly denied, is still very much with us and has left us an inheritance of guilt and anxiety. This perception has enabled her to portray with sympathy, accuracy and sharpness those segments of English society where the puritan tradition is strongest: 'liberal' intellectuals and the northern lower middle class." In addition, Drabble has portrayed her religious affinity in a more general way. She has stressed in interviews that her religious upbringing was very eclectic. The children attended Anglican services with their father because their mother, raised in the repressive fundamentalist tradition of the north, had become a devout atheist. Drabble also says that she "was very much affected by the Quakers" at her Quaker boarding school.

The Needle's Eye reflects both Drabble's deep interest in ethics and morality and her lack of orthodoxy. Like her, the novel's heroine, Rose Vassiliou, is unsure of her theology but possessed of a conviction that she must do right. As a young heiress she achieved a certain amount of notoriety by giving up her inheritance to marry Christopher Vassiliou, an unsavory and radical young immigrant. After their marriage, she infuriated Christopher by giving away a thirty-thousand-pound legacy to a rather dubious African charity and refusing to move out of their working class house into a more fashionable middle-class neighborhood when he began to make his own fortune. At the time of the novel, Rose is living in her house with her children and has divorced the violent Christopher, who is trying to get her back or to get custody of the children. After flirting with the idea of leaving the children to Christopher and going off to do missionary work in the Third World, Rose finally decides that Christopher is her fate, that the way to her salvation is to take him back and maintain the family. Drabble has commented that "Rose has several possibilities. She can stay with the children and continue to live as she does in a selfish state of grace that excludes the pains of the world. She can go off and become really martyred, an act which she is aware would produce a state of grace of another kind of selfishness, though one can be absolutely certain that if one does do something dramatic like go to help the starving, one will be redeemed in some way. A person like Rose might

have found a deep spiritual experience in quitting and going off, but Rose had to reject that, too, and what she accepts finally is no less painful."

Marion Vlastos Libby has written in *Contemporary Literature* that *The Needle's Eye* is a "complex and passionate evocation of a fatalism deriving from the human condition and the nature of the world" and that its greatness "lies in portraying the tension, real and agonizing, between the hounds of circumstance and the force of the individual will." This is certainly the book that shows the human will at its weakest and circumstance at its strongest. The best that Drabble can say for Rose is that she has been "weathered into identity" by the hostile forces that she confronts. In other words, she has developed a soul and found a way to grace, and in that sense she has won her battle. But she has "ruined her own nature against her own judgment, for Christopher's sake, for the children's sake. She had sold them for her own soul . . . the price she had to pay was the price of her own living death, her own conscious lying, her own lapsing, slowly, from grace." As Myer suggests, Drabble's fatalism constitutes a religious vision if looked at as a means to salvation: "For Margaret Drabble the true end of life is to reconcile flesh and spirit by accepting one's own nature and living with it, in a context of love and responsibility for others. While this is far from easy, and any accommodation achieved is costly, the reconciliation of instinct and morality remains as a possibility worth striving for. This reconciliation, the author hopes, can come about by involvement in society."

If *The Needle's Eye* represents the human will at its weakest and circumstance at its strongest, Drabble moved to the opposite extreme in *The Realms of Gold*. Its protagonist Frances Wingate is the apotheosis of the high-powered heroine. A celebrated archaeologist in her mid-thirties, she has divorced the wealthy man she married at an early age and is raising their four children on her own. She has a satisfying love affair with Karel Schmidt, a historian and survivor of the holocaust, whom she eventually marries. She is rich, accomplished, and a little smug. She recognizes in herself "amazing powers of survival and adaptation," and she admits to herself that she is a "vain, self-satisfied woman."

Frances has her frailties, particularly of the body. She suffers quite a bit from two tooth-aches in the course of the novel, and she worries that her body is deteriorating. She knows she drinks too much and fears that she may share the fate of her alcoholic brother. And she suffers from bouts of hereditary depression, what Drabble calls the "midlands sickness." The important fact about Frances, however, is that she is not affected by these limitations in any fundamental way, because she does not allow them to affect her. She is Drabble's quintessential personification of will: "I must be mad, she thought to herself. I imagine a city, and it exists. If I hadn't imagined it, it wouldn't have existed. All her life things had been like that. She had imagined herself doing well, and had done well. Marrying, and had married. Bearing children, and had borne them. Being rich, and had become rich. Being free and was free. Finding true love, and had found it. Losing it, and had lost it."

Not everyone finds Frances attractive. Fox-Genovese calls her a "fatuous, self-satisfied bitch; too good at everything by half, not to mention too rich and unencumbered." She is an obvious extreme, and Drabble sets her in opposition to the other extremes in the novel. While she makes her mark on her family, her profession, her society, even—in discovering a lost city in the desert—upon nature, she is surrounded by people who are destroyed by circumstances: environment, heredity, psychology, and, one might as well say it, fate. Her Aunt Constance has starved to death, left alone by an indifferent society. Her nephew has committed suicide, killing his baby daughter as well, because he cannot face the state of the world and does not want her to grow up in it. His anorexic wife is slowly starving herself toward the same escape. Less drastically, Frances's cousin is caught in a miserable marriage in a miserable midlands town and dreams that the gas main will blow up and deliver her from her fate. The list goes on. As Mary Moran has noted in *Margaret Drabble: Existing within Structures,* "Margaret Drabble's fiction portrays a bleak, often menacing universe, ruled over by a harsh deity who allows human beings very little free will." Drabble's emphatic statement in *The Realms of Gold,* however, is that the will does count for something, that what hope there is for survival lies precisely in the individual's exercise of will in the face of what may seem overwhelming external forces.

The two novels that followed, *The Ice Age* (1977) and *The Middle Ground* (1980), present what has become the typical struggle of the individual in Drabble's work to survive and to maintain an identity in the face of a disintegrating social order. Drabble has remarked that *The Ice Age* is in one sense a novel about money. Its protagonist, Anthony Keating, is a thoughtful man who made a fortune in real estate development during the boom times of the 1960s and lost it during the recession of the early 1970s. At the beginning of the novel he is recuperating from a heart attack and trying to come to terms with his new relation to life. Meanwhile the spoiled teenaged daughter of his fiancee, Alison Murray, has gotten herself into trouble in an eastern European country, and his former partner, Len, has landed himself in prison through his shady dealings. The novel is about money in many senses: about the failing British economy, about the effects that making a lot of money has on people, about the interaction of old money and new money, and about the class structures that underlie everyone's thinking about money. However, it is also about the forces that individuals in contemporary Britain are up against, from the natural fact of Alison's retarded younger daughter to the threat that an alien totalitarian government poses to her older one.

The interesting artistic fact about *The Ice Age* is that its narrative is not centered in one character, but is divided among Anthony, Alison, Len, and Len's girlfriend, Maureen. This is in part a reflection of the general disintegration going on in the world Drabble is presenting, in part a somewhat ironic move toward community. Not one of these characters has the force of will that makes Frances Wingate the central presence she is. Each of them is severely handicapped in some way, but they do manage to function in concert. There is some power in community.

The Middle Ground returns to a central character, a character who is very much like Frances Wingate. Kate Armstrong is a successful writer with teenaged children who lives a very comfortable expense-account life. Because she resides in the world of *The Ice Age,* however, Kate is less confident than Frances of her future. In one sense *The Middle Ground* is about middle age. After the ending of a ten-year love affair and the abortion of a fetus with spina bifida, Kate at forty-one is asking what is left for her to do with the rest of her life: "Work? Living for others? Just carrying on, from day to day, enjoying as much of it as one could? Responding to demands as they came, for come they would?" Faced with the decay of urban London, the realities of the Third World visited upon her in the shape of a house-guest called Mujid, the apparent failure of the women's movement, and the turning off of the youth in her world, Kate is not sure what course she should take. In the end she decides to steer a middle ground between her friend Evelyn, a self-sacrificing so-

cial worker, and Evelyn's husband and Kate's former lover Ted, a biologist who uses Darwin to justify his self-interest. Kate decides somewhat ambiguously to settle for being "a nice woman," and Drabble leaves her looking toward the future with anticipation and excitement, a woman in the middle of her life.

More recently, Drabble has written the first two novels of a planned trilogy that follows the lives of three women who began a friendship while they were students at Cambridge in the 1950s. In the first book, *The Radiant Way,* Drabble introduces Liz, a successful psychotherapist, Alix, an idealist whose socialistic principles have led her to work at low-paying, altruistic jobs, and Esther, a scholar whose main interest lies with minor artists of the Italian Renaissance. By following these three characters through the years in *The Radiant Way* and into their middle age in *A Natural Curiosity,* the author "also attempts to show us how a generation managed (or mismanaged) its hopes and dreams," comments Michiko Kakutani in the *New York Times.* Kakutani finds this approach similar to that of Mary McCarthy's *The Group,* a novel about former Vassar students, and criticizes the tendency in both books "to substitute exposition for storytelling, sociological observation for the development of character and drama." But in a *Newsweek* review by Laura Shapiro, the critic approves of Drabble's willingness to explore all the facets of her characters' lives "at a time when skimpy prose, skeletal characterizations, frail plots and a sense of human history that stops sometime around last summer have become the new standards for fiction." Shapiro concludes: "Drabble reminds us here as in all her books exactly why we still love to read."

There is still a small contingent of academic critics who fail to take her writing seriously, however. The main reason for this response is that she has chosen to write, as she says, "at the end of a dying tradition, which I admire, [rather] than at the beginning of a tradition which I deplore." As she has often reiterated in interviews, Drabble's models have been the great British novelists of the nineteenth century—George Eliot, the Brontes, Arnold Bennett, and to a lesser extent Jane Austen and Virginia Woolf—as well as Henry James. Elaine Showalter quotes her in *A Literature of Their Own* as saying, "I don't want to write an experimental novel to be read by people in fifty years, who will say, oh, well, yes, she foresaw what was coming. I'm just not interested."

It is this kind of thinking that has led Drabble to be seen, as Michael F. Harper has noted in *Contemporary Literature,* "as a late twentieth-century novelist who writes what many reviewers have taken to be good, solid nineteenth-century novels." One such critic, Morton Levitt, has said flatly that "her novels fail . . . for her work is founded on the same unyielding belief that Modernist experience in fiction is an irrelevancy and that an earlier Victorian form is most appropriate to convey the nuances of contemporary life." Harper disagrees with this conception of Drabble, suggesting that the judgment is misleading "insofar as it implies an unthinking, uncritical acceptance of Victorian conventions and techniques, for there are crucial differences between her novels and the tradition to which critics so quickly assign them."

The views of these two critics reflect basic critical disagreement over Drabble's ability as a realist to write novels that actually reflect the reality of human experience in the twentieth century. Levitt claims that Drabble's omniscient narrator "is at best an anachronism, unwittingly parodic, while at worst it undercuts, even destroys her intended post-Modernist themes of uncertainty and misdirection. This is Trollope revisited to be sure, but in the context of a new time for which his vision and narrative technique are woefully unsuited, it is also Trollope demeaned.'' Drabble's contemporary realism has been most eloquently defended by Harper, who says that "the form of Margaret Drabble's novels is not the result of unthinking acceptance of Victorian conventions, or of nostalgia for 'the riches of the past.' It is rather a working back to a reconstituted realism, in which Drabble begins with modernism and subjects it to a critique that is profound and contemporary." Drabble's realistic world, he says, "is something painfully and with difficulty constructed by the author and her characters, something not assumed but affirmed in an act of faith, achieved at the end of an odyssey of doubt and questioning of both the world and the self."

Bromberg goes a long way toward reconciling these two points of view in suggesting that Drabble is really a "post Romantic ironist who sees salvation not in imaginative communion with nature, but in the natural procreative immortality of the human generations." This view anchors Drabble's vision securely in the traditional realistic values of family and society and provides for both a transcendent vision of ultimate unity and an ironic vision of the inability of human society to achieve it. Bromberg holds that, in *The Realms of Gold,* Drabble has constructed "an ironic counter-myth to the journey toward poetic identity and paradise that [Wordsworth] describes in *The Prelude.*" She says, "Drabble suggests that Wordsworth's youthful faith in the poetic imagination failed him because it was too extravagant. . . . Moments [of joy] are found, not in Wordsworth's solitary confrontations with the imagination in its relationship to the natural world, but in human relationship and community."

Taken from this point of view, Drabble's work represents a critique of romanticism in the context of what is possible in the real world, a representation of the compromise that must take place when the ideal world of the imagination confronts the limitations of reality. Drabble's realism may very well be her personal mediation between two extreme visions that permeate her world: the vestigial yearning for a transformation of the ordinary into an ideal unity and the post-modernist view that contemporary society has disintegrated beyond the possibility of unity or coherence, beyond the possibility of even a coherent description of its disintegration. She continues to insist both on the reality of the writer and on the reality of the world she describes. And while she sees very clearly the extreme tensions in our society—from the contrary pulls on a talented woman who wants both to be a mother and to make her mark on the world to the economic and political forces that threaten the precarious stability of our social institutions—she continues to believe in the human striving for something transcendent, something spiritual or ideal. She has, finally, what she recognizes as a typically English faith in the human capacity for endurance: "You don't start throwing yourself out of the city windows when things go wrong. You just accept and carry on."

MEDIA ADAPTATIONS: The Millstone was adapted as a 1969 film entitled "A Touch of Love."

BIOGRAPHICAL/CRITICAL SOURCES:

BOOKS

Contemporary Literary Criticism, Gale, Volume 2, 1974, Volume 3, 1975, Volume 5, 1976, Volume 8, 1978, Volume 10, 1979, Volume 22, 1982, Volume 53, 1989.

Dictionary of Literary Biography, Volume 14: *British Novelists since 1960,* Gale, 1983.

Moran, Mary Hurley, *Margaret Drabble: Existing within Structures,* Southern Illinois University Press, 1983.

Myer, Valerie Grosvenor, *Margaret Drabble: Puritanism and Permissiveness,* Vision Press, 1974.

Rose, Ellen Cronan, *The Novels of Margaret Drabble: Equivocal Figures,* Barnes & Noble, 1980.

Schmidt, Dory and Jan Seale, editors, *Margaret Drabble: Golden Realms,* Pan American University, 1982.

Showalter, Elaine, *A Literature of Their Own,* Princeton University Press, 1977.

Staley, Thomas F., editor, *Twentieth Century Women Novelists,* Barnes & Noble, 1982.

Todd, Janet, *Gender and Literary Voice,* Holmes & Meier, 1980.

PERIODICALS

American Scholar, winter, 1973.

Atlantic, January, 1976, December, 1977, November, 1980.

Books and Bookmen, September, 1969.

Bookview, January, 1978.

Canadian Forum, November, 1977.

Chicago Tribune Book World, August 31, 1980.

CLA Journal, September, 1984.

College Literature, fall, 1982.

Commentary, December, 1977.

Commonweal, June 18, 1976, February 13, 1981.

Contemporary Literature, Volume 14, 1973, Volume 16, 1975, Volume 21, 1980, Volume 23, 1982.

Contemporary Review, April, 1972, January, 1976, January, 1978.

Critic, August, 1979.

Critique, Number 15, 1973, Number 21, 1980.

Detroit News, October 19, 1980.

Economist, July 13, 1974, February 14, 1976.

English Studies, Number 59, 1978.

Frontiers, Number 3, 1978.

Globe and Mail (Toronto), April 11, 1987, October 7, 1989.

Guardian Weekly, May 29, 1969, January 15, 1972, April 8, 1972, May 13, 1972, July 20, 1974, October 4, 1975, November 11, 1979, July 13, 1980.

Harper's, November, 1969, October, 1977, October, 1980.

History Today, March, 1980.

Hudson Review, winter, 1970, winter, 1973, summer, 1975, winter, 1975, spring, 1978, spring, 1981.

Journal of Narrative Technique, spring, 1981.

Los Angeles Times, December 28, 1980, November, 25, 1982, June 21, 1987, October 23, 1989.

Los Angeles Times Book Review, October 18, 1987, September 24, 1989.

Maclean's, September 29, 1980.

Midwest Quarterly, Volume 16, 1975.

Modern Fiction Studies, Volume 25, 1979-80.

Modern Language Review, April, 1971.

Ms., August, 1974, July, 1978, November, 1980.

Nation, October 23, 1972, April 5, 1975.

National Review, December 23, 1977, March 20, 1981.

New Leader, July 24, 1972, April 26, 1976, January 30, 1978, September 22, 1980.

New Republic, July 8, 1972, September 21, 1974, October 22, 1977.

New Statesman, May 23, 1969, March 31, 1972, July 12, 1974, September 26, 1975, March 19, 1976, September 9, 1977, December 7, 1979, July 11, 1980.

Newsweek, September 9, 1974, October 17, 1977, October 6, 1980, November 2, 1987.

New Yorker, October 4, 1969, December 16, 1972, December 23, 1974, January 12, 1976, December 26, 1977, July 11, 1980.

New York Review of Books, October 5, 1972, October 31, 1974, November 27, 1975, November 10, 1977, July 19, 1979, November 20, 1980.

New York Times, October 31, 1975, October 4, 1977, July 4, 1985, October 21, 1987, August 22, 1989.

New York Times Book Review, November 23, 1969, June 11, 1972, December 3, 1972, September 1, 1974, December 1, 1974, December 7, 1975, April 18, 1976, June 26, 1977, August 21, 1977, October 9, 1977, November 20, 1977, December 23, 1977, September 7, 1980, February 14, 1982, November 7, 1982, July 14, 1985, November 1, 1987, September 3, 1989.

New York Times Magazine, September 11, 1988.

Novel, Volume 11, 1978.

Observer, April 2, 1972, September 23, 1973, July 14, 1974, September 28, 1975, December 14, 1975, March 21, 1976, April 17, 1977, September 4, 1977, December 18, 1977, June 29, 1980, July 13, 1980.

Partisan Review, Number 46, 1979.

People, October 13, 1980.

Prairie Schooner, spring-summer, 1981.

Progressive, January, 1981.

Publishers Weekly, May 31, 1985.

Regionalism and the Female Imagination, Number 4, 1978.

Saturday Review, November 15, 1975, January 10, 1976, February 21, 1976, August 20, 1977, January 7, 1978.

Sewanee Review, January, 1977, April, 1978, January, 1982.

Southern Review, winter, 1983.

Spectator, April 1, 1972, July 20, 1974, September 27, 1975, February 7, 1976, February 14, 1976, July 5, 1980.

Studies in the Literary Imagination, Volume 11, 1978.

Time, September 9, 1974, November 3, 1975, June 26, 1976, October 17, 1977 September 15, 1980, November 16, 1987.

Times (London), June 30, 1980, April 25, 1985, April 27, 1987, April 30, 1987, July 8, 1987.

Times Literary Supplement, July 12, 1974, September 26, 1975, September 2, 1977, July 11, 1980, April 26, 1985, July 12, 1985, May 1, 1987, September 29, 1989.

Tribune Books (Chicago), November 8, 1987, August 20, 1989.

Victorian Studies, spring, 1978.

Village Voice, November 24, 1975, October 24, 1977.

Virginia Quarterly Review, spring, 1976, summer, 1976, summer, 1978.

Voice Literary Supplement, May, 1982.

Washington Post, January 1, 1980.

Washington Post Book World, September 14, 1980, June 2, 1985, September 21, 1986, October 25, 1987, August 27, 1989.

Women's Studies, Volume 6, 1979.

Yale Review, March, 1970, June, 1978.

* * *

DRAYHAM, James
See MENCKEN, H(enry) L(ouis)

* * *

DREISER, Theodore (Herman Albert)   1871-1945
(The Prophet)

PERSONAL: Born August 27, 1871, in Terre Haute, Ind.; died of a heart attack, December 28, 1945, in Los Angeles, Calif. (some sources say Hollywood, Calif.); son of John Paul and Sarah Schaenaeb Dreiser; married Sara Osborne White, December 28, 1898 (divorced, 1910); married Helen Patges Richardson,

June 13, 1944. *Education:* Attended Indiana University, 1889-1890.

CAREER: Writer. *Globe,* Chicago, Ill., reporter, 1892; worked as a reporter for *Globe-Democrat* and *Republic,* both St. Louis, Mo., 1892-93; *Dispatch,* Pittsburgh, Pa., reporter, 1894; *Ev'ry Month,* New York City, editor, 1895-97; free-lance writer, 1897-1905; *Smith's Magazine,* New York City, editor, 1905-06; *Broadway Magazine,* New York City, editor, 1906-07; *Delineator,* New York City, editor, 1907-10; *American Spectator,* New York City, co-editor, 1932-34.

AWARDS, HONORS: Finalist, Nobel Prize in Literature, 1930; Award of Merit, American Academy of Arts and Letters, 1945.

WRITINGS:

NOVELS

Sister Carrie (also see below), Doubleday, Page, 1900, reprinted, Bantam, 1982, abridged edition edited by Dreiser and Arthur Henry, Heinemann, 1901, Pennsylvania edition, edited by John C. Berkey and Alice M. Winters, University of Pennsylvania, 1981, reprinted without textual and historical notes, introduction by Alfred Kazin, Penguin Books, 1981.

Jennie Gerhardt (also see below), Harper, 1911, reprinted, Penguin, 1989.

The Financier (first novel in a trilogy; also see below), Harper, 1912, revised edition, Boni & Liveright (New York), 1927, reprinted, New American Library, 1967.

The Titan (second novel in a trilogy; also see below), John Lane (New York), 1914, reprinted, World Publishing, 1959.

The "Genius," John Lane, 1915, reprinted, New American Library, 1981.

An American Tragedy, Boni & Liveright, 1925, reprinted, New American Library, 1981, abridged edition edited and with introduction by George Mayberry, New American Library, 1949.

The Bulwark, Doubleday, 1946, reprinted, Chivers, 1973.

The Stoic (third novel in a trilogy; also see below), Doubleday, 1947, reprinted, Crowell, 1974.

Trilogy of Desire (contains *The Financier, The Titan,* and *The Stoic*), Crowell, 1974.

OTHER

(Author of first verse and chorus) Paul Dresser, *On the Banks of the Wabash Far Away,* Howley, Haviland (New York), 1897.

A Traveler at Forty, Century (New York), 1913.

(Author of introduction) Oswald Fritz Bilse, *Life in a Garrison Town,* John Lane, 1914.

Plays of the Natural and the Supernatural, John Lane, 1916, reprinted, Scholarly Press, 1970.

A Hoosier Holiday, John Lane, 1916, reprinted, Greenwood Press, 1974.

The Girl in the Coffin (play), first produced in New York at Comedy Theatre, December 3, 1917.

The Hand of the Potter (play; first produced in New York at the Provincetown Playhouse, December 3, 1917), Boni & Liveright, 1919, revised edition, 1927.

Free and Other Stories, Boni & Liveright, 1918, reprinted, Scholarly Press, 1971.

Twelve Men (short stories; also see below), Boni & Liveright, 1919, reprinted, Scholarly Press, 1971.

Hey Rub-a-Dub-Dub: A Book of the Mystery and Wonder and Terror of Life, Boni & Liveright, 1920, reprinted, University Microfilms (Ann Arbor, Mich.), 1973.

A Book about Myself, Boni & Liveright, 1922, published as *Newspaper Days,* Liveright, 1931, reprinted, Beekman Publishers, 1974.

The Color of a Great City, Boni & Liveright, 1923, reprinted, Fertig, 1987.

Moods: Cadenced and Declaimed (poems; also see below), Boni & Liveright, 1926, revised edition published as *Moods Philosophic and Emotional, Cadenced and Declaimed,* Simon & Schuster, 1935.

Chains: Lesser Novels and Stories by Theodore Dreiser, Boni & Liveright, 1927, reprinted, Fertig, 1987.

(Author of introduction) Dresser, *The Songs of Paul Dresser,* Boni & Liveright, 1927.

(Author of introduction) Frank Norris, *McTeague,* Doubleday, Doran, 1928.

Dreiser Looks at Russia, Liveright, 1928.

A Gallery of Women, Liveright, 1929.

Epitaph: A Poem, Heron Press (New York), 1929, reprinted, Norwood, 1977.

Dawn (autobiography), Liveright, 1931, reprinted, Fawcett Publications (Greenwich, Conn.), 1965.

Tragic America, Liveright, 1931.

(Author of introduction) *Harlan Miners Speak: Report on Terrorism in the Kentucky Coal Fields,* Harcourt, 1932, reprinted, Da Capo Press, 1970.

(Editor and author of introduction) Henry David Thoreau, *The Living Thoughts of Thoreau,* Longmans, Green, 1938.

America Is Worth Saving, Modern Age, 1941.

The Best Short Stories of Theodore Dreiser (also see below), edited and with introduction by Howard Fast, World Publishing, 1947, reprinted, Elephant Paperbacks, 1989.

Letters of Theodore Dreiser: A Selection, three volumes, edited and with preface and notes by Robert H. Elias, University of Pennsylvania Press, 1959.

Letters to Louise: Theodore Dreiser's Letters to Louise Campbell, edited and with commentary by Louise Campbell, University of Pennsylvania Press, 1959.

(Author of notes with Hy Craft) Borden Deal, *The Tobacco Men: A Novel Based on Notes By Theodore Dreiser and Hy Craft,* foreword by Craft, Bantam, 1965.

The Lost Phoebe and Other Stories (selections from *The Best Short Stories of Theodore Dreiser;* English language textbook with Japanese annotations), edited and with notes by Fujio Aoyama, Shimizu Shoin (Tokyo), 1967.

Selected Poems (from Moods), introduction and notes by Robert Palmer Saalbach, Exposition, 1969.

Notes on Life, edited by Marguerite Tjader and John J. McAleer, University of Alabama Press, 1974.

Theodore Dreiser: A Selection of Uncollected Prose, edited by Donald Pizer, Wayne State University Press, 1977.

Theodore Dreiser: American Diaries, 1902-1926, edited by Thomas P. Riggio and others, University of Pennsylvania Press, 1983.

An Amateur Laborer (autobiography), edited and introduced by Richard W. Dowell, with James L. W. West and Neda M. Westlake, University of Pennsylvania Press, 1983.

Selected Magazine Articles of Theodore Dreiser: Life and Art in the American 1890s, edited by Yoshinobu Hakutani, Fairleigh Dickinson University Press, 1985.

Dreiser-Mencken Letters: The Correspondence of Theodore Dreiser and H. L. Mencken, 1907-1945, edited by Riggio, University of Pennsylvania Press, 1986.

Sister Carrie; Jennie Gerhardt; Twelve Men (omnibus edition), Literary Classics of the United States, 1987.

Theodore Dreiser's "Heard in the Corridors" Articles and Related Writings, Iowa State University Press, 1988.
Journalism, University of Pennsylvania Press, 1988.

Contributor of articles and the column, "Reflections," under pseudonym The Prophet, to *Ev'ry Month.* Contributor to periodicals, including *Success.* Most of Dreiser's manuscripts are kept at the Theodore Dreiser Collection of the University of Pennsylvania Library; other collections are maintained in the Cornell University Library, the Lilly Library of Indiana University, the New York Public Library, the University of Texas Library, and the University of Virginia Library.

SIDELIGHTS: One of the most prominent naturalistic authors in the United States during the early twentieth century, Theodore Dreiser was an instrumental figure in promoting a realistic portrayal of life in America. In such novels as *Sister Carrie* and *An American Tragedy,* he described people who were motivated not by a higher sense of ethics, but rather by their own selfish impulses and the social class pressures that surrounded them. Many conservative critics like *Nation* contributor Stuart P. Sherman, who favored the gentility and Puritan moralism that was characteristic of most writing at the time, felt that such "a representation of the life of a man in contemporary society . . . is an artistic blunder"; criticism was often also aimed at Dreiser's poor command of language and style. The novelist's career was thus marked by his struggle to be accepted by the critical community. More recently, however, the author's significance in American literary history has been generally acknowledged. Joseph Warren Beach, author of *The Twentieth Century Novel: Studies in Technique,* asserted that what makes Dreiser a major American author is "his fearlessness, his honesty, his determination to have done with conventional posturings and evasions. It was extremely important that we should have some one bold enough to set down in the English language just as he saw it the unvarnished truth about American business life, American social life in its major reaches, and the sex-psychology of American men and women."

As recorded in his autobiography *Dawn,* Dreiser came from a poor Indiana farm family of German and Bohemian origin. Unlike many authors of his time, he never graduated from college—although he spent an unproductive year at Indiana University under the sponsorship of his high school English teacher—nor did he have easy access to books as a child. He did, however, gather a wealth of experience from his own family, which *Dictionary of Literary Biography* contributor Donald Pizer described as "poor, large, Catholic, ignorant, and superstitious. . . . The character and experiences of the Dreiser family in the years during which Theodore was growing up were later to supply the mature author with many of his themes. The underlying configuration of the family—the warm, forgiving, and loving mother; the narrow-minded, disciplinarian father; and the fun-loving, wayward, and seeking children—became that of Dreiser's fictional families."

Sister Carrie, Dreiser's first novel, was based on the experiences of his sister Emma, who had an affair with a married man and then fled with him to Canada after he had stolen thousands of dollars from his company's safe. Changing the names to Caroline Meeber and George Hurstwood, the young author soon composed a fictionalized account of his sister's adventures. He completed the book in 1900, with the help of his friend Arthur Henry and his wife Sara ("Jug"); but his efforts to publish the manuscript with Doubleday, Page, and Company resulted in "one of the most famous incidents in American literary history," according to Pizer. In its first edition, *Sister Carrie* sold only five hundred copies, and Dreiser blamed the poor sales on his publisher's refusal to promote the book.

"The story that Dreiser told and embroidered over the years," related Richard Lingman in the *Nation,* "was that publisher Frank Doubleday (or his wife, in later versions) read the typescript after it had already been accepted by other members of the house and found it immoral" because it portrays a sinful woman who escapes moral retribution and, by the story's conclusion, is even rewarded by becoming a rich and famous actress. "When Dreiser refused to release Doubleday, Page from its contract, the latter set out to bury the book." Because of this story, reported Pizer, "the actions of Doubleday, Page became to Dreiser and his supporters a major symbol of control of American culture by a puritan ethic, and Dreiser was celebrated as a figure who both suffered from this control and persevered nevertheless." But authorities like Lingman now recognize that it "did not happen quite that way." Doubleday actually followed the contract "to the letter" and even signed the agreement after telling Dreiser they had decided not to publish it.

The failure of *Sister Carrie* caused Dreiser to sink into a deep depression and even to consider committing suicide. Much of this low point in his life is recorded in *An American Laborer,* a journal that Dreiser kept during the early 1900s, but that was not published until 1983. Here, Dreiser writes about his years of desperate poverty when he gave up writing—believing his creative powers had abandoned him—and instead sought work as a laborer. Reduced to living in a Brooklyn slum, Dreiser by chance met his brother Paul Dresser, the successful composer of "My Gal Sal" and "On the Banks of the Wabash Far Away," who had changed his name for professional reasons. Paul sent his destitute brother to Muldoon's Sanatorium, a spa and retreat for the upper classes.

The sanatorium helped Dreiser recover mentally and physically, but it also taught him that he did not like the company of the rich any more than that of the poor. In a *New York Times Book Review* article, E. L. Doctorow related that for Dreiser the rich were "no more estimable or interesting or brilliant in their lives than the miserable wretches lying about the precincts of the Mills Hotel" where he had once stayed. Likewise, the author considered the working poor to be "generally unimaginative, unaspiring, [and] terribly reduced in liveliness by the deadly and repetitive rituals of their work." Doctorow surmised that because Dreiser could not identify with these societies he was able to regain his confidence as a writer by recovering his own "identity as an artist."

In 1907 Dreiser had *Sister Carrie* reprinted by B. W. Dodge with much better results. This, in turn, encouraged him to complete his second novel, *Jennie Gerhardt.* Although not as well-known today as its predecessor, *Jennie Gerhardt,* commented Jonathan Yardley in the *Washington Post Book World,* was "a considerable commercial success and firmly established Dreiser's standing as a novelist—though it did not still the furor over his treatment of sexual and moral questions that had been stirred by *Sister Carrie.*" Once again using one of his sisters as a model for his novel's protagonist, Dreiser writes about another "fallen woman" in *Jennie Gerhardt.* Jennie sins by having a child out of wedlock, but she is a very different character compared to Carrie. Philip L. Gerber explained in another *Dictionary of Literary Biography* entry: "Unlike Carrie, who is all calculation and no genuine human feeling, Jennie Gerhardt is wholly without self-interest. Her actions are governed by her emotional responses, and she is known for her fidelity to those she loves." But despite these admirable qualities, Dreiser ends her story on a

tragic note. By the novel's conclusion, Jennie has lost her child and the man she loves, but she overcomes her feelings of loss by adopting and caring for two children. Thus, wrote Gerber, she "never succumbs to self-pity, never *feels* victimized either by other human beings or by Life. In drawing such a portrait, Dreiser appears to suggest, as he does nowhere else, that one's perception of his fate can itself become a type of 'protective coloration' which will assist one to survive in a harsh world."

Dreiser's conception of the nature of life was strongly influenced by Herbert Spencer and Honore de Balzac. As Pizer disclosed, Spencerian philosophy "argues that there is no authority in supernaturally sanctioned moral codes, that only that which develops naturally through the struggle for existence, whether this struggle occurs in nature or society, is beneficial. And Balzac's novels . . . reaffirmed Dreiser's own belief that the seeker will find in the great city not only struggle, degradation, and destruction but also wonder, beauty, and fulfillment."

In revising his first two novels, however, Dreiser's faith that the strength of his characters would eventually bring them success is obscured. Initially in *Jennie Gerhardt,* the author planned to have Jennie marry her rich lover, Lester Kane, and have the couple live happily ever after despite Jennie's first affair with a senator that resulted in her pregnancy. But Dreiser had learned that such a conclusion would not have pleased moralistic readers, so, according to Kenneth S. Lynn in his *The Dream of Success: A Study of the Modern American Imagination,* the author rewrote the ending to "generate reader-sympathy for Jennie." The first conclusion for *Sister Carrie,* which was restored and published in the 1981 Pennsylvania edition of the novel, is even more revealing of Dreiser's Spencerian beliefs. In this version, the materialistic, unscrupulous Carrie meets a respectable Midwesterner, Bob Ames, after she and Hurstwood have gone their separate ways. She and Ames become attracted to one another with the "implication . . . that Carrie will ascend to the next rung of growth and perhaps marry Ames," reported Lingman. "In fact," the reviewer later added, "Dreiser created the possibility of a young woman who is immoral by all standards of polite society achieving the virtuous woman's ultimate reward: marrying the handsome, clean-cut young man rather than being punished." However, Dreiser's wife Jug, who played a large role in editing *Sister Carrie,* would not tolerate such an ending and persuaded her husband to change the book so that Carrie is condemned to living a lonely, chaste life of "dreamy solipsism." Even with these changes, though, many readers objected to the author's novels.

Having separated from his wife in 1910, Dreiser's later books were less influenced by others and therefore reflect his philosophy more clearly. Regarding his philosophical works, many critics found the author's expositions to be severely flawed, yet revealing. *Theodore Dreiser* author James Lindquist, for example, remarked that in books like *Hey, Rub-A-Dub-Dub!: A Book of the Mystery and Wonder and Terror of Life* "there are, along with many inconsistencies and much triteness, dozens of striking sentences, moods that are frequently charming, and reflections that occasionally make aspects of Dreiser's novels more understandable." Ronald E. Martin, author of *American Literature and the Universe of Force,* also opined that Dreiser's dogma was "shallow and inconsiderable stuff," although Dreiser himself felt his philosophizing brought him near "the brink of some great discovery." Martin and others have blamed Dreiser's intellectual sloppiness on his tendency to season his thought with his emotions and sense of wonder for life—"he arrived at an attitudinal sense of things rather than a consistent rational paradigm of the universe."

The *"Genius,"* whose main character, Eugene Witla, strongly represents "Dreiser's self-image," according to Lindquist, is a good example of the author's tendency to mix rational with fanciful thinking. The novel mirrors its author's own life very closely, with the exception that Witla is a painter rather than a writer; it also reflects Dreiser's love of science and metaphysics. Both of these aspects flaw *The "Genius"* significantly in a number of critics' views. Pizer asserted, "Literalness mars Dreiser's extremely long reprise of his life in *The "Genius"* from the beginning to the end of the novel." And Martin pondered, "What are we to make of the novel's strange mixture of mechanistic materialism and mystical idealism? Simply that Dreiser's own incomparable philosophical enthusiasms, which are always close to expression in this nearly autobiographical work, come through in the novel as an incoherent narrative approach."

Because of these problems, Gerber concluded that *"The "Genius"* is probably the least admired of Dreiser's major novels." When *The "Genius"* was first published in 1915, however, critical and popular reception was positive. But because Dreiser portrays Witla as an artist—and therefore somehow above conventional moral codes—the New York Society for the Supression of Vice, an influential censor at the time, attempted to exert its power to ban the novel. Many important authors such as Ezra Pound, Robert Frost, Sinclair Lewis, and H. G. Wells protested this attempt, resulting in the book's reissue in 1923 and a major defeat of censorship in the United States.

If the character of Eugene Witla was considered amoral, Dreiser's Frank Cowperwood, whose life is portrayed in the trilogy consisting of *The Financier, The Titan,* and *The Stoic* (later published together as *The Trilogy of Desire*), is even more so. "The idea that civilization is a sham," said Sherman, takes on its most Social Darwinistic note in these novels. "Mr. Dreiser drives home the great truth that man is essentially an animal, impelled by temperament, instinct, physics, chemistry—anything you please that is irrational and uncontrollable." Cowperwood is based upon the real-life nineteenth-century traction magnate, Charles T. Yerkes. In writing this trilogy, the author hoped to present "both an expose and a celebration of the world of finance capitalism," explained Michael Spindler, author of *American Literature and Social Change: William Dean Howells to Arthur Miller.* Dreiser chose Yerkes over other prominent industrialists like John D. Rockefeller because he saw in him the possibility "to endow the entrepreneur with epic dimensions—to make him, in fact, a colossus of the age. Dreiser's irony is directed . . . at the hypocrisy, as he saw it, of the public and private moral codes. It was Yerkes' lack of such hypocrisy, his unabashed practice of dishonesty, which appealed so strongly to Dreiser, providing him with a foil against which to set the hollow sentiments which were supposed to govern American business life."

The Financier, which relates Cowperwood's early years in Philadelphia, "remains the most impressive" book in the trilogy in *New York Times Book Review* critic Malcolm Cowley's opinion. Cowley described the book as "an interweaving of finance and politics with a love story that, besides being effective in itself, is also essential to the climax of the novel." In this volume, Cowperwood rises from a middle-class childhood to a man of immense wealth and influence through his ruthless deals in the stock market. His fall from power comes when he has an affair with Aileen Butler, the daughter of one of Philadelphia's political bosses who, although easily as immoral a businessman as Cowperwood, is extremely conservative when it comes to his family values. His "moral outrage against Cowperwood on family grounds," revealed Spindler, "is the real motivation for his determination to ruin the financier and bring him to trial for the embezzlement of Philadelphian City Council funds." Cowperwood is imprisoned for his crimes but receives a pardon from the governor, and, unrepentant, regains his fortune during the economic crisis of 1873. Once again a wealthy man, Cowperwood leaves Philadelphia with Aileen, thus proving his superiority over hypocrites such as Butler. "The moral of this story," summarized Walter Benn Michaels, a contributor to *American Realism: New Essays,* ". . . is the irrelevance of anything but strength in a world 'organized' so that the strong feed on the weak. Such a moral is, of course, congruent with the Spencerian's Social Darwinist tendency to find in natural law a justification for the robber-baron practices of the most predatory American businessmen."

Although, as Gerber pointed out, *The Financier* "appalled" some reviewers because of its "candid portrayal of a man who openly flouted all established conventions of morality" and was rewarded for it, the critic later observed that *"The Titan* raised a storm of protest considerably greater than that fomented by *The Financier."* This second book in the trilogy takes place in Chicago and chronicles Cowperwood's stream of successes and, again, his ultimate failure. A number of critics such as Cowley considered *The Titan* "inferior to its predecessor." Lynn went so far as to call *The Titan* "a fabulous bore," in which chapters about Cowperwood's financial exploits alternate repetitively with chapters about his romantic exploits. The novel concludes when Cowperwood's attempt to obtain a monopoly of the Chicago transportation system is thwarted by the resistance of a league of civic voters, "thus preserving the natural equilibrium toward which nature strive," remarked Gerber.

Despite the flaws in these two novels, Granville Hicks commented in his *The Great Tradition: An Interpretation of American Literature since the Civil War* that in Frank Cowperwood Dreiser had "succeeded in creating such a figure as had not previously appeared in our literature." The author, however, did not return to the story of the financier's life until over thirty years later when he completed *The Stoic.* This tremendous interim between books in the trilogy resulted in the completely different nature of *The Stoic* compared to the other books. The Great Depression, related Lynn, "absolutely convinced Dreiser that capitalism was through, that the American atmosphere of 'zest and go' which he so loved was now only a memory." This, and Dreiser's own financial problems which he suffered in the time between *The Titan* and *The Stoic,* had an "effect on Dreiser's art [that] was catastrophic," and the last two major novels that he wrote, *The Stoic* and *The Bulwark,* became "curious, hollow shells of books, utterly lacking in conviction."

Rather than focusing upon the physical world, these last works emphasize the spiritual side of life, a change that some have attributed to the influence of Dreiser's second wife, Helen, who was interested in spiritualism. Also, before Dreiser completed these projects, he had become fascinated with transcendentalism, Hinduism, and Quakerism. But although this new focus on the spiritual might seem to have promised a new, deeper insight in the author's writing, a number of critics noted a sense of ennui in Dreiser. Describing Cowperwood as he is portrayed in *The Stoic,* Lynn compared the character to his creator: "[Cowperwood] finds it is no fun to win anymore, no fun to smash any more shams. Having lost his will to power, the Cowperwood of *The Stoic* shortly loses his will to live. . . . Like his dead hero . . . Dreiser seemed to have no real heart for what he was writing." About *The Bulwark,* Pizer similarly felt that the novel "lacks both the density of life and the Dreiserian presence of Dreiser's most characteristic fiction." Nevertheless, according to Gerber this story about Solon Barnes, a religious man who wins his own spiritual battle even though he is engulfed by the overwhelming forces of capitalism, is "an outcry which stands among Dreiser's more poignant testimonies to the loss suffered by America in following its new, material ideals."

But Dreiser's most powerful outcry against overwhelming social forces came before his disillusionment with the American dream. In *An American Tragedy*, the author resolved to write about "a certain kind of crime which he believed was significantly expressive of American life," according to Pizer. Basing his story on the true murder of Grace Brown by Chester Gilette in 1906, Dreiser set out to explain how an ordinary, middle-class American could be driven to commit homicide because of a deluded faith in the American dream. The novel follows the life story of Clyde Griffiths, a man who has been indoctrinated since his childhood to believe that the ultimate aim in life is to achieve financial success and that anyone who tries hard enough can reach this end. Only Clyde, for some reason he cannot comprehend, has found this goal to be unattainable. Working in his rich uncle's factory, he becomes envious of his relatives (who are condescending toward him) and disliked by his neighbors (who associate him with his snobbish relatives). Clyde's chance comes when Sondra Finchley, a wealthy, beautiful woman who embodies all of Clyde's hopes for success, takes an interest in him. But by this time he has already become involved with Roberta Alden, a poor woman who bears Clyde's child. Caught between the pressure to marry Roberta and his desire to wed Sondra, he resolves to kill Roberta. He intends to drown her on a boating trip, but Dreiser instead has her die accidentally, creating an ambiguous situation that allows the author to focus on the methods by which society will determine Clyde's guilt or innocence. Without any firm proof, Dreiser shows how the jury finds Clyde guilty and condemns him to death solely because of their class and sex prejudices, for as Elizabeth Langland explained in her *Society and the Novel*, the author saw "morality [as] a function of social class."

Reaction to *An American Tragedy* was generally optimistic. In a *New Republic* article, Irving Howe called the novel "a masterpiece, nothing less," observing that in this work the author "mines his talent to its very depth." Beach asserted that *An American Tragedy* "is doubtless the most neatly constructed of all Dreiser's novels, as well as the best written." Still, a number of reviewers found flaws in the book, most of which concerned problems that a number of critics found in all of Dreiser's books. For example, Arnold Bennett, author of *The Savour of Life: Essays in Gusto*, withheld his recommendation of *An American Tragedy* because it "is written abominably, by a man who evidently despises style, elegance, clarity, even grammar. Dreiser simply does not know how to write, never did know, never wanted to know." *The Shape of Books to Come* author, J. Donald Adams, added that "Dreiser's thinking was never more confused and never more sentimental than it was in the writing of *An American Tragedy*."

Despite such criticism, the book was a popular success and brought Dreiser financial security until the Great Depression. But at least part of this popularity, attested Gerber, was because by the time of *An American Tragedy*'s publication—after World War I and the appearance of T. S. Eliot's *The Waste Land* and Sinclair Lewis's *Babbitt*—"the public was at last prepared for a book which would hold society itself accountable for the behavior of its individual members. Dreiser had not changed, but the times had caught up with him, and *An American Tragedy*, with its gloomy picture of the havoc worked on American youth by the nation's unquestioning embrace of the Success Myth, suddenly was *au courant*."

After *An American Tragedy*, it is generally believed that Dreiser did not write anything of great significance. E. L. Docotorow, for one, observed in the *New York Times Book Review*: "The more he wrote, and the wealthier his writings made him, the more insecure he and his reputation became." Even "almost 30 years after his death," commented Jack Salzman in a 1974 *Washington Post Book World* article, "Dreiser is little read." More recently, however, Pearl K. Bell announced in the *Times Literary Supplement* that "the wheel of appreciation has turned back to Dreiser for his haunting illumination of the way both society and character spin the rope that lashes a man to his tragic destiny." During his lifetime, the closest Dreiser got to winning a major literary award was when he was the runner-up for the 1930 Nobel Prize in literature. The award went instead to Sinclair Lewis, who acknowledged Dreiser in his acceptance speech quoted in the *Dictionary of Literary Biography Documentary Series:* "Dreiser more than any other man, marching alone, usually unappreciated, often hated, has cleared the trail from Victorian and Howellsian timidity and gentility in American fiction to honesty and boldness and passion of life. Without his pioneering, I doubt if any of us could, unless we liked to be sent to jail, seek to express life and beauty and terror."

MEDIA ADAPTATIONS: In 1951 a movie adaptation of *An American Tragedy* was produced by Paramount Pictures.

BIOGRAPHICAL/CRITICAL SOURCES:

BOOKS

Adams, J. Donald, *The Shape of Books to Come*, Viking, 1944.

Asselineau, Roger, *The Transcendentalist Constant in American Literature*, New York University Press, 1980.

Beach, Joseph Warren, *The Twentieth Century Novel: Studies in Technique*, Appleton-Century-Crofts, 1932.

Bennett, Arnold, *The Savour of Life: Essays in Gusto*, Doubleday, 1928.

Cabell, James Branch, *Some of Us: An Essay in Epitaphs*, Robert M. McBride & Company, 1930.

Cheit, Earl F., *The Business Establishment*, Wiley, 1964.

Concise Dictionary of American Literary Biography: Realism, Naturalism, and Local Color, 1865-1917, Gale, 1988.

Dictionary of Literary Biography, Gale, Volume 9: *American Novelists, 1910-1945*, 1981, Volume 12: *American Realists and Naturalists*, 1982.

Dictionary of Literary Biography Documentary Series, Gale, Volume 1, 1982.

Dreiser, Helen, *My Life with Dreiser*, World, 1951.

Dreiser, Theodore, *An American Tragedy*, World Publishing, 1946, Little, Brown, 1962.

Dreiser, Theodore, *The Best Short Stories of Theodore Dreiser*, World Publishing, 1956.

Dreiser, Theodore, *Letters of Theodore Dreiser: A Selection*, Volume 2, University of Pennsylvania Press, 1959.

Elias, Robert H., *Theodore Dreiser: Apostle of Nature*, Cornell University Press, 1970.

Fleischmann, Fritz, editor, *American Novelists Revisited: Essays in Feminist Criticism*, G. K. Hall, 1982.

Forgue, Guy J., editor, *Letters of H. L. Mencken*, Knopf, 1961.

Frank, Waldo, *Our America*, Boni & Liveright, 1919.

Gerber, Philip L., *Theodore Dreiser*, Twayne, 1964.

Hakutani, Yoshinobu, *Young Dreiser: A Critical Study*, Fairleigh Dickinson University Press, 1980.

Hicks, Granville, *The Great Tradition: An Interpretation of American Literature since the Civil War*, Macmillan, 1935.

Langland, Elizabeth, *Society in the Novel*, University of North Carolina Press, 1984.

Lundquist, James, *Theodore Dreiser,* Ungar, 1974.
Lydenberg, John, editor, *Dreiser: A Collection of Critical Essays,* Prentice-Hall, 1971.
Lynn, Kenneth S., *The Dream of Success: A Study of the Modern American Imagination,* Little, Brown, 1955.
Martin, Ronald E., *American Literature and the Universe of Force,* Duke University Press, 1981.
Pizer, Donald, *The Novels of Theodore Dreiser,* University of Minnesota Press, 1976.
Salzman, Jack, editor, *Theodore Dreiser: The Critical Reception,* David Lewis, 1972.
Sherman, Stuart P., *On Contemporary Literature,* Holt, 1917.
Spindler, Michael, *American Literature and Social Change: William Dean Howells to Arthur Miller,* Indiana University Press, 1983.
Swanberg, W. A., *Dreiser,* Scribners, 1965.
Sundquist, Eric J., editor, *American Realism: New Essays,* Johns Hopkins University Press, 1982.
Tjader, Marguerite, *Theodore Dreiser: A New Dimension,* Silvermine, 1965.
Twentieth Century Literary Criticism, Gale, Volume 10, 1983, Volume 18, 1985.

PERIODICALS

American Literature, March, 1981.
Arizona Quarterly, autumn, 1981.
Athenaeum, September 7, 1901.
Bookman, December, 1912.
Forum, February, 1929.
Literary Review, January 16, 1926.
Nation, July 11, 1981.
New Yorker, March 23, 1946.
New York Review of Books, February 26, 1987.
New York Times Book Review, October 26, 1919, November 23, 1947, November 20, 1977, May 31, 1981, August 22, 1982, December 4, 1983.
Scribner's Magazine, April, 1926.
Times Literary Supplement, September 24, 1982, February 21, 1986, July 17, 1987.
Village Voice, January 24, 1984.
Washington Post Book World, July 21, 1974, July 4, 1982, January 25, 1987.
World Union, March, 1976.

—*Sketch by Kevin S. Hile*

*   *   *

DRUMMOND, Walter
See SILVERBERG, Robert

*   *   *

Du BOIS, W(illiam) E(dward) B(urghardt) 1868-1963

PERSONAL: Born February 23, 1868, in Great Barrington, Mass.; immigrated to Ghana, 1960, naturalized Ghanian citizen, 1963; died August 27, 1963, in Accra, Ghana; buried in Accra; son of Alfred and Mary (Burghardt) Du Bois; married Nina Gomer, 1896 (died, 1950); married Shirley Graham (an author), 1951 (died, 1977); children: Burghardt (deceased), Yolande Du Bois Williams (deceased). *Education:* Fisk University, B.A., 1888; Harvard University, B.A. (cum laude) 1890, M.A., 1891, Ph.D., 1896; graduate study at University of Berlin, 1892-1894. *Politics:* Joined Communist Party, 1961.

CAREER: Wilberforce University, Wilberforce, Ohio, professor of Greek and Latin, 1894-96; University of Pennsylvania, Phila-

delphia, assistant instructor in sociology, 1896-97; Atlanta University, Atlanta, Ga., professor of history and economics, 1897-1910; National Association for the Advancement of Colored People (NAACP), New York City, director of publicity and research and editor of *Crisis,* 1910-1934; Atlanta University, professor and chairman of department of sociology, 1934-1944; NAACP, director of special research, 1944-1948; Peace Information Center, New York City, director, 1950. Co-founder and general secretary of Niagra Movement, 1905-09. Organizer of the Pan-African Congress, 1919. Vice-chairman of the Council of African Affairs, 1949. American Labor Party candidate for U.S. Senator from New York, 1950.

AWARDS, HONORS: Spingarn Medal from NAACP, 1932; elected to the National Institute of Arts and Letters, 1943; Lenin International Peace Prize, 1958; Knight Commander of the Liberian Humane Order of African Redemption conferred by the Liberian Government; Minister Plenipotentiary and Envoy Extraordinary conferred by President Calvin Coolidge; LL.D. from Howard University, 1930, and Atlanta University, 1938; Litt.D. from Fisk University, 1938; L.H.D. from Wilberforce University, 1940; honorary degrees from Morgan State College, University of Berlin, and Charles University (Prague).

WRITINGS:

NOVELS

The Quest of the Silver Fleece, A. C. McClurg, 1911, reprinted, Kraus Reprint, 1974.
Dark Princess: A Romance, Harcourt, 1928, reprinted, Kraus Reprint, 1974.
The Ordeal of Mansart (first novel in trilogy; also see below), Mainstream Publishers, 1957.
Mansart Builds a School (second novel in trilogy; also see below), Mainstream Publishers, 1959.
Worlds of Color (third novel in trilogy; also see below), Mainstream Publishers, 1961.
The Black Flame (trilogy; includes *The Ordeal of Mansart, Mansart Builds a School,* and *Worlds of Color*), Kraus Reprint, 1976.

POETRY

Selected Poems, Ghana University Press, c. 1964, reprinted, Panther House, 1971.

PLAYS

"Haiti," included in *Federal Theatre Plays,* edited by Pierre De Rohan, Works Progress Administration, 1938.

Also author of pageants, "The Christ of the Andes," "George Washington and Black Folk: A Pageant for the Centenary, 1732-1932," and "The Star of Ethiopia."

WORKS EDITED IN CONJUNCTION WITH THE ANNUAL CONFERENCE FOR THE STUDY OF NEGRO PROBLEMS; ALL ORIGINALLY PUBLISHED BY ATLANTA UNIVERSITY PRESS

Mortality Among Negroes in Cities, 1896, reprinted, Octagon, 1968.
Social and Physical Condition of Negroes in Cities, 1897, reprinted, Octagon, 1968.
Some Efforts of American Negroes for Their Own Social Benefit, 1898, reprinted, Octagon, 1968.
The Negro in Business, 1899, reprinted, AMS Press, 1971.
A Select Bibliography of the American Negro: For General Readers, 1901.
The Negro Common School, 1901, reprinted, Octagon, 1968.
The Negro Artisan, 1902, reprinted, Octagon, 1968.

The Negro Church, 1903, reprinted, Arno Press, 1968.

Some Notes on Negro Crime, Particularly in Georgia, 1904, reprinted, Octagon, 1968.

A Select Bibliography of the Negro American, 1905, reprinted, Octagon, 1968.

The Health and Physique of the Negro American, 1906, reprinted, Octagon, 1968.

Economic Co-operation among Negro Americans, 1907, reprinted, Russell & Russell, 1969.

The Negro American Family, 1908, reprinted, M.I.T. Press, 1970.

Efforts for Social Betterment Among Negro Americans, 1909, reprinted, Russell & Russell, 1969.

(With Augustus Granville Dill) *The College-Bred Negro American,* 1910, reprinted, Russell & Russell, 1969.

(With Dill) *The Common School and the Negro American,* 1911, reprinted, Russell & Russell, 1969.

(With Dill) *The Negro American Artisan,* 1912, reprinted, Russell & Russell, 1969.

(With Dill) *Morals and Manners among Negro Americans,* 1914, reprinted, Russell & Russell, 1969.

Atlanta University Publications, two volumes, Hippocrene, 1968.

NONFICTION

The Suppression of the African Slave-Trade to the United States of America, 1638-1870, Longmans, Green, 1896, reprinted, Kraus Reprint, 1973.

The Conservation of Races, American Negro Academy, 1897, reprinted, Arno Press, 1969.

The Philadelphia Negro: A Special Study, (bound with *A Special Report on Domestic Service,* by Isobel Eaton), University of Pennsylvania, 1899, reprinted, Kraus Reprint, 1973.

The Souls of Black Folk: Essays and Sketches (young adult), A. C. McClurg, 1903, reprinted, Buccaneer, 1986.

(With Booker Taliaferro Washington) *The Negro in the South: His Economic Progress in Relation to His Moral and Religious Development* (lectures), G. W. Jacobs, 1907, reprinted, Metro Books, 1972.

John Brown (biography), G. W. Jacobs, 1909, reprinted, Kraus Reprint, 1973, 2nd revised edition, International Publishing, 1974.

The Negro, Holt, 1915, reprinted, Kraus Reprint, 1975.

Darkwater: Voices from Within the Veil (semi-autobiographical), Harcourt, 1920, reprinted, Kraus Reprint, 1975.

The Gift of Black Folk: The Negroes in the Making of America, Stratford Co., 1924, reprinted, Kraus Reprint, 1975.

Africa: Its Geography, People and Products (also see below), Haldeman-Julius Publications, 1930.

Africa: Its Place in Modern History, Haldeman-Julius Publications, 1930, reprinted in a single volume with *Africa: Its Geography, People and Products,* Unipub-Kraus International, 1977.

Black Reconstruction: An Essay Toward a History of the Part Which Black Folk Played in the Attempt to Reconstruct Democracy in America, 1860-1880, Harcourt, 1935, reprinted, Kraus Reprint, 1976, published as *Black Reconstruction in America, 1860-1880,* Atheneum, 1969.

Black Folk, Then and Now: An Essay in the History and Sociology of the Negro Race, Holt, 1939, reprinted, Kraus Reprint, 1975.

Dusk of Dawn: An Essay Toward an Autobiography of a Race Concept, Harcourt, 1940, reprinted, Kraus Reprint, 1975.

Color and Democracy: Colonies and Peace, Harcourt, 1945, reprinted, Kraus Reprint, 1975.

The World and Africa: An Inquiry Into the Part Which Africa Has Played in World History, Viking, 1947, revised edition, 1965.

(Editor) *An Appeal to the World: A Statement on the Denial of Human Rights to Minorities in the Case of Citizens of Negro Descent in the United States of America and an Appeal to the United Nations for Redress,* [New York], 1947.

In Battle for Peace: The Story of My 83rd Birthday (autobiography), Masses and Mainstream, 1952, reprinted, Kraus Reprint, 1976.

The Autobiography of W. E. Burghardt Du Bois: A Soliloquy on Viewing My Life From the Last Decade of Its First Century, edited by Herbert Aptheker, International Publishers, 1968.

Black North in 1901: A Social Study, Ayer, 1970.

COLLECTIONS AND CORRESPONDENCE

An ABC of Color: Selections From Over Half a Century of the Writings of W. E. B. Du Bois, Seven Seas Publishers (Berlin), 1963.

Three Negro Classics, edited by John H. Franklin, Avon, 1965.

W. E. B. Du Bois Speaks: Speeches and Addresses, edited by Philip S. Foner, Pathfinder Press, 1970.

The Selected Writings of W. E. B. Du Bois, edited by Walter Wilson, New American Library, 1970.

W. E. B. Du Bois: A Reader, edited by Meyer Weinberg, Harper, 1970.

The Seventh Son: The Thought and Writings of W. E. B. Du Bois, edited by Julius Lester, Random House, 1971.

A W. E. B. Du Bois Reader, edited by Andrew G. Paschal, Macmillan, 1971.

W. E. B. Du Bois: The Crisis Writings, edited by Daniel Walden, Fawcett Publications, 1972.

The Emerging Thought of W. E. B. Du Bois: Essays and Editorials from "The Crisis," edited by Harvey Lee Moon, Simon & Schuster, 1972.

The Correspondence of W. E. B. Du Bois, edited by Aptheker, University of Massachusetts Press, Volume I: *1877-1934,* 1973, Volume II: *1934-1944,* 1976, Volume III: *1944-1963,* 1978.

The Education of Black People: Ten Critiques, 1906-1960, edited by Aptheker, University of Massachusetts Press, 1973.

The Writings of W. E. B. Du Bois, edited by Virginia Hamilton, Crowell, 1975.

Book Reviews, edited by Aptheker, KTO Press, 1977.

Prayers for Dark People, edited by Aptheker, University of Massachusetts Press, 1980.

(And editor) *Writings in Periodicals,* UNIPUB-Kraus International, 1985.

Creative Writings by W. E. B. Du Bois: A Pageant, Poems, Short Stories and Playlets, UNIPUB-Kraus International, 1985.

Pamphlets and Leaflets by W. E. B. Du Bois, UNIPUB-Kraus International, 1985.

Against Racism: Unpublished Essays, Papers, Addresses, 1887-1961, edited by Aptheker, University of Massachusetts Press, 1985.

W. E. B. Du Bois on Sociology and the Black Community, edited by Dan S. Greene and Edwin D. Driver, University of Chicago Press, 1987.

W. E. B. Writings, Library of America, 1987.

OTHER

Columnist for newspapers, including *Chicago Defender, Pittsburgh Courier, New York Amsterdam News,* and *San Francisco Chronicle.* Contributor to numerous periodicals, including *Atlantic Monthly* and *World's Work.* Founder and editor of numerous periodicals, including *Moon,* 1905-06, *Horizon,* 1908-10, *Brownies' Book,* 1920-21, and *Phylon Quarterly,* 1940. Editor in chief of *Encyclopedia of the Negro,* 1933-46. Director of *Encyclopaedia Africana.*

SIDELIGHTS: W. E. B. Du Bois was at the vanguard of the civil rights movement in America. Of French and African descent, Du Bois grew up in Massachusetts and did not begin to comprehend the problems of racial prejudice until he attended Fisk University in Tennessee. Later he was accepted at Harvard, but while he was at that institution he voluntarily segregated himself from white students. Trained as a sociologist, Du Bois began to document the oppression of black people and their strivings for equality in the 1890s. By 1903 he had learned enough to state in *The Souls of Black Folk* that "the problem of the twentieth century is the problem of the color line," and he spent the remainder of his long life trying to break down racial barriers.

The Souls of Black Folk was not well received when it first came out. Houston A. Baker, Jr. explained in his *Black Literature in America* that white Americans were not "ready to respond favorably to Du Bois's scrupulously accurate portrayal of the hypocrisy, hostility, and brutality of white America toward black America." Many blacks were also shocked by the book, for in it Du Bois announced his opposition to the conciliatory policy of Booker T. Washington and his followers, who argued for the gradual development of the Negro race through vocational training. Du Bois declared: "So far as Mr. Washington apologizes for injustice, North or South, does not rightly value the privilege and duty of voting, belittles the emasculating effects of caste distinctions, and opposes the higher training and ambition of our brighter minds—so far as he, the South, or the Nation, does this—we must unceasingly and firmly oppose him. By every civilized and peaceful method we must strive for the rights which the world accords to men." In retrospect, many scholars have pointed to *The Souls of Black Folk* as a prophetic work. Harold W. Cruse and Carolyn Gipson noted in the *New York Review of Books* that "nowhere else was DuBois's description of the Negro's experience in American Society to be given more succinct expression. . . . *Souls* is probably his greatest achievement as a writer. Indeed, his reputation may largely rest on this remarkable document, which had a profound effect on the minds of black people."

A few years after *The Souls of Black Folk* was published, Du Bois banded with other black leaders and began the Niagra Movement, which sought to abolish all distinctions based on race. Although this movement disintegrated, it served as the forerunner of the National Association for the Advancement of Colored People (NAACP). Du Bois helped to establish the NAACP and worked as its director of publicity and research for many years. As the editor of *Crisis,* a journal put out by the NAACP, he became a well-known spokesman for the black cause. In 1973 Henry Lee Moon gathered a number of essays and articles written by Du Bois for *Crisis* and published them in a book, *The Emerging Thought of W. E. B. Du Bois.*

In addition to the articles and editorials he wrote for *Crisis,* Du Bois produced a number of books on the history of the Negro race and on the problems of racial prejudice. In *Black Reconstruction,* Du Bois wrote about the role that blacks played in the Reconstruction, a role that had been hitherto ignored by white historians. The history of the black race in Africa and America was outlined in *Black Folk: Then and Now.* H. J. Seligmann found the book impressive in the *Saturday Review of Literature:* "No one can leave it without a deepened sense of the part the Negro peoples have played and must play in world history." An

even higher compliment was paid by Barrett Williams reviewing for the *Boston Transcript:* "Professor Du Bois has overlooked one of the strongest arguments against racial inferiority, namely, this book itself. In it, a man of color has proved himself, in the complex and exacting field of scholarship, the full equal of his white colleagues."

Although Du Bois's novels did not attract as much notice as his scholarly works, they also were concerned with the plight of the black race. His first novel, *The Quest of The Silver Fleece,* dramatizes the difficulties created by the low economic status of the Southern Negro. *Dark Princess* dealt with miscegenation. After reading *Dark Princess,* a reviewer for the *Springfield Republican* observed: "The truth is, of course, that DuBois is not a novelist at all, and that the book judged as a novel has only the slightest merit. As a document, as a program, as an exhortation, it has its interest and value."

Du Bois gradually grew disillusioned with the moderate policies of the NAACP and with the capitalistic system in the United States. When he advocated black autonomy and "non-discriminatory segregation" in 1934, he was forced to resign from his job at the NAACP. Later he returned to the NAACP and worked there until another rift developed between him and that organization's leaders in 1944. More serious conflicts arose between Du Bois and the U.S. government. Du Bois had become disenchanted with capitalism relatively early. In *Darkwater: Voices From Within the Veil,* he had depicted the majority of mankind as being subjugated by an imperialistic white race. In the 1940s he returned to this subject and examined it in more detail. *Color and Democracy: Colonies and Peace* presented a case against imperialism. "This book by Dr. Du Bois is a small volume of 143 pages," critic H. A. Overstreet observed in the *Saturday Review of Literature,* "but it contains enough dynamite to blow up the whole vicious system whereby we have comforted our white souls and lined the pockets of generations of freebooting capitalists." *The World and Africa* contained a further indictment of the treatment of colonials. Du Bois "does not seek exaggeration of Africa's role, but he insists the role must not be forgotten," Saul Carson remarked in the *New York Times.* "And his insistence is firm. It is persuasive, eloquent, moving. Considering the magnitude of the provocation, it is well-tempered, even gentle."

Du Bois not only wrote about his political beliefs; he acted upon them. He belonged to the Socialist party for a brief time in the early 1900s. Later he conceived a program of Pan-Africanism, a movement that he called "an organized protection of the Negro world led by American Negroes." In 1948 he campaigned for the Progressive Party in national elections, and in 1950 he ran for senator from New York on the American Labor Party ticket. Du Bois's radical political stance provoked some run-ins with the U.S. government, the first of which occurred in 1949, when he accepted an honorary position as vice-chairman of the Council on African affairs. This organization was labeled "subversive" by the attorney general. His work with the Peace Information Center, a society devoted to banning nuclear weapons, also embroiled him in controversy. Along with four other officers from the Peace Information Center, Du Bois was indicted for "failure to register as an agent of a foreign principal." The case was brought to trial in 1951 and the defendants were acquitted.

After the trial was over, Du Bois wanted to travel outside the United States, but he was denied a passport on the grounds that it was not in "the best interests of the United States" for him to journey abroad. Later the State Department refused to issue a passport to him unless he stated in writing that he was not a member of the Communist Party, a condition that Du Bois rejected. In 1958 the Supreme Court handed down a decision which declared that "Congress had never given the Department of State any authority to demand a political affidavit as prerequisite to issuing a passport." This decision enabled Du Bois and his wife to leave the country the same year. For several months they traveled in Europe, the U.S.S.R., and China.

Du Bois's travels abroad had a profound influence on his thinking. In 1961 he joined the Communist Party. He explained in his autobiography how he reached this decision: "I have studied socialism and communism long and carefully in lands where they are practiced and in conversation with their adherents, and with wide reading. I now state my conclusion frankly and clearly: I believe in communism. . . . I believe that all men should be employed according to their ability and that wealth and services should be distributed according to need. Once I thought that these ends could be attained under capitalism, means of production privately owned, and used in accord with free individual initiative. After earnest observation I now believe that private ownership of capital and free enterprise are leading the world to disaster."

After joining the Communist party, Du Bois moved to Ghana at the invitation of President Nkrumah. While there he served as the director of the *Encyclopaedia Africana* project. In August, 1963, the ninety-five-year-old leader inspired a protest march on the U.S. embassy in Accra to show support for the historic "March for Jobs and Freedom" taking place in Washington, D.C. that same month. Shortly afterward, Du Bois died. Although Du Bois was a controversial figure in his lifetime, his reputation has grown in the past decade. A large number of books and scholarly studies about him have recently appeared. In a discussion of the revival of interest in Du Bois, Cruse and Gipson wrote: "It is important to remember that he continued to plead for a truly pluralistic culture in a world where the superiority of whites is still an *a priori* assumption. In so far as he grasped the basic dilemma of Western blacks as being a people with 'two souls, two thoughts, two unreconciled strivings,' Du Bois's attitudes have been vindicated. He was, as we can now see, one of those unique men whose ideas are destined to be reviled and then revived, and then, no doubt, reviled again, haunting the popular mind long after his death."

Some of Du Bois's books have been published in French and Russian.

BIOGRAPHICAL/CRITICAL SOURCES:

BOOKS

Baker, Houston A., Jr., *Black Literature in America,* McGraw, 1971.
Black Writers, Gale, 1989.
Bone, Robert A., *The Negro Novel in America,* Yale University Press, revised edition, 1965.
Concise Dictionary of American Literary Biography: Realism, Naturalism, and Local Color, 1865-1917, Gale, 1988.
Contemporary Literary Criticism, Gale, Volume 1, 1973, Volume 2, 1974.
Dictionary of Literary Biography, Gale, Volume 47: *American Historians, 1866-1912,* 1986, Volume 50: *Afro-American Writers Before the Harlem Renaissance,* 1986.
Du Bois, Shirley Graham, *His Day Is Marching On: A Memoir of W. E. B. Du Bois,* Lippincott, 1971.
Du Bois, W. E. B., *Darkwater: Voices from Within the Veil,* Harcourt, 1920, reprinted, Kraus Reprint, 1975.

Du Bois, W. E. B., *Dusk of Dawn: An Essay Toward an Autobiography of Race Concept,* Harcourt, 1940, reprinted, Kraus Reprint, 1975.
Du Bois, W. E. B., *In Battle for Peace: The Story of My 83rd Birthday,* Masses & Mainstream, 1952, reprinted, Kraus Reprint, 1976.
Du Bois, W. E. B., *The Autobiography of W. E. B. Du Bois: A Soliloquy on Viewing My Life from the Last Decade of Its First Century,* International Publishers, 1968.
Hawkins, Hugh, editor, *Booker T. Washington and His Critics: Black Leadership in Crisis,* Heath, 1974.
Logan, Rayford W., editor, *W. E. B. Du Bois: A Profile,* Hill & Wang, 1971.
Rampersad, Arnold, *Art and Imagination of W. E. B. Du Bois,* Harvard University Press, 1976.
Rudwick, Elliott M., *W. E. B. Du Bois: Propagandist of the Negro Protest,* Atheneum, 1968.
Something About the Author, Volume 42, Gale, 1986.
Sterne, Emma Gelders, *His Was the Voice: The Life of W. E. B. Du Bois,* Crowell-Collier, 1971.

PERIODICALS

Boston Transcript, June 24, 1939.
Ebony, August, 1972, August, 1975.
Los Angeles Times Book Review, January 25, 1987.
New Republic, February 26, 1972.
Newsweek, August 23, 1971.
New York Review of Books, November 30, 1972.
New York Times, March 9, 1947, October 24, 1979.
New York Times Book Review, September 29, 1985.
Saturday Review of Literature, July 29, 1939, June 23, 1945.
Springfield Republican, May 28, 1928.

*   *   *

DUERRENMATT, Friedrich   1921-

PERSONAL: Born January 5, 1921, in Konolfingen, Bern, Switzerland; son of Rienhold (a Protestant minister) and Hulda (Zimmermann) Duerrenmatt; married Lotti Geissler (an actress), 1946, (died, 1983); married Charlotte Kerr (a journalist), 1984; children: (first marriage) Peter, Barbara, Ruth. *Education:* Attended University of Zurich, 1941-42, and University of Bern, 1942. *Avocational interests:* Painting, astronomy.

ADDRESSES: Home—Pertuis-du-Sault 34, Neuchatel, Switzerland.

CAREER: Playwright, novelist, short story writer, essayist, and critic.

MEMBER: Modern Language Association of America (honorary fellow).

AWARDS, HONORS: Welti-stiftung fuer das Drama, City of Bern, 1948, for *Es steht geschrieben;* Literaturpreis, City of Bern, 1954, for *Ein Engel kommt nach Babylon;* Hoerspielpreis der Kriegsblinden (Berlin), 1957, for *Die Panne;* Prix Italia, RAI (Venice), 1958, for *Abendstunde im Spaetherbst;* Preis zur Foerderung des Bernischen Schrifttums, 1959, for *Das Versprechen;* Schiller-Preis, City of Mannheim, 1959, for *Grieche sucht Griechin;* New York Drama Critics Circle Awards for best foreign play, 1959, for *The Visit;* Grillparzer-Preis, Oesterreich Akademie der Wissenschaften, 1968, for *Der Besuch der alten Dame;* Grosser Schiller-Preis, Schweizer Stiftung, 1969, for *Die Physiker;* Grosser Literaturpreis, Canton of Bern, 1969; doctor honoris causa, Temple University, 1969, Hebrew University, 1977, University of Nice, 1977, and University of Neuchatel,

1981; International Writers Prize, Welsh Arts Council, University of Wales, 1976; Buber-Rosenzweig-Medaille (Frankfort), 1977; Grosser Literaturpreis, City of Bern, 1979.

WRITINGS:

STAGE PLAYS

Es steht geschrieben: Ein Drama; mit zwei Zeichnungen vom Autor (title means "It Is Written"; first produced in Zurich, Switzerland, at Schauspielhaus, April 19, 1947), Schwabe (Basel), 1947, new version published as *Der Wiedertaeufer: Ein Komoedie in zwei Teilen* (title means "The Annabaptists"; first produced in Zurich at Schauspielhaus, March 16, 1967), Arche (Zurich), 1967.

Der Blinde: Ein Drama (title means "The Blind Man"; first produced in Basel, Switzerland, at Stadttheater, January 10, 1948), Buehnenverlag Block Erben (Berlin), 1947, revised edition, Arche, 1965.

Romulus der Grosse: Eine ungeschichtliche historische Komoedie in vier Akten (first produced in Basel at Stadttheater, April 25, 1949, new version produced in Zurich at Schauspielhaus, October 24, 1957), Arche, 1958, revised version, 1964, 2nd edition, 1968.

Die Ehe des Herrn Mississippi: Eine Komoedie (first produced in Munich, West Germany, at Kammerspiele, March 26, 1952, translation by E. Peters and R. Schnorr produced in London, England, at Arts Theatre, September 30, 1959, as *The Marriage of Mr. Mississippi*), Oprecht (Zurich), 1952, revised edition published as *Die Ehe des Herrn Mississippi: Buehnenfassung und Drehbuch,* Arche, 1966.

Ein Engel kommt nach Babylon: Eine Komoedie in drei Akten (first produced in Munich at Kammerspiele, December 22, 1953, new version produced in Zurich at Schauspielhaus, October 24, 1957), Arche, 1954, revised edition published as *Ein Engel kommt nach Babylon: Eine fragmentarishe Komoedie in drei Akten,* 1958, translation by George White (produced at University of California, 1962), published as *An Angel Comes to Babylon,* K. Hellmer, c. 1962.

Der Besuch der alten Dame: Ein tragische Komoedie; mit einem Nachwort (first produced in Zurich at Schauspielhaus, January 29, 1956, produced in New York City, May 5, 1958), Arche, 1956, translation published as *The Visit: A Play in Three Acts,* Random House, 1958, translation by Patrick Bowles published as *The Visit: A Tragi-Comedy,* Grove, 1962.

(With Paul Burkhard) *Frank der Fuenfte: Oper einer Privatbank* (satirical opera; title means "Frank the Fifth: Opera of a Private Bank"; first produced in Zurich at Schauspielhaus, March 19, 1959), music by Burkhard, Arche, 1960, published as *Frank der Fuenfte: Eine Komoedie,* Bochumer Fassung (Zurich), 1960, revised edition, Arche, 1964.

Die Physiker: Eine Komoedie in zwei Akten (first produced in Zurich at Schauspielhaus, February 20, 1962, produced in New York City at Martin Beck Theatre, October 13, 1964), Arche, 1962, translation by James Kirkup published as *The Physicists: A Play in Two Acts,* Samuel French, 1963, published as *The Physicists,* Grove, 1964.

Herkules und der Stall des Augias: Eine Komoedie (expanded version of radio play; first produced in Zurich at Schauspielhaus, March 20, 1963), Arche, 1963, translation by Agnes Hamilton published as *Hercules and the Augean Stables,* Dramatic Publishing, 1963.

An Angel Comes to Babylon [and] *Romulus the Great: Two Plays* (latter a translation of *Romulus der Grosse*), translated by William McElwee and Gerhard Nellhaus, respectively, Grove, 1964.

Four Plays, 1957-62 (contains *Romulus the Great, The Marriage of Mr. Mississippi, An Angel Comes to Babylon,* and *The Physicists;* bound with essay, "Problems of the Theatre"), translated by Gerhard Nellhaus and others, J. Cape, 1964, published as *Four Plays,* Grove, 1965.

Der Meteor: Eine Komoedie in zwei Akten (first produced in Zurich at Schauspielhaus, January 20, 1966), Arche, 1966, translation by James Kirkup published as *The Meteor,* Dramatic Publishing, 1966, published as *The Meteor: A Comedy in Two Acts,* J. Cape, 1973, Grove, 1974.

(Adaptor) *Koenig Johann: Nach Shakespeare* (first produced in Basel at Basles Theatres, September 18, 1968), Arche, 1968.

Play Strindberg: Totentanz nach August Strindberg (first produced in Basel at Basles Theatres, February 8, 1969), Arche, 1969, translation by James Kirkup (produced in New York City at Forum Theatre of Lincoln Center, June 3, 1971), published as *Play Strindberg: Choreographed by Friedrich Duerrenmatt,* Dramatic Publishing, 1970, published as *Play Strindberg: The Dance of Death Choreographed,* Grove, 1973.

(Adaptor) *Goethes Urfaust: Ergaenzt durch das Buch von Doktor Faustus aus dem Jahre 1589* (first produced in Zurich at Schauspielhaus, October 20, 1970), Diogenes, 1980.

Portraet eines Planeten (first produced in Dusseldorf, West Germany, at Kleines Haus, November 27, 1970), Arche, 1971.

(Adaptor) *Titus Andronicus: Eine Komoedie nach Shakespeare* (first produced in Dusseldorf at Schauspielhaus, December 12, 1970), Arche, 1970.

Der Mitmacher, ein Komplex: Text der Komoedie, Dramaturgie, Erfahrungen, Berichte, Erzaehlungen (includes play and commentary by Duerrenmatt), Arche, 1976, play published singularly as *Der Mitmacher: Eine Komoedie,* 1978.

Die Frist: Eine Komoedie (first produced in Zurich at Schauspielhaus, October 6, 1977), Arche, 1977.

Die Panne: Komoedie (adaptation of novel), Diogenes, 1979.

Koenig Johann [and] *Titus Andronicus: Shakespeare-Umarbeitungen,* Diogenes, 1980.

Der Meteor [and] *Dichterdaemmerung: Nobelpreistraegerstuecke,* Diogenes, 1980.

Achterloo: Eine Komoedie in zwei Akten (first produced in Zurich, 1983), Diogenes, 1983.

RADIO PLAYS

Herkules und der Stall des Augias: Mit Randnotizen eines Kugelschreibers, Arche, 1954.

Das Unternehmen der Wega: Ein Hoerspiel (title means "The Vega Enterprise"; broadcast in 1954), Arche, 1958, reprinted, 1974.

Naechtliches gespraech mit einem verachteten Menschen: Ein Kurs fuer Zeitgenossen, Arche, 1957, translation by Robert David Macdonald published as *Conversation at Night with a Despised Character: A Curriculum for Our Times,* Dramatic Publishing, 1957.

Der Prozess um des Esels Schatten: Ein Hoerspiel (nach Wieland—aber nicht sehr) (title means "The Trial of the Ass's Shadow"), Arche, 1958.

Stranitzky und der Nationalheld: Ein Hoerspiel (title means "Stranitzky and the National Hero"), Arche, 1959.

Abendstunde im Spaetherbst: Ein Hoerspiel (produced by British Broadcasting Corp., September 24, 1959), Arche, 1959 translation by Gabriel Karminski published as *Episode on an Autumn Evening,* Dramatic Publishing, 1959, different translation published as "Incident at Twilight" in *Postwar German Theatre,* edited by M. Benedikt and G. E. Wellworth, Macmillan, 1968.

Der Doppelgaenger: Ein Spiel, Arche, 1960.

Die Panne: Ein Hoerspiel (first published as novel), Arche, 1961, published as *Die Panne: Ein Hoerspiel und eine Komoedie,* Diogenes, 1980.

Drei Hoerspiele, edited by Henry Regensteiner, Hot, 1965.

Vier Hoerspiele, Volk & Welt (Berlin), 1967.

Naechtliches Gespraech mit einem verachteten Menschen [and] *Stranitzky und der Nationalheld* [and] *Das Unternehmen der Wega: Hoerspiele und Kabarett,* Diogenes, 1980.

Also author of "Sammelband," 1960.

FICTION

Pilatus (story), Vereinigung Oltner Buecherfreunde (Olten), 1949.

Der Nihilist (story), Holunderpresse (Horgen), 1950, reprinted as *Die Falle,* Arche, 1952.

Der Tunnel (story), Arche, 1952.

Das Bild des Sisyphos (story), Arche, 1952.

Die Stadt: Prosa I-IV (title means "The City"; story collection), Arche, 1952.

Der Richter und sein Henker (novel; originally serialized in *Der Beobachter,* 1950), Benziger (Einsiedeln), 1952, translation by Cyrus Brooks published as *The Judge and His Hangman,* Jenkins, 1954, translation by Theresa Pol under same title, Harper, 1955.

Der Verdacht (novel; originally serialized in *Der Beobachter*), Benziger, 1953, translation by Eva H. Morreale published as *The Quarry,* Grove, 1961.

Grieche sucht Griechin: Eine Prosakomoedie (novel), Arche, 1955, new edition, 1957, translation by Richard Winston and Clara Winston published as *Once a Greek. . . ,* Knopf, 1965.

Die Panne: Ein noch moegliche Geschichte (title means "The Breakdown"; novel), Arche, 1956, new edition, 1960, translation by R. Winston and C. Winston published as *Traps,* Knopf, 1960 (published in England as *A Dangerous Game,* J. Cape, 1960).

Das Versprechen: Requiem auf den Kriminalroman (novel; originally written as screenplay), Arche, 1958, translation by R. Winston and C. Winston published as *The Pledge,* Knopf, 1959.

Die Panne [and] *Der Tunnel,* edited by F. J. Alexander, Oxford University Press, 1967.

Der Richter und sein Henker [and] *Die Panne,* Volk & Welt, 1969.

Der Sturz (story), Arche, 1971.

Der Hund [and] *Der Tunnel* [and] *Die Panne: Erzaehlungen* (stories), Diogenes, 1980.

Grieche sucht Griechin [and] *Mister X macht Ferien* [and] *Nachrichten ueber den Stand des Zeitungswesens in der Steinzeit: Grotesken,* Diogenes, 1980.

The Judge and His Hangman [and] *The Quarry: Two Hans Barlach Mysteries,* afterword by George Stade, David Godine, 1983.

Justiz: Roman (novel), Diogenes, 1985.

Minotaurus: Eine Ballade (story), drawings by Duerrenmatt, Diogenes, 1985.

Der Auftrag; oder, Vom Beobachten des Beobachters der Beobachter: Novelle in vierundzwanzig Saetzen (novel), Diogenes, 1986, translation by Joel Agee published as *The Assignment: or, On the Observing of the Observer of the Observers,* Random House, 1988.

The Execution of Justice (novel), translated by John E. Wood, Random House, 1989.

NONFICTION

Theaterprobleme (essay), Arche, 1955, reprinted, 1973.

Friedrich Schiller: Eine Rede (speech), Arche, 1960.

(With Werner Weber) *Der Rest ist Dank* (speeches), Arche, 1961.

Theater-Schriften und Reden (essays and speeches), edited by Elisabeth Brock Sulzer, Arche, Volume 1: *Theater-Schriften und Reden,* 1966, Volume 2: *Dramaturgisches und Kritisches,* 1972, translation by H. M. Waidson published as *Writings on Theatre and Drama,* J. Cape, 1976.

Monstervortrag ueber Gerechtigkeit und Recht nebst einem helvetischen Zwischenspiel: Eine kleine Dramaturgie der Politik (lecture), Arche, 1969.

Saetze aus Amerika (travel book), Arche, 1970.

Zusammenhaenge: Essay ueber Israel; eine Konzeption, Arche, 1976.

Albert Einstein: Ein Vortrag (lecture), Diogenes, 1979.

Literature und Kunst: Essays, Gedichte und Reden, Diogenes, 1980.

Philosophie und Naturwissenschaft: Essays, Gedichte und Reden, Diogenes, 1980.

Politik: Essays, Gedichte und Reden, Diogenes, 1980.

Kritik: Kritiken und Zeichnungen, Diogenes, 1980.

Also author of *Israel: Eine Rede,* 1975.

EXHIBITION CATALOGS

(Author of introduction) Willy Guggenheim, *Varlin: Kunsthalle Basel, 28. Oktober-25. November 1967,* [Basel], 1967.

(With Giovanni Testor) *Varlin: Peintures; 12 fevrier-27 mars 1982,* Galerie Claude Berhard/Galerie Albert Loeb, 1982.

(With Andre Kamber) *"Hommage a Hurs Liechti": 28. June bis 13. August, 1983,* Medici (Solothurn), 1983.

(With Peter Selz) *Varlin, 1900-1977: Paintings; April 9-May 17, 1986,* Claude Bernard Gallery, 1986.

INTERVIEWS

Gertrun Simmerling and Christof Schmind, editors, *Literarische Werkstatt: Interview mit Friedrich Duerrenmatt,* R. Oldenbourg (Munich), 1972.

Gespraech mit Heinz Ludwig Arnold, Arche, 1976.

(With Dieter Fringeli) *Nachdenken mit and ueber Friedrich Duerrenmatt: Ein Gespraech,* Jeger-Moll (Breitenbach), 1977.

Die Welt als Labyrinth: Die Unsicherheit unserer Wirklichket; Franz Kreuzer, im Gespraech mit Friedrich Duerrenmatt und Paul Watzlawick, Dueticke (Vienna), 1982.

OMNIBUS EDITIONS

Komoedien (also see below), Arche, Volume 1: *Komoedien I,* 1957, 7th edition, 1965, Volume 2: *Komoedien II und fruehe Stuecke,* 1963, Volume 3: *Komoedien III,* 1970.

Gesammelte Hoerspiele (radio plays), Arche, 1961.

Komoedien, Deutsche Buch-Gemeinschaft (Berlin), 1968.

Werkausbage in dreissig Baenden: Das dramatische Werk, thirty volumes, Diogenes, 1981.

Friedrich Duerrenmatt: Plays and Essays, edited by Volkmar Sander, Continuum, 1982.

Friedrich Duerrenmatt: His Five Novels, Pan Books, 1985.

OTHER

Friedrich Duerrenmatt liest: "Herkules und der Stall des Augias" [and] *"Eine Kurzfassung der Komoedie"* (recording), Deutsche Grammophon Gesselschaft, 1957.

It Happened in Broad Daylight (screenplay version of *The Pledge*), Continental, 1960.

Die Ehe des Herrn Mississippi: Ein Drehbuch mit Szenenbildern (filmscript adaptation of stage play), Sanssouci (Zurich), 1961.

Naechtliches Gespraech (recording), Platern Club, 1963.

Die Heimat im Plakat: Ein Buch fuer Schweizer Kinder (satirical drawings), Diogenes, 1963.

Problems of the Theatre: An Essay Translated from the German by Gerhard Nellhaus (translation of *Theaterprobleme*) [and] *The Marriage of Mr. Mississippi: A Play Translated from the German by Mihael Bullock*, Grove, 1964.

(With Gore Vidal) *Romulus: The Broadway Adaptation, by Gore Vidal* [and] *The Original Romulus the Great, by Friedrich Duerrenmatt,* translated by G. Nellhaus, preface by Vidal, Grove, 1966.

Zeichnungen gerachtfertigt durch Friedrich Duerrenmatt, Diogenes, 1972.

(Author of introduction) Hans Falk, *Hans Falk,* ABC (Zurich), 1975.

Duerrenmatt: Bilder und Zeichnungen (paintings and drawings), edited by Christian Strich, Diogenes, 1978.

Lesebuch: Friedrich Duerrenmatt, Arche, 1978.

(Author of foreword) Tomi Ungerer, *Babylon,* Diogenes, 1979.

Herkules und der Stall des Augias [and] *Der Prozess um des Esels Schatten* [and] *Griechische Stuecke,* Diogenes, 1980.

Play Strindberg [and] *Portrait eines Planeten: Uebungsstucke fuer Schauspieler* (exercises for actors), Diogenes, 1980.

Stoffe I-III, Diogenes, 1981.

(With Dorothea Christ) *Hildi Hess: Mit Texten von Dorothea Christ und Friedrich Duerrenmatt,* edited by Daniel Keel, Diogenes, 1981.

Denken mit Duerrenmatt: Denkanstosse; ausgewahlt und zusammengestellt von Daniel Keel; mit sieben Zeichnungen des Dichters, drawings by Duerrenmatt, Diogenes, 1982.

Die Erde ist zu schoen. . . .: Die Physiker [and] *Der Tunnel* [and] *Das Unternehmen der Wega,* Arche, 1983.

(With wife, Charlotte Kerr) *Rollenspiele: Protokoll einer fiktiven Inszenierung und Achterloo III* (includes play, *Achterloo III*), Diogenes, 1986.

Also author of television adaptation of *The Judge and His Hangman,* 1957. Work appears in numerous anthologies, including *The Modern Theatre,* edited by R. W. Corrigan, Macmillan, 1946; *The Best Plays of 1964-65,* edited by O. L. Guernsey, Jr., Dodd, 1965; *Postwar German Theatre,* edited by M. Benedikt and G. E. Wellwarth, Macmillan, 1968; and *Die Besten klassischen und modernene Hundegeschichten,* Diogenes, 1973. Drama critic for *Die Weltwoche,* 1951-52.

MEDIA ADAPTATIONS: The Visit: A Drama in Three Acts was adapted by Maurice Valency from *Der Besuch der Alten Dame* and published by Samuel French, 1956; Valency's adaptation was later published as *The Visit: A Play in Three Acts,* Random House, 1958, and produced in New York City in 1958. *Fools Are Passing Through* was adapted by Maximilian Slater from *Die Ehe des Herrn Mississippi* and produced in New York City at Jan Hus Auditorium, April 2, 1958. *The Deadly Game* was adapted by James Yaffe from *Traps* and produced in New York City at Longacre Theatre, February 2, 1960; Yaffe's *The Deadly Game: A Play in Two Acts; Adapted from the Novel "Traps" by Friedrich Duerrenmatt* was published by Dramatists Play Service, 1966. *The Jackass* was adapted by George White from *Der Prozess um des Esels Schatten* and produced in New York City at Barbizon Plaza Theatre, March 23, 1960. *Romulus: A New Comedy* was adapted by Gore Vidal from *Romulus the Great* and produced

in New York City, 1962; Vidal's *Romulus: A New Comedy; Adapted from a Play of Friedrich Duerrenmatt* was published by Dramatists Play Service, 1962. *The Visit of the Old Lady: Opera in Three Acts by Gottfried von Einem* was adapted from *Der Besuch der Alten Dame* (English version by Norman Tucker) and published by Boosey & Hawkes, 1972. *Chicago Radio Theatre Production of Friedrich Duerrenmatt's Play Strindberg* was released as a cassette recording, Allmedia Dramatic Workshop, 1977.

A dramatization of *The Judge and His Hangman* was televised in the United States in 1956, and an adaptation of *The Deadly Game* in 1957. Duerrenmatt's works have also been adapted as motion pictures, including an adaptation of *The Visit* by Twentieth Century-Fox Film Corp., 1964, *Fools Are Passing Through* (an adaptation of *The Marriage of Mr. Mississippi*), 1961, and an adaptation of one of Duerrenmatt's short stories by Sergeo Amidei for an Italian film, 1972.

SIDELIGHTS: Acclaimed Swiss playwright and critic Friedrich Duerrenmatt is considered to be one of the most important German-language dramatists of the twentieth century. His most famous works include *Der Besuch der alten Dame* (*The Visit*), regarded by many to be his finest play, and *Der Physiker* (*The Physicists*), one of the most frequently performed plays of the German stage. *The Visit,* a huge success on Broadway in addition to Germany, is the story of a wealthy old woman who returns to her impoverished hometown with the intent of financially rewarding the townspeople if they enact revenge on an old suitor of the woman's. According to Frederick Lumley in *New Trends in Twentieth Century Drama, The Visit* "raises Duerrenmatt to the level of the leading playwright of our times. Not only is it a good play in itself, it is one of the most forceful statements ever made on the corruption of the power of money, a radical indictment of the values of our society and the hypocrisy on which it is built." The grotesque comedy *The Physicists* depicts three insane nuclear physicists in an asylum who believe they are Albert Einstein, Sir Isaac Newton, and August Ferdinand Moebius. Possessing the knowledge of how to destroy the world, each physicist goes as far as murdering others to prevent others from discovering what they know; the play raises questions regarding definitions of madness, in addition to the limits of scientific responsibility. A reviewer for the *Times Literary Supplement* comments that in both plays "drama is generated by the pursuit of a ruthless, absolute logic in the teeth of anarchy," while "success rests in part on the way in which a tragi-comic ambivalence of plot is carried through into the language and the stage-realization."

Duerrenmatt once summarized his approach to the theatre: "I would ask you not to look upon me as the spokesman of some specific movement in the theatre or of a certain dramatic technique, nor to believe that I knock at your door as the traveling salesman of one of the philosophies current on our stages today, whether as existentialist, nihilist, expressionist, or satirist, or any other label put on the compote dished up by literary criticism. For me, the stage is not a battlefield for theories, philosophies, and manifestos, but rather an instrument whose possibilities I seek to know by playing with it. . . . My plays are not for what people have to say: what is said is there because my plays deal with people, and thinking and believing and philosophizing are all, to some extent at least, a part of human behavior."

For Duerrenmatt, the playwright's task is to present a new, fantastic, even grotesque and bizarre world upon a stage by using everything at his command: language, irony, ideas, and what Adolf D. Klarmann calls "theatrical pyro-technics." Klarmann cites a few of these from Duerrenmatt's work: "Figures appear out of trap doors, enter through windows and clocks, scenery flies up and down in full view, torture wheels are outlines against the sky, moon dances are performed on roofs, angels alight on chandeliers, chickens run across the stage, in short, every conceivable trick of the trade of the theatre, of the cabaret, the burlesque, and the movies is applied with a lusty abandon."

Believing that true tragedy is impossible to create in a world, he calls his dramatic pieces comedies, though the comedy to be found therein is no more merry than gallows humor. Duerrenmatt writes: "The task of art, insofar as art can have a task at all, and hence also the task of drama today, is to create something concrete, something that has form. This can be accomplished best by comedy. . . . [But] we can achieve the tragic out of comedy. We can bring it forth as a frightening moment, as an abyss that opens suddenly. . . . [The conceit employed by comedy] easily transforms the crowd of theatregoers into a mass which can be attacked, deceived, outsmarted into listening to things it would otherwise not so readily listen to. Comedy is a mousetrap in which the public is easily caught and in which it will get caught over and over again. Tragedy on the other hand, predicates a true community, a kind of community whose existence in our day is but an embarrassing fiction."

Although he is primarily known as a dramatist, Duerrenmatt has also written acclaimed fiction and is best known for his mystery and detective novels, including *Der Richter und sein Henker* (*The Judge and His Hangman*) *Der Verdacht* (*The Quarry*), and *Das Versprechen* (*The Pledge*). *The Judge and His Hangman* was a German best-seller when it appeared in 1950 and, according to Saad Elkhadem in *International Fiction Review*, "is undoubtedly one of the most exciting and entertaining novels in German literature." Elkhadem contends that the novel's popularity is due mainly to "its gripping incidents and breath-taking plot," while "from a narrative point of view, [the] pure event-novel testifies to the remarkable talent of Duerrenmatt as an imaginative fabulist and beguiling storyteller." *Dictionary of Literary Biography* contributor Roger A. Crockett notes "there is a distinctly dramatic quality to Duerrenmatt's prose," adding that "the same pessimistic view of history, the same distrust of absolutes, and the same dominance of coincidence over rational planning which characterize his dramas also pervade his prose."

"Duerrenmatt is a disillusioned analyst of the human character," writes George Wellwarth in *The Theater of Protest and Paradox*. "Even the plays with political themes are ultimately about the human beings rather than issues. Like Ionesco, like Beckett, like all the writers of the dramatic avant-garde in fact, Duerrenmatt feels deep down in himself that the problems of humanity are insoluble. And so he takes refuge from this knowledge in a mordantly sardonic portrayal of life." Duerrenmatt's recurring themes, according to Wellwarth, are "the effect of the possession of power on the human souls," and the senselessness of death, which "renders human acts trivial." But, Wellwarth contends, "Duerrenmatt always implies that events must be resisted. Nothing is inevitable and determined in Duerrenmatt. The fact that things are insignificant from a cosmic viewpoint does not alter the fact that they are significant in the immediate present: it merely argues that they are finally insoluble and will always repeat themselves." Duerrenmatt once commented: "The universal escapes my grasp. I refuse to find the universal in a doctrine. The universal for me is chaos. The world (hence the stage which represents this world) is for me something monstrous, a riddle of misfortunes which must be accepted but before which one must not capitulate."

BIOGRAPHICAL/CRITICAL SOURCES:

BOOKS

Arnold, Armin, *Friedrich Duerrenmatt,* translated by Arnold with Sheila Johnson, Ungar, 1972.

Bauland, Peter, *The Hooded Eagle: Modern German Drama on the New York Stage,* Syracuse University Press, 1968.

Block, H. M., and H. Salinger, editors, *Creative Vision,* Evergreen, 1960.

Bogard, Travis, and William I. Oliver, editors, *Modern Drama,* Oxford University Press, 1965.

Cole, Toby, editor, *Playwrights on Playwriting,* Hill & Wang, 1961.

Contemporary Literary Criticism, Gale, Volume 1, 1973, Volume 4, 1975, Volume 8, 1978, Volume 11, 1979, Volume 15, 1980, Volume 43, 1987.

Corrigan, Robert W., *The Theatre in Search of a Fix,* Delacorte Press, 1973.

Daemmrich, Horst S., and Diether H. Haenicke, editors, *The Challenge of German Literature,* Wayne State University Press, 1971.

Dictionary of Literary Biography, Volume 69: *Contemporary German Fiction Writers, First Series,* Gale, 1988.

Esslin, Martin, *Reflections: Essays on Modern Theatre,* Doubleday, 1969.

Fickert, J. K., *To Heaven and Back,* University Press of Kentucky, 1972.

Hansel, J., *Friedrich Duerrenmatt: Bibliographie,* Gehlen, 1968.

Hayman, Ronald, editor, *The German Theatre: A Symposium,* Barnes & Noble, 1975.

Jenny, U., *Duerrenmatt: A Study of His Play,* Methuen, 1971.

Knapp, Gerhard P., *Friedrich Duerrenmatt: Studien zu seinem Werk,* Lother Stiehm, 1976.

Knapp, Gerhard P., and Gerd Labroisse, editors, *Facetten: Studien zum 60. Geburtstag Friedrich Duerrenmatt,* Peter Lang, 1981.

Lumley, Frederick, *New Trends in Twentieth Century Drama,* Oxford University Press, 1967.

Mayer, Hans, *Steppenwolf and Everyman,* translated and introduced by Jack D. Zipes, Crowell, 1971.

Peppard, Murray, *Friedrich Duerrenmatt,* Twayne, 1969.

Symons, Julian, *Mortal Consequences: A History; from the Detective Story to the Crime Novel,* Harper, 1972.

Tynan, Kenneth, *Curtains,* Atheneum, 1961.

Wager, Walter, editor, *The Playwrights Speak,* Delacorte Press, 1967.

Wellwarth, George, *The Theater of Protest and Paradox: Developments in the Avant-garde Drama,* New York University Press, 1964.

Whitton, Kenneth S., *The Theatre of Friedrich Duerrenmatt: A Study in the Possibility of Freedom,* Oswald Wolff, 1980.

Wilbert-Collins, E., *Bibliography of Four Contemporary Swiss-German Authors: Friedrich Duerrenmatt, Max Frisch, Robert Walser, Albin Zollinger,* Francke, 1967.

PERIODICALS

Books Abroad, autumn, 1967.

Christian Century, October 28, 1964.

Christian Science Monitor, July 22, 1965; August 7, 1965.

Comparative Drama, spring, 1982.

Contemporary Literature, autumn, 1966; summer, 1970.

Esquire, May, 1961.

Forum for Modern Language Studies, January, 1976.

Genre, December, 1975.

German Life and Letters, January, 1974.

German Quarterly, January, 1962.
International Fiction Review, July, 1977.
Maske und Kothurn, Volume 2, 1977.
Modern Drama, June, 1977.
Modern Fiction Studies, winter, 1971-72.
Monatshefte, spring, 1971.
Mosaic, spring, 1972.
Nation, January 9, 1960; May 4, 1963.
New York Times, October 18, 1964; July 10, 1965; June 4, 1971; February 5, 1989.
New York Times Book Review, June 13, 1965; August 6, 1989.
Renascence, winter, 1985.
Saturday Review, July 17, 1965.
Stage, January 20, 1972.
Time, December 10, 1973.
Times (London), June 29, 1989.
Times Literary Supplement, January 11, 1964; July 14, 1966; October 27, 1972; October 16, 1981; October 29, 1982; May 16, 1986.
Tribune Books (Chicago), March 6, 1988.
Voice Literary Supplement, February, 1984.
World Literature Today, winter, 1978; autumn, 1981; summer, 1982; summer, 1984; spring, 1986; summer, 1986; autumn, 1987.

* * *

DUFFY, Maureen 1933-

PERSONAL: Born October 21, 1933, in Worthing, Sussex, England; daughter of Cahia Patrick Duffy and Grace Rose Wright. *Education:* King's College, London, B.A. (with honors), 1956. *Politics:* Socialist. *Religion:* None.

ADDRESSES: Home—8 Roland Gardens, London SW7, England. *Agent*—Jonathan Clowes, 22 Prince Albert Rd., London NW1, England.

CAREER: Novelist. Teacher of creative writing in England in state schools and to adults 1951-53, 1956-60; has also taught adult classes more recently in Amherst and London.

MEMBER: Writers Guild of Great Britain (deputy chairman; joint chairman, 1978-79), British Copyright Council (vice chairman, 1980—), Authors Lending and Copyright Society (chairman, 1981—).

AWARDS, HONORS: City of London Festival Playwright's Award, 1961, for "The Lay-Off"; Arts Council of Great Britain scholarships, 1963, for drama, 1966, for literature.

WRITINGS:

"The Lay-Off" (play), produced at the City of London Festival, 1961.
That's How It Was, Hutchinson, 1962.
(Translator) Domenico Rea, *A Blush of Shame*, Barrie & Rockliff, 1963.
The Single Eye, Hutchinson, 1964.
The Microcosm, Simon & Schuster, 1966.
"The Silk Room" (play), produced in England at Watford Civic Theatre, 1966.
The Paradox Players, Hutchinson, 1967, Simon & Schuster, 1968.
Lyrics for the Dog Hour (poems), Hutchinson, 1968.
Wounds, Knopf, 1969.
Rites (play; produced by the National Theatre Repertory Co. in London at Jeannetta Cochrane Theatre, spring, 1969), Methuen, 1969.
"Solo, Olde Thyme" (play), produced in Cambridge, 1970.

Love Child, Knopf, 1971.
The Venus Touch (poems), Weidenfeld & Nicolson, 1971.
The Erotic World of Faery, Hodder & Stoughton, 1972.
All Heaven in a Rage, Knopf, 1973 (published in England as *I Want to Go to Moscow*, Hodder & Stoughton, 1973).
"A Nightingale in Bloomsbury Square" (play), produced at the Hampstead Theatre, 1974.
Capital, Braziller 1976.
The Passionate Shepherdess: Aphra Behn (biography), J. Cape, 1977.
(Editor with Alan Brownjohn) *New Poetry* (anthology), Arts Council of Great Britain, 1977.
Housespy (novel), Hamish Hamilton, 1978.
Memorials of the Quick and the Dead (poems), Hamish Hamilton, 1979.
Inherit the Earth (social history), Hamish Hamilton, 1980.
Gor Saga (novel), Viking, 1982.
Londoners (novel), Methuen, 1983.
Men and Beasts: An Animal Rights Handbook, Paladin, 1984.
Collected Poems, Hamish Hamilton, 1985.
(Editor) Aphra Behn, *Oroonoko and Other Stories*, Methuen, 1986.
Change, Methuen, 1987.
A Thousand Capricious Chances: A History of the Methuen List 1889-1989, Methuen, 1989.

Also author of *Evesong* (poems), published by Sappho Publications.

SIDELIGHTS: "British critics have compared [Maureen Duffy] to Virginia Woolf," writes a reviewer for *Time*, "noting that both have the knack of tuning the physical world precisely to the pitch of the characters' emotions. Miss Duffy has a special talent for describing landscape, seascape and weather." Duffy's ability to handle description and develop characters is perhaps most apparent in her fourth novel, *The Paradox Players*. David Lawson notes: "Miss Duffy's sparse, restrained style captures the brooding emptiness of river living, but the reader is ever aware of the pulse and flow of the life there." A critic for the *New Yorker* writes that "no one character in [*The Paradox Players*] is outstanding, although each human being and each animal is impeccably drawn and treated with thorough understanding. As a study in gray, animated and given sad meaning by the slow movement of gray figures, gray weather, and fateful gray light, her book is a work of art."

Some reviewers are disturbed, however, by what Frank Littler calls an "obstinate lack of focus" in Duffy's work. M. K. Margoshes suggests that "perhaps it was the author's intention to write in a disjointed and disorganized manner to convey the feeling of confusion that exists in the subjects' lives." The critic for the *Times Literary Supplement* regrets the uncertainty he finds in the "larger implications" of her work because, as he writes, she "handles detail so beautifully and can suggest what her characters see, imagine and remember with such precision and life." According to Piers Brendon, "Maureen Duffy has a muted voice, but its attenuated tones subtly invade the consciousness and linger echoing in the memory."

Valentine Cunningham comments on a more recent novel: "Duffy is as much interested in language as in story. . . . And *Capital*'s celebration of London doesn't just recollect the past but tries to recreate it in the styles of the past—one of the braver methods of Joyce—even if 222 pages isn't quite up to *Ulysses*'s scope. . . . The room Maureen Duffy's proceedings allows her for irony is immense, and opportunities for sly humour rarely go unexploited."

BIOGRAPHICAL/CRITICAL SOURCES:

BOOKS

Contemporary Literary Criticism, Volume 37, Gale, 1986.
Dictionary of Literary Biography, Volume 14: *British Novelists since 1960,* Gale, 1983.

PERIODICALS

Books and Bookmen, October, 1967, November, 1967.
Bookseller, March 27, 1971.
New Statesman, September 9, 1975.
New Yorker, October 5, 1968.
New York Times, August 17, 1969, March 19, 1976.
New York Times Book Review, August 17, 1969, May 27, 1973.
Observer, September 17, 1967.
Spectator, October 13, 1967, May 1, 1971, October 29, 1983.
Time, September 13, 1968.
Times Literary Supplement, May 26, 1966, September 28, 1967, July 3, 1969, July 5, 1971, November 10, 1972, June 8, 1973, September 19, 1975, April 7, 1978, November 6, 1981, October 7, 1983, May 15, 1987, August 11, 1989.
Washington Post Book World, April 11, 1971.

*   *   *

DUHAMEL, Georges   1884-1966
(Denis Thevenin)

PERSONAL: Born June 30, 1884, in Paris, France; died April 13, 1966, in Valmondois, France; married Blanche Albane (an actress); children: three sons. *Education:* University of Paris, M.D., 1907.

CAREER: Writer. Physician in private practice; worked as laboratory researcher, 1909-14. Co-founder and member of L'Abbaye (an artists' colony), 1906-07; director of French Radio Broadcasting during World War II. *Military service:* Military surgeon during World War I.

MEMBER: National Committee of Authors, French Academy (former acting secretary), Academy of Medicine.

AWARDS, HONORS: Prix Goncourt, 1918, for *Civilization.*

WRITINGS:

"VIE ET AVENTURES DE SALAVIN" SERIES; NOVELS

Confession de minuit (also see below), Mercure de France, 1920.
Deux Hommes (title means "Two Men") Mercure de France, 1924.
Journal de Salavin (also see below), Mercure de France, 1927.
Le Club de Lyonnais (also see below), Mercure de France, 1929.
Tel qu'en lui-meme (also see below), Mercure de France, 1932.
Salavin (contains *Confession at Midnight, Salavin's Journal, The Lyonnais Club, End of Illusion*), translated by Gladys Billings, Putnam, 1936, reprinted, Morley-Baker, 1969.

"LA CHRONIQUE DES PASQUIER" SERIES; NOVELS

Le Notaire du Havre (also see below), Mercure de France, 1933, translation by Beatrice de Holthoir published as *News From Havre,* Dent, 1934, translation by Samuel Putnam published as *Papa Pasquier,* Harper, 1934.
Le Jardin des betes sauvages (also see below), Mercure de France, 1934, translation by de Holthoir published as *Young Pasquier,* Dent, 1935.
Vue de la terre promise (also see below), Mercure de France, 1934, translation by de Holthoir published as *The Sight of the Promised Land,* Dent, 1935.

The Fortunes of the Pasquiers (contains *The Garden of the Wild Beasts* and *Canaan Glimpsed*), translated by Putnam, Harper, 1935.
La Nuit de la Saint Jean (also see below), Mercure de France, 1935.
Le Desert de Bievres (also see below), Mercure de France, 1937.
The Pasquier Chronicles (contains *News From Havre, Caged Beasts, In Sight of the Promised Land, St. John's Eve, The House in the Desert*), translation by de Holthoir, Dent, 1937, Holt, 1938.
Les Maitres (also see below), Mercure de France, 1937.
Cecile parmi nous (also see below), Mercure de France, 1938.
La Combat contre les ombres (also see below), Mercure de France, 1939.
Cecile Among the Pasquiers (contains *Pastors and Masters, Cecile, The Fight Against the Shadows*), translation by de Holthoir, Dent, 1940, published as *Cecile Pasquier,* Holt, 1940.
Suzanne et les jeunes hommes (also see below), Mercure de France, 1940.
La Passion de Joseph Pasquier (also see below), [Paris], 1941.
Suzanne and Joseph Pasquier (contains *Suzanne and the Young Men* and *The Passion of Joseph Pasquier*), translation by de Holthoir, Dent, 1946, published as *Suzanne, Joseph: Two Novels from the Pasquier Chronicles,* Holt, 1949.
Chronique des Pasquier (omnibus), ten volumes, French and European Publications, 1957-63.

POETRY

Des Legendes, des batailles, Editiond de L'Abbaye, 1907.
L'Homme en tete, Editions "Vers et Prose," 1909.
Selon ma loi, Figuiere, 1910.
Compagnons, Novelle Revue Francaise, 1912.
Elegies, Bloch, 1920.
Voix du vieux monde, [France], 1925.

PLAYS

La Lumiere (four-act; first produced at the Odeon in 1911), Figuiere, 1911, translation by Sasha Best published as *The Light,* [Boston], 1914.
Dans l'ombre des statues (three-act; first produced at the Odeon in 1912), Novelle Revue Francaise, translation by Best published as *In the Shadow of Statues,* R. G. Badger, 1914.
Le Combat (five-act; first produced at Theatre des Arts in 1913), Mercure de France, 1913, translation by Best published as *The Combat,* R. G. Badger, 1915.
L'Oeuvre des athletes (four-act; first produced at the Vieux Colombier, April 10, 1920) [and] *Lapointe et Ropiteau* (one-act; first produced in Geneva, 1920), Nouvelle Revue Francaise, 1920.
La Journee aux aveux (three-act; first produced at the Comedie des Champs-Elysees in 1923) [and] *Quand vous voudrez,* Mercure de France, 1924.

"LUMIERES SUR MA VIE" SERIES; MEMOIRS

Inventaire de l'abime, 1884-1901 (also see below), P. Hartmann, 1944.
Biographie de mes fantomes, 1901-1906 (also see below), P. Hartmann, 1944.
Le Temps de la recherche, P. Hartmann, 1947.
Light on My Days: An Autobiography (contains *Inventaire de l'abime, 1884-1901* and *Biographie de mes fantomes, 1901-1906*), translation by Basil Collier, Dent, 1948.
La Pesee des ames, 1914-1919, Mercure de France, 1949.
Les Espoirs et les epreuves, 1919-1928, Mercure de France, 1953.

OTHER

(With Charles Vildrac) *Notes sur la technique poetique* (nonfiction), [Paris], 1910.

Propos critiques (literary criticism), Figuiere, 1912.

Paul Claudel: Le Philosophe—le poete—l'ecrivan (literary criticism), Mercure de France, 1913, 9th edition, 1924.

Les Poetes et la poesie, 1812-1913, Mercure de France, 1914, revised and enlarged edition, 1922.

Vie des martyrs, 1914-1916 (war stories), Mercure de France, 1917, reprinted, 1966, translation by Florence Simmonds published as *The New Book of Martyrs,* Doran, 1918.

(Under pseudonym Denis Thevenin) *Civilisation, 1914-1917* (war stories), Mercure de France, 1918, translation by Eleanor Stimson Brooks published as *Civilization, 1914-1917,* Century Co., 1919, reprinted, Richard West, 1978.

Entretiens dans le tumulte: Chronique contemporaine, 1918-1919 (essays), Mercure de France, 1919.

Elevation et mort d'Armand Branche (fiction), B. Grasset (Paris), 1919.

La Possession du monde (essays), Mercure de France, 1919, reprinted, 1964, translation by Brooks published as *The Heart's Domain,* Century Co., 1919.

Guerre et litterature, [Paris], 1920.

Les Hommes abandonnes (short stories; title means "The Abandoned Men"), Mercure de France, 1921.

Trois journees de la tribu, Gallimard, 1921.

Les Plaisers et les jeux: Memoires du Cuib et du Tioup, Mercure de France, 1922, reprinted, 1946, translation by R. Wills Thomas published as *Days of Delight,* Andrew Dakers, 1939.

Lettres d'Aupasie, Sablier (Paris), 1922.

(Editor) *Anthologie de la poesie lyrique francaise de la fin du XV siecle a la fin du XIX siecle,* Insel Verlag (Leipzig), 1923.

Le Miracle: Suivi de la chambre de l'horlage, Stock (Paris), 1923.

Le Prince Jaffar (novel; title means "The Prince of Jaffar"), Mercure de France, 1924.

La Belle-Etoile, a l'enseigne de la porte etroite, Mercure de France, 1925.

Suite Hollandaise, Sablier, 1925.

Deliberations, Cahiers de Paris, 1925.

Essai sur le roman (literary criticism), M. Lesage (Paris), 1925.

Essai sur une renaissance dramatique (literary criticism), Editions Lapina (Paris), 1926.

Lettres au Patagon, Mercure de France, 1926.

Lettre sur les malades, [Paris], 1926.

La Pierre d'Horeb (novel; title means "Horeb's Stone"), Mercure de France, 1926, reprinted, Vialetay (Paris), 1973.

Maurice de Vlaminck, Les Ecrivans Reunis, 1927.

Le Voyage de Moscou (nonfiction), Mercure de France, 1927.

Memorial de Cauchois, Editions de la Belle Page, 1927.

Images de la Grece, Sablier, 1928.

Hommages et souvenirs, [Liege], 1928.

Les Sept Dernieres Plaies (title means "The Last Seven Wounds"), Mercure de France, 1928.

Entretien sur l'esprit europeen (essays), Aux Editions des Cahiers Libres, 1928.

La Nuit d'orage (novel; title means "The Stormy Night"), Mercure de France, 1928, reprinted, Harper, 1953.

Chant du nord, Sablier, 1929.

Scenes de la vie future (essays), Mercure de France, 1931, translation by Charles Miner Thompson published as *America: The Menace, Scenes from the Life of the Future,* Houghton, 1931, reprinted, Arno, 1974.

L'Alsace entrevue; ou, L'aveugle et le paralytique, Librairie de la Messange (Strasbourg), 1931.

Geographie cordiale de l'Europe (nonfiction), Mercure de France, 1931.

Pages de mon carnet (nonfiction), Aux Editions des Cahiers Libres, 1931.

Les Jumeaux de Vallangoujard, P. Hartmann, 1931.

Mon Royaume, [Paris], 1932.

Querelles de famille (essays), Mercure de France, 1932, reprinted, 1959.

L'Humaniste et l'automate (nonfiction), P. Hartmann, 1933.

Remarques sur les memoires imaginaires (literary criticism), Mercure de France, 1934.

Discours aux nuages, Editions du Siecle, 1934.

(With Charles Jules Henri Nicolle and others) *Responsabilites de la medecine,* [Paris], 1935.

Fables de mon jardin (nature studies), Mercure de France, 1936.

Defense des lettres: Biologie de mon metier, Mercure de France, 1936, translation by Ernest Franklin Bozman published as *In Defence of Letters,* Dent, 1938, Greystone Press, 1939, reprinted, Richard West, 1973.

Discours de reception de M. Georges Duhamel a l'Academie francaise, Mercure de France, 1936.

Deux patrons, suivi de Vie et mort d'un heros de roman, P. Hartmann, 1937.

Le Dernier voyage de Candide, suivi d'un choix de nouvelles, Fernand Sorlot, 1938.

Memorial de la guerre blanche, Mercure de France, 1938, translation by N. Hoppe published as *The White War of 1938,* Dent, 1939.

Au chevet de la civilisation (essays), Flammarion (Paris), 1938.

Positions francaises: Chronique de l'annee 1939, Mercure de France, 1940, translation by Basil Collier published as *Why France Fights,* Dent, 1940, published as *The French Position,* Dent, 1940.

Les Confessions sans penitence, suivi de trois autres entretiens: Rousseau, Montesquieu, Descartes, Pascal, Plon (Paris), 1941.

Chronique des saisons ameres, 1940-1943, P. Hartmann, 1944.

Civilisation francaise, Hachette (Paris), 1944.

La Musique consolatrice, Editions du Rocher (Monaco), 1944.

Lieu d'asile, Mercure de France, 1945.

Souvenirs de la vie du paradis, Mercure de France, 1946.

Paroles de medecin, Editions du Rocher, 1946.

Semailles au vent, Editions du Rocher, 1947.

(With Henri Mondor) *Entretien au bord du fleuve: Discours de reception a l'Academie francaise de Henri Mondor et reponse de Georges Duhamel,* Editions du Rocher, 1947.

Consultation aux pays d'Islam, Mercure de France, 1947.

Tribulations de l'esperance, Mercure de France, 1947.

Homere au XXe siecle: Croquis et lettres de voyage de Berthold Mahn, Union Latine d'Editions (Paris), 1947.

Le bestiaire et l'herbier, Mercure de France, 1948.

(Author of preface) *Paris,* M. J. Challamel, 1950.

Le Voyage de Patrice Periot (novel), Mercure de France, 1951, translation by Bozman published as *Patrice Periot,* Dent, 1952.

Cri de profondeurs (novel), Mercure de France, 1951, translation by Bozman published as *Cry out of the Depths,* Dent, 1953, Little, Brown, 1954.

Manuel du protestataire, Mercure de France, 1952.

Le Japon entre le tradition et l'avenir, Mercure de France, 1953.

La Turquie nouvelle, puissance d'Occident, Mercure de France, 1954.

Refuges de lecture, Mercure de France, 1954.

L'Archange de l'aventure (novel), Mercure de France, 1955.

Croisade contre le cancer, Jeheber (Geneva), 1955.

Les Compagnons de l'Apocalypse (novel), Mercure de France, 1956.

Les Voyageurs de l'Esperance, Gedalge (Paris), 1956.

Israel, clef de l'Orient, Mercure de France, 1957.

Les Livres du bonheur, Mercure de France, 1957.

Problemes de l'heure, Mercure de France, 1957.

Le Complexe de Theophile (novel), Mercure de France, 1958.

(Author of introduction) Georges Poisson, *Histoire et histoires de Sceaux,* Les Amis du Musee de l'Ile de France, 1959.

Travail, o mon seul repos!, Editions Wesmael-Charlier, 1959.

Nouvelles du sombre empire, Mercure de France, 1960.

Traite du depart, suivi de Fables de ma vie (also see below), Mercure de France, 1961.

Problemes de civilisation, precede de Traite du depart, Fables de ma vie, La Medecine au vingtieme siecle, Mercure de France, 1962.

Le Livre de l'amertume: Extraits du journal de Blanche et Georges Duhamel, Mercure de France, 1983.

Director of *Mercure de France,* a literary magazine, 1935-37.

SIDELIGHTS: While studying to be a doctor at the University of Paris, Georges Duhamel began developing an interest in literature. With several other young men, including Jules Romains, Rene Arcos, Charles Vildrac, Albert Gleizes, and Henri Martin, Duhamel founded an artists' colony, L'Abbaye. The experimental community was located in an old house on the shore of the Marne. Its members shared a belief in unanimism, a philosophy developed by Romains which held that the spirit of a group lends direction and energy to an individual's life. The community published several books as a joint venture but was forced to disband after fourteen months for economic reasons. After the failure of L'Abbaye, Duhamel worked as a researcher in a laboratory and wrote poetry and plays in his spare time. It was his plays that first brought him public recognition.

Duhamel's literary aspirations were temporarily shoved aside when World War I broke out. Duhamel worked as a military surgeon at the front for over four years. During that time he performed 2300 operations and took care of 4000 wounded soldiers. Having witnessed the ravages of war firsthand, Duhamel yearned for a world in which compassion and tolerance would prevail over the baser instincts of mankind. This longing for a better world was to guide his future writing. Boyd G. Carter noted that Duhamel's canon "demonstrates the continuity of his interest in permanent human values and his anxiety concerning their survival in an age of mechanical acceleration, fantastic destruction, and epochal transformation."

In *The New Book of Martyrs* and *Civilization,* written when Duhamel could snatch time from his duties at the front, he describes the anguish of the wounded and dying as well as the insensitivity of those who ran the military hospitals. "In the spiritual sense, the author of *Civilisation* is a great war casualty: he is a man who has never recovered from what he saw every day for four years," Francois Mauriac observed. "The essential gift of the man who wrote *Vie des Martyres* is imagination of the heart; he had the ability to share the suffering of others, to relive it in himself."

Following the war, Duhamel began work on his two famous novel cycles, "Salavin" and "The Pasquier Chronicles." The five novels that make up the "Salavin" series are now regarded as classics of world literature. Salavin is a mediocre yet introspective man who works for a pasteurized milk company. Although he wishes to improve himself and his circumstances, Salavin fails in most of his endeavors. Nonetheless, he is a likable character because he remains aware of his potential even though he never achieves it. Critics have praised Duhamel for the subtlety and psychological depth with which he portrays Salavin. Salavin, who searches for salvation outside of religion, is considered by many to be the prototype of the ordinary man of the twentieth century.

The "Salavin" cycle focuses on an individual, but "The Pasquier Chronicles" give a broader picture of French middle class life from the 1880s to World War I. The saga of the Pasquier family is based on Duhamel's own family. The head of the Pasquier clan, like Duhamel's father, studied medicine in middle age and became a practicing physician. Of the five Pasquier children, Duhamel most closely resembles Laurent, an urbane, successful, and stable man. "The Pasquier Chronicles" are not so highly regarded as the "Salavin" series. Some commentators found the long series boring, while others faulted Duhamel's subjective promotion of his own values. "Duhamel's humanism is sincere and his concern with the frustrations and joys of the man in the street is real, but the rather facile sentimentality of his approach, the naive ethical evangelism of his attitude, based on vague spiritual values, hamper the creative artist he might have been," Germaine Bree and Margaret Guiton wrote in *An Age of Fiction.*

For a man who had devoted his life and work to promoting harmony between people, Duhamel was forced to view an excessive amount of violence and suffering. Duhamel stayed in Paris during the German occupation in World War II, even though he had openly announced his opposition to Hitler. Duhamel's books were banned, three of his relatives were arrested, but he himself managed to evade the Nazi persecutors. Extremely proud of the French resistance movement, Duhamel contributed to *Les Lettres francaises,* an underground publication.

Duhamel's experiences in World War II did not drive him to despair; rather, they reinforced his belief in humanism. In a review of the French author's work, Henri Peyre remarked that Duhamel "is not blind to the disappointments that an optimist must endure, and all his novels display the gradual collapse of a rosy dream. He will not seek a solution in an easy catchword, tendered by Christianity, which he respected but never professed, or in science, which he always admired, though he was aware of its limitations. Friendship is the feeling of which he spoke most nobly (in *Deux Hommes* especially); like Romains, Vildrac, and later Malraux and Saint-Exupery, he would have liked to build a virile and warm regeneration of mankind upon friendship, that is, upon the most beautiful of all words and ideals proposed by humanism and by christianity-fraternity." Some of Duhamel's works have been translated into German, Spanish, Polish, and Arabic.

AVOCATIONAL INTERESTS: Flutist.

BIOGRAPHICAL/CRITICAL SOURCES:

BOOKS

Bree, Germaine, and Margaret Otis Guiton, *An Age of Fiction: The French Novel From Gide to Camus,* Rutgers University Press, 1957, published as *The French Novel: From Gide to Camus,* Harcourt, 1962.

Contemporary Literary Criticism, Volume 8, Gale, 1978.

Dictionary of Literary Biography, Volume 65: *French Novelists, 1900-1930,* Gale, 1988.

Hatzfeld, Helmut, *Trends and Styles in Twentieth Century French Literature,* Catholic University, 1957.

Keating, Louis Clark, *Critic of Civilization: Georges Duhamel and His Writings,* University of Kentucky Press, 1965.

Knapp, Bettina L., *Georges Duhamel,* Twayne, 1972.

Mauriac, Francois, *Second Thoughts,* World, 1961.

Michand, Regis, *Modern Thought and Literature in France,* Funk, 1934.

Peyre, Henri, *French Novelists of Today,* Oxford University Press, 1967.

PERIODICALS

Books Abroad, winter, 1946.
Contemporary Review, April, 1948.
National Review of Literature, July, 1948.

OBITUARIES:

PERIODICALS

Antiquarian Bookman, May 2, 1966.
Books Abroad, spring, 1967.
New York Times, April 14, 1966.
Publishers Weekly, April 25, 1966.

*   *   *

du MAURIER, Daphne   1907-1989

PERSONAL: Born May 13, 1907, in London, England; died April 19, 1989, in Par, Cornwall, England; cremated; daughter of Gerald (an actor and manager) and Muriel (an actress; maiden name, Beaumont) du Maurier; married Frederick Arthur Montague Browning (a lieutenant-general and former treasurer to the Duke of Edinburgh), July 19, 1932 (died, 1965); children: Tessa (Mrs. David Montgomery), Flavia Browning Tower, Christian. *Education:* Attended schools in London, England, Meudon, France, and Paris, France. *Politics:* "Center."

ADDRESSES: Home—Kilmairth, Par, Cornwall, England. *Agent*—Curtis Brown, 162-168 Regent St., London, England.

CAREER: Writer, 1931-89.

MEMBER: Bronte Society, Royal Society of Literature (fellow).

AWARDS, HONORS: National Book Award, 1938, for *Rebecca;* Dame Commander, Order of the British Empire, 1969.

WRITINGS:

The Loving Spirit, Doubleday, 1931, reprinted, Pan Books, 1976.
I'll Never Be Young Again, Doubleday, 1932, reprinted, Pan Books, 1975.
The Progress of Julius, Doubleday, 1933, reprinted, Avon, 1973.
Jamaica Inn (also see below), Doubleday, 1936, reprinted, Avon, 1977, abridged edition, edited by Jay E. Greene, bound with *The Thirty Nine Steps* by John Buchan, Globe Publications, 1951.
Rebecca (also see below), Doubleday, 1938, reprinted, Avon, 1978.
Frenchman's Creek (also see below), Gollancz, 1941, Doubleday, 1942, reprinted, Pan Books, 1976.
Hungry Hill (also see below), Doubleday, 1943, reprinted, Avon, 1974.
The King's General, Doubleday, 1946, reprinted, Avon, 1978, abridged edition, edited by Lee Wyndham, Garden City Books, 1954.
The Parasites, Gollancz, 1949, Doubleday, 1950, reprinted, Avon, 1974.
My Cousin Rachel (also see below), Gollancz, 1951, Doubleday, 1952, reprinted, Bentley, 1971.
Mary Anne (fictionalized biography of author's great-great grandmother), Doubleday, 1954, reprinted, Avon, 1973.
The Scapegoat, Doubleday, 1957, reprinted, Queen's House, 1977.

Three Romantic Novels: Rebecca, Frenchman's Creek, Jamaica Inn, Doubleday, 1961.
(With Arthur Quiller-Couch) *Castle d'Or,* Doubleday, 1962.
The Glass-Blowers, Doubleday, 1963.
The Flight of the Falcon, Doubleday, 1965.
The House on the Strand (Literary Guild selection), Doubleday, 1969.
Rule Britannia, Gollancz, 1972, Doubleday, 1973.
Four Great Cornish Novels (contains *Jamaica Inn, Rebecca, Frenchman's Creek,* and *My Cousin Rachel*), Gollancz, 1978.

SHORT STORY COLLECTIONS

Come Wind, Come Weather, Heinemann, 1940, Doubleday, 1941.
The Apple Tree: A Short Novel and Some Stories, Gollancz, 1952, published as *Kiss Me Again, Stranger: A Collection of Eight Stories, Long and Short,* Doubleday, 1953, reprinted, Avon, 1972 (published in England as *The Birds, and Other Stories,* Pan Books, 1977).
The Breaking Point, Doubleday, 1959 (published in England as *The Blue Lenses, and Other Stories,* Penguin, 1970).
Early Stories, Todd, 1959.
The Treasury of du Maurier Short Stories, Gollancz, 1960.
Don't Look Now, Doubleday, 1971 (published in England as *Not After Midnight,* Gollancz, 1971).
Echoes From the Macabre: Selected Stories, Gollancz, 1976. Doubleday, 1977.
The Rendezvous, and Other Stories, Gollancz, 1980.

PLAYS

Rebecca (three-act; based on author's novel of same title; produced on the West End at Queen's Theatre, April 5, 1940, produced on Broadway at Ethel Barrymore Theatre, January 18, 1945), Gollancz, 1940, Dramatists Play Service, 1943.
The Years Between (two-act; first produced in Manchester, England, 1944, produced on the West End at Wyndham's Theatre, January 10, 1945), Gollancz, 1945, Doubleday, 1946.
September Tide (three-act; produced on the West End at Aldwych Theatre, December 15, 1948), Gollancz, 1949, Doubleday, 1950.

OTHER

Gerald: A Portrait (biography of author's father), Gollancz, 1934, Doubleday, 1935, reprinted, Richard West, 1978.
The du Mauriers (family history and biography), Doubleday, 1937.
Happy Christmas, Doubleday, 1940.
Spring Picture, Todd, 1944.
(Coauthor) "Hungry Hill" (screenplay; based on author's novel of same title), Universal Pictures, 1947.
(Editor) *The Young George du Maurier: A Selection of His Letters, 1860-1867,* P. Davies, 1951, Doubleday, 1952.
The Infernal World of Branwell Bronte (biography), Gollancz, 1960, Doubleday, 1961.
(Editor) Phyllis Bottome, *Best Stories,* Faber, 1963.
Vanishing Cornwall (history and travel), Doubleday, 1967.
Golden Lads: Sir Francis Bacon, Anthony Bacon and Their Friends, Doubleday, 1975.
The Winding Stair: Francis Bacon, His Rise and Fall, Gollancz, 1976, Doubleday, 1977.
Myself When Young: The Shaping of a Writer (autobiography), Doubleday, 1977 (published in England as *Growing Pains: The Shaping of a Writer,* Gollancz, 1977).

The "Rebecca" Notebook, and Other Memories, Doubleday, 1980.

SIDELIGHTS: "Last night I dreamt I went to Manderley again." With these words, some of the most recognizable in twentieth-century fiction, Daphne du Maurier began her classic Gothic novel *Rebecca.* Described by the *Spectator*'s Kate O'Brien as "a Charlotte Bronte story minus Charlotte Bronte," *Rebecca* takes a familiar situation (the arrival of a second wife in her new husband's home) and turns it into an occasion for mystery, suspense, and violence. Its primary features—an enigmatic heroine in a cold and hostile environment, a brooding hero tormented by a guilty secret, and a rugged seacoast setting—are now virtual staples of modern romantic novels. Though reviewers point out (and du Maurier agrees) that she cannot take credit for inventing this formula, many of them believe that her personal gift for story-telling places her novels a cut above most other Gothic fiction.

Daughter of renowned actor Gerald du Maurier and granddaughter of artist and author George du Maurier (Trilby), young Daphne first turned to writing as a means of escape. Despite a happy and financially secure childhood, she always felt "inadequate" and desperately in need of solitude. She delighted in the imaginary world of books and play-acting and stubbornly resisted "growing up" until her late teens. After shunning the debutante scene and a chance at an acting career, du Maurier determined to succeed on her own terms—as a writer. During one ten-week stay at her parents' country home on the Cornish coast, the twenty-four-year-old Englishwoman wrote her first novel, *The Loving Spirit,* a romantic family chronicle. A best-seller that achieved a fair share of critical acclaim as well, *The Loving Spirit* so impressed a thirty-five-year-old major in the Grenadier Guards that he piloted his motor launch past the du Maurier home in the hope of meeting the author. Major Frederick "Boy" Browning eventually introduced himself as the son of a man who had known Gerald du Maurier at the Garrick Club in London. Daphne and Major Browning married a few months later, setting off by boat on a honeymoon "just like the couple in *The Loving Spirit,*" as Nicholas Wade points out in the *Times Literary Supplement.*

Perhaps because of the fairy-tale quality in her own life, du Maurier displayed a fondness for romance and intrigue throughout her entire writing career. While some critics feel her short stories ("The Birds" and "Don't Look Now" are probably two of the best-known ones) represent her best work in a literary sense, few dispute the fact that her novels form the basis of her immense popular success. As V. S. Pritchett remarks in a review of *Rebecca:* "Many a better novelist would give his eyes to be able to tell a story as Miss Du Maurier does, to make it move at such a pace and to go with such mastery from surprise to surprise. . . . From the first sinister rumors to the final conflagration the melodrama is excellent."

The *New York Times*'s M. F. Brown also comments on du Maurier's "ability to tell a good story and people it with twinkling reality," while John Patton of *Books* writes: "[*Rebecca*] is first and last and always a thrilling story. . . . Du Maurier's style in telling her story is exactly suited to her plot and her background, and creates the exact spirit and atmosphere of the novel. The rhythm quickens with the story, is always in measure with the story's beat. And the writing has an intensity, a heady beauty, which is itself the utterance of the story's mood." The *Manchester Guardian*'s J. D. Beresford agrees, stating that "the actual writing of [*Rebecca*] has the compelling quality that holds the at-

tention in thrall, keeping our interest unintermittently rapt in the story."

Among those who are less impressed by du Maurier's work (other than *Rebecca*) are critics who feel her novels exhibit too much melodrama, too many plot similarities, and too little character development and analysis. O'Brien describes *Frenchman's Creek,* for example, as "eighteenth century, flashy, wordy, and full of 'sunset and dark water effects.' " The *New Yorker*'s Clifton Fadiman terms it "lushly nonsensical," and Edward Weeks of the *Atlantic* believes the "drag in the dialogue," the "flatness in the characters," and the lack of an "inner spark" make this novel an inadequate follow-up to "the overpowering illusion in *Rebecca.*" Notes a *Springfield Republican* reviewer: "[*Frenchman's Creek*] lacks a proper tempo of excitement. Its plot seems artificial. . . . We see [the heroine] only as she is influenced by [her] strange adventurous love affair. . . . One who likes an exceedingly romantic love affair will read this story . . . with pleasure, but it has not the sort of stuff that made readers of *Rebecca* cling to that book until they had read the last page."

With the exception of *My Cousin Rachel,* a book several critics hail as another *Rebecca,* most of du Maurier's later novels seem to suffer in comparison to the work some view as a minor classic. The *Spectator*'s Paul Ableman, for instance, declares that her "plots creak and depend on either outrageous coincidence or shamelessly contrived mood," that her prose is "both sloppy and chaotic," and that her dialogue "consists of rent-a-line, prefabricated units for the nobs or weird demotic for the yokels." L. A. G. Strong, another *Spectator* critic, also notes the "facile, out-of-character lines that disfigure the often excellent dialogue," as well as a certain "laziness over detail" and a "mixture of careful with perfunctory work." In addition, insists Beatus T. Lucey of *Best Sellers,* "nowhere does the reader become engaged and involved in the action." Lucey also points out that du Maurier's people are mere "types," a view shared by the *Los Angeles Times*'s Marilyn Murray Willison, who says her male characters are all "creatures who bully—physically or psychologically."

Du Maurier herself admits that she is "not so much interested in people as in types—types who represent great forces of good or evil. I don't care very much whether John Smith likes Mary Robinson, goes to bed with Jane Brown and then refuses to pay the hotel bill. But I *am* passionately interested in human cruelty, human lust and human avarice—and, of course, their counterparts in the scale of virtue."

Despite the views of critics who complain about plot similarities and stereotyped characters, Jean Stubbs of *Books and Bookmen* remains convinced that a writer like du Maurier should "seek out his or her personal Wilderness or Eden and stay in it." "Daphne Du Maurier has the deserved reputation of being an outstanding storyteller," Stubbs writes. "She has the gift of conveying mystery and holding suspense, above all of suggesting the grip of the unknown on ordinary lives. . . . She is passionately devoted to Cornwall, and insists on our participation. Her sense of theatre creates some characters a little larger than life, and her commonsense surrounds them with people we have met and known, so that the eccentric and dramatic is enhanced."

Furthermore, as a writer for the *Times Literary Supplement* points out in a review of *Rebecca,* it may not be to anyone's benefit to approach du Maurier's work as one would approach great literature. He states: "If one chooses to read the book in a critical fashion—but only a tiresome reviewer is likely to do that—it becomes an obligation to take off one's hat to Miss du Maurier for the skill and assurance with which she sustains a highly improbable fiction. Whatever else she may lack, it is not the story-teller's flow of fancy. All thing considered, [hers] is an ingenious, exciting and engagingly romantic tale."

Concludes the *Chicago Tribune Book World*'s Anstiss Drake: "There is no doubt that Du Maurier, right at the start of her career, hit on a brilliant combination of ingredients that will continue to hold readers spellbound for a long time. . . . [Her characters] are as real to us as any of Dickens' creations. . . . She sweeps dust away and brings her stories alive. It is a rare talent. . . . In this century few English-speaking authors seem to keep that particular magic. Somerset Maugham was one, and Du Maurier is most definitely another."

MEDIA ADAPTATIONS: Several of Daphne du Maurier's novels and short stories have been adapted for film and television. Alfred Hitchcock directed *Jamaica Inn* for Paramount Pictures Corp. in 1939, *Rebecca* for United Artists Corp. in 1940 (it won an Academy Award for best motion picture as well as a citation by the Film Daily Poll as one of the ten best pictures of the year), and "The Birds" for Universal Pictures in 1963. *Frenchman's Creek* was filmed by Paramount in 1944, *Hungry Hill* by I. Arthur Rank in 1947, *My Cousin Rachel* by Metro-Goldwyn-Mayer, Inc., in 1953, *The Scapegoat* by Metro-Goldwyn-Mayer in 1959, and "Don't Look Now" by Paramount in 1973. In 1979, the British Broadcasting Corp. televised a new adaptation of *Rebecca*.

AVOCATIONAL INTERESTS: Walking, sailing, gardening, country life.

BIOGRAPHICAL/CRITICAL SOURCES:

BOOKS

Contemporary Literary Criticism, Gale, Volume 6, 1976, Volume 11, 1979.
du Maurier, Daphne, *Myself When Young: The Shaping of a Writer,* Doubleday, 1977 (published in England as *Growing Pains: The Shaping of a Writer,* Gollancz, 1977).

PERIODICALS

Atlantic, April, 1942.
Best Sellers, May 1, 1963, October 15, 1969.
Books, August 2, 1931, September 25, 1938, February 1, 1942.
Books and Bookmen, January, 1973.
Canadian Forum, October, 1938.
Chicago Tribune Book World, September 21, 1980.
Christian Science Monitor, September 14, 1938, October 2, 1969, September 21, 1977.
Commonweal, April 10, 1942.
Critic, September, 1978.
Detroit News, November 13, 1977.
Ladies' Home Journal, November, 1956.
Life, September 11, 1944, February 6, 1970.
Listener, June 9, 1977.
Los Angeles Times, October 3, 1980.
Manchester Guardian, January 10, 1936, August 5, 1938, September 19, 1941, August 3, 1951.
Nation, November 11, 1931.
New Statesman and Nation, March 14, 1931, August 11, 1951.
Newsweek, September 26, 1938, January 9, 1950, June 24, 1954.
New Yorker, February 7, 1942, February 9, 1952, September 23, 1967.
New York Herald Tribune Book Review, February 10, 1952.
New York Times, August 2, 1931, April 26, 1936, September 25, 1938, February 1, 1942, February 10, 1952.
New York Times Book Review, October 26, 1969, November 6, 1977, September 21, 1980.

Observer, July 16, 1967.
Outlook, August 5, 1931.
Publishers Weekly, February 18, 1939, January 31, 1948.
Saturday Review, February 28, 1931, April 24, 1937, September 24, 1938, June 19, 1943, January 12, 1946, February 7, 1948, January 7, 1950, February 9, 1952, July 19, 1952, March 14, 1953, February 23, 1957, October 11, 1969.
Saturday Review of Literature, December 12, 1931, April 25, 1936, September 24, 1938, February 14, 1942.
Spectator, February 28, 1931, January 24, 1936, August 12, 1938, September 19, 1941, August 10, 1951, May 14, 1977, November 15, 1980.
Springfield Republican, January 11, 1942.
Theatre Arts, March, 1945.
Time, November 3, 1947, January 16, 1950, February 11, 1952, June 21, 1954, February 25, 1957, February 23, 1962.
Times Literary Supplement, March 5, 1931, January 11, 1936, August 6, 1938, September 13, 1941, June 3, 1977, December 26, 1980.

OBITUARIES:

PERIODICALS

Chicago Tribune, April 20, 1989.
Los Angeles Times, April 20, 1989.
New York Times, April 20, 1989.
Times (London), April 20, 1989.
Washington Post, April 20, 1989, April 23, 1989.

*   *   *

DUNBAR, Alice
  See NELSON, Alice Ruth Moore Dunbar

*   *   *

DUNBAR, Alice Moore
  See NELSON, Alice Ruth Moore Dunbar

*   *   *

DUNBAR-NELSON, Alice
  See NELSON, Alice Ruth Moore Dunbar

*   *   *

DUNBAR-NELSON, Alice Moore
  See NELSON, Alice Ruth Moore Dunbar

*   *   *

DUNCAN, Robert (Edward)   1919-1988
(Robert Edward Symmes)

PERSONAL: Born January 7, 1919, in Oakland, Calif.; died January 7, 1988, of a heart attack in San Francisco, Calif.; name at birth, Edward Howard Duncan; son of Edward Howard (a day laborer) and Marguerite (Wesley) Duncan (who died at the time of his birth); adopted, March 10, 1920, by Edwin Joseph (an architect) and Minnehaha (Harris) Symmes; adopted name, Robert Edward Symmes; in 1941 he took the name Robert Duncan; companion of Jess Collins (a painter). *Education:* Attended University of California, Berkeley, 1936-38, 1948-50, studying the civilization of the Middle Ages under Ernst Kantorowicz.

ADDRESSES: c/o New Directions Publishing Corp., 333 Sixth Ave., New York, N.Y. 10014.

CAREER: Poet. Worked at various times as a dishwasher and typist. Organizer of poetry readings and workshops in San Francisco Bay area, California. *Experimental Review*, co-editor with Sanders Russell, publishing works of Henry Miller, Anais Nin, Lawrence Durrell, Kenneth Patchen, William Everson, Aurora Bligh (Mary Fabilli), Thomas Merton, Robert Horan, and Jack Johnson, 1940-41; *Berkeley Miscellany*, editor, 1948-49; lived in Banyalbufar, Majorca, 1955-56; taught at Black Mountain College, Black Mountain, N.C., spring and summer, 1956; assistant director of Poetry Center, San Francisco State College, under a Ford grant, 1956-57; associated with the Creative Writing Workshop, University of British Columbia, 1963; lecturer in Advanced Poetry Workshop, San Francisco State College, spring, 1965. *Military service:* U.S. Army, 1941; discharged on psychological grounds.

AWARDS, HONORS: Ford Foundation grant, 1956-57; Union League Civic and Arts Foundation Prize, *Poetry* magazine, 1957; Harriet Monroe Prize, *Poetry*, 1961; Guggenheim fellowship, 1963-64; Levinson Prize, *Poetry*, 1964; Miles Poetry Prize, 1964; National Endowment for the Arts grants, 1965, 1966-67; Eunice Tietjens Memorial Prize, *Poetry*, 1967; nomination for National Book Critics Circle Award, 1984, for *Ground Work: Before the War;* first recipient of National Poetry Award, 1985, in recognition of lifetime contribution to the art of poetry; Before Columbus Foundation American Book Award, 1986, for *Ground Work: Before the War;* Fred Cody Award for Lifetime Literary Excellence from Bay Area Book Reviewers Association, 1986.

WRITINGS:

Heavenly City, Earthly City (poems, 1945-46), drawings by Mary Fabilli, Bern Porter, 1947.

Medieval Scenes (poems, 1947), Centaur Press (San Francisco), 1950, reprinted with preface by Duncan and afterword by Robert Bertholf, Kent State University Libraries, 1978.

Poems, 1948-49 (actually written between November, 1947, and October, 1948), Berkeley Miscellany, 1950.

The Song of the Border-Guard (poem), Black Mountain Graphics Workshop, 1951.

The Artist's View, [San Francisco], 1952.

Fragments of a Disordered Devotion, privately printed, 1952, reprinted, Gnomon Press, 1966.

Faust Foutu: Act One of Four Acts, A Comic Mask, 1952-1954 (an entertainment in four parts; first produced in San Francisco, Calif., 1955; produced in New York, 1959-60), decorations by Duncan, Part 1, White Rabbit Press (San Francisco), 1958, reprinted, Station Hill Press, 1985, entire play published as *Faust Foutu*, Enkidu sur Rogate (Stinson Beach, Calif.), 1959.

Caesar's Gate: Poems, 1949-55, Divers Press (Majorca), 1956, 2nd edition, Sand Dollar, 1972.

Medea at Kolchis; [or] The Maiden Head (play; first produced at Black Mountain College, 1956), Oyez, 1965.

Letters (poems, 1953-56), drawings by Duncan, J. Williams (Highlands, N.C.), 1958.

Selected Poems (1942-50), City Lights Books, 1959.

The Opening of the Field (poems, 1956-59), Grove, 1960, revised edition, New Directions, 1973.

(Author of preface) Jess [Collins], *O!* (poems and collages), Hawk's Well Press (New York), 1960.

(Author of preface) Jonathan Williams, *Elegies and Celebrations*, Jargon, 1962.

On Poetry (radio interview, broadcast on WTIC, Hartford, Conn., May 31, 1964), Yale University, 1964.

Roots and Branches (poems, 1959-63), Scribner, 1964.

Writing Writing: A Composition Book of Madison 1953, Stein Imitations (poems and essays, 1953), Sumbooks, 1964.

As Testimony: The Poem and the Scene (essay, 1958), White Rabbit Press, 1964.

Wine, Auerhahn Press for Oyez Broadsheet Series (Berkeley), 1964.

Uprising (poems), Oyez, 1965.

The Sweetness and Greatness of Dante's "Divine Comedy," 1263-1965 (lecture presented at Dominican College of San Raphael, October 27, 1965), Open Space (San Francisco), 1965.

Adam's Way: A Play on Theosophical Themes, [San Francisco], 1966.

(Contributor) Howard Nemerov, editor, *Poets on Poetry*, Basic Books, 1966.

Of the War: Passages 22-27, Oyez, 1966.

A Book of Resemblances: Poems, 1950-53, drawings by Jess, Henry Wenning, 1966.

Six Prose Pieces, Perishable Press (Rochester, Mich.), 1966.

The Years as Catches: First Poems, 1939-46, Oyez, 1966.

Boob (poem), privately printed, 1966.

Audit/Robert Duncan (also published as special issue of *Audit/Poetry*, Volume 4, number 3), Audit/Poetry, 1967.

Christmas Present, Christmas Presence! (poem), Black Sparrow Press, 1967.

The Cat and the Blackbird (children's storybook), illustrations by Jess, White Rabbit Press, 1967.

Epilogos, Black Sparrow Press, 1967.

My Mother Would Be a Falconress (poem), Oyez, 1968.

Names of People (poems, 1952-53), illustrations by Jess, Black Sparrow Press, 1968.

The Truth and Life of Myth: An Essay in Essential Autobiography, House of Books (New York), 1968.

Bending the Bow (poems), New Directions, 1968.

The First Decade: Selected Poems, 1940-50, Fulcrum Press (London), 1968.

Derivations: Selected Poems, 1950-1956, Fulcrum Press, 1968.

Achilles Song, Phoenix, 1969.

Playtime, Pseudo Stein; 1942, A Story [and] A Fairy Play: From the Laboratory Records Notebook of 1953, A Tribute to Mother Carey's Chickens, Poet's Press, c.1969.

Notes on Grossinger's "Solar Journal: Oecological Sections," Black Sparrow Press, 1970.

A Selection of Sixty-Five Drawings from One Drawing Book, 1952-1956, Black Sparrow Press, 1970.

Tribunals: Passages 31-35, Black Sparrow Press, 1970.

Poetic Disturbances, Maya (San Francisco), 1970.

Bring It up from the Dark, Cody's Books, 1970.

(Contributor) Edwin Haviland Miller, editor, *The Artistic Legacy of Walt Whitman: A Tribute to Gay Wilson Allen*, New York University Press, 1970.

A Prospectus for the Prepublication of Ground Work to Certain Friends of the Poet, privately printed, 1971.

An Interview with George Bowering and Robert Hogg, April 19, 1969, Coach House Press, 1971.

Structure of Rime XXVIII; In Memoriam Wallace Stevens, University of Connecticut, 1972.

Poems from the Margins of Thom Gunn's Moly, privately printed, 1972.

A Seventeenth-Century Suite, privately printed, 1973.

(Contributor) Ian Young, editor, *The Male Muse: Gay Poetry Anthology*, Crossing Press, 1973.

Dante, Institute of Further Studies (New York), 1974.

(With Jack Spicer) *An Ode and Arcadia*, Ark Press, 1974.

The Venice Poem, Poet's Mimeo (Burlington, Vt.), 1978.

Veil, Turbine, Cord & Bird: Sets of Syllables, Sets of Words, Sets of Lines, Sets of Poems, Addressing . . ., J. Davies, c.1979.

Fictive Certainties: Five Essays in Essential Autobiography, New Directions, 1979.

The Five Songs, Friends of the University of California, San Diego Library, 1981.

Towards an Open Universe, Aquila Publishing, 1982.

Ground Work: Before the War, New Directions, 1984.

The Regulators, Station Hill Press, 1985.

Ground Work II: In the Dark, New Directions, 1987.

Also author of "The H.D. Book," a long work in several parts, published in literary journals. Represented in anthologies, including *Faber Book of Modern American Verse,* edited by W. H. Auden, 1956, *The New American Poetry: 1945-1960,* edited by Donald M. Allen, 1960, and many others. Contributor of poems, under the name Robert Edward Symmes, to *Phoenix* and *Ritual.* Contributor to *Atlantic, Poetry, Nation, Quarterly Review of Literature,* and other periodicals.

SIDELIGHTS: Though the name Robert Duncan is not well known outside the literary world, within that world it has become associated with a number of superlatives. Kenneth Rexroth, writing in *Assays,* named Duncan "one of the most accomplished, one of the most influential" of the postwar American poets. An important participant in the Black Mountain school of poetry led by Charles Olson, Duncan became "probably the figure with the richest natural genius" from among that group, suggests M. L. Rosenthal in *The New Poets: American and British Poetry since World War II.* Duncan was also, in Rosenthal's opinion, perhaps "the most intellectual of our poets from the point of view of the effect upon him of a wide, critically intelligent reading." In addition, "few poets have written more articulately and self-consciously about their own intentions and understanding of poetry," reports *Dictionary of Literary Biography* contributor George F. Butterick. The homosexual companion of San Francisco painter Jess Collins, Duncan was also one of the first poets to call for a new social consciousness that would accept homosexuality. Largely responsible for the establishment of San Francisco as the spiritual hub of contemporary American poetry, Duncan has left a significant contribution to American literature through the body of his writings and through the many poets who have felt the influence of the theory behind his poetics.

Duncan's poetics were formed by the events of his early life. His mother died while giving him birth, leaving his father, a day-laborer, to care for him. Six months later, he was adopted by a couple who selected him on the basis of his astrological configuration. Their reverence for the occult in general, and especially their belief in reincarnation, and other concepts from Hinduism, was a lasting and important influence on his poetic vision. Encouraged by a high school English teacher who saw poetry as an essential means of sustaining spiritual vigor, Duncan chose his vocation while still in his teens. Though his parents wanted him to have a European education in Medieval history, he remained in San Francisco, living as a recluse so as not to embarrass the academic figure who was his lover. He continued reading and writing, eventually became the student of Middle Ages historian Ernst Kantorowicz, and throughout his life "maintained a profound interest in occult matters as parallel to and informing his own theories of poetry," Michael Davidson reports in another *Dictionary of Literary Biography* essay.

Minnesota Review contributor Victor Contoski suggests that Duncan's essays in *The Truth and Life of Myth* may be "the best single introduction to his poetry," which, for Duncan, was closely related to mysticism. Duncan, says a London *Times* reporter, was primarily "concerned with poetry as what he called 'manipulative magic' and a 'magic ritual', and with the nature of what he thought of (in a markedly Freudian manner) as 'human bisexuality.' " Reports James Dickey in *Babel to Byzantium,* "Duncan has the old or pagan sense of the poem as a divine form of speech which works intimately with the animism of nature, of the renewals that believed-in ceremonials can be, and of the sacramental in experience; for these reasons and others that neither he nor I could give, there is at least part of a very good poet in him." While this emphasis on myth was an obstacle to some reviewers, critic Laurence Liebermann, writing in a *Poetry* review, said of *The Opening of the Field,* Duncan's first mature collection, that it "announced the birth of a surpassingly individual talent: a poet of mysticism, visionary terror, and high romance."

Duncan wrote some of the poems in *The Opening of the Field* in 1956 when he taught at Olson's Black Mountain College. Olson promoted projective verse, a poetry shaped by the rhythms of the poet's breath, which he defined as an extension of nature. These poems would find their own "open" forms unlike the prescribed measures and line lengths that ruled traditional poetry. "Following Olson's death Duncan became the leading spokesman for the poetry of open form in America," notes Butterick. Furthermore, say some critics, Duncan fulfilled Olson's dictum more fully than Olson had done; whereas Olson projected the poem into a space bounded by the poet's natural breath, Duncan carried this process farther, defining the poem as an open field without boundaries of any kind.

Duncan was a syncretist possessing "a bridge-building, time-binding, and space-binding imagination" in which "the Many are One, where all faces have their Original Being, and where Eternal Love encompasses all reality, both Good and Evil," writes Stephen Stepanchev in *American Poetry since 1945.* A Duncan poem, accordingly, is like a collage, "a compositional field where anything might enter: a prose quotation, a catalogue, a recipe, a dramatic monologue, a diatribe," Davidson explains. The poems draw together into one dense fabric materials from sources as diverse as works on ancient magic, Christian mysticism, and the *Oxford English Dictionary.* Writing in the *New York Times Book Review,* Jim Harrison calls the structure of a typical Duncan poem multi-layered and four-dimensional ("moving through time with the poet"), and compares it to "a block of weaving. . . . *Bending the Bow* is for the strenuous, the hyperactive reader of poetry; to read Duncan with any immediate grace would require Norman O. Brown's knowledge of the arcane mixed with Ezra Pound's grasp of poetics. . . . [Duncan] is personal rather than confessional and writes within a continuity of tradition. It simply helps to be familiar with Dante, [William] Blake, mythography, medieval history, H.D., William Carlos Williams, Pound, [Gertrude] Stein, [Louis] Zukofsky, Olson, [Robert] Creeley and [Denise] Levertov."

Process, not conclusion, drew Duncan's focus. In some pages from a notebook published in Donald Allen's *The New American Poetry: 1945-1960,* Duncan stated: "A longing grows to return to the open composition in which the accidents and imperfections of speech might awake intimations of human being. . . . There is a natural mystery in poetry. We do not understand all that we render up to understanding. . . . I study what I write as I study out any mystery. A poem, mine or another's, is an occult document, a body awaiting vivisection, analysis, X-rays." The poet, he explained, is an explorer more than a creator. "I work at language as a spring of water works at the rock, to find a course, and so, blindly. In this I am not a maker of things, but, if maker, a maker of a way. For the way is itself." As in the art of marquetry (the making of patterns by enhancing natural wood grains), the poet is aware of the possible meanings of words and merely brings them out. "I'm not *putting* a grain into the wood," he told Jack R. Cohn and Thomas J. O'Donnell in a *Contemporary Literature* interview. Later, he added, "I acquire language lore. What I am supplying is something like . . . grammar of design, or of the possibilities of design." The goal of composition, he wrote in a *Caterpillar* essay, was "not to reach conclusion but to keep our exposure to what we do not know."

Each Duncan poem builds itself by a series of organic digressions, in the manner of outward-reaching roots or branches. The order in his poems is not an imposed order, but a reflection of correspondences already present in nature or language. At times, the correspondences inherent in language become insistent so that the poet following an organic method of writing is in danger of merely recording what the language itself dictates as possible. Duncan was highly susceptible to impressions from other literature—perhaps too susceptible, he said in a *Boundary 2* interview. In several interviews, for example, Duncan referred to specific early poems as "received" from outside agents, "poems in which angels were present." After reading Rainer Marie Rilke's *Duino Elegies,* he came to dread what he called "any angelic invasion"—or insistent voice other than his own. One poem that expresses this preference is "Often I Am Permitted to Return to a Meadow," the first poem in *The Opening of the Field.* He told Cohn and O'Donnell, "When I wrote that opening line, . . . I recognized that this was my permission, and that this meadow, which I had not yet identified, would be the thematic center of the book. In other words, what's back of that opening proposition I understood immediately: twice *you* wanted to compel me to have a book that would have angels at the center, but *now* I am permitted, often you have permitted me, to return to a mere meadow." His originality consisted of his demand that the inner life of the poem be his own, not received from another spiritual or literary source. "Whether he is working from Dante's prose Renaissance meditative poems, or Thom Gunn's *Moly* sequence, he works *from* them and *to* what they leave open or unexamined," explains Thomas Parkinson in *Poets, Poems, Movements.*

At the same time, Duncan recognized his works as derivative literature for several reasons. He said, "I am a traditionalist, a seeker after origins, not an original," reports Herbert Mitgang in the *New York Times.* Often he claimed Walt Whitman as his literary father, seeking in poetry to celebrate the experiences common to all men and women of all times, trying to manifest in words the underlying unity of all things that was essential to his beliefs. Complete originality is not possible in such a cosmos. In fact, the use of language—an inherited system of given sounds and symbols—is itself an imitative activity that limits originality. Even so, the poet, he believed, must be as free as possible "from preconceived ideas, whether structural or thematic, and must allow the internal forces of the composition at hand to determine the final form," Robert C. Weber observes in *Concerning Poetry.* This position, Duncan recognized, was bequeathed to him by Whitman and Pound, who viewed a poet's life work as one continuous "unfinished book," Parkinson notes.

Duncan's works express social and political ideals conversant with his poetics. The ideal environment for the poet, Duncan believed, would be a society without boundaries. In poetry, Duncan found a vocation where there was no prohibition against homosexuality, James F. Mersmann observes in *Out of the Viet Nam Vortex: A Study of Poets and Poetry against the War.* Duncan's theory, he goes on, "not only claims that the poem unfolds according to its own law, but envisions a compatible cosmology in which it may do so. It is not the poem alone that must grow

as freely as the plant: the life of the person, the state, the species, and indeed the cosmos itself follows a parallel law. All must follow their own imperatives and volition; all activity must be free of external coercion."

Political commitment is the subject of *Bending the Bow.* Duncan was "one of the most astute observers of the malpractices of Western governments, power blocs, etc., who [was] always on the human side, the *right* side of such issues as war, poverty, civil rights, etc., and who therefore [did] not take an easy way out," though his general avoidance of closure sometimes weakened his case, Harriet Zinnes remarks in a *Prairie Schooner* review. Highly critical of the Viet Nam war, pollution, nuclear armament, and the exploitation of native peoples and natural resources, the poems in *Bending the Bow* include "Up-Rising," "one of the major political poems of our time," according to Davidson. For Duncan, the essayist continues, "the American attempt to secure *one* meaning of democracy by eliminating all others represents a massive violation of that vision of polis desired by John Adams and Thomas Jefferson and projected through Walt Whitman." Though such poems voice an "essentially negative vision," says Weber, "it is a critical part of Duncan's search for the nature of man since he cannot ignore what man has become. . . . These themes emerge from within the body of the tradition of the poetry he seeks to find; politics are a part of the broad field of the poet's life, and social considerations emerge from his concern with the nature of man."

The difference between organic and imposed order, for Duncan, says Mersmann, "is the difference between life and death. The dead matter of the universe science dissects into tidy stacktables; the living significance of creation, the angel with which the poet wrestles, is a volatile whirlwind of sharp knees and elbows thrashing with a grace beyond our knowledge of grace." The only law in a dancing universe, he goes on, is its inherent "love of the dance itself." Anything opposed to this dance of freedom is seen as evil. Both Duncan's poetics and his lifestyle stem from "a truly different kind of consciousness, either a very old or a very new spirituality," Mersmann concludes.

Duncan's method of composition based on this spirituality results in several difficulties for even the sympathetic reader. Duncan's "drifting conglomerations" are an exercise of poetic freedom that sometimes inspires, "but more often I feel suicidal about it," Dickey comments. Davidson notes that Duncan "never courted a readership but rather a special kind of reader, who grants the poet a wide latitude in developing his art, even in its most extreme moments. . . . The number of such readers is necessarily limited, but fierce in devotion." A large number of Duncan's poems are most accessible to an inner circle familiar with the personal and literary contexts of his writings, observes a *Times Literary Supplement* reviewer, who points out that "not everyone can live in California."

Duncan's method of composition presents some difficulties for the critic, as well. The eclectic nature of *Bending the Bow,* for example, remarks Hayden Carruth in the *Hudson Review,* excludes it from "questions of quality. I cannot imagine my friends, the poets who gather to dismember each other, asking of this book, as they would of the others in this review, those narrower in scope, smaller in style, 'Is it good or is it bad?' The question doesn't arise; not because Duncan is a good poet, though he is superb, but because the comprehensiveness of his imagination is too great for us."

After the publication of *Bending the Bow* in 1968, Duncan announced he would not publish a major collection for another fifteen years. During this hiatus he hoped to produce process-oriented poems instead of the "overcomposed" poems he wrote when he thought in terms of writing a book. In effect, this silence kept him from receiving the widespread critical attention or recognition he might otherwise have enjoyed. However, Duncan had a small but highly appreciative audience among writers who shared his concerns. Distraught when *Ground Work: Before the War,* the evidence of nearly twenty years of significant work, did not win the attention they thought it deserved from the publishing establishment, these poets founded the National Poetry Award and honored Duncan by making him the first recipient of the award in 1985. The award, described in a *Sagetrieb* article, was "a positive action affirming the admiration of the poetic community for the dedication and accomplishment of a grand poet."

BIOGRAPHICAL/CRITICAL SOURCES:

BOOKS

Allen, Donald M., *The New American Poetry, 1945-1960,* Grove, 1960.

Allen, Donald M., *The Poetics of the New American Poetry,* Grove, 1973.

Bertholf, Robert J., and Ian W. Reid, editors, *Robert Duncan: Scales of the Marvelous,* New Directions, 1979.

Charters, Samuel, *Some Poems/Poets: Studies in American Underground Poetry since 1945,* Oyez, 1971.

Contemporary Literary Criticism, Gale, Volume 1, 1973, Volume 2, 1974, Volume 4, 1975, Volume 7, 1977, Volume 15, 1980, Volume 41, 1987, Volume 55, 1989.

Dickey, James, *Babel to Byzantium,* Farrar, Straus, 1968.

Dictionary of Literary Biography, Gale, Volume 5: *American Poets since World War II,* 1980, Volume 16: *The Beats: Literary Bohemians in Postwar America,* 1983.

Faas, Ekbert, editor, *Towards a New American Poetics: Essays and Interviews,* Black Sparrow Press, 1978.

Fass, Ekbert, *Young Robert Duncan: Portrait of the Homosexual in Society,* Black Sparrow Press, 1983.

Fauchereau, Serge, *Lecture de la poesie americaine,* Editions de Minuit, 1969.

Mersmann, James F., *Out of the Viet Nam Vortex: A Study of Poets and Poetry against the War,* University Press of Kansas, 1974.

Parkinson, Thomas, *Poets, Poems, Movements,* University of Michigan Research Press, 1987.

Pearce, Roy Harvey, *Historicism Once More: Problems and Occasions for the American Scholar,* Princeton University Press, 1969.

Rexroth, Kenneth, *Assays,* New Directions, 1961.

Rexroth, Kenneth, *American Poetry in the Twentieth Century,* Herder and Herder, 1971.

Rosenthal, M. L., *The New Poets: American and British Poetry since World War II,* Oxford University Press, 1967.

Stepanchev, Stephen, *American Poetry since 1945,* Harper, 1965.

Tallman, Warren, *Godawful Streets of Man,* Coach House Press, 1976.

Weatherhead, Kingsley, *Edge of the Image: Marianne Moore, William Carlos Williams, and Some Other Poets,* University of Washington Press, 1967.

PERIODICALS

Agenda, autumn/winter, 1970.
Audit/Poetry, Number 3, 1967 (special Duncan issue).
Boundary 2, winter, 1980.
Caterpillar, number 8/9, 1969.
Centennial Review, fall, 1975, fall, 1985.
Concerning Poetry, spring, 1978.

Contemporary Literature, spring, 1975.
Hudson Review, summer, 1968.
Maps, 1974, (special Duncan issue).
Minnesota Review, fall, 1972.
New York Review of Books, June 3, 1965, May 7, 1970.
New York Times Book Review, December 20, 1964, September 29, 1968, August 4, 1985.
Poetry, March, 1968, April, 1969, May, 1970.
Sagetrieb, winter, 1983, fall/winter, 1985 (special Duncan issue).
Saturday Review, February 13, 1965, August 24, 1968.
Southern Review, spring, 1969, winter, 1985.
Sulfur 12, Volume 4, number 2, 1985.
Times Literary Supplement, May 1, 1969, July 23, 1971.
Unmuzzled Ox, February, 1977.
Voice Literary Supplement, November, 1984.

OBITUARIES:

PERIODICALS

New York Times, February 2, 1988.
Times (London), February 11, 1988.

*   *   *

DUNN, Douglas (Eaglesham) 1942-

PERSONAL: Born October 23, 1942, in Inchinnan, Renfrewshire, Scotland; son of William Douglas (a factory worker) and Margaret (McGowan) Dunn; married Lesley Balfour Wallace (senior keeper of an art gallery), November 26, 1964 (died March 13, 1981); married Lesley Jane Bathgate (a graphic designer and artist), August 10, 1985; children: one son. *Education:* Scottish School of Librarianship, A.L.A., 1962; University of Hull, B.A. (English; first class honors), 1969.

ADDRESSES: Home—Braeknowe, Grey St., Tayport, Fife DD6 8HU, Scotland. *Agent*—Pat Kavanagh, A. D. Peters & Co. Ltd., 10 Buckingham St., London WC2N 6BU, England.

CAREER: Renfrew County Library, Renfrewshire, Scotland, junior library assistant, 1959-62; University of Strathclyde, Andersonian Library, Glasgow, Scotland, library assistant, 1962-64; Akron Public Library, Akron, OH, assistant librarian, 1964-66; University of Glasgow, Chemistry Department Library, Glasgow, librarian, 1966; University of Hull, Brynmor Jones Library, Hull, England, assistant librarian, 1969-71, writer in residence, 1974-75; poet and free-lance writer. Writer in residence at University of New England (Australia), 1984, and Duncan of Jordanstone College of Art, Dundee District Library, 1986-88; University of Dundee, writer in residence, 1981-82, honorary visiting professor, 1987-89.

MEMBER: Royal Society of Literature (fellow), Scottish P.E.N., Society of Authors.

AWARDS, HONORS: Eric Gregory Award, Society of Authors, 1968, for manuscript collection; Scottish Arts Council Publication Award, 1970, and Somerset Maugham Award, Society of Authors, 1972, both for *Terry Street;* Scottish Arts Council Publication Award, 1975, and Geoffrey Faber Memorial Prize, 1976, both for *Love or Nothing;* Hawthornden Prize, 1982, for *St. Kilda's Parliament;* Whitbread Literary Awards for poetry and for book of the year, 1985, both for *Elegies;* honorary LL.D., University of Dundee, 1987.

WRITINGS:

POEMS

Terry Street, Faber, 1969, Chilmark, 1973.
Backwaters, The Review, 1971.

The Happier Life, Faber, 1972, Chilmark, 1973.
Love or Nothing, Faber, 1974.
Barbarians, Faber, 1979.
Europa's Lover, Bloodaxe Books, 1982.
St. Kilda's Parliament, Faber, 1982.
Elegies, Faber, 1985.
Selected Poems: 1964-1983, Faber, 1986.
Northlight, Faber, 1988.
New and Selected Poems, Nineteen Sixty-six to Nineteen Eighty-eight, Ecco Press, 1989.

EDITOR

New Poems, 1972-73: The P.E.N. Anthology, Hutchinson, 1973.
A Choice of Lord Byron's Verse, Faber, 1974.
Two Decades of Irish Writing, Carcanet Press, 1975.
What Is to Be Given: Selected Poems of Delmore Schwartz, Carcanet Press, 1976.
The Poetry of Scotland, Batsford, 1979.
Poetry Book Society Supplement, Poetry Book Society, 1979.
A Rumoured City: New Poets from Hull, Bloodaxe Books, 1982.
To Build a Bridge, Lincolnshire and Humberside Arts Association, 1982.

FOR RADIO AND TELEVISION

Scotsmen by Moonlight (play), BBC-Radio, 1977.
(Author of verse commentary) *Running,* BBC-TV, 1977.
Ploughman's Share (play), BBC-TV, 1979.
Wedderburn's Slave, BBC-Radio Scotland, 1980.
(Author of verse commentary) *Anon's People,* BBC-TV Scotland, 1984.
The Telescope Garden, BBC-Radio, c. 1985.

OTHER

Secret Villages (short stories), Dodd, Mead, 1985.

Contributor to *New Statesman, Poetry Nation, Times Literary Supplement, New Yorker, Punch, London Magazine, New Review,* and *Listener.* Poetry reviewer, *Encounter,* beginning 1971; special editor, "British Poetry Issue," *Antaeus 12,* 1973.

WORK IN PROGRESS: A book of short stories; a novel; editing *Faber Book of Twentieth-Century Scottish Poetry.*

BIOGRAPHICAL/CRITICAL SOURCES:

BOOKS

Contemporary Literary Criticism, Gale, Volume 6, 1976, Volume 40, 1986.
Dictionary of Literary Biography, Volume 40: *Poets of Great Britain and Ireland since 1960,* Gale, 1985.
Haffenden, John, *Viewpoints: Poets in Conversation with John Haffenden,* Faber, 1981.

PERIODICALS

Listener, August 9, 1973.
Los Angeles Times Book Review, July 28, 1985.
New Statesman, June 16, 1972, December 6, 1974.
Observer (London), July 2, 1972, October 20, 1974.
Oxford Poetry, Volume 2, number 2, 1985.
Spectator, July 22, 1972, January 4, 1975.
Times Literary Supplement, June 9, 1972, January 31, 1975, October 2, 1981, January 7, 1983, August 19, 1983, May 31, 1985, April 5, 1985, October 21-27, 1988.
Virginia Quarterly Review, spring, 1975.

du PERRY, Jean
See SIMENON, Georges (Jacques Christian)

*   *   *

DURANT, Will(iam James)   1885-1981

PERSONAL: Born November 5, 1885, in North Adams, Mass.; died November 7, 1981, in Los Angeles, Calif., of heart failure; son of Joseph (a superintendent of a Du Pont branch) and Marie (Allors) Durant; married Ariel Kaufman (a writer and researcher), October 31, 1913; children: Ethel Benvenuta (Mrs. Stanislas Kwasniewski), Louis R. (adopted). *Education:* St. Peter's College (Jersey City, N.J.), B.A., 1907, M.A., 1908; Columbia University, Ph.D., 1917. *Religion:* "Agnostic, formerly Catholic."

ADDRESSES: Home—5608 Briarcliff Rd., Los Angeles, Calif. 90028.

CAREER: Seton Hall College (now University), South Orange, N.J., instructor in Latin and French, 1907-11; Ferrer Modern School, New York City, teacher, 1911-13; Labor Temple School, New York City, director and lecturer, 1914-27; Columbia University, New York City, instructor in philosophy, 1917; University of California, Los Angeles, professor of philosophy, 1935; full-time writer. Reporter, *New York Evening Journal,* 1908. Lecturer.

MEMBER: National Institute of Arts and Letters.

AWARDS, HONORS: L.H.D., Syracuse University, 1930; with wife, Ariel K. Durant, Huntington Hartford Foundation award for literature, 1963, for *The Age of Louis XIV;* with A. K. Durant, Pulitzer Prize, 1968, for *Rousseau and Revolution;* with A. K. Durant, California Literature Medal Award, 1971, for *Interpretations of Life;* with A. K. Durant, Medal of Freedom, 1977.

WRITINGS:

Philosophy and the Social Problem, Macmillan, 1917.
The Story of Philosophy, Simon & Schuster, 1926, revised edition, 1933.
Transition: A Sentimental Story of One Mind and One Era (autobiographical novel), Simon & Schuster, 1927, reprinted, 1978.
(Editor) Arthur Schopenhauer, *Works,* Simon & Schuster, 1928, revised edition, Ungar, 1962.
Mansions of Philosophy: A Survey of Human Life and Destiny, Simon & Schuster, 1929, published as *The Pleasures of Philosophy: A Survey of Human Life and Destiny,* 1953.
The Case for India, Simon & Schuster, 1930.
Adventures in Genius (also see below; essays and articles; also see below), Simon & Schuster, 1931.
A Program for America, Simon & Schuster, 1931.
On the Meaning of Life (correspondence), R. R. Smith, 1932.
Tragedy of Russia: Impressions from a Brief Visit, Simon & Schuster, 1933.
100 Best Books for an Education (excerpt from *Adventures in Genius*), Simon & Schuster, 1933.
Great Men of Literature (excerpt from *Adventures in Genius*), Simon & Schuster, 1936.
The Story of Civilization, Simon & Schuster, Volume 1: *Our Oriental Heritage* (also see below), 1935, Volume 2: *The Life of Greece,* 1939, Volume 3: *Caesar and Christ: A History of Roman Civilization from Its Beginnings to A.D.337,* 1944, Volume 4: *The Age of Faith,* 1950, Volume 5: *The Renaissance,* 1953, Volume 6: *The Reformation,* 1957, Volume 7:

(with wife, Ariel K. Durant) *The Age of Reason Begins,* 1961, Volume 8: (with A. K. Durant) *The Age of Louis XIV,* 1963, Volume 9: (with A. K. Durant) *The Age of Voltaire,* 1965, Volume 10: (with A. K. Durant) *Rousseau and Revolution,* 1967, Volume 11: (with A. K. Durant) *The Age of Napoleon,* 1975.

The Foundations of Civilization (introduction to Volume 1 of *The Story of Civilization*), Simon & Schuster, 1936.

(With A. K. Durant) *The Lessons of History,* Simon & Schuster, 1968.

(With A. K. Durant) *Interpretations of Life,* Simon & Schuster, 1970.

(With A. K. Durant) *A Dual Autobiography,* Simon & Schuster, 1977.

SIDELIGHTS: In the eleven-volume *The Story of Civilization,* Will Durant, in collaboration with his wife, Ariel, endeavored to synthesize the developments in art, science, religion, politics, literature, and economics. It was an unusual approach, according to Bernard A. Weisberger in the *Washington Post Book World,* as these subjects and their progress are "usually treated separately." The Durants' purpose was to popularize history, to make a large and varied amount of information accessible and comprehensible to the average reader. Though their efforts were popular bestsellers, professional historians often insisted, as Weisberger reports, "that the attempt to handle sixty centuries of human history resulted fatally and inevitably in shallowness and error."

However, Weisberger contends that, notwithstanding the scholars' criticism, "the Durants fill a spiritual vacuum." He believes that "the key" to the popularity and success of *The Story of Civilization* was "[Will] Durant's late 19th-century faith in the simple concepts of history and civilization," his belief in "patterns and structures, tides and movements in history." The reviewer explains: "Somehow, out of chaos, civilizations emerged, and if one unravelled and went under in a civil war or a barbarian incursion, another painfully emerged. . . . People appear to need this assurance that there is a purposeful flow in the life of the whole human race; that their instant of existence matters in an overall scheme."

A *Time* critic argues that "the charge that [the Durants] are popularizers is meaningless. Of course they are popularizers—and great ones." Durant himself responded to his detractors in a *Publishers Weekly* interview with John F. Baker: "We're amateurs. . . . We want to make history meaningful for ordinary readers. . . . We need specialists who devote their time to research, and who work from first-hand materials, sure, but I reject the notion that only university professors can write history. There's room for an integral view, which looks at every aspect of an age—its art, its manners and morals, its philosophy, even its architecture—and shows how they all interrelate. That's how history works—it's not all in separate compartments."

BIOGRAPHICAL/CRITICAL SOURCES:

BOOKS

(With A. K. Durant) *A Dual Autobiography,* Simon & Schuster, 1977.

PERIODICALS

Book Week, September 15, 1963, October 10, 1965.
Christian Science Monitor, October 28, 1965, November 30, 1967.
Life, October 18, 1963.
National Review, January 16, 1968.

New Republic, October 2, 1965.
Newsweek, September 16, 1957, September 11, 1961, September 16, 1963.
New York Herald Tribune Book Review, October 25, 1953.
New York Times Book Review, September 15, 1963, September 19, 1965, October 15, 1967, February 5, 1978.
Publishers Weekly, November 24, 1975.
Reader's Digest, October, 1969.
Saturday Review, September 9, 1961, September 21, 1963, October 23, 1965, September 23, 1967.
Time, September 28, 1953, September 27, 1963, August 13, 1965, October 8, 1965, October 6, 1967.
Washington Post Book World, November 27, 1977.
Yale Review, December, 1963.

OBITUARIES:

PERIODICALS

Chicago Tribune, November 10, 1981.
Detroit News, November 15, 1981.
Newsweek, November 23, 1981.
New York Times, November 10, 1981.
Publishers Weekly, November 20, 1981.
Time, November 23, 1981.
Times (London), November 10, 1981.

*   *   *

DURAS, Marguerite   1914-

PERSONAL: Original name Marguerite Donnadieu; born April 4, 1914, near Saigon, Indochina (now Vietnam); daughter of Henri (a mathematics teacher) and Marie (Legrand) Donnadieu; divorced; children: one son. *Education:* Graduated from Lycee de Saigon; University of Paris, Sorbonne, licences in law and political science; also studied mathematics.

ADDRESSES: Home—5 rue Saint-Benoit, 75006 Paris, France.

CAREER: Novelist, screenwriter, playwright, and film director. Emigrated from Indochina to Paris at age seventeen; secretary at French Ministry of Colonies, Paris, 1935-41; began writing in 1943; directed the film versions of her "La Musica," originally a play, and "Detruire, dit-elle," originally a novel; directed her original filmscript, "Nathalie Granger."

AWARDS, HONORS: Prix Jean Cocteau, 1954; Prix Ibsen, 1970, for her play, "L'Amante anglaise"; Grand Prix Academy du Cinema, 1973; Prix Goncourt, 1984; Ritz Paris Hemingway Award, 1986.

WRITINGS:

NOVELS

Les Impudents, Plon, 1943.
La Vie tranquille, Gallimard, 1944.
Un Barrage contre le Pacifique, Gallimard, 1950, translation by Herma Briffault published as *The Sea Wall,* Pellegrini & Cudahy, 1952, reprinted, Farrar & Straus, 1985, same translation published with a preface by Germaine Bree, Farrar, Straus, 1967, translation by Antonia White published as *A Sea of Troubles,* Methuen, 1953.
Le Marin de Gibraltar, Gallimard, 1952, reprinted, Schoenhof, 1977, translation by Barbara Bray published as *The Sailor from Gibraltar,* Grove, 1966, reprinted, Pantheon, 1986.
Les Petits Chevaux de Tarquinia, Gallimard, 1953, translation by Peter DuBerg published as *The Little Horses of Tarquinia,* J. Calder, 1960, reprinted, Riverrun, 1986.

Le Square, Gallimard, 1955, translation by Sonia Pitt-Rivers and Irina Morduch published as *The Square,* Grove, 1959, French language edition, published under original French title, edited by Claude Morhange Begue, Macmillan, 1965.

Moderato Cantabile Editions de Minuit, 1958, translation by Richard Seaver published as *Moderato Cantabile,* Grove, 1960, French language edition, edited by Thomas Bishop, Prentice-Hall, 1968, another French language edition, edited by W. S. Strachan, Methuen, 1968, also published with supplemental material as *Moderato cantabile* [suivi de] *L'Univers romanesque de Marguerite Duras,* Plon, 1962.

Dix heures et demie du soir en ete, Gallimard, 1960, translation by Anne Borchardt published as *Ten-thirty on a Summer Night,* J. Calder, 1962, Grove, 1963.

L'Apres Midi de Monsieur Andesmas, Gallimard, 1962, translation by Borchardt published together with Bray's translation of "Les Eaux et forets" (play; also see below) as *The Afternoon of Monsieur Andesmas* [and] *The Rivers and Forests,* J. Calder, 1965.

Le Ravissement de Lol V. Stein, Gallimard, 1964, reprinted, Schoenhof, 1990, translation by Seaver published as *The Ravishing of Lol Stein,* Grove, 1966, reprinted, Pantheon, 1986, translation by Eileen Ellenbogen published as *The Rapture of Lol V. Stein,* Hamish Hamilton, 1967.

Four Novels (contains *The Square, Moderato Cantabile, Ten-thirty on a Summer Night,* and *The Afternoon of Monsieur Andesmas*), translations by Pitt-Rivers and others, introduction by Bree, Grove, 1965, reprinted, 1988.

Le Vice-consul, Gallimard, 1966, translation by Ellenbogen published as *The Vice-consul,* Hamish Hamilton, 1968, reprinted, Pantheon, 1990.

L'Amante anglaise, Gallimard, 1967, translation by Bray published as *L'Amante Anglaise,* Grove, 1968.

Detruire, dit-elle, Editions de Minuit, 1969, translation by Bray published as *Destroy, She Said,* Grove, 1970.

Abahn Sabana David, Gallimard, 1970.

L'Amour, Gallimard, 1972, translation published as *The Lover,* Pantheon, 1985.

(With Xaviere Gauthier) *Les Parleuses,* Editions de Minuit, 1974.

PLAYS

Les Viaducs de la Seine-et-Oise (translation by Bray produced as "The Viaduct" in Guildford, England, at Yvonne Arnaud Theatre, February, 1967), Gallimard, 1960.

(With James Lord) "La Bete dans la jungle" (adaptation of "The Beast in the Jungle," by Henry James), produced, 1962.

Theatre I (contains "Les Eaux et forets," "Le Square," and "La Musica"; "La Musica" produced Off-Off Broadway as "The Music," March, 1967), Gallimard, 1965.

Three Plays, translation by Bray and Sonia Orwell (contains "The Square," "Days in the Trees," and "The Viaducts of Seine-et-Oise"; "Days in the Trees" produced in Paris at Theatre de France, and on BBC-Television "Wednesday Play," 1967), Calder & Boyars, 1967.

Theatre II (contains "Suzanna Andler," "Des Journees entieres dan les arbres," "Yes, peut-etre," "Le Shaga," and "Un Homme est venue me voir"; "Suzanna Andler" first produced in Paris at Theatre Mathurins, December, 1969; translation by Bray produced on the West End at Aldwych Theatre, March 7, 1973), Gallimard, 1968.

"L'Amante anglaise" (adapted from her novel), produced in Paris at Theatre National Populaire, December, 1969, produced in French as "L'Amante Anglaise" on the West End at Royal Court Theatre, 1969, produced in French Off-

Broadway at Barbizon-Plaza Theatre, April 14, 1971, translation by Bray first produced as "A Place without Doors" in New Haven, Conn., at Long Wharf Theatre, November 21, 1970, produced Off-Broadway at Stairway Theatre, December 22, 1970, same translation produced as "Lovers of Viorne" on the West End at Royal Court Theatre, July 6, 1971.

Ah! Ernesto, F. Ruy-Vidal, 1971.

India Song, Gallimard, 1973, translation by Bray published under same title, Grove, 1976, reprinted, 1989.

SCREENPLAYS

Hiroshima mon amour: Scenario et dialogues (based on the novel by Alain Resnais; film produced in 1959), Gallimard, 1960, translation by Seaver published as *Hiroshima mon amour: Text by Marguerite Duras for the Film by Alain Resnais,* Grove, 1961, reprinted, 1987, same translation also published together with Barbara Wright's translation of *Une Aussi longue absence* (see below).

(With Gerard Jarlot) *Une Aussi longue absence* (based on the novel by Henri Colpi), Gallimard, 1961, translation by Wright published under original French title together with above translation as *Hiroshima mon amour* [and] *Une Aussi longue absence* (movie scripts), Calder & Boyars, 1966.

"Moderato Cantabile" (adapted from her novel), Royal Films International, 1964.

(With Jules Dassin) "Ten-thirty p.m. Summer" (adapted from her novel, *Ten-thirty on a Summer Night*), Lopert, 1966.

"Detruire, dit-elle" (adapted from her novel), Ancinex/Madeleine Films, 1970.

"La Musica" (adapted from her play), United Artists, 1970.

"Nathalie Granger" (Monelet & Co., 1972), published in *Nathalie Granger* [suive de] *La Femme du Grange,* Gallimard, 1973.

Also author of filmscript, "Jaune le soleil," 1971.

OTHER

Des Journees entieres dans les arbres (short stories), Gallimard, 1954.

(With Jacques Lacan and Maurice Blanclot) *Etude sur l'oeuvre litteraire, theatrale, et cinematographique de Marguerite Duras* (nonfiction), Albatros, 1976.

(With Michelle Porte) *Les Lieux de Marguerite Duras,* French and European, 1977.

Outside: Selected Writings, Beacon Press, 1988.

Contributor to *Vogue.*

SIDELIGHTS: "Marguerite Duras [is] an experimental novelist whose neglect in this country has been qualified chiefly by uneasy lip-service and a few cursory nods of identification," writes James R. Frakes. He believes that she is an important talent and deserves a wider reading. Germaine Bree writes, "Fiction, drama, cinema: These are her media." She has written more novels than plays or screenplays, "yet the hold the cinema has always had on her imagination is great and visibly affects her narrative techniques." Bree points out that Duras does not promote "esthetic theories and ideas. But she shares with her contemporaries the desire to discard many of the rather worn-out conventions of the traditional novel, conventions which she put to effective use in her first works. . . . Duras's major esthetic preoccupation," Bree states, is "to shape a story so that it achieves an emotional intensity and unity that goes beyond the limits of the outer events related."

Etienne Lalou states that Duras shows, as does Picasso, that to be faithful to oneself is to accept change and to understand the transformation in oneself. He finds unity in her work and an absence of contradiction even though she has progressed through three stages which he equates with the three states of life: childhood, adolescence, and maturity. In the first period he includes *Les Impudents, La Vie tranquille,* and *Un Barrage contre le Pacifique.* These novels have an epic realism similar to that found in American novelists. In the second period he places *Le Marin de Gibraltar* and *Les Petits Chevaux de Tarquinia,* which reveal a more personal vision of the world, and in which humor and nostalgia become dominant elements. The third period includes all subsequent novels.

George Craig believes that the work of Duras is "essentially cumulative." He finds the novels of the first stage "clotted and slow-moving, heavy with the presence of previous connoisseurs of the oppressive." In the novels of the second stage "she begins to find her own direction. More and more in these, conversation, no longer a predictable function of social living, takes on symbolic, almost therapeutic value."

Germaine Bree writes about *Un Barrage contre le Pacifique:* "The very title of the story suggests a dogged, unequal battle against a superhuman force. This was to remain one of Duras's basic themes: barrage against the immense solitude of human beings, barrage against the pain of all involvements, barrage against despair." A *Times Literary Supplement* reviewer comments: "The account of all this is one of almost unrelieved depression, and the misery of 'the mother,' as she is always called, is only equalled by the boredom of her son and daughter, the unrelenting rapacity of the local officials, and the degradation of the natives. Undeniably the novel has a certain power and its atmosphere carries conviction." Duras based this book on her memories of South Indochina.

The Sailor from Gibraltar represents a new direction in Duras's writing. "She writes about people and their moods with incomparable ease and sensuality. These qualities are nowhere more apparent than in *The Sailor from Gibraltar,* an expansive, leisurely novel . . . only recently translated," *Time* comments. Adele Silver writes: "The author deals in simple urgencies— love, loneliness, suspense, fear—and her imagination forces them into striking new shapes. Her story is told largely through dialogue, a technique nicely suited to her special gifts." There seems to be some resistance to the work of Duras; as Richard Mayne points out in his review of *The Sailor from Gibraltar,* "Few reviewers seemed to seize the essential point of this tender, funny, somnambulistic love story—the lifelong quest for purpose and communication between human beings." The *Times Literary Supplement* reviewer finds "sly genuflections in the direction of Ernest Hemingway," a point which other critics echo in comments on this and her earlier books. The mood is much lighter than that of earlier books; as *Time* says, "The book at its best has the sunny charm of one of Renoir's floating picnics."

From *The Little Horses of Tarquinia* onward, Marguerite Duras turns toward a more abstract and synthetic literature. There are now fewer characters, and they are concerned with one event or relationship. The novels are pared down, spare. "Though Marguerite . . . isolates what might appear as a fragment of existence," Germaine Bree writes, "she does not present fragments of experience, but within the limits set by the molding of the narrative, she reaches toward an essential moment when, in a flash of awareness, the inner truth of a situation comes to light in the form of pure emotion. . . . Love, the fierceness of love, the happiness, the pain, the compelling and destructive power of love is

Marguerite Duras's essential theme, and not, as is too often stressed, solitude." In *The Square,* Duras begins to experiment with what Bree calls "a new stylized form of storytelling which, without being analytical, would bring to light certain fundamental patterns of human feeling." With *The Square,* Bree believes, Duras "took front rank" among the new novelists who emerged during the fifties. *The Square* is "a novel of unusual depth and poetic beauty," Bree writes. "Perhaps it is the strictly controlled, quasi-musical form which the author has chosen, and preserved in an excellent translation . . . which keep the novel from yielding to a certain sentimentality. It is impeccably written and the impact is due to its restraint." J. M. Edelstein compares *The Square* to "the modern paintings in which the deliberate omission of any recognizable object or design may be discerned," because Duras "has written a novel of surfaces. It needs nothing else but the words that give it its body." "The fact that it depends upon dialogue rather than upon the careful description of objective facts," comments Vernon Hall, "gives it a warmth lacking" in the novels of Robbe-Grillet and other contemporaries. "The human voice cannot speak without emotional overtones. No matter how commonplace the content, the vibration of the spirit is always audible."

"*Moderato Cantabile* brought fame to Marguerite Duras," writes Henri Peyre. "She became, rather hastily, hailed as one of the practitioners of the 'new novel,' with which she has in fact nothing in common, and, because her recits were brief, written with simplicity and purity, harmless in their subjects. . . . *Moderato Cantabile* is built ingeniously according to a musical technique suggested by Diabelli's sonatina learned on the piano by the heroine's child; its vague and delicate tale of a woman dreaming of love 'strong as death' which she knows she cannot have is instinct with emotion and restrained tragedy." Bree calls the book "a modern restatement of the incompatibility of individual passion with the orderly mechanism of social decorum. . . . 'Moderato cantabile' suggests a tempo and lyrical mode that are in direct contradiction with the violence of the crime, with the fierce desire that engulfs Anne and Chauvin, and with the strange new detached mode of perception Anne acquires in her state of intoxication."

Armand Hoog calls *Moderato Cantabile* "a novel which hesitates, which fills back upon itself, a 'hesitating novel,' undecided and perplexed and perhaps for that very reason one of the most exciting novels its author has written. Neither completely of flesh and blood nor altogether disincarnate, it floats midway between geography and pure space. . . . Everything, in the end, is as if nonexistent and forgotten. And in the closing lines of the narrative nothing counts any more except the knowledge that it will rain tomorrow. But the evocative power of the story is so strong and so minutely specific that when the book is closed, the reader cannot tear himself away from its temporal spell."

"The strange, acute, yet different modes of perception reached through intoxication—another form of alienation," Bree states, "give *Ten-thirty on a Summer Night* its strange double structure. . . . A number of events, held in suspense, coincide to give the story its unique pattern. . . . [Here] in the baroque setting evoked, outer and inner events fuse, merge, and develop with a poetic inevitability. Death, love, desire, and violence mold the most banal of events: a man's infidelity to his wife." Kathleen Nott praises Duras for much the same reasons: "However strange, this is a beautifully coordinated work. Beautiful and brief, its poetry is not only in its language but in its structure. It takes all the advantage of an interesting even exciting action, to integrate sense and feeling: landscape, light, emotion, perception, all cohere. The characters are not just figures in a landscape, they are truly significant because of this chosen setting, so that the passions become genuinely universal and impersonal, which means also mature and objective." *The Afternoon of Monsieur Andesmas* is also a story of suspense, "but a suspense that evolves toward a disengagement from the passion of living—thereby from time—that human relationships reveal," Bree comments. "The thematic pattern of the story, its clarity and serenity, offer a striking contrast to the tormented, baroque design of the two preceding works."

Peter Buitenhuis finds Duras's technical work in *The Ravishing of Lol Stein* to be brilliant: "With her remarkable objective style, full of strange contrasts, sudden insights and haunting images, she shoots vertical shafts down into the dark morass of human love. She may not come up with any answers, but she does display to the reader's eye strange cut gems of the imagination that stay with him after the shape of the events themselves has begun to dissolve." There are those, however, who do not feel that Duras delves very deeply. Claire Tomalin writes: "She has her own way of plunging you into the non-world of her novel, and only when you shake off the drops dazedly at the end do you realize that you have never gone any deeper than that first drugged plunge. . . . It is partly Mme. Duras's ability to make poetry out of the ludicrous, to blandish the reader with inconsequential dialogue that seems always about to inform us of something but never does. It is also her power to conjure up dreamlike settings, precise appearances of people and places: precise but not quite real." Saul Maloff notes that Duras "seems less interested in the frail scaffolding of narrative than in the opportunities it provides for what she calls the 'cinema of Lol Stein,' the slow-motion sensuality of the strange triad of lovers, caught like dancers in balletic movement, an endless succession of pirouettes. The artist reaches for the moon and captures instead thin, rarefied air filled with sparkling but insubstantial fireflies—not lives caught and laid bare, but shadowy silhouettes cast upon a screen."

In her review of *The Vice-consul,* Nott again cites Duras's "many poetic gifts—structural imagery, of vividly concrete individualization, of the sense of nature as a real presence. But she cannot escape from the Russian (or French?) egg of the novel-within-the-novel." She sees the book as "beautifully and coldly written. . . . It is a mystery in the way of the later Kafka, I mean, the mystery is why there is a mystery." "Her manner is cool, oracular, mysterious," writes David Williams.

L'Amante anglaise, writes Bettina L. Knapp, "is a poetically and brilliantly spun tale which shuttles the reader back and forth from the world of the rational to that of the irrational. . . . Because of the musicality of Marguerite Duras's prose, the precision of her imagery, the sensitivity with which she describes the most subtle of emotions and feelings, the reader is increasingly captivated and embroiled in this drama in which the tenuous tine, carefully drawn at first, between the world of reality and irreality, sanity and insanity, grows ever slimmer and dimmer." A *Time* reviewer points out that the novel would make a good thriller, "but Duras is not interested in anything so crude as whodunit. She is concerned with subtler problems with the undercurrents and delicate nuances of emotion that underlie even the smallest action—in short, with questions that have no answers, or rather that have any number of answers. The snag is that when the characters are as boring, as predictable and unconvincing as Duras's, it is difficult to work up much interest in their motives, let alone their delicate nuances." Diane Leclercq, on the other hand, writes: "It is a dazzling book written to find and recreate the truth of a fictional crime, exploring the background, the distant past, the far-reaches of a mad mind. It is an open-ended book with a mesomeric fascination written in a bare, oddly lyri-

cal style cut like a diamond to glisten with the infinitely faceted ramifications of the characters and situations." The book purports to be the transcript of tape-recorded interviews with the three people centrally concerned with the crime; thus it is in dialogue form throughout.

Jack Kroll believes the novel's dramatization, produced as "A Place without Doors," to be "one of those chic, bloodless, sterile exercises in esthetic-philosophical algebra which are endemic among certain French writers." John Simon writes of the play, "Marguerite Duras also tries to study the causes of murder in vacuous human lives, and though her investigation at least has shrewdness to recommend it, it lacks dramatic structuring and sustained interest." The *Variety* reviewer, on the other hand, calls the play a "superb psychological suspenser" which is "intriguing on many levels. The why of the ghostly murder is what the questioner (who disavows ties to police and other official sources; presumably, he represents the vox populi) is after. . . . The search for motivation dogs the inquisitor as well as the audience." Walter Kerr comments: "Astonishingly, we are tied to it from beginning to almost end, . . . committed to an inquiry that we feel in our bones is going to be factually profitless. . . . The play rides on uncertainty alone, on sheer unsatisfied curiosity. . . . The chase is more important than the quarry, the play says. Call it right and wrong at once, and watch it work."

Melvin Maddocks writes of *Detruire, dit-elle:* "Mme. Duras has layers under her layers—she makes the old anti-novel seem crude. Book by complex book, the author . . . has evolved a new breed of fiction. She is that ultramodern. . . . She is not only an antiart artist, she is that newer invention, an antiintellectual intellectual. She admits to sharing with her son 'an almost irrepressible repulsion against knowledge and culture.' She dreams of 'creating a vacuum'—of getting back to 'absolute zero.' She longs to 'forget everything. So as to be able to start over.' "

Detruire, dit-elle deals with people in a political world which is no longer relevant, and with the human implications of such an existence. It takes place in a resort, where one sees people who seem to be recuperating, but one is never quite sure. Madeleine Chapsal asks if the work is concerned with insanity, and wonders who really are the insane—the people who exist in an intolerable system, or those who refuse to so exist and seek another way. As the novel progresses the main characters come closer together and eventually their ideas are interchangeable, it matters not which one expresses which idea; any one can speak for all. Duras said in an interview, "There are ten ways to read *Destroy;* that's what I wanted." She believes that her characters "are completely interchangeable."

Hiroshima mon amour, Bree writes, is "an excellent introduction" to Duras's writing, although the author does not usually write about historical subjects. Bree says that the dialogue has a "haunting, unobtrusive beauty." Frakes believes that "to recall [her] work on *Hiroshima mon amour* is to gain a fresh sense of the cinematic elements of her fiction. These are not only visual (dynamic lighting effects, slow dissolves, juxtaposition of startling images, rapid cuts) but aural. The murmur of voices is brilliantly counterpoised in each novel against the sounds of rain on a skylight, car motors, whistling, piano scales, scraps of melody from a phonograph, a blaring radio, the rustling of a bead curtain, the dry scraping of a dog's claws and a woman's fingernails, the creaking of wicker—masterfully orchestrated sound track that lacerates the nerves as it establishes a frame for the close-focus views of these intimate revolutions in private lives." Saul Maloff comments that Duras is known best in America for *Hiroshima mon amour* and says that "elusive, illusory states of consciousness are [her] specialty." Buitenhuis contends that the third dimension, for Duras, "is not space but time." He notes that she sees "people and landscapes in two-dimensional black and white," and he feels that this is because of her work with films. Silver comments on the "sharp visual sense" present in *The Sailor from Gibraltar*. Harold Hobson writes that "Une Aussi longue absence" "is one of the most moving films ever made." Duras told Chapsal, however, that she would rather write new screenplays than see the characters in her novels on screen, because people always compare the screenplay to the novel, and do not allow themselves the freedom to judge the films on their own merits. She says that her only interest in films is to portray interior situations because, she says, "je pense que le reste a ete fait."

Chapsal points out that Duras portrays women very differently than she does men. The women are drawn much more fully, and their unvoiced thoughts are more carefully developed; the men seem to be more fragile and tend to be maneuvered by the women. *Time* says that there is really a man in all her stories: "[He] is invariably of humble birth. He may be called the Demon Lover." The women are described as "a long line of broody ladies who are young no longer, neglected or betrayed by their husbands, obsessed with violent crime, ready to pick up the first available man." The man is usually a fugitive of some sort, or at least a dissident. Geoffrey Wolff writes: "Her heroines are frequently obsessed by erotic impulses which disgust them. These women live among alien objects; they are isolated in their queerness and by their fear." Duras says that the role of the child is very important in her novels. The child serves as a counterpoint to the action in the story. When the child appears he conceals the drama, in the sense that the drama ceases even if he is only present for a brief moment. The innocence of the child serves as a direct contrast to the intensity of the story. This is especially true in the relationship of mother and child in *Moderato Cantabile*.

Politically, Marguerite Duras is considered to be very definitely left wing. *Variety* reports that she had considerable trouble obtaining a visa to attend the New York Film Festival in 1969 for the showing of her film, "Detruire, dit-elle," "because she would not provide the 'concrete evidence of anti-Communist activities' that was required." Politics, however, is not at all the basis of her work. She said, in an interview with Harold Hobson: "There is, and there can be, . . . no Utopia. My novels are not a parable of humanity's need of a state of perfection. I do not believe that perfection can ever be attained. There is in life an amount of happiness which is irreducible, whatever the form of society may be. Nevertheless, things could be very much better than they are." Hobson notes that Duras emphasizes the distinction between her political and artistic interests, a separation which, Hobson comments, "has brought her some criticism from the intellectual French left." He also finds it clear that Duras "is no fanatic. She does not allow her political convictions to blind her to other, and perhaps more important, considerations. She can, as many Frenchmen cannot, with their rigid devotion to Cartesian logic, tolerate the other side. . . . As France's position in the world has improved, . . . her writers have in reaction lost all their certainty. The characteristic note of French literature now both in novels and in plays is one of doubt. French writers today do not pretend to certainty about even their own plots. The film 'L'Annee derniere a Marienbad' [by Robbe-Grillet] . . . is full of an unresolved ambiguity. . . . A similar ambiguity, with all its poetic overtones of beauty and sadness, is the basis of Madame Duras's work, and it militates against her popularity."

Marguerite Duras told Chapsal that Alain Resnais, the director of "Hiroshima mon amour," encouraged her to write, to let herself go. She finds writing a terrible drudgery, and when she is working, she writes as long as ten hours a day. But, she points out to Chapsal, there are also many months when she does nothing. She often gets ideas for her novels from very minute things—small bits of conversation, a story overheard—almost anything might give her something with which to work. Bree writes: "Very little is necessary to start her stories moving. The story of Mr. Andesmas was born . . . of a few 'words overheard': 'I have just bought a house. A very beautiful spot. Almost like Greece. The trees around the house belong to me. One of them is enormous and, in summer, will give so much shade that I'll never suffer from the heat. I am going to build a terrace. From that terrace at night you'll be able to see the lights of G.' Simple words overheard, from which it would seem was born the massive figure of seventy-eight-year-old Mr. Andesmas."

Duras also told Chapsal that she never considers herself a "woman writer," although she considers writing her most important work. She feels the same way about her work as a director. She told Claude Veillot that she directs films the same way a man would; she is not interested in making a woman's film.

John Elsom writes: "The excitement of Marguerite Duras's plays and novels is that she so nearly manages to make those moments of existential 'freedom' and uncertainty, the suspension of belief, humanly credible. . . . Marguerite Duras can create and describe the sensation, so central to romanticism, where innocence takes over from experience, and the myths of habit, duty, and responsibility fall away. We open our eyes-wide-once; and then half-close them: but we don't forget what the world was like when we could bear to look at it."

MEDIA ADAPTATIONS: Un Barrage contre le Pacifique was filmed as "The Sea Wall" by Columbia Pictures, 1958, and was also translated and adapted by Sofka Skipworth as "A Dam against an Ocean," for British Broadcasting Corp., 1962; *The Sailor from Gibraltar* was filmed by Lopert, 1967.

BIOGRAPHICAL/CRITICAL SOURCES:

BOOKS

Chapsal, Madeleine, *Quinze Ecrivains,* Rene Julliard, 1963.
Contemporary Literary Criticism, Gale, Volume 3, 1975, Volume 6, 1976, Volume 11, 1979, Volume 20, 1982, Volume 34, 1985, Volume 40, 1986.
Dictionary of Literary Biography, Volume 83: *French Novelists since 1960,* Gale, 1989.
Four Novels, introduction by Germaine Bree, Grove, 1965.
Moore, Harry T., *Twentieth Century French Literature since World War II,* Southern Illinois University Press, 1966.
Peyre, Henri, *French Novelists of Today,* Oxford University Press, 1967.

PERIODICALS

Atlantic, September, 1970.
Books Abroad, winter, 1967, spring, 1968, summer, 1969, spring, 1970.
Books and Bookmen, July, 1968.
Choice, October, 1970.
Christian Science Monitor, November 29, 1968, July 30, 1970.
Encounter, February, 1963.
Hudson Review, autumn, 1967.
Illustrated London News, January 14, 1967, February 4, 1967.
Kenyon Review, January, 1967.

L'Express, March 27-April 2, 1967, March 31-April 6, 1969, June 16-22, 1969, November 23-29, 1970.

Listener, October 5, 1967.

London Magazine, May, 1967, October, 1968.

Mercure de France, June, 1958.

Nation, March 16, 1963, January 11, 1971.

New Leader, August 14, 1967, February 8, 1971.

New Statesman, January 20, 1967, April 7, 1967, September 29, 1967, May 3, 1968, July 14, 1970, July 16, 1971.

Newsweek, January 16, 1967, January 11, 1971.

New York, January 11, 1971, May 3, 1971.

New Yorker, November 8, 1968.

New York Herald Tribune Book Review, February 7, 1960.

New York Times, March 15, 1953, September 14, 1969, August 23, 1970, January 3, 1971, September 7, 1972.

New York Times Book Review, November 8, 1959, February 19, 1967, July 2, 1967, November 17, 1968.

Observer, February 26, 1967, September 24, 1967, May 5, 1968, October 13, 1968, September 6, 1970.

Plays and Players, August, 1970, September, 1971, October, 1972.

Punch, January 11, 1967, November 6, 1968.

Saturday Review, November 23, 1968.

Stage, June 17, 1971, July 15, 1971, October 21, 1971, January 27, 1972.

Theatre Arts, November, 1963.

Time, July 7, 1967, November 1, 1968, December 14, 1970.

Times Literary Supplement, January 19, 1967, June 22, 1967, October 5, 1967, May 30, 1968, September 25, 1970, October 30, 1970.

Variety, October 1, 1969, October 8, 1969, December 9, 1970, December 16, 1970, January 13, 1971, April 12, 1971, April 14, 1971, July 21, 1971, August 25, 1971, September 6, 1972, March 28, 1973.

Village Voice, March 16, 1967.

Washington Post Book World, November 10, 1968.

Yale French Studies, summer, 1959.

*   *   *

DURRELL, Gerald (Malcolm) 1925-

PERSONAL: Surname accented on the first syllable; born January 7, 1925, in Jamshedpur, India; son of Lawrence Samuel (a civil engineer) and Louisa Florence (Dixie) Durrell; married Jacqueline Sonia Rasen, 1951 (divorced); married Lee Wilson McGeorge, 1979. *Education:* Educated privately in France, Italy, Switzerland, and Greece.

ADDRESSES: Home and office—Jersey Wildlife Preservation Trust, Les Augres Manor, Trinity, Jersey, Channel Islands. *Agent*—Curtis Brown Ltd., 162-168 Regent St., London W1R 5TA, England.

CAREER: Whipsnade Zoological Park, Whipsnade, Bedfordshire, England, student animal keeper, 1945-46; leader and underwriter of zoological expeditions to various parts of the world, including Cameroon, 1947, 1948, and 1956, Nigeria, 1948, Guyana, 1949, Argentina, 1953 and 1958, Paraguay, 1953, Australia, New Zealand, and Malaya, 1961, Sierra Leone, 1964, Mexico, 1968, Mauritius, 1976 and 1977, Assam, India, 1978, Malagasy Republic, 1981, and the Soviet Union, 1986; Jersey Wildlife Preservation Trust, Trinity, Jersey, Channel Islands, founder, 1958, director, 1964—. Founder and chairman, Wildlife Preservation Trust International, Philadelphia, Penn., 1972—; founder and president, Wildlife Preservation Trust Canada, Toronto, 1986—. Conductor of film expedition to Australia and New Zea-

land for British Broadcasting Corporation television series "Two in the Bush," 1962; host of television series "The Stationary Ark," "Ark on the Move," "The Amateur Naturalist," "Durrell in Russia," and "Ourselves and Other Animals."

MEMBER: International Institute of Arts and Letters (fellow), Royal Society of Literature (fellow), Royal Geographical Society (fellow), Fauna Preservation Society, American Zooparks Association, British Ornithologists Union, Australian Mammal Society, Nigerian Field Society, Malayan Nature Society, Zoological Society of London (fellow), Bombay Natural History Society.

AWARDS, HONORS: National Association of Independent Schools award, 1956, for *Three Tickets to Adventure;* D.H.L., Yale University, 1977; honorary D.Sc., University of Durham, 1988; Officer of the Order of the British Empire.

WRITINGS:

The Overloaded Ark, Viking, 1953.

Three Singles to Adventure, Hart-Davis, 1954, published as *Three Tickets to Adventure,* Viking, 1955.

The Bafut Beagles, Viking, 1954.

The New Noah (juvenile; also see below), Collins, 1955, Viking, 1964.

The Drunken Forest, Viking, 1956.

My Family and Other Animals (memoirs), Hart-Davis, 1956, Viking, 1957.

Encounters with Animals, Hart-Davis, 1958, Avon, 1970.

A Zoo in My Luggage, Viking, 1960.

Island Zoo, Collins, 1961, published as *Island Zoo: The Animals a Famous Collector Couldn't Part With,* Macrae Smith, 1963.

The Whispering Land, Hart-Davis, 1961, Viking, 1962.

Look at Zoos, Hamish Hamilton, 1961.

Menagerie Manor, Hart-Davis, 1964, Viking, 1965.

Two in the Bush (story of the filming of the British Broad-casting Corporation television series of the same title), Viking, 1966.

Birds, Beasts and Relatives (memoirs), Viking, 1969.

Fillets of Plaice (memoirs), Viking, 1971.

Catch Me a Colobus, Viking, 1972.

A Bevy of Beasts (memoirs), Simon & Schuster, 1973 (published in England as *Beasts in My Belfrey,* Collins, 1973).

The Stationary Ark, Simon & Schuster, 1976.

Golden Bats and Pink Pigeons, Simon & Schuster, 1977.

The Garden of the Gods (memoirs), Collins, 1978, published as *Fauna and Family,* Simon & Schuster, 1979.

(With wife, Lee Durrell) *The Amateur Naturalist: A Practical Guide to the Natural World,* Hamish Hamilton, 1982, Knopf, 1983.

Ark on the Move (story of the filming of the nature series of the same title), Coward-McCann, 1983.

How to Shoot an Amateur Naturalist (story of the filming of the television series "The Amateur Naturalist," starring Durrell), Little, Brown, 1984.

(With Lee Durrell) *Gerald and Lee Durrell in Russia* (story of the filming of the nature series "Durrell in Russia"), Simon & Schuster, 1986.

(With Peter Evans) *Ourselves and Other Animals,* Pantheon, 1987.

FICTION

(Compiler) *My Favourite Animal Stories,* Lutterworth, 1961, McGraw, 1962.

Rosy Is My Relative (novel), Viking, 1968.

The Donkey Rustlers (juvenile novel), Viking, 1968.

The Talking Parcel (juvenile fantasy), Collins, 1974, Lippincott, 1975.

The Picnic and Suchlike Pandemonium (short stories), Collins, 1979, published as *The Picnic and Other Inimitable Stories,* Simon & Schuster, 1980.

The Mockery Bird (novel), Collins, 1981, Simon & Schuster, 1982.

The Fantastic Flying Journey (juvenile fantasy), Conran Octopus, 1987.

OTHER

(Author of introduction) Bernard Heuvelmans, *On the Track of Unknown Animals,* Hill & Wang, 1958.

(Contributor) *Three Great Animal Stories* (includes *The New Noah*), Collins, 1966.

(Author of notes) Jacquie Durrell, *Beasts in My Bed,* Atheneum, 1967.

"Elephant Country" (television script), National Broadcasting Company, Inc., 1971.

(Contributor) Martin Boddey, editor, *The Twelfth Man,* Cassell, 1971.

(Author of introduction) Theodore Stephanides, *Island Trails,* Macdonald & Co., 1973.

(Author of foreword and contributor) *The Encyclopedia of Natural History,* Smith Publishers, 1978.

Contributor to newspapers and magazines in England, Canada, the United States, Australia, and New Zealand, including the *New York Times, Harper's, Mademoiselle, Atlantic, Holiday,* and *Show.*

SIDELIGHTS: Gerald Durrell "is famous for his work in preserving real wild animals and for his humorous and poignant books on the subject," says Brigitte Weeks in the *Washington Post Book World.* The youngest brother of novelist and poet Lawrence Durrell, and a respected naturalist and zoologist, he is "one of the best writers around for capturing the spirit of nature and travel," according to Jack Imes, Jr., in *Best Sellers.* His books about his travels in search of specimens for zoos, his chronicles of his own youth spent on the Greek island of Corfu, and his occasional revels in the realm of fiction have, in the opinion of London *Times* contributor Caroline Moorehead, "won him fame and readers in numbers surpassed perhaps only by James Herriott."

Although born in India, Gerald Durrell returned with his family to England in 1928. In 1933 the Durrells left for the continent, eventually settling on the Greek island of Corfu. There, under the instruction of Theodore Stephanides and others, Durrell developed the interest in zoology that was to become the consuming passion of his life. He describes this life in *My Family and Other Animals, Birds, Beasts, and Relatives,* and *The Gardens of the Gods,* three books that combine "reminiscence and natural history in a highly individual fashion," according to a reviewer in *Choice.* August Derleth, writing for the *Chicago Sunday Times,* reports that *My Family and Other Animals* "is an amusingly nostalgic account of a childhood notably different from most, replete with sympathetic characters (not excluding the nonhuman) who are more than just types." *New York Times Book Review* contributor Gavin Maxwell calls *Birds, Beasts, and Relatives* "a delightful book full of simple, long-known things: cicadas in the olive groves, lamp-fishing at night, the complexities of fish and animals but, above all, childhood molded by these things and recalled intimately in middle age."

In 1939, the Durrells left Corfu, driven by the onset of World War II. After returning to England, Gerald spent some time

working in a pet shop in London, then managed to obtain a position as a student animal keeper at the Whipsnade zoo, experiences which he chronicles in *Fillets of Plaice* and *A Bevy of Beasts. Fillets,* a title suggested by his brother Lawrence based on the latter's own book *Spirit of Place,* is a selection of five episodes from various points in Gerald's life. The stories are "not all zoological," according to Ronald Blythe in the *Listener,* "but it is a kind of decency learnt from animals which gives them their attractive flavour. They are youthful disasters and mystifications recollected in hilarity." *A Bevy of Beasts* tells of Durrell's yearlong stint as a student keeper of animals in the Whipsnade Zoological Park. "Involved, and yet objective, Mr. Durrell combines his personal passion with keen humour and no illusions," states Jean Stubbs in *Books and Bookmen.* "Gallivanting gnus, bumbling bears, looming giraffes, superior camels, and Billy the Goat," she continues, "come off the pages with all the engaging and lovely maddening qualities of Dickensian characters."

Durrell's first book, *The Overloaded Ark,* was written at the suggestion of his brother Lawrence. Telling of his adventures collecting animals in the British Cameroons, it broke with the genre's tradition of life-threatening situations and hair-raising thrills; lighthearted in tone and filled with humorous anecdotes, Durrell's work recounts not the dangers, but the delights of collecting animals. "There is nothing of the 'mighty hunter' in Durrell's book," declares M. L. J. Akeley in *Saturday Review.* "He carried a small gun, but never fired in self-defense." This book and its successors *The Bafut Beagles, Three Tickets to Adventure* and *The Drunken Forest,* all accounts of collecting trips to various exotic parts of the world, were well received by reviewers. For instance, *The Bafut Beagles* "is, first of all, a gay little book," remarks J. W. Krutch in the *New York Herald Tribune Book Review,* "—no charging rhinoceroses, no man-eaters lurking in the tall grass, no sinister drums subduing the sophisticated European with the hypnotism of Africa's dark beating heart." Similarly, he says of *The Drunken Forest,* "[Durrell's] books are as far as possible from either the earnestness of the I-am-a-humble-servant-of-science or the robustness of the bring-'em-back-alive schools." Marston Bates, writing in the *New York Times,* expresses the opinion that Durrell "has shown that an honest, straightforward account of such a trip [to British Guiana, in *Three Tickets to Adventure*], written by a person who likes words as well as animals, who can be amused at himself and the frustrations of his circumstances, is also never dull."

In 1958 Durrell established a zoological park on the channel island of Jersey for the purpose of breeding and caring for endangered species. *A Zoo in My Luggage, Menagerie Manor, Catch Me a Colobus,* and *The Stationary Ark* all tell of his efforts to begin and maintain populations of animals for other zoological gardens and for their eventual reintroduction into the wild. *Christian Science Monitor* contributor D. K. Willis calls Durrell "a writer who sees animals as individuals demanding nothing less than man's utmost care and respect—as fellow sharers of the earth, not to be diminished on the one hand, or set up on pedestals." "He writes with good breeding about breeding," says Neil Millar in the *Christian Science Monitor;* "he tells how the captivating are made captive and the cagy are caged. His enthusiasm is as infectious as a chuckle in a church." Peter Canby of *Saturday Review* states of *The Stationary Ark,* "On one level this book is about zoos, particularly the one that the renowned naturalist himself started on the island of Jersey. More profoundly, however, *The Stationary Ark* is about the misuse of wild animals in captivity."

Durrell also uses his interest in animals as the basis of his fiction. *Rosy Is My Relative,* the author's first novel, tells the story of

Adrian Rookwhistle's adventures while traveling across Edwardian England with Rosy, an elephant with an unfortunate penchant for alcohol. Peter Corodimas of *Best Sellers* describes this work as "a descendant of the traditional rambling, good-natured British novel which goes back at least as far as Smollett." *The Mockery Bird,* a later effort, concerns animal preservation and the destruction of habitat. The action takes place on the tropical island of Zenkali, a paradise which has been chosen as the site of a new British military base. Construction of the base will involve building a dam and hydroelectric plant, which in turn will mean the flooding of virgin jungle and many small valleys. Peter Foxglove, the new assistant to the political adviser of Zenkali's king, discovers a valley in the backwoods filled with mockery birds, a species supposed to have been extinct for many years. Eventually it is shown that the economy of the entire island depends on this species, and the valley is preserved. Durrell's goal, declares Vic Sussman of the *Washington Post Book World,* is to emphasize the importance of species preservation: "Long before there was a vigorous environmental movement, in fact, people like Durrell were devoting their lives to reversing the trend of extinction and exploitation." *The Mockery Bird,* he concludes, is intended "to convey [Durrell's] message of conservation and compassion."

Durrell's recent work in television and in the books based on his programs emphasizes the need for education in the natural sciences, yet still maintains the standards of his earlier work. *The Amateur Naturalist,* a handbook for the average animal collector, serves as an example. It inspired not only a television series, but another book as well: *How to Shoot an Amateur Naturalist,* based on Durrell's experiences while filming the series. *The Amateur Naturalist* "provides astonishing amounts of information," says James Kaufmann of the *Christian Science Monitor,* "which goes down as easily as if sugarcoated." However, he continues, the information it provides is only part of the book's attraction; Durrell has "a seemingly unlimited capacity for the appreciation of any plant or animal. He treats the common and the arcane with equal enthusiasm. Durrell's sense of wonder, his delight in telling stories, his love of nature are contagious." *Los Angeles Times Book Review* contributor Barbara Salzman expresses similar feelings: "Durrell has put together the perfect book for the budding dabbler, youthful or not. [The volume is] a wonderful primer, a bounty of material for those ready to observe and appreciate the teeming life around us, and the delicate strands that weave it together." Imes, writing about *How to Shoot an Amateur Naturalist,* states: "[Durrell] is an amateur only in the best sense of that word; a man with deep knowledge because of his vast interest in the magnificent mysteries of living things. [But] this book is no dull science documentary droning with a stern-voiced narrator. Instead, it is a romp." Although both *Washington Post Book World* contributor T. H. Watkins and *Times Literary Supplement* reviewer Stephen Mills charge Durrell with paying too much attention to people and not enough to the animals that are his subject, they both recommend the work; Watkins, for example, calls it "natural history writing at its graceful and entertaining best."

Gerald Durrell never loses sight of his objective in spite of his efforts to entertain. In the "Tailpiece" to his novel *The Mockery Bird,* he states that "the world and its wildlife [are] being steadily and ruthlessly decimated by what we call progress." At the Jersey Wildlife Trust, he continues, "we are endeavouring to build up colonies of almost extinct species, to save them, and to train people from different parts of the world in the arts of captive breeding, in order to help these animals that are being edged into oblivion by our unthinking rapaciousness. . . . We are pleading on behalf of these plants and creatures because they cannot plead for themselves, and it is, after all, your world which we are asking you to help preserve."

MEDIA ADAPTATIONS: The Amateur Naturalist: A Practical Guide to the Natural World was made into a BBC television series, featuring Durrell searching for animal life in a variety of locations. *My Family and Other Animals,* his most popular book, was filmed for a 12-part series by BBC television, and was screened in the U.K. in 1987.

AVOCATIONAL INTERESTS: Reading, photography, drawing, and swimming.

BIOGRAPHICAL/CRITICAL SOURCES:

BOOKS

Durrell, Gerald, *My Family and Other Animals,* Hart-Davis, 1956, Viking, 1957.

Durrell, Gerald, *Birds, Beasts and Relatives,* Viking, 1969.

Durrell, Gerald, *Fillets of Plaice,* Viking, 1971.

Durrell, Gerald, *A Bevy of Beasts,* Simon & Schuster, 1973 (published in England as *Beasts in My Belfrey,* Collins, 1973).

Durrell, Gerald, *The Garden of the Gods,* Collins, 1978, published as *Fauna and Family,* Simon & Schuster, 1979.

Durrell, Gerald, *The Mockery Bird,* Collins, 1981, Simon Schuster, 1982.

PERIODICALS

Antioch Review, winter, 1980.

Atlantic, December, 1953, February, 1962, February, 1967, October, 1969, December, 1971.

Best Sellers, April 15, 1965, June 1, 1968, September 15, 1969, February 1, 1972, June 1, 1973, January, 1978, January, 1981, June, 1982, December, 1985.

Books and Bookmen, November, 1968, September, 1971, September, 1972, March, 1974, January, 1977, December, 1977.

Chicago Sunday Tribune, April 7, 1957, January 28, 1962.

Chicago Tribune Book World, October 3, 1982.

Children's Book World, November 3, 1968.

Choice, March, 1970.

Christian Science Monitor, September 24, 1953, October 13, 1955, November 7, 1960, January 25, 1962, November 5, 1964, April 27, 1965, December 28, 1967, October 3, 1968, May 1, 1969, September 11, 1969, December 30, 1971, October 25, 1972, June 6, 1973, September 2, 1983, December 2, 1983, April 6, 1984.

Commonweal, October 16, 1953, November 6, 1964.

Economist, November 20, 1971, December 28, 1974.

Harper's, September, 1969, November, 1974.

International Wildlife, July/August, 1988.

Listener, August 19, 1971.

Los Angeles Times Book Review, November 4, 1979, November 20, 1983, December 14, 1986.

New Statesman, November 19, 1964, October 15, 1976.

New Statesman and Nation, October 20, 1956.

New Yorker, October 3, 1953, November 6, 1954, October 8, 1955, May 25, 1957, October 29, 1960, January 27, 1962, June 1, 1968, December 28, 1980, April 19, 1982, December 5, 1983.

New York Herald Tribune Book Review, November 7, 1954, October 9, 1955, October 28, 1956, May 26, 1957, November 6, 1960, February 11, 1962.

New York Review of Books, September 28, 1978.

New York Times, September 27, 1953, December 5, 1954, September 18, 1955, September 30, 1956, April 7, 1957, November 28, 1983, October 13, 1988.

New York Times Book Review, November 13, 1960, February 4, 1962, January 26, 1964, June 25, 1967, May 26, 1968, November 24, 1968, August 24, 1969, October 1, 1972, May 13, 1973, November 27, 1977, November 18, 1979, December 11, 1983, April 8, 1984.

People, March 15, 1982.

Quill and Quire, April, 1986.

San Francisco Chronicle, November 16, 1954, September 16, 1955, October 2, 1956, April 11, 1957, October 26, 1960, January 25, 1962.

Saturday Review, September 26, 1953, September 29, 1956, November 7, 1964, December 3, 1966, October 7, 1972, December 10, 1977.

Spectator, July 6, 1956, October 28, 1960, December 11, 1976.

Time, April 15, 1957, December 5, 1960, February 2, 1962, September 12, 1969, September 24, 1973, October 9, 1978, April 12, 1982.

Times (London), November 12, 1981, November 24, 1984.

Times Literary Supplement, September 4, 1953, March 26, 1954, December 3, 1954, May 18, 1956, December 21, 1956, November 4, 1960, November 10, 1961, November 23, 1962, January 12, 1967, February 1, 1967, October 3, 1968, November 6, 1969, December 1, 1972, September 21, 1973, December 6, 1974, March 22, 1985.

Virginia Quarterly Review, winter, 1970.

Washington Post, November 6, 1979.

Washington Post Book World, December 24, 1972, May 6, 1973, May 4, 1975, June 14, 1982, September 17, 1985.

*   *   *

DURRELL, Lawrence (George) 1912-
(Charles Norden, Gaffer Peeslake)

PERSONAL: Surname is accented on first syllable; born February 27, 1912, in Julundur, India, of Irish and English parents; son of Lawrence Samuel (an engineer) and Louise Florence (Dixie) Durrell; married Nancy Myers, 1935 (divorced, 1947); married Yvette Cohen, February 26, 1947 (divorced); married Claude Marie Vineenden (a writer), March 27, 1961 (died, 1967); children: (first marriage) Penelope Berengaria; (second marriage) Sappho-Jane. *Education:* Attended College of St. Joseph, Darjiling, India, and St. Edmund's School, Canterbury, England. *Religion:* "Of course I believe in God; but every kind of God. But I rather dread the word religion because I have a notion that the reality of it dissolves the minute it is uttered as a concept."

ADDRESSES: Home—Provence, France. *Agent*—c/o National and Grindlay's Bank, Parliament St., Whitehall, S.W.1, England.

CAREER: Held many odd jobs, including that of jazz pianist at the Blue Peter Night Club, London; also was automobile racer, jazz composer, real estate agent, and ran a photographic studio with his first wife; taught at British Institute in Athens, Greece, 1940; foreign press service officer in British Information Office, Cairo, Egypt, 1941-44; press attache, Alexandria, 1944-45; public relations director, Dodecanese Island, Greece, 1946-47; director of Institute, British Council in Cordoba, Argentina, 1947-48; press attache at British Legation, Belgrade, Yugoslavia, 1949-52; taught school, 1951; teacher of English, then director of public relations for British government in Cyprus during the 1950s; special correspondent for the *Economist,* Cyprus, 1953; moved to France and became full-time writer, 1957.

MEMBER: Royal Society of Literature (fellow, 1954).

AWARDS, HONORS: Duff Cooper Memorial Prize, 1957, for *Bitter Lemons;* Prix du Meilleur Livre Etranger (France), 1959, for *Justine,* and *Balthazar;* James Tait Black Memorial Prize, 1975, for *Monsieur; or, The Prince of Darkness; Constance; or, Solitary Practices* was shortlisted for the Booker Prize, 1981; Cholmondeley Award from the Society of Authors, 1986, for contributions to poetry.

WRITINGS:

Ten Poems, Caduceus Press, 1932.

Ballade of Slow Decay, [London], 1932.

(Under pseudonym Gaffer Peeslake) *Bromo Bombastes,* Caduceus Press, 1933.

Transition: Poems, Caduceus Press, 1934.

Pied Piper of Lovers (novel), Cassell, 1935.

(Under pseudonym Charles Norden) *Panic Spring,* Covici-Friede, 1937.

The Black Book, An Agon, Obelisk 1938, 2nd edition, Olympia Press, 1959, Dutton, 1960.

A Private Country (poems), Faber, 1943.

Prospero's Cell: A Guide to the Landscape and Manners of the Island of Corcyra, Faber, 1945 (published with *Reflections on a Marine Venus,* Dutton, 1960).

Cities, Plains, and People (poems), Faber, 1946.

(Translator) *Six Poems From the Greek of Sekilianos and Seferis,* [Rhodes], 1946.

Zero and Asylum in the Snow, [Rhodes], 1946, published in the United States as *Two Excursions Into Reality,* Circle Editions, 1947.

Cefalu (novel), Editions Poetry, 1947, reprinted with minor alterations as *The Dark Labyrinth,* Ace Books, 1958, Dutton, 1962.

On Seeming to Presume (poems), Faber, 1948.

(Translator, with Bernard Spencer and Nanos Valaoritis) George Seferis, *The King of Asine, and Other Poems,* Lehmann, 1948.

A Landmark Gone, [Los Angeles], 1949.

Deus Loci (poem), [Ischia], 1950.

Nemea, [London], 1950.

Sappho; A Play in Verse (broadcast on BBC, March 25, 1957; staged in Hamburg on November 21, 1959, in Edinburgh, summer, 1961), Faber, 1950, Dutton, 1958.

Key to Modern Poetry, Peter Nevill, 1952, published in the United States as *A Key to Modern British Poetry,* University of Oklahoma Press, 1952.

Reflections on a Marine Venus, Faber, 1953.

(Translator) Emmanuel Royidis, *Pope Joan: A Romantic Biography,* Verschoyle, 1954, revised edition, Deutsch, 1960, Dutton, 1961, Overlook Press, 1972.

Private Drafts, Proodos Press, 1955.

The Tree of Idleness, and Other Poems, Faber, 1955.

Selected Poems, Grove, 1956.

Bitter Lemons, Faber, 1957, Dutton, 1958.

Esprit de Corps: Sketches From Diplomatic Life, Faber, 1957, Dutton, 1958 (also see below).

Justine: A Novel, Dutton, 1957, 2nd edition, Faber, 1963 (also see below).

White Eagles Over Serbia (detective stories), Criterion, 1957, abridged edition, edited by G. A. Verdin, Chatto & Windus, 1961.

Balthazar: A Novel, Dutton, 1958 (also see below).

(Contributor, in French) *Hommage a Roy Campbell,* [Montpellier], 1958.

Mountolive: A Novel, Faber, 1958, Dutton, 1959 (also see below).

Stiff Upper Lip: Life Among the Diplomats, Faber, 1958, Dutton, 1959, published with *Esprit de Corps,* Dutton Everyman, 1961.

(Contributor) *Art and Outrage* (a correspondence about Henry Miller between Alfred Perles and Durrell, including letters by Miller), Putnam, 1959, Dutton, 1961.

(Editor and author of introduction) *The Henry Miller Reader,* New Directions, 1959, reprinted, Books for Libraries, 1972 (published in England as *The Best of Henry Miller,* Heinemann, 1960).

Clea: A Novel, Dutton, 1960 (also see below).

Collected Poems, Dutton, 1960, revised edition, Faber, 1968.

The Alexandria Quartet (contains *Justine, Balthazar, Mountolive,* and *Clea*), Dutton, 1961.

(Author of introduction) Georg Walther Groddeck, *The Book of the It,* [Wiesbaden], 1961.

Briefwechsel ueber Actes (correspondence between Durrell and Gustaf Gruendgens concerning *Acte*) Rowohlt Verlag, 1961.

The Poetry of Lawrence Durrell, Dutton, 1962.

(Editor) *New Poems, 1963: A P.E.N. Anthology of Contemporary Poetry,* Hutchinson, 1963, Harcourt, 1964.

Lawrence Durrell and Henry Miller: A Private Correspondence, edited by George Wickes, Dutton, 1963.

Beccafico (limited edition), [Montpellier], 1963.

An Irish Faustus: A Morality in Nine Scenes (produced in Hamburg, 1963), Dutton, 1964.

Selected Poems, 1935-1963, Faber, 1964.

Drei dramatische Dichtungen, Rohwohlt Verlag, 1964.

La descente du Styx (limited edition), [Montpellier], 1964, published in the United States as *Down the Styx,* Capricorn Press, 1971.

Acte (verse play; produced in Hamburg, 1962), Dutton, 1965.

The Icons, and Other Poems, Faber, 1966, Dutton, 1967.

Sauve qui peut (more sketches from diplomatic life), Faber, 1966, Dutton, 1967.

Nothing is Lost, Sweet Self (poem set to music by Wallace Southam), Turret Books, 1967.

Tunc: A Novel, Dutton, 1968.

In Arcadia (poem set to music by Southam), Turret Books, 1968.

(Author of introductory essay) Gyula Halasz Brassai, *Brassai,* Museum of Modern Art, 1968.

Spirit of Place: Letters and Essays on Travel, edited by Alan G. Thomas, Dutton, 1969.

Nunquam: A Novel (Book-of-the-Month Club selection), Dutton, 1970.

Red Limbo Lingo: A Poetry Notebook, Dutton, 1971.

On the Suchness of the Old Boy, Turret, 1972.

Vega and Other Poems, Faber, 1973.

The Plant Magic Man, Capra Press, 1973.

The Happy Rock (on Henry Miller), Village Press, 1973.

(Editor) *Wordsworth,* Penguin, 1973.

Lifelines, Tragara Press, 1974.

The Best of Antrobus, Faber, 1974.

Monsieur; or, The Prince of Darkness (novel), Faber, 1974, Viking, 1975.

Blue Thirst, Capra Press, 1975.

Selected Poems, edited by Alan Ross, Faber, 1977.

Sicilian Carousel, Viking, 1977.

The Greek Islands, Viking, 1978.

Livia; or, Buried Alive (novel), Faber, 1978, Viking, 1979.

Collected Poems, 1931-1974, edited by James A. Brigham, Penguin, 1980.

Constance; or, Solitary Practices, Penguin, 1982.

Antrobus Complete, Faber, 1985.

Quinx; or, The Ripper's Tale, Penguin, 1985.

Sebastian; or, Ruling Passions, revised edition, Penguin, 1985.

Also author of *A Smile in the Mind's Eye.* Author, with others, of screenplays *Cleopatra,* 1963, and *Judith,* 1966; author of television script *The Lonely Road,* 1971.

Contributor to *The Booster, Delta, New English Weekly, Geographical Magazine, Seven, Poetry* (London), *T'ien Hsia Monthly* (Shanghai), *Poetry World, Experimental Review, Furioso, View, Chimera, Counterpoint, Circle, Partisan Review, Neurotica, New Statesman, Time and Tide, Quarterly Review of Literature, Spectator, London Magazine, Encounter, Holiday, Mademoiselle, Esquire, New York Times Book Review, Realities* (Paris), and other publications. Edited, with Robin Fedden, *Personal Landscape,* in Cairo, 1941-44; edited, with Henry Miller and Alfred Perles, *The Booster,* later known as *Delta;* edited *Cyprus Review,* 1954-55.

MEDIA ADAPTATIONS: Film rights to both *Tunc* and *Nunquam* have been sold to American producer Ronald I. Kahn. An adaptation of *Stiff Upper Lip* was produced on BBC-TV in 1968. Durrell may be heard on several recordings: "Grecian Echoes," selections from *Bitter Lemons, Prospero's Cell,* and *Reflections on a Marine Venus;* "An Irish Faust"; and "The Love Poems of Lawrence Durrell," Spoken Arts.

SIDELIGHTS: Lawrence Durrell's baroque prose is reminiscent of that of Thomas De Quincey, Joseph Conrad, and more recently, Vladimir Nabokov. "The style," writes George Steiner, "is mosaic. Each word is set in its precise and luminous place. Touch by touch, Durrell builds his array of sensuous, rare expressions into patterns of image and idea so subtle and convoluted that the experience of reading becomes one of total sensual apprehension."

Principally Durrell is a poet, or what he calls a "hander on of sound." He told his *Paris Review* interviewer: "Poetry turned out to be an invaluable mistress. Because poetry is form, and the wooing and seduction of form is the whole game." His style and poetic vision he has termed "heraldic," transcending ordinary syntax and logic, invading "a realm where unreason reigns, and where the relations between ideas are sympathetic and mysterious—affective—rather than casual, objective, substitutional."

Durrell's magnum opus, *The Alexandria Quartet,* he calls "a yarn on one plane, and a sort of poetic parable on another. . . . Every good work should have a good deal of bone meal and manure mixed with it, or the cultural humus you manufacture won't be rich enough to allow for the growth of future flowers." The *Quartet* is principally an investigation of modern love. In it Durrell applies the principles of Einsteinian time, trying to create the idea of a continuum of words ("ideally, all four volumes should be read simultaneously," he once said). To answer the critics of this ambitious scheme he lightheartedly comments: "I'm trying to give you stereoscopic narrative with stereophonic personality, and if that doesn't mean anything to anybody at least it should be of interest to radio engineers."

Each of the novels in the *Quartet* is prefaced by a quotation from the Marquis de Sade who is for Durrell "the most typical figure of our century, with his ignorance and cruelty. I regard him as both a hero and a pygmy. . . . The very apotheosis of our infantile unconscious." He feels, however, that morality "should not have an explicit place in an art context; to the artist everyone is primally good, however bad or ignorant their actions. . . . [Art] doesn't read sermons, but teaches by example," urging people "to wake up by giving them the vicarious feel of the poetic illumination." Despite the references to Sade, Durrell's view of life is generally positive, unlike that of many of his contemporaries. Gerald Sykes notes the distinction between him and Samuel Beckett, for example: "Durrell celebrates life 'heraldically' as a blessing; Beckett wishes it had never been inflicted on him."

Durrell's longtime friend, Henry Miller, once observed that Durrell took his work seriously, but not himself. "Me change the world?" says Durrell. "Good Lord, no. Or only perhaps indirectly by persuading itself to see itself and relax; to tap the source of laughter in itself." And, he warns, "it's possible my ideas are altogether too explicit not to be suspect. Beware!"

Upon publication of *The Black Book,* the book and its author were praised by such people as Miller ("You are *the* master of the English language") and T.S. Eliot ("The first piece of work by a new English writer to give me any hope for the future of prose fiction"). Durrell himself does not regard this book as a good one. "There are parts of it which I think probably are a bit too obscene."

Though many consider the *Quartet* "the highest performance in the modern novel since Proust or Joyce," George Steiner has noted that other critics call Durrell "a pompous charlatan," "a mere word-spinner," a "gatherer of flamboyant cliches," a "late Victorian decadent," a "minor disciple of Henry Miller." He admits that he always feels he is overwriting, and that he has done a good deal of potboiling in his career. His comment on the latter: "Let them riddle me with arrows so long as I can keep it up and avoid jobs." In defense of Durrell's use of language, poet Hayden Carruth has written: "Durrell is a writer, embodying perhaps as well as any man alive all the refinements and conscientiousness that has been bred into the genus since antiquity, and his protests are well-fashioned, the products of as much intelligence as a very intelligent man can bring to bear; and they are beautiful as well."

About *Tunc* Sykes writes: "The author may be moving in a new direction. . . . One gets the impression that . . . Durrell has deliberately thrown overboard the charm that won him so many readers in *Justine.* . . . [Durrell] seems to be trying to come to grips, at least in concept, with 'the real world.'" Cassill reports of *Nunquam:* "One feels that Durrell has been alert to the whole significant culture of his time and grasps it with almost dismaying facility." And, comparing *Nunquam* with the *Quartet,* Durrell himself told an interviewer: "[It] is much more contemporary. It's no longer an historical dream of a city which gave us our sources; it's where we are now."

"A born writer," Miller calls him, though Durrell himself says he was driven to writing "by sheer ineptitude," perhaps recalling his futile attempts to get into Cambridge University "about eight times." Except for poetry, he writes on a typewriter, and writes prolifically and often rapidly: *Bitter Lemons* took six weeks; *Justine* about four months; *Balthazar* six weeks; *Mountolive* two months; *Clea* seven weeks.

Durrell's personal and literary sympathies lie with Miller (whom he greatly admired in the 1930s, while now it is Miller's turn to affirm Durrell's mastery), Henry de Montherlant, Marcel Proust, Nikos Kazantzakis, Jorge Luis Borges, and Italo Svevo. He has almost always been an expatriate, though H. T. Moore quotes him as saying, "I'm as English as Shakespeare's birthday." The Irish element "means the fire, the hysteria, the mental sluttishness, the sensuality and intuition." He told one interviewer: "With all my love-hate complex for England I keep in touch and try not to become a 'professional foreigner'."

AVOCATIONAL INTERESTS: Painting (he has been called an accomplished watercolorist), and though he refers to himself as a "dauber," he has said he would have preferred to be a painter rather than a writer; at one time listed travel, but he told the *Paris Review:* "You know I'm so travel-stained with fifteen or sixteen years of it—the great anxiety of being shot at in Cyprus, being bombed, being tormented by the Marxists in Yugoslavia—that now for the first time I've a yen for my tiny roof. Staying put is so refreshing that it's almost anguish to go into town for a movie."

BIOGRAPHICAL/CRITICAL SOURCES:

BOOKS

Contemporary Literary Criticism, Gale, Volume 1, 1973, Volume 4, 1975, Volume 6, 1976, Volume 8, 1978, Volume 13, 1980, Volume 27, 1984, Volume 41, 1987.
Dictionary of Literary Biography, Gale, Volume 15: *British Novelists, 1930-1959,* 1983, Volume 27: *Poets of Great Britain and Ireland, 1945-1960,* 1984.
Fraser, George Sutherland, *Lawrence Durrell: A Study* (with complete bibliography by Alan G. Thomas), Dutton, 1968.
Friedman, Allen Warren, *Lawrence Durrell and the Alexandria Quartet: Art for Love's Sake,* University of Oklahoma Press, 1970.
Moore, H. T., editor, *The World of Lawrence Durrell,* Southern Illinois University Press, 1962.
Perles, Alfred, *My Friend, Lawrence Durrell,* Scorpion Press, 1961.
Potter, Robert A. and Brooke Whiting, *Lawrence Durrell: A Checklist,* University of California Library, 1961.
Unterecker, John, *Lawrence Durrell* (essay with bibliography), Columbia University Press, 1964.
Weigel, John A., *Lawrence Durrell,* Twayne, 1966.

PERIODICALS

Books and Bookmen, February, 1960.
Detroit News, August 29, 1982, October 13, 1985.
Encounter, December, 1959.
Los Angeles Times Book Review, June 13, 1982, June 18, 1982, July 15, 1984, October 27, 1985, February 2, 1986.
Manchester Guardian, May 6, 1961.
Modern Fiction Studies, summer, 1971.
New York Times Book Review, April 14, 1968, August 1, 1982, December 2, 1982, April 1, 1984, September 15, 1985.
Paris Review, autumn-winter, 1959-60.
Saturday Review, March 21, 1964.
Shenandoah, winter, 1971.
Times (London), October 14, 1982, October 27, 1983, May 30, 1985.
Times Literary Supplement, May 22, 1969, October 15, 1982, October 28, 1983, May 31, 1985.
Virginia Quarterly Review, summer, 1967.
Washington Post, May 29, 1986.
Washington Post Book World, April 15, 1984, October 14, 1984, September 1, 1985.

*   *   *

DURRENMATT, Friedrich
    See DUERRENMATT, Friedrich

DWORKIN, Andrea 1946-

PERSONAL: Born September 26, 1946, in Camden, N.J.; daughter of Harry (a guidance counselor) and Sylvia (a secretary; maiden name, Spiegel) Dworkin. *Education:* Bennington College, B.A., 1968. *Politics:* Radical feminist.

ADDRESSES: Agent—Elaine Markson, 44 Greenwich Ave., New York, N.Y. 10011.

CAREER: Writer and lecturer. Has worked as a waitress, receptionist, secretary, typist, salesperson, factory worker, paid political organizer, and teacher.

MEMBER: P.E.N., American Society of Journalists and Authors, Women's Institute for Freedom of the Press, Authors Guild, Authors League of America.

WRITINGS:

Woman Hating: A Radical Look at Sexuality (nonfiction), Dutton, 1974.
Our Blood: Prophecies and Discourses on Sexual Politics (essays), Harper, 1976.
The New Womans Broken Heart (short stories), Frog in the Well, 1980.
(Contributor) *Take Back the Night: Women on Pornography,* Morrow, 1980.
Pornography: Men Possessing Women (nonfiction), Putnam, 1981.
Right-wing Women: The Politics of Domesticated Females (nonfiction), Putnam, 1983.
Ice and Fire (novel), Secker & Warburg, 1986.
Intercourse (nonfiction), Free Press, 1987.
(With Catharine A. MacKinnon) *Pornography and Civil Rights: A New Day for Women's Equality* (nonfiction), Organizing Against Pornography, 1988.
Letters from a War Zone (essays), Dutton, 1989.

Also author of the novel *Ruins.* Contributor to periodicals, including *Village Voice, Christopher Street, America Report, Gay Community News, Ms.,* and *Social Policy.*

SIDELIGHTS: "One of the most compelling voices in the Women's Movement" is that of Andrea Dworkin, according to Carole Rosenthal in *Ms.* Author and lecturer Dworkin is noted for expressing her radical politics with forceful style. She "writes like a Leon Trotsky of the sex war," states Stanley Reynolds in *Punch.* "Short, sharp sentences, full of repetitions but never boring. She is full of power and energy. She writes—dare I say it?—with an aggressive manner, like a man. Except that no men write with such utter conviction these days."

Woman Hating and *Our Blood,* Dworkin's first books, review some of the methods that she feels men have used to subjugate women. These include physical incapacitation, such as binding the feet; terrorism, in the form of witch-hunts; and social conditioning through fairy tales, myth, and pornography, which demonstrate the two choices men offer women: be passive and helpless and protected by men, or be strong and assertive and destroyed by men. In her 1983 book, *Right-wing Women,* Dworkin theorizes that fear of male violence has forced many women to seek protection by accepting the rigid, predetermined social order of conservatism, which promises "form, shelter, safety, rules, and love" in exchange for female subservience. Dworkin warns that this protection is bought at a high price, for in time, when laboratory reproduction is possible, the only role men will sanction for women is that of the prostitute. She envisions a "gynocide," or female holocaust, with survivors reduced to the status of worker ants in a brothel-ghetto. *Intercourse,* Dworkin's

1987 publication, is a "bitter, painful" book that depicts "the intrinsic connection of violence to sex," explains reviewer Naomi Black in the Toronto *Globe and Mail.* According to Dworkin, writes Black, "heterosexuality is necessarily exploitative" because of the typically dominant role of the male, and such exploitation extends throughout heterosexual society.

Some reviewers have taken exception to Dworkin's portrayal of men as uniformly enamored of violence and power. In order to fully accept her work, remarks Anne Tyler in *New Republic,* "you would have to accept its pervasive sense of a world where the sexes exist in an unremitting tooth and nail relationship; where men and women have absolutely no hope of any genuine connection with each other; where they have never once experienced a disinterested, kindly affection for each other." David Pannick claims in the *Listener* that Dworkin's generalizations about men amount to sexism: "What is offensive in Ms. Dworkin's work is the sexual stereotyping she adopts. She seems unaware that sexism consists in judging an individual by reference to his or her gender and not by reference to his or her individual attributes. The Marquis de Sade is, apparently, 'Everyman.' " However, Dworkin's strong convictions and passionate language usually impress even those reviewers who do not agree with her politics. Rosenthal states that although Dworkin's revolutionary demands are sometimes unrealistic, her "relentless courage" in calling for drastic social reform is admirable. "If she overstates her case, it is because she is a true revolutionary," notes Reynolds.

Dworkin believes that pornography is one of the primary weapons used by men to control women. In her opinion, pornography is not about sex; it is about male power. By portraying women as masochistic, submissive playthings for men, "it creates hostility and aggression toward women, causing both bigotry and sexual abuse," she told *CA.* Reynolds explains that Dworkin's book *Pornography: Men Possessing Women* analyzes numerous pornographic stories to illustrate that they "all—even those dealing with homosexuals—demonstrate the male lust for violence and power."

The book is "less a theoretical work than a book-length sermon, preached with a rhetorical flourish and a singleminded intensity that meet somewhere between poetry and rant," writes Ellen Willis in the *New York Times Book Review.* David Pannick feels that Dworkin's blanket condemnation of all pornographic material "considerably weakens the worth of this book. . . . An author who sees Nazi gas ovens when she looks at a picture in *Playboy* has exhausted the range of human disgust on the least unacceptable of publications, and is guilty, at least, of a lack of judgment." But Ruthann Robson in *New Pages* supports Dworkin's position. "Soft core pornography, such as *Playboy* and *Penthouse,* poses a more serious threat to females than hard core pornography because it is so insidious and it masquerades as serious," she points out.

Dworkin has not limited her crusade against pornography to her writings; she and lawyer Catharine A. MacKinnon, with whom she wrote *Pornography and Civil Rights: A New Day for Women's Equality* in 1988, are responsible for a controversial antipornography ordinance that has been passed in Indianapolis, was twice passed and twice vetoed in Minneapolis, and is being considered in many other cities. The ordinance defines pornography as a form of sex discrimination and allows any person who has been harried by pornography to sue its maker or seller. Dworkin explained the ordinance further in a letter to *CA:* "Every part of the law can be used by men, women, children, and transsexuals. A person can sue if she has been coerced into a pornographic performance, forced to watch pornography, assaulted or physically injured as a direct result of a specific piece of pornography, or she can bring a complaint against traffickers (makers, sellers, exhibitors, distributors), because they are part of a system of exploitation that keeps women in particular civilly inferior (though men, children, and transsexuals can also sue under this part, if they can show that pornography impacts on their civil status)."

Opponents of the legislation have said that it violates the First Amendment and restricts basic personal freedoms. Dworkin disagrees in *Ms.:* "The law really doesn't have anything to say about what people do in their private lives, unless they're forcing pornography on somebody or coercing somebody or assaulting somebody. If personal, private sexual practice involves the use of pornography that someone else has to produce, the question then is, do they have a right to that product no matter what it costs the people who have to produce it? When we look at what is really done to women to make that product, then who will say, 'Well, I have a right to that product because I need it in my sex life.' That's the most direct conflict I can see: somebody saying, 'I have private sexual rights that involve the use of pornography,' versus our claim that 'No, you don't actually have a right to use dispossessed and exploited people to have that product so that you can have sex.' "

Dworkin remarked to *CA* that even as a child, she believed that writing and legislation were two ways to "really change society. By writing, you did it by changing people's minds." The impact that Dworkin's writing carries is summarized in Rosenthal's review of *Our Blood:* "It is difficult to remain neutral or unmoved by such passionate language and conviction. But however strongly a reader agrees or takes issue with the essays in this book, Dworkin will never be found dull or dishonest or glib. She is a genuine visionary—bold, thoughtful, willing to take risks. *Our Blood* poses questions that enlighten us in exploring our lives; it constantly tugs and stretches at the imagination's boundaries. These are trailblazing essays. They can alter your mental map of the world."

BIOGRAPHICAL/CRITICAL SOURCES:

BOOKS

Contemporary Literary Criticism, Volume 43, Gale, 1987.

PERIODICALS

Choice, October, 1974.
Globe and Mail (Toronto), August 2, 1986, July 11, 1987.
Listener, December 3, 1981.
Los Angeles Times, August 10, 1983.
Los Angeles Times Book Review, May 3, 1987.
Ms., February, 1977, June, 1980, March, 1981, June, 1983, April, 1985.
New Pages, spring, 1982.
New Republic, February 21, 1983, June 25, 1984.
New Statesman, November 6, 1981, July 29, 1983.
Newsweek, March 18, 1985.
New Yorker, March 28, 1977.
New York Times Book Review, July 12, 1981, May 3, 1987, October 29, 1989.
Observer, May 16, 1982.
Publishers Weekly, February 25, 1974.
Punch, February 10, 1982.
Times (London), June 4, 1987, May 18, 1988.
Times Literary Supplement, January 1, 1982, June 6, 1986, October 16, 1987, June 3, 1988.
Village Voice, July 15-21, 1981.
Washington Post Book World, June 21, 1981.
West Coast Review of Books, March/April, 1983.

*   *   *

DWYER, Deanna
    See KOONTZ, Dean R(ay)

*   *   *

DWYER, K. R.
    See KOONTZ, Dean R(ay)